British and International Music Yearbook 2000

Editor: Louise Head
Assistant Editors: Henry Watson, Claire Throp

Twenty Sixth Edition

Rhinegold Publishing Limited
241 Shaftesbury Avenue
London WC2H 8EH
United Kingdom

Editorial: +44 (0)20 7333 1760
Book Sales: +44 (0)20 7333 1721 Advertising: +44 (0)20 7333 1748
Fax: +44 (0)20 7333 1769 Email: bmyb@rhinegold.co.uk Website: www.rhinegold.co.uk

Classical Search: www.classicalsearch.com

First published **1999** in Great Britain by
Rhinegold Publishing Ltd
241 Shaftesbury Avenue
London WC2H 8EH
United Kingdom
Tel: +44 (0)20 7333 1721

British Library Cataloguing in Publication Data.
A catalogue record for this book is available from the British Library.

ISBN 0-946890-83-8
ISSN 0306 5928

Printed in Great Britain by Perfectaprint, Byfleet, Surrey.

new london children's choir

Patrons:
Luciano Berio, Oliver Knussen

MUSICAL DIRECTOR:
RONALD CORP

Training choir age 8 upwards - no auditions
Senior choir - upper voices - auditions
Youth choir - SATB - auditions
Barbershop - New London Barbers

The New London Children's Choir was launched in September 1991 with the specific aim of performing a wide range of music, and with a special commitment to presenting new works.

Since its inauguration the choir has commissioned works from Diana Burrell, Gary Carpenter, Simon Bainbridge, Brian Chapple, Howard Skempton, Philip Cashian, Colin Huehns, Kevin Malone, David Horne, Laurence Hughes, Malcolm Lipkin, Elis Pehkonen, Douglas Weiland, Judith Bingham, David Knotts, Thoma Simaku, Joseph Phibbs, Jennifer Fowler, Param Vir, Bernard Hughes, Julian Philips, Oscar Bettison, Andrew Simpson, Gabriel Jackson, Nicholas Ansdell-Evans and Patrick Nunn.

Performances include Proms (Goehr, Stravinsky, Tavener, Berlioz, Tan Dun), Radio 3, Classic *f*M, and BBC TV (Krasa's *Brundibar*), concerts in Paris, Assisi, Seville and Brussels and in London with major orchestras. Recordings include film soundtracks for *Little Women, A Little Princess, The Hunchback of Notre Dame* and *Star Wars.* CDs include Tchaikovsky's *Nutcracker* (Jansons), Shostakovich (Ashkenazy), Prokofiev (Rostropovich), Mahler (Sinopoli), Britten's *St Nicolas* (Bedford). Cds of Britten's *Ceremony of Carols* and Betty Roe's *A Family Tree* are conducted by Ronald Corp.

The New London Children's Choir regularly performs with the New London Orchestra.

Photography by Dee Conway

Designed by GYRO

For further information about the Choir's availability or auditions, contact; Ronald Corp
41 Aberdare Gardens London NW6 3AL Tel 020 7625 4641 Fax 020 7625 4876

Stravinsky
Tippett
Goehr
Penderecki
Takemitsu
Bryars
Henze
Ligeti
Turnage
Rodrigo
Hindemith
Casken
Korngold
Grainger
Martland
Orff
Weill

CONTENTS

✦ Performance ✦

Artists and Agents

Competitions

Broadcasting

Venues and Promoters

✦ Education ✦

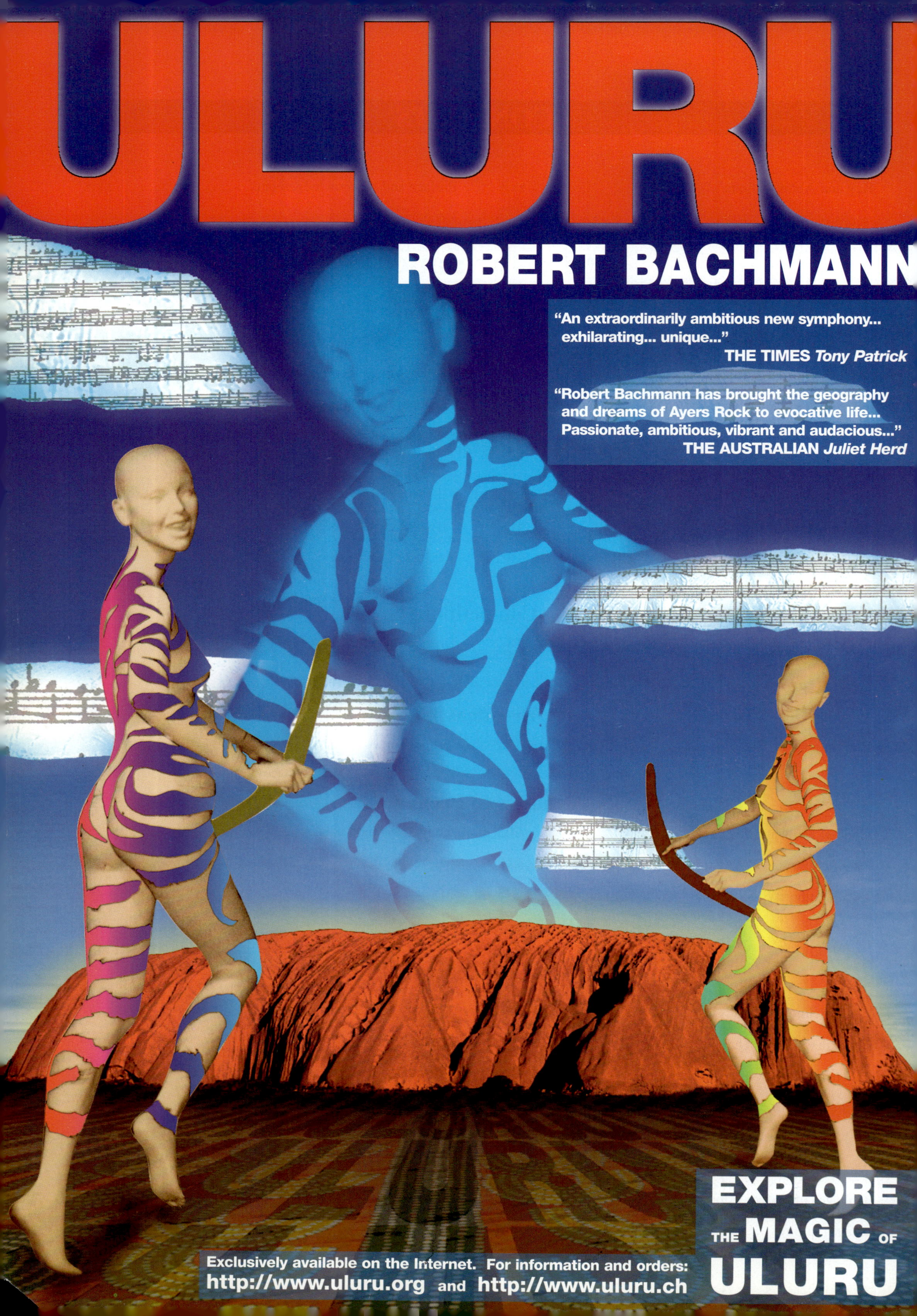
ULURU
ROBERT BACHMANN
"An extraordinarily ambitious new symphony... exhilarating... unique..."
THE TIMES Tony Patrick
"Robert Bachmann has brought the geography and dreams of Ayers Rock to evocative life... Passionate, ambitious, vibrant and audacious..."
THE AUSTRALIAN Juliet Herd
Exclusively available on the Internet. For information and orders:
http://www.uluru.org and http://www.uluru.ch
EXPLORE THE MAGIC OF ULURU

✦ Services ✦

Marketing

Suppliers and Services

Recording

✦ Organisations ✦

✦ International Directory ✦

✦ Indexes ✦

© Paul Maurer / Photo Courtesy Arquitectonica, Miami

Auditorium de Dijon, Dijon, France

© Georg Anderhub

Lucerne Culture and Congress Center, Lucerne, Switzerland

Key and Abbreviations

The geographical scope of the *British Music Yearbook* includes England, Scotland, Wales, Northern Ireland, the Isle of Man and the Channel Islands. In lists arranged in alphabetical order of places, London entries are grouped together at the beginning. The *International Directory* includes information from the rest of the world.

The postal address is followed by the full telephone, fax and email numbers. In the *British Music Yearbook* international telephone numbers are given complete wherever possible, with the UK international access code first, the country code, the local area code, followed by the subscribers number. (If dialling the number from within the relevant country, the international access code and country code are omitted and a zero is added at the front of the area code.) In the *International Directory* the UK international access code is omitted and replaced with a '+' sign.

In addition to conventional abbreviations, the following (referring mainly to voices, instruments and performing groups) are used throughout the book.

Musical Performance

acc	accompanist
bar	baritone
br	brass
bs	bass
bs-bar	bass-baritone
bsn	bassoon
cbsn	contrabassoon
chmbr	chamber
cl	clarinet
clvd	clavichord
con	contralto
cor	cor anglais
c-ten	counter-tenor
db	double-bass
eh	english horn
ens	ensemble
euph	euphonium
fl	flute
f-pno	fortepiano
gui	guitar
hn	horn
hp	harp
hpd	harpsichord
inst	instrument, instrumental
m-sop	mezzo-soprano
mus	music, musical
ob	oboe
ob d'am	oboe d'amore
orch	orchestra, orchestral
org	organ
perc	percussion
picc	piccolo
pno	piano
rcdr	recorder
sax	saxophone
sop	soprano
str	string
synth	synthesizer
tb	tuba
ten	tenor
timp	timpani
tpt	trumpet
trb	trombone
vc	violoncello
va	viola
va d'am	viola d'amore
vib	vibraphone
vn	violin
w/wind	woodwind

Organisations, Orchestras and Halls

ABRSM	Associated Board for the Royal Schools of Music
BBCPO	BBC Philharmonic
BBCSO	BBC Symphony Orchestra
BBCSSO	BBC Scottish Symphony Orchestra
BMIC	British Music Information Centre
CBSO	City of Birmingham Symphony Orchestra
ECO	English Chamber Orchestra
ENO	English National Opera
GSMD	Guildhall School of Music and Drama
LCM	London College of Music
LPO	London Philharmonic
LSO	London Symphony Orchestra
PO	Philharmonia Orchestra
QEH	Queen Elizabeth Hall
RAH	Royal Albert Hall
RAM	Royal Academy of Music
RCM	Royal College of Music
RFH	Royal Festival Hall
RLPO	Royal Liverpool Philharmonic Orchestra
RNCM	Royal Northern College of Music
ROH	Royal Opera House
RPO	Royal Philharmonic Orchestra
RSAMD	Royal Scottish Academy of Music and Drama
TCL	Trinity College London
WCMD	Welsh College of Music and Drama
WNO	Welsh National Opera

Positions

admin	administrator
arr	arranger, arranged by
asst	assistant
chmn	chairman
cond	conductor
co-ord	co-ordinator
dir	director
ed	editor
gen	general
mgr	manager, managing
mkt	marketing
offr	officer
sec	secretary
subs	subscription(s)

Other

accs	accessories
coll	collection
educ	education, educational
elec	electronic
ext	extension
jnr	junior
m/class	masterclass
snr	senior
tel	telephone number
w/end	weekend
w/shop	workshop

Click to the music

by Ashutosh Khandekar

GLOBAL MUSIC NETWORK's new website, GMN.com, is set to revolutionise the way we listen to music and interact with performers

RICHARD HAUGHTON

Movers and shakers at GMN: President David Atherton, Chairman and CEO Michael Lubin, and a recent addition to the 'family', Plácido Domingo

With its rapidly expanding resource of 300 hours of music and 100 hours of video, all accessible through its GMN.com website, Global Music Network has quickly established itself as the Internet's most dynamic site for live performances of classical music and jazz. The development of GMN.com is a rare example of a marriage between culture and technology that has extended the boundaries of both. What is more, the site also has an extraordinary interactive capacity, giving users unprecedented access to musicians, music-making and music appreciation that promises to revolutionise the way the music business as a whole, and the recording industry in particular, engages with its public.

As revolutions go, this one has gathered pace at an incredible rate since the first seeds were sown in the mid-1990s. Like many good ideas, it started with a group of lively minded people enjoying a casual drink together and trying to set the world to rights. The assembled company that laid the foundations for the development of GMN included conductor David Atherton, pianist Peter Donohoe and a leading technology entrepreneur and music fanatic Michael Lubin. In early 1996, the three found themselves in conversation in San Diego during the Mainly Mozart Festival, of which Atherton is Artistic Director and Lubin is a major sponsor. Talk centred on the demise of the music industry and, in particular, the marginalisation of classical music by record companies and broadcasters. As computer buffs, all three were interested in how the new and rapidly developing fields of information technology and communications might be harnessed to advance the work of musicians in a targeted, accessible way.

To begin with, the concept took shape as a non-profit making website for the promotion of artists, containing, for instance schedules, biographies and discographies, allowing musicians to make direct contact with their clients and audiences. By the late-1990s however, the full potential of the Internet as a global and highly interactive resource had become apparent, and once the possibility of delivering music on-line had been established, along with development of the Internet as an advertising medium, it became clear that the GMN website could become an important educational tool and a serious business proposition rather than merely a casual service.

Over the last two years, GMN.com has expanded in earnest, with Michael Lubin as Chairman and Chief Executive Officer and David Atherton as Artistic Director and President. Among the latest additions to the board is Plácido Domingo, who will also record for the company and act as Artistic Consultant. Domingo joins a growing roster of musicians from the classical and jazz world who are part of what Global Music Network calls its Family of Artists. Steve Long, who came on board in 1998 as a company Vice President responsible for production, explains what this 'family' is all about :'The great beauty of GMN.com is that it's musician-led – it was basically set up by musicians and music lovers, for musicians and music lovers. So at the core of our business, we have a group of artists who have signed an agreement that gives GMN.com exclusive rights to broadcast performances and recordings over the Internet. In return, these artists have given us a commitment to interact with people who use the website. So it's not just a question of listening to, say Tasmin Little playing a violin concerto with the Hong Kong Philharmonic, with David Atherton conducting. You'll actually be able to discuss the performance with the artists involved, click onto video clips and interviews, and generally become much more personally involved in the way music is made. It's all part of bringing music alive and giving

“GMN.com enables you to explore subtle relationships between musicians, their playing and the works that they perform, and it allows you to enhance your understanding of music by making links among the wealth of audio and textual information built into the website”

artists a chance to communicate their passion for what they do to millions of people, rather than the few hundred that can be contained in a concert hall at any one performance.'

Of the 300 hours of music (the amount is growing by the day) which can be downloaded from the GMN.com site, most has been commissioned by the company itself. 'We've also licensed recordings of our artists from record and broadcasting companies,' Steve Long adds. 'For example,

It's all part of bringing music alive and giving artists a chance to communicate their passion for what they do to millions of people, rather than the few hundred that can be contained in a concert hall at any one performance.

we have have a number of recordings from the ASV label and have negotiated to make those available directly from the site, so you can just download them and listen, and ASV get a royalty. Or you can order the CD from us and it'll be supplied through GMN's on-line distributors.'

The site will allow users to cross-reference with other music and recordings. So if you have enjoyed, say, David Goode's performance of Bach's Toccata and Fugue in D minor (and very fine it is too) you might be directed to other organ works performed by the same artist, or to music by Bach and his contemporaries that you might also enjoy, or recordings recommended by the artist himself. You can then download these works, or order a recording over the Internet.

Or there is a third, rather innovative option, says Long: 'In between buying a CD and downloading from the Internet, we'll be introducing a "customer compilation" option, where you can select a series of tracks from the site and we'll burn a CD of your chosen music and post it out to you as a one-off, bespoke recording.'

As well as being able to download music and videos of performances, a visit to GMN.com will enable you to find out more about the music itself. Contained on the website is the Grove Concise Dictionary of Music and Musicians in its entirety, giving access to huge body of historical notes, composer and performer biographies and general musical background. The site is also setting up links with international festivals and major venues such as the Wigmore Hall, so that you can be taken on a tour backstage or look up schedules for the forthcoming season. 'It's

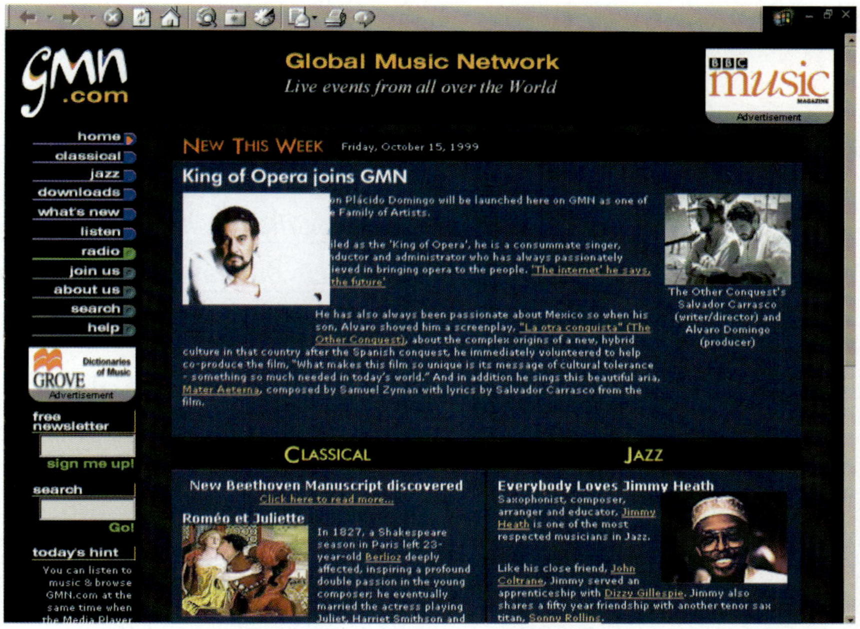

all part of – for want of a better word – "infotainment",' says Long, adding that he hopes the word never catches on. 'You listen, you look and you learn, and you're in complete control of any of these aspects of using the site.'

This educational dimension of 'infotainment' is something that the Internet handles supremely well: GMN.com enables you to explore subtle relationships between musicians, their playing and the works that they perform, and it allows you to enhance your understanding of music by making links among the wealth of audio and textual information built into the website. 'What we're aiming to do is entertain and educate,' says Long. 'But we're also looking to give classical and jazz musicians a superb showcase for their talents, and one that has been set up with both their artistic and commercial interests at heart'.

These commercial interests have been further enhanced by the launch of e-commerce, which will link users of GMN.com into a vast stock of goods which can be bought on line. 'We're aiming to give our users access to a database of around 400,000 recordings,' says Long. 'It's just like any other sort of shopping. You fill up your on-line shopping trolley, proceed to check out, pay and they all arrive in the post.' The long-term objective is to supply a wide range of products through e-commerce, encompassing such items as computers and hi-fi equipment; but initially, says Long, the aim is to focus on music-related products which complement the material available on GMN.com.

Keeping abreast of technology is another key factor in the development of Global Music Network. One of the company's guiding principles is that its website should be able to deliver complete symphonies and operas to users, not just extracts. 'What we want to be able to do is ensure that entire works can be downloaded quickly from the Net, without compromising on quality. That's something we're actively working on, and the technology is moving very rapidly.'

The quality of music downloaded from the Internet is already exceptionally high, although accessing CD-quality output will depend, of course, on your modem speed and ISP link. In the States, where cable modem is standard, you can download video excerpts of the same quality as a television broadcast. At present in Britain, modem access can get rather congested at peak hours, when downloading music and images can take a long time. Again, the pace of change means that this problem is likely to be eliminated in the near future as compression rates for audio and video signals improve.

The great beauty of GMN.com is that it's musician led - it was basically set up by musicians and music lovers, for musicians and music lovers

The next major step for GMN will be the advent of web television: 'I believe that web-tv will be a very normal way of accessing music in the home,' says Long. 'At the moment, I don't think that PCs are really integrated into people's living space – and when you listen to music, you want to incorporate it into your everyday life, in your living room. That's the beauty of television: it'll enable people to bring GMN.com off the web and into their lives. And we're not just talking about recordings. This is about the thrill of listening to music as it is made or watching an opera as it unfolds, live from St Petersburg, San Diego, Hong Kong or wherever in the world you want to go, from the comfort of your armchair.'

Engine Room

Report by Ashutosh Khandekar

Rhinegold Publishing's search engine for the music world, www.classicalsearch.com, has delivered fast, streamlined and comprehensive access to music-related websites all around the globe

We live, as we are so often reminded, in the Information Age. But as the Internet expands exponentially, the sheer amount of data from a vast range of sources is making it more and more difficult to pinpoint specific information and be sure of its accuracy. Performing a search on the web these days is becoming increasingly frustrating and bemusing: a single word can throw up hundreds of links, giving no inkling of which might be the most appropriate to one's needs.

The award-winning website, classicalsearch.com, has been developed by Rhinegold Publishing for the music world to address precisely this problem of 'information overload' on the web. It is a unique resource – a search engine that has been tailored specifically for music professionals and music lovers to give them fast, reliable access to websites that they will find useful and relevant. The idea for a guide to music-related websites grew out of the *British and International Music Yearbook*, already a hefty tome, which would have become unworkably cumbersome if it were to include all Internet sites that have proliferated in the music world over the previous year. At first, the idea was to create an on-line directory listing websites, which could then be updated through the year. After all, the thinking went, the best way to look for websites is through the web itself. But out of this solution to the *British Music Yearbook*'s immediate problems emerged a much more radical idea, as technology consultant Alan Kitcher, of AFK, explains: 'The Internet directory, which we called *Music on the Web*, had 2,300 British sites and it seemed to go down very well; but we soon discovered that we actually had a tiger by the tail – we realised that what we were dealing with was an embryonic search engine, and this is what developed and expanded into classicalsearch.com.'

All this linked up with what Kitcher had been reading in business journals about the Internet: 'The computer trade press was saying how nice it would be to have search engines which were not so all-encompassing, but were tailored to a certain area of activity. If you go into a popular search engine such as Yahoo or Excite, say, and look up 'orchestra', you're likely to get hundreds of hits, of which a fraction might contain the information you really want.'

The criticisms people have of these conventional search engines are that it is difficult to puzzle your way through the mass of links, and that once you click on the links, some of them don't work. Where more specific search engines do exist, they tend to be compiled on an amateur basis by enthusiasts in their spare time who cannot hope to be systematic in their approach. 'At Classical Search, we have set out to be totally methodical and comprehensive,' says Kitcher, 'without resorting to the indiscriminate "big is beautiful" policy of other search engines.'

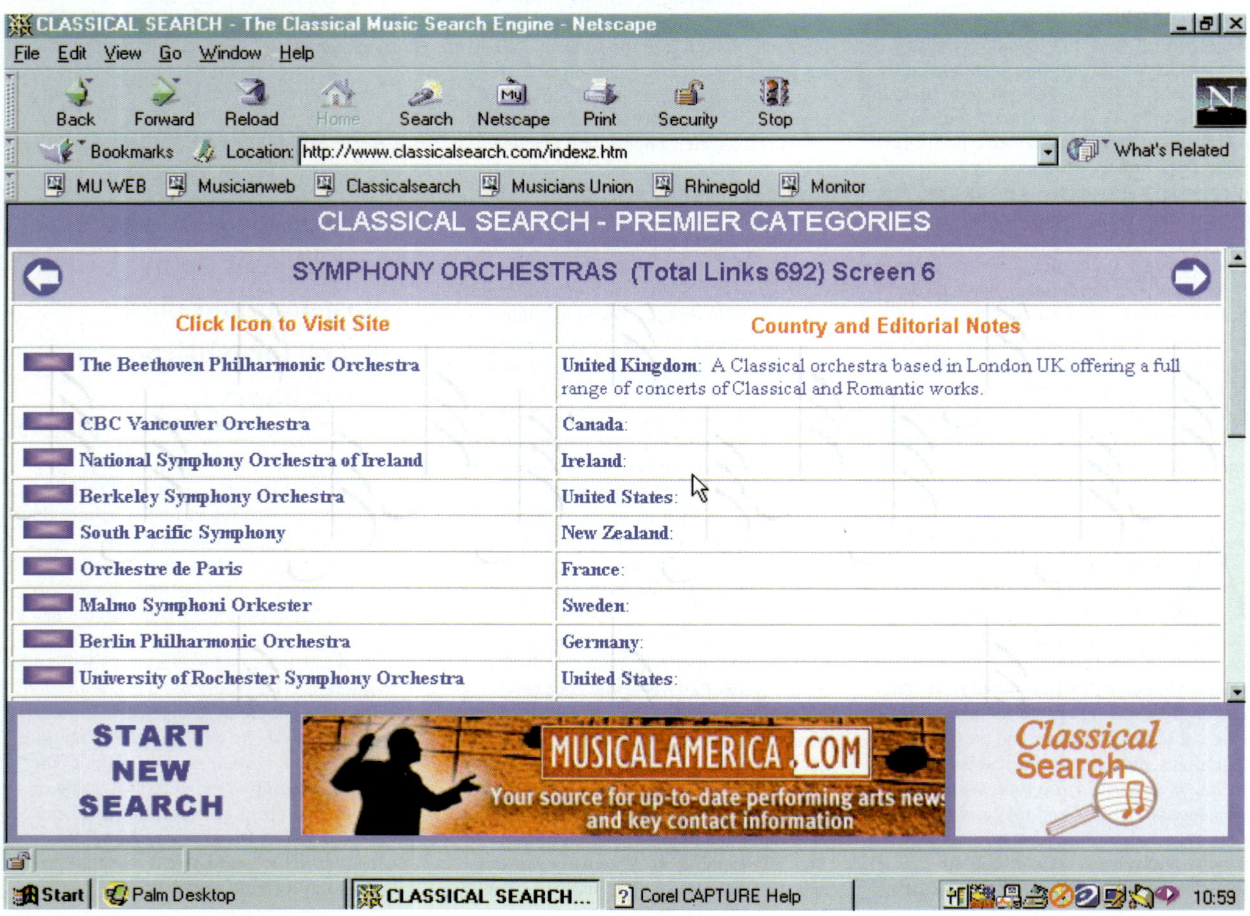

The site was launched with more than 15,000 links, and this has been growing by the day: 'In the first case we trawled around the web using conventional search engines. We called together thousands of relevant websites, then reviewed every one – one thing to note about Classical Search is you don't get on to it without being reviewed. We've also been asking people to submit their sites for validation and that's an on-going process, although in some areas, we really don't have too many more sites to add. For example, we now have the biggest aggregation of links to orchestras and to academic institutions for music of any search engine.' Furthermore, the Classical Search site is meticulously maintained: every link is checked each week to make sure it is still active and anything that appears to have gone out of use is reviewed manually. 'It's actually a way of encouraging people to maintain their website,' says Kitcher. 'Before we remove a site, we'll remind the person who submitted it that it needs to be updated and, if we've had to remove it, we'll go back and ask if they would like to resubmit their link.

Visiting classicalsearch.com enables the user to search the web in two very different ways. On one hand, there are the 'Premier Categories', a list of 13 search categories which include areas such as Performers, Organisations, Venues and Festivals, Products and Services, Management, Education, etc, most of which link into official websites containing factual information. The alternative to this is to access websites through the Music Appreciation facility, which offers a more informal forum for discussion, criticism, musical opinion and academic research. 'Music Appreciation is much more like a conventional search engine,' Kitcher explains. 'You put in your key words, but we give you themes to direct you – performance, recordings, e-zines. We'll give you the tools to try to narrow things down to what you're looking for.'

In designing the site, Kitcher looked for a somewhat different approach to the conventional search engine. 'The objective is to enable people to get as few links back as possible!' he says. 'That's a very big difference from the Alta Vistas, Excites and Yahoos of the world, who proudly boast there were tens of thousands of sites that match your criteria. We like to think that that's not what people want from a search engine, so we give our users the opportunity to narrow their search by region, by category of artist, business, voice-type, instrument, etc. These categories go down to quite a low level, 250 different ones. But we also acknowledge that some people might want more general access to a range of websites, so we've also built in the facility for people to browse more generally.'

Within weeks of its launch, classicalsearch.com received the MirandaRose Award for Educational Site of the Month in September 1999. The award is given by an association of teachers in America who are promoting the use of technology in education. And, education apart, the possibilities for Classical Search to adapt to the needs of musicians and music lovers are endless. Look out for links to sites that give details of employment opportunities in music, new record releases, and a whole range of sites which will deepen users' access to and understanding of the music world. In essence, however, the aim is that Classical Search should be a search engine that doesn't swamp you with a broad range of results, but produces results that work for you.

VALIDATING YOUR WEBSITE ON CLASSICAL SEARCH

How do you submit a website for inclusion on classicalsearch.com?

Visit **www.classicalsearch.com**. On the home page, there is a button which you can click on to in order to submit your site for inclusion. You will be asked to select a category for the site and provide a brief text description which will be displayed with the link. Your site will be validated **within a few working days**, unlike other search engines which can take several months to include a link to a new site. As far as possible, classicalsearch.com will only list a site once rather than dividing it up into individual pages. If you key in London Symphony, you'll get two entries: Orchestra and Choir. The aim is to be **as fast, simple and focused** as possible, so that you don't have to trawl your way through lots of subsidiary sites before you get to the one you want.

How do I know whether my site will be listed under the Premier Categories section or in Music Appreciation?

We are reasonably strict when it comes to including a site in the Premier Categories section. These should be submitted either by the subject of the site, or by somebody who has a professional interest in promoting them. So the link might come from an agent, a record company, a publisher or a professional body.

The Music Appreciation sector is for more informal sites which involve discussion and opinion. If you searched for, say, a composer under Premiere Categories, you would probably find an official society promoting his or her music. In the Music Appreciation site, there would be a great many more links, which might include reviews of performances and recordings or new academic research into that composer's work.

Why would a website not be included in classicalsearch.com?

As long as your site is music-related and fulfils the wide-ranging parameters of the criteria above, you should have no problem being included. If you fail to maintain your website, you will be reminded via email that the site needs updating. If this still does not happen, your site may be removed. Of course, if you are looking for a person or organisation on classicalsearch.com that does not have a website, your search will fail. That's where the **British and International Music Yearbook** remains indispensable.

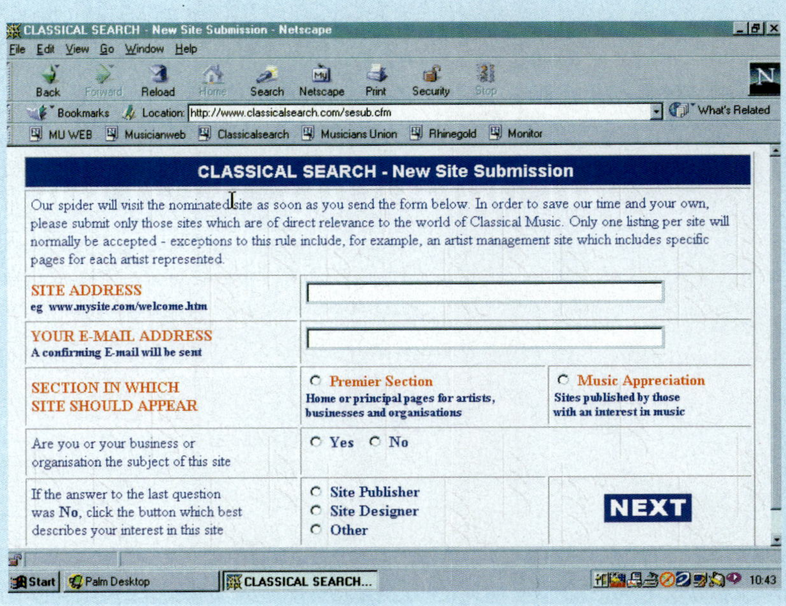

European Cities of Culture

by Simon Tait

Glasgow's arts scene continues to thrive following its year as European City of Culture in 1990

The phenomenon of the European Cities of Culture burst on the British in 1990, five years after the programme had started, when the British government was invited to nominate a city after asking for bids and Glasgow won the honour for this country against competition from the favoured Edinburgh. Now, 15 years after the programme was launched, Europe is celebrating the start of what it hopes will be a new era of co-operation and interaction between European cities, with not one but nine Cities of Culture: three from the north, three from the central regions, and three from the south. It is an integral cultural scheme unprecedented in Europe. Simultaneously, Avignon, Bergen, Bologna, Brussels, Helsinki, Krakow, Reykjavik, Prague and Santiago de Compostela are mounting arts festivals to hail the new millennium.

It is unlikely that its creators expected it to stretch across the centuries. The programme was born not in a smoke-filled room in Brussels but in a conversation between two ministers of culture, Melina Mercouri of Greece and Jack Lang of France, in 1984. "They believed culture should play a central part in a city's self-recognition," said Trevor Davies, the British director of one of the most successful years, Copenhagen's, in 1996. The European Union's cultural ministers were persuaded and the scheme got under way in 1985, "to open up to the European public particular aspects of the city, region and country concerned". The first City of Culture was Athens, followed by Florence, Amsterdam, Berlin, Paris, Glasgow, Dublin, Madrid, Antwerp, Lisbon, Luxembourg, Copenhagen, Thessaloniki, Stockholm and, in 1999, Weimar in Germany. The first to make a European theme of its year, rather than simply an arts festival was Berlin in 1988 with the Wall, coincidentally, trembling and then falling, but generally it had been seen as an excuse for a self-congratulatory pat on the back in the shape of a city festival for a few weeks of the year. "Then Glasgow in '90 showed you could use it to activate the whole city," said Mr Davies. "Glasgow put culture at the centre of politics, for the whole of the 12 months." Glasgow, a city well aware of the popular perception that its principal claims to fame seemed to be football and an inimitable brand of aggressive comedy, knew it had a great deal to offer and, despite Edinburgh's international cultural reputation through its annual festival, won the nomination.

Under the direction of Robert Palmer, Glasgow saw the opportunity to not only celebrate its outstanding, though for too many unsuspected, cultural excellence, but to bring tourists to the city. It managed to raise an unprecedented £40 million in sponsorship support, and the city has never looked back - this year it is Britain's City of Architecture.

"Glasgow changed the significance of the years of culture," said Mr Palmer, who now finds himself in charge of Brussels 2000, and so becomes something of a godfather to the concept conceived by Mercouri and Lang. "The programme started off in '85 as a celebration in a series of arts festivals, but Glasgow moved it on to utilise the opportunity to develop itself and involve its citizens." The concept, he said, has developed further to build a spirit of co-operation, manifested properly for the first time in 2000, and from an economic purpose as tourist attraction to social purpose as developing art and artists. At the height of 1990 Glasgow's population was multiplied ten fold, and tourism was 300 per cent up from 1989. That has been sustained, with Glaswegians now expressing a new-found pride in their city.

Copenhagen had a similarly low point of self-regard from which to build. "We've taken it as a cultural development project, taking up what needs to be supported, what needs to be nurtured in the city where some projects have been starved for years," Trevor Davies said at the time, and the legacy has been permanent infrastructure, including a contemporary art gallery, a new opera house and the Copenhagen Jazz House.

Now the scheme is projecting towards the horizon of 2019. Britain is due to get its chance again in 2008, and Culture Secretary Chris Smith has already called for bids. He is giving them two years to work up their submissions against criteria yet to be announced, but he has emphasised that he wants not simply a city that already has a pre-eminent cultural reputation, but one which, like Glasgow and Copenhagen, will use the title to develop and innovate. He will announce the winner in 2003, giving them five years to prepare.

"To be European Capital of Culture is an honour and an opportunity," Mr Smith said. "As a showcase for a city's cultural and creative life, it is second to none. As a way of getting the best possible results from cultural regeneration, the designation provides a real boost to the holder."

Mr Palmer has already received more than a dozen approaches from British cities interested in taking up the challenge, and anxious to know what the secret of Glasgow's success was. "I tell them it's belief in your city, the taxi-driver test – if the driver in the cab from the airport talks up the city's cultural attributes, it's got a good basis."

The idea of years shared between cities will continue in 2001 when the Cities of Culture are Rotterdam and Oporto, with Brugge and Salamanca in 2002, Graz by itself in 2003, and in 2004 Genoa and Lille. Then the title changes slightly to become European Capital of Culture, to reflect a more outward-looking approach to Europe which the European Union hopes cities will adopt. The cities have not yet been selected, but they will be in Ireland, Netherlands, Luxembourg again, United Kingdom, Austria, Germany, Finland, Portugal, France, Sweden, Belgium, Spain, Denmark, Greece and Italy.

However, there are concerns about funding for the future. In 1997 the European Commission allocated 200,000 Euros, (£133,000), in 1998 a total of 250,000 Euros (£166,000) and in 1999 a total of 350,000 Euros (£233,000) to the respective cities as a contribution to projects and other initiatives. Now, as the year 2000 is upon us, the nine Cities of Culture are extremely concerned about the possible EU budget for this programme. In the "First Framework Programme of the European Community in Support for Culture (2000-2004)" presented by the Commission in May 1998, the finance being proposed for the nine Cities of Culture of the year 2000 was only 2.5 million Euros (£1.6 million). This would amount to 277,777 Euros (£185,000) for each city, which is less than half the amount allocated to Stockholm in 1998 and Weimar in 1999 who, between them, received 600,000 Euros (£400,000).

With 'Kaleidoscope', the EC programme which funds the Cities of Culture, being wound up in 1999 to be succeeded by a wider-reaching scheme called Culture 2000, there are urgent discussions within the

ARNO DE LA CHAPELLE

Helsinki's Kide will form part of a sound and light tunnel

ONE LITTLE INDIAN RECORDS

Björk, the Icelandic pop star, heads Reykjavik's celebrations

Commission and with the cities on whether the estimated amount is unfair, whether it will create significant problems for each city and whether the EU may be in for serious embarrassment over a scheme which it has already committed to far into the future. Those discussions are likely to continue well into 2000, and until the Culture 2000 programme itself is fine-tuned.

It is not, according to Robert Palmer, so much the amount of the contribution, rather the importance of the gesture for Europe. The EC contribution works out at between three and five per cent of the costs, with the cities themselves contributing probably a third to a half of the costs, and the rest coming from sponsorship. Helsinki is a good example. The city's celebrations are costing 50 million Euros, (£33 million), which puts the EU contribution into perspective. It cites three sources for the financing: the city itself and its neighbours Espoo, Vantaa and Kauniainen; the Finnish Government; and the sponsorship of companies such as Finnair, the Helsinki Telephone Corporation, ICL and Nokia. What Helsinki wants out of the year is international awareness of its "lively culture and many-faceted know-how", and an improvement in the quality of everyday life for its citizens. "The EU contribution is so marginal as to be inconsequential, but the City of Culture has become very important to Europeans who will not be impressed if the EU are seen to be regarding it as too insignificant to allocate a respectable amount of money to," said Robert Palmer.

Meanwhile, the nine cities themselves are pressing on with programmes which both celebrate their indigenous cultural profiles, and joint initiatives with a communal will which should impress the EU. The sharing approach instituted for 2000 is a response to the policy expressed by the Council of Ministers, and announced when they designated the nine in November 1995. Despite disappointment over the level of funding, the nine have been co-operating closely and intensively since 1996 in a cultural collaboration unprecedented in Europe.

Helsinki has already set the spirit of communication alive with Kide, meaning crystal. This glass sound-and-light artwork, nine crystals each standing ten feet tall, twelve feet wide and six feet deep, but each with a different combination of colours and sounds, is Helsinki's greeting to the other Cities of Culture. In the autumn of 1999, one was sent to each of the partners to be displayed in the city's centre. The other eight sites will be visible in a monitor next to each Kide, and each one will react electronically to the environment and retain its reactions. At the turn of the millennium the crystals will return, with their unique records, to Helsinki where they will be put together to become a sound-and-light tunnel.

Helsinki's other events for the year include Spain's Placido Domingo at the Olympic stadium; an international festival of baroque music in which the other Cities of Culture will be represented by baroque ensembles from Prague and Bergen; the

Bergen, birth-place of Edvard Grieg, celebrates its cultural heritage in the next millennium

oldest symphonic orchestra in the United States, the Philadelphia Orchestra, will be performing as special guests - this was also the first American orchestra to perform Jean Sibelius's Symphonies No. 5, 6 and 7 giving Finland's greatest composer international credibility. A snow church is to be built (for the second time) in Helsinki's Senate Square, a scaled down version of the wooden Church of Ulrika Eleonora that originally stood on the site, and church services will be held inside.

Showing northern European cosmopolitanism, the organisers have christened the opening event of the sailing season 'Fish and Ships', a weekend-long event with sea shanties and accordion playing, jetty dances and sailings for the public. And a more contemporary art form is scheduled with Nouveau Cirque, a spectacular of street theatre, acrobatics, fireworks, joie de vivre and flavours of the Mediterranean with the French Cirque Plume group.

Reykjavik's transcendent contribution to Europe's contemporary popular culture has been the singer Björk, and the city's unique gift to Europeanism is to centre on her. Björk has been working with ten choristers aged from 16 to 23 from each of the nine countries, brought together as a choir which will make its debut at a New Year's Eve concert in Reykjavik, and later in the year will tour the other eight. Their repertoire is to consist of music from each venue, with the whole choir singing in the native language of each city. The distinguished Estonian composer Arvo Pärt has written a special anthem for them, and there will also be music by Björk herself.

Reykjavik is using its role as a European City of Culture to open new facilities. Reykjavik Municipal Art Museum opens a branch at the Harbour House. Museum House will bring together the city's library, archives and museum of photography. The City Theatre will get a new stage which will have the premiere of a play about Iceland's romantic poet Jonas Hallgrimson. And celebrity swimmers will open a thermal beach at Nautholsvik, where the unique geothermal system creates sea temperatures of 20 degrees.

Krakow's plans for Codex Calixtinus were presented in 1998 as the city's main event for 2000. The Association of European Cities of Culture and the other participants asked to be involved, making it a pan-European exploration of the musical past. The Codex is a 12th century manuscript housed, appropriately, in the Cathedral in Santiago which takes its name from Pope Calixtinus, who may have been the author of some fragments of the work. Its five books depict the legend of St James, but it also relates the alleged journey of Charlemagne and Roland to Santiago, and a description of routes leading to it through France and Spain. In other words, it is regarded as the first tourist guide.

But what the Codex also contains is a rich and comprehensive repertoire of liturgical songs designed for splendid ceremonies in honour of St James in July. The homage to the Codex which Krakow is to pay is in the form of a concert based on the historic annotation of the chants, led by Polish experts who have made a particular study of the manuscript and the music. Although no record has survived to explain how church music was performed 800 years ago, research has reconstructed it as closely as possible, and an international choir and soloists will give the concert in each of the nine cities in the course of the year.

Krakow also has a Beethoven Festival, a three-day street theatre event, a week of puppet theatre for children, and Café Europe, an international literary event. And the work of one of Krakow's most famous sons, the artist Tadeusz Kantor, who died in 1990, is to be celebrated with events and exhibitions throughout the year.

Bergen, essentially a maritime city, is presenting three projects which co-operate with other Cities of Culture. The first is Green Voyage in which students from all nine cities will examine the coast and waterways of Norway to make art. More focused is ArtNaust, for which six professional artists from the Nordic cities, Bergen, Helsinki and Reykjavik, will make a single work of art on the theme of the boathouse, arrival and departure, which will be seen in all three cities. Life by the North Atlantic Ocean is an exhibition mounted in co-operation with Reykjavik and Santiago about the development of the fisheries in the North Atlantic, and will be the first major show in the new Coastal Culture Centre. A highlight will be in April when the Polish composer Krzystof Penderecki conducts the Bergen Philharmonic in his own masterpiece, the St Luke Passion, with guest players from Krakow taking part. A highlight of a different kind will be Cleopatra's Needles, when 100 cassette radios and a saxophone quartet perform in the open around an ivy-clad cottage.

Prague is giving Telelink, an international electronic clearing house for all the cultural events associated with the Cities of Culture 2000 for television broadcasters anywhere, while Bologna has teamed up with Helsinki to give Europe Café Nine. This is an electronic café providing a platform for exchange on internet arts and new media projects of all kinds as they develop in the nine cities during 2000.

Prague sees itself as a City of Open Gates, a crossroads of cultural movements and influences, and its programme has been compiled to represent this. Its events include Le Complement, a drama project involving artists from several European counties; Opera North's production of Martinù's opera Julietta at Prague's National Theatre; the Transe Danse Europe project with dancers from the nine Cities of Culture 2000; and The New York Philharmonic Orchestra. One special event for Prague which is unlikely to be repeated elsewhere is an international congress of European bell founders, at which the first Czech mobile glockenspiel will be presented.

Brussels is to tackle head-on one of the principal concerns about the coming age: city life in the future. The city is the central subject for the year here, and a co-operation with the other cities of culture of the year 2000 focuses on urbanism and the role of the artist in the public space. Two separate projects are being developed. Walk About/Stalk, an artistic intervention in the urban space by two young dancers/choreographers, two young architects and two young musicians in Brussels, Helsinki, Bergen, Reykjavik, Krakow and, in lieu of Avignon, Marseilles. And for The House of the Nine Cities, nine young artists from one of the cities have been invited to present their work at the occasion of the opening weekend of Brussels 2000 in February.

Other important events in Brussels include a retrospective of the work of the composer Olivier Messiaen in four different venues, led by the British pianist Peter Donohoe. Another British artist, the choreographer William Forsythe, is creating a new ballet for the year, called Endless House, with the Ballet de Francfort, and jazz sessions are to take place in some of the least accessible venues in the city, under the title of Secret Public.

Santiago's border-crossing event is Faces of the Earth, an exhibition about Europe's contribution to the worldwide cartography in territory and ocean maps, and its influence on universal knowledge of the earth. This is being curated with help from Reykjavik, Krakow and Helsinki.

Santiago is also planning a music festival devised to illustrate not only the musical life of Compostela but also the city's communion with other cultures. A Cineuropa film festival is also planned, and the cultures of sport and circus combine for Clown Futbol, a serious piece of comedy theatre created by actors and technicians from Spain, Holland and Italy.

Bolgona is remodelling itself for the year, at a cost of 170 billion lire (£6 million). A Multimedia Library (Biblioteca Multimediale) is being created in the former stock exchange, the Sala Borsa; a tobacco factory has become a centre for exhibitions and workshops; public buildings in the Piazza Maggiore are being renovated, extended and even removed; a Music Museum has been installed at the Palazzo Sanguinetti; and a National Centre for Women has been created in the former Convento di Santa Cristina.

Communication is the theme for Bologna 2000, which has a scientific committee co-ordinated by the scientist and novelist Umberto Eco. The work of major European 20th century artists such as Munch, Bacon and Fontana will be displayed at Gallery of Modern Art, and Giacometti, Cézanne and Klee at the Morandi Museum. Film director Peter Greenaway will direct the light and sound installations from the city's Two Towers to San Luca's Church. Almost six hundred projects and initiatives have been chosen from nine hundred proposed by institutions, their joint aim being to promote Bologna both domestically and internationally, and to create opportunities for local institutions to grow.

Avignon is setting its first foot into the new age with a masked ball celebrating not just Europe but all six continents, and Avignon's associations with other cultures on the medieval ramparts of the ancient community. Six giant podiums bearing musicians offering music representing the six continents and commissioned by six musical magazines will create the inaugural atmosphere.

The city's own emblem for the year is Beauty, and in April Avignon is handed over to its children, the generation of the 21st century. In August a festival of theatre will fill the Palace of the Popes, and there is to be a new French-American film festival, while in September, a great feast will take place celebrating the harvesting of the grapes, and the famous cuisine of Provence.

The EU sees the year 2000 as an opportunity to move the concept of the year of culture forward, but also outward. Robert Palmer hopes that it will not become a victim of the kind of competition between cities that comes with sport. "I hope it retains the spirit of cultural capitals rather than cultural capital, a kind of Olympics in which making money is the vital factor," he said. "That's a danger that would distract from the original objective – make art and help make artists."

Preface and Acknowledgements

Welcome to the 2000 edition of the British and International Music Yearbook. Once again this volume of information has been revised, updated and amended, and I must begin by thanking all who ensured that proof forms were returned to us. A publication such as this very much depends on the goodwill of its entrants in ensuring that their own listings are kept up to date, so prompt returning of forms is very much appreciated.

With significant alterations made to the 1999 edition, the aim for the 2000 edition has been to keep changes to the layout and order of the book as minimal as possible. There are changes and improvements to the content, however, and these are outlined below.

With the new millennium come new telephone dialling codes. As of 22 April 2000, changes planned by OFTEL to some national and local dialling codes will be implemented, with six areas being affected: London, Southampton, Portsmouth, Coventry, Cardiff and Northern Ireland. New numbers will consist of an area code plus an eight-digit local number. The new national area codes have been working parallel to the old codes since June 1999, and this will continue until April 2000. However, for local numbers there is no period of parallel running of the old and new forms; instead there will be a flash change to the new eight-digit numbers at midnight 22 April 2000.

The telephone number changes are not limited just to national and local numbers; mobile telephone and pager numbers are being altered in order that these codes will begin 07. As with the national dialling codes, there is a period of parallel running of the new and old mobile and pager numbers - this will run from September 1999 to April 2001.

This edition of the yearbook incorporates all these new dialling codes, including the new mobile and pager codes. For further information regarding the new codes, please contact your telephone company or service provider.

Smaller changes to the 2000 edition include a new section on Wind Bands which can be found with the Military and Brass Bands. There is also a new international index which includes all international listings by country. We hope that this will make the section more user-friendly, and enable readers to see at a glance all entries for a particular country.

Staying with the international section, in the coming years we hope to raise the profile of the section by overhauling, improving and extending the listings. To bring an international flavour to this edition, however, we have included an article on the European Cities of Culture. To mark the millennium, instead of just one city of culture, nine cities have been selected. Turn to Simon Tait's article on page (xxiii) to find out more.

1999 saw significant developments to Rhinegold's web page, Music on the Web. What started as a practical solution to lack of space in the book has now been transformed into a comprehensive classical music search engine. Music on the Web was relaunched as Classical Search earlier this year as Ashutosh Khandekar explains on page (xx).

As always, a great deal of hard work has gone into making this book a success, and it only remains for me to thank all the people involved in producing this edition. My thanks go to the contributors, Simon Tait and Ashutosh Khandekar, and also to Alan Kitcher for his technical expertise in ensuring all the new telephone numbers have been incorporated correctly. Finally, special thanks go to Claire Throp and Henry Watson for their invaluable commitment and support.

Earlier this year, Julian Caedmon Diggle, a much-valued friend and colleague of the British Music Yearbook's team, lost his fight against cancer, aged 24. This edition is dedicated to his memory.

Louise Head
London 1999

Editor
Louise Head

Assistant Editors
Henry Watson
Claire Throp

Publishing Manager
Sarah Williams

Deputy Publishing Manager
Robert Holmes

Advertising Sales
Stuart Brightwell
Tim Holmes
James Geer

Advertising Administrator
Charlotte Dettmer

Advertising Production
Natalie Tayoro
Nick Watts

Head of Design
Sharon Gallagher

Designers
Steve Talkington
Hallam Bannister
Phil Wingrove

Book Sales Administrator
Penny Mills

Marketing Manager
Richard Thomas

Marketing Director
Keith Diggle

Managing Director
Tony Gamble

Performance

GABOR MESZAROS

IVANO TORRE

Strumentisti

ELISAVETA BLUMINA, piano
- •• MARIA LUISA CANTOS, piano
- • OLIVIER DARBELLAY, corno e violoncello - *french horn and cello*
- • BRUNO GROSSI, flauto

MARC LAFORET, piano
- • GABOR MESZAROS, fagotto - *bassoon*
- • HANNES MEYER, organo

BRANIMIR SLOKAR, trombone
- • MARC TEICHOLZ, chitarra - *guitar*

Attrazioni speciali

KOL SIMCHA, contemporary Klezmer, piano-clarinetto-flauto contrabbasso-percussioni
- • IVANO TORRE, percussioni e composizione, incontro-scontro-incrocio tra musica classica e jazz. Diversi ensembles: percussioni-saxofoni-violoncello-fisarmonica-tuba-trombone-clarinetto-conchiglie
- • QUARTETTO TORRES E LA MAYA, chitarra classica e danza

ENSEMBLE OF FOLK MUSIC DIVOGRAY, musica folcloristica, classica e moderna dall'Ucraina

TRIO OF BANDURA PLAYERS UKRAINKA, canti folcloristici e classici accompagnati con il "bandura"

Circolo Musicale
Emilia Tonolla-Rosa
6558 Lostallo
Switzerland
Tel. +41 91 / 830 12 88
Fax +41 91 / 830 15 55
etonolla@ticino.com

Ensembles

DUO EISENHOFFER-SLOKAR, arpa-trombone

21ST CENTURY DUO, piano-violoncello

JESS-TRIO-WIEN, piano-violino-violoncello

SPILLER TRIO, piano-violino-violoncello
- • TRIO ADORJÁN-CHUMACHENKO-LYSY, flauto-violino-viola
- • QUARTETTO TORRES, chitarre, *guitars*

SLOKAR QUARTET, tromboni
- • IL NONETTO SVIZZERO-THE SWISS NONET, violino-viola-violoncello-contrabasso-flauto oboe-clarinetto-fagotto-corno

I FIATI ITALIANI-SOLISTI TEATINI, oboi-clarinetti-fagotti-corni-pianoforte a quattro mani *oboes-clarinets-bassoons-horns-four-hands piano*

I CAMERISTI LOMBARDI, orchestra da camera

HUNGARIAN VIRTUOSI, orchestra da camera

KIEV CHAMBER ORCHESTRA, orchestra da camera

THE ZAGREB SOLOISTS, orchestra da camera

THE ZAGREB SOLOISTS

Conductor

PEI-YU CHANG

senza segno : in certi Paesi questi musicisti o ensembles sono rappresentati da altre agenzie. Diamo informazioni.
Unmarked : these musicians or ensembles are represented in some Countries by other agencies.Information on request
• : rappresentanza generale - general representative

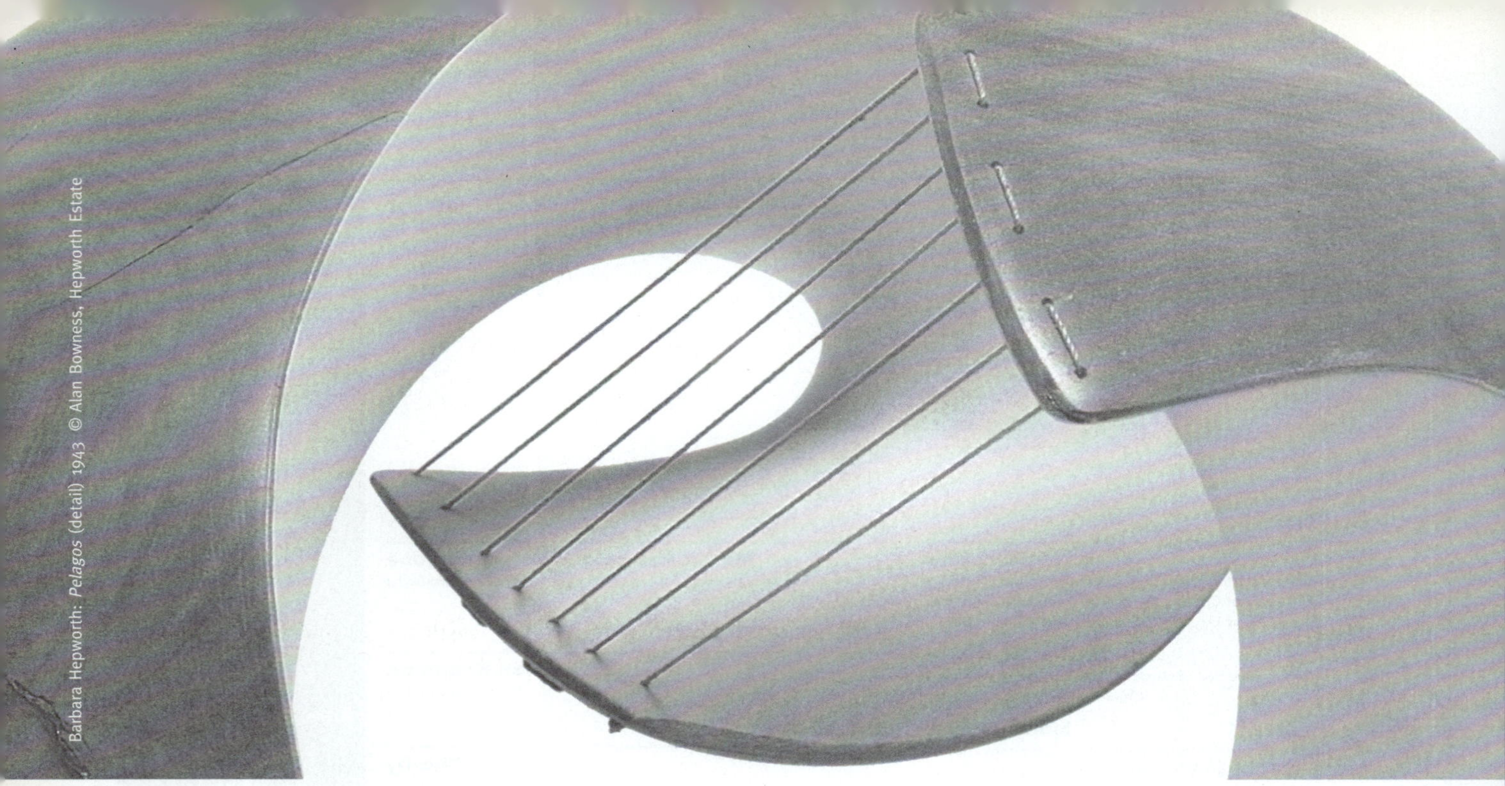

Barbara Hepworth: *Pelagos* (detail) 1943 © Alan Bowness, Hepworth Estate

Agents and Managers

Artists wishing to register with a concert agency or artist management company should be aware of what services an agent or manager can provide. All those listed below may assist with the administration of engagements already secured by the performer. Additionally, agents may find work on behalf of the artists they represent, and may also undertake to provide an employer (eg opera house, music club) with artists for a given performance. The agencies listed below all represent two or more classical artists or groups within the UK.

The **Incorporated Society of Musicians** (10 Stratford Pl, London W1N 9AE *tel:* 020 7629 4413 *fax:* 020 7408 1538 *email:* membership@ism.org *website:* www.ism.org) publishes an information sheet, free to members, on the artist/agent relationship and how to approach an agent or manager.

Membership of the **International Artist Managers' Association** (*formerly* BACA) (41a Lonsdale Rd, London W11 2BY *tel:* 020 7243 2598 *fax:* 020 7610 4994 *email:* iama@easynet.co.uk) is indicated by an asterisk.

ADM	AD Management
CDI	Concert Directory International
DCM	Daniels Concert Management
GIA	Georgina Ivor Associates
HP	Harrison Parrott
KDM	Karen Durant Management
LA	London Artists
LM	London Musicians
NBM	NB Management
NCCP	Neil Chaffey Concert Promotions
NWA	N W Artists
OCA	Opera and Concert Artists
OWM	Owen/White Management
PA	Performing Arts
PGM	Patrick Garvey Management
SJM	Sylvia Junge Management
SS	Simply Singers
SWA	Stephannie Williams Artists
THA	Terry Harrison Artists Management
VWM	Van Walsum Management
WWA	World Wide Artists
YCAT	Young Concert Artists Trust

ARTISTS' LIST 1999

ATHOLE STILL INTERNATIONAL MANAGEMENT LTD

CONDUCTORS

Guido Ajmone-Marsan	W
Dietfried Bernet	W
Noel Davies	W
Andrew Greenwood	W
Hilary Griffiths	W*
James Kelleher	W
Günter Neuhold	W*
Donald Runnicles	□

ENSEMBLES

Ensemble 415	W_4

SOPRANOS

Maria Abajan	W*
Georgina Benza	W
Elena Brilova	W
Raphaelle Farman	W
Helen Field	W
Jacquelyn Fugelle	W
Juliette Galstian	W
Cornelia Götz	W
Cynthia Haymon	W
Cynthia Makris	W*
Denia Mazzola	W
Karen Notare	W
Sue Patchell	W*
Nina Pavlovski	W*
Gail Pearson	W
Claire Primrose	W
Ashley Putnam	W_1
Nina Rautio	W
Soya Smolyaninova	W*
Penelope Thorn	W
Christine Weidinger	W

MEZZO SOPRANOS

Angela Hickey	W
Maria José Trullu	W_2
Natascha Petrinsky	W_3
Ilia Aramayo Sandivari	W
Cécile Van de Sant	W
Gabriella Sborgi	W_2
Patricia Spence	W
Nuala Willis	W

COUNTER TENOR

Ricard Bordas	W
Martin Oro	W

W = GENERAL MANAGEMENT
□ = GB/SUNDRY TERRITORIES
E = EUROPE
* = NON EXCLUSIVE

1 = ex USA/Canada
2 = ex Italy
3 = ex Germany/Austria
4 = ex Switzerland

STAGE DIRECTORS/DESIGNERS

Mike Ashman	W
Tim Coleman	W
Spyros Koskinas	W
Stefanos Lazaridis	W*
John Lloyd Davies	W
Stephen Medcalf	W
John Pascoe	W
Keith Warner	W

TENORS

Terje Andersen	W
Pietro Ballo	W*
Edmund Barham	W
Evan Bowers	W
John Duykers	E
Francis Egerton	W
Bruce Ford	W_1
Stuart Kale	W
Justin Lavender	W
Gianni Mongiardino	W
Shalva Mukeria	W
Patrick Power	W
Jorma Silvasti	W*
Graham Sanders	W_3
Ian Thompson	W
Bradley Williams	E
Alan Woodrow	W
Charles Workman	W
Boiko Zvetanov	W*

BARITONES

Lado Ataneli	W*
Sigmund Cowan	W_1
Mark Glanville	W
John Hancock	E
Carlos Marin	W
Anthony Marber	W
Daniel Mobbs	E
Louis Otey	W_1
Stephen Owen	W
Malcolm Rivers	W
Andrew Rupp	W
Russell Smythe	W

BASSES

Mark Beesley	W
Eric Garrett	W
Manfred Hemm	W*
Brian Jauhiainen	W_1
Jyrki Korhonen	W
Daniel Lewis Williams	W_2
Frode Olsen	W
Matti Salminen	W*
Giovanni Tarasconi	W*
Tómas Tómasson	W

ATHOLE STILL INTERNATIONAL MANAGEMENT LTD

FORESTERS HALL
25-27 WESTOW STREET
LONDON SE19 3RY
TEL: 0181 771 5271 (6 LINES)
FAX: 0181 771 8172
E-MAIL ADDRESS:
ATHOLE@DIAL.PIPEX.COM

AD Management. 68 High St, Malmesbury, Wilts SN16 9AT *tel:* 01666 824748 *fax:* 01666 824374. Alex Durston, mgr.

Alexander European Management. 38 Lytton Grove, Putney, London SW15 2HB *tel:* 020 8780 9377 *fax:* 020 8788 1481. David Bartleet, dir.

* **Allied Artists Agency.** 42 Montpelier Square, London SW7 1JZ *tel:* 020 7589 6243 *fax:* 020 7581 5269 *email:* info@alliedartists.co.uk. Andrew Rosner, Robert Slotover, partners.

Anglo-Swiss Artists' Management Ltd. Suite 35-37, Morley House, 320 Regent St, London W1R 5AD *tel:* 020 7323 2147 *fax:* 020 7323 1760. Susanne Baumgartner, artists mgr; Leor Segal, consultant.

Annon Music Services - Anne Hancox. 44 Cromwell Rd, Canterbury CT1 3LE *tel:* 01227 463867 *also fax;* 07970 855816 *email:* annon@clara.net. Anne Hancox, mgr.

Anthony Abbott Music Management. Medlar Cottage, Lodge Lane, Keymer, Hassocks, W Sussex BN6 8NA *tel:* 01273 843348 *fax:* 01273 846585. *Concert, tours and event management; personal representation.*

Anthony Purkiss. 35 Fonthill Rd, Hove, E Sussex BN3 6HB *tel:* 01273 774730 *also fax.*

Antony Pristavec. 79 Norbury Cres, London SW16 4JT *tel:* 020 8679 0369 *fax:* 020 8679 9399 *email:* Pristavec@aol.com. Antony Pristavec, dir.

Apollo Group of London. Gatekeepers, 77 Gordon Ave, Stanmore, Middx HA7 3QR *tel:* 020 8954 4646. Barbara Davies, Trevor Richards, dirs.

* **Askonas Holt Ltd.** Lonsdale Chambers, 27 Chancery Lane, London WC2A 1PF *tel:* 020 7400 1700 *fax:* 020 7400 1799 *email:* info@askonasholt.co.uk. Martin Campbell-White, Robert Rattray, chief execs.

* **Athole Still International Management Ltd.** Foresters Hall, 25-27 Westow St, London SE19 3RY *tel:* 020 8771 5271 *fax:* 020 8771 8172 *email:* athole@dial.pipex.com. Athole Still, mgr dir; Isobel Still, deputy mgr dir; Christopher Broom, Scott Cooper, Robert Haitink, Roxane Still, artists mgrs.

Barber *see* Valerie Barber PR & Personal Management Ltd.

Blythe *see* Jennie Blythe Artists' Management.

Boddy *see* John Boddy Agency.

Bray Artists Management. Savoia House, Bray Rd, Bray, Berks SL6 1UQ *tel:* 01628 630040 *fax:* 01628 673888. Roger Edwards, proprietor.

Brunskill Management Ltd. Suite 8a, 169 Queens Gate, London SW7 5HE *tel:* 020 7581 3388 *fax:* 020 7589 9460 *email:* contact@brunskill.com.

* **C & M Craig Services Limited (Mary Craig).** 3 Kersley St, London SW11 4PR *tel:* 020 7228 4855; 020 7978 4715 *fax:* 020 7223 2189 *email:* mary.craig@mcmail.com. Mary Craig, dir.

Camerata Artists (International Artists Management). 4 Margaret Rd, Birmingham B17 0EU *tel:* 0121 426 6208 *fax:* 0121 608 0676. John Humphreys.

Caroline Ireland Management. Uwchlaw'r Coed, Llanbedr, Gwynedd LL45 2NA *tel:* 01341 241532 *also fax; email:* caroline.ireland@virgin.net.

* **Caroline Phillips Management.** Tailor House, 63-65 High St, Whitwell, Herts SG4 8AH *tel:* 01438 871828 *fax:* 01438 871838 *email:* cphillips@caroline-phillips.co.uk. Caroline Phillips; Sylvia Carrasco-Oñate, artists mgr.

Carroll Artist Management. 11 Palmerston Place, Edinburgh EH12 5AF *tel:* 0131 225 2006 *also fax.* F J Carroll, dir.

Chameleon Arts Management. 32 St Michael's Rd, Sandhurst, Berks GU47 8HE *tel:* 01252 873313 *fax:* 01252 871517 *email:* CamArts@dial.pipex.com. Andrew Phillips, dir.

Charles McK Finch Artists' Management. 23 Farm Rd, Morden, Surrey SM4 6RA *tel:* 020 8648 8852 *fax:* 020 8687 1741.

* **Christa Phelps.** 6 Malvern Rd, London E8 3LT *tel:* 020 7254 1006 *fax:* 020 7254 1086 *email:* christa.phelps@talk21.com. Christa Phelps.

Christine Talbot-Cooper. Stoneville Cottage, Gretton Fields, Cheltenham, Glos GL54 5HH *tel:* 01242 620736 *also fax.* Christine Talbot-Cooper.

Chuck Julian Associates. Suite 51, 26 Charing Cross Rd, London WC2H 0DH *tel:* 020 7437 4248; 020 7240 1301 *fax:* 020 7240 1296 *email:* admin@cjagency.demon.co.uk. Chuck Julian, Sue Yager, Anita Alraun, associates.

* **Clarion/Seven Muses.** 47 Whitehall Park, London N19 3TW *tel:* 020 7272 4413/5125/8448 *fax:* 020 7281 9687 *email:* c7m@dircon.co.uk. Nicholas Curry, Caroline Oakes, partners, artists mgrs; Alan Coates, snr artists mgr; Costas Peristianis, artistic asst.

CMG Artists. 1st Floor, 105 Ferndale Rd, London SW4 7RL *tel:* 020 7207 3564 *fax:* 020 7652 0979 *email:* cmg@cgrist.demon.co.uk. Chris Grist, dir.

* **Columbia Artists Management Ltd.** 28 Cheverton Rd, London N19 3AY *tel:* 020 7272 8020 *fax:* 020 7272 8991. Judith Salpeter, dir; Sergei Selivanov, touring dir.

Concert Directory International (CDI). Lyndhurst, Denton Rd, Ben Rhydding, Ilkley, W Yorks LS29 8QR *tel:* 01943 607821 *fax:* 01943 817063. Catherine Scott, dir.

* **Connaught Artists Management Ltd.** 2 Molasses Row, Plantation Wharf, London SW11 3UX *tel:* 020 7738 0017 *fax:* 07070 603710 *email:* classicalmusic@connaughtartists.com. Jill Segal, Patrick Allen, dirs.

Craig ***see*** C & M Craig Services Limited (Mary Craig).

Cruickshank Cazenove Ltd. 97 Old South Lambeth Rd, London SW8 1XU *tel:* 020 7735 2933 *fax:* 020 7820 1081. Harriet Cruickshank, mgr dir. *Opera producers, choreographers and designers only.*

Daniels Concert Management (DCM). 63 Marlborough Mansions, Cannon Hill, London NW6 1JS *tel:* 020 7794 9108 *also fax; email:* m@woolf90.freeserve.co.uk. M Daniels, C Daniels, dirs.

Darren Ockert Management. The Young Vic, 66 The Cut, South Bank, London SE1 8LZ *tel:* 020 7928 8353 *fax:* 020 7928 8505 *email:* darrenockert@easynet.co.uk. Darren Ockert, mgr dir.

* **Denny Lyster Artists' Management.** 25 Courthope Rd, London NW3 2LE *tel:* 020 7485 5932 *fax:* 020 7267 0179. Denny Lyster, dir.

Donald Scrimgeour. 49 Springcroft Ave, London N2 9JH *tel:* 020 8444 6248 *fax:* 020 8883 9751. Donald E Scrimgeour, Valerie West. *Specialise in dance.*

Dyfel Management. 19 Fontwell Drive, Bromley, Kent BR2 8AB *tel:* 020 8467 9605 *fax:* 020 8249 1972 *email:* dyfel-for-music@mcmail.com.

* **ECAM Limited (European Cooperative Artists Management).** 130 Drayton Park, Highbury, London N5 1LX *tel:* 07973 156370 *fax:* 07070 605072 *email:* info@ecam-limited.com. J Cormac McGettigan, admin.

Ellison ***see*** J Audrey Ellison International Artists' Management.

Encore Concerts. Bibury House, 2 The Paddocks, Baunton, Cirencester, Glos GL7 7DL *tel:* 01285 640266 *fax:* 01285 640267. Elizabeth Goldfinch, dir.

Finch ***see*** Charles McK Finch Artists' Management.

Four A Music International. 47 Boscombe Rd, Wimbledon, London SW19 3AX *tel:* 020 8542 7610 *also fax; email:* faure@globalnet.co.uk. A Aarons, dir (UK); J Leibovici, dir (Australia).

GBZ Management. PO Box 11845, London SE21 8ZS *tel:* 020 8761 6565 *fax:* 020 8670 3195 *email:* gbz_mgmt@compuserve.com. Gwenneth Bransby-Zachary, dir.

* **Georgina Ivor Associates (GIA).** 28 Old Devonshire Rd, London SW12 9RB *tel:* 020 8673 7179 *fax:* 020 8675 8058 *email:* givor@aol.com. Georgina Ivor, dir; Melanie Harding, asst.

Gilder ***see*** Robert Gilder & Company.

HAYDN RAWSTRON

1999/2000 SEASON

Sopranos
Renate Behle
Katarina Dalayman
Gabriele Fontana
Dorothee Jansen
Hillevi Martinpelto
Jeanne Piland
Anne Schwanewilms

Mezzo Sopranos
Lani Poulson
Birgitta Svendén

Tenors
Heinz Kruse
Thomas Sunnegårdh
Rainer Trost
Roland Wagenführer

Baritones/Basses
Reinhard Dorn
Carlos Feller
Ronnie Johansen
Eike Wilm Schulte
Kristinn Sigmundsson
Alexandre Vassiliev

Conductors
Gregor Bühl
Peter Erckens
Johannes Fritzsch
Arnold Östman
Erich Wächter
Heinz Wallberg

Stage Directors/ Designers
Willy Decker
Andreas Homoki
Wolfgang Gussmann

ENQUIRIES MAY BE MADE TO HAYDN RAWSTRON (UK) LTD
36 STATION ROAD • LONDON • SE20 7BQ
TELEPHONE: (+44 181) 659 2659 FACSIMILE: (+44 181) 676 9119
E-MAIL: haydnraw@aol.com

Georgina Ivor Associates

INTERNATIONAL ARTIST MANAGEMENT
28 OLD DEVONSHIRE ROAD, LONDON SW12 9RB
TEL + 44 (020) 8673 7179 FAX + 44 (020) 8675 8058
E-MAIL GIvor@aol.com http://members.aol.com/givor

2000 - 2001 season

pianists

Nikolai Demidenko	*World*
Marc-André Hamelin	*World*
Piers Lane	*World (recitals)*
Vladimir Ovchinnikov	*World*
Graham Scott	*World*

bass baritone

Anatoli Safiulin	*UK & sun terr*

bass baritone & piano

Anatoli Safiulin & Nikolai Demidenko	*UK & sun terr*

Medici String Quartet *World*

music: the healing art

Schubert	Quartet in C minor D703 *Quartettsatz*
Nigel Osborne	Quartet No 1 *Medicinal Songs & Dances*
Beethoven	Quartet in A minor Op 132 *Heiliger Dankesang*

french connections

Saint-Saëns	Quartet No 1 in E minor Op 112
Debussy	Quartet in G minor Op 10
Ravel	Quartet in F

east meets west

Beethoven	Quartet in G Op 18 No 2
Wajahat Khan	Solo Sarod
Wajahat Khan	Raag Desh: Quintet for Sarod & String Quartet

A member of the International Artist Managers' Association (IAMA)

Giustiniani Artists. North Lodge, Potter Row, nr Great Missenden, Bucks HP16 9LT *tel:* 01494 868240 *fax:* 01494 868250 *email:* GArtists1 @aol.com. Kathy and Peter Bassano.

* **Grant Rogers Musical Artists' Management.** 64 Watling St, Radlett, Herts WD7 7NP *tel:* 01923 855753 *fax:* 01923 855584 *email:* nigel.rogers1@virgin.net.

Haferkorn Associates. 9 Belgrave Court, Wellesley Rd, Chiswick, London W4 4LG *tel:* 020 8987 8558 *fax:* 020 8987 8588 *email:* HaferkornJ@aol.com. Julia Haferkorn, dir.

* **Harlequin Agency Ltd.** 203 Fidlas Rd, Llanishen, Cardiff CF14 5NA *tel:* 029 2075 0821 *fax:* 029 2075 5971 *email:* admin@harlequin-agency.co.uk. Doreen O'Neill, mgr dir, artists mgr; Colin Ure, artists mgr, dir.

Harold Holt Ltd ***see*** Askonas Holt Ltd.

* **Harrison Parrott Ltd (HP).** 12 Penzance Place, London W11 4PA *tel:* 020 7229 9166 *fax:* 020 7221 5042 *email:* info@harrisonparrott.co.uk. Jasper Parrott, chmn, joint mgr dir; Linda Marks, joint mgr dir; Lydia Connolly, Ian Giddons, dirs.

Haydn Rawstron (UK) Ltd. 36 Station Rd, London SE20 7BQ *tel:* 020 8659 2659 *fax:* 020 8676 9119 *email:* haydnraw@aol.com. Chris Gray, dir.

* **Hazard Chase Ltd.** Richmond House, 16-20 Regent St, Cambridge CB2 1DB *tel:* 01223 312400 *fax:* 01223 460827 *email:* info@hazardchase.co.uk. James Brown, mgr dir; John Bickley, Elizabeth Jones, dirs; Lucy Rice, Sibylle Mager, Anne-Marie Norman, Chris Loake, Hilary Perrott, artist mgrs; Helen Poole, mkt; Hannah Pettit, admin; Zoe Owen, accounts.

* **Helen Sykes Artists' Management.** First Floor, Parkway House, London SW14 8LS *tel:* 020 8876 8276 *fax:* 020 8876 8277 *email:* helen@hsam.u-net.com. Helen Sykes, gen mgr; Sarah Mahon, admin; James Black, artists' mgr.

* **IMG Artists.** Media House, 3 Burlington Lane, London W4 2TH *tel:* 020 8233 5800 *fax:* 020 8233 5801 *email:* artistseurope@imgworld.com. Stephen Wright, mgr dir; Nicholas Mathias, dir, artist management; Kathryn Enticott, associate dir, artist management; Janie Garnon, press and publicity mgr; Tom Graham, vocal division dir; Anthony Howard, orch tours dir; Joan Cruickshank, associate orch tours dir; Gillian Newton, associate dir, dance.

* **Ingpen and Williams Ltd.** 26 Wadham Rd, London SW15 2LR *tel:* 020 8874 3222 *fax:* 020 8877 3113 *email:* info@ingpen.co.uk. David Sigall, Jonathan Groves, Thomas Hull, dirs.

* **Intermusica Artists' Management Ltd.** 16 Duncan Terrace, London N1 8BZ *tel:* 020 7278 5455 *fax:* 020 7278 8434 *email:* mail@intermusica.co.uk. Stephen Lumsden, mgr dir; Susie McLeod, dir, artists mgr; Kathy Schuman, promotions, artist mgr; Karen McDonald, associate; Peter Savory, dir, tours and projects; James Ross, artists' mgr.

Invisible Pilots Ltd. The Barony, 16 Sandringham Rd, Petersfield, Hants GU32 2AA *tel:* 01730 267341 *also fax; email:* invisiblepilots@classical-artists.com. Peter Thompson, dir, company sec.

Ireland ***see*** Caroline Ireland Management.

* **J Audrey Ellison International Artists' Management.** 135 Stevenage Rd, Fulham, London SW6 6PB *tel:* 020 7381 9751 *fax:* 020 7381 2406.

Janet Hughes Management. 76 Cross Oak Rd, Berkhamstead, Herts HP4 3HZ *tel:* 01442 878654 *also fax; email:* janet.hughes@music.globalnet.co.uk.

Jean Judge Artist Management. 7 Hayward Rd, Oxford OX2 8LN *tel:* 01865 515286 *also fax; email:* jjarts@msn.com. Jean Judge, dir; Peter Johnson, dir.

* **Jennie Blythe Artists' Management.** Sunnyside, Lower Swell, Glos GL54 1LG *tel:* 01451 830059 *fax:* 01451 832357 *email:* jennie.blythe@virgin.net. Jennie Blythe, dir; Liz Stevens, asst.

CADENZA CONCERTS LTD

40 Shorrolds Road
London SW6 7TP

TEL & FAX: 0171 381 4691
TEL: 0171 385 9171

Concert Promotion and Artist Management

Some of the groups we have worked with

Ladybones
Barrie Webb
The Hyde Sinfonia
Philharmonia Chorus
The Millennium Sinfonia
London Orpheus Orchestra
Performance The Arts Channel
The Feinstein Ensemble of London
The English Cornett and Sackbut Ensemble

Tel:- +44 (0)181 606 0030
Fax:- +44 (0)181 606 0037

For all your concert requirements

66 Hyde Way
Hayes
Middlesex
UB3 4PB

CONCERT SERVICES

ARBOREA MUSICA & FRIENDS
GERARD McDONALD (Artistic Director)
Baroque chamber music on period instruments

ARUNDO CLARINET QUARTET
JANET SPOTSWOOD, JILL SADLER, JOANNA ESTALL (Clarinets), **ANGELA CRISPE** (Bass Clarinet)
Light classical arrangements

THE BURGUNDIAN CADENCE
RUPERT DAMERELL (Counter-tenor), **SIMON BIAZEK** (Tenor), **MATTHEW WOOLHOUSE** (Tenor), **DAMIAN O'KEEFFE** (Baritone):
Early vocal & choral music

COPERNICUS PIANO TRIO
RAFAEL TODES (Violin), **JENNIFER JANSE** ('cello), **VIRGINIA HANSLIP** (Piano)

ENGLISH BRASS ENSEMBLE
PAUL ARCHIBALD (Artistic Director)
Contemporary & Classical Brass

CHAPELLE du ROI
ALISTAIR DIXON (Artistic Director)
A capella choral music from the Renaissance

JENNIFER JANSE ('cello) & **VIRGINIA HANSLIP** (Piano)

JENNIFER JANSE (Baroque 'cello) & **HELEN ROGERS** (Harpsichord)

GERARD McDONALD (Baroque Oboes, Flauto Traverso, Recorders) & **IAN SIMCOCK** (Harpsichord)

THE CHOIR OF PAMPLONA CATHEDRAL
PADRE AURELIO SAGASETA (Maestro de Capilia)
Spanish cathedral music at its best

MICHAEL HARROLD ARTIST MANAGEMENT
223, Kingston Road, LEATHERHEAD, Surrey, KT22 7PE, ENGLAND.
Telephone & Fax: (+44) (0)1372 375728
E-mail: angelus.organo@pmail.net
World Wide Web: http://www.angelus.co.uk

LISTING OF ARTISTS - 2000

GERVASE de PEYER (Clarinet) & **GWENNETH PRYOR** (Piano)

THE MELOS ENSEMBLE OF LONDON
GERVASE de PEYER (Artistic Director)
Classical, Romantic & Twentieth Century Chamber Music

VOCES SACRAE
JUDY MARTIN (Artistic Director)
Contemporary choral ensemble

VOCES STRING QUARTET
BUJOR PRELIPCEAN, ANTON DIACONU (Violins), **CONSTANTIN STANCIU** (Viola), **DAN PRELIPCEAN** ('cello)
World-class Romanian quartet

EDWIN ROXBURGH (Composer/Conductor/Lecturer)

MALCOLM BINNS (Piano)

JULIE AINSCOUGH (Organ)

ÓSCAR CANDENDO ZABALA (Organ)

GUILLIERMO DIEZ ARNÁIZ (Organ)

ANDREW PARNELL (Organ, Harmonium, Harpsichord, Conductor)

IAIN SIMCOCK (Organ, Harpsichord, Conductor)

GERARD McDONALD (Baroque Oboes, Flauto Traverso, Recorders)

GERVASE de PEYER (Solo Clarinet, Conductor)

Jenny Ricotti Music Management. Thimble Farm, Green Lane, Prestwood, Bucks HP16 0QE *tel:* 01494 865205 *also fax; email:* jenny@ricotti.force9.co.uk.

JLM Artists. 95 Oxford Gardens, London W10 6NF *tel:* 020 8993 8350 *fax:* 020 8969 5364. Joëlle Partner, dir.

John Boddy Agency. 10 Southfield Gardens, Twickenham, Middx TW1 4SZ *tel:* 020 8892 0133/8891 3809 *fax:* 020 8892 4283.

Judith Hendershott Arts Management. 4 Bennett Park, Blackheath, London SE3 9RB *tel:* 020 8852 0823.

* **Karen Durant Management (KDM).** 298 Nelson Rd, Whitton, Twickenham, Midd TW2 7BW *tel:* 020 8893 3172 *fax:* 020 8893 8090 *email:* kdm@karen-durant.co.uk. Karen Durant, dir.

Lies Askonas Ltd ***see*** Askonas Holt Ltd.

Lindsay Music. 23 Hitchin St, Biggleswade, Beds SG18 8AX *tel:* 01767 316521 *fax:* 01767 317221 *email:* lindsaymusic@clara.net. Rose Miles, admin.

* **London Artists (LA).** 3 Wheeler's Court, Scholars Lane, Stratford-upon-Avon, Warwicks CV37 6HE *tel:* 01789 261561 *fax:* 01789 261577 *email:* Londartist@aol.com. Michael Emmerson, dir.

* **London Musicians Ltd (LM).** Cedar House, Vine Lane, Hillingdon, Middx UB10 0BX *tel:* 01895 252555 *fax:* 01895 252556 *email:* mail@lonmus.demon.co.uk. Dave White, mgr dir; Sylvia Addison, orch mgr; Catherine Le Bris, artists mgr.

Lubbock ***see*** Sue Lubbock Artist Management.

Lunn ***see*** Maureen Lunn Management.

Maestoso Musicmakers Ltd. Milestone, St Nicholas Ave, Great Bookham, Surrey KT23 4AY *tel:* 01372 457755 *fax:* 01372 450525 *email:* maestoso@btinternet.com. Elizabeth Pryde, dir.

Manygate Management. 13 Cotswold Mews, 30 Battersea Square, London SW11 3RA *tel:* 020 7223 7265 *fax:* 020 7585 2830 *email:* manygate@easynet.co.uk. James Thomson, mgr dir; John Boyden, chmn.

Margaret Murphy Management. 28 Windsor Rd, Wanstead, London E11 3QU *tel:* 020 8989 1357 *also fax; email:* mmagent@freeuk.com.

Matthew Tullah Management. 301 Firs Lane, London N13 5QH *tel:* 020 8807 0343; 07956 318810 *fax:* 020 8807 3800 *email:* matttullah @compuserve.com.

Maureen Lunn Management. Top Farm, Parish Lane, Hedgerley, Bucks SL2 3JH *tel:* 01753 645008 *fax:* 01753 647431.

Michael Brewer. 8 Edward Court, 317 Hagley Rd, Birmingham B16 9LQ *tel:* 0121 454 3160 *fax:* 0121 454 0225 *email:* mbrewer@ mb-artists.ndirect.co.uk.

Michael Harrold Artist Management. 223 Kingston Rd, Leatherhead, Surrey KT22 7PE *tel:* 01372 375728 *also fax; email:* angelus.organo@pmail.net.

Mostylea Music Management. Grange Cottage, Grange Rd, Knightley, Staffs ST20 0JX *tel:* 01785 284433 *also fax.*

Murphy *see* Margaret Murphy Management

* **Music International.** 13 Ardilaun Rd, London N5 2QR *tel:* 020 7359 5183 *fax:* 020 7226 9792 *email:* music@musicint.demon.co.uk. Neil Dalrymple, mgr dir; Bernard Dickerson, artistic adviser; John McHugh, Andrew Comben.

Music Management. PO Box 1105, London SW1V 2DE *tel:* 020 7823 1111 *fax:* 020 7823 1001 *email:* mm@musicmanagement.demon.com.uk.

The Music Partnership Limited. 41 Aldebert Terrace, London SW8 1BH *tel:* 020 7787 0373 *fax:* 020 7787 0364 *email:* office@ themusicpartnership.ltd.uk. Louise Badger, Lawrence Kershaw, dirs.

Music Services Agency. 75 Claremont Rd, Tunbridge Wells, Kent TN1 1TE *tel:* 01892 527970 *also fax.* David Ebbage, dir; Avril Ebbage, sec; Andrew Laing, leader. *Light music specialists; themed events, concerts, entertainment, corporate business events, festivals.*

Musichall. Vicarage Way, Ringmer, E Sussex BN8 5LA *tel:* 01273 814240; 07885 227969 *fax:* 01273 813637 *email:* musichall@compuserve.com. Peter Hall, dir; Tim Aspeling, mgr.

* **Musicmakers.** Tailor House, 63-65 High St, Whitwell, Herts SG4 8AH *tel:* 01438 871708 *fax:* 01438 871777 *email:* 100620.2341@compuserve.com. Christopher Knowles, dir.

NB Management (NBM). PO Box 100, East Horsley, Surrey KT24 6WN *tel:* 01483 282666 *fax:* 01483 284777 *email:* nick@bomford.com. Nick Bomford, dir.

* **Neil Chaffey Concert Promotions (NCCP).** 9 Munts Meadow, Weston, Herts SG4 7AE *tel:* 01462 790919 *fax:* 01462 790920. Neil Chaffey, dir.

Nuns Meadow Productions. 20 New Rd, Ham Common, Richmond-upon-Thames, Surrey TW10 7HY *tel:* 020 8940 9006 *also fax.* James Bisgood, dir. *Specialists in early mus and period entertainments.*

N W Artists (NWA). 51 Tresco Rd, London SE15 3PY *tel:* 020 7635 7688 *fax:* 020 7635 6211. Nina Whitehurst, dir.

Ockert *see* Darren Ockert Management.

* **Olivia Ma Artists' Management.** 65 Campden St, London W8 7EL *tel:* 020 7221 3606 *fax:* 020 7221 3607 *email:* oliviama@omam.u-net.com. Olivia Ma, dir; Kathryn Naish, artists' asst.

Opera and Concert Artists (OCA). 75 Aberdare Gardens, London NW6 3AN *tel:* 020 7328 3097 *fax:* 020 7372 3537. Judith Newton, Andrew Dugdale.

Organisation. 17 Tressillian Cres, London SE4 1QJ *tel:* 07050 205588 *fax:* 020 8694 1476. Martin Baker, Joseph Cullen, Ann Elise Smoot, partners.

* **Owen/White Management (OWM).** 39 Hillfield Ave, London N8 7DS *tel:* 020 8340 9571 *fax:* 020 8340 4056 *email:* owenwhite@compuserve.com. John Owen, Trudy White.

* **Patrick Garvey Management (PGM).** Top Floor, 59 Lansdowne Place, Hove, E Sussex BN3 1FL *tel:* 01273 206623 *fax:* 01273 208484 *email:* patrick@patrickgarvey.demon.co.uk. Patrick Garvey, dir; Andrea McDermott, admin; Una Marchetti, project dir.

Patrick Voullaire. Park Offices, 121 Dora Rd, London SW19 7JT *tel:* 020 8946 8848 *fax:* 020 8944 1317.

* **Performing Arts (PA).** 6 Windmill St, London W1P 1HF *tel:* 020 7255 1362 *fax:* 020 7631 4631. Richard Haigh, proprietor.

Phillips *see* Caroline Phillips Management.

POEM (Performers of Early Music) ***A section of CDI.*** Lyndhurst, Denton Rd, Ben Rhydding, nr Ilkley, W Yorks LS29 8QR *tel:* 01943 607821 *fax:* 01943 817063 *email:* pca@mail.ndirect.co.uk.

* **Portland Wallis Artists' Management.** 50 Great Portland St, London W1N 5AH *tel:* 020 7636 6785 *fax:* 020 7636 6786. Alan Beavis, gen mgr; Daniel Stinson, artists mgr.

Pristavec *see* Anthony Pristavec

Pro Piano Management. 85 Jane St, New York, NY 10014, USA *tel:* +1 212 206 8794 *fax:* +1 212 613 1207 *email:* ricard@propiano.com. Ricard de La Rosa, exec dir, founder.

Prophet Music Ltd. 147 Drummond St, London NW1 2PB *tel:* 020 7383 5003 *fax:* 020 7383 5004 *email:* info@prophetmusic.co.uk. Jonathan Brigden, mgr dir.

Purkiss *see* Anthony Purkiss.

PVA Management. Hallow Park, Worcester WR2 6PG *tel:* 01905 640663 *fax:* 01905 641842 *email:* pvamanltd@aol.com. Paul Vaughan, mgr dir; Stephen Pink, company sec; Lisa Ventura-Whiting, sec; Irene Sanderson, mkt manager

Rawstron ***see*** Haydn Rawstron (UK) Ltd.

Ricard de La Rosa. 85 Jane St, New York, NY 10014, USA *tel:* +1 212 206 8794 *fax:* +1 212 613 1207 *email:* ricard@propiano.com.

* **Robert Gilder & Company.** Enterprise House, 59-65 Upper Ground, London SE1 9PQ *tel:* 020 7928 9008 *fax:* 020 7928 9755. Robert Gilder, dir.

* **Robert White Artist Management.** 182 Moselle Ave, London N22 6EX *tel:* 020 8881 6914 *fax:* 020 8888 9662 *email:* rwhiteam@aol.com. Robert White, dir.

Rondo Music. 59 Hauteville, St Peter Port, Guernsey, Channel Islands, GY1 1DQ *tel:* 01327 659176 *email:* rondoproms@compuserve.com. James Anderson, dir.

* **Rostrum Promotions.** 4 Ferniebank Brae, Bridge of Allan FK9 4PJ *tel:* 01786 834449 *fax:* 01786 833949 *email:* no-rostrum@compuserve.com. Fiona Paterson, mgr dir.

Roxane Houston Concert Agency. 8 Hartington Rd, Aldeburgh, Suffolk IP15 5HD *tel:* 01728 454048. Roxane Houston, dir; David Radford, associate.

Roy Baker Concert Management. 25 Lynors Ave, Rochester, Kent ME2 3NQ *tel:* 01634 714434 *also fax.* Audrey Banker, admin.

Scrimgeour ***see*** Donald Scrimgeour.

Seaview Music. 28 Mawson Rd, Cambridge CB1 2EA *tel:* 01223 508431 *fax:* 01223 508449 *email:* seaview@dial.pipex.com. Alison Page, mgr; Sarah Bruce, asst mgr.

Shauni McGregor. *tel:* 01608 642352 *fax:* 01608 643235 *email:* smcg @fixall.demon.co.uk.

Simply Singers (SS). 23 Freke Rd, London SW11 5PU *tel:* 020 7223 7327 *fax:* 020 7924 5730.

Singers Direct. 39 The Ridings, Surbiton, Surrey KT5 8HG *tel:* 020 8390 5375; 07889 153382 *fax:* 020 8390 9818 *email:* singersdirect@mrb.clara.net. Michael R Bundy. *Non-percentage driven co-operative.*

Sonata Limited. 11 North Park St, Glasgow G20 7AA *tel:* 0141 945 3553 *fax:* 0141 946 7034. Gregor Tassie, mgr dir.

* **Stafford Law.** 6 Barham Close, Weybridge, Surrey KT13 9PR *tel:* 01932 854489 *fax:* 01932 858521 *email:* staffordlaw@btinternet.com. Margherita Stafford, David Law, partners.

Stella Baker. Home Close, Sheep St, Winslow, Buckingham MK18 3HR *tel:* 01296 712411 *also fax; email:* m.s@lineone.net.

* **Stephannie Williams Artists (SWA).** 9 Central Chambers, Wood St, Stratford-upon-Avon, Warwicks CV37 6JQ *tel:* 01789 266272 *fax:* 01789 266467 *email:* enquiries@swartists.co.uk. Stephannie Williams, mgr; Martin Denny, concerts mgr; Jayne Rollason, concerts mgr.

Still ***see*** Athole Still International Management Ltd.

* **Sue Lubbock Artist Management.** 25 Courthope Rd, London NW3 2LE *tel:* 020 7485 5932 *fax:* 020 7267 0179. Sue Lubbock, dir.

Susie Wong Artists Management Ltd. 27 Old Gloucester St, London WC1N 3XX *tel:* 020 7633 9878 *also fax;* 07710 380838. Susie Wong, mgr; Iris Tse, sec.

Sykes ***see*** Helen Sykes Artists' Management.

Sylvia Junge Management (SJM). 7 Elton Close, Kingston upon Thames, Surrey KT1 4EE *tel:* 020 8977 9613 *also fax.*

Sympathetic Developments. 48 Bridle Way, Colehill, Wimborne, Dorset BH21 2UE *tel:* 01202 880331 *fax:* 01202 888037. Graham Stansfield, proprietor.

Talbot -Cooper *see* Christine Talbot-Cooper

* **Tennant Artists.** Unit 2, 39 Tadema Rd, London SW10 0PY *tel:* 020 7376 3758 *fax:* 020 7351 0679 *email:* info@tennantartists.demon.co.uk. Christopher Tennant, mgr dir; Angela Sulivan, dir.

Terry Harrison Artists Management (THA). The Orchard, Market St, Charlbury, Oxon OX7 3PJ *tel:* 01608 810330 *fax:* 01608 811331 *email:* artists@terryharrison.force9.co.uk. Helen Turner, mgr; Lynne Ness, Denise Bucknell, assts.

* **TransArt (UK) Ltd.** 8 Bristol Gardens, London W9 2JG *tel:* 020 7286 7526 *fax:* 020 7266 2687 *email:* transart@transartuk.com. Hervé Corre de Valmalète, dir; Sarah Trice, company sec; Bruno Ceccaldi, Angela Giouinazzo, artists mgrs.

* **Upbeat Management.** Sutton Business Centre, Restmor Way, Wallington, Surrey SM6 7AH *tel:* 020 8773 1223 *fax:* 020 8669 6752 *email:* classic@upbeat.co.uk. Maureen Phillips, Liz Biddle, dirs.

* **Valerie Barber PR & Personal Management Ltd.** Suite 300, Mappin House, 4 Winsley St, London W1N 7AR *tel:* 020 7436 1115/6 *fax:* 020 7436 5090 *email:* vbpr@compuserve.com.

* **Van Walsum Management (VWM).** 4 Addison Bridge Place, London W14 8XP *tel:* 020 7371 4343 *fax:* 020 7371 4344 *email:* vwm@vanwalsum.co.uk. Joeske van Walsum, mgr dir; Victoria Rowsell, deputy mgr dir; Roderick Thomson, Geoffrey Owen, Rachel Bostock, dirs.

Voullaire *see* Patrick Voullaire

* **Worldwide Artists (London) Ltd (WWA).** 12 Roseberry Ave, Thornton Heath, London CR7 8PT *tel:* 020 8771 3444 *fax:* 020 8771 3445 *email:* WWArtists@aol.com.

Wright Music Promotions Limited. 235 Streetsbrook Rd, Solihull, W Midlands B91 1HE *tel:* 0121 705 0098 *fax:* 0121 705 4815. Penelope Beaumont-Wright, dir.

* **Young Concert Artists Trust (YCAT).** 23 Garrick St, London WC2E 9AX *tel:* 020 7379 8477 *fax:* 020 7379 8467. Rosemary Pickering, chief exec; Susan Hudson, artists mgr. *Career management for outstanding young musicians; selected by audition.*

Symphony and Chamber Orchestras

In this section the conductor or musical director is given, together with the names of the chief administrative staff and the associated chamber groups. A list of officers responsible for booking orchestral players will be found under **Orchestral Contractors**. The number of performers is shown in parentheses; those of 15 and under are listed in **Ensembles**. An asterisk indicates membership of the **Association of British Orchestras** (*see* **Associations**). Youth orchestras are listed in the **Youth Orchestras and Bands** section.

Aberystwyth University Sinfonia (35). Music Centre, University of Wales, Aberystwyth, 10 Laura Place, Aberystwyth, Ceredigion SY23 2AU *tel:* 01970 622685 *fax:* 01970 622686 *email:* muswww @aber.ac.uk. David Russell Hulme, cond.

* **The Academy of Ancient Music** (3-180). 10 Brookside, Cambridge CB2 1JE *tel:* 01223 301509 *fax:* 01223 327377 *email:* administrator @aam.co.uk. Christopher Hogwood CBE, dir; Paul Goodwin, associate cond; Andrew Manze, associate dir and concert master; Christopher Lawrence, gen mgr; Fiona Seers, concerts and tours mgr; Madeleine Holmes, admin. *Associated choir is The Academy of Ancient Music Chorus.*

* **Academy of St Martin in the Fields** (8-80). Raine House, Raine St, London E1 9RG *tel:* 020 7702 1377 *fax:* 020 7481 0228 *email:* info@academysmif.co.uk. Sir Neville Marriner CBE, life president; Iona Brown OBE, artistic dir; Kenneth Sillito, artistic dir; Miss George Brown, gen mgr; Julia Seddon, head of mkt and development; Elise Akseralian, educ co-ord; Dawn Day, admin; Antony Delmege, financial admin. *Associated chmbr group is Academy of St Martin in the Fields Chamber Ensemble.*

Academy of the London Mozarteum (50). 7 Woodland Glade, Farnham Common, Bucks SL2 3RG *tel:* 01753 648113 *fax:* 01753 648114 *email:* rhamwee@clara.net. Robert Hamwee, artistic dir; Josefina Stabile, gen mgr.

Aeolian Sinfonia (23-70). 25 Roy Rd, Northwood, Middx HA6 1EQ *tel:* 01923 828055. Philip Gibson, mus dir.

All Souls Orchestra (35-110). All Souls Music Office, St Paul's Church, Robert Adam St, London W1M 5AH *tel:* 020 7487 3508 *fax:* 020 7224 6087. N H Tredinnick, mus dir and principal cond. *Associated chmbr groups are All Souls Sinfonietta, Band and Theatre Orchestra.*

Amadeus Orchestra (100). 41 Cahir St, London E14 3QR *tel:* 020 7537 2329 *fax:* 020 7379 5205. Philip Mackenzie, principal cond; Eric Handy, admin; Alastair King, composer-in-association; Odaline de la Martinez, president.

* **Ambache Chamber Orchestra** (16-30). 9 Beversbrook Rd, London N19 4QG *tel:* 020 7281 7880 *also fax; email:* polmear.ambache@telinco.co.uk. Diana Ambache, mus dir; Louise Brooksbank, gen mgr; Malcolm Wilson, fixer. *Associated chmbr group is the Ambache Chamber Ensemble.*

Amici. 23 The Moorings, Middlewich, Cheshire CW10 9ER *tel:* 01606 836292. Raymond Lomax, mus dir; Judith Lomax, admin.

Amici Chamber Orchestra (12-65). 20 Oakhill Drive, Welwyn, Herts AL6 9NW *tel:* 01438 715740 *also fax.* Nigel Springthorpe, principal cond; Karen Van Poznak, admin. *Associated chmbr group is Amici Wind Ensemble.*

Amsterdam Baroque Orchestra. c/o Hazard Chase Ltd, Richmond House, 16-20 Regent St, Cambridge CB2 1DB *tel:* 01223 312400 *fax:* 01223 460827 *email:* info@hazardchase.co.uk.

Apollo Chamber Orchestra (25-45). 43 Clifden Rd, London E5 0LL *tel:* 020 8986 4101 *also fax.* David Chernaik, cond; Elizabeth Pigram, leader; David Burke, admin.

Bach Chamber Orchestra. c/o Sonata, 11 North Park St, Glasgow G20 7AA *tel:* 0141 945 3553 *fax:* 0141 946 7034 *email:* gregor@sonata. Freeserve.co.uk.

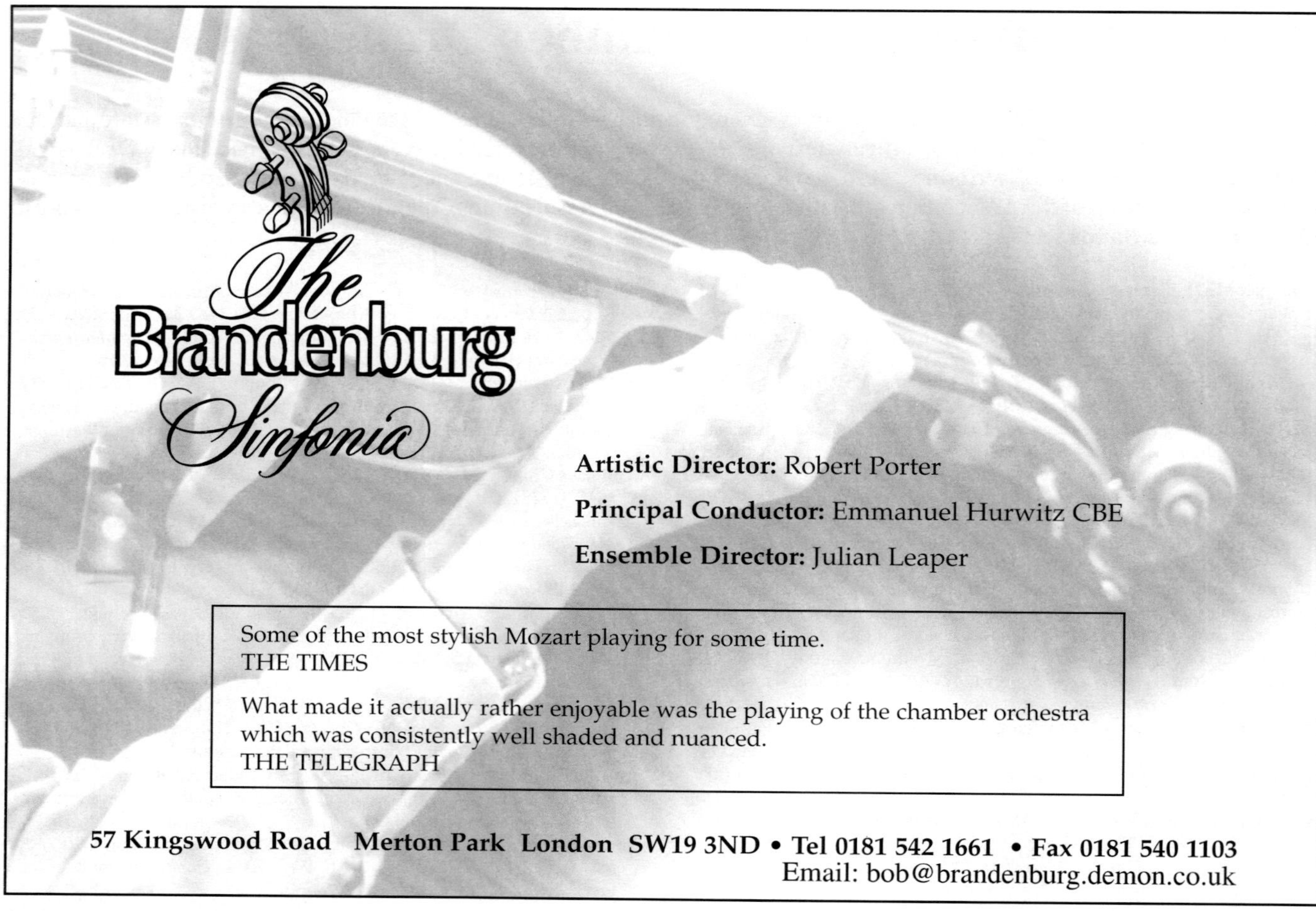
The Brandenburg Sinfonia
Artistic Director: Robert Porter
Principal Conductor: Emmanuel Hurwitz CBE
Ensemble Director: Julian Leaper
Some of the most stylish Mozart playing for some time.
THE TIMES
What made it actually rather enjoyable was the playing of the chamber orchestra which was consistently well shaded and nuanced.
THE TELEGRAPH
57 Kingswood Road Merton Park London SW19 3ND • Tel 0181 542 1661 • Fax 0181 540 1103
Email: bob@brandenburg.demon.co.uk

* **BBC Concert Orchestra** (56). The Hippodrome, North End Rd, Golders Green, London NW11 7RP *tel:* 020 7765 4010 *fax:* 020 7765 4929 *email:* concert.orch@bbc.co.uk. Barry Wordsworth, principal cond; Vernon Handley, principal guest cond; Ian Maclay, gen mgr; Adrian Evett, orch mgr; Jan Parr, asst orch mgr; Sarah Biggs, promotions and mkt mgr; Martin Ward, librarian.

* **BBC National Orchestra of Wales** (88). BBC Broadcasting House, Llandaff, Cardiff CF5 2YQ *tel:* 029 2032 2000 *fax:* 029 2032 2575 *email:* byron.jenkins@bbc.co.uk. Mark Wigglesworth, mus dir; Tadaaki Otaka, cond laureate; Richard Hickox, principal cond (from Aug 2000); Joseph Swensen, principal guest cond (from Aug 2000); Grant Llewellyn, cond in residence; Huw Tregelles Williams, dir; Byron Jenkins, orch mgr; Jeremy Garside, business mgr; Andrew Burke, educ offr; Joanna Sigsworth, mkt mgr; Philip Watts, development offr.

* **BBC Philharmonic** (89). New Broadcasting House, Oxford Rd, Manchester M60 1SJ *tel:* 0161 244 4001 *fax:* 0161 244 4010. Yan Pascal Tortelier, principal cond; Vassily Sinaisky, principal guest cond; Sir Peter Maxwell Davies, composer and cond; Sir Edward Downes, cond emeritus; Brian Pidgeon, gen mgr; Fiona McIntosh, orch mgr; Amanda Dorr, mkt mgr; Martin Maris, educ and community co-ord.

* **BBC Scottish Symphony Orchestra** (69). BBC Broadcasting House, Queen Margaret Drive, Glasgow G12 8DG *tel:* 0141 338 2606 *fax:* 0141 307 4312 *email:* bbcsso@bbc.co.uk. Osmo Vänskä, chief cond; Jerzy Maksymiuk, cond laureate; Martyn Brabbins, associate principal cond; Tan Dun, composer and cond; Stuart MacRae, composer in association; Hugh Macdonald, dir; Simon Lord, snr mus producer; Alan Davis, mgr; Marion Caldwell, asst mgr; Stephen Strugnell, mkt mgr; Chris Dale, promotions asst.

* **BBC Symphony Orchestra.** BBC Maida Vale Studios, Delaware Rd, London W9 2LG *tel:* 020 7765 5751 *fax:* 020 7286 3251. Andrew Davis CBE, chief cond; Günter Wand, chief guest cond; Jiri Belohlavek, principal guest cond; Paul Hughes, gen mgr; Ann McKay, chief producer; Richard Smith, orch mgr; Susanna Simmons, asst orch mgr; Marelle McCallum, concert mgr; Christine Bissat, mkt mgr.

Beethoven Philharmonic Orchestra (80). 24 New Cavendish St, London W1M 7LH *tel:* 020 7351 2439 *fax:* 020 7487 3971 *email:* maestrotod @aol.com. Michael Jameson, artistic advisor; David Todhunter, principal cond; John Hill, orch mgr.

Belmont Ensemble of London (16-35). 3 Princes Lodge, 16 Brightlingsea Place, Limehouse, London E14 8DB *tel:* 020 7531 1672 *fax:* 020 7531 9895 *email:* belmont@easynet.co.uk. Peter Gilbert-Dyson, mus dir; Rebekah Gilbert-Dyson, admin; Anna Bradley, leader.

Ben Uri Chamber Orchestra (20). 5 Bradby House, Carlton Hill, London NW8 9XE *tel:* 020 7624 1756. Sydney Fixman, cond and mus dir; David Richmond, personnel and orch mgr.

Birmingham Sinfonietta (24-45). 41 St Agnes Rd, Birmingham B13 9PJ *tel:* 0121 449 0225. Susan Savage, orch mgr; Jeremy Ballard, mus dir.

Boston Sinfonia (60). Holm Leigh, Station Rd, Hubberts Bridge, Boston, Lincs PE20 3QT *tel:* 01205 290301 *email:* bossin@ aemmmqdales.demon.co.uk. Michael Dales, admin; Nigel Morley, cond; Gary Sieling, cond; Anne Dales, leader; Owen Moorin, orch mgr.

* **Bournemouth Sinfonietta** (30). Bournemouth Orchestras, 2 Seldown Lane, Poole, Dorset BH15 1UF *tel:* 01202 670611 *fax:* 01202 687235. Alexander Polianichko, principal cond; Michael Henson, mgr dir; Cristina Rocca, gen mgr; Michael Marx, concerts dir; Bob Cator, orch mgr; Liz O'Neill, mkt dir; Jacky Thorne, head of sponsorship; Andrew Burn, educ dir.

* **Bournemouth Symphony Orchestra** (81). Bournemouth Orchestras, 2 Seldown Lane, Poole, Dorset BH15 1UF *tel:* 01202 670611 *fax:* 01202 687235. Yakov Kreizberg, principal cond; Paavo Berglund, cond emeritus; Andrew Litton, cond laureate; Kees Bakels, chief guest cond; Michael Henson, mgr dir; Cristina Rocca, gen mgr; Liz O'Neill, mkt dir; Jacky Thorne, head of sponsorship; Andrew Burn, educ dir.

* **The Brandenburg Consort** (14-30). 5 Cornfield View, Sleaford, Lincs NG34 7WF *tel:* 01529 304130 *fax:* 01529 304131 *email:* roy.goodman@virgin.net. Roy Goodman, mus dir; Steven Jones, admin. *Period insts.*

Brandenburg Opera Orchestra. 57 Kingswood Rd, Merton Park, London SW19 3ND *tel:* 020 8542 1661 *fax:* 020 8540 1103 *email:* bob@ brandenburg.demon.co.uk. Robert Porter, artistic dir; Wendy Warrilow, admin; Pat Unwin, finance dir.

Brandenburg Orchestra. 57 Kingswood Rd, Merton Park, London SW19 3ND *tel:* 020 8542 1661 *fax:* 020 8540 1103 *email:* bob@ brandenburg.demon.co.uk. Robert Porter, artistic dir; Emmanuel Hurwitz CBE, principal cond; Julian Leaper, ens dir; Wendy Warrilow, admin; Pat Unwin, finance dir.

The Brandenburg Orchestra (30-60). 5 Cornfield View, Sleaford, Lincs NG34 7WF *tel:* 01529 304130 *fax:* 01529 304131 *email:* roy.goodman@virgin.net. Roy Goodman, mus dir; Steven Jones, admin. *Period insts.*

Brandenburg Sinfonia. 57 Kingswood Rd, Merton Park, London SW19 3ND *tel:* 020 8542 1661 *fax:* 020 8540 1103 *email:* bob@brandenburg.demon.co.uk. Robert Porter, artistic dir; Emmanuel Hurwitz CBE, principal cond; Julian Leaper, ens dir; Wendy Warrilow, admin; Pat Unwin, finance dir.

Brighton Philharmonic Orchestra (80). 50 Grand Parade, Brighton BN2 2QA *tel:* 01273 622900 *fax:* 01273 697887. Barry Wordsworth, principal cond; Tony Woodhouse, gen mgr; Wilfred Goddard, orch mgr; Ronald Power, chmn; Emma Vallance, asst mgr and librarian; Glynis Leaney, accounts admin.

Bristol Philharmonic Orchestra *formerly* Philharmonia of Bristol (100). 11 Windsor Court, Victoria Terrace, Bristol BS8 4LJ *tel:* 0117 929 7597 *fax:* 0117 925 1301. Kenneth Gibbs, gen mgr; Anthony Pooley, orch mgr. *Associated chmbr group is Bristol Philharmonic Ensemble.*

British Concert Orchestra (30-80). 147 Haling Park Rd, Croydon, Surrey CR2 6NN *tel:* 020 8688 4605 *fax:* 020 8667 0607. Frank Renton, principal cond; Peter Craen, gen mgr.

British Police Symphony Orchestra. Woodbine House, 148 Crewe Rd, Alsager, Stoke-on-Trent ST7 2JA *tel:* 01270 884347 *also fax; email:* alexbpso@aol.com. Alex Roe, sec; Miki Volpe, orch mgr; Martyn Snell, concert mgr; Mike Botley, tour mgr. *Members of the orch are police personnel from all over the UK.*

* **The Britten Sinfonia** (14-50). 12d Kings Parade, Cambridge CB2 1SJ *tel:* 01223 300795 *fax:* 01223 302092 *email:* info@brittensinfonia.demon.co.uk. Nicholas Cleobury, artistic dir; Helen Busbridge, orch mgr; David Butcher, gen mgr; Helen Thompson, concert and mkt mgr; Jackie Inverdale, development dir; Glyn Evans, educ dir; Emma Martin, educ offr; Charles Barrington, chmn; David Matthews, composer-in-association. *Associated chmbr group is the Britten Sinfonia Ensemble directed by Nicholas Daniel, ob, and Pauline Lowbury, vn.*

Brunel Ensemble (4-90). 129 Hughenden Rd, High Wycombe, Bucks HP13 5PN *tel:* 01494 462048 *also fax; email:* deborah.keyser@virgin.net. Christopher Austin, artistic dir; Deborah Keyser, gen mgr; Tony Best, orch mgr; Sean T Rourke, mkt mgr; Robert Saxon, president; Malcolm Williamson CBE, patron. *Chmbr and symphony orch.*

Buxton Spa Orchestra. Riverside House, Chapel-en-le-Frith, High Peak SK23 0QQ *tel:* 01298 813813. Sylvia Goodborn, mgr; John Goodborn, stage mgr. *Associated chmbr groups are Buxton Spa Duo, Buxton Spa Quartet and Buxton Spa Quintet.*

Camerata of London *formerly* Surrey Sinfonietta (3-50). c/o 8 Birdhurst Ave, South Croydon, Surrey CR2 7DX *tel:* 020 8688 9166 *also fax; email:* gee.chris@schal.co.uk. Richard Milone, artistic dir; Hilary Dennis, orch mgr; Jane Healey, personnel mgr; Chris Gee, treasurer; David Benke, chmn.

Camerata Roman of Sweden. c/o Neil Chaffey Concert Promotions, 9 Munts Meadow, Weston, Herts SG4 7AE *tel:* 01462 790919 *fax:* 01462 790920.

* **CBSO (City of Birmingham Symphony Orchestra)** (101). CBSO Centre, Berkley St, Birmingham B1 2LF *tel:* 0121 616 6500 *fax:* 0121 616 6518 *email:* information@cbso.co.uk. Sakari Oramo, principal cond; Stephen Maddock, chief exec; Richard York, deputy chief exec; Natalie Cruse, concerts admin; Michael Buckley, gen mgr; Sir Michael Checkland, chmn; Judy Dolman, orch mgr; Ann Tennant, educ mgr; Sarah Gee, dir of mkt and development. *Associated chmbr group is Birmingham Contemporary Music Group.*

Chamber Orchestra of Europe (50). 8 Southampton Place, London WC1A 2EA *tel:* 020 7831 2326 *fax:* 020 7831 8248 *email:* redbird@coeurope.org. Claudio Abbado, artistic adviser; Peter Readman, chmn; June Megennis, gen mgr; Simon Fletcher, personnel and planning mgr; Christopher Smith-Gillard, tour mgr; Julie Pickles, travel and office mgr; Mollie Pearson, press offr. *Associated chmbr group is Wind Soloists of The Chamber Orchestra of Europe.*

Chamber Orchestra of London (26-60). COOL Music Productions, 20 Spruce Hills Rd, Walthamstow, London E17 4LD *tel:* 07768 570383 (business) *fax:* 020 8531 4962 *email:* coolmp@iname.com. Anthony Langrish, gen mgr. *Opera galas and concert performances. Associated groups include Trilogia (str trio).*

Charivari Agréable Simfonie. Oakley, 109 Windmill Rd, Oxford OX3 7DN *tel:* 01865 751928 *also fax; email:* Events.Manager@charivari.freeserve.co.uk. Kah-Ming Ng, mus dir; Lynda Sayce, artistic dir; Susanne Heinrich, admin dir.

Cheltenham Chamber Orchestra (40). 31 School Rd, Charlton King's, Cheltenham, Glos GL53 8BQ *tel:* 01242 517258 *email:* angela@hedgeways.freeserve.co.uk. Robin Proctor, Denise Ham, mus dirs;

Dorothy Roberts, press offr; Peter Tomlinson, orch mgr; Peter B Kerr, treasurer; Angela Walker, secretary.

City of Canterbury Symphony Orchestra. PO Box 600, Canterbury, Kent CT4 6NP *tel:* 01227 832154 *fax:* 01227 832254. P Jarvis, admin.

The City of London Chamber Players (3-50). Kenton Cottage, Burnt Hill Way, Farnham, Surrey GU10 4RP *tel:* 01252 795047 *also fax.* Brian Lloyd Wilson, dir, vn.

* **City of London Sinfonia** (16-50). 11 Drum St, London E1 1LH *tel:* 020 7480 7743 *fax:* 020 7488 2700 *email:* info@cls.co.uk. Stephen Carpenter, gen mgr; Alasdair Nicolson, composer-in-association; Richard Hickox, mus dir; Elaine Baines, admin; Sarah Guest, educ mgr; Jane Lomas, orch mgr; Catharine Pitt, mkt mgr; Liz Knock, development offr; Samantha Lodge, office mgr and librarian. *Associated chmbr group is Sinfonia Soloists.*

* **City of Oxford Orchestra** (70). Bury Knowle House, North Place, Headington, Oxford OX3 9HY *tel:* 01865 744457/739535 *also fax; fax:* 01865 744481. Lady Marks, hon president; Lindsay Sandison, chmn; Roger Payne, concert dir; Leo Phillips, leader, dir; Duncan Hinnells, associate cond. *Associated chmbr group is the Soloists of the City of Oxford Orchestra.*

City of Peterborough Symphony Orchestra (60). 55 Sapperton, Werrington, Peterborough PE4 5BS *tel:* 01733 576797 *fax:* 01733 755939. Antony Hopkins, president; Norman Beedie, cond; Jackie Over, sec.

City of Rochester Symphony Orchestra. 71 Aintree Rd, Lordswood, Chatham, Kent ME5 8PQ *tel:* 01634 684088 *email:* CRSO@dprothero.easynet.co.uk. Tracey Andrew, orch mgr; Warwick Potter, mus dir; Bernard Parris, chmn; Jill Cole, sec; Stan Gregory, treasurer.

Classic East Symphony Orchestra (50+). Marriotts Drove Farm, Ramsey Mereside, Huntingdon, Cambs PE17 1UF *tel:* 01733 844603 *also fax.* Norman Beedie, cond; Hilary Stafford-Clark, events co-ord; Robert Reynolds, mkt dir.

Classical Fanfare Orchestra. c/o Classical Management Services, Rhydyberi Cottages, Merthyr Cynog, Brecon, Powys LD3 9SA *tel:* 01874 690339 *fax:* 01874 690254. Fraser Goulding, cond; Brendan Wheatley, gen mgr; Bridget Gill, admin.

Collegium Musicum 90 (3-35). 71 Priory Rd, Kew, Surrey TW9 3DH *tel:* 020 8940 7086 *fax:* 020 8332 0879. Richard Hickox, mus dir; Simon Standage, mus dir; Francesca McManus, gen mgr.

Continuum Ensemble. 28 King Edward Gardens, London W3 9RG *tel:* 020 8993 1466 *also fax.* Douglas Finch, pno, co-artistic dir; Philip Headlam, cond, co-artistic dir.

Corinthian Orchestra (24+). 80 Hampton Lane, Solihull, W Midlands B91 2RS *tel:* 0121 704 4450 *fax:* 0121 704 9056. Elaine Donohoe, gen mgr; Peter Donohoe, artistic dir and principal cond.

Cornish Sinfonia (30-40). Chycara House, Carnon Valley, Carnon Downs, Truro, Cornwall TR3 6LG *tel:* 01872 865510 *fax:* 01872 863557 *email:* cs@woodwinds.demon.co.uk. David White, gen mgr; Ian Hughes, artistic dir.

* **Corydon Orchestra** (40-90). 24 Kirdford Rd, Arundel, W Sussex BN18 9EE *tel:* 01903 885465 *fax:* 01903 885466 *email:* corydon.office@btinternet.com. Matthew Best, artistic dir; Linda Osborne, gen mgr.

The Court Chamber Orchestra (42). Harewood, 22 Rooksmead Rd, Sunbury-on-Thames, Middx TW16 6PD *tel:* 01932 781577 *fax:* 01932 789822. Peter Clarke, cond.

The Cyprus Chamber Orchestra (37). 37 Cancell Rd, London SW9 6HP *tel:* 020 7735 1002 *also fax.* Roland Melia, artistic dir.

Dante Alighieri Orchestra (15-25). East West Arts Ltd, 93b Cambridge Gardens, N Kensington, London W10 6JE *tel:* 020 8960 5889 *fax:* 020 8968 5541. Anup Kumar Biswas, mus dir; Peter A Connell OBE, personnel and orch mgr. *Associated chmbr group is Guadagnini Piano Trio.*

* **East of England Orchestra (EOEO)** (40). Beaufort Business Centre, Beaufort St, Derby DE21 6AX *tel:* 01332 207570 *fax:* 01332 207569 *email:* orchestra@eoeo.freeserve.co.uk. Nicholas Kok, principal cond; Peter Helps, chief exec; David Hill, chmn; Naomi Wilds, mkt and admin; Siân Davies, educ mgr; Nick Cutts, orch mgr; Mimi Errington, development mgr; Adam Saunders, composer-in-association.

Elgar Camerata (31-50). The Elgar School of Music, 16-20 Deansway, Worcester WR1 2ES *tel:* 01905 28613 *fax:* 01905 723919. Donald Hunt OBE, cond; Louise Sharp, admin.

Emerald Ensemble (8-14). 29 Holmes Grove, Henleaze, Bristol BS9 4ED *tel:* 0117 962 4289 *also fax.* Roger Huckle, dir.

English Bach Festival Baroque Orchestra (20-30). 15 South Eaton Place, London SW1W 9ER *tel:* 020 7730 5925 *fax:* 020 7730 1456. Lina Lalandi OBE, dir.

English Baroque Orchestra (12-37). 57 Kingswood Rd, London SW19 3ND *tel:* 020 8542 1661 *fax:* 020 8540 1103. Leon Lovett, mus dir; Robert Porter, mgr. *Associated chmbr group is English Baroque Players.*

ESO

English *String* Orchestra
English *Symphony* Orchestra

William Boughton **Artistic Director**
Michael Bochmann **Concertmaster**

The English String Orchestra was founded in 1980 by William Boughton, who is still the Artistic and Music Director, and nine years later the English Symphony Orchestra was established.

"What can a music critic do in a concert when there is nothing to criticise."
Quote by Berner Oberlaender, Switzerland. 1994.

The orchestra's numerous best-selling recordings with Nimbus Records are played regularly on radio stations such as Classic FM. With the support of internationally acclaimed musicians including notably, the late Yehudi Menuhin, the ESO sustains a concert programme from its residency in the newly refurbished Malvern Theatres complex to national and international venues. Alongside its performance of standard repertoire the ESO is a dedicated exponent of English music, and particularly of the work of 20th Century English composers.

"The sheer commitment of the players shines through."
Quote by Classical Corner, UK. 1990.

To find out more concerning future concerts or how you can be a part of the ESO, please do not hesitate to contact us.

Administration.
William Boughton - Artistic/Music Director
Alison King - Finance Officer
Kate Hodson - Administrator
Cheryl Tyler - Publicity Officer

English Symphony Orchestra
Rockcliffe House, 40 Church Street, Malvern WR14 2AZ.
Telephone +44 (0)1684 560696, Fax +44 (0)1684 560656
email info@eso.co.uk Website http://www.eso.co.uk

ENGLISH STRING ORCHESTRA LTD. REGISTERED IN ENGLAND No. 1850234, REGISTERED CHARITY No. 293345

The Musician's Handbook

THE SURVIVAL KIT FOR THE PROFESSIONAL MUSICIAN

- Hardback
- 318 pages
- A5 format
- Price:£14.95 (plus p&p)

3RD EDITION OUT NOW

41 chapters covering every aspect of the music profession written by 31 acknowledged experts.

CREDIT CARD ORDERS
Tel: 020 7333 1721
(office hours)
Fax: 020 7333 1769

Postage & Packing charges
Please add £2.00 for 1 copy to UK addresses (then add £1.00 for each additional copy); £4.50 per copy Airmail Europe; £6.50 per copy Airmail outside Europe; £3.00 per copy Surface mail worldwide

OVERSEAS CUSTOMERS
Payment may be made by Eurocheque or by credit card. We cannot accept cheques in foreign currencies or sterling cheques drawn on overseas banks.

To obtain your copy please send a cheque (payable to *Rhinegold Publishing Ltd*) to: **Book Sales Dept, Rhinegold Publishing Ltd, FREEPOST, London WC2H 8BR. www.rhinegold.co.uk**

"...The best orchestra of its kind in the world." **Intermezzo, Paris.**

The Palm Court Theatre Orchestra & Company

"PUTTIN' ON THE RITZ"

A Sparkling Cavalcade
of 20th Century Popular Music
Original Orchestral Arrangements, Wit & Words;
Unique Concert & Theatre Entertainments

"... Superb showmanship allied to superb musicianship"
Chelmsford Cathedral Festival
"....Enchanting evening" **Illinois, USA**
"...The playing of light music became a specially cultivated art... The tradition has been continued by such sympathetic groups as the Palm Court Theatre Orchestra in England.."
The Oxford Companion to Popular Music

Also Cabaret or Elegant Background;
Big Band Hot Rhythm or Romantic Dance Orchestra;
Syncopated Twenties Razzamatazz,
Sophisticated Swing or Parisian Cafe Jazz;
Classical Ensemble or Tea Room Trio.

Stylish Art Deco Setting, Silver Palms,
Period Microphones, Superb Discreet Sound.

Palm Court Theatre Productions,
Winkton, Christchurch BH23 7AR Tel: 01202 484185
Fax: 01202 47 1920 Email: godwin@palm-court.demon.co.uk

* **English Baroque Soloists** (20-45). Monteverdi Choir and Orchestra Ltd, 61 Wandsworth High St, London SW18 2PT *tel:* 020 8871 4750 *fax:* 020 8871 4751 *email:* info@monteverdi.org.uk. Sir John Eliot Gardiner, artistic dir; Jan Normanton, admin; Howard Gough, acting gen mgr; David Adams, orch mgr; Andrew Hammond, project co-ord.

* **English Camerata** (35). 54 Pegholme Mill, Wharfebank Business Centre, Otley LS21 3JP *tel:* 01943 850853 *fax:* 0113 267 5821 *email:* english.camerata@virgin.net. Elizabeth Altman, artistic dir; Wendy Bowman, admin; Pamela Comber, admin asst. *Associated ensemble is the English Camerata Soloists.*

English Chamber Orchestra (35). 2 Coningsby Rd, London W5 4HR *tel:* 020 8840 6565 *fax:* 020 8567 7198 *email:* mail@e-c-orch.demon.co.uk. Jeffrey Tate, principal cond; Paul Goodwin, principal guest cond; Shuntaro Sato, associate cond; Quintin Ballardie, artistic dir; Pauline Gilbertson, dir.

* **English Classical Players** (15-70). 25b Epsom Lane South, Tadworth, Surrey KT20 5TA *tel:* 01737 813273 *fax:* 01737 215676. Jonathan Brett, artistic dir; Lyn Mumford, exec dir; Anwen Lewis, educ projects mgr.

The English Concert (20-36). 8 St George's Terrace, London NW1 8XJ *tel:* 020 7911 0905 *fax:* 020 7911 0904 *email:* ec@englishconcert.co.uk. Trevor Pinnock, artistic dir; Felix Warnock, gen mgr; Sarah Fenn, orch mgr; Victoria Atkinson, admin.

English Concert Orchestra (50). 6 Chailey Ave, Rottingdean, Brighton BN2 7GH *tel:* 01273 300894 *fax:* 01273 308394 *email:* engconorch@fastnet.co.uk. Roy Wales, mus dir; Christine Wales, admin.

English Festival Orchestra (15-75). 151 Mount View Rd, London N4 4JT *tel:* 020 8341 6408 *fax:* 020 8340 0021 *email:* tford151@aol.com. Trevor Ford, gen mgr; Marianne Barton, concerts mgr.

English Haydn Orchestra. c/o 24a St Mary's St, Newport, Shropshire TF10 7AB *tel:* 01952 825235/811829 *fax:* 01952 814734/812011. John Reid, mgr dir; Sandra Day, admin. *Period insts.*

The English Heritage Orchestra (10-100). Hollybank, 5 The Orchard, Kislingbury, Northants NN7 4BG *tel:* 01604 832461 *also fax*. Graham Mayo, mus dir; Jackie Mayo, admin.

* **English National Opera Orchestra** (91). London Coliseum, St Martin's Lane, London WC2N 4ES *tel:* 020 7836 0111 *fax:* 020 7845 9277 *email:* pdaniel@eno.org. Paul Daniel, mus dir; Ian Killik, orch and concerts dir; Barry Griffiths, orch leader; Nicholas Payne, gen dir; Ian Brignall, orch mgr; Jonathan Burton, librarian; Anthony Legge, head of mus; Terri-Jayne Griffin, production controller.

* **English Northern Philharmonia** (54). Opera North, Grand Theatre, Leeds LS1 6NU *tel:* 0113 243 9999 *fax:* 0113 244 0418. Richard Mantle, gen dir; Stephen Sloane, mus dir; David Greed, leader; Malcolm Warne Holland, orch and concerts mgr; Helen Stephens, mus sec; Andrew Fairley, snr librarian. *Associated chmbr groups are Yorkshire Classic Brass, Music Serenade.*

* **English Sinfonia** (35). 1 Wedgwood Court, Stevenage, Herts SG1 4QR *tel:* 01438 350990 *fax:* 01438 350930 *email:* EnglishSinfonia@tesco.net. Nicolae Moldoveanu, principal cond; Jacek Kaspszyk, principal guest cond; Graham Pfaff, chief exec; Trevor Ford, personnel mgr; Jonathan Hagger, chmn; David Bedford, composer-in-association; John Lill, president; Janice Graham, leader; Janet Wright, educ offr. *Associated chmbr group is English Sinfonia Ensemble (3-9 of the principal players).*

English Sinfonietta (25). The Barn, Layston Park, Royston, Herts SG8 9DS *tel:* 01763 242847 *fax:* 01763 248048. Steuart Bedford, principal cond; Graham Pfaff, gen mgr; Trevor Ford, personnel and orch mgr.

English String Orchestra (48-55). Rockliffe House, 40 Church St, Malvern, Worcs WR14 2AZ *tel:* 01684 560696 *fax:* 01684 560656 *email:* info@eso.co.uk. William Boughton, artistic and mus dir; Anthony Hampson, chmn of the board; Alison King, head of finance and admin; Kate Hodson, admin.

English Symphony Orchestra (48-55). Rockcliffe House, 40 Church St, Malvern, Worcs WR14 2AZ *tel:* 01684 560696 *fax:* 01684 560656 *email:* info@eso.co.uk. William Boughton, artistic and mus dir; Anthony Hampson, chmn of the board; Alison King, head of finance and admin; Kate Hodson, admin.

Eos (6-45). Ellesmere House, South St, Castle Cary, Somerset BA7 7EX *fax:* 01963 351446. Charles Hazlewood, mus dir; Philip Dukes, leader; Mark Dornford-May, producer.

Equinox (45). 1 Elmsted Court Cottages, Elmsted, Ashford, Kent TN25 5JN *tel:* 01233 750221 *also fax*. Richard Farnes, mus dir.

The Esterhazy Orchestra (17). 278 Kew Rd, Richmond, Surrey TW9 3EE *tel:* 020 8948 6140. Philip Trzebiatowski, admin; Martin Loveday, leader.

European Camerata. c/o TransArt (UK) Ltd, 8 Bristol Gardens, London W9 2JG *tel:* 020 7286 7526 *fax:* 020 7266 2687 *email:* transart@transartuk.com.

Ex Cathedra Baroque Orchestra (18-25). Suite 303, Jewellery Business Centre, 95 Spencer St, Birmingham B18 6DA *tel:* 0121 523 1025 *fax:* 0121 523 1026. Justin Lee, gen mgr; Micaela Comberti, leader; Jeffrey Skidmore, artistic dir.

Fine Arts Sinfonia (40). c/o Thornton Management, 24 Thornton Ave, London SW2 4HG *tel:* 020 8671 4408 *fax:* 020 8671 2848 *email:* admin@fasinfonia.freeserve.co.uk. Michael Nebe, mus dir; Peter Fisher, Martin Smith, leaders; John Austin, mgr (*tel:* 020 8313 1733).

Fiori Musicali. Bank Cottage, Preston Capes, Northants NN11 3TD *tel:* 01327 361380 *fax:* 01327 361415 *email:* emma@fiori-musicali.com. Penelope Rapson, dir; Kerstin Linder-Dewan, leader; Bernard Rapson, treasurer; Jonathan Asquith, chmn; Emma Abel, concert development (*tel:* 020 8679 9591).

* **Foundation Philharmonic Orchestra, Young Persons Concert Foundation** (30-94). PO Box 419, Enfield, Middx EN2 0ZB *tel:* 020 8367 0553; 01923 859388 *fax:* 020 8366 3535. William Starling, artistic dir; Sara Neighbour, orch mgr; Sally Needleman, special projects co-ord; David Gallagher, librarian. *Associated group is the Foundation Big Band.*

Franz Liszt Chamber Orchestra. c/o Hazard Chase Ltd, Richmond House, 16-20 Regent St, Cambridge CB2 1DB *tel:* 01223 312400 *fax:* 01223 460827 *email:* info@hazardchase.co.uk.

Gabrieli Consort and Players (12-70). Foresters Hall, 25-27 Westow St, London SE19 3RY *tel:* 020 8771 7974 *fax:* 020 8771 7973 *email:* gabrieliconsort@compuserve.com. Paul McCreesh, dir; Anita Crowe, gen mgr; Lucy Miller, admin; Dawn Rotheram, dir of development. *Renaissance and baroque insts.*

The Georgian Camerata (4-40). 2 Gastein Rd, London W6 8LU *tel:* 020 7381 2175 *also fax.* Jonathan Stallick, artistic dir; Sarah Baxter, orch mgr. *Specialists in baroque and classical repertoire.*

* **Glyndebourne Touring Opera Orchestra.** Lott's End, Highgate, Forest Row, E Sussex RH18 5BE *tel:* 01342 824536 *also fax; email:* nicholas.logie@virgin.net. Louis Langrée, mus dir; Nicholas Logie, orch mgr.

Goldberg Chamber Orchestra. 7 Rowsley Ave, West Didsbury, Manchester M20 2XD *tel:* 0161 448 0978 *also fax.* Malcolm Layfield, artistic dir.

Grieg Festival Orchestra (14-45). c/o Roy Baker Concert Management, 25 Lynors Ave, Rochester, Kent ME2 3NQ *tel:* 01634 714434 *also fax.* Roy Baker, mkt dir and publicity; David Burrowes, artistic dir and cond.

* **Guildford Philharmonic Orchestra** (70-75). Millmead House, Millmead, Guildford, Surrey GU2 5BB *tel:* 01483 444666 *fax:* 01483 444732 *email:* guildfordphil@guildford.gov.uk. En Shao, principal cond; Clare Lister, mus development; Nicola Goold, gen mgr; Peter Holt, mus admin. *Associated chmbr group is Guildford Philharmonic Chamber Orchestra.*

* **The Hallé Orchestra** (80). The Bridgewater Hall, Manchester M2 3WS *tel:* 0161 237 7000 *fax:* 0161 237 7029. Kent Nagano, mus dir and principal cond; John Summers, chief exec; Tom Baxter, orch mgr; Andy Ryans, dir of mkt; Lesley Tomlinson, dir of finance; Katharine Russell, dir of development; Richard Wigley, dir of educ.

Handel Festival Orchestra (45+). 34 Northend Rd, London W14 0SH *tel:* 020 7602 6818 *fax:* 020 7602 8162. Charles Farncombe CBE, mus dir; Rolf Wilson, leader; Sylvia Darley OBE, admin.

* **The Hanover Band.** The Old Market, Upper Market St, Hove, E Sussex BN3 1AS *tel:* 01273 206978 *fax:* 01273 329636 *email:* mailbox @hanoverband.co.uk. Caroline Brown, artistic dir; Stephen Neiman, exec dir; David Orams, mkt and communication mgr; Jane Saunders, PA to artistic dir; Kathy Avdiev, promotions mgr.

Havant Symphony Orchestra (70-90). 152 West St, Havant, Hants PO9 1LP *tel:* 023 9248 3228. Peter Craddock, mus dir; Sandra Craddock, admin; Helen Gutteridge, librarian. *Associated orch group is Havant Chamber Orchestra.*

Imperial Chamber Orchestra (35). 1 Imperial Manor, 34 Clifftown Parade, Southend-on-Sea, Essex SS1 1DL *tel:* 01702 332480 *fax:* 01702 339108. Miranda Hanbury, admin; Christopher Wood, principal cond.

Interpreti Veneziani (8-30). c/o Roy Baker Concert Management, 25 Lynors Ave, Rochester, Kent ME2 3NQ *tel:* 01634 714434 *also fax.* Paolo Cognolato, artistic dir; Giuliano Fontanella, leader.

Irish Chamber Orchestra. c/o Owen/White Management (OWM), 39 Hillfield Ave, London N8 7DS *tel:* 020 8340 9571 *fax:* 020 8340 4056 *email:* owenwhite@compuserve.com. Fionnuala Hunt, artistic dir; John Kelly, chief exec.

Isle of Wight Symphony Orchestra Society (60+). 2 Kingsway, Park Rd, Cowes, Isle of Wight PO31 7LU *tel:* 01983 290495. Jean Kirkpatrick, admin; Richard Scott, chmn; Malcolm Lawson, press offr; Jonathan Butcher, cond; Mark Fitzgerald, guest cond.

* **Jupiter Orchestra** (30-35). 57 White Horse Rd, London E1 0ND *tel:* 020 7790 5883 *fax:* 020 7265 9170 *email:* gregory-rose@tisl.co.uk. Gregory Rose, mus dir; John Jones, publicity offr. *Associated chmbr groups are Principal Winds of Jupiter Orchestra, Jupiter Brass and Jupiter Singers.*

Kiev Radio Symphony (105). c/o Sonata, 11 North Park St, Glasgow G20 7AA *tel:* 0141 945 3553 *fax:* 0141 946 7034 *email:* gregor@sonata.freeserve.co.uk. Vladimir Sirenko, cond; Yevgeni Semchenko, mgr.

The King's Consort (15-50). 34 St Mary's Grove, London W4 3LN *tel:* 020 8995 9994 *fax:* 020 8995 2115 *email:* info@the-kings-consort.org.uk. Robert King, artistic dir; Edward Hossack, artistic mgr; Nicky Oppenheimer, development dir; Eugenia Pino, tour mgr; Elizabeth Baines, admin. *Associated chmbr group and choir.*

Kreisler String Orchestra (17). 57 Sunnyside Rd, Chesham, Bucks HP5 2AR *tel:* 01494 792572 *also fax*. Robert Woollard, mgr; Helen Kamminga, admin. *Associated chmbr groups are Duke String Quartet, Diorama String Quartet and Kreisler String Quartet.*

Leicester Symphony Orchestra. 37 Cancell Rd, London SW9 6HP *tel:* 020 7735 1002 *also fax*. Roland Melia, artistic dir.

Lithuanian State Symphony (95). c/o Sonata, 11 North Park St, Glasgow G20 7AA *tel:* 0141 945 3553 *fax:* 0141 946 7034 *email:* gregor@sonata.freeserve.co.uk. Gintaras Rinkevicius, cond; Eugenijus Butvidas, mgr.

Little Symphony of London (35). 14 Beaumont Rd, Purley, Surrey CR8 2EG *tel:* 020 8668 5883 *also fax*. Darrell Davison, mus dir.

Liverpool Sinfonia (20-70). 117 Beresford Rd, Birkenhead, Merseyside CH43 2JD *tel:* 0151 653 4575 *fax:* 0151 653 5541. Graham Jordan Ellis, principal cond; Ferdinand Bush, admin; John Bratherton, leader.

London Bach Orchestra (8-40). c/o Malcolm Layfield Management, 1 Rowsley Ave, West Didsbury, Manchester M20 2XD *tel:* 0161 446 2170 *also fax*. Nicholas Kraemer, artistic dir. *Associated chmbr group is London Bach Ensemble.*

London Camerata (15-35). 21 Halstead Rd, Mountsorrel, Leics LE12 7HD *tel:* 0116 230 3674 *also fax*. Paul Hilliam, mus dir.

London Chamber Orchestra (6-45). c/o The London Chamber Society Ltd, 6 Hambalt Rd, London SW4 9EB *tel:* 020 8772 9741 *fax:* 020 8772 9742 *email:* info@lco.co.uk. Christopher Warren-Green, mus dir; Step Parikian, projects mgr; Jonathan Williams, artistic admin.

London Chamber Players (10-32). PO Box 84, London NW11 8AL *tel:* 020 8455 9200 *also fax*. Adrian Sunshine, mus dir; Sheila Genden, admin. *Various associated chmbr ensembles (quartets, quintets, sextets, etc).*

London Chamber Symphony (30+). Toynbee Studios, 28 Commercial St, London E1 6LS *tel:* 020 7247 2950 *fax:* 020 7247 2956. Odaline de la Martinez, cond and mus dir; Sophie Langdon, leader; Jan Hart, admin.

London City Chamber Orchestra (25). 3-5 Bridge St, Hadleigh, Suffolk IP7 6BY *tel:* 01473 822596 *fax:* 01473 824175. T L McIntosh, principal cond; Miranda H V Reckitt, gen mgr and admin; S Sowman, press offr. *Associated chmbr group is London City Chamber Orchestra Ensemble.*

London Concert Orchestra (30-80). 29-31 East Barnet Rd, New Barnet, Herts EN4 8RN *tel:* 020 8216 3000 *fax:* 020 8216 3001 *email:* info@raymond-gubbay.co.uk. Cathy Lewis, events co-ord; Raymond Gubbay, dir.

London Concert Sinfonia (13-45). 14 Frampton House, Frampton St, London NW8 8LY *tel:* 020 7724 7222 *also fax*. John Landor, mus dir; David Jermyn, gen asst.

London Concertante (18). 1st Floor, 105 Ferndale Rd, London SW4 7RL *tel:* 020 7207 3564 *fax:* 020 7652 0979 *email:* cmg@cgrist.demon.co.uk. Bjorn Bryn Petersen, cond; Chris Grist, gen mgr.

London Festival Orchestra (15-30). 13 Theed St, London SE1 8ST *tel:* 020 7928 9251 *fax:* 020 7928 9252 *email:* orchestra@lfo.co.uk. Ross Pople, artistic dir; Ian Pressland, gen mgr; Sarah Roseblade, educ and outreach offr; Elizabeth Szücs, exec mgr, The Warehouse. *Based at the Warehouse, Waterloo.*

London Gala Orchestra (20-70). 14 Lytton Rd, London E11 1JH *tel:* 020 8556 8294 *also fax*. Phillip Ellis, associate cond; Wilfred Goddard, gen mgr; Lynne Dore, admin. *Associated chmbr group is London Gala Soloists.*

London Lyric Orchestra. 4a Harewood Rd, South Croydon, Surrey CR2 7AL *tel:* 020 8688 2430 *also fax*. Judith Wordsworth, orch mgr.

London Metropolitan Orchestra (15-110). Timbers, Woburn Hill, Weybridge, Surrey KT15 2QG *tel:* 01932 853271/853273 *fax:* 01932 859233 *email:* andy@lmo.co.uk. Andrew Brown, mgr dir; Steven Fox, company sec; Rachel Bennett, orch mgr; Howard Chilvers, business development mgr.

* **London Mozart Players** (19-45). 92 Chatsworth Rd, Croydon, Surrey CR0 1HB *tel:* 020 8686 1996 *fax:* 020 8686 2187 *email:* info@lmp.org. Matthias Bamert, mus dir; Ian Lush, mgr dir; James Galway, principal guest cond; Fiona Emmerson, admin; David Wilson, orch mgr; Alice Walton, mkt mgr; Margaret Archibald, educ mgr. *Associated chmbr group is London Mozart Players Chamber Ensemble.*

London Musici. C134, Learning Resource Centre, Thames Valley University, St Mary's Rd, London W5 5RF *tel:* 020 8231 2319 *fax:* 020 8231 2316 *email:* london.musici@tvu.ac.uk. Mark Stephenson, mus dir; Trea Hubbard, admin; Wendy Hacker, orch mgr; Qasim Kazmi, mkt and development mgr.

* **London Musicians Orchestra** (25-80). Cedar House, Vine Lane, Hillingdon, Middx UB10 0BX *tel:* 01895 252555 *fax:* 01895 252556 *email:* mail@lonmus.demon.co.uk. Sylvia Addison, orch mgr.

London Orchestra da Camera (15-50). 15 Green St, Milton Malsor, Northampton NN7 3AT *tel:* 01604 859414 *fax:* 01604 859269. Nick Turner, chmn; Matthew Turner, concerts mgr; Angela Bartram, admin; Robert Williams, cond. *Baroque to contemporary mus; chmbr to full-size orch.*

London Orpheus Orchestra (50-60). 2 Tenby Mansions, Nottingham St, London W1M 3RD *tel:* 020 7486 1929. James Gaddarn, principal cond; Colin Evans, chmn; Judith Scammell, sec.

London Philanova Orchestra. 43 Briton Hill Rd, Sanderstead, Surrey CR2 0JJ *tel:* 020 8657 1662. Philip Winter, mus dir.

* **London Philharmonic Orchestra** (92). Riverside Building, Belvedere Rd, County Hall, London SE1 7PB *tel:* 020 7546 1600 *fax:* 020 7546 1601 *email:* email@lpo.org.uk. Bernard Haitink, president; Kurt Masur, principal conductor designate; Robert St John Wright, chmn; Serge Dorny, artistic dir and chief exec; Andrew Gambrell, gen mgr and finance dir; Ruth Sansom, artistic admin; Dominique Savelkoul, dir of mkt and development; Jacqueline Barsoux, mkt mgr.

London Pops Orchestra (18-80). 58 Alexandra Rd, London NW4 2RY *tel:* 020 8203 1747 *fax:* 020 8203 1064 *email:* londonpops@lineone.net. Ian McMillan, principal cond and artistic dir; Quentin Poole, exec dir; Tano Rea, gen mgr; Paul Elliott, concert/tours mgr; Becca Smithers, concert admin; Stephen Dinwoodie, personnel and orch mgr.

London Pro Arte Baroque Orchestra. 17b St Augustine's Ave, South Croydon, Surrey CR2 6JN *tel:* 020 8688 2890 *fax:* 020 8688 2901 *email:* proarte@dial.pipex.com. Murray Stewart, artistic dir; Richard Thomas, mgr.

* **London Pro Arte Orchestra** (14-60). 17b St Augustine's Ave, South Croydon, Surrey CR2 6JN *tel:* 020 8688 2890 *fax:* 020 8688 2901 *email:* proarte@dial.pipex.com. Murray Stewart, mus dir; John Cobb, orch mgr. *Associated chmbr groups are London Pro Arte Brass Ensemble and London Pro Arte Percussion Ensemble.*

London Schubert Players (14+). 72 Warwick Gardens, London W14 8PP *tel:* 020 7603 1396 *also fax; email:* schubert@dial.pipex.com. John Gritten, dir; Anda Anastasescu, mus dir; Jonathan Del Mar, principal cond. *Associated chmbr groups are London Schubert Players Piano Trio, Quartet, Quintet; string, wind quintet.*

London Sinfonia Ltd (34). 1 The Bridle Path, Coventry CV5 9QF *tel:* 024 7640 4696. Gordon Heard, mus dir; Noreen Mason, gen mgr. *Associated chmbr groups are Mozart Orchestra, London Wind Sinfonia.*

* **London Sinfonietta.** Dominion House, 101 Southwark St, London SE1 0JF *tel:* 020 7928 0828 *fax:* 020 7928 8557. Oliver Knussen CBE, mus dir; Gillian Moore MBE, artistic dir; Cathy Graham, mgr dir; Jane Williams, artistic admin; Sarah Holmes, concerts mgr; Tony Mackintosh, chmn of the council; Nick Reyland, mkt offr; Tabby Bowers-Broadbent, educ mgr; Patricia Mayes, personnel mgr; Penny Jonas, development mgr. *Associated chmbr groups are London Sinfonietta Voices and London Sinfonietta Chorus.*

London Soloists' Chamber Orchestra (14-43). 76 Sloane St, London SW1X 9SF *tel:* 020 7235 6378; 01483 282666 gen mgr *fax:* 020 7235 1615 *email:* nick.bomford@btinternet.com. David Josefowitz, principal cond; Nick Bomford, gen mgr; Maria Morphopoulos, sec.

London String Orchestra (16). 37 St Davids Rd, Clifton Campville, nr Tamworth, Staffs B79 0BA *tel:* 01827 373586. James Maddocks, mus dir; Joan Maddocks, mgr. *Associated chmbr group is Concordia Ensemble.*

* **London Symphony Orchestra** (100). Barbican Centre, Barbican, London EC2Y 8DS *tel:* 020 7588 1116 *fax:* 020 7374 0127 *email:* admin@lso.co.uk. Sir Colin Davis CBE, principal cond; Richard Hickox, associate cond; Michael Tilson Thomas, principal guest cond; André Previn, cond laureate; Clive Gillinson, mgr dir; Sue Mallet, concerts head; John Lawley, chmn; Karen Cardy, head of mkt; Alison Dunnett, head of development; Simon Wales, concerts mgr; Dvora Lewis, PR consultant.

London Theatre Orchestra. 210 Burnt Ash Hill, London SE12 0QE *tel:* 020 8857 1297. Peter Civil, cond.

* **Manchester Camerata** (30). Zion Arts Centre, Stretford Rd, Manchester M15 5ZA *tel:* 0161 226 8696 *fax:* 0161 226 8600 *email:* mancam@compuserve.com. Sachio Fujioka, principal cond; Richard Howarth, leader; Lucy Potter, gen mgr.

Manchester Concert Orchestra. Raymond Gubbay Ltd, Eaton Place, 114 Washway Rd, Sale, Cheshire M33 7RF *tel:* 0161 718 9208 *fax:* 0161 718 5947 *email:* cknowles@raymond-gubbay.co.uk. Christopher Knowles.

The Matrix Ensemble (5-35). 77 Thrale Rd, London SW16 1NU *tel:* 020 8769 4292 *fax:* 020 8696 7293 *email:* ziegler@matrixmusic.u-net.com. Robert Ziegler, mus dir; Nicky Webb, gen manager

national musicians

nmso

symphony orchestra

National Musicians Symphony Orchestra

Artistic Director James Blair

Flat 4,
11 Gunnersbury Avenue,
London W5 3NJ

Tel:	0208 993 3135
Fax:	0208 993 2635
Email:	nmso@dircon.co.uk
Homepage:	www.users.dircon.co.uk/~nmso

Auditions held throughout the UK and Ireland every year in January.

A total of three courses and workshops are held annually during easter, summer and autumn. Concerts are given in all major venues.

NMSO

Training the new generation of musicians

Unilever

Sponsored by Unilever

* **Milton Keynes City Orchestra** (25-60). 3 Theatre Walk, Central Milton Keynes MK9 3PX *tel:* 01908 692777 *fax:* 01908 230099 *email:* rodbirtles@cityorch.freeserve.co.uk. Hilary Davan Wetton, mus dir; Rod Birtles, gen mgr; Ian Brignall, personnel and orch mgr; Sue Smith, operations mgr.

Moray Chamber Orchestra (20-90). Kildonan, Young St, Elgin, Moray IV30 1TH *tel:* 01343 543531. Peter Zanrè, dir.

Mozart Orchestra Ltd (18-50). Sinfonia, The Bridle Path, Coventry CV5 9QF *tel:* 024 7640 4696. Gordon Heard, artistic dir; Cyril Horne, chmn.

Music Projects/London (10-50). 11 Elmwood Rd, Chiswick, London W4 3DY *tel:* 020 8994 9528 *fax:* 020 8994 9595 *email:* mpl.richard @bernas.demon.co.uk. Richard Bernas, Roger Williams, artistic dirs; Nancy Ruffer, concert mgr.

The Musicians of All Saints. 11 Cranedown, Lewes, E Sussex BN7 3NA *tel:* 01273 475544 *fax:* 01273 483561. Andrew Sherwood, mus dir; Jan Stammers, sec; Peter Copley, deputy mus dir.

National Chamber Orchestra of Wales (12-60). 40 Tudor Court, Murton, Swansea SA3 3BB *tel:* 01792 232387; 07860 725934 *fax:* 01792 234868 *email:* ncowales@hotmail.com. G J Harries, mgr.

National Musicians Symphony Orchestra. 11 Gunnersbury Ave, London W5 3NJ *tel:* 020 8993 3135 *fax:* 020 8993 2635 *email:* nmso @dircon.co.uk. James Blair, artistic dir.

National Philharmonic of Ukraine (Kharkov) (75). c/o Sonata, 11 North Park St, Glasgow G20 7AA *tel:* 0141 945 3553 *fax:* 0141 946 7034. Victoria Zhadko, cond; Nikolai Saltovsky, mgr.

The National Sinfonia (25-80). 15 Green St, Milton Malsor, Northampton NN7 3AT *tel:* 01604 859414 *fax:* 01604 859269. Nick Turner, gen mgr; Russell Thackeray, chmn; Matthew Turner, orch mgr; David Temple, cond. *Associated orch is The National Sinfonietta.*

The National Symphony Orchestra (60-100). Jumps Rd, Churt, Farnham, Surrey GU10 2JY *tel:* 01252 792315 *fax:* 01252 795120 *email:* enquiries@nso.co.uk. Martin Yates, principal cond; Anne Collis, joint artistic dir and mgr; Perry Montague-Mason, leader and artistic dir; Eileen Wellington, librarian. *Associated chmbr group is National Symphony Orchestra Virtuosi.*

New Chamber Orchestra. 130 High St, Oxford OX1 4DH *tel:* 01865 378514 *fax:* 01865 722953. Andrew Zreczycki, mus dir; Philip Vincent, chmn.

New English Concert Orchestra (45-50). 23 Hitchin St, Biggleswade, Beds SG18 8AX *tel:* 01767 316521 *fax:* 01767 317221 *email:* neco@lindsaymusic.co.uk. Douglas Coombes, mus dir; Rose Miles, gen mgr; Carole Lindsay-Douglas, concerts mgr. *Agent: Lindsay.*

New English Orchestra. 14 Woodbine Rd, Barbourne, Worcester WR1 3JB *tel:* 01905 613771. Nigel Swinford, artistic dir and principal cond; Alison Hawcutt, gen enquiries; Nick Gerrard, PR.

* **New London Orchestra** (15-80). 4 Lower Belgrave St, London SW1W 0LJ *tel:* 020 7823 5523 *fax:* 020 7823 6373. Ronald Corp, artistic dir; Celia Mike, general mgr; James Doherty, orch mgr; Elizabeth Harper, educ and community.

New London Sinfonia (12-75). 2 Cuckoo Close, North Waltham, Hants RG25 2BJ *tel:* 01256 397409 *also fax.* David Gibson, mus dir; Julian Leaper, leader.

New Mozart Orchestra (30). c/o Westcott House, 54 Walkford Rd, Walkford, Christchurch, Dorset BH23 5QF *tel:* 01425 277128. Clive Fairbairn, artistic dir; Andrew Foreman, finance dir; Ronald Swann, chmn and acting sec.

New Queen's Hall Orchestra (80). c/o Manygate Management, 13 Cotswold Mews, 30 Battersea Square, London SW11 3RA *tel:* 020 7223 7265 *fax:* 020 7585 2830 *email:* manygate@easynet.co.uk. John Boyden, artistic dir; James Thomson, gen admin; Edward Price, concerts mgr.

New Wind Symphony Orchestra (8-40). 119 Woolstone Rd, Forest Hill, London SE23 2TQ *tel:* 020 8699 1101 *fax:* 020 8699 2219. Catherine Pluygers, mus dir; Neil Thomson, principal cond; Jonathan Lindridge, admin; Mark Tromans, personnel and orch mgr.

North of England Chamber and Concert Orchestra. Northern Orchestral Enterprises Limited, Room 23, Dean Clough, Halifax HX3 5AX *tel:* 01422 330533 *fax:* 01422 348916. John Pryce-Jones, artistic dir; Sue Rosborough, admin; Jane Killian, admin asst.

Northern Chamber Orchestra (16-27). MMU, 799 Wilmslow Rd, Manchester M20 2RR *tel:* 0161 247 2220 *fax:* 0161 247 6899. Nicholas Ward, artistic dir; Jonathan Thackeray, development mgr.

* **Northern Sinfonia** (37). The Sinfonia Centre, 41 Jesmond Vale, Newcastle upon Tyne NE2 1PG *tel:* 0191 240 1812 *fax:* 0191 240 2668 *email:* nsinfonia@ndirect.co.uk. Richard Hickox, cond emeritus; Heinrich Schiff, hon guest cond; John Casken, composer-in-association; Andrew Bennett, chief exec; Stella Robson, chair. *Associated chmbr groups are The Sinfonia Ensemble and Vaganza.*

Northern Symphony Orchestra. 23 The Moorings, Middlewich, Cheshire CW10 9ER *tel:* 01606 836292. Raymond Lomax, mus dir; Judith Lomax, admin.

Oare String Orchestra (24). 25 Church Rd, Oare, Faversham, Kent ME13 0QA *tel:* 01795 535209 *fax:* 01795 533215 *email:* oso@dial.pipex.com. Don Goodsell, president; Peter Aviss, mus dir; Peter Colman, treasurer; Jonathan Chapter, sec; Michael F Clark, chmn.

* **Orchestra da Camera** (25-50). 41 Fishponds Rd, Kenilworth, Warwicks CV8 1EY *tel:* 01926 858187 *also fax; email:* RosPage1@aol.com. Brenda Page, personnel and orch mgr; David Wilkinson, chmn; Margaret Banwell, educ co-ord; Rosalind Page, concerts mgr, artistic adviser. *Associated chmbr group is Neue Wiener Ensemble.*

* **Orchestra of St John's, Smith Square** (12-80). The White House, Eltham College, Grove Park Rd, London SE9 4QF *tel:* 020 8857 8579 *fax:* 020 8857 9340. John Lubbock, artistic dir; Nicky Goulder, gen mgr; Anna Hall, educ and audience development mgr; Alison Atkinson, concerts dir; Helen Willis, mkt dir; John Woolrich, associate composer, 1999-2000; Deirdre Gribbin, associate composer 1999-2002. *Various associated chmbr groups and choir.*

* **Orchestra of The Age of Enlightenment.** Fifth Floor, Westcombe House, 56-58 Whitcomb St, London WC2H 7DN *tel:* 020 7930 0646 *fax:* 020 7930 0626 *email:* oae@premier.co.uk. Marshall Marcus, chmn; David Pickard, gen mgr; James Ellis, artistic admin; Philippa Brownsword, orch manager.

* **Orchestra of the Swan** (16-45). 66 West St, Stratford-upon-Avon, Warwicks CV37 6DR *tel:* 01789 267567 *also fax*. David Curtis, cond, artistic dir; Allan McKay, chmn; Sheila Bligh, sec of Friends.

* **Orchestre Révolutionnaire et Romantique** (45-70). Monteverdi Choir and Orchestra Ltd, 61 Wandsworth High St, London SW18 2PT *tel:* 020 8871 4750 *fax:* 020 8871 4751 *email:* info@monteverdi.org.uk. Sir John Eliot Gardiner, artistic dir; Jan Normanton, admin; Howard Gough, acting gen mgr; David Adams, orch mgr.

Oxford Philomusica. PO Box 5, 266 Banbury Rd, Oxford OX2 7DL *tel:* 0870 606 0804 *fax:* 020 8208 4239 *email:* oxfilmus@globalnet.co.uk. Vladimir Ashkenazy, patron; Marios Papadopoulos, mus dir; Philip Newman, chmn of the Oxford Philomusica Trust; David C Stone, chief exec; Julian Gallant, international liaison; James Lawson, mgr; Jeannette Warwick, social sec; Larissa Blackwood, Vanessa Friar, admin.

Palm Court Theatre Orchestra. Palm Court Theatre Productions, Winkton, Christchurch BH23 7AR *tel:* 01202 484185 *fax:* 01202 471920.

Pasadena Roof Orchestra. Priors, Tye Green, Elsenham, Herts CM22 6DY *tel:* 01279 813240/815593 *fax:* 01279 815895 *email:* procentral@aol.com. David Curtis, mgr.

* **Performing Arts Symphony Orchestra** (65). c/o Performing Arts Management Ltd, Canal 7, Clarence Mill, Bollington, Macclesfield, Cheshire SK10 5JZ *tel:* 01625 575681 *fax:* 01625 572839. Clare Scott, orch mgr; Nicholas Smith, cond.

Petersfield Orchestra. 1 Stable Flat, Uppark, South Harting, Petersfield GU31 5QR *tel:* 01730 825638. Judith Bailey, cond.

* **Philharmonia Orchestra** (93). 1st Floor, 125 High Holborn, London WC1V 6QA *tel:* 020 7242 5001 *fax:* 020 7242 4840 *email:* info@philharmonia.co.uk. Christoph von Dohnányi, principal cond; Leonard Slatkin, principal guest cond; Keith Bragg, chmn; David Whelton, mgr dir; Fiona Martin, deputy mgr dir; Nikola White, concerts dir; Emma Fergie Woods, development mgr; Jill Pridmore, sales and mkt mgr; Michael Elliston, finance dir; Mansel Bebb, personnel mgr. *Philharmonia Orchestra Library:* Unit LG10, Linton House, 164-180 Union St, London SE1 0LH *tel:* 020 7928 7682 *fax:* 020 7401 9098.

Philharmonic Concert Orchestra (35). 6 Victoria Grove, Fallowfield, Manchester M14 6BF *tel:* 0161 256 3686 *fax:* 0161 248 4435 *email:* joncordial@msn.com. Edward Peak, mus dir and principal cond; Matthew Scrivener, leader; Jonathan Thackeray, gen mgr.

Philomel Orchestra. 57 Grange Rd, Sutton, Surrey SM2 6SY *tel:* 020 8643 4425 *also fax*. Duke Dobing, mus dir. *Associated chmbr group is Philomel Ensemble.*

Philomusica of Aberystwyth (95). Maesarfor, Borth, Ceredigion SY24 5JP *tel:* 01970 871372 *email:* muswww@aber.ac.uk. David Russell Hulme, cond; Geraint Lewis, chmn of orch; Celia Matthews, sec.

The Portsmouth New Music Orchestra. The New Theatre Royal, Guildhall Walk, Portsmouth, Hants PO1 2DD *tel:* 023 9235 1815 *email:* pnmo_webber@yahoo.com. John Webber, dir of mus; Robert Blanken, dir of chmbr mus.

Primavera Chamber Orchestra (13-33). Horseshoe Barn, Cobbarn Farm, Groombridge Lane, Eridge, Tunbridge Wells TN3 9LA *tel:* 01892 864069 *also fax*. Paul Manley, mus dir. *Associated chmbr group is Primavera Chamber Ensemble.*

Purcell Orchestra (15-35). 86 Park Hill, Carshalton Beeches, Surrey SM5 3RZ *tel:* 020 8669 4358 *also fax; email:* purcell.orch@argonet.co.uk. Robin Page, artistic dir; Elizabeth Andrews, gen mgr; Rebecca Lacey, orch mgr.

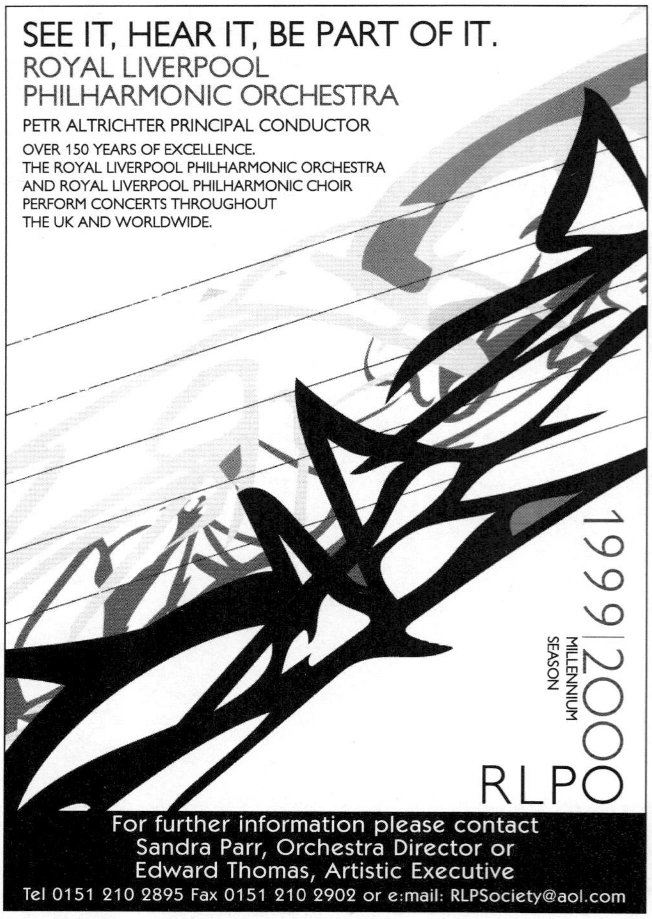
SEE IT, HEAR IT, BE PART OF IT.
ROYAL LIVERPOOL
PHILHARMONIC ORCHESTRA
PETR ALTRICHTER PRINCIPAL CONDUCTOR
OVER 150 YEARS OF EXCELLENCE.
THE ROYAL LIVERPOOL PHILHARMONIC ORCHESTRA
AND ROYAL LIVERPOOL PHILHARMONIC CHOIR
PERFORM CONCERTS THROUGHOUT
THE UK AND WORLDWIDE.
1999|2000
MILLENNIUM SEASON
RLPO
For further information please contact
Sandra Parr, Orchestra Director or
Edward Thomas, Artistic Executive
Tel 0151 210 2895 Fax 0151 210 2902 or e:mail: RLPSociety@aol.com

SUSSEX SYMPHONY ORCHESTRA
President **Sir Charles Mackerras CBE**
Principal Conductor **Mark Andrew-James**
Still making waves across the South
20 Hampton Place, Brighton, East Sussex BN1 3DD
Telephone: 01273 208680 Fax: 01273 777963
e-mail: ss0@goodger.demon.co.uk
web: www.goodger.demon.co.uk/sso/

Royal Philharmonic Orchestra
For concerts, tours,
recordings and film scores . . .
WITH BRILLIANCE AND PASSION
'RICH, FLUID and
BEAUTIFUL sound'
The Times
Please contact Sara Lom:
16 Clerkenwell Green, London ECIR 0QT
020 7608 2381 info@rpo.co.uk www.rpo.co.uk
Registered charity 244533

Raglan Baroque Players (9-40). 140 Muswell Hill Rd, London N10 3JD *tel:* 020 8444 2507 *fax:* 020 8444 1795 *email:* raglanadmin@compuserve.com. Nicholas Kraemer, mus dir; Vicky Miller, mgr. *Agent: Sykes.*

The Regent Sinfonia of London (14-60). 17 Parliament Hill, London NW3 2TA *tel:* 020 7435 5965 *fax:* 020 7435 9166. George Vass, artistic dir; Michael Moore, concerts mgr; Charlotte Edwards, leader.

Ripon St Cecilia Orchestra (30-100). Ashley House, Ure Bank, Ripon, N Yorks HG4 1JG *tel:* 01765 602856 *email:* RipStCec@hotmail.com. Xenophon Kelsey, mus dir. *Associated chmbr group is The Mowbray Ensemble.*

Rossini Chamber Orchestra (13-35). 10a Radipole Rd, London SW6 5DL *tel:* 020 7736 3821. Alexander Bryett, mus dir; Ian Bookey, gen mgr; John Biggin, concerts mgr.

Royal Ballet Sinfonia, the Orchestra of Birmingham Royal Ballet (45). Thorp St, Birmingham B5 4AU *tel:* 0121 622 2555 *fax:* 0121 689 3072 *email:* sinfonia@brb.org.uk. Barry Wordsworth, mus dir; Paul Murphy, principal cond; Philip Ellis, cond; John Beadle, mus admin; Andrew Bentley, orch mgr; Louise Robertson, mus asst/librarian.

* **The Royal Liverpool Philharmonic Orchestra** (90). Philharmonic Hall, Hope St, Liverpool L1 9BP *tel:* 0151 210 2895 *fax:* 0151 210 2902 *email:* rlpsociety@aol.com. Petr Altrichter, principal cond; Junichi Hirokami, principal guest cond; Antony Lewis-Crosby, chief exec; Robert Moon, finance dir; Ian Archer, dir of mkt; Sandra Parr, orch dir; Marion Mottram, orch mgr.

* **Royal Philharmonic Concert Orchestra** *formerly* Pops Orchestra (80). 16 Clerkenwell Green, London EC1R 0DP *tel:* 020 7608 2381 *fax:* 020 7608 1226 *email:* info@rpo.co.uk. Thomas Siracusa, mgr; John Manger, mgr dir; Andrew Sippings, chmn.

* **Royal Philharmonic Orchestra** (85). 16 Clerkenwell Green, London EC1R 0QT *tel:* 020 7608 2381 *fax:* 020 7608 1226 *email:* info@rpo.co.uk; Daniele Gatti, mus dir; Yuri Temirkanov, cond laureate; Sir Peter Maxwell Davies CBE, associate cond and composer; John Manger, mgr dir; Andrew Sippings, chmn; Tom Siracusa, head of RPCO; Sara Lom, development and mkt; Judith Webster, head of educ.

* **Royal Scottish National Orchestra** (87). 73 Claremont St, Glasgow G3 7JB *tel:* 0141 226 3868 *fax:* 0141 221 4317 *email:* admin@rsno.org.uk. Simon Crookall, chief exec; Julian de Ste. Croix, planning mgr; Paul Rissman, educ mgr; Jenny Black, finance mgr.

St James's Baroque Players (3-50). 200 Broomwood Rd, London SW11 6JY *tel:* 020 7228 6388 *fax:* 020 7738 1706. Ivor Bolton, mus dir; Delia Pye, mgr.

St Petersburg State Capella. c/o Sonata, 11 North Park St, Glasgow G20 7AA *tel:* 0141 945 3553 *fax:* 0141 946 7034. Vladislav Chernoushenko, cond; Vitali Lavrov, mgr.

Sarum Chamber Orchestra (20-30). 57 East St, Corfe Castle, Wareham, Dorset *tel:* 01929 481020 *also fax.* Howard Moody, artistic dir; Nancy Strike, admin; Daphne Handford, leader. *Associated chmbr groups are Eberle String Quartet, Banks Piano Trio.*

* **The Scottish Chamber Orchestra** (37). 4 Royal Terrace, Edinburgh EH7 5AB *tel:* 0131 557 6800 *fax:* 0131 557 6933 *email:* info@sco.org.uk. Joseph Swensen, principal cond; Sir Charles Mackerras, cond laureate; Sir Peter Maxwell Davies, composer laureate; James MacMillan, affiliate composer; Donald MacDonald, chmn; Roy McEwan, mgr dir; Tim Baker, mkt dir; Judith Colman, concerts dir; Fiona McLeod, business relations dir; Ben Larpint, orch mgr.

* **Sinfonia 21** (5-40). 14 Prince's Garden, London SW7 1NA *tel:* 020 7584 2759 *fax:* 020 7581 0970 *email:* info@sinfonia21.co.uk. Sir Dennis Stevenson CBE, chmn; Martyn Brabbins, principal cond; Sue Bottomley, chief exec; Claire Wright, concerts mgr; Katy Dent, development mgr (educ); Tamsin Currey, development asst, south east; Valerie Thorncroft, community programme co-ord.

Sinfonia da Camera (12-60). 105 Woodgrange Ave, London N12 0PT *tel:* 020 8445 4091 *also fax.* Brian Smith, artistic dir; L Rosner, finance dir.

* **Sinfonia Verdi** (21-42). 60 Cowper Rd, Harpenden, Herts AL5 5NG *tel:* 01582 462137 *also fax.* David Murphy, mus dir; Irene Boogerman, admin dir; Julia Barker, personnel mgr.

Slovene Radio Symphony Orchestra (60-120). c/o Antony Pristavec, 79 Norbury Cres, London SW16 4JT *tel:* 020 8679 0369 *fax:* 020 8679 9399 *email:* Pristavec@aol.com. Anton Nanut, principal cond.

Slovenian Chamber Orchestra. c/o Antony Pristavec, 79 Norbury Cres, London SW16 4JT *tel:* 020 8679 0369 *fax:* 020 8679 9399 *email:* Pristavec@aol.com. Andrej Petrac, art dir.

The Soloists Ensemble. Bradbourne Farmhouse, Sevenoaks, Kent TN13 3DH *tel:* 01732 455641 *fax:* 01732 465664 *email:* robert.turrell@btinternet.com. Robert Turrell, cond; Dame Gillian Weir, president.

South Yorkshire Symphony Orchestra (5-50). 1 Springfield Close, Eckington, Sheffield S21 4GS *tel:* 01246 431562 *email:* paulsyso88@aol.com. Paul Scott, mus dir.

Southampton Concert Orchestra. 1 Stable Flat, Uppark, South Harting, Petersfield GU31 5QR *tel:* 01730 825638. Judith Bailey, cond.

Southern Concert Brass (45). Garibaldi Rd, Redhill, Surrey RH1 6PB *tel:* 01737 763708; 07976 402178. Graham Ivory, dir.

Southern Festival Orchestra (30-35). 11 Juniper Ave, Bricket Wood, St Albans AL2 3LR *tel:* 01923 670278 *fax:* 01923 679184. Robin White, cond.

Southern Pro Musica. York House, 39 The Avenue, Fareham, Hants PO14 1PF *tel:* 01329 235474 *fax:* 01329 314101 *email:* spm@cwcom.net. Jonathan Willcocks, principal cond; Bryan Burdett, personnel and orch mgr.

Southern Sinfonia (3-36). 113 New Greenham Park, Newbury, Berks RG19 6HW *tel:* 01635 580035 *fax:* 01635 31311. Chris de Souza, Miranda Wilson, Steuart Bedford, artistic dirs; Amanda Richards, gen mgr and educ organiser.

Steinitz Bach Players (c 30). Bach House, 73 High St, Old Oxted, Surrey RH8 9LN *tel:* 01883 717372 *fax:* 01883 715851. Margaret Steinitz, mgr; Shauni McGregor, orch mgr. *Period insts only.*

Stockholm Chamber Orchestra. c/o Van Walsum Management, 4 Addison Bridge Place, London W14 8XP *tel:* 020 7371 4343 *fax:* 020 7371 4344 *email:* vwm@vanwalsum.demon.co.uk.

Stockport Festival Orchestra. 23 The Moorings, Middlewich, Cheshire CW10 9ER *tel:* 01606 836292. Raymond Lomax, mus dir.

Surrey Chamber Orchestra (27-40). 25b Epsom Lane South, Tadworth, Surrey KT20 5TA *tel:* 01737 813273 *fax:* 01737 215676. Jonathan Brett, mus dir; Lyn Mumford, admin.

Surrey Sinfonietta *see* **Camerata of London**.

Sussex Symphony Orchestra (105). 20 Hampton Place, Brighton BN1 3DD *tel:* 01273 777963 *also fax; email:* sso@goodger.demon.co.uk. Sir Charles Mackerras CBE, president; P B Ziolkowski, chmn; Mark Andrew-James, mus dir and cond; Nigel Simmons, concerts mgr; Philippa Bull, sec; Eileen Cook, PR and mkt; Richard Bramwell, librarian. *Associated chmbr groups are Sussex Symphony Chamber Orchestra, Sussex Wind, Pavilion Wind Ensemble, Sussex Symphony Opera Orchestra.*

Swedish Radio Symphony Orchestra. c/o Van Walsum Management Ltd, 4 Addison Bridge Place, London W14 8XP *tel:* 020 7371 4343 *fax:* 020 7371 4344 *email:* vwm@vanwalsum.demon.co.uk.

The Symphony of Harmony and Invention (20). First Floor, Enslow House, Station Rd, Enslow, Kidlington, Oxon OX5 3AX *tel:* 01869 331544/331711 *fax:* 01869 331011 *email:* info@thesixteen.org.uk. Harry Christophers, mus dir; Gijs Elsen, gen mgr; Alison Stillman, admin; Peter Burrows, development mgr. *Baroque, period inst ens. Associate orch of The Sixteen Choir.*

Symphony Orchestra of Russia (95). c/o Sonata, 11 North Park St, Glasgow G20 7AA *tel:* 0141 945 3553 *fax:* 0141 946 7034. Veronika Dudarova, cond; Mikhail Medvedev, mgr.

Taunton Sinfonietta (15-20). Weaver's Cottage, Hardington Moor, Yeovil, Somerset BA22 9NW *tel:* 01935 862339 *fax:* 01460 75707 *email:* robin.carpenter@virgin.net. Alan Schiller, president; Robin Carpenter, chmn; John Edwards, finance dir; Miranda Lisk, vice chmn; Anne Cleves, sec; Sheila Carpenter, librarian.

Taverner Players (5-60). Ibex House, 42-46 Minories, London EC3N 1DY *tel:* 020 7481 2103 *fax:* 020 7481 2865. Andrew Parrott, artistic dir; Malcolm Bruno, associate dir; Victoria Newbert, admin.

Tbilist Symphony (95). c/o Sonata, 11 North Park St, Glasgow G20 7AA *tel:* 0141 945 3553 *fax:* 0141 946 7034. Jansug Kakhidze, cond.

Thames Chamber Orchestra. 41 Shirley Drive, Hounslow, Middx TW3 2HD *tel:* 020 8894 2068 *also fax; email:* admin@thamesorch.demon.co.uk. Keith Marshall, artistic dir; Anthea Robinson, admin; Sarah Parfitt, concerts asst.

Thames Sinfonia (25-60). 86 Park Hill, Carshalton Beeches, Surrey SM5 3RZ *tel:* 020 8669 4358 *also fax; email:* thames.sinf@argonet.co.uk. Robin Page, mus dir and principal cond; Elizabeth Andrews, gen mgr; Rebecca Lacey, orch mgr.

Trianon Music Group. D'Arcy Gate, Tolleshunt D'Arcy, Essex CM9 8EL *tel:* 01621 860681 *fax:* 01621 868806 *email:* alison@keeps.net. Alison Keep, admin.

* **Ulster Orchestra** (64). Elmwood Hall at Queen's, 89 University Rd, Belfast BT7 1NF *tel:* 028 9066 4535 *fax:* 028 9066 2761. David J L Fisk, chief exec; James Stewart OBE, chmn; Dmitry Sitkovetsky, principal cond and art adviser; Lesley Hatfield, leader; Lara Stokes, orch mgr; Paul McKinley, librarian; Norma Sinte, mkt and sponsorship mgr; Elish Martin, press offr. *Associated chmbr groups are Adelphi String Quartet, Ulster Orchestra Jazz Ensemble, Ulster Brass Quintet, Belfast Wind Quintet, Big Bad Bass, Carousel, Elmwood Trio, Orion String Duo, Phoenix Duo/Trio, Ulster Brass Ensemble.*

Virtuosi of England (27). 14 Beaumont Rd, Purley, Surrey CR8 2EG *tel:* 020 8668 5883 *also fax.* Darrell Davison, mus dir.

Vivaldi Concertante. 35 Laurel Ave, Potters Bar, Herts EN6 2AB *tel:* 01707 650735 *also fax;* 01707 643366. Joseph Pilbery, cond and mus dir; Maurice Powell, chmn; Mary Pilbery, sec; Audrey Banker, admin. *Associated chmbr group is Giordani Ensemble.*

* **Welsh Chamber Orchestra** (12-42). 100 Ystrad Fawr, Bridgend, Mid-Glamorgan CF31 4HW *tel:* 01656 658891 *also fax.* Anthony Hose, mus dir and principal cond; Barbara Parish, admin; Paul Loveluck CBE, chmn.

Welsh National Opera Orchestra (64). c/o Welsh National Opera Ltd, John St, Cardiff CF10 5SP *tel:* 029 2046 4666 *fax:* 029 2048 3050. Carlo Rizzi, mus dir; Anthony Freud, gen dir; Geoffrey Rowe, dir of admin; Peter Harrap, orch and concerts mgr; Peter Bellingham, head of mkt and press; Julian Smith, head of mus; John Stein, leader; Anthony Burke, librarian.

Welsh Philharmonic Orchestra (85-95). 40 Tudor Court, Murton, Swansea SA3 3BB *tel:* 01792 232387; 07860 725934 *fax:* 01792 234868 *email:* griff.harries@virgin.net. G J Harries, gen mgr. *Associated chmbr groups are Welsh Symphonic Wind Orchestra and Gower Symphonic Wind.*

Western Sinfonia (12-30). Sarum House, Union Rd, Crediton, Devon EX17 3AL *tel:* 01363 773472. Scott Stroman, cond and mus dir; Isolde Summers, admin.

Westminster Chamber Orchestra (c 30). 152 Blackmoor Wood, North Ascot, Berks SL5 8EZ *tel:* 01344 884155. Peter Davis, mgr.

The Whitehall Orchestra. 24 Thornton Ave, London SW2 4HG *tel:* 020 8671 4408 *fax:* 020 8671 2848 *email:* admin@fasinfonia.freeserve.co.uk. Michael Nebe, cond; Paul Hayter, chmn; Darragh Morgan, leader. *The orch of the civil service.*

Worthing Symphony (60). Connaught Theatre, Union Place, Worthing, W Sussex BN11 1LG *tel:* 01903 231799 *fax:* 01903 215337. David Smith, orch admin; John Gibbons, principal cond.

Wren Baroque Orchestra. Wren Music, 8 Park Lane, Selsey, W Sussex PO20 0HD *tel:* 01243 604281 *fax:* 01243 604387 *email:* m.elliott@chihe.ac.uk. Martin Elliott, mus dir; Susan Carpenter-Jacobs, Julia Bishop, leaders.

Yorkshire Philharmonic Orchestras (12-61). Torridon House, 104 Bradford Rd, Wrenthorpe, Wakefield WF1 1BR *tel:* 01924 371496. Brian Greensmith, gen mgr; Magdalen Greensmith, company sec. *Incorporating Yorkshire Sinfonietta, Yorkshire Symphony Orchestra, Yorkshire Chamber Orchestra, Yorkshire Concert Orchestra.*

Opera, Dance and Music Theatre

The organisations listed here comprise companies presenting opera, ballet or mixed-media dramatic productions on a professional or mainly professional basis. An asterisk indicates membership of the **Opera and Music Theatre Forum (OMTF),** Pegasus House, 37-43 Sackville St, London W1X 2DL *tel:* 020 7287 7018 *fax:* 020 7287 9959 *email:* abo@orchestranet.co.uk, which represents the interest of small-scale opera and music theatre companies. The youth opera companies are also included in this chapter.

Alias Opera. 206 Amelia St, London SE17 3AS *tel:* 020 7701 6963 *email:* sg@mailbox.co.uk. Sabrina George, artistic dir.

* **Almeida Opera.** Almeida Theatre, Almeida St, London N1 1TA *tel:* 020 7226 7432 *fax:* 020 7704 9581 *email:* almeidatheatre@demon.co.uk. Jonathan Reekie, dir; Patrick Dickie, associate dir; John Woolrich, concerts dir; David Parry, mus dir. *Presents premieres of newly-commissioned operas and concerts.*

* **Bampton Classical Opera.** Holcot House, Market Square, Bampton, Oxon OX18 2JJ *tel:* 01993 851876; 020 7222 1173 *also fax; email:* bampton@onet.co.uk. Jeremy Gray, Gilly French, artistic dirs; Jennifer French, admin. *Principal venue: The Deanery Garden, Bampton, Oxon. Specialise in little-known opera of the late-baroque and classical periods.*

* **Broomhill Opera.** Wilton's Music Hall, 1 Grace's Alley, Wellclose Square, London E1 8JB *tel:* 020 7702 9555 *also fax; email:* opera@broomhill.demon.co.uk. Mark Dornford-May, artistic dir; Charles Hazlewood, mus dir; Flora Smith, producer.

* **Camberwell Pocket Opera.** 19 Nigel Rd, London SE15 4NP *tel:* 020 7635 8905; 07973 653960 *fax:* 020 7635 9331. Mark Tinkler, artistic dir; Jeremy Silver, mus dir; Annabel Lee, visual dir; Rachel Shipp, technical dir. *Broad-based repertoire including site-specific productions and performances of forgotten operas.*

Cambridge Opera Group. 50 Salisbury Mansions, St Ann's Rd, London N15 3TP *tel:* 020 8211 0569 *also fax.* Peter Davis, mus and ed dir; John Fulljames, Abigail Pogson, artistic dirs. *Touring company based in the East of England, specialising in 20th C opera and mus theatre.*

Castleward Opera. 737 Lisburn Rd, Belfast, N Ireland BT9 7GU *tel:* 028 9066 1090 *fax:* 028 9068 7081. Ian Urwin, Jack Smith, artistic dirs; R L Schierbeek, chmn; Hilda Logan, company mgr. *Principal venue: Castle Ward.*

Central Festival Opera Ltd. 411b Wellingborough Rd, Abington, Northampton NN1 4EY *tel:* 01604 233082 *fax:* 01604 627089. Tom Hawkes, artistic dir; Pierre Aumonier, admin; Jeffrey Greenwell CBE, chmn. *Principal venue: Derngate, Northampton.*

Champagne Opera. Burycroft Farm House, Crawley Rd, Witney, Oxon OX8 5TG *tel:* 01993 708294/708652 *fax:* 01993 708643.

* **City of Birmingham Touring Opera.** 205 The Argent Centre, 60 Frederick St, Birmingham B1 3HS *tel:* 0121 246 6644 *fax:* 0121 246 6633. Graham Vick, artistic dir; Andrew Bennett, admin; Simon Halsey, principal cond. *Touring company.*

Court Opera Productions. Durngate House, 3 Durngate St, Dorchester, Dorset DT1 1JP *tel:* 01305 264420 *fax:* 01305 269005 *email:* powell@copp29.freeserve.co.uk. Margaret Powell, artistic dir; Richard Morris, designer; Douglas Pinchin, stage mgr; Oliver Broome, mus dir; Peter Powell, technical dir. *Touring company. Auditions and rehearsals held in London area.*

Crystal Clear Opera. The Old Rectory, Grafham, Cambs PE18 0BB *tel:* 01480 810261 *fax:* 01480 812835 *email:* martin.mcevoy@virgin.net. Martin McEvoy, artistic dir; Ian Moorhouse, company mgr; Dominique Werner, European tour mgr; Anne Carrol, sec and corporate events mgr. *Mid-scale UK touring opera company. Under their international identity, London City Opera, the company has 1 major US tour per year (*The Magic Flute *in 2000,* Carmen *in 2001,* La Traviata *in 2002). Also regular tours throughout Europe.*

D'Oyly Carte Opera Company. The Powerhouse, 6 Sancroft St, London SE11 5UD *tel:* 020 7793 7100 *fax:* 020 7793 7300 *email:* mail@doylycarte.org.uk. Sir Michael Bishop CBE, chmn; John Owen Edwards, mus dir; Ian Martin, admin mgr; Jon Sherwood, technical mgr; Keith Nicholls, finance controller; Joseph Hollings, mus hire library. *Touring company.*

Diva Opera. 115 Princes Gardens, London W3 0LR *tel:* 020 8932 8555 *fax:* 020 8723 6357 *email:* divopra@aol.com. Bryan Evans MBE, mus dir; Anne Marabini Young, admin; Peter Coleman-Wright, artistic consultant. *International touring company, opera, concerts and recitals.*

Dorset Opera. 13 The Stables, Dragoon Way, Christchurch, Dorset BH23 2TY *tel:* 01202 481856; 07974 494412 *fax:* 01202 481858 *email:* Shelleypj@aol.com; dorsetopera@talk21.com. Patrick Shelley, mus dir; Gareth Jones, chorus master; Jennifer Coultas, chief repetiteur; Elisabeth Lang Brown, admin; Michael Burton Brown, treasurer; Sir Anthony Wilson, finance dir; Arthur Davies, personnel and orch mgr; Mary Glasby, mkt offr; The Lady Digby, president; Michael Beauchamp, dir; David Higgins, designer; Gill Vahey, costumes; A Scott Parr, stage mgr; Tim Lee, chmn. *Principal venue: Sherborne.*

Duchy Opera. Long View, Hillside Rd, Carharrack, Redruth, Cornwall TR16 5RZ *tel:* 01209 821972. Jenny Gardiner, admin; Cynthia Baxter, artistic dir; David Frost, mus dir. *Amateur touring company. Principal venue: Hall for Cornwall, Truro.*

* **Echo Reverb (branch of ECO).** 60c Kyverdale Rd, London N16 7AJ *tel:* 020 8806 4231/9996 *fax:* 020 8806 4465/1949 (dir) *email:* reverb@echopera.demon.co.uk. Darren Royston, dir. *Perform new opera and mus theatre. Aim to integrate physical skills into opera and encourage collaboration between composers and artists to produce new works. Recent work includes a dance theatre piece commissioned by the Austrian Cultural Institute.*

English Festival Opera. 27 Sea Ave, Rustington, Littlehampton, W Sussex BN16 2DQ *tel:* 01903 850432 *also fax*; 07973 596780/2. Pamela Haywood, mgr dir; Simon Gray, mus dir; Elizabeth Wall, finance dir; Ian Gledhill, technical dir; Alison Hoyland, orch mgr. *Touring company.*

English National Opera. London Coliseum, St Martin's Lane, London WC2N 4ES *tel:* 020 7836 0111 *fax:* 020 7836 8379 *email:* marketing@eno.org. Nicholas Payne, gen dir; Russell Willis Taylor, exec dir; Paul Daniel, mus dir; Laurence Holderness, technical dir; Maggie Sedwards, dir of PR; Jane Livingston, head of press; Graeme Wallace, financial controller. *Principal venue: London Coliseum.*

* **English Touring Opera.** 250a Kennington Lane, London SE11 5RD *tel:* 020 7820 1131/1141 *fax:* 020 7735 7008. Andrew Greenwood, mus dir; Katharine Herbert, chief exec; Peter Thompson, orch mgr; John Haywood, mkt mgr; Paul Reeve, educ mgr; Robert Chevara, production dir. *Touring company.*

Essex Opera (Amateur). 141 Inverness Ave, Westcliff-on-Sea, Essex SS0 9DU *tel:* 01702 349009. Isobel Tedstill, gen mgr. *Opera w/shops (beginners to aspiring professionals), concerts and opera performance. Self-funding.*

* **European Chamber Opera (ECHO).** 60c Kyverdale Rd, London N16 7AJ *tel:* 020 8806 4231/9996 *fax:* 020 8806 4465. Stefan Paul Sanchez, artistic dir; Emmanuel Siffert, Tommaso Placidi, Stuart Stratford, conds; Monserrat Caballé, patron; Lara Taylor, orch mgr. *International touring company.*

First Act Opera International. The Thatched House, West Farleigh, Maidstone, Kent ME15 0NJ *tel:* 01622 747762 *fax:* 01622 745276 *email:* figaro@globalnet.co.uk. Elaine Holden, principal; John von Nuding, producer; Kenneth Roberts, mus dir. *To promote increased appreciation and enjoyment of opera to a wider audience. Performances in theatres, private houses and stately homes.*

Gala Opera International. 8 The Squirrels, Welwyn Garden City, Herts AL7 2JH *tel:* 01707 321550 *also fax; email:* GalaOpera@aol.com. Mrs Kevin Harkins, gen dir; Sarah Wilkinson, mus dir. *Small-scale touring company.*

The Garden Opera Company. All Saints Church, 100 Prince of Wales Drive, London SW11 4BD *tel:* 020 7720 4627 *fax:* 020 7720 4212. Peter Bridges, artistic dir; Louise Hynd, company co-ord. *Touring company. Summer season, min of 30 outdoor performances; winter season, indoor performances, devised and educ work in various venues.*

* **Garsington Opera Ltd.** Garsington Manor, Garsington, Oxford OX44 9DH *tel:* 01865 368201 *fax:* 01865 361545. Leonard Ingrams, chmn; Rachel Dominy, associate dir; Clare Adams, PR.

Glyndebourne Festival Opera. Glyndebourne, Lewes, E Sussex BN8 5UU *tel:* 01273 812321 *fax:* 01273 812783. Andrew Davis CBE, mus dir; Graham Vick, dir of productions; Tecwyn Evans, chorus master; Nicholas Snowman, gen dir; Peter Horne, technical dir; Sarah Playfair, artistic admin dir; Alison Winkler, auditions sec; Katie Tearle, head of educ and community projects.

* **Glyndebourne Touring Opera.** Glyndebourne, Lewes, E Sussex BN8 5UU *tel:* 01273 812321 *fax:* 01273 812783. Louis Langrée, mus dir; Aidan Lang, dir of production; Helen McCarthy, admin; Bernard W

Davies, company mgr; Nicholas Logie, orch mgr; Katie Tearle, head of educ and community; Jenny Kilbride, appeals admin. *Touring company. Principal venue: Glyndebourne.*

Grange Park Opera. 1 Fleet Place, London EC4M 7WS *tel:* 020 7246 7567 *fax:* 020 7246 7569. Wasfi Kani, exec dir; Jessica Wanamaker, admin. *Small-scale opera company with summer festival at Grange Park, Hampshire.*

The Handel Opera Company. The Chestnuts, 56 Snakes Lane West, Woodford Green, Essex IG8 0DF *tel:* 020 8559 1983 *also fax; email:* nicolino.giacalone@virgin.net. Nicolino Giacalone, artistic dir, cond and vocal coach.

* **Hatstand Opera Ltd.** 3 Heber Rd, Cricklewood, London NW2 6AB *tel:* 020 8452 7042 *also fax;* 07774 133155 *email:* enqs@hatstand.dircon.co.uk. Kirsty Young, dir. *Touring company offering a wide range of innovative opera shows for small and mid-scale venues, private functions and open-air events. Also educ work with schools.*

Hillside Opera. 57 Gordon Ave, Portswood, Southampton, Hants SO14 6WH *tel:* 023 8055 1088 *also fax.* Jill Meager, artistic dir; Kaarina Manzur, business mgr. *Opera training company for singers preparing for a professional career. Principal venue: Nuffield Theatre, Southampton. Also touring company.*

Jigsaw Music Theatre. 38 Rectory Grove, London SW4 0EB *tel:* 020 7622 4794 *also fax; email:* jigsawopera@easicom.com. Sarah Jennings, artistic dir; William Pool, company mgr. *Touring company. Principal venue: Purcell Room. Specialists in 20th C mus theatre and opera; community opera w/shops.*

Jupiter Opera. 57 White Horse Rd, London E1 0ND *tel:* 020 7790 5883 *fax:* 020 7265 9170 *email:* gregory-rose@tisl.co.uk. Gregory Rose, mus dir; John Jones, publicity offr. *Touring company.*

La Brigata. Billington Manor, Billington, Leighton Buzzard LU7 9BJ *tel:* 01525 372516 *fax:* 01525 851649. Peter Syrus, mus dir. *13th-16th C English, French and Italian mus.*

London Opera Players. Broadmeade Copse, Westwood Lane, Wanborough, Surrey GU3 2JN *tel:* 01483 811004 *fax:* 01483 811721. Peter Gellhorn, mus dir; Elisabeth Parry, mgr dir; Robin Green, mus educ offr; Peter Andrews, mkt offr; Derek and Jennie Chappel, stage and lighting. *Touring company.*

Mayfield Chamber Opera. The Dormer Flat, High St, Mayfield TN20 6AL *tel:* 01435 872187 *also fax; email:* m.fields@cwcom.net. Michael Fields, artistic dir.

* **Mid Wales Opera.** Meifod, Powys SY22 6BY *tel:* 01938 500611 *fax:* 01938 500681. Barbara McGuire, gen dir; Keith Darlington, artistic dir. *Festival of opera, Theatr Hafren, Newtown, Powys (August). Extensive tour throughout England and Wales.*

* **Modern Music Theatre Troupe.** 10 Lime Grove, Blaby, Leicester LE8 4GS *tel:* 0116 278 8326 *also fax; email:* caro@mmtt.co.uk. Caroline Sharman, Christopher Newell, artistic dirs; Paul Barker, composer-in-association. *Small and medium-scale touring venues; new music theatre.*

* **Music Theatre London.** Chertsey Chambers, 12 Mercer St, London WC2H 9QD *tel:* 020 7240 0919 *fax:* 020 7240 0805. Tony Britten, artistic dir. *Touring company. Mid and large-scale venues, opera and mus theatre.*

* **New Chamber Opera.** 4 Mansfield Rd, Oxford OX1 3TA *tel:* 01865 279526 *fax:* 01865 279590 *email:* michael.burden@new.ox.ac.uk. Gary Cooper, mus dir; Michael Burden, dir. *Acts as a platform for young singers with 3-4 major productions pa.*

New Sussex Opera. 22 Bradford Rd, Lewes, E Sussex BN7 1RB *tel:* 01273 471851/486496 *fax:* 01273 471851. Michael Fulcher, mus dir; John Lloyd Davies, dir of productions; David James, dir of planning; Dick Passmore, secretary; Richard Pulham, gen admin; Roy Patten, treasurer. *Principal venues: The Dome, Brighton and The Old Market, Hove; also touring company.*

Nexus Opera. 17 Rookery Close, Kibworth Beauchamp, Leics LE8 0SD *tel:* 0116 279 1047 *email:* ianjarvis@netgates.co.uk. Ian R Jarvis, admin; Lionel Friend, Keith Warner, Delia Lindon, artistic dirs. *Touring company which runs w/shops for singers and actors. Educ work. No open auditions.*

Northern Opera Ltd. 24 Bankside, Morpeth, Northumberland NE61 1XD *tel:* 01670 514149 *also fax.* Roy Beasley, chmn and admin; Richard Bloodworth, mus dir; John Smedley, chorus dir; David Nicol, company sec; Ridley Stokoe, technical dir. *Pro-am productions with large amateur chorus in Newcastle upon Tyne. Touring concerts and small-scale productions in the North East and Cumbria. Principal venue Whitley Bay Playhouse.*

Opera 2000. Hereford House, 23/24 Smithfield St, London EC1A 9LF *tel:* 020 7489 1944 *fax:* 020 7489 1945 *email:* Opera2K@aol.com. Peter Walters, admin dir; Jonathan Bradshaw, business dir; Ian Hayter, artistic dir. *Specially formed to present innovative productions of seminal works for the beginning of the new millennium. Principal venue, Sadler's Wells, and on tour.*

Opera à la Carte. 82 Balcombe St, London NW1 6NE *tel:* 020 7724 2696 *also fax; email:* opera_a_la_carte@compuserve.com. Nicholas Heath, dir. *Touring company. Specialises in chmbr performances of large-scale operas.*

Opera Anglia/Artsanglia Ltd. 3-5 Bridge St, Hadleigh, Suffolk IP7 6BY *tel:* 01473 822596 *fax:* 01473 824175. Thomas McIntosh, artistic dir; M H V Reckitt, admin; S Sowman, asst. *Principal venue: The Old School, Hadleigh.*

* **The Opera Band.** 77 Godstone Rd, St Margaret's, Twickenham, Middx TW1 1JY *tel:* 020 8891 0143 *also fax; email:* colinriley@ndirect.co.uk. Colin Riley, John Ginman, artistic dirs. *Small-scale company presenting new work.*

* **Opera Box Ltd.** Rhydyberi Cottages, Merthyr Cynog, Brecon, Powys LD3 9SA *tel:* 01874 690339 *fax:* 01874 690254 *email:* opera-box@international.freeserve.co.uk. Brendan Wheatley, dir; Fraser Goulding, mus dir. *Touring company associated with English Heritage, giving outdoor performances of operas at historic venues and touring in theatres.*

Opera Brava. 67 Franklynn Rd, Haywards Heath, W Sussex RH16 4DT *tel:* 01444 443060. Simon Phillippo, mus dir; Bronek Pomorski, artistic dir, educ; Kate Weston, PR and mkt; Amanda Buckland, company sec; Jane Willis, admin. *Touring company. Visiting National Trust and other historic houses and theatres throughout the UK. Extensive educ programme. Also commissions operas.*

* **Opera Circus.** 1 Aberdeen House, 22 Highbury Grove, London N5 2EA *tel:* 020 7228 1222 *fax:* 020 7228 1220 *email:* operacircu@aol.com. Tina Ellen Lee, David Pearl, dirs; Tracey McAteer, gen mgr. *Physical opera, devised and newly-commissioned work. Touring company.*

Opera da Camera. 7 Meadow Rd, New Costessey, Norwich NR5 0NF *tel:* 01603 744584 *fax:* 01603 250599. Jeffrey Davies, gen dir and producer; Derek Barnes, mus dir and cond; John Aplin, cond and chorus master; Carol Thornton, sec; David Gwyn Harris, producer/designer. *Touring company.*

Opera Europa. 149 Woodhouse Ave, Perivale, Middx UB6 8LQ *tel:* 020 8991 5063 *fax:* 020 8810 7118. John Gibbons, mus dir; Romolo Bruni, artistic dir. *Anglo-Italian opera company.*

Opera Exclusive! 87 Sumatra Rd, London NW6 1PT *tel:* 020 7433 1058 *fax:* 020 7813 5486 *email:* opex2000@lineone.net. C Humphreys, mgr. *Opera concerts, opera dinner cabaret and specialised educ programmes for schools.*

Opera Experience. Marriotts Drove Farm, Ramsey Mereside, Huntingdon, Cambs PE17 1UF *tel:* 01733 844603 *also fax.* Norman Beedie, artistic dir; Diana Stuart, vocal consultant. *Regional touring company in East Anglia.*

* **Opera Holland Park.** Central Library, Phillimore Walk, Kensington, London W8 7RX *tel:* 020 7361 3058 *fax:* 020 7361 2976. John McEachen, head of libraries and arts; Ray Bingle, admin. *Principal venue: Holland Park Theatre.*

Opera in Cameo. c/o Roy Baker Management, 25 Lynors Ave, Rochester, Kent *tel:* 01634 714434 *also fax.* Matthew Craven, gen dir; Judith Buckle, mus dir. *Performances in a range of venues from private functions to theatres and historic houses.*

Opera Ireland. John Player House, 276-288 South Circular Rd, Dublin 8, Republic of Ireland *tel:* 00 353 1 453 5519/20 *fax:* 00 353 1 453 5521. David Collopy, gen mgr; Eileen O'Mara Walsh, chmn; Dieter Kaegi, artistic dir; Kay Keilthy, admin; Taragh Loughrey-Grant, mkt exec. *Principal venue: Gaiety Theatre, Dublin.*

Opera Italiana (incorporating the Rossini Society). 10a Radipole Rd, London SW6 5DL *tel:* 020 7736 3821. Alexander Bryett, artistic dir; Carol Wells, chorus master; Ian Bookey, admin dir; Rita Volante, admin. *Principal venue: Fulham Palace.*

* **Opera Live!** 20 Bull Stag Green, Hatfield, Herts AL9 5DE *tel:* 01707 267511 *also fax; email:* operalive@yahoo.com. Neil Simon, producer; Matthew Hough, mus dir; Susan Wright, educ offr. *Provides w/shops for schools using fully-trained professional singers. Also concert work.*

Opera North. Grand Theatre, 46 New Briggate, Leeds LS1 6NU *tel:* 0113 243 9999 *fax:* 0113 244 0418 *email:* rgreenon@aol.com. Richard Mantle, gen dir; Steven Sloane, mus dir; Christine Chibnall, controller of planning; Malcolm Warne Holland, orch and concerts mgr; James Holmes, head of mus; Jane Bonner, company mgr; Richard Whitehouse, head of mkt; Shona Galletly, press offr; Ric Green, tech dir. *Principal venues: Grand Theatre, Leeds; touring to Palace Theatre, Manchester; Hull New Theatre; Theatre Royal, Nottingham; Theatre Royal, Newcastle; Lyceum Theatre, Sheffield.*

Opera Omnibus. c/o Anne's Hatch, Hatch Lane, Kingsley Green, Haslemere, Surrey GU27 3LJ *tel:* 01428 656605 *fax:* 01428 641112. Jenny Hill, publicity mgr; John Braithwaite, chmn; John Miller, financial dir; Moyra Finlay, controller of opera planning; Peter Clarke, cond; Richard Gregson, dir. *Performs opera (in English) each Feb; also fully-staged concerts and recitals. Principal venue: Haslemere Hall, Surrey. No resident orch.*

The Opera Project. 6a St Julian's Farm Rd, London SE27 0JJ *tel:* 020 8670 1614. Richard Studer, artistic dir; Jonathan Lyness, mus dir. *Touring company, fully-staged in English with orch. Also, summer festival.*

Opera Rara. 134-146 Curtain Rd, London EC2A 3AR *tel:* 020 7613 2858 *fax:* 020 7613 2261 *email:* operarara@amity.co.uk. Patric Schmid, artistic dir; Robert Roberts, musicologist; Stephen Revell, mgr dir.

* **Opera Restor'd.** 54 Astonville St, London SW18 5AJ *tel:* 020 8870 7649 *fax:* 020 8516 6313. Peter Holman, mus dir; Peter Milne, gen mgr; Caroline Anderson, admin; Jack Edwards, stage dir. *Touring company. Specialises in 17th-18th C opera in English, fully-staged with small orch.*

Opera South East. 3 Manor Court, 20 De La Warr Rd, Bexhill-on-Sea, E Sussex TN40 2JA *tel:* 01424 223518 (sec), 434492 (art and theatre admin). Mary Ward, hon sec; Kenneth Roberts, mus dir; Betty Muffit, art and theatre admin; Pamela Bugden, mkt dir. *Registered office:* 111 Bohemia Rd, St Leonards on Sea TN37 6RL *tel:* 01424 712712. *Full orch and chorus. Principal venue: White Rock Theatre, Hastings.*

Opera West. Production Office, 14 Ashgrove St, Ayr KA7 3AQ *tel:* 01292 264489 *fax:* 01292 282424. Raymond Bramwell, Marilyn de Blieck, joint artistic dirs. *Productions with professional soloists, orch and quality amateur chorus with high level of community involvement. Project-only basis. Young artists' training. Principal venue: The Gaiety Theatre, Ayr.*

Operating Theatre. 47 Balmoral Rd, Colwick, Nottingham NG4 2GF *tel:* 0115 961 4182 *also fax; email:* kate.pallant@lineone.net. Stephen Williams, artistic dir; Michael Palin, mus dir; Kate Williams, company mgr. *Midlands-based opera and mus theatre specialising in rarely performed and new works. Small or medium venues.*

Pavilion Opera. Thorpe Tilney Hall, Thorpe Tilney, nr Lincoln LN4 3SL *tel:* 01526 378231 *fax:* 01526 378315. Peter Bailey, mus dir; Freddie Stockdale, gen mgr; Christine Baxter, admin.

* **Pegasus Opera Company Ltd.** The Brix, St Matthews, Brixton Hill, London SW2 1JF *tel:* 020 7501 9501 *also fax; email:* lloyd@ or admin@pegopera.org. Lloyd Newton, artistic dir; Douglas Mayo, admin; Allison Buchanan, asst artistic dir; Allyson Devenish, asst mus dir. *Touring company, small and mid-scale venues. Also educ work.*

* **Pimlico Opera.** 1 Fleet Place, London EC4M 7WS *tel:* 020 7246 7567/8 *fax:* 020 7246 7569. Wasfi Kani, artistic dir; Jessica Wanamaker, S Lindsay Getman, admin. *Small-scale touring company with own orch. Extensive co-productions with prisons.*

Pisa Opera Group. Flat 2, 79 Linden Gardens, London W2 4EU *tel:* 020 7229 7060. Stella J Wright, dir. *Gives advice concerning repertoire, etc, to young singers.*

Randazzo Opera. 24 Bladon Court, Barrow Rd, London SW16 5NE *tel:* 020 8677 8821 *also fax.* Arlene Randazzo, stage dir and admin. *On-going w/shops with 12 opera miniature performances pa. London-based.*

The Royal Opera. Royal Opera House, Covent Garden, London WC2E 9DD *tel:* 020 7240 1200 *fax:* 020 7212 9502. Bernard Haitink, mus dir; Richard Jarman, artistic dir; Peter Mario Katona, artistic admin; Amanda Jones, head of press; Ann Richards, press offr; Cormac Simms, company mgr; Terry Edwards, chorus dir; Dermot Agnew, chorus mgr.

Scottish Opera. 39 Elmbank Cres, Glasgow G2 4PT *tel:* 0141 248 4567 *fax:* 0141 221 8812. Richard Armstrong, mus dir; Derek Clark, head of mus; Ruth Mackenzie, gen dir; Fergus Shiel, chorus master; Jenny Slack, dir of planning; Jay Allen, orch and concerts mgr; Roberta Doyle, head of mkt and press; Jane Davidson, projects dir; Catriona Reynolds, head of fundraising and sponsorship. *Principal venue: Theatre Royal, Glasgow.*

* **Selfmade Music Theatre.** Basement Flat, 16d Hampstead Hill Gardens, London NW3 2PL *tel:* 020 7794 3610 *also fax.* Susannah Self, artistic dir; Michael Christie, artistic admin. *London-based mus theatre company; newly commissioned and devised works.*

Sounds Lyrical. c/o Diana Hirst PR, 55 Marmora Rd, London SE22 0RY *tel:* 020 8299 1914 *also fax; email:* Hirstpr@aol.com. John Upperton, artistic dir; Peter Crockford, Robyn Sevatos, Joan Taylor, mus dirs. *Janine Button, Alison Higham-Bell, sop; Lynne McAdam, Alenka Ponjavic, m-sop; Andrew Morton, John Upperton, ten; Trevor Alexander, Simon Neal, bs.*

Stowe Opera. 1 Poplar's Close, Preston Bissett, Bucks MK18 4LR *tel:* 01280 848275 *also fax.* Robert Secret.

Surrey Opera. 71 Gainsborough Rd, Tilgate, Crawley, W Sussex RH10 5LJ *tel:* 01293 532692. Jonathan Butcher, artistic dir; Anthea Hall, gen admin; Ian Clarke, finance dir; John Ingman, sponsorship dir; Christopher Glover, publicity offr. *Principal venues: Ashcroft Theatre, Croydon; Harlequin Theatre, Redhill; Stag Theatre, Sevenoaks.*

Tête à Tête Productions Ltd. 7 Richmond Ave, London N1 0NE *tel:* 020 7609 6656 *also fax.* Katie Price, admin; Richard van Allan, patron; Bill Bankes-Jones, artistic dir; Orlando Jopling, mus dir; Louise Grattan, Matthew Hart, Alan Moug, Lady Ravensdale, Philip Turner, dirs.

* **Vocem Electric Voice Theatre.** 39 Birnam Rd, London N4 3LJ *tel:* 020 7281 0672 *also fax; email:* frances@birnam39.freeserve.co.uk. Frances M Lynch, artistic dir; Charlotte McClelland, lighting design; Alan Burgess, Paul Bull, sound design. *Contemporary electronic and vocal mus theatre productions. Major educ projects. Film, TV, radio and multimedia projects. International tours.*

* **Welsh National Opera.** John St, Cardiff CF10 5SP *tel:* 029 2046 4666 *fax:* 029 2048 3050. Anthony Freud, gen dir; Carlo Rizzi, mus dir; Peter Bellingham, head of mkt; Geoffrey Rowe, dir of admin; Julian Smith, head of mus; Isabel Murphy, dir of opera planning; Lucy Stout, dir of development; Alan Parr, technical dir; Julia Carson Sims, stage mgr. *Principal venues include: New Theatre, Cardiff; Hippodrome, Bristol; Empire Theatre, Liverpool; Theatre Royal, Plymouth; Apollo, Oxford; Hippodrome, Birmingham; The Mayflower, Southampton.*

West End International Ltd. 15 Mount Pleasant, London WC1X 0AA *tel:* 020 7833 0884 *fax:* 020 7833 9883. Gary Brown, Martin Yates, dirs. *Worldwide presenters of* West End The Concert *and* Broadway The Concert, *concert performances of operas and musicals. Also international celebrity concerts.*

Youth Opera Companies

* **British Youth Opera.** South Bank University, 103 Borough Rd, London SE1 0AA *tel:* 020 7815 6090 *fax:* 020 7815 6094 *email:* byopera@mailbox.co.uk. Sir John Hannam, chmn; Timothy Dean, mus dir; Jamie Hayes, dir of productions; Mikel Toms, admin dir. *For singers aged 22-30, instrumentalists and repetiteurs aged 18-30. Auditions Nov-May, summer season mid Jul-mid Sep; also year-round programme.*

Live Culture and Live Wires Youth Opera Groups. c/o Baylis Programme, The ENO Works, 40 Pitfield St, London N1 6EU *tel:* 020 7739 5808 *fax:* 020 7729 8928. Tim Yealland, Jo de Waal, Tuula Jukola, artistic dirs. *Opera groups meet weekly Sep-Jun during term-time. Not purely singing based but looks at all aspects of opera including design and directing. Informal w/shop auditions in held annually. Live Culture, ages 12-16; Live Wires, ages 9-12.*

* **National Youth Music Theatre.** 5th Floor, The Palace Theatre, Shaftesbury Ave, London W1V 8AY *tel:* 020 7734 7478 *fax:* 020 7734 7515. Jeremy James Taylor, artistic dir; Jon Bromwich, gen mgr; Vivienne Hughes, outreach admin (auditions, w/shops); Susie Moor, admin; Jill Coggins, company mgr. *Touring mus theatre with 4 major productions pa and open w/shops for singers, actors, dancers (aged 11-19) and instrumentalists (aged 11-22). Open auditions for productions Oct-Dec. Also national residential and regional open access w/shops throughout the year.*

Dance and Ballet Companies

Alexander Roy London Ballet Theatre. North House, 69 Eton Ave, London NW3 3EU *tel:* 020 7586 2498 *fax:* 020 7722 9942. Alexander Roy, artistic dir; Christina Gallea, associate dir. *London-based company which performs original ballet-theatre. National and international tours.*

Birmingham Royal Ballet. Birmingham Hippodrome, Thorp St, Birmingham B5 4AU *tel:* 0121 622 2555 *fax:* 0121 689 3070. David Bintley, artistic dir; Derek Purnell, admin dir; John Beadle, mus admin; Su Matthewman, mkt mgr; Keith Longmore, communications dir; Sandy Robertson, dir, BRB trust. *Large-scale classical ballet company.*

City Ballet of London Trust Ltd. 3rd Floor, Lloyds Bank, 113 Leadenhall St, London EC3A 4AX *tel:* 020 7623 4737 *fax:* 020 7623 4738. Harold King, artistic dir; June Gamble, gen mgr; Sara Winnington, head of mkt, deputy gen mgr; Judith Pleasance, development dir; Sheila Ghelani, educ officer, mgr asst. *Touring neo-classical ballet company. Also educ outreach programmes and corporate training.*

The Companie of Dansers and Trabocchetti. 41 Talma Gardens, Twickenham, Middx TW2 7RB *tel:* 020 8892 9638 *also fax.* Madeleine Inglehearn, artistic dir; Jean McCreery, mus dir. *Baroque dance and mus.*

Dance For Everyone. 30 Sevington Rd, London NW4 3RX *tel:* 020 8202 7863 *also fax; email:* info@dfe.org.uk. Naomi Benari, artistic dir. *To entertain and educate, with special concern for new audiences and the deaf.*

Earthfall. Chapter, Market Rd, Cardiff CF5 1QE *tel:* 029 2022 1314 *fax:* 029 2034 2259. Jessica Cohen, Jim Ennis, artistic dirs. *Touring company with a policy to create innovative dance-theatre with live mus.*

English National Ballet. 39 Jay Mews, London SW7 2ES *tel:* 020 7581 1245 *fax:* 020 7225 0827 *email:* marketing@en-ballet.co.uk. Derek Deane, artistic dir; Carole McPhee, exec dir; Jack Haslam, finance dir; Alan Riches, technical dir; Neroli Hobbins, development dir; Richard Whitehouse, dir of public affairs. *Touring company. Principal venues: London Coliseum; Royal Albert Hall; Mayflower Theatre, Southampton; Palace Theatre, Manchester.*

Ludus Dance Company. Assembly Rooms, King St, Lancaster LA1 1RE *tel:* 01524 389901/35936 *fax:* 01524 847744 *email:* ludus@easynet.co.uk. Deborah Barnard, dir; Joan Dowthwaite, head of finance and admin; Jacqueline Greaves, head of touring. *Contemporary, touring, educ company.*

MZT. 1 Oast Cottage, Great Maxfield, Three Oaks, nr Hastings, E Sussex TN35 4NU *tel:* 01424 756114 *also fax; email:* spreston@bluetit.u-net.com. Stephen Preston, artistic dir; Sarah Cremer, rehearsal dir; Nikki Fido, admin. *Touring company.*

Northern Ballet Theatre. West Park Centre, Spen Lane, Leeds LS16 5BE *tel:* 0113 274 5355 *fax:* 0113 274 5381 *email:* press@nbtdance.demon.co.uk. Stefano Giannetti, artistic dir; Mark Skipper, exec dir; John Pryce-Jones, mus dir; Anna M D Izza, press and PR mgr; Katherine Scott, head of mkt; Barry Collarbone, orch and concerts mgr. *Dance, drama.*

Rambert Dance Company. 94 Chiswick High Rd, London W4 1SH *tel:* 020 8995 4246 *fax:* 020 8747 8323. Christopher Nourse, exec dir; Christopher Bruce, artistic dir; Paul Hoskins, mus dir; Geoff Hunt, finance/admin dir; Malcolm Glanville, technical dir; Jackie Friend, mkt dir; Ellen Plant, development mgr; Sarah Dekker, educ mgr. *Touring contemporary dance company.*

Richard Alston Dance Company. The Place, 17 Duke's Rd, London WC1H 9AB *tel:* 020 7387 0324 *fax:* 020 7482 5785 *email:* radc@theplace.org.uk. Richard Alston, artistic dir; Chris May, admin dir.

The Royal Ballet. Royal Opera House, Covent Garden, London WC2E 9DD *tel:* 020 7240 1200 *fax:* 020 7212 9121. Andrea Quinn, cond; Sir Anthony Dowell CBE, dir; Michael Kaiser, exec dir; John Seekings, development dir; Anthony Russell-Roberts, admin dir; Richard Shaw, dir of mkt, press and PR. *Touring company. Principal venue: The Royal Opera House, Covent Garden, London.*

Scottish Ballet. 261 West Princes St, Glasgow G4 9EE *tel:* 0141 331 2931 *fax:* 0141 331 2629 *email:* promo@scottishballet.co.uk. Robert North, artistic dir; Ken Burke, asst artistic dir; Alan Barker, mus dir; John Aitken, company mgr. *Classical (and contemporary) ballet. Principal venues: Theatre Royal, Glasgow; Edinburgh Festival Theatre.*

Choirs and Choruses

The following list of choirs includes only professional choirs and choirs with amateur membership which have achieved a national reputation through concerts, recordings and broadcasts.

Other amateur choirs can be contacted through the **National Federation of Music Societies** (Francis House, Francis St, London SW1P 1DE *tel:* 020 7828 7320 *fax:* 020 7828 5504 *email:* nfms@nfms.demon.co.uk) which operates a mailing service for artists and agents wishing to contact choirs and offers free advice to singers wanting to join a choir in their area. The **National Association of Choirs** (21 Charmouth Rd, Lower Weston, Bath BA1 3LJ *tel:* 01225 426713) represents the interests of amateur choirs in the United Kingdom.

Abbey Singers (45+). Beckstones, Orton, Penrith, Cumbria CA10 3RG *tel:* 01539 624695. Elizabeth Lamb, cond; Jay Norris, sec.

Aberystwyth University Choral Union (110). Music Centre, University of Wales, Aberystwyth, 10 Laura Place, Aberystwyth, Ceredigion SY23 2AU *tel.* 01970 622685 *fax:* 01970 622686 *email:* muswww@aber.ac.uk. David Russell Hulme, cond.

Academy of St Martin in the Fields Chorus (24-70). Raine House, Raine St, London E1 9RG *tel:* 020 7702 1377 *fax:* 020 7481 0228 *email:* info@academysmif.co.uk. Louise Allen, admin.

The Aeolian Singers (100). 34 Moorland Rd, Boxmoor, Hemel Hempstead, Herts HP1 1NH *tel:* 01442 257023. Stephen Jones, mus dir.

Aldwyn Voices (16-20). 42 Worcester Rd, Malvern, Worcs WR14 4AA *tel:* 01684 569721 *also fax*. Andrew Sackett, cond; Peter Smith, dir.

The Allegri Singers (30). 16 Hall Drive, Sydenham, London SE26 6XB *tel:* 020 8778 4760. Malcolm Gale, hon sec.

Ambrosian Opera Chorus (450). 4 Reynolds Rd, Beaconsfield, Bucks HP9 2NJ *tel:* 01494 680873 *fax:* 01494 680501. John McCarthy OBE, cond.

Ambrosian Singers (450). 4 Reynolds Rd, Beaconsfield, Bucks HP9 2NJ *tel:* 01494 680873 *fax:* 01494 680501. John McCarthy OBE, cond.

Amici (24). 23 The Moorings, Middlewich, Cheshire CW10 9ER *tel:* 01606 836292. Raymond Lomax, mus dir; Judith Lomax, admin.

Apollo Voices (4-100+). 106 Harborough Rd, London SW16 2XW *tel:* 020 8677 7997 *fax:* 020 8696 9783 *email:* chris@tisl.co.uk. Christopher Foster, Elizabeth Roberts, admin.

The Bach Choir (265). 30a Evelina Rd, London SE15 2DX *tel:* 020 7277 7100 *also fax; email:* richard@TheBachChoir.org.uk. David Hill, cond; Richard Sadler, general mgr.

Bath Camerata (25). Birch Tree Cottage, Nettlebridge, Oakhill, Somerset BA3 5AA *tel:* 01749 841086. Nigel Perrin, dir; Pauline Perrin, sec.

BBC National Chorus of Wales (165). BBC, Room E4101, Broadcasting House, Llandaff, Cardiff CF5 2YQ *tel:* 029 2032 2587 *fax:* 029 2032 2575 *email:* david.lawrence@bbc.co.uk. Simon Halsey, artistic dir; Adrian Partington, asst artistic dir; David Lawrence, chorus mgr.

BBC Singers (24). Room 24, BBC Studios, Delaware Rd, London W9 2LG *tel:* 020 7765 4370/3266 *fax:* 020 7765 2762 *email:* stephen.ashley-king@bbc.co.uk. Stephen Ashley-King, mgr; Stephen Cleobury, chief cond; Michael Emery, snr producer; Ruth Potter, co-ord.

BBC Symphony Chorus (150). BBC Studios, Delaware Rd, London W9 2LG *tel:* 020 7765 4715 *fax:* 020 7286 3251 *email:* bbcso@bbc.co.uk. Stephen Jackson, dir; Graham Wood, admin.

Birmingham Festival Choral Society (c 130). Fishers Castle, Sandy Lane, Harvington, nr Kidderminster, Worcs DY10 4NF *tel:* 01562 700771 *also fax; email:* Jeremy.Patterson@btinternet.com. Jeremy Patterson, mus dir; Anthony Bradbury, associate cond; James Bradbury, hon sec.

75

BBC SINGERS

The UK's only full-time professional choir

Chief Conductor: Stephen Cleobury

The BBC Singers are world-renowned for their breadth of repertoire, ranging from the Renaissance to the present day. Their busy schedule includes regular public concerts, broadcasts, recordings and soundtracks for films, documentaries and drama, both for the BBC and external promoters. Exceptional musicianship, including highly-skilled sight-reading and vocal ability, is the hallmark of the 24-voice ensemble.

For further enquiries please contact Stephen Ashley-King (General Manager)

Telephone 020 7765 4370

E-mail stephen.ashley-king@bbc.co.uk

or write to Room 24, BBC Studios, Delaware Road, London W9 2LG

BBC RADIO 3
90-93FM

"Any idea that unaccompanied choral music is austere and faintly ecclesiastical soon evaporates in the face of the Singers' astonishing precision and virtuosity"

Michael Oliver, *Daily Telegraph*

"The BBC Singers are arguably our finest professional choir"

Richard Morrison, *The Times*

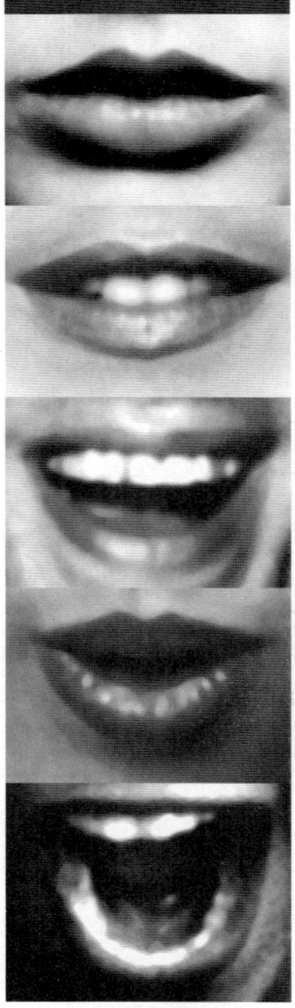

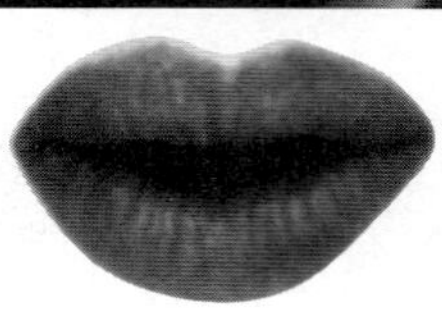

"Canzonetta...impeccably prepared by Jeffrey Wynn Davies."
Manchester Evening News – April 1999

"...this group knows how to generate real atmosphere."
Jane Glover

Canzonetta
chamber choir manchester

whether it be Dupré, Mozart or Vierne at the Bridgewater Hall, music club/society evenings or international festivals, Canzonetta's sheer versatility is unrivalled

director : jeffrey wynn davies
administration : fiona clucas
tel/fax : 0161 905 1218
email: flc@canzonetta.freeserve.co.uk

"Cappella Nova's focus, commitment and virtuosic a cappella singing would make it premier just about anywhere" THE BOSTON GLOBE

"Cappella Nova are exceptional interpreters and performers of early music" RUHR NACHRICHTEN

"Cappella Nova are as firm and round-toned in the flesh as they are on disc, and they obviously enjoy the drama of performing" THE SCOTSMAN

Scotland's professional vocal ensemble at the cutting-edge of stylish interpretation of early and modern repertoire, Cappella Nova ranges in size from 4 to 18 singers and offers unique, beautifully constructed programmes of Scottish Medieval, Renaissance and contemporary vocal music.

For full biographical details, discography, programmes and repertoire lists, contact:

Rebecca Tavener, Cappella Nova
172 Hyndland Road, GLASGOW G12 9HZ Scotland
T: 0141 552 0634 F: 0141 552 4053 email: alan.tavener@strath.ac.uk

Blackburn Music Society (c 90). 42 Royshaw Ave, Blackburn, Lancs BB1 8RJ *tel:* 01254 262293 *fax:* 01254 265640 *email:* esa@ukip.co.uk. Sylvia Alexander, chmn.

Bolshoi Theatre Children's Choir (60). Andrei Zaboronok, cond; Boris Dergachev, mgr. *Sonata*

Boston Choral Society (60). The Flat, Fulbeck Manor, Fulbeck, Grantham, Lincs NG32 3JN *tel:* 07889 569226. Gary Sieling, mus dir; Jennifer Oughton, chmn.

Bournemouth Sinfonietta Choir (25). 221 Queen's Park Ave, Bournemouth, Dorset BH8 9HD *tel:* 01202 393352. Howard Ionascu, cond; Pat Williams, sec.

Bournemouth Symphony Chorus (180). 7 Southbourne Coast Rd, Bournemouth BH6 4BE *tel:* 01202 423429 *also fax; email:* bschorus@dircon.co.uk. Neville Creed, chorus master; Carolyn Date, sec.

Bradford Festival Choral Society (140). Fairbank, Woodlands Grove, Ilkley, W Yorks LS29 9BX *tel:* 01943 600175 *also fax.* Michael Baker, chorus dir; John C Hammond, sec; Brian Kay, mus dir.

Brighton Festival Chorus (180). 42 High St, Tarring, Worthing, W Sussex BN14 7NR *tel:* 07010 706235 *fax:* 01903 601831. James Morgan, mus dir; Jane Davies, chmn; Robert Smith, chor admin; Gill Kay, artistic admin.

Bristol Choral Society (160). 10 Logan Rd, Bishopston, Bristol BS7 8DT *tel:* 0117 942 2719 *fax:* 020 8688 2901 *email:* proarte@dial.pipex.com. Murray Stewart, cond; Carla Murray, hon sec.

Britten-Pears Chamber Choir. Britten-Pears School for Advanced Musical Studies, High St, Aldeburgh, Suffolk IP15 5AX *tel:* 01728 452935 *fax:* 01728 452715 *email:* bps.admin@aldeburghfestivals.org. Joseph Cullen, cond; Ann Rawdon Smith, admin.

Britten Singers *formerly* BBC Northern Singers (16+). Simon Wright, cond; Jolyon Dodgson, mgr. *Denny Lyster*

Brno Academic Choir. *POEM*

Cambridge Taverner Choir (20). 29 Denton House, Bingham Court, Halton Rd, Islington, London N1 2AE *tel:* 020 7359 5960 *also fax; email:* helen.garrison@bbc.co.uk. Helen Garrison, admin; Owen Rees, dir.

Cambridge University Chamber Choir (c 35). Clare College, Cambridge CB2 1TL *tel:* 01223 333264 *fax:* 01223 333219 *email:* tcb21@hermes.cam.ac.uk. Timothy Brown, cond; David Lowe, associate cond.

Cambridge Voices (16-40). 200 Cambridge Rd, Great Shelford, Cambridge CB2 5JU *tel:* 01223 511510 *fax:* 01223 460817 *email:* ajt27@cam.ac.uk. Anthony Tootal, mgr; Ian de Massini, dir; Carl Rütti, president.

Cannock Chase Orpheus Male Choir (62). 78 Brooklands Ave, Great Wyrley, Walsall WS6 6LG *tel:* c/o 01922 419318/412094. Alan D Jones, mus dir; Alan Goodman, chmn; David Robinson, sec.

Canterbury Cathedral Choir (30). Christ Church Cathedral, 6 The Precincts, Canterbury CT1 2EE *tel:* 01227 765219 *fax:* 01227 865222 *email:* daocjaflood@email.msn.com. David Flood, choir master.

Canticum (30). Flat 2, 96 Westwood Hill, Sydenham, London SE26 6PD *tel:* 020 7632 8300. Mark Forkgen, cond; Angela Jones, admin.

Cantores ad vincula (14-18). 2 Child's Place, London SW5 9RX *tel:* 020 7373 3638. John Williams, dir.

Canzonetta (8-28). 266 Manor Ave, Sale, Cheshire M33 4NB *tel:* 0161 905 1218 *also fax; email:* canzonetta@freeserve.co.uk. Jeffrey Wynn Davies, dir; Fiona Clucas, admin.

Cappella Nova (3-18). 172 Hyndland Rd, Glasgow G12 9HZ *tel:* 0141 552 0634 *fax:* 0141 552 4053 *email:* alan.tavener@strath.ac.uk. Alan Tavener, dir; Rebecca Tavener, mgr.

Cardiff Polyphonic Choir (50). 148 Westbourne Rd, Penarth, Vale of Glamorgan CF64 5BQ *tel:* 029 2070 7827 *also fax.* Howard Goodfellow, mgr.

The Cecilian Singers (25). 23 Prince Edward Cres, Radcliffe-on-Trent, Nottingham NG12 2DX *tel:* 0115 933 2896 *also fax; email:* clive.holland@btinternet.com. Jeremy Jackman, mus dir; Lynne Holland, sec.

Chameleon Arts Chorus (20-80). Andrew Phillips, chorus master. *Chameleon*

Chandos Chamber Choir (30). 63 Mayford Rd, Balham, London SW12 8SE *tel:* 07973 630990. Piers Maxim, mus dir.

Chantry Singers of Bath (38-60). 22 First Avenue, Oldfield Park, Bath BA2 3NW *tel:* 01225 333253 *email:* kj.lush@ukonline.co.uk. Christine Warner, publicity offr; Elizabeth Bates, mus dir.

Chapelle du Roi (8). 10 Kensington Hall Gardens, Beaumont Ave, London W14 9LS *tel:* 020 7379 9361 *fax:* 020 7379 9636 *email:* chapelle@newrenaissance.co.uk. Alistair Dixon, dir; Jan Hart, admin. *Sonata*

Cheltenham Bach Choir (100). Cotteswold, Brockhampton Lane, Swindon Village, Cheltenham, Glos GL51 9RS *tel:* 01242 222853. Stephen Jackson, cond; Lesley Nicholls, sec.

"Inspiring performance..." *Daily Telegraph*

English Chamber Choir

conductor
Guy Protheroe

"...dedicated ensemble" *The independent*

This busy London-based Choir
- promotes its own annual concert series
- is frequently engaged by other promoters
- is well known for its commercial credits on television and film soundtracks
- sings further afield in Britain and abroad

ECC • 8 Alma Square • London NW8 9QD
Tel: 0171 286 3944 Fax: 0171 289 9081

Chapelle du Roi

"...their interpretation at times almost touches the visionary."

(Mary Berry, *Gramophone*)

Chapelle du Roi is a vocal ensemble of eight of London's most exciting young singers and is one of England's hottest new sensations in the world of Early Music. Directed by Alistair Dixon, *Chapelle du Roi* specialises in the performance of sacred music from the European Renaissance. With numerous radio appearances on Radio 3 and in the US and Europe, concert engagements in the UK, Belgium, Holland, and Czechoslovakia and seven CDs to its credit, *Chapelle du Roi* is rapidly gaining an enviable reputation for its interpretation of the Renaissance repertoire. The 1999/2000 season sees performances at the Royal Festival Hall, Warwick Arts Society, Birmingham Early Music Festival, the St Ceciliatide Festival and a two week tour of the USA in October 2000.

For further information please contact Jan Hart at:
10 Kensington Hall Gardens, Beaumont Avenue, London W14 9LS
Tel: +44 (0) 20 7 379 9361 Fax: +44 (0) 20 7 379 9362
E-mail: chapelle@newrenaissance.co.uk
Website: www.newrenaissance.co.uk

CROUCH END FESTIVAL CHORUS

Crouch End Festival Chorus

conductor David Temple

'the large choir of choice for contemporary music'
Evening Standard

'really imaginative programming'
Independent

'an exceptional concert – expertly performed and immensely enjoyable'
Ham & High

Why not join these musicians who have recently worked with the Chorus:

BBC Symphony Orchestra
Philip Glass
Martyn Brabbins
Academy of St Martin-in-the-Fields
Willard White
Brodsky Quartet
Wayne Marshall
Neil Hannon and The Divine Comedy
Lynne Dawson
John Harle

Works for 2000 include:
Philip Glass *Three Songs*
Stravinsky *Symphony of Psalms*
Brahms *Ein Deutsches Requiem*
Arvo Pärt *Credo*
Berlioz *Grande Messe des Morts*
Joby Talbot *A new commission*
Steve Reich *The Desert Music*

Interested in singing with us?
Contact Catherine Best
telephone 0181 444 4438

Interested in working with us?
Contact the chorus on
tel/fax 0181 374 4463

www.cefc.org.uk

A new recording by the chorus
is now available on double CD:

Will Todd *The Burning Road*
Britten *The Company of Heaven*
(narrated by Jonathan Pryce & Fiona Shaw)

National Sinfonia Conductor: David Temple
Silva Classics SILKD 6021

CEFC is a registered charity no. 803604

Choir of the Golden Age. *POEM*

Choir of Pamplona Cathedral. Padre Aurelio Sagaseta. *Michael Harrold*

The Choir of St John's College, Cambridge (16+14). Christopher Robinson, choir master. *SWA*

Choir of St Mary's Cathedral, Edinburgh (16+12). St Mary's Cathedral, Palmerston Place, Edinburgh EH12 5AW *tel:* 0131 225 6293 *fax:* 0131 225 3181. Simon Nieminski, asst organist. *Chameleon*

The Choir of St Paul's Cathedral, London. John Scott, dir. *Hazard*

City of Birmingham Symphony Chorus (200). CBSO Centre, Berkely St, Birmingham B1 2LF *tel:* 0121 616 6500 *fax:* 0121 616 6518 *email:* information@cbso.co.uk. Simon Halsey, chorus dir; Sir Simon Rattle CBE, artistic dir; Claire Walters, chorus mgr.

City Chamber Choir (29). 6 Barnfield Rd, St Albans, Herts AL4 9UP *tel:* 01727 864007 *fax:* 01727 845884 *email:* steve_sta@compuserve.com. Stephen Jones, mus dir.

The City of Glasgow Chorus (150). 14 Hyndland Rd, Glasgow G12 9UP *tel:* 0141 339 6153 *fax:* 0141 357 2186. Graham Taylor, chorus master.

City of London Choir (c 100). 81b Copleston Rd, London SE15 4AH *tel:* 020 7639 2873. Hilary Davan Wetton, dir of mus; Duncan Robertson, chair; Daniel Mansfield, membership sec.

City of London Sinfonia Singers *formerly* Richard Hickox Singers (28). 11 Drum St, London E1 1LH *tel:* 020 7480 7743 *fax:* 020 7488 2700 *email:* info@cls.co.uk. Richard Hickox, mus dir; Stephen Carpenter, gen mgr.

Collegium Musicum of London (30). 52 Finsbury Park Rd, London N4 2JX *tel:* 020 7359 3729. Peter Owens, chorus master; Barry Creasy, chmn; Ann Flett, sec.

Consortium (8-24). Edge Grove, Aldenham, Herts WD2 8BL *tel:* 07050 602518 *fax:* 07050 602519 *email:* consortium@churchmusic.co.uk. Edward Barbieri, dir.

Corydon Singers (35-100). 24 Kirdford Rd, Arundel, W Sussex BN18 9EE *tel:* 01903 885465 *fax:* 01903 885466 *email:* corydon.office@btinternet.com. Matthew Best, artistic dir; Linda Osborne, gen mgr.

Crouch End Festival Chorus (165). PO Box 17102, London N8 9WH *tel:* 020 8374 4463 *also fax; email:* gkemball@hgmp.mrc.ac.uk. David Temple, cond; Pauline Hoyle, chmn.

Croydon Philharmonic Choir (142). 29 Sundown Ave, Sanderstead, Surrey CR2 0RQ *tel:* 020 8657 1631. Janet Jalfon, chorus sec.

Croydon SDA Gospel Choir (35). 123 Cobden Rd, South Norwood, London SE25 5NU *tel:* 07956 395203; 07973 665175 *fax:* 020 8656 7748 *email:* sdagc@kenburton.com; sdagc@aol.com. Ken Burton, Herbie Joseph, dirs.

Cryes of London (40-60). 41 Greenham Rd, London N10 1LN *tel:* 020 8442 1748 *also fax*. David Temple, mus dir.

The Curate's Egg. St Faith's House, Shandy St, London E1 4ST *tel:* 020 7791 0330 *also fax*. Adey Grummet, dir; Lilla Grindlay, press and publicity; Mhairi Ellis, admin and librarian.

Derby Choral Union (110+). 36 Buttermere Drive, Allestree, Derby DE22 2SN *tel:* 01332 550968. Kenneth E Spruce, hon sec; David Fisher, mus dir.

Ditchling Choral Society (150). 11 Barrowfield, Cuckfield, W Sussex RH17 5ER *tel:* 01444 454091 *also fax; email:* dcs@choral.org.uk. Rosemary Pardey, hon sec; Janet Canetty-Clarke, cond.

Dunedin Consort (4-14). 11c Lauriston Gardens, Edinburgh EH3 9HH *tel:* 0131 228 3410 *fax:* 0131 622 0076 *email:* ben@dunedin-consort.org.uk. Ben Parry, mus dir; Susan Hamilton, associate dir.

Dyfed Choir (55-60). 6 Lawnswood, Ragged Staff, Saundersfoot, Dyfed SA69 9HX *tel:* 01834 811588 *also fax*. James Thomas, mus dir; Joyce Gallon, hon sec.

East London Chorus (55). 150 Greenvale Rd, London SE9 1PQ *tel:* 020 8859 8288 *fax:* 020 8859 8388 *email:* alibri@dial.pipex.com. Murray Stewart, mus dir; Brian Seaman, chair.

Edinburgh Festival Chorus (175). c/o Edinburgh Festival Society, The Hub - Edinburgh's Festival Centre, Castlehill, Royal Mile, Edinburgh EH1 2NE *tel:* 0131 473 2027 *fax:* 0131 473 2002 *email:* margery.ramsay@eif.co.uk. David Jones, chorus master; Margery Ramsay, chorus admin.

Edinburgh Royal Choral Union (c 120). 43 Inverleith Gardens, Edinburgh EH3 5PR *tel:* 0131 552 3874 *email:* ercu@jabd.abel.co.uk. Lilian Davidson; Robert Marshall, chorus master.

The Elysian Singers of London. 81 Milborough Cres, Lee, London SE12 0RP *tel:* 020 7499 8567; 020 8857 7991 *fax:* 020 7499 4795. Matthew Greenall, dir; Jessica Buchanan-Barrow, admin.

English Arts Chorale (75). 50a Cambridge Rd, New Malden, Surrey KT3 3QL *tel:* 01737 244407; 020 8942 4555 *fax:* 01737 241153. Leslie Olive, artistic dir; Hazel Timbrell, hon sec.

English Cathedral Singers. 3 The Square, Compton, W Sussex PO18 9HA *tel:* 023 9263 1369 *fax:* 023 9263 1786. Jonathan Willcocks, mus dir.

English Chamber Choir (40-45). 8 Alma Square, London NW8 9QD *tel.* 020 7286 3944 *fax:* 020 7289 9081 *email:* ecc.protheroe@btinternet.com. Guy Protheroe, cond; Ann Manly, admin.

English Concert Singers/English Concert Chorus (30-150). 6 Chailey Ave, Rottingdean, Brighton BN2 7GH *tel:* 01273 300894 *fax:* 01273 308394 *email:* engconsing@fastnet.co.uk. Roy Wales, dir; Christine Wales, admin.

English National Opera Chorus (68). London Coliseum, St Martin's Lane, London WC2N 4ES *tel:* 020 7836 0111 *fax:* 020 7836 8379. Stephen Harris, chorus master; Charles Kraus, chorus mgr.

English String Orchestra Choir (40-45). Caves Farm, Chatley, Droitwich, Worcs WR9 0AP *tel:* 01905 621215; 01600 890289 *fax:* 01905 621865. Adrian Partington, choir dir; Michael Foster, admin.

Estonian Philharmonic Chamber Choir. *HP*

Ex Cathedra (12-30). Suite 303, Jewellery Business Centre, 95 Spencer St, Birmingham B18 6DA *tel:* 0121 523 1025 *fax:* 0121 523 1026. Justin Lee, gen mgr; Jeffrey Skidmore, artistic dir.

Exmoor Singers (35). 104 Newlands Park, London SE26 5NB *tel:* 020 7724 5182 *fax:* 020 7594 8710 *email:* exmoor@dircon.co.uk. James Jarvis, cond; Carolyn Steel, chmn; Judy Elias, publicity.

Exon Singers (28). 6 Ashlake Rd, London SW16 2BB *tel:* 020 8677 0882. Matthew Owens, mus dir; Julian Poppleton, admin dir; Graham Wood, sec.

FineChants (12). The Flat, Fulbeck Manor, Fulbeck, Grantham, Lincs NG32 3JN *tel:* 07889 569226. Gary Sieling, mus dir.

Finzi Singers (12-24). 4 The Close, Lichfield, Staffs WS13 7LD *tel:* 01543 250627 *fax:* 01543 250970 *email:* paul.spicer@tisl.co.uk. Paul Spicer, dir; Elizabeth Dibben, admin.

Gentlemen of the Chappell. Peter Bassano, cond. *Giustiniani tel:* 01494 868240 *fax:* 01494 868250 *email:* GArtists1@aol.com.

Geoffrey Mitchell Choir. 49 Chelmsford Rd, Woodford, London E18 2PW *tel:* 020 8491 0962 *fax:* 020 8491 0956. Geoffrey Mitchell, cond.

Glinka State Choir of Saint Petersburg (72). Vladislav Chernoushenko, cond; Vitali Lavrov, mgr. *Sonata*

Glyndebourne Chorus. Glyndebourne Festival Opera, Glyndebourne, Lewes, E Sussex BN8 5UU *tel:* 01273 812321 *fax:* 01273 812783. Alison Winkler, auditions sec; Tecwyn Evans, chorus master.

Goldsmiths Choral Union (130). 25 Ashlyn Grove, Ardleigh Green, Hornchurch, Essex RM11 2EQ *tel:* 01708 472252 *also fax; email:* 106620.1575@compuserve.com. Brian Wright, mus dir and cond; Victoria Ware MBE, sec.

Gonville and Caius College Choir (21). Gonville and Caius College, Cambridge CB2 1TA *tel:* 01223 332448 *fax:* 01223 332456 *email:* gaw25@cam.ac.uk. Geoffrey Webber, dir of mus.

Grupo de Canto Coral. Nestor Andrenacci, dir. *Ellison*

Guildford Chamber Choir. 31 Yew Tree Rd, Dorking, Surrey *tel:* 01306 887054 *fax:* 01306 876266. Iain Macleod, chmn; Tim Horton, principal cond.

Guildford Choral Society (200). 42 Binscombe Cres, Farncombe, Godalming, Surrey GU7 3RB *tel:* 01483 416325 *fax:* 01483 450597. Hilary Davan Wetton, dir of mus; Nicola Fournel, sec.

Guildford Philharmonic Choir (140). 13 Vicarage Gate, Guildford, Surrey GU2 5QJ *tel:* 01483 566341 *fax:* 01483 444732. Jeremy Backhouse, chorus dir; John Trigg, chmn; Jeremy Filsell, accompanist.

Halifax Choral Society (150-160). Warren Wells, Woodbottom Lane, Brighouse, W Yorks HD6 2QW *tel:* 01484 713803 *also fax.* John Pryce-Jones, mus dir; Mrs B S Whitehead, gen admin.

Harlow Chorus (130). 7 Great Hyde Hall, Sawbridgeworth, Herts CM21 9JA *tel:* 01279 726806 *fax:* 01279 726603 *email:* philip.jones4@virgin.net. Val Brockbank, admin; Sarah Tenant-Flowers, mus dir.

Harrogate Choral Society (159). 18 Park Ave, Harrogate, N Yorks *tel:* 01423 530764 *fax:* 01423 556720 *email:* pridsea@cwcom.net. Ruth Pridmore, sec; Jeffrey Wynn Davies, cond; Brian Kay, principal guest cond.

Hertfordshire Chorus (130). 1 Tintern Close, Kinsbourne Green, Harpenden, Herts AL5 3NZ *tel:* 01582 763871 *also fax.* Michael Kibblewhite, mus dir; Shirley Thwaite, admin.

Highgate Choral Society (160). 31 Lanchester Rd, London N6 4SX *tel:* 020 8883 8740 *fax:* 020 8883 5961. Ronald Corp, mus dir; Andrew Frankl, chmn; Carolyn Pascall, sec.

Holst Singers (36). PO Box 16090, London EC4Y 7HS *tel:* 020 7936 4762 *fax:* 020 7936 4767 *email:* holst-singers@tisl.co.uk. Stephen Layton, cond; Liz de Lacey, artistic producer.

Huddersfield Choral Society (210). Jane Glover, principal guest cond; Martyn Brabbins, principal cond; Joseph Cullen, chorus master; Stephen Brook, sec. *Blythe*

Ionian Singers (c 35). 54 Holmdene Ave, London SE24 9LE *tel:* 020 7733 6719 *also fax; email:* ionsing@netcomuk.co.uk. Timothy Salter, cond; Ulla Gray, sec.

John McCarthy Singers (60). 4 Reynolds Rd, Beaconsfield, Bucks HP9 2NJ *tel:* 01494 680873 *fax:* 01494 680501. John McCarthy OBE, cond.

The Joyful Company of Singers (24-30). 452 Kings Rd, London SW10 0LQ *tel:* 020 7352 7050 *fax:* 020 7351 7058 *email:* rday@joyfulco.demon.co.uk. Peter Broadbent, cond; Rosemary Day, chmn.

Jupiter Singers (16-40). 57 White Horse Rd, London E1 0ND *tel:* 020 7790 5883 *fax.* 020 7265 9170 *email:* gregory-rose@tisl.co.uk. Gregory Rose, cond; John Jones, publicity agent.

Keele Bach Choir (c 60). The Library, Keele University, Keele, Staffs ST5 5BG *tel:* 01782 583637. Christopher Hand, mus dir; Kay Williams, sec.

Kiev Chamber Choir (20). Mykola Gobdych, artistic dir, cond; Nikolai Trofimov, mgr. *Sonata*

King's College Choir, Cambridge (16+14). King's College, Cambridge CB2 1ST *tel:* 01223 331224 *fax:* 01223 331890 *email:* choir@kings.cam.ac.uk. Stephen Cleobury, dir. *Intermusica*

Lancaster Singers (50). Music Dept, Lancaster University, Lancaster LA1 4YW *tel:* 01524 593777 *fax:* 01524 847298 *email:* r.hutchison@lancaster.ac.uk. Denis McCaldin, cond; Ruth Hutchison, sec.

Laudate (8-20). 81 Church Rd, Radley, Oxon OX14 3QF *tel:* 01235 543066 *fax:* 01235 543034 *email:* HJPI@radley.org.uk. Howard Ionascu, mus dir; Bella Pearson, admin.

Laudibus (National Youth Chamber Choir) (24). Michael Brewer, dir. *Chameleon*

Leeds Festival Chorus (160). 9 Ashleigh Rd, Leeds LS16 5AX *tel:* 0113 275 1628. Marie Holland, sec; Simon Wright, chorus master.

Leeds Philharmonic Chorus (200). 30 Jackman Drive, Horsforth, Leeds LS18 4HS *tel:* 0113 258 2744. Lady Groves, president; John Brodwell, sec.

Leicester Philharmonic Choir (165). 6 Hoby Rd, Ragdale, Melton Mowbray, Leics LE14 3PE *tel:* 01664 434393 *fax:* 01664 434962. A Geary, gen sec; Margaret Pearson, choir sec.

The Little Eagles of Siberia. Ludmilla Stebenjkova, chorus dir. *Gilder*

London Adventist Chorale (32). Ken Burton, artistic dir and principal cond; Tina Brooks, mus dir. *Ellison*

London Choral Society (140). 15 Aldersmead Rd, Beckenham, Kent BR3 1NA *tel:* 020 8659 1108 *fax:* 020 8325 3586 *email:* 106306.3704@compuserve.com; LondonChoralSociety@iname. com. Jane Glover, principal guest cond; Ronald Corp, mus dir; Anne Howick, admin; HRH Duke of Gloucester, patron.

London Concert Choir (100). 9 Cromwell Rd, Burgess Hill, W Sussex RH15 8QH *tel:* 01444 230779 *fax:* 01444 233699. Mark Forkgen, cond; Helen Houghton, development mgr.

London Contemporary Voices (16-24). 19a North Villas, Camden Square, London NW1 9BJ *tel:* 020 7267 8778 *also fax; fax:* 020 7813 4601 *email:* voices@camdenmusic.com. Andrew Skirrow, cond.

London Handel Choir (18-20). The Coach House, Drury Lane, Redmarley d'Abitot, Glos GL19 3JX *tel:* 01531 650616 *also fax.* Denys Darlow, cond.

London Philharmonic Choir (150). 13 Huntspill St, London SW17 0AA *tel:* 020 8947 4355 *also fax; email:* russ@dircon.com. Neville Creed, chorus dir; Jane Hanson, chmn; Anne Cotter, hon sec (*tel:* 020 8670 1635).

London Symphony Chorus (230). Richard Hickox, principal cond; Stephen Westrop, chorus dir; Pamela Barker, chmn; Susan Francis, admin. *Intermusica*

London Voices. 22 St Mary's Ave, London E11 2NP *tel:* 020 8989 4804 *fax:* 020 8989 7389. Terry Edwards, dir; Jacqueline Peet, sec.

Magnificat (8-24). 64 Ferry Rd, Marston, Oxford OX3 0EU *tel:* 01865 244801 *fax:* 01865 437238 *email:* magnificat@compuserve.com. Philip Cave, dir.

Malcolm Sargent Festival Choir (350). 34 North End Rd, London W14 0SH *tel:* 020 7352 6805/7602 6818 *fax:* 020 7376 3503/7602 8162 *email:* malcolm.sargent@virgin.net. Sylvia Darley OBE, admin.

Manchester Chorale (45). 5 Leslie Ave, Bury, Lancs BL9 8DL *tel:* 0161 767 9226 *also fax; email:* lesley.cavanagh@virgin.net. Lesley Cavanagh, sec; Jeffrey Wynn Davies, cond.

Minsk Chamber Choir (20). Igor Matyukhov, cond. *Sonata*

Monteverdi Choir (20-75). Monteverdi Choir and Orchestra Ltd, 61 Wandsworth High St, London SW18 2PT *tel:* 020 8871 4750 *fax:* 020 8871 4751 *email:* info@monteverdi.org.uk. Sir John Eliot Gardiner, artistic dir; Howard Gough; acting gen mgr; Jan Normanton, admin; Christopher Foster, choir mgr; Andrew Hammond, project co-ord.

Musica Contexta (16). 24 Fairfield Rd, Crouch End, London N8 9HG *tel:* 020 8347 9655 *also fax; email:* musica@hexachord.freeserve.co.uk. Simon Lillystone, admin; Simon Ravens, mus dir.

New London Chamber Choir (12-50). Bancroft, Rectory Lane, Fringford, Bicester, Oxon OX6 9DX *tel:* 01869 278392 *also fax; email:* nlcc@brailsford.demon.co.uk. James Wood, mus dir.

New London Singers (c 32). 8 Island House, Ravensbury Mill, Wandle Rd, Morden, Surrey SM4 6AU *tel:* 020 8646 6176 *email:* newlondonsingers@hotmail.com. Ivor Setterfield, cond; Julia Smallbone, sec.

Leeds Festival Chorus

Chorus Master
Simon Wright

The renowned Leeds Festival Chorus, 150 strong, was founded in 1858 to sing at the first Leeds Musical Festival. It now performs regularly in the Leeds International Concert Season and elsewhere with leading orchestras and conductors. Its repertoire is wide; it tours, broadcasts, records and commissions. Great works written for the Chorus include Elgar's Caractacus and Walton's Belshazzar's Feast, both premièred in Leeds Town Hall. The chorus is looking forward to its next commission, a major work for the Millennium by Dominic Muldowney

'....the finely disciplined Leeds Festival Chorus deserved its ovation....' *(Daily Telegraph)*
'....under Yan Pascal Tortelier each scene was vividly portrayed by the Leeds Festival Chorus....' *(Independent)*

For information about auditions for new members or about the choir's availability for concerts please contact the Secretary
Marie Holland 9 Ashleigh Road, Leeds LS16 5AX
Tel:0113 275 1628

The chorus is a registered charity

New members welcome, for further information contact Dorothy Wardhaugh on **0191 252 8093**

or write, c/o Northern Sinfonia, 41 Jesmond Vale, Newcastle upon Tyne, NE2 1PG

Charity No 235712, Company No 63918

Funded by THE ARTS COUNCIL OF ENGLAND

MALCOLM SARGENT FESTIVAL CHOIR

CHARLES FARNCOMBE CBE
Director of Music

SYLVIA DARLEY OBE
Chairman

The Malcolm Sargent Festival Choir often sings in aid of the Malcolm Sargent Cancer Fund for Children. The Choir is 26 years old this coming season and has a standing choir of 350 auditioned voices. They perform regularly at the Royal Albert Hall and many of the Cathedrals in this country, in Europe, as well as visits to Notre Dame, in Paris and St. Peter's, Rome.

The Festival Choir is drawn from members of Choirs from every part of England, from the South Coast to Newcastle in the North, from Bristol in the West to Aldeburgh in the East, after passing an audition. They pay all their own travel and personal expenses to rehearsals in London, however far afield the concerts are scheduled. The Choir performs voluntarily in order to raise substantial sums of money for children's charities.

New members always welcome.

Enquiries for Concerts and Auditions:
Malcolm Sargent Festival Choir
34 North End Road
London W14 0SH
Tel: 0171 352 6805 / 0171 602 6818
Fax: 0171 376 3503 / 0171 602 8162
Email: malcolm.sargent@virgin.net

Charity Registration no 1055426

Northern Symphony Chorus. 23 The Moorings, Middlewich, Cheshire CW10 9ER *tel:* 01606 836292. Raymond Lomax, mus dir; Judith Lomax, admin.

Nottingham Harmonic Society (220). 67 Holly Ave, Breaston, Derby DE72 3BR *tel:* 01332 872024. Neil Page, mus dir; Kathleen Jackson, gen sec.

Orchestra of the Renaissance. The Old Manse, Leafield, Witney, Oxon OX8 5NN *tel:* 01993 878200 *fax:* 01993 878375 *email:* oldmanse@compuserve.com. Richard Cheetham, dir; Mary Taylor, admin.

Oxford Bach Choir (200). 59 Southmoor Rd, Oxford OX2 6RF *tel:* 01865 556585 *also fax*. Nicholas Cleobury, cond; David Lowe, associate cond; Mrs C S Redman, chmn; Ruth Durbridge, mkt mgr; Martin Peters, artistic admin.

Oxford Pro Musica Singers (35). 15 Parkers Hill, Tetsworth, Oxford OX9 7AQ *tel:* 01844 281427 *also fax; email:* m.smedley.opms@lineone.net. Michael Smedley, cond.

Pamplona Cathedral Choir. *Michael Harrold*

The Philharmonia Chorus (180). 40 Carr Rd, Northolt, Middx UB5 4RA *tel:* 020 7333 1722 *email:* sales@rhinegold.co.uk. Richard Thomas, acting chmn; Robert Dean, chorus master; Hana Tiller, auditions sec.

The Philharmonic Choir (150). Hollybank, 5 The Orchard, Kislingbury, Northants NN7 4BG *tel:* 01604 830679 *also fax*. Graham Mayo, cond; Jackie Mayo, admin.

Polyhymnia (8-18). Flat 3, Paternoster House, Colebrook St, Winchester SO23 9LG *tel:* 01962 865617. Richard Lowell Childress, dir.

Polyphony (24). PO Box 16090, London EC4Y 7HS *tel:* 020 7936 4762 *fax:* 020 7936 4767 *email:* admin@polyphony.co.uk. Stephen Layton, cond. *Hazard*

Prague Radio Chamber Choir. *Sonata*

Pro Musica Chorus of London (120). 6 Durham Row, London E1 0NP *tel:* 020 7790 1004 *also fax*. William Ryder, admin.

Reading Festival Chorus (120). Acorn Cottage, The Old Orchard, Mill Lane, Kelcot, Reading RG31 7RF *tel:* 0118 941 0720 *also fax*. Jacques Cohen, cond; Mrs T Dodd, sec.

Regent's Singers (30). 32 Angel Rd, Harrow, Middx HA1 1JY *tel:* 020 8427 5409 *also fax*. Bernard Barker, cond.

The Renaissance Singers (34). 104 Whinney Lane, Blackburn, Lancs BB2 7DL *tel:* 01254 247407 *fax:* 01254 696361 *email:* lindsey@macdonald.demon.co.uk. Lindsey Cooper.

Rossica Choir of St Petersburg (26). 12 Warren Drive, Dorridge, Solihull, W Midlands B93 8JY *tel:* 01564 776376 *also fax; email:* jean.shearman@virgin.net. Jean Shearman, UK mgr.

Royal Choral Society (c 200). Unit 9, 92 Lots Rd, London SW10 0QD *tel:* 020 7376 3718 *fax:* 020 7376 3719 *email:* royalchoralsociety@compuserve.com. Helen Body, choir sec; Richard Cooke, cond.

Royal Liverpool Philharmonic Choir (175). Philharmonic Hall, Hope St, Liverpool L1 9BP *tel:* 0151 210 2895 *fax:* 0151 210 2902. Ian Tracey, choir master; Eleanor Wright, admin; Stuart Christie, chmn.

Royal Opera (Covent Garden) Chorus (44). Royal Opera House, Covent Garden, London WC2E 9DD *tel:* 020 7240 1200 *fax:* 020 7212 9444 *email:* operacompany@roh.org.uk. Terry Edwards, chorus dir; Dermot Agnew, chorus mgr.

Royal Scottish National Orchestra Chorus (190). 73 Claremont St, Glasgow G3 7HA *tel:* 0141 226 3868 *fax:* 0141 221 4317 *email:* admin@rsno.org.uk. Christopher Bell, chorus master; Jill Mitchell, chorus mgr.

Rundfunkchor Berlin. Robert Gritton, chief cond. *Gilder*

St Giles' Cathedral Choir (30). St Giles' Cathedral, High St, Edinburgh EH1 1RE *tel:* 01506 410477 *also fax; email:* m.harris@napier.ac.uk. Michael Harris, org, master of mus.

St Michael's Singers (25). St Michael's Vestry, Cornhill, London EC3V 9DS *tel:* 01737 244604; 020 7626 8841 *fax:* 01737 271128. Jonathan Rennert, mus dir.

St Petersburg Male Voice Choir (28). Vadim Afanasiev, cond. *Sonata*

Schola Cantorum of Oxford (30-40). c/o Faculty of Music, St Aldates, Oxford OX1 1DB *tel:* 01865 276147 *fax:* 01865 276128. Mark Shepherd, cond; Cathryn Miserandino-Gaherty, sec.

Schola Gregoriana Pragensis. *Sonata*

Scottish Chamber Orchestra Chorus (60). 4 Royal Terrace, Edinburgh EH7 5AB *tel:* 0131 557 6800 *fax:* 0131 557 6933. Ben Parry, chorus master.

Scottish Opera Chorus (34). Scottish Opera, 39 Elmbank Crescent, Glasgow G2 4PT *tel:* 0141 248 4567 *fax:* 0141 221 8812. Fergus Sheil, chorus master.

Sheffield Philharmonic Chorus (150). 15 Lumley Drive, Tickhill, Doncaster DN11 9QE *tel:* 01302 742049. Paul Tennant, gen sec; Keith Alford, chmn; Darius Battiwalla, chorus master.

The Sinfonia Chorus (60). The Sinfonia Centre, 41 Jesmond Vale, Newcastle upon Tyne NE2 1PG *tel:* 0191 240 1812 *fax:* 0191 240 2668 *email:* nsinfonia@ndirect.co.uk. Alan Fearon, chorus master.

The Sixteen (16+). First Floor, Enslow House, Station Rd, Enslow, Kidlington, Oxon OX5 3AX *tel:* 01869 331544 *fax:* 01869 331011 *email:* info@thesixteen.org.uk. Gijs Elsen, gen mgr; Harry Christophers, cond, mus dir; Alison Stillman, admin; Peter Burrows, development mgr.

Song Company. *Ellison*

Stockport Festival Chorus. PO Box 5, Disley Delivery Office, Cheshire SK12 2FA *tel:* 01663 747605 *email:* festivalchorus@cwcom.net. Raymond Lomax, mus dir; John Huw Davies, chorus master; Graham Eagland, admin.

Tallis Chamber Choir (13-60). c/o 13 Albury St, London SE8 3PT *tel:* 020 8691 8337 *also fax; email:* tcc@classical-artists.com. Philip Simms, dir; Deborah Sandringham, admin.

Taverner Choir and Consort (5-30). Taverner Concerts Ltd, Ibex House, 42-46 Minories, London EC3N 1DY *tel:* 020 7481 2103 *fax:* 020 7481 2865. Andrew Parrott, artistic dir; Malcolm Bruno, associate dir; Victoria Newbert, admin.

Tewksbury Abbey School Choir. *POEM*

Thames Philharmonic Choir (90-100). 7a Cromford Rd, London SW18 1NZ *tel:* 020 8870 8154 *also fax; email:* GabrielleRankin@compuserve.com. John Bate, artistic dir; Gabrielle Rankin, sec.

Thomas Tallis Society (40+). 13 Albury St, London SE8 3PT *tel:* 020 8691 8337 *also fax.* Philip Simms, dir; Deborah Sandringham, sec.

Trianon Music Group. D'Arcy Gate, Tolleshunt D'Arcy, Essex CM9 8EL *tel:* 01621 860681 *fax:* 01621 868806 *email:* alison@keeps.net. Alison Keep.

University of Warwick Chorus (350). Music Centre, University of Warwick, Coventry CV4 7AL *tel:* 024 7652 3799 *fax:* 024 7652 8136 *email:* musab@warwick.ac.uk. Colin Touchin, cond; Stuart Dunlop, asst cond.

Vasari Singers (25-35). 19 Norman Rd, Sutton, Surrey SM1 2TB *tel:* 020 8642 3233 *also fax; email:* jeremy.backhouse@50montacute.freeserve.co.uk. Jeremy Backhouse, cond; Janet Clucas, sec. *Ellison*

Voces Sacrae. Judy Martin, artistic dir. *Michael Harrold*

Vox dicentis (16). 14 Roselands Court, Chester Rd, Lavister, Wrexham LL12 0DD *tel:* 01244 571857 *also fax.* Marian Needham, admin.

Welsh National Opera Chorus (40). Welsh National Opera, John St, Cardiff CF10 5SP *tel:* 029 2046 4666 *fax:* 029 2048 3050.

Westminster Cathedral Choir (28-32). 42 Francis St, London SW1P 1QW *tel:* 020 7798 9066/9057 *fax:* 020 7798 9091 *email:* musicdepartment@westminstercathedral.org.uk. James O'Donnell, master of mus.

Whitehall Choir (80). 1 Midland Terrace, London NW2 6QH *tel:* 020 8452 4797. Heather Atkinson, chmn.

William Byrd Singers of Manchester (28). 9 Harboro Rd, Sale, Cheshire M33 5AE *tel:* 0161 976 6992.

Winchester Cathedral Choir. David Hill, org, choirmaster; Philip Scriven, sub-org. *Chameleon*

The Wooburn Singers (65). 3 Riversdale Court, Riversdale, Bourne End, Bucks SL8 5EB *tel:* 01628 532710. Jeremy Backhouse, mus dir; Roger Webber, treasurer.

Worcester Cathedral Choir. Adrian Lucas, master of the choristers; Daniel Phillips, asst organist. *Chameleon*

Worcester Festival Choral Society (206). The Cedars, 171 Oldbury Rd, Worcester WR2 6AR *fax:* 01905 611139. Adrian Lucas, mus dir; Marjorie Potts, sec.

Wren Singers of London. Wren Music, 8 Park Lane, Selsey, Chichester, W Sussex PO20 0HD *tel:* 01243 604281 *fax:* 01243 604387 *email:* m.elliott@chihe.ac.uk. Martin Elliott, artistic dir.

Yorkshire Bach Choir (35). 11 Bootham Terrace, York YO30 7DH *tel:* 01904 652799 *fax:* 01904 338349 *email:* ps22@york.ac.uk. Peter Seymour, cond.

The Zemel Choir (55-60). 26 Larch Close, Friern Barnet, London N11 3NN *tel:* 020 8361 3389 *also fax; email:* business-manager@the-zemel-choir.org. Marc Landsman, business mgr.

Military, Brass and Wind Bands

Military Bands

Most bands of the armed forces are standard 'military bands' of woodwind, brass and percussion (double bass is usually added when not on the march). The police, fire service and Royal British Legion have military bands and also some bands that follow the format of a conventional brass band. Some of the bands may also be able to provide orchestras. The list below consists of the best-known bands and their music directors, preceded by the address of their particular school of music.

Army

Royal Military School of Music Kneller Hall. Headquarters CAMus, Twickenham, Middx TW2 7DU *tel:* 020 8898 5533 ext 8625 *fax:* 020 8893 8746. Lt Col S A Watts LRAM psm, principal dir of mus.

Household Cavalry

Band of the Household Division Musician's Association. c/o The Adjutant's Office, The Royal Hospital, Chelsea, London SW3 4SR *tel:* 020 8660 8079 (sec); 01323 729936 (mus dir) *fax:* 020 7823 6871. J M Millard, band sec. G Broom, mus dir; S Lindley, personnel admin. *Comprised of concert band, dance band, str orch and ens of any number. Affiliated to the Household Division (Guards and Cavalry).*

Band of The Life Guards. Hyde Park Barracks, Knightsbridge, London SW7 1SE *tel:* 020 7414 2525 *fax:* 020 7414 2529. Maj M J Torrent LTCL LGSM psm, dir of mus.

The Blues & Royals (Royal Horse Guards and 1st Dragoons). Hyde Park Barracks, Knightsbridge, London SW7 1SE *tel:* 020 7414 2525 *fax:* 020 7414 2599. Dir of mus: Combermere Barracks, Windsor, Berks SL4 3DN *tel:* 01753 755209 *fax:* 01753 755281.

Royal Artillery

Royal Artillery Band. Royal Artillery Band Rooms, RA Barracks, Woolwich, London SE18 4BB *tel:* 020 8854 1508 *fax:* 020 8781 3178. Maj G A Kingston psm RA, dir of mus.

Royal Engineers

Band of the Corps of Royal Engineers (RE Band). Brompton Barracks, Chatham, Kent ME4 4UG *tel:* 01634 822321 *fax:* 01634 822837. Capt D Burton ARCM psm, dir of mus.

Royal Signals

Band of the Royal Corps of Signals. Blandford Garrison, Blandford Forum, Dorset DT11 8RH *tel:* 01258 482445; *also fax.* Capt P L Murrell psm, dir of mus.

Infantry: Guards Division

Coldstream Guards. Wellington Barracks, Birdcage Walk, London SW1E 6HQ *tel:* 020 7930 4466 ext 3269; 020 7414 3269 *fax:* 020 7414 3399. Maj D J Marshall ARCM LTCL BBCM psm, dir of mus.

Grenadier Guards. Wellington Barracks, Birdcage Walk, London SW1E 6HQ *tel.* 020 7414 3267 *fax:* 020 7414 3236. Lt Col P E Hills FLCM psm, dir of mus.

Irish Guards. Chelsea Barracks, London SW1W 8RF *tel:* 020 7414 4519 *fax:* 020 7414 4349. Maj A R Chatburn ARCM psm, dir of mus.

Scots Guards Band. Wellington Barracks, Birdcage Walk, London SW1E 6HQ *tel.* 020 7414 3266 *fax:* 020 7414 3011. Maj R J Owen ARCM, dir of mus.

Welsh Guards. Chelsea Barracks, London SW1W 8RF *tel:* 020 7414 4521 *fax:* 020 7414 4530. Capt P D Shannon MBE ARCM LRAM psm, dir of mus.

Miscellaneous Staff Bands

Band of the Adjutant General's Corps. Armstrong Block, AGC Centre, Winchester, Hants SO21 2RG *tel:* 01962 887938 *fax:* 01962 887720. Capt C R Meldrum LRSM ARCM ALCM psm, dir of mus.

Band of the Army Air Corps. School of Army Aviation, Middle Wallop, Stockbridge, Hants SO20 8DY *tel:* 01980 674545 *fax:* 01980 674144. Capt P R Clark psm AAC, dir of mus.

Band of the Brigade of Gurkhas. Queen Elizabeth Barracks, Church Crookham, Fleet, Hants GU13 0RJ *tel:* 01252 355171 *also fax.* Capt E H Keeley ARCM A(mus)LCM BBCM psm CAMus, dir of mus.

Band of the Corps of Royal Electrical and Mechanical Engineers. Rowcroft Barracks, Arborfield, Reading RG2 9NL *tel:* 0118 976 3279 *fax:* 0118 976 3466. Capt Ian R Peaple LRSM, dir of mus.

Band of the Royal Lancers. Stanley Barracks, Bovington Camp, Wareham, Dorset BH20 6JB *tel:* 01929 403339/403429 *fax:* 01929 403217. *Address from Feb 2000:* York Barrack, BFPO 17. Capt J R Young BA BBCM psm, dir of mus.

Band of the Royal Logistic Corps. The Princess Royal Barracks, Deepcut, Camberley, Surrey GU16 6RW *tel:* 01252 340833 *fax:* 01252 340628/340994. Capt J W Taylor ARCM ALCM BBCM psm, dir of mus.

Regimental Bands

Band of the Hussars and Light Dragoons. York Barracks, BFPO 17 *tel:* 00 49 251 927 2427 *fax:* 00 49 251 927 2426. Capt R Pennington MISM psm, dir of mus.

Band of the Light Division. Sir John Moore Barracks, Winchester, Hants SO22 6NQ *tel:* 01962 888315/888285 *fax:* 01962 888285 *email:* lightdivision.band@virgin.net. Capt G Jones MBE, dir of mus.

Band of the Parachute Regiment. RHQ Para, Browning Barracks, Aldershot, Hants GU11 2BU *tel:* 01252 347644 *also fax; email:* paraband@tesco.net. Capt I D McElligott, dir of mus.

The Band of the Prince of Wales' Division (Clive). Clive Barracks, Tern Hill, Market Drayton, Shrops TF9 3QE *tel:* 01630 698270/698273 *fax:* 01630 698233. Capt S C Barnwell BBCM psm, dir of mus.

Band of the Prince of Wales' Division (Lucknow). Jellalabad Barracks, Tidworth, Hants SP9 7AB *tel:* 01980 602814/602852/602853 *fax:* 01980 602831. Capt J A C Huggins ARCM psm, dir of mus.

The Band of the Royal Irish Regiment. St Patrick's Barracks, Ballymena, BFPO 808 *tel:* 028 2566 1122 *fax:* 028 2566 1262. Capt C C Attrill psm, dir of mus.

Highland Band of the Scottish Division. Dreghorn Barracks, Redford Rd, Edinburgh EH13 9QW *tel:* 0131 310 2735 *also fax.* Capt G D Rodger LRAM ARCM psm, dir of mus.

The King's Division Normandy Band. Weeton Barracks, Preston PR4 3JQ *tel:* 01772 260942 *fax:* 01772 260944. Capt K Hatton FTCL ARCM psm, dir of mus.

King's Division Waterloo Band. Piave Lines, Catterick Garrison, N Yorks DL9 3JS *tel:* 01748 873984/5 *fax:* 01748 872190. Capt C E Hicks LRAM ARCM LTCL psm, dir of mus.

The Lowland Band of the Scottish Division. Cavalry Barracks, Colinton Rd, Edinburgh EH13 0PP *tel:* 0131 310 5267 *fax:* 0131 310 5288. Capt C C Gray ARCM BBCM psm, dir of mus.

Minden Band. The Queen's Division, Oakington Barracks, Longstanton, Cambridge CB4 5EJ *tel:* 01223 205555 *fax:* 01223 205559. Capt C R Meldrum LRSM ARCM ALCM psm, dir of mus.

Normandy Band of the Queen's Division. Piave Lines, Leyburn Rd, Catterick Garrison, N Yorks DL9 3LR *tel:* 01748 874805 *fax:* 01748 874900. Capt J W Taylor ARCM ALCM BBCM psm CAMus, dir of mus.

Royal Air Force

Headquarters Music Services. RAF Uxbridge, Middx UB10 0RZ *tel:* 01895 237144 ext 6291 *fax:* 01895 810846. Wg Cdr R K Wiffin FTCL LRAM ARCM RAF, principal dir of mus. *All booking enquiries for RAF bands and mus services should be directed to the Engagement Co-ord at the above address. This covers the Central Band of the RAF, The Band of the RAF Regiment, the Band of the RAF College, the RAF Squadronnaires (Big Band), Fanfare Trumpeters and smaller ensembles including the Salon Orchestra of the RAF.*

Band of the Royal Air Force College. Cranwell, Sleaford, Lincs NG34 8HB *tel:* 01400 261201 ext 6040/6053. Sqn Ldr S L Stirling FTEL ARAM ARCM RAF, dir of mus.

Band of the RAF Regiment. Cranwell, Sleaford, Lincs NG34 8HB *tel:* 01400 261201 *fax:* 01400 261382. Flt Lt G J Bain LRAM ARCM RAF, dir of mus.

Central Band of the RAF. Uxbridge, Middx UB10 0RZ *tel:* 01895 237144 ext 6380 *fax:* 01895 810846. Flt Lt D W Compton ARCM RAF, dir of mus.

Royal Marines

Royal Marines School of Music. HMS Nelson, Queen St, Portsmouth PO1 3HH *tel:* 023 9272 6161 *fax:* 023 9272 6169. Lt Col R A Waterer LRAM, principal dir of mus.

Dartmouth: Band of HM Royal Marines. Britannia Royal Naval College, Dartmouth, Devon TQ6 0HJ *tel:* 01803 835788 *also fax.* Lt P F Watson LRAM ARCM RM, dir of mus.

Exmouth: Band of HM Royal Marines. Commando Training Centre Royal Marines, Lympstone, Devon EX8 5AR *tel:* 01392 414138 *fax:* 01392 414149. Lt P A Western LRSM ARCM, dir of mus; Bd Sgt M E Reynolds, sec.

Plymouth: Band of HM Royal Marines. HMS *Raleigh*, Torpoint, Cornwall PL11 2PD *tel:* 01752 811297 *fax:* 01752 811590. Capt B Mills LRAM ARCM RM, dir of mus.

Portsmouth: Band of HM Royal Marines. HMS *Nelson*, Portsmouth, Hants PO1 3HH *tel:* 023 9286 4069; 023 9287 6943 *also fax.* Major J R Perkins ARAM ARCM LGSM, dir of mus.

Rosyth: Band of HM Royal Marines Scotland. HMS *Caledonia*, Rosyth, Fife KY11 2XH *tel:* 01383 425418 *also fax.* Lt P Best LRAM RM, dir of mus.

Police Force

Band of An Garda Siochana (Irish Police). Garda HQ, Garda Depot, Phoenix Park, Dublin 8, Republic of Ireland *tel:* 00 353 1 666 2040/4 *fax:* 00 353 1 666 2045 *email:* dalyv@iol.ie. Ins William Byrne, dir of mus.

Greater Manchester Police Band. Greater Manchester Police, Chester House, Boyer St, Manchester M16 0RE *tel:* 0161 856 2243 *fax:* 0161 856 2259. Capt M S Hennis SB St J ARCM, dir of mus.

The Nottinghamshire Police Wind Orchestra. Public Relations Office, Sherwood Lodge, Arnold, Nottingham NG5 8PP *tel:* 0115 942 0999 *fax:* 01623 559106. Sgt Mark Wakeland, sec.

Fire Service

Band of the West Midlands Fire Service. Lancaster Circus, Queensway, Birmingham B4 7DE *tel:* 0121 380 6724 *fax:* 0121 380 7201. Wendy Williams, band mgr.

Suffolk Fire Service Band. Fire Service HQ, Colchester Rd, Ipswich, Suffolk IP4 4SS *tel:* 01473 588888 *email:* howells@ajec.flexnet.co.uk. A Brock, chmn.

Suffolk Fire Service Training Band. Fire Service HQ, Colchester Rd, Ipswich, Suffolk IP4 4SS *tel:* 01473 588888 *email:* howells@ajec.flexnet.co.uk. A Brock, chmn.

Royal British Legion

Central Band of The Royal British Legion. 4 Christopher Way, Emsworth, Hants PO10 7QZ *tel:* 01243 379594 *also fax; email:* twhealing@ntserver.britishlegion.org.uk. Capt E P Whealing MVO, dir of mus. *For information on other Royal British Legion Bands throughout the country contact the above address.*

Central Band of the Royal British Legion Scotland. New Haig House, Logie Green Rd, Edinburgh EH7 4HR *tel:* 0131 448 2786 *fax:* 0131 557 5819 *email:* Jean@roslindale.freeserve.co.uk. Capt B H S Rodgers LRAM ARCM, dir of mus.

Maghull Town Band (The Band of the Royal British Legion in Maghull). Beech Lodge, 51 Burscough Rd, Ormskirk, Lancs L39 2XE *tel:* 01695 572150. Bill Casey, sec.

Poynton Royal British Legion Concert Band. 24 Fawns Keep, Wilmslow Park, Wilmslow, Cheshire SK9 2BQ *tel:* 01625 520243. Peter Leary, mus dir.

Brass Bands

The following bands compete in various championships ('contesting bands'); their competition successes since 1998 and the section in which they will compete in 2000 are shown in italics. The number of members is given in parentheses. Additional information can be obtained from the **British Brass Band Registry** (c/o PO Box 349, Halifax, W Yorks HX3 5YJ *tel:* 01422 252245, Colin Johnson). For details and dates of the brass band competitions see **Competitions UK.**

The **British Federation of Brass Bands** (c/o PO Box 349, Halifax, W Yorks HX3 5YJ *tel:* 01422 252245) publishes a directory of British Brass Bands. *The British Bandsman,* a weekly publication, is available from Harold Charles House, 64a London End, Beaconsfield, Bucks HP9 2JD *tel:* 01494 674411 *fax:* 01494 670932 *email:* info@britishbandsman.com *website:* www.britishbandsman.com. *Brass Band World,* a monthly publication, is available from Caron Publications, Peak Press Building, Eccles Rd, Chapel-en-le-Frith, High Peak SK23 9RQ *tel:* 01298 812816 *fax:* 01298 815220 *email:* info@bbworld.com *website:* www.brassbandworld.com.

Armthorpe Elmfield Band (40). 36 Fernbank Drive, Armthorpe, Doncaster DN3 2HB *tel:* 01302 831646. Haydn Griffiths, mus dir; Roz Cox, sec (*tel:* 01302 833136). *3rd section. Yorkshire Area.*

Banavallum Brass (Horncastle) Band. Oriana, Bowl Alley Lane, Horncastle, Lincs LN9 54EQ. Miss W Sharp, treasurer; Elizabeth White, cond; Mark Tong, sec. *4th section.*

Beaumaris and District Silver Band (100). Boston Villa, Llanddaniel, Anglesey LL60 5DY. G Evans, cond. *Championship section.*

Besses o' th' Barn Band (30). 7 Yew Tree Grove, Lostock Hall, Preston PR5 5NP *tel:* 01772 316908. Jean Heyes, sec; Steven Beardmore, resident mus dir. *Championship section.*

Black Dyke Band (1855) Ltd (31). Bandroom, Sandbeds, Queensbury, Bradford BD13 1AB *tel:* 01274 814970 *fax:* 01274 814168 *email:* blackdyke@blackdykeband.co.uk. James Watson, mus dir; Robert Childs, cond; Geoffrey Whiteley, admin.

Blackburn and Darwen Band (35). 19 Ainsworth Hall Rd, Ainsworth, Bolton, Lancs BL2 5RY *tel:* 01204 526743. C Harrison, contest sec; Mrs C Baxter band sec; Eric Landon, cond. *1st section. 1999: area contest; Buxton contest; Rhyl contest; Rochdale contest; Preston & District contest.*

Blackley Band (25). 50b Chapelhill Drive, Blackley, Manchester M9 8FJ *tel:* 0161 795 9494; 01625 520243 *also fax.* Peter Leary, mus dir. *3rd section. Manchester and District (3rd); Buxton Contest (1st).*

The Bodmin Town Band (30). The Bodmin Town Band & Social Club, Honey St, Bodmin PL31 2DL *tel:* 01566 774903 *email:* dadobson@lineone.net. Nicholas Childs, cond; Mrs V A Dobson, sec. *Championship section. All England Masters.*

Boldon Colliery Brass Band (35). 20 Penhill Close, Ouston, Chester-le-Street, Co Durham DH2 1SF *tel:* 0191 410 9423. S Malcolm, mus dir; M Burr, sec. *1st section. Buxton Brass Band Festival; Wansbeck Entertainment contest; Whit Friday Marches; regional finalists, Harrogate.*

Brighouse and Rastrick Band (27). West Ridings, Finkil St, Brighouse HD6 2NY *tel:* 01484 400785. Ian J Dust, sec; Allan Withington, cond; David Hirst, mus dir. *Championship section. 1997-98 National Champions, 1998 European Champions, 1998 All England Masters Champions.*

Brighton Silver Band (35). 18 Flower Farm Close, Henfield, Sussex BN5 9QA *tel:* 01273 493469 *also fax; email:* sianxmartin@compuserve.com. Sian Buss, sec; Estelle Flood, mus dir; Geoffery Enefer, chmn. *1st section. National championships; London and Southern counties.*

British Steel Teesside Band (32). 26 Pritchett Rd, Ormesby, Middlesbrough, Cleveland TS3 0NG *tel:* 01642 291410/507859 *email:* Mplus40@aol.com. Paul Robinson, sec; Graham O'Connor, professional cond. *Championship section.*

Broxburn Public Band (35). 40 Station Rd, Broxburn, W Lothian EH52 5QX *tel:* 01506 852144. T White, sec; Michael Marzella, cond; D W Anderson, treasurer; A Chalmers, president. *Championship section. Scottish Championship winners, 1st section.*

Camborne Town Band (28). 1 Harveys Way, Hayle, Cornwall TR27 4PE *tel:* 01736 753779. Ruth Richards, sec; Reg Bennett, chmn. *Championship section.*

City of Birmingham (28). 65 Beeches Drive, Erdington, Birmingham B24 0DT *tel:* 0121 373 7237. Miss B J Dunscombe, sec and treasurer; Warren Belshaw, mus dir. *2nd section. 1998: Milton Keynes; Midlands Region; RHYL. 1999: Midlands Region.*

City of Stoke-on-Trent Brass Band (35). 104 Weston Coyney Rd, Longton, Stoke on Trent ST3 5NF *tel:* 01782 314742. Linsay Lawrie, mus dir; Lindsay Clowes, chmn; Alan Sargeant, sec. *2nd section. 1999: North East Midlands Brass Band Association Annual Contest (winner); Midlands Region (2nd).*

Cosham Concert Brass Band (27). 3 Sparsholt Close, Havant, Hants PO9 4AP *tel:* 023 9225 7867/9283 4040 *fax:* 023 9283 4076. Beryl Pearce, sec; Ted Howard, cond. *2nd section.*

Crystal Palace Band (35). 26 Clock House Rd, Beckenham, Kent BR3 4JP *tel:* 020 8658 9659 *email:* riz.bleach@btinternet.com. Rachel Bleach, hon sec; Michael Gray, mus dir. *2nd section. Southern Counties ABA 1st section; London & Southern Counties 2nd section.*

Cwmaman Institute Silver Band (30). 3 Foundry View, Godreaman, Aberdare, Mid Glamorgan CF44 6DW *tel:* 01685 879326. David Jones, president. *Championship section.*

David Urquart Travel Yorkshire Imperial (28). 32 Rose Ave, Haydock, St Helens WA11 0NF *tel:* 01942 714904. Neal McNulty, mgr. *Championship section.*

Deiniolen Band (32). Minafon, Clwtybont, Caernarfon, Gwynedd LL55 3DW *tel:* 01286 870452 *email:* deiniolenband@hotmail.com. M Jones; D W Williams, resident cond; R Wyatt, professional cond. *1st section. 1998: Welsh Regional contest 2nd section (2nd). 1999: Welsh Regional contest 2nd section(4th).*

Denham Hendon Brass (28). 5 Plover Close, Berkhamstead HP4 2HU *tel:* 01442 385840 *email:* Linsdavies@aol.com. Stewart Gaudion, cond; Lindsey Davies, sec. *Championship section. 1998: Winners of Harrow contest; Basildon area contest 1st section (3rd).*

Dobcross Silver Band (28). 5 Park View, Park Terrace, Mossley OL5 0AU *tel:* 01457 836223 *also fax.* F Hanley, president; Mrs J Lawless, sec; Simon Wood, mus dir. *1st section.*

Dodworth Colliery Band (35). 12 Meadow Croft, Outwood, Wakefield, W Yorks WF1 3TF *tel:* 01924 870981. G O'Connor, cond/mus dir; A Leicester, sec. *Championship section. Amber Valley Entertainment (1st); Grand Shield; Yorkshire Area Contest.*

Dunaskin Doon Band (30). 36 Strathayr Place, Ayr KA8 0AY *tel:* 01292 289868. Margaret Rae, sec. *Championship section.*

Elland Silver Band (34). 7 Elland Hall Farm, Exley Lane, Elland, W Yorks HX5 0SN *tel:* 01422 370880. Mrs K Harrison, sec; K Billington, treasurer. *2nd section.*

Elmsett Fellowship Brass Band (15). Homeland, Hadleigh Rd, Elmsett, Ipswich, Suffolk IP7 6ND *tel:* 01473 658658. Joy Sillitoe, membership sec; Malcom Cox, cond.

Enfield Co-Op Band (c 20). 33 Carlton Terrace, Edmonton, London N18 1PJ *tel:* 020 8807 2939. Les Watson, sec; Denis André, mus dir.

Ever Ready Band (35). 1 Goodrich Close, Lambton Rise, Philadelphia, Houghton-le-Spring, Tyne and Wear DH4 4XJ *tel:* 0191 512 0296 *fax:* 0191 512 0294 *email:* Les.Palmer@bt.com. L J Palmer, band mgr; S Malcolm, bandmaster. *Championship section. 1998: Harry Ramsden runners-up; Wansbeck contest champions; Camerons champions. 1999: Northern Area champions.*

Fodens (Courtois) Band. c/o 26 Horsefair Ave, Chapel-en-le-Frith, High Peak SK23 9SQ *tel:* 01298 812591 *also fax.* Nicholas Childs, mus dir; B Malcolm Brew, treasurer. *Championship section. 1998: French Open champions; North West Area champions.*

Foss Dyke Band (30). 12 Megs Lane, Navenby, Lincoln LN5 0TE *tel:* 01522 810992; 07798 538042 *email:* fossdyke@geocities.com. Simon D Oates, sec. *1st section.*

Friary Guildford Brass Band (30). 4 Ivybank, Nightingale Rd, Godalming, Surrey GU7 2JE *tel:* 01483 861129. M Yarham, sec; B Le Tissier, cond; N Winter, chmn. *1st section. Crawley Entertainment; Isle of Wight Entertainment. Folkestone, Brighton, Reading, Whit Friday.*

Frickley-South Elmsall Band (33). 1 Lincoln Cres, South Elmsall, Pontefract, W Yorks WF9 2TJ *tel:* 01977 643826. D Baxter, sec; K Raper, chmn; L Price, mus dir. *2nd section. 1998: Yorkshire Area Champions (3rd section).*

Fulham Brass Band (20). 6 Chaldon Rd, London SW6 7NJ *tel:* 020 7385 4092 *email:* angela@cua.ulsop.ac.uk. Guy Dawes, band sec; David Payn, dir of mus. *4th section. Sole remaining central London brass band.*

Gillingham Imperial Silver Band (37). 37 Bridgeclose, Gillingham, Dorset SP8 4LS *tel:* 01747 823550. N W Perrin, gen sec; R Sansom, contest sec; S F Tranter, mus dir. *2nd section.*

Greenhall Band. 2 Mortonhall Park Gardens, Edinburgh EH17 8SL *tel:* 0131 664 5125. John Robertson, sec. *2nd section.*

Grimethorpe Colliery Band (28). Acorn Centre, 512 High St, Grimethorpe, Barnsley, S Yorks S72 7BB *tel:* 01226 780981 *also fax.* Garry Cutt, mus dir; Terry Webster, sec. *Championship section.*

GUS Band (28). 90 Logan St, Market Harborough, Leics LE16 9AR *tel:* 01858 432444. Lisa Grimshaw, concert sec; Melvyn White, mus dir. *Championship section. All England Masters; British Open; National Championships.*

Hatherleigh Silver Band (35). 51 Market St, Hatherleigh, Devon EX20 3JP *tel:* 01837 810414. P Chandler, contest sec; R A Wonnacott, cond; Rebecca Entwistle, band sec. *4th section. Bristol Area; SWBB Annual; Bandsmens Festival.*

Horden Colliery Band (30). 9 Hazel Cres, Easington Colliery, Peterlee, County Durham SR8 3HP. Miss AT Rice, sec; Wilf Beddell, cond; Basil Rice, chmn. *2nd section.*

Hyde Band (60). 78 Phelipps Rd, Corfe Mullen, Wimborne, Dorset BH21 3NW *tel:* 01202 605083 *fax:* 01425 475044. G Cook, sec; Peter Wise, mus dir and cond. *1st section. 1999: West of England (1st).*

Ipswich Co-op Band (30). 4 Orchard Grove, Claydon, Ipswich, Suffolk IP6 0BZ *tel:* 01473 832242 *fax:* 01473 211417. Andrew Shipp, membership sec; Stephen Kenna, cond. *1st section. Stevenage Area; Milton Keynes Entertainment; Folkestone Open; Harrow.*

JJB Sports Leyland Band *formerly* The BNFL Band (28). 26 Offley Rd, Sandbach, Cheshire CW11 1GY *tel:* 01270 763906 *also fax.* Allan Littlemore, band mgr; Richard Evans, mus dir. *Championship section. 1998: Brass In Concert champions; All England Masters; British Open; National Championships.*

Kirkby Colliery Welfare Band (28). 31 Burton Rd, Sutton-in-Ashfield, Notts NG17 2EU *tel:* 01623 553715. Mrs V Wilkes, sec. *2nd section.*

Lewis Merthyr Brass Band (35). 1 Ashgrove, Nelson, Mid Glamorgan CF46 6LR *tel:* 01443 450380. Miss C Thomas, sec; Lawrence Harris, cond; Mrs F Davies, treasurer; Paul Williams, chmn. *1st Section.*

Littleport Brass Band (35). 37 Angoods Lane, Chatteris, Cambs PE16 6RG *tel:* 01354 692247. Andrew Frost, chmn; Mrs S Peacock, mus dir. *2nd section.*

Long Melford Silver Band (25-30). Thorncroft Batt Hall, Bulmer, Sudbury, Suffolk CO10 7EZ *tel:* 01787 372439. M Gore, membership sec; Roger Green, cond.

Lydbrook Band (58). c/o Cheristow, Stowfield, Lydbrook, Glos GL17 9PD *tel:* 01594 860944 *fax:* 01594 860394. R Morgan, sec. *1st section.*

Lydmet Lydney Band (30). 53 Highbury Rd, Bream, nr Lydney, Glos GL15 6EG *tel:* 01594 564490. Debbie Rulton, sec; Dave Bishop-Rowe, mus dir. *1st section.*

Marple Band (36). 21 Rushton Drive, Marple, Stockport SK6 7LS *tel:* 0161 427 3612. Mrs E M Murphy, sec; Garry E Cutt, cond. *Championship section. Qualifiers for National Finals; British Open. Also playing in Millennium Concert.*

Mount Charles Band (30+35). c/o 66 Pamear Parc Par, Cornwall PL24 2AU *tel:* 01726 812312. Gary Giles, publicity offr and engagement sec; Derek Thomas, band mgr. *Championship section. 1998: South West Area Finals (5th).*

Newtongrange Silver Band (35). 25 Carrick Cres, Easthouses, Dalkeith EH22 4HQ *tel:* 0131 663 1607. Grant O'Connor, sec; Tony Swainson, cond. *Championship section. Grand Shield competition; Carnegie Trust Invitation Contest.*

Ocean Brass (40). 8 Beechwood Cres, Chandler's Ford, Eastleigh, Hants SO53 5PA *tel:* 023 8025 4416 *fax:* 023 8027 3597. A J Hickson, sec; Leighton Rich, cond. *2nd section. National Brass Band Championships, SW area finals.*

Oldham Brass 97 (35). 9 The Sycamores, Lees, Oldham, Lancs OL4 3JP *tel:* 0161 620 7434. G Briggs, chmn. *2nd section. 1998 3rd section champions.*

Ovington Tynedale Band (25). First Cottage, West View, Acomb, Hexham, Northumberland NE46 4PP *tel:* 01434 608469. Phil Rutherford, sec. *3rd section.*

Point of Ayr Band. 1 Foxglove Close, Wistaston, Crewe, Cheshire CW2 6UD *tel:* 01270 569183 *also fax; email:* Pointcncrt@aol.com. T R Davies, concert mgr; Michael Rowles, md. *Championship section. 1998: European Championship (3rd). 1999: Welsh Championship (1st).*

RAF St Athan Voluntary Band (40). RAF St Athan, Barry, Vale of Glamorgan CF62 4WA *tel:* 01446 797318 *also fax;* 07775 800210 *email:* alan@statham.freeserve.co.uk. Alan R Bourne, mus dir. *2nd section. 3 times Royal National Eisteddfod of Wales winner. 1999 regional champions.*

Ratby Co-Operative Band (108). 20 Mill Drive, Ratby, Leics *tel:* 0116 238 6954. Kevin Steward, mus dir; Sheralyn Newman, sec. *1st section.*

Redbridge Brass Band (28). Colindale, Station Rd, Sawbridgeworth, Herts CM21 9JY *tel:* 01279 722338; 07973 313913 *email:* alan@redbridgebrass.freeserve.co.uk. Alan Roberts, band mgr. *All England Masters; National Championship qualifiers. Starred in* Brassed Off, *Royal National Theatre 1998.*

Regent Brass (30). 114 Wheatlands, Heston, Middx TW5 0SD *tel:* 020 8577 1752 *fax:* 020 8937 3484. Karen Hunt, band sec; Paul Fensom, mus dir; Paul Cosh, artistic dir. *Championship section.*

Rhodian Brass (28). 5 St Johns Close, Walton, Chesterfield, Derbys S42 7HH *tel:* 01246 567182/236773. R E Fawbert, sec; S Thompson, band mgr. *Championship section.*

Rothwell Temperance Band (34). 22 Knightscroft Drive, Rothwell, Leeds, W Yorks *tel:* 0113 282 5715. A Riley, sec; David Roberts, cond. *Championship section. 1998: 1st section Yorkshire Area Championship (1st), Malton Entertainments Contest (1st). 1999: Yorkshire Area Championship, Championship section (3rd).*

St Austell Kernow Band (100+). The Band Hall, East Hill, St Austell, Cornwall PL25 4TR *tel:* 01726 61008 *also fax;* 01726 69990. Trevor Hitchens, sec; Chris Norse, chmn. *Second section.*

St Austell Town Band (100+). The Band Hall, East Hill, St Austell, Cornwall PL25 4TR *tel:* 01726 61008 *also fax;* 01726 69990. Trevor Hitchens, sec; Chris Norse, chmn. *Championship section.*

St Dennis Band (55). Park Head, Hendra Rd, St Dennis, St Austell, Cornwall PL26 8EQ *tel:* 01726 824486. S Julian, sec; J Brush, mus dir. *4th section. 1998: Truro Contest (2nd).*

Seindorf Trefor Band (35). Bethlehem, Trefor, Caernarfon, Gwynedd LL54 5HN *tel:* 01286 660546. Ann Williams, sec; Geraint Jones, cond. *1999 3rd section; 2000 2nd section.*

Sellers International (36). Sellers International Ltd, International House, Chapel Hill, Huddersfield, W Yorks HD1 3EE *tel:* 01484 469620 /540006. Major Peter Parkes, mus dir; David Johnson, treasurer; Steve Jarvis, bandman, (*tel:* 0113 2866 230). *Championship section.*

Skipton Brass Band (35). 21 Raikeswood Drive, Skipton, N Yorks BD23 1NA *tel:* 01756 798435/700200 *fax:* 01756 700186. Andrew Eastwood, cond; C R Davies, sec. *Championship section.*

South Nottinghamshire Hussars Yeomanry Band (28). 4 Greenacre Ave, Heanor, Derbys DE75 7YR *tel:* 01773 710359. B Mousley, sec.

South West Trains Woodfalls Band (30). Mere, Oak Drive, Alderbury, Salisbury, Wilts *tel:* 01722 710074 *email:* woodfallsband@geocities.com. Brian Easterbrook, sec; D Hayward, resident cond. *Championship section. 1998: West of England Champions.*

Staffordshire Building Society Band (35-40). Ivy Cottage, 36 Camden St, Walsall Wood, Walsall WS9 9BQ *tel:* 01543 373193. Shaun Elliott, chmn; Andy Culshaw, mus dir. *Championship section. 1998: Regional Qualifying (2nd); WMBBA (1st).*

Thames Brass Band. 72 Nelson Road, Whitton, Twickenham, Middx TW2 7AU *tel:* 020 8898 5509 *fax:* 020 8408 9786 *email:* david.e.loftus@lineone.net. David E Loftus, hon sec. *2nd section. 1999: London & Southern Counties 2nd Section champions; SCABA Entertainment Contest Section 'A' (4th).*

Tredegar Band (35). 8 Dolwydellan Close, Grove Park, Blackwood, Gwent NP2 1GG *tel:* 01495 226510. D Powell, band mgr. *Championship section. 1998: Champion Band of Wales; Radio Wales Band of the Year; South Somerset champions. British Open Welsh Championship, runners-up.*

Tylorstown Band - Valley Lines (33). c/o 23 Elizabeth St, Pentre, Mid Glamorgan CF41 7JN *tel:* 01443 442504. Mrs R Evans, sec; W H Taylor, chmn; L Harries, cond. *1st section.*

Uckfield Concert Brass (28). 5 Silverdale Ave, Hove, E Sussex BN3 6FF *tel:* 01273 882539 *fax:* 0870 161 7291 *email:* andy@awooler.demon.co.uk. Andy Wooler, resident cond. *1st section. National Area Contest; Southern Counties Amateur Bands Association spring contest.*

Unison Kinneil Band. 31 Ochilview Rd, Bo'ness, W Lothian EH51 0LD *tel:* 01506 827761. Robert Doherty, sec. *Championship section.*

Unity Brass Band (The Band of Manchester Unity Friendly Society) (50+). 7 Harecroft Cres, Sapcote, Leics LE9 4FX *tel:* 01455 273184 *fax:* 01455 271464. Mrs R Walker, sec; Rob Boulter, cond. *Championship section.*

Wansbeck's Ashington Colliery Band. 98 Burnside, North Seaton, Ashington, Northumberland NE63 9UF *tel:* 01670 812823. J Dunn. *2nd section.*

Whitburn Band (40). Cumloden, Fauldhouse, W Lothian EH47 9EL *tel:* 01501 771616; 0141 429 7555 *fax:* 0141 429 7899 *email:* archie.simpson@lineone.net. Maj Peter Parkes, mus adviser and hon president; A Simpson, sec. *Championship section. 1999: Scottish champions.*

Williams Fairey Band (28). Fairey Engineering Ltd, PO Box 41, Crossley Rd, Heaton Chapel, Stockport SK4 5BD *tel:* 0161 432 0281 *fax:* 0161 431 3575 *email:* yatia@williamsfaireyband.co.uk. James Gourlay, mus dir; John Cresswell, mgr. *Championship section. 1998: British Open Champions.*

Wrentham Band (25). The Moorings, 153 Yarmouth Rd, Lowestoft, Suffolk NR32 4AF *tel:* 01502 561641. Mrs B Beevor; R Pearcey, cond. *4th section.*

Yeovil Town Band (45). 71 St Michaels Rd, Yeovil, Somerset BA21 5AH *tel:* 01935 471604. A J Lock, sec; S Syke, mus dir. *1st section. 1998: West of England Champions (1st section).*

Yiewsley & West Drayton Band (50). 30 Edgar Rd, Yiewsley, Middx UB7 8HW *tel:* 01895 854720 *also fax; email:* christopher@connect4free.net. Christopher Cole, mus dir; Mrs D Tubb, sec. *4th section (national). 3rd section (SCABA).*

Yorkshire Building Society Band (28). 48 Moorside Gardens, Eccleshill, Bradford, W Yorks BD2 3RE *tel:* 01274 632676 *fax:* 01274 626788. David King, principal cond; Richard Hirst, band mgr. *Championship section. 1999: European champions.*

Wind Bands

Most of the following bands are members of the **British Association of Symphonic Bands and Wind Ensembles (BASBWE)** (*see* **Associations**). The magazine *Winds* is published quarterly by BASBWE. Youth Wind Bands are listed in the **Youth Orchestras and Bands** section. School, college and university wind bands are not listed, unless membership of the band is open to external applicants.

Abington Wind Band. 14 Barnstaple Close, Northampton NN3 3BH *tel:* 01604 236936. Anthony Healey, sec. *Open to ages 20 and over.*

The Barnet Band. 17 Stanmore Rd, London N15 3PR *tel:* 020 8889 0689. Sue Dunn, sec; Jean Cotterell, mus dir. *Open to gr 5 and above; no age limit. Wed evening rehearsals.*

Bicester Concert Band. 45 Welland Croft, Bicester, Oxon OX6 8GD *tel:* 01869 600656. Rosalind Mason, chair. *Mainly adult members but all welcome. Rehearsals Tue, 7.45pm, St Edburg's Church Hall, Bicester. Repertoire includes jazz, popular, classical, film mus.*

Birmingham Symphonic Winds. Rose Cottage, Bonds End Lane, Sibford Gower, Oxon OX15 5RT *tel:* 01295 788499 *also fax; email:* bsw@bigfoot.com. Jayne Rollason, admin; Keith Allen, mus dir. *High performance skills necessary; membership by invitation; ages 18-35. Presents a series of concerts throughout the year at the CBSO Centre in central Birmingham, giving many premiere performances and working with international soloists and guest conds. Represented the UK at the 1997 WASBE conference in Austria.*

Bisham Concert Band. 1 Collyer Rd, Stokenchurch, Bucks HP14 3QG *tel:* 01494 482152. Beatrix Taylor, cond. *Community wind band; ages 8 and over.*

Bristol Concert Wind Band. 12 Brentry Rd, Fishponds, Bristol BS16 2AA *tel:* 0117 965 1796 *email:* harrisc@globalnet.co.uk. Chris Harris, mus dir. *Independent adult band: main band, gr 6 min; intermediate, gr 3 min; beginners. Band practice at St Bonaventure's Parish Hall, Wed, 7.45pm. The band is available for fundraising events.*

Burnham Concert Band (46). 674 Bath Rd, Taplow, Berks SL6 0NZ *tel:* 01628 604826. Peter Kenneth, sec. *Open to ages 16 and over; gr 4/5 min. Rehearsals each Wed, 7.45pm in Burnham Park Hall, Burnham.*

Cork Barrack Street Band (60+). 29 Reeds Square, Barrack St, Cork City, Ireland *tel:* +353 021 321212. Kevin Meldrum, cond; Billy O'Callaghan, chmn. *Divided into 2 bands - snr and youth. Eight part-time mus teachers provide on educ and appreciation of mus and its performance. All students must complete graded exams of Trinity College of Music, London in their respective insts before entering the Senior Band. Won the National Concert Band Championships in 1997 and 1998 and came second in 1999. Takes part in many events including The St Patrick's Day Parade and has featured in a documentary by RTE.*

Croydon Symphonic Band. 74 Ridge Langley, Sanderstead, Surrey CR2 0AR *tel:* 020 8657 8591 *also fax.* Derek Reeves, chmn. *Open to ages 16 and above, no auditions. A community band which regularly performs in the Fairfields Halls, Croydon.*

Edinburgh Concert Band. 16 Linden Place, Loanhead EH20 9RY *tel:* 0131 448 2583. Stephen Callaghan, band mgr, cond. *Community wind band open to ages 16 and above.*

Eynsford Concert Band. 55 Clarendon Way, Chislehurst, Kent BR7 6RG *tel:* 01689 822646 *fax:* 07970 082369 *email:* Dorianburt@hotmail.com. Chris Mowat, mus dir; Colin Palmer, asst mus dir. *Ages 13-70; gr 6 min. Annual tours abroad, competitions, concerts at the Royal Albert Hall and Queen Elizabeth Hall, London. CD also available.*

The Hanover Wind Band. The Old Market, Upper Market St, Hove, E Sussex BN3 1AS *tel:* 01273 206978 *fax:* 01273 329636 *email:* mailbox@hanoverband.co.uk. Caroline Brown, artistic dir. *Professional, period inst wind band specialising in mus c 1890. Ages 25-60; entry by audition.*

Harrow Concert Band. 128 Mill Way, Bushey, Herts WD2 2AQ *tel:* 01923 252396 *fax:* 01923 217794. Phil Price, treasurer. *Community band open to players of all ages and backgrounds; gr 3 or similar ability. Concerts played in royal parks, fêtes, etc.*

Herefordshire Symphonic Wind Band. Fairview, Eardsley, Hereford HR3 6PQ *tel:* 01544 327020 *email:* big.bill@online.net. Bill Griffiths, sec/admin; Kenneth Booth, mus dir. *Open to school-leaving age and above; gr 8 min. Plays for charitable organisations in Hereford and neighbouring counties; 6 concerts per year.*

Huntingdonshire Concert Band. c/o Sativus House, 3a High St, Saffron Walden, Essex CB10 1AT *tel:* 01799 526339. Gordon C Smith, sec. *Open to ages 16 and above; gr 6 approx. 6 engagements a year, usually for local charities. Annual w/shop held in Feb.*

Kew Wind Orchestra. 23 Ferrymoor, Ham, Richmond, Surrey TW10 7SD *tel:* 020 8940 0444. John Morrison, hon sec; Duncan Stubbs, cond. *Community band open to ages 16-65; gr 8 min. Performs locally in London parks; gold medal award winner in the community band section of the BASBWE wind festival, Manchester.*

La Ronde Concert Band of Jersey. 74 De Quetteville Court, St Saviour's Rd, St Helier, Jersey JE2 4GB *tel:* 01534 724937. Len Perkins, librarian. *Ages 16-78; gr 5 min.*

Maidstone Winds. Cream House, 7 Church St, Burham, Rochester ME1 3SB *tel:* 01634 660550 *email:* maidstone.winds@cwcom.net. Martin Farebrother, chmn; Brendon Le Page, mus dir. *Ages 17-70; gr 8 approx. Repertoire includes classics of international band mus and new compositions. Four concerts per year.*

Northampton Concert Band. 10 Laneside Hollow, E Hunsbury, Northampton NN4 0SR *tel:* 01604 700830 *email:* keith.crompton@btinternet.com. Keith Crompton, sec. *Open to ages 18 and above; gr 5 min. Rehearses once a week at Nene College, Northampton. Performs on average once or twice a month at concerts and events, many of which are for local charities and churches. Has won several awards in national wind band festivals.*

Nottingham Symphonic Winds. Windblowers, 75-7 Derby Rd, Nottingham NG1 5BA *tel:* 0115 941 0543 *fax:* 0115 947 4433. Margaret Frogson, band sec. *Community wind band, ages 16-60; entry by audition. Also training band (Nottingham Wind Ensemble).*

Rossendale Valley Sounds. 36 Anemone Drive, Haslingden, Lancs BB4 6NJ *tel:* 01706 216901 *also fax.* Christine Hudson, hon sec. *Community band open to all ages and abilities. Rehearsals at Alder Grange School, Thur.*

South Berks Concert Band. 25 Clover Field, Lychpit, Basingstoke, Hants RG24 8SR *tel:* 01256 356318 *also fax; email:* southberksconcertband@yahoo.com. Fran Hallet, treasurer. *Open to all ages; abilities range from gr 3 to gr 8+. Currently play mainly outdoor concerts. Repertoire consists of marches, medleys and more recent pieces composed specifically for wind bands.*

Southampton Concert Wind Band (c 50). 4 Lordswood Close, Bassett, Southampton SO16 6SB *tel:* 023 8079 0730. Honor Powrie, chair; Peter Hyland, mus dir. *Ages 17-70; gr 5 min. Repertoire includes classical, shows, traditional, swing, and jazz.*

Southwark Concert Band. 44 Red Post Hill, Herne Hill, London SE24 9JQ *tel:* 020 7733 4311 *fax:* 020 7736 4483. Paul Millington, treasurer; Judi Stockwell, chair; Robert Bridges, mus dir. *Community band open to* *ages 17+ with some mus ability and plenty of enthusiasm. Rehearse on Thur evening and perform a number of concerts during the year including two formal concerts and the London Marathon.*

Tutbury Band. 62 Station Rd, Rolleston on Dove, Burton-on-Trent, Staffs DE13 9AA *tel:* 01283 814703. Malcolm Heywood, mus dir; Barbara Harvey, sec. *Open to ages 8 and above, gr 3 min. Rehearse Sat mornings.*

West Bristol Concert Band (50). 19 Wintor Close, Chepstow, Gwent NP6 5LE *tel:* 01291 625552 *also fax.* Philip Sims, mus dir. *Open to ages 14 and above, gr 5 min. Part of the Community Music Centre organised by the Bristol Schools Music Service. Rehearse Mon evenings at Porterny Community School, Shirehampton, Bristol*

White Rose Concert Band. 14 Woodlands Close, Harrogate, N Yorks HG2 7AZ *tel:* 01423 885418. Isobel Beard, sec. *Main band is for w/wind, br and perc players of any age; performs at a variety of venues throughout the year and competes in local and national mus festivals. The training band is for players with basic mus skills, adult learners especially welcome.*

Woking Wind Orchestra. 46 Arthurs Bridge Rd, Horsell, Woking, Surrey GU21 4NT *tel:* 01483 769845 *also fax; email:* paulharris.19@virgin.net. Paul Harris, mus dir; Pat Page, admin. *Open to players aged 17 and above, of a high standard. Rehearsals Mon at St Pauls Church, Oriental Rd, Woking. 2 or 3 concerts performed each year, one of which is for charity. Young soloists are encouraged in their early years from mus colleges.*

Ensembles

Ensembles listed here are confined to those based in Britain or those bookable through a British concert agent. Agents are shown in italics at the end of the entry (*see* **Agents and Managers**). Entries are in alphabetical order, and where a partnership has no name except those of the individuals, the surnames are given in square brackets. Performers' names are given and the nature of the ensemble (string, vocal, etc) is indicated. A small number of ensembles combine music with the spoken word and these are listed at the end of this chapter under **Words and Music**.

A Man, a Woman and a Double Bass. Warwick House, 34 Warwick Rd, Coulsdon, Surrey CR5 2EE *tel:* 020 8660 7877 *fax:* 020 8763 0492 *email:* silvius@dial.pipex.com. Lowri Blake, voice, vc; Peter Buckoke, db. Classical Music Cabaret.

A1 Brass Ensemble. 26 Wattleton Rd, Beaconsfield, Bucks HP9 1TS *tel:* 01494 674692 *fax:* 01494 676428. Phillip Pickering, Chris White, tpt; Chris Many, hn; Simon Jack, trb; John Carr, euph, tb. Concerts, weddings, funerals, educ demonstrations, dinners, garden parties.

Abacus. 20 Spencer Gate, St Albans, Herts AL1 4AD *tel:* 01727 839516 *fax:* 01727 762407. Joanna West, vn; Angela Crispe, cl; Helen Edgar, vc; Karen Suter, pno.

The Abbott O'Gorman Duo. 40 Cubitt Terrace, London SW4 6AR *tel:* c/o 020 7720 8660 *also fax; email:* jocelyn_abbott@cubittmusic.freeserve.co.uk. Jocelyn Abbott and Laura O'Gorman, pno duo.

Aberdeen Sinfonietta. South House, 17 Kirk Brae, Cults, Aberdeen AB15 9QP *tel:* 01224 869615 *also fax; email:* violin@sreid.freeserve.co.uk. Bryan Dargie, dir; Mary Dargie, sec; Shelagh Reid, publicity/promotions mgr.

Aberdeen Trio. Morven, Crossroads, Strathdon, Aberdeen AB36 8XN *tel:* 019756 51284. Bryan Dargie, vn; Raymond Dodd, vc; Donald Hawksworth, pno.

Academia Wind Quintet of Prague. Jiri Marsalek, fl; Otto Trnka, ob; Petr Donek, cl; Frantisek Pok, hn; Josef Janda, bsn. *NCCP*

* **The Academy of Ancient Music.** 10 Brookside, Cambridge CB2 1JE *tel:* 01223 301509 *fax:* 01223 327377 *email:* administrator@aam.co.uk. Christopher Hogwood CBE, dir; Paul Goodwin, associate cond; Andrew Manze, associate dir, concert master; Christopher Lawrence, gen mgr; Fiona Seers, admin. Associated choir is The Academy of Ancient Music Chorus.

The Academy of Ancient Music Chamber Ensemble. 10 Brookside, Cambridge CB2 1JE *tel:* 01223 301509 *fax:* 01223 327377 *email:* administrator@aam.co.uk. Christopher Hogwood CBE, dir; Paul Goodwin, associate cond; Andrew Manze, associate dir, concert master; Christopher Lawrence, gen mgr; Fiona Seers, admin.

Academy of St Martin in the Fields Chamber Ensemble. Station House, Staverton, Totnes, Devon TQ9 6AG *tel:* 01803 762670 *fax:* 01803 762451. Kenneth Sillito, dir; Malcolm Latchem, mgr. Ens performs as str quintet, sextet and octet, mixed wind and str, pno quintet.

Accademia Wind Ensemble. c/o Arts Associates (Artists Management), 16 Manor Close, Baston, Peterborough PE6 9PM *tel:* c/o 01778 560511 *also fax; email:* ann@paulrodriguezmus.demon.co.uk. Ann Cherry, fl; Anthony Randall, hn; Brian Wightman, bsn; David Wilson, ob; Peter Thompson, cl.

Accolade Singers. 34 Guildford Rd, Croydon CR0 2HG *tel:* 020 8684 2422 *also fax;* 020 8309 1309 *email:* M.J.Akalay-Watkin@city.ac.uk. Marilyn Akalay-Watkin, Louise Hillier, Mark Evans, Ian Priestley. Versatile, professional singers (from solo plus pno to sextet). Varied repertoire, from opera to West End musicals.

Adam Trio. Eliyahu Shulman, vn; David Sella, vc; Morris Chernorudsky, pno. *Ellison*

Adelphi Saxophone Quartet. 3 Corran Close, Winton, Eccles M30 8LP *tel:* 0161 789 2092 *fax:* 0161 477 9835 *email:* martin@adelphisaxquartet.freeserve.co.uk. Sarah Markham, sop sax; Andrew Wilson, alto sax; Martin Kerrigan, ten sax; Alex Mitchell, bar sax.

Almira string quartet

"...The quartet's fine tone and exacting phrasing were admirable..." "...a delicate and stylish reading..."
The Strad

"...the very best of this concert was a really well prepared reading of the challenging Dissonance string quartet...for me it completely stole the show..."
The Birmingham Post

"...an evening of sublime music making..."
The Northern Scot

The Almira String Quartet, Wright Music Promotions.
235 Sreetsbrook Rd, Solihull. West Midlands. B91 1HE. UK
TELEPHONE: (+44) 0121 705 0098
FAX: (+44) 0121 705 4815
E-MAIL: ansi.chalk@lineone.co.uk

ARCHAEUS QUARTET

"The Archaeus Quartet gave a performance that was both sensitive and committed" "Exhilarating playing"
The Strad

A Life In Reverse: Minna Keal:
LORELT label

"Performances, production-values and presentation are all beyond reproach. Do try and investigate this bold, most stimulating release" **Gramophone**

***Enquiries:* 29 Chadwick Road, London SE15 4RA**
tel/fax: 0171 639 1203
hooleycole@compuserve.com

The Armonioso Quartet

"In both works the Quartet gave their all, demonstrating an excellent range of dynamic musicality"
(The Northern Scot)

Joanna Emerson Toby Turton Angela Jessopp Anete Graudina-Jeanette

This London based Quartet is passionate about chamber music, particularly when played in the intimate setting of a traditional drawing room.

Its repertoire ranges from the pre-classical to the contemporary.

Management – Christopher Emerson

Tel/Fax: 01309 690571 E-mail: 101325.645@Compuserve.com

THE BRUCE/LYTTELTON DUO

Margaret Bruce, piano
Adrian Lyttelton, reader

Recitals of poetry and piano solos

"The Romantic Imagination"
– inspired by the life and times of Goethe

"Time, Night and Music"
– a celebration of British Poetry and piano solos for the Millennium

Agent: Miranda Phipps
21 Foskett Rd; London SW6 3LY
phone: 0171 731 3782
fax: 0181 969 0820

Aeolian Duo. 14 Thaxted Drive, Stockport, Cheshire SK2 5XH *tel:* 0161 483 1327 *also fax.* Eira Lynn Jones, hp; David Sumbler, fl.

Aeolian Reeds. 4 Hillside Way, Bevendean, Brighton BN2 4TR *tel:* 01273 677588; 01293 871251. Sarah Cobby, ob; Nicola Hazelwood, cl; Sarah Hadfield, bsn.

Aeona Flute Quartet. 87a Queens Rd, East Grinstead, W Sussex RH19 1BG *tel:* 01342 300949 *email:* egsales@egnet.co.uk. Paul Cheneour, Claire Hope, Sinéad McCarthy, Kathryn Smith, fls.

Albion Brass Consort. 78 Jacksons Drive, Cheshunt, Waltham Cross, Herts EN7 6HW *tel:* 01992 637180 *fax:* 01992 429637 *email:* albion.brass@gmx.net. Paul Thornton, Peter Rudeforth, tpt; Christine Norsworthy, hn; David Whitehouse, trb; Marc Easener, tb.

Albion Ensemble. 29 Alston Rd, Barnet, Herts EN5 4EU *tel:* 020 8441 1107 *also fax; email:* sw_artists@msn.com. Michael Cox, fl; George Caird, ob; Angela Malsbury, cl; Gareth Newman, bsn; Peter Francomb, hn. *SWA*

Alibas. The Briars, The Green, Blakesley, Northants NN12 8RD *tel:* 01327 861150 *also fax;* 020/8533 1372 (diary) *email:* alibas@compuserve.com. Chmbr mus for fl.

Allandale Quartet. Torridon House, 104 Bradford Rd, Wrenthorpe, Wakefield, WF1 2AH *tel:* 01924 371496. Brian Greensmith, dir. Str and pno quartet. Mus for all occasions.

Allegri String Quartet. 5 The Barons, St Margarets, Twickenham, Middx TW1 2AN *tel:* 020 8892 3848 *also fax; email:* Allegri@moyse.demon.co.uk. Peter Carter, David Roth, Jonathan Barritt, Pál Banda. Sarah Moyse, admin.

Almira String Quartet. Simon Chalk, Ian Davidson, vn; David Aspin, va; Joseph Spooner, vc. *Wright*

Alshar Ensemble. *ECAM*

* **Amaryllis Consort.** 34 Lebanon Court, Richmond Rd, Twickenham, Middx TW1 3DA *tel:* 020 8892 3484 *also fax.* Charles Brett, dir, c-ten; Catherine Peacock, Juliet Schiemann, sop; Ian Thompson, ten; Stephen Roberts, bs.

The Ambache. 9 Beversbrook Rd, London N19 4QG *tel:* 020 7281 7880 *fax:* 020 7263 4027 *email:* polmear.ambache@telinco.co.uk. Diana Ambache, mus dir; Louise Brooksbank, gen mgr. 3-30 players. Pioneers revival of mus by women composers.

[Amos, Perrett]. 127 Armour Rd, Tilehurst, Reading RG31 6HD *tel:* c/o 0118 962 5443 *fax:* 020 7732 0653 *email:* sheridap@arizona.edu. Lisa-Maree Amos, fl; Danielle Perrett, hp.

* **The Amsterdam Baroque Orchestra.** Ton Koopman, cond. *Hazard*

Andrusier Ensemble. 80 Glenthorne Rd, Friern Barnet, London N11 3HJ *tel:* 020 8361 5209 *also fax; email:* ensemble@andrusier.demon.co.uk. Tamar Andrusier, artistic dir, pno; David Routledge, David Adams, vn; Scott Dickinson, va; Garry Walker, vc; Dov Goldberg, cl. Mus of Terezín.

Angelique String Quartet. *John Boddy*

The Angell Piano Trio. 2 St Donatts Rd, London SE14 6NR *tel:* 020 8691 0309 *also fax.* Jan Peter Schmolck, vn; Richard May, vc; Frances Angell, pno.

Angels of the North. 24 Lime Tree Drive, Farndon, Chester CH3 6PN *tel:* 07710 245777; 01642 466864 *also fax.* Hp, sop. Classical, jazz, musicals, popular.

* **Anna Magdalena.** 4 Conegra Rd, High Wycombe, Bucks HP13 6DY *tel:* 01494 524596 *also fax.* Gill Ross, Alastair Ross, dirs.

Apartment House. Anton Lukoszevieze, artistic dir. Flexible ens of 2-16 members. Specialises in the performance of avant-garde and experimental mus from around the world. *Haferkorn*

Apollo Brass Quintet. 1 Railway Cottages, Holland Lane, Oxted, Surrey RH8 9AZ *tel:* 01883 723072 *fax:* 01883 714481. Christopher Pigram, Timothy Hayward, tpt; Raul Diaz, hn; Simon Gunton, trb; David Powell, tb.

Apollo Saxophone Quartet. c/o Rob Buckland, 27 Birkdale Close, Tytherington, Macclesfield, Cheshire SK10 2UA *tel:* 01625 425840 *also fax*; 07976 728699. David Roach, Rob Buckland, Tim Redpath, Andy Scott.

Apollon Quartet. *Sonata*

[Appleton, Ryder]. 81 Chatsworth Rd, London E5 0LH *tel:* 020 8986 9197. Pno duo.

* **Arborea Musica & Friends.** Gerard McDonald, artistic dir. Baroque mus on period insts. *Michael Harrold*

* **Arcadia.** 60 Ashville Rd, London E11 4DT *tel:* 020 8558 7723. MaryAnn Tedstone, dir. 3-12 players specialising in renaissance dance mus and baroque.

* **The Arcadian Academy.** Nicholas McGegan, dir. *Clarion/Seven Muses*

Archaeus Quartet. 29 Chadwick Rd, Peckham, London SE15 4RA *tel:* 020 7639 1203 *also fax; email:* hooleycole@compuserve.com. Ann Hooley, Bridget Davey, vn; Elizabeth Turnbull, va; Martin Thomas, vc.

Archduke Trio. 99 Wimbledon Hill Rd, London SW19 7QT *tel:* 020 8946 6967 *fax:* 020 8946 6966 *email:* chris.hirons@which.net. Christopher Hirons, vn; Russell Davis, vc; James Walker, pno. Resident ens at University of Leicester.

L'Archibudelli. Trio. *TransArt*

[Ardagh-Walter, Jeffrey]. 40 Mossbury Rd, London SW11 2PB *tel:* 020 7223 2408 *also fax.* Catherine Ardagh-Walter, vc; Emily Jeffrey, pno.

Arditti Quartet. Irvine Arditti, Graeme Jennings, vn; Dov Scheindlin, va; Rohan de Saram, vc. *Haferkorn*

Arenstein-Hoy Guitar Duo. 78 Ridge Rd, London N8 9NR *tel:* 020 8348 3630. Colin Arenstein, Robert Hoy, gui.

Arethusa Oboe Quartet. Bearsden, 25 Hampstead Lane, London N6 4RT *tel:* 020 8348 8498 *also fax.* Graham Salter, ob; Emer Calthorpe, vn; Ian Rowbotham, va; Justin Pearson, vc.

Arietta. Fl, hp. *John Boddy*

The Armonioso Quartet. The Quillet, Findhorn, Forres, Moray IV36 3YJ *tel:* 01309 690571 *also fax; email:* 101325.645@compuserve.com. Also: 10 Eastholm, Hampstead Garden Suburb, London NW11 6LR *tel:* 020 8458 5542. Christopher Emerson, mgr; Anete Graudina-Jeannette, Angela Jessopp, vn; Joanna Emerson, va; Toby Turton, vc. Repertoire ranges from pre-classical to contemporary. Performances usually for charities.

* **Arrigoni Consort.** Baroque mus. *Murphy*

Arundo Clarinet Quartet. Woodside, Orestan Lane, Effingham, Surrey KT24 5SN *tel:* 01372 452513 *fax:* 01372 451416 *email:* Joanna@eatonclarinets.co.uk. Janet Spotswood, Jill Sadler, Angela Crispe, Joanna Estall, cl. *Michael Harrold*

Athena Ensemble. 91 Brands Hill Ave, High Wycombe, Bucks HP13 5PX *tel:* 01494 527826 *also fax.* Robert Jordan, dir. Wind and str ens.

Atlantic Winds. 10 Adria Rd, Didsbury, Manchester M20 6SG *tel:* 0161 434 6182 *also fax.* Laurence Perkins, mus dir.

Attacca. 37 Mount Pleasant Cres, Crouch Hill, London N4 4HP *tel:* 020 7272 6101 *also fax; email:* andrew.pink@btinternet.com. Andrew Pearce, Dale Loth, vn; Andrew Tait, va; Joseph Spooner, vc; Helen Fidler, ob; Jessica Rabin, tpt; Andrew Pink, dir; Michael Chapman, continuo.

Audubon Quartet. David Ehrlich, Akemi Takayama, vn; Doris Lederer, va, Thomas Shaw, vc. *NCCP*

Auer Quartet. *Tennant*

Aurelian Trio. Torridon House, 104 Bradford Rd, Wrenthorpe, W Yorks WF1 2AH *tel:* 01924 371496. Brian Greensmith, dir. Vn or fl, vc and pno. Mus for all occasions.

The Australian String Quartet. Peter Tanfield, James Cuddeford, vn; Keith Crellin, va; Niall Brown, vc. *Ellison*

* **The Avison Ensemble.** 3 Bentinck Place, Newcastle Upon Tyne NE4 6XN *tel:* 0191 226 0799 *fax:* 0191 273 7008 *email:* gordix@btclickfree.com. Gordon Dixon, mgr; Adrian Chandler (vn), Timothy Roberts (hpd), dirs. Baroque ens of up to 12 players. Specialises in performance of Avison and other British composers of the baroque period. Also educ programmes.

[Ax, Stern, Laredo, Ma]. Emanuel Ax, pno; Isaac Stern, vn; Jaime Laredo, va; Yo-Yo Ma, vc. *Askonas Holt*

* **Bach Ensemble.** Joshua Rifkin, dir. *Clarion/Seven Muses*

* **Badinage Ensemble.** Paul Carroll, bsn, fl, rcdr; Sally Civval, vc, va da gamba; David Rowland, hpd, org, f-pno. Baroque and classical repertoire on period insts. *Music Management*

* **The Baker Collection.** Kenton Cottage, Burnt Hill Way, Wrecclesham, Farnham, Surrey GU10 4RP *tel:* 01252 795047 *also fax.* The oldest English vn consort. 17th C mus on complete set of English 17th C insts. Brian Lloyd Wilson, Diane Terry, vns; Oliver Webber, va and vn; Laurie Ann Macleod, bs vn, 5-str vc, gamba; Alastair Ross, keyboards; Peter Trevelyan, presenter.

[Bannister, Smart]. Phillida Bannister, Alpin Smart. Contralto and gui. *Roxane Houston*

Barbican Piano Trio. 3 Campbell Rd, Bow, London E3 4DS *tel:* 020 8980 5711 *also fax; email:* jnjkirby@aol.com. Gabrielle Lester, vn; Robert Max, vc; James Kirby, pno.

* **Baroque Brass of London.** 39 Huntingdon St, London N1 1BP *tel:* 020 7609 1401 *also fax.* Mark Bennett, Michael Laird, Michael Harrison, Crispian Steele-Perkins, Stephen Saunders, Patrick Jackman, David Staff, Tom Lees, Colin Chapman, Robert Howes; Alison Glaister, mgr. Early br mus on period insts. 8 tpts, timpani and hpd.

Bassoon & Beyond. Bsn jazz quartet. Daniel Smith and others. *Michael Brewer*

Bax Duo. Gregory Sheppard, va; Graham Waugh-Bennett, pno. *Ellison*

The Beaufort Ensemble. Clare Bentley, fl; Deborah Rich, ob; Paul Saunders, cl; Elizabeth Mason, bsn; Jonathan Hassan, hn. *Chameleon*

Beaumont Reed Trio. 40 Calder Gardens, Edgware, Middx HA8 5PT *fax:* 020 7372 4883 *email:* brtrio@aol.com. Simon Dewhurst, ob; Rachel Elliott, cl; Hazel Granthier, bsn.

Beaux Arts Trio. c/o 35 Victoria Rd, Shoreham by Sea, W Sussex BN43 5LA *tel:* 01273 454310 *also fax.*

Bekova Sisters Piano Trio. 76 Honeybrook Rd, London SW12 0DN *tel:* 020 8675 6885 *fax:* 020 8673 8356. Elvira Bekova, vn; Eleonora Bekova, pno; Alfia Bekova, vc.

Belcea String Quartet. *YCAT*

Bella Opera. Finchingfield House, The Green, Finchingfield, Essex CM7 4JS *tel:* 01371 810289 *also fax.* Lorraine Patient, artistic dir. Highlights from popular operas.

Bellissima. 57 Canadian Ave, Hoole, Chester CH2 3HQ *tel:* 01244 400217 *also fax; email:* Janice@webb-ward.freeserve.co.uk. Janice Webb, admin, scripts, sop; Jane Route, sop; Janine Roebuck, sop; plus guests. Light-hearted scripted stage shows (2 or 3 sops) featuring opera, operetta, musicals.

[Bennetts, Bowman]. 4 Heathleigh Cottages, Maidstone Rd, Horsmonden, Kent TN12 8JL *tel:* 01892 723370 *also fax; email:* 101767.2724 @compuserve.com. Kathryn Bennetts, Peter Bowman, rcdrs. *Invisible Pilots*

Berg (Alban) Quartet. Guenter Pichler, Gerhard Schulz, vn; Thomas Kakuska, va; Valentin Erben, vc. *Intermusica*

* **[Berg, Slade-Lipkin].** 12 Freemasons Rd, Croydon, Surrey CR0 6PB *tel:* 020 8656 5412. Nicola Berg, sop; Heather Slade-Lipkin, pno, hpd, f-pno.

Bernard Roberts Piano Trio. Bernard Roberts, pno; Andrew Roberts, vn; Nicholas Roberts, vc. *Ireland*

[Beyer, Dagul]. 15 Birchmead Close, St Albans, Herts AL3 6BS *tel:* 01727 858485 *also fax; email:* mailbox@classical-artists.com. Isabel Beyer, Harvey Dagul, pno duettists.

[Bibby]. 73 Pirbright Rd, London SW18 5ND *tel:* 020 8874 6886 *fax:* 0151 625 5711. Alexandra and Nicola Bibby, pno duo.

Bingham String Quartet. 6 Munsons Lane, Feltwell, Norfolk IP26 4DE *tel:* 01842 828424 *also fax;* 07973 977704 *email:* bsq@con-brio.com. Stephen Bingham, Sally-Ann Weeks, vn; Brenda Stewart, va; James Halsey, vc.

Birmingham Contemporary Music Group. CBSO Centre, Berkley St, Birmingham B1 2LF *tel:* 0121 616 2616 *fax:* 0121 616 2622 *email:* bcmg@bcmg.org.uk. Simon Rattle, artistic adviser; Simon Clugston, artistic dir; Thomas Adès, mus dir; Jackie Newbould, gen mgr; Stephen Newbould, development mgr.

The Birmingham Ensemble. 16 Yew Tree Rd, Edgbaston, Birmingham B15 2LX *tel:* 0121 440 5164 *also fax.* Peter Thomas, artistic dir; Constanza Lezama, admin.

[Bishop, Hastings]. 12 Bramley Close, Wilmslow, Cheshire SK9 6EP *tel:* 01625 531240 *also fax;* 0161 881 0781. Sally Bishop, Anne-Marie Hastings, pno duo.

Black Hair. New Rectory, Everingham, York YO42 4JD *tel:* 01430 861954 *also fax; email:* rmm6@york.ac.uk. Roger Marsh, artistic dir; Anna Myatt, voice. Contemporary mus ens; vocal, inst and mus theatre.

The Bold Balladiers. 23 King Edward's Rd, Ruislip, Middx HA4 7AQ *tel:* 01895 635737 *also fax; email:* TheBoldBalladiers@bigfoot.com. Michael Goldthorpe, ten, dir; Wendy Eathorne, Roimata Templeton, Silva Vuckovic, sops; John Bradbury, Alice Pratley, vns; Christina Shillito, Martin Johnson, vc; Sam Kenyon, Rupert Widdows, fls; Peter Hewitt, Iain Ledingham, Harold Lester, Samantha Newbold, accompanists.

Borodin String Quartet. *VWM*

The Boros Gypsy Ensemble. 357 Kenton Rd, Harrow, Middx HA3 0XS *tel:* 020 8907 7953 *also fax; email:* borosensemble@breathemail.net.

[Bradshaw, Bennett]. 55 Compton Rd, London N1 2PB *tel:* 020 7226 8675. Susan Bradshaw, Richard Rodney Bennett, pnos.

Brahms Trio of London. 187c Devonshire Rd, London SE23 3NJ *tel:* 020 8291 2510. Peter Thompson, mus dir, cl; Anne Baker, vc; Timothy Barratt, pno.

* **The Brandenburg Consort.** 5 Cornfield View, Sleaford, Lincs NG34 7WF *tel:* 01529 304130 *fax:* 01529 304131 *email:* roy.goodman @virgin.net. Roy Goodman, mus dir; Steven Jones, admin.

Brass Belles. 47 Little Roke Ave, Kenley, Surrey CR8 5NP *tel:* 020 8763 2113. Marion Wilson, Claire Duncan, tpt; Tracey Golding, hn; Lorraine Temple, trb; Amanda Parkin, tb.

Brass Camerata. 2 Courtfield House, Baldwins Gardens, London EC1N 7SB *tel:* 020 7916 8461 *fax:* 020 7916 8462 *email:* img@msn.com. Ian Golding, dir. 2 tpts, hn, trb, tb and other ens as required.

Bravura. 32 Chandos Ave, London W5 4ER *tel:* 020 8847 0888 *also fax.* Fiona Firth-Spiller, sop; Martin Robson, bs; William Hancox, pno.

Brentano String Quartet. *VWM*

* **Brian Lloyd Wilson and the City of London Chamber Players.** Kenton Cottage, Burnt Hill Way, Wrecclesham, Farnham, Surrey GU10 4RP *tel:* 01252 795047 *also fax.* Brian Lloyd Wilson, dir and vn. Chmbr mus on period insts.

Bridge String Quartet. 12 Haslemere Ave, London W13 9UJ *tel:* 020 8579 4624 *also fax; email:* kaye@bridge-quartet.demon.co.uk. Catherine Schofield, Kaye Barker, vn; Michael Schofield, va; Lucy Wilding, vc.

The Abbott O'Gorman Duo

The Abbott O'Gorman Duo offer a wide range of musical evenings for four hands at one or two pianos. Their programmes range from a formal recital of the classical repertoire to a light entertainment featuring popular and nostalgic classics from the world of jazz and Broadway. Abbott & O'Gorman will tailor the evening to suit whatever theme is desired.

"They were a great success at the Windsor Festival. They played a dazzling programme of Classical Jazz which was beautifully introduced. We were delighted by them."
Director - Windsor Festival

Their CD - ***Ravel à Quatre Mains*** was hailed as:
"Excellent - a generous offering of five familiar works played by an expert piano duo."
Musical Opinion

Their new recording ***Classical Jazz à Quatre Mains*** featuring works by Bernstein and Gershwin including ***Rhapsody in Blue*** is available on the Cubitt Music label.

Cubitt Music Management
40 Cubitt Terrace London SW4 6AR UK

Tel/fax: +44 (0)20 7720 8660
Jocelyn_Abbott@cubittmusic.freeserve.co.uk
www.cubittmusic.freeserve.co.uk

Colour Blind Design 020 8771 3694

Bellissima

Two and three soprano scripted shows and concert items

Janice Webb

Janine Roebuck

Jane Route

Light-hearted scripted shows, featuring items from opera, musicals and musical comedy

Soprano arias, duets, trios, original musical arrangements and comedy items for concerts

Available for *theatre work*, *festivals*, *corporate entertainment*, *special events*, and as *guest artistes*

Tel/Fax: 01244-400217
or e-mail:-
Janice@webb-ward.freeserve.co.uk

HEBRIDES ENSEMBLE

James Clark Violin
Andrew Haveron Violin
Gillianne Haddow Viola
Catherine Marwood Viola
William Conway Cello
Rosemary Eliot Flute
Douglas Boyd Oboe
Ruth Ellis Clarinet
Ursula Leveaux Bassoon
Nigel Boddice Trumpet
Philippa Tunnell Harp
Peter Evans Piano

Scotland's international chamber ensemble with co-artistic directors William Conway and Peter Evans presents programmes of imagination and variety, covering a wide range of period and style and giving a particular emphasis to the music of the 20th century and contemporary Scottish composers.

"The peerless Hebrides Ensemble presented its group signature; enormous sound, huge confidence, flamboyant passion...a gripping performance"
(Guardian)

HEBRIDES ENSEMBLE MANAGEMENT
11 Palmerston Place, Edinburgh EH12 5AF
Tel/Fax: 0131 225 2006

'That REAL Gypsy Thing'

The Boros Ensemble

***Tomi Boros** Solo violin and director*

An 'Extravaganza' of Music

Ranging from 2 to an Assiette Gourmande of 12 versatile players and singers continuing a 230 year old tradition. The repertoire stretching from Hungarian & Eastern European Gypsy Music, Classical, the Viennese Classics, Romantic and Modern Master pieces.

Mission & Endorsements

'Superb violin playing, and players of classical & Hungarian Gypsy Music'
Anglo-Hungarian Mirror

'The cimbalom player of the Boros Ensemble plays Wonderfully'
Edit Adler, president of the Anglo-Hungarian Roman Catholic Association

Tel & Fax: 020 8 907 7953
email: borosensemble@breathemail.net
websites: www.borosensemble.com
www.gypsy-music.com

PHOTO:CARPENTER TURNER

Marianne Olyver & Her Orchestra

A highly acclaimed ensemble of 2 to 10 musicians

"Brilliant violinist Marianne Olyver has brought something new to the music scene by reviving something old; the tradition of European popular music played by a small Orchestra."
The Musician

"stunning...the thrill of the week!"
The Independent

Enquiries and CD:
Patrick Crooke
Georgius, The Street
Stoke-by-Clare
Suffolk CO10 8HR

Tel & Fax: 01787 277063
patrick@woodley.demon.co.uk
http://www.woodleyside.co.uk/olyver/

LOUISE JONES

VIOLIN

"...formidable technique and musical personality."
THE STRAD

"Louise Jones is a violinist whose musicianship shines out of every note..."
MUSICAL OPINION

CONCERTOS
RECITALS
CHAMBER MUSIC

Internationally acclaimed soloist and leader of the GLADSTONE STRING QUARTET. Many recordings include the complete works of Delius and Hoddinott for violin and piano (Meridian and Divine Art Labels).

"...devoted performances which enter Delius' elusive soundworld with rare sensitivity and insight." CLASSIC CD****

J.Audrey Ellison, International Artists Management,
135 Stevenage Rd, London SW6 6PB. T/F: 020 8450 1783.

Stella Dickinson

Oboe and Cor Anglais

Capital Oboe Quintet
Rita Manning-Violin
Bill Hawkes-Viola
James Potter-cello
Helen Tunstall-Harp

This combination has flexibility and infinite variety.

Programmes may include the Oboe Quartets of Mozart, Britten and/or Francaix, specially commissioned works and **exclusive repertoire from Stella's Solo debut C.D. Love's Lore** *WHL2118 ASV*

Programmes tailored to requirement, from three to eight performers.

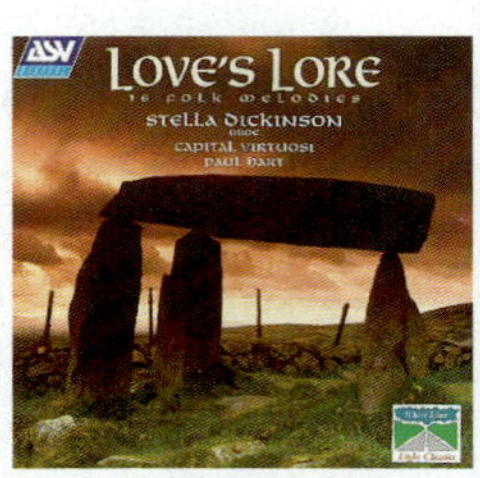

The Independent *16 British folk songs are given the virtuoso treatment rounded off to mesmerizing effect by Stella Dickinson's plaintive Oboe and Cor Anglais... "Early One Morning" "Scarborough Fair" "Blow the Wind Southerly" and others are translucently captured and immaculately played.*

(Bill Newman Hi Fi News)... *music making for all occasions, centered round Stella's wonderful range of timbres and instrumental technique-all performers singing their multi-coloured phrases in the best chamber music traditions ... This is a Peach of a disc.*

Whats on Magazine *This one should keep Classic FM listeners happy for many years to come, as it's the kind of music you might never tire of hearing. It is timeless, beautiful and evocative of earlier days.*

Stella is one of the most talented and versatile British oboists of her generation. Her performances are distinctive through her warmth of personality and ability to connect with her audience.

For more details contact:
130 St. James's Lane, Muswell Hill, London N10 3RH
Tel: 0181 883 0657 Fax: 0181 883 9970
Email: stellar1@stellar1.demon.co.uk www.musiciansgallery.com

QuintEssential

Sackbut and Cornett Ensemble

QuintEssential were magnificent throughout. Crisp articulation and taut rhythmic playing were their hallmark... The current musical appetite for the Baroque seems insatiable, and not surprising if there are young ensembles of this calibre.
Eastern Daily News

The splendid young sackbut and cornett ensemble QuintEssential..... purring like a rolls royce engine no less.
Early Music Today

For further details contact: Richard Thomas,
Tel & Fax 0208 855 8584 http://www.landini.org/quint
email: quintessential@gtemail.net

* **La Brigata.** Billington Manor, Billington, Leighton Buzzard LU7 9BJ *tel:* 01525 372516 *fax:* 01525 851649. Sue Tyson, sop; Kristine Szulik, alto; Philip Leech, ten; Peter Syrus, bs, mus dir. 13th-16th C English, French and Italian mus.

Brindley String Trio. *Michael Brewer*

British Chamber Ensemble. c/o Keown Artists Management, 62 Chestnut Rd, London SE27 9LE *tel:* 020 8761 4221 *also fax.* Celia Chambers, fl; Julian Shaw, va; Rachel Masters, hp.

British String Trio. c/o Keown Artists' Management, 62 Chestnut Rd, London SE27 9LE *tel:* 020 8761 4221 *also fax.* Jagdish Mistry, vn; Julian Shaw, va; Rhydian Shason, vc.

British Tuba Quartet. Meadowview, 10 Old Forge Rd, Fenny Drayton, Warwicks CV13 6BD *tel:* 01827 711964 *also fax;* 07971 843668 *email:* stevemead@compuserve.com. Steven Mead, David Thornton, euph; Richard Sandland, Stuart Birnie, tb.

* **Broadside Band.** 20 Leverton St, London NW5 2PJ *tel:* 020 7267 7176 *fax:* 020 7267 0127 *email:* jrmybarlow@aol.com. Jeremy Barlow, dir.

Brodsky Quartet. Delfina Studios, 50 Bermondsey St, London SE1 3UD *tel:* 020 7378 8033 *fax:* 020 7378 8034 *email:* brodskyquartet@compuserve.com.

* **The Brook Street Band.** 69 Tabley Rd, Islington, London N7 0NB *tel:* 020 7607 0185 *fax:* 020 7687 1586 *email:* tatty@easynet.co.uk. Tatty Theo, dir and baroque vc. Period inst chmbr mus ens.

Broomhill Opera. Wilton's Music Hall, 1 Grace's Alley, London E1 8JB *tel:* 020 7702 9555 *also fax; email:* opera@broomhill.demon.co.uk. Mark Dornford-May, artistic dir; Charles Hazlewood, mus dir.

BT Scottish Ensemble. 5 Newton Terrace Lane, Glasgow G3 7PB *tel:* 0141 221 2222 *fax:* 0141 221 4444 *email:* scottishensemble@yahoo.com. Heather Duncan, gen mgr; Clio Gould, artistic dir; Martin Ritchie, events mgr; Nicola Mutton, PA to dir.

Buckingham Duo. 1 Buckingham Rd, Leeds LS6 1BP *tel:* 0113 275 8509; 01227 261975. Anna Shuttleworth, vc; Elizabeth Altman, pno.

Bureau Piano Trio. 120 Belmont Rise, Sutton, Surrey SM2 6EE *tel:* 020 8642 5714. Richard Bureau, vn; Elizabeth Angel, vc; Carlina Carr, pno.

* **The Burgundian Cadence.** Rupert Damerell, c-ten; Simon Biazek, Matthew Woolhouse, tens; Damian O'Keeffe, bar. Early vocal and choral mus. *Michael Harrold*

* **Burlington Concerts.** 4 Gloucester Cottages, Croft Rd, Hastings, E Sussex TN34 3HN *tel:* 01424 715435 *also fax.* Robert Aldwinckle, Benedict Cruft, artistic dirs. Hpd, baroque and modern vn.

The Burlington Quartet. Allerton, Hawley Rd, Hawley, Dartford, Kent DA2 7RB *tel:* 01322 229837; 07973 303967 *fax:* 01322 270417 *email:* doug.burlington@lineone.net. Charles Tait, Susan Harrison, vns; Doug Blew, va; Sally Whale, vc. Str quartet specialising in the performance of classical and light background mus.

* **The Burning Bush.** c/o Lucie Skeaping, 19 Patshull Rd, London NW5 2JX *tel:* 020 7485 3957 *fax:* 020 7267 2957 *email:* lucieskeaping@hotmail.com. Lucie Skeaping, voice, rebec, vn; Robin Jeffrey, oud, lauto, perc; Roddy Skeaping, vn, lyra, yayli-tambor; Ben Harlan, cl, darabukka; Kevin Street, accordion, tpt; Robert Levy, db. Traditional Jewish music and songs from around the world.

* **Byzantium Duo.** c/o Cassell Entertainment, Lavington, Margery Lane, Lower Kingswood, Tadworth, Surrey KT20 7BG *tel:* 01737 242966 *also fax.* Pno and gui/lute duo. Baroque, classical, romantic, latin.

Calyx. Pno, vn, vc and cl. *JLM*

* **Cambiata.** 143 Aylesbury Rd, Wendover, Bucks HP22 6LJ *tel:* 01296 696795 *fax:* 01296 623410. Andrew Challinger, baroque ob, rcdr; Hazel Todd, baroque ob; Veronica Thomas, baroque bsn; John Dunnett, hpd. Performs in period costume for concerts and social functions.

* **Cambria Baroc.** 72 Gladsmuir Rd, London N19 3JU *tel:* 020 7281 9135. Elin Harries, sop; Nia Harries, baroque vc; Katharine May, hpd. Also vn. Sacred and secular mus, seasonal and themed programmes available.

Cambrian Brass Quintet. 16 Barrie Ave, Kidderminster, Worcs DY10 3AN *tel:* 01562 820737 *also fax; email:* cbq@ricadams.demon.co.uk. Richard Adams, Andrew Stone-Fewings, tpt; Simon Morgan, hn; Kevin Pitt, trb; Alan Inglis, tb.

* **Cambridge Baroque Camerata.** Jonathan Hellyer Jones, dir. *NCCP*

The Cambridge Scholars. Vocal ens. Neil Worsey, Robin Tyson, c-tens; Rupert Jennings, Tom Raskin, ten; Robert Rice, bar; Paul Grier, bs. *Chameleon*

CAMEO. 45a Cannon Hill, Southgate, London N14 6LH *tel:* 020 8882 5333 *also fax;* 07976 614429. Anthony Robb, Janet Larsson, fl; Richard Shaw, pno.

Camerata Brass. 75 Moor End Rd, Mellor, Stockport, Cheshire SK6 5PT *tel:* 0161 427 5482 *also fax; email:* gavin@gavinreid.netlineuk.net. Gavin Reid, David Carstairs, tpt; Naomi Atherton, French hn; Barry Daykin, trb; Phil Goodwin, tb.

Camerata Ensemble. 4 Kingston Rd, Handforth, Cheshire SK9 3JN *tel:* 01625 530792 *fax:* 01625 525331 *email:* ensemble@

major-minor.co.uk. Richard Howarth, dir; Luci Hanson, admin. All combinations of inst chmbr works.

* **Camerata of London.** 22 Derwentwater Rd, London W3 6DE *tel:* 020 8992 8973 *fax:* 020 8896 9826. Glenda Simpson, Barry Mason, dirs.

Camerata Roman of Sweden. *NCCP*

Camerata Singers. West Lea, Wylam Wood Rd, Wylam, Northumberland NE41 8HZ *tel:* 01661 852161 *also fax*. Percy Lovell, dir.

Camerata Vistula. *Finch*

Cameristi of London. 44 Gondar Gardens, London NW6 1HG *tel:* 020 7435 6232 *fax:* 020 7431 6843 *email:* cameristi@gondar.demon.co.uk. Luciano Iorio, artistic dir. Pno, str and wind in various combinations.

Campbell Trio. c/o Keown Artists' Management, 62 Chestnut Rd, London SE27 9LE *tel:* 020 8761 4221. David Campbell, cl; Julian Shaw, va; Andrew Ball, pno.

The Cann Twins. c/o GH Management, 5 Engleric, Chrishall, Royston, Herts SG8 8QZ *tel:* 01763 261535/837268 *fax:* 01763 261435. Claire and Antoinette Cann, pnos. Pno duo.

Cantabile. Richard Bryan, c-ten; Steve Trowell, Mark Fleming, ten; Michael Steffan, bs-bar. Humorous a cappella quartet. *Seaview*

Cantamen. Gate Cottage, High St, Hinxworth, Herts SG7 5HQ *tel:* 01462 743052 *also fax; email:* cole@which.net. Tim Lissimore, pno; Caroline Balding, vn; Jo Cole, vc; Will Sleath, fl; Joan Enric Lluna, cl.

* **Canterbury Clerkes.** Peveril, 5 Chapel Rd, Upton, Norwich, Norfolk NR13 6BT *tel:* 01493 751741 *also fax*. Peter Giles, c-ten; Martin Renshaw, Peter Haseldine Baker, ten; Antony Bussell, bass. *Annon*

Cantilena. 3 St Mark's Close, Hitchin, Herts SG5 1US *tel:* 01462 455835 *fax:* 01462 458544 *email:* elmitt@btinternet.com. Diana Levitas, vn; Catherine Wilmers, vc; Kate Elmitt, pno. Specialises in primary childrens' concerts and in playing for parties, weddings, etc.

* **Canzona.** 20 The Hill, Church Hill, Caterham, Surrey CR3 6SD *tel:* 01883 344031 *also fax; email:* jcaudle@cix.compulink.co.uk. Jill Caudle, gen mgr; Theresa Caudle, dir, baroque vn, cornett; Jean Paterson, baroque vn; Mark Caudle, baroque vc, va da gamba; Laurence Cummings, hpd, org; Elizabeth Kenny, theorbo.

* **Cappella Nova.** 172 Hyndland Rd, Glasgow G12 9HZ *tel:* 0141 552 0634 *fax:* 0141 552 4053 *email:* alan.tavener@strath.ac.uk. Alan Tavener, dir; Rebecca Tavener, mgr. Flexible vocal ens of 3-18 singers, plus insts as required.

Capriccio String Quartet. Marla McLennan, Nathaniel Vallois, Geoffrey Cole, William Bersey. *Chameleon*

Capricorn. c/o Flat 1, 14 Marius Rd, London SW17 7QQ *tel:* 020 8772 0710 *fax:* 020 8772 0711 *email:* capri@schubert-road.demon.co.uk. Ileana Ruhemann, fl; Christopher O'Neal, ob; Anthony Lamb, cl; Gareth Newman, bn; Stephen Stirling, hn; Rebecca Hirsch, vn; James Boyd, va; Enno Senft, db; Catherine Edwards, pno.

* **The Cardinall's Musick.** 1 Lorne Court, Whitehall Rd, Harrow-on-the-Hill, Middx HA1 3BH *tel:* 020 8422 3119 *fax:* 020 8423 9707 *email:* admin@cardinallsmusick.demon.co.uk. Andrew Carwood, David Skinner, artistic dirs; Irene Wears, admin. Vocal ens.

The Carducci Quartet. Matthew Denton, Julie Gillett-Smith, vn; Graham Broadbent,va; Emma Denton, vc. *Christine Talbot-Cooper*

Carlos Bonell Ensemble. Carlos Bonell, dir. *Upbeat*

The Carnival Band. Andy Watts, shawm, flemish bagpipes, cl, rcdrs, curtal, voice; Jub, db, voice; Giles Lewin, vn, medieval bagpipes, rcdrs, shawm, voice; Raf Mizraki, drums, perc, gui, vc, dulcimer, voice; Bill Badley, gui, banjo, mandolin, lute, vocals. *Seaview*

* **The Carolinian Consort.** 57 Glen Albyn Rd, Wimbledon, London SW19 6HB *tel:* 020 8789 5902 *also fax*. H Åberg, L Mazzarri, Clara Sonabras, sops; S Pauley, theorbo, gui; C Gibley, hpd, org. Specialising in 17th C Italian secular mus.

Casablanca Steps. *GBZ*

Castagneri String Quartet. *LM*

* **Catch!** 57a St Philip's Rd, Cambridge CB1 3DA *tel:* 01223 461143 *also fax; email:* mtargent@silverfe.demon.co.uk. William Summers, Melanie James, Helena Brown, Mark Argent. Baroque and modern chmbr mus.

Cause Celebre. 9 Cromwell Rd, Burgess Hill, W Sussex RH15 8QH *tel:* 01444 230779 *fax:* 01444 233699. Jenny Caws, ob, ob d'am, eh; James Shenton, vn, penny whistle; Nicholas Houghton, pno; Helen Houghton, mgr.

Cavatina. Hp and fl duo. *John Boddy*

* **Cavendish Consort.** Hedgeways, Ballast Quay Rd, Fingringhoe, Essex CO5 7DB *tel:* 01206 729582. Christopher Turner, org; Jackie Wallace, rcdr; Christopher Gibson, vn; Andrew Spencer, rcdr; Marcel Glover, baroque bsn. Medieval, renaissance and baroque mus on authentic insts.

Cavendish Trio. 10 Mill Rd, Waterbeach, Cambridge CB5 9RQ *tel:* 01223 862232 *also fax*. Elaine Hammonds, sop; Peter Thompson, cl; Adrian Hobbs, pno.

Cellos Ad Lib. Flat 6, 46 Onslow Square, London SW7 3NX *tel:* 020 7584 9845 *fax:* 020 7589 3432. Eve Harris, admin; Ferenc Szucs, Anne-Isobel Meyer, Eve Harris, vcs.

Chaconne Brass. PO Box 2677, Reading, Berks RG6 5XY *tel:* 0118 975 6295 *fax:* 0118 926 7754 *email:* chaconne@livmusic.globalnet.co.uk. Torbjorn Hultmark, Mark Kesel, tpt; Simon de Souza, hn; Chris Mitchell, trb; James Baker, tb.

The Chagall Trio. 28 Oak St, Hemel Hempstead, Herts HP3 9TT *tel:* 01442 244832 *also fax*. Nicoline Kraamwinkel, vn; Julian Rolton, pno; Siân Bell, vc. *Christine Talbot-Cooper*

* **Chalemie.** 49 Pitts Rd, Oxford OX3 8BA *tel:* 01865 761966 *also fax; email:* chalemie@matspring.demon.co.uk. Barbara Segal, Frank Perrenboom, baroque dance; Sara Stowe, sop, hpd, perc; Barry Grantham, commedia del'arte actor; Matthew Spring, hurdy-gurdy, gui, actor; Sharon Lindo, vn, rcdr.

The Chamber Ensemble of New York. *Pro Piano*

Chamber Domaine. Thomas Kemp, artistic dir. Str trio plus pno and voice; mixed chmbr mus and lieder. *Murphy*

The Chamber Music Company. 44 Melrose Ave, London NW2 4JS *tel:* 020 8452 8983 *fax:* 020 8450 0546. Mark Troop, artistic dir, pno; Patricia Rozario, sop; Jagdish Mistry, vn; Matthew Barley, vc; Joan-Enric Lluna, cl; Stephen Stirling, hn.

* **Chameleon.** 4 Station Cottages, Harby Lane, Stathern, Leics LE14 4HJ *tel:* 01949 861347 *also fax; email:* dwh@globalnet.co.uk. Douglas Hollick, hpd; Iva Junková, fl; Sarah Smythe, vn; Iva Fleischhansová, vn; Catherine Fleming, rcdr; Emma Skeaping, vc; Alison Smart, sop.

The Chameleon Ensemble. 115 Selsey Rd, Edgbaston, Birmingham B17 8JP *tel:* 0121 434 5440 *email:* MeanChloe@aol.com. Rachel Selvidge, fl; Simon Dewhurst, ob; Luan Ford, cl; Robert Percival, bsn; Tim Hill, hn; plus strs, wind and pno as required.

* **The Chandos Baroque Players.** c/o Maya Homburger/Barry Guy, Carrickmourne, Thomastown, Co Kilkenny, Ireland *email:* maya @tinet.ie. Rachel Beckett, fl, rcdr; Lorraine Wood, ob; Jeremy Ward, bsn; Maya Homburger, vn; David Watkin, Daniel Yeadon, vc; Malcolm Proud, hpd.

* **Chapelle du Roi.** 10 Kensington Hall Gardens, Beaumont Ave, London W14 9LS *tel:* 020 7379 9361 *fax:* 020 7379 9636 *email:* chapelle@ newrenaissance.co.uk. Alistair Dixon, dir; Jan Hart, admin. Vocal ens.

* **Charivari Agréable.** Oakley, 109 Windmill Rd, Oxford OX3 7DN *tel:* 01865 751928 *also fax; email:* EventsManager@charivari. freeserve.co.uk. Susanne Heinrich, viols, violone; Kah-Ming Ng, hpd, f-pno and org; Lynda Sayce, lutes, theorbo and baroque gui. Consort and continuo band.

The Charleston Chasers. 16 Chiswick End, Meldreth, Royston, Herts SG8 6LZ *tel:* 01763 260823 *also fax*. Terry Dash, mgr; Sean Bolan, cornett, band leader; Peter Rudeforth, tpt; Steve Shaw, trb; Nick Payton, Richard Exall, Robert Fowler, cl, alt and ten sax; Raina Reid, pno, vocals; Martin Wheatley, banjo, gui; Malcolm Sked, sousaphone; Debbie Arthurs, perc, vocals.

Charlie Barber + Band. c/o Sound Affairs, 62 Arran St, Roath, Cardiff CF24 3HT *tel:* 029 2049 7157 *also fax; email:* sound.affairs@tesco.net. Charlie Barber, dir. Wind, str and perc ens; 12 musicians.

[Charlier, Engerer]. Vn and pno. *TransArt*

Charme du Hautbois. 44 Perryfield Rd, Crawley, W Sussex RH11 8AB *tel:* 07850 914024. Mark Baigent, ob; Eileen Pearce-Davies, pno. Turn of the century mus with period ob.

Cherry Trio. c/o Arts Associates (Artists Management), 16 Manor Close, Baston, Peterborough PE6 9PM *tel:* c/o 01778 560511 *also fax*. Ann Cherry, fl; David Kennedy, cl; Raphael Terroni, pno.

* **Chiaroscuro.** 71 Priory Rd, Kew, Surrey TW9 3DH *tel:* 020 8940 7086 *fax:* 020 8332 0879. Nigel Rogers, dir; Francesca McManus, mgr. Vocal soloists and baroque inst ens.

Chilingirian Quartet. Levon Chilingirian, Charles Sewart, vn; Ásdís Valdímarsdottír, va; Philip De Groote, vc. *Intermusica*

Chinese Festival Ensemble. Chen Dacun, dir and Chinese fiddle; Cheng Yu, pipes; Xu Pingxin, dulcimer; Liu Xiaohu, bamboo fl. *Chameleon*

Chinook Clarinet Quartet. 31 Tanyard Rd, Oakes, Huddersfield HD3 4YW *tel:* 01484 325818 *also fax; email:* chinookquartet@hotmail.com. Teresa Whiffen, Maria Insua-Cao, Emily Gould, Howard Jacobs, cls.

Chopin Trio. *Finch*

The Chuckerbutty Ocarina Quartet. *Seaview*

* **Circa 1500.** 86 Avenue Rd, London N15 5DN *tel:* 020 8802 7873 *also fax*. Nancy Hadden, dir, fl, rcdr; Erin Headley, va da gamba; Dirk Freymuth, lute; Stephen Player, dancer, gui; Mhairi Lawson, sop. Renaissance mus and dance. *Upbeat*

Circle. 57 White Horse Rd, London E1 0ND *tel:* 020 7790 5883 *fax:* 020 7265 9170 *email:* gregory-rose@tisl.co.uk. Gregory Rose, dir. Contemporary inst ens.

* **The City Waites.** c/o Lucie Skeaping, 19 Patshull Rd, London NW5 2JX *tel:* 020 7485 3957 *fax:* 020 7267 2957 *email:* lucieskeaping @hotmail.com. Lucie Skeaping, Doug Wootton, Roddy Skeaping,

Michael Brain. Four voices, lute, cittern, fiddle, viol, shawm, rebecs, perc, etc. Popular mus and song from Tudor England, restoration and middle ages.

[Clark, McMahon]. 31 Velindre Rd, Whitchurch, Cardiff CF4 7JE *tel:* 029 2061 7180 *email:* mcmahonrb@wcmd.ac.uk. James Clark, vn; Richard McMahon, pno.

The Classic Buskers. Michael Copley, w/winds; Ian Moore, accordion. Arrangements and derangements of the world's mus masterpieces. *Seaview*

Classic Cocktail. Smallwood Productions, Bramleys, Tarrant Keyneston, DT11 9JE *tel:* 07974 191336. Voice, db, cl and pno. Heady mixture of virtuosity and verve.

Classic Rhythm. Helen O'Connell fl; Chris Brannick, perc; Adrian Sutcliffe, pno. *Chameleon*

* **Classical Rasumovsky.** 7 Fraser Gardens, Southbourne, nr Emsworth, Hants PO10 8PY *tel:* 01243 378300 *also fax.* Frances Mason, Marilyn Taylor, vn; Christopher Wellington, va; Christina Shillito, vc. *GBZ*

Clementi Piano Quartet. Blackland Farm, Stewkley, Leighton Buzzard, Beds LU7 0EU *tel:* 01525 240296 *fax:* 01525 240918 *email:* blacklands@compuserve.com. Maria Cooper, vn; Robert Smissen, va; Martin Loveday, vc; Sally Mellor, pno.

* **[Cole, North].** 83 Stanlake Rd, London W12 7HQ *tel:* 020 8749 1853 *fax:* 020 8742 9594. Maggie Cole, hpd, f-pno; Nigel North, lute, 19th C gui.

Collegiate Wind Ensemble. David Campbell, cond. Flexible wind ens, 8-16 players. *Janet Hughes*

* **Collegium Musicum 90.** 71 Priory Rd, Kew, Surrey TW9 3DH *tel:* 020 8940 7086 *fax:* 020 8332 0879. Simon Standage, Richard Hickox, mus dirs; Francesca McManus, gen mgr.

* **Combattimento.** c/o Diana Hirst PR, 55 Marmora Rd, London SE22 0RY *tel:* 020 8299 1914 *also fax; email:* Hirstpr@aol.com. David Roblou, dir; Kym Amps, Nicholas Clapton, Mark Tucker, Ian Caddy. Vocal and inst ens; 3-35 performers.

* **Commedia.** 411 Manhattan Building, Bow Quarter, Fairfield Rd, London E3 2UQ *tel:* 020 8981 7413 *also fax; email:* music@paulmharris.demon.co.uk. Lesley Holliday, fl; Chris Donnelly, cl; Paul Harris, bsn. Georgian mus on original insts in period dress.

The Composers Ensemble. 80 Highworth Rd, London N11 2SH *tel:* 020 8368 1211 *also fax.* John Woolrich, Mary Wiegold, dirs; Jenny Goodwin, admin.

Le Concert Impromptu. Wind quintet. *TransArt*

* **Concert Royal.** 25 Turners Croft, Heslington, York YO10 5EL *tel:* 01904 410298 *fax:* 01904 421109 *email:* conroy@classical-artists.com. Peter Harrison, fl; Margarette Ashton, sop; John Treherne, hpd; Rachel Gray, vc. 18th C vocal and inst mus. *Chameleon*

* **Concerto Caledonia.** 109 Randolph Rd, Glasgow G11 7DS *tel:* 0141 400 1219 *fax:* 0141 576 8009 *email:* marie.dunn@net.ntl.com. David McGuinness, dir; Marie Dunn, mgr; Lucy Russell, Sarah Bevan-Baker, vn; Katherine McGillivray, va; Alison McGillivray, vc; Paula Chateauneuf, lutes. Baroque chmbr ens.

* **Concerto Delle Donne.** 4 Conegra Rd, High Wycombe, Bucks HP13 6DY *tel:* 01494 524596 *also fax.* Donna Deam, Helen Parker, Gill Ross, sop; Alastair Ross, hpd, org. *Chameleon*

* **Les Concerts Royaux.** 12 Spenser Rd, Harpenden, Herts AL5 5NN *tel:* 01582 462024 *also fax; email:* terence@charlston.freeserve.co.uk. Terence Charlston, dir.

* **Concordia.** 46 Uplands Rd, London N8 9NL *tel:* 020 8348 4295 *fax:* 020 8292 7125 *email:* sarah.bm@btinternet.com. Mark Levy, Joanna Levine, Alison McGillivray, Emilia Benjamin, Daniel Yeadon, viols. *Clarion/Seven Muses*

* **The Consort of Musicke.** 13 Pages Lane, London N10 1PU *tel:* 020 8444 6565 *fax:* 020 8444 1008 *email:* consort@easynet.co.uk. Anthony Rooley, mus dir; Lindsay Richardson, admin.

* **The Consort of Twelve.** Ian Graham-Jones, dir, hpd. Baroque orch using period insts. *Purkiss*

* **The Consort of Twelve Baroque Singers.** Ian Graham-Jones, dir. *Purkiss*

Contemporary Music Ensemble of Wales. 30 Windsor Rd, Radyr, Cardiff CF15 8BQ *tel:* 029 2084 2718. Gordon Downie, dir.

Contraband. 4 Sunnybank, Shipley, W Yorks BD18 3RP *tel:* 01274 599379 *also fax.* Graham Coatman, dir. 20th C mus and mus theatre.

Contrasts. 799 Chester Rd, Erdington, Birmingham B24 0BX *tel:* 0121 373 0420; 07976 414663. Frank Allen, cl, admin, dir. Cl and str trio; popular classics for concerts, banquets and special occasions.

* **Convivium.** Elizabeth Wallfisch, vn; Richard Tunnicliffe, vc, va da gamba; Paul Nicholson, hpd, f-pno. Baroque and classical mus on authentic insts. *Sykes*

Cook and Stanley Piano Duet. Greystones, Pyrford Rd, West Byfleet, Surrey KT14 6QY *tel:* 01932 342187 *also fax;* 07850 917653 *email:* cook.stanley@classical-artists.com. Berendina Cook, Matthew Stanley.

The Copenhagen Trio. Søren Elbaek, vn; Troels Svane, vc; Morten Mogensen, pno. *SWA*

Copernicus Piano Trio. Rafael Todes, vn; Jennifer Janse, vc; Virginia Hanslip, pno. *Michael Harrold*

Cordial Company. 6 Victoria Grove, Fallowfield, Manchester M14 6BF *tel:* 0161 256 3686 *fax:* 0161 248 4435 *email:* joncordial@msn.com. Jennifer Hamilton, m-sop, celtic hp; Alan Beck, ten; Jonathan Thackeray, db; Susan Valentine, pno. Entertainments of mus and words on themes.

Coull String Quartet. Roger Coull, Philip Gallaway, vn; David Curtis, va; John Todd, vc. *SWA*

* **Courtlye Musick.** Hillside Cottage, Pound Lane, Dewlish, Dorchester, Dorset DT2 7LZ *tel:* 01258 837034. Phil Humphries, Anne Humphries, Martin Felton, Anita Felton. Renaissance wind and str insts. *Sympathetic*

Covent Garden String Quartet. *John Boddy*

[Cox, Latarche]. 33 Sandy Lane, Lymm, Cheshire WA13 9HP *tel:* 01925 756281 *fax:* c/o 0151 210 2902 *email:* nicox@eurobell.co.uk. Nicholas Cox, cl; Vanessa Latarche, pno.

Crayford Duo. 14 Azalea Walk, Old Eastcote, Pinner, Middx HA5 2EJ *tel:* 020 8868 0477 *also fax.* Marcia Crayford, vn; Helen Crayford, pno.

The Cremone Trio. 411 Manhattan Building, Bow Quarter, Fairfield Rd, London E3 2UQ *tel:* 020 8981 7413 *also fax; email:* music@paulmharris.demon.co.uk. Jo Shephard, ob; Gregor Laing, cl; Paul Harris, bsn. *Michael Brewer*

Crimson Twilight. R Theobald, con; J Briggs, pno. *Mostylea*

Critical Band. Bancroft, Rectory Lane, Fringford, Bicester, Oxon OX6 9DX *tel:* 01869 278392 *also fax; email:* cb@brailsf.demon.co.uk. James Wood, dir; Matthew Brailsford. Specialises in extended contemporary techniques such as microtonality and multiphonics as well as 20th C mus in general.

* **Cròmata.** 1 Queensgate Place, London SW7 5NS *tel:* 020 7584 6962; 020 8677 7798 *email:* gnuti@csi.com. Giulia Nuti, dir, hpd; Nicki Kennedy, dir, sop; Arno Peck, Andre Heinrich, lute; Jordi Domènech-Subiranas, c-ten. 17th C Italian vocal mus.

[Cross, Page, Webb]. Fiona Cross, cl; Kathryn Page, pno; Hugh Webb, hp. *NCCP*

The Crowther Wind Quintet. 10 Longport, Canterbury, Kent CT1 1PE *tel:* 01227 763965 *also fax; email:* ICrowther@compuserve.com. Ian Crowther, dir, ob; Rosemary Rathbone, fl; Carol Raby, cl; Simon Chiswell, bsn; Nick Morgan, French hn.

The Crusell Ensemble. 23 Manor House Rd, Wilsden, Bradford BD15 0EB *tel:* 01535 273033. Sally Robinson, vn; Nick Turner, cl; Sally Ladds, vc; Paul Freehan, pno. Chmbr mus for mixed ens.

!Cuatro! 78 Ridge Rd, London N8 9NR *tel:* 020 8348 3630. Colin Arenstein, dir. Mus for 4, 3, 2 and solo guis.

Cummings String Trio. 44 Gondar Gardens, London NW6 1HG *tel:* 020 7435 6232 *fax:* 020 7431 6843 *email:* trio@gondar.demon.co.uk. Diana Cummings, vn; Luciano Iorio, va; Gerard Le Feuvre, vc.

The Curate's Egg. St Faith's House, Shandy St, London E1 4ST *tel:* 020 7791 0330 *also fax.* Adey Grummet, dir; Lilla Grindlay, press and publicity; Mhairi Ellis, admin and librarian. All-female vocal ens specialising in 20th C and commissioned work.

Da Ponte Ensemble. 42 Kensington Park Gardens, London W11 2QT *tel:* 020 7243 1435 *fax:* 020 7221 5448. Luigi de Filippi, dir; Miranda Fulleylove, leader.

* **Da Rocha Pastorale.** 31 Minster Court, Hillcrest Rd, London W5 1HH *tel:* 020 8998 2392. Margaret Morrell, sop; William Morton, fl; Richard Hand, gui; Stephen Rose, pno, hpd. From Bach to Bernstein.

Dai-Chi and Valentin. 10 Mead Rd, Edgware, Middlesex HA8 6LJ *tel:* 020 8952 8245 *also fax; email:* daichi@yahoo.com. Dai-Chi Chiu, Valentin Schiedermair, pno duo and pno duet.

Danel String Quartet. Marc Danel, Gilles Millet, vn; Tony Nys, va; Guy Danel, vc. *NCCP*

Danish Chamber Ensemble. Hanne Holten, sop; Gitte Sørensen, fl; Kim Bak Dinitzen, vc; Eugene Asti, pno. *Roy Baker*

Dante Quartet. Str quartet. Krysia Osostowicz, Declan Daly, vns; Judith Busbridge, va; Alastair Blayden, vc. *Connaught*

Dartington Piano Trio. c/o Vicky Evans, Lakemead, Maudlin Rd, Totnes, Devon TQ9 5EX *tel:* 01803 863677. Frances Mason, vn; Michael Evans, vc; John Bryden, pno.

Davey String Quartet. 2 The Chilterns, Wookey Hole, Wells, Somerset BA5 1BS *tel:* 01749 677156. Juliet Davey, vn, leader.

[Davies], Helen and Harvey. 7 Menai Ville, Menai Bridge, Anglesey, North Wales LL59 5ES *tel:* 01248 713336 *fax:* 01248 715844 *email:* daviesfourhands@hotmail.com. Helen Davies, Harvey Davies. Pno duo.

Dazzling Digits. Beverley Davison, vn; Helen Crayford, pno. *Jean Judge*

De Saram Trio. 40 Greenford Ave, London W7 3QP *tel:* 020 8579 0420 *fax:* 020 8567 9832. Rohan de Saram, vc; Angela Malsbury, cl; David Pettit, pno.

the elizabethan
SINGERS OF LONDON

The Elizabethan Singers are one of the oldest established chamber choirs in London and have performed in many historic churches and buildings throughout the UK. Professional tours abroad have included Sweden, Luxembourg, Belgium and Germany.

Performances include a staged chamber opera in period costumes with a Baroque instrumental ensemble and also a 20th Century repertoire in modern dress. The style of the choir is ideally suited to events in stately homes, historic buildings, pageants & festivals.

For further information and to request a promotional video contact:
Anthony Ratcliffe, Administrator
Elder Cottage, Felixstowe Ferry,
Felixstowe
Suffolk IP11 9RZ, UK.
Tel/Fax: +44 (0)1394 282306
E-mail address: elizabethan@classical-artists.com
Or visit our **website** at http://www.classical-artists.com/elizabethan-singers

ENESCO TRIO

Elizabeth Layton, violin
Jane Atkins, viola
Paul Watkins, cello

Jenny Ricotti Music Management
Thimble Farm, Green Lane, Prestwood, Bucks HP16 0QE
Tel and Fax *+44 (0)1494 865205*
Website *www.classical-artists.com/enesco*

Deakin Piano Trio

Richard Deakin *violin*
Emma Ferrand *cello*
Catherine Dubois *piano*
with
Yuko Inoue *viola*

All enquiries to:
J Audrey Ellison International
135 Stevenage Road
London SW6 6PB
Tel: 0171 381 9571

CDs now available from all good music bookshops
Parry **Piano Trio in E minor • Piano Quartet in Ab major** *Meridian CDE 84248*
Parry **Piano Trios in B minor and G major** *Meridian CDE 84255*

Deakin Piano Trio. Richard Deakin, vn; Emma Ferrand, vc; Catherine Dubois, pno. *Ellison*

Debussy Trio. Susan Milan, fl; Yuko Inoue, va; Christina Rhys, hp. *Upbeat*

The Defoe String Quartet. 17 Fairfield Close, Harpenden, Herts AL5 5RZ *tel:* 01582 765322 *also fax.* Peter Fisher, Simon Perkins, vn; Andrew Byrt, va; Chris Fish, vc.

* **Deller Consort.** 2 Rural Terrace, Wye, Ashford, Kent TN25 5AP *tel:* 01233 812267 *fax:* 01227 781830. Olive Simpson, Elisabeth Priday, sop; Mark Deller, c-ten, dir; Charles Daniels, ten; James Ottaway, bar; Dorothy Linell, lute.

Delmé Quartet. 33 Whittingstall Rd, London SW6 4EA *tel:* 020 7736 7316 *fax:* 020 7371 7396; 01787 237970 *email:* jw@lco.co.uk. Galina Solodchin, John Trusler, vn; John Underwood, va; Jonathan Williams, vc. *NBM*

Delta Saxophone Quartet. 109 George Lane, Lewisham, London SE13 6HN *tel:* 020 8690 6071 *also fax; email:* steva@compuserve.com. Stephen Cottrell, Chris Caldwell, Peter Whyman, Gareth Brady.

Demon Barbers. Paul Thompson, alto; Andrew Phillips, Rob Scales, ten; Anthony Scales, bar; Jeremy Birchall, bs. *Chameleon*

Derbyshire String Quartet. 18 Oaklea Way, Old Tupton, Chesterfield, Derbys S42 6JD *tel:* 01246 863829. Nina Martin, Edward Boothroyd, vn; Patricia Curteis, va; Peter White, vc.

[Derwinger, Pontinen]. Love Derwinger, Roland Pontinen, pno duo. *Gilder*

The Devienne Ensemble. 168 Downs Rd, Hastings, E Sussex TN34 2DZ *tel.* 01424 440929; 07973 734572 *email:* WarwickMD@aol.com. Warwick Potter, bn; Joanne Gould, vn; John Murphy, va; Carolyn Richards, vc.

* **Diabolus in Musica.** 21 Oakfield Ave, Kingswinford, W Midlands DY6 8HJ *tel:* 01384 295210 *email:* paul@diabolus-in-musica.freeserve.co.uk. Paul Baker, rcdrs, renaissance winds, hurdy gurdy, bagpipes; Pam Smith, lute, cittern, gui, bagpipes, curtal; David Jarratt-Knock, cornett, natural tpt, rcdrs. Elizabethan costumed duo/trio.

Dittmer/Coulson Baroque to Modern Duo. 10 Pembroke Mews, London W8 6ER *tel:* 020 7937 0684 *also fax.* Petronella Dittmer, vns, sop; Richard Coulson, org, hpd. Mus from plainsong to the present day.

Divertimenti of London. 8 Hartington Rd, Aldeburgh, Suffolk IP15 5HD *tel:* 01728 454048. Courtney Kenny, mus dir; Roxane Houston, artistic dir; Lindsay Gowers, sop; Phillida Bannister, con; Richard Reaville, ten; Adrian Hutton, bs. Vocal and inst ens presenting mus from 16th-20th C, with emphasis on living composers' works. *Roxane Houston*

Divertimenti. 28 Rivermount, Walton-on-Thames, Surrey KT12 2PR *tel:* 01932 246796 *fax:* 01932 267188. Kathy Avdiev, mgr; Paul Barritt, Rachel Isserlis, vn; Jonathan Barritt, va; Sebastian Comberti, Josephine Horder, vc. Str quintet, expands to sextet and octet.

Divertimento. Trio. *John Boddy*

Dolezal String Quartet. Jiri Fiser, Vladimir Kucera, vn; Karel Dolezal, va; Vladan Koci, vc. *NCCP*

Double Image. 20 Standish Rd, London W6 9AL *tel:* 020 8748 0935 *also fax.* David Carhart, dir, pno; Phillipa Ibbotson, vn; Miriam Lowbury, vc; Andrew Sparling, cl; Carola Nielinger, fl.

Dragonsfire. Nigel Perona-Wright, dir. *Upbeat*

Dramatis Personae. The Old Rectory Coach House, High St, Bourton-on-the-Water, Glos GL54 2AP *tel:* 01451 821481 *also fax; email:* jane@lesleyjanerogers.demon.co.uk. Lesley-Jane Rogers, sop; Edward Peters, bar; Christopher Ross, pno. Concert-staged recitals on a chosen theme. Also performs with The Rosewood Ensemble.

Duette. 6 Munsons Lane, Feltwell, Norfolk IP26 4DE *tel:* 01842 828424 *also fax;* 07973 977704 *email:* duette@con-brio.com. Stephen Bingham, vn; Brenda Stewart, va.

* **The Dufay Collective.** 19 Hillfield Rd, Comberton, Cambridge CB3 7DB *tel:* 020 8488 3947 *also fax;* 01223 263023 *also fax; email:* admin@dufay.com. Paul Bevan, Giles Lewin, William Lyons, Susanna Pell, Peter Skuce.

Duke Quartet. Louisa Fuller, Rick Koster, vn; John Metcalfe, va; Ivan McCready, vc. *Hazard*

[Dukes, Rahman]. Philip Dukes, va; Sophia Rahman, pno. *NCCP*

[Dumay, Pires]. *Askonas Holt*

[Dumay, Pires, Wang]. *Askonas Holt*

Dunav Balkan Group. 77 Forest Rd, London E17 6HF *tel:* 020 8527 4896 *also fax; email:* dunav@classical-artists.com. Caroline Thomas. Traditional mus from SE Europe.

Duo Amati. 149 Howard Rd, London E17 4SG *tel:* 020 8520 7739. Elizabeth Ann Binks, vn; Christine Greig, pno.

* **Duo Basiliensis.** 58 Redhill Drive, Brighton BN1 5FL *tel:* 01273 552548 *fax:* 01273 389572 *email:* simmonds.mezger@cwcom.net. Marianne Mezger, rcdrs, fr flageolet, baroque musette de cour; Paul Simmonds, hpd; 16th-18th C mus.

Duo Cantaré. Michael Axtell, fl; Paul Brown, gui. *Dyfel*

Duo Dunamis. 47 Minsterley Ave, Shepperton, Middx TW17 8QS *tel:* 01932 770831 *also fax.* Christine Townsend, vn; Stephen Robbings, pno.

Duo Mandala. Alison Stephens, mandolin; Lauren Scott, hp. *Purkiss*

Duo Paganini. 2 Staik Hill, Lanark ML11 7PW *tel:* 01555 662645. Angus Ramsay, vn; Phillip Thorne, gui.

Duo Rosso. Alison Stephens, mandolin; Neil Smith, gui. *Purkiss*

Duo Soledad. 2 Shaftesbury House, Trinity St, London SE1 4JF *tel:* 020 7407 9243 *also fax; email:* david@viana.freeserve.co.uk. David Parsons, gui, lute; Raenelda MacKie, pno.

Dussek Piano Trio. 2 Morecambe Gardens, Stanmore, Middx HA7 4SP *tel:* 020 8958 6983 *also fax.* Gonzalo Acosta, vn; Margaret Powell, vc; Michael Dussek, pno.

Duty Free Bassoons. Hilltop, Gravel Hill, Chartham Hatch, Kent CT4 7NH *tel:* 01227 730923 *fax:* 01233 713833 *email:* music@wyvers.freeserve.co.uk. Aoileann Fidler, Sheilia Wyver, Warwick Potter, bsns.

Dynamix. 46 Albert Rd, London N22 7AH *tel:* 020 8881 1758 *also fax; email:* Dynamix@i.am. Patrick Nunn, artistic dir; Richard Souper, asst dir; Lewis Mitchell, admin.

Eberle String Quartet. 28 Pemberton Rd, Lyndhurst, Hants SO43 7AN *tel:* 023 8028 2376 *fax:* 01722 320072 *email:* eberle@labaster.demon.co.uk. Daphne Moody, Jennifer Gibbs, vn; Moira Alabaster, va; Muriel Daniels, vc.

The Ebony Quartet. Redwings, Linden Chase, Uckfield, E Sussex TN22 1EE *tel:* 01825 760046 *also fax; email:* turbettp@aol.com. Graeme Vinall, Philip Turbett, Trevor Barlow, Rodney Smith, cls and saxes.

Ecco. 503a Kingston Rd, Wimbledon Chase, London SW20 8JP *tel:* 020 8395 7433 *email:* artists@midman503a.freeserve.co.uk. Flexible chmbr ens based around Claire-Louise Lucas, voice, and Jonathan Darnborough, pno. Classical, contemporary and educ programmes. *Christine Talbot-Cooper*

Eden-Stell Guitar Duo. 78 Kent Rd, Orpington, Kent BR5 4AB *tel:* 01689 836605 *also fax.* Repertoire spans 17th to 20th centuries. Enthusiasm for baroque hpd transcriptions by Rameau, Couperin, Scarlatti and Bach. Repertoire also includes Brazilian mus.

Edinburgh Quartet. 119 Craigleith Rd, Edinburgh EH4 2EH *tel:* 0131 332 8691 *fax:* 0131 332 5084 *email:* edinburghquartet@compuserve.com. Jane Murdoch, Philip Burrin, vn; Michael Beeston, va; Mark Bailey, vc. *GBZ*

Edlian Piano Trio. 69 Rodenhurst Rd, London SW4 8AE *tel:* 020 8674 4804 *fax:* 020 8674 9685. Charlotte Edwards, vn; Babette Lichtenstein, vc; Tatiana Andrianova, pno.

The Eimer Trio. Nicola Eimer, pno; Matthew Denton, vn; Emma Denton, vc. *Christine Talbot-Cooper*

The Elastic Band. 77 St Albans Ave, East Ham, London E6 4HH *tel:* 020 8472 2057 *also fax;* 020 8452 8983 *fax:* 020 8450 0546 *email:* v.soames@clarind-classics.ndirect.co.uk. Victoria Soames, cl, artistic dir; Mark Troop, artistic dir, pno. Artists include: Nicolas Robert, vc; Patracia Rozario, sop; Carlos Bonell, gui.

Electric Phoenix. 22 St Mary's Ave, London E11 2NP *tel:* 020 8989 4804 *fax:* 020 8989 7389. Judith Rees, sop; Meriel Dickinson, m-sop; Daryl Runswick, ten; Terry Edwards, bs; John Whiting, elec.

Electro-Acoustic Ensemble. 26 Hopwood Close, Hull HU3 1QU *tel:* 01482 225663. John Stead, artistic dir, composer; Nigel Bartram, w/shop co-ord, keyboard; Stanislaw Hansel, pno, org, composer; Gordon Ross, composer, sound engineer.

Elanara. Elizabeth Nash, sop; Rose Andresier, gui. *DCM*

* **Elizabethan Consort of Viols.** 22 Crouch St, Banbury, Oxon OX16 9PP *tel:* 01295 277976 *also fax.* Peter Adams, Terence Pamplin, treble viol; Lars Payne, Martin Heath, ten viol; Brian Capleton, bs viol.

* **The Elizabethan Singers of London.** Elder Cottage, Felixstowe Ferry, Felixstowe, Suffolk IP11 9RZ *tel:* 01394 282306 *also fax; email:* elizabethan@classical-artists.com. Sam Laughton, artistic and mus dir, cond; Anthony Ratcliffe, admin. Secular and sacred mus and chmbr opera, 16-20 members. Performances in full period costume, including staged chmbr opera.

The Ellerdale Trio. *Mostylea*

[Elliott, Jones]. 45 Elms Rd, Sutton Coldfield, W Midlands B72 1JE *tel:* 0121 354 2905. Fleur Elliott, Michael Jones, pno duo.

Emerald Ensemble. 29 Holmes Grove, Henleaze, Bristol BS9 4ED *tel:* 0117 962 4289 *also fax.* Roger Huckle, vn; John Bishop, pno. All chmbr-size ens up to and including small chmbr orch.

Emerald String Quartet. 5 Aplin Way, Isleworth, Middx TW7 4RJ *tel:* 020 8847 2170. Rosemary Campton, Jonathan Acton, vn; Scott Newcombe, va; William Routledge, vc.

The Emerson String Quartet. *IMG*

The Emiro Ensemble. 35 Gibson's Hill, London SW16 3JR *tel:* 020 8764 4402 *also fax; email:* emiro.ensemble@usa.net. Sarah Miller, cl; Charlotte Eksteen, vc; Neil Roxburgh, pno.

"...each new Fibonacci programme is a joy – innovative repertoire played with passion and brilliant musicianship."

Barry Millington, The Times

THE FIBONACCI SEQUENCE, a flexible ensemble composed of soloists of international standing, has achieved recognition and renown in the musical world in an astonishingly short space of time.

THE FIBONACCI SEQUENCE

Kathron Sturrock *Piano*
James Clark *Violin*
Yuko Inoue *Viola*
Michael Stirling *Cello*
Duncan McTier *Bass*
Anna Noakes *Flute*
Christopher O'Neal *Oboe*
Julian Farrell *Clarinet*
Richard Skinner *Bassoon*
Stephen Stirling *Horn*
Paul Archibald *Trumpet*
Gillian Tingay *Harp*
Simon Limbrick *Percussion*

Described by one critic as 'a piece of history in the making', the Fibonacci Sequence is distinguished by the quality and high profile of its players and by the imagination and variety of its programming, making full use of the range and versatility of the chamber music repertoire.

Programmes can be devised to appeal to each individual audience and to suit each venue. The speciality of the Fibonacci Sequence is an 'Extravanza' programme, using different combinations of instruments and imaginative repertoire: this provides an evening of great variety and entertainment. For a genuine extravaganza – the *Assiette Gourmande* – the whole ensemble would be involved, but if space is limited successful programming on a smaller scale can easily be achieved.

Registered Charity No. SCOL3960

81 Lacy Road
London SW15 1NR
Tel 020 8780 3266
Fax 020 8780 0600
E-mail cicfib@easynet.co.uk
website www.classical-artists.com/fibonacci

English Serenata

"A top notch performance" *Daily Telegraph*

"Hugely enjoyable... meltingly beautiful and romantic."
BBC Music Magazine

Four musical programmes:
THE FRENCH COLLECTION
A NIGHT IN OLD VIENNA
SWEET SWAN OF AVON
KEW FOR MUSIC

Programmes for smaller venues are also available

Presenters include:
DAVID JACOBS, JOHN NETTLES,
JENNY AGUTTER and ANGELA RIPPON

Musical Director:
GABRIELLE BYAM-GROUNDS

Contact: ALL-ELECTRIC THEATRE PRODUCTIONS. UNIT 6. 94 CHARLTON ROAD. ANDOVER. HANTS SP10 3JY.
Tel: 01264 361924. Fax: 01264 337014

The Emperor String Quartet. 12 Winding Shott, Bramfield, Herts SG14 2QP *tel:* 01992 504049 *also fax.* Martin Burgess, Clare Hayes, vn; Fiona Bonds, va; William Schofield, vc. *Connaught*

The Emperor's New Clothes. c/o 52 St Kilda's Rd, Oldfield Park, Bath BA2 3QL *tel:* 01225 337722. Matthew Bale, mus dir, pno; Lorna Osbon, vn; Imogen Triner, ob. Contemporary mus ens.

Encore! 34 Princes Rd, Teddington, Middx *tel:* 020 8977 2133 *fax:* 020 8977 8568. Julia Dewhurst, sop; Zoë Haydn, m-sop; Leon Berger, baritone; Adrian Hobbs, pno. Opera and light mus.

Endellion String Quartet. Andrew Watkinson, Ralph de Souza, vn; Garfield Jackson, va; David Waterman, vc. *Hazard*

Endymion Ensemble. 55 Murchison Rd, London E10 6NA *tel:* 020 8556 2820 *also fax.* Carol Butler, admin; Helen Keen, fl; Melinda Maxwell, ob Mark Van de Wiel, cl; Stephen Stirling, hn; Bruce Nockles, tpt; Simon Wills, trb; Michael Dussek, pno; Simon Limbrick, perc; Krysia Osostowicz, Marshall Marcus, vns; Jane Salmon, vc; Chichi Nwanoku, db.

The Enesco Trio. Elizabeth Layton, vn; Jane Atkins, va; Paul Watkins, vc. *Jenny Ricotti*

* **English Baroque Orchestra.** 57 Kingswood Rd, London SW19 3ND *tel:* 020 8542 1661 *fax:* 020 8540 1103. Leon Lovett, mus dir; Robert Porter, mgr.

* **English Baroque Soloists.** Monteverdi Choir and Orchestra Ltd, 61 Wandsworth High St, London SW18 2PT *tel:* 020 8871 4750 *fax:* 020 8871 4751 *email:* info@monteverdi.co.uk. Sir John Eliot Gardiner, artistic dir; Jan Normanton, admin; Howard Gough, acting gen mgr; David Adams, orch mgr; Andrew Hammond, project co-ord.

English Brass Ensemble. Paul Archibald, artistic dir. Contemporary and classical br mus. *Michael Harrold*

English Camerata Soloists. 54 Pegholme Mill, Wharfebank Business Centre, Otley, LS21 3JP *tel:* 01943 850853 *fax:* 0113 267 5821 *email:* english.camerata@virgin.net. Elizabeth Altman, artistic dir. 18th-20th C chmbr mus classics.

English Chamber Orchestra Brass Ensemble. 2 Coningsby Rd, London W5 4HR *tel:* 020 8840 6565 *fax:* 020 8567 7198 *email:* mail@e-c-orch.demon.co.uk. Contact: Pauline Gilbertson. Min of 5 players.

English Chamber Orchestra Wind Ensemble. 2 Coningsby Rd, London W5 4HR *tel:* 020 8840 6565 *fax:* 020 8567 7198 *email:* mail@e-c-orch.demon.co.uk. Contact: Pauline Gilbertson. 6-13 players.

* **English Consort of Viols.** Consort mus with singer. *POEM*

* **The English Cornett and Sackbut Ensemble.** 3 High Rd, Willesden Green, London NW10 2TE *tel:* 020 8451 4712 *also fax;* 07961 177118 *email:* ecse@ecse.demon.co.uk. Adrian Woodward, Fiona Russell, cornetts; Abigail Newman, Tom Lees, Adrian France, sackbuts; Robert Howarth, chmbr org, hpd.

English Haydn Orchestra. c/o 24a St Mary's St, Newport, Shropshire TF10 7AB *tel:* 01952 825235/811829 *fax:* 01952 814734/812011. John Reid, mgr dir; Sandra Day, admin. Period insts.

English Horn Trio. 25 Quebec Rd, East Dereham, Norfolk NR19 2DR *tel:* 01362 694223. Richard Watkins, hn; Pauline Lowbury, vn; Christopher Green-Armytage, pno.

English Oboe Quartet. Imogen Triner, dir. *Roxane Houston*

English Piano Trio. Victoria House, The Green, Sarratt, Rickmansworth, Herts WD3 6AY *tel:* 01923 265066 *also fax; email:* ept@classical-artists.com. Jane Faulkner, vn; Justin Pearson, vc; Timothy Ravenscroft, pno.

English Serenata. Unit 6, All Electric Theatre Productions, 94 Charlton Rd, Andover, Hants SP10 3JY *tel:* 01264 361924; 07850 985550 *fax:* 01264 337014 *email:* all.electric@cwcom.net. Gabrielle Byam-Grounds, dir, fl. Wind, str, hp, pno, perc and celebrity narrators and singers.

English String Quartet. 44 Gondar Gardens, London NW6 1HG *tel:* 020 7435 6232 *fax:* 020 7431 6843 *email:* quartet@demon.co.uk. Diana Cummings, Keith Lewis, vn; Luciano Iorio, va; Gerard Le Feuvre, vc.

Ensemble 10:10. 33 Sandy Lane, Lymm, Cheshire WA13 9HP *tel:* 01925 756281 *fax:* c/o 0151 210 2902 *email:* nicox@eurobell.co.uk. Nicholas Cox, admin. 5-22 player contemporary mus group.

Ensemble Bash. Chris Brannick, Richard Benjafield, Stephen Hiscock, Andrew Martin. Perc quartet. *Chameleon*

Ensemble of the Bela Bartók Centre for Musicianship. 6 Frognal Court, Finchley Rd, London NW3 5HL *tel:* 020 7435 3685. Agnes Kory, dir. Voice, hpd, baroque vc, va da gamba, ten vn. Also chmbr choir and orch with modern insts.

Ensemble Clement Janequin. Dominic Visse, dir. *Sykes*

Ensemble QTR. 4 Heathleigh Cottages, Maidstone Rd, Horsmonden, Kent TN12 8JL *tel:* 01892 723370 *also fax; email:* peterbowman1@compuserve.com. Kathryn Bennetts, Peter Bowman, rcdrs; Damien Harron, perc; Roger Heaton, cl; Sara Stowe, sop; Barrie Webb, trb; Clive Williamson, keyboards, pno; Jos Zwaanenburg, fl; Donald Bousted, artistic dir.

Ensemble Triton. Fl, vc, pno. *Pristavec*

Ensemble X. 37 Coltman House, Welland St, London SE10 9DW *tel:* 020 8853 0818 *also fax.* Errollyn Wallen, dir. Mainly mus of Errollyn Wallen.

Eos. Ellesmere House, South St, Castle Cary, Somerset BA7 7EX *fax:* 01963 351446. Charles Hazlewood, mus dir; Philip Dukes, leader; Mark Dornford-May, producer.

Erard Ensemble. Susan Gill, cl; Siobhan Grealy, fl; Catherine Morgan, Steve Morris, vns; Richard May, vc; Lucy Wakeford, hp. *Encore*

The Erisian Brass Ensemble. 114a High St, Walkern, Stevenage, Herts SG2 7NU *tel:* 020 7715 8461 *fax:* 01923 249869. Andrew Humphries, tpt; William Watson, tpt; Edward Hodgson, hn; William Hodgson, trb; Jonathan Gale, tb.

* **Eroica String Quartet.** Peter Hanson, Lucy Howard, Gustav Clarkson, David Watkin. *Hazard*

* **[Esswood, Hubscher].** Paul Esswood, c-ten; Jurgens Hubscher, lute. *PGEM*

* **Estampie.** c/o PR Music Management, 5 Parramatta St, Rawtenstall, Rossendale, Lancs BB4 6AF *tel:* 01706 230084 *email:* annsmith@supp.freeserve.co.uk. Deborah Catterall, John Bryan, Susan Marshall, John Peel, Ian Richardson, voices; Ann Smith, insts. Medieval and renaissance mus on period insts.

The Esterhazy String Quartet. 278 Kew Rd, Richmond, Surrey TW9 3EE *tel:* 020 8948 6140. Martin Loveday, James Shenton, vns; Justin Ward, va; Philip Trzebiatowski, vc.

The Esterhazy String Trio. 11 Sandringham Rd, London NW11 9DR *tel:* 020 8458 2607. Brenda Cullity, vn; Irmeli Rawson, va; Jocelyn Gale, vc.

Ethos Percussion Group. *Clarion/Seven Muses*

The European Chamber Ensemble. 43 Norcott Rd, Stoke Newington, London N16 7EJ *tel:* 020 8806 7704 *fax:* 020 7502 6484 *email:* helen@wickham.u-net.com. Helen Leek, pno, dir; Ten-member mixed ens.

* **European Union Baroque Orchestra.** Hordley, Wootton, Woodstock OX20 1EP *tel:* 01993 812111 *fax:* 01993 812911 *email:* info@eubo.org.uk. Roy Goodman, mus dir; Paul James, gen admin; Emma Wilkinson, orch mgr; Nick Berry, development dir.

Eva Meier's 'Berlin' Cabaret Company. Eva Meier, sop; Conor Linehan, pno; Mary Keegan, speaker. *Michael Brewer*

* **Ex Cathedra.** Suite 303, Jewellery Business Centre, 95 Spencer St, Birmingham B18 6DA *tel:* 0121 523 1025 *fax:* 0121 523 1026. Jeffrey Skidmore, artistic dir; Justin Lee, gen mgr; Lyn Collin, business and educ development. Consort (12 singers) to chmbr choir.

* **Ex Cathedra Baroque Ensemble.** Suite 303, Jewellery Business Centre, 95 Spencer St, Birmingham B18 6DA *tel:* 0121 523 1025 *fax:* 0121 523 1026. Jeffrey Skidmore, artistic dir; Justin Lee, gen mgr; Micaela Comberti, leader.

Farinelli Ensemble. *Manygate*

Fermata. *NBM*

[Ferrand, Hare]. Emma Ferrand, vc; Ian Hare, org and hpd. *Ellison*

The Festival Soloists. 49 Clifton Rd, Newbury Park, Ilford, Essex IG2 7DG *tel:* 020 8491 4813 *also fax; email:* TheFestivalSoloists@tesco.net. Margaret-Mary Kane, sop; Louise Crane, con; Simon Curtis, ten; Ashley Thorburn, bs.

The Fibonacci Sequence. 81 Lacy Rd, London SW15 1NR *tel:* 020 8780 3266 *fax:* 020 8780 0600 *email:* cicfib@easynet.co.uk. Kathron Sturrock, pno; Jonathan Rees, vn; Yuko Inoue, va; Michael Stirling, vc; Duncan McTier, db; Anna Noakes, fl; Christopher O'Neal, ob; Julian Farrell, cl; Richard Skinner, bsn; Stephen Stirling, hn; Gillian Tingay, hp; Paul Archibald, tpt; Simon Limbrick, perc; Shelley Phillips, mgr (*tel:* 01892 870187).

Fiddlesticks. 10 Mill Rd, Waterbeach, Cambridge CB5 9RQ *tel:* 01223 862232 *also fax.* Ishani Bhoola, Sarah Ewins, vn; Ania Ullman, va; Joy Hawley, vc; Ann Clampit, admin.

Fidelio Trio. Flat 2, Raisbeck Court, 26 Rosendale Rd, West Dulwich SE21 8DR *tel:* 07956 916510 *fax:* 020 8761 6039 *email:* darraghm@hotmail.com. Darragh Morgan, vn; Andrew Skrimshire, vc; Mary Dullea, pno.

Fine Arts Brass Ensemble. 68 Sion Hill, Broadwaters, Kidderminster, Worcs DY10 2XS *tel:* 01562 515403 *also fax; email:* Rich@fabtuba.freeserve.co.uk. Simon Lenton, Angela Whelan, tpt; Stephen Roberts, hn; Simon Hogg, trb; Richard Sandland, tb, mgr.

* **Fiori Musicali.** Bank Cottage, Preston Capes, Northamptonshire NN11 3TD *tel:* 01327 361380 *fax:* 01327 361415 *email:* fiori@fiori-musicali.com. Penelope Rapson, dir; Kerstin Linder-Dewan, leader; Bernard Rapson, treasurer; Jonathan Asquith, chmn; Emma Abel, concert development (*tel:* 020 8679 9591).

Firebird. Station House, Station Rd, Haxby, York YO32 3LX *tel:* c/o 020 8606 0030; 01904 763765 *also fax; fax:* c/o 020 8606 0037. Barrie Webb, dir.

[Fisher, Lasserson]. Peter Fisher, vn; Nadia Lasserson, pno. *Ellison*

THE FIDELIO TRIO

"They are a tight-knit and highly musical bunch with something important to say"
THE STRAD

"The Fidelio Trio's playing was deftly coloured and responsive down to the lightest shadows of vapour"
THE IRISH TIMES

Piano – Mary Dullea
Violin – Darragh Morgan
Cello – Andrew Skrimshire

Flat 2, Raisbeck Court, 26 Rosendale Road, West Dulwich, London SE21 8DR – Tel: 07956 916510 – Fax: 0181 761 6039

FRETWORK

Wendy Gillespie, Richard Campbell, Julia Hodgson, Susanna Pell, Richard Boothby & William Hunt
viols

not just an ace viol consort but a vibrant performing ensemble commissioning composers of today whose works are programmed alongside masterpieces of England's golden age **Independent**

irresistibly diverse programme...highest level of performance **Times**

Management: Askonas Holt Ltd,
tel: 0207 400 1751 fax: 0207 400 1799

www.fretwork.co.uk

GOLDSTONE ~ & ~ CLEMMOW

LEADING PIANO DUO
TWO PIANOS / PIANO DUET

'One superlative after another' - **The Musical Times**
'Dazzling husband and wife team' - **Gramophone**
'A class act among piano duettists' - **Irish Times**
'Revelations such as this are rare in the concert hall these days' - **Charleston Post and Courier**

They have now completed transferring their unique, acclaimed seven-recital series of the really complete original piano duets of Schubert to seven CDs for Olympia, the revolutionary format of which ensures that all are varied and satisfying concert programmes, even to the extent of including encores (Schumann's rarely heard Schubert-inspired 1828 Polonaises). 'Haunted with the spirit of Schubert' - Luister, Netherlands. The duo's CDs number twenty one.

Concert enquiries to: Walcot Old Hall, Alkborough, N. Lincs. DN15 9JT, England
tel: 01724 720475; fax: 01724 721599

HAND/DUPRÉ DUO

"A Duo of World Rank"
Classical Guitar Magazine

HAND/DUPRÉ DUO

Newburn, Tatham Road, Abingdon Oxon OX14 1QD
Tel 01235 539 395 Fax 01235 539 483

Fitzwilliam Quartet. 10 Bootham Terrace, York YO30 7DH *tel:* 01904 658189 *also fax; email:* FitzQtet@aol.com. Lucy Russell, Jonathan Sparey, vn; Alan George, va; Daniel Yeadon, vc.

Florestan Piano Trio. Anthony Marwood, vn; Richard Lester, vc; Susan Tomes, pno. *Tennant*

* **Florilegium.** 53 Tresco Rd, London SE15 3PY *tel:* 020 7639 7376 *also fax; email:* florilegium@compuserve.com. Ashley Solomon, Neal Peres Da Costa, management. Baroque and classical chmbr and orch mus on period insts; also choir.

Flutes Fantastic. Trevor Wye. Fls and pno. Amusing recital with commentary. *Seaview*

* **Folies Bergeres.** 49 Pitts Rd, Oxford OX3 8BA *tel:* 01865 761966 *also fax; email:* foliesbergeres@matspring.demon.co.uk. Sara Stowe, sop, hpd; Jean-Pierre Rasle, musette, bagpipe; Matthew Spring, hurdy gurdy, gui, theorbo; Sharon Lindo, vn, rcdr, viol.

Four Strings Plus Piano. 75 Platts Lane, London NW3 7NL *tel:* 020 7435 0821. Lucy White, vn; Juliet Davey, pno and vn. Concerts for the sick and elderly.

Fourth Dimension String Quartet. 51 Salisbury Rd, Walthamstow, London E17 9JW *tel:* 020 8521 5398 *also fax; email:* 4d@nikpat.demon.co.uk. Sophie Langdon, Marjorie Hodge, vn; Catherine Musker, va; Miriam Lowbury, vc.

[Frankl, Pauk, Kirshbaum]. Peter Frankl, pno; György Pauk, vn; Ralph Kirshbaum, vc. *TransArt*

* **Fretwork.** 16 Teddington Park Rd, Teddington, Middx TW11 8ND *tel:* 020 8977 0924 *fax:* 020 8404 2414 *email:* 100636.1302@compuserve.com. Wendy Gillespie, Richard Campbell, Richard Boothby, Julia Hodgson, Susanna Pell, William Hunt, viols. 15th-18th C and contemporary mus for viols. *Askonas Holt*

* **Frottola.** 79 Humber Doucy Lane, Ipswich, Suffolk IP4 3NU *tel:* 01473 718811 *email:* frottola@btinternet.com. Jennie Cassidy, m-sop; Jacob Heringman, lute; Philip Thorby, viol, rcdr. Lute song trio, programmes of renaissance mus.

Full Circle. Str quintet. D Lewis, G Clarke, vns; M Giske, va; M Woodcock, vc. *Mostylea*

* **The Gabrieli Consort and Players.** Room 13 The Annexe, Shoreditch Town Hall, 380 Old St, London EC1V 9LT *tel:* 020 7613 4404 *fax:* 020 7613 4414 *email:* gabrieliconsort@compuserve.com. Paul McCreesh, dir; Anita Crowe, gen mgr; Lucy Miller, admin. Renaissance and baroque insts.

Gabrieli String Quartet. *Grant Rogers*

The Gagliano Trio. The Fountain, Tidebrook, Wadhurst, E Sussex TN5 6PF *tel:* 01892 782220 *also fax.* Roger Garland, vn; Brian Hawkins, va; Roger Smith, vc.

Galliard Ensemble (Wind Quintet). 39 Bushwood, London E11 3BW *tel:* 020 8518 8903; 07976 399828 *email:* malcolmjg@aol.com. Kathryn Thomas, dir, fl, picc; Owen Dennis, ob; Katherine Spencer, cl; Richard Bayliss, hn; Helen Simons, bsn. *Murphy*

Gamelan Sekar Petak. c/o Music Dept, University of York, Heslington, York YO10 5DD *tel:* 01904 432438 *fax:* 01904 432450 *email:* nfis1@york.ac.uk. Neil Sorrell, mus dir. Complete bronze javanese gamelan, played by past and present members of the York mus dept.

The Garden Consort. 36 Southside, Clapham Common, London SW4 9BS *tel:* 020 7627 1089 *also fax.* Vocal quartet and pno artists from the Royal Opera House. Glenys Roberts, sop; Jean Tredaway, m-sop; George Owen, ten; John Morgan, bar; Roy Gregory, pno. *Clifton Karim*

* **Gassenhauer Trio.** 17 Hayesford Park Drive, Bromley, Kent BR2 9DA *tel:* 020 8464 1645 *fax:* 020 8402 5859. Margaret Archibald, cl; Sebastian Comberti, vc; David Mason, pno.

The Gatsby Saxophone Quartet. 28b Heddington Grove, Islington, London N7 9SY *tel:* 020 7700 5431 *fax:* 07970 703753 *email:* nicky.baigent@freenet.co.uk. Nick White, sop sax; Nicola Baigent, alto sax; Katie Brown, ten sax; Susan White, bar sax. Mus from the 20s and 30s played on period insts.

Gemini. 137 Upland Rd, East Dulwich, London SE22 0DF *tel:* 020 8693 4694 *fax:* 020 8693 4426 *email:* gemini@themitchells.screaming.net. Ian Mitchell, cl, dir. Mixed chmbr ens; repertoire from 12th C to present day; regular educ projects for all levels and teachers. Ens in residence Goldsmith's College.

[Genova, Dimitrov]. Aglika Genova, Liuben Dimitrov. Pno duo. *Pristavec*

* **The Georgian Chamber Orchestra.** 25 Turners Croft, York YO10 5EL *tel:* 01904 410298 *fax:* 01904 421109. Peter Harrison, artistic dir; Iona Davies, leader.

* **The Georgian Music Room.** 33 Hartswood Rd, London W12 9NE *tel:* 020 8749 3365 *fax:* 020 8749 1201. Neil Jenkins, ten; Rachel Beckett, baroque fl, rcdr; Celia Harper, dir, hpd. Concerts of 17th-18th C mus in period costume with contemporary readings.

* **Gesualdo Consort.** 112 Wordsworth Rd, Hampton, Middx TW12 1ET *tel:* 020 8941 2684 *also fax; email:* venosa@ndirect.co.uk. Gerald Place, dir, singer; Amanda Morrison, Alison Place, Penny Vickers, Graham Titus, singers; Dorothy Linell, lute. *POEM*

Gilbert and Sullivan Ensemble. 10 Pembroke Mews, London W8 6ER *tel:* 020 7937 0684 *also fax.* Petronella Dittmer, vn; Christine Blair, pno, vc. Gilbert and Sullivan, palm court mus, light classics, dinner mus.

Gilde String Quartet. *Michael Brewer*

Giordani Ensemble. Mary Pilbery, mus dir, ob; Susan Edwards, ob; Glyn Williams, bsn; Stephen Warner, db; Nicholas Durcan, hpd, pno. *Roy Baker*

Giovanni Piano Trio. Tong Lee Head, Marsden HD7 6NJ *tel:* 01484 841868 *also fax.* Pno, vn, vc.

The Glinka Trio. Spencer Pitfield, cl; Risto Lauriala, pno; Antal Mojzer, bsn. *Ellison*

Gnessin Duet. *Sonata*

Gnessin Piano Trio. Katya Apekisheva, Anna Safonova, Alexei Sarkissov. *Sonata*

Goldberg Ensemble. 7 Rowsley Ave, West Didsbury, Manchester M20 2XD *tel:* 0161 448 0978 *also fax.* Malcolm Layfield, artistic dir. Str and chmbr ens, chmbr orch.

[Goldberg, Frith]. 28 Leicester Rd, London N2 9EA *tel:* 020 8444 5891 *fax:* 020 8444 3225 *email:* goldberg@dircon.co.uk. Nigel Goldberg, vn; Benjamin Frith, pno.

[Goldstone, Clemmow]. Walcot Old Hall, Alkborough, N Lincs DN15 9JT *tel:* 01724 720475 *fax:* 01724 721599. Anthony Goldstone, Caroline Clemmow, pno duo.

The Gonzaga Band. 48 Charles St, Enfield, Middx EN1 1LD *tel:* 020 8367 2097 *also fax;* 07889 334886 *email:* jsavan@freenet.co.uk. Jamie Savan, dir. Renaissance and early baroque mus for sackbuts, cornetts and continuo.

[Gough, Bottomley]. John Gough, Sally Ann Bottomley, pno duo. *NCCP*

Gould Piano Trio. Lucy Gould, vn; Martin Storey, vc; Benjamin Frith, pno. *Clarion/Seven Muses*

Graham Dalby and the Grahamophones. *Chameleon*

Graham Fitkin Group. c/o 38 Townfield, Rickmansworth, Herts WD3 2DD *tel:* 01923 493903 *also fax; email:* wardjmusic@aol.com. Ann Morfee, vn; Ben Davies, vc; Stephen Gibson, perc; Nick Moss, Simon Haram, sax; Graham Fitkin, keyboards. Also available with 9 players. Features mus of Graham Fitkin and other new mus composers.

Grand Union. Shoreditch Town Hall, 380 Old St, London EC1V 9LT *tel:* 020 7729 8729 *fax:* 020 7729 8789. Tony Haynes, artistic dir; Catherine Mummery, admin. Musicians include: Brian Abrahams, drums; Claude Deppa, tpt; Paul Jayasinha, tpt; Louise Elliott, fl, sax; Balu Shrivastav, sitar, tabla; Vladimir Vega, charango, panpipes; Brenda Rattray, voice, steel pans. Performed by professional musicians from different countries and ethnic backgrounds.

Grieg Trio. Pno trio. *Gilder*

* **[Griffett, Walker].** James Griffett, ten; Timothy Walker, lute, gui. *CDI*

* **[Griffett, Wright].** James Griffett, ten; Brian Wright, lute. *CDI/POEM*

Grupo de Canto Coral. Nestor Andrenacci, dir. *Ellison*

The Guadagnini Piano Trio. East West Arts Ltd, 93b Cambridge Gardens, N Kensington, London W10 6JE *tel:* 020 8960 5889 *fax:* 020 8968 5541. Christina Anghelescu, vn; Anup Kumar Biswas, vc; Stephen Gutman, pno.

Guarneri Quartet. *Ingpen*

Guarneri Trio Prague. Pno trio. *Judith Hendershott*

Guildhall Strings. 4 Addison Bridge Place, London W14 8XP *tel:* 020 7371 3755 *fax:* 020 7371 3756. Jeremy Woods, gen mgr; Robert Salter, mus dir. 11-piece str ens.

* **[Guimond, Cole].** Claire Guimond, baroque fl; Maggie Cole, hpd. *Robert White*

Guitaria. 35 Enmore Gardens, London SW14 8RF *tel:* 020 8876 6161 *also fax.* Marylyn Troth, sop; Michael Lewin, gui.

[Guy, Riley, Wachsmann]. 53 Tweedy Rd, Bromley, Kent BR1 3NH *tel:* 020 8290 5917. Phillip Wachsmann, vn; Barry Guy, db; Howard Riley, pno.

* **[Hadden, Carolan, Headley].** 86 Avenue Rd, London N15 5DN *tel:* 020 8802 7873 *also fax.* Nancy Hadden, renaissance and baroque fls; Lucy Carolan, hpd; Erin Headley, va da gamba. Solo, duo and trio programmes.

The Haffner Wind Ensemble of London. *Upbeat*

Hagen Quartet. Lukas Hagen, Rainer Schmidt, vn; Veronika Hagen, va; Clemens Hagen, vc. *Intermusica*

Hall Quartet. Parke View, Bovey Tracey, Devon TQ13 9AD *tel:* 01626 833223. Judith Hall, fl; str trio. *Michael Brewer*

[Hall, Webb]. Parke View, Bovey Tracey, Devon TQ13 9AD *tel:* 01626 833223. Judith Hall, fl; Hugh Webb, hp. *Michael Brewer*

Hammig String Quartet. 10 Meadow Close, Catford, London SE6 3NW *tel:* 020 8695 6004. David Burton, Paul Collen, vns; Jane Tyler, va; (tba), vc.

[Hammond]. 39b Carlton Ave, Kenton, Middx HA3 8AX *tel:* 020 8909 2687 *also fax; email:* mhammond@btinternet.com. Richard Hammond, tpt; Mark Hammond, org.

The Hilliard Ensemble

"famous for flawless intonation in both old and contemporary music alike.....it is always the 'sound' in particular which fascinates the audience" FRANKFURTER RUNDSCHAU

ALL enquiries to: Shauni McGregor
tel: 01608 642352
fax 01608 643235
email: smcg@fixall.demon.co.uk

INSTANT SUNSHINE

MUSIC AND HUMOUR
COMEDY CLASSIC

Their every second on stage is honed for comedy
The Scotsman

9 Ashdown Road, Epsom, Surrey KT17 3PL
Tel: 01372 720727

HARLEQUIN

wind quintet (and more)
commissions
music theatre

"a sparkling, vivid performance" Pan
"perfection and intimacy" Rhein-Neckar-Zeitung

Chromattica Artist Management
20 Summerhill Road
Dartford, Kent DA1 2LP
tel/fax 01322 287924

http://www.intune.co.uk/harlequin/
email: woodsinsummer@compuserve.com

[Hand, Dupré]. Newburn, Tatham Rd, Abingdon OX14 1QD *tel:* 01235 539395 *fax:* 01235 539483 *email:* dupre@dial.pipex.com. Richard Hand, Tom Dupré, gui duo.

* **The Hanover Band.** The Old Market, Upper Market St, Hove, E Sussex BN3 1AS *tel:* 01273 206978 *fax:* 01273 329636 *email:* mailbox@hanoverband.co.uk. HRH The Duke of Kent, KG, patron; Caroline Brown, artistic dir; Stephen Neiman, exec dir; David Orams, mkt and communications mgr; Jane Saunders, PA to artistic dir; Kathy Avdiev, promotions mgr.

The Harewood Duo. Harewood, 22 Rooksmead Rd, Sunbury-on-Thames, Middx TW16 6PD *tel:* 01932 781577. Ian Clarke, fl; Joyce Clarke, pno.

Harlequin. 20 Summerhill Rd, Dartford, Kent DA1 2LP *tel:* 01322 287924 *also fax.* Mark Underwood, fl; Bryony Otaki, ob; Graeme Vinall, cl; Glyn Williams, bsn; James Thomson, hn.

Harlequin Brass. Benjamin Lees, Oliver Preece, tpt; Clare Lintott, hn; Tracy Holloway, trb; Graham Sibley tb. *Chameleon*

* **Harmonious Murmur.** 25 Plasturton Ave, Cardiff CF1 9HL *tel:* 029 2022 8154 *also fax; email:* w-d@baynet.co.uk. Lucy Robinson, Alexandra Robinson, Gillian Stevens, viols; Andrew Wilson-Dickson, viols, keyboards; Dan Jones, baroque gui.

Harp to Harp. Lucy Wakeford, Alison Nicholls, hp duo. *NBM*

* **[Harries, Hurst].** 72 Gladsmuir Rd, London N19 3JU *tel:* 020 7281 9135. Elin Harries, sop; Andrew Hurst, lute, theorbo, baroque gui. Elizabethan and baroque mus; English and Italian sacred and secular mus.

The Hartley Piano Trio. Walcot Old Hall, Alkborough, N Lincs DN15 9JT *tel:* 01724 720475 *fax:* 01724 721599. Jacqueline Hartley, vn; Lionel Handy, vc; Caroline Clemmow, pno.

* **Hausmusik London.** Monica Huggett, Pavlo Beznosiuk, vn; Roger Chase, va; Richard Lester, vc; Chi-chi Nwanoku, db; Antony Pay, cl; Anthony Halstead, hn; Jeremy Ward, bsn. Romantic chmbr repertoire on period insts. *Judith Hendershott*

* **Haydn Baryton Trio.** Waye House, Alston Cross, Ashburton, S Devon TQ13 7ET *tel:* 01364 652114 *also fax; email:* roundelay@bigfoot.com. Oliver Brookes, baryton, dir; Roxanna Gundry, mgr; Tony Shorrocks, baroque va; Tatty Theo, baroque vc.

Heard String Trio. Robert Heard, vn; Christopher Yates, va; Richard Jenkinson, vc. *Michael Brewer*

The Hebrides Ensemble. Chmbr ens up to 16 players. Much 20th C and contemporary. William Conway, Peter Evans, artistic dirs; Frank Carroll, mgr. Pno, wind, str, br and perc. *Carroll*

Hegedos. Lajos Hollokoi, wind insts, bagpipes; Tamas Gombai, vn; Kalman Balogh, cembalom; Sandor Toth, va, voice, perc; Zsolt Kurtosi, db, accordian. Original inst Hungarian folk band. *Michael Brewer*

Helicon Trio and Helicon Players. Stonewalls, 1 Malt Lane, Syresham, Northants NN13 5YE *tel:* 01280 850102 *fax:* 01280 824498. Lisa-Maree Amos, artistic dir. Fl, str trio, hp.

Helios Duo. Jane Phillips, gui; Samantha Moore, fl. *Invisible Pilots*

[Hellsten, Ennis]. c/o Diana Hirst Arts Administration and PR, 55 Marmora Rd, London SE22 0RY *tel:* 020 8299 1914 *also fax; email:* Hirstpr@aol.com. Dominique Hellsten, sop; Catherine Ennis, org. Transcriptions of symphonic song cycles and Wagner operatic arias.

* **Henry's Eight.** 70a Stondon Park, London SE23 1JZ *tel:* 020 8699 8060 *also fax; email:* jonathan@henrys-eight.co.uk. Jonathan Brown, dir.

Henschel Quartet. Christoph and Markus Henschel, vns; Monika Henschel, va; Mathias D Beyer, vc. *Connaught*

Heritage Ensemble. 47 Hambalt Rd, London SW4 9EQ *tel:* 020 8675 3877 *email:* stephen.bennett@telia.com. Stephen Bennett, artistic dir.

[Hill, Wiltschinsky]. c/o 3 Kintyre Drive, Ladybridge, Bolton, Lancs BL3 4PE *tel:* c/o 01204 63055 *fax:* 01204 658028. Robin Hill, Peter Wiltschinsky, guis.

* **The Hilliard Ensemble.** David James, c-ten; Rogers Covey-Crump, John Potter, ten; Gordon Jones, bar. Vocal ens. *Shauni McGregor*

[Hirst, Potter]. Linda Hirst, sop; John Potter, ten. Early and contemporary mus. *Robert White*

* **His Majestys Sagbutts and Cornetts.** 80 Vancouver Rd, London SE23 2AJ *tel:* 020 8473 0444 *fax:* 020 8699 6926 *email:* j.west@ic.ac.uk. Jeremy West, David Staff, Susan Addison, Abigail Newman, Adam Woolf, Stephen Saunders, Timothy Roberts.

* **Holbein Consort.** 1 Boston Farm Cottage, Swyncombe Ave, London W5 4DT *tel:* 020 8568 1445. Tudor wind ens.

[Holliger]. Heinz Holliger, ob; Ursula Holliger, hp. *Ingpen*

* **[Holmes].** Holly Lodge, 231 Worlds End Lane, Chelsfield Park, Orpington, Kent BR6 7SS *tel:* 01689 857533 *fax:* 01689 854566 *email:* pholmes@tcm.ac.uk. Richard Holmes, vc; Patricia Holmes, pno, hpd.

* **[Holton, Staff, Egarr].** Ruth Holton, sop; David Staff, tpt; Richard Egarr, keyboard. *POEM*

Holywell Ensemble. 53 Stapleton Rd, Headington, Oxford OX3 7LX *tel:* 01865 766565 *also fax; email:* jjarts@msn.com. Margaret Ozanne, pno; Kate Bailey, Kiera Lyness, vn; Daniel Lyness, va; Peter Nichols, cl; Spike Wilson, vc; Miles Hewitt, hn. *Jean Judge*

* **[Hooker, Pollock].** Helen Hooker, rcdrs; David Pollock, hpd. *Purkiss*

[Hopkins, Presland, Madzar]. Louise Hopkins, vc; Carole Presland, pno; Aleksandar Madzar, pno. *NCCP*

Horn Belles. Mill Farm, Farlow, Kidderminster, Worcs DY14 0LP *tel:* 01746 718727 *fax:* 01746 718540 *email:* the.pigpen@dial.pipex.com.uk. Gillian Jones, Stella Disney, Allyson Roper, Nicola Daw, hns.

Hornflakes. 51 Lausanne Rd, London N8 0HJ *tel:* 020 8347 7358. Richard Steggall, Rachel Bunyan, Martin Grainger, Adam Walters. Hn quartet.

* **Hortus Musarum.** 18 Mare St, London E8 4RT *tel:* 020 8533 6404 *also fax.* Lewis Jones, dir.

[Hoskuldsson, Kopelman]. Stefan Ragnar Höskuldsson, Elizaveta Kopelman. Fl and pno duo. *Roxane Houston*

Hot Strings. Beverley Davison, artistic dir. Europe's first all-female str orch. Concets range from classics to Gershwin, Glen Miller, Sondheim, Scott Joplin and Michael Nyman. *Jean Judge*

The Houghton Consort. 9 Cromwell Rd, Burgess Hill, W Sussex RH15 8QH *tel:* 01444 230779 *fax:* 01444 233699. Nicholas Houghton, artistic dir; Helen Houghton, mgr.

hr-brass. Brass section of the Frankfurt Radio Symphony Orchestra. *Pristavec*

Hugo Wolf String Quartet. *Lubbock*

Humphrey Lyttelton and his Band. *John Boddy*

* **I Fagiolini.** 24 Salisbury Close, Princes Risborough, Bucks HP27 0JF *tel:* 01844 345957 *also fax; email:* robert.hollingworth@virgin.net. Robert Hollingworth, dir; Anna Crookes, Rachel Elliott, Carys Lane, sops; William Purefoy, Richard Wyn-Roberts, c-ten; James Gilchrist, Hugh Wilson, Nicholas Hurndall Smith, tens; Roderick Williams, bar; Matthew Brook, bs. Renaissance and baroque solo-voice ens mus. *Clarion/Seven Muses*

I Musicanti. 8a Manor Rd, Tring, Herts HP23 5DA *tel:* 01442 823796 *also fax; email:* bosch@iaxnet.co.uk. Str, wind and pno chmbr ens.

Icebreaker. 26 Stadium St, London SW10 0PT *tel:* 020 7351 6519 *also fax; email:* admin@icebreaker.org.uk. James Poke, artistic dir; Lewis Mitchell, admin. 11-member amplified contemporary mus ens.

Ifeka Saunders Duo. Althea Ifeka, ob; Dominic Saunders, pno. *Ellison*

Il Giardino Armonico. *Askonas Holt*

Incontro di Solisti. Pno quartet. *ECAM*

Instant Sunshine. 9 Ashdown Rd, Epsom, Surrey KT17 3PL *tel:* 01372 720727. David Barlow, Peter Christie, Alan Maryon-Davis; Tom Barlow, db. Guis, banjos, db, perc.

Interfusion. 38 Denman Rd, London SE15 5NR *tel:* 020 7701 6438 *also fax; email:* interfusion@brailsford.demon.co.uk. Matthew Brailsford, admin; Judith Mitchell, dir, vc; Clive Williamson, pno, keyboards. Electric-acoustic ens performing with sound projection 20th C works for vc and pno, keyboards and electronics.

* **Interpreti Veneziani.** Paolo Cognolato, artistic dir; Giuliano Fontanella, leader. Baroque strs and keyboard. Period insts. *Roy Baker*

* **Invocation.** 1 Wroxham Mansions, 38 Canfield Gardens, London NW6 3LB *tel:* 020 7604 4704 *fax:* 020 7328 8014 *email:* timroberts@Talk21.com. Timothy Roberts, dir, keyboard; Frances Kelly, hp; Julia Gooding, Ana-María Rincón, Rufus Müller, Charles Daniels, Christopher Purves, vocalists.

Isis Piano Trio. 70 Midhurst Rd, Ealing, London W13 9XR *tel:* 020 8579 1740 *also fax; email:* kaye@bridge-quartet.demon.co.uk. Kaye Barker, vn; Kevin Faux, vc; Timothy Murray, pno.

Israel Piano Trio. Menahem Breuer, vn; Marcel Bergman, vc; Alexander Volkov, pno. *Christine Talbot-Cooper*

Israel String Quartet. Yigal Tunch, vn; Elyakum Saltzman, vn; Robert Mozes, va; Alexander Kaganovsky, vc. *Ellison*

* **The Italian Madrigal Group.** 11 York Rd, Watford Fields, Watford WD1 8BE *tel:* 020 8771 5954; 01923 491290 *fax:* 01923 244234 *email:* italianmadrigalgroup@btinternet.com. Julian Stocker, Simon Haynes, dirs; Helen Groves, sop; Margaret Cameron, m-sop; Julian Stocker, Simon Haynes, ten; Thomas Barnard, bs. Madrigals, duets, dialogues, arias, and inst mus from Italy 1500-1643. Larger-scale works for strs, cornetts, sackbuts and continuo.

IXION. 57b Station Rd, Willesden, London NW10 4UX *tel:* 020 8961 1051 *also fax; email:* andrewtoovey@tooveyworld.freeserve.co.uk. Andrew Toovey, dir; Charles Mutter, leader; Michael Finnissy, cond. Contemporary mus.

[Jackson, McAllister]. Robin Jackson, Maureen McAllister. Org duo. *Invisible Pilots*

Jacques Loussier Trio. *John Boddy*

Janacek String Quartet. *Lubbock*

Jane's Minstrels. 2 Wilton Square, London N1 3DL *tel:* 020 7359 1593 *fax:* 020 7226 4369 *email:* jane@wiltonsq.demon.co.uk. Jane Manning, artistic dir; Roger Montgomery, cond. Mixed ens: 4-18 insts plus occasional vocals and Jane Manning, sop.

[Janse, Hanslip]. Jennifer Janse, vc; Virginia Hanslip, pno. *Michael Harrold*

* **[Janse, Rogers].** Jennifer Janse, baroque vc; Helen Rogers, hpd. *Michael Harrold*

The Isis Trio

Kaye Barker - *violin*
Kevin Faux - *cello*
Timothy Murray - *piano*

"...good by any standards"

The Independent

"...the artists displayed extremes of musicianship and virtuosity throughout this masterpiece."

Bridport & Lyme Regis News

Enquiries to:
Kaye Barker 70 Midhurst Road,
Ealing, London W13 9XR
Tel/Fax: 020 8579 1740

JANE'S MINSTRELS

Artistic Director JANE MANNING OBE
2 WILTON SQUARE LONDON N1 3DL
Tel: 0171-359 1593 Fax: 0171-226 4369
Email: jane@wiltonsq.demon.co.uk

"der Erzengel aller Avantgardesängerinnen" WIENER ZEITUNG

JANE MANNING with ROGER MONTGOMERY (conductor/horn) FENELLA BARTON (violin) and DOMINIC SAUNDERS (piano) at the ULTIMA Festival in Oslo

"Jane Manning's performances with her own ensemble 'Jane's Minstrels' were as near perfect as could be wished for, with phrasing, and balance intuitively grasped." **THE INDEPENDENT**

"Eloquently phrased, amply expressive, refined of sound... Gratefully and enthusiastically recommended." **THE GRAMOPHONE**

Available for Concerts, Festivals, Workshops and Master-Classes

CONDUCTOR: ROGER MONTGOMERY
27 AVINGTON GROVE
LONDON SE20 8RY
TEL/FAX: 0181 778 9411

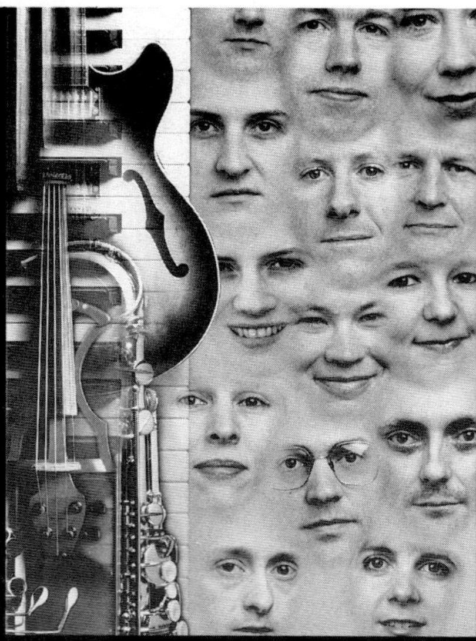

London's uniquely electrifying 11-piece ensemble Icebreaker delivers an unstoppable wall of sounds beyond the cutting edge. Icebreaker is high octane crossover, delivering what the *Musical Times* described as a 'monumental sonic assault'.

***Trance* by hip New Yorker Michael Gordon, the centrepiece of their current touring programme, is a 52-minute work that combines the driving rock/jazz sound of Icebreaker with an ambient spiritual sensibility that includes digital samples of pygmies, Buddhist monks, and sheikhs singing together. With its many points of entry *Trance* will appeal to those interested in minimal classical, ambient, alternative rock, contemporary jazz, world-beat and new age spirituality.**

ICEBREAKER

collective virtuosity Stephen Pettit *The Times*

unabashedly virtuosic Alan Kozinn *The New York Times*

adrenalin-pumping tour de force Michael Stewart *Gramophone*

brilliant...superb Joshua Kosmann *San Francisco Chronicle*

raunchy sonorities Meirion Bowen *The Guardian*

Music by
Louis Andriessen
Damian le Gassick
Michael Gordon
David Lang
Lukas Ligeti
Conlon Nancarrow
Michael Torke
Diderik Wagenaar
Frank Zappa

Lewis Mitchell
Administrator
26 Stadium Street
London SW10 0PT
T&F 0171 351 6519

James Poke
Artistic Director
Amy Coffey
General Manager

Website
www.icebreaker.org.uk
E mail
admin@icebreaker.org.uk

Trance is available on CD Argo 455 662-2

Japan Music Pool. 27 Heber Rd, London NW2 6AB *tel:* 020 8452 9234 *also fax.* Takako Selby-Okamoto, sop, dir; Lyn McLarin, fl; Yuri Nagai, vn; Julia Walker, vc; Keiko Tokunaga, pno; Harold Lester, pno, hpd; Mike Selby, sec.

The Jeruslam Quartet. *HP*

Jeux. 30 Woodsome Rd, London NW5 1RY *tel:* 020 7485 1903 *also fax.* Imogen Barford, artistic dir; Gillian Tingay, hp; Ileana Ruhemann, fl; Rebecca Hirsch, vn; Martin Outram, va; Julia Vohralik, vc. Chmbr mus with hp.

[Jewel, Slater]. 49 Exeter Rd, London NW2 4SE *tel:* 020 8452 6843. Carol Slater, vn; Ian Jewel, va.

Joachim Piano Trio. John Lenehan, Rebecca Hirsch, Caroline Dearnley. *Upbeat*

* **Joglaresa.** c/o Belinda Sykes, 31a Vestry Rd, London SE5 8PG *tel:* 020 7708 3529 *also fax; email:* belinda.sykes@btinternet.com. Belinda Sykes, voice; Ben Davis, Stuart Hall, Paul Clarvis, insts.

Julian Joseph Big Band. *HP*

Jupiter Brass. 57 White Horse Rd, London E1 0ND *tel:* 020 7790 5883 *fax:* 020 7265 9170 *email:* gregory-rose@tisl.co.uk. Gregory Rose, dir.

The Jupiter Ensemble. Cornubia, 16 Edenfield, Orton Longueville, Peterborough PE2 7HY *tel:* 01733 235888 *email:* gpcasey@compuserve.com. Graham Casey, admin. Chmbr ens of mixed insts. *Invisible Pilots*

Kaleidoscope Wind. 188a Squires Lane, Finchley, London N3 2QT *tel:* 020 8346 0203 *email:* kal-wind@pop3.poptel.org.uk. Ferencz Diczku, dir, cond. Double wind quintet. Fls, obs, cls, hns, bsns, db. Classical, contemporary and popular mus.

[Kalichstein, Laredo, Robinson]. Joseph Kalichstein, pno; Jaime Laredo, vn; Sharon Robinson, vc. *Askonas Holt*

Kandinsky String Quartet. Hathaway, Surrey Gardens, Effingham, Surrey KT24 5HS *tel:* 01483 282445 *also fax.* Jenny Godson, Jane Carwardine, vn; Rachel Bolt, va; Shuna Wilson, vc.

Karelia Brass. 52 Pymers Mead, West Dulwich, London SE21 8NH *tel:* 020 8244 5036 *also fax*; 07973 956079. Martin Evans, Matt Warren, tpt; Richard Steggall, hn; Adam Woolf, trb; Richard Halliday, tb. Mus entertainment for recitals, corporate functions, and educ presentations.

Katin Piano Trio. Krzysztof Smietana, vn; Pal Banda, vc; Peter Katin, pno. *Purkiss*

Katona Twins. Gui duo. *YCAT*

Kegelstatt Trio. Fiona Cross, cl; Rosemary Sanderson, va; Nigel Clayton, pno. *NCCP*

Keller Quartet. Andras Keller, Janos Pilz, vn; Zoltan Gal, va; Judit Szabó, vc. *Tennant*

The Kempf Trio. *Grant Rogers*

[Kennedy, Harrell]. Nigel Kennedy, Lynn Harrell. *IMG*

* **Kensington Gore Singers.** 10 Pembroke Mews, London W8 6ER *tel:* 020 7937 0684 *also fax.* Petronella Dittmer, dir. 3-16 singers. Sacred and secular mus.

Kenwood Ensemble. West Byres Cottage, Balmerino, Fife DD6 8SB *tel:* 01382 330883. Yvonne Howard, sop; Duncan Prescott, cl; Ivan McCready, vc; Scott Mitchell, pno.

* **The King's Consort.** 34 St Mary's Grove, London W4 3LN *tel:* 020 8995 9994 *fax:* 020 8995 2115 *email:* info@the-kings-consort.org.uk. Robert King, artistic dir; Edward Hossack, artistic mgr; Elizabeth Baines, admin; Nicky Oppenheimer, development dir; Eugenia Pino, tour mgr. Vocal and inst baroque ens. Baroque and early classical on period insts; can also be with choir and soloists. Chmbr ens 8-14 players.

The King's Singers. Nigel Short, David Hurley, c-ten; Paul Phoenix, ten; Philip Lawson, Gabriel Crouch, bar; Stephen Connolly, bs. *IMG*

* **[King, Heringman].** Catherine King, m-sop; Jacob Heringman, lute, vihuela. *POEM*

[Kipling, Packwood]. Flat 10, Towerside, 144 Wapping High St, London E1 9XF *tel:* 020 7488 3490 *also fax;* 020 8533 1372 *email:* SimonCTimK@compuserve.com. Timothy Kipling, fl; Mark Packwood, pno.

[Kipling, Perrett]. Flat 10, Towerside, 144 Wapping High St, London E1 9XF *tel:* 020 7488 3490 *also fax;* 020 8533 1372 *email:* SimonCTimK@compuserve.com. Timothy Kipling, fl; Danielle Perrett, hp.

[Kirby, Parnell]. 22 Chestnut Ave, Hornsey, London N8 8NY *tel:* 020 8340 2983 *also fax; email:* bparnell@tutte.demon.co.uk. Michael Kirby, cl; Brian-Michael Parnell, pno.

Klarinettenharmonie. 24 Clarence Rd, Malvern WR14 3EH *tel:* 01684 575771. Cl quartet. Elizabeth Rozelaar, Richard Percy, Rosemary Harrington, Antony Dean.

Klaviola. Duo. *John Boddy*

Kocian Quartet. Str quartet. *Judith Hendershott*

KODO. *HP*

Kol Simcha. Klezmer band. *Upbeat*

Kontraste. 8 Pit Farm Rd, Guildford, Surrey GU1 2JH *tel:* 01483 563096 *also fax.* Martin Feinstein, fl, rcdr; Marina Solarek, vn; Penelope Cave, hpd.

Kreutzer Quartet. Peter Sheppard, Gordon MacKay, Bridget Carie, Neil Heyde. *Manygate*

Kutrowatz Piano Duo. Eduard and Johannes Kutrowatz. *Ellison*

[Labèque]. Katia and Marielle Labèque, pno. *TransArt*

Lacock Abbey Chamber Ensemble. 10 Pembroke Mews, London W8 6ER *tel:* 020 7937 0684 *also fax.* Group of 4-24 musicians. Petronella Dittmer, dir, vn.

* **Ladybones.** c/o B & B Concert Services, 66 Hyde Way, Hayes, Middx UB3 4PB *tel:* 020 8606 0030 *fax:* 020 8606 0037 *email:* roderick_burnett@compuserve.com. Sarah Williams, Abigail Newman, Jayne Murrill, Tracey Holloway, trbs; Carole Marnoch, sop; Roderick Burnett, mgr dir. Trb quartet and voice. Offers introduction to lower br insts, demonstrations of various mus styles, detailed lecture recitals, children's w/shops.

Lake Piano Trio. 157 Ferndale Rd, London SW4 7RU *tel:* 020 7738 7391 *also fax.* Grigori Zhislin, vn; Douglas Cummings, vc; Ian Lake, pno.

* **Lammas.** California Farm, Priests Way, Swanage, Dorset BH19 2RS *tel:* 01929 426091 *email:* dcd@dial.pipex.com. Sarah Deere-Jones and Phil Williams. English hp and English bagpipes, gemshorn, mandola, psaltery, cup-bells. Medieval mus.

* **Lecosaldi Ensemble.** 10 Javelin Court, Streatham Common North, London SW16 3HL *tel:* 020 8769 2677 *also fax;* 020 7606 4986; 01297 553620 *email:* englund@cape.com. Peter Lea-Cox, dir; Rev Ronald Englund, admin. Singers and insts; mainly 18th C mus, specialising in Bach cantatas.

* **Legrand Ensemble.** James Bowman, Charles Brett, c-ten; John Turner, David Pugsley, rcdr; Jonathan Price, vc; Keith Elcombe, hpd. *Upbeat*

Lehar Schrammel. 68 Lysia St, London SW6 6NG *tel:* 020 7385 0182 *fax:* 020 7381 1155. John Leach, dir, zither; Jake Rea, vn; Rodney Stewart, bs; Laurence Joyce, fl; Colin Courtenay, cl; Judd Procter, gui; Tracey Goldsmith, accordion. *GBZ*

Leodian String Quartet. 34 Stainburn Cres, Moortown, Leeds LS17 6NS *tel:* 0113 266 0602 *also fax.* Douglas Reid, Raymond Sidebottom, vn; Brian Carlile, va; Roger Ladds, vc.

[Lewis, Pearson, Jones]. Oliver Lewis, vn; Justin Pearson, vc; Ian Jones, pno. *Sympathetic*

The Lindsays. Peter Cropper, Ronald Birks, vn; Robin Ireland, va; Bernard Gregor-Smith, vc. *Ingpen*

Liverpool Music Group. 4 Windermere Terrace, Liverpool L8 3SB *tel:* 0151 727 2727 *fax:* 0151 727 7272. Fritz Spiegl, dir.

Locke Brass Consort of London. 55 Heather Rd, Grove Park, London SE12 0UG *tel:* 020 8857 4152 *also fax; email:* llake@fundraising.co.uk. Leslie Lake, mus dir. Available from quintet to symphonic br and perc ens.

* **The Loki Ensemble.** 10 Viking Court, Beaver Close, Hampton, Middx TW12 2BZ *tel:* 020 8941 4917 *also fax; email:* wsummers@dircon.co.uk. William Summers (early fl, rcdr), Heidi Pegler (sop) Richard Partridge (viol), co-directors. Other insts as required.

London Adventist Chorale. Ken Burton, principal cond and artistic consultant; Tina Brooks, dir. *Ellison*

* **London Baroque.** Brick Kiln Cottages, Hollington, Newbury, Berks RG20 9XX *tel:* 01635 254331 *fax:* 01635 253629 *email:* c.medlam@btinternet.com. Ingrid Seifert, Irmgard Schaller, vn; Richard Gwilt, vn, va; Charles Medlam, vc, va da gamba; Terence Charlston, keyboard.

London Baroque Soloists. 34 Fernwood Ave, London SW16 1RD *tel:* 020 8769 4158 *also fax; email:* EastRevolution@compuserve.com. Angela East, artistic dir, vc; Julia Bishop, Adrian Butterfield, vn; Alistair Ross, hpd. Chmbr ens to small baroque orch, on period insts.

London Baroque Trio. 122 Wigmore St, London W1H 9FE *tel:* 020 7935 1270. Christopher Ball, rcdrs; Paul Arden Taylor, ob, rcdr; Alan Wilson, hpd.

London Beethoven Trio. 100 Harvist Rd, London NW6 6HL *tel:* 020 8960 4780 *fax:* 020 8964 5510. Catherine Manson, vn; Thomas Carroll, vc; Leslie Howard, pno.

London Brass. 42 Norbiton Ave, Kingston-upon-Thames, Surrey KT1 3QR *tel:* 020 8974 5660 *also fax; email:* london-brass@easynet.co.uk. David Purser, mgr; Andrew Crowley, Paul Beniston, John Barclay, Anne McAneney, tpt; Richard Bissill, hn; Lindsay Shilling, Richard Edwards, David Purser, David Stewart, trb.

London Brass Virtuosi. 194 Muswell Hill Rd, Muswell Hill, London N10 3NG *tel:* 020 8444 0246 *also fax;* 020 8883 7395. David Honeyball, mus dir; Janice Ballard, orch mgr and admin; Nicholas Betts, principal tpt; Ian Brignall, gen mgr.

London Chamber Ensemble. 41 Queen's Gardens, London W2 3AA *tel:* 020 7402 0014 *fax:* 020 7402 3134. Madeleine Mitchell, artistic dir, vn. Flexible group up to 12 insts.

London Classics String Quartet. *John Boddy*

London Gabrieli Brass Ensemble. 22 Athenaeum Rd, London N20 9AE *tel:* 020 8445 3016 *also fax*. Christopher Larkin, dir. *Sykes*

London Grieg Ensemble. Jonathan Carney, Janice Graham, Colin Callow, vn; Stephen Shakeshaft, va; David Burrowes, vc; Tony Hougham, bs; Martin Ennis, pno, hpd; Jennifer Stinton, fl. *Roy Baker*

The London Guitar Duo. 41 Arkwright Rd, Sanderhead, Surrey CR2 0LP *tel:* 020 8657 5840 *also fax*. Harvey Hope, Martin Byatt, gui. Popular classics.

London Harpsichord Ensemble. 10 Avenue Rd, London N6 5DW *tel:* 020 8340 5461 *fax:* 020 8347 5907. Sarah Francis, ob, dir; Graham Mayger, fl; Peter Stevens, vn; Margaret Powell, vc; Jane Dodd, hpd.

London Metropolitan Ensemble. Timbers, Woburn Hill, Weybridge, Surrey KT15 2QG *tel:* 01932 853271/3 *fax:* 01932 859233 *email:* andy@lmo.co.uk. Rosemary Furniss, vn; Andrew Brown, va; Caroline Dale, vc; Dave Heath, fl; Melinda Maxwell, ob; David Campbell, cl; Barrington Pheloung, gui; Sally Heath, pno; Gillian Tingay, hp.

London Mozart Players Chamber Ensemble. 92 Chatsworth Rd, Croydon, London CR0 1HB *tel:* 020 8686 1996 *fax:* 020 8686 2187 *email:* info@lmp.org. Ens of mixed insts from 5 to 14 players.

London Mozart Trio. 50 Lowlands Rd, Harrow, Middx HA1 3AN *tel:* 020 8423 3915 *fax:* 020 8933 0249. Krzysztof Smietana, vn; Colin Stone, pno; Leonid Gorokhov, vc. *Manygate*

London Music Phoenix. 20 Courtnell St, London W2 5BX *tel:* 020 7229 4185 *fax:* 020 7727 2036. Keith Puddy, cl; Hugh Bean, vn; Lionel Handy, vc; Shelagh Sutherland, pno.

The London Piano Quartet. 15a Tredegar Terrace, London E3 5AH *tel:* c/o 01643 831370 *also fax; email:* adie.exmoor@btinternet.com. Nona Liddell, vn; Elizabeth Turnbull, va; David Kenedy, vc; Philip Fowke, pno.

London Pro Arte Brass Ensemble. 17b St Augustine's Ave, South Croydon, Surrey CR2 6JN *tel:* 020 8688 2890 *fax:* 020 8688 2901 *email:* proarte@dial.pipex.com. Murray Stewart, artistic dir; John Cobb, mgr.

London Pro Arte Percussion Ensemble. 17b St Augustine's Ave, South Croydon, Surrey CR2 6JN *tel:* 020 8688 2890 *fax:* 020 8688 2901 *email:* proarte@dial.pipex.com. Murray Stewart, Tristan Fry, artistic dirs; John Cobb, mgr.

* **London Pro Musica.** 15 Rock St, Brighton, E Sussex BN2 1NF *tel:* 01273 692974 *fax:* 01273 622792. Bernard Thomas, dir. Shawms, cornetts, sackbuts, etc.

London Serpent Trio. Cantax House, Lacock, Chippenham, Wilts SN15 2JZ *tel:* 01249 730468 *also fax*. Andrew van der Beek, Clifford Bevan, Phil Humphries, serpents.

London Soloists Chamber Orchestra. *NBM*

London Sonata Group. Susan Milan, fl; Nicholas Ward, vn; John Heley, vc; Ian Watson, pno, hpd. *Upbeat*

The London String Ensemble. 133 Victoria Way, Charlton, London SE7 7NX *tel:* 020 8858 7384 *fax:* 020 8858 1369 *email:* rushlse97@aol.com. Celeste Rush, artistic dir.

London String Soloists. 6 Munsons Lane, Feltwell, Norfolk IP26 4DE *tel:* 01842 828424; 07973 977704 *email:* lss@con-brio.com. Stephen Bingham, artistic dir. Str chmbr ens with or without hpd. Performs all types of repertoire.

London Voices. 22 St Mary's Ave, London E11 2NP *tel:* 020 8989 4804 *fax:* 020 8989 7389. Terry Edwards, dir; Jacqueline Peet, sec.

The London Wind Quartet. Kathy Seabrook, fl, sax; Susan Frost, ob, sax; Graham Quilter, cl, sax; Michael Rear, bn, sax. *Chameleon*

London Wind Trio. 20 Courtnell St, London W2 5BX *tel:* 020 7229 4185 *fax:* 020 7727 2036. Neil Black. ob; Keith Puddy, cl; Roger Birnstingl, bsn.

London Winds. Michael Collins, dir. *Intermusica*

Lontano. Toynbee Studios, 28 Commercial St, London E1 6LS *tel:* 020 7247 2950 *fax:* 020 7247 2956. Odaline de la Martinez, dir; Jan Hart, admin.

Lydian Trio. The Brew House, Radwell, Baldock, Herts SG7 5ES *tel:* 01462 730490 *also fax; email:* ccwilmers@bigfoot.com. Anna Dryer-Beers, vn; Catherine Wilmers, vc; Thea King, pno.

Lyriades. Steven Cupitt, fl; Adrian Smith, va; Patrizia Meier, hp. *Chameleon*

The Lyric Quartet. Patricia Calnan, Harriet Davies, vn; Nick Barr, va; David Daniels, vc. *Jenny Ricotti*

[McDonald, Simcock]. Gerard McDonald, baroque obs, flauto traverso, rcdrs; Iain Simcock, hpd. *Michael Harrold*

[McNaught, Tong]. Flat 4, Hillside, 41 St Mary's Rd, Long Ditton, Surrey KT6 5HB *tel:* 020 8398 8231 *also fax*. Fiona McNaught, vn; Daniel Tong, pno.

[McVicker, Barham]. 31 Colvin Gardens, Wanstead, London E11 2DD *tel:* 020 8530 4491; 020 8299 1971 *email:* wrmcvicker@aol.com. William McVicker, Jeremy Barham, org duo.

[**Mackie, Hooper**]. 70 Broadwood Ave, Ruislip, Middx HA4 7XR *tel:* 01895 632115 *fax:* 01895 625765 *email:* neil@mackies.freeserve.co.uk. Neil Mackie, ten; Nicholas Hooper, gui.

[**Mackie, North**]. 70 Broadwood Ave, Ruislip, Middx HA4 7XR *tel:* 01895 632115 *fax:* 01895 625765 *email:* neil@mackies.freeserve.co.uk. Neil Mackie, ten; Nigel North, lutes.

* [**Mackintosh, Cole**]. Catherine Mackintosh, baroque vn; Maggie Cole, hpd. *Robert White*

* **Maggie Cole & Friends.** Hpd and f-pno with other insts and soloists. *Robert White*

Maggini String Quartet. 138b St Thomas's Rd, London N4 2QP *tel:* 020 7359 8861 *also fax; email:* maggini@cableinet.co.uk. Laurence Jackson, David Angel, vn; Martin Outram, va; Michal Kaznowski, vc.

Mandelring Quartet. Str quartet. Sebastian Schmidt, Nanette Schmidt, vns; Roland Glassi, va; Bernhard Schmidt, vc. *Connaught*

[**Manning, Guy**]. 2 Wilton Square, London N1 3DL *tel:* 020 7359 1593 *fax:* 020 7226 4369 *email:* jane@wiltonsq.demon.co.uk. Jane Manning, sop; Barry Guy, db.

Mardi Brass. 15 Jerome Court, 59-65 The Limes Ave, New Southgate, London N11 1RF *tel:* 020 8368 8223. Richard Hammond, Edward Maxwell, tpt; Jonathan Boswell, hn; Kenneth McGregor, trb; Jeff Miller, tb. *Chameleon*

Marianne Olyver And Her Orchestra. Georgius, The Street, Stoke by Clare, Suffolk CO10 8HR *tel:* 01787 277063 *also fax; email:* patrick@woodley.demon.co.uk. Patrick Crooke, admin. 2-24 piece. Gypsy, Viennese and romantic mus played by virtuosi.

The Martin Loveday Palm Court Trio. 41 Summerfield Ave, London NW6 6JT *tel:* 020 8933 7615 *fax:* 020 8969 1975. Christine Blair, pno; Martin Loveday, vn; Philip Trzebiatowski, vc.

The Matrix Ensemble. 77 Thrale Rd, London SW16 1NU *tel:* 020 8769 7002 *fax:* 020 8696 7293 *email:* ziegler@matrixmusic.u-net.com. Robert Ziegler, mus dir; Nicky Webb, gen mgr. 20th C mus and mus theatre.

Maurizi Ensemble. 1 Poplar's Close, Preston Bissett, Bucks MK18 4LR *tel:* 01280 848275 *also fax.* Robert Secret, artistic dir. Str or pno quartet, quintet or octet. Mixed chmbr mus.

Mazaika. *Seaview*

Medici String Quartet. Paul Robertson, Stephen Morris, vn; Ivo-Jan van der Werff, va; Anthony Lewis, vc. *GIA*

Melisma. 29 Doods Rd, Reigate, Surrey RH2 0NT *tel:* 01737 249839 *also fax; email:* sarah-jane@melisma.freeserve.co.uk. Sarah-Jane Dale, sop; Susan Legg, m-sop; Andrew Morris, ten; Audrey Hyland, pno.

* **The Mellstock Band.** 22 Swinbourne Rd, Littlemore, Oxford OX4 4PQ *tel:* 01258 837034; 01865 714778 *fax:* 01865 749428 *email:* mellstock@aol.com. David Townsend, concertina, vn, dir; Tim Hill, cl; Philip Humphries, serpent; Charles Spicer, ob, vox humana. Authentic performance of early 19th C west-gallery church mus and other village band mus; also available with small choir. Mus of Hardy's Wessex with period insts and costume.

Melos Ensemble of London. Gervase de Peyer, artistic dir. Classical, romantic and 20th C chmbr mus. *Michael Harrold*

Melos Quartet. *Ingpen*

Mendelssohn Quartet. Str quartet. *Gilder*

Metalworks Gamelan. 1 St Anne's Rd, Caversham, Reading RG4 7PA *tel:* 0118 947 7170 *also fax; email:* janet@metalworks.org. Contemporary perc group, mus from Java, Bali, USA and UK.

Metamorphosis. Pno, wind, str, perc. *CMG*

Micallef-Inanga Piano Duo. c/o Siva Oke Music Management, 13 Riversdale Rd, Thames Ditton, Surrey KT7 0QL *tel:* 020 8398 1586 *fax:* 020 8339 0981 *email:* soke@somm-recordings.demon.co.uk.

Michael Thompson Wind Quintet. *PGM*

* **Midland Baroque.** 3 Abbey Mill End, St Albans, Herts AL3 4HN *tel:* 01727 843656 *also fax.* Diane Terry, baroque vn; Pam Cresswell, baroque va; Laurie Ann MacLeod, baroque vc, va da gamba; Katharine May, hpd. Baroque mus on original insts.

[**Milan, Brown**]. Susan Milan, fl; Ian Brown, pno. *Upbeat*

Millennia Strings. *Prophet Music Ltd*

Mistral Saxophone Quartet. 3 Villiers Rd, West Bridgford, Nottingham NG2 6FR *tel:* 07973 541364 *fax:* 07970 702679 *email:* alistairparnell@connectfree.co.uk. Alistair Parnell, sop sax; Kyle Horch, alto sax; Malcolm Pritchard, ten sax; Sarah Parnell, bar sax.

Mobius. Field House, The Haven, Fulbourn, Cambridge CB1 5BG *tel:* 01223 882354 *also fax; email:* mobiusmail@aol.com. Philippe Honoré, Kanako Ito, vn; Lorna McGhee, fl; Alison Nicholls, hp; Ashan Pillai, va; Robert Plane, cl; Martin Storey, vc. *Connaught*

Montague/Mead Piano Plus. 2 Ryland Rd, London NW5 3EA *tel:* 020 7267 5416 *also fax; email:* srmontague@aol.com. Philip Mead, pno; Linda Merrick, cl; Stephen Montague, live electronics. Performs contemporary works for pno, cl and electronics.

Moray Piano Trio. Kildonan, Young St, Elgin, Moray IV30 1TH *tel:* 01343 543531. Peter Zanrè, vn; Gareth John, vc; Brian Anderson, pno.

Moray String Quartet. Kildonan, Young St, Elgin, Moray IV30 1TH *tel:* 01343 543531. Peter Zanrè, James Alexander, vn; Rachel Mackison, va; Gareth John, vc.

Moscow Rachmaninov Trio. Mikhail Tsinman, vn; Natalia Savinova, vc, Viktor Yampolsky, pno. *Ellison*

Mountain Piano Trio. 93 Park Rd, Bingley, W Yorks BD16 4BY *tel:* 01274 568762 *fax:* 01274 220884 *email:* mountain@which.net. Peter Mountain, vn; Jeanette Mountain, vc; Angela Mountain, pno.

The Mowbray Ensemble. Ashley House, Ure Bank, Ripon, N Yorks HG4 1JG *tel:* 01765 602856 *email:* MowbEns@hotmail.com. Xenophon Kelsey, mus dir. Wind and str players of the Ripon St Cecilia Orchestra.

Mugenkyo. Japanese Taiko drum performance group. *Chameleon*

The Mühlfeld Ensemble. 77 St Albans Ave, East Ham, London E6 4HH *tel:* 020 8472 2057 *also fax; email:* v.soames@clarinet-classics.ndirect.co.uk. Victoria Soames, cl; Richard Friedman, vn; Nicholas Roberts, vc; Mark Troop, pno.

The Mullova Ensemble. *Askonas Holt*

* **The Music Collection.** 38 Fairhazel Gardens, London NW6 3SJ *tel:* 020 7328 9347 *fax:* 020 7328 4689 *email:* max@musicol.demon.co.uk. Jessica Max, mgr; Susan Alexander-Max, dir, f-pno; Micaela Comberti, vn; Pal Banda, vc. Ens featuring mus of the late 18th and early 19th C as well as new commissions.

Music of the Fuchsia. c/o Flat 4, 2 Albany Rd, Ealing, London W13 8PG *tel:* 020 8998 2294 *also fax; email:* paulayres@clara.net. Rosemary Forbes-Butler, sop; Paul Ayres, pno.

Music Projects/London. 11 Elmwood Rd, London W4 3DY *tel:* 020 8994 9528 *fax:* 020 8994 9595 *email:* mplrichard@bernas.demon.co.uk. Richard Bernas, Roger Williams, artistic dirs.

The Music Serenade. 7 Clarence Grove, Horsforth, Leeds, W Yorks LS18 4LA *tel:* 0113 258 1300 *also fax; email:* bob.ashworth@dial.pipex.com. Wind and str players of the English Northern Philharmonia, the orchestra of Opera North.

Music Theatre Wales Ensemble. 5 Llandaff Rd, Cardiff CF11 9NF *tel:* 029 2023 0833 *fax:* 029 2034 2046. Michael Rafferty, mus dir.

Music à la Carte. 2 Falkland Ave, Newton Mearns, Glasgow G77 5DR *tel:* 0141 639 3176 *also fax; email:* sheilaosborne@connectfreeco.uk. Sheila Osborne, admin, m-sop and accompanist; plus additional artists as required. Gypsy, Viennese, Russian, dance, opera and film themes.

* **Musica Antiqua of London.** 87 Olive Rd, London NW2 6UR *tel:* 020 8452 3254 *also fax; email:* alison.crum@which.net. Philip Thorby, dir; Alison Crum, admin; John Bryan, viols, rcdrs, crumhorns, harp, shawms, rebecs, etc; Jacob Heingman, lute; guest singers.

* **Musica Contexta.** 24 Fairfield Rd, Crouch End, London N8 9HG *tel:* 020 8347 9655 *email:* musica_contexta@hexachord.freeserve.co.uk. Simon Ravens, dir; Simon Lillystone, admin. Vocal ens.

* **Musica Dolce.** Redwings, Linden Chase, Uckfield, E Sussex TN22 1EE *tel:* 01825 760046 *also fax; email:* turbettl@aol.com. Donna Deam, sop; Linda Brand, rcdr, ob; Joanna Levine, vc; Helena Brown, hpd.

Musica Domestica. Pno, fl, vc. *Ellison*

* **Musica Fiammante.** Kate Eckersley, sop; Katharine Sharman, vc; Timothy Roberts, hpd. *Ellison*

* **Musica Secreta.** 9 Chalkers Lane, Hurstpierpoint, W Sussex BN6 9LR *tel:* 01273 833950 *also fax; email:* 101565.3033@compuserve.com. Deborah Roberts, Tessa Bonner, sops; Mary Nichols, alto; John Toll, hpd, org; David Miller, lute, theorbo. Sacred and secular mus for women's voices including 16th and 17th C convent mus.

* **Musical Offering.** Darnholme, 14 Bristow Close, Westbrook, Warrington, Cheshire WA5 5EU *tel:* 01925 710454. Rachel Brown, baroque fl, rcdr; Pauline Nobes, baroque vn; Jonathan Price, baroque vc; David Francis, hpd.

* **Musiche Delightes.** c/o Lyric Production, 41 Arkwright Rd, Sanderstead, Surrey CR2 0LP *tel:* 020 8657 5840 *also fax.* Lutes, viols, guis, clvds, rcdrs, sackbuts, serpents and crumhorns.

Musicians of the Globe. 12 Vathouse, Regents Bridge Gardens, London SW8 1HD *tel:* 020 7735 8154 *fax:* 020 7820 0801 *email:* philip.pickett@btinternet.com. Philip Pickett, dir. Associate early mus ens at Shakespeare's Globe Theatre. *Allied*

Musicians of the Royal Exchange. Walcot Old Hall, Alkborough, N Lincs DN15 9JT *tel:* 01724 720475 *fax:* 01724 721599. Anthony Goldstone, dir. Pno, wind, strs.

* **The Musicke Companye.** Phillippa Hyde, sop; Paul Esswood, c-ten; Jennifer Janse, baroque vc; Helen Rogers, hpd. *NCCP*

* **Músicos de Cámara.** 19 Linton St, London N1 7DU *tel:* 020 7354 2973 *also fax; email:* mjyakeley@callnetuk.com. June Yakeley, dir. Baroque mus (especially Spanish) with voices and early guis.

Musique Oblique. *Gilder*

orchestra of the
RENAISSANCE

Richard Cheetham, *Director*

"An absolutely exquisite debut disc...stunning in its impact."
Continuo

"Quite glorious...consistently fresh and challenging...thoroughly recommended."
Gramophone

"The Orchestra of the Renaissance...turned this normally reverential music into a devastating avowal of passion. A group to watch."
The Times

Richard Cheetham
Director
Flat 4, 111 Bulwer Road
London E11 1BU
tel: 0181 539 8125
fax: 0181 539 8125

Mary Taylor, Administrator
The Old Manse
Leafield, Witney
Oxon OX8 5NN
tel: 01993 878200
fax: 01993 878375
e-mail: oldmanse@compuserve.com

Oxford Concert Party!

Director: ARne Richards

PETER KING

Vivaldi to Piazzolla, French café music, Argentinian tango, O'Carolan, Scott-Skinner, Finnish polkas...

300 years of music from around the world - turned upside-down!

'Pick of the Fringe' Edinburgh Festival

'A bunch of superb musicians' Daily Telegraph

'Unbelievable!' Ned Sherrin

'F*ing great'** Inmates of H.M.Prison Whitemoor

Oxford Concert Party, 31 Borrowmead Road, Oxford OX3 9QP
Tel/Fax 01865 763834
Email: oxparty@clara.co.uk
www.classical-artists.com/oxford-concert-party

OffStage Brass

ROBERT CARPENTER TURNER

Phone Music for Special Events on **01628-781094** fax 01628-672884 for details

Mwynion Mai Flute & Harp Duo. 244 Cathedral Rd, Cardiff CF11 9JG *tel:* 029 2039 7714 *fax:* 029 2039 7713 *email:* duo@mwynion-mai.co.uk. Tim Griffiths, mgr; Jane Groves, fl; Eluned Scourfield, hp. Specialises in traditional Welsh mus.

* **MZT.** 1 Oast Cottage, Great Maxfield, Three Oaks, nr Hastings, E Sussex TN35 4NU *tel:* 01424 756114 *also fax; email:* spreston@bluetit.u.net.com. Stephen Preston, artistic dir; Sarah Cremer, rehearsal dir; Nikki Fido, admin.

Nash Ensemble of London. 14 Cedars Close, London NW4 1TR *tel:* 020 8203 3025 *fax:* 020 8203 9540. Amelia Freedman MBE, artistic dir; Alison Rae, admin co-ord. Pno, wind, str, hp, perc.

Nemo Brass Quintet. Andrew Dallimore, Craig Patterson, tpt; Matt Cooke, hn; Simon Johnson, trb; Mark Heron, tb. *GBZ*

[Nettle, Markham]. The Old Power House, Atherton St, London SW11 2JE *tel:* 020 7738 2765 *also fax.* David Nettle, Richard Markham, pnos.

* **New London Consort.** 12 Vathouse, Regents Bridge Gardens, London SW8 1HD *tel:* 020 7735 8154 *fax:* 020 7820 0801 *email:* philip.pickett@btinternet.com. Philip Pickett, dir. Medieval, renaissance and baroque insts with solo voices. Associate early mus ens of the Royal Festival Hall. *Allied*

New Pro Arte Guitar Trio. Raymond Burley, Cornelius Bruinsma, Mark Ashford. *Chameleon*

New Queen's Hall Chamber Ensemble. Richard Friedman, Clive Hughes, Graeme Scott, Ferens Szuks, Clare Tyack, Roger Montgomery, Keith Puddy, Gareth Newman. *Manygate*

New Queen's Hall Quartet. Richard Friedman, Clive Hughes, vn; Graeme Scott, va; Ferens Szuks, vc. *Manygate*

New Sussex Wind Ensemble. 1 Hillmead, Gossops Green, Crawley, W Sussex *tel:* 01293 546762 *fax:* 01273 703280. Alison Letschka, fl; Sarah Ionides, ob; Andrew Sutton, cl; Alan Newnham, hn; Alison Wills, bsn.

[Newbold, Moore]. Sarah Newbold, fl; Angela Moore, hp. *GBZ*

* **Noise of Minstrels.** 19 Burke St, Harrogate, N Yorks HG1 4NR *tel:* 01423 500351 *also fax;* 07860 955347 *email:* anlu@globalnet.co.uk. Michael Sargeant, bagpipes, rcdrs, shawm, crumhorn, three-hole pipe, drum; James Tribble, vn, vielle, rebec, spinet, voice; David Chatterley, hurdy-gurdy, perc, gui, lute, voice; Ray Attfield, perc, hurdy-gurdy, voice. Concerts and shows including period dance.

North Sea Project. 122 Underhill Rd, London SE22 0QJ *tel:* 020 8693 4292 William Purefoy, c-ten; Harry van Berne, Matthew Vine, ten; Harry van der Kamp, bs. Anglo-Dutch vocal ens.

Northern Saxophone Quartet. 31 Agbrigg Rd, Sandal Magna, Wakefield WF1 5AB *tel:* 01924 257826 *fax:* 01924 219272. Richard Ingham, sop sax; Julia Mills, alto sax; Tony Davis, ten sax; Nick Turner, bar sax.

* **Norwich Waits.** The Old Station, Kimberley, Wymondham, Norfolk NR18 9HB *tel:* 01953 850711. Six musicians, shawms, curtals, rauschpfeifen, crumhorns, hurdy-gurdy, bagpipes, lute, viol, cittern, rcdrs, org. Costumed entertainments of 16th and 17th C mus on period wind and str insts with readings and dialogue.

Michael Nyman Band. c/o Serious Ltd, Chapel House, 18 Hatton Place, London EC1N 8RU *tel:* 020 7405 9900 *fax:* 020 7405 9911 *email:* nyman@seriousltd.demon.co.uk. Michael Nyman, dir.

* **Odyssey.** Gwespyr, 6 Hallcroft Lane, Copmanthorpe, York YO23 3UQ *tel:* 01904 701459; 01502 724020. Yvonne Robert, sop; Maurice Ridge, pno; Graham Roberts, reader.

Off Stage Brass. 15 Cherington Gate, Pinkneys Green, Maidenhead, Berks SL6 6RU *tel:* 01628 781094 *fax:* 01628 672884. Tim Hawes.

Onyx. Tong Lee Head, Marsden HD7 6NJ *tel:* 01484 841868 *also fax.* Pno, cl, vc.

Onyx Brass. Christopher Horn, Niall Keatley, tpt; Andrew Sutton, hn; Amos Miller, trb; David Gordon-Shute, tb. *NCCP*

Opera Cocktail. c/o Michael Carey, Godre'r Grogwy, Rhoshill, Cardigan, Pembs SA43 2TX *tel:* 01239 841461 *fax:* 01239 621851 *email:* info@buddug.co.uk. Wyn Davies, pno; Carol Smith, sop; Buddug Verona James, m-sop; Huw Rhys Evans, ten; Richard Morris, bar. Opera and mus ens semi-staged.

Opera Diva and Three Tenors. 14 Kings Crescent East, Boughton, Chester, Cheshire CH3 5TH *tel:* c/o 01244 319981 *fax:* 01244 315662. Sara Hindley, promoter. 3 sops and 3 tens. Variable programmes including opera, West End opera, operetta, movies, musicals.

Opera Diva - The Three Sopranos. 14 Kings Crescent East, Boughton, Chester, Cheshire CH3 5TH *tel:* c/o 01244 319981 *fax:* 01244 315662. Sara Hindley, promoter. Variable programmes including opera, musicals and show pieces. Also original material and arrangements.

* **Opera Restor'd.** 54 Astonville St, London SW18 5AJ *tel:* 020 8870 7649 *fax:* 020 8516 6313. Peter Holman, mus dir; Jack Edwards, stage dir. Revival and performance of 17th-18th C opera; fully-staged, small orch.

Operantics. Ruth Gomme, sop; Jeanette Ager, m-sop; Ben Cooper, ten; Robert Rice, bar; Helen Vickery, pno. *Chameleon*

Opus 20. 75 New Rd, Brentford, Middx TW8 0NU *tel:* 020 8560 2920 *also fax;* 020 7354 5539 *email:* op20@aol.com. Ann Morfee, mgr; Scott Stroman, cond. 20th C mus for strs.

* **Opus Anglicanum.** 92 St Thomas St, Wells, Somerset BA5 2UZ *tel:* 01749 677903 *fax:* 01749 675131. Stephen Tilton, c-ten; William Lee, Nicholas Todd, ten; Roland Robertson, bar; John Rowlands-Pritchard, bs; John Touhey, narrator.

Oracle. Del Bearfoot, voice; Carol Wells, pno. *Dyfel*

Original Blend. Barber shop quartet. *John Boddy*

The Orbestra Ensemble. 1 South St, Middle Barton, Chipping Norton, Oxon OX7 7BU *tel:* 01869 340951; 0771 281 5338 *fax:* 01869 349084 *email:* orbestra@excite.com.

* **The Orchestra of the Golden Age.** *POEM*

Orchestra of the 18th Century. *Askonas Holt*

* **Orchestra of the Age of Enlightenment.** 5th Floor, Westcombe House, 56-58 Whitcomb St, London WC2H 7DN *tel:* 020 7930 0646 *fax:* 020 7930 0626 *email:* oae@premier.co.uk.

* **Orchestra of the Renaissance.** The Old Manse, Leafield, Witney, Oxon OX8 5NN *tel:* 01993 878200 *fax:* 01993 878375 *email:* oldmanse@compuserve.com. Richard Cheetham, dir; Mary Taylor, admin. Voice, shawms, sackbuts, dulcians, lutes, hp, org. 16th C sacred mus.

Orfeo Chamber Opera Company. *Sonata*

Orion Quartet. *Ingpen*

* **Orlando Consort.** 124 Westway, London SW20 9LS *tel:* 020 8540 1633 *fax:* 020 8542 8215 *email:* angussmithl@compuserve.com. Robert Harre-Jones, alto; Charles Daniels, Angus Smith, ten; Donald Greig, bar.

The Orphean Ensemble. 47 Boscombe Rd, London SW19 3AX *tel:* 020 8542 7610 *also fax; email:* faure@globalnet.co.uk. Gabrielle Fisher, sop; Anthony Aarons, tpt; Andrew Arthur, org; David Wickham, pno.

Osiris Trio. Pno trio. *Gilder*

Ovid Ensemble. Flat 1, 238 Nether St, Finchley, London N3 1HU *tel:* 020 8343 4221 *also fax.* Alun Darbyshire, ob; Mia Cooper, vn; David Adams, va; Alice Neary, vc; Jeremy Young, pno.

* **Oxford Baroque.** 70 Hayfield Rd, Oxford OX2 6TU *tel:* 01865 559771 *also fax.* Guy Williams, artistic dir, fl; Jean Paterson, vn; Gabriel Amherst, vc; Martin Souter, hpd.

Oxford Concert Party. 31 Borrowmead Rd, Oxford OX3 9QP *tel:* 01865 763834 *also fax; email:* oxparty@clara.co.uk. Arne Richards, hpd, accordion, dir; Isabel Knowland, Greg Warren Wilson, vn; James Sleigh, va; Justin Pearson, vc; Lucy Hare, db. Baroque and tango orch with a special commitment to performing in hospitals and prisons.

Palazzo String Quartet. 1 Ravensdon St, Kennington, London SE11 4AQ *tel:* 020 7735 2160 *also fax.* Wide repertoire of mus for special occasions. Michael Hall, leader, mgr.

* **Palladian Ensemble.** Pamela Thorby, rcdr; Rachel Podger, vn; Susanne Heinrich, va da gamba; William Carter, lutes, gui. Baroque chmbr quartet. *Hazard*

Panocha Quartet. Str quartet. *Judith Hendershott*

The Paradise Quartet. 87a Queens Rd, East Grinstead, W Sussex RH19 1BG *tel:* c/o 01342 300949 *email:* egsales@egnet.co.uk. Paul Cheneour, fl; Martin Sonnaveld, vn; Anna Marie Sonnaveld, va; Ben Hess, vc.

Paradisi Quartet. 11 York Rd, Watford Fields, Watford, Herts WD1 8BF *tel:* 01628 635534. Susan Piggott, sop; Margaret Cameron, m-sop; Julian Stocker, ten; Matthew Brook, bs. Soloists specialising in Oratorio.

Paragon Ensemble Scotland. 1 Bowmont Gardens, Glasgow G12 9LR *tel:* 0141 342 4242 *fax:* 0141 342 4442 *email:* admin@paragon.sol.co.uk. David Davies, artistic dir; Andrew Logan, gen mgr; Karyn Mackie, admin. Chmbr ens performing new and contemporary works.

* **The Parley of Instruments.** Peter Holman, dir, hpd, chmbr org; Judy Tarling, vn; Theresa Caudle, vn, va; Mark Caudle, bs vn, vc, bs viol. Baroque and renaissance strs and continuo. Also classical and baroque orchs. *Sykes*

The Parlour Quartet. 63 Hemstal Rd, London NW6 2AD *tel:* 020 7624 2225 *fax:* 020 7624 7731 *email:* robert.turner@ndirect.co.uk. Jacqueline Evill, sop; Angela Vernon Bates, m-sop; Robert Carpenter Turner, bar; Augustus Fortesque, pno. Victorian and Edwardian songs and ballads. *Pristavec*

* **The Parnassian Ensemble.** Sophie Middleditch, baroque fl, rcdr; Helen Hooker, rcdr; Susan Glossop, baroque vc; David Pollock, hpd. *Purkiss*

* **[Partridge, Cuckston].** Ian Partridge, ten; Alan Cuckston, f-pno. *POEM*

* **Passacaglia.** 5 Sackville Rd, Sutton, Surrey SM2 6HS *tel:* 020 8643 9344 *also fax; email:* passacaglia@ndirect.co.uk. Annabel Knight. Baroque inst quartet: rcdrs, fls, va da gamba, hpd. *NBM*

Pastorella. c/o Anglo-Links, 10 Mill Rd, Queens Park, Waterbeach, Cambridge CB5 9RQ *tel:* 01223 862232 *also fax.* Norma Ritchie, m-sop, clarsach; Elaine Hammonds, sop, rcdr.

Paul Cheneour and Dilly Meah. 87a Queens Rd, East Grinstead, W Sussex RH19 1BG *tel:* c/o 01342 300949 *fax:* 01342 410846 *email:* egsales@egnet.co.uk. Paul Cheneour, fls; Dilly Meah, tabla.

Pavilion Music. 1 Riverside Mews, Millgate, Thirsk, N Yorks YO7 1AE *tel:* 01845 525207. Jean Hotton, dir. Duo, trio or quartet of strs, w/wind and keyboards.

[Pearce, Drake]. Alison Pearce, sop; Susan Drake, hp. *Sympathetic*

Perfect Harmony. c/o Finchingfield House, The Green, Finchingfield, Essex CM7 4JS *tel:* 01371 810289 *also fax.* Lorraine Daniels, Ralph Meanley, voice; David Mackie, pno.

[Perkins, Hancock]. Laurence Perkins, bsn; Michael Hancock, pno. *Ellison*

[Pertis, Egri]. Attila Pertis, Monika Egri; pno duo. *Ellison*

Petersen Quartet. *Tennant*

* **La Petite Bande.** *Allied*

Petits Fours. 143 Aylesbury Rd, Wendover, Bucks HP22 6LJ *tel:* 01296 696795 *fax:* 01296 623410. Peter Noble, fl; Paul Copas, cl, sax; Andrew Challinger, ob; Veronica Thomas, bsn. Light mus for social functions.

[Petrou, Papageorgiou]. Pno duo. George Petrou, Christos Papageorgiou. *Ellison*

[Peyer, Pryor]. Gervase de Peyer, cl; Gwenneth Pryor, pno. *Michael Harrold*

* **Phantasm.** 32g Belsize Park, London NW3 4DX *tel:* 020 7435 5970 *fax:* 020 7794 8272 *email:* dreyfus@phantasm.org.uk. Laurence Dreyfus, Wendy Gillespie, Jonathan Manson, Markku Luolajan-Mikkola, viols.

Philomel Ensemble. 57 Grange Rd, Sutton, Surrey SM2 6SY *tel:* 020 8643 4425 *also fax.* Duke Dobing, mus dir.

Phoenix Arts Connection. 13 Poplar Close, Oversley Green, Alcester, Warwicks B49 6PL *tel:* 01789 762343 *also fax.* Libby Bennett, fl; Audrey Douglas, hp.

Phoenix String Quartet. *John Boddy*

Piano Circus. 20 Mentmore Terrace, Hackney, London E8 3PN *tel:* 020 8533 4027 *also fax; email:* studio@pianocircus.demon.co.uk. Kirsteen Davidson Kelly, Richard Harris, David Appleton, Kate Heath, Catherine Larkin, Richard Saxel, pnos.

Piano Plus. 16 Ashmere Grove, London SW2 5UJ *tel:* 020 7274 0054 *fax:* 020 7733 7684 *email:* Juliet.Edwards@btinternet.com. Juliet Edwards, pno; Emma Bell, sop; Belinda Dunn, fl; Emma Feilding, ob; Chi-Yu Mo, cl; Philip Gibbon, bsn; Jorge Renteria, hn; Catherine Martin, vn; Nikos Zarb, va; Anna Holmes, vc.

Pipe Dreams. 55 Rokesly Ave, London N8 8NH *tel:* 020 8340 3789 *fax:* 020 8341 6073. Anna Pope, Nancy Ruffer, fl; Helen Crayford, pno.

Pirasti Trio. Rutland House, The Ridge, Woking, Surrey GU22 7EE *tel:* 01483 771361 *also fax;* 07973 222882 *email:* jsharkey@compuserve.com. Nicholas Miller, vn; Alison Wells, vc; Jeffrey Sharkey, pno.

Plaegan Piano Quartet. Woodcott, Church Rd, Shepperton, Middx TW17 9JT *tel:* 01932 228012. Michelle Carte, vn; Amber Bonham-Carter, va; Michael Nebe, vc; Peter Croser, pno.

The Plane-Dukes-Rahman Trio. Robert Plane, cl; Philip Dukes, va; Sophia Rahman, pno. *Purkiss*

* **Platform 4.** G Clarke, vn; R Theobald, con; D Francis, hpd. Classical, experimental, chmbr ens. *Mostylea*

PM Music Ensemble. 46 Richmond Rd, Roath, Cardiff CF24 3AT *tel:* 029 2048 2183 *also fax.* Peter Reynolds, dir. Contemporary mus ens.

Poetica Musica. *Anthony Abbott*

Polly and the Phonics. 25 Hailstone Close, Rowley Regis B65 8LJ *tel:* 01384 252632 *also fax; email:* polly@hecate.freeserve.co.uk. Kate Buttolph, Alison Sabedoria, Heather Wastie. Original material - vocal harmony with a twist.

Polmear Ambache Duo. 9 Beversbrook Rd, London N19 4QG *tel:* 020 7263 4027 *also fax; email:* polmear.ambache@telinco.co.uk. Jeremy Polmear, ob; Diana Ambache, pno.

* **Polyhymnia.** Flat 3, Paternoster House, Colebrook St, Winchester SO23 9LG *tel:* 01962 865617. Richard Lowell Childress, dir. Vocal ens of 8-18 members, mixed or all-male, usually unaccompanied.

* **Praetorius Consort of London.** 122 Wigmore St, London W1H 9FE *tel:* 020 7935 1270. Christopher Ball, dir, renaissance wind; Paul Arden Taylor, Philip Thorby, wind; Alan Wilson, spinet; Peter Vel, bs viol; Michael Lewin, lute.

Prazak Quartet. *Olivia Ma*

The Prelude Ensemble. Richard Deakin, vn; Yuko Inoue, va; Emma Ferrand, vc; Duncan McTier, db; Alan Schiller, pno; Ryland Davies, ten. *Ellison*

Primavera Chamber Ensemble. Horseshoe Barn, Cobbarn Farm, Groombridge Lane, Eridge TN3 9LA *tel:* 01892 864069 *also fax.* Paul Manley, artistic dir. 3-8 players in varying combinations.

Prime Brass. 22 Lovell Rd, Cambridge CB4 6BW *tel:* 01223 561744 *email:* prime_brass@yahoo.com. Paul Garner, Tim Judges, tpt; Guy Llewellyn, hn; Alex Hewins, trb; Christopher Lawrence, tb.

Priory Concertante of London. 43 Beech Rd, Branston, Lincoln LN4 1PP *tel:* 01522 791662. Frank Stiles, principal cond. 14-40 players.

Pro Arte Antiqua Praha. *Sonata*

Pro Arte Guitar Trio. Richard Hand, requinto; Tom Dupre, gui; Peter Rueffer, 8-str gui. *NCCP*

* **Pro Cantione Antiqua.** Timothy Penrose, Robin Tyson, Paul Esswood, c-ten; James Griffett, Ian Partridge, Andrew King, Joseph Cornwell, ten; Michael George, Stephen Roberts, David Beavan, Adrian Peacock, bar. Vocal ens. *CDI/POEM*

Prospero Chamber Ensemble. 35 Priory Walk, Tonbridge, Kent TN9 2AL *tel:* 01732 369041 *also fax;* 07767 780563. Jennifer Stinton, fl; Caroline Balding, vn; Judith Busbridge, Susan Knight, va; Alastair Blayden, vc; Alison Nicholls, hp.

Psappha - New Music Specialists from Manchester. 57 Ingleton Rd, Stockport, Cheshire SK3 9NN *tel:* 0161 480 5922 *fax:* 0161 291 8974 *email:* t.williams@psappha.nwnet.co.uk. Tim Williams, artistic dir, perc; Claire O'Neill, fl; Dov Goldberg, cl; Richard Casey, pno; David Routledge, vn; Heather Wallington, va; Jennifer Langridge, vc. Ens of 7-20 players.

Purcell Consort of Voices. The Spinney, 5 Park Lane, Histon, Cambridge CB4 9JJ *tel:* 01223 237317. Grayston Burgess, dir.

Quartet Caravaggio. c/o National Symphony Orchestra, Jumps Rd, Churt, Surrey GU10 2JY *tel:* 01252 792315 *fax:* 01252 795120 *email:* annecollis@aol.com. Perry Montague-Mason, Rita Manning, vn; Kate Musker, va; Justin Pearson, vc.

Quartet DOM. 48 Morningside Park, Edinburgh EH10 5HA *tel:* 0131 447 0284 *also fax.* Kathryn Greeley, Paul Jourdan, vn; Kathryn Jourdan, va; Juliet Welchman, vc.

* **Quatuor Mosaïques.** Str quartet. *Judith Hendershott*

Quatuor Parisii. Thierry Brodard, vn; Jean-Michel Berrette, vn; Dominique Lobet, va; Jean-Philippe Martignoni, vc. *Clarion/Seven Muses*

Quatuor Sine Nomine, Lausanne. *Ingpen*

[Queffélec, Cooper]. Anne Queffélec, Imogen Cooper, pno duo. *Tennant*

Quintaria. Flat 2, 2 Great North Rd, Highgate, London N6 *tel:* 07956 431449. Ian Judson, fl; Huw Clement-Evans, ob; Nicola Baigent, cl; Philip Gibbon, bsn; Tom Ainger, hn.

Quintessence. The Little House, 14 Windhill, Bishops Stortford, Herts CM23 2NG *tel:* 01279 651856. Anna Lethieullier, sop; Carol Leatherby, m-sop; John Terry, David Waters, ten; Alan Lamb, bar; Carol Wells, pno. Victorian and Edwardian drawing room entertainment: opera, operetta and musicals.

Quintessence. 79 Royal Hill, Greenwich, London SE10 8SE *tel:* 020 8692 3795 *fax:* 020 8692 6524 *email:* susiehw@connectfree.co.uk. Susie Hodder-Williams, fl; Victoria Cornet, cl; Rebecca Wood, ob; Alison Bryce, hn; Jo Turner, bsn.

* **QuintEssential Sackbut and Cornett Ensemble.** 10 King's Highway, Plumstead Common, London SE18 2NL *tel:* 020 8855 8584 *also fax; email:* quintessential@gtemail.net. Richard Thomas, dir.

Quintessential Opera. c/o Anness and Partners, Hamilton House, Cobblers Green, Felsted, Great Dunmow, Essex CM6 3LX *tel:* 01371 820382 *fax:* 01371 821100. Antoine Mitchell, dir.

Quintette Moraguès. Wind quintet. *Clarion/Seven Muses*

Quorum. 21 Allendale Close, London SE5 8SG *tel:* 020 7703 7372. Julia Munn, cl, sax; Martin Pring, vn, va; Hugh McDowell, vc; Andrew Spiceley, pno, perc.

The Rachmaninov Trio. 537 Sauchiehall St, Glasgow G3 7PQ *tel:* 0141 248 1611 *fax:* 0141 248 1989 *email:* phillipsilver@allegro.demon.co.uk. Lev Atlas, vn and va; Alexander Volpov, vc; Phillip Silver, pno.

[Ránki, Klukon]. Dezsö Ránki and Edit Klukon, pno duo. *Lubbock*

Raphael Ensemble. James Clark, Catherine Manson, vn; Ralf Ehlers, Louise Williams, va; Andrea Hess, Timothy Gill, vc. String sextet. *Tennant*

Rasumovsky String Quartet. 7 Fraser Gardens, Southbourne, nr Emsworth, Hants PO10 8PY *tel:* 01243 378300 *also fax.* Frances Mason, Marilyn Taylor vn; Christopher Wellington, va; Christina Shillito, vc. *GBZ*

Raw Goods. c/o Sound Affairs, 62 Arran St, Roath, Cardiff CF24 3HT *tel:* 029 2049 7157 *also fax; email:* sound.affairs@tesco.net. Charlie Barber, dir. Contemporary mus and new dance.

* **Red Byrd.** John Potter, ten; Richard Wistreich, bs; and other voices, insts. Early and contemporary mus. *Robert White*

* **Red Priest.** Piers Adams, dir, rcdrs. *Upbeat*

Redbridge Brass Band. Colindale, Station Rd, Sawbridgeworth, Herts CM21 9JY *tel:* 01279 722338; 07973 313913 *email:* alan@redbridgebrass.freeserve.co.uk. Alan Roberts, mgr. Starred in *Brassed Off,* Royal National Theatre 1998.

Regular Music II. 13c Grove Park, London SE5 8LR *tel:* 020 7733 3808 *also fax.* Jeremy Peyton Jones, dir. Amplified chmbr ens. Contemporary mus.

[Reid, Stewart]. 21 Hyacinth Close, Haslingden, Lancs BB4 6JU *tel:* 01706 212753 *also fax; email:* gordon@stewartmusic.freeserve.co.uk. Gavin Reid, tpt; Gordon Stewart, org.

The Rembrandt Piano Trio. Valerie Tryon, pno; Gerard Kantarjian, vn; Coenraad Bloemendal, vc. *Ellison*

Renaissance 2000. c/o Jonathan Freeman-Attwood, Royal Academy of Music, Marylebone Rd, London NW1 5HT *tel:* 020 7873 7351 *fax:* 020 7873 7314 *email:* j.freeman-attwood@ram.ac.uk. Jonathan Freeman-Attwood, tpt; Colm Carey, org.

* **The Renaissance Ensemble.** 49 Dalmeny Ave, London SW16 4RS *tel:* 020 8764 5563 *fax:* 020 8679 8300. Joseph Cornwell, ten; Andrew King, dir and ten; Simon Grant, bs; Monica Huggett, Emilia Benjamin, vns; Catherine Finnis, gamba; David Miller, lute; Alan Wilson, hpd and organ. Renaissance and baroque specialists.

Reservoir. Mikel Toms, dir. Contemporary mus ens, largely late 20th C repertoire. *Haferkorn*

ReSound. 47 Boscombe Rd, Wimbledon, London SW19 3AX *tel:* 020 8542 7610 *also fax; email:* faure@globalnet.co.uk. Anthony Aarons, tpt; Tim Palmer, perc; Andrew Lovett, electronics.

* **The Restoration Academy.** *POEM*

Review-Revue. Nuala Willis, m-sop; Courtney Kenny, pno. Present and old gems from mus shows. *Roxane Houston*

* **The Revolutionary Drawing Room.** 34 Fernwood Ave, London SW16 1RD *tel:* 020 8769 4158 *also fax; email:* EastRevolution@compuserve.com. Adrian Butterfield, Oliver Webber, vns; Rachel Stott, va; Angela East, vc; Judith Evans, db; Rachel Brown, fl; Frank de Bruine, ob; Colin Lawson, cl; Alastair Mitchell, bsn; Roger Montgomery, hn; Geoffrey Govier, pno. Chmbr mus on period insts. *Upbeat*

The Revolutionary String Quartet. 34 Fernwood Ave, London SW16 1RD *tel:* 020 8769 4158 *also fax; email:* EastRevolution@compuserve.com. Adrian Butterfield, Oliver Webber, vns; Rachel Stott, va; Angela East, vc.

Reyjkavik Wind Quintet. *Rostrum*

[Riley, Rubenstein]. 9 St George's Ave, London N7 0HB *tel:* 020 7609 2976 *email:* rubyrich@compuserve.com. Catherine Riley and Robin Rubenstein, pno duo and duet.

[Riley, Tippett]. 53 Tweedy Rd, Bromley, Kent BR1 3NH *tel:* 020 8290 5917. Howard Riley, Keith Tippett, pno duo.

The Rogeri Trio. Yoshiko Endo, pno; Nadia Myerscough, vn; Peter Adams, vc. *Christine Talbot-Cooper*

The Romantic Chamber Group of London. Brick Kiln Cottages, Hollington, Newbury, Berks RG20 9XX *tel:* 01635 254331 *fax:* 01635 253629 *email:* c.medlam@btinternet.com. Paul Barritt, vn; Charles Medlam, vc; James Lisney, pno. *SWA*

The Rondel Ensemble. Tickerage Castle, Pound Lane, Framfield, Uckfield, E Sussex TN22 5RT *tel:* 01825 890348. Melanie Wall, sop; Leonard Paice, Kathleen Moy, fl, picc; Catherine Pluygers, Marcia Ferran, ob, eh; Catherine Morphett, Angela Crispe, cl, bs-cl; Anna Meadows, Barbara Lake, bsn, double-bsn; Lance Baker, hn, tam-tam.

Roquefort Duo. 19 Crossway, Harpenden, Herts AL5 4RA *tel:* 01582 462668 *fax:* 01582 623418. Gerard Le Feuvre, vc; Nigel Clayton, pno.

[Roscoe, Donohoe]. Martin Roscoe, Peter Donohoe, pno. *Hazard*

* **Rose Consort of Viols.** 28 Wentworth Rd, Scarcroft Hill, York YO24 1DG *tel:* 01904 652736 *also fax; fax:* 020 8452 3254 *email:* j.h.bryan@hud.ac.uk. John Bryan, Alison Crum, Sarah Groser, Roy Marks, Peter Wendland, viols.

Rosehill Instruments. The Old House, 64 London End, Beaconsfield, Bucks HP9 2JD *tel:* 01494 671717 *fax:* 01494 676428 *email:* rosehillmi@aol.com. Neville Griffiths, Ken Tinsley, tpt; Pamela Wise, hn; Nigel Barr, trb; Trevor Austin, tb.

* **The Rosewood Ensemble.** The Old Rectory Coach House, High St, Bourton-on-the-Water, Glos GL54 2AP *tel:* 01451 821481 *also fax; email:* jane@lesleyjanerogers.demon.co.uk. Lesley-Jane Rogers, sop; Jan Waterfield, hpd; Melanie Woodcock, baroque vc; plus other insts.

Rossetti Cartledge Duo. Dario Rossetti-Bonell, gui; Nicholas Cartledge, fl. *Chameleon*

Les Rossignols. 111c St Mark's Rd, London W10 6NP *tel:* 020 8969 8707. Ian Judson, fl; Joseph Asghar, gui.

Rothwell Band (Leeds). *Chameleon*

* **Roundelay.** Waye House, Alston Cross, Ashburton, Devon TQ13 7ET *tel:* 01364 652114 *also fax; email:* roundelay@bigfoot.com. Oliver Brookes, early str; Roxana Gundry, voice, lutes, early insts.

Rubio String Quartet. *Manygate*

Ruskin Trio and Ensemble. 26 Common View, Rusthall, Tunbridge Wells, Kent TN4 8RG *tel:* 01892 540576 *also fax; email:* ruskin@radiosite.freeserve.co.uk. Jane Gomm, dir, vn. Mixed chmbr group: strs, wind, pno, gui.

Saba Brown Duo. Barn Hill House, Stamford, Lincolnshire PE9 2AE *tel:* 01780 482432 *fax:* 01780 482433 *email:* geoffrey.saba@hotmail.com. Geoffrey Saba, Jeremy Brown, pno.

Safri Duo. *IMG*

* **St James's Baroque Players.** 200 Broomwood Rd, London SW11 6JY *tel:* 020 7228 6388 *fax:* 020 7738 1706. Ivor Bolton, mus dir; Delia Pye, mgr. Period insts.

St Magnus Trio. 61 Clock House Rd, Beckenham, Kent BR3 4JU *tel:* 020 8650 9990 *email:* john@blakelys.freeserve.co.uk. Neil Mackie, ten; Richard Watkins, hn; John Blakely, pno.

St Petersburg Piano Trio. *Sonata*

St Petersburg String Quartet. *Upbeat*

Sajori Ensemble. 131 Heol-y-deri, Rhiwbina, Cardiff CF4 6UH *tel:* 029 2062 0469 *also fax;* 07768 233369 *email:* w-d@baynet.co.uk. Sara Clethero, m-sop; Richard Wiegold, vc; Andrew Wilson-Dickson, pno.

* **Salomon String Quartet.** 71 Priory Rd, Kew, Surrey TW9 3DH *tel:* 020 8940 7086 *fax:* 020 8332 0879. Simon Standage, Micaela Comberti, vn; Trevor Jones, va; Jennifer Ward Clarke, vc; Francesca McManus, mgr.

San Francisco Saxophone Quartet. *Gilder*

* **San Petronio Players.** 119 Canal Lane, Stanley, Wakefield, W Yorks *tel:* 01924 827337 *fax:* 01484 689408. Duncan Druce, Kenneth Mitchell, vn; Rachel Gray, vc; Keith Elcombe, hpd, org.

[Sanderson, Clayton]. Rosemary Sanderson, va; Nigel Clayton, pno. *NCCP*

* **Sarabande.** 8 Elmslack Lane, Silverdale, Carnforth, Lancs LA5 *tel:* 01524 701623. Ann Bond, hpd; Elizabeth Dodd, va da gamba; Philip Gruar, baroque fl and rcdr. Mostly French baroque repertoire; recitals include baroque dance.

* **Sarband.** Vladimir Ivanoff, artistic dir. Ens specialising in links between European, Islamic and Jewish mus. Early mus to avantgarde. *Pristavec*

Saxology Quartet. 15 Hemmings Court, Maldon, Essex CM9 6UW *tel:* 01621 852844 *fax:* 01245 450192. Jeffery Wilson, ten sax; Denis Hill, alto sax; Fiona Dermit, sop sax; Tracey Bridgeman, bar sax.

Saxpak. Peter Davis, Richard Addison, Peter Ripper, Tim Holmes, Stan Sulzman, Andy Findon, Dave White, sax septet; Ted White, mus dir. *LM*

Saxtet. 4 Elm Park Rd, Winchmore Hill, London N21 2HN *tel:* 020 8350 7139 *also fax*; 07973 692497. Luke Ansley, saxes, cl; Richard Exall, saxes, cl; Jamie Anderson, saxes, cl, perc; Karen Street, saxes, accordion, fl; Andrew Tweed, saxes, cl, bs cl. Saxophone quintet playing mostly original compositions with the inclusion of other insts.

The Scandinavian Flute Quartet. Tine Jensen, fl; Andrea Rebekka Alsted, vn; Uffe Willemoes-Wissing, va; Eugene Hye-Knudsen, vc. *Purkiss*

Scarampella Quartet. c/o Jean Calder Concerts Management, 4 Pottery Court, Church Rd, Dartmouth TQ6 9SN *tel:* 01803 833018. Malcolm Stewart, Martin Richardson, vn; David Greenlees, va; Betsy Taylor, vc.

Schidlof Quartet. 28 Springfield Rd, Stoneygate, Leicester LE2 3BA *tel:* 0116 270 6528 *also fax; email:* schidlof@dircon.co.uk. Ofer Falk, Rafael Todes, vn; Graham Oppenheimer, va; Bridget MacRae, vc.

Schubert Ensemble of London. c/o Ann Senior, 32 Wolverton Gardens, London W6 7DY *tel:* 020 8563 0618 *fax:* 020 8741 5233 *email:* senior.mgt@dial.pipex.com.

[Scott, Chard]. VAMP, Ealing House, 33 Hanger Lane, London W5 3HJ *tel:* 020 8992 1571 *also fax*; 07961 837418. Andy Scott, gui; Verona Chard, sop and narrator.

* **Sequentia.** Benjamin Bagby and others, 12th-13th C vocal and inst mus. *Hazard*

Seraphim Ensemble. c/o Jean Calder Concerts Management, 4 Pottery Court, Church Rd, Dartmouth TQ6 9SN *tel:* 01803 833018. Iain King, vn; David Greenlees, va; Clive Greensmith, vc; Aaron Shorr, pno; and others.

Seraphim Trio. M-sop, vn, hp. *CMG*

Serenata. 20 Bull Stag Green, Hatfield, Herts AL9 5DE *tel:* 01707 267511 *also fax; email:* Serenatamusicforvoiceandguitar@yahoo.com. Neil Simon, ten, gui; Susan Wright, sop; Amanda Cook, gui.

The Serenata of London. Woodhouse Cottage, Marsh, nr Aylesbury, Bucks HP17 8SP *tel:* 01296 614647 *fax:* 01296 614648. Anthea Cox. Quintets to small chmbr orch.

* **La Serenissima.** 23 Burbage Rd, London SE24 9HJ *tel:* 020 7737 4484 *fax:* 020 7326 0712 *email:* 10061.1412@compuserve.com. Adrian Chandler, dir and vn. Baroque orch specialising in the mus of Vivaldi and Venice contemporaries.

Sheherazade. VAMP, Ealing House, 33 Hanger Lane, London W5 3HJ *tel:* 020 8992 1571 *also fax;* 07961 837418. Denise Dance, fl; Verona Chard, sop; Fiona Clifton Welker, hp.

Sheridan Brass Ensemble. 13 Summerhouse Rd, London N16 0NA *tel:* 020 7249 3233; 01372 745584. Ben Lees, Richard Hammond, Nick Baker, Matthew Booth, tpts; Clare Lintott, hn; Tony Boorer, Tony Neal, Tracy Holloway, Tony Leggett, trbs; Graham Sibley, tb. *Chameleon*

Sheridan Duo. Stonewalls, 1 Malt Lane, Syresham, Northants NN13 5YE *tel:* 01280 850102 *fax:* 01280 824408. Peter Sheridan, fl, picc, alto fl; Lisa Maree Amos, fl, picc, alto fl.

Shika. 27 Heber Rd, London NW2 6AB *tel:* 020 8452 9234 *also fax*. Philip Booth, pno, dir; Takako Selby-Okamoto, sop; plus various insts.

Shiraz. 139 Churchill Rd, London NW2 5EH *tel:* 020 8459 6462. Nia Harries, vc; Fenella Barton, vn; Pamela Lidiard, pno.

Shiva Nova. Peregrine, Grange Rd, St Michaels, Tenterden, Kent TN30 6TJ *tel:* 01580 764258; 020 8354 0619 (admin) *also fax; fax:* 01580 763500 *email:* shivanova@aol.com. Priti Paintal, artistic dir. Euro-asian mus group: Indian, African Jazz, western classical insts, mus theatre.

Shostakovich Quartet. *Sonata*

Silk and Steel. 39 Water View Park, Leigh, Lancs WN7 4JP *tel:* 01942 680941 *also fax;* 07973 787663. John Powell, euph; Susie Hodder-Williams, fl; Stuart Death, pno.

The Silver Duo. 4 May Terrace, Glasgow G42 9XF *tel:* 0141 569 6319 *email:* Phillip_Silver@umit.maine.edu. Phillip Silver, pno; Noreen Silver, vc.

* **The Simon Mayor Mandolin Quartet.** Simon Mayor, mandolin, mandola, mandocello; Gerald Garcia, gui; Hilary James, vocals, mandobass; Richard Collins, mandola, mandolin, gui, vocals. *Jean Judge*

Singcircle. 57 White Horse Rd, London E1 0ND *tel:* 020 7790 5883 *fax:* 020 7265 9170 *email:* gregory-rose@tisl.co.uk. Gregory Rose, mus dir. Contemporary vocal ens.

Singers Two. 14 The Crescent, S Harrow, Middx HA2 0PJ *tel:* 020 8864 1802 *also fax.* Lynne Hirst, sop; Kenneth Fraser Annand, bar; Timothy Barratt, acc.

Singers Unlimited. Jennifer Partridge, mus dir; Beryl Korman, sop; Julia Meadows, m-sop. Vocal ens with pno. *Upbeat*

Singphoniker. Alfons Brandl, Christof Rösel, Ludwig Thomas, Berno Scharpf, Gunnar Mühling, Christian Schmidt. *Ellison*

* **Sirinu.** Sara Stowe, sop, keyboards; Henry Stobart, rcdrs, shawm, bagpipes; Jon Banks, hp, dulcimer, sackbut; Matthew Spring, lutes, vihuela, guis, hurdy-gurdy. Early and world mus. *Seaview*

* **The Sixteen.** First Floor, Enslow House, Station Rd, Enslow, Kidlington, Oxon OX5 3AX *tel:* 01869 331544 *fax:* 01869 331011 *email:* info@thesixteen.org.uk. Harry Christophers, cond; Gijs Elsen, gen mgr; Alison Stillman, admin; Peter Burrows, development mgr. Choral ens performing also with period orch, The Symphony of Harmony and Invention.

Škampa Quartet. *Barber*

Slowind. Cl, fl, hn. *Pristavec*

[Smietana, Gibb]. Krzysztof Smietana, vn; James Gibb, pno. *Purkiss*

The Smith Quartet. 6 Elfindale Rd, London SE24 9NW *tel:* 020 7564 5676 *also fax; email:* njm@musicon.demon.co.uk. Nick Morrison, mgr; Ian Humphries, vn; Charles Mutter, vn; Nic Pendlebury, va; Philip Sheppard, vc.

[Smith, Rowland-Jones]. 8 Heath Close, London NW11 7DX *tel:* 020 8458 4827 *email:* srj@easynet.co.uk. Maureen Smith, vn; Simon Rowland-Jones, va.

Solarek Piano Trio. 30 Chandos Rd, London NW2 4LU *tel:* 020 8208 0277 *also fax; email:* solarek@aol.com. Marina Solarek, vn; Kim Mackrell, vc; Angela Zanders, pno.

Solaris String Quartet. *Margaret Murphy*

The Soloists' Ensemble. *Denny Lyster*

The Songmakers' Almanac. 25 Fournier St, Spitalfields, London E1 6QE *tel:* 020 7247 7219 *fax:* 020 7247 6094. Graham Johnson, dir; Carolyn Humphreys, admin.

* **Sonnerie.** 71 Priory Rd, Kew, Richmond, Surrey TW9 3DH *tel:* 020 8940 7086 *fax:* 020 8332 0879. Monica Huggett, mus dir, vn; Francesca McManus, mgr. 3-15 members. *Hazard*

Sorrel String Quartet. *Christa Phelps*

Sounds for Silents. John Lenehan, mus dir, pno. Mus for classic silent films. *Upbeat*

Sounds Positive. 28 Cavendish Ave, London N3 3QN *tel:* 020 8349 2317 *fax:* 020 8346 8257. David Sutton-Anderson, cond; Simon Desorgher, fl; Linda Merrick, cl; Edwin Roxburgh, ob; Anthony Aarons, tpt; Sally Mays, sax; Steve Cottrel, trb; Alan Tomlinson, Avril Anderson, co-ord.

Southern Concert Brass. 45 Garibaldi Rd, Redhill, Surrey RH1 6PB *tel:* 01737 763708; 07976 402178. Robin Woollams, Ken Bache, tpt; Graham Ivory, hn and dir; Alison Knight, trb; Robin Tweddle, tb.

Spectrum. 8 Alma Square, London NW8 9QD *tel:* 020 7286 3944 *fax:* 020 7289 9081 *email:* guy.protheroe@btinternet.com. Guy Protheroe, Ann Manly, dirs. Contemporary mus ens.

[Spencer, Hollingworth]. Kirstin Spencer, vc; Leslie Hollingworth, pno. *Chameleon*

[Spratt, Holden]. 14a Mount Villas, London SE27 0NU *tel:* 020 8766 6557 *fax:* 020 7252 5279 *email:* kirstenspratt@compuserve.com. Kirsten Spratt, fl; Ruth Holden, hp.

* **[Staff, Egarr].** David Staff, tpt, cornetto; Richard Egarr, org, hpd. *POEM*

Stamic Quartet of Prague. Str quartet. *Gilder*

[Stanzeleit, Jacobson]. 217a Milkwood Rd, London SE24 0JE *tel:* 020 7738 5356 *also fax.* Susanne Stanzeleit, vn; Julian Jacobson, pno.

Status Cymbal. Paul Costin, Gill Austin, Paul Appleyard, Diane Porteous. Str quartet. *Chameleon*

[Steele, Sherbourne]. 1 St Anne's Rd, Caversham, Reading RG4 7PA *tel:* 0118 947 7170 *also fax; email:* janet@metalworks.org. Jan Steele, sax, fl, cl; Janet Sherbourne, pno, vocals. Contemporary mus and jazz duo.

[Stenstadvold, Blewett]. Erik Stenstadvold, gui; Brenda Blewett, f-pno. *Ellison*

Sterling Quartet. 7 Fernleigh Rd, Winchmore Hill, London N21 3AN *tel:* 020 8886 5290; 01372 273358 *fax:* 01372 278369. Megan Pound, Rebecca Jones, vn; Alistair Scahill, va; Brian Mullan, vc.

Steve Martland Band. Steve Martland, cond. Saxes, guis, keyboards, br, drums. *Hazard*

Steve Reich and Musicians. *Allied*

[Stigmer, Lenehan]. Jan Stigmer, vn; John Lenehan, pno. *NCCP*

Stockhausen Group. *Allied*

STORM. Beverley Davison, artistic dir, vn; Lucy Hare, db, bs gui; plus perc and keyboard. *Jean Judge*

String Sound. 15 Hawkhurst Way, West Wickham, Kent BR4 9PE *tel:* 020 8777 6414. Clive Lander, vn; Lesley Shrigley Jones, vc; Max Brittain, gui; Roy Chilton, db.

Stringendo. Str quartet. *Annon*

Stringfactory. 21 Hamlet Rd, Upper Norwood, London SE19 2AD *tel:* 020 8771 7164 *also fax.* Nic Pendlebury, Colin Riley, artistic dirs; 2-16 player str ens.

Stringtalk. 29 Chadwick Rd, Peckham, London SE15 4RA *tel:* 020 7639 1203 *also fax; email:* hooleycole@compuserve.com. Ann Hooley, Elizabeth Turnbull.

Sun Music. 51b Dartmouth Rd, London NW2 4EP *tel:* 020 8208 1541 *also fax.* Tony Gray, admin. Ens promoting Australian mus and musicians in the UK.

Sweet and Low. 278 Monega Rd, London E12 6TS *tel:* 020 8552 7149 *also fax;* 07889 988312. Jessica Grant, m-sop; Carol Ann Leatherby, m-con; David Mackie, pno.

The Swingle Singers. *HP*

Sylfanome. 76 Lower Oldfield Park, Bath, Somerset BA2 3HP *tel:* 01225 313531. Richard Carder, dir. Flexible w/wind group of fls and cls, including alto and bass.

* **The Symphony of Harmony and Invention.** First Floor, Enslow House, Station Rd, Enslow, Kidlington, Oxon OX5 3AX *tel:* 01869 331544 *fax:* 01869 331011 *email:* info@the sixteen.org.uk. Harry Christophers, cond. Period orch.

Synergy. 44 Howard Rd, London E17 4SJ *tel:* 020 8923 0265 *also fax; email:* micaela@synergyvocals.com. Micaela Haslam, mus dir.

Syrinx Ensemble. 1 Wickham Hall Cottages, Langford Rd, Wickham Bishops, Essex CM8 3JQ *tel:* 01621 892229 *email:* syrinxmusic @talk21.com. Stephen Rumsey, mus dir. Mixed ens from str, wind, perc, keyboard, voice.

Syrinx Wind Quintet. 411 Manhattan Building, Bow Quarter, Fairfield Rd, Bow, London E3 2UQ *tel:* 020 8981 7413 *also fax; email:* music@paulmharris.demon.co.uk. Tracey Stewart, fl; Jane Finch, ob; David Coyle, cl; Paul Harris, bsn; Stephen Flower, hn.

Szabó Quartet. Attila Szabó, Zarko Mickovic, vn; Margit Szabó, va; Gertraud Hajdany, vc. *Ellison*

Takacs String Quartet. *Christa Phelps*

Take 2. The Old Station, Kimberley, Wymondham, Norfolk NR18 9HB *tel:* 01953 850711. Sax and pno.

Take Two. c/o Lyric Production, 41 Arkwright Rd, Sanderstead, Surrey CR2 0LP *tel:* 020 8657 5840 *also fax.* Classical and elec gui, mandolin, balalaiki, bazouki, etc.

* **The Tallis Scholars.** Peter Phillips, dir; Sibylle Mager, admin. *Hazard*

Tamarisk. Anthony Abbott, admin; Janet Howd, sop; Dona Lee Croft, vn; Martin Pacey, Alvin Moisey, pno. *Anthony Abbott*

Tambourin. Fiona Masters, fl; Peter Howe, gui. *Purkiss*

[Tan, Brautigam]. Melvyn Tan, Ronald Brautigam, pno, f-pno. *Barber*

Tapestry. 113 High Rd, Wilmington, Dartford, Kent DA2 7BW *tel:* 01322 224085 *fax:* 01322 409269 *email:* tapestry@cwcom.net. Sandra Lissenden, sop; Andrew Sparling, cl; Tony Gray, pno.

* **Tarleton's Jig.** 20 New Rd, Ham Common, Richmond-upon-Thames, Surrey TW10 7HY *tel:* 020 8940 9006 *also fax.* James Bisgood, dir, strs, vocals, perc, hurdy-gurdy; Jeremy West, cornett, bagpipes; Keith Thompson, Keith McGowan, Nick Perry, Martin Pope, William Lyons, wind; Lewis Gibson, vn. Renaissance wind band. Street mus and ballads. *Music Management*

Tarrega Trio. 32 South Grove, Sale, Cheshire M33 3AU *tel:* 0161 969 5772. Margaret Duffy, vn; Valerie Hayward, vc; Wendy Jackson, gui. Classical and light mus for all occasions.

Tate Music Group of London. 101 Queens Park Ave, Bournemouth, Dorset BH8 9LJ *tel:* 01202 394955 *also fax; email:* rstudt@cwcom.net. Richard Studt, dir and vn.

* **Taverner Consort, Choir and Players.** Ibex House, 42-46 Minories, London EC3N 1DY *tel:* 020 7481 2103 *fax:* 020 7481 2865. Andrew

Parrott, artistic dir; Malcolm Bruno, associate dir; Victoria Newbert, admin. Medieval, renaissance and baroque insts with voices.

Tchaikovsky Quartet. *Sonata*

* **Telemann Players of London.** Redwings, Linden Chase, Uckfield, E Sussex TN22 1EE *tel:* 01825 760046 *also fax; email:* turbettl@aol.com. Linda Brand, rcdr, ob; Philip Turbett, baroque bsn; Helena Brown, hpd.

Tempo 2000. Garden Flat, 89 Chippenham Rd, London, W9 2AB *tel:* 020 7266 1895 *also fax; email:* T2000JFK@aol.com. Julian Knight, dir. Mixed ens of 5-15 players.

Temps Contre Temps. c/o Diana Hirst Arts Administration and PR, 55 Marmora Rd, London SE22 0RY *tel:* 020 8299 1914 *also fax; email:* Hirstpr@aol.com. Dominique Hellsten, sop; David Roblou, hpd, f-pno and pno. Semi-staged 18th, 19th and 20th C vocal and keyboard mus.

Terroni Piano Trio. Raphael Terroni, pno; John Trussler, vn; Fiona Murphy, vc. *Grant Rogers*

Tetra Guitar Quartet. Stephen Goss, Peter Howe, Richard Storry, Graham Roberts, gui. *Purkiss/Chameleon*

Thames Fanfare Brass. 26 Cartmel Rd, Bexleyheath, Kent DA7 5EA *tel:* 01322 430779 *fax:* 01322 448416 *email:* rbilham@wallacebrass.u-net.com. Br group, dixie band, herald tpts.

Three Down One Across. 105 Priory Park Rd, London NW6 7UY *tel:* 020 7372 7311 *fax:* 020 8537 9665 *email:* sarafreedman@freeuk.com. Sara Freedman, mus dir. W/wind quartet; fl, ob, cl and bsn and doubling insts. Specialise in lecture recitals with mus ranging from baroque to 20th C, including Irish and jazz.

Three Reeds. The Old Meeting House, St James, Shaftesbury, Dorset SP7 8HF *tel:* 01747 854999. Gillian Carter, Elisabeth Jacoby, Jennifer Porcas; concerts include ob, ob d'amore, eh, bs ob, bsn.

Thurston Clarinet Quartet. Alex Allen, John Bradbury, Douglas Mitchell, Paul Richards, cl. *KDM*

Tirami Su. 7 Queensdown Rd, London E5 8NN *tel:* 020 8985 2802 *also fax; email:* 106325.1610@compuserve.com. Erin Headley, dir; Milos Valent, Peter Spissky, vn; Keren Bruce, Juraj Kovak, va da gamba; Erin Headley, va da gamba, lirone; Laurie Reviol, sop; Harry van der Kamp, bs. 17th C mus for strs and voices, including Monteverdi, Schütz and Purcell.

* **Tirata.** 4 Heathleigh Cottages, Maidstone Rd, Horsmonden, Kent TN12 8JL *tel:* 01892 723370 *also fax; email:* 101767.2724@compuserve.com. Peter Bowman, Kathryn Bennetts, rcdrs; Laurie Ann MacLeod, vc, va da gamba; Yeo Yat-Soon, hpd.

Tokyo String Quartet. Mikhail Kopelman, Kikuei Ikeda, vn; Kazuhide Isomura, va; Clive Greensmith, vc. *Intermusica*

Tonus Peregrinus. The Welcome Stranger, High St, Flimwell, E Sussex TN5 7PB *tel:* 07771 692024 *fax:* 01580 879369 *email:* tonusperegrinus@yahoo.com. Joanna Forbes, Rebecca Parkyns, sop; Kathryn Oswald, alto; Alexander L'Estrange, c-ten; Benjamin Rayfield, Alexander Hickey, ten; Antony Pitts, bar and dir; Francis Brett, bs. Vocal and inst ens.

Touchwood. Piano quartet. Fiona McCapra, vn; Judith Busbridge, va; Andrew Bradbury, vc; Andrew West, pno. *NCCP*

Tradewinds Clarinet Quartet. 4 Vallentin Rd, Walthamstow, London E17 3JH *tel:* 020 8520 8682 *also fax;* 07976 350062; 01636 830881 *email:* clare@wassermann.demon.co.uk. Sarah Lewington, Clare Wassermann, James Wolfe, Gary Holdsworth, cl; plus saxes. Classical and light jazz. Weddings, parties, exhibitions.

Trafalgar Brass. 11 Haslemere Close, Wallington, Surrey SM6 8LT *tel:* 020 8680 8645. Dave McCallum, Martyn Lewington, tpt; Alan Jones, hn; Danny Scott, trb; Kevin Morgan, tb. *Charlton*

Triangulus. 15 Wilton Place, London SW1X 8RL *tel:* 020 7235 2729 *fax:* 020 7823 2209. Pno trio. Roland Roberts, vn; Alison Moncrieff Kelly, vc; Lyn Garland, pno.

* **Trio Basiliensis.** 58 Redhill Drive, Brighton BN1 5FL *tel:* 01273 552548 *fax:* 01273 389572 *email:* simmonds.mezger@cwcom.net. Marianne Mezger, rcdr, baroque musette de cour and fr flageolet; Ekkehard Weber, va da gamba, Paul Simmonds, hpd. 16th-18th C chmbr mus.

Trio Cantabile. c/o Catherine Wilmers, The Brew House, Radwell, Baldock, Herts SG7 5ES *tel:* 01462 730490 *also fax; email:* ccwilmers@bigfoot.com. Irene Cooper, sop; Catherine Wilmers, vc; Nicholas Durcan, pno.

Trio Fibonacci. 65 Craigerne Rd, London SE3 8SN *tel:* 020 8853 0353 *email:* trio_fibonacci@yahoo.com. Julie-Anne Derome, vn; Gabriel Prynn, vc; André Ristic, pno. Pno trio specialising in contemporary mus.

Trio Gemelli. c/o Diana Lashmore, 11 Lefroy Rd, London W12 9LF *tel:* 020 8743 0457 *also fax.* John Bradbury, cl; Adrian Bradbury, vc; Emily Segal, pno.

* **Trio Holloway, ter Linden, Mortensen.** The Old Manse, Leafield, Witney, Oxon OX8 5NN *tel:* 01993 878200 *fax:* 01993 878375 *email:* oldmanse@compuserve.com. John Holloway, vn; Jaap ter Linden, va da gamba; Lars Ulrik Mortensen, hpd.

Trio Krosta. Mere Cottage, Ashmansworth, nr Newbury, Berks RG20 9SJ *tel:* 01635 253031. Sylvia Bowden, pno; Celia Redgate, fl; Christopher Redgate, ob.

Trio Serenata. 21 Lynn Drive, Eaglesham, Glasgow G76 0JJ *tel:* 01355 302869. Alison Donaldson, sop; George Macilwham, fl; David Murray, pno. Victorian, Viennese, French, Burns and Scottish programmes.

Trio Wanderer. Vincent Coq, pno; Jean-Marc Phillips, vn; Raphael Pidoux, vc. *Hazard*

Trio Zingara. c/o 102 Totteridge Lane, London N20 8JH *tel:* 020 8445 4485 *also fax.* Felix Schmidt, vc; Annette Cole, pno.

Triple Echo. 17 Keele Rd, Newcastle-under-Lyme, Staffs ST5 2JT *tel:* 01782 618156. Jane Ginsborg, sop; Philip Edwards, cl; George Nicholson, pno.

Triptych. c/o Little Corner, Cross Oak Rd, Berkhamsted, Herts HP4 3NA *tel:* 01442 863263. Christopher Hughes, pno; Ruth Scott, ob; Sarah Burnett, bsn.

Triptych Piano Trio. c/o 27 London Rd, Tonbridge, Kent TN10 3AB *tel:* 01732 353944 *fax:* 01732 362356. Ruth Herbert, pno; Oliver Lewis, vn; Jonathan Few, vc. Broad repertoire, accessible commissions.

Les Trois. 14a Mount Villas, London SE27 0NU *tel:* 020 8766 6557 *fax:* 020 7225 5279 *email:* kirstenspratt@compuserve.com. Kirsten Spratt, fl; Rachel Bolt, va; Ruth Holden, hp.

* **Trompette.** The Old Station, Kimberley, Wymondham, Norfolk NR18 9HB *tel:* 01953 850711. 2 costumed entertainers of medieval, renaissance and baroque mus.

* **The Troubadours.** Tudor Lodge, Pymoor Lane, Pymoor, nr Ely, Cambs CB6 2EE *tel:* 01353 698084 *email:* ancestral@cambs.net. Costumed demonstrations and concerts with medieval and renaissance w/winds, strs, br, perc, bagpipe duo, hurdy-gurdies.

Tuba Magna. 95 Parklands Ave, Leamington Spa CV32 7BP *tel:* 01926 451550 *email:* tuba-magna@classical-artists.com. Andrew Stone-Fewings, tpt; Colin Druce, org.

Tubalaté. 15 Muirfield Close, Wilmslow, Cheshire SK9 2QT *tel:* 01625 532932 *also fax*; 07710 311771. John Powell, Paul Walton, euph; Ian Anstee, Ryan Breen, tb.

* **[Tubb, Fiels].** Evelyn Tubb, sop; Michael Fiels, lute. *POEM*

Two Gentlemen and Verona. VAMP, Ealing House, 33 Hanger Lane, London W5 3HJ *tel:* 020 8992 1571 *also fax*; 07961 837418. Sop, ten, bs and pno. Opera, light opera, songs from the shows.

Two's Company. 25 The Village, Powick, Worcester, Worcs WR2 4QR *tel:* 01905 831817 *also fax; email:* two's.company@virgin.net. Wendy Nieper, m-sop; Stephen Watkins, pno. Classical/contemporary recitals and educ w/shops.

Umea Chamber Orchestra of Sweden. *NCCP*

Uroboros Ensemble. 13 Nevil Rd, Bishopston, Bristol BS7 9EG *tel:* 0117 924 7537 *also fax; email:* gp.ck@virgin.net. Wind, str, hp, pno and perc ens. *Camerata*

Vale Wind Quintet. 50 Parc-y-Coed, Creigiau, Cardiff CF15 9LY *tel:* 029 2089 2388 *also fax.* Christopher Vale, bsn; Jonathan Burgess, fl; Celia Craig, ob; John Cooper, cl; Angus West, hn.

Vallis-Davies Music for TV. PO Box 2288, Glastonbury BA6 9YJ *tel:* 020 8943 5329 *also fax; email:* formedia@vallis-davies.freeserve.co.uk. Nicholas and Sian Vallis Davies, fl and ob.

[Van Spaendonck, Queyras, Tharaud]. Ronald Van Spaendonck, cl; Jean-Guihen Queyras, vc; Alexandre Tharaud, pno. *LM*

Vanbrugh String Quartet. Gregory Ellis, Elizabeth Charleson, vn; Simon Aspell, va; Christopher Marwood, vc. *Christa Phelps*

Vasari Singers. *Ellison*

Vellinger String Quartet. Stephanie Gonley, Harvey de Souza, vn; Tim Boulton, va; Sally Pendlebury, vc. *Tennant*

Vermeer String Quartet. *Allied*

Vernicelli Cello Quartet. Justin Pearson, Adrian Bradbury, Tony Hinnegan, Penny Bradshaw. *Sympathetic*

Verona Jazz. VAMP, Ealing House, 33 Hanger Lane, London W5 3HJ *tel:* 020 8992 1571 *also fax*; 07961 837418. Voice and insts.

Victoriana. 278 Monega Rd, London E12 6TS *tel:* 020 8552 7149 *also fax*; 020 8559 1696; 07889 988312. Carol Ann Leatherby, dir: Victorian mus entertainment in costume.

The Victorians. *Mostylea*

Vienna Brahms Trio. Yuri Smirnov, pno; Boris Kuschnir, vn; Orfeo Mandozzi, vc. *Anglo-Swiss*

Vivaldi Concertante. 35 Laurel Ave, Potters Bar, Herts EN6 2AB *tel:* 01707 650735 *also fax;* 01707 643366. Joseph Pilbery, mus dir. Str ens with hpd and wind.

Voces String Quartet. Bujor Prelipcean, Anton Diaconu, vn; Constantin Stanciu, va; Dan Prelipcean, vc. *Michael Harrold*

Vogler Quartet. *Clarion/Seven Muses*

* **The Wallace Collection.** 26 Cartmel Rd, Bexleyheath, Kent DA7 5EA *tel:* 01322 430779 *fax:* 01322 448416 *email:* rbilham@wallacebrass.u-net.com. Roy Bilham, gen mgr. Br ens. *Denny Lyster*

Weingarten Ensemble. 13 Ravenscroft Ave, London NW11 0SA *tel:* 020 8458 0980 *also fax; email:* jmduk@hotmail.com. Noa Lachman, concert mgr; David Kenedy, vc; Jane Finch, ob; William Hancox, pno; guest artists.

[Weinmeister, Dimitrova]. Hanna Weinmeister, vn; Lora Dimitrova, pno. *Annon*

* **[West, Roberts].** Jeremy West, cornetto; Timothy Roberts, org, hpd. *POEM*

Westbourne Concordia. Forge House, River St, Westbourne, nr Emsworth, Hants PO10 8TG *tel:* 01243 375841 *also fax.* Ursula Snow, artistic dir. Str trio.

Westminster Glee Singers. Male voices from London Cathedrals. *Sympathetic*

Westminster Piano Trio. c/o Merlin Cottage, 13a Merlin Haven, Wotton under Edge, Glos GL12 7BA *tel:* 01453 521091. Justine Tomlinson.

Wharfdale Wind Quintet. P Drummond, fl; R Theobald, ob; Richard Griffiths, cl; Lynne Bottomley, hn; F Theobald, bsn *Mostylea*

Whistlebinkies. G1, 13 Lawrence St, Glasgow G11 5HH *tel:* 0141 334 8580. Eddie McGuire. Traditional Scottish mus.

Wihan Quartet or Prague. c/o Pamela Majaro, 52d Maresfield Gardens, London NW3 5RX *tel:* 020 7435 8479 *fax:* 020 7431 2737 *email:* majaro@clara.net

[Williams, Goss]. Jenevora Williams, sop; Stephen Goss, gui. *Chameleon*

Wind and Company. Bell House, Widford, Ware, Herts SG12 8SH *tel:* 01279 842632. Graham Knight, dir; Judith Knight, co-dir. Wind octet and other combinations.

Wind Soloists of The Chamber Orchestra of Europe. *Lubbock*

Winds of the Southern Cross II. Paul Dean, cl; Leesa Dean, bsn; Peter Luff, hn; Kevin Power, pno; Margaret Schindler, sop; Duncan Tolmie, ob. *Ellison*

* **The Windsor Box & Fir Co.** 64 Frances Rd, Windsor, Berks SL4 3AJ *tel:* 01753 831064 *also fax.* Jenny Thomas, fl; Michael Sanderson, voice and violin; Ian Gammie, bs viol and gui; Katharine May, hpd and square pno.

Wolfgang Bauer Consort. Tpt, vns, va, basso continuo. *Pristavec*

The Wood Sisters. Ob, vn and vc. *NBM*

* **Wren Baroque Orchestra.** Wren Music, 8 Park Lane, Selsey, Chichester, W Sussex PO20 0HD *tel:* 01243 604281 *fax:* 01243 604387 *email:* m.elliott@chihe.ac.uk. Martin Elliott, dir; Susan Carpenter-Jacobs, Julia Bishop, leaders.

* **Wren Baroque Soloists.** Wren Music, 8 Park Lane, Selsey, Chichester, W Sussex PO20 0HD *tel:* 01243 604281 *fax:* 01243 604387 *email:* m.elliott@chihe.ac.uk. Lesley-Jane Rogers, Nicola Jenkin, sop; Frances Jellard, alto; Simon Davies, ten; Martin Elliott, bs; Melanie Woodcock, baroque vc; Jan Waterfield, hpd, org, virginals.

* **Wren Consort.** Wren Music, 8 Park Lane, Selsey, Chichester, W Sussex PO20 0HD *tel:* 01243 604281 *fax:* 01243 604387 *email:* m.elliott@chihe.ac.uk. Alison Pearce, sop; Martin Elliott, bs-bar; Steven Keogh, Paul Thomas, tpt; Andrew Lumsden, org, hpd; Christopher Ross, pno.

* **Wren Singers of London.** Wren Music, 8 Park Lane, Selsey, Chichester, W Sussex PO20 0HD *tel:* 01243 604281 *fax:* 01243 604387 *email:* m.elliott@chihe.ac.uk. Martin Elliott, artistic dir.

Yggdrasil Quartet. Fredrik Paulsson, Per Öman, vn; Robert Westlund, va; Per Nyström, vc. *Clarion/Seven Muses*

* **The York Waits.** c/o PR Music Management, 5 Parramatta St, Rawtenstall, Rossendale, Lancs BB4 6AF *tel:* c/o 01706 230084 *email:* annsmith@supp.freeserve.co.uk. James Merryweather, Tim Bayley, Anthony Barton, William Marshall, Ian and Roger Richardson, shawms, cornetts, sackbuts, curtals, rcdrs, bagpipes, hurdy-gurdies, etc.

* **Yorkshire Baroque Soloists.** 11 Bootham Terrace, York YO30 7DH *tel:* 01904 652799 *fax:* 01904 338349 *email:* ps22@york.ac.uk. Peter Seymour, dir. Voices, str, wind, keyboard.

Yorkshire Classic Brass. 32 Heaton Grove, Heaton, Bradford BD9 4DZ *tel:* 01274 487078 *also fax.* Br sextet with perc.

Ysaye String Quartet. *Christa Phelps*

Zagreb Guitar Trio. Darko Petrinjak, István Römer, Goran Listeš. *GBZ*

The Zagreb Quartet. Str quartet. *ECAM*

Zehetmair Quartet. *Lubbock*

Zephyr. *IMG*

[Zolinsky, Le Page, Sheppard]. Andrew Zolinsky, pno; David Le Page, vn; Phillip Sheppard, vc. *Sympathetic*

The Zurich String Trio. Boris Livschitz, vn; Zvi Livschitz, va; Pi-Chin Chien, vc. *Pristavec/Ellison*

Words and Music

A Breath of Fresh Air. Station View, St Mary's St, Penistone, Sheffield S36 6AD *tel:* 01226 767759. Catherine Baker, Mark Pollard, Alan Asquith, bsns; Jeremy Fisher, pno; Patrick Moody, narrator.

* **Airs & Graces.** 33 Lancaster Rd, London N4 4PJ *tel:* 020 7281 6949 *fax:* 020 7272 8854 *email:* norburnc@dircon.co.uk. Clare Norburn, sop; Steven Devine, hpd, f-pno. Patience Tomlinson, actress; David Timson, actor.

All Things English. Blackthorn Lodge, The Common, Happisburgh, Norfolk NR12 0RT *tel:* 01692 583002. Jack Barratt, ten, actor, insts; Marjorie Barratt, pno, actress, sop. Celebration of English life.

An Evening with Queen Victoria. Prunella Scales; Ian Partridge, ten; Richard Burnett, pno. *Clarion/Seven Muses*

As Time Goes By. Smallwood Productions, Bramleys, Tarrant Keyneston DT11 9JE *tel:* 07974 191336. A celebration of Britain.

Ball and Chain. 3 St Mark's Close, Hitchin, Herts SG5 1US *tel:* 01462 455835 *fax:* 01462 458544 *email:* elmitt@btinternet.com. Bob Wilkins, singer/story teller; Kate Elmitt, pno. Wacky, adult, irreverent, sophisticated cabaret.

Belle and Two Beaux. 41 Newlands Close, Walton on Thames, Surrey KT12 4PW *tel:* 01932 242805 *also fax.* Janet Shell, m-sop; Mark Oldfield, bar; John Flinders, pno. An evening in the company of Victoria and Albert.

The Bruce/Lyttelton Duo. Walshaw, Hebden Bridge, W Yorks HX7 7AX *tel:* c/o 020 7731 3782 *fax:* 020 8948 5428. Poetry and pno solos.

[Garcia, Sussman]. Pilar Garcia, narrator; David Sussman, gui. *NCCP*

The Gentle Art. 41 Newlands Close, Walton on Thames, Surrey KT12 4PW *tel:* 01932 242805 *also fax.* Janet Shell, m-sop; Christopher Goldsack, bar; John Flinders, pno. A portrait of Henry J Wood, founder of the Proms, cond and acc. Also other song recital programmes.

The Georgian Music Room. 33 Hartswood Rd, London W12 9NE *tel:* 020 8749 3365 *fax:* 020 8749 1201 *email:* celia.harper@dial.pipex.com. Neil Jenkins, ten; Rachel Beckett, baroque fl, rcdr; Celia Harper, dir, hpd. Concerts in period costume with contemporary readings.

Geraldine McEwan's Jane Austen. Geraldine McEwan; Danielle Perrett, hp. *Clarion/Seven Muses*

Jane Austen and Colette. Maggie Cole, pno with sop and speaker. *Robert White*

Jill Balcon and the Rasumovsky String Quartet. 7 Fraser Gardens, Southbourne, nr Emsworth, Hants PO10 8PY *tel:* 01243 378300. Jill Balcon, speaker; Frances Mason, Marilyn Taylor, vn; Christopher Wellington, va; Christina Shillito, vc. Two programmes, 'The Sunlight on the Garden' and 'Know'st thou the land where lemon trees bloom'. *GBZ*

Lyricanta. 20 Oakhill Drive, Welwyn, Herts AL6 9NW *tel:* 01438 715740 *also fax.* Karen Van Poznak, Nigel Springthorpe, artistic dirs.

The Menagerie. *tel:* c/o 020 8773 1223. Concert entertainment with an animal theme. Nicholas Daniel, ob; Julius Drake, pno; invited guest. *Upbeat*

Musical Miscellany. Beechwood House, High Bickington, Umberleigh, N Devon EX37 9BQ *tel:* 01769 560348. Jenny Goldsmith, actress; Stella Searson, pno, hpd. Dramatised costumed entertainment of words and mus.

* **Odyssey.** Gwespyr, 6 Hallcroft Lane, Copmanthorpe, York YO23 3UQ *tel:* 01904 701459; 01502 724020. Yvonne Robert, sop; Maurice Ridge, pno; Graham Roberts, reader.

Opus Anglicanum. 92 St Thomas St, Wells, Somerset BA5 2UZ *tel:* 01749 677903 *fax:* 01749 675131. Stephen Tilton, c-ten; William Lee, ten; Nicholas Todd, ten; Roland Robertson, bar; John Rowlands-Pritchard, bs; John Touhey, narrator.

Philip Fowke. Talks at the pno. *NBM*

Playing - with Words. Katharina Wolpe and Corin Redgrave, poetry and pno. *Michael Brewer*

Rags to Riches. c/o Matthew Brailsford, 2a Harefield Rd, London SE4 1LR *tel:* 020 8691 7385 *fax:* 020 8692 1066. Helen Crayford, pno. 6 shows tracing the development of ragtime and jazz.

Tête à Tête. Flat 21, 5 Elm Park Gardens, London SW10 9QQ *tel:* 020 7352 8271. Ian Edwards, Jennifer Rice, two voices and gui. Themed entertainments in words and mus; international folk songs and 'nostalgia' of twenties, thirties and forties.

Things We Found Under the Sofa. St Faith's House, Shandy St, London E1 4ST *tel:* 020 7791 0330 *also fax.* Adey Grummet, sop; Graham Coatman, pno. A diva and her encores.

Turner Fish Smith Trio. Brownson House, Grenofen, Tavistock, Devon PL19 9ER *tel:* 01822 615730 *also fax; email:* adrian_vernon.Fish@virgin.net. Rosemary Turner, sop; Adrian Vernon Fish, pno; Will Smith, narrator. Themed entertainments with appropriate stage sets.

Voice and Verse. 69 Park Ave, Palmers Green, London N13 5PH *tel:* 020 8882 2106. Garry Humphreys, dir. Anthology entertainments on specific themes with 2 speakers, 2 singers and pno.

Voices-go-Round. 8 Ashwood Villas, Leeds LS6 2EJ *tel:* 0113 278 0827 *fax:* 0113 230 6114 *email:* virginia@ashwood.u-net.com. Virginia Rushton, sop; David Rowland, hpd, f-pno, pno; Clive Brown, vn. Mus and literary programmes.

Words and Music. 16 Highbury Park, London N5 2AB *tel:* 020 7359 0707 *also fax; email:* songful@compuserve.com. Sally Bradshaw. Programmes on particular themes involving actors, singer and insts.

Solo Performers

The artists listed in this section are confined to those living in Britain and/or bookable through a British concert agent. Chorus-masters are included under Conductors. Instrumentalists are listed according to instrument in the following order: organ, solo piano, harpsichord, accompanists and coaches, violin, viola and viola d'amore, cello, double bass, woodwind, brass, harp, guitar and lute, percussion and miscellaneous. Singers are sub-divided according to voice.

Where an artist's services may be booked through an agent or manager, that agent or manager is named in abbreviated form. Those which are not self-explanatory are listed below. *The agent is not necessarily that artist's exclusive agent,* however, and may not represent the artist outside Britain. See **Agents and Managers** for addresses and telephone numbers. Where the artist is currently or has been associated with a major opera company, then that company is given as the contact, see **Opera, Dance and Music Theatre** for addresses and telephone numbers. Reference to an opera company does not necessarily imply that the company has any control of, or present interest in, the availability of the artist. Artists without named agents are either listed with a personal telephone or a number preceded by *c/o* which denotes a personal manager through which the artist may be contacted.

The *Register of Performers and Composers* published by the **Incorporated Society of Musicians** (10 Stratford Place, London W1N 9AE *tel:* 0120 7629 4413) gives addresses as well as telephone numbers for its members who may be soloists or members of an ensemble or orchestra. Many other instrumentalists are members of the **Musicians' Union** (60-62 Clapham Rd, London SW9 0JJ *tel:* 020 7582 5566). Many singers are members of the **British Actors' Equity Association** (Guild House, Upper St Martin's La, London WC2H 9EG *tel:* 020 7379 6000). A list of artists represented by artist managers and concert agents who are members of the **International Artist Managers' Association** is available from 4 Addison Bridge Place, London W14 8XP *tel:* 020 7610 4884.

Agents' Abbreviations

ADM	AD Management	OCA	Opera and Concert Artists
CDI	Concert Directory International	OWM	Owen/White Management
DCM	Daniels Concert Management	PA	Performing Arts
GIA	Georgina Ivor Associates	PGM	Patrick Garvey Management
HP	Harrison Parrott	SJM	Sylvia Junge Management
KDM	Karen Durant Management	SS	Simply Singers
LA	London Artists	SWA	Stephannie Williams Artists
LM	London Musicians	THA	Terry Harrison Artists Management
NBM	NB Management	VWM	Van Walsum Management
NCCP	Neil Chaffey Concert Promotions	WWA	World Wide Artists
NWA	N W Artists	YCAT	Young Concert Artists Trust

Conductors

Choral directors and chorus-masters are included in this list.

Abbado, Claudio – *Askonas Holt*
Abel, Yves – *Askonas Holt*
Adams, John – *HP*
Adey, Christopher – *PA*
Ajmone-Marsan, Guido – *Still*
Alldis, John – *Allied*
Alsop, Marin – *Intermusica*
Altrichter, Petr – *Hazard*
Alwyn, Kenneth – 01403 741348
André, Martin – *Ingpen*
Andrew-James, Mark – 01273 208680 *fax:* 01273 777963
Andrews, Matthew – 01206 576347; 07973 712262
Angus, David – *PGM*
Anissimov, Alexander – *Askonas Holt*
Armstrong, Richard – *Ingpen*
Armstrong, Stephen – 01494 528664 *also fax; email:* 106506.1555@compuserve.com
Arnic, Lovrenc – *Pristavec*
Arundel Timms, T – 01237 473887
Asbury, Stefan – *HP*
Ashcroft, Michael – 020 8761 3439 *fax:* 020 8299 9258
Ashkenazy, Vladimir – *HP*
Atherton, David – *Askonas Holt*
Atzmon, Moshe – *PGM*
Auguin, Philippe – *Askonas Holt*
Bachmann, Robert – 01624 624822 *fax:* 01624 624243 *email:* rcb@orbitex.ch
Backhouse, Jeremy – 020 8690 1278 *fax:* 020 8690 4462 *email:* jeremy.backhouse@50montacute.freeserve.co.uk
Badea, Christian – *Transart*
Bainbridge, Simon – c/o 020 7434 0066 *fax:* 020 7287 6329
Bakels, Kees – *IMG*
Balcombe, Richard – 01279 831821 *fax:* 01279 724299 *email:* rbalcombe@aol.com
Bale, Matthew – 01225 337722
Balkwill, Bryan – 020 8947 4250
Ball, Christopher – 020 7935 1270
Ball, Timothy – 020 8871 0317 *fax:* 020 8488 4965 *email:* timball@sudlow.demon.co.uk
Bamert, Matthias – *Intermusica*
Barber, Graham – 0113 263 1890 *fax:* 0113 263 7178 *email:* g.d.barber@leeds.ac.uk
Barbieri, Edward – 07050 602518 *fax:* 07050 602519 *email:* ceb@royal.net
Barenboim, Daniel – *Askonas Holt*
Barham, Stuart – 020 7622 8864
Barker, Bernard – 020 8427 5409 *also fax*
Barker, John – 020 8224 0514
Barlow, Alan – 01639 849497
Barlow, Jeremy – 020 7267 7176 *fax:* 020 7267 0127 *email:* jrmybarlow@aol.com
Barlow, Stephen – *Musichall*
Barnes, Derek – c/o 020 7287 9000
Barnes, Richard – 01243 776325 *fax:* 01243 539604 *email:* Cathedral_Music@compuserve.com
Barrios, Enrique – *LA*
Barshai, Rudolf – *Askonas Holt*

Barton, Christopher – 01633 266708 *also fax; email:* stworg@aol.com
Bassano, Peter – *Giustiniani – 01494 868240 fax:* 01494 868250 *email:* GArtists1@aol.com
Bate, John – 020 8940 8930 *fax:* 020 8547 7400 *email:* j.bate@kingston.ac.uk
Bateman, Paul – c/o 020 8444 4088 *email:* paul@b8man.swinternet.co.uk
Bates, Kevin – 01449 741707
Beaven, Peter – 01483 475506 *fax:* 01483 475184 *email:* pmsnet@argonet.co.uk
Bedford, Steuart – *HP*
Beedie, Norman – 01733 844603 *also fax*
Bell, Christopher – *Gilder*
Bending, Arthur – 01626 890242
Benjamin, George – *Askonas Holt*
Berio, Luciano – *Allied*
Bernard, André – *Gilder*
Bernas, Richard – *Gilder*
Bernet, Dietfried – *Still*
Best, Matthew – *IMG*
Bethell, John – 01624 832870 *also fax*
Bicket, Harry – *Askonas Holt*
Birtwistle, Harrison – *Allied*
Black OBE, Stanley – 020 7586 5958 *fax:* 020 7586 3524
Bolton, Ivor – *Ingpen*
Bond, Graham – 01892 536944 *also fax;* c/o 00 45 33 696933
Bond, Rupert – 020 8691 0691 *also fax*
Bonynge OBE, Richard – *Ingpen*
Boughton, William – 01684 567522 *also fax; email:* William.Boughton@eso.co.uk
Boulez, Pierre – *Ingpen*
Bourgeois, Derek – 020 8748 6027 *also fax; email:* dbourgeois@tramuntana.demon.co.uk; Derek.Bourgeois@SPGS.org
Bourne, Alan R – 01446 797318 *also fax;* 01446 751446 *email:* alan@stathan.freeserve.co.uk
Brabbins, Martyn – *Allied*
Bradbury, John – 020 8422 1456
Braithwaite, Nicholas – *Tennant*
Brett, Jonathan – c/o 01737 813273 *fax:* 01737 215676
Broadbent, Peter – *LM – 020 8360 7281 also fax; email:* pb@jcos.demon.co.uk
Brooker, Stephen – *LM*
Brown, Adrian – *Finch*
Brown, Ian – *Manygate – 020 8459 3589*
Brown, Iona – *IMG*
Brown, Justin – *IMG*
Brown, Mark – *POEM*
Brown, Timothy – 01223 333264 *fax:* 01223 333219 *email:* tcb21@hermes.cam.ac.uk
Brüggen, Frans – *Askonas Holt*
Brunton, Barry – 01366 386589 *fax:* 01366 386590
Brydon, Roderick – *Mus Int*
Bryett, Alexander – 020 7736 3821
Buckley, Richard – *Gilder*
Bugaj, Tomasz – *PGM*
Bühl, Gregor – *Rawstron*
Burgess-Ellis, Richard – 020 7495 3122
Burton, Ken – *Ellison*
Butcher, Jonathan Charles – c/o 01883 713183; 020 8654 9306 *also fax;* 07802 645384 *fax:* c/o 01883 717446
Butterworth MBE, Arthur – 01756 792968
Cambreling, Sylvain – *Allied*
Canetty-Clarke, Janet – 01444 811243 *fax:* 01444 811171 *email:* janet@orphic.demon.co.uk
Caradon, Richard – 01225 313531
Carewe, John – c/o 00 49 40 2805 2227 *fax:* 00 49 40 2805 2228
Carignani, Paolo – *HP*
Chadwick, Eric – 0161 370 3547
Chaslin, Frédéric – *Allied*
Chernaik, David – 020 8986 4101 *also fax*
Chmura, Gabriel – *Transart*
Christie, Michael – *IMG*
Christie, William – *IMG*
Christophers, Harry – *HP*
Civil, Peter – 020 8857 1297
Clarke, Peter – 01932 781577 *fax:* 01932 789822
Clayton, Julian – *Grant Rogers*
Clayton, Kenny – *Brunskill*
Cleobury, Nicholas – *Allied*
Cleobury, Stephen – *Hazard*
Cleve, George – *THA*
Cohen, Brad – *Lubbock*
Cohen, Jacques – 020 8368 8956 *also fax; email:* jacquescohen@easynet.co.uk
Collis, Peter – c/o 01426 253439 *fax:* 01924 832006 *email:* pec29@tutor.open.ac.uk
Constantine, Andrew – *PGM*
Conway, William – 0131 667 4630 *also fax*
Cooke, Richard – *Musicmakers*
Coombes, Douglas – *Lindsay*
Corp, Ronald – 020 7625 4641 *fax:* 020 7625 4876 *email:* reynaldo@angkor.demon.co.uk
Corti, Francesco – *Allied*
Crabb, Michael – 01702 298314
Cripps, David – *Manygate*
Cuckston, Alan – 01757 638238 *also fax; email:* alancuckston@iname.com
Cullen, Joseph – c/o 020 8299 1914 *email:* Hirstpr@aol.com
Daniel, Paul – *Ingpen*
Dankworth CBE, John – *Clarion/Seven Muses*
Daras, Yannis – *Finch*
Darlow, Denys – c/o 020 8563 0618
Dausgaard, Thomas – *IMG*
Davan Wetton, Hilary – *PA*

Nigel Boddice

Contemporary, Mainstream and Specialised Children's Concerts

".....inspirational to the young..."
(Herald)

".....taut and sonorous..... highly entertaining..."
(Scotsman)

7 Orleans Avenue, Jordanhill, Glasgow G14 9LA
Tel/Fax: 0141-959 1825 Mobile: 0850 223496
Email: nboddice@aol.com

Graham Lea-Cox

Conductor

<gleacox@hotmail.com>

"... but the highest praise for this recording is due to the players of the Hanover Band and to the conductor, Graham Lea-Cox ..."

Anthony Burton, BBC Radio 3, 'Record Review', June 1998
[William Boyce: The Secular Masque, recorded on ASV (CD GAU 176)]

Enquiries to:
Christine Gray
Haydn Rawstron (UK) Limited
36 Station Road, London SE20 7BQ
ENGLAND

Telephone: + 44 181 659 2659
Facsimile: + 44 181 676 9119
E-Mail: haydnraw@aol.com
****

Simon Lindley

organist

a player of distinctive style - accompaniment, continuo and orchestral work a speciality

17 Fulneck, Pudsey
West Yorkshire, LS28 8NT
(0113) 255-6143 (telephone and facsimile)

Recent Recordings by Simon Lindley include

HANDEL CONCERTOS
(Northern Sinfonia & Bradley Creswick)
NAXOS 8.553835

TOWN HALL ORGAN CLASSICS
(Leeds Town Hall)
OXRECS OXCD-71

DANIEL IN BABYLON
FRANCIS JACKSON
with JOHN STUART ANDERSON
and ST PETER'S SINGERS
(Simon Lindley, conductor)
recorded in Leeds Parish Church
- experience this unique monodrama with music on Amphion PHI CD 145

VICTOR MORRIS

INTERNATIONAL VOCAL COACH

former AUDITIONS SUPREMO at ENO is available to work with

PROFESSIONAL SINGERS

in ENGLAND and AUSTRALIA on the preparation of operatic repertoire for performance and/or audition

Consultations by arrangement

Opera masterclasses for singers and repetiteurs
Aria classes for specific voice groups
Repetiteur classes and study days

Fees and other information on application

LONDON STUDIO: 45 Madrid Rd, SW13 9PQ
Tel: 020 8748 4544 Fax: 020 8748 1703
SYDNEY STUDIO: 171 Albion St, Surry Hills, NSW 2010
Tel: 00 612 9360 4049 Fax: 00 612 9332 1585

Artistic Director — **RONALD DOWD NATIONAL SUMMER SCHOOL FOR SINGERS, AUSTRALIA**

Davie, Anthony – 020 8670 9839
Davies, Noel – *Still*
Davies, Wyn – *PA*
Davis CBE, Sir Andrew – *Askonas Holt*
Davis, Carl – 01494 431667 *fax:* 01494 431714 *email:* paulwing@englandmail.com
Davis CBE, Sir Colin – *Columbia*
Dawes, Alistair – *Gilder*
De Carlo, Nicholas – *Brunskill*
de Peyer, Gervase – *Michael Harrold*
DePreist, James – *Transart*
De Rivera, Edward – 0870 740 4059 *fax:* 0870 740 4061
Dean, Robert – *Musichall*
Del Mar, Jonathan – 020 7622 2000 *also fax*
Delogu, Gaetano – *Connaught*
Deneve, Stephane – *Stafford*
Diemecke, Enrique – *Music Partnership*
Dobing, Duke – 020 8643 4425 *also fax*
Dohnányi, Christoph von – *HP*
Downes CBE, Sir Edward – *Ingpen*
Drummond, David – 020 8861 1511 *also fax; email:* david_liz_drummond@compuserve.com
Dufallo, Richard – *Allied*
Dunk, Roderick – *Manygate*
Dunner, Leslie B – *Gilder*
Eberle, Christoph – *Tennant*
Edwards, Sian – *Ingpen*
Edwards, Terry – 01707 268576 *fax:* 020 8989 7389
Elder CBE, Mark – *Ingpen*
Ellis, Graham Jordan – 0151 653 5541 *also fax*; 07778 876448
Ellis, Philip – *Music Partnership*
Eötvös, Peter – *Allied*
Epple, Roger – *Phillips*
Erckens, Peter – *Rawstron*
Ermler, Mark – *Allied*
Eschenbach, Christoph – *Columbia*
Fagen, Arthur – *Gilder*
Fardell, Andrew – 01206 765591 *fax:* 01206 575708 *email:* andrew@fardell.demon.co.uk
Farncombe CBE, Charles – 01600 780233; 020 7402 8664 *also fax*
Farnes, Richard – *Ingpen*
Farnon, Robert – c/o 020 7828 6533 *email:* rbfarnon@guernsey.net
Farrell, Kevin – *Brunskill*
Fedoseyev, Vladimir – *Gilder*
Ferland, Janos – *JLM*
Fifield, Christopher – 020 8289 6786 *also fax; email:* cgfifield@aol.com
Fisch, Asher – *Askonas Holt*
Fischer, Adam – *Askonas Holt*
Fischer, Ivan – *HP*
Fischer, Raymond – 020 8748 4702 *also fax*
Fischer-Dieskau, Dietrich – *Askonas Holt*
Fisher, David – 0116 224 0144 *fax:* 0116 291 0677
Fixman, Sydney – 020 7624 1756
Flor, Claus Peter – *Intermusica*
Fontanelli, Simone – *ECAM*
Forkgen, Mark – *Gilder*
Foster, Lawrence – *HP*
Fournillier, Patrick – *Music Partnership*
Fox, James – c/o 01206 393848 *fax:* 01206 393847 *email:* JFox744095@aol.com
Fraillon, Nicolette – *Gilder*
Francis, Alun – *LA*
Franck, Mikko – *HP*
Fredman, Myer – *Grant Rogers*
Frémaux, Louis – *Tennant*
Friend, Lionel – *Gilder*
Fritzsch, Johannes – *Rawstron*
Frühbeck de Burgos, Rafael – *Askonas Holt*
Fujioka, Sachio – *IMG*
Furrer, Patrick – *Gilder*
Fürst, János – *IMG*
Gaddarn, James – 020 7486 1929
Gamba, Rumon – *HP*
Gammon, Philip – 020 8866 3260 *fax:* 020 8248 2906
Gardiner CBE, Sir John Eliot – *IMG*
Garforth, David – 07050 374838 *fax:* 07050 374839 *email:* garforth@compuserve.com
Gayford, Christopher – 020 7722 5948 *also fax; email:* c.gayford@talk21.com
Gee, Leon – 01923 827404 *also fax*
Gellhorn, Peter – 020 8876 3949
Gelmetti, Gianluigi – *Music Partnership*
Geringas, David – *Connaught*
Gibbons, John – *Connaught*
Gibson, David – 01256 397409 *also fax*
Gibson, Philip – 01923 828055
Gielen, Michael – *Ingpen*
Gilbert, Alan – *IMG*
Gilbert-Dyson, Peter – *Manygate – 020 7531 1672; 07976 278476 fax:* 020 7531 9895 *email:* belmont@easynet.co.uk
Gill, Jonathan – *Craig*
Glover, Jane – *Askonas Holt*
Goodman, Roy – 01529 304130 *fax:* 01529 304131 *email:* roy.goodman@virgin.net
Goodwin, Paul – *Askonas Holt*
Goulding, Fraser – 01945 880314 *also fax*
Graf, Hans – *Tennant*
Graubart, Michael – 020 8265 5504
Gray, Simon – 01273 724817 *fax:* 01273 722716
Greenwood, Andrew – *Still*
Griffiths, Hilary – *Mus Int/Still*
Gritton, Robin – 01737 243058 *fax:* 01737 246623
Gruber, Heinz Karl – *Intermusica*
Guidarini, Marco – *Allied*
Hadjinikos, George – 0161 928 3329 *fax:* 00 301 361 9373
Haitink KBE, Bernard – *Askonas Holt*
Hale, Paul – 01636 812228 *also fax; email:* PaulHale@diaphone.clara.net
Halsey, Louis – 020 8942 7597 *also fax*
Halsey, Simon – *Hazard*
Halstead, Anthony – *PGM*
Hamm, Michael – 0151 625 9980 *also fax*
Hamwee, Robert – 01753 648113 *fax:* 01753 648114 *email:* rhamwee@clara.net
Hand, Christopher – 01905 351292
Handley, Vernon – *VWM*
Hanson, Geoffrey – 020 8444 9214 *also fax; email:* geoffreyhanson@btinternet.com
Harding, Daniel – *Askonas Holt*
Harries, Clive – 01609 881552 *fax:* 01609 881110 *email:* cliveharries@compuserve.com
Hartman, Thomas – 020 7737 6770 *email:* cmbski@aol.com
Hazeldine, Alan – 020 8341 0567 *also fax; email:* alan.hazeldine@mcmail.com
Hazlewood, Charles – *ADM*
Headlam, Philip – 020 8993 1466 *also fax*
Heard, Gordon – 024 7640 4696
Hellewell, David – 01202 551440
Henzold, Olaf – *Gilder*
Herbig, Günther – *THA*
Herrick, Christopher – 020 8546 8966 *fax:* 020 8541 0034
Hickox, Richard – *Intermusica*
Higgins, Tom – 020 8390 1020 *also fax*
Hill, David – *Phillips*
Hilliam, Paul – 0116 230 3674 *fax:* c/o 01202 251450
Hirokami, Junichi – *THA*
Hoban, John – 020 8946 8852
Hogwood CBE, Christopher – 01223 363975 *fax:* 01223 327377 *email:* chogwood@compuserve.com
Holliger, Heinz – *Ingpen*
Holmes, Richard – 01444 257427 *also fax*; 07802 250510
Honeck, Manfred – *IMG*
Hose, Anthony – *Ellison*
Hoskins, Paul – *Connaught – 020 8450 4857 also fax*
Houghton, Nicholas – 01444 230779 *fax:* 01444 233699
Howarth, Elgar – *Allied*
Hoyland, David – *Roxane Houston*
Hughes, Owain Arwel – *Voullaire*
Humphris, Ian – 020 8747 1025
Hunt OBE, Donald – 01905 756329 *fax:* 01905 755142 *email:* dhunt2126@aol.com
Hurwitz CBE, Emanuel – 020 8346 3936 *fax:* 020 8343 1595
Hutchinson, Stuart – *Mus Int*
Inbal, Eliahu – *Askonas Holt*
Inglis, Anthony – *Connaught*
Ingram, Alex – *Portland*
Inouye, Derrick – *Gilder*
Ioannides, Sarah – *Ellison*
Iwaki, Hiroyuki – *Transart*
Jackman, Jeremy – 020 8341 3408 *also fax; email:* jeremy@jackman.primex.co.uk
Jackson, Graham – 0117 962 3850 *also fax*
Jacobson, Julian – 020 8694 9525 *fax:* 020 8692 7065 *email:* julian.jacobson@breathemail.net
Janowski, Marek – *IMG*
Jansons, Mariss – *IMG*
Jarre, Maurice – *Encore Concerts*
Järvi, Kristjan – *VWM*
Järvi, Neeme – *Columbia*
Järvi, Paavo – *HP*
Jenkins, Graeme – *Askonas Holt*
Joel, Emmanuel – *Allied*
Joly, Simon – 020 8785 9617 *also fax*
Jones, David – *VWM*
Jones, Gareth – *Harlequin*
Jones, Kenneth Victor – 01323 894377
Jones, Stephen – 01727 864007 *fax:* 01727 845884 *email:* steve_sta@compuserve.com
Judd, James – *LA*
Karpe, Stefan – *VWM*
Kaspszyk, Jacek – *Music Partnership*
Keable, Russell – 01223 290410 *email:* rkeable@bigfoot.com
Keeffe, Bernard – 020 8699 3672 *also fax; email:* bernard@batons.demon.co.uk
Kelleher, James – *Still*
Kelsey, Xenophon – 01765 602856
Kennaway, George – 0113 266 3966 *also fax; email:* george@knwy.freeserve.co.uk
Keyes, Colin – *Brunskill*
Keys, Robert – 01963 362999
Kikuchi, Yoshinori – *Stafford*
King, Robert – *HP*
Knight, Barry – 01707 662903 *fax:* 01707 654817
Knussen, Oliver – *HP*
Koivula, Hannu – *PGM*
Kok, Nicholas – *Allied*
Koopman, Ton – *Hazard*
Korsten, Gérard – *Lubbock*
Kovacevich, Stephen – *VWM*
Kraemer, Nicholas – *Phillips*
Kreizberg, Yakov – *HP*
Krivine, Emmanuel – *Askonas Holt*
Kyzlink, Jaroslav – *POEM*
Lade, Stephen – *Scrimgeour*
Lamminmäki, Juhani – *Ellison*
Landor, John – 020 7724 7222 *also fax*
Latham-Koenig, Jan – *Askonas Holt*
Lawrence, David – 07973 686963; 0116 239 0741 *also fax; email:* david@lawrence-music.co.uk
Layton, Stephen – *Hazard*
Lazarev, Alexander – *Tennant*
Lea-Cox, Graham – *Rawstron*
Leaper, Adrian – *Olivia Ma*
Ledger CBE, Sir Philip – c/o 0141 332 4101 *fax:* 0141 332 8901

Legge, Harry – 020 7624 1221 *fax:* 020 7328 2511
Leonard, Lawrence – 01306 883413
Leppard CBE, Raymond – *Clarion/Seven Muses*
Levy, Alastair – 020 7586 7910
Liebreich, Alexander – *HP*
Ligeti, András – *Music Partnership*
Lindley, Simon – 0113 255 6143 *also fax; email:* simonlin@nascr.net
Litton, Andrew – *IMG*
Llewellyn, Grant – *Hazard*
Llewellyn MBE, William – 01297 552414 *also fax; email:* wll@mcmail.com
Lloyd, Michael – *Gilder*
Lloyd-Jones, David – *Allied*
Lockhart, James – *Portland*
Longden, Lee – 0161 225 0445 *fax:* 0161 224 4530 *email:* lee.longden@music-services.demon.co.uk
Lopez-Cobos, Jesus – *THA*
Loughran, James – *Interartists BV* (*see* International Agents, Netherlands) – 0141 337 2091 *fax:* 0141 357 0643
Lü, Jia – *IMG*
Lü, Shao-Chia – *Olivia Ma*
Lubbock, John – 01865 858310
McCaldin, Denis – 01524 593750 *fax:* 01524 847298 *email:* d.mccaldin@lancaster.ac.uk
McCarthy OBE, John – 01494 680873 *fax:* 01494 680501
McCreesh, Paul – *Intermusica*
McGegan, Nicholas – *Allied*
McGonigal, Dominic – 020 7603 1728 *also fax*
McGrath, Paul – *Musicmakers*
McIntosh, Thomas – 01473 822596 *fax:* 01473 824175
McLeod, Callum – *LM*
McLeod, John – 0131 441 3035 *fax:* 0131 441 5218 *email:* john.mcleod@btinternet.com
McMillan, Ian – 01494 758595 *also fax*
MacMillan, James – *Intermusica*
Mackenzie, Philip – 020 7537 2329 *fax:* 020 7379 5205
Mackerras, Sir Charles – *Askonas Holt*
Mägi, Paul – *Gilder*
Maksymiuk, Jerzy – *IMG*
Mandeäl, Cristian – *Connaught*
Mann, Paul – *HP*
Manson, Anne – *Ingpen*
Mansur, Cem – *PGM*
Marin, Ion – *Askonas Holt*
Märkl, Jun – *Allied*
Markson, Gerhard – *Anglo-Swiss*
Marshall, Wayne – *Askonas Holt*
Martinez, Odaline de la – c/o 020 8208 2480 *fax:* 020 8208 2490 *email:* dkantor.kcm@webstar.co.uk
Masson, Diego – *Ingpen*
Max, Robert – 020 8458 2839 *also fax; email:* RobandZoe@aol.com
Maxwell Davies, Sir Peter – c/o 020 7370 2328 *fax:* 020 7373 6730 *email:* j.arnold@maxopus.com
Mayer, Uri – *Anglo-Swiss*
Mayo, Graham – 01604 830679
Medlam, Charles – 01635 254331 *fax:* 01635 253629 *email:* c.medlam@btinternet.com
Mehta, Zubin – *Askonas Holt*
Merry, Martin – 01305 848710 *also fax; email:* martinmerry@hotmail.com
Metters, Colin – *Scrimgeour*
Metzmacher, Ingo – *Intermusica*
Miller, Antony – 01608 652192
Minczuk, Roberto – *LA*
Mitchell, Antoine – 01371 820382 *fax:* 01371 821100
Mitchell, Geoffrey – 020 8491 0962 *fax:* 020 8491 0956 *email:* 113073.654@compuserve.com
Mogrelia, Andrew – *Gilder*
Moldoveanu, Nicolae – *Clarion/Seven Muses*
Montgomery, Kenneth – *Voullaire*
Moody, Howard – 01342 851053 *also fax*
Morris, Andrew – 01234 365520 *fax:* 01234 362283
Morris, Victor – 020 8748 4544 *fax:* 020 8748 1703
Murphy, David – 01582 462137 *also fax; email:* david@firstmaestro.com
Mustonen, Olli – *HP*
Nagano, Kent – *VWM*
Neary, Martin – 020 7736 5268 *fax:* 020 7610 6995 *email:* PJNeary@compuserve.com
Nebe, Michael – c/o 020 8671 4408 *fax:* c/o 020 8671 2848 *email:* admin@fasinfonia.freeserve.co.uk
Nelson, John – *IMG*
Neschling, John – *LA*
Neuhold, Günter – *Still*
Ng, Kah-Ming – 01865 751928 *also fax; email:* Kah-MingNg@charivari.freeserve.co.uk
Nicolls, Christopher – *Scrimgeour*
Niquet, Hervé – *Portland*
Norrington CBE, Sir Roger – 01635 37231 *fax:* 01635 34681
Ogden, David – 0117 951 4687 *fax:* 0117 973 8263 *email:* david.ogden@gifford.co.uk
Ollila, Tuomas – *PGM*
Olmi, Paolo – *IMG*
Ono, Kazushi – *IMG*
Ooi, Chean See – *IMG*
Oramo, Sakari – *HP*
Östman, Arnold – *Rawstron*
Otaka, Tadaaki – *Askonas Holt*
Oue, Eiji – *IMG*
Owen Edwards, John – *Musicmakers*
Oxley, Harrison – 01284 787533 *also fax*
Padmore, Andrew – 0113 273 1120 *also fax*
Paemurru, Peter – *Ellison*
Page, Neil – 01572 747412
Page, Robin – 020 8669 4358 *also fax; email:* robinpage1@compuserve.com
Papadopoulos, Marios – 020 8450 2714 *fax:* 020 8450 0087 *email:* marios@apple-uk.net
Parnell, Andrew – *Michael Harrold*
Parrott, Andrew – *Allied*
Parry, David – *Allied*
Patrick, Nicholas – 020 8521 5398 *also fax; email:* NicholasPatrick@nikpat.demon.co.uk
Pay, Antony – *Allied*
Payton, Paul – c/o 01257 267262 *also fax; email:* paytonpj@aol.com
Peacock, Adrian – *POEM*
Peebles, Charles – *Music Partnership*
Pešek, Libor – *IMG*
Pesko, Zoltan – *Allied*
Petersen, Bj¢rn Bryn – *Ellison/CMG*
Pichler, Guenter – *Intermusica*
Pickett, Philip – *Allied – 020 7735 8154* *fax:* 020 7820 0801 *email:* philip.pickett@btinternet.com
Pilbery, Joseph – 01707 650735 *also fax;* 01707 643366
Pink, Andrew – 020 7272 6101 *also fax; email:* andrew.pink@btinternet.com
Pinnock CBE, Trevor – *Askonas Holt*
Placidi, Tommaso – *Gilder*
Plasson, Michel – *IMG*
Pletnev, Mikhail – *Columbia*
Polianichko, Alexander – *Ingpen*
Politchuk, Alexander – *NWA*
Pomphrey, John – 0161 428 5456 *also fax*
Ponsford, David – 01285 651995 *also fax*
Pont, Kenneth H – 01892 835164
Pople, Ross – 01539 560304 *fax:* 01539 561483
Porcelijn, David – *PGM*
Post, Arthur – *LM*
Potter, Warwick – 01424 440929; 07973 734572 *email:* WarwickMD@aol.com
Proost, Walter – *WWA*
Protheroe, Guy – 020 7286 3944 *fax:* 020 7289 9081 *email:* guy.protheroe@btinternet.com
Pryce-Jones, John – 01422 825594 *also fax;* 07768 352399
Quinn, Andrea – *Clarion/Seven Muses*
Rafferty, Michael – c/o 029 2023 0833 *fax:* 029 2034 2046
Rahbari, Alexander – *Anglo-Swiss*
Rampal, Jean-Pierre – *Transart*
Rands, Bernard – *Allied*
Rasilainen, Ari – *Allied*
Rattle CBE, Sir Simon – *Askonas Holt*
Reason, Michael – *Ellison*
Redmond, Timothy – 020 8361 5209 *also fax; email:* tredmond@andrusier.demon.co.uk
Reed, Philip – *Roxane Houston*
Renes, Lawrence – *HP*
Rennert, Jonathan – 01737 244604 *fax:* 01737 271128
Rennert, Wolfgang – *Allied*
Renzetti, Donato – *Allied*
Rescigno, Joseph – *Gilder*
Reymond, Valentin – *Mus Int*
Rhodes, Burt – 020 8371 9896 *also fax*
Rickenbacher, Karl Anton – *Transart*
Ridley, Anthony – 0151 677 8708
Rifkin, Joshua – *Clarion/Seven Muses*
Rizzi, Carlo – *Allied*
Roberts, Kenneth – 01233 740560 *email:* oldsalieri@aol.com
Robertson, Stewart – *Gilder*
Robinson, Christopher – *SWA*
Robinson, Peter – *Voullaire*
Roblou, David – c/o 020 8299 1914 *also fax; email:* Hirstpr@aol.com
Rochester, Marc – 01252 783172 *also fax; email:* marcroc@pc.jaring.my
Romano, Marco – 0141 551 8789 *also fax*
Romanos, Simon – *ECAM*
Ros Marbá, Antoní – *Ingpen*
Rose, Gregory – 020 7790 5883 *fax:* 020 7265 9170 *email:* gregory-rose@tisl.co.uk
Roseberry, Eric – 01225 891410
Ross, James – 01865 251510 *also fax*; 07768 810354 *fax:* 020 8864 4746 *email:* james.ross@christ-church.ox.ac.uk
Rostropovich, Mstislav – c/o 020 7794 0987 *fax:* 020 7431 2531
Roth, Alec – 020 7497 3754 *also fax*
Rothstein, Jack – c/o 020 8459 1475 *fax:* 020 8459 1642
Rowe, Tony – 0161 928 8640 *fax:* 0161 929 6808
Roxburgh, Edwin – *Michael Harrold*
Rozhdestvensky, Gennadi – *Allied*
Rudel, Julius – *VWM*
Rudland, Malcolm – 020 7589 9595 *also fax; email:* malcolmrudland@ndirect.co.uk
Rumble, Andy – *Brunskill*
Rumsey, Stephen – c/o 01621 892229 *email:* syrinxmusic@talk21.com
Rumstadt, Guido Johannes – *Gilder*
Runnicles, Donald – *Still*
Ruud, Ole Kristian – *VWM*
Saccani, Rico – *Stafford*
Sado, Yutaka – *Transart*
Salonen, Esa-Pekka – *VWM*
Salter, Lionel – 020 8458 3568 *also fax*
Salter, Timothy – 020 8318 2031 *also fax; email:* ugm@netcomuk.co.uk
Sander, Alexander – *Mus Int*
Sanderling, Kurt – *Music Partnership*
Sanderling, Thomas – *Music Partnership*

Saraste, Jukka-Pekka – *VWM*
Sato, Shuntaro – c/o *Sarah Gordon Mgt* 020 7483 2681 *fax:* 020 7586 5343
Schiff, Heinrich – *Intermusica*
Schirmer, Ulf – *HP*
Schmidt, Ole – *PGM*
Schønwandt, Michael – *Ingpen*
Schwarz, Gerard – *Columbia*
Scimone, Claudio – *Transart*
Scott, Christopher – *ADM*
Scott, John – *Hazard*
Scott, Paul – 01246 431562; 07801 510872 *email:* paulsyso88@aol.com
Seaman, Christopher – *HP*
Secret, Robert – 01280 848275 *also fax*
Segal, Uriel – *Olivia Ma*
Segerstam, Leif – *PGM*
Semkow, Jerzy – *Transart*
Shallon, David – *HP*
Shao, En – *IMG*
Shelley, Howard – c/o 020 8444 9003 *also fax*
Shipway, Frank – 01981 580363 *fax:* 01981 580578
Shostakovich, Maxim – *Pristavec*
Shulman, Andrew – 01420 472206 *fax:* 01420 478690 *email:* andrew.shulman@lineone.net
Sieling, Gary – 07889 569226
Simcock, Iain – *Michael Harrold*
Simms, Philip – c/o 020 8692 3037; 020 8691 8337 *also fax*
Simon, Geoffrey – 020 8883 7306 *fax:* 020 8365 3388 *email:* geoffreysimon@compuserve.com
Simonov, Yuri – *Allied*
Simons, Dennis – *Manygate*
Sinaisky, Vassily – *IMG*
Singer, Malcolm – 020 8992 2318 *fax:* 020 8896 2556
Sitkovetsky, Dmitry – *IMG*
Skidmore, Jeffrey – c/o 0121 523 1025 *fax:* 0121 523 1026
Skrowaczewski, Stanislaw – *Intermusica*
Slater, Christopher – 01372 454963 *also fax; email:* c.h.slater@cwcom.net
Slatkin, Leonard – *Askonas Holt*
Sloane, Steven – *Allied*
Snashall, John – 01983 753527
Spano, Robert – *HP*
Spearing, Robert – 01981 250849; 01974 282631
Spicer, Paul – 01543 250627 *fax:* 01543 250970 *email:* paul.spicer@tisl.co.uk
Squires, Chris – c/o 0141 248 4567; 07966 416765 *fax:* 0141 221 8812
Stanger, Peter – 01273 390351 *also fax*
Stapleton, Robin – *Stafford*
Stark, Peter – 020 8208 1709 *also fax; email:* peterstark_conductor@compuserve.com
Steadman Robert – 0115 917 4546 *also fax; email:* robsteadman@hotmail.com
Steinberg, Pinchas – *Intermusica*
Stenz, Markus – *Ingpen*
Stephens, Richard – 01437 760269 *fax:* 01437 768939
Stephenson, Mark – c/o 020 8231 2319 *fax:* 020 8231 2316 *email:* london.musici@tvu.ac.uk
Stern, Michael – *Transart*
Stewart, Murray – *Mus Int*
Stones, Joseph – 0113 275 2348
Studt, Richard – 01202 394955 *also fax; email:* rstudt@cwcom.net
Sturman, Paul – 023 8026 0342 *also fax*
Summers, Patrick – *Askonas Holt*
Sunshine, Adrian – c/o *Sheila Genden* 020 8455 9200 *also fax*
Sutherland, Iain – 020 8428 2998
Sutton-Anderson, David – 020 8349 2317 *fax:* 020 8346 8257
Swensen, Joseph – *VWM*
Tabachnik, Michel – *PGM*
Talmi, Yoav – *Anglo-Swiss*
Taylor, Graham – 0141 334 9588 *fax:* 0141 357 2116 *email:* grataylorglas@btinternet.com
Taylor, Matthew – 01892 511570 *also fax*
Tear CBE, Robert – *Askonas Holt*
Temirkanov, Yuri – *IMG*
Temple, David – 020 8442 1748 *also fax*
Tenant-Flowers, Sarah – 01235 850488 *also fax; email:* info@thesixteen.org.uk
Thorp, Sigmund – *Anthony Abbott*
Tilbrook, Jonathan – 020 8521 7657 *also fax*
Tilson Thomas, Michael – *VWM*
Tirimo, Martino – *Music Partnership*
Toms, Mikel – *Haferkorn*
Tongue, Alan – *Manygate*
Tortelier, Yan Pascal – *IMG*
Touchin, Colin – 024 7667 0211 *also fax;* 024 7652 3799 (office) *fax:* 024 7652 8136 (office) *email:* musab@warwick.ac.uk
Townend, Richard – 020 7589 1206 *fax:* 020 7589 5925
Tracey, Ian – 0151 708 8471 *also fax*
Trautmann, Marc – *Stafford*
Treacher, Graham – 0117 974 3279
Tredinnick, Noël – 020 7487 3508 *fax:* 020 7224 6087
Trifan, Marioara – *Gilder*
Trory, Robert – *NWA*
Truslove, David – 01962 861887 *also fax*; 07889 702376
Turner, Bruno – *POEM*
Valdes, Maximiano – *HP*
van Steen, Jac – *Music Partnership*
Vandernoot, Joseph – 020 7385 5432
Vann, Stanley – 01780 782192
Vänskä, Osmo – *HP*
Varga, Gilbert – *Intermusica*
Vasáry, Támás – *IMG*
Vass, George – 020 7435 5965 *fax:* 020 7435 9166
Veis, Daniel – c/o 020 8788 2710 *fax:* 020 8788 4282
Venzago, Mario – *Tennant*
Verdernikov, Alexander – *Askonas Holt*
Viotti, Marcello – *Askonas Holt*
Volkov, Ilan – *VWM*
Von Dohnányi, Oliver – *Mus Int*
Vonk, Hans – *Intermusica*
Waart, Edo de – *HP*
Wächter, Erich – *Rawstron*
Wagner, Jan – *PGM*
Wales, Roy – 01273 300894 *fax:* 01273 308394 *email:* BritChorInst@fastnet.co.uk
Wallberg, Heinz – *Rawstron*
Walter, Alfred – *Finch*
Warren, Edward – *Hazard – 0151 336 4039 also fax; email:* Edward_Warren@msn.com
Warren-Green, Christopher – c/o 020 8772 9741 *fax:* 020 8772 9742 *email:* cwg@lco.co.uk
Webb, Barrie – c/o 020 8606 0030 *fax:* 020 8606 0037
Webb, Jonathan – *Mus Int*
Webb, William – 01202 757847 *also fax; email:* chaselodge@hotmail.com
Wehner, Nigel – *JLM*
Weil, Bruno – *Ingpen*
Weller, Walter – *HP*
Welser-Möst, Franz – *IMG*
West, Martin – 020 8785 4142 *also fax;* 07966 196996 *email:* martin.west@virgin.net
Wheeler, Dominic – *Musicmakers*
White, Robin – 01923 670278 *fax:* 01923 679184
Wigglesworth, Mark – *Askonas Holt*
Wilder, Stephen – 020 8886 0421/8372 2478 *fax:* 01296 614828 *email:* k.wilder@btinternet.com
Willcocks CBE, Sir David – 01223 359559 *fax:* 01223 355947
Willcocks, Jonathan – 023 9263 1369 *fax:* 023 9263 1786 *email:* jwillcocks@argonet.co.uk
Willén, Niklas – *PGM*
Williams, Elwyn – 029 2061 1435
Williams, Howard – *Connaught*
Williams MBE, John Hywel – 01554 772979 *also fax*
Williams, Roger – 01224 272570 *fax:* 01224 272515
Williams, Simon – 01923 770543 *also fax*
Williamson, Julian – 020 8579 5643
Wilson, John – *Clarion/Seven Muses*
Wit, Antoni – *WWA*
Wolff, Hugh – *VWM*
Wood, Christopher – 01702 332480 *fax:* 01702 339108
Woods, Thomas – *Hazard*
Woolfenden, Guy – *SWA*
Wright, Simon – *Denny Lyster*
Wroe, David – *Transart*
Wulstan, David – 01974 241229 *email:* dww@aber.ac.uk
Yershon, Gary – *Chuck Julian*
Yinon, Israel – *Connaught*
Young, Emanuel – 020 8886 1144
Yuasa, Takuo – *PGM*
Zambelli, Marco – *Musichall*
Zander, Benjamin – *IMG*
Zehetmair, Thomas – *Lubbock*
Zender, Hans – *Allied*
Ziegler, Robert – c/o 020 8769 4292 *fax:* 020 8696 7293 *email:* ziegler@matrixmusic.u-net.com
Zinman, David – *HP*
Zreczycki, Andrew – *Encore Concerts*
Zweden, Jaap van – *IMG*

Pianist

Conductor

Vocal Coach

Stephen Wilder

Graduate of The Royal College of Music, 7 seasons with Glyndebourne Festival Touring Opera, 16 years with The Royal Opera House. Much sought-after for his extensive knowledge of chamber music and complete classical vocal repertoire. Professor at the Royal College of Music.

Management:
K. Gilbert
Tel: 01296-61-2331
Fax: 01296-61-4828

Address:
39 Ulleswater Road
Southgate
London N14 7BL
Tel: 0181-886-0421
e-mail:
k.wilder@btinternet.com

Douglas Hollick

Organist and Harpsichordist

From press reviews:

A musician of substantial worth...
The West Australian

... A masterly performance
Hampshire Chronicle

Played with flair and conviction...this was a jewel in the University early music series...
Nottingham Evening Post

With international acclaim as an outstanding player, Douglas Hollick is recognised for his vibrant and musical performances and has been heard in many UK festivals, Dresden, Prague and Australia. He also teaches at a number of universities, and is available for masterclasses. His Supraphon CD *The Young Bach* drew the comment *'vivid, exciting and imaginative'* from Choir and Organ magazine. Programmes include such delights as *'Fantasy, inebriation and madness...'* 'Bach 250 celebration' ones like *Bach, family and friends...'*, or vocal and instrumental chamber music from his early music group *Chameleon.*

See http://www.classical-artists.com/douglas-hollick or contact:

4 Station Cottages, Harby Lane, Stathern, Leics. LE14 4HJ.
Tel/Fax 01949 861347
E-Mail: dwh@globalnet.co.uk

© Photo: Malcolm Crowthers

NEW CD WHITLOCK – Organ Music ASV QS 6233

"Jennifer Bate's lyrical approach and sensitive registration is a constant delight, and it is a pleasure to hear the right music on the right instrument in the right hands". The Organ, August 1999

Visit her web page to hear this and other Special CD offers
http://www.classsical-artists.com/jbate

Jennifer Bate

* Recitals * Lectures *
* Concertos * Masterclasses *
* Education and outreach projects *
* * * * * * * * * * * *

For availability please contact:
John Boyden or Edward Price,
ManyGate
13 Cotswold Mews,
30 Battersea Square,
London, SW11 3RA
Tel:020 7223 7265
Fax:020 7585 2830
e-mail: manygate@easynet.co.uk

International Management
Kunstleragentur Dr Raab & Dr Böhm,
Plankengasse 7,
A-1010 Wien, Austria
Tel:(+43 1) 512 0501
Fax:(+43 1) 512 7743
e-mail: raab.boehm@magnet.at

in co-operation for France & sundry territories with
Bureau de Concerts Maurice Werner,
7, rue Richepance,
75008 Paris, France
Tel:(+33 1) 47 03 13 60
Fax:(+33 1) 49 26 05 07
e-mail: werner@gofornet.com

Instrumentalists

Organ

The artists marked with an asterisk also perform as accompanists.

Ainscough, Julie – *Michael Harrold*
Alain, Marie-Claire – *TransArt*
* Archer, Malcolm – 01749 674483 *fax:* 01749 677360
Arnáiz, Guilliermo Diez – *Michael Harrold*
Ashfield, Robert – 01634 841508
* Aubrey-Drew, Helen – 01824 704582 *also fax; email:* helemuse@aol.com
* Ayres, Paul – 020 8998 2294 *also fax; email:* paulayres@clara.net
* Baden Fuller, Stephen – 01455 552009 *also fax*
* Baker, Alison – 01206 575825 *also fax;* 07850 241637 *email:* alisonbaker@aspects.net
Baker, Cyril – 01595 692632
* Ball, Timothy – 020 8871 0317 *fax:* 020 8488 4965 *email:* timball@sudlow.demon.co.uk
* Barber, Graham – 0113 263 1890 *fax:* 0113 263 7178 *email:* g.d.barber@leeds.ac.uk
* Barbieri, Edward – 07050 602518 *fax:* 07050 602519 *email:* ceb@royal.net
* Barham, Jeremy – 01483 505309 *also fax; email:* jbarham@tcm.ac.uk
* Barker, Bernard – 020 8427 5409 *also fax*
* Barnes, Gerald – 020 8346 6637
* Barnes, Richard – 01243 776325 *fax:* 01243 539604 *email:* Cathedral_Music@compuserve.com
* Barton, Christopher – 01633 266708 *also fax; email:* stworg@aol.com
Bate, Jennifer – *Manygate*
Beaumont, Kerry – 01765 600237 *fax:* 01765 690530 *email:* kerrybeaum@lineone.net
* Beaven, Peter – 01483 475506 *fax:* 01483 475184 *email:* pmsnet@argonet.co.uk
* Beechey, Gwilym – 01482 508910
Bending, Arthur – 01626 890242
Bielby, Jonathan – 01924 378841 *fax:* 01924 215054
* Binnington, Stephen – 01258 820087 *fax:* 01747 854684
* Bishop, John – 0117 942 3373
Bonaventure, Michael – 0131 657 4631
Bond, Timothy – 020 8670 3308 *fax:* 00 49 4295 400 *email:* tmbond@t-online.de
Bowen, Geraint – 01437 720128 *fax:* 01437 721813 *email:* grlbowen@aol.com
Bowyer, Kevin – c/o 01608 677417
Bruce-Payne, David – 0121 454 6222
* Byram-Wigfield, Timothy – c/o 01223 339339
* Carey, Colm – 020 8426 5961 *also fax; email:* careycolm@aol.com
* Carter, Roger – 01582 720095
Carter, Stanley – *JLM*
* Charlston, Terence – 01582 462024 *also fax; email:* terence@charlston.freeserve.co.uk
Cleobury, Stephen – *Hazard* – 01223 331224 *fax:* 01233 331890 *email:* choir@kings.cam.ac.uk
* Coulson, Richard – 01932 229171
Cullen, Joseph – *Organisation*
* Curley, Carlo – *PVA*
* Curror, Ian – 020 7730 7395 *email:* curror@usa.net
Darlington, Stephen – 01865 276195 *fax:* 01865 286581
* Davies, Stephen Robert – 020 8656 1732
Disley, Stephen – 020 7407 4515 *also fax; email:* Stephen.Disley@virgin.net
* Druce, Colin – 01926 451550
* Duro, Stephen Howard – 01895 232055 *also fax*
Eccles, Graham – 01745 583429
Elcombe, Keith – 0161 445 6661
Ennis, Catherine – *Blythe*
* Etherington, Carleton – 01684 298177 *fax:* 01684 293113
* Farrell, Scott – 01353 663715; 07771 883802 *fax:* 01353 665658 *email:* farrell@ely-organist.freeserve.co.uk
* Farrell, Timothy – 020 7286 5181
Filsell, Jeremy – *Chameleon*
Fiseisky, Alexander – *Ellison*
* Fletcher, Andrew – 0121 706 5708 *fax:* 0121 608 2990 *email:* AIF001@aol.com
* Foreman, Robert – 0116 286 1216
* Gaze, Nigel – 01253 591869
Goodwin, Andrew – 01248 714194/354015 *fax:* 01248 352466
Gower, Christopher – 01733 891333 *fax:* 01733 565165
Gower, Robert – 01738 880219 *also fax*
* Green, Gareth David – 01924 376848 *fax:* 01924 380182
Greenway, Kenneth – 01902 754529
* Hale, Paul – 01636 812228 *also fax; email:* PaulHale@diaphone.clara.net
Hanson, Geoffrey – 020 8444 9214 *also fax; email:* geoffreyhanson@btinternet.com
* Hare, Ian – *Ellison* – 01768 773342 *also fax*
* Harper, Norman – 020 7274 1712 *also fax; email:* norman.harper@cwcom.net
* Harries, Clive – 01609 881552 *fax:* 01609 881110 *email:* cliveharries@compuserve.com
* Harris, Michael – 01506 410477 *also fax; email:* m.harris@napier.ac.uk
* Heath-Downey, Susan – 020 7231 1423
Hekimova, Yanka – *PVA*
Herrick, Christopher – 020 8546 8966 *fax:* 020 8541 0034
Higginbottom, Edward – 01865 279519 *fax:* 01865 279590 *email:* edward.higginbottom@new.ox.ac.uk
* Hoeg, Michael Erling – 029 2056 3179 *fax:* 029 2056 7752
Hollick, Douglas – 01949 861347 *also fax; email:* dwh@globalnet.co.uk
* Hone, Timothy – 0191 261 4505 *fax:* 0191 230 0735
* Houghton, Nicholas – 01444 230779 *fax:* 01444 233699
* Howell, Alison – 0117 951 4692
Hoyland, David – *Roxane Houston*
* Hughes, Trevor – *Lindsay*
* Hunt OBE, Donald – 01905 756329 *fax:* 01905 755142 *email:* dhunt2126@aol.com
* Jackson, Carl – 020 8686 4297 *also fax; email:* carl_jackson@ccis.org.uk
Jackson, Graham – 0117 962 3850 *also fax*
Jarvis, Keith – 01484 683159
* John, Keith – 01234 708029
Jones, Jonathan Hellyer – 01223 515688
* Kemp-Luck, Edward – 020 7226 1218 *fax:* 020 7919 7644 *email:* edward.kemp-luck@virgin.net
Kerry, Nigel – 01223 350787 *fax:* 01223 360180 *email:* NPK@city32.freeserve.co.uk
King, David – 020 7976 6805 *also fax;* 07957 440574 *email:* DavidKing9@aol.com
* Kitchen, John P – 0131 650 2432 *fax:* 0131 650 2425 *email:* j.kitchen@music.ed.ac.uk
Koopman, Ton – *Hazard*
Kynaston, Nicolas – 020 8878 4455 *fax:* 020 8392 9314
Lancelot, James – 0191 386 4766
Leach, Simon Peter – 0161 861 9246
* Ledger CBE, Sir Philip – c/o 0141 332 4101 *fax:* 0141 332 8901
Lehtonen, Maija – *Ellison*
* Leith, Ronald – 01224 634427
Leonhardt, Gustav – *Allied*
Liddle, David – 020 8444 4454
* Lindley, Simon – *CDI* – 0113 255 6143 *also fax; email:* simonlin@nascr.net
* Longden, Lee – 0161 225 0445 *fax:* 0161 224 4530 *email:* lee.longden@music-services.demon.co.uk
* Luke, Philip – 01449 711511
* Lumsden, Andrew – 01543 306200 *fax:* 01543 306205
McAllister, Maureen – *Invisible Pilots*
* McGregor, Simon – 020 7987 5110
* McPhee MBE, George – 0141 889 3528 *fax:* 0141 840 4906
* McVicker, William – 020 8299 1971 *also fax; email:* wrmcvicker@aol.com
* Marsden Thomas, Anne – 020 7638 3052 *fax:* 020 7638 8285 *email:* AMT@organschool.com
Marshall, Wayne – *Askonas Holt*
* Matthews, Charles – 01386 438078 *also fax*
Melinkova, Ekaterina – *Finch*
* Missin, Russell – 0191 281 1513 *email:* mim2@callnetuk.com
* Moore, Adrian – 01926 883615
Moroney, Davitt – *LM*
Morris, Andrew – 01234 365520 *fax:* 01234 362283
Neary, Martin – 020 7736 5268 *fax:* 020 7610 6995 *email:* PJNeary@compuserve.com
* Nevill, Barry StJohn – 01323 417006 *also fax;* 07721 373734
* Newberry, Andrew – 01243 830695
* Nickol, Christopher – 0141 558 6555 *also fax; email:* kingnickol@aol.com
Nolan-Cain, Joseph – *Ellison*
* Overbury, Michael – 01636 702054
* Page, Anne, org, harmonium – 01223 240026 *fax:* 01223 573663
Parker-Smith, Jane – 020 7262 9259 *also fax; email:* jane@parker-smith.demon.co.uk
Parnell, Andrew, org, harmonium – *Michael Harrold*
* Parry, Martyn – 020 8980 9735 *also fax; email:* mp@antillroad.demon.co.uk
* Parsons, James – 01832 273447 *fax:* 01832 272026 *email:* OIF@btinternet.com
* Patrick, David Kinnear – 020 8449 4873 *email:* DeeKayPea@argonet.co.uk
Patrick, David M – 01392 275078
* Pearce, Geoffrey – 01977 681831
* Phillips, Margaret – 01963 250899
* Pilliner, Richard – 020 8651 3728
* Pink, Andrew – 020 7272 6101 *also fax; email:* andrew.pink@btinternet.com
* Ponsford, David – 01285 651995 *also fax*

GARY SIELING

ORGAN & HARPSICHORD

"...brilliant and elegant playing..." **Folkebladet Denmark**
"...very accomplished musician..." **NWZ Oldenburg**
"...a magnificent performance..." **Nottingham Evening Post**

162 LANGDALE ROAD, DUNSTABLE, BEDS LU6 3BT
07889 569226
email: garysieling@finemusic.freeserve.co.uk

Photo: Robert Barber

EVA-MARIA ALEXANDRE

Pianist

First Prizewinner
East-West Artists' International Competition, New York
Pro Musicis International Competition, Paris
South East Arts 'Young Musicians' Platform, London

"PATRICIAN OF THE KEYS - qualities that set her apart... dark foreboding, dreaminess and fiery brilliance with flair"
THE TIMES

"An artist who compels attention. Everything fell into place with majestic inevitability"
MUSICAL OPINION

"Power in reserve...intimate and engaging performances..."
THE BOSTON GLOBE

"Top notch pianist... dramatic and highly virtuosic..."
THE NEW YORK TIMES

Please contact:
Brahma Artists Management
Tel: 07931 121 243 • Fax: 0181 948 8895 • Email: brahma@talk21.com

Early music today

The magazine for everyone involved with the performance, promotion, study or sheer enjoyment of early music

- PROFILES
- NEWS
- MUSEUMS
- CONCERTS
- RECORDINGS
- INSTRUMENT MAKERS
- UK & OVERSEAS LISTINGS

Published bi-monthly
Annual UK subscription: £14.40
Telephone 020 7333 1720
for details of our
TRIAL SUBSCRIPTION OFFER
www.rhinegold.co.uk

* Popplewell, Richard – 020 8332 7301
* Price, David J C – 023 9243 0811 *fax:* 023 9229 5480 *email:* pennyport@aol.com
* Proud, Malcolm – 00 353 56 61497 *also fax*
* Rathbone, Christopher – 0113 274 7716 *also fax*
* Rees-Williams, Jonathan – *Musicmakers*
* Rennert, Jonathan – 01737 244604 *fax:* 01737 271128
* Riddle, Ian – 01782 661723
* Rochester, Marc – 07770 388001 *fax:* 01252 783172 *email:* marcroc@pc.jaring.my
Rogg, Lionel – *Denny Lyster*
* Roseberry, Eric – 01225 891410
Rowland, David – *Music Management*
* Rudland, Malcolm – 020 7589 9595 *also fax; email:* malcolmrudland@ndirect.co.uk
Saint, David – 0121 454 8529
Sanger, David – 017687 76628 *also fax*
* Sayer, Roger – 01634 849683 *fax:* 01634 401410
Scott, John – *Hazard*
* Seymour, Peter – 01904 652799 *fax:* 01904 338349 *email:* ps22@york.ac.uk
* Sieling, Gary – 07889 569226
Simcock, Iain – *Michael Harrold*
Smedley, Peter – 0115 929 1308
* Smith, Michael – 01262 670869 *also fax; email:* admin@mtsmith.newnet.co.uk
Souter, Martin – 01865 722552 *fax:* 01865 243388 *email:* martinsouter@mcmail.com
Stokes, Christopher – 0161 833 2220 *fax:* 0161 839 6226 *email:* christopher.stokes@btinternet.com
Stout, Alastair – 020 7490 0248 *pager:* 07625 631757
Tanner, Richard – 01254 51491 *fax:* 01254 699963 *email:* richard.tanner@blackburn.anglican.org
* Tebbet, Roger D – 01904 416219 *fax:* 01904 424898 *email:* roger.tebbet@which.net
* Thomas, James L – 01874 658313; 07971 403856 *fax:* 01874 658597
Titterington, David – *Denny Lyster*
Townend, Richard – 020 7589 1206 *fax:* 020 7589 5925
Townhill OBE, Dennis – 0131 225 1116 *fax:* 0131 225 3181
* Tracey, Ian – 0151 708 8471 *also fax*
Trinkwon, D'Arcy – 01227 280241 *also fax;* 07956 182113 *email:* altrinkwon@aol.com
Trotter, Thomas - 01753 859265
* Underwood, Philip – 0161 456 9037
* Walsh, Colin – 01522 532877 *fax:* 01522 511307
* Ward Russell, Gillian – 01621 853237
Watts, Jane – 01525 222729 *also fax*
Weir DBE, Dame Gillian – *Denny Lyster*
* White, Martin John – 028 3752 4110 *fax:* 028 3839 4525 *email:* martin.white14@virgin.net
* Williams, Roger Bevan – 01224 272570 *fax:* 01224 272515
* Williams, Simon – 01923 770543 *also fax*
Wills OBE, Arthur – 01353 662084 *also fax;* 07774 680716 *email:* artwill@argonet.co.uk
Winpenny, Keith – 01204 852466
* Wright, Simon – *Denny Lyster*
Zabala, Óscar Candendo – *Michael Harrold*

Solo Piano

The artists listed below are soloists; those indicated with an asterisk also perform as accompanists. Other accompanists and coaches are listed in a separate section. This list includes players of the forte-piano, whilst harpsichordists are listed in the following section.

* Aarons, Mignonette – 020 8204 8778
Achúcarro, Joaquín – *Olivia Ma*
Adams, John Christopher – *Ellison*
* Adni, Daniel – 020 7794 4076 *also fax*
Aimard, Pierre-Laurent – *HP*
Aldwell, Edward – *Pro Piano*
Alexandre, Eva-Maria – 07931 121243 *fax:* 020 8948 8895 *email:* brahma@talk21.com
Alexeev, Dmitri – *IMG*
Alexeyev, Anya – *HP*
* Allen, Juliet – 020 8404 0284; 07958 977625
Altman, Elizabeth – 01943 850853 *fax:* 0113 267 5821
Alvanis, Louis Demetrius – *JLM*
Ambache, Diana – 020 7263 4027 *also fax; email:* polmear.ambache@telinco.co.uk
Anastasescu, Anda – 020 7603 1396 *also fax; email:* aajg@btinternet.com
Anderszewski, Piotr – *Askonas Holt*
Andsnes, Leif Ove – *IMG*
Angelich, Nicholas – *TransArt*
Apekisheva, Katya – *Sonata*
Appleton, David – 020 8986 9197
Ardakov, Alexander – *Ellison* – 01494 724461 *also fax; fax:* 01494 581144 *email:* ardakov@hotmail.com
Armstrong, Paul – 020 7603 8431
Ashkenazy, Vladimir – *HP*
Aubakirova, Jania – *ADM*
Ax, Emanuel – *Askonas Holt*
Babayan, Sergei – *Pro Piano*
Badura-Skoda, Paul – *Connaught*
* Bailie, Eleanor – 020 8788 5270
* Baker, Alison – 01206 575825 *also fax;* 07850 241637 *email:* alisonbaker@aspects.net
* Bale, Matthew – 01225 337722
Ball, Andrew – 020 7732 1405 *also fax*
* Bamford, Stephanie – 0151 652 2033
Banowetz, Joseph – *Camerata*
Barenboim, Daniel – *Askonas Holt*
Barnes, Philippa – 01638 714534
Barthold, Kenneth van – 01747 838318 *also fax*
Barto, Tzimon – *Olivia Ma*
Bartoli, Sandro Ivo – *Clarion/Seven Muses*
Bashkirov, Dmitri – *Columbia*
Bavouzet, Jean-Efflam – *Gilder*
* Beament, Jane – 01279 436570
Bebbington, Mark – *SWA*
* Beechey, Gwilym – 01482 508910
Beedie, Norman – 01733 844603 *also fax*
Bekova, Eleonora – 020 8675 6885 *fax:* 020 8673 8356
Belinkaya, Noemy – *Ellison*
Belliere, Krystian – *Purkiss*
Bellucci, Giovanni – *TransArt*
Ben-Or, Nelly – 01923 822268 *also fax*
Bennett CBE, Sir Richard Rodney – *Clarion/Seven Muses*
* Benselin, Margaret – 01737 843792
* Benson, Clifford – 01732 364204 *also fax*
* Bentley, Keith – 0161 798 4329
Berezovsky, Boris – *IMG*
Berman, Boris – *Askonas Holt*
Berman, Lazar – *TransArt*
Béroff, Michel – *TransArt*
* Betteridge, Stephen – 01727 811443
Beyer, Isabel – 01727 858485 *also fax*
Bielicki, Richard – *SJM*
* Billington, Vincent – 01723 364241
Bingham, John – 0114 230 8113 *also fax;* 020 8289 3067
Binns, Malcolm – *Michael Harrold*
Biret, Idil – *Purkiss*
* Black, Richard – 020 7277 7068 *fax:* 020 7277 8354 *email:* 100115.3701@compuserve.com
Block, Michel – *Pro Piano*
Bloss, Nicholas van – *Ellison*
Boardman, Bruce – *John Boddy*
Bottrill, Andrew – 01865 712763 *also fax; email:* aeb29@yahoo.co.uk
* Bradley-Fulgoni, Peter – *Talbot-Cooper*
* Bradshaw, Susan – 020 7226 8675 *also fax*
Bratke, Marcelo – *Connaught*
Brautigam, Ronald – *Lubbock*
Brendel KBE, Alfred – *Ingpen*
* Brewster-Franzetti, Allison G – *Ellison*
Briggs, Sarah Beth – 01904 787011 *fax:* 01904 331906 *email:* enquiries@sarahbethbriggspianist.co.uk
* Broster, Eileen – 020 8551 0439 *also fax;* 07931 173727
* Brown, Alan – 01737 354642
Brown, Ian – *Manygate*
Browning, John – *PGM*
Brownridge, Angela – *Manygate*
* Bruce, Margaret – c/o 020 7731 3782 *fax:* 020 8948 5428
* Bruzon, John, keyboards – 01273 304450
Buckley, Geoffrey – 01600 780354 *also fax*
Budiardjo, Esther – *Pro Piano*
Burato, Cristiano – *Pristavec*
Burke, Paul – 01226 752504 *also fax; email:* paul.burke@ndirect.co.uk
Burmester, Pedro – *Gilder*
Burnett, Richard, f-pno – 01580 211702 *fax:* 01580 211007 *email:* finchcocks@argonet.co.uk
Burns MBE, Joan – 0161 998 3715
* Burnside, Iain – *VWM*
Burwell, Kim – *Purkiss*
* Byberg, Beth Elin – *Roy Baker*
* Byram-Wigfield, Timothy – c/o 01223 339339
* Canetty-Clarke, Janet – 01444 811243 *fax:* 01444 811171 *email:* janet@orphic.demon.co.uk
Canino, Bruno – *Allied*
Carlock, Sandra – *Ellison*
* Carter, Jeremy – *Invisible Pilots* – c/o 01452 857859 *also fax; email:* jjcarter@clara.co.uk
Cascioli, Gianluca – *Ingpen*
* Casén, Petra – 020 8941 9778
* Caskie, Graham – 020 8422 3016 *also fax;* 07930 984401
Cassard, Philippe – *OWM*
Chaushian, Anahit – *NBM*
Chen, Gwyneth – *Pro Piano*
* Chiu, Dai-Chi – 020 8952 8245 *also fax; email:* daichi@yahoo.com
Choi, Vivian – *Ellison*
Chudinovich, Evgenia – *Connaught*
* Clayton, Nigel – 020 8462 5702 *also fax*
Clegg, John – *Ellison*
* Clemmow, Caroline – 01724 720475 *fax:* 01724 721599
Cohen, Arnaldo – *Grant Rogers*

RAGS TO RICHES

Helen Crayford traces the story of Ragtime and its transformation into the 'riches' of early jazz between 1890 and 1940.

Helen performs a wide range of virtuoso piano works ranging from familiar names such as Scott Joplin and George Gershwin through to such outrageous characters as 'Jelly Roll' Morton and 'Fats' Waller.

The personalities behind the music are portrayed with lively commentary and anecdote, which can be presented in several European languages.

There are six informative and highly entertaining programmes:

- Maple Leaf Centenary
- Lady, Be Good!
- Striding thro' Harlem
- Cakewalks to Concert Halls
- Americans in Paris
- Fascinatin' Rhythms

"Crayford's playing took on the joyous assertiveness of the great stride pianists" The Independent

For fees and availability, contact:
Jean Judge Artist Management
Tel/Fax: +44 (0)1865 515286
e-mail:jjarts@msn.com
http://website.lineone.net/~matthew.brailsford

Photography by James Caldwell

Christopher Langdown

Piano

"A strong performance built on a rigorous technique..." *Birmingham Post*
"Thoughtful...with a beautiful sound. Crisp and controlled..." *Birmingham Post*
"...impressive with a powerful, yet delicate touch. Like the entire programme, his playing was a delight to the ear." *Richmond & Twickenham Times*

Contact:
Wright Music Promotions Limited
235 Streetsbrook Road
Solihull
West Midlands B91 1HE
Tel: (+44) 0121 705 0098 Fax: (+44) 0121 705 4815

Recitals & Masterclasses UK / Europe during 2000/2001.

Recently released CD of piano works by Beethoven, Brahms, Chopin, Poulenc and Bridge available upon request.

DAVID ELWIN

pianist/accompanist

PHOTO: HANYA CHLALA

Recitalist
solo, vocal & instrumental

Auditions
& recording

Coaching

"Fine touch and stylistic awareness"

14 Princes Road
Wimbledon
London SW19 8RB

020 8540 8426

Appearing on 10th February 2000 at St John's Smith Square with The Revolutionary Drawing Room chamber ensemble performing works of Schubert, Rossini and rare Donizetti and Liszt piano music

"...a performance of artistic stature..."
(The Birmingham Post)

NORMAN OLSFANGER
Piano

Enquiries to:
35 Falkland Road
London NW5 2PU
Tel/Fax 0207 485 1508

* Cole, Annette – 020 8445 4485 *also fax*
Cole, Maggie, f-pno – *Robert White*
Collard, Jean-Philippe – *Tennant*
Colvill, Robin – 01727 848123; 07979 598508 *fax:* 01727 854910 *email:* colvillconcerts@cwcom.net
Coombs, Stephen – 01273 685849 *fax:* 01273 703850 *email:* scriptory@compuserve.com
Cooper, Imogen – *VWM*
Costa, Sequeira – *Ellison*
Cousin, Martin – *Pristavec*
* Crayford, Helen – 020 8863 4659 *fax:* 020 8863 9223
* Croser, Peter – 01932 228012
* Crossland, Jill – 020 8579 4394
* Crossland, Neil – *Murphy/Purkiss* *email:* shaun.margaret.murphy@virgin.net
Crossley, Paul – *Connaught*
* Cuckston Alan – 01757 638238 *also fax; email:* alancuckston@iname.com
D'Ascoli, Bernard – *Clarion/Seven Muses*
Dagul, Harvey – 01727 858485 *also fax*
Dalberto, Michel – *TransArt*
Darnborough, Jonathan – 020 8395 7433 *email:* artists@midman503a.freeserve.co.uk
Davidovich, Bella – *Tennant*
Davies, Eiluned – 020 8368 8202
* Davies, Helen – 01248 713336 *email:* daviesfourhands@hotmail.com
de Larrocha, Alicia – *Christa Phelps*
De Maria, Pietro – *TransArt*
De Pledge, Stephen – 020 8670 3115 *also fax*
de Quetteville, Timothy – 01534 879082 *fax:* 01534 629147
de Saram, Druvi – *Stella Baker*
de Waal, Rian – *Gilder*
* Deering, Richard – 020 8656 6222 *also fax; email:* richard@malacca.demon.co.uk
Demidenko, Nikolai – *GIA*
Dick, James – *Camerata*
* Dickinson, Peter – 01728 454540 *email:* peterdickinson@foxborough.demon.co.uk
* Dimitrova, Lora – *Annon* *email:* watsona@aol.com
Dimitrova, Nina – *Michael Brewer*
* Dodd, Jane – 020 8642 5418
Donohoe, Peter – *Askonas Holt*
Douglas, Barry – *IMG*
Dowdeswell, Gretel – 020 8292 2132 *also fax; fax:* 020 8350 4579
Dudnik, Olga – *Sonata*
* Durran, Katharine – 01484 841868 *also fax*
* Dussek, Michael – 020 8958 6983 *also fax*
Dyson, Phillip – c/o 020 8786 8830 *also fax*
* Earl, David – 01223 303857
El Bacha, Abdel Rahman – *TransArt*
Elias-José, Vanya – 020 8878 0980 *fax:* 020 8392 9546 *email:* vanya@eliast.swinternet.co.uk
Elton, Christopher – 020 8455 6587 *fax:* 020 8381 4797 *email:* christopher@parkdr.demon.co.uk; c.elton@ram.ac.uk
* Elwin, David – 020 8540 8426
Endo, Yoshiko – *GBZ*
Engerer, Brigitte – *TransArt*
Evans, Clifford – c/o Marycliff Productions 01473 253217 *email:* recitals@marycliff.co.uk
* Evans, Patricia – 01604 603323
* Evans, Peter – 0131 447 6414 *also fax*
Evans, Richard – *Dyfel*
Fear, Margaret – 01923 661159
Feghali, José – *Olivia Ma*
Feinberg, Alan – *Tennant*
Fellner, Till – *Ingpen*
* Fenyö, Gusztáv – 0141 339 2708 *fax:* 0141 337 6923
Fergus-Thompson, Gordon – 020 8202 5861 *also fax*
Fialkowska, Janina – *Ingpen*
* Filsell, Jeremy – *Chameleon*
Fingerhut, Margaret – c/o 01444 230779 *fax:* 01444 233699
* Fischer, Raymond – 020 8748 4702 *also fax*
Fisher, Norma – *Ellison*
Fong, William – 01400 250972 *email:* william.fong@lineone.net
Ford, Gillian – 020 8643 0275 also fax; 07970 723301
Forey, Edmund – *Mostylea*
Fountain, Ian – *Connaught*
Fowke, Philip – *PGM* – 020 7935 5773 *fax:* 020 8980 3679 *email:* pfowke@xva.u-net.com
Francesch, Homero – *Anglo-Swiss*
Franceschetti, Davide – *OWM*
Frankl, Peter – *TransArt*
* Freyhan, Michael, f-pno – 020 8459 6825 *also fax; email:* michael@freyhan.freeserve.co.uk
* Frith, Benjamin – 01909 562395 *also fax*
* Gammon, Philip – 020 8866 3260 *fax:* 020 8248 2906
Gampel, Alan – *THA*
Garzón, Maria – *Ellison*
Gasser, Mark – *Camerata*
Gavrilov, Andrei – *Hazard*
Gelber, Bruno Leonardo – *TransArt*
* Gellhorn, Peter – 020 8876 3949
Geniushas, Petras – *Ellison*
Gibb, James – *Purkiss*
Gibbons, Jack – *NBM*
Gillespie, Rhondda – 01424 715167 *fax:* 01424 712214 *email:* 100723.510@compuserve.com
Goerner, Nelson – *Christa Phelps*
Golan, Itamar – *Askonas Holt*
Goldstone, Anthony – 01724 720475 *fax:* 01724 721599
Goode, Richard – *Intermusica*
* Govier, Geoffrey, f-pno – 020 8922 0587 *also fax*
Graf, Enrique – *Ellison*
Gräsbeck, Folke – *Ellison*
* Gray, Antony – *Blythe* *email:* gray-dupuy@mcmail.com
Green-Armytage, Christopher – 01362 694223
* Greenwood, Richard – 020 8748 6203
Gruenberg, Joanna – *Intermusica*
* Gulley, Margaret – 01392 874761
* Gutman, Stephen – 020 7254 7763 *also fax*
Guy, François-Frédéric – *VWM*
Hadjinikos, George – 0161 928 3329 *fax:* 00 301 361 9373
Haefliger, Andreas – *Intermusica*
* Hall, Garth – 01730 231765 *fax:* 01730 304337 *email:* GHall111@aol.com
Hamelin, Marc André – *GIA*
Hamilton, Kenneth – *Camerata*
* Hancox, William – 07956 833337 *fax:* 020 8458 0980
Harding, Elizabeth – 01690 710523
Harris, Jeffery – 01737 355245 *also fax*
* Harte, Ruth – 020 8650 2929 *also fax*
Harvey, Jean – 01428 642230
* Hattingh, Michael – c/o 020 8802 2719
Haywood, Sam – 07961 178026 *email:* sam@haywood.u-net.com
Hazeldine, Alan – 020 8341 0567 *also fax; email:* alan.hazeldine@mcmail.com
Hazlehurst, Marjorie – 0121 454 0771
Hegedüs, Endre – *Ellison*
Herskowitz, Matthew – *Pro Piano*
Hewitt, Angela – c/o 01242 578893
* Hewson, James – 01572 767653 *email:* J.Hewson@scm.brad.ac.uk
Hickman, Carl – 0121 454 8431
* Hill, Barbara – 020 7435 9210
* Hill, Peter – 0114 230 2309 *fax:* 0114 263 0231
Hind, Rolf – *Clarion/Seven Muses*
Hobson, Ian – c/o 020 8894 0391 *fax:* 020 8287 9428 *email:* howard@howardgreenwood.freeserve.co.uk
Hodges, Nicolas – *fax:* 0870 052 3240 *email:* info@nicolashodges.demon.co.uk
Honeybourne, Duncan – *Camerata*
Horsley OBE, Colin – 01624 813095
Hough, Stephen – *HP*
Houlihan, Phillip – 020 8947 0484
* Howard, Leslie – c/o 020 8960 4780 *fax:* 020 8964 5510
Howard, William – 01453 872478 *fax:* 01453 872173 *email:* william.howard@dial.pipex.com
* Howat, Roy – 020 8648 1700 *also fax; email:* howat_hiscocks@compuserve.com
Howells, David – 020 7794 2077
Hoyland, John – *Roxane Houston*
* Humphrey, Graeme – 020 8690 6264 *fax:* 020 8314 1550
Humphreys, John – *Camerata*
Hursey, John – *Annon*
* Hurton, Amanda – 020 8390 6951 *fax:* 020 8395 5374 *email:* ahurton@msn.com
Hutchison, Nigel – 020 8340 5217 *also fax*
Igoshina, Valentina – *Ingpen*
Immelman, Niel – 020 8947 7201 *fax:* 020 8946 8846
* Innes, Audrey – 0131 620 0380 *fax:* 0131 620 0379 *email:* 100777.2721@compuserve.com
Iruzun, Clélia – *NCCP* – 020 7916 2410 *fax:* 020 7916 2448 *email:* clelia.iruzun@virgin.net
Jablonski, Peter – *HP*
* Jacobs, Peter – 020 8943 2918
Jacobson, Julian – 020 8694 9525 *fax:* 020 8692 7065 *email:* julian.jacobson@breathemail.net
Janusz – 01765 605508 *fax:* 01765 606688
* Jeffrey, Emily – 020 7223 2408 *also fax*
Jhlig, Florian – *Michael Brewer*
Jiménez, Raúl – *NBM*
Jones, Martin – *OWM*
Jones, Michael – 01384 393706 *also fax*
* Jones, Rosalind – 020 8743 3744 *also fax*
Joseph, Julian – *HP*
Kahane, Jeffrey – *IMG*
Kalichstein, Joseph – *HP*
Kaplan, Benjamin – 020 8458 1018 *fax:* 020 8209 0265
Katin, Peter – *TransArt*
Katsaris, Cyprien – *TransArt*
Kazakevich, Mikhail – *LM*
Keeley, Robert – 020 8968 3625; 020 7848 2486 *email:* robert.keeley@kcl.ac.uk
Kempf, Frederick – *Grant Rogers*
Kendall, Marie-Noëlle – *Ellison*
Kenner, Kevin – *Connaught*
* Kenny, Courtney – *Upbeat*
Kerri – c/o 020 8521 2424 *fax:* 020 8521 4343
* Kingsley, Colin – 0131 669 2070
Kirby, James – 020 8980 5711 *also fax; email:* jnjkirby@aol.com
Kissin, Evgeny – *Askonas Holt*
Klansky, Ivan – *Judith Hendershott*
Kodama, Mari – *OWM*
Kodjabashia, Nikola – *ECAM*
Kopelman, Elizaveta – *YCAT*
Kotok, Carolyn – *Invisible Pilots*
Koumis, Matthew – 01962 624148 *fax:* 01962 864727 *email:* telos@dial.pipex.com
Kovacevich, Stephen – *VWM*
Krausz, Adrienne – *TransArt*
Kravtchenko, Anna – *Christa Phelps*

BERNARD ROBERTS

Pianist

... "the audience were priveleged to hear one of the most powerful, utterly compelling interpretations of the Beethoven Sonata op.111 around the present time and come face to face with possibly this country's most serious Beethoven interpreter, Bernard Roberts". *DAILY TELEGRAPH*

"The interpretations are beyond criticism, more than worthy company for those by the most celebrated names." (Beethoven's last three Piano Sonatas) *CLASSIC CD*

Caroline Ireland Management

Caroline Ireland Management
Uwchlaw'r Coed, Llanbedr, Gwynedd LL45 2NA
Tel/fax 01341 241532
e-mail caroline.ireland@virgin.net
http://freespace.virgin.net/caroline.ireland

LOUISE JONES

VIOLIN

"...formidable technique and musical personality." THE STRAD

"Louise Jones is a violinist whose musicianship shines out of every note..." MUSICAL OPINION

CONCERTOS
RECITALS
CHAMBER MUSIC

Internationally acclaimed soloist and leader of the GLADSTONE STRING QUARTET. Many recordings include the complete works of Delius and Hoddinott for violin and piano (Meridian and Divine Art Labels).

"...devoted performances which enter Delius' elusive soundworld with rare sensitivity and insight." CLASSIC CD****

J.Audrey Ellison, International Artists Management, 135 Stevenage Rd, London SW6 6PB. T/F: 020 8450 1783.

Mary Mei-Loc Wu

piano

"... a poetical quality to her playing... totally involved with the music... captivates her audiences"
THE LORD MENUHIN O.M., K.B.E.

"One of the most gifted of her generation"
VLADO PERLEMUTER

"Superb technique combined with aggression, wit and poetry"
THE TIMES

"Throughout, one recognised Wu's brilliance. She captured the essence of each composer, convincing listeners of her commitment to modern French and Romantic German music."
HONG KONG STANDARD

Contact:
J Audrey Ellison International Artists' Management
135 Stevenage Road, Fulham, London, SW6 6PB
Tel: 0171 381 9751 Fax: 0171 381 2406

CD now available on the PARADISUM label
The Chinese Pianoforte
PDS-CD5

Kuerti, Anton – *Pro Piano*
Kvapil, Radoslav – *Murphy*
Lane, Piers – *PGM (concertos)/GIA (recitals)*
Langdown, Christopher – *Wright*
* Latarche, Vanessa – 01932 786625; 07831 656827 *fax:* 01932 788808 *email:* vanessa@illumiere.demon.co.uk
* Latimer, Mark – *SS*
Lauriala, Risto – *Ellison*
Law, John – *JLM*
* Lawson, Peter – 01457 862555 *also fax*
Lazaridis, George-Emmanuel – *Gilder*
Lazie, Dejan – *Lubbock*
* Lear, Angela – *Ellison*
* Ledger CBE, Philip – c/o 0141 332 4101 *fax:* 0141 332 8901 *email:* p.ledger@rsamd.ac.uk
* Lee, Dennis – 020 8969 7468 *also fax; email:* dleepiano@aol.com
* Leek, Helen – 020 8806 7704 *fax:* 020 7502 6484 *email:* helen.wickham.u-net.com
* Lenehan, John – 01494 531862 *also fax*
Levin, Muriel – 020 8947 5538
Lewis, Paul – *Ingpen*
Liberg, Hans – c/o 01363 866665 *fax:* 01363 866667
Lill OBE, John – *Askonas Holt*
* Lin, You-Chiung – 020 8381 4736 *also fax; email:* youchiung@hotmail.com
* Lion, Margaret – 020 7263 2365 *also fax*
Lisney, James – *SWA*
Llewellyn-Jones, Iwan – *Ellison*
* Long, Shirley – 020 7436 0914; 07770 983295 *email:* shirleysmusic@yahoo.co.uk
Loriod, Yvonne – *Allied*
Lortie, Louis – *Intermusica*
* Lowe, Timothy – 01892 535040
Lupu, Radu – *THA*
Lythgoe, Clive – *Grant Rogers*
* McArthur, David – *Maestoso*
McCabe, John – 020 8574 5039 *also fax*
McCawley, Leon – *Askonas Holt*
MacGregor, Joanna – *Ingpen*
McIntosh, Thomas – 01473 822596 *fax:* 01473 824175
* McKay, Elizabeth – 01993 881910 *fax:* 01993 881278
* McLachlan, Murray – *Chameleon*
* McMahon, Richard – 029 2061 7180 *email:* mcmahonrb@wcmd.ac.uk
* Macnamara, Hilary – 020 8341 2811 *also fax*
Madzar, Aleksandar – *HP*
Magill, Ronan – 020 7584 3795
Mallett, Charles – *Roxane Houston*
Mantas, Santiago – *Ellison*
Markham, Richard – 020 7738 1480 *fax:* 020 7738 2765
Markland, Anna – *Denny Lyster*
* Marshall, Mark – 01722 325313 *also fax*
Marshall, Wayne – *Askonas Holt*
Marshev, Oleg – *Maestoso*
Martin, Philip – 01249 812508 *also fax; email:* pmandppj@globalnet.co.uk
Martin-Davis, Ann – 01993 813620 *also fax*
Matsuzawa, Yuki – *ADM*
* Matthews, Charles – 01386 438078 *also fax*
* Maxwell, Dorothy – *Purkiss*
Meacock, David – 01753 886005 *also fax; email:* David.G.Meacock@btinternet.com
Mead, Philip – 01223 357431 *also fax*
Meecham, Nicola – c/o 01225 832192 *also fax; email:* nicola@meecham.demon.co.uk
Melnikov, Alexander – *IMG*
Menuhin, Jeremy – *Upbeat*
Merscher, Kristin – *Finch*
Meshulam, Benita – *Ellison*
Meyrick, Richard – *Invisible Pilots*
* Milford, Julian – 020 7720 8377 *fax:* 020 7720 5309 *email:* julian@milfordj.freeserve.co.uk
Milic-Apostolovic, Marina – 01727 825320 *also fax*
Milne, Hamish – 020 8946 9268 *fax:* 020 8296 8603
* Mobbs, Kenneth – 0117 973 3613 *also fax*
Monetti, Mariaclara – *Manygate*
Moravec, Ivan – *VWM*
* Mosley, Kathryn – 020 7430 1668 *fax:* 020 7430 1672
Mursky, Eugene – *Pristavec*
Mustonen, Olli – *HP*
Myers, Thalia – c/o 020 7733 6719 *also fax; email:* ugm@netcomuk.co.uk
Nakajima, Sanae – 01865 558392 *also fax*
Naoumoff, Emile – *TransArt*
Nettle, David – 020 7738 9427 *fax:* 020 7738 2765
* Neugarten, Steven – 020 8312 2070 *also fax; email:* steven.neugarten@excite.com
Nguyen, Tra – *Finch*
* Nicholls, Simon, pno, f-pno – 020 8446 0812
Nicholson, Tessa – 020 7624 2336
Nissman, Barbara – *Ellison*
* Norris, David Owen – *Clarion/Seven Muses*
O'Hagan, Peter – c/o 020 8960 4780 *fax:* 020 8964 5510
O'Hora, Ronan – *Gilder*
Ogawa, Noriko – *Clarion/Seven Muses*
Ogdon, Brenda Lucas – *Ellison*
Okada, Hiromi – *Ellison*
Okashiro, Chitose – *Pro Piano*
Olechowski, Jósef – *LA*
Olsfanger, Norman – c/o 020 7485 1508 *also fax*
Ortiz, Cristina – *HP*
Osborne, Steven – *Tennant*
Ousset, Cécile – *Intermusica*
Ovchinikov, Vladimir – *GIA*
Ozolins, Arthur – *Gilder*
* Pace, Ian – *Haferkorn* – 020 8948 6615 *also fax; email:* ian.pace@virgin.net
Palmer, Phyllis – 01223 354338

Evelyn Sargent

Solo performance concerts, Chamber Music

155 Southborough Lane,
Bromley, Kent
Tel: 0181 – 467 1810

RICHARD SHAW

Pianist

RECITALS •
(chamber, vocal & instrumental)
MASTERCLASSES •
RECORDINGS •
AUDITIONS •
COACHING •

- *"What a wonderful pianist"* **Felix Aprahamian**
- *"Incisive and sensitive"* **The Independent**
- *"Excellent support"* **The Times**
- *"The colour and clarity of Richard Shaw's playing was a pleasure in its own right"* **Bath Chronicle**
- *"A fervent, intensely moving performance"* **The Strad**
- *"At the Wigmore Hall the Russian bass-baritone Vassily Savenko was most ably accompanied by Richard Shaw"* **Opera Now**

45a Cannon Hill, Southgate, London N14 6LH
Tel/Fax: 020 8882 5333
Mobile: 07976 614 429
email: richard.shawpiano@btinternet.com

Mûza Rubackyté - Pianist

More than 30 different recital programs and more than 35 concerti

Laureate of International Competition of Vilnius, Tallinn, ALL-UNION, Budapest (Liszt-Bartock) Paris (Grands Maîtres Français)

Portrait through some music press reviews

The Newport Music Festival Saved The Best Pianist For Last. Mûza Rubackyté was back for another lesson in just how the piano should be played.
The Providence USA, July 1996

The Wigmore Hall was alive with the virility of her performance without any sense of noise or excessive volume-a rare treat of a rare talent. She will be welcome back at any time.
Musical Opinion London, June 1996

She let loose the full force of her temperament, playing with complete abandon and finally humor. Her huge intrepid performances, fulminating and girlishly whimsical by turns, brought people shouting to their feet at the end of each piece.
Boston Globe USA, July 1995

Were the gods angered that a mere mortal could play the piano so well? No just a fireworks display in the skies over Rosecliff, as Lithuanian pianist Mûza Rubackyté made her american debut. She turned out to be the real thing, though, a pianist with a ferocious technique, coupled with the soul of poet.
The Providence USA, July 1995

Muza Rubackyté is clearly a musician of rare talent.
Gramophone, February 1995

The present performance are abreath with that spirit, bringing forcefully to mind the young Argerich in Chopin… Now hearing Mûza Rubackyté, an artist of phenomenal powers who must be counted among the most gifted pianists of her generation… Turning up amid the plethora of mediocre recitals by young hope fuls attempting to recreate The Legend, Rubackyté's recent LISZT program revealed the astounding and «consistent combinaison of power and shimmer, intensity and radiance, élan, and urbanity» comprising her unique sound - a sort of prismatically tinted ecstasy. Enthusiastically Recommended.
Fanfare-USA, September-October, 1994

Here is something remarkable-the lightning reflexes of a Lazar Berman wedded to the tonal fitness of a Barenboim or Bolet in a sultry, unknown Lithuanian Beauty. Mûza Rubackyté is a born LISZT player with an instinctive grasp of the way that flourishes and fioriture, rippling arpeggios, tremolos, and massive chords call for color… Enthusiastically Recommended.
Fanfare-USA, January-February 1994

No barnstroming here. Mûza Rubackyté's selfless poetry makes Liszt even more exciting. An excellent Lithuanian pianist, Mûza Rubackyté is an accomplished virtuoso who makes no show of virtuosity. Even in the formidable Erlkönig, bravura is entirely subordinated to musical gesture, with exciting and chilling results.
Classic CD, UK, March 1994

Managements : UK Mr. Ivan Beal 88 Fortis Green Rd. Muswell Hill London N10 3HN Tel: 0181-365-3063 Fax: 0181-444-0415
Gen. Mng.: France-Benelux Represt. Lithuanian National Philharmonic. Mr A. Shvaloff 16 rue Vernier 75015 Paris France tel: 3301-4574-0343 Fax: 3301-4574-6461

Papadopoulos, Marios – 020 8450 2714 *fax:* 020 8450 0087 *email:* marios@apple-uk.net
Parham, Lucy – *Voullaire*
Parker, Jon Kimura – *HP*
Parkin, Eric – 0118 947 4421 *also fax*
Partridge, Jennifer – *Upbeat*
* Peake, Timothy – 020 8969 7004
Peebles, Antony – 020 8788 8162 *fax:* 020 8788 0488
* Pendlebury, Karl, keyboards – 01932 703569 *also fax;* 07956 208131
Perahia, Murray – *Askonas Holt*
Perl, Alfredo – *Askonas Holt*
Pertis, Attila – *Ellison*
Petrov, Marina – *John Boddy*
Pettersson, Mikael – *Michael Brewer*
* Phillips, Jean – 01227 767282
Phillips, Jonathan – 020 8743 6958 *also fax*; 07973 621738
* Phillips, Lois – 020 7722 7815
Piatti, Polo – 020 8514 3998; 07956 251858 *email:* piatti@globalnet.co.uk
Pires, Maria João – *Askonas Holt*
Pizarro, Artur – *Hazard*
Plessis, Herbert du – *Ellison*
Pletnev, Mikhail – *Columbia*
Plowright, Jonathan – 01273 674457 *also fax; email:* jdplowright@hotmail.com
Pludermacher, Georges – *TransArt*
* Plummer, Paul – 07973 915053 *fax:* 020 7370 5767 *email:* plums@psiona.demon.co.uk
Pogorelich, Ivo – *Columbia* – c/o 020 8208 2480 *fax:* 020 8208 2490 *email.* dkantor.kcm@webstar.co.uk
Pollini, Maurizio – *HP*
Pöntinen, Roland – *Gilder*
Portugheis, Alberto – *Murphy*
Postnikova, Viktoria – *Allied*
* Pott, Francis – 01962 885874 *also fax; email:* fpott@argonet.co.uk
Pratt, Awadagin – *Anglo-Swiss*
Pressler, Menahem – c/o 01273 454310 *also fax*
* Preston, Gary – 020 8651 3548
* Prior, Gary – *Purkiss*
* Pruslin, Stephen – 020 8948 7404 *also fax*
Pryor, Gwenneth – c/o 020 8906 4464 *fax:* 020 8906 1180 *email:* rlstone@compuserve.com
* Purkiss, Anthony – 01273 774730 *also fax*
Queffélec, Anne – *Tennant*
* Rahman, Sophia – *Purkiss*
Ránki, Dezsö – *Lubbock*
Rathbone, Joyce – 020 7229 0219 *also fax email:* jrathbone@cwcom.net
* Riddle, Ian – 01782 661723
Rifkin, Joshua – *Clarion/Seven Muses*
Riley, Howard – 020 8290 5917
Riu, Elena – *GBZ*
Roberts, Bernard – *Ireland*
Roberts, Ken – *Annon*
Roberts, Paul – *Lunn*
Robertson, Caryl – 020 7435 7978 *fax:* 020 7916 8830
Rogé, Pascal – *Clarion/Seven Muses*
Roll, Michael – *THA*
* Rolton, Julian – 01442 244832 *also fax*
Romero, Patricia – 020 8288 1432 *also fax*
Roscoe, Martin – *Hazard*
Rosen, Charles – *OWM*
* Roskell, Penelope – 020 8806 5969 *also fax*
* Rowlands, Maxim – 020 8468 7794 *email:* rowlandsmx@aol.com
Rubackytė, Mûza – c/o 020 8348 6144 *fax:* 020 8348 6145 *email:* ivan8renee@aol.com
Rudy, Mikhaïl – *HP*
Rumessen, Vardo – *Pro Piano*
Rutherford, Jonathan – 01728 688484 *also fax*
Saba, Geoffrey – 01780 482432 *fax:* 01780 482433 *email:* geoffrey.saba@hotmail.com
Sager, Christopher Czaja – *Ellison*
* Salter, Lionel – 020 8458 3568 *also fax*
Sarkissova, Oksana – *Sonata*
* Schiedermair, Valentin – 020 8952 8245 *also fax; email:* Valentin_Schiedermair@yahoo.com
Schiff, András – *THA*
Schiller, Allan – *Manygate*
Schönfeld, Avi – *Ellison*
Scott, Christopher – *ADM*
Scott, Graham – *GIA*
* Searson, Stella – 01769 560348
* Seed, Christopher, pno, left-handed f-pno – 01962 715134 *email:* lefthandpiano@msn.com
* Seferinova, Valentina – 023 9226 5910 *also fax*
Seivewright, Peter – 01555 820369 *fax:* 01555 820840
Seow, Yitkin – 020 7584 5393 *also fax*
Serkin, Peter – *Ingpen*
Servadei, Annette – 01227 369501 *also fax; email:* anet-mike@servasiv.freeserve.co.uk
* Seymour, Peter, f-pno – 01904 652799 *fax:* 01904 338349 *email:* ps22@york.ac.uk
* Sharkey, Jeffrey – 01923 331177 *also fax; email:* jsharkey@compuserve.com
Sheppard, Craig – *ECAM*
* Sherbourne, Janet – 0118 947 7170 *email:* janet@metalworks.org
* Sherlaw-Johnson, Robert – 01993 891318 *fax:* 01865 276128 *email:* robert.sherlaw-johnson@music.ox.ac.uk; robert.sherlaw-johnson@worc.ox.ac.uk
* Shewring, Simon – 029 2089 2107
* Shimizu, Hisayo – 020 8458 5817 *also fax*
Shorr, Aaron – *NBM*
* Silkoff, David – 020 8501 3115
Skanavi, Katia – *Pro Piano*

Simon Shewring

Pianist

"...played not only with virtuosity but, even more laudably, with modesty and impeccable taste."

"The Times"
(Solo Recital at Purcell Room)

"...Ravel's 'Jeux d'Eau' was brilliantly and sensitively dispatched and finally Rachmaniov's two Kreisler transcriptions, as it were, programmed the delightful encores. Simon Shewring is an excellent and finished player and this recital was further proof of his admirable qualities."

"Musical Opinion"
(Solo Recital at St John's Smith Square)

134 Parc-y-Fro, Creigiau, Cardiff. CF15 9SB

KATHARINE MAY

HARPSICHORD

"The evening's feisty and urbane harpsichordist"
The Times

"The performance was a delight to the mind, heart, and ear"
Nottingham Evening Post

46, CANNON COURT ROAD, MAIDENHEAD,
BERKSHIRE, SL6 7QN
TEL/FAX: 01628 783272

Skoumal, Adam – *Sonata*
* Slade, Vyvyenne – 020 8883 3195 *fax:* 020 7265 1642
* Smith, Philip – *Maestoso* – 020 8690 5504 *fax:* 020 8690 9972 *email:* ph.smith@virgin.net
Smith, Ronald – *Purkiss*
Soifertis, Evgeny – *Murphy*
Sokolov, Grigory – *Tennant*
Solzhenitsyn, Ignat – *Columbia*
Sowden, Janine – *NWA*
Spanswick, Melanie – *Bray*
Spottiswoode, Daphne – *Ellison*
Steen-Nökleberg, Einar – *Roy Baker*
Steuerman, Jean Louis – *LA*
* Stevens, Eric – 020 8942 7706
* Stevenson, Ronald – *Camerata*
* Stirling, Ian – 020 8455 0288 *also fax*
* Stoker, Richard – 020 8852 9608 *also fax; email:* gps5@tutor.open.ac.uk
Stone, Colin – *Dyfel*
* Stone, Robin – 01206 272587
Stott, Kathryn – *Askonas Holt*
* Sturrock, Kathron – 020 8780 3266 *fax:* 020 8780 0600 *email:* cicfib@easynet.co.uk
Swartzentruber, Mark – c/o 020 7272 7911 *fax:* 020 8372 6189 *email:* 106777.73@compuserve.com
Tan, Melvyn, f-pno, pno – *Barber*
* Tanner, Mark Philip – 01823 324439 *fax:* 01823 349201 *email:* markptanner@compuserve.com
Taylor, Kendall – *Ellison*
Terroni, Raphael – *Purkiss*
Thalmann, Michael – *Ellison*
Tharaud, Alexandre – *LM*
Thwaites, Penelope – 020 7794 5090 *also fax; email:* thwaites.jackson@virgin.net
Tiempo, Sergio – *Pro Piano*
Tirimo, Martino – *Music Partnership*
* Toh, Chee-Hung – 020 8969 7468 *also fax; email:* toh@clarionmusic.com; TohcheeH@aol.com
Tong, Daniel – 020 8398 8231 *also fax*
Toradze, Alexander – *Askonas Holt*
* Townsend, Ian – 020 8668 5191 *also fax;* 07808 021792
* Tozer, Geoffrey – c/o 023 8073 3674
* Troon, Vivian – 020 8907 8428 *also fax*
Tryon, Valerie – c/o 020 8894 0391 *fax:* 020 8287 9428 *email:* howard@howardgreenwood.freeserve.co.uk
Tuck, Rosemary – 020 8203 5723 *also fax*
Uchida, Mitsuko – *VWM*
Uhlig, Florian – *Michael Brewer*
Valesova, Lada – *CDI*
Vásáry, Tamás – *IMG*
Ventura, Alba – *YCAT*
Viardo, Vladimir – *Pro Piano/TransArt (Europe)*
Vogt, Lars – *Askonas Holt*
Volodos, Arcadi – *Columbia*
Vriend, Jan – 01453 751213 *also fax; email:* JNMV@tinyonline.co.uk
* Walker, Nicholas – 01722 333147 *also fax*
* Ward, David, f-pno – 020 8874 4938 *also fax; email:* 106224.2623@compuserve.com
Wass, Ashley – *Pristavec*
* Waters, Marian – 01737 245252
Wells, Carol – *Dyfel*
* Werry, Elizabeth – 020 8693 7869 *also fax*
West, Andrew – *NCCP*
White, Emily – *Ellison*
* Whitworth, Geoffrey – 020 8458 4281
Wibaut, Frank – *Camerata*
Wild, Earl – *Gilder*
Wilde, David – *Ellison*
Williams, Oliver – *Invisible Pilots*
* Williamson, Clive – 020 8647 3781 *fax:* 020 8699 2772 *email:* c.williamson@surrey.ac.uk
Wilson, Malcolm – *Camerata*
* Wilson-Dickson, Andrew – 029 2022 8154 *also fax; email:* w-d@baynet.co.uk
Wolff, Marguerite – *Ellison*
Wolfram, William – *Encore Concerts*
Wolpe, Katharina – *Michael Brewer*
Woo, Betty – *Susie Wong*
Woodward, Roger – *ECAM*
Woyke, Andreas – *Finch*
* Wray, David – 00 353 1 454 7971 *also fax; email:* dwray@tinet.ie
* Wray, Steven – *Chameleon*
Wright, Rosemarie, f-pno – 01424 423260 *also fax*
Wu, Mary Mei-Loc – *Ellison*
Yablonskaya, Oxana – *Pro Piano*
Yampolsky, Viktor – *Ellison*
* Zebaida, Robin – 020 7286 0242 *also fax*
Zellan-Smith, Georgina – c/o 020 8946 6690
Zilberstein, Lilya – *TransArt*
Zimerman, Krystian – *HP*
Zwingenberger, Axel – c/o 01363 866665 *fax:* 01363 866667

Harpsichord

This list includes players of the clavichord, spinet, virginals, etc. The artists marked with an asterisk also perform as accompanists.

* Aldwinckle, Robert – 01424 715435 *also fax*
Bale, Matthew – 01225 337722
Barber, Graham – 0113 263 1890 *fax:* 0113 263 7178 *email:* g.d.barber@leeds.ac.uk
* Barlow, Jeremy – 020 7267 7176 *fax:* 020 7267 0127 *email:* jrmybarlow@aol.com
* Beechey Gwilym – 01482 508910
* Bond, Ann – 01524 701623
* Booth, Colin – 01749 870516 *also fax*
Bowyer, Kevin – c/o 01608 677417; 07774 657010
* Brown, Helena – 020 8580 8429 *also fax; fax:* 020 8580 8430 *email:* helenam-b@zetnet.co.uk
* Byram-Wigfield, Timothy – c/o 01223 339339
* Cave, Penelope – 01483 563096 *also fax*
Chapman, Jane – 020 8997 7621 *also fax*
* Charlston, Terence – 01582 462024 *also fax; email:* terence@charlston.freeserve.co.uk
Cole, Maggie – *Robert White*
* Coulson Richard – 01932 229171
* Cuckston, Alan – *POEM* – 01757 638238 *also fax; email:* alancuckston@iname.com
Devine, Steven – 01580 212635 *also fax; email:* sdevine@argonet.co.uk
* Dodd, Jane – 020 8642 5418
Elcombe, Keith – 0161 445 6661
* Farrell, Timothy – 020 7286 5181
* Francis, David – 01925 710454
* Freyhan Michael – 020 8459 6825 *also fax; email:* michael@freyhan.freeserve.co.uk
* Gould, Sharon – 01722 712449 *fax:* 01722 712901 *email:* sg@contech.force9.co.uk
Griffiths, Clare – 01233 663775 *fax:* 01233 611942
Hare, Ian – *Ellison*
* Harper, Celia, hpd, chmbr org – *Blythe*
* Harries, Clive – 01609 881552 *fax:* 01609 881110 *email:* cliveharries@compuserve.com
Harris, Richard Leigh – 01865 243306
* Heath-Downey, Susan – 020 7231 1423
Heilbron, Annette, f-pno – 01223 315681
* Hill, Barbara – 020 7435 9210
Hollick, Douglas – 01949 861347 *also fax; email:* dwh@globalnet.co.uk
Hoyland, David – *Roxane Houston*
* Kenny, Courtney – *Upbeat*
* Kitchen, John P – 0131 650 2432 *fax:* 0131 650 2425 *email:* j.kitchen@music.ed.ac.uk
Klosiewicz, Wladislaw – *Finch*
Koopman, Ton – *Hazard*
Leach, Simon Peter – 0161 861 9246
Leonhardt, Gustav – *Allied*
Lester, Harold, f-pno – *Sympathetic*
McGuinness, David – 0141 339 0605 *also fax; email:* concal@btinternet.com
* May, Katharine – 0115 925 7851; 01628 622903
* Mobbs, Kenneth – 0117 973 3613 *also fax*
* Moody, Howard – 01342 851053 *also fax*
Moroney, Davitt – *LM*
* Ng, Kah-Ming – 01865 751928 *also fax; email:* Kah-MingNg@charivari.freeserve.co.uk
Nicholson, Paul – 020 8364 6353 *also fax*
* Overbury, Michael – 01636 702054
Parnell, Andrew – *Michael Harrold*
Parry, Martyn – 020 8980 9735 *also fax; email:* mp@antillroad.demon.co.uk
* Patrick, David Kinnear – 020 8449 4873 *email:* DeeKayPea@argonet.co.uk
* Phillips, Jean – 01227 767282
* Phillips, Margaret – 01963 250899 *fax:* 01963 250999
Pinnock CBE, Trevor – *Askonas Holt*
Pollock, David – *Purkiss*
* Ponsford, David – *Camerata* – 01285 651995 *also fax*
* Proud, Malcolm – 00 353 56 61497 *also fax*
* Pruslin, Stephen – 020 8948 7404 *also fax*
Puyana, Rafael – c/o 020 7722 7142 *fax:* 020 7911 0904
* Roblou, David – 020 8690 5652/8299 1914 *also fax; fax:* 020 8244 5789 *email:* david@siskat.demon.co.uk; Hirstpr@aol.com
Rowland, David, f-pno – *Music Management*
Rowland, Gilbert – *SJM*
* Salter, Lionel – 020 8458 3568 *also fax*
* Seymour, Peter – 01904 652799 *fax:* 01904 338349 *email:* ps22@york.ac.uk
* Sieling, Gary – 07889 569226
Simcock, Iain – *Michael Harrold*
* Simmonds, Paul, hpd, clvd – 01273 552548 *fax:* 01273 389572 *email:* simmonds.mezger@cwcom.net
Skuce, Peter – 020 8488 3947 *also fax; email:* peter.skuce@dufay.com
Souter, Martin – 01865 722552 *fax:* 01865 243388 *email:* martinsouter@mcmail.com

Beryl Chempin

FTCL LRAM ARCM LTCL ABSM Hon FBC

Music Lecturer and Piano Teacher

Enquiries are welcome from music students and teachers for piano master classes, adjudicating, training for professional musicians and for writing sleeve notes for CD's.

Having been on the staff of Birmingham Conservatoire for a number of years, Beryl has gained world-wide experience in piano pedagogy. During the six years of the *"Young Midland Musician of the Year"* competition, she produced winners on four occasions and finalists in each year. She has given master classes in Brisbane, Cape Town, Helsinki, Hong Kong, Melbourne, Tasmania and the UK, and most recently, gave a series of lectures on piano pedagogy and interpretation in Australia.

For consultations, please telephone or fax 0121 449 3055 or write to 10 Russell Road, Moseley, Birmingham B13 8RD, UK

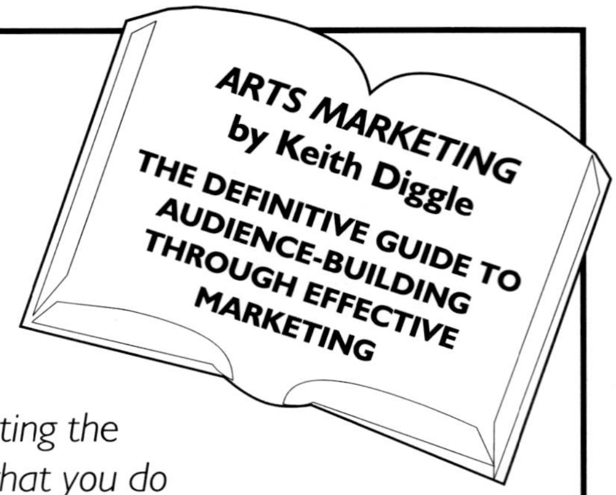

If marketing the arts is what you do for a living this book will help you do that job better.

It will give you know-how and it will give you confidence

Hardback • 293 pages • PRICE: £15.00

Postage and packing is FREE to UK addresses and to overseas addresses by surface mail. Please add £1 per copy for airmail to Europe and £4 per copy outside Europe.
To obtain your copy please send a cheque (payable to Rhinegold Publishing Ltd) to: **Book Sales Dept, Rhinegold Publishing Ltd, FREEPOST, London WC2H 8BR**.
CREDIT CARD ORDERS
Tel: 020 7333 1721 Fax: 020 7333 1769

www.rhinegold.co.uk

Johann Sebastian Bach's Sonatas and Partitas for solo violin played by Benedict Cruft

Johann Sebastian Bach's set of six works for unaccompanied violin is the only set of music by a great composer for a solo violin. While other composers have written unaccompanied violin music that has great interest and merit, Bach's three Sonatas and three Partitas tower in stature, complexity and beauty over everything written before or since for this medium.

Sadly, audiences are unfamiliar with hearing these works performed as a set, the myth having arisen of their being too hard to appreciate. Loving the works, and with this in mind, Benedict Cruft has been performing the complete set as a pair of concerts since 1987, in China, Vietnam, Macau and Hong Kong as well as Britain. Confounding the belief that a concert of solo Bach would be too difficult for them, audiences have been captivated, finding the works easier to understand, with the result that he has been invited to repeat them in succeeding years in the same place, including every year since 1989 at the Brighton Festival.

In October 1998 **Benedict Cruft** recorded **Bach's Sonatas and Partitas** for solo violin over six successive nights in Binham Priory, Norfolk, where he has performed the works many times. This will be released on CD and in the new 5.1 format, used for cinema sound, which reproduces amazingly the wonderful acoustics of Binham's surviving Norman nave.

For the last ten years **Benedict Cruft** with **Robert Aldwinckle** has also been performing **Bach's six sonatas for Violin and Keyboard** in one concert, both on the baroque violin with harpsichord, and on the modern violin with piano.

Benedict Cruft 23 Dorset Road, Vauxhall, London SW8 1EF
tel: 0207 735 4203. fax: 0207 735 8900. E-mail: katia@cruft.demon.co.uk

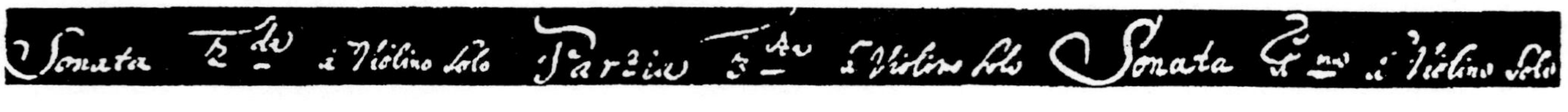

* Steer, Maxwell – 01747 870070 *fax:* 01747 871451 *email:* msteer@freeuk.com
* Townend, Richard – 020 7589 1206 *fax:* 020 7589 5925
* Tracey, Ian – 0151 708 8471 *also fax*
* Ward, David – 020 8874 4938 *also fax; email:* 106224:2623@compuserve.com
* Waterfield, Jan – 0131 553 5038; 07970 968885
Weir DBE, Dame Gillian – *Denny Lyster*
Williams, Roger Bevan – 01224 272570 *fax:* 01224 272515
* Woolley, Robert – 020 8398 6085 *also fax*

Accompanists and Coaches

Many solo pianists and organists are also accompanists, see the lists above.

Allbright, Terence – 01428 707658 *also fax*
Angell, Frances – 020 8691 0309 *also fax*; 07768 053690
Arkadiev, Mikhail – *Askonas Holt*
Arnold, Timothy – 01444 400643 *also fax; email:* timjarnold@aol.com
Asti, Eugene – *Harlequin*
Balcombe, Richard – 01279 831821 *fax:* 01279 724299 *email:* rbalcombe@aol.com
Ball, Timothy – 020 8871 0317 *fax:* 020 8488 4965 *email:* timball@sudlow.demon.co.uk
Barber, Graham – 0113 263 1890 *fax:* 0113 263 7178 *email:* g.d.barber@leeds.ac.uk
Barker, Bernard – 020 8427 5409 *also fax*
Barnes, Richard – 01243 776325 *fax:* 01243 539604 *email:* Cathedral_Music@compuserve.com
Barrow, Gretta – 020 8644 1579; 01908 662975
Barton, Christopher – 01633 266708 *also fax; email:* stworg@aol.com
Beechey, Gwilym – 01482 508910
Bishop, John – 0117 942 3373
Black, Richard – 020 7277 7068 *fax:* 020 7277 8354 *email:* 100115.3701@compuserve.com
Blakely, John – 020 8650 9990 *email:* john@blakelys.freeserve.co.uk
Blewett, Brenda – *Ellison*
Bolt, Anne – 020 8699 1691 *also fax; email:* anne@aethomas.clara.net
Burnside, Iain – *VWM*
Canetty-Clarke, Janet – 01444 811243 *fax:* 01444 811171 *email:* janet@orphic.demon.co.uk
Capra, Glen – 01273 700494
Cawthorne, Helen – 01730 261297; 07976 283444
Chempin, Beryl – 0121 449 3055 *also fax*
Clarke, Joyce – 01932 781577 *fax:* 01932 789822
Cleveland, Kenneth – 020 8994 2768 *also fax*
Cooley, Nancy – 01424 441116
Copestake, Margaret – 01954 231482 *also fax*
Crawford, Anne – 0141 942 2905
Crayford, Helen – 020 8863 4659 *fax:* 020 8863 9223
Dalby, John – 020 8992 1269 *fax:* 020 8992 1346 *email:* john@newlovemakepeace.demon.co.uk
Dean, Timothy – c/o 0141 332 4101 *fax:* 0141 353 0372 *email:* t.dean@rsamd.ac.uk
Deutsch, Helmut – *IMG*
Dewey, Thomas – *Gilder*
Dodd, Jane – 020 8642 5418
Drake, Julius – *IMG* – 020 8960 2821 *fax:* 020 8964 5261
Dubery, David – 0161 740 2762 *email:* david.dubery@argonet.co.uk
Dussek, Michael – 020 8958 6983 *also fax*
Fenyö, Gusztáv – 0141 339 2708 *fax:* 0141 337 6923
Fifield, Christopher – 020 8289 6786 *also fax; email:* cjfifield@aol.com
Fischer, Gyorgy – *Askonas Holt*
Flinders, John – 020 8659 4458
Ford, Gillian – 020 8643 0725 *also fax*; 07970 723301
Foster, Nigel – 020 8879 0323 *also fax;* 07973 292992
Furnish, Alfred – 01858 462034
Gammon, Philip – 020 8866 3260 *fax:* 020 8248 2906
Gergieva, Larissa – *Askonas Holt*
Gibbons, John – 020 8991 5063 *fax:* 020 8810 7118 *email:* johng@tisl.co.uk
Gilchrist, Iain – 0131 346 0975
Graham Smith, Susan – 01992 503896 *fax:* 01707 324052
Gulyas, Marta – *Michael Brewer*
Hancock, Michael – *Ellison*
Hancox, William – 07956 833337 *fax:* 020 8458 0980
Herbert, Philip – *Ellison*
Hill, Mary – 020 7262 9023 *also fax; email:* maryhill32@hotmail.com
Hillman (Glass), Jennifer – 020 8455 1106 *also fax*
Hipkin, Murray – 01628 810491 *also fax*; 020 7836 0111 (work); 07966 513187
Holmes, Patricia – 01689 857533 *fax:* 01689 854566 *email:* pholmes@tcm.ac.uk
Holt, Rebecca – 01494 771594 *fax:* 01494 773919
Hose, Anthony – *Ellison*
Ireland, Helen – 020 7790 5883 *fax:* 020 7265 9170 *email:* gregory-rose@tisl.co.uk
Isepp, Martin – 020 7722 3085 *fax:* 020 7483 0653
Johnson OBE, Graham – *Askonas Holt*
Jones, Rosalind – 020 8743 3744 *also fax*
Jones, Stephen – 01727 864007 *fax:* 01727 845884 *email:* steve_sta@compuserve.com
Keaney, Jack – 0141 334 3763
Kenny, Courtney – *Upbeat*
Kersey, John – 020 8363 0403
Keys, Robert – 01963 362999
Kirkwood, Gordon – 020 8203 2562 *fax:* 020 7320 1098 *email:* kirkwood@lgu.ac.uk
Knight, Dennis – 020 8886 1094
Lawrence, David – 020 8954 1079
Legge, Anthony – 020 8992 2133
Lenton, Suzanne – 0113 252 4778
Lloyd, David – *Lunn* – 01803 525806
Locock, Victoria – 01283 813816 *email:* marekt@aol.com
Mackie, David – 020 8946 7892 *also fax*
Mallett, Charles – *Roxane Houston*
Martineau, Malcolm – *Askonas Holt*
Massocchi, Jeanette – 01600 780354 *also fax*
Mitchell, Scott – 01382 330883; 07710 960923
Moody, Howard, f-pno – 01342 851053 *also fax*
Moore, Adrian – 01926 883615
Morris, Victor – 020 8748 4544 *fax:* 020 8748 1703
Nash, Mary – 020 7586 3897
Naylor, Steven – 020 8692 4771 *also fax*
Nicholson, George – 01782 618156 *email:* g.nicholson@sheffield.ac.uk
Ogonovsky, Antonia – 01225 334894
Orfenova, Ljouba – *Gilder*
Oxley, Harrison – 01284 787533 *also fax*
Pace, Ian – 020 8948 6615 *also fax; email:* ian.pace@virgin.net
Parnell, Brian-Michael – 020 8340 2983 *also fax; email:* bparnell@tutte.demon.co.uk
Partridge, Jennifer – *Upbeat*
Peacock, Gary – 020 8840 2539
Pettit, David – 020 8579 0420 *fax:* 020 8567 9832
Pilkington, Michael – 01737 556346 *also fax*
Pink, Andrew – 020 7272 6101 *also fax; email:* andrew.pink@btinternet.com
Pollock, Michael – 029 2048 5968 *also fax*
Pont, Kenneth – 01892 835164
Pratley, Geoffrey – 01279 870907 *fax:* 01279 870991
Rhodes, Paul – 01737 779697
Richter, Julia – 020 7328 1653 *also fax*; 07976 230012
Roberts, Christopher – 020 7352 6643
Roblou, David – 020 8690 5652/8299 1914 *also fax*
Rose, Stephen – 020 8579 3108
Salter, Timothy – 020 8318 2031 *also fax; email:* ugm@netcomuk.co.uk
Saunders, Antony – 01935 873199 *also fax*
Seeley, Paul – 01274 544847
Shannon, Philip – 020 8692 1795
Sharpe, Neil – 0115 929 2784 *email:* pianonas@eggconnect.net
Shaw, Richard – 020 8882 5333 *also fax;* 07976 614429
Shea, John – 020 8947 6706; 07976 233713 *email:* john.shea@bbc.co.uk
Silver, Phillip – 0141 569 6319 *fax:* 0141 569 6322 *email:* Phillip-Silver@unit.maine.edu
Smith, Maureen – 01603 618903
Smith, Sandra – 020 8451 2810
Smith, Simon – 020 8574 2743
Smith, Stuart – 01926 339002 *fax:* 01926 772667 *email:* rforbes@primex.co.uk
Solomon, Zoë – 020 8458 2839 *also fax; email:* robandzoe@aol.com
Squires, Chris – c/o 0141 248 4567; 07966 416765 *fax:* 0141 221 8812
Stanger, Peter – 01273 390351 *also fax*
Surgenor, Ingrid – *Harlequin/WWA*
Tarlton, Sally – 01446 796733
Teed, Roy – 01206 870839
Thomas, Hugh – 01550 720978 *also fax*
Tillett, Michael – 01622 754814
Tomlinson, Charlotte – 020 8766 0399 *also fax*
Upchurch, Elizabeth – 07956 811020
Vignoles, Roger – *Ingpen*
Ward, David – 020 8874 4938 *also fax; email:* 106224.2623@compuserve.com
Ward Russell, Gillian – 01621 853237
Waterfield, Jan – 0131 553 5038; 07970 968885
Wickham, David – 020 8699 3611; 07976 302389 *fax:* 020 8291 4427 *email:* david.wickham@talk21.com
Wilder, Stephen – 020 8886 0421/8372 2478 *fax:* 01296 614828 *email:* k.wilder@btinternet.com
Wilkinson, Nigel – 01628 825676 *fax:* 01628 540655
Woods (Williams), Beryl – 01494 881837
Wright, Diana – 020 7625 4692
Yarr, Sharon – 028 9059 0995

CHRIS. CHRISTODOULOU

Iwona Boesche

'Iwona is not just a good violinist, she is also a fine musician'

Trevor Pinnock

Full virtuoso repertoire: concertos/ sonatas etc. Prize winner of international competitions in Mexico and Poland

During Yr 2000

Spring – Haslemere Bach Festival
7th April – St John's, Smith Square, London 7.30
30th May – St Martin-in the-fields 1.00
and much more

For details contact Dennis Day
01462-451044

A player of enviable accomplishment and immaculate presentation, "The Strad"

Tel: 01568 613027

PETRONELLA DITTMER

VIOLINIST AND SOPRANO

"...her playing shows humour, vitality and an exceptionally beautiful tone"

2000 presents further national and international venues where Petronella will perform her unusual and extensive repertoire of music from early plainsong, to the present day including some recent commissions. She uses period and modern instruments.

All enquiries to: 10 Pembroke Mews, London W8 6ER Fax and tel: + 44 20 7937-0684 (24 hours)

Violin

Accardo, Salvatore – *VWM*
Alleson, Robin – *Blythe*
Alvanis, Adonis – *JLM*
Amoyal, Pierre – *Voullaire*
Arditti, Irvine – *Haferkorn*
Atherton, Joan – 020 8455 0658
Barritt, Paul – 01442 822732 *also fax; email:* 101765.465@compuserve.com
Barton, James – 01446 735028
Batiashvili, Elizabeth – *HP*
Bekova, Elvira – 01276 505357 *fax:* 01276 509558
Belkin, Boris – *THA*
Bell, Joshua – *IMG*
Bernard, Andrew – c/o 020 8533 1372
Boros, Tomi – 020 8907 7953 *email:* borosensemble@breathemail.net
Bradbury, John – 020 8422 1456
Carte, Michelle – 020 8540 3035
Carter, Peter – 020 8789 2649 *also fax; email:* carterp@allegri2000.freeserve.co.uk
Caudle, Theresa, va, va d'am – 01264 736565 *also fax*
Chandler, Adrian – 020 8664 7314 *fax:* 020 7326 0712
Charlier, Olivier – *TransArt*
Chen, Leland – *Upbeat*
Christocoulou, Efi – 020 8800 5483 *fax:* 020 8800 9423 *email:* efi@classical-artists.com
Clarke, Pip – *Encore Concerts*
Cohen, Raymond – 020 8452 3493
Contzen, Mirijam – *NBM*
Cowdrey, Elizabeth – 01869 340951 *fax:* 01869 349084 *email:* orbestra@excite.com
Croft, Dona Lee – *Anthony Abbott*
Cruft, Benedict – 020 7735 4203 *fax:* 020 7735 8900
Cummings, Diana – 020 7435 5408 *fax:* 020 7431 6843 *email:* cummings@gondar.demon.co.uk
Davies, Edward – 01248 713336
Davis, Howard – 01279 431337 *also fax*
Deakin, Richard – 01768 483443 *fax:* 01768 483904
Demeterová, Gabriela – *Ellison*
Derome, Julie-Anne – 020 8853 0353 *email:* jaderome@yahoo.com
Dittmer, Petronella, vn, baroque vn – 020 7937 0684 *also fax*
Doll, Barbara – *ADM*
Dumay, Augustin – *Askonas Holt*
Edvaldsdottir, Sigrun – *SWA*
Ewart, George – 01568 613027
Faust, Isabelle – *Hazard*
Fischer, Simon – 020 7722 1889 *also fax; email:* simonfischer@violin-basics.co.uk
Fisher, Peter – *CMG/Ellison*
Fourmy, Ruth – 020 8904 9106
Friedman, Erick – c/o Stephen Redrobe 020 8444 5169 *also fax;* 07973 694881
Frowde, Paul – 01582 840753; 07802 402646 *fax:* 01582 840991
Fujikawa, Mayumi – *THA*
Gamalova, Devorina – 020 8648 2822 *also fax*
Gibbs, Robert – 020 8891 2174 *also fax*
Gomyo, Karen – *VWM*
Gonley, Stephanie – *Gilder*
Graffin, Philippe – *Grant Rogers*
Gräsbeck, Manfred – *Ellison*
Graudina-Jeannet, Anete – 020 8458 5542; 07931 902923
Grimal, David – *TransArt*
Grindenko, Tatiana – c/o 020 8540 4533
Gruenberg, Erich – *Intermusica*
Gulli, Franco – *OWM*
Haendel, Ida – *Askonas Holt*
Hahn, Hilary – *IMG*
Hancox, Ben – *Annon*
Harte, Benjamin – 023 8078 0305 *pager:* 07654 250396 *email:* benharte@tesco.net
Harvey, Jean – 01428 642230
Hatfield, Lesley – 028 4483 1156 *also fax;* c/o 01622 757814 *email:* gbain@aol.com
Haveron, Andrew – *NBM*
Hirons, Christopher – 020 8946 6967 *fax:* 020 8946 6966 *email:* chris.hirons@which.net
Hoelscher, Ulf – *Connaught*
Holloway, John – 01993 878200 *fax:* 01993 878375 *email:* oldmanse@compuserve.com
Howick, Clare – 020 8390 1561 *also fax;* 07710 424767
Huckle, Roger – 0117 962 4289 *also fax*
Huehns, Colin – 020 8204 7369
Huggett, Monica – *Hazard*
Hunt, Fionnuala – *OWM*
Hurwitz CBE, Emanuel – 020 8346 3936 *fax:* 020 8343 1595
Hydle, Eli – *Roy Baker*
Jeal, Lucy – *THA*
Jones, Louise – *Ellison*
Josefowicz, Leila – *IMG*
Juillet, Chantal – *Clarion/Seven Muses*
Kalnits, Yuri – *Talbot-Cooper*
Kang, Dong-Suk – *Clarion/Seven Muses*
Kanga, Homi – 020 8205 4973
Kanno, Mieko – 020 8830 1627 *also fax*
Kaplan, Mark – *Tennant*
Kavakos, Leonidas – *Intermusica*

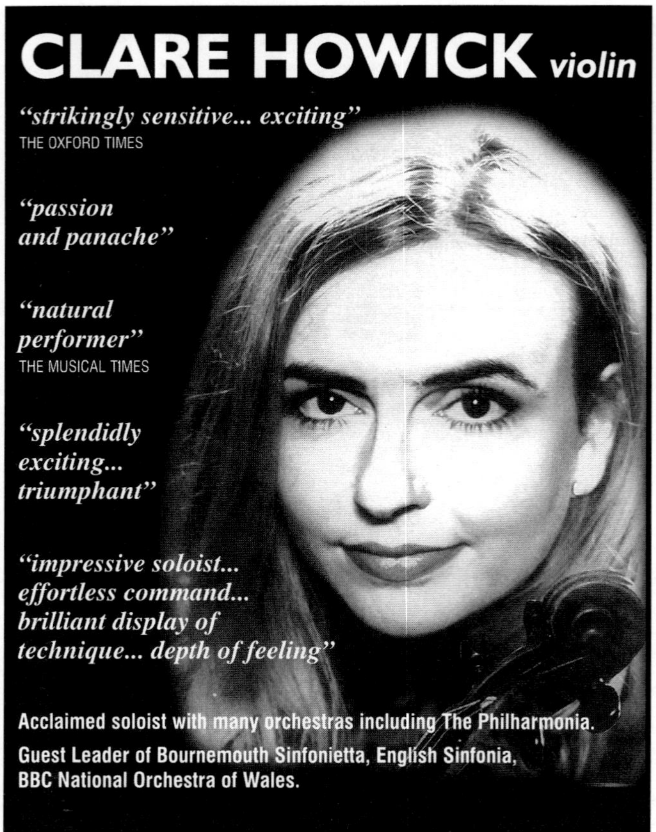

CLARE HOWICK violin

"strikingly sensitive... exciting"
THE OXFORD TIMES

"passion and panache"

"natural performer"
THE MUSICAL TIMES

"splendidly exciting... triumphant"

"impressive soloist... effortless command... brilliant display of technique... depth of feeling"

Acclaimed soloist with many orchestras including The Philharmonia.
Guest Leader of Bournemouth Sinfonietta, English Sinfonia, BBC National Orchestra of Wales.

SOLOIST - LEADER - RECITALIST
ENQUIRIES: TEL/FAX 0181 390 1561 OR 0410 424767

MADELEINE MITCHELL

VIOLIN

"One of the most enjoyable was Madeleine Mitchell's fastidious and original programme" *Sunday Times*

◆◆◆

"Assured technical brilliance and impressive musicality" *Canberra Times 1999*
(International Chamber Festival, Australia – return invitation 2000)

◆◆◆

"An affecting performance, rapt in concentration"
(BBC Proms) *Daily Telegraph*

◆◆◆

Telephone 0207 402 0014 fax 0207 402 3134
Email:madeleinemitchell@zyworld.com
www.classical-artists.com/madeleinemitchell

photo: Leon Martin

0171 266 3596

MIRIAM KRAMER

violin

"a violinist of superior natural talent, an exceptionally sensitive interpreter, and a phrase maker of uncommon expressivity."
Henry Roth, THE STRAD

NEW CD RELEASES
ASV December 1999
NAXOS February 2000

Kelly, Alison – 020 8855 1040 *also fax*; 07973 660785
Kemp, Thomas – 020 8342 8619 *also fax*
Kim, So-Ock – *Lubbock*
Kino, Masayuki – 020 8882 2695
Kovacic, Ernst – *Clarion/Seven Muses*
Kovats, Peter – *Ellison*
Kramer, Miriam – 020 7266 3596 *also fax*
Krysa, Oleh – *Connaught*
Kuijken, Sigiswald – *Allied*
Kun, Hu – *Gilder*
Kuusisto, Pekka – *HP*
Kym, Min-Jin – c/o 01189 761003
Laredo, Jaime – *Askonas Holt*
Layton, Elizabeth – 01923 770445
Leprince, Franck – 07000 001812; 01202 757373; 07808 299413
Lewis, Oliver – *Ellison/Roxane Houston/Sympathetic* – 020 8643 6154
Liddell MBE, Nona – 020 8441 7703
Little, Tasmin – *Askonas Holt*
Load, Nicola – *PGM*
Lomeiko Natalia – *Sonata* – 020 7727 7806 *also fax*
Lowbury, Pauline – 020 8991 5975 *also fax*
Lubotsky, Mark, Violin – *Encore Concerts*
McAslan, Lorraine – 020 8440 0574 *fax:* 020 8440 0632
McCormack, Gina – 020 8761 7637; 07970 804802 *fax:* c/o 020 8761 7845
McDuffie, Robert – *Gilder*
McNaught, Fiona – 020 8398 8231 *also fax*
Malikian, Ara – *Connaught*
Manley, Paul – 01892 864069 *also fax*
Marinkovic, Mateja – 020 8450 2367 *also fax; email:* mateja@marinkovic.freeserve.co.uk
Markov, Alexander – *TransArt*
Marwood, Anthony – *OWM*
Mészáros, Susie – 020 8343 8935
Milanova, Stoika – *THA*
Mitchell, Madeleine – 020 7402 0014 *fax:* 020 7402 3134
Mitchell, Priya – *Ingpen*
Morgan, Darragh – 020 8761 6039 *also fax;* 07956 916510; 01306 500011 (diary) *email:* darraghm@hotmail.com
Mullova, Viktoria – *Askonas Holt*
Myerscough, Clarence – 020 7272 2547 *also fax*
Myerscough, Nadia – 020 7375 2602 *also fax*
Neaman OBE, Yfrah – 020 7837 4455 *fax:* 020 7833 0268
Nikkanen, Kurt – *HP*
Noval, Tara – *Murphy*
Oleg, Raphael – *VWM*
Olyver, Marianne – 01787 460296 *also fax; email:* patrick@woodley.demon.co.uk
Osbon, Lorna – 01225 337722
Osostowicz, Krysia – *Connaught*
Perlman, Itzhak – *Askonas Holt*
Piggott, Mike – 01403 256064 *also fax*
Poole, Peter – *Dyfel*
Quo, Qing – *Susie Wong*
Rachlin, Julian – *Columbia*
Read, Christine – 020 8348 4938
Redrobe, Stephen – 020 8444 5169 *also fax;* 07973 694881
Reid, Edmund – 020 8644 1579; 01908 662975
Renwick, Clare – 020 8883 2334
Repin, Vadim – *IMG*
Ricci, Ruggiero – *Intermusica*
Roth, David – 020 8452 7376 *email:* drroth@lineone.net
Rozhdestvensky, Sasha – *Columbia*
Safonova, Anna – *Sonata*
Schnarch, Ani – 020 7244 7623 *also fax*
Shaham, Gil – *HP*
Shaham, Hagai – 020 7631 4420 *also fax; email:* 106400.206@compuserve.com
Sheppard, Peter – *Manygate*
Shih, Patricia – *WWA*
Shiokawa, Yuuko – *THA*
Simons, Marijn – *Music Partnership*
Sitkovetsky, Dmitry – *IMG*
Slater, Carol – 020 8452 6843
Smietana, Krzysztof – *Purkiss* – 020 7254 8876 *fax:* 020 7254 8860
Smith, Maureen – 020 8458 4827
Soh, Tomotada – 020 7723 1446 *fax:* 020 7706 4154
Stanzeleit, Susanne – *Jean Judge*
Steinberg, Mark – *VWM*
Stern, Isaac – *Askonas Holt*
Stigmer, Jan – *NCCP*
Stowell, Robin – 029 2075 2001 *fax:* 029 2087 4379 *email:* stowell@cardiff.ac.uk
Strange, Alison – *Murphy*
Studt, Richard – 01202 394955 *also fax; email:* rstudt@cwcom.net
Sturdy, Kathleen – 020 8458 2983
Suk, Josef – *TransArt*
Sushanskaya, Rimma – *SWA*
Szabadi, Vilmos – *Michael Brewer*
Tetzlaff, Christian – *HP*
Thomas, Peter – *Camerata*
Thorn, Jennifer – 020 8969 9403
Tonson-Ward, Maxwell – 01476 577554; 020 8883 2334
Tretyakov, Victor – *Askonas Holt*
Trusler, Matthew – *VWM*
Tsuji, Mifune – 01223 368951 *also fax; email:* mifune@netmatters.co.uk
Tsukahara, Ruriko – *Finch*
Ughi, Uto – *Music Partnership*
Van Keulen, Isabelle – *Intermusica*
Vengerov, Maxim – *Askonas Holt*
Wanami, Takayoshi – *Manygate*
Warren-Green, Christopher – c/o 020 8772 9741 *fax:* 020 8772 9742 *email:* cwg@lco.co.uk

MIFUNE TSUJI

"... unconditional proof of her outstanding talent. Her warm intonation in Bach's 2nd Partita was a perfect foil to her excellent technique."
GEERT VAN DEN DUNGEN

"I had thought the only musicians who could play my music *authentically* were those with whom I had worked for years. I realised my error as soon as I heard Mifune Tsuji lead the Xenakis Ensemble in a wonderful performance of my work."
MICHAEL NYMAN

"To Mifune, with friendship and gratitude for her work."
JOHN CAGE

"She's a wonderful violinist allying technical mastery with an exceptional musicianship. She's a really velvety interpreter of traditional and today's European music."
IANNIS XENAKIS

VIOLIN

Repertoire: from Bach to Xenakis
tel/fax: **01223 368951**
e-mail: mifune@netmatters.co.uk

BARRY WILDE

SOLOIST - LEADER - DIRECTOR

"One of Europe's finest violinists"
Henryk Szeryng.

Also available with the
Serenata of London

A superb chamber group with whom he has directed many highly acclaimed CDs.

17A Rhenish Mansion
84, Bonham Road
Hong Kong
Tel: (852) 2547 8539
Fax: (852) 2547 8867

4, Montague Road
Wimbledon
London SW19 1SY
Tel: 0181 542 0310
Fax: 0181 543 9346

JOBS! JOBS! JOBS!

* **Management**
* **Marketing**
* **Teaching**
* **Playing**

FOR A TRIAL SUBSCRIPTION Telephone 020 7333 1720 during office hours

They're all in Classical Music magazine

CLASSICAL music

The music industry's noticeboard

Special 6-month subscription £30

Fortnightly £3.10

CREDIT CARD SUBSCRIPTIONS
Tel: 01474 334500 (office hours)
Fax: 01474 325557
www.rhinegold.co.uk

ELIZABETH WATSON

VIOLA D'AMORE

instruments: Bohemian C18 and Viennese, restored France C19
with

JANE DODD

HARPSICHORD - PIANO

PHOTO: FRITZ CURZON

Music by Milandre, Marais, Petzold, Rust, Telemann, Stamitz... Hindemith, Velisek, Tonson...

Concerto performances in Germany with Telemann-Kammerorchester and Purcell Room with London Harpsichord Ensemble - also on Unicorn-Kanchana CD: Telemann Triple Concerto - "full of joy and sparkle... nicely judged expressive feeling" - Penguin Guide to Compact discs.

Viola and Piano Duo with Geoffrey Pratley

Music by Bach, Schubert, Brahms, Rebecca Clarke, Bliss, Shostakovich, Baciewicz, Dodgson...

"a born chamber music player... fluently musical throughout"
The Times - after Wigmore Hall recital with Andrew Davis

Winner Lionel Tertis Open Competition

Enquiries to Elizabeth Watson 0208 876 1445
3 Ormonde Road, London SW14 7BE

Waterman, Ruth – 020 8994 7442 *also fax;* 020 8806 0885 *fax:* 020 8806 8520 *email:* ianpressland@compuserve.com
Wei, Xue – *Upbeat*
Weithaas, Antje – *HP*
Wilde, Barry – 020 8542 0310 *fax:* 020 8543 9346
Wilson, Brian Lloyd – 01252 795047 *also fax*
Yasuraoka, Yu – *Finch*
Zazofsky, Peter – *Gilder*
Zehetmair, Thomas – *Lubbock*
Zhislin, Grigori – *Ellison* – 020 8993 8223 *fax:* 020 8993 8295
Zhislin, Yuri – *Bray/Sonata*
Zivoni, Yossi – *Anglo-Swiss*

Viola and Viola d'Amore

Bashmet, Yuri – *VWM*
Bassano, Kathy, va, va d'am – *Giustiniani* – 01494 868240 *fax:* 01494 868250 *email:* GArtists1@aol.com
Beeston, Michael – 0131 332 8691 *fax:* 0131 332 5084 *email:* edinburghquartet@compuserve.com
Bigley, Roger – 0161 224 9522 *also fax*
Boulton, Timothy – 020 8670 3086 *also fax*
Brown, Andrew – 01932 853271/853273 *fax:* 01932 859233 *email:* andy@lmo.co.uk
Caussé, Gérard – *TransArt*
Cornford, Dan – *JLM*
Crabtree, Richard – *CMG*
Dittmer, Petronella – 020 7937 0684 *also fax*
Dukes, Philip – *NCCP/Purkiss*
Ebsworth, Phyllis – 020 7431 2846
Erblich, Ferdinand – *NWA*
Gamalova, Devorina – 020 8648 2822 *also fax*
Geldard, Esther – 020 8291 3648 *also fax;* 01306 500011(diary) *email:* esthergeldard@ndirect.co.uk
Golani, Rivka – c/o 020 7701 3107 *fax:* 020 7701 6918 *email:* foxjones@compuserve.com; 113461.2714@compuserve.com
Greenlees, David – c/o 01803 833018 *also fax*
Gunes, Rusen – *Finch*
Harte, Francis – 023 8078 0305 *pager:* 07626 247299
Hawkins, Brian – 020 8946 4511 *fax:* 020 8946 9183 *email:* violahawk@aol.com
Holbrook, Elizabeth – 01263 733487
Imai, Nobuko – 020 7482 5610 *also fax*
Inoue, Yuko – *Upbeat*
Iorio, Luciano, va, va d'am – 020 7435 5408 *fax:* 020 7431 6843 *email:* iorio@gondar.demon.co.uk
Jewel, Ian – 020 8452 6843
Karni, Gilad – *Ellison*
Logie, Nicholas – 01342 824536 *also fax; email:* nicholas.logie@virgin.net
Oppenheimer, Graham – 0116 270 6528 *also fax; email:* schidlof@dircon.co.uk
Ponder, Michael – 020 8444 2541 *also fax*
Rowland-Jones, Simon – 020 8948 2345 *email:* srj@easynet.co.uk
Sanderson, Rosemary – *NCCP*
Schiele, Brian – c/o 020 7733 6719
Scott, Graeme – 020 8423 0067
Secret, Robert – 01280 848275 *also fax*
Shaw, Julian – 020 8761 4221 *also fax*
Silverthorne, Paul – *Gilder*
Tomter, Lars Anders – *SWA*
Tonson-Ward, Maxwell, va, va d'am – 01476 577554; 020 8883 2334
Van Keulen, Isabelle – *Intermusica*
Watson, Elizabeth, va, va d'am – 020 8876 1445
Wellington, Christopher, va, va d'am – *GBZ*
White, John – 01279 422567 *also fax*
Williams, Louise – 020 7352 8588 *fax:* 020 7352 8511 *email:* louiserla@aol.com
Wilson, Brian Lloyd – 01252 795047 *also fax*
Zhislin, Grigori – *Ellison*
Zimmermann, Tabea – *HP*

Cello

Abrahamson, Liam – *Ellison*
Adams, Peter – 01295 277976 *also fax*
Ardagh-Walter, Catherine – 0121 777 6643 *also fax; email:* sjcaw@btinternet.com
Attwood, Elspeth – 01604 414828
Baillie, Alexander – *TransArt*
Banda, Pál – *Purkiss* – 020 8343 8935 *also fax; email:* palbanda@freenet.co.uk
Barta, Jiri – *Sonata*
Blake, Lowri – 020 8660 7877 *fax:* 020 8763 0492 *email:* silvius@dial.pipex.com
Bylsma, Anner – *TransArt*
Carr, Colin – *Clarion/Seven Muses*
Christie, Michael – 020 7435 0914 *fax:* 020 7794 3610
Clein, Natalie – *Askonas Holt* – 01202 707209 *also fax*
Comberti, Sebastian – 020 8444 6358 *also fax; email:* comberti@mailbox.co.uk
Conway, William – 0131 667 4630 *also fax*
Croxford, Eileen – 020 8878 4286
de Saram, Rohan – *Stella Baker*
Del Mar, Pauline E – 020 7937 7346 *also fax*
Deniz, Clare – 07956 137942
East, Angela – 020 8769 4158 *also fax; email:* EastRevolution@compuserve.com
Fan, Felix – *Music Partnership*
Feigelson, Yosif – *Ellison*
Ferrand, Emma – *Ellison*
Fukacová, Michaela – *Judith Hendershott*
Georgian, Karine – *Olivia Ma*
Gerhardt, Alban – *Tennant*
Geringas, David – *Connaught*
Gledhill, Oliver – 020 8455 7211 *also fax*
Gorokhov, Leonid – 020 8771 6765 *also fax; email:* leonid@cello1.freeserve.co.uk
Green, Nancy – *CMG*
Greenlees, Patrick – 01803 833018 *also fax*
Grist, Chris – *CMG*
Gruber, Emmanuel – *Ellison*
Gwilt, John – 01562 851630
Haimovitz, Matt – *TransArt*
Hall, Joy – 01297 678365
Harrell, Lynn – *IMG*
Harries, Nia – 020 8459 6462
Harwood, Richard – 023 9226 5831 *fax:* 023 9225 5595
Heinen, Ulrich – *Camerata*
Henderson, Veronica – 01223 413234 *also fax*
Hoffman, Gary – *Olivia Ma*
Holmes, Richard – 01689 857533 *fax:* 01689 854566 *email:* pholmes@tcm.ac.uk
Hopkins, Louise – *NCCP*
Horsch, Gregor – *Gilder*
Isserlis, Steven – *HP*
Jenkinson, Richard – *Michael Brewer*
Kirshbaum, Ralph – *Ingpen*
Kitchen, Jonathan – 020 8325 7649; 07973 204642 *email:* kitch@cwcom.net
Le Feuvre, Gerard – 01582 462668 *fax:* 01582 623418
Lee, Angela – *Susie Wong*
Lee, Daniel – *Manygate*
Lester, Richard – 020 8455 3538 *also fax*
Liwei, Qin – *YCAT*
Lloyd Webber, Julian – *IMG*
Lovett OBE, Martin – 020 7794 9898 *fax:* 020 7794 6699 *email:* martinlovett@compuserve.com
Lynex, Penelope – 020 8340 0897 *fax:* 020 8341 5292
Ma, Yo-Yo – *Askonas Holt*
MacLeod, Marie – 01728 746301 *also fax*
Maisky, Mischa – *Intermusica*
Markevitch, Dimitry – *Ellison*
Max, Robert – 020 8458 2839 *also fax; email:* RobandZoe@aol.com
Medlam, Charles – 01635 254331 *fax:* 01635 253629 *email:* c.medlam@btinternet.com
Meneses, Antonio – *Lubbock*
Merz, Juliet – 020 8542 2412; 020 8533 1372 (diary)
Mitchell, Judith – 020 7701 6438 *also fax; email:* ccs@brailsford.demon.co.uk
Mørk, Truls – *HP*
Müller-Schott, Daniel – *HP*
Nakipbekova, Alfia – 020 7226 8412 *also fax*
Neary, Alice – 020 8343 4221 *also fax*
Nebe, Michael – 020 8671 4408 *fax:* 020 8671 2848 *email:* admin@fasinfonia.freeserve.co.uk
Noras, Arto – *PGM*
Onczay, Csaba – *Michael Brewer*
Pearson, Justin – *Sympathetic*
Perenyi, Miklós – *THA*
Pergamenshikov, Boris – *Columbia*
Powell, Margaret – 020 8958 6983 *also fax*
Price, Kathryn – *Connaught*
Prynn, Gabriel – 020 8853 0353 *email:* gabrielprynn@yahoo.com
Queyras, Jean-Guihen – *LM*
Rolland, Sophie – 020 8995 3572 *fax:* 020 8747 3255
Rostropovich, Mstislav – c/o 020 7794 0987 *fax:* 020 7431 2531
Rummel, Martin – *Talbot-Cooper*
Salmon, Jane – 020 8246 6674/8563 0618 *fax:* 020 8246 6827/8741 5233 *email:* jane@jsalmon.demon.co.uk
Sanderling, Michael – *WWA*
Sarkissov, Alexei – *Sonata*
Schiff, Heinrich – *Intermusica*
Schmidt, Felix – 020 8445 4485 *also fax*
Sheppard, Philip – 020 8560 4091; 07767 810560 *email:* bluesnow@easynet.co.uk
* Shrigley Jones, Lesley, vc, va da gamba, baroque vc – c/o 020 8977 9690 *fax:* 020 8255 3852
Shulman, Andrew – 01420 472206 *fax:* 01420 478690 *email:* andrew.shulman@lineone.net
Shuttleworth, Anna – 0113 275 8509; 01227 261975
Silver, Noreen – 0141 569 6319 *fax:* 0141 569 6322 *email:* phillip_silver@umit.maine.edu
Smith, Roger – 01892 782220 *also fax; email:* fountmus@aol.com
Starker, Janos – *TransArt*
Taylor, Betsy – c/o 01803 833018 *also fax*
Teulières-Sommer, Geneviève – 020 7586 9730 *fax:* 020 7586 8815 *email:* rgsommer@cableinet.co.uk
Thedéen, Torleif – *Gilder*

Graham Casey

Clarinet

Graham has recently been focusing on performances of the clarinet concertos by Gerald Finzi and Robin Holloway. He is the Administrator of the Jupiter Ensemble and is clarinet tutor at Anglia University and Homerton College, Cambridge. His lively, entertaining style of presentation makes one of his recitals an event to be remembered.

All Enquiries to:
(Concertos, Chamber Music, Recitals)

"Cornubia"
16 Edenfield
Orton Longueville
Peterborough
PE2 7HY
Telephone: 01733 235888
E-mail: gpcasey@compuserve.com

The Jupiter Ensemble

Nicholas Cox

Clarinet

Truly lovely playing by Nicholas Cox.
Stephen Johnson The Independent

Photo: Stuart Hastain

Superb playing The Gramophone

The ideal Mozart experience lay in Nicholas Cox's playing of the Clarinet Concerto on the darker-toned basset clarinet. The result was exquisite and as good as anything in the present recording catalogue. Wonderful, mellifluous, apparently effortless playing of the type an audience can dream of, but so rarely gets to such a degree. A combination of perfect intonation and phrasing to make the spine tingle.
Joe Riley Liverpool Echo

Of his duo with Vanessa Latarche:
Technical accomplishment, stylistic insight and interpretative discernment... An exhilarating evening & a duo to watch.
Geoffrey Norris Daily Telegraph

A brilliantly conceived and technically sparkling display.
Rex Bawden Liverpool Post

Bliss Clarinet Quintet Recording (RR010)

beautifully rendered by Nicholas Cox and the Redcliffe Ensemble and the elegaic slow movement is most movingly delivered too. The Gramophone

Nicholas Cox
Principal Clarinet RLPO and MKCO
Artistic Director Ensemble 10:10
Clarinet Tutor RNCM Manchester

For Concertos, Chamber music, Recitals and Master-classes contact:

NICHOLAS COX Tel: 01925-756281
33, Sandy Lane, Lymm, Cheshire, WA13 9HP
or Morgensterns on 0181-533 1372 E-mail: nicox@eurobell.co.uk

---

FIONA CROSS CLARINET

'Charismatic musicianship'
THE GUARDIAN

'Wide tonal range ...adding ornaments and cadenza-like flourishes with winning ease'
THE GUARDIAN

'Variety of tones of voice and subtlety of dynamic grading she brought to even the most tongue-twisting passages'
THE TIMES

Further enquiries:
Neil Chaffey, 9 Hunts Meadow, Weston, Herts SG4 7AE
Tel: 01462 790919 Fax: 01462 790920

Concerto Soloist

Regular performances of concerti and cantatas by Albinoni, Bach, Marcello and Vivaldi with the **Milton Keynes City Orchestra** and the **Bath City Orchestra** at Marble Hill Park, St John's Smith Square, Milton Keynes and Bath. 1996 British Premiere of "The Songs of the Magi" (Adolphus Hailstork, 1988) for **Black and Classic** at St James's Piccadilly.

DUO with Katharine May, harpsichord

Recitals for music clubs throughout the UK and EIRE. Broadcasts for **Classic fM** and **RTE FM3**. Former scholars on the Countess of Munster Musical Trust Recital Scheme.

DUO with Dominic Saunders, piano

Classical, Romantic and 20th Century music for Oboe and Piano

ALTHEA IFEKA oboe

Concertos and recitals from Baroque to Berio
020 8591 4285 – 00 61 2 6295 1683
01628 783 272

"Althea Ifeka was superb in the Albinoni Concerto"
Bath Chronicle

"A sensitive and stylish performer"
Canberra Times

Thoday, Gillian – 020 8447 0858
Thompson, Ross – 020 8303 9770
Tunnell, Charles – 020 8892 6837
Veis, Daniel – c/o 020 8788 2710 *fax:* 020 8788 4282
Vigay, Denis – 020 8346 3670
Wallfisch, Raphael – *Clarion/Seven Muses*
Wang, Jian – *Askonas Holt*
Ward Clarke, Jennifer, vc, baroque vc – 020 7228 7059 *also fax*
Warner, Wendy – *Encore Concerts*
Wells, Alison – 01923 331177 *also fax; email:* JSharkey@compuserve.com
Welsh, Moray – *Olivia Ma*
Wiegold, Richard – 029 2062 0469 *also fax;* 07768 233369 *email:* wiegold@compuserve.com
Wilmers, Catherine – 01462 730490 *also fax; email:* ccwilmers@bigfoot.com
Wispelwey, Pieter – *Lubbock*

Double Bass

Boros, Gabor – 020 8907 7953 *email:* borosensemble@breathemail.net
Canonici, Corrado – 020 7281 3822 *also fax; email:* canonicibass@compuserve.com
Drucker, Gerald – 020 8427 4730 *also fax*
Fejervary, Zsolt – *Michael Brewer*
Hartley, Keith – 020 8393 6385 *fax:* 020 8786 7429
Heyes, David – 01252 319610 *also fax;* 07831 192772 *email:* bibf@classical-artists.com
McTier, Duncan – 020 8894 5381 *fax:* 020 8898 4591 *email:* mctier@globalnet.co.uk
Marder, Marc – *TransArt*
Naish, Bronwen – 020 8299 2931 *fax:* 01766 530356 *email:* NaishB@aol.com
Seldis, Dominic – 01594 844895 *fax:* 01594 844995 *email:* dominic@seldis.netkonect.co.uk
Williams, Stephen – 020 8991 5975 *also fax;* 01306 880669

Woodwind

Adams, Piers, rcdr – *Upbeat*
Allen, Alex, cl – *KDM*
Allen, Frank, cl, bs cl – 0121 373 0420; 07976 414653
Allen, Geraldine, cl – 020 8444 8587 *fax:* 020 8245 0358 *email:* impulse@impulse-music.co.uk
Amos, Lisa-Maree, fl – 01280 850102 *fax:* 01280 824408 *email:* lisa_maree_a@hotmail.com
Andrew-James, Mark, ob, eh – 01273 208680 *fax:* 01273 777963
Archibald, Margaret, cl – 020 8464 1645; 01306 880669 *fax:* 020 8402 5859 *email:* Margaretxy@aol.com
Arden-Taylor, Paul, ob, rcdr – 01562 710801 *also fax*
Ashkenazy, Dimitri, cl – *HP*
Axtell, Michael, fl – *Dyfel*
Bacchus, Peter, fl – *Ellison*
Baigent, Mark, ob, baroque ob, classical ob – 07850 914024
Ball, Christopher, rcdr, early wind insts – 020 7935 1270
Bass, Alexandra, fl, picc – 01327 861150 *also fax;* 020 8533 1372 (diary) *email:* alibas@compuserve.com
Bennett, Stephen, cl – 020 8675 3877 *email:* stephen.bennett@telia.com
Bennett OBE, William, fl – 020 7498 9807 *fax:* 020 7498 1155 *email:* wibb@doghousemail.com
Bennetts, Kathryn, rcdr – 01892 723370 *also fax; email:* 101767.2724@compuserve.com
Berent, Fritz, bsn, contra bsn – 020 8504 3001
Beynon, Emily, fl – *YCAT*
Bisengaliev, Stina, fl – *ADM*
Bourgue, Maurice, ob – *Ingpen*
Bowman, Peter, rcdr – 01892 723370 *also fax; email:* peterbowman1@compuserve.com
Bradbury, Colin, cl – 020 8997 4300 *fax:* 020 8991 5982 *email:* bradbury@clarinet.demon.co.uk
Browne, Jacqueline, cl – 01239 698602 *fax:* 01239 612200
Brymer OBE, Jack, cl – *Lunn*
Bucknall, Nicholas, cl – 020 8771 0390 *fax:* 020 8768 1800
Butt, David, fl – 01372 724488 *also fax*
Caird, George, ob – c/o 0121 331 5910 *fax:* 0121 331 5906 *email:* george.caird@uce.ac.uk
Campbell, David, cl – *Janet Hughes/NBM*
Campbell, Margaret, fl – 020 8998 6246 *also fax;* 01306 500022 *email:* MagCampbel@aol.com
Carpenter, Nicholas, cl – *Maestoso*
Carr, Jennifer, fl – 020 8876 1756
Carroll, Paul, bsn – *Music Management*
Casey, Graham, cl, bs cl – 01733 235888 *email:* gpcasey@compuserve.com
Cheneour, Paul, fl, alto fl, picc, bs fl, arab fl, indian fl – c/o 01342 300949 *email:* egsales@egnet.co.uk
Cherry, Ann, fl – 020 8802 5984 *fax:* 020 8809 7436 *email:* ann@paulrodriguezmus.demon.co.uk
Clarke, Dennis, fl – 01293 862464
Collins, Michael, cl – *Intermusica*
Copley, Michael, rcdr, fl, panpipes, ocarina – *Seaview*
Cottrell, Stephen, sax – 020 8690 6071 *also fax; email:* steva@compuserve.com
Cox, Nicholas, cl – 01925 756281; 020 8533 1372 *fax:* c/o 0151 210 2902 *email:* nicox@eurobell.co.uk
Crew, Paul, ob, cor – 020 8891 1162 *also fax*
Cross, Fiona, cl – *NCCP*
Daniel, Nicholas, ob – *Upbeat*
Dankworth CBE, John, sax, cl – 01908 583151 *fax:* 01908 584414
Davies, Philippa, fl – 020 7431 8317 *fax:* 020 7435 8535 *email:* flute@pipdavies.freeserve.co.uk
de Peyer, Gervase, cl – *Michael Harrold*
Dobing, Duke, fl – 020 8643 4425 *also fax*
Dobrée, Georgina, cl, basset hn – 01462 455929
Drew, Elisabeth, cl – *CMG*
Dundas-Grant, Deirdre, bsn – 020 8946 6875
Durán, Elena, fl – *LA*
Edwards, Philip, cl, sax – 01424 773038 *email:* mu802rpe@gold.ac.uk
Eggleden, Janet, cl – 020 8959 5433
Estall, Joanna, cl – 01372 452513 *fax:* 01372 451416 *email:* Joanna@eatonclarinets.co.uk
Evans, Janine, fl – *SJM*
Fairbairn, Zoë, cl – 020 8524 3898
Feilding, Emma, ob, cor – 020 8693 1481; 07971 829660; 020 8533 1372 (diary)
Ferran, Marcia, ob – 020 8348 8879
Field, Martin, bsn, contra bsn – 07970 924308; c/o 01306 880669 (diary)
Fitzgerald, David – 01603 632444 *also fax;* 07768 573284 *email:* davidftz@aol.com
Ford, Luan, cl – 0121 434 5440 *email:* LuanFord@aol.com
Francis, Sarah, ob, ob d'amore, cor – 020 8340 5461 *fax:* 020 8347 5907
Fuest, John, cl – 0161 905 2144
Fussell, Angela, cl, sax – 020 8907 8428; 07710 520539 *fax:* 020 8907 8428
Galway OBE, James, fl – *IMG*
Galway, Jeanne, fl – *IMG*
Georgie, Esther, cl – 01638 714534
Gerrard, Nicola J, baroque fl, fl – 01925 752795; 07774 151145
Gill, Susan, cl – *Encore Concerts*
Glaser, Susan, fl – *Ellison*
Godsell, Edward, cl, sax – 020 8769 4118
Goodman, Robert, fl – 01273 687555; 07930 483839 *fax:* 01273 687554 *email:* robert.goodman@dial.pipex.com
Granados, Marco, fl – *Grant Rogers*
Hadden, Nancy, renaissance, baroque fl, rcdr – 020 8802 7873 *also fax*
Hall, Judith, fl – *Michael Brewer*
Harle, John, sax – *IMG*
Harris, Paul, bsn – 020 8981 7413 *also fax;* 020 8533 1372 *email:* music@paulmharris.demon.co.uk
Harris, Paul, cl – 01280 813144 *also fax; email:* paulharris@easynet.co.uk
Hazelwood, Nicola, cl – 01273 677588
Heau, Florent, cl – *TransArt*
Hilton, Janet, cl – *Gilder*
Hinson, Nigel – 0115 985 6343 *also fax*
Hirst, Michael, fl – 020 8693 1086
Holliger, Heinz, ob – *Ingpen*
Hooker, Helen, rcdr – *Purkiss*
Hoskins, Clare, ob, eh – 020 8450 4857 *also fax;* 020 8533 1372 (diary)
Höskuldsson, Stefán Ragnar, fl – *Roxane Houston*
Hyde-Smith, Christopher, fl – 020 8642 5418
Ifeka, Althea, ob – *Ellison* – 020 8591 4285
Johnson, Emma, cl – *Christa Phelps*
Keates, Nigel, cl, bs cl, eb cl – 020 8291 5176 *fax:* 020 8766 8689 *email:* nigekeates@aol.com
Kemp, Jill, rcdr – *Grant Rogers*
Kerkezos, Theodoros D, sax – *Ellison*
Khouri, Murray, cl – *Camerata*
Kingdon Ward, Martha, cl, basset hn – 0118 986 0905; 0118 978 5989 *fax:* c/o 0118 975 3365; 0118 989 1251 *email:* llsshkey@rdg.ac.uk
Kipling, Timothy, fl, picc, alto fl, rcdrs, chinese fls – 020 7488 3490 *also fax;* 020 8533 1372 *email:* simonctimk@compuserve.com
Kirby, Michael, cl – 01989 564101 *fax:* 00 34 922 68 24 37
Lawson, Colin, cl – 020 8866 3557 *also fax*
Lee, Michelle, fl, rcdr – c/o 01245 471291; 00 33 4 68 43 59 77 *also fax*
Lluna, Joan Enric, ob – *Ellison*
Logan, Alistair, cl – 0115 921 2909
Maberly, Vanessa, ob – *CMG*
McChrystal, Gerard, sax – *Upbeat*
McDonald, Gerard, baroque fl, baroque ob, ob d'am, rcdrs – *Michael Harrold*

TIMOTHY KIPLING

FLUTE, PICCOLO, ALTO FLUTE, CHINESE FLUTES

Orchestral ***Flute and harp*** ***flute and piano***
(with Danielle Perrett) (with Mark Packwood)

TEL/FAX (0207) 488 3490
DIARY: MORGENSTERN'S (0208) 533 1372

Photo: David Gough

Recital venues include St. John's Smith Square, St. Martin in the Fields, St. James's Piccadilly and the Fairfield Hall.

"The programme was extremely well chosen…a performance of great musicality, imagination and style with fine technical ability and sensitivity. The harmonious cominbination of flute and harp was shown to beautiful effect"
PAUL DAVIES, General Manger, St. John's, Smith Square

"Timothy plays with great technical facility. He produces a well focused sound, and phrases with sensitivity and imagination."
JAMES HOLMES, Head of Music, Opera North.

KATE WALSH

FLUTE/PICCOLO/FLUTES D'AMORE

CONCERTOS RECITALS FUNCTIONS

Kate is a player with style, charisma and a passion for the flute which she is keen to share. Her wide-ranging repertoire can cater for every audience. Let her introduce you to the rich, warm sound of the flute d'amore

99 DEFOE HOUSE, BARBICAN
LONDON EC2Y 8ND

TEL/FAX: 020 7588 0195
EMAIL: RICKAT@GLOBALNET.CO.UK
MOBILE: 0589 716181

Julian Baker

Horn Teacher

- *20 years a Professor at the RCM*
- *Former pupils include members of leading orchestras – in Britain and abroad*
- *Preparation for college and orchestral auditions*

59 Hargrave Park, London N19 5JW
telephone/fax 0171-272-6789

Steven Mead

Euphonium Soloist

The most sought after euphonium soloist in the World today; performs with Orchestras, Brass and Wind bands, Piano, Percussion and Electronics.

Twice voted "Euphonium Player of the Year"
"His recital was a tour-de-force of flawless technique, incredible virtuosity and a refined and appropriate sense of good taste and true musicianship" British Bandsman

Contact: 10 Old Forge Road,
Fenny Drayton, Warks, CV13 6BD
Tel/Fax: 01827 711964 Mobile: 07971 843668
Email: stevemead@compuserve.com
Website: www.euphonium.net

McGuire, Colin, cl – 020 8367 0212 *fax:* 020 8351 4670
McLarin, Lyn, fl – 0117 952 0619 *email:* wildmusic@msn.com
Maguire, Conor, fl – 020 8968 6857 *also fax; email:* Conor2you@aol.com
Malsbury, Angela, cl – 020 8579 0420 *fax:* 020 8567 9832
Marriner, Andrew, cl – *Ingpen*
Maxwell, Melinda, ob – 020 8549 9178 *fax:* 020 8974 5660
Meryon, Angus, cl – *Wright*
Mezger, Marianne, rcdr, fr flageolet, baroque musette – 01273 552548 *fax:* 01273 389572 *email:* simmonds.mezger@cwcom.net
Middleditch, Sophie, rcdr, baroque fl – *Purkiss*
Milan, Susan, fl – *Upbeat*
Miller, Tess, ob – 020 8392 2408
Mitchell, Ian, cl, bs cl – 020 8693 4694 *fax:* 020 8693 4426 *email:* ian@themitchells.screaming.net
Moraguès, Pascal, cl – *Clarion/Seven Muses*
Murphy, Emma, rcdr – 020 8960 7625 *also fax*
Muskett, Michael, rcdr, cl, musette, hurdy-gurdy, fujara – 01300 345412 *email:* hurdyplay@aol.com
Nelsen, Lisa, fl – *Purkiss*
O'Neal, Christopher, ob – *Manygate* – 020 8772 0710 *fax:* 020 8772 0711 *email:* chris@schubert-road.demon.co.uk
Pahud, Emmanuel, fl – *Askonas Holt*
Palmer, Hilary, ob – 020 8366 4846; 01732 355045 *email:* Hubpal@aol.com
Parr, Colin, cl – *Camerata*
Pay, Antony, cl – *Allied*
Percy, Richard, cl – 01684 567501 *email:* richard@rama4.freeserve.co.uk
Perkins, Laurence, bsn – *Ellison* – 0161 434 6182 *also fax*
Peterkova, Ludmila, cl – *Sonata*
Pfaff, Graham, ob – 01763 242847 *fax:* 01763 243048
Pilbery, Mary, ob – 01707 650735 *also fax;* 01707 643366
Plane, Robert, cl – *Purkiss*
Plowman, Lynne, fl – 029 2023 9198
Pluygers, Catherine, ob – 020 8699 1101 *fax:* 020 8699 2219
Polmear, Jeremy, ob – 020 7263 4027 *also fax; email:* polmear.ambache@telinco.co.uk
Pope, Anna, fl – 020 8340 3789
Porcas, Jennifer, ob, ob d'amore, eh – 01747 854999
Potter, Warwick, bsn, baritone sax, contra – 01424 440929; 07973 734572 *email:* WarwickMD@aol.com
Preston, Stephen, baroque, classical, romantic fls – 01424 756114 *also fax*
Puddy, Keith, cl – 020 7229 4185 *fax:* 020 7727 2036
Rampal, Jean-Pierre, fl – *TransArt*
Robinson, Julie, ob, eh – 024 7640 5283 *also fax*
Robson, Barnaby, cl – *Camerata/Annon*
Rubach, Keith, bsn – 01889 566608 *fax:* 01889 562649
Salter, Graham, ob, cor – 020 8348 8498 *also fax*; 07976 830309; 01306 500022 (diary)
Schatzberger, Lesley, cl, basset hn – 01904 658189 *also fax; email:* jessiefund@aol.com
Schuelein, Rainer, fl, rcdr – 020 7722 5744 *also fax*
Scott, Ruth, ob – 020 8453 1823; 020 8533 1372 (diary)
Sewell, Brian, bsn – 020 8540 0670 *fax:* 020 8241 1280 *email:* brisew@globalnet.co.uk
Smith, Daniel, bsn – *Michael Brewer*
Smith, Kenneth, fl – 020 8675 4220; 01202 671621
Smith, Rachel, fl – *Dyfel*
Smith, Tommy, tenor sax – 07710 585231 *email:* music@tommysmith.demon.co.uk
Snowden, Jonathan, fl – *LM*
Soames, Victoria, cl – c/o 020 8472 2057 *also fax; email:* v.soames@clarinet-classics.ndirect.co.uk
Solomon, Ashley, baroque fl, fl, rcdr – 020 8346 2896 *also fax; email:* ashleysolomon@compuserve.com
Sørensen, Gitte, fl – *Roy Baker*
Southworth, Clare, fl – 01923 260721 *also fax; email:* clareflute@aol.com
Sparling, Andrew, cl – 020 8503 2364 *also fax*
Spratt, Kirsten, fl – 020 8766 6557 *fax:* 020 7252 5279 *email:* kirstenspratt@compuserve.com
Stinton, Jennifer, fl – 01732 369041 *also fax*; 07767 780563
Theodore, David, ob – 020 8886 4950
Thomas, Kathryn, fl, alto fl, picc – *Murphy*
Thompson, Peter, cl – 020 8291 2510
Thorby, Pamela, rcdr – *Hazard*
Todd, Hazel, ob, baroque ob – 0118 978 5866
Touchin, Colin, cl, rcdr – 024 7667 0211 *also fax; email:* musab@warwick.ac.uk
Trier, Stephen, cl, sax – 020 8748 4711 *fax:* 020 8932 0261
Triner, Imogen, ob – *Roxane Houston*
Turbett, Philip, bsn – 01825 760046 *also fax; email:* turbettp@aol.com
Underwood, Mark, fl, bs fl, alto fl, picc – 01322 287924 *also fax*
Vallis-Davies, Nicholas, fl – 020 8943 5329 *also fax; email:* formedia@vallis-davies.freeserve.co.uk
Vallis-Davies, Sian, ob – 020 8943 5329 *also fax; email:* formedia@vallis-davies.freeserve.co.uk
Van Spaendonck, Ronald, cl – *LM*
Viscardi, Giulio Giannelli, fl – *GBZ*
Walker, Elizabeth, renaissance, baroque fl, fl, rcdr – 020 7226 8141 *fax:* 020 7226 9732
Walsh, Kate, fl, alto fl, bs fl, fl d'amore – 020 7588 0195 *also fax;* 01306 500022 *email:* rickat@globalnet.co.uk
Wang, Jian – *Askonas Holt*
Waterhouse, William, bsn, cbsn, baroque cbsn – 020 8340 8362 *fax:* 020 8341 7616 *email:* wwaterhouse@ndirect.co.uk
Weigall, Richard, ob – *Camerata*
Weinberg, Anton, cl – 020 8672 5903
van de Wiel, Mark, cl – 020 7704 8079 *also fax*
Williams, Averil, fl – 020 8946 6857 *also fax*
Williams, Glyn, bsn, sax – 020 8341 3556; 07956 318794
Wilson, David, ob – 07958 651878
Wilson, Jeffery, cl, sax – 01245 450192 *also fax*
Winters, Ross, rcdr – 01263 512605
Wye, Trevor, fl – *Seaview* *email:* trevorwye@compuserve.com
Zukerman, George, bsn – *Gilder*

Brass

Aarons, Anthony, tpt – 020 8542 7610 *also fax; email:* faure@globalnet.co.uk
Adams, Richard, tpt – 029 2049 5237 *also fax; fax:* 0870 164 1457 *email:* adamsrj@hotmail.com
Allen, Bryan, tpt – 0141 332 4101 ext 274 *email:* b.allen@rsamd.ac.uk
Antonsen, Ole Edvard, tpt – *Askonas Holt*
Ashton, Graham, tpt – *LM*
Ashworth, Robert, hn, hand hn, baroque hn – 0113 258 1300 *also fax; email:* bob.ashworth@dial.pipex.com
Bauer, Wolfgang, tpt – *Pristavec*
Bevan, Clifford, ophicleide, serpent – 01962 864755 *also fax;* 020 7724 3250
Caudle, Theresa, cornett – 01264 736565 *also fax*
Fulkerson, James, trb – *SJM*
Griffiths, Chris, hn, natural hn – 0191 251 0146
Halstead, Anthony, hn – 020 8348 0447; 07973 421626 *email:* halstead@globalnet.co.uk
Hazelgrove, Bernard, tpt – 01733 239072 *fax:* 01733 235462
Hendrie, Andrew – 020 8769 6204 *fax:* 020 8664 7326
Hogg, Simon, trb – 01926 497887 *fax:* 01926 419701 *email:* shogg@aol.com
Houghton, William, tpt – 01494 837390 *also fax*
Jenkins, Huw, hn – 07973 268331; 01483 723644
Kenny, John, trb, sackbut, rcdr, carnyx, voice, alphorn – 0131 447 3707 *also fax; email:* carnyx@mcmail.com
Laird, Michael, tpt, natural tpt – 020 8946 2700 *fax:* 020 8946 7272
Lindberg, Christian, trb – *Clarion/Seven Muses*
Lumsden, Alan, trb, serpent, ophicleide – 01452 750253 *fax:* 01452 750585 *email:* music@beauchamp.demon.co.uk
Mason, David, tpt – 020 8864 9056
Mead, Steven, euph – 01827 711964 *also fax;* 07971 843668 *email:* stevemead@compuserve.com
Mowat, Christopher, trb – 020 8398 0057 *fax:* 020 8398 7559 *email:* cmowat@btinternet.com
Murphy, Maurice, tpt – 020 8959 1372
Parsons, Anthony, trb – 020 8340 4109 *also fax; email:* lerncurv@aol.com
Picton, Wendy, euph – *Ellison*
Pigneguy, John, hn, Wagner tuba, tenor hn – 020 7373 8915; 01483 723644
Powell, John, euph, ten tb, bs tpt – 01942 680941 *also fax;* 07973 787663
Pyatt, David, hn – *Askonas Holt*
Ruske, Eric, hn – *TransArt*
Shifrin, Ken, trb, alto trb, euph, bs tpt – 0121 778 4912 *fax:* 0121 778 5569
Smith, Malcolm, tpt – 020 8291 5939 *fax:* 020 8291 2205
Steele-Perkins, Crispian, tpt, natural tpt – *Anglo-Swiss*
Stirling, Stephen, hn – 020 8202 2050 *also fax;* 01892 870187 (manager) *also fax; email:* concertmanagement@dial.pipex.com
Thompson, Michael, hn, natural hn, wagner tuba – *PGM*
Vlatkovic, Radovan, hn – *Ingpen*
Wallace, John, tpt – *Denny Lyster*
Watkins, Richard, hn – *Christa Phelps*
Weale, Malcolm, tpt, cnt – 01202 298795 *also fax*
Webb, Barrie, trb – c/o 020 8606 0030 *fax:* c/o 020 8606 0037
Wiggins, Bram, tpt – 01280 812408

KEN SHIFRIN

Tenor & Alto Trombone/Euphonium & Bass Trumpet

"The soloist Ken Shifrin played brilliantly with almost unbelievable beauty of tone, artistry and elegance. A seemingly effortless rendition full of effects, technical bravura and feeling." THE VIENNA KURIER

"Not only is he one of the most able trombonists in my experience but also an intelligent and wide-ranging musician." SIR SIMON RATTLE

"A one-man tour-de-force." COLONEL L.B. SHELBURNE, JR
United States Army Band, Leader and Commander

"Ken Shifrin demonstrated outstanding instrumental ability as well as excellent qualities of musicianship."
CHARLES DUTOIT

"An extremely good performer."
IANNIS XENAKIS

"A superb performance by this marvellous player."
JOSEPH HOROWITZ

also available with

from Baroque to Broadway

Posaune Voce Trio

Trombone ● Voice ● Piano

STEPHEN STIRLING

"Stephen Stirling is one of the most original talents I have experienced. He is a player with the utmost sensitivity and imagination, which is shown through the beautiful way he shapes musical phrases and the extraordinary range of colours he employs"
Richard Hickox

Latest Release:
Mozart's Horn Concertos 1-5 on Classic FM label
Catalogue no: 75605570252 (CD)
75605570254 (Cassette)

Listen to Stephen on: www.classical-artists.com/stephen-stirling

For further details, please contact Shelley Phillips at Concerto Management, Little Moorden, Leigh, Kent, TN11 8HU
Tel/Fax: 01892 870187 Email: concertomanagement@dial.pipex.com

NORRIS TURNER

SIONED WILLIAMS

Internationally renowned soloist and chamber musician.
Extensive repertoire from 17th Century to present day.
TV and radio broadcaster.
CD recordings include Hyperion, Meridian, Collins Classics.
Principal Harpist BBC Symphony Orchestra.

60 Friern Mount Drive
Whetstone, London N20 9DL
Tel: 020 8446 1346
Fax: 020 8446 9379

SUCCESS IN THIS BUSINESS IS ALL ABOUT CONTACTS

Your comprehensive guide to venues, performing companies, arts festivals, suppliers and services, education and training, arts councils, regional arts boards and support organisations.

British Performing Arts Yearbook

Price £24.95 (plus p&p)

NEXT EDITION PUBLISHED JUNE '2000

ORDER YOUR COPY TODAY
Please send your cheque
(made payable to Rhinegold Publishing Ltd)
to:
Book Sales Dept,
Rhinegold Publishing Ltd,
FREEPOST, London WC2H 8BR
(no stamp needed in the UK).

CREDIT CARD ORDERS
Tel: 020 7333 1721
Fax: 020 7333 1769 **www.rhinegold.co.uk**

Harp

Baldry, Elizabeth Jane – 01647 433635; 01273 204064 *email:* ejbharp@btinternet.com
Barford, Imogen – 020 7485 1903 *also fax*
Beattie, Maria – 020 8519 5474 *fax:* 020 8555 3040 *email:* mdb-harpoonprod@clara.net
Bennett, Elinor – *Ellison* – 01286 830010 *fax:* 01286 831265 *email:* elinorbennett@email.wales.com
Bennett, Janet, hp, Celtic hp – 0191 276 3019 *email:* janetbennettharp@hotmail.com
Bevis, Suzanne, hp, Irish hp – 023 8025 4238 *also fax*
Boden, Daphne – 020 8346 5706 *fax:* 020 8346 0121
Brewer, Aline – *OWM*
Deere-Jones, Sarah, concert/Celtic hp – 01929 426091 *also fax*
Doris, Clíona – 028 4461 3856 *fax:* 028 4461 7740 *email:* doris@unite.co.uk
Drake, Susan – *Sympathetic*
Ellis CBE, Osian – 020 8445 7896 *also fax;* 0175 861 2501
Englichova, Katerina – *Sonata*
Gondry, Jeannette – *John Boddy*
Goossens OBE, Sidonie – 01306 611283
Graham, Emma – 01392 833813 *email:* emgharp@onet.co.uk
Granger, Emma – 020 8847 4880
Holliger, Ursula – *Ingpen*
Jenkins, Nia – *John Boddy*
Jones, Ieuan – 020 8563 2239 *fax:* 020 8563 2249
Jones, Rebeca – 020 7924 2436
Keogh, Miriam, hp, Celtic hp – 020 8349 4067 *also fax; email:* mikecello@which.net
Liston, Jane – *John Boddy*
Master, Rachel – *John Boddy*
Meier, Patrizia – *NCCP*
Moore, Angela – 020 8291 9535
Nicholls, Alison – 01223 882354 *also fax; email:* alisonn@aol.com
Nordmann, Marielle – *TransArt*
Perrett, Danielle – c/o 01189 625443 *fax:* 020 7732 0653 *email:* delbravo@lineone.net
Robles, Marisa – *Clarion/Seven Muses*
Roth, Rebecca – *John Boddy*
Rothstein, Sue – 020 8202 4769
Salo, Satu – 01753 525249 *also fax; email:* bosleykssg@msn.com
Seale, Charlotte – 020 7254 0419
Thomas, Caryl – *LM*
Wakeford, Lucy – *YCAT*
Watts, Sheila – *John Boddy*
Webb, Hugh – 020 7837 4954 *fax:* 020 7833 8155
White, Catherine – *John Boddy*
Williams, Sioned – 020 8446 1346 *also fax*
Wilson, Kate – 01829 271271 *also fax*

Guitar, Lute, etc

Andresier, Rose – *DCM*
Arenstein, Colin – 020 8348 3630
Auchterlonie, Domingo, flamenco gui – 01905 424083
Barrueco, Manuel – *HP*
Biberian, Gilbert – 01242 581457 *also fax; email:* gbiberian@aol.com
Bonell, Carlos – *Upbeat*
Bream CBE, Julian – *Hazard*
Brightmore, Robert – 01455 635851 *also fax*
Brown, Paul – *Dyfel*
Burgess, Edward – 01256 763764
Burley, Raymond – *Chameleon*
Byrne, John – 01928 577596 *also fax*
Chadwick, Roland – 020 8579 4287 *email:* roland_chadwick@hotmail.com
Chapman, Richard – *Manygate*
* Chateauneuf, Paula, lute, theorbo, early gui – 020 8771 2152 *also fax*
Chaurand, Anne – 0141 334 5691 *also fax; email:* ChaurandA@aol.com
Dimakopoulos, Dimitris – *Ellison*
Durrant, Richard – 01273 465371 *email:* richard@longman-records.com
Elsner, Kasia, lute, baroque gui, theorbo – 020 7354 5883 *also fax*
Fierens, Guillermo – *Gilder*
Fisk, Eliot – *Pristavec*
Garcia, Gerald, gui, vihuela – 01865 725929 *fax:* 01865 725811 *email:* geraldgarcia@compuserve.com
Gibb, Steve, gui, banjo, mandolin, bs, dobro, electric gui – 07702 648015; 020 8986 5718 *also fax; email:* sbgibb@globalnet.co.uk
Gregory, Paul – c/o 01273 736377
Grigoryan, Slava – c/o 00 61 2 9371 0022 *fax:* 00 61 2 9371 6886 *email:* michael@gtmgt.com.au

NEIL
SMITH
guitar
"It was really a spectacular experience to watch this very fine musician perform."
LOS ANGELES VALLEY STAR
"Neil Smith has an extremely accomplished technique and his grasp of the instrument is masterly"
THE DAILY TELEGRAPH
"Das war ein Konzert der Meisterklasse"
BERLINER MORGENPOST
"He belongs to the very front rank of guitarists."
CLASSICAL GUITAR
Representation:
BDA(UK) : 01925 766655
HLM(EUROPE) : 0031 263615444

A renowned professional guitarist, fully experienced in many diverse musical forms, John has performed on BBC television & radio, Classic FM and major festivals, including performances for Princess Anne and Tony Blair.
A former pupil and teacher at the RNCM, John is equally at home on the 'classical' concert platform, or on the rock stage, as he was formerly lead guitarist with the Liverpool band the LAs, who had a worldwide hit with "There she goes".
BAROQUE
SPANISH
JAZZ
CLASSICAL
CONTEMPORY
POPULAR
GNRCM
John Byrne
Guitarist
For further information, phone or fax
01928 577596
or mobile: 0421 316567

"An exhilarating experience..." - Independent on Sunday, London
"music at its most spontaneous, vibrant and sensual." - South China Morning Post
"electrifying impact of these superb performances" - Soundscapes, Australia
"astonishing individuality ... he munipulated fragments in a way that built excitement" - The Washington Post
"indeed a most welcome change from the usual run of today's instrumental music" - The Statesman, New Delhi
"a unity of spiritual well-being that was expressed in an exuberant standing ovation." - Huddersfield Daily
"The evening was a resounding success." - Hong Kong Standard
Wajahat Khan
sarod, sitar, surbahar
Indian classical music
"one of the leading Sarod players of India."
– Evening Standard, London
Universally recognised as a leading sarod player of India. One of the most dynamic performers of his generation. Son of legendary Ustad Imrat Khan, belongs to one of the first and foremost Indian musical dynasties. Tours frequently, has performed and broadcast worldwide, in major venues/festivals including Smithsonian - Washington DC, the Kremlin - Moscow, Suntory Hall - Tokyo, Queen Elizabeth Hall and BBC Proms - Royal Albert Hall - London. As composer most recently has written a sarod quintet playing with the Medici string quartet, and has also accomplished numerous successful world music collaborations.
Personal Managers: Miriam Nelken / Anita Rogan
141 Carlton Avenue East, London HA9 8PU
Tel: 020 8904 2833 Fax 020 8904 2833
Email: wkmanagement@wajahatkhan.com
Agent:
Neil Chaffey Concert Promotions
Tel: 01462 790919 Fax: 01462 790920
Website: www.wajahatkhan.com

Hand, Richard – 020 7724 3806 *also fax*
* Harris, Ian, gui, mandolin, mandola, mandocello, mandobass – 01273 565589 *also fax; email:* 100754.3674@compuserve.com
* Harrison, Fiona, gui – 020 8932 6876 *email:* fiona.harrison.mus.92@aya.yale.edu
Hartman, Thomas, gui, vihuela – 020 7737 6770 *email:* cmbski@aol.com
Hill, Robin – c/o 01204 63055 *fax:* c/o 01204 658023
Hope, Harvxey – 020 8657 5840 *also fa*
Howe, Peter – *Purkiss*
Isbin, Sharon – *Music Partnership*
Jackson, Andy, gui, guitarra portuguesa – 01388 607060; 01670 516997
Jeffrey, Robin, lute, oud – 01892 852878 *also fax; email:* Peshref@aol.com
Keeping, Andrew – 020 8420 7467 *also fax; email:* akeeping@globalnet.co.uk
Kerstens, Tom – c/o 020 7831 0345 *fax:* 020 7831 0346
Kilvington, Chris – 01223 276763 *fax:* 01223 277980 *email:* chriskilvi.cmw@argonet.co.uk
Kotzia, Eleftheria – *Purkiss*
* Lamb, Antony, lute, oud – 029 2079 9184 *also fax; email:* lambyork@globalnet.co.uk
Lewin, Michael, gui, lute – 020 8876 6161 *also fax*
Linell, Dorothy, lute, gui, theorbo – 01923 822934 *also fax;* 020 7580 8764 *email:* Dlinell@aol.com
Lund, Vegard, gui, lute – *Roy Baker*
Mackenzie, John – c/o 01347 878746 *email:* john.mackenzie@lineone.net
McLaughlin, John – *TransArt*
* Madeley, Selina, gui, lute – 01785 211218 *also fax; email:* selina@staffordguitar.com
Marchionda, Stephen – *Camerata*
Marcos, flamenco gui – c/o 01865 243663
Martin, Juan – c/o 020 8346 4500 *fax:* 020 8346 2488 *email:* www.hvmartin@dircon.co.uk
Meryon, Tom – *Wright*
Mills, John – c/o 01435 872391 *also fax*
Nockalls, Martin, gui – 01302 772677 *also fax; email:* ambrosmus@aol.com
Ogden, Craig – *SWA*
Parsons, David, gui, lute – 020 7407 9243 *also fax; email:* david@viana.freeserve.co.uk
Pells, Timothy, gui – 01206 298256 *fax:* 01206 299528
Perkins, Brian, gui, lute – 01902 333237 *email:* guitarville@freeserve.co.uk
Phillips, Freddie – 020 8393 6251
Ramirez, Alexander Sergei – *Annon*
Richards, Jonathan – 01492 544259
Romero, Pepe – *Anglo-Swiss*
Rooley, Anthony, lute – 020 8444 6565 *fax:* 020 8444 1008 *email:* consort@easynet.co.uk
Salfield, Jon, flamenco gui – 01209 713426 *email:* jonsalfield@edda.freeserve.co.uk
* Sayce, Lynda, lute – 01235 816158 *also fax*
Smith, Neil – c/o 0113 239 2222 *fax:* 0113 239 2016
Spooner, Terry – 01279 418015
Spring, Matthew – 01865 761966 *also fax; email:* matthewspring@matspring.demon.co.uk
Stephens, Alison, mandolin – 07973 111690 *email:* AliMSteph@aol.com
Stimpson, Michael – 01722 780671 *also fax*
Taylor, Frances, mandolin – *Murphy*
Thodey, Robin, lute – *Ellison*
Thomas, Alan – 020 8699 1691 *also fax; email:* aethomas@clara.net
Tursi, Sante – *Pristavec*
Vale, Galina – 0161 226 8273 *also fax*
Wade, Graham – 0113 275 2456 *also fax*
Walker, Timothy, gui, lute – *CDI*
Watson, Malcolm – 0131 447 4951 *also fax; email:* jmalcw@lineone.net
Wheatley, Martin, gui, banjo, ukelele, hawaiian gui – c/o 020 8532 2923
Williams, John – *Askonas Holt*
Willmott, Roderick, gui, lute – 01905 427026
Wiltschinsky, Peter – c/o 01204 63055 *fax:* 01204 658028
Woodhouse, Nigel, mandolin, gui, tenor banjo – 01727 865164 *also fax*; 07970 840927
Zanon, Fabio – *Grant Rogers*
Zaradin, John – 01234 720018; 07970 650322 *fax:* 01234 720090 *email:* 101662.557@compuserve.com

Percussion

Auchterlonie, Delphine Daigane, castanets, platillos, conchas – 01905 424083
Balogh, Kalman, cimbalom – *Michael Brewer*
Benjafield, Richard – 01483 533892 *also fax; email:* benjafield@argonet.co.uk
Corbett, Heather, tuned perc, cimbalom, timpani – 0141 772 3152 *also fax;* 07050 168772 *email:* Heather_Corbett@hotmail.com
Currie, Colin – *Intermusica*
Glennie, Evelyn – *IMG*
Goedicke, Kurt-Hans, timpani – 020 8866 1845
Holland, James – 01494 677436
Limbrick, Simon – 020 7732 4590; 07768 514353 *email:* pslimbrick@aol.com
Shipway, Nigel – c/o 01306 500022
Szakály, Agnes, cimbalom – *Ellison*
Warburton, Julian – *YCAT*
Whettam, Andrew, marimba, etc – *Talbot-Cooper*
Wright, Tim – 020 8690 4429; 07889 410597 *fax:* 07070 800382

Miscellaneous

Baigent, Mark, digeridoo, ethnic shawms – 07850 914024
Boros, Gabor, cimbalom – 020 8907 7953 *email:* borosensemble@breathemail.net
* Broadway, Michael, pianola – 020 7254 6145 *fax:* 020 7249 0130
Crabb, James, accordion – *Ingpen*
Glennie, Evelyn, Great Highland bagpipes – *IMG email:* Greg@evelyn.co.uk
* Gupta, Punita, sitar – 020 8427 3530 *fax:* 020 8248 5138
Huehns, Colin, erhu, Mongolian horsehead fiddle – 020 8204 7369
Kalsi, Johnny, dhol – *SJM*
Khan, Imrat, sitar, subahar – 020 8904 2833 *also fax*
Khan, Wajahat, sarod, sitar, surbahar – c/o 020 8904 2833 *also fax*
Leach, John, zither – 020 7385 0182 *fax:* 020 7381 1155
Leith, Ronald, carillon, clavichord – 01224 634427 *fax:* 01224 639096
Malloy, Alasdair, glass harmonica, bagpipes – *LM*
Millar, Cynthia, ondes martenot – *OWM*
Murray, Owen, classical accordion – *Denny Lyster*
Muskett, Michael, hurdy-gurdy, fujara – 01300 345412 *email:* hurdyplay@aol.com
Naish, Bronwen, musical saw – 020 8299 2931 *fax:* 01766 530356 *email:* NaishB@aol.com
* Perkins, John, sitar, surbahar – 01803 868687 *also fax*
Petric, Joseph, concert accordion – *NCCP*
Pruslin, Stephen, celesta, chmbr org – 020 8948 7404 *also fax*
Roth, Alec, Javanese gamelan – 020 7497 3754 *also fax*
Sahai, Vishnu 'Sanju', Tabla – 020 8737 3582 *also fax*
Shankar, Ravi, sitar – *Tennant*
Shrivastav, Baluji, sitar, tabla, Indian vocal, dicruba – 020 7354 5709; 0777 5851845 *fax:* 020 7503 5270
Spring, Matthew, hurdy-gurdy, sinfonye – 01865 761966 *also fax; email:* matthewspring@matspring.demon.co.uk
* Srikantha Rajah, Arunthathy, veena – 020 8543 2126 *also fax; fax:* 020 8540 3442
Townsend, David, English concertina, bar concertina, bs concertina – 01865 714778 *fax:* 01865 749228 *email:* dtctina@aol.com
Wilson, Malcolm C, handbells – 01786 825387 *also fax; email:* claganach@easynet.co.uk
Xu, Pingxin, Chinese dulcimer – *Ellison*

Early Music Instrumentalists

Performers who have made a special study of early instrumental technique and performance practice are listed below under three broad categories: strings (bowed and plucked), wind and keyboard. A telephone number is given for each artist; where an agent is named, details will be found in the **Agents and Managers** section.

Strings (bowed and plucked)

Adams, Peter, va da gamba, treble and bs – 01295 277976 *also fax*
Barford, Imogen, early hps – 020 7485 1903 *also fax*
Bassano, Kathy, va, renaissance, baroque, classical, va d'am – 01494 868240 *fax:* 01494 868250 *email:* GArtists1@aol.com – *Giustiniani Artists*
Capleton, Brian, va da gamba – 01685 891156 *email:* brian@asclepius.u-net.com
Caudle, Theresa, baroque vn, baroque va – 01264 736565 *also fax*
Chandler, Adrian, baroque vn – 020 8664 7314
Chateauneuf, Paula, lutes, theorbos, early guis – 020 8771 2152 *also fax*
Civval, Sally, va da gamba, baroque vc – *Music Management*
Comberti, Micaela, baroque vn – 020 8349 3580 *fax:* 020 8346 7490
Crum, Alison, viols, violone, hp, early strs, sackbut – 020 8452 3254 *also fax; email:* alison.crum@which.net
Davis, Howard, baroque vn – 01279 431337 *also fax*
Deere-Jones, Sarah, concert/celtic hp – 01929 426091 *also fax*
Dittmer, Petronella, baroque vn, baroque va – 020 7937 0684 *also fax*
Dolmetsch, Marguerite, bs viol – 01428 651473 *also fax*
East, Angela, classical and baroque vc, va da gamba, bs vn – 020 8769 4158 *also fax; email:* EastRevolution@compuserve.com
Elsner, Kasia, theorbo, lute, baroque gui – 020 7354 5883 *also fax*
Glenton, Robert, baroque vc – *POEM*
Hanson, Peter, baroque vn – *POEM*
Harper, Celia, double hp, hpd, chmbr org – *Blythe*
Harris, Ian, gui, mandolin, mandola, mandocello, mandobass – 01273 565589 *also fax; email:* 100754.3674@compuserve.com
Heinrich, Susanne, viols, violone, va da gamba – 01865 751928 *also fax; email:* SusanneHeinrich@charivari.freeserve.co.uk
Hope, Harvey, baroque gui – 020 8657 5840 *also fax*
Jeffrey, Robin, lute, theorbo, baroque gui, oud – 01892 852878 *also fax; email:* Peshref@aol.com
Kerstens, Tom, vihuela, baroque gui – 07071 201111 *also fax; email:* igf@guitarfestivalin.demon.co.uk
Kuijken, Sigiswald, vn – *Allied*
Kuijkin, Wieland, va da gamba – *Allied*
Levine, Joanna, vc, va da gamba, violone – 020 8348 4295 *fax:* 020 8292 7125
Levy, Mark, va da gamba, violone, lirone – 020 8348 4295 *fax:* 020 8292 7125
Lewin, Michael, lute, archlute, theorbo – 020 8876 6161 *also fax*
Linell, Dorothy, lute, theorbo – 01923 822934 *also fax;* 020 7580 8764 *email:* Dlinell@aol.com
Lund, Vegard, baroque gui, lute – *Roy Baker*
MacLeod, Laurie Ann, baroque and classical vc, bs viol, bs vn, ten vn – 01252 795047 *also fax*
Marks, Roy, viols, lutes, violone, theorbo – 020 8452 3254 *also fax; email:* alison.crum@which.net
Medlam, Charles, baroque vc, va da gamba – 01635 254331 *fax:* 01635 253629 *email:* c.medlam@btinternet.com
Muskett, Michael, hurdy-gurdy – 01300 345412 *email:* hurdyplay@aol.com
Parsons, David, lute, gui, theorbo – 020 7407 9243 *also fax; email:* david@viana.freeserve.co.uk
Partridge, Richard, va da gamba – 020 8318 6638 *email:* richard.partridge1@virgin.net
Rogers, Cornelia, va da gamba, baroque vn – 01323 734207 *also fax*
Rogers, Maurice, viols – 01323 734207 *also fax*
Rooley, Anthony, lute – 020 7229 5142 *fax:* 020 7221 1282 *email:* consort@easynet.co.uk
Sayce, Lynda, lute, baroque gui, theorbos, baroque mandolin – 01235 816158 *also fax*
Skeaping, Roderick, baroque vn, rebecs, viols – 020 7485 6668 *fax:* 020 7267 2957 *email:* Roddyskeaping@hotmail.com
Skuce, Peter, medieval hp – 020 8488 3947 *also fax; email:* peter.skuce@dufay.com
Spring, Matthew, lute, guis, theorbo, hurdy-gurdy, viols – 01865 761966 *also fax; email:* matthewspring@matspring.demon.co.uk
Stowell, Robin, baroque vn – 029 2075 2001 *fax:* 029 2087 4379 *email:* stowell@cardiff.ac.uk
Taylor, Frances, mandolin – *Murphy*
Theo, Tatty, baroque vc – 020 7607 0185 *fax:* 020 7687 1586 *email:* tatty@easynet.co.uk
Wallfisch, Elizabeth, baroque vn – *Sykes*
Willmott, Roderick, gui, lute – 01905 427026
Wilson, Brian Lloyd, baroque, classical, romantic vn, va, va d'am – 01252 795047 *also fax*
Wright, Brian, lute – *POEM*

Wind

Adams, Piers, rcdr – *Upbeat*
Arden-Taylor, Paul, rcdr, early reeds, ob – 01562 710801 *also fax*
Baker, Paul, rcdrs, hurdy-gurdy, renaissance winds, bagpipes – 01384 295210 *email:* paul@diabolus-in-musica.freeserve.co.uk
Ball, Christopher, rcdr, early wind insts – 020 7935 1270
Barlow, Jeremy, fl, rcdr, pipe and tabor – 020 7267 7176 *fax:* 020 7267 0127 *email:* jrmybarlow@aol.com
Bennetts, Kathryn, rcdr – 01892 723370 *also fax; email:* 101767.2724@compuserve.com
Booth, Jane, cl, chalumeau – 020 8942 1519; 07711 724138 *fax:* 020 8287 9284
Bowman, Peter, rcdr – 01892 723370 *also fax; email:* peterbowman1@compuserve.com
Brown, Barnaby, early Highland bagpipes – 07041 564142 *email:* barnaby.b@which.net
Carroll, Paul, baroque and classical bsn, baroque fl, rcdr, baroque ob, chalumeau – *Music Management*
Dolmetsch, Marguerite, rcdr – 01428 651473 *also fax*
Donnelly, Christopher, cl – 01296 334272
Halstead, Anthony, natural hn – 020 8348 0447; 07973 421626 *email:* halstead@globalnet.co.uk
Harris, Paul, baroque and classical bsn – 020 8981 7413 *also fax;* 020 8533 1372 *email:* music@paulmharris.demon.co.uk
Jarratt-Knock, David, cornetto – 01564 773532 *email:* david@jarratt-knock.freeserve.co.uk
Kuijken, Barthold, transverse fl – *Allied*
Laird, Michael, natural tpt, cornetto – 020 8946 2700 *fax:* 020 8946 7272
Lawson, Colin, cl, chalumeau, basset hn – 020 8866 3557 *also fax*
Lumsden, Alan, sackbut, serpent, ophicleide, rcdr – 01452 750253 *fax:* 01452 750585 *email:* music@beauchamp.demon.co.uk
Macdonald, Gerard, flauto traverso, baroque ob, rcdr – *Michael Harrold*
Merryweather, James, shawms, curtal, medieval, renaissance bagpipes, baroque bsn – 01904 432878/431328 *fax:* 01904 432860 *email:* jwm5@york.ac.uk
Mezger, Marianne, rcdrs, fr flageolet, baroque musette – 01273 552548 *fax:* 01273 389572 *email:* simmonds.mezger@cwcom.net
Muskett, Michael, rcdr, cl, musette, hurdy-gurdy – 01300 345412 *email:* hurdyplay@aol.com
Nallen, Evelyn, rcdrs – 01223 561331 *also fax; email:* r.groove@dial.pipex.com
Pickett, Philip, rcdr, early winds – 020 7735 8154 *fax:* 020 7820 0801 *email:* philip.pickett@btinternet.com
Preston, Stephen, cl, romantic and baroque fl – 01424 756114 *also fax; email:* spreston@bluetit.u-net.com
Puddy, Keith, cl, basset hn, chalumeau – 020 7229 4185 *fax:* 020 7727 2036
Rogers, Cornelia, rcdr – 01323 734207 *also fax*

Early music today
Carole Cerasi on playing Elisabeth Jacquet de la Guerre

Schuelein, Rainer, fl, rcdr – 020 7722 5744 *also fax*
Solomon, Ashley, rcdr, baroque and classical fl – 020 8346 2896 *also fax; email:* ashleysolomon@compuserve.com
Staff, David, baroque, classical tpt, cornetto – *POEM*
Steele-Perkins, Crispian, tpt, natural tpt – *Anglo-Swiss*
Summers, William, early fl, rcdr – 020 8941 4917 *also fax; email:* wsummers@dircon.co.uk
Thomas, Jenny, baroque, classical fl – 01753 831064 *also fax*
Thompson, Michael, natural hn – *PGM*
Thorby, Pamela, rcdr – 020 7607 9541 *also fax – Hazard*
van der Beek, Andrew, sackbut, serpent – 01249 730468 *also fax*
Walker, Elizabeth, renaissance, baroque and classical fl, rcdr – 020 7226 8141 *fax:* 020 7226 9732
Wallace, John, tpt, natural tpt – *Denny Lyster*
West, Jeremy, cornetto – *POEM*

Keyboard

Ainscough, Julie, org – *Michael Harrold*
Aldwinckle, Robert, hpd, chmbr org – 01424 715435 *also fax*
Alexander-Max, Susan, f-pno, clvd – 020 7328 9347 *fax:* 020 7328 4689 *email:* max@musicol.demon.co.uk
Arnáiz, Gulliermo Diez, org – *Michael Harrold*
Barber, Graham, hpd, org – 0113 263 1890 *fax:* 0113 263 7178 *email:* g.d.barber@leeds.ac.uk
Barlow, Jeremy, hpd – 020 7267 7176 *fax:* 020 7267 0127 *email:* jrmybarlow@aol.com
Barthold, Kenneth van, f-pno – 01747 838318 *also fax*
Bate, Jennifer, org *email:* jenniferbate@classical-artists.com – *Manygate*
Beechey, Gwilym, hpd – 01482 508910
Black, Virginia, hpd – 01279 431337 *also fax*
Bond, Ann, hpd, org – 01524 701623
Booth, Colin, hpd – 01749 870516 *also fax*
Burnett, Richard, f-pno – 01580 211702 *fax:* 01580 211007 *email:* finchcocks@argonet.co.uk
Carey, Colm, org – 020 8426 5961 *also fax; email:* careycolm@aol.com
Cave, Penelope, hpd, virginals – 01483 563096 *also fax*
Chapman, Jane, hpd – 020 8997 7621 *also fax*
Cole, Maggie, hpd, f-pno – *Robert White*
Coulson, Richard, hpd, org – 01932 229171
Cuckston, Alan, hpd, org – 01757 638238 *also fax; email:* alancuckston@iname.com – *POEM*
Egarr, Richard, org, hpd – *POEM*
Elcombe, Keith, hpd – 0161 445 6661
Francis, David, hpd, chmbr org – 01925 710454
Gordon, David – 01923 239038 *also fax*
Gould, Sharon, hpd – 01722 712449 *fax:* 01722 712901 *email:* sg@contech.force9.co.uk
Griffiths, Clare, hpd – 01233 663775 *fax:* 01233 611942
Harris, Richard Leigh, hpd – 01865 243306
Heilbron, Annette, hpd, f-pno – 01223 315681
Henry, John, hpd, clvd – 020 7586 7216
Hollick, Douglas, hpd, org, f-pno – 01949 861347 *also fax; email:* dwh@globalnet.co.uk
Hoyland, David, hpd – *Roxane Houston*
Jones, Stephen, hpd, org, harmonium – 01727 864007 *fax:* 01727 845884 *email:* steve_sta@compuserve.com
Kenny, Courtney, hpd – *Roxane Houston*
King, Robert, hpd *email:* info@the-kings-consort.org.uk – *HP*
Klosiewicz, Wladislaw, hpd – *Finch*
Koopman, Ton, hpd, org – *Hazard*
Leigh, David, hpd, f-pno – 01865 244197; 01608 810607
Leonhardt, Gustav, hpd – *Allied*
May, Katharine, hpd – 0115 925 7851; 01628 622903
Mobbs, Kenneth, f-pno, hpd – 0117 973 3613 *also fax*
Moroney, Davitt, hpd, org – *LM*
Nash, Pamela, hpd – 01270 567895 *also fax*
Ng, Kah-Ming, hpd – 01865 751928 *also fax; email:* Kah-MingNg@charivari.freeserve.co.uk
Nicholls, Simon, f-pno – 020 8446 0812
Overbury, Michael, hpd, org – 01636 702054
Parnell, Andrew, harmonium, hpd – *Michael Harrold*
Parry, Martyn, hpd, org – 020 8980 9735 *also fax; email:* mp@antillroad.demon.co.uk
Patrick, David Kinnear, hpd – 020 8449 4873 *email:* DeeKayPea@argonet.co.uk
Phillips, Margaret, org, hpd – 01963 250899
Pinnock CBE, Trevor, hpd – *Askonas Holt*
Ponsford, David, hpd, org – 01285 651995 *also fax – Camerata*
Proud, Malcolm, hpd, org – 00 353 56 61497 *also fax*
Pruslin, Stephen, hpd, chmbr org, f-pno, regal – 020 8948 7404 *also fax*
Puyana, Rafael, hpd – c/o 020 7722 7142 *fax:* 020 7911 0904
Rennert, Jonathan, hpd, chmbr org – 01737 244604 *fax:* 01737 271128
Rifkin, Joshua, hpd – *Clarion/Seven Muses*
Roberts, Timothy, org, hpd – *POEM*
Roberts, Timothy, hpd, org, f-pno, clvd – 020 7604 4704 *fax:* 020 7328 8014 *email:* timroberts@Talk21.com
Roblou, David, hpd, org, pno – c/o 020 8299 1914 *also fax; email:* Hirstpr@aol.com
Rogg, Lionel, org – *Denny Lyster*
Rowland, David, hpd, org, f-pno – *Music Management*
Rowland, Gilbert, hpd – *SJM*
Simcock, Ian, org, hpd – *Michael Harrold*
Simmonds, Paul, hpd, clvd, chmbr org – 01273 552548 *fax:* 01273 389572 *email:* simmonds.mezger@cwcom.net
Skuce, Peter, early keyboards – 020 8488 3947 *also fax; email:* peter.skuce @dufay.com
Souter, Martin, hpd, org – 01865 722552 *fax:* 01865 243388 *email:* martinsouter@mcmail.com
Titterington, David, org – *Denny Lyster*
Townend, Richard, hpd – 020 7589 1206 *fax:* 020 7589 5925
Tverskaya, Olga, f-pno – *Talbot-Cooper*
Ward, David, f-pno, hpd – 020 8874 4938 *also fax; email:* 106224.2623 @compuserve.com
Ward Russell, Gillian, org – 01621 853237
Waterfield, Jan, hpd, chmbr org – 0131 553 5038 *also fax*; 07970 968885
Weir, Dame Gillian, org – *Denny Lyster*
Wilson-Dickson, Andrew, hpd, org – 029 2022 8154 *also fax; email:* w-d@baynet.co.uk
Zabala, Oscar Candendo, org – *Michael Harrold*

SINGERS DIRECT

SOLOISTS MAKING YOUR LIFE EASIER

SINGERS DIRECT is a network of eight of Britain's most popular and established oratorio singers, who combine many years' experience with a desire to simplify booking procedures between choral society and soloist

Shelley Everall

Diane Atherton

Susanna Spicer

Jennifer Higgins

John Bowley

Andrew Carwood

Christopher Foster

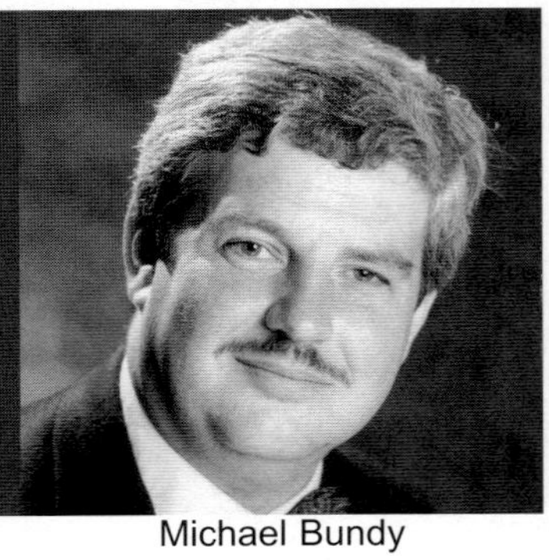
Michael Bundy

ONE CALL BOOKS ALL

One call books all **24 hour service** **No overheads**

Musical compatibility **Easily approachable**

Make **one call** to a member singer, **anytime**. That singer will then engage and liaise with any other members you wish to book. **All the advantages of an agency** are provided including contracts and replacement singers in the event of illness, but there are **no overheads, procedures are streamlined** and you have **direct access to your soloists**, however many you need, when it suits you

SHELLEY EVERALL
Soprano
0208 947 2124

DIANE ATHERTON
Soprano
0208 864 7616

JENNIFER HIGGINS
Mezzo-Soprano
01438 221918

ANDREW CARWOOD
Tenor
0208 423 7671

SUSANNA SPICER
Mezzo-Soprano
0208 671 4112

JOHN BOWLEY
Tenor
0208 664 6078

CHRISTOPHER FOSTER
Bass-Baritone
0208 677 7997

MICHAEL BUNDY
Bass-Baritone
0208 390 5375

Email: singers@singersdirect.freeserve.co.uk - Web: http://www.singersdirect.freeserve.co.uk

Singers

Singers with their own accompaniment

Bennett, Janet, hp, celtic hp – 0191 276 3019 *email:* janetbennettharp@hotmail.com
Bevis, Suzanne, hp, Irish hp – 023 8025 4238 *also fax*
Deere-Jones, Sarah, hp, celtic hp – 01929 426091 *also fax; email:* dcd@dial.pipex.com
Edwards, Jacqueline, m-sop, pno – 01904 763876
Ellis CBE, Osian, hp – 020 8445 7896; 01758 612501
Hambleton-Smith, Sandra, gui – 020 8699 8342 *email:* hsmiths@compuserve.com
Pearcey, Leonard, gui – 020 8947 2555
Sherry, Rachel, hp, clarsach, Irish hp – 01908 261903 *fax:* 01908 266031

The singers in the following list are sub-divided according to voice category

Sopranos

Abajan, Maria – *Still*
Ablaberdyeva, Alla – *Ellison*
Acworth, Rachel – 07970 443598 *fax:* 020 7603 5380
Adellita, Antonia – *Ellison*
Aghova, Livia – *Mus Int*
Aikin, Laura – *Ingpen*
Aitken, Mary-Louise – *Askonas Holt*
Aldridge, Anne – 020 8445 7698 *also fax;* 020 8449 1882
Alexander, Roberta – *Music Partnership*
Allen, Giselle – *Mus Int*
Amit, Sheila – *Annon*
Amou, Akie – *Portland*
Anderson, June – *Askonas Holt*
Anderson, Lorna – *Askonas Holt*
Anderson, Valdine – *Ingpen*
Andreyeva, Marina – *Gilder*
Angel, Marie – *Allied*
Archibald, Ann – *Mus Int*
Argenta, Nancy – *Askonas Holt*
Armitstead, Melanie – *Gilder*
Arnesen, Bodil – *Roy Baker*
Arthars, Rosemarie – *Grant Rogers*
Arthur, Jillian – *Roxane Houston*
Ashe, Rosie – *Sykes*
Ashton, Caroline – 020 8740 1567
Astrid, Helen – 020 8993 8822 *also fax*
Atherton, Diane – *Singers Direct* – 020 8896 3492; 07721 007860
Auyanet Yolande – *Music Partnership*
Back, Andrée – *CDI*
Baird, Janice – *Portland*
Baker, Zena – 01449 760315
Bakic, Cynthia Hansell – *Pristavec*
Barron, Jacqueline – *LM*
Barry, Elaine – 020 7928 6291 *also fax*
Barry, Una – *CDI/Roxane Houston* – 020 8981 4648 *also fax*
Barstad, Ingeborg – *Roy Baker*
Barstow Dame Josephine – *Askonas Holt*
Bartha, Clarry – *IMG*
Bates, Susan – 020 8208 2272; 07958 616503
Battle, Kathleen – *Askonas Holt*
Bechly, Daniela – *Mus Int*
Behle, Renate – *Rawstron*
Bell, Emma – *Askonas Holt*
Benza, Georgina – *Still*
Berg, Nicola – 020 8656 5412
Bern, Jeni – *Musicmakers*
Biriouccv, Lada – *IMG*
Birve, Marie – *OCA*
Bishop, Hilary – 01243 842150 *fax:* 01243 583914
Björklund, Ingegerd – *Ellison*
Black, Susan – *CDI*
Blackwell, Harolyn – *Gilder*
Bonner, Tessa – 020 8676 0270 *also fax; email:* Tessa@Bonnard.freeserve.co.uk
Bonney, Barbara – *IMG*
Booth, Juliet – *Craig*
Bortolot, Susan – *OCA*
Bott, Catherine – *Music Partnership*
Bott, Paula – c/o 020 8567 1909 *also fax*
Bowen, Miriam – *CDI*
Boylan, Orla – *HP*
Boynton, Patricia – 01252 629348
Bradshaw, Sally – 020 7359 0707 *email:* songful@compuserve.com
Braga, Sola – *Gilder*
Brathwaite, Maureen – *Harlequin*
Bremer, Jacqueline – *OCA*
Brewer, Christine – *Askonas Holt*
Bridge, Debbie – 01273 732121 *fax:* 01273 728797 *email:* debbiebridge@bigfoot.com
Bright, Alma – 01527 852806
Brilova, Elena – *Still*
Brodie, Sarah – *Dyfel*
Broome, Gillian – 01732 461893 *also fax*
Buchanan, Alison – *Portland*
Buckle, Judith – *Annon*
Buffle, Christine – *Mus Int*
Bullock, Susan – *HP*
Bunning, Christine – *Mus Int*
Bureau, Karen – *Gilder*
Burgin Lister, Gabrielle – 01777 702400 *fax:* 01777 869529
Cahill, Teresa – c/o 020 8208 2480 *fax:* 020 8208 2490 *email:* dkantor.kcm@webstar.co.uk
Caine, Rebecca – *Askonas Holt*
Cameron, Fiona – 01483 537592 *also fax*
Cantelo, April – 01235 848994
Cardnell, Valerie – 020 8399 9158
Carewe, Mary – *LM*
Carpenter, Jayne – 01625 431450 *also fax*
Carroll, Joan – 01622 745346
Chadwick, Carolyn – 01743 362015 *also fax; email:* carolyn_chadwick@hotmail.com
Chadwick, Suzanne – 0113 293 1384 *email:* chad.max@worldnet.att.net
Chalmers, Penelope – *Gilder*
Chard, Verona – 020 8992 1571
Charlton-West, Alison – 01487 830521
Chickering, Carol – *Gilder*
Chilcott, Susan – *Ingpen*
Christie, Nan – 020 8769 6204 *fax:* 020 8664 7326
Christie, Natalie – *Askonas Holt*
Chuchrova, Liubov – *Mus Int*
Clague, Deborah – 01604 710736 *also fax; email:* varivox@aol.com
Clarke, Elisabeth – 020 8989 6852 *also fax; email:* elisclarke@ndirect.co.uk
Clarke, Suzannah – 07710 245777 *fax:* 01642 466864
Claycomb, Laura – *IMG*
Clifton-Griffith, Natalie – *Sykes: Concerts*
Close, Shirley – *Gilder*
Coku, Alexandra – *Portland*
Cole, Joanna – *Connaught*
Cole, Rosamund – *Mus Int*
Coles, Priti – *Gilder*
Collier, Christina – *Brunskill*
Colpos, Mariana – *Mus Int*
Colwell, Georgina Anne – 01932 244038 *fax:* 01932 889186 *email:* georgina@musicair.demon.co.uk
Connell, Elizabeth – *IMG*
Connors, Ann-Marie – *ADM*
Coombes, Susan – 020 8446 6872 *fax:* 020 8201 8071
Copley, Rebecca – *Stafford*
Cotterill, Marianne – *Ellison* – c/o 020 7794 8598 *also fax*
Criswell, Kim – *Askonas Holt*
Cullagh, Majella – *IMG*
Cullis, Rita – *Askonas Holt*
da Cunha, Viola – 020 8368 4789
Daguerre, Florence – 01323 815737 *fax:* 01323 815736
Dalayman, Katarina – *Rawstron*
Dale, Sarah-Jane – 01737 249839 *also fax; email:* sarah-jane@melisma.freeserve.co.uk
Dalton, Julie – c/o 020 7388 8772 *also fax; email:* tall_diva@hotmail.com
Dam-Jensen, Inger – *HP*
Dames-Longworth, Phillippa – *Portland*
Daneman, Sophie – *Phillips*
d'Aragnes, Maria – *Stafford*
Davies, Lynne – 020 7586 2184 *fax:* 020 7813 1907
Dawson, Lynne – *IMG*
Deam, Donna – 01483 768790
de Arellano, Margarita – *Gilder*
Delahunt, Colette – *Musichall*
Dewhurst, Julia – *Maestoso*
Dexter, Joanne – *CDI*
Dimitrova, Ghena – *Stafford*
Dittmer, Petronella – 020 7937 0684 *also fax*
Dives, Tamsin – *Musichall*
Dobie, Fiona – 01865 246718
Dobronravova, Svetlana – *Sonata*
Donaldson, Alison – 01355 302869
Drummond, Irene – *Carroll*
Dugdale, Sandra – *Mus Int*
Dunwoodie, Christina – *Sonata*
Eckersley, Kate – *Ellison/SJM*
Edwards, Yvonne – *SS*
Eibenova, Gabriela – *POEM*
Eikenes, Adele – *VWM*
Einarsdottir, Thora – *Gilder*
Errington, Helen – 07860 164662 *email:* helen@syederrington.freeserve.com
Evans, Anne – *Ingpen*
Evans, Rebecca – *Harlequin*
Everall, Shelley – *Singers Direct* – 020 8947 2124 *also fax*
Falcon, Ruth – *Gilder*
Fandrey, Birgit – *Gilder*

CHAMELEON
ARTS
MANAGEMENT

Chameleon Singers 2000

Soprano

Katharine Fuge
Anna Margolis
Claire Seaton
Jenevora Williams
Anna-Louise Wood

Mezzo Soprano

Serena Kay

Countertenor

David Clegg
Charles Humphries
Robin Tyson

Tenor

Stephen Douse
Rupert Jennings
Roy Rashbrook
Christopher Watson

Baritone

Robert Rice
Leandros Taliotis

Bass Baritone

Simon Birchall

For further details and a free brochure contact:

Andrew Phillips
Chameleon Arts Management
32 St Michael's Road
SANDHURST
Berkshire GU47 8HE

Tel: +44 (0) 1252 873313
Fax: +44 (0) 1252 871517
Email: CamArts@dial.pipex.com
Web:http://www.chameleon-arts.co.uk

EQUITY.....

is the organisation that represents singers from across the industry.

Thousands of concert, session, pop, opera singers and choristers belong to Equity and take advantage of the services and peace of mind this brings them:

singers' rates • singers' agreements • singers' task force • singers' committee • singers' register • singers' newsletter • experienced staff who know about singers' needs and issues • information for agents • pension schemes • free insurance cover for accident, public liability and backstage cover • free legal help • free welfare advice • job information service, and many more.

If you are working professionally as a singer and are not yet a member please call one of our six offices, or see our website for details on joining your union:

www.equity.org.uk
London & S. East: 0207 670 0253
North East: 01142 305 294
Scotland & N Ireland: 0141 248 2472
North West: 0161 832 3183
Midlands: 01926 408 638
Wales & S. West: 02920 387 971

.....EQUITY

Catherine Françoise

Soprano

PROFESSIONAL EXPERIENCE INCLUDES:
Opera, Operetta, Gilbert & Sullivan, West End Musical Theatre, Oratorio, Recital (especially French and Russian Song), Concert work and Gala Events.

...Catherine Françoise was admirable, impressive in her solos...
Trouble in Tahiti – THE INDEPENDENT

There were vocal contributions from first-rate singers. Catherine Françoise sang 'A Fors e Lui' from Verdi's La Raviata with full tone, contrasting strongly with the following 'Sempre Libera'
HERALD EXPRESS TORQUAY

Catherine Françoise sparkled as the Queen of the night...
(The Magic Flute) – SURREY HERALD

Catherine Françoise was most impresive, giving a firm assured performance throughout, but particularly in the very lovely Laudate Dominum.
(Mozart – Solomn Vespers) – CHATHAM, ROCHESTER & GILLINGHAM News

FURTHER INFORMATION & DEMONSTRATION TAPE from

Tel: 01753 882646 / 0850 617 775 Fax: 01753 408089
71 Leachcroft, Chalfront St Peter, Bucks SL9 9LD

Farman, Raphaelle – *Still*
Fernandez, Wilhelmenia – *Voullaire/TransArt*
Ferrari, Elena – *Craig*
Ferrarini, Alida – *Stafford*
Field, Helen – *Still*
Field, Pamela – 01685 875392
Filip, Felicia – *Stafford*
Fink, Deborah – 020 8802 6748 *also fax*
Firth-Spiller, Fiona – 020 8847 0888 *also fax*
Fisher, Gabrielle – 020 8542 7610 *also fax; email:* faure@globalnet.co.uk
Fleming, Renée – *IMG*
Flowers, Kate – *Musicmakers*
Flowers, Suzanne – *CDI*
Focile, Nuccia – *Askonas Holt*
Fontana, Gabriele – *Rawstron*
Ford, Sandra – *Mus Int*
Fortuna, Maria – *Portland*
Foster, Catherine – *Harlequin*
Foulkes, Carolyn – *CDI*
Françoise, Catherine – 01753 882646 *fax:* 01753 408089
Freiberg, Christine – *Mus Int*
Frittoli, Barbara – *Askonas Holt*
Frowde, Judi Merri – 01582 840753; 07802 402597 *fax:* 01582 840991
Fuge, Katharine – *Chameleon*
Fugelle, Jacquelyn – *Still* – 01243 779664
Gain, Sally June – *Stafford*
Galante, Inessa – *Ellison*
Gale, Elizabeth – *Musichall*
Galloway, Catherine – *Murphy*
Galstian, Juliet – *Still*
Gannon, Kate – *Rondo*
Garrett, Lesley – *Music Partnership*
Gasztowt-Adams, Helen – 020 7625 8903 *also fax*
Gerrard, Linda – 01949 81014 *also fax*; 07710 866048 *email:* lindaroe@compuserve.com
Gill, Bridgett – 01874 690339 *fax:* 01874 690254
Ginsborg, Jane – 01782 618156
Glanville, Susannah – *Askonas Holt*
Glennon, Jean – *Sykes*
Goerke, Christine – *Ingpen*
Gomez, Jill – *Grant Rogers* – 020 8348 4193 *also fax*
Goodwin, Harriet – *CDI*
Gorchakova, Galina – *Askonas Holt*
Gormley, Clare – *Askonas Holt*
Götz, Cornelia – *Still*
Gowers, Lindsay – *Roxane Houston*
Grahn, Jenny – *Stafford*
Gritton, Susan – *Askonas Holt*
Grummet, Adey – *Craig*
Guleghina, Maria – *Askonas Holt*
Gustafson, Nancy – *IMG*
Gutteridge, Karmel – *KDM*
Hagley, Alison – *IMG*
Hammonds, Elaine – 020 8540 5780
Hamvasi, Sylvia – *Ingpen*
Hanley, Regina – *Mus Int*
Hannigan, Barbara – *OWM*
Hardwick, Helen – *Purkiss*
Hardy, Janet – *Mus Int*
Hardy, Rosemary – *Portland*
Hargreaves, Carolyn – *Grant Rogers*
Harman, Lynne – *Mus Int*
Harper, Catherine – *OCA*
Harrhy, Eiddwen – *Phillips*
Harries, Kathryn – *Ingpen*
Harris, Brenda – *Gilder*
Harrison, Sally – *Gilder*
Harvey, Naomi – *Stafford*
Haslam, Micaela – *CDI*
Havranova, Jana – *Mus Int/Sonata*
Hawkins, Cheryl – 01525 261950 *also fax*
Haymon, Cynthia – *Still*
Hayward Segal, Marie – 020 8346 8975 *also fax; email:* marie@angelicvoices.demon.co.uk
Heath, Karen – 01889 882097
Heath-Welch, Anne – c/o 020 7328 1378 *fax:* 020 7328 6021 *email:* heath-welch@marecon.co.uk
Heaton-Wright, Susan – 01707 267511 *also fax; email:* susanheatonwright@yahoo.com
Hegarty, Mary – *Musichall*
Heller-Jones, Cathy – 01727 865768 *also fax; email:* hellerjone@aol.com
Hellgren, Marianne – *Sykes*
Hellsten, Dominique – c/o 020 8299 1914 *also fax; email:* Hirstpr@aol.com
Helton, Melanie – *Gilder*
Hemington Jones, Susan – 01664 822965 *fax:* 01664 823773
Hendricks, Barbara – *Ingpen*
Herman, Natalie – 020 8681 2938
Herrmann, Anke – *Gilder*
Hetherington, Elizabeth – *Gilder*
Hetherington, Marie-Anne – *SS*
Higham-Bell, Alison – 020 8451 3051 *also fax;* 07768 685469
Hill Smith, Marilyn – *Mus Int*
Hillier, Helen – 020 8675 6172 *fax:* 020 8675 9781
Hodges, Anne – 01992 461535 *also fax*
Hollyman, Nicola – 029 2075 4032; 07970 496987
Holmes-Drewry, Margaret – 020 7794 3842 *fax:* 020 8922 3645
Holton, Ruth – *CDI/POEM*
Hooper, Patricia – 020 8858 4293
Horriben, Alison – 01344 883847 *email:* mpwatson@hotmail.com
Horrocks, Luise – *CDI*
Howarth, Judith – *Askonas Holt*

NICOLINO GIACALONE
Bass-Baritone

International Classical Singer

"The protagonist, Diocles, played and sung by Nicolino Giacalone at first appeared merely the earnest stolid figure that Fletcher (the playwright) had parroted from his sources. Very soon, however, this imposing actor began to glimpse the absurd possibilities in the part – his moral inconsistencies, which could either shock or amuse, or both. He played with the audience like an accomplished comedian, so that our laughter felt almost forbidden: we experienced the double pleasures of delight and shame."
Peter Pagnell, *The Independent*, London, England, UK. (Critique of performance of Purcell's semi-opera Dioclesian)

"He made the art songs seem real. He has a way of conveying the spirit of the art songs by careful attention to the text, while the arias and Broadway show tunes rounded out the program. Giacalone reminded the listeners of how great songs like Richard Strauss' Morgen and Zueignung really are"
Charles Ward, *Houston Chronicle*, Texas, USA.

"... his potential has been fully realised in all ways, from the warmth and generosity of his personality to the deep vibrancy and spell-binding quality of his singing"
E. Forrest-O'Driscoll, *Irish International Arts Centre*, Ireland.

International Singing Instructor

"His genius as a teacher emerged as he coached the participating singers in a knowledgeable way, frequently making suggestions which caused immediate and obvious improvement in the participants' presentations. In addition to learning a great deal, the singers and audience members laughed a lot and had a good time. His cheerful, bouyant, and witty demeanour made it fun to be part of this experience"
Suzanne Marion, Concert Secretary and Past President, Houston Tuesday Musical Club Member, Houston, Texas, USA.

"He is a brilliant and persuasive teacher who combines professional exactness with a charismatic personality. The result is a profound learning experience"
Keith Taylor, *Stephen Sondheim Society*, Westminster University, London, England, UK.

"I would not hesitate to recommend Mr. Giacalone. Proper breathing, voice placement, posture and accurate movement of the articulators (i.e. jaw, tongue) were and integral part of each lesson. I feel that his method of teaching would facilitate the transfer of proper vocal use from speech to singing."
Leslie P. Suite, M.Sc. Reg. OSLA, CCC-SLP, Speech-Language Pathologist, Canada.

The Chestnuts, 56 Snakes Lane West, Woodford Green, Essex, IG8 ODF, England, United Kingdom.
Tel: (+44) 020 8559 1983 Mobile: 0468 838 494 Website: http://vzone.virgin.net/nicolino.giacalone Email: nicolino.giacalone@virgin.net
Management: J. Audrey Ellison International Artists' Management, 135 Stevenage Road, Fulham, London, SW6 6PB, England, United Kingdom.
Tel: (+44) 020 7381 9751 Fax: (+44) 020 7381 2406 Email: Audrey@Ellison-Intl.freeserve.co.uk

SARA HINDLEY PRESENTS...

THREE *British* TENORS

EXCERPTS FROM OPERAS AND SONGS FROM THE MUSICALS DELIVERED WITH STYLE & ORIGINALITY

I am at a loss to think of a superlative adequate to describe their performance - it was magnificent! [DIRECTOR-NORTH OF ENG. FESTIVAL]

The standing ovation was a well-deserved end to one of the best shows around for a long time. [THE LYNN NEWS]

TEL: 01244 319981 FAX: 01244 315662

JOY NAYLOR

soprano

Opera

Operetta

Oratorio

Recital

Voice Coach

" ... provided a stylish and masterly performance."

Birmingham Post

" ... sang beautifully as Norina."

Opera Magazine

Solo engagements with: CBSO, ESO, ON, CBTO

Joy Naylor
01606 836284
Newton Hall, St Ann's Road
Middlewich, Cheshire
CW10 9BN

Helen Miles *Soprano*

"the delightful voice of Helen Miles" **(The Stage)**

"female lead enjoyably taken by Helen Miles" **(Opera)**

"firm, sweet tone to her delivery" **(Opera)**

"an excellent Mozartian voice" **(Bucks Free Press)**

Available for Opera, Oratorios, Orchestral Concerts

Recitals with Adrian Boynton (piano)

All enquiries to: Robert Phillips, 42 Granes End,
Great Linford, Milton Keynes, Buckinghamshire MK14 5DX.
Tel/Fax: 01908 691 487
E-mail: robertphillips.ltd@virgin.net

helen pritchard

soprano

oratorio specialist

'It was a privilege to work with such a singer'
...Hugh Bean, orchestra leader.
Elgar *The Kingdom* at Dorking Halls.

'Lucid, piano, unaccompanied singing and yet with the ability to soar above the full orchestra in the fortissimo passages.'
Dvorak *Requiem* ... April 1999.

'...her rich voice beautifully coloured the text'.

'Helen...sang with power and tonal beauty'
Haydn *Creation.*

'great musicianship'

'Helen Pritchard's beautifully clear soprano voice gave ultimate credibility to her character' ... 'heart-achingly beautiful' ...Surrey Advertiser.
Dido in Purcell's *Dido and Aeneas.*

The Mount, Rookery Hill, Ashtead Park, Ashtead, Surrey. KT21 1HY.
Tel: 01372 273420
Fax: 01372 279475
email: gammack@aol.com

Howd, Janet – 020 8747 5072 *also fax; email:* jan@jbat.demon.co.uk
Hulse, Eileen – 020 8886 6534 *also fax*
Illing, Rosamund – *Gilder*
Irving, Eloise – *Clarion/Seven Muses*
Isokoski, Soile – *IMG*
Itami, Naomi – *Mus Int*
James, Catherine – *Camerata*
Jansen, Dorothee – *Rawstron*
Jeffers, Gweneth-Ann – *Askonas Holt*
Jenkin, Kathryn – 020 8861 0065
Jenkin, Nicola – 020 7735 7636 *also fax; email:* nicola@njenkin.freeserve.co.uk
Jenkins, Angela – 020 8560 5988 *also fax*
Jenkins, Merril – 020 8579 3108
Jenkins, Susan Anne – 01832 710447
Jo, Sumi – *Askonas Holt*
Johnson, Harriet – 020 8942 2887
Jones, Natalie – *Craig*
Joshua, Rosemary – *Askonas Holt*
Kalinina, Galina – *Stafford*
Kaupova, Helena – *Mus Int*
Kazimierczuk, Angela – *Camerata*
Keen, Olivia – 020 8889 7990 *also fax*
Keetch, Maureen – 020 8458 4723
Kelly, Janis – *Musichall*
Kemmer, Mariette – *Mus Int*
Kemp, Nicola Jane – *Mus Int*
Kendall-Davies, Barbara – 020 8954 4646
Kendrick, Jeanne – *KDM*
Kennard, Julie – *CDI*
Kennedy, Nicki – *Sykes*
Kennedy-Richardson, Louisa – *OCA*
Kenny, Yvonne – *Askonas Holt*
Kerr, Virginia – *Musichall*
Kesselman, Maria – *Brunskill*
Khalemskaia, Marianna – *Harlequin*
Khoklova, Elvira – *Gilder*
King, Catherine – *CDI/POEM*
King, Tracey Anne – *Dyfel*
Kirkby, Emma – 020 8444 6565 *fax:* 020 8444 1008 *email:* consort@easynet.co.uk
Kitchen, Linda – *Musichall*
Korman, Beryl – *Upbeat*
Korondi, Anna – *Askonas Holt*
Kringelborn, Solveig – *IMG*
Ladner, Kate – *Gilder*
Lancaster, Jane – *Roxane Houston*
Lane, Elizabeth – *CDI*
Langston, Candida – *KDM*
Lapina, Marina – *Gilder*
Lascarro, Juanita – *HP*
Lawrence, Susan – 0121 472 2728
Lawson, Mhairi – *Sykes*
Leeks, Caroline – 01793 700298 *also fax*
Leighton, Lesley – *Portland*
Lenton-Ward, Caroline – 020 8299 6866
Leonard, Helena – *KDM*
Leonard, Sarah – *Allied*
Levitt, Marina – *Gilder*
Lindsay-Douglas, Carole – *Lindsay*
Lissenden, Sandra – 01322 224085 *fax:* 01322 409269 *email:* tapestry@cwcom.net
Livingstone, Kathleen – 01895 632115 *fax:* 01895 625765 *email:* kath@mackies.freeserve.co.uk
Lloyd, Julie-Dawn – *KDM*
Lloyd, Prudence – 020 8449 4873 *email:* DeeKayPea@argonet.co.uk
Lloyd Davies, Mary – *Harlequin*
Logan, Catriona – *KDM* – 01279 439902 *also fax*
Lott DBE, Felicity – *Askonas Holt*
Lucey, Frances – *Mus Int*
Luxon, Rachel – *Stafford*
Lynch, Frances M – 020 7281 0672 *also fax; email:* frances@birnam39.freeserve.co.uk
Lyness, Kiera – *Jean Judge*
McCarthy, Fionnuala – *Mus Int*
McCormick, Phyllida – 01444 484382 *also fax*
McCulloch, Susan – *Gilder*
McCusker, Kathryn – *Ingpen*
McFadden, Claron – *Portland*
McGreevy, Geraldine – *Askonas Holt*
McGuiness, Cheryl – *Dyfel*
McLaren, Morag – c/o 020 7839 4433/4 *fax:* 020 7930 5738
McLaughlin, Marie – *IMG*
McLaughlin, Victoria – *KDM*
McNair, Sylvia – *Askonas Holt*
Mackay, Ann – *NBM*
Mackenzie, Jane Leslie – *Mus Int*
Maine, Margaret – c/o 01777 703603 *fax:* c/o 01777 708145
Major, Dame Malvina – *Gilder*
Makris, Cynthia – *Still*
Malmberg, Myrra – *LM*
Maney, Carla – *CDI*
Manly, Ann – 020 7286 3944 *fax:* 020 7289 9081 *email:* annmanly.protheroe@btinternet.com
Manning OBE, Jane – 020 7359 1593 *fax:* 020 7226 4369 *email:* jane@wiltonsq.demon.co.uk
Mannion, Rosa – *IMG*
Margolis, Anna – *Chameleon* – 020 8340 4084 *email:* bluelava@compuserve.com
Marshall, Margaret – *Allied*
Martin, Clara – *KDM*
Martin-Smith, Penelope – 01993 832352 *also fax*
Martinez, Ana – *Roy Baker*
Martinez-Galdos, Itziar – *Gilder*
Martinpelto, Hillevi – *Rawstron*
Masterson, Valerie – *Mus Int*
Mattila, Karita – *IMG*
May-Sysum, Jayne – c/o 01926 428419 *also fax*
Mayfield, Elizabeth – 01274 826226
Mazzola, Denia – *Still*
Medlyn, Margaret – *Sykes*
van der Meer, Mariká – *Dyfel*
Melinek, Julia – *Gilder* – c/o 020 8723 6984 *also fax*
Mellor, Alwyn – *Ingpen*
Melnik, Natalia – *Mus Int*
Meloy, Laure – 01707 321550 *also fax; email:* KHGarts@aol.com
Merrett, Louise – 020 7284 2156
Mescheriakova, Marina – *Gilder*
Methven, Jean – 01494 524007
Meyerhoff, Helen – *CDI*
Miles, Gaynor – 020 8452 1336
Miles, Helen – 01908 691487 *also fax*
Mills, Bronwen – *CDI*
Mills, Rachael – 020 8668 5898; 01403 257729
Milne, Lisa – *Askonas Holt*
Minns, Giselle – *Craig* – 020 8964 0920 *also fax*
Moffat, Julie – *OWM*
Moorhouse, Maryrose – 01924 830461
Morgan, Nicola – 029 2048 3063; 07970 480155
Morley, Debra – *SS*
Morrison, Amanda – 020 8567 6823 *also fax;* 07973 781145 *email:* amanda@martin1997.freeserve.co.uk
Mulholland, Denise – *Musicmakers*
Munro, Janet – 020 8473 3756 *email:* janet.munro@which.net
Murphy, Heidi Grant – *Askonas Holt*
Murphy, Suzanne – *Ingpen*
Myers, Deborah – *Sykes*
Nadelman, Noemi – *Mus Int*
Naglestad, Catherine – *Mus Int*
Nash, Elizabeth – 01932 857520 *also fax*
Naylor, Joy – 01606 836284
Nelson, Mary – *YCAT*
Nicholson, Evelyn – *CDI* – 01753 821956 *also fax*
Noack, Romana – *Mus Int*
Norburn, Clare – 020 7281 6949 *fax:* 020 7272 8854 *email:* norburnc@dircon.co.uk
Nordin, Lena – *Allied*
Notare, Karen – *Still*
Novis, Constance – *Sykes*
Nunn, Toni – *SS*
O'Neill, Fiona – *OCA*
O'Sullivan, Cara – *Harlequin*
O'Sullivan, Paula – 01273 708250 *also fax*
Olafimihan, Tinuke – *Stafford*
Orde, Corinne – 020 7987 9600 *also fax; email:* orde@compuserve.com
Padmore, Elaine – *SS*
Page, Charlotte – *Mus Int*
Palmerston, Diana – *CDI*
Panichi, Gabriella – *Ockert*
Papikian, Emma – *Grant Rogers*
Parker, Jaqueline – *KDM*
Parry, Pamela Jane – 01273 608726 *fax:* 01273 687290
Passow, Sabine – *Mus Int*
Patchell, Sue – *Still*
Patrick, Yvonne – 01273 777417 *also fax;* 07768 224576
Patterson, Caroline – *KDM*
Pavlovski, Nina – *Still*
Pearce, Alison – CDI – 020 7836 7556 *also fax*
Pearson, Gail – *Still*
Peate, Zoe – *Purkiss*
Pegler, Heidi – 020 8758 9422 *fax:* 020 8758 9865 *email:* langers@cableinet.co.uk
Pierard, Catherine – 020 8995 3226 *fax:* 020 8742 7476 *email:* kate@rubecat.demon.co.uk
Pierce, Judith – 01795 533523
Piland, Jeanne – *Rawstron*
Pinkarchevski, Eileen – 0118 942 7055
Platt, Rachel – 020 8778 2629 *fax:* 020 8325 9098
Plazas, Mary – *OWM*
Pollet, Françoise – *TransArt*
Polydorou, Margarita – *Sonata*
Poole, Sarah – 01252 319610 *also fax;* 07860 251232
Pope, Cathryn – 01932 248518 *also fax*
Porackova, Joanna – *Stafford*
Pratschke, Sinéad – *Sykes*
Preece, Margaret – *Craig*
Price, Janet – 0117 924 8456
Price Jones, Penelope – 01249 812508 *also fax; email:* pmandppj@globalnet.co.uk
Primrose, Claire – *Still*
Pritchard, Helen – 01372 273420 *fax:* 01372 279475
Pritchett, Bernadine – 020 8527 7163 *fax:* 020 8491 2801
Prokina, Elena – *Askonas Holt*
Putnam, Ashley – *Still*
Quigley, Jennifer – *GBZ*
Radovan, Norina – *Pristavec*
Rae-Walker, Gillian – *Sonata* – 0141 848 5411 *also fax*
Randle, Katie – *CDI*
Rautio, Nina – *Still*
Rees, Judith – 01707 268576
Rhodes, Sarah – *Connaught*
Richardson, Linda – *VWM*
Richardson, Lynda – 020 7482 0415 *also fax;* 07956 371232 *email:* simlynrichbridge@compuserve.com
Ridehalgh, Helen – 01253 892698; 07970 904603
Riedel, Deborah – *IMG*
Robert, Yvonne – 01904 701459; 01502 724020
Roberts, Deborah – 01273 833950 *also fax; email:* 101565.3033@compuserve.com
Roberts, Elizabeth – 020 8677 7997 *fax:* 020 8696 9783 *email:* liz@tisl.co.uk
Rodgers, Joan – *Ingpen*

Virginia Rushton
soprano

"this fine singer"

- **oratorio** "outstanding...full rounded tone up to a brilliant top D" *Oxford Mail*
- **recitals with harpsichord, fortepiano, piano** "artistic gifts of an uncommon order" *Yorkshire Post*
- **duo recitals with John Mills, guitar** "a well-planned programme...obvious enjoyment was infectious" *Nottingham Evening Post*
- **programmes of readings and music on Jane Austen, Rudyard Kipling, Lewis Carroll, and the Brontë sisters**
- **specialist programmes with organ for churches MAN OF SORROWS and SING OH, MY LOVE**

Further details and enquiries:
Allegro Artists Management
Conifers, Roselands Avenue, Mayfield, E. Sussex TN20 6EB
Tel/Fax: 01435 872391
http://www.cdj.co.uk/impulse/rushton.htm

ALISON SMART

Soprano

'the literally transcendental virtuosity of soloists Alan Opie and Alison Smart' ***The Times***

'the taxing vocal lines were handled with ease and sensitivity...lovely tone quality' ***Henley Standard***

'exquisitely sung...Her characterisation was without blemish' ***The Stage***

- wide experience in oratorio, opera, concert, recital
- Baroque, Classical and 20th-century repertoire

For bookings and further details please contact:
Alison Smart at 327 Long Lane, London N2 8JW
Tel: 0208 349 0824 and 0973 350396 Fax: 0208 343 1850
Email: alison_smart@long-lane.demon.co.uk
Website: http://www.long-lane.demon.co.uk
or phone Helen Sykes Artists' Management on 0208 876 8276

CLARISSA STEDMAN

Dramatic Coloratura
Experienced soloist in Opera, Oratorio and Recital
Contact: 01227 712694 0385 587139

Rachel Payne

Contralto

from
1999-2000

Albert Herring - Britten
Songs of Sunset - Delius
Child of our time - Tippett

...La Bonne Chanson comprises a variety of moods and these Rachel Payne captured quite admirably. *Recital - Daily Telegraph*

...the depth and constant variety of colour made her singing an unfailing delight. *Messiah - Michael Ball*

...of the soloists, Rachel Payne, a light but firmly focussed contralto, was outstanding. *Dixit Dominus - Manchester Evening News*

...made a wonderful witch...everything about it was superbly imaginative. *Hansel and Gretel - Howard Williams*

CONCERT DIRECTORY INTERNATIONAL
Tel: 01943 607821
Fax: 01943 817063

Amari Cottage
Great Barrow
Chester CH3 7JJ
Tel: 01829 740246

Roebuck, Janine – *Mus Int*
Rogers, Lesley-Jane – 01451 821481 *also fax; email:* jane@lesleyjanerogers.demon.co.uk
Roocroft, Amanda – *Ingpen*
Röschmann, Dorothea – *Askonas Holt*
Rose, Fiona – 020 8870 9591 *also fax*
Rothschild, Charlotte de – 020 7730 4465 *fax:* 020 7730 0166 *email:* cderoth@aol.com
Rowley, Laura – *SJM*
Roy, Helen – 01798 874721
Rozario, Patricia – *Askonas Holt*
Rubtsova, Irina – *Gilder*
Rudakova, Larissa – *Askonas Holt*
Rushton, Virginia – c/o 01435 872391 *email:* virginia@ashwood.u-net.com
Russell, Lynda – *Connaught*
Rutter, Claire – *Askonas Holt*
Ryberg, Anna – *Portland*
Salmon Trutz, Caroline – 020 8343 2197 *also fax*
Sand, Malmfrid – *Gilder*
Sauphanor, Simone – *OWM*
Savova, Galina – *Stafford*
Schäfer, Christine – *IMG*
Schwanewilms, Anne – *Rawstron*
Scott, Vanessa – 01353 663894
Seaton, Claire – *Chameleon*
Secunde, Nadine – *Ingpen*
Selby-Okamoto, Takako – 020 8452 9234 *also fax*
Seymour, Yvonne – *CDI*
Shade, Ellen – *IMG*
Shafajinskaia, Anna – *Gilder*
Shaw, Penelope – *SS*
Shelley, Rosamund – c/o 020 8444 4088
Shepherson, Sally-Ann – *SS*
Sheppard, Honor – 0161 928 4727
Sheppard, Kerrie – *Harlequin*
Sheridan, Anne – 020 8748 4159; 01527 525954
Sherry, Rachel – 01908 261903 *fax:* 01908 266031
Simons, Lyndy – *Craig*
Sinclair, Jeannette – 020 8959 6651
Skornicková, Lenka – c/o 024 7630 6106 *also fax; email:* cees_van_dorland@talk21.com
Slepneva, Ludmila – *Gilder*
Smart, Alison – *Sykes*
Smith, Carol – *Mus Int*
Smith, Jennifer – *Sykes*
Smolyaninova, Soya – *Still*
Stacey, Susan – *Musicmakers*
Starr, Christine – *CDI*
Stedman, Clarissa – 01227 712694 *email:* cr13@canterbury.ac.uk
Stefanescu, Ana Camelia – *IMG*
Steffan, Katherine – *Sykes*
Stefiuk, Maria – *Sonata*
Stetsiun, Maria – *Sonata*
Stowe, Sara – 01865 761966 *also fax; email:* sarastowe@matspring.demon.co.uk
Streeton, Jane – *SS*
Stuart, Diana – 01733 844603 *also fax*
Sutherland, Rosalind – *IMG*
Sweeting, Sarah – 020 8444 7647 *also fax; email:* sarah_sweeting@hotmail.com
Swenson, Ruth Ann – *Askonas Holt*
Szreter, Anya – 020 8882 5935; 07711 322368
Te Kanawa DBE, Kiri – c/o 020 8332 9829 *fax:* 020 8332 7049; 00 4141 320 1915
Teare, Christine – *Stafford*
Thiébaud, Dominique – 01727 848335 *fax:* 01727 847664
Thomas, Caroline – *Gilder*
Thomas, Gwyneth – 01789 763509
Thorn, Penelope – *Still*
Tibbels, Nicole – *Allied*
Tierney, Vivian – *VWM*
Tilling, Camilla – *IMG*
Tinsley, Pauline – *Mus Int*
Todd Howarth, Anne – 0118 926 4401 *also fax*
Tovey, Rachael – *Phillips*
Trainor, Joan – 0191 267 9164 *fax:* 0191 267 5366
Troth, Marylyn – 020 8876 6161 *also fax*
Tsydypova, Valentina – *Askonas Holt*
Tubb, Evelyn – *CDI/POEM*
Tucapská, Beryl – 020 8200 5200
Turri, Ida-Maria – *OCA*
Tuvas, Linda – *Mus Int*
Tynan, Kathleen – *Sykes*
Unwin, Julie – *Musicmakers*
Upshaw, Dawn – *IMG*
Urbanova, Eva – *Mus Int*
Vaduva, Leontina – *Stafford*
Vaice, Sonora – *Portland*
Van Poznak, Karen – 01438 715740 *also fax*
Vaness, Carol – *IMG*
Varady, Julia – *Askonas Holt*
Varsey, Jacqueline – *Mus Int*
Vassiliou, Marie – *Craig*
Velichko, Lydia – *Sonata*
Vernon, Susannah – 020 8847 4476 *email:* susannah.vernon@lineone.net
Vivian, Diana – *Pristavec*
Voigt, Deborah – *IMG*
Voss, Ealynn – *Gilder*
Waite, Nicola – *Gilder*
Wall, Melanie – *Roxane Houston*
Walmsley-Clark, Penelope – *Allied*
Walsh, Louise – *Mus Int*
Wardell, Annette – *Craig*
Watanabe, Yoko – *Stafford*
Waters, Rosalind – 020 8947 5386; 07778 020730
Watson, Janice – *Askonas Holt*
Watson, Lillian – *IMG*
Watts, Linda – *Dyfel*
Watts, Valerie – 01704 567907 *fax:* 0151 227 5953
Wayman, Lynne – 0115 962 0258 *fax:* 0115 841 0243
Webster, Jane – *Sykes*
Weidinger, Christine – *Still*
Wells, Alison – 020 8980 9735 *also fax; email:* agw@antillroad.demon.co.uk
Whaley, Rosemary – *SS*
Wheatley, Rachel – 01664 840291 *also fax*
Whelan, Franzita – *YCAT*
Whitehouse, Elizabeth – *Craig*
Whittlesey, Christine – *Ingpen*
Wiegold, Mary – 020 8368 1211 *also fax*
Wilkes, Sandra – 020 8979 6266
Williams, Helen – *Musichall*
Williams, Jenevora – *Chameleon*
Williams-King, Anne – *Alexander*
Winter, Sidonie – 020 8503 1841 *also fax*
Witney, Kate – 01673 885058 *email:* kate.witney@lineone.net
Wold, Helene – *Roy Baker*
Wood, Anna-Louise – *Chameleon*
Woodhouse, Karen – 01923 491290 *fax:* 01923 244234 *email:* stockerwoodhouse@btinternet.com
Woods, Elizabeth – *Craig*
Woollett, Elizabeth – *Alexander*
Wright, Chloe – *Mus Int*
Wright, Patricia – c/o 020 8969 3579 *also fax*
Wyn-Davies, Catrin – *HP*
York, Deborah – *IMG*
Yuen, Nancy – *Sykes*
Zabiliasta, Lydia – *Sonata*
Zagorinskaia, Natalia – *Gilder*
Zakhartchuk, Tatiana – *Sonata*
Zelenskaya, Elena – *Gilder*
Zeltzer, Sandra – *Ingpen*
Zhang, Li Ping – *Stafford*
Ziesak, Ruth – *IMG*
Zoratti, Maria – *Mus Int*

Mezzo Sopranos and Contraltos

Aarons, Mignonette – 020 8204 8778
Adams, Lynn – *Invisible Pilots* – 01223 873018 *fax:* 01223 870029 *email:* Lynnsings@dial.pipex.com
Ager, Jeanette – 07976 397642
Aksenova, Sofia – *Gilder*
Anthony, Mary – *Annon*
Araya, Graciela – *Gilder*
Arkhipova, Irina – *Askonas Holt*
Ash, Pauline – 01207 542832
Asher, Nadine – *Mus Int*
Ashley, Susan – *SS*
Attfield, Helen – *CDI*
Ayers, Angela – 01865 340777
Bainbridge, Elizabeth – *Mus Int*
Balleys, Brigitte – *Mus Int*
Bannister, Phillida – *Roxane Houston*
Bardon, Patricia – *Ingpen*
Barr, Catriona – *Craig*
Barton, Alison – 0141 551 8789 *also fax*
Bartram, Claire – 0121 426 4318 *email:* CBartram1@aol.com
Beckley, Nicola – 020 8670 2948 *email:* NicolaBeckley@bigfoot.com
Begg, Heather – *Gilder*
Bellamy, Marcia – *OCA*
Benackova, Marta – *Mus Int*
Berganza, Teresa – *Askonas Holt*
Bickley, Susan – *Allied*
Blythe, Stephanie – *IMG*
Borodina, Olga – *Askonas Holt*
Botes, Christine – *Gilder*
Bradley, Zena – *OCA*
Bradley Bailey, Bonnie – c/o 01803 834619 *email:* B3Cantobel@aol.com
Bradshaw, Claire – *Phillips*
Bramley, Lindsay – 01628 484860; 0780 1104666 *email:* l_c_bramley@hotmail.com
Brillembourg, Fredrika – *Gilder*
Brookes, Frances Anne – 020 8521 3818; 01472 874761
Browner, Alison – *Mus Int*
Buchheister, Utta – *Stafford*
Budge, Bridget – *CDI*
Burford, Anna – *Portland*
Burgess, Sally – *IMG*
Burnett, Yvonne – *Mus Int*
Busby, Joan – c/o 020 8202 1731 *fax:* 01875 341011
Cable, Margaret – *Musicmakers/POEM*
Cairncross, Heather – *SS*
Cairns, Christine – *Carroll*
Cals, Isabelle – *Askonas Holt*
Campbell, Fiona – *Musichall*
Cassidy, Jennifer – 01473 718811 *email:* Jennie.Cassidy@btinternet.com
Castle, Elizabeth – 01306 730511 *also fax; email:* jcastle@cdcssb.demon.co.uk
Castle, Sarah – *Gilder*
Cheeseman, Jenny – 023 9286 3422
Christova, Plama – *Alexander*
Ciurca, Cleopatra – *Stafford*
Clayton, Beth – *IMG*
Clennell, Claire – 01624 832713
Clethero, Sara – 0121 454 3087 *also fax*; 07976 388523

Collins, Anne – *Askonas Holt*
Connolly, Sarah – *Askonas Holt*
Cook, Kathryn – *CDI*
Coote, Alice – *IMG*
Crane, Louise – *Sykes*
Cullen, Susan – c/o 020 7433 1058 *fax:* 020 7813 5486 *email:* su@lineone.net
Cummings, Yvette – *SS*
da Cunha, Viola – 020 8368 4789
Dalley, Tamsin – 020 7274 5337; 07973 503051
Daniels, Lorraine – 01371 810289 *also fax*
Davies, Menai – *Harlequin*
Davies, Rebecca de Pont – *Gilder*
de Blieck, Marilyn – *SS/Camerata*
DeYoung, Michelle – *Askonas Holt*
Dean, Amanda – 020 8202 3804 *also fax; email:* Amandaj.dean@btinternet.com
Denley, Catherine – *CDI/POEM*
Didonato, Joyce – *IMG*
D'Intino, Luciana – *Allied*
Dix, Barbara – 01704 530903 *also fax*
Dolzhenko, Irina – *Gilder*
Doufexis, Stella – *Askonas Holt*
Dragojevic, Katija – *Mus Int*
Drumm, Imelda – *VWM*
Duckworth, Margaret – 01709 583461
Duguid, Alison – *Gilder*
Durseneva, Alexandra – *Gilder*
Edmunds, Janet – 01295 711000
Edwards, Jacqueline – 01904 763876
Finnie, Linda – *Stafford*
Firestone, Adria – *Stafford*
Fisher, Rachel – *Roxane Houston*
Fontane, Yvonne – *KDM*
Forrester, Oenone – 020 8952 2148
Foster, Beryl – 01727 863477
Foster, Caroline – 0161 226 4098
Fox, Jacqueline – 01932 267607 *email:* jfox@tron.clara.net
Fryer, Heather – *KDM*
Fryer, Sarah – *Mus Int*
Fulgoni, Sara – *HP*
Gorton, Susan – *Harlequin*
Graham, Sharon – *Stafford*
Graham, Susan – *IMG*
Gravas, Alexandra – *Grant Rogers*
Grayston, Jean – 020 7286 4133 *fax:* 020 7266 4398
Grech, Sophia – *Bray*
Groop, Monica – *IMG*
Grose, Cynthia – *Gilder*
Gushina, Elena – *Gilder*
Hadda, Natanya – 020 8743 6958 *also fax*; 07973 621738
Harris, Michelle – 020 8245 0328; 07931 756459
Hawksley, Deborah – *Mus Int*
Haydn, Zoe – *Dyfel*
Hellekant, Charlotte – *IMG*
Henry, Claire – *Mus Int*
Henschel, Jane – *Askonas Holt*
Hibberd, Linda – *OCA*
Hickey, Angela – *Still*
Higgins, Jennifer – *Singers Direct* – 01438 221918 *email:* singers@singersdirect.freeserve.co.uk
Higgins, Suzanne – 020 8471 7739
Hillerud, Margareta – *Mus Int*
Hirst, Linda – 020 7481 1345 *fax:* 020 7680 0665 *email:* hirstcraig@compuserve.com
Hoffman, Paula – *Gilder*
Holden, Elisabeth – 0116 270 6430
Howard, Ann – *Stafford*
Howard, Yvonne – *Musichall*
Howells, Anne – *IMG*
Hughes, Alexandra – *Gilder*
Humble, Deborah – *KDM*
Hunt, Lorraine – *IMG*
Innes, Louise – *Musichall*
Irwin, Jane – *Ingpen*
James, Buddug Verona – *Sykes*
James, Eirian – *Musichall*
Janes, Fiona – *Gilder*
Januszajtis, Iwona – 01932 229412 *fax:* 020 8871 9416 *email:* 100631.1755@compuserve.com
Jennings, Sarah – 020 7622 4794 *also fax; email:* sarahlou@easicom.com
Jidkova, Elena – *Askonas Holt*
Jones, Della – *Mus Int*
Jones, Leah-Marian – *Harlequin*
Jones, Nerys – *Musichall*
Jose Trullu, Maria – *Still*
Juniku, Marita – *Pristavec*
Karnéus, Katarina – *Ingpen*
Kay, Serena – *Chameleon*
Keeble, Gaynor – 01676 533072 *also fax*
Keegan, Liane – *Connaught*
Keen, Catherine – *IMG*
Kettlewell, Alison – *Pristavec*
Kimm, Fiona – *Connaught*
King, Catherine – *CDI*
King, Mary – *Craig*
Kozená, Magdalena – *Askonas Holt*
Kubrick, Anya – *CMG*
Langfield, Mary Rose – *KDM*
Lapworth, Jane – 01702 711146 *also fax*
Larmore, Jennifer – *IMG*
Laurence, Elizabeth – *Gilder*
Lea, Yvonne – *Portland*
Leatherby, Carol Ann – 020 8552 7149 *also fax*; 07889 988312
Legg, Susan – 01243 552389 *also fax*
Lewis, Katharine – *Annon*
Lindop, Rachel – *KDM*
Lipovsek, Marjana – *Askonas Holt*
Lofthouse, Susan – 020 7720 4973
Lucas, Claire-Louise – 020 8395 7433 *email:* artists@midman503a.freeserve.co.uk
Lytting, Katja – *Allied*
McAdam, Lynne – *SS*
McCafferty, Frances – *Mus Int*
McCarney, Kate – *Musicmakers*
McCormack, Elizabeth – *Musichall*
McCormick, Mary Ann – *Gilder*
McDonald, Margaret – *Musicmakers*
McGahon, Colette – *Craig*
McIlwraith, Gillian – *Portland*
Maguire, Margaret – *Roxane Houston*
Marchione, Lydia – 020 7603 9820 *also fax*
Marshall, Melanie – c/o 020 7436 4626 *fax:* 020 7436 4627
Mason, Anne – *Phillips*
Meadows, Julia – *Upbeat*
Meek, Clarissa – *Musichall*
Melnikova, Ekaterina – *Gilder*
Michael, Beth – *OCA*
Michael, Nadja – *Askonas Holt*
Michelow, Sybil – 020 8459 2027
Miles-Johnson, Deborah – *CDI/Grant Rogers*
Millburn-Fryer, Cherith – *CDI*
Mills, Beverley – *Mus Int*
Mishura, Irina – *Askonas Holt*
Montague, Diana – *IMG*
Morloc, Renee – *Gilder*
Mott, Louise – *Portland*
Murray, Ann – *Askonas Holt*
Nichiteanu, Liliana – *Gilder*
Nicholls, Hyacinth – *Sykes*
Nichols, Mary – 01263 721552 *fax:* 01263 720320
Nikolova, Zlatomira – *Pristavec*
Obraztsova, Elena – *Askonas Holt*
Olsen, Marion – 01932 874405
Ormiston, Linda – *Mus Int*
Owens, Anne-Marie – *IMG*
Pantos, Pamela – *Alexander*
Parker, Gloria – *Gilder*
Parry, Susan – *IMG*
Payne, Rachel – *CDI* – 01829 740246
Peel, Ruth – *Musichall*
Petrie, Mollie – 01275 830733 *fax:* 01275 838426
Petrinsky, Natascha – *Still*
Philogene, Ruby – *Askonas Holt*
Pierard, Catherine – 020 8995 3226 *fax:* 020 8742 7476 *email:* kate@rubecat.demon.co.uk
Pinto, Mireia – *Askonas Holt*
Place, Alison – 020 8941 2684 *also fax*
Poulson, Lani – *Rawstron*
Pring, Sarah – *Musicmakers*
Quittmeyer, Susan – *Askonas Holt*
Randova, Edita – *Sonata*
Randova, Eva – *Askonas Holt*
Rappé, Jadwiga – *Finch*
Rearick, Barbara – *OWM*
Reid, Valerie – *OCA*
Rice, Christine – *Portland*
Richardson, Lindsay – 020 8884 1278
Rigby, Jean – *Askonas Holt*
Risley, Patricia – *IMG*
Robbin, Catherine – *Phillips*
Robinson, Ethna – *OWM*
Romanenko, Elena – *Sonata*
Romanova, Nina – *Gilder*
Rorholm, Marianne – *Ingpen*
Rowlands, Carol – 01323 491082
Sandivari, Ilia Aramayo – *Still*
Sborgi, Gabriella – *Still*
Schaufer, Lucy – *Musichall*
Schimmack, Susanne – *Askonas Holt*
Schneiderman, Helene – *Gilder*
Sciannimanico, Lucia – *CDI*
Sebron, Carolyn – *Gilder*
Self, Susannah – *Musicmakers*
Selway, Emma – *OWM*
Shaw, Teresa – *Stafford*
Shearer, Clare – *Portland*
Shell, Janet – *Gilder/CDI*
Sherman, Alexandra – *Musicmakers*
Shilling, Phyllis Kirian – *Roy Baker*
Slater, Judy – 01444 257009 *also fax*
Slepkovska, Denisa – *Mus Int*
Sotgiu, Antonia – *Portland*
Soulis, Maria – *Gilder*
Spence, Patricia – *Still*
Spicer, Susanna – *Singers Direct* – 020 8671 4112; 07976 987831 *fax:* 020 8671 0210
Squires, Shelagh – 01892 524099
Stafford, Dianne – 01776 870272 *also fax*
Steinfeld, Josephine – *SS*
Stene, Randi – *Askonas Holt*
Stephen, Pamela Helen – *Mus Int*
Stuart, Debra – *Gilder*
Stutzmann, Nathalie – *IMG*
Summers, Hilary – *Ingpen*
Sutton, Alison Mary – *CDI*
Svenden, Birgitta – *Rawstron*
Sykes, Belinda – 020 7708 3529 *also fax; email:* belinda.sykes@btinternet.com
Taylor, Ann – *Ingpen*
Tchistjakova, Irina – *Askonas Holt*
te Brummelstroete, Wilke – *OWM*
Theobald, Ruth – *Mostylea*
Thomas, Margaret – 01768 341437
Toczyska, Stefania – *Stafford*
Tomlinson, Margaret – 01326 241049
Tucker, Louise – *Alexander*
Turpin, Kathryn – *Sykes*
Uleman, Klara – *Stafford*
Unsworth, Beatrice – 029 2076 5177
Van Nes, Jard – *Askonas Holt*
Van de Sant, Cécile – *Still*
Vaughan, Elizabeth – *IMG*
Vizin, Viktoria – *Craig*
von Otter, Anne Sofie – *IMG*
Walker, Penelope – *Gilder*
Walker CBE, Sarah – *Askonas Holt*
Walker Smith, Nicola – 01249 660938 *also fax; email:* the.smiths1@virgin.net
Wallewik, Mathilde – *Connaught*

Walton, Michelle – *OWM*
Watkins, Helen – 020 8660 2786
Wendel, Renate Maria – 020 7277 7068 *fax:* 020 7277 8354 *email:* 100115.3701@compuserve.com
Westbrook, Kate – 01752 830589 *fax:* 01752 830539 *email:* smiths_academy@hotmail.com
Westwood, Jennifer – 0114 266 6132; 07973 765849 *email:* Jennifer@springvale95.freeserve.co.uk
Wilkens, Anne – *IMG*
Williams, Harriet – *Harlequin*
Williams, Tania Marie – *Annon*
Williamson, Josephine – *Pristavec*
Williamson, Vanessa – *CDI/POEM*
Willis, Nuala – *Still/Roxane Houston*
Wilson, Christina – *Connaught*
Winkler, Jutta – *Stafford*
Winter, Louise – *Askonas Holt*
Wood, Hazel – 020 8878 9714 *also fax; email:* hazel.wood@easynet.co.uk
Woodhouse, Kim-Marie – *CDI*
Woodruff, Kathryn – *CDI*
Woolford, Delia – 01428 642653 *also fax*
Wyn-Rogers, Catherine – *Askonas Holt*
Yang, Guang – *Harlequin*
Zajick, Dolora – *HP*

Counter Tenors and Falsettists

Angel, Ryland – *Gilder*
Asawa, Brian – *Askonas Holt*
Blaze, Robin – *Phillips*
Bordas, Ricard – *Still*
Bowman, James – 01737 767520 *fax:* 01737 779690
Brett, Charles – 020 8892 3484 *also fax*
Buwalda, Sytse – *Sykes*
Chance, Michael – *Ingpen*
Chavner, Robert – 01732 452462 *also fax*
Cheng-Jim, Tay – 020 7720 6928
Clapton, Nicholas – 01865 244207 *also fax*
Clegg, David – *Chameleon*
Clifford, Christopher John – 020 8543 7633; 07768 908486 *fax:* 020 8543 9600 *email:* cjcliffordct@bodytreats.com
Daniels, David – *Askonas Holt*
Domènech-Subiranas, Jordi – *OCA*
Esswood, Paul – *CDI/POEM*
Gay, Simon – *Sympathetic* – 020 8761 2779
Giles, Peter – *Annon*
Harper, Michael – *Mus Int*
Harre-Jones, Robert – 01753 853573 *also fax*
Hill, Simon – 020 8995 2757
Howells, Vaughan – 020 8683 1659 *also fax; email:* vaughan-howells@hotmail.com
Humphries, Charles – *Chameleon*
James, David – *Hazard*
Jeffries, James Huw – *Mus Int (opera)/Sykes (concerts)*
Josey, Christopher – *Musicmakers*
Kenny, Jonathan Peter – *Musichall*
Kusel, Paul – 01255 506377 *also fax*
Lakey, Denis – *Connaught*
McLusky, Fergus – 020 7403 7474 *also fax*
Missin, William – 020 8553 3247 *also fax; email:* willmissin@btinternet.com
Nicholson, Paul – *CDI/POEM*
Ogden, Robert – *CDI*
Oro, Martin – *Still*
Penrose, Timothy – *CDI/POEM*
Purefoy, William – *Portland*
Ragin, Derek Lee – *Askonas Holt*
Robson, Christopher – *Mus Int*
Royall, Christopher – 020 8292 5987 *also fax*
Sanderson, James – 020 7791 1730 *fax:* 020 7791 2618 *email:* james@musico.net
Scholl, Andreas – *HP*
Stafford, Ashley – *OCA*
Stefanowicz, Artur – *Sykes*
Taylor, Daniel – *HP*
Tyson, Robin – *Allied/Chameleon/CDI*
Van Goethem, Patrick – *Sykes*
Wallace, Stephen – *HP*
Watts, Andrew – *Mus Int*
Whitworth, John – 01509 413327 *email:* piewhit@globalnet.co.uk
Wyn Roberts, Richard – 01372 739985 *also fax; email:* rwynrob@aol.com
Zazzo, Lawrence – *Portland*

Tenors

Ackerman, Neville – *Gilder*
Agafonov, Mikhail – *Gilder*
Agnew, Paul – *Hazard*
Ainsley, John Mark – *Askonas Holt*
Aler, John – *Askonas Holt*
Alexander, Rein – *Roy Baker*
Allen, Stephen – *Portland*
Anderson, Terje – *Still*
Anderson-Hall, Alexander – *OCA*
Aragall, Giacomo – *Stafford*
Arden-Griffith, Paul – *Brunskill*
Arvidsson, Bjorn – *Sykes*
Ashmore-Turner, David – *KDM*
Austin-Kelly, Paul – *IMG*
Auty, Peter – *Ingpen*
Badea, Alexandro – *Mus Int*
Ballo, Pietro – *Still*
Bamber, Peter – *CDI*
Banks, Barry – *HP*
Bantick, John – 01438 812761 *also fax*
Barham, Edmund – *Still*
Barratt, Jack – 01692 583002
Barrett, Brent – *Askonas Holt*
Bartleet, David – *Alexander*
Bartolini, Lando – *Stafford*
Beck, Alan – *Connaught*
Begley, Kim – *IMG*
Berkeley-Steele, Richard – *Gilder*
Berridge, Simon – *CDI*
Beuron, Yann – *IMG*
Blinkhof, Jan – *IMG*
Boe, Alfred – *Askonas Holt*
Bomstein, Leonid – *Gilder*
Bostridge, Ian – *Askonas Holt*
Bottone, Bonaventura – *Stafford*
Bowen, John – *Phillips*
Bowers, Evan – *Still*
Bowley, John – *Singers Direct* – 020 8664 6078
Boydall, Steven – *Mus Int*
Bronder, Peter – *Allied*
Bruni, Romolo – 020 8992 0527; 07770 303422
Burden, Andrew – *Musicmakers*
Burden, William – *Askonas Holt*
Burt, Robert – *Musichall*
Busher, Andrew – *SS*
Butterfield, Peter – *Mus Int*
Buxton, Nicholas – *KDM*
Caley, Ian – *Ingpen*
Calleja, Joseph – *Allied*
Campbell, Rory – *Dyfel*
Carwood, Andrew – *Singers Direct* – 020 8423 7671 *fax:* 020 8423 7653 *email:* andrewcarwood@oratory.demon.co.uk
Cave, Philip – 01865 244801 *fax:* 01865 437238 *email:* magnificat@compuserve.com
Cazalet, Hal – *Mus Int*
Chaundy, Stephen – *Gilder*
Clark, Graham – *Ingpen*
Clarke, Paul Charles – *Askonas Holt*
Cogram, John – *Craig*
Conrad, Andreas – *Mus Int*
Conyers, David – 01768 341783 *also fax*
Cornwell, Joseph – *Sykes/CDI/POEM*
Covey-Crump, Rogers – *Hazard*
Coxon, Richard – *IMG*
Cresswell, Jeffrey – *CDI*
Croft, Richard – *Askonas Holt*
Crowe, Robert W – 01764 684535 *also fax; email:* crowe@castledunning.freeserve.co.uk
Cupido, Alberto – *Stafford*
Curtis, Mark – *Mus Int*
Curtis, Simon – 020 8491 4813 *also fax; email:* Simon.Curtis@tesco.net
Daggett, Philip – *SS*
Daley, Bradley – *Craig*
Daniels, Charles – *Hazard*
Daszak, John – *IMG*
Davies, Arthur – *Stafford*
Davies, Maldwyn – *Gilder/CDI*
Davies, Ryland – *IMG*
Davies, Simon – 020 7732 7389 *fax:* 020 7642 5310 *email:* sghdavies@cwcom.net
Dawidoff, Mikhail – *Gilder*
Daymond, Karl – *Askonas Holt*
del Pozo, Rodrigo – *Sykes*
del Valle, Fernando – *Gilder*
Dodd, Geraint – *Harlequin*
Donets, Sergei – *Gilder*
Douglas, Nigel – *Mus Int*
Douse, Stephen – *Chameleon*
Dowd, Jeffrey – *Portland*
Downes, Craig – *Sykes*
Duykers, John – *Still*
Egerton, Francis – *Still*
Elias, Jorge – *IMG*
Elliott, Paul – *CDI/POEM*
Ellis, Tomos – 020 8445 7896 *also fax*
Elming, Poul – *Ingpen*
Evans, Huw Rhys – *Sykes: Concerts*
Evans, Joseph – *Mus Int*
Evans, Wynford – *CDI*
Evans, Wynne – *Harlequin*
Evans-Jones, Timothy – *Musichall*
Eve, Philip – 020 7265 1384 *also fax; email:* philip@carltoneve.freeserve.co.uk

Farrington, Paul – *SS*
Fedderly, Greg – *Askonas Holt*
Flint, Ivor – 020 8968 9605 *fax:* 020 8354 2631 *email:* ivor.flint@virgin.net
Forbes, Rupert Oliver – *Mus Int*
Forbes-Lane, Andrew – *Mus Int*
Ford, Bruce – *Still*
Fouchécourt, Jean Paul – *Askonas Holt*
Fox, Darren – *KDM*
Frederick, James – *Rondo*
Fryatt, John – *Mus Int*
Gardner, Lyndon – *CDI* – 01509 236281 *also fax*
Garfield Henry, Antoni – *Mus Int*
Gavin, Julian – *IMG*
Gedda, Nicolai – *Clarion/Seven Muses*
George, Donald – *Stafford*
Gibbs, Robert – 01843 842996 *email:* bobgibbs@mistral.co.uk; bob@cant.ac.uk
Gietz, Gordon – *IMG*
Gilchrist, James – *Portland*
Gillett, Christopher – *IMG*
Goldberg, Reiner – *Allied*
Goldthorpe, Michael – *CDI/Mus Int/Roxane Houston* *email:* mgoldthorpe@x-stream.co.uk
Graham-Hall, John – *Musichall*
Gray, George – *Portland*
Green, Robin – *KDM/CDI* *email:* robin.green@netmatters.co.uk
Griffett, James – *CDI/POEM*
Grivnov, Vsevolod – *Askonas Holt*
Gubsky, Mikhail – *Gilder*
Hall, Aled – *Harlequin*
Hall, Peter – *CDI*
Hand, Christopher – 01905 351292
Harrison, Martyn – 01268 282221 *also fax; email:* mhrson@yahoo.com
Hart-Davis, Michael – *Musicmakers*
Haskin, Howard – *Stafford*
Hibberd, Russell – *KDM*
Hill, Martyn – *OWM*
Hillman, David – *Ellison*
Hindmarsh, Martin – *CDI*
Hoare, Peter – *Harlequin*
Honeyman, Ian – 01229 432956
Horgan, Breffni – *Craig*
Hudson, John – *Ingpen*
Ireland, Richard – *CDI*
Jeffes, Peter – *Connaught*
Jenkins, Neil – *Mus Int*
Jenkins, Terry – *Mus Int*
Jennings, Rupert – *Chameleon*
Jensen, Julian – *Mus Int*
Johnson, Alexander – *Gilder*
Johnston, Robert – *Musicmakers*
Jones, Doug – *Gilder*
Jones, Gwyn Hughes – *Harlequin*
Kaasch, Donald – *IMG*
Kale, Stuart – *Still*
Kaufmann, Jonas – *IMG*
Kelly, Declan – *Sykes*
Kim, Shane Shinuk – *Stafford*
King, Andrew – *CDI/POEM*
Kirk, Vernon – *Grant Rogers*
König, Klaus – *Allied*
König, Michael – *IMG*
Kouzmenko, Vladimir – *Allied*
Kruse, Heinz – *Rawstron*
Kuebler, David – *IMG*
La Pierre, John – *Mus Int*
Langridge, Philip – *Allied*
Lavender, Justin – *Still*
Lawton, Jeffrey – *Mus Int*
Leggate, Robin – *Askonas Holt*
Lentz, Jeffrey – *Gilder*
Levinsky, Ilya – *Askonas Holt*
Lewis, Keith – *IMG*
Lima, Luis – *Stafford*
Lincoln, Christopher – *Harlequin*
Lindskog, Pär – *VWM*
Lloyd-Roberts, Jeffrey – *Musichall*
Lombardo, Luca – *Gilder*
Lopez-Yanez, Jorge – *Gilder*
Lorimer, Glenn C – 01920 461915; 07801 65785
Ludha, Ludovit – *Mus Int*
McCann, Paul – *Gilder*
MacDougall, Jamie – *Musichall*
MacKenzie, Neil – *CDI*
Mackenzie-Wicks, Andrew – 01273 474635 *also fax*
McKerracher, Colin – 020 8445 6646; 01324 626441
McLean-Mair, Kevin – *SS/Sykes*
MacMaster, John – *Gilder*
Macias, Reinaldo – *Stafford*
Mackie, Neil – *Askonas Holt*
Maisuradze, Badri – *Askonas Holt*
Malagnini, Mario – *Gilder*
Margita, Stefan – *Mus Int*
Marlton, Hilton – *Craig*
Marsden, John – *Portland*
Martin, Adrian – *Mus Int*
Martinucci, Nicola – *Stafford*
Maxwell Anderson, David – *Allied*
Mayall, Alan – 020 8680 8287 *also fax*; 07973 641305
Meades, Daniel – *Craig*
Mee, Anthony – *Harlequin*
Meirion, Rhys – *Askonas Holt*
Merritt, Chris – *Askonas Holt*
Mitchinson, John – *CDI/Camerata*
Mok, Warren – *Mus Int*
Mongiardino, Gianni – *Still*
Monks, Jonathan – *Ockert*
Morris, Andrew – 01737 249839 *also fax; email:* andrewmorris@melisma.freeserve.co.uk
Morton, Richard – 01865 372045
Moss, Henry – *Allied*
Mulkaria, Shalva – *Still*
Müller, Rufus – *OWM*
Murgatroyd, Andrew – *CDI*
Murray, John Horton – *IMG*
Mussard, Timothy – *Gilder*
Nagore, Antonio – *Gilder*
Natoli, Dominic – *Mus Int*
Nelson, James – *Mus Int*
Newton, Lloyd B A – 020 8659 3289 *also fax; email:* lloydnewton@pegopera.org
Nicoll, Harry – *Musicmakers*
Nilon, Paul – *Ingpen*
Norman, Daniel – *Askonas Holt*
Norton, Anthony – *Craig*
O'Beirne, Gerard – 01923 774485
O'Neill, Dennis – *Ingpen*
Oke, Alan – *Musichall*
Oliver, Alexander – *IMG*
Ovenden, Jeremy – *Phillips*
Owen, David – *Gilder*
Oxley, Benjamin – *Dyfel*
Oxley, James – *Allied*
Padmore, Mark – *VWM*
Partridge CBE, Ian – *Clarion/Seven Muses/CDI*
Paton, Iain – *Askonas Holt*
Pike, Julian – *Camerata*
Pita, Jorgie Antonio – *Stafford*
Place, Gerald – 020 8941 2684 *also fax*
Podbolotov, Alexandre – *Gilder*
Popov, Valery – *Sonata*
Potter, John – *Robert White*
Powell, Michael – 01993 708652 *fax:* 01993 708643 *email:* michael.powell@btinternet.com
Power, Patrick – *Still*
Prégardien, Christoph – *Askonas Holt*
Priday, Huw – *CDI/Gilder*
Priest, Richard – 0121 643 7553 *fax:* 0121 633 4773 *email:* richard.priest@allegro.co.uk
Prunell-Friend, Agustin – *Mus Int*
Pullin, Gordon – 01449 741414
Rahme, Edmondo – *Dyfel*
Randle, Thomas – *IMG*
Rashbrook, Roy – *Chameleon*
Ray, Dennis – 01922 408571 *fax:* 0121 455 0859 *email:* ent@ear-ltd.co.uk
Reaville, Richard – *CDI/Roxane Houston*
Rendall, David – *IMG*
Renshaw, Martin – *Annon*
Richards, Timothy – *Harlequin*
Roberts, Gareth – 020 8907 3022 *also fax*
Robinson, Timothy – *Askonas Holt*
Robson, Nigel – *Ingpen*
Rodriguez, Luis – *Craig*
Rogers, Nigel – 01635 253319 *also fax*
Rojas, Rafael – *IMG*
Rolfe Johnson, Anthony – *Askonas Holt*
Rooke, Stephen – *Harlequin*
Sadé, Gabriel – *Gilder*
Saetre, William – *Gilder*
Salmon, Philip – *Gilder*
Saunders, Christopher – *Harlequin*
Schade, Michael – *IMG*
Scherbakov, Vladimir – *Gilder*
Schreier, Peter – *Askonas Holt*
Sears, Nicholas – *Askonas Holt/IMG*
Sharpe, Ivan – *Portland*
Sheffield, Philip – *Musicmakers*
Shtoda, Daniil – *Askonas Holt*
Silvasti, Jorma – *Still*
Slane, Philip – *Annon*
Solodovnikov, Vladimir – *Gilder*
Spence, Toby – *Askonas Holt*
Stephenson, Donald – 01597 840204 *fax:* 01597 840608 *email:* donaldstephenson@compuserve.com
Stewart, Jeffrey – *IMG*
Stocker, Julian – 01923 491290 *fax:* 01923 244234 *email:* stockerwoodhouse@btinternet.com
Storey, Ian – *Music Centre* (*see* International Agents, Italy) – c/o 00 392 4870 2828; 01568 760206 *also fax; email:* istoreyuk@aol.com
Streit, Kurt – *IMG*
Sunnegårdh, Thomas – *Rawstron*
Tear CBE, Robert – *Askonas Holt*
Tevis, Mark – *Gilder*
Thomas, Matthew Elton – *Craig*
Thompson, Adrian – *Phillips*
Thompson, Alastair – 01865 558501 *also fax*
Thompson, Ian – *Still/CDI*
Thompson, Robert – *CDI* – 01765 604775 *email:* robert_thompson@tenor1.demon.co.uk
Tolley, Phillip – 01252 548275 *email:* philliptolley@colcanto.co.uk
Treleaven, John – *Alexander/OCA*
Trost, Rainer – *Rawstron*
Trotter, Paul – *CDI*
Tucker, Mark – *HP*
Uhlenhopp, John – *Gilder*
Upperton, John – c/o 020 8299 1914
van Rensberg, Kobie – *Allied*
Ventre, Carlo – *IMG*
Ventris, Christopher – *IMG*
Vine, Matthew – 020 8693 4292
Vodicka, Leo-Marian – *Mus Int*
Voinorowski, Vjacheslav – *Gilder*
Vostriakov, Alexander – *Sonata*
Wagenführer, Roland – *Rawstron*
Warden, Mark – 020 8761 4853; 07971 080194
Watson, Christopher – *Chameleon*
Webb, Barry – 020 7430 1373
Wedd, Peter – *Mus Int*
White, Melvyn – 0114 258 0148 *also fax*
Wilde, Mark – *Sykes*

Williams, Bradley – *Still*
Williams, Tom Emlyn – 020 8944 1402; 00 31 20 625 1750 *fax:* 020 8879 1498 *email:* tomemlyn@xs4all.nl
Wilson, Gordon – *Portland*
Wilson, Hugh – 01923 237261 *also fax; email:* hwilson@vcmeasom.u-net.com
Winsor, Michael – *LM*
Woodrow, Alan – *Still*
Workman, Charles – *Still*
Woroniecki, Robert – *Gilder*
Zamparino, Cesare – *Gilder*
Zaplechny, Vadim – *Gilder*
Zvetanov, Boiko – *Still*

Baritones, Bass-Baritones and Basses

Abdrasakov, Askar – *Askonas Holt*
Agache Alexandru – *Stafford*
Albert, Laurence – *CDI/POEM*
Alder, Stephen – 020 8540 6795 *also fax*
Aleksashkin, Sergei – *Askonas Holt*
Alexancer, Trevor – *Alexander/Roxane Houston*
Allan, Lewis – 0141 639 5433; 07885 423214
Allen, Thomas – *Askonas Holt*
Allenby William – *Craig*
Anderson, Barry – *Stafford*
Angas, Richard – *Musichall*
Anisimov, Alexander – *Askonas Holt*
Antonov, Andrey – *Gilder*
Arnold, Jonathan – 01865 874791
Ashman David – 01273 687555; 07703 537472 *fax:* 01273 687554 *email.* david.ashman@dial.pipex.com
Ashworth, James – 01274 499062 *also fax; email.* JamesRAshworth@prunepark.idps.co.uk
Ataneli, Lado – *Allied/Still*
Ayldon, John – *Mus Int*
Bailey, Norman – *Gilder*
Baker, Alisdair – *SS*
Bamford, Alistair – 020 8742 0858
Bannatyne-Scott, Brian – *Musicmakers*
Bär, Olaf – *IMG*
Barrell, David – *Allied*
Baturkin, Andrei – *Gilder*
Bayley, Clive – *IMG*
Beavan, David – *CDI/POEM*
Beaven, Peter – 01483 475506 *fax:* 01483 475184 *email:* pmsnet@argonet.co.uk
Beesley, Mark – *Still*
Belsey, Ian – *Dyfel*
Berg, Nathan – *IMG*
Berger, Leon – 020 7485 8702 *also fax; email:* leon.berger@virgin.net
Bernays, John – *KDM*
Best, Jonathan – *Musichall*
Best, Matthew – *IMG*
Bindley, Justin – *SS* – 01242 239049
Birchall, Jeremy – *SS*
Birchall, Simon – *Chameleon/CDI*
Black, Jeffrey – *IMG*
Bland, Benjamin – *OWM*
Bleiker, D'Arcy – *Portland*
Boldyrev, Vladimir – *Sonata*
Booth-Jones, Christopher – *Sykes*
Bork, Robert – *Gilder*
Borowski Daniel – *Portland*
Boughton Ian – 01462 434318; 07703 584152
Braun, Russell – *IMG*
Braun, Victor – *Ingpen*
Broad, Daniel – *Portland*
Broadbent, Graeme – *Askonas Holt*
Bronikowski, Marcin – *Gilder*
Brown, Quentin – *CDI*
Bryson, Roger – *Mus Int*
Bundy, Michael – *Singers Direct* – 020 8390 5375; 07889 153382 *fax:* 020 8390 9818 *email:* mrb@clara.net
Burchuladze, Paata – *Askonas Holt*
Burns, Dominic – *CDI*
Burton, Nigel – 0118 931 8414 *fax:* 0118 931 8412 *email:* n.m.burton@reading.ac.uk
Bussell, Antony – *Annon*
Butler, James Elliot – 01383 872049
Caddy, Ian – *CDI/POEM/Mus Int*
Campbell, David – 01279 862172
Caproni, Bruno – *Portland*
Carolis, Natale de – *Askonas Holt*
Carpenter Turner, Robert – *CDI*
Carr, Gavin – *Sykes: Concerts*
Cashmore, John – *Alexander*
Caswell, Edward – 020 8674 9861 *also fax*
Cato, Ralph – *Dyfel*
Cavallier, Nicolas – *Gilder*
Clarke, Adrian – *Musicmakers*
Clarkson, Julian – *CDI/POEM*
Cleverdon, Roger – 020 8946 8904
Cleverton, James – *KDM*
Cliffe, Nigel – 01793 700298
Coad, Conal – *Musichall*
Cold, Ulrik – *Allied*
Coleman-Wright, Peter – *HP*
Collis, Andrew – *VWM*
Comboy, Ian – *Mus Int*
Cook, Brian Rayner – *CDI* – 020 8368 3010
Corbett, Joseph – 020 7624 6280 *fax:* 020 7372 3317
Cowan, Sigmund – *Still*
Croft, Howard Quilla – *Stafford*
Crown, David – *Portland*
Dale Forbes, Andrew – *Mus Int*
Danby, Graeme – *Stafford*
Daniluk, Pavel – *Gilder*
Davies, Christopher – 020 8954 4646
Davies, Meurig – *OWM*
Davies, Neal – *Askonas Holt*
Davis, Stephen – 01494 773919 *also fax;* 07774 461600 *email:* sdavisbass@aol.com
Dazeley, William – *Askonas Holt*
De Costa, Michael – *Pristavec*
de Jong, Lucas – *Sykes*
Dean, Mikel – *Mus Int*
Dean, Stafford – *IMG*
Delrez, Gerard – *Annon*
Dewis, Michael – *Harlequin*
Diaz, Justino – *Stafford*
Dickson, Grant – *Harlequin*
Dolton, Geoffrey – *Allied*
Donnelly, Malcolm – *Gilder*
Dore, Michael – *LM*
Dorn, Reinhard – *Rawstron*
Doyle, Grant – *Gilder*
Druiett, Michael – *IMG*
Ducarel, Michael – 020 7582 1052 *also fax; email:* morrice@cix.co.uk
Duesing, Dale – *Askonas Holt*
Duisburg, Johannes von – *Gilder*
Dulieu, John – *Brunskill*
Earle, Roderick – *Musichall*
Ebrahim, Omar – *Allied*
Edelmann, Peter – *Gilder*
Edwards-Lowe, John – 0115 959 9966
Elliot, Brian Newton – 0161 773 2266
Elliott, Martin – *CDI/POEM* – c/o 01243 604281 *fax:* 01243 604387 *email:* m.elliott@chihe.ac.uk
Ellis, David – *Portland*
Ely, Dean – *Mus Int*
Ens, Phillip – *IMG*
Evans, Bryn – 020 8891 1308; 07711 351718
Evgenij, Dmitriev – *Stafford*
Ewing, Alan – *Allied*
Fair, Nigel – *OCA*
Fairs, Alan – *OCA/CDI*
Feller, Carlos – *Rawstron*
Field, Christopher – 020 8858 6510
Finley, Gerald – *IMG*
Finney, Jonathan – *CMG*
Fissore, Enrico – *Gilder*
Fitchew, Michael – 020 8523 1054
Flanagan, John Michael – 01273 478268
Flanagan, Leslie John – *Harlequin*
Fletcher, John – *Sykes*
Folwell, Nicholas – *Mus Int*
Foster, Andrew – *Phillips*
Foster, Christopher – *Singers Direct* – 020 8677 7997 *fax:* 020 8696 9783 *email:* chris@tisl.co.uk
Francke, Donald – 020 8769 0423; 020 7328 0864 *fax:* 020 7328 0684
Fraser Annand, Kenneth – 01209 820890
Freedman, David – *SS*
Galla, Jan – *Mus Int*
Garner, Stephen – *Craig*
Garrett, Eric – *Still*
Garrett, Nicholas – *Gilder*
George, Michael – *IMG*
Gerello, Vassily – *Askonas Holt*
Giacalone, Nicolino – *Ellison* – 020 8559 1983 *also fax; email:* nicolino.giacalone@virgin.net
Gilfry, Rodney – *Askonas Holt*
Glanville, Mark – *Still*
Gluschak, Vladimir – *Gilder*
Goldsack, Christopher – *Gilder*
Golesorkhi, Anooshah – *Stafford*
Gombrich, Carl – *OCA*
Greenan, Andrew – *Gilder*
Guedes, Hector – *Gilder*
Gunn, Nathan – *Ingpen*
Gunthorpe, Jonathan – *Sykes: Concerts*
Haenen, Tom – *Gilder*
Hagegård, Håkan – *IMG*
Hagen, Reinhard – *Allied*
Halfvarson, Eric – *IMG*
Halton, Richard – *Musichall*
Hammond-Stroud OBE, Derek – 020 8883 2120
Hampson, Thomas – *IMG*
Hancock, John – *Still*
Hancorn, John – *Sykes*
Harbottle, Guy – *KDM*
Hargreaves, Glenville – *CDI/Musichall*
Hargreaves, Matthew – *Harlequin*
Harrison, Devon – *Dyfel*
Harvey, Peter – *Hazard*
Haugland, Aage – *Askonas Holt*
Hawlata, Franz – *IMG*
Hayes, Quentin – *Portland*
Hayward, Robert – *Ingpen*
Hearne, John – 01651 882274 *also fax*
Held, Alan – *Askonas Holt*
Hemm, Manfred – *Still*
Henschel, Dietrich – *IMG*
Herford, Henry – *CDI* – 01865 300884 *also fax*
Holl, Robert – *Ingpen*
Holland, Ashley – *IMG*
Holland, Mark – *Gilder*
Holzmair, Wolfgang – *VWM*
Hoult, David – 0161 427 7255 *email:* d.hoult@leedscolmusic.ac.uk
Howard, Jason – *IMG*
Howell CBE, Gwynne – *Ingpen*
Hudson, Paul – *Alexander*
Humphreys, Garry – 020 8882 2106
Hunt, Tom – *CDI*
Hutton, Adrian – *Roxane Houston*

NICOLINO GIACALONE
Bass-Baritone

International Classical Singer

"The protagonist, Diocles, played and sung by Nicolino Giacalone at first appeared merely the earnest stolid figure that Fletcher (the playwright) had parroted from his sources. Very soon, however, this imposing actor began to glimpse the absurd possibilities in the part – his moral inconsistencies, which could either shock or amuse, or both. He played with the audience like an accomplished comedian, so that our laughter felt almost forbidden: we experienced the double pleasures of delight and shame."
Peter Pagnell, *The Independent*, London, England, UK. (Critique of performance of Purcell's semi-opera Dioclesian)

"He made the art songs seem real. He has a way of conveying the spirit of the art songs by careful attention to the text, while the arias and Broadway show tunes rounded out the program. Giacalone reminded the listeners of how great songs like Richard Strauss' Morgen and Zueignung really are"
Charles Ward, *Houston Chronicle*, Texas, USA.

"... his potential has been fully realised in all ways, from the warmth and generosity of his personality to the deep vibrancy and spell-binding quality of his singing"
E. Forrest-O'Driscoll, *Irish International Arts Centre*, Ireland.

International Singing Instructor

"His genius as a teacher emerged as he coached the participating singers in a knowledgeable way, frequently making suggestions which caused immediate and obvious improvement in the participants' presentations. In addition to learning a great deal, the singers and audience members laughed a lot and had a good time. His cheerful, bouyant, and witty demeanour made it fun to be part of this experience"
Suzanne Marion, Concert Secretary and Past President, Houston Tuesday Musical Club Member, Houston, Texas, USA.

"He is a brilliant and persuasive teacher who combines professional exactness with a charismatic personality. The result is a profound learning experience"
Keith Taylor, *Stephen Sondheim Society*, Westminster University, London, England, UK.

"I would not hesitate to recommend Mr. Giacalone. Proper breathing, voice placement, posture and accurate movement of the articulators (i.e. jaw, tongue) were and integral part of each lesson. I feel that his method of teaching would facilitate the transfer of proper vocal use from speech to singing."
Leslie P. Suite, M.Sc. Reg. OSLA, CCC-SLP, Speech-Language Pathologist, Canada.

The Chestnuts, 56 Snakes Lane West, Woodford Green, Essex, IG8 ODF, England, United Kingdom.
Tel: (+44) 020 8559 1983 Mobile: 0468 838 494 Website: http://vzone.virgin.net/nicolino.giacalone Email: nicolino.giacalone@virgin.net
Management: J. Audrey Ellison International Artists' Management, 135 Stevenage Road, Fulham, London, SW6 6PB, England, United Kingdom.
Tel: (+44) 020 7381 9751 Fax: (+44) 020 7381 2406 Email: Audrey@Ellison-Intl.freeserve.co.uk

JOHN EDWARDS-LOWE

Bass-Baritone

"He sang with an exciting, full, rich voice in bel canto tradition, which one might never tire of hearing. His baritone voice with deep bass resonances must rank him amongst the best in his generation..."
D G Hambleton, Greenwich Festival 1990

"Formerly a student with John Noble among others, Mr Lowe has a handsome bass-baritone voice, and his opening group of Vaughan Williams songs revealed a marked feeling for colour and nuance."
St Mary's Church Recital, Nottingham Evening Post

2 Pendle Crescent, Mapperley, Nottingham NG3 3EZ
Telephone: 0115 9599966

Oratorio
Opera
Recital
Recording
Adjudication
Master Classes
Teaching
Radio/TV
Musicals
Cabaret

GRAHAM TREW
Baritone

"The voice is a pleasure to hear, he uses it with great artistry and variety, while his diction is quite remarkable." *'Gramophone'*

61 Sydner Road, London N16 7UF
Tel/Fax 0207 275 8260
e mail: trwlew@globalnet.co.uk

International Who's Who in Music
(1996–97 Edition p.943)

Hvorostovsky, Dmitri – *Askonas Holt*
Hynninen, Jorma – *Allied*
Jackson, Richard – *Phillips*
Jaffe, Monte – *Ingpen*
Jauhiainan, Brian – *Still*
Johansen, Ronnie – *Rawstron*
Johnston, Charles – *Mus Int*
Joll, Philip – *IMG*
Kanevsky, Dmitry – *Gilder*
Keenlyside, Simon – *Askonas Holt*
Kempster, David – *Harlequin*
Kennedy, Roderick – *Mus Int*
Kesselman, Bryan – 020 8868 8912
Keyte, Christopher – *CDI*
Kharitonov, Dimitri – *Allied*
Kirby-Ashmore, David – *Craig*
Kirkbride, Simon – *Allied*
Kit, Mikhail – *Askonas Holt*
Koc, Jozik – *Mus Int*
Konstantinov, Julian – *Askonas Holt*
Korhonen, Jyrki – *Still*
Kovats Kolos – *Mus Int*
Kraft, David – 020 8807 4973
Kubiak, Laurence – *Ellison*
Kusjner, Ivan – *Mus Int*
Lamb, Alan – 01279 651856
Langford, Roger – *Gilder*
Langley, John – c/o 020 7836 9377 *fax:* c/o 020 7836 9388
email: langers@cableinet.co.uk
Latham, Keith – *Stafford*
Leiferkus, Sergei – *Allied*
Lewis Williams, Daniel – *Still*
Linnenbank, René – *Gilder*
Lloyd, Robert – *Askonas Holt*
Lloyd-Morgan, Richard – *Gilder*
Loges, Stephan – *VWM*
Lowe, John – 0115 959 9966
McElroy, Sam – *Harlequin*
McIntyre, Sir Donald – *Ingpen*
McVeigh, Tom – *KDM*
Mackie, William – *CDI (concerts only)*
Magee, Garry – *HP*
Maltman, Christopher – *Askonas Holt*
Mann, Noel – *Mus Int*
Mannov, Johannes – *Gilder*
Marber, Anthony – *Still*
Marin, Carlos – *Still*
Marsh, David – *Mus Int*
Martirossian, Tigran – *Askonas Holt*
Massis, René – *Gilder*
Masterton-Smith, Simon – *Chuck Julian*
Matiukhin, Igor – *Gilder*
Matorin, Vladimir – *Gilder/Allied*
Matthews, Hubert – *CDI*
Maxwell, Donald – *Mus Int*
May, Jonathan – *Stafford*
Mayor, Andrew – *SS*
Mazura, Franz – *Ingpen*
Meanley, Ralph – *SS*
Melrose, Leigh – *IMG*
Michaels-Moore, Anthony – *IMG*
Mikhailov, Maxim – *Gilder*
Mikulas, Peter – *Mus Int*
Miller, Niven – 01372 275430
email: nivnmiller@aol.com
Milne, John – 020 8806 1872
Milnes, Sherrill – *Ingpen*
Mobbs, Daniel – *Still*
Moll, Kurt – *Askonas Holt*
Morgan, Arwel Huw – *Ingpen*
Morgan, John – *Alexander*
Morgan, Tim – *Mus Int*
Morris, Colin – *Mus Int*
Morris, James – *Askonas Holt*
Morris, Richard – *OCA*
Morrison, Richard – *Craig*
Moses, Geoffrey – *Phillips*
Mosley, George – *Gilder*
Motchalov, Alexei – *Gilder*
Mozhayev, Flodor – *Sonata*
Murzaev, Sergei – *Gilder*
Neal, Simon – *Sykes*
Nechaev, Yuri – *Gilder*
Nelson, Martin – *Chuck Julian*
Nesterenko, Evgeny – *Allied*
Newman, Henry – *Alexander*
Noble, John – *CDI*
Noble, Timothy – *IMG*
Norris, James – *SS*
O'Brien, Philip – *KDM*
O'Connor, Gerard – *Mus Int*
O'Donnell, Kevin – *LM*
O'Keefe, David – *KDM*
Ognev, Vladimir – *Gilder*
Ognovenko, Vladimir – *Allied*
Okerlund, David – *Harlequin*
Oldfield, Mark – *Gilder*
Olsen, Frode – *Still*
Opie, Alan – *Allied*
Otey, Louis – *Still*
Ottaway, James – *CDI*
Owen, Stephen – *Still*
Page, Steven – *Stafford*
Pape, René – *Allied*
Parfitt, Paul – *Mus Int*
Park, Kenneth – 01205 351733
Patriarco, Earle – *Askonas Holt*
Peacock, Adrian – *CDI/POEM*
Peaker, Jeremy – *Mus Int*
Pearce, Michael – *KDM*
Peel, William – *Gilder*
Pencarreg, Wyn – *Musichall*
Perroni, Jacques – *OCA*
Platt, Ian – *Gilder*
Polegato, Brett – *IMG*
Polhamus, John – *Roxane Houston/Dyfel*
Polikanin, Evgeny – *Gilder*
Ponomarenko, Ivan – *Sonata*
Pott, Charles – 01923 234669

Poulton, Robert – *Musicmakers*
Prey, Hermann – *Askonas Holt*
Purves, Christopher – *Mus Int*
Putilin, Nikolai – *Askonas Holt*
Quilico, Gino – *IMG*
Quinn, Gerard – *Alexander*
Raffell, Anthony – c/o 01235 525412 *fax:* 01235 559722 *email:* Suse@SKManagement.freeserve.co.uk
Ramey, Samuel – *IMG*
Rath, John – *Alexander*
Rathbone, Harvey – 020 8340 3693 *also fax;* 01502 578360
Reeves, Paul – 07976 694067 *fax:* 020 8679 1812 *email:* pauledwardreeves@yahoo.com
Relyea, John – *Askonas Holt*
Rice, Robert – *Chameleon*
Richardson, Mark – *Gilder*
Richardson, Stephen – *HP*
Rivers, Malcolm – *Still*
Roberts, Stephen – *IMG/CDI*
Robertson, Christopher – *Askonas Holt*
Robinson, Dean – *Harlequin*
Robson, Martin – *Sykes* – 020 8847 0888 *also fax*
Robson, Richard – *Gilder*
Rock, Philip – *Mus Int*
Rootering, Jan-Hendrik – *Ingpen*
Rose, Peter – *Askonas Holt*
Rouillon, Philippe – *Allied*
Rowlands-Pritchard, John – 01749 677903 *fax:* 01749 675131
Rowlinson, Mark – 01625 527628 *fax:* 0161 244 4231 *email:* mark.rowlinson@bbc.co.uk
Rupp, Andrew – *Still*
Russell, Christopher – 020 8940 4484
Rutherford, James – *Harlequin*
Safiulin, Anatoli – *GIA*
St John, Del – *Dyfel*
Saks, Gidon – *Harlequin*
Salminen, Matti – *Ingpen/Still*
Sandison, Gordon – *Portland*
Sarrazin, Lionel – *Stafford*
Savenko, Vassily – c/o 01684 892343 *fax:* 01684 572734 *email:* m.rolle@medtner.freeserve.co.uk
Savidge, Peter – *Musicmakers*
Scales, Anthony – *Camerata*
Scattriti, Roberto – *IMG*
Schelomianski, Michail – *IMG*
Schenk, Orlando – *KDM*
Schmidt, Andreas – *IMG*
Schöne, Wolfgang – *Ingpen*
Schulte, Eike Wilm – *Rawstron*
Schwets, Stanislaw – *Askonas Holt*
Sedov, Denis – *Allied*
Shilling, Eric – 020 8989 7093
Shimell, William – *IMG*
Shirley-Quirk, John – *Mus Int*
Shore, Andrew – *Ingpen*
Sidhom, Peter – *Allied*
Sigmundsson, Kristinn – *Rawstron*
Sigurdarson, Olafur – *Phillips*
Simonetti, Riccardo – *IMG*
Sims, Toby – c/o 01273 472548
Singer, Malcolm – 01582 727248
Skinner, Philip – *Gilder*
Slater, Andrew – 01246 566243 *also fax; email:* andrew_slater@talk21.com
Smit, Henk – *Gilder*
Smith, Craig – *Portland*
Smythe, Russell – *Still*
Snipp, Peter – *Gilder*
Stamm, Harald – *Allied*
Stephenson, David – *Portland*
Stone, Graham – *Mus Int*
Stone, Mark – *Musichall*
Strauch, Jacek – *Grant Rogers*
Strivens, Richard – 0161 881 6852 *also fax*
Struckmann, Falk – *Mus Int*
Stuart-Lloyd, Anthony – *Harlequin*
Suart, Richard – *Musichall*
Sulzenko, Jiri – *Mus Int*
Sutin, Daniel – *Gilder*
Sylvan, Sanford – *Allied*
Taliotis, Leandros – *Chameleon*
Tarasconi, Giovanni – *Still*
Tattersall, Norman – 01206 867462 *also fax*
Terfel, Bryn – *Harlequin*
Thomas, David – *Allied*
Thomas, Gwion – *KDM*
Thorpe, Simon – *OWM*
Todorovic, Nicholas – *Craig*
Tómasson, Tómas – *Still*
Tomlinson, John – *Mus Int*
Tovey, Julian – *CDI/Mus Int*
Tranter, John – *Mus Int*
Trew, Graham – 020 7275 8260 *also fax; email:* trwlew@globalnet.co.uk
Tschammer, Hans – *Allied*
Tumagian, Eduardo – *Stafford*
Tumanyan, Barseg – *Askonas Holt*
Underwood, Christopher – *CDI*
Van Allan, Richard – *Askonas Holt*
Van Ast, Jochem – *Mus Int*
Van Dam, Jose – *Askonas Holt*
Varcoe, Stephen – *Phillips*
Vassiliev, Alexandre – *Rawstron*
Veira, Jonathan – *Sykes*
Villa-Lobos, Carlos Almaguer – *Gilder*
Vincent, Chris – *Ockert*
Vinogradov, Jeremy – *KDM*
Volle, Michael – *Allied*
Waddington, Henry – *Ingpen*
Wade, Eddie – *OCA*
Washington, Daniel – *Mus Int*
Watson, Keel – *Sykes*
Watt, Alan – *Carroll*
Wegner, John – *Mus Int*
Weston, Richard – 01865 883840 *also fax*
Wheatley, Brendan – 01874 690339 *fax:* 01874 690254
Whelan, Paul – *IMG*
White, Brian – 01622 756660 *also fax; email:* drbdwhite@hotmail.com
White, Jeremy – *Musicmakers/Portland*
White, Willard – *IMG*
Whitehouse, Richard – *Mus Int*
Wickens, Nigel – 01223 248812
Wickham, Henry – 020 8788 0158 *fax:* 020 8780 9838
Wiegold, Richard – 029 2062 0469 *also fax;* 07768 233369 *email:* wiegold@compuserve.com
Wilding, Simon – *Mus Int*
Wildman, Mark – *Sympathetic*
Williams, Cleveland – *Roy Baker*
Williams, Jeremy Huw – *SWA*
Williams, Roderick – *VWM*
Wilson-Johnson, David – *Askonas Holt*
Windmüller, Yaron – *Anglo-Swiss*
Wistreich, Richard – *Robert White*
Wlaschiha, Ekkehard – *Allied*
Woodall, Richard – *Grant Rogers*
Zancanaro, Giorgio – *Stafford*
Zethner-Møller, Jacob – *KDM*

Opera Producers

Addresses and telephone numbers of agents listed below will be found under **Agents and Managers**.

Abulafia, John – *Craig*
Albery, Tim – *Cruickshank*
Alden, David – *IMG*
Anderson, Gordon – *Cruickshank*
Ashman, Mike – *Still*
Bailey, Lucy – c/o 020 7287 4550 *fax:* 020 7287 9128
Bedford, Peter Lehmann – 020 8361 9648
Bertman, Dmitry – *Gilder*
Brown, Kate – 020 8674 3069 *also fax; email:* amfiparnaso@cockaigne.demon.co.uk
Burden, Michael – 01865 279526 *fax:* 01865 279590 *email:* michael.burden@new.ox.ac.uk
Burge, Stuart – *Cruickshank*
Caddy, Ian – *POEM*
Caird, John – 020 8348 1996 *fax:* 020 8340 5030
Cairns, Tom – *Cruickshank*
Callow, Simon – *Cruickshank*
Carsen, Robert – *IMG*
Chevara, Robert – *PA*
Cocker, Jonathan – 020 7249 0887 *also fax; email:* jonathan.cocker@virgin.net
Coleman, Tim – *Still*
Collins, Aletta – *Cruickshank*
Conway, James – *PA*
Cox, John – *Askonas Holt*
Dane, John – *Scrimgeour*
de Mallet Burgess, Thomas – c/o 020 8670 8968 *also fax*
Decker, Willy – *Rawstron*
Dew, John – *Still*
Dooner, Daniel – 01273 476700
Douglas, Nigel – *Mus Int*
Duncan, Martin – *Askonas Holt*
Edwards, David – 020 7625 8903 *also fax; email:* DEDWARDSVERBATIM @compuserve.com
Fettes, Christopher – *Cruickshank*
Fielding, David – *Cruickshank*
Freeman, David – *Allied*
Fuchs, Olivia – 020 7732 1900 *fax:* 020 7564 8286 *email:* olivia.fuchs@lineone.net – *Musichall*
Gibson, Jane – *Allied*
Gilbert, Terry – *Scrimgeour*
Godefroid, Philippe – *Gilder*
Graham, Colin – c/o 020 7727 0601
Hands, Terry – *Allied*
Hausman, Leah – *PA*
Havergal, Giles – c/o 0141 429 5561 *fax:* 0141 429 7374 *email:* boxoffice@citz.co.uk
Hawkes, Tom – *OCA*
Heyland, Michael – c/o 020 8789 0776 *fax:* 020 8789 1192
Himmelmann, Philipp – *Gilder*
Hollander, Julia – *Ingpen*
Homoki, Andreas – *Rawstron*
Hytner, Nicholas – *Askonas Holt*
Ibelhauptaite, Dalia – *Cruickshank*
Jacobs, Sally – *PA*
Judd, Wilfred – c/o 020 8894 2277 *fax:* 020 8894 7952
Judge, Ian – c/o 020 7434 9167 *fax:* 020 7494 2887
Koskinas, Spyros – *Still*
Kraus, Mary Anne – *PA*
Kuningas, Neeme – *Gilder*
Kupfer, Harry – *Allied*
Lang, Aidan – *Musichall*
Lawless, Stephen – *Askonas Holt*
Lazaridis, Stefanos – *Still*
Lloyd, Matthew – *Cruickshank*
Lloyd, Phyllida – c/o 020 7734 0626 *fax:* 020 7434 2346
Lloyd Davies, John – *Still*
Lowery, Nigel – *Cruickshank*
MacDonald, James – *Cruickshank*
McVicar, David – *PA*
Mason, Patrick – c/o 020 7287 5131 *fax:* 020 7287 5161
Medcalf, Stephen – 01737 764115 *fax:* 01737 771337 – *Still*
Meitlis, Rebecca – 01273 477990 *email:* meitlis@ndirect.co.uk
Melbye, Mikael – *Askonas Holt*
Miller, Jonathan – *IMG*
Molnár, Nicolette – *PA*
Moore, Jonathan – *Ingpen*
Mound, Vernon – *Gilder*
Mumford, Peter – *Cruickshank*
Negrin, Francisco – *IMG*
Nunn, Trevor – 020 7452 3333 *fax:* 020 7452 3350
Parr, Philip – 020 8555 2154 *also fax; email:* regisseur@hotmail.com
Pascoe, John – *Still*
Pimlott, Steven – *Cruickshank*
Pountney, David – *IMG*
Prowse, Philip – *Cruickshank*
Ramsay, Alasdair – 01256 323073 *fax:* 01256 357130 *email:* dreampark@compuserve.com
Richardson, Matthew – *Cruickshank*
Ritch, David – c/o 020 8741 3794; 020 7836 0111 *fax:* 020 7240 4629
Robinson, James – *Gilder*
Schaaf, Johannes – *IMG*
Sharman, Caroline – 0116 278 8326 *also fax; email:* caro@mmtt.co.uk
Sinclair, Andrew – *Gilder*
Smith, Tom – 020 7482 1351 – *PA*
Spink, Ian – *Cruickshank*
Stripf, Markus – 020 8444 1410
Sulkin, David – 020 7434 0406 *fax:* 020 7439 1237 *email:* sulkin@compuserve.com
Sutcliffe, Jeremy – c/o 020 7240 1200 *fax:* 020 7212 9549 – *PA*
Sutherland, Malcolm – *Cruickshank*
Tambosi, Olivier – *IMG*
Tebbutt, Robin – c/o 029 2046 4666
Tinkler, Mark – 020 7635 8905 *fax:* 020 7635 9331
Trevis, Di – *Allied*
Venables, Clare – *Cruickshank*
Vick, Graham – *Ingpen*
von Nuding, John – 01622 747762 *fax:* 01622 745276 *email:* figaro@globalnet.co.uk
Warner, Deborah – *Askonas Holt*
Warner, Keith – *Still*
Watson, Peter – 020 8985 7712 *also fax*
Wright, Rennie – *Askonas Holt*

DAVID ARDITTI

Composer of beautiful music in the true classical tradition for the 20th and 21st centuries

CHORAL
SONGS
FILM
CHAMBER
ORCHESTRAL

Publishers: Oriana Publications
Musica21 (Florida)
Menelik Music

WWW.DARDITTI.COM

Symphony No.1 (1957)
Recorded by MUNICH SYMPHONY ORCHESTRA
(Douglas Bostock)
(The British Symphonic Collection)
Classico Records (Denmark) – CLASSCD 274

Symphony No.2 (1965)
(Sibelius/Nielsen centenary)

Symphony No.3 (1979)
("Sinfonia Borealis")

Symphony No.4 (1986)

– Music of the English tradition –

Orchestral and chamber music; wind band, brass band, vocal and educational music
Peters Edition, Comus Edition,
Boosey & Hawkes – and other publishers

"Pohjola", Embsay, Skipton, BD 23 6PE
North Yorkshire
01756 792968
http://www.edu.coventry.ac.uk/mus/buttera/

from **Longship**
MUSIC BY
JOHN HEARNE

❖❖❖

"LÆTATUS SUM" for soloists (SATB)
and chorus SSSAAATTTBBB
(featured in 1999 Eton Choral Course)

❖

QUINTET for Alto Saxophone
and String Quartet

❖

SOLEMN AND STRANGE MUSIC
Piano Duet
(Winner of 1998 Gregynog Composers' Award of Wales)

❖

"LJÓS" (Light) *(Isaiah 60:1)* for 16 voices
(Commissioned by Michael Brewer for Laudibus)

❖

"ENDURSPEGLA" (Reflection)
for solo instrument (treble) and piano

❖❖❖

Longship music
"Smiðskot", Fawells,
Keith-hall, INVERURIE
AB51 0LN Tel/fax: 01651 88 22 74
http://www.impulse-music.co.uk/hearne.htm

Jonathan Rutherford

composer & pianist

Recent commissions include:
'Gospelsong' for brass quintet (1998)
'Three Advent Carols' for choir & organ (1998)
Oboe Quartet (1999)
&
'An Intake of Breath' for musical saw, violin & soprano (1999)
which has been described as inspirational & is to be
recorded for CD

His solo piano recital, which opened the 1999 Queille festival & included Schumann's Carnaval, "set a tone & quality which moved us all & pervaded the entire atmosphere thereafter".

Woodlands, Sandy Lane, Iken,
Woodbridge, Suffolk IP12 2EU
Tel/Fax: 01728 688484
e-mail: jonruth@argonet.co.uk

Composers

Most of the composers listed belong to the **British Academy of Composers and Songwriters** (*see* **Associations**). This incorporates the Composers' Guild of Great Britain, the Association of Professional Composers and the British Academy of Songwriters, Composers and Authors. Composers living overseas are not included unless they belong to this organisation. Each composer's contact address is followed by a listing of his/her music publisher(s) in alphabetical order. Contact information for these publishers may be found under **Music Publishers** and **Subsidiary Music Publishers**. Those not listed may be contacted through the **Music Publishers Association,** 3rd Floor, Strandgate, 18-20 York Buildings, London WC2N 6JU *tel:* 020 7839 7779 *email:* mpa@musicpublishers.co.uk.

Publishers' Abbreviations

AA	Anglo-American (USA)	Free	H Freeman & Co	Ric	Ricordi & Co (London) Ltd
AAK	Alfred A Kalmus	Gal	Galliard Ltd	Rob	Roberton Publications St
ABd	Associated Board of the Royal Schools of Music	GS	Schirmer (G) Ltd	RSCM	Royal School of Church Music
B	Bosworth & Co Ltd	Hin	Hinrichsen Edition Ltd	SB	Stainer & Bell Ltd
Belwin	Belwin-Mills Ltd	IMC	International Music Co	SMIC	Scottish Music Information Centre
BH	Boosey & Hawkes Ltd	IMP	International Music Publications	Sph	Sphemusations
Breit	Breitkopf	JW	Joseph Williams Ltd	TP	Thames Publishing
Ches	Chester Music	KM	Kevin Mayhew Ltd	UE	Universal Edition
CUP	Cambridge University Press	Leng	Alfred Lengnick & Co Ltd	UMP	United Music Publishers Ltd
Elk	Elkin & Co Ltd (see Novello & Co Ltd)	ME	Mozart Edition (Great Britain) Ltd	Wein	Josef Weinberger Ltd
Eul	Ernst Eulenberg Ltd	Mod Ed	Modern Edition	Wolfe	de Wolfe Ltd
F-E	Fraser-Enoch Publications	Nov	Novello & Co Ltd	WC	Warner Chappell
Feld	Feldman & Co Ltd	NWM	New Wind Music Co	WR	Wright & Round Ltd
For	Forsyth Brothers Ltd	Oec	Oecumuse		
		OUP	Oxford University Press		
		PP	Paterson's Publications Ltd		

Aaron, Bernard. 8 Townfield Gardens, Altrincham, Cheshire WA14 4DT *tel:* 0161 941 1138. *Playwrights Press (Canada), Tayborn Publishing, Waterloo Music (Canada). Classical gui, songs, children's theatre scores.*

Adams, John. c/o Boosey & Hawkes Music Publishers Ltd, 295 Regent St, London W1R 8JH *tel:* 020 7580 2060 *fax:* 020 7637 3490 *email:* composers@boosey.com. *Opera, chmbr, orch, vocal and ens.*

Adès, Thomas. c/o Faber Music Ltd, 3 Queen Square, London WC1N 3AU *tel:* 020 7833 7911/2 *fax:* 020 7833 7939 *email:* promotion @fabermusic.co.uk. *Faber. Inst, orch, chmbr, vocal, opera.*

Aho, Kalevi. c/o Boosey & Hawkes Music Publishers Ltd, 295 Regent St, London W1R 8JH *tel:* 020 7580 2060 *fax:* 020 7637 3490 *email:* composers@boosey.com. *Opera, orch, concertos, chmbr.*

Alberga, Eleanor. 166 Bethnal Green Rd, London E2 6DL *tel:* 020 7729 8362 *also fax. Chmbr mus, choral and orch works, film scores.*

Alexander, Christian. 26 New Rd, Kingham, Oxon OX7 6YP *tel:* 01608 659558 *email:* c.alexander@clara.net. *Leng. Concert mus.*

Allbright, Terence. Greyhound, Petworth, W Sussex GU28 9ND *tel:* 01428 707658 *also fax.*

Alvarez, Geoffrey. 5 Rensburg Rd, Walthamstow, London E17 7HL *tel:* 020 3521 7642. *Symphony, opera, chmbr.*

Alvarez, Javier. 26 Wolseley Rd, London N22 4TW *tel:* 020 8352 3282 *email:* j.alvarez@herts.ac.uk. *Faber. Chmbr, orch, film, electro-acoustic.*

Amos, Keith. c/o CMA Publications, 10 Avenue Rd, Kingston, Surrey KT1 2RB *tel:* 020 8541 0857 *fax:* 020 8974 8120 *email:* cmagrp@dircon.co.uk. *CMA. Orch, chmbr mus, wind, br band, choral.*

Anderson, Avril. 28 Cavendish Ave, London N3 3QN *tel:* 020 8349 2317 *fax:* 020 8346 8257. *Andresier, OUP, ABd. Orch, inst, vocal, mus for dance, educ mus.*

Anderson, Julian. c/o Faber Music Ltd, 3 Queen Square, London WC1N 3AU *tel.* 020 7833 7911/2 *fax:* 020 7833 7939 *email:* promotion@ fabermusic.co.uk. *Faber. Inst, orch, chmbr, vocal.*

Andrews, Mark. c/o Penelope Manuel, 11 Beldham Rd, Farnham, Surrey GU9 8TW *tel:* 01252 724131. *BH, Fand. Inst, orch, choral, ens, chmbr, children s.*

Andriessen, Louis. c/o Boosey & Hawkes Music Publishers Ltd, 295 Regent St, London W1R 8JH *tel:* 020 7580 2060 *fax:* 020 7637 3490 *email:* composers@boosey.com. *Opera, works for large ens, theatre, jazz singers and ens, chmbr.*

Anstey, Marjolijn. Belvedere, Seymer Rd, Swanage, Dorset BH19 2AL *tel:* 01929 422908. *Leng. Chmbr mus, oratorio, vocal, opera.*

ApIvor, Denis. 9 Ashurst Ave, Saltdean, E Sussex BN2 8DR *tel:* 01273 301587. *Bèrben (Milan), Doorns (USA), For, Hans Pero (Vienna), Musical New Services (Bimport), OUP, Schott, Sikesdi (Canada), Warwick. Ballet, opera, inst, symphonic and songs, gui.*

Archer, Malcolm. 15 Vicars Close, Wells, Somerset BA5 2UJ *tel:* 01749 674483 *fax:* 01749 677360. *Hinshaw (USA), KM, OUP. Choral, org, educ and musicals.*

Arditti, David. Menelik Music, 16 Menelik Rd, London NW2 3RP *tel:* 020 7431 2964 *also fax; email:* darditti@darditti.com. *Oriana, Musica21 Publishing, Menelik Music (sp). Songs, chmbr, orch, choral, film mus.*

Arenstein, Colin. 78 Ridge Rd, London N8 9NR *tel:* 020 8348 3630.

Argento, Dominick. c/o Boosey & Hawkes Music Publishers Ltd, 295 Regent St, London W1R 8JH *tel:* 020 7580 2060 *fax:* 020 7637 3490 *email:* composers@boosey.com. *Opera, voice and orch, chorus and orch.*

* **Arnell, Richard.** Benhall Lodge, Benhall, Saxmundham, Suffolk IP17 1JD *tel:* 01728 602014 *fax:* 01728 603256. *Broadbent and Dunn, Leng, Peer-Southern (USA), Peters, Schott. Symphonic and chmbr works, opera, ballet mus, film and TV, electro-acoustic, mus theatre.*

* **Arnold CBE, Sir Malcolm.** 26 Springfields, Attleborough, Norfolk NR17 2PA *tel:* 01953 455420 *also fax. EMI, Faber, Leng, Molenaar, Nov, Rob, Studio. Symphony, wind band, military band, br band, ens, opera, ballet, orch and chmbr works, film and TV scores. Composer's representative:* Diana Hirst (*tel:* 020 8299 1914).

Arundel Timms, T. 10 Moreton Park Rd, Bideford, N Devon EX39 3AU *tel:* 01237 473887. *EMI, Rob. Vocal, orch, choral, solo inst.*

Ascough, Richard. 118 Summer Rd, Thames Ditton, Surrey *tel:* 020 8398 7863 *email:* richardascough@hotmail.com. *EMC, Frontier.*

Aston, Peter. 9 Bourne Close, Long Stratton, Norwich NR15 2RW *tel:* 01508 530644. *AA, Asch, Banks, Chappell, CUP, Hinshaw, Nov, OUP, Pavane, RSCM, SB, WC. Choral, orch, chmbr, church mus, opera.*

Aubrey-Drew, Helen. Hafod, Llanbedr DC, Ruthin, Clwyd LL15 1YG *tel:* 01824 704582 *also fax; email:* helemuse@aol.com. *PP, Kerygma. Opera, orch, org, choral, church.*

* **Aviss, Peter R F.** 77 St Nicholas Rd, Littlestone, New Romney, Kent TN28 8QA *tel:* 01797 361490 *email:* peter@aviss.freeserve.co.uk. *Shaftesbury Edition (sp). Orch, choral, chmbr, educ.*

Ayres, Paul. Flat 4, 2 Albany Rd, Ealing, London W13 8PG *tel:* 020 8998 2294 *also fax; email:* paulayres@clara.net. *Gordon Thompson Music (WC). Choral, vocal, mus for theatre, inst.*

Bachmann, Robert. Orbitex Ltd, 4 Mona Terrace, Finch Rd, Douglas, Isle of Man IM1 3NA *tel:* 01624 624822 *fax:* 01624 624243 *email:* rcb@orbitex.ch.

Back, Peter. 5 St Martin's House, Lewes Rd, Ringmer, E Sussex BN8 5QB *tel:* 01273 812159. *PP, A & C Black. Musicals.*

* **Bailey, Judith.** 1 Stable Flat, Uppark, South Harting, Petersfield GU31 5QR *tel:* 01730 825638. *Composers Library, Da Capo, Goodmusic, Modus, Samuel King, Sarnia Music, Mayhew. Orch, chmbr, inst, br band, vocal, wind band.*

Bailey, Keith McDonald. 194a Straight Rd, Harold Hill, Romford, Essex RM3 8XR *tel:* 01708 371936. *WC, Music Sales Ltd. Pno, vocal.*

Bainbridge, Simon. c/o Novello & Co Ltd, 8-9 Frith St, London W1V 5TZ *tel:* 020 7434 0066 *fax:* 020 7287 6329 *email:* music@musicsales.co.uk. *Nov, UMP. Contemporary classical mus.*

* **Baird, John.** 121 St James's Drive, Wandsworth Common, London SW17 7RP *tel:* 020 8672 0423 *also fax. Camden. Choral mus, operas, orch mus.*

Baker, Lance. 2 Cavendish Rd, Woking, Surrey GU22 0EP *tel:* 01483 715474. *(sp). Wind mus (composer and arranger).*

Ball, Christopher. 122 Wigmore St, London W1H 9FE *tel:* 020 7935 1270. *Belwin, Columbia Pictures, E & S Mus, Nova, Peacock Press. Chmbr, concertos for wind, orch, symphony, ballet.*

Ball, Timothy. 12a Sudlow Rd, London SW18 1HP *tel:* 020 8871 0317 *fax:* 020 8488 4695 *email:* timball@sudlow.demon.co.uk. *SB, (sp). Choral, church, songs, mus theatre.*

Bamford, Adrian. 4 Bells End Rd, Walton-on-Trent, Swadlincote, Derbys DE12 8ND *tel:* 01283 712942 *email:* adrian.bamford@onet.co.uk. *ACB Notation (sp). Chmbr, choral, solo, orch, vocal.*

Bannan, Nicholas. 21 Reading Rd, Woodley, Berks RG5 3DA *tel:* 01189 696035 *fax:* 01189 352080 *email:* n.j.c.bannan@reading.ac.uk. *Choral, ens, educ.*

Barber, Charlie. 62 Arran St, Roath, Cardiff CF24 3HT *tel:* 029 2049 7157 *also fax; email:* sound.affairs@tesco.net. *(sp). Concert, mus theatre, dance, film.*

Barbour, Freeland. 44 Beauchamp Rd, Edinburgh EH16 6LU *tel:* 0131 666 1024 *also fax;* 07775 504123. *Traditional and folk mus, educ, film and TV, theatre.*

Barker, Paul. Flat 3, 33 Hopton Rd, London SW16 2EH *tel:* 020 8677 9880/3224 *email:* paul@mmtt.co.uk. *(Sp). Opera, vocal, orch, inst mus, dance, theatre mus. Educ projects.*

Barnard, Keith. 34 Longberrys, Cricklewood Lane, London NW2 2TE *tel:* 07970 971513. *Chmbr, orch, pno, vc concerto, vocal, chmbr opera, choral.*

* **Barnes, Derek.** 56 Further Green Rd, Catford, London SE6 1JH *tel:* 020 8698 8480 *fax:* 020 8698 1673 *email:* derekbarnes@coryphaeus.demon.co.uk. *Agent: London Management. BH, (sp). Mus theatre, br band, reduced orchestrations for opera and mus theatre, incidental mus for the theatre.*

Barratt, Jack. Blackthorn Lodge, The Common, Happisburgh, Norwich, Norfolk NR12 0RT *tel:* 01692 583002. *Cadenza. Inst, choral, ens, oratorio, mus theatre, br band.*

* **Barrell, Bernard.** 62 Hotson Rd, Southwold, Suffolk IP18 6BP *tel:* 01502 722269. *Anglian, Brunton, F-E, Goodmusic, MSM, Nov, Oec, Piper, Ric, Rob, SB, R Schauer, Sph, UE, Wise Owl. Contemporary, schools, adult, church.*

Barrett, Richard. c/o United Music Publishers Ltd, 42 Rivington St, London EC2A 3BN *tel:* 020 7729 4700 *fax:* 020 7739 6549 *email:* ump@compuserve.com. *UMP. Inst, chmbr, vocal, orch, electronic, mus theatre.*

* **Barron, Christine.** 27 Madeira Croft, Coventry, Warwicks CV5 8NX *tel:* 024 7667 9827 *also fax; email:* angbaron@dircon.co.uk. *BH, Carlin, EMI, Standard Music Ltd, WC. Library mus, film, TV and radio scores, advertisements, theatre, orch, electro-acoustic, educ mus.*

Barry, Gerald. c/o Oxford University Press, Repertoire Promotion, 70 Baker St, London W1M 1DJ *tel:* 020 7616 5900 *fax:* 020 7616 5901 *email:* repertoire.promotion@oup.co.uk. *OUP. Opera, pno, chmbr mus.*

Bartlett, John. c/o Great Stave Publications, Sycamore Lodge, Lower Peryers, E Horsley, Surrey KT24 6SD *tel:* 01483 284207. *(Sp). Vocal, choral, chmbr, orch, org, inst, pno.*

Bate, Jennifer. 35 Collingwood Ave, Muswell Hill, London N10 3EH *tel:* 020 8883 3811 *fax:* 020 8444 3695 *email:* jenniferbate@classical-artists.com. *Banks, Nov. Solo inst (org).*

Bauld, Alison. 6 Dungarvan Ave, London SW15 5QU *tel:* 020 8876 3008. *Nov. Opera, chmbr, vocal, radio, theatre.*

* **Bayford, Frank.** 21 Canonbury Rd, Enfield, Middx EN1 3LW *tel:* 020 8363 2663. *Modus, Mayola. Concert works, pno, cl, w/wind, chmbr mus, vocal, str orch, etc.*

* **Bayliss, Colin.** c/o Da Capo Music Ltd, 26 Stanway Rd, Whitefield, Manchester M45 8EG *tel:* 0161 766 5950. *Da Capo, Fentone. Chmbr, orch, insts, pno.*

Beat, Janet. c/o Scottish Music Information Centre, 1 Bowmont Gardens, Glasgow G12 9LR *tel:* 0141 334 6393 *email:* jbeat@music.gla.ac.uk. *Ches, Faber, Furore Verlag, Nov. Classical electro-acoustic and chmbr mus.*

Beaumont, Adrian. 73 Kings Drive, Bishopston, Bristol BS7 8JQ *tel:* 0117 924 8456. *Vanderbeek. Choral, orch, chmbr.*

* **Bedford, David.** 12 Oakwood Rd, Henleaze, Bristol BS9 4NR *tel:* 0117 962 4202 *also fax; email:* dvbmus@aol.com. *Camden, G & M Brand, Nov, UE, (sp). Concert mus, film and TV.*

Beechey, Gwilym. 15 Hamlyn Ave, Hull HU4 6BT *tel:* 01482 508910. *Augsburg, Concordia, Oec, SB. Church, org mus.*

Beeson, Jack. c/o Boosey & Hawkes Music Publishers Ltd, 295 Regent St, London W1R 8JH *tel:* 020 7580 2060 *fax:* 020 7637 3490 *email:* composers@boosey.com. *Opera, orch, choral, pno.*

Benjamin, George. c/o Faber Music Ltd, 3 Queen Square, London WC1N 3AU *tel:* 020 7833 7911/2 *fax:* 020 7833 7939 *email:* promotion@fabermusic.co.uk. *Faber. Inst, orch, chmbr, vocal mus.*

Bennett, Richard Rodney. c/o Novello & Co Ltd, 8-9 Frith St, London W1V 5TZ *tel:* 020 7434 0066 *fax:* 020 7287 6329 *email:* music@musicsales.co.uk. *Nov. Concert works, film and TV.*

Bergman, Erik. c/o Boosey & Hawkes Music Publishers Ltd, 295 Regent St, London W1R 8JH *tel:* 020 7580 2060 *fax:* 020 7637 3490 *email:* composers@boosey.com. *Orch, voices and orch, choral.*

Berio, Luciano. c/o Universal Edition (London) Ltd, 48 Gt Marlborough St, London W1V 2BN *tel:* 020 7437 6880 *fax:* 020 7437 6115 *email:* miranda@ue-london.demon.co.uk. *UE.*

Berkeley, Michael. c/o Oxford University Press, Repertoire Promotion, 70 Baker St, London W1M 1DJ *tel:* 020 7616 5900 *fax:* 020 7616 5901 *email:* repertoire.promotion@oup.co.uk. *OUP. Orch, chmbr, choral, opera.*

Best, Christopher. Pump Cottage, 1 Old Hazard, Higher Plymouth Rd, nr Totnes, Devon TQ9 7LN *tel:* 01803 868582. *Inst, orch, chmbr, contemporary dance mus, mus theatre, electro-acoustic mus.*

* **Betro, Denis.** Houseboat Alma, Scotland Bridge Lock, Weybridge, Surrey KT15 3HL *tel:* 01932 350575. *Orch, film and TV scores, concertos, symphonies.*

Bettison, Oscar. 3 Grove House, 66 British Grove, London W4 2NL *tel:* 020 8741 0392 *also fax; email:* oscar@obettison.screaming.net. *Orch, chmbr, vocal, arrangements.*

Bevan, Clifford. 10 Clifton Terrace, Winchester, Hants SO22 5BJ *tel:* 01962 864755 *also fax;* 020 7724 3250. *BC, Carlin, Columbia, Feld, Piccolo. Chmbr mus, pno, vocal, band and choral.*

Biberian, Gilbert. 49 Copt Elm Rd, Charlton Kings, Cheltenham, Glos GL53 8AG *tel:* 01242 581457 *also fax; email:* gbiberian@aol.com. *Belwin, Bèrben, Ches, Cramer, Editions Orphée, Nouran Enterprises (sp), Nov, Rob, Van Poppel.*

* **Bicât, Nick.** c/o London Management (Marc Berlin), 2-4 Noel St, London W1V 3RB *tel:* 020 7287 9000 *fax:* 020 7287 3236 *email:* info@nickbicat.com. *Film scores, songs, opera, choral and orch mus, mus theatre.*

* **Biggin, Tony.** 63 Leyland Rd, Southport, Merseyside PR9 9JA *tel:* 01704 535740 *fax:* 01704 500957 *email:* biggint@mail.cybase.co.uk. *SB. Film and TV scores, choral, orch.*

Bingham, Judith. c/o Maecenas Music Ltd, 5 Bushey Close, Old Barn Lane, Kenley, Surrey CR8 5AU *tel:* 020 8660 4766 *fax:* 020 8668 5273. *Maecenas, Nov. Orch, choral, chmbr, vocal, inst.*

Birney, Anthony. 17 The Drive, Gosforth, Newcastle upon Tyne NE3 4AH *tel:* 0191 285 2120. *Oratorios, opera, musicals.*

Biro, Daniel. 6 Maryland Walk, Popham St, London N1 8QZ *tel:* 020 7359 7825 *also fax; email:* daniel@sargasso.com. *Acoustic and electronic chmbr mus; dance, film, theatre, vocal, inst.*

* **Birtwistle, Harrison.** c/o Allied Artists Agency, 42 Montpelier Square, London SW7 1JZ *tel:* 020 7589 6243 *fax:* 020 7581 5269. *BH, UE. Opera, orch, concertos, ens, chmbr.*

* **Black OBE, Stanley.** 43 Viceroy Court, Prince Albert Rd, London NW8 7PR *tel:* 020 7586 5958 *fax:* 020 7586 3524. *Film scores.*

* **Blackford, Richard.** c/o London Management, Noel House, 2-4 Noel St, London W1V 3RB *tel:* 020 7287 9000 *fax:* 020 7287 3236 *email:* richard@blackford.co.uk. *London Music Ltd. Film, TV, opera, theatre, concert.*

Blake, David. Mill Gill, Askrigg, Leyburn, N Yorks DL8 3HR *tel:* 01969 650364. *Nov, OUP, Schott, University of York. Opera, orch, choral, solo cantata, chmbr, young people's mus, etc.*

* **Blake OBE, Howard.** Studio 6, 18 Kensington Court Place, London W8 5BJ *tel:* 020 7937 1966 *fax:* 020 7938 1969 *email:* tax@hogbens.co.uk (attn Richard Wadhams, business mgr). *Britannia, Chappell, Ches, EMI, Faber, Highbridge, Leng, Mercury, OUP, Paramount, Rank, Studio Music, Warner, Wein. Concert mus, orch concerto, choral, inst, film and TV scores, opera, ballet, theatre.*

Blake, Michael. c/o Bardic Edition, 6 Fairfax Cres, Aylesbury, Bucks HP20 2ES *tel:* 01296 428609 *also fax. Bardic. Chmbr, inst, choral, orch.*

* **Blunt, Marcus.** Craigs Cottage, Lochmaben, Lockerbie, DG11 1RW *tel:* 01387 811949. *Emerson, Modus.*

* **Blyton, Carey.** Howans, Pytches Rd, Woodbridge, Suffolk IP12 1EY *tel:* 01394 383468 *fax:* 01394 385834. *ABC Book Publishing, AV Music, Bardic, Belwin, Bèrben, BH, Ches, Fand, Fox, F-E, GS, HaMaR, IMP, Maurer, Modus, Nov, NWM, Oec, OUP, Rob, UE, Wein. Film and TV scores, opera, songs, chmbr, schools mus, orch, insts.*

Bonsor, Brian. 37 Weensland Rd, Hawick, Roxburghshire TD9 9NW *tel:* 01450 372643. *Faber, IMP, Rob, Schott, UE, (sp). Rcdr, educ mus.*

* **Bourgeois, Derek.** 43 Bute Gardens, London W6 7DR *tel:* 020 8748 6027 *also fax; email:* dbourgeois@tramuntana.demon.co.uk; Derek.Bourgeois @spgs.org. *Brass Wind, Ches, Fentone, G & M Brand Publications, Hafabra Music, Obrasso, Marc Reift, Rose Hill, R Smith, Samuel French, Vanderbeek, Warwick, WR, Yorke. Symphonies, orch, concertos, br, wind band, choral, chmbr, org; film, TV and stage scores, opera.*

Bousted, Donald. Camberley, 75 Canbury Ave, Kingston, Surrey KT2 6JR *tel:* 020 8546 1424 *email:* donaldbousted@compuserve.com. *Composer Press Recorder Series Dist, Recorder Music Mail. Moeck Concert mus, mus for stage and TV, rcdr.*

* **Bower, Neville.** 1 Freeford Gardens, Lichfield, Staffs WS14 9RJ *tel:* 01543 256930. *BH, Frontier, (sp). Orch, chmbr mus, educ mus, choral, org, pno, solo song-cycles.*

* **Boyle, Rory.** Firs Cottage, College Grove, Malvern, Worcs WR14 3HP *tel:* 01684 573710 *also fax. ABd, BH, Ches. Orch, chmbr, choral, TV mus.*

Brandon, Patrick C. 53 Broad St, Ely, Cambs CB7 4BD *tel:* 01353 664253. *Ric. Chmbr, songs, orch and educ mus.*

* **Broughton, Julian.** Eridge Cottage, Tower Ride, Uckfield, E Sussex TN22 1SD *tel:* 01825 765416. *Choral, orch, pno and chmbr.*

* **Brown, Christopher.** 6 Station Rd, Catworth, Huntingdon, Cambs PE18 0PE *tel.* 01832 710227 *also fax; email:* chris@musography.freeserve.co.uk. *AA, ABd, Ches, Forsyth, Musography, OUP, Rob. Choral mus, opera, orch and chmbr.*

Brown, James. 29 Vesper Gate Drive, Leeds LS5 3NH. *Banks, OUP. Choral, org, vocal, pno, chmbr, orch, operetta.*

* **Brown, James Francis.** 99 Frenches Rd, Redhill, Surrey RH1 2HS *tel:* 01737 768597 *also fax. Music Haven. Concert mus.*

Bruce, Stuart. 5 Brook Drive, Kinoulton, Nottingham NG12 3RA *tel:* 01949 81682 *also fax. Film and TV, concert works.*

Bryan, Paul. Five Bells, High St, Over, Cambridge CB4 5NB *tel:* 01954 231117 *email:* paul10a@hotmail.com. *Animus, Banks, Hope Publishing (USA), Jubilate Hymns, KM.*

* **Buckeridge, Corin.** Flat B, 140 Kennington Lane, London SE11 4UZ *tel:* 020 7207 6863 *email:* corin@lcbuckeridge.freeserve.co.uk. *Theatre mus.*

* **Bullard, Alan.** 11 Christ Church Court, Ireton Rd, Colchester, Essex CO3 3AU *tel:* 01206 562607 *email:* alan.bullard@colch-inst.ac.uk. *ABd, Banks, BH, Colne (sp), For, Harlequin, Nov, Nova, Oec, OUP, Presser, RSCM, Schott, UE. Concert mus, educ mus, choral mus for adults and children.*

Buller, John. c/o Oxford University Press, Repertoire Promotion, 70 Baker St, London W1M 1DJ *tel:* 020 7616 5900 *fax:* 020 7616 5901 *email:* repertoire.promotion@oup.co.uk. *OUP. Orch, chmbr, opera, mus theatre, film.*

* **Burgon, Geoffrey.** c/o Chester Music, 8-9 Frith St, London W1V 5TZ *tel:* 020 7434 0066 *fax:* 020 7287 6329 *email:* music@musicsales.co.uk. *Ches. Concert, opera, film and TV mus.*

Burn, Chris. 11 Marks Ave, Ongar, Essex CM5 9AY *tel:* 01277 362416 *also fax; email:* jbacta@msn.com. *ACTA. Contemporary mus.*

* **Burrell, Diana.** c/o United Music Publishers Ltd, 42 Rivington St, London EC2A 3BN *tel:* 020 7729 4700 *fax:* 020 7739 6549 *email:* ump@ compuserve.com. *UMP. Inst, chmbr, orch, opera, choral and vocal mus.*

Burtch, Mervyn. 5 Oakfield St, Ystrad Mynach, Hengoed, Caerphilly County Borough CF82 7AF *tel:* 01443 812100 *also fax. Ashdown, Banks, Curiad, Griffiths, Gwynn, Rob, Vanderbeek, WC, WMIC. Children's opera, choral, chmbr mus.*

* **Burton, Jonathan.** 12 Corner Green, Blackheath, London SE3 9JJ *tel:* 020 8852 7599 *also fax.*

Burton, Ken. c/o J Audrey Ellison International Artists' Management, 135 Stevenage Rd, Fulham, London SW6 6PB *tel:* 020 7381 9751 *fax:* 020 7381 2406 *email:* Audrey@Ellison.Intl.freeserve.co.uk.

Bush, Glyn. Spring Cottage, Ilsington Farm, Tincleton, Dorchester, Dorset DT2 8QW *tel:* 01305 848026 *email:* biggabush@hotmail.com. *Film and TV documentary scores, musicals, drama, jingles, signature, children's, youth radio and TV, electronic mus, sample and sound manipulation, samba.*

Butler, Martin. c/o Oxford University Press, Repertoire Promotion, 70 Baker St, London W1M 1DJ *tel:* 020 7616 5900 *fax:* 020 7616 5901 *email:* repertoire.promotion@oup.co.uk. *OUP. Orch, chmbr, opera.*

Butt, James. 12 Northfield Rd, Onehouse, Stowmarket, Suffolk IP14 3HF *tel:* 01449 613388. *BC, Belwin, BH, Cramer, EMI, OUP, SB, Sph, TP, WC. Film, TV, opera, musicals, chmbr, orch, choral, educ, mus for children.*

Butterworth MBE, Arthur. Pohjola, Dales Ave, Embsay, Skipton, N Yorks BD23 6PE *tel:* 01756 792968. *BH, Brass Wind, Ches, Comus, Feld, For, Léduc, Molenaar, Nov, Peters, Smith, Vanderbeek. Orch, symphonic, br band, chmbr mus.*

* **Butterworth, Neil.** 1 Roderick Place, West Linton, Peebleshire EH46 7ES *tel:* 01968 661112. *Ashgate, Banks, Belwin, Brunton, Cathedral, Chiltern, Fentone, Francis, Garland (US), Nova, Nov, NWM, Oec, Ric, Rob, WC. Orch, choral, insts.*

* **Byrchmore, Ruth.** Flat D, Kerry House, 67b Kelvin Rd, Highbury, London N5 2PQ *tel:* 020 7359 2931 *fax:* 020 7873 7374 *email:* r.byrchmore@ram.ac.uk. *Faber.*

* **Cannon, Philip.** 25 Ansdell St, London W8 5BN *tel:* 020 7937 6768. *Kronos (sp). Opera, symphonies, choral, chmbr.*

* **Caradon, Sulyen R.** 76 Lower Oldfield Park, Bath BA2 3HP *tel:* 01225 313531. *Da Capo, (sp), Phyloscopus, Handlo. W/wind, vocal, choral, ecological and spiritual mus.*

Carcas, Gillian. Yarne Cottage, Tower Hill, Horsham, W Sussex RH13 7JT *tel:* 01403 263591 *fax:* 01403 211014 *email:* gillrc@yahoo.com.

* **Carhart, David.** 20 Standish Rd, London W6 9AL *tel:* 020 8748 0935 *also fax. Ric. Orch, pno, chmbr, songs.*

Carpenter, Gary. 11 Gerard Rd, West Kirby, Wirral CH48 4ES *tel:* 0151 625 4151; 07976 775561 *fax:* 0151 625 4152 *email:* gary.carpenter@ btinternet.com. *BH, Camden, Donemus, Ric, Sparta Florida, Wein. Br, ens, inst, band.*

Carter, Andrew. c/o Oxford University Press, Repertoire Promotion, 70 Baker St, London W1M 1DJ *tel:* 020 7616 5900 *fax:* 020 7616 5901 *email:* repertoire.promotion@oup.co.uk. *Banks, OUP, RSCM. Choral, choral/orch, org.*

Carter, Elliott. c/o Boosey & Hawkes Music Publishers Ltd, 295 Regent St, London W1R 8JH *tel:* 020 7580 2060 *fax:* 020 7637 3490 *email:* composers@boosey.com. *Chmbr mus, orch, vocal, ens, concertos.*

* **Cary, Tristram.** 30 Fowlers Rd, Glen Osmond, SA 5064, Australia *tel:* 00 61 8 8338 1094 *also fax; fax:* www.amcoz.com.au *email:* tcary@ pa.adelaide.edu.au. *Nov, OUP, Peters, SB, The Southern Dot Factory (sp). Inst, electro-acoustic, film, theatre, TV, radio.*

Cashian, Philip. c/o New Voices, BMIC, 10 Stratford Place, London W1N 9AE *tel:* 020 7499 8567 *fax:* 020 7499 4795 *email:* newvoices @bmic.co.uk.

Cashmore, Donald. Cottage End, 27 King Alfred Way, Newton Poppleford, Sidmouth EX10 0DG *tel:* 01395 567923. *Nov, OUP. Cantatas, anthems, songs, carols.*

Casken, John. Craigside, Reservoir Rd, Whaley Bridge, High Peak, Derbys SK23 7BW *email:* john.casken@man.ac.uk. *Schott.*

Catán, Daniel. c/o Boosey & Hawkes Music Publishers Ltd, 295 Regent St, London W1R 8JH *tel:* 020 7580 2060 *fax:* 020 7637 3490 *email:* composers@boosey.com. *Opera, voice, orch.*

Chadwick, Roland. 47 Sydney Rd, Ealing, London W13 9EZ *tel:* 020 8579 4782 *email:* roland_chadwick@hotmail.com. *Orch, chmbr, gui.*

Chapple, Brian. 31 Warwick Rd, New Barnet, Herts EN5 5EQ *tel:* 020 8449 8610. *AA, ABd, B, Ches, OUP. Choral, orch, inst.*

Cheshire, John B. 3 Maes Yr Hafod, Llanfairtalhaiarn, Abergele, Clwyd LL22 8SA *tel:* 01745 720708.

Chilcott, Bob. c/o Oxford University Press, Repertoire Promotion, 70 Baker St, London W1M 1DJ *tel:* 020 7616 5900 *fax:* 020 7616 5901 *email:* repertoire.promotion@oup.co.uk. *OUP. Choral, inst.*

Chin, Unsuk. c/o Boosey & Hawkes Music Publishers Ltd, 295 Regent St, London W1R 8JH *tel:* 020 7580 2060 *fax:* 020 7637 3490 *email:* composers@boosey.com. *Orch, ens, chmbr, electronic, pno.*

Christie, Michael. Basement Flat, 16d Hampstead Hill Gardens, London NW3 2PL *tel:* 020 7435 0914 *fax:* 020 7794 3610. *Opera, mus theatre, film scores, inst mus, songs, educ mus.*

* **Churches, Richard.** 36 Riverdale Rd, Plumstead, London SE18 1NZ *tel:* 020 8473 2213; 0795 7171 391. *Andresier, Frontier. Contemporary and educ mus.*

Clark, Philip. 96a Wandsworth Bridge Rd, London SW6 2TF *tel:* 020 7731 0973 *also fax. Orch, ens, chmbr, inst, jazz.*

* **Clarke, Nigel.** 57 St Clair Drive, Worcester Park, Surrey KT4 8UG *tel:* 020 8337 8229 *email:* nigel.clarke1@virgin.net. *Brass Wind, Maecenas, Nov. Contemporary mus, studio mus.*

* **Claxton, Andrew.** Ivony, Cumnor Hill, Oxford OX2 9JA *tel:* 01865 865654 *fax:* 01865 865653. *Momentum Music, Andrew Music. TV and film scores, concertos.*

* **Clemson, Gareth.** Tillywhally Cottage, Milnathort, Kinross-shire KY13 0RN *tel:* 01577 864297 *email:* Thora.Clemsonclyne@nationwideish. net. *Tillywhally Arts (sp). Chmbr mus, pno, orch, songs.*

Cloke, Geoffrey. 88 Park Rd, Exeter EX1 2HT *tel:* 01392 490387. *Orch, chmbr, vocal, opera.*

Clucas, Humphrey. 19 Norman Rd, Sutton, Surrey *tel:* 020 8642 3233. *Animus, Kirklees, KM, Leng, Oec, OUP. Choral, org mus, inst.*

Coatman, Graham. 4 Sunny Bank, Shipley, W Yorks BD18 3RP *tel:* 01274 599379 *also fax. Opera, mus theatre, songs, orch, chmbr, choral, educ.*

* **Coe, Michael.** Merlyn Cottage, The Cross, Eyam, Derbys S32 5QH *tel:* 01433 630324. *Chandos, Hope, HRGB. Choral, orch, wind band, handbells, educ.*

Cohen, Jacques. 14b Carlton Rd, London N11 3EX *tel:* 020 8368 8956 *also fax;* 07958 312679 *email:* jacquescohen@easynet.co.uk. *Orch, mus for youth/amateur orchs, choral arrangements, opera.*

Coker, Tim. 22a High St, Stanwell Village, Middx TW19 7JS *tel:* 01784 243529 *email:* timcoker@hotmail.com. *Symphonic, chmbr, choral, theatre/dance mus.*

* **Collier, Graham.** 38 Shell Rd, London SE13 7TW *tel:* 020 8692 6250 *fax:* 020 8692 5213 *email:* graham@jazzcontinuum.com. *Film and TV scores, jazz.*

* **Collins Rice, Hugh.** c/o Alfred Lengnick & Co, 27 Grove Rd, Beaconsfield, Bucks HP9 1UR *tel:* 01494 681216 *fax:* 01494 670443 *email:* gbmuswill@aol.com. *Orch, chmbr, vocal.*

Cook, Douglas. Ding Dong Cottage, Boskednan, Newmill, Penzance, Cornwall TR20 8XX *tel:* 01736 363677 *fax:* 01736 366925 *email:* douglascook@globalnet.co.uk. *Schott. Pno, fl, br quintet, vc, jazz pieces, film scores, TV, orch.*

Cooke, Mervyn. Music Dept, University of Nottingham, Nottingham NG7 2RD *tel:* 0115 951 4762 *fax:* 0115 951 4756 *email:* mervyn.cooke @nottingham.ac.uk.

* **Coombes, Douglas.** 23 Hitchin St, Biggleswade, Beds SG18 8AX *tel:* 01767 316521 *fax:* 01767 317221 *email:* coombes @lindsaymusic.co.uk. *BBC, Brass Wind, EMI, Early Learning, Lindsay, Music Sales, OUP, Rob. Orch, opera, musicals, choral, educ, vocal, ens.*

Cooney, John. 86 Bromfelde Rd, London SW4 6PR *tel:* 020 7498 2643 *also fax. Orch, ens, ballet, educ.*

Cooper, David. 12 Cornmill Cres, Norristhorpe, Liversedge, W Yorks WF15 7DU *tel:* 01924 409051 *fax:* 01132 332583 *email:* d.g.cooper@leeds.ac.uk. *Samuel King, (sp). Inst, vocal, electronic, film.*

Copley, Peter. 93 Goldstone Rd, Hove, E Sussex BN3 3RG *tel:* 01273 208851. *Ric, TP. Orch, choral, pno solo, gui, chmbr, film.*

Corp, Ronald. 41 Aberdare Gardens, London NW6 3AL *tel:* 020 7625 4641 *fax:* 020 7625 4876 *email:* reynaldo@angkor.demon.co.uk. *Nov, OUP, SB. Choral and orch.*

* **Cowdell, Alexander.** 8 Blendon Terrace, Plumstead Common, London SE18 7RR *tel:* 020 8854 5167. *Frontier. Pno, vocal, ens, orch.*

Cowdrey, Peter. 1 South St, Middle Barton, Oxon OX7 7BU *tel:* 01869 340951; 0771 281 5338 *fax:* 01869 349084 *email:* orbestra@excite.com.

Cowdrey, Peter. 1 South St, Middle Barton, Oxon OX7 7BU *tel:* 01869 340951; 0771 281 5338 *fax:* 01869 349084 *email:* orbestra@excite.com.

Cowie, Edward. c/o Dartington College of Arts, Totnes, Devon TQ9 6EJ *tel:* 01364 643028 *also fax; email:* e.cowie@dartington.ac.uk. *Ches, Schott. Multimedia, orch, opera, ballet, chmbr mus.*

Cowles, Colin E. Keens Barn Cottage, Keens Lane, Othery, Bridgwater, Somerset TA7 0PU *tel:* 01823 698162. *BH, Cascade, Ches, Chiltern, Cottage Harmony, Fentone, Griffiths, Headline, PP, Polyphonic, Ric, Spartan, Studio. Orch, choral and chmbr mus.*

Coxon, Christopher. 18 St Julian's Rd, St Alban's, Herts AL1 2AZ.

Crane, Laurence. Flat 4, 17 Harecourt Rd, London N1 2LW *tel:* 020 7704 6541 *fax:* 020 7688 0839.

* **Crawford, Robert.** 12 Inverleith Terrace, Edinburgh EH3 5NS *tel:* 0131 556 3600. *Chmbr mus, pno, orch.*

* **Cresswell, Lyell.** 4 Leslie Place, Edinburgh EH4 1NQ *tel:* 0131 332 9181 *also fax. Promethean Editions Ltd, Wai-te-ta Press. Orch, chmbr, choral and vocal.*

Crosse, Gordon. c/o Oxford University Press, Repertoire Promotion, 70 Baker St, London W1M 1DJ *tel:* 020 7616 5900 *fax:* 020 7616 5901 *email:* repertoire.promotion@oup.co.uk. *OUP. Orch, chmbr, choral, vocal, opera, works for children.*

Crossland, Neil. c/o Margaret Murphy Management, 28 Windsor Rd, London E11 3QU *tel:* 020 8989 1357 *also fax; email:* mmagent@freeuk.com. *Pno, orch, chmbr, solo inst.*

Crumb, George. c/o Peters Edition Ltd, 10-12 Baches St, London N1 6DN *tel:* 020 7553 4030 *fax:* 020 7490 4921 *email:* newmusic@ uk.edition-peters.com.

* **Crump, Peter.** 21 Kingsway Rd, Evington, Leicester LE5 5TL *tel:* 0116 273 6257. *Crump Music (sp), TP. Chmbr, songs, pno, choral.*

Curtis, Matthew. 152 Granville Rd, London NW2 2LD *tel:* 020 8458 2492. *(Sp). Symphonic, light orch, songs, choral mus.*

Dakin, Charles. Lane Cottage, Norbury, Bishops Castle, Shropshire SY9 5DX *tel:* 01588 650307 *also fax. BH, Dorn, Hin, (sp). Orch, chmbr, educ.*

Dalbavie, Marc-André. c/o Van Walsum Management, 4 Addison Bridge Place, London W14 8XP *tel:* c/o 020 7371 4343 *fax:* 020 7371 4344.

* **Dalby, John.** 63 Gunnersbury Lane, London W3 8HG *tel:* 020 8992 1269 *fax:* 020 8992 1346 *email:* john@newlovemakepeace.demon.co.uk. *WC. Film and TV scores, musicals.*

* **Dalby, Martin.** 23 Muirpark Way, Drymen, Stirlingshire G63 0DX *tel:* 01360 660427 *fax:* 01360 660397 *email:* pescatore@dial.pipex.com. *BH, Ches, Leng, Nov, OUP. Concert mus, film and TV.*

Dale, Gordon. c/o 6 Fleming Court, Mytton Priory, Leegomery, Telford, Shropshire TF1 4DR *tel:* 01952 255851. *EMI, For, Piper. Mus for schools, colleges, amateurs and professional musicians.*

* **Dankworth CBE, John.** The Old Rectory, Wavendon, Milton Keynes, Bucks MK17 8LT *tel:* 01908 583151 *fax:* 01908 584414. *Jazz, orch, film scores.*

Darlow, Denys. The Coach House, Drury Lane, Redmarley, D'Abitot, Glos GL19 3JX *tel:* 01531 650616 *also fax. Banks, Lorenz, Nov, OUP. Choral and orch.*

Darnborough, Jonathan. 503a Kingston Rd, Wimbledon Chase, London SW20 8JP *tel:* 020 8395 7433 *email:* artists@midman503a.freeserve.co.uk. *Solo pno, vocal, chmbr, orch.*

Daugherty, Michael. c/o Faber Music Ltd, 3 Queen Square, London WC1N 3AU *tel:* 020 7833 7911/2 *fax:* 020 7833 7939 *email:* promotion@fabermusic.co.uk. *Faber, Peermusic. Opera, inst, orch, chmbr, vocal.*

Davies, Eiluned. 40 The Limes Ave, New Southgate, London N11 1RH *tel:* 020 8368 8202. *Bardic, Gwynn, Guild for the Promotion of Welsh Music. Solo songs, part songs, pno arrangements.*

Davies, Hugh. 25 Albert Rd, London N4 3RR *tel:* 020 7272 5508. *(Sp). Avant-garde electronic and inst mus.*

* **Davies, Terry.** 8 Heyford Ave, London SW8 1ED *tel:* 020 7735 8950 *also fax; email:* terrydavieslondon@compuserve.com. *Film, TV, theatre.*

* **Davis, Carl.** c/o Faber Music Ltd, 3 Queen Square, London WC1N 3AU *tel:* 020 7833 7911/2 *fax:* 020 7833 7939 *email:* promotion @fabermusic.co.uk. *EMI, Euston, Faber, Leeds, Threefold. Film, TV, musicals, ballets, concert works.*

* **de Souza, Christopher.** Westbrook Farm Cottage, Boxford, Newbury, Berks RG20 8DL *tel:* 01488 608010 *also fax; email:* chris.desouza@talk21.com. *Orch, choral, chmbr, radio, TV.*

Deacon, Nigel. 56 Arbor Rd, Croft, Leics LE9 3GD *tel:* 01455 284096 *fax:* 0116 223 1999. *Sutton Elms Publications (sp). Pno solo, original compositions and folk-tune arrangements.*

Dean, Roger. 23 Westfield Terrace, Longford, Gloucester GL2 9BA *tel:* 01452 522379 *fax:* 00 61 2 527 2139 *email:* r.dean@hri.edu.au *Crayson, Frog Peak, Harwood, Open University Press, Some Recording, Sounds Australian, Red House, Tall Poppies Recording, Rufus Records. Contemporary, electro-acoustic mus.*

* **Dedman, Malcolm.** 27 Pentland Ave, Thornbury, Bristol BS35 2YB *tel:* 01454 413917. *Anglian, Obelisk. Contemporary, children's mus.*

Del Tredici, David. c/o Boosey & Hawkes Music Publishers Ltd, 295 Regent St, London W1R 8JH *tel:* 020 7580 2060 *fax:* 020 7637 3490 *email:* composers@boosey.com. *Solo voice and orch, solo voice and ens, orch, pno.*

Dench, Chris. c/o United Music Publishers Ltd, 42 Rivington St, London EC2A 3BN *tel:* 020 7729 4700 *fax:* 020 7739 6549 *email:* ump @compuserve.com. *Australian Music Centre, BMG (Rome), UMP. Inst, chmbr, vocal and orch.*

Denny, Louise. Arun House, 58 Seddlescombe Rd South, St Leonards on Sea, E Sussex TN38 0TJ *tel:* 01424 714222. *Bandleader, Bardic, Military, light orch mus.*

* **Denwood, Russell.** Greenhills, East Heslerton, Malton, N Yorks YO17 8RW *tel:* 01944 728217. *BH, Emerson, Kendor, ME, Muzika, Phoenix, Phylloscopus. Educ mus, wind ens, w/wind, chmbr, pno, strs.*

Diamond, Eileen. Flat 7, Allington Court, Allington St, London SW1E 5ED *tel:* 020 7828 1335. *Black, IMP, UE, Ward Lock Educational, WC. Educ, songs, perc, rounds, musicals for children. Schools, radio and TV.*

Dickinson, Peter. Foxborough House, Aldeburgh, Suffolk IP15 5QP *tel:* 01728 454540 *email:* peterdickinson@foxborough.demon.co.uk. *Nov.*

Dillon, James. c/o Peters Edition Ltd, 10-12 Baches St, London N1 6DN *tel:* 020 7553 4030 *fax:* 020 7490 4921 *email:* newmusic@uk edition-peters.com.

Dillon, Shaun. 34 Richmond St, Aberdeen AB25 4TR *tel:* 01224 630954 *Lomond, Music to Measure, SB. All mus including Scottish traditional.*

Dodgson, Stephen. 4 Scarth Rd, London SW13 0ND *tel:* 020 8876 6901 *ABd, Bèrben, BH, Ches, Eschig, Möseler, Nogatz, Nov, OUP, Ric, SB, Schott, WC.*

* **Don, Nigel.** 12 Kelso Place, Dundee DD2 1SL *tel:* 01382 667251 *fax:* 01382 640775 *email:* donmusic@rmplc.co.uk. *Church mus, inst, vocal, concert mus.*

* **Dorward, David.** Dovecot House, Preston Rd, Prestonpans EH32 9JZ *tel:* 01875 810 512 *email:* dorward@argonet.co.uk. *Curwen, Gal, GMC, OUP, SB. Radio, film, TV, concert works, opera, musicals.*

* **Douglas, James.** c/o Eschenbach Editions, 28 Dalrymple Cres, Edinburgh EH9 2NX *tel:* 0131 667 3633 *also fax. Caritas, Eschenbach. Orch, choral, inst, chmbr, pno, org, songs, opera, ballet.*

Douglas, Johnny. 39 Tadorne Rd, Tadworth, Surrey KT20 5TF *tel:* 01737 812922 *also fax. Anglia, EMI, Fil, KPM, Marlyn, Wein, WC. Film, TV, musicals.*

* **Dove, Jonathan.** c/o Peters Edition Ltd, 10-12 Baches St, London N1 6DN *tel:* 020 7553 4030 *fax:* 020 7490 7421 *email:* newmusic@uk.edition-peters.com.

* **Downes, Professor Andrew.** 2 Church St, West Hagley, W Midlands DY9 0NA *tel:* 01562 886625 *fax:* 0121 331 5906 *email:* downlyn@globalnet.co.uk. *Lynwood. Orch, choral, chmbr mus, songs, small ens, solo inst, voice.*

Downie, Gordon. 30 Windsor Rd, Radyr, Cardiff CF15 8BQ *tel:* 029 2084 2718. *Editio Musica Budapest.*

Downing, Jaemus. Stables Cottage, Bannadon Farm, Broadbury, Okehampton, Devon EX20 4LQ *tel:* 01837 871547. *Treborne (sp), Trelaske (sp). Choral, chmbr mus, carols.*

Drakeford, Richard. 30 Dovehouse Close, Upper Wolvercote, N Oxford OX2 8BG *tel:* 01865 554836. *Elk, Nov, Oec, Schott. Songs, chmbr (br, wind, str), choral, pno, org, church opera.*

Drayton, Paul. 73 Polmear Parc, Par, Cornwall PL24 2AU *tel:* 01726 813529. *Hinshaw (USA), KS Music, Nov, OUP, Ramsey. Vocal, choral, opera, inst, educ mus.*

* **Druce, Duncan.** Westfield House, 155 West End, Netherthong, Huddersfield HD7 2YJ *tel:* 01484 683158 *fax:* 01484 689408. *Corda Music, For, Nov. Orch, chmbr, choral, reconstructions and transcriptions of classical mus.*

Duarte, John. 25 Brunswick Grove, London N11 1HN *tel:* 020 8361 2731. *Bèrben, Broekmans, Chappell, Ches, Columbia, Corda, Criterion, Eschig, Gendai, Hampton, Lemoine, Margaux, Melbay, Norsk Musik, Nov, Novascribe, Ric, Schirmer, Schott, UE, Wise, Yolotl, Zanibon, Zimmerman. Gui mus.*

Dubery, David Leigh. 2 Boardman Rd, Higher Crumpsall, Manchester M8 4WJ *tel.* 0161 740 2762 *email:* david.dubery@argonet.co.uk. *For, MSM, Rob, Sunshine Music Co. English song, chmbr, musicals.*

Dubugnon, Richard. c/o Alfred Lengnick & Co, 27 Grove Rd, Beaconsfield, Bucks HP9 1UR *tel:* 01494 681216 *fax:* 01494 670443 *email:* gbmuswill@aol.com. *Orch, chmbr, vocal.*

* **Dunkin Wedd, F L.** 114 Woodside Rd, Tonbridge, Kent TN9 2PB *tel:* 01732 357648 *email:* dunkinwed@geocities.com. *(Sp). Voice, choral, inst.*

* **Duro, Stephen.** 33 Belmont Close, Uxbridge, Middx UB8 1RF *tel:* 01895 232055 *also fax. ABd, Chappell, Spartan, Stanza. Inst, jazz, band mus, choral.*

* **Duxbury, Rosemary.** 74 Stoneygate Rd, Leicester LE2 2BN *tel:* 0116 270 2255 *email:* raduxbury@aol.com. *Chmbr, pno, vocal, choral, orch and film.*

Earl, David. Flat 1, 26a Newmarket Rd, Cambridge CB5 8DT *tel:* 01223 303857. *Nov. Symphonic, ballet, chmbr, film, choral.*

Earle, Melvyn Stuart. 53 The Street, Blundeston, Suffolk NR32 5AA. *Orch, chmbr, inst, ens.*

East, Harold. 11 Bettridge Rd, London SW6 3QH *tel:* 020 7736 6109. *Brass Wind, Ches, Ric, Wolfe.*

Edwards, Paul C. 28 Green End, Great Barford, Beds MK44 3HA. *BBMP, Jubilate Hymns, Oec, RSCM. Church mus.*

* **Elias, Brian.** c/o Chester Music, 8-9 Frith St, London W1V 5TZ *tel:* 020 7434 0066 *fax:* 020 7287 6329 *email:* music@musicsales.co.uk. *Ches. Chmbr, orch, vocal, dance.*

* **Ellis, David.** 14 Patch Lane, Bramhall, Cheshire SK7 1JB *tel:* 0161 440 9007 *also fax; email:* paratactile.asc@btinternet.com. *Birnbach, Da Capo, For, Gal, Leng, Nov, Wein, Yorke. Contemporary classical, educ, jazz orch.*

Ellis, James Antony. 6 The Street, Kingston, nr Lewes, E Sussex BN7 3PB *tel:* 01273 471586 *email:* jamesandhonor@hotmail.com. *Opera, vocal, inst, film scores.*

* **Elton, Antony.** Badger Bungalow, 41 Findon Ave, Witton Gilbert, Durham DH7 6RF *tel:* 0191 371 2522. *Essex, Leeds, Nov, Scores, Toad (sp). Songs, song cycles, pno suites, mus for drama, ballet, choral, chmbr mus including w/wind quartets and str quartets, semi-improvisation.*

* **Elwyn-Edwards, Dilys.** Caerwys, 48 Cae Gwyn, Caernarfon, Gwynedd LL55 1LL *tel:* 01286 672820. *Curiad, Guild for the Promotion of Welsh Music, Gwasg Gwynedd, Gwynn, Pantycelyn, Rob. Songs, choral works.*

* **Emmans, Les.** 23 Welwyn Ave, Allestree, Derby DE22 2JR *tel:* 01332 552519 *fax:* 01332 556045 *email:* les@emmans.prestel.co.uk. *Beccam, Lindens Music (sp). Ballad operas, schools, church, songs, chmbr, inst.*

* **Emmerson, Simon.** 15 Holligrave Rd, Bromley, Kent BR1 3PJ *tel:* 020 8460 4997 *fax:* 020 8460 0540 *email:* s.emmerson@city.ac.uk. *Live electro-acoustic mus.*

Emsley, Richard. 168 Carlyle Rd, London W5 4BJ *tel:* 020 8847 5074 *email:* richardemsley@argonet.co.uk. *(sp). Chmbr, solo.*

Endrich, Archer (Tom). 12 Goodwood Way, Cepen Park South, Chippenham, Wilts SN14 0SY *tel:* 01249 461361 *email:* archer@trans4um.demon.co.uk. *Eul, Kunz. Chmbr, electronic, orch, vocal, theatrical.*

Erber, James. 127 Grange Rd, London SE25 6TQ *tel:* 020 8771 5184 *also fax; email:* jerber1031@aol.com.

Evans, Colin. 30 Ravensroost, Beulah Hill, London SE19 3LN *tel:* 020 8771 7467 *also fax; email:* colinevans@hotmail.com. *Belwin, BH, Ches, Choral Web, Nov, OUP, Paxton, Schott. School choral, orch and educ mus.*

Ewers, Tim. 79 Erlanger Rd, London SE14 5TQ *tel:* 020 7635 7038 *also fax; email:* timewers@nuxg.freeserve.co.uk. *Forward. Concert mus.*

* **Fanshawe, David.** Fanshawe One World Music, PO Box 574, Marlborough, Wilts SN8 2SP *tel:* 01672 520211 *fax:* 01672 521151 *email:* fanshaweuk@cwcom.net. *IMC, OUP, WC. Choral, orch, pno, vocal, film, TV, ethnic mus recordings.*

Farnon, Robert. La Falaise, St Martins, Guernsey, Channel Islands *tel:* 01481 38986 *fax:* 01481 38087 *email:* rbfarnon@guernsey.net. *Carlin, Feld, Leeds, R Smith, Rediffusion, WC, Zomba.*

FeBland, Jonathan. 19 Manor Park Cres, Edgware, Middx HA8 7NH *fax:* 020 8951 1005/5219 *email:* jonfeb@befnojj.freeserve.co.uk. *Bardic, Samuel King, UE. Contemporary, educ and film mus.*

Feeney, Philip. c/o Robert White Artist Management, 182 Moselle Ave, London N22 6EX *tel:* 020 8881 6914 *fax:* 020 8888 9662 *email:* rwhiteam@aol.com. *Concert mus, dance and ballet scores.*

* **Fenton, George.** 1 Barrett St, London W1M 5HG *tel:* 020 7486 6676 *fax:* 020 7486 0789 *email:* george.fenton@virgin.net. *Shogun. Film, TV and theatre scores.*

* **Ferguson, Howard.** 51 Barton Rd, Cambridge CB3 9LG *tel:* 01223 359206. *ABd, BH, OUP. Orch, choral, chmbr mus, pno, songs.*

Fernández, Agustín. Dept of Music, University of Newcastle, Newcastle upon Tyne NE1 7RU *tel:* 0191 222 7636 *email:* agustin.fernandez@newcastle.ac.uk. *Chmbr, orch, electro-acoustic, opera.*

Ferneyhough, Brian. c/o Peters Edition Ltd, 10-12 Baches St, London N1 6DN *tel:* 020 7553 4030 *fax:* 020 7490 4921 *email:* newmusic@uk.edition-peters.com.

* **Fiddy, John.** Fruit Farm House, Foxton, Cambridge CB2 6RT *tel:* 01763 208610 *fax:* 01763 208241 *email:* johnfiddymusic@dial.pipex.com. *John Fiddy Music (sp).*

Field, Robin. 4 Ellergreen, Burneside, Kendal, Cumbria LA9 5SD *tel:* 01539 729226. *(sp). Choral, chmbr, orch, electro-acoustic, vocal.*

Finnerty, Adrian J. 10 Brandon Drive, Bearsden, Glasgow G61 3LN *tel:* 0141 943 1517.

Firsova, Elena. c/o Boosey & Hawkes Music Publishers Ltd, 295 Regent St, London W1R 8JH *tel:* 020 7580 2060 *fax:* 020 7637 3490 *email:* composers@boosey.com. *Orch, ens, chmbr, vocal.*

* **Fish, Adrian Vernon.** Brownson House, Grenofen, Tavistock, Devon PL19 9ER *tel:* 01822 615730 *also fax; email:* adrian_vernon.fish@virgin.net. *Brunton, KM, Oec, RSCM, Sermersuaq (sp), Creative and Expressive Arts in Education. Orch, choral, chmbr, liturgical; also Greenlandic mus editions.*

* **Fisher, David.** Holly Tree House, 13 Braunstone Lane East, Leicester LE3 2FD *tel:* 0116 224 0144 *fax:* 0116 291 0677. *Oriana, Rob. Choral, vocal, chmbr and mus for children.*

Fitkin, Graham. 4 Lisbon Terrace, St Buryan, W Cornwall *tel:* 01736 810927 *email:* www.fitkin.com. *(sp).*

Fleming, Tim. 17 Huddersfield Rd, Brighouse, W Yorks HD6 1NP *tel:* 01484 717173 *also fax. Choral, musicals, oratorios, TV drama, mus for special needs, br band.*

Fletcher, Andrew. 230 The Avenue, Acocks Green, Birmingham B27 6NU *tel:* 0121 706 5708 *fax:* 0121 608 2990 *email:* AIF001@aol.com. *KM, Oec, OUP (New York), RSCM. Church and org mus.*

* **Fligg, David.** 32 High Moor Cres, Moortown, Leeds LS17 6DU *tel:* 0113 268 7440 *email:* d.fligg@leedscolmusic.ac.uk.

Flood, Philip. 39 Kynaston Rd, Stoke Newington, London N16 0EA *tel:* 020 7249 7208 *fax:* 020 7306 5950 *email:* philipflood@hotmail.com. *CMC, Haven, Warwick. Orch, chmbr, electro-acoustic, dance.*

Floyd, Carlisle. c/o Boosey & Hawkes Music Publishers Ltd, 295 Regent St, London W1R 8JH *tel:* 020 7580 2060 *fax:* 020 7637 3490 *email:* composers@boosey.com. *Opera, mus drama, voice, orch.*

Fontanelli, Simone. c/o ECAM Limited, 130 Drayton Park, London N5 1LX *tel:* 07973 156370 *fax:* 07070 605072 *email:* info@ecam-limited.com.

* **Forbes, Sebastian.** Octave House, Boughton Hall Ave, Send, Woking, Surrey GU23 7DF *tel:* 01483 211785/259317 *fax:* 01483 259386 *email:* s.forbes@surrey.ac.uk. *ABd, Bosworth, Cathedral, Ches, Nov, OUP, SB, Yorke. Orch, chmbr, choral.*

* **Forshaw, David Campbell.** 40 Howards Lane, Eccleston, St Helens, Merseyside WA10 5HY *tel:* 01744 28456 *email:* david@dforshaw.demon.co.uk. *Da Capo, Forsyths. Choral, orch, chmbr, educ, pno.*

Foss, Lukas. c/o Boosey & Hawkes Music Publishers Ltd, 295 Regent St, London W1R 8JH *tel:* 020 7580 2060 *fax:* 020 7637 3490 *email:* composers@boosey.com. *Opera, orch, concertos, chmbr, vocal.*

* **Foster, Anthony.** 1 Cawley Rd, Chichester, W Sussex PO19 1UZ *tel:* 01243 780134. *Belwin, Brunton, Epworth, Free, Oec, OUP. Sacred, keyboard, musicals.*

Foster, Derek. 41 Gloucester Court, Kew Rd, Kew, Richmond, Surrey TW9 3EA *tel:* 020 8940 8373. *Modus.*

* **Fowler, Jennifer.** 21 Deodar Rd, London SW15 2NP *tel:* 020 8788 7156 *email:* 100611.2060@compuserve.com. *Sounds Australian, UE.*

Fox, Christopher. 3 Old Moor Lane, York YO24 1QE *tel:* 01904 704645 *email:* p.c.fox@hud.ac.uk. *Fox Edition (sp).*

* **Fox, Erika.** 78 Peterborough Rd, London SW6 3EB *tel:* 020 7736 7707 *email:* Erika@rossini.demon.co.uk. *Chmbr, theatre, solo inst, vocal, opera.*

Francis, Alun. c/o London Artists (LA), 3 Wheelers Court, Scholars Lane, Stratford-upon-Avon, Warwicks CV37 6HE *tel:* 01789 261561 *fax:* 01789 261577 *email:* londartist@aol.com. *Bote & Bock, Peters, Wein. Symphony, chmbr mus, film and TV scores.*

* **Fraser, Bruce.** 32 Bankton Park, Kingskettle, Fife KY15 7PY *tel:* 01337 830974 *fax:* 01337 830653 *email:* bruce.fraser@zetnet.co.uk. *Bandleader, Ches, Fortune, Kirklees Music, Lomond Music, Obrasso (Switzerland), Smith & Co, Studio.*

* **Freedman, Latif.** 163 Gwydir St, Cambridge CB1 2LJ *tel:* 01223 322712. *Mercia. Vocal, choral, inst, solo, ens, drama, ballet.*

* **Freeman, Roland.** Brockswood, Canal Lane, Alderbury, Salisbury SP5 3NY *tel:* 01722 710190. *(sp), Trumph (Sweden). Orch, choral, church, chmbr, pno, org, vocal.*

Fribbins, Peter. 44 Rosecroft Drive, Watford, Herts WD1 3JQ *tel:* 01923 223581 *fax:* 01923 334696. *Edward Kassner Ltd, Music Haven.*

* **Gange, Kenneth.** 129 Dartmouth Ave, Cannock, Staffs WS11 1EJ *tel:* 01543 577447. *B, Banks, Cramer, Nov, Oec, OUP, Piper, Rob.*

Garcia, Gerald. 16 Parker St, Oxford OX14 1TD *tel:* 01865 725929 *fax:* 01865 725811 *email:* geraldgarcia@compuserve.com.

Gardiner, Ian. 11 Hampden Rd, Higher Tranmere, Birkenhead CH42 5LH *tel:* 0151 647 8022 *also fax; email:* i.gardiner@lipa.ac.uk. *Concert mus, mus for silent film, TV mus, arranging.*

* **Gardner, Robert Neil.** Slip Cottage, Hawkley, Liss, Hants GU33 6NH *tel:* 01730 827315. *Inst, orch, chmbr mus.*

* **Garrett, Michael.** 68 Devonshire Rd, Colliers Wood, London SW19 2EF *tel:* 020 8543 7734. *Terrano Gruppo Editoriale (Italy). Film, orch, inst, vocal.*

Gates, Philip. Woods Corner, Cliddesden, Hants RG25 2JF *tel:* 01256 466854. *Camden, Fentone, Phylloscopus. Ens.*

Gaze, Nigel. 11 Norbreck Court, Norcliffe Rd, Blackpool, Lancs FY2 9BN *tel:* 01253 591869. *Brunton, Oec. Choral, org.*

Geddes, John Maxwell. 20 Baronald Drive, Glasgow G12 0HZ *tel:* 0141 357 2941. *Bèrben (Italy), Periwinkle, Peterson (California). Chmbr, symphonic, film and TV, orch, band.*

Geesin, Ron. Headrest, Street End Lane, Broadoak, Heathfield, E Sussex TN21 8TU *tel:* 01435 863994 *fax:* 01435 867027 *email:* ron@geesin.demon.co.uk. *Installations, (sp). Ballet, opera, film scores, radio mus.*

Gibbs, Alan. 8 St Margaret's Drive, Twickenham, Middx TW1 1QN *tel:* 020 8892 9888 *fax:* 020 8891 2174. *B, Bardic, Lawson-Gould, RSCM, WC. Choral, org, chmbr, orch, radio drama.*

Gibson, Stephen. 40 Campbell Close, Streatham, London SW16 6NJ *tel:* 020 8677 8473 *fax:* 020 8877 3494 *email:* stephen@gibmusic.freeserve.co.uk. *Ararat (sp), R Smith, EMI. Mus theatre, concert mus.*

Gifford, Keith. 77 Gayton House, Knapp Rd, London E3 4BY *tel:* 020 7987 2887 *also fax. Orch, chmbr.*

* **Gilbert, Anthony.** 4 Oak Brow Cottages, Altrincham Rd, Styal, Cheshire SK9 4JE *tel:* 01625 536462 *fax:* 0161 273 7611. *For, Schott, UP, University of York Music Press. Mus theatre, orch, chmbr, vocal, ens.*

Gilder, Eric. 21 Fieldend, Twickenham, Middx TW1 4TF *tel:* 020 8892 0742. *Cramer, Curwen, Evans, French, Gay, Manor, Ric. Musicals, orch, choral, chmbr, songs.*

Glanert, Detlev. c/o Boosey & Hawkes Music Publishers Ltd, 295 Regent St, London W1R 8JH *tel:* 020 7580 2060 *fax:* 020 7637 3490 *email:* composers@boosey.com. *Opera, orch, concertos, ens, chmbr.*

Glass (Hillman), Jennifer. 24 Hill Top, London NW11 6EE *tel:* 020 8455 1106 *also fax. Emerson, Griffiths. Inst, vocal mus.*

Glass, Philip. c/o Chester Music, 8-9 Frith St, London W1V 5TZ *tel:* 020 7434 0066 *fax:* 020 7287 6329 *email:* music@musicsales.co.uk.

* **Glasser, Stanley.** 46 Weigall Rd, Lee, London SE12 8HE *tel:* 020 8852 1997 *fax:* 020 8318 7417. *B, Essex, Faber, Griffiths, Lemmel, MR, Piers, Ric, Woza. Orch, choral, theatre mus, educ.*

Globokar, Vinko. c/o Allied Artists Agency, 42 Montpelier Square, London SW7 1JZ *tel:* 020 7589 6243 *fax:* 020 7581 5269. *Peters.*

Goddard, Mark. Old Brewery House, Redbrook, Monmouth NP5 4LU *tel:* 01600 71248/712482 *fax:* 01600 712483. *Ric, Spartan, Trinity College London. Educ mus, flexible mus.*

Godfrey, Paul Corfield. 4 Craiglee Drive, Atlantic Wharf, Cardiff CF10 5BN *tel:* 029 2045 4717 *also fax. Zarathustra, Black Mountain Records. Operas, symphonies, choral, orch, chmbr, songs, pno.*

* **Golightly, David.** c/o Modrana Music Publishers, 41 Parklands Way, Poynton, Cheshire SK12 1AL *tel:* 01625 875389 *also fax; email:* david.f.golightly@btinternet.com. *MM, Piccolo. TV and film, theatre incidental mus.*

* **Goodall, Howard.** PBJ Management, 5 Soho Square, London W1V 5DE *tel:* 020 7287 1112 *fax:* 020 7287 1448 *email:* howardg@argonet.co.uk. *Choral, opera, musicals, TV and film.*

* **Goodwin, Ron.** Blacknest Cottage, Brimpton Common, Reading, Berks RG7 4RP *tel:* 0118 981 5147 *fax:* 0118 981 0770. *Chandos, EMI, KPM, G & M Brand, WC. Film scores.*

Gorb, Adam. 138 Salcott Rd, London SW11 6DG *tel:* 020 7223 5843 *also fax; email:* adam@gorb.demon.co.uk. *Brass Wind, Corda, G & M Brand Leng, Maecenas. Orch, chmbr, wind band, choral, ballet, pno, educ.*

Gordon, Christopher. 22 Ivybridge Close, Twickenham, Middx TW1 1EA *tel:* 020 8892 1833 *also fax; email:* stoffg@hotmail.com. *Janus Studio, Peacock. Mus for children, wind and chmbr mus, pno, ens, choral songs, duos, trios, quartets, especially mus for fl and cl.*

Gordon, Morgan. 127 Grange Rd, London SE25 6TQ *tel:* 020 8771 5184 *also fax; email:* mor3411404@aol.com. *Theatre (incidental mus to plays and songs), concert works.*

Górecki, Henryk Mikolaj. c/o Boosey & Hawkes Music Publishers Ltd, 295 Regent St, London W1R 8JH *tel:* 020 7637 3490 *fax:* 020 7580 2060 *email:* composers@boosey.com. *Works for solo voice and orch, br and str mus, orch, chmbr, choir.*

Graebner, Ric. Resurge Studio, 30 Dyke Rd Drive, Brighton BN1 6AJ *tel:* 01273 541816 *fax:* 023 8059 3197. *(sp). Electronic, opera, multimedia, vocal, inst, dance.*

Grange, Philip. c/o Maecenas Music Ltd, 5 Bushey Close, Old Barn Lane, Kenley, Surrey CR8 5AU *tel:* 020 8660 4766 *fax:* 020 8668 5273. *Maecenas. Orch, chmbr, vocal, br band, wind band, etc.*

* **Grant, Julian.** 7 Thackeray House, Herbrand St, London WC1N 1HN *tel:* 020 7278 5263 *also fax;* 00 852 2849 2992 *fax:* 00 852 2849 2990 *email:* jmgpr1@hknet.com. *Opera, inst, chmbr, vocal.*

Grant, Robin. 46 Austin St, Whitmore Reans, Wolverhampton WV6 0NW *tel:* 01902 423685. *ABd, BH, Brass Wind, Ches, Emerson, Faber, Goodmusic. Concert, educ, opera.*

* **Graubart, Michael.** 18 Laitwood Rd, London SW12 9QL *tel:* 020 8265 5504. *Chmbr, vocal, choral, orch.*

* **Greenway, Kenneth.** 6 Buttermere Close, Tettenhall, Wolverhampton WV6 9DN *tel:* 01902 754529. *Rob. Org and choral mus.*

Gregson, Edward. c/o Royal Northern College of Music, 124 Oxford Rd, Manchester M13 9RD *tel:* 0161 907 5273 *fax:* 0161 273 8188. *BH, Brass Wind, Emerson, Maecenas, Nov, OUP, Smith, Studio, WC. Concert mus.*

Grier, Francis. 22 Rydal Gardens, Wembley, Middx HA9 8RZ *tel:* 020 8904 2422 *also fax; email:* francis@fgrier.freeserve.co.uk. *Banks, Faber, OUP. Opera, choral, chmbr, church, inst.*

* **Grossner, Sonja.** 85 Maple Rd, Loughborough, Leics LE11 2JN *tel:* 01509 215960. *Da Capo. Chmbr, orch, vocal, pno, vn.*

Gruber, H K. c/o Intermusica Artists' Management Ltd, 16 Duncan Terrace, London N1 8BZ *tel:* 020 7278 5455 *fax:* 020 7278 8434. *BH. Opera, orch, concertos.*

Gruss, René. 2 St Richard's Court, Ashburnham Rd, Richmond, Surrey TW10 7NS *tel:* 020 8940 3680 *email:* rene.gruss@newklassical.com.

Gubaidulina, Sofia. c/o Boosey & Hawkes Music Publishers Ltd, 295 Regent St, London W1R 8JH *tel:* 020 7580 2060 *fax:* 020 7637 3490 *email:* composers@boosey.com. *Orch, concerto, ens, chmbr.*

Gundry, Inglis. 11 Winterstoke Gardens, London NW7 2RA *tel:* 020 8959 1744. *BH, Hin, OUP, TP. Opera, song-cycle, hp mus, orch.*

* **Guy, Barry.** Griffinstown, Skeoughvosteen, nr Borris, Co Kilkenny, Ireland *email:* maya@tinet.ie. *Nov. Concert mus, chmbr, jazz, film.*

* **Haines, David Charles.** 88 Higher Brimley, Teignmouth, Devon TQ14 8JU *tel:* 01626 779690 *email:* puzjig@aol.com. *Operas, musicals, children's mus, theatre mus, secular oratorios, community projects.*

Hall, John. c/o Mrs Kaye, 11 Bleasdale Ave, Thornton-Cleveleys, Lancs FY5 3QZ *tel:* 01253 856606. Also at: St Leger de Montbrillais, F-86120 Les Trois Moutiers, France *tel:* 00 33 05 49 22 93 06 *also fax. Yorke.*

Hallett, Sylvia. 33 Summerhill Rd, London N15 4HF *tel:* 020 8802 0094 *also fax. Mash. Contemporary dance, film, educ, theatre mus, vocal, inst, electro-acoustic.*

Halsey, Louis. 8 Beechcroft Ave, New Malden, Surrey KT3 3EG *tel:* 020 8942 7597 *also fax. Encore, Faber, Kirklees, Nov, OUP, TP. Choral.*

Hamilton, Iain. Flat 4, 85 Cornwall Gardens, London SW7 4XY *tel:* 020 7589 4788. *AAK (Presser), Schott, UE. Opera, orch, chmbr, choral, solo inst.*

Hand, Colin. 9 Manor Close, Sibsey, Boston, Lincs PE22 0SL *tel:* 01205 750135. *Asch, BH, Curwen, Elk, Eul, Faber, Gal, KM, Nova, Nov, Oec, OUP, Piper, Ric, Schott. Choral, orch, pno, org, rcdr.*

Hansel, Stanislaw. 38 West Parade, Peterborough, Cambs PE3 6BD *tel:* 01733 341068 *email:* hansel@cix.co.uk. *(sp), Writers' Forum. Sound poetry, sound installations, opera, keyboard and pno, ens.*

Hanson, Geoffrey. 22 New Ash Close, London N2 8DQ *tel:* 020 8444 9214 *also fax; email:* geoffreyhanson@btinternet.com. *Rob. Orch, choral and opera.*

* **Hardy, John.** Ael Y Garth, 3 Iron Bridge Rd, Tongwynlais, Cardiff CF15 7NJ *tel:* 029 2081 0655 *fax:* 029 2081 0653. *EMI, Pocket. Opera, mus theatre, orch, concert, chmbr, choral, solo, film and TV, dance, educ, theatre.*

Harle, John. c/o Chester Music, 8-9 Frith St, London W1V 5TZ *tel:* 020 7434 0066 *fax:* 020 7287 6329 *email:* music@musicsales.co.uk. *Ches. Opera, orch, chmbr, film scores.*

* **Harper, Edward.** 7 Morningside Park, Edinburgh EH10 5HD *tel:* 0131 447 5366. *OUP. Opera, orch, choral, chmbr.*

* **Harrex, Patrick.** 21 Preston Drove, Brighton BN1 6LA *tel:* 01273 501758. *Schott, (sp). Chmbr, choral.*

Harris, Max. Checkmate, Chequers Lane, Walton on the Hill, Tadworth, Surrey KT20 7RB *tel:* 01737 812744. *Amphonic Music, ATV Music, Bruton Music, EMI, Essex, Music Sales, WC. Film and TV scores.*

Harris, Paul. 15 Mallard Drive, Buckingham, Bucks MK18 1GJ *tel:* 01280 813144 *also fax; email:* paulharris@easynet.co.uk. *ABd, BH, Camden Music, CUP, Ebony, Faber, Fentone, Nov, OUP, Ric. Educ mus.*

* **Harris, Philip.** 52 Dean Rd West, Hinckley, Leics LE10 1QB *tel:* 01455 634945 *email:* phil@beacon-hky.demon.co.uk. *(sp). Religious mus, Christian worship songs.*

Harris, William Lewarne. 26 Park Court, Park Hall Rd, London SE21 8DZ *tel:* 020 8761 6460. *Cornish Music Guild, Leduc, OUP, TP. Operas, orch, chmbr, songs, choral.*

Hart, Don. Cottage Farm, The Hollow, Westbury-sub-Mendip, nr Wells, Somerset BA5 1HH *tel:* 01749 870351 *fax:* 01749 870994 *email:* hart@hartmusic.freeserve.co.uk. *Orch, choral, chmbr, Christian worship songs, video.*

Hartman, Thomas. 319 City Rd, London EC1V 1LJ *tel:* 020 7737 6770 *email:* cmbski@aol.com. *Arlington, Bèrben (Italy), Ches. Orch, choral, opera, ballet, gui, film scores, jazz.*

* **Harvey, Frank.** 26 Waite Meads Close, Purton, nr Swindon, Wilts SN5 9ET *tel:* 01793 770139. *School, orch, choral, chmbr.*

* **Harvey, Jonathan.** 35 Houndean Rise, Lewes, E Sussex BN7 1EQ *tel:* 01273 471241 *also fax; email:* jharvey@solutions-inc.co.uk. *Faber, Nov, Schott. Chmbr, orch, vocal, choral, opera, electronic. Agent: PGM*

Harvey, Paul. 36 Alton Gardens, Twickenham, Middx TW2 7PD *tel:* 020 8898 4869 *also fax. BH, Breit, Ches, Egon, Emerson, Fentone, Harlequin, Kahn & Averill, Kjos, KM, Maurer, Music Sales, Nov, NWM, Ric, Roncorp, Schott, Shallumo, Sou, Studio, Universal, WC, Warwick. W/wind mus.*

Harvey, Richard. Fireworks Music Ltd, Snake Ranch Studios, 90 Lots Rd, London SW10 0QD *tel:* 020 7351 7448 *fax:* 020 7351 7442 *email:* fwx@fireworksmusic.co.uk. *Film and TV scores.*

Hasse, Jean. 10 Woodlands, Clapham Common North Side, London SW4 0RJ *tel:* 020 7627 4961 *fax:* 020 7720 5426 *email:* visible.music @argonet.co.uk. *Visible Music (sp). Choral, chmbr, inst, ens, orch.*

* **Hawkins, John B.** 94 Greenham Rd, London N10 1LP *tel:* 020 8245 7990 *email:* manuscript49@hotmail.com. *BH. Orch, vocal, chmbr, educ.*

Haynes, Tony. c/o Grand Union, Shoreditch Town Hall, 380 Old Street, London EC1V 9LT *tel:* 020 7729 8729 *fax:* 020 7729 8789. *Large-scale cross-cultural works.*

Head, Raymond. The Firs, 10 Worcester Rd, Chipping Norton, Oxon OX7 5XX *tel:* 01608 642025. *(sp). Inst, choral, wind band, ens, orch.*

* **Hearne, John.** Smidskot, Fawells, Keithhall, Inverurie AB51 0LN *tel:* 01651 882274 *also fax. Adlais, Longship (sp), Sph. Vocal, chmbr, choral, orch, br, org.*

* **Heathcock, Marcus Tristan (Mikhail Teterev).** c/o 50 Bowling Green Rd, Stourbridge, W Midlands DY8 3RZ *tel:* 01384 832264 *fax:* 01384 372044 *email:* mthpop@hotmail.com. *Banks. Orch, electro-acoustic, chmbr, choral, film mus, musical.*

Hedger, Alison. Hinton House, Hinton, Christchurch, Dorset BH23 7EA *tel:* 01425 274993 *also fax. Golden Apple. Children's educ mus.*

* **Hedges, Anthony.** Malt Shovel Cottage, 76 Old Walkergate, Beverley, E Yorks HU17 9ER *tel:* 01482 860580 *email:* ahedges@ westfieldmusic.karoo.co.uk. *Fentone, Rob, Samuel King, UE, Westfield (sp). Chmbr, orch, choral, educ, opera.*

Heininen, Paavo. c/o Boosey & Hawkes Music Publishers Ltd, 295 Regent St, London W1R 8JH *tel:* 020 7580 2060 *fax:* 020 7637 3490 *email:* composers@boosey.com. *Opera, orch and ens mus.*

Hellawell, Piers. 94 Carmel St, Belfast BT7 1QF *tel:* 028 9024 7064 *also fax; email:* p.hellawell@qub.ac.uk; P.Hellawell@freenet.co.uk. *Maecenas. Orch, chmbr, vocal.*

Hellewell, David. c/o M-D Music, 57 Lansdowne Rd, Bournemouth BH1 1RN *tel:* 01202 551440. *Editio Musica Budapest, M-D Music (sp).*

Henshall, Dalwyn James. Beverlie Cottage, Shrub Hill Rd, Chestfield, Kent CT5 3NZ *tel:* 01227 792641 *email:* d.j.henshall@canterbury.ac.uk. *Aureus, Curiad. Choral, chmbr, orch.*

Hensher, Ray. 134 Millhouses Lane, Sheffield S7 2HB *tel:* 0114 235 0096. *Emerson, Fentone. Wind ens, br ens, solo insts, school band mus.*

* **Henshilwood, Donald.** 130 Frankby Rd, Newton, West Kirby, Wirral CH48 9UX *tel:* 0151 625 6742. *Orch, band, chmbr, electronic, theatre.*

Henze, Hans Werner. c/o Schott & Co Ltd, 48 Gt Marlborough St, London W1V 2BN *tel:* 020 7494 1487 *fax:* 020 7287 1529 *email:* schottcontemporarymusic@compuserve.com. *Schott. Opera, symphony, chmbr.*

Herbert, Philip. c/o J Audrey Ellison International Artists' Management, 135 Stevenage Rd, Fulham, London SW6 6PB *tel:* 020 7381 9751 *fax:* 020 7381 2406. *Augsburg. Choral, chmbr mus.*

* **Herschmann, Heinz.** 32 Ellerdale Rd, London NW3 6BB *tel:* 020 7435 5255 *fax:* 020 7431 0621. *Kunzelmann, Obelisk. Light orch, background.*

Hill, Richard George. c/o Ennismor, 19 Huggincraig Rd, Newmilns, Ayrshire KA16 9EW *tel:* 01560 320881 *fax:* c/o 01851 880216 *email:* richard@ossion1.freeserve.co.uk. *Ossion Music, Vanderbeek and Imrie. Chmbr, choral, ens, orch, incidental mus, film.*

* **Hinchliffe, Robert.** 4 The Jays, Nightingale Wood, Uckfield, E Sussex TN22 5YG *tel:* 01825 767149. *Ebony, Faber, Fentone, OUP. Chmbr mus.*

Hind O'Malley, Pamela. 23 Nightingale Ave, Cambridge CB1 4SG *tel:* 01223 247885. *SB, SJ Music. Pno, chmbr, vocal.*

Hinton, Alistair. The Sorabji Archive, Easton Dene, Bailbrook Lane, Bath BA1 7AA *tel:* 01225 852323 *fax:* 01225 852523 *email:* alistair-hinton@compuserve.com; 100775.2716@compuserve. com. *Inst, pno, vocal, org, orch.*

Hiscocks, Wendy. 26 Morden Court, Morden, Surrey SM4 5HN *tel:* 020 8648 1700 *also fax; email:* howat_hiscocks@compuserve.com. *Australian Music Centre, Creativity & Music (sp), Currency (Sydney), Editions Combre (France), Frontier, Hovea (Perth). Songs, chmbr, pno mus, choral, orch.*

Hobbs, Christopher. 34 Baldwin Rd, Leicester LE2 6HA *tel:* 0116 281 1278 *email:* assembly1@btinternet.com. *Forward, (sp). Concert mus, theatre, electronic.*

Hoddinott, Alun. Tan-y-Rhiw, 64 Gowerton Rd, Three Crosses, Swansea SA4 3PX *tel:* 01792 873702. *Aureus, Brass Wind, Leng, OUP, Oriana, Paraclete. Opera, incidental mus for film, TV, radio, stage, choral, orch, inst, vocal and chmbr.*

Hodkinson, Juliana. 11 Hammond Croft Way, Alphington, Exeter EX2 8FZ *tel:* 01392 278217 *email:* julianahodkinson@hotmail.com. *Chmbr mus, orch, mus theatre.*

Hodson, Maud. 6 Joseph Priestley House, Canrobert St, London E2 0BQ *tel:* 020 7729 0489 *also fax; email:* maud@maud.co.uk. *Chmbr, orch, educ.*

Hofmann-Engl, Ludger. 12 Essenden Rd, Sanderstead, Surrey CR2 0BU *tel:* 020 8651 5832 *also fax; email:* hofmannengl@netscape.net. *Maecenas. Orch, pno, chmbr, vocal.*

Hold, Trevor. Dovecote House, Wadenhoe, Oundle, Northants, via Peterborough PE8 5SU *tel:* 01832 720279 *also fax. Ramsey, TP. Concert mus, opera.*

Höller, York. c/o Boosey & Hawkes Music Publishers Ltd, 295 Regent St, London W1R 8JH *tel:* 020 7580 2060 *fax:* 020 7637 3490 *email:* composers@boosey.com. *Opera, concertos, orch and tape, chmbr.*

* **Holloway, Laurie.** Elgin, Fishery Rd, Bray, Berkshire SL6 1UP *tel:* 01628 637715 *fax:* 01628 776232 *email:* LaurenceHolloway@compuserve.com. *TV and film scores.*

Holloway, Robin. c/o Boosey & Hawkes Music Publishers Ltd, 295 Regent St, London W1R 8JH *tel:* 020 7580 2060 *fax:* 020 7436 5675 *email:* composers@boosey.com. *Opera, orch, concertos, ens and chmbr.*

Holt, Simon. c/o Chester Music, 8-9 Frith St, London W1V 5TZ *tel:* 020 7434 0066 *fax:* 020 7287 6329 *email:* music@musicsales.co.uk. *AAK, Ches, UE. Contemporary classical mus.*

* **Hooper, Nicholas.** Muffities, The Ridings, Stonesfield, Witney, Oxon OX8 8EA *tel:* 01993 891313 *fax:* 01993 891085. *BMG, Carlin, EMI, Trackdown. Film and TV scores.*

* **Hope, Peter.** Toller Mill, Toller Porcorum, Dorchester, Dorset DT2 0DQ *tel:* 01300 320826 *fax:* 01300 321131. *AA, Arc, ME, Wein.*

Hopkins CBE, Antony. Woodyard Cottage, Ashridge, Berkhamsted, Herts HP4 1PS *tel:* 01442 842257. *Agent: Lunn, Wright. Ches, Wein, Bardic, Schott. Mus for radio features, drama, film, opera, choral, ballet.*

Horne, David. c/o Boosey & Hawkes Music Publishers Ltd, 295 Regent St, London W1R 8JH *tel:* 020 7580 2060 *fax:* 020 7436 5675 *email:* composers@boosey.com. *Opera, concerto, ens, chmbr.*

* **Horovitz, Joseph.** 7 Dawson Place, London W2 4TD *tel:* 020 7229 5333 *also fax. ABd, Belwin, BH, Ches, Emerson, Molenaar, Nov, OUP, Schott, Smith, Studio.*

Hough, Lester. c/o Da Capo Music Ltd, 26 Stanway Rd, Whitefield, Manchester M45 8EG *tel:* 0161 766 5950. *Solo, chmbr, choral, orch.*

Hoyland, David. c/o Roxane Houston Concert Agency, 8 Hartington Rd, Aldeburgh, Suffolk IP15 5HD *tel:* 01728 454048. *Opera, drama, chmbr, songs, choral, orch.*

Hubicki MBE, Margaret (Katharine Lovell). Flat 1, 14 Abbey Gardens, London NW8 9AT *tel:* 020 7624 1031. *B, Braydeston, Faber, Hin, Schott. Vocal, inst (vn, vc, fl, pno), educ.*

* **Hudes, Eric.** The Old White Horse, Parsonage St, Halstead, Essex CO9 2JZ *tel:* 01787 475845. *Anglian (sp), B, For, Simrock, TP. Concert mus, theatre mus.*

Huehns, Colin. 18 Crundale Ave, London NW9 9PL *tel:* 020 8204 7369. *Opera, vocal, inst, chmbr, choral.*

Hughes, Edward Dudley. 36 Dorset St, Bath BA2 3RA *tel:* 01225 471541 *also fax; email:* e_d_hughes@compuserve.com.

Hughes, Eric. 65 Mount Pleasant, S Ruislip, Middx HA4 9HQ *tel:* 020 8841 2880. *Emerson, Griffiths, Harlequin, Schauer, Studio, WC. Musicals, arranging (especially br and military bands).*

Hugill, Andrew. De Montfort University, Hawthorn Building, Room 00.11, 1 The Gateway, Leicester LE1 9BH *tel:* 0116 250 6146 *fax:* 0116 257 7583 *email:* ahu@dmu.ac.uk. *Cymbalum Pataphysicum, Forward, Rubble. Concert works, mus theatre, TV, film, electronic.*

* **Hugill, Robert C.** 36 Torrens Rd, Brixton, London SW2 5BT *tel:* 020 7274 3600 *email:* hugill@hugill.demon.co.uk. *Bardic, Da Capo. Choral, vocal, orch.*

Humpage, David. The Church, Toft-Next-Newton, Lincolnshire LN8 3NE *tel:* 01673 878719 *email:* david.humpage@zetnet.co.uk. *(sp). Orch, chmbr, opera, theatre, film, image-related mus.*

Humphris, Ian. 21 Brackley Rd, London W4 2HW *tel:* 020 8747 1025. *Nov. Choral arr, orch, mus for children.*

Hunt, Geoffrey. 52 Wolsey Rd, Ashford, Middx TW15 2RB. *Da Capo. Chmbr, gui, educ.*

* **Hunt, Oliver.** 35 Salisbury Rd, Harrow, Middx HA1 1NU *tel:* 020 8863 8275 *also fax. Guitar Solo Publications, Music Sales, Revelo-Cornish, Schott, (sp). Educ, inst, electronic mus.*

Hurd, Michael. 4 Church St, W Liss, Hants GU33 6JX *tel:* 01730 893378. *Nov. Choral, orch, chmbr, opera, film.*

* **Hush, David.** 170 Windsor St, Paddington, Sydney NSW 2021, Australia *tel:* 00 612 9328 1685 *also fax; email:* hush@tig.com.au. *Hush Edition (sp). Orch, inst, chmbr and concert mus.*

Iliff, James. Eithin Tewion, Cilycwm, Llandovery, Caerfyrddin SA20 0TF *tel:* 01550 720021. *(sp). Momentum in mus.*

Ingman, Nick. 9 Elizabeth Court, Ferris Rd, London SE22 9NP *tel:* 020 8693 5608 *fax:* 020 8693 9576 *email:* ningman@yahoo.com. *Film, TV, records.*

Inwood, Paul. 3 Marlborough Park, Havant, Hants PO9 2PP *tel:* 023 9249 8388. *Chapman/Cassell, GIA (USA), Magnificat, McCrimmon, OCP (USA), Willow (Aus), WLP (USA). Liturgical and choral mus.*

* **Ives, Grayston.** Potmans Heath Cottage, Wittersham, Tenterden, Kent TN30 7PU *tel:* 01797 270347. *Banks, Curwen, Faber, Nov, OUP, Ric, Rob, RSCM, SB. Choral mus.*

* **Jackson, Andy.** 13 West Road, Bishop Auckland, Durham DL14 7PP *tel:* 01388 607060. *Durham County Books, Schott, Hampton, Ric. Choral, ens, dance, gui mus, mus theatre, opera, orch, br band, composer in educ, soundtracks.*

Jackson, Antony. c/o Redhill Cottage, Hookagate, Shrewsbury, Shropshire SY5 8BP *tel:* 01743 860726. *(sp). Orch, chmbr, gui, choral, educ.*

Jackson OBE, Francis. Nether Garth, East Acklam, Malton, N Yorks YO17 9RG *tel:* 01653 658395. *Asch, Banks, Nov, OUP, Paraclete, RSCM. Org, church mus, monodramas.*

Jackson, Gabriel. Basement Flat, 10 Comeragh Rd, London W14 9HP *tel:* 020 7381 4326 *also fax; email:* comera@globalnet.co.uk. *ABd. Orch, chmbr, inst, vocal, choral.*

Jacobson, Julian. 34 St Margaret's Rd, London SE4 1YU *tel:* 020 8694 9525 *fax:* 020 8692 7065 *email:* julian.jacobson@breathemail.net. *Bardic. Inst, chmbr, pno, songs, film.*

* **Jacques, Michael.** 22 Stephen's Rd, Tunbridge Wells, Kent TN4 9JE *tel:* 01892 537764 *fax:* 01892 511352. *ABd, B, Oec, OUP, Quavers Rest (sp), Ramsey, Ric, Rob, SB, Studio. Educ, concert.*

* **Janovicky, Karel.** 18 Muswell Ave, London N10 2EG *tel:* 020 8883 6351 *also fax; email:* simsova@simsova.demon.co.uk. *Orch, chmbr, songs, children's mus, opera, org, pno.*

Jenkins, Clive. 9 Fircroft Rd, Beacon Park, Plymouth, Devon PL2 3JU *tel:* 01752 709236. *Oec, Hohner (sp). Orch, choral, concert band, br band.*

Jenkins, Karl. c/o Boosey & Hawkes Music Publishers Ltd, 295 Regent St, London W1R 8JH *tel:* 020 7580 2060 *fax:* 020 7637 3490 *email:* composers@boosey.com. *Orch, choral, chmbr, TV and film.*

Johnson, Christopher. The Blue Coat School, Somerset Rd, Harborne, Edgbaston, Birmingham B17 0HR *tel:* 0121 454 1425; 07958 900006. *(sp). Film and TV scores, educ mus.*

* **Jones, Kenneth Victor.** Cleavers, Bishopstone Village, Seaford, E Sussex BN25 2UD *tel:* 01323 894377. *ABd, Ches, Nov. Concert works, film scores.*

* **Jordan, John.** 3 Famet Close, Purley, Surrey CR8 2DX *tel:* 020 8660 1542. *Bardic, Kahn & Averill, Roeginga Edition. Chmbr, orch, choral, songs, opera.*

Joseph, Jeffrey. 15 Selsdon Rd, London SE27 0PQ *tel:* 020 8766 6668 *fax:* 020 7486 6018. *Orch, vocal, ens, inst, incidental mus, chmbr.*

* **Joubert, John.** 63 School Rd, Moseley, Birmingham B13 9TF *tel:* 0121 449 4997. *Nov. Opera, orch, choral, chmbr, vocal, inst.*

Judd, Garry. 30 Kingsway, Ware, Herts SG12 0QT *tel:* 01920 487823 *also fax; email:* aaron@artcorp.co.uk. *Artful Music. Film, TV, radio, concert, musicals.*

Kagel, Mauricio. c/o Peters Edition Ltd, 10-12 Baches St, London N1 6DN *tel:* 020 7553 4030 *fax:* 020 7490 4921 *email:* newmusic@uk.edition-peters.com.

Kancheli, Giya. c/o Boosey & Hawkes Music Publishers Ltd, 295 Regent St, London W1R 8JH *tel:* 020 7580 2060 *fax:* 020 7637 3490 *email:* composers@boosey.com. *Orch, concerto, ens.*

* **Kay, Norman Forber.** The Summer House, St Donats, nr Llantwit Major, S Wales CF61 1ZB *tel:* 01446 794775 *also fax. Apollo, BH, Emerson, OUP, Polygram. Orch, opera, chmbr, film and TV.*

Keeley, Robert. 38 Wakeman Rd, London NW10 5DE *tel:* 020 8968 3625; 020 7848 2486 *email:* robert.keeley@kcl.ac.uk. *Orch, chmbr, choral, vocal.*

Keeling, Andrew. 15 Marsh Rd, Thornton-Cleveleys, Lancs FY5 2SE *tel:* 01253 825927 *email:* andrew@keelings.u-net.com. *Crimson Music. Orch, chmbr, choral, vocal.*

Kell, Richard. 18 Rectory Grove, Gosforth, Newcastle upon Tyne NE3 1AL *tel:* 0191 284 2017. *Solo, small ens, orch.*

* **Kendell, Iain.** Mousehole Cottage, 1-32 Park Rd, Swanage, Dorset BH19 2AD *tel:* 01929 422739. *Arnold, Ches, Keysworth Press (sp as Mousehole Publications). TV and radio, chmbr, songs, pno, choral, orch.*

Kenny, John. 69 Spottiswoode St, Edinburgh EH9 1DL *tel:* 0131 447 3707 *also fax; email:* carnyx@mcmail.com. *Tezak Verlag (Cologne), Warwick. Mus theatre, dance, ens, orch, film, TV.*

* **Kiernan, Catherine.** 33 Arun Vale, Coldwaltham, Pulborough, W Sussex RH20 1LP *tel:* 01798 872 978. *Planet Music (sp). Chmbr, orch, choral.*

Kilvington, Chris. 40 Thornton Rd, Cambridge CB3 0NW *tel:* 01223 276763 *fax:* 01223 277980 *email:* chriskilvi.cmw@argonet.co.uk. *Cambridge Music Works, Corda, Edition Transatlantique, Hampton, KM, Ric, Verlag Nogatz. Gui mus.*

* **Kimpton, Geoffrey.** 52 Hillingdon Rd, Stretford, Manchester M32 8PJ *tel:* 0161 865 1201. *(sp). Orch, chmbr, choral, solo vocal, and inst mus.*

King, Denis. 55 Parliament Hill, London NW3 *tel:* 020 7794 5110. *Deekers. Film and TV scores.*

King, Geoffrey. c/o Hazel Sheppard, 16 Clerwood Gardens, Edinburgh EH12 8PT *tel:* 0131 539 8877 *fax:* 0131 539 2211.

King, Matthew. Brook Garden Cottage, Troy Town Lane, Brook, Ashford, Kent TN25 5PQ *tel:* 01233 813066 *also fax; email:* matthew.king@argonet.co.uk. *Chmbr, choral, opera, ens, pno, vocal, orch, educ mus theatre, pno.*

* **Kinsey, Tony.** 5 The Pennards, Sunbury-on-Thames, Middx TW16 5JZ *tel:* 01932 783160. *APC, BH, KPM, WC. TV and film scores.*

Kirby, Kenneth. 18 Silvertree Close, Walton on Thames, Surrey KT12 1NN *tel:* 01932 228635. *Light classics.*

Kirkwood, Antoinette. 56 Sutherland St, London SW1V 4JZ *tel:* 020 7828 1683 *fax:* 020 7828 7907. *Andresier, Bardic. Orch, chmbr mus, songs.*

* **Kiszko, Martin.** 29 Wellington Park, Clifton, Bristol BS8 2UW *tel:* 0117 973 1267 *fax:* 0117 973 8170. *Film and TV, stage.*

Knight, Tim. The Lodge, 178 Ottey Rd, West Park, Leeds LS8 1PE *tel:* 0113 289 9010 *also fax. Corda, Phylloscopus, Oec, Parish, Parkfield, Sam King. Inst, ens, choral.*

Knotts, David. 48a Oakdale Rd, Streatham, London SW16 2HL *tel:* 020 8677 3047. *Chmbr, ens, choral, inst, opera, vocal.*

Knussen, Oliver. c/o Faber Music Ltd, 3 Queen Square, London WC1N 3AU *tel:* 020 7833 7911/2 *fax:* 020 7833 7939 *email:* promotion@fabermusic.co.uk. *Faber. Opera, inst, orch, chmbr, vocal.*

Kodjabashia, Nikola. c/o ECAM Limited, 130 Drayton Park, Highbury, London N5 1LX *tel:* 020 7354 3844 *fax:* 07070 605072 *email:* info@ecam-limited.com. *Orch, chmbr, opera, theatre, film, live electronic.*

Kolb, Barbara. c/o Boosey & Hawkes Music Publishers Ltd, 295 Regent St, London W1R 8JH *tel:* 020 7580 2060 *fax:* 020 7637 3490 *email:* composers@boosey.com. *Orch, chmbr, pno, pre-recorded tapes.*

Kurtág, György. c/o Boosey & Hawkes Music Publishers Ltd, 295 Regent St, London W1R 8JH *tel:* 020 7580 2060 *fax:* 020 7637 3490 *email:* composers@boosey.com. *Orch, ens, chmbr, vocal, pno.*

Laing, Alan. Barnham Lodge, Townend Rd, Walkington, E Yorks HU17 8SY *tel:* 01482 870210. *Da Capo, Fentone, (sp). Theatrical mus, pno, vn, va, orch, chmbr, choral, inst.*

Lamb, Peter. 5 Silchester Close, Bournemouth BH2 6PY *tel:* 01202 295034. *BH.*

* **Lambert, Edward.** The Old Rectory, Smannell, Andover SP11 6JW *tel:* 01264 338700 *fax:* 01264 345696 *email:* lambert@which.net. *Concert mus, theatre, TV, educ.*

* **Lambros, Simon.** Elmina, Old Dashwood Hill, Studley Green, Bucks HP14 3XD *tel:* 01494 483524 *also fax; email:* cimbam @lmps.freeserve.co.uk. *Charo Pubs, KM. Film and TV, concert mus, theatre mus.*

* **Lane, Philip.** 10 Trafalgar St, Cheltenham, Glos GL50 1UH *tel:* 01242 226101 *also fax. Banks, Bourne, Fentone, Fulcrum, KM, KPM, Lorenz, Nov, OUP, Rob, Smith, Studio, UE, Wein, WR. Orch, choral, chmbr, TV and radio.*

Last OBE, Joan. 11 St Mary's Close, Littlehampton, W Sussex BN17 5PZ *tel:* 01903 713522. *AA, B, BH, Cramer, Curwen, EMI, For, GMC, JW, LGB, Lorenz (USA), MSM, Nov, OUP, SB, WC.*

* **Laurence, Zack.** 1 Glanleam Rd, Stanmore, Middx HA7 4NW *tel:* 020 8954 2025 *also fax. Miriamusic. Music House: Production Music. TV, film scores and jingles.*

Lawrance, Peter A. 7 Reading Ave, Nuneaton, Warwicks CV11 6HE *tel:* 024 7637 3250. *Alders, Arnold, Brass Wind, Ches, Fortune, Frontier, Keynote, Practical Teacher, Thomas Nelson. Musicals, educ, wind mus, br ens, br band, vocal, orch.*

Lawrence, Mark. 88 Belmont Rd, St Andrews, Bristol BS6 5AU *tel:* 0117 942 3775 *fax:* 0117 942 3526. *Vocal, choral, children's and community opera, theatre and radio.*

Lawson, Gordon. Braeside, 32 College Place, Brighton BN2 1HN *tel:* 01273 705426. *Cathedral, Emerson, F-E, Kenwood (USA), Nov, Oec, RSCM, Selah (USA), TP. Choral, pno, inst, org, songs, chmbr, concertos.*

Laycock, Jolyon. Music Dept, University of Bath, Avon BA2 7AY *tel:* 01225 826431 *also fax; email:* j.laycock@bath.ac.uk. *Opera, chmbr, solo.*

Leach, John. 68 Lysia St, London SW6 6NG *tel:* 020 7385 0182 *fax:* 020 7381 1155. *Bruton, Editio Musica Budapest, KPM, Rob, Studio G, Parry Music (Canada), WC, Wein, Wolfe, Yorke. Film mus.*

Leadbetter, Martin. Ivy Lodge, 2 Priory Lane, Little Wymondley, Herts SG4 7HE *tel:* 01438 359292 *fax:* 01438 759113. *Con Moto, Fentone, Mostyn. Inst, vocal, choral, orch.*

* **Lee, Clifford.** 21 Lawn Lane, Springfield, Chelmsford, Essex CM1 6NP *tel:* 01245 357539. *Melandra (sp). Concert and chmbr mus.*

Lees, Benjamin. c/o Boosey & Hawkes Music Publishers Ltd, 295 Regent St, London W1R 8JH *tel:* 020 7580 2060 *fax:* 020 7637 3490 *email:* composers@boosey.com. *Orch, concertos.*

le Fleming, Antony. c/o Diana Hirst PR, 55 Marmora Rd, London SE22 0RY *tel:* 020 8299 1914 *also fax; email:* Hirstpr@aol.com. *Roberton, Samuel King, CWM Music.*

Lesser, David. 351 Station Rd, Dorridge, Solihull, W Midlands B93 8EY *tel:* 01564 772402 *also fax; email:* dtlesser@aol.com. *Chmbr, inst and vocal.*

* **Lewis, Jeffrey.** Crafnant, Park Cres, Llanfairfechan, Gwynedd LL33 0AU *tel:* 01248 680776. *Nov, Rob, Curiad. Orch, chmbr, choral, vocal, solo.*

* **Lewis, Paul.** 9 Westbourne St, Hove, E Sussex BN3 5PE *tel:* 01273 204064 *also fax. Studio G, de Wolfe. TV, production library, concert.*

Liddle, David. 9 Western Rd, East Finchley, London N2 9JB *tel:* 020 8444 4454. *Nov, (sp). Org mus.*

Lindberg, Magnus. c/o Boosey & Hawkes Music Publishers Ltd, 295 Regent St, London W1R 8JH *tel:* 020 7580 2060 *fax:* 020 7637 3490 *email:* composers@boosey.com. *Orch, concertos, ens, chmbr.*

Lindley, Simon. 17 Fulneck, Pudsey, Leeds LS28 8NT *tel:* 0113 255 6143 *also fax; email:* simonlin@nascr.net. *Banks, OUP, Ramsey, RSCM. Church mus.*

* **Lipkin, Malcolm.** Penlan, Crowborough Hill, Crowborough, E Sussex TN6 2EA *tel:* 01892 652454. *Ches, (sp). Symphonies, concertos, chmbr, inst, choral, vocal.*

Llewellyn MBE, William. Forecourt, Queens Square, Colyton, Devon EX24 6JX *tel:* 01297 552414 *also fax; email:* wll@mcmail.com. *Nov, OUP, RSCM. Choral, educ mus, hymn tunes.*

Lloyd, Jonathan. c/o Boosey & Hawkes Music Publishers Ltd, 295 Regent St, London W1R 8JH *tel:* 020 7580 2060 *fax:* 020 7436 5675 *email:* composers@boosey.com. *Orch, concertos, chmbr, ens.*

Lloyd, Richard. Refail Newydd, Pentraeth, Anglesey LL75 8YF *tel:* 01248 450220. *Banks, Basil Ramsey, Cathedral, Encore, Kirklees Cathedral Music, KM, Leng, Lorenz, Nov, RSCM. Church mus.*

Lloyd-Howells, David. 26 Bevelin Hall, Saundersfoot, Pembrokeshire SA69 9PG *tel:* 01834 814894 *email:* 100622.3205@compuserve.com. *DLH Productions (sp), Five Lines. Sonic art mus concept and protoscores all media. I.D.E.A.*

* **Lloyd Webber, Andrew.** The Really Useful Group Ltd, 22 Tower St, London WC2H 9NS *tel:* 020 7240 0880 *fax:* 020 7240 1204. *Really Useful Group.*

* **Lord, David.** c/o Terra Incognita, 1 Walcot Gate, Bath BA1 5UG *tel:* 01225 462286 *also fax; email:* dlord@easynet.co.uk. *Cary, Chapman, Ches, OUP, UE. Film and TV scores.*

* **Lovett, Andrew.** 1 George's Terrace, Halifax Rd, Cambridge CB4 3PY *tel:* 01223 369641 *fax:* 01223 740736 *email:* acl29@cam.ac.uk. *(sp). Electro-acoustic mus, chmbr, opera, theatre.*

Lowe, Jez. 60 Maritime Cres, Horden, Peterlee, Co Durham SR8 3SX *tel:* 0191 586 1938 *also fax; email:* jez.lowe@lineone.net. *Lowe Life Music (sp). Folk mus.*

* **Luff, Enid.** 12 Heol Tyn Y Cae, Cardiff CF14 6DJ *tel:* 029 2061 6023 *also fax; email:* luff@globalnet.co.uk. *Primavera (sp). Chmbr, orch, church anthems, dance and pno.*

* **Lyon, David.** 1 St Rumbolds Rd, Shaftesbury, Dorset SP7 8NE *tel:* 01747 855903. *ABd, Ches, Fulcrum, ME, Studio, WC. Orch, choral, educ, mus theatre, children's mus events.*

* **McBain, Hugh.** 1 Munro Rd, Glasgow G13 1SQ *tel:* 0141 959 1966. *SMIC. Mus theatre, symphony, chmbr, pno, concerto.*

* **McCabe, John.** 49 Burns Ave, Southall, Middx UB1 2LR *tel:* 020 8574 5039 *also fax. Nov, OUP.*

* **McCartney, Sir Paul.** c/o MPL Communications Ltd, 1 Soho Square, London W1 *tel:* 020 7534 4000 *fax:* 020 7439 1492.

McDevitt, Robert. c/o Bardic Edition, 6 Fairfax Cres, Aylesbury, Bucks HP20 2ES *tel:* 01296 428609 *also fax; email:* 101464.2670@ compuserve.com. *Bardic. Pno, inst.*

* **McDowall, Cecilia.** 58 Abinger Rd, London W4 1EX *tel:* 020 8994 8639 *also fax; email:* mcdowall@argonet.co.uk. *Gemini, Hunt, Nova, Pan Educational. Chmbr mus, choral, songs, children's mus.*

McGowan, Peter. c/o Caroline Ireland Management, Uwchlaw'r Coed, Llanbedr, Gwynedd LL45 2NA *tel:* 01341 241532 *also fax; email:* caroline.ireland@virgin.net. *Film, ballet scores, chmbr mus, mus theatre.*

McGregor, Richard Ewan. c/o Performing Arts Dept, St Martin's College, Bowerham Rd, Lancaster LA1 3JD *tel:* 01524 384234/384339 *fax:* 01524 384593 *email:* r.mcgregor@ucsm.ac.uk.

* **McGuire, Eddie.** 13 Lawrence St, Glasgow G11 5HH *tel:* 0141 334 8580. *Opera, ballet, orch, solo.*

MacIlwham, George. 25 Ravelston Rd, Bearsden, Glasgow G61 1AW *tel:* 0141 942 6779. *SMIC, WC. Orch, choral, chmbr, songs, bagpipe, Scottish mus.*

McIntosh, John M. Stamford, 55 Royal Cres, Dunoon, Argyll PA23 7AQ *tel:* 01369 703304 *email:* mcintosh@maura.demon.co.uk. *Choral, arrangements.*

Mackey, Steven. c/o Boosey & Hawkes Music Publishers Ltd, 295 Regent St, London W1R 8JH *tel:* 020 7580 2060 *fax:* 020 7637 3490 *email:* composers@boosey.com. *Chmbr, orch, voice and str quartet.*

Mackmin, Norman. 17 Bazehill Rd, Rottingdean, E Sussex BN2 7DB *tel:* 01273 302033. *Film and TV, songs, light classical, musicals.*

McLain, John (J A Lain). 42 Osidge Lane, Southgate, London N14 5JG *tel:* 020 8368 2759. *Bardic (Copperplate). Vocal, inst, pno, choral, humour, ballads.*

McLelland-Young, Thomas. 2 Onslow Gardens, Sanderstead, Surrey CR2 9AB *tel:* 020 8651 0072. *KM, Nov, Oec. Choral, org, song cycles, ballet, orch, pno, chmbr.*

* **McLeod, John.** Hill House, 9 Redford Cres, Edinburgh EH13 0BS *tel:* 0131 441 3035 *fax:* 0131 441 5218 *email:* john.mcleod@ btinternet.com. *For, Griffin, Sparta Florida. Choral, orch, chmbr, inst mus, film and TV.*

MacMillan, James. c/o Boosey & Hawkes Music Publishers Ltd, 295 Regent St, London W1R 8JH *tel:* 020 7580 2060 *fax:* 020 7637 3490 *email:* composers@boosey.com. *Opera, orch, concertos, choral, chmbr. Also contact:* Intermusica Artists' Management Ltd, 16 Duncan Terrace, London N1 8BZ *tel:* 020 7278 5455 *fax:* 020 7278 8434.

* **McNeff, Stephen.** 131 Melbourne Grove, London SE22 8RR *tel:* 020 8693 8388 *fax:* 020 8516 6134 *email:* stephen_mcneff@lineone.net.

Brassworks (Toronto), Samuel French. Opera, mus theatre, theatre songs, chmbr.

McPhee MBE, George. 17 Main Rd, Castlehead, Paisley, Renfrewshire PA2 6AJ *tel:* 0141 889 3528 *fax:* 0141 840 4906. *Oec. Church and choral mus.*

* **McQueen, Ian.** 159 Newport Rd, Leyton, London E10 6PG *tel:* 020 8926 1867 *fax:* 020 8926 1862 *email:* ianmcqueen@compongo.freeserve.co.uk. *Ric. Opera, orch, vocal and chmbr mus.*

Magill, Ronan. 22 Princes Gate Mews, London SW7 2PS *tel:* 020 7584 3795.

Mallett, Charles. c/o Roxane Houston Concert Agency, 8 Hartington Rd, Aldeburgh, Suffolk IP15 5HD *tel:* 01728 454048. *Opera, chmbr, songs, orch, pno.*

Malone, Kevin. Dept of Music, University of Manchester, Denmark Rd, Manchester M15 6HY *tel:* 0161 275 4987 *fax:* 0161 275 4994 *email:* KHMalone@aol.com. *OUP, For, Dorn. Orch, chmbr, electro-acoustic, multimedia, theatre, dance.*

* **Manduell CBE, Sir John.** Chesham, High Bentham, Lancaster LA2 7JY *tel:* 0161 273 8111 *fax:* 0161 273 8222 *email:* mailbox@eoperac.org.uk. *For, Nov.*

Markham, Karen. Flat 1, 88 Brantingham Rd, Whalley Range, Manchester M16 8LZ *tel:* 0161 881 7795. *Ens, orch, inst, chmbr, vocal, choral.*

Marsh, Roger. c/o Music Dept, University of York, Heslington, York YO10 5DD *tel:* 01904 432432 *fax:* 01904 432450. *Maecenas, Nov. Orch, ens, vocal, mus theatre.*

Martelli, Carlo. 215 Burrage Rd, London SE18 7JZ *tel:* 020 8316 7905. *Broadbent & Dunn, Leng. Inst, opera and film scores.*

* **Martin, David Charles.** 27 Nimrod Rd, London SW16 6SZ *tel:* 020 8769 6537 *email:* MusicDCM@incipit.force9.co.uk. *(sp). Mus theatre, opera, chmbr.*

* **Martin, Philip.** Chapel House, Theobald's Green, Calstone, nr Calne, Wilts SN11 8QE *tel:* 01249 812508 *also fax; email:* pmandppj@globalnet.co.uk. *BH, Bosworths, Irish Contemporary Music Centre. Symphony, concertos, chmbr, choral.*

Martinez, Odaline de la. c/o Lontano Trust, Toynbee Studios, 28 Commercial St, London E1 6LS *tel:* 020 7247 2950 *fax:* 020 7247 2956 *email:* odaline@hanita.demon.co.uk. *Opera, chmbr, inst, vocal, choral.*

Martland, Steve. c/o Schott & Co Ltd, 48 Gt Marlborough St, London W1V 2BN *tel:* 020 7494 1487 *fax:* 020 7287 1529 *email:* schottcontemporarymusic@compuserve.com. *Schott.*

Mason, Douglas Gerald. Chetham's School of Music, Long Millgate, Manchester M3 1SB *tel:* 0161 838 7220. *Encore.*

Matthew-Walker, Robert. 1 Exford Rd, London SE12 9HD *tel:* 020 8857 1582 *also fax. Arena, BH, Leng, OUP, Ramsey.*

Matthews, Colin. 3 Manchuria Rd, London SW11 6AF *tel:* 020 7228 5591 *fax:* 020 7228 2358. *Faber, Nov.*

* **Matthews, David.** 12 Woodlands, Clapham Common North Side, London SW4 0RJ *tel:* 020 7622 1607 *fax:* 020 7720 5426. *BH, Faber.*

Maw, Nicholas. c/o Faber Music Ltd, 3 Queen Square, London WC1N 3AU *tel:* 020 7833 7911/2 *fax:* 020 7833 7939 *email:* promotion@fabermusic.co.uk. *BH, Ches, Faber, Nov, OUP. Opera, inst, orch, chmbr, vocal.*

Maxwell Davies, Sir Peter. c/o Mrs J Arnold, Flat 3, 50 Hogarth Rd, London SW5 0PU *tel:* 020 7370 2328 *fax:* 020 7373 6730 *email:* j.arnold@maxopus.com. *BH, Ches, Schott.*

Mayer, John. 27 Hermitage Rd, London N4 1DF *tel:* 020 8802 2421 *also fax; email:* indojazz@compuserve.com. *Leng, Lopes, Preston Stevens, Paragon, Schott, Simrock. Musicals, orch, chmbr, radio and film mus.*

* **Messervy, George.** Flat 20, Hautmont Close, Mont Millais, St Helier, Jersey JE2 4XS *tel:* 01534 610055. *Chmbr, inst, choral, orch, vocal.*

Metcalf, John. Ty Yfory, Llanfair Rd, Lampeter, Ceredigion SA48 8JZ *tel:* 01570 493576 *fax:* 01570 493636 *email:* john@metcalf.demon.co.uk. *Curiad.*

* **Michelmore, Guy.** Atlantic Studios, 65 Jeddo Rd, London W12 9ED *tel:* 020 8740 7727 *fax:* 020 8743 2523 *email:* guy@mftv.co.uk. *Music for Television. TV and film scores.*

Miller, Charles. c/o Darren Ockert Management, The Young Vic, 66 The Cut, South Bank, London SE1 8LZ *tel:* 020 7928 8353 *fax:* 020 7928 8505 *email:* darrenockert@easynet.co.uk. *Mus theatre.*

Mills, Alan. 87 Palmerston Rd, Wood Green, London N22 4QS *tel:* 020 8888 8214. *Material Productions, Music Haven, Warwick. Concert, vocal, choral.*

* **Mitcham, David.** 1 Lyons Green Cottages, Shillinglee Rd, Plaistow, W Sussex RH14 0PH *tel:* 01403 871297 *fax:* 01403 871303 *email:* david@lyonsgreen.demon.co.uk. *Brass Wind, Carlin, WC, Wein. Film scores and concert mus.*

Mitchell, John. Woodstock, Pett Bottom, Canterbury, Kent CT4 5PB *tel:* 01227 832871. *Mayola, Modus, TP. Handbell mus.*

Mitchell-Davidson, Paul. 25 Bannerman Ave, Prestwich, Manchester M25 1DZ *tel:* 0161 798 9604 *also fax; email:* pm-d@muse.telinco.co.uk. *Kamela, Maurice Wray. Chmbr, dance, jazz, orch, radio, theatre, TV, educ.*

Monk, Peter Anthony. Fir Tree House, 169b St James's Rd, Croydon, Surrey CR0 2BY *tel:* 020 8689 9268 *fax:* 020 8689 4739. *Belpaire (sp), Suv. Solo inst and voice, full ens, film mus, chmbr mus, br and songs.*

* **Montague, Stephen.** 2 Ryland Rd, London NW5 3EA *tel:* 020 7267 5416 *also fax; email:* srmontague@aol.com. *Mod Ed, UMP. Concert mus, electro-acoustic mus, dance, ballet.*

Moody, Ivan. c/o Vanderbeek & Imrie Ltd, 15 Marvig, Lochs, Isle of Lewis HS2 9QP *tel:* 01851 880216 *also fax. Vanderbeek. Choral, orch, religious, chmbr, inst.*

* **Moore, Timothy.** 86 Chesterton Rd, Cambridge CB4 1ER *tel:* 01223 564933/363731 (answerphone). *Editions BIM, Elkin, For, Frontier Press, Nov, Oriel Library, Schott, Westerleigh. Chmbr, orch, choral, vocal.*

Morgan, Glen. c/o Anthony Abbott Music Management, Medlar Cottage, Lodge Lane, Keymer, Hassocks, W Sussex BN6 8NA *tel:* 01273 843348 *fax:* 01273 846585 *email:* glenmorgan@gemtones.demon.co.uk. *Soundscapes UK. Br band, choral, classical gui, orch, songs.*

Morris, Keith. 5 Bentinck Rd, Newcastle upon Tyne NE4 6UT *tel:* 0191 273 5326. *Br band, choral, jazz, contemporary classical, dance, film and TV, theatre, educ.*

Morris, Peter. 56 Gloucester Place, London W1H 3HL *tel:* 020 7486 3297 *also fax; email:* amewiscal@aol.com. *Film, library, concert.*

Musgrave, Thea. c/o Novello & Co Ltd, 8-9 Frith St, London W1V 5TZ *tel:* 020 7434 0066 *fax:* 020 7287 6329 *email:* music@musicsales.co.uk.

* **Naylor, Peter.** Greenacres, Brady Rd, Lyminge, Folkestone, Kent CT18 8HA *tel:* 01303 863284. *Nov, Oec, Ramsey. Opera, vocal, orch and inst mus.*

Nelson, Peter. Faculty of Music, Edinburgh University, Alison House, Nicolson Square, Edinburgh EH8 9DF *tel:* 0131 650 2433 *fax:* 0131 650 2425 *email:* p.nelson@music.ed.ac.uk. *SMIC. Orch, chmbr, electro-acoustic.*

* **Nevens, David.** Trengale, Piccadilly, Llanblethian, Cowbridge, Vale of Glamorgan CF71 7JL *tel:* 01446 771317 *also fax;* 00 968 544747 *also fax; email:* rgoroslb@gto.net.om. *Welsh Music Information Centre, Cyhaeadiadau Curiad. TV and film scores, educ mus. Also at: PO Box 18, SEEB 121, Oman.*

* **Neville, Paul.** 9 Greenfield Rd, Eastbourne, E Sussex BN21 1JJ *tel:* 01323 640067 *fax:* 01323 644699 *email:* music@greenfield.prestel.co.uk. *Orch, ens, film, TV, theatre.*

Newson, George. Chapel Cottage, Stone in Oxney, nr Tenterden, Kent TN30 7JL *tel:* 01233 758227 *also fax. Leng, Schott. Orch, chmbr, vocal, opera.*

* **Newton, Rodney.** c/o London International Film School, 24 Shelton St, London WC2H 9HP *tel:* 020 7240 0168 *fax:* 020 7497 3718 *email:* lifs@dial.pipex.com. *Chandos, Cranz/UMP, Marc Reift, Rosehill, WR. Film, TV, br and wind band.*

Nicholls, David. Dept of Music, Keele University, Keele, Staffs ST5 5BG *tel:* 01782 583462 *fax:* 01782 583295 *email:* mua02@cc.keele.ac.uk. *Chmbr mus.*

* **Nicholson, George.** 17 Keele Rd, Newcastle under Lyme, Staffs ST5 2JT *tel:* 01782 618156 *email:* g.nicholson@sheffield.ac.uk. *For, University of York. Warwick. Concert work.*

Nockalls, Martin. Charnwood House, High St, Wroot, Doncaster DN9 2BT *tel:* 01302 772677 *also fax; email:* ambrosmus@aol.com. *Amber Rose, Hampton, Wise Owl. Gui mus.*

* **Norris, Michael.** 31 Hawthorn Ave, Glasgow G61 3NG *tel:* 0141 942 5527. *Camden, Sirron Publications (sp), Yorke. Orch, inst, chmbr mus, mus theatre, vocal, youth opera.*

* **North, Roger.** 24 Strand on the Green, London W4 3PH *tel:* 020 8995 9174. *Ches, (sp). Film and TV (electro-acoustic), opera, chmbr, orch.*

* **Nunn, Patrick.** 46 Albert Rd, London N22 7AH *tel:* 020 8881 1758 *also fax; email:* patricknunn@i.am.

* **Nutman, Carey.** Rosegarth, Hetton Rd, Houghton-le-Spring, Durham DH5 8JN *tel:* 0191 584 4141 *also fax; email:* cnutmanmps@compuserve.com. *Electro-acoustic, computer mus, chmbr.*

Nye, Richard. c/o Cascade Music Publishing, 30 College Green, Bristol BS1 5TB *tel:* 01454 323608 *also fax; email:* atticmusic@hotmail.com. *Andresier, Attic (sp), Cascade. Choral, orch, inst, chmbr and ens.*

Nyman, Michael. c/o Chester Music, 8-9 Frith St, London W1V 5TZ *tel:* 020 7434 0066 *fax:* 020 7287 6329. *Publisher: Ches. Manager:* Elizabeth Lloyd, Michael Nyman Ltd, 83 Pulborough Rd, London SW18 5UL *tel:* 020 8870 8961 *fax:* 020 8875 9377 *email:* 106703.1172@compuserve.com. *Film, TV, chmbr mus, songs, orch, opera and choral.*

O'Neill, Nicholas E B. 74 New Bond St, London W1Y 9DD *tel:* 07831 751956 *fax:* 020 7629 5206 *email:* info@noneill.freeserve.co.uk. *Choral, inst.*

Oehring, Helmut. c/o Boosey & Hawkes Music Publishers Ltd, 295 Regent St, London W1R 8JH *tel:* 020 7580 2060 *fax:* 020 7637 3490 *email:* composers@boosey.com. *Chmbr, ens, orch, mus theatre.*

* **Omer, Michael.** 12 Belsize Lane, London NW3 5AB *tel:* 07000 784928; 020 7794 6834; 07836 262457 *email:* michael@musictopicture.com. *A & C Black, Music to Picture Company (sp), TVS Music, Walt Disney Company/Buena Vista. TV and film scores, musicals, concert works.*

Omran, Farid. 14 Eleanor House, Queen Caroline St, Hammersmith, London W6 9RE *tel:* 020 8746 3526 *also fax. Rudaki Publications.*

* **Orr CBE, Robin.** 16 Cranmer Rd, Cambridge CB3 9BL *tel:* 01223 352858. *AA, For, Hin, Nov, OUP, Paraclete, Peters, Schott, SMIC, WC. Opera, orch, chmbr and church mus.*

Orton, Richard. 21 West Moor Lane, Heslington, York YO10 5ER *tel:* 01904 416312 *also fax; email:* orton_richard@hotmail.com. *University of York. Inst, electro-acoustic, orch, vocal; algorithmic computer mus.*

Osbon, David. The Tithe Barn, Ashwell Farm, Windsor Lane, Little Kingshill, Bucks HP16 0DZ *tel:* 01494 866462 *email:* dosbon@sas.upenn.edu. *Contemporary concert.*

* **Osborne, Tony.** 42 Parkland Ave, Slough, Berks SL3 7LQ *tel:* 01753 541818 *also fax; email:* adamo@vossnet.co.uk. *BH, Faber, Piper, Recital, Yorke. Concert, film and TV, educ mus.*

* **Owen, Albert Alan.** Melindwr, Ponterwyd, Aberystwyth, Dyfed SY23 3JY *tel:* 01970 890603 *fax:* 020 7580 4754 *email:* aaocompose@aol.com. *Amphonic, BTW, Chordsongs, Emeryson (sp), Obelisk and New Experience, Vigiesse (Italy). Film, TV and recording.*

Owen Thomas, Janet. c/o Maecenas Music Ltd, 5 Bushey Close, Old Barn Lane, Kenley, Surrey CR8 5AU *tel:* 020 8660 4766 *fax:* 020 8668 5273. *Maecenas, Nov. Concert, ens, chmbr, inst, vocal.*

Oxley, Harrison. 1 Conyers Way, Gt Barton, Bury St Edmunds, Suffolk IP31 2RL *tel:* 01284 787533 *also fax. KM, Nov, OUP, RSCM, Ramsey, Rob. Church, choral, org mus.*

* **Özdil, Sidika.** 31 Cromwell Ave, London N6 5HN *tel:* 020 8341 4671 *also fax. Les Editions de Lestang (France). Orch, chmbr, vocal, choral.*

Paintal, Priti. Peregrine, Grange Rd, St Michaels, Tenterden, Kent TN30 6TS *tel:* 01580 764258 *fax:* 01580 763500 *email:* ppaintal@aol.com. *Opera, orch, chmbr, solo works and works for Western, Asian, African and jazz insts using improvisation.*

Painter, Christopher. 33 Southminster Rd, Penylan, Cardiff CF23 5AT *tel:* 029 2049 1585 *fax:* 029 2049 9970 *email:* painter@aubade.freeserve.co.uk. *Oriana, Vanderbeek. Classical.*

Palmer, Geoffrey. c/o J Audrey Ellison International Artists Management, 135 Stevenage Rd, Fulham, London SW6 6PB *tel:* 020 7381 9751 *fax:* 020 7381 2406. *Music Haven. Song, choral, chmbr, chmbr orch.*

Palmer, John. 70 Western Way, Barnet EN5 2BT *tel:* 020 8275 0693 *also fax; email:* j.palmer@herts.ac.uk. *Inst, orch, chmbr, vocal, electro-acoustic mus.*

* **Panufnik, Roxanna.** c/o Helen Sykes Artists' Management, 1st Floor, Parkway House, Sheen Lane, London SW14 8LS *tel:* 020 8876 8276 *fax:* 020 8876 8277. *AAK. Orch, chmbr, vocal, choral, dance, opera, mus theatre, arranging, TV and film.*

Papastávrou, Krinió. Stackwood Cottage, Monks Eleigh, Ipswich, Suffolk IP7 7BD *tel:* 01449 740321. *Bardic, Lyra. Opera, cantatas, pno, w/wind, songs, str mus.*

* **Parfrey, Raymond.** 53 Longley Rd, Harrow, Middx HA1 4TG *tel:* 020 8427 5267. *AV, Bardic, Cascade, Chapman, Cinque Port, Comus, Con Moto, Cramer, Da Capo, Emerson, Griffiths, Harlequin, Kendor, Longley, Oec, Piccolo, Samuel King, Studio. Wind and br ens, pno, str, choral.*

* **Parker, Alan.** Whistler's Wood, The Ridge, Woldingham, Surrey *tel:* 01883 653147 *fax:* 01883 652579. *Amphonic, ASP, De Wolfe, Golden Eagle, KPM, Music House, Rondor, Themes International. Film and TV scores.*

Parker, Jim. 16 Laurel Rd, London SW13 0EE *tel:* 020 8876 8442 *also fax. BH, Brass Wind Educational, Ches, Faber, IMP, Studio. Film and TV, concert works.*

Parrott, Ian. Henblas Abermad, nr Aberystwyth, Ceredigion SY23 4ES *tel:* 01974 241660. *Banks, BH, Ches, Elk, EMI, For, Griffiths, Gwynn, Leng, MR, Nov, Oec, Samuel King, Schott, PP, TP, UWP, Weekes.*

Parsons, Michael. 148 Fellows Rd, London NW3 3JH *tel:* 020 7722 0054. *EMC, Forward. Vocal, inst, electronic.*

Pärt, Arvo. c/o Universal Edition (London) Ltd, 48 Gt Marlborough St, London W1V 2BN *tel:* 020 7437 6880 *fax:* 020 7437 6115 *email:* miranda@ue-london.demon.co.uk. *UE. Contemporary classical mus.*

Paterson, Wilma. Dalvrecht Manse, Tomintoul, Ballindalloch AB37 9HN *tel:* 01807 580270 *fax:* 01807 580760 *email:* wilma.paterson@virgin.net. *Vocal, chmbr, incidental.*

* **Patten, James.** 1 Crown Cottages, Cats Ash, Shepton Mallet, Somerset BA4 5EL *tel:* 01749 344859 *fax:* 01963 351133 *email:* pattenjames@hotmail.com. *B, KM. Orch, inst ens, inst solo, vocal, military band, TV scores, incidental mus, theatre mus, children's opera.*

Patterson, Paul. 31 Cromwell Ave, London N6 5HN *tel:* 020 8348 3711 *fax:* 020 8340 6489 *email:* p.patterson@ram.ac.uk. *UE, Wein.*

* **Payne, Anthony.** 2 Wilton Square, London N1 3DL *tel:* 020 7359 1593 *fax:* 020 7226 4369 *email:* tony@wiltonsq.demon.co.uk.

Peacock, Bob. 52 Reeth Rd, Linthorpe, Middlesbrough, Cleveland TS5 5JX *tel:* 01642 815943. *Jazz educ, incidental mus.*

Pearce, Malcolm N. 26 The Warren, Abingdon, Oxon OX14 3XD *tel:* 01235 201329. *Camden.*

Peck, Dennis. 167 Woodstock Rd, Oxford OX2 7NA *tel:* 01865 553694. *Opera, songs.*

* **Peggie, Andrew.** 4 Colchester Ave, London E12 5LE *tel:* 020 8514 2219 *fax:* 020 8478 7141. *Wein. Mus theatre, opera, oratorio, multi-ens community productions.*

* **Penri-Evans, David.** 23a High St, Esher, Surrey KT10 9RN *tel:* 01372 471193 *also fax; email:* dpe@penrievans.idps.co.uk. *Bryntirion (sp), Da Capo, UMI (USA). Orch, chmbr, opera, film scores, contemporary dance.*

Perrin, Glyn. 4 Rochester House, Rushcroft Rd, London SW2 17R *tel:* 020 7326 1096 *also fax. University of York. Concert, dance, electro-acoustic scores.*

* **Pert, Morris.** The Chalet, 189 Balchrick, Kinlochbervie, Sutherland IV27 4RU *tel:* 01971 521314. *Wein. Orch, symphonic, inst, electronic, educ, jazz and rock.*

Peyton Jones, Jeremy. 13c Grove Park, London SE5 8LR *tel:* 020 7733 3808 *also fax. Chmbr, dance, film, mus theatre, orch, vocal.*

* **Pheloung, Barrington.** 41 Imperial Ave, Westcliff on Sea, Essex SS0 8NQ *tel:* 01702 342404 *fax:* 01702 331176 *email:* bpheloung@aol.com. *Polygram. Orch, film and TV scores, musicals, ballets.*

Philips, Julian. The Granary, 19 Green End, Comberton, Cambridgeshire CB3 7DY *tel:* 01223 264210 *also fax; email:* granary@argonet.co.uk. *Choral, ens, inst, vocal, orch, theatre, opera, film.*

Phillips, Freddie. 178 Chessington Rd, West Ewell, Surrey KT19 9XA *tel:* 020 8393 6251. *Wein. Film and TV scores.*

Piatti, Polo. 157 Capel Rd, London E7 0JT *tel:* 020 8514 3998; 07956 251858 *email:* piatti@globalnet.co.uk. *Film, theatre, dance, elec inst.*

Pickard, John. c/o Bardic Edition, 6 Fairfax Cres, Aylesbury, Bucks HP20 2ES *tel:* 01296 428609 *also fax; email:* 101464.2670@compuserve.com. *Bardic. Orch, choral, inst and chmbr.*

* **Pike, Jeremy.** 84 Southdown Cres, Cheadle Hulme, Cheadle, Cheshire SK8 6HA *tel:* 0161 486 0742 *fax:* 0161 369 3609 *email:* fjpike@globalnet.co.uk. *Da Capo. Orch, choral, chmbr, inst and vocal works.*

Pittas, Christos. 4 Hendham Rd, London SW17 7DQ *tel:* 020 8767 4451. *Theatre and ballet mus.*

Plowman, Lynne. 175 Malefant St, Cathays, Cardiff CF2 4QG *tel:* 029 2023 9198. *Orch, opera, chmbr, inst, vocal, theatre, dance.*

Pont, Kenneth H. Old Mullions, Queen St, Paddock Wood, Kent TN12 6NT *tel:* 01892 835164. *OUP. Inst and vocal arrangements for schools, church mus.*

Pook, Jocelyn. c/o Chester Music, 8-9 Frith St, London W1V 5TZ *tel:* 020 7434 0066 *fax:* 020 7287 6329 *email:* music@musicsales.co.uk. *Ches. Inst, film, chmbr.*

* **Poole, Geoffrey.** Woodlands, 19 Grange Ave, Levenshulme, Manchester M19 2EY *tel:* 0161 224 3224 *fax:* 0161 275 4994 *email:* grpkpbw@aol.com. *Maecenas, (sp). Contemporary classical.*

Poppy, Andrew. 22c Breakspears Rd, London SE4 1UW *tel:* 020 8691 8646. *Concert, dance, theatre, film and TV scores.*

* **Pott, Francis.** Thurlows, Main Rd, Littleton, Winchester, Hants SO22 6PS *tel:* 01962 885874 *also fax; email:* fpott@argonet.co.uk. *Cathedral, Fand, Kirklees, Nov, UMP. Org, pno, religious choral, chmbr, orch.*

* **Powers, Anthony.** c/o Oxford University Press, Repertoire Promotion, 70 Baker St, London W1M 1DJ *tel:* 020 7616 5900 *fax:* 020 7616 5901 *email:* repertoire.promotion@oup.co.uk. *OUP. Orch, chmbr, vocal, choral.*

Pratt, Stephen. c/o Music Department, Liverpool Hope University College, Hope Park, Liverpool L16 9JD *fax:* 0151 291 3170 *email:* pratts@hope.ac.uk.

Pritchard, Gwyn. 13 Nevil Rd, Bishopston, Bristol BS7 9EG *tel:* 0117 924 7537 *also fax; email:* gp.ck@virgin.net. *Orch, inst, vocal. Agent: Camerata.*

Proctor, Simon. 8 Henbane Close, Grove Green, Maidstone, Kent ME14 5UW *tel:* 01622 734003 *also fax; email:* simonproctor@tinyonline.co.uk. *Brass Wind, Cathedral, Heavy Metal (USA), Musicland, School Sheet Music, Spring Tree (USA), Studio, Warwick. Concertos, choral, chmbr, musicals.*

Purkiss, Anthony. 35 Fonthill Rd, Hove, E Sussex BN3 6HB *tel:* 01273 774730 *also fax.*

Puumala, Veli-Matti. c/o Boosey & Hawkes Music Publishers Ltd, 295 Regent St, London W1R 8JH *tel:* 020 7580 2060 *fax:* 020 7637 3490 *email:* composers@boosey.com. *Orch and ens.*

* **Rabinowitz MBE, Harry.** 11 Mead Rd, Cranleigh, Surrey GU6 7BG *tel:* 01483 278676 *email:* mitziscott@aol.com. *BH, EMI, Essex, Key, KPM, Mood Music, Songways, Sou, Standard, Virgin, Weekend, Wein. TV, radio and film. Mus for children.*

* **Rae, Charles Bodman.** 25 Priory St, Bowdon, Cheshire WA14 3BQ *tel:* 0161 941 5266 *email:* charles.bodman.rae@rncm.ac.uk.

* **Ramskill, Robert.** 142 Woodside Ave South, Green Lane, Coventry CV3 6BE *tel:* 024 7641 0325 *also fax. BH, Brass Wind. Concert pieces, educ mus.*

Randalls, Jeremy S. 3 Luss Brae, Hamilton, ML3 9UW *tel:* 00 39 091 528516 *also fax; email:* jerryrandalls@cheerful.com. *Caliban Press. Orch, wind band, chmbr, vocal, fl, picc, vocal, songs, jazz, blues, dixie, light music, educ.*

Rathbone, Jonathan. c/o Kikapust Music, 61 Clarendon Rd, London E17 9AY *tel:* 020 8520 7648 *fax:* 020 8520 0662 *email:* rathbone@kikapust.com. *Choral, orch musicals and film.*

Rautavaara, Einojuhani. c/o Boosey & Hawkes Music Publishers Ltd, 295 Regent St, London W1R 8JH *tel:* 020 7580 2060 *fax:* 020 7637 3490 *email:* composers@boosey.com. *Opera, orch and concertos.*

* **Read, Martin.** 7 Gladstone St, Winchester, Hants SO23 8TQ *tel:* 01962 860886 *also fax; email:* martin.read1@virgin.net. *Banks, Editions A Coeur Joie (Lyon), Fand, Noteworks, (sp). TV and video scores, chmbr, choral, inst, orch.*

Reade, Paul. 30 Platts Lane, London NW3 7NS *tel:* 020 7431 8317 *fax:* 020 7435 8535. *ABd, Faber, Nova, Simrock, Studio, Wein. Ballet, concert, TV.*

Redgate, Roger. 29 Ladas Rd, West Norwood, London SE27 0UP *tel:* 020 8670 5761 *also fax; email:* r.redgate@gold.ac.uk. *Editions Henry Lemoine (Paris), UMP, ABd. Concert, film and TV scores.*

Reed, William L. Upper Suite 22, The Quadrangle, Morden College, London SE3 0PW *tel:* 020 8305 0380. *Blandford, Cassell, SB. Chmbr, vocal, orch, musicals, film mus.*

* **Reeman, John.** 6 Grenville Ave, Lytham St Annes, Lancs FY8 2RR *tel:* 01253 726681. *KM, Nov, SB, Spartan, Studio Music, UE. Concert.*

* **Regan, Michael.** 85 Northwood Way, Northwood, Middx HA6 1RT *tel:* 01923 825955 *also fax. Animus, Brunton, Duettino, Phylloscopus, Piccolo, Power, Samuel King, SB, Schott, Spartan, Vanderbeek. Educ, inst, songs, choral.*

Reich, Steve. c/o Allied Artists Agency, 42 Montpelier Square, London SW7 1JZ *tel:* 020 7589 6243 *fax:* 020 7581 5269. *BH.*

Reichard-Gross, Clara. 17 Finlay St, London SW6 6HE *tel:* 020 7736 1977. *Opera, concertos, ens, orch.*

Reynolds, Peter. 46 Richmond Rd, Roath, Cardiff CF24 3AT *tel:* 029 2048 2183 *also fax.*

Reynolds, Roger. c/o Peters Edition Ltd, 10-12 Baches St, London N1 6DN *tel:* 020 7553 4030 *fax:* 020 7490 4921 *email:* newmusic@uk.edition-peters.com.

* **Rhys, John Marlow.** 26 Cresswell Rd, Twickenham, Middx TW1 2DZ *tel:* 020 8892 0759. *Orch, chmbr, mus theatre.*

* **Richman, Eddie.** Flat 13, Birchington Court, West End Lane, London NW6 4PB *tel:* 020 7328 2205. *Bardic. Vocal, inst.*

Rihm, Wolfgang. c/o Universal Edition (London) Ltd, 48 Gt Marlborough St, London W1V 2BN *tel:* 020 7437 6880 *fax:* 020 7437 6115 *email:* miranda@ue-london.demon.co.uk. *UE. Contemporary classical mus.*

Riley, Colin. 77 Godstone Rd, St Margarets, Twickenham, Middx TW1 1JY *tel:* 020 8891 0143 *also fax; email:* colinriley@ndirect.co.uk. *Inst, opera, orch, dance.*

Riley, Howard. 53 Tweedy Rd, Bromley, Kent BR1 3NH *tel:* 020 8290 5917. *Notated inst works, jazz for small and large ens.*

Roberts, Kenneth. The Thatched House, West Farleigh, Maidstone, Kent ME15 0NJ *tel:* 01233 740560 *also fax; email:* oldsalieri@aol.com. *Opera, orch, musical, choral, pno.*

Robinson, Paul. 5 Box House, Luddenden, Halifax, W Yorks HX2 6QA *tel:* 01422 883408 *also fax; email:* paul@box-house.demon.co.uk. *Film, orch, chmbr, dance.*

* **Roderick Jones, Richard.** 2 Primrose Court, Moreton-in-Marsh, Glos GL56 0JG *tel:* 01608 651097/652453. *Curiad Music (Caernarvon), The Guild for the Promotion of Welsh Music. Opera, choral, ballet, symphonic, concerto, br band, chmbr, TV and theatre mus.*

* **Rodgers, Sarah.** 18 Hillfield Park, Muswell Hill, London N10 3QS *tel:* 020 8444 8587 *fax:* 020 8245 0358 *email:* impulse@impulse-music.co.uk. *English Music Press (sp), Impulse, Methodist, SB. Orch, choral, chmbr, film, cross-cultural mus, liturgical mus.*

* **Roe, Betty.** 14 Barlby Rd, London W10 6AR *tel:* 020 8969 3579 *also fax. Chanterelle, KM, Recital, TP, Yorke. Solo vocal, choral, opera, inst, mus for children, inst and vocal mus for special needs.*

Roe, Helen. Little Greystones, West End, Launton, nr Bicester, Oxon OX6 0DF *tel:* 01869 252658 *also fax; email:* timms-roe@greystones99.swinternet.co.uk. *Chmbr and orch mus.*

Rogers, Timothy. 22 Tonbridge Rd, Hildenborough, Kent TN11 9BS *tel:* 01732 832783 *fax:* 01732 832706 *email:* tim.rogers5@virgin.net. *Encore, SB. Choral, org.*

* **Roper, Antony.** 72 Doxey, Stafford ST16 1EE *tel:* 01785 253289. *(sp), Studio. Orch, chmbr, pno, songs.*

Rorem, Ned. c/o Boosey & Hawkes Music Publishers Ltd, 295 Regent St, London W1R 8JH *tel:* 020 7580 2060 *fax:* 020 7637 3490 *email:* composers@boosey.com. *Orch, chmbr, songs.*

Rose, Gregory. 57 White Horse Rd, London E1 0ND *tel:* 020 7790 5883 *fax:* 020 7265 9170 *email:* gregory-rose@tisl.co.uk. *Altaria Editions, BH, Nov, OUP. Orch, choral, vocal, inst, ens.*

* **Rose, John.** 42 Killermont Rd, Bearsden, Glasgow G61 2JA *tel:* 0141 942 3089. *Bardic, Eden Music (sp), EMU, Nov, SMIC. Sacred choral, pno, org, choral, educ, songs, br ens, str quartet.*

* **Rose, John Luke.** Kalon, 113 Farnham Rd, Guildford, Surrey GU2 5PF. *BH, Gal, JW. Symphonic, concertos, opera, musicals, pno, songs, chmbr, choral, educ, church.*

* **Roth, Alec.** H13 Peabody Buildings, Wild St, London WC2B 4BJ *tel:* 020 7497 3754 *also fax.*

Rothstein, Sue. 37 Sydney Grove, Hendon, London NW4 2EJ *tel:* 020 8202 4769. *Sclvi. Inst, songs.*

Rourke, Sean. 296 Hughenden Rd, High Wycombe, Bucks HP13 5PE *tel:* 01494 526052/461177 *fax:* 01494 461188 *email:* sean@strmmm.com. *Forward.*

Rouse, Christopher. c/o Boosey & Hawkes Music Publishers Ltd, 295 Regent St, London W1R 8JH *tel:* 020 7580 2060 *fax:* 020 7637 3490 *email:* composers@boosey.com. *Orch, concerto, ens.*

Routh, Francis. 68 Barrowgate Rd, London W4 4QU *tel:* 020 8995 1223 *also fax. Leng, Redcliffe.*

Rowland-Jones, Simon. 77 The Vineyard, Richmond, Surrey TW10 6AS *tel:* 020 8948 2345 *also fax; email:* srj@easynet.co.uk. *(sp). Va, chmbr mus.*

* **Roxburgh, Edwin.** Springside, Forest Rd, E Horsley, Surrey KT24 5AZ *tel:* 01483 282995 *also fax. IMC, Ric, UMP. Agent: Michael Harrold.*

Rudland, Malcolm. 32a Chipperfield House, Cale St, London SW3 3SA *tel:* 020 7589 9595 *also fax; email:* malcolmrudland@ndirect.co.uk. *TP.*

* **Runswick, Daryl.** 34a Garthorne Rd, Honor Oak, London SE23 1EW *tel:* 020 7639 6006 *fax:* 020 7639 6007 *email:* runswick@btinternet.com; promotion@fabermusic.co.uk. *Faber, Improvised Music, Dazzle/Bucks Music. Opera, concert mus, community works, film, TV.*

Russell, James. 30 Lithos Rd, London NW3 6EF *tel:* 020 7431 1512. *Member of Scottish Society of Composers. Orch, pno mus and film scores; electro-acoustic mus, songs.*

Rutherford, Jonathan. Woodlands, Sandy Lane, Iken, Woodbridge, Suffolk IP12 2EU *tel:* 01728 688484 *also fax.*

* **Rutter, John.** Old Laceys, St John's St, Duxford, Cambridge CB2 4RA *tel:* 01223 832474 *fax:* 01223 836723. *OUP.*

Saariaho, Kaija. c/o Chester Music, 8-9 Frith St, London W1V 5TZ *tel:* 020 7434 0066 *fax:* 020 7287 6329 *email:* music@musicsales.co.uk. *Ches.*

Sackman, Nicholas. 19 Selby Rd, West Bridgford, Nottingham NG2 7BP *tel:* 0115 981 9528 *fax:* 0115 951 4756 *email:* nick.sackman@nottingham.ac.uk. *Schott. Contemporary classical - all genres.*

* **Sainsbury, Lionel.** Boot Cottage, Brook End, Chadlington, Chipping Norton, Oxon OX7 3NF *tel:* 01608 676486 *also fax. Nov. Vn concerto, pno mus, str.*

Sallinen, Aulis. c/o Novello & Co Ltd, 8-9 Frith St, London W1V 5TZ *tel:* 020 7434 0066 *fax:* 020 7287 6329 *email:* music@musicsales.co.uk.

Salter, Lionel. 26 Woodstock Rd, London NW11 8ER *tel:* 020 8458 3568 *also fax. ABd, Asch, BH, Emerson, Faber, Gal, Leng, OUP, Ric, Wein.*

* **Salter, Timothy.** 26 Caterham Rd, London SE13 5AR *tel:* 020 8318 2031 *also fax; email:* ugm@netcomuk.co.uk. *ABd, Obelisk, Usk. Inst, chmbr, orch, choral, songs.*

* **Salzedo, Leonard.** 363 Bideford Green, Leighton Buzzard, Beds LU7 7TX *tel:* 01525 371126. *Amoris, Ches, Lopés. Ballet, film, chmbr mus for perc and br, orch, vocal.*

* **Sander, Peter.** 73 The Avenue, London NW6 7NS *tel:* 020 8459 1781 *fax:* 020 8459 4990 *email:* peter@psander.demon.co.uk. *B, Bèrben, BH, Carlton, Ches, Eul (Zurich), KPM, Kunzelmann, Lemmel, Record Supervision, Schmitt, Sou. Film and TV scores, commercial and serious concert mus, opera.*

Sanders, John. Ridge Cottage, Upton Bishop, Ross-on-Wye, Herefords HR9 7UD *tel:* 01989 780482. *Kirklees, KM, McCrimmon, Nov, Oec, Presser, Roger Dean, RSCM. Choral, orch, vocal, church mus.*

Saunders, Rebecca. c/o Peters Edition Ltd, 10-12 Baches St, London N1 6DN *tel:* 020 7553 4030 *fax:* 020 7490 4921 *email:* newmusic@uk.edition-peters.com.

* **Savaskan, Sinan.** 27 Dorchester Court, Herne Hill, London SE24 9QX *tel:* 020 7737 5777 *also fax;* 020 7963 1123 *email:* s@sav777.demon.co.uk; scs9027@westminster.org.uk. *Independent Composers Catalogue, IMC, Society of New Musics. Contemporary classical, dance, electro-acoustic, incidental mus.*

Sawer, David. c/o Universal Edition (London) Ltd, 48 Gt Marlborough St, London W1V 2BN *tel:* 020 7437 6880 *fax:* 020 7437 6115 *email:* miranda@ue-london.demon.co.uk. *UE. Contemporary classical mus.*

Sawyers, Philip. c/o NWA Artists, 51 Tresco Rd, London SE15 3PY *tel:* 020 7635 7688 *fax:* 020 7635 6211.

Saxton, Robert. c/o Chester Music, 8-9 Frith St, London W1V 5TZ *tel:* 020 7434 0066 *fax:* 020 7287 6329 *email:* music@musicsales.co.uk. *Ches. Orch, chmbr, opera, choral.*

Schlünz, Annette. c/o Boosey & Hawkes Music Publishers Ltd, 295 Regent St, London W1R 8JH *tel:* 020 7580 2060 *fax:* 020 7637 3490 *email:* composers@boosey.com. *Chmbr, ens, opera, orch.*

Schofield, Ian. c/o Caddy Publishing, Convent Lodge, Andover Down, Hants SP11 6LR *tel:* 01264 337205 *fax:* 01264 350823.

Schultz, Andrew. Head of Composition of Music Studies, Guildhall School of Music and Drama, Silk St, Barbican, London EC2Y 8OT *tel:* 020 7382 7255 *fax:* 020 7382 2313 *email:* andrew.schultz@lineone.net. *ABC, Red House, AMC, La Trobe University Press.*

Schweinitz, Wolfgang von. c/o Boosey & Hawkes Music Publishers Ltd, 295 Regent St, London W1R 8JH *tel:* 020 7580 2060 *fax:* 020 7637 3490 *email:* composers@boosey.com. *Works for soloists, chorus and orch, vc and orch, ens.*

Schwertsik, Kurt. c/o Boosey & Hawkes Music Publishers Ltd, 295 Regent St, London W1R 8JH *tel:* 020 7580 2060 *fax:* 020 7637 3490 *email:* composers@boosey.com. *Opera, orch, vn concerto, songs.*

Scott, Anthony. 18 Spin Hill, Market Lavington, Devizes, Wilts SN10 4NR *tel:* 01380 813689. *BH, Basil Ramsey, KM. Mus for small chmbr ens, org, vn, pno, operas, songs.*

* **Scott, Stuart.** 6 Colville Grove, Sale, Cheshire M33 4FW *tel:* 0161 972 0327 *email:* sjs@stuartscott.demon.co.uk. *Da Capo, Elbeck, Frontier, MSM, Phylloscopus, Piccolo, Southern (USA), (sp). Choral, orch, chmbr, inst, pno, opera, educ, vocal.*

Sculthorpe, Peter. c/o Faber Music Ltd, 3 Queen Square, London WC1N 3AU *tel:* 020 7833 7911/2 *fax:* 020 7833 7939 *email:* promotion@fabermusic.co.uk. *Faber. Inst, orch, chmbr, vocal, opera, mus for theatre, film.*

Seaman, Barry. PO Box 11845, London SE21 8ZS *tel:* 020 8761 6565 *fax:* 020 8670 3195 *email:* gbz_mgmt@compuserve.com. *OUP. Inst, orch, chmbr, vocal, choral, mus theatre, dance.*

Segger, Jill. 32 Holland Park, Cheveley, Newmarket, Suffolk CB8 9DL *tel:* 01638 730006 *also fax. AV, KM, Phylloscopus. Vocal, choral, liturgical, wind mus, pno.*

Self, Adrian. 4 Rawlinson St, Dalton-in-Furness LA15 8AL *tel:* 01229 467432. *AA, Nov, Oec, RSCM. Choral, org, inst.*

Self, Geoffrey. 13 Rosevean Ave, Camborne, Cornwall TR14 8UG *tel:* 01209 713427. *Animus, Nov. Songs, carols, chmbr, choral, org and orch.*

Self, George. 10 Bassett Close, Southampton SO16 7PE *tel:* 023 8076 9143. *Nov, UE. Tape, computer mus, educ mus.*

Selwyn, David. 8 Barrow Court, Barrow Gurney, Bristol BS48 3RW *tel:* 01275 463421. *Opera, vocal, chmbr mus.*

* **Senator, Ronald.** 20 Denbigh Gardens, Richmond, Surrey TW10 6EN *tel:* 020 8940 8831 *also fax. Albert, BH, Cary, GS, Leng, SB. Opera, oratorio, symphonic, concerto, chmbr, pno, TV mus.*

Sharkey, Jeffrey. West Lodge House, The Purcell School, Aldenham Rd, Bushey, Herts WD2 3TS *tel:* 01923 331177 *also fax; email:* jsharkey@compuserve.com. *Orch, chmbr, vocal and solo.*

Sharma, Elizabeth. 18 Thirlmere Ave, Perivale, Middx UB6 8EF *tel:* 020 8998 6896 *fax:* 020 8991 9141. *Multicultural mus w/shops, children's mus stories, inst, vocal, mus and songs for shows.*

* **Shaw, Francis Richard.** 5 Mall Studios, Tasker Rd, London NW3 2YS *tel:* 020 7284 4450 *also fax; email:* francis.shaw@virgin.net. *Ches, Leng, Music Sales, Nov. Concert mus, film and TV scores.*

* **Shephard, Richard.** The Minster School, Deangate, York YO1 7JA *tel:* 01904 557230 *fax:* 01904 557232. *OUP, RSCM, St James Press (Kentuckey, USA). Orch, church, musicals.*

Sheppard, Philip. 20 Downs View, Isleworth, Middx TW7 5HF *tel:* 020 8560 4091; 07767 810560 *email:* bluesnow@easynet.co.uk.

Sherbourne, Janet. 1 St Anne's Rd, Caversham, Reading RG4 7PA *tel:* 0118 947 7170 *also fax; email:* janet@metalworks.org. *Practical (sp).*

* **Sherlaw Johnson, Robert.** Malton Croft, Woodlands Rise, Stonesfield, Oxon OX8 8PL *tel:* 01993 891318 *fax:* 01865 276128 *email:* robert.sherlaw-johnson@music.ox.ac.uk. *Faber, Nov, OUP. Pno, chmbr, choral, song cycles, orch, opera.*

* **Short, Michael.** Dassells, Priory Rd, Hastings, E Sussex TN34 3JS *tel:* 01424 442729 *also fax; email:* mshort@dassells.free-online.co.uk. *Bandleader, BH, Blackwell, Consort, Crouch (sp), Dolmetsch, Goodmusic, Oriel, OUP, Rob, SB, Studio, TP, WC.*

* **Shrapnel, Hugh.** 27a Shooters Hill Rd, Blackheath, London SE3 7AS *tel:* 020 8858 7123. *Forward, Music Now. Chmbr mus, songs, pno.*

* **Singer, Malcolm J.** 29 Goldsmith Ave, London W3 6HR *tel:* 020 8992 2318 *fax:* 020 8896 2556.

Sisson, Richard. The Mill, Breachwood Green, nr Hitchin, Herts SG4 8PH *tel:* 01438 833801 *email:* richard.sisson@virgin.net. *Ballet, chmbr, oratorio, vocal.*

Skeet, Andrew. c/o Prophet Music Ltd, 147 Drummond St, London NW1 2PB *tel:* 020 7383 5003 *fax:* 020 7383 5004 *email:* info@prophetmusic.co.uk.

* **Skempton, Howard.** c/o Oxford University Press, Repertoire Promotion, 70 Baker St, London W1M 1DJ *tel:* 020 7616 5900 *fax:* 020 7616 5901 *email:* repertoire.promotion@oup.co.uk. *OUP. Chmbr, orch, solo, ballet.*

Skene, Hugh Crawford. Crowhills, Quarter, by Hamilton, Lanarks ML3 7XP *tel:* 01357 300303. *Member of Scottish Society of Composers. Concerto, symphony, vocal and inst.*

Smalley, Denis. Dept of Music, City University, Northampton Square, London EC1V 0HB *tel:* 020 7477 8270 *fax:* 020 7477 8576 *email:* d.smalley@city.ac.uk. *Electro-acoustic mus.*

Smirnov, Dmitri. c/o Boosey & Hawkes Music Publishers Ltd, 295 Regent St, London W1R 8JH *tel:* 020 7580 2060 *fax:* 020 7637 3490 *email:* composers@boosey.com. *Opera, orch, ens, chmbr.*

Smith, Dave. 61a Farleigh Rd, London N16 7TD *tel:* 020 7241 1909 *also fax. Pno, inst mus.*

* **Smith, Gavin.** 36 Linden Grove, Hartlepool, Cleveland TS26 9PY *tel:* 01429 260916. *Studio. Br band, wind orch, big band, solo, ens, orch.*

Smith, Geoff. 25 Exeter Close, Chippenham, Wilts SN14 0YG *tel:* 01249 660938 *also fax; email:* the.smiths1@virgin.net. *EMI.*

Smith, Peter R. 20 Northcote Ave, Holgate, York YO2 4JD *tel:* 01904 782279. *WD10 Records. Classic mus, concertos, chmbr mus, symphonies.*

Smith, Tommy. Smythe Music, PO Box 3743, Lanark ML11 9WD *tel:* 07710 585231 *email:* music@tommysmith.demon.co.uk.

Sohal, Naresh. 55 Drakefell Rd, London SE14 5SH *tel:* 020 7635 5132. *Nov, Music Production Company. Orch, chmbr mus, opera, ballet, mus theatre, film and TV.*

* **Speare, Simon.** 31 Chester Rd, Walthamstow, London E17 7HP *tel:* 020 8521 5259. *Ens, chmbr, orch, choral, pno, vocal, theatre, ballet.*

Spearing, Robert. Ty-wrth-y-Coed, Cwmystwyth, Aberystwyth, Ceredigion *tel:* 01981 250849; 01974 282631. *Nov, Faber Music, Paraclete. Orch, choral, chmbr, solo vocal, incidental mus, mus theatre.*

* **Spedding, Frank.** 17 Digby Ave, Mapperley, Nottingham NG3 6DS *tel:* 0115 960 5964. *TV, film, symphony and chmbr mus.*

Spicer, Paul. 4 The Close, Lichfield, Staffs WS13 7LD *tel:* 01543 250627 *fax:* 01543 250970 *email:* paul.spicer@tisl.co.uk. *Editions Billaudot, For, Nov, Ramsey. Choral, inst, vocal, orch.*

Spratling, Huw. c/o Siva Oke Music Management, 13 Riversdale Rd, Thames Ditton, Surrey KT7 0QL *tel:* 020 8398 1586 *fax:* 020 8339 0981 *email:* soke@somm-recordings.demon.co.uk. *Opera, orch, choral, chmbr, vocal, solo, inst.*

Sproston, Darren. 3 Woodhill Close, Wombourne, Wolverhampton, Staffs WV5 0ET *tel:* 01902 326567. *Inst, ens, theatre mus.*

Stacey, Peter. 7 Pitman St, Pontcanna, Cardiff CF1 9DJ *tel:* 029 2064 1727 *email:* peter@stacey-wells.demon.co.uk. *Multi-cultural mus.*

Standford, Patric. 17 Bradford Rd, St John's, Wakefield, Yorks WF1 2RF *tel:* 01924 370454 *email:* standford@rtsmusic.demon.co.uk. *Fentone, Leng, Nov, SB. Concert/recital, film and TV.*

Stead, John. 26 Hopwood Close, Hull HU3 1QU *tel:* 01482 225663 *email:* wooler@cix.compulink.co.uk. *(sp). Son et lumières, celebratory openings, electro-acoustic, sacred mus.*

* **Steadman, Robert.** 36 Trafalgar Rd, Beeston Rylands, Nottingham NG9 1LB *tel:* 0115 917 4546 *also fax; email:* robsteadman@hotmail.com. *Con Moto, Piccolo, TVS, Vanderbeek. Concert, theatre, educ.*

Steel, Alan. 324 Desborough Ave, High Wycombe, Bucks HP11 2TJ *tel:* 01494 528380 *fax:* 01494 464125. *Choral works.*

Steele, Jan. 1 St Anne's Rd, Caversham, Reading RG4 7PA *tel:* 0118 947 7170 *also fax; email:* jan@metalworks.org. *Practical (sp). Jazz, classical, Indian light mus.*

Steer, Maxwell. 125 Duck St, Tisbury, Wilts SP3 6LJ *tel:* 01747 870070 *fax:* 01747 871451 *email:* mms@enterprise.net; msteer@freeuk.com. *Kings, Nov. Experimental mus drama, educ mus.*

Steinke, Gunter. c/o Boosey & Hawkes Music Publishers Ltd, 295 Regent St, London W1R 8JH *tel:* 020 7580 2060 *fax:* 020 7637 3490 *email:* composers@boosey.com. *Orch, ens, chmbr.*

* **Stevenson, Ronald.** Townfoot House, West Linton, Peeblesshire EH46 7EE *tel:* 01968 60511 *fax:* 0131 229 9298 *email:* rss@medeco.co.uk. *Altarus, BH, EMI, Henmar, Hyperion, Klavar, Marco Polo, Nov, Olympia, OUP, Peters, Rob, Ronald Stevenson Society, Schott, UMP. Vocal, chmbr, choral, orch and pno.*

* **Stiles, Frank.** 43 Beech Rd, Branston, Lincoln LN4 1PP *tel:* 01522 791662 *email:* frankstiles@callnetuk.com. *Anglian, Cramer, Mixolydian. Orch, choral, inst, opera.*

* **Stimpson, Michael.** Bridge House, Bishopstone, nr Salisbury, Wilts SP5 4DB *tel:* 01722 780671 *also fax; email:* mstim57565@aol.com. *OUP, Ric. Orch, chmbr, vocal, inst.*

* **Stocken, Frederick.** 3 Goodhope House, Poplar High St, London E14 0AQ *tel:* 020 7537 4951 *also fax; email:* fstocken@argonet.co.uk. *Orch, choral, chmbr, ballet.*

* **Stoker, Richard.** 38 Lee Rd, Blackheath, London SE3 9RU *tel:* 020 8852 9608 *also fax; email:* gps5@tutor.open.ac.uk. *ACS, Anchor, ASC, Bèrben, BH, Breit, Brunton, CMP, Evans Bros, Fentone, Forward, Hin, Leeds, MCA, Merlin, Minerva, Oec, OUP, Outposts, Ric, TP, Triumph, UZA, WC. Concert mus, vocal, choral, opera, film, TV, musicals.*

* **Stoll, David M.** 4 Cranford Ave, London N13 4PA *tel:* 020 8882 1358 *fax:* 020 8886 7095 *email:* stoll.dm@argonet.co.uk. *Concert, film, TV, theatre, children's mus.*

* **Stone, David E.** Lammasbank, 26 Chalk Rd, Godalming, Surrey GU7 3AP *tel:* 01483 423298. *BH, Goodmusic, Nov, Piccolo. Orch, band, chmbr, educ mus.*

Stone, Robin. Kerkyra, Straight Rd, Boxted, nr Colchester, Essex *tel:* 01206 272587.

* **Stout, Alastair.** Wesley's Chapel, 49 City Rd, London EC1Y 1AU *tel:* 020 7490 0248 *pager:* 07625 631757. *Oec. Contemporary classical mus, org, choral; arrangements, copying.*

Streatfield, Valma. Valley View, Sulhamstead Hill, Sulhamstead, Reading RG7 4DE *tel:* 0118 930 2859 *fax:* 0118 930 3339 *email:* marquee @ash-mon.demon.co.uk. *Children's songs, mus comedy, chmbr mus, pno, org, rcdr mus, hymns.*

Stripf, Markus. 148 Muswell Hill Broadway, London N10 3SA *tel:* 020 8444 1410. *Composer and mus producer focusing on classical, pop, rock and dance.*

* **Strutt, D A L.** 27 Dunedin Rd, Rainham, Essex RM13 8HA *tel:* 01708 520779 *email:* 10664.2024@compuserve.com. *Roeginga Edition. Chmbr, vocal, inst, choral.*

Stuart, Amanda. ZigZag Music Productions, Croeso, Church Lane, Hilton, Huntingdon, Cambs PE18 9NH *tel:* 01480 830073 *also fax. Film, TV, video, theatre, radio, ballet, opera, educ.*

Sturman, Paul. 44 Harvest Rd, Chandlers Ford, Hants SO53 4HF *tel:* 023 8026 0342. *Ashdown, EMI, Feld, Longman. Educ mus, choral, orch, keyboard.*

Summers, Al. 61 Bratton Rd, Westbury, Wilts BA13 3ES *tel:* 01373 864721. *Chmbr, incidental, choral.*

Sutton-Anderson, David. 28 Cavendish Ave, London N3 3QN *tel:* 020 8349 2317 *fax:* 020 8346 8257. *Andresier, Camden. Orch, chmbr, dance, educ.*

Swayne, Giles. c/o Performing Arts, 6 Windmill St, London W1P 1HF *tel:* 020 7255 1362 *fax:* 020 7631 4631. *Nov. Orch, choral, chmbr, opera, TV.*

Szymanski, Pawel. c/o Chester Music, 8-9 Frith St, London W1V 5TZ *tel:* 020 7434 0066 *fax:* 020 7287 6329 *email:* music@musicsales.co.uk. *Ches.*

Tamblyn, William. Malting Cottage, Church Rd, Peldon, Colchester CO5 7PU *tel:* 01206 735770 *also fax; email:* bill.tamblyn@aspects.net. *BH, Chapman, Chiswick, CTS, Faber, Jabulani (USA), Nov, OCP (USA), OUP, St Thomas More Group. Liturgical mus.*

Tanaka, Karen. c/o Chester Music, 8-9 Frith St, London W1V 5TZ *tel:* 020 7434 0066 *fax:* 020 7287 6329 *email:* music@musicsales.co.uk. *Ches.*

Tavener, John. c/o Chester Music, 8-9 Frith St, London W1V 5TZ *tel:* 020 7434 0066 *fax:* 020 7287 6329 *email:* music@musicsales.co.uk. *Ches. Orch, choral, chmbr, opera, vocal.*

Taylor, Matthew. 7 East Cliff Rd, Tunbridge Wells, Kent TN4 9AD *tel:* 01892 511570 *also fax. Maecenas.*

Taylor, Philip. The Manse, Aith, Bixter, Shetland ZE2 9NB *tel:* 01595 810472 *also fax; email:* philip@camille.demon.co.uk.

Taylor, Richard. 11 Garnet Terrace, Stutton, Tadcaster, N Yorks LS24 9BB *tel:* 0161 446 2163 *also fax; email:* richard@richardtaylor.demon.co.uk. *Musicland, Wein. Mus theatre, concert hall.*

Taylor, Timothy. Dept of Music, Cardiff University, Corbett Rd, Cardiff CF1 3EB *tel:* 029 2087 4816 *fax:* 029 2087 4379 *email:* taylortn@cf.ac.uk. *UCC.*

* **Teed, Roy.** 63 Egret Cres, Longridge Park, Colchester, Essex CO4 3FP *tel:* 01206 870839. *ABd, Ches, Curwen, Ric, Rob. Vocal, chmbr, orch, opera, film, pno.*

Thomas, David. Arunvale House, 10 Kingsmead Rd, Broadbridge Heath, W Sussex RH12 3LL *tel:* 01403 269378. *UE. Song cycles, school musicals, cantatas.*

Thomas, Jane. Arunvale House, 10 Kingsmead Rd, Broadbridge Heath, W Sussex RH12 3LL *tel:* 01403 269378. *UE. Song cycles, school musicals, cantatas.*

* **Thomas, John Ashton.** 22a Chesterton Rd, London W10 5LX *tel:* 020 8964 5410 *email:* jathomasuk@yahoo.com. *Bruton. Film and TV, orch.*

Thomas, Wyndham. Dept of Music, University of Bristol, Bristol BS8 1SA *tel:* 0117 954 5028 *fax:* 0117 954 5027 *email:* wyndham.thomas@bris.ac.uk. *Antico, Imrie, Medieval Editions, Vanderbeek. Org, choral, chmbr mus.*

Thompson, Peter. The Barony, 16 Sandringham Rd, Petersfield, Hants GU32 2AA *tel:* 01730 267341. *Fand. Vocal, chmbr, choral, orch, pno.*

* **Thompson, Terence J.** 58 Willenhall Rd, Bilston, W Midlands WV14 6NW *tel:* 01902 495646. *Schott, Studio, WC. Solo inst, ens, sax quartets, educ, band, orch.*

Thwaites, Penelope. 23 Lyndale Ave, Child's Hill, London NW2 2QB *tel:* 020 7794 5090 *also fax; email:* thwaites.jackson@virgin.net. *Bardic. Songs, musicals, inst.*

* **Tipler, Brian.** 24 Catherine Rd, Bredbury Green, Romiley, Stockport, Cheshire SK6 3DH *tel:* 0161 430 6046. *Orch, operetta, ens, choral.*

Tocher, Gordon. 54 Glenburn Drive, Inverness IV2 4NE *tel:* 01463 232345. *Corda. Inst, choral mus, gui quartet.*

Todd, Paul. 3 Rosehart Mews, 165a Westbourne Grove, London W11 3JN *tel:* 020 7229 9776 *fax:* 020 7243 4751. *Musicals, theatre mus.*

* **Tomlinson, Ernest.** Lancaster Farm, Chipping Lane, Longridge, Preston PR3 2NB *tel:* 01772 783646 *fax:* 01772 786026. *BH, Electrophonic, EMI, ME, Nov, Wein. Light orch, symphonic jazz, library mus, songs, choir mus, br band, wind band and org.*

Toovey, Andrew. 57b Station Rd, Willesden, London NW10 4UX *tel:* 020 8961 1051 *also fax; email:* andrewtoovey@tooveyworld.freeserve.co.uk. *BH. Orch, opera, chmbr mus. Agent: YCAT.*

Torke, Michael. c/o Boosey & Hawkes Music Publishers Ltd, 295 Regent St, London W1R 8JH *tel:* 020 7580 2060 *fax:* 020 7637 3490 *email:* composers@boosey.com. *Ballet, orch, chmbr, br, keyboard, perc.*

Tormis, Veljo. c/o Boosey & Hawkes Music Publishers Ltd, 295 Regent St, London W1R 8JH *tel:* 020 7580 2060 *fax:* 020 7637 3490 *email:* composers@boosey.com. *Vocal, choral.*

* **Torphichen, Pamela.** c/o Bardic Edition, 6 Fairfax Cres, Aylesbury, Bucks HP20 2ES *tel:* 01296 428609 *also fax; email:* 101464.2670@compuserve.com. *Bardic. Vocal, inst.*

Touchin, Colin. 17 Kensington Rd, Earlsdon, Coventry CV5 6GG *tel:* 024 7667 0211 *also fax; email:* musab@warwick.ac.uk. *Tomus (sp). Orch, choral, chmbr, wind ens.*

Treacher, Graham. 33 Royal York Cres, Bristol BS8 4JU *tel:* 0117 974 3279. *BH, OUP, Schott.*

* **Tucapsky, Antonin.** 50 Birchen Grove, London NW9 8SA *tel:* 020 8200 5200. *Ed A Coeur Joie (Lyon), Ric, Rob. Opera, choral, songs, chmbr, orch.*

Turnage, Mark-Anthony. c/o Schott & Co Ltd, 48 Gt Marlborough St, London W1V 2BN *tel:* 020 7494 1487 *fax:* 020 7287 1529 *email:* schottcontemporarymusic@compuserve.com. *Schott. Contact also:* Van Walsum Management, 4 Addison Bridge Place, London W14 8XP *tel:* 020 7371 4343 *fax:* 020 7371 4344.

Turner, Barrie Carson. 2 Redbrick Cottages, Little Green, Burgate, Diss, Norfolk IP22 1QG *tel:* 01379 783277 *fax:* 01379 783177. *Educ, mus for children.*

Tüür, Erkki-Sven. c/o Peters Edition Ltd, 10-12 Baches St, London N1 6DN *tel.* 020 7553 4030 *fax:* 020 7490 4921 *email:* newmusic@uk.edition-peters.com.

Twigg, David. 15 Wentworth Park Ave, Harborne, Birmingham B17 9QU *tel:* 0121 427 7343. *Oec, Ramsey. Church, org mus, songs, pno mus, musicals.*

* **Tyrrell, Andrew.** 29 Castle Hill, Banwell, N Somerset BS29 6NX *tel:* 01934 822857 *also fax; email:* ajt@tyrrellfam.demon.co.uk. *(sp). Educ, orch, choral.*

Underwood, Mark. 20 Summerhill Rd, Dartford, Kent DA1 2LP *tel:* 01322 287924 *also fax. Pan Educational.*

* **Usher, Julia.** 11 Langham Place, Highwoods, Colchester, Essex CO4 4GB *tel:* 01206 751522 *email:* rodusher@lineone.net. *Primavera (sp). Chmbr, mus theatre, choral, orch, cross-media.*

Ustvolskaya, Galina. c/o Boosey & Hawkes Music Publishers Ltd, 295 Regent St, London W1R 8JH *tel:* 020 7580 2060 *fax:* 020 7637 3490 *email:* composers@boosey.com. *Orch, ens, chmbr.*

* **Vale, Sydney.** 3 Albany Mews, Fourth Ave, Hove, E Sussex BN3 2PQ *tel:* 01273 775630. *Modus, (sp). Opera, orch, inst, film scores, vocal.*

Vann, Stanley. Holly Tree Cottage, Wansford, Peterborough, Cambs PE8 6PL *tel:* 01780 782192. *AA, Lorenz, KM, Oec, OUP, Ramsey, Rob, RSCM. Choral, vocal, org, inst.*

Vaughan, Mike. 36 Windmill Drive, St Audlem, Cheshire CW3 0AH *tel:* 01270 811589 *fax:* 01782 583295 *email:* m.p.vaughan@keele.ac.uk. *Contemporary chmbr, electro-acoustic.*

* **Veale, John.** 7 Nourse Close, Woodeaton, Oxford OX3 9TJ *tel:* 01865 558156. *Leng. Concert mus, film and TV.*

Venables, Ian. Turrall House, 2 Turrall St, Barbourne, Worcester WR3 8AJ *tel:* 01905 611570. *Enigma, Headline. Orch, chmbr, pno, songs, solo inst, choral, br.*

Vinao, Alejandro. Flat 3, 27 Coolhurst Rd, London N8 8ET *tel:* 020 8340 4664 *fax:* 020 8374 1021 *email:* alej@vinao.u-net.com. *Serious mus, opera, film and TV scores.*

Vincent, Simon. 8 Milton Ave, London N6 5QE *tel:* 020 8342 8687 *also fax; email:* simon.vincent@v-o-s.dircon.co.uk. *Vision of Sound (sp). Electro-acoustic, choral, inst.*

Vine, Carl. c/o Faber Music Ltd, 3 Queen Square, London WC1N 3AU *tel:* 020 7833 7911/2 *fax:* 020 7833 7939 *email:* promotion@fabermusic.co.uk. *Faber. Inst, orch, chmbr, vocal, media, film, electronic.*

* **Vishnick, Martin Lawrence.** 12 Watling St, St Albans, Herts AL1 2PX *tel:* 01727 866507 *also fax; email:* MVishnick@st.albans.herts.sch.uk. *Corda. Concert, chmbr, film and TV, opera, theatre, electro-acoustic.*

Volans, Kevin. c/o Chester Music, 8-9 Frith St, London W1V 5TZ *tel:* 020 7434 0066 *fax:* 020 7287 6329 *email:* music@musicsales.co.uk. *Ches. Orch, pno, chmbr, opera, dance.*

Vriend, Jan. 22 Pooles Lane, Selsley, Stroud, Glos GL5 5JT *tel:* 01453 751213 *also fax; email:* jnmv@tinyonline.co.uk. *Donemus (Amsterdam). Orch, inst, vocal.*

* **Wadsworth, Derek.** 22 Gerard Rd, London SW13 9RG *tel:* 020 8748 5868 *fax:* 020 8846 9349. *Film, TV, orch, electronic.*

* **Wai-On, Ho.** 25 Wellington Rd, London E11 2AS *tel:* 020 8530 5687 *also fax. Vocal, inst, orch, choral, ens, mus for dance, mus theatre, electro-acoustic, film, cross-cultural and combined arts.*

Wakefield, Anthony. 115 Village Way, Ashford, Middx TW15 2JY *tel:* 01784 252958 *also fax. Carlin, Harlequin, KPM, Patterdale, Studio. Orch, inst, chmbr, wind band, br band, big band, arrangements and orchestral reductions.*

Walker, Eldon. 1 Ashford Ave, off Ashton Rd, Lancaster LA1 5BA *tel:* 01524 39141. *Anglia. Chmbr, orch mus, songs, big band, jazz arrangements.*

Walker, James. The Brooklands, 57 Shottery, Stratford upon Avon CV37 9HD *tel:* 01789 204315. *GS, Polyphonic, Studio, Wein. Chmbr, wind, vocal, theatre.*

* **Wallen, Errollyn.** 37 Coltman House, Welland St, London SE10 9DW *tel:* 020 8853 0818 *also fax. Orch, ens, opera, ballet, theatre, popular songs, radio, film and TV.*

Walters, Gareth. 31 Beauchamp Rd, E Molesey, Surrey KT8 0PA *tel:* 020 8979 3202 *fax:* 020 8979 5806. *AA, BH, Hohner, OUP, Ric, SB.*

Ward, David. c/o SMIC, 1 Bowmont Gardens, Glasgow G12 9LR *tel:* 0141 334 6393 *fax:* 0141 337 1161 *email:* smic@glasgow.almac.co.uk. *SMIC, Vanderbeek. Chmbr, opera, orch, vocal.*

* **Ward, Stuart.** c/o Roxane Houston Concert Agency, 8 Hartington Rd, Aldeburgh, Suffolk IP15 5HD *tel:* 01728 454048. *Choral, orch, chmbr, songs, gui.*

Warlow, Wayne. The Haven, Ocean View, West Drive, Porthcawl CF36 3HT *tel:* 01656 773389 *also fax; email:* wayne@buffettwarlow.freeserve.co.uk. *Film, TV scores, orch, ballet, chmbr, jazz orch.*

* **Warren, Raymond.** 9 Cabot Rise, Portishead, Bristol BS20 6NX *tel:* 01275 844289. *Nov. Opera, symphony, chmbr, cantatas.*

* **Watkins, Michael Blake.** Acacia House, Uxbridge Rd, Hillingdon, Middx UB10 0LF *tel:* 01895 238689 *also fax. Nov.*

Watkins, Roderick. 44 Tile Kiln Hill, Blean, Canterbury, Kent CT2 9EE *tel:* 01227 458456 *also fax; email:* r.watkins@cant.ac.uk. *Orch, chmbr, opera, ens, electro-acoustic.*

* **Watkinson, Fabian.** 8 Stoneleigh Terrace, London N19 5TY *tel:* 020 7561 0576. *New Essex. Opera, songs, vocal.*

Watson, Stephen. c/o Alfred Lengnick & Co, Pigeon House Meadow, 27 Grove Rd, Beaconsfield, Bucks HP9 1UR *tel:* 01494 681216 *fax:* 01494 670443. *Symphony, choral, band.*

* **Watt, Howard.** Y Graig, 17 Coryton Cres, Whitchurch, Cardiff CF14 7EQ *tel:* 029 2069 1811. *Oriana.*

* **Webb, John.** 30 Coleman Rd, Camberwell, London SE5 7TG *tel:* 020 7701 8038 *also fax; email:* j.webb@camberwell.free-online.co.uk. *New Voices (BMIC). Chmbr, ens, orch, choral.*

Webber, John. 88 Balfour Rd, North End, Portsmouth PO2 0NH *tel:* 023 9235 1816 *also fax; email:* pnmo-webber@yahoo.com. *AA, Arsis (USA), Webber. Orch, chmbr and vocal.*

Weeks, John Ralph. 120 Kylepark Drive, Uddingston, Glasgow G71 7DE *tel:* 01698 813723. *Britannia, Oec, Rob. Solo inst, chmbr mus, vocal, org.*

Weiland, Douglas. The Punch Bowl, Old Beetley, Norfolk NR20 4AB *tel:* 01362 861096.

* **Weir, Judith.** c/o Chester Music, 8-9 Frith St, London W1V 5TZ *tel:* 020 7434 0066 *fax:* 020 7287 6329 *email:* music@musicsales.co.uk. *Ches, Nov. Orch, chmbr, opera.*

* **Wells, Jane.** Lion Cottage, 2 High St, Wighton, Wells-next-the-Sea, Norfolk NR23 1AL *tel:* 01328 820917 *also fax. Concert mus, mus with dance and film.*

Westbrook, Mike. Brent House, Holbeton, nr Plymouth PL8 1LX *tel:* 01752 830589 *fax:* 01752 830539 *email:* smiths_academy@hotmail.com. *Metisse (Paris). Jazz and classical ens, radio, TV, theatre, opera, dance and cinema.*

Wetherell, Eric. 24 The Crescent, Bristol BS9 4RW *tel:* 0117 962 8652. *Anglo-Continental, Banks, Kirklees, KPM, ME, Molenaar, Rob, Sou, TP.*

* **Whettam, Graham.** Silverwood House, Woolaston, nr Lydney, Glos GL15 6PJ *tel:* 01594 529026 *fax:* 01594 529027. *Meriden (sp), Theodore Presser (USA). Orch, str orch, inst, ens, chmbr, choral mus, songs.*

White, Brian. c/o Prophet Music Ltd, 147 Drummond St, London NW1 2PB *tel:* 020 7383 5003 *fax:* 020 7383 5004 *email:* info@prophetmusic.co.uk.

* **Wickens, Dennis.** Candleshoe, Manor Rd, Wantage, Oxon OX12 8NE *tel:* 01235 763598. *Nov, OUP. Choral, orch, chmbr, vocal, br band.*

Wiegold, Peter. 82 Lordship Park, London N16 5UA *tel:* 020 8802 9646 *also fax. UE. Some works include improvisation.*

* **Wiggins, Christopher D.** Tilsdown Lodge, Dursley, Glos GL11 5QQ *tel:* 01453 543132; 00 49 172 3261971. *AA, Concordia, Emerson Horn Editions (USA), Kjos, Neuschel, Oec, Phoenix (NL), Ric, Studio. Educ, choral, orch, chmbr, pop.*

Wilby, Philip. c/o Chester Music, 8-9 Frith St, London W1V 5TZ *tel:* 020 7434 0066 *fax:* 020 7287 6329 *email:* music@musicsales.co.uk. *Ches, Nov. Orch, chmbr, wind and br band, choral.*

Wilde, David. c/o J Audrey Ellison International Artists' Management, 135 Stevenage Rd, Fulham, London SW6 6PB *tel:* c/o 020 7381 9751 *fax:* 020 7381 2406. *Chmbr, opera, vocal.*

Wilens, Greta. 333 Russell Court, Woburn Place, London WC1H 0NG *tel:* 020 7837 6001. *B, EMI. Military marches, classical mus, vocal.*

Wilkins, Margaret Lucy. 4 Church St, Golcar, Huddersfield HD7 4AH *tel:* 01484 652762 *fax:* 01484 472656 *email:* m.l.wilkins@hud.ac.uk. *For, Hildegard (USA), Satanic Mills (sp). Concert mus, orch, chmbr, solo, contemporary dance, acoustic, electro-acoustic, choral, vocal, br band.*

Wilkinson, Philip. Lyndhurst, Avenue Rd, Cranleigh, Surrey GU6 7LE *tel:* 01483 273813. *Arnold, Asch, Nov, OUP, WC. Educ mus.*

Willcocks, Jonathan. 3 The Square, Compton, W Sussex PO18 9HA *tel:* 023 9263 1369 *fax:* 023 9263 1786 *email:* jwillcocks@argonet.co.uk. *Lorenz, OUP. Classical, vocal, inst.*

Willett, Susan Anne. 9 Westfield Oval, Yeadon, Leeds LS19 7NR *tel:* 0113 250 4989. *Ballet.*

* **Williams, Adrian.** c/o Editions Max Eschig, 215 Rue du Faubourg Saint Honoré, F-75008 Paris, France *tel:* 00 33 1 42 89 17 13 *fax:* 00 33 1 45 63 62 91 *email:* adrian.williams@virgin.net. *Eschig (Paris). Orch, chmbr, choral, vocal, film and TV. Agent: NCCP.*

Williams, Chris. 11 Great Bridge Cottages, Headborough Rd, Ashburton, Devon TQ13 7QW *tel:* 01364 653603. *Choral, mus theatre, mus for young people.*

Williams, Graham. 48 Etheldene Ave, Muswell Hill, London N10 3QH *tel:* 020 8365 2952 *fax:* 020 8444 5014. *Chmbr, orch.*

Williams, Roger Bevan. c/o University Music, Powis Gate, College Bounds, Old Aberdeen AB24 3UG *tel:* 01224 272570 *fax:* 01224 272515. *Choral, pno, org, gui, hpd, orch.*

Williams, Tom. 7 Lingfield Terrace, Northampton NN2 7HT *tel:* 01604 792010 *email:* tom@twills.demon.co.uk. *Electro-acoustic mus, vocal, chmbr, orch.*

Williams-Morgan, Ralph. c/o RWM Music, PO Box 166, Northwood, Middx HA6 2FL *tel:* 01923 841645 *fax:* 01923 841785 *email:* ralph@rwmmusic.com. *RWM Music (sp).*

* **Williamson, John Ramsden.** 31a Aberconway Rd, Prestatyn, Denbighshire, N Wales LL19 9HL *tel:* 01745 852067. *Curiad, Da Capo, Gwynn. Orch, chmbr, pno, vocal, choral, symphony, concerto.*

Williamson CBE AO, Malcolm. c/o J Audrey Ellison International Artists' Management, 135 Stevenage Rd, Fulham, London SW6 6PB *tel:* c/o 020 7381 9751 *fax:* 020 7381 2406. *BH, Campion, Wein. Agent: Ellison.*

* **Wills OBE, Arthur.** 26 New Barns Rd, Ely, Cambs CB7 4PN *tel:* 01353 662084 *also fax;* 07774 680716 *email:* artwill@argonet.co.uk. *ABd, Banks, BB, Bèrben, BH, Brunton, Cramer, Fentone, Nov, Nova, Oec, OUP, Ric, Rob, RSCM, Warwick, WC, Wein. Choral, opera, org, vocal.*

Wilson, Ian. c/o Universal Edition (London) Ltd, 48 Great Marlborough St, London W1V 2BN *tel:* 020 7437 6880 *fax:* 020 7437 6115 *email:* miranda@ue-london.demon.co.uk. *Camden, Irish Contemporary Music Centre, UE. Orch, chmbr mus.*

Wilson, Jeffery. 5 Church Green, Boreham Village, Essex CM3 3EH *tel:* 01245 450192 *also fax. Camden, Environ Music, LCD, Royal Ballet School, GSMD Publications. Chmbr mus, jazz, opera, orch.*

Wilson, Malcolm C. Claganach, 1a Stirling Rd, Dunblane, Perthshire FK15 9EP *tel:* 01786 825387 *also fax; email:* claganach@easynet.co.uk. *AGEHR, Member of ASCAP. Deeay, Flagstaff, Flammer, Hope, HRGB, Jeffers, Lorenz, National. Handbells.*

* **Wilson CBE, Thomas.** 120 Dowanhill St, Glasgow, Scotland G12 9DN *tel:* 0141 339 1699 *also fax. Bèrben, Queensgate (sp), SMIC, WC. Opera, symphony, orch, choral, vocal, chmbr, inst including concertos for gui, pno, va, vn.*

Wilson-Dickson, Andrew. 25 Plasturton Ave, Cardiff CF1 9HL *tel:* 029 2022 8154 *also fax; email:* w-d@baynet.co.uk. *Banks, Griffiths. Opera, classical scores, church mus.*

Wimhurst, Karen. c/o Clarke Agency, 39 Birnam Rd, Islington N4 3LJ *tel:* 020 7281 0672 *also fax. Opera, choral, mus theatre, br bands, dance.*

* **Winters, Geoffrey.** Brett Cottage, Ash St, Semer, Ipswich IP7 6QZ *tel:* 01449 740613. *Brett (sp), Ches, For, OUP, Nov, Nova, Simrock, UE, WC.*

Wishart, Trevor. 83 Heslington Rd, York YO10 5AX *tel:* 01904 630143. *Realspace (sp), University of York. Voice, electro-acoustics, mus theatre, educ and computer mus.*

* **Witchell, Peter J.** Old School House, Owston Rd, Knossington, Oakham LE15 8LX *tel:* 01664 454469. *RSCM. Musicals, orch, choral, inst, ballet.*

Wood, David. c/o Casarotto Ramsay and Associates Ltd, National House, 60-66 Wardour St, London W1V 4ND *tel:* 020 7287 4450 *fax:* 020 7287 9128. *Samuel French. Musical plays for children.*

* **Wood, Gareth Haydn.** 57 Marishal Rd, London SE13 5LE *tel:* 020 8318 3312 *also fax. BH, Maecenas, Rosehill, Smith, Warwick.*

Wood, Hugh. c/o Chester Music, 8-9 Frith St, London W1V 5TZ *tel:* 020 7434 0066 *fax:* 020 7287 6329 *email:* music@musicsales.co.uk. *Ches. Orch, pno, chmbr, inst.*

Wood, James. Bancroft, Rectory Lane, Fringford, Bicester, Oxon OX6 9DX *tel:* 01869 278392 *also fax; email:* jw@rogosanti.demon.co.uk. *(sp). Chmbr ens, chmbr orch, vocal, choir, electronic mus, perc solo and ens.*

* **Wood, Philip.** Derwent Mews, Papcastle, Cockermouth, Cumbria CA13 0JN *tel:* 01900 821251. *Da Capo. Solo inst, orch, educ mus, chmbr, br, wind band, choral.*

Woolfenden, Guy. Malvern House, Sibford Ferris, Banbury, Oxon OX15 5RG *tel:* 01295 780679 *fax:* 01295 788630 *email:* guy@arielmusic.demon.co.uk. *Ariel, Brass Wind, R Smith, Warwick. Theatre mus, ballet, opera, film and TV, concert, chmbr mus.*

Woolrich, John. c/o Faber Music Ltd, 3 Queen Square, London WC1N 3AU *tel:* 020 7833 7911/2 *fax:* 020 7833 7939 *email:* promotion@fabermusic.co.uk. *Faber. Inst, orch, chmbr, vocal, opera.*

Worby, Robert. 30a Spencer Place, Leeds, W Yorks LS7 4BR *tel:* 0113 262 7302 *fax:* 0113 262 2766 *email:* worby@sontec.demon.co.uk. *Low Noise Music. Contemporary dance, film, TV, educ, electro-acoustic mus.*

* **Wright, Christopher George.** Greenways, 46 Duke's Drive, Halesworth, Suffolk IP19 8DR *tel:* 01986 872050. *Animus, BH, Harlequin. Br, w/wind, inst and pno, vocal, choral, symphony.*

* **Wright, Geoffrey.** Shrub Wood Cottage, East Barton, Bury St Edmunds, Suffolk IP31 2QY *tel:* 01284 787316. *AA, BC, Ches. Musicals, films, theatre, chmbr, songs, symphony.*

Wulstan, David. Ty Isaf, Llanilar, nr Aberystwyth, Cardiganshire SY23 4NP *tel:* 01974 241229 *email:* dww@aber.ac.uk. *Ches.*

Wuorinen, Charles. c/o Peters Edition Ltd, 10-12 Baches St, London N1 6DN *tel:* 020 7553 4030 *fax:* 020 7490 4921 *email:* newmusic@uk.edition-peters.com.

Yershon, Gary. c/o Chuck Julian Associates, Suite 51, 26 Charing Cross Rd, London WC2H 0DH *tel:* 020 7437 4248; 020 7240 1301 *fax:* 020 7240 1296. *Theatre, TV, radio, educ, film.*

Young, Derek. 1 Hive Cottages, North St, Cambridge CB4 3QW *tel:* 01223 560067. *Lynwood.*

Yu, Julian. c/o Universal Edition (London) Ltd, 48 Gt Marlborough St, London W1V 2BN *tel:* 020 7437 6880 *fax:* 020 7437 6115 *email:* miranda@ue-london.demon.co.uk. *UE. Contemporary classical mus.*

Zehm, Norbert. 31 Cavendish Rd, Southport, Merseyside PR8 4RT *tel:* 01704 568155 *also fax; email:* norbert@zehm.freeserve.co.uk.

Librettists and Translators

Writers whose operatic work has been professionally performed and/or has been published (in score or libretto form) are listed below. Only those resident in the UK are included, plus some overseas-based translators whose translations are used by British opera companies. Composers who have written librettos only for their own works are excluded. Translators' languages are listed alphabetically in italics after each entry.

Andrews, John. 101 Western Rd, Lewes, E Sussex BN7 1RS *tel:* 01273 473910. *Librettist.*

Apter, Ronnie. 5748 West Brooks Rd, Shepherd, Michigan 48883-9202, USA *tel:* 00 1 517 828 6987 *email:* herman.apter@sensible-net.com. *Librettist and translator. Anglo-Saxon, Czech, French, German, Greek, Italian, Latin, Old Provençal, Russian, Spanish.*

Ashurst, David. 76 Gilbey Rd, London SW17 0QG *tel:* 020 8767 1358 *also fax; email:* d.ashurst@english.bbk.ac.uk. *Librettist.*

Barzetti, Marcella. 8 Hawthorn Rd, Hatfield Peverel, Essex CM3 2SE *tel:* 01245 382349 *fax:* 01245 382223. *Translator. French, German, Italian.*

Black, Leo. 112 Chetwynd Rd, London NW5 1DH *tel:* 020 7485 1211 *also fax. Translator. German.*

Bloxam, Monica. 13 Glasslyn Rd, London N8 8RJ *tel:* 020 8348 5137 *fax:* 020 8348 5101 *email:* 106025.30@compuserve.com. *Translator. French, German, Italian, Romanian, Russian, Spanish.*

Branscombe, Peter. 32 North St, St Andrews, Fife KY16 9AQ *tel:* 01334 473367 *email:* pjb7@st-and.ac.uk. *Translator. French, German.*

Burton, Jonathan. 12 Corner Green, Blackheath, London SE3 9JJ *tel:* 020 8852 7599 *also fax. Translator. French, German, Italian (also Czech, Latin, Russian).*

Carstairs, Adam. 19 Highgate Ave, London N6 5SB *tel:* 020 8340 0547 *fax:* 020 8347 6733. *Translator. French, German.*

Chater, James. 56 Sistova Rd, London SW12 9QS *tel:* 020 8333 1440; 07771 780664 *fax:* 020 8355 4696 *email:* JMChater@aol.com. *Translator. Dutch, French, German, Italian.*

Clarke, Peter. Harewood, 22 Rooksmead Rd, Sunbury-on-Thames, Middx TW16 6PD *tel:* 01932 781577 *fax:* 01932 789822. *Librettist and translator. French, Italian.*

Criswick, Mary. 94 Kidmore Rd, Reading RG4 7NB *tel:* 0118 947 2627 *email:* marycriswick@magic.fr. *Translator. French to English.*

Cruickshank, Marty. c/o Janet Fillingham Associates, 52 Lowther Rd, London SW13 9NU *tel:* 020 8748 5594 *fax:* 020 8748 7374 *email:* jfillassocs@aol.com. *Librettist.*

Daguerre de Hureaux, Florence. 16 Laughton Lodge, Laughton, E Sussex BN8 6BY *tel:* 01323 815737 *fax:* 01323 815736. *Translator. French.*

Dawson, David. 10 Glen Rd, Eldwick, Bingley, W Yorks BD16 3ET *tel:* 01274 562007 *also fax. Translator. French, Italian.*

Dunnett, Roderic. 4 Warwick Court, Michaelmas Rd, Coventry CV3 6HD *tel:* 024 7650 2749 *also fax. Librettist and translator. Bulgarian, Dutch, French, German, Greek, Italian, Latin.*

Farncombe CBE, Charles. c/o Werner Kühnly, Woerthstr 31, D-70563 Stuttgart, Germany *tel:* 00 49 711 780 2764 *fax:* 00 49 711 780 4403. *Translator. German, Italian.*

Forbes, Elizabeth. Flat 3, 1 Bryanston Square, London W1H 7FE *tel:* 020 7262 0266 *also fax. Translator. French, German, Italian, Swedish.*

Gledhill, Ian. 29 Over St, Brighton BN1 4EE *tel:* 01273 689657 *email:* i.angle@virgin.net. *Translator. Czech, French, German.*

Harriott, Ted. Belvedere, Seymer Rd, Swanage, Dorset BH19 2AL *tel:* 01929 422908. *Librettist.*

Herman, Mark. 5748 West Brooks Rd, Shepherd, Michigan 48883-9202, USA *tel:* 00 1 517 828 6987 *email:* herman.apter@sensible-net.com. *Librettist and translator. Anglo-Saxon, Czech, French, German, Greek, Italian, Latin, Old Provençal, Russian, Spanish.*

Houston, Roxanne. 8 Hartington Rd, Aldeburgh, Suffolk IP15 5HD *tel:* 01728 454048. *Librettist.*

Jones, Andrew V. Selwyn College, Cambridge CB3 9DQ *tel:* 01223 335866 *fax:* 01223 335837 *email:* avj1000@cam.ac.uk. *Translator. Italian (Handel operas).*

Kennedy, Paula. 37 Swainstone Rd, Reading RG2 0DX *tel:* 0118 975 0981 *also fax; email:* shortkennedy@compuserve.com. *Translator. Czech, Hungarian. Also surtitler (Focon system).*

Keys, Robert. Red Lion Court, Stalbridge, Sturminster Newton, Dorset DT10 2LR *tel:* 01963 362999. *Translator. German, Italian.*

Lenz-Mulligan, Gundhild. 15 Sandbourne Ave, Merton Park, London SW19 3EW *tel:* 020 8544 0983 *fax:* 020 8543 8909 *email:* glenz-mulligan@dial.pipex.com. *Translator. German.*

Levy, Jonathan. 444 Mooney Hill Rd, Patterson, New York, NY 12563, USA *tel:* 00 1 914 878 6064 *also fax. Librettist and translator. French, Italian.*

Lindsay CBE, Maurice. 7 Milton Hill, Milton, Dumbarton G82 2TS *tel:* 01389 762655. *Librettist.*

Macdonald, Hugh. c/o Dept of Music, Washington University, St Louis, MO 63130, USA *tel:* 00 1 314 863 6621 *fax:* 00 1 314 863 7231 *email:* hjmacdon@artsci.wustl.edu. *Translator. French, German, Italian.*

Maresova, Eva. 40 Campbell Close, London SW16 6NG *tel:* 020 8677 8473. *Translator. Czech.*

Mertl, Michael. 81 Chambers Lane, Willesden Green, London NW10 2RN *tel:* 020 8459 5023 *also fax; email:* mmertl@compuserve.com. *Translator. German.*

Minchin, Leslie. 11 Parkhill Rd, London NW3 2YH *tel:* 020 7722 8022. *Translator. German.*

Mitchell, Adrian. c/o Peters, Fraser & Dunlop Scripts Ltd, 5th Floor, The Chambers, Chelsea Harbour, Lots Rd, London SW10 0XF *tel:* 020 7376 7676. *Librettist and adaptor from foreign language literal translations.*

Morgan, Edwin. 19 Whittingehame Court, Glasgow G12 0BG *tel:* 0141 339 6260 *fax:* 0141 357 4977. *Librettist and translator. French.*

Morley, Christopher. 16 Melbourne Rd, Halesowen B63 3NB *tel:* 0121 550 4482 *also fax; email:* cfmorley@breathemail.net. *Translator. French, German, Italian.*

Mugridge, Pat. 19 Mount Pleasant Drive, Belper, Derbys DE56 2TQ *tel:* 01773 824770. *Librettist.*

Novelli, Florence. 8 Townfield Gardens, Altrincham, Cheshire WA14 4DT *tel:* 0161 941 1138. *Librettist.*

Phillips, Gordon. 28 Ridgeway, Fenham, Newcastle upon Tyne NE4 9UL *tel:* 0191 274 7803. *Librettist.*

Platt, Norman. Pembles Cross, Egerton, Ashford, Kent TN27 9BN *tel:* 01233 756237 *fax:* 01233 756704. *Librettist and translator. French, German, Italian.*

Presland, Eric. 17 Hathway House, Gibbon Rd, London SE15 2AU *tel:* 020 7277 5014 *also fax. Librettos for opera, mus theatre, musicals and other large and small-scale choral works. Also individual classical and cabaret songs. Translations from French, Italian and German.*

Rae, Charles Bodman. 25 Priory St, Bowdon, Cheshire WA14 3BQ *tel:* 0161 941 5266 *email:* charles.bodman.rae@rncm.ac.uk. *Translator. French, German, Polish.*

Redmond, Patrick. 1 Ashmore Rd, Coundon, Coventry CV6 1LH *tel:* 024 7659 3931. *Translator. French, German, Italian.*

Rees, Simon. Dramaturg, Welsh National Opera, John St, Cardiff CF10 5SP *tel:* 029 2046 4666 *fax:* 029 2048 3050 *email:* simon.rees@wno.org.uk. *Librettist and translator. French, German, Italian. Specialises in Focon surtitle system.*

Roberts, Don. Dale House, Marshborough, nr Sandwich, Kent CT13 0PG *tel:* 01304 812576. *Librettist.*

Salter, Lionel. 26 Woodstock Rd, London NW11 8ER *tel:* 020 8458 3568 *also fax. Translator. French, German, Italian, Spanish.*

Shaw, Jean. 38 Hazlewell Rd, London SW15 6LR *tel:* 020 8788 0680. *Translator. French, German, Italian.*

Smith, Rosemary. 11 Oxdowne Close, Cobham, Surrey KT11 2SZ *tel:* 01372 844271 *fax:* 01372 843854 *email:* rosemary.smith@btinternet.com. *Translator. French, German. Books, concert programmes, texts and pronunciation texts for choral and solo singers.*

Stilnovo Associates. 1 College St, Bury St Edmunds, Suffolk IP33 1NH *tel:* 01284 724516 *also fax; email:* stilnovian@aol.com. Paola Bortolotti, mgr dir. *Translation: French, Italian, Spanish; interpreting: Italian.*

Taylor, Philip. 112 Main Rd, Wilby, Northants NN8 2UE *tel:* 01933 223301 *also fax; email:* 100661.1355@compuserve.com. *Translator. Russian.*

Tracey, Edmund. 58 Ripplevale Grove, London N1 1HT *tel:* 020 7607 4116. *Librettist and translator. French, Italian, German.*

Trowell, Brian. Faculty of Music, University of Oxford, St Aldate's, Oxford OX1 1DB *tel:* 01865 276126 *fax:* 01865 276128 *email:* office@music.ox.ac.uk. *Translator. French, German, Italian, Latin, Spanish.*

Tunnicliffe, Stephen. Clairmont, The Square, Clun, Shropshire SY7 8JA *tel:* 01588 640398 *fax:* 01588 640107 *email:* tunnicliffe@btinternet.com. *Librettist.*

Venables, Clare. c/o Cruickshank Cazenove Ltd, 97 Old South Lambeth Rd, London SW8 1XU *tel:* 020 7735 2933 *fax:* 020 7820 1081. *Librettist.*

Warburton, Ernest. 10a Park Ave, St Albans, Herts AL1 4PB *tel:* 01727 852589 *also fax. Translator. Czech, French, German, Italian, Russian.*

Warrack, John. Beck House, Rievaulx, Helmsley, York YO62 5LB *tel:* 01439 798322 *also fax; email:* warrack@beckho.demon.co.uk. *Translator. French, German, Italian, Russian.*

Watt, Jill. 1a Warwick Chambers, Pater St, London W8 6EN *tel:* 020 7937 0636 *fax:* 020 7938 4778. *Librettist and translator. French, German.*

Webber, Stephen. 2 Waterside Cottages, Mill Green, Hatfield, Herts AL9 5NY *tel:* 01707 263385. *Librettist and translator. French, Italian.*

Wendel, Renate Maria. c/o Friary Music Services, 142b Friary Rd, London SE15 5UW *tel:* 020 7277 7068 *fax:* 020 7277 8354 *email:* 100115.3701@compuserve.com. *Translator. German.*

White, Michael. 16 Willow Rd, London NW3 ITJ *tel:* 020 7431 1618. *Librettist and translator.*

Wright, Stella J. Flat 2, 79 Linden Gardens, London W2 4EU *tel:* 020 7229 7060. *Translator. French.*

Jazz and Light Music Agencies

These agencies operate along similar lines to the concert and opera agencies listed under **Agents and Managers**.

Acker's International Jazz Agency/Apricot Music. 53 Cambridge Mansions, Cambridge Rd, London SW11 4RX *tel:* 020 7978 5885/6 *fax:* 020 7978 5882. Pamela F Sutton, mgr; Leslie S Squires, associate. *Personal mgr and exclusive agent for Aker Bilk and his Paramount Jazzband.*

Allied Talent Agency. Mansfield House, 9 Great Chapel St, London *tel:* 020 7437 2551; 01582 831443 *fax:* 020 7437 2295. Jan Cotton, mgr dir; Livvy Stainer, booking agent.

Associated Artists Music Agency. 57 Wix's Lane, London SW4 0AH *tel:* 020 7228 9390 *also fax; email:* aama@belcanto.demon.co.uk. Bernadette Keeffe, proprietor.

BPR. 36 Como St, Romford, Essex RM7 7DR *tel:* 01708 725330 *fax:* 01708 725322 *email:* bprmusic@compuserve.com. Brian Theobald, Ina Dittke, dirs; Vicki Horrigan, mgr.

Cassell Entertainment & Leisure Consultants. Lavington, Margery Lane, Lower Kingswood, Tadworth, Surrey KT20 7BG *tel:* 01737 242966 *also fax.* Edna Cassell, principal.

Cromwell Management. 4-5 High St, Huntingdon, Cambs PE18 6TE *tel:* 01480 435600 *fax:* 01480 356250 *email:* tricvic@lineone.net. Vic Gibbons and Tricia Gibbons, managing partners.

Ernie Garside Productions. 2 Musbury Ave, Cheadle Hulme, Cheshire SK8 7AT *tel:* 0161 485 6538 *also fax.* Ernie Garside, mgr dir.

Europa Jazz Live. 6 Belgrove, Tunbridge Wells, Kent TN1 1YW *tel:* 01892 516722 *fax:* 01892 536080 *email:* e.j.i@talk21.com. David E Jacobs, proprietor. *Mgt for Tina May and her various ens.*

Gordon Poole Agency Ltd. The Limes, Brockley, Bristol BS48 3BB *tel:* 01275 463222 *fax:* 01275 462252 *email:* agents@gordonpoole.com. Gordon Poole, mgr dir. *Musicians and bands provided for hotels and corporate functions.*

Graham Dalby Artists Ltd. 116a Penwith Rd, London SW18 4QE *tel:* 020 8874 3587 *fax:* 020 8871 9869 *email:* grahamdalby@compuserve.com.

Ibis Productions. PO Box 11009, Banchory AB31 6YB *tel:* 01330 844456 *fax:* 01330 844435 *email:* ibis@prods.demon.co.uk. Ian Middleton.

Jazz & Arts Directions. PO Box 118, Newport NP19 8XJ *tel:* 01633 211368 *fax:* 01633 220422. John Minnion, mgr; Barbara Bowman, bookings mgr. *Specialises in classic traditional jazz nationwide.*

Jazz Expo. 8 Lucas Place, Leeds LS6 2JB *tel:* 0113 245 5439; 01484 604392; 07768 013937. Jon Taylor, mgr. *Provides musicians for concerts, functions, promotions, weddings, etc.*

Jim Crawshaw Agency. 26 Westcombe Drive, Bury, Lancs BL8 1DN *tel:* 0161 764 3697 *also fax.* Jim Crawshaw, proprietor. *Represents The Syd Lawrence Orchestra.*

John Boddy Agency. 10 Southfield Gardens, Twickenham, Middx TW1 4SZ *tel:* 020 8892 0133/8891 3809 *fax:* 020 8892 4283.

Kaleidoscope Music Services. 75 Fernhurst Rd, Portsmouth, Hants PO4 8AA *tel:* 023 9229 7210 *also fax; email:* kaleidoscope@fsbdial.co.uk.

Live Music UK. 43 Northover Rd, Westbury on Trym, Bristol BS9 3LN *tel:* 0117 950 6744 *fax:* 0117 959 0299 *email:* chris@lmuk.co.uk. Chris Pope, snr partner. *Mus for corporate and private hospitality.*

Music Plus. 78 Croydon Rd, Reigate, Surrey RH2 0NH *tel:* 01737 226670 *fax:* 01737 225600. Mark Walmsley, dir. *Private and corporate entertainment consultancy with limited artists' management.*

Music Services Agency. The Chalet, 75 Claremont Rd, Tunbridge Wells, Kent TN1 1TE *tel:* 01892 527970 *also fax.* David Ebbage, dir. *Spa Palm Court Orchestra; Spa Palm Court Trio; Claude Bolling and Jacques Louissier Jazz Quartet; dance band, jazz trio, swing band, and theatre orchestra.*

Renaissance Music Agency. PO Box 154, Congleton, Cheshire CW12 4FT. Richard Lythall, mgr dir. *Established to provide opportunities of performance experience for young semi-professional musicians. Specialises in mus theatre; singers almost exclusively perform 'Songs from the Shows' while inst players have wider repertoire. Trains young people in the essential principles demanded by the mus industry.*

Robert Masters Artistes' Personal Management. Lower Marshay, Pennymoor, Tiverton EX16 8LZ *tel:* 01363 866665 *fax:* 01363 866667. Robert Masters, proprietor.

Sympathetic Developments. 48 Bridle Way, Colehill, Wimborne, Dorset BH21 2UE *tel:* 01202 880331 *fax:* 01202 888037. Graham Stansfield, proprietor.

Upbeat Management. Sutton Business Centre, Restmor Way, Wallington, Surrey SM6 7AH *tel:* 020 8773 1223 *fax:* 020 8669 6752 *email:* info@upbeat.co.uk. Liz Biddle, Beryl Korman, mgrs.

Wienerwald Entertainments. 52 Helen Ave, Feltham, Middx TW14 9LB *tel:* 020 8751 0417 *also fax.* Keith Harmon, mgr dir.

zZob. 9 Wyndham Rd, Kingston KT2 5JR *tel:* 020 8546 8269 *email:* mark@zzob.com. Mark Narayn, Dillon Tonkin.

Regional Jazz Organisations

Administrative organisations have been set up to sponsor, co-ordinate and encourage jazz activities in their particular region. They are funded through a variety of sources, one of which is the **Arts Council of England** (Rajan Hooper, jazz officer, Music Department, Arts Council of England, 14 Great Peter Street, London SW1P 3NQ *tel:* 020 7333 0100 *fax:* 020 7973 6590).

Jazz Action. 9 Dunbar Drive, Eaglescliffe, Stockton on Tees TS16 9EG *tel:* 01642 805016 *also fax.* Adrian Tilbrook, jazz development offr. *Covers Yorkshire and the North.*

Jazz Education Projects. 10 Wiston Ave, Chichester, W Sussex PO19 4RJ *tel:* 01243 533752. Adrian Kendon, admin. *Covers the South of England.*

Jazz North West. 2a Church St, Malpas, Cheshire SY14 8NZ *tel:* 01948 861050 *fax:* 01948 861066. *Covers the North West.*

Jazz Services. Room 518, Africa House, 64 Kingsway, London WC2B 6BD *tel:* 020 7405 0737/47/57 *fax:* 020 7405 0828 *email:* admin@jazzservices.org.uk. Chris Hodgkins, dir; Celia Wood, information offr. *Promotes the growth and development of jazz within the UK and provides services in marketing, touring, information, education, communication and jazz newspapers.*

South West Jazz. Bradninch Place, Gandy St, Exeter EX4 3LS *tel:* 01392 218368 *fax:* 01392 420442 *email:* rosie@ejjarvis.demon.co.uk. Rosie Jarvis, admin. *This organisation acts as an advisory and information centre and contact for jazz groups in SW England.*

Welsh Jazz Society Ltd (Cardiff). 26 The Balcony, Castle Arcade, Cardiff CF1 2BY *tel:* 029 2034 0591 *fax:* 029 2066 5160 *email:* jazzwale@compuserve.com. Brian Hennessey, dir. *Covers Wales.*

Competitions

Competitions are annual unless otherwise stated and are listed in alphabetical order of title. Some of these, such as the Kathleen Ferrier Award, have their final stages as public events like competitions and are listed in both **Scholarships and Grants** and **Competitions**.The closing date for applications is usually several months in advance of the competition date.

Competitions for Performers and Conductors

Admira Young Classical Guitarist of the Year Competition. Newton Park, Newton St Loe, Bath BA2 9BN *tel:* 01225 875522 *fax:* 01225 875444 *email:* e.ginn@bathspa.ac.uk. Emmanuelle Ginn, bookings admin. *Jul 2000, applications by Jun. Open to all aged under 20 on day of competition, of any nationality. Application fee £30. First prize £1000.*

Anglo-Czechoslovak Trust. 23 Stonefield St, London N1 0HW *tel:* 020 7278 8459 *also fax; email:* nataia@actrust.freeserve.co.uk. N Newton, treasurer. *Apr-May, applications by 10 Jan. 7 categories: str, w/wind, br, keyboard, singers, gui, ens. For young professional musicians and mus students. Works by Czech and Slovak composers included. No age limit. Application fee £15 (solo), £25 (ens). First prize: 2 return flights to Prague, accommodation for 4 people, and possibility of performance in Prague.*

Association of English Singers and Speakers Prize. 16a Cromwell Ave, Highgate, London N6 5HL *tel:* 020 7347 6889 *fax:* 01234 355787. Jacob de Vries, chmn. *Open to students under the age of 30 at all UK institutions of HE where singing and speech are taught and who are nominated by their institution. Aims to encourage singing and speaking of English. Candidates are required to introduce and sing a recital in English of up to 20 mins duration. Applications by 1 Mar for first round at end Mar. Competition in Apr. Application fee £5. First prize £1000; accompanist prize £100.*

Bath Spa International Guitar Competition. Newton Park, Newton St Loe, Bath BA2 9BN *tel:* 01225 875522 *fax:* 01225 875444 *email:* e.ginn@bathspa.ac.uk. Emmanuelle Ginn, bookings admin. *4th week of July 2000, applications by 4 Jun. Open to all nationalities. For ages 30 and under. Application fee £50. First prize £3000.*

Bayreuth Bursary Competition. c/o The Wagner Society, 45 Frankfield Rise, Tunbridge Wells, Kent TN2 5LF *tel:* 01892 539781. Roger Temple, admin. *Travel bursary to Bayreuth Festival awarded annually, for young Wagnerian singers of all voices who are based in Britain. Aged 35 and under. Preliminary auditions held in London during Nov, applications by 31 Oct. Public final in London in Jan. First prize of tickets for performances at Bayreuth Festival with travel and accommodation.*

BBC Young Musicians. BBC Classical Music TV, EG30 East Tower, Television Centre, Wood Lane, London W12 7RJ *tel:* 020 8895 6143 *fax:* 020 8895 6146 *email:* young.musicians@bbc.co.uk. Jessica Brennan, admin. *Jul 1999-Mar 2000. Str, w/wind, br, perc, keyboard. Open to UK citizens aged 19 and under on 1 Jan 2000. Must have gr 8. £2000 prize for each concerto finalist.*

British Contemporary Piano Competition. 31 Lingholme Close, Cambridge CB4 3HW *tel:* 01223 357431. Philip Mead, ARAM founder and artistic dir. *Triennial. Next Nov 2000. Open to pianists aged 18-40. Repertoire entirely 20th C. Application fee £25. First prize £1200 and 10 engagements.*

British Reserve Insurance Conducting Prize/Seminar. National Association of Youth Orchestras, Ainslie House, 11 St Colme St, Edinburgh EH3 6AG *tel:* 0131 539 1087 *fax:* 0131 539 1069 *email:* admin@nayo.org.uk. Carol Main, dir. *Biennial, next 2001. Ages 18-26. First prize £500.*

Bromsgrove Festival Young Musicians' Platform. c/o 10 Evertons Close, Droitwich Spa, Worcs WR9 8AE *tel:* 01527 575441 *fax:* 01527 575366 *email:* lgharris@compuserve.com. Andrew Harris, hon

UK & EIRE COMPOSITION PLATFORM

WORKS FOR VIOLIN & PIANO DUO
Chairman of Jury – Yfrah Neaman OBE
Artistic Director – Adam Summerhayes

PRIZES

- **Performance in Purcell Room Platform : 12 Dec 2000**
- **Release on CD to be recorded and distributed by Sargasso records.**
- **Jury's Prize: £1000**
- **Critic's Prize £1000**
- **Audience Prize: £1000**

Composers will be asked to submit works that utilize the violin and piano in any way that catches their imagination, but will also be invited to search for the beauty and expressiveness of tone and timbre inherent in the combination of instruments, as well as the possibilities for dramatic expression.

It is important to understand that works in any idiom will be welcomed and that "beauty and expressiveness of tone" is not intended to mean that the music must be either melodic or tonal. Equally, works that take no account of the above will have in no way jeopardized their chances for consideration and selection – the invitation is intended as a starting point, to be taken or rejected as the composer chooses.

The deadline for submissions for the first platform is May 21st 2000.

The next platform will be held in December 2002.

Composers must be nationals of the UK or Eire, or should have been resident for over five years.
There are no age restrictions.
Submitted works should be of anything from 5 – 15 minutes duration.
Submitted works must not have received a previous public performance.
Submitted works should be for violin and piano only, used acoustically.
An administration fee will be charged: one score - £15, or two scores - £20.

For full details of prizes and conditions please send an s.a.e. to
The Administrator, UK & Eire Composition Platform, 6 Vicary Lane, Woodhouse, Loughborough, Leics. LE12 8UL

Great Elm Vocal Awards

24, 25, 26 October 2000

Three Prizes: £2,000, £1,000, £500

sponsored by the Rosemary Bugden Charitable Trust

and promoted by

JACKDAWS
Educational Trust

The competition is open to singers between 22 and 32 years of age inclusive. The repertoire is a song or aria by Handel, a song or aria by Peter Wishart and a song or aria of the competitor's own choice.

The application deadline is 25 September 2000. For more information and a form, please contact Jackdaws, Bridge House, Great Elm, Frome, Somerset BA11 3NY.
Tel: 01373 812383 or Fax: 01373 812083

July 2000
New Millennium Competition
at the LLANGOLLEN INTERNATIONAL MUSICAL EISTEDDFOD

LLANGOLLEN INTERNATIONAL Singer

A new and exciting competition for the Millennium with a first prize of £15,000. The competition will attract the best of the world's singers who are at the beginning of their professional careers.

The competition will take place in the Royal International Pavilion in two competitive sessions on Monday 3rd July and the final will be held in the Pavilion on the evening of Friday 7th July 2000.

The minimum age of entry will be 18 years and the upper age limit will be 26 on the day of the competition. Only twenty singers can be accommodated in the competition. The closing date for all applications is the 1st February 2000.

The twenty semi-finalists will be announced by the 1st April 2000.

For further details and application form contact:
Llangollen International Musical Eisteddfod, Music Office, Royal International Pavilion, Llangollen, North Wales LL20 8SW
Tel: 01978 860236 Fax: 01978 861300 E-mail: music@lime.uk.com Internet: www.lime.uk.com

organiser. *Apr-May, applications by Feb. For young performers of any nationality aged 17-25 (any inst or voice) of gr 8 distinction standard.*

C B Oldman Prize. Faculty of Music Library, Oxford University, St Aldate's Oxford OX1 1DB *tel:* 01865 286263 *fax:* 01865 286260 *email:* julie.crawley@music.ox.ac.uk. Julie Crawley, mus librarian. *Annual award of £200 for an outstanding work of mus bibliography, mus reference or mus librarianship by an author resident in the UK.*

Caerphilly County Borough Council Schools' Young Musician of the Year Competition. Caerphilly County Borough Council, Caerphilly Music Service, Ashfield Rd, Newbridge NP1 4QZ *tel:* 01495 246037 *fax:* 01495 243232. Keith Ellerington, principal mus offr. *Pno, singing, str, w/wind, br, tuned perc and composition. Open to those attending a Caerphilly County Borough Council secondary school or college. Maximum age of 19 at competition in Mar. Applications by 31 Jan. First prize £100 and 7 class prizes of £35 each. Prizewinners' schools receive matching cash prizes.*

Cardiff Singer of the World Competition. BBC Wales, Broadcasting House, Llandaff, Cardiff CF5 2YQ *tel:* 01437 563834 *also fax.* Anna Williams, admin. *Biennial competition organised by BBC Wales. Next 17-23 Jun 2001, applications by 24 Sep 2000. Singers aged 18 and above, must be recommended by national opera company, broadcasting organisation or principal of Conservatory of Music. First prize £10,000.*

Beryl Chempin Bach Prize for Pianists. 10 Russell Rd, Moseley, Birmingham B13 8RD *tel:* 0121 449 3055. Malcolm Wilson, competition organiser. *Annual competition in Jan, applications by Dec. Open to Conservatoire u/grads (except 1st years). Substantial prize. Programme 20-25 mins duration of original keyboard works by J S Bach.*

Beryl Chempin Beethoven Prize for Pianists. 10 Russell Rd, Moseley, Birmingham B13 8RD *tel:* 0121 449 3055. Malcolm Wilson, competition organiser. *Annual competition in Dec, applications by Nov. Open to Conservatoire u/grads (except 1st years). Substantial prize. Programme 25-30 mins duration of Beethoven works. Winner goes forward to Inter-collegiate Beethoven Competition in Dec.*

Beryl Chempin Postgraduate Keyboard Prize. 10 Russell Rd, Moseley, Birmingham B13 8RD *tel:* 0121 449 3055 *also fax.* Malcolm Wilson, David Saint, Lucy Carolan, competition organisers. *Annual prize awarded in June. Open to pianists, organists and harpsichordists on MA and PGDip courses only. Candidates must present programme of max 30 mins duration.*

Clonter Opera Theatre Inter-Conservatoire Opera Prize. Clonter Opera Theatre, Swettenham Heath, Congleton, Cheshire CW12 2LR *tel:* 01260 224638 *fax:* 01260 224742. Leana Isaac, admin. *Apr 2000, applications Oct. Annual inter-conservatoire opera prize worth £1500, 2nd prize £250. Open to singers of UK residence aged 20-35 nominated by heads of conservatoires for audition. No unsolicited applications please.*

Donatella Flick Conducting Competition. 47 Brunswick Gardens, London W8 4AW *tel:* 020 7792 2885 *fax:* 020 7792 2574. Judy Strang, admin. *Biennial. Next 21-23 Oct 2000, applications by 16 May. Award of £15,000 to subsidise period of up to one year as asst cond with London Symphony Orchestra, specialist study and concert engagements. Open to European Community nationals under 35. Application fee £35. Final at the Barbican with the LSO.*

E T Bryant Memorial Prize. Faculty of Music Library, Oxford University, St Aldate's, Oxford OX1 1DB *tel:* 01865 286263 *fax:* 01865 286260 *email:* julie.crawley@music.ox.ac.uk. Julie Crawley, mus librarian. *Prize of £200 to be awarded annually for a significant contribution to the literature of mus librarianship. Entries are invited from students of Library and Information Science and librarians within their first 5 yrs in mus librarianship.*

Eastbourne Symphony Orchestra Young Soloists Competition. 7 Prideaux Rd, Eastbourne, E Sussex BN21 2NW *tel:* 01323 724763. Brian Knights, awards admin. *Feb-Mar, applications by Dec. Concerto competition for young soloists of any nationality aged under 24. First prize £450 and an opportunity to play a concerto with the orch. Application fee £20.*

Essex Young Musician of the Year. Ongar Music Club, Corbetts House, Norwood End, Fyfield, Chipping Ongar, Essex CM5 0RW *tel:* 01277 899337 *also fax.* Jean Hall, admin. *1-2 Jul 2000, applications by 31 May. Total prize money £1725. Winner receives £500, plus recitals for Ongar Music Club and others, and an invitation to appear at a leading London venue. Age limit 25, with two prizes for those aged 18 and under. Open to instrumentalists (except organists) and singers who were born, live or attend school or college in the Essex postal area. Application fee £25.*

Gerald Moore Award. Courtyard House, Neopardy, Crediton, Devon EX17 5EP. Katie Avey, admin. *Biennial prize for UK pno accompanists (residents or studying full-time) of the song repertoire. Next competition spring 2000, applications by Dec 1999. Majority of entrants are nominations from colleges. A few outside places for pianists residing or*

studying full-time in the UK under the age of 29. Auditions in London. Independent candidates selected from written applications. Award £2000.

Great Elm Music Festival Vocal Awards. Bridge House, Great Elm, Frome, Somerset BA11 3NY *tel:* 01373 812383 *fax:* 01373 812083. Maureen Lehane Wishart, organiser. *Oct, entries by 31 Jul. Ages 22-32.*

Haverhill Sinfonia Soloist Competition. 8 Templars Court, Haverhill, Suffolk CB9 9AJ *tel:* 01440 763799 *also fax.* Kevin Hill, mus dir; Deena Shypitka, admin. *23 Sep 2000, applications by 24 Aug. W/wind, br, str, pno and singers. No age limit and any nationality. Administration fee £10. In 1999 there were 6 prizes totalling £1520. First prize included solo performances with City of London Sinfonia and Haverhill Sinfonia, solo recitals in Colchester, Glasgow, Gainsborough and Haverhill broadcast by BBC Radio Suffolk. Also performance prizes for remaining prize-winners. For details send SAE from Apr.*

Howarth Clarinet Competition. London College of Music and Media Room TC 308, Thames Valley University, St Mary's Rd, Ealing, London W5 5RF *tel:* 020 8231 2692 *fax:* 020 8231 2546 *email:* clare.beckett@tvu.ac.uk. Clare Beckett, mkt mgr. *Open to any clarinettist currently studying mus full-time at Higher Education level. Next competition spring 2000. Contact for further details.*

International Early Music Network Young Artists' Competition. The Early Music Network, 31 Abdale Rd, London W12 7ER *tel:* 020 8743 0302 *fax:* 020 8743 0996 *email:* glyn@earlymusicnet.demon.co.uk. Glyn Russ, admin. *Biennial. Next Jul 2001. Open to vocal and inst ens (min 3 persons) aged 17-30 (17-35 for singers) who specialise in repertoire from the Middle Ages to the 19th C and use the playing techniques and stylistic conventions of early mus. Prizes in the form of concerts with the Early Music Network, and possibilities of recording/broadcasting. Traditionally part of the York Early Music Festival*

Isle of Wight International Oboe Competition. c/o Island Partners Ltd, Alpine House, 13 Alpine Rd, Ventnor, Isle of Wight P038 1BT *tel:* 01983 853411 *fax:* 01983 856411 *email:* oboecomp@islandpartners.co.uk. Julia Holofcener, event producer. *Biennial. Next 8-13 May 2001, entries by 1 Dec 2000. For oboists who have not won an international competition and are aged 30 or under on date of finals (13 May 2001). Competition includes chmbr mus at semi-final stage. First prize is a London debut and £1000, second prize £800, third prize £500. Application fee £30.*

Kathleen Ferrier Awards. Kathleen Ferrier Memorial Scholarship Fund, 52 Rosebank, Holyport Rd, London SW6 6LY *tel:* 020 7381 0985 *also fax.* Shirley Barr, admin. *10-14 Apr 2000, entries by 1 Feb. Open to British singers (and those from the British Commonwealth and Republic of Ireland) aged 21-28. Application fee £25. First prize: £10,000 (from total prize money of £17,500), and Wigmore Hall recital.*

Leeds Conductors' Competition. Music Dept, Leeds Leisure Services, Leeds Town Hall, Leeds LS1 3AD *tel:* 0113 247 8335/6 *fax:* 0113 247 8397 *email:* matthew.sims@leeds.gov.uk. Matthew Sims, principal mus offr. *Triennial. Next 6-10 Jul 2002. British-born conds aged under 35. Application fee £50. First prize £1500 and numerous prestigious engagements.*

Leeds International Pianoforte Competition. The Piano Competition Office, University of Leeds, Leeds LS2 9JT *tel:* 0113 244 6586 *also fax; email:* info@leedspiano.bdx.co.uk. Paul Holloway, admin. *Triennial. Next Sep 2000, applications by 15 Mar. Competition for pianists of all nationalities aged 32 and under. Application fee £50. First prize £12,000 from total prize money c £55,000.*

Lionel Tertis International Viola Competition. The Secretariat, Erin Arts Centre, Victoria Square, Port Erin, Isle of Man IM9 6LD *tel:* 01624 835858 *fax:* 01624 836658 *email:* erinartscentre@enterprise.net. Martin Norbury, admin. *Triennial. Next 19-26 Aug 2000, entries by 31 Mar. Open to any nationality; aged 30 and under. First prize £3000 and Wigmore Hall recital. Application fee £54.*

Llangollen International Singer. Llangollen International Musical Eisteddfod, Royal International Pavilion, Llangollen, Denbighshire LL20 8SW *tel:* 01978 860236 *fax:* 01978 861300 *email:* music@lime.uk.com. Contact: Music Administrator. *Annual, early Jul. Applications by 1 Feb 2000. Competition for singers in the early stages of a professional career, ages 18-26. Semi finals held at Royan International Pavilion, Llangollen on 3 Jul 2000. Final on 7 Jul 2000. First prize £15,000.*

London International String Quartet Competition. 62 High St, Fareham, Hants PO16 7BG *tel:* 01329 283603 *fax:* 01329 281969 *email:* lsqf@compuserve.com. Dennis Sayer, admin. *Triennial. Next 10-16 Apr 2000, entries by 1 Dec. Open to str quartets of all nationalities, average age 30 or under and total age of players not exceeding 120 yrs. Application fee £50 per quartet. First prize £8000.*

Maggie Teyte/Miriam Licette Awards. 2 Keats Grove, London NW3 2RT *tel:* 020 7435 5861 *fax:* 020 7431 5706. Felicity Guinness, admin.

Leeds International Pianoforte Competition 2000

SPONSORED BY

HALIFAX

6 - 23 September 2000

Finals on 22 and 23 September
with the City of Birmingham Symphony Orchestra
conducted by Sir Simon Rattle
BBC Television and Radio

Closing date for applications: 15 March 2000
Prizes to be awarded: First Prize £12,000.
Total Prizes £57,000

Large number of national and international engagements including all British Orchestras and national and international Festivals

Address: Leeds International Pianoforte Competition, Piano Competition Office, The University of Leeds, GB-Leeds LS2 9JT
Phone and Fax: (44/113) 244 6586
E-mail: info@leedspiano.bdx.co.uk
Website: http://www/leedspiano.com

Patron:
Mrs Lionel Tertis

Honorary President:
Yuri Bashmet

Jury:
Yuri Bashmet *Russia*
Sally Beamish *UK*
Wolfram Christ *Germany*
Masao Kawasaki *Japan*
Irina Morozova *Australia*
Bruno Pasquier *France*
Howard Snell *UK (Chairman)*

Lionel Tertis International Viola Competition and Workshop

Lionel Tertis Internationaler Wettbewerb und Seminar für Bratsche

Lionel Tertis Concours et Séminaire International d'alto

Lionel Tertis Concorso e Seminario Internazionale per Viola

Лионель Тертис Международный Конкурс и Семинар по Альту

Isle of Man, British Isles
August 19th - 26th 2000

Masterclasses, recitals, lectures with:
Yuri Bashmet, Man-Seng Chan, Wolfram Christ, Helen Davies, Philip Dukes, Olga Eggert, Garfield Jackson, Masao Kawasaki, Garth Knox, Katherine McGillivray, Irina Morozova, Mikhail Muntian, Bruno Pasquier, Robert Plane, Tully Potter, Carole Presland, Sophia Rahman, Wilfred Saunders, Christopher Wellington, John White

Further information from:
Lionel Tertis Secretariat,
Erin Arts Centre,
Victoria Square,
Port Erin,
Isle of Man,
IM9 6LD
British Isles

Telephone: +44 (0) 1624 835858
Fax: +44 (0) 1624 836658
Website: http://homepages.enterprise.net/erinartscentre

Administered by the Erin Arts Centre. Registered Office: Victoria Square, Port Erin, Isle of Man, IM9 6LD, British Isles.
Incorporated at Douglas Isle of Man Number 068137C (Limited By Guarantee). Charity Registration Number 236A. VAT Registration Number 001 3251 51.

Newport International Competition for Young Pianists 2000

Preliminary Auditions
Royal Academy of Music, London
July 2000

Finals
Newport (South Wales) October 2000
(Free airfare and accommodation available for Finalists - see guidelines for full details).

Full guidelines and an application form available from Iain Varah (Hon Sec) Civic Centre, Newport, South Wales NP20 4UR or from our website
www.newport.gov.uk/piano

Entrance fee £50
Closing Date - 1 May 2000
(entrants must be 25 or under on 1 September 2000)

supported by
Diana
Princess of Wales Memorial Fund
THE WORK CONTINUES

The **Williams-Morgan Piano** Competition
Alpine Symphony
2000
WAM Awards

WAM AWARD FIRST
2000
could be your opportunity for a
RECORDING CONTRACT

For 2000 Entry Form
&
COMPETITION KIT details
REGISTER TODAY
YOUR NAME & ADDRESS

THE WILLIAMS-MORGAN PIANO COMPETITION
RWM Music
P O Box 166, Northwood, Middlesex, HA6 2FL
Tel: 01923 841 645 Fax: 01923 841 785
E-mail: wmpc2000@rwmmusic.com http://www.rwmmusic.com
Freephone 0500 30 56 30

Or

To listen to the music first, send for
the CD-Alpine Symphony £13.99 inc p&p
School purchase concession
£10 inc p&p – Schools send no money now
payment 90 days from invoice
Order by Freephone – Fax – E-mail

Annual. Jan, applications by 1 Dec. Registration fee £18. Aged 30 and under. Maggie Teyte Prize of £2000 awarded together with a recital in association with the Friends of the Royal Opera House and the Covent Garden Festival. Open to female singers aged 30 and under. Registration fee £18. Miriam Licette Scholarship £5000. Megan Foster Accompanists Prize £250. Send sae for application form.

Moeck/Society of Recorder Players Solo Recorder Playing Competition. 20 The Coppice, Impington, Cambridge CB4 9PP *tel:* 01223 234791. Mrs P Davies, competition admin. *Biennial, next 2001. For young performers of any nationality aged under 30. To encourage talented young players with their professional aspirations. First round cassettes by end of Jan, final recitals during International Exhibition of Early Music, London. Prizes include Wigmore Hall and other recitals, cash and commemorative scroll. Solo rcdr players, with and without accompaniment, are required to show the ability to sustain a whole recital programme, providing a cross section of the different facets of the rcdr and its repertoire.*

Musicale Young Instrumentalist Competition. Musicale plc, 20 Salisbury Ave, Harpenden, Herts AL5 2QG *tel:* 01582 460978 *fax:* 01582 767343 *email:* HMusicale@aol.com. Gillian and David Johnston, dirs. *Jan/Feb 2000. Players aged 11-16 of gr 5 and above. A series of concerts takes place, culminating in a final with cash prizes for the winner and runner-up. The winner also has concerto performance with the National Children's Chamber Orchestra at a major concert venue.*

National Concert Band Festival. c/o 7 Dingle Close, Tytherington, Macclesfield SK10 2UT *tel:* 01625 430807 *also fax; email:* lizwinter@aol.com. Liz Winter, festival admin. *Symphonic wind band categories: beginners (aged 14 and under), school, youth (aged 19 and under), community, open. Three big band categories: school, youth, open. Regionals Nov-Dec, finals held the following Mar/Apr at the RNCM, Manchester.*

National Mozart Competition. 66 Talbot St, Southport, Merseyside PR8 1LU *tel:* 01704 530903 *also fax.* Barbara Dix, competition admin; Dame Kiri Te Kanawa, patron. *Annual. 1-2 Dec 2000, applications by 9 Oct. For singers of any nationality, aged under 33 on 2 Dec 2000. Preliminary rounds at end of Oct in London, Manchester, Glasgow and Dublin. Application fee £30. Prize money of £3250 plus engagements. Also Verdi/Wagner prize of £250 for best performance by a male singer of a Verdi or Wagner aria; Tenor Prize £250 and for female singers the David Kelly (Oratorio) £250 prize.*

Newport International Competition for Young Pianists. Civic Centre, Newport, South Wales NP20 4UR *tel:* 01633 232604 *fax:* 01633 232808. Iain Varah, hon sec. *Triennial. Next Oct 2000. Open to pianists aged under 25. Entry fee £50. First prize £5000.*

The Noble Award. Scottish Opera, 39 Elmbank Cres, Glasgow G2 4PT *tel:* 0141 248 4567 *fax:* 0141 221 8812. Margaret Sloan, auditions sec. *Biennial. Next Mar 2000. Applications by 5 Feb 2000. Award to singer of Scottish origin, residence or training. Applicants aged 18 and above who are in early stages of career. Application fee £20. Auditions held in London and Glasgow. First prize £2000.*

Norfolk Young Musician Competition. Music at Saint George's, Wahnfried, 4 Church Close, Buxton, Norwich NR10 5ER *tel:* 01603 279742 *also fax.* Ivor R Hosgood, chmn and sec. *Nov, entries by 30 Sep. For gr 8+ singers and instrumentalists aged 21 and under who either work, receive tuition or are resident in Norfolk. Three cash prizes plus sponsorship for public concerts including one in the Norfolk and Norwich Festival the following year.*

Parkhouse Award. c/o GBZ Management, PO Box 11845, London SE21 8ZS *tel:* 020 8761 6565 *fax:* 020 8670 3195 *email:* gbz_mgmt @compuserve.com. Gwenneth Bransby-Zachary, admin. *Biennial. Next spring 2001. Open to pno-based str ens, duos, trios and pno quartets only, age range 18-32. Applications by 1 Dec 2000. First prize: two concerts in prestigious London venues. Application fee £35.*

The Pro Piano New York Recital Series. 85 Jane St, New York, NY 10014, USA *tel:* +1 212 206 8794 *fax:* +1 212 633 1207 *email:* ricard@propiano.com. Ricard de La Rosa, exec dir, founder; Chitose Okashiro, artistic dir. *26-29 May 2000. Pianists, chmbr groups with piano. No age limit. Prize includes cash, recital, possible recording contract.*

RCO Performer of the Year. 7 St Andrew St, London EC4A 3LQ *tel:* 020 7936 3606 *fax:* 020 7353 8244 *email:* poty@rco.org.uk. Alan Dear, snr exec. *Org competition open to all members of the RCO.*

Richard Tauber Prize. Anglo-Austrian Music Society, 46 Queen Anne's Gate, London SW1H 9AU *tel:* 020 7222 0366 *fax:* 020 7233 0293. Tony Fessler, gen sec. *Biennial. Next spring 2000, applications by Feb 2000. Travel bursary and public London recital. Open to British and Austrian singers aged 21-30 (women), 21-32 (men). Application fee £20. First prize £2500.*

Robert William and Florence Amy Brant Pianoforte Competition. 83 Windsor Rd, Oldbury, W Midlands B68 8PB. Miss G L Brant, organiser and trustee. *3, 4 and 10 Jun 2000, applications by 1 Apr. Awarded to pianists of any nationality, aged 20-30 and resident in the UK. Entry fee £35. First prize £1200, second £600, third £300. Adjudicators John Barstow, Vanessa Latarche, Guy Woolfenden.*

Rowena Ferguson Memorial Piano Competition. 26 Pentland Cres, Edinburgh EH10 6NP *tel:* 0131 445 2044 *email:* rfmpc@commonsensemusic.com. Nicholas Hind, dir. *28-29 Apr 2001, open to pianists of all ages, nationalities and musical backgrounds; prizes awarded for outstanding solo pno performance. Emphasis placed on passion and performer-audience relations as well as technique. Pianists performing their own work also welcome.*

Royal Over-Seas League Annual Music Competition. Royal Over-Seas League, Park Place, St James's St, London SW1A 1LR *tel:* 020 7408 0214 ext 219 *fax:* 020 7499 6738 *email:* culture@rosl.org.uk. Roderick Lakin, dir of arts. *Auditions Feb-Apr, applications by 14 Jan. Open to commonwealth citizens. Aged 28 or under (insts), 30 or under (singers), also ens. Application fee £20 (insts and ens). £4000 first prize and gold medal; £3000 for ens. £25,000 in prizes including awards for overseas students and performance opportunities.*

Sainsbury's Choir of the Year. c/o Kallaway Ltd, 2 Portland Rd, Holland Park, London W11 4LA *tel:* 020 7221 7883 *fax:* 020 7229 4595 *email:* kate.jones@kallaway.co.uk. Kate Jones, mgr. *Biennial. Next 2000, entries by Dec 1999. Open to amateur choirs of 20-100 members. Auditions Mar-May 2000; semi-finals in Buxton, 10-12 Nov 2000; final at Royal Albert Hall, 3 Dec 2000 and televised on BBC2. New Children's Choir category, age 13 or under.*

St Albans International Organ Festival Competition. PO Box 80, St Albans, Herts AL3 4HR *tel:* 01727 844765 *also fax.* Ken Chaproniere, gen mgr. *Biennial. Next Jul 2001, applications by 12 Mar. Two competitions: Interpretation and Improvisation. Taped elimination rounds. Open to organists of all nationalities.*

St John's Festival Choir. 71 Pevensey Rd, Forest Gate, London E7 0HF *tel:* 020 8519 6491 *also fax; email:* SingComp@pnms.co.uk. Philip Norman, dir. *Annual. Finals, 13 May 2000. Applications by end Mar 2000. Solo singing competition at St John's Church, Loughton. Entry fee £5 per class. Three 1st prizes of £100 plus concerts and auditions.*

Scottish International Piano Competition. c/o RSAMD, 100 Renfrew St, Glasgow G2 3DB *tel:* 0141 332 4101 ext 243 *fax:* 0141 332 8901 *email:* r.barr@rsamd.ac.uk. Robin Barr, hon sec. *Triennial. Next competition held at RSAMD, Glasgow, 5-16 Sep 2001, applications by 31 Mar 2001. Open to pianists of all nationalities. Aged 30 or under. Application fee £30. First prize £10,000.*

Shell LSO Music Scholarship. c/o The Scholarship Administrator, London Symphony Orchestra, Barbican Centre, Barbican, London EC2Y 8DS *tel:* 020 7588 1116 *fax:* 020 7374 0127 *email:* shell@lso.co.uk. Helen Smith, admin. *Information available Oct, entries by mid-Dec. Orch instrumentalists aged 14-22. Insts vary; 2000 timp and perc; 2001 w/wind. £6000 annual scholarship. Auditions, w/shops and m/classes with LSO principals.*

South East Musicians' Platform. South East Music Schemes, 19 Bourne Rd, London N8 9HJ *tel:* 020 8340 4116 *fax:* 020 8348 8894 *email:* bcandordarees@compuserve.com. Deborah Rees, dir. *Annually open to soloists and ens aged under 30 and working in classical mus. Closing date 19 May 2000, 18 May 2001. Public Final in prestigious regional venue. First prize of concerts in London and the South East, and opportunity to bid for funds for commissions and recordings. Funded by South East Arts. Application fee £15. Send SAE/email requesting PLATFORM details for further information and application form, from Mar.*

Texaco Young Musician of Wales. 1 Westferry Circus, Canary Wharf, London E14 4HA *tel:* 020 7719 3000; 020 8549 7660 *fax:* 020 7719 5175. June P McCullough. *Biennial event organised in partnership with Côr Meibion De Cymru (South Wales Male Choir). Preliminary rounds and regional finals held autumn, final Mar. Open to instrumentalists aged 14-19 who have lived or studied in Wales for a minimum of 3 years. Final is broadcast on television and the winner receives the Texaco Young Musician of Wales trophy and a prize of £1000. Second prize £750; third prize £500; 3 runner-up prizes £250 each. Application fee of £10 refunded on attendance at preliminary rounds. For application forms contact Ken Crowle* tel: *01222 843631 or June McCullough* tel: *0181 549 7660.*

Thames Valley Young Musicians' Platform. Kencot Lodge, Kencot, Lechlade, Glos GL7 3QX *tel:* 01367 860588 *fax:* 01367 860619 *email:* chrisyapp@btconnect.com. Chris Yapp, dir. *Jul 2000, applications by mid-Jun. Ages 20-26 (instrumentalists), 20-28 (singers). Candidates born, educated, living or working in Oxfordshire or Berkshire. Prizes for selected soloists/groups: subsidised recitals.*

Tunbridge Wells International Young Concert Artists Competition. TWIYCA, Competition Office, PO Box 10, Tunbridge Wells North, Kent TN2 5ZQ *tel:* 01892 616844 *also fax; email:* twiyca@aol.com. Arthur Boyd, chmn. *Biennial. Next Jul 2000, entries by Feb 2000. Aged under 24 on date of final. Three sections: pno, str, wind. First prize £4000. Total prize money available £10,500 plus London recital. Application fee £45.*

Wells Double Bass Competition. Wells Cathedral School, The Coach House, New St, Wells, Somerset BA5 2LQ *tel:* 01252 319610 *also fax.* David Heyes, dir. *Oct. Open to bassists of school age. Prizes: £250, £150, £100.*

Welsh Singers' Competition. Live Music Now! - Wales, 1 Miles Court, Gwaelod y Garth, Cardiff CF4 8SR *tel:* 029 2081 3398; 01437 563834 (admin) *fax:* 029 2081 3380. Gillian Green, dir, Live Music Now! - Wales. Anna Williams, admin. *Biennial. Next 30 Oct 2000, information and application forms available from 1 Mar. Open to those born and educated in Wales or living and/or working in Wales. For singers at the beginning of their professional careers. First prize £2000. Sponsored by HSBC.*

West Belfast Classical Music Bursary Award. 56 Oakhurst Ave, Blacks Rd, Dunmurry, Belfast BT10 0PE *tel:* 028 9062 6269 *also fax.* Una Downey, sec. *Annual Easter event in Belfast for musicians born in Northern or Southern Ireland. Applications by Feb. New ens section.*

Wigmore Hall International Song Competition. Room 609 Langham House, 308 Regent St, London W1R 5AL *tel:* 020 7637 8515 *fax:* 020 7637 8516 *email:* whisc@compuserve.com. Virginia Harding, admin. *Biennial, third competition Sep 2001. Open to singers and pianists of all nationalities, aged 32 or under. Pianists will only be considered as part of a duo. Entrance fee £30. Detailed brochure available May 2000.*

The Williams-Morgan Piano Competition. RWM Music, PO Box 166, Northwood, Middx HA6 2FL *tel:* 01923 841645 *fax:* 01923 841785 *email:* wmpc2000@rwmmusic.com. Graham Watkins, educ and competition dir; Rosalind Morgan, admin mgr. *Dec 2000, entries by 1 Nov. Open to pianists. Set mus composed by Williams-Morgan. 2 classes, under and over the age of 18. Combined entry fee and competition kit (including a book and CD recording of the set mus) £40. First prize for each class - a recording contract.*

World Piano Competition London. 28 Wallace Rd, London N1 2PG *tel:* 020 7354 1087 *fax:* 020 7704 1053 *email:* ldn-ipc@dircon.co.uk. S Aronovsky, chmn and artistic controller. *Triennial. Next 2nd half of Apr 2000, Grand Final on 29 Apr with the Philharmonic Orchestra, entries by Jan. Pianists of all nationalities aged 29 and under. Application fee £50 (provisional). First prize in 1997 was £10,000.*

Yehudi Menuhin International Competition for Young Violinists. 8 St Georges Terrace, London NW1 8XJ *tel:* 020 7911 0901 *fax:* 020 7911 0903. Kim Gaynor, admin. *14-22 Apr 2000 in Folkestone. Two sections: under 16 (jnr), under 22 (snr). First prizes £3000 (jnr) and £4000 (snr) plus performance at gala concert. Apply in writing for application form.*

Young Artists Platform. Tillett Trust, Courtyard House, Neopardy, Crediton, Devon EX17 5EP. Katie Avey, admin. *Entry forms available in Oct, applications by Nov, auditions in Jan-Feb, competition spring 2000. Open to musicians residing or studying full-time in the British Isles. Age limits: inst soloists 20-25, singers 23-28, ens of up to 6 players, all members must be within same age limits. Application fee £10, returned at audition. No cash prizes. Successful candidates given concerts including Fairfield, Croydon and Blackheath concert halls, plus a demo tape, publicity photos and a publicity brochure.*

Competitions for Composers

Bath Spa International Guitar Competition. Newton Park, Newton St Loe, Bath BA2 9BN *tel:* 01225 875522 *fax:* 01225 875444 *email:* e.ginn@bathspa.ac.uk. Emmanuelle Ginn, bookings admin. *4th week of Jul 2000, applications by 4 Jun. Competition for composers for the gui. First prize: publication, recording and performance of winning piece.*

Clements Memorial Chamber Music Competition. Fernside, Copthall Green, Upshire, Waltham Abbey, Essex EN9 3SZ *Last Clements Memorial Prize in 2000, entries by 1 Oct. Chmbr composition (3-8 players); min length 15 mins. Entry fee £4. First prize £750. Send sae for details.*

The Galliard Ensemble Wind Quintet Composition Competition. c/o 39 Bushwood, London E11 3BW *tel:* 020 8518 8903; 07976 399828

email: malcolmjg@aol.com. c/o Kathryn Thomas. *Spring 2000, entries by 1 Mar. Compositions for wind quintet (fl, ob, cl, hn, bsn plus standard orch doublings) in any style invited from professional, amateur and student composers of any age and nationality (school age section available for age 18 and under in full-time education). Entries should comprise full score plus parts and may include a tape if desired. Recommended duration up to 15 mins. Winning pieces in both categories to be performed at the Woodford and Wanstead Festival of Chamber Music. For further details please send SAE or see website.*

Gregynog Composers Award of Wales. Festival Office, Gregynog, Newtown, Powys SY16 3PW *tel:* 01686 620224 *fax:* 01686 650656. Nia Price, festival organiser. *Entries by Apr. Open to all nationalities, no age limits. Special award available for composers aged 22 and under. Composition criteria to be confirmed.*

Dr Harold Smart Competition. Royal School of Church Music, Cleveland Lodge, Westhumble St, Westhumble, Dorking, Surrey RH5 6BW *tel:* 01306 877676 *fax:* 01306 887260 *email:* dg@rscm.com. John Harper, dir gen. *Competition for short anthems; deadline for applications Jan. Prize of £100 plus publication by RSCM.*

The Kathryn Thomas Composition Competition for Flute. c/o Malcolm Galloway, 39 Bushwood, London E11 3BW *tel:* 020 8518 8903; 07976 399828 *email:* malcolmjg@aol.com. *Compositions for solo fl, fl and pno or fl and gui are eligible. Submission deadline 5 Feb 2000. Entries judged in two categories: adult and school age (under 18 and in full-time education). Winning pieces performed at the Wanstead and Woodford Festival of Chamber Music, spring 2000 or later date. To apply send SAE or see website.*

Masterprize International Competition for Composition. PO Box 248, Barnet EN4 9ZU *tel:* 020 8447 1677 *also fax; email:* masterpriz @aol.com. Louise Burton, competition mgr; Madeleine Milne, asst mgr. *Triennial. Registration 30 March 2000. Completed manuscripts by end July 2000. Final May 2001, Lincoln Centre, New York. New composition of between 6 and 15 mins scored for normal symphonic forces; works including voice or in concerto form will not be accepted. No age or geographical limit. First prize $60,000 and recording release. Multiple radio broadcasts worldwide at semi-final stage and final stage. CD covermount with BBC Music Magazine at final stage. In collaboration with BBC Radio 3, BBC Worldservice, EMI, LSO and BBC Music Magazine.*

Millennium Competition for Composers. The Organist, New College, Oxford OX1 3BN *tel:* 01865 279519. *Motet or anthem on text appropriate to Feast of Pentecost. First prize: £2000. Applications by 31 Jan 2000. Ages 30 or under.*

Royal Philharmonic Society Composition Prize. 10 Stratford Place, London W1N 9AE *tel:* 020 7491 8110 *fax:* 020 7493 7463 *email:* admin@rps-uk.demon.co.uk. Rosemary Johnson, gen admin. *Annual award of £5000. Open to registered students past or present of any conservatoire or university within the UK, aged 28 and under on closing date. Application fee £20 (free to RPS members).*

Stephen Oliver Prize. Stephen Oliver Trust, c/o P W Productions, 7 Leicester Place, London WC2H 7BP *Biennial. Next 2000. The Trust was set up in 1993 in memory of Stephen Oliver and aims to encourage young people working in contemporary opera. Entrants aged 35 and under. First prize of £10,000 awarded for the composition of a chmbr opera. Format for future prizes may change so for further info send SAE to above address.*

Vivian Ellis Prize. Gloucester Mansions, 140a Shaftesbury Ave, London WC2 *tel:* 020 7836 7732 *fax:* 020 7836 8787 *email:* chris.grady @newmusicals.co.uk. Chris Grady, admin. *A national competition to encourage new composers, lyricists and librettists for the musical theatre. Entries by 4 Feb for summer/autumn w/shop and showcase. Application fee £30. Writers must be British resident. No age restriction. £4000 prize money plus a series of other benefits are shared by the finalists. Supported by PRS, The Stage, Stoll Moss Theatres, Tiffany & Co, Warner/Chappell Music Ltd and BBC Wales.*

Dr William Baird Ross Prize for Composition in Church Music. Horseshoe Cottage, Old Greenlaw Farm, Duns, Berwickshire TD10 6UP *tel:* 01361 810206. Dr I Coy, trustee. *Triennial. Next 2002, closing date 31 Aug. Open to composers of any age, resident and working in Scotland. First prize £250, second prize £175, third prize £100.*

Yorkshire Arts Young Composers' Award. Huddersfield Contemporary Music Festival, Music Dept, Huddersfield University, Queensgate, Huddersfield HD1 3DH *tel:* 01484 425082/472103 *fax:* 01484 472957 *email:* hcmf@hud.ac.uk. Alison Porey, asst admin. *Nov, entries by 28 Sep. New compositions for varied instrumentation. Open to British citizens or residents in the UK. Aged 30 or under. Application fee £7. Prizes totalling £600. Shortlisted works performed at festival.*

Brass Band Championships

All England Masters Brass Band Championship. 21 The Coppice, Impington, Cambridge CB4 4PP *tel:* 01223 234090 *also fax; email:* philipbiggs@bandstand.demon.co.uk. Philip Biggs, Richard Franklin, organisers. *May at Corn Exchange, Cambridge. First prize £3500.*

Boosey & Hawkes National Brass Band Championships of Great Britain. 13 The Paddocks, Penarth, South Glamorgan CF64 5BW *tel:* 029 2070 1246/2022 9759 *fax:* 029 2022 7537. Philip Morris, contest admin dir. *Finals 21-23 Oct 2000 at Royal Albert Hall. Winners receive the Boosey & Hawkes National Challenge Trophy and £2000.*

Boosey & Hawkes National Youth Brass Band Championships of Great Britain. c/o Brass Band Heritage Trust, Room 112 E Mill, Dean Clough, Halifax HX3 5YJ *tel:* 01422 250323 *fax:* 01422 252246. Peter Denton, development offr. *Feb at University of Salford, applications by end Nov. Jnr (aged 16 and under), intermediate, advanced and open (aged 19 and under) classes. First prize and trophy in each class. Application fee £45.*

British Open Brass Band Championship. Flat 3, 50 Ladbroke Grove, London W11 2PA *tel:* 020 7229 1129. Mrs M Mortimer, contest organiser. *All British-based br bands, insts and perc. No age limit. Invitation only - issued mid-June.*

Radio and Television

British Broadcasting Corporation

BBC Broadcast. Television Centre, Wood Lane, London W12 7RJ *tel:* 020 8743 8000. Will Wyatt, chief exec, broadcast; Alan Yentob, dir of television; David Docherty, deputy dir of television; Mark Thompson, controller, BBC2; Peter Salmon, controller, BBC1.

BBC Corporate Headquarters. Broadcasting House, Portland Place, London W1A 1AA *tel:* 020 7580 4468. Sir Christopher Bland, chmn; John Birt, dir general (to be succeeded by Greg Dyke).

BBC Local Radio. BBC Regional Broadcasting, Room 704, Henry Wood House, 3 & 6 Langham Place, London W1A 1AA *tel:* 020 7765 2795 *fax:* 020 7765 5838.

BBC World Service. Bush House, Strand, London WC2B 4PH *tel:* 020 7240 3456 *fax:* 020 7379 3984. Jenny Bild, exec producer, classical mus.

BBC Worldwide. Woodlands, 80 Wood Lane, London W12 0TT *tel:* 020 8576 2000 *fax:* 020 8749 0538. Rupert Gavin, chief exec. *Magazines, books, videos, spoken word, audio, CD-ROM, commercial website, programme licensing, channels mgt, online services, mus publishing and licensing.*

BBC Radio Principal Music Executives

Radio 1. Yalding House, London W1N 6AJ *tel:* 020 7580 4468. Andy Parfitt, controller; Trevor Dann, head of mus entertainment.

Radio 2. 99 Great Portland St, London W1A 1AA *tel:* 020 7765 3436 *fax:* 020 7765 3416 *email:* radio2@bbc.co.uk. Jim Moir, controller; Lesley Douglas, mgr ed; Geoff Mullin, head of mus; Alan Dedicoat, ed.

Radio 3. Broadcasting House, London W1 1AA *tel:* 020 7580 4468. Nicholas Kenyon, controller; Brian Barfield, mgr ed; John Evans, head of mus. Martyn Westerman, commissioning ed mus (live); Andrew Kuroski, specialist mus ed; Graham Dixon, EBU/ World Service/Multimedia mus ed; Andrew Lyle, sequences and talks ed; Edward Blakeman, snr producer, BBC Proms; Ann McKay, chief producer, BBC SO; Michael Emery, snr producer, BBC Singers; Cathy Wearing, head of presentation.

Radio 4. Broadcasting House, London W1 1AA *tel:* 020 7580 4468

Radio 5 Live. Broadcasting House, London W1A 1AA *tel:* 020 7580 4458. Roger Mosey, controller.

BBC Radio Production Centres Outside London

North BBC Entertainment Features. BBC North, PO Box 27, Oxford Rd, Manchester M60 1SJ *tel:* 0161 200 2020 *fax:* 0161 236 1005. Mario Dubois, business mgr; Paul Hindmarsh, snr producer (*tel:* 0161 244 4216); Mark Rowlinson, snr producer (*tel:* 0161 244 4215); Edwina Wolstencroft, snr producer (*tel:* 0161 244 4236).

Scotland. BBC Radio Scotland, Broadcasting House, Queen Margaret Drive, Glasgow G12 8DG *tel:* 0141 339 8844 *fax:* 0141 357 1283. Hugh Macdonald, dir BBC SSO.

Wales. BBC Radio Wales and Radio Cymru, Broadcasting House, Llantrisant Rd, Llandaff, Cardiff CF5 2YQ *tel:* 029 2032 2000 *fax:* 029 2055 2973. Nick Evans, Aled Glynne Davies, eds; Huw Tregelles Williams, dir of mus; Phil George, head, arts, music and features.

BBC Staff Orchestras and Choirs

Information on the BBC staff orchestras and choirs can be found under BBC in the **Symphony and Chamber Orchestras** and **Choirs and Choruses**.

BBC Local Radio Stations

The BBC Local Radio Stations are listed below. Additional information can be obtained from **BBC Regional Broadcasting Headquarters**, Room 715, Henry Wood House, 3 and 6 Langham Place, London W1A 1AA *tel:* 020 7765 2795.

BBC Asian Network. Epic House, Charles St, Leicester LE1 3SH *tel:* 0116 251 6688. Pebble Mill Rd, Birmingham B5 7SD. Vijay Sharma, ed.

BBC Coventry and Warwickshire. 25 Warwick Rd, Coventry CV1 2WR *tel:* 024 7655 9911 *fax:* 024 7657 0100. David Robey, ed.

BBC Essex. 198 New London Rd, Chelmsford, Essex CM2 9XB *tel:* 01245 616000 *fax:* 01245 490703 *email:* essex@nc.bbc.co.uk. Margaret Hyde, mgr ed.

BBC GLR. 35c Marylebone High St, London W1A 4LG *tel:* 020 7224 2424 *fax:* 020 7935 3535. Steve Panton, mgr ed.

BBC GMR. PO Box 951, Oxford Rd, Manchester M60 1SD *tel:* 0161 244 3002 *fax:* 0161 236 5804. Mike Briscoe, acting ed.

BBC Hereford and Worcestershire. Hylton Rd, Worcester WR2 5WW *tel:* 01905 748485 *fax:* 01905 748321. Anita Bhalla, acting ed.

BBC Radio Bristol. PO Box 194, Bristol BS99 7QT *tel:* 0117 974 1111 *fax:* 0117 923 8323. Jenny Lacey, mgr ed.

BBC Radio Cambridgeshire. Broadcasting House, 104 Hills Rd, Cambridge CB2 1LD *tel:* 01223 259696 *fax:* 01223 460832. Andrew Wilson, mgr ed.

BBC Radio Cleveland. PO Box 95FM, Newport Rd, Middlesbrough TS1 5DG *tel:* 01642 225211 *fax:* 01642 211356. David Peel, mgr ed.

BBC Radio Cornwall. Phoenix Wharf, Truro, Cornwall TR1 1UA *tel:* 01872 275421 *fax:* 01872 240679. Pauline Causey, mgr ed.

BBC Radio Cumbria. Annetwell St, Carlisle, Cumbria CA3 8BB *tel:* 01228 592444 *fax:* 01228 511195. Nigel Dyson, mgr ed.

BBC Radio Derby. PO Box 269, Derby DE1 3HL *tel:* 01332 361111 *fax:* 01332 290794 *email:* radio.derby@bbc.co.uk. Mike Bettison, ed.

BBC Radio Devon. PO Box 5, Broadcasting House, Seymour Rd, Mannamead, Plymouth PL3 5BD *tel:* 01752 260323 *fax:* 01752 234599. John Lilley, mgr ed.

BBC Radio Foyle. 8 Northland Rd, Londonderry BT48 7JD *tel:* 028 7126 2244 *fax:* 028 7137 8666. Ana Leddy, ed.

BBC Radio Gloucestershire. London Rd, Gloucester GL1 1SW *tel:* 01452 308585 *fax:* 01452 309491 *email:* radio.gloucestershire@bbc.co.uk. Bob Lloyd-Smith, ed.

BBC Radio Guernsey. Commerce House, Les Banques, St Peter Port GY1 2HS, Guernsey, Channel Islands *tel:* 01481 728977 *fax:* 01481 713557. Denzil Dudley, mgr ed.

BBC Radio Humberside. 9 Chapel St, Hull HU1 3NU *tel:* 01482 323232 *fax:* 01482 326038. Barrie Stephenson, ed.

BBC Radio Jersey. 18 Parade Rd, St Helier JE2 3PL, Jersey, Channel Islands *tel:* 01534 870000 *fax:* 01534 32569. Denzil Dudley, mgr ed; Murray Norton, presenter/producer.

BBC Radio Kent. Sun Pier, Chatham, Kent ME4 4EZ *tel:* 01634 803505 *fax:* 01634 803573.

BBC Radio Lancashire. 26 Darwen St, Blackburn, Lancs BB2 2EA *tel:* 01254 262411 *fax:* 01254 841043. Steve Taylor, mgr ed.

BBC Radio Leeds. Broadcasting House, Woodhouse Lane, Leeds LS2 9PN *tel:* 0113 244 2131 *fax:* 0113 242 0652. Ashley Peatfield, mgr ed.

BBC Radio Leicester. Epic House, Charles St, Leicester LE1 3SH *tel:* 01162 516688 *fax:* 01162 513632. Mark Shardlow, mgr ed.

BBC Radio Lincolnshire. PO Box 219, Newport, Lincoln LN1 3XY *tel:* 01522 511411 *fax:* 01522 511058. Charlie Partridge, mgr ed.

BBC Radio Merseyside. 55 Paradise St, Liverpool L1 3BP *tel:* 0151 708 5500 *fax:* 0151 794 0909 (news); 0151 794 0988 (general). Mick Ord, ed.

BBC Radio nan Gaidheal. 7 Culduthel Rd, Inverness IV2 4AD *tel:* 01463 720720 *fax:* 01463 236125. Ishbel MacLennan, ed.

BBC Radio Newcastle. Broadcasting Centre, Barrack Rd, Newcastle upon Tyne NE99 1RN *tel:* 0191 232 4141 *fax:* 0191 232 5082. Sarah Drummond, ed.

BBC Radio Norfolk. Norfolk Tower, Surrey St, Norwich NR1 3PA *tel:* 01603 617411. David Calyton, mgr ed.

BBC Radio Northampton. Broadcasting House, Abington St, Northampton NN1 2BH *tel:* 01604 239100 *fax:* 01604 233027. Claire Paul, mgr ed.

BBC Radio Nottingham. York House, Mansfield Rd, Nottingham NG1 3JB *tel:* 0115 955 0500 *fax:* 0115 955 0571. Kate Squire, ed.

BBC Radio Scotland. Queen Margaret Drive, Glasgow G12 8DG *tel:* 0141 339 8844 *fax:* 0141 337 1402.

BBC Radio Sheffield. Ashdell Grove, 60 Westbourne Rd, Sheffield S10 2QU *tel:* 0114 268 6185 *fax:* 0114 266 5102 *email:* radio.sheffield@bbc.co.uk. Emma Gilliam, acting ed.

BBC Radio Shropshire. 2-4 Boscobel Drive, Shrewsbury, Shropshire SY1 3TT *tel:* 01743 248484 *fax:* 01743 271702. Tony Fish, mgr ed.

BBC Radio Solent. Broadcasting House, Havelock Rd, Southampton SO14 7PW *tel:* 023 8063 1311 *fax:* 023 8033 9648. Chris van Schaick, mgr ed.

BBC Radio Stoke. Cheapside, Hanley, Stoke-on-Trent, Staffs ST1 1JJ *tel:* 01782 208080 *fax:* 01782 289115. Mark Hurrell, ed; Mary Fox, snr producer.

BBC Radio Suffolk. Broadcasting House, St Matthews St, Ipswich IP1 3EP *tel:* 01473 250000 *fax:* 01473 210767 *email:* suffolk@bbc.co.uk. Keith Beech, ed.

BBC Radio Ulster. Broadcasting House, Ormeau Ave, Belfast BT2 8HQ *tel:* 01232 338000 *fax:* 01232 338814.

BBC Radio Wales. Broadcasting House, Llandaff, Cardiff CF5 2YG *tel:* 01222 322000 *fax:* 01222 552973.

BBC Radio WM. Pebble Mill Rd, Birmingham B5 7SD *tel:* 0121 414 8484 *fax:* 0121 472 3174. David Robey, mgr ed.

BBC Radio York. 20 Bootham Row, York YO3 7BR *tel:* 01904 641351 *fax:* 01904 613108. Jane Sampson, mgr eds.

BBC Solent for Dorset. Broadcasting House, Havelock Rd, Southampton SO14 7PW *tel:* 01305 269654. Chris Van Schaick, ed.

BBC Somerset Sound. 14-15 Paul St, Taunton, Somerset TA1 3PF *tel:* 01823 252437 *fax:* 01823 238323. Jenny Lacey, mgr ed.

BBC Southern Counties Radio. Broadcasting Centre, Guildford GU2 5AP *tel:* 01483 306306 *fax:* 01483 304952. Mike Hapgood, ed.

BBC Thames Valley FM. 269 Banbury Rd, Oxford OX2 7DW *tel:* 01865 311444. Phil Ashworth, ed.

BBC Three Counties Radio. PO Box 3CR, Luton, Beds LU1 5XL *tel:* 01582 637400. Mark Norman, mgr ed.

BBC Wiltshire Sound. Broadcasting House, Prospect Place, Swindon, Wilts SN1 3RW *tel:* 01793 513626 *fax:* 01793 513650 *email:* bbc.wiltshire.sound@dial.pipex.com. Sandy Milne, mgr ed.

National Independent Radio Stations

Atlantic 252. 74 Newman St, London W1P 3LA *tel:* 020 7637 5252 *fax:* 020 7637 3925. Travis Baster, mgr dir; Al Dunne, programme dir; Steve Johnson, sales controller.

Classic FM. Academic House, 24-28 Oval Rd, London NW1 7DQ *tel:* 020 7284 3000 *fax:* 020 7713 2630 *email:* enquiries@classicfm.co.uk. Murray Dudgeon, mgr dir; Steve Orchard, dir of programmes; Simon Ward, sales and mkt dir; Ralph Bernard, chief exec.

Virgin Radio. 1 Golden Square, London W1R 4DJ *tel:* 020 7434 1215 *fax:* 020 7434 1197 *email:* reception@ginger.com. David Campbell, chief exec, Ginger media group; John Pearson, chief exec, Virgin Radio; Henry Owens, programme dir; Kathryn Jacobs, sales dir.

Independent Local Radio

Independent Local Radio (ILR) provides a daytime mix of information, education and entertainment, and the evening programmes are frequently of specialist or minority interest. International and national news is supplied by the Independent Radio News. Organisations concerned with independent broadcasting are to be found below and under *Independent Television.* Enquiries and comments concerning individual programmes should be addressed to the Press Office of the local ITV or ILR company. Complaints specifically concerning unfair or unjust treatment, or infringement of privacy should be made to the **Broadcasting Standards Commission**, 7 The Sanctuary, London SW1P 3JS *tel:* 020 7233 0544 *fax:* 020 7233 0397.

Radio Advertising Bureau (RAB). 77 Shaftesbury Ave, London W1V 7AD *tel:* 020 7306 2500 *fax:* 020 7306 2505 *email:* rab@rab.co.uk. *RAB, the marketing company of commercial radio industry, provides an independent information service to advertisers. Also involved in publication of marketing material and organising consumer research.*

The Radio Authority. Holbrook House, 14 Great Queen St, London WC2B 5DG *tel:* 020 7430 2724 *fax:* 020 7405 7062. Tracey Mullins, press offr. *Licenses and regulates all Independent Radio Services. Plans frequencies; appoints licensees with a view to widening listener choice; regulates programming and advertising.*

Local Radio Stations

The area of transmission of the radio station is shown in italics after each entry.

1152 Capital Gold AM. Radio House, Aston Rd North, Birmingham B6 4BX *tel:* 0121 359 4481 *fax:* 0121 359 1117 *email:* programmes@brmb.co.uk; sales@brmb.co.uk; news@brmb.co.uk. Julie Fair, station dir. *Birmingham and Black Country.*

1458 Lite AM. PO Box 1458, Quay West, Trafford Park, Manchester M17 1FL *tel:* 0161 872 1458 *fax:* 0161 872 0206. John Bateson, chmn; Michael Connolly, chief exec; Anthony Dewhurst, mgr dir; Andy Garner, head of sales; Kris Burford, programme dir; Gillian Clyne, head of news; Paul Fairclough, head of mus. *Manchester.*

2CR FM/Classic Gold 828. 5-7 Southcote Rd, Bournemouth BH1 3LR *tel:* 01202 259259 *fax:* 01202 255244 *email:* steve@2crfm.musicradio.com. Robin Haycock, chmn; Jeremy Lewis, mgr dir; Steve Woods, programme controller 2CR FM; John Panteny, sales dir. *Dorset and Hampshire.*

2-Ten FM/Classic Gold 1431/1485. PO Box 2020, Reading RG31 7FG *tel:* 0118 454400 *fax:* 0118 288456. Richard Palmer, chmn; Jeff Lee, mgr dir; Jana Rangooni, programme controller; Adrian Olney, sales dir. *Reading.*

95.8 Capital Gold FM. 30 Leicester Square, London WC2H 7LA *tel:* 020 7766 6000 *fax:* 020 7766 6100. Richard Park, programme dir; Fru Hazlitt, sales dir; Tara Barun, press offr. *Greater London.*

96.3 Aire FM. PO Box 2000, 51 Burley Rd, Leeds LS3 1LR *tel:* 0113 283 5500 *fax:* 0113 283 5501. John O'Hara, programme dir; Stephen King, mgr dir. *Leeds.*

96.3 Q FM. 26 Lady Lane, Paisley PA1 2LG *tel:* 0141 887 9630 *fax:* 0141 887 0963 *email:* admin@qfmclassichits.co.uk. Harry McNab OBE, chmn; Carol-Ann Morrison, mgr dir; Mike Arthur, programme controller. *Paisley.*

96.4 FM BRMB. 9 Brindley Place, Birmingham B1 2BL *tel:* 0121 359 4481 *fax:* 0121 359 1117 *email:* programmes@brmb.co.uk; sales@brmb.co.uk; news@brmb.co.uk. Julie Fair, station dir; David Andrews, head of mkt; Paul Jackson, programme controller; Jane Turnbull, head of sales. *Birmingham.*

96.4 FM The Wave. Victoria Rd, Gowerton, Swansea SA4 3AB *tel:* 01792 511964 *fax:* 01792 511965. Terry Mann, mgr dir; Esther Morton, sales dir; Andy Griffiths, programme controller. *Swansea.*

96.6 Oasis FM. 9 Christopher Place Shopping Centre, St Albans, Herts AL3 5DQ *tel:* 01727 831966 *fax:* 01727 834456 *email:* studios@oasisfm.co.uk. Sue Roscoe, station dir; Steve George, programme controller. *St Albans, Watford, Rickmansworth, Hemel Hempstead, Hatfield.*

97.2 Stray FM. PO Box 972, Harrogate HG1 5YF *tel:* 01423 522972 *fax:* 01423 522922 *email:* programmes@972strayfm.co.uk. Erik Thompson, chmn; Ann Dyson, mgr dir; Steve Parsley, news ed; Les Gunn, programme controller. *N and W Yorkshire (Harrogate, Ripon, Nidderdale, Wetherby).*

Alpha 103.2. Radio House, 11 Woodland Rd, Darlington, Co Durham DL3 7BJ *tel:* 01325 255552 *fax:* 01325 255551 *email:* progs@alpharadio.demon.co.uk. Graham Ledger, mgr dir; Lisa Marrey, programme mgr; Denise Dickinson, sales mgr; Debb Evans, news ed. *Darlington, Newton Aycliffe and Sedgefield.*

B97 Chiltern FM. 55 Goldington Rd, Bedford, Beds MK40 3LS *tel:* 01234 272400 *fax:* 01234 218580. Sheila Mallett, mgr dir; Derek Flood, programme controller; Ian Wootton, sales dir.

The Bay. PO Box 969, St George's Quay, Lancaster LA1 3LD *tel:* 01524 848747 *fax:* 01524 848787 *email:* bay969@aol.com. Kenni James, mgr dir; John Gillmore, programme dir; Emma Barton, sales dir; Chris Hornby, head of mus and news ed. *N Lancashire and S Cumbria.*

The Breeze. Radio House, Clifftown Rd, Southend-on-Sea, Essex SS1 1SX *tel:* 01702 333711 *fax:* 01702 345224 *email:* breeze@netforce.net. Rob van Pooss, mgr dir; Paul Chantler, programme dir. *Southend.*

Cable Radio Milton Keynes (CRMK). 14 Vincent Ave, Crownhill, Milton Keynes MK8 0AB *tel:* 01908 265266 *fax:* 01908 564893. M J Barry, mgr dir; T White, station mgr; N Craske, head of mus. *Milton Keynes.*

Capital Gold. Radio House, Whittle Ave, Segensworth West, Fareham, Hants PO15 5SH *tel:* 01489 589911 *fax:* 01489 587754. Radio House, PO Box 2000, Brighton BN41 2SS. Bob Hoad, Jane Finden, station dirs (Brighton and Portsmouth); Mark Sadler, programme controller. *Portsmouth, Southampton, Winchester, Brighton.*

Century Radio. Century House, PO Box 100, Gateshead NE8 2YY *tel:* 0191 477 6666 *fax:* 0191 477 5660 *email:* reception@centurynortheast.com. Jeff Stevenson, mgr dir; John Caine, programme controller; Michael Dobson, sales dir. *North East.*

CFM. PO Box 964, Carlisle, Cumbria CA1 3NG *tel:* 01228 818964 *fax:* 01228 819444. Darrell Thomas, mgr dir; Gill Garston, head of news; Simon Monk, programme controller; Denise Pape, station admin; Kerry Dawes, sales mgr. *Carlisle and W Cumbria.*

Channel Travel Radio. Main Control Building, Eurotunnel UK Terminal, PO Box 2000, Folkestone, Kent CT18 8XY *tel:* 01303 283873 *fax:* 01303 283874. Michaëla Segol, station mgr. *Along the M20 towards Folkestone and the Kent Channel ports.*

Chiltern FM. Chiltern Rd, Dunstable, Beds LU6 1HQ *tel:* 01582 676200 *fax:* 01582 676201. Sharon Davies, station dir; Kevin Snowden, sales dir; Trevor James, programme controller.

Clyde 1/Clyde 2. Clydebank Business Park, Clydebank, Glasgow G81 2RX *tel:* 0141 565 2200 *fax:* 0141 565 2265. James S Gordon CBE, chmn, Scottish Radio Holdings; Alex Dickson OBE, mgr dir, Radio Clyde. *Glasgow.*

Coast FM 96.3. 41 Conwy Rd, Colwyn Bay, Conwy LL28 5AB *tel:* 01492 534555/530999 *fax:* 01492 535248 *email:* mfm.radio@ukonline.co.uk. Martin Thomas QC OBE, chmn; Godfrey W Williams, mgr dir and deputy chmn; Terry Underhill, programme dir; Eira Davies, station dir; Brian Cullen, community liaison offr. *North Wales Coast.*

Cool FM. PO Box 974, Belfast BT1 1RT *tel:* 028 9181 7181 *fax:* 028 9181 4974 *email:* music@coolfm.co.uk. John Paul Ballantine, head of mus and promotions; Joanne Steen, programming asst. *Belfast.*

Delta FM 102. Prospect Place, Mill Lane, Alton, Hants GU34 2SY *tel:* 01420 544444 *fax:* 01420 544044 *email:* studio@delta102.freeserve.co.uk. David Way, mgr dir and programme controller; James Metherill, journalist/producer; Kevin Huffer, station mgr.

Downtown Radio. Newtownards, Co Down BT23 4ES *tel:* 028 9181 5555 *fax:* 028 9181 5252 *email:* programmes@downtown.co.uk. James T Donnelly, chmn; David Sloan MBE, mgr dir; John Rosborough, head of programming. *Northern Ireland.*

Eleven Seventy AM. PO Box 1170, High Wycombe, Bucks HP13 6YT *tel:* 01494 446611 *fax:* 01494 445400. Jim Leftwich, chmn; Andy Muir, station mgr; Jill Barter, head of sales. *High Wycombe.*

Essex FM. Radio House, Clifftown Rd, Southend-on-Sea, Essex SS1 1SX *tel:* 01702 333711 *fax:* 01702 345224 *email:* essexfm@netforce net. Rob van Pooss, mgr dir; Paul Chantler, programme dir. *Southend.*

FM 103 Horizon. Broadcast Centre, Crownhill, Milton Keynes MK8 0AB *tel:* 01908 269111 *fax:* 01908 564893 *email:* johns@ musicradio.com. Richard Godber, chmn; John Sanderson, station dir; Trevor Marshall, programme controller. *Milton Keynes.*

Forth AM/Forth FM. Forth House, Forth St, Edinburgh EH1 3LF *tel:* 0131 556 9255 *fax:* 0131 558 3277 *email:* forth@srh.co.uk. Tom Steele, mgr dir; Jay Crawford, head of mus. *Edinburgh.*

Fox FM. Brush House, Pony Rd, Cowley, Oxford OX4 2XR *tel:* 01865 871000 *fax:* 01865 871036 *email:* fox@foxfm.co.uk. Lyn Long, mgr dir; Sally Oldham, acting chmn; Alex Roland, programme controller. *Oxfordshire.*

Galaxy 101. PO Box 1010, Bristol *tel:* 0117 901 0101 *fax:* 0117 901 4555. PO Box 1010, Cardiff. Tony McVoy, chmn; Mark Flanagan, mgr dir; John Dash, programme dir; Sarah Bernard, sales controller. *S Wales and the West.*

Galaxy 102. PO Box 102, Manchester M60 1GJ *tel:* 0161 228 0102 *fax:* 0161 228 1020. Henry Owens, mgr dir; Paul Saunders, programme dir; John Chapman, sales mgr. *Greater Manchester.*

Galaxy 102.2. 1 The Square, 111 Broad St, Birmingham B15 1AS *tel:* 0121 695 0000 *fax:* 0121 696 1007 *email:* mail@galaxy1022.co.uk. Paul Fairburn, mgr dir; Dianne Hall, sales dir. *Birmingham.*

Gemini AM. Hawthorn House, Exeter Business Park, Exeter, Devon EX1 3QS *tel:* 01392 444444 *fax:* 01392 444433. David Rodgers, mgr dir; Iwerne Cameron, chmn; Colin Slade, programme mgr AM; Mike O'Brien, head of sales; Adrian Webster, head of news; Stephanie Warner, arts producer. *Exeter, E and mid-Devon, Torbay.*

Goldbeat 828 AM. 2c Park Ave, Cookstown, Co Tyrone BT80 8AH *tel:* 028 8676 4828 *fax:* 028 8676 3828. Nigel Ringland, mgr; Kenni Sames, production and programme controller. *Mid Ulster.*

GWR FM (East). PO Box 2000, Swindon, Wilts SN4 7EX *tel:* 01793 842600 *fax:* 01793 842602. Neil Cooper, station dir and sales dir; Steve Fountain, programme controller. *Swindon and Wiltshire.*

GWR FM (West). PO Box 2000, Bristol BS99 7SN *tel:* 0117 984 3200 *fax:* 0117 984 3202. Jonathan Bradley, station dir; Mark Beever, programme controller. *Bristol.*

Hallam FM/Magic AM. Radio House, 900 Herries Rd, Hillsborough, Sheffield S6 1RH *tel:* 0114 285 3333 *fax:* 0114 285 3159 *email:* programmes@hallamfm.co.uk. Tony McKenzie, programme controller; Helen Scholefield, news and sport mgr. *Sheffield, Rotherham, Barnsley, Doncaster.*

Heart FM. PO Box 1007, 1 The Square, 111 Broad St, Edgbaston, Birmingham B15 1AS *tel:* 0121 626 1007 *also fax.* Viscountess Cobham, chmn; Philip Riley, mgr dir; Don Thomson, commercial dir; Paul Fairburn, programme dir. *W Midlands.*

Heartland FM. Lower Oakfield, Pitlochry, Perthshire PH16 5HQ *tel:* 01796 474040 *fax:* 01796 474007. Michael Dobson, chmn; Martin Hobson, technical dir; Brian Smith, programme controller; Brendan Murphy, sales dir. *Pitlochry and Aberfeldy.*

Island FM. 12 Westerbrook, St Sampson, GY2 4QQ, Guernsey *tel:* 01481 42000 *fax:* 01481 49676 *email:* kevin@islandfm.guernsey.net. Kevin Stewart, mgr dir; Nick Creed, news ed; Carl Ward, programme controller; Vikki Stewart, head of promotions. *Guernsey.*

Isle of Wight Radio. Dodnor Park, Newport, Isle of Wight PO30 5XE *tel:* 01983 822557 *fax:* 01983 821690 *email:* admin@iwradio.co.uk. Andy Shier, mgr dir; Stuart McGinley, programme mgr. *Isle of Wight.*

Jazz FM 100.4. The World Trade Centre, Exchange Quay, Manchester M5 3EJ *tel:* 0161 877 1004 *fax:* 0161 877 1005. Richard Wheatly, chief exec; Mick Carter, regional mkg dir. *North West.*

KCBC 107.4 FM. Centre 2000, Unit 1, Robinson Close, Telford Way Industrial Estate, Kettering, Northants NN16 8UP *tel:* 01536 412413 *fax:* 01536 517390 *email:* 107.4fm@kcbc.co.uk. Bill Johnston, mgr dir; Richard Oliff, news ed; Charmian Wright, admin mgr; Dougie King, programme controller. *Kettering, Corby, Wellingborough.*

Key 103 FM. Castlequay, Castlefield, Manchester M1 4PR *tel:* 0161 288 5000 *fax:* 0161 288 5001. David Lincoln, mgr dir; Dave Shearer, programme dir; Barbara Gardner, sales dir. *Greater Manchester.*

Kiss 100 FM. Kiss House, 80 Holloway Rd, London N7 8JG *tel:* 020 7700 6100 *fax:* 020 7700 3979. Mike Soutar, mgr dir; Mark Matthews, programme controller. *Greater London.*

Kix 96. PO Box 962, Coventry CV1 4XX *tel:* 024 7652 5656 *fax:* 024 7655 1744 *email:* kix962@aol.com. Chris Brooks, programme controller; Ginny Murfin, mgr dir. *Coventry and Warwickshire.*

KLFM 96.7. PO Box 77, 18 Blackfriars St, King's Lynn, Norfolk PE30 1NN *tel:* 01553 772777 *fax:* 01553 766453 *email:* info@klfmradio.co.uk. Nigel Sutcliffe, mgr dir; Jason Smith, sales mgr; Dave King, programme controller. *W Norfolk.*

Lantern FM. The Light House, Market Place, Bideford, N Devon EX39 2DR *tel:* 01237 424444 *fax:* 01237 423333. John Greenstreet, mgr dir; Paul Hopper, head of mus; Bob McCreadie, programme controller. *N Devon.*

LBC 1152 AM. 200 Gray's Inn Rd, London WC1X 8XZ *tel:* 020 7973 1152 *fax:* 020 7312 8565. Nigel Reeve, mgr dir; Tony Robinson, sales mgr. *Greater London.*

London Greek Radio. Florentia Village, Vale Rd, London N4 1TD *tel:* 020 8800 8001 *fax:* 020 8800 8005 *email:* sales@lgr.co.uk. A Yerolemou, mgr dir; G Gregoriou, programme controller; C Harmanda, sales dir; G Lefteri, finance dir. *Haringey.*

Magic 828. PO Box 2000, 51 Burley Rd, Leeds LS3 1LR *tel:* 0113 283 5500 *fax:* 0113 283 5501. Steve King, mgr dir; John O'Hara, programme dir. *Leeds.*

Magic 1152. Longrigg Swalwell, Newcastle upon Tyne NE99 1BB *tel:* 0191 496 0505. Phil Roberts, mgr dir; Sean Marley, programme dir; Cath Ellington, sales dir. *Northumberland, Tyne and Wear, Co Durham.*

Mercury FM. The Stanley Centre, Kelvin Way, Crawley, W Sussex RH10 2SE *tel:* 01293 519161 *fax:* 01293 565663. Sara Atkinson, station dir; Jeff Graham, programme dir; Clive Douthwaite, sales dir. *Reigate and Crawley.*

Millennium 106.8 FM. The Company Offices, Harrow Manor Way, Thamesmead South, London SE2 9XH *tel:* 020 8311 3112 *fax:* 020 8312 1930. Rodney Collins, mgr dir; Sammy Bell, station mgr; Jon Lucas, programme mgr, snr presenter; Walter McDonald, sales mgr. *SE London, NW Kent and Essex.*

Mix 96. Friars Square Studios, 11 Bourbon St, Aylesbury, Bucks HP20 2PZ *tel:* 01296 399396 *fax:* 01296 398988 *email:* mix@mix96.demon.co.uk. Richard Morris-Adams, chmn; Avril Davies, dir; Henry Aubrey-Fletcher, dir; Erika Sorby-Firth, mgr dir. *Aylesbury.*

Moray Firth Radio Ltd. PO Box 271, Inverness IV3 8UJ *tel:* 01463 224433 *fax:* 01463 243224 *email:* presentersfirstname@mfr.co.uk. Thomas Prag, mgr dir; Ray Atkinson, programme controller; Tich McCooey, head of mus. *N Scotland.*

Nevis Radio. Inverlochy, Fort William, Inverness-shire PH33 6LU *tel:* 01397 700007 *fax:* 01397 701007 *email:* nevisradio@lochaber.sol.co.uk. Ian Sykes, chmn; Geoff Wright, studio mgr; Gina Kennedy, sales. *Lochaber, West Coast of Scotland.*

News Direct 97.3. 200 Gray's Inn Rd, London WC1X 8XC *tel:* 020 7973 1152 *fax:* 020 7312 8565. Nigel Reeve, mgr dir; Tony Robinson, sales mgr. *Greater London.*

Northants 96/Classic Gold 1557. 19-21 St Edmunds Rd, Northampton NN1 5DY *tel:* 01604 795600 *fax:* 01604 795601 *email:* reception@northants96.musicradio.com. Mark Lee, mgr dir; Mark Jeeves, programme controller. *Northampton, Kettering.*

Ocean FM. Radio House, Whittle Ave, Segensworth West, Fareham, Hants PO15 5SH *tel:* 01489 589911 *fax:* 01489 587754 *email:* info@oceanradio.co.uk. Jane Finden, station dir; Mark Sadler, programme controller; Alison Fry, sales mgr. *Portsmouth, Southampton, Winchester.*

Orchard FM. Haygrove House, Shoreditch, Taunton, Somerset TA3 7BT *tel:* 01823 338448 *fax:* 01823 321044. Howard Bowles, mgr dir; Bob McCreadie, programme dir; Alan Jennings, news ed. *Yeovil and Taunton.*

Piccadilly Radio/Key 103. Castlequay, Castlefield, Manchester M5 4PR *tel:* 0161 288 5000 *fax:* 0161 288 5001. Dave Shearer, programme dir; David Ditchfield, head of mus; Dave Lincoln, mgr dir. *Greater Manchester.*

Pirate FM. Cam Brea Studios, Wilson Way, Redruth, Cornwall TR15 3XX *tel:* 01209 314400 *fax:* 01209 314345. James St Aubyn, chmn; Joseph Swain, mgr dir; Ed Goodridge, programme and operations mgr. *Cornwall, Plymouth and W Devon.*

Power FM. Radio House, Whittle Ave, Segensworth West, Fareham, Hants PO15 5SH *tel:* 01489 589911 *fax:* 01489 587754. Jane Finden, station dir; Anthony Brook, chmn; Karyn Head, sales mgr. *Portsmouth, Southampton, Winchester.*

Premier Christian Radio. PO Box 13000, London SW1E 5PP *tel:* 020 7316 1300 *fax:* 020 7233 6706 *email:* premier@premier.org.uk. Peter Kerridge, mgr dir; David Heron, chmn. *Greater London.*

The Pulse. Forster Square, Bradford BD1 5NE *tel:* 01274 203040 *fax:* 01274 203130 *email:* general@pulse.co.uk. Neil S Robinson, chmn; Mick Hall, mgr dir; Lee Connell, programme dir; Steve South, sales dir. *Bradford, Huddersfield, Halifax.*

Q102.9. The Old Waterside Railway Station, Duke St, Waterside, Londonderry BT47 6DH *tel:* 028 7134 4449/7134 6666/7131 1000 *fax:* 028 7131 1177. Frank McLaughlin, mgr dir, programme controller; Steve Kirk, head of mus; John O'Connor, head of sales; Susan Mawhinney, accounts mgr. *Londonderry.*

Radio Borders. Tweedside Park, Galashiels, Selkirkshire TD1 3TD *tel:* 01896 759444 *fax:* 01896 759494. Danny Gallagher, mgr dir. *Borders, N Northumberland.*

Radio Ceredigion. Yr Hen Ysgol Gymraeg, Ffordd Alexandra, Aberystwyth SY23 1LF *tel:* 01970 627999 *fax:* 01970 627206. Ellen ap Gwynn, gen mgr; Geraint Davies, chmn; Victor Edwards, head of sales. *Aberystwyth.*

Radio City 96.7/Magic 1548. 8-10 Stanley St, Liverpoool L1 6AF *tel:* 0151 227 5100 *fax:* 0151 471 0330. Terry D Smith, chmn; Tom Hunter, mgr dir; Paul Jordan, programme dir. *Liverpool.*

Radio Maldwyn. The Studios, The Park, Newtown, Powys SY16 2NZ *tel:* 01686 623555 *fax:* 01686 623666 *email:* radio.maldwyn@ukonline.co.uk. Kenn Morris, chmn and station mgr; Martin Adams, sales; Luci Anscombe, news ed; Austin Powell, programme controller. *Mid Wales and the borders.*

Scot FM. Number 1 Shed, Albert Quay, Leith, Edinburgh EH6 7DN *tel:* 0131 554 6677 *fax:* 0131 554 2266. Michael J Connolly, chmn; Mike Bawden, mgr dir; James Curran, head of mus. *Central Scotland.*

Severn Sound FM/ Classic Gold 774. Old Talbot House, Southgate St, Gloucester GL1 2DQ *tel:* 01452 423791 *fax:* 01452 423008. Penelope Holton, mgr dir; Jo Littlehales, programme controller. *Gloucester and Cheltenham.*

SGR Colchester. Abbeygate Two, 9 Whitewell Rd, Colchester CO2 7DE *tel:* 01206 575859 *fax:* 01206 561199. Mike Stewart, mgr dir; Ian Wooton, sales dir; Ian Puckey, news ed. *Colchester, Clacton, Harwich.*

SGR FM (Ipswich). Radio House, Alpha Business Park, White House Rd, Ipswich, Suffolk IP1 5LT *tel:* 01473 461000 *fax:* 01473 741200. Mike Stewart, mgr dir; Ian Wooton, sales dir; Mark Pryke, programme dir; David Cargill, chmn. *Ipswich.*

Shetland Islands Broadcasting Company (SIBC). Market St, Lerwick, Shetland ZE1 0JN *tel:* 01595 695299 *fax:* 01595 695696 *email:* info@sibc.co.uk. Inga Walterson, head of mus.

Signal FM. Regent House, Heaton Lane, Stockport SK4 1BX *tel:* 0161 285 4545 *fax:* 0161 285 1010 *email:* sales@signal1049.com. Glyn Owen, mgr dir; Mark Chivers, programme dir. *S Manchester and Cheshire.*

South West Sound. Campbell House, Bankend Rd, Dumfries DT1 4TH *tel:* 01387 50999 *fax:* 01387 65629. Paul Conry, mgr dir; Gordon McArthur, programme dir; Fiona Blackwood, station dir; Gordon Cassius, snr presenter. *Dumfries and Galloway.*

Southern FM. Radio House, PO Box 2000, Brighton BN41 2SS *tel:* 01273 430111 *fax:* 01273 424783. Alex Roland, programme controller; Bob Hoad, station dir. *Sussex.*

Spire FM. City Hall Studios, Malthouse Lane, Salisbury, Wilts SP2 7QQ *tel:* 01722 416644 *fax:* 01722 415102 *email:* studio@spirefm.co.uk. Tim Butcher, head of mus; Gary Haberfield, station dir; Ceri Hurford-Jones, sales mgr. *Salisbury.*

Spirit FM. Dukes Court, Bognor Rd, Chichester, W Sussex PO19 2FX *tel:* 01243 773600 *fax:* 01243 786464 *email:* spiritfm@argonet.co.uk. Stephen Oates, mgr dir; Iain Meadows, programme mgr; Jacqui Renwick, local sales mgr; Adam Porter, news ed. *Chichester, Bognor Regis, Littlehampton, Arundel.*

Sun FM 103.4. PO Box 1034, Sunderland SR1 3YZ *tel:* 0191 567 3333 *fax:* 0191 567 0888. Jon Henson, mgr dir; Dave Lee, programme controller; Michelle Napier, sales mgr. *Sunderland.*

Sunshine 855. Waterside, Ludlow, Shropshire SY8 1PE *tel:* 01584 877855 (studio); 01584 873795 (office) *fax:* 01584 875900. Austin Powell, dir; Mark Edwards, programme controller. *Ludlow.*

Swansea Sound/The Wave. Victoria Rd, Gowerton, Swansea, W Glamorgan SA4 3AB *tel:* 01792 511170/511964 *fax:* 01792 511171/511965 *email:* admin@swanseasound.co.uk; admin@thewave.co.uk. Terry Mann, mgr, programme dir; Andy Griffiths, FM programme mgr; Lynn Courtney, head of news; Esther Morton, sales and mkt dir. *Swansea.*

Ten 17. Radio House, 19-20 Clifftown Rd, Southend-on-Sea, Essex SS1 1SX *tel:* 01702 333711 *fax:* 01702 345224 *email:* studios@essexradio.co.uk. *Harlow.*

Trent FM. 29-31 Castle Gate, Nottingham NG1 7AP *tel:* 0115 952 7000 *fax:* 0115 912 9333. Chris Hughes, mgr dir; Dick Stone, programme controller. *Nottingham.*

Vale FM. Longmead, Shaftesbury, Dorset SP7 8QQ *tel:* 01747 855711 *fax:* 01747 855722 *email:* studio@valefm.co.uk. David Jeffery, chmn; Martin Lee, programme controller.

The Wave 96.5. 965 Mowbray Drive, Blackpool, Lancs FY3 7JR *tel:* 01253 304965 *fax:* 01253 301965. Glyn Owen, mgr dir; Simon Tate, programme dir; Matthew Allitt, sales dir. *Blackpool.*

Wessex FM. Radio House, Trinity St, Dorchester, Dorset DT1 1DJ *tel:* 01305 250333 *fax:* 01305 250052. Ian Acton, regional dir; John Baker, general mgr; Peter Bolton, chmn; Gordon McRae, news ed. *Weymouth and Dorchester.*

West Sound Radio plc. Radio House, Holmston Rd, Ayr KA7 3BE *tel:* 01292 283662 *fax:* 01292 283665. Paul Cooney, mgr dir; Gordon McArthur, programme dir and head of news; Kenny Campbell, head of mus. *Ayrshire, Dumfries and Galloway.*

West Yorkshire's Classic Gold. Forster Square, Bradford BD1 5NE *tel:* 01274 203040 *fax:* 01274 203130 *email:* general@pulse.co.uk. Mick Hall, mgr dir; Lee Cornell, programme dir; Steve South, commercial dir; Geoff Hemming, programme mgr. *W Yorkshire.*

BBC Television Principal Music Executives

BBC Television. Television Centre, Wood Lane, London W12 7RJ *tel:* 020 8743 8000. Will Wyatt, chief exec, broadcast; Alan Yentob, dir of television; David Docherty, deputy dir of television; Mark Thompson, controller BBC2; Peter Salmon, controller BBC1; Keith Samuel, controller, press and PR, broadcast; Kim Evans, head of arts; Trevor Dann, head of mus entertainment; Roger Wright, head of classical mus; Avril MacRory, head of classical mus television.

Independent Television

Organisations concerned with independent television broadcasting are listed below, followed by the independent television and production companies. The area of transmission is indicated in italics.

Independent Television Commission. 33 Foley St, London W1P 7LB *tel:* 020 7255 3000 *fax:* 020 7306 7800 *email:* publicaffairs@itc.org.uk. Sir Robin Biggam, chmn; Lord Holme of Cheltenham, deputy chmn; Peter Rogers, chief exec. *Under the terms of the Broadcasting Act 1996, the ITC is the public body responsible for licensing and regulating all commercially-funded television in the United Kingdom through codes on programme content, advertising, sponsorship and technical standards.*

ITC East of England. 24 Castle Meadow, Norwich NR1 3DH *tel:* 01603 623533 *fax:* 01603 633631 *email:* monteith.p@itc.org.uk. Peter Monteith, head of ITC (East).

ITC Midlands. 10-11 Poultry, Nottingham NG1 2HW *tel:* 0115 952 7333 *fax:* 0115 952 7353 *email:* wootton.j@itc.org.uk. Janet Wootton, head of ITC (Midlands).

ITC North-East England, The Borders and Isle of Man. 3 Collingwood St, Newcastle upon Tyne NE1 1JS *tel:* 0191 261 0148 *fax:* 0191 261 1158. Robert Conlon, head of ITC (North East and Borders).

ITC North of England. The Workstation, 15 Paternoster Row, Sheffield S1 2BX *tel:* 0114 276 9091 *fax:* 0114 276 9089. Michael Fay, head of ITC (North).

ITC North-West England. Television House, Mount St, Manchester M2 5WT *tel:* 0161 834 2707 *fax:* 0161 835 3513. Louise Bennett, head of ITC (NorthWest).

ITC Northern Ireland. Albany House, 75 Great Victoria St, Belfast BT2 7AF *tel:* 028 9024 8733 *fax:* 028 9032 2828. Denis Wolinski, head of ITC (Northern Ireland).

ITC Scotland. 123 Blythswood St, Glasgow G2 4AN *tel:* 0141 226 4436 *fax:* 0141 226 4682. Brian Marjoribanks, head of ITC (Scotland); Alan Stewart, deputy head.

ITC South and The Channel Islands. Kings Worthy Court, Kings Worthy, Winchester SO23 7QA *tel:* 01962 883950 *fax:* 01962 848657. Jean Young, head of ITC (South).

ITC South-West England. 153 Armada Way, Plymouth PL1 1HY *tel:* 01752 663031 *fax:* 01752 662490. Nicholas Bull, head of ITC (South West).

ITC Wales and West of England. 2nd Floor, Elgin House, 106 St Mary St, Cardiff CF1 1PA *tel:* 029 2038 4541 *fax:* 029 2022 3157. Stella Mair Thomas, head of ITC (Wales and West).

Producers Alliance for Cinema and Television (PACT). 45 Mortimer St, London W1N 7TD *tel:* 020 7331 6000 *fax:* 020 7331 6700. Shaun Williams, chief exec. *Trade association and employers' body for film and independent TV producers.*

Royal Television Society (RTS). Holborn Hall, 100 Gray's Inn Rd, London WC1X 8AL *tel:* 020 7430 1000 *fax:* 020 7430 0924 *email:* publications@rts.org.uk. Peter Fiddick, ed; Louise Bishop, deputy ed; Sue Griffith, production ed. *Independent forum for discussions on all aspects of television open to all working in or with an interest in television. Magazine published 10 times a year covering all aspects of the industry.*

Independent Television Companies

National Companies

British Sky Broadcasting Ltd. 6 Centaurs Business Park, Grant Way, Isleworth, Middx TW7 5QD *tel:* 020 7705 3000 *fax:* 020 7705 3030. Mark Booth, chief exec; Rupert Murdoch, chmn.

Channel Four Television Corporation. 124 Horseferry Rd, London SW1P 2TX *tel:* 020 7396 4444 *fax:* 020 7306 8366. Vanni Treves, chmn; Michael Jackson, chief exec. *National.*

Channel Five Broadcasting Ltd. 22 Long Acre, London WC2E 9LP *tel:* 020 7550 5555 *fax:* 020 7550 5554. David Elstein, chief exec.

GMTV Ltd. London Television Centre, Upper Ground, London SE1 9TT *tel:* 020 7827 7000 *fax:* 020 7827 7001 *email:* talk2us@gmtv.co.uk. Charles Allen, chmn; Christopher Stoddart, mgr dir. *National breakfast-time.*

ITN. 200 Gray's Inn Rd, London WC1X 8XZ *tel:* 020 7833 3000 *fax:* 020 7430 4228. Mark Wood, chmn; Stewart Purvis, chief exec. *Provides the main national and international news for the UK's three commercial terrestrial television channels.*

Regional Companies

Anglia Television Ltd. Anglia House, Norwich NR1 3JG *tel:* 01603 615151 *fax:* 01603 631032. 48 Leicester Square, London WC2H 7FB. Graham Creelman, mgr dir. *E of England.*

Border Television plc. The Television Centre, Durranhill, Carlisle, Cumbria CA1 3NT *tel:* 01228 525101 *fax:* 01228 5141384. James Graham OBE, chmn; Peter Brownlow, mgr dir; Neil Robinson, head of programmes; Paul Corley, chief exec. *Scottish Borders, Isle of Man and most of Cumbria.*

Carlton Television. 101 St Martin's Lane, London WC2N 4AZ *tel:* 020 7240 4000 *fax:* 020 7240 4171. Nigel Walmsley, chmn; Clive Jones, chief exec. *London weekday.*

Central Broadcasting. Central Court, Gas St, Birmingham B1 2JT *tel:* 0121 643 9898 *fax:* 0121 634 4740. 35-38 Portman Square, London W1A 9AH. Ian Squires, mgr dir. *E, W and S Midlands.*

Channel Television. The Television Centre, St Helier, Jersey JE1 3ZD, Channel Islands *tel:* 01534 816816 *fax:* 01534 816817 *email:* broadcast@channeltv.co.uk. John Henwood MBE, chief exec; Michael Lucas, mgr dir. *Channel Islands.*

Grampian Television. Queens Cross, Aberdeen AB15 2XJ *tel:* 01224 846846 *fax:* 01224 846800 *email:* gtv@grampiantv.co.uk. Calum Macleod CBE, chmn; *N Scotland to Shetland and Western Isles.*

Granada Television Ltd. Granada TV Centre, Quay St, Manchester M60 9EA *tel:* 0161 832 7211 *fax:* 0161 827 2180. 36 Golden Square, London W1R 4AH. Charles Allen, chmn; Steve Morrison, chief exec. *NW England.*

HTV (Cymru) Wales. The Television Centre, Culverhouse Cross, Cardiff CF5 6XJ *tel:* 029 2059 0590 *fax:* 029 2059 7183 *email:* htv@htv-wales.co.uk. Gerald Davies, chmn; Menna Richards, mgr dir. *Wales and W England.*

HTV Ltd. The Television Centre, Bath Rd, Bristol BS4 3HG *tel:* 0117 972 2722 *fax:* 0117 972 2400. Jeremy Payne, mgr dir. *Avon, parts of Gloucestershire, Somerset and Wiltshire.*

London Weekend Television Ltd. The London Television Centre, Upper Ground, London SE1 9LT *tel:* 020 7620 1620 *fax:* 020 7261 1290. Charles Allen, chmn. *London weekend.*

Meridian Broadcasting Ltd. Television Centre, Southampton SO14 0PZ *tel:* 023 8022 2555 *fax:* 023 8033 5050. Bill Cotton CBE, chmn; Mary McAnally, mgr dir. *S and SE England.*

S4C (Sianel Pedwar Cymru). Welsh Fourth Channel Authority, Parc Ty Glas, Llanishen, Cardiff CF4 5DU *tel:* 029 2074 7444 *fax:* 029 2075 4444 *email:* gwifren@s4c.co.uk. Elan Closs Stephens, chair; Huw Jones, chief exec. *Wales (also available throughout UK via satellite). S4C is the broadcasting service transmitted on the fourth channel in Wales. On analogue, it broadcasts c 32 hrs in Welsh and for the remainder of the time reschedules Channel 4's English language programmes. S4C Digital is a Welsh-language service, broadcasting 12 hours a day.*

Scottish Television. Cowcaddens, Glasgow G2 3PR *tel:* 0141 300 3000 *fax:* 0141 300 3030. 20 Lincoln's Inn Fields, London WC2A 3ED. Calum MacLeod, acting chmn; Andrew Flanagan, chief exec. *Central Scotland.*

Teletext Ltd. 101 Farm Lane, Fulham, London SW6 1QJ *tel:* 020 7386 5000 *fax:* 020 7386 5002. Mike Stewart, mgr dir; Roger Gilbert, chmn. *Teletext service for ITV and Channel 4.*

Tyne Tees Television Ltd. Television Centre, City Rd, Newcastle upon Tyne NE1 2AL *tel:* 0191 261 0181 *fax:* 0191 261 2302 *email:* tttv.regional.affairs@gmg.co.uk. Charles Allen, chmn; Margaret Fay, mgr dir. *NE England and N Yorkshire.*

Ulster Television plc. Havelock House, Ormeau Rd, Belfast BT7 1EB *tel:* 028 9032 8122 *fax:* 028 9024 6695 *email:* info@utv.live.com. Television Sales and Marketing (TSMS), West World, Westgate, Ealing, London W5 1EH. John B McGuckian, chmn; Desmond Smyth, mgr dir. *Northern Ireland.*

Westcountry Television Ltd. Western Wood Way, Langage Science Park, Plymouth PL7 5BG *tel:* 01752 333333 *fax:* 01752 333444. Clive Jones, chmn; Mark Haskell, mgr dir; Jane McCloskey, dir of programmes; Caroline Righton, controller of features and programme development. *SW England.*

Yorkshire Television Ltd. The Television Centre, Leeds LS3 1JS *tel:* 0113 243 8283 *fax:* 0113 244 5107. Charles Allen, chmn; Richard Gregory, mgr dir. *Yorkshire.*

Independent Production Companies

Classic Arts Productions Ltd. The Old Farmhouse, Wilcox Farm, Moreton Morrell, Warwicks CV35 9AN *tel:* 01926 651247 *fax:* 01926 651886 *email:* classart@dircon.co.uk. Wendy Thompson, exec dir. *Specialist in classical mus and arts-related productions.*

Hazard Chase Productions. Richmond House, 16-20 Regent St, Cambridge CB2 1DB *tel:* 01223 312400 *fax:* 01223 460827 *email:* info@hazardchase.co.uk. Patrick Allen, John Bickley, James Brown, John Willan, exec producers. *Location recording and production, specialising in classical mus (live concerts and studio sessions) for radio broadcast, demonstration recordings, samplers, TV and film soundtracks and CD production. Complete packages for CD and DVD manufacture. CD-ROM and CD-EXTRA programming and production.*

Heavy Entertainment Ltd. 222 Kensal Rd, London W10 5BN *tel:* 020 8960 9001/2 *fax:* 020 8960 9003 *email:* info@heavy-entertainment.co.uk. Nick St George, David Roper, company dirs; Matthew Thompson, production mgr. *TV and radio production company specialising in arts and mus.*

Peartree Productions. PO Box 325, Worcester WR5 2YR *tel:* 01905 351748 *also fax; email:* scott@peartree.softnet.co.uk. David Scott, audio and programme mgr; Shirley Scott, exec producer.

Powerline Productions. Unit 23, Winston Close, Romford, Essex RM7 8LL *tel:* 01708 724544; 0800 074 2367 *fax:* 01708 744166 *email:* info@powerlineproductions.com. Peter Walters. *Promotional and PR videos. Opera/concert performances. Tour videos. All kinds of mus/theatre performance and documentary production for TV.*

Streetwise TV. 11-15 Betterton St, Covent Garden, London WC2H 9PB *tel:* 020 7470 8825 *fax:* 020 7470 8826 *email:* streetwise_tv@hotmail.com. Ian Whittingham, creative and development producer; Linda Duff, producer.

Symphony Films. First Floor, 38 Russell Rd, London W14 8HT *tel:* 020 7460 1697 *email:* enquiries@symphonyfilms.demon.co.uk. Martin Phillips, dir. *Full programme production with musically trained producer (RCM). Shooting on Digi-Beta, Beta SP and SX and DV. Non-linear editing (media 100xr) and access to composers and session bands.*

Concert Halls and Theatres

This section includes concert halls and theatres where at least six professional classical music, opera or ballet performances are held per annum, or venues which are almost exclusively used for professional performances of classical music. London venues are listed first followed by the rest of England, Scotland, Wales and Northern Ireland. The venues are listed alphabetically in town order. Detailed information for over 1200 venues is contained in the *British Performing Arts Yearbook 1999/2000* which is also available from Rhinegold Publishing Ltd.

Inner London

BAC Grand Hall. Battersea Town Hall, Lavender Hill, London SW11 5TS *admin:* 020 7326 8211 *fax:* 020 7978 5207. Audrey Helps, hall and events manager. *Capacity:* 500.

Barbican Centre. Silk Street, Barbican, London EC2Y 8DS *admin:* 020 7638 4141/7628 3351 *box office:* 020 7638 8891 *fax:* 020 7920 9648/7374 0818/7382 7270 (box office). John Tusa, managing director; Graham Sheffield, artistic director; Adrian Noble, artistic director RSC; Ruth Hasnip, director of public affairs. *Barbican Hall Capacity:* 1,989; *Barbican Theatre Capacity:* 1,156; *The Pit Capacity:* 200.

Blackheath Halls. 23 Lee Road, Blackheath, London SE3 9RQ *admin:* 020 8318 9758 *box office:* 020 8463 0100 *fax:* 020 8852 5154 *email:* mail@blackheathhalls.com. Sarah Keel, administrative director; Peter Conway, artistic director. *Great Hall Capacity:* 700; *Recital Room Capacity:* 200.

Bloomsbury Theatre. 15 Gordon Street, London WC1H 0AH *admin:* 020 7679 2777 *box office:* 020 7388 8822 *fax:* 020 7383 4080 *email:* blooms.theatre@ucl.ac.uk. Michael Freeman, general manager; Mark Feakins, administrator; Gareth James, house manager. *Capacity:* 550.

Brixton Academy. 211 Stockwell Road, Brixton, London SW9 9SL *admin:* 020 7771 3000 *box office:* 020 7771 2000 *fax:* 020 7738 4427. McKenzie Group, management: Steve Forster, general manager; Salome Scott, group marketing co-ordinator. *Capacity:* 2,154.

Broadgate Arena. c/o Exchange House, 12 Exchange Square, London EC2A 2BQ *admin:* 020 7505 4000 *fax:* 020 7382 9854. Christine Purdie, events manager; Mark Smith, assistant events manager. *Arena/Ice Rink Capacity:* 3,000; *Exchange Square Capacity:* 3,000.

Conway Hall. Red Lion Square, Holborn WC1R 4RL *admin:* 020 7242 8032 *fax:* 020 7242 8036. Peter Vlachos, manager. *Main Hall Capacity:* 500; *Small Hall Capacity:* 100.

Hackney Empire. 291 Mare Street, Hackney, London E8 1EJ *admin:* 020 8986 0171 *box office:* 020 8985 2424 (6 lines) *fax:* 020 8985 4781 (admin)/9997 (technicians) *email:* cm@hackemp.demon.co.uk. Roland Muldoon, theatre director; Simon Thomsett, general manager. *Capacity:* 1,200

Holland Park Theatre. Central Library, Phillimore Walk, London W8 7RX *admin:* 020 7361 3058 *box office:* 020 7602 7856 *fax:* 020 7361 2976. John McEachen, head of libraries and arts; Laura Taub, theatre manager (technical and operation). *Capacity:* 827.

Lewisham Theatre & The Studio Theatre. Rushey Green, Catford, London SE6 4RU *admin:* 020 8690 2317 *box office:* 020 8690 0002 *fax:* 020 8314 3144 *email:* 100316.1453@compuserve.com. Martin Costello, general manager; Kathleen O'Sullivan, theatre technician; Linda Logue, box office manager. *Theatre Capacity:* 845; *The Studio Theatre Capacity:* 102.

London Apollo. Queen Caroline Street, Hammersmith, London W6 9QH *admin:* 020 8748 8660 *box office:* 0870 606 3400 *fax:* 020 8846 9320 admin. Graham Gilmore, general manager. *Capacity:* 3,271.

London Coliseum. St Martin's Lane, London WC2N 4ES *admin:* 020 7836 0111 *box office:* 020 7632 8300 *fax:* 020 7836 8379 *email:* marketing@eno.org. Nicholas Payne, general director; Paul Daniel, music director; Russell Willis Taylor, executive director. *Capacity:* 2,358.

Lyceum Theatre. 21 Wellington Street, Strand, London WC2E 7DA *admin:* 020 7420 8191 *box office:* 020 7420 8114/3/2 *fax:* 020 7240 4155 (admin)/4346 (box office). Debbie Garrick, manager. *Capacity:* 2,107.

Peacock Theatre. Portugal Street, off Kingsway, London WC2A 2HT *admin:* 020 7314 8950 *box office:* 020 7314 8800 *fax:* 020 7314 9004. Paula Gillespie, general manager; Damian Ball, theatre manager; Mark Dawson, chief technician. *Capacity:* 1,000.

Round Chapel. Lower Clapton Road, Hackney, London E5 *admin:* 020 8986 0029 *fax:* 020 8986 0029 *email:* roundchapel@pop3.poptel.org.uk. Jill Truman. *Capacity:* 400.

Royal Albert Hall. Kensington Gore, London SW7 2AP *admin:* 020 7589 3203 *box office:* 020 7589 8212 *fax:* 020 7823 7725 *email:* admin @royalalberthall.com. D Elliott, chief executive; E Hewitt, sales director; R Flower, show department manager. *Capacity:* 5,092.

Royal Festival Hall on The South Bank. London SE1 8XX *admin:* 020 7921 0600 *box office:* 020 7960 4242 *fax:* 020 7928 0063. Jodi Myers, director of performing arts; Nigel March, head of production; Kevin Wilson, head of marketing. *Royal Festival Hall Capacity:* 2,895; *Queen Elizabeth Hall Capacity:* 915; *Purcell Room Capacity:* 368.

Royal Opera House. Covent Garden, London WC2E 9DD *admin:* 020 7240 1200. Sir Colin Southgate, chairman; Michael Kaiser, executive director; Richard Jarman, artistic director.

St John's, Smith Square. Smith Square, London SW1P 3HA *admin:* 020 7222 2168 *box office:* 020 7222 1061 *fax:* 020 7233 1618. Paul Davies, general manager; Laura Curtis, assistant manager. *Capacity:* 780.

Savoy Theatre. The Strand, London WC2R 0ET *admin:* 020 7828 0600 *box office:* 020 7836 8888 *fax:* 020 7379 7322. Kevin Chapple, theatre manager; Thomas Bondanetzky, general manager. *Capacity:* 1,158.

Shaftesbury Theatre. Shaftesbury Avenue, London WC2H 8DP *admin:* 020 7379 3345 *box office:* 020 7379 5399 *fax:* 020 7836 8181 *email:* ALeigh@TOC.DLTentertainment.co.uk. Andrew Leigh, chief executive; Christopher Flatman, theatre manager. *Capacity:* 1,405.

Spitalfields Market Opera. Old Spitalfields Market, Brushfield St, London E1 6AA *admin:* 020 7375 2637 *box office:* 020 7247 2558 *fax:* 020 7247 2559. Andrew Hammond, general manager; Tyrrell Burgess, chair. *Capacity:* 297 *Capacity:* 460.

Westminster Central Hall. Storey's Gate, Westminster, London SW1H 9NH *admin:* 020 7222 8010 *fax:* 020 7222 6883 *email:* events@wch.co.uk. Michael Sharp, general manager. *Great Hall Capacity:* 2,350; *Lecture Hall Capacity:* 500.

Wigmore Hall. 36 Wigmore Street, London W1H 0BP *admin:* 020 7486 1907 *box office:* 020 7935 2141 *fax:* 020 7224 3800 (admin); 020 7935 3344 (box office) *email:* info@wigmorehall.org.uk. William Lyne MBE, director; Marion Friend, general administrator. *Capacity:* 538.

Outer London

Acton Town Hall. High Street, London W3 6NE *admin:* 020 8758 5624 *box office:* 020 8579 5436 *fax:* 020 8566 5008 *email:* handm@ealing.gov.uk. Mark Hand, halls manager; Maureen Biancardi, town hall manager. *Capacity:* 812.

Alexandra Palace. Alexandra Palace Way, Wood Green, London N22 4AY *admin:* 020 8365 2121 *fax:* 020 8883 3999 *email:* alexandrapalace@dial.pipex.com. Sarah Freds. *Great Hall Capacity:* 7,008; *West Hall Capacity:* 2,500.

Beck Theatre. Grange Road, Hayes, Middx UB3 2UE *admin:* 020 8561 7506 *box office:* 020 8561 8371 *fax:* 020 8569 1072. Apollo Leisure (UK) Ltd, management; Graham Bradbury, general manager. *Main Theatre Capacity:* 600; *Foyer Performance Area Capacity:* 150.

Churchill Theatre. High Street, Bromley, Kent BR1 1HA *admin:* 020 8464 7131 *box office:* 020 8460 6677 *fax:* 020 8290 6968 (admin); 020 8460 7043 (technical) *email:* churchill-th@mail.bogo.co.uk (admin). Ian Ross, producer; Colin Hilton, marketing and publicity; Liz Gentry, financial controller. *Capacity:* 785.

Crystal Palace Concert Bowl. Crystal Palace Park, Thicket Road, Penge, London SE20 8UT *admin:* 020 8778 9612/7148 *fax:* 020 8659 8397. Peter Beale, marketing manager. *Capacity:* 17,500.

Fairfield Halls. Fairfield (Croydon) Ltd, Park Lane, Croydon, Surrey CR9 1DG *admin:* 020 8681 0821 *box office:* 020 8688 9291 *fax:* 020 8760 0835 *email:* dbarr@fairfield.co.uk. Derek Barr, chief executive. *Concert Hall Capacity:* 1,700.

Great Hall. Kentish Way, Bromley, Kent BR1 3UH *admin:* 020 8313 4495 *fax:* 020 8313 4440. Tony Ardley, halls manager; Roz Crabtree, marketing and publicity. *Capacity:* 650.

Greenford Hall. Ruislip Road, Greenford, Middx UB6 9QN *admin:* 020 8758 5624 *box office:* 020 8579 5436 *fax:* 020 8566 5008 *email:* handm@ealing.gov.uk. Mark Hand, halls manager; Jud O'Connor, hall supervisor. *Capacity:* 580.

Harrow Arts Centre. Uxbridge Road, Hatch End, Middx HA5 4EA *admin:* 020 8428 0123 *box office:* 020 8428 0124 *fax:* 020 8428 0121. Ann Dooley, education manager; Sophie Mason, programming manager. *Elliot Hall Capacity:* 585; *Travellers' Studio Capacity:* 130.

Hippodrome. North End Road, Golders Green, London NW11 7RP *admin:* 020 8765 4066 *box office:* 020 7765 3200 *fax:* 020 7765 3201 *email:* nathan.clapton@bbc.co.uk. Nathan Clapton, account manager; Rachel Stubbs, marketing manager. *Circle Capacity:* 520; *Stage Capacity:* 180.

Queen's Theatre. Billet Lane, Hornchurch, Essex RM11 1QT *admin:* 01708 456118 *box office:* 01708 443333 *fax:* 01708 452348 *email:* queens@globalnet.co.uk. Bob Carlton, artistic director; Matt Devitt, associate director; Margaret Smith, finance officer. *Capacity:* 503.

Richmond Theatre. The Green, Richmond upon Thames, Surrey TW9 1QJ *admin:* 020 8940 0220 *box office:* 020 8940 0088 *fax:* 020 8948 3601; 020 8940 1041 (box office) *email:* rtheatre@dircon.co.uk. John Young, technical manager; Neil Keane, chief electrician; Lucy Dale, marketing manager. *Capacity:* 840.

Walthamstow Assembly Hall. Town Hall Complex, Forest Road, Walthamstow, London E17 4SY *admin:* 020 8527 5544 ext 4568 *box office:* 020 8521 7111 *fax:* 020 8925 5640. Andrew Lamarque, house manager; John Richardson, halls technician; E O'Machail, entertainments manager. *Capacity:* 1,150.

Wembley Grand Hall. Wembley Conference and Exhibition Centre, Empire Way, Wembley, Middx HA9 0DW *admin:* 020 8902 8833 *box office:* 020 8902 0902 *fax:* 020 8585 3879 *email:* petert@wembley.co.uk. Peter Tudor, senior sales manager; David Thomson, senior operations manager; Hasmita Mistry, marketing manager. *Capacity:* 2,636.

Wembley Stadium. Wembley Complex, Wembley, Middx HA9 0DW *admin:* 020 8902 8833 *box office:* 020 8902 0902 *fax:* 020 8900 1045. Mike Potter, managing director; Paul Sergeant, stadium director; Charles Shun, sales. *Capacity:* 83,000.

Wimbledon Theatre. The Broadway, Wimbledon, London SW19 1QG *admin:* 020 8543 4549 *box office:* 020 8540 0362 *fax:* 020 8543 6637. Anthony Radford, general manager; Jem Nicholson, production and technical manager; Robin Cooper, press officer. *Capacity:* 1,670.

England

Aylesbury. Civic Centre. Market Square, Aylesbury, Bucks HP20 1UF *admin:* 01296 585858 ext 5526 *box office:* 01296 486009 *fax:* 01296 392091. Sam McCaffrey, ext 585541, programming manager; John Braley, ext 585528, house manager; Andree Abbott, ext 5526, administration manager. *Reg Maxwell Hall Capacity:* 700.

Barnstaple. Queen's Theatre. Boutport Street, Barnstaple, Devon EX31 1SY *admin:* 01271 327357 *box office:* 01271 324242 *fax:* 01271 326412. Darran Regan, theatre manager; Chris Sawle, financial director; Karen Turner, programming director. *Capacity:* 688.

Basingstoke. Anvil. Churchill Way, Basingstoke, Hants RG21 7QR *admin:* 01256 819797 *box office:* 01256 844244 *fax:* 01256 331733 (admin)/329726 (box office) *email:* christine.bradwell@dial.pipex.com. Christine Bradwell, chief executive; Matthew Cleaver, marketing director. *Concert Hall Capacity:* 1,400; *The Forge Capacity:* 100.

Bath. Assembly Rooms. Bennett Street, Bath BA1 2QH *admin:* 01225 477782 *fax:* 01225 477476 *email:* ruth.warren@bathnes.gov.uk. Ruth Warren, sales officer. *Ballroom Capacity:* 425; *Tea Room Capacity:* 200.

Bath. Sir Michael Tippett Centre. Bath Spa University College, Newton Park, Bath BA2 9BN *admin:* 01225 826431/875696 *fax:* 01225 874123 *email:* m.linley@bathspa.ac.uk. Jolyon Laycock, concert administrator; Matthew Linley, arts manager. *Sir Michael Tippett Centre Capacity:* 250; *Assembly Hall Capacity:* 250.

Bath. Theatre Royal. Sawclose, Bath BA1 1ET *admin:* 01225 448815 *box office:* 01225 448844 *fax:* 01225 444080. Danny Moar, theatre director; Simon Payne, finance director. *Main House Capacity:* 900; *Studio Capacity:* 145.

Bedford. Corn Exchange. St Paul's Square, Bedford MK40 1SL *admin:* 01234 344813 *box office:* 01234 269519 *fax:* 01234 325358. Sue Reeves, finance and reception manager; Carl Amos, business manager, operations; Andrew Jacques, events manager. *Corn Exchange Capacity:* 820; *Harpur Suite Capacity:* 200.

Bedworth. Civic Hall. High Street, Bedworth, Warwicks CV12 8NF *admin:* 024 7637 6705 *box office:* 024 7637 6707 *fax:* 024 7637 6730. David Matthews, general manager and licensee; Colin Whitmore, production and technical manager; Lisa Parnell, marketing and development officer. *Main Auditorium Capacity:* 813; *Small Hall Capacity:* 100.

Bexhill-on-Sea. De La Warr Pavilion. Marina, Bexhill-on-Sea, E Sussex TN40 1DP *admin:* 01424 787900 *box office:* 01424 787949 *fax:* 01424 787940. Caroline Collier, general manager; Linda Lewis, assistant manager (programming); Tony Williams, senior technician. *Capacity:* 1,016.

Birmingham. Adrian Boult Hall. Birmingham Conservatoire, Paradise Place, Birmingham B3 3HG *admin:* 0121 331 5909 *box office:* 0121 236 5622 *fax:* 0121 331 5908. Claire Britcliffe, publicity manager; Sally Frankish, Kerryn Withers Green, hire and concerts manager. *Capacity:* 525.

Birmingham. Birmingham Hippodrome. Hurst Street, Birmingham B5 4TB *admin:* 0121 689 3030 *box office:* 0121 689 3000 *fax:* 0121 622 1433 (admin)/6506 (box office) *email:* admin@birmingham-hippodrome.co.uk. Peter Tod, theatre director; Barry Hopson, theatre manager; James Prescott, head of finances and resources. *Capacity:* 1,887.

Birmingham. Symphony Hall. Broad Street, Birmingham B1 2EA *admin:* 0121 200 2000 *box office:* 0121 212 3333 *fax:* 0121 212 1982 *email:* symphony-hall@necgroup.co.uk. Andrew Jowett, director; Chris Baldock, operations manager; Michael Rye, technical manager. *Capacity:* 2,200.

Blackburn. King George's Hall. Northgate, Blackburn, Lancs BB2 1AA *admin:* 01254 582579 *box office:* 01254 582582 *fax:* 01254 667277 *email:* geoff.peake@blackburn.gov.uk. Geoff Peake, general manager; Howard Alderson-Perkins, production and technical manager; Steve Burch, marketing and publicity. *The Concert Hall Capacity:* 1,853; *Windsor Suite Capacity:* 584.

Blackpool. Grand Theatre. Church Street, Blackpool FY1 1HT *admin:* 01253 290111 *box office:* 01253 290190 *fax:* 01253 751767/752981 *email:* generalmanager@blackpoolgrand.co.uk. Stephanie Sirr, general manager; Neil Thomson, deputy general manager; Sarah Ogle, head of press and marketing. *Main House Capacity:* 1,192; *Studio Capacity:* 80.

Blandford Forum. Bryanston Arts Centre. Blandford, Dorset DT11 0PX *admin:* 01258 456533 *box office:* 01258 456533 *fax:* 01258 484506 *email:* bac@bryanston.co.uk. Sarah Moore, administrator; Stuart Myles, technical manager; Richard Boswell, artistic director. *Coade Hall Capacity:* 600.

Bolton. Albert Halls Complex. Room 100, Town Hall, Bolton, Lancs BL1 1RU *admin:* 01204 522311 ext 1064 *box office:* 01204 364333 *fax:* 01204 399928. Phil Smith, entertainments and marketing; Jannette Mason, technical manager. *Albert Hall Capacity:* 670; *Festival Hall Capacity:* 375.

Bournemouth. Bournemouth International Centre. Exeter Road, Bournemouth, Dorset BH2 5BH *admin:* 01202 456400 *box office:* 01202 456456. Kevin Sheehan, director; Rob Zuradzki, entertainments and events manager. *Windsor Hall Capacity:* 3,500; *Tregonwell Hall Capacity:* 1,000.

Bournemouth. Pavilion Theatre. Westover Road, Bournemouth, Dorset BH1 2BX *admin:* 01202 456400 *box office:* 01202 456456. Kevin Sheehan, director. *Theatre Capacity:* 1,518; *Pavilion Ballroom Capacity:* 950.

Bournemouth. Winter Gardens. Exeter Road, Bournemouth BH2 5BH *admin:* 01202 456400 *box office:* 01202 456456 *fax:* 01202 451024. Rob Zuradzki, entertainments and events manager; Kevin Sheehan, director. *Capacity:* 1,818.

Bradford. Alhambra Theatre. Morley Street, Bradford, W Yorks BD7 1AJ *admin:* 01274 752375 *box office:* 01274 752000 *fax:* 01274 752185. John Botteley, general manager; Iain Bloomfield, head of community and education; Gerry Clifford, head of customer services. *Main House Capacity:* 1,464; *Studio Capacity:* 200.

Bradford. St George's Hall. Bridge Street, Bradford, W Yorks BD1 1JS *admin:* 01274 752374 *box office:* 01274 752000. Gerry Clifford, manager, St George's. *Capacity:* 1,700.

Brentwood. Brentwood Centre. Doddinghurst Road, Brentwood, Essex CM15 9NN *admin:* 01277 215151 *box office:* 01277 262616 *fax:* 01277 229694. Steve Allen, ext 381, concerts promotion manager; Lynn Barhan, ext 744, events manager. *International Hall Capacity:* 1,936.

Bridgnorth. Bridgnorth Leisure Centre. North Gate, Bridgnorth, Shropshire WV16 4ER *admin:* 01746 761541/2. M Burnell, manager. *Capacity:* 650.

Bridlington. Leisure World. The Promenade, Bridlington, E Riding YO15 2QQ *admin:* 01262 606715 *fax:* 01262 673458. Amanda Eustace, public relations. *Capacity:* 700.

Bridlington. Spa Hall and Spa Theatre. South Marine Drive, Bridlington, E Riding YO15 3JH *admin:* 01262 678257 *box office:* 01262 678258 *fax:* 01262 401769. Eric Heath, director, service organisation; I Cook, assistant leisure unit manager; R Clutterham, senior facilities manager. *Capacity:* 2,000.

Brighton. Brighton Dome. Brighton BN1 1UG *admin:* 01273 700747 *box office:* 01273 709709 *fax:* 01273 707505. John Lucas, general manager. *Dome Theatre Capacity:* 2,102; *Corn Exchange Capacity:* 1,200; *Pavilion Theatre Capacity:* 230.

Brighton. Theatre Royal, Brighton. New Road, Brighton BN1 1SD *admin:* 01273 327480 *box office:* 01273 328488 *fax:* 01273 777156. Roger Neil, general manager. *Capacity:* 951.

Bristol. Bristol Hippodrome. St Augustine's Parade, Bristol BS1 4UZ *admin:* 0117 926 5524 *box office:* 0870 607 7500 *fax:* 0117 925 1661. Apollo Leisure (UK) Ltd, proprietors; P R Gregg, managing director; John Wood, general manager. *Capacity:* 1,977.

Bristol. Colston Hall. Colston Street, Bristol BS1 5AR *admin:* 0117 922 3693/3673 *box office:* 0117 922 3682 *fax:* 0117 922 3681 *email:* paul_preager@bristol-city.gov.uk. Ken Lovell, general manager; Paul Preager, concert planning; Daniel Wood, hall manager. *Colston Hall Capacity:* 2,121.

Bristol. St George's Brandon Hill. Bristol BS1 5PZ *admin:* 0117 929 4929 *box office:* 0117 923 0359 *fax:* 0117 927 6537. Jonathan Stracey, director; Catherine Freda, administrator; Suzanne Clatworthy, marketing and development. *Capacity:* 500.

Bristol. Victoria Rooms. Department of Music, Queen's Road, Clifton, Bristol BS8 1SA *admin:* 0117 954 5035 *fax:* 0117 954 5011. Lesley Mason, client services manager. *Capacity:* 745.

Buxton. Buxton Opera House. Water Street, Buxton, Derbyshire SK17 6XN *admin:* 01298 72050 *box office:* 01298 72190 *fax:* 01298 27563 *email:* admin@buxton-opera.co.uk. Andrew Aughton, theatre director; Guy Dunk, technical manager; Chris Nelson, box office manager. *Capacity:* 937.

Buxton. Octagon Hall. Pavilion Gardens, St John's Road, Buxton SK17 6XN *admin:* 01298 23114 *fax:* 01298 27622. Maurice Roberts, general manager. *Capacity:* 1,000.

Cambridge. Arts Theatre. 6 St Edward's Passage, Cambridge CB2 3PJ *admin:* 01223 578922/33 *box office:* 01223 503333 *fax:* 01223 578929 *email:* theatre@cambarts.co.uk. Ian Ross, general manager; Raymond Cross head of operations; Nicola Upson, marketing manager. *Capacity:* 671.

Cambridge. Cambridge Corn Exchange. Wheeler Street, Cambridge CB2 3QB *admin:* 01223 457555 *box office:* 01223 357851 *fax:* 01223 457559 *email:* technical.cornex@cambridge.gov.uk. Robert Sanderson, director; Graham Saxby, business manager; Mick Gray, entertainments and events. *Capacity:* 1,462.

Canterbury. Marlowe Theatre. The Friars, Canterbury, Kent CT1 2AS *admin:* 01227 763262 *box office:* 01227 787787 *fax:* 01227 781802. Mark Everett, theatre director; Peter Walker, theatre manager; Martin Smith, chief electrician. *Capacity:* 993.

Chatham. Central Theatre. 170 High Street, Chatham, Kent ME4 4AS *admin:* 01634 848584 *box office:* 01634 403868 *fax:* 01634 827711. Tony Hill, theatre manager; Emma Cooper-Hammond, assistant manager; Andrew Cook, FOH manager. *Capacity:* 945.

Chelmsford. Civic Theatre. Fairfield Road, Chelmsford, Essex CM1 1JG *admin:* 01245 606635 *box office:* 01245 606505. Bernard Mellar, head, leisure services; Jim Gillies, arts and entertainment manager; Andy Chafer, technical. *Capacity:* 525.

Cheltenham. Dean Close School New Theatre. Dean Close School, Cheltenham, Glos GL51 5HE *admin:* 01242 258002 *also box office; fax:* 01242 258007 *email:* mcv.theatre@btinternet.com. Marian Venn, theatre administrator. *Main Auditorium Capacity:* 550; *Orangery Capacity:* 100; *Prince Michael Hall Capacity:* 120.

Cheltenham. Everyman Theatre. Regent Street, Cheltenham, Glos GL50 1HQ *admin:* 01242 512515 *box office:* 01242 572573 *fax:* 01242 224305 *email:* admin@everyman.u-net.com. Michelle Draine, administrative co-ordinator; Philip Bernays, chief executive; Rachel Stafford, marketing manager. *Main Auditorium Capacity:* 658; *The Other Space Studio Theatre Capacity:* 60.

Cheltenham. Town Hall. Imperial Square, Cheltenham, Glos GL50 1QA *admin:* 01242 521621 *box office:* 01242 227979 *fax:* 01242 573902 *email:* TownHall@cheltenham.gov.uk. Jeremy Tyndall, head of festivals and entertainments; Tim Hulse, entertainments and marketing manager; Shelagh Daley, customer services manager. *Capacity:* 1,008.

Chesterfield. Winding Wheel. 13 Holywell Street, Chesterfield, Derbyshire S41 7AY *admin:* 01246 345333 *box office:* 01246 345334 *fax.* 01246 345330. Chris Norcliffe, community entertainments; Sue Barham, DSO manager; G Cass, recreation officer. *Auditorium Capacity:* 1,000; *Ballroom Capacity:* 200.

Chichester. Chichester Festival Theatre. Oaklands Park, Chichester, W Sussex PO19 4AP *admin:* 01243 784437 *box office:* 01243 781312 *fax:* 01243 787288 *email:* admin@cft.org.uk. Andrew Welch, theatre director; Kate Mosse, administrative director. *Main House Capacity:* 1,374; *Minerva Theatre Capacity:* 278.

Colchester. Charter Hall. Colchester Leisure World, Cowdray Avenue, Colchester, Essex CO1 1YH *admin:* 01206 282946 *box office:* 01206 282020 *fax:* 01206 282916. Claire Jackson, events co-ordinator; Carol Jolly, events assistant. *Event Hall Capacity:* 1,216.

Colne. Colne Municipal Hall. Albert Road, Colne, Lancs BB8 0BP *admin:* 01282 661216 *box office:* 01282 661234 *fax:* 01282 661221. Gary Hood, principal leisure services officer; Steve Doleman, technical and stage manager. *Capacity:* 611.

Corby. Festival Hall Complex. George Street, Corby, Northants NN17 1QB *admin:* 01536 402551 *box office:* 01536 402233 *fax:* 01536 403748. Ted Blair, manager; Janice Tilley, administrator; Richard Glen, technical. *Festival Hall Capacity:* 964; *Civic Theatre Capacity:* 490.

Coventry. Warwick Arts Centre. University of Warwick, Coventry CV4 7AL *admin:* 024 7652 3734 *box office:* 024 7652 4524 *fax:* 024 7652 3883 *email:* Arts.Centre@warwick.ac.uk. Stella Hall, director; Alan Rivett, deputy; Howard Potts, technical director. *Theatre Capacity:* 573; *Studio Capacity:* 150; *Concert Hall Capacity:* 1,471.

Crewe. Lyceum Theatre. Heath Street, Crewe, Cheshire CW1 2DA *admin:* 01270 537243 *box office:* 01270 537333 *fax:* 01270 537322. Cliff Stansfield, general manager; Emma McDermott, marketing manager; Steve O'Brien, technical manager. *Capacity:* 693.

Darlington. Darlington Civic Theatre. Parkgate, Darlington DL1 1RR *admin:* 01325 468006 *box office:* 01325 486555 *fax:* 01325 368278. Peter Cutchie, theatre director; Sarah Richards, theatre manager; Adam Nix, technical manager. *Capacity:* 901.

Dartford. Orchard. Home Gardens, Dartford, Kent DA1 1ED *admin:* 01322 220099 *box office:* 01322 220000 *fax:* 01322 227122. Beverley Davies, publicity manager; Steve Easey, stage director; Peter Harper, educational liaison officer. *Proscenium Capacity:* 959; *In Round Capacity:* 1,017.

Derby. Assembly Rooms. Market Place, Derby DE1 3AH *admin:* 01332 255443 *box office:* 01332 255800 *fax:* 01332 255788. Chris Ward-Brown, general manager. *Great Hall Capacity:* 1,742; *Darwin Suite Capacity:* 330.

Dewsbury. Dewsbury Town Hall. Wakefield Old Road, Dewsbury, W Yorks WF12 8DQ *admin:* 01924 324502 *box office:* 01924 324501 *fax:* 01924 324529 *email:* cultural-hq@geo2.poptel.org.uk. Julia Robinson, venues manager; John McPherson, marketing and press officer; David Long, technical manager. *Capacity:* 690.

Doncaster. Civic Theatre. Waterdale, Doncaster, S Yorks DN1 3ET *admin:* 01302 735600 *box office:* 01302 342349 *fax:* 01302 367223. J Hartill, theatre manager; R Barsby, theatre superintendant; L Walker, theatre technician. *Capacity:* 500.

Dorking. Dorking Halls. Reigate Road, Dorking, Surrey RH4 1SG *admin:* 01306 879200 *box office:* 01306 881717 *fax:* 01306 877277. Vanessa Hart, general manager. *Grand Hall Capacity:* 801; *Martineau Hall Capacity:* 252.

Dudley. Dudley Town Hall. St James's Road, Dudley, W Midlands DY1 1HF *admin:* 01384 815544 *box office:* 01384 812812 *fax:* 01384 815534 (admin)/815539 (technician). Andrew Grimshaw, manager; Rosemary Amos, principal arts officer; Martin Jones, halls and arts technician. *Capacity:* 1,060.

Dunstable. Queensway Hall. Vernon Place, Dunstable, Beds LU5 4EU *admin:* 01582 609620 *box office:* 01582 603326 *fax:* 01582 471190. Yvonne Mullens, general manager; Ann Northwood, box office receptionist. *Capacity:* 900.

Eastbourne. Congress Theatre. Carlisle Road, Eastbourne, E Sussex BN21 4BP *admin:* 01323 415500 *box office:* 01323 412000; cc 411555 *fax:* 01323 727369. Ian Alexander, general manager; Gavin Davis, operations manager. *Capacity:* 1,689.

Ellesmere Port. Ellesmere Port Civic Hall. Civic Way, Ellesmere Port, South Wirral, Cheshire L65 0BE *admin:* 0151 356 6780 *box office:* 0151 355 7652 *fax:* 0151 355 0508. Miles Veitch, administrator. *Main Hall Capacity:* 636; *Annexe Capacity:* 120.

Exeter. Exeter University Great Hall. Stocker Road, Exeter EX4 4PZ *admin:* 01392 215566 *fax:* 01392 263512 *email:* m.v.carter@exeter.ac.uk. Derek Phillips, director, domestic services; Marilyn Carter, bookings. *Capacity:* 1,435.

Exeter. St George's Hall. George Street, Exeter EX1 1BU *admin:* 01392 265866 *fax:* 01392 422137 *email:* markets.halls@exeter.gov.uk. David Lewis, manager, halls and events; Dave Avery, halls supervisor. *Capacity:* 500.

Fareham. Ferneham Hall. Osborn Road, Fareham, Hants PO16 7DB *admin:* 01329 824864 *box office:* 01329 231942 *fax:* 01329 281528 *email:* boxoffice@fareham.gov.uk. Russell Davies, arts and entertainments manager. *Solent-Meon Hall Capacity:* 1,022.

Frimley Green. Lakeside Country Club. Wharf Road, Frimley Green, nr Camberley, Surrey GU16 6PT *admin:* 01252 836464 *fax:* 01252 836777. Bob Potter, managing director; Austin Brown, promotional manager; Rob Goodwin, technical manager. *Lakeside Cabaret Suite Capacity:* 1,170; *Canal Suite Capacity:* 500.

Glyndebourne. Glyndebourne Opera House. Glyndebourne, Lewes, E Sussex BN8 5UU *admin:* 01273 812321 *box office:* 01273 813813 *fax:* 01273 812783 *email:* info@glyndebourne.com. Nicholas Snowman, general director; Andrew Davis, music director; Graham Vick, director of productions. *Capacity:* 1,200.

Gravesend. Woodville Halls. Woodville Place, Gravesend, Kent *admin:* 01474 337456 *box office:* 01474 337459/60/61 *fax:* 01474 337458 *email:* woodville.halls@gravesham.gov.uk. Brian N Tourle, arts entertainments manager; Rob Allen, theatre manager. *Main Hall Capacity:* 835.

Grays. Thurrock Civic Hall. Blackshots Lane, Grays, Essex RM16 2JU *admin:* 01375 652397 *box office:* 01375 383961. M Allinson, general manager. *Capacity:* 747.

Great Comp. Great Comp. Comp Lane, Great Comp, nr Borough Green, Kent TN15 8QS *box office:* 01797 222363. Pamela Bruxner, administrator. *Capacity:* 80.

Guildford. Guildford Civic. London Road, Guildford, Surrey GU1 2AA *admin:* 01483 444720/1 *box office:* 01483 444555 *fax:* 01483 301982 *email:* info@guildford-civic.co.uk. John Holmes, general manager; Jez Pipkin, technical manager; Max Hort, house manager. *Main Hall Capacity:* 1,150; *County Suite Capacity:* 160.

Guildford. Yvonne Arnaud Theatre. Millbrook, Guildford, Surrey GU1 3UX *admin:* 01483 440077 *box office:* 01483 440000 *fax:* 01483 564071. James Barber, director; John Bostock, finance officer; David Lindsey, general manager. *Capacity:* 590.

Halifax. Piece Hall. Halifax, W Yorks HX1 1RE *admin:* 01422 358087 *fax:* 01422 349310. Mark Humphreys, commercial manager. *Capacity:* 2,000; *Outdoor Capacity:* 7,000.

Halifax. Victoria Theatre. Wards End, Halifax, W Yorks HX1 1BU *admin:* 01422 351156 *box office:* 01422 351158 *fax:* 01422 320552 *email:* victoria@legend.co.uk. George Candler, principal entertainments manager; Alison Metcalfe, customer services manager; Tim Fagan, technical manager. *Main Hall Capacity:* 1,585.

Harrogate. Harrogate International Conference Centre. King's Road, Harrogate, N Yorks HG1 5LA *admin:* 01423 500500 *box office:* 01423 537230 *fax:* 01432 537210 (admin)/537240 (technical). P Lewis, director; S Quin, deputy director; C Weston, head of operations. *Capacity:* 2,009.

Harrogate. Harrogate Theatre. Oxford Street, Harrogate, N Yorks HG1 1QF *admin:* 01423 502710 *box office:* 01423 502116 *fax:* 01423 563205 *email:* hgte-theatre@pop3.poptel.org.uk. Sheena Wrigley, executive director; Rob Swain, artistic director; Phil Day, production manager. *Theatre Capacity:* 500; *Studio Capacity:* 50.

Harrogate. Royal Hall. Ripon Road, Harrogate, N Yorks HG1 2RD *admin:* 01423 500500 *box office:* 01423 537230 *fax:* 01432 537210. P Lewis, director; S Quin, deputy director; Colin Weston, head of operations. *Grand Hall Capacity:* 1,260.

Hartlepool. Borough Hall. Middlegate, Hartlepool TS24 0JD *box office:* 01429 890000 *fax:* 01429 863029. Garry Marshall, manager. *Capacity:* 1,300.

Hastings. White Rock Theatre. White Rock, Hastings, E Sussex TN34 1JX *admin:* 01424 781010 *box office:* 01424 781000 *fax:* 01424 781170. A Mould, general manager; P Higson, technical manager; A Mould, box office manager. *Capacity:* 1,102.

Hemel Hempstead. Dacorum Pavilion. Marlowes, Hemel Hempstead, Herts HP1 1HA *admin:* 01442 228727 *box office:* 01442 228700 *fax:* 01442 228735 *email:* dacorumpavilion@hemelhempstead.freeserve.co.uk. Nick Mowat, general manager; Louise Cecil, programme manager; Eve White, box office and administration manager. *Main Hall Capacity:* 1,055; *Snooks, The Pub in the Pavilion Capacity:* 120.

Herne Bay. King's Hall. The Downs, Herne Bay, Kent *admin:* 01227 374188 *also box office; fax:* 01227 371514. L Fenlon, hall manager; Margaret Pamplin, administration. *Capacity:* 646.

Hertford. Castle Hall. The Wash, Hertford SG14 1PS *admin:* 01992 589024 *box office:* 01992 589026 *fax:* 01992 589025. T Brooke-Auty, operations manager; Eoin Baird, general manager. *Seated Capacity:* 500; *Standing Capacity:* 700.

High Wycombe. Wycombe Swan. St Mary Street, High Wycombe, Bucks HP11 2XE *admin:* 01494 514444 *box office:* 01494 512000 *fax:* 01494 538080. Stuart Griffiths, general manager; Roger Keele, assistant general manager; Carlos Queiroz, technical manager. *Theatre Capacity:* 1,076; *Town Hall Capacity:* 400; *Oak Room Capacity:* 130.

Horsham. Christ's Hospital Theatre. Christ's Hospital, Horsham, W Sussex RH13 7LW *admin:* 01403 267005 *box office:* 01403 252709 *fax:* 01403 255283. Jeffrey Mayhew, director of drama; Dominic Gibson, technical manager; Jackie Davies, publicity and box office. *Capacity:* 500.

Hove. Hove Town Hall. Norton Road, Hove, E Sussex BN3 4AH *admin:* 01273 292903 *fax:* 01273 292936. Chris Jones, general manager. *Great Hall Capacity:* 1,200.

Huddersfield. Huddersfield Town Hall. Ramsden Street, Huddersfield, W Yorks HD1 2TA *admin:* 01484 221900/221947/221902 *box office:* 01484 223200 *fax:* 01484 221541. Gary Ellis, bookings officer; Julia Robinson, venues manager; John McPherson, press officer. *Capacity:* 1,100.

Hull. Middleton Hall. University of Hull, Cottingham Road, Hull, East Riding of Yorks, HU6 7RX *admin:* 01482 466540 *fax:* 01482 466511 *email:* M.Bucknell@admin.hull.ac.uk. P Martin, campus services officer; M Bucknell, secretary. *Capacity:* 514.

Ilfracombe. Ilfracombe Landmark Theatre and Pavilion. Wilder Road, Ilfracombe, Devon *admin:* 01271 865655 *box office:* 01271 324242 *fax:* 01271 867707 *email:* northdevon.theatres@sosi.net. Erick Muzard, manager; Jo Lock, publicity officer; Karen Turner, programming director. *Theatre Capacity:* 483; *Pavilion Capacity:* 150.

Ilkley. King's Hall and Winter Gardens. Station Road, Ilkley, W Yorks LS29 8HA *admin:* 01943 751576. Mark Davies, general manager; Ian Powell, caretaker. *King's Hall Capacity:* 745; *Winter Gardens Capacity:* 300.

Ipswich. Corn Exchange. King Street, Ipswich 1P1 1DH *admin:* 01473 433133 *box office:* 01473 433100 *fax:* 01473 433450 (admin)/433499 (publicity) *email:* corn@ipswich-ents.co.uk. Billy Brennan, general manager; Craig Oldfield, operations manager; Hazel Clover, publicity officer. *Grand Hall (seated) Capacity:* 893; *Grand Hall (standing) Capacity:* 993.

Ipswich. Ipswich Regent. 3 St Helen's Street, Ipswich, Suffolk IP4 1HE *admin:* 01473 433555 *box office:* 01473 433100 *fax:* 01473 433727 (admin)/433499 (publicity) *email:* regent@ipswich-ents.co.uk. Roy Stephenson, general manager; Hazel Clover, publicity officer. *Capacity:* 1,781.

Kendal. Kendal Leisure Centre. Burton Road, Kendal, Cumbria LA9 7HX *admin:* 01539 729511 *box office:* 01539 729702 *fax:* 01539 731135 *email:* leisure.centre@kencomp.net. P Stewart, manager; D Garnett, special events officer. *Westmorland Hall Capacity:* 932.

King's Lynn. King's Lynn Corn Exchange. Tuesday Market Place, King's Lynn, Norfolk PE30 1JW *admin:* 01553 765565 *box office:* 01553 764864 *fax:* 01553 762141 *email:* howard.barnes@dial.pipex.com. Howard Barnes, general manager; Paul Pomfret, senior stage and technical manager; Ellen McPhillips, assistant general manager. *Seating Capacity:* 738; *Standing Capacity:* 1,200.

Kirkby in Ashfield. Festival Hall. Festival Hall Leisure Centre, Hodgkinson Road, Kirkby in Ashfield, Notts NG17 7DJ *admin:* 01623 457101 *box office:* 01623 457100 *fax:* 01623 457099. Denis Nicholls, centre manager; Peter Lamb, Alan Jones, Russell Webster, assistant managers. *Capacity:* 520.

Lancaster. Ashton Hall. Lancaster Town Hall, Dalton Square, Lancaster LA1 1PJ *admin:* 01524 582512. Mike Derham, manager; E Dugdale, town hall keeper; S Hall, buildings supervisor. *Capacity:* 800.

Lancaster. Great Hall. Dept of Music, University, Lancaster LA1 4YW *admin:* 01524 593777 *box office:* 01524 593729 *fax:* 01524 847298 *email:* D.McCaldin@lancaster.ac.uk; S.Birchall@lancaster. Denis McCaldin, artistic director; Stella Birchall, administrator. *Great Hall Capacity:* 1,100; *Jack Hylton Room Capacity:* 250.

Leamington Spa. Royal Spa Centre. Newbold Terrace, Leamington Spa, Warwicks CV32 4HN *admin:* 01926 334418 *also box office; fax:* 01926 832054. Peter B Nicholson, manager; David F Phillips, assistant manager. *Avon Hall Capacity:* 800; *Newbold Hall Capacity:* 200; *Jephson Room Capacity:* 40.

Leatherhead. Leatherhead Leisure Centre. Guildford Road, Leatherhead, Surrey KT22 9BL *admin:* 01372 386564 *box office:* 01372 377674 *fax:* 01372 386749. T Ward, general manager; Elena Glynn, conference manager. *Sports Hall Capacity:* 1,200; *Tyllney Room/Mariners Suite Capacity:* 350; *Mole Barn Capacity:* 600.

Leeds. Civic Theatre. Cookridge Street, Leeds LS2 8BH *admin:* 0113 245 6343 *box office:* 0113 214 5315 *fax:* 0113 234 7973. Steven Cartwright, general manager; Vivien Simpson, assistant manager; Peter Waddicor, chief technician. *Capacity:* 521.

Leeds. Leeds Grand Theatre and Opera House. 46 New Briggate, Leeds LS1 6NZ *admin:* 0113 245 6014 *box office:* 0113 222 6222 *fax:* 0113 246 5906. Warren Smith, general manager; Anne Baxendale, house manager. *Main Auditorium Capacity:* 1,550; *Assembly Rooms Capacity:* 600; *Studio Capacity:* 160.

Leeds. Victoria Hall. Town Hall, The Headrow, Leeds LS1 3AD *admin:* 0113 247 7989/8 *box office:* 0113 247 6962/245 5565 *fax:* 0113 247 4810 *email:* chrisaldred@leeds.gov.uk. *Capacity:* 1,500.

Leicester. De Montfort Hall. Granville Road, Leicester LE1 7RU *admin:* 0116 233 3113 *box office:* 0116 233 3111 *fax:* 0116 233 3182. Nick Hallam, marketing manager. *Capacity:* 1,974.

Leicester. Haymarket Theatre. Belgrave Gate, Leicester LE1 3YQ *admin:* 0116 253 0021 *box office:* 0116 253 9797 *fax:* 0116 251 3310 (admin); 0116 252 9043 (technical). Kathleen Hamilton, executive director; Paul Kerryson, artistic director. *Main Capacity:* 752; *Studio Capacity:* 120.

Liverpool. Methodist Mission Central Hall. Renshaw Street, Liverpool L1 2SS *admin:* 0151 709 4435/6. Mr Gardam, general manager. *Great Hall Capacity:* 985 *Capacity:* 250.

Liverpool. Philharmonic Hall. Hope Street, Liverpool L1 9BP *admin:* 0151 210 2895 *box office:* 0151 709 3789 *fax:* 0151 210 2902 *email:* RLPSociety@aol.com. Antony Lewis-Crosby, chief executive; Petr Altrichter, principal conductor, RLPO. *Capacity:* 1,700.

Liverpool. Royal Court. Roe Street, Liverpool L1 1HL *admin:* 0151 709 1808 *box office:* 0151 709 4321 *fax:* 0151 709 2678. Richard Maides, manager. *Capacity:* 1,525.

Liverpool. St George's Hall. William Brown Street, Liverpool L1 1JJ *admin:* 0151 707 2391 *fax:* 0151 709 2252. John Davies, director leisure services; Keith Davies, head of tourism, arts and heritage; Fiona Taylor, acting manager. *Great Hall Capacity:* 1,000.

Loughborough. Loughborough Town Hall. Market Place, Loughborough, Leics LE11 3EB *admin:* 01509 634775 *box office:* 01509 231914 *also fax*. Geoff Rowe, programme and marketing manager; Ian Stephens, general manager. *Theatre Capacity:* 528; *Victoria Room Capacity:* 350.

Lowestoft. Marina Theatre. The Marina, Lowestoft, Suffolk NR32 1HH *admin:* 01502 523444 *box office:* 01502 573318 *fax:* 01502 538179. David Shepheard, theatre manager; Darryl Franklin, technical manager. *Capacity:* 751.

Malvern. Malvern Theatres. Grange Road, Malvern, Worcs WR14 3HB *admin:* 01684 569256 *box office:* 01684 892277 *fax:* 01684 893300 *email:* post@malvern-theatres.co.uk. E Nicolas Lloyd, chief executive; Dorothy Warner, development manager; Stuart Davis, technical manager. *Festival Theatre Capacity:* 850; *New Space Capacity:* 500; *Cinema Capacity:* 380.

Manchester. Bridgewater Hall. Lower Mosley Street, Manchester M2 3WS *admin:* 0161 950 0000 *box office:* 0161 907 9000 *fax:* 0161 950 0001 (admin); 0161 907 9001 (box office) *email:* admin@bridgewater-hall.co.uk; box@bridgewater-hall.co.uk. Sue Vanden, director of sales and marketing; Howard Raynor, chief executive; Chris Wright, technical manager. *Concert Hall Capacity:* 2,330.

Manchester. Manchester Town Hall. Albert Square, Manchester M60 2LA *admin:* 0161 234 3039/234 5000 *fax:* 0161 234 3242. Lis Monson, facilities co-ordinator; John Henstock, buildings manager. *Great Hall Capacity:* 500.

Manchester. Palace Theatre. Oxford Street, Manchester M1 6FT *admin:* 0161 228 6255 *box office:* 0161 242 2503 *fax:* 0161 237 5746. Apollo Leisure (UK) Ltd, proprietors; Peter Evans, general manager. *Capacity:* 2,000.

Manchester. Royal Exchange Theatre. St Ann's Square, Manchester M2 7DH *admin:* 0161 833 9333 *box office:* 0161 833 9833 *fax:* 0161 832 0881 *email:* administration@royalexchange.co.uk. Braham Murray, Greg Hersov, Matthew Lloyd, artistic directors; Valerie Hawkin, financial controller. *Main Theatre Capacity:* 750; *Studio Capacity:* 120.

Manchester. Royal Northern College of Music. 124 Oxford Road, Manchester M13 9RD *admin:* 0161 907 5200 *box office:* 0161 907 5278/5279 *fax:* 0161 273 7611 *email:* allan.taylor@rncm.ac.uk. Edward Gregson, principal; Philip Jones, promotions co-ordinator; Allan Taylor, events manager (for hirings). *Opera Theatre Capacity:* 620; *Concert Hall Capacity:* 475.

Mansfield. Palace Theatre. Leeming Street, Mansfield, Notts NG18 1NG *admin:* 01623 412950 *box office:* 01623 633133 *fax:* 01623 412922. Andrew Tucker, cultural services manager; Louise Whitbread, marketing officer; David Longford, education outreach officer. *Capacity:* 586.

Margate. Winter Gardens. Fort Crescent, Margate, Kent CT9 1HX *admin:* 01843 296111/292795 *box office:* 01843 292795 *fax:* 01843 292795. Christopher Wolfe, general manager; Steven Davis, food and beverages manager. *Main Hall Capacity:* 1,400; *Queen's Hall Capacity:* 550.

Middlesbrough. Middlesbrough Town Hall. Albert Road, PO Box 69, Middlesbrough *admin:* 01642 263848 *box office:* 01642 242561 *fax:* 01642 221866. Jean Hewitt, Town Hall manager. *Town Hall Capacity:* 1,190; *Town Hall Crypt Capacity:* 450.

Middleton. Middleton Civic Hall. Fountain Street, Middleton, Manchester M24 1AF *admin:* 0161 643 2470 *box office:* 0161 643 2389 *fax:* 0161 643 3618. Brian Johnson, manager. *Capacity:* 589.

Newark. Palace Theatre. Appletongate, Newark, Notts NG24 1JY *admin:* 01636 671636 *box office:* 01636 671156 *fax:* 01636 701402 *email:* palace@newark-sherwooddc.gov.uk. David Piper, theatre director; Mark Noutch, resident stage manager; Jean Rushforth, box office. *Capacity:* 607.

Newcastle-under-Lyme. New Vic Theatre. Etruria Road, Newcastle-under-Lyme, Staffs ST5 0JG *admin:* 01782 717954 *box office:* 01782 717962 *fax:* 01782 712885 *email:* victheatre@aol.com. Ludo Keston, general manager. *New Vic Theatre Capacity:* 597; *Stephen Joseph Studio Capacity:* 100.

Newcastle upon Tyne. Newcastle City Hall. Northumberland Road, Newcastle upon Tyne NE1 8SF *admin:* 0191 222 1778 *box office:* 0191 261 2606 *fax:* 0191 261 8102. P J Brennan, general manager; D Hawkins, production and technical manager; J Slater, box office manager. *Capacity:* 2,133.

Newcastle upon Tyne. Newcastle Playhouse. Barras Bridge, Newcastle upon Tyne NE1 7RH *admin:* 0191 232 3366 *box office:* 0191 230 5151 *fax:* 0191 261 8093 *email:* info@northernstage.com. Alan Lyddiard, artistic director; Mandy Stewart, executive director; Edmund Nickols, director of operations. *Capacity:* 510.

Newcastle upon Tyne. Theatre Royal. Grey Street, Newcastle upon Tyne, NE1 6BR *admin:* 0191 232 0997 *box office:* 0191 232 2061 *fax:* 0191 261 1906. Peter Sarah, general manager; J J McMullen, stage manager; Andy Kent, chief LX. *Capacity:* 1,294.

Northampton. Derngate. 19-21 Guildhall Road, Northampton NN1 1DP *admin:* 01604 626222 *box office:* 01604 624811 *fax:* 01604 250901 (admin); 01604 233095 (box office) *email:* postbox@derngate.demon.co.uk. Roger Hopwood, general manager; Neil Smith, company secretary; Rosemary Jones, programming manager. *Concert Capacity:* 1,550; *Lyric Capacity:* 1,200.

Northampton. Spinney Hill Concert Hall. Northampton School for Girls, Spinney Hill Road, Northampton NN3 6DG *admin:* 01604 499311 *box office:* 01604 496996 *fax:* 01604 496996. Robin Hopkins, bookings. *Capacity:* 750.

Norwich. St Andrew's & Blackfriars Halls. St Andrew's Plain, Norwich, Norfolk NR3 1AU *admin:* 01603 628477 *fax:* 01603 762182 *email:* taldous.ncc.sah@gtnet.gov.uk. Timothy Aldous, general manager. *St Andrew's Hall Capacity:* 900; *Blackfriars Hall Capacity:* 370.

Norwich. Theatre Royal. Theatre Street, Norwich, Norfolk NR2 1RL *admin:* 01603 623562 *box office:* 01603 630000 *fax:* 01603 762904 *email:* admin@theatreroyalnorwich.co.uk. Peter Wilson, chief executive; Roger Richardson, programming and operations director; Norman Cullingford, finance manager. *Main House Capacity:* 1,314.

Nottingham. Albert Hall. North Circus Street, Nottingham *admin:* 0115 950 0411 *fax:* 0115 947 6512. Sally Robinson, general manager. *Great Hall Capacity:* 700; *Osborne Suite Capacity:* 200; *Balmoral Gallery Capacity:* 60.

Nottingham. East Midlands Conference Centre. University Park, Nottingham NG7 2RJ *admin:* 0115 951 5000 *fax:* 0115 951 5009. Malcolm Youngson, conference manager; Colin Zachura, deputy manager; Diane Foster, assistant manager. *Auditorium Capacity:* 550.

Nottingham. Royal Concert & Conference Hall. Theatre Square, Nottingham NG1 5ND *admin:* 0115 989 5500 *box office:* 0115 989 5555 *fax:* 0115 947 4218 *email:* m.grayson@royalcentre.co.uk. J Michael Grayson, managing director; James Ashworth, operations director; Nic Parr, marketing manager. *Capacity:* 2,496.

Nottingham. Theatre Royal. Theatre Square, Nottingham NG1 5ND *admin:* 0115 989 5500 *box office:* 0115 989 5555 *fax:* 0115 947 4218 *email:* m.grayson@royalcentre.co.uk. J Michael Grayson, director; Ken Marshall, technical manager; James Ashworth, operations director. *Capacity:* 1,186.

Oldham. Queen Elizabeth Hall. PO Box 66, West Street, Oldham, Lancs OL1 1UT *admin:* 0161 911 4070 *box office:* 0161 911 4072 *fax:* 0161 911 3057. Jasmine Hendry, arts and entertainments manager; Julia Turpin, entertainments officer; Brenda Lumley, senior venue manager. *Queen Elizabeth Hall Capacity:* 832; *Chadderton Suite Capacity:* 250; *Failsworth Suite Capacity:* 160.

Oxford. Apollo Theatre. George Street, Oxford OX1 2AG *admin:* 01865 243041 *box office:* 0870 606 3501 *fax:* 01865 791976. Apollo Leisure (UK) Ltd, proprietors; P R Gregg, managing director; Louise Clifford, general manager. *Capacity:* 1,826.

Oxford. Jacqueline du Pré Music Building. St Hilda's College, Oxford OX4 1DY *admin:* 01865 276821 *fax:* 01865 286174 *email:* jdp@st-hildas.ox.ac.uk. Marie-Alice Frappat, manager; Barbara Levick, chairman. *Capacity:* 200.

Oxford. Oxford Playhouse. Beaumont Street, Oxford OX1 2LW *admin:* 01865 247134 *box office:* 01865 798600 *fax:* 01865 793748 *email:* admin@oxfordplayhouse.demon.co.uk. Tish Francis, Hedda Beeby, joint theatre directors. *Capacity:* 613.

Oxford. Oxford Town Hall. St Aldate's, Oxford OX1 1BX *fax:* 01965 252388 *email:* rcharlett@oxvoed.gov.uk. Rosemary Charlett, bookings; David Clark, town hall manager. *Main Hall Capacity:* 742; *Assembly Room Capacity:* 200.

Oxford. Sheldonian Theatre. Broad Street, Oxford OX1 3AZ *admin:* 01865 277299 *fax:* 01865 277295. Sue Waldman, administrator. *Capacity:* 1,000.

Plymouth. Plymouth Pavilions. Millbay Road, Plymouth, Devon PL1 3LF *admin:* 01752 222200 *box office:* 01752 229922 *fax:* 01752 262226 (operations). Margaret Garcia, general manager; Liam Smith, marketing manager; Dave Cottrell, technical co-ordinator. *Arena Capacity:* 2,500.

Plymouth. Theatre Royal. Royal Parade, Plymouth, Devon PL1 2TR *admin:* 01752 668282 *box office:* 01752 267222 *fax:* 01752 671179 (admin)/221267 (mkt)/225985 (tech) *email:* education@theatreroyal.demon.co.uk. Adrian Vinken, chief executive; Simon Stokes, artistic director; Alan Finch, general manager theatre services. *Theatre Royal Capacity:* 1,296; *Drum Theatre Capacity:* 200.

Poole. Poole Arts Centre. Kingland Road, Poole, Dorset BH15 1UG *admin:* 01202 665334 *box office:* 01202 685222 *fax:* 01202 670016. Ruth Eastwood, chief executive; Alistair Wilkinson, programme director; Sarah Chapman, marketing manager. *Wessex Hall Capacity:* 1,473; *Towngate Theatre Capacity:* 669.

Preston. Guild Hall Centre. Lancaster Road, Preston, Lancs PR1 1HT *admin:* 01772 203456 *box office:* 01772 258858 *fax:* 01772 881716. John Shedwick, general manager. *Charter Theatre Capacity:* 780; *Guild Hall Capacity:* 2,020.

Reading. Hexagon. Queens Walk, Reading RG1 7UA *admin:* 0118 939 0390 *box office:* 0118 960 6060 *fax:* 0118 939 0028 *email:* hexagon@beta.reading-bc.gov.uk. Andrew Ormston, head of arts and theatres; William Brooker, operation manager; Paul Kennedy, technical manager. *Capacity:* 1,200.

Ryde. Ryde Theatre. Lind Street, Ryde, Isle of Wight, PO33 2NL *admin:* 01983 568099 *also fax.* Malcolm Bennett, Sarah Clark, administrators. *Capacity:* 502.

St Albans. Alban Arena. Civic Centre, St Albans, Herts AL1 3LD *admin:* 01727 861078 *box office:* 01727 844488 *fax:* 01727 865755 *email:* arena@relaxionaa.co.uk. Roger Cramer, Alban Arena manager; Tony Ayre, technical manager; Dave Mead, deputy technical manager. *Capacity:* 858.

St Helens. Theatre Royal. Corporation Street, St Helens, Lancs WA10 1LQ *box office:* 01744 451175 *fax:* 01744 613267. Mike Littlewood, technical manager. *Capacity:* 704.

St Ives. St Ivo Recreation Centre. Westwood Road, St Ives, Cambs PE17 4WU *admin:* 01480 388500 *also box office; fax:* 01480 388513 *email:* ian.cousins@hintsdc.gov.uk. I C Cousins, centre manager. *Burgess Hall Capacity:* 600; *Drama Theatre Capacity:* 250.

Salisbury. City Hall. Malthouse Lane, Salisbury, Wilts SP2 7TU *admin:* 01722 334432 *box office:* 01722 327676 *fax:* 01722 337059. Phillip Smith, general manager. *Auditorium Capacity:* 953.

Scarborough. Spa Grand Hall. Spa Complex, South Bay, Scarborough, N Yorks *admin:* 01723 376774 *also box office; fax:* 01723 355821. Peter Dahl, director of tourism and leisure services; Keith Norton, Spa and conference manager; B J Sheerin, Carol Mills, assistant managers. *Grand Hall Capacity:* 1,825.

Scunthorpe. Baths Hall. 59 Doncaster Road, Scunthorpe, S Humberside DN15 7RG *admin:* 01724 297861 *box office:* 01724 842332 *fax:* 01724 861341. Terry Wincott, entertainments manager; Janice Oliver, assistant entertainments manager. *Main Hall Capacity:* 600; *Apollo Room Capacity:* 200.

Sheffield. Lyceum Theatre. 55 Norfolk Street, Sheffield S1 1DA *admin:* 0114 249 5999 (Crucible) *box office:* 0114 249 6000 (Crucible) *fax:* 0114 249 6003 (admin); 0114 201 3830 (marketing) *email:* sheff-theatres@pop3.poptel.org.uk. Grahame Morris, chief executive; Deborah Paige, artistic director; Andrew Snelling, finance director. *Capacity:* 1,099.

Sheffield. Sheffield City Hall. Barkers Pool, Sheffield S1 2JA *admin:* 0114 273 4550 *box office:* 0114 278 9789 *fax:* 0114 276 9866. Maire McCarthy, general manager; Richard Hunter, events and operations manager; Donna Linehan, marketing and sales manager. *Oval Hall Capacity:* 2,346; *Memorial Hall Capacity:* 522; *Central Suite Capacity:* 850.

Skegness. Embassy Centre. Grand Parade, Skegness, Lincs PE25 2UG *admin:* 01754 768444 *box office:* 01754 768333 *fax:* 01754 761737. Steve Wattam, manager; Steve Rushforth, technical manager; Keith Morrison, publicity manager. *Capacity:* 1,158.

Snape. Snape Maltings Concert Hall. c/o Aldeburgh Productions, High Street, Aldeburgh, Suffolk IP15 5AX *admin:* 01728 452935 *box office:* 01728 453543 *fax:* 01728 452715 *email:* enquiries@aldeburghfestivals.org. Clare Lovell, general administrator; Jonathan Reekie, chief executive; Sharon Goddard, manager, artists and concerts. *Snape Maltings Concert Hall Capacity:* 832; *Britten Pears School Capacity:* 120.

Southampton. Mayflower Theatre. Commercial Road, Southampton SO15 1GE *admin:* 023 8071 1800 *box office:* 023 8071 1811 *fax:* 023 8071 1801. Dennis L J Hall, director; Wycliffe Musuku, financial controller; Paul Lewis, head of marketing and operations. *Capacity:* 2,299.

Southampton. Southampton Guildhall. Southampton City Council, Civic Centre, Southampton SO14 7LP *admin:* 023 8083 2453 *box office:* 023 8063 2601 *fax:* 023 8023 3359 (admin); 023 8082 3137 (technical) *email:* h.richardson@southampton.gov.uk. Sue Cheriton, manager; Heather Richardson, sales and marketing manager. *Guildhall Capacity:* 1,749; *Solent Suite Capacity:* 250; *Lecture Theatre Capacity:* 118.

Southampton. Turner Sims Concert Hall. University of Southampton, Southampton SO17 1BJ *admin:* 023 8059 2223 *box office:* 023 8059 5151 *fax:* 023 8059 2505 *email:* turnsims@soton.ac.uk. Peter Bolton, concert hall manager. *Capacity:* 461.

Southend on Sea. Cliffs Pavilion. Station Road, Southend on Sea, Essex SS0 7RA *admin:* 01702 331852 *box office:* 01702 351135 *fax:* 01702 433015. Charles Mumford, general manager; Paul Driscoll, marketing manager; Mark Homer, building operations officer. *Capacity:* 1,630.

Southport. Floral Hall. The Promenade, Southport, Merseyside PR9 0DZ *admin:* 01704 540454 *box office:* 01704 540404 *fax:* 01704 536841. Lisa Chu, general manager. *Floral Hall Capacity:* 1,200.

Southsea. Kings Theatre. Albert Road, Southsea, Hants PO5 2QJ *admin:* 023 9281 1394 *box office:* 023 9282 8282 *fax:* 023 9273 5242. J N Cooper, I S Barnes, co-lessees; Vanessa Dowling, general manager; John Pike, stage manager. *Capacity:* 1,450.

Spalding. South Holland Centre. Market Place, Spalding, Lincs PE11 1SS *admin:* 01775 711133 *box office:* 01775 725031 *fax:* 01775 712804. Nigel Hawkins, arts manager; Barbara Gorton, centre manager. *Function Hall Capacity:* 500; *Auditorium Capacity:* 153.

Stafford. Stafford Gatehouse. Eastgate Street, Stafford, Staffs ST16 2LT *admin:* 01785 253595 *box office:* 01785 254653 *fax:* 01785 225622. Daniel Shaw, manager, licensee; Lynn Elkin, administration manager. *Gatehouse Theatre Capacity:* 570; *Malcolm Edwards Theatre Studio Capacity:* 120.

Stevenage. Gordon Craig Theatre. Stevenage Arts/Leisure Centre, Lytton Way, Stevenage, Herts SG1 1LZ *admin:* 01438 242642/242649 *box office:* 01438 242866 *fax:* 01438 242342. Bob Bustance, arts and entertainments manager. *Theatre Capacity:* 506; *Concert Hall Capacity:* 1,500.

Stoke-on-Trent. King's Hall and Jubilee Hall. PO Box 757, Civic Centre, Glebe Street, Stoke-on-Trent, Staffs ST4 1RT *admin:* 01782 234567 *fax:* 01782 232592. Tony Meigh, venues and catering manager; David Powell, duty manager. *King's Hall Capacity:* 1,372; *Jubilee Hall Capacity:* 300.

Stoke-on-Trent. Victoria Hall. Bagnall Street, Hanley, Stoke-on-Trent, Staffs ST1 3AD *admin:* 01782 211201 *box office:* 01782 213800 *fax:* 01782 214738 *email:* suewilkinson@technocom.com. Ambassador Theatre Group: Richard Wingate, chief executive; David Brownlee, marketing manager. *Capacity:* 1,349.

Sunderland. Empire Theatre, Sunderland. High Street West, Sunderland SR1 3EX *admin:* 0191 510 0545 *box office:* 0191 514 2517 *fax:* 0191 553 7427. Symon Easton, managing director; Stuart Anderson, finance and deputy managing director; Christabel Brett, operations manager. *Main Auditorium Capacity:* 1,875.

Swindon. Wyvern Theatre. Theatre Square, Swindon, Wilts SN1 1QN *admin:* 01793 535534 *box office:* 01793 524481 *fax:* 01793 480278. Lizzie Jones, general manager; David Hollingworth, deputy manager; David Wicks, stage manager. *Theatre Capacity:* 617.

Telford. Oakengates Theatre. Limes Walk, Oakengates, Telford TF2 6EP *admin:* 01952 610163 *box office:* 01952 619020 *fax:* 01952 610164. Chris Maddocks, theatre manager; Valerie Ballantyne, marketing and publicity. *Capacity:* 650.

Torquay. Babbacombe Theatre. Babbacombe Downs, Torquay, Devon TQ1 3LU *admin:* 01803 322233 *box office:* 01803 328385 *fax:* 01803 322244 *email:* matpro@btinternet.com. Margaret Brooks, theatre manager; Colin Matthews, director; Rebecca McDonald, marketing. *Capacity:* 600.

Torquay. Princess Theatre. Torbay Road, Torquay TQ2 5EZ *admin:* 01803 290288 *box office:* 01803 290290 *fax:* 01803 290170. Apollo Leisure (UK) Ltd, management: P R Gregg, chairman; Mike Adamson, managing director entertainment division. *Capacity:* 1,494.

Torquay. Riviera Centre. Chestnut Avenue, Torquay, Devon TQ2 5LZ *admin:* 01803 299992 *box office:* 01803 206333 *fax:* 01803 206310 *email:* erc@torbay.gov.uk. Barry Cole, general manager; Nicky Harding, new business development manager. *Forum Capacity:* 1,800; *Arena Capacity:* 1,800.

Truro. Hall for Cornwall. Back Quay, Truro, Cornwall TR1 2LL *admin:* 01872 262465 *box office:* 01872 262466 *fax:* 01872 260246 *email:* hallforcornwall@enterprise.net. Tim German, general manager; Chris Warner, artistic director; Trevor Gardiner, marketing manager. *Theatre Capacity:* 1,000; *Rock concert Capacity:* 1,700.

Tunbridge Wells. Assembly Hall Theatre. Crescent Road, Tunbridge Wells, Kent TN1 2LU *admin:* 01892 526121 *box office:* 01892 530613 *fax:* 01892 525203 *email:* info@t-wells.gov.uk. Brian McAteer, business manager; Pat Casey, theatre manager; Sheila Ryall, marketing and publicity manager. *Capacity:* 940.

Ulverston. Coronation Hall Theatre. County Square, Ulverston, Cumbria LA12 7LZ *admin:* 01229 582610 *box office:* 01229 587140 (TIC); 587120 *fax:* 01229 582610 *email:* corohall@furness.co.uk. Janet Ridal, hall manager; Gordon Crayston, technical manager; James Croasdale, senior caretaker. *Capacity:* 636.

Wakefield. Theatre Royal and Opera House. Drury Lane, Wakefield, W Yorks WF1 2TE *admin:* 01924 215531 *box office:* 01924 211311 *fax:* 01924 215525. Murray Edwards, general manager. *Capacity:* 509.

Walsall. Bloxwich Leisure Centre. High Street, Bloxwich, Walsall, W Midlands WS3 2DA *admin:* 01922 710295 *fax:* 01922 495925. Ishbel Bibby, service manager; S Wood, team leader; G Headley, D Brewer, B Gwilt, duty managers. *Function Hall Capacity:* 400.

Walsall. Walsall Town Hall. Leicester Street, Walsall, W Midlands WS1 1TZ *admin:* 01922 653170 *box office:* 01922 653183/653195 *fax:* 01922 721682. Brian Elwood, curator; Antonia Pompa, promotions and events manager; Sunita Lal-Kooner, bookings and administration. *Town Hall Capacity:* 1,000; *Lily Hall Capacity:* 100.

Warrington. Parr Hall. Palmyra Square, Warrington, Cheshire WA1 1BL *admin:* 01925 651178 *box office:* 01925 634958 *fax:* 01925 234144 *email:* parrhall@warrington.gov.uk. John Perry, manager; Richard Fleming, hallkeeper; Delphine Corcoran, house manager. *Capacity:* 1,100.

Watford. Colosseum. Rickmansworth Road, Watford, Herts WD1 7JN *admin:* 01923 445300 *box office:* 01923 445000 *fax:* 01923 445225. John Wallace, Paul Scarborough, management; Ollie Smith, director; James Delanoy, marketing and publicity. *Large Hall Capacity:* 1,440.

Watford. Palace Theatre. Clarendon Road, Watford, Herts WD1 1JZ *admin:* 01923 235455 *box office:* 01923 225671 *fax:* 01923 819664. Giles Croft, artistic director; Alastair Moir, administrative director; Yvonne Elston, marketing manager. *Capacity:* 643.

Wellingborough. Castle. Castle Way, Wellingborough, Northants NN8 1XA *admin:* 01933 229022 *box office:* 01933 270007 *fax:* 01933 229888 *email:* info@thecastle.org.uk. Graham Brown, executive director; Pat Souster, administrator; Gordon Glass, marketing manager. *Main House Capacity:* 505; *Studio Theatre Capacity:* 84.

West Bromwich. West Bromwich Town Hall. High Street, West Bromwich, W Midlands B70 8DX *admin:* 0121 569 3940 *fax:* 0121 569 3948. Ron Hughes, curator; Joy Thompson, bookings. *Main Hall Capacity:* 700.

Weston-Super-Mare. Playhouse Theatre. High Street, Weston-Super-Mare, N Somerset BS23 1HP *admin:* 01934 627457 *box office:* 01934 645544 *fax:* 01934 622888 *email:* playhouse@n-somerset.gov.uk. Murray Macdonald, general manager; Peter Magor, technical manager; William Pritchard, marketing manager. *Capacity:* 658.

Weston-Super-Mare. Winter Gardens Pavilion. Royal Parade, Weston-Super-Mare, N Somerset BS23 1AQ *admin:* 01934 417117 *box office:* 01934 645544 *fax:* 01934 612323. Vivienne Thomson, general manager; Flan Ball, customer services manager; David Gentle, technical manager. *Ballroom Capacity:* 550; *Prince Consort Hall Capacity:* 500.

Whitley Bay. Whitley Bay Playhouse. Marine Avenue, Whitley Bay NE26 1LZ *admin:* 0191 252 6857 *box office:* 0191 252 3505 *fax:* 0191 251 4949. Tim Flood, general manager; Gloria Frier, assistant manager; Alexis Greener, marketing. *Capacity:* 746.

Windsor. Theatre Royal. Thames Street, Windsor, Berks SL4 1PS *admin:* 01753 863444 *box office:* 01753 853888 *fax:* 01753 831673. Bill Kenwright, executive producer; Mark Piper, executive director; Rob Gale, production manager. *Capacity:* 633.

Woking. New Victoria Theatre. The Ambassadors, Peacocks, Woking, Surrey GU21 1GQ *box office:* 01483 761144 *fax:* 01483 770477. David Blyth, chief executive; Richard Wingate, general manager; Pat Westwell, marketing manager. *Capacity:* 1,338.

Wolverhampton. Civic Hall/Wulfrun Hall. North Street, Wolverhampton, WV1 1RQ *admin:* 01902 552122 *box office:* 01902 552121 *fax:* 01902 552123 *email:* wolvescivicwulfrun@dial.pipex.com. Andy Bennett, entertainments manager; Diane Rhodes, administrator; Mark Blackstock, general manager. *Civic Hall Capacity:* 2,040; *Wulfrun Hall Capacity:* 672.

Wolverhampton. Grand Theatre. Lichfield Street, Wolverhampton, W Midlands WV1 1DE *admin:* 01902 573300 *box office:* 01902 429212 *fax:* 01902 573301. Brian Goddard, chief executive; Tony Pugh, general manager; Gary Postins, financial controller. *Capacity:* 1,200.

Worthing. Assembly Hall. Stoke Abbott Road, Worthing, W Sussex BN11 1HQ *admin:* 01903 239999 ext 2502/3 *box office:* 01903 820500 *fax:* 01903 821124. Peter Bailey, theatre manager; Trevor Gray, business development manager; Louise Sommerstein, marketing manager. *Capacity:* 930.

Worthing. Connaught Theatre. Union Place, Worthing, W Sussex BN11 1LG *admin:* 01903 231799 *box office:* 01903 235333 *fax:* 01903 215337. David Smith, theatre administrator; Glenda Harkess, deputy theatre administrator; Derek Oakley, technical manager. *Main House Capacity:* 514; *Ritz Capacity:* 225.

Worthing. Pavilion Theatre. Marine Parade, Worthing, W Sussex BN11 3PX *admin:* 01903 239999 ext 2502 *box office:* 01903 820500 *fax:* 01903 821124. Peter Bailey, theatres manager; Trevor Gray, business development manager; Louise Sommerstein, marketing manager. *Capacity:* 850.

Yeovil. Octagon Theatre. Hendford, Yeovil, Somerset BA20 1UX *admin:* 01935 422836 *box office:* 01935 422884 *fax:* 01935 475281. John G White, general manager. *Capacity:* 625.

York. Grand Opera House. Cumberland Street, York YO1 9SW *admin:* 01904 655441 *box office:* 01904 671818 *fax:* 01904 671858. Ian Sime, general manager; Charlotte Rose, PA to general manager; David Turner, deputy manager. *Capacity:* 1,032.

York. Theatre Royal. St Leonard's Place, York YO1 7HD *admin:* 01904 658162 *box office:* 01904 623568 *fax:* 01904 611534. Elizabeth Jones, executive director; Damian Cruden, artistic director. *Capacity:* 863.

York. York Barbican Centre. Paragon Street, York YO10 4NT *admin:* 01904 628991 *box office:* 01904 656688 *fax:* 01904 628227 *email:* 100530.1026@compuserve.com. Daniel Brookes, assistant technical services manager. *Main Hall Capacity:* 1,500.

Channel Islands and Isle of Man

St Helier. Fort Regent Leisure Centre. Fort Regent Road, St Helier, Jersey JE2 4UX, Channel Islands *admin:* 01534 500200 *box office:* 01534 500227 *fax:* 01534 500225. Vic Bourgoise, chief officer; Tony Allman, technical supervisor; Allyson Holmes, leisure and recreation officer. *Gloucester Hall Capacity:* 1,974; *Queen's Hall Capacity:* 1,050.

St Peter Port. St James. College Street, St Peter Port, Guernsey GY1 2NZ, Channel Islands *admin:* 01481 711360 *box office:* 01481 711361 *fax:* 01481 711364. Kirstin R Simon, director. *Capacity:* 480.

Douglas. Gaiety Theatre. Harris Promenade, Douglas, Isle of Man *admin:* 01624 620046 *box office:* 01624 625001 *fax:* 01624 629028 *email:* gaietytheatre@iom.com. Mervin Russell Stokes, artistic director; Seamus Shea, technical contact; Annette Christian, house manager. *Capacity:* 869.

Douglas. Villa Marina. Harris Promenade, Douglas, Isle of Man *admin:* 01624 674171 *box office:* 01624 628855 *fax:* 01624 612119. Martin Blackburn, general manager; Viv Lennon, administrative officer; Iain Wylie, stage manager. *Royal Hall Capacity:* 1,573; *Garden Room Capacity:* 320.

Port Erin. Erin Arts Centre, Victoria Square, Port Erin, Isle of Man IM9 6LD *admin:* 01624 835858 *box office:* 01624 832662 *fax:* 01624 836658 *email:* erinartscentre@enterprise.net. John Bethell, artistic director; Martin Norbury, administrator. *Capacity:* 180.

Scotland

Aberdeen. Aberdeen Music Hall. Union Street, Aberdeen AB10 1QS *admin:* 01224 632080 ext 220 *box office:* 01224 641122 *fax:* 01224 632400 *email:* abzmusichall@dial.pipex.com. Duncan Hendry, general manager. *Capacity:* 1,282.

Aberdeen. Cowdray Hall. Schoolhill, Aberdeen, Grampian AB10 1FQ *admin:* 01224 646333 *box office:* 01224 641122 *fax:* 01224 632133 (Aberdeen Art Gallery). Duncan Hendry, operations manager; Karen McDonald, bookings. *Capacity:* 300.

Aberdeen. His Majesty's Theatre. Rosemount Viaduct, Aberdeen *admin:* 01224 637788 *box office:* 01224 641122 *fax:* 01224 632519 *email:* katns@arts-rec.aberdeen.net.uk. Martin Milne, operations manager; Lena Dowell, technical manager; Alison Lubek, sales and marketing manager. *Capacity:* 1,445.

Aberdeen. Lemon Tree. 5 West North Street, Aberdeen AB24 5AT *admin:* 01224 647999 *box office:* 01224 642230 *fax:* 01224 630888. Shona Powell, director; Andy Catlin, marketing officer; Simon Gane, technical manager. *Café Theatre Capacity:* 500; *Studio Theatre Capacity:* 150.

Ayr. Ayr Town Hall. New Bridge Street, Ayr KA7 1LX *admin:* 01292 612448 *fax:* 01292 612143. Graham Peterkin, director of support services; Andrew Bohan, hall keeper. *Capacity:* 712.

Ayr. Gaiety Theatre. Carrick Street, Ayr KA7 1NU *admin:* 01292 617400 *box office:* 01292 611222 *fax:* 01292 880044. Gordon Taylor, theatre manager; John Seaman, technical manager; Mary Townsend, box office manager. *Capacity:* 584.

Clydebank. Clydebank Town Hall. Dumbarton Road, Clydebank, Strathclyde G81 *admin:* 0141 952 1243 (hall); 01389 738660 *box office:* 01389 738537 *fax:* 0141 952 1243; 01389 738595. Billy McCabe, principal amenities officer. *Large Hall Capacity:* 522; *Lesser Hall Capacity:* 170.

Dundee. Caird Hall. City Square, Dundee DD1 3BB *admin:* 01382 434451 *also fax; box office:* 01382 434940. Susan Pasfield, Caird Hall manager. *Caird Hall Capacity:* 2,400; *Marryat Hall Capacity:* 400.

Dunfermline. Carnegie Hall. East Port, Dunfermline, Fife KY12 7JA *admin:* 01383 314110 *box office:* 01383 314127 *fax:* 01383 314131. Lesley O'Hare, arts co-ordinator. *Capacity:* 590.

Dunoon. Queen's Hall. Argyll Street, Dunoon, Argyll & Bute *admin:* 01369 702800 *fax:* 01369 705150. J Anderson, leisure services manager; Lorna White, assistant leisure services manager. *Main Hall Capacity:* 888.

Edinburgh. Assembly Rooms and Music Hall. 54 George Street, Edinburgh EH2 2LR *admin:* 0131 220 4348 *box office:* 0131 220 4349 *fax:* 0131 220 6812 *email:* assemblyrooms@dial.pipex.com. Simon Robson, general manager. *Assembly Room Capacity:* 450; *Music Hall Capacity:* 730; *Supper Room Capacity:* 150.

Edinburgh. Edinburgh Festival Theatre. 13-29 Nicolson Street, Edinburgh EH8 9FT *admin:* 0131 662 1112 *box office:* 0131 529 6000 *fax:* 0131 667 0744 (admin); 0131 662 1199 (box office) *email:* empire@edfestth.demon.co.uk. Stephen Barry, general manager; Helen Bates, finance manager. *Capacity:* 1,913.

Edinburgh. King's Theatre. 2 Leven Street, Edinburgh EH3 9LQ *admin:* 0131 662 1112 *box office:* 0131 529 6000. Staff as Edinburgh Festival Theatre. *Capacity:* 1,336.

Edinburgh. Playhouse Theatre. 18-22 Greenside Place, Edinburgh EH1 3AA *admin:* 0131 557 2692 *box office:* 0131 557 2590 *fax:* 0131 557 6520. Apollo Leisure (UK) Ltd, proprietors; P R Gregg, managing director; Andy Lyst, general manager. *Theatre Capacity:* 3,056.

Edinburgh. Queen's Hall. Clerk Street, Edinburgh EH8 9JG *admin:* 0131 668 3456 *box office:* 0131 668 2019 *fax:* 0131 668 2656 *email:* queenshall@cableinet.com. Beth Cavanagh, general manager; Gwen Orr, hall manager. *Main Auditorium Capacity:* 800.

Edinburgh. Reid Concert Hall. 14 Bristo Square, Teviot Place, Edinburgh EH8 9AH *admin:* 0131 650 2423 *fax:* 0131 650 2425. D R B Kimbell, dean, faculty of music; Fiona Donaldson, concert secretary. *Capacity:* 300.

Edinburgh. Ross Theatre. Princes Street Gardens, Edinburgh *admin:* 0131 228 8616 *fax:* 0131 228 8848. Moira McKenzie, administration; James Hulligan, technical. *Capacity:* 1,500.

Edinburgh. Usher Hall. Lothian Road, Edinburgh EH1 2EA *admin:* 0131 228 8616 *box office:* 0131 228 1155 *fax:* 0131 228 8848. Moira McKenzie, manager; Fiona Easton, assistant. *Capacity:* 2,215.

Elgin. Elgin Town Hall. 5 Trinity Place, Elgin, Grampian IV30 1VL *admin:* 01343 563403 *box office:* 01343 562600 *fax:* 01343 562610 *email:* macraed@techleis.moray.gov.uk. Duncan Macrae, manager; William McCook, caretaker. *Capacity:* 692.

Falkirk. Falkirk Town Hall. c/o Community and Leisure Services, Kilns House, Kilns Road, Falkirk FK1 5SA *admin:* 01324 506176 *box office:* 01324 506850 *fax:* 01324 506171. A Craig Murray, entertainments manager; Jane Clark, entertainments officer; Morag Cochrane, assistant entertainments officer. *Main Hall Capacity:* 900; *Lesser Hall Capacity:* 200.

Forfar. Reid Hall. Castle Street, Forfar, Tayside DD8 5JX *admin:* 01307 461460 *fax:* 01307 462590. Sandy Thomson, arts officer. *Capacity:* 829.

Fort William. Marco's An Aird. An Aird, Fort William PH33 6AN *admin:* 01397 700707 *also box office; fax:* 01397 700708. Barry I Mason, centre manager. *An Aird Hall Capacity:* 1,700; *Lounge Capacity:* 500.

Galashiels. Volunteer Hall. St John Street, Galashiels, Selkirkshire *admin:* 01896 754751. D Harrison, hall manager; John Brotherston, caretaker. *Capacity:* 553.

Glasgow. City Hall. Candleriggs, Glasgow G1 1NQ *admin:* 0141 287 5005 *box office:* 0141 287 5511. Bridget McConnell, director, cultural and leisure service; S Miller, ticket centre manager; Susan Deighan, arts programming manager. *Grand Hall Capacity:* 1,216.

Glasgow. Glasgow Royal Concert Hall. 2 Sauchiehall Street, Glasgow G2 3NY *admin:* 0141 332 6633 *box office:* 0141 287 5511 *fax:* 0141 333 9123 (admin); 0141 353 4150 (stage dept) *email:* grch@grchscotnet.co.uk. Louise Mitchell, director; Arthur Laird, finance and administration; Phil Smith, production. *Concert Hall Capacity:* 2,417; *Strathclyde Suite Capacity:* 500.

Glasgow. Henry Wood Hall. RSNO Centre, 73 Claremont Street, Glasgow G3 7JB *admin:* 0141 225 3555 *fax:* 0141 221 4317 *email:* rsno@glasgow.almac.co.uk. Simon Crookall, manager; Ann Elliott, administrator. *Capacity:* 500.

Glasgow. King's Theatre. Bath Street, Glasgow G2 4JN *admin:* 0141 287 5429 *box office:* 0141 287 5511 *fax:* 0141 287 5533. Bridget McConnell, director; Edward O'Toole, stage manager; Pauline Murphy, programmer. *Capacity:* 1,785.

Glasgow. Theatre Royal. 282 Hope Street, Glasgow G2 3QA *admin:* 0141 332 3321 *box office:* 0141 332 9000 *fax:* 0141 332 4477 *email:* scotoptech@compuserve.com (Chief LX). Diane Long, theatre manager; Roberta Doyle, press and marketing director; Julian Sleath, technical director. *Capacity:* 1,445.

Glasgow. Tramway. 25 Albert Drive, Glasgow G41 2PE *admin:* 0141 287 3921/2/3/4 *box office:* 0141 287 3900 *fax:* 0141 422 2021. Susan Deighan, Steve Slater, performing arts programming; Alexia Holt, visual arts programming. *Tramway 1 Capacity:* 600; *Tramway 2 Capacity:* 1,500; *Tramway 4 Capacity:* 115.

Glenrothes. Rothes Halls. Kingdom Centre, Rothes Square, Glenrothes, Fife KY7 5NX *admin:* 01592 612121 *box office:* 01592 611101 *fax:* 01592 612220 *email:* rothes_halls@dial.pipex.com. Frank Chinn, halls manager; Nick Weeks, technical manager. *Hall A Capacity:* 720; *Hall B Capacity:* 204.

Hawick. Hawick Town Hall. High Street, Hawick TD9 9EF. Alister Murdie, hall manager. *Capacity:* 634.

Inverness. Eden Court Theatre. Bishop's Road, Inverness IV3 5SA *admin:* 01463 239841 *box office:* 01463 234234 *fax:* 01463 713810 *email:* ecmail@cali.co.uk. Colin Marr, theatre director; Jim Clark, technical manager; Kirsten MacDougall, marketing manager. *Capacity:* 814.

Kilmarnock. Grand Hall. London Road, Kilmarnock *admin:* 01563 537710 *box office:* 01563 523590 *fax:* 01563 573047. Bruce Gilmour, theatre manager. *Capacity:* 900.

Kilmarnock. Palace Theatre. 9 Green Street, Kilmarnock KA1 3BN *admin:* 01563 537710 *box office:* 01563 523590 *fax:* 01563 573047. Bruce Gilmour, theatre manager. *Capacity:* 503.

Kirkwall. Phoenix Cinema. Junction Road, Kirkwall, Orkney KW15 1AX *admin:* 01856 873535 ext 2404 *fax:* 01856 870302. William Scolley, cinema manager. *Capacity:* 520.

Lerwick. Clickimin Centre. Lochside, Lerwick, Shetland ZE1 0PJ *admin:* 01595 741000 *also fax*. Shona Nisbet, centre manager; Robert Leask, Maurice Haining, assistant managers; David Leslie. *Capacity:* 1,200.

Lerwick. Lerwick Town Hall. Hillhead, Lerwick, Mainland, Shetland ZE1 0HB *admin:* 01595 744500 *fax:* 01595 744509. Hazel Anderson, executive office manager. *Capacity:* 200.

Motherwell. Motherwell Theatre and Concert Hall. PO Box 14, Civic Centre, Motherwell, Lanarkshire ML1 1TW *admin:* 01698 267515 *also box office; fax:* 01698 268806. Ann Malloy, head of cultural services; Lizanne McMurrich, arts and venues manager; Stuart Archibald, technical manager. *Concert Hall Capacity:* 1,008; *Theatre Capacity:* 395.

Perth. Perth City Hall. King Edward Street, Perth, Perthshire PH1 5UG *admin:* 01738 624055 *fax:* 01738 630566. Drew Scott, general manager; Nikki Annand, lettings officer. *Large City Hall Capacity:* 1,600; *Lesser City Hall Capacity:* 300.

Pitlochry. Festival Theatre. Port-na-craig, Pitlochry, Perthshire PH16 5DR *admin:* 01796 484600 *box office:* 01796 484626 *fax:* 01796 484616 *email:* admin@pitlochry.org.uk. Clive Perry, festival director; Sheila Harborth, festival administrator. *Capacity:* 544.

Rothesay. Pavilion. 45 Argyle Street, Rothesay, Isle of Bute PA20 0A *admin:* 01700 504250. D McCombe, theatre manager; George Harper, director, development and environment. *Main Hall Capacity:* 1,250.

St Andrews. Younger Graduation Hall. University of St Andrews, North Street, St Andrews KY16 9AJ *admin:* 01334 462226 *fax:* 01334 462570 *email:* music@st-andrews.ac.uk. Alison Malcolm, administrator. *Capacity:* 968.

Stirling. Albert Halls. Albert Place, Dumbarton Road, Stirling FK8 2QL *admin:* 01786 473544 *also box office; fax:* 01786 448933 *email:* mccarthya@stirling.gov.uk. Anne Marie McCarthy, venues manager; Diane Rae, box office manager; Willie Mason, operations. *Main Hall Capacity:* 883; *Lesser Hall Capacity:* 150.

Stirling. Macrobert Arts Centre. University of Stirling, Stirling FK9 4LA *admin:* 01786 467155 *box office:* 01786 461081. Elizabeth Moran, director; Bill Armitage, general manager; Colin Proudfoot, technical manager. *Main Theatre Capacity:* 500; *Studio Capacity:* 140.

Wales

Aberdare. Coliseum. Mount Pleasant Street, Trecynon, Aberdare CF44 8NG *admin:* 01685 882380 *box office:* 01685 881188 *fax:* 01685 883000. Adrian Williams, general manager and licensee; Ioan Wynne, technical manager. *Capacity:* 617.

Aberystwyth. Aberystwyth Arts Centre. University of Wales Aberystwyth, Penglais, Aberystwyth, Ceredigion SY23 3DE *admin:* 01970 622882 *box office:* 01970 623232 *fax:* 01970 622883 *email:* lla@aber.ac.uk. Alan Hewson, director; Maris Davies, administrator; Louise Amery, marketing manager. *Theatre Capacity:* 327; *Concert Hall Capacity:* 900; *Studio Theatre Capacity:* 120.

Barry. Memorial Hall Theatre. Gladstone Road, Barry, S Glamorgan CF62 8NA *admin:* 01446 738663 *fax:* 01446 741626. I J Harris, executive officer. *Main Hall Capacity:* 1,111; *Glamorgan Suite Capacity:* 150; *Bedwas Hall Capacity:* 150.

Cardiff. Cardiff International Arena. Mary Ann Street, Cardiff CF1 2EQ *admin:* 029 2023 4500 *box office:* 029 2022 4488 *fax:* 029 2023 4501. Paul Latham, divisional manager; Graham Walters, general manager; Sharon Phillips, sales manager. *Arena Capacity:* 5,500; *Conference Suite Capacity:* 400; *Novello/Langley Suite Capacity:* 336.

Cardiff. Great Hall/Terminal 396. University Union, Park Place, Cathays, Cardiff CF1 3QN *admin:* 029 2078 1456 *box office:* 029 2038 7421 *fax:* 029 2078 1407 *email:* ssucw@cf.ac.uk. Vanesa Thomas, administration manager; Chrissy Woodman, entertainments manager; Roy Bryan, finance manager. *Great Hall Capacity:* 1,350; *Terminal 396 Capacity:* 1,600; *Finistere Capacity:* 300.

Cardiff. New Theatre. Park Place, Cardiff CF10 3LN *admin:* 029 2087 8787 *box office:* 029 2087 8889 *fax:* 029 2087 8788. Giles Ballisat, general manager; Judi Richards, head of arts and cultural services; Michael Gremsted, head of marketing. *Capacity:* 1,156.

Cardiff. St David's Hall. The Hayes, Cardiff CF10 1SH *admin:* 029 2087 8500 *box office:* 029 2087 8444 *fax:* 029 2087 8517. Judi Richards, head of arts and cultural services; Tony Williams, operations manager. *Capacity:* 1,956.

Cardiff. University Concert Hall. Department of Music, University of Wales, Corbett Road, Cardiff CF10 3EB *admin:* 029 2087 4816 *fax:* 029 2087 4379 *email:* RobertsAJI@cardiff.ac.uk. *Capacity:* 250.

Carmarthen. Lyric Theatre. King Street, Carmarthen, Camarthenshire SA31 *admin:* 01267 238685 *box office:* 01267 232632 *fax:* 01267 234559. Elizabeth Evans, artistic and theatre director; David Evans, technical manager. *Capacity:* 740.

Llandrindod Wells. Pavilion. Spa Road, Llandrindod Wells, Powys LD1 5EY *admin:* 01597 823532 *fax:* 01597 824413 *email:* pavilion @powys.gov.uk. Carolyn Flynn, manager. *Capacity:* 565.

Llandudno. North Wales Theatre & Conference Centre. The Promenade, Llandudno LL30 1BB *admin:* 01492 879771 *box office:* 01492 872000 *fax:* 01492 860790 *email:* info@nwtheatre.co.uk. Nick Reed (ext 1202), general manager; Bridget Jones (ext 1203), operations manager; Huw Roberts (ext 1233), marketing officer. *North Wales Theatre Capacity:* 1,500; *North Wales Conference Centre Capacity:* 970.

Llangollen. Royal International Pavilion. Abbey Road, Llangollen, LL20 8SW *admin:* 01978 860111 *fax:* 01978 860046 *email:* jeremy.miles@denbighshire.gov.uk. Jeremy Miles, general manager; Christine Griffith, Carol Ann Evans, duty officer team. *Arena Capacity:* 1,495; *Main Hall Capacity:* 400.

Mold. Clwyd Theatr Cymru. Mold, Flintshire CH7 1YA *admin:* 01352 756331 *box office:* 01352 755114 *fax:* 01352 758323 *email:* drama@celtic.co.uk. Terry Hands, director; Sarah Holmes, general manager; Ann Williams, marketing manager. *Anthony Hopkins Theatre Capacity:* 580; *Emlyn Williams Theatre Capacity:* 200; *Clwyd Room Capacity:* 300.

Neath. Gwyn Hall. Orchard Street, Neath, SA11 1BN *admin:* 01639 635013 (Council) *box office:* 01639 642019 *fax:* 01639 620230. Angie Dickinson, halls manager. *Main Hall Capacity:* 686.

Newport. Newport Centre. Kingsway, Newport NP9 1UH *admin:* 01633 662663 *box office:* 01633 662666 *fax:* 01633 662675. Roger Broome, events officer; Glenys Hawkes, box office manager; Simon Jones, general manager. *Main Hall Capacity:* 2,024; *Riverside Suite Capacity:* 400.

Newtown. Theatr Hafren. Llanidloes Road, Newtown, Powys SY16 4HU *admin:* 01686 625447 *box office:* 01686 625007 *fax:* 01686 625446 *email:* th-marketing@coleg-powys.ac.uk. Sara Clutton, administrator; Iain Kempton, marketing manager; Barbara Jones, house manager. *Capacity:* 568.

Pontardawe. Theatr Cwmtawe. Pontardawe Leisure Centre, Herbert St, Pontardawe, Swansea SA8 4ED *admin:* 01792 863722. Jacqueline Michelle Barker, general manager. *Theatre Capacity:* 460; *Sports Hall Capacity:* 600.

Porthcawl. Grand Pavilion. The Esplanade, Porthcawl CF36 3YW *admin:* 01656 783860 *box office:* 01656 786996 *fax:* 01656 772111. Jason Crook, manager. *Main Hall Capacity:* 637.

Rhyl. Coliseum Theatre. West Promenade, Rhyl, Denbighshire LL18 1H *admin:* 01745 351126 *also box office; fax:* 01745 351126. Aubrey Phillips, theatre director; D Denver, production and technical manager; Patrick Newley, press officer. *Capacity:* 630.

Rhyl. Pavilion Theatre. Promenade, Rhyl LL18 3AQ *admin:* 01745 332414 *box office:* 01745 330000 *fax:* 01745 339819 *email:* gareth.owen@denbighshire.gov.uk. Gareth Owen, theatre manager; Andrew Hughes, technical manager. *Capacity:* 1,032.

Swansea. Brangwyn Hall. Guildhall, Swansea SA1 4PN *admin:* 01792 635489. Sean Keir, general manager. *Capacity:* 1,198.

Swansea. Grand Theatre. Singleton Street, Swansea, SA1 3QJ *admin:* 01792 475242 *box office:* 01792 475715 *fax:* 01792 475379. Gary Iles, general manager. *Capacity:* 1,019.

Swansea. Penyrheol Theatre. Pontarddulais Road, Swansea, West Glamorgon, SA4 4FG *admin:* 01792 897039 *also box office; fax:* 01792 894931. David Osborne, manager. *Penyrheol Theatre Capacity:* 600; *Dance Studio Capacity:* 50.

Treorchy. Park & Dare Theatre. Station Road, Treorchy, Mid-Glamorgan, CF42 6NL *admin:* 01443 776689/472461 *box office:* 01443 773112 *fax:* 01443 776922. E Bowen, manager. *Theatre Capacity:* 750; *Theatre Lounge Capacity:* 150.

Northern Ireland

Ballymena. Ballymena Town Hall. Bridge Street, Ballymena, Co Antrim BT42 5AE *admin:* 028 2565 6262 *fax:* 028 2566 0400. Rosalind Lowry, arts officer, Ballymena BC. *Main Hall Capacity:* 670; *Minor Hall Capacity:* 200.

Belfast. Belfast Waterfront Hall. Lanyon Place, Belfast, Co Antrim *admin:* 028 9033 4400 *box office:* 028 9033 4455 *fax:* 028 9024 9862 *email:* kyle@belfastcity.gov.uk. Tim Husbands, general manager; Andrew Kyle, sales and marketing manager; Mark McBride, finance and administration manager. *Main Auditorium Capacity:* 2,235; *BT Studio Capacity:* 500; *Foyer Performance Space Capacity:* 100.

Belfast. Elmwood Hall at Queen's. 89 University Road, Belfast, Co Antrim BT7 1NF *admin:* 028 9066 4535 *fax:* 028 9066 2761. Barbara McKinley, Elmwood Hall manager; Kenneth Dennis, caretaker. *Capacity:* 518.

Belfast. Grand Opera House. Great Victoria Street, Belfast, Co Antrim BT2 7HR *admin:* 028 9024 0411 *box office:* 028 9024 1919 (ticket shop) *fax:* 028 9023 6842. Derek Nicholls, theatre director. *Capacity:* 1,001.

Belfast. Queen's University Concert Halls. University Road, Belfast, Co Antrim BT7 1NN *admin:* 028 9024 5133 ext 3052 *fax:* 028 9066 3733. Robert Agnew (ext 4286), festival executive director; Pauline Banna, assistant secretary of estates office; Elizabeth Moore, bookings. *Whitla Hall Capacity:* 1,224; *Harty Room Capacity:* 200.

Belfast. Ulster Hall. Bedford Street, Belfast, Co Antrim BT2 7FF *admin:* 028 9032 3900 *fax:* 028 9024 7199. P Falls, manager. *Capacity:* 1,600.

Coleraine. Diamond. University of Ulster, Cromore Road, Coleraine BT52 1GA *admin:* 028 7032 3058 *fax:* 028 7032 4160 *email:* u.donnelly@ulst.ac.uk. Una Donnelly, Laura Hernberg, bookings; David Simpson (*tel:* 01265 324247), technical; Dr Irena Adams (*tel:* 01265 324072), university arts administrator. *The Diamond Capacity:* 1,200; *The Octagon Capacity:* 400.

Derry. Guildhall. Shipquay Place, Derry, Co Londonderry, BT48 6DQ *admin:* 028 7137 7335 *box office:* 028 7126 0516/2567 *fax:* 028 7137 9757. John Keanie, town clerk and chief executive; Damien McMahon, city secretary and solicitor; Cathal Logue, director, recreation and leisure. *Main Hall Capacity:* 571; *Minor Hall Capacity:* 100.

Derry. Rialto Entertainment Centre. Market Street, Derry, Co Londonderry, BT48 6EF *admin:* 028 7126 4177 *box office:* 028 7126 0516 *fax:* 028 7126 0688. David McLaughlin, venues manager; Johnny Murray, FOH and box office manager; Paula Bradley, administration and promotions officer. *Capacity:* 988.

Downpatrick. Down Leisure Centre. 114 Market Street, Downpatrick, Co Down BT30 6LZ *admin:* 028 4461 3426 *fax:* 01395 616905. Macartan Bryce, general manager. *Main Hall Capacity:* 650.

Irvinestown. Bawnacre Centre. Irvinestown, Co Fermanagh BT94 1EE *admin:* 028 6862 1177 *fax:* 028 6862 8082 *email:* georgebeacom @fermanagh.gov.uk. George Beacom, centre manager. *Main Hall Capacity:* 800; *Minor Hall Capacity:* 300.

Newry. Newry Town Hall. Bank Parade, Newry, Co Down BT35 6HP *admin:* 028 3026 6232 *also box office; fax:* 028 3026 6177. Mark Hughes, artistic director. *Capacity:* 500.

Newtownabbey. Assembly Hall. University of Ulster, Jordanstown, Shore Road, Newtownabbey, BT37 0QB *admin:* 028 7032 3058 *fax:* 028 7032 4160 *email:* u.donnelly@ulst.ac.uk. Una Donnelly, conference manager. *Assembly Hall Capacity:* 1,100; *Dalriada Hall Capacity:* 500.

Omagh. Omagh Leisure Centre. Old Mountfield Road, Omagh, Co Tyrone BT79 7BL *admin:* 028 8224 6711 *fax:* 028 8225 1926. Philip Faithfull, chief contract services officer; Frank Sweeny, recreation officer, arts. *Main Hall Capacity:* 550; *Small Hall Capacity:* 200.

Music in Places of Worship

This section covers both the use of places of worship for regular concert series and the integral part played by music within the services of each denomination.

Lunchtime Concert Venues

Some of the following churches have a long-standing tradition of lunchtime or evening concert promotion; others offer infrequent performance opportunities. An asterisk indicates that a regular concert series takes place at the church. *The London Organ Concerts Guide* provides information about organ concerts in Greater London and is available from Catherine Ennis, 27 Southwood Ave, London N6 5SA.

Greater London

* **Grosvenor Chapel.** South Audley St, London W1 *tel:* 01923 828522 *also fax;* 020 7499 1684. Richard Hobson, org. *Fortnightly, Tue lunchtime. Mostly org and early mus.*

* **St Anne & St Agnes.** Gresham St, London EC2 7BX *tel:* 020 7606 4986 *fax:* 020 7600 8984 *email:* 74434.152@compuserve.com. Peter Lea-Cox, cantor. *Weekly, Mon 1.10pm; token fee; ens preferred (pro, semi-pro). Grand pno, org, power-points, changing room.*

* **St Bride's Church.** Fleet St, London EC4Y 8AU *tel:* 020 7353 1301 *fax:* 020 7583 4867. Matthew Busby, admin. *3 times weekly, 1.15pm; max 40 musicians (students, semi-pro, pro). Org, grand pno, power-points, changing rooms.*

* **St George's Church, Bloomsbury.** c/o 66 Hyde Way, Hayes, Middx UB3 4PB *tel:* 020 8606 0030 *fax:* 020 8606 0037. Rod Burnett, concerts consultant. *Tue 1.10pm and Sun 5pm (Sun only in summer). Grand pno. Enquiries in writing to 20 Tuckett Rd, Woodhouse Eaves, Leics LE12 8SE.*

* **St James's Church.** 197 Piccadilly, London W1V 0LL *tel:* 020 7381 0441 *also fax.* Sarah Baxter, concert mgr. *Lunchtime recitals 1-1.55pm; Mon, Wed, Fri. Capacity 10 singers. Evening concerts Thu, Fri, Sat. Capacity 30 singers plus orch of 30, 10 at lunch time. Concert lighting, org, chmbr org, grand pno, power-points, changing rooms.*

* **St John's, Smith Square.** London SW1P 3HA *tel:* 020 7222 1061 *fax:* 020 7233 1618. *Alternate Thu, Oct-Jul, 1pm.*

* **St John's, Waterloo Road.** Waterloo Rd, London SE1 8TY *tel:* 020 7366 9279 *fax:* 0870 111 8391 *email:* livemusic@lineone.net. *Weekly, Wed 1.10pm. Chmbr recitals. Written enquiries to Live Music, 12 Bradbury House, Commercial St, London E1 7NX.*

* **St Lawrence Jewry next Guildhall.** London EC2V 5AA *tel:* 020 7600 9478. James Common, admin. *Weekly, Mon 1-1.45pm (pno recitals), Tue 1-1.45pm (org recitals); expenses; changing facilities. Mus festival in Aug.*

* **St Margaret Lothbury.** London EC2R 7HH *tel:* c/o 020 7589 1206 *fax:* 020 7589 5925. Richard Townend, artistic dir; John Budgen, chmn. *Lunchtime lecture recitals, Thu 1.10pm; also lectures and tutorials on the org and an annual series of international celebrity org and choral concerts.*

* **St Martin-in-the-Fields Church.** Trafalgar Square, London WC2N 4JJ *tel:* 020 7839 1930 *fax:* 020 7839 5163. Paul Stubbings, master of the mus. *Weekly; Mon, Tue, Fri 1.05pm; large and small ens, soloists (auditions). Org, chmbr org, Blüthner concert grand, power-points, changing facilities, restaurant.*

* **St Martin-within-Ludgate Church.** Ludgate Hill, London EC4M 7DR *tel:* 020 7248 6054 *also fax.* Douglas Nurse, mus maker. *Weekly, Tue and Wed 1.15-1.45pm; choirs up to 25, ens up to sextet, soloists (pro, semi-pro); org, Bechstein grand pno.*

* **St Mary Abbots.** Kensington High St, London W8 4LA *tel:* 020 7937 5136. Denny Lyster, concerts mgr. *Fri 1.10-1.50pm. No fees. Grand pno. Singers, instrumentalists, small ens. Young artists preferred.*

St Mary-at-Hill Church. Lovat Lane, off Eastcheap, London EC3R 8EE *tel:* 01737 244604 *fax:* 01737 271128. Jonathan Rennert, dir of mus. *Approximately monthly, Tue 1pm. Performance of a Bach cantata(s) with the St Mary-at-Hill Baroque Players and Soloists. Other concerts by special arrangement. Grand piano, movable seating.*

* **St Mary-le-Strand.** Strand, London WC2R 1EP. Paul Weaver, dir of mus. *Lunchtime recitals throughout the year except during Lent. Church also available for hire. Semi-pro, pro groups, students and individuals. Org, baby grand pno, power-points, toilet, kitchen area, mus stands. Application by letter only.*

* **St Michael's Church.** Cornhill, London EC3V 9DS *tel:* 020 7626 8841; 01737 244604 *fax:* 01737 271128. Jonathan Rennert, dir of mus. *Weekly org recitals, Mon 1pm (except public holidays); other occasional concerts, times by arrangement; organists, specialists in British mus preferred. Org, chmbr org, upright pno, power-points, changing rooms.*

* **St Olave's Church.** 8 Hart St, London EC3R TNB *tel:* 020 7488 4318 *fax:* 020 7702 0811. Rev John Cowling, rector. *Weekly; Wed, Thu 1.05pm; expenses; young pro pianists and ens preferred. Org, power-points.*

* **Southwark Cathedral.** Montague Close, London SE1 9DA *tel:* 020 7367 6700 *fax:* 020 7367 6725 *email:* cathedral@dswark.org.uk. Rose Harding *tel:* 020 7367 6722. *Weekly (outside term-time of mus colleges when concerts are given by mus students); Tue 1.10pm-1.50pm; retiring collection. Grand pno, power-points, changing rooms.*

The Temple Church. PO Box 16090, London EC4Y 7HS *tel:* 020 7936 4766 *fax:* 020 7936 4767 *email:* directorofmusic@templechurch.com. Stephen Layton, dir of mus and organist; James Vivian, sub organist.

Westminster Abbey. c/o Chapter Office, 20 Deans Yard, London SW1P 3PA *tel:* 020 7222 5152 *fax:* 020 7233 2072 *email:* music@westminster-abbey.org. *Free org recitals, Sun 5.45pm.*

England, Scotland and Wales

* **Birmingham.** Birmingham Cathedral, Colmore Row, Birmingham B3 2QB *tel:* 0121 236 4333/6323 *fax:* 0121 212 0868. *Weekly org recitals, Mon 1pm. Mus recitals (org, chmbr mus, etc), Fri 1.10pm.*

* **Blackburn.** Blackburn Cathedral, Cathedral Close, Blackburn BB1 5AA *tel:* 01254 51491 *fax:* 01254 699963 *email:* richard.tanner@blackburn.anglican.org. *Lunchtime concerts, Wed 1pm, Oct-Jul.*

Bridlington. The Priory, 36 St Columba Rd, Bridlington, E Yorks YO16 6QX *tel:* 01262 670869 *also fax; email:* admin@mtsmith.newnet.co.uk. *Summer recital series, Wed 7.30pm, Jul-Aug.*

* **Bristol.** Bristol Cathedral, Bristol BS1 5TJ *tel:* 0117 926 4879 *fax:* 0117 925 3678. *Term-time, Tue 1.15pm.*

Bristol. Clifton Cathedral, Clifton Park, Bristol BS8 3BX *tel:* 0117 946 7456 *fax:* 0117 973 8263. Monsignor William Mitchell, admin; David Ogden, dir of mus. *Twice monthly, Sat 4pm; fees occasionally paid, otherwise hire charge. Rieger 3-manual org, Schiedermayer grand pno, power-points, changing and rehearsal rooms.*

Canterbury. Christ Church Cathedral, 6 The Precincts, Canterbury CT1 2EE *tel:* 01227 762862 *fax:* 01227 865222. David Flood, organist; Revd Kevin Goss, precentor. *Informal recitals by visiting choirs, many from overseas; a cappella, sacred mus. 12 noon.*

* **Chester.** Chester Cathedral, c/o The Cathedral Office, 12 Abbey Square, Chester CH1 2HU *tel:* 01244 324756 *fax:* 01244 341110. Nicholas Fry, visitors offr. *Org recitals; Thu 1.10pm.*

* **Chichester.** Chichester Cathedral, 2 St Richard's Walk, Chichester, W Sussex PO19 1QA *tel:* 01243 784790 *fax:* 01243 536190. *Term-time; Tue 1.10pm*

* **Coventry Cathedral.** 7 Priory Row, Coventry CV1 5ES *tel:* 024 7622 7597 *fax:* 024 7663 1448 *email:* music@coventrycathedral.org. *Org recitals; Mon 1pm; May-Sep.*

* **Dunblane.** Dunblane Cathedral, The Cross, Dunblane FK15 0AQ *tel:* 01786 870657. Matthew Beetscher. *Sat 12 noon, Jun-Sep. Mostly org recitals (1990 Flentrop org).*

* **Edinburgh.** St Giles' Cathedral, High St, Edinburgh EH1 1RE *tel:* 0131 225 9442 *fax:* 0131 220 4763 *email:* DramAHic@aol.com. Jan-Andrew Henderson, visitor services mgr. *Apr-Jun; Thu 1.10pm, Sep-Oct, org recitals. Frequent choral recitals, weekdays 12.15pm.*

Falmouth. Parish Church of King Charles the Martyr, Oyster Cottage, Helford Passage, Mawnan Smith, Falmouth TR11 5LA *tel:* 01326 250638. Robert Bates. *Capacity 450, 3-manual org, pno, power-points, changing rooms. Concerts by arrangement.*

Gloucester. Gloucester Cathedral, Chapter Office, 17 College Green, Gloucester *tel:* 01452 528695 *also fax. Monthly, Sat 12.30pm, May-Oct. Summer org recitals.*

* **Grimsby.** Grimsby Parish Church, The Parish Office, St James' House, St James Square, Grimsby, N E Lincs DN31 1EP *tel:* 01472 358610 *fax:* 01472 250751 *email:* parishoffice@saintjames.freeserve.co.uk. Steven J Maxson, organist. *Org recitals, first Fri of each month, 1pm.*

Leamington Spa. All Saints Parish Church, PO Box 163, Bath St, Leamington Spa, Warwicks CV31 1AA *tel:* 01926 429169 *also fax; email:* allsaints@ukf.net. Richard Taulbut, sec. *4-manual org; pnos; changing/rehearsal rooms. Bank Holiday Monday org recital 11am. Choral and inst concerts; occasional fees or hire charge.*

* **Leicester.** Leicester Cathedral, St Martin's, Leicester LE1 5FX *tel:* 0116 262 5294 *fax:* 0116 262 5295. *Term-time, Mon 1.05pm; Jul-Aug, Tue 8pm.*

* **Newcastle.** Cathedral Church of St Nicholas, Newcastle upon Tyne NE1 1PF *tel:* 0191 261 4505 *fax:* 0191 230 0735. Timothy Hone, dir of mus. *Weekly (Easter-Autumn), Mon 1pm; expenses; usually organists (students and young professionals). 4-manual Nicholson org, changing rooms, refectory facilities.*

* **Norwich.** St Peter Mancroft, 56a The Close, Norwich, Norfolk NR1 4EH *tel:* 01603 614305. Roger Rayner, sec and publicity. *Fri lunchtime concert series, usually 2nd and 4th of month, May-Oct. Mainly org recitals on outstanding classical org. Refreshments always available.*

Rochester Cathedral. The Cathedral Office, Garth House, The Precinct, Rochester, Kent ME1 1SX *tel:* 01634 849683 *fax:* 01634 401410. *Org recitals; occasional Sats 6.30pm, Apr-Sep.*

St Davids. St Davids Cathedral, The Organist's Lodgings, Cathedral Close, St Davids, Pembs SA62 6PE *tel:* 01437 720128 *fax:* 01437 721813 *email:* grlbowen@aol.com. *Weekly org recitals, Tue 8.15pm, Jul-Aug.*

Southwell. Southwell Cathedral, 4 Vicars' Court, Southwell, Notts NG25 0HP *tel:* 01636 812228 *also fax; email:* rectorchori@diaphone.clara.net. Paul R Hale, mus dir. *Bank holidays; org recitals 3.30pm, Apr-Aug; free admission.*

* **Tewkesbury.** Tewkesbury Abbey, 40 Church St, Tewkesbury, Glos GL20 5SN *tel:* 01684 298177/850959 *fax:* 01684 273113. *Tue 1pm, Jul-Sep.*

* **Truro.** Truro Cathedral, 21 Old Bridge St, Truro, Cornwall TR1 2AH *tel:* 01872 276782 *fax:* 01872 277788. Andrew Nethsingha, organist. *Org recitals; Fri 1.10pm, Apr-Oct.*

* **Winchester.** Winchester Cathedral, 1 The Close, Winchester SO23 9LS *tel:* 01962 857200 *fax:* 01962 857201 *email:* cathedral.office@winchester-cathedral.org.uk; sandy.davis@winchester-cathedral.org.uk. *Tue 1.10pm, Jun-Sep.*

Organisations

Church Music Society. 17 Fulneck, Pudsey, W Yorks LS28 8NT *tel:* 0113 255 6143 *also fax; email:* simonlin@nascr.net. Simon Lindley, hon sec.

Friends of Cathedral Music. Aeron House, Llangeitho, Tregaron, Dyfed SY25 6SU. M J Cooke, hon sec; Alan Thurlow, chmn.

Gregorian Association. 26 The Grove, London W5 5LH *tel:* 020 8840 5832. Grey Macartney, chmn; Peter Wilton, mus dir.

Guild of Church Musicians. Hillbrow, Godstone Rd, Blechingley, Surrey RH1 4PJ *tel:* 01883 741854 *also fax; fax:* 01883 740570. John Ewington OBE, gen sec.

Royal School of Church Music. Cleveland Lodge, Westhumble, Dorking RH5 6BW *tel:* 01306 872800 *fax:* 01306 887260 *email:* cl@rscm.com. Geoffrey Weaver, dir of studies; Jane Hiley, courses admin; John Wardle (01892 661722), Gordon Appleton (01765 606260), David Ogden (0117 946 7456), course dirs.

Society of St Gregory. 40 Cranwell Drive, Wide Open, Newcastle upon Tyne NE13 6AS *tel:* 0191 236 3855 *fax:* 0191 230 0735 *email:* alan@ssg-online.demon.co.uk. Lesley Wright, hon sec.

Anglican Church

Cathedrals and Collegiate Foundations

London

Chapel Royal (Hampton Court). Hampton Court Palace, East Molesey, Surrey KT8 9AU *tel:* 020 8781 9597 *fax:* 020 8977 4771 *email:* carl_jackson@ccis.org.uk. Carl Jackson, dir of mus; Alexander Mason, asst organist.

Chapel Royal (St James's). St James's Palace SW1 *tel:* 020 7930 3007. Richard Popplewell.

St Paul's Cathedral. 5b Amen Court, London EC4M 7BU *tel:* 020 7236 6883 *fax:* 020 7248 2817 *email:* music.stpauls@dial.pipex.com. John Scott, org and dir of mus; Huw Williams, sub org; Jane Ruthven, mus co-ord.

Southwark Cathedral. Montague Close, London SE1 9DA *tel:* 020 7367 6700 *fax:* 020 7367 6725 *email:* cathedral@dswark.org.uk. Peter Wright, dir of mus.

St Stephen's Vocal Arts. St Stephen's Church Vestry, Southwell Gardens, London SW7 4JL *tel:* 020 7370 5767 *also fax; email:* plums@psiona.demon.co.uk. Paul Plummer, dir of mus; Clare Almond, mus asst.

Temple Church. Temple Church Music Office, PO Box 16090, London EC4Y 7HS *tel:* 020 7936 4766 *fax:* 020 7936 4767 *email:* directorofmusic@templechurch.com. Stephen Layton, dir of mus and org; James Vivian, sub org.

Westminster Abbey. c/o Organist and Master of the Choristers, Chapter Office, 20 Deans Yard, London SW1P 3PA *tel:* 020 7222 5152 *fax:* 020 7233 2072 *email:* music@westminster-abbey.org.

Birmingham. Birmingham Cathedral. Colmore Row, Birmingham B3 2QB *tel:* 0121 236 4333/6323 *fax:* 0121 212 0868. Marcus Huxley, org.

Blackburn. Blackburn Cathedral. Cathedral Close, Blackburn BB1 5AA *tel:* 01254 51491 *fax:* 01254 699963 *email:* richard.tanner @blackburn.anglican.org. Richard Tanner, dir of mus; Timothy Cooke, asst dir of mus.

Bradford. St Peter's Cathedral. 1 Stott Hill, Bradford, W Yorks BD1 4EH *tel:* 01274 777720 *fax:* 01274 777730. Alan Horsey, org and choirmaster.

Bridlington. The Priory. 36 St Columba Rd, Bridlington, E Yorks YO16 6QX *tel:* 01262 670869 *also fax; email:* admin@mtsmith.newnet.co.uk. Michael T Smith.

Brighton. St George's Church. St George's Rd, Brighton BN2 1DE *tel:* 01273 279448 *also fax.* Fr Andrew Manson-Brailsford, parish priest; Malcolm Kemp, dir of mus.

Bristol. Bristol Cathedral. Bristol BS1 5TJ *tel:* 0117 926 4879 *fax:* 0117 925 3678. Mark Lee, org.

Bury St Edmunds. St Edmundsbury Cathedral. Abbey House, Angel Hill, Bury St Edmunds, Suffolk IP33 1LS *tel:* 01284 754933 *fax:* 01284 768655 *email:* cathedral@btconnect.com. James T Thomas, dir of mus (*tel:* 01284 756520); Michael Bawtree, asst dir of mus.

Cambridge. Jesus College. Cambridge CB5 8BL *tel:* 01223 339448 *fax:* 01223 324910. Julian Thomas, snr org scholar; Timothy Byram-Wigfield, dir of college mus; Thomas Corns, jnr org scholar.

Cambridge. King's College. Cambridge CB2 1ST *tel:* 01223 331224 *fax:* 01223 331890 *email:* choir@kings.cam.ac.uk. Stephen Cleobury, org.

Cambridge. St John's College. Cambridge CB2 1TP *tel:* 01223 338612/338765 *fax:* 01223 337720. Christopher Robinson, org.

Canterbury. Christ Church Cathedral. 6 The Precincts, Canterbury CT1 2EE *tel:* 01227 765219 *fax:* 01227 865222 *email:* daocjaflood @email.msn.com. David Flood, org and dir of mus.

Carlisle. Carlisle Cathedral. 6 The Abbey, Carlisle CA3 8TZ *tel:* 01228 526646 *fax:* 01228 547049. Jeremy Suter.

Chelmsford. Chelmsford Cathedral. Cathedral Office, New St, Chelmsford, Essex CM1 1TY *tel:* 01245 294485 *fax:* 01245 496802 *email:* music@chelmsford.anglican.org. Graham Elliott, org; Neil Weston, asst org.

Chester. Chester Cathedral. The Music Office, 1 Abbey Square, Chester CH1 2HU *tel:* 01244 351024 *fax:* 01244 341110 *email:* cathedral7@chesternet.co.uk. David Poulter, dir of mus; Benjamin Saunders, asst dir of mus; Edward Wellman, asst org.

Chichester. Chichester Cathedral. 2 St Richard's Walk, Chichester, W Sussex PO19 1QA *tel:* 01243 784790 *fax:* 01243 536190. Alan Thurlow, org.

Coventry. Coventry Cathedral. 7 Priory Row, Coventry CV1 5ES *tel:* 024 7667 3633 *also fax*. Rupert Jeffcoat, dir of mus; Daniel Moult, org.

Derby. Derby Cathedral. 3 Cathedral View, Littleover, Derby DE22 3HR *tel:* 01332 366692 *fax:* 01332 203991. Peter Gould, org.

Durham. Durham Cathedral. 6 The College, Durham DH1 3EQ *tel:* 0191 386 4766 *fax:* 0191 386 4267. James Lancelot, org; Keith Wright, sub-organist.

Ely. Ely Cathedral. The Old Sacristy, The College, Ely, Cambs CB7 4JU *tel:* 01353 665669 *fax:* 01353 665658 *email:* paul@stretto.demon.co.uk. Paul Trepte, org.

Exeter. Exeter Cathedral. 11 The Close, Exeter EX1 1EZ *tel:* 01392 277521. Andrew Millington, Paul Morgan, Stephen Tanner.

Gloucester. Gloucester Cathedral. Chapter Office, 17 College Green, Gloucester GL1 2BN *tel:* 01452 528095 *also fax*. David Briggs, dir of mus.

Hexham. Hexham Abbey. Beaumont St, Hexham, Northumberland NE46 3NB *tel:* 01434 602031 *fax:* 01434 606116. John C Green, dir of mus; Henry Wallace, asst org.

Leeds. St Peter-at-Leeds, Kirkgate (Leeds Parish Church). 3 St Peter's House, Kirkgate, Leeds LS2 7DJ *tel:* 0113 247 8334 *also fax;* 0113 245 4012 *fax:* 0113 243 9731 *email:* simonlin@nascr.net. Simon Lindley, org, master of mus.

Leicester. Leicester Cathedral. St Martin's, Leicester LE1 5FX *tel:* 0116 262 5294 *fax:* 0116 262 5295 *email:* cathedral@leicester.anglican.org. Jonathan Gregory, org and master of mus.

Lichfield. Lichfield Cathedral. 19a The Close, Lichfield, Staffs WS13 7LD *tel:* 01543 306100 *fax:* 01543 306109 *email:* lich.cath@virgin.net. Andrew Lumsden, org.

Lincoln. Lincoln Cathedral. 12 Minster Yard, Lincoln LN2 1PJ *tel:* 01522 532877 *fax:* 01522 511307. Colin Walsh, org; Jeffrey Makinson, asst org.

Liverpool. Liverpool Cathedral. 6 Cathedral Close, Liverpool L1 7BR *tel:* 0151 708 8471 *also fax*. Ian Tracey, org and master of choristers.

Manchester. Manchester Cathedral. Cathedral Yard, Manchester M3 1SX *tel:* 0161 833 2220 *fax:* 0161 839 6226. Christopher Stokes, org, dir of mus.

Newcastle. St Nicholas' Cathedral. Newcastle upon Tyne NE1 1PF *tel:* 0191 261 4505 *fax:* 0191 230 0735. Timothy Hone, dir of mus.

Norwich. Norwich Cathedral. 53a The Close, Norwich NR1 4EG *tel:* 01603 626589 *fax:* 01603 766032. David Dunnett, org and master of the mus.

Oxford. Christ Church Cathedral. Oxford OX1 1DP *tel:* 01865 276195 *fax:* 01865 286581 *email:* stephen.darlington@christ-church.oxford.ac.uk. Stephen Darlington, org.

Oxford. Magdalen College. Oxford OX1 4AU *tel:* 01865 276007 *fax:* 01865 276094 *email:* bill.ives@magd.ox.ac.uk. Grayston Ives, dir of mus.

Oxford. New College. Oxford OX1 3BN *tel:* 01865 279519 *fax:* 01865 279590 *email:* edward.higginbottom@new.ox.ac.uk. Edward Higginbottom, org.

Peterborough. Peterborough Cathedral. The Choir House, Laurel Court, Minster Precincts, Peterborough PE1 1XX *tel:* 01733 891333 *fax:* 01733 565165. Christopher Gower, org; Mark Duthie, asst org; Tom Moore, second asst.

Portsmouth. Portsmouth Cathedral. Chantry House, Lombard St, Old Portsmouth, Hants PO1 2HY *tel:* 023 9243 0811 *fax:* 023 9229 5480 *email:* pennyport@aol.com. David Price, org; David Thorne, asst org; Jenny Stoggles, mus sec.

Ripon. Ripon Cathedral. Minster Rd, Ripon, N Yorks HG4 1QT *tel:* 01765 603462 *fax:* 01765 690530 *email:* postmaster@riponcathedral.org.uk. Kerry Beaumont, org.

Rochester. Rochester Cathedral. Cathedral Office, Garth House, The Precinct, Rochester, Kent ME1 1SX *tel:* 01634 843366 *fax:* 01634 401410. Roger Sayer, org; Séan Farrell, asst org.

St Albans. St Albans Cathedral and Abbey Church. 31 Abbey Mill Lane, St Albans, Herts AL3 4HA *tel:* 01727 851810 *also fax; email:* AndrewL01@aol.com. Andrew Lucas, master of mus; Andrew Parnell, asst master of mus (*tel:* 01727 867818); Simon Bell, org scholar (*tel:* 01727 857725).

Salisbury. Salisbury Cathedral. Ladywell, 33 The Close, Salisbury, Wilts SP1 2EJ *tel:* 01722 555125 *fax:* 01722 555117 *email:* ladywell33@aol.com. Simon Lole, dir of mus; David Halls, asst org.

Selby. Selby Abbey. The Crescent, Selby, N Yorks YO8 0PU *tel:* 01757 703123 *fax:* 01757 708878. R D Tebbet, dir of mus.

Sheffield. Sheffield Cathedral. Sheffield S1 1HA *tel:* 0114 275 3434 *fax:* 0114 278 0244 *email:* sheffmusic@aol.com. Neil Taylor, master of mus; Mark Pybus, asst master of mus.

Southwell. Southwell Cathedral. 4 Vicars' Court, Southwell, Notts NG25 0HP *tel:* 01636 812649; 01636 812228 *also fax; email:* RectorChori@diaphone.clara.net. Paul Hale, org; Philip Rushforth, asst org (*tel:* 01636 814385).

Tewkesbury. Tewkesbury Abbey. 40 Church St, Tewkesbury, Glos GL20 5SN *tel:* 01684 298177/850959 *fax:* 01684 273113. Carleton Etherington, org.

Truro. Truro Cathedral. 21 Old Bridge St, Truro, Cornwall TR1 2AH *tel:* 01872 276782 *fax:* 01872 277788. Andrew Nethsingha, org; Simon Morley, asst org.

Wakefield. Wakefield Cathedral. Womack Cottage, Heath, Wakefield, W Yorks WF1 5SN *tel:* 01924 378841(home); 01924 373923 (office) *fax:* 01924 215054. Jonathan Bielby, org and master of the mus; Louise Marsh, asst org and dir of girls choir (*tel:* 01924 210006).

Wells. Wells Cathedral. 15 Vicars' Close, Wells BA5 2UJ *tel:* 01749 674483 *fax:* 01749 677360. Malcolm Archer, org and master of the choristers; Rupert Gough, asst org; Dawn Bonham, mus dept sec.

Winchester. Winchester Cathedral. 1 The Close, Winchester SO23 9LS *tel:* 01962 857200 *fax:* 01962 857201. David Hill, org (*tel:* 01962 857218).

Windsor. St George's Chapel. 25 The Cloisters, Windsor Castle, Berks SL4 1NJ *tel:* 01753 864529/865538 *fax:* 01753 620165. Jonathan Rees-Williams.

Worcester. Worcester Cathedral. 10a College Green, Worcester WR1 2LH *tel:* 01905 28854 *fax:* 01905 611139 *email:* worcestercathedral@compuserve.com. Adrian Lucas, dir of mus; Daniel Phillips, org.

York. York Minster. Church House, Ogleforth, York YO1 7JN *tel:* 01904 557206 *fax:* 01904 557201. Philip Moore, org and master of the mus; John Scott Whiteley, asst org; Jonathan Wainwright, asst choir trainer.

Scotland (Episcopal Church)

Aberdeen. St Andrew's Cathedral (Scottish Episcopal Church). 21a Deemount Rd, Aberdeen AB11 6TY *tel:* 01224 581151 *fax:* 01224 210259 *email:* a.morrisson@rgu.ac.uk. Andrew Morrisson, org.

Dundee. St Paul's Episcopal Cathedral. Castlehill, Dundee DD1 1TD *tel:* 01382 224486 *email:* MatthewEdwards@dundeecathedral.freeserve.co.uk. Matthew J Edwards, org, master of the choristers.

Edinburgh. St Mary's Episcopal Cathedral. The Cathedral Office, Palmerston Place, Edinburgh EH12 5AW *tel:* 0131 225 6293 *fax:* 0131 225 3181. Master of Music; Carol Wood, cathedral office.

Glasgow. St Mary's Cathedral. 300 Great Western Rd, Glasgow G4 9JB *tel:* 0141 339 6691 *also fax*. Fridrik Walker, dir of mus.

Oban. St John the Divine. Oban *tel:* 01631 710335. Norman Nicholson, org and choirmaster.

Perth. St Ninian's Cathedral. North Methven St, Perth PH1 5PP *tel:* 01738 626874/627982 *also fax*. James N Laird, org and master of the choristers.

Wales

Bangor. Bangor Cathedral. The Cathedral Office, The Deanery, Clos y Gadeirlan, Bangor, Gwynedd LL57 1LH *tel:* 01248 354015/353983 *fax:* 01248 352466. Andrew Goodwin, org and dir of mus; Martin Brown, James Griffiths, asst orgs.

Brecon. Brecon Cathedral. Garth Cottage, 29 Pendre, Brecon, Powys LD3 9EA *tel:* 01874 622442 *fax:* 01874 623716 *email:* cathedral@trinity.prestel.co.uk. David Gedge, org.

Llandaff. Llandaff Cathedral. 1 St Mary's, The Cathedral Green, Llandaff, Cardiff CF5 2EB *tel:* 029 2056 5880. Michael Smith, org.

Newport. St Woolos' Cathedral. 7 Macaulay Gardens, Newport, South Wales NP20 3JZ *tel:* 01633 266708 *also fax; email:* stworg@aol.com. Christopher Barton, org; Timothy Phillips, asst org.

St Asaph. St Asaph Cathedral. Cathedral Office, High St, St Asaph, Denbighshire LL17 0RD *tel:* 01745 583429. Graham Eccles, org and master of the choristers.

St Davids. St Davids Cathedral. The Organist's Lodgings, Cathedral Close, St Davids, Pembs SA62 6PE *tel:* 01437 720128 *fax:* 01437 721813 *email:* grlbowen@aol.com. Geraint Bowen, org; Simon Pearce, asst org.

Northern Ireland

Armagh. St Patrick's Cathedral. 50 Mullaghbane Rd, Armagh BT61 9HW *tel:* 028 3752 4110 *fax:* 028 3839 4525 *email:* martin.white14@virgin.net. Martin White, org.

Belfast. St Anne's Cathedral. Donegall St, Belfast BT1 2HB *tel:* 028 9032 8332 *fax:* 028 9023 8855. David Drinkell, org.

Londonderry. St Columb's Cathedral. 2 London St, Londonderry BT48 6PT *tel:* 028 7126 2412. Timothy Allen, org.

Churches

London. All Saints' Margaret Street. London W1N 8JQ *tel:* 020 7636 1788 *fax:* 020 7436 4470 *email:* AStsMgtSt@aol.com. Harry Bramma, org and dir of mus.

Church of the Annunciation. Bryanston St, Marble Arch, London W1 *tel:* 020 7262 4329 *email:* saward@compuserve.com. Christopher Saward, org.

Grosvenor Chapel. South Audley St, London W1Y 5DL *tel:* 01923 828522 *also fax;* 020 7499 1684 *also fax.* Richard Hobson, dir of mus.

Hampstead Parish Church. Church Row, London NW3 6UU *tel:* 020 7794 5808 *also fax; email:* vestry@hampstead-parish.demon.co.uk. Lee Ward, org and dir of mus.

The Queen's Chapel of the Savoy. Savoy Hill, Strand, London WC2R 0DA *tel:* 020 7836 7221 *fax:* 020 7379 8088. Philip Berg, master of the mus; James Cryer, asst org.

St Alban's. Brooke St, Holborn, London EC1 7RD *tel:* 020 7405 1831 *fax:* 020 7430 2551. Michael Fleming.

St Barnabas. 40 Calton Ave, Dulwich, London SE21 7DG *tel:* 020 8693 1524 *fax:* 020 8693 0203 *email:* wrmcvicker@aol.com. William McVicker, dir of mus; Clare Stevens, choir sec; Judith Hunter, treasurer.

St Bartholomew the Great. W Smithfield, London EC1A 7JQ *tel:* 020 7606 5171 *fax:* 020 7600 6909. David Trendell, dir of mus.

St Bride's. Fleet St, London EC4Y 8AU *tel:* 020 7353 1301; 01753 853573 *fax:* 020 7583 4867. Robert Jones, dir of mus; Matthew Morley, asst dir of mus.

St Clement Danes. Strand, London WC2 *tel:* 020 7242 8282 *fax:* 020 7404 2129. Peter Long, org and dir of mus.

St George's Hanover Square, London W1 *tel:* 020 7629 0874. Denys Darlow, dir of mus; Simon Williams, asst org.

St Giles-without-Cripplegate. Fore St, Barbican, London EC2Y 8DA *tel:* 020 7638 3052 *fax:* 020 7638 8285 *email:* AMT@organschool.com. Anne Marsden Thomas.

St James's. 197 Piccadilly, London W1V 0LL *tel:* 020 7381 0441 *also fax.* Ian Watson, org; Sarah Baxter, concert mgr.

St John's Wood Church. Lord's Roundabout, St John's Wood, London NW8 *tel:* 020 7722 2855. Robert Greenhill, dir of mus.

St Lawrence Jewry next Guildhall. London EC2 5AA *tel:* 020 7600 9478. Catherine Ennis, org; Rev D Burgess, admin.

St Luke's Church. Redcliffe Square, London SW10 9HF *tel:* 020 7370 0338 *fax:* 020 7341 9549 *email:* st.lukes.church@virgin.net.

St Martin-in-the-Fields, Royal Parish Church of. Trafalgar Square, London WC2N 4JJ *tel:* 020 7930 1538 *fax:* 020 7839 5163. Paul Stubbings, org and master of the mus; Nicholas Danks, asst org.

St Mary Abbots. Kensington Church St, London W8 4LA *tel:* 020 7937 5136 *fax:* 020 7938 4317. Mark Uglow, dir of mus; Denny Lyster, sub org.

St Mary-at-Hill Church. Lovat Lane, off Eastcheap, London EC3R 8EE *tel:* 01737 244604 *fax:* 01737 271128. Jonathan Rennert, dir of mus.

St Mary-le-Strand. 171 Strand, London WC2R 1EP. Paul Weaver, dir of mus.

St Mary the Virgin. Bourne St, London SW1W 8JJ *tel:* 020 7730 2423 *fax:* 020 7730 7455. Shane Fletcher, dir of mus.

St Michael's Church. Cornhill, London EC3V 9DS *tel:* 020 7626 8841; 01737 244604 *fax:* 01737 271128. Jonathan Rennert, dir of mus.

St Paul's. 32a Wilton Place, London SW1X 8SH *tel:* 020 7235 3460 *also fax.* James Morgan, org; Tony Kraus, asst org.

St Peter's. 119 Eaton Square, London SW1W 9AL *tel:* 020 7823 1205 *also fax; email:* acjsmith@hotmail.com. Andrew Smith, dir of mus; Christopher Glynn, asst dir of mus.

St Simon Zelotes. Milner St, London SW3 *tel:* 020 7359 1919 *also fax.* Anthony Herschel Hill, mus dir and org; Martin Ball, asst.

Bath. Bath Abbey. The Abbey Office, 13 Kingston Buildings, Bath BA1 1LT *tel:* 01225 422462 *fax:* 01225 429990. Peter King, dir of mus.

Brighton. St Bartholomew. Ann St, Brighton BN1 4GP *tel:* 01273 620491/492076. Derek Barnes, dir of mus.

Grimsby. Grimsby Parish Church. The Parish Office, St James' House, St James' Square, Grimsby, NE Lincs DN31 1EP *tel:* 01472 358610 *fax:* 01472 250751 *email:* parishoffice@saintjames.freeserve.co.uk. Steven J Maxson, org and master of choristers; Barry Whitfield, asst org.

Kenton. St Mary the Virgin. Kenton Rd, Kenton, Middx HA3 8EJ *tel:* 020 8907 2914. E M Singleton, dir of mus.

Northampton. All Saints Church. Mercers Row, Northampton NN1 1SF *tel:* 01604 632845 *also fax.* Simon Johnson, dir of mus.

Nottingham. St Mary the Virgin. High Pavement, Nottingham NG1 1HF *tel:* 0115 947 2476. John Keys, dir of mus and arts.

Military Chapels

London. Chapel of the Royal Hospital. Chelsea, London SW3 4SR *tel:* 020 7730 7395 *fax:* 020 7823 6871 *email:* curror@usa.net. Ian Curror, org.

Royal Military Chapel (Guards Chapel). Wellington Barracks, Birdcage Walk, London SW1E 6HQ *tel:* 020 7414 3228/9 *fax:* 020 7414 3414. Andrew Gant, org and master of the choir.

Roman Catholic Church

Cathedrals and Churches

London. Brompton Oratory. Brompton Rd, London SW7 2RP *tel:* 020 7589 4811 *fax:* 020 7584 1095. Patrick Russill, org; Neil Wright, asst org.

Christ the King Priory. Bramley Rd, London N14 4HE *tel:* 020 8449 6648 *fax:* 020 8449 2338.

Church of the Immaculate Conception. 114 Mount St, Farm St, London W1Y 6AH *tel:* 020 7493 7811 *fax:* 020 7495 6685. David Graham, org; Martyn Parry, choirmaster.

Corpus Christi Church. Maiden Lane, London WC2E 7NA *tel:* 020 7836 4700. Canon John McDonald.

Ealing Abbey (English Benedictine Congregation). Charlbury Grove, London W5 2DY *tel:* 020 8862 2157 *fax:* 020 8862 2206 *email:* ealingmonk@aol.com; philip.nunn@st-benets.ox.ac.uk. Richard Nicholson, dir; Kerry Prest, asst dir; Cherry-Willow Paul, org.

English Martyrs. 2 Mitcham Lane, London SW16 6NN *tel:* 020 8769 6268 *fax:* 020 8769 6714. G A Brine, org.

Holy Redeemer and St Thomas More. Cheyne Row, London SW3 5HS *tel:* 020 7352 0777; 01749 345924. David Bevan, org.

Our Lady. Lisson Grove, St John's Wood, London NW8 8LA *tel:* 020 7286 3214. Claude Crozet, dir of mus.

Our Lady of Grace and St Edward. 247 Chiswick High Rd, London W4 4PU *tel:* 020 8994 2877 *fax:* 020 8987 8332. Lucy Innes, dir of mus and choirmistress.

Our Lady of Mount Carmel and St Simon Stock. 41 Kensington Church St, London W8 4BB *tel:* 020 7937 9866; 01494 680873 *fax:* 01494 680501. John McCarthy OBE, dir of mus; Bruce Ogston, org.

Our Lady of the Assumption and St Gregory. Warwick St, London W1R 3PA *tel:* 020 7437 1525. Nicholas Attwater, dir of mus.

Our Lady of the Rosary. Old Marylebone Rd, London NW1 5QT *tel:* 020 7723 5101 (church); 020 7267 5858 (dir of mus) *fax:* 020 7258 0307 (church); 020 7284 1148 (dir of mus). Roy Emerson, dir of mus.

Our Lady of Victories. 235a Kensington High St, London W8 *tel:* 020 7937 4778 *fax:* 020 7937 4221. Christopher Scott, dir of mus; Charles Cole, org and asst dir.

Sacred Heart. Edge Hill, London SW19 *tel:* 020 8946 0305 *fax:* 020 8946 9130 *email:* sheartwim@aol.com. Robert Rathbone; Michael Newton.

St Anselm and St Cecilia. Kingsway, London WC2A 3JA *tel:* 020 7405 0376. Gerdi Troskie, choirmaster; Kevin Vockerodt, org.

St Augustine. 55 Fulham Palace Rd, London W6 8AU *tel:* 020 8748 3788.

St Etheldreda RC Church. Ely Place, London EC1 *tel:* 020 7405 1061 *fax:* 020 7405 7440. Paul Gillham, dir of mus; John McGreal, org.

St George's. 970 Harrow Rd, Sudbury, Wembley, Middx HA0 2QE *tel:* 020 8904 2552 *fax:* 020 8904 0774 *email:* sudgeorge@aol.com. Michael Crilly, dir of mus.

St James's. Spanish Place, 22 George St, London W1H 5RB *tel:* 020 7935 0943 *email:* tgworroll@osajibola.demon.uk. Terry Worroll, Gerald Pieti.

St Luke. 28 Love Lane, Pinner, Middx *tel:* 020 8866 7489. Vivien J Matthews, choral dir.

St Mary. Cadogan St, London SW3 2QR *tel:* 020 7589 5487 *fax:* 020 7581 5727. Malcolm Cottle, org and choirmaster.

Westminster Cathedral. 42 Francis St, London SW1P 1QW *tel:* 020 7798 9066/7798 9057 *fax:* 020 7798 9091 *email:* musicdepartment @westminstercathedral.org.uk. James O'Donnell, master of mus.

Aberdeen. St Mary's Cathedral. 20 Huntly St, Aberdeen AB1 1GH *tel:* 01224 634427/640160. Ronald Leith, dir of mus and org.

Beckenham. St Edmund of Canterbury. Village Way, Beckenham, Kent BR3 3NP *tel:* 020 8650 0970/1502 *fax:* 020 8249 3316. Michael Stannard.

Birmingham. Metropolitan Cathedral. St Chad's Queensway, Birmingham B4 6EU *tel:* 0121 236 2251 *fax:* 0121 233 9266. David Saint, dir of mus.

Brentwood. Brentwood RC Cathedral. Cathedral Church of St Mary and St Helen, Music Office, Cathedral House, Ingrave Rd, Brentwood, Essex CM15 8AT *tel:* 01277 261310 *fax:* 01277 234103. Andrew Wright, master of mus; Stephen King, org.

Bristol. Clifton Cathedral. Clifton Park, Bristol BS8 3BX *tel:* 0117 946 7456 *fax:* 0117 973 8263 *email:* cmd@gifford.co.uk. David Ogden, dir of mus; Mark Holt, Richard Jeffrey-Gray, orgs.

Cambridge. Our Lady and the English Martyrs. Catholic Rectory, Hills Rd, Cambridge CB2 1JR *tel:* 01223 350787 *fax:* 01223 360180 *email:* NPK@city32.freeserve.co.uk. Nigel Kerry, dir of mus.

Croydon. Our Lady of the Annunciation. Bingham Rd, Addiscombe, Croydon CR0 7EN *tel:* 020 8653 2373 *fax:* 020 7622 5459 *email:* jwoodhouse@mail.coynet.com. John Woodhouse, org.

Edinburgh. St Mary's Metropolitan Cathedral. Broughton St, Edinburgh EH1 3JD *tel:* 0131 556 1798/0027 *fax:* 0131 556 4821, dir of mus.

Erith. Our Lady of the Angels. Carlton Rd, Erith, Kent DA8 1DN *tel:* 01322 338984 *fax:* 01322 402694 *email:* olamusic@mcmail.com. Martin Hall, org.

Lancaster. Lancaster Cathedral. Balmoral Rd, Lancaster LA1 3BT *tel:* 01524 61860. Stephen Davies, org.

Leeds. Leeds Cathedral. Great George St, Leeds LS2 8BE *tel:* 0113 244 8634 *fax:* 0113 245 3626 *email:* LeedsCath@aol.com. Stuart Thompson, dir of mus (*mobile:* 07973 213901); Julie Crosby, org; Sally Barnes, vocal trainer.

Liverpool. Metropolitan Cathedral. Mount Pleasant, Liverpool L3 5TQ *tel:* 0151 708 7283 *fax:* 0151 708 7274 *email:* metcathedral @cwcom.net. Mervyn Cousins, dir of mus; Richard Lea, asst dir of mus; Chris McElroy, org scholar.

Manchester. Church of the Holy Name. Oxford Rd, Manchester M13 9PG *tel:* 0161 273 2435. Rosemarie Darby, dir of mus; Stephen Mann, org.

Nottingham. Nottingham Cathedral. Derby Rd, Nottingham NG1 5AE *tel:* 0115 953 9839 *fax:* 0115 953 9840. Peter Smedley, dir of mus; Graeme Vernon, sub-org.

Oxford. The Oratory Church of St Aloysius. Woodstock Rd, Oxford *tel:* 01844 338393; 01865 315800 *fax:* 01865 310470. Edward de Rivera, dir of mus.

Portsmouth. St John's Cathedral. Edinburgh Rd, Portsmouth PO1 3HG *tel:* 023 9287 0348 *fax:* 023 9283 9143 *email:* music@ portsmouth-dio.org.uk. Paul Inwood, diocesan and cathedral dir of mus.

Monastic Foundations

The following Abbeys have a strong choral tradition.

Bath. Downside Abbey. Stratton-on-the-Fosse, Bath BA3 4RJ *tel:* 01761 235100 *fax:* 01761 235105 *email:* downside@rmplc.co.uk. Christopher Tambling, dir of mus (*tel:* 01761 235146).

Buckfastleigh. Buckfast Abbey. Buckfastleigh, Devon TQ11 0EE *tel:* 01364 642519 *fax:* 01364 643891 *email:* buckabb @cix.compulink.co.uk. Dom Sebastian Wolff, monastic org; Trevor Jarvis, lay org.

Chelmsford. New Hall Convent of the Holy Sepulchre. Boreham, Chelmsford, Essex CM3 3HT *tel:* 01245 467588 *fax:* 01245 464348 *email:* fardell@newhallschool.co.uk. Andrew Fardell, dir of mus.

Crawley. Worth Abbey. Paddockhurst Rd, Turners Hill, Crawley, W Sussex RH10 4SB *tel:* 01342 710343 *fax:* 01342 710311 *email:* worth.abbey@ukonline.co.uk. Dom Philip Gaisford OSB, org and choirmaster.

Farnborough. St Michael's Abbey. The Coombes, Farnborough, Hants GU14 7NQ *tel:* 01252 546105 *fax:* 01252 372822.

Gloucester. Prinknash Abbey. Cranham, Gloucester GL4 8EX *tel:* 01452 812455 *fax:* 01452 813305. Dom Charles Watson OSB, precentor.

Leicester. Mount St Bernard Abbey. Coalville, Leicester LE67 5UL *tel:* 01530 832298/832022 *fax:* 01530 814608. Fr Peter Craddy, dir of mus.

London. Ealing Abbey (English Benedictine Congregation). Charlbury Grove, London W5 2DY *tel:* 020 8862 2100 *fax:* 020 8862 2206 *email:* ealingmonk@aol.com. Dom Stanislaus Hobbs, monastic choirmaster; Cherry-Willow Paul, org.

Reading. Douai Abbey. Upper Woolhampton, Reading RG7 5TQ *tel:* 0118 971 5300; 01635 44630 *also fax; fax:* 0118 971 5203. Dom Benedict Thompson, monastic choirmaster; John Rowntree, org, asst choirmaster, dir of abbey choir.

Ryde. Quarr Abbey. Ryde, Isle of Wight PO33 4ES *tel:* 01983 882420 *fax:* 01983 884402. Brother Denis Bradley, choirmaster; Brother David McCulloch, choirmaster.

Worcester. Stanbrook Abbey. Callow End, Worcester WR2 4TD *tel:* 01905 830209 *fax:* 01905 831737. Sister Margaret Truran OSB, choirmistress and org.

York. Ampleforth Abbey. York YO62 4ER *tel:* 01439 766701 *also fax.* Ian Little, choirmaster of Schola Cantorum.

Non-Conformist Churches

Baptist Church

Bristol. Baptist Music Network. c/o 19 Limefields Way, East Hunsbury, Northampton NN4 0SA *tel:* 01604 760928. Paul Lavender, chmn and training offr; Lesley Goulbourne, admin.

Bristol. Broadmead Baptist Church. 1 Whippington Court, The Horse Fair, Bristol BS1 3HY *tel:* 0117 929 1387 *also fax.* Derek Chivers, dir of mus.

London. Bloomsbury Central Baptist Church. 235 Shaftesbury Ave, London WC2H 8EL *tel:* 01449 711511 *fax:* 020 7836 6843. Philip Luke.

Church of Scotland

Aberdeen. St Machar's Cathedral. The Chanonry, Old Aberdeen AB24 1RQ *tel:* 01224 485988 *fax:* 01224 483688 *email:* stmachar@ifb.co.uk. James G Lobban, org and choirmaster; Michael Thomson, asst org.

Dunblane. Dunblane Cathedral. The Cross, Dunblane FK15 0AQ *tel:* 01786 870657. Matthew Beetschen, org and choirmaster.

Edinburgh. St Giles' Cathedral. High St, Edinburgh EH1 1RE *tel:* 0131 225 4363 *fax:* 0131 220 4763 *email:* m.harris@napier.ac.uk. Michael Harris, org and master of mus.

Glasgow. Glasgow Cathedral (St Mungo's). Castle St, Glasgow G4 0QZ *tel:* 0141 634 7775. John R Turner, org and dir of mus.

London. St Columba's. Pont St, London SW1X 0BD *tel:* 020 8346 6637 *fax:* 020 7584 5446. Gerald Barnes, org.

Paisley. Paisley Abbey. 17 Main Rd, Castlehead, Paisley PA2 6AJ *tel:* 0141 889 3528 *fax:* 0141 840 4906. George McPhee MBE.

Lutheran Church

St Anne & St Agnes. Gresham St, London EC2V 7BX *tel:* 020 7606 4986 *fax:* 020 7600 8984 *email:* 74434.1521 @compuserve.com. Peter Lea-Cox, cantor and dir of mus.

Methodist Church

British Methodist Youth Choir. 35 Westwood Rd, Sutton Coldfield, W Midlands B73 6UP *tel:* 0121 605 8766 *also fax; email:* gjones@ mcmail.com. Gilbert E Jones, admin; Ashley Thompson, mus dir.

Hinde Street Methodist Church. 19 Thayer St, London W1M 5LJ *tel:* 020 7935 6179. Robin Walker, dir of mus.

Methodist Church Music Society. 23a The Quadrant, Totley, Sheffield S17 4DB *tel:* 0114 235 1085. John Bailey, sec.

United Reformed Church

URC Musicians' Guild. 'Rainbow's End', 105 Humber Doucy Lane, Ipswich IP4 3NU *tel:* 01473 725075. John Harding, hon gen sec.

Other Free Churches

Church of Christ, Scientist

Enquiries should be directed to Alan Grayson, district mgr, Christian Science Committees on Publication, 2 Elysium Gate, 126 New Kings Rd, London SW6 4LZ *tel:* 020 7371 0600.

Salvation Army

Salvation Army. Territorial Headquarters, 101 Queen Victoria St, London EC4P 4EP *tel:* 020 7236 5222 *fax:* 020 7248 2575. Captain Peter Ayling, territorial mus sec; Richard Phillips, head of mus editorial.

Unitarian Church

The Unitarian Church Music Society. Underscar, Brigsteer, nr Kendal, Cumbria LA8 8AN *tel:* 015395 68631. Mrs J L Rogers, sec and treasurer.

Jewish Religion

Choirs

Jewish Heritage Youth Choir. PO Box 232, Harrow, Middx HA1 2NN *tel:* 020 8909 2445 *fax:* 020 8909 1030 *email:* singing@jmht.org. Vivienne Bellos, mus dir.

Zemel Choir. 26 Larch Close, Friern Barnet, London N11 3NN *tel:* 020 8361 3389 *also fax; email:* business-manager@the-zemel-choir.org. Marc Landsman, business mgr.

Orthodox Synagogues

London. Bevis Marks Synagogue. Bevis Marks, London EC3 *tel:* 020 7626 1274; 020 8371 9775 *fax:* 020 7283 8825. Maurice Martin, choirmaster.

Cricklewood Synagogue. 131 Walm Lane, London NW2 3AU *tel:* 020 8452 1739. Revd G Glausiusz, minister/cantor.

Edgware United Synagogue. Parnell Close, Edgware, Middx HA8 8YE *tel:* 020 8958 1323 *also fax; email:* sirobins@dircon.co.uk. Revd Stephen Robins, cantor.

Finchley Synagogue. Kinloss Gardens, London N3 3DU *tel:* 020 8346 8551.

Hampstead Synagogue. 1 Dennington Park Rd, London NW6 1AX *tel:* 020 7435 1518 *fax:* 020 7431 8369. Revd Stanley I Brickman, cantor.

Hendon Synagogue. 18 Raleigh Close, London NW4 2TA *tel:* 020 8202 6924 *fax:* 020 8202 1720. Alan Freedman, choirmaster; Rabbi Shmuel Neuman, cantor.

Ilford Synagogue. 22 Beehive Lane, Ilford, Essex IG1 3RT *tel:* 020 8554 5969. Arthur Poznanski, choirmaster.

New London Synagogue. 33 Abbey Rd, London NW8 0AT *tel:* 020 7328 1026 *fax:* 020 7372 3142. W W Scharf, choirmaster.

New West End Synagogue. 10 St Petersburgh Place, London W2 4JT *tel:* 020 7229 2631 *fax:* 020 7229 2355. Elliot Burman, choirmaster.

Palmers Green and Southgate Synagogue. Brownlow Rd, London N11 2BN *tel:* 020 8881 0037. Revd Brian Segal, cantor.

St John's Wood Synagogue. 37-41 Grove End Rd, London NW8 9NA *tel:* 020 7286 3838. Cantor Moshe Heschel (*tel:* 0171 483 1017).

Wembley United Synagogue. Forty Ave, Wembley, Middx HA9 8JW *tel:* 020 8904 6565 *fax:* 020 8903 2820 *email:* gamestheory@clara.net. Stephen Games, choirmaster.

Willesden Synagogue. 143 Brondesbury Park, London NW2 5JL *tel:* 020 8459 1083. Revd J Landenberg.

Woodside Park Synagogue. Woodside Park Rd, London N12 8RZ *tel:* 020 8445 2860/4236 *also fax*. Revd Michael Plaskow MBE.

Yeshurun Federation Synagogue. Fernhurst Gardens, Edgware, Middx HA8 7PH *tel:* 020 7797 8910 *fax:* 020 7797 8929 *email:* msimon @dnet.co.uk. Revd M Simon, cantor.

Leeds. United Hebrew Congregation. 151 Shadwell Lane, Leeds LS17 8DW *tel:* 0113 269 6141/283 2500 (choir bookings) *fax:* 0113 245 9412. Jack Fixman, choirmaster; Alan M Baker, bookings.

Salford. Higher Crumpsall and Higher Broughton Synagogue. Bury Old Rd, Salford M7 4PX *tel:* 0161 740 1210. A M Isaacs, dir of mus.

Reform Synagogues

London. Edgware and District Reform Synagogue. 118 Stonegrove, Edgware, Middx HA8 8AB *tel:* 020 8958 9782/8449 9240 *fax:* 020 8905 4710/8364 8452. Alan Kutner, dir of mus; Ann Sadan, choirmistress.

Hendon Reform Synagogue. Danescroft Ave, Hendon, London NW4 *tel:* 020 8203 4168 *fax:* 020 8203 9385.

North Western Reform Synagogue. Alyth Gardens, London NW11 *tel:* 020 8455 6763 *fax:* 020 8458 2469 *email:* viv@alyth.demon.co.uk. Vivienne Bellos, dir of mus; John Ringer, org.

West London Synagogue. 33 Seymour Place, London W1H 5AP *tel:* 020 7723 4404. Sydney Fixman, dir of mus; C Bowers-Broadbent, org.

Manchester. Reform Synagogue. Jacksons Row, Manchester M2 5WD *tel:* 0161 834 0514 *fax:* 0161 834 0415. Rabbi Dr R M Silverman, minister; Cedric Young, choirmaster and organization

Liberal Synagogues

London. Belsize Square Synagogue. 51 Belsize Square, London NW3 4HX *tel:* 020 7794 3949 *fax:* 020 7431 4559. Revd Lawrence Fine, cantor and dir of Institute of Prayer.

The Liberal Jewish Synagogue. 28 St John's Wood Rd, London NW8 7HA *tel:* 020 7286 5181 *fax:* 020 7266 3591. Cathy Heller-Jones, dir of mus; Timothy Farrell, org.

North London Progressive Synagogue. 100 Amhurst Park, London N16 5AR *tel:* 020 8800 8931 *fax:* 020 8800 0416. Malcolm Cottle, org and dir of mus.

Local Authority Promoters

This section comprises the local authority promoters in England, Wales, Scotland, Northern Ireland and the Isle of Man. The promoters are listed in county order preceded by London. With the exception of London, county entries are headed by the county council and followed by a list of borough and district councils in alphabetical order.

Inner London

City of Westminster Borough Council. Arts Unit, 18th Floor, City Hall, 64 Victoria Street, London SW1E 6QP *tel:* 020 7641 2498/7641 2814 *fax:* 020 7641 8083 *minicom:* 020 7641 2948 *email:* jgray@westminster.gov.uk. Joanne Gray and Cheryl Harris, manager and arts officer.

Hackney Borough Council. Arts and Cultural Services, Edith Cavell Building, Enfield Road, London N1 5BA *tel:* 020 8356 7308. Shweta Otiv, senior arts and cultural services officer.

Hammersmith and Fulham Borough Council. Community Learning and Leisure Service, Town Hall, King Street, London W6 9JU *tel:* 020 7736 1724. Jackie Sullivan, curricular leader - arts.

Kensington and Chelsea, Royal Borough of. Central Library, Hornton Street, London W8 7RX *tel:* 020 7937 2542 *fax:* 020 7361 2976. C J Koster, director of libraries and arts.

Lambeth Borough Council. Libraries and Leisure Services, 1st Floor, Mary Seacole House, 91 Clapham High Street, London SW4 7TF *tel:* 020 7926 0750. Caroline Jenkinson, arts development officer.

Lewisham Borough Council. Lewisham Arts Service, 199-201 Lewisham High Street, London SE13 6LG *tel:* 020 8297 8521. Norman Goodman, principal arts officer.

Southwark, London Borough of. Southwark Art and Leisure, 15 Spa Road, London SE16 3QW *tel:* 020 7525 1993 *fax:* 020 7525 1505. Adrian Olsen, head of arts, libraries and museums.

Tower Hamlets Borough Council. Mulberry Place, 5 Clove Crescent, London E14 2BG *tel:* 020 7364 5000. Brian Oakaby, arts and events officer.

Outer London

Barking and Dagenham Borough Council. Broadway Theatre, Broadway, Barking, Essex IG11 7LS *tel:* 020 8591 9662 *also fax.* Carol Oatham, theatre manager.

Barnet Council. Recreation, Leisure and Arts, Educational Services, Friern Barnet Lane, London N11 3DL *tel:* 020 8359 3152 *fax:* 020 8359 3246. Lloyd Gee, principal arts officer.

Croydon, London Borough of. Croydon Clocktower, Katharine Street, Croydon CR9 1ET *tel:* 020 8760 5400 ext 1034 *email:* arts@croydon.gov.uk. Laura Dyer, head of arts.

Ealing, London Borough of. Perceval House, 14-16 Uxbridge Road, Ealing, London W5 2HL *tel:* 020 8758 5743 *email:* farrara@ealing.gov.uk. Adam Farrar, events manager.

Enfield, London Borough of. Civic Centre, Silver Street, Enfield EN1 0XJ *tel:* 020 8379 3659 *fax:* 020 8982 5497. Claire Chidley, cultural services manager.

Harrow Borough Council. PO Box 22, Civic Centre, Harrow, Middx HA1 2UW *tel:* 020 8424 1906. Carol Stewart, arts and leisure service manager.

Havering Borough Council. Arts Office, Broxhill Centre, Broxhill Road, Romford, Essex RM4 1XN *tel:* 01708 773950 *email:* colec@havering.gov.uk. Chris Cole, arts officer.

Hillingdon Borough Council. Compass Theatre and Arts Centre, Glebe Ave, Ickenham, Middx UB10 8PD *tel:* 01895 632488 *email:* compass@lbhill.gov.uk. Bryony Flanagan, arts service manager.

Kingston, Royal Borough of. Cultural Services, Kingston Library, Fairfield Road, Kingston upon Thames, Surrey KT1 2PS *tel:* 020 8547 6416 *fax:* 020 8547 6426. Colin Bloxham, arts development officer.

Merton Borough Council. Civic Centre, London Road, Morden, Surrey SM4 5DX *tel:* 020 8545 3571 *email:* 106001.2536@compuserve.com. Jo Anne Hawley, arts development officer.

Newham Borough Council. Arts/Entertainments/Leisure Service, 292 Barking Road, East Ham, London E6 3BA *tel:* 020 8557 8648 *fax:* 020 8215 1029 *email:* david.curtis@newham.gov.uk. David Curtis, arts and events manager.

Redbridge, London Borough of. Borough Arts Office, Lynton House, High Rd, Ilford, Essex *tel:* 020 8478 3020.

Richmond upon Thames Borough Council. Langholm Lodge, 146 Petersham Road, Richmond TW10 6UX *tel:* 020 8831 6138 *fax:* 020 8940 7568 *email:* leisure@richmond.gov.uk. Nigel Cutting, principal arts officer.

Waltham Forest, London Borough of. Sycamore House, Town Hall, Forest Road, London E17 *tel:* 020 8527 5544 ext 4798. Helen Tredoux, arts and tourism officer.

England

Bath & North East Somerset

Bath and North East Somerset Council. Pump Room, Bath BA1 1LZ *tel:* 01225 477782 *email:* ruth_warren@bathnes.gov.uk. Ruth Warren, sales officer.

Bedfordshire

Bedford Borough Council. Arts and Leisure Unit, Room 550, Town Hall, St Paul's Square, Bedford, Beds MK40 1SJ *tel:* 01234 267422 *fax:* 01234 221606. Gilly Love, principal arts officer.

Luton Borough Council. Leisure and Cultural Services, Arts Unit, 146 Old Bedford Road, Luton LU2 7HH *tel:* 01582 876084 *fax:* 01582 876009. Leslie Hampson, arts development manager.

Mid Bedfordshire District Council. The Limes, 12 Dunstable St, Ampthill, Beds MK45 2JU *tel:* 01525 842244 *fax:* 01525 842209 *email:* hilary.western@midbeds.gov.uk. Hilary Western, arts worker.

South Bedfordshire District Council. The District Offices, High Street North, Dunstable, Beds LU6 1LF *tel:* 01582 472222 *fax:* 01582 474009. Catherine Doherty, corporate service manager (community and leisure).

Berkshire

Bracknell Forest Borough Council. Leisure Services Dept, Edward Elgar House, Skimped Hill Lane, Bracknell, Berks RG12 1LR *tel:* 01344 354181 *email:* vincent.paliczka@bracknell-forest.gov.uk. Vincent Paliczka, director of leisure services.

Reading Borough Council. The Hexagon, Queen's Walk, Reading RG1 7UA *tel:* 0118 939 0123 *fax:* 0118 939 0028 *email:* the.hexagon@reading.gov.uk. c/o Ann Brown, programme co-ordinator.

Slough Borough Council. Town Hall, Bath Road, Slough, Berks SL1 3UQ *tel:* 01753 875576. Andrew Lee, arts development promotion officer.

Windsor and Maidenhead, Royal Borough of. Town Hall, St Ives Road, Maidenhead, Berks SL6 1RF *tel:* 01628 796100 *fax:* 01628 796738. Kath Shackleton, arts development officer.

Bristol City Council

Bristol City Council. Dept of Leisure Services, Colston Hall, Colston Street, Bristol BS1 5AR *tel:* 0117 922 3698 *fax:* 0117 922 3681 *email:* paul_preager@bristol-city.gov.uk. Paul Preager, concert planning and promotions manager.

Buckinghamshire

Buckinghamshire County Council. Education Dept, County Hall, Aylesbury, Bucks HP20 1UZ *tel:* 01296 383549. Alan Noble, education officer.

Aylesbury Vale District Council. Bearbrook House, Oxford Road, Aylesbury, Bucks HP21 3RJ *tel:* 01296 585206. Dan Clucas, arts development officer.

Chiltern District Council. Council Offices, King George V Road, Amersham, Bucks HP6 5AW *tel:* 01494 732759. David Gardner, community arts officer.

South Bucks District Council. Council Offices, Windsor Road, Slough, Bucks SL1 2HN *tel:* 01753 533333 ext 347 *fax:* 01753 676214 *email:* artsofficer@southbucks.gov.uk.

Wycombe District Council. Leisure Dept, Queen Victoria Road, High Wycombe, Bucks HP11 1BB *tel:* 01494 421887 *fax:* 421808. Richard Sockett, arts development officer.

Cambridgeshire

Cambridgeshire County Council. Education, Libraries and Heritage, Shire Hall, Cambridge CB3 0AP *tel:* 01223 718134 *email:* steve.hollier@education.camcnty.gov.uk. Steve Hollier, county arts officer; Frances Williams, general inspector (music).

Cambridge City Council. Leisure Services, The Guildhall, Cambridge CB2 3QJ *tel:* 01223 457521 *email:* marketing@cambridge.gov.uk. Tim Holt, marketing and press manager.

East Cambridgeshire District Council. Arts Development in E Cambridgeshire, Artspace, 15 Fore Hill, Ely, Cambs CB7 4AA *tel:* 01353 669022 *fax:* 01353 669052 *email:* adec@dial.pipex.com. Angela Fordham, Chris Mathod, administrators.

Fenland District Council. Fenland Hall, March, Cambs PE15 8NQ *tel:* 01354 622346 *email:* andyohanlon@dl.fenland.gov.uk. Andrew O'Hanlon, arts development officer.

Huntingdonshire District Council. Pathfinder House, St Mary's Street, Huntingdon, Cambs PE18 6TN *tel:* 01480 388057 *email:* vpeters @huntsdc.gov.uk. Vivien Peters, arts and cultural services manager.

South Cambridgeshire District Council. South Cambridgeshire Hall, 9-11 Hills Road, Cambridge CB2 1PB *tel:* 01223 443018 *fax:* 01223 443149 *email:* celia.bell@scambs.gov.uk. Celia Bell, arts development officer.

Cheshire

Cheshire County Council. Arts Services, Goldsmith House, Hamilton Place, Chester CH1 1SE *tel:* 01244 602839. Jane Dawson, principal arts officer.

Congleton Borough Council. Westfields, Middlewich Road, Sandbach, Cheshire CW1 1HZ *tel:* 01270 763231. Carol MacGregor, arts development officer.

Crewe and Nantwich Borough Council. Victoria Community Centre, West Street, Crewe, Cheshire CW1 2PZ *tel:* 01270 211422 *fax:* 01270 537960. E McGahn, manager.

Halton Borough Council. Arts Development Team, Cultural and Leisure Services, Town Hall, Heath Road, Runcorn, Cheshire WA7 5TD *tel:* 0151 424 2061 ext 4063. Christina Christou, arts development manager.

Macclesfield Borough Council. Leisure Services Dept, Town Hall, Macclesfield, Cheshire SK10 1EA *tel:* 01625 504506 *fax:* 01625 504515 *email:* it_@macclesfield.gov.uk. Mark Wheelton, senior community activities officer.

Vale Royal Borough Council. Leisure Services, Community Services Directorate, Wyvern House, The Drumber, Winsford, Cheshire CW7 1AH *tel:* 01606 867533 *fax:* 01606 862100. Sue Gillett, events and entertainments officer.

Warrington Borough Council. Arts Development Unit, Newton House, Buttermarket Street, Warrington WA1 2NH *tel:* 01925 442885 *fax:* 01925 442888 *email:* gthorne@warrington.gov.uk. Gail Thorne, arts services manager.

Cornwall

Cornwall County Council. Chief Executive's Office, County Hall, Truro, Cornwall TR1 3AY *tel:* 01872 323465 *fax:* 01872 323836 *email:* arts@ceo.cornwall.gov.uk. Jenefer Lowe, arts officer.

Carrick District Council. Princess Pavilion, Falmouth, Cornwall TR11 4AR *tel:* 01326 311277 *fax:* 01326 315382 *email:* 306fips@aol.com. R H D Phipps, entertainments manager.

Kerrier District Council. Council Offices, Dolcoath Avenue, Camborne, Cornwall TR14 8SX *tel:* 01209 614000 *fax:* 01209 614491 *email:* ceo@kerrier.gov.uk. G Johns, leisure services officer.

Penwith District Council. Council Offices, St Clare, Penzance, Cornwall TR18 3QW *tel:* 01736 364823. Pauline Sheppard, arts development officer.

Restormel Borough Council. Restormel Borough Offices, 39 Penwinnick Road, St Austell, Cornwall PL25 5DR *tel:* 01726 74466/223300 *email:* rbc@restormel.gov.uk. Bryan Arthur, director of economic and community development.

Cumbria

Cumbria County Council. Arroyo Block, The Castle, Carlisle, Cumbria CA3 8UR *tel:* 01228 607292 *fax:* 01228 607299 *email:* herithq@ dial.pipex.com. Joe Hendry, heritage services officer.

Allerdale Borough Council. Cultural Services Unit, Helena Thompson Museum, Park End Road, Workington, Cumbria CA14 4DE *tel:* 01900 326257 *fax:* 01900 326256. Catherine Coulthard, cultural services officer.

Barrow-in-Furness Borough Council. Arts and Museums Service, Town Hall, Duke Street, Barrow-in-Furness, Cumbria LA14 2LD *tel:* 01229 894752 *also fax;* 01229 894942. Sue Jenkins, arts and museums manager.

Carlisle City Council. The Sands Centre, The Sands, Carlisle, Cumbria CA1 1JQ *tel:* 01228 810208 *fax:* 01228 514547. Nicky Appleby, arts, events and entertainments manager.

Copeland Borough Council. Whitehaven Civic Hall, Lowther Street, Whitehaven, Cumbria CA28 7SH *tel:* 01946 852821 ext 24/26. Dorothy Graham, hall manager.

Eden District Council. c/o Eden Arts Trust, 2 Sandgate, Penrith, Cumbria CA11 7TP *tel:* 01768 899444 *fax:* 01768 895920 *email:* edenarts @aol.com. Nick Jones, arts development officer.

Derbyshire

Derbyshire County Council. Libraries and Heritage Dept, County Hall, Matlock, Derbyshire DE4 3AG *tel:* 01629 580000 ext 6502 *email:* jaci.brumwell@derbyshire.gov.uk. Jaci Brumwell, deputy director, dept of libraries and heritage.

Amber Valley Borough Council. Borough Services, Leisure Development Unit, PO Box 19, Town Hall, Ripley, Derbys DE5 3SZ *tel:* 01773 841419 *fax:* 01773 841466 *email:* leisure-arts-sports@ ambervalley.gov.uk. Vicki Campbell, Alison Foote, arts development officers.

Bolsover (The District of). Sherwood Lodge, Bolsover, Chesterfield, Derbyshire S44 6NF *tel:* 01246 242320 *fax:* 01246 242424 *email:* leisure@bolsover.gov.uk. Steven Singleton, leisure and tourism officer.

Chesterfield Borough Council. North Lodge, Queen's Park, Chesterfield, Derbys S40 2LD *tel:* 01246 345111 *fax:* 01246 345110. G Cass, borough recreation and leisure officer.

Derby City Council. Leisure Services Dept, Derby City Council, Heritage Gate, Derby DE1 1LS *tel:* 01332 715515 *fax:* 01332 716215. Alf Fullerton, assistant director (arts and recreation).

Derbyshire Dales District Council. Town Hall, Matlock, Derbys DE4 3NN *tel:* 01629 580580 ext 2841 *email:* development@ derbydales.gov.uk. Roma Gee, arts development officer.

Erewash Borough Council. Town Hall, Derby Road, Long Eaton, Notts NG10 1HU *tel:* 0115 907 2321. R G Walters, leisure development manager.

High Peak Borough Council. Environmental Health and Leisure Dept, Howard Town House, High Street East, Glossop, Derbys SK13 8DA *tel:* 01457 851635. Bob Hall, chief leisure and services officer.

South Derbyshire District Council. Civic Offices, Civic Way, Swadlincote, Burton-on-Trent, Derbys DE11 0AH *tel:* 01283 228072 *fax:* 01283 550128. Rachel Walker, arts development officer.

Devon

East Devon District Council. Council Offices, Knowle, Sidmouth, Devon EX10 8HL *tel:* 01395 516551. Mary Schwarz, arts development officer.

Mid Devon District Council. Leisure Services Division, Ailsa House, Tidcombe Lane, Tiverton, Devon EX16 4DZ *tel:* 01884 255255 ext 4367/4330. Rob Kelley, leisure services officer.

North Devon District Council. Civic Centre, Barnstaple, Devon EX31 1EA *tel:* 01271 388325. Rosemarie Lyons, arts manager.

Plymouth City Council. Heritage and Leisure Dept, Plymouth, Devon PL1 2AA *tel:* 01752 307000 *fax:* 01752 307139. Paul Kelly, principal arts development officer.

South Hams District Council. Follaton House, Plymouth Road, Totnes, Devon TQ9 5NE *tel:* 01803 861234. Mike Thomas, principal leisure and parks officer.

Teignbridge District Council. Forde House, Newton Abbott, Devon TQ12 4XX *tel:* 01626 361101 ext 2607 *fax:* 01626 330162. Doff Pollard, arts development officer.

Torbay Borough Council. Strategic Services Directorate, Torhill House, Castle Circus, Torquay, Devon *tel:* 01803 546870. A Davies, events and entertainments manager.

Torridge District Council. Riverbank House, Bideford, Devon EX39 2QG *tel:* 01237 476711 *fax:* 01237 478849 *email:* david.pinney@torridge.gov.uk. David Pinney, director of planning and technical services.

West Devon Borough Council. Borough Council Offices, Tavistock, Devon PL19 0BZ *tel:* 01822 615911. Claire Stein, arts development officer.

Dorset

Dorset County Council. Dorset County Library Headquarters, Colliton Park, Dorchester, Dorset DT1 1XJ *tel:* 01305 224455 *fax:* 01305 224344. Ann Evans, professional support librarian.

Christchurch Borough Council. Civic Offices, Bridge Street, Christchurch, Dorset BH23 1AZ *tel:* 01202 495000 *email:* post@christchurch.gov.uk. Chris Horn, leisure services manager.

North Dorset District Council. Nordon, Salisbury Road, Blandford Forum, Dorset DT11 7LL *tel:* 01258 484034. Kate Montefiore, arts development officer.

Poole, Borough of. Poole Arts Centre, Kingland Road, Poole, Dorset BH15 1UG *tel:* 01202 665334 *fax:* 01202 670016. Polly Hamilton, arts development officer.

Purbeck District Council. Westport House, Wareham, Dorset BH20 4PP *tel:* 01929 556561 *fax:* 01929 557348. Debbie Anderson, tourism marketing and administration officer.

West Dorset District Council. Stratton House, High West Street, Dorchester, Dorset DT1 1UZ *tel:* 01305 252261. Patricia Jackson, arts development officer.

Weymouth and Portland Borough Council. The Pavilion Complex, The Esplanade, Weymouth, Dorset DT4 8ED *tel:* 01305 765218. Stephen Young, Pavilion Complex manager.

County Durham

Durham County Council. DLI Museum and Durham Art Gallery, Aykley Heads, Durham DH1 5TU *tel:* 0191 384 2214 *fax:* 0191 386 1770 *email:* help@durham.gov.uk. Zoe Channing, arts development manager.

Chester-le-Street District Council. Civic Centre, Newcastle Road, Chester-le-Street, Co Durham DH3 3UT *tel:* 0191 387 1919. Bill Lightburn, community leisure manager.

Darlington Borough Council. Civic Theatre, Parkgate, Darlington, Co Durham DL1 1RR *tel:* 01325 468006. Peter Cutchie, head of theatre and arts.

Derwentside District Council. Leisure Services Division, Civic Centre, Medomsley Road, Consett, Co Durham DH8 5JA *tel:* 01207 218438 *fax:* 01207 218432. Martin Weston, leisure development officer (arts).

Easington District Council. Seaside Lane, Easington, Co Durham SR8 3TN *tel:* 0191 527 0501 *email:* adam.sutherland@easington.gov.uk. A Sutherland, senior cultural development officer.

Sedgefield Borough Council. Green Lane, Spennymoor, Co Durham DL16 6JQ *tel:* 01388 816166 *fax:* 01388 815374. Pauline Murray, arts development officer.

Teesdale District Council. Teesdale House, Galgate, Barnard Castle, Co Durham DL12 8EL *tel:* 01833 690000 *fax:* 01833 637269 *email:* arts@teesdale.co.uk. Rosie Cross, arts development officer.

Wear Valley District Council. Leisure and Marketing Dept, Civic Centre, Crook, Co Durham DL15 9ES *tel:* 01388 765555 ext 215. David Plews, arts development officer.

East Riding of Yorkshire

East Riding of Yorkshire Council. Education, Leisure and Libraries Dept, County Hall, Beverley, E Yorks HU17 9BA *tel:* 01482 887700. June Mitchell, museums and arts officer.

East Sussex

East Sussex County Council. 44 St Anne's Crescent, Lewes, E Sussex BN7 1SQ *tel:* 01273 481871 *fax:* 01273 480092. Hilary Lane, arts officer.

Brighton & Hove Council. Royal Pavilion, Libraries and Museums, 4/5 Pavilion Buildings, Brighton BN1 1EE *tel:* 01273 290900. Anne Burrill, head of marketing and visitor development.

Eastbourne Borough Council. Eastbourne Theatres, Winter Garden, Eastbourne, E Sussex BN21 4BP *tel:* 01323 415500. Ian Alexander, general manager.

Hastings Borough Council. Directorate of Community and Leisure, Hastings Museum and Art Gallery, Bohemia Rd, Hastings, E Sussex TN34 1ET *tel:* 01424 781154 *fax:* 01424 781165. Paul Ackerley, arts development officer.

Rother District Council. De La Warr Pavilion, Bexhill-on-Sea, E Sussex TN40 1DP *tel:* 01424 787900. Linda Lewis, assistant manager.

Wealden District Council. Leisure Services Dept, Pine Grove, Crowborough, E Sussex TN6 1DH *tel:* 01892 602000 *email:* sussexcountry@wealden.gov.uk. Sarah Pascoe, arts officer.

Essex

Essex County Council. Learning Services, PO Box 47, Chelmsford, Essex CM2 6WN *tel:* 01245 436825 *fax:* 01245 436841 *email:* tim.freathy@essexcc.gov.uk. Tim Freathy, cultural services manager.

Braintree District Council. Town Hall Centre, Market Square, Braintree, Essex CM7 3YG *tel:* 01376 557776/340803 *email:* nicola@bdctownh.demon.co.uk. Nicola Deller, Alison Dando, arts development officers.

Brentwood Borough Council. Council Offices, Ingrave Road, Brentwood, Essex CM15 8AY *tel:* 01277 261111 *fax:* 01277 200152. Kim Anderson, promotions, community services directorate.

Chelmsford Borough Council. Civic Centre, Duke Street, Chelmsford, Essex CM1 1JE *tel:* 01245 606636 *email:* jimgillies@chelmsfordbc.gov.uk. Jim Gillies, arts and entertainments manager.

Colchester Borough Council. PO Box 331, Town Hall, Colchester, Essex CO1 1GL *tel:* 01206 282946 *email:* claire.jackson@colchester.gov.uk. Claire Jackson, event co-ordinator.

Epping Forest District Council. Epping Forest Arts, The House, rear of Loughton Pool, Traps Hill, Loughton, Essex IG10 1SZ *tel:* 020 8532 1105 *fax:* 020 8532 1106. Carien Meijer, arts officer.

Rochford District Council. Council Offices, South Street, Rochford, Essex SS4 1BW *tel:* 01702 546366. P Warren, corporate director (services).

Southend-on-Sea Borough Council. PO Box 6, Civic Centre, Victoria Avenue, Southend-on-Sea, Essex SS2 6ER *tel:* 01702 215436 *fax:* 01702 215110 *email:* rosemarypennington@southend.gov.uk. Rosemary Pennington, principal arts officer.

Tendring District Council. Town Hall, Station Road, Clacton-on-Sea, Essex CO15 1SE *tel:* 01255 253208. Robert Foster, entertainments officer.

Thurrock Borough Council. Thameside Theatre, Orsett Road, Grays, Essex RM17 5DX *tel:* 01375 382555. M Allinson, arts leisure manager.

Uttlesford District Council. Council Offices, London Road, Saffron Walden, Essex CB11 4ER *tel:* 01799 510560. Sarah McLagan, head of leisure and amenities.

Gloucestershire

Cheltenham Borough Council. Dept of Festivals and Entertainment, Town Hall, Imperial Square, Cheltenham, Glos GL50 1QA *tel:* 01242 521621 *fax:* 01242 573902 *email:* townhall@cheltenham.gov.uk. Jeremy Tyndall, head of festivals and entertainments.

Cotswold District Council. Corinium Museum, Park Street, Cirencester, Glos GL7 2BX *tel:* 01285 655611 *fax:* 01285 643286. Margaret Mernagh, cultural services manager.

Forest of Dean District Council. Council Offices, Coleford, Glos GL16 8HG *tel:* 01594 812381 *fax:* 01594 812314. G Derbyshire, entertainments officer.

Gloucester City Council. Leisure Management Services, Herbert Warehouse, The Docks, Gloucester GL1 2EQ *tel:* 01452 396620. Jon Hogan, promotions and events officer.

Stroud District Council. Ebley Mill, Westward Road, Stroud, Glos GL5 4UB *tel:* 01453 754312 *fax:* 01453 754955 *email:* alan.caig@stroud.gov.uk. Alan Caig, head of leisure.

Tewkesbury Borough Council. Council Offices, Gloucester Road, Tewkesbury, Glos GL20 5TT *tel:* 01684 295010/272091. Douglas Weldon, head of leisure and tourism.

Greater Manchester (Metropolitan County Area)

Bolton Metropolitan Borough Council. The Albert Hall, Room 100 The Albert Hall, Victoria Square, Bolton BL1 1RU *tel:* 01204 522311 ext 1065 *fax:* 01204 399928. Phil Smith, entertainments manager.

Bury Metropolitan Borough Council. Athenaeum House, Market Street, Bury, Lancs BL9 0BP *tel:* 0161 253 5869 *fax:* 0161 253 5915. Tony Trehy, principal arts officer.

Oldham Metropolitan District Council. PO Box 40, Civic Centre, West Street, Oldham OL1 1XJ *tel:* 0161 911 4080 *fax:* 0161 911 4220. Paul Barnett, head of arts, education and leisure services.

Rochdale Metropolitan Borough Council. Recreation and Community Services, PO Box 122, Municipal Offices, Smith Street, Rochdale, Lancs OL16 1YB *tel:* 01706 647474 *fax:* 01706 864104. Andy Wiggans, director, recreation and community services.

Salford City Council. Vulcan House, Albion Place, The Crescent, Salford M5 4NL *tel:* 0161 736 9448 *fax:* 0161 745 7806 *email:* ted.tootill @salford.gov.uk. Ted Tootill, arts and leisure manager.

Tameside Metropolitan District Council. Education and Leisure Services Dept, Council Offices, Wellington Road, Ashton-under-Lyne OL6 6DL *tel:* 0161 342 3310 *fax:* 0161 342 3744.

Wigan Metropolitan Borough Council. Dept of Leisure Services, The Indoor Sports Complex, Loire Drive, Robin Park, Wigan WN5 0UL *tel:* 01942 828560 *email:* p.gascoigne@wiganmbc.gov.uk. Pete Gascoigne, community development and planning manager.

Hampshire

Hampshire County Council. County Arts Office, Mottisfont Court, High Street, Winchester, Hants SO23 8ZD *tel:* 01962 846965 *email:* artsmf@hants.gov.uk. Michael Fuller, senior arts officer.

Basingstoke and Deane Borough Council. Civic Offices, London Road, Basingstoke, Hants RG21 4AH *tel:* 01256 845736 *fax:* 01256 845642 *email:* d.fraser@basingstoke.gov.uk. Daryl Fraser, arts and heritage manager.

East Hampshire District Council. Penn's Place, Petersfield, Hants GU31 4EX *tel:* 01730 234391 *fax:* 01730 234385 *email:* liz_panton@easthants.gov.uk. Liz Panton, community and arts development officer.

Eastleigh Borough Council. Civic Offices, Leigh Road, Eastleigh, Hants SO50 9YN *tel:* 023 8062 2187 *fax:* 023 8062 9466 *email:* cherylbutler@eastleigh.gov.uk. Cheryl Butler, tourism and arts manager.

Fareham Borough Council. Ferneham Hall, Osborn Road, Fareham, Hants PO16 7DB *tel:* 01329 824864 *fax:* 01329 281528 *email:* boxoffice@fareham.gov.uk. Russell Davies, arts and entertainments manager.

Gosport Borough Council. Town Hall, Gosport, Hants PO12 1EB *tel:* 023 9252 9129 *fax:* 023 9251 1856. Helen Payne, arts development officer.

Hart District Council. Civic Offices, Harlington Way, Fleet, Hants GU13 8AE *tel:* 01252 622122. Paul Dimmock, head of leisure services.

Havant Borough Council. Leisure and Community Service, Civic Offices, Civic Centre Road, Havant, Hants PO9 2AX *tel:* 023 9247 4174 *fax:* 023 9248 0263. Stephen Kerr, head of leisure and community services.

New Forest District Council. Appletree Court, Lyndhurst, Hants SO43 7PA *tel:* 023 8028 5474. Martin Devine, assistant director, leisure services.

Portsmouth City Council. City Arts, Guildhall, Portsmouth PO1 2AD *tel:* 023 9283 4182 *fax:* 023 9283 4904 *email:* clooney @portsmouthcc.gov.uk. Chris Carrell, city arts officer.

Rushmoor Borough Council. Rushmoor Leisure Services, Council Offices, Farnborough Road, Farnborough, Hants GU14 7JU *tel:* 01252 398743 *fax:* 01252 398765 *email:* rmann@rushmoor.gov.uk. Richard Mann, arts and cultural officer.

Southampton City Council. Cultural Services, Leisure/City Services, Civic Centre, Southampton SO14 7LP *tel:* 023 8083 2730 *fax:* 023 8033 7594 *email:* c.rawnsley@southampton.gov.uk. Christine Rawnsley, arts development officer.

Test Valley Borough Council. Leisure Services, Beech Hurst, Weyhill Road, Andover, Hants SP10 3AJ *tel:* 01264 343204 *fax:* 01264 332214. Michael Johnson, arts officer.

Hartlepool

Hartlepool Borough Council. Dept of Community Services, Civic Centre, Victoria Road, Hartlepool TS24 8AY *tel:* 01429 266522 ext 3417. John Mennear, cultural services officer.

Herefordshire

Herefordshire Council. PO Box 44, Leominster HR6 8ZD *tel:* 01432 260732 *email:* nsilver@herefordshire.gov.uk. Natalia Silver, cultural services manager.

Hertfordshire

Broxbourne Borough Council. Bishops' College, Churchgate, Cheshunt, Herts EN8 9XF *tel:* 01992 785555 ext 5906 *fax:* 01992 785578. Melanie Gifkins, promotions officer.

Hertsmere Borough Council. Hertsmere Leisure, Rudolph Road, Bushey, Herts WD2 3DU *tel:* 020 8386 4044 *fax:* 020 8420 4621. Mark Homer, arts development officer.

North Hertfordshire District Council. Council Offices, Gernon Road, Letchworth, Herts SG6 3JF *tel:* 01462 474274 *fax:* 01462 474546. Alan Fleck, arts and museums officer.

St Albans District Council. District Council Offices, Civic Centre, St Peter's Street, St Albans, Herts AL1 3JE *tel:* 01727 866100 *email:* f.bugg@stalbans.gov.uk. Fran Bugg, arts development officer.

Three Rivers District Council. Watersmeet Theatre, 17-23 High Street, Rickmansworth, Herts WD3 1HJ *tel:* 01923 896484 *fax:* 01923 710121. Sandra Bruce-Gordon, general manager.

Watford Borough Council. Watford Museum, 194 High Street, Watford, Herts WD1 2HG *tel:* 01923 213971. Paul Roach, arts development manager.

Welwyn Hatfield Council. Community Leisure, Campus West Complex, The Campus, Welwyn Garden City, Herts AL8 6BX *tel:* 01707 357174 *fax:* 01707 357185 *email:* J.Wilson@welhat.gov.uk. Joanne Wilson, community arts officer.

Kent

Kent County Council. Partnership Section, Springfield, Maidstone, Kent ME14 2LH *tel:* 01622 696498 *fax:* 01622 696419 *email:* john.brazier@kent.gov.uk. John Brazier, head of partnership.

Ashford Borough Council. Civic Centre, Tannery Lane, Ashford, Kent TN23 1PL *tel:* 01233 330228 *fax:* 01233 330620. Christina Fuller, arts development officer.

Canterbury City Council. Council Offices, Military Road, Canterbury, Kent CT1 1YW *tel:* 01227 763763 *email:* alison.haywood @canterbury.gov.uk. Alison Haywood, arts development officer.

Dartford Borough Council. Civic Centre, Home Gardens, Dartford, Kent DA1 1DR *tel:* 01322 343402. Chris Oliver, director of environment and leisure.

Dover District Council. Dover Town Hall, High Street, Dover, Kent CT16 1DL *tel:* 01304 201200 *also fax*. Trevor S Jones, general manager, Dover Town Hall.

Gravesham Borough Council. c/o Woodville Halls Theatre, Woodville Place, Gravesend, Kent DA12 1DD *tel:* 01474 337 6111. Rob Allen, theatre manager.

Sevenoaks District Council. Leisure Section, Community Services Dept, Argyle Road, Sevenoaks, Kent TN13 1HG *tel:* 01732 741222 ext 297 *fax:* 01732 742339 *email:* sdc.leisure@virgin.net. Allison Wright, arts development officer.

Shepway District Council. Civic Centre, Castle Hill Avenue, Folkestone, Kent CT20 2QY *tel:* 01303 852363.

Thanet District Council. Council Offices, Cecil Street, Margate, Kent CT9 1XZ *tel:* 01843 296111 *fax:* 01843 292795. Chris Wolfe, general manager, entertainments and catering.

Tonbridge and Malling Borough Council. Lesser Building, Gibson Drive, Kings Hill, West Malling, Kent ME19 4LZ *tel:* 01732 876169 *email:* shirley.franklin@tmbc.gov.uk. Shirley Franklin, arts development officer.

Tunbridge Wells Borough Council. Assembly Hall Theatre, Crescent Road, Tunbridge Wells, Kent TN1 2LU *tel:* 01892 526121/510971 *fax:* 01892 525203 *email:* info@t-wells.gov.uk. Pat Casey, theatre manager.

Kingston Upon Hull

Kingston upon Hull City Council. Central Library, Albion St, Kingston upon Hull HU1 3TF *tel:* 01482 883091/883106 *fax:* 01482 883080. Paul Holloway, city arts officer.

Lancashire

Lancashire County Council. Arts Unit, Education and Cultural Services, PO Box 61, County Hall, Preston, Lancs PR1 8RJ *tel:* 01772 263584 *fax:* 01772 264880 *email:* pruel@lb.lancscc.gov.uk. Linda Prue, county arts officer.

Blackburn with Darwen Borough Council. King George's Hall, Northgate, Blackburn, Lancs BB2 1AA *tel:* 01254 582579 *email:* geoff.peake@blackburn.gov.uk. Geoff Peake, general manager.

Blackpool Borough Council. Tourism Dept, 1 Clifton Street, Blackpool FY1 1LY *tel:* 01253 478203 *fax:* 01253 478210 *email:* blackpool.tourism@dial.pipex.com. Jane Seddon, head of tourism.

Fylde Borough Council. Tourism and Leisure Offices, 290 Clifton Drive South, Lytham St Annes, Lancs FY8 1LH *tel:* 01253 724141 *email:* pauln@fylde.gov.uk. P Norris, tourism and arts officer.

Hyndburn Borough Council. Town Hall, Blackburn Road, Accrington, Lancs BB5 1LA *tel:* 01254 380296 *email:* peterba@hyndburnbc.gov.uk. Peter Baron, promotions officer.

Lancaster City Council. Arts and Events Dept, Station Buildings, Central Promenade, Morecambe LA4 4DB *tel:* 01524 582801 *fax:* 01524 582323. Jon Harris, head of arts and events.

Pendle Borough Council. Bank House, Albert Road, Colne, Lancs BB8 0BP *tel:* 01282 661220 *fax:* 01282 661221. Gary Hood, principal leisure services officer.

Preston Borough Council. Guild Hall and Charter Theatre, Lancaster Road, Preston, Lancs PR1 1HT *tel:* 01772 203456. John Shedwick, general manager.

Ribble Valley Borough Council. Platform Gallery, Station Road, Clitheroe, Lancs BB7 2JT *tel:* 01200 443071 *fax:* 01200 452556 *email:* platform-gallery@ribblevalley.gov.uk. Elaine Sagar, arts development officer.

West Lancashire District Council. 52 Derby Street, Ormskirk, Lancs L39 2DF *tel:* 01695 577177. Kim Graham, arts officer.

Wyre Borough Council. Civic Centre, Brack Road, Poulton-le-Fylde, Lancs FY6 7PU *tel:* 01253 891000 ext 440 *fax:* 01253 899000. Vicky Tindall, events manager.

Leicestershire

Leicestershire County Council. Museums, Arts and Records Service, County Hall, Glenfield, Leicester LE3 8TB *tel:* 01530 510851 *fax:* 01530 813301 *email:* museums@leics.gov.uk. G Kelly, arts development officer.

Blaby District Council. Council Offices, Desford Road, Narborough, Leics LE9 5EP *tel:* 0116 275 0555 *fax:* 0116 275 0368. Ian Potter, leisure development officer.

Charnwood Borough Council. Loughborough Town Hall, Market Place, Loughborough, Leics *tel:* 01509 634775. I Stephens, general manager, Loughborough Town Hall.

Harborough District Council. Council Offices, Adam and Eve Street, Market Harborough, Leics LE16 7AG *tel:* 01858 821286.

Leicester City Council. De Montfort Hall, Granville Road, Leicester LE1 7RU *tel:* 0116 233 3138 *fax:* 0116 233 3182 *email:* harga001@leicester.gov.uk. Alvin Hargreaves, operations manager.

Melton Borough Council. Council Offices, Nottingham Road, Melton Mowbray, Leics LE13 0UL *tel:* 01664 502332 *fax:* 01664 410283. Leigh Thomas, arts assistant, client and leisure services.

North West Leicestershire District Council. Council Offices, Coalville, Leics LE6 3FJ *tel:* 01530 833333 ext 379 *fax:* 01530 815841. Tessa Massey, arts development officer.

Oadby and Wigston Borough Council. Council Offices, Station Road, Wigston, Leics LE18 2DR *tel:* 0116 288 8961. Jo Dacombe, arts and heritage officer.

Lincolnshire

Lincolnshire County Council. County Offices, Newland, Lincoln LN1 1YL *tel:* 01522 552831 *fax:* 01522 552811 *email:* david.lambert@lincolnshire.gov.uk. David M Lambert, county arts development officer.

Boston Borough Council. Municipal Buildings, West Street, Boston, Lincs PE21 8QR *tel:* 01205 314 2000 ext 590 *fax:* 01205 359401. Barrie Higham, tourism and arts officer.

East Lindsey District Council. Chief Executives Dept, Manby Park, Louth, Lincs LN11 8UP *tel:* 01507 601111 *fax:* 01507 327149. E A Clarke, recreation and arts officer.

Lincoln City Council. City Hall, Beaumont Fee, Lincoln LN1 1DJ *tel:* 01522 881188 ext 514 *email:* liz.wilson@lincoln.gov.uk. Liz Wilson, arts officer.

South Kesteven District Council. Council Offices, St Peter's Hill, Grantham, Lincs NG31 6PZ *tel:* 01476 406080 *fax:* 01476 406000 *email:* skdc@dial.pipex.com. Ken Ross, arts manager.

West Lindsey District Council. 26 Spital Terrace, Gainsborough, Lincs DN21 2HG *tel:* 01427 615411. Louise Samouelle, tourism and arts officer.

Merseyside (Metropolitan County Area)

Knowsley Metropolitan Borough Council. The Conference Centre, 219 Knowsley Lane, Huyton, Knowsley, Merseyside L36 8HW *tel:* 0151 443 5619. David Wycherley, arts officer.

Sefton Metropolitan Borough Council. PO Box 25, Southport, Merseyside PR9 0DZ *tel:* 0151 934 2416 *fax:* 0151 934 2418. Ken Wainman, chief economic development and tourism officer.

St Helens Metropolitan Borough Council. Education and Leisure Services Dept, Service Promotion Section, The Rivington Centre, Rivington Road, St Helens, Merseyside WA10 4ND *tel:* 01744 456349. Lorraine Simpson.

Wirral, Metropolitan Borough of. Dept of Leisure Services and Tourism, HQ2 The Hamilton Quarter, 43 Hamilton Street, Birkenhead, Wirral L41 5AA *tel:* 0151 666 5060 *fax:* 0151 666 5070 *email:* dlstrob@wir-mbc.u-net.com. Rob Smith, arts and creative industries development manager.

Middlesbrough

Middlesbrough Borough Council. Education and Leisure Dept, PO Box 69, Vancouver House, Middlesbrough TS1 1EL *tel:* 01642 263849 *fax:* 01642 221866. Christine Harforth, festival and events officer.

Milton Keynes

Milton Keynes Council. Saxon Court, 502 Avebury Boulevard, Milton Keynes MK9 2HS *tel:* 01908 253698 *email:* pauline.scottgarrett@milton-keynes.gov.uk. Pauline Scott-Garrett, arts and museums manager.

Norfolk

Norfolk County Council. Cultural Services, County Hall, Martineau Lane, Norwich NR1 2DH *tel:* 01603 222269 *fax:* 01603 222941 *email:* mari.martin.lib@norfolk.gov.uk. Mari Martin, county arts officer.

Broadland District Council. Thorpe Lodge, Yarmouth Road, Norwich NR7 0DU *tel:* 01603 703265. S Harris, leisure officer.

Great Yarmouth Borough Council. Town Hall, Great Yarmouth, Norfolk NR30 2QF *tel:* 01493 846488 *fax:* 01493 846365 *email:* arts@great-yarmouth.gov.uk. Arts Adviser, The Seachange Trust *tel:* 01493 853233.

King's Lynn and West Norfolk, Borough Council of. Leisure and Tourism Dept, Valentine Road, Hunstanton, Norfolk PE36 5EZ *tel:* 01485 532516 *fax:* 01485 533090 *email:* jane.falkner@west-norfolk.gov.uk. Jane Falkner, arts development officer.

North Norfolk District Council. PO Box 3, Council Offices, Holt Road, Cromer, Norfolk NR27 9EL *tel:* 01263 516053 *fax:* 01263 515042 *email:* arts@north-norfolk.gov.uk. Jan Legge, arts officer.

Norwich City Council. Gladstone House, 28 St Giles Street, Norwich NR2 1TQ *tel:* 01603 212137 *fax:* 01603 213003. Helen Selleck, arts and events officer.

South Norfolk Council. South Norfolk House, Long Stratton, Norfolk NR15 2XE *tel:* 01508 533681 *fax:* 01508 533695 *email:* snc.swan@gtnet.gov.uk. Alex Andrews, head of leisure.

North East Lincolnshire

North East Lincolnshire Council. Civic Offices, Knoll Street, Cleethorpes, NE Lincs DN35 8LN *tel:* 01472 323000 *email:* jonesc@nelincs.gov.uk. Chris Jones, principal arts development officer.

North Somerset

North Somerset Council. Playhouse Theatre, High Street, Weston-Super-Mare, North Somerset BS23 1HP *tel:* 01934 627457 *email:* playhouse@n.somerset.gov.uk. Murray Macdonald, general manager.

North Yorkshire

Craven District Council. Council Offices, Granville St, Skipton, N Yorks BD23 1PS *tel:* 01756 706408. Lorraine Greenald, arts development officer.

Hambleton District Council. Civic Centre, Stonecross, Northallerton, N Yorks DL6 2UU *tel:* 01609 779977 *fax:* 01609 780817. David Goodwin, head of leisure services.

Harrogate Borough Council. Harrogate International Centre, Kings Road, Harrogate, N Yorks HG1 5LA *tel:* 01423 500500 *fax:* 01423 537210. P Lewis, director.

Richmondshire District Council. Friars Wynd, Richmond, N Yorks DL10 4RT *tel:* 01748 829100 *fax:* 01748 850897. Tony Clark, leisure and economic development unit manager.

Ryedale District Council. Ryedale House, Malton, N Yorks YO17 7HH *tel:* 01653 600666 ext 240 *fax:* 01653 696801 *email:* elsadmin@ryedaledc.onyxnet.co.uk. Clare Slater, community services officer.

Scarborough Borough Council. Londesborough Lodge, The Crescent, Scarborough, N Yorks YO11 2PW *tel:* 01723 232323 *fax:* 01723 376941. Peter H Dahl, director of tourism and leisure services.

Northamptonshire

Corby Borough Council. Festival Hall Complex, George Street, Corby, Northants NN17 1QB *tel:* 01536 402551. Ted Blair, manager.

Daventry District Council. Leisure and Community Services, Lodge Road, Daventry, Northants NN11 5AF *tel:* 01327 302482 *fax:* 01327 703823 *email:* shawes@daventrydc.gov.uk. Sonia Hawes, arts officer.

East Northamptonshire Council. East Northamptonshire House, Cedar Drive, Thrapston, Northants NN14 4LZ *tel:* 01832 742045 *email:* cs@east-northamptonshire.gov.uk. Leisure Assistant, community services dept.

Kettering Borough Council. Municipal Offices, Bowling Green Road, Kettering, Northants NN15 7QX *tel:* 01536 410333 *fax:* 01536 410795. Annie McLachlan, community development worker (arts/events).

South Northamptonshire Council. Council Offices, Springfields, Towcester, Northants NN12 6AE *tel:* 01327 350211 ext 214 *fax:* 01327 359219. Anna Hayward, arts manager.

Wellingborough Borough Council. Council Offices, Swanspool, Wellingborough, Northants NN8 1BP *tel:* 01933 229777 ext 4425. Peter Morrall, head of leisure services.

Northumberland

Northumberland County Council. Central Library HQ, The Willows, Morpeth, Northumberland NE61 1TA *tel:* 01670 533000 *fax:* 01670 534521 *email:* amenities@northumberland.gov.uk. Dave Bonser, divisional director, libraries, arts and heritage.

Alnwick District Council. Allerburn House, Alnwick, Northumberland NE66 1YY *tel:* 01665 510505 ext 251 *fax:* 01665 605099.

Berwick-upon-Tweed Borough Council. Wallace Green, Berwick-upon-Tweed, Northumberland TD15 1SD *tel:* 01289 330044 ext 440 *email:* amenities@berwickc.demon.co.uk. Claire Burrow, borough amenities manager.

Blyth Valley Borough Council. Council Offices, Seaton Delaval, Whitley Bay, Northumberland NE25 0DX *tel:* 01670 542348 *fax:* 01670 542344. David Garrett, cultural development officer.

Tynedale Council. Prospect House, Hexham, Northumberland NE46 3NH *tel:* 01434 652200. Lynn Turner, chief leisure and tourism officer.

Wansbeck District Council. Leisure Dept, East View, Stakeford, Choppington, Northumberland NE62 5TR *tel:* 01670 819802 *fax:* 01670 520457. Nicholas Baumfield, cultural services manager.

Nottinghamshire

Nottinghamshire County Council. Community Services, Trent Bridge House, Fox Road, West Bridgford, Nottingham NG2 6BJ *tel:* 0115 977 4289 *fax:* 0115 977 2428 *email:* arts@is.nottscc.gov.uk. Tim Harris, head of arts.

Ashfield District Council. Community Leisure Dept, Urban Rd, Kirkby-in-Ashfield, Notts NG17 8DA *tel:* 01623 450000 ext 4456 *fax:* 01623 457530. Sarah Midgley, arts development officer.

Broxtowe Borough Council. Directorate, Technical and Leisure, Council Offices, Foster Avenue, Beeston, Nottingham NG9 1AB *tel:* 0115 917 7777 ext 3626 *fax:* 0115 917 3600 *email:* starr@broxbc.demon.co.uk. Simon Starr, assistant director, leisure.

Gedling Borough Council. Civic Centre, Arnot Hill Park, Arnold, Nottingham NG5 6UL *tel:* 0115 901 3901/3713 *fax:* 0115 901 3928 *email:* leisure@gedling.gov.uk. Alison Clark, arts development officer.

Newark and Sherwood District Council. Kelham Hall, Newark, Notts NG23 5QX *tel:* 01636 605111 *fax:* 01636 708267. Simon Fitch, strategic arts officer.

Nottingham City Council. 51-57 Castle Gate, Nottingham NG1 6AF *tel:* 0115 915 3560 *fax:* 0115 915 3599 *email:* tourism@nottinghamcity.gov.uk. June Whiteside, arts and events office, leisure and community services.

Rushcliffe Borough Council. The Civic Centre, Pavilion Road, West Bridgford, Nottingham NG2 5FE *tel:* 0115 981 9911 ext 517 *fax:* 0115 945 5882 *email:* info@rushcliffe.gov.uk. Nicola Tompkins, arts development officer.

Oxfordshire

Oxfordshire County Council. County Music Service, Oxford School, Glanville Rd, Oxford OX4 2XP *tel:* 01865 779959 *fax:* 01865 712438. Richard Hallam, director of music.

Cherwell District Council. Bodicote House, Bodicote, Banbury, Oxon OX15 4AA *tel:* 01295 252535 ext 4348. Vicky Hope-Walker, arts and tourism manager.

Oxford City Council. Leisure Dept, 109-113 St Aldate's, Oxford OX1 1DS *tel:* 01865 252838/232843. Alan Brown, events organisers.

South Oxfordshire District Council. PO Box 140, Council Offices, Crowmarsh, Wallingford, Oxon OX10 8QX *tel:* 01491 823717 *fax:* 01491 823015. Emma Marino, community services manager.

Vale of White Horse District Council. The Abbey House, Abingdon, Oxon OX14 3JE *tel:* 01235 520202 *fax:* 01235 554960. Graeme Surtees, arts and tourism manager.

West Oxfordshire District Council. Council Offices, Woodgreen, Witney, Oxon OX8 6NB *tel:* 01993 770384 *fax:* 01993 770388 *email:* heather.mcculloch@westoxon.gov.uk. Heather McCulloch, arts development officer.

Redcar & Cleveland

Redcar and Cleveland Borough Council. Community Leisure, Libraries and Tourism, Kirkleatham Street, Redcar TS10 1XX *tel:* 01642 444306. Bill Sinclair, arts development officer.

Shropshire

Shropshire County Council. Arts Service, Column House, London Road, Shrewsbury, Shropshire SY2 6NW *tel:* 01743 255077/8 *fax:* 01743 255078 *email:* arts.service@shropshire-cc.gov.uk. Jenna Kumiega, head of arts service.

Bridgnorth District Council. Westgate, Bridgnorth, Shropshire WV16 5AA *tel:* 01746 713191. Su Barber, arts development officer.

North Shropshire District Council. Edinburgh House, New Street, Wem, Shrewsbury, Shropshire SY4 5DB *tel:* 01939 238436. Rod Owens, director of legal and administrative services.

Shrewsbury and Atcham Borough Council. The Music Hall, The Square, Shrewsbury, Shropshire SY1 1LH *tel:* 01743 352019 *email:* lpicton@musichall.demon.co.uk. Lezley Picton, general manager.

Telford and Wrekin Council. Leisure/Culture and Community, PO Box 211, Darby House, Telford, Shropshire TF3 4LA *tel:* 01952 202532 *fax:* 01952 290628 *email:* lcc@wrekin.gov.uk. Jean Escott, arts and entertainments manager.

Somerset

Mendip District Council. Council Offices, Cannards Grave Road, Shepton Mallet, Somerset BA4 5BT *tel:* 01749 343399 ext 335 *fax:* 01749 344050. Nicola Epps, arts development officer.

Sedgemoor District Council. Bridgwater House, King Square, Bridgwater, Somerset TA6 3AR *tel:* 01278 435275. Chris Sidaway, marketing and arts development officer.

South Somerset District Council. Area West Offices, Holyrood Lace Mill, Holyrood Street, Chard, Somerset TA20 2YA *tel:* 01460 260358 *fax:* 01460 260345. Mark Etherington, arts development officer.

Taunton Deane Borough Council. The Deane House, Belvedere Road, Taunton, Somerset TA1 1HE *tel:* 01823 356521 *email:* arts@tauntondeane.gov.uk. Richard Crowe, Matt Hinks, arts development officers.

West Somerset District Council. Council Offices, 20 Fore Street, Williton, Taunton, Somerset TA4 4QA *tel:* 01984 632291. Maureen Winnall, arts development officer.

South Gloucestershire

South Gloucestershire Council. Leisure and Community Resources, Broad Lane, Engine Common, Yate, Bristol BS17 5PN *tel:* 01454 868686 *fax:* 01454 865819. Trish McGrath, arts and tourism officer.

South Yorkshire (Metropolitan County Area)

Barnsley Metropolitan Borough Council. Dept of Education and Leisure, Central Library, Shambles Street, Barnsley, S Yorks S70 2JF *tel:* 01226 773601 *email:* grahamnoble@barnsley.gov.uk. Graham Noble, head of libraries and cultural services.

Rotherham Metropolitan Borough Council. Rotherham Arts Centre, Walker Place, Rotherham, S Yorks S65 1JH *tel:* 01709 823666 *email:* jane.glaister@rotherham.gov.uk. Jane Glaister, head of culture, countryside and amenity services.

Staffordshire

Staffordshire County Council. Arts and Museum Service, Shugborough, Milford, Stafford ST17 0XB *tel:* 01889 881388 *fax:* 01889 882461. Rosalind Shipsides, county arts and museums officer.

Cannock Chase District Council. Civic Offices, PO Box 28, Beecroft Road, Cannock, Staffs WS11 1BG *tel:* 01543 462621. D W Lowndes, head of leisure services.

East Staffordshire Borough Council. Leisure and Community Services, Midland Grain Warehouse, Derby Street, Burton-on-Trent, Staffs DE14 2JJ *tel:* 01283 508656. Alison Betteridge, promotions officer.

Newcastle-under-Lyme Borough Council. Civic Offices, Merrial Street, Newcastle-under-Lyme, Staffs ST5 2AG *tel:* 01782 717717. J W Martin, head of leisure and amenity services.

South Staffordshire District Council. Council Offices, Codsall, Wolverhampton, Staffs WV8 1PX *tel:* 01902 696534 *email:* d.heywood@sstaffs.gov.uk. Sheena Lucas, arts development officer.

Stafford Borough Council. c/o Stafford Gatehouse, Eastgate Street, Stafford ST16 2LT *tel:* 01785 253595 *fax:* 01785 225622. Daniel Shaw, manager.

Staffordshire Moorlands District Council. Leisure Section, Moorlands House, Stockwell Street, Leek, Staffs ST13 6HQ *tel:* 01538 483732/483451 *fax:* 01538 483733. Nicola Shipley, arts development officer.

Stoke-on-Trent City Council. Leisure and Cultural Services, PO Box 816, Civic Centre, Glebe Street, Stoke-on-Trent, Staffs ST4 1HF *tel:* 01782 236926 *fax:* 01782 232544. Clair Birkett, assistant cultural development officer.

Tamworth Borough Council. Marmion House, Lichfield Street, Tamworth, Staffs B79 7BZ. Sue Finnigan, head of arts and media.

Stockton on Tees

Stockton-on-Tees Borough Council. Leisure Services, 72 Church Road, Stockton-on-Tees, Cleveland TS18 1YB *tel:* 01642 393939. Kevin McAuley, Community Services; Andrea Barker, cultural services.

Suffolk

Babergh District Council. Corks Lane, Hadleigh, Ipswich, Suffolk IP7 6SJ *tel:* 01473 825718 *email:* mutum@babergh-south-suffolk.gov.uk. Tim Mutum, head of leisure services.

Forest Heath District Council. District Offices, College Heath Road, Mildenhall, Suffolk IP28 7EY *tel:* 01638 719217. A Bass, leisure services manager.

Mid-Suffolk District Council. Council Offices, Needham Market, Suffolk IP6 8DL *tel:* 01449 720711 *fax:* 01449 721946. Chris Fry, head of leisure.

Suffolk Coastal District Council. Council Offices, Melton Hill, Woodbridge, Suffolk IP12 1AU *tel:* 01394 444321 *fax:* 01394 385100 *email:* scdc@suffolkcoastal.gov.uk. Tony Osmanski, assistant director (leisure and tourism).

Waveney District Council. The Marina Theatre, The Mariner, Lowestoft, Suffolk NR32 1HH *tel:* 01502 523443 *email:* info@marinatheatre.co.uk. David Shepheard, venues/theatre manager.

Surrey

Surrey County Council. County Arts Unit, Westfield School, Bonsey Lane, Woking, Surrey GU22 9PR *tel:* 01483 776246 *email:* arts.officer@surreycc.gov.uk. Imogen Haig, arts officer.

Epsom and Ewell Borough Council. Epsom Playhouse, Ashley Avenue, Epsom, Surrey KT18 5AL *tel:* 01372 742226/739351 *fax:* 01372 726228. Trevor Mitchell, Playhouse manager.

Guildford Borough Council. Dept of Leisure Services, Millmead House, Millmead, Guildford, Surrey GU2 5BB *tel:* 01483 444767 *fax:* 01483 444717. Nickola Moore, arts development officer.

Mole Valley District Council. Pippbrook, Dorking, Surrey RH4 1SJ *tel:* 01306 879200 *fax:* 01306 877277 *email:* dorking.halls @mole-valley.gov.uk. Keith Garrow, general manager, Dorking Halls.

Reigate and Banstead Borough Council. The Harlequin, Warwick Quadrant, Redhill, Surrey RH1 1NN *tel:* 01737 773721 *fax:* 01737 765549. Tom Kealey, Harlequin manager.

Runnymede Borough Council. Civic Offices, Station Road, Addlestone, Surrey KT15 2AH *tel:* 01932 705445 *email:* ronnie @runnymede.gov.uk. Ronnie Fleming, head of leisure services.

Waverley Borough Council. The Burys, Godalming, Surrey GU7 1HR *tel:* 01483 869390 *fax:* 01483 860643 *email:* lsalway@waverley.gov.uk. Linda Salway, arts manager.

Woking Borough Council. Civic Offices, Gloucester Square, Woking, Surrey GU21 1YL *tel:* 01483 743807 *email:* wokbc@woking.gov.uk. David Vince, arts and events officer.

Tyne and Wear (Metropolitan County Area)

Gateshead Metropolitan District Council. Central Library, Prince Consort Road, Gateshead NE8 4LN *tel:* 0191 477 3478. Mike White, assistant director (arts).

Newcastle City Council. Enterprise, Environment and Culture Directorate, Rm 811, Civic Centre, Newcastle upon Tyne NE1 8QN *tel:* 0191 211 5610 *fax:* 0191 211 4935. Andrew Rothwell, city arts officer.

North Tyneside Arts. Buddle Arts Centre, 258b Station Road, Wallsend NE28 8RH *tel:* 0191 200 7132 *fax:* 0191 200 7142 *email:* ntynearts.demon.co.uk. Mike Campbell, principal arts officer.

South Tyneside Metropolitan Borough Council. Central Library, Prince George Square, South Shields NE33 2PE *tel:* 0191 427 1717 ext 2059 *fax:* 0191 427 0469. Richard Jago, senior recreation assistant.

Warwickshire

North Warwickshire Borough Council. Leisure Services Division, Council House, South Street, Atherstone, Warwicks CV9 1BD *tel:* 01827 719207. Barry J McLoughlin, area recreation officer.

Rugby Borough Council. Town Hall, Rugby, Warwicks CV21 2LB *tel:* 01788 533533 *fax:* 01788 533778. Mary Ferrier, principal recreation officer.

Stratford upon Avon Town Council. Civic Hall, 14 Rother Street, Stratford upon Avon, Warwicks CV37 6LU *tel:* 01789 269332 *fax:* 01789 297072 *email:* manager@civichall.co.uk. Mike Simkiss, halls manager.

Warwick District Council. Royal Spa Centre, Newbold Terrace, Leamington Spa, Warwicks CV32 4HN *tel:* 01926 334418 *fax:* 01926 832054. Peter B Nicholson, entertainments manager.

West Midlands (Metropolitan County Area)

Birmingham City Council. Birmingham Museum and Art Gallery, Chamberlain Square, Birmingham B3 3DH *tel:* 0121 303 2919 *fax:* 0121 303 1394. Anthony Sargent, head of arts and entertainments.

Coventry City Council. Leisure Services Dept, Spire House, New Union Street, Coventry CV1 2PS *tel:* 024 7683 2399 *fax:* 024 7683 2361. Debbie Kingsley, arts officer.

Dudley Metropolitan Borough Council. Dudley Planning and Leisure Dept, Claughton House, Blowers Green Road, Dudley, W Midlands DY2 8UZ *tel:* 01384 815513 *email:* arts.pls@mbc.dudley.gov.uk. Rosemary Amos, principal arts officer.

Solihull Metropolitan Borough Council. Education, Libraries and Arts Dept, Central Library, Homer Road, Solihull, W Midlands B91 3RG *tel:* 0121 704 6961 *fax:* 0121 704 8195. Lawrence Smith, arts and entertainments manager.

Walsall Metropolitan Borough Council. Leisure and Community Services, PO Box 42, Civic Centre, Darwall Street, Walsall WS1 1TZ *tel:* 01922 653170 *fax:* 01922 721682. Antonia Pompa, promotions and events manager.

Wolverhampton Metropolitan District Council. Civic Hall, North Street, Wolverhampton, W Midlands WV1 1RQ *tel:* 01902 552122 *fax:* 01902 552123. Mark Blackstock, civic halls and outdoor events manager.

West Sussex

West Sussex County Council. County Hall, Chichester, W Sussex PO19 1RQ *tel:* 01243 777902 *fax:* 01243 777952. John Godfrey, assistant county secretary.

Adur District Council. Commerce Way, Lancing, W Sussex BN15 8TA *tel:* 01273 455566 *fax:* 01903 751140 *email:* devserv@adurdc.gov.uk. Jacqui Bladen, marketing and development officer; Louise Durrant, arts development officer.

Arun District Council. Civic Centre, Littlehampton, W Sussex BN17 5LF *tel:* 01903 716133. John Stride, head of leisure services.

Chichester District Council. East Pallant House, East Pallant, Chichester, W Sussex PO19 1TY *tel:* 01243 785166 *fax:* 01243 776766. Anne Bone, arts and heritage development manager.

Crawley Borough Council. The Hawth, Crawley, W Sussex RH10 6YZ *tel:* 01293 552941 *email:* hawth@enterprise.net. Kevin Eason, theatre and arts manager.

Horsham District Council. Horsham Arts Centre, North Street, Horsham, W Sussex RH12 1RL *tel:* 01403 259708 *fax:* 01403 211502. Kevin Parker, arts centre manager.

Mid Sussex District Council. Leisure and Amenities Dept, Oaklands, Haywards Heath, W Sussex RH16 1SS *tel:* 01444 458166 ext 2275 *fax:* 01444 414669 *email:* sarahe@midsussex.gov.uk. Sarah Elderkin, community arts development officer.

Worthing Borough Council. c/o Pavilion Theatre, Marine Parade, Worthing, W Sussex BN11 3PX *tel:* 01903 239999 ext 2502. Peter Bailey, theatre manager.

West Yorkshire (Metropolitan County Area)

City of Bradford Metropolitan District Council. Recreation Service, Jacob's Well, Bradford, W Yorks BD1 5RW *tel:* 01274 752646 *fax:* 01244 754676. Jim Mackay, head of recreation.

Kirklees Metropolitan Council. Kirklees Cultural Services, Red Doles Lane, Huddersfield, W Yorks HD2 1YF *tel:* 01484 226300 ext 6361 *fax:* 01484 226342 *email:* cultural-hq@geo2.poptel.org.uk. Richard Bealing, assistant head of cultural services.

Leeds City Council. Leisure Services, Leeds Town Hall, The Headrow, Leeds, W Yorks LS1 3AD *tel:* 0113 247 8337. Denise Preston, acting director, Leeds leisure services.

Wakefield Metropolitan District Council. Museums and Arts, Chantry House, 123 Kirkgate, Wakefield, W Yorks WF1 1ZS *tel:* 01924 305799 *fax:* 01924 305793. Adele Poppleton, senior development officer.

Wiltshire

Kennet District Council. Browfort, Bath Road, Devizes, Wilts SN10 2AT *tel:* 01380 724911 ext 674. Ruth Hecht, arts development officer.

North Wiltshire District Council. Leisure Services, The Citadel, Bath Road, Chippenham, Wilts SN15 2AA *tel:* 01249 706496.

Swindon Borough Council. Community and Leisure, Premier House, Station Road, Swindon, Wilts SN1 1TZ *tel:* 01793 466544. Ann Cullis, principal arts and strategy officer.

Worcestershire

Worcestershire County Council. County Hall, Spetchley Road, Worcester WR5 2NP *tel:* 01905 763763 *fax:* 01905 766244. Steve Boffy, county arts officer.

Malvern Hills District Council. The Council House, Avenue Road, Malvern, Worcs WR14 3AF *tel:* 01684 862412 *email:* warwick.toone @malvernhills.gov. Warwick Toone, tourism and arts officer.

Redditch Borough Council. Town Hall, Alcester Street, Redditch, Worcs B98 8AH *tel:* 01527 64252 ext 3300. Paul Patten, head of leisure services.

Worcester City Council. Orchard House, Farrier Street, Worcester WR1 3BW *tel:* 01905 722322 *fax:* 01905 722350. Liz Dart, arts development officer.

Wyre Forest District Council. 99 Coventry Street, Kidderminster, Worcs DY10 2BL *tel:* 01562 732664 *fax:* 01562 732625. Karen Curry, arts and lottery officer.

York

City of York Council. Leisure Services, 18 Back Swinegate, Swinegate Court, York YO1 8ZD *tel:* 01904 613161 ext 3387 *fax:* 01904 553378 *email:* peter.boardman@york.gov.uk. Peter Boardman, service commissioner, arts and culture.

Channel Islands

Bailiwick of Guernsey. States Arts Committee, Sir Charles Frossard House, PO Box 43, St Peter Port, Channel Islands GY1 1FH *tel:* 01481 717000 *fax:* 01481 712520 *email:* davidsavident@gov.gg. D M Savident, secretary.

Isle of Man

Douglas Borough Council. Entertainments Dept, Villa Marina, Douglas, Isle of Man *tel:* 01624 674171. Martin Blackburn, general manager.

Isle of Wight

Isle of Wight Council. Guildhall, Newport, Isle of Wight PO30 1TY *tel:* 01983 823822. Lorna Brown, arts development manager.

Isles of Scilly

Isles of Scilly Council. Town Hall, St Mary's, Isles of Scilly TR21 0LW *tel:* 01720 423371 *fax:* 01720 422049 *email:* steve@scilly.demon.co.uk. Steve Watt, tourism, development and maritime officer.

Scotland

Aberdeen City Council. Arts and Recreation Dept, St Nicholas House, Broad Street, Aberdeen AB10 1XJ *tel:* 01224 522472 *fax:* 01224 648256. Brian Woodcock, director of arts and recreation.

Aberdeenshire Council, Central Division. Gordon House, Blackhall Road, Inverurie AB51 3WA *tel:* 01467 628379. Sheila Waterhouse, arts development officer, recreation service.

Angus Council. Cultural Services, County Buildings, Forfar, Angus DD8 3WF *tel:* 01307 461460 ext 3256 *fax:* 01307 462590 *email:* cultural@angus.gov.uk. Colin Dakers, support services manager.

Clackmannanshire Council. Lime Tree House, Castle Street, Alloa FK10 1EX *tel:* 01259 450000/452486. Rosa Macpherson, team leader, arts, arts education; Karen Kirkwood, events and entertainments officer.

Dumfries and Galloway Council. Arts Team, Gracefield Arts Centre, 28 Edinburgh Rd, Dumfries DG1 1NW *tel:* 01387 262084 *fax:* 01387 255173. Rebecca Coggins, arts development officer for community resources.

Dundee City Council. Arts and Heritage Dept, Dundee Contemporary Arts, 152 Nethergate, Dundee DD1 4DY *tel:* 01382 432286 *fax:* 01382 432252 *email:* arts.heritage@dundeecity.gov.uk. Andrea Stark, chief arts officer.

East Dunbartonshire Council. Kilmardinny Arts Centre, 50 Kilmardinny Avenue, Bearsden, Glasgow G61 3NN *tel:* 0141 931 5084 *fax:* 0141 931 5085. Joan Riddell, arts and events manager.

East Lothian Council. Brunton Hall, Ladywell Way, Musselburgh, E Lothian EH21 6AA *tel:* 0131 665 9900. Lesley Smith, principal arts officer.

Edinburgh City Council. Directorate of Recreation, 17 Waterloo Place, Edinburgh EH1 3BG *tel:* 0131 529 7736 *fax:* 0131 529 7846. Herbert Coutts, acting director of recreation.

Falkirk Council. Community and Environmental Services, Kilns House, Kilns Road, Falkirk FK1 5SA *tel:* 01324 506070. Jack Sanderson, museum manager.

Glasgow City Council. City Chambers, George Square, Glasgow G2 1DU *tel:* 0141 287 2000 *fax:* 0141 287 5666 *email:* pr@glasgow.gov.uk. James Andrews, chief executive.

Highland Council, Inverness Area. Cultural and Leisure Services, Town House, Inverness IV1 1JJ *tel:* 01463 724261 *fax:* 01463 712850. Adrian Clark, arts officer.

Highland Council, Nairn Area. The Court House, High Street, Nairn IV12 4AU *tel:* 01667 458513 *fax:* 01667 458533. Phil Swainson, sports and arts development officer.

Highland Council, Sutherland Area. Council Offices, Main Street, Golspie KW10 6RB *tel:* 01408 633033 *fax:* 01408 633120 *email:* jim.poyner@highland.gov.uk. Jim Poyner, recreation officer.

Inverclyde Council. Education Services, 105 Dalrymple Street, Greenock PA15 1HT *tel:* 01475 712850 *fax:* 01475 712875. J Monteith, head of service.

Moray Council. Council Office, High Street, Elgin IV30 1BX *tel:* 01343 563403 *fax:* 01343 563410 *email:* mcgille@techleis.moray.gov.uk. Eric McGillivray, arts development officer.

North Lanarkshire Council. Leisure Services, Buchanan Tower, Buchanan Business Park, Cumbernauld Road, Stepps, Glasgow G33 6HR *tel:* 0141 304 1800. Ann Malloy, head of cultural and care services.

Perth and Kinross Council. Perth Museum and Art Gallery, George Street, Perth PH1 5LB *tel:* 01738 632488. Lynn Baxter, principal officer, community arts.

Renfrewshire Council. Paisley Arts Centre, New Street, Paisley *tel:* 0141 887 1010 *fax:* 0141 887 6300 *email:* renlib8@cqm.co.uk. John Harding, manager.

Scottish Borders Council. Council Headquarters, Newtown Street, Newtown St Boswells, Melrose TD6 0SA *tel:* 01835 824000. Iain Macaulay, arts development officer.

South Lanarkshire Council. Council Offices, South Vennel, Lanark ML11 7JT *tel:* 01555 661331 ext 281 *fax:* 01555 664260. Colin McAllister, arts officer (rural).

Stirling Council. Heritage and Cultural Services, Viewforth, Stirling FK8 2ET *tel:* 01786 443241 *email:* hendersone@stirling.gov.uk. Evan Henderson, events officer.

West Dunbartonshire Council. Education and Leisure Services, Arts and Leisure Development, 6-14 Bridge Street, Dumbarton G82 1NT *tel:* 01389 737073 *fax:* 01389 737075. Gill Graham, senior arts development officer.

Western Isles Islands Council

Comhairle Nan Eilean Siar. Lionacleit Education Centre, Benbecula, Western Isles HS7 5PJ *tel:* 01870 602043 *fax:* 01870 602053. Donald W Morrison, arts development officer.

Wales

Blaenau Gwent County Borough. Community Services Dept, c/o The Beaufort Theatre, Beaufort, Ebbw Vale NP23 5QQ *tel:* 01495 308996 *also fax.* Geoff Cripps, arts development manager.

Caerphilly County Borough Council. Blackwood Miners Institute, High Street, Blackwood NP2 1BB *tel:* 01495 224425 *fax:* 01495 226457. Lyn Evans, leisure development officer.

Cardiff County Council. Sports and Leisure Dept, County Hall, Atlantic Wharf, Cardiff CF1 5UW *tel:* 029 2087 3936/2087 3904. Paul Jenkins, director of sports and leisure.

Carmarthenshire County Council. Public Library, St Peters Street, Carmarthen, Dyfed SA31 1LN *tel:* 01267 224834. Phil Alder, arts officer.

Denbighshire County Council. Russell House, Churton Road, Rhyl, Denbighshire LL18 3DP *tel:* 01824 706409 *fax:* 01824 344516. Gareth Owen, theatre manager.

Gwynedd Council. Dept of Education and Culture, Swyddfa'r Cyngor, Caernarfon, Gwynedd LL55 1SH *tel:* 01286 679089 *email:* GarethHaulfryn@gwynedd.gov.uk. Gareth Haulfryn Williams, assistant director, culture.

Isle of Anglesey County Council. Leisure and Heritage Dept, Swyddfa'r Sir, Llangefni, Isle of Anglesey LL77 7TW *tel:* 01248 752021 *fax:* 01248 750365. E A Mitcheson, director of leisure and heritage.

Newport County Borough Council. Education Dept, Civic Centre, Newport NP9 4UR *tel:* 01633 233431 *fax:* 01633 233376. Alun D Williams, music adviser.

Pembrokeshire County Council. Scolton Manor Museum, Spittal, Haverfordwest, Pembrokeshire *tel:* 01437 731328 *fax:* 01437 731743. Tracey Morris, arts officer, cultural services division.

Rhondda Cynon Taff County Borough Council. Education Dept, Grawen Street, Porth, Rhondda CF39 0BU *tel:* 01443 687666 *fax:* 01443 680286. Gareth Newton, County Borough community education officer.

Swansea, City and County of. The Guildhall, Swansea SA1 4PE *tel:* 01792 302491 *email:* dave.evans@swansea.gov.uk. D Evans, director of leisure services.

Torfaen County Borough Council. Civic Centre, Pontypool, Gwent NP4 6YB *tel:* 01495 762200 *fax:* 01495 755513. David Congreve, head of leisure, youth and culture.

Wrexham County Borough Council. Memorial Hall, Bodhyfryd, Wrexham LL12 7AG *tel:* 01978 292683. G A Lacy, arts and entertainment officer.

Northern Ireland

Antrim

Antrim Borough Council. c/o Clotworthy Arts Centre, Randalstown Road, Antrim, Co Antrim *tel:* 028 9442 8000 *fax:* 028 9446 0360. G Shaw, arts and heritage development officer.

Ballymena Borough Council. 80 Galgorm Road, Ballymena, Co Antrim BT42 1AB *tel:* 028 2566 0300 ext 319. Rosalind Lowry, arts officer.

Ballymoney Borough Council. Riada House, Charles Street, Ballymoney, Co Antrim BT53 6DZ *tel:* 028 2766 2280 *fax:* 028 2766 7659. Ms M Higgins, cultural services officer.

Larne Borough Council. Smiley Buildings, Victoria Road, Larne, Co Antrim BT40 1RU *tel:* 028 2827 2313. H G Francis, secretary.

Lisburn Borough Council. Harmony Hill Arts Centre, Clonmore House, 54 Harmony Hill, Lisburn, Co Antrim BT27 4ES *tel:* 028 9267 8219 *fax:* 028 9266 2679. Siobhan Stewart, arts development officer.

Armagh

Armagh City and District Council. The Market Place, Armagh Theatre and Arts Centre, Market Street, Armagh *tel:* 028 3752 1805 *fax:* 028 3751 0180 *email:* armagh.arts@dnet.co.uk. Kate Bond, arts manager.

Craigavon Borough Council. Pinebank Arts and Resource Centre, Tullygally Road, Craigavon, Co Armagh BT65 5BY *tel:* 028 3834 1618 *fax:* 028 3834 2402. Rosaleen McMullan, arts development officer.

Down

Down District Council. Down County Museum, The Mall, Downpatrick, Co Down BT30 6AH *tel:* 028 4461 5218 ext 250 *fax:* 028 4461 5590. Jill Holmes, arts officer.

Ards Borough Council. Ards Arts Centre, Scrabo High School, Scrabo Road, Newtownards, Co Down BT23 4NP *tel:* 028 9181 0803 *fax:* 028 9182 3131 *email:* ards@ards-council.gov.uk. Eilis O Baoill, arts officer.

North Down Borough Council. Town Hall, Bangor, Co Down BT20 4BT *tel:* 028 9127 8032. Paula Clamp, Lorna Hastings, arts officers.

Londonderry

Derry City Council. Performing Arts, Rialto Entertainment Centre, 5 Market Street, Derry, Co Londonderry BT48 6EF *tel:* 028 7126 4177 *fax:* 028 7126 0688. David McLaughlin, venues manager.

Limavady Borough Council. 7 Connell Street, Limavady, Co Londonderry BT49 0HA *tel:* 028 7776 0304. S T McGregor, chief recreation officer.

Tyrone

Omagh District Council. Council Offices, The Grange, Mountjoy Road, Omagh, Co Tyrone BT79 7BL *tel:* 028 8224 5321 ext 316 *email:* jean.brennan@omagh.gov.uk. Jean Brennan, arts development officer.

Strabane District Council. District Council Offices, 47 Derry Road, Strabane, Co Tyrone BT82 8DY *tel:* 028 7138 2204 *fax:* 028 7138 2264 *email:* strabanecouncil@easynet.co.uk. Karen McFarland, community services officer.

Concert Promoters

The following organisations, including the cultural institutes of certain Commonwealth and foreign governments, promote concerts regularly using private funds, money from public funding bodies, or a mixture of the two. They act as principals in selecting, engaging, promoting and paying artists and take financial responsibility for the outcome.

Additional concert promoters are listed in the following sections: **Local Authority Promoters, Music Clubs and Societies** and **Associations.**

Adrian Hopkins Promotions. 24 Fulham Palace Rd, Hammersmith, London W6 9PH *tel:* 020 8741 9910 *fax:* 020 8741 9914.

Alternative Arts. 47a Brushfield St, Spitalfields, London E1 6AA *tel:* 020 7375 0441 *fax:* 020 7375 0484. Maggie Pinhorn, dir. *Jazz, opera, classical, contemporary.*

Anglo-Argentine Society. 2 Belgrave Square, London SW1X 8PJ *tel:* 020 7235 9505 *also fax; email:* angloarg@dircon.co.uk. T J Rumboll, sec. *Argentine mus and composers.*

Anglo-Austrian Music Society. 46 Queen Anne's Gate, London SW1H 9AU *tel:* 020 7222 0366 *fax:* 020 7233 0293. Tony Fessler, gen sec. *Promotes concerts which have a connection with Austria.*

Arthur Davison Family Concerts. 14 Beaumont Rd, Purley, Surrey CR8 2EG *tel:* 020 8668 5883 *also fax.* Darrell Davison, mus dir.

Asian Music Circuit. Unit F (Ground Floor), West Point, 33-34 Warple Way, Acton, London W3 0RG *tel:* 020 8742 9911 *fax:* 020 8749 3948. Kuldeep Jalf, sec; Penny King, programme co-ord; Alistair Will, educ co-ord. *UK touring organisation promoting mus from the Indian subcontinent, SE Asia, central Asia and the Far East.*

Austrian Cultural Institute. 28 Rutland Gate, London SW7 1PQ *tel:* 020 7584 8653 *fax:* 020 7225 0470 *email:* austrcul@dircon.co.uk. Andrea Rauter, mus offr. *Classical and contemporary, mostly chmbr mus; jazz.*

Beejays Promotions. 136 Pottinger St, Ashton-under-Lyne, Lancs OL7 0HQ *tel:* 0161 344 1610 *also fax.* John Burke, mgr. *Concert promoters, entertainment agents, artist management.*

Brighton & Hove Philharmonic Society. 50 Grand Parade, Brighton BN2 2QA *tel:* 01273 622900 *fax:* 01273 697887. Tony Woodhouse, gen mgr. *Presents annual orch concert series.*

British Music Information Centre. 10 Stratford Place, London W1N 9AE *tel:* 020 7499 8567 *fax:* 020 7499 4795 *email:* bmic@bmic.co.uk. Matthew Greenall, dir; Vanessa Reed, promotions asst. *Presents concerts of classical mus (mostly 20th C British) twice weekly; also lectures and discussions.*

La Colombe du Paradis. 16 Church St, South Brent, Devon TQ10 9AB *tel:* 01364 72522. Roland Mason, snr partner. *Mainly charity concerts.*

CPP Music Productions. 28 Tonmead Rd, Northampton NN3 8HX *tel:* 01604 412922 *email:* cppmusic@hotmail.com. Li Jiang, dir; Ket Y-Chiu, admin. *Promotion of traditional Chinese mus and cultural events.*

Danish Cultural Institute. 3 Doune Terrace, Edinburgh EH3 6DY *tel:* 0131 225 7189 *fax:* 0131 220 6162 *email:* fa@dancult.demon.co.uk. Mette Bligaard, dir. *Concerts throughout UK for Danish soloists and ens.*

Dartington Arts. The Gallery, Dartington Hall, Totnes, Devon TQ9 6DE *tel:* 01803 865864 (admin); 01803 863073 (box office) *fax:* 01803 868108 *email:* paul@dissorg.u-net.com. Paul Goddard, arts development, programme mgr; Lewis Riley, mus programmer; Kamya O'Keefe, mkt mgr. *Classical, world mus, folk, jazz, contemporary, improvised.*

La Dolca Musica. 47 Elmfield Ave, Teddington, Middx TW11 8BX *tel:* 020 8977 7497 *also fax.* June Allison, mgr dir. *Dedicated to providing a platform from which highly talented 23-25 year old instrumentalists can be introduced to the public. Two annual awards made.*

Early Music Network. 31 Abdale Rd, London W12 7ER *tel:* 020 8743 0302 *fax:* 020 8743 0996 *email:* glyn@earlymusicnet.demon.co.uk. Glyn Russ, admin. *Early mus, particularly young professional musicians, those with strong educational skills and those able to reach new audiences.*

ECAT (Edinburgh Contemporary Arts Trust). 16 Clerwood Gardens, Edinburgh EH12 8PT *tel:* 0131 539 8877 *fax:* 0131 539 2211. Hazel Sheppard, admin; Stephen Deazley, outreach offr. *Contemporary mus.*

Flamencovision. 54 Windsor Rd, London N3 3SS *tel:* 020 8346 4500 *fax:* 020 8346 2488 *email:* hvmartin@dircon.co.uk. Helen Martin, mgr. *Flamenco gui and dance.*

Fun with Music. PO Box 16975, London NW8 6ZL *tel:* 020 7722 9828 *fax:* 020 7722 7981. Iain Kerr, admin. *Children's and family concerts.*

Influence. Disraeli Mews, 137b Outney High St, London SW15 1SU *tel:* 020 8789 0776 *fax:* 020 8789 1192. Michael Heyland, events consultant. *Promotes concerts and international tours, particularly choral and operatic. Other entertainment has included open-air carol concerts at Covent Garden and jazz festivals in Battersea Park.*

Invisible Pilots Ltd. The Barony, 16 Sandringham Rd, Petersfield, Hants GU32 2AA *tel:* 01730 267341 *also fax; email:* invisiblepilots @classical-artists.com. Peter Thompson, proprietor. *Classical recitals.*

Jewish Music Heritage Trust. PO Box 232, Harrow, Middx HA1 2NN *tel:* 020 8909 2445 *fax:* 020 8909 1030 *email:* jewishmusic@jmht.org. Geraldine Auerbach, dir. *Promotes concerts and recitals of mus of Jewish significance.*

Kirckman Concert Society Ltd. 29 Northway, London NW11 6PB *tel:* 020 8458 7961. Neil Black, mus dir. Sarah Gordon Concert Management *tel:* 020 7483 2681. *London recitals for young artists chosen at audition.*

LACCS (Latin American and Caribbean Cultural Society). PO Box 30, London N12 0PR *tel:* 020 8446 6416 *fax:* 020 8446 5547. J R Monroy, dir; J L Sylvester, project mgr. *Latin American, classical, popular and folk mus; also worldwide mus and arts.*

Lancaster Concerts. University of Lancaster, Music Dept, Lancaster, Lancs LA1 4YW *tel:* 01524 593777/593729 (box office) *fax:* 01524 847298 *email:* dmccaldin@lancaster.ac.uk. Denis McCaldin, dir; Stella Birchall, admin. *Symphony orch, chmbr orch, choral, chmbr mus, chmbr opera, early mus, contemporary mus, jazz.*

Leeds International Concert Season. Leeds Leisure Services, Leeds Town Hall, Leeds LS1 3AD *tel:* 0113 247 8335 *fax:* 0113 247 8397 *email:* matthew.sims@leeds.gov.uk. Matthew Sims, principal mus offr. *Orch, chmbr, jazz, br, org and children's concerts.*

London Bach Society. Bach House, 73 High St, Old Oxted, Surrey RH8 9LN *tel:* 01883 717372 *fax:* 01883 715851. Margaret Steinitz, sec. *Promotes London Bach Festival annually in Oct-Nov as well as other events throughout the year.*

Manchester Midday Concerts Society. 134 Kingsbrook Rd, Manchester M16 8WG *tel:* 0161 881 9320 *also fax.* Carolyn Howlett, admin; Christopher Yates, dir of concerts. *Lunchtime chmbr mus concerts.*

Michael Webber Promotions. 23a Alma Rd, Cheltenham, Glos GL51 5LU *tel:* 01242 578893 *also fax. Jazz, classical (orch and chmbr), br band and opera.*

Minstrel Productions. 3-5 Bridge St, Hadleigh, Suffolk IP7 6BY *tel:* 01473 822596 *fax:* 01473 824175. *Classical chmbr and symphonic concerts. Solo inst concerts.*

Molto International Promotions Ltd. PO Box 256, Harrow HA2 0YH *tel:* 020 8357 0009 *fax:* 020 8933 9436 *email:* frances.dennys @dial.pipex.com. Gerald Drucker, artistic dir; Frances Dennys, artist mgt.

Music at Leicester University. University Rd, Leicester LE1 7RH *tel:* 0116 252 2781 *fax:* 0116 252 2782 *email:* ap1@leicester.ac.uk. Anthony Pither, dir of mus; Margaret Rose, admin. *Evening and lunchtime concerts; symphonic orch, chmbr orch, wind band, choral, chmbr mus, early and contemporary mus.*

Music at Oxford. Elms Court, Oxford OX2 9LP *tel:* 01865 242865 *fax:* 01865 242867 *email:* info@musicatoxford.demon.co.uk. Melinda Jordan, gen mgr; Jennifer Johns, artistic admin; Georgia Rivers, mkt mgr. Lindsey Glen, development offr. *Classical and light concerts in and around Oxford. Also manage concerts for other promoters.*

Music For All Occasions. Torridon House, 104 Bradford Rd, Wrenthorpe, Wakefield, W Yorks WF1 2AH *tel:* 01924 371496. Brian Greensmith, mgr dir; Magdalen Greensmith, company sec. *Symphony and light orch. Str quartets, fl/vn, vc, pno. Pno trios. Dance bands, jazz bands, etc. Specialise in events and functions.*

Musicon. The Music School, Palace Green, Durham DH1 3RL *tel:* 0191 374 3210 *fax:* 0191 374 3219 *email:* karen.scott@durham.ac.uk. Helen Dayananda, admin. *University professional concert series, contemporary emphasis.*

Newcastle City Orchestral Subscription Concerts. Room 811, Civic Centre, Barras Bridge, Newcastle upon Tyne NE1 *tel:* 0191 232 8520 *fax:* 0191 211 4935. Andrew Rothwell, city arts offr.

Orbestra Music. 1 South St, Middle Barton, Oxon OX7 7BU *tel:* 01865 340951; 0771 281 5338 *fax:* 01869 349084 *email:* orbestra@excite.com. Suzanne Tharani, admin; Peter Cowdrey, dir. *World and contemporary mus, especially cross-overs between the two.*

Pan Concerts for Children. Masters Yard, 180a South St, Dorking, Surrey RH4 2ES *tel:* 01306 508100 *fax:* 01306 880038 *email:* richard @maslink.co.uk. Richard Smith, promoter. *Children's educ concerts.*

Parkfield Music. 178 Otley Rd, West Park, Leeds LS16 5LG *tel:* 0113 289 9010 *also fax.*

Performing Arts Management. Canal 7, Clarence Mill, Bollington, Macclesfield, Cheshire SK10 5JZ *tel:* 01625 575681 *fax:* 01625 572839. Fifi Butler, PR. *Specialists in promotion and management of large-scale open-air orch concerts with fireworks.*

Philip Biggs Brass Festivals. 21 The Coppice, Impington, Cambridge CB4 4PP *tel:* 01223 234090 *also fax; email:* philipbiggs@bandstand. demon.co.uk. Philip Biggs, organiser. *Presents and promotes br bands and br soloists. Also specialises in event management and artist engagement.*

Polish Cultural Institute. 34 Portland Place, London W1N 4HQ *tel:* 020 7636 6032 *fax:* 020 7637 2190. Aleksandra Czapiewska, dir. *Promotion of Polish mus and concerts by Polish artists in the UK.*

Polish Social and Cultural Association Ltd. 238-246 King St, London W6 0RF *tel:* 020 8741 1940 *fax:* 020 8746 3798. Adam Ostaszewski, arts co-ord. *Classical, evening and afternoon concerts involving Polish composers and musicians.*

Pro Arte Enterprises Ltd. 27 Kendal Steps, St George's Fields, London W2 2YE *tel:* 020 7402 7860 *fax:* 020 7402 7172 *email:* p.a@ argonet.co.uk. Paul Appleyard. *London Schubert Orchestra, Statuz Cymbal.*

Raymond Gubbay Ltd. Knight House, 29-31 East Barnet Rd, New Barnet, Herts EN4 8RN *tel:* 020 8216 3000 *fax:* 020 8216 3001. Raymond Gubbay, mgr dir; Anthony Findlay, events dir. *Classical concerts, classical spectaculars, opera galas, opera spectaculars, ballet, jazz, dance and special events.*

Redcliffe Concerts. 68 Barrowgate Rd, London W4 4QU *tel:* 020 8995 1223 *also fax.* Francis Routh, artistic dir. *British mus.*

Rhinosaurus Records Ltd. 7 Springfields, Somerset Rd, New Barnet, Herts EN5 1SG *tel:* 020 8440 0183 *fax:* 020 8440 8169. Colin Middleton, producer; Richard Jacob, chief sound engineer. *Concert promotion and artist management.*

St George's Music Trust. St George's Brandon Hill, Bristol BS1 5PZ *tel:* 0117 929 4929 *fax:* 0117 927 6537. Jonathan Stracey, dir. *Promotes classical chmbr mus, opera and jazz.*

Sara Hindley Promotions. 59 Brook St, Chester, Cheshire CH1 3DZ *tel:* 01244 319981 *fax:* 01244 315662. Sara Hindley, proprietor; Rebecca Perez, mkt. *Personal mgt, concert mgt, publicity material, supply of artistes, programmes.*

Serious Ltd. Chapel House, 18 Hatton Place, London EC1N 8RU *tel:* 020 7405 9900 *fax:* 020 7405 9911 *email:* info@seriousltd.demon.co.uk. John Cumming, David Jones, Claire Whitaker, dirs. *Specialises in 20th C and new mus.*

Shropshire Music Trust. Wood Lane, Cressage, Shrops SY5 6DY *tel:* 01952 510375 *fax:* 01952 510350. Kate Hogwood, dir. *Shropshire Music Season: mainly classical with some folk, jazz and ethnic.*

Sonicity 2000. 24 Kensington Rd, Arundel Park, Chichester, W Sussex PO19 2XN *tel:* 01243 787740 *fax:* 01243 531610 *email:* 100622.3205@compuserve.com. David Lloyd-Howells, artistic dir. *Sonic art mus for mus clubs, societies, etc.*

Sound Affairs. 62 Arran St, Roath, Cardiff CF24 3HT *tel:* 029 2049 7157 *also fax; email:* sound.affairs@tesco.net. Charlie Barber, artistic dir. *New mus and multimedia.*

South Place Sunday Concerts. Conway Hall Humanist Centre, Red Lion Square, London WC1R 4RL *tel:* 01494 726106 *fax:* 01494 724230. Lionel Elton, hon sec. *Chmbr mus.*

spnm - promoting new music. Francis House, Francis St, London SW1P 1DE *tel:* 020 7828 9696 *fax:* 020 7931 9928 *email:* spnm@spnm.org.uk. Gill Graham, exec dir; Katy Bignold, admin; Sarah Gibbon, educ consultant. *Concerts of spnm shortlisted works and other British contemporary mus.*

Stevenage Leisure Ltd. Stevenage Arts & Leisure Centre, Lytton Way, Stevenage, Herts *tel:* 01438 766866. M McCardle, mgr dir.

Stoke and Newcastle Music. Brunswick House, 14-20 Brunswick St, Hanley, Stoke-on-Trent, ST1 1DR *tel:* 01781 206000 *fax:* 01782 213432. Mike Lloyd, dir. *Orch concerts, pno recitals, jazz concerts, etc.*

Thames Concerts Society. 56 Heath Ridge Green, Cobham, Surrey KT11 2QJ *tel:* 01372 843292. Bill Littlejohn, hon sec. *Professional classical orch concerts.*

Victor Hochhauser. 4 Oak Hill Way, London NW3 7LR *tel:* 020 7794 0987 *fax:* 020 7431 2531.

Wavendon Allmusic Plan. The Stables, Wavendon, Milton Keynes, Bucks MK17 8LT *tel:* 01908 582522 *fax:* 01908 281024 *email:* stables@ powernet.co.uk. Jacky Scott, gen mgr; John Dankworth, Cleo Laine, joint presidents. *Promotes all mus including jazz, classical, folk, country, rock, roots, world and blues.*

West End International Ltd. 15 Mount Pleasant, London WC1X 0AA *tel:* 020 7833 0884 *fax:* 020 7833 9883. Gary Brown, Martin Yates, dirs. *Opera: concert performances, mus theatre concerts (West End, Broadway), celebrity concerts and special events.*

Westbourne Music. 31 Westbourne Gardens, Glasgow G12 *tel:* 0141 334 3743. Stephen Strugnell, admin. *Promotes fortnightly lunchtime concert series in Glasgow.*

Wingfield Arts. College Yard, Wingfield, Eye, Suffolk IP21 5RA *tel:* 01379 384048 *fax:* 01379 384034 *email:* wingfield@easynet.co.uk. Ian Chance, arts dir. *Annual events in E Anglia, Mar-Dec.*

Special Promotion for Youth

The following organisations sponsor recitals and promote professional engagements. Many regional arts boards run schemes for those born or living in the area.

Cushion Concerts for Children. The Brew House, Radwell, Baldock, Herts SG7 5ES *tel:* 01462 730490 *also fax; email:* ccwilmers@ bigfoot.com. Catherine Wilmers.

Live Music Now! 4 Lower Belgrave St, London SW1W 0LJ *tel:* 020 7730 2205 *fax:* 020 7730 3641 *email:* lmnlondon@compuserve.com. Virginia Renshaw, UK dir; Katherine Potter, asst dir; Cate Cox, admin. *Mus charity founded by the late Yehudi Menuhin which provides performances and w/shops for young professional musicians and those with special needs who have little access to live mus. Concerts held at various venues within the community.*

National Federation of Music Societies. Francis House, Francis St, London SW1P 1DE *tel:* 020 7828 7320 *fax:* 020 7828 5504 *email:* postmaster@nfms.demon.co.uk. Robin Osterley, chief exec; Kate Fearnley, award admin; Chris Wright, membership and operating mgr. *NFMS Young Concert Artists Award. Young artists' platforms. NFMS concert promoters network.*

Yorkshire Youth & Music. Dean Clough, Halifax HX3 5AX *tel:* 01422 383130 *fax:* 01422 321823. Jan Hinde, dir. *Promotes region-wide series of mus events ('Family Funday Concerts') for 4-11 yr olds and their families. Central to this work is the building not only of young people's listening skills but also their creative and artistic potential.*

Young Persons Concert Foundation. PO Box 419, Enfield, Middx EN2 0ZB *tel:* 020 8367 0553; 01923 859388 *fax:* 020 8366 3535. William A J Starling, artistic dir; Sally Needleman, special projects co-ord. *Concerts for children and general public.*

Music Clubs and Societies

The clubs and societies listed here promote mainly professional concerts for members and visitors. Most belong to the **National Federation of Music Societies (NFMS)**, Francis House, Francis St, London SW1P 1DE *tel:* 020 7828 7320 *fax:* 020 7828 5504 *email:* enquiries@nfms.org.uk. The **NFMS** operates a mailing service for artists and agents wishing to contact the societies as well as free advice to those wishing to join their local society. School and College music societies are not listed unless they belong to the **NFMS**. To facilitate tour planning, this list is arranged according to the reorganised Regional Arts Boards.

England

London Arts Board

This includes all 32 London Boroughs and the City of London.

Barnes Music Society. c/o 28 Denehurst Gardens, Richmond, Surrey TW10 5DL *tel:* 020 8876 3919. Sheila Kearvell, hon recitals sec.

Bromley Music Society. 32 Repton Rd, Orpington, Kent BR6 9HS *tel:* 01689 839044 *email:* vhitchman@rics.org.uk. Valerie Hitchman, hon sec.

The Chopin Society. 44 Bassett Rd, London W10 6JL *tel:* 020 8960 6717 *also fax; email:* info@chopin-society.org.uk. Lady Rose Cholmondeley, president; Gill Newman, sec.

City Music Society. 16 Chase Court Gardens, Enfield EN2 8DH *tel:* 020 8363 4203 *also fax*. Leslie East, chmn.

Clarinet Heritage Society. 47 Hambalt Rd, London SW4 9EQ *tel:* 020 8675 3877 *email:* stephen.bennett@telia.com. Stephen Bennett, sec.

The John Lewis Partnership Music Society. John Lewis plc, 171 Victoria St, London SW1E 5NN *tel:* 020 7592 6265 *fax:* 020 7592 6589 *email:* mr@locumgroup.co.uk. M Spinner, sec; D M Wilson, chmn; M S Rattan, mus dir.

Mill Hill Music Club. 99 Kingsley Way, London N2 0EL *tel:* 020 8458 4720 *fax:* 020 8455 1363 *email:* walterfelman@compuserve.com. Walter Felman, chmn.

Music in Muswell Hill. 27 Weston Court, Farnham Close, London N20 9PQ *tel:* 020 8445 8391. Geoffrey Powell, chmn.

The Organ Club. Rothes Glen Hotel, Rothes, Morayshire AB38 7AQ *tel:* 020 7226 1218 (Adrian Gunning). Frederic Symonds, membership sec; Adrian Gunning, president.

Richmond Concert Society. 10 Hampton Rd, Hampton Hill, Middx TW12 1JN *tel:* 020 8977 4268 *fax:* 020 8287 9428. Peter King, hon sec.

St Anne's Music Society. Church of St Anne and St Agnes, Gresham St, London EC2V 7BX *tel:* 020 7606 4986 *fax:* 020 7600 8984 *email:* 74434.1521@compuserve.com. Rev Paul D Schmiege, admin; P Lea-Cox, cantor.

St Margaret Lothbury Organ Music Society. c/o 22 Moore St, London SW3 2QW *tel:* 020 7589 1206 *fax:* 020 7589 5925. Richard Townend.

Schubert Society of Britain. c/o The General Secretary, German YMCA, 35 Craven Terrace, London W2 3EL *tel:* 020 7723 9276 *fax:* 020 7706 2870 *email:* y-services@g-ymca.ndirect.co.uk. B Hildebrandt, gen sec.

Sutton House Music Society. 2-4 Homerton High St, Hackney, London E9 6JQ. Penelope Roskell, artistic dir.

East Midlands Arts

This covers Nottinghamshire, Derbyshire (excluding High Peak), Leicestershire, Lincolnshire and Northamptonshire.

Boston Concert Club. The Pharmacy, High St, Swineshead, nr Boston, Lincs PE20 3LH *tel:* 01205 820304. J Wilson.

East Lincolnshire Arts. 5 Lifeboat Ave, Skegness, Lincs PE25 3EW *tel:* 01754 763891. Peter Emmens, chmn.

Hinckley Music Club. Yew Tree Lodge, Main St, Higham on the Hill CV13 6AJ *tel:* 01455 212799 *also fax*. Michael Cox.

Leicester University. Department of Music, Leicester LE1 7RH *tel:* 0116 252 2781 *fax:* 0116 252 2782 *email:* mer@leicester.ac.uk. Margaret Rose.

Louth and District Concert Society. Glendale, Station Rd, Legbourne, Louth, Lincs LN11 8LH *tel:* 01507 609901. M Smith.

Matlock Music Society. Plantation Cottage, Hallmoor Rd, Darley Dale, Matlock, Derbys DE4 2HF *tel:* 01629 732072. E J Stuart, sec.

Music at Duffield. 14 Chevin Rd, Duffield, Derbys DE56 4DS *tel:* 01332 840817 (h); 01332 382233 (w) *fax:* 01332 291988 *email:* mikealexander@14chevinrd.freeserve.co.uk. Mike Alexander, concerts org.

Newark and District Music Club. 141 Main St, Old Balderton, Newark, Notts NG24 1PB *tel:* 01636 704975. Miss E A Whistler, chmn.

Nottingham Music Society. 12 Old Manor Close, Woodborough, Notts NG14 6DJ *tel:* 0115 965 3132. P V Trotman.

Peak Music Society. Ringwood, Eaton Drive, Baslow, Bakewell, Derbys DE45 1SE *tel:* 01246 582229. E J Grossman, hon sec.

Repton School Subscription Concerts Society. The Music School, Burton Rd, Repton, Derbys DE65 4FH *tel:* 01283 703374 (h); 01283 559319 (w) *fax:* 01283 559318 *email:* NCM@repton.org.uk. Neil Millensted, artistic dir.

South Holland Concerts. 19 Ladywood Rd, Spalding, Lincs PE11 2DA *tel:* 01775 766145 *fax:* 01775 713695 *email:* pvcase@cwcom.net. David Jones, chmn.

Uppingham Concerts. Uppingham School, Uppingham, Rutland LE15 9QU *tel:* 01572 822267 *fax:* 01572 822792 *email:* at@uppingham.co.uk. Alex Tester.

Worksop Music. Worksop College, Worksop, Notts *tel:* 01909 537143 *fax:* 01909 537102. David Evans, dir of mus.

Eastern Arts

This covers Bedfordshire, Cambridgeshire, Hertfordshire (other than the London Borough overlap), Norfolk, Essex and Suffolk.

Beccles and District Arts Society. 22 Lowestoft Rd, Worlingham, Suffolk NR34 7EH *tel:* 01502 714337. K J Cowburn.

Bedford Music Club. 2 Keats Close, Bedford MK40 2AR *tel:* 01234 354082 *email:* xyo55@dial.pipex.com. Roland Hoskins.

Berkhamsted Music Society. 1 Haynes Mead, Berkhamsted, Herts HP4 1BU *tel:* 01442 865384. Mrs M I Dudlyke, sec.

Brentwood Musical Society. 25 Crow Green Rd, Pilgrims Hatch, Brentwood, Essex CM15 9RB *tel:* 01277 373292. Mrs F Morris, hon sec.

Bury St Edmunds Concert Club. Felsham House, Bury St Edmunds, Suffolk IP30 0QG *tel:* 01449 736326 *fax:* 01449 737226. Mrs C M Erskine, chmn.

Colchester New Music Promotion. 32c Military Rd, Colchester, Essex CO1 2AJ *tel:* 01206 510784. Alan Parsons, mus dir.

Cuffley Concert Club. 50 Brookside Cres, Cuffley, Potters Bar, Herts EN6 4QN *tel:* 01707 873401. Mrs J Platt, chmn.

Felsted School Concert Club. Felsted School, Felsted, Gt Dunmow, Essex CM6 3JJ *tel:* 01371 820497 *fax:* 01371 821179. Jasper Thorogood, dir, school of mus.

Gainsborough Music Club. 13a Kirton Rd, Blyton, Gainsborough DN21 3LB *tel:* 01427 628260. Alan Sergent.

Grantham Music Club. 21 Parklands Drive, Harlaxton, Grantham, Lincs NG32 1HX *tel:* 01476 564345. Mrs M J Rowe.

Haverhill Sinfonia. 8 Templars Court, Haverhill, Suffolk CB9 9AJ *tel:* 01440 763799 *also fax*. Kevin Hill, mus dir.

Herts and Essex Concert Club. 12 Elm Rd, Bishop's Stortford, Herts CM23 2SS *tel:* 01279 651031. R J Phelps, hon treasurer.

Hoddesdon Music Club. 11 St David's Drive, Broxbourne, Herts EN10 7LS *tel:* 01992 462528 *also fax*. Felicity Foster, chmn.

Ipswich Arts Association. Town Hall, Cornhill, Ipswich IP1 1BZ *tel:* 01473 252552. B S Salmon, sec.

Ipswich Chamber Music Society. 16 Warrington Rd, Ipswich IP1 3QU *tel:* 01473 258218. Joyce Salmon, hon sec.

Ipswich Orchestral Society. 6 Borrowdale Ave, Ipswich, Suffolk IP4 2TN *tel:* 01473 408305 (w); 01473 251152 (h) *fax:* 01473 400058. Gareth D R Jones, chmn.

Kimbolton Music Society. 19 Newtown, Kimbolton, Huntingdon, Cambs PE18 0HY *tel:* 01480 860513. K W Laflin, chmn.

Leighton Buzzard Music Club. 11 Lomond Drive, Linslade, Leighton Buzzard, Beds LU7 7XH *tel:* 01525 371219. M Ward, hon sec.

Letchworth Music Club. 4 Greenside Drive, Hitchin, Herts SG5 2LP *tel:* 01462 456725. Dorothy Sault, gen sec.

Little Gaddesden and District Music Club. 7 Little Gaddesden, Berkhamsted, Herts HP4 1PA *tel:* 01442 843386. A C Cassell.

Luton Music Club. Carts Farm, Gravenhurst, Bedford MK45 4JB *tel:* 01462 711327 *email:* christhomas@nfmseast.freeserve.co.uk. Chris Thomas, chmn.

Music in Peterborough. 4 Robins Wood, Wansford, Peterborough PE8 6JQ *tel:* 01780 782972. Michael Hudson-Peacock, sec.

Norfolk and Norwich Music Club. 60 Park Lane, Norwich NR2 3EF *tel:* 01603 621169 *also fax; email:* rrowe@paston.co.uk. Roger Rowe, hon sec.

Ongar Music Club. Corbetts House, Norwood End, Fyfield, Ongar CM5 0RW *tel:* 01277 899337 *also fax*. Mrs Jean Hall, chmn.

Redbridge Music Society. 14 Morrab Gardens, Seven Kings, Ilford, Essex IG3 9HL *tel:* 020 8599 1578 *email:* cpmusic@compuserve.com. Patricia Waddle, hon sec.

Saffron Walden and District Music Club. 2 Chalklands, Saffron Walden, Essex CB10 2ER *tel:* 01799 527980. George Culling, deputy chmn.

Saxmundham Music and Arts. Benhall Lodge, Benhall, Saxmundham, Suffolk IP17 1JD. Richard Arnell, president.

Sleaford Music Club. 14 Kirkdale Close, Leasingham, Sleaford NG34 8NN *tel:* 01529 304389. Mrs B Lyon.

Southend Council Concert Club. PO Box 6, Civic Centre, Victoria Ave, Southend on Sea, Essex SS2 6ER *tel:* 01702 215436 *fax:* 01702 215110. Rosemary Pennington, dir.

Stour Valley Arts and Music Society. 13 Fiddlers Lane, East Bergholt, Colchester CO7 6SJ *tel:* 01206 298718. C H Willett, hon sec.

Stowmarket Concert Society. 24 Church Walk, Stowmarket, Suffolk IP14 1ET *tel:* 01449 612105. Arthur Winchester, hon sec.

Theydon Bois Music Society. 8 Slade End, Theydon Bois, Epping, Essex CM16 7EP *tel:* 01992 813270. Joyce Eynon, chmn.

Three Rivers Music Society. 71 Harefield Rd, Rickmansworth, Herts WD3 1ND *tel:* 01923 775623. Mrs S Murdoch, hon sec.

Trianon Music Group. D'Arcy Gate, Tolleshunt D'Arcy, Essex CM9 8EL *tel:* 01621 860681 *fax:* 01621 868806 *email:* alison@keeps.net. Alison Keep, admin.

University of Essex Concerts. Arts Office, University of Essex, Wivenhoe Park, Colchester CO4 3SQ *tel:* 01206 873718 *fax:* 01206 873702 *email:* cholden@essex.ac.uk. Christopher Holden, arts offr.

Watford Octagon Music Society. 3 The Hollies, Long Lane, Bovingdon Green, Hemel Hempstead, Herts HP3 0ND *tel:* 01442 834157. Mrs P Harborne.

Welwyn Garden Concert Club. 11 Roundwood Drive, Welwyn Garden City, Herts AL8 7JZ *tel:* 01707 323840. Margaret Wood, hon sec.

Wisbech Music Society. Rose Mount, Mount Drive, Wisbech, Cambs PE13 2BG *tel:* 01945 585921. Derek Walker, sec.

North West Arts

This covers Cheshire, Greater Manchester, High Peak (Derbyshire), Lancashire and Merseyside.

Chester Music Society Celebrity Concerts. Stone Bridge House, Balmoral Park, Chester CH1 4BQ *tel:* 01244 371134. G Hallett, hon sec.

Clitheroe Concerts Society. 11 Denbigh Drive, Clitheroe BB7 2BH *tel:* 01200 427551. G Hood, hon sec.

Clitheroe Parish Church Organ Society. 84 Woodbine Rd, Blackburn, Lancs BB2 6JZ *tel:* 01254 262107.

Concordia Concert Society. Liverpool Hope University College, Hope Park, Liverpool L16 9JD *tel:* 0151 291 3457 *fax:* 0151 291 3170 *email:* pratts@hope.ac.uk. Stephen Pratt.

Congleton Society for Music and Art. Mossley House, Mossley, Congleton, Cheshire CW12 3LQ *tel:* 01260 272946. Miss E D Chappell.

Douglas Music Society. 16 Coxfield Grove, Shevington, Wigan WN6 8DW *tel:* 01257 254635. Mrs A Lee.

Friends of the Phil. Philharmonic Hall, Hope St, Liverpool L1 9BP *tel:* 0151 210 3798 *fax:* 0151 210 2902 *email:* rlpsociety@aol.com. Betty Green.

Hallé Concerts Society. The Bridgewater Hall, Manchester M2 3WS *tel:* 0161 237 7000 *fax:* 0161 237 7029. Deborah Sullivan, press/mkt offr; Kent Nagano, mus dir, principal cond; Mark Elder, mus dir/principal cond designate; John Summers, chief exec.

Harris Music Club. 1 Barnacre View, High St, Garstang, Preston, Lancs PR3 1EB *tel:* 01995 606020 *also fax* (until June 2000); 01772 744714 (after June 2000). Mrs R Rogers (until June 2000), Mrs J Izatt (after June 2000).

Holmes Chapel Music Society. 4 Ironbridge Drive, Holmes Chapel, Crewe, Cheshire CW4 7DD *tel:* 01477 537769. J Perrins, hon sec.

Hoylake Chamber Concert Society. 10 Macdona Drive, West Kirby, Wirral, Merseyside CH48 3JD *tel:* 0151 625 1777. Ivor Fowler, chmn.

Lancaster Concerts. University of Lancaster, Music Dept, Lancaster, Lancs LA1 4YW *tel:* 01524 593777/593729 (box office) *fax:* 01524 847298 *email:* d.mccaldin@lancaster.ac.uk. Denis McCaldin, dir; Stella Birchall, admin.

Leigh Music Society. 19 Crowood Rd, Lowton, Warrington WA3 2EJ *tel:* 01942 725976. Miss M Halliwell, concert sec.

Liverpool Metropolitan Cathedral Concerts Society. c/o Cathedral House, Metropolitan Cathedral, Liverpool L3 5TQ *tel:* 0151 708 7283 *fax:* 0151 708 7274. J Moseley, chmn; P Dobbins, sec.

Macclesfield Music Society. Rulow House, Buxton Old Rd, Macclesfield, Cheshire SK11 0AG *tel:* 01625 611594. Shirley Jarvis, hon sec.

Manchester Chamber Concerts Society. Preston Cottage, Brook Lane, Alderley Edge, Cheshire SK9 7QQ *tel:* 01625 582349 *fax:* 01625 582308 *email:* margaret_m.stanley@virgin.net. Greta Stanley, sec; Alison Reade-Jahn, publicity offr.

Manchester Mid-day Concerts Society. 134 Kingsbrook Rd, Manchester M16 8WG *tel:* 0161 881 9320 *also fax*. Carolyn Howlett, admin.

Rochdale Music Society. 13 The Meadows, Grotton, nr Oldham, Lancs OL4 4LR *tel:* 0161 620 8156 (h); 0161 273 6283 (w). David Young, chmn.

Rossall Concert Society. Rossall School, Fleetwood, Lancs FY7 8JW *tel:* 01253 774217 *fax:* 01253 772052. John Foster.

Saddleworth Chamber Concerts Society. 42 Spring Meadow Lane, Uppermill, Oldham, Lancs OL3 6HL *tel:* 01457 872986. Mrs R Gillespie.

Northern Arts

This covers Cumbria, County Durham, Hartlepool, Middlesbrough, Northumberland, Redcar and Cleveland, Stockton-on-Tees, Tyne and Wear.

Cockermouth Music Society. Fell Edge, High Ireby, Carlisle, Cumbria CA5 1HF *tel:* 01697 371397. Susan Allison, hon sec.

Concerts on Campus. c/o University of Sunderland, Langham Tower, Ryhope Rd, Sunderland SR2 7EE *tel:* 0191 515 2180 *fax:* 0191 515 3375. Judith Hills.

Grange-over-Sands and District Concert Club. Glenside, Oxenholme, Kendal, Cumbria LA9 7RF *tel:* 01539 734375 *fax:* 01539 734378. Edna Jeffers, hon sec.

Kendal Midday Concert Club. 8 Castle Grove, Kendal LA9 7AY *tel:* 01539 725768. Elizabeth Howe, artists sec.

Keswick Music Society. Skald How, Applethwaite, Keswick, Cumbria CA12 4PP *tel:* 01768 772245. Gillian Edmonds, hon sec.

Lakeland Sinfonia Concert Society. High Ghyll, Newby Bridge Rd, Windermere, Cumbria LA23 3LW *tel:* 01539 448980. David Potts, hon sec.

Music in the Cathedral Society. 6 The Abbey, Carlisle CA3 8TZ *tel:* 01228 526646 *fax:* 01228 547049. J L Suter, chmn.

Newcastle International Chamber Music Series. 8 High Laws Newcastle upon Tyne NE3 1RQ *tel:* 0191 284 7421 *also fax.* Pat Kremer, hon sec; Tony Cullen, programming; George Fox, treasurer.

North Cumbria Recitals. 155 Greystone Rd, Carlisle *tel:* 01228 43666. Mrs M L Hall.

Penrith Music Club. 37 Frenchfield Gardens, Penrith, Cumbria CA11 8TX *tel:* 01768 863538 *also fax.* John Upson.

Sunderland Pianoforte Society. 85 Woodburn Square, Whitley Bay NE26 3JD *tel:* 0191 252 5396. Mrs L Scott, hon sec.

Teesside Music Society. 44 Church Lane, Acklam, Middlesbrough TS5 7EB *tel:* 01642 817097. Mrs M Bolton, sec.

South East Arts

This covers Kent, Surrey, East and West Sussex.

Ashford Music Society. Bumbles, The Lees, Boughton Aluph, Ashford, Kent TN25 4HX *tel:* 01233 622971 *also fax.* Mrs B D McCormack BEM.

Brighton & Hove Philharmonic Society. 50 Grand Parade, Brighton BN2 2QA *tel:* 01273 622900 *fax:* 01273 697887. Tony Woodhouse, gen mgr.

Broadstairs Music Club. 2 Edge End Rd, Broadstairs, Kent CT10 2AH *tel:* 01843 864788 *fax:* 01843 867416. Mrs J Fox.

Canterbury Music Club. 130 Salisbury Rd, Canterbury, Kent CT2 7SE *tel:* 01227 462029. Mrs G Waters, sec.

Charterhouse Celebrity Concerts. Charterhouse, Godalming, Surrey GU7 2DX *tel:* 01483 291696. David Wright, hon sec.

Cranbrook School and District Music Club. The Slatings, Hartley Rd, Cranbrook, Kent TN17 3QX *tel:* 01580 712369. Mrs L Stacey, hon sec.

Dorking Halls Concertgoers Society. Hythe Lodge, Knoll Rd, Dorking, Surrey RH4 3EP *tel:* 01306 887390 *fax:* 01306 884766. Gordon Coton.

Elmbridge Music Club. 40 Winchester Rd, Walton-on-Thames, Surrey KT12 2RH *tel:* 01932 225049 *also fax.* Kenneth J Uffen, hon sec.

Farnham and Bourne Music Club. 33 Aveley Lane, Farnham, Surrey GU9 8PR *tel:* 01252 713946. June Fielding.

Haywards Heath Music Society. Little Dormers, West Common, Haywards Heath, W Sussex *tel:* 01444 412949. Alan Gunson, chmn.

Herne Bay Music Club. 4 Hilary Close, Herne Bay, Kent CT6 6LH *tel:* 01227 373687. Mrs M Wallace.

HHH Concerts (Haslemere). Leith Court, East St, Amberley, W Sussex BN18 9NN *tel:* 01798 831242 *fax:* 01798 831970. Anna Hill, chmn.

Horsham Music Circle. 5 Worthing Rd, Horsham, W Sussex RH12 1SQ *tel:* 01403 252602. Miss J V Elsworthy, hon sec.

Nicholas Yonge Society. 22 Houndean Rise, Lewes, E Sussex BN7 1EQ *tel:* 01273 477662. Michael Marwod, concert sec.

Reigate Philharmonic Society. 9 Ridgeway House, The Crescent, Horley RH6 7NP *tel:* 01293 782119. Shirley Knights.

Seaford Music Society. 26 Southdown Rd, Seaford, E Sussex *tel:* 01323 895812. Mrs Jean McCapra.

Sevenoaks Music Club. 1 Bessels Way, Sevenoaks, Kent TN13 2QG *tel:* 01732 457191 *email:* terence_hall@compuserve.com. Margaret Hall, NFMS representative.

Steyning Music Society. 20 Middle Mead, Steyning, W Sussex BN44 3EG *tel:* 01903 812662. Zoë Peate, sec.

Sutton Valence Music Society. The Music School, Sutton Valence School, Sutton Valence, Maidstone, Kent ME17 3HL *tel:* 01622 844092 *also fax; email:* suttonvs@rmlpc.co.uk. Adrian Leang, dir of mus.

Tonbridge Music Club. The Old House, Philpots Lane, Hildenborough, Kent TN11 8PA *tel:* 01732 833140. Mrs C Vignoles, sec; Mrs S Broomfield, treasurer.

Uckfield Music Club. 38 Lashbrooks Rd, Uckfield, E Sussex TN22 2AZ *tel:* 01825 764214. Alan Weller.

Vinehall School Music Society. Vinehall School, Robertsbridge, E Sussex TN32 5JL *tel:* 01580 880413 *fax:* 01580 882119 *email:* vinehall @rmplc.co.uk. Geoffrey Whitehead, sec.

Woking Concert Society. Langley, Hockering Rd, Woking, Surrey GU22 7HG *tel:* 01483 762703 *fax:* 01483 725711 *email:* vhedley@ dial.pipex.com. Mrs V Hedley, concert sec.

South West Arts

This covers Bath and North East Somerset, Bristol, Dorset (other than Bournemouth), Cornwall, Devon, Gloucestershire, North Somerset, Somerset, South Gloucestershire.

Beauchamp Music Group. Beauchamp House, Churcham, Glos GL2 8AA *tel:* 01452 750382 *fax:* 01452 750585. Margaret Nelson, admin.

Bideford Music Club. Little Hill Cottage, Weare Giffard, Bideford, N Devon EX39 4QW *tel:* 01237 476286. E Hodgson, sec.

Bridport and West Dorset Music Club. 9 Hardy Rd, Bridport, Dorset DT6 3AZ *tel:* 01308 459278. Philip and Gillian Saunders.

Bude Music Society. Marlborough House, Poundstock, Bude, Devon EX23 0EE *tel:* 01840 230697. Mrs J D Cox, hon sec.

Cheltenham Music Society. 31 Longway Ave, Charlton Kings, Cheltenham, Glos GL53 9JH *tel:* 01242 576482 *also fax.* Paul Smith.

Chipping Sodbury Music Society. 24 Rockwood House, Gravel Hill Rd, Chipping Sodbury BS37 7BW *email:* cantalirica@breathemail.net. Judith Sheridan.

Curry Rivel Music Club. Coombstock House, Curry Rivel, nr Langport, Somerset TA10 0EY *tel:* 01458 251295. Mrs J Watson-Baker, hon sec; A Bladen, chmn.

Dartington Arts. The Gallery, Dartington Hall, Totnes, Devon TQ9 6DE *tel:* 01803 865864/863073 (box office) *fax:* 01803 868108 *email:* paul@dissorg.u-net.com. Paul Goddard, arts mgr.

Dorset County Museum Music Society. Hillview, Buckland Newton, Dorchester, Dorset DT2 7BS *tel:* 01300 345415. Gillian Frost.

Forde Abbey Concert Society. Merrivale, Holbear Rd, Forton, Chard, Somerset *tel:* 01460 220231/61487 *fax:* 01460 220296. Mrs B Hambleton, sec.

Gloucester Music Society. 'Bramfield', Edge, Stroud, Glos GL6 6NE *tel:* 01452 813910. Mrs R Ricketts.

Helston and Kerrier Music Society. 8 Marconi Close, Helston, Cornwall TR13 8PD *tel:* 01326 572389 *also fax.* G Oaten.

Kelly College Music Society. Kelly College, Tavistock, Devon PL19 0HZ *tel:* 01822 612010 *fax:* 01822 616628 *email:* 100432.3050@compuserve.com. Andrew Wilson, chmn.

Minehead and West Somerset Arts Society. The Outlook, Vicarage Rd, Minehead, Somerset TA24 5RR *tel:* 01643 702095 *also fax; email:* ianoutlook@tinyonline.ac.uk. Ken Francis.

Monkton Combe Concerts Society. Monkton Combe School, Bath BA2 7HG *tel:* 01225 721129 *fax:* 01225 723930. B J Newman.

Newton Abbot and District Society of Arts. Riverside, Preston, Kingsteignton, Devon TQ12 3PP *tel:* 01626 368496; 01647 277276 *email:* ric@riverside7.demon.co.uk. Richard Chambers, programme sec; Janet Power, hon sec.

Painswick Music Society. Westmorland House, Kingsmead, Edge Rd, Painswick, Glos GL6 6US *tel:* 01452 813259 *fax:* 01452 814043. Mrs B V A Kenber.

Rainbow over Bath. c/o Music Office, Bath University, Claverton Down, Bath BA2 7AY *tel:* 01225 826431 *also fax; email:* adsjol@bath.ac.uk; j.laycock@bath.ac.uk. Jolyon Laycock, programme dir.

St Boniface Concert Society. Sarum House, Union Rd, Crediton. Isolde Summers.

Seaton and District Music Club. Stoney House, Stoney Lane, Axminster, Devon EX13 5BU *tel:* 01297 33416 *fax:* 01297 631165. Hilary Juster, programme sec.

Summer Music Society of Dorset. Minterne, Dorchester, Dorset DT2 7AU *tel:* 01300 341370 *fax:* 01300 341747. The Lady Digby DBE DL, chmn and hon sec.

Thornbury Choral Society. 48 Waterford Close, Thornbury, Bristol, S Glos BS35 2HU *tel:* 01454 884177. Jennie Morris, sec.

Yatton Music Society. 4 Church Close, Yatton, Bristol BS49 4HG *tel:* 01934 834444 *also fax; email:* roger.lawrence@btinternet.com. Roger Lawrence, programme planner.

Southern Arts

This covers part of Dorset (Bournemouth, Christchurch and Poole), Hampshire, Berkshire, Buckinghamshire, Oxfordshire, Wiltshire and the Isle of Wight.

Amersham Concert Club. 9 Lime Tree Walk, Amersham, Bucks HP7 9HY *tel:* 01494 765420 *also fax.* Jenny Faulkner, hon sec.

Balliol College Musical Society. Balliol College, Oxford OX1 3BJ *tel:* 01865 277777 *fax:* 01865 277803 *email:* mathias.aspelin@balliol.ox.ac.uk. Mathias Aspelin, Louise Archer, secs.

Basingstoke Concert Club. 7 Hook Rd, Kingsclere, Newbury, Berks RG20 5PD *tel:* 01635 298866. J M Sentinella, chmn.

Beaconsfield Music Society. 89 Hotspur Top Lane, Beaconsfield, Bucks HP9 1DT *tel:* 01494 681649 *also fax; email:* gbmuswill@aol.com. Simon Howat, artists selection; Sally Willison, chmn.

Bognor Regis Music Club. 11 The Crescent, Felpham, Bognor Regis, W Sussex PO22 7HB *tel:* 01243 822757 *fax:* 01243 840563 *email:* info@bognorregis.inuk.com.

Brockenhurst Music Society. Eden Lodge, Partridge Rd, Brockenhurst, Hants SO42 7RZ *tel:* 01590 623383. K J A Crampton.

Chiltern Music Society. Abbey Farmhouse, Church St, Gt Missenden, Bucks HP16 0AZ *tel:* 01494 862767. Mrs N F Pearce.

Eton College Subscription Concerts. c/o Music Schools, Eton College, Windsor, Berks SL4 6EW *tel:* 01753 671169 *fax:* 01753 671170. Leila Clarke.

Gosport and Fareham Music Society. 124 Anmore Rd, Denmead, Waterlooville, Hants PO7 6NZ *tel:* 023 9224 1812. Hazel Clift.

Lacock Abbey Recitals. The Box Office, Lacock Abbey, Chippenham, Wilts SN15 2LG *tel:* 01249 730042. Petronella Dittmer, dir.

Lyndhurst Music Society. 16 Forest Gardens, Lyndhurst, Hants SO43 7AF *tel:* 023 8028 2851 *fax:* 023 8028 3260 *email:* abardoni@msn.com. Avril Bardoni, hon programme sec.

Maidenhead Music Society. Southwood, Burchetts Green, Maidenhead, Berks SL6 6QS *tel:* 01628 823340. David Ouvry.

Marlborough College Subscription Concerts. Marlborough College, Marlborough, Wilts SN8 1PA *tel:* 01672 892481. I G Crabbe.

Oxford Chamber Music Society. 19 Essex St, Oxford OX4 3AW *tel:* 01865 722991 *also fax.* Joan Fraser, hon sec.

Oxford University Music Society. Faculty of Music, St Aldate's, Oxford OX1 1DB *email:* oums@sable.ox.ac.uk.

Pangbourne College Arts Society. 5 Short St, Pangbourne, Reading RG8 7NE *tel:* 0118 984 3330 *also fax; email:* catherine_side@compuserve.com. Catherine E Side. *Scheduled to reopen in Jan 2000.*

Portsmouth Music Club. 38 Battenburg Ave, North End, Portsmouth PO2 0SJ *tel:* 023 9266 2151. Miss D E Lloyd, hon sec.

The Southern Orchestral Concert Society. Trees Cottage, Froxfield, Petersfield, Hants GU32 1DN *tel:* 01730 827317 *also fax.* Elizabeth Gotto, concert sec.

Tithe Barn Music and Drama Society. Shiplake College, Henley-on-Thames, Oxon RG9 4BW *tel:* 0118 940 2455 *fax:* 0118 940 5204. C A M Lowndes, sec.

University Concerts. University of Reading, Dept of Music, 35 Upper Redlands Rd, Reading RG1 5JE *tel:* 0118 931 6696 (am only) *fax:* 0118 931 8412 *email:* c.n.warner@reading.ac.uk. Caroline Warner.

Wolfson College Music Society. Wolfson College, Linton Rd, Oxford OX2 6UD *tel:* 01865 274108 *email:* linda.taft@wolfson.ox.ac.uk. Linda Taft, common room secretary.

West Midlands Arts

This covers Herefordshire, Shropshire, Staffordshire, Warwickshire, West Midlands and Worcestershire.

Abbotsholme Arts Society. c/o Lichfield Festival Office, 7 The Close, Lichfield, Staffs WS13 7LD *tel:* 01543 257298 *fax:* 01543 415137 *email:* abbotsholme.arts@lichfield-arts.org.uk. Paul Spicer, artistic dir, Claire Tetley, sec.

Birmingham Chamber Music Society. 101 Walmley Rd, Sutton Coldfield, W Midlands B76 1QL *tel:* 0121 240 7942 *also fax; email:* jhoad@compuserve.com. Bill Hoad, hon sec.

Bromsgrove Concerts. Coombe Cottage, Finstall, Bromsgrove, Worcs B60 1EW *tel:* 01527 872422. Jennie McGregor-Smith, chmn.

Bromsgrove Family Music. 16 Chestnut Drive, Cofton Hackett, Birmingham B45 8AQ *tel:* 0121 445 4309 *also fax.* Mrs D Marchand, sec.

Droitwich Concert Club. 40 Victoria Ave, Droitwich Spa, Worcs WR9 7DF *tel:* 01905 775246. Mrs S M Marsh.

Evesham and District Music Club. The Hayes, Drakes Bridge Rd, Eckington, Pershore, Worcs WR10 3DN *tel:* 01386 750416. Lylah Goodwin.

Friends of All Saints Music. All Saints Parish Church, PO Box 163, Bath St, Leamington Spa, Warwicks CV31 1AA *tel:* 01926 429169 *also fax; email:* allsaints@ukf.net. Richard Taulbut, sec.

Hereford Concert Society. Church Cottage, Michaelchurch Escley, Hereford HR2 0JW *tel:* 01981 510263 *also fax; email:* lfa@bulmer.com. Miss L F Arnold.

Keele Concerts Society. c/o Dept of Music, Keele University, Keele, Staffs ST5 5BG *tel:* 01782 714897 (Mon) *fax:* 01782 583295 *email:* keele.concerts.society@afsoc.keele.ac.uk. Alexandra Scott, artistic dir.

Ludlow Music Society. Glebe House, Caynham, Ludlow, Shropshire SY8 3BN *tel:* 01584 876141. Mrs R Caird.

Malvern Concert Club. 5 North Hill Court, Newtown Rd, Malvern WR14 1PD *tel:* 01684 565996. Catherine Freeman.

Market Drayton Music Club. 30 Mortimer Rd, Buntingsdale Park, Market Drayton, Shrops TF9 2EP *tel:* 01630 638818. Colin Bates, sec.

Newport Music Club. 19b Marsh Rd, Edgmond, Newport, Shropshire TF10 8EP *tel:* 01952 810244 *fax:* 01952 811722. Norah Bleloch, chmn; Roger Dixon, sec.

Redditch Music Society. 227 Birchfield Rd, Redditch, Worcs B97 4LX *tel:* 01527 546056. Miss A M Davis.

Shrewsbury School Concerts. The Schools, Shrewsbury SY3 7BB *tel:* 01743 344135 *fax:* 01743 243107 *email:* JohnMoore@Severnview.freeserve.co.uk. John Moore, dir of mus; Lisa Lowarch, concerts sec.

Stratford-upon-Avon Chamber Music Society. School House Flat, 41 Broad St, Stratford-upon-Avon, Warwicks CV37 6HN. Nicholas K Manley, hon sec.

Walsall Music Circle. 10 Knighton Close, Four Oaks, Sutton Coldfield B74 4BA *tel:* 0121 308 1677 *email:* bev@bevwragg.freeserve.co.uk. B Wragg.

Yorkshire Arts

This covers Kingston upon Hull, North East Lincolnshire, North Lincolnshire, East Riding of Yorkshire, South, West and North Yorkshire.

Ackworth Concert Society. Tenter Ings House, 83 Pontefract Rd, High Ackworth, Pontefract, W Yorks WF7 7LN *tel:* 01977 794500. John R P Gardham.

Bradford Chamber Concerts. 22 Sunset Drive, Ilkley, W Yorks LS29 8LS *tel:* 01943 609744 *also fax*. David Pyett, chmn.

British Music Society of York. 6 Bishopgate St, York YO23 1JH *tel:* 01904 637984. N J Dick, hon sec.

Cathedral Concert Society. St John's House, Sharow Lane, Sharow, Ripon HG4 5BN *tel:* 01765 605771. Mrs R Grenfell, hon sec.

Elland and District Music Society. 7 Crestfield Cres, Elland, W Yorks HX5 0LS *tel:* 01422 373191. Mrs J A Haigh, hon sec.

Goole Concert Society. Beech House, Low St, Swinefleet, Goole DN14 8BX *tel:* 01405 704358. Mrs M Shipley.

Grantley Hall Concert Society. 173 Leeds Rd, Harrogate HG2 8HQ *tel:* 01765 602691 *fax:* 01765 600516. Mrs M J R Davies.

Grimsby Wintringham Concerts. 133 Chichester Rd, Cleethorpes, N E Lincs DN35 0JL *tel:* 01472 501585. Eifion Griffiths, hon concert sec.

Halifax Philharmonic Club. Dunelm, 3 Church Lane, Shepley, Huddersfield HD8 8AF *tel:* 01484 604512. Miss A Mace, sec.

Harewood Subscription Concerts. Moor House, Harewood, Leeds LS17 9LQ *tel:* 0113 288 6331 *fax:* 0113 288 6467 *email:* business@harewood.org. Terence Suthers.

Huddersfield Music Society. 2 Sunny Bank Rd, Edgerton, Huddersfield HD3 3DE *tel:* 01484 422612 *fax:* 01484 432443. Mrs M S Glendinning.

Hull Chamber Music Club. Dept of Mathematics, University of Hull, Hull HU6 7RX *tel:* 01482 465827/465885 *fax:* 01482 466218 *email:* j.p.sproston@maths.hull.ac.uk. Peter Sproston.

Hull Philharmonic Society. 22 Westcott St, Hull HU8 8LR *tel:* 01482 702568 *fax:* 01482 641243. John Watson, sec; Andrew Penny, mus dir.

Ilkley Concert Club. 22 Sunset Drive, Ilkley, W Yorks LS29 8LS *tel:* 01943 609744 *also fax*. David Pyett, chmn.

Music for Lunch. c/o Fellow in Music, Bradford University, Bradford BD7 1DP *tel:* 01274 233191 *fax:* 01274 235495 *email:* a.n.hall@bradford.ac.uk. Antony Hall, fellow in mus.

Richmondshire Subscription Concerts. Manor End, 7 Greenacres, Hunton, Bedale, N Yorks DL8 1QZ *tel:* 01677 450366. Nora Dale.

Scunthorpe and North Lincolnshire Concert Society. 4 Mill Hill Drive, Bottesford, Scunthorpe, N Lincs DN16 3QY *tel:* 01724 866911. Mrs B M Hipkins.

Skipton Music Society. Lythe Cottage, Grassington, Skipton, N Yorks BD23 5DA *tel:* 01756 752288 *fax:* 01756 752917. Rowena Leder.

Scotland

Aberdeen University Recitals. University Music, Powis Gate, College Bounds, Old Aberdeen AB24 3UG *tel:* 01224 272571 *fax:* 01224 272515. R B Williams, dir of mus.

Ayr Music Club. 9 Shawfield Ave, Ayr KA7 4RE *tel:* 01292 442086. Pamela Martin, hon secretary.

Biggar Music Club. 16 Coulter Rd, Biggar, Lanarkshire ML12 6EP *tel:* 01899 220119 *email:* john_filshie@compuserve.com. Margaret H Filshie, hon sec.

Cowal Music Club. 'The Moorings', 183 Marine Parade, Hunter's Quay, Dunoon, Argyll *tel:* 01369 702466. Jess Hamilton.

Cumnock Music Club. 14 Bank Ave, Cumnock, Ayrshire *tel:* 01290 421492. Isabel Crawford, sec.

Dollar Music Society. 10 Sorley's Brae, Dollar, Clackmannanshire FK14 7AS. Andrea Ross, sec.

Dumfries Music Club. 29 Ardwall Rd, Dumfries DG1 3AQ. Lynn Otty, concerts sec.

Dunblane Cathedral Arts Guild. Applegarth, Glen Rd, Dunblane *tel:* 01786 825448 *email:* s.bamforth@which.net. R Bamforth, chmn.

Dunfermline Arts Guild. 13 Park Place, Dunfermline KY12 7QL *tel:* 01383 722368. Fay Mann.

Dunkeld and Birnam Music Club. Cluain, Tomnacroich, Aberfeldy, Perthshire PH15 2LJ *tel:* 01887 830298. Susan E Hoare, hon concerts sec.

Glenalmond Concert Society. Glenalmond College, Perthshire PH1 3RY *tel:* 01738 880340 *also fax*. N Smith, asst dir of mus.

Glenkens and District Music Club. 4 Throughgate, Dalry, Castle Douglas, Kirkcudbrightshire DG7 3UU *tel:* 01644 430352 *email:* gdmc@bohrhead.freeuk.com. Isobel Jackson, sec.

Gordonstoun Concerts Society. Gordonstoun School, Elgin, Morayshire *tel:* 01343 837894 *fax:* 01343 830074. M J Appleford.

Hawick Music Club. 5a Lanton Place, Hawick TD9 7QL *tel:* 01450 372404. Jean H Armstrong, programme sec.

Helensburgh Music Society. Upton, 15 Queen St, Helensburgh G84 9QJ *tel:* 01436 671969. David Menzies.

Heriot-Watt University Music Society. Musician in Residence, Heriot-Watt University, Riccarton, Edinburgh EH14 4AS *tel:* 0131 451 3705. Steve King, musician in residence.

Kelso Music Society. Maxwellheugh Cottage, Jedburgh Rd, Kelso, Roxburghshire TD5 8AZ *tel:* 01573 224753. Isabel Gordon.

Kintyre Music Club. Seabank, Low Askomil, Campbeltown, Argyll PA28 6EP *tel:* 01586 552500. John Kerr, sec.

Loretto Concert Society. Loretto School, Musselburgh, Midlothian EH21 7RE *tel:* 0131 653 4420 *fax:* 0131 653 4445. W E Coleman, dir of mus.

Melrose Music Society. Setter, Aldie Cres, Melrose, Scottish Borders TD6 9AY *tel:* 01896 822368. Miss M Paterson.

Music in Peebles. Newton Bank, Frankscroft, Peebles EH45 9DX *tel:* 01721 720583 *also fax; email:* AJFRussel@aol.com. S Russel, hon sec.

Perth Chamber Music Society. Embden House, Blairgowrie, Perthshire PH10 6SO *tel:* 01250 873810. Alice Gray, hon sec.

Pollok House Arts Society. 1 Hughenden Terrace, Glasgow G12 9XR *tel:* 0141 334 9174. I McGlashan.

Reid Concerts. Faculty of Music, University of Edinburgh, 12 Nicolson Square, Edinburgh EH8 9DF *tel:* 0131 650 2423 *fax:* 0131 650 2425 *email:* music@ed.ac.uk. Miss F Donaldson.

St Andrews Music Club. 66 Main St, Strathkinness KY16 9SA *tel:* 01334 850560 *email:* j.galbraithe@tay.ac.uk. Jill Galbraith, sec.

St Andrews University Music Society. Music Centre, Younger Hall, North St, St Andrews, Fife KY16 9AJ *tel:* 01334 462226 *fax:* 01334 462570 *email:* mussoc@st-andrews.ac.uk. Gareth Baynham-Hughes, president.

Stonehaven Music Club. Rutlands, Stonehaven, Kincardineshire AB39 2EH *tel:* 01569 762712. A Watt MBE.

Stranraer Music Association Music for All. 35 London Rd, Stranraer DG9 8AF *tel:* 01776 702311. Kate Murdoch, sec.

Thurso Live Music Association. Skinandi, Braal, Halkirk, Caithness KW12 6XE *tel:* 01847 831437. Barbara Myatt.

University of Glasgow. 2001 Development Office, 2 The Square, Glasgow G12 8QQ *tel:* 0141 330 4092 *fax:* 0141 330 4905 *email:* concerts@mis.gla.ac.uk. Ms A Cumberland, concerts organiser.

University of Strathclyde Music Society. University of Strathclyde, Livingstone Tower, Richmond St, Glasgow G1 1XH *tel:* 0141 548 3444 *fax:* 0141 552 4053 *email:* alan.taverner@strath.ac.uk. Alan Tavener, dir of mus.

Wales

Celyn Music Society. Coed y Celyn Hall, Betws-y-Coed, Gwynedd *tel:* 01690 710280. Barbara Carter, sec.

Dolgellau Music Club. Coleg Meirion-Dwyfor, Dolgellau, Gwynedd LL40 2SW *tel:* 01341 422827 *fax:* 01341 422393 *email:* b.ridler@meirion-dwyfor.ac.uk. Ben Ridler, sec.

Maelor Music Society. Walnut House, Bangor-on-Dee, Wrexham LL13 0AY *tel:* 01978 780246. Mrs C Peters, hon sec.

Rhyl Music Club. 15 Park Drive, Rhyl, Sir Ddinbych LL18 4DB *tel:* 01745 334255 *fax:* 01745 344094 *email:* derek_bartley@msn.com. Derek Bartley, concert organiser.

Welshpool Music Club. Bodynfoel, Guilsfield, Powys SY21 9BX *tel:* 01938 552350. Mrs G Finney.

Northern Ireland

Belfast Music Society. 7 Highgrove Ave, Ballyclare BT39 9XL *tel:* 028 9335 2912 *also fax*. Margaret Langhammer, concert mgr.

Music in Armagh. c/o Tourist Information Centre, 40 English St, Armagh BT61 7BA *tel:* 028 3752 1805 *fax:* 028 3751 0180. Katharine Bond, arts offr.

Photo: Graham Hussey

Ian Judson
flute

Joseph Asghar
guitar

Recitals of Classical, South American and Contemporary music as performed at Purcell Room, Fairfield Hall, Bath Pump Room and Conway Hall. Featuring world premiers of pieces composed for the duo.

Available now

Les Rossignols debut CD ***Concert d'aujourd'hui***

Les Rossignols, 111c St Marks Road, London W10 6NP

0181-969 8707 0956-431 449

Leith Hill Musical Festival 2000

Reg Charity No 275176

Festival Conductor: Brian Kay

DORKING HALLS March – April

The Annual Bach Passion Concert

Saturday March 11th 7.00pm	**Bach** *St John Passion* **Canzona**	Huw Rhys-Evans *Evangelist* Simon Birchall *Christus* Sally Matthews Diana Moore Andrew Kennedy Richard Burkhard

THE FESTIVAL

Competitions 9am – Concerts 7.30pm

Thursday April 27th 7.30pm	**Spring from The Seasons** ***Haydn*** **A Cotswold Romance** ***Vaughan Williams***	Donna Bateman Andrew Kennedy Christian Immler **English Festival Orchestra**
Friday April 28th 7.30pm	**Judas Maccabeus** ***Handel***	Caroline Childe Arlene Rolph Darren Abrahams Richard Burkhard **English Festival Orchestra**
Saturday April 29th 7.30pm	**Kyrie & Gloria from Mass in B Minor** ***Bach*** **Cantate Domino** ***Antony le Fleming***	Katharine Fuge Leigh Woolf Christopher Saunders Edward Caswell

Tickets £4 - £12.50 from LHMF Box Office 24 Raglan Road, Reigate, Surrey RH2 0DP. 01737 243931. Cheques payable to LHMF. Sae please. and Dorking Halls Box Office 01306 881717. Season Tickets from LHMF Box Office only.

The Chantry Singers' BACH FESTIVAL

250th Anniversary Celebrations

21 Events

***in* BATH**

21-28 October 2000

Artistic Director: Elizabeth Bates

- **PERFORMERS**
  The Chantry Singers
  Bath Abbey Choir
  London Festival Players
  London Harpsichord Ensemble
- **MUSIC**
  St Matthew Passion (complete)
  Christmas Oratorio
  Mass in B Minor
  Organ, harpsichord, piano recitals
  Concertos
  Masterclasses and workshops
- **SOLOISTS INCLUDE**
  Catherine Bott
  Margaret Cable
  Peter King
  Neil Mackie
  Roderick Williams
  and other distinguished artists
- **BROCHURES**
  Send now for a free brochure *(available April 2000)* enclosing SAE:
  The Chantry Singers' Bach Festival
  9 Ullswater Drive, Bath BA1 6NA
  Tel: 01225 333527

Bath Festivals Trust

is working to establish Bath as a *Festivals City* through a wide-ranging portfolio including...

Bath International Music Festival
Bath Literature Festival
Contemporary Art Programme
Education & Community Programme
Arts Support & Box Office Services

Photo: Damian Duncan

2000 Bath International Music Festival
19 May – 4 June

Bath Literature Festival
26 February – 5 March

Administration: 5 Broad Street, Bath BA1 5LJ
Tel: 01225 462231 Fax: 01225 445551

Box Office: 2 Church Street, Abbey Green, Bath BA1 1NL
Tel: 01225 463362 Fax: 01225 310377

Director: Tim Joss

Bath Festivals Trust

celebrating 50 Festivals

Music Festivals

The following list of festivals, which are wholly or considerably devoted to musical performance, are listed alphabetically by location. Certain major summer orchestral series are also included. A number of festivals are members of the **British Arts Festivals Association** (3rd Floor, Whitechapel Library, 77 Whitechapel High St, London E1 7QX *tel:* 020 7247 4667 *fax:* 020 7247 5010 *email:* bafa@netcomuk.co.uk *website:* www.artsfestivals.co.uk. Gwyn Rhydderch, co-ord) which produces arts festivals listings and a website directory, and organises conferences and festival meetings.

London

Almeida Opera. Almeida Theatre, Almeida Street, London N1 1TA *admin:* 020 7226 7432 *box office:* 020 7359 4404 *fax:* 020 7704 9581 *email:* pdickie@almeidatheatre.demon.co.uk. Jonathan Reekie, Artistic Director; Patrick Dickie, Associate Director. *Annual. June/July.*

BBC Henry Wood Promenade Concerts. Room 4088, BBC Broadcasting House, London W1A 1AA *admin:* 020 7765 5575 *box office:* 020 7589 8212 *fax:* 020 7765 0619 *email:* proms@bbc.co.uk. Nicholas Kenyon, Artistic Director. *14 July-9 September 2000.*

BOC Covent Garden Festival. Unit 47, The Market, The Piazza, Covent Garden, London WC2E 8RF *admin:* 020 7379 0870 *fax:* 020 7379 0876 *email:* diva@cgf.co.uk. Kenneth Richardson, Artistic Director; Anna Simpson, Festival Administrator. *15 May-3 June 2000.*

City of London Festival. City of London Festival, Bishopsgate Hall, 230 Bishopsgate, London EC2M 4HW *admin:* 020 7377 0540 *box office:* 020 7638 8891 *fax:* 020 7377 1972 *email:* cityfest@dircon.co.uk. Michael MacLeod, Director. *20 June-13 July 2000.*

Colourscape Festival. 30 Penwortham Road, Sanderstead, Surrey CR2 0QS *admin:* 020 8763 9298. Simon Desorgher, Festival Organiser. *September.*

Ealing Summer Festival. Perceval House, 14-16 Uxbridge Road, Ealing, London W5 2HL *admin:* 020 8758 5743 *box office:* 020 8579 2424 *fax:* 020 8566 5088 *email:* farrara@ealing.gov.uk. Adam Farrar, Events Manager. *July-August.*

Evening Standard Holland Park Theatre Festival. Central Library, Phillimore Walk, Kensington, London W8 7RX *admin:* 020 7361 2295 *box office:* 020 7602 7856. Michael Volpe, Marketing Manager. *June-August.*

Festival of Central European Culture. Bloomsbury Theatre, 15 Gordon Street, London WC1 *admin:* 020 7584 8653 *box office:* 020 7388 8822. *June-July.*

Greenwich and Docklands Festivals. Festival Office, 6 College Approach, Greenwich, London SE10 9HY *admin:* 020 8305 1818 *press desk:* 020 8305 1717 *box office:* 0870 900 0355 *fax:* 020 8305 1188 *email:* greendock@globalnet.co.uk. Bradley Hemmings, Artistic Director; Ms Sam McAuley, Marketing Manager. *July.*

Jewish Music Festival - London International. PO Box 232, Harrow, Middx HA1 2NN *admin:* 020 8909 2445 *fax:* 020 8909 1030 *email:* jewishmusic@jmht.org. Geraldine Auerbach, Festival Director. *June/July 2000 (biennial).*

London Bach Festival. Bach House, 73 High Street, Old Oxted, Surrey RH8 9LN *admin:* 01883 717372 *also box office; fax:* 01883 715851. Margaret Steinitz, Artistic Director; Margaret Steinitz, Founder, Director. *28 October-11 November 2000.*

London Festival of Chamber Music. 44 Gondar Gardens, London NW6 1HG *admin:* 020 7435 6232 *fax:* 020 7431 6843 *email:* festival@gondar.demon.co.uk. Luciano Iorio, Artistic Director; Eve Harris, Administrator. *26 September-21 October 2000.*

London Handel Festival. 265 Croxted Road, London SE21 8NN *admin:* 020 8244 2308. Denys Darlow and Paul Nicholson, Artistic Directors; Catherine Hodgson, Administrator. *March-April.*

Lufthansa Festival of Baroque Music. 200 Broomwood Road, London SW11 6JY *admin:* 020 7228 6388 *box office:* 020 7222 1061 *fax:* 020 7738 1706. Kate Bolton, Artistic Director; Delia Pye, Manager. *June-July.*

Music on a Summer Evening. English Heritage, Savile Row, London W1 *admin:* 020 7973 3438 *fax:* 020 7973 3425. Ann Christie, Head of Concerts. *July-September.*

National Festival of Music for Youth. Music for Youth, 102 Point Pleasant, London SW18 1PP *admin:* 020 8870 9624 *fax:* 020 8870 9935 *email:* mfy@globalnet.co.uk. Larry Westland CBE, Artistic Director; Lucy Riley, Assistant Director. *July.*

Park Lane Group Young Artists New Year Series. Langham House, 308 Regent Street, London W1R 5AL *admin:* 020 7255 1025 *box office:* 020 7928 8800 *fax:* 020 7255 1890. John Woolf, Director. *January.*

Pro Piano New York Recital Series. 85 Jane St, New York, NY 10014, USA *admin:* +1 212 206 8794 *fax:* +1 212 633 1207 *email:* classicmus@aol.com. Chitose Okashiro, Artistic Director; Ricard de La Rosa, Executive Director.

St Ceciliatide International Festival of Music. Saint Cecilia Limited, Bank Cottage, Old Forge Lane, Preston Capes, Northants NN11 3TD *admin:* 01327 361380 *also box office; fax:* 01327 361415 *email:* cecilia@st-ceciliatide.com. Penelope Rapson, Artistic Director. *18-26 November 2000.*

St Mary's Music Festival. 1 Lorne Court, Whitehall Road, Harrow on the Hill, Middx HA1 3BH *admin:* 020 8422 3119 *also box office; fax:* 020 8423 9707. Irene Wears, Festival Director. *3-20 May 2000.*

Soho Jazz and Heritage Festival. 29 Romilly Street, London W1V 6HP *admin:* 020 7437 6437 *fax:* 020 7434 1214. Peter Boizot, Artistic Director; Administrator, Soho Jazz Festival. *September-October.*

Southwark Festival. 16 Winchester Walk, London SE1 9AQ *admin:* 020 7403 7474 *also fax; box office:* 020 7403 7400 *email:* southwarkfestival.org.uk. Michele McLusky, Director. *October.*

Spitalfields Festival. 75 Brushfield Street, Spitalfields, London E1 6AA *admin:* 020 7377 0287 *box office:* 020 7377 1362 *fax:* 020 7247 0494 *email:* spitfest@easynet.co.uk. Judith Weir CBE, Artistic Director; Judith Serota, Festival Manager. *5-23 June and 18-22 December 2000.*

State of The Nation. c/o London Sinfonietta, Dominion House, 101 Southwark St, London SE1 0JF *admin:* 020 7928 0828 *box office:* 020 7960 4242 *fax:* 020 7928 8557 *email:* londonsinfonietta@atlas.co.uk. Gillian Moore MBE, Artistic Director; Cathy Graham, Managing Director. *15-16 April 2000.*

Sunbury and Shepperton Arts Festival. Riverside Arts Centre, 59 Thames Street, Sunbury-on-Thames, Middx TW16 5QF *admin:* 01932 782345/222240 *box office:* 01932 782400 *email:* ssaa@barclays.net. Catherine Black, Chairman; Dr Millan Sachania, Vice-Chairman and Publicity. *Last 10 days of July, annually.*

Wanstead and Woodford Festival of Chamber Music. 39 Bushwood, London E11 3BW *admin:* 020 8518 8903 *email:* malcolmjg@aol.com. Malcolm Galloway, Chairman. *Spring 2000.*

England

Abbotsbury Music Festival. 9a West Street, Abbotsbury, Dorset DT3 4JT *admin:* 01305 871475 *also fax and box office; email:* francesca@wdi.co.uk. Marina Tafur, Artistic Director; Francesca Radcliffe. *29 May-3 June 2000, The Legend of St Catherine.*

Aldeburgh - Snape Proms. Aldeburgh Productions, High Street, Aldeburgh, Suffolk IP15 5AX *admin:* 01728 452935 *box office:* 01728 453543 *fax:* 01728 452715 *email:* enquiries@aldeburghfestivals.org. Jonathan Reekie, Chief Executive. *1-31 August 2000.*

Aldeburgh Festival of Music and The Arts. Aldeburgh Productions, High Street, Aldeburgh, Suffolk IP15 5AX *admin:* 01728 452935 *box office:* 01728 453543 *fax:* 01728 452715 *email:* enquiries@aldeburghfestivals.org. Thomas Adès, Artistic Director; Jonathan Reekie, Chief Executive. *9-25 June 2000.*

Ambleside - Lake District Summer Music. Stricklandgate House, 92 Stricklandgate, Kendal, Cumbria LA9 4PU *admin:* 01539 733411 *box office:* 01539 724441 *fax:* 01539 724441 *email:* info@ldsm.org.uk. Christopher Rowland, Artistic Director; Andrew Lucas, Administrator. *5-19 August 2000.*

Appleby Jazz Festival. Bongate Mill, Appleby, Cumbria CA16 6UR *admin:* 01768 351052 *box office:* 01768 353332 *fax:* 01768 353824 *email:* jazz@bongate-mill.u-net.com. Neil Ferber, Artistic Director. *June.*

Arundel Festival. The Arundel Festival Society Ltd, The Mary Gate, Arundel, W Sussex BN18 9AT *admin:* 01903 883690 *fax:* 01903 884243 *email:* arundel.festival@argonet.co.uk. Anthony Phillips, Artistic Director; Victoria Moles, Festival Co-ordinator. *August-September.*

Banstead Arts Festival. 28 Greenhayes Avenue, Banstead, Surrey SM7 2JE *admin:* 01737 353738 *also box office*. Rowena Cox, Artistic Director; E W Foulser, Hon Secretary. *28 April-14 May 2000.*

Bath Bach Festival. 13 Pera Place, Camden, Bath BA1 5NX *admin:* 01225 333527 *box office:* 01225 463362 *fax:* 01225 310377 *email:* k.j.lush@ukonline.co.uk. Elizabeth Bates, Artistic Director. *21-28 October 2000.*

Bath - Iford Opera. The Bullpit, Bradford on Avon, Wilts BA15 1NB *admin:* 01225 868124 *fax:* 01225 867471 *email:* panagri@compuserve.com. Judy Eglington, Artistic Director; John Edwards, Administrator. *July.*

Bath International Guitar Festival. Newton Park, Newton St Loe, Bath BA2 9BN *admin:* 01225 875522 *box office:* 01225 463362 *fax:* 01225 875444 *email:* e.ginn@bathspa.ac.uk. Tom Kerstens, Artistic Director; Emmanuelle Ginn, Bookings Administrator. *24 July-4 August 2000.*

Bath International Music Festival. Bath Festivals Trust, 5 Broad St, Bath BA1 5LJ *admin:* 01225 462231 *box office:* 01225 463362 *fax:* 01225 445551 *email:* bathfestivals@btconnect.com. Tim Joss, Artistic Director; Tim Martienssen, Head of Marketing and Community Relations. *19 May-4 June 2000.*

Bath Mozartfest. 110 Gloucester Avenue, London NW1 8HX *admin:* 020 7483 2681 *fax:* 020 7586 5343. Amelia Freedman, Artistic Director; Sarah Gordon, Administrator. *November.*

Battle Festival. Southdene, 10 North Trade Rd, Battle, E Sussex TN33 0HB *admin:* 01424 772454. Judy Warrington, Artistic Director; Judith White, Festival Secretary. *30 June-15 July 2000.*

Beverley Chamber Music Festival. Hazard Chase Ltd, Richmond House, 16-20 Regent Street, Cambridge CB2 1DB *admin:* 01223 312400 *box office:* 01482 867430 *fax:* 01223 460827 *email:* info@hazardchase.co.uk. Martin Roscoe, Artistic Director; Helen Poole, James Brown. *September 2000.*

Beverley and East Riding Early Music Festival. PO Box 226, York YO30 5ZU *admin:* 01904 645738 *box office:* 01482 885296 *fax:* 01904 612631 *email:* yemf@netcomuk.co.uk. Delma Tomlin, Administrative Director. *25-29 May 2000.*

Beverley and East Riding Folk Festival. 2 Star Row, North Dalton, Driffield, E Yorks YO25 9UR *admin:* 01377 217662 *also box office; box office:* 01482 867430 *fax:* 01377 217754 *email:* adastra@adastey.demon.co.uk. Chris Wade, Artistic Director. *16-18 June 2000.*

Birkenhead - Guitar Festival of Great Britain. HQ2, 43 Hamilton Street, The Hamilton Quarter, Birkenhead, Wirral L41 5AA *admin:* 0151 666 5060 *box office:* 0151 666 5023 *fax:* 0151 666 5070 *email:* dlstrob@wirral.gov.uk. Rob Smith, Festival Director. *November.*

Birmingham Early Music Festival. 42 Beech Avenue, Worcester WR3 8PY *admin:* 01905 452692 *also box office; fax:* 01905 452629 *email:* csb@beech2.demon.co.uk. Carol Bawden, Festival Administrator. *October-November.*

HMV Birmingham International Jazz Festival. PO Box 944, Birmingham B16 8UT *admin:* 0121 454 7020 *fax:* 0121 454 9996 *email:* bigbearmusic@compuserve.com. Jim Simpson, Director. *July.*

Birmingham - Voices In The City. c/o Cadbury Ltd, PO Box 12, Bournville, Birmingham B30 2LU *admin:* 0121 451 4038 *fax:* 0121 451 4395 *email:* b.g.chapman@voicesinthecity.freeserve.co.uk. Simon Halsey, Artistic Director; Basil Chapman, General Manager. *October 2000.*

Bolton Festival. The Central Library, Le Mans Crescent, Bolton, Lancs BL1 1SE *admin:* 01204 382627 *fax:* 01204 363224. F N Parker, Hon Secretary. *August-September.*

Boroughbridge - The Northern Aldborough Festival. The Festival Office, Aldborough Manor, Boroughbridge, N Yorks YO51 9EP *admin:* 01423 324899 *also box office; fax:* 01423 323223 *email:* festival@aldborough.com. Martin Dreyer, Artistic Director; Andrew Lawson-Tancred. *July.*

Boughton Aluph - Stour Music. Stour Music, 2 Rural Terrace, Wye, Ashford, Kent TN25 5AP *admin:* 01233 812267 *box office:* 01227 455600. Mark Deller, Festival Director. *16-25 June 2000.*

Boxgrove - Music At Boxgrove. Westfield Cottage, Ashford Hill, Thatcham, Berks RG19 8BQ *admin:* 01189 813190 *box office:* 01243 536240 *fax:* 01189 810218. John Wright, Artistic Director; Devina Cameron, Administrator. *7-10 June 2000.*

Bradford Festival. Bradford Festival Ltd, Wool Exchange, Hustlergate, Bradford BD1 1RE *admin:* 01274 309199 *fax:* 01274 724213 *email:* info@bradfordfestival.yorks.com. Mark Fielding, Artistic Director; Rob Walsh, Press Officer. *June-July.*

Bridgenorth - The English Haydn Festival. Festival Box Office, 24a St Mary's St, Newport, Shrops TF10 7AB *admin:* 01952 811829/812922 *info:* 01952 810430 *box office:* 01952 810428/812922 *fax:* 01952

812011. H C Robbins Landon, Artistic Director; John Reid, Festival Director; Sandra Day, Assistant. *26 May-4 June 2000.*

Brighton Festival. Festival Office, 12a Pavilion Buildings, Castle Square, Brighton BN1 1EL *admin:* 01273 700747 *box office:* 01273 709709 *fax:* 01273 707505 *email:* info@brighton-festival.org.uk. Christopher Barron, Artistic Director; John Lucas, General Manager. *May 2000.*

Bromsgrove Festival. 10 Evertons Close, Droitwich, Worcs WR9 8AE *admin:* 01905 779852 (home); 01527 575441 (work) *fax:* 01527 575366. A D Harris, Hon Secretary. *29 April-13 May 2000.*

Buckingham Summer Festival. 1 Poplars Close, Preston Bissett, Buckingham MK18 4LR *admin:* 01280 848275. Robert Secret, Artistic Director. *July.*

Bude Jazz Festival. PO Box 118, Newport NP19 8XY *admin:* 01633 211368 (organiser); 01288 356360 (admin - Bude Visitor Centre, The Crescent, Bude EX23 8LE) *box office:* 01288 356360 *also fax.* John Minnion, Artistic Director; Jean Manuel, Diana Ohlson, Administrators. *26 August-2 September 2000.*

Bury St Edmunds Festival. Borough Offices, Angel Hill, Bury St Edmunds, Suffolk IP33 1XB *admin:* 01284 756933 *box office:* 01284 769505 *fax:* 01284 756932 *email:* kevin.appleby@burybo.stedsbc.gov.uk. Kevin Appleby, Artistic Director. *12-28 May 2000.*

Bushey Festival. 21 Grange Road, Bushey, Watford, Herts WD2 2LQ *admin:* 01923 220272 (Treasurer). 8-22 July 2000.

Buxton Festival. 1 Crescent View, Hall Bank, Buxton, Derbys SK17 6EN *admin:* 01298 70395 *box office:* 01298 72190 *fax:* 01298 72289 *email:* info@buxtonfestival.freeserve.co.uk. Aidan Lang, Artistic Director; Glyn Foley, General Manager. *13-23 July 2000.*

Cambridge Music Festival. 10 Gurney Way, Cambridge CB4 2ED *admin:* 01223 350544 *also fax; box office:* 01223 357851 *email:* cammusic@enterprise.net. Gillian Perkins, Festival Administrator. *July.*

Cambridge Summer Recitals, Cambridge Summer Music Festival. 10 Victoria Road, Oundle, Peterborough PE8 4AY *admin:* 01832 272284; 01832 275231 *also fax; box office:* 01223 503333 *email:* abrahamson@enterprise.net. Juliet Abrahamson, Director. *Mid July-mid August 2000.*

Canterbury Festival. Festival Office, Christ Church Gate, The Precincts, Canterbury, Kent CT1 2EE *admin:* 01227 452853 *box office:* 01227 455600 *fax:* 01227 781830. Mark Deller, Festival Director. *14-28 October 2000.*

Chard Festival of Women In Music. 3 Howards Row, Chard, Somerset TA20 1PH *admin:* 01460 66048. Angela Willes, Artistic Director. *26-29 May 2000.*

Charleston Manor Festival. 4 Peak Dean Close, Friston, Eastbourne, E Sussex BN20 0JA *admin:* 01323 423565 *also fax and box office.* Robert Cohen, Artistic Director. *11-18 June 2000.*

Chelmsford Cathedral Festival. Festival Office, Guy Harlings, New Street, Chelmsford, Essex CM1 1AT *admin:* 01245 359890 *box office:* 01245 606505 *fax:* 01245 280456. Graham Elliott, Artistic Director; Hilary Simmonds, Administrator. *10-20 May 2000.*

Chelmsford Spectacular. Chelmsford Borough Council, Duke Street, Chelmsford, Essex CM1 1JE *admin:* 01245 606985/6/7 *box office:* 01245 606505 *fax:* 01245 606977. Heather Taylor, Events Manager. *August Bank Holiday weekend 2000.*

Cheltenham International Festival of Music. Town Hall, Imperial Square, Cheltenham, Glos GL50 1QA *admin:* 01242 521621 *box office:* 01242 227979 *fax:* 01242 573902 *email:* townhall@cheltenham.gov.uk. Michael Berkeley, Artistic Director; Toby Smith, Festival Organiser. *1-16 July 2000.*

Cheltenham International Jazz Festival. The Mews, Mitcheldean, Glos GL17 0SL *admin:* 01594 544446 *box office:* 01242 227979 *fax:* 01594 544448 *email:* 101555.2016@compuserve.com. Jim Smith, Director.

Chester International Children's Choral Festival. c/o 5 Kennedy Close, Newton, Chester, Cheshire CH2 2PL *admin:* 01244 351003 *also fax.* Martin Cook, Artistic Director; P Dayananda, Administrator. *8 July 2000.*

Chester Summer Music Festival. Festival Office, 8 Abbey Square, Chester CH1 2HU *admin:* 01244 320722 *box office:* 01244 320700 *fax:* 01244 341200 *email:* csmf@dial.pipex.com. Andrew Burn, Artistic Director; Fiona England, Administrator. *July.*

Chichester Festivities. Canon Gate House, South Street, Chichester, W Sussex PO19 1PU *admin:* 01243 785718 *box office:* 01243 780192 *fax:* 01243 528356 *email:* chi.fest@argonet.co.uk. Amanda Sharp, Festival Administrator. *July 2000.*

Chiddingly Festival. Laurel House, Chiddingly, nr Lewes, E Sussex BN8 6HE *admin:* 01825 872338 (home) *box office:* 01825 872401 *fax:* 01825 872733. Noel Hardy, Chair. *September-October.*

Church Stretton and South Shropshire Arts Festival. The Marches, Westfields, Church Stretton, Shropshire SY6 7AF *admin:* 01694 724273 *box office:* 01694 723402. Trevor Johnson, Music Events Organiser. *July-August 2000.*

Clacton Jazz Festival. Tendring District Council, Town Hall, Clacton, Essex *admin:* 01255 253208 *box office:* 01255 423400 *fax:* 01255 253200. Bob Foster, Artistic Director. *August.*

Cressing Temple Festival. Cultural Services, ECC Learning Services, PO Box 47, Chelmsford, Essex CM2 6WN *admin:* 01245 436825 *box office:* 01245 606505 *email:* nikki.beckett@essexcc.gov.uk. Tim Freathy, Artistic Director; Nikki Beckett, Cultural Services Assistant. *Last two weekends in July.*

Dartington International Summer School. Dartington Hall, Totnes, Devon TQ9 6DE *admin:* 01803 867068 *box office:* 01803 865988 *fax:* 01803 868108 *email:* brochure@dissorg.u-net.com. Gavin Henderson, Artistic Director; Lisa Warren, Administrator.

Deal Summer Music Festival. 12 Woodlands, Clapham Common North Side, London SW4 0RJ *admin:* 020 7622 1607 *box office:* 01304 366077 *fax:* 01304 612292 *email:* dealmusic@yahoo.co.uk. David Matthews, Artistic Director. *23 July-6 August 2000.*

Devizes Festival. 34 Long Street, Devizes, Wilts SN10 1NT *admin:* 01380 728151. Stephen Brazier, Chair. *June 2000.*

Dorking - Leith Hill Musical Festival. 24 Raglan Road, Reigate, Surrey RH2 0DP *admin:* 01737 243931 *also box office.* Brian Kay, Artistic Director; Deirdre Hicks, Chair. *27-29 April 2000.*

East Coast Jazz Festival. Norwich Arts Centre, Reeves Yard, St Benedict's Street, Norwich NR2 4PG *admin:* 01603 660387 *box office:* 01603 660352 *also fax.* Pam Reekie, Director. *November.*

East Horsely - Concerto Festival (London Soloists). PO Box 100, East Horsley KT24 6WN *admin:* 01483 282666 *fax:* 01483 284777 *email:* nick@bomford.com. David Josefowitz, Artistic Director; Nick Bomford. *February-December 2001.*

Exeter Festival. 4.46, Civic Centre, Dix's Field, Exeter, Devon EX1 1JN *admin:* 01392 265210 *fax:* 01392 265366. Lesley Maynard, Organiser. *July.*

Felsted Arts Festival. Felsted School, Felsted, Dunmow, Essex CM6 3JG *admin:* 01371 820258 (school office) *fax:* 01371 821232 *email:* dre@felsted.essex.sch.uk. David Everett, Director of Festival. *12-19 March 2000.*

Fenland Colourscape Festival. c/o 30 Penwortham Road, Sanderstead, Surrey CR2 0QS *admin:* 020 8763 9298. Simon Desorgher. *October.*

Garsington Opera. Garsington Opera, Garsington, Oxon OX44 9DH *admin:* 01865 368201 *box office:* 01865 361636 *fax:* 01865 361545. Leonard Ingrams, Chair; Clare Adams, PR. *June-July 2000.*

Glyndebourne Festival Opera. Glyndebourne, Lewes, E Sussex BN8 5UU *admin:* 01273 812321 *information:* 01273 815000 *box office:* 01273 813813 *fax:* 01273 812783. *May-August.*

Gorleston - St Andrew's Festival of Music and The Arts. 1 Middleton Gardens, Gorleston, Great Yarmouth, Norfolk NR31 7AE *admin:* 01493 601167. Kathleen Plane. *November 2000.*

Goudhurst - Finchcocks Festival. Finchcocks, Goudhurst, Kent TN17 1HH *admin:* 01580 211702 *also box office; fax:* 01580 211007. Katrina and Richard Burnett, Directors. *Weekends throughout September.*

Grassington Festival. Lythe Cottage, Grassington, nr Skipton, N Yorks BD23 5DA *admin:* 01756 752288 *box office:* 01756 753093 *fax:* 01756 752917. Rowena Leder, Artistic Director. *16 June-1 July 2000.*

Grimsby - International Jazz Festival. Leisure Services Department, The Knoll, Cleethorpes, NE Lincs DN35 8LN *admin:* 01472 323007 *box office:* 01472 311311 *fax:* 01472 323005. Lynne Conlan, Arts and Cultural Development Officer. *July.*

Guiting Festival. Langley Lodge, Langley, Winchcombe, Glos GL54 5AB *admin:* 01242 603912 *also fax and box office; email:* duncan.westerman@virgin.net. Duncan Westerman, Artistic Director. *July.*

Halifax - National Young Musicians Chamber Music Festival. Nanholme Centre, Shaw Wood Road, Todmorden, Lancs OL14 6DA *admin:* 01706 817633 *box office:* 01422 349422 *fax:* 01706 818948 *email:* ymcmf.festival@virgin.net. Douglas Jarman, Artistic Director; Angela Jarman, Festival Co-ordinator. *5-13 May 2000, Apr/May annually.*

Harpenden Musicale Summer Music Festival. The Bourne, 20 Salisbury Ave, Harpenden, Herts AL5 2QG *admin:* 01582 460978 *also box office; fax:* 01582 767343 *email:* HMusicale@aol.com. David Johnston, Director. *August 2000.*

Harrogate International Festival. 1 Victoria Ave, Harrogate, N Yorks HG1 1EQ *admin:* 01423 562303 *box office:* 01423 537230 *fax:* 01423 521264 *email:* info@harrogate-festival.org.uk. William Culver Dodds, Artistic Director; Fiona Goh, Administrator. *20 July-5 August 2000.*

Harrogate International Youth Music Festival. Deepdene Lodge, Deepdene Avenue, Dorking, Surrey RH5 4AZ *admin:* 01306 744360 *box office:* 01423 537231 *fax:* 01306 744361 *email:* smb.peurope@kuoni.co.uk. E Jon de Revere, Artistic Director; Sharon Brewster, Festival Manager. *21-28 April 2000.*

Lichfield International Arts Festival

6th -16th July 2000

An inspiring context for one of the UK's leading Arts Festivals.

The *Bach 250* anniversary, the Millennium and the 1300th anniversary of the founding of Lichfield Cathedral by St. Chad provide the main focus.

Special features include The Lichfield Mystery Plays over the first weekend, The New London Consort performing all Bach's Brandenburg Concertos. Alfred Brendel, Kennedy and Lynn Harrell, the Endellion Quartet in a *Words and Music* series including Andrew Motion reading his new *Seven Last Words from the Cross* to Haydn's music, and a major new *Easter Oratorio* by Paul Spicer commissioned for the Festival.

In addition, there is jazz. light entertainment, drama, films, exhibitions, walks, talks, open gardens, children's events, a huge Medieval Market and Spectacular Fireworks. There are wonderful venues from Lichfield Cathedral to beautiful country churches in hidden corners of Staffordshire. July is an exciting time to be in Lichfield.

Full details of all events will be available in mid-April from:
The Festival Office, 7 The Close, Lichfield, Staffordshire WS13 7LD.
Tel: 01543 257298; Fax: 01543 415137.
e-mail: lichfield.fest@lichfield-arts.org.uk
website: www.lichfieldfestival.org

2000 Oundle

Oundle International Festival and Summer School for Young Organists

'an essential and inspiring experience for all serious students of the organ'

Course dates for 2000:

7 - 9 April Pulling Out the Stops

- A weekend course for beginner organ ists, or those who would like to start (aged 10 to 14).

16 - 23 July Oundle International Summer School for Young Organists

'An established must in the world of organ studies'

- Organists aged 14 - 24 are taught in a non-competitive atmosphere by some of the greatest names in the organ world.
- Valuable recital awards available at prestigious venues throughout the UK.
- Special provision for advanced players, who will spend three days resident in Cambridge.

For full details and brochures, please contact the Festival office:

Phone/fax 01832 272026

Email OIF@btinternet.com

Oundle International Festival
The Old Crown, Glapthorn,
Oundle, Peterborough PE8 5BJ

op♮

The Oxford Philomusica

Patron Vladimir Ashkenazy

The 2nd Oxford Philomusica International Piano Festival

In association with EPTA

August 2000

Malcolm Troup	Festival President
Julian Gallant	Director
Marios Papadopoulos	Artistic Director
Patricia Powell	Festival Co-ordinator

"The Pianist the Musician"

Internationally distinguished professors and lecturers have included Oxana Yablonskaya, Jean-Bernard Pommier, Peter Katin and Michael Young. Classes, lectures and performance opportunities at the Jacqueline du Pré Music Building and the Oxford University Faculty of Music. Week's full board available at St Hilda's College. Daily observers welcome. Discounts for EPTA members.

For further details write to:
The Oxford Philomusica International Piano Festival
The Oxford Philomusica
PO Box 5, 266 Banbury Road
Oxford, OX2 7DL
Tel: 0870 60 60 804
Email: oxfilmus@globalnet.co.uk
www.oxfordphil.com

RYEDALE FESTIVAL 2000

15th – 30th July

Two weeks of wonderful concerts and spectacular events set in some of the most beautiful locations in England

Artistic Director – Malcom Layfield

For details contact
The Ryedale Festival Office
The Old Meeting House
Helmsley York YO62 5DW
Tel/Fax 01439 771518

Harvington Festival. Harvington Hall, nr Kidderminster, Worcs DY10 4LR *admin:* 01562 777846 *also box office; fax:* 01562 777190. *July.*

Haslemere Festival. Festival Office, Jesses, Grayswood Road, Haslemere, Surrey GU27 2BS *admin:* 01483 416143 *also fax; box office:* 01428 642161 *fax:* 01428 651473 *email:* brian@be-blood.demon.co.uk. Jeanne Dolmetsch, Artistic Director; Marguerite Dolmetsch, Assistant Artistic Director. *July.*

Haverhill Summer Music. 8 Templars Court, Haverhill, Suffolk CB9 9AJ *admin:* 01440 763799 *also fax.* Kevin Hill, Artistic Director; Deena Shypitka, Administrator. *9, 12, 15, 19, 23 July 2000.*

Henley Festival of Music and The Arts. 14 Friday St, Henley-on-Thames, Oxon RG9 1AH *admin:* 01491 843400 *box office:* 01491 843404 *fax:* 01491 410482 *email:* info@henley-festival.co.uk. Stewart Collins, Artistic Director; Sam Gordon Clark, Chief Executive. *5-9 July 2000; 11-15 July 2001; 10-14 July 2002.*

Hexham Abbey Festival. Parish Centre, Beaumont Street, Hexham, Northumberland NE46 3NB *admin:* 01661 843347 (Artistic Director) *box office:* 01434 607272 *fax:* 01434 606043 *email:* kevin@kevinstephens.free-online.co.uk. Kevin Stephens, Artistic Director. *17-25 September 2000.*

Honiton Festival. Fermain House, Dolphin Street, Colyton, Devon EX24 6LU *admin:* 01297 552272 *fax:* 01297 553744 *email:* euco@compuserve.com. Ambrose Miller, Music Director. *2000 (biennial).*

Huddersfield Contemporary Music Festival. Festival Office, Department of Music, University of Huddersfield, Queensgate, Huddersfield, W Yorks HD1 3DH *admin:* 01484 472103/425082 *also fax; box office:* 01484 430528 *email:* hcmf@hud.ac.uk. Luke O'Shaughnessy, General Manager.

International East Anglian Summer Music Festival. 3-5 Bridge Street, Hadleigh, Suffolk IP7 6BY *admin:* 01473 822596 *fax:* 01473 824175. Thomas McIntosh, Artistic Director; Stacey Sowman, Assistant. *July-August.*

Isleworth Festival. 77 Godstone Rd, St Margaret's, Twickenham, Middx TW1 1JY *admin:* 020 8891 0143 *also fax; email:* colinriley@ndirect.co.uk. Colin Riley, Nic Pendlebury, Artistic Directors. *May.*

Kendal - Mary Wakefield Westmorland Festival. Moresdale Hall, Lambrigg, Kendal, Cumbria LA8 0DH *admin:* 01539 824696 *fax:* 01539 824084. K Pottinger, Secretary. *Biennial. Next 24-31 March 2001.*

Kendal - On The Edge: A Celebration of Adventurous Music. Brewery Arts Centre, Highgate, Kendal, Cumbria LA9 4HE *admin:* 01539 725133 *also box office; fax:* 01539 730257 *email:* brewery@ lakesnet.co.uk. Stuart Johnson, Music Officer. *November.*

Keswick Jazz Festival. PO Box 118, Newport NP19 8XJ *admin:* 01633 211368 *box office:* 01900 602122 *fax:* 01900 65143. John Minnion, Artistic Director; Paul Sherwin, Administrator. *14-21 May 2000.*

King's Lynn Festival. 27 King Street, King's Lynn, Norfolk PE30 1ET *admin:* 01553 767557 *also box office; fax:* 01553 767688 *email:* jo@kl-festival.freeserve.co.uk. Ambrose Miller, Artistic Director; Joanne Rutterford, Administrator. *20-29 July 2000.*

Lacock Abbey Festival. Lacock Abbey, nr Chippenham, Wilts SN15 2LG *admin:* 01249 730042 *also box office.* Petronella Dittmer, Artistic Director. *Easter and last week in July (provisional).*

Lake District Summer Music International Festival and Summer School. Stricklandgate House, 92 Stricklandgate, Kendal, Cumbria LA9 4PU *admin:* 01539 733411 *box office:* 01539 724441 *also fax; email:* info@ldsm.org.uk. Christopher Rowland, Artistic Director; Andrew Lucas, Administrator. *5-19 August 2000 (provisional).*

Leicester International Music Festival. New Walk Museum, 53 New Walk, Leicester LE1 7EA *admin:* 0116 247 3043 *also fax; box office:* 0116 255 4854 (Phoenix Arts). Graham Oppenheimer, Artistic Director; Sue Carverhill, Administrative Director. *16-25 June 2000.*

Leominster Festival. Fircroft, Hereford Road, Leominster, Hereford HR6 8JU *admin:* 01568 612874 *box office:* 01568 613477 *fax:* 01568 760254 *email:* leofest@ajmorris.globalnet.co.uk. Chris Sansom, Chair. *June.*

Leonard Stanley - Music At The Priory. Kingston House, Leonard Stanley, Stonehouse, Glos GL10 3NX *admin:* 01453 822299 *box office:* 01453 823152. Robert A Hutchings, Chair. *22 June-16 July 2000.*

Lichfield Festival. 7 The Close, Lichfield, Staffs WS13 7LD *admin:* 01543 257298 *box office:* 01543 257557 *fax:* 01543 415137 *email:* lichfield.fest@lichfield-arts.org.uk. Paul Spicer, Festival Director. *7-16 July 2000.*

Little Missenden Festival of Music and The Arts. 30 Dovehouse Close, Upper Wolvercote, N Oxford OX2 8BG *admin:* 01865 554836 *box office:* 01494 862816. Richard Drakeford, Musical Adviser. *October.*

Longborough Festival Opera. New Banks Fee, Longborough, Glos GL56 0QF *admin:* 01451 830292 *also box office fax:* 01451 830605. Martin Graham, Director. *June-July.*

Madley Festival. Woodman's Cottage, Stockley Hill, Peterchurch, Hereford HR2 0ST *admin:* 01981 550293 *box office:* 01981 250891. Charles Farncombe, Artistic Director; Denys Blainey. *8-16 July 2000.*

Malvern - Autumn in Malvern Festival. 42 Worcester Road, Great Malvern, Worcs WR14 4AA *admin:* 01684 569721 *also fax; box office:* 01684 892277. Peter Smith, Artistic Director. *October 2000 (w/ends).*

Manchester - Glories of The Keyboard. RNCM Broadwood International Festival, Festival Office, 134 Kingsbrook Rd, Manchester M16 8WG *admin:* 0161 881 9320 *also fax; box office:* 0161 273 4504. Renna Kellaway, Artistic Director; Carolyn Howlett, Administrator. *Next 2001 (biennial).*

Manchester - Hallé Proms Festival. Hallé Concerts Society, The Bridgewater Hall, Manchester M3 3WS *admin:* 0161 237 7000 *box office:* 0161 907 9000 *fax:* 0161 237 7029. Kent Nagano, Artistic Director; Leslie Robinson, Chief Executive. *June-July.*

Manchester - RNCM International Cello Festival. The Grange, Clay Lane, Handforth, Cheshire SK9 3NR *admin:* 01625 530140 *also fax; box office:* 0161 907 5278. Ralph Kirshbaum, Artistic Director; Alison Godlee, Administrator. *2-6 May 2001.*

Manchester - RNCM Quartet Fest 2000. The Grange, Clay Lane, Handforth, Cheshire SK9 3NR *admin:* 01625 530140 *also fax; box office:* 0161 907 5278. Christopher Rowland, Artistic Director; Alison Godlee, Festival Administrator. *13-16 January 2000.*

Marsden Jazz Festival. Marsden Mechanics, Peel Street, Marsden, Huddersfield, W Yorks HD7 6BW *admin:* 01484 843701 *also fax and box office; email:* mikron-theatre@pop3.poptel.org.uk. Mike Lucas, Co-ordinator. *13-15 October 2000.*

Mayfield Festival of Music and The Arts. Festival Office, The Old Palace, High Street, Mayfield, E Sussex TN20 6PH *admin:* 01435 873055 *box office:* 01435 873382 *fax:* 01435 872627. Kenneth Pont, Festival Director. *29 April-14 May 2000 (biennial).*

Milton Abbey Music Festival. Sweetwell, Fiddleford, Sturminster Newton, Dorset DT10 2BX *admin:* 01258 473139. Trevor Doar, Artistic Director; Hugh Hay, Administrator. *August.*

Minehead and Exmoor Festival. Sidella, Whitegate Road, Minehead, Somerset TA24 5SP *admin:* 01643 702353 *box office:* 01643 702624. David Yates. *July.*

Nailsworth Festival. Sesame House, Watledge, Nailsworth, Glos GL6 0AU *admin:* 01453 836350 *also fax.* Sue Reed. *22 April-1 May 2000.*

Newbury Spring Festival. 1 Bridge Street, Newbury, Berks RG14 5BE *admin:* 01635 32421/528766 *box office:* 01635 522733 *fax:* 01635 528690. Mark Eynon, Artistic Director; Bronwen Sutton, Administrator. *6-20 May 2000.*

Norfolk and Norwich Festival. 42-58 St George's Street, Norwich, Norfolk NR3 1AB *admin:* 01603 614921 *box office:* 01603 764764 *fax:* 01603 632303 *email:* info@nnfest.eastern-arts.co.uk. Marcus Davey, Artistic Director; Fiona Carter. *October.*

Norwich Festival of Contemporary Church Music. 53a The Close, Norwich NR1 4EG *admin:* 01603 626589/764383 *fax:* 01603 766032. David Dunnett, Cathedral Organist. *Next 2000 (every 2 or 3 years).*

Nottingham - Now 99. Nottingham City Council, 51-57 Castle Gate, Nottingham NG1 7AT *admin:* 0115 915 3534 *box office:* 0115 941 9741 *fax:* 0115 915 3599 *email:* xdg@dial.pipex.com. Andrew Caleya Chetty, Artistic Director. *October-November.*

Oundle International Festival. The Old Crown, Glapthorn, Oundle, Peterborough PE8 5BJ *admin:* 01832 272026 *also fax and box office; email:* OIF@btinternet.com. James Parsons, Director; Trisha Ryan, Administrator. *14-23 July 2000.*

Oxford - Charivari Agréable Summer Festival. Oakley, 109 Windmill Rd, Oxford OX3 7DN *admin:* 01865 751928 *also fax; email:* eventsmanager@charivari.freeserve.co.uk. Lynda Sayce, Artistic Director; Susanne Heinrich, Administrative Director. *Mid July-mid September.*

Oxford Festival of Contemporary Music. 25a Cave Street, Oxford OX4 1BA *admin:* 01865 791355 *box office:* 01865 798600 *fax:* 01865 432674 *email:* davidbass@ofcm.ndirect.co.uk. Philip Cashian, Stefan Asbury, Artistic Directors; David Bass, General Manager. *April/June, October/December.*

Petersfield Musical Festival. Mill House, Pulens Lane, Petersfield, Hants GU31 4BZ *admin:* 01730 264131 *box office:* 01730 266605. Ruth Firth, Secretary. *18-25 March 2000.*

Pickering Jazz Festival. 2 Leonard's Court, Pickering, N Yorks YO18 8DN *admin:* 01751 473524 *box office:* 01751 473843 *also fax.* Joe Passey, Artistic Director; Ann Bowley, Secretary. *July-August.*

Plaxtol Music Festival. Plaxtol Vineyard, Plaxtol, Sevenoaks, Kent TN15 0QF *admin:* 01732 810618 *also fax; fax:* 01732 811036 *email:* Carbonimedia@compuserve.com. Marius Carboni, Director.

Reigate Summer Music. Flat 2, 24 Castle Walk, Reigate, Surrey RH2 9PX *admin:* 01737 244407 *also box office; fax:* 01737 241153. Leslie Olive, Artistic Director; David Everett, Administrator.

Ripon Festival. The Firs, Spring Bank Close, Ripon, N Yorks HG4 1ER *admin:* 01765 690318 *fax:* 01765 692291 *email:* RiponFest@aol.com. Hazel Purvis, Festival Director.

Rochester - Music at Restoration House. 15 Brunswick Street, London E17 9NB *admin:* 020 8520 1463 *also fax*. Olga Tverskaya, Artistic Director; Robert Tucker, Administrator. *23-25 June; 1-2 and 7-9 July; 1-3 December.*

Ross and District Festival of The Arts. Ty Croeso, Aston Bank, Aston Ingham, Ross-on-Wye, Herefords HR9 7LS *admin:* 01989 720478 *also box office; email:* anthonybutcher@ukonline.co.uk. Chris Green, Artistic Director; Anthony Butcher, Hon Secretary. *June 2000.*

Ross-on-Wye International Festival. The Mews, Mitcheldean, Glos GL17 0SL *admin:* 01594 544446 *box office:* 01989 563330 *fax:* 01594 544448 *email:* Ross_Festival@compuserve.com. Helen Wragg, Artistic Director; Jim Smith. *17-28 August 2000.*

Ryedale Festival. The Festival Office, The Old Meeting House, Helmsley, York YO62 5DW *admin:* 01439 771518 *also fax; email:* ryefest @btconnect.com. Malcolm Layfield, Artistic Director. *14-29 July 2000.*

St Albans International Organ Festival. PO Box 80, St Albans, Herts AL3 4HR *admin:* 01727 844765 *box office:* 01727 846126 *fax:* 01727 844765 *email:* iofs@aol.com. Peter Hewitt, Artistic Director; Ken Chaproniere, General Manager. *Next 2001 (biennial).*

St Endellion Easter and Summer Festivals of Music. Churchtown Farmhouse, Michaelstow, Bodmin, Cornwall PL30 3PD *admin:* 01208 850463 *also box office*. Richard Hickox, Artistic Director; Anne Spicer, Publicity Officer. *April, July-August.*

Salisbury Festival. 75 New Street, Salisbury, Wilts SP1 2PH *admin:* 01722 323883 *box office:* 01722 320333 *fax:* 01722 410552 *email:* info@salisburyfestival.co.uk. Helen Marriage, Festival Director. *May-June.*

Sevenoaks Summer Festival. Sevenoaks School, Sevenoaks, Kent TN13 1HU *admin:* 01732 740480 *also box office; fax:* 01732 456143. Roger Woodward, Artistic Director; Eileen Williams, Festival Administrator. *June.*

Sheffield Music in the Round May Festival. Music in the Round, Unit 317, The Workstation, 15 Paternoster Row, Sheffield S1 2BX *admin:* 0114 221 2182 *box office:* 0114 276 9922 *fax:* 0114 221 2183 *email:* mitr@workstation.org.uk. Peter Cropper, Artistic Director; Tracey Waters, Administrator. *May.*

Shrewsbury - Music at Leasowes Bank. Leasowes Bank Farm, Ratlinghope, nr Shrewsbury, Shropshire SY5 0SW *admin:* 01743 790769 *also fax*. Frances Williams, Festival Director. *Last two weeks of July.*

Sidmouth Arts Festival. Gliddons Maisonette, Sheffield House, Devon EX10 8LX *admin:* 01395 579239. Philip Riley. *11-25 June 2000.*

Southern Cathedrals Festival. 33 The Close, Salisbury, Wilts SP1 2EQ *admin:* 01722 555125 *fax:* 01722 555116. David Hill, Artistic Director. *July 2000 (Salisbury).*

Stately Homes Festival of Early Music. Beechcroft, 33 The Drive, Esher, Surrey KT10 8DH *admin:* 020 8398 2882 *also fax;* 07785 936076. Douglas Reed, Artistic Director. *June-September 2000.*

Stogumber Music. Mill Close, Stogumber, Taunton, Somerset TA4 3TL *admin:* 01984 656202 *also fax*. V K Metters, Director. *August.*

Stour Music. 65 Oxenturn Road, Wye, Ashford, Kent TN25 5AY *admin:* 01233 812740 *box office:* 01227 455600 *fax:* 01227 781830. Mark Deller, Artistic Director; Valerie Paterson, Secretary. *June.*

Stratford-upon-Avon - The English Music Festival. 34 Scholars Lane, Stratford-upon-Avon, Warwicks CV37 6HE *admin:* 01789 261561 *fax:* 01789 261577 *email:* Londartist@aol.com. Michael Emmerson, Artistic Director. *6-15 October 2000.*

Stratford-upon-Avon International Flute Festival. PO Box 7, Stratford-upon-Avon, Warwicks CV37 9GB *admin:* 01789 261561 *fax:* 01789 261577 *email:* Stratflute@aol.com. Elena Durán, Artistic Director; Michael Emmerson, Chair. *24 July-5 August 2000.*

Stroud Festival. PO Box 92, Stonehouse, Glos GL10 3YN *admin:* 01453 827717 *email:* stroudfest@suetorres.demon.co.uk. Sue Bearder and Sue Torres, Artistic Directors. *September.*

Suffolk Villages Festival. 50 Halstead Road, Lexden, Colchester, Essex CO3 5AF *admin:* 01206 767895 *box office:* 01473 827718. Peter Holman, Artistic Director; Josephine Pearson, Publicity Manager. *25-28 August 2000.*

Sutton Bonington, Leics - National Folk Music Festival. 5 Church Street, Aylesbury, Bucks HP20 2QP *admin:* 01296 415333 *also box office; fax:* 01296 397092. John Heydon, Artistic Director. *28-30 April 2000.*

Swaledale Festival. Thornborough Hall, Leyburn, N Yorks DL8 5AB *admin:* 01969 622217 *box office:* 01969 623069. Elizabeth Carter, Director. *May-June.*

Swanage Jazz Festival. 4 Hardy Court, Marshall Row, Swanage, Dorset BH19 2AF *admin:* 01929 425053/425371 *box office:* 01929 422885. Fred Lindop, Artistic Director. *2nd weekend in July 2000.*

Thaxted Festival. Clarance House, Thaxted, Essex CM6 2PJ *admin:* 01371 831421 *also fax and box office.* Gareth Stainer, Artistic Director, Administrator. *23 June-16 July 2000 (weekends only).*

Three Choirs Festival. Festival Office, The Canon's House Flat, The Close, Hereford HR1 2NG *admin:* 01432 274455. Elizabeth Pooley, Administrator. *19-25 August 2000 (Hereford 2000; Gloucester 2001).*

Tilford Bach Festival. Old Quarry House, Seale, Farnham, Surrey GU10 1LD *admin:* 01252 782167. Denys Darlow, Paul Nicholson, Artistic Director; Helen Malyon, Hon Secretary. *May 2000.*

Tudeley Festival. Postern Park Oast, Tonbridge, Kent TN11 0QT *admin:* 01732 773322 *also box office; fax:* 01732 773344. Stephen Coles, Artistic Director. *December 1999-July 2000.*

Wallingford - Music At St Peter's. 55 The Street, Crowmarsh Gifford, Wallingford, Oxon OX10 8EA *admin:* 01491 825421 *fax:* 01491 824581 *email:* glynne.stackhouse@lineone.net. Glynne Stackhouse, Artistic Director. *May to September 2000.*

Wardour Music Festival. Festival Office, 7 Berwick Courtyard, Berwick St Leonard, Salisbury, Wilts SP3 5SN *admin:* 01747 820872 *also box office; fax:* 01747 820410. Robert Churchill, Artistic Director; Sean Rourke, Marketing Director. *June.*

Warwick & Leamington Festival. Warwick Arts Society, Northgate, Warwick CV34 4JL *admin:* 01926 410747 *box office:* 01926 496277 *fax:* 01926 407606. Richard Phillips, Festival Director. *1-16 July 2000.*

Weston Park Music Festival. Weston Park, nr Shifnal, Shropshire TF11 8LE *admin:* 01952 850207 *also box office; fax:* 01952 850430. Catherine Lloyd, PR and Park Development Officer. *August.*

Wimborne Arts Festival. 48 Bridle Way, Colehill, Wimborne, Dorset BH21 2UE *admin:* 01202 880331 *fax:* 01202 888037. Graham Stansfield, Artistic Director. *End September-early October.*

Winchester Early Music Festival. 3 Paternoster House, Colebrook St, Winchester, Hants SO23 9LG *admin:* 01962 865617 *box office:* 01962 877977 *email:* rlc@wemf.screaming.net. Richard Lowell Childress, Artistic Director; Angela Ryde-Weller, Secretary. *21-24 September 2000.*

Windsor Festival. Windsor Festival Society Ltd, 60 Ashworth Mansions, London W9 1LW *admin:* 020 7286 8811 *box office:* 01753 623400 *fax:* 020 7286 0866. Jane Krivine, Festival Director. *September-October.*

Wooburn Festival. Wooburn Festival Society Ltd, 14 Holtspur Lane, Wooburn Green, High Wycombe, Bucks HP10 0AA *admin:* 01628 531793 *box office:* 01628 524243 *email:* Info@wooburn.com. Liz Freeth, Secretary. *October.*

Woolacombe - Nick Holt's Most Excellent Jazz Weekends. 9 Forches Avenue, Barnstaple, Devon *admin:* 01271 72064 (home). Nick Holt. *Weekend before Easter and weekend in mid-October.*

Worthing - West Sussex International Youth Music Festival. Deepdene Lodge, Deepdene Avenue, Dorking, Surrey RH5 4AZ *admin:* 01306 744360 *fax:* 01306 744361 *email:* peurope@kuoni.co.uk. E Jon de Revere, Artistic Director; Wendy Good, Festival Manager. *19-25 April 2000.*

Wycombe Arts Festival. Edgehill, Upper Stanley Road, High Wycombe, Bucks HP12 4DB *admin:* 01494 523697. J W Beaumont, Chair. *May.*

York Colourscape Festival. c/o 30 Penworthan Road, Sandestead, Surrey CR2 0QS *admin:* 020 8763 9298. Simon Desorgher. *August.*

York Early Music Christmas Festival. PO Box 226, York YO30 5ZU *admin:* 01904 645738 *box office:* 01937 584123 *fax:* 01904 612631 *email:* yemf@netcomuk.co.uk. Delma Tomlin, Artistic Director. *15-17 December 2000.*

York Early Music Festival. PO Box 226, York YO30 5ZU *admin:* 01904 658338 *box office:* 01937 584123 *fax:* 01904 612631 *email:* yemf @netcomuk.co.uk. Delma Tomlin, Administrative Director. *7-16 July 2000.*

York Late Music Festival. 18 Glen Avenue, YO31 0XN *admin:* 01904 426372 *email:* david.power3@virgin.net. Steve Crowther, David Power, Administrators. *October/November.*

Channel Islands and Isle of Man

Jersey World Music Festival. 5 Sunshine Avenue, St Savious, Jersey JE2 7TS *admin:* 01534 607860 *box office:* 01534 873767 *email:* worldmus@itl.net. Gerry Jackson, Chair. *5-8 October 2000.*

Port Erin - Mananan International Festival of Music and The Arts. Mananan Festival Office, Port Erin, Isle of Man IM9 6LD *admin:* 01624 835858 *box office:* 01624 832662 *fax:* 01624 836658 *email:* erinartscentre@enterprise.net. John Bethell, Director. *24 June-2 July 2000.*

Scotland

Aberdeen International Youth Festival. 3 Nutborn House, Clifton Road, London SW19 4QT *admin:* 020 8946 2995 *box office:* 01224 641122 *fax:* 020 8944 6507 *email:* nicola.wallis@virgin.net. Nicola Wallis, Festival Director. *2-12 August 2000.*

Berwickshire - Summer Music at Paxton House. 17 North Gardner Street, Glasgow G11 5BU *admin:* 0141 339 2708 *also box office; fax:* 0141 337 6923. Gusztáv Fenyö, Artistic Director; Jeanette Fenyö, Administrator. *7-16 July 2000.*

Clackmannanshire Arts Festival. Team Leader, Arts, Room 28, Lime Tree House, Castle Street, Alloa FK10 1EX *admin:* 01259 452487 *box office:* 01259 213131 *fax:* 01259 452440. Rosa Macpherson, Festival Co-ordinator. *May.*

Dumfries and Galloway Arts Festival. Gracefield Arts Centre, 28 Edinburgh Road, Dumfries DG1 1NW *admin:* 01387 260447 *also fax; box office:* 01387 247780. Beryl Jago MBE, Artistic Director; Sheena Widdall, Administrative Assistant. *May-June.*

Dunkeld and Birnam Arts Festival. Old Manse of Strathbraan, Trochry, by Dunkeld, Perthshire PH8 0DY *admin:* 01350 723205. Sonja Arbuthnott, Artistic Director. *June.*

Edinburgh and Glasgow - Festival of British Youth Orchestras. NAYO, Ainslie House, 11 St Colme Street, Edinburgh EH3 6AG *admin:* 0131 539 1087; 0141 332 5057 (RSAMD box office) *box office:* 0131 226 5138 *fax:* 0131 539 1069 *email:* admin@nayo.org.uk. Carol Main, Director. *12 August-3 September 2000.*

Edinburgh Harp Festival. 7a Learmonth Court, Edinburgh EH4 1PD *admin:* 0131 332 8692. Sheila Kirk, Artistic Director; Sharon Quinn. *14-19 April 2000.*

Edinburgh International Festival. The Hub, Edinburgh's Festival Centre, Castlehill, Royal Mile, Edinburgh EH1 2NE *admin:* 0131 473 2099 *box office:* 0131 473 2000 *fax:* 0131 473 2002 *email:* eif@eif.co.uk. Brian McMaster, Festival Director; James Waters, Associate Director. *August-September.*

Edinburgh International Jazz and Blues Festival. 29 St Stephen Street, Edinburgh EH3 5AN *admin:* 0131 225 2202 *box office:* 0131 667 7776 *fax:* 0131 225 3321. Mike Hart, Artistic Director; Roger Spence, Fiona Alexander, Promoters. *July-August.*

Highland Festival. 40 Huntly Street, Inverness IV3 5HR *admin:* 01463 719000 *box office:* 01463 711112 *fax:* 01463 716777 *email:* info@highlandfestival.org.uk. Alastair McDonald, Artistic Director; Morven MacLeod, Administrator. *26 May-10 June 2000.*

Mendelssohn On Mull Trust Festival. 10 Gloucester Place, Edinburgh EH3 6EF *admin:* 0131 225 8282 *fax:* 0131 225 6889 *email:* m.jeffcoat@ukonline.co.uk. Angus Ramsay, Artistic Director; Marilyn Jeffcoat, Administrator. *1-8 July 2000.*

Northlands Festival. Northlands Festival Office, Whitechapel Rd, Wick KW1 4EA *admin:* 01955 606660. Mary Miller, Artistic Director; Sally Body, Festival Manager. *2nd week of September.*

Orkney Islands - St Magnus Festival. Strandal, Nicolson Street, Kirkwall, Orkney KW15 1BD *admin:* 01856 872669 *fax:* 01856 871170. Glenys Hughes, Artistic Director; Dorothy Rushbrook, Administrator. *16-21 June 2000.*

Perth Festival of The Arts. 3-5 High Street, Perth PH1 5JS *admin:* 01738 475295 *also fax; email:* artsfestival@perth.org.uk. Sandra Ralston, Administrator. *May.*

ScottishPower Proms. Royal Scottish National Orchestra, 73 Claremont Street, Glasgow G3 7JB *admin:* 0141 225 3550 *fax:* 0141 221 4317 *email:* admin@rsno.org.uk. Simon Crookall, Chief Executive. *May-June.*

Wales

Aberystwyth - Musicfest - International Music Festival and Summer School. Aberystwyth Arts Centre, Penglais, Aberystwyth, Ceredigion SY23 3DE *admin:* 01970 622882 *box office:* 01970 623232 *fax:* 01970 622883 *email:* lla@aber.ac.uk. Nicholas Jones, Artistic Director; Louise Amery, Marketing Manager. *17-31 July 2000.*

Barmouth Arts Festival. 1 Epworth Terrace, Barmouth, Gwynedd LL42 1PN *admin:* 01341 280392 *also box office.* Mair Jones, Secretary. *3-9 September 2000.*

Brecon Jazz. Jazz Festival Offices, Watton Chambers, Brecon, Powys LD3 7EF *admin:* 01874 625557 *also box office; fax:* 01874 622387. Jed Williams, Artistic Director; Deborah Anthony, Co-ordinator. *August.*

Cardiff Summer Festival. Cardiff County Council, Sports and Leisure Dept, County Hall, Atlantic Wharf, Cardiff CF1 5UW *admin:* 029 2087 3913/2087 3906 *fax:* 029 2087 3937/2087 3920. Helen Kitchen, Events Manager. *July-August.*

Denbigh Festival. Vale St, Denbigh, Denbighshire *admin:* 01244 319981 *fax:* 01244 315662. Sara Hindley, Promoter. *15-22 August 2000.*

Ewenny Early Summer Festival. c/o The Vicarage, Southerndown Road, St Bride's Major, Vale of Glamorgan CF32 0SD *admin:* 01656 880108 *also fax; email:* lambyork@globalnet.co.uk. Anthony Lamb, Artistic Director; Wendy York, Co-ordinator. *19-27 May 2000.*

Fishguard International Music Festival. Festival Office, Fishguard, Pembrokeshire SA65 9BJ *admin:* 01348 873612 *also fax and box office; email:* fishguard-imf@cwcom.net. John S Davies, Artistic Director; Marion Butler, Festival Co-ordinator. *22-29 July 2000.*

Gower Festival. 58 Hendrefoilan Road, Tycoch, Swansea SA2 9LU *admin:* 01792 207924 *box office:* 01792 468321 *fax:* 01792 390404 *email:* gowerfestival@hotmail.com. Maurice Broady, Publicity Manager. *July.*

Gregynog - Gwyl Gregynog Festival. Gregynog, nr Newtown, Powys SY16 3PW *admin:* 01686 650224 *box office:* 01686 650101 *fax:* 01686 650656. Anthony Rolfe Johnson, Artistic Director. *June.*

Llandudno October Festival. Festival Admin, c/o Ambassador Hotel, Llandudno LL30 2NR *admin:* 01492 876886 *box office:* 01492 872000 *fax:* 01492 860790. Anthony Hose, Artistic Director. *13-20 October 2000.*

Llangollen International Jazz Festival. Blazeahead Ltd, Farthings, Rivacre Road, Hooton Park, S Wirral CH65 1AS *admin:* 0151 339 3367 *also fax and box office; email:* 100524.2563@compuserve.com. Roy Potts, Festival Director. *12-14 May 2000.*

Llangollen International Musical Eisteddfod. Eisteddfod Office, Llangollen, Denbighshire LL20 8NG *admin:* 01978 860236 *box office:* 01978 861501 *fax:* 01978 861300 *email:* info@lime.uk.com. Miss Gwawr Owen, Artistic Director; Maureen A Jones, Marketing Director. *3-9 July 2000.*

Llantilio Crossenny Festival of Music and Drama. Treadam Farm, Llantilio Crossenny, Abergavenny, Monmouthshire NP7 8TA *admin:* 01600 780233 *box office:* 01873 856928 *email:* llantilio@btinternet.com. Charles Farncombe CBE, Artistic Director; Selby Milner. *May 2000.*

Lower Machen Festival. 46 Richmond Road, Roath, Cardiff CF24 3AT *admin:* 029 2048 2183 *fax:* 029 2048 2183. Peter Reynolds, Artistic Director. *26-30 June 2000.*

Machynlleth Festival. Y Tabernacl, Heol Penrallt, Machynlleth, Powys SY20 8AJ *admin:* 01654 703355 *also box office; fax:* 01654 702160. Ruth Lambert, Chairman. *20-27 August 2000.*

Presteigne Festival of Music and The Arts. 17 Parliament Hill, London NW3 2TA *admin:* 020 7435 5965 *box office:* 01544 267800 *fax:* 020 7435 9166. George Vass, Artistic Director. *24-29 August 2000.*

St Asaph - North Wales International Music Festival. Festival Office, High Street, St Asaph, Denbighshire LL17 0RD *admin:* 01745 584508 *also fax and box office; email:* musicfestival@ st_asaph-n_wales. demon.co.uk. Geraint Lewis, Artistic Director; Jill Mort, Administrator. *23-30 September 2000.*

St Davids Cathedral Festival. Gwyl Eglwys Gadeiriol Tyddewi, 65 Goat Street, St Davids, Pembrokeshire SA62 6RQ *admin:* 01437 720271/721885 *also fax; box office:* 01437 720835/720804 *email:* festival@stdavidscathedral.org.uk. Geraint Bowen, Artistic Director; Llywela Harris, Administrator. *27 May-4 June 2000.*

Swansea Festival of Music and The Arts. 9 Gabalfa Road, Sketty, Swansea *admin:* 01792 411570 *box office:* 01792 475715 *fax:* 01570 493636. John Metcalf, Artistic Director; Susan Croall, Administrator. *7-21 October 2000.*

Vale of Glamorgan Festival. St Donats Arts Centre, St Donats Castle, Llantwit Major, Vale of Glamorgan CF61 1WF *admin:* 01446 792151 *box office:* 01446 794848 *fax:* 01446 794711. John Metcalf, Artistic Director; David Ambrose, Director. *September.*

Wrexham Arts Festival. Memorial Hall, Bodhyfryd, Wrexham LL12 7AG *admin:* 01978 292683 *box office:* 01978 292015. G A Lacy, Artistic Director. *May.*

Northern Ireland

Armagh Arts Festival. c/o Tourist Information Centre, 40 English Street, Armagh BT61 7BA *admin:* 028 3752 1805 *box office:* 028 3752 1800 *fax:* 028 3751 0180 *email:* armagh.arts@dnet.co.uk. Kate Bond, Arts Officer. *May.*

Belfast - Festival of Early Music. School of Music, Queen's University of Belfast, Belfast BT7 1NN *admin:* 028 9033 5105 *also box office; fax:* 028 9023 8484 *email:* c.fegan@qub.ac.uk. Ian Woodfield, Chairman.

Belfast Festival at Queen's. Festival House, 25 College Gardens, Belfast BT9 6BS *admin:* 028 9066 7687 *box office:* 028 9066 5577 *fax:* 028 9066 3733. Robert Agnew, Executive Director. *27 October-12 November 2000.*

Belfast - Sonorities. School of Music, Queen's University, Belfast BT7 1NN *admin:* 028 9033 5105 *also box office; fax:* 028 9023 8484 *email:* c.fegan@qub.ac.uk. Michael Alcorn, Committee Chair. *April-May 2000.*

Castleward Opera Festival. 61 Marlborough Park North, Belfast BT9 6HL *admin:* 028 9066 1090 *fax:* 028 9068 7081. Ian Urwin and Jack Smith, Artistic Directors; Hilda Logan, Company Manager. *June.*

Derry - Banks of The Foyle Halloween Carnival. Recreation and Leisure Dept, Derry City Council, 98 Strand Road, Derry, Co Londonderry BT48 7NN *admin:* 028 7136 5151 *box office:* 028 7126 0516 *fax:* 028 7137 0080 *email:* festivals.dcc@btinternet.com. Nuala McGee, Festivals Officer; Claire Lundy, Press Officer. *26 October-6 November 2000.*

Derry - Two Cathedrals Festival. 2 St Columb's Court, Derry, Co Londonderry BT48 6PT *admin:* 028 7126 2412 *box office:* 028 7126 0516. Timothy Allen and Donal Doherty, Artistic Directors. *October.*

Portstewart - Flowerfield Arts Festival. Flowerfield Arts Centre, 185 Coleraine Road, Portstewart, Co Londonderry BT55 7HU *admin:* 028 7083 3959. Malcolm Murchison, Arts Organiser. *October.*

Education

SALISBURY CATHEDRAL
CHORISTERS

Voice trials for both boy and girl choristers (age 7 - 10) are held annually in January and February for admission to

Salisbury Cathedral School

in the following September.

Choristers all receive a full Preparatory School education at the Cathedral School.

For boy choristers, the Dean and Chapter provide scholarships which are worth half the full boarding fee.

Details regarding scholarships and bursaries for girl choristers are available on request.

For details apply to:
The Secretary (Dept. VT/CM)
Salisbury Cathedral School
1 The Close, Salisbury, SP1 2EQ.
Tel: 01722 555300

KING'S COLLEGE CAMBRIDGE

Generous Scholarships of at least two-thirds of boarding and tuition fees at King's College School are available for boys who would enjoy singing in the Chapel Choir and are between 6 and 8.

Choristers receive a first-class academic and musical education and most win valuable music scholarships at 13-plus to top schools.

Stephen Cleobury, Director of Music, is pleased to see prospective candidates at any time.

Full details may be obtained from him at King's College, Cambridge CB2 1ST.
Telephone: 01223 331224

MUSIC AWARDS AT INDEPENDENT SENIOR SCHOOLS 2000

(produced in association with HMC, GSA and SHMIS)

A comprehensive annual guide to music scholarships

which includes

- *detailed profiles of 177 schools*
- *listings of 164 further schools*
- *articles and advice on music scholarship procedures*
- *schools listed by type and location.*

Price £7.99 **Publication** September 1999

Available from leading music stores, or by mail at £9.50 (incl. p & p) from **MMA Awards Book, 'Wayfaring' Smithers Lane, Hale Street, Tonbridge, Kent TN12 5HT.**

(Cheques must accompany order and be made payable to the M.M.A.)

Write now for your copy of the 2000 edition

MMA ***The Professional Forum for Teachers of Music***

CANTERBURY CATHEDRAL CHOIR

CHORISTERS

VOICE TRIALS

for boys aged 7 & 8 will be held in

November 2000

Substantial scholarships are awarded and choristers enjoy the superb and extensive facilities of St Edmund's School.

The Master of the Choristers, David Flood, is always pleased to meet and advise parents and their sons.

For further details please telephone:

01227 865242

Choir Schools

The schools listed below provide choristers for cathedral choirs and some parish church choirs. They are primarily independent schools and most are members of the **Choir Schools' Association** (The Minster School, Deangate, York YO1 2JA *tel:* 01904 624900, Wendy Jackson, admin).

Preparatory Schools (age 7-13)

Abbey School. Church St, Tewkesbury, Glos GL20 5PD *tel:* 01684 294460 *fax:* 01684 290797. J H Milton, head; Andrew Sackett, dir of mus.

Cathedral Choir School. Whitcliffe Lane, Ripon, N Yorks HG4 2LA *tel:* 01765 602134 *fax:* 01765 608760 *email:* admin@choirschool.demon.co.uk. R H Moore, head; A J Bryden, dir of mus.

The Cathedral School (Llandaff). Cardiff Rd, Llandaff, Cardiff CF5 2YH *tel:* 029 2056 3179 *fax:* 029 2056 7752 *email:* plg@caliemus.demon.co.uk. Lindsay Gray, head; Michael Hoeg, dir of mus.

Cathedral School (Salisbury). 1 The Close, Salisbury, Wilts SP1 2EQ *tel:* 01722 555300 *fax:* 01722 410910 *email*: aspire@salisbury.enterprise-plc.com. Mr R M Thackray, head; David Halls, dir of mus.

The Chorister School. Durham DH1 3EL *tel:* 0191 384 2935. Stephen Drew, head; Mrs J Tasker, dir of mus.

Christ Church Cathedral School. 3 Brewer St, Oxford OX1 1QW *tel:* 01865 242561 *fax:* 01865 202945. Allan Mottram, head; Simon Whalley, dir of mus.

Exeter Cathedral School. The Chantry, Palace Gate, Exeter, Devon EX1 1HX *tel:* 01392 255298 *fax:* 01392 422718 *email:* exetercs@aol.com. C I S Dickinson, head; S W Tanner, dir of mus.

King's College School. West Rd, Cambridge CB3 9DN *tel:* 01223 365814 *fax:* 01223 461388 *email:* office@kingscam.demon.co.uk. N J Robinson, head; Charmian Farmer, dir of mus.

King's School Junior School. Ely, Cambs CB7 4DB *tel:* 01353 660730 *fax:* 01353 665281. M Anderson, head; N Porter-Thaw, head of mus.

Lanesborough School. Maori Rd, Guildford, Surrey GU1 2EL *tel:* 01483 880650 *fax:* 01483 880651 *email*: goodr@lanesboroughps.surrey.cabletel-schools.org.uk. S Deller, head; S Watts, dir of mus.

Lichfield Cathedral School (St Chad's). The Palace, Lichfield, Staffs WS13 7LH *tel:* 01543 306170 *also fax.* A F Walters, head; R W Dingle, dir of mus.

Lincoln Minster School. Eastgate, Lincoln LN2 1QG *tel:* 01522 523769 *fax:* 01522 514778 *email:* lms@legend.co.uk. Clive Rickart, head; Linda Hepburn-Booth, mus dir; Colin Walsh, master of the choristers.

The Minster School. Deangate, York YO1 7JA *tel:* 01904 625217 *fax:* 01904 632418. Richard Shephard, head; Jill Bowman, dir of mus.

New College School. Savile Rd, Oxford OX1 3UA *tel:* 01865 243657 *fax:* 01865 209116. J Edmunds, head; R W Allen, dir of mus.

The Pilgrims' School. 3 The Close, Winchester, Hants SO23 9LT *tel:* 01962 854189 *fax:* 01962 843610. Rev B A Rees, head; Miss Hilary Brooks, dir of mus.

Polwhele House School. Truro, Cornwall TR4 9AE *tel:* 01872 273011 *also fax; email:* polwhele@rmplc.co.uk. Richard White, head and dir of mus.

The Prebendal School. 53 West St, Chichester, W Sussex PO19 1RT *tel:* 01243 782026 *fax:* 01243 771821. Revd Canon G C Hall, head; Mark Wardell, dir of mus.

Queen Elizabeth Grammar Junior School. 158 Northgate, Wakefield, W Yorks WF1 3QY *tel:* 01924 373821 *fax:* 01924 366246. M M Bisset, head; David Turmeau, dir of mus.

St Edmund's Junior School. Canterbury, Kent CT2 8HU *tel:* 01227 454575 *fax:* 01227 471083. R G Bacon, head; Ian Sutcliffe, dir of mus.

St Edward's Junior School. Sandfield Park, Liverpool L12 1LF *tel:* 0151 281 2300 *fax:* 0151 281 4900. Philip Sweeney, head; Brenda Bixter, dir of mus.

St George's School. Windsor Castle, Berks SL4 1QF *tel:* 01753 865553 *fax:* 01753 842093 *email:* StGeoScho@aol.com. Revd R P Marsh, head; J C Young, dir of mus.

St John's College School. 73 Grange Rd, Cambridge CB3 9AB *tel:* 01223 353532 *fax:* 01223 315535 *email:* enquiry@sjcs.demon.co.uk. K L Jones, head; E P Bryan, dir of mus.

St Mary's Preparatory and Choir School. Chart Lane, Reigate, Surrey RH2 7RN *tel:* 01737 244880 *fax:* 01737 221540. David Tidmarsh, head; Marion Holmes, dir of mus; Jonathan Rennert, master of choristers.

St Paul's Cathedral School. 2 New Change, London EC4M 9AD *tel:* 020 7248 5156 *fax:* 020 7329 6568. Stephen A Sides, head; John Scott, Cathedral dir of mus.

Westminster Abbey Choir School. Dean's Yard, London SW1P 3NY *tel:* 020 7222 6151 *fax:* 020 7222 1548. Roger Overend, head; Stephen Le Prevost, mus master.

Independent and Maintained Secondary Schools (age 7-18)

Bristol Cathedral School. College Square, Bristol BS1 5TS *tel:* 0117 929 1872 *fax:* 0117 930 4219 *email:* webmaster@cathedral.demon.co.uk. K J Riley, head; Simon Holt, dir of mus.

Chetham's School of Music *see* **Specialist Music Schools.**

Hereford Cathedral School. Old Deanery, Cathedral Close, Hereford HR1 2NG *tel:* 01432 363522 (snr school) *fax:* 01432 363525. H C Tomlinson, head of snr school; T R Lowe, head of prep school; J M Williams, dir of mus.

King's School (Gloucester). Pitt St, Gloucester GL1 2BG *tel:* 01452 521251 *fax:* 01452 385275. Peter Lacey, head; Ian Fox, dir of mus.

King's School (Peterborough). Park Rd, Peterborough, Cambs PE1 2UE *tel:* 01733 751541 *fax:* 01733 751542 *email:* Kings_School_peterboro@compuserve.com. G L Longman, head; N C Kerrison, dir of mus.

King's School (Rochester). Satis House, Boley Hill, Rochester, Kent ME1 1TE *tel:* 01634 843913 *fax:* 01634 832493. I R Walker, head; G R Williams, dir of mus.

King's School (Worcester). College Green, Worcester WR1 2LH *tel:* 01905 23016 *fax:* 01905 25511. T H Keyes, head; D E Brookshaw, dir of mus.

Lincoln Minster School *see* **Preparatory Schools (age 7-13).**

Magdalen College School. Cowley Place, Oxford OX4 1DZ *tel:* 01865 242191 *fax:* 01865 240379. A D Halls, head; C J G Ives, organist; M N Pearce, dir of mus.

The Minster School. Nottingham Rd, Southwell, Notts NG25 0LG *tel:* 01636 814000/812911 (24 hr choir info) *fax:* 01636 814788. P J Blinston, head; Gill Baker, dir of mus.

Norwich School. The Close, Norwich NR1 4DQ *tel:* 01603 623194 *fax:* 01603 627036. C D Brown, head; Colin Dowdeswell, dir of mus.

St Edward's College. Sandfield Park, Liverpool L12 1LF *tel:* 0151 281 1999 *fax:* 0151 281 1909. John Waszek, head; John Moseley, dir of mus.

St James' School. 22 Bargate, Grimsby, S Humberside DN34 4SY *tel:* 01472 503260 *fax:* 01472 503275 *email:* stjamesschool@compuserve.com. D J Berisford, head; Adrian King, dir of mus.

St Mary's Music School. Coates Hall, 25 Grosvenor Cres, Edinburgh EH12 5EL *tel:* 0131 538 7766 *fax:* 0131 467 7289. Jennifer Rimer, head; John Grundy, dir of mus.

Wells Cathedral School. Wells, Somerset BA5 2ST *tel:* 01749 672117 *fax:* 01749 670724 *email:* wellscs@rmplc.co.uk. J S Baxter, head; Roger Durston, dir of mus.

Roman Catholic Choir Schools

St Edward's Junior School. Sandfield Park, Liverpool L12 1LF *tel:* 0151 281 2300 *fax:* 0151 281 4900. Philip Sweeney, head; Brenda Bixter, dir of mus; Mervyn Cousins, dir of cathedral mus.

Westminster Cathedral Choir School. Ambrosden Ave, London SW1P 1QH *tel:* 020 7798 9081 *fax:* 020 7798 9090. C Foulds, head; J O'Donnell, master of mus.

THE LONDON ORATORY SCHOOL

HEADMASTER:
John McIntosh OBE MA FRSA

The London Oratory School is a Roman Catholic voluntary-aided non fee-paying school under the trusteeship of the Fathers of the Oratory, London.

The Junior House of the school provides a specialist musical education with a strong emphasis on Catholic liturgical music for 80 boys between the ages of 7 and 10.

20 boys are admitted annually with up to 10 being offered places as choristers. Applicants are tested for general ability and musical aptitude and for choral aptitude if they are prospective choristers. The tests, auditions and interviews for admissions in September 2000 will be held during the Lent term 2000.

For further information and times for visiting the school please contact:
The Junior House Registrar, The London Oratory School, Seagrave Road, London SW6 1RX
Telephone: 020 7385 0102 Facsimile: 020 7381 3836

ST MARY'S MUSIC SCHOOL

Coates Hall, 25 Grosvenor Crescent,
Edinburgh EH12 5EL
Tel: 0131-538 7766 Fax: 0131-467 7289

SCOTLAND'S SPECIALIST MUSIC SCHOOL

ALL UK ENTRANTS QUALIFY FOR AIDED PLACES OR BURSARIES.

ENTRY BY AUDITION

SEND FOR OUR PROSPECTUS.

Scotland's independent specialist music school and the choir school of St Mary's Cathedral, offering music and academic education to young musicians, aged 9–19.

Headteacher: Jennifer Rimer Registered Charity SC014611 Director of Music: John Grundy

The Yehudi Menuhin School

developing musical potential in young string players and pianists aged 8 to 18 from all over the world

- An extended family of young musicians
- Excellent GCSE and A level results
- UK residents qualify for a substantial bursary
- Sample our unique atmosphere at one of our Open Days.
- Find out more about us by writing to:

Nicolas Chisholm, Headmaster
The Yehudi Menuhin School
Stoke d'Abernon, COBHAM,
Surrey, KT11 3QQ.
Tel: 01932 864739 Fax: 01932 864633

The Yehudi Menuhin School is a Registered Charity and exists to educate gifted young people.
Charity No: 312010

Specialist Music Schools

The schools listed below are especially devoted to the training of musically gifted children. A full list of entry requirements may be found in the *Music Education Yearbook 1999/2000* which is also available from Rhinegold Publishing Ltd.

Chetham's School of Music. Long Millgate, Manchester M3 1SB *tel:* 0161 834 9644 *fax:* 0161 839 3609. Canon Peter F Hullah, head; Stephen Threlfall, dir of mus.

The City of Edinburgh Music School. Broughton High School, Carrington Rd, Edinburgh EH4 1EG *tel:* 0131 332 7805 *fax:* 0131 343 3296 *email:* admin@broughtonhigh.edin.sch.uk. Tudor Morris, dir of mus.

London Oratory School. Seagrave Rd, London SW6 1RX *tel:* 020 7385 0102 *fax:* 020 7381 3836. John McIntosh, headmaster; Lee Ward, head of mus.

Music School of Douglas Academy. Mains Estate, Milngavie, Glasgow G62 7HL *tel:* 0141 956 2281 *fax:* 0141 956 1533. Gordon Wilson, head teacher; Ronald McIntosh, course dir (mus).

Pimlico School. Lupus St, London SW1V 3AT *tel:* 020 7828 0881/7821 1717 *fax:* 020 7931 0549 *email:* btaylorl@rmplc.co.uk. Philip Barnard, head; David Murphy, dir of mus.

Purcell School. Aldenham Rd, Bushey, Herts WD2 3TS *tel:* 01923 331100 *fax:* 01923 331166 *email:* purcell.school@btinternet.com. John Tolputt, head; Jeffrey Sharkey, dir of mus.

St Mary's Music School. Coates Hall, 25 Grosvenor Cres, Edinburgh EH12 5EL *tel:* 0131 538 7766 *fax:* 0131 467 7289. Jennifer Rimer, head; John Grundy, dir of mus; Hazel Sheppard, admin.

Wells Cathedral School. Wells, Somerset BA5 2ST *tel:* 01749 672117 *fax:* 01749 670724 *email:* wellscs@rmplc.co.uk. John Baxter, head; Roger Durston, dir of mus.

Yehudi Menuhin School. Cobham Rd, Stoke d'Abernon, Cobham, Surrey KT11 3QQ *tel:* 01932 864739 *fax:* 01932 864633 *email:* menuhinschool@intonet.co.uk. Nicolas Chisholm, head; Malcolm Singer, dir of mus.

Independent Schools Offering Music Scholarships

All the schools listed below offer music scholarships on the basis of musical ability. For full information on scholarships offered and all musical activities see the *Music Education Yearbook 1999/2000,* available from Rhinegold Publishing Ltd.

Abbots Bromley (School of SS Mary and Anne) (Girls). Abbots Bromley, Staffs WS15 3BW *tel:* 01283 840232 *fax:* 01283 840988 *email:* abgirls@compuserve.com. Mrs M Steel, head; Alison Evans, dir of mus.

Abbotsholme School (Co-Ed). Rocester, Uttoxeter, Staffs ST14 5BS *tel:* 01889 590217 *fax:* 01889 591001. Timothy Moon, dir of mus.

Abingdon School (Boys). Abingdon, Oxon OX14 1DE *tel:* 01235 521563 *fax:* 01235 536449. M St John Parker, head; Michael Stinton, dir of mus.

Ackworth School (Co-Ed). Ackworth, Pontefract, W Yorks WF7 7LT *tel:* 01977 611401 *fax:* 01977 616225 *email:* Ackworthq@aol.com. Martin Dickinson, head; Richard Ellis, dir of mus.

Aldenham School (Boys). Elstree, Herts WD6 3AJ *tel:* 01923 858122 *fax:* 01923 854410 *email:* admissions@aldenham.com. S R Borthwick, head; G J Barker, J Wyatt, dirs of mus.

Alleyn's School (Co-Ed). Townley Rd, Dulwich, London SE22 8SU *tel:* 020 8557 1460 *fax:* 020 8557 1467 *email:* music.alleyns@rmplc.co.uk. C H R Niven, head; A T Kermode, dir of mus.

Allhallows College (Co-Ed). Rousdon, Nr Lyme Regis, Dorset DT7 3RA *tel:* 01297 626110 *fax:* 01297 626114. K R Moore, head; Mrs M L Banting, dir of mus.

Ampleforth College (Boys). York YO62 4ER *tel:* 01439 788000 *fax:* 01439 788330 *email:* admiss@ampleforth.org.uk. Rev G F L Chamberlain, head; Ian Little, dir of mus.

Ardingly College (Co-Ed). Haywards Heath, W Sussex RH17 6SQ *tel:* 01444 892577 *fax:* 01444 892266. J R Franklin, head; Robert Hammersley, dir of mus.

Ashford School (Girls). East Hill, Ashford, Kent TN24 8PB *tel:* 01233 625171 *fax:* 01233 647185. Mrs J Burnett, head; J Fehr, dir of mus.

Badminton School (Girls). Westbury on Trym, Bristol BS9 3BA *tel:* 0117 905 5200 *fax:* 0117 962 8963 *email:* badminton.office@dial.pipex.com. Mrs J Scarrow, head; C Francis, dir of mus.

Bancroft's School (Co-Ed). Woodford Green, Essex IG8 0RF *tel:* 020 8505 4821 *fax:* 020 8559 0032. P R Scott, head; R M Bluff, dir of mus.

Barnard Castle School (Co-Ed). Barnard Castle, Co Durham DL12 8UN *tel:* 01833 690222 *fax:* 01833 638985 *email:* secretary@barneyschool.org.uk. M D Featherstone, head; Paul Harrison, dir of mus.

Bearwood College (Co-Ed). Wokingham, Berks RG41 5BG *tel:* 0118 978 6915 *fax:* 0118 977 3186. R J Belcher, head; A R I Cummings, dir of mus.

Bedales School (Co-Ed). Church Rd, Steep, Petersfield, Hants GU32 2DG *tel:* 01730 300100 *fax:* 01730 300500 *email:* registra@bedales.org.uk. D Strutt, admissions tutor; Alison Willcocks, head; Nicholas Gleed, dir of mus.

Bedford School (Boys). De Parys Ave, Bedford MK40 2TU *tel:* 01234 362200 *fax:* 01234 362283. I P Evans OBE, head; Andrew Morris, dir of mus.

Bedgebury School (Girls). Bedgebury Park, Goudhurst, Cranbrook, Kent TN17 2SH *tel:* 01580 211954 *fax:* 01580 212252 *email:* info@bedgebury.ndirect.co.uk. Mrs L J Griffin, head; Bryan Gipps, dir of mus.

Benenden School (Girls). Cranbrook, Kent TN17 4AA *tel:* 01580 240592 *fax:* 01580 240280 *email:* schooloffice@benenden.kent.sch.uk. Mrs G duCharme, head; Patricia M Gane, dir of mus.

Berkhamsted Collegiate School (Boys). Castle Campus, Castle St, Berkhamsted, Herts HP4 2BB *tel:* 01442 863236 *fax:* 01442 877657. Christopher McDade, dir of mus.

Berkhamsted Collegiate School (Girls). Kings Campus, Kings Rd, Berkhamsted, Herts HP4 3BG *tel:* 01442 862168 *fax:* 01442 876732. Christopher McDade, dir of mus.

Bethany School (Co-Ed). Goudhurst, Cranbrook, Kent TN17 1LB *tel:* 01580 211273 *fax:* 01580 211151 *email:* admin@bethany.demon.co.uk. N D B Dorey, head; R Fitzgerald, dir of mus.

Birkdale School (Boys). Oakholme Rd, Sheffield S10 2DH *tel:* 0114 266 8408 *fax:* 0114 267 1947 *email:* birkdalesc@aol.com. Robert Court, head; Andrew Sanderson, dir of mus.

Bishop's Stortford College (Co-Ed). Bishop's Stortford, Herts CM23 2PJ *tel:* 01279 838575 *fax:* 01279 836570. J G Trotman, head.

Bloxham School (Co-Ed). Banbury, Oxon OX15 4PE *tel:* 01295 720222 *fax:* 01295 721897. David K Exham, head; Christopher Fletcher-Campbell, dir of mus.

Blundell's School (Co-Ed). Tiverton, Devon EX16 4DN *tel:* 01884 252543 *fax:* 01884 243232 *email:* blundadmin@aol.com. J Leigh, head; A H Barlow, dir of mus.

Bootham School (Co-Ed). York YO30 7BU *tel:* 01904 623261 *fax:* 01904 652106. Ian M Small, head; Alasdair Jamieson, dir of mus.

Bradfield College (Boys). Reading, Berks RG7 6AU *tel:* 0118 974 4203 *fax:* 0118 974 4195. P B Smith, head; M R Harding, dir of mus.

Brentwood School (Co-Ed). Ingrave Rd, Brentwood, Essex CM15 8AS *tel:* 01277 212271 *fax:* 01277 262218. J A B Kelsall, head; David Pickthall, dir of mus.

Brighton College (Co-Ed). Eastern Rd, Brighton BN2 2AL *tel:* 01273 704202 *fax:* 01273 704204 *email:* admissions@brightoncollege.demon.co.uk. A F Seldon, head; C G Sandercock, dir of mus.

Bristol Cathedral School (Boys). College Square, Bristol BS1 5TS *tel:* 0117 929 1872 *fax:* 0117 930 4219. K J Riley, head; S D Holt, dir of mus.

Bristol Grammar School (Co-Ed). University Rd, Bristol BS8 1SR *tel:* 0117 973 6006 *fax:* 0117 946 7485. C E Martin, head; J Gadsden, dir of mus.

British School of Brussels, The (Co-Ed). Leuvensesteenweg 19, B-3080 Tervuren, Belgium *tel:* 00 32 2 766 0430 *fax:* 00 32 2 767 8070. Jennifer Bray, principal; David Iliff, dir of mus.

Bromsgrove School (Co-Ed). Worcester Rd, Bromsgrove, Worcs B61 7DU *tel:* 01527 579679 *fax:* 01527 576177. T M Taylor, head; A E Bird, dir of mus.

Bryanston School (Co-Ed). Blandford, Dorset DT11 0PO *tel:* 01258 452411 *fax:* 01258 484661 *email:* headmaster@bryanston.co.uk. T D Wheare, head; P A Lattimer, dir of mus.

Burgess Hill School (Girls). Keymer Rd, Burgess Hill, W Sussex RH15 0EG *tel:* 01444 241050 *fax:* 01444 870314 *email:* staffnet@rmplc.co.uk. Rosemary Lewis, head; C R B Haslam, dir of mus.

Campbell College (Boys). Belmont Rd, Belfast BT4 2ND *tel:* 028 9076 3076 *fax:* 028 9076 1894 *email:* ccb@zetnet.co.uk. R J I Pollock, head; D Catherwood, dir of mus.

Canford School (Co-Ed). Canford Magna, Wimborne, Dorset BH21 3AD *tel:* 01202 841254 *fax:* 01202 881009. J D Lever, head; D A Warwick, dir of mus.

Casterton School (Girls). Kirkby Lonsdale, Carnforth, Lancs LA6 2SG *tel:* 01524 279200 *fax:* 01524 279208. A F Thomas, head; D C Chapman, dir of mus.

Caterham School (Co-Ed). Harestone Valley, Caterham, Surrey CR3 6YA *tel:* 01883 343028 *fax:* 01883 347795. R A E Davey, head; Adrian Goss, dir of mus.

Charterhouse (Boys). Godalming, Surrey GU7 2DX *tel:* 01483 291695/6 *fax:* 01483 291637. Revd John Witheridge, head; Robin Wells, dir of mus.

Cheltenham College (Co-Ed). Bath Rd, Cheltenham, Glos GL53 7LD *tel:* 01242 513540 *fax:* 01242 265630 *email:* college@cheltcoll.gloucs.sch.uk. P A Chamberlain, head; G S Busbridge, dir of mus.

The Cheltenham Ladies' College (Girls). Bayshill Rd, Cheltenham, Glos GL50 3EP *tel:* 01242 520691 *fax:* 01242 227882 *email:* registrar@cheltladiescollege.org. Mrs V Tuck, head; A Lowen, dir of mus.

Chigwell School (Co-Ed). Chigwell, Essex IG7 6QF *tel:* 020 8501 5700/8501 5745 mus dept; 020 8501 5760 *fax:* 020 8500 6232. D F Gibbs, head; Benjamin Charles, dir of mus.

Christ College (Co-Ed). Brecon, Powys LD3 8AG *tel:* 01874 623359/611603 (mus dept) *fax:* 01874 611478. D P Jones, head; James L Thomas, dir of mus.

Christ's Hospital (Co-Ed). Horsham, W Sussex RH13 7LS *tel:* 01403 247438 *fax:* 01403 276470 *email:* pa@christs-hospital.org.uk. P C D Southern, head; Peter Allwood, dir of mus.

City of London Freemen's School (Co-Ed). Ashtead Park, Ashtead, Surrey KT21 1ET *tel:* 01372 277933 *fax:* 01372 276165. D C Haywood, head; P M Dodds, dir of mus.

City of London School (Boys). Queen Victoria St, London EC4V 3AL *tel:* 020 7489 0291 *fax:* 020 7329 6887. W Duggan, head; M Smedley, dir of mus.

Clifton COLLEGE

Music Scholarships for 2000

BOARDING AND DAY CO-EDUCATIONAL 13 – 18

A number of scholarships will be awarded to girls and boys with musical talent and potential for entry at 13+ and 16+

All awards include free instrument tuition and may be augmented by a bursary in cases of proven need

Clifton has a strong musical tradition and a large and lively music department

The school also has an outstanding academic record – over twenty each year go on to Oxford or Cambridge universities

For further details, application forms, or to arrange a visit, please contact:

Philip Hallworth, Director of Admissions, Clifton College, 32 College Road, Clifton, Bristol BS8 3JH
Tel (0117) 973 9187

CLIFTON COLLEGE IS A CHARITABLE TRUST PROVIDING BOARDING AND DAY EDUCATION FOR GIRLS AND BOYS AGED 3 – 18 YEARS

VERBUM DEI LUCERNA

DEAN CLOSE SCHOOLS

BROADEN OPPORTUNITIES

• BRAND NEW HI-TECH MUSIC SCHOOL •
• MUSIC SCHOLARSHIPS AVAILABLE •
• CO-EDUCATIONAL • BOARDING AND DAY • AGES 2½–18 •

CHELTENHAM, GLOUCESTERSHIRE
TELEPHONE: 01242 522640 WEBSITE: www.deanclose.org.uk

DENSTONE COLLEGE

MUSIC SCHOLARSHIPS

Denstone College offers Scholarships, up to 50%, to talented and promising musicians for entry at 11+, 13+ and on entry into the Sixth Form.

The Music Department boasts excellent facilities including a large teaching room, a newly built keyboard laboratory, 10 teaching/practice rooms, a Schimmel Grand Piano in the Schoolroom and a 3 manual Ahlborn organ in the magnificent Chapel.

Musicians are encouraged to participate in the College ensembles which include a Chapel Choir, Concert Band, Jazz Band, Percussion Ensemble, Saxophone Group, Guitar Group, Recorder Consort and other smaller ensembles.

The Director of Music, Christopher McDade, will be pleased to meet parents and prospective candidates at any time.

Telephone: 01889 590484. Fax: 01889 590744
E-Mail: *chris.mcdade@denstone.staffs.sch.uk*
E-Mail: *headmaster@denstone.staffs.sch.uk*
Website: http://www.denstone.staffs.sch.uk
A Woodard School Registered Charity No 269671

City of London School for Girls (Girls). St Giles' Terrace, Barbican, London EC2Y 8BB *tel:* 020 7628 0841 *fax:* 020 7638 3212. Y A Burne, head; Mrs M Donnelly, dir of mus.

Claremont Fan Court School (Co-Ed). Claremont Drive, Esher, Surrey KT10 9LY *tel:* 01372 467841 *fax:* 01372 471109 *email:* claremont@intonet.co.uk. Patricia Farrrar, principal; Alan Hitchcock, dir of mus.

Clayesmore School (Co-Ed). Iwerne Minster, Blandford, Dorset DT11 8LL *tel:* 01747 812122 *fax:* 01747 811343 *email:* music@clayesmore-sch.co.uk. D J Beeby, head; D K Pigot, dir of mus.

Clifton College (Co-Ed). Clifton, Bristol BS8 3JH *tel:* 0117 973 9187 *fax:* 0117 946 6826 *email:* admissions@clifton-college.avon.sch.uk. A H Monro, head; J C Heritage, dir of mus.

Clifton High School (Girls). Bristol BS8 3JD *tel:* 0117 973 0201 *fax:* 0117 923 8962 *email:* clifton@rmplc.co.uk. Mrs C Culligan, head; Jonathan Palmer, dir of mus.

Colston's Collegiate School (Co-Ed). Stapleton, Bristol BS16 1BJ *tel:* 0117 965 5207 *fax:* 0117 958 5652. D G Crawford, head; I R Holmes, dir of mus.

Colston's Girls' School (Girls). Cheltenham Rd, Bristol, Avon BS6 5RD *tel:* 0117 942 4328 *fax:* 0117 942 6933 *email:* cggadmin@aol.com. Judith Franklin, head; Alistair Mackenzie, dir of mus.

Cranbrook School (Co-Ed). Waterloo Rd, Cranbrook, Kent TN17 3JD *tel:* 01580 712163/712554 *fax:* 01580 715365 *email:* registrar@cranbrook.kent.sch.uk. P A Close, head; Malcolm K Riley, dir of mus.

Cranleigh School (Boys). Cranleigh, Surrey GU6 8QQ *tel:* 01483 273666 *fax:* 01483 267398. Guy Waller, head.

Culford School (Co-Ed). Bury St Edmunds, Suffolk IP28 6TX *tel:* 01284 728615 *fax:* 01284 728631 *email:* culford_edu@msn.com. John Richardson, head; John Humphries, registrar; James Recknell, dir of mus.

Dauntsey's School (Co-Ed). W Lavington, Nr Devizes, Wilts SN10 4HE *tel:* 01380 818441 *fax:* 01380 813620. S B Roberts, head; C B Thompson, dir of mus.

Dean Close School (Co-Ed). Shelburne Rd, Cheltenham, Glos GL51 6HE *tel:* 01242 522640 *fax:* 01242 258003. Timothy M Hastie-Smith, head; R O Knight, dir of mus.

Denstone College (Co-Ed). Uttoxeter, Staffs ST14 5HN *tel:* 01889 590484 *fax:* 01889 591295 *email:* headmaster@denstone.staffs.sch.uk. D M Derbyshire, head.

Dover College (Co-Ed). Dover, Kent CT17 9RH *tel:* 01304 205969 *fax:* 01304 242208 *email:* club@dcollege.demon.co.uk. H W Blackett, head; Roderick Spencer, dir of mus.

Downe House (Girls). Cold Ash, Hermitage Rd, Thatcham, Berks RG18 9JJ *tel:* 01635 200286 *fax:* 01635 202026. Mrs E McKendrick, head; A Cain, dir of mus.

Downside School (Boys). Stratton on the Fosse, Bath, Somerset BA3 4RJ *tel:* 01761 235100 *fax:* 01761 235105 *email:* downside@rmplc.co.uk. Dom Antony Sutch, head; Chris Tambling, dir of mus.

Dulwich College (Boys). Dulwich Common, London SE21 7LD *tel:* 020 8693 3601; 020 8299 9256/8 *also fax*. G G Able, master; M Ashcroft, dir of mus.

Dunottar School (Girls). High Trees Rd, Reigate, Surrey RH2 7EL *tel:* 01737 761945 *fax:* 01737 779450. Margaret Skinner, head; Terry Lamont, dir of mus.

Durham School (Co-Ed). Durham City, Co Durham DH1 4SZ *tel:* 0191 384 7977/386 6572 (mus school) *fax:* 0191 383 1025. N G Kern, head; Roger Muttitt, dir of mus.

Eastbourne College (Co-Ed). Old Wish Rd, Eastbourne, E Sussex BN21 4JX *tel:* 01323 452320 *fax:* 01323 452327. C M P Bush, head; Graham Jones, dir of mus.

Edgbaston High School for Girls (Girls). Westbourne Rd, Birmingham B15 3TS *tel:* 0121 454 5831 *fax:* 0121 454 2363. Miss E M Mullenger, head; Miss M Harper, dir of mus.

The Edinburgh Academy (Boys). Henderson Row, Edinburgh EH3 5BL *tel:* 0131 556 4603 *fax:* 0131 556 9353. J V Light, rector; P N Coad, dir of mus.

Elizabeth College (Boys). Guernsey, Channel Islands *tel:* 01481 726544 *fax:* 01481 714839. D E Toze, head; P C Harris, dir of mus.

Ellesmere College (Co-Ed). Ellesmere, Shropshire SY12 9AB *tel:* 01691 622321 *fax:* 01691 623286. B J Wignall, head; Christopher Deakin, dir of mus.

Emanuel School (Co-Ed). Battersea Rise, London SW11 1HS *tel:* 020 8870 4171 *fax:* 020 8877 1424 *email:* gmh@emanuel.org.uk. Anne-Marie Sutcliffe, head; J S Holmes, dir of mus.

Epsom College (Co-Ed). Epsom, Surrey KT17 4JQ *tel:* 01372 821234 *fax:* 01372 821005. Anthony Beadles, head; Ian Holiday, dir of mus.

Eton College (Boys). Windsor, Berks SL4 6DW *tel:* 01753 671000 *fax:* 01753 671159. J E Lewis, head; R Allwood, dir of mus.

The GODOLPHIN School

Independent boarding and day school for 400 girls aged 11-18

Music Scholarships

Scholarships are offered to talented musicians for entry at 11+, 12+, 13+ and Sixth Form

Major performing arts centre

Choirs, orchestras, bands, ensembles

Professional workshops and masterclasses

Foreign music tours

The Director of Music, Mrs Eileen Sharp, is always pleased to meet and advise prospective pupils and their parents.

Further information from: The Admissions Secretary, The Godolphin School, Milford Hill, Salisbury, Wiltshire SP1 2RA
Tel: 01722 333059 Fax: 01722 411700
www.godolphin.org

Reg. Charity No. CR 309488

GUILDFORD HIGH SCHOOL

(Church Schools Company. Registered Charity No. 1016538)

The Music Department offers:

✶ Music Scholarships at 11+ and Sixth Form

✶ Structured courses leading to GCSE, A level and university/college entrance, with encouragement of composing

✶ New facilities including Concert Hall and Music Technology Studio

✶ Choirs, orchestras, bands and smaller instrumental ensembles. Performance of choral works and large-scale musicals with Parents' Choir and school orchestra. Foreign tours. National competitions

✶ An experienced staff of instrumental teachers

For further details and a prospectus, contact the Registrar,
Guildford High School, London Road, Guildford, Surrey.
01483 450240

FETTES COLLEGE, EDINBURGH MUSIC SCHOLARSHIPS

Fettes College is able to offer a large number of Music Scholarships, including several major scholarships of up to 50% of school fees plus tuition on two instruments, to candidates entering the school at any age from 10 to 16 years.

Music thrives at Fettes, where school musicians are placed enviably for a lively involvement with the musical life of Scotland's capital city. The college boasts 3 orchestras, 4 choirs and numerous smaller ensembles coached by experienced staff (4 full time and 25 part time), all taking part in weekly musical events.

The Director of Music, David Goodenough, will be pleased to meet parents and prospective candidates at any time.
Telephone: 0131 311 6706
Fax: 0131 332 3081

Exeter School (Co-Ed). Exeter, Devon EX2 4NS *tel:* 01392 273679 *fax:* 01392 498144 *email:* exeter.se@campus.bt.com. N W Gamble, head; S D Foxall, dir of mus.

Farlington School (Girls). Strood Park, Horsham, Sussex RH12 3PN *tel:* 01403 254967 *fax:* 01403 272258. P M Mawer, head; Coralie Moult, dir of mus.

Felsted School (Co-Ed). Dunmow, Essex CM6 3JJ *tel:* 01371 820258/820497 (mus school) *fax:* 01371 821179. Stephen Roberts, head; Jasper Thorogood, dir of mus.

Fettes College (Co-Ed). Carrington Rd, Edinburgh EH4 1QX *tel:* 0131 332 2281 *fax:* 0131 332 3081. Michael Spens, head; David Goodenough, dir of mus.

Forest Girls' School (Girls). Snaresbrook, London E17 3PY *tel:* 020 8521 7477 *fax:* 020 8520 7381. Mrs R Martin, head; M D Palmer, dir of mus.

Forest School (Boys). Snaresbrook, London E17 3PY *tel:* 020 8520 1744 *fax:* 020 8520 3656. A G Boggis, warden; M D Palmer, dir of mus.

Framlingham College (Co-Ed). Framlingham, Suffolk IP13 9EY *tel:* 01728 723789 *fax:* 01728 724546. G M Randall, head; R Rogers, dir of mus.

Frensham Heights (Co-Ed). Rowledge, Farnham, Surrey GU10 4EA *tel:* 01252 792134 *fax:* 01252 794335 *email:* headmaster@frensham-heights.org.uk. Peter M de Voil, head; Edwin Rolles, dir of mus.

George Watson's College (Co-Ed). Colinton Rd, Edinburgh EH10 5EG *tel:* 0131 447 7931 *fax:* 0131 452 8594 *email:* n.mitchell@watsons.edin.sch.uk. F E Gerstenberg, principal; Norman Mitchell, dir of mus *Tel:* 0131 446 6031.

Giggleswick School (Co-Ed). Giggleswick, Settle, N Yorks BD24 0DE *tel:* 01729 823545 *fax:* 01729 824187. A P Millard, head; Tim Harvey, dir of mus.

Glenalmond College (Co-Ed). Glenalmond, Perthshire PH1 3RY *tel:* 01738 880442/880340 (mus dept) *fax:* 01738 880410 *email:* registrar@glencoll.demon.co.uk. Ian Templeton, warden; Robert Gower, dir of mus.

The Godolphin School (Girls). Milford Hill, Salisbury, Wilts SP1 2RA *tel:* 01722 333059 *fax:* 01722 411700. Jill Horsburgh, head; Eileen Sharp, dir of mus.

Gordonstoun School (Co-Ed). Elgin, Morayshire IV30 5RF *tel:* 01343 837894/837895/830264 (mus dept) *fax:* 01343 837808 *email:* mja@gordstoun.org.uk. M C S-R Pyper, head; M J Appleford, dir of mus.

Gresham's School (Co-Ed). Holt, Norfolk NR25 6EA *tel:* 01263 713271 *fax:* 01263 712028 *email:* headmaster@holtsch.demon.co.uk. John Arkell, head; Mark Jones, dir of mus.

Guildford High School (Girls). London Rd, Guildford, Surrey GU1 1SJ *tel:* 01483 561440 *fax:* 01483 306516. Mrs S H Singer, head; Graham Thorp, dir of mus.

Haberdashers' Aske's School (Boys). Butterfly Lane, Elstree, Borehamwood, Herts WD6 3AF *tel:* 020 8266 1700 *fax:* 020 8266 1800. J W R Goulding, head; C Muhley, dir of mus.

Haberdashers' Monmouth School for Girls (Girls). Hereford Rd, Monmouth NP5 3XT *tel:* 01600 711100 *fax:* 01600 711233 *Contact:* admissions secretary.

Haileybury (Co-Ed). Hertford, Herts SG13 7NU *tel:* 01992 463353 *fax:* 01992 467603 *email:* stuartw@haileybury.herts.sch.uk. S A Westley, master; Alexander Anderson, dir of mus.

Hampton School (Boys). Hanworth Rd, Hampton, Middx TW12 3HD *tel:* 020 8979 5526 *fax:* 020 8941 7368. B R Martin, head; Iain Donald, dir of mus.

Harrogate Ladies' College (Girls). Harrogate, Yorks HG1 2QG *tel:* 01423 504543 *fax:* 01423 568893 *email:* enquire@hlc.org.uk. Margaret J Hustler, head; David Andrews, dir of mus.

Harrow School (Boys). Harrow on the Hill, Middx HA1 3HW *tel:* 020 8869 1231 *fax:* 020 8423 3112 *email:* harrwmus@rmplc.co.uk. B Lenon, head; R H Walker, dir of mus.

Hereford Cathedral School (Co-Ed). Old Deanery, Cathedral Close, Hereford HR1 2NG *tel:* 01432 363522 *fax:* 01432 363525 *email:* enquiry@cathedralschool.hereford.sch.uk. H C Tomlinson, head; J M Williams, dir of mus.

Highgate School (Boys). North Rd, London N6 4AY *tel:* 020 8340 1524 *fax:* 020 8340 7674. R P Kennedy, head; John March, dir of mus.

Howells School (Girls). Denbigh, N Wales LL16 3EN *tel:* 01745 813631 *fax:* 01745 814443. Sandra Gordon, head; Morwen Blythin, head of mus.

Hurstpierpoint College (Co-Ed). Hassocks, W Sussex BN6 9JS *tel:* 01273 833636 *fax:* 01273 835257 *email:* info@hurstpierpoint.w-sussex.sch.uk. S D A Meek, head; R A Burton, dir of mus.

Hutchesons' Grammar School (Co-Ed). 21 Beaton Rd, Glasgow G41 4NW *tel:* 0141 423 2933 *fax:* 0141 424 0251 *email:* rector@hutchie.demon.co.uk. David Ward, head.

Ibstock Place (Co-Ed). Clarence Lane, Roehampton, London SW15 5PY *tel:* 020 8876 9991 *fax:* 020 8878 4897. Franciska Bayliss, head; Chris Artley, dir of mus.

Ipswich High School for Girls (Girls). Woolverstone, Ipswich IP9 1AZ *tel:* 01473 780201 *fax:* 01473 780985. Miss V C MacCuish, head; Peter Clayton, dir of mus.

Ipswich School (Co-Ed). Henley Rd, Ipswich, Suffolk IP1 3SG *tel:* 01473 408300 *fax:* 01473 400058 *email:* registrar@ipswich.suffolk.sch.uk. I G Galbraith, head; A D Leach, dir of mus.

James Allen's Girls' School (Girls). East Dulwich Grove, London SE22 8TE *tel:* 020 8693 1181; 020 7924 9578 *also fax* (mus dept) *fax:* 020 8693 7842 *email:* postmaster@jags.demon.co.uk. Marion Gibbs, head; Rupert Bond, dir of mus.

The John Lyon School (Boys). Middle Rd, Harrow, Middx HA2 0HN *tel:* 020 8422 2046 *fax:* 020 8422 5008. T J Wright, head; Stuart Miles, dir of mus.

Kelly College (Co-Ed). Tavistock, Devon PL19 0HZ *tel:* 01822 613005 *fax:* 01822 612050 *email:* kirwinc@aol.com. M Turner, head; Andrew Wilson, dir of mus.

Kent College (Co-Ed). Canterbury, Kent CT2 9TD *tel:* 01227 763231 *fax:* 01227 764777 *email:* kcollege@rmplc.co.uk. E Halse, head; R Johnston, dir of mus.

Kent College Pembury (Girls). Old Church Rd, Pembury, Tunbridge Wells TN2 4AX *tel:* 01892 822006 *fax:* 01892 820221 *email:* kentcoll@rmplc.co.uk. Barbara Crompton, head; Jenifer Horbury, dir of mus.

King Edward VI School (Co-Ed). Kellett Rd, Southampton SO15 7UQ *tel:* 023 8070 4561 *fax:* 023 8070 5937 *email:* registrar@kes.hants.sch.uk. P B Hamilton, head; M C Hall, dir of mus.

King Edward's School (Birmingham) (Boys). Edgbaston Park Rd, Birmingham B15 2UA *tel:* 0121 472 1672/471 1640 (mus dept) *fax:* 0121 415 4327 *email:* registrar@kes.bham.sch.uk. R M Dancey, chief master; M J Monks, dir of mus.

King Henry VIII School (Co-Ed). Warwick Rd, Coventry CV3 6AQ *tel:* 024 7667 3442 *fax:* 024 7667 7102 *email:* kinghenry8@rmplc.co.uk. T J Vardon, head; Richard Hollingdale, dir of mus.

King William's College (Co-Ed). Castletown, Isle of Man IM9 1TP *tel:* 01624 822551 *fax:* 01624 824287. P Kerr Fulton-Peebles, principal; A T Roberts, dir of mus.

King's College (Co-Ed). Taunton, Somerset TA1 3DX *tel:* 01823 328204 *fax:* 01823 328202 *email:* kingscol@aol.com. R S Funnell, head; C K Holmes, dir of mus.

King's College School (Boys). Wimbledon Common, London SW19 4TT *tel:* 020 8255 5300 *fax:* 020 8255 5309 *email:* admissions@kcs.org.uk. A C V Evans, head; M D Jenkins, dir of mus.

King's School (Bruton) (Co-Ed). Bruton, Somerset BA10 0ED *tel:* 01749 813326 *fax:* 01749 813426 *email:* kingshm@kingsbruton.somerset.sch.uk. R I Smyth, head; J P S Chesney, dir of mus.

King's School (Canterbury) (Co-Ed). Canterbury, Kent CT1 2ES *tel:* 01227 595501/595556 *also fax* (mus dept) *email:* music@kings-school.co.uk. Revd K H Wilkinson, head; Stefan Anderson, dir of mus.

King's School (Ely) (Co-Ed). Ely, Cambs CB7 4DB *tel:* 01353 660741/2 *fax:* 01353 662187/667485. R H Youdale, head; G P L Griggs, dir of mus.

King's School (Gloucester) (Co-Ed). Pitt St, Gloucester GL1 2BG *tel:* 01452 521251/2/3/4 *fax:* 01452 385275 *email:* hm@thekingsschool.co.uk. Peter Lacey, head; Ian Fox, dir of mus.

The King's School in Macclesfield (Co-Ed). Macclesfield, Cheshire SK10 1DA *tel:* 01625 260000 *fax:* 01625 260009. A G Silcock, head; Andrew K Green, dir of mus.

King's School (Rochester) (Co-Ed). Rochester, Kent ME1 1TE *tel:* 01634 843913 *fax:* 01634 832493 *email:* kingsroc@rmplc.co.uk. I R Walker, head; G R Williams, dir of mus.

King's School (Worcester) (Co-Ed). College Green, Worcester, Worcs WR1 2LH *tel:* 01905 23016 *fax:* 01905 25511. T H Keyes, head; D E Brookshaw, dir of mus.

Kingston Grammar School (Co-Ed). 70-72 London Rd, Kingston upon Thames, Surrey KT2 6PY *tel:* 020 8546 5875 *fax:* 020 8974 5177 *email:* registrar@kingston-grammar.surrey.sch.uk. C D Baxter, head; C A Jackson, dir of mus.

The Lady Eleanor Holles School (Girls). Hanworth Rd, Hampton, Middx TW12 3HF *tel:* 020 8979 1601 *fax:* 020 8941 8291. Miss E M Candy, head; Phoebe Woollam, dir of mus.

Lancing College (Boys). Lancing, W Sussex BN15 0RW *tel:* 01273 452213 *fax:* 01273 464720 *email:* lancingmus@aol.com. P M Tinniswood, head; P E Lewis, D N Cox, dirs of mus.

Langley School (Co-Ed). Langley Park, Norwich NR14 6BJ *tel:* 01508 520210 *fax:* 01508 528058 *email:* langley.school@dial.pipex.com. J G Malcolm, head; John Shooter, dir of mus.

MALVERN GIRLS' COLLEGE

Since 1893 Malvern Girls' College has been developing the individual potential of its pupils. Apart from its deserved academic reputation, the College has a long tradition of excellence in Music.

Music Scholarships & Exhibitions

(worth 50% and 25% respectively, plus FREE tuition in 3 instruments)

are available at ages 11, 12, 13 and Sixth Form entry.

Musicians benefit from individual programmes of study. Our music ranges from Plainsong to Jazz Band and Music Technology.
Regular masterclasses by distinguished musicians supplement teaching and ensemble work of the highest calibre.

For further information please contact

The Registrar, Malvern Girls' College,
Avenue Road, Great Malvern,
Worcestershire WR14 3BA

Telephone: (01684) 892288
Fax: (01684) 566204
Email: registrar@mgc.worcs.sch.uk

Malvern Girls' College is a Registered Charity No. 527513

Developed for Excellence

LORETTO SCHOOL

- *The independent Day and Boarding School from 8–18 yrs*
- *98% of leavers progress to Higher Education*
- *A full range of scholarships, bursaries and awards available – for an informal visit call Fiona Mackie 0131 653 4455*

LORETTO mind body spirit

Loretto School, Musselburgh, East Lothian, Scotland EH21 7RE
Facsimile 0131 653 4445 www.loretto.lothian.sch.uk
email.hcalldridge@loretto.lothian.sch.uk
Loretto School is a registered educational charity (No.32383)

Haberdashers' Monmouth Schools

MUSIC SCHOLARSHIPS (50% fees and free instrumental tuition) and other awards are made at 11+,13+ and 16+

OUTSTANDING MUSICAL REPUTATION is based on

FLOURISHING CHOIR STRUCTURE
Choral Society, Chamber Choir, Trebles' Choir and Barbershop.
Many high profile performances including:
Handel's Messiah (2000)
Carmina Burana at St David's Hall Cardiff with Welsh National Opera
Choral Tours (USA 1998, Italy 2001)

ORCHESTRAS
including Symphony Orchestra & two String Orchestras.
Orchestral Tours (Paris & Vienna 2000)

HIGHLY SUCCESSFUL WIND BANDS
Finalists for five years in B&H National Wind Band Competition.

HIGH QUALITY CHAMBER MUSIC
Finalists in National Chamber Music Trust Competition for seven consecutive years.

CELEBRITY MASTERCLASSES
Recent ones include:
Richard Rodney Bennett & Jane Glover.

Haberdashers' Monmouth Schools

Enquiries initially to the Admissions Secretaries at:

Monmouth School, boys 11-18, boarding & day
Tel: 01600 713143

Haberdashers' Monmouth School for Girls, girls 11-18, boarding & day
Tel: 01600 711104

The Directors of Music are always delighted to meet informally with parents and their children in advance of the Scholarship auditions.

Latymer Upper School (Boys). King St, Hammersmith, London W6 9LR *tel:* 020 8741 1851 *fax:* 020 8748 5212. C Diggory, head; Tony Henwood, dir of mus.

Leeds Girls' High School (Girls). Headingley Lane, Leeds, W Yorks LS6 1BN *tel:* 0113 274 4000 *fax:* 0113 275 2217 *email:* postmaster@lghs.demon.co.uk. Sue Fishburn, head; Margaret Smith, dir of mus.

Leicester Grammar School (Co-Ed). 8 Peacock Lane, Leicester LE1 5PX *tel:* 0116 222 0400 *fax:* 0116 291 0505. John B Sugden, head; David M T Whittle, dir of mus.

Leighton Park School (Co-Ed). Shinfield Rd, Reading, Berks RG2 7ED *tel:* 0118 987 9600 *fax:* 0118 987 9625 *email:* head@lps.i-way.co.uk. John Dunston, head; Stuart Beer, dir of mus.

The Leys School (Co-Ed). Cambridge, CB2 2AD *tel:* 01223 508900 *fax:* 01223 505303 *email:* office@theleys.cambs.sch.uk. J C A Barrett, head; Peter Noyce, dir of mus.

Llandovery College (Co-Ed). Llandovery, Carmarthenshire SA20 0EE *tel:* 01550 723000 *fax:* 01550 723049 *email:* llan.coll@virgin.net. Claude Evans, head; Richard Whitehead, dir of mus.

Lomond School (Co-Ed). 10 Stafford St, Helensburgh, Argyll & Bute G84 9JX *tel:* 01436 672476 *fax:* 01436 678320 *email:* admin@lomond-school.demon.co.uk. A D Macdonald, head; Anne Lyon, head of mus.

Lord Wandsworth College (Boys). Long Sutton, Hook, Hants RG29 1TB *tel:* 01256 862482 *fax:* 01256 862563. I G Power, head; R W Goodrich, head of mus.

Loretto School (Co-Ed). Musselburgh, Midlothian EH21 7RE *tel:* 0131 653 4455 *fax:* 0131 653 4445. Keith J Budge, head; Timothy Goulter, dir of mus; Hamish Alldridge, admissions dir.

Loughborough Grammar School (Boys). Burton Walks, Loughborough, Leics LE11 2DU *tel:* 01509 233233 *fax:* 01509 210486 *email:* hmpa@loughboroughgs.demon.co.uk. P J Underwood, dir of mus.

Magdalen College School (Boys). Oxford OX4 1DZ *tel:* 01865 242191 *fax:* 01865 240379. A D Halls, head; M N Pearce, dir of mus.

Malvern College (Co-Ed). College Rd, Malvern, Worcs WR14 3DF *tel:* 01684 892333 *fax:* 01684 572398 *email:* inquiry@malcol.worcs.sch.uk. H C K Carson, head; Rory Boyle, dir of mus.

Malvern Girls' College (Girls). 15 Avenue Rd, Malvern, Worcs WR14 3BA *tel:* 01684 892288 *fax:* 01684 566204 *email:* admin@mgc.worcs.sch.uk. Philippa M C Leggate, head; P K Redfern, dir of mus.

Marlborough College (Co-Ed). Marlborough, Wilts SN8 1PA *tel:* 01672 892300 *fax:* 01672 892307 *email:* mcadmiss@aol.com. E J H Gould, master; R W Nelson, dir of mus.

Mary Erskine School, The (Girls). Ravelston, Edinburgh EH4 3NT *tel:* 0131 337 2391 *fax:* 0131 346 1137. P F J Tobin, principal; Helen Mitchell, head of mus.

The Maynard School (Girls). Exeter EX1 1SJ *tel:* 01392 273417 *fax:* 01392 496199 *email:* office@maynard.co.uk. Miss F Murdin, head; N Horton, dir of mus.

Merchant Taylors' School (Boys). Sandy Lodge, Northwood, Middx HA6 2HT *tel:* 01923 820644 *fax:* 01923 835110 *email:* admissions@mtsn.org.uk. J R Gabitass, head; Richard Hobson, dir of mus.

Merchiston Castle School (Boys). Colinton, Edinburgh EH13 0PU *tel:* 0131 312 2200 *fax:* 0131 441 6060 *email:* adsec@mcsch.org.uk. A R Hunter, head; P K Rossiter, dir of mus.

Methodist College (Co-Ed). 1 Malone Rd, Belfast BT9 6BY *tel:* 028 9020 5205 *fax:* 028 9020 5230 *email:* school@mcb.rmplc.co.uk. T W Mulryne, head; J McKee, dir of mus.

Mill Hill School (Co-Ed). Mill Hill Village, London NW7 1QS *tel:* 020 8959 1221 *fax:* 020 8906 2614. W R Winfield, head; Richard Allain, dir of mus.

Millfield School (Co-Ed). Street, Somerset BA16 0YD *tel:* 01458 442291 *fax:* 01458 447276 *email:* admissions@millfield.somerset.sch.uk. P M Johnson, head; S D Pinnock, dir of mus.

Milton Abbey School (Boys). Nr Blandford, Dorset DT11 0BZ *tel:* 01258 880484 *fax:* 01258 881194. Jonathan Hughes-D'Aeth, head; Y F S Day, dir of mus.

Moira House School (Girls). Upper Carlisle Rd, Eastbourne, Sussex BN20 7TE *tel:* 01323 644144 *fax:* 01323 649720 *email:*head@moirahouse.e-sussex.sch.uk. A Harris, head; J Pendry, dir of mus.

Monmouth School (Boys). Monmouth NP5 3XP *tel:* 01600 713143 *fax:* 01600 772701 *email:* admissions@monmouth.monm.sch.uk. Tim H P Haynes, head; Jeffrey Gray, dir of mus.

Moreton Hall (Girls). Weston Rhyn, Oswestry, Shrops SY11 3EW *tel:* 01691 773671 *fax:* 01691 778552. Jonathan Forster, principal; Richard Meyer, head of mus.

The Mount School (Girls). Dalton Terrace, York YO2 4DD *tel:* 01904 667500 *fax:* 01904 667524. Barbara Windle, head; Derek Chivers, dir of mus.

New Hall School (Girls). Chelmsford, Essex CM3 3HT *tel:* 01245 467588 *fax:* 01245 464348. Sister Anne-Marie, head; A Fardell, dir of mus.

Norwich High School for Girls GDST (Girls). 95 Newmarket Rd, Norwich NR2 2HU *tel:* 01603 453265 *fax:* 01603 259891. Mrs V C Bidwell, head; Mrs H Weiland, dir of mus.

Notting Hill and Ealing High School (Girls). 2 Cleveland Rd, Ealing, London W13 8AX *tel:* 020 8799 8400 *fax:* 020 8810 6891. Susan Whitfield, head; Andrew Phillips, dir of mus.

Oakham School (Co-Ed). Chapel Close, Oakham, Rutland, Leics LE15 6DT *tel:* 01572 722487 *fax:* 01572 755786 *email:* registrar@oakham.rutland.sch.uk. A Little, head; D N Woodcock, dir of mus.

The Oratory School (Boys). Woodcote, Nr Reading, Berks RG8 0PJ *tel:* 01491 680207 *fax:* 01491 680020. S W Barrow, head; M J Crump, dir of mus.

Oswestry School (Co-Ed). Oswestry, Shropshire SY11 2TL *tel:* 01691 655711 *fax:* 01691 671194 *email:* osschoolhm@aol.com. P K Smith, head; S J Morris, dir of mus.

Oundle School (Co-Ed). North Street, Oundle, Peterborough PE8 4AS *tel:* 01832 277132 *fax:* 01832 277131. Dr R Townsend, head; Andrew Cleary, dir of mus.

Pangbourne College (Co-Ed). Pangbourne, Reading, Berks RG8 8LA *tel:* 0118 984 2101 *fax:* 0118 984 5443. A B E Hudson, head; R J Barsby, dir of mus.

The Park School (Co-Ed). Yeovil, Somerset BA20 1DH *tel:* 01935 423514/475468 *fax:* 01935 411257 *email:* admin@parkschool.com. P W Bate, head; Mrs Jo Jones, head of mus.

Plymouth College (Co-Ed). Ford Park, Plymouth PL4 6RN *tel:* 01752 203300 ext 36 (mus dept) *fax:* 01752 203246. A J Morsley, head; S J Oxley, dir of mus.

Pocklington School (Co-Ed). West Green, Pocklington, York YO4 2NJ *tel:* 01759 303125 *fax:* 01759 306366 *email:* pocklington.school@dial.pipex.com. J N D Gray, head; J P Bird, dir of mus.

Polam Hall (Girls). Darlington, Co Durham DL1 5PA *tel:* 01325 463383 *fax:* 01325 383539. Mrs H Hamilton, head; Mrs E Sleightholme, dir of mus.

The Portsmouth Grammar School (Co-Ed). High St, Portsmouth, Hants PO1 2LN *tel:* 023 9281 9125 *fax:* 023 9287 0184. T R Hands, head; D J Swinson, dir of mus.

The Princess Helena College (Girls). Preston, Hitchin, Herts SG4 7RT *tel:* 01462 432100 *fax:* 01462 431497 *email:* head@phc.herts.co.uk. A-M Hodgkiss, head; Cynthia Neaum, dir of mus.

Prior Park College (Co-Ed). Bath, Avon BA2 5AH *tel:* 01225 835353 *fax:* 01225 835753 *email:* info@priorpark.co.uk. Giles Mercer, head; Roland Robertson, dir of mus.

Prior's Field School (Girls). Godalming, Surrey GU7 2RH *tel:* 01483 810551 *fax:* 01483 810180 *email:* admin@priorsfield.demon.co.uk. Mrs J M McCallum, head; Mrs M R Thorne, dir of mus.

Queen Anne's School (Girls). Caversham, Reading, Berks RG4 6DX *tel:* 0118 947 1582 *fax:* 0118 946 1498. Mrs D Forbes, head; Miss F Brewitt-Taylor, dir of mus.

Queen Elizabeth's Grammar School (Boys). Blackburn, Lancs BB2 6DF *tel:* 01254 59911 *fax:* 01254 692314 *email:* qegs.blackburn@campus.bt.com. D S Hempsall, head; G R Hill, dir of mus.

Queen Elizabeth's Hospital School (Boys). Berkeley Place, Clifton, Bristol BS8 1JX *tel:* 0117 929 1856 *fax:* 0117 929 3106 *email:* admin@qehbristol.co.uk. R Gliddon, head; Richard Jones, dir of mus.

Queen Ethelburga's College (Girls). Thorpe Underwood Hall, Ouseburn, York YO5 9SZ *tel:* 01423 331480 *fax:* 01423 331007 *email:* remember@compuserve.com. Mrs E I E Taylor, principal; S Jandrell, dir of mus.

Queen Margaret's School (Girls). Escrick Park, York YO4 6EU *tel:* 01904 728261 *fax:* 01904 728150. G Chapman, head; S Nettleship, dir of mus.

Queen Mary's School (Girls). Baldersby Park, Topcliffe, Thirsk, N Yorks YO7 3BZ *tel:* 01845 577425 *fax:* 01845 577368. Margaret and Ian Angus, heads; N Carter, dir of mus.

Queen's College (Taunton) (Co-Ed). Taunton, Somerset TA1 4QS *tel:* 01823 272559 *fax:* 01823 338430. C T Bradnock, head; S C Bell, dir of mus.

Queenswood School (Girls). Shepherds Way, Brookmans Park, Hatfield, Herts AL9 6NS *tel:* 01707 652262 *fax:* 01707 602597 *email:* registry@queenswood.herts.sch.uk. Clarissa Farr, principal; Neil Bell, dir of mus.

Radley College (Boys). Abingdon, Oxon OX14 2HR *tel:* 01235 543000 *fax:* 01235 543106. Richard Morgan, warden; John Madden, dir of mus.

Reading Blue Coat School (Boys). Holme Park, Sonning, Reading RG4 6SU *tel:* 0118 944 1005 *fax:* 0118 944 2690. S J W McArthur, head; Jonathan Bowler, dir of mus.

Red Maids' School (Girls). Westbury-on-Trym, Bristol BS9 3AW *tel:* 0117 962 2641 *fax:* 0117 962 1687. Stephen J M Browne, dir of mus.

Redland High School for Girls (Girls). Redland Court, Bristol BS6 7EF *tel:* 0117 924 5796 *fax:* 0117 924 1127. Carol Lear, head; Nigel Davies, dir of mus.

Reed's School (Boys). Cobham, Surrey KT11 2ES *tel:* 01932 863076 *fax:* 01932 869046 *email:* reedsadmit@compuserve.com. David Jarrett, head; Richard Coulson, dir of mus.

Rendcomb College (Co-Ed). Cirencester, Glos GL7 7HA *tel:* 01285 831213 *fax:* 01285 831331. J N Tolputt, head; David White, dir of mus.

Repton School (Co-Ed). Repton, Derbys DE65 6FH *tel:* 01283 559200 *fax:* 01283 559210 *email:* postmaster@repton.org.uk. G E Jones, head; Richard Dacey, dir of mus.

Roedean School (Girls). Roedean Way, Brighton BN2 5RQ *tel:* 01273 603181 *fax:* 01273 680791 *email:* roedean@offiah.demon.co.uk. Patricia Metham, head; Veronica Fewkes, head of academic mus.

Rossall School (Co-Ed). Fleetwood, Lancs FY7 8JW *tel:* 01253 774200 *fax:* 01253 772052. R D W Rhodes, head; Stephen H Carleston, dir of mus.

Royal Grammar School (Worcester) (Boys). Upper Tything, Worcester WR1 1HP *tel:* 01905 613391 *fax:* 01905 726892 *email:* rgsw2@aol.com. W A Jones, head; J E Smith, dir of mus.

Royal Grammar School (Guildford) (Boys). High St, Guildford, Surrey GU1 3BB *tel:* 01483 880600 *fax:* 01483 306127 *email:* bwright @mail.rgs.netkonect.co.uk. Tim Young, head; Peter White, dir of mus.

The Royal High School, GDST (Girls). Lansdown Rd, Bath BA1 5SZ *tel:* 01225 313877. Margaret Winfield, head.

Royal Hospital School (Co-Ed). Ipswich IP9 2RX *tel:* 01473 326200 *fax:* 01473 326213. Nicholas Ward, head; Peter Crompton, dir of mus.

Royal Wolverhampton School (Co-Ed). Penn Rd, Wolverhampton, W Midlands WV3 0EG *tel:* 01902 341230 *fax:* 01902 344496. Mrs B A Evans, head; Mrs C Fellows, dir of mus.

Rugby School (Co-Ed). Rugby, Warwicks CV22 5EH *tel:* 01788 543465 *fax:* 01788 579745. Michael Mavor, head; Peter Crook, dir of mus.

Rydal Penrhos Co-educational Division (Co-Ed). Pwllycrochan Ave, Colwyn Bay, N Wales LL29 7BT *tel:* 01492 530155 *fax:* 01492 531872 *email:* rydal@rmplc.co.uk. N W Thorne, head; Mrs M Ireland, dir of mus.

Rydal Penrhos Senior Girls' Division (Girls). Colwyn Bay, N Wales LL28 4DA *tel:* 01492 530333 *fax:* 01492 533198 *email:* penrhos @rmplc.co.uk. C M J Allen, head; C Enston, dir of mus.

St Albans High School (Girls). 3 Townsend Ave, St Albans, Herts AL1 3SJ *tel:* 01727 853800 *fax:* 01727 845011. Mrs C Y Daly, head; Nigel Springthorpe, dir of mus.

St Antony's-Leweston School (Girls). Sherborne, Dorset DT9 6EN *tel:* 01963 210691 *fax:* 01963 210786 *email:* st.antony@virgin.net. Miss B King, head; Jane Stein, dir of mus.

St Bede's (Co-Ed). The Dicker, Hailsham, E Sussex *tel:* 01323 843252 *fax:* 01323 442628 *email:* school.office@stbedes.e-sussex.sch.uk. Andrew Barclay, dir of mus.

St Bees School (Co-Ed). St Bees, Cumbria CA27 0DS *tel:* 01946 822263 *fax:* 01946 823657 *email:* mailbox@st-bees-school. Mrs J D Pickering, head; H M Turpin, dir of mus.

St Catherine's School (Girls). Bramley, Guildford, Surrey GU5 0DF *tel:* 01483 893363 *fax:* 01483 893003. Mrs C M Oulton, head; R E Gillman, dir of mus.

St David's College (Boys). Llandudno, N Wales LL30 1RD *tel:* 01492 875974 *fax:* 01492 870383 *email:* sdc@llandudno.co.uk. William Seymour, head; Marion Horley, head of mus.

St Dunstan's College (Co-Ed). Stanstead Rd, Catford, London SE6 4TY *tel:* 020 8516 7200 *fax:* 020 8516 7300 *email:* stduncol@ mail.rmplc.co.uk. D I Davies, head; Norman Harper, dir of mus.

St Edmund's School (Co-Ed). Canterbury CT2 8HU *tel:* 01227 475600 *fax:* 01227 471083. A N Ridley, head; I P Sutcliffe, dir of mus.

St Edward's College *see* **Choir Schools (Co-Ed).**

St Edward's School (Co-Ed). Woodstock Rd, Oxford OX2 7NN *tel:* 01865 319200 *fax:* 01865 319202 *email:* administrator@stedward.oxon.sch.uk. D Christie, warden; Anthony Kerr-Dineen, dir of mus.

St Elphin's School (Girls). Darley Dale, Matlock, Derbys DE4 2HA *tel:* 01629 733263 *fax:* 01629 733956 *email:* admin@st-elphins.co.uk. Mrs V Fisher, head; A Teague, dir of mus.

St Felix School (Girls). Southwold, Suffolk IP18 6SD *tel:* 01502 722175 *fax:* 01502 722641 *email:* stfelix@rmplc.co.uk. Mr R W Williams, head; V Scott, dir of mus.

St George's School, Edgbaston *formerly* **Edgbaston Church of England College for Girls (Co-Ed).** 31 Calthorpe Road, Birmingham B15 1RX *tel:* 0121 625 0398 *fax:* 0121 625 3340. Mrs A Varley-Tipton, head; Sarah Russell, dir of mus; Nigel Morley.

St John's School (Boys). Leatherhead, Surrey KT22 8SP *tel:* 01372 372021 *fax:* 01372 386606. C H Tongue, head; B Noithip, dir of mus.

Shrewsbury School Music

SHREWSBURY SCHOOL
MUSIC SCHOLARSHIPS

Up to four or more Music Scholarships are awarded annually at 13+ after competitive examination held in February. Scholarships are graded in value according to need and considerable flexibility is exercised in their award. Two further scholarships are available for sixth form entrants, one of which may be for an organist.

Music scholars are expected to play a full and proactive part in the lively musical life of the school and in return receive free tuition on their first and second study instruments.

At Shrewsbury, which is shortly to build a new and innovative music facility, there are three orchestras, concert Band, Big Band, Choral Society, chamber and chapel choirs, extensive chamber coaching in all major areas and regular instrumental competitions. Lunchtime concerts and informal evening concerts complement the more formal large school events in providing numerous opportunities for regular performance; the school also has the Maginni Quartet as a visiting quartet three times a year for concerts and coaching. There are 25 visiting teachers in addition to the full-time members of the department. All instruments are taught by specialists, often performers in their own right.

Applicants should show real potential on their principal instrument and clearly demonstrate a lively overall enthusiasm for the subject. Successful candidates for audition will be expected to perform on their principal instruments/voice and to show general musical aptitude through a series of aural tests and sight-reading. There is also an interview with both headmaster and full-time members of the music department.

John Moore, the Director of Music, is happy to see potential applicants at any time prior to audition, and candidates are encouraged to make regular visits to the school in preparation for the scholarship.

For further details please apply to the Registrar, The Schools, Shrewsbury SY3 7BA. Tel. 01743 280552/email: registrar@shrewsbury.org.uk or contact the Music Department Secretary, Lisa Lowarch on 01743 280580/581 to make an appointment.

Outstanding Academic Success

Excellent Academic & Sporting Reputation

Generous Provision of Scholarships
and Solihull School Assisted Places

Continuity of Education for
Boys 7–18 years, Girls 16–18 years

Solihull School

...a tradition of excellence

MUSIC SCHOLARSHIPS

available for Boys 11–13 years and for Boys and Girls entering the Sixth Form

The Borough's leading private independent school.

Nationally praised by the Daily Telegraph in their Good Schools Guide:
"...challenging, lively and admirably attuned to the needs of highly able pupils".

Guided tours available.

For further information please contact the Admissions Secretary on **0121-705 4273**

Solihull School

Solihull School is a registered charity providing education for boys and Sixth Form girls

St Lawrence College (Co-Ed). Ramsgate, Kent CT11 7AE *tel:* 01843 592680 *fax:* 01843 851123 *email:* slcthanet@aol.com. M Slater, head; S A Clarkson, dir of mus.

St Leonards-Mayfield School (Girls). Convent of the Holy Child, The Old Palace, Mayfield, E Sussex TN20 6PH *tel:* 01435 873652 *fax:* 01435 872627. Jean Sinclair, head; Kenneth Pont, dir of mus.

St Leonards School (Girls). St Andrews, Fife KY16 9QU *tel:* 01334 472126/476345 (mus school) *fax:* 01334 476152. Mrs M James, head; Marilyn Cleobury-Jones, dir of mus.

St Margaret's School for Girls (Girls). 147 Magdalen Rd, Exeter EX2 4TS *tel:* 01392 273197 (head)/491699 (admissions) *fax:* 01392 251402. Mrs M D'Albertanson, head; Miranda Ashe, dir of mus.

St Mary's School (Ascot) (Girls). Ascot, Berks SL5 9JF *tel:* 01344 293607 *fax:* 01344 873281. Sister Frances Orchard, head; Gareth Lloyd, dir of mus.

St Mary's (Calne) (Girls). Calne, Wilts SN11 0DF *tel:* 01249 857200 *fax:* 01249 857207. Mrs C J Shaw, head; Keith Abrams, dir of mus.

St Mary's School (Gerrards Cross) (Girls). Gerrards Cross, Bucks SL9 8JQ *tel:* 01753 883370 *fax:* 01753 890966. Rosemary Millward, dir of mus.

St Mary's School (Wantage) (Girls). Wantage, Oxon OX12 8BZ *tel:* 01235 763571 *fax:* 01235 760467 *email:* stmarysw@rmplc.co.uk. Mrs S Bodinham, head; Ms F Eagar, dir of mus.

St Mary's Westbrook (Co-Ed). Ravenlea Rd, Folkestone, Kent CT20 2JU *tel:* 01303 851222 *fax:* 01303 249901 *email:* hm@st-marys-westbrook.co.uk. Christopher FitzGerald, head; George Sharman, dir of mus.

St Paul's Girls' School (Girls). Brook Green, Hammersmith, London W6 7BS *tel:* 020 7603 2288 *fax:* 020 7602 9932. Elizabeth Diggory, high mistress; Derek Bourgeois, dir of mus; Mrs R E Hayward, school sec.

St Paul's School (Boys). Lonsdale Rd, Barnes, London SW13 9JT *tel:* 020 8748 9162 *fax:* 020 8748 9557 *email:* pmt@stpauls.richmond.sch.uk. Stephen Baldock, high master; Mark Tatlow, dir of mus.

St Peter's School (Co-Ed). York YO30 6AB *tel:* 01904 623213 *fax:* 01904 640973. A F Trotman, head; Andrew Wright, dir of mus.

St Swithun's School (Girls). Winchester, Hants SO21 1HA *tel:* 01962 835700 *fax:* 01962 835779. H L Harvey, head; R Brett, dir of mus.

St Teresa's School (Girls). Effingham Hill, Dorking, Surrey RH5 6ST *tel:* 01372 452037 *fax:* 01372 450311 *email:* stteresa@rmplc.co.uk. Mary Prescott, head; Mrs J S Bolton, dir of mus.

Seaford College (Co-Ed). Petworth, W Sussex GU28 0NB *tel:* 01798 867392 *fax:* 01798 867606. T J Mullins, head; Martin Essex, dir of mus.

Sedbergh School (Boys). Sedbergh, Cumbria LA10 5HG *tel:* 01539 620535 *fax:* 01539 621301 *email:* sedsch@rmplc.co.uk. C H Hirst, headmaster; D M Andrew, dir of mus.

Sevenoaks School (Co-Ed). High St, Sevenoaks, Kent TN13 1HU *tel:* 01732 455133 *fax:* 01732 456143 *email:* regist@admin.soaks.kent.sch.uk. T R Cookson, head; Andrew Forbes, dir of mus.

Sherborne School (Boys). Sherborne, Dorset DT9 3AP *tel:* 01935 812030 (mus school) *fax:* 01935 816628. P H Lapping, head; Paul Ellis, dir of mus.

Sherborne School for Girls (Girls). Sherborne, Dorset DT9 3QN *tel:* 01935 812245 *fax:* 01935 818290 *email:* anner@ssg.compulink.co.uk. Miss J M Taylor, head; John Jenkins, dir of mus.

Shrewsbury School (Boys). Shrewsbury, Shrops SY3 7BB *tel:* 01743 344537/344135 (mus dept) *fax:* 01743 243107. F E Maidment, head; John Moore, dir of mus.

Sibford School (Co-Ed). Sibford Ferris, Banbury, Oxon OX15 5QL *tel:* 01295 781200 *fax:* 01295 781204 *email:* sibfordschool@dial.pipex.com. Susan Freestone, head; Matthew Smallwood.

Sidcot School (Co-Ed). Winscombe, N Somerset BS25 1PD *tel:* 01934 843102 *fax:* 01934 844181 *email:* sidcotad@aol.com. Angus Slesser, head; Timothy Bailey, dir of mus.

Silcoates School (Co-Ed). Wrenthorpe, Wakefield, W Yorks WF2 0PD *tel:* 01924 291614 *fax:* 01924 368690. A P Spillane, head; G L Cox, dir of mus.

Solihull School (Boys). Warwick Rd, Solihull, W Midlands B91 3DJ *tel:* 0121 705 4273 *fax:* 0121 711 4439 *email:* solsch@argonet.co.uk. P S J Derham, head; Stephen J Perrins, dir of mus.

Stamford High School (Girls). St Martin's, Stamford, Lincs PE9 2LJ *tel:* 01780 484200 *fax:* 01780 484201 *email:* music@shs.lincs.sch.uk. Patricia Clark, head; Paul White, dir of mus; John Worthington, deputy dir of mus.

Stamford School (Boys). St Paul's St, Stamford, Lincs PE9 2BS *tel:* 01780 750300 *fax:* 01780 750336 *email:* music@stamfordschool.lines.sch.uk. J Hale, head; Paul White, dir of mus; David Lovell Brown, dir of chapel mus.

Stewart's Melville College (Boys). Queensferry Rd, Edinburgh EH4 3EZ *tel:* 0131 332 7925 *fax:* 0131 343 2432. P F J Tobin, principal; Roger Askew, dir of mus.

Stockport Grammar School (Co-Ed). Buxton Rd, Stockport, Cheshire SK2 7AF *tel:* 0161 456 9000 *fax:* 0161 419 2407 *email:* suggest@stockportgrammar.co.uk. I Mellor, head; Jackson Towers, dir of mus.

Stonar School (Girls). Cottles Park, Atworth, Melksham, Wilts SN12 8NT *tel:* 01225 702309/702795 *fax:* 01225 790830 *email:* office@stonar.wilts.sch.uk. Caroline Homan, head; Nick Goodall, dir of mus.

Stonyhurst College (Co-Ed). Stonyhurst, Lancs BB7 9PZ *tel:* 01254 826345 *fax:* 01254 826370 *email:* admissions@stonyhurst.ac.uk. A J F Aylward, head; R A Highcock, dir of mus.

Stover School (Girls). Newton Abbot, Devon TQ12 6QG *tel:* 01626 54505 *fax:* 01626 335240. P E Bujak, head; Mrs S Farleigh, dir of mus.

Stowe School (Boys). Buckingham, Bucks MK18 5EH *tel:* 01280 813164 *fax:* 01280 822769. Jeremy Nichols, head; John Cooper Green, dir of mus.

Strathallan School (Co-Ed). Forgandenny, Perth PH2 9EG *tel:* 01738 812546 *fax:* 01738 812549. A W McPhail, head; D G Read, dir of mus.

Sutton Valence School (Co-Ed). Sutton Valence, Maidstone, Kent ME17 3HL *tel:* 01622 842281/844092 (mus dept) *fax:* 01622 844093. N A Sampson, head; Adrian Leang, dir of mus.

Talbot Heath (Girls). Rothesay Rd, Bournemouth, Dorset BH4 9NJ *tel:* 01202 761881 *fax:* 01202 768155. Christine Dipple, head; A P Hill, mus dept.

Taunton School (Co-Ed). Taunton, Somerset TA2 6AD *tel:* 01823 349200/349224 *fax:* 01823 349201. J P Whiteley, head; Philip Tyack, dir of mus.

Teesside High School (Girls). The Avenue, Eaglescliffe, Stockton on Tees TS16 9AT *tel:* 01642 782095 *fax:* 01642 791207. Miss J F Hamilton, head; Miss S Lloyd-Jones, dir of mus.

Tettenhall College (Co-Ed). Wood Hall, Tettenhall, Wolverhampton, W Midlands WV6 8QX *tel:* 01902 751119/741627 *fax:* 01902 747283/741940. P C Bodkin, head; I F Wass, dir of mus.

Tonbridge School (Boys). Tonbridge, Kent TN9 1JP *tel:* 01732 365555 *fax:* 01732 770853/363424 *email:* tonbschl@demon.co.uk. J M Hammond, head; Hilary Davan Wetton, dir of mus.

Tormead School (Girls). Cranley Rd, Guildford, Surrey GU1 2JD *tel:* 01483 575101 *fax:* 01483 450592. Mrs H E M Alleyne, head; Timothy Ball, dir of mus; James Marr, asst.

Trent College (Co-Ed). Long Eaton, Nottingham, Notts NG10 4AD *tel:* 0115 973 2737 *fax:* 0115 946 3284 *email:* pithsh@trentcollege.nott.sch.uk. J S Lee, head; P D Redfearn, dir of mus.

Trinity School (Boys). Shirley Park, Croydon CR9 7AT *tel:* 020 8656 9541 *fax:* 020 8655 0522. B Lenon, head; David Squibb, dir of mus.

Truro School (Co-Ed). Truro, Cornwall TR1 1TH *tel:* 01872 272763 ext 271 (mus school) *fax:* 01872 223431. G A G Dodd, head; D J Spedding, dir of mus.

University College School (Boys). Frognal, Hampstead, London NW3 6XH *tel:* 020 7435 2215 *fax:* 020 7431 4385 *email:* seniorschool@ucsonline.demon.co.uk. K J Durham, head; Colin Myles, dir of mus.

Uppingham School (Boys). Rutland, Leics LE15 9QE *tel:* 01572 822267 *fax:* 01572 822792. Stephen Winkley, head; Neil Page, dir of mus.

Walthamstow Hall (Girls). Sevenoaks, Kent TN13 3UL *tel:* 01732 451334 *fax:* 01732 740439. Mrs J S Lang, head; T J Daniell, dir of mus.

Warwick School (Boys). Myton Rd, Warwick CV34 6PP *tel:* 01926 776400 *fax:* 01926 401259 *email:* enquiries@warwick.warwks.sch.uk. P J Cheshire, head; Trevor G Barr, dir of mus.

Wellingborough School (Co-Ed). Irthlingborough Rd, Wellingborough, Northants NN8 2BX *tel:* 01933 222427 *fax:* 01933 271986. F R Ullmann, head; P R Marshall, dir of mus.

Wellington College (Boys). Crowthorne, Berks RG45 7PU *tel:* 01344 772639 *fax:* 01344 771725. C J Driver, head; J D Holloway, dir of mus.

Wentworth College (Girls). College Rd, Bournemouth, Dorset BH5 2DY *tel:* 01202 423266/422584 (mus dept) *fax:* 01202 418030. Miss S Coe, head; Mary Goodman, dir of mus.

West Buckland School (Co-Ed). Barnstaple, Devon EX32 0SX *tel:* 01598 760281 *fax:* 01598 760546 *email:* vick@westbuckland.devon.sch.uk. John Vick, head; Mark Richards, dir of mus.

Westminster School (Boys). 17 Dean's Yard, London SW1P 3PB *tel:* 020 7963 1003 *fax:* 020 7963 1006 *email:* headmaster@westminster.org.uk. Tristram Jones-Parry, head; Guy Hopkins, dir of mus.

Westonbirt School (Girls). Tetbury, Glos GL8 8QG *tel:* 01666 880333 *fax:* 01666 880364 *email:* head@westonbirt.gloucs.sch.uk. Mrs G Hylson-Smith, head; Malcolm Pike, dir of mus.

Whitgift School (Boys). Haling Park, S Croydon CR2 6YT *tel:* 020 8688 9222 *fax:* 020 8760 0682. C A Barnett, head; C G Tinker, dir of mus.

Winchester College (Boys). Winchester, Hants SO23 9NA *tel:* 01962 621122 *fax:* 01962 621123 *email:* kmp@wincoll.ac.uk. J P Sabben-Clare, head; Keith Pusey, master of mus.

Wolverhampton Grammar School (Co-Ed). Compton Rd, Wolverhampton WV3 9RB *tel:* 01902 421326 *fax:* 01902 421819. Bernard Trafford, head; Andrew Proverbs, dir of mus.

Woodbridge School (Co-Ed). Woodbridge, Suffolk IP12 4JH *tel:* 01394 385547 *fax:* 01394 380944 *email:* e-mail@woodbridge.suffolk.sch.uk. Stephen H Cole, head; John R Penny, dir of mus.

Woodhouse Grove School (Co-Ed). Apperley Bridge, Bradford BD10 0NR *tel:* 0113 250 2477 *fax:* 0113 250 5290 *email:* enquiries @woodhouse-grove.demon.co.uk. D C Humphreys, head; Mrs J Johnston, dir of mus.

Worth School (Boys). Paddockhurst Rd, Turners Hill, W Sussex RH10 4SD *tel:* 01342 710200 *fax:* 01342 710201. Father Christopher Jamison, head; Michael Oakley, dir of mus.

Wrekin College (Co-Ed). Wellington, Telford, Shrops TF1 3BG *tel:* 01952 242305 *fax:* 01952 240338. Stephen G Drew, head; Francis Murton, dir of mus.

Wycliffe College (Co-Ed). Stonehouse, Glos GL10 2JQ *tel:* 01453 822432 *fax:* 01453 827634 *email:* senior@wycliffe.co.uk. R A C Collins, head; C G Swain, dir of mus.

Wycombe Abbey School (Girls). High Wycombe, Bucks HP11 1PE *tel:* 01494 520381 *fax:* 01494 473836. Mrs P E Davies, head.

Yarm School (Boys). The Friarage, Yarm, Cleveland TS15 9EJ *tel:* 01642 786023 *fax:* 01642 789216. R N Tate, head; D M Dunn, head Ben Wilson, dir of mus.

Junior Departments at the Conservatoires

In most cases partial or full local authority funding is available for especially talented children to attend their nearest conservatoire; travelling expenses may also be payable.

Birmingham Conservatoire. Junior School, Paradise Place, Birmingham B3 3HG *tel:* 0121 331 5905 *fax:* 0121 331 5906 *email:* conservatoire@uce.ac.uk. Heather Slade-Lipkin, head of jnr dept; Christine Lees, str co-ord; Luan Ford, w/wind and br co-ord; Andrea Calladine, vocal co-ord; John Leach, academic co-ord; snr conservatoire staff, CBSO players; Katherine Tomlinson, sec.

Guildhall School of Music and Drama. Junior School, Barbican, London EC2Y 8DT *tel:* 020 7382 7160 *fax:* 020 7382 7212 *email:* twait@gsmd.ac.uk. Derek Rodgers, head of jnr school; Robert Pell, head of middle school; Valerie Kampmeier, head of lower school; Frederick Applethwaite, head of orch studies; Detlef Hahn, head of strs; Robert Porter, head of w/wind and perc; John Miller, br co-ord; Susan Tomes, head of keyboard studies; Mollie Petrie, head of singing; Faith Whiteley, head of prep course; Margaret Powell, head of chmbr mus; Heather Steedman, perc co-ord.

London College of Music and Media at Thames Valley University. Junior Music School, St Mary's Rd, Ealing, London W5 5RF *tel:* 020 8231 2304/2677 *fax:* 020 8231 2546 *email:* peter.cook@tvu.ac.uk. Peter Cook, dir; Peter Turnton, head of strs; Christina Bailey, head of vocal studies; Jeremy Davis, head of keyboard; Martin Vishnick, head of composition; Philip Cunningham, head of GCSE/A-level; Russell Hepworth-Sawyer, head of mus tech.

Royal Academy of Music. Junior Academy, Marylebone Rd, London NW1 5HT *tel:* 020 7873 7380 *fax:* 020 7873 7374. Jonathon Willcocks, dir.

Royal College of Music. Junior Dept, Prince Consort Rd, London SW7 2BS *tel:* 020 7591 4334 *fax:* 020 7589 7740 *email:* jd@rcm.ac.uk. Peter Hewitt, dir; Elisabeth Cook, asst dir; Andrea Robins, admin asst; John Mitchell, orch mgr and librarian.

Royal Northern College of Music. The Junior School of Music, 124 Oxford Rd, Manchester M13 9RD *tel:* 0161 273 6283/907 5264 *fax:* 0161 273 7611 *email:* postmaster@fsi.rncm.ac.uk; Karen Humphreys, admin.

Royal Scottish Academy of Music and Drama. Junior Academy of Music, 100 Renfrew St, Glasgow G2 3DB *tel:* 0141 332 4101 *fax:* 0141 353 0372 *email:* s.mcguire@rsamd.ac.uk. Anne Strachan, head of dept; Sharon McGuire, sec.

Trinity College of Music. Junior Dept and Foundation Studies, Mandeville Place, London W1M 6AQ *tel:* 020 7487 9602/3 *fax:* 020 7224 6278 *email:* mray@tcm.ac.uk. Mark Ray, dir of jnr dept and foundation studies; Christopher Caine, snr asst and co-ord; Lettice Stuart, creative mus consultant; Janet Lasky, admin and concerts mgr; Ann Cherry, co-ord, w/wind and br; Gordon Pringle, str co-ord; Philip Colman, co-ord, vocal and choral; Peter Wade, admin.

Welsh College of Music and Drama. Junior Music and Access Studies Dept, Castle Grounds, Cathays Park, Cardiff CF1 3ER *tel:* 029 2039 4665 *fax:* 029 2034 4906 *email:* jmas@wcmd.ac.uk. James Walker, head of jnr mus and access studies; Sally Craven, admin mgr, jnr mus.

Colleges of Further Education

Aberdeen College. Balgownie Centre, Hutcheon Gardens, Aberdeen AB23 8HA *tel:* 01224 272739. Dorothy Carnegie, course leader.

Accrington and Rossendale College of FE. Rawtenstall Centre, Haslingden Rd, Rawtenstall, Lancs *tel:* 01254 354202/3. Martin Cosgrif, acting team leader, performing arts.

Alton College. Old Odiham Rd, Alton, Hants GU34 2LX *tel:* 01420 88118 *fax:* 01420 80012 *email:* altoncollege@campus.bt.com. Martin Read, head of mus; Sylvia Harper, concerts co-ord.

Barking College. Dagenham Rd, Romford, Essex RM7 0XU *tel:* 01708 766841 ext 247 *fax:* 01708 731067. Heather Carmel, head of mus.

Boston College. Sam Newsom Music Centre, South St, Boston, Lincs PE21 6HT *tel:* 01205 365701 ext 350 *fax:* 01205 311478. David Forde, head of mus.

Bournemouth and Poole College of FE. Constitution Hill Rd, Parkstone, Poole, Dorset BH14 0QA *tel:* 01202 465733/747600 *fax:* 01202 205468. Mark Bellis, dir of mus.

Brockenhurst College. Lyndhurst Rd, Brockenhurst, Hants *tel:* 01590 625555 *fax:* 01590 625526. M C Newton, head of performing arts and media.

Bury College. Peel Centre, Parliament St, Bury, Lancs BL9 0TE *tel:* 0161 280 8280 *fax:* 0161 280 8228. Rob Nash, mus co-ord.

Chichester College of Arts, Science and Technology. Visual and Performing Arts, Dept of Music, Westgate Fields, Chichester, W Sussex PO19 1SB *tel:* 01243 786321 *fax:* 01243 775783 *email:* mdobson @inetgw. chichester.ac.uk. Martin Seath, head of dept; Mike Dobson, head of school of mus.

Clarendon College. New College Nottingham, Pelham Ave, Mansfield Rd, Nottingham NG5 1AL *tel:* 0115 953 4351 *email:* h.gelhaus@clarendon.ac.uk. H Gelhaus, curriculum team mgr, mus tech.

Colchester Institute. Centre for Music and Performance Arts, Sheepen Rd, Colchester, Essex CO3 3LL *tel:* 01206 518633 *also fax; email:* colinst@rmplc.co.uk. Bill Tamblyn, prof, dir of centre for music and performance arts.

Community Music Ltd. 35 Union St, London SE1 1SD *tel:* 020 7234 0900.

Coventry University Performing Arts. Leasowes Ave, Coventry CV3 6BH *tel:* 024 7641 8868 *fax:* 024 7669 2374. Sarah Whately, head of performing arts.

Cricklade College. Charlton Rd, Andover, Hants SP10 1EJ *tel:* 01264 363311 *fax:* 01264 332088 *email:* info@cricklade.ac.uk. Robert Taylor, dir of mus; Mark Osborne, Janet Weston, lecturers in mus.

Croydon College. Fairfield, College Rd, Croydon CR9 1DX *tel:* 020 8686 5700 *fax:* 020 8760 5880. John Parkes, programme mgr.

Estover Community College. Miller Way, Estover, Plymouth, Devon PL6 8UN *tel:* 01752 207888 *fax:* 01752 206058 *email:* pjs39@tutor.open.ac.uk. Alex Christaki, tutor in mus and tech; Phil Stevens, vice-principal; Dave Perrett, head of mus; Anita Wiseman, soundhouse mgr; Dave Puttick, development co-ord; Sam Dungey, training resources co-ord.

Exeter College. Hele Rd, Exeter EX4 4JS *tel:* 01392 205250. Iorwerth Pugh, head of mus.

Fareham College. Bishopsfield Rd, Fareham, Hants PO13 1NH *tel:* 01329 815200 *fax:* 01329 822483. Shirley Taylor, head of performing arts.

Gorseinon College. Belgrave Rd, Swansea SA4 6RD *tel:* 01792 890700/890723 *fax:* 01792 898729 *email:* p.ryan@gorseinon.ac.uk. Penelope Ryan, principal; Leslie Ryan, John Quirk, Simon Prothero, Heather James, mus dept.

Guildford School of Acting (GSA). Millmead Terrace, Guildford, Surrey GU2 5AT *tel:* 01483 560701 *fax:* 01483 535431. Gordon McDougall, principal.

Gwent Tertiary College (Newport). Crosskeys Centre, Newport, Gwent NP1 7ZA *tel:* 01495 333438 *fax:* 01495 333386. David Price, dir of mus, head of performing arts.

Huddersfield Technical College. New North Rd, Huddersfield HD1 5NN *tel:* 01484 536521 *fax:* 01484 511885 *email:* htcstaff@htcflex8.demon.co.uk. Mark Ellis, head of mus; Rick Cocker, tutor, mus tech and popular mus.

Kensington and Chelsea College. Faculty of Performing Arts, Sports, Health and Food, Hortensia Rd, London SW10 0QS *tel:* 020 7573 5233 *fax:* 020 7351 0956. Sally Martin, head of mus.

Kidderminster College. Dept of Community Studies, Hoo Rd, Kidderminster, Worcs DY10 1LX *tel:* 01562 820811 *fax:* 01562 748504 *email:* music@kidderminster.ac.uk. J Shepherd, lecturer in mus; J Bates, lecturer in mus and audio engineering; K Gammond, lecturer in mus industry management.

Kingsway College. Regents Park Centre, Longford St, London NW1 3HB *tel:* 020 7306 5700 *fax:* 020 7306 5950; Philip Flood, head of mus.

Langside College. 50 Prospecthill Rd, Glasgow G42 9LB *tel:* 0141 649 4991 *fax:* 0141 632 5252. Anna Young, head of school, languages and communication.

Leeds College of Music. 3 Quarry Hill, Leeds LS2 7PD *tel:* 0113 222 3400 *fax:* 0113 243 8798. Peter Whitfield, head of FE programmes; Ian Smith, asst head of FE programmes.

Lewisham College of FE *formerly* **South East London College.** Lewisham Way, London SE4 1UT *tel:* 020 8692 0353 *fax:* 020 8692 6258. T Cronin, programme area leader.

The Arts Centre. Liverpool Community College, 9 Myrtle St, Liverpool L7 7JA *tel:* 0151 252 1515. Brian Wishaw, head of mus.

Manchester College of Arts and Technology (MANCAT). Centre for Music and Performance Skills, 65-67 Lever St, Manchester M1 1FL *tel:* 0800 068 8585 (free course enquiry line) *fax:* 0161 953 2259 *email:* mail@mancat.ac.uk. Anne Bourner, head of mus and performance skills.

Middlesbrough College. Acklam Campus, Hall Drive, Acklam, Middlesbrough, Cleveland TS5 7DY *tel:* 01642 333398 *fax:* 01642 333310. L Harrison, mus co-ord, lecturer; E Round, lecturer in mus.

Neath College. Dwr Y Felin Rd, Neath, W Glamorgan SA10 7RF *tel:* 01639 634271 ext 253 *fax:* 01639 637453 *email:* alan.good@neath.ac.uk. Alan Good, course co-ord.

Nelson and Colne College of FE. Scotland Rd, Nelson, Lancs BB9 7YT *tel:* 01282 440200 *fax:* 01282 440274. Alison Birkinshaw, head of creative arts; Rosemary White, lecturer in mus.

Newcastle College. School of Music and Performing Arts, Rye Hill Campus, Scotswood Road, Newcastle upon Tyne NE4 7SA *tel:* 0191 200 4000 *fax:* 0191 200 4729/4675. Vee Wilkinson, dir of school.

North Devon College. Old Sticklepath Hill, Barnstaple, Devon EX31 2BQ *tel:* 01271 388164 *fax:* 01271 388121. Steve Edwards, head of dept of arts and sciences.

North East Surrey College of Technology. Reigate Rd, Ewell, Surrey KT17 3DS *tel:* 020 8394 3245. J Fincham, head of arts media and gen educ.

North Hertfordshire College. Cambridge Rd, Hitchin, Herts SG4 0JD *tel:* 01462 424242 *fax:* 01462 424380. Helen Corkill, co-ord for mus.

North Shropshire College. College Rd, Oswestry, Shrops SY11 2SA *tel:* 01691 688000 *fax:* 01691 688001. Ruth Loveluck, head of mus.

North Warwickshire and Hinckley College. Performing Art & Media Centre, London Rd, Hinckley, Leics LE10 1HQ *tel:* 024 7624 3000 ext 3002 *fax:* 01455 633930. Simon Edwards, head of popular mus; Ian Wynd, head of media production; Vince Brosnan, head of performance arts.

North Warwickshire College of Technology and Arts. Hinckley Rd, Nuneaton, Warwicks CV11 6BH *tel:* 024 7634 9321 *fax:* 024 7632 9056. Judith Norden, head of f/t mus studies.

Norwich City College of FE and HE. Ipswich Rd, Norwich NR2 2LJ *tel:* 01603 773162/3. David Morgan, head of dept.

Oldham College. Rochdale Rd, Oldham OL9 6AA *tel:* 0161 785 4070 *fax:* 0161 785 4064 *email:* nick.middleton@oldham.ac.uk. Nick Middleton, head of mus.

Perth College. Faculty of Arts, School of Music and Audio Engineering, Crieff Rd, Perth PH1 2NX *tel:* 01738 621171 *fax:* 01738 440050. Pamela McLean, head of faculty of arts.

Peter Symonds' College. Owens Rd, Winchester, Hants SO22 6RX *tel:* 01962 852764 *fax:* 01962 849372. Anna Bennetts, head of mus, including Hampshire specialist mus course.

Peterborough Regional College. Park Cres, Peterborough, Cambs PE1 4DZ *tel:* 01733 767366. Ian Burton, dir of mus.

Preston College. Park School, Moor Park Ave, Preston, Lancs PR1 6AP *tel:* 01772 225006. C H Pollington, head of mus.

Queen Mary's College. Cliddesden Rd, Basingstoke, Hants RG21 3HF *tel:* 01256 20861. David Coggins, head of mus.

Redcar and Cleveland College. Corporation Rd, Redcar, Cleveland TS10 1EZ *tel:* 01642 473132 *fax:* 01642 490856. Mike Heal, head of mus.

Richmond upon Thames College. Egerton Rd, Twickenham, Middx TW2 7SJ *tel:* 020 8607 8221. Chris Mitchell, head of mus; Peter Garvey, Justin Patterson, Paul Jenkins, lecturers in mus.

Rotherham College of Arts and Technology. Eastwood Lane, Rotherham, S Yorks S65 1EG *tel:* 01709 360765. Peter Goodwin, programme co-ord, popular mus.

Rugby College of FE. Rugby, Warwicks CV21 3QS *tel:* 01788 338602 *fax:* 01788 338574. Linda Wainscot, curriculum mgr, performing arts.

South Cheshire College. Dane Bank Ave, Crewe, Cheshire CW2 8AB *tel:* 01270 654654 *fax:* 01270 651515. J R Pyatt, head of mus dept.

South Devon College. Newton Rd, Torquay TQ2 5BY *tel:* 01803 386235/386381 *fax:* 01803 386403. Ian Bentley, principal.

South Downs College. College Rd, Purbrook Way, Havant, Hants *tel:* 023 9225 7011. Peter Rhodes, head of mus.

South East Derbyshire College. Cavendish Centre, Ilkeston, Derbys DE7 5AN *tel:* 0115 930 2942 *fax:* 0115 944 7181. Steve McAlone, programme co-ord, mus and performing arts.

South East Essex College. Carnarvon Rd, Southend-on-Sea, Essex SS2 6LS *tel:* 01702 220400/220639 *fax:* 01702 432320. Mark Vinall, head of media and performing arts.

Southgate College. High St, Southgate, London N14 6BS *tel:* 020 8886 6521/8982 5069 *fax:* 020 8982 5051. Neil Cloake, head of school of performance; Daniel Harding, co-ord jnr arts centre.

Stevenson College of FE. Carrickvale Centre, Stenhouse St West, Edinburgh EH11 3EP *tel:* 0131 535 4621 *fax:* 0131 535 4622. A D Knight, snr lecturer; Morag Campbell, head of section.

Stockton-Billingham Technical College. The Causeway, Billingham, Cleveland TS23 2DB *tel:* 01642 552101 *fax:* 01642 551194. Sara Fitzgerald, head of performing arts, head of dance; Andrew McIntyre, head of mus, First Diploma course tutor; Gordon Steel, head of drama/GNVQ course tutor.

Stoke-on-Trent College. Art, Design and Performing Arts, Burslem Campus, J Block, Moorland Rd, Burslem, Stoke-on-Trent ST6 1JJ *tel:* 01782 208208 *fax:* 01782 603103. Richard Longden, programme mgr (mus).

Stratford upon Avon College. The Willows, Alcester Rd, Stratford upon Avon CV37 9QR *tel:* 01789 266245. Christopher Long, head of mus.

Strode College. Church Rd, Street, Somerset BA16 0AB *tel:* 01458 844400 *fax:* 01458 844411. Tess Baber, head of creative arts and design; James Phippen, lecturer in charge of mus.

Taunton's College. Hill Lane, Southampton SO15 5RL *tel:* 023 8051 1811 *fax:* 023 8051 1991 *email:* higginj@tauntons.ac.uk. Jane Higgins, dir of mus.

Wakefield College. School of Music, Thornes Park Centre, Horbury Rd, Wakefield WF2 8QZ *tel:* 01924 789874 *fax:* 01924 789875 *email:* t.davis@wakcoll.ac.uk. Tony Davis, dir of mus; Andy Cholerton, head of classical mus; Kevin Dearden, head of popular mus; Sean Hodgson, jazz co-ord.

West Cheshire College. Handbridge Centre, Eaton Rd, Handbridge, Chester CH4 7ER *tel:* 01244 677677 (reception); 670403 (mus) *fax:* 01244 680131. Peter Southcott, Nicola Cunliffe.

West Herts College. Watford Campus, Hempstead Rd, Watford, Herts WD1 3EZ *tel:* 01923 812000 *fax:* 01923 812480. G. Warner, mus lecturer.

West Kent College. Brook St, Tonbridge, Kent *tel:* 01732 358101 *fax:* 01732 771415. Nigel Scaife, head of mus.

Wigan and Leigh College. Leigh Campus, Railway Rd, Leigh, Lancs WN7 4AH *tel:* 01942 761726 *fax:* 01942 761771. Mrs A J Boardman, centre mgr, performing arts.

Wirral Metropolitan College. Performing Arts and Media Studies, Borough Rd, Birkenhead, Wirral, Merseyside L42 9QD *tel:* 0151 551 7583 *fax:* 0151 551 7401 *email:* greg.williams@wmc.ac.uk. Greg Williams, head of school, arts and design.

Yale College (Coleg Iâl). Grove Park Rd, Wrexham, Clwyd LL12 7AA *tel:* 01978 311794 ext 2271 *fax:* 01978 291569 *email:* nbrowning@yale.ac.uk. Emlyn R Jones, principal; Sam Wyse, co-ord for performing arts.

Yeovil College. Hollands Campus, Mudford Rd, Yeovil, Somerset BA21 4DR *tel:* 01935 23921 ext 312 *fax:* 01935 429962 *email:* oayeovil@rmplc.co.uk. Andy Collyer, head of mus.

Music Degrees and Diplomas

The following are generally recognised music qualifications. It should be noted that some refer to institutions which are no longer in existence.

University Degrees

AMusM	*master of musical arts of Nottingham University*
AMusD	*doctor of musical arts of Nottingham University*
BA	*bachelor of arts*
BA(QTS)	*bachelor of arts (qualified teacher status)*
BEd	*bachelor of education*
BHum	*bachelor of humanities*
BMus	*bachelor of music*
BPhil	*bachelor of philosophy*
Dmus	*doctor of music*
Dphil	*doctor of philosophy*
MA	*master of arts*
MEd	*master of education*
MLitt	*master of letters*
MMus	*master of music*
MMusRCM	*master of music of the Royal College of Music*
MPhil	*master of philosophy*
MusB	*bachelor of music*
MusBac	*bachelor of music*
MusDoc	*doctor of music*
MusD	*doctor of music*
MusM	*master of music*
PhD	*doctor of philosophy*

Diplomas of Graduate Status

Several institutions have power to grant 'graduate diplomas', as they are usually styled. The following selection is of those diplomas most commonly awarded.

DipMusEd (RSAM)	*diploma in musical education of the Royal Scottish Academy of Music and Drama*
FRCO	*fellow of the Royal College of Organists*
GBSM	*graduate of the Birmingham School of Music*
GCLCM(LightMusic)	*graduate of the City of Leeds College of Music (Light Music)*
GDBM	*graduate diploma in Band Musicianship, University of Salford*
GDWCMD	*graduate diploma of the Welsh College of Music and Drama*
GGSM	*graduate of the Guildhall School of Music and Drama*
GLCM	*graduate of the London College of Music*
GNSM	*graduate of the (former) Northern School of Music*
GRNCM	*graduate of the Royal Northern College of Music*
GRSM	*graduate of the Royal Schools of Music*
GTSM	*graduate of Trinity College of Music*
GTCL	graduate of Trinity College of Music

Other Diplomas

These are usually awarded for either performing or teaching, and cover a wide range of subjects and instruments. Special qualifications may be additionally designated, e.g. TD for 'teaching diploma'.

ABCA	*associate of the British College of Accordionists*
ABSM	*associate of the Birmingham School of Music*
ACertCM	*Archbishop's certificate in church music*
ADCM	*Archbishop's diploma in church music*
AGSM	*associate of the Guildhall School of Music and Drama*
ALCM	*associate of the London College of Music*
AMusLCM	*associate in general musicianship of the London College of Music*
AMusNCM	*associate in theory of music of the National College of Music*
AMusTCL	*associate in compositional techniques of Trinity College of Music*
AMusTS	*associate in general musicianship of the Tonic Sol-Fa College of Music*
ANCM	*associate of the National College of Music*
ANSM	*associate of the (former) Northern School of Music*
ARCM	*associate of the Royal College of Music*
ARCO	*associate of the Royal College of Organists*
ARCO(CHM)	*associate of the Royal College of Organists, choirmaster's diploma*
ARMCM	*associate of the (former) Royal Manchester College of Music*
ARNCM	*associate of the Royal Northern College of Music*
ATCL	*associate of Trinity College of Music*
ATSC	*associate of the Tonic Sol-Fa College of music*
DipEd	*diploma in education (various institutions)*
DipMusEd	*diploma in musical education (various institutions)*
DipRAM	*recital diploma of the Royal Academy of Music*
DipTMus	*Scottish music teaching diploma*
DPLM	*diploma of proficiency in light music of the City of Leeds College of Music*
DRSAM	*diploma in music of the Royal Scottish Academy of Music and Drama*
FGCM	*fellowship of the Guild of Church Musicians*
FLCM	*fellow of the London College of Music*
FRCO(CHM)	*fellow of the Royal College of Organists, choirmaster's diploma*
FRMCM	*fellow of the (former) Royal Manchester College of Music*
FTCL	*fellow of Trinity College of Music*
FTSC	*fellow of the Tonic Sol-Fa College of Music*
LBCA	*licentiate of the British College of Accordionists*
LGSM	*licentiate of the Guildhall School of Music and Drama*
LLCM	*licentiate of the London College of Music*
LMusLCM	*licentiate in general musicianship of the London College of Music*
LMusNCM	*licentiate in theory of music of the National College of Music*
LMusTCL	*licentiate in compositional techniques of Trinity College of Music*
LMusTSC	*licentiate in general musicianship of the Tonic Sol-Fa College of Music*
LNCM	*licentiate of the National College of Music*
LRAM	*licentiate of the Royal Academy of Music*
LRSM	*licentiate of the Royal Schools of Music*
LTCL	*licentiate of Trinity College of Music*
LTCL(GMT)	*licentiate in general musicianship (teachers) of Trinity College of Music*

LTSC *licentiate of the Tonic Sol-Fa College of Music*
LWCMD *licentiate of the Welsh College of Music and Drama*
PDBM *professional diploma in band musicianship, University of Salford*
PDBM(PMR) *professional diploma in band musicianship (popular music with recording), University of Salford*
PGCC(Band) *postgraduate higher certificate in band conducting, University of Salford*
PPRNCM *professional performer of the Royal Northern College of Music*

Honorary Awards

These awards are in addition to certain university degrees listed above.

ARAM *associate of the Royal Academy of Music*
ARSCM *associate of the Royal School of Church Music*
DMus (Cantuar) *doctor of music, awarded by the Archbishop of Canterbury*
FBSM *fellow of the Birmingham School of Music*
FGSM *fellow of the Guildhall School of Music and Drama*
FNCM *fellow of the National College of Music*
FNSM *fellow of the (former) Northern School of Music*
FRAM *fellow of the Royal Academy of Music*
FRCM *fellow of the Royal College of Music*
FRNCM *fellow of the Royal Northern College of Music*
FRSAMD *fellow of the Royal Scottish Academy of Music and Drama*
FRSCM *fellow of the Royal School of Church Music*
FWCMD *fellow of the Welsh College of Music and Drama*
Hon ARAM *honorary associate of the Royal Academy of Music*
Hon ARCM *honorary associate of the Royal College of Music*
Hon FGCM *honorary fellow of the Guild of Church Musicians*
Hon FGSM *honorary fellow of the Guildhall School of Music and Drama*
Hon FRAM *honorary fellow of the Royal Academy of Music*
Hon FTCL *honorary fellow of Trinity College of Music*
Hon FTSC *honorary fellow of the Tonic Sol-Fa College of Music*
Hon GDBM *honorary graduate in band musicianship, Salford College of Technology*
Hon GSM *honorary member of the Guildhall School of Music and Drama*
Hon GCM *honorary member of the Guild of Church Musicians*
Hon LCM *honorary member of the London College of Music*
Hon RAM *honorary member of the Royal Academy of Music*
Hon RCM *honorary member of the Royal College of Music*
Hon RSCM *honorary member of the Royal School of Church Music*
Hon TSC *honorary member of the Tonic Sol-Fa College of Music*

Colleges of Higher Education

Colleges of Higher Education Students should apply for admission to colleges of higher education through the **Universities and Colleges Admissions Service (UCAS)**, Rosehill, New Barn Lane, Cheltenham, Glos GL52 3LZ *tel:* 01242 227788. Higher education establishments which have become University Colleges can now be found in the Universities section.

Barnsley College. Church St, Barnsley, S Yorkshire *tel:* 01226 730191 *email:* music@barnsley.ac.uk.

The Chichester Institute of HE. Music Dept, Bishop Otter Campus, College Lane, Chichester PO19 4PE *tel:* 01243 816000 *fax:* 01243 816080 *email:* a.robson@chihe.ac.uk. Arthur Robson, head of mus.

Christ Church College. School of Music, North Holmes Rd, Canterbury, Kent CT1 1QU *tel:* 01227 767700 *fax:* 01227 782244 *email:* g.r.hancox@canterburk.ac.uk. Grenville Hancox, head of dept; Dalwyn Henshall, dir joint hons; Roderick Watkins, dir single hons; Derek Hyde, dir p/grad studies; Faith Whiteley, str consultant; David Campbell, head of w/wind; Benjamin Luxon, vocal studies consultant; Ronald Smith, pno consultant.

City College Manchester. Arden Centre, Sale Rd, Manchester M23 0DD *tel:* 0161 957 1790 *fax:* 0161 945 9488. Adrian Armstrong, snr curriculum mgr; Emma Jarman, head of performing arts; Richard Hollywood, head of performance tech; Dennis Freedman, HND jazz course leader; Jason Brown, HND/ND popular mus course; Martin Moscrop, mus tech course leader; Phil Ellis, HND mus and new media management course leader.

Colchester Institute. Centre for Music and Performance Arts, Sheepen Rd, Colchester, Essex CO3 3LL *tel:* 01206 518633/518000 *fax:* 01206 518633. Bill Tamblyn, prof and dir; Mark Messenger, head of strs; Charles Hine, head of w/wind; Jennifer Lilleystone, head of vocal studies; Lesley Young, head of keyboard studies; Alan Bullard, head of composition; Christopher Phelps, BA course leader; Ian Ray, Foundation (ND) course leader; Andrew Allen, teacher in charge, CAMS; Gerard Essex, Foundation (pop) course leader.

Dartington College of Arts. Music Dept, Totnes, Devon TQ9 6EJ *tel:* 01803 862224 *fax:* 01803 863569 *email:* registry@dartington.ac.uk. Trevor Wiggins, dir of mus; Prof Kevin Thompson, principal.

King Alfred's College. Sparkford Rd, Winchester, Hants SO22 4NR *tel:* 01962 841515 *fax:* 01962 842280 *email:* malcolmf@virgo.wkac.ac.uk. June Boyce-Tillman, reader; Malcolm Floyd, head of dept; Ernest Piper; Jay Deeble; Francis Silkstone.

Liverpool Institute of Performing Arts. Mount St, Liverpool L1 9HF *tel:* 0151 330 3095 *fax:* 0151 330 3131. Arthur Bernstein, head of mus; Jill Halstead, admissions tutor.

North Hertfordshire College. Hitchin Centre, Cambridge Rd, Hitchin, Herts SG4 0JD *tel:* 01462 424242 *fax:* 01462 424580. Helen Corkill, co-ord for mus.

University College Northampton. Music Dept, Moulton Park, Northampton NN2 7AL *tel:* 01604 735500 *fax:* 01604 720636. J L Cranmer, course leader, snr lecturer; J Le Cocq, T Williams, L Reim, lecturers.

Perth College. Faculty of Arts, School of Music and Audio Engineering, Crieff Rd, Perth PH1 2NX *tel:* 01738 621171 *fax:* 01738 440050. Pamela McLean, head of faculty of arts.

Roehampton Institute London. Dept of Music, Southlands College, Roehampton Lane, London SW15 5SL *tel:* 020 8392 3432 *fax:* 020 8392 3435 *email:* music@roehampton.ac.uk. Damian Day, mus programme convener.

> Be the Future
In 2001, Trinity College of Music re-locates to the Royal Naval College at Greenwich to continue its excellence in provision of performance-based training.
To request the new prospectus of undergraduate, postgraduate and foundation courses, contact The Registry, Trinity College of Music 11-13 Mandeville Place London W1M 6AQ Tel +44 (0)171 935 5773 Fax +44 (0)171 224 6278 E-mail registry@tcm.ac.uk or visit the web site http://www.tcm.ac.uk
TRINITY
college of music
Registered Charity No. 309998

Conservatoires

Applications for places are made directly to the registrar of the establishment concerned who will forward the necessary forms.

Birmingham Conservatoire. Faculty of the University of Central England in Birmingham, Paradise Place, Birmingham B3 3HG *tel:* 0121 331 5901/2 *fax:* 0121 331 5906 *email:* conservatoire@uce.ac.uk. Prof George Caird, principal; Prof Alastair Pearce, vice-principal; Michael Harris, head of w/wind; Prof Keith Darlington, head of vocal studies; Prof Malcolm Wilson, head of keyboard studies; Reginald Reid, head of br; Prof Andrew Downes, head of composition and creative studies; Prof Jacqueline Ross, head of inst studies; James Strebing, head of perc; Mark Racz, head of u/grad studies; Peter Johnson, head of p/grad studies.

Guildhall School of Music and Drama. Silk St, Barbican, London EC2Y 8DT *tel:* 020 7628 2571 *fax:* 020 7256 9438. Ian Horsbrugh, principal; Damian Cranmer, dir of mus; Bernard Lanskey, asst dir of mus; Andrew Schultz, head of mus studies; David Takeno, head of strs; Peter Gane, head of wind and perc; Iain Burnside, head of keyboard studies; Robin Bowman, head of vocal studies; Yfrah Neaman, head of advanced studies; Clive Timms, head of opera studies; Scott Stroman, head of jazz.

Leeds College of Music. Mrs A Spatcher-Johnson, Head of mkt and development, 3 Quarry Hill, Leeds LS2 7PD *tel:* 0113 222 3400 *fax:* 0113 243 8798 *email:* Enquiries@leedscolmusic.ac.uk. David Hoult, principal; Graham Hearn, p/grad certificate course leader; Jonty Stockdale, head of HE programmes; Peter Whitfield, head of FE programmes; Philip Greenwood, head of tech programmes; Roger Ladds, head of community educ dept; David Smith, head of performance studies; Anthony Langford, head of academic studies and quality assurance.

London College of Music and Media at Thames Valley University. St Mary's Rd, Ealing, London W5 5RF *tel:* 020 8231 2304 *fax:* 020 8231 2546. Patricia Thompson, dean and dir; Linda Merrick, head of mus; Donald Ellman, programme leader, p/grad studies; Charles Ford, pathway leader, u/grad studies; Nigel Clarke, head of w/wind, br and perc; Pamela Bowden, head of vocal studies; Raphael Terroni, head of keyboard studies; Peter Sheppard Skaerved, head of strs; Martin Ellerby, head of composition.

National Opera Studio. Morley College, 61 Westminster Bridge Rd, London SE1 7HT *tel:* 020 7928 6833/7261 9267 *fax:* 020 7928 1810. Richard Van Allan, dir; Roy Laughlin, head of mus; Isobel Flinn, head of studies; Hugh Lloyd, admin.

Royal Academy of Music. Marylebone Rd, London NW1 5HT *tel:* 020 7873 7373 *fax:* 020 7873 7374. Curtis Price, principal; Jonathan Freeman-Attwood, vice-principal, dir of studies; John Wallace, head of br; David Strange, head of strs; Christopher Elton, head of keyboard studies; Robert Saxton, head of composition and contemporary mus; Mark Wildman, head of vocal studies; Sebastian Bell, head of w/wind; Laurence Cummings, head of historical performance; Kurt-Hans Goedicke, head of timpani and perc.

Royal College of Music. Prince Consort Rd, London SW7 2BS *tel:* 020 7589 3643 *fax:* 020 7589 7740. Janet Ritterman, dir; Jeremy Cox, dean and deputy dir; Elisabeth Cook, a/head of u/grad studies; David Wright, head of p/grad programmes; Graham Caldbeck, head of individual studies; Brian Hawkins, head of strs; Michael Rosewell, dir of opera; Neil Mackie, head of vocal studies; Janet Hilton, head of w/wind; Peter Bassano, head of br; Kevin Hathway, head of perc; Simon Channing, head of performance mgt; Peter Hewitt, dir of jnr dept; Paul Banks, research development fellow.

Royal Northern College of Music. 124 Oxford Rd, Manchester M13 9RD *tel:* 0161 907 5200 *fax:* 0161 273 7611. Edward Gregson, principal; Christopher Yates, vice-principal; Colin Beeson, dir of development; Charles Bodman Rea, dir of studies, head of school of academic studies; Anthony Gilbert, head of composition and contemporary mus; Rodney Slatford, head of strs; Renna Kellaway, head of keyboard studies; Patrick McGuigan, head of vocal and opera studies; James Gourlay, acting head of wind and perc; David Young, academic registrar.

Royal Scottish Academy of Music and Drama. 100 Renfrew St, Glasgow G2 3DB *tel:* 0141 332 4101 *fax:* 0141 332 8901/353 0372 *email:* registry@rsamd.ac.uk. Philip Ledger CBE, principal; Rita McAllister, dir of mus; Walter Blair, associate dir of mus; Christopher Underwood,

head of vocal studies; Philip Jenkins, head of keyboard studies; David Davies, head of orch studies and w/wind; Bryan Allen, head of br; Martin Hughes, head of strs; Timothy Dean, head of opera; Peter Inness, head of academic studies.

Trinity College of Music. 11-13 Mandeville Place, London W1M 6AQ *tel:* 020 7935 5773 *fax:* 020 7224 6278 *email:* info@tcm.ac.uk. Gavin Henderson, principal; Derek Aviss, deputy principal; Roger Pope, warden; Philip Meaden, dir of studies and academic development; Simon Young, dir of performance, head of composition and cond; Maureen Hanke, dir of continuing educ; Mark Ray, dir of jnr and foundation studies; Philip Fowke, head of keyboard studies; Linda Hirst, head of vocal studies; Paul Goodey, head of wind, br and perc; Elizabeth Turnbull, head of strs.

Welsh College of Music and Drama. Castle Grounds, Cathays Park, Cardiff CF1 3ER *tel:* 029 2034 2854/2064 0054 *fax:* 029 2034 4906 *email:* music.admissions@wcmd.ac.uk. Edmond Fivet, principal; Malcolm Goldring, asst principal; Jeremy Ward, head of performance studies; Richard Adams, head of w/wind, br and perc studies; Roger Butler, head of mus tech; Peter Esswood, head of str studies and orch training; Richard McMahon, head of keyboard studies; John Hugh Thomas, acting head of vocal studies; James Walker, head of jnr mus and access studies; Lucy Robinson, BA/MA course leader; Timothy Raymond, LWCMD/AD course leader.

Universities

Degree courses in music are offered at the following universities. Applications for admission to undergraduate courses at all of the following, except the Open University, are made through the **Universities and Colleges Admission Service (UCAS)**, Rosehill, New Barn Lane, Cheltenham, Glos GL52 3LZ *tel:* 01242 227788.

Anglia Polytechnic University. Music and Performing Arts Division, East Rd, Cambridge CB1 1PT *tel:* 01223 363271 *fax:* 01223 352935. Paul Jackson, head of dept; David Crilly, dir of research, MA mus course leader; Richard Hoadley, BA mus field leader; Alan Rochford, admissions tutor; Nicholas Toller, international degree access course leader; Paul Jackson, dir of practical studies; Helen Odell-Miller, course leader, MA mus therapy.

Bangor, University of Wales. Dept of Music, College Rd, Bangor, Gwynedd LL57 2DG *tel:* 01248 382181 *fax:* 01248 370297 *email:* mus014@bangor.ac.uk. Robert Pascall, head of dept; Stephen Rees, admissions tutor; Bruce Wood, David Evans, snr lecturers; Wyn Thomas, dir of studies; Suzi Collick, academic mgr.

Bath Spa University College *formerly* **Bath College of HE**. Newton St Loe, Bath BA2 9BN *tel:* 01225 875875 *fax:* 01225 875444. Alan Carter, dean of faculty of art and mus; Keith Bennett, course dir BA mus; Geoff Smith, course dir BA creative mus tech.

Birmingham University. Dept of Music, Barber Institute of Fine Arts, Edgbaston, Birmingham B15 2TT *tel:* 0121 414 5782 *fax:* 0121 414 5781 *email:* s.weldon@bham.ac.uk. Robert Meikle, head of dept; John Whenham, dir of p/grad studies; Vic Hoyland, u/grad admissions tutor.

Bretton Hall (College of the University of Leeds). West Bretton, Nr Wakefield, W Yorks WF4 4LG *tel:* 01924 830261 *fax:* 01924 832006.

Brighton University. Grand Parade, Brighton BN2 2JY *tel:* 01273 600900. Billie Cowie, course leader (mus).

Bristol University. Dept of Music, Victoria Rooms, Queens Rd, Clifton, Bristol BS8 1SA *tel:* 0117 954 5028 *fax:* 0117 954 5027 *email:* m.e.peirson@bris.ac.uk. Wyndham Thomas, head of dept; T J Samson, prof of mus; A Beaumont, reader in composition; W G Jenkins, snr lecturer in mus; J Irving, J Cross, E Dillon, J Pickard, lecturers in mus.

Brunel University. Faculty of Arts, Dept of Performing Arts, Uxbridge Campus *email:* arts-faculty@brunel.ac.uk. Peter Rudnick, snr tutor and course leader; Christine Bentham, faculty mkt offr; Sheila McQuattie, mus admin office; Marina English, admissions.

Cambridge University. University Music School, West Rd, Cambridge CB3 9DP *tel:* 01223 335176 *fax:* 01223 335067 *email:* admin@mus.cam.ac.uk. Alexander Goehr, prof of mus; Susan Rankin, chmn of faculty board; Sue Round, sec of faculty board; Martin Ennis, sec of degree committee; Roger Bowers, John Butt, Stefano Castelvecchi, Ian Cross, Laura Davey, Ruth Davis, Iain Fenlon, Robin Holloway, Andrew Jones, Hugh Wood, Dean Sutcliffe.

Cardiff, University of Wales. Dept of Music, Cardiff CF1 3EB *tel:* 029 2087 4816 *fax:* 029 2087 4379. Adrian Thomas, prof and head of dept; Robin Stowell, prof; Stephen Walsh, reader; David Wyn Jones, Richard Elfyn Jones, snr lecturers; Derek Carew, Kenneth Gloag, David Humphreys, Caroline Rae, lecturers; Stephen Price, Timothy Taylor, tutors.

University of Central England in Birmingham *see* **Birmingham Conservatoire** *in* **Conservatoires** *section.*

City University. Dept of Music, Northampton Square, London EC1V 0HB *tel:* 020 7477 8284 *fax:* 020 7477 8576 *email:* music@city.ac.uk. Denis Smalley, head of dept; Steve Stanton, BMus/BSc admissions tutor; Jim Grant, Dip/MIT dir; Annegret Fauser, MA dir; Simon Emmerson, research dir; Susannah Marsden, admin.

Coventry University. Performing Arts, Leasowes Ave, Coventry CV3 6BH *tel:* 024 7641 8868 *fax:* 024 7669 2374. Sarah Whatley, head of performing arts.

Derby University. School of Art and Design, Western Rd, Mickleover, Derby DE3 5GX *tel:* 01332 622222 *fax:* 01332 514323. Richard Hodges, head of mus.

Durham University. Dept of Music, The Music School, Palace Green, Durham DH1 3RL *tel:* 0191 374 3221 *fax:* 0191 374 3219 *email:* karen.scott@durham.ac.uk. Jeremy Dibble, chmn of dept; Michael Spitzer, admissions tutor.

University of East Anglia. School of Music, Norwich NR4 7TJ *tel:* 01603 592452 *fax:* 01603 250454 *email:* e.varge@uea.ac.uk. Peter Aston, professorial fellow; David Chadd, head of dept, snr lecturer in mus; Sharon Choa, Simon Waters, Anthony Gritten, lecturers in mus.

Edge Hill University College. St Helens Rd, Ormskirk, Lancs L39 4QP *tel:* 01695 575171 *fax:* 01695 579997 *email:* biggint@staff.ehche.ac.uk. Tony Biggin, head of subject; Avril Yisdall, snr lecturer; Lauren Goldthorpe, lecturer.

Edinburgh University. Faculty of Music, Alison House, Nicolson Square, Edinburgh EH8 9DF *tel:* 0131 650 2427 *fax:* 0131 650 2425 *email:* music@ed.ac.uk. D R B Kimbell, head of dept and prof; N Osborne, prof; E J Harper, R J Monelle, readers; J P Kitchen, P W Nelson, T N O'Regan, T M Turnbull, snr lecturers; L Coates, E Sheinberg, lecturers; A M Trewin, ethnomusicology; A Myers, G G O'Brien, organology.

Exeter University. Music Dept, Knightley, Streatham Drive, Exeter, Devon EX4 4PD *tel:* 01392 263810 *fax:* 01392 263815. Nicholas Sandon, prof of mus; Richard Langham Smith, reader; Philip R Grange, reader in composition; Timothy Jones, lecturer; Alan Street, lecturer and admissions tutor; Peter C Allsop, lecturer in mus; Paul Morgan, Ian Mitchell, p/t lecturer.

Glasgow University. Dept of Music, 14 University Gardens, Glasgow G12 8QH *tel:* 0141 330 4093 *fax:* 0141 330 3518 *email:* marjorie@music.gla.ac.uk. Graham Hair, composition; Marjorie Rycroft, head of dept, baroque and classical mus; Warwick Edwards, medieval and renaissance mus; Carola Böhm, mus tech; Stephen Arnold, contemporary composition, computer mus; Stuart Campbell, Russian and Soviet mus.

Goldsmiths College. Music Dept, University of London, New Cross, London SE14 6NW *tel:* 020 7919 7640 *fax:* 020 7919 7644 *email:* music@gold.ac.uk. Simon McVeigh, head of dept, head of p/grad studies; Roger Wibberley, deputy head of dept; Colin Lawson, chair of performance studies; John Baily, reader in ethnomusicology, p/grad admissions; Frank Dobbins, reader; Keith Potter, snr lecturer, international offr; Craig Ayrey, Peter Driver, Sadie Harrison, Anthony Pryer, lecturers; Roger Redgate, lecturer, u/grad admissions; Benedict Sarnaker, head of u/grad studies; Noelle Mann, head of Centre for Russian Music; Katharine Norman, dir of electronic mus studio.

University of Hertfordshire. College Lane, Hatfield, Herts AL10 9AB *tel:* 01707 284441 *fax:* 01707 285098. Howard Burrell, prof of mus and head of dept; Martyn Parry, head of academic studies; John Palmer, head of research.

Huddersfield University. Dept of Music, Queensgate, Huddersfield HD1 3DH *tel:* 01484 472003 *fax:* 01484 472656 *email:* music@hud.ac.uk. Peter Lawson, head of dept; Michael Holloway, admissions offr; John Bryan, performance leader; Margaret Lucy Wilkins, composition leader; Michael Clarke, electro-acoustic mus leader; Graham Cummings, musicology leader.

Hull University. Dept of Music, Hull University, Hull HU6 7RX *tel:* 01482 465998. Brian Newbould, prof of mus; Ian Denley, head of w/wind; Delia Fletcher, head of vocal studies; Ann Airton, head of keyboard studies; Richard Quick, head of strs.

Keele University. Dept of Music, Keele University, Keele, Staffs ST5 5BG *tel:* 01782 583295 *also fax email:* mua09@mus.keele.ac.uk. David Nicholls, prof; Mike Vaughan, head of dept and snr lecturer; Jane Manning, hon prof; Raymond Fearn, Rajmil Fischman, Philip Jones, Barbara Kelly, Sohrab Uduman, Alastair Williams, lecturers.

King's College, London. Dept of Music, Strand, London WC2R 2LS *tel:* 020 7873 2029 *fax:* 020 7873 2326 *email:* irene.auerbach@kcl.ac.uk. Laurence Dreyfus, head of dept, prof of performance studies; Michael Fend, mus history, dir of u/grad studies; Sir Harrison Birtwistle, prof of composition; John Deathridge, prof of mus, mus history; Cliff Eisen, Daniel Leech-Wilkinson, mus history; Tim Crawford, applied computing and mus; Daniel Chua, Christopher Wintle, mus analysis; Robert Keeley, composition; Silvina Milstein, composition, mus analysis; David Trendell, mus history, college organist; Irene Auerbach, dept sec.

Kingston University. School of Music, Kingston Hill Centre, Kingston on Thames, Surrey KT2 7LB *tel:* 020 8547 7149 *fax:* 020 8547 7118. Edward Ho, prof, head of school of mus; Roger Beeson, principal lecturer; Kevin Jones, reader; John Bate, Carol Gartrell, Michael Searby, principal lecturers; Gloria Toplis, Maria Busen-Smith, snr lecturers.

Lancaster University. Music Dept, Bailrigg, Lancaster LA1 4YW *tel:* 01524 65201 *fax:* 01524 593939. Roger Bray, prof, head of dept.

Leeds Metropolitan University. Calverley St, Leeds LS1 3HE *tel:* 0113 283 5912 *fax:* 0113 283 3110 *email:* j.hardman@lmu.ac.uk. R Ward, P Greenwood, course leaders; P Conway, course mgr.

University of Leeds. Dept of Music, Leeds LS2 9JT *tel:* 0113 233 2583 *fax:* 0113 233 2586 *email:* music.dept@leeds.ac.uk. Julian Rushton, prof of mus; Graham Barber, head of dept, prof of performance studies; David Cooper, dir of electronic studio; Ewan Stefani, electronic mus; Richard Rastall, musicology; Philip Wilby, composition; Kate Daubney, film mus, u/grad admissions; Steve Sweeney-Turner, popular mus, p/grad admissions; Luke Windsor, perception and cognition; Simon Baines, Joanne Fairley, performance; Kia Ng, research fellow.

Liverpool Hope University College. Music Dept, Hope Park, Liverpool L16 9JD *tel:* 0151 291 3457/3459 *fax:* 0151 291 3170. Stephen Pratt, head of mus; Mary Black, Robin Hartwell, Jonathan Powles, Ian Sharp.

Liverpool University. Music Dept, PO Box 147, Liverpool L69 3BX *tel:* 0151 794 3096 *fax:* 0151 794 3141 *email:* music@liv.ac.uk. John Williamson, head of dept; Robert Orledge; David Horn, popular mus dir; Colin Iveson, head of vocal studies; James Wishart, head of composition and electronic studio; John Gough, head of keyboard studies; Tony Shorrocks, head of performance studies.

University of London Institute of Education. Dept of Music, 20 Bedford Way, London WC1H 0AL *tel:* 020 7612 6740 *fax:* 020 7612 6741. Lucy Green, head of group; Keith Swanwick, prof of mus educ.

Manchester Metropolitan University (Crewe and Alsager Faculty). Hassall Rd, Alsager, Cheshire ST7 2HL *tel:* 0161 247 5302 *fax:* 0161 247 6377. Grahame Shrubsole, head of mus.

Manchester University. Dept of Music, Denmark Rd, Manchester M15 6HY *tel:* 0161 275 4987 *fax:* 0161 275 4994. John Casken, prof of mus; Keith Elcombe, head of dept; David Fallows, prof, admissions offr; Julie Bray, lecturer; Barry Cooper, snr lecturer, p/grad admissions; David Fanning, snr lecturer; Crawford Howie, lecturer; Geoffrey Poole, snr lecturer.

Napier University. The Ian Tomlin School of Music, Craighouse Campus, Craighouse Rd, Edinburgh EH10 5LG *tel:* 0131 455 6200 *fax:* 0131 455 6211 *email:* p.sawyer@napier.ac.uk. Philip Sawyer, head of School of Music; Anna Butterworth, snr lecturer; Nicholas Ashton, Andrew Doig, Frederick Frayling-Kelly, Michael Harris, lecturers; Jim Doyle, technician.

Newcastle University. Dept of Music, Armstrong Building, Newcastle upon Tyne NE1 7RU *tel:* 0191 222 6736 *fax:* 0191 222 5242 *email:* susan.lloyd@ncl.ac.uk. Eric Cross; Richard Middleton, head of dept; David Clarke; Agustín Fernández; Ian Biddle; Magnus Williamson.

Nottingham University. Dept of Music, University Park, Nottingham NG7 2RD *tel:* 0115 951 4755 *fax:* 0115 951 4756. Mervyn Cooke, head of dept, Britten, jazz, composition, film mus, ethnomusicology; John Morehen, conducting and musicology; Peter Wright, composition, medieval, renaissance, contemporary; Nick Sackman, composition and contemporary mus; Anthony Pople, analysis; Philip Weller, 18th C opera, 19th and 20th C song.

Open University. Walton Hall, Milton Keynes MK7 6AA *tel:* 01908 274066. Donald Burrows, prof, head of mus dept; Trevor Herbert, prof, staff tutor; David Rowland, snr lecturer; J Barrie Jones, David Mateer, Robert Samuels, Fiona Richards, Martin Clayton, Patricia Howard, lecturers; Kevin Dawe, staff tutor.

Oxford Brookes University. Music Dept, School of Art, Publishing and Music, Music and Publishing, Gipsy Lane, Headington, Oxford OX3 0BP *tel:* 01865 484986 *fax:* 01865 484952. Dai Griffiths, principal lecturer, head of mus; Christina Bashford, snr lecturer in musicology; Tim Howle, snr lecturer, studio mgr; Michael Young, snr lecturer in composition.

Oxford University. Faculty of Music, St Aldate's, Oxford OX1 1DB *tel:* 01865 276125 *fax:* 01865 276128 *email:* office@music.ox.ac.uk. Reinhard Strohm, Heather prof of mus; Roger Parker, prof; Bojan Bujic, reader, fellow of Magdalen College; John Caldwell, reader; Stephen Darlington, organist at Christ Church; Peter Franklin, reader, fellow of St Catherine's College; Edward Higginbottom, organist at New College; Harry Johnstone, fellow of St Anne's College; Hélène La Rue, curator of the Bate Collection.

Queen's University. School of Music, Belfast BT7 1NN *tel:* 028 9033 5105 *fax:* 028 9023 8484 *email:* c.fegan@qub.ac.uk. Ian Woodfield, dir, u/grad admissions; Jan Smaczny, p/grad admissions.

Reading University. Dept of Music, 35 Upper Redlands Rd, Reading RG1 5JE *tel:* 0118 931 8411 *fax:* 0118 931 8412. Jonathan Dunsby, head of dept.

University College of Ripon and York St John. The Ripon Campus, College Rd, Ripon HG4 2QX *tel:* 01765 602691 *fax:* 01765 600516. Marilynne J R Davies, head of performance studies; Bonnie Martin, David Lancaster, snr lecturers in mus; Josephine Peach, snr lecturer in mus p/t; Bruce Cole, Ralph Bateman, lecturers in mus p/t.

Royal Holloway. University of London, Egham Hill, Egham, Surrey TW20 0EX *tel:* 01784 434455 *fax:* 01784 439441 *email:* t.carter@rhbnc.ac.uk. Tim Carter, prof of mus, head of dept; David Charlton, Andrew Wathey, readers in mus; John Rink, reader in mus, p/grad admissions; Geoffrey Chew, Lionel Pike, snr lecturers in mus; Erik Levi, snr lecturer in mus, u/grad admissions; Julie Brown, James Dack, Katharine Ellis, lecturers in mus; Simon Holt, p/t lecturer in composition.

University College of St Martin. Lancaster LA1 3JD *tel:* 01524 384335 *fax:* 01524 384593 *email:* r.mcgregor@ucsm.ac.uk. Richard McGregor, head of performing arts; Gillian Cummins, Gerard Doyle, snr lecturers in mus; Kevin Hamel, lecturer in mus; Clive Walkely, lecturer (p/t).

University of Salford. Faculty of Media and Music, Dept of Music, Adelphi, Peru St, Salford, Manchester M3 6EQ *tel:* 0161 295 5000 *fax:* 0161 295 6106. Keith Wilson, dean of faculty; Derek Scott, head of dept and prof of mus; Mick Wilson, head of band musicianship; Robin Dewhurst, head of popular mus; David King, head of performance; Sheila Whiteley, associate dir of Institute for Social Research, reader in pop mus.

School of Oriental and African Studies. University of London, Dept of Music, Thornhaugh St, Russell Square, London WC1H 0XG *tel:* 020 7637 6182 Dept of Music, *also fax; email:* music@soas.ac.uk. Richard Widdess, head of dept; Keith Howard, snr lecturer in Korean Studies and music; David Hughes, admissions tutor (MMus), snr lecturer in Ethnomusicology; Owen Wright, admissions tutor (MPhil), prof of Musicology of the Middle East; Lucy Durán, admissions tutor (BA), lecturer in African mus; Alexander Knapp, Joe Loss lecturer in Jewish mus.

Sheffield University. Dept of Music, Western Bank, Sheffield S10 2TN *tel:* 0114 222 0470 *fax:* 0114 266 8053 *email:* v.r.messenger@sheffield.ac.uk. Eric Clarke, head of dept; A F Bennett, A M Brown, J W Davidson, P H A W Hill, M J Hindmarsh, A Moore, G Nicholson, J Stock.

Southampton University. Dept of Music, Highfield, Southampton SO17 1BJ *tel:* 023 8059 3425 *fax:* 023 8059 3197 *email:* musicbox@soton.ac.uk. Mark Everist, prof of mus, head of dept; Nicholas Cook, Anthony Pople, profs of mus; William Drabkin, snr lecturer and u/grad co-ord; José Bowen, lecturer in mus and p/grad co-ord; Julie Brown, Jeanice Brooks, Robynn Stilwell, Marina Frolova-Walker, lecturers in mus; Laurie Stras, lecturer in performance studies; Peter Collyer, head of early mus studies; Pete Thomas, head of jazz and popular mus studies.

University of Sunderland. School of Arts, Design and Media, Ashburne House, Ryhope Rd, Sunderland SR2 7EE *tel:* 0191 515 2180 *fax:* 0191 515 3375. Judith Hills, Elizabeth Holden, snr lecturers in mus.

University of Surrey. Dept of Music, Guildford, Surrey GU2 5XH *tel:* 01483 300800/259317 *fax:* 01483 259386. Thomas Messenger, head of dept, renaissance and baroque mus; Sebastian Forbes, prof, dir of mus, composition; Dave Fisher, dir of Tonmeister studies; Nicholas Conran, conducting, opera, jazz, Feldenkrais technique; Stephen Downes, 19th-20th C mus and aesthetics; Christopher Mark, analysis, 18th and 20th C mus; Francis Rumsey, digital audio tech; George Mowat-Brown, composition, 20th C mus; Tim Brookes, acoustics, psycho-acoustics, mus tech; Matthew Head, late baroque and classical, gender and sexuality.

Sussex University. Faculty of Music, Falmer, Brighton BN1 9QR *tel:* 01273 678019 *fax:* 01273 678466. Martin Butler, chair of mus, reader in mus; Michael Finnissy, research fellow (mus); Donald Mitchell, visiting prof in mus; David Osmond-Smith, prof of mus; Julian Johnson, lecturer in mus; Robert Adlington, lecturer in mus.

Thames Valley University. London College of Music and Media, St Mary's Rd, Ealing, London W5 5RF *tel:* 020 8579 5000 *fax:* 020 8566 1353. Keith Beniston, mus admissions, chief examiner; Patricia Thompson, dean and dir; Linda Merrick, head of mus; Donald Ellman, principal lecturer academic studies; Charles Ford, Allan Moore, snr lecturers.

Ulster University. Dept of Music, Shore Rd, Newtownabbey, Co Antrim BT37 0QB *tel:* 028 9036 6690 *fax:* 028 9036 6870 *email:* hm.bracefield@ulst.ac.uk. Mrs H M Bracefield, head of mus.

Westminster University. Commercial Music Dept, Watford Rd, Northwick Park, Harrow, Middx HA1 3TP *tel:* 020 7911 5000 ext 4033 *fax:* 020 7911 5934. Norton York, course leader; John Eacott, Keith Harris, Allan Dumbreck, Mykael Riley, Simon Pitt, Helen Reddington, course tutors.

University of Wolverhampton. School of Education, Sport and Performance Studies, Gorway Rd, Walsall WS1 3BD *tel:* 01902 323236

fax: 01902 323230. John Pymm, principal lecturer, head of mus; Kevin Stannard, snr lecturer, mus; Shirley Thompson, baroque mus, research co-ord; Gay Leese, head of w/wind; Hilary Middleton, head of keyboard studies; Malcom Procter.

York University. Dept of Music, York University, York YO1 5DD *tel:* 01904 432446 *fax:* 01904 432450 *email:* music@york.ac.uk. Nicola LeFanu, head of mus and composition; David Blake, composition; Bruce Cole, community mus; Ambrose Field, computer mus, mus educ; Tim Howell, analysis; Nicky Losseff, medieval polyphony, gender and mus, performance; Roger Marsh, mus theatre, composition; Tony Myatt, computer mus composition; John Potter, vocal performance, contemporary mus; Neil Sorrell, world mus, ethnomusicology and composition; Peter Seymour, performance; Jonathan Wainwright, renaissance and early baroque mus.

External Examining Institutions

Principal Examining Institutions

Associated Board of the Royal Schools of Music. 14 Bedford Square, London WC1B 3JG *tel:* 020 7636 5400 *fax:* 020 7637 0234 *email:* abrsm@abrsm.ac.uk. Richard Morris, chief exec. *Preparatory test, theory and practical graded exams, professional diplomas; performance assessment for adults. CT ABRSM professional development course for inst and singing teachers.*

Guildhall School of Music and Drama. Examinations Service, 3 Lauderdale Place, Barbican, London EC2Y 8EN *tel:* 020 7382 7167 *fax:* 020 7382 7212 *email:* exams@gsmd.ac.uk. Eric Hollis, dir. *Distinctive curriculum based syllabuses and publications that develop imaginative thinking through practical mus making. The School's Clear Marking System and professional examiners are setting standards for mus and drama around the world.*

London College of Music Examinations. Thames Valley University, St Mary's Rd, London W5 5RF *tel:* 020 8231 2364 *fax:* 020 8231 2433 *email:* lcm.exams@tvu.ac.uk. Gillian Patch, exams mgr; Keith Beniston, chief examiner in mus. *All insts, singing, sacred mus, mus theatre, duets and ens. Pre-preparatory, steps, leisure play, grs 1-8, certificate in advanced performance, ALCM, ALCM(TD), LLCM, LLCM(TD), FLCM (theory, composition, mus tech, cond). AMusLCM, LMusLCM.*

Trinity College London. 16 Park Cres, London W1N 4AP *tel:* 020 7323 2328 *fax:* 020 7323 5201 *email:* info@trinitycollege.co.uk. Mark Stringer, dir of mus and drama exams; Roger Bowers, chief exec; Nicholas King, chief examiner (mus). *Graded exams in all insts from initial to grs 1-8. First Concert Certificate (Brass), Performers Certificate, ATCL, AMusTCL, LTCL in Performance, Instrumental Teaching, Compositional Techniques, LMusTCL, ATCL (MusEd) and LTCL (MusEd), Certificate in Music Education, FTCL in Performance, Composition, F(MusEd)TCL.*

Other Examining Institutions

Birmingham Conservatoire. University of Central England in Birmingham, Paradise Place, Birmingham B3 3HG *tel:* 0121 331 5901/2 *fax:* 0121 331 5906 *email:* conservatoire@uce.ac.uk. George Caird, principal. *ADBC, LDBC, FBC. Teachers', performers', fellowship diplomas.*

Faculty of Church Music. 27 Sutton Park, Blunsdon, Swindon SN2 4BB *tel:* 020 8675 0180. Rev G Gleed, registrar. *Examinations for the grade of Associate, Licentiate and Fellow open to church musicians of any denomination.*

Guild of Church Musicians. St Katharine Cree, 86 Leadenhall St, London EC3A 3DH *tel:* 01883 743168 *fax:* 01883 741854. John Ewington OBE, gen sec; Michael Nicholas, exams sec. *Membership is open to church musicians of all Christian denominations. The Guild administers the exams for the Archbishops' Award in Church Music; Archbishops' Certificate in Music (ACertCM); Fellowship of the Guild of Church Musicians (FGCM).*

Independent Contemporary Music Awards (ICMA). PO Box 134, Witney, Oxon OX8 7FS *tel:* 07000 780728 *also fax*; 07774 59969824 hrs *email:* icmusa@compuserve.com. Margaret Woolway, registrar. *Diploma and grade exams in all traditional insts, plus electric org, electric keyboard, mus tech, composition, conducting, church mus, accordion, gui, rock gui, kit drumming, contemporary vocals and musicianship. Regular competitive festivals. Examinations are held throughout the year at times and venues chosen by applicants. Approved*

by the Secretary for State for Education and Employment under Section 400 of the Education Reform Act 1996.

National College of Brass. 242 Grimsby Rd, Cleethorpes, NE Lincs DN35 7EY *tel:* 01472 691623. Andrew White, chmn; J Hall, dir of exams. *Grs 1-8 practical for br; also theory. Diploma in performing, theory, conducting.*

National College of Music. 4 Duffield Rd, Chelmsford, Essex CM2 9RY *tel:* 01245 354596. Eric Hayward, gen sec. *Grs 1-8; bronze, silver and gold medal exams; associate diploma (ANCM), licentiate diploma (LNCM), fellowship diploma (FNCM). All syllabuses approved by the Secretary of State for Examinations in Schools.*

Phillips College. PO Box 107, Manchester M14 7SL *tel:* 0161 225 0445 *fax:* 0161 224 4530 *email:* examinations@music-services.demon.co.uk. Lee P Longden, dir; Nicholas Groves, academic dean; Ian Roche, admin dean. *The examination division of the Cambridge Society of Musicians, offering certificate, diploma and advanced diploma in band musicianship, bandmastership, popular mus studies (rock, jazz and pop stylings), mus educ for classroom teachers, choir training, arranging and musicology.*

Rockschool/Trinity Graded Examinations for Guitar, Bass and Drums. Rockschool Ltd, Broomfield Rd, Richmond, Surrey TW9 3HS *tel:* 0870 333 6303 *fax:* 020 8332 6297. Norton York, chmn; Richard Beadle, examinations mgr. *Grs 1-6 and 8 available in electric gui, bass gui and drums for solo players. Mus theory diploma exam (AMusTCL) available for rock guis, bass players and drummers. Performance diploma (ATCL) and Teaching Diploma (LTCL) available.*

Royal College of Music. Prince Consort Rd, London SW7 2BS *tel:* 020 7589 3643 *fax:* 020 7589 7740. David Harpham, registry offr. *ARCM (performers).*

Royal College of Organists. 7 St Andrew St, London EC4A 3LQ *tel:* 020 7936 3606 *fax:* 020 7353 8244. Alan Dear, snr exec. *Membership open to any interested person; corporate membership is also available to groups. Those wishing to take any diploma must first apply for membership. ARCO, FRCO; the Choir-training Diploma (Dip CHM) and Organ Teaching Diploma (Dip TCR) may be added to either of these. The Preliminary Certificate may be taken by members or jnr members.*

Royal School of Church Music. Cleveland Lodge, Westhumble, Dorking, Surrey RH5 6BW *tel:* 01306 872800 *fax:* 01306 887260 *email:* education@rscm.com. Geoff Weaver, dir of studies. *Foundation Certificate in Church Music Studies, a modular course for church musicians; Organist Training Scheme, focusing on service accompaniment; St Nicholas and St Cecilia Awards, qualifications for advanced singers. Proficiency Certificate for Church Choir; Archbishops' Diploma in Church Music, advanced award for church mus directors.*

Victoria College of Music. 9 Staple Inn, London WC1V 7QH *tel:* 020 7405 6483 *also fax; email:* exams@vcm.telme.com. Jeffery Tillett, dir of exams; Sir Malcolm Arnold CBE, hon president; Martin Ellerby, principal. *AVCM, LVCM (teachers and performers), FVCM, AMusVCM, LMusVCM, grs 1-8, jnr bronze, silver and gold medals. All insts including electric keyboard.*

Specialist Courses

Alexander Technique Training Courses

The **Society of Teachers of the Alexander Technique** can provide a full list of members who teach in the UK. The society can be contacted at 20 London House, 266 Fulham Rd, London SW10 9EL *tel:* 020 7351 0828 *email:* info@stat.org.uk.

Brighton Alexander Training Centre. 57 Beaconsfield Villas, Brighton, E Sussex BN1 6HB *tel:* 01273 501612 *fax:* 01273 552002 *email:* nicholls@pavilion.co.uk. J Nicholls, dir; C Nicholls, co-dir.

Bristol Alexander Technique Training School Association. 37 Bellevue Cres, Cliftonwood, Bristol BS8 4TF *tel:* 0117 987 2989 *also fax.* Ali Burrows, head of training; Linda Jordan, asst.

Centre for the Alexander Technique. 46 Stevenage Rd, London SW6 6HA *tel:* 020 7731 6348. P Ribeaux, Mrs E Ribeaux, dirs.

Constructive Teaching Centre. 18 Lansdowne Rd, London W11 3LL *tel:* 020 7727 7222. W H M Carrington, D M G Carrington, dirs.

Essex Alexander School. 65 Norfolk Rd, Ilford, Essex IG3 8LJ *tel:* 020 8220 1630. Ken Thompson, dir.

Hampstead Alexander Centre. 4 Marty's Yard, Hampstead High St, London NW3 1QW *tel:* 020 7435 4940 *fax:* 020 7794 2652 *email:* robinsimmons@btinternet.com. R J Simmons, dir.

Headington Alexander Training School. 10 York Rd, Headington, Oxford OX3 8NW *tel:* 01865 765511 *fax:* 01865 454112 *email:* s.c@btinternet.com. Stephen Cooper, dir.

North London Alexander Technique Teachers Training Centre. 10 Elmcroft Ave, London NW11 0RR *tel:* 020 8455 3938. M Magidov, dir.

North of England Teaching Centre for the F M Alexander Technique. Flat 3, Park House, 39 Hanover Square, Leeds LS3 1BQ *tel:* 0113 244 9713 *fax:* 0113 246 7240. Margaret Rakusen, dir.

Oxford Alexander Technique Teaching Centre. 63 Chalfont Rd, Oxford OX2 6TJ *tel:* 01865 558477. Mrs Walker, dir.

West Sussex Centre for Alexander Technique. 5 Coates Castle, Pulborough, W Sussex *tel:* 01798 865503. A and R Nott, dirs.

Arts Administration Courses

Anglia Polytechnic University. East Rd, Cambridge CB1 1PT *tel:* 01223 363271 *fax:* 01223 352900. Barbara Mornin, course admin; Tony Smith, pathway leader.

Buckinghamshire University College. Wellesbourne Campus, Kingshill Rd, High Wycombe, Bucks HP13 5BB *tel:* 01494 522141 *fax:* 01494 465432 *email:* md@rncb.ac.uk. John Beaven, course leader.

City University. Dept of Arts Policy and Management, Level 12, Frobisher Cres, Barbican, London EC2Y 8HB *tel:* 020 7477 8751/3 *fax:* 020 7477 8887 *email:* artspol@city.ac.uk. Eric Moody, prof, head of dept; Ursula Hedgley, admissions; Mary Dines, admin.

Durham University Business School. Mill Hill Lane, Durham DH1 3LB *tel:* 0191 374 2233 *fax:* 0191 374 1230 *email:* mba.ft@durham.ac.uk. A M Nevin, C Cumming, MBA programme mgrs.

Moray House Institute. Chessel's Land, Heriot-Watt University, Edinburgh EH8 8AQ *tel:* 0131 558 6506 *fax:* 0131 558 6505.

Roehampton Institute London. Roehampton Lane, London SW15 5PH *tel:* 020 8392 3269 *fax:* 020 8392 3289 *email:* p.reynolds@roehampton.ac.uk. Peter Reynolds, head of drama and theatre studies; Pauline Barrie, programme convener, arts management.

University College, Warrington. Padgate Campus, Fearnhead Lane, Warrington WA2 0DB *tel:* 01925 494494 *fax:* 01925 816077. David Grimshaw, snr lecturer.

Warwick University. Centre for the Study of Cultural Policy, School of Theatre Studies, Coventry CV4 7AL *tel:* 024 7652 3020 *fax:* 024 7652 4446. Oliver Bennett, dir, MA cultural policy.

Instrument Making and Repair Courses

Leeds College of Music. 3 Quarry Hill, Leeds LS2 7PD *tel:* 0113 222 3400 *fax:* 0113 243 8798. Angela Spatcher-Johnson, head of mkt and development; Philip Greenwood, head of tech programmes; Edward Lee, asst head of tech programmes.

London Guildhall University. Sir John Cass Dept of Design and Technology, 41 Commercial Rd, London E1 1LA *tel:* 020 7320 1842/1000 *fax:* 020 7320 1830.

Merton College. London Rd, Morden, Surrey SM4 5QX *tel:* 020 8640 3001 ext 1812 *fax:* 020 8640 0835. T Head, K Graves, tutors.

Newark and Sherwood College. School of Violin, Woodwind and Piano Technology, Friary Rd, Newark on Trent, Notts NG24 1PB *tel:* 01636 680680 *fax:* 01636 680681 *email:* mhunt@newark.ac.uk. Malcolm Hunt, college mgr; Kerry Boylan, J Lord, G Else, R Summerfield, A Lucas, course tutors.

Royal National College for the Blind. Piano Tuning and Repairs, College Rd, Hereford HR1 1EB *tel:* 01432 265725 *fax:* 01432 353478 *email:* md@rncb.ac.uk. Michael Wigmore, deputy head of creative arts.

Stevenson College. Carrickvale Centre, Stenhouse St West, Edinburgh EH11 3EP *tel:* 0131 535 4621 *fax:* 0131 535 4622. Andrew Knight, snr lecturer, mus inst tech; Ken Thomson, course mgr, orch inst tech; Morag Campbell, head of section.

West Dean College. West Dean, Chichester, W Sussex PO18 0QZ *tel:* 01243 811301 *fax:* 01243 811343 *email:* westdean@pavilion.co.uk. Roger Rose, course tutor.

Professional Development Courses for Private Music Teachers

Associated Board of the Royal Schools of Music. 14 Bedford Square, London WC1B 3JG *tel:* 020 7467 8257 *also fax; email:* profdev@abrsm.ac.uk. Richard Crozier, professional development dir.

Bela Bartók Centre for Musicianship. 6 Frognal Court, 158 Finchley Rd, London NW3 5HL *tel:* 020 7435 3685 *email:* agnes.kory@kcl.ac.uk. Agnes Kory, dir.

British Suzuki Institute. 39 High St, Wheathampstead, Herts AL4 9BB *tel:* 01582 832424 *fax:* 01582 834488 *email:* bsi@suzukimusic.force9.co.uk. Birte Kelly, gen sec.

Goldsmiths. University of London, New Cross, London SE14 6NW *tel:* 020 7919 7229 *fax:* 020 7919 7223. Jeremy Peyton Jones, mus programme co-ord.

University of Reading. International Centre for Research in Music Education, Bulmershe Court, Reading RG6 1HY *tel:* 0118 931 8843/8837 *fax:* 0118 935 2080. Anthony Kemp, professor of mus educ.

Psychology for Musical Performance Courses

Psychology for Music Teaching, Learning and Performing. 28 Glebe Place, London SW3 5LD *tel:* 020 7352 1666 *also fax; email:* musicmindmovement@btinternet.com. Lucinda Mackworth-Young, consultant in psychology.

Recording and Technology Courses

Bangor, University of Wales. Dept of Music, College Rd, Bangor, Gwynedd LL57 2DG *tel:* 01248 382181 *fax:* 01248 370297 *email:* mus018@bangor.ac.uk. Robert Pascall, head of dept; Jochen Eisentraut, Andy Lewis, course organisers.

Bath Spa University College. Newton St Loe, Bath BA2 9BN *tel:* 01225 875875 *fax:* 01225 875444. Geoff Smith, course dir.

Bournemouth University. School of Media Arts and Communication, Poole House, Talbot Campus, Fern Barrow, Poole, Dorset BH12 5BB *tel:* 01202 524111/595469. Stephen Deutsch, course dir.

City University. Northampton Square, London EC1V 0BH *tel:* 020 7477 8284 *fax:* 020 7477 8576 *email:* music@city.ac.uk. Anna Woodward, course admin.

De Montfort University. Dept of Media and Cultural Production, Gateway House, Leicester LE1 9BH *tel:* 0116 255 1551 *fax:* 0116 250 6199. Andrew Hugill, head of dept.

University of Derby. Western Rd, Mickleover, Derby DE3 5GX *tel:* 01332 622222 ext 2066 *fax:* 01332 514323. Richard Hodges, programme co-ord.

Edinburgh University. Faculty of Music, Alison House, Nicolson Square, Edinburgh EH8 9DF *tel:* 0131 650 2423 *fax:* 0131 650 2425 *email:* music@ed.ac.uk.

Gateway School of Recording, Music Technology and Music Business Studies. Kingston Hill Centre, Kingston-upon-Thames, Surrey KT2 7LB *tel:* 020 8549 0014 *fax:* 020 8547 7337. Andrew Gower, dir of courses.

Glasgow University. Dept of Music, 14 University Gardens, Glasgow G12 8QH *tel:* 0141 330 4093 *fax:* 0141 330 3518 *email:* stephen@music.gla.ac.uk. Stephen Arnold, dir of computer mus studies; Carola Boehm, lecturer in mus tech.

Goldsmiths College. University of London, Professional and Community Education, New Cross, London SE14 6NW *tel:* 020 7919 7200/7229 *fax:* 020 7919 7223 *email:* cen01cce@gold.ac.uk. Jeremy Peyton Jones, mus programme co-ord.

Keele University. Dept of Music, Keele, Staffs ST5 5BG *tel:* 01782 583295 *also fax; email:* mua09@mus.keele.ac.uk. Michael Vaughan, head of dept.

Kidderminster College. Dept of Community Studies, Hoo Rd, Kidderminster, Worcs DY10 1LX *tel:* 01562 820811. J Shepherd, lecturer in mus; Jon Bates, lecturer in mus tech; Kevyn Gammond, lecturer in mus industry mgt.

London College of Music at Thames Valley University. St Mary's Rd, London W5 5RF *tel:* 020 8231 2304 *fax:* 020 8231 2546. Jolyon Forward, programme leader, lecturer (sound, multimedia); Lezli-An Barrett, lecturer (video).

London Guildhall University. Sir John Cass Dept of Design and Technology, 41 Commercial Rd, London E1 1LA *tel:* 020 7320 1842/1000 *fax:* 020 7320 1830.

Media Production Facilities. Bon Marche Building, Ferndale Rd, London SW9 8EJ *tel:* 020 7737 7152 *fax:* 020 7738 5428 *email:* mpf@media-production.demon.co.uk. Paul Halpin, head of media training.

Newark and Sherwood College. Chauntry Park, Friary Rd, Newark on Trent, Notts NG24 1PB *tel:* 01636 680680 *fax:* 01636 680681. Colin Boothman.

Newcastle College. School of Music and Performing Arts, Rye Hill Campus, Scotswood Rd, Newcastle upon Tyne NE4 7SA *tel:* 0191 200 4211 *fax:* 0191 200 4729 *email:* enquiries@ncl-coll.ac.uk. Vee Wilkinson, dir of school; A Hooper, curriculum co-ord, mus.

University of North London. School of Communications Technology and Mathematical Sciences, 166-220 Holloway Rd, London N7 8DB *tel:* 020 7607 2789 *fax:* 020 7753 7002. P C Prigmore, course admin.

Perth College. Faculty of Arts, School of Music and Audio Engineering, Crieff Rd, Perth PH1 2NX *tel:* 01738 621171 ext 128 *fax:* 01738 440050. Pamela McLean, head of faculty of arts.

Peterborough Regional College. Music Dept, Park Cres, Peterborough, Cambs PE1 4DZ *tel:* 01733 67366. Ian Burton, dir of mus.

Queen's University. Music Dept, Belfast BT17 1NN *tel:* 028 9033 5105 *fax:* 028 9023 8484 *email:* c.fegan@qub.ac.uk. Michael Alcorn.

Rose Bruford College. School of Production, Lamorbey Park, Sidcup, Kent DA15 9DF *tel:* 020 8300 3024 *fax:* 020 8308 0542 *email:* admiss@bruford.ac.uk. Mark Constable, course tutor.

Royal National College for the Blind. College Rd, Hereford HR1 1EB *tel:* 01432 265725 *fax:* 01432 353478 *email:* md@rncb.ac.uk. Martin Sayer, course tutor/leader; Paul Cobbold, lecturer in sound engineering.

SAE Technology College *formerly* **School of Audio Engineering.** United House, North Rd, Islington, London N7 9DP *tel:* 020 7609 2653 *fax:* 020 7609 6944 *email:* enquiries@sael.demon.co.uk.

University of Salford. Dept of Music, Adelphi, Peru St, Salford, Manchester M3 6EQ *tel:* 0161 834 6633 *fax:* 0161 834 3327. Derek B Scott, prof of mus, head of dept; Mark Grimshaw, head of mus tech and studio production.

South Derbyshire College. Cavendish Centre, Music Dept, Cavendish Rd, Ilkeston, Derby DE7 5AN *tel:* 0115 930 2942 *fax:* 0115 944 7181. Steve McAlone, programme co-ord, mus and performing arts.

South East Essex College. Carnarvon Rd, Southend-on-Sea, Essex SS2 6LS *tel:* 01702 220400/220639 *fax:* 01702 432230. Mark Vinall, head of media and performing arts.

Surrey University. Dept of Music, Guildford, Surrey GU2 5XH *tel:* 01483 300800/259317 *fax:* 01483 259386. Dave Fisher, Tonmeister course dir.

Wakefield College. School of Music, Thornes Park Centre, Horbury Rd, Wakefield WF2 8QZ *tel:* 01924 789789 *fax:* 01924 789821 *email:* t.davis@wakcoll.ac.uk. Tony Davis, dir of mus; Andy Cholerton, head of classical mus; Kevin Dearden, head of popular mus; Sean Hodgson, jazz co-ord.

University of York. Graduate Office, Dept of Music, Heslington, York YO10 5DD *tel:* 01904 432142 *fax:* 01904 432450 *email:* music@york.ac.uk. Ambrose Field, mus tech admissions tutor.

Services Schools of Music

Royal Air Force Headquarters Music Services. RAF Uxbridge, Middx UB10 0RZ *tel:* 01895 237144 ext 6345/6286 *fax:* 01895 810846. Flt Lt D J G Stubbs, dir of mus.

Royal Marines School of Music. HMS Nelson, Queen St, Portsmouth PO1 3HH *tel:* 023 9272 2351. Lt-Col R A Waterer, principal dir of mus; Maj K G Lamb, chief instructor.

Royal Military School of Music. Kneller Hall, Twickenham, Middx TW2 7DU *tel:* 020 8898 5533 ext 8623 *fax:* 020 8898 7906. Lt-Col S A Watts, principal dir of mus (army); Major K G Lamb, chief instructor.

Colleges of Bagpipe Music

College of Piping. 16-24 Otago St, Glasgow G12 8JH *tel:* 0141 334 3587 *fax:* 0141 337 3024 *email:* info@piping.scot.net. Dugald MacNeill, acting principal.

Royal Scottish Band Association College. 45 Washington St, Glasgow G3 8AZ *tel:* 0141 221 5414 *fax:* 0141 221 1561. Iain M White, exec offr.

Scholarships and Grants

The Department of Education and Science publishes leaflets on state scholarships. The **Musicians Benevolent Fund** publishes annually the *Handbook of Music Awards and Scholarships,* available from 16 Ogle St, London W1P 8JB *tel:* 020 7636 4481.

The Directory of Grant-Making Trusts is published by CAF and is available from Biblios, Star Rd, Partridge Green, W Sussex RH13 8LD *tel:* 01403 710851 and *The Grants Register* is published by Macmillan and is available from Macmillan Reference Ltd, 23 Eccleston Place, London SW1W 9NF *tel:* 020 7881 8027. Scholarships tenable at UK universities by UK and/or other Commonwealth graduates are contained in *Awards for Postgraduate Study at Commonwealth Universities,* which is available from Publications Sales, Association of Commonwealth Universities, 36 Gordon Square, London WC1H 0PF *tel:* 020 7387 8572.

Unless otherwise stated, scholarships for study and research are available to British and Commonwealth students only. For details of low-interest loans for young professional musicians towards the purchase of instruments, apply to The Secretary, **Loan Fund for Musical Instruments**, 16 Ogle St, London W1P 8JB *tel:* 020 7436 4816. There is also a **Loan Scheme for Musical Instruments;** enquiries to Jenny Dann, Benslow Musical Instrument Loan Scheme, Little Benslow Hills, off Benslow Lane, Hitchin, Herts SG4 9RB *tel:* 01462 420748 *fax:* 01462 440171 *email:* LoanSch@aol.com.

A K Holland Award. c/o Rushworths Music of Liverpool Ltd, 42-46 Whitechapel, Liverpool L1 6EF *tel:* 0151 709 9071 *fax:* 0151 709 9073. W D C Rushworth, sec. *Small awards for choral societies and solo singers living within a 60-mile radius of Liverpool.*

Abbado European Young Musicians Trust. Speechly Bircham, Bouverie House, 154 Fleet St, London EC4A 2HX *tel:* 020 7353 3290 *fax:* 020 7353 4825 *email:* speechlys@speechlys.co.uk. J V Hughes. *Loans (usually interest free) to assist young instrumentalists in buying suitable insts. Applications to be supported with details of specific inst. Available for those aged 30 or under.*

Alfreda Hodgson Bursary/Raymond Fox Bursary. c/o NFMS, Francis House, Francis St, London SW1P 1DE *tel:* 020 7976 4930 *fax:* 020 7828 5504. Kate Fearnley, award admin. *Award in alternate years for singers and instrumentalists respectively as part of the NFMS Award for Young Concert Artists. Applications are invited from EU citizens aged 21-30 (singers) or 21-27 (instrumentalists) who are at the beginning of their professional careers in mus and normally resident in the UK. Application forms available early Jan. Annual auditions in spring.*

Allcard Grants. The Worshipful Company of Musicians, Allcard Grants, 74-75 Watling St, London EC4M 9BJ *tel:* 020 7489 8888 *fax:* 020 7489 1614. *Singers, str players, pno accompanists and (in exceptional circumstances) wind players; for three p/grad scholarships of £3000 for an advanced course of performance study within the EU. Applications only through the heads of conservatoires or university mus depts. Nominations by 30 Apr, final selection by audition and interview in May/Jun.*

Sir Arthur Bliss Memorial Scholarship. The Secretariat, Royal College of Music, Prince Consort Rd, London SW7 2BS *tel:* 020 7589 3643 *fax:* 020 7589 7740. Development Officer (*tel:* 020 7591 4331). *1-year p/grad scholarship, tenable at the RCM in alternate years (next award Sep 2002). Open competition for composers of any age (usually under 25) and of all nationalities after acceptance at RCM. Applications by 1 Dec. Award of c £3200.*

Australian Music Foundation. c/o Richards Butler, Beaufort House, 15 St Botolph St, London EC3A 7EE *tel:* 020 7247 6555 *fax:* 020 7247 5091 *email:* jfe@richardsbutler.com. John F Emmott, hon sec. *Major award for Australian singers and instrumentalists of p/grad or equivalent standard for advanced course of study in Europe. Age 30 or under on 31 Dec prior to application in Apr.*

Awards for Advanced Study in Music. Arts Council of Wales, Artform Development Division, 9 Museum Place, Cardiff CF10 3NX *tel:* 029 2037 6500 *fax:* 029 2022 1447 *email:* information@ccc-acw.org.uk. *Awards have been made to musicians under 28, born and educated in Wales; also open to those now permanently resident in Wales and normally having lived in Wales for 2 years. Applications by 1 Feb annually. Award of c £2000.*

Benslow Musical Instrument Loan Scheme. Little Benslow Hills, off Benslow Lane, Hitchin, Herts SG4 9RB *tel:* 01462 420748 *fax:* 01462 440171 *email:* LoanSch@aol.com. Jenny Dann, sec; Sara Hewitt, mkt sec. *Applicants must be in f/t educ and a recommendation from instrumental teacher is required. Age range 5-25.*

Bob Harding Bursary. c/o 152 West St, Havant, Hants PO9 1LP *tel:* 023 9248 3228. Peter Craddock, mus dir. *Opportunity for young cond to assist in and observe rehearsals and concerts of the Havant Symphony Orchestra throughout a season. Must be under 30, on an advanced conducting course and resident in UK. Travel and subsistence grant up to £350. Selection by audition; open to candidates nominated by London mus colleges. Applications by Jun annually.*

Boise Foundation Scholarship. c/o Royal Academy of Music, Marylebone Rd, London NW1 5HT. Jean Shannon, hon sec. *Biennial award worth £5000 (next 2001) for performers aged 30 and under at closing date who are resident in the UK or Ireland. Applicants must be nominated by heads of mus colleges, etc. Application fee £10. Auditions Apr, applications by Mar. Enquiries in writing only.*

Professor Charles Leggett Awards for Young Wind and Brass Players. c/o Musicians Benevolent Fund, 16 Ogle St, London W1P 8JB *tel:* 020 7636 4481 *fax:* 020 7637 4307 *email:* sdolton@mbf.org.uk. Contact: awards and trusts administrator. *Annual awards of £4000 for wind and br players. Applications from Oct. Application fee £10.*

The Countess of Munster Musical Trust. Wormley Hill, Godalming, Surrey GU8 5SG *tel:* 01428 685427 *fax:* 01428 685064 *email:* munstertrust@compuserve.com. Gillian Ure, sec. *Tuition and maintenance grants for UK and Commonwealth students, tenable at home or abroad. Ages 18-25 for instrumentalists, 18-27 for female singers and 18-28 for male singers. Interest-free loans available for inst purchase to young professional musicians aged 28 and under. Applications by 31 Jan, auditions Apr-Jun.*

Craxton Memorial Trust. 15 Cambridge Rd, Uxbridge, Middx UB8 1BQ. Jane Craxton, hon sec. *Biennial awards worth £300-700 for outstanding young pianists and instrumentalists (excluding org, perc and hpd) ages 17-25. Send sae for application form. Application fee £5. Auditions late spring, applications by 31 Jan 2001.*

Denis Matthews Trust Scholarships for Pianists. 10 Russell Rd, Moseley, Birmingham B13 8RD *tel:* 0121 449 3055 *also fax. Annual scholarships to students of Birmingham Conservatoire. Two u/grad scholarships and a p/grad scholarship are awarded by audition at the end of first year's study.*

Donald Tovey Memorial Prize. Board of the Faculty of Music, University Offices, Wellington Square, Oxford OX1 2JD *tel:* 01865 270001 *fax:* 01865 270708. E Marston, sec, board of the faculty of mus. *Awarded irregularly for research in philosophy, history or understanding of mus. May also be awarded to assist publication of research already completed. Awards normally for post-doctoral or advanced work.*

Emanuel Hurwitz Chamber Music Charitable Trust. 44 Church Cres, London N3 1BJ. Miriam Keogh, founder and admin. *Bursaries for str players to further their studies in chmbr mus (college/university fees will not be paid). UK citizens only. Must apply in writing with sae. Applications by 1 Jun; fee £15.*

Emily English Award. c/o Musicians Benevolent Fund, 16 Ogle St, London W1P 8JB *tel:* 020 7637 4481 *fax:* 020 7637 4307 *email:* sdolton@mbf.org.uk. Contact: awards and trusts administrator. *Award of £10,000 to assist young vn p/grad students aged 24 and under. Applications open Nov for auditions in Apr. Application fee £10.*

English-Speaking Union Music Scholarships. Cultural Affairs, The English-Speaking Union, Dartmouth House, 37 Charles St, London W1X 8AB *tel:* 020 7493 3328 *fax:* 020 7495 6108 *email:* esu@esu.org. Contact: Lucy Passmore. *The English-Speaking Union offers the following mus scholarships to musicians aged 30 or under from Britain* *or the Commonwealth, and students or graduates from RSAMD, REM, GSMD, RNCM, Trinity College, RSM, Birmingham Conservatoire or equivalent institutions to study at summer schools in the UK: International Musicians Seminar (Cornwall). Applications by mid-Nov for placements the following year. Tuition, board and lodgings and any relevant flight costs.*

Eric Thompson Trust. c/o The Royal Philharmonic Society, 10 Stratford Place, London W1N 9AE *tel:* 020 7491 8110 *fax:* 020 7493 7463. Richard Fisher, clerk to the trustees. *Modest cash awards given at the Trustees' discretion to help aspiring professional organists. No fixed age range, but younger applicants preferred. Applications in writing (with details of training, career and two references from organists of standing) by 30 Jun and 31 Dec annually.*

ESTA Nannie Jamieson Nutshell Fund. 6 Ember Lane, Esher, Surrey KT10 8ER *tel:* 020 8398 4691 *also fax.* Sylvia Palmer, hon sec. *European String Teachers Association, British Branch. Modest bursaries awarded annually for students and teachers of str insts (ESTA members) for help to attend w/shops, conferences and teaching courses. Applications by 1 May.*

Francis Chagrin Fund. c/o spnm, Francis House, Francis St, London SW1P 1DE *tel:* 020 7828 9696 *fax:* 020 7931 9928 *email:* spnm@spnm.org.uk. Katy Bignold, admin. *Grants available towards cost of reproducing performance materials of unperformed works by British composers and composers resident in Britain of any age (pieces must have scheduled date for performance). Applications considered monthly; max £250.*

Grace Williams Music Prize. 6 The Chantry, Llandaff, Cardiff CF5 2NN *tel:* 029 2055 3622. Roy Bohana, trustee. *Awards for advanced study to singers and instrumentalists aged 14-30, born and educated in Wales. Closing date 1 Jun 2000. Award worth £750-1000.*

Graucob Music Awards. 34 Chiltern Drive, Hale, Altrincham, Cheshire WA15 9PN *tel:* 0161 941 1522. Sharon Martin, admin. *10 annual awards of up to £750 each. Open to young musicians with gr 8+, aged 18 and under on 1 May and living in Greater Manchester, W Yorks, Lancs and Cheshire LEAs. Applications by 31 Mar.*

Guilhermina Suggia Gift for the Cello. c/o Musicians Benevolent Fund, 16 Ogle St, London W1P 8JB *tel:* 020 7636 4481 *fax:* 020 7637 4307 *email:* sdolton@mbf.org.uk. Contact: awards and trusts administrator. *Award of £2000 to assist exceptionally talented vc students aged 21 and under. Applications from Nov-Mar for auditions in Apr. Application fee £10.*

H A Thew Fund. c/o Rushworths of Liverpool Ltd, Whitechapel, Liverpool L1 6EF *tel:* 0151 709 9071 *fax:* 0151 709 9073. W D C Rushworth, sec. *Small awards made to mus students and organisations in Merseyside. Must be based within 60-mile radius of Liverpool.*

H J C Stevens Organ Scholarship. St Bride's Church, Fleet St, London EC4Y 8AU *tel:* 020 7353 1301 *fax:* 020 7583 4867. Canon John Oates, rector; Robert Jones, mus dir. *Award to 2nd or 3rd year org student at London mus college or university; p/grad student applications also considered.*

Harriet Cohen Memorial Music Awards Trust. Manches & Co, Aldwych House, 81 Aldwych, London WC2 *tel:* 020 7404 4433 *fax:* 020 7430 1133. John Rubinstein, admin trustee. *Discretionary annual awards to max £1500 made to British performers, composers, academics or singers of outstanding excellence and promise. Open to those aged 18-30. No individual applications will be considered; candidates will be nominated by main mus institutions upon invitation only and will be auditioned and interviewed.*

Hattori Foundation For Young Musicians. 72e Leopold Rd, London SW19 7JQ *tel:* 020 8944 5319 *fax:* 020 8946 6970. Kim Gaynor, admin. *Awards up to £7000. Aims to assist exceptionally talented instrumentalists (ages 15-20 and 21-27) to pursue a solo career. Also awards to ens with average age under 27. Awards are not for tuition fees in f/t study courses. Open to UK residents and foreign nationals studying in the UK subject to certain conditions. Applications by 30 Apr for snrs and at any time for jnrs.*

Sir Henry Richardson Awards. c/o Musicians Benevolent Fund, 16 Ogle St, London W1P 8JB *tel:* 020 7636 4481 *fax:* 020 7637 4307 *email:* sdolton@mbf.org.uk. Contact: awards and trusts administrator. *Annual award of £8000 available alternately to accompanists and repetiteurs aged under 30 (repetiteurs in 2000). Applications from Jan for auditions in May. Application fee £10.*

Hinrichsen Foundation. 10-12 Baches St, London N1 6DN. Lesley Adamson, admin. *Awards only in the areas of contemporary composition and its performance and musicological research. Costs of degree and study courses, recordings and the purchase of insts and equipment excluded. Preference shown to UK applicants. Applications by 1 Jan, 1 Apr, 1 Jun, 1 Oct (subject to change).*

Holst Foundation. 43 Alderbrook Rd, London SW12 8AD *tel:* 020 8673 4215 *fax:* 020 7228 2358. *Funds available to applicants of any age, primarily for the performance of contemporary mus.*

Ian Fleming Music Education Awards. c/o Musicians Benevolent Fund, 16 Ogle St, London W1P 8JB *tel:* 020 7636 4481 *fax:* 020 7637 4307. *Awards for mus educ and help with inst purchase to outstanding young musicians beginning a career. Aged 26 and under (instrumentalists), 30 and under (singers). Applications from Oct-Feb for auditions in Mar. Application fee £10.*

Ida Carroll Research Fellowship. Royal Northern College of Music, 124 Oxford Rd, Manchester M13 9RD *tel:* 0161 907 5200 *fax:* 0161 273 7611 *email:* info@rncm.ac.uk. Colin Beeson, vice-principal. *1-year award worth £8000 for research at doctoral or post-doctoral level, tenable at the RNCM.*

Sir James Caird's Travelling Scholarships Trust. Thorntons Solicitors, 50 Castle St, Dundee DD1 3RU *tel:* 01382 229111 *fax:* 01382 202288. A F McDonald, M Black, admin and sec. *Grants and scholarships of up to £3500 available to Scottish p/grad students. Scholarships are tenable for 1 year but may be renewed for up to 2 further years. Wiseman Prize (£600) for best performance and Joseph Bloch LRAM Prize (£200) for best str player. Auditions in Mar or Apr in London and Glasgow, applications by 31 Jan.*

The James Pantyfedwen Foundation. 9 Market St, Aberystwyth SY23 1DL *tel:* 01970 612806 *also fax.* Richard Morgan, exec sec. *For Welsh students requiring support for approved courses, excluding private study. Applications by 31 Jul annually.*

John Tunnell Trust. 4 Royal Terrace, Edinburgh EH7 5AB *tel:* 0131 556 4043 *fax:* 0131 556 3969. Jonathan Tunnell, chmn. *Awards in form of paid engagements in conjunction with Scottish mus societies to young professional inst chmbr ens (max 8 players). Preference given to British-based groups aged 27 or under. Application forms supported by tapes. Applications by Jun each year for following season.*

Julius Isserlis Scholarship. Royal Philharmonic Society, 10 Stratford Place, London W1N 9AE *tel:* 020 7491 8110 *fax:* 020 7493 7463 *email:* admin@rps-uk.demon.co.uk. Rosemary Johnson, gen admin. *Scholarship worth £20,000 over two years to fund study abroad. Awarded biennially by competition in selected performing categories to students aged 15-25 (of any nationality) permanently resident in the UK. Next scholarship May 2001. Entry fee £20.*

Lake District Summer Music Trust. Stricklandgate House, 92 Stricklandgate, Kendal, Cumbria LA9 4PU *tel:* 01539 733411 *fax:* 01539 724441 *email:* info@ldsm.org.uk. Sir John Manduell, chmn; Andrew Lucas, admin. *Bursaries and scholarships to help students receive specialist inst and chmbr mus training at Lake District Summer Music International Summer School (conservatoire and young professional level) and Young String Venture (ages 6-18). See* **Summer Schools.** *1999 awards amounted to over £8000.*

Loan Fund for Musical Instruments. 16 Ogle St, London W1P 8JB *tel:* 020 7436 4816 *fax:* 020 7637 4307. Marjorie Dickinson, sec. *Low-interest loans to talented young professional musicians towards the purchase of fine insts. Further details and application form available from the secretary.*

London Arts Board/NFMS Special Activities Fund. c/o NFMS, Francis House, Francis St, London SW1P 1DE *tel:* 020 7976 4930 *fax:* 020 7828 5504 *email:* nfms@nfms.org.uk. Gail Brand, training and development offr, London; Robin Osterley, chief exec.

Maisie Lewis Young Artists Fund. Musicians' Company Concerts, 6 Pembridge Cres, London W11 3DT *tel:* 020 7229 2610 *also fax; email:* janandali@aol.com. Jan Lowy, admin. *Assists singers (under 30) and instrumentalists (under 25) of British residency to gain experience on the concert platform. Application forms available from 1 May for completion by 31 July. Award: concert.*

Manoug Parikian Award. c/o Musicians Benevolent Fund, 16 Ogle St, London W1P 8JB *tel:* 020 7636 4881 *fax:* 020 7637 4307 *email:* sdolton@mbf.org.uk. Contact: awards and trusts administrator. *Award of £4000 to assist young vn students aged 21 and under of any nationality. Applications from Nov-Mar for auditions in Apr. Application fee £10.*

The Mario Lanza Educational Foundation. 646 Portway, Avonmouth, Bristol BS11 9NZ. Carol Jacobs, sec. *Various awards for students who are engaged in a f/t course of classical singing at a college or conservatoire. Age 18 and over.*

Mendelssohn Scholarship Foundation. c/o Royal Academy of Music, Marylebone Rd, London NW1 5HT. Jean Shannon, hon sec. *Award min £5000 for composers aged 30 and under at closing date, of any nationality but resident in the UK or Republic of Ireland. Application fee £10. Applications by Mar 2000. Enquiries in writing only.*

Michael Tippett Musical Foundation. 1 Dean Farrar St, London SW1H 0DY. Gwyn Rhydderch, sec. *Individual study or research costs are not* *funded. Leaflet available giving guidelines on performance and educ project policy.*

Miriam Licette Scholarship. c/o Maggie Teyte Prize Administrator, 2 Keats Grove, London NW3 2RT *tel:* 020 7435 5861. Felicity Guinness. *Scholarship of £5000 to assist a female student (aged 18-30) of French Song. Next award Apr 2000.*

Muriel Taylor Scholarship. The Warehouse, 13 Theed St, London SE1 8ST *tel:* 020 7928 9251 *fax:* 020 7928 9252 *email:* murieltaylor @lfo.co.uk. Kate Beresford, sec. *£2000 awarded annually to cellist aged 17-23 for advanced study. Send sae for further details. Application fee £15. Applications by 31 Jan.*

The Music Experience. NFMS, Francis House, Francis St, London SW1P 1DE *tel:* 020 7976 4930 *fax:* 020 7828 5504 *email:* tme@nfms.org.uk. Duncan Barker, projects offr; Robin Osterley, chief exec. *Funded by the Arts Council of England and BT, 1998-2001, offers voluntary mus societies:* Developing Music Life *awards up to £1500 for community development activities such as audience and performance development and society access;* New Horizons *Education and New Music Tours; the* Young Promoters *scheme to allow pupils to promote live mus in schools;* Come and Sing Days *to encourage first-time singers. Applications taken for all strands of the project throughout the year.*

The Musicas Fund. 18c Lambolle Place, London NW3 4PG *tel:* 020 7813 3539 *also fax; email:* musicas@compuserve.com. Vivienne Dimant, admin. *Annual awards for individual instrumentalists aged 5-18 for tuition fees, courses, inst purchase, travel. Applications by 31 Mar for auditions in spring.*

Music Sound Foundation. c/o 4 Tenterden St, Hanover Square, London W1A 2AY *tel:* 020 7355 4848 *fax:* 020 7355 4494. Janie Orr, admin. *Charitable trust aiming to provide funds for the educ of the public, and young people in particular, in all aspects of mus. Trustees meet twice a year, Mar and Sep.*

Myra Hess Trust. c/o Musicians Benevolent Fund, 16 Ogle St, London W1P 8JB *tel:* 020 7636 4481 *fax:* 020 7637 4307 *email:* sdolton@mbf.org.uk. Contact: awards and trusts administrator. *Limited number of awards towards p/grad fees, cost of inst or recital debut for exceptional young str players and pianists aged 20-28 beginning a performing career. Applications open from Nov for auditions in Jun. Application fee £10.*

The Nicholas Danby Trust. 72 Wandsworth Common Westside, London SW18 2ED *tel:* 020 8874 2757 *also fax.* Mrs M Danby, sec, admin. Robert Vincent, James O'Donnell, Patrick Russill, Catherine Ennis, John Ramsey, Mary Danby Calvert, Hal Danby, trustees. *Up to £5000 annually to be awarded biennially to an organ student of outstanding promise for p/grad conservatoire study outside their home tradition. Open to students from UK mus colleges for study elsewhere in Europe, and to conservatoire students from other European countries for study in UK. Applications by 31 May in year of award.*

Oppenheim-John Downes Memorial Trust. Reference 13, 36 Whitefriars St, London EC4Y 8BH. *Makes awards each Dec to deserving artists who are unable to pursue their vocation by reason of their poverty. Awards restricted to persons who are natural born British subjects, of parents both of whom are British subjects. Age range 30+. Closing date for applications 31 Oct.*

Peter Whittingham Awards. c/o Musicians Benevolent Fund, 16 Ogle St, London W1P 8JB *tel:* 020 7636 4481 *fax:* 020 7637 4307 *email: sdolton @mbf.org.uk. Contact: awards and trusts administrator. Annual award of £5000 open to individuals for projects in popular mus or jazz. Applications for course fees not accepted. Applications from Jul-Oct, interviews Nov; fee £10.*

Pocklington Apprenticeship Trust. RB of Kensington and Chelsea, Room 250, Town Hall, Hornton St, London W8 7NX *tel:* 020 7361 2239 *fax:* 020 7361 2764 *email:* socsho@rbkc.gov.uk. Susan Hollendoner, funding programmes admin. *Small educ awards for young people aged 21 and under in financial need, born and/or living in the Royal Borough for 10 years. Max grant awarded £300.*

Sir Richard Stapley Educational Trust. PO Box 57, Tonbridge, Kent TN9 1ZT. *Small grants worth £250-1000. For graduates aged over 24 on 1 Oct of the proposed academic year, with a first or upper-second class degree studying for higher degrees at a university in the UK, or courses considered to be equivalent to a higher degree by the university or conservatoire, and who are not in receipt of local authority, research council, British Academy or other similar public bodies awards. Send sae for application form. Applications to arrive between 1 Mar and 31 Mar, with two academic references in sealed envelopes.*

Royal College of Organists. 7 St Andrew St, Holborn, London EC4A 3LQ *tel:* 020 7936 3606 *fax:* 020 7353 8244 *email:* grants@rco.org.uk. Alan Dear, snr exec. *A number of trusts available to organists who are members of the College (non-members considered in exceptional circumstances). No age limit. Awards between £200 and £1200.*

Royal Hospital Millennium Church Music Scholarship. The Organist, 22 West Rd, Royal Hospital, Chelsea, London SW3 4SR *tel:* 020 7730 7395 *email:* curror@usa.net. Ian Curror, organist. *New annual scholarship (£3000) providing an aspiring young church musician with an opportunity to receive practical guidance, support and experience. Available to full-time mus students, aged 18-26, at recognised institutions of higher educ, living within easy reach of central London. Tenable for one academic year (Sep-Jul). Closing date for applications Mar 2000. Auditions and interviews May 2000.*

RVW Trust. 7th Floor, Manfield House, 1 Southampton St, London WC2 0LR *tel:* 020 7379 6547 *fax:* 020 7240 6333. Bernard Benoliel, admin and sec. *Founder, Ralph Vaughan Williams. Corporate Trustee, Musicians' Benevolent Fund. Assists with the cost of first Master's Degrees in mus composition (non electro-acoustic or screen) for British applicants or those of British residency. Does not consider applications towards cost of other degrees, summer courses or PhDs. Applications by early May.*

Ryan Davies Memorial Awards. 1 Squire Court, The Marina, Swansea SA1 3XB *tel:* 01792 301500 *also fax.* Michael Evans, sec. *Awards worth £500-2000 to assist young Welsh post-grads aged 16-30 in mus and drama. Applications by 30 May.*

Schools Music Association Founder's Fund. 71 Margaret Rd, New Barnet, Herts EN4 9NT *tel:* 020 8440 6919 *also fax.* Maxwell Pryce, hon sec, chief exec. *Small awards made to help with purchase costs of mus insts and summer schools available to British school pupils and students in FE and HE, aged 18 and under.*

Scottish Arts Council Travel and Training Bursaries. Performing Arts Dept (Music), 12 Manor Place, Edinburgh EH3 7DD *tel:* 0131 226 6051 *fax:* 0131 225 9833 *email:* helen.jamieson.sac@artsfb.org.uk. Helen Jamieson, mus offr. *Bursaries (usually up to £1500) for instrumentalists, singers, composers and conds to extend skills (f/t study excluded). Applicants of any age, must be based in Scotland and have worked in the profession for 2 years. Full details and application forms from the mus offr.*

Scottish International Education Trust. 22 Manor Place, Edinburgh EH3 7DS *tel:* 0131 225 1113 *also fax.* J F McClellan, dir. *Grants to promote individual Scottish talent or for projects contributing to the quality of life in Scotland. Over school age. Applications in writing to above address.*

Shell LSO Music Scholarship. London Symphony Orchestra, Barbican Centre, Barbican, London EC2Y 8DS *tel:* 020 7588 1116 *fax:* 020 7374 0127 *email:* shell@lso.co.uk. Helen Smith, admin. *Annual competition with a first prize of £6000 for orch instrumentalists aged 14-22. Auditions, w/shops and m/classes with LSO principals. 2000: perc. Applications by Dec.*

Awards for Advanced Study. South East Music Schemes, 19 Bourne Rd, London N8 9HJ *tel:* 020 8340 4116 *fax:* 020 8348 8894 *email:* hcandordarees@compuserve.com. Deborah Rees, dir. *Awards of up to £1000 for p/grad singers, instrumentalists and composers based in the SE Arts region, who may not receive mandatory awards towards further study in the UK or abroad. Aged 30 and under. Applications by 19 May 2000, 18 May 2001. Send sae or email for application form from Mar. Funded by South East Arts. Application fee (non-refundable) £15.*

Stephen Arlen Memorial Fund. London Coliseum, St Martin's Lane, London WC2N 4ES *tel:* 020 7845 9355 *fax:* 020 7845 9274. Teresa Howell, admin. *Autumn, applications by end of Feb 2000. Annual award of £3000 (may be split) to a UK resident aged 18-30, following a career in opera, mus, dance or drama for a specific project. This is specifically not intended for the funding of study or educ of any kind.*

Sybil Tutton Awards. c/o Musicians Benevolent Fund, 16 Ogle St, London W1P 8JB *tel:* 020 7636 4481 *fax:* 020 7637 4307. *Awards to assist exceptionally talented opera students aged 18-30 with the cost of training on a recognised course. Applications from Nov-Apr for auditions in May. Application fee £10.*

Tait Memorial Trust. 4/80 Elm Park Gardens, London SW10 9PD *tel:* 020 7351 0561 *fax:* 020 7349 0531. Isla Baring, chmn. *Awards for p/grad performance opportunities and general help in the furtherance of the careers of Australian musicians resident in the UK. Apply (include SAE) with tape, full CV and 2 references by 28 Mar. Awarded in May.*

Thalben-Ball Memorial Awards. St Michael's Vestry, Cornhill, London EC3V 9DS *tel:* 01737 244604; 020 7626 8841 *fax:* 01737 271128. Jonathan Rennert, trustee, hon sec. *Annual grants ranging from £100 to £2500 for young organists and church musicians of any nationality studying in the UK. Age limit usually 26. Applications by 1 Apr annually. Also funds available for annual scholarship for Assistant Organist at St Michael's Church, Cornhill, City of London. No fee for application.*

Sir Thomas Beecham Trust. 15 North Pallant, Chichester, W Sussex PO19 1TQ *tel:* 01243 789855. Lady Beecham, trustee. *Scholarships, tenable for 3 years, established in partnership with certain universities. Available to 1st year students studying for a mus degree and nominated by the university.*

Sir Thomas White's Educational Foundation. General Charities City of Coventry, Old Bablake, Hill St, Coventry CV1 4AN *tel:* 024 7622 2769 *also fax. Mus scholarship, tenable in a HE institution approved by*

Trustees. For students with local connections only. Ages 18-25. Advertised annually in local press.

Tillett Trust. Courtyard House, Neopardy, Crediton, Devon EX17 5EP. Katie Avey, admin. *Limited financial assistance to young professional musicians, usually aged under 30, of exceptional talent, to further their performing careers. British or residing f/t in British Isles. Award normally in £100 to £1000 range. No application forms available but write giving full CV, references and details of budget for project. Funds* not *available for the purchase of insts, for normal u/grad or p/grad courses, for funding commissions or commercial recordings.*

W T Best Memorial Scholarship. Worshipful Company of Musicians, 74-75 Watling Street, London EC4M 9BJ *tel:* 020 7489 8888 *fax:* 020 7489 1614. S F N Waley, clerk. *Provides financial assistance (£3000 a year for a maximum of 3 years) to an org scholar, aged 18-25, showing exceptional promise. Nominations from certain professors or principals of mus colleges.*

West Belfast Classical Bursary Award. 56 Oakhurst Ave, Blacks Rd, Dunmurry, Belfast BT10 0PF *tel:* 028 9062 6269 *also fax.* Una Downey, admin. *Open to all classical musicians born on the island of Ireland. Ages: 17-23 (instrumentalists); 18-30 (vocal) on 8 Mar. Entry by 12 Feb; entrance fee £7. Prize £10,000; BBC and RTE studio recordings; lunchtime concerts in Belfast plus concerts in Munich and Brussels. Bursary dates 26-29 Apr; finalists concert 29 Apr 2000.*

William Cox Memorial Fund for Young Singers. Badger Bungalow, 41 Findon Ave, Witton Gilbert, Durham DH7 6RF. Antony Elton, hon admin, hon trustee. *Grants to help very talented advanced students of professional solo singing to purchase scores, etc. For ages 19-29 inclusive. Trustees normally meet Mar, Jun and Oct. Awards at discretion of trustees and dependent on resources. Enquiries and applications by post only; those not sending sae will be ignored. No application fee.*

William Rushworth Memorial Trust. c/o Rushworths of Liverpool Ltd, 42-46 Whitechapel, Liverpool L1 6EF *tel:* 0151 709 9071 *fax:* 0151 709 9073. W D C Rushworth, sec. *For instrumentalists. Small awards for societies and individuals within 60-mile radius of Liverpool.*

Wingate Scholarships. 38 Curzon St, London W1Y 8EY. Jane Reid, admin. *Awards of up to £10,000 pa made to people undertaking original work in almost any field and to outstanding musicians for advanced training. Open to citizens of the UK, Commonwealth, Ireland or Israel resident in British Isles during period of application, and to EU citizens who have been resident in the UK for at least 5 years. All applicants should be aged 24 or over on 1 Sep. Applications by 1 Feb. Shortlisted candidates auditioned/interviewed in London during May and results announced in Jun.*

Worshipful Company of Musicians. 1st Floor, 74/75 Watling St, London EC4M 9BJ *tel:* 020 7489 8888 *fax:* 020 7489 1614 *email:* margareta@wcom.freeserve.co.uk. S F N Waley, clerk.

Yamaha Music Foundation of Europe. Yamaha-Kemble Music (UK) Ltd, Sherbourne Drive, Tilbrook, Milton Keynes MK7 8BL *tel:* 01908 366700 *fax:* 01908 368872 *email:* sian_monahan@infomta.post.yamaha.co.jp. Siân Monahan, co-ord. *3 scholarships of £2000 awarded annually to UK and international student performers on f/t courses at UK conservatoires, universities and tertiary educ colleges.*

Young Musicians' Recording Trust. 26 Cleveland Square, London W2 6DD *tel:* 020 7262 9066 *fax:* 020 7262 3235. Mark Sutton, admin. *Student recording scheme open to final year instrumentalist and singing students. Nominations from heads of mus colleges only.*

Scholarships for Study Abroad

Organisations

It is advisable to contact the Embassy or High Commission in Britain of the country in which you wish to study. The organisations below can provide information on opportunities in certain countries.

Association of Commonwealth Universities. Publication Sales, John Foster House, 36 Gordon Square, London WC1H 0PF *tel:* 020 7387 8572 *fax:* 020 7387 2655 *email:* info@acu.ac.uk. Sue Kirkland, head of mkt development. *Students and staff wishing to study in a country other than their own, primarily, but not exclusively, within the Commonwealth, should refer to the following publications available from the above address: Awards for First Degree Study at Commonwealth Universities; Awards for Postgraduate Study at Commonwealth Universities; Awards for University Teachers and Research Workers; Awards for University Administrators and Librarians.*

British Council. MIRC Overseas Appointments Services, Bridgewater House, 58 Whitworth St, Manchester M1 6BB *tel:* 0161 957 7755. Mark Hepworth, applications offr. *The British Council itself does not offer scholarships to attend courses outside the UK. The funds administered by the British Council are channelled through schemes which enable overseas students to study in Britain. For information about scholarships offered by the Chinese government, write to: British Embassy, 4th Floor Landmark Building, 8 North Dongsamhuan Rd, Chaoyang District, Peking 100026, PRC.*

Czech Ministry of Culture. Foreign Relations Dept, Milady Horákové 139 160 41, CZ-118 11 Praha 6, Czech Republic *tel:* 00 420 2 5708 5294 *fax:* 00 420 2 2432 4282 *email:* romanovr@mkcr.cz. Renata Romanova, British head desk offr. *Czech artists, agents or representatives may seek support directly from the Ministry of Culture of the Czech Republic. The Ministry of Culture liaises with the Embassy's Cultural Dept.*

Embassy of Brazil. 32 Green St, London W1Y 4AT *tel:* 020 7499 0877 *fax:* 020 7493 5105 *email:* ademar@infolondres.org.uk. Ademar Seabra da Cruz Junior, head of cultural section. *All requests for support should be addressed to the head of the Cultural Section at the Brazilian Embassy, which has a budget for support towards Brazilian cultural activity in the UK. The type and level of support is determined by each application. Proposals should be presented in writing or by fax and interviews will be arranged where appropriate. The cultural section of the Embassy can advise on sponsorship opportunities. It is essential that such requests be presented at least six months before the intended date of the recital or concert.*

Embassy of Mexico. Cultural Section, 42 Hertford St, London W1Y 7TF *tel:* 020 7499 8586 *fax:* 020 7495 4035. Juan Manuel Santin, minister for cultural affairs. *As part of a co-operative programme between the Mexican and British governments, the Mexican government offers student scholarships for Masters, PhDs, research, advanced conferences, high-level courses, residencies for collaborative academic research projects. Application deadlines vary. Students and researchers must establish individual contact with the appropriate university or institution and obtain written confirmation of their acceptance on their chosen course of study. More information can be found at these websites:* www.sre.gob.mx; www.sep.gob.mx/becas/dgri; www.anuies.mex; www.edumexico.org; www.studymexico; www.conacyt.mx; www.serpiente.dgsca.unam.mx; www.unam.mx/post-grado.

Embassy of Peru. 52 Sloane St, London SW1X 9SP *tel:* 020 7235 3802 *fax:* 020 7235 4463. Luis Escalante, cultural attaché. *The Peruvian Embassy does not have a budget to support the UK presentation of arts from Peru but can offer limited support, such as publicity in the Embassy's press releases, for selected projects. It cannot offer financial assistance directly to the promoter but can give selective advice on sponsorship opportunities. The Instituto Nacional de Cultura (INC) at Jiron Ancash 390, Lima 1, Peru, and the Ministry of Foreign Affairs can also advise on potential sources of private funding and sponsorship opportunities.*

Embassy of Venezuela. Bolívar Hall, 58 Grafton Way, London W1P 5LB *tel:* 020 7388 5788 *fax:* 020 7383 3253 *email:* embvenuk-ccm@dial.pipex.com. Gloria Carnevali, cultural attaché. *UK promoters seeking advice or support for projects should contact the Cultural Centre, which can liaise with the relevant Ministry in Venezuela. The Cultural Centre has a small budget to supplement some of the costs of projects involving the presentation of the Venezuelan arts in the UK. In order to qualify for a grant the project must be supported by an institution or an official body.*

German Academic Exchange Service. 34 Belgrave Square, London SW1X 8QB *tel:* 020 7235 1736 *fax:* 020 7235 9602 *email:* info@daad.org.uk. *Offers scholarships to p/grad students based at UK institutions of HE to study in Germany.*

The Italian Institute. The Bursary Dept, 39 Belgrave Square, London SW1X 8NX *tel:* 020 7235 1461 *fax:* 020 7235 4618 *email:* ici@italcultur.org.uk. Silvana Prosdocimo, educ offr. *Courses at art academies and mus conservatories. A final diploma in mus or art is required.*

Japan Information and Cultural Centre. The Embassy of Japan, 101-104 Piccadilly, London W1V 9FN *tel:* 020 7465 6500 *fax:* 020 7491 9347 *email:* jicc@jicc.demon.co.uk. Susan Meehan, educ offr. *The Embassy deals directly with the Japanese Ministry of Education (Monbusho) scholarship, which is annual and open to all UK passport holders aged 35 and under who have a first degree in any discipline. Scholarships are held for 18 months to 2 years, tenable from Apr or Oct. Participants spend the first 6 months on an intensive Japanese course, then pursue their specialist subject. Living expenses, a return air ticket and university fees are covered by the Japanese Government. Application forms available from Mar for scholarships taken up the following year. A maximum of 20 scholarships offered annually.*

The Polish Embassy. Education Officer, 34 Portland Place, London W1N 4HQ *tel:* 020 7636 6032 *fax:* 020 7637 2190 *email:* pci-lond@pcidir.demon.co.uk. *Provides details of study in Poland and administers the Polish Government Postgraduate Scholarship Scheme. This scheme enables exchanges to take place in the fields of sciences, humanities and arts, lasting from 3-9 months. The scholarship provides exemption from tuition fees, free medical care and book grants, but does not cover travel costs between the UK and Poland. Candidates must be British citizens aged under 35, and should hold at least a BA, BSc or equivalent degree. Application forms must be submitted by the end of Dec for the following year. 5 Polish government scholarships are available annually for 4-week 'Polonicum' Polish language courses held at the University of Warsaw, Jagiellonian University in Cracow and the Marie Curie-Sklodowska University in Lublin during the summer. Short visits to Poland are also available for individuals aged under 50 wishing to visit Poland for professional or academic purposes. Visits normally last 7-30 days and proposals should be submitted not later than 12 weeks prior to the proposed arrival date. Funding covers internal travel, accommodation and daily subsistence costs, but does not cover travel to and from Poland.*

Scholarships

Grants and Scholarships for Commonwealth students are listed in the *Awards for Postgraduate Study at Commonwealth Universities*, available from the Publications Dept, Association of Commonwealth Universities (*see* **Organisations for Study Abroad**). Some principal scholarships for study abroad are listed below, along with certain British educational trusts which provide scholarships for those wishing to study abroad.

Anna Instone Memorial Award. Capital Radio, 30 Leicester Square, London WC2H 7LA. Kevin Appleby, admin. *Award of £5000 for a p/grad student at a London mus college who must be nominated by the principal. Applications through nominators only by 1 Mar. Award may be used for study abroad.*

Arts Council of Wales Awards for Advanced Study in Music. Artform Development Division, 9 Museum Place, Cardiff CF10 3NX *tel:* 029 2037 6500 *Minicom:* 029 2039 0027 *fax:* 029 2022 1447 *email:* information@ccc-acw.org.uk. *Awards made to musicians aged 28 and under, born and educated in Wales. Also open to those now permanently resident in Wales and who, usually, have lived in Wales for 2 years. May be used for study in UK or abroad. Applications by 1 Feb annually.*

Australian Music Foundation. Beaufort House, 15 St Botolph St, London EC3A 7EE *tel:* 020 7247 6555 *fax:* 020 7247 5091 *email:* jfe@richardsbutler.com. John F Emmott, hon sec. *Major award for Australian singers and instrumentalists of p/grad or equivalent standard for advanced course of study in Europe. Aged under 30 on 31 Dec prior to application in Apr.*

Brandon University Graduate Assistantships. School of Music, Brandon University, Brandon, Manitoba, Canada R7A 6A9 *tel:* 00 1 204 727 9631 *fax:* 00 1 204 728 6839 *email:* music@brandonu.ca. *4-6 awards annually with value up to $C6,500, tenable at Brandon University for one year. For study leading to Master of Music degree. Applications by 1 May.*

ESTA Nannie Jamieson Nutshell Fund. 6 Ember Lane, Esher, Surrey KT10 8ER *tel:* 020 8398 4691 *also fax.* Sylvia Palmer, hon sec. *European String Teachers Association, British Branch. Modest bursaries awarded annually for students and teachers of str insts (ESTA members) for help to attend w/shops, conferences and teaching courses. May be used abroad. Applications by 1 May.*

Emanuel Hurwitz Chamber Music Charitable Trust. 44 Church Cres, London N3 1BJ. Miriam Keogh, founder, admin. *Bursaries for str players to further their studies in chmbr mus at home or abroad; college/university fees will not be paid although there is some help available with fees at RAM, RCM, RNCM, and Guildhall. Applications will only be accepted in writing with sae. Applications by 1 Jun, £15 fee. UK citizens only.*

English-Speaking Union Scholarships. The English-Speaking Union, Dartmouth House, 37 Charles St, London W1X 8AB, UK *tel:* 020 7493 3328 *fax:* 020 7495 6108 *email:* lucy_passmore@esu.org. Lucy Passmore, cultural affairs offr. *The ESU offers the following mus scholarships, varying from 3 to 9 weeks, to musicians of outstanding ability to study at summer schools in America, Canada and Europe: Aspen Music School, Tanglewood Music Center, Yale University School of Music (Norfolk Chamber Music Festival), Banff Centre for the Arts, Académie Internationale de Musique Maurice Ravel (France), Sándor Vegh International Chamber Music Academy (Prague) and IMS Prussia Cove. Applications in Nov for placements the following year.*

Fulbright Scholarships. Fulbright Commission, Fulbright House, 62 Doughty St, London WC1N 2LS *tel:* 020 7404 6880 *fax:* 020 7404 6834. Contact: programme dir. *Scholarships for 1st year of p/grad academic study and research in the US. Any discipline, must have or expect a 2:1 degree, possess UK citizenship and be able to demonstrate leadership qualities; deadline for submission of application forms is early Nov. Benefits include tuition fees and maintenance allowance including round-trip travel. Distinguished scholar awards are awarded to established or potential leaders in any field for a minimum of 10 months lecturing or research in the US. Applicants must be UK citizens. Application forms should be submitted by mid March. Benefits include £15,000 and limited health insurance. Also Fulbright Chester Shirmer Fellowship in Music Composition, to enable a young British composer to spend time in the US extending his/her artistic experience and developing an international reputation. P/grad educ must have been completed at least 2 years prior to application. Benefits include up to £12,000 pro rata (minimum stay 4 months), plus round trip travel. Further information and application forms for any of the above can be obtained by visiting the Commission's website or send large (A4) sae (for 100g) to British Programme Administrator for application form, stating clearly the award for which details are required.*

Harriet Cohen Memorial Music Awards Trust. Manches & Co, Aldwych House, 81 Aldwych, London WC2 *tel:* 020 7404 4433 *fax:* 020 7430 1133. John Rubinstein, admin trustee. *Annual awards to young British professional musicians which may be used for study or performances abroad. Aged under 30. Trust invites nominations from main mus institutions in rotation. No individual applications considered. Candidates will be auditioned and interviewed.*

Ian Fleming Music Education Awards. c/o Musicians Benevolent Fund, 16 Ogle St, London W1P 7LG *tel:* 020 7636 4481 *fax:* 020 7637 4307 *email:* sdolton@mbf.org.uk. Contact: awards and trusts administrator. *Awards for mus educ and help with inst purchase to outstanding young musicians beginning their career. May be used for study abroad. Aged under 25 (instrumentalists), 29 (singers). Application fee £10. Applications from Nov, auditions Apr.*

Julius Isserlis Scholarship. Royal Philharmonic Society, 10 Stratford Place, London W1N 9AE *tel:* 020 7491 8110 *fax:* 020 7493 7463 *email:* admin@rps-uk.demon.co.uk. Rosemary Johnson, gen admin. *Awarded biennially by competition to students aged 15-25, of any nationality, permanently resident in the UK. Selected performing categories: 2001, piano. For study abroad. Value £20,000 over 2 years. Entry fee £20. May 2001.*

Nadia and Lili Boulanger International Foundation. 25 ave des Gobelins, F-75013 Paris, France *tel:* 00 33 1 47 07 05 93 *fax:* 00 33 1 45 35 09 43. Alexandra Laederich, sec. *Scholarships are awarded to musicians of all nationalities studying in France and to scholars who propose research into the history or theory of mus who have shown ability for musical achievement and creativity. Open to those aged 20-35.*

The Nicholas Danby Trust. 72 Wandsworth Common Westside, London SW18 2ED *tel:* 020 8874 2757 *also fax.* Magaret Danby, chmn. *Applications by 31 May. Biennial award for an org student of outstanding promise for p/grad conservatoire study outside their home tradition. Open to UK students for study in the EU and EU students for study in the UK. Also help successful candidates to establish concert careers.*

Richard Tauber Prize. Anglo-Austrian Music Society, 46 Queen Anne's Gate, London SW1H 9AU *tel:* 020 7222 0366 *fax:* 020 7233 0293. Tony Fessler, gen sec. *Travel bursary and public recital in London open to British or Austrian singers. Next prize awarded in spring 2000.*

Scottish Arts Council Travel and Training Bursaries. Performing Arts Dept (Music), 12 Manor Place, Edinburgh EH3 7DD *tel:* 0131 226 6051 *fax:* 0131 225 9833 *email:* sac@artsfb.org.uk. Helen Jamieson, mus offr. *Bursaries to professional instrumentalists, singers, composers and conductors to extend expertise through study in UK or abroad. Bursaries cannot be made in connection with f/t study or training. Applicants must be Scottish based and have worked in the profession for 2 years. Awards unlikely to exceed £1500.*

South East Music Schemes. 19 Bourne Rd, London N8 9HJ *tel:* 020 8340 4116 *fax:* 020 8348 8894 *email:* hcandordarees@compuserve.com. Deborah Rees, dir. *Awards for p/grad singers, instrumentalists and composers who live (or have lived) in the South East Arts region and who may not receive mandatory awards towards further study in the UK or abroad. Aged 30 or under. Applications from Mar 2000 with sae closing date 19 May. Funded by South East Arts. Application fee (non-refundable) £15.*

Sybil Tutton Awards. c/o Musicians Benevolent Fund, 16 Ogle St, London W1P 8JB *tel:* 020 7636 4481 *fax:* 020 7637 4307 *email:* sdolton@mbf.org.uk. Contact: awards and trusts administrator. *Awards to assist exceptionally talented opera students at p/grad level aged under 30; intended primarily for maintenance. May be used for study abroad. Applications from Nov for auditions in Apr. Application fee £10.*

Winston Churchill Memorial Trust. 15 Queen's Gate Terrace, London SW7 5PR *tel:* 020 7584 9315 *fax:* 020 7581 0410 *email:* office@wcmt.org.uk. Miss R Conner, mgr. *Travelling fellowships in arts subjects, not necessarily mus. Applications June-Oct.*

Yamaha Music Foundation of Europe. Yamaha-Kemble Music (UK) Ltd, Sherbourne Drive, Tillbrook, Milton Keynes MK7 8BL *tel:* 01908 369235 *fax:* 01908 368872. R Bird. *3 scholarships of £2000 each; disciplines rotate annually.*

Youth Orchestras and Bands

This section is divided into lists of orchestras, wind bands and brass bands. Each list is subdivided under international, national, and regional and local headings. This subdivision is based upon the method and scope of the audition procedure, and from where the majority of players are drawn. Other orchestras which hold annual courses, but who do not audition and whose personnel change every year, are listed under **Summer Schools and Short Courses.** School, music college and university groups are not listed unless membership of the group is open to external applicants. Details of those county youth orchestras administered by local education authorities which are not listed here can be obtained from the Local Music Education Adviser.

An asterisk indicates membership of the **National Association of Youth Orchestras**, Ainslie House, 11 St Colme St, Edinburgh EH3 6AG *tel:* 0131 539 1087 *fax:* 0131 539 1069, which draws its members from both independent and LEA-run orchestras.

Youth Orchestras

International

European Union Baroque Orchestra. Hordley, Wootton, Woodstock OX20 1EP *tel:* 01993 812111 *fax:* 01993 812911 *email:* info@eubo.org.uk. Roy Goodman, mus dir; Paul James, gen admin; Emma Wilkinson, mgr; Nick Berry, development dir.

European Union Youth Orchestra. 65 Sloane St, London SW1X 9SH *tel:* 020 7235 7671 *fax:* 020 7235 7370 *email:* info@euyo.org.uk. Bernard Haitink, mus dir; Joy Bryer, gen sec.

Southbank International Youth Orchestra. c/o Southbank AIS, 36-38 Kensington Park, London W11 3BU *tel:* 020 7229 8230 *email:* bso @southbank.org. Beverly Sortland, dir.

Youth Orchestras - National

Britten-Pears Orchestra and Baroque Orchestra. Britten-Pears School for Advanced Musical Studies, High St, Aldeburgh, Suffolk IP15 5AX *tel:* 01728 452935 *fax:* 01728 452715 *email:* bps.admin@aldeburghfestivals.org. Elizabeth Webb, school dir; Ann Rawdon Smith, admin; Julia Robinson, asst admin.

* **Camerata Scotland.** NYOS, 13 Somerset Place, Glasgow G3 7JT *tel:* 0141 332 8311 *fax:* 0141 332 3915 *email:* nyos@cqm.co.uk. Richard Chester, dir.

* **ESO Children's Orchestra.** Rockliffe House, 40 Church St, Malvern, Worcs WR14 2AZ *tel:* 01684 560696 *fax:* 01684 560656 *email:* info@eso.co.uk. William Boughton, artistic/mus dir.

Guildhall School of Music and Drama, Junior Guildhall Symphony Orchestra. Junior School, Guildhall School of Music and Drama, Silk St, Barbican, London EC2Y 8DT *tel:* 020 7382 7160 *fax:* 020 7382 7212 *email:* junior@gsmd.ac.uk. Derek Rodgers, head; Frederick Applewhite, cond.

Jewish Youth Orchestra of Great Britain. 5 Bradby House, Carlton Hill, London NW8 9XE *tel:* 020 7624 1756. Sidney Fixman, dir of mus.

The London Philharmonic Youth Orchestra. County Hall, Riverside Building, Westminster Bridge Rd, London SE1 7PB *tel:* 020 7546 1600 *fax:* 020 7546 1601. Maria Smith, educ, Youth Orch admin.

London Schools Symphony Orchestra. Centre for Young Musicians, Morley College, 61 Westminster Bridge Rd, London SE1 7HT *tel:* 020 7928 3844 *fax:* 020 7928 3454. Oliver Butterworth, artistic dir, LSSO.

Methodist Association of Youth Clubs Orchestra. 25 Marylebone Rd, London NW1 5JR *tel:* 020 7486 5502 *fax:* 020 7935 1507 *email:* admin@mayc.mln.co.uk. Craig McLeish, dir.

National Children's Chamber Orchestra of Great Britain. The Bourne, 20 Salisbury Ave, Harpenden, Herts AL5 2QG *tel:* 01582 760014 *fax:* 01582 767343 *email:* HMusicale@aol.com. Gillian Johnston, David Johnston, mus dirs; Caroline Marriott, admin; Melanie Ragge, associate dir.

* **National Children's Orchestra.** 157 Craddocks Ave, Ashtead, Surrey KT21 1NU *tel:* 01372 276857 *fax:* 01372 271407 *email:* mail@ ncoorch.demon.co.uk. Vivienne Price MBE, dir of mus; Elisabeth Humphreys, admin.

* **The National Children's Orchestra of Scotland.** NYOS, 13 Somerset Place, Glasgow G3 7JT *tel:* 0141 332 8311 *fax:* 0141 332 3915 *email:* nyos@cqm.co.uk. Richard Chester, dir.

National Musicians Symphony Orchestra. 11 Gunnersbury Ave, London W5 3NJ *tel:* 020 8993 3135 *fax:* 020 8993 2635 *email:* nmso @dircon.co.uk. James Blair, artistic dir, principal cond.

National Youth Jazz Orchestra of Great Britain. 11 Victor Rd, Harrow, Middx HA2 6PT *tel:* 020 8863 2717 *fax:* 020 8863 8685 *email:* bill.ashton@virgin.net. Bill Ashton, dir of mus.

* **National Youth Jazz Orchestra of Scotland.** NYOS, 13 Somerset Place, Glasgow G3 7JT *tel:* 0141 332 8311 *fax:* 0141 332 3915 *email:* nyos@cqm.co.uk. Richard Chester, dir.

National Youth Music Theatre Orchestra. Fifth Floor, Palace Theatre, Shaftesbury Ave, London W1V 8AY *tel:* 020 7734 7478 *fax:* 020 7734 7515. Jeremy James Taylor, artistic dir; Jon Bromwich, gen mgr; Vivienne Hughes, outreach admin.

* **National Youth Orchestra of Great Britain.** 32 Old School House, Britannia Rd, Bristol BS15 8DB *tel:* 0117 960 0477 *fax:* 0117 950 0376 *email:* nyo@btinternet.com. Jill White, dir of mus; Michael de Grey, chief exec.

* **National Youth Orchestra of Scotland.** 13 Somerset Place, Glasgow G3 7JT *tel:* 0141 332 8311 *fax:* 0141 332 3915 *email:* nyos@cqm.co.uk. Richard Chester, dir.

* **National Youth Orchestra of Wales.** Welsh Joint Education Committee, 245 Western Ave, Cardiff CF5 2YX *tel:* 029 2026 5047 *fax:* 029 2057 5894 *email:* p.crossley@wjec.co.uk. Beryl Jones, admin; Pauline Crossley, expressive arts offr.

National Youth String Orchestra and String Training Orchestra of Scotland. Scottish Amateur Music Association, 18 Craigton Cres, Alva, Clackmannanshire FK12 5DS *tel:* 01259 760249 *email:* secretary @sama.org.uk. Margaret Simpson, hon sec; Mark Duncan, dir of mus.

* **National Youth Wind Orchestra of Great Britain.** 2 High Green, Woodham Village, Aycliffe, Co Durham DL5 4RZ *tel:* 01325 308893 *also fax.* Kit Shepherd, exec dir.

Pro Corda (The National School For Young Chamber Music Players). Leiston Abbey House, Theberton Rd, Leiston, Suffolk IP16 4TB *tel:* 01728 831354 *fax:* 01728 832500 *email:* procorda@procorda.demon.co.uk. Robert Max, mus dir; Sir Colin Davis, president; Pamela Spofforth MBE, dir emeritus; Mererid Crump, admin.

Rehearsal Orchestra. 60-62 Clapham Rd, London SW9 0JJ *tel:* 020 7820 9994 *email:* admin@rehearsal-orchestra.org. Katie Lang, admin; Harry Legge OBE, artistic dir.

Royal College of Music Junior Dept Symphony Orchestra. Junior Dept, Royal College of Music, Prince Consort Rd, London SW7 2BS *tel:* 020 7591 4334 *fax:* 020 7589 7740 *email:* phewitt@rcm.ac.uk. Peter Hewitt, dir, jnr dept; Neil Thomson, cond.

* **Royal Scottish Academy of Music and Drama Junior Academy Orchestra.** Junior Academy, Royal Scottish Academy of Music and Drama, 100 Renfrew St, Glasgow G2 3DB *tel:* 0141 332 4101 *fax:* 0141 353 0372 *email:* registry@rsamd.ac.uk. Anne Strachan, head of jnr academy.

Vacation Chamber Orchestras. Ashley House, Ure Bank, Ripon, N Yorks HG4 1JG *tel:* 01765 602856 *email:* vaco@bronco.co.uk. Xenophon Kelsey, mus dir.

Youth Orchestras - Regional and Local

Bedfordshire County Youth Orchestras. Emerald Court, Pilgrim Centre, 20 Brickhill Drive, Bedford MK41 7PZ *tel:* 01234 213439 *fax:* 01234 363516. John Shayler, asst mus service mgr.

* **Brighton Youth Orchestra.** Brighton Youth Orchestra Trust, University of Brighton, Falmer, Brighton BN1 9PH *tel:* 01273 643450 *fax:* 01273 643534 *email:* byo@bton.ac.uk. Andrew Sherwood, dir of mus, cond.

* **Bromley Youth Chamber Orchestra.** Bromley Youth Music Trust, Southborough Lane, Bromley, Kent BR2 8AA *tel:* 020 8467 1566 *fax:* 020 8468 7595. Nicholas Woodall.

* **Bromley Youth Symphony Orchestra.** Bromley Youth Music Centre, Southborough Lane, Bromley BR2 8AA *tel:* 020 8467 1566 *fax:* 020 8468 7595. Peter M Mawson, principal.

* **Cambridgeshire County Youth Orchestra.** CIMA, Ermine St North, The Old School, Papworth Everard, Cambs CB3 8RH *tel:* 01480 831695 *fax:* 01480 831696 *email:* peter.britton@education.camcnty.gov.uk. Peter Britton, dir.

* **Cardiff County and Vale of Glamorgan Youth Orchestra.** The Friary Centre, The Friary, Cardiff CF1 4AA *tel:* 029 2064 0950/1 *fax:* 029 2022 7471. Eric Phillips, mus dir; Stuart Burrows, president.

* **Cheshire Youth Orchestra.** Cheshire School of Music, Woodford Lodge Professional Centre, Woodford Lane West, Winsford, Cheshire CW7 4EH *tel:* 01606 557328 *fax:* 01606 862113. Valerie Hayward, orch dir; Timothy Redmond, principal cond.

* **City of Coventry Youth Orchestra.** Performing Arts Service Office, Leasowes Ave, Coventry CV3 6BH *tel:* 024 7669 2348 *fax:* 024 7669 2717. Brian Chappell, dir.

* **City of Hull Youth Symphony Orchestra.** The Albemarle Music Centre, Ferensway, Hull HU2 8LZ *tel:* 01482 223941 *fax:* 01482 320565. Chris Maynard, head of performing arts.

City of Sheffield Youth Orchestra. The Cottage, Park Head, Birds Edge, Huddersfield HD8 8XW *tel:* 01484 606114 *also fax; email:* woodh@cwcom.net. Edward Woodhead, dir; Christopher Gayford, cond.

* **Colchester Youth Chamber Orchestra.** Weltevreden, Mount Pleasant, Hundon, nr Sudbury, Suffolk CO10 8DW *tel:* 01440 786337 *also fax.* George Reynolds, dir of mus; Edna Robson, hon sec.

* **Cornwall Youth Orchestra.** c/o The Music Service, Dalvenie, County Hall, Truro TR1 3BA *tel:* 01872 323476 *fax:* 01872 225041. John A Harries, head of mus service.

Derbyshire City & County Youth Orchestra. Music Activities, Advisory and Inspection Service, John Hadfield House, Dale Rd, Matlock DE4 3RD *tel:* 01629 580000 ext 2771 *fax:* 01629 585466 *email:* dais.dcc@ukonline.co.uk. Philip King, adviser; Peter Stark, guest cond.

* **Dorset Youth Orchestras.** Dorset Music Service, Carter Community School, Blandford Close, Hamworthy, Poole BH15 4BQ *tel:* 01202 678233 *fax:* 01202 679381 *email:* dms@dorsetmusicservice.freeserve.co.uk. David Kenyon, dir.

* **Dudley Schools Symphony Orchestra.** Dudley Music Centre, Lawnwood Rd, Wordsley, Stourbridge DY8 5PQ *tel:* 01384 813865 *fax:* 01384 813866 *email:* keith.horsfall@nayo.org.uk. Gerald Johnson, head of service; Keith Horsfall, deputy head of service; Geoffrey Thomas, mus inspector.

* **Dundee Schools Symphony Orchestra.** Dundee City Council, Gardyne Rd, Dundee DD5 1NY *tel:* 01382 462857 *fax:* 01382 462862 *email:* advisers@educational-development-service.dundeecity.sch.uk. Charles Maynes, dir.

* **Edinburgh Youth Orchestra.** 92 St Alban's Rd, Edinburgh EH9 2PG *tel:* 0131 667 4648 *fax:* 0131 662 9169 *email:* marjory@ednet.co.uk. Marjory Dougal, admin; Christopher Adey, cond.

Enfield Young Symphony Orchestra. Enfield Arts Support Service, Aylward School, Windmill Rd, Edmonton, London N18 1NB *tel:* 020 8807 8881 *fax:* 020 8807 8213. Kim Kirk, orch mgr; Stephen Block, cond.

* **Fife Youth Jazz Orchestra.** Beath High School, Cowdenbeath, Fife *tel:* 01383 512114 *fax:* 01383 610589. Richard Michael, cond; Jim O'Malley, Denis Boyd, asst conds.

* **Fife Youth Orchestra.** Auchterderran Centre, Woodend Rd, Cardenden KY5 0NE *tel:* 01592 414785 *fax:* 01592 414641 *email:* gwilson@itasdarc.demon.co.uk. Graeme Wilson, adviser in mus, Fife Council.

Four Counties Youth Chamber Orchestra. c/o Rhondda Cynon Taff Education Department, The Education Centre, Grawen St, Porth CF39 0BU *tel:* 01443 687666 *fax:* 01443 680286. Simon Thomas, cond.

Four Counties Youth Orchestra. c/o ESIS, G5, Treforest Industrial Estate, Pontypridd CF37 5YL *tel:* 01443 845400 *fax:* 01443 842639 *email:* esis@aol.com. Kevin Adams, cond.

* **Goldsmiths' Youth Orchestras.** PACE, Goldsmiths College, University of London, Lewisham Way, London SE14 6NW *tel:* 020 7919 7171 *fax:* 020 7919 7223. Elinor Corp, cond.

* **Grimsby, Cleethorpes and District Youth Orchestra.** 102 Woodhall Drive, Waltham, Grimsby DN37 0UT *tel:* 01472 827661. Mrs S Parr, sec; Leo Solomon, chmn.

* **Hackney Youth Orchestras.** c/o Stoke Newington School, Clissold Rd, London N16 *tel:* 020 7286 4897. Mladen Stankovic, dir.

Hemsted Forest Youth Orchestra. Music Dept, Benenden School, Cranbrook, Kent TN17 4AA *tel:* 01580 242030 *fax:* 01580 240280. Patricia M Gane, dir of mus, cond.

Hull Philharmonic Youth Orchestra. 11 Lynwood Ave, Anlaby, Hull HU10 7DP *tel:* 01482 651128. J B Harston, sec.

Jordan Junior Strings. 17 Meadow Cottages, Little Kingshill, Great Missenden, Bucks HP16 0DX *tel:* 01494 862861 *email:* elaine.jordan@virgin.net. Elaine Bonner, dir.

* **Lydian Orchestra.** 1 Molyneux Park Gardens, Tunbridge Wells, Kent TN4 8DL *tel:* 01892 530548. Victor Clements, chmn.

* **Merseyside Youth Orchestra.** Philharmonic Hall, Hope St, Liverpool L1 9BP *tel:* 0151 210 2895 *fax:* 0151 210 2902. L Clark Rundell, mus dir; Andrew Bentley, dir of community educ.

* **Midland Youth Orchestra.** c/o 3 Armour Close, Burbage, Hinckley, Leics LE10 2QW *tel:* 01455 890528. Stephen Williams, mus dir; Anthony Bradbury, principal cond; James Ross, associate cond; Caroline Jephcott, sec.

Milton Keynes Symphony Orchestra. Milton Keynes Music Centre, Stantonbury Campus, Stantonbury, Milton Keynes MK14 6BN *tel:* 01908 224250 *fax:* 01908 224201.

North Lincolnshire Schools Orchestras. North Lincolnshire Music Support Service, c/o John Leggott College, West Common Lane, Scunthorpe DN17 1DS *tel:* 01724 297157 *fax:* 01724 863907. S Fareham, head of service; E Hardy, deputy head of service; S Russell, co-ord.

North Norfolk Youth Orchestra. 11 Cromwell Close, Cromer, Norfolk NR27 0DE *tel:* 01263 511433/512129 *fax:* 01263 515378 *email:* rbaker@rbaker.free-online.co.uk. Richard Baker, dir; Keith Paterson, treasurer; Norman Moor, Alan Morris, associate conds.

Northamptonshire County Youth Orchestra. Northamptonshire County Music Service, 125-129 Kettering Rd, Northampton NN1 4AZ *tel:* 01604 637117 *fax:* 01604 603070. Peter Dunkley, cond, head of mus service.

* **Perth Youth Orchestra.** 20 Spoutwells Rd, Scone PH2 6RW *tel:* 01738 551162. Hazel Mackinnon, sec.

Reading Youth Orchestra. 69 Bulmershe Rd, Reading RG1 5RP *tel:* 0118 926 1506/926 1828 *fax:* 0118 926 3070. Rupert D'Cruze, dir.

Ripon Youth String Ensemble. Ashley House, Ure Bank, Ripon, N Yorks HG4 1JG *tel:* 01765 602856. Xenophon Kelsey, mus dir.

Solihull Youth Orchestras. Education Dept, Council House, Solihull, W Midlands B91 3QU *tel:* 0121 704 6619 *fax:* 0121 704 8065. Joyce Rothschild, mus inspector; Tim Low, head of mus service; Richard Hart, asst head of service.

South East Surrey Area Youth Orchestra. South East Surrey Music Centre, Longmead Adult Education Centre, Holland Close, Redhill, Surrey RH1 1HT *tel:* 01737 778890 *fax:* 01737 780380 *email:* musarts@sympa.org.uk. Christopher Pratt, cond.

* **Southampton Youth Orchestra.** Southampton Music Service, 5th Floor Frobisher House, Nelson Gate, Southampton SO15 1GX *tel:* 023 8083 3635 *fax:* 023 8083 3324 *email:* plitchfield@sccms.freeserve.co.uk. Keith Smith, mus dir, cond.

* **Stoneleigh Youth Orchestra.** 52 Manor Rd, Teddington, Middx TW11 8AB *tel:* 020 8943 2661 *fax:* 020 8977 4653. Christine Blake, admin.

* **Strathclyde Youth Jazz Orchestra.** Dept of Applied Arts, University of Strathclyde, Jordanhill Campus, 76 Southbrae Drive, Glasgow G13 1PP *tel:* 0141 950 3476 *fax:* 0141 950 3314. Bobby Wishart, mus dir, admin.

* **Suffolk Youth Orchestra.** County Music Service, Northgate Arts Centre, Sidegate Lane West, Ipswich, Suffolk IP4 3DF *tel:* 01473 281866 *fax:* 01473 286068 *email:* philip.shaw@educ.suffolkcc.gov.uk. Philip Shaw, head of county mus service, cond.

Swale Youth String Orchestra. Swale Music Centre, Highsted School, Highsted Rd, Sittingbourne, Kent ME10 4PT *tel:* 01795 420586. Alan Parris, head of Swale Music Centre.

Symphony Orchestra. Milton Keynes Music Centre, Milton Keynes Music Service, Stantonbury Campus, Stantonbury, Milton Keynes MK14 6BN *tel:* 01908 224250 *fax:* 01908 225271.

Thames Vale Youth Orchestra. 6 Park Rd, Abingdon OX14 1DS *tel:* 01235 530774 *fax:* 01865 267749 *email:* tvyo@aol.com. J Elloway, chmn; M Stinton, dir of mus.

Ulster Youth Orchestra. Chamber of Commerce House, 22 Gt Victoria St, Belfast BT2 7LX *tel:* 028 9027 8287 *fax:* 028 9033 3845. Helen Henson, gen mgr.

Warrington and District Youth Orchestra. 338 London Rd, Appleton, Warrington, Cheshire WA4 5PW *tel:* 01925 265456. Mrs J Bingham, chmn.

* **Warwickshire County Youth Orchestra.** Education Office, 22 Northgate St, Warwick CV34 4SR *tel:* 01926 412803 *also fax; email:* cms@warwickshire.gov.uk. Ray Hutchinson, head of youth mus.

* **West Norfolk Jubilee Youth Orchestra.** The Dairies, Stoney Rd, Roydon, King's Lynn, Norfolk *tel:* 01485 600792. S Corbett, sec; Joan Hooke, head of orch; Robin Norman, head of band.

* **West of England Schools' Symphony Orchestra.** Education School Services, PO Box 25 Riverside, Keynsham, Bristol BS31 1DN *tel:* 01225 395119 *fax:* 01225 395147. J L Fowles, orch co-ord.

Wirral Schools' Orchestras. Education Centre, Acre Lane, Bromborough, Wirral L62 7BZ *tel:* 0151 343 1783 *fax:* 0151 343 9352 *email:* philchapman@yahoo.com. Philip Chapman, dir.

York Area Schools Symphony Orchestra. Whitecross Lodge, 150 Haxby Rd, York YO31 8JN *tel:* 01904 673436 *also fax*. Alison Goffin, head of mus centre; Gill Cooper, mgr of performing arts service.

* **Young Sinfonia.** The Sinfonia Centre, 41 Jesmond Vale, Newcastle upon Tyne NE2 1PG *tel:* 0191 240 1812 *fax:* 0191 240 2668 *email:* nsinfonia@ndirect.co.uk. Baldur Brönnimann, cond; Andrea Stafford, gen manager

Wind Bands - National

National Children's Wind Ensemble of Great Britain. The Bourne, 20 Salisbury Ave, Harpenden, Herts AL5 2QG *tel:* 01582 760014 *fax:* 01582 767343 *email:* HMusicale@aol.com. Gillian and David Johnston, dirs; Caroline Marriott, admin; Melanie Ragge, associate dir.

National Children's Wind Orchestra of Great Britain. The Bourne, 20 Salisbury Ave, Harpenden, Herts AL5 2QG *tel:* 01582 760014 *fax:* 01582 767343 *email:* HMusicale@aol.com. Gillian Johnston, David Johnston, mus dirs; Caroline Marriott, admin.

National Youth Wind Ensemble and Wind Band of Scotland. Scottish Amateur Music Association, 18 Craigton Cres, Alva, Clackmannanshire FK12 5DS *tel:* 01259 760249. Margaret Simpson, hon sec; Charles Maynes, dir of mus.

Wind Bands - Regional and Local

Ashford Youth Wind Orchestra. c/o Kent Music School, The Master's House, College Rd, Maidstone, Kent ME15 6IQ *tel:* 01622 691212 *fax:* 01622 688544 *email:* kmsho@cix.compulink.co.uk. Tony Spencer, dir.

BYMT West Berkshire Concert Band. Trinity School, Church Rd, Newbury, Berks RG13 2DU *tel:* 01635 48814 *fax:* 01635 522732 *email:* Simon_Salisbury@bymt.ccmail.compuserve.com. Simon Salisbury.

* **Barnet Schools Wind Orchestra.** Music Office, Educational Services, Friern Barnet Lane, London N11 3DL *tel:* 020 8359 3111 *fax:* 020 8359 3105. James Williams, dir of mus and cond.

Bedfordshire County Bands. Emerald Court, Pilgrim Centre, 20 Brickhill Drive, Bedford MK41 7PZ *tel:* 01234 213439 *fax:* 01234 363516. John Shayler, asst mus service mgr (courses).

Birmingham Schools Wind Orchestra. Music Centre, Martineau Education Centre, Balden Rd, Harborne, Birmingham B32 2EH *tel:* 0121 303 1175 *fax:* 0121 303 8304. John Wesley-Barker, cond, admin.

Bodmin Community College Band. Lostwithiel Rd, Bodmin, Cornwall PL31 1DD *tel:* 01208 72114 *fax:* 01208 78680. Adrian Evans, dir of mus.

* **Bromley Youth Concert Band.** Bromley Youth Music Centre, Southborough Lane, Bromley BR2 8AA *tel:* 020 8467 1566 *fax:* 020 8468 7595. Peter Mawson, cond.

Canterbury Music Centre. 1 Pound Lane, Canterbury, Kent CT1 2BZ. Kerry Boyle.

Cardiff County and Vale of Glamorgan Youth Wind Band. The Friary Centre, The Friary, Cardiff CF1 4AA *tel:* 029 2064 0950/1 *fax:* 029 2022 7471. Peter Knight, mus dir.

Derbyshire City & County Youth Wind Band. Music Activities, Advisory and Inspection Service, John Hadfield House, Dale Rd, Matlock DE4 3RD *tel:* 01629 580000 ext 2771. Philip King, adviser; Murray Slater, cond.

Dorset Youth Concert Band. Dorset Music Service, Carter Community School, Blandford Close, Hamworthy, Poole, Dorset BH15 4BQ *tel:* 01202 678233 *fax:* 01202 679381 *email:* d.kenyon@rmplc.co.uk. David Kenyon, head of Dorset Music.

Durham County Wind Ensemble. 63 Mowbray Rd, Catterick Village, N Yorks DL10 7LB *tel:* 01748 818585. Steve Down, mus dir.

Enfield Youth Wind Band. Enfield Arts Support Service, Windmill Rd, Edmonton, London N18 1NB *tel:* 020 8807 8881 *fax:* 020 8807 8213. Helen Jenkins, activities co-ord.

* **Fife Youth Concert Band.** Auchterderran Centre, Woodend Rd, Cardenden KY5 0NE *tel:* 01592 414785 *fax:* 01592 414641 *email:* gwilson@itasdarc.demon.co.uk. Graeme Wilson, adviser in mus, Fife Council.

Four Counties Youth Wind Band. Education and Leisure Services, Sunnyside, Bridgend CF31 4AR *tel:* 01656 642658 *fax:* 01656 642646. David Hughes, cond.

Hampshire County Youth Wind Orchestra. Hampshire Music Centre, Gordon Rd, Winchester SO23 7DD *tel:* 01962 861502 *fax:* 01962 863690 *email:* edmsmcla@hants.gov.uk. Jill Larner, snr mgr; David Woodgates, cond.

Harrogate and Skipton Area Schools Concert Band. 3 Royd Place, Cononley, Keighley, W Yorks BD20 8JT *tel:* 01535 636823. Bernard G Tierney, dir of mus.

High Wycombe Music Centre Concert Band. Sands Middle School, Mill End Rd, High Wycombe, Bucks *tel:* 01494 445947 *fax:* 01494 442773. Andy Rogers, cond.

Highbury Area Band. 19 Brunswick Gardens, Bedhampton Havant, Hants PO9 3HZ *tel:* 023 9246 2614 *fax:* 023 9259 5799. B H Strugnell, chmn; Mrs B Boyer, mgr.

Isle of Wight Youth Concert Band. 9 Elm Close, Ryde, Isle of Wight PO33 1ED *tel:* 01983 565675 *also fax*. Martyn Stroud, dir of mus.

Kent Youth Wind Orchestra. Kent Music School, College Rd, Maidstone, Kent ME15 6YQ *tel:* 01622 691212 *fax:* 01622 661318 *email:* kmsho@cix.compulink.co.uk. Alan Hutt, dir of mus; Phillip Hyde, mgr.

Mancunian Winds. Zion Arts Centre, Stretford Rd, Manchester M15 5ZA *tel:* 0161 226 4411/22 *fax:* 0161 226 1010 *email:* musicservice@manchester.gov.uk. Allan Jones, head of mus service.

Milton Keynes Music Centre Wind Orchestra. Milton Keynes Music Service, Stantonbury Campus, Stantonbury, Milton Keynes MK14 6BN *tel:* 01908 224250 *fax:* 01908 225271.

North Tyneside Concert Band. School Services, Stephenson House, Stephenson St, North Shields NE30 1QA *tel:* 0191 200 5025 *fax:* 0191 200 6091 *email:* nteaiv@rmplc.co.uk. R Harrison, cond.

Northallerton Area Wind Orchestra. Northallerton Music Centre Office, c/o Bedale High School, Fitzalan Rd, Bedale, N Yorks DL8 2EQ *tel:* 01677 422070. Trevor Wilson, dir.

Shrewsbury Concert Band. 9 Greyfriars Rd, Longden Coleham, Shrewsbury SY3 7EN *tel:* 01743 367482 *fax:* 01743 340412. Mike Dutton, chmn; Shelley Holloway, sec.

Solihull Youth Wind Band. Lyndon Music Centre, Daylesford Rd, Solihull, W Midlands B92 8EJ *tel:* 0121 743 2483 *fax:* 0121 743 5682. Tim Low, head of mus service; Clive Allsopp, inst teacher.

South East Surrey Area Wind Band. South East Surrey Music Centre, Longmead Adult Education Centre, Holland Close, Redhill, Surrey RH1 1HT *tel:* 01737 778890 *fax:* 01737 780380 *email:* musarts@sympa.org.uk. Hugh Craig, cond.

* **Suffolk Youth Wind Band.** County Music Service, Northgate Arts Centre, Sidegate Lane West, Ipswich, Suffolk IP4 3DF *tel:* 01473 281866 *fax:* 01473 286068 *email:* philip.shaw@educ.suffolkcc.gov.uk. Philip Shaw, head of county mus service; Sue Taylor, cond.

Surrey County Youth Wind Orchestra. South East Surrey County Music Centre, Longmead Adult Education Centre, Holland Close, Redhill, Surrey RH1 1HT *tel:* 01737 778890 *fax:* 01737 780380 *email:* scywo@netcomuk.co.uk. Hugh Craig, cond.

Swale Youth Wind Orchestra. Swale Music Centre, Highsted School, Highsted Rd, Sittingbourne, Kent ME10 4PT *tel:* 01795 420586. Alan Parris, head of Swale mus centre.

Trafford Youth Concert Band. 17 Abington Rd, Sale, Cheshire M33 3DL *tel:* 0161 969 3301 *email:* enquiry@tyos.freeserve.co.uk. Anthony Houghton, cond.

Tutbury Junior Band. 62 Station Rd, Rolleston on Dove, Burton upon Trent DE13 9AA *tel:* 01283 814703. Malcolm Heywood, cond; Barbara Harvey, sec.

Warwickshire County Youth Wind Band. 22 Northgate St, Warwick CV34 4SP *tel:* 01926 412803 *also fax*. Jim Norden, dir.

West of England Schools' Symphonic Wind Band and Orchestra. Education School Services, PO Box 25 Riverside, Keynsham, Bristol BS31 1DN *tel:* 01225 395119 *fax:* 01225 395147. J L Fowles, orch co-ord.

West Kent Youth Wind Band. Kent Music School, The Master's House, College Rd, Maidstone, Kent ME15 6YQ *tel:* 01622 765072. Alun Cook, faculty head of w/wind.

West Wiltshire Concert Band. Wiltshire Music Centre, Ashley Rd, Bradford-on-Avon, Wilts BA15 1DZ *tel:* 01225 860116 *fax:* 01225 860117. V S Blay, mus dir.

Wirral Schools' Concert Band. Education Office, Hamilton Building, Conway St, Birkenhead CH41 4FD *tel:* 0151 666 4324 *fax:* 0151 666 4207. David Straughan, school mus inspector.

York Area Schools' Senior Concert Band. White Cross Lodge, 150 Haxby Rd, York YO31 8JN *tel:* 01904 673436 *also fax*. Gill Cooper, mgr of performing arts.

Brass Bands - National

National Youth Brass Band of Great Britain. 21 The Coppice, Impington, Cambridge CB4 4PP *tel:* 01223 234090 *also fax;* 07710 505689 *email:* nybbgb@bandstand.demon.co.uk. Philip Biggs, admin; Roy Newsome, mus dir.

National Youth Brass Band of Scotland. Scottish Amateur Music Association, 18 Craigton Cres, Alva, Clackmannanshire FK12 5DS *tel:* 01259 760249 *email:* secretary@sama.org.uk. Margaret Simpson, hon sec; Neil Cross, dir of mus.

National Youth Brass Band of Wales. c/o Welsh Amateur Music Federation, Ty Cerdd, 15 Mount Stuart Square, Cardiff CF10 5DP *tel:* 029 2046 5700 *fax:* 029 2046 2733. Keith Griffin, admin; Edward Gregson, president; James Watson, mus adviser.

Brass Bands - Regional and Local

Beaumaris and District Youth Band. Boston Villa, Llanddaniel, Anglesey LL60 5DY *tel:* 01248 421509. G Evans.

Cardiff County and Vale of Glamorgan Youth Brass Band. The Friary Centre, The Friary, Cardiff CF1 4AA *tel:* 029 2064 0950/1 *fax:* 029 2022 7471. Keith Griffin, mus dir.

Cheshire Youth Brass Band. Cheshire School of Music, The Professional Centre, Woodford Lodge, Woodford Lane West, Winsford, Cheshire CW7 4EH *tel:* 01606 557328 *fax:* 01606 862113. Sandy Blair, dir.

Dobcross Youth Band. 42 Sandy Lane, Dobcross, Oldham, Lancs OL3 5AG *tel:* 01457 870895. Jenny Wood, sec.

East Riding Youth Brass Band. South Cattleholmes, Wansford, Driffield, E Riding of Yorks YO25 8NW *tel:* 01377 254293. Mrs M A Buckton, sec.

Greater Gwent Youth Brass Band. Gwent Music Support Service, Melfort Rd, Newport, South Wales NP20 3FP *tel:* 01633 223196 *fax:* 01633 252051. Alun F Williams.

Guildhall School of Music and Drama Brass Band. Junior School, Guildhall School of Music and Drama, Silk St, Barbican, London EC2Y 8DT *tel:* 020 7382 7160 *fax:* 020 7382 7212 *email:* junior@gsmd.ac.uk. Derek Rodgers, head; John Miller, cond.

Hampshire County Youth Band. Hampshire Music Centre, Gordon Rd, Winchester, Hants SO23 7DD *tel:* 01962 861502 *fax:* 01962 863690 *email:* edmsmclr@hants.gov.uk. Leighton Rich, cond.

Hathern Youth Band. 10 St Peters Ave, Hathern, Loughborough, Leics LE12 5JL *tel:* 01509 842813. Mrs M Spencer, sec.

Northamptonshire County Youth Brass Band. Northamptonshire County Music Service, 125-129 Kettering Rd, Northampton NN1 4AZ *tel:* 01604 637117 *fax:* 01604 603070. Rachel Coles, cond; Peter Dunkley, head of mus service.

Oldham Music Centre Youth Band. Oldham Music Centre, Lyceum Building, Union St, Oldham, Lancs OL1 1QG *tel:* 0161 627 2332 *fax:* 0161 620 0259. M Evans, head of br teaching.

Poynton Youth Brass Band. 21 Hollymount Gardens, Offerton, Stockport, Cheshire SK2 7NE *tel:* 0161 487 1989. F Cox.

Ratby Co-operative Junior Band. 12 Oxford Rd, Desford, Leics LE9 9JN *tel:* 01455 823883. Mrs L Plant.

Rotherham Schools Youth Brass Band. Parkhurst Teachers Centre, Doncaster Rd, Rotherham, S Yorks S65 2BL *tel:* 01709 828191 *fax:* 01709 379601 *email:* music.rmbc@btinternet.com. Jeremy Wade, cond.

St Helens Youth Brass Band, Training Band and Beginners Band. 20 Birchwood Drive, Lower Peover, Knutsford, Cheshire WA16 9QJ *tel:* 01565 722590 *also fax*. Miss L Nicholson, cond.

Spennymoor Youth Band. 12 Co-operative Terrace, Coxhoe, Co Durham DH6 4DQ *tel:* 0191 377 0454. Mrs E M Jackson.

Stantonbury Brass Band. Milton Keynes Music Service, Stantonbury Campus, Stantonbury, Milton Keynes MK14 6BN *tel:* 01908 224250 *fax:* 01908 225271.

Stockport Schools' Senior and Intermediate Bands. 6 Oakland Ave, Dialstone Lane, Stockport SK2 6AX *tel:* 0161 285 0869 *also fax*. Gill Scourfield, admin.

Wakefield Metropolitan Band and Schools Band. Band Room 1-2, Manygates Adult Education Centre, Manygates Lane, Wakefield *tel:* 01924 257643 *also fax; email:* roybusby@aol.com. R Busby, mgr.

Wirral Schools' Brass Band. Professional Development Centre, Acre Lane, Bromborough, Wirral CH62 7BZ *tel:* 0151 343 1783 *fax:* 0151 343 9352 *email:* AMBrass1@aol.com. A Milnes, head of br teaching.

Youth Choirs

The Youth Choirs listed below are divided under national, regional and local headings, depending on the method and scope of the audition procedure and from where the majority of performers are drawn. A list of **Youth Opera and Music Theatre** companies appears at the end of the section.

National

British Methodist Youth Choir. 35 Westwood Rd, Sutton Coldfield, W Midlands B73 6UP *tel:* 0121 605 8766 *also fax; email:* gjones@mcmail.com. Gilbert Jones, admin; Ashley Thompson, cond.

Laudibus - The National Youth Chamber Choir. c/o Chameleon Arts Management, 32 St Michael's Rd, Sandhurst, Berks GU47 8HE *tel:* 01252 873313 *fax:* 01252 871517 *email:* camarts@dial.pipex.com. Mike Brewer, mus dir.

National Children's Choir of Great Britain. PO Box 1628, Andover, Hants SP10 1NU *fax:* 01264 710768. Lissa Gray, mus dir; Rhonda Smith, development dir; Sue Milton, admin.

National Youth Choirs of Great Britain. PO Box 67, Holmfirth, Huddersfield, W Yorks HD7 1GQ *tel:* 01484 687023 *fax:* 01484 681635. Carl Browning, exec dir; Michael Brewer OBE, mus dir; Danny Curtis, choir admin.

National Youth Choir of Scotland and Chamber Choir. 18 Polmont Park, Falkirk FK2 0XT *tel:* 01324 711749 *fax:* 01324 713746 *email:* nycos@ednet.co.uk. Robert Tait, admin; Christopher Bell, artistic dir, cond.

National Youth Choir of Wales. Welsh Amateur Music Federation, Ty Cerdd, 15 Mount Stuart Square, Cardiff CF10 5DP *tel:* 029 2046 5700 *fax:* 029 2046 2733. Keith Griffin, dir; Bryn Terfel, president; Jean Stanley Jones.

The Rodolfus Choir. The Shepherd's Cottage, Great Shelford, Cambridge CB2 5JX *tel:* 01223 845685 *fax:* 01223 841980 *email:* r.allwood@etoncollege.org.uk. Ralph Allwood, cond; Lydia Smallwood, admin.

Regional and Local

Alicia Bardsley Singers. 22 Greek St, Stockport SK3 8AB *tel:* 0161 429 7413 *also fax.* K Mullen, admin; Alicia Bardsley, cond.

Berkshire Boys' Choir. Berkshire Young Musicians Trust, Stoneham Court, 100 Cockney Hill, Reading RG30 4EZ *tel:* 0118 901 2350 *fax:* 0118 901 2351. Gillian Dibden, cond.

Berkshire Girls' Choir. Berkshire Young Musicians Trust, Stoneham Court, 100 Cockney Hill, Reading RG30 4EZ *tel:* 0118 901 2350 *fax:* 0118 901 2351. Gillian Dibden, dir.

Berkshire Youth Choir. Berkshire Young Musicians Trust, Stoneham Court, 100 Cockney Hill, Reading, Berks RG30 4EZ *tel:* 0118 901 2350 *fax:* 0118 901 2351. Gillian Dibden, choral dir.

Boden Show Choir. 6-12 Windmill Hill, Enfield, Middx EN2 6SA *tel:* 020 8367 2692 *fax:* 020 8367 1836 *email:* aboden2387@aol.com. Adam Boden, choral dir; Robert Hyman, choirmaster.

The Bradford Choristers. 8 Moorcroft, Eldwick, nr Bingley, Yorkshire BD16 3DR *tel:* 01274 774758. Ann Foster, sec; Richard Darke, mus dir.

Bridgwater Young People's Choir. 11 Morgans Rise, Bishops Hull, Taunton, Somerset TA1 5HW *tel:* 01823 252658 *also fax.* Andrew Maddocks, cond; Ann Fisher, sec.

Bromley Youth Choir. Bromley Youth Music Trust, Bromley Youth Music Centre, Southborough Lane, Bromley, Kent BR2 8AA *tel:* 020 8467 1566 *fax:* 020 8468 7595. Charles Vignoles, dir of choral studies, cond BYCC; Lesley Cooper, cond BYSC, BYJC.

Caerphilly Children's Choir. Plasyfelin Junior School, Churchill Park, Caerphilly CF83 3FT *tel:* 029 2085 2523. Nigel Jones, mus dir.

Calne Girls' Choir. 18 Wyvern Ave, Calne, Wilts SN11 8NZ *tel:* 01249 817470 *also fax.* Geoffrey Field, dir.

Cambridgeshire Boys' Choir. 35 Acorn Ave, Bar Hill, Cambridge CB3 8DT *tel:* 01954 780307 *also fax;* 07785 597837 *email:* cambridgeshire.boys.choir@dial.pipex.com. Nicholas Bergstrom-Allen, dir.

Cantamus. c/o Camerata, 4 Margaret Rd, Birmingham B17 0EU *tel:* 0121 426 6208 *fax:* 0121 608 0676. Sheila Haslam, sec; Pamela Cook MBE, dir.

Cantate Youth Choir. 106 Potter St, Harlow, Essex CM17 9AW *tel:* 01279 304746 *also fax; email:* cantatechoir@compuserve.com. Michael Kibblewhite, mus dir; Dawn Helder, gen mgr; Jan Eke, mkt mgr.

Cantores Novae. 269 Dobcroft Rd, Sheffield S11 9LG *tel:* 0114 235 0993 *fax:* 0114 235 1883. Vivien Pike, cond.

Capital Arts Children's Choirs. Wyllyotts Centre, Wyllyotts Place, Darkes Lane, Potters Bar, Herts EN6 2HN *tel:* 020 8449 2342; 01707 653800 *also fax.* Kathleen Shanks, mus dir; Pamela Horsepool, sec.

Capital Arts Show Choir. Wyllyotts Centre, Wyllyotts Place, Darkes Lane, Potters Bar, Herts EN6 2HN *tel:* 020 8449 2342; 01707 653800 *also fax.* Kathleen Shanks, mus dir; Pamela Horsepool, sec.

Cardiff County and Vale of Glamorgan Youth Choir. The Friary Centre, The Friary, Cardiff CF1 4AA *tel:* 029 2064 0950/1 *fax:* 029 2022 7471. Kelvin Thomas, mus dir.

Central Berkshire Girls' Choir. Central Berkshire Music Office, Stoneham Court, 100 Cockney Hill, Reading RG30 4EZ *tel:* 0118 901 2370 *fax:* 0118 901 2371. Michael Wood, dir, cond; Mrs E Bartley, admin.

Chamber Choir of The Arts Educational School. Tring Park, Tring, Herts HP23 5LX *tel:* 01442 824255 *fax:* 01442 891069. Vaughan Meakins, cond.

Chelmer Youth Choir. 34 Longmead Ave, Great Baddow, Chelmsford CM2 7EG *tel:* 01245 471649 *also fax.* Eric Withams, cond.

Chelmsford Star Children's Choir. 34 Longmead Ave, Great Baddow, Chelmsford CM2 7EG *tel:* 01245 471649 *also fax.* Eric Withams, cond.

Cheshire Youth Chamber Choir. Hadfield House, County Hall, Chester CH1 1SQ *tel:* 01244 602319 *fax:* 01244 603813. Beverley Stanton, admin; Mervyn Williams, dir.

Cheshire Youth Choir. Hadfield House, County Hall, Chester CH1 1SQ *tel:* 01244 602319 *fax:* 01244 603813. Beverley Stanton, admin; Martin Cooke, dir.

Chester Music Society Junior Choir. c/o 5 Kennedy Close, Newton, Chester CH2 2PL *tel:* 01244 351003 *also fax.* Pat Dayananda, admin; Martin Cook, cond.

Children's Voices of Enfield. 20 Brycedale Cres, Southgate, London N14 7EY *tel:* 020 8882 0630 *also fax.* June Keyte, dir.

City of Birmingham Symphony Youth Chorus. CBSO Centre, Berkely St, Birmingham B1 2LF *tel:* 0121 616 6500 *fax:* 0121 616 6518 *email:* information@cbso.co.uk. Simon Halsey, chorus dir; Claire Walters, chorus mgr; Hilary Parfitt, vocal coach; Shirley Court, cond jnr chorus; Adrian Partington, cond snr chorus.

City of Birmingham Young Voices. CBSO Centre, Berkely St, Birmingham B1 2LF *tel:* 0121 616 6500 *fax:* 0121 616 6518. Simon Halsey, chorus dir; Claire Walters, chorus mgr; David Lawrence, cond.

City of Sheffield Young Choirs. 17 Ladysmith Ave, Sheffield S7 1SF *tel:* 0114 281 8330. Andrew Nimmo, cond.

Durham County Youth Choir. Darlington Music Centre, Borough Rd, Darlington DL1 1SG *tel:* 01325 380757 *fax:* 01325 352473. John Allen, admin; Matthew Grehan-Bradley, cond.

Ealing Youth Choir. 169 Murray Rd, Ealing, London W5 4DD *tel:* 020 8560 4532 *also fax.* John Compton, chmn; Paul Ayres, cond.

Farnham Youth Choirs. 21 Firgrove Hill, Farnham, Surrey GU9 8LH *tel:* 01252 717173 *also fax; email:* fyc@which.net. David Victor-Smith MBE, dir; Catherine Watts, associate cond.

Fife Youth Choir. Auchterderran Centre, Woodend Rd, Cardenden KY5 0NE *tel:* 01592 414785 *fax:* 01592 414641 *email:* gwilson@itasdarc.demon.co.uk. Graeme Wilson, adviser in mus, Fife Council.

Finchley Children's Music Group. 69 Etchingham Park Rd, Finchley, London N3 2ED *tel:* 020 8343 3847 *also fax.* Lucy Harris, admin; Nicholas Wilks, mus dir.

Four Counties Youth Choir. c/o Caerphilly County Borough Council, Caerphilly Music Service, Ashfield Rd, Newbridge NP1 4QZ *tel:* 01495 246037 *fax:* 01495 243232. Keith Ellerington, cond.

Glasgow Youth Choir. 47 Westfields, Bishopbriggs, Glasgow G64 3PL *tel:* 0141 563 6699 *also fax.* Isobel McInnes, choir sec.

Guildford Chorale. c/o Royal Grammar School, High St, Guildford, Surrey GU1 3BB *tel:* 01483 880600 *fax:* 01483 306127. Andrew Wilson, cond, admin.

Hampshire County Children's Choir. c/o Hampshire Music Service, Gordon Rd, Winchester, Hants SO23 7DD *tel:* 01962 861502 *fax:* 01962 863690 *email:* edmsmcla@hants.gov.uk. Lissa Gray, mus dir, cond.

Hampshire County Youth Choir. Hampshire Music Service, Gordon Rd, Winchester, Hants SO23 7DD *tel:* 01962 861502 *fax:* 01962 863690 *email:* edmsmcla@hants.gov.uk. Keith Clark, mus dir, cond.

Hartlepool Youth Choir. 9 Granville Ave, Hartlepool TS26 8ND *tel:* 01429 261124 *fax:* 01429 232235. Christopher J Simmons, mus dir; Daniel Raine, mgr.

Hywel Girls' Choir and Hywel Boy Singers. 6 Harries Ave, Llanelli, Carmarthenshire SA15 3LF *tel:* 01554 772979 *also fax; email:* jeremywilliams@photosound.co.uk. John Hywel Williams MBE, dir of mus; Lady Mary Mansel Lewis OBE, president; Stuart Burrows, vice-president.

Ipswich Girls' Choir. County Music Service, Northgate Arts Centre, Sidegate Lane West, Ipswich, Suffolk IP4 3DF *tel:* 01473 281866 *fax:* 01473 286068 *email:* philip.shaw@educ.suffolkcc.gov.uk. Philip Shaw, head of county mus service; David Bramhall, cond.

Jersey Boys' Choir. Professional Development Centre, c/o PO Box 142, Jersey, Channel Islands, JE4 8QJ *tel:* 01534 509491 *fax:* 01534 509300. Malcolm Whittell, dir.

Jewish Heritage Youth Choir. PO Box 232, Harrow, Middx HA1 2NN *tel:* 020 8909 2445 *fax:* 020 8909 1030 *email:* singing@jmht.org. Geraldine Auerbach, dir, Jewish Music Heritage Trust.

Kent County Junior Choir. Kent Music School, The Masters House, College Rd, Maidstone ME15 6YQ *tel:* 01622 691212 *fax:* 01622 661318 *email:* kmsho@cix.compulink.co.uk. Andrew Larner, dir of mus.

Kent County Junior Singers. Kent Music School, The Masters House, College Rd, Maidstone ME15 6YQ *tel:* 01622 691212 *fax:* 01622 661318 *email:* kmsho@cix.compulink.co.uk. Andrew Larner, dir of mus.

Kent Youth Chamber Choir. Kent Music School, The Masters House, College Rd, Maidstone ME15 6YQ *tel:* 01622 691212 *fax:* 01622 661318 *email:* kmsho@cix.compulink.co.uk. Andrew Larner, dir of mus.

Kent Youth Choir. Kent Music School, The Masters House, College Rd, Maidstone ME15 6YQ *tel:* 01622 691212 *fax:* 01622 661318 *email:* kmsho@cix.compulink.co.uk. Andrew Larner, dir of mus.

Kent Youth Singers. Kent Music School, The Masters House, College Rd, Maidstone ME15 6YQ *tel:* 01622 691212 *fax:* 01622 661318 *email:* kmsho@cix.compulink.co.uk. Andrew Larner, dir of mus.

The Manchester Boys' Choir. Zion Arts Centre, Stretford Rd, Manchester M15 5ZA *tel:* 0161 226 4411 *fax:* 0161 226 1010. Adrian P Jessett, founder dir.

Manchester Boys' Chorus. Zion Arts Centre, Stretford Rd, Manchester M15 5ZA *tel:* 0161 226 4411 *fax:* 0161 226 1010. Adrian P Jessett, founder dir.

Manx Youth Choir. Music Centre, Lord St, Douglas, Isle of Man IM1 1LE *tel:* 01624 686555 *fax:* 01624 686557.

Maureen Hunter Singers. 14 Vine Close, Cottingham, E Yorks HU16 5RF *tel:* 01482 843344 *also fax.* J Graham Hunter, mgr.

Methodist Association Youth Club Singers and Orchestra. 25 Marylebone Rd, London NW1 5JR *tel:* 020 7486 5502 *fax:* 020 7935 1507. Craig McLeish, dir.

New London Children's Choir. 41 Aberdare Gardens, London NW6 3AL *tel:* 020 7625 4641 *fax:* 020 7625 4876 *email:* reynaldo@angkor.co.uk. Ronald Corp, cond.

Northants County Youth Choirs. c/o Music Services, 125-129 Kettering Rd, Northampton NN1 4AZ *tel:* 01604 637117 *fax:* 01604 603070. Peter Dunkley, head of mus service.

Nottingham Choral Trust Youth Choir. 2 Trinity Cottages, Stapleford Woods, Lincs LN6 9LE *tel:* 01522 789245 *also fax.* Angela Kay, cond; Susan Hatherly, sec.

Oldham Boys' Choirs. Oldham Metropolitan Borough Music Centre, The Lyceum Building, Union St, Oldham OL1 1QG *tel:* 0161 627 2332 *fax:* 0161 620 0259. Eileen Bentley, cond, snr choir; Wendy Andrew, cond, jnr choir.

Oldham Girls' Choirs. Oldham Metropolitan Borough Music Centre, The Lyceum Building, Union St, Oldham OL1 1QG *tel:* 0161 627 2332 *fax:* 0161 620 0259. Eileen Bentley, cond, snr choir; Jacqui Hamlett, cond, jnr choir.

Oxford Girls' Choirs. The Old Manse, Leafield, Witney, Oxon OX8 5NN *tel:* 01993 878200 *fax:* 01993 878375 *email:* oldmanse@compuserve.com. Mary Taylor, admin.

Royal Scottish National Orchestra Junior Chorus. Royal Scottish National Orchestra, 73 Claremont St, Glasgow G3 7JB *tel:* 0141 225 3553 *fax:* 0141 221 4317 *email:* admin@rsno.org.uk. Christopher Bell, chorus master; Jill Mitchell, chorus mgr.

St Catherine's Chamber Choir. St Catherine's School, Bramley, Guildford, Surrey *tel:* 01483 893363 *fax:* 01483 893003. Robert Gillman, cond, admin.

Southend Boys' Choir. PO Box 6, Civic Centre, Southend on Sea, Essex *tel:* 01702 215436 *fax:* 01702 215110. Roger Humphrey, cond.

Southend Girls' Choir. PO Box 6, Civic Centre, Southend on Sea, Essex *tel:* 01702 215436 *fax:* 01702 215110. Roger Humphrey, cond.

Stockport Youth Choirs and The Maia Singers. 23 Buttermere Rd, Gatley, Cheadle, Cheshire SK8 4RH *tel:* 0161 428 5456. John Pomphrey, dir; Lynda Whitney, admin.

Suffolk Jubilee Choir. County Music Service, Northgate Arts Centre, Sidegate Lane West, Ipswich, Suffolk IP4 3DF *tel:* 01473 281866 *fax:* 01473 286068 *email:* philipshaw@educ.suffolkcc.gov.uk. Philip Shaw, head of county mus service; David Bramhall, cond.

Vivace Girls' Choir. c/o 7 Park Lane, Charvil, Reading RG10 9TR *tel:* 0118 934 0589. Miss S Newman, mus dir.

The Voice Squad. Fish and Bell Management, PO Box 175, Bury St Edmunds, Suffolk IP32 7DY *tel:* 01359 270034 *email:* fishbell @aol.com. Birgitta Kenyon, dir.

West Sussex Girls' Choir. Crawley Area Music Centre, c/o Hazelwick School, Mill Lane, Three Bridges, Crawley, W Sussex RH10 1SX *tel:* 01293 537197. Janet McCleery, cond.

Youth Opera and Music Theatre

British Youth Opera. South Bank University, 103 Borough Rd, London SE1 0AA *tel:* 020 7815 6090 *fax:* 020 7815 6094 *email:* byopera @mailbox.co.uk. Timothy Dean, mus dir; Sir John Hannam, chmn; Mikel Toms, admin dir.

Hillside Opera. 57 Gordon Ave, Portswood, Southampton SO14 6WH *tel:* 023 8055 1088 *also fax.* Jill Meager, artistic dir; Kaarina Manzur, business mgr.

Music Box Children's Opera Group. 88 Belmont Rd, St Andrews, Bristol BS6 5AU *tel:* 0117 942 3775 *fax:* 0117 942 3526. Mark Lawrence, mus dir; Margaret Abels, membership sec.

National Youth Music Theatre. 5th Floor, Palace Theatre, Shaftesbury Ave, London W1V 8AY *tel:* 020 7734 7478 *fax:* 020 7734 7515. Jeremy James Taylor, artistic dir; Jon Bromwich, gen mgr; Vivienne Hughes, outreach admin, auditions.

Organisations for Young Performers

The organisations listed below exist to promote excellence in performance for school-age musicians and singers.

Association of British Choral Directors (ABCD). 46 Albert St, Tring, Herts HP23 6AU *tel:* 01422 891633 *also fax; email:* marie.louise.petit@abcd.org.uk. Howard Layfield, chair; Marie-Louise Petit, gen sec. *Choral conducting training for young people, teachers and directors at all levels. Student membership available.*

British Choral Institute. 6 Chailey Ave, Rottingdean, Brighton BN2 7GH *tel:* 01273 300894 *fax:* 01273 308394 *email:* britchorinst@fastnet.co.uk. Roy Wales, dir; Christine Wales, admin. *A national organisation established as an advisory, promotional, educ and training body for choral singers, conds, choral administrators and organisers from all sectors of the choral community with a special emphasis on developing international choral projects.*

British Federation of Young Choirs (BFYC). Devonshire House, Devonshire Square, Loughborough, Leics LE11 3DW *tel:* 01509 211664 *fax:* 01509 260630 *email:* admin@bfyc.demon.co.uk. Susan Lansdale, chief exec; Andrew Fairbairn, hon sec. *Choral events for young people and training courses for teachers, conds and singers. 450 members (180 choirs and 270 individuals). Choral animateurs in Scotland, Northern Ireland, East Anglia, London, W and E Midlands.*

British Reserve Insurance Youth Orchestra Awards. NAYO, Ainslie House, 11 St Colme St, Edinburgh EH3 6AG *tel:* 0131 539 1087 *fax:* 0131 539 1069 *email:* admin@nayo.org.uk. Carol Main, dir. *5 awards of £500 each will be made to youth orchs within NAYO's membership towards a project to enhance the orchs' activities. Deadline for applications Apr. Previous winners may reapply after an interval of one year.*

Essex Young Musicians' Trust. Loom House, Royal Square, Dedham, Essex CO7 6AA *tel:* 01206 322938 *also fax.* Judith A Fowle, trustee. *Aims to give young musicians in Essex access to mus educ and experience as a member of one of the county youth orchs. Full fee and tour bursaries plus occasional discretionary awards available only after auditions and interviews.*

The International Handchime Circle. Hillcroft, Northbrook Ave, Winchester, Hants SO23 0JU *tel:* 01962 856404 *also fax.* Sue Richardson, dir. *W/shops, courses and demonstration team for concerts. CDs available.*

Music for Youth. 102 Point Pleasant, London SW18 1PP *tel:* 020 8870 9624 *fax:* 020 8870 9935 *email:* mfy@globalnet.co.uk. Larry Westland CBE, exec dir; Pippa Cleve, Lucy Riley, asst dirs. *Charity dedicated to providing regional and national platforms for young musicians.*

National Association of Choirs. 21 Charmouth Rd, Lower Weston, Bath BA1 3LJ *tel:* 01225 426713. John Robbins, gen sec.

National Association of Youth Orchestras (NAYO). Ainslie House, 11 St Colme St, Edinburgh EH3 6AG *tel:* 0131 539 1087 *fax:* 0131 539 1069 *email:* admin@nayo.org.uk. Carol Main, dir. *Has members from independent and LEA run orchs. Organises the Festival of British Youth Orchestras in Edinburgh and Glasgow, Anglo-German Youth Music Week, British Reserve Insurance Youth Orchestra Awards and the British Reserve Insurance Conducting Prize. Organises various Silver Baton award schemes in association with business sponsors. Publishes a newsletter* Full Orchestra *three times pa. Also the Marion Semple Weir library of chmbr mus, free hire to members. In preparation:* Directory of Youth and Student Orchestras.

Sing for Pleasure. Nortonthorpe Mills, Wakefield Rd, Scissett, Huddersfield HD8 9LA *tel:* 01484 860404 *email:* choral@sfp.cix.co.uk. Alan Jefferis, dir. *Wide variety of day and residential courses for young singers and conds. Singing day for children and INSET courses for teachers. Choir repertoire available from above address.*

Festivals for Young Performers

Aberdeen International Youth Festival. 3 Nutborn House, Clifton Rd, London SW19 4QT *tel:* 020 8946 2995 *fax:* 020 8944 6507 *email:* nicola.wallis@virgin.net. Nicola Wallis, festival dir. *2-12 Aug 2000. Youth orchs, choirs, jazz and rock groups, dance and theatre groups from all over the world. Mainly amateur, but some professional input.*

The Festival of British Youth Orchestras in Edinburgh and Glasgow. NAYO, Ainslie House, 11 St Colme St, Edinburgh EH3 6AG *tel:* 0131 539 1087 *fax:* 0131 539 1069 *email:* admin@nayo.org.uk. Carol Main, dir. *12 Aug-3 Sep 2000.* RSAMD box office *tel:* 0141 332 5057; Central Hall box office *tel:* 0131 229 7937 (during festival period only).

Harrogate International Youth Music Festival. Perform Europe (Incoming), Deepdene Lodge, Deepdene Ave, Dorking, Surrey RH5 4AZ *tel:* 01306 744360 *fax:* 01306 744361 *email:* smb.peurope@kuoni.co.uk. Sharon Brewster, festivals mgr. *Apr. Celebrating its 28th year in 2000, the festival features varied and exciting performances from local and international choirs, bands, orchs and dance groups.*

The National Festival of Music for Youth. 102 Point Pleasant, London SW18 1PP *tel:* 020 8870 9624 *fax:* 020 8870 9935 *email:* mfy@globalnet.co.uk. Larry Westland CBE, exec dir; Lucy Riley, asst dir.

Music For Youth Schools Prom. Music for Youth, 102 Point Pleasant, London SW18 1PP *tel:* 020 8870 9624 *fax:* 020 8870 9935 *email:* cleevep@mfy.globalnet.co.uk. Larry Westland CBE, exec dir; Pippa Cleeve, asst dir.

West Sussex International Youth Music Festival. Perform Europe (Incoming), Deepdene Lodge, Deepdene Ave, Dorking, Surrey RH5 4AZ *tel:* 01306 744360 *fax:* 01306 744361 *email:* smb.peurope@kuoni.co.uk. Sharon Brewster, festival mgr. *Apr. Celebrating its 9th year in 2000. Non-competitive festival taking place in various venues throughout W Sussex and on the South coast, including Arundel Cathedral and Worthing Assembly Hall. Attracts both local and international bands, orchs, choirs and dance groups.*

Summer Schools and Short Courses

Courses held in the holidays, at weekends and in the evenings are listed here with the address for applications and the venue (if different from the first address). The **Benslow Music Trust** (*see entry below*) maintains a permanent short-term residential centre and presents courses throughout the year for amateur musicians of all types and standards.

A detailed list of music courses held throughout the year can be found in the February issue of *Music Teacher* and a summer school supplement is published in a January issue of *Classical Music.* Both magazines are available from Rhinegold Publishing Ltd. The **National Institute of Adult Continuing Education** (21 De Montfort St, Leicester LE1 7GE *tel:* 0116 255 1451 *fax:* 0116 285 4514) produces a bi-annual publication '*Time To Learn*' detailing a wide range of residential courses.

Abingdon Summer School for Solo Singers. Pencots, Northmoor, Oxon OX8 1AX *tel:* 01865 300884 *also fax.* Henry Herford, Robin Bowman, dirs; Lindsay John, admin. *6-13 Aug 2000, apply by Jun. Ages 18 and above. Fees: £445 (tbc).*

ACE Study Tours. Babraham, Cambridge CB2 4AP *tel:* 01223 835055 *fax:* 01223 837394 *email:* ace@study-tours.org. Hugh Barnes, mgr. *Programme of study tours, residential courses in UK and worldwide, including visits to Haydn Festival in Eisenstadt, Schubert at Feldkirch, Tanglewood in New England, Three Choirs Festival, Kuhmo Music Festival, Dresden Music Festival, etc. Average age 40-75. Fees: £600-1800.*

Alexander Technique for Pianists. 50 Weston Way, Weston Favell, Northampton NN3 3BN *tel:* 01604 401862 *also fax; email:* john.n@virgin.net. John Naylor, admin. *Courses on the application of Alexander Technique to pno study and performance. Individual and group tuition in both pno and Alexander Technique. Dates on application. Aged 16 and above.*

Alpha-Beta-Cello. 33 Romsey Rd, Cambridge CB1 3DD *tel:* 01223 413234 *also fax. Non-residential 1-day w/shops for cellists (min gr 5-advanced). Performance opportunity in non-competitive environment. Vc ens participation and discussion encouraged. Also exploration of musicians' health issues, good practice habits, etc. Fee: £20.*

Alston Hall College. Alston Lane, Longridge, Preston, Lancs PR3 3BP *tel:* 01772 784661 *fax:* 01772 785835 *email:* info@alstonhall.u-net.com. Graham Wilkinson, principal. *Courses include, Music Appreciation, Chamber Music and Choral Singing. Fees: w/ends from £87, summer schools from £175, day courses from £17. Free programme on application. Aged 18 and above.*

The Amadeus Chorus and Orchestra Summer School. 41 Cahir St, London E14 3QR *tel:* 020 7537 2329 *fax:* 020 7379 5205. Philip Mackenzie, dir; Odaline de la Martinez, president. *16-23 Jul 2000 in Gloucestershire. For players aged 18-30 min gr 8 (higher for wind, br and perc). Also places for 4 conductors (u/grads). Repertoire includes Barber's* Adagio *and* Cello Concerto *(soloist: Steven Isserlis) and Stravinsky's* The Rite of Spring. *Fees: £105 (half-price bursaries are available).*

Amadeus Summer Course. 100 Harvist Rd, London NW6 6HL *tel:* 020 8960 4780 *fax:* 020 8964 5510. Robin Anderton, admin. *24 Jul-5 Aug 2000 at the RAM, apply by end of Apr (some scholarships available). For p/grad and young professional str quartets, aged 18-30. 1-2 weeks concentrated study of the quartet repertoire, with members of the Amadeus Quartet. Fees: on application.*

Anglo-German Youth Music Week. NAYO, c/o The Band of the RAF Regiment, Royal Air Force Cranwell, Sleaford, Lincs NG34 8MB *tel:* 07050 622403 *fax:* 07020 934902 *email:* malcolm.goodman@nayo.org.uk. Malcolm Goodman, NAYO course admin. *28 Jul-6 Aug 2000 in Münster, Germany. Annual residential mus week, alternately in Germany and the UK. Wide range of orch and chmbr mus with students from other European countries. Full symphony orch also forming 2 chmbr orchs. For age 15-25 of gr 7-8+ standard on first inst. Fees: £260.*

Association of British Choral Directors. 46 Albert St, Tring HP23 6AU *tel:* 01442 891633 *also fax; email:* marie.louise.petit@abcd.org.uk. Marie-Louise Petit, gen sec; Howard Layfield, chair. *Regional and national events including choral conducting training w/shops (beginners, intermediate, advanced), m/classes, open rehearsals, discussion forums, repertoire and vocal technique seminars, residential convention. Non-members welcome. Annual Choral Directors' Convention in Chester, 25-27 Aug 2000; fees on application; open to any age.*

Bass-Fest 1999. The British and International Bass Forum, Studio Ten, Farnham Maltings, Farnham, Surrey GU9 7QR *tel:* 01252 319610 *also fax; email:* bibf@classical-artists.com. David Heyes, dir. *6-12 Aug 2000 at Leighton Park School, Reading, Berks. A convention/course for db players of all ages and abilities. Involves quartet coaching, individual lessons, jazz, bass orch, improvisation, m/class, orch technique, recitals, warm-ups, 'All Stars' concert, mus and CD shop, etc. Emphasis on enjoyment and informality. Fees: from c £150 (non-residential); £220 (residential); auditors £30 per day.*

Bath Spa International Guitar Festival. Newton Park, Newton St Loe, Bath BA2 9BN *tel:* 01225 875522 *fax:* 01225 875444 *email:* e.ginn@bathspa.ac.uk. Emmanuelle Ginn, bookings admin. *3rd and 4th week of Jul 2000 at Bath Spa University College, applications by 15 Jun. Top performers and teachers in all styles of gui, classical, flamenco, rock, jazz and blues. All levels and ages welcomed for m/classes, lectures, seminars and study modules. Full concert series, three major competitions for performers: Bath International Guitar Competition, Admira Young Classical Guitarist of the Year and Takamine Young Acoustic Guitarist of the Year. Accommodation available, as well as some scholarships. Fees: £430-450. No age limit.*

Beauchamp House Holiday Music Courses. Churcham, Gloucester GL2 8AA *tel:* 01452 750382 *fax:* 01452 750585 *email:* music@beauchamp.demon.co.uk. Alan and Caroline Lumsden, dirs; Margaret Nelson, admin. *3-day and 1-week w/shops, for children throughout school holidays including orch courses (jnr, intermediate, snr and international chmbr), big band, international mus theatre week, jnr choir, gr 5 theory. Beginners up to gr 8+, aged 8 and above. Also early mus week and chmbr mus course for adults. Residential fees: £61-255 pw.*

Beechwood Easter Guitar Course. Elizabeth's Cottage, The Green, Leigh, Tonbridge, Kent TN11 8QW *tel:* 01732 832459. Raymond Love. *Apr 2000, applications by Mar. 4-day residential course for classical gui; solo and ens playing. Emphasis on ens playing and concerts. Aged 16 and above. Fees: £150-160.*

Bela Bartók Centre for Musicianship. 6 Frognal Court, 158 Finchley Rd, London NW3 5HL *tel:* 020 7435 3685 *email:* agnes.kory@kcl.ac.uk. Agnes Kory, dir. *Professional, amateur and children's classes focus on comprehensive mus educ including the Kodály system, history, analysis and performance skills. Regular classes and occasional intensive holiday courses. Ages 4-adult. Summer course for cellists, July 2000, London. Fees £180. Also running course in Bayreuth on Wagner, Liszt, Bartok and Kodály, July 2000. Fee: £200.*

Benslow Music Trust. Little Benslow Hills, off Benslow Lane, Hitchin, Herts SG4 9RB *tel:* 01462 459446 *fax:* 01462 440171 *email:* BMusicT@aol.com. Helen Marshall, mus mgr. *Residential w/end and holiday courses for amateur musicians, students and teachers, aged 16 and above. Annual programme of over 100 different courses includes many for chmbr mus (strs, wind, pno and combinations), orchs of different standards, rcdrs, solo singing and insts, early mus, Alexander Technique, etc. Summer programme includes weeks and w/ends for viol, str quartet, hp, big band (tbc), banjo (tbc), str orch, wind chmbr mus, wind ens and London Brass Summer School (tbc).*

Bochmann String Courses. BMCC, The Barns, Village Farm, Ford, Cheltenham, Glos GL54 5RU *tel:* 01386 584539 *also fax.* Gina Bochmann, admin; Michael Bochmann, dir. *Courses throughout the year for students, p/grads and young professionals aged 18 and above. For str ens and solo vn with or without pno. Dates and duration arranged according to mutual convenience.*

Border Marches Early Music Forum. 3 Upper Linney, Ludlow, Shropshire SY8 1EF *tel:* 01584 876175. Jenny Sayer, sec; Alison James, newsheet distribution. *Day w/shops held on Sundays in Leominster, Herefordshire, approximately 6 times pa, vocal and inst from medieval to baroque. Baroque Chamber Music for Wind and Strings, 25 Apr 2000; tutor: Jeremy Barlow. Lassus and Andrea Gabrieli - for singers and instrumentalists, 18 Jun 2000; tutor: Alan Lumsden. Fees: £8.50 (members); £10 (non-members).*

Brass Band Summer School. 21 The Coppice, Impington, Cambridge CB4 9PP *tel:* 01223 234090 *also fax;* 07710 505689 *email:* philipbiggs@bandstand.demon.co.uk. Philip Biggs, admin. *Aug at Oxford Brookes University. All ages welcome. Applications by Mar 2000. Fees: £280.*

The British Kodály Academy. c/o 13 Midmoor Rd, London SW19 4JD *tel:* 020 8946 6528 *fax:* 020 8946 6561 *email:* enquiries@britishkodalyac.demon.co.uk. Celia Cviic, treasurer and courses sec; Jane Lee, chmn. *Adult diploma courses, certificate in Kodály mus educ, w/end courses, w/shops and INSET throughout the UK. Summer school in Cheltenham, 13-20 Aug 2000 studying the Kodály approach to musicianship, classroom techniques and choral conducting. Special course for singers. Tutors from Hungary and the UK. W/end intensive course, 15-16 Apr 2000. Musicianship courses, 3 levels, London (elementary only), Bath, Manchester. All courses credit bearing for Trinity LTCL and Cert-Ed.*

British Suzuki Institute. 39 High St, Wheathampstead, Herts AL4 8BB *tel:* 01582 832424 *fax:* 01582 834488 *email:* courses@suzukimusic.force9.co.uk. Suzanne Porter, gen sec. *Suzuki teacher training in vn, pno, vc and fl. P/t courses lead to Diploma of European Suzuki Association. Regular p/t courses open to observers. New academic year from Apr 2000; applications by 10 Dec 1999.*

British Youth Opera. South Bank University, 103 Borough Rd, London SE1 0AA *tel:* 020 7815 6090 *fax:* 020 7815 6094 *email:* byopera@mailbox.co.uk. Timothy Dean, mus dir; Sir John Hannam, chmn; Mikel Toms, admin dir. *Summer season 15 Jul-15 Sep; also year round programme. Auditions from Nov, singers apply by Dec, orchs by Apr. Ages 18-30. Performances in London and other locations.*

Britten-Pears School for Advanced Musical Studies. High St, Aldeburgh, Suffolk IP15 5AX *tel:* 01728 452935 *fax:* 01728 452715 *email:* bps.admin@aldeburghfestivals.org. Elizabeth Webb, dir; Ann Rawdon Smith, admin; Julia Robinson, asst admin. *10-day residential m/class advanced courses and opera courses organised from Apr-Oct for instrumentalists and singers. Various courses available with small number of places on each; entry by audition only (Jan), usually advanced students and young professionals. Courses for singers include fully staged opera, Brahms duos, Weill songs, Bel Canto, Handel oratorio; inst courses including str quartets, baroque ens, br ens, vn and vc m/classes. Prospectus published Oct, and available on request. Also Britten-Pears Orchestra; advanced national training orch and Britten-Pears Baroque Orchestra meeting for short courses. Applications by mid-Dec.*

Bryanston Summer School. London Suzuki Group, 96 Farm Lane, London SW6 1QH *tel:* 020 7386 8006 *also fax; email:* lsg@pullinger.prestel.co.uk. Nicholas Pullinger, admin. *Aug. Age range 5-16. Individual and group lessons for Suzuki vn, va, vc and pno students. Four levels of orch, chmbr mus, choirs, Dalcroze, Kodály and theory. Residential. Fees: £235-320, parents £295. Non-residential and observer rates available. BSI teacher training*

Bude Jazz Summer School. South West Jazz, c/o Exeter and Devon Arts Centre, Gandy St, Exeter EX4 3LS *tel:* 01392 218368 *fax:* 01392 420442. Kevin Buckland, regional development offr. *Aug. An intensive but fun week of courses for musicians who have already acquired a reasonable level of musical ability with their voice or chosen inst, either as sight readers or by ear. W/shops developing understanding, interpretation and improvisation; m/classes, public performances. Courses suitable for various levels of experience in jazz skills, including beginners.*

Burton Manor. Burton, S Wirral, Cheshire L64 5SJ *tel:* 0151 336 5172 *fax:* 0151 336 6586. Janet Hooper, course admin. *Classical Guitar w/shop 16-18 Jun 2000. Fees: £108; tutor: John Mills; concert 16 Jun (tickets £7). Bach's Harpsichord Music 20 Feb 2000. Fee: £26.*

Cambridge Early Music Summer Schools. Trinity Hall, Cambridge CB2 1TJ *tel:* 01223 847330 *also fax; email:* cemss@btinternet.com. Selene Mills, admin. *Hilliard Summer Festival Aug 2000 (The Hilliard Ensemble); applications by 31 May 2000. For ens singers aged 16 and above. Course emphasis is on performance, focusing on early and contemporary vocal ens mus. Basic fees: £525 (residential) or £415 (non-residential). Surcharges for small groups, discounts for large groups. Renaissance Music Course Jul 2000 (Musica Antiqua of London). For Renaissance insts and voices. Fees: £495 (residential) or £395 (non-residential). Baroque Music of the Holy Roman Empire Aug 2000 (The Parley of Instruments). Masses, motets, orch works, and vocal and inst chmbr mus, focusing on mus by Schmelzer, Biber, Fux, Zelenka and early Haydn. Fees: £510 (residential) or £405 (non-residential). Also summer concert series.*

Cambridge School of Music. Maple House, Westley Waterless, nr Newmarket, Suffolk CB8 0RH *tel:* 01638 508577 *fax:* 01638 508578 *email:* barkerfour@aol.com. Mrs Barker, course dir. *Residential orch course 24-30 Jul 2000, applications by 15 Jun. Age 7 to adult (gr 1-5). Fees: £260.*

University of Cambridge. Board of Continuing Education, Madingley Hall, Madingley, Cambridge CB3 8AQ *tel:* 01954 210636 *fax:* 01954 210677. Sue Hoskins, courses registrar. *W/end appreciation courses and coaching for str players aged 18 and above. Fees: £125 (w/end), £390 (week).*

Canford Summer School of Music. 5 Bushey Close, Old Barn Lane, Kenley, Surrey CR8 5AU *tel:* 020 8660 4766 *fax:* 020 8668 5273 *email:* oakcroft@msn.com. Malcolm Binney, mus dir. *30 Jul-20 Aug 2000, applications by early Jul. Aged 16 and above. Orch, wind band and choral conducting, chmbr mus for w/wind and str, composition, jazz, m/class for pno, pno accompaniment and voice, wind orch, choirs, br band, opera, orchs, str orch, perc, and mus teaching techniques. Fees: c £350 pw.*

Centre For Young Musicians. Morley College, 61 Westminster Bridge Rd, London SE1 7HT *tel:* 020 7928 3844 *fax:* 020 7928 3454 *email:* hc@cymlondon.demon.co.uk. Victoria Sweatman. *3-4 day courses during the school holidays at venues around London. Courses include: London Schools Concert Band, London Schools Symphonic Band, snr str ens, intermediate str ens, jnr w/wind, jnr strs, jnr rcdrs, jnr guis, jnr perc, rcdr ens, jnr musicianship, jnr br.*

The Chalemie Summer School of Early Music, Dance and Commedia. 3 Thornhill Square, London N1 1BQ *tel:* 020 7700 4293 *fax:* 020 7700 5877 *email:* chalemie@thorn.demon.co.uk. Sara Stowe; Barbara Segal, summer school organiser. *8-13 Aug 2000, applications by end Jul. All ages. Held at Bath Spa University College, Newton Park. Mus, dance and commedia from the 17th/18th centuries.*

chamber@chase. Chase Lodge, Herbert Rd, Bournemouth, Dorset BH4 8HD *tel:* 01202 757847 *also fax; email:* chaselodge@hotmail.com. William Webb, dir; Colin Callow, artistic dir; Jean Shannon, admin. *Residential chmbr mus courses for advanced players of all ages throughout the year. Courses designed for ens which are either newly-formed or established. Distinguished tutors.*

Chamber Music Holidays and Festivals. 57 Chatsworth Rd, Bournemouth, Dorset BH8 8SL *tel:* 01202 528328 *fax:* 01202 524081 *email:* vivpit@mcmail.com. Vivienne Pittendrigh. *23 May-6 Jun Vienna, Esterhaza, Budapest; 25 Jun-6 Jul Bournemouth, London; 29 Aug-9 Sep Prague String Quartet Festival; 13-27 Sep Corfu. Holidays for chmbr mus players and listeners. Scheduled playing, m/classes, concerts and various festival activities in historically and scenically interesting places.*

Charterhouse Summer School of Music. Music Office, Charterhouse, Godalming, Surrey GU7 2DX *tel:* 01483 291696. Robin Wells, dir of mus. *Late Jul 2000, applications by 1 Apr. Age 18 and above. Symphony, str and chmbr orchs, chmbr mus, gui, accompaniment, solo and choral singing, org. Special Vaughan Williams Symposium.*

Choral Workshop. 6 Clive Rd, Balsall Common, Coventry CV7 7DW *tel:* 01676 532436 *fax:* 0121 743 5682. Jill Pacey, admin. *21-22 Oct 2000. Choral w/end for age 16 and above with professional artists and orch for singers. Mendelssohn,* Elijah *at the Warwick Arts Centre. Some bursaries available.*

The City Lit. Music Dept, Keeley House, Keeley St, London WC2B 4BA *tel:* 020 7430 0546 *fax:* 020 7831 8508. Moira Hayward, head of mus section; Della Rhodes, jazz co-ord. *Adult educ courses from beginner to advanced level in inst, vocal, opera, musicianship, ens, jazz and classical appreciation and mus tech. Enrolment Jul-Sep for year courses. Students may join throughout academic year subject to vacancies. Ages 18 and over; fees £3.50 ph or £174 per year (1.5 hrs a week).*

Clarinetwise. Pengribyn, Cilrehydn, Llanfyrnach, Pembs SA35 0AA *tel:* 01239 698602. Jacqueline Browne, events organiser; Michael Collins, president. *Regular cl w/shops, courses and m/classes. Quarterly journal available. Workshop in central England includes playing sessions, classical, jazz, w/shops, demos, talks, m/classes, recitals. All ages and standards welcome. Membership £12 pa; w/shops from £15 per day. W/wind w/shop in late Nov 2000; applications by Oct.*

Clonter Opera Theatre. Swettenham Heath, Congleton, Cheshire CW12 2LR *tel:* 01260 224638 *fax:* 01260 224742. Jeffery Lockett, artistic dir; Leonard Hancock, mus dir. *Two residential opera studios culminating in public performances for singers aged 20-35. Applications by end Sep for the following year. Performance fees and travel costs paid; free board and lodging.*

Coleg Harlech. Harlech, Gwynedd LL46 2PU *tel:* 01766 780363 *fax:* 01766 780169 *email:* ifans@harlech.ac.uk. M Ifans. *Aug. Orch mus summer school for ages 16 and above. Fees: £270 (concessions for students).*

Colin Fleming Flute Summer School. Liverpool Hope University College, Dept of Music, Hope Park, Liverpool L16 9JD *tel:* 0151 291 3457 *fax:* 0151 291 3170 *email:* walterd@livhope.ac.uk. David Walters, snr instrumental tutor. *Jul, Liverpool Hope College; applications by Jun. Offers full range of participatory classes for fl players. Ages 12 and above. As well as technique, repertoire and performance classes, there will also be lessons in fl making and repairing. Runs concurrently with the Leblanc Clarinet School.*

Colla Voce Enterprises. Ridgeside, Eastfield Rd, Redhill, Surrey RH1 4DY *tel:* 01737 763292 *also fax; email:* scook@netcomuk.co.uk. Sue Cook, business dir. *Jul/Aug 2000, applications by 31 May. General and*

advanced summer schools held at Leighton Park, Reading and directed by Alison Pearce, Professor of the Royal Academy of Music, accompanied by teams of international tutors. Aged 16 and above. Courses for singers and accompanists focusing on the essential skills needed for performance and presentation including voice, drama, personal presentation, interpretation and posture.

Colourstrings/Colourkeys Course for Teachers. The Szilvay Foundation, 4 Ullswater Close, Kingston Vale, London SW15 3RF *tel:* 020 8547 3073 *also fax; email:* colourstrings@compuserve.com. Pat Wislocki, Deborah Harris, dirs. *Annual residential/day courses including mus kindergarten and primary school mus (4-7), pre-instrumental mus, vn, vc, mini-bass, pno and gui teaching methods. Kodály-based, using relative sol-fa to train the inner ear prior to learning an inst and continuing this approach in inst tuition. Musicianship and Dalcroze Eurhythmics classes included. All 5-day courses are credit bearing for the LTCL (MusEd) and Cert (MusEd).*

Conspiracy of Flutes. 41 Devon Ave, Twickenham TW2 6PN *tel:* 020 8241 7572 *also fax.* Julie Wright. *A booster course for adult flautists of all levels, directed by Julie Wright.*

Contemporary Music-Making for Amateurs (COMA). Toynbee Studios, 28 Commercial St, London E1 6LS *tel:* 020 7247 7736 *fax:* 020 7247 7732 *email:* coma@coma.org. Chris Shurety, dir; Gill Redfern, admin. *Residential summer school, late Jul/early Aug at Bretton Hall, Yorkshire. W/shops for age 18 and above in composition, improvisation, contemporary inst, vocal and electro-acoustic techniques, ens and orchs, concerts of commissioned and students' works, recording and computer facilities, invitation public concert series. Tutors include Michael Finnissy, Deirdre Gribbin, Joanna MacGregor and Gregory Rose. Fees: on application. Early application recommended.*

Countrywide Holidays Association. Grove House, Wilmslow Rd, Didsbury, Manchester M20 2HU *tel:* 0161 448 7112; 0161 446 2226 (reservations) *fax:* 0161 448 7113 *email:* info@countrywide-walking.org. Patricia Percival, reservations mgr. *Various musical courses (including singing, orch and opera) throughout the year.*

Creative Dance Artists Trust. 15b Lauriston Rd, London SW19 4TJ *tel:* 020 8946 3444 *fax:* 020 8879 0642. Gale Law, admin. *2 weeks in Jul, applications by Mar. International course for professional choreographers and composers. Fosters creative collaboration between essential elements of dance, mus and movement. Participants are selected by committee. No age restriction, but evidence of talent in a professional context required.*

Cumbria College of Art and Design. Brampton Rd, Carlisle CA3 9AY *tel:* 01228 400300 *fax:* 01228 514491 *email:* q@cumbriacad.ac.uk. Judith Todd, mkt. *Please telephone for summer school information.*

Dalcroze Society. 41a Woodmansterne Rd, Coulsdon, Surrey CR5 2DJ *tel:* 020 8645 0714 *also fax.* Mrs P Piqué, sec. *31 Jul-4 Aug 2000. Summer course of mus educ through movement for adults.*

Dartington International Summer School. Dartington Hall, Totnes, Devon TQ9 6DE *tel:* 01803 865988/867068 *fax:* 01803 868108 *email:* brochure@dissorg.u-net.com. Gavin Henderson, artistic dir; Lisa Warren, admin. *Jul-Aug. Summer course for those of any age, with opportunity for advanced tuition and m/classes, informal mus-making, plus concerts, talks, etc. Composer in residence; mus theatre, masque and opera. Fees: £195-715 per week.*

Dolmetsch Summer School. Heartsease, Grayswood Rd, Haslemere, Surrey GU27 2BS *tel:* 01428 643235/651473 *fax:* 01428 654920/651473 *email:* brian@dolmetsch.com. Dr Blood, course sec. *Aug, applications by 30 Jul. For any age group. Bishop Otter College, Chichester, W Sussex. Rcdr; also optional classes for viols, chmbr orch, classroom techniques, choir, rcdr orch, conducting and composition. Fees: £420 (residential); £210 (non-residential). Discounts for Society of Recorder Players.*

Double Bass Summer Holiday Course *see* **Oxford Cello School.**

Double Bass Summer School. 7 St Clair Drive, Worcester Park, Surrey KT4 8UG *tel:* 020 8330 3188 *also fax; email:* peter.emery@kcl.ac.uk. P W Emery, hon sec. *Aug, applications by 1 Aug. Separate courses for beginners, intermediate and advanced db players aged 8-25. Ens playing, m/classes, technique classes and chmbr mus. Fees: £180.*

The Earnley Concourse. Earnley, Chichester, W Sussex PO20 7JL *tel:* 01243 670392 *fax:* 01243 670832 *email:* info@earnley.co.uk. *W/end and week-long study courses for ages 16 and above, featuring mus history, chmbr and singers' w/shops. Fees: c £160-310 (w/end); c £415 (week) inclusive of accommodation, meals and tuition. Includes amongst others: 14-16 Jan 2000, Stravinsky; 28 Jul-4 Aug, Summer School for Singers; 25-28 Aug, Vaughan Williams - The Symphonies.*

East Anglia Summer Music School. c/o Opera da Camera, 7 Meadow Rd, New Costessey, Norwich NR5 0NF *tel:* 01603 744584 *fax:* 01603 250599 *email:* c.l.thornton@uea.ac.uk. Jeffrey Davies, organiser and dir. *Aug, applications by Jul 20. Residential and w/end classes for ages 17 and above at the University of East Anglia, covering concert repertoire, opera and technique. M/classes, opera w/shops and w/shops for singers and accompanists. Fees: £115 (residential), £65 (non-residential).*

Edinburgh University Centre for Continuing Education. 11 Buccleuch Place, Edinburgh EH8 9LW *tel:* 0131 650 4400/662 0783 *fax:* 0131 667 6097 *email:* cce@ed.ac.uk. Bridget Stevens, admin dir, dir of international summer courses. *Weekly classes in mus theory and appreciation. For ages 18 and above. Applications taken until one month before start date. Also Piano w/shop 9-27 Aug 2000. Music at the Edinburgh Festival. Music, Theatre and Dance at the Edinburgh International Festival 21 Aug-4 Sep 2000. Fees: £230 pw (including concert tickets).*

Edrom House Summer Schools. Edrom House, Duns, Berwickshire TD11 3PX *tel:* 0189 081 8277; 020 8340 0897 *fax:* 020 8341 5292. Christopher Cowan, Lucy Cowan, Penelope Lynex. *Chmbr mus, vn and vc courses. Aged 11 and above. Apr, Jul, Aug and Sep. Fees: £170-215.*

Eton Choral Courses. The Shepherd's Cottage, Gt Shelford, Cambridge CB2 5JX *tel:* 01223 845685 *fax:* 01223 841980 *email:* rallwood@netcomuk.co.uk. Ralph Allwood, dir; Lydia Smallwood, admin. *3 courses at Eton College; 4th course at Liverpool Anglican Cathedral; applications by 30 Apr. Aged 16-20. Fees: £330-35.*

European Piano Teachers' Association UK (EPTA). 1 Wildgoose Drive, Horsham, W Sussex RH12 1TU *tel:* 01403 267761 *also fax; email:* eptauk@hotmail.com. Frances Bryan, admin; Frank Martin, chmn. *EPTA has 32 regional centres throughout the UK which organise regular seminars, w/shops, m/classes, pupils' and teachers' concerts. Annual pno pedagogy courses. Annual residential summer conference Aug with m/classes, pno teaching, recitals, lectures. Open to non-members. Ages 18 and above.*

European String Teachers' Association (ESTA). 105 Perryfield Way, Richmond, Surrey TW10 7SN *tel:* 020 8940 4640 *fax:* 020 8940 4300. Marion Seymour, admin. *27 Aug-1 Sep 2000, applications by 15 Jul. For ages 18 and above. Fees: tba. Venue: St Mary's School, Wantage.*

European Youth Summer Music. Festivals House, 198 Park Lane, Macclesfield, Cheshire SK11 6UD *tel:* 01625 428297 *fax:* 01625 503229 *email:* liz@festivals.demon.co.uk. Liz Whitehead, course organiser. *A summer orch course for young musicians aged 11-21. Applications by 1 Jul. Fees: c £265.*

Fantasia Music School. 5 Aspen Way, Middleton on Sea, W Sussex PO22 6PW *tel:* 01243 586068. Mrs M Sutton, admin. *3 summer courses held at Dorset House School, nr Arundel for young musicians aged 6-18. Residential and day; Aug.*

Fawley Court Music Courses. 4b Marshall Parade, Coldharbour Rd, Pyrford, Surrey GU22 8SW *tel:* 01932 351839 *also fax.* Pippa Dice, admin; Michael Procter. *W/end courses near Henley on Thames, Guildford and Salisbury for singers with good sight-reading abilities.*

Fife Summer Jazz Course. Fife Council Arts, The Tower Block, Auchterderran Centre, Woodend Rd, Cardenden KY5 0NE *tel:* 01592 414714 *fax:* 01592 414727. Anne Chalk, support services offr. *Jul, applications by Jun. For all ages. Jazz Course directed by Richard Michael. Aims to improve and develop standards of playing, public performance and improvisation. Fees: £40-240.*

Flutewise Residential Courses. 9 Beaconsfield Rd, Portslade, E Sussex BN41 1XA *tel:* 01273 702367 *fax:* 01273 888864 *email:* mail@flutewise.com. Liz Goodwin, Christine Mead, admin. *Courses for fl players aged 7 and above. Feb 2000, w/end with Jeanne Galway; Mar 2000, w/end Improve Your Playing. Fees: £2120 (members); £135 (non-members).*

Folkworks Youth Summer School. 69 Westgate Road, Newcastle upon Tyne NE1 1SG *tel:* 0191 222 1717 *fax:* 0191 230 2484 *email:* folkworks@folkworks.demon.co.uk. Pam Hobson, admin asst. *7-12 Aug 2000 (tbc), applications by 28 Jul. Annual summer school in trad mus, song and dance. Held at College of St Hild and St Bede, Durham City. Age range 12-25. W/shops cover individual insts as well as bands for mixed insts. Performance opportunities at the Durham Gathering Festival. Residential and non-residential places available. Also Folkworks Adult Summer School for ages 20 and over, held at Elvet Methodist Church and surrounding venues, Durham City. Details as for Youth summer school. Camping and B&B available locally.*

Royal Festival Hall Gamelan Programme. Royal Festival Hall, London SE7 8XX *tel:* 020 7921 0848 *fax:* 020 7928 2049 *email:* rwelch@rfh.org.uk. Robert Welch, gamelan co-ord. *Regular evening classes in mus and dance; course for beginners, children aged 7 and above, and more advanced players. Courses begin 17 Jan 2000, 1 May, Sep; applications 2 weeks before each term. Fees: from £55 per term. W/shops with teachers packs also available.*

Gathering of the Clans. c/o The Villa, Tollerson, York YO61 1QQ *tel:* 01347 838273. *Courses and m/classes for cellists aged 14 and above. Various venues around the country.*

Glamorgan Summer School. The Summer School Office, University of Glamorgan, Pontypridd, South Wales CF37 1DL *tel:* 01443 482828 *fax:* 01443 482941 *email:* ggiles@glam.ac.uk. Gill Giles, events offr. *24*

Jul-4 Aug 2000, applications by 21 Jul. Ages 18 and above. Mus summer school held at University of Glamorgan, Treforest, Pontypridd. Includes courses on jazz, classical and rock gui, keyboards and pno.

Glasgow University. Dept of Adult and Continuing Education, 57-61 Oakfield Ave, Glasgow G12 8LW *tel:* 0141 339 8855 ext 4394 *fax:* 0141 307 8025. J G Macdonald, deputy dir. *Joint study days with Scottish Opera. Also mus appreciation and theory, 8, 10 and 20 week courses from Oct. For ages 18 and above. Fees: from £40 for 10 week courses.*

Gloucestershire Choral Weekend. Cotswold House, Naunton, Cheltenham, Glos GL54 3AA *tel:* 01451 850796. Cedric Virgin, organiser; Geoffrey Mitchell, mus dir. *14-16 Apr 2000, applications by 31 Mar. No age limit. Study of choral works by Palestrina, Bruckner, Josquin, Finzi and others, for mixed voices at Wycliffe College in Gloucestershire. Fees: c £95 (residential), c £62 (non-residential), both prices include meals and hire of mus. Usually 70-80 singers attend.*

Gloucestershire Summer Orchestral Course. Colwell Centre for Arts in Education, Derby Rd, Gloucester GL1 4AD *tel:* 01452 330300 *fax:* 01452 330311 *email:* glosmusic@cableinet.co.uk. Brenda Whitwell, office mgr. *23-30 Jul 2000, applications by 1 Jul. Residential orch summer course for instrumentalists aged 9-18. Caters for all grades, but min gr 1 required for entry.*

Goldsmiths College. University of London, Professional and Community Education, New Cross, London SE14 6NW *tel:* 020 7919 7200/7229 *fax:* 020 7919 7223 *email:* cen01cce@gold.ac.uk. Jeremy Peyton Jones, mus programme co-ord. *P/t and w/end courses throughout the year in a wide variety of styles and at a range of levels from beginners to advanced standard. Certificate courses giving access to HE. Professional development courses for musicians and mus teachers. Courses include mus theory, mus history and analysis, composition and arranging, jazz and pop, gospel singing, mus tech, mus for film, theatre and dance, mus therapy, world mus, inst and vocal classes, jazz and classical ens. Certificate courses in Music Workshop Skills, Music Teaching to Adults, Music Studies, Jazz and Popular Music. Aged 18 and above.*

Guildhall Summer School. Guildhall School of Music and Drama, Silk St, Barbican, London EC2Y 8DT *tel:* 01702 714733 (answerphone). Heather Swain, mgr. *2-week jazz, rock, studio and world mus summer school Jul 2000, ages 12-70. Fees: £70 (intro to jazz w/end); £90 (mus tech w/end); £200 (jazz, rock and studio 1 week); £350 (jazz, rock and studio 2 weeks); £160 (singers week).*

H F Holidays Ltd. Imperial House, Edgware Rd, London NW9 5AL *tel:* 020 8905 9558; 020 8905 9388 (24 hr brochure line) *fax:* 020 8205 0506 *email:* hfholidays@compuserve.com. *Wide variety of mus-making and appreciation holidays with expert tuition throughout the year. Courses include Elgar in the Dales, Composers of Gloucestershire, Monteverdi to Mozart, Choral Music in England, Singing for Beginners, Gilbert and Sullivan, Singing for Pleasure.*

Harrogate Woodwind/Horns Chamber-Music Course. c/o Lindsey Music, 42 St Mary's Park, Louth, Lincs LN11 0EF *tel:* 01507 605244 *email:* jeff@wwplus.freeserve.co.uk. Jeff Brown, events organiser. *Aug 2000; for students, adults; apply by Jul.*

Haworth Chamber Music Weekend. 14 Dunstarn Drive, Leeds LS16 8EH *tel:* 0113 267 5821 *also fax.* Elizabeth Altman. *April 2000, applications by mid-March. Residential w/end course of m/classes and coaching for students and adults in strs, w/wind and pno. Arrangements for repertory carefully designed and course includes walks, participants' concerts and professional concert. Also B&B accommodation in character village cottages. Meals and rehearsals in historic buildings. Wealth of activity for non-playing partners. Bursaries offered. Groups and individuals welcome. Fees: £170 inc meals and accommodation. Further information also available from Haworth Tourist Information Centre* tel: *01535 642329.*

Headington Summer School. 1/1 Corrennie Drive, Edinburgh EH10 6EQ *tel:* 0131 447 1557. Heather Thomson, sec; E King, treasurer. *Jul at Headington School, Oxford. M/classes for solo singers and accompanists and ens singing. Peter Gellhorn, David Coleman, Paul Hamburger and Jean Allister.*

Hereford International Summer School. Flat 1, 54 Lullingstone Lane, Hither Green, London SE13 6UH *tel:* 020 8695 1685. David Battersby, admin. *Aug. For ages 13 and above. Courses for choral singers, choral conducting, solo singers, pno performance, young pianists, adult pno and pno accompaniment. Fees: £350.*

Higham Hall College. Bassenthwaite Lake, Cockermouth, Cumbria CA13 9SH *tel:* 01768 776276 *fax:* 01768 776013 *email:* higham.hall@dial.pipex.com. A Galbraith, dir. *Jazz ens, Aug. Also various courses throughout year for ages 18 and above. Fees: from £105.*

Hindhead Music Centre. Hindhead Rd, Hindhead, Surrey GU26 6BA *tel:* 01428 604941 *fax:* 01428 607871 *email:* info@hindheadmusiccentre.co.uk. Ann Hughes-Chamberlain, dir. *Summer mus m/class courses with international artists.*

Holiday Music. 34 Stanton Rd, London SW20 8RJ *tel:* 020 8947 5538. Muriel Levin, dir. *'Piano Plus' day and residential courses for pianists and others (str, w/wind, vocal) aged 15 and above. Recitals, w/shops. Further details on application.*

Incorporated Association of Organists Festival and Summer School. 11 Stonehill Drive, Bromyard, Herefordshire HR7 4XB *tel:* 01885 483155 *fax:* 01885 488609. Richard Popple MBE, sec; Margaret Phillips, president. *Annual summer school held in Birmingham for a w/end in late Jul including recitals, lectures and m/classes. Open to all who study or enjoy org mus. Applications by May. Fees: c £150. Bursaries available for f/t students.*

Incorporated Society of Musicians (ISM). 10 Stratford Place, London W1N 9AE *tel:* 020 7629 4413 *fax:* 020 7408 1538 *email:* membership@ism.org. Neil Hoyle, chief exec. *Annual conference 27 Apr-1 May 2000, Aberdeen; Apr 2001, Greenwich. Conferences of special interest to school and private teachers, performers and composers. Also w/shops, seminars, lecture recitals at various regional centres. Open to non-members.*

The Inner Voice. The White House, Aston Hill, Aston Rowant, Watlington, Oxon OX9 5SG *tel:* 01844 351561 *fax:* 01844 354891 *email:* elisabeth@innervoice.demon.co.uk. Elisabeth Wingfield; Ali Gordon-Creed. *Courses designed to help performers free themselves of problems associated with nerves, lack of self-confidence and the inner critic. Training enables performers to use their potential more effectively and reduce the negative effects of stress. Also, psychology for musical performance courses in England and Italy for teachers, students, professional singers and musicians.*

The International Brass Band Summer School. Sedbergh School, Sedbergh, Cumbria LA10 5HG *tel:* 01539 622246 (day); 01539 622218 (eve) *also fax; email:* sedsch@rmplc.co.uk. Chris Cooper, course admin; Alan Lewis, course dir. *Jul, apply by 30 Jun. Annual summer school at Sedbergh School, open to br and perc players of all abilities and ages. Wide repertoire of band and ens mus, optional theory classes and inst tutorials. Fees: £260-320.*

The International Handchime Circle. Hillcroft, Northbrook Ave, Winchester, Hants SO23 0JW *tel:* 01962 856404 *also fax.* Sue Richardson, dir. *W/shops and short courses (residential and non-residential) in handchime ringing for leisure. All ages welcome. Speciality is Christmas Carol w/shops.*

International Musicians Seminar. IMS, Prussia Cove, 32 Grafton Square, London SW4 0DB *tel:* 020 7720 9020 *fax:* 020 7720 9033. Rosanna Yeatman, sec. *3-23 Apr 2000, applications by 10 Dec 1999. M/classes in Cornwall given by eminent musicians (Steven Isserlis, Ralph Kirshbaum, Andras Schiff), for str players, pianists and chmbr ens aged 16-30. Fees: c £675 per 10-day course.*

International Piano Teachers Consultants (IPTEC). 29 Beaumont Rd, Chiswick, London W4 5AL *tel:* 020 8994 4288. Meriel Jefferson, hon sec. *Jul 2000, apply by Jun. Seminar for pno teachers, Beachern Wood, Brockenhurst, Hants. Aged 16 and above. 1-day courses, consultations available in specialist subjects.*

International Society for Study of Tension in Performance (ISSTIP). School of Music, Kingston University, c/o 28 Emperor's Gate, London SW7 4HS *tel:* 020 7373 7307 *fax:* 020 7373 5440. Carola Grindea, chmn; Pamela Bowden, co-dir London Performing Arts Clinic. *Annual 1-day w/shops and seminars open to non-members. Special courses on prevention of physical injuries and pyschological problems. For ages 18 and above. Performing Arts Clinic 1st and 3rd Weds at London College of Music.*

Islington Arts Factory. 2 Parkhurst Rd, London N7 0SF *tel:* 020 7607 0561 *fax:* 020 7700 7229. Licy Clayden, office mgr. *Arts centre offering courses and w/shops for adults and children. Vocal classes, drumming. Waged/concession rate. Fees: from £20 per 3-month term.*

J S Arts. 31 Sidney Rd, Staines, Middx TW18 4LP *tel:* 01784 880937. Joanne Smith, proprietor. *Intensive technique courses in British traditional mus for vn, mandolin, gui, small-pipes. Also art/pottery. Tutors are drawn from leading professionals. Various dates. Full-board based in rural South Wales. Limited to a maximum of ten students. Fees: £245 (residential only).*

Jackdaws Educational Trust. Bridge House, Great Elm, nr Frome, Somerset BA11 3NY *tel:* 01373 812383 *fax:* 01373 812083. Maureen Lehane Wishart, mus dir. *Residential w/end mus courses offered every w/end all year round, catering for students, proficient amateurs, mus teachers and professional musicians. Young people of a required standard are encouraged and appropriate concessions in course fees are made. Fees: residential w/ends £105 plus B&B at £16 per person per night; for age 14 or under, £50 plus B&B; for age 15-22, £75 plus B&B.*

Jazz Academy. c/o 12 Castle St, Berkhamsted, Herts HP4 2BQ *tel:* 01442 864989 *fax:* 01442 384493. Michael Garrick, dir. *Piano People, Hereford, 23-26 Apr 2000; Summer Jazz, Tunbridge Wells 20-26 Aug 2000. Fees on application. For any age. Applications by 7 Apr and 14 Aug.*

JACKDAWS • Educational Trust

Bridge House • Great Elm
Frome • Somerset • BA11 3NY
Tel: 01373 812383 • Fax: 01373 812083
Musical Director • Maureen Lehane Wishart

WEEKEND MUSIC COURSES
for just £105 plus B&B

Jackdaws Educational Trust invites music lovers of every level to find peace and inspiration on a Jackdaws music weekend. We offer high quality tuition by top musicians and teachers in a rural setting of great beauty.

Courses are offered for singers and instrumentalists of all ages and levels. A warm welcome, delicious meals and like-minded company make these hard-working courses a sociable and relaxing experience.

Interested? If so, call us on 01373 812383 and we'll send you a brochure post haste. Discounts are available for children, students and multiple bookings. B&Bs in local homes can be arranged for just £16 per night.

KENNETH VAN BARTHOLD
PIANO

Workshop Course
established 1966

uniquely INTENSIVE
2 tutors to 12 students; working from 9am to 6pm daily; 12 practice studios; recording facilities; closed circuit TV; full use of faculty library and record collection; final public recitals on Steinway Concert Grand.

7th - 25th August 2000
in Edinburgh, the Athens of the North, during the International Festival of Music, Theatre, and Films presented in association with the University of Edinburgh Music Faculty and Centre for Continuing Education.

write or ring:
Kenneth van Barthold, Arvensis,
Stour Lane, Stour Row,
Shaftesbury, Dorset SP7 0QJ
Tel/Fax: 01747 838318

Singing at Morley

Courses for adults

including:
Opera School
Singers' Workshops
(beginners to advanced)
Large Choirs
Chamber Choir
Choral Workshops
Languages for Singers
Music reading
Jazz Singing, Pop Singing

Further information & enrolment from

Morley College
61 Westminster Bridge Road, London SE1 7HT
Tel: 0171 450 9238 • Fax: 0171 928 4074
Waterloo Mainline/Lambeth North Tube

Morley College Ltd is a Company limited by guarantee registered in England No. 2829836. Reg. Charity N. 1023523

Junior Bass-Fest. The British and International Bass Forum, Studio Ten, Farnham Maltings, Farnham, Surrey GU9 7QR *tel:* 01252 319610 *also fax; email:* bibf@classical-artists.com. David Heyes, dir; Cathy Elliott, jnr Bass-Fest dir; Elizabeth Hosford, tutor. *8-12 Aug 2000, Leighton Park School, Reading. For db players aged 7-14. Emphasis placed on informality and enjoyment and will include full programme of supervised free-time activities alongside bass orch, ens coaching, individual lessons, jazz, contemporary and improvisation. Fees: from £120 (non-residential); from £140 (residential).*

Kato Havas One-Day Workshop for Strings. 72 Victoria Rd, Oxford OX2 7QE *tel:* 01865 514094 *also fax.* Kato Havas, sec. *Jul. Release of Tension and Stage Fright in Performance, held at St Edmund Hall, Oxford. Fees: £10 (Khana members); £30 (non-members).*

Keele Summer Schools. Centre for Continuing and Professional Education, Keele University, Keele, Staffs ST5 5BG *tel:* 01782 583436 *fax:* 01782 583248 *email:* ada02@cc.keele.ac.uk. Helen McGarry, course sec. *26 Aug-2 Sep 2000, applications by 26 May. Chamber Music Summer School, for amateurs, students and teachers aged 18 and above.*

Kenneth van Barthold Intensive Piano Workshop. Arvenis, Stour Lane, Stour Row, Shaftesbury, Dorset SP7 0QJ *tel:* 01747 838318 *also fax.* Kenneth van Barthold. *7-25 Aug 2000. 2 tutors for 12 students, 12 practice rooms, recording facilities, final public recitals on Steinway concert grand. Presented in association with the University of Edinburgh Music Faculty and Centre for Continuing Education.*

The Kodály Institute of Britain. 133 Queen's Gate, London SW7 5LE *tel:* 020 7823 7371 *fax:* 020 7584 7691. Mary Skone-Roberts, admin. *International summer school in Edinburgh. Courses for kindergarten, primary, secondary and tertiary educators, singers and pno teachers. Musicianship training for all. M/classes and recitals. 1-year p/t courses in musicianship according to the Kodály Principles at 3 levels: elementary, intermediate, advanced, begin late Sep in London and Edinburgh, credit bearing for Trinity College LTCL (Mus Ed) Cert and Dip. W/end courses in early childhood, primary and secondary mus educ.*

Lacock Summer School. Cantax House, Lacock, Chippenham, Wilts SN15 2JZ *tel:* 01249 730468 *also fax.* Andrew van der Beek. *16-21 Jul, 23-28 Jul 2000. For singers and players of renaissance and baroque insts. All ages. Fees: £230, £140 (aged 25 and under).*

Lake District Summer Music. Stricklandgate House, 92 Stricklandgate, Kendal, Cumbria LA9 4PU *tel:* 01539 733411 *fax:* 01539 724441 *email:* info@ldsm.org.uk. Christopher Rowland, summer schools dir; Andrew Lucas, admin. *5-19 Aug 2000. Residential summer school, classes and individual coaching with international artists and tutors. For ens, str players and pianists at conservatoire and young professional level. Public performance opportunities. Free tickets to Festival concerts. Children's w/shops (ages 6-12) and Young String Venture (ages 10-18). See* **Young String Venture** *for str players aged 6-18.*

Lambent Books. 4 Coombe Gardens, New Malden, Surrey KT3 4AA *tel:* 020 8715 2560 *also fax; email:* lambent@well.com. Joseph O'Connor. *Courses and individual consultations for performers and teachers on performance anxiety, communication skills and psychology of learning.*

Lancaster Rehearsal Orchestra. Dept of Music, University of Lancaster, Lancaster LA1 4YW *tel:* 01524 593777/593013 *fax:* 01524 847298 *email:* d.mccaldin@lancaster.ac.uk. Denis McCaldin, cond; Ronald Adelson, sec. *1-day symphony orch courses 3 times pa. Alwyn,* Symphony No 3, *6 Feb 2000; Prokofiev,* Symphony No 7, *30 Apr 2000; Bax,* Symphony No 4, *13 Nov 2000. Entry by audition, aged 16 and above. Applications by 6 weeks before event. Fees: £8 per session (reductions for students).*

Latour International Festival of Music and the Arts (France). c/o Mananan Festival Office, Erin Arts Centre, Port Erin, Isle of Man IM9 6LD *tel:* 01624 835858 *fax:* 01624 836658 *email:* erinartscentre@enterprise.net. John Bethell, dir. *23-29 Jul 2000, applications by 1 May. Vocal and opera study courses with Jeffrey Lawton for professionals and amateurs aged 19-35. Opportunity to appear in opera performance.*

Lauderdale House Music. 22 Gresley Rd, London N19 3JZ *tel:* 020 7272 5664 *also fax.* Murray Gordon, mus chmn. *M/classes for pno, voice, vc, gui, vn, fl. Concerts, gui society, Singers Guild, Suzuki, U3A, etc.*

Learn at Leisure (Continuing Education). University of Nottingham, Cherry Tree Buildings, Nottingham NG7 2RD *tel:* 0115 951 6526 *fax:* 0115 951 6556 *email:* ce.residential@nottingham.ac.uk. Sylvia Stephens, residential courses admin. *Residential courses for adults. CBSO in Birmingham, 3-5 Mar; WNO in Llandudno: Carmen and Der Rosenkavalier, 23-25 Jun; Warsaw Mozart Festival, 8-15 Jul; Music of Robert Schumann, 1-3 Sep; Prague Music, 23-30 Sep; Glyndebourne w/end, 20-22 Oct. Fees: tbc.*

Leblanc Clarinet Summer School. Liverpool Hope University College, Hope Park, Liverpool L16 9JD *tel:* 0151 291 3457 *fax:* 0151 291 3170 *email:* walterd@livhope.ac.uk; AJRLeblanc@aol.com. David Walters, snr instrumental tutor; Andrew Roberts, (Leblanc). *Jul, applications by Jun; open to gr 8+; no age limit. M/classes and chmbr groups with UK's leading players. Some integration with the Colin Fleming Flute School. Further details from David Walters* tel: *0151 291 3457.*

Leeds College of Music. 3 Quarry Hill, Leeds LS2 7PD *tel:* 0113 222 3400 *fax:* 0113 222 3455 *email:* enquiries@leedscolmusic.ac.uk. Angela Spatcher-Johnson, head of mkt and commercial development. *Aug 2000. Annual residential jazz summer school for all standards, grouped by experience. Maximum number around 60. DJ 2-week summer school, grouped by experience. Non-residential. Ages 14 and above.*

Lights, Music, Action. Fish & Bell Management, PO Box 175, Bury St Edmunds, Suffolk IP32 7DY *tel:* 01359 270034 *email:* fishbelluk@aol.com. Phil Robson, course dir. *Annual residential summer school, Aug. Auditions by arrangement. Held in Suffolk. Ages 9-18. Jazz musicians (gr 4+); drama, dance and mus theatre (all standards, grouped by experience); backstagers training (make-up, scenery, costume). Large-scale final production. Fees: £242 full board, 10% discount for additional family members.*

Lionel Tertis International Viola Workshop. Erin Arts Centre, Victoria Square, Port Erin, Isle of Man IM9 6LD *tel:* 01624 835858 *fax:* 01624 836658 *email:* erinartscentre@enterprise.net. Martin Norbury, admin. *19-26 Aug 2000, applications by 31 Mar. Study courses and m/classes for professional and amateur va players of all ages. Fees: £90 plus £15 registration.*

Llandaff Summer Music Course. 50 Parc-y-Coed, Creigiau, Cardiff CF15 9LY *tel:* 029 2089 2388 *also fax.* Jenny Vale, admin; Christopher Vale, course dir. *Jul/Aug. Orch course for ages 10-17; Jun orch course for ages 8-12; pno course for ages 8-17.*

London Masterclasses. 5 Lyndhurst Gardens, London N3 1TA *tel:* 020 8346 7088 *fax:* 020 8343 3669 *email:* info@lmc.ftech.co.uk. B Saipe, dir. *Summer 2000; apply by mid-May; aged 18 and above. Fees: £350.*

MAC (Midlands Arts Centre). Education Dept, Cannon Hill Park, Birmingham B12 9QH *tel:* 0121 440 4221 ext 266/7 *fax:* 0121 446 4372. Gabrielle Oliver, educ programmer. *Specialist mus w/end courses for all ages including jazz and early mus. Mus courses for adults and children (Western and Asian insts and styles) during term-time and holidays. Jazz w/end, autumn half-term (date tbc); apply by 1 Oct.*

Manchester University. Centre for Continuing Education (CCE), Faculty of Arts, Humanities Building, Oxford Rd, Manchester M13 9PL *tel:* 0161 275 3290 *fax:* 0161 275 3300 *email:* angela.grandey@man.ac.uk. Glyn Davies, Programme head for mus. *Jan-Jun; Oct-Dec. Learning for pleasure: 1 and 2-term courses on variety of mus topics. Residential w/end courses at Chancellors: choral, orchestral and mus appreciation. Ages 18 and above. Fees: from £37-50 per term and £80-100 for residential courses.*

Marlborough College Summer School. Marlborough, Wilts SN8 1PA *tel:* 01672 892388 *fax:* 01672 892476. Alex Scott, sec. *Jul-Aug. Weekly courses for residents and non-residents of all ages: singing, pno for beginners and improvers, gui, choral w/shop, Unlock Your Voice, jazz improvisation, big bands, the History of Music From Cylinders to CDs, Classical Music Through the Centuries. Plus over 180 different courses for all the family. Fees: from £85 (tbc).*

Mid-Pennine Arts. Yorke St, Burnley BB11 1HD *tel:* 01282 421986 *fax:* 01282 429513 *email:* midpen@midpenninearts.demon.co.uk. Nick Hunt, dir. *Arts Development Agency for Burnley, Hyndburn, Pendle, Rossendale, Todmorden. Various mus in educ projects.*

Missenden Abbey. Great Missenden, Bucks HP16 0BD *tel:* 01494 862904 *fax:* 01494 890087 *email:* enquiries@missendenabbey.ac.uk. Rosa Maria Welsh, educ co-ord. *W/end courses all year round including mus appreciation and singing. Aged 16 and above. Fees: £165.60 (residential); £116.60 (tuition and meals); £71.60 (non-residential). Summer school, Aug. Fees: £499 (residential); £154 (non-residential).*

Morland Choristers' Camp. Garden Flat, Morland, Penrith, Cumbria CA10 3AZ *tel:* 01931 714654. Revd Canon Gervase W Markham, camp chief. *30 Jul-6 Aug 2000, apply by 30 Jun. A residential course approved by the Royal School of Church Music for ages 9-18 who are members of church choirs or school choirs. Church mus, secular mus and outdoor activities. Fees: £180.*

Morley College. 61 Westminster Bridge Rd, London SE1 7HT *tel:* 020 7450 9238 *fax:* 020 7928 4074. Robert Hanson, dir of mus; Helen Simpson, Mus Access co-ord. *Large range of adult educ courses, including ens, solo performance, singing, electronic mus, history and theory; all levels from beginners to advanced. Special theme days held regularly.*

Mostly Music. 28 Carlisle Close, Mobberley, Knutsford, Cheshire WA16 7HD *tel:* 01565 872650 *also fax; email:* mostlymusic@btinternet.com. Roger Wilkes. *Courses and events throughout the year, in Greater Manchester and NW England: choral, rcdr, early mus, study courses, church mus, private and correspondence tuition. Singing holidays at home and abroad (spring, summer). For all ages; apply by 12 days before each event.*

Music at the Edinburgh Festival *see* **Edinburgh University Centre for Continuing Education.**

Music at Madingley. Board of Continuing Education, University of Cambridge, Madingley Hall, Madingley, Cambs CB3 8AQ *tel:* 01954 280280 *fax:* 01954 280200 *email:* laf22@cam.ac.uk. Linda Fisher, programmes mgr. *Various w/end and week-long residential practical courses for ages 18 and above. Alberni m/classes, 21-28 Apr 2000. Fees: £413 (residential), £295 (non-residential).*

Music at Rendcomb. 2/228 London Rd, Cheltenham GL52 6HW *tel:* 01242 244200 *also fax; email:* ams@228sundridge.freeserve.co.uk. Alison Mary Sutton, dir; Richard Sharpe, admin. *Solo singing course in operatic art, including operetta. Singers of all standards welcome, although some experience preferred. Coaching sessions, voice clinics to address specific technical problems, dramatic techniques and improvisation. Plus daily yoga linking relaxation with breathing and sound. 29 May-4 Jun 2000, Rendcomb, Cirencester. Fees: £395 residential, £325 non-residential.*

Music Summer School. Wedgwood Memorial College, Barlaston, Stoke-on-Trent ST12 9DG *tel:* 01782 372105 *fax:* 01782 372393 *email:* wedgwood.college@staffordshire.gov.uk. D Tatton. *Short courses throughout the year including mus tutorial w/ends from Sep 2000-Mar 2001.*

Musicale Holidays. The Bourne, 20 Salisbury Ave, Harpenden, Herts AL5 2QG *tel:* 01582 460978 (24 hrs) *fax:* 01582 767343 *email:* HMusicale@aol.com. David Johnston, Gillian Johnston, dirs. *Residential course (Musicale Young Artists' Programme) at Harpenden for high-standard orch and symphonic wind orch players, plus other non-residential courses held at venues throughout UK during Jul and Aug. Caters for instrumentalists aged 5-18 of all standards and non-instrumentalists aged 5-9 in the form of a mus activity course. Applications welcome until opening date of course.*

Musicfest International Summer School. Aberystwyth Arts Centre, Penglais, Aberystwyth, Ceredigion SY23 3DE *tel:* 01970 622882 *fax:* 01970 622883 *email:* lla@aber.ac.uk. Louise Amery, mkt mgr; Nicholas Jones, artistic dir. *17-31 Jul 2000, applications by Jul. Runs in conjunction with Musicfest, Aberystwyth International Music Festival. Provides the opportunity for children over 14, mus students, professional and amateur adults to work on chmbr mus and solo repertoire and to play in orchs with a team of British chmbr musicians of international standing.*

Musicosophia United Kingdom. PO Box 3030, Littlehampton, W Sussex BN17 6GA *tel:* 01273 327712 *also fax;* 01903 786745 *email:* ics@pavilion.co.uk. Catherine Brophy, dir. *Organises courses for listeners, aged 6 and above, as part of an international movement for music lovers. Beethoven: Symphonies, 6-7 May 2000; Bach: 250th Anniversary, 1-3 Aug (£120, resident); Mendelssohn:* A Midsummer Night's Dream, *24-25 Jun. Various 1-day courses and children's Sat morning w/shops. Fees: £25-150 (concessions available). Applications by two weeks before course begins.*

National Chamber Music Course. 3 Grand Ave, London N10 3AY *tel:* 020 8442 0326 *fax:* 020 8372 6465 *email:* ncmc@btinternet.com. Caroline Stone, dir admin; Elisabeth Waterhouse, dir. *Aug, applications by end Apr. Held at Temple Dinsley, Herts. Chmbr mus course for str players aged 10-18. (2 chmbr ens, inst classes, orch and choir). Fees: £320.*

The National Children's Chamber Orchestra of Great Britain. The Bourne, 20 Salisbury Ave, Harpenden, Herts AL5 2QG *tel:* 01582 760014 *fax:* 01582 767343 *email:* HMusicale@aol.com. Gillian and David Johnston, dirs; Caroline Marriott, admin; Melanie Ragge, associate dir. *For str players aged 10-16 at gr 7 and above. The players will play in quartets and in a chmbr orch combining with wind players from the National Children's Wind Orchestra of Great Britain. Entry is by audition during the autumn term for a residential course at Easter - concerts at major venues around the country later in the year. Also training str orch for promising younger players. BBC Albert Hall Proms concert, 12 Aug 2000.*

National Children's Music Camps. 61 Crown Rd, Sutton, Surrey SM1 1RT *tel:* 020 8715 4048 *also fax; email:* ncmc@edcrown.demon.co.uk. Avril Dankworth, founder-president; David Edwards, campers' admin. *Aug, applications by Feb. Annual mus camps for ages 8-17 in the grounds of the Old Rectory, Wavendon, Bucks. Fees: £183 (teenage), £168 (jnr) (tbc).*

National Children's Orchestra. 157 Craddocks Ave, Ashtead, Surrey KT21 1NU *tel:* 01372 276857 *fax:* 01372 271407 *email:* mail @ncoorch.demon.co.uk. Vivienne Price MBE, dir of mus; Elisabeth Humphreys, admin. *Easter and summer holidays. Auditions in autumn. 5 orchs divided into age groups: Main orch, under 13, under 12, under 11 (2 orchs). 2000: main orch, 14-22 Apr, Worksop College; 4-12 Aug, Ackworth School, Pontefract; 17 Dec, QEH, London. Under-13 orch, 14-22 Apr, Ackworth School; 20-28 Aug, Ackworth; 17 Dec, QEH, London. Under-12 orch, 12-19 Aug, Ackworth School and w/wind, br and perc course. Training and introductory orchs, 28 Jul-4 Aug, Ackworth School.*

National Children's Orchestra of Scotland. 13 Somerset Place, Glasgow G3 7JT *tel:* 0141 332 8311 *fax:* 0141 332 3915 *email:* nyos@cqm.co.uk. Richard Chester, dir. *Apr 2000, residential courses providing tuition from professional musicians prior to public performance. Ages 8-14; apply by Nov. Applicants must be resident in Scotland.*

The National Children's Wind Orchestra of Great Britain. The Bourne, 20 Salisbury Ave, Harpenden, Herts AL5 2QG *tel:* 01582 760014 *fax:* 01582 767343 *email:* HMusicale@aol.com. Gillian and David Johnston, dirs; Caroline Marriott, admin; Melanie Ragge, associate dir. *For w/wind, br and perc players aged 10-15 at gr 5 and above. A 1-player-per-part wind ens and 2 wind orchs are formed. Entry by audition during the autumn term for a residential course at Easter and concerts at major venues around the country later in the year. Study includes standard repertoire, new commissions and chmbr mus. Albert Hall Proms concert scheduled for the Wind Ensemble, 12 Aug 2000.*

National Isis Strings Academy. 2a Chapel Close, Brookman's Park, Hatfield, Herts AL9 6NY *tel:* 01707 642244 *also fax; email:* vrnisa@queenswood.herts.sch.uk. Viviane Ronchetti, mus dir; Sir Neville Marriner CBE, patron. *High-quality chmbr orch training for str players gr 7+ and aged 11-19. Residential course at Queenswood School, Hatfield. Feb w/end; 14-18 Apr; 15-22 Jul; Oct w/end; applications by Dec 1999. Fees: £210 (week); £95(w/end).*

National Junior Music Club of Great Britain. 23 Hitchin St, Biggleswade, Beds SG18 8AX *tel:* 01767 316521 *fax:* 01767 317221 *email:* courses@lindsaymusic.co.uk. Douglas Coombes, dir; Carole Lindsay-Douglas, organiser. *Available for INSET bookings.*

National Operatic and Dramatic Association (NODA). NODA House, 1 Crestfield St, London WC1H 8AU *tel:* 020 7837 5655 *fax:* 020 7833 0609. Mark Thorburn, chief executive. *Aug, applications by 31 Jul. Residential week-long theatre training course for ages 18 and above. University of Warwick in Coventry.*

National Scout and Guide Symphony Orchestra Course. c/o Youth Programme Section, Guide Association, 17-19 Buckingham Palace Rd, London SW1W 0PT *tel:* 020 7834 6242 *fax:* 020 7828 8317 *email:* chq@guides.org.uk. Katie Hillier, youth programme asst. *Aug 2000 in London and South East for one week then one week touring overseas. Applicants must be aged 13-26, members of the Scout or Guide Associations and proficient in at least one orch inst. Fees: tbc.*

National Youth Choir of Scotland. 18 Polmont Park, Polmont By Falkirk FK2 0XT *tel:* 01324 711749 *fax:* 01324 713746 *email:* nycos@ ednet.co.uk. Robert W Tait, admin; Christopher Bell, artistic dir and cond. *Residential courses for the Training Choir (ages 14-17), Easter 2000 and NYCOS (ages 16-24), Jul 2000. Fees: £250-300. Children's choirs in W Lothian and Edinburgh for ages 8-9; entry by audition; meet weekly; fee: £30 pa.*

National Youth Choirs of Great Britain. PO Box 67, Holmfirth, Huddersfield, W Yorks HD7 1GQ *tel:* 01484 687023 *fax:* 01484 681635 *email:* nycgb@compuserve.com; nycgb@tesco.net. Carl Browning, exec dir; Michael Brewer OBE, mus dir; Anna Tonkin, choir admin. *Residential courses for members of the National Youth Choirs. Auditions held annually in Jun, Jul, Oct and Nov for ages 12-19 (training choir) and 16-22 (main choir). Courses at New Year, Easter and summer. Fees: £240-300 (course), £20 (audition).*

National Youth Jazz Orchestra of Scotland. 13 Somerset Place, Glasgow G3 7JT *tel:* 0141 332 8311 *fax:* 0141 332 3915 *email:* nyos@cqm.co.uk. Richard Chester, dir. *Residential summer course with tuition from experienced tutors followed by public performances. Ages 12-21. Applicants must be resident in Scotland.*

National Youth Music Theatre. 5th Floor, The Palace Theatre, Shaftesbury Ave, London W1V 8AY *tel:* 020 7734 7478 *fax:* 020 7734 7515. Jeremy James Taylor, artistic dir; Uon Bromwich, gen mgr; Vivienne Hughes, outreach admin/auditions. *Application by Sep for open access mus theatre w/shops, national (residential) and regional. Auditions Oct-Dec for singer/actor/dancers (ages 11-19), musicians (11-22) and stage management (16-19) for 4 major mus theatre productions pa. Courses are residential and non-residential, usually during school holidays and w/ends. Please phone for further details.*

National Youth Orchestra of Great Britain. 32 Old School House, Britannia Rd, Bristol BS15 8DB *tel:* 0117 960 0477 *fax:* 0117 960 0376 *email:* nyo@btinternet.com. Michael de Grey, chief exec; Jill White, dir of mus. *Residential courses 3 times pa. In 2000 the NYO will perform in major venues throughout the UK, including Symphony Hall, Birmingham; The Anvil, Basingstoke; The Barbican, London; Victoria Hall, Hanley and The Royal Albert Hall, London. Auditions annually for players aged 13-19 (gr 8 dist standard, applicants need not have taken exams). Applications for 2001 orch by 31 Jul 2000. Fees: £225. Grants available. 31 Jul-18 Aug, Wycombe Abbey, Bucks.*

National Youth Orchestra of Scotland. 13 Somerset Place, Glasgow G3 7JT *tel:* 0141 332 8311 *fax:* 0141 332 3915 *email:* nyos@cqm.co.uk. Richard Chester, dir. *Winter and summer residential courses providing tuition from professional musicians and rehearsals with internationally renowned conds and soloists prior to concert tours. Easter residential training course. Ages 12-21. Summer residential courses in Jun-Jul followed by public performances. Annual auditions held in Jan-Feb for courses at Easter, in Jul-Aug and Dec-Jan; application deadline Nov. Applicants must be resident in Scotland.*

National Youth Wind Orchestra of Great Britain. 2 High Green, Woodham Village, Aycliffe, Co Durham DL5 4RZ *tel:* 01325 308893 *also fax; email:* kits@nywo.freeserve.co.uk. Kit Shepherd, exec dir. *5-16 Apr 2000, Staffs; 31 Jul-12 Aug, Berks. Auditions for membership of orch held every autumn. Residential courses for main orch. Courses and w/shops; outreach days and m/classes. Age 15-21 at gr 8+. Fees: £350 main orch; £250 focus courses.*

Nelly Ben-Or Piano Courses Incorporating the Alexander Technique. 23 Rofant Rd, Northwood, Middlesex HA6 3BD *tel:* 01923 822268 *also fax.* Roger Clynes, course sec; Nelly Ben-Or, dir. *7-9 Jan 2000, mid-July 2000. International courses in London for pianists, teachers and advanced students. Individual sessions at the keyboard and in the Alexander Technique. The courses apply the principles of the Alexander Technique to aspects of pno playing and creative study of mus for performance.*

Nonsuch Summer School. 101 St Stephens Rd, Canterbury CT2 7JT *tel:* 01227 462871 *also fax.* Sian Jones, admin. *Jul/Aug 2000 at Hockerill School, Bishops Stortford. W European court dances of 12th-19th C. Fully residential. Aged 16 and above. Fees: £120-450.*

North East Early Music Forum (NEEMF). 43 Beckett's Park Cres, Leeds LS6 3PH *tel:* 0113 278 6886 *fax:* 0113 230 7818 *email:* bmb6jlj@bmb.leeds.ac.uk. Jillian Johnson, hon sec. *Day w/shops throughout year in performance and interpretation of early mus for ages 16 and above. Residential w/end at the University of Leeds for singers and instrumentalists, apply by 1 Sep. Fees: £95-145 (some student bursary funding).*

Northern Junior Philharmonic Orchestra Course. Moorcroft, South Rd, Prudhoe, Northumberland NE42 5LB *tel:* 01661 832605 *fax:* 01661 833526. Peter Swan, organising sec. *Jul-Aug, auditions Apr, applications by Feb. Orch course for instrumentalists aged 12-23 of gr 8 standard. Sir Michael Tippett Award (£500) available for the most promising musician(s) on the course.*

Northern Recorder Course. 41 Grosvenor Rd, Sale, Cheshire M33 6WL *tel:* 0161 973 2050. D A Bamforth. *Held at Chester College, 13-20 Apr 2000. St Matthews Hall, Stretford, 21 Oct 2000. Any age.*

Northern Sax Course (Harrogate). c/o Lindsey Music, 42 St Mary's Park, Louth, Lincs LN11 0EF *tel:* 01507 605244 *email:* jeff@wwplus.freeserve.co.uk. Jeff Brown, events organiser. *25-28 Apr 2000; apply by Apr; for adults/students.*

Northumbrian Recorder and Viol School (NORVIS). 5 Birchgrove Ave, Gilesgate Moor, Durham DH1 1DE *tel:* 0191 386 4782 *email:* marlene.austin@durham.ac.uk. Marlene Austin, admin. *22-29 Jul 2000 held at College of St Hild and St Bede, Durham. Course for any age covers all aspects of early mus: rcdrs, viols, baroque strs, renaissance insts, plucked insts, keyboard, singing and dancing.*

Oakham International Summer School. PO Box 992, Waterbeach, Cambridge CB5 9SQ *tel:* 01223 522411 *fax:* 08700 548706 *email:* info@laplaya.co.uk. Juliet Allan, gen mgr; Peter Phillips, artistic dir; David Woodcock, associate dir. *9-15 Jul 2000; applications by 31 Jan; ages 16 and over. Choral course directed by Peter Phillips (director of The Tallis Scholars) at Oakham School in Rutland. Fees: £950 (£300 bursary available for UK students).*

The Old Rectory Music Courses. Fittleworth, Pulborough, W Sussex RH20 1HU *tel:* 01798 865306 *also fax; email:* oldrectory@mistral.co.uk. Tony and Sue Dawkins, principals. *Wide range of week, w/end and mid-week courses in singing, hpd, mus appreciation, handbells, rcdr, etc.*

Opera Mint. 278 Gillott Rd, Edgbaston, Birmingham B16 0RU *tel:* 0121 454 3087 *also fax.* Sara Clethero, artistic dir; John Challenor, hon treasurer. *Trains individual student singers of all ages to as near professional standards as possible. Provides dramatic and vocal training in a group setting. W/end w/shops and classes in movement, singing technique, Alexander Technique and staging operatic productions, choral work and m/classes. Fees: £60 (w/end). Also summer school for adult choral and solo singers, ages 18-35. 22-29 Jul 2000, applications by 16 Jul. Fees: £315 (inc board).*

The Opera School (Wales). Rhydyberi Cottages, Merthyr Cynog, Brecon, Powys LD3 9SA *tel:* 01874 690339 *fax:* 01874 690254. Bridgett Gill, dir. *1-22 Apr 2000, apply by Oct. Intensive 3-week spring course for young professional singers, ages 20-35, combining stage and vocal training, make-up and stage-fighting instruction, culminating in several fully-staged performances with orch ens, touring theatres in Wales and London. Fees: £350, bursaries available.*

Orff Society (UK). 7 Rothesay Ave, Richmond, Surrey TW10 5EB *tel:* 020 8876 1944 *also fax.* Margaret Murray, hon sec. *Creative mus courses mainly for teachers in primary and middle schools. Basic Orff, 18-19 Apr 2000, London; Putting Theory into Practice, 10-11 Jun, Richmond; Hands on Music, 29 Jul-4 Aug, Huddersfield University.*

Oundle International Festival and Summer School for Young Organists. The Old Crown, Glapthorn, Oundle, Peterborough PE8 5BJ *tel:* 01832 272026 *also fax; email:* OIF@btinternet.com. James Parsons, dir; Trisha Ryan, admin. *16-23 Jul 2000, applications by 1 Apr. Summer School for 60 organists based in Oundle, Northants. Ages 14-24. Fees: c £400. Four courses offered, with international faculty of org tutors; valuable recital awards and week of festival events. Special courses for prospective university org scholars and intensive advanced tuition for students already at conservatoire. 7-9 Apr 2000, Pulling Out the Stops, w/end course for beginner organists ages 10-14. Applications by 1 Feb 2000. Fees: c £150.*

Oxford Baroque Chamber Music Week. c/o 13 Brackley Rd, Monton Green, Eccles, Manchester M30 9LG *tel:* 0161 281 2502 *fax:* 01223 461143 *email:* baroquew@silverfe.demon.co.uk. Peter Collier, course dir. *Aug 2000 at Headington School, Oxford. Course for wind, str and keyboard players of baroque or modern insts at old or modern pitch. A secure technique and good sight-reading is required. No age limit.*

Oxford Cello School. 67 Oxford Rd, Abingdon, Oxon OX14 2AA *tel:* 01235 530572 *fax:* 01235 555952 *email:* cello@oxfordcelloschool.freeserve.co.uk. Marianne Gottfeldt, dir; Stephen Gottfeldt, course dir. *Residential and non-residential summer schools for vc in Jul and Aug. Technique m/classes, individual lessons, scales, video analysis, improvisation, ens, vc orch and choir. Gr 6-8 aural training and theory for the younger student. Solo performance with orch for performance students. Performance course for post gr 8 students, adult improvers course and AEB Advanced Certificate.*

Oxford Chamber Music Courses. 80 St Bernard's Rd, Oxford OX2 6EJ *tel:* 01865 553892. Tom Patterson. *3-day meetings. 2000: 13-16, 17-20 Apr, plus two 3-day meetings in Aug; apply by six weeks before each meeting. Fees: £155 (residential), £120 (non-residential), reduction for students in f/t educ (£35). For any age group.*

Oxford Flute Summer School. 26 Hyde Green, Beaconsfield HP9 2ER *tel:* 01494 681566 *fax:* 0118 950 7865 *email:* ofss@compuserve.com. Clive Conway, Janet Way, dirs; Katie Bycroft, admin. *Mid-Aug 2000. Annual course for fl players of all standards ages 14 and above, held at The Queen's College, Oxford. Concerts, classes, ens and individual tuition. Four options offered: general course for players of all ages and standards; intensive course, 3 individual lessons and public performance; audition course for young students auditioning for mus colleges and universities; seminar course for advanced small group tuition. Fees: £240 (general), £320 (intensive, audition and seminar).*

Oxford University Department for Continuing Education. 1 Wellington Square, Oxford OX1 2JA *tel:* 01865 270396 *fax:* 01865 270309 *email:* oussa@conted.ox.ac.uk. Anna Sandham, co-ord (summer school); Jonathan Darnborough, associate tutor in mus (day/week classes). *Wide-ranging programme of weekly courses and day schools in Oxford and surrounding area, for ages 18 and above. Fees: from £24. Also runs a number of 1-week summer schools for adults in aspects of mus appreciation, 15 Jul-19 Aug 2000; applications by Jun. Provisional fees: from £275 p/week (non-residential); from £500 p/week (full board). Also Association for Learning Technology international conference, Sep.*

Pendrell Hall College. Codsall Wood, Wolverhampton, Staffs WV8 1QP *tel:* 01902 434112 *fax:* 01902 434113 *email:* pendrell.college@staffordshire.gov.uk. David Evans, principal; Linda Reeve, admin offr. *Mus study w/ends for ages 18-80. Includes light mus, classical mus, rcdr playing and early mus. 2000: Recorders, 28 Feb-1 Mar; Life and Music of Brahms, 24-26 Mar; Recorder Playing, 9-11 May.*

Pipers' Guild. 121 Hallam Way, West Hallam, Derbys DE7 6LP *tel:* 0115 930 8323 *email:* margent@rmplc.co.uk. Stephanie Payne, sec; Mary Argent, chmn; Betty Roe, president. *Summer school, Aug at Royal School for the Deaf in Derby.*

Practical Psychology for Instrumental and Vocal Music Teachers and Performers. Music, Mind and Movement, 28 Glebe Place, London SW3 5LD *tel:* 020 7352 1666 *also fax; email:* musicmindmovement@btinternet.com. Lucinda Mackworth-Young, dir. *17-20 Jul 2000, apply by 3 Jun. Practical psychology for inst and vocal mus teaching, learning and performing, including teacher-pupil-parent relationships, emotions and motivation, teaching styles and learning strategies, practice, problem pupils, communication and anxiety in performance. Also Eurhythmics, Dance through the Ages, Improvisation and related disciplines. Also w/end courses in Apr, Nov 2000 and Apr 2001, Norfolk and 1-day courses throughout the year. Courses bear credit towards the ATCL and LTCL (Mus Educ) and Certificate of Music Education of Trinity College, London.*

Pro Corda Trust (National School for Young Chamber Music Players). Leiston Abbey House, Theberton Rd, Leiston, Suffolk IP16 4TB *tel:* 01728 831354 *fax:* 01728 832500 *email:* procorda@procorda.demon.co.uk. Sir Colin Davis, president; Robert Max, mus dir; Mererid Crump, admin; Pamela Spofforth, founder; M Parrington, T Boulton, course dirs. *Residential courses during school holidays for young str players and pianists aged 8-18 attending twice yearly at preparatory, primary, jnr, intermediate and snr levels. Specialist ens tuition under the direction of distinguished musicians. Entry by audition. Application forms from Administrator at above address.*

Randazzo Opera. 24 Bladon Court, Barrow Rd, London SW16 5NE *tel:* 020 8677 8821/8309 1309. Arlene Randazzo, admin and stage dir. *Jul 2000, Hylands House, Chelmsford, Essex. W/shops start in Mar with performances in Jun and Jul throughout London. All ages. Auditions in winter. Fees: £300 per term including all performances.*

Rathbone-Dickson Chamber Music Course. 31 Chepstow Place, London W2 4TT *tel:* 020 7229 0219 *also fax; email:* rdcourse@cwcom.net. Joyce Rathbone, David Waterman, dirs. *Aug. Held at Westonbirt School, Tetbury, Glos. Pno and str players aged 16-26.*

Recorder Summer School. 113 Birchwood Rd, Marton, Middlesbrough TS7 8DE *tel:* 01642 310628. Miss S Foxall, sec. *29 Jul-5 Aug 2000 at Bretton Hall, Wakefield. Classes and ens for rcdr players aged 16 and above (age 15 accepted if accompanied by an adult on the course). All grades including beginners. Renaissance band, baroque chmbr mus, concert and mus shops.*

The Rehearsal Orchestra. 60-62 Clapham Rd, London SW9 0JJ *tel:* 020 7820 9994 *email:* bwhyte@rehearsal-orchestra.org. Harry Legge OBE, artistic dir; Katie Lang, admin. *Advanced orch training for students and young professionals, teachers and experienced players. Wide range of orch repertoire studied, including new mus. 1 and 2-day sessions throughout the year, plus residential week in Edinburgh during the festival. Ages 16 and above with good sight-reading. Student and non-student rates given on application.*

Royal College of Organists. 7 St Andrew St, Holborn, London EC4A 3LQ *tel:* 020 7936 3606 *fax:* 020 7353 8244 *email:* events@rco.org.uk. Alan Dear, snr exec; Simon Williams, educ and events offr. *Residential course for organists.*

Royal School of Church Music. Cleveland Lodge, Westhumble, Dorking RH5 6BW *tel:* 01306 872800 *fax:* 01306 887260 *email:* education@rscm.com. Geoffrey Weaver, dir of studies; Jane Hiley, courses admin. *1-day and longer residential courses for singers and instrumentalists aged 9+ at many locations around the country. Training events for choristers of all ages during Easter (applications by 1 Mar) and summer holidays (applications by 1 Jun). Fees: £65-400. Brochure available.*

Royal School of Church Music Harwich Summer Courses. Cherry Trees, 23 Stanley Rd, Wivenhoe, Essex CO7 9EN *tel:* 01206 824036. Graham Wadley, admin. *Boys' and girls' courses; students' course.*

Royal Scottish Pipe Band Association. 45 Washington St, Glasgow G3 8AZ *tel:* 0141 221 5414 *fax:* 0141 221 1561. Iain M White, exec offr. *Organises educ classes run by 12 branches. Annual summer school, 16-21 Jul 2000; apply by 31 May. All ages.*

St Andrews International Flute Summer School. 3/9 Canada Court, 81 Miller St, Glasgow G1 1EB *tel:* 0141 248 5756 *also fax; email:* ruthmorley@ndirect.co.uk. Ruth Morley, dir. *Jul at St Leonard's School, St Andrews. Annual course for fl players to study with Peter Lloyd, including m/classes, chmbr mus, student concerts, daily warm-up/technique class, performance skills, tone development. May be attended by performers, participants or observers. Details on application.*

Sarum College Courses. Sarum College, 19 The Close, Salisbury, Wilts SP1 2EE *tel:* 01722 424800 *fax:* 01722 338508 *email:* rcf@sarum.ac.uk. Robert Fielding, dir of mus. *Residential courses held in Salisbury. Study week for organists, choir trainers and singers, 3-7 Apr 2000; applications by 31 Mar; fee £195; no age limit. Summer course for young composers, 25-29 Jul 2000; applications by 15 Jul; fee £150; 10 places; ages c 11-23. Summer course for young organists, 14-18 Aug 2000; applications by 7 Aug; fee £150; ages c 11-23.*

Schools Music Association of Great Britain. 71 Margaret Rd, New Barnet, Herts EN4 9NT *tel:* 020 8440 6919 *also fax.* Maxwell Pryce, hon sec and chief exec. *20-22 Oct 2000. Annual residential course and conference on mus in schools. Courses for mus teachers at regional centres throughout year.*

Scottish Amateur Music Association. 18 Craigton Cres, Alva, Clackmannanshire FK12 5DS *tel:* 01259 760249 *email:* secretary@sama.org.uk. Margaret Simpson, hon sec. *Summer courses include Traditional Fiddle School, National Youth Wind Ensemble of Scotland, National Youth Brass Band of Scotland, National Youth String Orchestra of Scotland (and Training School), Aug 2000; National Recorder School of Scotland, Sep 2000.*

Scottish Schools Orchestra Trust. 11 Melville Place, Edinburgh EH3 7PR *tel:* 0131 226 3392 *also fax; email:* jean@11mp.freeserve.co.uk. Jean Murray, dir. *Annual 1-week residential course held in a different part of Scotland each Jul. Orch and wind band playing for ages 9-15, including sports, arts, crafts and entertainments. Occasional Play Away days throughout the year for younger, less experienced players.*

Sheffield University Division of Adult Continuing Education. 196-198 West St, Sheffield S1 4ET *tel:* 0114 222 7000 *fax:* 0114 222 7001 *email:* adultconted@sheffield.ac.uk. Adam White, mus co-ord. *Courses in mus theory, pop mus, women in mus, mus appreciation, improvisation, composition. Sep-May, applications by Sep. Particularly suited to those over age 18 who wish to study mus without the need to give up work. Modules are accredited and validated by the University of Sheffield. Fees: £31.50-126 per 20 credit modules (24 weeks), or £360 pa (concessions also available). Also p/t certificate in Music Studies (120 credits), two years.*

Sing for Pleasure. Nortonthorpe Mills, Wakefield Rd, Scissett, Huddersfield HD8 9LA *tel:* 01484 860404 *also fax; email:* choral@sfp.cix.co.uk. Allan Jefferis, dir. *Residential and day courses for children, teachers, singers and choral conductors of all ages, throughout the country. International festivals through the 'A Coeur Joie' movement. Publishes repertoire suitable for schools and choral groups.*

Southend Summer School for the Performing Arts. PO Box 63, Southend-on-Sea, Essex SS1 3FE *tel:* 01702 588700/541595/586790 *fax:* 01702 586790. Roger Humphrey, dir; Rosemary Pennington, co-dir. *Intensive week-long summer school for ages 8-16, Aug. Mus, drama, dance, arts and crafts. Mus with specialist tutors includes strs, w/wind groups, perc, composition, keyboard. All activities culminate in a final public performance and demonstration. Fees: £40.*

Spode Music Week. 66 Cornish House, Green Dragon Lane, Brentford, Middx TW8 0DF *tel:* 020 8568 1072 *email:* IMS@moose.co.uk. Ian Saxton, bursar. *17-24 Aug 2000, applications by 5 Aug. Choir, orch, children's orch, lectures, recitals. Informal mus-making encouraged and families welcomed; children under 14 must be accompanied by an adult. Creche facilities and bursaries available. Fees (full board): adults £300, children 12-15 £190, children under 12 free.*

Stratford-upon-Avon International Flute Festival. 2 Windsor Court, Windsor St, Stratford-upon-Avon CV37 6LF *tel:* 01789 261561 *fax:* 01789 261577 *email:* stratflute@aol.com. Elena Durán, dir; Michael Emmerson, chmn. *24 Jul-5 Aug 2000, applications by 1 Jul. Annual m/classes for flautists of all ages and levels at King Edward VI School, Stratford upon Avon. Emphasis on performance; special sessions for young flautists. Fees: £500 (residential); £300 (non-residential).*

Stringwise. 3 Dresden Rd, London N19 3BE *tel:* 020 7561 0864 *also fax.* Cecily Mendelssohn. *A team of specialists, led by Sheila Nelson, offering professional development courses for all str teachers with emphasis on musicianship and freedom of movement in playing.*

Summer Music Summer School. 70 Surrenden Cres, Brighton BN1 6WF *tel:* 01273 884186 *also fax; email:* hinden-j@pavilion.co.uk. Jacqueline Froom, organiser. *Renowned internationally for solo singing courses. Also offers courses for choral singers and accompanists.*

Summer School for Piano Teachers. Ian Tomlin School of Music, Napier University, Craighouse Campus, Queens Craig, Edinburgh EH10 5LG *tel:* 0131 455 6200 *fax:* 0131 455 6211 *email:* a.butterworth@napier.ac.uk. Anna Butterworth, dir. *Aug 2000.*

Sussex University. Centre for Continuing Education, Education Development Building, Falmer, Brighton BN1 9RG *tel:* 01273 678040 *fax:* 01273 678848 *email:* cce@sussex.ac.uk. F Gray, dir. *P/t certificate in mus; day schools and weekly classes for adults throughout the year.*

Temple Dinsley Summer School. 86 Cromwell Ave, London N6 5HQ *tel:* 020 8340 8362 *fax:* 020 8341 7616 *email:* e.waterhouse@btinternet.com. Elisabeth Waterhouse, dir. *Aug, applications by 1 Jul. Suzuki camp in Herts for children aged 3-10 playing vn, vc or pno. Inst lessons, group lessons and related activities.*

Trinity College of Music. Continuing Education Dept, 11-13 Mandeville Place, London W1M 6AQ *tel:* 020 7487 9623; 020 7224 1626 *fax:* 020 7487 5717 *email:* ehardy@tcm.ac.uk. Maureen Hanke, dir for continuing educ; Elaine Hardy, snr admin. *Vacation course for teachers. Week one: 24-28 Jul 2000, SEN - The Performiing Arts; Piano Summer School. Week two: 31 Jul-4 Aug 2000, Composing and Improvising; 1-3 Aug, Preparing for FTCL. Fees: £200 p/week (non-residential). Also runs programmes of courses during half-term and Easter holidays.*

Urchfont Manor. Devizes, Wilts SN10 4RG *tel:* 01380 840495 *fax:* 01380 840005. Patricia Howell, dir. *Courses for adults. Apply by one month before each course. Fees: c £106 per w/end.*

Vacation Chamber Orchestras. Ashley House, Ure Bank, Ripon, N Yorkshire HG4 1JG *tel:* 01765 602856 *email:* vaco@bronco.co.uk. Xenophon Kelsey, mus dir. *Residential courses each vacation for advanced players. Frequent concerts in Yorkshire Dales, North York*

Moors, Northern Pennines, etc. Ages 16-22 with gr 8 or above. 2000: 22-26 Apr; European tour, 29 Jul-12 Aug; 14-19 and 21-26 Aug; 27-30 Dec. Fee: c £75 per course.

Wansfell College. Theydon Bois, Epping, Essex CM16 7LF *tel:* 01992 813027 *fax:* 01992 814761. Marilyn Taylor, principal. *W/end and midweek courses throughout year in all subjects including mus, mus appreciation, history and performance. Aged 18 and above. Fees: from £87.*

Wavendon Allmusic Plan. The Stables, Wavendon, Milton Keynes MK17 8LT *tel:* 01908 582522/583928 *fax:* 01908 281024 *email:* stables@powernet.co.uk. Jacky Scott, gen mgr; John Dankworth, Dame Cleo Laine, presidents. *W/shops, m/classes and courses running all year for all types of mus and all ages. Mus summer camps and courses for those aged 8-16.*

Wells Double Bass Weekend. Wells Cathedral School, The Coach House, New St, Wells, Somerset BA5 2LQ *tel:* 01252 319610 *also fax.* David Heyes, dir; Mette Hanskov, guest soloist and tutor. *Oct. Bass quartet coaching, bass orch, individual lessons, concerts and m/classes and is aimed at bassist of all ages and abilities. Emphasis on enjoyment and informality.*

Wessex Band Courses. 7 High Bank, Thurlstone, Sheffield S36 9QH *tel:* 01226 765579 *also fax.* John Grinnell, Margaret Grinnell, organisers. *31 Jul-6 Aug 2000; apply by end of Apr. Fees: c £50. Courses held at Sturminster Newton, Dorset, for br and wind band players. All ages - families encouraged. Snr (gr 4+) and jnr (pre gr 3-4 standard).*

West Dean College. West Dean, Chichester, W Sussex PO18 0QZ *tel:* 01243 811301 *fax:* 01243 811343 *email:* westdean@pavilion.co.uk. Rosemary Marley, mus course organiser. *7-9 Jan 2000, viol consort music; tutor: Alison Crum. 17-19 Mar, Renaissance music weekend; tutor: Nancy Hadden. 24-26 Mar, w/end for solo singers; tutor: Lena Phillips. Tba, new vocal repertory; tutor: Jane Manning. Summer schools in Jul/Aug: fl m/classes with Susan Milan; Chilingirian String Quartet course; Early Music Performance - for singers and instrumentalists. Aged 16 and above. Apply by 4 weeks before course.*

William Bennett Flute Summer School. 50 Lansdowne Gardens, London SW8 2EF *tel:* 020 7498 9807 *fax:* 020 7498 1155 *email:* mmichie@email.msn.com. Michie Bennett, sec.

Winchester Summer Music Course. 37 St David's Rd, Clifton Campville, nr Tamworth, Staffs B79 0BA *tel:* 01827 373586. James Maddocks, dir; Joan Maddocks, sec. *6-13 Aug 2000. Aged 14 and above.*

Wind Band Courses. 12 Brentry Rd, Fishponds, Bristol BS16 2AA *tel:* 0117 965 1796. Chris Harris, sec. *27-29 Oct 2000, applications by Jul. Wind Band Festival for all able wind band players at Queens Hotel, Southsea.*

Workers' Music Association Summer School. 71 Greenfield Gardens, London NW2 1HU *tel:* 020 8458 2321. L J Bielby, admin; J R Horrocks, chair. *5-12 Aug 2000. Participatory courses held at Wortley Hall, Yorks, for amateur musicians. Br band, orch, chmbr mus, folk, jazz, wind band, choral, solo and ens singing. Fees: £290 (residential), £205 (day student), £120 (external student).*

Wycombe Music Summer School. c/o New London Music Society, 5 Thame Rd, Sydenham, Chinnor, Oxon OX9 4LA *tel:* 01844 354083. Philip Meaden, dir; Cynthia Gomme, admin. *Aug 2000, applications by 31 May. For ages 16 and above. Symphony and intermediate orchs, choir, late learner ens, br and w/wind courses, all held at Queenswood School, Brookman's Park, Herts.*

Young String Venture. Stricklandgate House, 92 Stricklandgate, Kendal, Cumbria LA9 4PU *tel:* 01539 733411 *fax:* 01539 724441 *email:* info@ldsm.org.uk. Christopher Rowland, summer schools dir; Penny Stirling, Rachel Moore, course dirs; Andrew Lucas, admin. *6-11 Aug 2000. Summer chmbr mus course for str players aged 6-18. Coaching with specialist tutors includes Dalcroze eurythmics and orch training: children's w/shop, intermediate and advanced levels. New residential Advanced course option. End of course concerts. Application form from the administrator. See also* **Lake District Summer Music.**

Youth Music Centre Summer School. 58 Cyprus Ave, Finchley, London N3 1SR *tel:* 020 8343 1940. Jane Barnett, sec. *23-29 Jul 2000, applications by 15 May. Held at Farleigh School, Andover, Hants. For str and wind players aged 9-17, orch, chmbr mus and choir. Also included tuition in English for Japanese students. Fees: £240.*

Services

Marketing, Fundraising and Related Services

This section provides information on the resources necessary for the successful marketing of music and musicians, and on fundraising, whether in the form of patronage or sponsorship.

Marketing and Organisational Management

Entrants listed here usually offer a comprehensive service which may include guidance on market research, marketing planning, advertising, public and media relations, design and print, sales and sales promotion, pricing, personnel selection and training; some offer an event management service and some will provide an interim management service for organisations. There are also some organisations, closely allied in terms of their function, who specialise in arranging and promoting concerts; these are Concert Managements and are listed in the next sub-section. Readers seeking a service should first look here and then move on to the specialist sub-sections which follow. If uncertain as to which service is required, do not hesitate to make preliminary enquiries by telephone. There now exists a membership organisation for practitioners in arts marketing, the **Arts Marketing Association,** Bolton's Warehouse, 23 Tenison Rd, Cambridge CB1 2DG *tel:* 01223 578078 *fax:* 01223 578079 *email:* info@a-m-a.co.uk.

Anderton, Robin. 100 Harvist Rd, London NW6 6HL *tel:* 020 8960 4780 *fax:* 020 8964 5510. *Administration for w/shops, courses and auditions. Concert management.*

Anna Hassan Arts Marketing. 54 Elm Rd, Hale, Altrincham, Cheshire WA15 9QP *tel:* 0161 928 3085 *fax:* 0161 929 9648 *email:* ahassan@easynet.co.uk. *Freelance arts marketing and administration consultant.*

Arts About Manchester. 23 New Mount St, Manchester M4 4DE *tel:* 0161 953 4035 *fax:* 0161 953 4106 *email:* arts-mcr@mcrl.poptel.org.uk. Andrew McIntyre, asst dir. *Specialist market research into the attitudes, perceptions and motivations of classical mus attenders. UK-wide at subsidised rates.*

Arts and Business. Nutmeg House, 60 Gainsford St, Butler's Wharf, London SE1 2NY *tel:* 020 7378 8143 *fax:* 020 7407 7527 *email:* head.office@AandB.org.uk. Colin Tweedy, chief exec. *National association promoting partnerships between business and the arts.*

The Arts Business Ltd (ABL). 38 St Martin's Lane, London WC2N 4ER *tel:* 020 7420 9700 *fax:* 020 7420 9701. Jessica Robinson, new projects and sales co-ord. *Arts management consultancy specialising in arts, heritage, entertainment, media and crafts. Offers detailed sector knowledge, research and consultation expertise and market research.*

Arts Management Services. Bolton's Warehouse, 23 Tenison Rd, Cambridge CB1 2DG *tel:* 01223 578077 *fax:* 01223 578079. Anne Roberts. *Management of arts projects.*

Arts Marketing East. 50 The Street, Melton, Woodbridge, Suffolk IP12 1PW *tel:* 01394 388029 *fax:* 01394 386511 *email:* eo@audience.co.uk. Eric Orme, dir; Mary Ann Bartlet, publicity mgr. *Arts marketing services and consultancy for concert promoters. Clients include local authorities, RABs and many different arts organisations.*

Arts Marketing Hampshire. Mottisfont Court, High St, Winchester, Hants SO23 8ZD *tel:* 01962 865383 *fax:* 01962 841644 *email:* artsamh@hantsnet.hants.gov.uk. Julie Eaglen, dir; Matthew Carwardine-Palmer, mkt mgr. *Audience development initiatives, market research, marketing advice and consultancy, training, publications and distribution.*

Bill Clancy Arts Marketing. 67 Broadbottom Rd, Mottram-in-Longdendale, Cheshire SK14 6JA *tel:* 01457 765877 *also fax; email:* billaidmot@aol.com. Bill Clancy, Adrienne Pye, dirs. *Arts marketing consultants; promoters (mus and literary events).*

Cardiff Arts Marketing Ltd. 2 Market House, Market Rd, Canton, Cardiff CF5 1QE *tel:* 029 2037 3736 *fax:* 029 2038 4141. Peter Reynolds, mkt mgr. *Market research, database services, print distribution, project management, consultancy and marketing services.*

Chuck Julian Associates. Suite 51, 26 Charing Cross Rd, London WC2H 0DH *tel:* 020 7437 4248 *fax:* 020 7240 1296. C Julian, S Yager, A Alraun, associates. *Management and marketing.*

David Allthorpe Management Services. 21 Launcelyn Close, North Baddesly, Romsey, Hants SO52 9NP *tel:* 023 8073 7505. *Market research and management consultancy.*

European Marketing Consultants Ltd. 22-24 Worple Rd, London SW19 4DD *tel:* 020 8879 3033 *fax:* 020 8947 9042 *email:* info@emc-europr.com. Richard Price, mgr dir. *PR agency with specialist arts expertise.*

Gillian Perkins, Arts Consultant. 10 Gurney Way, Cambridge CB4 2ED *tel:* 01223 350544 *also fax; email:* cammusic@enterprise.net. *Fundraising, concert management, educ project advice, organisation and evaluation.*

Helen Fraser Arts Management. Normansland, Dymock, Glos GL18 2BE *tel:* 01531 890589 *also fax; email:* hf@artsland.demon.co.uk. *Business planning, funding, organising events, concert management.*

Impulse Music Consultants. 18 Hillfield Park, Muswell Hill, London N10 3QS *tel:* 020 8444 8587 *fax:* 020 8245 0358 *email:* impulse@impulse-music.co.uk. Geraldine Allen, Sarah Rodgers. *Mus consultants for professional mus-making in every context. Specialists in project co-ordination, copyright advice and internet services.*

Kallaway Ltd. 2 Portland Rd, Holland Park, London W11 4LA *tel:* 020 7221 7883 *fax:* 020 7229 4595. William Kallaway, mgr dir. *Communications and marketing through sponsored arts events. Services include consultancy, event production and management, promotion and media planning.*

Kivity, Sharon. 19b Albert Rd, Teddington, Middx TW11 0BD *tel:* 020 8977 2961 *fax:* 020 8977 6281 *email:* sharonarts@btinternet.com. Sharon Kivity, snr consultant; Alexandra Curran, consultant. *Training, promotion, publicity and PR services. Event management. Festival programming and organisation.*

McCann Matthews Millman Ltd. Marine House, 23 Mount Stuart Square, Cardiff Bay, Cardiff CF1 6DP *tel:* 029 2046 2121 *fax:* 029 2046 2122 *email:* office@mcmatmil.co.uk. John Matthews, dir. London office: Friars' House, 157-168 Blackfriars' Rd, London SE1 8EZ *tel:* 020 7401 2225 *fax:* 020 7401 3773. Roger McCann, dir. *Specialist consultants in strategic planning, feasibility studies, research and training for the arts.*

Maestoso Musicmakers Ltd. 'Milestone', St Nicholas Ave, Gt Bookham, Surrey KT23 4AY *tel:* 01372 457755 *fax:* 01372 450525 *email:* maestoso@btinternet.com. Elizabeth Pryde, dir. *Consultants in arts management and sponsorship.*

The Management Centre. 366 Kennington Rd, London SE11 4DB *tel:* 020 7820 1100 *fax:* 020 7820 3828 *email:* tmc@managementcentre.co.uk. Bernard Ross, Clare Segal, dirs. *Provides management training, fundraising and sponsorship, open and in-house programmes for not-for-profit organisations. Also carries out consultancy.*

Manygate Management. 13 Cotswold Mews, 30 Battersea Square, London SW11 3RA *tel:* 020 7223 7265 *fax:* 020 7585 2830 *email:* manygate@easynet.co.uk. *Sponsorship and fundraising for orchs, recordings, festivals and concerts. Concert management, marketing strategies, concepts, research, TV and satellite hook-ups.*

Midlands Arts Marketing. 4 Russell Place, Nottingham NG1 5HJ *tel:* 0115 948 3344 *fax:* 0115 948 3343 *email:* mam@agency-net.co.uk. Heather Maitland, chief exec. *Comprehensive arts marketing consultancy service, including design and print, audience development, distribution and market analysis.*

Millward Brown Market Research Ltd. Olympus Ave, Tachbrook Park, Warwick CV34 6RJ *tel:* 01926 452233 *fax:* 01926 833600 *email:* bob.barnes@uk.millwardbrown.com. Bob Barnes, charts dir. *Specialist in market research for arts, sponsorship, audience development. Compilers of the official record industry charts.*

Nicky Webb Associates. 82 Kempshott Rd, London SW16 5LH *tel:* 020 8679 9303 *fax:* 020 8679 9306. Nicky Webb, Beverley Etkin, Maggie Jones. *Specialist marketing and PR for the arts.*

Organisation for Arts and Media. 5 Dryden St, London WC2E 9NW *tel:* 020 7829 8456 *fax:* 020 7240 5600 *email:* jackie-artsorg@cwcom.net. Jackie Elliman. *Administration, development, marketing and event services for the arts and media.*

Riley Sinclair Events/Project Management. 10 Greystone Ave, Chorlton, Manchester M21 7RP *tel:* 0161 881 0156 *also fax; email:* bobriley5572@yahoo.com. Bob Riley, Fiona Sinclair. *Administrative, planning and management service for a wide range of musical events, specialising in festival management and corporate entertainment.*

Spero Communications Ltd. Grampian House, Meridian Gate, Marsh Wall, London E14 9XT *tel:* 020 7538 9946 *fax:* 020 7538 4747 *email:* spero@sperocom.co.uk. Connie Brighton, dir. *Interactive marketing programmes which combine innovation with sound business objectives.*

STR Music Marketing and Management. 296 Hughenden Rd, High Wycombe, Bucks HP13 5PE *tel:* 01494 461177 *fax:* 01494 461188 *email:* admin@strmmm.com. Sean Rourke, mgr dir. *Strategic planning, comprehensive marketing campaigns and sponsorship consultant, lottery assessments and feasibility studies.*

Tom Petzal and Associates. Pantiles Chambers, 85 High St, Tunbridge Wells, Kent TN1 1YG *tel:* 01892 506968 *fax:* 01892 547120 *email:* pantilesbc@compuserve.com. Tom Petzal, mgr dir. *Management, promotion, fundraising advice, PR services, feasibility studies and National Lottery application expertise.*

Web Projects. The Studio, 78 Croydon Rd, Reigate, Surrey RH2 0NH *tel:* 01737 222008 *fax:* 01737 225600 *email:* mwalmsley@webprojects.co.uk. Mark Walmsley, mgr dir; Ben Sauer, mkt mgr. *Specialist consultants in classical mus internet marketing and publishing.*

Concert and Personal Management

This sub-section includes organisations specialising in the marketing and overall management of concerts, tours, festivals and music for special occasions; the service offered will frequently include booking of venues, concert programme production, organisation of press and other receptions. This sub-section also includes organisations providing a personal PR service and/or a representation/agency service for musicians. Concert Managements do not act as principals, i.e. they are not risk-takers. *See also* **Marketing and Organisational Management.**

Anglo-European Arts. 25 Fournier St, Spitalfields, London E1 6QE *tel:* 020 7247 7219 *fax:* 020 7247 6094. Carolyn Humphreys, dir. *Concert, event and festival management, PR consultant.*

Anthony Abbott Music Management. Medlar Cottage, Lodge Lane, Keymer, Hassocks, W Sussex BN6 8NA *tel:* 01273 843348 *fax:* 01273 846585. *Concert, tours and event management, plus personal representation.*

Antony Pristavec. 79 Norbury Cres, London SW16 4JT *tel:* 020 8679 0369 *fax:* 020 8679 9399 *email:* Pristavec@aol.com. Antony Pristavec, dir. *Personal, concert, festival and tour management.*

B & B Concert Services. 66 Hyde Way, Hayes, Middx UB3 4PB *tel:* 020 8606 0030 *fax:* 020 8606 0037 *email:* roderick_burnett@compuserve.com. Roderick Burnett, mgr dir.

Cabaret International Ltd. Suite 1, The Clarendon Suites, 2 Stirling Rd, Edgbaston, Birmingham B16 9SB *tel:* 0121 454 2918 *fax:* 0121 455 0859 *email:* ent@ear-ltd.co.uk. Maureen Potter, mgr and secretary. *Concert and personal management, tour and event management, organisers.*

Caroline Ireland Management. Uwchlaw'r Coed, Llanbedr, Gwynedd LL45 2NA *tel:* 01341 241532 *also fax; email:* caroline.ireland@virgin.net. *Personal and concert management.*

Clare Edwards, Music and Arts Project Management and Development. 7a Mary Rd, Stechford, Birmingham B33 8AR *tel:* 0121 244 3834; 07973 694913 *fax:* 0121 604 0522 *email:* c.edwards@bassoon.demon.co.uk.

Classic Music Management. 35 Cannonside, Fetcham, Leatherhead, Surrey KT22 9LE *tel:* 01372 375939 *fax:* 01372 379095 *email:* classicman@mailexcite.com. Graham Bolton, mgr. *Musicians' management service, contracting freelance musicians for private, corporate and charity events.*

Fox Jones & Associates. 54 Crofton Rd, London SE5 8NB *tel:* 020 7701 3107 *fax:* 020 7701 6918 *email:* foxjones@compuserve.com; foxjones@inforamp.net. Jeremy Fox, president; Margaret Barkman, mgr. *Management consulting, artist management.*

GBZ Management. PO Box 11845, London SE21 8ZS *tel:* 020 8761 6565 *fax:* 020 8670 3195 *email:* gbz_mgmt@compuserve.com. Gwenneth Bransby-Zachary, dir. *PR, personal and concert management.*

Hazard Chase Ltd. Richmond House, 16-20 Regent St, Cambridge CB2 1DB *tel:* 01223 312400 *fax:* 01223 460827 *email:* helen.poole@hazardchase.co.uk. Helen Poole, events and mkt mgr. *Concert and event management and marketing for solo artists and ens.*

Helen Fraser Arts Management. Normansland, Dymock, Glos GL18 2BE *tel:* 01531 890589 *also fax; email:* hf@artsland.demon.co.uk. *Organises events, tour co-ordination, concert management.*

Influence. Disraeli Mews, 137b Putney High St, London SW15 1SU *tel:* 020 8789 0776 *fax:* 020 8789 1192. Michael Heyland, events consultant. *Events consultant, specialising in charity and corporate events here and abroad, from concerts and conferences to rallies and wine tastings.*

JLM Artists. 95 Oxford Gardens, London W10 6NF *tel:* 020 8993 8350 *fax:* 020 8969 5364. Joëlle Partner, dir. *Concert management, career consultation and promotion. Profile enhancement.*

Jones, Jill. 3 Willow Close, Woodham, Addlestone, Surrey KT15 3SB *tel:* 01932 348908. *Freelance consultant and trainer, providing a personal resource for small to medium-sized organisations which want to improve business performance.*

Judith Hendershott Arts Management. 4 Bennett Park, London SE3 9RB *tel:* 020 8852 0823. *PR, personal management, press service. Concert, event and project management.*

Kantor Concert Management and Public Relations. 67 Teignmouth Rd, London NW2 4EA *tel:* 020 8208 2480 *fax:* 020 8208 2490 *email:* dkantor.kcm@webstar.co.uk. Denise Kantor, proprietor. *PR and publicity, concert management, mus secretariat, brochure and leaflet design. Also large database of song texts and translations.*

Kathy Avdiev. 28 Rivermount, Walton-on-Thames, Surrey KT12 2PR *tel:* 01932 246796 *fax:* 01932 267188 *email:* pitcairn@globalnet.co.uk. *Artist, concert and project management; also programme advertising sales.*

Ken Chaproniere Arts and Events Management. 3 The Clock House, Little Brickhill, Milton Keynes MK17 9NR *tel:* 01525 261670 *fax:* 01525 261291 *email:* kenchaproniere@compuserve.com. Ken Chaproniere. *Marketing, fundraising, event management and strategic planning within the arts and entertainment industry, specialising in mus.*

Keown Artists' Management. 62 Chestnut Rd, London SE27 9LE *tel:* 020 8761 4221 *also fax.* Sarah Keown. *Concert and personal management.*

Lisa Peacock Concert Management. 23a Holland Rd, London W14 8HJ *tel:* 020 7602 1416 *fax:* 020 7371 2726 *email:* lisapeacok@aol.com. Lisa Peacock. *Concert management.*

Louise Naftalin Management. 537 Sauchiehall St, Glasgow G3 7PQ *tel:* 0141 248 1611 *fax:* 0141 248 1989. *PR, concert and event management.*

McLusky, Michèle. Borough Market, London SE1 *tel:* 020 7793 7948. *Administration, publicity, concert and festival management.*

Maestoso Musicmakers Ltd. Milestone, St Nicholas Ave, Gt Bookham, Surrey KT23 4AY *tel:* 01372 457755 *fax:* 01372 450525 *email:* maestoso@btinternet.com. Elizabeth Pryde, dir. *Management for single events and tours.*

Matthew Tullah Management. PO Box 3379, London N13 5RA *tel:* 020 8807 0343 *fax:* 020 8807 3800 *email:* matttullah@compuserve.com. *Artist management, concert and event management, production and marketing services.*

Maureen Lunn Management. Top Farm, Parish Lane, Hedgerley, Bucks SL2 3JH *tel:* 01753 645008 *fax:* 01753 647431. *Concert management.*

Music Management (UK) Ltd. PO Box 1105, London SW1V 2DE *tel:* 020 7823 1111 *fax:* 020 7823 1001 *email:* mm@musicmanagement.demon.co.uk. *Corporate entertainment specialists and concert promotion.*

NB Management. PO Box 100, East Horsley, Surrey KT24 6WN *tel:* 01483 282666 *fax:* 01483 284777 *email:* nick@bomford.com. Nick Bomford. *Concert management and administration for orchs, ens and mus-theatre companies.*

Pascall Promotions. 31 Lanchester Rd, London N6 4SX *tel:* 020 8883 8740 *fax:* 020 8883 5961 *email:* cdpascall@aol.com. Carolyn Pascall, dir. *Concert management and promotion for inst and vocal ens, and event management for corporate sponsors. Brochure and leaflet design and PR. Admin and promotion for conds and composers.*

Performing Arts Management. Canal 7, Clarence Mill, Bollington, Macclesfield, Cheshire SK10 5JZ *tel:* 01625 575681 *fax:* 01625 572839. Sally Smith. *Specialists in promotion and management of large-scale, open-air orch concerts.*

Peter Zander Artist and Concert Management. 22 Romilly St, London W1V 5TG *tel:* 020 7437 4767. Peter Zander, dir. *Promotion, PR and sponsorship for festivals, concerts and recitals. Supervision of leaflet, brochure, poster and advertising design and distribution. Artist management.*

Prelude. The Old Stables, 10 Timber Lane, Caterham, Surrey CR3 6LZ *tel:* 01883 344300 *fax:* 01883 347712 *email:* prelud@globalnet.co.uk. Philippa Lunn, dir; Julianne Basten, client co-ord. *Mus events and other entertainment for corporate and marketing events.*

Roy Baker Concert Management. 25 Lynors Ave, Rochester, Kent ME2 3NQ *tel:* 01634 714434 *also fax. Specialist with Nordic mus and artists. Arranges and promotes concerts, special events, educ projects and tours on behalf of charity organisations and foreign embassies.*

Sarah Gordon Concert Management. 110 Gloucester Ave, London NW1 8JA *tel:* 020 7483 2681 *fax:* 020 7586 5343 *email:* sarah.gordon @easynet.com. *Concert management and mus festival administration. Some artist management.*

Siva Oke Music Management. 13 Riversdale Rd, Thames Ditton, Surrey KT7 0QL *tel:* 020 8398 1586 *fax:* 020 8339 0981 *email:* soke@ somm-recordings.demon.co.uk. K H Oke, admin. *Concert management, programme and leaflet design, PR and marketing consultancy for the mus and record industry.*

Smith, Amanda. 25 Prospect Park, Southborough, Tunbridge Wells, Kent TN4 0EQ *tel:* 01892 534525 *also fax; email:* amandasmith @toadinthehole.freeserve.co.uk. *Orch, tour and concert management.*

South West Jazz. c/o Exeter and Devon Arts Centre, Gandy St, Exeter EX4 3LS *tel:* 01392 218368 *fax:* 01392 420442. Kevin Buckland, regional development offr. *Jazz touring, concerts, festival and educ project development and management services.*

STR Music Marketing and Management. 296 Hughenden Rd, High Wycombe, Bucks HP13 5PE *tel:* 01494 461177 *fax:* 01494 461188 *email:* admin@strmmm.com. Sean T Rourke, mgr dir. *Marketing, publicity, PR consultant, personal and concert management, media focus and mailing service. Lottery assessments.*

Valerie Barber PR and Personal Management. Suite 300, Mappin House, 4 Winsley St, London W1N 7AR *tel:* 020 7436 1115/6 *fax:* 020 7436 5090 *email:* vbpr@compuserve.com; 106653.1112@compuserve.com. *General management of Melvyn Tan and UK, Australia and New Zealand management of Skampa quartet.*

Public and Media Relations

These organisations help musicians and music organisations create public awareness of themselves via newspapers, magazines, radio and TV; their work often inter-relates with that of organisations listed in other sub-sections. *See also* **Marketing and Organisational Management.**

Adams, Clare. Clattercote House, Claydon, nr Banbury, Oxon OX17 1ES *tel:* 01295 690344 *fax:* 01295 690413 *email:* adamsarts@aol.com. *Freelance PR consultant.*

Anglo-European Arts. 25 Fournier St, Spitalfields, London E1 6QE *tel:* 020 7247 7219 *fax:* 020 7247 6094. Carolyn Humphreys, dir. *Concert, event and festival management, PR consultant.*

Annon Music Services. 44 Cromwell Rd, Canterbury, Kent CT1 3LF *tel:* 01227 463867 *also fax; email:* annon@clara.net. Anne Hancox. *Agency working on behalf of musicians and singers.*

Arts Council of England Press and Public Affairs. 14 Gt Peter St, London SW1P 3NQ *tel:* 020 7973 6565 *fax:* 020 7973 6560 *email:* info. press@artscouncil.org.uk. *Co-ordination service aimed at avoiding clashes between daytime arts press conferences nationwide. Press contacts and mailing list available, price £28. List is supplied in both book and disc format.*

Birdsong Public Relations. 12 Penzance Place, London W11 4PA *tel:* 020 7229 9166 *fax:* 020 7221 5042 *email:* db.birdsong@harrisonparrott.co.uk. Debra Boraston, associate dir, mgr; Kate Gedge, snr account dir; Lorna Neill, account dir (Europe); Georgina Langdale, account dir. *Wide-ranging PR and marketing for the arts in the UK and Europe.*

Bolton and Quinn Ltd. 8 Pottery Lane, Holland Park, London W11 4LZ *tel:* 020 7221 5000 *fax:* 020 7221 8100. Erica Bolton, Jane Quinn, dirs. *Media relations consultants.*

Brown, Peter J. 25 Fair Acres, Roehampton Lane, London SW15 5LX *tel:* 020 8876 9011 *also fax.* Peter Brown, chief exec; Christopher Brown, account supervisor. *PR and marketing consultant for mus organisations and artists.*

Carboni Classical Media. PO Box 308, Sevenoaks, Kent TN15 0ZW *tel:* 01732 811036 *also fax; email:* Carbonimedia@compuserve.com. Marius Carboni, mgr. *Marketing and TV, radio and news print, mus and corporate press and promotion for all types of classical mus projects.*

Carlson, Mary De Camp. 9 Campden Hill Square, London W8 7LB *tel:* 020 7221 6444 *fax:* 020 7229 1275 *email:* mearlson@cwcom.net. *Specialist in PR for the classical mus industry.*

Clarke Agency. 39 Birnam Rd, Islington, London N4 3LJ *tel:* 020 7281 0672 *also fax; email:* herbie@birnam39.freeserve.co.uk. Herbie Clarke, mgr dir. *Freelance public and media relations for musicians and performing artists.*

Day, Elizabeth. 15 Grove Court, Circus Rd, London NW8 9EN *tel:* 020 7286 5390. *Specialist media relations for all the arts.*

Gilbert, Valerie. 23 Burbage Rd, London SE24 9HJ *tel:* 020 7737 4484 *fax:* 020 7326 0712 *email:* 10061.1412@compuserve.com. *Publicity, management and writing, marketing and features.*

Graham-Dixon, Suzanne and Elizabeth. Maskets Manor, Nutley, East Sussex TN22 3HD *tel:* 01825 712719 *fax:* 01825 712241. Suzanne Graham-Dixon; Elizabeth Graham-Dixon, partners. *Press and PR for opera houses and mus festivals in Europe.*

Diana Hirst Public Relations. 55 Marmora Rd, Honor Oak, London SE22 0RY *tel:* 020 8299 1914 *fax:* 020 8299 1914 *email:* Hirstpr@aol.com. Diana Hirst; Lynne Ellis, project associate. *PR for singers, musicians and educ establishments; advice surgeries on PR and building your network.*

information communication ltd. 6 Hornsey Lane Gardens, Highgate, London N6 5PB *tel:* 020 8374 6040 *email:* infocom@dial.pipex.com. Michael Thorne, mgr dir. *Internet marketing solutions, publicity, promotion, proof-reading, event organisation and marketing services for both the mus and media industries.*

Jackson Quigg Associates Ltd. 26 Astral Ave, Hipperholme, Halifax, W Yorks HX3 8NN *tel:* 01422 204405; 07770 303952 *fax:* 01422 200183 *email:* JacksonQuigg@compuserve.com. Piers Jackson, Anne-Marie Quigg, dirs. *Arts and media management, business planning, fundraising, media campaigns, feasibility studies, profile raising, strategic planning.*

James Parker Associates. 67 Richmond Park Rd, London SW14 8JY *tel:* 020 8876 1918 *also fax.* Jim Parker, proprietor. *Marketing, promotion, sales activities (field operatives), distribution of publicity literature, support management, mailings to coach trade and groups market.*

Judith Hendershott Arts Management. 4 Bennett Park, London SE3 9RB *tel:* 020 8852 0823. *PR, personal management, press service. Concert, event and project management.*

Kantor Concert Management and Public Relations. 67 Teignmouth Rd, London NW2 4EA *tel:* 020 8208 2480 *fax:* 020 8208 2490 *email:* dkantor.kcm@webstar.co.uk. Denise Kantor, proprietor. *Press and PR for one-off or long-term projects. Mus secretariat, freelance publicist, concert management, brochure and leaflet design.*

Katherine Howard Promotions. Hope Cottage, Pettaugh Lane, Gosbeck, Suffolk IP6 9SD *tel:* 01473 892007 *fax:* 01473 892006 *email:* KHP@mithian.demon.co.uk. *Specialising in all areas of UK media - classical, jazz, contemporary and mainstream projects. Clients include record companies, artists, arts events, book publishing and personalities.*

LAP International Public Relations and Marketing. Strategy House, 51a Westgate, Almondbury, Huddersfield, W Yorks HD5 8XF *tel:* 01484 426000 *fax:* 01484 421209 *email:* roz@lap.u-net.com. Rosamund Edwards, principal. *Public relations and marketing for the arts.*

Lewis, Dvora. 12 Pilgrim's Lane, London NW3 1SN *tel:* 020 7435 9257 *fax:* 020 7435 1417 *email:* dvoralewis@compuserve.com. *Freelance PR consultant.*

Macbeth Media Relations. Suite 3 Mountfort House, 15-16 Barnsbury Square, London N1 1JL *tel:* 020 7700 5959 *fax:* 020 7700 1329 *email:* macbethg@btinternet.com. Ginny Macbeth, Lisa Knowles, Anne White. *UK and international press for soloists, orchs, festivals and record companies.*

Music Management (UK) Ltd. PO Box 1105, London SW1V 2DE *tel:* 020 7823 1111 *fax:* 020 7823 1001. *Corporate entertainment specialists and concert promotion.*

Music Services Agency. The Chalet, 75 Claremont Rd, Tunbridge Wells, Kent TN1 1TE *tel:* 01892 527970 *also fax.* David Ebbage, dir; Avril Ebbage, admin. *Light classical mus freelance PR. Concert and artist management. Mus theatre.*

Nicky Webb Associates. 82 Kempshott Rd, London SW16 5LH *tel:* 020 8769 7002 *fax:* 020 8696 7293. Nicky Webb, Maggie Jones. *Specialist marketing and PR for the arts.*

Phillips, Richard. Northgate Music, Northgate, Warwick CV34 4JL *tel:* 01926 492468 *fax:* 01926 407606. *Freelance publicist and sponsorship expert.*

Rosemary Rogers Public Relations. 10 Stanhope Rd, St Albans, Herts AL1 5BL *tel:* 01727 848420 *fax:* 01727 845640 *email:* rosemary.rogers@lineone.net. Rosemary Rogers. *Freelance PR consultant.*

Simon Blake and Co. PO Box 60, Teddington, Middx TW11 8XF *tel:* 020 8943 2661 *fax:* 020 8977 4653. *Press and PR, newsletter production and direct mail.*

Siva Oke Music Management. 13 Riversdale Rd, Thames Ditton, Surrey KT7 0QL *tel:* 020 8398 1586 *fax:* 020 8339 0981 *email:* soke@somm-recordings.demon.co.uk. *Promotion, PR, marketing and publicity. Specialist marketing in mus and record industry.*

STR Music Marketing and Management. 296 Hughenden Rd, High Wycombe, Bucks HP13 5PE *tel:* 01494 461177 *fax:* 01494 641188 *email:* admin@strmmm.com. Sean T Rourke, mgr dir. *PR consultant for festivals, orchs and local authorities. Sponsor liaison services. Lottery assessments.*

Tom Petzal and Associates. Pantiles Chambers, 85 High St, Tunbridge Wells, Kent TN1 1YG *tel:* 01892 506968 *fax:* 01892 547120 *email:* pantilesbc@compuserve.com. Tom Petzal, mgr dir. *Management, fundraising, promotion, project management, National Lottery application advice and feasibility studies.*

Tony Barlow Associates. 3 Choumert Square, London SE15 4RE *tel:* 020 7358 9291 *also fax. Concert management; marketing and press for mus, dance and theatre; fundraising.*

Valerie Barber PR and Personal Management. Suite 300, Mappin House, 4 Winsley St, London W1N 7AR *tel:* 020 7436 1115/6 *fax:* 020 7436 5090 *email:* vbpr@compuserve.com; 106653.1112@compuserve.com. *PR consultancy specialising in UK and European media coverage, including jazz and world mus.*

Web Projects. The Studio, 78 Croydon Rd, Reigate, Surrey RH2 0NH *tel:* 01737 222008 *fax:* 01737 225600 *email:* mwalmsley@webprojects.co.uk. Mark Walmsley, mgr dir; Ben Sauer, mkt mgr. *Internet website design, hosting, promotion and maintenance. Internet marketing consultancy.*

Advertising: Agencies, Media Buying and Media Sales

Organisations listed here will advise on the advertising content of a marketing campaign and will buy advertising space for clients; some specialise in selling advertising on behalf of clients in concert programmes. *See also* **Marketing and Organisational Management.**

Brian Shilling Associates. 12 Clayfield Mews, Newcomen Rd, Tunbridge Wells, Kent TN4 9PA *tel:* 01892 677740 *fax:* 01892 677743. Brian Shilling. *Advertising sales contractor for South Bank Centre, Philharmonia Orchestra, Barbican Centre mus programmes and NFMS News.*

Cabbell Publishing Limited. 31 Hartfield Cres, Wimbledon, London SW19 3SG *tel:* 020 8545 8300; 020 8395 3808 *fax:* 020 8395 3999 *email:* cabbell@cableinet.co.uk. Andrew Todd, mgr dir; Catherine Hawkins, ad mgr. *Specialist in opera, classical mus, festival and theatre advertising. Souvenir brochures, booking brochures and performance programmes.*

Concert Publications. Clifford Place, Clifford, Herefords HR3 5HJ *tel:* 01497 831238 *fax:* 01497 831716 *email:* Concertiuk@aol.com. Rhona Lyle, partner. *Advertising sales contractor and sponsorship consultant specialising in mus, theatre, festivals and charity events.*

Dewynters PLC. 48 Leicester Square, London WC2H 7QD *tel:* 020 7321 0488 *fax:* 020 7321 0104.

Haymarket Advertising Ltd. 41 Great Windmill St, London W1V 7PA *tel:* 020 7437 7206 *fax:* 020 7734 4835. *Media buying, design and production.*

Radford Advertising Marketing Ltd. 1st Floor, Blackfriars House, Parsonage, Manchester M3 2JA *tel:* 0161 832 8807 *fax:* 0161 832 2460 *email:* ads@radford-ad.demon.co.uk. Catherine Warrington, account dir. *Marketing-led approach. Services include all forms of media advertising, direct mail, promotions, video, broadcast and events management.*

Unit Communications Group. 1 Canal St, Manchester M1 3HE *tel:* 0161 236 8002 *fax:* 0161 228 6258 *email:* dmh@unitcomms.co.uk. Denise Hitchen, deputy mgr dir. *Specialist in arts and entertainment.*

Design and Print

See also **Marketing and Organisational Management.**

Battley Brothers Printers. 37 Old Town, Clapham, London SW4 0JN *tel:* 020 7622 3401 *fax:* 020 7498 1497 *email:* battleys@dial.pipex.com. Bernard Battley, chmn. *Award-winning arts print and design company. Multimedia consultancy, mailing facilities and advertising sales.*

Colophon. 9a New Road, Watlington, Oxon OX9 5QS *tel:* 01491 614499 *fax:* 01491 614488. Ross Speirs. *Information design for business and the arts.*

DC Graphics. 2 Gatestone Rd, London SE19 3AT *tel:* 020 8771 7767 *also fax;* 07971 965867 *email:* david.canning@ukonline.co.uk. David Canning, graphic designer. *Promotion through the design of publicity, brochure, leaflet, poster and/or website.*

The Design Stage. 21 West Bute St, Cardiff CF10 5EP *tel:* 029 2046 5366 *fax:* 029 2049 0104 *email:* steve@design-stage.co.uk. Steve Allison, mgr dir. *Graphic design consultants specialising in the arts and leisure industries.*

Digital Support Ltd. 164-180 Union St, London SE1 0LH *tel:* 020 7401 8692 *fax:* 020 7261 1328. Sean Sainsbury, mgr dir; Mark Alford, mgr dir. *Design and artwork for print, internet and CD-ROM creation and database publishing.*

John Good Holbrook Ltd. Elm Place, Old Witney Rd, Eynsham, Oxford OX8 1PU *tel:* 01865 885400 *fax:* 01865 885401 *email:* jghox@globalnet.co.uk. Caroline Good, mgr dir; Joanna Lever, sales and mkt dir. *Publishers of programmes, posters and leaflets for theatres, lyric companies, concerts and festivals throughout the UK. Extensive in-house design and print capability.*

John Spencer Posters, Calligraphy. Stamford Arcade, Ashton under Lyne, Lancs OL6 6JY *tel:* 0161 330 4666 *also fax. Poster design and print. Presentation certificates, invitations, place cards, etc professionally hand-lettered in italic script.*

Maggs, Leo. 7 Bridge Wharf, 156 Caledonian Rd, London N1 9UU *tel:* 020 7278 6005 *fax:* 020 7833 8902. Leo Maggs, snr partner; B A Maggs, partner. *Designer and print buyer.*

Nickol, Peter. 50 St Leonards Rd, Exeter EX2 4LS *tel:* 01392 255512 *also fax; email:* PNickol@ninoakes.freeserve.co.uk. Peter Nickol. *Editing, writing, design and typesetting. Copyright clearance. Mus educ specialist.*

Oldacres. 62 Hatton Garden, London EC1N 8LR *tel:* 020 7242 3242 *fax:* 020 7831 9095. Mr Brown, Mrs Clement. *Printers and photographic services.*

Presto Copying Service. Basement Office, Gatesden Flats, Cromer St, London WC1H 8EA *tel:* 020 7916 1657 *also fax.* Les Bamford. *Photocopying, hand copying.*

Printing Administration Ltd. Unit E, Lombard Business Park, 20-26 Purley Way, Croydon, Surrey CR0 3JP *tel:* 020 8683 3245 *fax:* 020 8684 0254. *Printing, photocopying, binding, artwork and mailing.*

Publicity and Display Ltd. Douglas Drive, Godalming, Surrey GU7 1HJ *tel:* 01483 428326 *fax:* 01483 424566.

Thumb Design Partnership. 53 Corsica St, London N5 1JT *tel:* 020 7704 6000 *fax:* 020 7226 6482. David Porthouse. *Graphic design consultancy involved in all aspects of design including concert programmes and posters.*

Vargas Organisation. 8 Templeton Place, London SW5 9LZ *tel:* 020 7370 7976 *also fax; email:* vargas@dial.pipex.com. Anthony Auerbach. *Designers specialising in needs of musicians and the mus business. Concert and festival programmes, posters, CD packaging, publishing, marketing and fundraising strategies, personal and corporate presentation, internet.*

Vers Ltd. 34b Altenburg Gardens, London SW11 1JJ *tel:* 020 7585 0701. Ralph Varcoe. *Design and print of all programmes, posters, flyers and other literature.*

Web Projects. 78 Croydon Rd, Reigate, Surrey RH2 0NH *tel:* 01737 222008 *fax:* 01737 225600 *email:* mwalmsley@webprojects.co.uk. Mark Walmsley, mgr dir; Ben Sauer, mkt mgr. *Internet website design, hosting, promotion and maintenance. CD-ROM brochure creation.*

Zincpark Screen Printers. Kaymar Industrial Estate, Trout St, Preston, Lancs PR1 4AL *tel:* 01772 562211 *fax:* 01772 257813. Jennifer Stead. *Posters and leaflets for the entertainment industry.*

photographer

28 Woowich Road

Greenwich

London SE10 0JU

Tel: 0181 853 2291

Fax: 0181 858 5388

Mobile: 0973 669370

Robert Carpenter Turner ~ Photographer

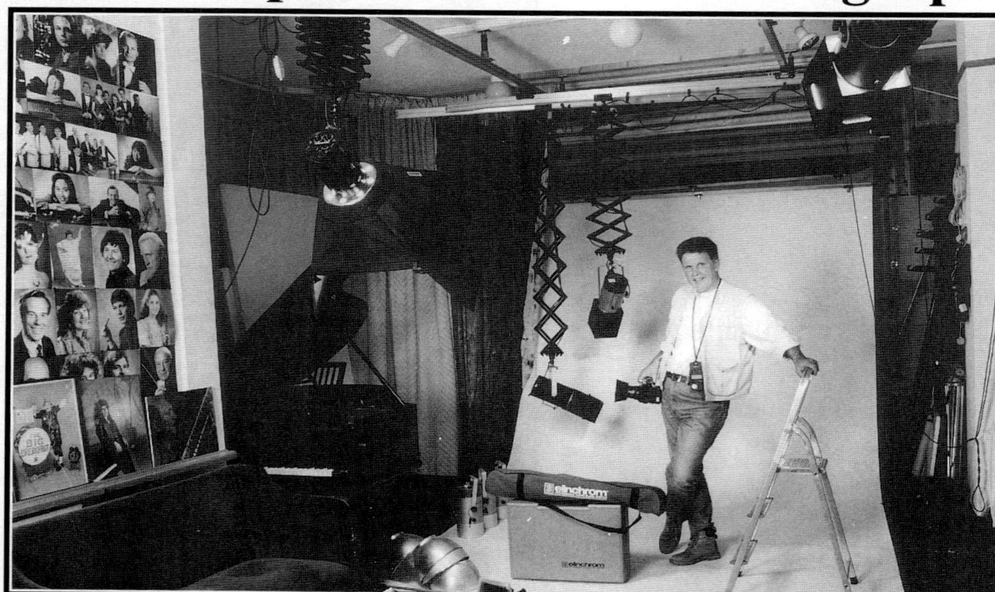

Specialising in promotional pictures for musicians

Fully equipped large studio with separate changing/make-up room. Location work. Express 2 hour processing available.
Grand piano in studio. 5 minutes West Hampstead tube and railway stations.
On street free parking. Credit cards accepted. No casual callers. Phone or fax for illustrated price list.

The Studio, 63 Hemstal Road, West Hampstead, London NW6 2AD
Telephone: 0207-624 2225 ***Facsimile:*** **0207-624 7731 Email: robert.turner@ndirect.co.uk**

Photographers and Photograph Libraries

Alan Wood Photography. 36a Park Field Rd, Oldbury, W Midlands B68 8PS *tel:* 0121 552 4374. *Specialist in mus, theatre and arts photography including press and PR.*

Arena Images Ltd. 11 Blackfriars Foundry, 156 Blackfriars Rd, London SE1 8EN *tel:* 020 7721 8540 *fax:* 020 7721 8541 *email:* arena.images@dial.pipex.com. Rachel Hughes, mgr. *Agency representing top mus photographers: Hanya Chlala, Keith Saunders, Richard Mildenhall, Eric Richmond and Colin Willoughby. Commissions and full library service available.*

Ashmore, Catherine. 4b Moore Park Rd, London SW6 2JT *tel:* 020 7381 0007 *fax:* 020 7381 0008. *Photographer of the entertainment world. Library containing 250,000 colour and b/w.*

Bache, David. 25 Carmalt Gardens, London SW15 6NE *tel:* 020 8789 5589 *fax:* 020 8780 9399 *email:* bache.photography@virgin.net. *Portraits for press and publicity uses.*

Barda, Clive. 50 Agate Rd, London W6 0AH *tel:* 020 8741 0805 *fax:* 020 8563 0538 *email:* clivebarda@pobox.com. *Publicity, portrait and stage photography; comprehensive mus, opera, drama and ballet photo library.*

Batten, John. 72 Woodland Rise, London N10 3UJ *tel:* 020 8883 9153 *fax:* 020 8444 4480 *email:* johnbatten@easynet.co.uk. *Publicity, portrait, corporate brochures, TV and film stills.*

Burn, Sisi. Hermitage House, Church Terrace, Richmond, Surrey TW10 6SE *tel:* 020 8332 7958 *fax:* 020 8287 8448. *Music images for musicians, contemporary, classical, jazz. Documentary, performance and portraits.*

Burns, Laurence. 244 Clapham Rd, Stockwell, London SW9 0PZ *tel:* 020 7735 7906 *also fax. Specialist photographer of the Performance Arts for display publicity and all related media.*

Carpenter Turner, Robert. The Studio Shop, 63 Hemstal Rd, W Hampstead, London NW6 2AD *tel:* 020 7624 2225 *fax:* 020 7624 7731 *email:* robert.turner@ndirect.co.uk. *Comprehensively fitted studio specialising in the needs of professional musicians. On site processing available.*

Chlala, Hanya. c/o Arena Images, 11 Blackfriars Foundry, 156 Blackfriars Rd, London SE1 8EN *tel:* c/o 020 7721 8540 *fax:* c/o 020 7721 8541 *email:* arena.images@dial.pipex.com. Rachel Hughes, agent. *Specialist in the arts. Location and studio shots, photojournalism, publicity and extensive picture library available.*

Dominic Old. 6 Lingwood Walk, Bassett, Southampton SO1 7GL *tel:* 023 8076 8218 *also fax; fax:* 07970 119731 *email:* DPOld@bigfoot.com. *Specialises in documentary and portrait assignments.*

Dominic Photography. 4b Moore Park Rd, London SW6 2JT *tel:* 020 7381 0007 *fax:* 020 7381 0008. Zoe Dominic, Catherine Ashmore. *Photographer of the entertainment world. Library containing 250,000 colour and b/w.*

Donnier-Valentin, Christine. The Glassworks, 1 The Yard, Pegasus Place, London SE11 5SD *tel:* 020 7735 5454; 07850 025254 *fax:* 020 7735 9273 *email:* christine@theglassworks.co.uk. *Single and group portraits.*

Four, Jim. 28 Woolwich Rd, Greenwich, London SE10 0JU *tel:* 020 8853 2291; 07973 669370 *fax:* 020 8858 5388. *Photo documentary specialist, covering all aspects, formal and informal, of classical mus.*

Haddon Davies Photography. Unit 37a, Monument Industrial Park, Chalgrove, Oxford OX44 7RW *tel:* 01865 891900 *also fax. Commercial studio and location photography. Specialist in effective portraiture, colour and b/w, for marketing and promotional purposes.*

Keenan, Jonathan. 121 Princess St, Manchester M1 7AD *tel:* 0161 236 8283 *also fax*; 07802 182319. Nick Hunt, assisting photographer. *Nationwide creative photographic services with particular understanding of musicians' needs. Location or studio.*

Keith Saunders Photography. 39 Stoneleigh St, London W11 4DU *tel:* 020 7727 6770 *fax:* 020 7727 7814. *Studio and location publicity, promotion and press photography.*

Lamplight Photographers. 8 Cleveland Grove, Lupset Park, Wakefield, W Yorks WF2 8LD *tel:* 01924 379573 *also fax.* Paul Stafford, Steve Anstey, partners. *Location, studio and performance photography for solo artists and bands.*

Lance. 45 Redbourne Ave, London N3 2BP *tel:* 020 8922 5156. *Individuals, groups and ens. Studio and location. Portfolio of distinguished sitters available for inspection.*

The Lebrecht Collection. 58b Carlton Hill, London NW8 0RJ *tel:* 020 7625 5341 *also fax;* 020 7372 8233 *email:* lebrecht.coll@clara.net.

SUZIE MAEDER
0171 602 5699
PORTRAIT
STILL LIFE
REPORTAGE
& MUSIC
IMAGES
WITH A
DIFFERENCE

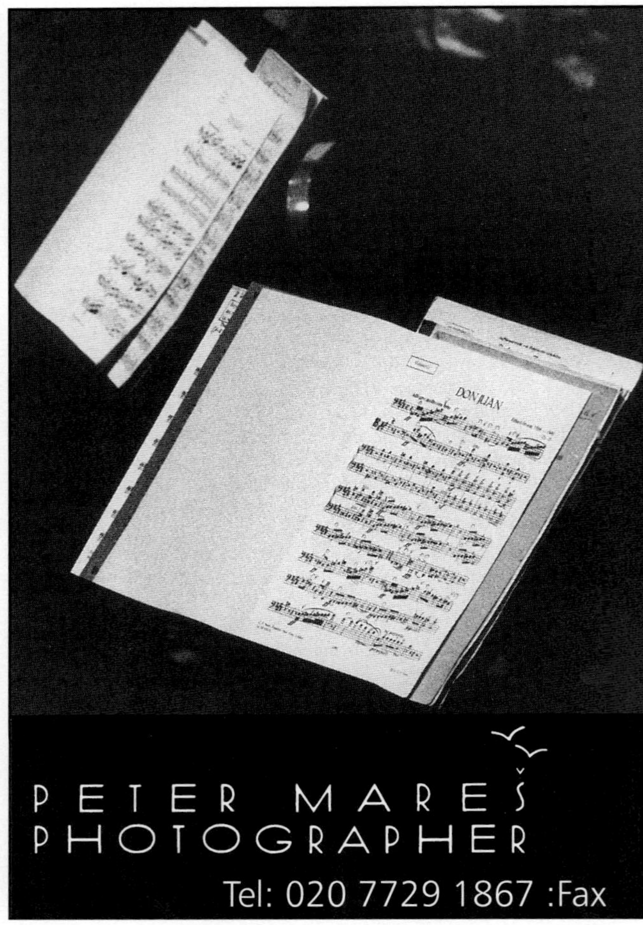
PETER MAREŠ
PHOTOGRAPHER
Tel: 020 7729 1867 :Fax

GERALD PLACE
PROMOTIONAL PHOTOGRAPHY FOR THE ARTS
112 WORDSWORTH RD HAMPTON TW12 1ET
Tel & Fax 020 8941 2684 venosa@ndirect.co.uk
PHOTO: THE CLERKES GROUP

ARTS MARKETING
by Keith Diggle
THE DEFINITIVE GUIDE TO AUDIENCE-BUILDING THROUGH EFFECTIVE MARKETING
If marketing the arts is what you do for a living this book will help you do that job better.
It will give you know-how and it will give you confidence
Hardback • 293 pages • PRICE: £15.00
Postage and packing is FREE to UK addresses and to overseas addresses by surface mail. Please add £1 per copy for airmail to Europe and £4 per copy outside Europe.
To obtain your copy please send a cheque (payable to Rhinegold Publishing Ltd) to: Book Sales Dept,
Rhinegold Publishing Ltd, FREEPOST, London WC2H 8BR.
CREDIT CARD ORDERS
Tel: 020 7333 1721 Fax: 020 7333 1769
www.rhinegold.co.uk

Picture library for classical mus: paintings, engravings and photographs from early antiquity to post-minimalism.

Leon Martin Photography. 3j Stuart Tower, 105 Maida Vale, London W9 1UE *tel:* 020 7266 3596. *Classic and innovative photography for the performing arts.*

Linda Chapman Photography. 69 Rectory Grove, London SW4 0DS *tel:* 020 7627 1208 *also fax*; 07931 592560. *Specialist in the performing arts. Studio, location, rehearsal or performance pictures for promotion, publicity, portfolios and brochures in colour or black and white.*

Luckhurst, Nigel. 40 Orchard Estate, Cherry Hinton, Cambridge CB1 3JP *tel:* 01223 246990 *also fax. Specialist in portrait session photography.*

Maeder, Suzie. 26 Batoum Gardens, London W6 7QD *tel:* 020 7602 5966 *also fax. Specialist portrait and innovative photography.*

Mares, Peter. Studio B, 8 French Place, London E1 6JB *tel:* 020 7729 1867 *also fax;* 07836 252804. *Specialist photography for classical and jazz musicians; portrait portfolio shots. Studio or location. Live action stills. In-house b/w processing and printing.*

Mary Robert Photoworks. 47 Creffield Rd, London W5 3RR *tel:* 020 8993 4378 *fax:* 020 8993 3984 *email:* robertm@richmond.ac.uk. *Photographic portraits of individuals and groups for all publicity purposes. Studio and location including action shots.*

Performing Arts Library. 52 Agate Rd, London W6 0AH *tel:* 020 8748 2002 *fax:* 020 8563 0538 *email:* performingartslibrary@pobox.com. Harriet Orr, Ed Miller, Anna Parrick. *Specialist photo library covering all aspects of the performing arts; extensive collection of contemporary and archive images of opera, ballet, drama productions, classical musicians, composers, venues, performances and related subjects.*

PhotoWork. 71 Jersey Rd, Wolverton, Milton Keynes MK12 5BQ *tel:* 01908 311142 *also fax;* 07885 213449 *email:* Stuart.PhotoWork@btinternet.com. Stuart Isaac, photographer. *Mus specialist. Soloists to orchs, PR and marketing portfolios, opera, insts, competitions, corporate sponsored events. Layout and design.*

The Photographic Service. The University of Warwick, Westwood, Coventry CV4 8AL *tel:* 024 7652 4445 *fax:* 024 7652 4566. Michael Gould, mgr. *Comprehensive photographic service specialising in Midlands venues. Creative studio and performance photography. Digital imaging. Quick turn around.*

Photography by Selwyn Green. 53 Baslow Grove, Heaton, Bradford, W Yorks BD9 5JA *tel:* 01274 494998 *also fax; email:* selwyn_green@talk21.com. *Location pictures, publicity portraits, photo library. Large choirs a speciality.*

Place, Gerald. Studio Venosa, 112 Wordsworth Rd, Hampton, Middx TW12 1ET *tel:* 020 8941 2684 *also fax. Promotional photography for the arts; studio or location.*

PR Pictures. Park House, 15-23 Greenhill Cres, Watford WD1 8QU *tel:* 0800 585092 *fax:* 0800 454442 *email:* info@prpics.com. *Creative photography, professional laboratory, digital imaging, guaranteed service times, free collection and delivery.*

Redferns Music Picture Library. 7 Bramley Rd, London W10 6SZ *tel:* 020 7792 9914 *fax:* 020 7792 0921 *email:* info@redferns.com. Dede Millar, David Redfern, partners. *Comprehensive mus picture library with artists from 1920s to current top ten, plus insts, crowds, festivals, generics. Free catalogue available.*

S L Chai. 20 Beulah Cres, Thornton Heath, Surrey CR7 8JL *tel:* 020 8771 3970 *fax:* 020 8239 0444 *email:* slchai@colourblind.com. *Photography, graphic and web design, production of all printed materials. View portfolio on web site.*

Shane Edgar Photographic. Peartree Studio, 47 Clifford St, Chudleigh, Devon TQ13 0LE *tel:* 01626 853931 *email:* shane.edgar@mail.eclipse.co.uk. *Professional photographic, graphic and internet page design services to the performing and visual arts, both studio and location.*

Sharples, Steve. Fotobrew Picture Library, 54 Platts Cres, Amblecote, Stourbridge, W Midlands DY8 4YZ *tel:* 01384 376557; 01625 511551 *email:* steve.sharples@fotobrew.demon.co.uk. *Classic photography for musicians, singers and dancers for PR and marketing portfolios, taken in studio, rehearsal, performance or chosen venue.*

3rd Millennium Music Ltd. 22 Avon, Hockley, Tamworth, Staffs B77 5QA *tel:* 01827 286086 *also fax; email:* Neil3MMLtd@aol.com. Neil Williams, mgr dir. *Picture archive specialising in classical mus ephemera, particularly portraits of composers, musicians, conds and opera singers and any references to them including monuments, museums, etc. Rare photographs, postcards, prints, stamps, concert programmes. Subjects also include mus insts, concert halls, opera houses, manuscripts and 'music in art'.*

Vandyck, Katie. 15 Mauleverer Rd, Brixton, London SW2 5DR *tel:* 020 7733 9297 *also fax. Specialises in photographing musicians. Studio, location, during sessions.*

Visualeyes Imaging Services. 24 West St, off Cambridge Circus, London WC2H 9NA *tel:* 020 7836 3004 *fax:* 020 7240 0050 *email:* imaging@visualeyes.ltd.uk. *Premier photographic and duping services provider to the entertainment industry. Full range of digital services including drum scanning and image database systems.*

Window on the World Ltd. 124 Cornwall Rd, London SE1 8TQ *tel:* 020 7928 3448; 07831 289190 *fax:* 020 7620 0350 *email:* usill@winworld.co.uk. David Usill, photographer; Judith Stewart, stylist. *Photography and graphic design studio. Portraits (studio or location), publicity material (brochures, programmes, posters, etc).*

Workman, Robert. Studio 103b, The Business Village, 3-9 Broomhill Rd, Wandsworth, London SW18 4JQ *tel:* 020 7385 5442 *email:* bob@robertworkman.demon.co.uk. *Publicity, portrait and stage photography; actors and singers photo library.*

Zuboff, Tatjana. Hill Cottage, Chapel Lane, Forest Row, E Sussex RH18 5BU *tel:* 01342 824929 *also fax; email:* TZuboff@aol.com. *Portrait and stage photography.*

Leaflet Distributors

Artscene Magazine Despatch Service. c/o Artscene, Dean Clough Office Park, Dean Clough, Halifax HX3 5AX *tel:* 01422 322527 *fax:* 01422 322518 *email:* artscene@compuserve.com. Vic Allen, ed; David Nesbitt, commercial mgr. *Arts and public venues across Yorkshire and the humber region, linked to distribution of free local what's on magazine.*

Brochure Display Ltd. Century Point, Halifax Rd, Cressex, High Wycombe, Bucks HP12 3SL *tel:* 01494 888500 *fax:* 01494 436914. Catherine Dixon, sales dir. *Display and distribution service for promotional brochures throughout London, the home counties and the Midlands.*

Cardiff Arts Marketing Ltd. 2 Market House, Market Rd, Canton, Cardiff CF5 1QE *tel:* 029 2037 3730 *fax:* 029 2038 4141. Peter Reynolds, mkt mgr; Tony Lloyd, distribution mgr. *Market research, database services, print distribution, project management, consultancy and marketing services.*

Edinburgh Arts and Entertainments Ltd. 11 Pirrie St, Edinburgh EH6 5HY *tel:* 0131 555 1897 *fax:* 0131 555 2905 *email:* info@eae.co.uk. Glen Bennett, mgr dir. *Posters, leaflets, brochures, programmes, distributed nationwide. 5800 display sites. Precision targeting to reach any audience. Europe's first virtual leaflet rack.*

Parade Direct Marketing Ltd. Parade House, Rovex Business Park, Birmingham B11 2AF *tel:* 0121 706 2020 *fax:* 0121 706 9942 *email:* sales@paradedirect.co.uk. Rachael See, dir; Deirdre Leahy, account mgr; Clive Urwin, mgr dir. *Printer, packer and distributor of promotional literature for the mus industry.*

spnm - promoting new music. Francis House, Francis St, London SW1P 1DE *tel:* 020 7828 9696 *fax:* 020 7931 9928 *email:* spnm@spnm.org.uk. Rachel Duncombe, publications offr. *New mus leaflet distribution with* new notes *magazine.*

Theatre Despatch. Azof Hall, Azof St, London SE10 0EG *tel:* 020 8853 0750 *fax:* 020 8293 4861 *email:* info@theatre.org. Philip Ormond, dir. *Comprehensive distribution service including 1,500 display racks, 6,000 other regularly serviced outlets throughout Greater London, poster distribution, mailing service and an arts and entertainments database.*

Box Office Services

Galathea. 54-62 Regent St, London W1R 5PJ *tel:* 020 7734 2299 *fax:* 020 7287 6728 *email:* bruce@globaltickets.com. Richard Leggatt, gen mgr; Suzannah Zody, sales mgr; Bruce Moore, mkt co-ord. *Produces event management system software used for ticketing and marketing operations.*

Harlands. Numbered Products Division, Land of Green Ginger House, Springfield Way, Anlaby HU10 6RN *tel:* 01482 574408 *fax:* 01482 574945. Suzie Dunnington, Beryl Hutchinson, execs. *Long-established manufacturer and distributor of printed tickets and labels.*

Just Tickets. Unit 2, Empstead Works, Greys Rd, Henley-on-Thames, Oxon RG9 2EF *tel:* 01491 413150 *fax:* 01491 413152. C Mooring, works mgr; J Birney, mgr dir; C Birney, financial dir. *Theatrical and leisure ticket printers. 2 sizes vertical tickets, 3 sizes horizontal tickets. Dot matrix or laser printed.*

Performance Ticket Printers. Freepost, The Smithy, Brownlow Heath, Congleton, Cheshire CW12 4AT *tel:* 01260 276164 *fax:* 01260 270984 *email:* tickets@timewell.com. Keith Arnold, mgr. *Low-cost computer printed perforated tickets.*

Select Ticketing Systems Ltd. City Gate, 17 Victoria St, St Albans, Herts AL1 3JJ *tel:* 01727 834303 *fax:* 01727 859515 *email:* sales@select-info.co.uk. Jo Shinner, mkt mgr; Robert Edwards, sales mgr. *PASS, a computerised ticketing and marketing system used by venues worldwide to control all types of ticketed events and handle all marketing.*

Synchro Systems Ltd. International House, Stubbs Gate, Newcastle-under-Lyme, Staffs ST5 1LU *tel:* 01782 741999 *fax:* 01782 742999 *email:* sales@synchro.co.uk. S W Vernon, sales mgr. *A complete box office and marketing computerised system with fast ticketing and extensive database for profiling customers.*

Ticketmaster UK Ltd. 48 Leicester Square, London WC2H 7LR *tel:* 020 7344 4000 *fax:* 020 7915 0411 *email:* jules.boardman@ticketmaster.co.uk. Jules Boardman, mgr dir; N Blackburn, sales dir. *Entertainment ticket retailer providing computerisation, retail and marketing services. 24-hr credit card booking, group booking service, nationwide outlet network.*

Tickets Please! PO Box 13, Droylsden, Manchester M43 6TL *tel:* 0161 371 0439 *also fax.* Philip Royle. *Ticket printing for arts centres, theatres, etc. Suppliers of tickets for computerised box office systems.*

TOR Systems Ltd. 58 Longton Rd, Trentham, Stoke on Trent, Staffs ST4 8YZ *tel:* 01782 644755 *fax:* 01782 644346 *email:* tor@torsystems.co.uk. Stephen Hale, sales exec; Ian Perry, sales dir. *Supplier of admissions, reservations, high-speed ticketing systems. Services range from improvement advice to commissioning networked systems.*

Fundraising and Sponsorship

Many, if not most, music organisations need money from sources other than ticket sales and hope to raise it in the form of grants from official funding bodies, gifts from charities, commercial companies and private individuals and sponsorship (which has been defined as a *quid pro quo* relationship between a sponsoring company and a music organisation under which both parties benefit). Organisations listed here may be involved in raising money for music in a variety of ways; some work directly on behalf of the music organisation by actively seeking money on its behalf; some offer advice; some prefer to work exclusively with commercial companies that choose to sponsor musical events. A preliminary telephone call is recommended to determine precisely what service is offered.

Arts and Business. Nutmeg House, 60 Gainsford St, Butler's Wharf, London SE1 2NY *tel:* 020 7378 8143 *fax:* 020 7407 7527 *email:* head.office@AandB.org.uk. Paul Brown, head of mkt. *To promote and encourage partnerships between the private sector and the arts to their mutual benefit and to that of the community at large.*

Andrew de Mille Fundraising Consultants. Hedsordene, Cookham, Berks SL6 9HW *tel:* 01628 527753 *fax:* 01628 529938 *email:* andrew@demille.co.uk. Andrew de Mille, partner; Patrick Boggon, snr consultant. *Fundraising and organisational development consultants, particularly capital fundraising campaigns. Fundraising reviews, management studies, feasibility studies and training. Not event sponsorship.*

Brakeley Europe. Paramount House, 162-170 Wardour St, London W1V 4AB *tel:* 020 7287 3361 *fax:* 020 7287 8705 *email:* johnkelly_brakeley@compuserve.com. John G Kelly, mgr dir. *Specialists in major-gift fundraising, offering strategic advice on all aspects of fundraising and external relations to not-for-profit clients worldwide.*

Crowcroft and Partners. 62 Britton St, London EC1M 5PJ *tel:* 020 7251 1191 *fax:* 020 7251 1151. Chris Crowcroft, snr partner. *Specialist sponsorship consultancy focusing on arts and educ.*

The Factory Ltd. The Coach House, 2 Upper York St, Bristol BS2 8QN *tel:* 0117 924 0663 *fax:* 0117 944 6262 *email:* TheFactory@compuserve.com. Angela Hope, mkt dir; Nicola Ramsden, mgr dir; Robin Jones, research dir. *Donor/sponsor research service for fundraisers and development managers in the arts, charity and educ.*

The Friedland Group. 15 Queens Gate Place, London SW7 5NX *tel:* 020 7581 5567 *fax:* 020 7823 7757 *email:* mail@friedland.demon.co.uk. Freda G Wooldridge, mgr dir. *Fundraising and sponsorship as part of strategic development and financial planning. Lottery applications and feasibility studies.*

Kallaway Ltd. 2 Portland Rd, Holland Park, London W11 4LA *tel:* 020 7221 7883 *fax:* 020 7229 4595 *email:* info@kallaway.co.uk. William Kallaway, mgr dir; Vanessa Swann, account dir. *Communications and marketing through sponsored arts, educ and community programmes. Services include consultancy, event production and management, promotion and media planning.*

Maestoso Musicmakers Ltd. St Nicholas Ave, Great Bookham, Surrey KT23 4AY *tel:* 01372 457755 *fax:* 01372 450525 *email:* maestoso@btinternet.com. Elizabeth Pryde, dir. *Consultants in arts management and sponsorship.*

The Management Centre. 366 Kennington Rd, London SE11 4DB *tel:* 020 7820 1100 *fax:* 020 7820 3828 *email:* tmc@managementcentre.co.uk. Clare Segal, dir; Bernard Ross, dir. *Fundraising and sponsorship, open and in-house management development programmes for not-for-profit organisations.*

Manygate Management. 13 Cotswold Mews, 30 Battersea Square, London SW11 3RA *tel:* 020 7223 7265 *fax:* 020 7585 2830.

PB Communications International. 25 Fair Acres, Roehampton Lane, London SW15 5LX *tel:* 020 8876 9011 *also fax.* Peter Brown, chief exec. *Management and sponsorship consultants, public and media relations.*

Tom Petzal and Associates. Pantiles Chambers, 85 High St, Tunbridge Wells, Kent TN1 1YG *tel:* 01892 506968 *fax:* 01892 547120 *email:* pantilesbc@compuserve.com. Tom Petzal, chief exec. *Arts sponsorship and fundraising advice, appeals, events, strategic planning, promotion and PR, feasibility studies.*

Virtuosi Society. 70 South Lambeth Rd, London SW8 1RL *tel:* 020 7582 0994 *fax:* 020 7587 1277. Wendy Stephenson, mgr dir. *Charity.*

Orchestral Contractors

The list below includes the orchestral managers/contractors of professional orchestras and freelance contractors. The address given is either a personal address or that of the orchestra if contracting is done only from the orchestra's offices. The orchestras (or types of freelance booking) for which the person named is responsible are listed at the end of the entry.

Arthur Dakin Organisation. The Old Post House, Hammond St, Mappowder, Dorset DT10 2EH *tel:* 01258 817802 *fax:* 01258 817844. *Arthur Dakin Orchestra. TV sessions, light, MOR, pop backing orchs, recording sessions.*

B & B Concert Services. 66 Hyde Way, Hayes, Middx UB3 4PB *tel:* 020 8606 0030 *fax:* 020 8606 0037 *email:* roderick_burnett@compuserve.com. *The Millennium Sinfonia, The Hyde Sinfonia, The Mandeville Players, The Virtuosi of London, The Croydon Philharmonic.*

Baxter, Thomas. RLPO Orchestra Manager, Philharmonic Hall, Hope St, Liverpool L1 9BP *tel:* 0151 210 2895/3805 *fax:* 0151 210 2902 *email:* tomrbaxter@aol.com. *Royal Liverpool Philharmonic Orchestra.*

Baxter, Tom. Orchestra Manager, c/o Hallé Orchestra, The Bridgewater Hall, Manchester M2 3WS *tel:* 0161 237 7000 *fax:* 0161 237 7029 *email:* tombaxter@halle.co.uk. *Hallé Orchestra.*

Bebb, Mansel. Flat 2, 42 Gipsy Hill, Upper Norwood, London SE19 1NL *tel:* 020 8655 7255 *also fax. The Philharmonia Orchestra.*

Bentley, Andrew. c/o Birmingham Royal Ballet, Birmingham Hippodrome, Thorp St, Birmingham B5 4AU *tel:* 0121 689 3074 *fax:* 0121 689 3072 *email:* andrewbentley@brb.org.uk. *Royal Ballet Sinfonia, The Orchestra of Birmingham Royal Ballet.*

Bomford, Nick. PO Box 100, E Horsley, Surrey KT24 6WN *tel:* 01483 282666 *fax:* 01483 284777 *email:* nick@bomford.com. *London Soloists' Chamber Orchestra. Freelance orch booking.*

Cator, Robert Paul. 27 Victoria Rd, Upper Parkstone, Poole, Dorset BH12 3BA *tel:* 01202 748435. *Bournemouth Sinfonietta.*

Chameleon Arts Management. 32 St Michael's Rd, Sandhurst, Berks GU47 8HE *tel:* 01252 873313 *fax:* 01252 871517 *email:* camarts@dial.pipex.com. *Chameleon Arts Orchestra. Films, recordings, choral society accompaniment.*

Classic Music Management. 35 Cannonside, Fetcham, Leatherhead, Surrey KT22 9LE *tel:* 01372 375939 *fax:* 01372 379095 *email:* classicman@mailexcite.com. *City Ballet of London Orchestra, freelance orchs for concerts, charity galas, opera and ballet.*

Cobb, John. 19 Thorkhill Gardens, Thames Ditton, Surrey KT7 0UP *tel:* 020 8398 6468. *London Pro Arte Orchestra.*

Cool Music Productions. 20 Spruce Hills Rd, Walthamstow, London E17 4LD *tel:* 07768 570383 *fax:* 020 8531 4962 *email:* coolmp@iname.com. *Chamber Orchestra of London, British Chamber Orchestra, Opera Europa. Bookings of all types of groups or individuals from harpists to rock bands.*

Dolman, Judy. CBSO, Berkley St, Birmingham B1 2LF *tel:* 0121 236 1555 *fax:* 0121 233 2423 *email:* jd@cbso.co.uk. *City of Birmingham Symphony Orchestra.*

Ford, Trevor. 151 Mount View Rd, London N4 4JT *tel:* 020 8341 6408 *fax:* 020 8340 0021 *email:* tfordandco@aol.com. *English Festival Orchestra, English Sinfonia, Philomusica of London. TV, film, library, pop sessions.*

Goddard, Wilfred. 14 Lytton Rd, London E11 *tel:* 020 8556 8294 *also fax. Brighton Philharmonic Orchestra, London Gala Orchestra.*

Goold, Nicola. Millmead House, Millmead, Guildford, Surrey GU2 5BB *tel:* 01483 444666 *fax:* 01483 444732. *Guildford Philharmonic Orchestra.*

Harries, Griff. 40 Tudor Court, Murton, Swansea SA3 3BB *tel:* 01792 232387; 07860 725934 *fax:* 01792 234868 *email:* griff.harries@virgin.net. *TV, radio, concerts, light music, pantomime, Opera Box, National Chamber Orchestra of Wales.*

Holmes, Sarah. 40 Spring Park Ave, Shirley, nr Croydon, Surrey CR0 5EG *tel:* 020 8655 1306 *also fax. Freelance orch and session booking.*

Holt, Peter. 9 Weylea Ave, Burpham, Guildford, Surrey GU4 7YN *tel:* 01483 573705 *email:* holtp@guildford.gov.uk. *Langham Chamber Orchestra. Freelance orch and session booking.*

Johnny Douglas Enterprises Ltd. 39 Tadorne Rd, Tadworth, Surrey KT20 5TF *tel:* 01737 812922 *also fax. Norma Camby, dir.*

Jones, Catherine. 49 Dukes Ave, Muswell Hill, London N10 2PX *tel:* 020 8444 6008 *fax:* 020 8444 1864 *email:* katyj2@aol.com. *Academy of St Martin-in-the-Fields.*

Killik, Ian. Orchestra and Concerts Director, English National Opera, London Coliseum, St Martin's Lane, London WC2N 4ES *tel:* 020 7845 9428; 07778 158024 *fax:* 020 7845 9277 *email:* ikillik@eno.org. *Orchestra of English National Opera, New Symphony Orchestra.*

The King's Consort. 34 St Mary's Grove, London W4 3LN *tel:* 020 8995 9994 *fax:* 020 8995 2115 *email:* info@the-kings-consort.org.uk. *Freelance booking for baroque performers.*

Larpent, Ben. 4 Royal Terrace, Edinburgh EH7 5AB *tel:* 0131 478 8336 *fax:* 0131 557 6933. *Scottish Chamber Orchestra.*

Logie, Nicholas. Lott's End, Highgate, Forest Row, E Sussex RH18 5BE *tel:* 01342 824536 *also fax; email:* nicholas.logie@virgin.net. *Glyndebourne Touring Opera Orchestra.*

London Musicians Ltd. Cedar House, Vine Lane, Hillingdon, Middx UB10 0BX *tel:* 01895 252555 *fax:* 01895 252556 *email:* mail@lonmus.demon.co.uk. *Freelance orch booking, sessions, management, West End shows.*

McGregor, Shauni. Fenton House, Banbury Rd, Chipping Norton, Oxon OX7 5AW *tel:* 01608 642352 *fax:* 01608 643235. *Steinitz Bach Players. Freelance orch booking (baroque).*

Manly, Ann. 8 Alma Square, London NW8 9QD *tel:* 020 7286 3944 *fax:* 020 7289 9081 *email:* annmanly.proTherve@btinternet.com. *English Chamber Choir, English Players. Freelance orch and choral booking, sessions.*

Moss, Jane. 16 Clerkenwell Green, London EC1R 0QT *tel:* 020 7608 2381 *fax:* 020 7608 1226 *email:* info@rpo.co.uk. *Royal Philharmonic Orchestra and Royal Philharmonic Concert Orchestra; concerts, TV, film, library sessions.*

National Symphony Orchestra. Dragon Lodge, Jumps Rd, Churt, Surrey GU10 2JY *tel:* 01252 792315 *fax:* 01252 795120 *email:* enquiries@NSO.co.uk. *National Symphony Orchestra.*

Neiman, Stephen. The Old Market, 11a Upper Market St, Hove, E Sussex BN3 1AS *tel:* 01273 206978 *fax:* 01273 329636 *email:* mailbox@hanoverband.co.uk. *The Hanover Band.*

Prophet Music Ltd. 147 Drummond St, London NW1 2PB *tel:* 020 7383 5003 *fax:* 020 7383 5004 *email:* info@prophetmusic.co.uk. *Jonathan Brigden, mgr dir. Freelance orch bookings.*

Province, Hazel. Royal Opera House, Covent Garden, London WC2E 9DD *tel:* 020 7212 9381 *fax:* 020 7240 1673 *email:* hazel.province@roh.org.uk. *Orchestra of the Royal Opera House.*

Pye, Delia. 200 Broomwood Rd, London SW11 6JY *tel:* 020 7228 6388 *fax:* 020 7738 1706. *St James's Baroque Players. Freelance booking for period inst performers.*

Raymond Gubbay Ltd. Knight House, 29-31 East Barnet Rd, New Barnet, Herts EN4 8RN *tel:* 020 8216 3000 *fax:* 020 8216 3001 *email:* info@raymond-gubbay.co.uk. *London Concert Orchestra, Johann Strauss Orchestra, Mozart Festival Orchestra, Manchester Concert Orchestra.*

Scott, Paul. 1 Springfield Close, Eckington, Sheffield S21 4GS *tel:* 01246 431562; 07801 510872 *email:* paulsyso88@aol.com. *South Yorkshire Symphony Orchestra, Sheffield Bach Players.*

Sessions International (UK). 14 Woodmansterne Rd, Carshalton Beeches, Surrey SM5 4JL *tel:* 020 8643 6154 *fax:* 020 8770 0622 *email:* megamusic@compuserve.com. Oliver Lewis, dir. *Northern Aldborough Festival Chamber Orchestra. TV, film, pop sessions/orchs, jingles, West End shows.*

Smith, Richard. BBC Maida Vale Studios, Delaware Rd, London W9 2LG *tel:* 020 7765 5401 *fax:* 020 7286 3251 *email:* bbcso@bbc.co.uk. *BBC Symphony Orchestra.*

Studt, Richard. 101 Queens Park Ave, Bournemouth BH8 9JL *tel:* 01202 394955 *also fax; email:* rstudt@cwcom.net. *Tate Music Group of London.*

Williams OBE, Huw Tregelles. BBC Broadcasting House, Llandaff, Cardiff CF5 2YQ *tel:* 029 2032 2442 *fax:* 029 2032 2575 *email:* huwtregelles.williams@bbc.co.uk. *BBC National Orchestra of Wales.*

Willison, Peter. Pigeon House Meadow, 27 Grove Rd, Beaconsfield, Bucks HP9 1UR *tel:* 01494 677934 *fax:* 01494 670443 *email:* gbmuswill@aol.com. *Sinfonia of London. Recording and film-scoring.*

Wilson, David. 92 Chatsworth Rd, Croydon CR0 1HB *tel:* 020 8686 1996 *fax:* 020 8686 2187 *email:* info@lmp.org. *London Mozart Players.*

Wing, Paul. 16 Highland Rd, Amersham, Bucks HP7 9AU *tel:* 01494 431667 *fax:* 01494 431714. *Freelance session, orch, film, TV booking.*

Wordsworth, Judith S. 4a Harewood Rd, South Croydon, Surrey CR2 7AL *tel:* 020 8688 2430 *also fax. London Lyric Orchestra. Film and stage sessions, functions, promotions, freelance jazz and classical booking from soloists to full-size orch.*

Music Publishers

This list contains British publishers of mainly classical music and is divided into two parts. Major and independent publishers are listed first, and the second part (**Subsidiary Publishers**) lists major foreign and some UK companies whose interests are represented by another firm in the UK. Many publishers are members (indicated by an asterisk) of the **Music Publishers' Association Ltd**, 3rd Floor, Strandgate, 18-20 York Buildings, London WC2N 6JU *tel:* 020 7839 7779 *email:* mpa@musicpublishers.co.uk.

A & C Black Publishers Ltd. 35 Bedford Row, London WC1R 4JH *tel:* 020 7242 0946 *fax:* 020 7831 8478 *email:* enquiries@acblack.co.uk. *Children's, educ mus, song books, classroom resources, inst tutors and repertoire.*

Academic & University Publishers. 1 Gower St, London WC1E 6HA *tel:* 020 7580 3994 *fax:* 020 7580 3995.

Acuta Music. Hambrook, Ledbury HR8 2PX *tel:* 01531 670634 *also fax. Late Elgar works, w/wind ens.*

Ad-Chorel Music Ltd. 40 Sciennes, Edinburgh *tel:* 0131 668 3366 *fax:* 0131 662 4463 *email:* rel@relrecords.co.uk. *All types of mus projects.*

Alan Hawkshaw Music Ltd. c/o Music House International Ltd, 143 Charing Cross Rd, London WC2H 0EE *email:* bigal@globalnet.co.uk. *S/publishing company for Alan Hawkshaw.*

* **Alan Simmons Music.** PO Box 7, Scissett, Huddersfield, W Yorks HD8 9YZ *tel:* 01484 860755 *fax:* 01484 860756. *Choral and educ.*

Alchemy Records. PO Box 393, Maidstone, Kent ME14 5XU *tel:* 01622 729593.

Alfred A Kalmus Ltd/Universal Edition (London) Ltd. 38 Eldon Way, Paddock Wood, Kent TN12 6BE *tel:* 01892 833422 *fax:* 01892 836038. *Solo, ens, wind band, school orch, choir; school mus, orch, vocal, books.*

Alfred Lengnick & Co (division of Complete Music Ltd). 27 Grove Rd, Beaconsfield, Bucks HP9 1UR *tel:* 01494 681216 *fax:* 01494 670443 *email:* gbmuswill@aol.com. *Classical symphonies, chmbr, choral, vocal, inst, educ books, World Renowned series.*

* **Alfred Publishing Co (UK) Ltd.** 7 Amber Business Village, Tamworth, Staffs B77 4RP *tel:* 01827 311553 *fax:* 01827 313011 *email:* music@alfredpublishing.demon.co.uk. *All insts, especially pno and gui; band, orch, choral and vocal mus. Exclusive distributors: Music Exchange.*

Alison Hedger Children's Music. Hinton House, Hinton, Christchurch, Dorset BH23 7EA *tel:* 01425 274993 *also fax. Children's educ mus.*

Amber Rose Music. Nockalls, Charnwood House, High St, Wroot, Doncaster DN9 2BT *tel:* 01302 772677 *also fax; email:* ambrosmus@aol.com. *Gui mus.*

* **Amphonic Music Ltd.** Kerchesters, Waterhouse Lane, Kingswood, Surrey KT20 6HT *tel:* 01737 832837 *fax:* 01737 833812 *email:* music@amphonic.co.uk.

Anderson Guitar Publications. 4 The Close, Upton, Southwell, Notts NG23 5SS *tel:* 01636 813405.

Andresier Editions. 63 Marlborough Mansions, Cannon Hill, West Hampstead, London NW6 1JS *tel:* 020 7794 9108 *also fax; fax:* 01296 428609 *email:* 101464.2670@compuserve.com. *Solo, ens (gui only).*

Anglian Edition. The Old White Horse, 34 Parsonage St, Halstead, Essex CO9 2JZ *tel:* 01787 475845. *S/publishing company for Eric Hudes and Alan Parsons (see* **Composers***).*

Animus. 4 Rawlinson St, Dalton-in-Furness, Cumbria LA15 8AL *tel:* 01229 467432. *Choral, org, gui, vocal.*

Antico Edition. PO Box 1, Moretonhampstead, Newton Abbot, Devon TQ13 8UA *fax:* 01647 252085. *Medieval, renaissance, sacred and secular mus.*

Alfred
"Music for a lifetime"
Alfred's Basic Piano Library
Prep Course
Alfred Choral Designs 1999-2000
A collection of 2-part, SSA, SAB, TTB and SATB choral pieces,
Pumping Nylon
"...a recommended source for improving all aspects of Technique and Musicality"
In the pursuit of musical excellence, place the...
Accent on Achievement
ALFRED PUBLISHING
"The Best in Music Education"
Strictly Strings
Add another String to your Bow
A complete series of books to introduce your student to ensemble playing, developing their skills and preparing them for orchestral performances
ALFRED PUBLISHING
"The Best in Music Education"
Alfred
Alfred Publishing (UK) Ltd
7 Amber Business Village, Tamworth, Staffs, B77 4RP
Tel: 01827 311553 Fax: 01827 313011
Email: music@alfredpublishing.demon.co.uk

Ararat Music. 40 Campbell Close, Streatham, London SW16 6NJ *tel:* 020 8677 8473 *fax:* 020 8877 3494 *email:* stephen@gibmusic.freeserve.co.uk. *S/publishing company of Stephen Gibson (see* **Composers**).

* **Ariel Music.** Sibford Ferris, Banbury, Oxon OX15 5RG *tel:* 01295 780679 *fax:* 01295 788630 *email:* jane@arielmusic.demon.co.uk. *Concert and chmbr mus, ballets, operas, musicals, incidental mus for theatre.*

Aristocrat Music Ltd. Clarendon House, Shenley Rd, Borehamwood WD6 1AG *tel:* 020 8207 7006 *fax:* 020 8207 5460.

Arpeggio Music. 25 Latchmoor Way, Gerrards Cross, Bucks SL9 8LS *tel:* 01753 884810 *also fax; fax:* 01753 864910. *Orch, big band and latin jazz.*

Asclepius Editions. The Coach House, Blackheath Way, Malvern, Worcs WR14 4DR *tel:* 01684 891156 *email:* editors@asclepius.u-net.com. *Academic performing editions of lesser-known renaissance, baroque and contemporary mus, esp for viols, rcdr and small ens.*

* **Ashley Mark Publishing Co.** 1-2 Vance Court, Trans-Britannia Enterprise, Bladon on Tyne NE21 5NH *tel:* 0191 414 9000 *fax:* 0191 414 9001. Simon Turnbull, mkt. *Gui mus.*

* **The Associated Board of the Royal Schools of Music (Publishing) Ltd.** 14 Bedford Square, London WC1B 3JG *tel:* 020 7636 5400 *fax:* 020 7637 0234 *email:* publishing@abrsm.ac.uk. *Keyboard, classical inst, theory of mus textbooks and exam material; educ inst.*

Aureus Publishing. 24 Mafeking Rd, Cardiff CF23 5DQ *tel:* 029 2045 5200 *also fax; email:* meurynhughes@aureus.co.uk. *Concert and chmbr mus, operas, musicals, vocal, inst, children's mus, educ, choral, ens. Mus for hire.*

AV Music. 51 Cannon Lane, Pinner, Middx HA5 1HN *tel:* 020 8866 3401 *fax:* 020 8866 5929. *Wind, br mus.*

* **Banks Music Publications.** The Old Forge, Sand Hutton, York YO41 1LB *tel:* 01904 468472 *fax:* 01904 468679 *email:* banksramsay@cwcom.net. *Choral and inst mus.*

Bardic Edition. 6 Fairfax Cres, Aylesbury, Bucks HP20 2ES *tel:* 01296 428609 *also fax; email:* 101464.2670@compuserve.com. *Choral, educ, inst, pno, vocal, band and orch mus.*

* **Bärenreiter Ltd.** Burnt Mill, Elizabeth Way, Harlow, Essex CM20 2HX *tel:* 01279 828930 *fax:* 01279 828931 *email:* baerenreiter@dial.pipex.com. *Solo, ens, str, wind, pno, org, choir, opera; complete editions, facsimilies, mus books. Choral and orch performance material. Vocal and study scores.*

Baroque Publications. Treadam Farm, Llantilio Crossenny, Abergavenny, Monmouthshire NP7 8TA *tel:* 01600 780233. *Orch parts and vocal scores for baroque operas, mainly Handel, edited for the Handel Opera Society; 18th and 19th C ballet mus with pno scores and orch parts; reduced scores for some Mozart and Rossini operas, and* Hansel and Gretel *(Humperdinck).*

Barry Brunton Music Publisher. 52a Broad St, Ely, Cambs CB7 4AH *tel:* 01353 663252 *fax:* 01353 663371. *Choral, keyboard, solo song, ens.*

Bartholomew Music Publications. 105 Bartholomew Rd, Kentish Town, London NW5 2AR *tel:* 020 7267 0437 *also fax. Specialising in mus for teachers and students of db.*

Basil Ramsey Publisher of Music Ltd. 604 Rayleigh Rd, Eastwood, Leigh-on-Sea, Essex SS9 5HU *tel:* 01702 524305 *fax:* 01702 526142 *email:* basilmusic@freeserve.co.uk. *Choral, inst, church mus.*

BBC Educational Publishing. BBC White City, 201 Wood Lane, London W12 7TS *tel:* 020 8752 5263 *fax:* 020 8752 5340 *email:* edinfo@bbc.co.uk. *BBC Primary Music Course: Song Tree; Time and Tune; Music Workshop.*

Bearsongs. PO Box 944, Edgbaston, Birmingham B16 8UT *tel:* 0121 454 7020 *fax:* 0121 454 9996. *Jazz, blues, swing, R & B.*

The Beauchamp Press. Churcham, Gloucester GL2 8AA *tel:* 01452 750253 *fax:* 01452 750585 *email:* music@beauchamp.demon.co.uk. *Renaissance and baroque vocal and inst mus.*

BGS Music Publications. Bath Spa University College, Newton Park, Newton St Loe, Bath BA2 9BN *tel:* 01225 875609 *fax:* 01225 875444 *email:* t.kerstens@bathspa.ac.uk. Tom Kerstens. *Bath Guitar Series publishing arm of the International Guitar Festival. Dedicated to publication of new work for gui.*

* **Bocu Music Ltd.** 1 Wyndham Yard, Wyndham Place, London W1H 1AR *tel:* 020 7402 7433 *fax:* 020 7402 2866. *All types.*

Bonsormusic. Grove House, 37 Weensland Rd, Hawick, Roxburghshire TD9 9NW *tel:* 01450 372643. *Educ mus and concert items for rcdr groups.*

* **Boosey & Hawkes Music Publishers Ltd.** 295 Regent St, London W1R 8JH *tel:* 020 7580 2060 *fax:* 020 7291 7109/7637 3490 (promotion)/7291 7199 (sales) *email:* composers@boosey.com. *Classical, leisure, educ and media mus. Catalogues available: mus for schools, keyboard, str, w/wind, br, perc, ens, symphonic band, vocal, choral, MIDI software and CD-ROMs. Also Bote & Bock, Editio Musica Budapest, Fazer, Guildhall, Ricordi and Itchy Fingers publications.*

* **Bosworth & Co Ltd.** 8-9 Frith St, London W1V 5TZ *tel:* 020 7434 0066 *fax:* 020 7287 6329 *email:* Howard.Friend@musicsales.co.uk. *Solo, ens, wind band, school orch, choir, rcdr, str and orch scores.*

* **Brass Wind Publications.** 4 St Mary's Rd, Manton, Oakham, Rutland LE15 8SU *tel:* 01572 737210/737409 *also fax; email:* brasswnd@globalnet.co.uk. *Solo, br ens, w/wind ens, mixed ens (catalogue).*

* **Breitkopf & Härtel.** Broome Cottage, The Street, Suffield, Norwich NR11 7EQ *tel:* 01263 768732 *fax:* 01263 768733. *Renaissance, baroque, classical, romantic, contemporary, collected editions, inst, orch, vocal, choral.*

Britannia Publishing Company. 156 Hatfield Rd, St Albans, Herts AL1 4JD *tel:* 01727 846055 *fax:* 01727 811164. David Blyth. *Specialist publisher of w/wind mus for solo and chmbr combinations.*

* **Broadbent & Dunn Ltd.** 12 Tudor Court, London E17 8ET *tel:* 020 8521 4275 *fax:* 020 8520 8994. *Solo and ens mus for br, w/wind, strs and pno.*

* **BTW Music.** 106 Westpole Ave, Cockfosters, Herts EN4 0BB *tel:* 020 8449 6110 *also fax. Inst library mus, children's songs.*

Caddy Publishing. Convent Lodge, Andover Down, Hants SP11 6LR *tel:* 01264 337205 *fax:* 01264 350823. *Choral, orch, str quartet, songs, books.*

Cambridge University Press. The Edinburgh Building, Shaftesbury Rd, Cambridge CB2 2RU *tel:* 01223 312393 *fax:* 01223 315052. *Mus journals and books.*

Camden Music. 19a North Villas, Camden Square, London NW1 9BJ *tel:* 020 7267 8778 *fax:* 020 7813 4601 *email:* info@camdenmusic.com. *Orch, wind, br, vocal, urtext editions, educ.*

Campion Press. Sandon, Buntingford, Herts SG9 0QW *tel:* 01763 247287 *fax:* 01763 249984. *Mus by Malcolm Williamson and Elizabeth Poston. Orch, choral, opera, songs, chmbr and inst mus.*

Canterbury Press Norwich. St Mary's Works, St Mary's Plain, Norwich NR3 3BH *tel:* 01603 612914 *fax:* 01603 624483. *Hymn and worship song books.*

Cantiones Press. 10 Kensington Hall Gardens, Beaumont Ave, London W14 9LS *tel:* 020 7379 9361 *fax:* 020 7379 9636 *email:* cantiones@newrenaissance.co.uk. *Sacred renaissance mus.*

Caritas Music Publishing. 28 Dalrymple Cres, Edinburgh EH9 2NX *tel:* 0131 667 3633 *also fax; email:* caritas@caritas-music.co.uk. *All genres.*

Cascade Music Publishing. 30 College Green, Bristol BS1 5TB *tel:* 01454 323608 *also fax; email:* cascademusic@hotmail.com. *Classical and jazz-based pieces for w/wind and br solo and ens.*

* **Cathedral Music.** Maudlin House, Westhampnett, Chichester, W Sussex PO18 0PB *tel:* 01243 776325 *fax:* 01243 539604 *email:* cathedral_music@compuserve.com. *Classical, particularly choral.*

Chandos Music Ltd. Chandos House, Commerce Way, Colchester, Essex CO2 8HQ *tel:* 01206 225200 *fax:* 01206 225201 *email:* enquiries@chandos-records.com. *Br band, vocal, hp mus.*

Chapman (Geoffrey). Wellington House, 125 Strand, London WC2R 0BB *tel:* 020 7420 5555 *fax:* 020 7240 8531. *Church mus specialists.*

* **Chester Music.** Hire and Distribution, Newmarket Rd, Bury St Edmunds, Suffolk IP33 3YB *tel:* 01284 702600 *fax:* 01284 768301. *Contemporary mus, classroom mus, inst solo and ens, str orch, school orch, wind band, br ens, vocal, choral, scores and books; also graded pno pieces.*

Chilmark Publications. 1000 Westbury Rd, Little Cheverell, Devizes, Wilts SN10 4JW *tel:* 01380 816338 *fax:* 01380 816467 *email:* wessex.music@easynet.co.uk. *Br mus, specialising in trb.*

Chiswick Music. Malting Cottage, Church Rd, Peldon, Colchester CO5 7PU *tel:* 01206 735770 *also fax; email:* bill.tamblyn@aspects.net. *Recordings of liturgical mus. S/publishing company for William Tamblyn (see* **Composers**).

Cinque Port Music Publishers. Bank House, Queen St, Deal, Kent CT14 6ET *tel:* 01304 362181 *fax:* 01304 362181. *Military and br band mus and tutors.*

Clairmont Press. Clairmont, The Square, Clun, Shropshire SY7 8JA *tel:* 01588 640398 *fax:* 01588 640107. *Early stages, vc and pno course books and ens packs.*

Clyde, R. 6 Whitelands Ave, Chorleywood, Rickmansworth, Herts WD3 5RD *tel:* 01923 283600 *also fax; email:* r.clyde@dial.pipex.com. Roger Harris, proprietor. *Mus by Arthur Sullivan.*

* **CMA Publications.** 10 Avenue Rd, Kingston upon Thames, Surrey KT1 2RB *tel:* 020 8541 0857 *fax:* 020 8974 8120 *email:* cmagrp@dircon.co.uk. *Inst, orch, ens, choral, wind band and br band.*

Colne Edition. 11 Christ Church Court, Ireton Rd, Colchester, Essex CO3 3AU *tel:* 01206 562607 *email:* allan.bullard@colch-inst.ac.uk. *Solo, ens, br band, wind band, orch, choral mus for adults and children. S/publishing company for Alan Bullard (see* **Composers**).

Composer Press Recorder Series. c/o Recorder MusicMail, Scout Bottom Farm, Mytholmroyd, Hebden Bridge, W Yorks HX7 5JS *tel:* 01422 882751 *fax:* 01422 886157 *email:* ruth@recordermail.demon.co.uk. *Mus for rcdr.*

Composers Library. 106 High St, Bildeston, Suffolk IP7 7EB *tel:* 01449 741707. *Contemporary composers, solo, ens, orch, choir.*

* **Comus Edition.** Leach Cottage, Heirs House Lane, Colne, Lancs BB8 9TA *tel:* 01282 864985 *fax:* 01282 860770 *email:* wmd@comusic.demon.co.uk. *Ens, br, w/wind, va mus.*

Con Moto Publications UK. 17 Mostyn St, Dukinfield, Cheshire SK16 5JS *tel:* 0161 303 0963 *fax:* 0161 343 2423 *email:* tony@mostynmusic.com. *Br, w/wind mus.*

* **Concord Partnership.** 5 Bushey Close, Old Barn Lane, Kenley, Surrey CR8 5AU *tel:* 020 8660 4766 *fax:* 020 8668 5273 *email:* oakcroft @msn.com. *Concord Music Hire Library, Maecenas Music Ltd, Maecenas Contemporary Composers, EF Kalmus Wind Band (catalogue), Masters Music Wind Band (catalogue), Warner Chappell Music Hire Library, GIA Publications Inc, LSO Explorer, Music Unlimited Limited, Warner Bros Publications, Belwin Kalmus Library.*

Corda Music Publications. 183 Beech Rd, St Albans, Herts AL3 5AN *tel:* 01727 852752 *also fax; email:* orders@cordamus.demon.co.uk. *Mus for schools and private tuition, str ens, guis, specialist early mus.*

Cottage Harmony Productions. Evelyn Stephens, Keens Barn Cottage, Keens Lane, Othery, nr Bridgwater, Somerset TA7 0PU *tel:* 01823 698162; 01296 424455. *Ens mus, pno, solo instrumentation.*

* **Cramer Music.** 23 Garrick St, London WC2E 9AX *tel:* 020 7240 1612 *fax:* 020 7240 2639. *Catalogue includes Middle Eight Music and Portland Publications. Also hire catalogue.*

* **Curiad.** The Old Library, County Rd, Pen-y-Groes, Caernarfon, Gwynedd LL54 6EY *tel:* 01286 882166 *fax:* 01286 882692 *email:* curiad@curiad.co.uk. *Vocal, choral, orch and inst mus.*

Da Camera Music. 1 Boston Farm Cottages, Swyncombe Ave, London W5 4DT *tel:* 020 8568 1445. *Gui mus.*

Da Capo Music Ltd. 26 Stanway Rd, Whitefield, Manchester M45 8EG *tel:* 0161 766 5950. *British contemporary classical mus. Catalogue of c 500 titles. Also M Karkoff (Sweden).*

Dolce Edition. 15 Rock St, Brighton BN2 1NF *tel:* 01273 692974 *fax:* 01273 622792. *Rcdr mus only.*

Duettino Publications. Ardencaple, 16 Batchworth Heath, Rickmansworth, Herts WD3 1QB *tel:* 01923 825625. *Arrangements for pno duet.*

Ebony Edition. Redwings, Linden Chase, Uckfield, E Sussex TN22 1EE *tel:* 01825 760046 *also fax; email:* turbettp@aol.com. *Specialises in mus for w/wind.*

Eden Music Publishing. 42 Killermont Rd, Bearsden, Glasgow G61 2JA *tel:* 0141 942 3089. *S/publishing company for John Rose (see* **Composers**). *Choral, educ, songs, pno, str quartet.*

* **EG Music Ltd.** 63a Kings Rd, London SW3 4NT *tel:* 020 7730 2162 *fax:* 020 7730 1330. *Popular, rock, world mus.*

Electrophonic Music Company. Lancaster Farm, Chipping Lane, Longridge, Preston PR3 2NB *tel:* 01772 783646 *fax:* 01772 786026. *S/publishing company for Ernest Tomlinson (see* **Composers**). *Orch, band, songs and choral mus.*

* **Emerson Edition Ltd.** Windmill Farm, Ampleforth, York YO62 4HF *tel:* 01439 788324 *fax:* 01439 788715 *email:* juneemerson@compuserve.com. *W/wind, solo, ens.*

Emeryson Music Press. Melindwr, Ponterwyd, Aberystwyth, Dyfed SY23 3JY *tel:* 01970 890603 *fax:* 020 7580 4754 *email:* tecartpro@aol.com. *S/publishing company for Albert Alan Owen (see* **Composers**). *Also mus prod company, Techno Arts Productions (TAP Records).*

Encore Publications. 22 Tonbridge Rd, Hildenborough, Kent TN11 9BS *tel:* 01732 832783 *fax:* 01732 832706 *email:* info@ encorepublications.co.uk. *Choral and org.*

English Folk Dance & Song Society. Cecil Sharp House, 2 Regents Park Rd, London NW1 7AY *tel:* 020 7485 2206 *fax:* 020 7284 0534. *Folk song and dance mus.*

Environ Music. 5 Church Green, Boreham Village, Essex CM3 3EH *tel:* 01245 450192. *S/publishing company for Jeffery J Wilson (see* **Composers**). *Educ, wind band, orch and jazz mus.*

* **Eschenbach Editions.** 28 Dalrymple Cres, Edinburgh EH9 2NX *tel:* 0131 667 3633 *also fax; email:* eschenbach@caritas-music.co.uk. *Solo, ens, str orch, orch, choir, org, songs, choral, opera, ballet, chmbr mus.*

European Music Archive. 33a Chestnut Lane, Amersham, Bucks HP6 6EN *tel:* 01494 722602. *17th-18th C inst mus.*

Evening Star Music. 223 Windsor Rd, Carlton-in-Lindrick, Notts S81 9DH *tel:* 01909 733690 *fax:* 01909 732565 *email:* Music @EveningStarMusic.freeserve.co.uk.

* **Evita Music Ltd.** Elsinore House, 77 Fulham Palace Rd, London W6 8JA *tel:* 020 8741 8686 *fax:* 020 8741 8646. *Stage musical mus.*

* **Faber Music Ltd.** 3 Queen Square, London WC1N 3AU *tel:* 020 7278 7436 *fax:* 020 7833 7939 *email:* information@fabermusic.co.uk. Distribution and Sales: Burnt Mill, Elizabeth Way, Harlow, Essex CM20 2HX *tel:* 01279 828989 *fax:* 01279 828990. *Contemporary concert and media composers, choral, educ, jazz, tutors/repertoire for pno, keyboard, strs, w/wind, br, etc.*

Fand Music Press. Blumleins, 7a Dragon St, Petersfield, Hants GU31 4JN *tel:* 01730 266605 *fax:* 01730 262961 *email:* fandmusicpress@printed-music.com. *Pno, vocal, chmbr, choral and orch mus.*

* **Fentone Music Ltd.** Fleming Rd, Earlstrees, Corby, Northants NN17 4SN *tel:* 01536 260981 *fax:* 01536 401075 *email:* music@fentone.com. *Educ, solo, pno, vocal, w/wind, br, gui, strs (especially quartet), orch. Catalogue available.*

* **Fireworks Music Ltd.** Snake Ranch Studios, 90 Lots Rd, London SW10 0QD *tel:* 020 7351 7448 *fax:* 020 7351 7442 *email:* fwx@fireworksmusic.co.uk. *Film, TV, library, classical.*

Folktracks and Soundpost Publications. 16 Brunswick Square, Gloucester GL1 1UG *tel:* 01452 415110 *email:* peter@folktrax.demon.co.uk. *Traditional mus.*

Formedia Virtuosi Ltd. PO Box 2288, Glastonbury, Somerset BA6 9YJ *tel:* 020 8943 5329 *email:* formedia@vallis-davies.freeserve.co.uk. *Nicholas and Sian Vallis-Davies. Classical/folk mus for TV and radio. Mus books with CDs.*

* **Forsyth Brothers Ltd.** 126 Deansgate, Manchester M3 2GR *tel:* 0161 834 3281 *fax:* 0161 834 0630 *email:* forsythmus@aol.com. *Educ, classical.*

Forward Music Ltd. 72 Verdant Lane, London SE6 1LF *tel:* 020 8461 5353 *fax:* 020 8244 7951. *Contemporary mus.*

Fretwork. 16 Teddington Park Rd, Teddington, Middx TW11 8ND *tel:* 020 8977 0924 *fax:* 020 8404 2414 *email:* 100636.1302@compuserve.com. *Mus for viols.*

Friendly Music. PO Box 53, Cranbrook, Kent TN17 3ZX *tel:* 01580 713281. *Collections of solos and duets for w/wind insts; also cl quartets, wind quintets and mus for other wind groups.*

Frontier Press. 36 Riverdale Rd, Plumstead, London SE18 1NZ *tel:* 020 8473 2213. *Contemporary mus, British Contemporary Music Anthology.*

Fulcrum Music Publications. 10 Trafalgar St, Cheltenham, Glos GL50 1UH *tel:* 01242 226101 *also fax. Orch, br band, chmbr and educ mus.*

G & M Brand Publications Ltd. PO Box 367, Aylesbury, Bucks HP22 4LJ *tel:* 01296 682220 *fax:* 01296 681989 *email:* info@rsmith.co.uk.

Gee Music Group. 7 Fleetsbridge Business Centre, Upton Rd, Poole, Dorset BH17 7AF *tel:* 01202 686368 *fax:* 01202 686363. *Including Music Forte, Music Gifts Co and Musigraphic Publishers. Edwin F Kalmus Orchestral, Music Gifts, Masters, Southern, Peanuts Piano Course, Wynn School Orchestral and Band.*

* **Golden Apple Productions.** Chester Music, 8-9 Frith St, London W1V 5TZ *tel:* 020 7434 0066 *fax:* 020 7287 6329. Distribution: Newmarket Rd, Bury St Edmunds, Suffolk IP33 3YB *tel:* 01284 702600 *fax:* 01284 768301. *Children's mus, educ mus.*

* **Goodmusic.** PO Box 100, Tewkesbury, Glos GL20 7YQ *tel:* 01684 773883 *fax:* 01684 773884 *email:* sales@goodmusic-uk.com. *Educ, inst, orch, choral.*

Grail Publications. Grail Centre, 125 Waxwell Lane, Pinner, Middx HA5 3ER *tel:* 020 8866 2195/8866 0505 *fax:* 020 8866 1408 *email:* waxwell@compuserve.com. *Gelineau psalmody; children's musical, religious dramas.*

Grainger Society Edition. 6 Fairfax Cres, Aylesbury, Bucks HP20 2ES *tel:* 01296 428609 *also fax; email:* 101464.2670@compuserve.com. *Mus by Percy Grainger, original compositions and arrangements by others.*

Griffin Music. Hill House, 9 Redford Cres, Edinburgh EH13 0BS *tel:* 0131 441 3035 *fax:* 0131 441 5218 *email:* griffin.music@btinternet.com. *Works by John McLeod.*

Griffiths Edition. 21 Cefn Coed, Bridgend, Mid Glamorgan CF31 4PH *tel:* 01656 649351 *also fax. Pno, strs, hp, w/wind, br, br band, orch, choral and church mus. Also greetings cards.*

Gwynn Publishing Co (Cwmni Cyhoeddi Gwynn Cyf). Y Gerlan, Heol-y-Dwr, Penygroes, Caernarfon, Gwynedd LL54 6LR *tel:* 01286 881797. *Vocal and choral.*

Hallamshire Music. Bank End, N Somercotes, Louth, Lincs LN11 7LN *tel:* 01507 358141 *fax:* 01507 358034. *Solo, ens, br band, wind band and school band.*

The Hardie Press. 17 Harrison Gardens, Edinburgh EH11 1SE *tel:* 0131 313 1383 *fax:* 0131 313 1388. *Scottish mus: solo inst, vocal and baroque. Publishers for The Liszt Society.*

Harlequin Music. 69 Eversden Rd, Harlton, Cambridge CB3 7ET *tel:* 01223 263795 *also fax. Br and wind mus, solo, ens, wind band, perc, jazz ens.*

Harper Collins Religious. 77-85 Fulham Palace Rd, Hammersmith, London W6 8JB *tel:* 020 8741 7070 *fax:* 020 8307 4440. *Christian mus, hymn books.*

Harwood Academic Publishers. c/o IPD, PO Box 90, Reading, Berks RG1 8JL *tel:* 0118 956 0080 *fax:* 0118 956 8211 *email:* info@gbhap.com. *Mus archive publications.*

Hawthorns Music. The Hawthorns, Hawthorn Drive, Wheaton Aston, Staffs ST19 9NG *tel:* 01785 840186 *fax:* 01785 840476 *email:* hawthorn@g0nen.demon.co.uk. *Specialising in editions of early mus, particularly medieval mus and rcdr ens.*

Hughes a'i Fab. S4C International, 50 Lambourne Crescent, Cardiff Business Park, Llanishen, Cardiff CF14 5GG *tel:* 029 2074 1440 *fax:* 029 2075 4444 *email:* luned_whelan@s4c.co.uk. *Traditional and hymn mus, Welsh language.*

Hungerford Music. 9 Bray Close, Crewe, Cheshire CW1 5LJ

Hunt Edition. 40 Portland Rd, London W11 4LG *tel:* 020 7727 5965 *email:* simonhunt@spartanpress.co.uk. *Wind mus for recreation and educ.*

Hymns Ancient & Modern Ltd. St Mary's Works, St Mary's Plain, Norwich NR3 3BH *tel:* 01603 612914 *fax:* 01603 624483. *Hymn books.*

Impulse Edition. 18 Hillfield Park, Muswell Hill, London N10 3QS *tel:* 020 8444 8587 *fax:* 020 8245 0358 *email:* impulse@impulse-music.co.uk. *Contemporary mus: solo, chmbr, orch, choral, liturgical, cross-cultural.*

Isa Music. 27-29 Carnoustie Place, Scotland St, Glasgow G5 8PH *tel:* 0141 420 1881 *fax:* 0141 420 1892 *email:* lismor@lismor.co.uk. *Traditional Scottish pipe mus; all other styles.*

J & C Richard Enterprises. 17 Finlay St, London SW6 6HE *tel:* 020 7736 1977. *Classical mus.*

Jacks, Pipes and Hammers. Bridge View, Garrigill, Alston, Cumbria CA9 3DU *tel:* 01434 381583 *also fax; email:* edjacksph@btinternet.com. *Facsimile of 17th and 18th C English mus.*

James Pass & Co Ltd. 71 Smallbrook Queensway, Birmingham B5 4HX *tel:* 0121 643 7623 *also fax; email:* info@euromusicweb.com. *Choral mus.*

Janus Music. 22 Ivybridge Close, Twickenham, Middx TW1 1EA *tel:* 020 8892 1833 *also fax; email:* janus@printed-music.com. *W/wind, rcdr; specialises in duos, trios and quartets.*

Jazzwise Publications. 2b Gleneagle Mews, Ambleside Ave, London SW16 6AE *tel:* 020 8769 7725 *fax:* 020 8677 7128. *Publisher and distributor of printed mus and study materials for jazz.*

Jewish Music Distribution. PO Box 67, Hailsham BN27 4UW *tel:* 01323 832863 *email:* jmduk@hotmail.com. Noa Lachman, partner. *Distributors and suppliers of Jewish and Israeli mus and recordings from around the world.*

John Fiddy Music. Fruit Farm House, Foxton, Cambridge CB2 6RT *tel:* 01763 208610 *fax:* 01763 208241 *email:* johnfiddymusic@dial.pipex.com. *Production mus library.*

Josef Weinberger Ltd. 12-14 Mortimer St, London W1N 7RD *tel:* 020 7580 2827 *fax:* 020 7436 9616 *email:* wendyh@jwmail.co.uk. *Mus theatre, classical, light, educ and religious mus.*

Jubilate Hymns. 4 Thorne Park Rd, Chelston, Torquay TQ2 6RX *tel:* 01803 607754 *fax:* 01803 605682 *email:* JubilateMW@aol.com. *Hymns, psalms and worship song material. Member of the Christian Music Publishers' Association.*

K B Productions. 72 Waverley Rd, Rayners Lane, Harrow, Middx HA2 9RD *tel:* 020 8866 4158. *Choral service mus, org mus.*

Kerroy Music (Division of Kerroy Group Ltd). PO Box 16975, London NW8 6ZL *tel:* 020 7722 9828 *fax:* 020 7722 9886.

Kevin Mayhew Ltd. Buxhall, Stowmarket, Suffolk IP14 3DJ *tel:* 01449 737978 *fax:* 01449 737834 *email:* info@kevinmayhewltd.com. *Church, org and choral mus; pno and inst; educ materials; recordings.*

Keysworth Press. 4 Kennart Rd, Poole, Dorset BH17 7AP *tel:* 01202 668525 *email:* music@keysworth.ndirect.co.uk. Michael Moorsom, Rosemary Fraser, partners. *Str: solo, quartets, orch.*

King's Music GMC. Redcroft, Banks End, Wyton, Huntingdon, Cambs PE17 2AA *tel:* 01480 52076 *fax:* 01480 450821 *email:* cbkings@ibm.net. *Facsimiles and editions of early mus.*

Kingsway's Thankyou Music Ltd. PO Box 75, Eastbourne, E Sussex BN23 6NW *tel:* 01323 437700 ext 306/316 *fax:* 01323 411970 *email:* music@kingsway.co.uk. *Christian mus.*

* **Kirklees Music.** 609 Bradford Rd, Bailiff Bridge, Brighouse HD6 4DN *tel:* 01484 722855 *also fax. Br and wind band, educ mus.*

Kronos Press. 25 Ansdell St, London W8 5BN *tel:* 020 7937 6768. *S/publishing company for Philip Cannon* (*see* **Composers**).

Leicestershire Music Publications. 1 Garth Heads, Beast Banks, Kendal LA9 4JL *tel:* 01539 736038 *also fax; email:* info@lmp.net1.co.uk. *Materials for teachers: activities, schemes of work and policy documentation on ringbinder, booklets and/or discs, literacy and mus developed by advisers, inspectors and teachers in Leics.*

* **Leosong Copyright Services Ltd.** Independent House, 54 Larkshall Rd, Chingford, London E4 6PD *tel:* 020 8523 9000 *fax:* 020 8523 8888.

* **Light Music Ltd.** 23 Bryanston Court, George St, London W1H 7HA *tel:* 020 7402 4810 *fax:* 020 7262 4296. *S/publishing company for Trevor Lyttleton.*

* **Lindsay Music.** 23 Hitchin St, Biggleswade, Beds SG18 8AX *tel:* 01767 316521 *fax:* 01767 317221 *email:* sales@lindsaymusic.co.uk. *Educ, choral, songbooks, mus giftware.*

Lipkin, Malcolm. Penlan, Crowborough Hill, Crowborough, E Sussex TN6 2EA *tel:* 01892 652454. *S/publishing company of Malcolm Lipkin* (*see* **Composers**).

Llonnod. Frogwy Fawr, Llangwyllog, Llangefni, Anglesey LL77 7PX *tel:* 01248 750418 *email:* gareth@llonnod.demon.co.uk. *S/publishing company for Gareth Glyn.*

Logorhythm Music. 6-10 Lexington St, London W1R 3HS *tel:* 020 7734 7443 *fax:* 020 7439 7057. *Film and TV scores.*

Lomond Music. 32 Bankton Park, Kingskettle, Fife KY15 7PY *tel:* 01337 830974 *fax:* 01337 830653 *email:* bruce.fraser@zetnet.co.uk. *Br band, wind band mus; educ, ens mus (br, w/wind, str), choral.*

London Gabrieli Brass Edition. PO Box 1825, London N20 9NU *tel:* 020 8445 3016 *also fax. Rare, mainly 19th C br.*

London Music (Publishing) Ltd. 2 Noel St, London W1V 3RB *tel:* 020 7287 9000 *fax:* 020 7433 3295. *Choral and orch mus.*

London Pro Musica Edition. 15 Rock St, Brighton BN2 1NF *tel:* 01273 692974 *fax:* 01273 622792. *Medieval, renaissance and baroque mus.*

Longship Music. Smidskot, Fawells, Keith Hall, Inverurie AB51 0LN *tel:* 01651 882274 *also fax. S/publishing company for John Hearne* (*see* **Composers**).

Lopés Edition Ltd. 363 Bideford Green, Leighton Buzzard, Beds LU7 7TX *tel:* 01525 371126. *Contemporary mus.*

Lovely Music. 17 Westgate, Tadcaster, N Yorks LS24 9JB *tel:* 01937 832946 *fax:* 01937 835696. *Educ mus and books. Agents for Holdstock & Mayflower publications.*

Lynwood Music. 2 Church St, West Hagley, W Midlands DY9 0NA *tel:* 01562 886625 *email:* downlyn@globalnet.co.uk. *Mus of contemporary British and European composers.*

McCrimmon Publishing Co Ltd. 10-12 High St, Great Wakering, Essex SS3 0EQ *tel:* 01702 218956 *fax:* 01702 216082 *email:* mccrimmons @dial.pipex.com. *Hymn books, psalm collections, mus for schools.*

McTier Music. 106 Hounslow Rd, Twickenham, Middx TW2 7HB *tel:* 020 8894 5381 *fax:* 020 8898 4591 *email:* music@mctier.globalnet.co.uk. *Db mus.*

* **Maecenas Europe.** 5 Bushey Close, Old Barn Lane, Kenley, Surrey CR8 5AU *tel:* 020 8660 3914 *fax:* 020 8668 5273 *email:* oakcroft@msn.com. *Educ, solo, ens, choral, wind band, orch, pno, org, gui, jazz, jazz ens, str, wind, perc, vocal.*

* **Maecenas Music Ltd.** 5 Bushey Close, Old Barn Lane, Kenley, Surrey CR8 5AU *tel:* 020 8660 3914 *fax:* 020 8668 5273 *email:* oakcroft @msn.com. *Educ, classical, gui, keyboard, perc, wind, jazz, str, br, orch, wind band, br band, marching band, jazz ens, choral, vocal, textbooks.*

Magick Musick Ltd. Philip Houlihan, PO Box 17930, London SW19 7WA *tel:* c/o 020 8947 0484. *Educ mus.*

Magnificat Music. Bishop's House, Edinburgh Rd, Portsmouth PO1 3HG *tel:* 023 9287 0348 *fax:* 023 9283 9143 *email:* Magnimus@aol.com. *Liturgical mus and recordings; specialises in the mus of Paul Inwood* (*see* **Composers**).

Mahayana Music. 91 Portland St, Southport, Merseyside PR8 6QZ *tel:* 01704 548737; 0121 555 5103 *email:* simon@mahayana. demon.co.uk. *Contemporary and educ. Specialists in young composers.*

Mansel Thomas Trust. Ty Cerbyd, Station Rd, Ponthir, Newport NP18 1GQ *tel:* 01633 421299 *email:* grace.gilmore-james@solutia.com. *Publishes the works of the late Mansel Thomas.*

Mapa Mundi. 15 Marvig, Lochs, Isle of Lewis, Scotland HS2 9QP *tel:* 01851 880216 *also fax; email:* mapamundi@aol.com. *Renaissance choral mus.*

Masterclass Music. 12 Kelso Place, Dundee DD2 1SL *tel:* 01382 667251 *fax:* 01382 640775 *email:* donmusic@rmplc.co.uk. *Inst arrangements for secondary schools.*

* **Mautoglade Music Ltd.** 22 Denmark St, London WC2H 8NA *tel:* 020 7836 5996 *fax:* 020 7379 5205 *email:* cmac@mautogladeмusic. demon.co.uk.

* **MCA Music Ltd.** Unit 9, Elsinore House, 77 Fulham Palace Rd, London W6 8JA *tel:* 020 8741 8686 *fax:* 020 8741 8646. *Stage musicals and popular mus.*

* **Memory Lane Music Ltd.** 22 Denmark St, London WC2H 8NA *tel:* 020 7240 5349 *fax:* 020 7379 5205 *email:* cmac@mautogladeмusic.demon.co.uk.

* **Meriden Music.** Silverwood House, Woolaston, nr Lydney, Glos GL15 6PJ *tel:* 01594 529026 *fax:* 01594 529027. *S/publishing company for Graham Whettam (see* **Composers**).

Merton Music. 8 Wilton Grove, London SW19 3QX *tel:* 020 8540 2708 *also fax; email:* mertonmusic@argonet.co.uk. *Str chmbr mus.*

Methodist Publishing House. 20 Ivatt Way, Peterborough PE3 7PG *tel:* 01733 332202 *fax:* 01733 331201 *email:* chief.exec@mph.org.uk. *Hymn books, choral mus, religious musical dramas.*

Mister D Music (Publications). 57 Landsdowne Rd, Bournemouth BH1 1RN *tel:* 01202 551440. *Solo, ens, str orch, school orch; also electric keyboard mus. S/publishing company for David Hellewell (see* **Composers**).

Modus Music. 21 Canonbury Rd, Enfield, Middx EN1 3LW *tel:* 020 8363 2663. *Composers' publishing co-operative.*

Moeck UK. 38 Manningham Lane, Bradford BD1 3EA *tel:* 01274 721646 *fax:* 01274 393516.

* **Moggie Music Ltd.** 101 Hazelwood Lane, London N13 5HQ *tel:* 020 8886 2801 *fax:* 020 8882 7380. *Commercial popular mus.*

Mozart Edition (GB) Ltd. c/o Somerset & Co, 19 Woburn Place, London WC1H 0LU *tel:* 020 7278 3615 *fax:* 020 7837 6029. *Light orch mus and recorded mus library.*

* **MPL Communications Ltd.** 1 Soho Square, London W1V 6BQ *tel:* 020 7439 1492 *also fax. Big band, br band, military band, musicals, choral and vocal.*

* **MSM & LGB Music Publishers.** Gilbert House, 406 Roding Lane South, off Woodford Ave, Woodford Green, Essex IG8 8EY *tel:* 020 8551 1282 *fax:* 020 8550 8377. *Incorporates Leonard, Gould & Bottler. Solo, ens, choir (catalogue).*

Music Dynamics Ltd. PO Box 340, Cheltenham, Glos GL52 4ZP *tel:* 01242 679379 *also fax; email:* music@museco.demon.co.uk. Sue Lloyd, sales mgr. *Originator and producer of the* ChoraLine *range of hi-tech rehearsal cassettes for choral singers (SATB).*

* **Music Exchange (Manchester) Ltd.** Claverton Rd, Wythenshawe, Manchester M23 9ZA *tel:* 0161 946 1234 *fax:* 0161 946 1195 *email:* mail@music-exchange.co.uk. *Publishes educ, classical and pop mus; also distributors.*

Music for Brass Ltd. Unit 1, Warneford Ave, Dewsbury Rd, Ossett WF5 9NJ *tel:* 01924 261154 *fax:* 01924 280310. *Br and wind band.*

Music for Television. Atlantic Studios, 65 Jeddo Rd, London W12 9ED *tel:* 020 8740 7727 *fax:* 020 8743 2523 *email:* guy@mftv.co.uk. *Library mus publisher and s/publishing company for Guy Michelmore (see* **Composers**).

Music Haven Publishing. 61 Silk Mill Rd, Oxhey, Herts WD1 4JW *tel:* 01923 334696 *also fax. Contemporary, (classical).*

Musica Baltica Ltd. 16 Chase Court Gardens, Enfield, Middx EN2 8DH *tel:* 020 8363 4203 *also fax. Latvian contemporary, choral, inst and educ mus.*

Musicland Ltd. Beauchamp House, Churcham, Glos GL2 8AA *tel:* 01452 750253 *fax:* 01452 750585 *email:* music@beauchamp.demon.co.uk. *Educ mus for children.*

* **Musisca Publishing.** 34 Strand, Topsham, Exeter EX3 0AY *tel:* 01392 877737 *also fax; fax:* 01453 751911 *email:* musisca@printed-music.com. *Solo (vc), str quartet.*

Muskett Music. The Old Mill, Duntish, Dorchester, Dorset DT2 7DR *tel:* 01300 345412 *also fax; email:* hurdyplay@aol.com. *Teaching methods and early inst mus.*

Musography. 6 Station Rd, Catworth, Huntingdon, Cambs PE18 0PE *tel:* 01832 710227 *also fax; email:* chris@musography.freeserve.co.uk. *S/publishing company of Christopher Brown (see* **Composers**).

Mute Song Ltd. 429 Harrow Rd, London W10 4RE *tel:* 020 8969 8866 *fax:* 020 8968 6983 *email:* scampbell@muteha.co.uk. *All types of mus.*

New Wind Music Co. 11 Park Chase, Wembley Park, Middx HA9 8EQ *tel:* 020 8902 2073. *Wind mus (solo and ens).*

* **Novello & Co Ltd.** 8-9 Frith St, London W1V 5TZ *tel:* 020 7434 0066 *fax:* 020 7287 6329; 020 7439 2848 *email:* music@musicsales.co.uk. *Contemporary classical, educ, choral.*

* **Obelisk Music.** 32 Ellerdale Rd, London NW3 6BB *tel:* 020 7435 5255 *fax:* 020 7431 0621. *Classical, inst, light mus.*

* **Odyssey Music Ltd.** 20 Watford Rd, Radlett, Herts WD7 8LE *tel:* 01923 857792 *fax:* 01923 858052 *email:* songs@odysseymusic.co.uk.

Oecumuse. 52a Broad St, Ely, Cambs CB7 4AH *tel:* 01353 663252 *fax:* 01353 663371. *Choral, org.*

Oliver Brockway Music. 53 Oakley St, London SW3 5HB. *Specialist publications for hn.*

Oriana Publications. 33 Southminster Rd, Penylan, Cardiff CF23 5AT *tel:* 029 2025 4768 *fax:* 029 2049 9970 *email:* info@orianapub. freeseve.co.uk. *Contemporary, historical, educ, wind and br, catalogues available, hire library.*

Oriel Library. 32 The Burgage, Market Drayton TF9 1EG *tel:* 01630 653802 *email:* oriellibrary@compuserve.com. *Rcdr, viol and vocal consort mus.*

* **Oxford University Press Music Department.** Great Clarendon St, Oxford OX2 6DP *tel:* 01865 556767 *fax:* 01865 267749 *email:* music.enquiry@oup.co.uk. Trade orders: Saxon Way West, Corby, Northants NN18 9ES. *20th C, choral, orch, educ, easy and tutorial, opera, inst, church, etc.*

* **Oxford University Press/New Music Promotion.** 70 Baker St, London W1M 1DJ *tel:* 020 7616 5900 *fax:* 020 7616 5901 *email:* repertoire.promotion@oup.co.uk. *Also Early Music Journal. British contemporary composers.*

Pan Educational Music. 40 Portland Rd, London W11 4LG *tel:* 020 7727 5965 *email:* simonhunt@spartanpress.co.uk. *Specialists in wind mus.*

* **Panache Music Ltd.** Regent House, 1 Pratt Mews, Camden, London NW1 0AD *tel:* 020 7267 6899 *fax:* 020 7267 6746.

Parish Publications. 28 Tom Price Close, Cheltenham, Glos GL52 2LF *tel:* 01242 230455 *also fax; email:* parish@lineone.net. *Church, choral, org, pno, vocal, inst mus.*

Pathway Music. 2a Grosvenor Ave, London N5 2NR *tel:* 020 7359 0970 *fax:* 020 7226 8958. *Pop and jazz. Spoken word.*

Paul Rodriguez Music Ltd. 61 Queen's Drive, London N4 2BG *tel:* 020 8802 5984 *fax:* 020 8809 7436 *email:* paul@paulrodriguezmus.demon.co.uk. *Classical, pop, jazz.*

Peacock Press. Scout Bottom Farm, Mytholmroyd, Hebden Bridge, W Yorks HX7 5JS *tel:* 01422 882751 *fax:* 01422 886157 *email:* ruth@recordermail.demon.co.uk. *Publishers of rcdr mus.*

Pendragon Press. Crag House, Witherslack, Grange-over-Sands, Cumbria LA11 6RW *tel:* 01539 552286 *fax:* 01539 552013 *email:* musicbks@rdooley.demon.co.uk. *Facsimiles of 18th-19th C French operas.*

Perfect Songs Ltd. 42-46 St Luke's Mews, London W11 1DG *tel:* 020 7221 5101 *fax:* 020 7221 3374.

* **Peters Edition Ltd.** 10-12 Baches St, London N1 6DN *tel:* 020 7553 4000 *fax:* 020 7490 4921 *email:* info@edition-peters.com. *Classical.*

Phaidon Press Ltd. Regent's Wharf, All Saints St, London N1 9PA *tel:* 020 7843 1000 *fax:* 020 7843 1010.

* **Phoenix Music.** Bryn Golau, Saron, Denbighshire LL16 4TH *tel:* 01745 550317 *fax:* 01745 550560 *email:* phoenixmus@aol.com. *Variable ens, inst ens, mus for schools.*

Photoplay Music Ltd. 23 Bryanston Court, George St, London W1H 7HA *tel:* 020 7402 4810 *fax:* 020 7262 4296. *Library mus.*

Phylloscopus Publications. 92 Aldcliffe Rd, Lancaster LA1 5BE *tel:* 01524 67498 *email:* a.malloch@lancaster.ac.uk. *Chmbr mus for wind insts.*

Piccolo Press. 10 Clifton Terrace, Winchester, Hants SO22 5BJ *tel:* 01962 864755 *also fax;* 020 7724 3250. *Mainly mus for unusual ens and soloists. Also books on insts.*

Piers Press. Overthorpe Hall Lodge, Banbury, Oxon *tel:* 01295 257722 *fax:* 01295 263733. *Classical sheet mus.*

* **Pink Floyd Music Publishers Ltd.** 27 Noel St, London W1V 3RD *tel:* 020 7734 6892 *fax:* 020 7439 4613 *email:* info@noelstreet.com.

Piper Publications. Dochroyle Farm, Barrhill by Girvan, Ayrshire KA26 0QG *tel:* 01465 821377 *email:* piperpub@dircon.co.uk. *Educ, vocal (including cantatas and mus plays), inst (solo and ens), orch; text books and mus linked project packs; steelpan handbook; Piper New Classics.*

* **Power Music Ltd (Arrensdorff Edition).** 1 Station Rd, Harecroft, Wilsden, Bradford BD15 0BS *tel:* 01535 272905 *fax:* 01535 273520 *email:* power.music@btinternet.com. *Educ and w/wind mus specialists. Jazz, sax quartet, br quartet, fl/cl quartet, str quartet and ens series.*

Practical Music. 1 St Anne's Rd, Caversham, Reading RG4 7PA *tel:* 0118 947 7170 *also fax; email:* jsherbourne@bigfoot.com. *S/publishing company for Janet Sherbourne, Jan Steele (see* **Composers**).

Primavera. 11 Langham Place, Highwoods, Colchester, Essex CO4 4GB *tel:* 01206 751522 *email:* rodusher@lineone.net. *Contemporary mus. Also solo, str, orch, choir, ABRSM pieces.*

Quavers Rest Music. 22 Stephen's Rd, Tunbridge Wells, Kent TN4 9JE *tel:* 01892 537764 *fax:* 01892 511352. *Pno, choral, inst. S/publishing company for Michael Jacques (see* **Composers**).

Queen's Temple Publications. 15 Mallard Drive, Buckingham, Bucks MK18 1GJ *tel:* 01280 813144 *also fax. Educ, wind ens, minority wind insts.*

Realspace Music. 83 Heslington Rd, York YO10 5AX *tel:* 01904 630143. *Inst, vocal, electro-acoustic, educ mus games, multimedia participatory projects. S/publishing company for Trevor Wishart (see* **Composers**).

Recital Music. Studio Ten, Farnham Maltings, Farnham, Surrey GU9 7QR *tel:* 01252 319610 *also fax; email:* recital@printed-music.com. *Specialist publications for db. Also other insts.*

Redcliffe Edition. 68 Barrowgate Rd, London W4 4QU *tel:* 020 8995 1223 *also fax. British composers.*

Redgold Music. c/o Grand Union Shoreditch Town Hall, 380 Old St, London EC1V 9LT *tel:* 020 7729 8729 *fax:* 020 7729 8789. *S/publishing company for Tony Haynes (see* **Composers**) *and Grand Union.*

Revelo-Cornish Music. 35 Salisbury Rd, Harrow, Middx HA1 1NU *tel:* 020 8863 8275 *also fax. Elec, inst, educ. S/publishing company for Oliver Hunt (see* **Composers**).

RG Editions. 23 The Croft, Hungerford, Berks RG17 0HY *tel:* 01488 682994 *fax:* 01488 686341 *email:* rg.editions@argonet.co.uk. *Specialists in 17th and 18th C str chmbr mus, working from original editions and autograph manuscripts.*

Ricordi & Co (London) Ltd. Bedford House, 69-79 Fulham High Street, London SW6 3JW *tel:* 020 7384 8180/8195 *fax:* 020 371 7270/384 8167 *email:* Miranda.Jackson@bmg.co.uk. *Opera, ballet, inst, ens, br band, orch, vocal, choral, school mus.*

Roanna Music. 141 Manor Rd North, Thames Ditton, Surrey KT7 0BQ *tel:* 020 8224 6493. *Easy listening.*

* **Roberton Publications.** The Windmill, Wendover, Aylesbury, Bucks HP22 6JJ *tel:* 01296 623107. *Standard classical, vocal, choral and inst mus.*

Ronald Stevenson Society. 3 Chamberlain Rd, Edinburgh EH10 4DL *fax:* 0131 229 9298 *email:* rss@medeco.co.uk. *Publishing company for Ronald Stevenson (see* **Composers**).

Rosehill Music Publishing Co Ltd. Harold Charles House, 64a London End, Beaconsfield, Bucks HP9 2JD *tel:* 01494 674411 *fax:* 01494 670932. *Br.*

Rosewood Publications. 61 Oak Hill, Surbiton, Surrey KT6 6DY *tel:* 020 8390 3236 *email:* michael@bryant14.demon.co.uk. *New works and previously unpublished or rare chmbr mus for wind and pno, wind, strs and pno, wind and strs and wind alone.*

Routledge Ltd. Christoph Chesher, 11 New Fetter Lane, London EC4P 4EE *tel:* 020 7583 9855 *fax:* 020 7842 2298. *Authorship and copyright, history of mus and of British Publishing, rock and pop mus, world mus, mus therapy.*

* **Royal School of Church Music.** Publications Dept, Cleveland Lodge, Westhumble St, Westhumble, Dorking, Surrey RH5 6BW *tel:* 01306 872811 *fax:* 01306 887240 *email:* musicsupplies@rscm.com. *Choral mus, plus reference material for the church musician.*

RTL Music. White House Farm, Pipe Gate, Shropshire TF9 4HA *tel:* 01630 647374 *fax:* 01630 647612.

RTS Music Partnership. 17 Bradford Rd, St Johns, Wakefield, W Yorks WF1 2RF *tel:* 01924 370454 *email:* standford@rtsmusic.demon.co.uk. *British composers, educ, light, publishers for Patric Standford (see* **Composers**).

St Gregory Publishing Co. 64 Pineheath Rd, High Kelling, Holt, Norfolk NR25 6RH *tel:* 01263 712288. *Church, org, vocal, educ mus.*

Salvationist Publishing & Supplies Ltd. 117-121 Judd St, London WC1H 9NN *tel:* 020 7387 1656 *fax:* 020 7383 3420. *Religious vocal mus for children and adults, br band mus.*

Salvi Publications. 58 Hopton St, London SE1 9JH *tel:* 020 7928 8451 *fax:* 020 7928 8284. *Hp mus only.*

Samuel French Ltd. 52 Fitzroy St, London W1P 6JR *tel:* 020 7387 9373 *fax:* 020 7387 2161 *email:* theatre@samuelfrench-london.co.uk. *Musical plays and school mus.*

* **Samuel King Music Publishers.** PO Box 17, Cardigan, Ceredigion SA43 1HZ *tel:* 01239 621292 *also fax; email:* samuel.king@btinternet.com. *W/wind, br, wind band, choral and vocal, str orch. Catalogue and demo tapes available.*

Satanic Mills Press. 4 Church St, Golcar, Huddersfield HD7 4AH *tel:* 01484 652762 *fax:* 01484 472656 *email:* m.l.wilkins@hud.ac.uk. *S/publishing company for Margaret Lucy Wilkins (see* **Composers**). *Orch, chmbr, solo, inst, vocal, choral.*

Saxtet Publications. 15 Paignton Rd, Edgbaston, Birmingham B16 0JX *tel:* 0121 565 5484 *also fax; email:* saxtetpublications@saxwood.demon.co.uk. *Sax, cl, fl mus.*

Sceptre Publishers. 97 Elton Rd, Stibbington, Peterborough PE8 6JX *tel:* 01780 782093 *fax:* 01780 783159. *Solo elec org.*

* **Schauer & May Ltd.** Simrock House, 220 The Vale, London NW11 8HZ *tel:* 020 8731 6665 *fax:* 020 8731 6667. *Classical and educ mus.*

Schirmer (G) Ltd. 8-9 Frith St, London W1V 5TZ *tel:* 020 7434 0066 *fax:* 020 7287 6329 *email:* music@musicsales.co.uk.

* **Schott & Co Ltd.** 48 Great Marlborough St, London W1V 2BN *tel:* 020 7494 1487 *fax:* 020 7287 1529. *Mkt & Sales Dept:* Brunswick Rd, Ashford, Kent TN23 1EH *tel:* 01233 628987 *fax:* 01233 610232. *Solo, ens, wind band, str orch, school orch, choir; also rcdr, Orff-Schulwerk; contemporary.*

Sea Dream Music. PO Box 13533, London E7 0SG *tel:* 020 8534 8500 *fax:* 07070 718613. *Legal texts on mus, christian songs.*

Seresta Music Ltd. 410a Hessle Rd, Hull, E Yorks HU3 3SD *tel:* 01482 210743 *also fax; email:* davidashbridge@yahoo.com. *Sullivan, Chieftain, Burgess, chmbr, orch. For all enquiries, including hire, contact William Elkin Music Services*

* **SGO Music Publishing Ltd.** PO Box 26022, London SW10 0FY *tel:* 07071 226822 *fax:* 07071 225119 *email:* sgomusic@aol.com. *Complete spectrum of pop mus.*

Shaftesbury Edition. 16 Mitcham Rd, Dymchurch, Kent TN29 0TH *tel:* 01303 874449. *S/publishing company for Peter Aviss (see* **Composers**).

* **SJ Music.** 23 Leys Rd, Cambridge CB4 2AP *tel:* 01223 314771 *fax:* 01223 560353. *Str and chmbr mus.*

Snell & Sons. 68 West Cross Lane, West Cross, Swansea SA3 5LU *tel:* 01792 405727 *email:* snell's@welshmusic.demon.co.uk. *Welsh mus.*

Sound Music. 25 Turners Croft, Heslington, York YO10 5EL *tel:* 01904 410298 *fax:* 01904 421109. *Specialising in musicals for primary schools.*

Spanish Guitar Centre. 44 Nottingham Rd, New Basford, Nottingham NG7 7AE *tel:* 0115 962 2709 *fax:* 0115 962 5368 *email:* sales@spanishguitar.com. *Specialist classical gui mus.*

Spartan Press Music Publishers Ltd. Old Brewery House, Redbrook, Monmouth NP25 4LU *tel:* 01600 712482 *fax:* 01600 712483 *email:* spartanpress@compuserve.com. *Solo, duets, flexible ens, str orch, br ens, pno, group teaching.*

Sphemusations. 12 Northfield Rd, Onehouse, Stowmarket, Suffolk IP14 3HF *tel:* 01449 613388. *Contemporary mus including choral, orch and chmbr.*

Spin Publications. 24 Beresford Rd, Wallasey, Merseyside L45 0JJ *tel:* 0151 639 3559.

Springpark Music. 10 Princess Mews, London NW3 5AP *tel:* 020 7431 1771 *fax:* 020 7431 8422.

Springthyme Music. Balmalcolm House, Kingskettle, Fife KY15 7TJ *tel:* 01337 830773 *fax:* 01337 831773 *email:* music@springthyme.co.uk. *Folk and traditional mus.*

* **Stainer & Bell Ltd.** PO Box 110, Victoria House, 23 Gruneisen Rd, London N3 1DZ *tel:* 020 8343 3303 *fax:* 020 8343 3024 *email:* post@stainer.co.uk. *Solo, ens, wind band, str orch, school orch, choral.*

Stanley Thornes (Publishers) Ltd. Ellenborough House, Wellington St, Cheltenham, Glos GL50 1YW *tel:* 01242 228888 *fax:* 01242 221914 *email:* cservice@thornes.co.uk. *Sounds of Music, Silver Burdett Music, Blueprints Music. Curriculum mus materials.*

Stanza Music. 11 Victor Rd, Harrow, Middx HA2 6PT *tel:* 020 8863 2717 *fax:* 020 8863 8685 *email:* bill.ashton@virgin.net. *Big band and small jazz ens; also standard-type songs. Full catalogue available.*

* **State Music Ltd.** 20 Watford Rd, Radlett, Herts WD7 8LE *tel:* 01923 857792 *fax:* 01923 858052 *email:* songs@statemusic.co.uk.

* **Studio Music Co.** 77-79 Dudden Hill Lane, London NW10 1BD *tel:* 020 8459 6194; 020 8830 0110 (sales) *fax:* 020 8451 6470. *General educ (inst and vocal); br, wind, jazz band, orch.*

Studium Classica. Ffair Rhos, Ceredigion SY25 6BS *tel:* 01974 831391 *fax:* 01974 831320 *email:* studium_classica@lineone.net. *Pno mus.*

Sutton Elms Publications. 56 Arbor Rd, Croft, Leics LE9 3GD *tel:* 01455 284096. *Mus of Nigel Deacon (see* **Composers**).

* **Sweet 'n' Sour Songs Ltd.** 2-3 Fitzroy Mews, London W1P 5DQ *tel:* 020 7383 7767 *fax:* 020 7383 3020. *Musicals, pop.*

Take Note Publishing Ltd. 54 Lincolns Mead, Lingfield, Surrey RH7 6TA *tel:* 01342 836689 *also fax; email:* editor@takenote.co.uk. *Mus for w/wind, strs, gui, pno and keyboard; theory, mus educ software.*

Tecla Editions. PO Box 7567, London NW3 2LJ *tel:* 020 7435 5077 *also fax; email:* tecla@tecla.com. *Solo.*

* **Television Music Ltd.** Television Centre, Kirkstall Rd, Leeds LS3 1JS *tel:* 0113 243 8283 *fax:* 0113 244 5107.

Thames Publishing. 14 Barlby Rd, London W10 6AR *tel:* 020 8969 3579 *also fax. Serious solo vocal, choral and inst. Also books.*

Tinderbox Music. 93 Stradella Rd, London SE24 9HL *tel:* 020 7274 5314. *Resource material for specialist and non-specialist teachers; primary, song books, rcdr, classroom insts. Ethnic and world mus.*

Tobin Music/Helicon Press. The Old Malthouse, Knight St, Sawbridgeworth, Herts CM21 9AX *tel:* 01279 726625 *email:* candidatobin@compuserve.com. *Educ.*

Tomus Publications. 17 Kensington Rd, Earlsdon, Coventry CV5 6GG *tel:* 024 7667 0211 *also fax. Rcdr and wind mus.*

Tristan Music Ltd. 22 Denmark St, London WC2H 8NA *tel:* 020 7836 5996 *fax:* 020 7379 5205 *email:* cmac@mautogladeмusic.demon.co.uk.

Tyne Music. 38 Westmorland Rd, Newcastle-upon-Tyne NE1 4EN *tel:* 0191 232 2479 *also fax. Br band, choir, mus plays (8-15 yrs), br, w/wind, ens; also modern original musicals for adults and new Christmas songs.*

* **United Music Publishers Ltd (UMP).** 42 Rivington St, London EC2A 3BN *tel:* 020 7729 4700 *fax:* 020 7739 6549 *email:* ump@compuserve.com. *Classical mus.*

* **Universal Edition (London) Ltd/Alfred Kalmus Ltd.** 48 Great Marlborough St, London W1V 2BN *tel:* 0800 525566 *fax:* 0800 525567. Also at: 38 Eldon Way, Paddock Wood, Kent TN12 6BE *tel:* 01892 833422 *fax:* 01892 836038.

University of York Music Press Ltd. Department of Music, University of York, Heslington, York YO10 5DD *tel:* 01904 432434 *fax:* 01904 432450 *email:* uymp@york.ac.uk. *Contemporary mus.*

Useful Music. Old Brewery House, Redbrook, Monmouth NP5 4LU *tel:* 01600 712482 *fax:* 01600 712483 *email:* spartanpress@compuserve.com. *Distributed by Spartan Press.*

Utopia Music Ltd. 7 Chalcot Rd, London NW1 8LH *tel:* 020 7586 3434 *fax:* 020 7586 3438. *Pop, folk, jazz.*

* **Valentine Music Group Ltd.** 7 Garrick St, London WC2E 9AR *tel:* 020 7240 1628 *fax:* 020 7497 9242 *email:* valentine@bandleader.co.uk. *MOR and country mus.*

* **Valley Music Ltd.** Elsinore House, 77 Fulham Palace Rd, London W6 8JA *tel:* 020 8741 8686 *fax:* 020 8741 8646. *Pop mus.*

* **Vanderbeek & Imrie Ltd.** 15 Marvig, Lochs, Isle of Lewis HS2 9QP *tel:* 01851 880216 *also fax; email:* mapamundi@aol.com. *Renaissance choral mus and 20th C mus.*

Viking Publications (Whittaker Centenary Fund). The Oast House, Goddards Green, Benenden, Cranbrook, Kent TN17 4AR *tel:* 01580 240377. *Mus by WG Whittaker (1876-1944).*

Virgo Music Publishers. PO Box 1068, Knowle, Solihull, W Midlands B94 6DT *tel:* 0121 778 5569 *also fax. Specialists in br, sax, easy jazz, educ mus and orch excerpt series.*

Visible Music. c/o Studio Music Company, 77-79 Dudden Hill Lane, London NW10 1BD *tel:* 020 8830 0110 *fax:* 020 8451 6470. *S/publishing company for Jean Hasse (see* **Composers**).

Voicebox. 16 Teddington Park Rd, Teddington, Middx TW11 8ND *tel:* 020 8977 0924 *fax:* 020 8404 2414 *email:* 100636.1302@compuserve.com *Vocal mus.*

Warwick Music. Holloway House, The Market Place, Warwick CV34 4SJ *tel:* 01926 497887 *fax:* 01926 419701 *email:* info@warwickmusic.com. *Specialists in all br mus.*

Welsh Music Information Centre. Ty Cerdd, 15 Mount Stuart Square, Cardiff CF10 5DP *tel:* 029 2046 2855 *fax:* 029 2046 2733. *Mus by Welsh composers (limited editions) otherwise unavailable. Enquiries by correspondence only.*

Westfield Music. Malt Shovel Cottage, 76 Old Walkergate, Beverley, East Yorks HU17 9ER *tel:* 01482 860580 *email:* ahedges@westfieldmusic.karoo.co.uk. *S/publishing company for Anthony Hedges (see* **Composers**).

William Elkin Music Services. Station Rd Industrial Estate, Salhouse, Norwich NR13 6NS *tel:* 01603 721302 *fax:* 01603 721801 *email:* sales@elkinmusic.demon.co.uk. *Distributors.*

Wind Mail Associates. The South Wing, Lullingstone Castle, Eynsford, Kent DA4 0JA *tel:* 01322 862455 *fax:* 01322 866154. *Distributors and m/order company. Publishers of The Wind Band Catalogue and The Jazz and Stage Band Catalogue.*

Woodwind Plus. 42 St Mary's Park, Louth, Lincs LN11 0EF *email:* jeff@wwplus.freeserve.co.uk. *Chmbr mus for w/wind, saxes, hns, strs.*

Woza Music. 46 Weigell Rd, Lee, London SE12 8HE *tel:* 020 8852 1997 *fax:* 020 8318 7417. *S/publishing company for Stanley Glasser (see* **Composers**).

Wright & Round Ltd. The Cornet Office, PO Box 157, Gloucester GL1 1LW *tel:* 01452 523438 *fax:* 01452 385631 *email:* wright-and-round@interactive-sciences.co.uk. *Br band, solo, ens.*

* **Yorke Edition.** 31 Thornhill Square, London N1 1BQ *tel:* 020 7607 0849 *fax:* 020 7700 4577 *email:* sales@yorkedition.co.uk. *Db.*

Subsidiary Music Publishers

Certain major foreign editions are available through publishers in the United Kingdom. These are listed below along with some UK editions that are represented by another publisher.

A Piacere (UK) – *Boosey*
ABRSM – *OUP (distributors)*
Akkord Music Publishers (Budapest) – *Schauer*
Alfred Publishing – *Music Exchange*
Alkor-Edition (Kassel) – *Bärenreiter*
Allans (Australia) – *Elkin*
Alphonse Leduc & Cie (Paris) – *UMP*
Alsbach (Holland) – *Fentone*
Amadeus Verlag – *Schott*
Amphion Editions Musicales (Paris) – *UMP*
Anglo-Soviet Music Press Ltd – *Boosey*
Anton J Benjamin – *Schauer*
Ashley – *Elkin*
Attic Music Publishing – *Cascade*
Aug Zurfluh (Paris) – *UMP*
Augener Edition Ltd – *Stainer*
Bardic Edition – *Schott*
Bärenreiter (UK) Ltd – *Faber*
Barry & Cia (Argentina) – *Boosey*
Belle Music (Jersey) – *Spanish Guitar Centre*
Belmont Music Publishers (LA) – *Kalmus*
Belwin Kalmus – *Concord*
Belwin Mills Publishing Corporation – *Concord*
Berandol (Canada) – *Kalmus*
Bèrben, Edizioni (Italy) – *Fentone*
Bessel, W (Germany) – *Breitkopf and Härtel*
Boccaccini & Spada (Rome) – *Kalmus*
Boelke-Bomart Inc (New York) – *Kalmus*
Bold Strummer – *Elkin*
Bornemann, Editions (Paris) – *UMP*
Bosse Verlag (Regensburg) – *Bärenreiter*
Bote & Bock (Berlin) – *Boosey*
Bourne Music (USA) – *Kalmus*
Braydeston Press – *Elkin*
British Standard Music Company – *Schauer*
Broekmans & Van Poppel (Amsterdam) – *Kalmus*
C F Kahnt – *Peters*
Camden Music – *Spartan Press*
Carisch SA – *Elkin/Boosey (hire of symphonic works)*
Carl Fischer (USA) – *Boosey/Schott*
Carl Gehrmans Musikforlag – *Elkin/Boosey (hire of symphonic works)*
Cavendish Music Ltd – *Boosey*
Chant du Monde, Editions (France) – *UMP*
Chanterelle (Germany) – *Spanish Guitar Centre*
Chantraine (Belgium) – *UMP*
Chappell (Choral) – *Elkin*
Chiltern Music – *Cathedral Music*
Choudens, Editions (Paris) – *UMP*
Christian Music Ministries – *Elkin*
CIS Soviet Publishing – *Elkin*
Colin – *Elkin*
Combre, Editions (Paris) – *UMP*
Complete Music – *Elkin*
Consortium Musical (Paris) – *UMP*
Cool Music – *Fentone*
Coppelia – *Elkin*
Coppenrath – *Elkin*
Copperplate Music (UK) – *Bardic*
Costallat, Editions (Paris) – *UMP*
CPP/Belwin Inc – *Concord*
Cranz – *UMP*
Creative Concepts – *Elkin*
Curci, Edizioni (Italy) – *Weinberger/Elkin*
D Rahter – *Schauer*
Da Camera Music (UK) – *Spanish Guitar Centre*
Daehn Publications (USA) – *Bardic*
Daminus Edition (Germany) – *Spanish Guitar Centre*
Deutscher Verlag für Musik (Germany) – *Breitkopf and Härtel*
Dilia – *Boosey (operas and ballets)*
Doberman-Yppan (Canada) – *Spanish Guitar Centre*
Doblinger Musikverlag (Vienna) – *Kalmus*
Dominis Music (Canada) – *UMP*
DR Downing Music – *Kalmus*
Drumblade Music (UK) – *Bardic*
Duettino Publications – *Elkin*
Durand, Editions (Paris) – *UMP*
E C Schirmer Music Co (Boston, Mass, USA) – *Elkin*
E F Kalmus (wind band) – *Concord*
Earlham Press Ltd – *Fentone*
Early English Church Music – *Stainer*
Editio Musica Budapest – *Boosey*
Editio Supraphon Prague – *Bärenreiter*
Edition HH (Oxford) – *Schott*
Edition Margaux (Germany) – *Spanish Guitar Centre*
Edition Schwann (Germany) – *Peters*
Éditions Marc Reift (Switzerland) – *Schauer*
Edwin Ashdown – *Elkin*
EFM (Paris) – *UMP*
Elgo Productions (Holland) – *Fentone*
Elisabeth Thomi-Berg (Germany) – *Fentone*
Elkan-Vogel (USA) – *UMP*
Enoch & Cie (Paris) – *UMP*
Eschig, Editions max (Paris) – *UMP*
Eurobeat (UK) – *Classic Editions*
European American Music (USA) – *Kalmus*
European Music Archive – *Spartan Press*
Fazer Music Estonia – *Boosey*
Fazer Music Inc (Helsinki) – *Boosey*
Fenette Music – *Fentone*
Forberg, Robert – *Peters*
Fountain Publications – *Elkin*
Fraser-Enoch Publications – *Kalmus*
Freeman Easy – *Elkin*
Fretful (Australia) – *UMP*
Friedrich Hofmeister (Leipzig) – *Elkin*
Furore Edition (Germany) – *Kalmus*
Furstner, Edition – *Boosey*
G Delrieu – *Elkin*
G Ricordi & Co – *Boosey*
Galliard Ltd – *Stainer*
Garden Music (UK) – *Spanish Guitar Centre*
Gendai Guitar (Japan) – *Spanish Guitar Centre*
Gérard Billaudot (Paris) – *UMP*
GIA Publications Inc – *Concord*
Gitarre & Laute Verlag (Germany) – *Spanish Guitar Centre*
Glocken Verlag Ltd – *Weinberger*
Goldfeder – *Elkin*
Grafton Classics – *Elkin*
Grainger Society Edition (UK) – *Bardic*
Guildhall School of Music & Drama (UK) – *Boosey*
Gutheil, Edition – *Boosey*
Hal Leonard (Choral) – *Elkin/Music Sales*
Halali Horns (USA) – *Oliver Brockway Music*
Hamelle (Paris) – *UMP*
Hammond Publications – *Elkin*
Hans Gerig (Germany) – *Breitkopf and Härtel*
Hargail Press – *Elkin*
Harmonia (Holland) – *Kalmus*
Harpress (California) – *Sphemusations*
Hawkes & Son (London) Ltd – *Boosey*
Heinrichschofen Edition (Germany) – *Peters*
Heinrichschofen Edition (USA) – *Peters*
Hendon Music – *Boosey*
Henle Verlag (Munich) – *Schott*
Henmar Press – *Peters*
Henn, Editions (Switzerland) – *UMP*
Henry Lemoine Editions (Paris) – *UMP*
Heugel & Cie (Paris) – *UMP*
Highbridge Music (Howard Blake) – *Faber*
Hinnenthal Verlag (Germany) – *Bärenreiter*
Hinrichsen – *Peters*
Hinshaw – *Elkin*
Hornmusik International – *Oliver Brockway Music*
HUG Musikverlage (Switzerland) – *Kalmus*
Huguenin (Switzerland) – *UMP*
Hunt Edition – *Spartan Press*
International Music Co (New York) – *Kalmus*
Iota Music Publishers (UK) – *Amphonic*
Israel Brass Woodwind Publications (Israel) – *Schauer*
Itchy Fingers Publications – *Boosey*
J Curwen & Sons Ltd – *Elkin/Music Sales*
Joad Press – *Elkin*
Joaquin Rodrigo Ediciones (Spain) – *Spanish Guitar Centre/Schott*
Jobert, Editions (Paris) – *UMP*
Joel Rothman – *Elkin*
Josef Weinberger – *Elkin*
Joseph Patelson – *Elkin*
Joseph Williams Ltd – *Stainer*
Kahn & Averill – *Elkin*
Karamar – *Elkin*
Karg-Elert Society – *Cathedral Music*
Karthause - Schmülling (Germany) – *Hardie Press*
Kendor Music – *Elkin*
Kneusslin (Switzerland) – *Peters*
Kosinus Music Library (France) – *Amphonic*
Koussevitzky Editions – *Boosey*
Kunzelmann, Edition (Switzerland) – *Peters*
Lafleur Music Ltd – *Boosey*
Latham Music Enterprises (USA) – *Fentone*
Lawson Gould – *Elkin*
LCT Publications – *Schauer*
Lengnick – *Elkin/Schauer (Simrock Editions)*
Les Productions d'Oz (Canada) – *Spanish Guitar Centre*
Leslie Music Supply (Ontario) – *Roberton*
Lienau, Robert – *Peters*
Litolff Henry Verlag (Frankfurt) – *Peters*
London Orchestral Series – *Fentone*
Lorenz Music Corp – *Elkin*
LSO Music Explorer – *Concord*
Lucks Music Library (USA) – *Fentone*
Lyche (Norway) – *Peters*
M P Belaieff Editions – *Peters*
McGinnis & Marx (New York) – *Bärenreiter*
Magnamausic Distributors Inc – *Schott*
Mannheimer Musikverlag – *Schauer*
Mansem Music (UK) – *Classic Editions*
Marais, Editions (Paris) – *UMP*
Margaux – *Elkin*
Masters Music (wind band) – *Concord*
Max Brockhaus (Germany) – *Schauer*
Mel Bay (UK distribution) – *Kevin Mayhew*
Melodie – *Elkin*
Meredith – *Elkin*
Metro Music Library (USA) – *Amphonic*
Mimram – *Fentone*
Minster Music – *Cathedral Music*

Minstrel Press – *Elkin*
MMB Music (St Louis, USA) – *Schott*
Modern Music – *Cascade*
Moeck Verlag (Germany) – *Kalmus (hire materials only)*
Molenaar – *Elkin*
Music 70 – *Elkin*
Music Box Dancer – *Elkin*
Music Concepts – *Fentone*
Music Exchange Publications – *Music Exchange*
Music Express (USA) – *Schauer*
Music Unlimited Limited – *Concord*
Musica Britannica – *Stainer*
Musica Rara (Montreux) – *Kalmus*
Musica Russica – *Boosey*
Musicales Yolotyl Ediciones (Mexico) – *Spanish Guitar Centre*
Musicus (Edition) (USA) – *Schauer*
Musikverlag City – *Schauer*
Musikverlag Georg Bratfisch (Germany) – *Schauer*
Musikverlag McNaughton – *Schauer*
Musikverlag Pan (Switzerland) – *Schauer*
Musikwissenschaftlicher Verlag (Vienna) – *Kalmus*
Musisca – *Schott*
N Simrock – *Schauer*
Nagels Verlag (Germany) – *Bärenreiter*
No Boyfriend Music Library (USA) – *Amphonic*
Noga Music (Israel) – *Schauer*
Norsk Musikforlag A/S (Norway) – *Fentone*
Norton Books – *Elkin*
Nova Music – *Spartan Press*
Nova Music Ltd – *Faber*
OGM/Professional Line (USA) – *Amphonic*
Opera Rara (USA) – *Weinberger*
Opera Tres Ediciones Musicales (Spain) – *Spanish Guitar Centre*
Opus (former Czechoslovakia) – *Classic Editions*
Or-Tav Music Publications (Israel) – *Schauer*
Orphée Editions (USA) – *Spanish Guitar Centre*
Otto Wrede-Regina Verlag (Germany) – *Schauer*
Out of the Ark Music – *Music Exchange*
Ouvrières (Paris) – *UMP*
Oxenford Imprint – *Cathedral Music*
Pan Educational Music – *Spartan Press*
Panton (Prague) – *Schott*
Papagrigoriou, C - H Nakas Co (Greece) – *Spanish Guitar Centre*
Paraclete Press – *Elkin*
Philharmonia Miniature Scores – *Kalmus*
Plymouth Music Co – *Elkin*
Power Music Co Ltd – *Kalmus*
PP Music – *Elkin*
Pro Musica (Leipzig) – *Schott*
PWM (Warsaw) – *Kalmus*
Real Musical (Spain) – *Fentone*
Regina Music Publishing – *Music Exchange*
Richard Schauer – *Schauer*
Ricordi, G & Co – *Boosey (sales)*
Rideau-Rouge (Paris) – *UMP*
Robert King Music for Brass (USA) – *UMP*
Robert Lienau (Germany) – *Kalmus*
Robert Martin Editions (France) – *UMP*
Rodrigo (Spain) – *UMP*
Roger Dean – *Elkin*
Royal Scottish Country Dance Society (UK) – *Hardie Press*
Russe de Musique, Edition – *Boosey*
Sacred Music Press – *Elkin*
Salabert, Editions (Paris) – *UMP*
Sam Fox – *Elkin*
Scala Productions (Holland) – *Fentone*
Schola Cantorum (Switzerland) – *UMP*
Schott Freres (Brussels) – *Schott*
Sedim (Paris) – *UMP*
Seresta Music – *Elkin*
Sher – *Elkin*
Sikorski (Germany) – *Elkin/Kalmus*
Sound Stage Production Music (UK) – *Amphonic*
Souvenir Press – *Elkin*
Spratt – *Elkin*
Staff Music Publishing – *Elkin*
Star Nine Publishing – *Elkin*
Subject Publications – *Music Exchange*
Süddeutscher Musikverlag Willy Müller – *Bärenreiter*
Suivini Zerboni, Editions – *Elkin*
Summy Birchard – *Concord*
Sunshine Music Company – *Spartan Press*
Suzuki – *Concord*
Tayborn Publishing – *Music Exchange*
Tecla – *Elkin*
Tezakverlag (Germany) – *Schauer*
Thames – *Elkin*
Theodore Presser Co (USA) – *Kalmus*
Toccata Press – *Elkin*
Transatlantiques, Editions Musicales (Paris) – *UMP*
Trinity College London – *Music Exchange*
TRO – *Elkin*
UCCP – *Elkin*
Universal Edition (London, Vienna) – *Kalmus*
Useful Music – *Spartan Press*
Varney Music HB (Sweden) – *Spanish Guitar Centre*
Verlag Hubertus Nogatz (Germany) – *Spanish Guitar Centre*
Verlag Neue Musik (Germany) – *Spanish Guitar Centre*
Virgo Music Publishers – *Kalmus*
W W Norton Music Books – *Peters*
Walsh – *Fentone*
Walton Music Corp – *Elkin*
Waltons (Dublin) – *Hardie Press*
Warner Bros Publication Inc – *Concord*
Warner Bros (Choral and Organ) – *Elkin*
Warner Chappell Scandinavia – *Boosey*
West Wind Music (USA) – *Bardic*
Wiener Urtext Edition – *Kalmus*
Wiener Waldhorn Verein, Verlag (Austria) – *Oliver Brockway Music*
Willemsen (Holland) – *Fentone*
William Grant Still Music (USA) – *Bardic*
Winthrop Rogers Ltd – *Boosey*
Wollenweber (Switzerland) – *Peters*
World Music Press (USA) – *Lindsay Music*
XYZ International (Holland) – *Fentone*
Zen-on – *Boosey*
Zimmermann (Germany) – *Elkin/Kalmus*

Book Publishers

Listed below are the publishers of academic, educational and general interest books about music. Information on the publications available is shown after each entry; for educational publishers the education level is specified.

A & C Black (Publishers) Ltd. Music Dept, 35 Bedford Row, London WC1R 4JH *tel:* 020 7242 0946 *fax:* 020 7831 7489 *email:* music@acblack.co.uk. Sheena Roberts, Jane Sebba, Ana Sanderson, commissioning eds. *Primary, secondary, songbooks, classroom mus, inst tutors and repertoire.*

Amadeus Press. 2-4 Station Rd, Swavesey, Cambridge CB4 5QJ *tel:* 01954 232959 *fax:* 01954 206040 *email:* timberpressuk@btinternet.com. Pam Segers, mkt mgr (UK). *Specialist books on classical mus and musicians. Biographies of major figures such as Jussi Björling, Rosa Ponselle, Beethoven, Boulez, Korngold, etc.*

Ashgate Publishing Ltd. Gower House, Croft Rd, Aldershot, Hants GU11 3HR *tel:* 01252 331551 *fax:* 01252 344405 *email:* info@ashgatepub.co.uk. Sarah Noble, mkt mgr; Rachel Lynch, commissioning ed. *Academic studies in mus, biographies, bibliographies and monographs. U/grad and p/grad level.*

Blackwell Publishers. 108 Cowley Rd, Oxford OX4 1JF *tel:* 01865 791100 *fax:* 01865 791347 *email:* lberrett@blackwellpublishers.co.uk. Lorna Berrett, mkt mgr. *Publishers of Music Analysis Journal and various mus reference titles including Blackwell History of Music in Britain, Early Twentieth Century Music, Music Before 1600 and Blackwell Guide to Recorded Jazz.*

Boosey & Hawkes Music Publishers Ltd. 295 Regent St, London W1R 8JH *tel:* 020 7580 2060 *fax:* 020 7291 7199 *email:* sales@boosey.com. *Catalogues available: mus for schools, keyboard, str, w/wind, br, perc, ens, symphonic band, vocal, choral, midi software and CD-ROMs. Also Bote & Bock, Editio Musica Budapest, Fazer, Guildhall, Ricordi and Itchy Fingers publications.*

The British Library. Publishing Office, 96 Euston Rd, London NW1 2DB *tel:* 020 7412 7535 *fax:* 020 7412 7768. *Wide range of mus publications.*

Cambridge University Press. Edinburgh Building, Shaftesbury Rd, Cambridge CB2 2RU *tel:* 01223 312393 *fax:* 01223 315052 *email:* information @cup.cam.ac.uk. Penny Souster, snr commissioning ed, academic group; Victoria Cooper, commissioning ed, academic group; Susan Taylor, commissioning ed, educ group. *Primary and secondary educ mus books; gen mus books; books for scholars and students on the history of mus, mus performance, theory and analysis, popular mus and opera. Books series include Cambridge Companions to Music, Cambridge Music Handbooks, Musical Lives, Music in the Twentieth Century, Cambridge Studies in Opera and Cambridge Opera Handbooks. Also publishes a range of mus journals including British Journal of Music Education, Cambridge Opera Journal and Popular Music.*

Cassell plc. Wellington House, 125 Strand, London WC2R 0BB *tel:* 020 7420 5555 *fax:* 020 7240 7261 *email:* cassellacad@msn.com. Philip Sturrock, mgr dir; Anthony Haynes, commissioning ed for educ. *Primary. Professional.*

Cork University Press. Crawford Business Park, Crosses Green, Cork, Ireland *tel:* 021 902980 *fax:* 021 315329 *email:* corkunip@www.ucc.ie. *Selection of books covering Irish mus, traditions and culture.*

Evans Brothers Ltd. 2a Portman Mansions, Chiltern St, London W1M 1LE *tel:* 020 7935 7160 *fax:* 020 7487 5034 *email:* sales@evansbrothers.co.uk. S Pawley, mgr dir; B Jones, international publishing dir; S Swallow, UK publishing dir; J Hole, UK sales mgr. *World of Music (book and CD), Tell Us About Mozart and Tell Us About Chopin.*

Faber & Faber Ltd. 3 Queen Square, London WC1N 3AU *tel:* 020 7465 0045 *fax:* 020 7465 0034. Belinda Matthews, mus ed. *Gen mus books, including Composers Remembered series, biographies and letters, history, criticism, theory, reference, popular mus titles.*

First and Best in Education Ltd. Earlstrees Court, Earlstrees Rd, Corby, Northants NN17 4AX *tel:* 01536 399011 (orders)/399004 (editorial) *fax:* 01536 399012 *email:* firstbest9@aol.com. Katy Charge, snr ed; Julia Perkins, Linda Robinson, editorial assts. *Books geared towards schools' mus departments including Listening to Music for GCSE and Music: The Perfect Classroom.*

Golden Cockerel Press. 16 Barter St, London WC1A 2AH *tel:* 020 7405 7979 *fax:* 020 7404 3598 *email:* lindesay@btinternet.com. Andrew H Lindesay. *Two imprints: Associated University Presses and Cygnus Arts. Wide range of mus titles including the Great Composers series.*

Gresham Books Ltd. The Gresham Press, PO Box 61, Henley-on-Thames, Oxon RG9 3LQ *tel:* 0118 940 3789 *also fax; email:* greshambks@aol.com. Mary Green, mgr dir; Lewis Green, liaison offr; Liz O'Brian, copyright mgr. *Approx 25 hymn books (standard, special, school) pa. Words only, melody and full mus editions; prayer books (special), orch and choir portfolios.*

Grove's Dictionaries of Music. 25 Eccleston Place, London SW1W 9NF *tel:* 020 7881 8024 *fax:* 020 7881 8109 *email:* grove@macmillan.co.uk. Catherine Jones, humanities mkt mgr; Rachel Boase, humanities mkt exec; Tony Grimes, internet mkt exec. *The New Grove Dictionary of Music and Musicians (20 vols, paperback, 'Special Editions' and on-line), The New Grove Dictionary of Opera (4 vols, hardback and paperback), The New Grove Dictionary of Jazz (2 vols, hardback), The New Grove Dictionary of Musical Instruments (3 vols, hardback), The New Grove Dictionary of American Music (4 vols, hardback), The Grove Concise Dictionary of Music, The Encyclopedia of Popular Music (8 vols, hardback).*

Guinness Publishing. 338 Euston Rd, London NW1 3BP *tel:* 020 7891 4567 *fax:* 020 7891 4501 *email:* guinness_publishing@guinness.com. Ian Castello-Cortes, publishing dir; Michael Feldman, dir of TV; Karen O'Brien, David Roberts, projects mgrs. *The Guinness Book of British Hit Singles; The Guinness Book of British Hit Albums; Guinness Rockopedia; Guinness Classical 1000; Guinness Guide to Classical Music.*

Harwood Academic Publishers. c/o IPD, PO Box 90, Reading, Berks R61 8JL *tel:* 0118 956 0080 *fax:* 0118 956 8211 *email:* info@gbhap.com. Robert Robertson, snr commissioning ed. *Books for students, academics, professionals and the general public on all aspects/periods of mus.*

Heinemann Educational. Halley Court, Jordan Hill, Oxford OX2 8EJ *tel:* 01865 314130 *fax:* 01865 314140 *email:* sue.walton@repp.co.uk. Sue Walton, mus publisher. *Curriculum materials for primary and secondary schools.*

Hodder & Stoughton. 338 Euston Rd, London NW1 3BH *tel:* 020 7873 6000 *fax:* 020 7873 6099. Philip Walters, mgr dir; Jan Mitchener, mkt mgr. *Hodder & Stoughton Educational, Essential Guide To Music (GNVQ/BTEC) and What Primary Teachers Should Know About Music. Teach Yourself series.*

Holt, Rinehart & Winston Ltd. Harcourt Brace & Company Ltd, 24-28 Oval Rd, London NW1 7DX *tel:* 020 7424 4200 *fax:* 020 7482 2293 *email:* college@hbuk.co.uk. Madelene Hyde, college mkt mgr. *Small list covering mus theory and methods of teaching mus.*

Holt-Saunders Ltd *see* **Holt, Rinehart & Winston Ltd.**

Indiana University Press. Combined Academic Publishers Ltd, 27 Devonshire Close, Amersham, Bucks HP6 5JG *tel:* 01494 581601 *fax:* 01494 581602 *email:* nickesson@combinedacademic.demon.co.uk. *Academic books for students, academics and professionals. Specialisms include publications of The Early Music Institute, American mus history, 17th and 18th C mus, Russian and 20th C mus, voice and song, and practical reference volumes for musicians. Distributed by Open University Press.*

International Music Publications Ltd. Griffin House, 161 Hammersmith Rd, London W6 8BS *tel:* 020 8222 9222 *fax:* 020 8222 9264 (editorial). Peter Woodhead, mgr dir; Mark Mumford, head of publishing; Sadie Cook, mgr ed; Paul Smith, dir of sales and mkt; Mike Bufton, dir of international sales. *Classical, jazz, pop and rock publications, tutors, mus for schools. Series include In Session With, Take the Lead, Jam With. Educ range includes Music About Us, Sing It And Say It, Key Club and Let's Make Music Fun.*

Jessica Kingsley Publishers. 116 Pentonville Rd, London N1 9JB *tel:* 020 7833 2307 *fax:* 020 7837 2917 *email:* post@jkp.com. *Mus therapy, mus for children with special needs, mus and health. Mus therapy and palliative care.*

Little, Brown & Company (UK). Brettenham House, Lancaster Place, London WC2E 7EN *tel:* 020 7911 8000 *fax:* 020 7911 8100. Philippa Harrison, chief exec and publisher; David Young, mgr dir; Alan Samson, Barbara Boote, editorial dirs. *Selected titles of interest to musicians, including reference guides and numerous popular mus titles.*

Melrose Press Ltd. Trade Dept, St Thomas Place, Ely, Cambs CB7 4GG *tel:* 01353 646600 *fax:* 01353 646601 *email:* info@melrosepress.co.uk. Nicholas S Law, mgr dir; Jean Pearson, chief exec; Jon Gifford, ed. *International Who's Who in Music; Musicians' Directory Vol 1 (classical); International Who's Who in Music Vol 2 (Popular Music).*

Open University Press. Celtic Court, 22 Ballmoor, Buckingham, Bucks MK18 1XW *tel:* 01280 823388 *fax:* 01280 823233 *email:* enquiries@openup.co.uk. *Academic books for students, academics and professionals. Popular Music in Britain series focuses on the history of popular mus culture.*

Oxford University Press (OUP). Great Clarendon St, Oxford OX2 6DP *tel:* 01865 556767 *fax:* 01865 556646 *email:* fosterh@oup.co.uk. *Academic, general, reference, college, paperbacks and Master Musicians series. Education/Trade: Saxon Way West, Corby, Northants*

NN18 9ES tel: *01536 741519* fax: *01536 746337. Choral, orch, educ, courses, tutors, insts, church mus, etc.*

Pendragon Press. Crag House, Witherslack, Grange-over-Sands, Cumbria LA11 6RW *tel:* 01539 552286 *fax:* 01539 552013 *email:* musicbks@rdooley.demon.co.uk. Rosemary Dooley, UK distributor. *Aesthetics, dance and mus, Liszt, French opera, analysis, Czech mus, performance guides, thematic catalogues, mus history.*

Penguin Books Ltd. Bath Rd, Harmondsworth, Middx UB7 0DA *tel:* 020 8757 4000 *fax:* 020 8757 4099. Clare Fletcher, mkt dir; Helen Drake, mkt mgr. *Reference books on mus, including Penguin Guide to Compact Discs, Penguin Guide to Compact Discs Yearbook, Penguin Opera Guide, Penguin Price Guide for Record and CD Collectors.*

Phaidon Press. Regent's Wharf, All Saints St, London N1 9PA *tel:* 020 7843 1234 *fax:* 020 7843 1111. *20th C composers series of biographies and other titles, including a new translation and commentary of Der Ring des Nibelungen by Rudolph Sabor.*

Random House UK. 20 Vauxhall Bridge Rd, London SW1V 2SA *tel:* 020 7840 8400 *fax:* 020 7828 6681. *Encyclopaedia, opera, history.*

Rhinegold Publishing Ltd. 241 Shaftesbury Ave, London WC2H 8EH *tel:* 020 7333 1721 *fax:* 020 7333 1769 *email:* sales@rhinegold.co.uk. Tony Gamble, mgr dir; Keith Diggle, mkt dir; Sarah Williams, publishing mgr; Richard Thomas, mkt mgr. *Publishes magazines and reference books for the arts, specialising in the mus industry. The company began with the magazine Classical Music and has expanded to include Music Teacher, Piano, Early Music Today, The Singer, and Opera Now. Works of reference include the British and International Music Yearbook, Music Education Yearbook and British Performing Arts Yearbook. Other books include The Musician's Handbook, Arts Marketing, Healthy Practice for Musicians and Analysis Matters.*

Robert Hale Ltd. 45-47 Clerkenwell House, Clerkenwell Green, London EC1R 0HT *tel:* 020 7251 2661 *fax:* 020 7490 4958. Martin Kendall, mkt dir; Paula Whitworth, promotions mgr. *Various books including reference, Christmas carols, classical mus guides, violin-making, etc.*

Royal Musical Association. Crag House, Witherslack, Grange-over-Sands, Cumbria LA11 6RW *tel:* 01539 552286 *fax:* 01539 552013 *email:* musicbks@rdooley.demon.co.uk. Rosemary Dooley, RMA distributor. *RMA monographs series. 8 titles to date.*

Schofield & Sims Ltd. Dogley Mill, Fenay Bridge, Huddersfield HD8 0NQ *tel:* 01484 607080 *fax:* 01484 606815 *email:* 100641.252@compuserve.com. Jack Brierley, sales dir. *Primary and parent/child use at home.*

Shelwing Ltd. 4 Pleydell Gardens, Folkestone, Kent CT20 2DN *tel:* 01303 850501 *fax:* 01303 850162 *email:* info@shelwing.com. Eileen Marshall, publicity mgr; Iris Farrar, book sales. *Sole agents for Scarecrow, McFarland cats. Secondary and above. General mus books including biography and religious.*

Showcase Publications Ltd. 38c The Broadway, London N8 9SU *tel:* 020 8348 2332 *fax:* 020 8340 3750. Kay Chestnutt, ed; Tony Tillmanns, sales and mkt. *Showcase International Music Book (formerly Kemps International Music Book).*

Sounds Write. 56 Baswich Crest, Stafford ST17 0HJ *tel:* 01785 250405 *also fax.* Keith Baskett, mgr of mkt and sales. *Theory work books for young beginners to gr 3 following the ABRSM syllabus. Material offers a structured and fun approach through its child-centred method of teaching. Applicable to any inst and does not require keyboard skills. Free brochure available.*

Stanley Thornes (Publishers) Ltd. Ellenborough House, Wellington St, Cheltenham, Glos GL50 1YD *tel:* 01242 267280 *fax:* 01242 221914 *email:* cservice@thornes.co.uk. Mark Pritchard, primary mkt mgr; Mary Maggs, list development mgr. *Sounds of Music: National Curriculum mus scheme for nursery and primary teachers. Silver Burdett Music: mus scheme for teachers of 4 to 14 year olds. Blueprints Music: curriculum resource books for primary teachers.*

Sweet & Maxwell Ltd. Customer Services, 100 Avenue Rd, London NW3 3PF *tel:* 020 7449 1111 *fax:* 020 7449 1144. *Copyright, EC directive on rental, lending rights and piracy, entertainment law, legal books on mus and private video copying.*

Ward Lock Educational Co Ltd. BIC Ling Kee House, 1 Christopher Rd, East Grinstead, W Sussex RH19 3BT *tel:* 01342 318980 *fax:* 01342 410980. Penny Kitchenham. *Mus and song books for young children.*

Warner Books. Brettenham House, Lancaster Place, London WC2 7EW *tel:* 020 7911 8000 *fax:* 020 7911 8100 *email:* u16@littlebrown.com. Philippa Harrison, chief exec and publisher; David Young, mgr dir; Alan Samson, Barbara Boote, editorial dirs. *Various reference publications and popular mus titles.*

Woodwind Plus. 42 St Mary's Park, Louth, Lincs LN11 0EF *email:* jeff@wwplus.freeserve.co.uk. *Mus for w/wind ens, w/wind and pno, saxes. Tutorial publications.*

Writers and Readers Ltd. 35 Brittania Row, London N1 8QH *tel:* 020 7226 3377 *fax:* 020 7359 1406 *email:* begin@writersandreaders.com. *For Beginners Documentary Comic Book series presents complex subjects to readers in an entertaining and accessible way. Titles include Opera For Beginners, Classical Music For Beginners, Jazz For Beginners and Popular Music For Beginners.*

WW Norton & Company Ltd. 10 Coptic St, London WC1A 1PU *tel:* 020 7323 1579 *fax:* 020 7436 4553 *email:* office@wwnorton.co.uk. Alan Cameron, mgr dir; Victoria Keown-Boyd, mkt mgr. *Norton Introduction to Music History, Norton History of Music, Marsalis on Music, musicology titles, Norton Critical Scores series and Grout: History of Western Music.*

Orchestral Hire Libraries

Listed below are the main commercial libraries that deal in the hire of orchestral scores and parts. The works of most well-known composers are available from nearly all the libraries, and the information after each entry indicates the specific composers and editions which are only available from that library. Some orchestral sets of works that are no longer in copyright may be available from larger music libraries.

Alfred A Kalmus Ltd Hire Library *see* **Music Distribution Services Hire Library.**

Banks Music Publications Hire Library. The Old Forge, Sand Hutton, York YO41 1LB *tel:* 01904 468472 *fax:* 01904 468679 *email:* banksramsay@cwcom.net. Jeremy Warnes, hire library mgr. *Mus of James Brown, Gerald Finzi, Francis Jackson, Philip Marshall.*

Bardic Edition. 6 Fairfax Cres, Aylesbury, Bucks HP20 2ES *tel:* 01296 428609 *also fax; email:* 101464.2670@compuserve.com. *Mus of Percy Grainger, Christopher Headington, John Pickard.*

Baroque Publications Ltd Hire Library. Treadam Farm, Llantilio-Crossenny, Abergavenny, Gwent NP7 8TA *tel:* 01600 780233. Sally Felps, hire library mgr. *Mainly mus of Handel (orch parts and vocal scores of operas, separate arias available). Reduced orchestration (10 insts) of some Mozart and Rossini operas. Also Hansel and Gretel (Humperdinck).*

Boosey & Hawkes Music Publishers Ltd Hire Library. 295 Regent St, London W1R 8JH *tel:* 020 7580 2060 *fax:* 020 7580 5815. Bruce MacRae, hire library mgr; Angharad Evans, snr admin. *Mus of Adams (since 1986), Andriessen, Bartók (some), Bernstein, Blacher, Britten (until 1963), Birtwistle (since 1994), Carter (since 1981), Copland, Delius (some), Druckman, Einem, Finzi, Firsova, Floyd, Gerhard (until 1960), Ginastera, Glanert, Goldschmidt, Górecki (some), Gubaidulina, Gruber, Holloway, Höller (since 1983), Jenkins, Kodály (some), Kurtág, Lindberg (since 1996), MacMillan, Martinu (some), Maxwell Davies (some), Panufnik, Prokofiev, Rachmaninoff, Rautavaara, Reich, Rouse, Schnittke, Schwertsik, Shostakovich, Strauss, Stravinsky, Torke, Xenakis (until 1969), Yun. Editions: Bote & Bock/Berlin, Carisch/Milan, Carl Fischer/USA, Dilia/Czech Republic, EMB/Budapest, Gehrmans Musikforlag/Sweden, Margun Music/USA, Moscow State Edition, Roberto Barry/South America, Warner Chappell/Scandinavia, Zen-on Music/Japan.*

Chandos Music Ltd. Chandos House, Commerce Way, Colchester, Essex CO2 8HQ *tel:* 01206 225200 *fax:* 01206 225201 *email:* shogger@chandos-records.com.

Chester Music Ltd Hire Library (division of Music Sales Limited). Newmarket Rd, Bury St Edmunds, Suffolk IP33 3YB *tel:* 01284 705705 *fax:* 01284 703401. Paul Narey, hire library mgr; Janet Atkinson, Jeremy Harding, Adam Harvey, hire librarians. *Editions: Associated Music Publishers, Bosworth & Co Ltd, Chester Music, J Curwen & Sons Ltd, Dunvagen, Edwin Ashdown Ltd, A Lengnick & Co, MCA, Nordiska, Norsk Musikforlag As, Really Useful Group plc, Ricordi, G Schirmer Inc, G Schirmer (Australia) Pty Ltd, Union Musical Ediciones, Wilhelm Hansen Edition, Zanibon.*

Clyde, R. 6 Whitelands Ave, Chorleywood, Rickmansworth, Herts WD3 5RD *tel:* 01923 283600 *also fax; email:* r.clyde@dial.pipex.com. Roger Harris, proprietor. *Works for orch, voices and orch, operas by Sullivan.*

Concord Music Hire Library. 5 Bushey Close, Old Barn Lane, Kenley, Surrey CR8 5AU *tel:* 020 8660 4766 *fax:* 020 8668 5273 *email:* oakcroft@msn.com. Ray Lee, hire library mgr. *Mus of Judith Bingham, Martin Ellerby, Philip Grange, Piers Hellawell, Daniel Jones, Clark McAlister, Geoffrey Poole, Matthew Taylor, Gareth Wood. Editions: Maecenas Music, Maecenas Contemporary Composers Ltd, Warner Chappell Music Hire Library.*

D'Oyly Carte Music Library. The Powerhouse, 6 Sancroft St, London SE11 5UD *tel:* 020 7793 7700/7100 *fax:* 020 7793 7205/7300 *email:* mail@doylycarte.org.uk. Joseph Hollings, mus library mgr. *Gilbert & Sullivan operettas, Sullivan & Co, J Strauss, Offenbach.*

Faber Music Hire Library. 3 Queen Square, London WC1N 3AU *tel:* 020 7833 7907 *fax:* 020 7833 7934 *email:* chris_norris@fabermusic.co.uk. Chris Norris, performance and hire library mgr; Hannah Luxton, asst hire librarian. *Mus of T Adès, J Anderson, M Arnold (some), G Benjamin, H Blake, Britten (some), M Daugherty, C Davis, J Harvey (late works), O Knussen, C Matthews, D Matthews (some), N Maw (late works), D Muldowney (some), P Sculthorpe, R Smalley, J Woolrich. Editions: Alkor, Bärenreiter, Highbridge Music, Peer Southern, Threefold Music, Supraphon.*

Fentone Music Ltd Hire Library. Fleming Rd, Earlstrees, Corby, Northants NN17 4SN *tel:* 01536 260981 *fax:* 01536 401075 *email:* music@fentone.com. Mark Coull, hire library mgr. *Editions: Berben, London Orchestral Series, Norsk Musikforlag, Real Musical, XYZ International.*

Josef Weinberger Ltd Hire Library. 12-14 Mortimer St, London W1N 7RD *tel:* 020 7927 7312 *fax:* 020 7436 9616 *email:* hirelibrary@jwmail.co.uk. Christopher Moss, hire library mgr; Timothy Seddon, ed. *Music Theatre International and Rodgers and Hammerstein concert libraries, Kurt Weill American shows, mus of Emmérich Kálmán, Wilfred Josephs (some), Mahler (some), Paul Patterson (some), Morris Pert (some), André Tchaikovsky, Ernst Von Dohnanyi (some), Malcolm Williamson (some), Ermanno Wolf-Ferrari (some).*

Music Distribution Services Hire Library. 38 Eldon Way, Paddock Wood, Kent TN12 6BE *tel:* 01892 838083 *fax:* 01892 836038 *email:* rod.taylor@schott-ue-hire.demon.co.uk. Rod Taylor, hire library mgr; Sarah Benson, Jonathan Penny, hire assts. *Mus of Birtwistle, Bryars, Casken, Goehr, Henze, Holt, Ligeti, Orff, Roxanna Panufnik, Takemitsu, Tippett, Turnage. Editions: Boelke Bomart, Breitkopf & Härtel, Casa Musicale Sonzogno, Czech Music Fund, European American Music/Helicon Inc, Israel Music Institute, PWM, Schott/London/Mainz/Japan, Theodore Presser, Universal Edition/London/Vienna.*

Novello Co Ltd Hire Library (division of Music Sales Ltd). Newmarket Rd, Bury St Edmunds, Suffolk IP33 3YB *tel:* 01284 705705 *fax:* 01284 703401. Paul Narey, hire library mgr; Janet Atkinson, Jeremy Harding, Adam Harvey, hire librarians. *Mus of Malcolm Arnold (some), Arthur Bliss, Richard Rodney Bennett, Herbert Howells, Tristan Keuris, John McCabe, Thea Musgrave, Stephen Oliver, Aulis Sallinen, Giles Swayne, Judith Weir (some). Editions: Arnold, Belwin Mills, Donemus, Elkin, EMI, Goodwin & Tabb, Paterson, Paxton, Bosworth.*

Oxford University Press Hire Library. Gt Clarendon St, Oxford OX2 6DP *tel:* 01865 267699 *fax:* 01865 267767 *email:* music.hire@oup.co.uk. Simon Wright, hire library mgr; Simon Lay, hire librarian; Kathryn Elson, hire library asst; Cheryl Hitchman, accounts clerk. *Mus of Gerald Barry, Michael Berkeley, John Buller, Martin Butler, Richard Causton, Bob Chilcott, Gordon Crosse, Michael Finnissy (from 1988), Edward Harper, Constant Lambert (some), William Mathias, Anthony Powers, John Rutter, Robert Sherlaw Johnson, Howard Skempton, Ralph Vaughan Williams (from 1926), William Walton.*

Peters Edition Ltd Hire Library. 10-12 Baches St, London N1 6DN *tel:* 020 7553 4020 *fax:* 020 7490 4921 *email:* hire@uk.edition-peters.com. Fiona Flower, dir, hire and copyright; Stephen Murphy, hire library mgr; Helen Rowlands, hire library asst. *Mus of John Cage, George Crumb, James Dillon, Jonathan Dove, Morton Feldman (some), Brian Ferneyhough, Alan Hovhaness, Mauricio Kagel, György Ligeti (some), Roger Reynolds, Rebecca Saunders, Erkki-Sven Tüür. Editions: M P Belaieff, Edition Kunzelmann, Edition Schwann, Heinrichshofen, Henry Litolff, Hinrichsen Edition, C F Kahnt, F E C Leuckart, Robert Lienau, Lyche, C F Peters/London/New York/Frankfurt/Leipzig, Robert Forberg Musikverlag, Tischer & Jagenberg, Christian Vieweg, Zimmermann.*

Queensgate Music Hire Library. 120 Dowanhill St, Glasgow G12 9DN *tel:* 0141 339 1699 *also fax. Mus of Thomas Wilson only.*

Richard Schauer Hire Library. Simrock House, 220 The Vale, London NW11 8HZ *tel:* 020 8731 6665 *fax:* 020 8731 6667. T R Gill, hire library mgr; Irene Retford, mgr dir. *Editions: Anton J Benjamin, Bartolf Senff, Brockhaus/Germany, Musicus/USA, McNaughtan (David)/Germany, Mannheimer Musikverlag/Germany, D Rahter, Reift (Mark) Editions/Switzerland, N Simrock, Wrede (Otto)/Germany.*

Schott & Co Ltd Hire Library *see* **Music Distribution Services Hire Library**.

Stainer & Bell Ltd Hire Library. PO Box 110, Victoria House, Gruneisen Rd, London N3 1DZ *tel:* 020 8343 3303 *fax:* 020 8343 3024 *email:* post@stainer.co.uk. Erica Jeal, hire library mgr. *Agents for UK and rest of Europe for the hire library of ECS Publishing, Boston, USA.*

United Music Publishers Ltd Hire Library. 42 Rivington St, London EC2A 3BN *tel:* 020 7729 4700 *fax:* 020 7739 6549 *email:* ump@compuserve.com. Claire Bowdler, hire library mgr; Shirley Ranger, mgr dir. *Mus of Simon Bainbridge (some), Richard Barrett, Havergal Brian, Diana Burrell, Chris Dench (some), Petr Eben (some), Naji Hakim (some), Stephen Montague (some), Edwin Roxburgh (some). Editions (all France unless otherwise stated): Amphion, Billaudot, Bornemann, Carus-Verlag (Germany), Chant du Monde, Chantraine (Belgium), Choudens, Combre, Costallat, Dominis (Canada), Durand, EFM, Elkan-Vogel (USA), Enoch, Eschig, Hamelle, Henn (Switzerland),*

Heugel, Jobert, Leduc, Lemoine, Marais, R Martin, Ouvrières, Rideau-Rouge, Salabert, Schola Cantorum, SEDIM, Transatlantiques, UMP (UK), Wiscasset (USA), Zurfluh.

Warner Chappell Music Ltd Hire Library. 5 Bushey Close, Old Barn Lane, Kenley, Surrey CR8 5AU *tel:* 020 7660 4766 *fax:* 020 7668 5273 *email:* oakcroft@msn.com. Ray Lee, librarian. Administered by the Concord Music Hire Library. *Mus of Arnold Bax, Eric Coates, George Gershwin. Editions: Asherberg Hopwood and Crew, Chappell, Warner Brothers.*

William Elkin Music Services Hire Library. Station Rd Industrial Estate, Salhouse, Norwich NR13 6NS *tel:* 01603 721302 *fax:* 01603 721801 *email:* richard@elkinmusic.demon.co.uk. Cindy Hazard, hire library mgr; N Everett, accounts clerk. *Editions: Braydeston Press, Curwen, Hofmeister, Lawson-Gould, Sikorski.*

Copyright Organisations

Listed below are the main organisations concerned with musical copyright in the UK. The Copyright Laws are extremely complex and details should be checked carefully with the institution concerned.

Butterworths. Halsbury House, 35 Chancery Lane, London WC2A 1EL *tel:* 020 7400 2500 *fax:* 020 7400 2842. *Legal texts, copyright.*

Christian Copyright Licensing (Europe) Ltd. PO Box 1339, Eastbourne, E Sussex BN21 4YF *tel:* 01323 417711 *fax:* 01323 417722 *email:* info@ccli.co.uk. *Issues and administrates the Church Copyright Licence (CCL) and the Music Reproduction Licence (MRL). The CCL allows the copying of the words of copyright songs and hymns to schools, churches and Christian organisations. The MRL allows the photocopying of words and mus from a wide range of mus books. Also, by exclusive arrangement with MCPS, the CCL includes video and audio cassette recordings and issues the Private Function Filming Licence and 'Dubbings' licence.*

International Federation of the Phonographic Industry. IFPI Secretariat, 54 Regent St, London W1R 5PJ *tel:* 020 7878 7900 *fax:* 020 7878 7950 *email:* info@ifpi.org. *Promotes and defends the copyright interests of its members in sound recordings and music videos.*

Mechanical-Copyright Protection Society Ltd (MCPS). Elgar House, 41 Streatham High Rd, London SW16 1ER *tel:* 020 8664 4400 *fax:* 020 8769 8792. *An organisation of mus publishers and composers, which collects and distributes mechanical royalties due from the recording of their copyright musical works.*

Music and Copyright. FT Media and Telecoms, Maple House, 149 Tottenham Court Rd, London W1P 9LL *tel:* 020 7896 2236 *fax:* 020 7896 2256 *email:* info@ftmedia.com. *Annual subscription £695 ($1182) for 23 issues. Information on legislation, corporate analysis, industry news, contracts, piracy, national trends, market structures and technical developments.*

Music Publishers Association. 3rd Floor, Strandgate, 18-20 York Buildings, London WC2N 6JU *tel:* 020 7839 7779 *fax:* 020 7839 7776 *email:* mpa@musicpublishers.co.uk. *Represents mus publishers in the UK. Advises and assists members in the promotion and protection of mus copyright.*

Performing Right Society. 29-33 Berners St, London W1P 4AA *tel:* 020 7580 5544 *fax:* 020 7306 4050 *email:* info@prs.co.uk. John Hutchinson, chief exec. *Protects, promotes and administers the public performance and broadcasting rights of composers, songwriters and mus publishers.*

Music Journalism

Newspapers

The following list of major newspapers all carry regular coverage of classical music. The editor, the chief music critics and additional music and arts critics are listed below.

The Birmingham Post. 28 Colmore Circus, Queensway, Birmingham B4 6AX *tel:* 0121 236 3366 *fax:* 0121 233 0271. Nigel Hastilow, ed; Terry Grimley, arts ed; Christopher Morley, chief mus critic. David Hart, David Williams, Clare Mackney, John Bradshaw, Aprella Fitch, Richard Leigh Harris, mus critics.

The Daily Telegraph. 1 Canada Square, Canary Wharf, London E14 5DT *tel:* 020 7538 5000 *fax:* 020 7538 7650. Charles Moore, ed; Geoffrey Norris, chief mus critic; Sarah Crompton, arts ed. Norman Lebrecht, mus correspondent; Rupert Christiansen, opera critic.

Evening Express (Mon-Sat). PO Box 43, Lang Stracht, Mastrick, Aberdeen AB15 6DF *tel:* 01224 690222 *fax:* 01224 699575 *email:* editor@ee.ajl.co.uk. Donald Martin, ed; Ron Ferrier, features ed. *27p.*

Evening Press (Mon-Sat). PO Box 29, 76-86 Walmgate, York YO1 1YN *tel:* 01904 653051 *fax:* 01904 612853 *email:* yorknewsdesk@york.newsquest.co.uk. Liz Page, ed; Charles Hutchinson, mus ed. *30p. Evening paper serving York and N Yorkshire.*

The Evening Standard. Northcliffe House, 2 Derry St, Kensington, London W8 5EE *tel:* 020 7938 6000 *fax:* 020 7937 2648. Max Hastings, ed; Alison Roberts, arts ed.

The Financial Times. 1 Southwark Bridge, London SE1 9HL *tel:* 020 7873 3000 *fax:* 020 7407 5700. Richard Lambert, ed; Max Loppert, mus and opera critic; Richard Fairman, mus critic; Annalena McAfee, arts ed. *70p. Arts section daily plus in the Weekend FT.*

The Guardian. 119 Farringdon Rd, London EC1R 3ER *tel:* 020 7278 2332 *fax:* 020 7837 2114. Alan Rusbridger, ed; Claire Armitstead, arts ed; Andrew Clements, chief mus and opera critic. Adrian Searle, art critic; Dan Glaister, arts correspondent.

The Herald (Mon-Sat). 195 Albion St, Glasgow G1 1QP *tel:* 0141 552 6255 *fax:* 0141 552 2288. Harry Reid, ed; Michael Tumelty, chief mus critic. *48p.*

The Independent. Newspaper Publishing plc, 1 Canada Square, Canary Wharf, London E14 5DL *tel:* 020 7293 2000 *fax:* 020 7293 2451. Simon Kellner, ed; Chris Maume, arts ed. The Independent on Sunday: Michael White, chief mus critic.

The News (Mon-Sat). The News Centre, Hilsea, Portsmouth, Hants PO2 9SX *tel:* 023 9266 4488 *fax:* 023 9267 3363. Geoff Elliott, ed; Mike Allen, mus critic; Barry Rutter, pop music. *29p.*

The Observer (Sun). 119 Farringdon Rd, London EC1R 3ER *tel:* 020 7278 2332 *fax:* 020 7713 4225. Will Hutton, ed; Fiona Maddocks, mus correspondent; Jane Ferguson, arts ed.

The Scotsman. 20 Northbridge, Edinburgh EH1 1YT *tel:* 0131 225 2468 *fax:* 0131 243 3686. Alan Ruddock, ed; Robert Dawson Scott, arts ed; Steven Johnston, mus critic. Fiona Shepherd, rock and pop critic. *42p. 50p Sat.*

The Sunday Telegraph. 1 Canada Square, Canary Wharf, London E14 5AR *tel:* 020 7538 5000 *fax:* 020 7513 2504. Dominic Lawson, ed; John Preston, arts ed; Michael Kennedy, opera critic.

The Sunday Times. 1 Pennington St, London E1 9XW *tel:* 020 7481 4100 *fax:* 020 7782 5776. John Witherow, ed; Hugh Canning, Paul Driver, mus critics; Helen Hawkins, arts ed.

The Times. 1 Pennington St, London E1 9XW *tel:* 020 7782 5000 *fax:* 020 7782 5748. Sarah Vine, arts ed; Rodney Milnes, chief opera critic; Barry Millington, Hilary Finch, John Allison, Gerald Larner, mus critics.

The Times Educational Supplement (weekly). Admiral House, 66-68 East Smithfield, London E1 9XY *tel:* 020 7782 3000 *fax:* 020 7782 3200 *email:* friday@tes.co.uk. Caroline St John-Brooks, ed; Heather Neill, arts and literature ed; Philippa Davidson, chief mus critic. *£1.10.*

Yorkshire Post. United Provincial Newspapers Ltd, Wellington St, Leeds LS1 1RF *tel:* 0113 243 2701 *fax:* 0113 238 8537. Tony Watson, ed; Eric Roberts, arts ed; David Denton, Patric Standford, Donald Webster, mus critics.

Music Periodicals

Periodicals devoted to classical music or of specific music interest are listed alphabetically, followed by the number of issues per annum and the name of the editor.

ABO News (4). Pegasus House, 37-43 Sackville St, London W1X 1DB *tel:* 020 7333 0371 *fax:* 020 7287 9959 *email:* info@abo.org.uk. Alison White, admin. *Issued free to Association of British Orchestras members.*

Acoustic Guitar (12). 1-2 Vance Court, Trans Britannia Enterprise Park, Blaydon on Tyne NE21 5NH *tel:* 0191 414 9000 *fax:* 0191 414 9001. Jeffrey Pepper Rodgers, ed. *£2.95.*

BBC Music Magazine (12). Room A1004, Woodlands, 80 Wood Lane, London W12 0TT *tel:* 020 8576 3283 (ed); 020 8576 2022 (ad) *fax:* 020 8576 3292 *email:* music.magazine@bbc.co.uk. Helen Wallace, ed. *£3.95; £45.00 pa (UK).*

Braille Music Magazine (12). Royal National Institute for the Blind, 224 Great Portland St, London W1N 6AA *tel:* 020 7388 1266 ext 2318 *fax:* 020 7388 2034 *email:* rfirman@rnib.org.uk. Roger Firman, ed. *66p per issue. Original commissioned articles including CD reviews and items from print magazines. Specialising in classical mus.*

Brass Band World (10). Caron Publications, Peak Press Building, Eccles Rd, Chapel-en-le-Frith, High Peak SK23 9RQ *tel:* 01298 812816 *fax:* 01298 815220 *email:* info@bbworld.u-net.com. Robert Mulholland, ed; Liz Winter, ad mgr; Gillian Smith, head of subs. *£2.95; £29.50 pa. Illustrated magazine with informative coverage of the br band scene, with articles by leading authorities and up-to-date news.*

Brio (2). The Library, Royal Northern College of Music, 124 Oxford Rd, Manchester M13 9RD *tel:* 0161 273 6283 *fax:* 0161 273 7611 *email:* geoff@rncm.ac.uk. Geoffrey Thomason, ed; Christopher Grogan, reviews ed. *Membership £32 (individual), £46 (institutions). Sub £28. Journal of International Association of Music Libraries, Archives and Documentation Centres UK Branch. Articles on mus bibliography/librarianship. Reviews of books and mus.*

British Bandsman (52). Harold Charles House, 64a London End, Beaconsfield, Bucks HP9 2JP *tel:* 01494 674411 *fax:* 01494 670932 *email:* info@britishbandsman.com. Peter Wilson, ed. *70p.*

British Institute of Organ Studies, Journal of the (1). 17 Wheeleys Rd, Edgbaston, Birmingham B15 2LD *tel:* 0121 440 5491 *also fax.* Rels Plark, publicity offr. *£20. Scholarly research into the history of the org.*

British Journal of Music Education (3). Journals Dept, CUP, Edinburgh Building, Shaftesbury Rd, Cambridge CB2 2RU *tel:* 01223 312393 *fax:* 01223 315052 *email:* journals-subscriptions@cup.cam.ac.uk. William Salaman, Piers Spencer, eds. *£49 (institutions), £30 (individuals), £23 (students) pa. Aims to provide clear, stimulating and readable accounts of current issues in mus educ worldwide. Covers classroom mus teaching, individual inst teaching, group teaching, mus in higher educ, international comparative mus educ and teacher educ.*

British Journal of Music Therapy (2). 25 Rosslyn Ave, East Barnet, Herts EN4 8DH *tel:* 020 8368 8879 *also fax; email:* Denize@bsmt.demon.co.uk. Nicky Barber, G Ansdell, eds. *£55.*

British Music Yearbook (1). Rhinegold Publishing Ltd, 241 Shaftesbury Ave, London WC2H 8EH *tel:* 020 7333 1760 (ed); 020 7333 1748 (ad) *fax:* 020 7333 1769 (ed); 020 7333 1736 (ad) *email:* bmyb@rhinegold.co.uk. Louise Head, ed. *£23.95. The directory of the classical mus industry.*

British Performing Arts Yearbook (1). Rhinegold Publishing, 241 Shaftesbury Ave, London WC2H 8EH *tel:* 020 7333 1762 (ed); 020 7333 1733 (ad) *fax:* 020 7333 1769 (ed); 020 7333 1736 (ad) *email:* bpay1@rhinegold.co.uk. Henry Watson, ed. *£24.95. Annual directory of performing arts in Britain. Includes venues, companies, solo performers, symphony and chmbr orchs, arts festivals, educ and*

training, arts councils, regional arts boards, support associations, local authorities, suppliers and services.

The Bruckner Journal (3). 2 Rivergreen Close, Beeston, Nottingham NG9 3ES *tel:* 0115 928 8300 (ed/ad); 01384 566383 (sub) *fax:* 0161 275 4994 *email:* crawfhowie@aol.com. Peter Palmer, ed; Crawford Howie, associate ed; Raymond Cox, mgr ed. *£9 (UK), £10 (Europe), £12 (world) pa.*

Cambridge Opera Journal (3). Journals Dept, CUP, The Edinburgh Building, Shaftesbury Rd, Cambridge CB2 2RU *tel:* 01223 312393 *fax:* 01223 315052 *email:* journals-subscriptions@cup.cam.ac.uk. Mary Hunter, ed. *£51 (institutions), £31 (individuals) pa. Articles across the whole opera repertoire.*

Cerddoriaeth Cymru *see* **Welsh Music.**

Choir & Organ (6). Orpheus Publications Ltd, 7 St John's Rd, Harrow, Middx HA1 2EE *tel:* 020 8863 2020 *fax:* 020 8863 2444 *email:* choirandorgan@orphpl.com. Matthew Power, ed; Shirley Ratcliffe, choral ed; Katinka Welz, asst ed. *£3.25. Features and news on choral mus and singing, orgs and org mus.*

Church Music Quarterly (4). 151 Mount View Rd, London N4 4JT *tel:* 020 8341 6408 *fax:* 020 8340 0021 *email:* cmqeditor@aol.com. Trevor Ford, ed; Marianne Barton, associate ed; Anne Hastings, ad mgr. *No cover price, issued to Royal School of Church Music members only.*

Classic CD (13). Beauford Court, 30 Monmouth St, Bath, Avon BA1 2BW *tel:* 01225 442244 *fax:* 01225 732353 *email:* nevans@futurenet.co.uk. Neil Evans, ed; Daniel Jaffé, reviews ed; Mark Funnell, news and production ed. *£3.95; £45 pa. Features, news and reviews of classical mus releases and concerts, with a cover-mounted CD of extracts.*

Classic FM Magazine (12). John Brown Contract Publishing Ltd, The New Boathouse, 136-142 Bramley Rd, London W10 6SR *tel:* 020 7565 3228/3223 *fax:* 020 7565 3062 *email:* classicfm@johnbrown.co.uk. Lucy Hall, ed. *£3.75.*

Classical Guitar (12). 1-2 Vance Court, Trans Britannia Enterprise Park, Blaydon on Tyne NE21 5NH *tel:* 0191 414 9000 *fax:* 0191 414 9001 *email:* mail@ashleymark.co.uk. Colin Cooper, ed. *£2.95; £40.95 pa.*

Classical Music (26). Rhinegold Publishing Ltd, 241 Shaftesbury Ave, London WC2H 8EH *tel:* 020 7333 1742 (ed); 020 7333 1733 (ad) *fax:* 020 7333 1769 (ed); 020 7333 1736 (ad) *email:* classical.music@rhinegold.co.uk. Keith Clarke, ed; Rebecca Agnew, deputy ed. *£3.10; £63 pa.*

The Conductor (4). Marrey, 7 Carr View Rd, Hepworth, Huddersfield HD7 7HN *tel:* 01484 683793 *fax:* 01484 686209. Jeffrey Turner, ed. *£2. Journal of the NABBC.*

The Consort (Journal of the Dolmetsch Foundation) (1). 272 Lewisham Rd, London SE13 7LB *tel:* 020 8318 6638 *email:* richard.partridge1@virgin.net. Richard Partridge, ed. *£22.50 pa (overseas), £18 (UK), £7 (student) including general membership and newsletter* Bulletin *(3).*

Contemporary Music News (3). Peters Edition Ltd, 10-12 Baches St, London N1 6DN *tel:* 020 7553 4030 *fax:* 020 7490 4921 *email:* newmusic@uk.edition-peters.com. Jo Shaw, ed. *Free. Activities of contemporary composers published in Edition Peters.*

Contemporary Music Review (4). Harwood Academic Publishers, PO Box 90, Reading RG1 8JL *tel:* 0118 956 0080 *fax:* 0118 956 8211 *email:* info@gbhap.com. Nigel Osborne, Peter Nelson, eds. *£200 (plus p&p) (libraries and institutions), £60 (individuals). A forum for the discussion of contemporary composition.*

Early Music (4). Oxford University Press, 70 Baker St, London W1M 1DJ *tel:* 020 7616 5902/7352 6400 (ad) *fax:* 020 7616 5901 *email:* jnl.early-music@oup.co.uk. Tess Knighton, ed; David Roberts, asst ed. *£10.50; £42 pa (individuals), £72 (institutions). Articles on medieval, renaissance, baroque and pre-classical mus with special reference to performance practice. Book, mus and recording reviews.*

Early Music History (1). Journals Dept, CUP, Edinburgh Building, Shaftesbury Rd, Cambridge CB2 2RU *tel:* 01223 312393 *fax:* 01223 315052 *email:* journals-subscriptions@cup.cam.ac.uk. Iain Fenlon, ed. *£56 (institutions), £37 (individuals). Devoted to the study of mus from the early Middle Ages to the 17th C.*

Early Music News (10). Forever Green, 3 Onslow House, Castle Rd, The Common, Tunbridge Wells, Kent TN4 8BY *tel:* 01892 511652 *also fax; email:* foreverg@dircon.co.uk. Robin Hillier, ed. *Free in the UK. Listings of concerts, broadcasts and CD releases.*

Early Music Review (10). King's Music, Redcroft, Bank's End, Wyton, Huntingdon PE17 2AA *tel:* 01480 52076 *fax:* 01480 450821 *email:* cbkings@ibm.net. Clifford Bartlett, ed; Brian Clark, associate ed; Elaine Bartlett, admin. *£2; £15 pa. For all concerned with the performance, study and enjoyment of early mus throughout the world.*

Early Music Today (6). Rhinegold Publishing Ltd, 241 Shaftesbury Ave, London WC2H 8EH *tel:* 020 7333 1744 (ed); 020 7333 1733 (ad) *fax:* 020 7333 1769 (ed); 020 7333 1736 (ad) *email:* emt@rhinegold.co.uk. Lucien Jenkins, ed; Sara Cunningham, asst ed. *£2.40; £14.40 pa. News magazine reporting on performers, insts, broadcasting, events, books, mus, CDs and the early mus scene in the UK and abroad.*

Early Music Yearbook (1). National Early Music Association, Southside Cottage, Brook Hill, Albury, Guildford GU5 9DJ *tel:* 01483 202159 *fax:* 01483 203088 *email:* Lutesoc@aol.com. *£14.50 (plus p&p). List of individuals and ens, directory of useful addresses, buyers' guide.*

Ensemble (The Music Masters' and Mistresses' Association) (3). Wayfaring, Smithers Lane, East Peckham, Tonbridge, Kent TN12 5HT *tel:* 01622 871576 *also fax; email:* gary@woodl.demon.co.uk. Katharine Le Page, admin; Gary Beauchamp, ed (*tel:* 01222 459098); *£3.50. Members and general sale.*

The First National Directory of Community Music. Sound Sense, c/o The Arts Business, 38 St Martins Lane, London WC2N 4ER *tel:* 020 7420 9700 *fax:* 020 7420 9701 *email:* info@artsbusiness.co.uk. Peter Budge, publications mgr. *£5.95 (plus £2 p&p)*

Flamenco International Magazine (4). PO Box 15085, London N8 7WD *tel:* 020 8348 3777 *fax:* 020 8348 0562.

Flutewise (4). 9 Beaconsfield Rd, Portslade by Sea, E Sussex BN41 1XA *tel:* 01273 702367 *fax:* 01273 888864 *email:* mail@flutewise.com. James Galway, president; Liz Goodwin, ed. *£15 pa. Quarterly magazine for all fl players, especially the young, featuring articles, quizzes, competitions and events.*

Folk Music Journal (1). English Folk Dance and Song Society, 2 Regents Park Rd, London NW1 7AY *tel:* 020 7485 2206 *fax:* 020 7284 0523 *email:* michael.heaney@ulib.ox.ac.uk. Michael Heaney, ed. *£7.50, £21 including individual membership of EFDSS.*

Footloose in London Magazine (52). 39 Bushwood, London E11 3BW *tel:* 020 8518 8903; 07976 399828 *email:* malcolmjg@aol.com. Malcolm Galloway, classical mus critic. *Free. Arts, entertainments and review magazine. Highlights classical mus CDs and concerts.*

The Full Score (4). Chester Music Limited, 8-9 Frith St, London W1V 5TZ *tel:* 020 7434 0066 *fax:* 020 7287 6329 *email:* music@musicsales.co.uk. Nick Kimberley, ed; Catherine Manners, head of promotion. *Free. Quarterly newsletter for Chester Music, Novello & Co, Edition Wilhelm Hansen and G Schirmer Inc.*

The Galpin Society Journal (1). The Coach House, 55a High St, Long Crendon, Aylesbury, Bucks HP18 9AL *tel:* 01844 208234 *fax:* 01844 202613 *email:* charles.mould@stx.ox.ac.uk. Graham Wells, chmn; Pauline Holden, sec; Charles Mould, ed; Andrew Pinnock, reviews ed. *£18 (UK), £24 (Europe), £28 (elsewhere), £30 (institutions and non-members), inclusive of Journal and Bulletins (study of mus insts).*

Gramophone (12). Gramophone Publications Ltd, 135 Greenford Rd, Sudbury Hill, Harrow, Middx HA1 3YD *tel:* 020 8422 4562 *fax:* 020 8869 8400 *email:* editor@gramophone.co.uk. James Jolly, ed; C Pollard, editorial dir. *£3.40. Monthly; features and reviews.*

Hallmark (4). Hallé Concerts Society, The Bridgewater Hall, Manchester M2 3WS *tel:* 0161 237 7000 *fax:* 0161 237 7029. Richard Grange, Patsy Lawler, eds. *Free to members, press and sponsors. News of fundraising, sponsorship, educ and other activities.*

Haydn Society Journal (1). Music Dept, Lancaster University, Lancaster LA1 4YW *tel:* 01524 593777 *fax:* 01524 847298 *email:* dmccaldin@lancaster.ac.uk. Denis McCaldin, dir; Stella Birchall, admin. *£5 pa. Articles, reviews, forthcoming events concerning Joseph Haydn and his circle.*

Hi-Fi News & Record Review (12). Link House Magazines Ltd, Link House, Dingwall Ave, Croydon CR9 2TA *tel:* 020 8686 2599 *fax:* 020 8760 0973. Steve Harris, ed; Christopher Breunig, mus ed. *£3.10; £35.40 pa (UK), $80 (US), £43.10 (Europe and Eire).*

The Horn Magazine (3). 15 Hailey Croft, Chinnor, Oxon OX9 4TS *tel:* 01844 353025 *also fax; email:* 101353.1656@compuserve.com. Ian Wagstaff, publisher and ed. *A magazine for horn players by horn players, published for the British Horn Society.*

International Arts Manager (10). Arts Publishing International Ltd, Lime Wharf, Vyner St, London E2 9DJ *tel:* 020 8709 9050 *fax:* 020 7247 9080 *email:* editorial@api.co.uk. Jane Morris, ed; Flemmich Webb, news ed. *£40 pa, or £65 for two years (UK); £45 pa, or £70 for two years (outside UK).*

International Journal of Music Education (2). ISME, International Centre for Research in Music Education, University of Reading, Bulmershe Court, Reading RG6 1HY *tel:* 0118 931 8846 *also fax; fax:* 0118 935 2080 *email:* e.smith@reading.ac.uk. Elizabeth Smith, admin. *£8.75. Articles covering a wide range of issues concerning mus educ worldwide and book reviews.*

International Trombone Association Journal (4). 3 Cumbria Close, Coventry CV1 3PG *tel:* 024 7623 0900 *fax:* 024 7623 0901 *email:* kagarice@gte.net. Vern Kagarice, ed; Paul Hunt, president; Mark Nightingale, 2nd vice-president. *Quarterly publication for trombonists. £6 per issue or free to ITA members.*

ISM Register of Musicians in Education (1). Incorporated Society of Musicians, 10 Stratford Place, London W1N 9AE *tel:* 020 7629 4413; 01376 563811 (ad) *fax:* 020 7408 1538; 01376 562453 (ad) *email:* membership@ism.org. Helen Houghton, head of professional policy; Kim Davenport Gee, production; PRN Media Ltd, ad sales. *£10. Directory and classified lists of ISM members working in or for educ establishments.*

ISM Register of Professional Private Music Teachers (1). Incorporated Society of Musicians, 10 Stratford Place, London W1N 9AE *tel:* 020 7629 4413; 01376 563811 (ad) *fax:* 020 7408 1538; 01376 562453 (ad) *email:* membership@ism.org. Helen Houghton, head of professional policy; Kim Davenport Gee, production; PRN Media Ltd, ad sales. *£16. Classified directory, by insts and geographical location, of ISM registered private teachers.*

ISM Yearbook (1). Incorporated Society of Musicians, 10 Stratford Place, London W1N 9AE *tel:* 020 7629 4413; 01376 563811 (ad) *fax:* 020 7408 1538; 01376 562453 (ad) *email:* membership@ism.org. Neil Hoyle, chief exec and ed; Kim Davenport Gee, production; PRN Media Ltd, ad sales. *£26. Gives contact details for the ISM's 5000 members, reports on the previous year's activities and describes the Society's services.*

ISSTIP Journal (1). School of Music, Kingston University, c/o 28 Emperor's Gate, London SW7 4HS *tel:* 020 7373 7307 *fax:* 020 7373 5440. Carola Grindea, ed. *£3.50 (including p&p); free to ISSTIP members. Articles on musicians' physical and psychological problems by specialists in the field as well as various techniques for coping with stress and anxiety in performance.*

Jazz Journal International (12). 3 and 3a Forest Rd, Loughton, Essex IG10 1DR *tel:* 020 8532 0456/0678 *fax:* 020 8532 0440. Eddie Cook, publisher and ed in chief; Janet Cook, company sec and associate publisher; Ivan Etherington, circulation mgr. *£3; £35 pa (UK). A magazine for jazz record collectors.*

Jazz UK (6). South West Jazz, Bradninch Place, Gandy St, Exeter EX4 3LS *tel:* 01392 218368 *email:* rosie@ejjarvis.demon.co.uk. Rosie Jarvis, regional ed, listings, ad, info. *£10 including membership of National Jazz Card Scheme. Comprehensive listings of forthcoming concerts and events. Editorial commentary on jazz in the UK.*

Jazzwise Magazine (10). Jazzwise Publications, 2b Gleneagle Mews, London SW16 6AE *tel:* 020 8769 7725 *fax:* 020 8677 6128. Charles Alexander, publisher; Stephen Graham, ed. *£2.75; £27.50 pa (UK). Covers all styles and periods of jazz, with emphasis on current activity. Includes features, news, CD reviews, concert reviews, technical articles.*

Journal into Melody (4). Stone Gables, Upton Lane, Seavington St Michael, Ilminster, Somerset TA19 0PZ *tel:* 01460 242226 *also fax. £10 pa (Robert Farnon Society).*

The Lute (1). c/o The Lute Society, Southside Cottage, Brook Hill, Albury, Guildford, Surrey GU5 9DJ *tel:* 01483 202159 *fax:* 01483 203088 *email:* lutesoc@aol.com. Christopher Goodwin, sec and ed. *£27. Subscribers also receive the quarterly magazine* Lute News. *Covers all aspects of the lute and related insts and their mus.*

The Mix (13). 30 Monmouth St, Bath BA1 2BW *tel:* 01225 442244 *fax:* 01225 732353. Chris Kempster, ed. *£3.99. Mus production and recording magazine with covermount CD. Interviews with musicians, producers and sound engineers. Reviews of mus recording equipment.*

Music Analysis (3). Blackwell Publishers, 108 Cowley Rd, Oxford OX4 1JF *tel:* 01865 791100 *fax:* 01865 791347 *email:* Jninfo@blackwellpublishers.co.uk. Anthony Pople, ed. *UK: £59 pa for individuals; £178 institutions; £39 students. World: £76 pa for individuals; £220 institutions; £47 students. Forum for the promotion of new writing focused on works and repertoires.*

Music and Letters (4). Music Dept, Royal Holloway and Bedford New College, Egham, Surrey TW20 0EX *tel:* 01784 443532 *fax:* 01784 439441. Nigel Fortune, Jeanice Brooks, Katharine Ellis, eds. *UK/Europe £40 (individuals), £68 (institutions).*

Music and Liturgy (5). 33 Brockenhurst Rd, Addiscombe, Croydon CR0 7DR *tel:* 020 8654 3379 *also fax.* Ann Moynihan, ed. *£20 pa (concessions £15) (UK); £21 (Europe); £23 (rest of world).*

Music Archive Publications. Harwood Academic Publications, c/o IPD PO Box 90, Reading RG1 8JL *tel:* 0118 956 0080 *fax:* 0118 956 8211 *email:* info@gbhap.com. Andrew Hansen, international sales dir.

Music Business (12). The Swan Agency, 35 High St, Marlow, Bucks SL7 1AU *tel:* 01628 487821; 020 8950 4984 (ad) *fax:* 01628 890209 (ed); 020 8950 0302 (ad) *email:* 101765.2626@compuserve.com. Gez Kahan, ed; Sandie Smith, ad mgr. *£18 pa. Trade magazine for mus inst industry, including annual directory (published in Feb).*

Music Business International. Miller Freeman Entertainment, 8 Montague Close, London Bridge, London SE1 9UR *tel:* 020 7620 3636 *fax:* 020 7401 8035. *£110 pa including free MBI directory.*

Music Education Yearbook (1). Rhinegold Publishing Ltd, 241 Shaftesbury Ave, London WC2H 8EH *tel:* 020 7333 1761 (ed); 020 7333 1718 (ad) *fax:* 020 7333 1769 (ed); 020 7333 1736 (ad) *email:* meyb@rhinegold.co.uk. Louise Head, ed; Claire Throp, asst ed. *£16.50. Guide to mus in educ for parents, teachers, students and musicians. Provides contact information, course details, scholarship policy and entry requirements for independent schools, colleges and universities in Britain. Also sections on world mus, publishers, exam syllabuses, mus information technology, youth orchs and choirs, teachers' resources and others.*

Music Journal (12). Incorporated Society of Musicians, 10 Stratford Place, London W1N 9AE *tel:* 020 7629 4413; 01376 563811 (ad) *fax:* 020 7408 1538; 01376 562453 (ad) *email:* membership@ism.org. Neil Hoyle, ed; Kim Davenport Gee, production; PRN Media Ltd, ad sales. *£2.50, £25 pa. Details of ISM members' activities and the ISM's work, plus news and views from the world of professional mus.*

Music, Opera, Dance and Drama in Asia, the Pacific and North America. Arts Publishing International Ltd, Lime Wharf, Vyner St, London E2 9DJ *tel:* 020 8709 9050 *email:* editorial@api.co.uk. Martin Huber, publisher; Shizuka Yokomizo, Anal Laura, Lopez-de la Torre, eds; Marion Qazi, ed admin. *£33.*

Music Review (4). Black Bear Press, King's Hedges Rd, Cambridge CB4 2PQ *tel:* 01223 424571. A F Leighton Thomas, ed. *£15.25; £52.50 pa.*

Music Teacher (12). Rhinegold Publishing Ltd, 241 Shaftesbury Ave, London WC2H 8EH *tel:* 020 7333 1747 (ed); 020 7333 1733 (ad) *fax:* 020 7333 1769 *email:* music.teacher@rhinegold.co.uk. Lucien Jenkins, ed; Sara Cunningham, asst ed. *£3.45; £40 pa. News and features on mus technology, A-level and GCSE history and analysis, insts and teaching choices; book, mus and video reviews. Regular special topic guides.*

Music Week and Music Week Directory (52). Miller Freeman Entertainment, 8 Montague Close, London Bridge, London SE1 9UR *tel:* 020 7620 3636 *fax:* 020 7401 8035. Steve Redmond, ed in chief. *Mus industry trade publication, including news, new release listings and official CIN charts. £3.50; £135 pa including* Music Week Directory.

Musical Opinion (4). 2 Princes Rd, St Leonards-on-Sea, E Sussex TN37 6EL *tel:* 01424 715167 *fax:* 01424 712214 *email:* musical_opinion@mcmail.com. Denby Richards, ed; Caroline Bendell, asst ed. *Also 8 supplements. £3.50; £24 pa (UK), £36 pa (overseas).*

Musical Performance (4). Harwood Academic Publishers, 197 Knightsbridge, 8th Floor North, London SW7 1RB *tel:* 020 7586 7676 *fax:* 020 7823 7969 *email:* tschaikov@dial.pipex.com. Basil Tschaikov, ed in chief. *£12 (paper); £50 pa (paper); £182 pa (cloth). International journal for composers, musicians and their audiences.*

The Musical Times (4). 63b Jamestown Rd, London NW1 7DB *tel:* 020 7482 5697 (ed) *also fax*; 020 7613 0717 (ad). Antony Bye, ed; Brian R Hook, ad mgr. *£8.*

New Music News (3). Irish Contemporary Music Centre, 95 Lower Baggot St, Dublin 2, Ireland *tel:* 00 353 1 661 2105 *fax:* 00 353 1 676 2639 *email:* info@cmc.ie. Eve O'Kelly, ed. *Free.*

new notes (11). c/o spnm, Francis House, Francis St, London SW1P IDE *tel:* 020 7630 0950 *fax:* 020 7931 9928 *email:* spnm@spnm.org.uk. Rachel Duncombe, publications offr. *Free. New mus concerts listings plus spnm news.*

NODA National News (4). NODA House, 1 Crestfield St, London WC1H 8AU *tel:* 020 7837 5655 *fax:* 020 7833 0609. Mark Thorburn, mgr ed. *£2; free to members of National Operatic and Dramatic Association.*

Opera (13). 1a Mountgrove Rd, London N5 2LU *tel:* 020 7359 1037 *fax:* 020 7354 2700 *email:* operamag@clara.co.uk. Rodney Milnes, ed. *£3.15. Ad mgrs:* Cabbell Publishing Ltd (*tel:* 020 8395 3808).

Opera Now (6). Rhinegold Publishing Ltd, 241 Shaftesbury Ave, London WC2H 8EH *tel:* 020 7333 1740 (ed); 020 7333 1733 (ad) *fax:* 020 7333 1769 (ed); 020 7333 1736 (ad) *email:* opera.now@rhinegold.co.uk. Ashutosh Khandekar, ed; Antonia Couling, deputy ed; Matthew Peacock, asst ed. *£4.95; £29.70 pa.*

The Organ (4). 5 Aldborough Rd, St Leonards-on-Sea, E Sussex TN37 6SE *tel:* 01424 422225 *fax:* 01424 712214. Brian Hick, ed. *£3.50; £17 pa (UK), £23 (elsewhere). Magazine for organists, org builders and general listeners, covering all types of org mus and orgs.*

Organ Club Journal (6). 152 Graham Rd, London SW19 3SJ *tel:* 020 8543 5861 *also fax; email:* david.gammie@virgin.net; edward.kemp-luck@virgin.net. David Gammie, Edward Kemp-Luck, eds. *Features on insts, composers and repertoire, news and reviews, reports of club activities. Distributed free to members of The Organ Club.*

Organ and Keyboard Cavalcade (12). Sceptre Promotions, 97 Elton Rd, Stibbington, Peterborough PE8 6JX *tel:* 01780 782093 *fax:* 01780 783159. Grant Neal, ed. *£16 pa. Monthly magazine covering all things electronic org and home keyboard: tutorial, news, reviews, concerts, classifieds, etc.*

Organised Sound (3 +CD). Journals Dept, CUP, Edinburgh Building, Shaftesbury Rd, Cambridge CB2 2RU *tel:* 01223 312393 *fax:* 01223 315052 *email:* journals-subscriptions@cup.cam.ac.uk. Ross Kirk, Leigh Landy, Tony Myatt, Richard Orton, eds. *£69 (institutions print plus electronic), £39 (individuals print only), £27 (students). Issues arising from the use of contemporary technology in fields of multimedia, performance art, sound sculpture and electronic composition.*

Organists' Review (4). 4 Vicars' Court, Southwell, Notts NG25 0HP *tel:* 01636 812228 *also fax;* 01245 259120 *email:* OrganistsReview @diaphone.clara.net. Paul Hale, ed; Marcus Knight, ad mgr; Roger Fisher, features ed. *£4. Articles on orgs, org and choral mus, org playing. Major review section.*

Performing Arts Yearbook for Europe (PAYE) (1). Arts Publishing International Ltd, Lime Wharf, Vyner St, London E2 9DJ *tel:* 020 8709 9050 *email:* editorial@api.co.uk; post@api.co.uk. Martin Huber, publisher; Anal Laura Lopez-de la Torre, ed, Wiebke Müller, consultant ed; Karin Junker, deputy ed. *£43 (UK); £51.*

Phono. Morgan Freeman Entertainment, 8 Montague Close, London Bridge, London SE1 9UR *tel:* 020 7620 3636 *fax:* 020 7401 8035. *£128 pa*

Phono. Morgan Freeman Entertainment, 8 Montague Close, London Bridge, London SE1 9UR *tel:* 020 7620 3636 *fax:* 020 7401 8035.

Piano (6). Rhinegold Publishing Ltd, 241 Shaftesbury Ave, London WC2H 8EH *tel:* 020 7333 1724 (ed); 020 7333 1733 (ad) *fax:* 020 7333 1769 (ed); 020 7333 1736 (ad) *email:* piano@rhinegold.co.uk. Jeremy Siepman, ed; Matthew Peacock, deputy ed. *£2.40; £14.40 pa.*

Piano Journal (3). 28 Emperor's Gate, London SW7 4HS *tel:* 020 7373 7307 *fax:* 020 7373 5440. Malcolm Troup, ed; Carola Grindea, consultant. *Free to members of the European Piano Teachers Association (UK) and associate members (outside Europe). Interviews, articles on repertoire, pno teaching, technique, etc; book, mus and CD reviews.*

Piano Tuners Quarterly (4). RNIB, PO Box 173, Peterborough PE2 6WS *tel:* 01733 370777 *fax:* 01733 371555 *email:* ebury@rnib.org.uk. Elizabeth Bury, publications ed. *£1.25 (UK); £1.85 (overseas). News and articles about pno tuning.*

Plainsong and Medieval Music (2). Journals Dept, CUP, Edinburgh Building, Shaftesbury Rd, Cambridge CB2 2RU *tel:* 01223 312393 *fax:* 01223 315052 *email:* journals-subscriptions@cup.cam.ac.uk. Joseph Dyer, Christopher Page, eds. *£46 (institutions), £28 (individuals). Liturgical chant of any period, monophonic and polyphonic in East and West.*

Popular Music (3). Journals Dept, CUP, The Edinburgh Building, Shaftesbury Rd, Cambridge CB2 2RU *tel:* 01223 312393 *fax:* 01223 315052. Lucy Green, Dave Laing, co-ord eds. *£70 (institutions); £39 (individuals); £30 (students). A multi-disciplinary journal covering all aspects of popular mus.*

Radio Times (51). BBC Worldwide Ltd, 80 Wood Lane, London W12 0TT *tel:* 0870 608 4455 *fax:* 020 8576 3160 *email:* radio.times@bbc.co.uk. Sue Robinson, ed. *79p.*

The Record Collector (4). 111 Longshots Close, Broomfield, Chelmsford CM1 7DU *tel:* 01245 441661 *fax:* 01245 443642 *email:* larrylusti @aol.com. Larry Lustig, ed. *£20 by subscription.*

The Recorder Magazine (4). Scout Bottom Farm, Mytholmroyd, Hebden Bridge, W Yorks HX7 5JS *tel:* 01422 882751 *fax:* 01422 886157 *email:* ruth@recordermail.demon.co.uk. Andrew Mayes, ed. *£3.75.*

Rhythm (13). 30 Monmouth St, Bath BA1 2BW *tel:* 01225 442244 *fax:* 01225 732285 *email:* rhythm@dial.pipex.com. Ronan Macdonald, ed; Louise King, deputy ed; Kevin Lowery, artistic ed, Helen Bavester, ad mgr. *£2.95. Magazine for drummers and percussionists, covering a wide range of mus from jazz to world mus.*

The Ringing World (52). Ringing World Ltd, Penmark House, Guildford, Surrey GU1 1BL *tel:* 01483 569535 *fax:* 01483 567876 *email:* ringingw@luna.co.uk. Miss T R Stoecklin, ed. *£1.15; £39 pa.*

Royal Musical Association, Journal of the (2). Dept of Music, Royal Holloway, University of London, Egham, Surrey TW20 0EX *tel:* 01784 443806/443532 *fax:* 01784 439441 *email:* a.wathey@uk.ac.rhbnc.vax. Andrew Wathey, ed. *£53 pa (UK and EU), US$95 (elsewhere).*

Royal Musical Association Research Chronicle (1). Dept of Music, University of York, Heslington, York YO10 5DD *tel:* 01904 661016 *fax:* 01904 432450 *email:* jpw6@york.ac.uk. Jonathan Wainwright, ed. *Approx £30. Emphasis on the raw materials of musicology; indexes, categories, inventories, etc.*

Scottish Folk Directory (1). Scottish Folk Arts Group, Blackfriars Music, 49 Blackfriars St, Edinburgh EH1 1NB *tel:* 0131 557 3090 *also fax; email:* scotfolk@compuserve.com. Willie Haines, ed. *£2.95. A contact resource for all involved in Scottish folk mus and arts.*

Sheet Music (4). Press House, Godinton Rd, Ashford, Kent TN23 1LJ *tel:* 01233 643574 *fax:* 01233 641816. Paul Smith, ed; Julie Robinson, sales mgr. *For musicians, teachers and all who buy and sell sheet mus.*

Showcase International Music Book (1). Showcase Publications Ltd, 38c The Broadway, London N8 9SU *tel:* 020 8348 2332 *fax:* 020 8340 3750. Kay Chestnutt, ed; Tony Tillmanns, ad sales and mkt. *£40 (EEC), £47 (other). Mus production guide for the UK and Europe published annually in Jan. Also available on CD-ROM £49.95 including VAT.*

The Singer (6). Rhinegold Publishing Ltd, 241 Shaftesbury Ave, London WC2H 8EH *tel:* 020 7333 1746 (ed); 020 7333 1733 (ad) *fax:* 020 7333 1769 (ed); 020 7333 1736 (ad) *email:* the.singer@rhinegold.co.uk. Antonia Couling, ed; Matthew Peacock, asst ed. *£2.40; £14.40 pa. For anyone with a serious, wide-ranging enthusiasm for vocal mus, from choral and lieder to opera, jazz, cabaret and mus theatre.*

Sounding Board (4). Sound Sense, Riverside House, Rattlesden, Bury St Edmunds IP30 0SF *tel:* 01449 736287 *fax:* 01449 737649 *email:* 100256.30@compuserve.com. Kathryn Deane, ed. *Quarterly journal for those interested in participatory mus-making. Subscription ranges from £10 to £65 pa and includes membership of Sound Sense.*

Sounds Great! (10). Bright Horizons Publications, PO Box 1572, Ascot, Berks SL5 0PF *tel:* 01344 291398 *fax:* 01344 621021 *email:* jb@soundsgreat.co.uk. Joan Brightwell, ed. *£18.50 pa. Comprehensive guide to live classical events in over 800 venues in London and the home counties.*

South West Jazz Newsletters. South West Jazz, Bradninch Place, Gandy St, Exeter, Devon EX4 3LS *tel:* 01392 218368 *fax:* 01392 420442 *email:* rosie@ejjarvis.demon.co.uk. Rosie Jarvis, ed. *Quarterly newsletters for musicians, bands, venues, promoters and amateur musicians.*

The Stage (52). Stage House, 47 Bermondsey St, London SE1 3XT *tel:* 020 7403 1818 *fax:* 020 7403 1418 *email:* info@thestage.co.uk. Brian Attwood, ed. *90p.*

The Strad (12). Orpheus Publications, 7 St John's Rd, Harrow, Middx HA1 2EE *tel:* 020 8863 2020 *fax:* 020 8863 2444 *email:* thestrad@orphpl.com; subs@orphpl.com; advertising@orphpl.com. Joanna Pieters, ed; Juliette Barber, deputy ed; Naomi Sadler, asst ed. *£3.50; £38.50 pa (UK). For performers, teachers, students, makers and enthusiasts of bowed str insts.*

Studio Sound (12). 8 Montague Close, London Bridge, London SE1 9UR *tel:* 020 7620 3636 *fax:* 020 7401 8036. Tim Goodyer, ed; Zenon Schoepe, exec ed. *£3.75. Controlled circulation journal serving professional recording, post-production and broadcast industry.*

Tempo (4). Boosey & Hawkes Ltd, 295 Regent St, London W1R 8JH *tel:* 020 7580 2060 *fax:* 020 7436 5675 *email:* tempo2@boosey.com. Calum MacDonald, ed; Arthur Boyers, ad mgr; Sue Rose, subs mgr. *£3.50; £17.50 pa.*

Unknown Public (4). PO Box 354, Reading RG1 5TX *tel:* 0118 931 2580 *fax:* 0118 931 2582 *email:* walters@gn.apc.org. John L Walters, ed; Laurence Aston, publisher. *£55 (individual), £90 (institutions). Audio journal of contemporary creative mus on CD or MC.*

Welsh Music (2). 17 Penyrheol Drive, Llanelli, Carmarthenshire SA15 3NX *tel:* 01554 774188. A J Heward Rees, ed. *£3.*

What Hi-fi? (13). Haymarket Magazines Ltd, 38-42 Hampton Rd, Teddington, Middx TW11 0JE *tel:* 020 8943 5000 *fax:* 020 8943 5019 *email:* jez@whf1.demon.co.uk. Jez Ford, ed; Andrew Clough, deputy ed; Andrew Everard, technical ed. Frank Foster, art ed. *£2.75. Hi-fi buyers' guide with reviews of hi-fi and home cinema equipment plus hi-fi news and related features.*

What's On In London (52). 182 Pentonville Rd, London N1 9LB *tel:* 020 7278 4393 *fax:* 020 7837 5838. Michael Darvell, classical and opera ed; Danny Scott, rock and pop ed. *£1.20. Rock, pop, jazz, folk, world mus as well as classical. Weekly listings of all mus in London including features, previews, album reviews, opera reviews and other entertainment coverage of the arts.*

The White Book (1). Bank House, 23 Warwick Rd, Coventry CV1 2EW *tel:* 024 7655 9658 *fax:* 024 7663 1185 *email:* whitebook@ dial.pipex.com. Sarah Hutchinson, ed. *£65 (UK). Production directory to the entertainment industry.*

Winds (4). Wayfaring, Smithers Lane, East Peckham, Tonbridge TN12 5HT *tel:* 01622 872758 *also fax; email:* editor@winds.org.uk. Timothy Reynish, chmn; Brendon Le Page, ed. *£3; £10 pa. Articles on repertoire analysis, conducting, inst teaching, jazz, plus news and reviews. Incorporating the journal of the British Association of Symphonic Bands and Wind Ensembles (BASBWE).*

Instrument Manufacturers

Listed here are the principal manufacturers and repairers of modern instruments, with their area of expertise given in italics after each entry. A list of early musical instrument makers will be found under **Early Music Instrument Manufacturers**. For repairs of standard instruments, refer to the manufacturers listed below or to the **Retailers** section. Specialist repairers can be found under **Instrument Technicians.**

A Noterman Ltd. 11 Broughton Ave, Aylesbury, Bucks HP20 1NN *tel:* 01296 489847 *also fax. Pipe orgs.*

Acorn (Percussion) Ltd. Unit 33, Abbey Business Centre, Ingate Place, London SW8 3NS *tel:* 020 7720 2243 (24 hrs) *fax:* 020 7627 8883. Richard Benson, dir. *Perc inst manufacture, import and supplies: pre-school to secondary school and hospitals, mainstream and multicultural, mus books.*

AD Guitars. 39 Chatsworth Rd, Brighton BN1 5DA *tel:* 01273 550055. *Guis.*

Adam Whone. 86 Mill Hill Rd, Acton, London W3 8JJ *tel:* 020 8992 0619 *fax:* 020 8992 8891 *email:* awhonevns@aol.com. Hiroko Whone. *Dealer, restorer and maker of fine vns, vas, vcs and bows. Also valuations and sales.*

Alfred Knight Ltd. 154 Clapham Park Rd, London SW4 7DE *tel:* 020 7978 2444 *fax:* 020 7978 2347. *Pnos.*

Allen Organ Studios (London) Ltd. Trada Business Campus, Stocking Lane, Hughenden Valley, High Wycombe, Bucks HP14 4ND *tel:* 01494 563833 *fax:* 01494 563546 *email:* sales@allenorgans.co.uk. David Shepherd, sales mgr.

Amadeus Performance Equipment Ltd. Great Beech Barn, Kane Hythe Rd, Battle, E Sussex TN33 9QU *tel:* 01424 775867 *fax:* 01424 775866 *email:* info@amadeus-equipment.co.uk. *Accs.*

Arbiter Group plc. Wilberforce Rd, London NW9 6AX *tel:* 020 8202 1199 *fax:* 020 8202 7076 *email:* info@arbitergroup.com. Dave Glover, mkt mgr. *Fender guis, amps, perc, band insts, mus technology.*

Ardival Harps Ltd. Orchard House, Castle Leod, Strathpeffer, Ross-shire IV14 9AA *tel:* 01997 421260 *also fax; email:* ardival@netmatters.co.uk. *Historical and trad Scottish hps.*

Bach *see* **Vincent Bach International Ltd.**

Barnes & Mullins Ltd. 155 Grays Inn Rd, London WC1X 8UF *tel:* 020 7278 4631/2/3 *fax:* 020 7837 2184/6928. Bruce Perrin, dir. *Range of guis, vns, saxes, amps and all mus accs.*

Bentley Piano Co Ltd. 154 Clapham Park Rd, London SW4 7DE *tel:* 020 7978 2444 *fax:* 020 7978 2347. *Pnos. Also manufacture under names of Rogers, Hopkinson, Gerh Steinberg and Rich Lipp and Sohn.*

Bigio, Robert. 1 Doveridge Gardens, London N13 5BJ *tel:* 020 8882 2627 *fax:* 020 8882 2728 *email:* robert@bigio.demon.co.uk. *Boehm system fls and piccs (wood and silver).*

Bishop and Son. 38 Bolton Lane, Ipswich, Suffolk IP4 2BT *tel:* 01473 255165 *also fax.* E J Bailey, mgr. *Org builders; new pipe orgs; also org restoration, repair and tuning.*

Blüthner Pianos, Whelpdale Maxwell & Codd Ltd. 154 Clapham Park Rd, London SW4 7DE *tel:* 020 7978 2444 *fax:* 020 7978 2347. *Distributor for Blüthner and Haessler pnos.*

Boardman, Peter. 33a Hogstown Rd, Donaghadee, Co Down BT21 0NH *tel:* 028 9188 3474. *Vns, vas and vcs.*

Bolton, Tarquin. 33 Quebec St, Langley Park, Durham DH7 9UU *tel:* 0191 373 4906. *Vns and bows.*

Bontempi-Comus (UK) Ltd. 12 Churchill Way, Lomeshaye Industrial Estate, Nelson, Lancs BB9 6RT *tel:* 01282 606600 *fax:* 01282 606660 *email:* bontempi@comus-uk.demon.co.uk. *Elec keyboards, educ insts, mus toys.*

Boosey & Hawkes Musical Instruments Ltd. Deansbrook Rd, Edgware, Middx HA8 9BB *tel:* 020 8429 7511 *fax:* 020 8429 7556 *email:* MI.Edgware@boosey.com. *Br, w/wind, str.*

Border Harps. Waterloo Cottages, Letton, Hereford HR3 6DN *tel:* 01544 327352 *also fax.* M C Saunders, S R Saunders, partners. *Hps, hp kits, parts and strs.*

Bösendorfer Pianos. 142 Edgware Rd, London W2 2DZ *tel:* 020 7935 7378 *fax:* 020 7224 8692. Terence Lewis, mgr dir. *Pnos. Sales, hire, tuning, servicing, practice rooms.*

Bradley, James. Stockwell Studios, McCall Close, Stockwell SW4 6PT *W/wind repairs.*

The Bridge Fiddler. Riverside House, Chapel Milton, Chapel-en-le-Frith, High Peak SK23 0QQ *tel:* 01298 813813. *Str insts, bows and accs supplied; repairs and restoration.*

Broadwood Pianos Ltd. 154 Clapham Park Rd, London SW4 7DE *tel:* 020 7720 3559 *fax:* 020 7978 2347. *Pnos.*

Cambridge Pianola Co & J V Pianos. The Limes, Landbeach, Cambridge CB4 4DR *tel:* 01223 861348 *fax:* 01223 441276. F Thomas Poole, proprietor. *Pianolas, pianocorders, nickelodeons; also retail.*

Canter, Kenneth J. 54 Maltings Garth, Thurston, Bury St Edmunds, Suffolk IP31 3PP *tel:* 01359 230694. *Orgs.*

Casio Electronics Co Ltd. Unit 6, 1000 North Circular Rd, London NW2 7JD *tel:* 020 8450 9131 *fax:* 020 8452 6323. *Elec keyboards, digital pnos.*

Centrepiece Music. PO Box 1601, Newport Pagnell, Bucks MK16 8PD *tel:* 01908 218003 *fax:* 01908 211828. *Wholesaler and distributor of speciality accs for w/wind: mouthpieces, reeds, etc; Neotech sax and gui slings and straps; m/order.*

Chappell Piano Co Ltd *see* **Kemble & Co Ltd.**

The Clarke Tin Whistle Co Ltd. The Old Joinery, Whetsted Rd, Five Oak Green, Kent TN12 6RS *tel:* 01892 835632 *fax:* 01892 838086 *email:* jim@clarketinwhistle.com. *Manufacturers of the 'Clarke' tin whistle.*

Clive Morley Harps Ltd. Goodfellows, Filkins, Nr Lechdale, Glos GL7 3JG *tel:* 01367 860493 *fax:* 01367 860659 *email:* morley@harps.demon.co.uk.

Cohen, Brian. Soundpost, The Old Glassworks, Alexandra Place, Guildford, Surrey GU1 3QH *tel:* 01483 456022 *also fax; email:* strings@soundpost.co.uk. *Guis, vns, vcs.*

Copeman Hart & Company Ltd. Finedon Rd, Irthlingborough, Northants NN9 5TZ *tel:* 01933 652600 *fax:* 01933 652288 *email:* info@copemanhart.co.uk. E C Hart, I J Rees, C C Hart, dirs. *Church org builders.*

David R Ouvry Violin Maker. Southwood, Burchetts Green, Maidenhead, Berks SL6 6QS *tel:* 01628 823340. *Vns.*

David Wells Organ Builders. Cathedral Works, 52 Westminster Rd, Kirkdale, Liverpool L4 4LT *tel:* 0151 207 9200 *fax:* 0151 207 9201 *email:* dwob@compuserve.com. *Pipe org builder and restorer.*

Derek Roberts Violins. 185 Leam Terrace, Leamington Spa, Warwicks CV31 1DW *tel:* 01926 428313 *also fax; email:* roberts@violins.demon.co.uk. *Modern and baroque vn, va, vc maker and restorer.*

Doe, Roger. Mount St Laurence, High St, Cranbrook, Kent TN17 3EW *tel:* 01580 712330. *Silver and gold mounted bows. French styles and English Hill pattern bows.*

Dolmetsch Musical Instruments. Unicorn Trading Estate, Weydown Rd, Haslemere, Surrey GU27 1DN *tel:* 01428 643235 *fax:* 01428 654920 *email:* brian@dolmetsch.com. *Viols, rcdrs in wood and plastic, hpds, clvds and spinets.*

Eaton, Peter. Woodside, Orestan Lane, Effingham, Surrey KT24 5SN *tel:* 01372 452513 *fax:* 01372 451416 *email:* Peter@eatonclarinets.co.uk. *Cls and cl mouthpieces.*

Edgar, Alan. 43 Beverley Rd, Hessle, N Humberside *tel:* 01482 640330. *Hpds, clvds, hps.*

Elysian Pianos. Robert Morley & Co Ltd, 34 Engate St, London SE13 7HA *tel:* 020 8318 5838 *fax:* 020 8297 0720 *email:* www.yell.co.uk/sites/morley. Julia Morley. *Grand and upright pnos; also stools.*

F H Browne & Sons (Organ Builders). Old Cartwright School, The Street, Ash, Canterbury, Kent CT3 2AA *tel:* 01304 813146 *also fax. Orgs.*

Farfisa (UK) Ltd. 12 Churchill Way, Lomeshaye Industrial Estate, Nelson, Lancs BB9 6RT *tel:* 01282 606600 *fax:* 01282 606660. *Elec keyboards.*

Fazioli. The Music Studios, 29 Marylebone Lane, London W1M 5FH *tel:* 020 7486 0025 *fax:* 020 7935 8454.

Flutemakers Guild Ltd. 10 Shacklewell Rd, London N16 7TA *tel:* 020 7254 7175 *also fax. W/wind (fls, piccs, etc).*

Forrest Pianos. 9 Ravenscar Terrace, Oakwood, Leeds, W Yorks LS8 4AU *tel:* 0113 248 4448. *Pnos (Laurence and Nash); also tuning and repairs.*

Gordon Stevenson Violins. 6 Barclay Terrace, Bruntsfield, Edinburgh EH10 4HP *tel:* 0131 229 2051 *fax:* 0131 229 9298. *Vns.*

Graham Wright Violin Maker. 20 Renfrew St, Glasgow G2 3BW *tel:* 0141 332 4513 *fax:* 0141 400 1513 *email:* GW@Slantsix.prestel.co.uk. *Vns.*

Green, Miranda. 21 Wathen Rd, Dorking, Surrey RH4 1JY *tel:* 01306 886199. *Vns and vas.*

Grotrian-Steinweg Pianos. Robert Morley & Co Ltd, 34 Engate St, London SE13 7HA *tel:* 020 8318 5838 *fax:* 020 8297 0720. Julia Morley. *Grand and upright pnos.*

Roger Hansell Violins. Ulshaw House, Coverbridge, Leyburn, N Yorks DL8 5PU *tel:* 01969 623048 *fax:* 01969 624416. *Vns, vas, vcs; also fine inst fittings.*

State of the Art.

80 YEARS OF EXCELLENCE
1919 THOMASTIK-INFELD 1999

THOMASTIK-INFELD
V I E N N A

visit our website... http://www.thomastik-infeld.com
A-1051 Wien, Diehlgasse 27, Tel. +43-1-545 12 62,
Fax +43-1-545 30 42

Harrison & Harrison Ltd. St John's Rd, Meadowfield, Durham DH7 8YH *tel:* 0191 378 2222 *fax:* 0191 378 3388 *email:* h.h@btinternet.com. Mark Venning, mgr dir. *Pipe orgs.*

Hawkins (Organ Builders) Ltd. Unit 6, Greenhough Rd, Lichfield, Staffs WS13 7AU *tel:* 01543 255135.

Hele & Co Ltd. The Tower, Lower Port View, Saltash, Cornwall PL12 4BY *tel:* 01752 842027 *also fax. Org builders.*

Henry Willis & Sons Ltd. 87-91 Rushes Rd, Petersfield, Hants GU32 3AT *tel:* 01730 263141 *fax:* 01730 262151 *email:* dw@willis-organs.demon.co.uk. *Pipe orgs. IBO accredited.*

Sir Herbert Marshall & Sons Ltd. 154 Clapham Park Rd, London SW4 7DE *tel:* 020 7978 2444 *fax:* 020 7978 2347. *Pnos.*

Hibernian Violins. 24 Players Ave, Malvern Link, Worcs WR14 1DU *tel:* 01684 562947 *also fax.* Padraig Ó Dubhlaoidh. *Vn and viol family insts, bows.*

Holywell Music Ltd. 58 Hopton St, London SE1 9JH *tel:* 020 7928 8451 *fax:* 020 7928 8284 *email:* holywell@netcomuk.co.uk. *Salvi and Lyon & Healy concert and non-pedal hps.*

Huggett, Martin. The Old Library, Stour St, Manningtree, Essex CO11 1BE *tel:* 01206 396354 *also fax. Artcase pno restoration and rebuilding including all decorative work. Carving, gilding, painting, marquetry, and all associated areas of expertise.*

Impact Percussion. 120-122 Bermondsey St, London SE1 3TX *tel:* 020 7403 5900 *fax:* 020 7403 5910 *email:* impactperc@msn.com. *Tubular bells, bass bells, bass drums, custom manufacture of perc insts and touring trolleys.*

Irish Organ Co Ltd. Steeple Rd Industrial Estate, Antrim, Co Antrim BT41 1AB *tel:* 028 9446 7954 *also fax; email:* colin@davidsonc.freeserve.co.uk. *Pipe orgs.*

J P Guivier & Co Ltd. 99 Mortimer St, London W1N 7TA *tel:* 020 7580 2560 *fax:* 020 7436 1461 *email:* violins@guivier.com. *Restorers and dealers of insts, bows and accs of the vn family.*

J W Walker & Sons Ltd. Wimbledon Ave, Brandon, Suffolk IP27 0NF *tel:* 01842 810296 *fax:* 01842 813124 *email:* organs@jwwalker.co.uk. *Pipe orgs.*

J Wood & Sons Ltd. 38 Manningham Lane, Bradford BD1 3EA *tel:* 01274 307636 *fax:* 01274 393516 *email:* sales@earlyms.demon.co.uk. *Orgs, celestas, pnos, keyboards, early w/wind insts.*

Jack Hayward Harps. 5 Sun Gardens, Burghfield Common, Reading RG7 3JB *tel:* 0118 983 3922 *fax:* 0118 983 3868. *Celtic and concert hps, accs, insurance, gut and nylon strings.*

Jacques Samuel Pianos Ltd. 142 Edgware Rd, London W2 2DZ *tel:* 020 7723 8818 *fax:* 020 7224 8692. *Pnos, repairs, removals, sale and hire. Practice rooms.*

John Brinsmead Pianoforte Manufacturers Ltd *see* **Kemble & Co Ltd.**

John Hornby Skewes & Co Ltd. Salem House, Parkinson Approach, Garforth, Leeds LS25 2HR *tel:* 0113 286 5381 *fax:* 0113 286 8515 *email:* info@jhs.co.uk. *Manufacturer, wholesaler and distributor of mus insts, associated accs, inst amplification and pro-audio equipment.*

Keith S Bance. 72 Waverley Rd, Rayners Lane, Harrow, Middx HA2 9RD *tel:* 020 8866 4158. *Organ builders, tonal consultants, voicers.*

Kemble & Co Ltd. Mount Ave, Bletchley, Milton Keynes MK1 1JE *tel:* 01908 371771 *fax:* 01908 270448 *email:* 100601.2045@compuserve.com. *Upright pnos, silent pnos.*

KGB Musical Instruments. 61 Derby Rd, Tranmere, Birkenhead, Merseyside CH42 7HA *tel:* 0151 647 3268 *email:* keith@kgb-music.co.uk. *Guis and fretted insts; parts and accs.*

Langer Piano Actions Ltd. Stapleford Rd, Trowell, Notts NG9 3QE *tel:* 0115 932 1214 *fax:* 0115 932 1215. *Pno actions, keys, spare parts.*

Lodge, J M. Fiddlers Folly, Baughurst Rd, Ramsdell, Basingstoke, Hants *tel:* 01256 850140. *Vn, va, vc, db, gui, bows.*

Lowes Woodwind. 102 Greenwich South St, London SE10 8UN *tel:* 020 8691 6944 *fax:* 020 8694 2503 *email:* jlowe@dircon.co.uk. Jeremy Lowe, proprietor; Michael Edwards, repairer. *Cl mouthpieces, barrels; cl design.*

Lyons Musicale Ltd. The Bourne, 20 Salisbury Ave, Harpenden, Herts AL5 2QG *tel:* 01582 460978 *fax:* 01582 767343 *email:* HMusicale@aol.com. David Johnston, mgr dir. *Lyons 'c' cl, lightweight easy stretch cl for the young beginner.*

McQueens Musical Instruments. Sunset Business Centre, Manchester Rd, Kearsley, Bolton BL4 8RT *tel:* 01204 794600 *also fax. Bugles, cavalry tpts, post horns, herald tpts. Also repairs. Contractors to MOD.*

Makin Organs Ltd. Compton House, Franklin St, Oldham, Lancs OL1 2DP *tel:* 0161 626 5666 *fax:* 0161 665 2284 *email:* david@makinorgans.co.uk. David Clegg, dir and gen mgr. *Classical orgs, digital pnos, MIDI expanders. Also distributors and nationwide hire service.*

Mark Norris Harps. Old School, Stobo, Peebles, Peeblesshire EH45 8NU *tel:* 01721 760298 *also fax; email:* norris.harps@virgin.net. *Non-pedal hps with professional semitone levers.*

Michael Johnson Violin Maker/Restorer/Dealer. Upper Sunnyside, Lowther St, Penrith, Cumbria CA11 7UW *tel:* 01768 864424 *also fax. Vns, vas, vcs, basses and bows. Visitors by appointment.*

The Midland Organ Company. The Manufactory, PO Box 5269, Melton Mowbray, Leics LE13 1WW *tel:* 01664 569208 *also fax; email:* midorgco@telinco.com. Christopher Gray, mgr dir. *Manufacture of chmbr and continuo pipe orgs. Supplier of quality restored historic insts.*

Moeck UK. 38 Manningham Lane, Bradford, W Yorks BD1 3EA *tel:* 01274 721646 *fax:* 01274 393516. *Rcdrs and historical w/wind.*

Monington and Weston Pianos. Robert Morley & Co Ltd, 34 Engate St, Lewisham, London SE13 7HA *tel:* 020 8318 5838 *fax:* 020 8297 0720. Julia Morley. *Upright and grand pnos; also stools.*

N P Mander Ltd. St Peter's Organ Works, St Peter's Square, Warner Place, Hackney Rd, London E2 7AF *tel:* 020 7739 4747 *fax:* 020 7729 4718 *email:* manderuk@compuserve.com. *Pipe orgs.*

Nicholls, Colin. 316 Church Rd, Northolt, Middx UB5 5AP *tel:* 020 8845 1092 *also fax. Vns, vas and vcs.*

Norman Hall & Sons Organ Builders. 39 Sturton St, Cambridge CB1 2QG *tel:* 01223 350516 *also fax.*

Norwich Organs. Bidwell Rd, Rackheath, Norfolk NR13 6LH *tel:* 01603 720360 (24 hrs) *fax:* 01603 720746. *Classical elec orgs.*

Nowak, Steffen. 12 Windsor Terrace, Totterdown, Bristol BS3 4UF *tel:* 0117 977 7141. *Modern and baroque vn, va and vc.*

Oakwood Instruments. 8 Ladywood Rd, Leeds LS8 2QF *tel:* 0113 265 8585 *fax:* 0113 293 3011 *email:* oakwood@magpie.demon.co.uk. *Electric vns, mandolins, mandolas, bouzoukis, citterns, guis, banjos, hammer dulcimers, hps, melodeons.*

Ocarina Workshop. PO Box 56, Kettering, Northants NN15 5LX *tel:* 01536 485963 *fax:* 01536 485051 *email:* ocarina@compuserve.com. *Ocarinas, duet ocarinas, poly-oc, ocarina mus (also m/order).*

The Orchestration Workshop. Springwood Music Workshops, Water St, Huddersfield HD1 4BB *tel:* 01484 422300 *fax:* 01484 305303 *email:* drl@musiclink.co.uk. David R Leach, proprietor. *Mechanical org design, manufacture and restoration, fine wood pipework and perforated card mus.*

Oxley, Jon. 39 Eaton Rd, West Kirby, Wirral L48 3HE *tel:* 0151 625 8613.

Paxman Musical Instruments Ltd. Linton House, 164-180 Union St, London SE1 0LH *tel:* 020 7620 2077 *fax:* 020 7620 1688 *email:* info@paxman.co.uk. *Hns.*

Peavey Electronics Ltd. Great Folds Rd, Oakley Hay, Corby, Northants NN18 9ET *tel:* 01536 461234 *fax:* 01536 747222. *Guis, basses, drums, keyboards, amps and sound equipment.*

Percussion Plus. The Mill, Great Bowden Rd, Market Harborough, Leics LE16 7DE *tel:* 01858 433124 *fax:* 01858 462218. *Perc inst manufacturer and distributor.*

Peter Collins Ltd. 42 Pate Rd, Melton Mowbray, Leics LE13 0DG *tel:* 01664 410555 *fax:* 01664 410535. Peter Collins, mgr dir; Alan Goulding, gen mgr. *Pipe org builders and restorers.*

Peter Conacher & Co Ltd. Springwood Organ Works, Water St, Huddersfield HD1 4BB *tel:* 01484 530053 *fax:* 01484 305303 *email:* admin@musiclink.co.uk. *Orgs, harmoniums, reed orgs; repair, restoration and tuning.*

Phil Parker Ltd (Wholesale). 106a Crawford St, London W1H 1AL *tel:* 020 7723 6909 *fax:* 020 7935 6686 *email:* sales@philparker.co.uk. *W/wind, br, educ strs, gig bags and accs.*

Phil Rees Music Tech. Unit 2 Clarendon Court, Park St, Charlbury, Oxford OX7 3PT *tel:* 01608 811215 *fax:* 01608 811227. Sheila Cantlay, sales mgr; Philip Rees. *Manufacturers of electronic mus accs. Specialists in MIDI.*

Philip Brown Violins. 85a Northbrook Street, Newbury, Berks RG14 IAE *tel:* 01635 35465 *also fax.* Phil Brown. *Sale and manufacture of vns, vcs and vas.*

The Piano Warehouse. 30 Highgate Rd, London NW5 1NS *tel:* 020 7267 9229 *fax:* 020 7284 0083 *email:* rs@piano-workshop.co.uk. *Distributor of Young Chang, Weber, Steinmater, Ritmuller pnos; pno stools.*

Pilgrim Harps. Stansted House, Tilburstow Hill Rd, South Godstone, Surrey RH9 8NA *tel:* 01342 893242 *fax:* 01342 892646 *email:* info@pilgrimharps.co.uk. *Pedal and non-pedal hps.*

Premier Percussion Ltd. Blaby Rd, Wigston, Leics LE18 4DF *tel:* 0116 277 3121 *fax:* 0116 277 6627. *Perc insts and accs.*

R A J Bower & Co. Wellgrove Organ Manufactory, Weston Longville, Norwich NR9 5JJ *tel:* 01603 881189 *fax:* 01603 881222 *email:* rbower@albatross.co.uk. *Orgs, pedal pnos.*

Richard Smith Musical Instruments. 110 The Vale, London N14 6AY *tel:* 020 8882 1580 *fax:* 020 8447 8567 *email:* smithwatkins@rsmi.u-net.com. *Designers and makers of Smith-Watkins tpts, cornets and flugel hns.*

Robert Morley & Co Ltd. 34 Engate St, Lewisham, London SE13 7HA *tel:* 020 8318 5838 *fax:* 020 8297 0720. Julia Morley. *Pnos, hpds, spinets, clvds, virginals and celestes.*

Roger Hansell Violins. Ulshaw House, Coverbridge, Middleham, Leyburn, N Yorks DL8 4PU *tel:* 01969 623048; 01969 624416 *also fax. Vns, vas, vcs; also pegs and fittings. Visitors' centre.*

Roland (UK) Ltd. Atlantic Close, Swansea Enterprise Park, Swansea, W Glamorgan SA7 9FJ *tel:* 01792 702701 *fax:* 01792 700130; 01792 799644 (sales). *Distributor and manufacturer of elec mus insts and computer mus peripherals.*

Rosetti Ltd. 4 Tamdown Way, Springwood Industrial Estate, Braintree, Essex CM7 2QL *tel:* 01376 550033 *fax:* 01376 550042. *Str, br, w/wind, guis, perc, gui accs, amps.*

Rotosound Marketing Ltd. Unit 3b, Morewood Close, Sevenoaks, Kent TN13 2HU *tel:* 01732 450838/9 *fax:* 01732 458994 *email:* jason@rotosound.co.uk. *Strings for gui, bs gui, vn and db and all other str insts.* Rotosound USA, 19000 Lake Rd, Suite 8708, Rocky River, Ohio, 44116, USA *tel:* 001 440 895 9467 *fax:* 001 440 895 9966 *email:* rsusa@gateway.net.

Rushworth & Dreaper Ltd (incorporating Compton Pipe Organs). 72 St Anne St, Liverpool L3 3DY *tel:* 0151 207 5252 *also fax.* Alastair J M Rushworth, chmn and mgr dir. *Pipe orgs; cathedral, church and concert hall.*

Schimmel Pianos. Forsyth Bros Ltd (Distributor), 126 Deansgate, Manchester M3 2GR *tel:* 0161 834 3281 ext 225 *fax:* 0161 834 0630 *email:* forsythmus@aol.com. Kathryn Howard. *Pno.*

Simon Watkin Violins. 2 North Green, Coates, Peterborough, Cambs PE7 2BQ *tel:* 01733 840235 *also fax; email:* scdw@cix.compulink.co. *Vns.*

Sloan Ray Bagpipes. North Tyne Works Wall, Hexham, Northumberland NE46 4DZ *tel:* 01434 681122 *also fax; email:* ray@ray-sloan.com. *Bagpipes, wooden fls, Scottish smallpipes, Irish uilleann pipes, other wind insts.*

Smith-Watkins Brass. 110 The Vale, Southgate, London N14 6AY *tel:* 020 8882 1580 *fax:* 020 8447 8567 *email:* smithwatkins@rsmi.u-net.com. *Designers/makers of tpts, cornets and flugel hns.*

Soar Valley Music. 3 Waldron Court, Prince William Rd, Loughborough, Leics LE11 5GU *tel:* 01509 269629 *fax:* 01509 269206. *Folk inst wholesaler (w/wind, perc), Latin and African perc.*

Solid State Logic Organ Systems. 21-22 Putney Close, Brandon, Suffolk IP27 0PA *tel:* 01842 813813 *fax:* 01842 813802 *email:* organs@solid-state-logic.com. *Elec switching and piston capture systems for the pipe org.*

Stagg, John W. 10 Christmas Steps, Bristol BS1 5BS *tel:* 0117 925 4538 *also fax; email:* johnstagg.bows@tesco.net. *Bow maker and restorer.*

Starfish Designs. Unit 4, Old Ferry Rd, North Ballachulish, by Fort William, Inverness-shire PH33 6SA *tel:* 01855 821429 *also fax; email:* stingray@starfish.f9.co.uk. *Makers and repairers of Celtic hps (26, 31 and 34 string models) and electric bowed insts (Stingray electric vns, vas; Dolphon electric vcs; Orca electric dbs).*

Steinway & Sons (UK). Steinway Hall, 44 Marylebone Lane, Wigmore St, London W1M 6EN *tel:* 020 7487 3391 *fax:* 020 7935 0466. *Pnos.*

Stentor Music Co Ltd. Albert Rd North, Reigate, Surrey RH2 9EZ *tel:* 01737 240226 *fax:* 01737 242748 *email:* stentor@stentor-music.com. *Str, br, w/wind and gui wholesaler.*

Stephen Wessel. Millbrook House, Alhampton, Shepton Mallet, Somerset BA4 6PX *tel:* 01749 860047 *also fax. Fl maker, repairs and alteration.*

Stoppani, George. 6 Needham Ave, Chorlton cum Hardy, Manchester M21 8AA *tel:* 0161 860 7386/256 1173. *Str family insts, db.*

Strings & Things Ltd. Unit 3, 202-210 Brighton Rd, Shoreham-by-Sea, W Sussex BN43 6RJ *tel:* 01273 440442 *fax:* 01273 440278 *email:* strings@stringsandthings.co.uk. *Str, accs.*

Summerfield. 1-2 Vance Court, Trans Britannia Enterprise Park, Blaydon on Tyne NE21 5NH *tel:* 0191 414 9000 *fax:* 0191 414 9001 *email:* summerfield@ashleymark.co.uk. *Guis and fretted insts.*

T W Howarth & Co Ltd. 31-35 Chiltern St, London W1M 1HG *tel:* 020 7935 2407 *fax:* 020 7224 2564 *email:* sales@howarth.demon.co.uk. Nigel Clark, mgr dir. *Cls, obs, ob d'am, ehs, bsns.*

Taylor, Eric J. 17 Orton Drive, Witchford, Ely, Cambs CB6 2JG *tel:* 01353 667422. *Pnos, repairs.*

Technics Musical Instruments. Panasonic UK, Panasonic House, Willoughby Rd, Bracknell, Berks RG12 8FP *tel:* 01344 853177 *fax:* 01344 853389 *email:* emio@mail.panasonic.co.uk. *Elec orgs, digital pnos, keyboards.*

Terry Riley Ocarina Maker. 183 Glen Rd, Oadby, Leicester LE2 4RJ *tel:* 0116 271 9784. *Concert ocarinas and vessel fls using English fingering system.*

Thibouville-Lamy & Co Ltd. Gilbert House, 406 Roding Lane South, (off Woodford Ave), Woodford Green, Essex IG8 8EY *tel:* 020 8551 1282 *fax:* 020 8550 8377. *Importer and wholesaler of mus insts and accs.*

Trevor J James & Co. 4-6 Buckland Rd, Maidstone, Kent ME16 0SL *tel:* 01622 692119 *fax:* 01622 692438 *email:* tjjco@kentnet.co.uk. *W/wind, br and accs manufacture and distribution.*

DON'T BUY A PIANO...
...UNTIL YOU'VE TRIED A
ROLAND DIGITAL PIANO
"We have been delighted with our choice of Roland instruments for our Keyboard Skills Course. We were swayed by the quality of excellent touch and response, as well as the quality of the tone. Week by week, the students and staff are continually persuaded by the musical qualities of these instruments."
DAVID GRAHAM, ROYAL COLLEGE OF MUSIC.
• 3 Year Warranty
• Superb tone quality
• Prices start from £899
• 11 models to choose from
• MIDI and computer interface
• Excellent touch and response
• 2 Headphone sockets for silent practice
• 88 note superior hammer action keyboards
ROYAL COLLEGE OF MUSIC
Roland
THE BEST IN ANY CLASS
For further information about Roland products please call
Roland Customer Service:- 01792 515009
Roland (UK) Limited, Atlantic Close, Swansea. SA7 9FJ.
Visit our web site at http://www.roland.co.uk
Call Roland Customer Service for a free demonstration CD

gentle on strings
gentle on bows
left in a natural state,
made of natural materials
tested for harmful substances
MADE IN GERMANY
Royal Oak
Kolophonium
Rosin
NOT AGRESSIVE TO BOW AND STRINGS
Royal Oak Comp.
Distribution Agency Germany
63768 Hösbach, Siemensstraße 8
Tel. ++49 (0) 60 21/59 27-08
Fax. ++49 (0) 60 21/59 27-09

Tunnicliffe, Brian. 53 Crescent Wood Rd, Upper Sydenham, London SE26 6SA *tel:* 020 8693 7785. *Insts; also bows for vn, va, vc, db and the baroque family of bows.*

Unison Strings. 113 The Custard Factory, Gibb St, Birmingham B9 4AA *tel:* 0121 693 1214 *fax:* 0121 693 0933. David Bruce Johnson; Francois Bignon. *Makers, restorers and dealers of vns, vas, vcs and dbs. Also bows and accs.*

Vincent Bach International Ltd. Unit 71, Capitol Park Industrial Estate, Capitol Way, Edgware Rd, London NW9 0EW *tel:* 020 8358 8800 *fax:* 020 8905 9149 *email:* e-mail@bach.ndirect.co.uk. *W/wind, br, orch str insts and related accs.*

Violectra. 113 The Custard Factory, Gibb St, Birmingham B9 4AA *tel:* 0121 693 0933 *also fax; email:* info@violectra.co.uk. David Bruce Johnson. *Electric vns, vas and vcs handmade to order. 4, 5, 6, and 7 str models.*

W P Williams & Co. 2 Boscombe Mews, Boscombe Rd, Southend on Sea SS2 5JD *tel:* 01702 610981 *fax:* 01702 325049. *Pipe orgs, br shallots.*

Ward, Alan. St Andrews, 27 Plomer Hill, Downley, High Wycombe, Bucks HP13 5JG *tel:* 01494 523371. *Modern and baroque vn, va, vc maker, restorer, repairer.*

Ward & Winterbourn. 75 Alexandra Rd, London NW4 2RX *tel:* 020 8203 2678. *W/wind.*

Wells-Kennedy Partnership Ltd. 85-87 Gregg St, Lisburn, Co Antrim BT27 5AW *tel:* 028 9266 4257 *fax:* 028 9260 3722 *email:* wellskennedy@dnet.co.uk. David H McElderry, dir. *Orgs.*

Welmar Pianos Ltd. 154 Clapham Park Rd, London SW4 7DE *tel:* 020 7978 2444 *fax:* 020 7978 2347. *Pnos.*

Whelpdale, Maxwell & Codd Ltd. 154 Clapham Park Rd, London SW4 7DE *tel:* 020 7978 2444 *fax:* 020 7978 2347. *Pnos. Also manufacture under the names of Welmar, Marshall and Rose, Knight, Broadwood, Bentley, and distributor for Blüthner, Haessler and Eavestaff.*

Wood of Huddersfield. St Andrews Rd, Huddersfield, W Yorks HD1 6RZ *tel:* 01484 533374 *also fax; email:* woodorgan@huddersfield11.freeserve.co.uk. Philip Wood, David Wood. *Org builders.*

Wooderson, Andrew. 5 Bourne Rd, Bexley, Kent DA5 1LG *tel:* 01322 558326/525558 *also fax. All types of hpds, spinets, virginals, clvds, early pnos; also tuning, maintenance, restoration, repairs and hire.*

Woolrich, A P. Canal Side, Huntworth, Bridgwater, Somerset TA7 0AJ *tel:* 01278 663020 *fax:* 01278 663913 *email:* apw@ap-woolrich.co.uk. *Manufacturer of ironmongery for keyboard insts.*

Wyvern Classical Organs Ltd. Station Rd, Chobham, Woking, Surrey GU24 8AQ *tel:* 01276 856363 *fax:* 01276 855241. *Orgs.*

Yamaha-Kemble Music (UK) Ltd. Sherbourne Drive, Tilbrook, Milton Keynes MK7 8BL *tel:* 01908 366700 *fax:* 01908 368872. *Br, w/wind, elec keyboards, hi-tech, pro audio, pnos, guis, cymbals and drums.*

REID-SOHN PIANOS

As chosen by the UK's leading music colleges, schools and universities

including:
Royal Academy of Music, London
Christ College, Cambridge
Surrey University
Saint Peters School, York
City of London School
Sevenoaks School, Kent
Kings College, Cambridge
Stallbridge County Primary School
Hazelwood School, Surrey
Yarlet Hall, Staford
Truro High School, Truro
Saint Catherines College, Cambridge
Royal Alexander & Albert School, Surrey
Ipswich Preparatory School, Ipswich
Saint Anthony's Convent School, Ipswich
Temple Primary School, Dorset
Hazelwood School, Surrey
Newbold College, Berkshire
Tremough Convent School, Cornwall
Grove Primary School, Lowestoft
Saint John's College, Cambridge

UPRIGHT & GRAND PIANOS CAN BE VIEWED AT GOOD MUSIC SHOPS THROUGHOUT THE UK.
FOR DETAILS OF YOUR NEAREST STOCKIST TEL: 0181 800 6907

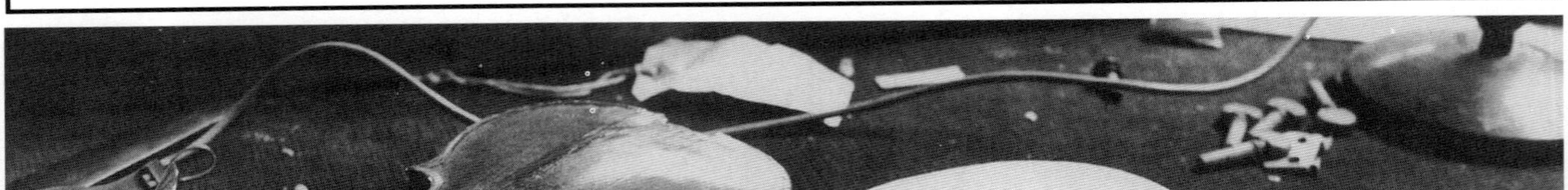

56 Lammas Park Road, Ealing, London W5 5JB • Telephone/Fax 0181-567-3464
(from June 1999 Nat. dialing code changed to 0208)

Early Music Instrument Manufacturers

This list of manufacturers of instruments for early music and authentic performance is divided into five broad categories: strings (bowed and plucked instruments); wind (woodwind and brass); keyboard (harpsichord, organ, etc); percussion; materials. Different manufacturers often use different spellings for particular instruments. To avoid confusion, spelling has been standardised in the entries below.

Strings

Ancestral Instruments. Tudor Lodge, Pymoor Lane, Pymoor, nr Ely, Cambs CB6 2EE *tel:* 01353 698084 *email:* ancestral@cambs.net. David Marshall. *Medieval fiddles, rebec, tromba marina, citole.*

Attwood, Merion David. 16a Queens Rd, Berkhamsted, Herts HP4 3HU *tel:* 01442 878019 *email:* instruments@merion.co.uk. *Viols, vns, bows.*

Baker, Paul. 21 Oakfield Ave, Kingswinford, W Midlands DY6 8HJ *tel:* 01384 295210 *email:* paul@diabolus-in-musica.freeserve.co.uk. Paul Baker, David Jarratt-Knock. *Medieval and renaissance plucked and bowed strs, natural tpts, cornetti.*

Batov, Alexander. 18 Devonshire Place, Brighton BN2 1QA *tel:* 01273 684781. *Lutes, viols, baroque and modern vns. Also restoration and repair.*

Border Harps. Waterloo Cottages, Letton, Hereford HR3 6DN *tel:* 01544 327352 *also fax.* M C Saunders, S R Saunders, partners. *Non-pedal hps, hp kits, parts and strings.*

Bowers, Martin. 101 Wantz Rd, Maldon, Essex CM9 5DD *tel:* 01621 853376. Martin Bowers, proprietor. Chitarrones, theorbos, archlutes, liuto attiorbato, renaissance and baroque lutes, guis, vn family, oud. Repairs and restorations.

Brescia Viols. Eastwood Lodge, Mathern, Chepstow NP16 6HY *tel:* 01291 623012 *email:* evolutionarts@compuserve.com. Dominic Shann, bow maker, Jenny Shann, viol maker. *Student viols and bows.*

Bridgewood, Gary D. 146 Stoke Newington Church St, London N16 0UA *tel:* 020 7249 9398 *fax:* 020 7275 9330 *email:* ViolinsBN@aol.com. *Vas da gamba, violones, baroque vns, vcs, etc.*

Cohen, Brian. Soundpost, The Old Glassworks, Alexandra Place, Guildford GU1 3QH *tel:* 01483 456422 *also fax; email:* strings@soundpost.co.uk. *Guis, lutes, violas da gamba, vns, vcs.*

Coltman, Matthew. 153 Acton Lane, Chiswick, London W4 5HN *tel:* 020 8742 7934 *also fax.* Andrew Riley, vn maker. *Bowmaker, specialising in baroque and classical. Also strings and accs. M/order.*

Demetriou, Andrew. 39 Chatsworth Rd, Brighton BN1 5DA *tel:* 01273 550055. *Guis.*

Doe, Roger. Mount St Laurence, High St, Cranbrook, Kent TN17 3EW *tel:* 01580 712330. *Bows for baroque and classical insts, including viols.*

Early Music Shop. 38 Manningham Lane, Bradford BD1 3EA *tel:* 01274 393753 *fax:* 01274 393516 *email:* sales@earlyms.demon.co.uk. *Viol family, lutes, psalteries (bowed, plucked), medieval fiddles, hourglass dulcimers, hps, hurdy-gurdies; also available in kit form.*

Edgar, Alan. Northwood, 43 Beverley Rd, Hessle, E Yorks HU13 9AE *tel:* 01482 640330. *Small hps, mus stands.*

Edwards, David Van. The Smokehouse, 6 Whitwell Rd, Norwich, Norfolk NR1 4HB *tel:* 01603 629899 *email:* vanedwar@dircon.co.uk. *Medieval, renaissance and baroque lutes, chitarrones and theorbos, renaissance and baroque bows for vn, va da gamba inst families.*

Ellis, Bernard. The Forge, Wigmore, nr Leominster, Herefords HR6 9UA *tel:* 01568 770462 *fax:* 01568 770505 *email:* ellisium@mcmail.com. Bernard Ellis, Megan Ellis, partners. *Medieval to baroque strs, plucked and bowed.*

Eyland, Robert. 6 Birchwood Close, Totnes, Devon TQ9 5GB *tel:* 01803 864040 *fax:* 01803 868014. Robert Eyland, luthier. *Vas da gamba, violones, baroque dbs and vcs.*

Fleming, Michael. 13 Upland Park Rd, Oxford OX2 7RU *tel:* 01865 512807 *also fax. Viols (wide range, especially early 17th C English), vn family (16th-17th C), viol maintenance and restoration or conservation, fixed-frog and other bows.*

Forrester, Peter S. Sunflower House, 20 Beechwood Ave, Aylmerton, Norfolk NR11 8QQ *tel:* 01263 837711. *Early guis, citterns, bandoras, orpharions, mandores, lutes and associated, more exotic, plucked strs.*

Frood, Roger. Dove Workshops, Barton Rd, Butleigh, Glastonbury, Somerset BA6 8TL *tel:* 01458 850682 *also fax. Hammered dulcimers and accs.*

Glover, Marcel. Norton Cottage, Colchester Rd, Wivenhoe, Colchester, Essex CO7 9HT *tel:* 01206 826342 *email:* marcelg@aspects.net. *Rebec, psaltaries, fiddles, pochettes.*

Hadaway, Robert. Cwm Meiarth, Bwlch-Llan, Lampeter, Dyfed SA48 8QR *tel:* 01974 821248. Robert Hadaway, luthier, hp maker and organologist. *Renaissance and baroque str insts, special and unusual insts, single and chromatic hps, bandora family, lutes, citterns, lyra, renaissance and early baroque viols, fidel, rebec, crwth, early vns, lectures and consultancy.*

Haycock, Martin. 2 Charlton Mill, Charlton, Chichester, W Sussex PO18 0HY *tel:* 01243 811545. *Lutes.*

Heale, Michael. 8 Pit Farm Rd, Guildford, Surrey GU1 2JH *tel:* 01483 563096 *also fax. Baroque and modern str insts (va da gamba, hpd), restoration.*

Jack Hayward Harps. 5 Sun Gardens, Burghfield Common, Reading RG7 3JB *tel:* 0118 983 3922 *fax:* 0118 983 3868. *Celtic hps, hp strings, accs, insurance.*

Jones, Lewis. 18 Mare St, London E8 4RT *tel:* 020 8533 6404 *also fax. Hps, other medieval and renaissance str insts.*

Julier, Jane. Old Trickey's Farmhouse, Blackborough, Devon EX15 2HZ *tel:* 01823 681012 *also fax. Vas da gamba.*

Maynard, Bryan. Teviot House, Fishers Brae, Coldingham, Berwickshire TD14 5NJ *tel:* 01890 771235. *Renaissance and baroque vns, vas, vcs, viols and violones.*

Northern Renaissance Instruments. 6 Needham Ave, Chorlton cum Hardy, Manchester M21 8AA *tel:* 0161 881 8134 *also fax; email:* post@nrinstruments.demon.co.uk. E and Y Segerman, partners. *Medieval, renaissance, baroque lutes, guis, mid-16th C and Jacobean viols, va d'am, citterns, bandoras, strs and varnish materials.*

Nowak, Steffen. 12 Windsor Terrace, Totterdown, Bristol BS3 4UF *tel:* 0117 977 7141 *email:* steffen@nowakviolins.free-online.co.uk. *Vn, va, vc, baroque and modern.*

O'Kelly, Joseph M. 2 Middleton Rd, London E8 4BL *tel:* 020 7254 7074 *also fax; email:* boxes@globalnet.co.uk. *Baroque lutes and guis, ouds, theorbos, vihuelas, chitarrones, calasciones. Also restoration.*

Oakwood Instruments. 8 Ladywood Rd, Leeds LS8 2QF *tel:* 0113 265 8585 *fax:* 0113 293 3011 *email:* oakwood@magpie.demon.co.uk. Martyn Banks, dir. *Hps, hammer dulcimers, guis, citterns, mandolins, banjos, bouzoukis, mandolas.*

Pilgrim Harps. Stansted House, Tilburstow Hill Rd, South Godstone, Surrey RH9 8NA *tel:* 01342 893242 *fax:* 01342 892646. *Non-pedal and pedal hps, accs. Insurance.*

Plant, Michael. The Coach House, Monyash Rd, Bakewell, Derbys DE45 1FG *tel:* 01629 815294. *Viols.*

Robb, Arthur. 79 Gloucester Rd, Malmesbury, Wilts SN16 0AJ *tel:* 01666 822945 *email:* artlute@argonet.co.uk. *Renaissance lutes.*

Rose, Roger. West Dean Musical Inst Workshop, c/o West Dean College, Chichester, W Sussex PO18 0QZ *tel:* 01243 811301/818235. *Viols, baroque vns, vcs and bows.*

Stoppani, George. 6 Needham Ave, Chorlton cum Hardy, Manchester M21 8AA *tel:* 0161 860 7386 (w/shop); 0161 256 1173 (home). *Period vns, vas, vcs, bass vns, violones. Gut str for period insts.*

Tunnicliffe, Brian. 53 Crescent Wood Rd, Upper Sydenham, London SE26 6SA *tel:* 020 8693 7785. *Bowmaker for vn, va, vc and db, and the baroque family of bows.*

Ward, Alan. St Andrews, 27 Plomer Hill, Downley, High Wycombe, Bucks HP13 5JG *tel:* 01494 523371. *Baroque and modern vns, vas, vcs. Also restoration and repairs.*

MORLEY

Robert MORLEY Co Ltd

020•8318•5838

http://www.yell.co.uk/sites/morley

John Morley Clavichords, Spinets, Harpsichords, Virginals & Celestes

Antique, Modern & New, Rental, Repairs, Sales lists & colour brochures on request.

Grand & Upright Pianos by Elysian, Grotrian-Steinweg, Bechstein, Monington & Weston and other famous makers.

Robert **MORLEY** *& Co Ltd.*
Piano & Harpsichord Makers
Established 1881

34 ENGATE St. LONDON SE13 7HA

ROBIN JENNINGS

Chamber & Continuo
Organ Builder

Instruments built to
individual specifications

The English Organ Museum Workshop
83 Church Street
Milborne Port, Sherborne
Dorset DT9 5DJ

Telephone & Fax: 01963 250999
E-mail: robin@jennings-organs.co.uk
Web Site: www.jennings-organs.co.uk

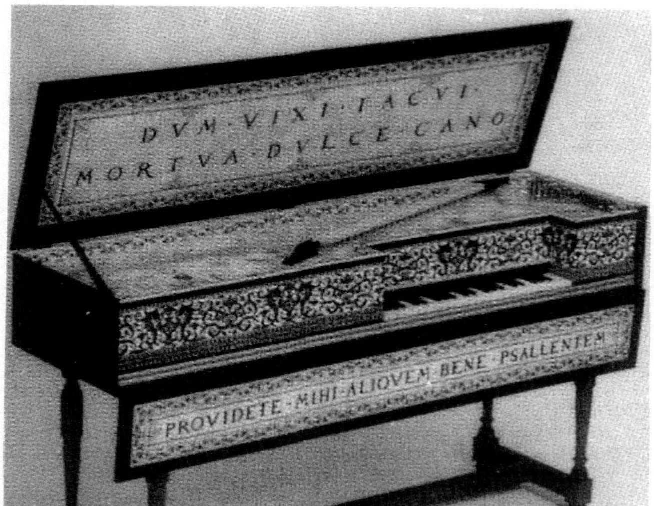

D. Jacques Way & Marc Ducornet
facteurs de clavecins

Zuckermann Harpsichords, Inc.
Kits for all early keyboard instruments

For full colour brochure and prices, contact
Malcolm Greenhalgh
48 Lordship Park, London N16 5UD
Tel/Fax: 0181 800 6176

EARLY BRASS

- *English & German Baroque Trumpets*
- *English Flatt Trumpets*
- *Medieval Straight Trumpets*
- *Alto, Tenor & Bass Sackbutts*
- *Sackbutt in A*

All instruments feature bells made by traditional methods and utilise the acoustic principles of the period to re-create, as near as possible, the original sound.

Full details on request from:
FRANK TOMES
25 CHURCH PATH
MERTON PARK
LONDON SW19 3HJ. U.K.
telephone: 0181-542 4942

Brass instrument maker for the late Christopher Monk

Wind

Ackerman, Brian. 70 Portland Rd, Hove, E Sussex BN3 5DL *tel:* 01273 702444 *also fax; email:* ackerman@mistral.co.uk. *Cls (also mouthpieces), fls, chalumeaux.*

Ancestral Instruments. Tudor Lodge, Pymoor Lane, Pymoor, nr Ely, Cambs CB6 2EE *tel:* 01353 698084 *email:* ancestral@cambs.net. David Marshall. *Reedpipes, hornpipes, medieval and renaissance bagpipes, small shawms.*

Browning, Stephen. 28 Lawrence Close, Basingstoke, Hants RG24 9DP *tel:* 01256 461507. *Cornetts.*

Christopher Monk Instruments. Workshop 4, 30-32 Devonshire Rd, London SE23 3SR *tel:* 020 8291 6900 *fax:* 020 8291 0709. Jeremy West, Keith Rogers, Dick Earle, partners. *Cornetts, serpents, baroque obs, 3-hole pipes.*

Dart, Mathew. 45 Bonnington Square, London SW8 1TF *tel:* 020 7735 0479 (home); 020 7787 2614 (w/shop) *email:* mathdart@aol.com. *Baroque fls, bsns, classical bsns.*

Dolmetsch Musical Instruments. Unicorn Trading Estate, Weydown Rd, Haslemere, Surrey GU27 1DN *tel:* 01428 643235 *fax:* 01428 654920 *email:* brian@dolmetsch.com. Brian Blood, mgr and sales dir. *Rcdrs.*

Early Brass. 25 Church Path, Merton Park, London SW19 3HJ *tel:* 020 8542 4942 *fax:* 020 8287 9528. Frank Tomes. *English and German baroque and medieval tpts; sackbutts.*

Early Music Shop. 38 Manningham Lane, Bradford BD1 3EA *tel:* 01274 393753 *fax:* 01274 393516 *email:* sales@earlyms.demon.co.uk. *Crumhorns, cornamuse, racketts, bagpipes (also available in kit form), sordunes, curtals, baroque bsns.*

Gruar, Philip. Brook Cottage, Burton Rd, Holme, via Carnforth, Lancs LA6 1QN *tel:* 01524 781601 *email:* philip@gruar.clara.net. *Northumbrian and Scottish small-pipes, baroque fls; also restoration work.*

Harding, David. 56 Netherton Rd, Appleton, Abingdon, Oxon OX13 5JZ *tel:* 01865 863673. *Serpents.*

Heriot & Allan. 28 Fairfield Green, West Monkseaton, Whitley Bay, Tyne and Wear NE25 9SD *tel:* 0191 251 3845. R A Greensitt, owner; A H Sessoms, asst. *Northumbrian and Scottish small-pipes.*

Jones, Lewis. 18 Mare Street, London E8 4RT *tel:* 020 8533 6404 *also fax. Renaissance transverse fls.*

Julian Goodacre - Bagpipe Maker. 4 Elcho St, Peebles EH45 8LQ *tel:* 01721 722539 *email:* goodacres@cwcom.net. Julian Goodacre, bagpipe maker. *Historical and folk bagpipes: English medieval bagpipes and Leicestershire small-pipes, Cornish double pipes, Scottish bellows, small-pipes, Border bagpipes. Also repairs and restores.*

Lewin, Greg. The Hawthorns, Hawthorn Drive, Wheaton Aston, Staffs ST19 9NG *tel:* 01785 840186 *fax:* 01785 840476 *email:* greg@g0nen.demon.co.uk. *Crumhorns, cornamuse, kortholts, racketts, schreierpfeifen (schryarii), sordunes.*

Lyndon-Jones, G & M. 20 Queen St, St Albans, Herts AL3 4PJ *tel:* 01727 853951. *Curtals (dulcians).*

Moeck UK. 38 Manningham Lane, Bradford BD1 3EA *tel:* 01274 721646 *fax:* 01274 393516. *Crumhorns, cornamuse, dulcians, shawms, cornetts, fls, obs, bsns, racketts, chalumeaux.*

Moulder, A Eric. 175 Buxton Rd, Leek, Staffs ST13 6NF *tel:* 01538 386867 *also fax. Renaissance reed insts, chorist-fagotts, cornamuse, crumhorns, dulcians, (curtals), shawms, rauschpfeifen, etc.*

Recorder and Woodwind Centre. 5 Dorset St, London W1H 3FE *tel:* 020 7935 3339. Jane Vickers, rcdr sales specialist. *Rcdrs, baroque fls, various ethnic wind insts.*

Saunders Recorders. 205 Whiteladies Rd, Blackboy Hill, Clifton, Bristol BS8 2XT *tel:* 0117 973 5149 *also fax.* John Everingham, mgr. *Specialist rcdr dealer.*

Songstone Studios. Fern House, Fern Rd, Buxton, Derbys SK17 9NP *tel:* 01298 26993 *fax:* 01298 79229 *email:* langley@fenetre.co.uk. *Concert ocarinas, polyoc, songstones, spiral didjeridoos.*

Stanley, Barbara. 21 Broad St, Clifton, Beds SG17 5RJ *tel:* 01462 814981 *fax:* 01462 629218 *email:* b.stanley@net.ntl.com. *Baroque bsns, renaissance fls, reeds.*

Theatrum Instrumentorum. 393 Bradford Rd, Huddersfield, W Yorks HD2 2QY *tel:* 01484 427870. John Cousen. *Rcdrs (Virdung and Praetorius), renaissance and baroque fls, chalumeaux.*

Wells, Charles. 32 Manor Rd, Hatfield, Doncaster, S Yorks DN7 6SD *tel:* 01302 846492 *also fax. Renaissance, baroque and classical fls, obs, cls, flageolets, tabor pipes, restoration, repairs.*

Keyboard

Bavington, Peter. Unit B114, 8-10 Creekside, London SE8 3DX *tel:* 020 8694 1477 *email:* peterbav@nildram.co.uk. *Clvds and hpds.*

Bolton, D H. 44 Church Lane, Acklam, Middlesbrough TS5 7EB *tel:* 01642 817097 *fax:* 01642 284178 *email:* dhbolton@cwcom.net. *Custom-built hpds, spinets, virginals, clvds, also in kit form with many components sold separately.*

Booth, Colin. Mount Pleasant, Westbury-sub-Mendip, Wells BA5 1HU *tel:* 01749 870516 *also fax. Hpds, virginals.*

Coad, Lucy. Workshop 3, Greenway Farm, Bath Rd, Wick, nr Bristol BS30 5RL *tel:* 0117 937 4949 *also fax; email:* lucy@squarepiano.demon.co.uk. *Square pno conservation and repairs; wound bass strings.*

Cole, Michael. Little Tatchley, 334 Prestbury Rd, Cheltenham Spa, Glos GL52 3DD *tel:* 01242 517192 *fax:* 01242 570383. *Hpds, f-pnos.*

Dolmetsch Musical Instruments. Unicorn Trading Estate, Weydown Rd, Haslemere, Surrey GU27 1DN *tel:* 01428 643235 *fax:* 01428 654920 *email:* brian@dolmetsch.com. Brian Blood, mgr and sales dir. *Hpds, clvds, spinets.*

Early Keyboard Agency. Heyford Galleries, High St, Upper Heyford, Oxon OX6 3LE *tel:* 01869 232282. Martin, Stuart and Barry Robertson, proprietors. *Hpds, virginals, spinets, clvds, restoration, tuning; specialists in all types of early and modern overspun strs. Humidifiers and dehumidifiers.*

Early Music Shop. 38 Manningham Lane, Bradford BD1 3EA *tel:* 01274 393753 *fax:* 01274 393516 *email:* sales@earlyms.demon.co.uk. *Spinets, clvds, hpds (also in kit form).*

Edgar, Alan. Northwood, 43 Beverley Rd, Hessle, E Yorks HU13 9AE *tel:* 01482 640330. *Hpds, spinets, virginals, clvds, mus stands.*

Garlick, Andrew. Madgeon Wood House, Buckland St Mary, Chard, Somerset TA20 3QF *tel:* 01460 234221 *fax:* 01460 234782. *Hpds, spinets, virginals.*

George Veness Workshop. Stanhope Studio, Donald Way, Winchelsea, E Sussex TN36 4NH *tel:* 01797 225878. Marcus Weeks, pno tuner, technician, restorer. *Clavichord maker and restorer.*

Glover, Marcel. Norton Cottage, Colchester Rd, Wivenhoe, Colchester, Essex CO7 9HT *tel:* 01206 826342 *email:* marcelg@aspects.net. *Virginals.*

Goetze, Martin and Dominic Gwynn. 5 The Tan Gallop, Welbeck Abbey Estate, Worksop, Notts S80 3LW *tel:* 01909 485635 *also fax; email:* gg@creswell.co.uk. *Church and chmbr orgs in period styles; also restoration work.*

Gotto, Alan. 5 Bessemer Rd, Norwich NR4 6DQ *tel:* 01603 620102 *also fax; email:* agotto@dsn.co.uk. *Hpds, virginals, spinets.*

Greenhalgh, Malcolm. 48 Lordship Park, London N16 5UD *tel:* 020 8800 6176 *email:* greenhalgh@gpo.sonnet.co.uk. *UK agents for the Paris Workshop. All early keyboard insts, kits and repairs.*

Handy, Edmund. 5 Bourne Rd, Bexley, Kent DA5 1LG *tel:* 01322 527366; 020 8300 2715. *Square pno restoration; tuning, maintenance of early keyboard insts. Also reconditioning.*

Hellon, Miles F. Unit B114, 8-10 Creekside, London SE8 3DX *tel:* 020 8694 1477. *Hpds, spinets, virginals.*

Hollick, Douglas. 4 Station Cottages, Harby Lane, Stathern, Leics LE14 4HJ *tel:* 01949 861347 *also fax; email:* dwh@globalnet.co.uk. *Hpds, virginals, clvds, also restoration work.*

Huggett, Martin. The Old Library, Stour St, Manningtree, Essex CO11 1BE *tel:* 01206 396354 *also fax. Hpds, clvds, spinets; mus stands, chmbr orgs and harmoniums. Also materials. Specialist artcase pno restorations, including carving, gilding, all art and decorative work, recreated and restored.*

Hugh Craig Harpsichords. Sugarcroft, Lower Southfield Lane, Bosbury, Ledbury, Herefords HR8 1NH *tel:* 01531 640046. *Hpds, spinets, clvds.*

Jennings, Robin. English Organ Museum Workshop, 83 Church St, Milborne Port, Sherborne, Dorset DT9 5DJ *tel:* 01963 250999 *also fax; email:* robin@jennings-organs.co.uk. *Chmbr and continuo orgs, early keyboard insts including keyed glockenspiel.*

John Storrs Workshop. 125 Culham I Site, Culham, Abingdon, Oxon OX14 3DA *tel:* 01865 407085 *also fax; email:* jsw@storrs.demon.co.uk. John Storrs. *Hpds, spinets, clvds, kits.*

Jones, Lewis. 18 Mare St, London E8 4RT *tel:* 020 8533 6404 *also fax. Hpds, spinets, virginals, clvds, clavicytheria, lute-hpds, also specialist restoration work.*

Julia Morley, Robert Morley and Co Ltd. 34 Engate St, London SE13 7HA *tel:* 020 8318 5838 *fax:* 020 8297 0720. Julia Morley, mgr. *Hpds,*

clvds, spinets, virginals, celestes. Also repairs, rentals, sales and restoration work.

Keen, Nicholas. Lamel Towers, 81 Hull Rd, York YO10 3JS *tel:* 01904 411873. *Hpds, clvds, spinets, virginals, f-pnos, pedalboard insts and orgs.*

Leigh-Flanders, Xavier. 4 Carbery Lane, Southbourne-on-Sea, Dorset BH6 3QG *tel:* 01202 428835 *also fax; email:* xl-f@harpsichords.prestel.co.uk. *Hpds, virginals.*

Mackinnon & Waitzman. Early Keyboard Workshop, 85 Cholmley Gardens, Fortune Green Rd, London NW6 1UN *tel:* 020 7431 5507 *fax:* 020 7794 1350. Mimi Waitzman. *Hpds, clvd; also conservation, assessments, repair.*

Mander, N P. St Peter's Organ Works, St Peter's Square, London E2 7AF *tel:* 020 7739 4747 *fax:* 020 7729 4718 *email:* manderuk@compuserve.com. John Pike Mander, mgr dir. *Portatives, regals, chmbr orgs, pipe orgs.*

Minns, Michael. 22a Davenant Rd, Oxford OX2 8BX *tel:* 01865 556368 *fax:* 01865 316876 *email:* michael@minnsox.freeserve.co.uk. *Hpds, spinets, virginals.*

Mitchell, William. 4 Carbery Lane, Southbourne-on-Sea, Dorset BH6 3QG *tel:* 01202 428835 *also fax; email:* wm@harpsichords.prestel.co.uk. *Hpds, virginals, claviorganum.*

Nimblejack Ltd. 24 Alexandra Rd, Windsor, Berks SL4 1HN *tel:* 01753 853724. Alan Whear. *Portable clavicytheria, hpd maintenance, gen inst repairs.*

Peter Collins Ltd. 42 Pate Rd, Melton Mowbray, Leics LE13 0DG *tel:* 01664 410555 *fax:* 01664 410535. Peter Collins, mgr dir; Alan Goulding, gen mgr. *New pipe orgs of all sizes, restoration; continuo org for hire.*

R A J Bower & Co. Wellgrove Organ Manufactory, Weston Longville, Norwich NR9 5JJ *tel:* 01603 881189 *fax:* 01603 881222 *email:* rbower@albatross.co.uk. *Early orgs, practice orgs, continuo orgs, church and chmbr orgs, pipe orgs.*

Ransom, Mark. 130 Westbourne Terrace Mews, London W2 6QG *tel:* 020 7723 9650 *also fax. Hpds, virginals, spinets.*

Richter, Karin. The Workshop, English Passage, Lewes, E Sussex BN7 2AP *tel:* 01273 481010 *also fax. Clvds, restoration of keyboard insts.*

Robert Deegan Harpsichords. Tonnage Warehouse, St Georges Quay, Lancaster LA1 1RB *tel:* 01524 60186 *also fax.* Robert Deegan, proprietor. *Hpds, virginals, spinets, clvds. Also concert hire, tuning, maintenance, restoration and repairs.*

Robert Goble & Son Ltd. Greatstones, Kiln Lane, Headington, Oxford OX3 8HQ *tel:* 01865 761685 *also fax.* Edward Goble, dir. *Hpds, spinets.*

Robert Shaftoe Organbuilder. 58 High St, Pavenham, Bedford MK43 7PE *tel:* 01234 823609 (evenings). Robert Shaftoe. *Orgs, spinets.*

Rogers, Sandy. Warren House, Stone St, Faversham, Kent ME13 8PS *tel:* 01795 532437. *Hpd, clvd (insts and kits).*

Rose, Malcolm. The Workshop, English Passage, Lewes, E Sussex BN7 2AP *tel:* 01273 481010 *also fax. Hpd maker, repairer and conservator. Maker of iron and brass wires for keyboard insts up to 1850.*

Temple, Alex. Platt Lodge, 61 Barton Rd, Worsley, Manchester M28 2GX *tel:* 0161 794 3717 *email:* alextemple@compuserve.com. *Hpds, clvds; also hire and maintenance.*

W P Williams & Co. 2 Boscombe Mews, Boscombe Rd, Southend-on-Sea, Dorset SS2 5JD *tel:* 01702 610981 *fax:* 01702 352049. Robin Stannard. *Pipe orgs, reeds and shallots.*

Wells-Kennedy Partnership Ltd. 85-87 Gregg St, Lisburn, Co Antrim BT27 5AW *tel:* 028 9266 4257 *fax:* 028 9260 3722 *email:* wellskennedy@dnet.co.uk. David H McElderry, dir. *Chmbr orgs and pipe orgs.*

Whale & Martin. 156 Broadgate, Weston Hills, Spalding, Lincs PE12 6DQ *tel:* 01406 380731. *Hpds, clvds.*

Wooderson, Andrew. 5 Bourne Rd, Bexley, Kent DA5 1LG *tel:* 01322 558326/525558 *also fax. All types of hpds, spinets, virginals, clvds, early pnos; also tuning, maintenance, restoration, repairs and hire.*

Woolley, Dennis. Tubhole Barn, Dent, Sedbergh, W Riding, Yorks LA10 5RE *tel:* 01539 625361. *F-pno, hpd.*

Percussion

Early Music Shop. 38 Manningham Lane, Bradford BD1 3EA *tel:* 01274 393753 *fax:* 01274 393516 *email:* sales@earlyms.demon.co.uk. *Timbrels, tabors, nakers, drums and timpani (also in kit form).*

Glover, Marcel. Norton Cottage, Colchester Rd, Wivenhoe, Colchester, Essex CO7 9HT *tel:* 01206 826342 *email:* marcelg@aspects.net. *Nakers, tabors, triangles.*

Materials

Aubrey, A B. The Willows, Crudwell, Malmesbury, Wilts SN16 9EL *tel:* 01666 577451 *also fax. Specialist in boxwood and blackwood for mus inst makers.*

Huggett, Martin. The Old Library, Stour St, Manningtree, Essex CO11 1BE *tel:* 01206 396354 *also fax. All early keyboard insts, clvd, hpd, spinet, org and harmonium. Specialist inlaying and marquetry, high-class cabinet making, mus stands.*

Woolrich, A P. Canal Side, Huntworth, Bridgewater, Somerset TA7 0AJ *tel:* 01278 663020 *fax:* 01278 663913 *email:* apw@ap-woolrich.co.uk. *Ironmongery; tuning hammers, wrest pins, itch pins, hpd stop levers, stop mechanisms, etc.*

Retailers

This list is arranged by county, with Greater London first, followed by England, Channel Islands, Isle of Man, Scotland, Wales and Northern Ireland. Shops listed consist of dealers in printed music and musical instruments. The list does not claim to be exhaustive and excludes multiple stores whose larger branches occasionally stock instruments or accessories. A list of record shops specialising in classical recordings will be found under **Specialist Record Dealers**. Many **Music Publishers** also have a retail counter.

Greater London

Acoustic Centre. 131 Wapping High St, London E1 9NQ *tel:* 020 7265 1366 *fax:* 020 7488 3530. *Acoustic guis, amps, accs, books and videos. Valuations and appraisals, experts on vintage guis.*

All Flutes Plus. 5 Dorset St, London W1H 3FE *tel:* 020 7935 3339 *fax:* 020 7224 2053 *email:* afp@allflutesplus.co.uk. Gavin Tate-Lovery. *Fl specialists; w/wind, mus, rcdrs, repairs, rentals.*

ASM Music. 318a Kennington Rd, London SE11 4LD *tel:* 020 7735 1932 *fax:* 020 7582 6128 *email:* asmmusic@btinternet.com. *Keyboards, hi-tech, home recording, PA equipment.*

Baldrey's Music Centre. 19 Cheam Common Rd, N Cheam, Surrey KT4 8TL *tel:* 020 8337 6283. N F Baldrey, proprietor. *Insts, mus, accs.*

Barbican Music Shop. Cromwell Tower, Silk St, Barbican, London EC2Y 8DD *tel:* 020 7588 9242 *fax:* 020 7628 1080 *email:* barbicanmusic @compuserve.com. *Books, mus, insts, CDs, accs.*

The Bass Cellar. 22 Denmark St, London WC2H 8NA *tel:* 020 7240 3483. *Bs guis, bs amps, effects and accs.*

The Bass Centre Ltd. 131 Wapping High St, London E1 9NQ *tel:* 020 7265 1567 *fax:* 020 7488 3530. *Bs gui, bs amps, accs.*

Bell Percussion Ltd. 6 Greenock Rd, Acton, London W3 8DU *tel:* 020 8896 1200 *fax:* 020 8896 0100. *Percussion retail, hire and repairs. Yamaha 5.5 octave celeste. West London Sibelius Software dealer.*

Blackburn Stringed Instruments. 75 Harrington Gardens, London SW7 4JZ *tel:* 020 7373 2474 *fax:* 020 7373 5141. *Vns, vas, bows, vcs; also restoration and evaluation. Buying and selling of str insts.*

Blanks Music Store. 271-273 Kilburn High Rd, London NW6 7JR *tel:* 020 7624 7777 *fax:* 020 7624 1260. *Guis, amps, drums, sax, fls, mandolins, perc, servicing (within 24 hrs), books, etc.*

Blüthners. 18 Aintree Rd, Perivale, Middx UB6 7LA *tel:* 020 8997 4785 *fax:* 020 8997 6485.

Blüthners. 8 Berkeley Square, London W1X 5HF *tel:* 020 7753 0533 *fax:* 020 7753 0535. J B T Howard, retail sales mgr. *Leading makes of grand and upright pnos (Blüthner, Broadwood, Bentley, Knight, Welmar, Eavestaff); tuning and repairs.*

Blüthners. 154 Clapham Park Rd, London SW4 7DE *tel:* 020 7622 1402 *fax:* 020 7978 2347. *Pnos.*

Books Etc. Royal Festival Hall, Belvedere Rd, South Bank, London SE1 8XX *tel:* 020 7620 0403 *fax:* 020 7620 0426. *Biographies, analyses, histories, libretti, scores.*

Boosey & Hawkes Music Shop. 295 Regent St, London W1R 8JH *tel:* 020 7291 7255 *fax:* 020 7436 2850 *email:* musicshop@boosey.com. *Books, mus, accs; m/order (catalogue), credit cards.*

Bridgewood and Neitzert. 146 Stoke Newington Church St, London N16 0UH *tel:* 020 7249 9398 *fax:* 020 7275 9330 *email:* ViolinsBN@aol.com. *Vn, va, vc, db, bows; maker, restorer and dealer. Strings for period insts.*

Britten's Music Ltd. 136 George Lane, South Woodford, London E18 1AY *tel:* 020 8530 6432. K Moorcraft, mgr. *Mus, insts, accs.*

Bush Books & Records. 113 Shepherds Bush Centre, London W12 8PP *tel:* 020 8740 5342 *fax:* 020 8749 7652. *Books, cassettes, CDs.*

BLACKBURN

stringed instruments
(Established 1969)

75 Harrington Gardens,
London SW7 4JZ

Telephone: 0171-373 2474
Fax: 0171-373 5141
(near to Royal College of Music).

VIOLINS, VIOLAS, 'CELLOS & their bows.

We offer an honourable and dedicated service to musicians throughout the country, from the advancing student of limited financial means to the top professional player.

● ● ●

If you are looking for an instrument of quality, why not try us?

● ● ●

Our service also includes valuations, restorations and repairs of quality, Insurance advice, free approvals.

● ● ●

PLEASE ASK FOR A FREE CATALOGUE.

● ● ●

Please telephone for an appointment in the first instance, evenings and weekends are often available.

Holywell Music Ltd.

For all your musical needs -

Salvi

Harps

Music

Strings

Accessories

LYON & HEALY

BOW BRAND

58 Hopton Street London SE1 9JH
Tel: (020) 7928 8451 Fax: (020) 7928 8284
Email: Holywell@Holywell.co.uk

J. Thibouville-Lamy & Co. LTD

Wholesale Only

Gilbert House, 406 Roding Lane South
Woodford Green, Essex IG8 8EY
Tel: 0181 551 1282 Fax: 0181 550 8377
Telephone orders welcome
Trade callers by appointment

STOCKISTS OF:-
DR. THOMASTIK INFELD

KÜNSTLER-SEIL-SAITEN OTTO INFELD

Dominant Precision
Spirocore Superflex

D'Addario Range of Strings
Helicore – Prelude – Pro Arte
Golden Spiral
Golden Spiral Solo
and Zyex

Super-Sensitive® Musical String Co.

Red Lable, Old Fiddler, Stellar, Sensicore, Supreme and Pinnacle.

Corelli

SAVAREZ

Crystal, Alliance, Consept and Corelli Mini Bass Strings.

WOLF MUSIC PRODUCTS

1886VA	Forte Secondo Viola (new)
1696N	Wolf Forte Primo Violin Rest
1886N	Wolf Forte Secondo Violin Rest
18861/2N	Wolf Secondo Violin Rest 1/2 Size
1698N	Wolf Forte Primo Viola Rest
1697N	Violin/Viola Superflexible
481	Huber Shoulder Pad

SPARE PARTS AVAILABLE
PLAY ON AIR SHOULDER RESTS

510	Deluxe, fits violin and viola
509	Standard, fits violin and viola
508	Junior, fits violin 1/16 - 1/2

KUN SHOULDER REST

492VA	Viola
492 4/4 3/4	Violin 4/4 to 3/4
492 1/2 1/4	Violin 1/2 to 1/4
492 1/8 1/16	Violin 1/8 to 1/16
4929	Violin Grande Collapsible

RESONANS

592	Resonans Violin Shoulder Rests Sizes – 1, 2, 3
593	Resonans Viola Shoulder Rests Sizes – 1, 2, 3

WINTER CASES
VIOLIN, VIOLA AND CELLO CASES MADE IN A NEW MOULD WITH A DIFFERENT HARD WEARING PLASTIC COMPOUND

WITTNER METRONOMES
MAELZEL QUARTZ WOODEN PYRAMID CASING, COMPLETE WITH EARPHONE AND BATTERY. TAKTELL PRELUDE IN BLACK PLASTIC MODERN CASING.

TOP WIND
Telephone: 0171 401 8787
Facsimile: 0171 401 8788
Email: topwind@topwind.com
Website: www.topwind.com

Chandler Guitars. 300-302 Sandycombe Rd, Kew, Richmond, Surrey TW9 3NG *tel:* 020 8940 5874 *fax:* 020 8948 8203 *email:* sales@chandlerguitars.co.uk. *Fretted insts, amps, effects; sales and repairs.*

Chappell of Bond Street. 50 New Bond St, London W1Y 9HA *tel:* 020 7491 2777 *fax:* 020 7491 0133. *Insts, mus, pnos, keyboards, books, school mus.*

Chas E Foote Ltd. 10 Golden Square, London W1R 3AF *tel:* 020 7437 1811 *fax:* 020 7734 3095 *email:* footesdrums@msn.com. *W/wind, br, str and perc.*

Chimes Music Shop. 44 Marylebone High St, London W1M 3AD *tel:* 020 7935 1587/7486 1303 *fax:* 020 7935 0457 *email:* chimesmusic@compuserve.com. Ling Sam, mgr. *Books, insts, mus, CDs, sheet mus (comprises majority of stock), bargain books. Also m/order.*

Discurio. 9 Gillingham St, London SW1V 1HN *tel:* 020 7828 7963 *also fax. Books, records, videos, CDs and LPs; military mus.*

The Drum Cellar. 28 Denmark St, London WC2H 8NJ *tel:* 020 7240 3483. *Acoustic and electric drums, wide range of ethnic perc.*

The Dulwich Music Shop. 2 Croxted Rd, Dulwich, London SE21 8SW *tel:* 020 8766 0202 *fax:* 020 8766 8689 *email:* dulwichmus@aol.com. *Printed mus, books, CDs, cassettes, mus gifts and novelties, insts-exchange, rental, repairs.*

Ealing Strings. 4 Station Parade, Uxbridge Rd, London W5 3LD *tel:* 020 8992 5222/3993. *Books, str insts, accs. Suppliers and restorers.*

Ebony & Ivory. 11 Varley Parade, Edgware Rd, Colindale, London NW9 6RR *tel:* 020 8200 5510 *fax:* 020 8205 1907. *New and second-hand pnos. Concert hire services.*

Electrohill. 124-126 Green Lanes, London N13 5UN *tel:* 020 8886 9426 *fax:* 020 8886 9356 *email:* sales@electrohill.co.uk. *Specialists in guis, amps, effects and PA equipment.*

ENO Shop. MDC Classic Music, 31 St Martin's Lane, London WC2N 4ER *tel:* 020 7240 0270 *email:* classic@mdcmusic.co.uk. James Skeggs, mgr. *Books on opera, dance and ballet. CDs, videos and gifts.*

Eric Lindsey Ltd. 20-22 Rushey Green, Catford, London SE6 4AS *tel:* 020 8690 8621 *fax:* 020 8690 7064. *Guis, drums, keyboards, recording and PA equipment.*

Fazioli. The Music Studios Ltd, 29 Marylebone Lane, London W1M 5FH *tel:* 020 7486 0025 *fax:* 020 7935 8454. *Distributor of Fazioli pnos, retail, restoration of fine makes.*

Frederick Phelps Ltd, Violins. 67 Fortess Rd, London NW5 1AG *tel:* 020 7482 0316 *fax:* 020 7813 4589. Rachel Douglas, dir. *Vns, vas, vcs, accs; also restoration and bow repairs.*

Freedmans Musical Instruments. 631 Leytonstone High Rd, London E11 4PA *tel:* 020 8539 0288 *also fax. Group and electric insts, PA, w/wind insts, guis, amps, books.*

Gigsounds Ltd. 86-88 Mitcham Lane, Streatham, London SW16 6NR *tel:* 020 8769 6496; 0800 092 1410 *fax:* 020 8769 9530. *Electric/acoustic/wind, etc, insts and accs.*

Hampstead Pianos. 133 Abbey Rd, London NW6 4SL *tel:* 020 7624 8895 *fax:* 020 8245 4653. Tom Walter, mgr. *Acoustic pnos, restoration, tuning, removals and unique pno designs.*

Hanks Acoustics. 24 Denmark St, London WC2H 8NE *tel:* 020 7379 1139. *Acoustic and semi-acoustic insts, harmonica specialists.*

Harpsichord Workshop. 130 Westbourne Terrace Mews, London W2 6QG *tel:* 020 7723 9650 *also fax.* Mark Ransom, mgr. *Tuning, repair and renovation, short and long-term hire, insts for sale. Agent for well-known makers.*

Harrods Ltd (Piano and Musical Instruments Department). Knightsbridge, London SW1X 7XL *tel:* 020 7730 1234 *fax:* 020 7225 6565. Jeff Charlton, buyer. *Upright and grand pnos, w/wind and br insts, electric keyboards, sheet mus, guis, hps, hpds, spinets, orgs and accs.*

Hobgoblin Music. 24 Rathbone Place, London W1P 1DG *tel:* 020 7323 9040 *fax:* 020 7323 1606 *email:* london@hobgoblin.co.uk. *Folk and acoustic inst specialist; also CDs, books, mus and repairs.*

Holywell Music Ltd. 58 Hopton St, London SE1 9JH *tel:* 020 7928 8451 *fax:* 020 7928 8284 *email:* holywell@netcomuk.co.uk. David Williams, gen mgr; Rebecca Jones, mus dept. *Salvi and Lyon & Healy concert and non-pedal hps, hp mus, str, recordings and accs.*

Impact Percussion. 120-122 Bermondsey St, London SE1 3TX *tel:* 020 7403 5900 *fax:* 020 7403 5910 *email:* impactperc@msn.com. Paul Hagen, proprietor. *Orch and latin perc and kits; also repairs and hire.*

Islington Music. 6 Shillingford St, off Cross St, London N1 2DP *tel:* 020 7354 3195 *also fax. Sheet mus, books, tapes, accs, gifts, insts sales and hire, m/order.*

Ivor Mairants Musicentre. 56 Rathbone Place, London W1P 1AB *tel:* 020 7636 1481 *fax:* 020 7580 6272. Dennis Drumm, mgr. *Acoustic, classical, electric guis, m/order, repairs.*

J & A Beare Ltd. 7 Broadwick St, London W1 *tel:* 020 7437 1449 *fax:* 020 7439 4520. Peter Beare. *Dealers, restorers and makers of vn, va, vc.*

J P Guivier & Co Ltd. 99 Mortimer St, London W1N 7TA *tel:* 020 7580 2560/7636 6499 *fax:* 020 7436 1461 *email:* violins@guivier.com. Richard White, Robin Hamilton, dirs. *Dealers and restorers of insts and bows of the vn family. Also cases, accs and valuations.*

J Reid Pianos. 184 St Annes Rd, Tottenham, London N15 5RP *tel:* 020 8800 6907 *fax:* 020 8809 0767. *Pnos, repairs, restoration, educ discounts, retail and wholesale supplier.*

Jaques Samuel Pianos Ltd. 142 Edgware Rd, London W2 2DZ *tel:* 020 7723 8818 *fax:* 020 7224 8692. *Agents for Bechstein and Bösendorfer. Concert and show hire, tuning, servicing, transport. Practice rooms.*

Jewish Music Distribution. PO Box 67, Hailsham BN27 4UW *tel:* 01323 832863; 020 8458 0980 *also fax; email:* jmduk@hotmail.com. William Hancox, Noa Lachman, partners. *Suppliers of Jewish and Israeli mus from around the world. CDs, books and sheet mus.*

Kensington Music Shop. 9 Harrington Rd, London SW7 3ES *tel:* 020 7589 9054 *fax:* 020 7225 2662 *email:* kensingtonmusic@compuserve.com. *Mus, books, insts, accs.*

Knightsbridge Pianos. 88 Old Brompton Rd, London SW7 3LQ *tel:* 020 7584 2581. *New and reconditioned uprights and grands for rental or purchase.*

Len Stiles Musical Instruments Ltd. 268 Lewisham High St, London SE13 6JX *tel:* 020 8690 2958; 020 8690 7771 *also fax. Mus, keyboards, digital pnos, synthesizers, orch, group gear, accs, repairs. Digital pnos.*

Les Aldrich. 98 Fortis Green Rd, London N10 3BH *tel:* 020 8883 5631 *fax:* 020 8444 9805 *email:* simon@lesaldrich.demon.co.uk. *Books, insts, mus, classical CDs, tapes, opera videos, inst repairs.*

Lowes Woodwind. 102 Greenwich South St, London SE10 8UN *tel:* 020 8691 6944 *fax:* 020 8694 2503 *email:* jlowe@dircon.co.uk. Jeremy Lowe, proprietor. *W/wind insts, repairs, design. Cl mouthpieces and barrels.*

M and J Healey Violins. 12 Rosehill, Sutton, Surrey SM1 3EU *tel:* 020 8644 4700 *also fax;* 020 8644 3419. *Str insts, accs.*

Macari's Ltd. 92-94 Charing Cross Rd, London WC2H 0BP *tel:* 020 7836 9149 *fax:* 020 7379 8762. *Acoustic and electric guis, strs, amps, br, w/wind, accs.*

Markson Pianos. 36-38 Artillery Place, Woolwich, London SE18 4AB *tel:* 020 8854 4517 *fax:* 020 8317 1076. Judith Parker, mgr. *Pno sales, hire, restoration, tuning, maintenance, transport, concert hire, educ discounts.*

Markson Pianos Ltd. 8 Chester Court, Albany St, London NW1 4BU *tel:* 020 7935 8682 *fax:* 020 7224 0957 *email:* marksonpianos@compuserve.com. *Pno sales, hire, tuning, repairs, restoration, transport; acoustic and electric. 24-hr concert hire service.*

Media Tools. 12 Flitcroft St, London WC2 *tel:* 020 7379 3555 *fax:* 020 7497 0690 *email:* mediatools@co.uk. *Professional and audio-visual equipment.*

Michael White. 11 Queens Parade, Queens Drive, Ealing, London W5 3HU *tel:* 020 8997 4088 *fax:* 020 8566 9379. *W/wind and br sales and repairs.*

Music Sales Ltd. Music Book Centre, 8-9 Frith St, London W1V 5TZ *tel:* 020 7434 0066 *fax:* 020 7439 2848 *email:* music@musicsales.co.uk. *Books, mus, karaoke, interactive MIDI mus software.*

Musical Instruments (Cheltenham). 52 Winchcombe St, Cheltenham, Glos GL52 2ND *tel:* 01242 517635 *fax:* 01242 250794. *Pnos.*

Normans Eltham Music House. 32 Well Hall Rd, London SE9 6SF *tel:* 020 8850 1263. *Books, insts, mus, guis, keyboards, amps, educ insts.*

Paxman Musical Instruments Ltd. Unit B4, Linton House, 164-180 Union St, London SE1 0LH *tel:* 020 7620 2077 *fax:* 020 7620 1688 *email:* info@paxman.co.uk. *Hns, mus, repairs, accs.*

Peter Vel Fine String Instruments and Bows. 164 Camden Rd, London NW1 9HJ *tel:* 020 7813 7981 *fax:* 020 7267 3418 *email:* camden@globalnet.co.uk. *Sales and repairs.*

Peters Music Shop. c/o Boosey & Hawkes, 295 Regent St, London W1R 8JH *tel:* 020 7291 7244. *Stocks mus in Peters Edition and agencies.*

Phelps Pianos. 49 Fortess Rd, London NW5 1AD *tel:* 020 7485 2042 *fax:* 020 7284 1404. *Selection of new, nearly new, second-hand and reconditioned pnos for sale or hire. Tuning, repairs, restoration and free advice.*

Phil Parker. 106a Crawford St, London W1H 1AL *tel:* 020 7486 8206 *fax:* 020 7935 6686 *email:* sales@philparker.co.uk. *Br insts, accs, repairs and mus.*

The Piano Workshop. 30 Highgate Rd, London NW5 1NS *tel:* 020 7267 7671 *fax:* 020 7284 0083 *email:* pw@piano-workshop.co.uk. *Insts, pno specialists (new and restored), sales, hire, restoration and tuning.*

Professional Percussion. 205 Kentish Town Rd, London NW5 2JU *tel:* 020 7485 0822/4434 *fax:* 020 7485 9745. *All areas of perc: drum kits and accs, cymbals, electric drums, tuned, latin and marching perc.*

Protape. 15 Percy St, London W1P 0EE *tel:* 020 7323 0277 *fax:* 020 7580 6852.

Ransom, Mark. 130 Westbourne Terrace Mews, London W2 6QG *tel:* 020 7723 9650 *also fax. Hpds, virginals.*

Ray Man. 54 Chalk Farm Rd, London NW1 8AN *tel:* 020 7692 6261 *fax:* 020 7692 5765. *Eastern mus insts, recordings, tuition, hire.*

Rhodes Music Ltd. 21 Denmark St, London WC2H 8NA *tel:* 020 7240 7696 *fax:* 020 7379 3398. *All mus insts and recording equipment.*

Rhodes Music II. 22 Denmark St, London WC2H 8NA *tel:* 020 7497 1178. *All types of second-hand mus equipment - classic and contemporary.*

Ritz Music Ltd. 3a Lacy Rd, Putney, London SW15 1NH *tel:* 020 8788 5000 *also fax. Drums, perc, guis, amps, books, educ insts and PA.*

Robert Morley & Co Ltd. 34 Engate St, London SE13 7HA *tel:* 020 8318 5838. Julia Morley. *Spinets, virginals, clvds, hpds, pnos; stools, cabinets, mus stands; sales and rental, tuning, repairs. (Catalogue).*

Roka's Musical Instruments. 5 Denmark St, London WC2H 8LP *tel:* 020 7240 2610 *fax:* 020 7836 3257. *Acoustic and electric guis, basses, repairs.*

Rose-Morris London's 6-Floor Music Store. 11 Denmark St, London WC2H 8LS *tel:* 020 7836 0991 (inst); 020 7836 4766 (mus) *fax:* 020 7240 9874. *Acoustic, electric and bs guis; amps, mixers, mus stands, sheet mus, computer accs, cassettes, CDs, harmonicas, keyboards, software, synthesizers, sound libraries, videos.*

Salvationist Publishing and Supplies Ltd. 117-121 Judd St, London WC1H 9NN *tel:* 020 7387 1656 *fax:* 020 7383 3420. *Salvation Army vocal and inst mus.*

Schott/Universal Edition. 48 Great Marlborough St, London W1V 2BN *tel:* 0800 525566 *fax:* 0800 525567 *email:*schottcontemporarymusic @compuserve.com. Eric Forder, mgr. *Classical mus.*

Soho Soundhouse Ltd/Turnkey. 114-116 Charing Cross Rd, London WC2H 0DT *tel:* 020 7379 5148 *fax:* 020 7379 0093 *email:* sales@turnkey.demon.co.uk. *Electric and electronic mus insts. Digital and analogue recording and processing, multimedia, studio supplies, PA equipment, installation.*

Southgate Music Shop. 110 Chase Side, London N14 5PH *tel:* 020 8886 9901 *fax:* 020 8886 3426. Robert Phelps, mgr. *Sheet mus, insts for sale and hire, keyboards, accs and repairs; also second-hand insts.*

Spanish Guitar Centre. 36 Cranbourn St, London WC2H 7AD *tel:* 020 7240 0754 *also fax. Classical and flamenco guis, accs, mus, CDs, tuition.*

Steinway & Sons. 44 Marylebone Lane, London W1M 6EN *tel:* 020 7487 3391 *fax:* 020 7935 0466. G Oakley, mgr dir. *New and refurbished pnos, tuning, rebuilds and repairs, concert hire.*

Supreme Drums. 206-208 Forest Rd, London E17 6JG *tel:* 020 8520 3873 *fax:* 020 8923 9020. *Kit drums, specialists in vintage drums, custom-made concert drums, cymbals, spares, repairs, re-covering.*

T W Howarth & Co Ltd. 31 Chiltern St, London W1M 1HG *tel:* 020 7935 2407 *fax:* 020 7224 2564 *email:* sales@howarth.demon.co.uk. *W/wind, sheet mus, w/wind repairs and accs, inst hire, m/order.*

Talking Book Shop. 11 Wigmore St, London W1H 9LB *tel:* 020 7491 4117 *fax:* 020 7629 1966. *Educational cassettes.*

Top Wind. 2 Lower Marsh, London SE1 7RJ *tel:* 020 7401 8787 *fax:* 020 7401 8788 *email:* topwind@topwind.com. *Fl specialists. Also repairs and suppliers to schools and colleges. Full range of student and professional insts, sheet mus, rentals, books, accs and expert advice.*

Tune Inn. 124-126 St Mildreds Rd, London SE12 0RG *tel:* 020 8698 8743; 020 8698 4446 *also fax. Keyboards, guis, electric equipment, saxs.*

Turnkey. 114-116 Charing Cross Rd, London WC2H 0DT *tel:* 020 7379 5148 *fax:* 020 7379 0093 *email:* sales@turnkey.demon.co.uk. *Hi-tech insts, recording equipment, computers, PC, Macintosh and Acorn computer mus, PA systems, guis, amps, basses, home keyboards and digital pnos.*

Two-5 Music. 25 Denmark St, London WC2H 8NJ *tel:* 020 7836 5354. *Vintage, rare and second-hand insts bought, sold and traded.*

Walthamstow Music. 116 Hoe St, Walthamstow, London E17 4QR *tel:* 020 8520 2163/5448 *fax:* 020 8509 3005 *email:* @walthamstowmusic.demon.co.uk. *Br, w/wind, str, keyboard and hi-tech insts. Sheet mus, repairs, hire.*

Whone, Adam. 86 Mill Hill Rd, London W3 8JJ *tel:* 020 8992 0619 *fax:* 020 8992 8891 *email:* awhonevns@aol.com. *Vn restorers, makers and experts. Also vas, vcs and bows.*

World of Pianos. 8 Denmark St, London WC2H 8LP *tel:* 020 7240 5555 *fax:* 020 7379 3398. *Digital pnos, mus software, home keyboards, br and w/wind insts.*

England

Bath and North East Somerset

Bath

Bath Music Centre Ltd. 20-22 Monmouth Place, Bath BA1 2AY *tel:* 01225 335154. *Insts, sheet mus.*

C Milsom & Son Ltd/Duck Son & Pinker Ltd. Northgate, Bath BA1 5AS *tel:* 01225 465975 *fax:* 01225 316750. *Books, insts, mus, recordings, hi-fi.*

Duck Son & Pinker Ltd. 9-12 Bridge St, Pulteney Bridge, Bath BA2 4AU *tel:* 01225 465975 *fax:* 01225 316750. *Insts, books, recordings.*

Bedfordshire

Biggleswade

Lindsay Music. 23 Hitchin St, Biggleswade, Beds SG18 8AX *tel:* 01767 316521 *fax:* 01767 317221 *email:* sales@lindsaymusic.co.uk. *Books, mus, accs (strs, reeds, etc), mus gifts.*

Kempston

Tema Music. 34-36 High St, Kempston, Beds MK42 7AL *tel:* 01234 856465 *also fax. Insts, mus, accs.*

Leighton Buzzard

Graham Webb Music. 6-8 Bridge St, Leighton Buzzard, Beds LU7 7AL *tel:* 01525 376622 *fax:* 01525 850628 *email:* grahamwebbmusic @clara.co.uk. *Books, insts, keyboards, orgs, guis, mus, accs; also servicing and m/order.*

Berkshire

Langley

Guitar Centre. 126 Meadfield Rd, Langley, Berks SL3 8JF *tel:* 01753 542720 *also fax. All mus insts, recording equipment and rehearsal studio, PA and mus hire service, pnos.*

Maidenhead

Dawkes Music Ltd. 652 Bath Rd, Taplow, nr Maidenhead, Berks SL6 0NZ *tel:* 01628 604407/4 *fax:* 01628 604336 *email:* sales@dawkes.co.uk. *Wind insts (w/wind, sax specialists, br) and repairs.*

Just Woodwind. Basement, 40 Queen St, Maidenhead, Berks SL6 1HZ *tel:* 01628 674707. *Mus, insts, ABRSM exam mus, US jazz educ books and recordings.*

Sheargold Pianos Ltd. 53 King St, Maidenhead, Berks SL6 1DU *tel:* 01628 771400 *fax:* 01628 771483 *email:* graham@sheargold.demon.co.uk. *New and second-hand pnos, digital pnos, pno hire, sheet mus. Removals, tuning, part-exchange, 0% credit.*

Sound of Music. The Bishop Centre, Taplow, Maidenhead, Berks SL6 0NY *tel:* 01628 661155 *also fax. Elec orgs and keyboards, digital pnos, mus repairs.*

Windcraft Ltd. Riverside, Mill Lane, Taplow, Maidenhead, Berks SL6 0AA *tel:* 01628 778377 *fax:* 01628 777466 *email:* sales@windcraft.co.uk. *Wind inst spares, accs (m/order), repair materials and tools.*

Newbury

Hogan Music. 3 Craven Rd, Newbury, Berks RG14 5NG *tel:* 01635 37868 *fax:* 01635 524595 *email:* hoganmusic@compuserve.com. *Educ mus insts, accs; specialist gui amps; PA equipment; sheet mus; pedal steel gui specialists.*

Reading

Hickies Ltd. 153 Friar St, Reading RG1 1HG *tel:* 0118 957 5771 *fax:* 0118 957 5775. *Insts, pnos, restorations, mus, CDs.*

Sandhurst

In Tune Music. 410-412 Yorktown Rd, College Town, Sandhurst, Berks GU47 0PR *tel:* 01276 34800. *Guis, amps, all types of trad insts. Exam mus and mus albums.*

Bristol, City of

Bristol

Arnolfini/Bristol. 16 Narrow Quay, Bristol BS1 4QA *tel:* 0117 929 9191 *fax:* 0117 925 3876. *Books, art magazines, jewellery, cards.*

Bristol Music Shop. 30 College Green, Bristol BS1 5TB *tel:* 0117 929 0390 *also fax. Orch insts, keyboards, mus, restorations, MIDI songfiles, accs.*

Bristol Musical. 88 Horfield Rd, Bristol BS2 8EQ *tel:* 0117 929 2758 *also fax. New and used electric guis, basses; accs, equipment, PA systems.*

Bristol Piano Co. 85 Bristol Rd, Whitchurch, Bristol BS14 0PS *tel:* 01275 834141. *New and reconditioned pnos, repairs, rebuilds, tuning, polishing.*

The Bristol Violin Shop. 12 Upper Maudlin St, Bristol BS2 8DJ *tel:* 0117 925 9990 *also fax; email:* sales@bristol-violin-shop.co.uk. *Makers and repairers of bowed str insts; insts bought and sold; accs and specialist str mus; m/order.*

Cremona House Violin Shop. 7 Perry Rd (Park Row), Bristol BS1 5BQ *tel:* 0117 926 4617 *also fax; email:* violins@bigfoot.com. *Richard Bristow. Vns, vcs, vas; repairs; valuations, old insts bought and sold; bows, accs; advice, insurance. Also m/order and sheet mus service (cat).*

The Drumstore. 125 St Georges Rd, Hotwells, Bristol BS1 5UW *tel:* 0117 929 8540. *Specialists in drums and perc.*

Emis. The Old School House, Cossham St, Mangotsfield, Bristol BS16 9EN *tel:* 0117 956 1855 *also fax; email:* sales@emismusic.com. *Keyboards, synths, hi-tech, digital pnos, sheet mus, software.*

Hamilton Caswell Violins. 9-11 Perry Rd (Park Row), Bristol BS1 5BG *tel:* 0117 929 4642. *Vns, vas, vcs, dbs, bows, cases, accs. Free m/order catalogue available. Valuations and insurances.*

Heron Music. 158 Whitehall Rd, St George, Bristol BS5 9BP *tel:* 0117 955 3763. *Guis, amps, basses, PA, accs.*

Hobgoblin Music. 30 College Green, Bristol BS1 5TB *tel:* 0117 929 0902 *fax:* 0117 929 3431 *email:* post@hobgoblin.co.uk. *Specialists in traditional, folk, and acoustic insts: fretted, stringed, pipes, w/wind, free reed, perc. Books, accs, spares and strings.*

Mickleburgh Ltd. 1-9 Stokes Croft, Bristol BS1 3PL *tel:* 0117 924 1151 *fax:* 0117 924 4158. *Insts, pnos, keyboards, mus, pno hire for concerts, pno repairs and tuning.*

Saunders Recorders. 205 Whiteladies Rd, Blackboy Hill, Clifton, Bristol BS8 2XT *tel:* 0117 973 5149 *also fax. Insts, mus, rcdr specialist.*

Spanish Guitar Centre. 103 Coldharbour Rd, Westbury Park, Bristol BS6 7SD *tel:* 0117 942 0479 *fax:* 0117 914 6685 *email:* bristol@ spanish-guitar.co.uk. *Insts, mus, tuition.*

Trevor Jones Brass and Woodwind Ltd. 13 Christmas Steps, Bristol BS1 5BS *tel:* 0117 922 7402 *also fax. Insts, mus, accs, rentals, repairs, m/order.*

Buckinghamshire

Beaconsfield

Rosehill Instruments Ltd. 64 London End, Beaconsfield, Bucks HP9 2JD *tel:* 01494 671717 *fax:* 01494 676428 *email:* rosehillmi@aol.com. *Insts, mus, electronic pnos.*

Strings. 66 London End, Beaconsfield, Bucks HP9 2JD *tel:* 01494 676968. *Str insts; sales, accs, repairs.*

Chesham

Perfect Pitch. 72 The Broadway, Chesham, Bucks HP5 1EG *tel:* 01494 774826 *fax:* 01494 778353. *Mus, insts, repairs, rental scheme, accs.*

Hazlemere

Countrywide Piano Centre Ltd. 194 Penn Rd, Hazlemere, High Wycombe, Bucks HP15 7NU *tel:* 01494 813388 *fax:* 01494 813994. *Pnos (new and second-hand), repairs, tuning, restorations. School, churches, educ discount.*

High Wycombe

Allen Organ Studios (London) Ltd. Trada Business Campus, Stocking Lane, Hughenden Valley, High Wycombe HP14 4ND *tel:* 01494 563833 *fax:* 01494 563546 *email:* sales@allenorgans.co.uk. *Allen classical and theatre orgs.*

Kingfisher Music Company. 909 London Rd, Loudwater, High Wycombe, Bucks HP1 9TB *tel:* 01494 520837. *Guis, amps, drums, PA, recording.*

Percy Prior (Rosehill Instruments) Ltd. 31 The Arcade, The Octagon, High Wycombe, Bucks HP11 2HT *tel:* 01494 443418/448899 *fax:* 01494 463353 *email:* ppriors@aol.com. *Insts, repairs, hi-tech, mus.*

Milton Keynes

Chappell of Bond Street. 21 Silbury Arcade, The Shopping Centre, Central Milton Keynes MK9 3AG *tel:* 01908 663366 *fax:* 01908 606414 *email:* david_meek@chappell-bond-st.co.uk. *Insts, keyboards, studio, PA, mus, CDs, tuning, repairs, hire, pnos.*

Hammond Suzuki (UK) Ltd. 19 Presley Way, Crownhill, Milton Keynes MK8 0ES *tel:* 01908 263990 *fax:* 01908 265955. *Orgs, digital pnos, keyboards, harmonicas, rcdrs.*

Yamaha-Kemble Music Ltd. Sherbourne Drive, Tilbrook, Milton Keynes MK7 8BL *tel:* 01908 366700. David Jones, educ mgr. *Yamaha mus insts, synths, portable keyboards, Clavinova digital pnos, br, w/wind, drums, guis.*

Cambridgeshire

Cambridge

1066 Pianos. 20-22 Pierce Lane, Fulbourn, Cambridge CB1 5DL *tel:* 01223 881691. *Rebuilt grand and upright pnos, rebuilding. Nationwide delivery and estimates.*

Brian Jordan. 10 Green St, Cambridge CB2 3JU *tel:* 01223 322368 *fax:* 01223 302654. *Mus, books, facsimiles.*

Cambridge Music Shop. 1a All Saints' Passage, Cambridge CB2 3LT *tel:* 01223 351786 *fax:* 01223 464178. *Mus, books, facsimiles, insts, m/order.*

Cambridge Pianoforte Centre. 12 Kings Hedges Rd, Cambridge CB4 2PA *tel:* 01223 424007 *fax:* 01223 425599. *Full range of new and previously owned grand and upright pnos.*

Ken Stevens (Music and Instruments). 12 Sussex St, Cambridge CB1 1PW *tel:* 01223 367758 *fax:* 01223 362480 *email:* info@millers.demon.co.uk. *Insts, pnos, keyboards, mus, CDs, cassettes; also school supply specialists.*

Miller's Music Centre Ltd. 12 Sussex St, Cambridge CB1 1PW *tel:* 01223 354452 *fax:* 01223 362480 *email:* info@millers.demon.co.uk. *Insts, mus, records, pnos, orgs, keyboards, school supply specialists, CDs, cassettes.*

Music Village. 86 Mill Rd, Cambridge CB1 2AS *tel:* 01223 316091/324536 *fax:* 01223 353857 *email:* cbridgemu@aol.com.

Reeds Direct Cambridge. Freepost, Cambridge CB2 1YA *tel:* 0800 096 9440 (orders) *fax:* 01223 576231 *email:* shop@reeds-direct.co.uk. *M/order cl and sax reeds.*

Wood, Wind and Reed. Russell St, Cambridge CB2 1HU *tel:* 01223 500442 *fax:* 01223 576231 *email:* shop@wwr.co.uk. *W/wind and br insts and accs, sheet mus; valuations, repairs and restoration, m/order.*

Peterborough

Stamford Music Shop. 4 Cattlemarket Rd, Peterborough PE1 1TW *tel:* 01733 345385 *fax:* 01733 559158. *Mus, insts, repairs, accs, mail order.*

Cheshire

Altrincham

Concert Systems. Unit 4d, Stag Industrial Estate, Atlantic St, Altrincham, Cheshire WA14 5DW *tel:* 0161 927 7700 *fax:* 0161 927 7722. *Sound equipment, PA, repairs, m/order.*

H Wright Greaves Ltd. 11 Goose Green, Altrincham, Cheshire WA14 1DW *tel:* 0161 929 6949 *fax:* 0161 926 8280 *email:* martinwgreaves@h-wrightgreaves.u-net.com. *Mus, books, accs, gifts, m/order.*

Cheadle

Sounds Great. 182 Wilmslow Rd, Heald Green, Cheadle, Cheshire SK8 3BG *tel:* 0161 436 4799 *fax:* 0161 436 1307 *email:* soundsgreat@btinternet.com. *Insts, br, w/wind, guis, amps, keyboards, digital and acoustic pnos, mus.*

Chester

Bookland Music Shop. 12 Bridge St, Chester CH1 1NQ *tel:* 01244 313281 *fax:* 01244 341868 *email:* music@bookland.co.uk. *Printed mus, books, mus gifts, accs.*

Curzon Music (Mail Order). 82b Hough Green, Chester CH4 8JW *tel:* 01244 683457 *also fax. Educ and classical mus, m/order.*

Knutsford

Mostly Music. 28 Carlisle Close, Mobberley, Knutsford, Cheshire WA16 7HD *tel:* 01565 872650 *also fax; email:* mostlymusic@btinternet.com. *M/order books, mus, recordings, tapes, CDs.*

Macclesfield

Macclesfield Organ Centre. 15 Mill Lane, Macclesfield, Cheshire SK11 7NN *tel:* 01625 427062 *fax:* 01625 619507. *Keyboards, digital pnos, orgs, mus insts.*

Margin Music. 3 Market Place, Macclesfield, Cheshire SK10 1EB *tel:* 01625 619013 *fax:* 01625 269015. *Keyboards, guis, br, w/wind, amps, books, accs.*

Stockport

Music Exchange. 9 St Petersgate, Stockport, Cheshire SK1 1EB *tel:* 0161 474 7104. *Insts, mus, accs.*

Warrington

Dawsons Music Ltd. 65 Sankey St, Warrington, Cheshire WA1 1SU *tel:* 01925 632591 *fax:* 01925 417812 *email:* education@dawsons.co.uk. *Books, insts, mus, hi-tech equipment, pnos.*

Cornwall

Camborne

Trevada Music. 9 Chapel St, Camborne, Cornwall TR14 8EF *tel:* 01209 714353 *fax:* 01209 718708 *email:* trevada@netcomuk.co.uk. Also at: 18 Wind St, Ammanford SA18 3DN *tel:* 01269 596607. *Pnos, keyboards, br, w/wind, perc, str, sheet mus, repairs, rental scheme.*

Launceston

Tottle's Music Shop. 30 Westgate St, Launceston, Cornwall PL15 7AE *tel:* 01566 772512. *Books, mus, records; w/wind, br, str, perc insts; gui, amps, orgs, keyboards, pnos.*

Redruth

John Oliver. 33 Fore St, Redruth, Cornwall TR15 2AE *tel:* 01209 216494 *fax:* 01209 213999. *Records, CDs, Laserdisc, cassettes, mus, small insts, accs, videos.*

Truro

Tottles Music Shop. 2 Highshore House, Newbridge St, Truro, Cornwall TR1 2AA *tel:* 01872 278501. *W/wind, br, str insts; mus, orgs, pnos, rental scheme.*

Wadebridge

West Country Accordion Centre. Polmorla House, Polmorla Walk, Wadebridge, Cornwall PL27 7NS *tel:* 01208 812230. *Accordions and folk insts.*

Cumbria

Alston

Jacks, Pipes & Hammers. Bridge View, Garrigill, Alston, Cumbria CA9 3DU *tel:* 01434 381583 *also fax; email:* edjacksph@btinternet.com. *Mus for keyboard, org, vocal, trio sonatas, quadros, solos. Specialists in 17th-18th C mus and books. Publishers of 17th-18th C mus in facsimile.*

Barrow in Furness

The New Kelly's Music Shop. 105 Church St, Barrow in Furness, Cumbria LA14 2HW *tel:* 01229 822973. *Books, mus, guis, br, wind, str, perc, keyboards, accs.*

Brampton

Omega Music. Town Foot Estate, Brampton, Cumbria CA8 1SW *tel:* 016977 3067 *fax:* 016977 41018. *Insts, perc, pno showroom.*

Kendal

Sound of Music. Unit 8, Library Rd, Kendal, Cumbria LA9 4QB *tel:* 01539 721009.

Derbyshire

Chesterfield

C E Hudson & Son Ltd. 5 Market Place, Chesterfield, Derbys S40 1TJ *tel:* 01246 271177 *fax:* 01246 211631. *Keyboards, guis (elec and acoustic), amps, sheet mus, elec pnos; br, w/wind, str insts. CDs, cassettes, videos, records.*

Palfreymans Music. 171 Chatsworth Rd, Chesterfield, Derbys S40 2AU *tel:* 01246 271737. *Keyboards, drums, guis, digital pnos, sheet mus, rcdrs, harmonicas, folk insts, amps. Repairs and hire. Teaching.*

Derby

Chas Foulds & Son (Derby) Ltd. 40 Irongate, Derby DE1 3GA *tel:* 01332 344842/342654 *fax:* 01332 294415. *Pnos, insts, sheet mus, guis.*

Neville Bros. 74 Babington Lane, Derby DE1 1SX *tel:* 01332 290762 *also fax. Guis, amps, br, w/wind, repairs.*

Play It Again Sam. 77-79 Osmaston Rd, Derby DE1 2JH *tel:* 01332 348156 *fax:* 01332 341414. *Keyboards, elec guis, accs, basses, computers, amps, PA.*

Ilkeston

Zebra Muzik. 336 Nottingham Rd, Ilkeston, Derbys DE7 5BD *tel:* 0115 930 8362 *fax:* 0115 944 1936 *email:* 113744.2000@compuserve.com. *Peavey, Marshall, Yamaha, Fender. All leading brands.*

Devon

Barnstaple

Soundpad. Rolle Quay House, Rolle Quay, Barnstaple, Devon EX31 1JE *tel:* 01271 23686 *also fax. Guis, amplification, perc, keyboards, disco, lighting, recording equipment.*

Exeter

Bill Greenhalgh Ltd. 125-127 Fore St, Exeter EX4 3JQ *tel:* 01392 430008. *Insts, keyboards, mus, pnos, amps.*

LMS Music Supplies. 154 Sidwell St, Exeter EX4 6RT *tel:* 01392 428108 *fax:* 01392 412521 *email:* lmsmusic@compuserve.com. *Educ m/order mus insts and books.*

Music Lines. 1 Bartholomew St West, Exeter EX4 3AJ *tel:* 01392 433748 *also fax. Sheet mus and m/order.*

Exeter Music Shop. 154 Sidwell St, Exeter EX4 6RT *tel:* 01392 436258 *fax:* 01392 438447. *Mus, books, orch insts, keyboards, pnos, orgs, guis, accs, tuition, m/order.*

Newton Abbot

Rossner Pianos. Shute House, Denbury, Newton Abbot, Devon TQ12 6EB *tel:* 01803 813149.

Plymouth

Make Music. 423 Crown Hill Rd, West Park, Plymouth, Devon PL5 2LJ *tel:* 01752 364900.

South Molton

Studio Music Shop. 5 East St, South Molton, Devon EX36 3BU *tel:* 01769 574346 *also fax.*

Tavistock

Maestros (including Mainly Music). 19 Market St, Tavistock, Devon PL19 0DE *tel:* 01822 614074. *Insts, books, repairs, accs, m/order.*

Torquay

Soundpad - Torquay. 65 Market St, Torquay TQ1 3AW *tel:* 01803 295488.

Capital Mamba (Gig). PO Box 158, Torquay, Devon TQ2 5NZ *tel:* 01803 299493. *Custom-made covers and soft cases for insts and accs.*

Dorset

Bournemouth

Eddie Moors Music Ltd. 679 Christchurch Rd, Boscombe, Bournemouth, Dorset BH7 6AE *tel:* 01202 395135 *fax:* 01202 397622. *Hi-tech*

recording studio equipment, classical insts, perc, keyboards, digital pnos.

Poole

Achille Roma. 456 Ashley Rd, Parkstone, Poole, Dorset BH14 0AD *tel:* 01202 743654 *also fax. All insts, sheet mus, accs, MIDI, PA equipment.*

Poole Music Centre. Unit 14 Towngate Centre, High St, Poole, Dorset BH15 1ER *tel:* 01202 682700 *fax:* 01202 660755. *Printed mus, Yamaha keyboards and guis, Technics pnos, keyboards and orgs, Casio keyboards, Fender guis and amps; Zoom, Fostek, Gibson and Epiphone guis.*

County Durham

Darlington

Williams. Blackwellgate, Darlington, Co Durham DL1 5HH *tel:* 01325 466224 *fax:* 01325 383644. *Mus, keyboards, pnos, orgs, insts, guis.*

East Riding of Yorkshire

Beverley

Beverley Music Centre. 14 Norwood, Beverley, East Yorks HU17 9EZ *tel:* 01482 881584 *fax:* 01482 867653. *Dealers and restorers of vns, vas, vcs, bows and accs. Br, w/wind, guis. Educ insts. Printed mus. Postal service.*

East Sussex

Battle

Amadeus Performance Equipment Ltd. Great Beech Barn, Kane Hythe Rd, Battle, E Sussex TN33 9QU *tel:* 01424 775867 *fax:* 01424 775866 *email:* info@amadeus-equipment.co.uk. *Mus stands, musician posture chairs, inst racks, portable staging, acoustically designed rehearsal rooms, other performing arts furniture, accs.*

Bexhill

Marten's Music. 15 London Rd, Bexhill, E Sussex TN39 3JR *tel:* 01424 222560 *fax:* 01424 222542. *New and reconditioned pnos, tuning, repairs, keyboards, w/wind, br, strs, mus.*

Brighton

The Brighton Violin Shop Ltd. 131-133 Edward St, Brighton BN2 2JL *tel:* 01273 673200. *Str insts, accs, mus, repairs.*

The Brighton Woodwind and Brass Shop. 131-133 Edward St, Brighton BN2 2JL *tel:* 01273 626012. *W/wind, br, accs, repairs, rentals.*

Music Scene. 90 Western Rd, Brighton BN1 2LB *tel:* 01273 775607. *Insts (clavinovas, keyboards, guis), mus, accs, educ.*

Total Percussion Centre. 102 North Rd, Brighton BN1 1YE *tel:* 01273 698593. *Perc specialists.*

Eastbourne

Bonners Ltd. 31-34 Grove Rd, Eastbourne, E Sussex BN21 4TT *tel:* 01323 639335/645775/639339 *fax:* 01323 649100. *Keyboards, pnos, elec pnos, guis, amps, hi-tech, orgs, drums, br, w/wind, str, PA.*

Seaford Music. 24 Pevensey Rd, Eastbourne, E Sussex BN21 3HP *tel:* 01323 732553 *fax:* 01323 417455 *email:* seafordmus@aol.com. *Mus, educ books, inst accs, classical CDs, cassettes.*

Hastings

B & T Keyboards. 9-10 Claremont, Hastings, E Sussex TN34 1HA *tel:* 01424 434480 *also fax. All mus insts, mus albums, repairs and tuition in all insts.*

Hove

Ackerman and Reynolds. 70 Portland Rd, Hove, E Sussex BN3 5DL *tel:* 01273 702444 *also fax; email:* ackerman@mistral.co.uk. *Specialists in wind and str sales and repairs.*

Lewes

Academy Music incorporating Cornelius Edition. 29 Lansdown Place, Lewes, E Sussex BN7 2JU *tel:* 01273 473278 *also fax. Mus, insts.*

Winchelsea

George Veness. Stanhope Studio, Donald Way, Winchelsea, E Sussex TN36 4NH *tel:* 01797 225878. *Mus stands, clvd and hpd maker.*

Essex

Chelmsford

James Dace & Son Ltd. 33 Moulsham St, Chelmsford, Essex CM2 0HX *tel:* 01245 352133 *fax:* 01245 262841. *Insts, mus, accs, CDs.*

Colchester

Allegro Music. 1 Centurion House, St John's St, Colchester, Essex CO2 7AH *tel:* 01206 579886. *Pnos, orgs, keyboards, insts.*

Axe Music. 95-96 High St, Colchester, Essex CO1 1TH *tel:* 01206 765652 *fax:* 01206 764110 *email:* axe.music@dial.pipex.com. *Guis, amps, recording equipment, accs, cassettes.*

Mann's Music. 123 High St, Colchester, Essex CO1 1SZ *tel:* 01206 572783 *also fax; email:* 100762.471@compuserve.com. *Br, w/wind, str, perc, keyboards, pnos, guis, sheet mus. Repairs, hire and m/order.*

Musicland. 37 St Botolph's St, Colchester, Essex CO2 7EA *tel:* 01206 577463 *fax:* 01206 765701. *Full range of Yamaha, Technics, Casio, Roland keyboards, digital pnos, orgs. Also guis, amps, mus and accs.*

Harlow

Machinehead Music. 2 Bush House, Bush Fair, Harlow, Essex CM18 6NS *tel:* 01279 421744/453092 *fax:* 01279 421744. Jason Ward. *Group insts, guis, accs.*

Hornchurch

Advance Music Ltd. 79 Station Lane, Hornchurch, Essex RM12 6JU *tel:* 01708 442748 *fax:* 01708 452727 *email:* music@advancemusic.co.uk. *Insts, mus, pnos, classical CDs.*

Maldon

Zings Music Ltd. Wycke Hill Business Park, Wycke Hill, Maldon, Essex CM9 6UZ *tel:* 01621 853990 *fax:* 01621 840556 *email:* sales@zings-music.co.uk.

Romford

The Music Village. 10 High Rd, Chadwell Heath, Romford, Essex RM6 6PR *tel:* 020 8598 9506.

Musicland. 54 North St, Romford, Essex RM1 1UT *tel:* 01708 737977; 01268 763100.

Southend-on-Sea

Allegro Music. 252-254 London Rd, Westcliff-on-Sea, Southend-on-Sea, Essex SS0 7JG *tel:* 01702 348476 *also fax. Gen mus insts specialising in keyboards, pnos, orgs.*

Musicland. 98 Hamlet Court Rd, Westcliff-on-Sea, Southend-on-Sea, Essex SS0 7LP *tel:* 01702 334488.

Tim Gentle Music. 39-45 Grainger Rd Ind Estate, Southend-on-Sea, Essex SS2 5DD *tel:* 070 7171 7777 *fax:* 070 7122 6231. *Mus insts and accs.*

Gloucestershire

Cheltenham

Cheltenham Soundhouse. 295a High St, Cheltenham, Glos GL50 3HL *tel:* 01242 525967. *Drums, guis, amps, mus, keyboards, brass, w/wind.*

Musical Instruments (Cheltenham). 52 Winchcombe St, Cheltenham, Glos GL52 2ND *tel:* 01242 517635 *fax:* 01242 250794. *Pnos, insts, mus, accs.*

Sounds Good. 26 Clarence St, Cheltenham, Glos GL50 3NU *tel:* 01242 234604 *fax:* 01242 253030. *CDs (classical, folk, world, blues, country, jazz); videos (opera, ballet); DVDs.*

Cirencester

Tower Sounds. 9 Market Place, Cirencester, Glos *tel:* 01285 654283. *Insts, mus, records, cassettes, CDs, videos.*

Gloucester

Duck Son & Pinker Ltd. 52-56 Southgate St, Gloucester GL1 2DR *tel:* 01452 521061. *Insts, pnos, keyboards, mus.*

Gloucester Music Co. 84 Westgate St, Gloucester GL1 2NZ *tel:* 01452 501457 *fax:* 01452 505881. *All insts except pnos.*

Gloucester Soundhouse. 49 Westgate St, Gloucester GL1 2NW *tel:* 01452 417429 *also fax. Drums, guis, amps, keyboards, br, w/wind, mus.*

Lechlade

Clive Morley Harps Ltd. Goodfellows, Filkins, nr Lechlade, Glos GL7 3JG *tel:* 01367 860493 *fax:* 01367 860659 *email:* morley@harps.demon.co.uk. *Concert and folk hps, antique insts, restorations, hp strings, mus.*

Ruardean

Frank Fidler. Rosehill Instruments, The Old Dairy, The Square, Ruardean, Glos GL17 9TJ *tel:* 01594 544053. *Br, w/wind sales and repairs, accs.*

Stroud

Harley Musical Instruments. 4 Market St, Nailsworth, Stroud, Glos GL6 0BX *tel:* 01453 833000 *also fax. Pnos, mus insts, sheet mus, repairs, tuning.*

Musisca Ltd. Piccadilly Mill, Lower St, Stroud, Glos GL5 2HT *tel:* 01453 751911 *also fax. Mus stands, pno stools and lighting, cond stands, desk stands.*

Stroud Music Centre. 48-49 London Rd, Stroud, Glos GL5 2AD *tel:* 01453 763587/765662 *also fax; email:* lesliehanson@compuserve.com. *Pnos, orgs, keyboards, accordions, w/wind, str insts, sheet mus.*

Tewkesbury

Goodmusic. PO Box 100, Tewkesbury, Glos GL20 7YQ *tel:* 01684 773883 *fax:* 01684 773884 *email:* sales@goodmusic-uk.com. *M/order only. Mus, books.*

Greater Manchester

Cadishead

Woodwind & Co. 208 Liverpool Rd, Cadishead, Greater Manchester M44 5DB *tel:* 0161 775 1842 *fax:* 0161 775 4149 *email:* woodwindco@tesco.net. *W/wind specialists.*

Denton

Howorth Wrightson Ltd. Unit 2, Cricket St, Denton, Manchester M34 3DR *tel:* 0161 335 0220. *Manufacturers of own design of mus stands.*

Quicksilver. Broom Grove Lane, Denton, Manchester M34 3DU *tel:* 0161 320 7232 *fax:* 0161 335 9871 *email:* sales@quicksilver-uk.demon.co.uk. *UK distributors of Howorth Wrightson mus stands.*

Eccles

The Drum Centre. Bridgewater Mill, Legh St, Eccles, Manchester M30 0RT *tel:* 0161 789 4415 *also fax. Perc and drums specialist. Insts, cases, accs, tutor books, spare parts, repairs.*

Fallowfield

Alan Gregory Music. 196 Moseley Rd, Fallowfield, Manchester M14 6PB *tel:* 0161 224 8915 *fax:* 0161 248 4032. *Str insts, bows, w/wind, br, guis, sales and repairs, accs, mus.*

Manchester

Forsyth Brothers Ltd. 126 Deansgate, Manchester M3 2GR *tel:* 0161 834 3281 *fax:* 0161 834 0630 *email:* forsythmus@aol.com. *Mus, books, orch insts, guis, keyboards, digital pnos, grand and upright pnos (new and second-hand), etc. Tuning, repair, hire. CDs, cassettes, videos, talking books, m/order.*

Music Exchange (Manchester) Ltd. 12 St Peter's Square, Manchester M2 3DF *tel:* 0161 236 1766. *Books, mus, insts, accs, mus novelties. M/order.*

Swan's Music Ltd. 3 Plymouth Court Business Centre, 166 Plymouth Grove, Manchester M13 0AF *tel:* 0161 273 3232 *fax:* 0161 274 4111 *email:* swansmusicltd@btinternet.com. *Mus, insts, orgs, pnos, keyboards, amps, accs; hire and repairs.*

Hampshire

Aldershot

George Potter & Co (Musical Instruments) Ltd. 26 Grosvenor Rd, Aldershot, Hants GU11 3DP *tel:* 01252 323226 *fax:* 01252 342921. *Books, insts, mus.*

Percy Prior's Music. 45 Station Rd, Aldershot, Hants GU11 1BD *tel:* 01252 343085 *fax:* 01252 25560. *Mus insts and accs for br and military bands and orchs. W/shop for br and w/wind.*

Basingstoke

Modern Music (Basingstoke) Ltd. 3-4 Chelsea House, Town Centre, Basingstoke, Hants RG21 7JR *tel:* 01256 464663 *fax:* 01256 818113. *Insts, mus, pnos, orgs, hi-tech.*

Eastleigh

Bandsound. 26 Mitre Copse, Eastleigh, Hants SO50 8QE *tel:* 023 8060 0444 *also fax. Mus educ products.*

Fareham

Kimbers Keyboards and Musical Instruments. 179a West St, Fareham, Hants PO16 0EF *tel:* 01329 286535 *fax:* 01329 285826. *Keyboards, elec pnos, orgs, guis, amps, accs, mus.*

Fleet

Kingfisher Music Co. 20 Kings Rd, Fleet, Hants GU13 9AD *tel:* 01252 621210/621554 *fax:* 01252 620129 *email:* kathy@kingfish.demon.co.uk. *Guis, amps, drums, hi-tech, recording.*

Petersfield

Blumein's. 7a Dragon St, Petersfield, Hants GU31 4JN *tel:* 01730 266605 *fax:* 01730 262961 *email:* blumein@talk21.com. *CDs, cassettes, mus, books, m/order.*

Portsmouth

Nevada Music. 189 London Rd, North End, Portsmouth PO2 9AE *tel:* 023 9266 0036 *fax:* 023 9269 0626 *email:* music@nevada.co.uk. *Guis, amps, keyboards. PA effects, repairs and hire.*

Ringwood

Oasis Musical Instruments Ltd. 3 West St, Ringwood, Hants BH24 1EN *tel:* 01425 478135; 0800 627621 *fax:* 01425 480595. *Guis, basses, amps, PA, br, w/wind, sheet mus, effects, repairs, PA hire.*

Venables Pianos. 1 Monmouth Court, Ringwood, Hants BH24 1HE *tel:* 01425 476644 *fax:* 01425 476645. *New and second-hand pnos, uprights, specialising in grands; clavinovas, electronic keyboards.*

Southampton

Beckett's Music Shop. 56 Commercial Rd, Southampton SO15 1GD *tel:* 023 8022 4827 *fax:* 023 8032 2046 *email:* becketts@btinternet.com. *W/wind, br, guis, keyboards, perc, repairs, mus, computer software, accs, educ insts, rental scheme, m/order.*

Fret Music Co Ltd. 11-13 Church St, Southampton SO15 5LG *tel:* 023 8077 4433 *fax:* 023 8070 4116 *email:* sales@fretmusic.co.uk. *Guis, drums, amps, accs, effects, 4-track recording, hire service, PA.*

Music Store. Civic Centre Rd, Southampton SO14 7SL *tel:* 023 8033 1844. *Guis, elec pnos, orgs, keyboards, sheet mus, harmonicas, accordions, br, w/wind, strs.*

Teville Music Centre. 68 East St Centre, Southampton SO14 3HX *tel:* 023 8022 0728 *also fax. Digital pnos, guis, orgs, strs, accs, keyboards, mus.*

Southsea

Courtney and Walker Ltd. 82-86 Elm Grove, Southsea, Hants PO5 1LN *tel:* 023 9282 2036 *fax:* 023 9278 0799 *email:* business@spectrum.newnet.co.uk. *Br, w/wind, strs, pno, perc, sheet mus, PA and PA installation.*

Winchester

Martin Restall Violins. Stonemasons Court, Parchment St, Winchester, Hants *tel:* 01962 841514 *also fax. Vns, vas, vcs, accs, also repairs.*

Whitwams Music. 70 High St, Winchester, Hants SO23 9DE *tel:* 01962 865253 *fax:* 01962 842064 *email:* music@whitwams.co.uk. *Printed mus specialists, recordings, digital pnos, keyboards, all insts, guis, amps, accs, rental service, school supply, m/order.*

Herefordshire

Hay-on-Wye

Hancock & Monks. 15 Broad St, Hay-on-Wye, Herefords HR3 5DB *tel:* 01497 821784 *fax:* 01591 610555 *email:* haymusic@compuserve.com. *Classical cassettes, CDs, videos, second-hand books on mus.*

Hereford

Allegro Music. 5 Commercial Rd, Hereford HR1 2BB *tel:* 01432 270069. *Technics and Yamaha keyboards, Technics digital pnos.*

Music Plus Ltd. 29a Union St, Hereford HR1 1SY *tel:* 01432 356194 *fax:* 01432 353872. *Keyboards, pnos, guis, accs, printed mus.*

Leominster

Capriole Music and Syrinx Records. 4 High St, Leominster, Herefords HR6 8LZ *tel:* 01568 613477 *also fax; email:* syrinx1@freeserve.co.uk. *Mus, books, insts, repairs.*

Capriole Music and the Violin Shop. 11 Buttercross Arcade, Leominster, Herefords HR6 8BN *tel:* 01568 613477 *also fax. Vns, insts, sheet mus (early mus specialists), repairs, cassettes, CDs.*

Trevor Davies Music. 87 Etnam St, Leominster, Herefords HR6 8AE *tel:* 01568 613611. *Insts, amps, mus, accs.*

Hertfordshire

Berkhamsted

Graham Webb Music. 39 Lower Kings Rd, Berkhamsted, Herts HP4 2AB *tel:* 01442 871758. *Keyboards, guis, mus, accs; also servicing.*

Broxbourne

Three Jay & Co. 8a Nazeing Glass Works, Nazing New Rd, Broxbourne, Herts EN10 6SF *tel:* 01992 442974 *fax:* 01992 449339 *email:* choirmusic@3jay.globalnet.co.uk. *Choral mus for choirs.*

Cockfosters

Make Music. 109 Cockfosters Rd, Cockfosters, Herts EN4 0DA *tel:* 020 8441 1050 *fax:* 020 8441 8254.

Harpenden

Musicale plc. 20 Salisbury Ave, Harpenden, Herts AL5 2QG *tel:* 01582 769712 *fax:* 01582 767343 *email:* HMusicale@aol.com. *Books, nationwide inst trial and purchase scheme, mus, accs, m/order, repairs. Commission for teachers and mus depts.*

Hitchin

Machinehead Music. 10 Bucklersbury, Hitchin, Herts ST5 1BB *tel:* 01462 433305/457686 *fax:* 01462 458880. *Guis.*

Myatt (John) Woodwind and Brass. 57 Nightingale Rd, Hitchin, Herts SG5 1RQ *tel:* 01462 420057 *fax:* 01462 435464 *email:* shop@myatt.co.uk. *New and second-hand wind insts, accs, CDs, T-shirts, repairs.*

Richard Reason Pianos. 94 Tilehouse St, Hitchin, Herts SG5 2DW *tel:* 01462 454244 *fax:* 01462 450367. *New and reconditioned pnos, restorations, second-hand mus.*

Hoddesdon

George Stokes Music Ltd. 5a Tower Centre, Hoddesdon, Herts EN11 8UB *tel:* 01992 451019 *fax:* 01992 446793 *email:* GSMusic@yahoo.com. *Digital pnos and keyboards (Yamaha, Korg, Casio), guis, amplification, w/wind, accs, mus.*

St Albans

Britannia Music Shop. 156 Hatfield Rd, St Albans, Herts AL1 4JD *tel:* 01727 846055 *fax:* 01727 811164. *W/wind, br, str insts, sheet mus, reeds, accs. Second-hand inst list available.*

St Albans Music Centre. 20 Holywell Hill, St Albans, Herts AL1 1DD *tel:* 01727 852717. *Mus, insts, accs, books.*

Stevenage

Coda Music. 51 High St, Stevenage, Herts SG1 3AH *tel:* 01438 350815 *fax:* 01438 747006. *Wide range of guis, amps and gui related products.*

Ware

Make Music Ltd. 31 Baldock St, Ware, Herts SG12 9DH *tel:* 01920 460646 *fax:* 01920 464601 *email:* makemusic@btinternet.com. *Keyboards, orgs, digital pnos.*

Watford

Thwaites. 33 Chalk Hill, Oxhey, Watford WD1 4BL *tel:* 01923 232412 *also fax; email:* sales@thwaites.com. *Str insts, repairs, restoration.*

Viscount Organs Ltd. 5 Caxton Way, Watford Business Park, Watford WD1 8UA *tel:* 01923 247437 *fax:* 01923 249345. *Classical church and theatre orgs, digital pnos.*

Isle of Wight

Newport

W Teague & Co Ltd. 34 Orchard St, Newport, Isle of Wight PO30 1AU *tel:* 01983 523460 *fax:* 01983 525171. *Mus, orgs, pnos (elec and acoustic), keyboards, br, w/wind, str insts, perc, accs.*

Kent

Bexley

Wooderson, Andrew. 5 Bourne Rd, Bexley, Kent DA5 1LG *tel:* 01322 558326/525558 *also fax. All types of hpds, spinets, virginals, clvds, early pnos; also tuning, maintenance, restoration, repairs and hire.*

Bromley

Reid-Sohn Pianos. 216 High St, Bromley, Kent BR1 1PW *tel:* 020 8460 0165.

Unisound. 171 Widmore Rd, Bromley, Kent BR1 3AX *tel:* 020 8313 1161. *Guis, drums, amps, br, w/wind, mus.*

Canterbury

Crowthers of Canterbury. 10 Longport, Canterbury, Kent CT1 1PE *tel:* 01227 763965 *also fax; email:* crowther@compuserve.com. *Lorée obs, w/wind insts, accs, mus, rentals, repairs.*

Forwoods Music. 35-37 Palace St, Canterbury, Kent CT1 2DZ *tel:* 01227 464741 *fax:* 01227 762836 *email:* forwoods.music@btinternet.com. *Insts, mus, books; also m/order.*

Chatham

Musicland. 98 High St, Chatham, Kent ME4 4DS *tel:* 01634 408989 *fax:* 01634 817591. *Orgs, keyboards, digital elec pnos, guis, amps, brass, w/wind, mus accs, sheet mus.*

Chislehurst

Derek Cadde Pianos Ltd. Walden Parade, Walden Rd, Chislehurst, Kent BR7 5DW *tel:* 020 8468 7972 *fax:* 01689 817014. *New and reconditioned pnos, tuning, repairs, removals and polishing.*

Deal

Make Music (Kent). 114 High St, Deal, Kent CT14 6BB *tel:* 01304 375028.

Gillingham

Sharon Music. 95 Watling St, Gillingham, Kent ME7 2YX *tel:* 01634 850058 *fax:* 01634 570823. *Guis, keyboards, clavinovas, sheet mus, accs.*

Herne Bay

Music Bay. 144 Mortimer St, Herne Bay, Kent CT6 5DX *tel:* 01227 373364 *fax:* 01227 367704. *Guis, keyboards, amps, w/wind, sheet mus, accs.*

Maidstone

Sharon Music. 65 High St, Maidstone, Kent ME14 1SR *tel:* 01622 761649 *fax:* 01622 685935. *Insts, w/wind, br, guis, educ supplies, accs, mus, pnos, keyboards.*

Sittingbourne

Newington Strings. 39 High St, Newington, Sittingbourne, Kent ME9 7JR *tel:* 01795 843822 *fax:* 01795 842838. *Str insts and accs, guis, sheet mus. Repairs, hire, m/order.*

Tonbridge

Beat 'N' Track Music Co. 7 Quarry Hill Parade, Tonbridge, Kent TN9 2HR *tel:* 01732 366455. *Group insts, keyboards, drums, br, w/wind, PA systems, amps, mus.*

Black Cat Music. Bankside House, Vale Rd, Tonbridge, Kent TN9 1SJ *tel:* 01732 367123 *fax:* 01732 367755. *Mus equipment, mus stands, chairs, staging, acoustic rooms.*

Tunbridge Wells

Classic Violins Ltd. 1 Northfields, Speldhurst, Tunbridge Wells, Kent TN3 0PL *tel:* 01892 870319/863748 *fax:* 01892 870966. *Vns, vas, vcs, dbs, bows (baroque, classical and modern). Also restorers, valuers.*

JB's Music Stores. 108-110 St James Rd, Tunbridge Wells, Kent TN1 2HH *tel:* 01892 515007/522141 *fax:* 01892 515602. *Mus insts, PA, DJ supplies.*

Newingtons Music Centre. Grove Hill Rd, Tunbridge Wells, Kent TN1 1RZ *tel:* 01892 526659 *fax:* 01892 540611. *Insts, keyboards, pnos, mus, cassettes, CDs, videos, books, accs, restoration and repair, m/order.*

Underground Sounds Ltd. 108-110 St James Rd, Tunbridge Wells, Kent TN1 2HH *tel:* 01892 533778 *fax:* 01892 515026. *Classical guis, drums, br, w/wind, printed mus, software.*

Kingston upon Hull

Hull

Antone's Guitars. 326 Beverley Rd, Hull HU5 1BA *tel:* 01482 448733 *fax:* 01482 343007 *email:* tony@antones.co.uk. *Guis, amps, vintage section, repairs, home recording, acoustic insts.*

Big Rock Basement. 13-15 Savile St, Hull HU1 3EH *tel:* 01482 326525 *fax:* 01482 587598. *Guis, amps, drums, PA, hi-tech, accs.*

Lancashire

Accrington

Music Box. 16 Whalley Rd, Accrington, Lancs BB5 1AA *tel:* 01254 383571. *Insts, mus, repairs, pawnbrokers.*

Blackburn

Time and Tune (Blackburn). Eldon Place, 53 Preston New Rd, Blackburn, Lancs BB2 6AY *tel:* 01254 697460 *also fax. Mus, pnos, str, w/wind, br insts, CDs, repairs, tuning, rentals.*

Blackpool

Tower Music. 46-48 Topping St, Blackpool, Lancs FY1 3AQ *tel:* 01253 27359 *also fax. Amps, PA, keyboards, guis, mus, educ, br, w/wind.*

Bolton

Booth's Music. 17 Churchgate, Bolton, Lancs BL1 1HU *tel:* 01204 522908 *fax:* 01204 399244. *Insts, mus, repairs, hire.*

Harker & Howarth (Music) Ltd. Folds Rd, Bolton, Lancs BL1 1UN *tel:* 01204 526623 *fax:* 01204 364220. *Pnos, keyboards, orgs, insts, mus. Mus school.*

McQueens Musical Instruments. Sunset Business Centre, Manchester Rd, Kearsley, Bolton BL4 8RT *tel:* 01204 794600 *also fax. Br and w/wind insts, new and second-hand; repairs; manufacturers of bugles, cavalry tpts, post hns, herald tpts.*

Burnley

Dawsons Music Ltd. 20 Standish St, Burnley, Lancs BB11 1AP *tel:* 01282 425829. *Orch insts, pnos, orgs, keyboards, guis, amps, synths, hi-tech equipment.*

Bury

Read Franklin and Heywood Ltd. 11 Broad St, Bury, Lancs BL9 0DA *tel:* 0161 764 4624 *fax:* 0161 764 9424. *Keyboards, orgs, guis, insts, mus, tuition, elec pnos.*

Leyland

Rimmers Music Ltd. 20 Chapel Brow, Leyland, Lancs PR5 2NE *tel:* 01772 433281 *fax:* 01772 623075. *Keyboards, digital pnos, orgs, guis, PA, FX, amps, br and w/wind. Accs, mus and tuition.*

Lytham St Annes

Raymond Wallbank. 42 Woodlands Rd, Ansdell, Lytham St Annes, Lancs FY8 4BX *tel:* 01253 736462 *also fax. Insts, mus, accs.*

Mossley

Derek Hossle Woodwind. 26 Andrew St, Mossley, Lancs OL5 0DN *tel:* 01457 835656 *email:* derekjo.hossle@btinternet.com. *W/wind, repairs, restoration.*

Harry Ash. 58 Quickedge Rd, Mossley, Lancs OL5 0PH *tel:* 01457 834922 *also fax;* 07721 585997 *email:* tarisio@compuserve.com. *Vns, vas, vcs, all accs, repairs, valuations, bow repairs, insurance facilities, strs by m/order.*

Oldham

Keys Musical Instruments Ltd. 71 Henshaw St, Oldham, Lancs OL1 2AA *tel:* 0161 627 0614 *fax:* 0161 620 0614 *email:* peter.braid@gconnect.com. *Keyboards, hi-tech, pnos, orgs, guis, PA, br, w/wind.*

Preston

A&C Hamilton. 946-950 Blackpool Rd, Preston, Lancs PR2 1XN *tel:* 01772 722468 *email:* sales@achamilton.co.uk. *Keyboards, pnos, digital pnos, orgs, guis, amplification, mus, accs.*

Music Cellar, Preston. 12 Fox St, Preston, Lancs PR1 2AB *tel:* 01772 251407 *fax:* 01772 251412 *email:* themusiccellar@btinternet.com. *Orch insts, pnos, clavinovas, keyboards, mus.*

St Anne's-on-Sea

Thelma's Music Shop. St Anne's School of Music, Victoria Rd, St Annes-on-Sea, Lancs FY8 5LE *tel:* 01253 727444. *Mus, guis, insts, accs.*

Leicestershire

Leicester

City Music. 66 London Rd, Leicester LE2 0QD *tel:* 0116 254 4441. *Printed mus specialists; m/order.*

David Snelling Violins. 11 Cross St, Blaby, Leicester LE8 4FD *tel:* 0116 278 4444. *Sales of vns and bows; also rentals, valuations, insurance, repairs.*

Sheehan's Music Services. 50 London Rd, Leicester LE2 0QD *tel:* 0116 255 7492 *fax:* 0116 285 5932 *email:* noel@sheehans.com. *W/wind, br, electro-acoustic and classical gui, folk insts, books, accs, repairs.*

Market Harborough

Keyboard Kavern. Adam & Eve St, Market Harborough, Leics LE16 7LT *tel:* 01858 434516 *fax:* 01858 434716 *email:* geoffkey@aol.com. *Keyboards, pnos, br, w/wind, perc, etc.*

Melton Mowbray

Mel-Tone. 58 King St, Melton Mowbray, Leics LE13 1XB *tel:* 01664 568000 *fax:* 01664 480722. *Insts, mus, guis, amps, drums, br, w/wind, strs, mus books, tuition, repairs.*

Lincolnshire

Boston

Harmony Music. 78-84 West St, Boston, Lincs PE21 8QN *tel:* 01205 355366 *also fax. Br and w/wind specialists, orgs, pnos, keyboards, perc, sheet mus, repairs.*

Lincoln

Counterpoint Music Shop. 38 Grantham St, Lincoln LN2 1LW *tel:* 01522 560065 *email:* eileen@counterpointmusic.co.uk. *Sheet mus, books, CDs, cassettes, educ specialist, m/order.*

Fox's Music. 161-162 High St, Lincoln LN5 7AF *tel:* 01522 537141 *also fax; email:* enquiries@foxmusic.co.uk. *Yamaha, Technics, Marshall, Fender, Roland. Keyboards, guis, amps, mus.*

The Music Cabin. 453 High St, Lincoln LN5 8JA *tel:* 01522 525104 *also fax. Insts, repairs, mus.*

Spalding

Portass & Carter Entertainments. 26 Bridge Rd, Sutton Bridge, Spalding, Lincs PE12 9UA *tel:* 01406 350407/350266. *New, second-hand insts.*

Stamford

Stamford Music Shop. 11 St Mary's Hill, Stamford, Lincs *tel:* 01780 751275 *fax:* 01780 752245. *Mus, insts, cassettes, CDs.*

Merseyside

Birkenhead

Hammersound. 49-51 Grange Rd West, Birkenhead, Merseyside CH41 4BZ *tel:* 0151 652 7454. *Guis, drums, keyboards, accs, PA.*

KGB Musical Instruments. 61 Derby Rd, Birkenhead, Merseyside CH42 7HA *tel:* 0151 647 3268 *email:* keith@kgb-music.co.uk. *Guis, gui parts, strs, accs.*

Liverpool

Graham C Johns Percussion. 17 Burnham Rd, Calderstones, Liverpool L18 6JU *tel:* 0151 724 1072 *fax:* 0151 729 0592 *email:* gcjperc@aol.com. *Retailing specialists of classical perc insts. Large stock of timpani, xylophones, marimbas, sticks, mallets, cymbals, educ perc insts. M/order welcome.*

The Music Store (Cranes). 87 Hanover St, Liverpool L1 3DZ *tel:* 0151 709 4714 *fax:* 0151 709 8013. *Guis, digital pnos, pnos, mus, keyboards.*

Richard Behrend. 8 Greenbank Rd, off Smithdown Rd, Liverpool L18 1HN *tel:* 0151 733 2213. *Mus, br and w/wind insts, accs, repairs.*

Rushworths of Liverpool. 42-46 Whitechapel, Liverpool L1 6EF *tel:* 0151 709 9071 *fax:* 0151 709 9073.

Southport

Music Shop. 37 Tulketh St, Southport, Merseyside PR8 1AG *tel:* 01704 533315 *also fax. Books, insts, mus, accs.*

Rimmers Music Ltd. 173-175 Eastbank St, Southport, Merseyside PR8 6TH *tel:* 01704 532145. *Keyboards, pnos, orgs, guis, w/wind, mus, strs, accs.*

Middlesbrough, City of

Middlesbrough

The Middlesbrough Music Centre. 15 Gilkes St, Middlesbrough TS1 5ET *tel:* 01642 226977 *fax:* 01642 253698. *Mus, insts, amps, keyboards, sheet mus, perc.*

Williams Music People. Unit 2, Corporation House, 28 Corporation Rd, Middlesbrough TS1 2RX *tel:* 01642 232373 *also fax. Orgs, pnos, keyboards, br, w/wind, guis, sheet mus, educ products. Repairs, hire, m/order.*

Middlesex

Edgware

Don Mackrill's Woodwind and Brass. 3-5 Station Rd, Edgware, Middx HA8 7JE *tel:* 020 8952 5813 *fax:* 020 8951 5248 *email:* donmac@dircon.co.uk. *Br, w/wind, guis, amps; also educ insts, books and school rentals; repairs.*

Harrow

Harrow Music Centre. 52 Greenhill Way, Harrow HA1 1LE *tel:* 020 8427 2250 *fax:* 020 8863 1167. *Insts, mus, amps, PA.*

Herga Music. 2a-4 High St, Wealdstone, Harrow HA3 7AA *tel:* 020 8861 1590 *fax:* 020 8861 5501. *Sheet mus, br, w/wind, str insts, guis, pnos, keyboards, educ products, mus books, gifts, hire, m/order.*

Shaftesbury Music. 2 Shaftesbury Ave, Kenton, Harrow, Middx HA3 0QX *tel:* 020 8907 1376 *fax:* 020 8933 6282. *Sheet mus (mail order).*

Hayes

Make Music. 670-674 Uxbridge Rd, Hayes, Middx UB4 0RY *tel:* 020 8756 1079 *fax:* 020 8813 6384. *Elec orgs, digital pnos, keyboards, br, w/wind, guis, hi-tech, software, accs.*

Hounslow

Project Music. 433-437 Great West Rd, Hounslow, Middx TW5 0BY *tel:* 020 8570 4444 *fax:* 020 8577 5818. *Keyboards, guis, elec equipment, drums, PA.*

Perivale

Bluthners. 18 Aintree Rd, Perivale, Middx UB6 7LA *tel:* 020 8997 4785 *fax:* 020 8997 6485. *Pnos.*

Twickenham

Albert's Music Shop Ltd. 138-140 Heath Rd, Twickenham, Middx TW1 4BN *tel:* 020 8892 7634 *fax:* 020 8891 1781. *Insts, mus, keyboards.*

The Way Out West Music Co. 47 London Rd, Twickenham, Middx TW1 3SA *tel:* 020 8744 1040/50 *fax:* 020 8744 1095 *email:* info@wowmusic.demon.co.uk. *Mus, insts, pro-audio recording equipment, digital audio editing.*

Norfolk

Great Yarmouth

Soundgear Music. 11 Southdown Rd, Great Yarmouth, Norfolk NR31 0HU *tel:* 01493 603746 *also fax. Guis, drums, amplification, br, w/wind, etc.*

Kings Lynn

Lynn Music. 23 Norfolk St, Kings Lynn PE30 1AN *tel:* 01553 774390. *Orgs, keyboards, digital pnos, br, w/wind, guis, drums, accs, sheet mus. Repairs and hire.*

Norwich

A W Cooke & Son (Music) Ltd. 19 St Benedicts St, Norwich NR2 4PE *tel:* 01603 625970 *fax:* 01603 630598. *Pnos, orgs, keyboards, accordions.*

Aldens Pianos. 107 Gloucester St, Norwich NR2 2DY *tel:* 01603 625331. *Pnos (new, re-conditioned, second-hand and as traded in), Korg electric pnos, pno stools, accs. Tuning, polishing, repairs, hire.*

Cooke's Band Instruments. 34 St Benedicts St, Norwich NR2 4AQ *tel:* 01603 623563 *fax:* 01603 626675 *email:* theteam@cookes.co.uk. *Guis, amps, drums, PA, stage and effects lighting.*

Elkin Music. 31 Exchange St, Norwich NR2 1DP *tel:* 01603 666332 *also fax. Books, mus, mus gifts.*

Gibson Music. 5 St John Maddermarket, Norwich NR2 1DN *tel:* 01603 663262 *also fax. Orch insts, guis, sheet mus, accs, repairs, rentals.*

Jack White Music. 48-50 St Benedicts St, Norwich NR2 4AR *tel:* 01603 613678. *Keyboards, elec pnos, orgs, mus, amplification, tuition.*

Klef Music Ltd. 118 Magdalen St, Norwich *tel:* 01603 612396. *New and second-hand guis, amps, repairs, accs.*

St Benedict's Music (incorporating Cooke's Orchestral Supplies). 2-4 St Benedict's St, Norwich NR2 4AG *tel:* 01603 627863 *fax:* 01603 762510. *Insts, mus.*

St George's Music Shop. 17-19 St George's St, Norwich NR3 1AB *tel:* 01603 626414 *fax:* 01603 618811 *email:* sales@stgeorgesmusic.co.uk. *Comprehensive selection of classical sheet mus, books, accs and insts supplying many schools and colleges. Also m/order.*

Salhouse

William Elkin Music Services. Station Rd Industrial Estate, Salhouse, Norwich, Norfolk NR13 6NS *tel:* 01603 721302. *Books, mus, mus gifts, m/order.*

North East Lincolnshire

Grimsby

Music For You. 12 High St, Waltham, Grimsby DN37 0LL *tel:* 01472 828524 *fax:* 01472 828681. *Mus, insts, bows, accs, educ suppliers, m/order, sheet mus.*

North Lincolnshire

Scunthorpe

Pauls Music Shop. 15 Laneham St, Scunthorpe, N Lincs DN15 6LJ *tel:* 01724 867650.

North Somerset

Clevedon

Clevedon Music Shop. 19 Alexandra Rd, Clevedon, BS21 7QH *tel:* 01275 791181/342090 *also fax. Insts, pnos, mus, books, accs, repairs, CDs, sheet mus. Recording equipment, PAs.*

North Yorkshire

Ampleforth

June Emerson Wind Music. Ampleforth, York Y062 4HF *tel:* 01439 788324 *fax:* 01439 788715 *email:* juneemerson@compuserve.com. *Mus for wind insts.*

Harrogate

Arcadia Music. 27 Cheltenham Cres, Harrogate, N Yorks HG1 1DH *tel:* 01423 565110 *also fax. Insts, mus, accs, gifts, repairs.*

Knock on Wood. Unit 131, Glasshouses Mill, Harrogate, N Yorks HG3 5QH *tel:* 01423 712712 *also fax; email:* kow@globalnet.co.uk. *M/order multicultural supplies of insts, recordings, books and teaching resources.*

Musicmakers of Harrogate. 16 Oxford St, Harrogate, N Yorks HG1 1SN *tel:* 01423 566238 *fax:* 01423 524650. *Insts, mus, books, accs.*

Selby

Bob Crossland Music. The Shop, Scott Rd, Selby, N Yorks Y08 4BL *tel:* 01757 703228. *Mus, br and w/wind insts, keyboards, drums, acoustic and elec guis, amps, mics.*

Skipton

Tapp (Music) Ltd. 14-16 Otley St, Skipton, N Yorks BD23 1DZ *tel:* 01756 797513 *fax:* 01756 701215 *email:* sales@tappmusic.freeserve.co.uk. *Mus, m/order, specialist pno catalogue.*

Time and Tune. 14-16 Otley St, Skipton, N Yorks BD23 1DZ *tel:* 01756 798515 *fax:* 01756 701215. *Mus, pnos, str, w/wind, br insts, CDs, repairs, tuning, rentals.*

Tadcaster

Lovely Music. 17 Westgate, Tadcaster, N Yorks LS24 9JB *tel:* 01937 832946 *fax:* 01937 835696. *Mus, educ mus and books, choral, orch, wind band.*

Northamptonshire

Northampton

St Giles Music. 16 St Giles Terrace, Northampton NN1 2BN *tel:* 01604 250905 *fax:* 01604 234864. *Yamaha main agent. Teaching studio, orgs, digital pnos, keyboards; elec keyboards (Casio and Technics); Technics digital pnos; w/wind, strs, guis, sheet mus.*

Oundle

Oundle Music. R Keightley, 13 West St, Oundle, Peterborough PE8 4EJ *tel:* 01832 273669 *also fax. Mus, insts, accs, repairs, m/order service.*

Northumberland

Bedlington

Dennis Todd Music. 86 Front St, Bedlington, Northumberland NE22 5AE *tel:* 01670 822085 *fax:* 01670 820592. *Br, w/wind, perc, electronic keyboards, guis, sheet mus, educ inst and mus, rental plan, repairs.*

Corbridge

John Ross (Pianos). St Helen's St, Corbridge, Northumberland NE45 5BE *tel:* 01434 632968 *fax:* 01434 632245. *Insts, pnos, mus, accs.*

Nottinghamshire

Mansfield

Music Scene. 9a Albert St, Mansfield, Notts NG18 1EA *tel:* 01623 631174 *fax:* 01623 654544. *Keyboards, orgs, pnos, digital pnos, br, w/wind, guis, amps, mus, accs; tuition.*

Newark

The Music Shop. 20 Barnby Gate, Newark, Notts NG24 1PZ *tel:* 01636 610588 *also fax. New and second-hand insts, accs, mus, repairs.*

Trent Music Centre. 1a Pelham St, Newark, Notts NG24 4XD *tel:* 01636 677626. *Mus, books, insts, amps, keyboards, repairs, tuition; goods made to order, guild and jazz gui stockist.*

Nottingham

Academy of Sound. 9-13 Hockley, Nottingham NG1 1FH *tel:* 0115 958 1888 *fax:* 0115 958 0033. *Multimedia equipment, keyboards, recording, guis, drums, PA.*

Farnsworth Musical Supplies Ltd. 126 Nottingham Rd, Sherwood Rise, Nottingham NG7 7AH *tel:* 0115 960 8955 *email:* farnsworth.musical@tesco.net. *Insts, mus, accs.*

Fox's Music. 246 Victoria Centre, Nottingham NG1 3QQ *tel:* 0115 947 4221 *fax:* 0115 924 3292. *Clavinovas, elec orgs, pnos, mus, accs, guis, amplification, br, w/wind, teaching.*

S & E M Turner Violins. 1-5 Lily Grove, Beeston, Nottingham *tel:* 0115 943 0333 *fax:* 0115 943 0444 *email:* turnerviolins@compuserve.com. *Vns, db, vas, vcs, repairs, accs, valuations, rentals, export, commission.*

Spanish Guitar Centre. 44 Nottingham Rd, New Basford, Nottingham NG7 7AE *tel:* 0115 962 2709 *fax:* 0115 962 5368 *email:* sales@spanishguitar.com. *Guis, gui mus, accs, m/order, tuition.*

Windblowers. 75-77 Derby Rd, Nottingham NG1 5BA *tel:* 0115 941 0543 *fax:* 0115 947 4433. *Br and w/wind insts and accs; all types of sheet mus.*

Worksop

Berry's Music. 23 Bridge Place, Worksop, Notts S80 1DT *tel:* 01909 473532 *fax:* 01909 530609. *Mus, insts, accs.*

Oxfordshire

Bicester

Early Keyboard Agency. Heyford Galleries, High St, Upper Heyford, Bicester, Oxon OX6 3LE *tel:* 01869 232282. *Hpds, spinets, virginals, clvds, stools, tuners, covers, wound strings, humidification equipment; also reconditioning, maintenance.*

Henley-on-Thames

Henley Piano Galleries. 24 Duke St, Henley-on-Thames, Oxon RG9 1UP *tel:* 01491 413019 *fax:* 01491 411361. *New and restored pnos (Rud. Ibach Sohn, Broadwood, Weinbach).*

Oxford

Allegro Oxford Ltd. 404 Marston Rd, Marston, Oxford OX3 0JE *tel:* 01865 798165 *fax:* 01865 407662. *Specialists in w/wind and br; repairs.*

Blackwell's Music Library Services. Hythe Bridge St, Oxford OX1 2ET *tel:* 01865 792792 *fax:* 01865 261395 *email:* lbdmus@blackwell.co.uk. *M/order suppliers to mus libraries, colleges and orchs; books, printed mus, recordings.*

Blackwell's Music Shop. 38 Holywell St, Oxford OX1 3SW *tel:* 01865 792792 *fax:* 01865 248833 *email:* music@blackwellbookshops.co.uk. *New and second-hand books and mus, CDs, cassettes, videos, gifts; also m/order.*

Lighting Sound and Equipment. 118 Cowley Rd, Oxford OX4 1JE *tel:* 01865 722027 *fax:* 01865 202454. *PA, lighting, hire and sales.*

Oxford University Press Bookshop. 116-117 High St, Oxford OX1 4BZ *tel:* 01865 242913 *fax:* 01865 241701 *email:* bookshop@oup.co.uk. *Books, sheet mus.*

Russell Acott Ltd. 124 High St, Oxford OX1 4DE *tel:* 01865 241195 *fax:* 01865 798256 *email:* shop@russellacott.demon.co.uk. *Insts, mus, pnos.*

Witney

Shackell Pianos. Burford Rd, Minster Lovell, Witney, Oxon OX8 5RB *tel:* 01993 703375 *fax:* 01993 700867 *email:* sales@shackell-pianos.demon.co.uk. *Yamaha and Steinway; sales, service and hire.*

Redcar and Cleveland

Guisborough

Greensleeves. 21 Chaloner St, Guisborough, Redcar and Cleveland TS14 6QD *tel:* 01287 636028 *also fax. Mus, insts, str, w/wind, br, perc, keyboards, guis, amps, CDs, cassettes, accs.*

Shropshire

Oswestry

Hidersine Co Ltd. Middleton Rd, Oswestry, Shropshire SY11 2RB *tel:* 01691 657921 *fax:* 01691 679403 *email:* barnhide@enterprise.net. *Rosin and strs.*

Music Makers. 2 Leg St, Oswestry, Shropshire SY11 2NL *tel:* 01691 654510. *Mus, insts, accs.*

Shrewsbury

Brattons Pianos Ltd. Bratton House, 23 Dogpole, Shrewsbury, Shropshire SY1 1ES *tel:* 01743 362133. *Books, insts, mus; m/order.*

Salop Music Centre. St Michaels St, Shrewsbury, Shropshire SY1 2DE *tel:* 01743 365561/364111 *fax:* 01743 245127. *Sheet mus, br, w/wind, keyboards, orch str, educ perc, gui specialists, hi-tech, PA, folk; schools discount; repairs.*

Windband. 9 Greyfriars Rd, Shrewsbury, Shropshire SY3 7EN *tel:* 01743 367482 *also fax; fax:* 01743 340412 *email:* windband@cableinet.co.uk. *W/wind and br specialist, folk and early insts, mus and accs, m/order, rental purchase, inst hire schemes, repairs.*

Telford

Telford Musical Instruments. 7 Bell St, Wellington, Telford, Shropshire TF1 1LS *tel:* 01952 255310 *also fax. Insts, mus.*

Somerset

Frome

Sounds of Frome. 5 Bath St, Frome, Somerset BA11 1DH *tel:* 01373 462083 *fax:* 01373 453164. *Pnos, keyboards, guis, amps, multi-track recorders, sheet mus.*

Taunton

Gillian Greig Music. 44 Kingston Rd, Taunton, Somerset TA2 7SG *tel:* 01823 333317 *fax:* 01823 338454. *Books, mus, cassettes, CDs.*

John Packer Ltd. 1 Portland St, Taunton, Somerset TA1 1UY *tel:* 01823 282386 *fax:* 01823 337653. *Suppliers and repairers of wind and br insts. Educ contractor.*

Westside Music Centre. 24-26 Bridge St, Taunton, Somerset TA1 1UB *tel:* 01823 283307. *Electronic orgs, keyboards, guis, amps, drums, hi-tech.*

South Yorkshire

Carcroft

Carcroft Organs. Old Co-Op, 39a Skellow Rd, Carcroft, Doncaster, S Yorks DN6 8HQ *tel:* 01302 338445/727974 *also fax.*

Doncaster

Dodds of Doncaster Ltd. 55 Christ Church Rd, Doncaster, S Yorks *tel:* 01302 366008 *fax:* 01302 816000 *email:* doddsmusic@aol.com. *Strs, br, w/wind, keyboards, perc, mus, accs, repairs.*

E Smedley & Sons. 19 Printing Office St, Doncaster, S Yorks DN1 1TS *tel:* 01302 323248 *also fax. Mus, portable keyboards, guis, accs.*

Sheffield

The Music Box. 31, The Lanes (by the Oasis), Meadowhall, Sheffield S9 1EP *tel:* 0114 256 9089 *email:* ask@themusicbox.co.uk. *Insts, mus, accs, gifts, etc.*

Wilson Peck Ltd. 13 Rockingham Gate, Sheffield S1 4JD *tel:* 0114 275 0808 *fax:* 0114 278 7795 *email:* wilsonpeck@fax.co.uk. *Acoustic pnos, digital pnos (main dealer Kawai & Korg), insts, sheet mus, classical CDs, cassettes. By appointment, agent for Steinway and Boston.*

Sheffield Music Shop. 136 Whitham Rd, Sheffield S10 2SR *tel:* 0114 266 1000 *also fax. Vns, vcs, vas, w/wind insts; mus.*

Staffordshire

Burton-on-Trent

Eric Reynolds Ltd. 88 High St, Burton-on-Trent, Staffs DE14 1LJ *tel:* 01283 565869/565086/517997 *fax:* 01283 512330 *email:* ereynolds@reconjappianos.demon.co.uk. *New and rebuilt pnos, elec orgs and keyboards, guis, sheet mus, accs. Repairs and hire. Also wholesaler of imported used pnos.*

Normans Ltd. Unit 1, Moor St, Burton-on-Trent, Staffs DE14 3SU *tel:* 01283 535333 *fax:* 01283 515572. *Books, band and orch insts, mus, m/order.*

Lichfield

S & J Music. 13 Dam St, Lichfield, Staffs WS13 6AE *tel:* 01543 268909 *fax:* 01543 417736. *Insts, mus, accs.*

Stoke-on-Trent

Music Control Ltd. Chapel Mews, 68 Crewe Rd, Alsager, Stoke-on-Trent, Staffs ST7 2HA *tel:* 01270 883779 *fax:* 01270 883847. *Professional audio equipment, specialising in selling and locating second-hand analogue synths.*

Robert Keyes Music Centre. 211 London Rd, Stoke-on-Trent, Staffs ST4 5RW *tel:* 01782 745111.

Suffolk

Beccles

Morlings Ltd. 18 New Market, Beccles, Suffolk NR34 9HB *tel:* 01502 713143 *fax:* 01502 711410. *Mus, cassettes, CDs, video, DVD.*

Bury St Edmunds

Balaam's Music. 103 Risbygate St, Bury St Edmunds, Suffolk IP33 3AA *tel:* 01284 766933 *fax:* 01284 701605 *email:* balaams-music @cwcom.net. *Mus, insts, books, repairs, insurance.*

Mail Order Music. Dettinger Way, Bury St Edmunds, Suffolk IP33 3YB *tel:* 01284 725725/703097 *fax:* 01284 702592 *email:* mailorder @musicsales.co.uk; enquiry@musicsales.co.uk. *Sheet mus: classroom, solo, ens, choral, musical shows, new media. Catalogues include Chester Music, Novello, Golden Apple, Shawnee Press, G Schirmer, UME and Youngsongs.*

Music In Print (Head Office). Newmarket Rd, Bury St Edmunds, Suffolk IP33 3YB *tel:* 01284 767019 *fax:* 01284 723235. *Printed mus, insts and mus accs franchisers.*

Ipswich

Amberstone Bookshop. 49 Upper Orwell St, Ipswich, Suffolk IP4 1HP *tel:* 01473 250675 *fax:* 01473 226980 *email:* amber@anglianet.co.uk. *Books, classical CDs, cassettes.*

East End Music. 142 Felixstowe Rd, Ipswich IP3 8EF *tel:* 01473 725961. *Insts, amps (new and second-hand).*

Haven Keyboards. 486 Felixstowe Rd, Ipswich *tel:* 01473 710051. *Keyboards, digital pnos, orgs, sheet mus. Hammond specialists.*

Jack White Music. 92 Fore Hamlet, Ipswich IP3 8AF *tel:* 01473 257223 *fax:* 01473 254070. *Orgs, keyboards, pnos, synthesizers, MIDI, modules, guis, accs, tuition.*

Keysounds. 37 Upper Orwell St, Ipswich, Suffolk IP4 1HP *tel:* 01473 213494 *also fax. Keyboards, digital pnos, amps, orgs, guis, mus books, repairs, m/order.*

Music World. 16 Queen St, Ipswich *tel:* 01473 253666 *fax:* 01473 213091. *Insts, sheet mus.*

Lowestoft

Morlings Ltd. 149-151 London Rd North, Lowestoft, Suffolk NR32 1NG *tel:* 01502 565491/2 *fax:* 01502 589839. *Books, insts, mus, keyboards.*

Surrey

Banstead

Banstead Music Shop. 8 High St, Banstead, Surrey SM7 3HE *tel:* 01737 373333 *also fax. Mus, w/wind, br, strs, guis, amps, keyboards, drums. M/order.*

Cobham

Sheargold Pianos Ltd. 162 Anyards Rd, Cobham, Surrey KT11 2LH *tel:* 01932 866577 *fax:* 01932 868178 *email:* anthony@ SheargoldPianos.com. *Uprights, grands (new and reconditioned); digital pnos, pno rental, removals, sheet mus, tuning, repairs.*

Croydon

Gigsounds Ltd. 195 London Rd, Croydon, Surrey CR0 2RJ *tel:* 0800 092 1420; 020 8686 4546 *fax:* 020 8681 5755. *Electric, acoustic, wind, etc insts and accs.*

H & R Cloake Ltd. 29 High St, Croydon, Surrey CR0 1QB *tel:* 020 8686 1336/8686 3965. *Large classical dept, CDs.*

H Lane & Son Pianos. 326 Brighton Rd, South Croydon, Surrey CR2 6AJ *tel:* 020 8688 3513 *fax:* 020 8688 4804 *email:* abrizga@cocoon.co.uk. *New and reconditioned upright and grand pnos.*

Jonathan Myall Music/Just Flutes. 46 South End, Croydon, Surrey CR0 1DP *tel:* 020 8662 8424 *fax:* 020 8662 8404 *email:* enquiries@ justflutes.com. *Mus, books, insts, recordings, cassettes, accs, m/order, repairs.*

Martin Phelps Music Ltd. 9 South End, Croydon, Surrey CR0 1BE *tel:* 020 8680 9747 *fax:* 020 8680 9471. *Pnos, orgs, digital pnos, keyboards, guis. Sheet mus, amps, accs, computer mus software.*

Willson & Newman. High Bank, Hook Hill, Sanderstead, Croydon CR2 0LA, Surrey *tel:* 020 8657 5817. *Pno tuning and repairs.*

Dorking

Royal School of Church Music. Cleveland Lodge, Westhumble, Dorking RH5 6BW *tel:* 01306 872811 *fax:* 01306 887240 *email:* musicsupplies @rscm.com. *Org and choral mus.*

Epsom

Bootleg Musical Instruments. 5-7 South St, Epsom, Surrey KT18 7PJ *tel:* 01372 724528 *fax:* 01372 729703. *Mus insts, educ suppliers.*

Esher

ABC Music Ltd. 85 High St, Esher, Surrey KT10 9QA *tel:* 01372 466195 *fax:* 01372 470445 *email:* abc@enterprise.net. *Insts, mus, CDs, pnos.*

Farnham

Lloyd & Keyworth Music. 6-7 Downing St, Farnham, Surrey GU9 7PE *tel:* 01252 710666 *fax:* 01252 711159 *email:* 101636.3600@ compuserve.com. *Pnos, Roland pnos, keyboards, w/wind, br, strs, sheet mus, Roland Music Learning Centre.*

Guildford

Albert's Music Shop Ltd. 9 Market St, Guildford, Surrey GU1 4LB *tel:* 01483 440188 *fax:* 01483 440823. *Mus insts, accs, sheet mus.*

Andertons Music Co. 58-59 Woodbridge Rd, Guildford, Surrey GU1 4RF *tel:* 01483 456777 (sales); 01483 456888 (educ) *fax:* 01483 456722 *email:* sales@andertons.co.uk. *Guis, keyboards, perc, computers, recording equipment, educ equipment, PA, repairs, amps, accs.*

Haslemere

Chamberlain Music. Weyhill, Haslemere, Surrey GU27 1HN *tel:* 01428 658806 *fax:* 01428 658807 *email:* info@chamberlainmusic.co.uk. *Strs, w/wind, br, Yamaha pnos; specialists in sheet mus and school supplies; Grove dictionaries.*

Dolmetsch Musical Instruments. Unicorn Trading Estate, Weydown Rd, Haslemere, Surrey GU27 1DN *tel:* 01428 643235 *fax:* 01428 654920 *email:* brian@dolmetsch.com. *Rcdrs in wood and plastic, early keyboard insts, accs, viols.*

Kew

ABC Music Ltd. 9 Royal Parade, Station Approach, Kew Gardens, Surrey TW9 3QD *tel:* 020 8940 1892 *fax:* 01372 470445 *email:* abc@enterprise.net. *Insts, pnos, sheet mus, gifts, CDs, accs, software.*

Kingston-upon-Thames

Hands Keyboards. 14 Eden Street, Kingston-upon-Thames, Surrey KT1 1BB *tel:* 020 8547 0944 *fax:* 020 8549 4151 *email:* handsmusic @callnetuk.com. *Keyboards, digital pnos and orgs, teaching school.*

Hands Music. 5 The Griffin Centre, Market Place, Kingston-upon-Thames, Surrey KT1 1JT *tel:* 020 8546 9630 *fax:* 020 8546 7771 *email:* music@tabfine.freeserve.co.uk. *Sheet mus, albums, educ, exam mus.*

Hands Music. 6 The Griffin Centre, Market Place, Kingston-upon-Thames, Surrey KT1 1JQ *tel:* 020 8546 9156 *fax:* 020 8546 7771 *email:* music@tabfine.freeserve.co.uk. *Classical, orch, ethnic insts bought and sold. Guis, amps, rental, repairs.*

Merstham

David and Emma Newton Violins, at Potters Music Shop Ltd. 16 High St, Merstham, Surrey RH1 3EA *tel:* 01737 645065 *fax:* 01737 645808. *Bowed str insts, repairs, bow-makers.*

Emma Newton Electric Violins at Potters Music Shop (Croydon) Ltd. 16 High St, Merstham, Surrey RH1 3EA *tel:* 01737 645065 *fax:* 01737 645808 *email:* newt@rainbow30.freeserve.co.uk. *Electric vns, vas, vcs, dbs. Accs.*

Reigate

Eric Lindsey Ltd. 12 West St, Reigate RH2 9BS *tel:* 01737 221481 *fax:* 01737 223584. *Guis, drums, keyboards, recording, PA equipment.*

Stentor Music Co Ltd. Albert Rd North, Reigate, Surrey RH2 9EZ *tel:* 01737 240226 *fax:* 01737 242748 *email:* stentor@stentor- music.com. *Wholesale specialist str inst supplier; also br, w/wind and guis.*

Touchstone Tonewoods Ltd. 44 Albert Rd North, Reigate, Surrey RH2 9EZ *tel:* 01737 221064 *fax:* 01737 242748 *email:* tt@stentor-music.com. *Supplier to makers and repairers.*

Richmond

Chandler Guitars. 300-302 Sandycombe Rd, Kew, Richmond, Surrey TW9 3NG *tel:* 020 8940 5874 *fax:* 020 8948 8203 *email:* sales@ chandlerguitars.co.uk. *Elec and acoustic guis, amps and accs.*

Richmond Music Shop Ltd. Red Lion St, Richmond, Surrey TW9 1RW *tel:* 020 8332 6220 *fax:* 020 8332 0552 *email:* richmondmusic@ compuserve.com.

Sanderstead

Willson & Newman. High Bank, Hook Hill, Sanderstead, S Croydon CR2 0LA *tel:* 020 8657 5817. *Pno tuning and repairs.*

Surbiton

The Piano Workshop. 111-113 Ewell Rd, Surbiton, Surrey KT6 6AL *tel:* 020 8399 4110 *fax:* 020 8390 1688 *email:* sales@piano-workshop.co.uk. *Upright and grand pnos, Yamaha grand centre, digital pnos.*

Sutton

Music Education Supplies. 101 Banstead Rd South, Sutton, Surrey SM2 5LH *tel:* 020 8770 3866 *fax:* 020 8770 3554. *Agents of Sonor school perc and suppliers of Suzuki handchimes and perc, Nordoff-Robbins reed hns, Aulos rcdrs, books, insts, etc.*

Sutton Music Centre. 64 Haddon Rd, Sutton, Surrey SM1 1RN *tel:* 020 8642 2838 *fax:* 020 8643 2500. *Insts, mus.*

West Byfleet

Britten's Music Ltd. 3-4 Station Approach, West Byfleet, Surrey KT14 6NG *tel:* 01932 351165/351614 *also fax; email:* sales@britten.co.uk. *Sheet mus, insts, accs, digital pnos, keyboards, software, m/order.*

Woking

Surrey Music Store. 76 High St, Horsell, Woking, Surrey GU21 4SZ *tel:* 01483 729319 *fax:* 01483 747719 *email:* sales@surreymusic.co.uk. *Insts to rent or buy, accs, mus books including ABRSM exam mus, classical CDs, m/order.*

Tyne and Wear

Blaydon-on-Tyne

George Harrison Organs. 7 The Precinct, Blaydon-on-Tyne, Tyne and Wear NE21 5DT *tel:* 0191 414 4333 *fax:* 0191 414 5158.

Gateshead

Williams the Music People. 16 Garden Walk, Metro Centre (Yellow Quadrant), Gateshead, Tyne and Wear *tel:* 0191 493 2244 *fax:* 0191 460 2422 *email:* enquiries@williams-music.co.uk. *Mus, insts, keyboards, pnos, orgs, sheet mus, guis, amps and electric.*

Newcastle upon Tyne

Andy Lee Woodwind. 195 Osborne Rd, Jesmond, Newcastle upon Tyne *tel:* 0191 281 3585 *also fax. W/wind repairs, second-hand refurbished stocks of all w/wind insts, specialising in sax.*

Newcastle Music. 71 Westgate Rd, Newcastle upon Tyne NE1 1SG *tel:* 0191 221 0595 *fax:* 01661 820755. *W/wind, br, strs, folk insts. Repairs and rental scheme.*

Saxophone Emporium. 2 Causey Building, Newcastle upon Tyne NE3 4DL *tel:* 0191 285 4177. *New and second-hand saxes and accs.*

Warwickshire

Leamington Spa

Derek Roberts Violins. 185 Leam Terrace, Leamington Spa, Warwicks CV31 1DW *tel:* 01926 428313 *also fax; email:* derek.roberts@violins.demon.co.uk. *Orch strs, cases, bows, accs; also maker and restorer.*

Presto Music. 23 Portland St, Leamington Spa, Warwicks CV32 5EZ *tel:* 01926 317020 *email:* presto@city2000.net. *Insts, mus, CDs, cassettes, m/order.*

R B Mew. 1 Park St, Leamington Spa, Warwicks CV32 4QN *tel:* 01926 424949. *Pnos, keyboards, insts and accs, tuning and repairs.*

Nuneaton

Abbey Music Studios. 114 Abbey St, Nuneaton, Warwicks CV11 5BX *tel:* 024 7664 1915 *also fax. Orgs, pnos, keyboards, mus, insts, tuition.*

Leisure Music (Head Office). 43-44 Abbey St, Nuneaton, Warwicks CV11 5BT *tel:* 024 7634 8702 *also fax. Orgs, pnos, keyboards, guis, w/wind, br; educ insts; m/order.*

Rugby

Freeman & Neale's Music Shop. 40-42 Lawford Rd, Rugby, Warwicks CV21 2DY *tel:* 01788 577064 *fax:* 01788 541612 *email:* freenmusic@aol.com. *Insts, mus.*

Stratford-upon-Avon

The Music House. 27 Greenhill St, Stratford-upon-Avon, Warwicks CV37 6LE *tel:* 01789 268515 *also fax. Mus, insts, accs.*

West Midlands

Bearwood

Classical Guitar Centre Ltd. 51a St Mary's Rd, Bearwood, W Midlands B67 5DH *tel:* 0121 429 7446 *fax:* 0121 429 4211. *Guis, mus, accs.*

Birmingham

Allegro Music. 82 Suffolk St, Queensway, Birmingham B1 1TA *tel:* 0121 643 7553 *fax:* 0121 633 4773 *email:* sales@allegro.co.uk. *Books, mus, m/order.*

Birmingham Piano Warehouse/Moseley Pianos. Unit L, 68 Wyrley Rd, Witton, Birmingham B6 7BN *tel:* 0121 327 2701 *also fax;* 07970 989373. *Wholesale and retail. Restored trad and modern upright and grand pnos. All styles and cabinets. 50 in stock. Restoration, removal, hire, valuations.*

James Pass & Co Ltd. 71 Smallbrook Queensway, Birmingham B5 4HX *tel:* 0121 643 7623 *also fax; email:* info@euromusic.web.com. *Books, insts, mus, educ videos and cassettes, m/order.*

Midland Music. 1070 Stratford Rd, Hall Green, Birmingham B28 8AD *tel:* 0121 777 3188 *fax:* 0121 702 2683. *Mus, books, br, w/wind, str insts, guis, accs, novelties, educ mus; m/order; tuition centre.*

Musical Exchanges. 89 Old Snow Hill, Birmingham B4 6HX *tel:* 0121 248 5868 *fax:* 0121 233 9127. *Guis, keyboards, drums, br, PA, w/wind, repairs.*

Sydney Evans Ltd. Unit 204, The Argent Centre, 60 Frederick St, Birmingham B1 3HS *tel:* 0121 233 1741 *fax:* 0121 233 1220. *Accs for str insts.*

Coventry

MB Sunderland Music. 62 Earlsdon St, Coventry CV5 6EJ *tel:* 024 7671 4272 *also fax; email:* music@mbsunderlandmusic.freeserve.co.uk. *Insts, mus, classical CDs, cassettes.*

Halesowen

Musical Instrument Repairs & Sales. Hereward Rise, Halesowen Industrial Park, Halesowen, W Midlands B62 8AN *tel:* 0121 550 9707 *fax:* 0121 501 3873 *email:* mirsales@aol.com. *New and second-hand insts, repairs.*

Solihull

Express Music (Solihull). 382 Stratford Rd, Shirley, Solihull, W Midlands B90 4AQ *tel:* 0121 745 8122 *email:* sales@atozmusic.co.uk. *Insts, amps, accs, software, free tuition.*

The Music Store. 130 Station Rd, Knowle, Solihull, W Midlands B93 0EP *tel:* 01564 773100 *fax:* 01564 777530. *Insts, mus, m/order. Gui specialists.*

Sutton Coldfield

Colbecks. 26-28 Chester Rd, New Oscott, Sutton Coldfield, Birmingham B73 5DA *tel:* 0121 321 3909 *fax:* 0121 321 1815. *Pnos, keyboards, insts, sheet mus.*

Walsall

TR Music. 233-236 Stafford St, Walsall, W Midlands WS2 8DF *tel:* 01922 613101. *Guis, PA, amps, electric repairs, str insts, cl, fl, drums, mus books, accs, recording equipment, lighting, pyrotechnics.*

Wolverhampton

Make Music. 46 School St, Wolverhampton WV1 4LF *tel:* 01902 425284 *fax:* 01902 427630 *email:* makemusic@schoolst.freeserve.co.uk. *Insts, keyboards, hi-tec, mus.*

The Music House. 122-123 Salop St, Wolverhampton WV3 0RX *tel:* 01902 425900 *fax:* 01902 424094.

Roden's Music. Unit 1 (1st floor) Hampton Walk, Wolverhampton WV1 1TQ *tel:* 01902 428459; 0800 328 5742 *fax:* 01902 425600. *Books, mus, insts, repairs, tuition.*

West Sussex

Burgess Hill

The Rock Shop. 21 Junction Rd, Burgess Hill, W Sussex RH15 0HR *tel:* 01444 241167. *Guis, amps, keyboards, w/wind insts, drums, repairs, mus, m/order, accs.*

Chichester

Berns Music. 42 West St, Chichester, W Sussex PO19 1RP *tel:* 01243 781844 *also fax; email:* bernsmusic@btinternet.com. *Sheet mus: classical, popular and educ. W/wind, br, str insts, rental with option to buy, repairs, accs, gifts.*

Cathedral Music. Maudlin House, Westhampnett, Chichester, W Sussex PO18 0PB *tel:* 01243 776325 *fax:* 01243 539604. *Mus (m/order); visitors by appointment.*

The Chichester Music Centre. 4 Eastgate Square, Chichester, W Sussex PO19 1ED *tel:* 01243 780536.

Crawley

The Guitar Makers. 87 Gales Drive, Three Bridges, Crawley, W Sussex RH10 1QA *tel:* 01293 543055 *also fax; email:* mail@guitarmakers.freeserve.co.uk. *Custom-made guis, accs, amps, repairs, Gibsons, Fenders Aria, etc.*

Hobgoblin Music. 17 The Parade, Northgate, Crawley, W Sussex RH10 2DT *tel:* 01293 515858 *fax:* 01293 561602 *email:* post@hobgoblin.co.uk. *Folk insts.*

Haywards Heath

Peter Voigt Ltd. 71 High St, Lindfield, Haywards Heath, W Sussex RH16 2HN *tel:* 01444 483206 *also fax. Vn family insts and accs.*

Horsham

Musique. 36a East St, Horsham, W Sussex RH12 1HL *tel:* 01403 254880 *fax:* 01403 259800. *Sheet mus, accs, insts, repairs, hire, m/order.*

Rustington

Macaulay Library Supply Co Ltd. The Studio, Waverley Rd, Rustington, W Sussex BN16 2DY *tel:* 01903 785966 *fax:* 01903 775950. *Suppliers of books and recorded mus to libraries and schools.*

Steyning

Macdonald Music Service (MMS). 14 High St, Steyning, W Sussex BN44 3GG *tel:* 01903 816120 *also fax. Books, mus, speciality org mus.*

Worthing

Music Supplies Ltd. 33 Warwick St, Worthing, W Sussex BN11 3DQ *tel:* 01903 208[illegible]92 *fax:* 01903 239004. *Books, mus, insts, br, w/wind, keyboards, studio equipment, PA, computers, accs, m/order, educ supplier, rental*

S M C Pianos and Keyboards. 57-59 Brighton Rd, Worthing, W Sussex BN11 3EE *tel:* 01903 211181.

West Yorkshire

Bradford

A to G Woodwind & Brass. 68 Morley St, Bradford BD7 1AQ *tel:* 01274 307207 *also fax. W/wind and br insts sales and repairs.*

Early Music Shop. 38 Manningham Lane, Bradford BD1 3EA *tel:* 01274 393753 *fax:* 01274 393516 *email:* sales@earlyms.demon.co.uk. *Insts, inst kits, rcdrs, mus.*

J Wood & Sons Ltd. 38 Manningham Lane, Bradford BD1 3EA *tel:* 01274 307636 *fax:* 01274 393516 *email:* sales@earlyms.demon.co.uk. *Insts, mus, pnos, orgs, keyboards, strs, sheet mus, CDs.*

Michael Rath Brass Sales and Repairs and Trombone Manufacture. 38 Manningham Lane, Bradford BD1 3EA *tel:* 01274 721894 *fax:* 01274 735325. *Br sales and repairs. Also manufacture trbs.*

Minstrels Music Shop. 38 Sunbridge Rd, Bradford BD1 2AA *tel:* 01274 390847 *also fax; email:* mail@minstrels-music.co.uk. *Acoustic and elec guis, vns, w/wind, harmonicas, printed mus, videos, repairs. M/order service for strs, harmonicas, etc.*

Renaissance Workshop Company Ltd. 38 Manningham Lane, Bradford BD1 3EA *tel:* 01274 201752 *fax:* 01274 201753 *email:* sales@renwks.com. *Early mus insts, inst kits and inst plans.*

The Woodwind Exchange. 38 Manningham Lane, Bradford BD1 3EA *tel:* 01274 7218[illegible]1 *fax:* 01274 393516. *New and second-hand w/wind insts.*

Castleford

Rock Factory. Wheldon Rd, Castleford, W Yorks WF10 2SD *tel:* 01977 513643 *fax:* 01977 513644. *Guis, amps, drums, PA, group equipment.*

Halifax

GSG Pianos. Grove House, Wade House Rd, Shelf, Halifax HX3 7PX *tel:* 01274 677450 *fax:* 01274 677450. *New and reconditioned pnos and digital pnos.*

Maestro Music. 25 The Piece Hall, Halifax HX1 1RE *tel:* 01422 349359. *Guis, keyboards, mus books, w/wind, br, accs, effects (zoom).*

Huddersfield

Normans Ltd. 9 Mini Park, Leeds Rd, Huddersfield, W Yorks HD1 6PA *tel:* 01484 514961 *fax:* 01484 514963. *Br and w/wind insts, perc, repairs, mus, accs, also m/order.*

R E Wood & Sons Ltd. 11 Market St, Huddersfield, W Yorks *tel:* 01484 427455 *fax:* 01484 427355. *Insts, mus, records, pnos, orgs, TV, hi-fi, keyboards.*

Ilkley

Time and Tune. 10 The Grove, Ilkley, W Yorks LS29 9EG *tel:* 01943 817301 *also fax. Mus, CDs, insts.*

Leeds

Fox's Music. 97-99 Vicar Lane, Leeds LS1 6PJ *tel:* 0113 245 0350 *fax:* 0113 245 8897 *email:* enquiries@foxmusic.co.uk. *Guis, PA, hi-tech, keyboards, accs, mus, pnos, digital pnos.*

J Scheerer & Sons Ltd. 88-90 Merrion Centre, Leeds LS2 8NG *tel:* 0113 244 9592/0444; 0113 243 2401 *fax:* 0113 245 0347 *email:* sales@scheerers.co.uk. *Insts, br, w/wind, strs, mus, perc, electric guis.*

Knock on Wood. Granary Wharf, Leeds LS1 4BR *tel:* 0113 242 9146 *fax:* 0113 245 9878 *email:* kow@globalnet.co.uk. *Insts, books and recordings from around the world.*

Ossett

Music for Brass Ltd. Unit 1, Warneford Ave, Dewsbury Rd, Ossett, W Yorks WF5 9NJ *tel:* 01924 261154 *fax:* 01924 280310. *Own titles (br and wind band).*

Wakefield

R E Wood & Son Ltd. 20 Cross St, Wakefield, W Yorks WF1 3BW *tel:* 01924 374446 *fax:* 01924 291807.

Wiltshire

Heytesbury

The Sound Post. Heytesbury Mill, Heytesbury, Wilts BA12 0HE *tel:* 01985 841244 *fax:* 01985 841266 *email:* bimy@thesoundpost.co.uk. *Vns, vas, vcs and strs. Wholesalers.*

Melksham

In Tune Music. Unit G21, Avonside Enterprise Park, Melksham, Wilts SN12 8BS *tel:* 01225 709710. *Elec orgs and keyboards, digital pnos, sheet mus, repairs.*

Pewsey

Warblers. Embrook House, Hilcot, Pewsey, Wilts SN9 6LE *tel:* 01672 851317 *also fax. M/order vocal mus.*

Salisbury

Percy Prior's Music. 5 Catherine St, Salisbury SP1 2DF *tel:* 01722 322278; 01722 328181 (sheet mus dept). *Electric pnos, keyboards, insts, sheet mus specialists, repairs.*

Swindon

Duck Son & Pinker Ltd. 59-60 Bridge St, Swindon, Wilts SN1 1BT *tel:* 01793 522018/522220. *Mus, books, insts, pnos, orgs, hire, educ mus, CDs, cassettes, records.*

Holmes Music. 21-23 Faringdon Rd, Swindon, Wilts SN1 5AR *tel:* 01793 520948/534095 *fax:* 01793 542436 *email:* holmes_music@compuserve.com. *Mus, elec orgs, keyboards, pnos, synths, guis, amps, drums, records, educ insts.*

Kempster & Son (The Music Shop). 98 Commercial Rd, Swindon, Wilts SN1 5PL *tel:* 01793 535523 *fax:* 01793 526375. *Group and PA gear, multi-track recording, educ insts.*

Make Music Leisure Centres. 22-23 Victoria Rd, Swindon, Wilts SN1 3AW *tel:* 01793 644181 *also fax. Group equipment, disco and club.*

Worcestershire

Evesham

Vine Music. Vine Court, 7 Vine St, Evesham, Worcs WR11 4RE *tel:* 01386 442548. *Insts, accs, lighting, PA installation, books, tutorials.*

Malvern

Hibernian Violins. 24 Players Ave, Malvern Link, Worcs WR14 1DU *tel:* 01684 562947 *also fax. Vns, bows, accs, repairs, restoration.*

Malvern Bookshop. 7 Abbey Rd, Malvern, Worcs WR14 3ES *tel:* 01684 575915 *fax:* 01684 577357 *email:* jona@malvernbooks.demon.co.uk. Jonathan Gibbs. *Second-hand books, vocal scores, minature and full scores, sheet mus.*

Worcester

Music City. 5 Charles St, Worcester WR1 2AQ *tel:* 01905 26600 *also fax. Guis, amps, drums, effects units, home recording.*

Musical Instrument Repairs and Sales. 57 Martley Rd, St John's, Worcester WR2 6HH *tel:* 01905 420241 *also fax. Br, w/wind, str, guis, printed mus, finance schemes.*

York, City of

York

Banks & Son (Music) Ltd. 18 Lendal, York YO1 8AU *tel:* 01904 658836 *fax:* 01904 629547 *email:* banksmusic@dial.pipex.com. *Printed mus, mus text books, classical CDs, mus insts, accs, software, mus gifts.*

Classical Harpsichords and Classical Organs. Lamel Towers, 81 Hull Rd, York YO10 3JS *tel:* 01904 411873. *Mainly demo insts and work done to order.*

Philip Martin Music Books. 38 Fossgate, York YO1 2TF *tel:* 01904 636111 *fax:* 01904 658889 *email:* musicbooks@philipmartin.demon.co.uk. *Books, mus; also m/order.*

York Music Services. 9 Museum St, York YO1 2DT *tel:* 01904 636721 *fax:* 01904 672392. *Books, mus, accs, insts.*

Channel Islands

Jersey

Easy Play Music. 11-13 New St, St Helier, Jersey JE2 3RA, Channel Islands *tel:* 01534 879570 *fax:* 01534 878901 *email:* offsure@itl.net. *Roland, Technics, Yamaha, Casio, Korg.*

Isle of Man

Douglas

Peter Norris Music. Villa Marina Arcade, Douglas, Isle of Man IM1 2HN *tel:* 01624 661794 *fax:* 01624 622540. *Insts, mus, amplification.*

Scotland

Aberdeen, City of

Aberdeen

Bruce Millers. 363 Union St, Aberdeen AB9 1EN *tel:* 01224 592211 *fax:* 01224 580085. *Insts, keyboards, pnos, mus, recordings, books, tuning, repairs, hi-fi, accs, TV videos.*

Dundee, City of

Dundee

Rainbow Music. 35 Cowgate, Dundee DD1 2JF *tel:* 01382 201405 *fax:* 01382 225183. *Insts, PA and recording equipment.*

East Ayrshire

Kilmarnock

RGM. 24 Nelson St, Kilmarnock KA1 1BA *tel:* 01563 537711 *fax:* 01563 530209. *Guis, perc, mus, insts, lighting, repairs.*

Edinburgh, City of

Edinburgh

The Bagpipe Centre. 49 Blackfriars St, Edinburgh EH1 1NB *tel:* 0131 577 3090 *also fax; email:* scotfolk@compuserve.com. *Bagpipe products.*

Edinburgh Organ Studio. 98 Canongate, The Royal Mile, Edinburgh EH8 8DD *tel:* 0131 556 3005 *fax:* 0131 556 8445. *Orgs, church orgs, keyboards, digital pnos. Repairs, tuition.*

Gordon Stevenson Violin Maker and Restorer. 6 Barclay Terrace, Bruntsfield, Edinburgh EH10 4HP *tel:* 0131 229 2051 *fax:* 0131 229 9298. *Str insts for sale; restoration of vns.*

Live Music. 48 Elm Row, Leith Walk, Edinburgh EH7 4AH *tel:* 0131 556 9956 *fax:* 0131 558 7575. *Guis (elec, acoustic, bass), amps, PAs. Vintage and used equipment specialists. Spares and repairs.*

Mev Taylor's Music Shop. 212 Morrison St, Edinburgh EH3 8AE *tel:* 0131 229 7454. *Br and w/wind specialists.*

Music Shop. 22 Grindlay St, Edinburgh EH3 9AP *tel:* 0131 229 8392 *also fax; email:* pagano@globalnet.co.uk. *Insts, elec.*

Rae Macintosh Music Ltd. 6 Queensferry St, Edinburgh EH2 4PA *tel:* 0131 225 1171 *fax:* 0131 225 9447. *Mus, videos, m/order.*

Scayles Music. 50 St Patrick Square, Edinburgh EH8 9ES *tel:* 0131 667 8241 *fax:* 0131 558 7575. *Guis (elec, acoustic, bass), br, w/wind, drums, perc, bouzoukis, mandolas, mandolins, books, spares, repairs, PA hire, amplification.*

Sheena McNeil. 7 Barclay Terrace, Edinburgh EH10 4HP *tel:* 0131 228 3666 *fax:* 0131 228 3966 *email:* sales@sheenamcneil.freeserve.co.uk. *Books, mus.*

Sheila Barnes. 3 East Castle Rd, Edinburgh EH10 5AP *tel:* 0131 229 8018. *W/shop drawings and information for builders of early keyboard insts, clvd kits (portable 18th C design), hpd and spinet kits. Covered strings for clvds and square pnos.*

Falkirk, City of

Falkirk

Normans Ltd. The Studio, Burnfoot Lane, Falkirk *tel:* 01324 611895 *fax:* 01324 634611. *Br, w/wind, str, perc.*

Fife

Dunfermline

Sound Control. The Elgin Works, Dunfermline, Fife KY12 7SD *tel:* 01383 732273 *fax:* 01383 725733. *Hi-tech, recording, PA, guis, keyboards.*

Glasgow, City of

Glasgow

Band Supplies (Scotland). 5 Old Dumbarton Rd, Glasgow G3 8QY *tel:* 0141 339 9400 *fax:* 0141 334 8157. *Sax specialists, insts (br, w/wind, perc), mus, recordings; also repairs.*

Biggars - Music for All. 273 Sauchiehall St, Glasgow G2 3HH *tel:* 0141 332 8676 *fax:* 0141 352 7408. *Orgs, pnos, digital pnos, keyboards, orch and band insts, mus, synthesizers, guis, sheet mus.*

Drum Shop. 15 Blackie St, Glasgow G3 8TN *tel:* 0141 339 4497 *also fax. Perc.*

McCormack's Music Ltd. 29-35 Bath St, Glasgow G2 1HT *tel:* 0141 332 6644 *fax:* 0141 353 3095 *email:* 106251.2710@compuserve.com. *Guis, drums and ethnic perc, keyboards, br, w/wind, amps, PA systems, mics, educ supplies, accs, mus.*

Sound Control - Direct. Jamaica St, Glasgow G1 4NN *tel:* 0800 525260 *fax:* 0141 204 0614 *email:* direct@soundcontrol.co.uk.

Highland

Beauly

Serenade for Strings. South Teavarran, Foxhole, Kiltarlity, Beauly, Inverness-shire IV4 7HT *tel:* 01463 741651 *also fax; email:* serenade.strings@virgin.net. *Specialises in sheet mus for strs, including current syllabuses for the exam boards. Post-free service for mus not in stock.*

Dingwall

Maitland Music. Tulloch St, Dingwall, Ross-shire IV15 9JY *tel:* 01349 863191 *also fax; email:* sales@maitlandmusic.co.uk. *Insts, sheet mus, amps, accs, repairs, educ supplies, rentals, m/order.*

Inverness

The Music Shop. 27 Church St, Inverness IV1 1DY *tel:* 01463 233374 *fax:* 01463 713983. *Books, insts including bagpipes and bodhrans, sheet mus, accs. Educ discount.*

Perth and Kinross

Perth

Wilkie's Music House. Charterhouse Lane, Canal Cres, Perth PH2 8HT *tel:* 01738 623041 *fax:* 01738 633173. *Mus, guis, pnos, keyboards, insts, accs.*

Renfrewshire

Paisley

Music Centre. 8 Wellmeadow St, Paisley PA1 2EF *tel:* 0141 848 1033. *Keyboards, guis, mus, insts.*

Peter Smith & Sons. 60 Back Sneddon St, Paisley PA3 2BY *tel:* 0141 887 6160.

Scottish Borders

Galashiels

Waverley Piano Co. 4 Chapel St, Galashiels, Selkirkshire TD1 1BU *tel:* 01896 752308. *Upright and grand pnos; also restoration, tuning and reconditioning.*

South Ayrshire

Ayr

Billy McEwen Organ Ltd. Keyboard and Piano Centre, 31-35 Fort St, Ayr KA7 1DG *tel:* 01292 269667 *fax:* 01292 289597. *Orgs, pnos, digital pnos, keyboards, synths, guis, accs, amps.*

South Lanarkshire

Auldhouse

Just Music. 246 Auldhouse Rd, East Kilbride G75 9DX *tel:* 01355 245674 *fax:* 01355 231020 *email:* Just.Music.Scotland@zetnet.co.uk. *Mus (m/order), br and wind band specialist.*

Hamilton

Music Centre. 75 Cadzow St, Hamilton ML3 8DZ *tel:* 01698 283325 *fax:* 01698 283330. *Insts, amps, mus.*

Stirling, City of

Stirling

Roadshow. 64 Upper Craigs, Stirling FK8 2DS *tel:* 01786 471323 *also fax. PA, guis, amps, drums, lighting, sales, tuition, hire, repairs.*

West Dunbartonshire

Wishaw

Magnum Sound. 67 Stewarton St, Wishaw ML2 8AG *tel:* 01698 358761 *fax:* 01698 359745. *PA, insts, installation, accs, mus.*

Wales

Caerphilly County Borough

Caerphilly

Christopher Music Stores. 24 Cardiff Rd, Caerphilly CF83 1JP *tel:* 029 2088 8788.

Cardiff County Borough

Cardiff

Cranes Musical Instruments. 5a High St, Cardiff CF10 1AW *tel:* 029 2039 8215 *fax:* 029 2066 7017. *Pnos, guis, amps, keyboards, br, w/wind, str, drums, mus.*

Eric Lewin Pianos. 147 Crwys Rd, Cardiff CF24 4NH *tel:* 029 2064 4558. *Grand and upright pnos, new and second-hand. Repairs and hire.*

G M Music. 2 Wharton St, Cardiff CF10 1AG *tel:* 029 2023 1606 *also fax. Orch and group insts, equipment.*

Gamlin's Music Centre. 56 St Mary St, Cardiff CF10 1FE *tel:* 029 2023 1290/2022 0828 *fax:* 029 2023 7616. *Sheet mus, br, w/wind, str, pno, keyboards, guis, amps, hire, repairs.*

Music Direct. 33 Tydfil Place, Roath Park, Cardiff CF23 5HP *tel:* 029 2049 6080 *fax:* 029 2049 6080. *Printed mus and books; specialist catalogues on request. UK and export.*

Musicland and Sound Centre. 148-154 North Rd, Cardiff CF14 3BH *tel:* 029 2062 1715 *fax:* 029 2062 1285.

Rowlands Music Ltd. 19 High St, Arcade, Cardiff CF1 2QR *tel:* 029 2022 6935. *Sheet, exam, choral, educ mus, m/order.*

San Domenico Stringed Instruments. 175 Kings Rd, Cardiff CF11 9DF *tel:* 029 2023 5881 *fax:* 029 2034 4510 *email:* hmorgan@san-domenico.co.uk. *Fine vns, vcs, bows, accs. Bow repairs, restoration, insurance, expert appraisals.*

Cwmbran

Soundwave Music Centre. 46 Court Rd Ind Est, Cwmbran, Gwent NP44 3AS *tel:* 01633 482501/874251. *Guis, amps, PAs, books, second-hand records, full repair w/shop, PA installation.*

Carmarthenshire

Ammanford

Trevada Music. Shoppers World, 18 Wind St, Ammanford, Carmarthenshire SA18 3DN *tel:* 01269 596607 *fax:* 01269 596608 *email:* trevada@netcomuk.co.uk. *Insts, amplification, repairs, mus.*

Newcastle Emlyn

Christian Savage Violins. Danyrhelyg Isaf, Danyrhelyg, Newcastle Emlyn, Carmarthenshire SA38 *tel:* 01239 710036. *New and second-hand vns, vas, vcs, dbs. Also bows and accs.*

Ceredigion

Aberystwyth

Music Warehouse. 10 Northgate St, Aberystwyth, Ceredigion SY23 2JS *tel:* 01970 612349. *Books, insts, mus, recordings.*

Clwyd

Colwyn Bay

Music Makers. 12 Penrhyn Rd, Colwyn Bay, Clwyd LL29 8LG *tel:* 01492 534834. *Orgs, keyboards, pnos, guis, str, br, w/wind insts, sheet mus, accs, educ products, inst repair and hire, m/order, tuition facilities.*

Llandudno

Gog's Music Ltd. 6a Vaughan St, Llandudno LL30 1AB *tel:* 01492 876649 *also fax.*

Newport District

Abergavenny

Abergavenny Music. 23 Cross St, Abergavenny, Monmouthshire NP7 5EW *tel:* 01873 853394 *fax:* 01873 859525 *email:* abermusic@compuserve.com. *Sheet mus, books, CDs, tapes, videos, gifts, accs, m/order.*

Newport

G M Music. 14 Upper Dock St, Newport, Gwent *tel:* 01633 840606 *also fax. Orch and group insts, equipment. PA specialists.*

Gamlins Music Centre. 107 Commercial St, Newport, Gwent NP20 1LU *tel:* 01633 263867.

Speed Music Cool Blue Enterprise Ltd. 177 Upper Dock St, Newport, Gwent NP9 1DY *tel:* 01633 220390. *General mus inst store with PA dept, digital recording, school inst hire (everything except acoustic pno and org).*

Pembrokeshire

Haverfordwest

Swales Music Centre Ltd. 2-6 High St, Haverfordwest, Pembrokeshire *tel:* 01437 762059 *fax:* 01437 760872 *email:* musician@swalesmusic.co.uk. *Mus, books, cassettes, CDs, insts, accs.*

Pembroke Dock

The Music Centre. 38 Meyrick St, Pembroke Dock, Pembrokeshire SA72 6UT *tel:* 01646 682811 *also fax. Insts, accs, mus, CDs, videos.*

Powys

Newtown

Mid Wales Music Centre. Lion Works, Pool Rd, Newtown, Powys SY16 3AG *tel:* 01686 622161 *also fax. Guis, amps, PA specialists, perc, br, w/wind, keyboards, printed mus.*

Swansea County

Swansea

Music Station. Phoenix Way, Enterprise Park, Swansea *tel:* 01792 775751 *fax:* 01792 702141. *Orgs, keyboards, pnos, hi-tech, synths, guis, PA systems, etc.*

Wilks Music Stores Ltd. 32-33 St Helens Rd, Swansea SA1 4AY *tel:* 01792 655953 *also fax. Insts; also restoration, repairs, pno showroom, large mus showroom.*

Vale of Glamorgan

Barry

Christophers Music Stores. 1 High St, Barry, S Glamorgan CF62 7DZ *tel:* 01446 735914 *fax:* 01446 720488. *Mus, CDs, insts, guis, cassettes, imports.*

Bridgend

Carrington's World of Music. 39 Wyndham St, Bridgend CF31 1EB *tel:* 01656 661095 *also fax. Full range of insts and printed mus.*

Wrexham County Borough

Wrexham

Music Place. 30 Brook St, Wrexham LL13 7LL *tel:* 01978 265308. *Orgs, keyboards, guis, str, br, w/wind, sheet mus.*

Northern Ireland

County Antrim

Belfast

Drum Sounds. 96 Sandy Row, Belfast BT12 5EX *tel:* 028 9024 2684. *Fl band specialist.*

Marcus Musical Instruments Ltd. 125 Royal Ave, Belfast BT1 1FF *tel:* 028 9032 2871 *fax:* 028 9043 9955 *email:* musicman@marcus.dnet.co.uk. *All types of mus inst.*

County Derry

Portstewart

Dempseys of Portstewart. 36 The Promenade, Portstewart BT55 7AE, Co Derry *tel:* 028 7083 3005 *also fax.*

County Londonderry

Coleraine

McMeekin's (Music) Ltd. 6 Abbey St, Coleraine, Co Londonderry BT52 1DS *tel:* 028 7034 3045 *also fax.*

Antiquarian and Specialist Music Booksellers

Alba Secondhand Music. The Courtyard, 61 Otago St, Glasgow G12 8PQ *tel:* 0141 357 1795. Robert Lay, proprietor. *Inst and vocal printed mus, some antiquarian; vinyl records. Collections purchased Mon-Sat, 11am-5.30pm.*

Archive Bookstore. 83 Bell St, Marylebone, London NW1 6TB *tel:* 020 7402 8212. Tim and Michele Meaker. *19th C, second-hand and-out-of print books and mus bought and sold, including pop song sheets, vocal scores, ens and chmbr mus, etc. Library surplus purchased: rarities and collections of books and printed mus. Mon-Sat, 10.30am-6pm.*

Baron, H. 76 Fortune Green Rd, London NW6 IDS *tel:* 020 7794 4041 *fax:* 020 8459 2035. *Antiquarian mus, books, autographs, mss, prints. Open Fri and Sat, 1-6pm; also m/order.*

Bingham, Tony. 11 Pond St, London NW3 2PN *tel:* 020 7794 1596 *fax:* 020 7433 3662. *Old insts, reference books.*

Dooley, Rosemary M S. Crag House, Witherslack, Grange-over-Sands, Cumbria LA11 6RW *tel:* 01539 552286 *fax:* 01539 552013 *email: musicbks@rdooley.demon.co.uk. Second-hand books on mus. Catalogues issued. Worldwide distributor for Royal Musical Association. UK distributor for Pendragon Press (US).*

Gilham Books. 44 St Austell Rd, London SE13 7EQ *tel:* 020 8852 1905 *also fax. Second-hand mus books. 2000 vols. 2 catalogues pa.*

Goodden, Peter. 7 Clarendon Villas, Widcombe Hill, Bath BA2 6AG *tel:* 01225 310986. *Rare, second-hand, out-of-print books.*

Haas, Otto A and M Rosenthal. 49 Belsize Park Gardens, London NW3 4JL *tel:* 020 7722 1488 *fax:* 020 7722 2364. *Mss, rare mus books and eds. By appointment only.*

Lisa Cox Music. 20 Old Tiverton Rd, Exeter, Devon EX4 6LG *tel:* 01392 255776 *fax:* 01392 435871 *email: 100541.2220@compuserve.com; music@lisacoxmusic.free-online.co.uk. Rare printed and ms mus, autographs and ephemera.*

Macdonald, Charles. 14 High St, Steyning, W Sussex BN44 3GG *tel:* 01903 816120 *also fax. Org mus and books.*

May & May Ltd. Whitebridge, Semley, Shaftesbury SP7 9QP *tel:* 01747 830034 *fax:* 01747 830035. *Large stock of books on mus in many languages. Catalogues issued. Visitors welcome by appointment. Search service.*

Paramor, C D. 25 St Mary's Square, Newmarket, Suffolk CB8 0HZ *tel:* 01638 664416 *also fax. Gilbert & Sullivan, mus and theatre. Catalogues issued.*

Tamarisk Books. 80 High St, Hastings, E Sussex TN34 3EL *tel:* 01424 420591. *Second-hand books on mus, mainly classical, approx 4000. Miniature and other scores. Catalogues issued: 4-6 pa.*

Travis & Emery. 17 Cecil Court, London WC2N 4EZ *tel:* 020 7240 2129 *fax:* 020 7497 0790. *Antiquarian and second-hand mus, new and second-hand books, programmes, playbills. Catalogues issued.*

Trotman, F. Farrs, 3 Whitcombe Rd, Beaminster, Dorset DT8 3NB *tel:* 01308 862293/863336 (24 hr ans) *fax:* 01308 863673 *email: trotman.books@cwcom.net. Mus books (approx 2000) on all aspects of classical mus. Catalogues issued. Booksearch service.*

Wood, Peter. 20 Stone Hill Rd, Great Shelford, Cambridge CB2 5JL *tel:* 01223 842419 *also fax. Specialist in books on performing arts, including mus and opera.*

Woodlands Books. 65 Gledhow Wood Rd, Leeds LS8 4DG *tel:* 0113 266 7834. W F and V W Astbury. *Out-of-print and second-hand books on mus and musicians. Catalogues issued. M/order only.*

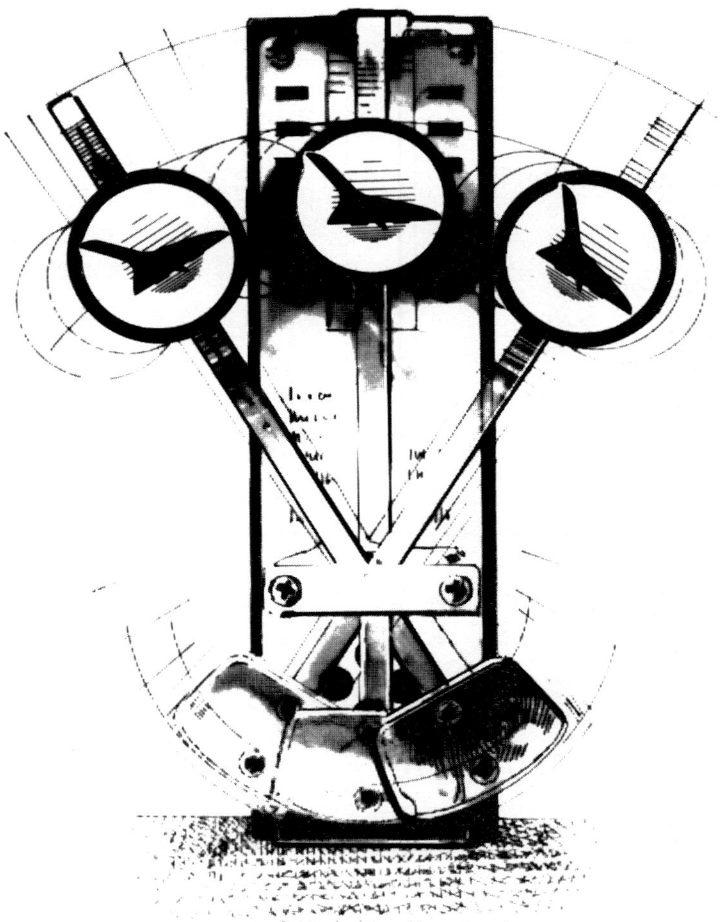

Musician Services

Accessory Distributors

American Percussion. 120-122 Bermondsey St, London SE1 3TX *tel:* 020 7403 3200 *fax:* 020 7403 5910. *Distributor of drums, sticks, accs.*

Britannia Reeds and Regency Reeds. 156 Hatfield Rd, St Albans, Herts AL1 4JA *tel:* 01727 846055 *fax:* 01727 811164. *Specialist manufacturers and sales of ob reeds, cane and accs; m/order worldwide.*

Centrepiece Music. PO Box 1601, Newport Pagnell, Bucks MK16 8PD *tel:* 01908 218003 *fax:* 01908 211828. Glenda Smith. *Wholesaler and distributor of accs for w/wind: mouthpieces, reeds, etc; Neotech sax and gui slings and straps; m/order.*

Impact Percussion. 120-122 Bermondsey St, London SE1 3TX *tel:* 020 7403 5900 *fax:* 020 7403 5910 *email:* impactperc@msn.com. Paul Hagen. *Importer of orch perc and accs.*

Riverside Reeds. 49 Fairway, Raynes Park, London SW20 9DN *tel:* 020 8540 0670 *fax:* 020 8241 1280 *email:* brisew@globalnet.co.uk; pbeew@globalnet.co.uk. Brian Sewell, Peter Williams. *Bsn reeds and cane supplied at all stages. Bespoke shapes specialists.*

Rosetti Ltd. 4 Tamdown Way, Springwood Industrial Estate, Braintree, Essex CM7 2QL *tel:* 01376 550033 *fax:* 01376 550042. *Str, br, w/wind, guis, perc, accs.*

T W Howarth & Co Ltd. 31 Chiltern St, London W1M 1HG *tel:* 020 7935 2407 *fax:* 020 7224 2564 *email:* sales@howarth.demon.co.uk. *Manufacturers and wholesale importers of w/wind accs.*

Accountancy and Taxation Services

Artistes Accountable. 29 Ravenshurst Ave, London NW4 4EG *tel:* 020 8202 3804 *also fax. Amanda Dean ATII. Personal tax returns, accounts and tax planning for musicians and other creative and performing artists. Member of the Chartered Institute of Taxation and Equity Union.*

Beechams Chartered Accountants. 3 Bedford Row, London WC1R 4BU *tel:* 0800 146075 freephone *fax:* 020 7242 5624 *email:* paul.davis @beechams.com. Paul Davis (MU member). *Tailored accounting manuals for musicians, making your book-keeping work easy. Act for several musicians and teachers already.*

Bruton Charles Chartered Accountants. 60 Valley Rd, Henley-on-Thames RG9 1RR *tel:* 01491 411322 *fax:* 01491 410951 *email:* 101565.2202 @compuserve.com. Jonathan Lawrence-Archer, Henley partner; Mark Lynskey, London partner. *Tax and accounts, VAT returns and personal financial planning.*

Bruton Charles Chartered Accountants. Ashland House, 20 Moxon St, Marylebone High St, London W1M 3JE *tel:* 020 7935 7872 *fax:* 020 7486 7639. *Tax and accounts, VAT returns and personal financial planning.*

Chantrey Vellacott. Derngate Mews, Derngate, Northampton NN1 1UE *tel:* 01604 639257 *fax:* 01604 231460 *email:* eharris@cvdfk.com. Elliot Harris. *Auditing and accounting services; personal financial planning and taxation.*

Chantrey Vellacott. Russell Square House, 10-12 Russell Square, London WC1B 5LF *tel:* 020 7509 9000 *fax:* 020 7436 8884. Chris Jones. *Auditing and accounting services; personal financial planning and taxation.*

David Smith & Co. 41 Welbeck St, London W1M 8HH *tel:* 020 7224 1004 *fax:* 020 7486 8705 *email:* dcsmithcd@aol.com. D C Smith, practitioner; R Shah, qualified snr. *Accounts preparation and taxation advice to self-employed musicians and teachers. Clients need not be local.*

Guy Rippon Organization. 24 Pepper St, London SE1 0EB *tel:* 020 7928 9777 *fax:* 020 7928 9222. Guy Rippon, snr partner. *Chartered certified accountants. Comprehensive accountancy services to the mus industry. Also registered auditors.*

Ivan Sopher & Co. 5 Elstree Gate, Elstree Way, Borehamwood, Herts WD6 1JD *tel:* 020 8207 0602 *fax:* 020 8207 6758.

John Seeley & Co. 1 Upper Saint Mary's Rd, Bearwood, Warley, W Midlands B67 5JR *tel:* 0121 429 1504 *fax:* 0121 429 3121. John Seeley, principal. *Full range of accountancy and taxation services for the mus industry. Free financial guide for musicians available on request.*

Lloyd Piggott Chartered Accountants. Blackfriars House, Parsonage, Manchester M3 2JA *tel:* 0161 833 0346 *fax:* 0161 832 0045 *email:* accs@lloydpiggott.u-net.com. Colin Lomas, snr partner; Gary Dodds, Christopher Swallow, partners. *Accountancy and taxation services for musicians throughout the UK.*

Martin Greene Ravden. 55 Loudoun Rd, St John's Wood, London NW8 0DL *tel:* 020 7625 4545 *fax:* 020 7625 5265 *email:* mgr@mgr.co.uk. Lionel Martin, David Ravden, Steve Daniel, Ed Grossman, Harish Shah, partners. *Business management, tour accounting and admin, inter-nation tax clearances, VAT, royalty examinations, litigation support and other financial services.*

Nyman Libson Paul Chartered Accountants. Regina House, 124 Finchley Rd, London NW3 5JS *tel:* 020 7794 5611 *fax:* 020 7431 1109 *email:* mail@nymanlibsonpaul.co.uk. Amin Saleh, partner (mus division). *Specialist knowledge of the entertainment and mus industry.*

Pearson & Co (Chartered Accountants). 113 Smug Oak Business Centre, Lye Lane, Bricket Wood, St Albans, Herts AL2 3UG *tel:* 01923 894404 *fax:* 01923 894990 *email:* musbus@pearson.nw2000.co.uk. Richard Pearson, partner. *Accountancy, audits, taxation and financial management services.*

Pryor, Begent, Fry & Co. The Great Barn Studio, Cippenham Lane, Slough SL1 5AU *tel:* 01753 554613 *fax:* 01753 553520. *Accountants.*

Trevor Ford & Co. 151 Mount View Rd, London N4 4JT *tel:* 020 8341 6408 *fax:* 020 8340 0021 *email:* tfordandco@aol.com. *Client list full at present.*

Willott Kingston Smith and Associates. Quadrant House, Air St Entrance, 80-82 Regent St, London W1R 5PA *tel:* 020 7304 4646 *fax:* 020 7304 4647 *email:* gh@kingsmith.co.uk. Cliff Ireton, Geraint Howells, partners; Paul Moore, taxation snr. *Financial management, contract reviews, litigation support, international tax, personal financial planning, audit and accounting, taxation, VAT, royalty auditing.*

Computer Systems Consultants

Artifax Software Ltd. 38 Ridgeway, Epsom, Surrey KT19 8LB *tel:* 01372 810081 *fax:* 01372 743390 *email:* admin@artifaxsoftware.com. Timothy Nathan, Nina Kaye, dirs; Bob Chase, sales; Ben Curthoys, Andrew Dunford, development; Tim Coleman, Geoffrey Dallamore, technical support. *Computer programs: ARTIFAX Event - for venue management to handle bookings, technical resources, personnel management, etc; ARTIFAX Festival - to manage festivals for performing arts; ARTIFAX Agent - designed for artists managers and concert agencies to handle all admin.*

DMT Associates. The Banda, Clifford Rd, Barnet, Herts EN5 5NY *tel:* 020 8440 4070 *fax:* 020 8447 0903 *email:* dmt@compuserve.com. Dinah Molloy, mgr dir. *Custom-designed software and services for mus organisations.*

Express Music (Solihull). 382 Stratford Rd, Shirley, Solihull, W Midlands B90 4AQ *tel:* 0121 745 8122. Peter Brown. *Computer software. Specialist media awareness courses on AVID, Cakewalk Cubase Logic, mus sequencing, Powerpoint, Word 6, Publisher.*

New Notations Computer Services. Unit A8, Friston Business Centre, Aldeburgh Rd, Friston, Saxmundham, Suffolk IP17 1NP *tel:* 01728 604906 *also fax; email:* stevef@newnotations.free-online.co.uk. Stephen Ferre, proprietor. *Consultancy and hardware/software sales. Mus notation. Custom-built computer workstations.*

New Notations London. 40 Campbell Close, London SW16 6NG *tel:* 020 8677 8473 *fax:* 020 8877 3494 *email:* nnlondon@gibmusic.freeserve.co.uk. Stephen Gibson, proprietor. *Software sales and consultancy. Mus notation, MIDI specialists. Distributors of Score mus publishing system.*

PRIAM. Nene House, Drayton Way, Drayton Fields Industrial Estate, Daventry, Northants NN11 5EA *tel:* 01327 702785 *fax:* 01327 311110. Andrew Kypri, technical adviser. *Supply Priam computer system covering accounts, stock, point of sales, marketing, order processing and copyright for mus retailers, m/order, record shops and distributors. Also provide bespoke systems.*

Sibelius Software Ltd. 75 Burleigh St, Cambridge CB1 1DJ *tel:* 01223 302765 *fax:* 01223 351947 *email:* infoUK@sibelius.com. Ben Finn, mgr dir; Jonathan Finn, development mgr. *Developer and distributor of the mus notation programmes, Sibelius for Windows and Sibelius for Mac.*

Software Partners. Oak Tree House, Station Rd, Claverdon, Warwicks CV35 8PE *tel:* 01926 842998 *fax:* 01926 842384 *email:* info@software-partners.co.uk. Richard Blundell. *Distributors of capella mus notation software, Capriccio (MIDI sequencer) tonica harmony and analysis software and Capella-scan and Midiscan mus scanning software.*

Diary and Answering Services

These organisations keep copies of their clients' diaries and will take bookings on behalf of freelance musicians who might otherwise be difficult to contact. Whilst they are in a position to notify managements of the availability of clients they cannot act in the capacity of an agent by promoting particular players. Subscription to a diary service is, therefore, no guarantee of increased work unless a player has already established a list of contacts.

Bakers Diary Service. 10 Send Rd, Send, Woking, Surrey GU23 7ET *tel:* 01483 723644 *fax:* 01483 723662. Sandy Wells, principal.

Morgenstern's Diary Service. 34 Thistlewaite Rd, London E5 0QQ *tel:* 020 8533 1372 *fax:* 020 8533 1367 *email:* morgensterns@dial.pipex.com. Julian Morgenstern, mgr. *Personal management and answering services for orch and session musicians.*

Musicians Answering Service. Masters Yard, 180a South St, Dorking, Surrey, RH4 2ES *tel:* 01306 500000 *fax:* 01306 888041 *email:* mas@maslink.co.uk. Richard Smith, mgr dir; Isobel Collins, mgr. *Estd 1976; session and orch musicians; permanent or temporary; reduced rate pagers; 8am-midnight, 7 days per week.*

Equipment Hire

Arthur Dakin Organisation. The Old Post House, Hammond St, Mappowder, Dorset DT10 2EH *tel:* 01258 817802 *fax:* 01258 817866. *Lit mus stands for hire.*

Dreamhire. Unit 5, Chapmans Park Ind Est, 378-388 High Rd, London NW10 2DY *tel:* 020 8451 5544 *fax:* 020 8451 6464. Keith Knowles, gen mgr; Bruce Robins, product mgr. *Professional audio equipment hire; 24-hr service.*

Express Music (Solihull). 382 Stratford Rd, Shirley, Solihull, W Midlands B90 4AQ *tel:* 0121 745 8122. Peter Brown. *PAs, amplification, digital pnos and keyboards, lighting, guis, br, w/wind, vns, new and used. All equipment available for sales or hire. Also computer software.*

FX Rentals Ltd. 38-40 Telford Way, London W3 7XS *tel:* 020 8746 2121 *fax:* 020 8746 4100 *email:* fx@fxrentals.co.uk. Nick Harris, mgr dir; Roger Evan, chmn. *Professional audio and inst equipment hire. Open 24 hours every day of the year.*

John Henry Enterprises. 16-24 Brewery Rd, London N7 9NH *tel:* 020 7609 9181 *fax:* 020 7700 7040 *email:* hiredept@jhe.co.uk. John Henry, mgr dir. *Musical equipment and sound reinforcement rental.*

Laser Magic. LM House, No 2 Church St, Seaford, E Sussex BN25 1HD *tel:* 01323 890752 *fax:* 01323 898311 *email:* 100563.325@compuserve.com. Malcolm Harvey, sales dir; Steve Harvey, mgr dir. *Laser display consultants; laser lighting specialists, fireworks, special effects, pyrotechnics displays, video projection, sound systems, large-format slide projection.*

Whitwams SV. 70 High St, Winchester, Hants SO23 9DE *tel:* 01962 870408 *fax:* 01962 850820 *email:* hire@whitwams.co.uk. David Harding, dir; Steve Birnage, snr mgr. *Sound and vision equipment, hire and sales.*

Equipment Manufacturers

Amadeus Performance Equipment Ltd. Great Beech Barn, Kane Hythe Rd, Battle, E Sussex TN33 9QU *tel:* 01424 775867 *fax:* 01424 775866 *email:* info@amadeus-equipment.co.uk. Anne Holliday, mgr dir. *Musician posture chairs, inst racks, mus stands, portable staging, acoustically designed rehearsal rooms, mus stand banners, performing arts furniture, accs.*

Covernote. 17 Lime Ave, Alton, Hants GU34 2AD *tel:* 01420 84449 *also fax.* Lindy Wiltshire. *Custom-made covers and cases for insts and related equipment.*

George Veness Workshop. Stanhope Studio, Donald Way, Winchelsea, E Sussex TN36 4NH *tel:* 01797 225878. Marcus Weeks, pno tuner, technician, restorer. *Wooden mus stands.*

Hostess Furniture. Vulcan Rd, Bilston, W Midlands WV14 7JR *tel:* 01902 493681 *fax:* 01902 353185 *email:* johncave@globalnet.co.uk. *Range of orch seating, musicians' chairs, ergonomically designed to address the postural and health problems suffered by musicians.*

John Henry Enterprises. 16-24 Brewery Rd, London N7 9NH *tel:* 020 7609 9181 *fax:* 020 7700 7040. John Henry, mgr dir; Robert Harding, audio mgr. *Mus equipment, staging, flight cases, mus stands.*

Midland Flight Cases. 59 Sibson Rd, Birstall, Leicester LE4 4DX *tel:* 0116 267 1122 *also fax.* Stuart Ashby, proprietor. *Custom-built flight cases for all types of equipment. Also rack cases, perc cases.*

Musisca Ltd. Piccadilly Mill, Lower St, Stroud, Glos GL5 2HT *tel:* 01453 751911 *also fax.* Marc Oboussier, dir. *Mus stands, conductor stands, pno stools, lights, desk stands.*

Mutronics Ltd. 27 Britton St, Farringdon, London EC1M 5UD *tel:* 020 7608 3636/7251 2376 *fax:* 020 7490 0474 *email:* sarah@theaudionet.ltd.uk. Mark Lusardi. *Manufacturer of analogue audio equipment.*

Paxman Cases. 3 Tudor Court, Harold Court Rd, Romford RM3 0AE *tel:* 01708 345415 *also fax.*

RAT (Music Stands) Ltd. 16 Melville Rd, London SW13 9RJ *tel:* 020 8741 4804 *fax:* 020 8741 8949 *email:* sales@ratstands.com. A C Michell, dir. *Mus stands, with or without lamps.*

Information Services

Jazz Services Ltd. Room 518, Africa House, 64 Kingsway, London WC2B 6BD *tel:* 020 7405 0737/47/57 *fax:* 020 7405 0828 *email:* admin@jazzservices.org.uk. Celia Wood, publications mgr; Chris Hodgkins, dir. *Information on all jazz matters.*

The Music Information Consultancy. 13 York St, Harborne, Birmingham, B17 0HG *tel:* 0121 427 9376 *also fax; email:* musicinfo@clara.net. Ian Ledsham, dir; Ann Lee, training consultant. *Offers training and professional development courses, cataloguing services, music bibliography, stock editing and advice, consultancy and research services.*

National Piano Centre and Information Service. 5 Summerfield Rd, London W5 1ND *tel:* 020 8997 1793 *also fax; email:* info@pianocentre.co.uk. Jonathan Ranger, dir. *Impartial advice and information on pnos: ownership, use and maintenance, buying and selling, positioning, climate control, etc.*

Renaissance Music Consultation. P O Box 154, Congleton, Cheshire CW12 4FT. Richard Lythall, mgr dir; James Critchlow, finance mgr; Ruth Bywater, research dept head. *Specialist subjects include mus exams, perspectives on the concept and definition of mus and teaching. Compares products and services and gathers information through an extensive research team. Enclose SAE with enquiries.*

South West Jazz. Bradninch Place, Gandy St, Exeter EX4 3LS *tel:* 01392 218368 *fax:* 01392 420442 *email:* rosie@ejjarvis.demon.co.uk. Rosie Jarvis, admin. *Information services to amateur and professional musicians, promoters, educators, public, local authorities and business.*

Instrument Auctioneers

Bonhams. Montpelier St, London SW7 1HH *tel:* 020 7393 3958 *fax:* 020 7393 3905. Peter Horner, Elisabeth Tölken.

Christies. 85 Old Brompton Rd, London SW7 3LD *tel:* 020 7321 3471 *fax:* 020 7321 3321. Kerry Keane, international head of dept.

Phillips Fine Art Auctioneers. 101 New Bond St, London W1Y 0AS *tel:* 020 7468 8380/7629 6602 *fax:* 020 7465 0223. Philip A Scott, dir, mus insts. *Auctions of vns, vas, vcs, bows; antique and modern pnos.*

Sotheby's. Musical Instruments Dept, 34-35 New Bond St, London W1A 2AA *tel:* 020 7293 5342 *fax:* 020 7293 5942 *email:* tim.ingles@sothebys.com. Tim Ingles, dir, mus insts.

Instrument Hire

Many **Retailers** operate schemes for the hire of student instruments. The firms and individuals listed below are concerned with the hire of professional concert instruments, generally for one concert or tour within the UK only.

Abinger Organ Hire. Little Hoe, Hoe Lane, Abinger Hammer, Dorking, Surrey RH5 6RH *tel:* 01306 730277 *fax:* 01306 731483 *email:* Liz@Abinger.globalnet.co.uk. Peter Flatau, Elizabeth Matthews, Simon Flatau. *Orgs, harmoniums, hpds and elec pnos for sale and hire.*

Allen Organ Studios (London) Ltd. Trada Business Campus, Stocking Lane, Hughenden Valley, High Wycombe, Bucks HP14 4ND *tel:* 01494 563833 *fax:* 01494 563546 *email:* hires@allenorgans.co.uk. Jeremy Meager, UK hires mgr.

Banquet of Musick. Hillview Cochno Rd, Hardgate, Clydebank, Dunbartonshire G81 6PT *tel:* 01389 875996. Robert Lay. *Chmbr org and hpds for hire and standby for concerts and recording. Tuning.*

Bell Percussion Ltd. 6 Greenock Rd, London W3 8DU *tel:* 020 8896 1200 *fax:* 020 8896 0100. *Perc hire.*

Booth, Colin. Mount Pleasant, Westbury sub Mendip, Wells BA5 1HU *tel:* 01749 870516 *also fax; email:* colinbooth@harpsichords.demon.co.uk. *Early keyboard insts. Full service for concerts and recordings.*

Bösendorfer Piano Hire Services. 142 Edgware Rd, London W2 2DF *tel:* 020 7723 8818/9 *fax:* 020 7224 8692; Elizabeth Mooney, hire manager. *Concert pno hire, tuning and servicing all areas. Practice rooms.*

Cambridge Reed Organs. 18 Hill Close, Newmarket, Suffolk CB8 0NR *tel:* 01638 660531 *also fax.* Bruce Dracott, proprietor. *Harmoniums and celeste for hire.*

Cochrane, Maurice. Coach House, Chetwynd Rd, London NW5 1BH *tel:* 020 7267 1710 *also fax;* 07860 297970. *Historical keyboards including hpds, virginals, chmbr orgs, f-pnos. Voicing, tuning, hire.*

Cole, Michael. Little Tatchley, 334 Prestbury Rd, Cheltenham, Glos GL52 3DD *tel:* 01242 517192 *fax:* 01242 570383. *Hpd and f-pno hire. Concert tuning.*

Forsyth Brothers Ltd. 126 Deansgate, Manchester M3 2GR *tel:* 0161 834 3281 *fax:* 0161 834 0630 *email:* forsythmus@aol.com. *Pno hire and tuning.*

FX Rentals Ltd. 38-40 Telford Way, London W3 7XS *tel:* 020 8746 2121 *fax:* 020 8746 4100 *email:* fx@fxrentals.co.uk. Nick Harris, mgr dir; Roger Evans, chmn. *Professional audio and inst equipment hire. Open 24 hours every day of the year.*

Greenhalgh, Malcolm. 48 Lordship Park, London N16 5UD *tel:* 020 8800 6176 *email:* greenhalgh@gpo.sonnet.co.uk. *Hpds, orgs, f-pnos for concerts and recordings.*

Hammett, Claire. 19 Buxton Rd, E Sheen, London SW14 8SY *tel:* 020 8876 1496 *also fax;* 07973 659212 *email:* claire.hammett@btinternet.com. *Hpds and orgs for concert and recording hire, also transport and tuning.*

Harmonium Services. 6 Albert Terrace, Saltaire, Shipley, W Yorks BD18 4PS *tel:* 01274 585601; 07976 535980 *email:* phil@harmoniumservice.demon.co.uk. Phil Fluke, proprietor. *Harmoniums for hire. Also street org on hand cart for hire.*

Harpsichord Workshop. 130 Westbourne Terrace Mews, London W2 6QG *tel:* 020 7723 9650 *also fax.* Mark Ransom. *Short and long term hire.*

Hickies Ltd. 153 Friar St, Reading RG1 1HG *tel:* 0118 957 5771 *fax:* 0118 957 5775. *Grand and upright pnos for concert hire.*

Horniblow Harpsichord Hire. 23 Hamilton Rd, Reading RG1 5RA *tel:* 0118 926 1480. John Horniblow.

Impact Percussion. 120-122 Bermondsey St, London SE1 3TX *tel:* 020 7403 5900 *fax:* 020 7403 5910 *email:* impactperc@msn.com. *Large perc hire fleet, worldwide delivery. Also sales and repair.*

Jaques Samuel Pianos Ltd. 142 Edgware Rd, London W2 2DZ *tel:* 020 7723 8818 *fax:* 020 7224 8692. Elizabeth Mooney, concert and show hire. *Pnos for concert and show hire and sale. Tuning, transport, servicing. Practice rooms.*

John Henry Enterprises. 16-24 Brewery Rd, London N7 9NH *tel:* 020 7609 9181 *fax:* 020 7700 7040 *email:* hiredept@jhe.co.uk. John Henry, mgr dir. *Insts and PA.*

Jones, Stephen. 6 Barnfield Rd, St Albans, Herts AL4 9UP *tel:* 01727 864007 *fax:* 01727 845884 *email:* steve_sta@compuserve.com. *Hpd, harmonium.*

Justin Sillman & Co. 6 Tomlins Grove, Bow, London E3 4NX *tel:* 020 8981 9800 *fax:* 020 8981 2800 *email:* justin@justin.idiscover.co.uk. *Orgs.*

Ken Smith Music Services Ltd. 6 The Maltings, High St, Henlow, Beds SG16 6AQ *tel:* 01462 811244 *fax:* 01462 851801. Kenneth Smith, mgr dir; Alyda Smith, company sec. *Supplier, tuner and transporter of hpds, pipe orgs, f-pnos and harmoniums. Orchestral transport.*

Makin Organs Ltd. Compton House, Franklin St, Oldham, Lancs OL1 2DP *tel:* 0161 626 5666 *fax:* 0161 665 2284 *email:* davidc@makinorgans.co.uk. David Clegg, dir. *Classical orgs, digital pnos, MIDI expanders, nationwide hire service.*

Markson Pianos. 8 Chester Court, Albany St, London NW1 4BU *tel:* 020 7935 8682 *fax:* 020 7224 0957 *email:* marksonpianos@compuserve.com. Julian Markson, Simon Markson, partners. *Pno sale, hire with option to buy, concert and recording hire, tuning and repairs, restoration, free advice.*

Maxima Music. 20 Wolseley Gardens, London W4 3LP *tel:* 020 8995 2757. Simon Hill. *Chmbr org.*

Neal, Simon. 10 Hamilton Rd, London NW10 1NY *tel:* 020 8452 1556 *fax:* 020 8452 3467 *email:* simonneal.harpsichords@btinternet.com. *Short-term hire of early keyboard insts (hpds, f-pnos, chmbr orgs); also transport and tuning for rehearsals, concerts, tours and recording.*

Peter Conacher & Co Ltd. Springwood Organ Works, Water St, Huddersfield, W Yorks HD1 4BB *tel:* 01484 530053 *fax:* 01484 305303 *email:* admin@musiclink.co.uk. J Sinclair Willis, mgr dir. *Pipe orgs for hire UK only, tunings and stand-by for concerts and recordings. Reed orgs, harmoniums, fairground orgs and hand-turned orgs for hire, UK only.*

Pro Piano Inc. 85 Jane St, New York, NY 10014, USA *tel:* +1 212 206 8794 *fax:* +1 212 633 1207 *email:* ricard@propiano.com. Ricard de La Rosa, dir. *Hamburg Steinway, Kanai, Yamaha concert pno. Perc, assorted insts available.*

Ransom, Mark. 130 Westbourne Terrace Mews, London W2 6QG *tel:* 020 7723 9650 *also fax. Hpd hire, tuning, maintenance and transport.*

Robert Deegan Harpsichords. Tonnage Warehouse, St Georges Quay, Lancaster LA1 1RB *tel:* 01524 60186 *also fax.* Robert Deegan, proprietor. *Hpd maker, hpd concert hire, tuning, maintenance, restoration, repairs.*

Robert Morley & Co Ltd. 34 Engate St, London SE13 7HA *tel:* 020 8318 5838 *fax:* 020 8297 0720. Julia Morley. *Long-term home rental of pnos, f-pnos, hpds, spinets, clvds, virginals, celestes.*

Shackell Pianos. Burford Rd, Minster Lovell, Witney, Oxon OX8 5RB *tel:* 01993 703375 *fax:* 01993 700867 *email:* sales@shackell-pianos.demon.co.uk. *Steinway concert grands available for hire.*

T W Howarth & Co Ltd. 31 Chiltern St, London W1M 1HG *tel:* 020 7935 2407 *fax:* 020 7224 2564 *email:* sales@howarth.demon.co.uk. *Hire scheme for student w/wind insts and short-term hire of w/wind for orch concerts.*

Temple, Alex. Platt Lodge, 61 Barton Rd, Worsley, Manchester M28 2GX *tel:* 0161 794 3717 *email:* alextemple@compuserve.com. *Hpd, clvd concert hire.*

Wooderson, Andrew. 5 Bourne Rd, Bexley, Kent DA5 1LG *tel:* 01322 558326/525558 *also fax. All types of hpds, spinets, virginals, clvds, early pnos. Construction, repair, restoration, tuning, hire.*

Instrument Technicians

Those listed below offer a more specialised service than the general repairers listed in the **Retailers** section.

Allen Organ Studios (London) Ltd. Trada Business Campus, Stocking Lane, Hughenden Valley, High Wycombe, Bucks HP14 4ND *tel:* 01494 563833 *fax:* 01494 563546 *email:* service@allenorgans.co.uk. Paul Arkwright, UK service mgr.

Andrew Lamb, Musical Instrument Conservation. 30 Maple House, Idonia St, Deptford, London SE8 4LS *tel:* 020 8691 6537. *Conservation and restoration of historical mus insts.*

Bishop and Son. 38 Bolton Lane, Ipswich, Suffolk IP4 2BT *tel:* 01473 255165. *Org builders.*

Booth, Colin. Mount Pleasant, Westbury sub Mendip, Wells BA5 1HU *tel:* 01749 870516 *also fax. Early keyboard insts: tuning, maintenance, repair, restoration.*

The Bridge Fiddler. Riverside House, Chapel Milton, Chapel-en-le-Frith, High Peak SK23 0QQ *tel:* 01298 813813. John Goodborn, proprietor. *Str inst and bow repairer and supplier of str insts and accs. Specialists in restoration.*

Cambridge Pianola Co & J V Pianos. The Limes, Landbeach, Cambridge CB4 4DR *tel:* 01223 861348 *fax:* 01223 441276. F T Poole, proprietor. *Pno and pianola restoration, sales and rentals.*

Cambridge Reed Organs. 18 Hill Close, Newmarket, Suffolk CB8 0NR *tel:* 01638 660531 *also fax.* Bruce Dracott, proprietor. *Harmonium restoration, repair, tuning and hire.*

Cavalier Music. 145 Barncroft Way, Havant, Hants PO9 3AF *tel:* 023 9247 5923. B L Boughton. *Br and w/wind repairs, specialist alterations. Insts bought and sold.*

Chandler Guitars. 300-302 Sandycombe Rd, Kew, Richmond, Surrey TW9 3NG *tel:* 020 8940 5874 *email:* repairs@chandlerguitars.co.uk. Charlie Chandler, dir; Ian Allerton, Simon Piggott, B Schwarz; David Petersen, amplifier repairs. *Repairs.*

Clive Morley Harps. Goodfellows, Filkins, nr Lechlade, Glos GL7 3JG *tel:* 01367 860493 *fax:* 01367 860659 *email:* morley@harps.demon.co.uk. *Hp servicing and repair.*

Coad, Lucy. Workshop 3, Greenway Farm, Bath Rd, Wick, nr Bristol BS15 1RL *tel:* 0117 937 4949 *also fax; email:* lucy@squarepiano.demon.co.uk. *Square pno repairs and conservation.*

Cochrane, Maurice. Coach House, Chetwynd Rd, London NW5 1BH *tel:* 020 7267 1710 *also fax;* 07860 297970. *Early-keyboard maintenance, preparation, gen advice.*

David Corey Piano Tuning & Repairs. 18 Woodside Ave, Ainsdale, Southport, Merseyside PR8 3UE *tel:* 01704 574610; 07971 422601.

David Corey. *Member of Pianoforte Tuners' Association. Concert tuning, full re-stringing, restoration.*

Davies, Peter. The Woodwind Workshop, 36 Byram Arcade, Westgate, Huddersfield HD1 1ND *tel:* 01484 533053 *also fax*. Peter Davies, mgr. *Specialist repair and restoration of ob family of insts. Repairs, insurance, sales (new and second-hand), accs, mus for w/wind.*

Derek Roberts Violins. 185 Leam Terrace, Leamington Spa, Warwicks CV31 1DW *tel:* 01926 428313 *also fax; email:* roberts@violins.demon.co.uk. *Vn maker and restorer.*

Frith, Stephen C. 22 Ewhurst Close, W Green, Crawley, Sussex RH11 7EZ *tel:* 01293 543055 *also fax; email:* mail@guitarmakers.freeserve.co.uk. Stephen Frith, luthier; Sherrie Frith, mgr. *Maker and repairer of classical concert guis. Custom-built electric guis and advisory service.*

Gittins, Roy. Hollebeke House, Gore End Rd, Ball Hill, Newbury, Berks RG20 0PD *tel:* 01635 253566 *also fax. Br mus insts repairs and overhauls.*

Gordon Stevenson Violins. 6 Barclay Terrace, Bruntsfield, Edinburgh EH10 4HP *tel:* 0131 229 2051 *fax:* 0131 229 9298. *Maker and restorer of vns.*

Hammett, Claire. 19 Buxton Rd, E Sheen, London SW14 8SY *tel:* 020 8876 1496 *also fax;* 07973 659212 *email:* claire.hammett@btinternet.com. *Hpd tuner and technician; also clvds, f-pnos.*

Handy, Edmund. 5 Bourne Rd, Bexley, Kent DA5 1LG *tel:* 01322 527366; 020 8300 2715. *Tuning, maintenance and repair of hpds, clvds and early pnos. Celeste maintenance and repair. Square pno restorations. Reconditioned insts for sale.*

Hansford, Neil. The Bristol Violin Shop, 12 Upper Maudlin St, Bristol BS2 8DJ *tel:* 0117 925 9990 *also fax. Viols; Eng, Fr, Ger, It baroque vcs.*

Harmonium Services. 6 Albert Terrace, Saltaire, Shipley, W Yorks BD18 4PS *tel:* 01274 585601; 07976 535980 *email:* phil@harmoniumservice.demon.co.uk. Phil Fluke, proprietor. *Restoration work using original materials wherever possible. Parts and reeds for sale. Insts bought and sold.*

The Harpsichord Workshop. 130 Westbourne Terrace Mews, London W2 6QG *tel:* 020 7723 9650 *also fax*. Mark Ransom. *Tuning, repair, renovation, hire.*

Henley Piano Galleries Ltd. 24 Duke St, Henley-on-Thames, Oxon RG9 1UP *tel:* 01491 413019 *fax:* 01491 411361. *Concert services for pianists, concert grand maintenance and specialist servicing, complete restorations of fine European insts.*

Hibernian Violins. 24 Players Ave, Malvern, Worcs WR14 1DU *tel:* 01684 562947 *also fax*. Padraig O Dubhlaoidh, proprietor, inst conservator-restorer. *W/shop for str insts and bows.*

Hickies Ltd. 153 Friar St, Reading RG1 1HG *tel:* 0118 957 5771 *fax:* 0118 957 5775. *Pno repairs and restoration.*

Hossle, Derek. 26 Andrew St, Mossley, Lancs OL5 0DN *tel:* 01457 835656 *email:* derekjo.hossle@btinternet.com. *W/wind inst restoration.*

Huggett, Martin. The Old Library, Stour St, Manningtree, Essex CO11 1BE *tel:* 01206 396354 *also fax. Repairer, restorer, tuner of historic and modern keyboard insts. Also cabinet work.*

Impact Percussion. 120-122 Bermondsey St, London SE1 3TX *tel:* 020 7403 5900 *fax:* 020 7403 5910 *email:* impactperc@msn.com. *Repair and custom manufacture of perc insts and stands. Also hire and sales.*

J & A Beare Ltd. 7 Broadwick St, London W1V 1FJ *tel:* 020 7437 1449 *fax:* 020 7439 4520. C Beare, P Beare, F Gillham, D Morris, S Morris, S Smith, dirs. *Dealers, restorers and makers of fine vns, vas and vcs.*

John Coppen Woodwind Repairs. Unit 7, The Leathermarket, Weston St, London SE1 3ER *tel:* 020 7378 1952. *Hand-made keywork, extensions to all cls, tuning for all w/wind, new and commission sales. Reeds m/order service. Wooden bass cl bells.*

Krattenmacher, Stefan Johann. Sinclair Rd, West Kensington, London W14 0NS *tel:* 020 7602 8869 *also fax. Maker and restorer of vns, vas, vcs and dbs. Consultant. Accs, bows, plus small selection of fine old insts. By appointment only.*

Lowes Woodwind. 102 Greenwich South St, London SE10 8UN *tel:* 020 8691 6944 *fax:* 020 8694 2503 *email:* jlowe@dircon.co.uk. Jeremy Lowe, proprietor. *Cl, sax and fl repairs, cl mouthpieces and barrels.*

M and J Healey Violins. 12 Rosehill, Sutton, Surrey SM1 3EU *tel:* 020 8644 4700 *also fax;* 020 8644 3419. *Strs.*

Markson Pianos. 8 Chester Court, Albany St, London NW1 4BU *tel:* 020 7935 8682 *fax:* 020 7224 0957 *email:* marksonpianos@compuserve.com. Simon Markson, Julian Markson. *Pno sale, hire, restoration, repair, tuning, maintenance, transport. Concert and recording hire; hire with option to buy. 24-hour concert hire service.*

Marshall McGurk Musical Services. Elm House Farm, Crosby, Maryport, Cumbria CA15 6SH *tel:* 01900 813200 *also fax; email:* steve@marshallmcgurk.freeserve.co.uk. Allison McGurk, Steve Marshall, partners. *W/wind specialists, especially sax, cl. Also pno tuning and other insts .*

Martyn Booth Guitar Services. Unit 4, Old Brickworks, Chapel Lane, Little Cornard, Sudbury, Suffolk CO10 0PB *tel:* 01787 370192 *also fax. Repairs and customisation of all types of gui.*

The Midland Organ Company. The Manufactory, PO Box 5269, Melton Mowbray, Leics LE13 1WW *tel:* 01664 569208 *also fax; email:* midorgco@telinco.com. Christopher Gray, mgr dir. *Repair, rebuilding and restoration of all types of pipe org; tuning service, blowing plant, humidifier service.*

Music For You. 12 High St, Waltham, Grimsby, S Humberside, DN37 0LL *tel:* 01472 828524 *fax:* 01472 828681. Roger and Elaine Huggett, proprietors. *Vn maker and repairer. Sheet mus suppliers.*

National Association of Musical Instrument Repairers. Gracefield House, 13 Cawdor Cres, Boston Manor, London W7 2DA *tel:* 020 8567 2969 *email:* markjmoran@compuserve.com. Mark Moran, secretary; Gale Lawson, chmn; Rachel White, publicity offr, editor. *Can provide contact information for members of the association. Encourages high standard of workmanship and customer care, provides info on techniques and parts availability, technical back-up. Acts as arbitrator in the event of a dispute between repairer and customer.*

Nimblejack Ltd. 24 Alexandra Rd, Windsor, Berks SL4 1HN *tel:* 01753 853724. Alan Whear. *Pno and hpd tuning, maintenance and repair. Gen repairs.*

Pro Piano Inc. 85 Jane St, New York, NY 10014, USA *tel:* +1 212 206 8794 *fax:* +1 212 633 1207 *email:* ricard@propiano.com. Ricard de La Rosa, dir.

Ranger, Jon (Pianos and Harpsichords). 5 Summerfield Rd, London W5 1ND *tel:* 020 8997 1793 *also fax; email:* jranger@pianocentre.co.uk. Jonathan Ranger. *Restoration, conservation, tuning and maintenance of historic and modern pnos, hpds, squares, f-pnos, spinets, clvds, virginals. Information service.*

Ransom, Mark. 130 Westbourne Terrace Mews, London W2 6QG *tel:* 020 7723 9650 *also fax. Tuning, maintenance, hire, transport of hpds.*

Reg Thorp Woodwind Repair. 13 Pinewood Way, Midhurst, W Sussex GU29 9LN *tel:* 01730 814782 *email:* saxmechanic@compuserve.com. Reg Thorp, proprietor. *W/wind repair and renovation. Keymaking, tuning, customising, alterations, mouthpiece refacing, silver plating, etc.*

Ricard de la Rosa. Pro Piano, 85 Jane St, New York, NY 10014, USA *tel:* +1 212 206 8794 *fax:* +1 212 633 1207 *email:* ricard@propiano.com.

Robert Morley & Co Ltd. 34 Engate St, London SE13 7HA *tel:* 020 8318 5838 *fax:* 020 8297 0720. Julia Morley. *Repair, restoration and tuning of pnos, f-pnos, hpds, spinets, clvds, virginals, celestes.*

Royal National College of the Blind. College Rd, Hereford HR1 1EB *tel:* 01432 265725 *fax:* 01432 353478. *Pno tuning and repairs.*

Stevens, Mike. 272 Louth Rd, Scartho, Grimsby DN33 2LF *tel:* 01472 824138 *email:* mijan.stev63@virgin.uk. *Repairs for str, w/wind, br, etc. Replacements made for any part of any inst, modifications for the disabled. Rebuilt second-hand insts for sale.*

T W Howarth & Co Ltd. 31 Chiltern St, London W1M 1HG *tel:* 020 7935 2407 *fax:* 020 7224 2564 *email:* sales@howarth.demon.co.uk. *Specialist repair of all w/wind insts, including restoration of old and authentic insts.*

Temple, Alex. Platt Lodge, 61 Barton Rd, Worsley, Manchester M28 2GX *tel:* 0161 794 3717 *email:* alextemple@compuserve.com. *Hpd, clvd, tuning, repairs and hire.*

Top Wind. 2 Lower Marsh, London SE1 7RJ *tel:* 020 7928 8181 *fax:* 020 7401 8788 *email:* jon@topwind.com. Jon Dodd. *Specialist fl and picc repairs.*

Trainor, Brian. 15 Stanmore Cres, Lanark ML11 7DF *tel:* 01555 664024 *email:* brian.trainor@btinternet.com. *Br, str and w/wind inst repairs.*

Ward, Alan. St Andrews, 27 Plomer Hill, Downley, High Wycombe, Bucks HP13 5JG *tel:* 01494 523371. *Str restorer and repairer.*

Whitham, J S. Faraway, Llandegla, Denbighshire LL11 3BG *tel:* 01978 790238 *also fax; email:* jswhit@ptfoods.demon.co.uk. *Repairs to all orch insts, also mobile service.*

Whittaker, Helen. Dawsons Music Ltd, 30 Pepper St, Chester CH1 1DF *tel:* 01244 348606. Helen Whittaker, repairer. *W/wind, str, br inst repairs.*

Wooderson, Andrew. 5 Bourne Rd, Bexley, Kent DA5 1LG *tel:* 01322 558326/525558 *also fax. Tuning, maintenance, repair and restoration of early keyboard insts. Hand-built insts made to order.*

Woolley, Dennis. Tubhole Barn, Dent, Sedbergh, W Yorks LA10 5RE *tel:* 01539 625361. *F-pno, hpd. Tuning, regulation and restoration of early keyboard insts.*

Woolrich, A P. Canal Side, Huntworth, Bridgwater, Somerset TA7 0AJ *tel:* 01278 663020 *fax:* 01278 663913 *email:* apw@ap-woolrich.co.uk. *Reproduction ironmongery for keyboard insts.*

BRITISH RESERVE
– supporting Musicians
Specialist insurer of classical musical instruments.
Why not join our many satisfied customers?
Ranging from amateurs to world renowned professionals, from young players to the U.K.'s leading symphony orchestras.
Premiums from £20
For a quotation please contact your usual dealer or call us on
01892 515244 stating Ref: BMY
(Fax: 01892 511080)
British Reserve Insurance Co. Ltd.
Musical Instruments Department
Cornhill House, 6 Vale Avenue
Tunbridge Wells, Kent TN1 1EH
Internet address: http://www.britishreserve.co.uk
British Reserve is part of the Cornhill group
SC1775

N.W. BROWN
MUSIC DIVISION
Registered Insurance Brokers
Richmond House, 16-20 Regent Street, Cambridge, CB2 1DB
tel: 01223 357131 email: richard.rampley@nwbrown.co.uk

Insurance and Financial Services

Adam Brothers Contingency Ltd. 12 Camomile St, London EC3A 7BP *tel:* 020 7638 3211 *fax:* 020 7374 0726.

AON Entertainment Risk Services Ltd. Pinewood Studios, Pinewood Rd, Iver, Bucks SL0 0NH *tel:* 01753 658200 *fax:* 01753 653152. James B T Davies, Mark Wilkins, account execs. *Cover for promoters, exhibitors, festival organisers, backers, artists, agents, radio and TV companies and others.*

Brass Band Insurance Services. 312 High St, Harlington, Hayes, Middx UB3 5BT *tel:* 020 8759 0825 *fax:* 020 8564 9063. Mr and Mrs J Beeston, admins. *Insurers of bands, orchs, ens and individual musicians.*

British Reserve Insurance Co Ltd. Musical Instruments Dept, Cornhill House, 6 Vale Ave, Tunbridge Wells, Kent TN1 1EH *tel:* 01892 515244 *fax:* 01892 511080. Dilys Killick, account handler. *Specialist insurers of mus insts.*

Entertainment & Leisure Insurance Services Ltd. Thorpe Underwood Hall, Ouseburn, York YO26 9SZ *tel:* 01423 330711 *fax:* 01423 331008 *email:* remember@compuserve.com. Lorraine Illingworth, head of quotations dept. *All-risks cover for insts, br bands and equipment.*

Equity Insurance Services. 131 New London Rd, Chelmsford, Essex CM2 0QZ *tel:* 01245 357854 *fax:* 01245 491641.

Galaxy 7 Policies (Underwriting Agents). 1st-3rd Floor Office Suite, 21 Market Place, Abbey Gate, Nuneaton CV11 5UH *tel:* 024 7632 6128.

Harrison-Beaumont (Insurance Brokers) Ltd. 2 Des Roches Square, Witney, Oxon OX8 6BE *tel:* 01993 700200 *fax:* 01993 700502 *email:* info@hbinsurance.co.uk. *Specialists in providing injury and travel insurance to performers.*

Hencilla Canworth Insurance Group. 27-29 Brighton Rd, South Croydon, Surrey CR2 6EB *tel:* 020 8686 5050 *fax:* 020 8686 5559. Kevin Harding, dir; Rob Hart, account exec. *Specialists in all types of insurance for those involved in the entertainment industry.*

Hibernian Violins. 24 Players Ave, Malvern Link, Worcs WR14 1DU *tel:* 01684 562947 *also fax.* Padraig O' Dubhlaoidh. *Advice on insuring str insts, bows.*

Homematch. 15 Castle St, Worcester WR1 3AD *tel:* 01905 22007; 07836 361232 *fax:* 01905 724972. Chris Catchpole. *Mortgages for musicians.*

Jack Hayward Harps. Harp Strings Insurance, 5 Sun Gardens, Burghfield Common, Reading RG7 3JB *tel:* 0118 983 3922 *fax:* 0118 983 3868. Jack Hayward, proprietor. *All-risks insurance for all mus insts. UK to worldwide cover.*

La Playa. PO Box 992, Waterbeach, Cambridge CB5 9SQ *tel:* 01223 522411 *fax:* 08700 548706 *email:* mark.boon@laplaya.co.uk. Mark Boon, mgr dir. *Specialist insurance for the mus and media industries. Cover includes insts, equipment, touring, cancellation, property and liabilities.*

N W Brown Music Division. Richmond House, 16-20 Regent St, Cambridge CB2 1DB *tel:* 01223 357131 *fax:* 01223 353705 *email:* music@nwbrown.co.uk. Richard Rampley, dir. *Specialists in the provision of insurance services to the classical mus industry.*

P J Jenkins & Co. Bristan House, Colham Mill Rd, West Drayton, Middx UB7 7AE *tel:* 01895 431448 *fax:* 01895 434055. *Specialist insurance service for musicians. Inst insurance, liability, travel, etc.*

Shepherd Finance Ltd. 2 The Hall, Turners Green Rd, Wadhurst, E Sussex TN5 6TR *tel:* 01892 785010 *fax:* 01892 785023. B J Branson, dir. *Specialists in finance for mus insts.*

Internet and Website Services

Abbey Road Interactive. Abbey Road Studios, 3 Abbey Rd, St John's Wood, London NW8 9AY *tel:* 020 7266 7236 *fax:* 020 7266 7250 *email:* interactive@abbeyroad.co.uk *website:* www.abbeyroad.co.uk. Sam Harvey, creative dir; Sarah Bradley, digital video mgr. *New media for the entertainment and mus industries. Authoring individually tailored to clients needs. Areas of expertise are websites, Enhanced CDs, DVDs, MPEG and Digital Video Services.*

ARA Associates (Web Design). Flat 6, 54 Lullingstone Lane, Lewisham SE13 6UH *tel:* 020 8695 6948 *fax:* 020 8695 6986 *email:* ara@dircon.co.uk *website:* www.ara.gold.ac.uk. *Specialist website design and management for the classical mus industry; also academic and educ websites and on-line database solutions.*

Cadenza. 25 Oxford Rd, Ealing, London W5 3SP *tel:* 020 8840 1564 *fax:* 0870 056 2196 *email:* music@cadenza.org *website:* www.cadenza.org. Keith Bramich. *Various free resources, including adverts, concert listings and directory entries, which can be set up by visiting the website, faxing or sending text, concert leaflets and biographies.*

Classical Artists Worldwide. 19a North Villas, London NW1 9BJ *tel:* 020 7267 8778 *fax:* 020 7813 4601 *email:* info@classical-artists.com *website:* www.classical-artists.com. Andrew Skirrow, Ronny Adsetts, Andrew Saunders, partners. *Website design/hosting service and internet index for classical musicians and the classical mus industry. Subsidiary of Camden Music.*

Classical London. *website:* members.aol.com/malcolmjg/Page1.html. *Email discussion group and listings for classical music in London.*

Global Music Network (GMN). 61 Harley St, London W1N 1DD *tel:* 020 7636 2112 *fax:* 020 7 636 8130 *email:* info@gmn.com *website:* www.gmn.com. *Website features live performances and video interviews of classical and jazz artists.*

Impulse. 18 Hillfield Park, Muswell Hill, London N10 3QS *tel:* 020 8444 8587 *fax:* 020 8245 0358 *email:* impulse@impulse-music.co.uk *website:* www.impulse-music.co.uk. Geraldine Allen, mkt and PR; Sarah Rodgers, design and technical. *Impulse Classical Music Website: established 1997 to promote musicians, recordings and composer catalogues on the internet. Web page design, internet consultancy and copyright advice.*

Intune. 20 Beulah Cres, Thornton Heath, Surrey CR7 8JL *tel:* 020 8239 0444 *also fax; email:* info@intune.co.uk *website:* www.intune.co.uk. S L Chai. *Internet directory of UK musicians and related organisations. Join or advertise free online or phone/fax.*

Opera Data. Rhinegold Publishing Ltd, 241 Shaftesbury Ave, London WC2H 8EH *tel:* 020 7333 1766 *fax:* 020 7333 1736 *email:* database@operadata.co.uk *website:* www.operadata.co.uk. *Internet service for agents, companies and artists within the opera industry.*

Orion Computer Consultants Ltd. 25 Oxford Rd, London W5 3SP *tel:* 020 8840 1564 *fax:* 0870 056 2196 *email:* enquiries@orion-arts.com *website:* www.orion-arts.com. Keith Bramich, mgr dir. *Internet website design and consultancy for the arts.*

spacehoppa.com. 10 Kites Nest Lane, Stroud, Glos GL5 3PQ *tel:* 01453 750481 *fax:* 01453 767770 *email:* info@spacehoppa.com *website:* www.spacehoppa.com. Ruth Arnold. *Low-cost website design and internet consultancy for the arts.*

Vargas Organisation. 8 Templeton Place, London SW5 9LZ *tel:* 020 7370 7976 *also fax; email:* vargas@dial.pipex.com. Anthony Auerbach. *Designers specialising in needs of musicians and the mus business.*

Web Projects. The Studio, 78 Croydon Rd, Reigate, Surrey RH2 0NH *tel:* 01737 222008 *fax:* 01737 225600 *email:* mwalmsley@webprojects.co.uk *website:* www.webprojects.co.uk. Mark Walmsley, mgr dir; Greg Watson, exec; Ben Sauer, mkt mgr. *Internet consultancy and training, website design, promotion and maintenance. Clients include Philharmonia, Associated Board, CBSO, Gramophone Magazine. See www.classicalmusic.co.uk.*

Medical Support Organisations

Arts Psychology Consultants. 29 Argyll Mansions, Hammersmith Rd, London W14 8QQ *tel:* 020 7602 2707 *fax:* 020 7602 8441 *email:* arts.psychology@cwcom.net. Andy Evans, dir. *A confidential counselling and careers service for musicians and industry staff dealing with performance problems, stage fright, career guidance and personal issues. Psychologists have professional mus backgrounds.*

British Performing Arts Medicine Trust. 196 Shaftesbury Ave, London WC2H 8JL *tel:* 020 7240 4500 (helpline)/020 7240 3331 (admin); 0845 602 0235 *fax:* 020 7240 3335 *email:* bpamt@dial.pipex.com. Eileen Quilter Williams, gen admin; Angelina Spurrier, asst admin; Yinka Fasawe, helpline co-ord. *A charity founded in 1984 which tries by its helpline, clinics and contacts to put performers in touch with medical expertise, both physical and psychiatric, conventional and alternative practitioners, who may be able to help them overcome or reduce injury and illness.*

Mary Howard Stress Management and Hypnotherapy Services. 94 Spencer St, Norwich NR3 4PE *tel:* 01603 627449 *email:* mary.howard@virgin.uk. *A registered practitioner working with all* *stress-related problems including phobias and performance nerves. Confidentiality assured.*

Musicians' and Keyboard Clinic. 152 Harley St, London W1N 1HH *tel:* 020 7359 8533 *fax:* 020 7354 1501 *email:* richard.pe@which.net. Dr R M Pearson, consultant. *Non-NHS clinic for the medical problems of inst musicians and keyboard operators, including muscle overuse, movement disorders and rehabilitation after injuries. Also NHS via: Dr R M Pearson, Consultant Physician, Harold Wood Hospital, Romford, Essex RM3 0BE.*

North Dorset Centre for the Alexander Technique. Sheriffs Mead, Telegraph St, Iwerne Courtney, Dorset DT11 8QQ *tel:* 01258 861856 *also fax.* Frances Robinson, dir. *Introductory groups, individual lessons and custom-made courses.*

Performing Arts Counselling Service (PAX Northwest). Beechwood, 9 Harboro Rd, Sale, Cheshire M33 5AE *tel:* 0161 976 6992. Delyth Wilkinson, counsellor/voice consultant. *UKRC Reg Ind Counsellor, BAPAM trained. Welcomes music and/or voice-related psychological concerns. Private practice.*

Potters Bar Osteopathic Clinic. 3 Highfield Way, Potters Bar, Herts EN6 1UL *tel:* 01707 662813. J Goh, osteopath. *Treatment, preventative advice, talks and lectures on avoiding injury while playing.*

Renaissance Couselling Service. PO Box 154, Congleton, Cheshire CW12 4FT. Richard Lythall, mgr dir. *Confidential postal counselling service for musicians.*

Westminster Alexander Centre. 8 Hop Gardens, off St Martin's Lane, London WC2N 4EH *tel:* 020 7240 2118 *email:* wac@alextech.demon.co.uk. John Hunter, co-ord; Aideen Curtis, Paola Corteen, teachers. *Introductory courses, private lessons, refresher classes in the Alexander Technique, including application to insts, respiration, voice, performance and dealing with injury.*

Music Copyists, Setters, Engravers and Printers

Acoustic Art. 2 Milton House, 25 Short St, Waterloo, London SE1 8LH *tel:* 020 7928 1216 *fax:* 020 7976 5408 *email:* less@enterprise.net. James Burden. *Professional computerised mus copying and processing. Full production service. Transposition, orchestration and arranging services available.*

Acuta Music. Hambrook, Ledbury, Herefordshire HR8 2PX *tel:* 01531 670634 *also fax.* Robert Kay. *Computerised mus setting, hand-copying, proof-reading.*

Allegro Reproductions. 33 Belmont Close, Uxbridge, Middx UB8 1RF *tel:* 01895 232055 *also fax.* Stephen Duro, Beryl Duro, dirs. *Computerised mus engraving. Also editing, arranging, orchestrating, transposing, part extraction.*

Animus. 4 Rawlinson St, Dalton-in-Furness, Cumbria LA15 8AL *tel:* 01229 467432. Adrian and Pamela Self. *Computerised mus setting. Transposition, arranging. Choral and org mus a speciality.*

Arnold Reproduction Co. 77 Dudden Hill Lane, London NW10 1BD *tel:* 020 8459 6194 *fax:* 020 8459 1184. Peter Hunt, print mgr. *Sheet mus printers.*

Barnes Music Engraving Ltd. Sheepwash Farm, Sheepwash Lane, Blackboys, E Sussex TN22 4HA *tel:* 01825 830751 *fax:* 01825 830311. Simon Mortimer, dir. *Mus setting, mus and text origination, arranging, transcription, programming and editorial services.*

Barry Peter Ould Music Services. 6 Fairfax Cres, Aylesbury, Bucks HP20 2ES *tel:* 01296 428609 *also fax; email:* bpo1@compuserve.com. Barry Peter Ould. *Computerised mus setting, design, typesetting and photocopying service.*

Boase, Bernard. 38 Mansfield Rd, London NW3 2HP *tel:* 020 7485 3366 *email:* b.boase@bcs.org.uk. Bernard Boase. *Transcription of ms mus to high-quality print or computer file using Sibelius software.*

Bowden, Elizabeth. 4 Pitt Court, Nymet Rowland, Crediton, Devon EX17 6AN *tel:* 01363 83515. *Mus copyist, computer setting (Sibelius 7).*

Cabot Music Productions. 29 Long Mead, Brimsham Park, Yate, Bristol BS37 7YT *tel:* 01454 326509 *email:* cabotmus@compuserve.com. David Kear, proprietor. *Computerised mus typesetting using Coda Finale. Arranging and transcription services available (PVGs, gui tablature, rock and pop scores, big band transcriptions).*

Caligraving Ltd. Brunel Way, Thetford, Norfolk IP24 1HP *tel:* 01842 752116 *fax:* 01842 755512. Oliver W Makings, sales and mkt dir. *Mus printing and book binding. Full note setting and studio facilities available.*

web?

Who did these organisations turn to?

www.abrsm.ac.uk
(Associated Board of the Royal Schools of Music)

www.cbso.co.uk
(City of Birmingham Symphony Orchestra)

www.classicalmusic.co.uk
(Classical Music UK)

www.orchestranet.co.uk
(Association of British Orchestras)

www.philharmonia.co.uk
(Philharmonia Orchestra)

WEB PROJECTS

The classical music internet specialists.
www.classicalmusic.co.uk
www.webprojects.co.uk

Telephone: 01737 222 008

mwalmsley@webprojects.co.uk

How do you make contact with thousands of working musicians via your computer?

www.musicianweb.co.uk

The website for promoters and fixers that can put you in touch with professional musicians of every musical genre, throughout Britain, all of whom are willing to be contacted about engagements.

The solution to your problems may just be a click away.

MUSICIANS' UNION WEB NETWORK

For more information telephone 0207 333 1723

M.E. DAPHNE FOSTER

M.P. Ac.A., M.P. C..H.A., M.Hk.Ac.A.

REGISTERED PRACTITIONER OF COMPLEMENTARY MEDICINE

Member of the Fook Sang Acupuncture and Chinese Medical Herbal Practitioners Association, Member of Chinese Acupucture Association Hong Kong, Fellow of British Reflexology Assoc. Treatment of back, shoulder, hip and joint pains, stress, digestion, sleep and menstrual problems, anxiety. Eye, nose, ear problems and headaches etc.

SOLE PRACTITIONER
Please Contact
M.E. Daphne Foster
140 Harley Street
London W1N 1AH
Telephone: 0207 224 2628
Mobile: 0385 988578

MUSICLINK

www.musiclink.co.uk

From a single page to a complete web site - we create and maintain a world-wide Internet presence for our clients from only £20.00 a year.

INTERNET ADVERTISING

Springwood Music Workshops
Water Street, Springwood
HUDDERSFIELD HD1 4BB

Tel: 01484 530053 Fax: 01484 305303
E-mail: sales@musiclink.co.uk

The Affordable Internet Solution
WORLD-WIDE

Camden Music. 19a North Villas, Camden Square, London NW1 9BJ *tel:* 020 7267 8778 *fax:* 020 7813 4601 *email:* info@camdenmusic.com. Andrew Skirrow, dir. *Specialist computerised mus typesetting service, media mus, internet development and website design.*

Chalmers Enterprises. 48 Bonaly Rise, Edinburgh EH13 0QX *tel:* 0131 441 3488 *fax:* 0131 441 6029 *email:* music@cbnews.demon.co.uk. *Computerised mus typesetting using Coda Finale.*

Cowdrey, Elizabeth. 1 South St, Middle Barton, Oxon OX7 7BU *tel:* 01869 340951 *fax:* 01869 349084 *email:* orbestra@excite.com. *Hand transcription. Special interest in world mus, vn, fiddle mus.*

Craig-McFeely, Julia. 41 Freelands Rd, Oxford OX4 4BS *tel:* 01865 241323 *fax:* 01865 437582 *email:* julia.craig-mcfeely@music.oxford.ac.uk. Julia Craig-McFeely. *Typesetting of all types of mus, specialising in unusual notational requirements: editing includes early mus notations. Proof-reading and copy-editing.*

Crofton, Robin. 8 Wynbury Drive, Totteridge, High Wycombe, Bucks HP13 7QB *tel:* 01494 533775. *Computerised mus setting (Sibelius 7).*

Curiad. The Old Library, County Rd, Pen-y-Groes, Caernarfon, Gwynedd LL54 6EY *tel:* 01286 882166 *fax:* 01286 882692 *email:* curiad@curiad.co.uk. *Full mus publishing consultancy by computerised mus copying with editing, design and print service.*

Da Capo Music Ltd. 26 Stanway Rd, Whitefield, Manchester M45 8EG *tel:* 0161 766 5950. *Computerised mus setting and processing.*

Dale, Simon. 26 Leicester Rd, Lewes, E Sussex BN7 1SX *tel:* 01273 486389 *also fax; email:* simondale@compuserve.com. *Computer typesetting. Orchestration, arranging, pno reductions.*

Discantus Music. 83 Oakfield Rd, London N14 6LT *tel:* 020 8882 5976. Blaise Compton, mgr. *Gen mus copying, early mus editions to order, archive research.*

Donald Bousted Studio. 75 Canbury Ave, Kingston-upon-Thames, Surrey KT2 6JR *tel:* 020 8546 1424 *email:* donaldbousted@compuserve.com. Donald Bousted, dir. *Computer engraving using Finale software.*

Enigma Music Production Services. 44 Grove Rd, Amersham, Bucks HP6 6NE *tel:* 01494 431663 *also fax.* B R Wilson. *Mus engraving (Sibelius 7).*

Fand Music Press. Blumleins, 7a Dragon St, Petersfield GU31 4JN *tel:* 01730 266605 *fax:* 01730 262961 *email:* fandmusicpress@printed-music.com. *Pno, vocal, chmbr, choral, orch mus.*

Final Score. Cecilia Cottage, 47 Brighton Rd, Horsham, W Sussex RH13 6EZ *tel:* 01403 264798 *also fax; email:* finalscore@mistral.co.uk. Michael and Helen McCabe. *Mus typesetting and printing; publication layout and graphic design; CRC or full-scale production service.*

Fly Music Inc. 11 Sheldon Court, Lower Edgeborough Rd, Guildford, Surrey GU1 2DU *tel:* 01483 533892 *also fax; email:* Benjafield@argonet.co.uk. Ursula John; Richard Benjafield. *Mus copying, typesetting, editing and publishing on Sibelius UMP. Contemporary mus a speciality.*

Frontier Music Services. 36 Riverdale Rd, Plumstead, London SE18 1NZ *tel:* 020 8473 2213. Jennifer Churches, proprietor. *Computerised typesetting service.*

Gibson, Stephen. 40 Campbell Close, London SW16 6NJ *tel:* 020 8677 8473 *fax:* 020 8877 3494 *email:* stephen@gibmusic.freeserve.co.uk. *Mus typesetting, orchestration, arranging, vocal reductions.*

Ginn, Jeffrey. 11 Haycroft, Wootton, Bedford, Beds MK43 9PB *tel:* 01234 765602; 07778 896721 *fax:* 01234 765367 *email:* jeff@ginn-mus.demon.co.uk. *Mus typesetting to laser or film. Sibelius 7 recording service.*

Gordon, Christopher. 22 Ivybridge Close, Twickenham, Middx TW1 1EA *tel:* 020 8892 1833 *also fax; email:* stoffg@hotmail.com. Christopher Gordon. *Computerised mus setting, hand copying. Special rates for educ clients.*

Halstan & Co Ltd. 2-10 Plantation Rd, Amersham, Bucks HP6 6HJ *tel:* 01494 725525 *fax:* 01494 432305 *email:* sales@halstan.co.uk. Christopher Smith, mgr dir. *Mus process engraving, computerised mus setting, design service, mus printing and binding.*

Harlequin Music. 69 Eversden Rd, Harlton, Cambridge CB3 7ET *tel:* 01223 263795 *also fax. Computerised mus setting and copying (Sibelius 7).*

Harman, Mrs M. 48 Huxley Rd, Welling, Kent DA16 2EW. *Preparation for printing of mastercopies of mus from composers' manuscripts.*

Hinkins, Chris and Gail. 66 Spilsby Rd, Horncastle, Lincs LN9 6AW *tel:* 01507 526531 *also fax. High-quality computer mus engraving.*

Hodson, Maud. 6 Joseph Priestley House, Canrobert St, London E2 0BQ *tel:* 020 7729 0489 *also fax; email:* maud@maud.co.uk. *Computerised mus typesetting (Sibelius 7). Also arranging, pno reductions, orchestrations.*

Kanon Music Solutions. PO Box 14750, Dunfermline KY11 4WF *tel:* 01383 738267 *also fax; email:* dw@kanon.demon.co.uk. D Watson, owner. *Computer typesetting (Sibelius). Preparation for commercial publication. Short run DTP where commercial runs not viable.*

Keysworth Press. 4 Kennart Rd, Poole, Dorset BH17 7AP *tel:* 01202 668525 *email:* music@keysworth.ndirect.co.uk. Michael Moorsom, Rosemary Fraser, partners. *Computer mus engraving and printing using Score and Sibelius software.*

King's Music. Redcroft, Banks End, Wyton, Huntingdon, Cambs PE17 2AA *tel:* 01480 52076 *fax:* 01480 450821 *email:* cbkings@ibm.net. Clifford Bartlett, Brian Clark. *Photocopying, mus and text typesetting, programme production (including writing and printing notes).*

Langley, John. 77 Braybourne Drive, Isleworth, Middx TW7 5DZ *tel:* 020 8758 9422 *fax:* 020 8758 9865 *email:* langers@cableinet.co.uk. *Computer typesetting and editing (Sibelius), transposing, transcribing, sequencing, arranging, DTP, proof-reading, ms sourcing, orch librarian and trouble-shooting service.*

Laser Music Ltd. 6 Lytham Close, Chippenham, Wilts SN15 3XW *tel:* 01249 444858 *also fax; email:* lasermusic@argonet.co.uk. Gareth Bennett, principal associate. *Computerised mus setting and mus copying.*

Lawrence Music. 55 Borough Rd, Darlington, Co Durham DL1 1SR *tel:* 01325 464609 *also fax.* Peter Lawrence, proprietor; Hazel Lawrence. *Computerised mus setting (Sibelius 7), laser printing, binding, recording.*

Linda Lancaster Music Setting. 19 Far View, Almondbury, Huddersfield HD5 8ER *tel:* 01484 546490 *also fax.* Paul Lancaster, partner. *Computerised mus and text setting.*

Lipkin, Malcolm. Penlan, Crowborough Hill, Crowborough, Sussex TN6 2EA *tel:* 01892 652454. *Computerised mus setting, artwork and editing.*

Loft Music. 103 Stubbington Ave, North End, Portsmouth, Hants PO2 0JE *tel:* 023 9269 0894 *also fax. Computer mus transcription, mus editing.*

Longship Music. 'Smidskot', Fawells, Keith-Hall, Inverurie, Aberdeenshire AB51 0LN *tel:* 01651 882274 *also fax.* John Hearne. *Mus copying and typesetting (Sibelius 7). Full service including binding in card covers, title pages, etc. Phone for quotation.*

Lowdell, Robert. 29 Montana Rd, London SW17 8SN *tel:* 020 8672 8020 *fax:* 020 8682 3647. *Computerised mus copying (Sibelius 7).*

Maestro Music Services. Ivy Cottage, Chapel Rd, Beaumont-cum-Moze, Essex CO16 0AK *tel:* 01255 860502 *also fax; email:* mms@aspects.net. Sarah Williams, principal. *Computerised mus copying from ms or MIDI files; part extractions, transposition, score reduction, arrangements.*

MME (Marrington Musical Enterprises). 9 Mount Pleasant Ave, Leeds LS8 4EF *tel:* 0113 226 5943. Mark Marrington. *Computerised mus typesetting (Sibelius 7), transposition, transcription, arranging.*

MSS Studios. Rhiwlas, Cae Deintur, Dolgellau, Gwynedd LL40 2YS *tel:* 01341 422115 *fax:* 01341 422127 *email:* 100273.673@compuserve.com. Mr King, snr partner. *Mus engravers with 20 years experience.*

Music Reprographics. 34 Hollingworth Court, Ashford Rd, Maidstone, Kent ME14 5PP *tel:* 01622 683884 *fax:* 01622 661919. R Shipley, dir. *Full range of printing and publishing services.*

Music To Measure. New House, Ballachulish, Argyll PA39 4JR *tel:* 01855 811507 *also fax; email:* 100272.2253@compuserve.com. Mary Anne Alburger, dir. *Computerised mus and text typesetting to print and film; DTP services.*

Music Works. 2 Queens Gardens, Benton, Newcastle upon Tyne NE12 9PL *tel:* 0191 266 7991/292 0014 *also fax; email:* ipk@musicworks2000.freeserve.co.uk. Ian Phillips-Kerr, dir. *Computerised mus production, Sibelius, A3 laser printers. Scores, parts, binding, mus examples, incidental and background mus.*

Musicleigh Inklined. 35 Kirtle Rd, Chesham, Bucks HP5 1AD *tel:* 01494 771872. Jackie Leigh. *Computerised mus typesetting (Sibelius), artwork productions, laser printing.*

Musography. 6 Station Rd, Catworth, Huntingdon, Cambs PE18 0PE *tel:* 01832 710227 *also fax; email:* chris@musography.freeserve.co.uk. Christopher Brown. *Computerised mus typesetting (SCORE), specialising in complex contemporary scores and baroque mus.*

Needham, Marian. 14 Roselands Court, Chester Rd, Lavister, Wrexham LL12 0DD *tel:* 01244 571857 *also fax; email:* M.Needham@btinternet.com. *Quality computerised mus setting service from ms to camera-ready using Score and Sibelius.*

New Notations Computer Services. Unit A8, Friston Business Centre, Aldeburgh Rd, Friston, Saxmundham, Suffolk IP17 1NP *tel:* 01728 604906 *also fax; email:* sales@newnotations.free-online.co.uk. *Stephen Ferre, proprietor. Advanced computerised mus typesetting, mus and text integration, etc. Specialists in large projects, fast turnaround. Consultancy and custom-built computer workstations and software sales.*

Orphean Press Ltd. c/o 100 Botham Hall Rd, Longwood, Huddersfield, W Yorks HD3 4RH *tel:* 01206 761942 *also fax; email:* info@orphean-press.demon.co.uk. Cheryl Jessop, mgr dir. *Mus engraving, typesetting, publishing and design. Preparation of performing editions.*

Parfrey, Raymond. 53 Longley Rd, Harrow, Middx HA1 4TG *tel:* 020 8427 5267. *High-class notation by hand.*

Parish Publications. 28 Tom Price Close, Cheltenham, Glos GL52 2LF *tel:* 01242 230455 *also fax; email:* parish@lineone.net. Ian and Janine Higginson, dirs. *Computerised mus setting, composition, transposition, arranging, orchestrating, part extraction. Proof-reading. Typesetting of all types of mus.*

Phillips, Sally. 10 Quayside Close, Nottingham NG2 3BP *tel:* 0115 986 3386 *email:* sally.phillips@ntu.ac.uk. *Hand copying, transposition, binding, secretarial services, website design.*

Pilkington, Michael. 268 Coulsdon Rd, Old Coulsdon, Surrey CR5 1EB *tel:* 01737 556346 *also fax. Computerised mus copying, transposition, part extraction.*

Richmond House Music. 33 Southminster Rd, Penylan, Cardiff CF23 5AT *tel:* 029 2049 9970 *also fax; email:* rhmusic@cerddor.freeserve.co.uk. Chris Painter. *Computerised typesetting (Coda Finale and Sibelius) on Power Macintosh and Pentium II. Brochure design and printing. Web page design. Digital printing (up to A3) on laser photocopiers.*

RM Music. Ivydene, 37 West Pastures, Fallowfield, Ashington, Northumberland NE63 8LB *tel:* 01670 521570 *also fax. Specialist in br and wind band.*

Rob Danter Computer Music Typesetting. 18 Clydesdale Rd, Box, Corsham, Wilts SN13 8EN *tel:* 01225 742424. Rob Danter. *Computerised mus typesetting (Sibelius). Special interest in church and org mus.*

RTS Music Partnership. 17 Bradford Rd, St John's, Wakefield, W Yorks WF1 2RF *tel:* 01924 370454 *email:* standford@rtsmusic.demon.co.uk. Patric Standford, dir. *Composition, arranging, computer copying, editing, revision and tutorial support; work for TV and concert, schools and amateurs.*

Scoreprint. 12b Anstey Way, Cambridge CB2 2JE *tel:* 01223 841721. *Mus process engraving.*

SFZ Professional Music Arranging & Typesetting Services. 86 Newark St, Whitechapel, London E1 2ES *tel:* 020 7426 0340 *email:* jay-glover@compuserve.com. Jason Glover, dir. *Computerised mus typesetting. Arranging and dictation.*

Silverfen. 57a St Philip's Rd, Cambridge CB1 3DA *tel:* 01223 461143 *also fax; email:* mtargent@silverfe.demon.co.uk. Timothy Argent, dir. *Mus setting, design, typesetting.*

SJ Music. 23 Leys Rd, Cambridge CB4 2AP *tel:* 01223 314771 *fax:* 01223 560353. Judith Rattenbury, principal; Susan Otty, associate. *Computerised mus typesetting and transposition.*

Smith, Andrew. c/o 27 Reeth Rd, Richmond, N Yorks DL10 4EH *tel:* 01748 823948. *Hand and computer transcription.*

Snell, Piers. 1a All Saints' Passage, Cambridge CB2 3LT *tel:* 01223 460818 *fax:* 01223 464178 *email:* cmsrecords@compuserve.com. Piers Snell. *Advanced computerised mus engraving.*

Software Partners. Oak Tree House, Station Rd, Claverdon, Warwicks CV35 8PE *tel:* 01926 842998 *fax:* 01926 842384 *email:* info@software-partners.co.uk. Richard Blundell. *Distributors for Capella (mus notation), Capriccio (MIDI sequencer), Tonica (harmony and composition), Capella-scan and MIDISCAN (mus OCR software).*

Southgate Music. 2 Canute Rd, Winchester, Hants SO23 0PW *tel:* 01962 851210 *also fax; email:* 106041.3464@compuserve.com. Nick Morris, proprietor. *Computerised mus engraving.*

Spartan Press Ltd. Old Brewery House, Redbrook, Monmouth NP5 4LU *tel:* 01600 712482 *fax:* 01600 712483 *email:* spartanpress@compuserve.com. Mark Goddard, mgr dir; Ken Harris, press mgr; Jonathan Kershaw, sales co-ord; Mark Pulman, sales rep. *Mus typesetting, laser and offset printing services.*

Steadman, Robert. 36 Trafalgar Rd, Beeston Rylands, Nottingham NG9 1LB *tel:* 0115 917 4546 *also fax; email:* robsteadman@hotmail.com. *Computerised mus copying and typesetting. Transposition and orchestration services available.*

Sulian Music. Kynance, Millards Hill, Midsomer Norton, Bath BA3 2UX *tel:* 01761 418331 *also fax.* David Simmonds, James Simmonds, partners. *Computerised mus setting (Sibelius 7, Sibelius for Windows), camera-ready artwork, linotronic film or bromides, printing service. Transcriptions, arrangements, orchestrations.*

Top Type Music Bureau. 78 St Laurence Rd, Chapelizod, Dublin 20, Republic of Ireland *tel:* 00 353 1 6261409 *also fax; email:* dmtrstry@indigo.ie. Deborah Metrustry, Simon Trezise, mgrs. *Computerised mus typesetting, DTP and camera-ready text and mus.*

Vann, Esther. Hambrook Cottage, Hambrook, Ledbury, Herefordshire, HR8 2PX *tel:* 01531 670634 *also fax. Hand and computerised copying and notesetting.*

Vinson, P. 36 Rosetta Rd, Spixworth, Norwich NR10 3NW *tel:* 01603 898722 *also fax. Computer mus setting and hand copying.*

Wakefield, Anthony. 115 Village Way, Ashford, Middx TW15 2JY *tel:* 01784 252958 *also fax. Orchestration, arranging, reductions/enlargements for film or similar media projects.*

Music Typesetting Service

Symphonic - Choral - Piano - Windband
Brass Band - Bagpipe - Quintets.

RM *Music Copy Specialist*

RM MUSIC produce quality Typeset Manuscripts. We have thirty years experience in the music industry and produce Scores and instrumental parts at very competitive rates.

Every Typeset Score is expertly finished.
For further information, and a comprehensive sample package, please contact. .

Roy McCluskey
RM MUSIC
Ivydene - 37 West Pastures - Fallowfield
ASHINGTON - Northumberland - NE63 8LB
Tel/Fax: (01670) 521570 (24 hrs)

SILVERFE

The printed music production company
helping clients meet their publishing goals

Quality design, typesetting and printing of sheet music

Typesetting to the highest standards
Design of publications
Writing of typefaces
Printing and print buying
Web site design

Our service covers all forms of music:
from scholarly editions of mediæval
works in original-style notation
to contemporary music,
from teaching music
to critical editions
– all matching the finest nineteenth
and twentieth century music engraving.

57a St Philip's Road, Cambridge, CB1 3DA. Tel/fax 01223 461143
email: info@silverfe.demon.co.uk

For the retail trade and everybody interested in music

MUSIC NOTABLES

57 Amberwood
Ferndown
Dorset
BH22 9JT

Telefax: 01202 855955
email: info@musicnotables.co.uk

The leading company
for a wide range of exclusive
British high quality music-related gifts.
Aprons, tote bags, oven mitts, china mugs,
bookmarks and stationery etc
(plus various tea towels, including the
hilarious "Nota Bene for Musicians")

Giftware much sought-after by musicians and music lovers

Greetings Cards
Manuscript
Notepapers
&
MUSIC

MUSICAL EXPRESSIONS

Phone for catalogue:

(01449) 741707

Musical Expressions Ltd.
106 High St., Bildeston, Suffolk IP7 7EB.

Webber, John. 88 Balfour Rd, North End, Portsmouth PO2 0NH *tel:* 023 9235 1816 *also fax; email:* webber_pnmo@yahoo.com. *Mus arranged, transcribed, typeset.*

Wessex Music Services. 1000 Westbury Rd, Little Cheverell, Devizes, Wilts SN10 4JW *tel:* 01380 816338 *fax:* 01380 816467 *email:* wessex.music@easynet.co.uk. John Bickerton, proprietor. *Computerised mus typesetting, laser printing, arrangements, transposition.*

Wilson, Jenny. 10 Hogan Way, Stafford, Staffs ST16 3YN *tel:* 01785 228871 *also fax; email:* jenny.wilson@which.net. Jenny Wilson, Proprietor. *Computerised mus setting and printing (Sibelius 7 software).*

Musical Giftware and Novelties Manufacturers and Retailers

Barnes and Mullins. 155 Grays Inn Rd, London WC1X 8UF *tel:* 020 7278 4631 *fax:* 020 7837 2184/6928. Bruce Perrin, Sandra Fowler, dirs. *Musical inst and acc manufacture and distribution.*

Instrumental Furniture. 128 Brondesbury Villas, London NW6 6AE *tel:* 020 7328 0058 *fax:* 020 7328 4101. John Hammond, designer, dir. *Vc and pno shape coffee tables, note hooks, vn and gui shape chopping boards, sax and db shape CD racks, lamps, garden things. Over 40 musical designs.*

Lindsay Music. 23 Hitchin St, Biggleswade, Beds SG18 8AX *tel:* 01767 316521 *fax:* 01767 317221 *email:* sales@lindsaymusic.co.uk. Carole Lindsay-Douglas, dir. *Tea-towels, thimbles, display plates, mus bags.*

MAK Enterprises. 195 Poplar Grove, Kennington, Oxford OX1 5QT *tel:* 01865 730671 *also fax. Manufacturers and producers of branded mus merchandise for all sections of mus retailing.*

The Music Box. 31 The Lanes (by the Oasis), Meadowhall, Sheffield S9 1EP *tel:* 0114 256 9089 *email:* ask@themusicbox.co.uk.

Music Gifts Co (Poole) Ltd. 7 Fleetsbridge Business Centre, Upton Rd, Poole, Dorset BH17 7AF *tel:* 01202 686368 *fax:* 01202 686363. David Gee, mgr dir; Len de Silva, sales mgr. *Silk apparel, stationery, mugs, coasters, keyrings, pewter, bone china, textiles, chopping boards, clocks, greetings cards. Large collection of British-made gifts.*

Music Notables. 57 Amberwood, Ferndown, Dorset BH22 9JT *tel:* 01202 855955 *also fax; email:* info@musicnotables.co.uk. Edouard Sefton, Veronica Sefton, partners. *A range of exclusive British innovative mus-related giftware: tea-towels, aprons, tote bags, oven mitts, china mugs, bookmarks, stationery, etc.*

Musical Expressions Ltd. 106 High St, Bildeston, Suffolk IP7 7EB *tel:* 01449 741707. Kevin Bates, dir; Jackie Bates, sales. *'Musical Expressions' greetings cards and mus stationery manufacturers.*

The Musical Gift Catalogue. 51 Fortess Rd, London NW5 1AD *tel:* 0990 275124 *fax:* 020 7284 1404. *M/order of stationery, insts, jewellery, accs, novelties, clothing, household goods.*

Spartan Press Music Publishers Ltd. Old Brewery House, Redbrook, Monmouth NP5 4LU *tel:* 01600 712482 *fax:* 01600 712483. Mark Goddard, mgr dir; Ken Harris, Phil Goddard, production; Jonathan Kershaw, Mark Pulman, sales. *Greetings cards, cartoon books, ms books.*

William Elkin Music Services. Station Rd Industrial Estate, Salhouse, Norwich NR13 6NS *tel:* 01603 721302 *fax:* 01603 721801 *email:* sales@elkinmusic.demon.co.uk. Cindy Hazard, sales. *Giftware including jewellery, clothing, umbrellas, stationery, clocks and household goods.*

Practice Studios

Amadeus Centre. 50 Shirland Rd, London W9 2JA *tel:* 020 7286 1686 *fax:* 020 7266 1225 *email:* TheAmadeusCentre@amadeuscentre.co.uk. Raynier Platings, gen mgr. *2 rehearsal halls and café. Upper hall up to 50 players with grand pno; lower hall up to 20 players. Suitable for auditions and concerts.*

Bell Studios. 6 Greenock Rd, London W3 8DU *tel:* 020 8896 1200 *fax:* 020 8896 0100. *3 purpose-built studios, Yamaha grand pno, easy access and free parking. On site perc hire.*

Belsize Music Rooms. 67 Belsize Lane, Hampstead, London NW3 5AX *tel:* 020 7916 0111 *fax:* 020 7916 0222 *email:* belsize.music.rooms@dial.pipex.com. Clare Howells, David Howells. *3 air-controlled and sound-proofed mus rooms with Steinway, Bösendorfer and Ibach pnos and a concert hpd. Quality new upright pnos for sale. Also waiting room, outside relaxation area, refreshment facilities.*

Bösendorfer (UK Principal Dealer). Jaques Samuel Pianos Ltd, 142 Edgware Rd, London W2 2DF *tel:* 020 7723 8818/9 *fax:* 020 7224 8692; Elizabeth Mooney, hire mgr. *Pno hire, tuning, servicing, transport. Practice rooms.*

Bromley Youth Music Centre. Southborough Lane, Bromley, Kent BR2 8AA *tel:* 020 8467 1566 *fax:* 020 8468 7595. Peter Mawson, principal. *Large hall, up to 70 players. Yamaha grand pno, 12 other rooms with uprights.*

Cecil Sharp House. 2 Regent's Park Rd, London NW1 7AY *tel:* 020 7485 2206 *fax:* 020 7284 0534. Dee Swain, lettings mgr. *2 large rehearsal halls; upper hall seats 500 with grand pno. 2 committee rooms and studio. Facilities include café, bar, PAs.*

The Clarendon Suites. 2 Stirling Rd, Edgbaston, Birmingham B16 9SB *tel:* 0121 454 2918 *fax:* 0121 455 0859 *email:* sales@ear-ltd.co.uk. Maureen Potter, mgr; Mo Hadley, duty mgr; Martin Robinson, Stuart Perry. *Nine rooms suitable for rehearsals of any kind; plus nine for vocalists.*

Craxton Studios. 14 Kidderpore Ave, London NW3 7SU *tel:* 020 7435 2965 *fax:* 020 7431 1579. Jane Craxton. *Rehearsals, auditions, filming, recording. Large studio: double-height, wood-panelled, 2 concert grand pnos, up to 30 (orch) or 50 (choir). 2nd studio: grand pno, up to 7 players.*

John Henry Enterprises. 16-24 Brewery Rd, London N7 9NH *tel:* 020 7609 9181 *fax:* 020 7700 7040 *email:* hiredept@jhe.co.uk. John Henry, mgr dir. *Rehearsal studios.*

Music Dynamics Ltd. PO Box 340, Cheltenham, Glos GL52 4ZP *tel:* 01242 679379 *also fax; email:* music@museco.demon.co.uk. Sue Lloyd, sales mgr. *Originator and producer of the ChoraLine range of high-tech rehearsal cassettes for choral singers. Cassettes are SATB, signposted throughout and provide individual control of target voice against remaining parts. Sound is neutral ensuring the choral director keeps full control of interpretation, tempo and dynamics.*

The Music Room. 49 Great Ormond St, London WC1N 3HZ *tel:* 020 7405 9848. Alec Forshaw.

Music Services (MSA). The Chalet, 75 Claremont Rd, Tunbridge Wells, Kent TN1 1TE *tel:* 01892 52790. David Ebbage, dir. *Studio with two pnos for hire. Arranging, transposition, mus written for special events.*

Pro Piano Inc. 85 Jane St, New York, NY 10014, USA *tel:* +1 212 206 8794 *fax:* +1 212 633 1207 *email:* ricard@propiano.com. Ricard de La Rosa, dir.

Terminal 24 Rehearsal Ltd. 4-10 Lamb Walk, London Bridge, London SE1 3TT *tel:* 020 7403 3050 *fax:* 020 7407 6123. Charlie Barrett, dir. *Large Turbosound-equipped studios, central London, parking. Comprehensive equipment hire on site, showcase and production rooms. Café and production office. Storage cages.*

The Warehouse Waterloo. London Festival Orchestra, 13 Theed St, London SE1 8ST *tel:* 020 7928 9251 *fax:* 020 7928 9252 *email:* orchestra@lfo.co.uk. *2 rehearsal halls; large hall up to 60 players, small hall up to 35 players. Steinway and Rönich grand pnos.*

Wembley Park Practice Studios. 9 Hillcroft Cres, Wembley Park, Middx HA9 8EE *tel:* 020 8903 2759. Marian Treece, Ulle Sachs, mgrs. *Garden studio with Steinway grand; additional studio with new Young Chang upright. Well-appointed rooms, reasonable hire charges.*

Wigmore Hall. 36 Wigmore St, London W1H 0BP *tel:* 020 7486 1907 *fax:* 020 7224 3800 *email:* info@wigmorehall.org.uk. Marion Friend, gen admin. *Contact the management office. Rehearsal room with upright Bösendorfer pno. Main hall available for rehearsal auditions. Bechstein Room available for talks and receptions.*

Cecil Sharp House

Regent's Park, NW1

Attractive, undisturbed and spacious halls for rehearsals, auditions and concerts

Facilities include:
2 grand pianos
Large hall 500 capacity
Superb acoustics
Cafe and licensed bar
Staging
Walled garden
PA systems

For more details, please contact
Dee Swain at Cecil Sharp House
2, Regent's Park Road, NW1 7AY
Tel: 0171 485 2206 Fax: 0171 284 0534

THE DEFINITIVE GUIDE TO AUDIENCE-BUILDING THROUGH EFFECTIVE MARKETING

ARTS MARKETING

by Keith Diggle

Hardback • 293 pages • PRICE: £15.00

Postage and packing is FREE to UK addresses and to overseas addresses by surface mail. Please add £1 per copy for airmail to Europe and £4 per copy outside Europe.

To obtain your copy please send a cheque (payable to Rhinegold Publishing Ltd) to: **Book Sales Dept, Rhinegold Publishing Ltd, FREEPOST, London WC2H 8BR.**

CREDIT CARD ORDERS
Tel: 020 7333 1721 Fax: 020 7333 1769

www.rhinegold.co.uk

BELSIZE MUSIC ROOMS

London's most comfortable rehearsal and audition venue for classical musicians. Renowned for its superb location, soundproofed and air controlled rooms - all equipped with high quality pianos. Regular users include soloists, chamber groups, orchestral and opera companies, teachers and concert agents.

Room 1 (11' x 10') - Steinway upright piano. Ideal for individual rehearsal, teaching and warm-up.

Room 2 (15' x 10') - Ibach grand piano. Ideal for chamber music, meetings and examinations.

Room 3 (28' x 16') - Bösendorfer grand piano and Goble concert harpsichord. Ideal for group rehearsals of up to 20 musicians, seminars up to 50 people, auditions, examinations, TV filming, photography and recording.

High quality upright pianos, stools, music stands and cabinets for sale.

Close to Finchley Road & Swiss Cottage tube. Prices from £8 an hour.
Monday to Friday 9am to 9pm, Saturday 9am to 4pm, Sundays by appointment.

67 BELSIZE LANE . HAMPSTEAD . LONDON NW3 5AX
TEL: 0171 916 0111 FAX: 0171 916 0222
http://www.belsize-music-rooms.co.uk

Programme and Sleeve Notes

Ades, David. Stone Gables, Upton Lane, Seavington St Michael, Ilminster, Somerset TA19 0PZ *tel:* 01460 242226 *also fax. Compiler and sleeve note writer.*

Allen, Kevin. 23 Benbow Close, Malvern Wells, Worcs WR14 4JJ *tel:* 01684 569643.

Avis, Peter Graham. 91 Cambridge Rd, New Malden, Surrey KT3 3QP *tel:* 020 8336 1656 *fax:* 020 8336 1742. *Programme and sleeve notes, more anecdotal than technical.*

Barfoot, Terry. 25 Mulberry Lane, Cosham, Portsmouth PO6 2QU *tel:* 023 9238 3356 *also fax. Programme and sleeve notes.*

Bartlett, Clifford. Redcroft, Banks End, Wyton, Huntingdon, Cambs PE17 2AA *tel:* 01480 52076 *fax:* 01480 450821 *email:* cbkings@ibm.net. *Programme notes.*

The Basil Ramsey Programme Note Library. 604 Rayleigh Rd, Eastwood, Leigh-on-Sea, Essex SS9 5HU *tel:* 01702 524305 *fax:* 01702 526142 *email:* basilmusic@freeserve.co.uk. Basil Ramsey, Keith Bramich, dirs. *Library of classical mus programme notes by various authors. Works can be requested by phone or email.*

Bishop, David. Curls Farmhouse, Ripe, Lewes, E Sussex BN8 6AP *tel:* 01323 811654. *Programme and sleeve notes.*

Bryant, Michael. 61 Oak Hill, Surbiton, Surrey KT6 6DY *tel:* 020 8390 3236 *email:* michael@bryant14.demon.co.uk. *Specialising in Czech and Slovak mus and all chmbr and wind repertoire.*

Bullamore, Tim. 25 Brock St, Bath BA1 2LN *tel:* 01225 330037 *also fax;* 07836 617030 *email:* TBullamore@aol.com. *Programme notes for concerts, festivals, recordings, etc. Author of Fifty Festivals, the history of the Bath Festival.*

Burton, Anthony. 19 Capel Rd, E Barnet, Herts EN4 8JD *tel:* 020 8440 4380. *Programme and CD notes.*

Butterworth, Neil. 1 Roderick Place, West Linton, Peeblesshire EH46 7ES *tel:* 01968 661112. *Programme and sleeve notes, any level/length.*

Carroll, Brendan G. 2 Southbank Rd, Grassendale, Liverpool, L19 9AR *tel:* 0151 427 1181; 020 7681 3890 *also fax; fax:* 0151 494 3589 *email:* brendan_carroll@compuserve.com. *Programme notes, sleeve notes, reviews of recordings and books. Specialises in early 20th C mus, especially opera, film mus and Korngold.*

Carson, Ian. Yew Trees, Comeytrowe Rise, Taunton TA1 5JA *tel:* 01823 272764 *also fax; email:* ian.carson@tesco.net. *Programme and liner notes, extensive library, reviews and articles.*

Chater, James. 56 Sistova Rd, London SW12 9QS *tel:* 020 8333 1440 *fax:* 020 8355 4696 *email:* JMChater@aol.com.

Clark, Jayne. 7 Purbeck Rd, Chatham, Kent ME4 6ED *tel:* 01634 849674. *Programme notes.*

Conway, Joe. 22 Brook Court, Harrow Rd, London E11 3PP *tel:* 020 8539 5933. *Programme and sleeve notes. Also reviews and mus journalism.*

Daw, Stephen. 6 Parkland Drive, Darlington, Co Durham DL3 9DU *tel:* 01325 350244. *Specialist interest in Bach.*

Duchen, Jessica. 7 Leinster Ave, London SW14 7JW *tel:* 020 8876 5774 *also fax.*

Fligg, David. 32 High Moor Cres, Moortown, Leeds LS17 6DU *tel:* 0113 268 7440 *email:* d.fligg@leedscolmusic.ac.uk. *Programme and sleeve notes.*

Frontier Music Services. 36 Riverdale Rd, Plumstead, London SE18 1NZ *tel:* 020 8473 2213. Jennifer Churches, proprietor. *Copywriting, sleeve notes and part-writing.*

Gault, Dermot. 4 Stormont Court, Belfast BT4 3LE *tel:* 01232 410584 *fax:* 01232 418980 *email:* dermot@drmg.freeserve.co.uk. *Programme notes dispatched in any format (hard copy, email, disc, fax) as required.*

George, Alan. 10 BoothamTerrace, York YO30 7DH *tel:* 01904 658189 *also fax; email:* FitzQtet@aol.com. *Any classical, romantic, early 20th C repertoire, str quartets, Shostakovich.*

Green, Christopher OBE. 25 The Avenue, Braintree, Essex CM7 3HY *tel:* 01376 324079 *also fax. Programme and sleeve notes.*

Humphreys, Garry. 69 Park Ave, Palmers Green, London N13 5PH *tel:* 020 8882 2106. *Specialist in British mus.*

Humphries, John. 24 Aragon Ave, East Ewell, Epsom, Surrey KT17 2QG *tel:* 020 8393 6067 *also fax. Informed notes on orch, chmbr, choral and early mus. Specialist in br and wind mus.*

Joseph, Jeffrey. 15 Selsdon Rd, London SE27 0PQ *tel:* 020 8766 6668 *fax:* 020 7486 6018. *Programme and sleeve notes.*

Kennedy, Paula. 37 Swainstone Rd, Reading RG2 0DX *tel:* 0118 975 0981 *also fax; email:* shortkennedy@compuserve.com. *Programme and sleeve notes. Specialising in Czech and Hungarian mus.*

Langley, John. 77 Braybourne Drive, Middx TW7 5DZ *tel:* 020 8758 9422 *fax:* 020 8758 9865 *email:* langers@cableinet.co.uk.

Lawrence, Richard. 115 Camberwell Grove, London SE5 8JH *tel:* 020 7701 1896 *also fax. Programme and sleeve notes.*

Lillystone, Simon. 24 Fairfield Rd, London N8 9HG *tel:* 020 8347 9655 *email:* simon@lillystones.freeserve.co.uk. *Programme and sleeve notes.*

Manly, Ann. 8 Alma Square, London NW8 9QD *tel:* 020 7286 3944 *fax:* 020 7289 9081 *email:* annmanly.protheroe@btinternet.com. *Programme notes, liner notes, editorial services.*

Mayhew, John. Norman Cottages, 36 Suez Rd, Cambridge CB1 3QB *tel:* 01223 249864 *also fax; email:* john-mayhew@cambridge.softnet.co.uk. *Liner notes, programme notes, record reviews.*

Morley, Christopher. 16 Melbourne Rd, Halesowen B63 3NB *tel:* 0121 550 4482 *also fax; email:* cfmorley@breathemail.net. *Programme and sleeve notes.*

Ng, Kah-Ming. Oakley, 109 Windmill Rd, Oxford OX3 7DN *tel:* 01865 751928 *also fax; email:* Kah-MingNg@charivari.freeserve.co.uk.

Notes in Edge-Wise. 38 Heyes Lane, Alderley Edge, Cheshire SK9 7JY *tel:* 01625 585378 *fax:* 01625 590175 *email:* edgewise@dircon.co.uk. Lynne Walker. *Agency providing all types of programme or liner material; also editing any arts publications.*

Oldland, Marie. 65 Byfield Rise, Worcester, Worcs WR5 1BA *tel:* 01905 26113 *email:* moldland@aol.com. Marie Oldland, writer. *English mus specialist.*

Pott, Francis. Thurlows, Main Rd, Littleton, Winchester, Hants SO22 6PS *tel:* 01962 885874 *email:* fpott@argonet.co.uk. *Regular contributor of concert programme notes and sleeve notes to record companies and major concert venues.*

Pro Piano Records. 85 Jane St, New York, NY 10014, USA *tel:* +1 212 206 8794 *fax:* +1 212 633 1207 *email:* ricard@propiano.com. Ricard de La Rosa, classical division head; Chitose Okashiro, A&R.

Purkiss, Anthony J. 35 Fonthill Rd, Hove, E Sussex BN3 6HB *tel:* 01273 774730 *also fax. Programme notes and record sleeves.*

Rast, Nicholas. 47 Borrowdale Drive, Norwich NR1 4LY *tel:* 01603 433935 *fax:* 01603 403400. *Especially Franz Schubert.*

Saba, Thérèse Wassily. 9 Methuen Park, Muswell Hill, London N10 2JR *tel:* 020 8442 1489 *also fax; email:* 106665.3500@compuserve.com. *Programme and sleeve notes, especially Arabic, Spanish and Latin-American mus, gui mus. News ed of Classical Guitar magazine, ed of Flamenco International Magazine.*

Sara Hindley Promotions. 59 Brook St, Chester, Cheshire CH1 3DZ *tel:* 01244 319981 *fax:* 01244 315662. Maria King, writer; Rebecca Perez, mkt. *Programme notes, sleeve notes, press releases.*

Standford, Patric. 17 Bradford Rd, St John's, Wakefield, W Yorks WF1 2RF *tel:* 01924 370454 *email:* standford@rtsmusic.demon.co.uk. *Yorkshire Post mus critic, reviews, features.*

Steadman, Robert. 36 Trafalgar Rd, Beeston Rylands, Nottingham NG9 1LB *tel:* 0115 917 4546 *also fax; email:* robsteadman@hotmail.com. *Including reviews, specialising in 20th C repertoire.*

Stewart, Andrew. 46 Schoolbell Mews, Arbery Rd, London E3 5BZ *tel:* 020 8983 0011 *also fax; email:* AndrewStewart1@compuserve.com. *Specialist in choral, song and early mus. Essays supplied for festival programme books, recordings, videos, etc. Extensive resource of existing notes available.*

Stowell, Robin. 43 Woodvale Ave, Cyncoed, Cardiff CF23 6SP *tel:* 029 2075 2001 *fax:* 029 2087 4379 *email:* stowell@cardiff.ac.uk. *Programme and sleeve notes, especially mus for strs.*

Taylor, Philip. 112 Main Rd, Wilby, Northants NN8 2UE *tel:* 01933 223301 *also fax; email:* 100661.1355@compuserve.com. *Specialist in Russian mus.*

3rd Millennium Music Ltd. 22 Avon, Hockley, Tamworth, Staffs B77 5QA *tel:* 01827 286086 *also fax; email:* Neil3MMLtd@aol.com. Neil Williams, mgr dir. *Programme and sleeve notes, especially for composers, conds and musicians; also picture archive.*

Thomas, Janet Owen. Flat 3, 88 Holgate Rd, York YO24 4AB *tel:* 01904 654283. *Programme and sleeve notes. Record, concert and book reviews, especially contemporary mus, mus educ and org mus.*

Ward Russell, Gillian. 10 New Street, Maldon, Essex CM9 6AQ *tel:* 01621 853237. *Programme and sleeve notes.*

Wheeler, Mike. 20 Sudbury St, Derby DE1 1LU *tel:* 01332 362194. *Programme and sleeve notes. Also proof-reading and copy-editing.*

Wright, Simon. 6 Warneford Place, Moreton-in-Marsh, Glos GL56 0LR *tel:* 01608 651409. *Programme and sleeve note writing (especially French and Latin-American mus).*

Solicitors

Howell-Jones & Partners. 19a Wimbledon Bridge, London SW19 7NH *tel:* 020 8947 7991 *fax:* 020 8947 8725. Peter Scott, partner. *Solicitors with 25 years' experience in the mus industry.*

Marshall Hatchick Solicitors. 17 Bentinck St, London W1M 5RL *tel:* 020 7935 3272 *fax:* 020 7224 1592 *email:* mhat@compuserve.com. Keith Hatchick, Nicholas Marshall, partners. *General arts law advice, particularly sponsorship and lottery applications.*

Teacher Stern Selby. 37-41 Bedford Row, London WC1R 4JH *tel:* 020 7242 3191 *fax:* 020 7242 1156 *email:* gs@tsslaw.co.uk. Graham Shear, partner. *Specialists in the entertainment, mus, film and TV industries, including production and distribution, licences, recording, management, agency, publishing, copyright, multimedia agreements; litigation in all areas.*

Tods Murray WS. 66 Queen St, Edinburgh EH2 4NE *tel:* 0131 226 4771 *fax:* 0131 624 7170 *email:* richard.findlay@todsmurray.co.uk. Richard Findlay, entertainment law partner; David Smith, entertainment lawyer. *Specialist entertainment and media lawyers.*

Tour and Travel Companies

ABC Executive Travel. Tower Bridge Piazza, Butlers Wharf, London SE1 2LH *tel:* 020 7357 8322 *fax:* 020 7357 8323 *email:* info@abc-extra.co.uk. Andreas Schwalbe, gen mgr. *Complete tour arrangements for individuals, orchs and choirs, including air and international rail tickets, aircraft charter, ground handling, accommodation, transfers, passport and visa service.*

ACFEA Tour Consultants. 12-15 Hanger Green, London W5 3EL *tel:* 020 8799 8360 *fax:* 020 8998 7965 *email:* admin@stlon.com. Matthew Grocutt, operations mgr. *Organises concert tours in UK, Europe, the Baltic States, S Africa, USA, Australia and Japan for youth and adult choirs, bands and orchs.*

Aircraft Chartering Services Ltd. 7 High St, Ewell, Epsom, Surrey KT17 1SG *tel:* 020 8394 2795 *fax:* 020 8393 6154 *email:* sales@aircraft-chartering.co.uk. Mark Hugo, mgr dir; Ian Browne, Andrew Richley, touring mgrs. *Charter of aircraft for touring orchs.*

Albion Services. 17 Cleevelands Ave, Cheltenham, Glos GL50 4PY *tel:* 01242 254771 *fax:* 01242 527728. Ian Bird, mgr; Linda Hack, accounts. *Specialist in handling all accommodation requirements inc hotels, self-catering, B&Bs and guest houses for all types and sizes of touring groups. Long term lets arranged, group and individual bookings for all ferry crossings.*

Cameron Logistics. 80 Keswick Rd, East Kilbride, Glasgow G75 8QX *tel:* 07973 504492 *fax:* 01355 265737. Stephen Cameron, proprietor. *Vans to 45' stepframe trailers, one-off performances, festivals and tours in UK and Europe. Also supply 7-seater Chrysler Grand Voyager people-carriers.*

Club Europe Concert Tours. Fairway House, 53 Dartmouth Rd, London SE23 3HN *tel:* 020 8699 7788 *fax:* 020 8699 7770 *email:* music@club-europe.co.uk. Lucy Szymonski, concert tours product development mgr. *International concert tours throughout Europe for amateur adult, youth and school groups.*

Congress Travel. 20 Tuckett Rd, Woodhouse Eaves, Leics LE12 8SE *tel:* 01509 891131 *fax:* 01509 891151 *email:* artsman@btinternet.com. Anthony Goodchild, UK representative. *Performing tours, exchanges, festivals worldwide. Specialises in USA and Canada.*

Edwin Doran Music Travel. 54 King St, Twickenham, Middx TW1 3SH *tel:* 020 8288 2931 *fax:* 020 8288 2955. Edwin Doran. *Specialist in mus and educ tours.*

Euro-Academy Ltd. 77a George St, Croydon, Surrey CR0 1LD *tel:* 020 8686 2363 *fax:* 020 8681 8850 *email:* euroacademy@btinternet.com. Mrs M B Malone, dir. *Mus tours to Germany, Holland and Austria for schools, youth orchs and choirs, br bands, folk groups, etc.*

Gower Music International. 2 High St, Studley, Warwicks B80 7HJ *tel:* 01527 851414 *fax:* 01527 851417 *email:* gower@gowstrav.demon.co.uk. Peter Cook, gen mgr; Catherine Neale, sales and mkt.

Specialist tour operator arranging performance tours and festivals abroad for choirs, bands and orchs.

HF Holidays. Imperial House, Edgware Rd, London NW9 5AL *tel:* 020 8905 9558 (reservations); 020 8905 9388 (brochure line) *fax:* 020 8205 0506 *email:* hfholidays@compuserve.com. Christine Helps, media relations exec; Erica Looney, media relations asst. *Wide range of mus holidays including orch and choral weeks, opera w/shops, mus appreciation and festivals.*

Hotelink (UK) Ltd. Silver House, Church Lane, Lower Fyfield, Marlborough, Wilts SN8 1PY *tel:* 01672 861111 *fax:* 01672 861100 *email:* hotelink@compuserve.com. Jean and John Grant-Silver, dirs. *Specialist in negotiating best quality hotel accommodation at lowest rates for orchs and other groups on tour in the UK or abroad.*

Interchange. Interchange House, 27 Stafford Rd, Croydon, Surrey CR0 4NG *tel:* 020 8681 3612 *fax:* 020 8760 0031 *email:* interchange @interchange.uk.com. Gordon Burnett, mgr dir. *Specialist in group tours worldwide catering to individual group requests.*

Legato Music Tours. 8 Meadow Lane, Alvechurch, Birmingham B48 7LH *tel:* 0121 445 4938 *also fax.* Christine Read, Nigel Morley, dirs. *Specialist mus tours throughout Europe for schools, youth groups, choirs, bands and orchs.*

Maestro Travel & Touring Company. 6th Floor, 32 Hanover St, Liverpool L1 4AA *tel:* 0151 707 1234 *fax:* 0151 707 1747 *email:* maestro@compuserve.com. Ken Grundy, Nigel Foo. *International travel arrangements for the classical mus business from individual artists to ens and full-scale orch touring.*

Martin Randall Travel Ltd. 10 Barley Mow Passage, Chiswick, London W4 4PA *tel:* 020 8742 3355 *fax:* 020 8742 7766 *email:* info@ martinrandall.co.uk. Martin Randall, dir. *Special lecture tours to European festivals and opera houses.*

Music and Travel Ltd. 124 Village Way, Beckenham, Kent BR3 3PA *tel:* 020 8663 3037 *fax:* 020 8663 3012 *email:* info@music-and-travel.co.uk. David Horsburgh, dir. *Travel and tour arrangements specialising in Europe and N America. Tailor-made tours, festivals and exchanges.*

Musica Europa. 7a Farm Rd, Maidenhead, Berks SL6 5HX *tel:* 01628 776795 *fax:* 01628 632112 *email:* bengunner@musica-europa.com. Ben Gunner, dir. *Organises concert tours, w/shops, courses, exchanges and visits to the European festivals for all types of amateur choirs and orchs.*

NST Music Tours. Chiltern House, 181 Bristol Ave, Blackpool, Lancs FY2 0FA *tel:* 01253 503008 *fax:* 01253 356955 *email:* nmartin @nstgroup.co.uk. Sarah Foden, mus tours mgr. *Tailor-made performance tours for bands, choirs and orchs throughout Europe and N America. Arrangements for travel and accommodation only also available.*

Onyx International Travel Services Ltd. 26 Woodford Close, Caversham, Reading RG4 7HN *tel:* 0118 947 2830 *fax:* 0118 946 3104. *Specialists in orch and choir travel including flight, hotel bookings worldwide, air charter and tailor-made tours.*

Perform Europe. Deepdene Lodge, Deepdene Ave, Dorking, Surrey RH5 4AZ *tel:* 01306 744360 *fax:* 01306 744361 *email:* peurope@ kuoni.co.uk. Sharon Brewster, festival and operations mgr. *Specialist tour operator run by musicians for musicians. Performance tours worldwide. Agent for the Bournemouth Music Makers Festival, performance opportunities at the Sydney 2000 Olympics. Organisers of Harrogate and W Sussex International Youth Music Festivals.*

Progressive Tours Ltd. 12 Porchester Place, London W2 2BS *tel:* 020 7262 1676 *fax:* 020 7724 6941 *email:* 101533.513@compuserve.com. L R Temple, mgr. *Specialist in travel to former USSR, most European countries, Cuba and South Africa for choirs, orchs, cultural groups, etc. Exchange enquiries welcome.*

Rayburn Tours Ltd. Rayburn House, Parcel Terrace, Derby DE1 1LY *tel:* 01332 347828 *fax:* 01332 371298 *email:* enquiries @rayburntours.co.uk. Julian Edwards, sales mgr; Catherine Astle, senior tours organiser; Daniel Carriett, mus tours mgr. *Tailor-made concert tours to worldwide destinations for all types of amateur youth and adult bands, choirs, orchs and ens.*

St Albans Travel Service. 4a Spencer St, St Albans, Herts AL3 5EQ *tel:* 01727 842276/866533 *fax:* 01727 847418. Carole Simpson, mgr. *UK and international travel service, hotel and theatre bookings, many discounts.*

School Rail. PO Box 1, St Albans, Herts AL1 4ED *tel:* 01727 834475 *fax:* 01727 851676 *email:* schoolrail@aol.com. Pat Kearley, mgr. *Educ tours, reduced rail travel, overnight accommodation, ticket bookings, lecture and tour arrangements. Theatre and mus events. Worldwide tours for choirs, orchs, etc.*

Specialised Travel Ltd. 12-15 Hanger Green, Park Royal, London W5 3EL *tel:* 020 8799 8360 *fax:* 020 8998 7965 *email:* admin@stlon.com. Richard Savage, chmn; David Beaumont, dir business development. *ABTA, IATA*

and CAA bonded travel consultant to the mus industry since 1955. Competitive quotes for travel to any part of the world. Concert tours organised to E and W Europe, USA, Canada, Japan, South Africa, China.

Tempo Touring Productions Ltd. Meadow House, Mill Lane, Hildenborough, nr Tonbridge, Kent TN11 9LX *tel:* 01732 833141 *also fax.* Brian Martineau, mgr dir; Nick Milburn, transportation mgr. *Long haul budget specialist: USA, Asia, Australia. Current projects in Chicago, Singapore, Australia. Youth, school, university and amateur choirs. Tailor-made tours.*

Travel for the Arts. 117 Regent's Park Rd, London NW1 8UR *tel:* 020 7483 4466 *fax:* 020 7586 0639 *email:* enquiries@travelforthearts.co.uk. Clare Temple, mgr. *Operates a programme of visits to opera houses and summer festivals for opera, ballet and mus lovers.*

Upbeat Tours. 29 High St, Llandovery, Carms SA20 0PU *tel:* 01550 720978 *also fax.* Meryl Goodwin, Hugh Thomas, dirs. *Specialist in concert tours of France for choirs, orchs and chmbr musicians.*

Wyvern Schooltours Ltd. 28 Westbourne Gardens, Trowbridge, Wilts BA14 9AW *tel:* 01225 766346 *fax:* 01225 777936 *email:* nigel@wyverntours.co.uk. Ashley Scarlett, operations dir. *Tailor-made tours to W Europe for orch, inst and choral groups.*

Young Travellers Ltd. Dept Music and Leisure, Travel House, 34 Station Rd, London SE20 7BQ *tel:* 020 8778 6850 *fax:* 020 8778 9754 *email:* musicleisure@young-travellers.co.uk. S Williamson, dir; A McIntyre, programme consultant. *Transportation by coach and air of orchs and choirs in the UK and abroad, including accommodation arrangements if required.*

Video Companies

Colmar Video Productions. 36 Planton Way, Brightlingsea, Colchester, Essex CO7 0LB *tel:* 01206 303764 *fax:* 01206 305027. Colin Sadler, partner. *Concert and recital videos.*

Documentary Video Associates Ltd. 7 Campbell Court, Bramley, Tadley, Hants RG26 5EG *tel:* 01256 882032 *fax:* 01256 882024.

Heavy Entertainment Ltd. 222 Kensal Rd, London W10 5BN *tel:* 020 8960 9001/2 *fax:* 020 8960 9003 *email:* info@heavy-entertainment.co.uk. Nick St George, David Roper, company dirs; Matthew Thompson, production mgr. *TV and radio producers. Commercials, direct-mail CDs and cassettes, promotional video and audio, electronic press kits, video news releases, media training, event staging, showreels (audio and video).*

Music Mall. 1 Upper James St, London W1R 3HG *tel:* 020 7534 1444 *fax:* 020 7534 1440 *email:* post@musmall.demon.co.uk. Roger Drage, mgr dir; Jason Simms, mkt exec. *Sourcing, tracing, clearance, duplication, programme development for mus video.*

Powerline Productions. Unit 23, Winston Close, Romford, Essex RM7 8LL *tel:* 01708 724544; 0800 074 2367 *fax:* 01708 744166 *email:* info@powerlineproductions.com. Peter Walters. *Promotional and PR videos. Opera/concert performances. Tour videos. All kinds of mus/theatre performance and documentary production for TV.*

Symphony Films. First Floor, 38 Russell Rd, London W14 8HT *tel:* 020 7460 1697 *email:* enquiries@symphonyfilms.demon.co.uk. Martin Phillips, dir. *Full programme production. Promotional videos, video press-releases, tour videos, demo tapes, self-observance videos, audition tapes, concert and recital videos. USA conversions, duplication to any quantity.*

Word Processing and Editorial Services

Better English. Suite 22, Sparkford House, Battersea Church Rd, Battersea, London SW11 3NQ *tel:* 020 7350 0661 *also fax; email:* infocom@dial.pipex.com. Michael Thorne, mgr dir. *Sub-editing and proof-reading services for press releases, websites, annual reports, etc.*

Cadenza Consultants. 40 Shorrolds Rd, London SW6 7TP *tel:* 020 7385 9171 *fax:* 020 7381 4691. *High-quality letters, mailings, reports, theses, CVs, etc and business computing.*

Classique Arts Administration. 118 Craigmount Ave North, Edinburgh EH4 8HJ *tel:* 0131 339 7663 *email:* carolanwood@hotmail.com. Carol Wood. *Audio-typing of correspondence, CVs, dissertations, brochures, fliers, programmes, mailshots, etc. Organisation of concerts and recitals.*

Complete Secretarial Services. Milestone, St Nicholas Ave, Great Bookham, Surrey KT23 4AY *tel:* 01372 457755 *fax:* 01372 450525 *email:* maestoso@btinternet.com. Elizabeth McArthur. *Service includes typing letters, mailings, reports, theses, CV preparation, address labels for mailshots, accounts and book-keeping for artists and small businesses, the organisation of conferences, special events, travel arrangements, etc.*

Compro. 63 Charles St, Epping, Essex CM16 7AX *tel:* 01992 572805 *also fax.* Genevieve Pearson, dir. *Laser address labels of concert promoters, UK and abroad. Complete mailshots and mailmerge.*

Friary Music Services. 142b Friary Rd, London SE15 5UW *tel:* 020 7277 7068 *fax:* 020 7277 8354 *email:* 100115.3701@compuserve.com. *Editorial services, proof-reading (English and German).*

Key Support. Ivy Cottage, Chapel Rd, Beaumont-cum-Moze, Essex CO16 0AR *tel:* 01255 860502 *also fax; email:* keysupport@aspects.net. Sarah Williams, principal. *CVs, reports, theses, dissertations, general word processing and admin.*

Lees, Tracy. 35 Hamilton Rd, Wimbledon, London SW19 1JG *tel:* 020 8540 9857 *also fax. Secretarial and admin service.*

Manly, Ann. 8 Alma Square, London NW8 9QD *tel:* 020 7286 3944 *fax:* 020 7289 9081 *email:* annmanly.protheroe@btinternet.com. *DTP, design, word-processing, programme notes.*

SMG Secretarial Services. 39 Parkwood Ave, Esher, Surrey KT10 8DE *tel:* 020 8398 8541 *fax:* 020 8339 0625. Susan Garratt, proprietor. *Typing of general correspondence, CV preparation, reports, theses, mailshots, proof-reading, laser printing, photocopying, fax.*

Sprint. 10 Quayside Close, Nottingham NG2 3BP *tel:* 0115 986 3386 *email:* sally.phillips@ntu.ac.uk. Sally Phillips, mgr. *Typing, reports, CV preparation, mailshots, laser printing, data processing, binding, leaflets, website design.*

Wessex Music Services. 1000 Westbury Rd, Little Cheverell, Devizes, Wilts SN10 4JW *tel:* 01380 816338 *fax:* 01380 816467 *email:* wessex.music@easynet.co.uk. John Bickerton, proprietor. *Word processing and typing services, especially text with mus examples.*

Record Companies

The following is a list of classical record companies. As many classical records are manufactured abroad, the importers or distributors of these are also listed, indicated by an asterisk. Membership of the **British Phonographic Industry (BPI)**, 25 Savile Row, London W1X 1AA *tel:* 020 7287 4422 is indicated after each entry.

Abbey Records/SCS Music Ltd. 4 Newtec Place, Magdalen Rd, Oxford OX4 1RE *tel:* 01865 244557 *fax:* 0870 056 8880. Steve C Smith, mgr dir.

Acta Records. 28 Alymer Rd, London W12 9LQ *tel:* 020 8740 1349 *email:* JBacta@msn.com.

Albany Records. PO Box 12, Carnforth, Lancs LA5 9PD *tel:* 01524 735873. William Lloyd, mgr dir. Label: Albany.

Alchemy Records and Fetish Records. PO Box 393, Maidstone, Kent ME14 5XU *tel:* 01622 729593.

* **Alpha Records (Oxford) Ltd.** 1 Abbey St, Eynsham, Oxford OX8 1HR *tel:* 01865 880240 *also fax.* H F Mudd, mgr dir; A J Wilson, press offr. Label: Alpha. *BPI*

Altarus Records. Easton Dene, Bailbrook Lane, Bath BA1 7AA *tel:* 01225 852323 *fax:* 01225 852523 *email:* 100775.2716@compuserve.com; alistair_hinton@compuserve.com. Chris Rice, president; Alistair Hinton, UK office mgr. UK Distributor: Kingdom Records.

Amon Ra Records. Chipping Manor, The Chipping, Wotton-under-Edge, Glos GL12 7AD *tel:* 01453 845036 *fax:* 01453 521056 *email:* saydisc@aol.com. Gef Lucena, mgr dir; Arwen Lucena, mkt offr. Labels: Amon Ra, Saydisc.

Apollo Sound. 32 Ellerdale Rd, London NW3 6BB *tel:* 020 7435 5255 *fax:* 020 7431 0621. H Herschmann, mgr dir. Label: Apollo Sound. *BPI*

* **Appian Publications & Recordings (APR).** PO Box 1, Wark, Hexham, Northumberland NE48 3EW *tel:* 01434 220627 *fax:* 01434 220628 *email:* aprrecordings.co.uk. Edwin Alan, mgr. Label: APR. *Specialises in historic releases.*

ARC Music. PO Box 111, East Grinstead, W Sussex RH19 2FZ *tel:* 01342 328567 *fax:* 01342 315958 *email:* info@arcmusic.co.uk. *World and folk mus.*

* **Arembe.** 84 Filsham Rd, Hastings, E Sussex TN38 0PG *tel:* 01424 423260 *also fax.* Margaret Brand, mkt dir. Label: Arembe Records.

ASV Ltd. 1 Beaumont Ave, London W14 9LP *tel:* 020 7381 8747 *fax:* 020 7385 2653. Hywel Davies, mgr dir; Ray Crick, mkt mgr; Richard Harrison, sales mgr; Johanna Knowles, press and promotions mgr. Labels: ASV, COE, Gaudeamus, Living Era, Quicksilva, White Line. *BPI*

Athene Records. 7 Felden St, London SW6 5AE *tel:* 020 7736 9485 *fax:* 020 7371 7087. Labels: Athene (period square pnos), Athene-Minerva (modern insts).

* **Audio Book and Music Company (ABM) (Distributors).** 24 Somerton Rd, London NW2 1SA *tel:* 020 8830 7224 *fax:* 020 8830 7225. John Cooper, mgr dir; Melinda Sandell, publishing mgr. Label: ABM.

Bandleader Music. Modern Publicity Services Ltd, 9 Gillingham St, London SW1V 1HN *tel:* 020 7233 7801 *fax:* 020 7233 7802.

Belltree Records. 9 Hillside Rd, Ashtead, Surrey KT21 1RZ *tel:* 01372 277703 *fax:* 01372 278406 *email:* dragonsfire@btinternet.com. Nigel Perona-Wright, partner. Label: Belltree Records.

Beulah. 66 Rochester Way, Crowborough, E Sussex TN6 2DU *tel:* 01892 652413. *BPI*

BGS Records. Bath Spa University College, Newton Park, Newton St Loe, Bath BA2 9BN *tel:* 01225 875609 *fax:* 01225 875444 *email:* t.kerstens@bathspa.ac.uk. Tom Kerstens, dir. *In partnership with Black Box Music. Label is dedicated to presentation of new or rediscovered work and/or new artists.*

* **Biddulph Recordings.** 34 St George St, Hanover Square, London W1R 0ND *tel:* 020 7408 2458 *fax:* 020 7495 6501 *email:* jlaredo.biddulph@btinternet.com. Eric Wen, producer; Jennifer Laredo, mkt mgr.

Bitter and Twisted Records. 22c Breakspears Rd, London SE4 1UW *tel:* 020 8691 8646 *email:* btrap@argonet.co.uk. Andrew Poppy, mgr dir; Frederick Ruby, label mgr; Grant Bardsley, mkt.

Black Box Music Ltd. PO Box 28, Orpington, Kent BR5 1TQ *tel:* 01689 898154 *fax:* 01689 898155 *email:* info@bbmusic.demon.co.uk. Chris Craker, dir. *Classical and jazz.*

Black Mountain Ltd. 1 Squire Court, The Marina, Swansea SA1 3XB *tel:* 01792 301500 *also fax.* Mike Evans, dir. Label: Black Mountain.

Blue Snow Records. 20 Downs View, Isleworth, Mddx TW7 5HF *tel:* 07767 810560 *email:* bluesnow@easynet.co.uk. Philip Sheppard, dir. *Contemporary classical and improvised mus.*

BMG Conifer. 69-79 Fulham High St, London SW6 3JW *tel:* 020 7384 7500 *fax:* 020 7371 9571 *email:* conifer@enteract.co.uk. Alison Wenham, mgr dir; Richard Dinnadge, mkt dir; Brian Hopkins, business development dir; Nicole Rochman, A&R co-ord. Labels: Catalyst, Conifer Classics, Deutsche Harmonia Mundi, Melodiya, RCA Classics Navigator, RCA Gold Seal, RCA Red Seal, RCA Victor, Royal Opera House Records, Telarc, Classic for Full Works. *BPI*

BMP Broken Music Publishing (UK) Ltd. Ripe Recordings, B9, FUN, BMP, Riverbank House, 1 Putney Bridge Approach, London SW6 3JD *tel:* 020 7371 0022 *fax:* 020 7371 0099 *email:* ripe@compuserve.com. Jurgen Dramm, mgr dir.

Brewhouse Music. Breeds Farm, 57 High St, Wicken, Cambs CB7 5XR *tel:* 01353 720309 *fax:* 01353 723364 *email:* brewhouse@bigfoot.com. Eric Cowell, Ray Cowell, partners. Labels: Brewhouse, Calle Classics, Home Brew. *BPI*

* **British Music Society.** 7 Tudor Gardens, Upminster, Essex RM14 3DE *tel:* 01708 224795. S C Trowell, hon treasurer. *Only distributes the society's own productions.*

* **Cadillac Jazz Distribution.** 61-71 Collier St, London N1 9BE *tel:* 020 7278 7391 *fax:* 020 7278 7394. John Jack, mgr dir. Labels: Arbors, BvHaast, Cadillac, Caprice, Dragon, FMP, Gemini, Ogun, Phontastic, Reservior, Storyville and a large list of jazz labels. Cadillac Music and Publishing own Cadillac Dawn Club record labels.

Cala Records. 17 Shakespeare Gardens, London N2 9LJ *tel:* 020 8883 7306 *fax:* 020 8365 3388 *email:* music@calarecords.com. Geoffrey Simon, artistic dir; Daniel Schiffman, exec producer; Jeremy Swerling, Matthew Daines, mkt; Matt Hall, mgr. Labels: Cala Artists, Cala Cascade, Cala Records, Cala-The Edge, Cala-United.

* **Campion Cameo.** 1st and 2nd Floors, 7 High St, Cheadle, Cheshire SK8 1AX *tel:* 0161 491 6655 *fax:* 0161 491 6688 *email:* didistr@aol.com. Alan Wilson, mgr dir. Label: Campion.

Cantoris Records. Exchequer Gate, Lincoln LN2 1PZ *tel:* 01522 536981 *fax:* 01522 560550 *email:* sales@cantoris.co.uk. Paul Pinchbeck, proprietor. Label: Cantoris. *Specialise in Cathedral, choral, and org mus as well as general classical and crossover.*

Cardinal. 216 Evering Rd, London E5 8AJ *tel:* 020 8806 0555 *also fax.* Sarah Marsh, Martin Carling, mkt dept.

* **Caritas Records.** 28 Dalrymple Cres, Edinburgh EH9 2HX *tel:* 0131 667 3633 *also fax; email:* caritas-records@caritas-music.co.uk. Katharine Douglas, professional mgr; James Douglas, dir. Labels: Caritas, Caritas Classics, Caritas Music Library. *BPI*

Castle Communications PLC. Unit A29, Barwell Business Park, Leatherhead Rd, Chessington, Surrey KT9 2NY *tel:* 020 8974 1021. Lee Simmonds, head of budget audio. Label: Cirrus, Pulse. *BPI*

* **Chandos Records Ltd.** Chandos House, Commerce Way, Colchester, Essex CO2 8HQ *tel:* 01206 225200 *fax:* 01206 225201 *email:* enquiries@chandosrecords.com. Brian Couzens, mgr dir; S Revill, finance dir; Ralph Couzens, operations dir; Ginny Cooper, sales mgr; Jeff Coventry, mkt mgr; Paul Westcott, press offr. Labels: Chaconne, Chandos, Brass, Collect, Opera in English, Enchant, New Direction, 2-4-1. *BPI*

Clarinet Classics. 77 St Albans Ave, London E6 4HH *tel:* 020 8472 2057 *also fax; email:* enquiries@clarinet-classics.ndirect.co.uk. Victoria and Nicolas Soames, partners; Richard Ralph, sales and mkt.

Classical Communications. Hamilton House, Howard St, Oxford OX4 3AY *tel:* 01865 722552 *fax:* 01865 243388. Frances Sunderland, Martin Souter, dirs.

Claudio Records Ltd. Studio 17, The Promenade, Peacehaven, E Sussex BN10 8PU *tel:* 01273 580250 *fax:* 01273 583530 *email:* info@claudio-records.ltd.uk. Colin Attwell, William Attwell, mgr dirs. Labels: Bohema, Claudio, Claudio Contemporary.

* **CM Distribution.** Hookstone Park, Harrogate HG2 7DB *tel:* 01423 888979 *fax:* 01423 885761.

Collegium Records. PO Box 172, Whittlesford, Cambridge CB2 4QZ *tel:* 01223 832474 *fax:* 01223 836723 *email:* info@collegium.co.uk. John Rutter, mgr dir; Joanna Holland, mkt offr. Label: Collegium. *BPI*

The Complete Record Co. 22 Prescott Place, London SW4 6BT *tel:* 020 7498 9666 *fax:* 020 7498 1828. *BPI*

Consort Records. 34 St Mary's Grove, London W4 3LN *tel:* 020 8995 9994 *fax:* 020 8995 2115 *email:* info@the-kings-consort.org.uk.

CRD Records Ltd. PO Box 26, Stanmore, Middx HA7 4XB *tel:* 020 8958 7695 *fax:* 020 8958 1415. Graham Pauncefort, mgr dir. Label: CRD.

Darmo Records. Arvensis, Stour Lane, Shaftesbury, Dorset SP7 0QJ *tel:* 01747 838318 *also fax.* Kenneth van Barthold, proprietor.

* **Decca UK (PolyGram UK Ltd).** 22 St Peters Square, London W6 9NW *tel:* 020 8910 5000 *fax:* 020 8910 5411. Dickson Stainer, head of Decca UK; Chrissie Wild, press offr. Labels: Argo, Decca, L'Oiseau-Lyre. *BPI*

Dell'Arte Records. PO Box 26, Hampton, Middx TW12 2NL *tel:* 020 8979 2479. Philip Moores, mgr dir; R G Dominy, remastering. Label: Dell'Arte.

* **Delta Music PLC.** 222 Cray Ave, Orpington, Kent BR5 3PZ *tel:* 01689 888888 *fax:* 01689 888800 *email:* info@deltamusic.co.uk. L J Adams, dir; N Kellas, product mgr. Labels: Audiophile Classics, Bella Voce, Blue Nite, Capriccio, Gala, Lake, Laserlight, Live at EJ's, Memoir Classical, Upbeat Recordings.

* **Deutsche Grammophon (PolyGram UK Ltd).** 22 St Peter's Square, London W6 9NW *tel:* 020 8910 5000. Karen Schrader, head of mkt; Terri Griffin, press offr. *BPI*

Deux-Elles Ltd. 63 Culver Lane, Reading RG6 1DX *tel:* 0118 901 2827 *also fax; email:* info@deux-elles.com. Patrick Naylor, mgr dir. Label: Deux-Elles.

* **DI Music.** 1st and 2nd Floors, 7 High St, Cheadle, Cheshire SK8 1AX *tel:* 0161 491 6655 *fax:* 0161 491 6688 *email:* didistr@aol.com. I T Wilson, chmn; A I Wilson, mgr dir; F Langton, gen mgr. Label: Campion, Cameo.

* **DI Music (Distribution).** 1st and 2nd Floors, 7 High St, Cheadle, Cheshire SK8 1AX *tel:* 0161 491 6655 *fax:* 0161 491 6688 *email:* didistr@aol.com. Jacquiline Holmes, distribution mgr. Labels: Butterfly, Cambria, Campion, Campion Cameo, Classico, EMEC, EDA-Edition Abseit, ERI-Elyseum, Essay, Gallo, JMP, Mastersound, Newport Classics, Newport Premier, Panton, ZUK Records.

* **Discovery Records.** The Old Church Mission Room, King's Corner, Pewsey, Wilts SN9 5BS *tel:* 01672 563931 *fax:* 01672 563934. Mike Cox, gen mgr; Martin Cobb, commercial mgr; Bill Trythall, sales mgr. Labels: Accord, Ades, Andre Charlin, Arion, Atrium, Chesky, Christophorus, Classical Collector, Col Legno, Cypres, Danacord, Elan, Ensayo, Four Hands Music, Fy, Gaiete Lyrique, Harmonic, Ivory Classics, Kontrapunkt, Lammas, Ligia, Lorelt, Ode, Oliverius, Pierre Verany, Quantum, Ricercar, Skarbo, Solstice, Studio SM, Symphonia, Tactus, 3D Classics.

* **Divine Art Ltd.** Tindle House, 31 Beach Rd, South Shields, Tyne and Wear NE33 2QX *tel:* 0191 456 1837 *fax:* 0191 455 2954 *email:* divinearts@aol.com. Stephen Sutton, mgr dir. Label: The Divine Art, Pilgrim's Star. *Also non-classical label (distributor), Dansing.*

Doyen Recordings. Doyen Centre, Vulcan St, Oldham, Lancs OL1 4EP *tel:* 0161 628 3799 *fax:* 0161 628 0177 *email:* sales@doyen-recordings.co.uk. N J Childs, mgr dir; A Childs, dir.

Ember Records. PO Box 130, Hove, E Sussex BN3 6QU *tel:* 01273 550088 *fax:* 01273 540969 *email:* tkomusicgroup.co.uk. Adam Clavering, dir.

EMI Classics. 64 Baker St, London W1M 1DJ *tel:* 020 7467 2000 *fax:* 020 7467 2200. Richard Lyttelton, president; Peter Alward, vice-president, A&R; Theo Lap, vice-president, mkt; John King, vice-president, finance. *BPI*

EMI Gold. 43 Brook Green, Hammersmith, London W6 7EF *tel:* 020 7605 5000. Paul Holland, dir, EMI Gold and cat; Steve Woof, repertoire mgr. Labels: EMI Gold, Music for Pleasure, Spoken Word. *BPI*

* **Fand Music Recordings Ltd.** Blumlein's, 7a Dragon St, Petersfield, Hants GU31 4JN *tel:* 01730 266605 *fax:* 01730 262961 *email:* fand-music-recordings@classical-artists.com. Peter Thompson.

Flamencovision. 54 Windsor Rd, London N3 3SS *tel:* 020 8346 4500 *fax:* 020 8346 2488 *email:* humartin@dircon.co.uk. Helen Martin, mgr. Label: Flamencovision.

Fly Records. Onward House, 11 Uxbridge St, London W8 7TQ *tel:* 020 7221 4275 *fax:* 020 7229 6893 *email:* info@bucksmusicgroup.co.uk. *BPI*

* **Forsyth Brothers Ltd (Distributor).** 126 Deansgate, Manchester M3 2GR *tel:* 0161 834 3281 *fax:* 0161 834 0630 *email:* forsythmus@aol.com. D R Loat, mgr dir; Jean Colter, trade mgr. Label: Music Minus One.

Four Hands Music. 15 Birchmead Close, St Albans, Herts AL3 6BS *tel:* 01727 858485 *also fax.* Isabel Beyer, Harvey Dagul, partners. Label: FHM.

Gemini Sound. Church Path, Hook, Hants RG27 9LZ *tel:* 01256 762605 *fax:* 01256 763706 *email:* 106133.1066@compuserve.com. David Wright, proprietor. Label: Libra.

Gimell Records Ltd. 4 Newtec Place, Magdalen Rd, Oxford OX4 1RE *tel:* 01865 244557 *fax:* 0870 056 8880 *email:* info@gimell.com. Steve C Smith, mgr dir. Label: Gimell. Press and mkt: Universal Classics. *BPI*

Grasmere Music. 59 Marlpit Lane, Coulsdon, Surrey CR5 2HF *tel:* 020 8666 0201 *fax:* 020 8667 0037. Bob Barratt, mkt. Label: Grasmere Records.

Grosvenor Records. 16 Grosvenor Rd, Handsworth Wood, Birmingham B20 3NP *tel:* 0121 356 9636 *also fax.*

Guildhall Recording. 17 Haven Hall, South Square, Boston, Lincs PE21 6HX *tel:* 01205 365340. Philip Towell, mgr dir. Label: Guildhall.

* **Guitar Masters Records.** 1-2 Vance Court, Trans Britannia Enterprise Park, Blaydon on Tyne NE21 5NH *tel:* 0191 414 9000 *fax:* 0191 414 9001 *email:* mail@ashleymark.co.uk.

Hallmark Music and Entertainment. 25-26 Ivor Place, London NW1 6HR *tel:* 020 7616 8100 *fax:* 020 7616 8146. Richard Hodkinson, classical label mgr. Labels: Carlton Classics, Hallmark Classics, IMP Classics, LSO Doubles.

* **Harlequin Recording.** Elgar House, Rufford, Tamworth, Staffs *tel:* 01827 53553 *also fax.* Geoffrey Poulton, owner and dir. Label: Harlequin.

* **Harmonia Mundi (UK) Ltd.** 19-21 Nile St, London N1 7LL *tel:* 020 7253 0865 *fax:* 020 7253 3237 *email:* info.uk@harmoniamundi.com. Serge Rousset, mgr dir; Ian Lambert, commercial mgr; Celia Ballantyne, press offr. Labels: Alienor, APR, Arbiter, Atma, Auvidis, Babel, Calliope, Forlane, Glossa, Harmonia Mundi, Hat Hut, Le Chant du Monde, Mandala, Mode, Music & Arts, Network, New Albion, New World, Pearl/Pavilion, Praga, Preiser, Russian Season, Salabert Actuel, Saydisc, Unicorn-Kanchana, Wergo, Winter and Winter. *BPI*

* **Herald Audio Visual Publications.** The Studio, 29 Alfred Rd, Farnham, Surrey GU9 8ND *tel:* 01252 725349 *fax:* 01252 735567. Brian Johnson, studio mgr.

Heritage Recordings. 50 Bessborough Place, London SW1V 3SG *tel:* 020 7828 1055 *fax:* 020 7376 5705. Hugh MacPherson, mgr dir.

* **Horatio Nelson Records & Tapes Ltd.** 76 Carlisle Mansion, Carlisle Place, London SW1 1HZ *tel:* 020 7828 6533 *fax:* 020 7828 1271. Derek Boulton, mgr; Siv Boulton, mkt offr. Label: Horatio Nelson. *BPI*

Hyperion Records Ltd. PO Box 25, London SE9 1AX *tel:* 020 8294 1166 *fax:* 020 8294 1161 *email:* info@hyperion-records.co.uk. Ted Perry, mgr dir; Mike Spring, sales mgr; Jenny Wegg, press and promotions mgr; Simon Perry, recording mgr; Richard Howard, production mgr. Labels: Helios, Hyperion. *BPI*

* **Impetus Distribution.** 10 High St, Skigersta, Ness, Isle of Lewis, Outer Hebrides, HS2 0TS *tel:* 01851 810808 *fax:* 01851 810809. Labels include: Phono Suecia, Crystal, Jaro, Innova, Content, Alice.

Isis Records. Hamilton House, Howard St, Oxford OX4 3AY *tel:* 01865 726553 *fax:* 01865 243388. Frances Sunderland, business mgr.

* **Jammy Music.** The Beeches, 244 Anniesland Rd, Glasgow G13 1XA *tel:* 0141 954 1873 *fax:* 0141 954 6341.

Jewish Music Heritage Recordings. PO Box 232, Harrow, Middx HA1 2NN *tel:* 020 8909 2445 *fax:* 020 8909 1030 *email:* jewishmusic@jmht.org. Geraldine Auerbach, trust dir.

* **K B Productions.** 72 Waverley Rd, Rayners Lane, Harrow, Middx HA2 9RD *tel:* 020 8866 4158. Keith S Bance. Labels: Hortus (Paris).

Keyboard Records. 418 Brockley Rd, Brockley, London SE4 2DH *tel:* 020 8699 2549. Gilbert Rowland, mgr dir. Label: Keyboard.

* **Kingdom Records Ltd.** Clarendon House, Shenley Rd, Boreham Wood, Herts WD6 1AG *tel:* 020 8207 7006 *fax:* 020 8207 5460 *email:* kingdomrec@aol.com. Terry King, mgr dir; Geoffrey Gunther-Smythe, sales mgr; Jeff Summers, press offr. Labels: Altarus, Bella Musica/Antes Concerto, Brioso, Cavalier, CBC, Iron Needle, Istituo Discografico Italiano, Killerwatt, Kingdom, Kingdom Jazz, KLT, Mantra, Minerva, Pavane, Piano Library, PMF, Promised Land, Sirio, Sonora, Strings Record Co, Submarine, Thorofon, Twinkle, Vista Vera, Vocal Archives, Wolf.

* **Kingsway Music.** 26-28 Lottbridge Drove, Eastbourne, E Sussex BN23 6NT *tel:* 01323 437700 *fax:* 01323 411970 *email:* music@kingsway.co.uk. Stuart Townend, head of mus division; Les Moir, A&R mgr.

* **Koch International.** Charlotte House, 87 Little Ealing Lane, London W5 4EH *tel:* 020 8832 1800 *fax:* 020 8832 1813. Rashmi Patani, mgr dir; Simon Carver, sales and mkt mgr; Michael K Jones, label mgr. Labels: Acoustic Disc, Acoustic Records, Black Lion, Bridge Records, Burnside Records, Century Media, Channel Classics, Charly, Compass Records, Consonance, Deluge, Diehard, Empress, Etcetera, Inside Out, King-snake, Koch International Classics, Koch Schwann, Koch UK, Modern Music, Moment Records, Naim Audio, Nightingale, Noise, Razor and Tie, Red House, Russian Disc, See For Miles, Shpraphon, Silva Screen, Smithsonian Folkways Records, SPV, Start Records, Ter, Triton. *BPI*

* **Linn Records.** 257 Drakemire Drive, Castlemilk, Glasgow G45 9SZ *tel:* 0141 303 5027/5029 *fax:* 0141 631 1485. Philip Hobbs, label mgr; Yvonne Tipping, admin; Claire Logue, press offr. Label: Linn. *BPI*

* **Lismor Recordings Ltd.** 27-29 Carnoustie Place, Scotland St, Glasgow G5 8PH *tel:* 0141 420 1881 *fax:* 0141 420 1892 *email:* lismor@lismor.co.uk. Ronnie Simpson, dir.

Longman Records. PO Box 2649, Brighton BN2 3PP *tel:* 01273 465371 *email:* sales@longman-records.com. Richard Durrant, dir; Louise Brattle, promotional mgr; Michael Munday, designer. *Longman is an acoustic mus label covering classical material.*

Lorelt (Lontano Records Ltd). Toynbee Studios, 28 Commercial St, London E1 6LS *tel:* 020 7247 2950 *fax:* 020 7247 2956. Odaline de la Martinez, mgr dir; Jan Hart, admin. Label: Lorelt.

Lyric Production. 41 Arkwright Rd, Sanderstead, Surrey CR2 0LP *tel:* 020 8657 5840 *also fax.* H T Hope, mgr dir; Norma Dyer, exec producer. Label: Lyric.

Lyrita Recorded Edition. 99 Green Lane, Burnham, Slough SL1 8EG *tel:* 01628 604208. A R Itter, proprietor. Label: Lyrita. *BPI*

* **Maxsound Ltd.** 6 Stainbeck Lane, Leeds LS7 3QY *tel:* 0113 237 0441 *fax:* 0113 237 0218. Max Rapaport, mgr dir. Label: Maxsound.

Melcot Music. PO Box 2404, New Milton, Hants BH25 7XZ *tel:* 01425 611924 *also fax.* Label: Melcot Music. *Specialise in classical org.*

Meridian Records. PO Box 317, Eltham, London SE9 4SF *tel:* 020 8857 3213 *fax:* 020 8857 0731. John Shuttleworth, mgr dir; Richard Hughes, mgr/engineer. Labels: Duo, Meridian.

* **Merlin Classics.** The Old Rectory, Church Lane, Exning, nr Newmarket, Suffolk CB8 7HF *tel:* 01638 577324 *fax:* 01638 577106. Trygg Tryggvason, Marian Freeman, partners. Labels: Merlin Label, UEA Records.

Metier Sound & Vision. PO Box 270, Preston, Lancs PR2 3LZ *tel:* 01772 866178 *email:* lefeber@enterprise.net. David Lefeber. Label: Metier (specialising in contemporary mus). Distributor: Priory Records.

Metronome Recordings Ltd. Carrick Business Centre, Beacon House, Commercial Rd, Penryn, Cornwall TR10 8AR *tel:* 01326 377738/ 378737 *fax:* 01326 378643 *email:* 106504.2417@compuserve.com. Tim Smithies, mgr dir. Label: Metronome.

* **Michele International Ltd.** Michele House, The Acorn Centre, Roebuck Rd, Hainault, Essex IG6 3TU *tel:* 020 8500 1819 *fax:* 020 8500 1745 *email:* michele_int@compuserve.com. Terry Denoff, sales dir. Label: Michele International, Scarborough Classics, Stradivari Classics.

Minstral Records. 3-5 Bridge St, Hadleigh, Ipswich, Suffolk IP7 6BY *tel:* 01473 822596 *fax:* 01473 824175. T L McIntosh, mgr dir; S Sowman, asst. Label: Minstral.

Montague Music. East Wing, Southwick Hall, Peterborough PE8 5BL *tel:* 01832 274790.

MPS Music and Video. Rosegarth, Hetton Rd, Houghton-le-Spring, Durham DH5 8JN *tel:* 0191 584 4141 *also fax; email:* cnutmanmps@ compuserve.com. C Nutman, studio mgr. *Contemporary mus, especially electro-acoustic and experimental mus.*

* **Music Collection International Ltd.** 72-74 Dean St, London W1V 5HB *tel:* 020 7396 8899 *fax:* 020 7396 8900/1 *email:* info@mcimusic.co.uk. Ian Foster, mgr dir; Danny Keene, mkt dir; Adrian Sear, commercial dir. Labels: Music Club, Nascente, Gallerie, Emporio, e2, Music Club US, Harmless, DCI, Startrax, Reflection, Showtime, Westside. *BPI*

* **Music Masters Ltd.** Orchard End, Upper Oddington, Moreton-in-Marsh, Glos GL56 0XH *tel:* 01451 870701 *fax:* 01451 870702. Nicholas John, mgr dir.

* **Neuschel Publications.** 15 Hailey Croft, Chinner, Oxon OX9 4TS *tel:* 01844 353025 *also fax; email:* 101353.1656@compuserve.com. Ian and Gillian Wagstaff, proprietors. *Br mus specialists.*

* **New Note Distribution Ltd.** Electron House, Cray Ave, Orpington, Kent BR5 3RJ *tel:* 01689 877884 *fax:* 01689 877891 *email:* mail@newnote.com. Eddie Wilkinson, Graham Griffiths, joint mgr dirs. Labels: ASC Classics, ECM New Series, Millenium Classics, and various jazz labels. *BPI*

* **Nimbus Records.** Wyastone Leys, Monmouth, Gwent NP5 3SR *tel:* 01600 890682 *fax:* 01600 890779 *email:* sales@nimbus.ltd.uk. Gerald Reynolds, chmn; Adrian Farmer, deputy chmn; Alf Goodrich, head of press and PR; Carl Wade, sales and mkt mgr; Colin Chambers, label mgr. Labels: Delos, Hermes, Lyrita, Meridian, MusicMasters, Nimbus, Prima Voce. *BPI*

NMC Recordings Ltd. Francis House, Francis St, London SW1P 1DE *tel:* 020 7828 3432 *also fax; email:* nmc@nmcrec.co.uk. Hannah Vlcek, admin; Jennifer Goodwin, consultant; Colin Matthews, exec producer. *Label devoted to contemporary British classical mus. BPI*

Novelbond Limited. Soverign House, 212-224 Shaftesbury Ave, London WC2H 8HQ *tel:* 020 7240 5821 *fax:* 020 7240 5827. Peter Watts, dir. Label: Novelbond.

NPC Records. PO Box 274, Barnsley S74 8YX *tel:* 0191 285 4098/2219 *also fax; email:* info@nutcracker-productions.com. Edward Marsh, Andrew Platts, dirs. Labels: NPC Records, Mirabilis. Interest in choral, org, hpd and br mus.

Olympia Compact Discs Ltd. The Courtyard, Evelyn Rd, London W4 5JL *tel:* 020 8995 8080 *fax:* 020 8995 8012 *email:* sales@olympia-cd.com. Jackie Campbell, label dir. Label: Olympia.

Opera Omnia Productions. Bunyan Rd, Biggleswade, Beds SG18 8QQ *tel:* 01767 314668 *fax:* 01767 601037. Patrick Allen, mgr dir. Label: Opera Omnia.

* **Opera Rara.** 134-146 Curtain Rd, London EC2A 3AR *tel:* 020 7613 2858 *fax:* 020 7613 2261 *email:* operarara@amity.co.uk. Patric Schmid, artistic dir; Stephen Revell, mgr dir; Robert Roberts, musicologist. Label: Opera Rara.

The Opus Magnum Record Group. 63 London Rd, Brighton BN1 4JE *tel:* 01273 604371/608444/608445 *fax:* 01273 626495/604813 *email:* postmaster@jwps.demon.co.uk. Jonathan R Wearn, chmn; Robert Harding, mgr dir. Labels: OM, OM Classics, OM Archive.

* **OxRecs Digital.** Magdalen Farm Cottage, Standlake, Witney, Oxon OX8 7RN *tel:* 01865 300347 *email:* info@oxrecs.com. Bernard Martin, mgr dir.

Paradisum Records (Hayter & Shone Ltd). 19 Grove Hill, South Woodford, London E18 2JB *tel:* 020 8989 3706 *fax:* 020 8491 0898 *email:* paradisum@aol.com. Ian Hayter, Fred Shone, dirs. Labels: Jongleur, Paradisum. Distributor: Grapevine Distribution via PolyGram Telesales.

Pavilion Records Ltd. Sparrows Green, Wadhurst, E Sussex TN5 6SJ *tel:* 01892 783591 *fax:* 01892 784156 *email:* pearl@pavilionrecords.com. John Waite, mgr dir. Labels: Flapper (jazz, humour, nostalgia, light music), Opal (classical, documentary, historical), Pearl (classical, historical), Topaz (jazz). *BPI*

Peartree Productions. PO Box 325, Worcester WR5 2YR *tel:* 01905 351748 *also fax; email:* scott@peartree.softnet.co.uk. David Scott, audio and programme mgr; Shirley Scott, exec producer. Label: Peartree.

* **Pentacone.** 4 Cross Bank Road, Batley, W Yorks WF14 8PJ *tel:* 01924 445039 *also fax; email:* pentacone@hotmail.com. Peter Sheehan, proprietor; Dot Andrews, mkt. Labels: Opus3, Prophone, Proprius, Swedish Society.

Philips Music Group. 22 St Peter's Square, London W6 9NW *tel:* 020 8910 5000 *fax:* 020 8910 3130. Mark Wilkinson, head of mkt; Lucy Hall-Smith, press offr; Yvonne Gerrard, product mgr. Labels: Gimell, Imaginary Road, Philips Classics, Point Music.

Pianissimo. Ridgway Rd, Pyrford, Woking, Surrey GU22 8PR *tel:* 01932 345371. Joe Laredo, proprietor.

* **Pinnacle Records.** Electron House, Cray Ave, St Mary Cray, Orpington, Kent BR5 3RJ *tel:* 01689 870622 *fax:* 01689 878269. Steve Mason, chmn; Sean Sullivan, dir; Tony Powell, mgr dir; Alan King, dir of operations. *BPI*

* **Plankton Records.** PO Box 13533, London E7 0SG *tel:* 020 8534 8500 *fax:* 07070 718613. Simon Law, snr partner; Nigel Palmer, recording supervisor; Keith Dixon, mkt and A&R. Labels: Embryo Arts, Gutta, It Stinks, Plankton, Sarepta, Sea Dream.

Polyphonic Reproductions Ltd. 77-79 Dudden Hill Lane, London NW10 1BD *tel:* 020 8459 6194/5 *fax:* 020 8451 6470. Stan Kitchen, mgr dir; Paul Williams, mkt offr; Shirley Kitchen, press offr. Label: Polyphonic. *BPI*

* **Practical Music.** 1 Staines Rd, Caversham, Reading RG4 7PA *tel:* 0118 947 7170 *also fax.* Jan Steele, Janet Sherbourne, partners. Label: Practical.

President Records Ltd. Exmouth House, 11 Pine St, London EC1R 0JH *tel:* 020 7837 5020 *fax:* 020 7837 4795 *email:* hits@president-records.co.uk. David Kassner, mgr dir. Label: President. *BPI*

* **Presto Music.** 19 Portland St, Royal Leamington Spa, Warwickshire CV32 5EZ *tel:* 01926 317025 *email:* presto@city2000.net. Jean Rainbow, mgr.

* **Priory Records Ltd.** 9b Upper Wingbury Courtyard, Wingrave, Aylesbury, Bucks *tel:* 01296 682255 *fax:* 01296 682275 *email:* sales@priory.org.uk. Neil V R Collier, mgr dir; Caroline Paschalides, A&R mgr, snr producer; Callum Ross, mgr finance and sales. Labels: Albany, Amphion, Athene, Audite, Beulah, British Music Society, Calig, Datum, Doneuw, Dynamic, Festivo, Guild, Ikon, Isis, Malibran, Kevin Mayhew, Metier, Motette, Multisonic, Olympia, Pan, Priory, Shellwood, Signum (GB), Signum (Germany), Somm, Sterling, Stradivarius, Tahra, Tower Hill, Tring RPO International, Vox.

Pro Piano Records. 85 Jane St, New York, NY 10014, USA *tel:* +1 212 206 8794 *fax:* +1 212 633 1207 *email:* ricard@propiano.com. Ricard de La Rosa, classical division head; Chitose Okashiro, A&R.

R & A Recording. 28 Venn St, London SW4 0AT *tel:* 020 7720 8887 *also fax; email:* RDamerell@msn.com. Rupert Damerell, producer. Label: Zenobia.

Recording Associates. October's End Studio, 34 Ryhill Way, Shinfield, Reading RG6 4AZ *tel:* 0118 986 6142 *also fax;* 07977 596661; *email* recordingassociates@compuserve.com. Geoff Addis, dir; Antony Hodgson, Kate Addis, producers. Labels: Unicorn-Kanchana, ASV, Olympia, Helios, Rose, Havoc, Classical Elegance, Dial (Malta).

* **Red Hedgehog Music Ltd.** PO Box 25, Shepshed, Loughborough, Leics LE12 9ZB *tel:* 01509 829301 *fax:* 01509 829302 *email:* info@ red-hedgehog.co.uk. Nigel Judson, mgr dir; Janice Judson, company sec. Labels: Hungaroton, CD Accord, Novalis, Slovart, La Ma Del Guido, Gega New, Lyrichord, Garton.

Redcliffe Recordings. 68 Barrowgate Rd, London W4 4QU *tel:* 020 8995 1223 *also fax;*. John Rushby-Smith, producer.

* **Regent Records.** PO Box 528, Wolverhampton WV3 9YW *tel:* 01902 424377 *fax:* 01902 717661 *email:* regent.records@btinternet.com. Gary Cole, producer; Pippa Cole, admin. Label: Regent.

Rhinosaurus Records Ltd. 42 Chase Side, Southgate, London N14 5PO *tel:* 020 8440 0183 *fax:* 020 8440 8169. Colin Middleton, producer; Richard Jacob, chief sound engineer. Distributor: Classical Elite.

River Productions. Aaron House, Bardolph Rd, Richmond, Surrey TW9 2LS *tel:* 020 8332 7300 *fax:* 020 8332 9233.

* **RTL Music.** White House Farm, Shropshire TF9 4HA *tel:* 01630 647374 *fax:* 01630 647612. Ron Lee, producer; Xavier Lee, producer; Tanya Lee, A&R; Catherine Lee, international A&R. Label: Check.

S & R Cressidia. PO Box 2077, Poole, Dorset BH16 5YR *tel:* 01202 632703 *fax:* 01202 608619 *email:* s&r@cressidia.com. Toby Richards, dir; Jane Child, press offr; David Singleton, mgr dir. Label: Cressidia Classics.

* **Sain (Recordiau) Cyf.** Llandwrog, Caernarfon, Gwynedd LL54 5TG *tel:* 01286 831111 *fax:* 01286 831497 *email:* xxx@sain.wales.com. D Iwan, mgr dir (audio); O P Huws, mgr dir (video); E B Davies, studio mgr. Labels: Crai, Sain.

Sargasso. PO Box 10565, London N1 8SR *tel:* 020 7359 7825 *also fax; email:* info@sargasso.com. Veronique Joly, mgr. *Contemporary classical and experimental mus.*

Saydisc Records. Chipping Manor, The Chipping, Wotton-under-Edge, Glos GL12 7AD *tel:* 01453 845036 *fax:* 01453 521056 *email:* saydisc@aol.com. Gef Lucena, mgr; Arwen Lucena, mkt. Labels: Amon Ra, Saydisc.

SCS Music Ltd. 4 Newtec Place, Magdalen Rd, Oxford OX4 1RE *tel:* 01865 244557 *fax:* 0870 056 8880. S C Smith, mgr dir.

* **Seaford Music.** 24 Pevensey Rd, Eastbourne, E Sussex BN21 3HP *tel:* 01323 732553 *fax:* 01323 417455 *email:* seafordmus@aol.com. Labels: Cedille, Divox, Mediaphon, Morrison & Co Trust, Partridge, Pro-Piano, Sonpact, Talent, Tall Poppies, Aurora, Hemera, Bergen Studio, Grappa, NFK, Vest-Norsic, Victoria.

Signum Records. 10 Kensington Hall Gardens, Beaumont Ave, London W14 9LS *tel:* 020 7379 9361 *fax:* 020 7379 9636; *email:* signum@newrenaissance.co.uk. Alistair Dixon, Steve Long, mgr dirs; Jan Hart, production and mkt mgr.

* **Silver Sounds (CD) Ltd.** Unit 7, Peerglow Estate, Queensway, Ponders End, Enfield EN3 4SN *tel:* 020 8364 7711 *fax:* 020 8805 1135 *email:* ssounds@dresscircle.co.uk. Murray Allan, mgr dir; Dominique Matica, sales exec; Phil Crank, sales mgr. Various jazz labels. Cam (Italian and French Soundtracks). *Worldwide imports and exports.*

Solo Records. 40 Osborne Rd, London N4 3SD *tel:* 020 7272 7911 *fax:* 020 8372 6189.

Soma Records. Brown Packaging, 257 Liverpool Rd, London N1 *tel:* 020 7607 9034 *fax:* 020 7700 5673. Roger T Dean, mgr dir. Label: Soma.

Somm Recordings. 13 Riversdale Rd, Thames Ditton, Surrey KT7 0QL *tel:* 020 8398 1586 *fax:* 020 8339 0981 *email:* sales@somm-recordings.demon.co.uk. Siva Oke, dir; K H Oke, admin. Label: Somm. *BPI*

* **Sony Classical.** Sony Music Entertainment (UK) Ltd, 10 Gt Marlborough St, London W1V 2LP *tel:* 020 7911 8251 *fax:* 020 7911 8792. Chris Black, dir, Sony Classical & Jazz UK; Alun Taylor, mkt mgr; Beatrice Blades, mkt asst; Carol Lowry, press and PR mgr; Nigel Robins, retail development mgr. Label: Sony Classical. *BPI*

Soundboard. Mount Pleasant, Westbury sub Mendip, Wells BA5 1HU *tel:* 01749 870516 *also fax; email:* colin@harpsichords.demon.co.uk. Colin Booth, proprietor. Mus for hpd. Label: Soundboard.

Sphemusations. 12 Northfield Rd, Onehouse, Stowmarket, Suffolk IP14 3HF *tel:* 01449 613388.

Springthyme Records. Balmalcolm House, Kingskettle, Fife KY15 7TJ *tel:* 01337 830773 *fax:* 01337 831773 *email:* springthyme@zetnet.co.uk. Peter Shepheard, mgr dir. Label: Springthyme. Scottish folk and traditional mus.

Start Audio and Video Ltd. 3 Warmair House, Green Lane, Northwood, Middx HA6 2QB *tel:* 01923 841414 *fax:* 01923 842223 *email:* startav@compuserve.com. Brian Gibbon, mgr dir; Nicholas Dicker, gen mgr. Labels: Focus, Musketeer, Parade, Platinum Collection, Start Classics. *BPI*

State Records. 20 Watford Rd, Radlett, Herts WD7 8LE *tel:* 01923 857792 *fax:* 01923 858052 *email:* recordings@staterecords.co.uk. Label: State Prima. *BPI*

Sutton Sound. 26 Cleveland Square, London W2 6DD *tel:* 020 7262 9066 *fax:* 020 7262 3235 *email:* marktsutton@compuserve.com.

* **Symposium Records.** 110 Derwent Ave, East Barnet, Herts EN4 8LZ *tel:* 020 8368 8667 *also fax email:* symposium@cwcom.net. Eliot B Levin. Label: Symposium. *BPI*

* **Thames Distributors.** 12 Mill Farm Business Park, Millfield Rd, Hounslow, Middx TW4 5PY *tel:* 020 8898 2227 *fax:* 020 8898 2228 *email:* thames_uk@compuserve.com. Labels: APR, Beecham, Biddulph, Castle, Decca, Dell'Arte, Dutton, EMI, Lab, Linn, MCI, Pickwick, Proudsound, Start Audio, Testament, Tring. *BPI*

That's Entertainment Records Ltd/Jay Productions Ltd. 107 Kentish Town Rd, London NW1 8PD *tel:* 020 7485 9593 *fax:* 020 7485 2282. John Yap, mgr dir; Jessica Lim, gen mgr. Label: Ter Classics. *BPI*

Timbre Records. PO Box 3698, London NW2 6ZA *tel:* 020 8450 9087 *fax:* 020 7691 7632 *email:* dmhtimbre@aol.com. Neil Gibbons, Diane M Hinds, dirs.

* **TKO Licensing Ltd.** PO Box 130, Hove, E Sussex BN3 6QU *tel:* 01273 550088 *fax:* 01273 540969 *email:* licencing@tkogroup.com. Adam Clavering, licensing mgr. Label: Great Voices of the Century, Bulldog Records, Emsen Records, Energy Records. Importer and distributor: Magnum Music.

Top Note Music. 123 Crown St, Aberdeen AB11 6HN *tel:* 01224 210259 *also fax; email:* topnote@ifb.co.uk.

* **Topic Records Ltd.** 50 Stroud Green Rd, London N4 3EF *tel:* 020 7263 1240 *fax:* 020 7281 5671. Tony Engle, mgr dir; David Kuznets, sales and accounts mgr; Harriet Simms, head of press and promotion.

Tremula Records. 11 Hordern Close, Haddenham, Bucks HP17 8NA *tel:* 01844 299005. Kenrick Dance, proprietor. Label: Tremula.

TSC Enterprises. 5 Sanderson St, Sheffield S9 2UA *tel:* 0114 244 2424 *fax:* 0114 243 4312 *email:* pab@abgroup.demon.co.uk. *Mainly choral mus.*

* **Unicorn-Kanchana Records.** PO Box 339, London W8 7SJ. Nigel Brandt, dir. Label: Unicorn-Kanchana. *BPI*

* **Universal Classics and Jazz.** PO Box 1420, 22 St Peters Square, London W6 9NW *tel:* 020 8910 5000 *fax:* 020 8910 3130. John Kennedy, chmn; Bill Holland, division dir; Dickson Stainer, head of Decca; Chrissie Wilde, press offr Decca; Mark Wilkinson, mkt mgr Deutsche Grammophon and Philips; Lucy Hall-Smith, press offr, Deutsche Grammophon and Philips; Nathan Graves, head of jazz. Labels: Decca, Deutsche Grammophon, Philips, Verve, GRP, Belart. *BPI*

Upbeat Recordings Ltd. Sutton Business Centre, Restmor Way, Wallington, Surrey SM6 7AH *tel:* 020 8773 1223 *fax:* 020 8669 6752 *email:* info@upbeat.co.uk. Liz Biddle, mgr dir; Maureen Philips, dir; Beryl Korman, press and PR dir. Labels: Upbeat Classics, Upbeat Jazz, Upbeat Showbiz, Ossia Classics. *BPI*

Usk Recordings. 26 Caterham Rd, London SE13 5AR *tel:* 020 8318 2031 *fax:* 020 7737 0063 *email:* usk@netcomuk.co.uk. Timothy Salter, dir. Label: Usk Recordings.

Utopia Music Ltd. 7 Chalcot Rd, London NW1 8LH *tel:* 020 7586 3434 *fax:* 020 7586 3438. *Pop, folk, jazz.*

Valentine Music Group. 7 Garrick St, London WC2E 9AR *tel:* 020 7240 1628 *fax:* 020 7497 9242 *email:* valentine@bandleader.co.uk. John Nice, mgr dir. Labels: Valentine.

Veloce Classics Recording Company. 30a Mapperley Hall Drive, Mapperley Park, Nottingham NG3 5EY *tel:* 0115 985 6343 *also fax.*

Verve Music Group. 22 St Peters Square, London W6 9NW *tel:* 020 8910 3115 *fax:* 020 8910 3131 *email:* nathan.graves@umusic.com. Nathan Graves, mkt mgr; Becky Stevenson, press offr.

Virgin Classics Ltd. 64 Baker St, London W1M 1DJ *tel:* 020 7467 2100 *fax:* 020 7467 2243. Alain Lanceron, president; Alison Kiln, international promotion mgr; Bertrand Schmitt, mkt dir; Stéphane Charpentier, jnr production mgr. Labels: Veritas, Virgin Classics.

* **Warner Classics UK.** The Warner Building, 28 Kensington Church St, London W8 4EP *tel:* 020 7937 8844 *fax:* 020 7938 3986. Matthew Cosgrove, gen mgr; Talia Hull, press offr; Jane Carter, mkt mgr. Labels: Erato, Finlandia, Nonesuch, Teldec. *BPI*

* **Words and Music Ltd.** 58-62 High St, Billingshurst, W Sussex RH14 9NY *tel:* 01403 785131 *fax:* 01403 700546. Jean Lawson, mgr director

Recording Studios

Studios are arranged by town, with Greater London listed first. Scotland, Wales and Northern Ireland can be found at the end of the section. Studios are indicated as being 8, 16, 24 track, etc, with a note of how many performers each can accommodate. Membership of the **Association of Professional Recording Services (APRS)**, PO Box 111, Ukfield, E Sussex TN22 SWQ *tel:* 01803 868600 *fax:* 01803 868444 *email:* info@aprs.co.uk, is indicated by an asterisk. **Location Recording Studios** are listed under **Recording and Sound Duplication**.

Greater London

* Abbey Road Studios. 3 Abbey Rd, London NW8 9AY *tel:* 020 7266 7000 *fax:* 020 7266 7228 *email:* bookings@abbeyroad.co.uk. Chris Buchanan, dir of operations; Colette Barber, studio operations mgr. *Studio 1: capacity 150, Neve VRP Legend 64 CH. Studio 2: capacity 55, Neve VRP Legend 60 CH. Studio 3: large control room, SSL G series desk, 72 CH. Penthouse Neve Capricorn digital desk. Post-production DMM and lacquer cutting, CD preparation and PQ encoding, digital duplication and tape copying from all formats. Apple Mac-based multimedia production studio.*

* Air-Edel Recording Studios Ltd. 18 Rodmarton St, London W1H 3FW *tel:* 020 7486 6466 *fax:* 020 7224 0344. Trevor Best, studio mgr. *Specialise in mus to picture and voice-over recordings. 24 track analogue recorder, fully -automated desk, full sync to picture facilities. 3 newly furnished studios; main studio capacity 25.*

* Air Studios. Lyndhurst Hall, Lyndhurst Rd, Hampstead, London NW3 5NG *tel:* 020 7794 0660 *fax:* 020 7794 8518 *email:* alison@airstudios.com. Alison Burton, bookings mgr. *Lyndhurst Hall: 400 sq m orch studio, capacity over 100. Neve VRP console. Studio 1: 140 sq m, capacity 40. Custom Neve console. Studio 2: mixing room with SSL 8000 G Plus console and Ultimation. Studio 3: Mixing room with 4 x 48 input AMS Logic Two console.*

Angel Recording Studios Ltd. 311 Upper St, London N1 2TU *tel:* 020 7354 2525 *fax:* 020 7226 9624. *2 large studios, capacity up to 85. Studio 1: Neve VR60 with flying faders and KEF monitoring. Studio 3: AMS Neve VXS 60-channel desk with flying faders and ATC customised monitoring. 1 small studio with Soundtracks Jade 48-channel desk and Quested monitoring. Studer A800 tape machines. All studios have facilities for recording to picture and Dolby Surround.*

The Audio Workshop. 217 Askew Rd, London W12 9AZ *tel:* 020 8742 9242/9449 *fax:* 020 8743 4231. Martin Cook, dir. *Voice work, soundtrack compilation, audio books, language courses.*

Backtrack Studio. Acacia Cottage, Princess Rd, Croydon CR0 2QS *tel:* 020 8683 2492 *fax:* 020 8239 6992. *Analogue 16 track; digital 8 track. Capacity 8.*

* Battery Studios. 1 Maybury Gardens, London NW10 2NB *tel:* 020 8967 0013 *fax:* 020 8459 8732. Amanda Todd, studio mgr. *2 SSL studios, 1 Neve, 1 DDA, 48/48/48/24 track. Programming suite. Accommodation and restaurant.*

* Beethoven St Studios. The Yellow Building, 56 Beethoven St, London W10 4LG *tel:* 020 8960 1088 *fax:* 020 8969 5231. *1 studio, 24 track, digital, analogue.*

* Berwick St Studios. 8 Berwick St, London W1V 3RG *tel:* 020 7292 0000 *fax:* 020 7292 0010. Alex Jones, studio mgr. *3 studios. Studio 1: 56 track analogue/digital; 24 track analogue and 32 track Akai DR16 Hard Disk Recorder. Studio 2: 32 track Akai DR16 Hard Disk Recorder. Studio 3: Protools digital editing and CD mastering.*

Boyden Associates. 13 Cotswold Mews, 30 Battersea Square, London SW11 3RA *tel:* 020 7223 7265 *fax:* 020 7585 2830. John Boyden. *Location recording service.*

* Britannia Row Recording. 3 Bridge Studios, 318-326 Wandsworth Bridge Rd, London SW6 2TZ *tel:* 020 7371 5872 *fax:* 020 7371 8641

email: bookings@britanniarowstudios.co.uk. *Studio 1: Neve 60-channel. Studio 2: Mackie 56 -channel. Studio 3: DDA DMR 12 32:24, 56-channel. Residential.*

Chiswick Reach Ltd. Lamb House, Church St, Chiswick, London W4 2PD *tel:* 020 8995 2647 *fax:* 020 8995 0441. Nigel Woodward, dir. *Studio 1: 300 sq ft, control room, Yamaha acoustic pno, 8 and 24 track tape machines, equalisers, Atari 1040 ST, 28-channel hand-built valve console.*

* CTS Studios. Engineers Way, Wembley, Middx HA9 0DR *tel:* 020 8903 4611 *fax:* 020 8903 7130 *email:* info@cts-lansdowne.co.uk. Pat Dodd, studio operations mgr. *Studio service.*

* Eden Studios. 20-24 Beaumont Rd, London W4 5AP *tel:* 020 8995 5432 *fax:* 020 8747 1931 *email:* eden@edenstudios.com. Beth Shuttleworth, studio mgr. *2 x 48 track SSL studios, 1 x 24 track pre-production room.*

* The Exchange. 42 Bruges Place, Randolph St, London NW1 0TX *tel:* 020 7485 0530 *fax:* 020 7482 4588.

Flintworks Protocol Studios. 23a Benwell Rd, London N7 7BW *tel:* 020 7686 0044 *fax:* 020 7686 0050 *email:* david@flintworks.com. David Richardson, studio mgr. *2 studios, 24 track, ProTools 24 Mix Plus; capacity 30.*

* Gateway Studio. The School of Music, Kingston Hill Centre, Surrey KT2 7LB *tel:* 020 8547 8167 *also fax; email:* gateway@eosound.co.uk. Andy Smith, Jason Edge, studio mgrs; Steve Lowe, house engineer and producer. *1 studio, 24 track analogue and digital mastering, teaching facilities. Also location recording service.*

Hear No Evil. 6 Lillie Yard, London SW6 1UB *tel:* 020 7385 8244 *fax:* 020 7385 0700 *email:* traxx@cix.compulink.co.uk. *Large live room, capacity 40, orch, scoring, commercials.*

Henry Wood Hall Ltd. Trinity Church Square, London SE1 4HU *tel:* 020 7403 0118 *fax:* 020 7378 8294. Andrew Stevens, mgr. *Ens to full symphony orch. One large hall, studio only, 2 control rooms.*

KD's Studio. 78 Church Path, Fletcher Rd, London W4 5BJ *tel:* 020 8994 3142 *fax:* 020 8995 5006. *1 studio, 24 track (with Bechstein grand and cassette duplication facilities); ProTools/Logic.*

* Lansdowne Recording Studios. Lansdowne House, Lansdowne Rd, London W11 3LP *tel:* 020 7727 0041/2/3 *fax:* 020 7792 8904 *email:* cts-lansdowne@cts-lansdowne.co.uk. Chris Dibble, studio mgr; Lucy Jones, bookings. *1 studio, 48 track, digital, analogue, Neve 72-channel VXS with flying faders; capacity 35. Video transfers for composers and digital audio post-production.*

* Livingston Studios Ltd. Brook Rd, Wood Green, London N22 6TR *tel:* 020 8889 6558 *fax:* 020 8888 2698. Jerry Boys, studio mgr. *Studio for up to 30 people. SSL 4056E and G series, Amek Rembrandt.*

Mark Angelo Recording Studio. 27 Britton St, London EC1M 5UD *tel:* 020 7251 2376; 020 8443 1523 *fax:* 020 7490 0474 *email:* sarah@theaudionet.ltd.uk. Sarah Ozelle, mgr. *Studio recording service. 24 track, producers, re-mixers, soundscape hard disc digital editing; capacity 12.*

Master Rock Studios. 248 Kilburn High Rd, Kilburn, London NW6 2BS *tel:* 020 7372 1101 *fax:* 020 7328 6368 *email:* master.rock@dial.pipex.com. Miriam Gottlieb, Maryke Van Duin, studio mgrs. *2 studios, 48 track, analogue, Dolby surround, 48 track Sony and 48 Dolby SR, consoles (focusrite and SSL), Otari Radar II; capacity 40.*

Matrix Studios. 35 Little Russell St, London WC1A 2HH *tel:* 020 7580 9956 *fax:* 020 7636 1069.

* Olympic Studios. 117 Church Rd, Barnes, London SW13 9HL *tel:* 020 8286 8600 *fax:* 020 8286 8625. *5 studios. 1 x SSL G series, 1 x 35 orch capacity; 1 x SSL J series, 60 orch capacity; 1 with SSL G 72-channels, 1 with SSL G 64-channels, 1 with AMEK 9098i 56-channels.*

Pathway Studios. 2a Grosvenor Ave, London N5 2NR *tel:* 020 7359 0970 *fax:* 020 7226 8958. M I Finesilver, studio mgr. *1 studio, capacity 6, 8 track, digital, analogue.*

Pisces Studios. 20 Middle Row, London W10 5AT *tel:* 020 8964 4555 *fax:* 020 8964 4666 *email:* hq@pisces.uk.com. Morgan Khan, mgr dir. *2 studios, 24 track (with automation), digital pre-production and programming suite.*

* R G Jones Recording Studios. Beulah Rd, London SW19 3SB *tel:* 020 8540 9881 *fax:* 020 8542 4368. Gerry Kitchingham, studio mgr. *1 studio, console SSL 4000E series, 32 track digital, 24 track A827 analogue tape machine; capacity 30. Wide range of microphones.*

* RAK Recording Studios. 42-48 Charlbert St, London NW8 7BU *tel:* 020 7586 2012 *fax:* 020 7722 5823 *email:* trisha@rakstudios.co.uk. Trisha Wegg, studio admin. *3 studios. 2 API desks, 1 SSL 4056 (G series computer).*

Redwood Studios. 1 Falconberg Court, London W1V 5FG *tel:* 020 7287 3799 *fax:* 020 7287 3751 *email:* redwood@onet.co.uk. André Jacquemin, studio mgr and producer. *Studio and location recording service; hard disc recording. Studio 1 for 5 musicians, Digital Mackie d8b mixing console, full outboard equipment list on request.*

* Rewind Studios. The Media Centre, 131-151 Great Titchfield St, London W1P 8AE *tel:* 020 7665 8202 *fax:* 020 7665 8201.

RMS Studios. 43-45 Clifton Rd, London SE25 6PX *tel:* 020 8653 4965 *also fax.* Andy Le Vien, studio mgr; Alan Jones, bookings mgr. *Studio 1: 2 inch 16 track Studer, Soundcraft 1600, grand pno, capacity 8. Studio 2: 16 track ADAT XT, AHB Saber, MIDI facilities, capacity 6. Studio 3: SADIE digital editing, copying.*

* Sarm Studios (West) Ltd. 8-10 Basing St, London W11 1ET *tel:* 020 7229 1229 *fax:* 020 7221 9247/3374 *email:* lolasarm@aol.com. Lola Weidner, studio mgr. *4 studios, SSLJ series and surround sound. Easy on-site parking, catering and apartments.*

SD Post. 7 Chalcot Rd, Unit 11, Utopia Village, London NW1 8LH *tel:* 020 7586 1271 *fax:* 020 7586 4488.

* Snake Ranch Studio. 90 Lots Rd, London SW10 0QD *tel:* 020 7351 7888 *fax:* 020 7352 5194. Gerry O'Riordan, studio mgr. *2 studios, 24 track, analogue, video sync; capacity 25.*

Sound-Suite Recording Studios Ltd. 92 Camden Mews, London NW1 9AG *tel:* 020 7485 4881 *fax:* 020 7482 2210. *Audio visual post-production and mus recording facility. Amek Hendrix desk, Otari MTR90 multitrack, Tascam DA88s, all machines locked to picture Quested & Genelec monitoring. Bechstein grand pno, synths and sequencers available. DAWN digital editing. Sound design and foley recording, voice-overs, CD copying.*

SRL Cassettes. 47 High St, Pinner, Middx HA5 5PJ *tel:* 020 8868 5555 *fax:* 020 8866 5555 *email:* srl@btinternet.com. John Bales, studio mgr. *2 track digital and analogue; spoken word specialists.*

* Stanley House Studios. 39 Stanley Gardens, London W3 7SY *tel:* 020 8735 0280 *fax:* 020 8743 6365 *email:* andy-morris@stanley-house.demon.co.uk. Verity Boys. *SSL J series 56 channel console; Quested and Genelec monitoring; multitracks, Studer A800 mk3, Otari Radar.*

* The Town House Studios. 150 Goldhawk Rd, London W12 8HH *tel:* 020 8932 3200 *fax:* 020 8932 3207. *Studio 1: SSL 4072 G Plus with ultimation. Studio 2: SSL 9072 J series. Studio 4: SSL 4072E.*

The Warehouse Waterloo. London Festival Orchestra, 13 Theed St, London SE1 8ST *tel:* 020 7928 9251 *fax:* 020 7928 9252 *email:* orchestra@lfo.co.uk. *2 studios: large (capacity 60), small (capacity 35). Steinway grand pno. SADIE digital editing. Mackie 8 busdesk, etc.*

* West Side Studios. Olaf Centre, 10 Olaf St, London W11 4BE *tel:* 020 7221 9494 *fax:* 020 7727 0008 *email:* info@westsidestudios.co.uk. *Studios: Neve VR72, Solid State logic 4048E with G series computer.*

* Whitfield St Recording Studios. 31-37 Whitfield St, London W1P 5RE *tel:* 020 7636 3434 *fax:* 020 7580 0543. Matthew Villa, dir; Denise Love, bookings mgr. *3 studios, capacity 90, 2, 6; 24 and 48 track.*

* The Workhouse Studios. 488-490 Old Kent Rd, London SE1 5AG *tel:* 020 7237 1737 *fax:* 020 7231 7658. Ian Tompson, studio mgr and bookings. *Studio 1: 48 track, analogue, SSL E Series 4048. Studio 2: 24 track analogue, DDA DMR 12.*

England

Berkshire

Reading

Recording Associates. October's End Studio, 34 Ryhill Way, Shinfield, Reading RG6 4AZ *tel:* 0118 986 6142 *also fax;* 07977 596661 *email:* recordingassociates@compuserve.com. Geoff Addis, dir; Antony Hodgson, Kate Addis, producers. *Digital audio, video and surround-sound recording and editing.*

Bristol, City of

Bristol

Christ Church Studios. 38 Portland St, Clifton, Bristol BS8 4JB *tel:* 0117 946 6765. Paul Rummer.

St George's Brandon Hill. Bristol BS1 5PZ *tel:* 0117 929 4929 *fax:* 0117 927 6537. Jonathan Stracey, dir; Catherine Freda, admin. *Converted Georgian church with recording facilities suitable for soloists, chmbr mus, small orchs, choirs. Also houses permanently equipped BBC control room for concert and CD session recording, mastering to DAT and digital multi-track; SADIE and Sonic Solutions digital editing. Further details: BBC Resources* tel: *0117 974 2167.*

Sound Conception. 82-84 York Rd, Bedminster, Bristol BS3 4AL *tel:* 0117 966 2932 *fax:* 0117 963 5059. Ken Wheeler, studio mgr; Alis Bligh, bookings. *1 studio, 24 track analogue, 8 track digital (hard disc); capacity 16.*

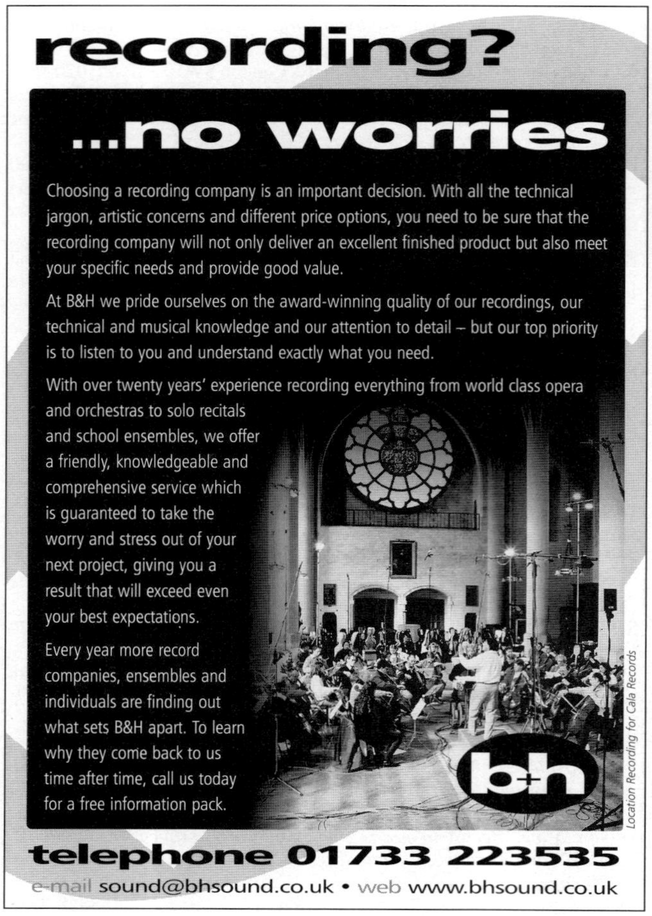
recording?
...no worries
Choosing a recording company is an important decision. With all the technical jargon, artistic concerns and different price options, you need to be sure that the recording company will not only deliver an excellent finished product but also meet your specific needs and provide good value.
At B&H we pride ourselves on the award-winning quality of our recordings, our technical and musical knowledge and our attention to detail – but our top priority is to listen to you and understand exactly what you need.
With over twenty years' experience recording everything from world class opera and orchestras to solo recitals and school ensembles, we offer a friendly, knowledgeable and comprehensive service which is guaranteed to take the worry and stress out of your next project, giving you a result that will exceed even your best expectations.
Every year more record companies, ensembles and individuals are finding out what sets B&H apart. To learn why they come back to us time after time, call us today for a free information pack.
b+h
Location Recording for Cala Records
telephone 01733 223535
e-mail sound@bhsound.co.uk • web www.bhsound.co.uk

Claudio
Records Ltd
The Natural Choice For Your Recording Requirements
Established Since 1974
CD's Released Through One of Our Three Labels
Claudio Records
Claudio Contemporary
Claudio Bohema
Digital Location Recording
Concert Recordings - All Major London Venues
Speech Recording
Full Post Production Facilities
Digital Editing & Mastering
CD Production & Duplication
Broadcast Production
Archiving
Artwork & Design
Competitive Rates
Web site: www.claudio-records.ltd.uk
Further Information: Studio 17, The Promenade, Peacehaven, East Sussex, BN10 8PU Tel: (+44) 01273 580 250
Fax: (+44) 01273 583 530 Email: info@claudio-records.ltd.uk

The Sound Studio
24 Track Recording Studio
2 inch 24T Analogue
ADAT XT 24T Digital
Pro Tools 24 Mix
Digital Recording Mixing & Editing
THE RECORDING SPECIALISTS
0171 249 6640
info@sound-uk.demon.co.uk

POSTERN PARK DIGITAL
LOW COST RECORDINGS FOR CLASSICAL MUSICIANS
Chamber Organ Harpsichord Fortepiano available without hire charge
Bösendorfer Concert Grand Piano
Chagall Church Recording Venue
20 bit recording · SADiE editing
CD · CDR · MD · Cassette
Postern Park DIGITAL
POSTERN PARK OAST
TONBRIDGE
KENT TN11 0QT
TELEPHONE
01732 773322

Buckinghamshire

Seer Green

Bucks Audio Recordings. Clear Croft, Bottom Lane, Seer Green, Bucks HP9 2UH *tel:* 01494 675900 *also fax.* Alan Smyth, proprietor. *Digital recording, editing, dubbing, CD mastering and production. Cassette duplication, recording and editing on SADIE, editing from score. Kawai Concert Grand. Capacity 2. Studio and location recording. Yamaha, Sennheisser, Tascam, Sony, Alesis, Akai, etc. A/c parking.*

Cambridgeshire

Peterborough

B & H Sound Services Ltd. The Old School Studio, Crowland Rd, Eye, Peterborough, Cambs PE6 7TN *tel:* 01733 223535 *fax:* 01733 223545 *email:* studio@bhsound.co.uk. Matt Parkin, recording services mgr. *24 track digital studio with MIDI suite; capacity 5. Stereo and multitrack mobile recording rigs; digital editing and mastering; CD and cassette manufacture; equipment hire.*

St Ives

* SRT Sound Recording Technology Ltd. Edison Rd, Audio House, St Ives, Cambs PE17 4LF *tel:* 01480 461880; 020 8446 3218 *fax:* 01480 496100 *email:* srt@btinternet.com. Nick Watson, studios mgr; Sarah Richardson, dir. *5 studios; HDCD, 1630 PCM Umatic, Exabyte, Sony SDP 1000, analogue Dolby A/SR; cassette and CD duplication.*

Cheshire

Sale

Stockport

Cavalier Studios Ltd. 280 Wellington Rd South, Stockport, Cheshire SK2 6ND *tel:* 0161 480 6073 *fax:* 0161 429 8492. Arny Sage, studio mgr. *1 studio, 24 track, analogue, digital mastering, Cubase, Yamaha grand pno; capacity 10.*

Dorset

Poole

Active Music Recording Studio. 7c Bank Chambers, Penn Hill Ave, Lower Parkstone, Poole, Dorset BH14 9NB *tel:* 01202 746049 *also fax; email:* martin@active-music.demon.co.uk. *Ampex 124.24 track, Ampex ATR 100, Raindirk series 3 desk, ATC 100A monitors, digital editing available, large selection of mics.*

East Sussex

Eastbourne

* ICC Studios. 4 Regency Mews, Silverdale, Eastbourne, E Sussex BN20 7AB *tel:* 01323 643341 *fax:* 01323 649240 *email:* studio@icc.org.uk. H Kaufmann, mgr dir; Gayle Price, bookings. *3 studio complex. Studio 1: 24 track residential, Radar II Digital Recorder and vintage mics. Studio 2: Budget 24 track 1" or A-dat Digital. Studio 3: Digital editing and CD mastering.*

Peacehaven

Claudio Records Ltd. Studio 17, The Promenade, Peacehaven, E Sussex BN10 8PU *tel:* 01273 580250 *fax:* 01273 583530 *email:* info@claudio-records.ltd.uk. Colin Attwell, William Attwell, studio mgrs. *Studio recording, digital editing and CD production.*

Essex

Chelmsford

Frinton-on-Sea

East Anglian Productions. 21-23 Walton Rd, Frinton-on-Sea, Essex CO13 0AA *tel:* 01255 676252 *fax:* 01255 850528.

Hertfordshire

Knebworth

* Select Sound Studio. Big M House, 1 Stevenage Rd, Knebworth, Herts SG3 6AN *tel:* 01438 814433 *fax:* 01438 815252 *email:* select@bigmgroup.co.uk. *DDA DCM232, 48 track ProTools, Studer tape machines, programming suite.*

Ware

John Kehoe Music Production. 201 River Meads, Stanstead Abbotts, Ware, Herts SG12 8EK *tel:* 01920 877021 *also fax; message service:* 0941 114766 *email:* jkehoe@globalnet.co.uk. John Kehoe, proprietor. *Executive producer services and project management in classical recording. Classical mus general consultancy.*

Watford

EQ Studios. 10 Stanley Rd, Watford, Herts *tel:* 01923 247879 *fax:* 01923 210917. *1 studio, 16 track (MIDI-based).*

Kent

Tonbridge

Postern Park Digital. Postern Park Oast, Tonbridge, Kent TN11 0QT *tel:* 01732 773322 *fax:* 01732 773344. *20 bit recording, SADIE editing. Church and location personal recording service.*

Kingston upon Hull

Hull

Fairview Studios. Great Gutter Lane West, Willerby, Hull HU10 6DP *tel:* 01482 653116 *fax:* 01482 654667 *email:* keith@fairview-music.demon.co.uk. Jackie Herd, sales and accounts; Phil Parker, artwork. *1 studio, analogue 2" tape 24 track; capacity 10.*

Leicestershire

Leicester

The Sound Studio at Q Broadcast. 1487 Melton Rd, Queniborough, Leicester LE7 3FP *tel:* 0116 260 8813 *fax:* 0116 260 8329 *email:* qbroadcast@dial.pipex.com. Rob Nugent, studio mgr. *2 studios, one for 50+ players, the other for overdubs and vocals; soundcraft DC2000 32F mixing desk; mastering with various DATs. S/Craft 400W active nearfield monitoring. Limited location facilities (stereo only).*

Merseyside

Liverpool

Parr Street Studios. 35-45 Parr St, Liverpool L1 4JN *tel:* 0151 707 1050 *fax:* 0151 707 1813 *email:* parr.street@dial.pipex.com. Anne Lewis, mgr; Paul Lewis, bookings mgr. *Residential studio complex, 3 studios, located in Liverpool city centre. Tracking and mixing facilities to suit all budgets. Professional assistants and 2 full-time maintenance engineers.*

Nottinghamshire

Nottingham

Network Studios (Nohponex Ltd). 22a Forest Rd West, Nottingham NG7 4EQ *tel:* 0115 978 4714 *fax:* 0115 942 4183. *1 studio, 32 digital tracks; capacity 35.*

Shropshire

Shrewsbury

Shropshire Youth Arts Network (SHYAN). 5 Belmont, Shrewsbury SY1 1TE *tel:* 01743 243755 *fax:* 01743 344773. Diana Walton; Jonathan Tritton, studio mgr. *8 track, digital, 24/48 channel desk; large live room.*

Staffordshire

Keele

Clock House Recording Studio. Keele, Staffs ST5 5BG *tel:* 01782 583301 *also fax; email:* mua00@mus.keele.ac.uk. Cliff Bradbury, studio mgr. *3 studios, ProTools multitrack. Digital, analogue, digital mastering and editing, CD preparation; capacity 20.*

Rugeley

Abbey Sound Studios. The Abbey, Heron Court, Heron St, Rugeley, Staffs WS15 2DZ *tel:* 01889 579494 *fax:* 01889 881462 *email:* lbedd1sc@stokecoll.ac.uk. Lee Beddow, mgr, engineer. *8 track studio with large live room.*

Stoke-on-Trent

Sub Sound Studio. 54 Oxford St, Penkull, Stoke-on-Trent ST4 7EE *tel:* 01782 416306. Gordon Lee. *Analogue/digital multitrack editing, mastering. Valve/computer-based multitrack studio. On-site automated CDR duplication/on disc print.*

Surrey

Addlestone Moor

Hatch Farm Recording Studios. Unit 16, Hatch Farm, Chertsey Rd, Addlestone Moor, Surrey KT15 2EH *tel:* 01932 828715 *fax:* 01932 828717.

Dorking

* Ridge Farm Studios. Rusper Rd, Capel, Dorking, Surrey RH5 5HG *tel:* 01306 711202 *fax:* 01306 711626 *email:* info@ridgefarmstudio.com. Frank Andrews, mgr dir; Ann Needham, bookings and admin. *Studio (residential): main recording area 48 sq m. SSL 9000J console. 2 Studer A800 MkII multi-track recorders.*

Farnham

Keynote Audio Services. Wishanger Lane, Churt, Farnham, Surrey GU10 2QJ *tel:* 01252 794253 *fax:* 01252 792642 *email:* keynote@dial.pipex.com. *1*

studio, 24 track; capacity 10. Digital, analogue, digital editing and mastering, audio post-production, sound to picture sync.

Woldingham

The Factory. Toftrees, Church Rd, Woldingham, Surrey CR3 7JH *tel:* 01883 652386 *fax:* 01883 652457 *email:* mackaydc@aol.com. *1 studio, 48 track, digital sync to video; capacity 15.*

Tyne and Wear

Wallsend

Impulse Sound Recording Studios. 71 High St East, Wallsend, Tyne and Wear NE28 7RJ *tel:* 0191 262 4999 *fax:* 0191 263 7082 *email:* mdwood33@aol.com. Peter Carr, studio mgr. *24 track studio, 32 input desk, DAT mastering.*

Warwickshire

Coventry

Leamington Spa

Woodbine Street Recording Studio. 1 St Marys Cres, Leamington Spa CV31 1JC *tel:* 01926 338971. John Rivers. *24 track master; large studio with live area; fully automated. DDA DCM 232 console. Accommodation available.*

West Midlands

Birmingham

ARC Studio. 17 Yewtree Rd, Edgbaston, Birmingham B15 2LX *tel:* 0121 4400635. Bob Wilson. *Studio only.*

Grosvenor Recording Studios. 16 Grosvenor Rd, Birmingham B20 3NP *tel:* 0121 356 9636 *also fax. 2 studios, 16 track; capacity 40 and 15.*

Hollick & Taylor Recording Company Ltd. 16 Grovesnor Rd, Handsworth Wood, Birmingham B230 3NP *tel:* 0121 356 9636 *also fax.* John Taylor. *2 studios; 16 track; capacity 40 and 15.*

Ninth Wave Audio. PO Box 5517, Birmingham B13 8QW *tel:* 0121 442 2276; 07770 364464 *fax:* 0121 689 1902 *email:* ninthwave@dial.pipex.com. Tony Wass, studio mgr. *Studio specialising in classical mus for CD and radio broadcast. Full BBC broadcast facilities and mastering including short run CD production.*

Rich Bitch Studio. 505 Bristol Rd, Selly Oak, Birmingham B29 6AU *tel:* 0121 471 1339 *fax:* 0121 471 2070. Rob Bruce, Veegee Lyn. *16 track studio, 24 track studio, plus 11 fully-equipped rehearsal rooms.*

The Sound and Picture House. 2 Greenfield Cres, Edgbaston, Birmingham B15 3BE *tel:* 0121 456 1429 *fax:* 0121 454 6427 *email:* spictureh@aol.com. *1 studio, 16 track.*

Kingswinford

Diabolus in Musica Recording Services. 21 Oakfield Ave, Kingswinford, W Midlands DY6 8HJ *tel:* 01384 295210 *email:* paul@diabolus-in-musica.freeserve.co.uk. Paul Baker. *Specialist digital recording of soloists and ens in studio or on location. DAT mastering for CD and cassette.*

Solihull

Made To Measure Music. 21 Fernhill Rd, Olton, Solihull, W Midlands B92 9PX *tel:* 0121 706 3621 *also fax.* Andrew Sparkes. *16 track analogue; digital mastering; live room; arrangement and production services; duplication.*

Worcester

Kempsey

The Old Smithy Recording Studio. 1 Post Office Lane, Kempsey, Worcester WR5 3NS *tel:* 01905 820659 *fax:* 01905 820015 *email:* muff.murfin@virgin.net. Jan Allsop, bookings. *3 studios, 24 tracks, digital, analogue, video production, cassette duplication, full MIDI sequencing and sampling hardware; capacity 24. Visual broadcast facilities. Accommodation.*

Scotland

Glasgow, City of

Glasgow

The Audiomobile. 49 Derby St, Glasgow G3 7TU *tel:* 0141 334 5099 *fax:* 0141 339 0271 *email:* HClark4422@aol.com. Helen Clark, admin. *48 or 24 track continuous, fully air-conditioned, sync to picture. Full interface with all standard broadcast applications.*

Ca Va Sound Workshops. 30 Bentinck St, Glasgow G3 7TU *tel:* 0141 334 5099 *fax:* 0141 339 0271 *email:* HClark4422@aol.com. Helen Clark, admin. *4 studios; Neve VR Legend with flying faders plus total recall; 48 and 24 track analogue plus 16 tracks of hard disc recording on Digidesign ProTools III, 24 track demo studio, 16 track programming studio, digital editing and mastering with Digidesign ProTools III, CAP 50-100 (ST1). Sync to picture facilities in studios 1, 2 and 3.*

* Scotty's Sound Studio. Newtown St, Kilsyth, Glasgow G65 0JX *tel:* 01236 823291 *fax:* 01236 826900 *email:* nscott@scotdisc.co.uk. Bill Garden, dir. *1 studio, 24 track and 2 track, digital, analogue.*

Lanarkshire

Bellshill

Mara Recordings. 52 Strathview Rd, Lochview Estate, Bellshill, Scotland ML4 2UY *tel:* 01698 747751. Duncan Mackay, production. *Location recording service: digital classical recording and editing.*

Wales

Gwynedd

Bangor

Stiwdio Cantor - Music Department. Main Arts Building, University of Wales, Bangor, Gwynedd LL57 2DG *tel:* 01248 383827 *fax:* 01248 370297. Bryn Jones, studio dir. *1 studio, 2 concert halls, 12 tracks digital, DAT mastering, digital editing, video post-production, Bösendorfer and Steinway pnos, Apple Mac, PC; capacity 600.*

Monmouthshire

Caerleon

Loco Studios. Plas Llecha, Llanhennock, Caerleon, Newport, Monmouthshire NP6 1LU *tel:* 01633 450603 *fax:* 01633 450666, John Payne, Geoff Downes.

Monmouth

* Rockfield Studios. Amberley Court, Monmouth, South Wales NP5 4ET *tel:* 01600 712449 *fax:* 01600 714421 *email:* rockfieldstudios@compuserve.com.

Northern Ireland

County Down

Newtownards

Downtown Radio. Newtownards, Co Down BT23 4ES *tel:* 028 9181 5555 *fax:* 028 9181 8913 *email:* music@coolfm.co.uk. David Sloan, mgr dir. *Soundcraft TS12 console, Orban 8TK digital editor, Sony DATs, Studer A80 quarter inch, compressors, gates and effects, Neuman and AKG mics, ISDN PRIMA 120 & APT X, control room 29 sq m, studio 23 sq m. Speciality audio for radio and TV commercials.*

Recording and Sound Duplication

Location Recording and Production Services

Some recording studios also have sound duplication facilities. Membership of the **Association of Professional Recording Services** is indicated by an asterisk.

A2D Remote Recordings. Warrens Lee, Bell Lane, Nutley, E Sussex TH22 3PD *tel:* 01825 712724 *also fax; email:* a2dremote@aol.com. Doug Hopkins. *Location recording anywhere in mainland Europe, including classical recording.*

* **Abbey Road Mobiles.** 3 Abbey Rd, London NW8 9AY *tel:* 020 7266 7236 *fax:* 020 7266 7250. Colette Barber, mgr, studio operations. *Worldwide location recording to all current digital formats.*

Allen, Patrick. 3 Bunyan Rd, Biggleswade, Beds SG18 8QQ *tel:* 01767 314668; 07971 829212 *fax:* 01767 601037 *email:* PatrickAllen@msn.com. *Location recording service specialising in classical mus for broadcast and CD production. Concert recordings, demo recordings. Complete packages for cassette and CD manufacture. High bit rate digital recording, editing and mastering.*

Astounding Sounds. 7 Birkbeck Way, Greenford, Middx UB6 8NY *tel:* 020 8578 7714. Jonathan Haskell. *Classical mus specialists. Digital location recording of concerts, sessions and demos, editing, cassette duplication and CD production.*

The Attic. 95 Ashfield St, London E1 2HA *tel:* 020 7247 6442. Stephen Evans, studio mgr. *Digital recording and editing. Inlay design service available.*

B & H Sound Services Ltd. The Old School Studio, Crowland Rd, Eye, Peterborough PE6 7TN *tel:* 01733 223535 *fax:* 01733 223545 *email:* studio@bhsound.co.uk. Matt Parkin, recording services mgr. *Stereo and multi-track location recording facilities, including complete classical production service; digital editing and mastering; CD and cassette manufacture; equipment hire.*

* **BBC Live Music Mobile.** Room 407 Western House, 99 Great Portland St, London W1A 1AA *tel:* 020 7765 5747 *fax:* 020 7765 0787 *email:* john.pearson@bbc.co.uk. John Pearson, mobile recording mgr. *Location recording for the broadcast and mus industries, specialising in all types of live mus including classical.*

* **Beethoven St Mastering.** The Yellow Building, 56 Beethoven St, London W10 4LG *tel:* 020 8960 1088 *fax:* 020 8969 5231. *CD duplication, mastering.*

Black Box Music Ltd. PO Box 28, Orpington, Kent BR5 1TQ *tel:* 01689 898154 *fax:* 01689 898155 *email:* info@bbmusic.demon.co.uk. Chris Craker, dir. *Digital location recordings, digital editing, production, classical and jazz record labels.*

BMP Recording. The Red House, Aswardby, Spilsby, Lincs PE23 4JU *tel:* 01790 754400 *also fax; email:* bmpuk@compuserve.com. Ken Blair, Sara Blair-Manning, partners. *Location and studio recording, digital editing and mastering, CD production.*

* **The Church Studios.** 145h Crouch Hill, London N8 9QH *tel:* 020 8340 9779 *fax:* 020 8348 3346. Lise Price, studio mgr. *24 and 48 track SSL 56 CH G series. All major recording formats.*

Circle Sound Services. Circle House, 14 Waveney Close, Bicester, Oxon OX6 8GP *tel:* 01869 240051 *also fax; email:* sound@circle.force9.net. John Willett, studio mgr. *Location recording unit, hard disc digital editing and mastering, CD preparation, CD-R recording. Specialises in classical mus, choirs, etc.*

The Classical Recording Co. 16-17 Wolsey Mews, London NW5 2DX *tel:* 020 7482 2303; 07850 666531 *fax:* 020 7482 2302 *email:* info@classicalrecording.com. S Weir, producer, engineer; C Hughes, engineer; Beth Hammond, production mgr. *20-bit digital location recording and post-production. CD mastering and cassette*

duplication. Archive recording and broadcast production to BBC standards.

Classical Recording Service. 11 Romsley Hill Grange, Farley Lane, Romsley, nr Halesowen, W Midlands B62 0LN *tel:* 01562 710801 *also fax*. Paul Arden-Taylor, dir. *Location digital recording, digital editing, CD and cassette production.*

Claudio Records Ltd. Studio 17, The Promenade, Peacehaven BN10 8PU *tel:* 01273 580250 *fax:* 01273 583530 *email:* info@claudio-records.ltd.uk. Colin and William Attwell, studio mgrs. *Classical location and studio recording, digital editing, CD production.*

Clive Cowan Recording (CCR). 27 Stirling Ave, Leigh-on-Sea, Essex SS9 3PP *tel:* 01702 420609; 07625 397858. Clive Cowan. *Location recording in London and the south east, especially for film, video and television. Professional audio equipment sales.*

Condor Music Ltd. Mayfair House, 72 New Bond St, London W1Y 9DD *tel:* 020 7514 5813 *fax:* 020 7499 3417. Roman Rowlands, dir; Peter Murray, dir, sec. *Recording service for orchestral mus. Includes studio hire, sound engineer, conductor, Moscow State Radio and TV Symphony Orchestra. Studio and concert recordings, mus to picture recordings.*

CreativeDialogue Ltd. 24 Highbury Grove, London N5 2DQ *tel:* 020 7359 7122 *fax:* 020 7359 7110 *email:* creativedialogueltd@btinternet.com. *Production, engineering, mastering, research and development.*

* **CTS Studios Ltd.** Engineers Way, Wembley, Middx HA9 0DR *tel:* 020 8903 4611 *fax:* 020 8903 7130 *email:* pf@cts-lansdowne.co.uk. Pat Dodd, studio operations mgr. *Studio service.*

D & J Recording Ltd. 7 Felden St, London SW6 5AE *tel:* 020 7736 9485 *also fax*. Joanna Leach. *Classical digital location recording, digital editing for CD and cassette production.*

Emerson, Roy. 80 Darwin Court, Gloucester Ave, London NW1 7BQ *tel:* 020 7267 5858; 07973 517788 *fax:* 020 7284 1148. Roy Emerson. *Independent classical record producer and television sound director; location recording and editing facilities to full international standard including 20-bit digital equipment.*

Emglow Records. Norton Cottage, Colchester Rd, Wivenhoe, Colchester, Essex CO7 9HT *tel:* 01206 826342 *email:* marcelg@aspects.net. Marcel Glover. *Location recording and small-scale cassette and CD production for light, classical and early mus.*

Euphonia. Trinity Mews, Cambridge Gardens, London W10 6JA *tel:* 020 8960 8128 *fax:* 020 8968 0341 *email:* nickm@teddbear.co.uk. Nick Morgan, project co-ord; Iestyn Rees, snr engineer. *Classical mus specialists. Sony Award-winning recordings. 16 and 20-bit mobile recording units. Live sound for broadcast or recording for CD release.*

* **The Exchange.** 42 Bruge Place, Randolph St, London NW1 0TX *tel:* 020 7485 0530. Graeme Durham, Mike Marsh, dirs; Alex Lowe, studio mgr. *Vinyl and CD mastering.*

Friary Music Services. 142b Friary Rd, London SE15 5UW *tel:* 020 7277 7068 *fax:* 020 7277 8354 *email:* 100115.3701@compuserve.com. Richard Black, producer. *Location recording, including highest quality, lowest cost demos with free pianist, and complete CD projects. Classical mus only.*

* **Gateway Studio.** The School of Music, Kingston Hill Centre, Kingston KT2 7LB *tel:* 020 8547 8167 *also fax; email:* gateway@eosound.co.uk. Andy Smith, Jason Edge, mgrs; Steve Lowe, house engineer, producer. *Studio and location recording service.*

Ginn, Jeffrey. 11 Haycroft, Wootton, Bedford, Beds MK43 9PB *tel:* 01234 765602; 07778 896721 *fax:* 01234 765367 *email:* jeff@ginn-mus.demon.co.uk. *Location recording service and post-production studios. Classical recording, digital editing and mastering.*

Green Room Productions. The Laurels, New Park Rd, Harefield, Middx UB9 6EQ *tel:* 01895 822771 *fax:* 01895 824880 *email:* tony@greenroom2.demon.co.uk. Tony Faulkner, proprietor. *Classical mus location, high-resolution sound and video recording.*

Grosvenor Recording Studios. 16 Grosvenor Rd, Birmingham B20 3NP *tel:* 0121 356 9636 *also fax. Location recording service.*

Hazard Chase Productions. Richmond House, 16-20 Regent St, Cambridge CB2 1DB *tel:* 01223 312400 *fax:* 01223 460827 *email:* info@hazardchase.co.uk. Patrick Allen, John Bickley, James Brown, John Willan; exec producers. *Location recording and production, specialising in classical mus (live concerts and studio sessions) for radio broadcast, demonstration recordings, samplers, TV and film soundtracks and CD production. Complete packages for CD and DVD manufacture. CD ROM and CD EXTRA programming and production.*

Hear No Evil. 6 Lillie Yard, London SW6 1UB *tel:* 020 7385 8244 *fax:* 020 7385 0700 *email:* traxx@cix.co.uk. Steve Parr, Sharon Rose, mgr dirs. *Hard disc editing; specialists in orch and film scoring. Surround-sound mixing.*

Herald Audio Visual Publications. The Studio, 29 Alfred Rd, Farnham, Surrey GU9 8ND *tel:* 01252 725349 *fax:* 01252 735567. Brian Johnson,

mgr dir. *Specialists in choral, org, early church mus and gregorian chants. Digital, analogue.*

Impulse Sound Recording Studios. 71 High St East, Wallsend, Tyne and Wear NE28 7RJ *tel:* 0191 262 4999 *fax:* 0191 263 7082. Peter Carr, chief engineer. *Studio and location recording; 24 track recording. All mus styles.*

Instant Records. 14 Moorend Cres, Cheltenham, Glos GL53 0EL *tel:* 01242 523304. Martin Mitchell, mgr dir. *Mobile digital stereo recording service for orchs, choirs and small ens. Also cassette and CD manufacture.*

* **Jacob's Studios Ltd.** Ridgway House, Runwick Lane, Farnham, Surrey GU10 5EE *tel:* 01252 715546/723518 *fax:* 01252 712846. Andy Fernbach, studio mgr. *2 studios (fully-residential), 1 Neve VR and 1 SSL.*

K & A Productions. 5 Wyllyotts Place, Potters Bar, Herts EN6 2HN *tel:* 01707 661200 *fax:* 01707 661400 *email:* andrew@kaproductions.demon.co.uk. Andrew Walton, dir. *Digital location recording, 16/20-bit surround including production, engineering, editing, mastering and cover design. Project supervision including replication and A&R consultation. Classical mus.*

Loco Studios. Plas Llecha, Llanhennock, Caerleon, Newport, Monmouthshire NP6 1LU *tel:* 01633 450603 *fax:* 01633 450666. John Payne, Geoff Downes, studio mgrs. *Residential recording studio.*

Manygate Management Ltd. 13 Cotswold Mews, 30 Battersea Square, London SW11 3RA *tel:* 020 7223 7265 *fax:* 020 7585 2830. John Boyden. *Independent classical recording production, location recording and editing; also packaging and marketing consultants.*

Metier Sound & Vision. PO Box 270, Preston, Lancs PR2 3LZ *tel:* 01772 866178 *email:* lefeber@enterprise.net. David Lefeber, producer and engineer. *Digital location recording for classical record industry; digital editing; demos; broadcast TV sound specialist; mus and arts video and radio production; CD PQ mastering; one-off CD-Rs.*

The Mobile Recording Company. 3 South Meadow, South Horrington, Wells, Somerset BA5 3DJ *tel:* 01749 676544 *also fax; email:* enquire@mobilerecording.co.uk. David Finch. *16 and 20-bit digital location recording, digital hard disc editing and mastering, CD production. Low-cost self-promotion packages available.*

* **Modus Music.** The Old Rectory, Church Lane, Exning, nr Newmarket, Suffolk CB8 7HF *tel:* 01638 577324 *fax:* 01638 577106 *email:* marian@modus.force9.net. Trygg Tryggvason, Marian Freeman, partners. *Full independent location recording, production and editing for classical CD market.*

Musical Cocktails Ltd. 561 Kenton Lane, Harrow Weald, Middx HA3 7LB *tel:* 020 8427 5918 *fax:* 020 8863 7826 *email:* sales@musicalcocktails.com. Dieter Hester, mgr dir; Martin Hart, Karen Cormican. *Classical location recording, digital editing, mastering and remastering, CD production and duplication.*

Ninth Wave Audio. PO Box 5517, Birmingham B13 8QW *tel:* 0121 442 2276; 07770 364464 *fax:* 0121 689 1902 *email:* ninthwave@dial.pipex.com. Tony Wass, studio owner. *Location recording and post-production specialising in classical mus for CD and radio broadcast. Full BBC broadcast facilities, editing and disc mastering including short run CD production. Equipment: 24-track capable mobile, fully-digital 24-bit, ATC monitoring, Schoeps, Sennheiser and AGK mics, Lexicon 300 reverb, Tascam 8 tracks, Sony PCM 700 DAT, Genex M-0 24-bit 96khz, video links and BBC communications. Sonic Solutions digital editing with CD-R and Mediaform duplicating.*

Orientis Recording Services. 54 Sycamore Rd, London SW19 4TP *tel:* 020 8286 6943 *also fax.* Simon Vout, gen mgr. *Specialists in digital location recording for classical musicians, full CD and cassette production, digital editing and mastering, artwork design and print facilities.*

OxRecs DIGITAL. Magdalen Farm Cottage, Standlake, Witney, Oxon OX8 7RN *tel:* 01865 300347 *email:* info@oxrecs.com. Bernard Martin, dir. *Location classical recording specialising in orgs, chmbr orchs and choirs; digital editing, CD mastering, typesetting and design service.*

Panda Productions. 7 Arlington Rd, Surbiton, Surrey KT6 6BW *tel:* 020 8390 6951 *fax:* 020 8395 5374. Amanda Hurton, producer. *Production, editing and mastering of digital location recordings. Specialist in classical orch, chmbr and inst repertoire.*

Parish Recordings. 28 Tom Price Close, Cheltenham, Glos GL52 2LF *tel:* 01242 230455 *also fax; email:* parish@lineone.net. Ian and Janine Higginson, dirs. *Digital location recording service run by trained classical musicians. Complete packages for cassette and CD manufacture. Fully-digital recording, editing, mastering and full colour printing. Also live concerts and demo tapes.*

R & A Recording. 28 Venn Street, London SW4 OAT *tel:* 020 7720 88887 *also fax; email:* RDamerell@msn.com. Rupert Damerell, producer. Digital location recording, editing and CD mastering. Concert, session and demo recordings. Spcial production packages.

Ray Harvey Productions Ltd. 34 Riefield Rd, London SE9 2QA *tel:* 020 8850 5788 *fax:* 020 8294 2072. *Thirty years recording and producing mus for BBC Radio. Location digital recording, stereo to multitrack, digital editing, CD mastering, free project appraisals.*

Raymer Sound. Apsley House, Courtland Rd, Wellington, Somerset TA21 8ND *tel:* 01823 662160 *fax:* 01823 664055 *email:* neil@raymer.swinternet.co.uk. Neil Raybould, recording engineer, record producer. *Studio and location recording: 8 track digital. National distribution of own-label product. Mobile recording, CD mastering and replication, cassette duplication. Jazz, folk, choral, orch, br bands.*

Redbridge Recordings. 23 Bethell Ave, Cranbrook, Ilford, Essex IG1 4UX *tel:* 020 8518 6342 *fax:* 020 8518 0286 *email:* 101456.1034@compuserve.com. Frank Wilson, engineer; Roderick Elms, producer. *Specialist classical location recording. Recitals, concerts, special productions, CDs, cassettes, digital editing suite, artwork preparation.*

Redwood Studios Ltd. 1-6 Falconberg Court, London W1V 5FG *tel:* 020 7287 3799 *fax:* 020 7287 3751 *email:* redwood@onet.co.uk. André Jacquemin, mgr. *Digital hard disc recording using ProTools 24 system, film post-production suite, Dolby SR and A, large sound effects library. Toscam DA88-DA38 Mackie digital mixing console d8b.*

Regent Records. PO Box 528, Wolverhampton WV3 9YW *tel:* 01902 424377 *fax:* 01902 717661 *email:* regent.records@btinternet.com. Gary Cole, producer and engineer. *Classical location recording and production, post-production, 16 and 20-bit digital editing on Sonic Solutions. One-off and full custom CD service, demonstration and concert recordings.*

Rhinosaurus Records Limited. 7 Springfields, Somerset Rd, New Barnet, Herts EN5 1SG *tel:* 020 8440 0183 *fax:* 020 8440 8169. Colin Middleton, producer; Richard Jacob, chief sound engineer. *Digital location recording.*

Simon Fox Gál. 15 Chelmsford Square, London NW10 3AP *tel:* 020 8357 9625 *also fax; email:* simonfox@onet.co.uk. Simon Fox Gál. *Location recording, production and editing for the classical CD market. High-end equipment rig for solo, chmbr and orch work. Specialist in the mus/artistic aspects of the recording process.*

Sound Moves. The Oaks, Cross Lane, Smallfield, Surrey RH6 9SA *tel:* 01342 844190 *fax:* 01342 844290 *email:* steve@sound-moves.com. Steve Williams, owner. *Classic analogue, digital stereo or multi-track. Recording, live broadcast and post-production for all types of mus.*

Spiritus. Yew Trees, Comeytrowe Rise, Taunton TA1 5JA *tel:* 01823 272764 *also fax; email:* ian.carson@tesco.net. Ian Carson, producer. *Classical mus production for broadcasting and CDs; org, choirs, chmbr mus, contemporary worship mus.*

Vers Ltd. 34b Altenburg Gardens, London SW11 1JJ *tel:* 020 7585 0701. Ralph Varcoe, dir. *Location recording and production, live or studio. Digital mastering, editing, tape duplication, CD pressing, inert design and printing.*

Wearn, Jonathan R. 2 Eastern Terrace, Brighton BN2 1DJ *tel:* 01273 604371 *fax:* 01273 626495.

Record Pressing, Cassette Duplication, CD Mastering

* **Ablex Audio Video Ltd.** Halesfield 14, Telford, Shropshire TF7 4QR *tel:* 01952 680131 *fax:* 01952 583501 *email:* online@ablex.co.uk. Martine Tatman, sales dir. *Cassette duplication; CD replication and pre-mastering. All types of mus.*

* **Accurate Sound Ltd.** Queniborough Industrial Estate, Melton Rd, Queniborough, Leicester LE7 8FP *tel:* 0116 260 2064 *fax:* 0116 260 0108 *email:* as@accuratesound.demon.co.uk. William and Paul Komedera, dirs. *All aspects of audio cassette duplication and CD manufacture.*

Adrenalin Manufacturing Ltd. 252-253 Argyll Ave, Slough, Berks SL1 4HA *tel:* 01753 523200 *fax:* 01753 692243.

AWL Compact Disc Co Ltd. 356 Scraptoft Lane, Leicester LE5 1PB *tel:* 0116 241 3979 *fax:* 0116 243 3760. Andrew W Lipinski, mgr dir. *CD mastering and replication.*

* **Damont Audio Ltd.** Blyth Rd, Hayes, Middx UB3 1BY *tel:* 020 8573 5122 *fax:* 020 8561 0979. Chris Rose, mgr dir; Ian Ramsden, finance; Malcolm Pearce, sales mgr. *Manufacture vinyl 7" and 12" records; audio cassette duplication including classical.*

Euphonia. Trinity Mews, Cambridge Gardens, London W10 6JA *tel:* 020 8960 8128 *fax:* 020 8968 0341 *email:* nickm@teddbear.co.uk. Nick Morgan; Iesten Rees. *Digital editing and mastering services for cassette and CD. Analogue and digital format transfers. Real-time cassette and CD-R duplication.*

Filterbond Ltd (JBS Records Division). 19 Sadlers Way, Hertford, Herts SG14 2DZ *tel:* 01992 500101 *also fax*. John B Schefel, mgr dir; David F J Reeve, dir and sec. *Quality cassette duplication and blanks 1-1000. Computer printed cassette labels. Solo, 1/4" reel, Sony Betamax or R-DAT recording.*

Fine Tuning. Curls Farmhouse, Ripe, Lewes, E Sussex BN8 6AS *tel:* 01323 811604; 07831 614292 *fax:* 01323 811136 *email:* piers@finetuning.demon.co.uk. Piers Bishop. *Digital location recording and post-production. Radio OBs; microwave links.*

* **Finesplice Ltd.** 1 Summerhouse Lane, Harmondsworth, West Drayton, Middx UB7 0AW *tel:* 020 8564 7839 *fax:* 020 8759 9629 *email:* finespl@dircon.co.uk. Ben Turner, mgr dir; Julia Thomas, snr engineer. *Studios for mus editing, audio restoration, CD pre-mastering, and CD duplication. All types of mus.*

First Sound and Vision. 4-10 North Rd, London N7 9HN *tel:* 020 7865 3800 *fax:* 020 7865 3803 *email:* sales@fsv.co.uk. Keith Lloyd, mgr dir; Andrew Reynolds, Peter Culshaw, dirs. *Cassette duplication, CD replication and vinyl pressing.*

Ginn, Jeffrey. 11 Haycroft, Wootton, Bedford, Beds MK43 9PB *tel:* 01234 765602; 07778 896721 *fax:* 01234 765367 *email:* jeff@ginn-mus.demon.co.uk. *Location recording service and post-production studios. Classical recording, digital editing and SADIE mastering. SADIE hard-disc editor, DAT, CDR, Exabyte, Genex, Lexicon.*

* **ICC Duplication.** Unit 27, Hawthorn Road Industrial Estate, Lottbridge Drive, Eastbourne, E Sussex BN23 6QA *tel:* 01323 647880 *fax:* 01323 643095 *email:* duplication@icc.org.uk. Geoff Durrant, customer service mgr; Andy Thorpe, sales and development mgr. Andy Hooper, production mgr. *Professional cassette duplication, blank cassettes, CD replication, CD pre-mastering, video duplication, video blanks.*

* **Isis Duplicating Co Ltd.** Unit 11, Shaftesbury Industrial Centre, The Runnings, Cheltenham, Glos GL51 9NH *tel:* 01242 571818 *fax:* 01242 571315. Glyn Ellis Evans, sales mgr. *Recording, editing, mastering, high-speed cassette duplication.*

* **ITD Cassettes.** Unit 21 Faraday Rd, Rabans Lane, Aylesbury, Bucks HP19 3RY *tel:* 01296 427211 *fax:* 01296 392019 *email:* itdcassets@aol.com. R P Jackson-Moore, mgr dir; M A McLoughlin, technical dir. *Audio and video cassette duplication.*

James Yorke Ltd. Yorke House, Corpus St, Cheltenham, Glos GL52 6XH *tel:* 01242 584222 *fax:* 01242 222445 *email:* ken@jamesyorke.co.uk. Ken Leeks, mgr dir. *Loop-bin duplication for cassettes.*

K & A Productions. 5 Wyllyotts Place, Potters Bar, Herts EN6 2HN *tel:* 01707 661200 *fax:* 01707 661400 *email:* andrew@kaproductions.demon.co.uk. Andrew Walton, dir. *Digital editing, restoration and CD and cassette mastering to Exabyte or CD-R. One-off CDs. Cover and inlay design and layout. Project supervision to pressing stage. Classical mus.*

Keynote Cassettes. Wishanger Lane, Churt, Farnham, Surrey GU10 2QJ *tel:* 01252 794253 *fax:* 01252 792642 *email:* keynote@dial.pipex.com. Tim Wheatley. *Cassette and CD-R duplicators and CD brokers.*

* **KG Engineering Ltd.** Unit 6, Ipplepen Business Park, Edgelands Lane, Ipplepen, Newton Abbot TQ12 5UG *tel:* 01803 813833 *fax:* 01803 813141. Keith Gould, mgr dir; Jackie M Turner, production mgr. *CD mastering, cassette duplication. Recording studio and CD production.*

* **Nimbus Manufacturing (UK) Ltd.** Llantarnam Park, Cwmbran, Gwent NP44 3AB *tel:* 01633 465000 *fax:* 01633 876131. Howard Nash, mgr dir; Bill Warhurst, associate dir, CD-audio; Emil Dudek, dir CD-ROM. *Pre-mastering, mastering and manufacture of all CD, CD-ROM, DVD and other optical discs. Also video with compression (MPEG, Quicktime, etc), full printing and packaging services.*

The Old Smithy Recording Studio. 1 Post Office Lane, Kempsey, Worcester WR5 3NS *tel:* 01905 820659 *fax:* 01905 820015 *email:* muff.murfin@virgin.net. Janet Allsopp, bookings mgr. *Cassette duplication, MIDI sequencing and sampling hardware.*

Portfolio CDs - Brochures in Sound. PO Box 2288, Glastonbury, Somerset BA6 9YJ *tel:* 020 8943 5329 *also fax*. Nicholas Vallis-Davies; Sian Vallis-Davies. *Organisation specialising in putting audition pieces on CD with full production, artwork and distribution services.*

PR Records Ltd. Hamilton House, Endeavour Way, Wimbledon, London SW19 8UH *tel:* 020 8241 9000; 01423 888979 *fax:* 020 8241 2226; 01423 885761. Ray Young, mgr dir. *Vinyl, cassette and CD manufacturing.*

Pro Piano Records. 85 Jane St, New York, NY 10014, USA *tel:* +1 212 206 8714 *fax:* +1 212 633 1207 *email:* ricard@propaino.com. Ricard de La Rosa, classical division head; Chitose Okashire, dir, A&R. *Location recording for classical pno.*

Raymer Sound. Apsley House, Courtland Rd, Wellington, Somerset TA21 8ND *tel:* 01823 662160 *fax:* 01823 664055. Neil Raybould, recording engineer. *Mobile recording, CD mastering, cassette duplication for classical mus.*

Reflex Media Group Ltd. Unit 5, Cirrus, Glebe Rd, Huntingdon, Cambs PE18 7DX *tel:* 01480 434333 *fax:* 01480 411441. John Garrad, dir; Roger Masterson, dir. *Editing and post-production, mastering for CD and MC, CD pressing and MC duplication.*

Rhinosaurus Records Limited. 7 Springfields, Somerset Rd, New Barnet, Herts EN5 1SG *tel:* 020 8440 0183 *fax:* 020 8440 8169. Colin Middleton, producer; Richard Jacobs, chief sound engineer. *Mastering, cassette duplication, CD manufacture.*

* **RTS, One Stop.** Unit M2, Albany Rd, Prescot, Merseyside L34 2SH *tel:* 0151 430 9001 *fax:* 0151 430 7441.

Selecta Sound. 5 Margaret Rd, Romford, Essex RM2 5SH *tel:* 01708 453424 *fax:* 01708 455565 *email:* select@classiques.demon.co.uk. John and Carol Smailes; Nigel Davidson, technical mgr. *Audio and video duplication; CD replication; blank tape supply. PA systems, lighting line.*

* **Sounds Good Ltd.** 12 Chiltern Enterprise Centre, Station Rd, Theale, Berks RG7 4AA *tel:* 0118 930 2600 *fax:* 0118 930 3181. Martin Maynard, dir; Alison Marshall, client mgr. *Cassette duplication, CD mastering and digital editing, CD pressing, inlay print. CD-R duplication; CD-ROM; design and reprographics.*

Speech Plus Recordings. Unit 32, 19 Pages Walk, London SE1 4SB *tel:* 020 7231 0961.

SRL Cassettes. 47 High St, Pinner, Middx HA5 5PJ *tel:* 020 8868 5555 *fax:* 020 8866 5555 *email:* srl@btinternet.com. J Bales, production mgr. *High-quality audio cassette and CD duplication of all types of mus; classical, pop and speech. Quantity 100-30,000.*

SRT Sound Recording Technology Ltd. Edison Rd, Audio House, St Ives, Cambridge PE17 4LF *tel:* 01480 461880; 020 8446 3218 *fax:* 01480 496100. Matthew Dilley, classical mgr. *CD manufacturer and 6 studios. Full classical service including restoration and multi-session discs.*

WNE. Unit 7, Sovereign Centre, Lichfield Rd Industrial Estate, Tamworth, Staffs B79 7XA *tel:* 01827 310052 *fax:* 01827 60868. *Cassette duplication, min run 250.*

Sound Recovery and Restoration

Abbey Road Studios. 3 Abbey Rd, St Johns Wood, London NW8 9AY *tel:* 020 7266 7237 *fax:* 020 7266 7250. Lucy Launder. *Award-winning archive restoration engineers using Sonic Solutions No-Noise or CEDAR systems for optimum retrieval of audio information. Transfer can be made from virtually any format.*

Euphonia. Trinity Mews, Cambridge Gardens, London W10 6JA *tel:* 020 8960 8128 *fax:* 020 8968 0341 *email:* nickm@teddbear.co.uk. Simon Heyworth, chief sound engineer. *Sonic Solutions No-Noise TM and de-clicking systems. Restoration of old and damaged recordings from all sources. Full range of digital and analogue processing and format transfer equipment available. Specialist services for legal and forensic work and film sound restoration.*

Friary Music Services. 142b Friary Rd, London SE15 5UW *tel:* 020 7277 7068 *fax:* 020 7277 8354 *email:* 100115.3701@compuserve.com. Richard Black, producer. *Highest quality transcription of all 78, 45 and 33 rpm records and analogue tape recordings. Classical mus only.*

John R T Davies. 1 Walnut Tree Cottage, Burnham, Bucks SL1 8DH *tel:* 01628 604811. *Recovery and restoration of sound from ancient and defective recordings.*

K & A Productions. 5 Wyllyotts Place, Potters Bar, Herts EN6 2HN *tel:* 01707 661200 *fax:* 01707 661400 *email:* andrew@kaproductions.demon.co.uk. Andrew Walton, dir. *Restoration using Sonic Solutions No-Noise. Transfer off any format. Full EQ, Dynamics and Reverberation processing. Classical mus.*

Pro Piano Records. 85 Jane St, New York, NY 10014, USA *tel:* +1 212 206 8714 *fax:* +1 212 633 1207 *email:* ricard@propiano.com. Ricard de La Rosa, classical division head; Chitose Okashire, A&R.

Specialist Record Dealers

Many record shops carry recordings of classical music as a small proportion of their total stock. In the following list, retailers with exclusive or large sections devoted to classical music or jazz are grouped alphabetically by county. Greater London is listed first followed by the rest of England. Scotland and Wales are located at the end of this section.

Greater London

Barbican Music Shop. Cromwell Tower, Silk St, Barbican, London EC2Y 8DD *tel:* 020 7588 9242 *fax:* 020 7628 1080 *email:* barbicanmusic @compuserve.com. *Mus, CDs, inst accs, books.*

Bargain Records. 9 The Arcade, High St, Eltham, London SE9 1BE *tel:* 020 8859 5836. *Second-hand classical records, CDs.*

Consort Records. 34 St Mary's Grove, London W4 3LN *tel:* 020 8995 9994 *fax:* 020 8995 2115 *email:* info@the-kings-consort.org.uk. *M/order early mus recordings.*

Dress Circle. 57-59 Monmouth St, Upper St Martin's Lane, London WC2H 9DG *tel:* 020 7240 2227 *fax:* 020 7379 8540 *email:* online@dresscircle.co.uk. *CDs, cassettes, books, videos.*

ENO Shop, MDC Classic Music. 31 St Martin's Lane, London WC2N 4ER *tel:* 020 7240 0270 *also fax; email:* classic@mdcmusic.co.uk. *CDs, videos and gifts. Books on opera, dance and ballet.*

Farringdons Records. 64-72 Leadenhall Market, London EC3V 1LT *tel:* 020 7623 9605 *fax:* 020 7626 2891. *Classical specialist.*

Farringdons Records. Royal Festival Hall, South Bank Centre, London SE1 8XX *tel:* 020 7620 0198 *fax:* 020 7928 0063. *Classical CDs, videos, jazz films, shows and world mus.*

HMV Shop (HMV UK Ltd). 150 Oxford St, London W1N 0DJ *tel:* 020 7631 3423 *fax:* 020 7580 6648. *Audio recordings (all formats), videos, computers and video games, mus merchandise and accs.*

HMV Shop. 363 Oxford St, London W1R 2BJ *tel:* 020 7629 1240/7499 9014 *fax:* 020 7495 0261. *Classical, jazz, blues, easy listening, rock and pop, soul, dance, films and shows, world mus, folk, country, new age, spoken word, games, videos.*

HMV Shop. 81 (Unit 66) The Mall, Broadway Shopping Centre, Bexleyheath DA6 7JJ *tel:* 020 8298 0876.

HMV Shop. Unit Y11A, Brent Cross Centre, Brent Cross, London NW4 3FG *tel:* 020 8201 5430.

HMV Shop. 90-92 High St, Bromley, Kent BR1 1EY *tel:* 020 8313 0727.

HMV Shop. 2 Arcadia Centre, Ealing Broadway, London W5 2ND *tel:* 020 8566 2590. *CDs, cassettes and videos.*

HMV Shop. 11-13 Church St, Enfield EN2 6AF *tel:* 020 8363 0184. *CDs, cassettes and videos.*

HMV Shop. 332-334 North End Rd, Fulham, London SW6 1NF *tel:* 020 7386 5256. *CDs, cassettes, vinyl and videos.*

HMV Shop. Trocadero, Coventry St, London W1V 7FD *tel:* 020 7439 0447.

Koolman Records. 7 Gilmore Rd, London SE13 5AD *tel:* 020 8852 5727 *fax:* 020 8297 9214. *Rare and bargain classical LPs in mint condition.*

Mole Jazz. 311 Gray's Inn Rd, London WC1X 8PX *tel:* 020 7278 0703 *fax:* 020 7833 1029 *email:* jazz@molejazz.co.uk. *Jazz specialists, new and second-hand CDs, LPs, books. M/order worldwide, free mailing lists, auctions of rare LPs.*

Music Discount Centre. 124 Camden High St, London NW1 0LU *tel:* 020 7482 7097 *fax:* 020 7482 6888.

Music Discount Centre. 58 Ludgate Hill, London EC4M 7HX *tel:* 020 7489 8077. *Records, CDs, mini discs.*

Music Discount Centre. 33-34 Rathbone Place, London W1P 1AD *tel:* 020 7637 4700. *Classical CDs, live and historical opera.*

Music Discount Centre. 437 Strand, London WC2R 0QN *tel:* 020 7240 2157. *Cassettes, CDs.*

Music Discount Centre. 46 Thurloe St, London SW7 2LT *tel:* 020 7584 3338.

Ray's Jazz Shop. Incorporating Ray's Blues & Roots, 180 Shaftesbury Ave, London WC2 8JS *tel:* 020 7240 3969 *fax:* 020 7240 7375 *email:* rays.jazz@dial.pipex.com. *Jazz, blues, world, folk and country. CDs, records (vinyl) new and second-hand, cassettes, 78s, books, magazines, videos.*

Reckless Records. 30 Berwick St, London W1V 3RF *tel:* 020 7437 4271 *email:* rarities@reckless.co.uk. *CDs, vinyl, second-hand specialists.*

Reckless Records. 79 Upper St, London N1 0NU *tel:* 020 7359 0501/7359 2222 *fax:* 020 7359 9509 *email:* rarities@reckless.co.uk. *Buy, sell and exchange CDs, vinyl, tapes. Rock, soul, pop, dance. Rarities by m/order.*

Thomas (Michael G). 5a Norfolk Place, London W2 1QN *tel:* 020 7723 4935. *Records, cassettes, CDs, m/order. Archive documents. Mengelberg Edition.*

Tower Records. 162 Camden High St, London NW1 0NE *tel:* 020 7424 2800 *fax:* 020 7424 2801. *CDs, cassettes, mini discs, vinyl, books, DVD.*

Tower Records. 62-64 Kensington High St, London W8 4PE *tel:* 020 7938 3625 *fax:* 020 7937 5024. *Records, cassettes, CDs.*

Tower Records. Swan & Edgar Building, 1 Piccadilly Circus, London W1R 8TR *tel:* 020 7439 2500 *fax:* 020 7434 2766 *email:* tower@easynet.co.uk. *Classical, opera, jazz, international, new age, folk, country, blues, rock & pop, alternative, soul, rap, swing. CD singles, films and shows, easy listening and vocals, comedy, books and magazines, laser discs, videos.*

Tower Records. Whiteleys of Bayswater, Unit 001b, London W2 4YR *tel:* 020 7229 4550 *fax:* 020 7792 0075. *Cassettes, CDs, videos and books.*

Trehantiri. 365-367 Green Lanes, London N4 1DY *tel:* 020 8802 6530 *also fax; email:* trehanti@greekmus.demon.co.uk. *Specialists in Greek, Middle Eastern and Eurovision.*

Vinyl Connections. 22 Hilltop Rd, London NW6 2PY *tel:* 020 7625 8966 *also fax. Specialists in original 1950s-1970s classical LP records: symphony, chmbr, inst, operatic, vocal, etc. Most labels. Collections bought for cash; record cleaning service; quality vintage turntables and cartridges supplied.*

Virgin Megastore. 14-16 Oxford St, London W1N 9FL *tel:* 020 7631 1234 *fax:* 020 7580 9546. *Books, records, cassettes, CDs, sheet mus.*

England

Bath and North East Somerset

Bath

Bath Compact Discs. 11 Broad St, Bath, Avon BA1 5LJ *tel:* 01225 464766 *fax:* 01225 482275 *email:* bathcds@btinternet.com. *Classical CDs and videos, also m/order (post free in UK).*

HMV Shop. 13-15 Stall St, Bath BA1 1QE *tel:* 01225 466681 *fax:* 01225 330820.

Bedfordshire

Luton

HMV Shop. 146 Arndale Centre, Luton, Beds LU1 2TG *tel:* 01582 401414.

Berkshire

Reading

Hickies Ltd. 153 Friar St, Reading RG1 1HG *tel:* 0118 957 5771 *fax:* 0118 957 5775. *Cassettes, Cds.*

Bristol, City of

Bristol

Bristol Classical Discs. 59 Broad St, Bristol BS1 2EJ *tel:* 0117 927 6536. *CDs, classical specialist.*

Rayners Compact Discs. 84 Park St, Bristol BS1 5LA *tel:* 0117 927 3936. *CDs and cassettes.*

Buckinghamshire

Aylesbury

HMV Shop. Unit 6, 7 Friars Square, Aylesbury, Bucks HP20 2SP *tel:* 01296 399 290.

Cambridgeshire

Cambridge

CMS Records. 1a All Saints' Passage, Cambridge CB2 3LT *tel:* 01223 460818 *fax:* 01223 464178 *email:* cmsrecords@compuserve.com. *Classical CDs, cassettes, videos, m/order.*

Garon Records. 70 King St, Cambridge CB1 1LN *tel:* 01223 362086. *Records, cassettes, CDs, classical, jazz, folk, blues, ethnic, second-hand and new.*

HMV Shop. 12-15 Lion Yard, Cambridge CB2 3NA *tel:* 01223 319090 *fax:* 01223 319091. *CDs, cassettes and videos.*

Peterborough

HMV Shop. 4 Cathedral Square, Peterborough, Cambs PE1 1XH *tel:* 01733 347642. *CDs and cassettes.*

Cheshire

Wilmslow

D.I. Music Direct. 13 Bank Square, Wilmslow, Cheshire SK9 1AN *tel:* 01625 527844 *fax:* 01625 536101 *email:* dimus@aol.com. *Records, cassettes, CDs; classical, jazz, opera, nostalgia, spoken word, classical videos. M/order only.*

Derbyshire

Derby

HMV Shop. 2 Albion St, Derby DE1 2AL *tel:* 01332 201902.

MDT Classics. 6 Old Blacksmiths Yard, Sadler Gate, Derby DE1 3PD *tel:* 01332 368251 *fax:* 01332 383594 *email:* info@mdt.co.uk. *CDs (classical only), m/order.*

Devon

Exeter

HMV Shop. 191 High St, Exeter EX4 3DU *tel:* 01392 420190. *Records, cassettes, CDs, books.*

Opus Classical. 14a Guildhall Centre, Exeter, Devon EX4 3HW *tel:* 01392 214044 *fax:* 01392 496196 *email:* enquiries@opus-classical.com. *CDs, cassettes, books, videos.*

Plymouth

HMV Shop. 30-32 New George St, Plymouth PL1 1RW *tel:* 01752 228181. *Records, cassettes, CDs.*

Sidmouth

Acorn Music Inc (Peter Russell's Hot Record Store). PO Box 17, Sidmouth, Devon EX10 9EH *tel:* 01395 578145 *fax:* 01395 578080. *Records (jazz, blues, big band, dance band, nostalgia, Latin-American, stage and screen); m/order only.*

Dorset

Bournemouth

HMV Shop. 5-6 The Avenue, Commercial Rd, Bournemouth BH2 5RP *tel:* 01202 556297. *CDs, cassettes and videos.*

East Sussex

Brighton

Classics. 28a Tidy St, Brighton BN1 4EL *tel:* 01273 694229. *Second-hand records, cassettes, CDs, videos (classical, opera, jazz, stage shows, vocal, big band, rock, pop, etc), bought and sold.*

HMV Shop. 61-62 Western Rd, Brighton BN1 2HA *tel:* 01273 747221.

Eastbourne

C G Robson Imports. 39 Winchcombe Rd, Eastbourne, E Sussex BN22 8DE *tel:* 01323 725376 *also fax. Customer order only. American and UK CDs, cassettes and some videos. Worldwide postal service. Supply American Schwann Opus and Artist catalogues (classical) and Schwann Spectrum catalogue (popular); also Fanfare review.*

Seaford Music. 24 Pevensey Rd, Eastbourne, E Sussex BN21 3HP *tel:* 01323 732553 *fax:* 01323 417455 *email:* seafordmus@aol.com. *Classical CDs, cassettes, videos.*

Hove

Fine Records. 32 George St, Hove, E Sussex BN3 3YB *tel:* 01273 723345 *fax:* 01273 748717. *Classical specialist; many rare deletions on cassette, record and CD.*

Essex

Chelmsford

HMV Store. Unit 2 High Chelmer Shopping Centre, Chelmsford, Essex CM1 1XG *tel:* 01245 351641.

Epping

Chew & Osborne. 148 High St, Epping, Essex CM16 4AG *tel:* 01992 574242 *fax:* 01992 572300 *email:* c&o@eppinc148.demon.co.uk. *CDs, classical specialists.*

Saffron Walden

Chew & Osborne. 26 King St, Saffron Walden, Essex CB10 1ES *tel:* 01799 523728. *CDs, classical specialists and hi-fi.*

Southend

HMV Shop. 8-14 Queens Rd, Southend, Essex SS1 1LU *tel:* 01702 435158.

West Thurrock.

HMV Shop. Unit 281 Lakeside Shopping Centre, West Thurrock Way, West Thurrock, Grays, Essex RM16 1WT *tel:* 01708 860110.

Gloucestershire

Cheltenham

HMV Shop. 111-113 High Street, Cheltenham, Glos GL50 1DW *tel:* 01242 230930.

Sounds Good. 26 Clarence St, Cheltenham, Glos GL50 3NU *tel:* 01242 234604 *fax:* 01242 253030 *email:* cds@soundsgood.demon.co.uk. *Classical, folk, world, jazz, blues and country CDs. Also opera and ballet videos and DVDs.*

Gloucester

Audiosonic (Gloucester) Ltd. 6 College St, Gloucester GL1 2NE *tel:* 01452 302280 *fax:* 01452 302202. *Cassettes, CDs, m/order. Classical mus specialists. Videos, sheet mus; also second-hand CDs.*

Folktracks (Audio and Video) International. The Traditions Library, 16 Brunswick Square, Gloucester GL1 1UG *tel:* 01452 415110 *email:* peter@folktrax.demon.co.uk. Peter Kennedy, Beryl Kennedy, mgrs. *Cassettes, CDs and videos of traditional mus and customs of the world.*

HMV Shop. 18-20 Kings Walk, Gloucester GL1 1RW *tel:* 01522 539349. *Records, cassettes, CDs, videos.*

Greater Manchester

Manchester

Forsyth Bros Ltd. 126 Deansgate, Manchester M3 2GR *tel:* 0161 834 3281 *fax:* 0161 834 0630 *email:* forsythmus@aol.com. *Classical, jazz, world, spoken word. CDs, cassettes, mus videos, m/order.*

HMV Shop. 90-100 Market St, Manchester M1 1PD *tel:* 0161 834 8550. *CDs, cassettes, videos.*

Virgin Megastore. 52-56 Market St, Manchester M1 1PW *tel:* 0161 833 1111 *fax:* 0161 832 2765. *CDs, cassettes, records, videos, books, games, clothing.*

Hampshire

Basingstoke

HMV Shop. 2 Old Basing Mall, Basingstoke, Hants RG21 1AW *tel:* 01256 816 707.

Portsmouth

HMV Shop. 183-187 Commercial Rd, Portsmouth PO1 1EA *tel:* 023 9282 9678. *Records, cassettes, CDs.*

Southampton

HMV Shop. 56-58 Above Bar St, Southampton SO14 7DS *tel:* 023 8033 8398. *Records, cassettes, CDs and videos, mini discs and laser discs.*

Southsea

Orpheus Music. 27 Marmion Rd, Southsea, Hants *tel:* 023 9281 2397 *fax:* 023 9286 5421. *Records, cassettes, CDs (classical, jazz, big band, folk and new world), new and second-hand.*

Winchester

Whitwams Music. 70 High St, Winchester, Hants SO23 9DE *tel:* 01962 865253 *fax:* 01962 842064 *email:* music@whitwams.co.uk. *CDs, cassettes, videos; classical specialists, m/order.*

Herefordshire

Hay-on-Wye

Hancock & Monks. 15 Broad St, Hay-on-Wye, Herefordshire HR3 5DB *tel:* 01497 821784 *fax:* 01591 610555 *email:* haymusic@compuserve.com. *Specialists in classical cassettes, CDs, videos. Second-hand books on mus; sheet mus.*

Isle of Wight

Newport

HMV Shop. 62 High St, Newport PO39 1BA *tel:* 01983 522533.

Kent

Maidstone

HMV Shop. 34 Week St, Maidstone, Kent ME14 1RP *tel:* 01622 751 650.

West Wickham

Showells Record Centre. 94 High St, West Wickham, Kent BR4 0NF *tel:* 020 8777 5255. *Cassettes, CDs, videos.*

Kingston upon Hull

Hull

HMV Shop. 51 Whitefriargate, Hull HU1 2HT *tel:* 01482 620880. *CDs, cassettes and videos.*

Lancashire

Blackpool

HMV Shop. Unit 1, Tower Shopping Centre, Bank Hey St, Blackpool FY1 4RZ *tel:* 01253 291393 *fax:* 01253 299874. *Records, cassettes, CDs, books, magazines and videos.*

Bolton

HMV Shop. 3-5 Exchange St, Bolton BL1 1RS *tel:* 01204 524641 *fax:* 01204 522547. *CDs, cassettes and videos, computer games, books, clothing.*

Oldham

HMV Shop. 29 Town Square Shopping Centre, Oldham OL1 1XE *tel:* 0161 633 7332.

St Annes on Sea

Squires Gate Music Centre. Rear of 13 St Andrew's Road South, St Annes on Sea, Lancs FY8 1SX *tel:* 01253 782588 *fax:* 01253 782985. *Cassettes, CDs.*

Leicestershire

Leicester

Classic Tracks. 21 East Bond St, Leicester LE1 4SX *tel:* 0116 253 7700 *fax:* 0116 252 3553. *Classical mus, film soundtracks, shows and musicals.*

HMV Shop. 9-17 High St, Leicester LE1 4FP *tel:* 0116 253 9638. *Records, cassettes, CDs, books.*

Virgin Megastore. 8 Churchgate, Leicester LE1 4AJ *tel:* 0116 242 5969 *fax:* 0116 253 0136.

Merseyside

Liverpool

HMV Shop. 22-36 Church St, Liverpool L1 3AW *tel:* 0151 709 1088 *fax:* 0151 707 2368. *Records, cassettes, CDs, video games.*

Middlesbrough

Middlesbrough

HMV Shop. 33 Centre Mall, Cleveland Centre, Middlesbrough TS1 2NR *tel:* 01642 242322. *CDs, cassettes and videos.*

Middlesex

Harrow

Jewish Music Distribution. PO Box 32, Harrow, Middx HA1 2NN *tel:* 020 8209 2445 *fax:* 020 8909 1030 *email:* jmd@jmht.org. *Retail and wholesale suppliers of Jewish recorded and printed mus. Main agent for Israel's major recording and sheet mus companies.*

Milton Keynes, City of

Milton Keynes

Chappell of Bond Street. 21 Silbury Arcade, The Shopping Centre, Central Milton Keynes MK9 3AG *tel:* 01908 663366 *fax:* 01908 606414 *email:* mandi_meek@chappell-bond-st.co.uk. *CDs, mus, m/order.*

Norfolk

Norwich

HMV Shop. 21 Gentleman's Walk, Norwich NR2 1NA *tel:* 01603 622329.

Prelude Records. 25b St Giles St, Norwich NR2 1JN *tel:* 01603 628319 *also fax; fax:* 01603 620170 *email:* sales@prelude-records.co.uk. *CDs, cassettes, videos, mini discs; classical specialist.*

Northamptonshire

Kettering

HMV Shop. 32a Newlands Centre, Kettering NN16 8JB *tel:* 01536 519101. *Cassettes, CDs and videos.*

Northampton

HMV Shop. 2-6 Princes Walk, Grosvenor Centre, Northampton, NN1 2EL *tel:* 01604 232662.

Spinadiscs. 75a Abington St, Northampton NN1 2BH *tel:* 01604 631144 *fax:* 01604 624418. *CDs, cassettes, records.*

Nottinghamshire

Mansfield

HMV Shop. 24 Four Seasons Centre, Mansfield, Notts NG18 1FU *tel:* 01623 420666. *Cassettes, CDs and videos.*

Nottingham

HMV Shop. 38 Listergate, Nottingham NG1 7EE *tel:* 0115 950 2841 *fax:* 0115 950 4785. *Records, cassettes, CDs, books.*

HMV Shop. 134 Victoria Centre, Nottingham NG1 3QE *tel:* 0115 941 5525. *Cassettes, CDs, videos.*

Virgin Megastore. 6-8 Wheelergate, Nottingham NG1 2NB *tel:* 0115 947 6126 *fax:* 0115 948 3857.

Oxfordshire

Oxford

HMV Shop. 43-46 Cornmarket St, Oxford OX1 3HA *tel:* 01865 728190. *CDs, cassettes.*

South Yorkshire

Doncaster

HMV Shop. 10 Frenchgate, Doncaster DN1 1QQ *tel:* 01302 340484.

Sheffield

HMV Shop. 34 High St, Meadowhall Centre, Sheffield S9 1EN *tel:* 0114 256 8138. *CDs, cassettes.*

HMV Shop. 121-123 Pinstone St, Sheffield S1 2HL *tel:* 0114 275 1445.

Virgin Megastore. 3 Orchard Square, Fargate, Sheffield S1 2FB *tel:* 0114 273 1175 *fax:* 0114 275 1831.

Staffordshire

Hanley

HMV Store. 212 The Potteries Shopping Centre, Market Square, Hanley, Staffs ST1 1PS *tel:* 01782 283232.

Suffolk

Felixstowe

Ian's Music and Video. 111 Hamilton Rd, Felixstowe IP11 7BL *tel:* 01394 279442 *also fax; email:* ianmusic@anglianet.co.uk. *CDs. M/order rarities.*

Ipswich

Amberstone Bookshop. 49 Upper Orwell St, Ipswich, Suffolk IP4 1HP *tel:* 01473 250675 *fax:* 01473 226980 *email:* amber@anglianet.co.uk. *Books, classical CDs, cassettes.*

Andy's Records. Unit 8, The Buttermarket Centre, St Stephens Lane, Ipswich IP1 1DW *tel:* 01473 258933.

HMV Shop. 20 Tavern St, Ipswich IP1 3AY *tel:* 01473 213127.

Ipswich Record and Tape Exchange. 34 Upper Orwell St, Ipswich *tel:* 01473 230207. *New and second-hand records and CDs.*

Sudbury

Compact Music. North St, Sudbury, Suffolk CO10 6RB *tel:* 01787 881160 *fax:* 01787 880909. *CDs, cassettes, vinyl, videos, mini disc; classical, jazz and easy listening. Order service.*

Surrey

Cobham

Threshold Compact Discs. 53-55 High St, Cobham, Surrey KT11 3DP *tel:* 01932 865678 *also fax; email:* sales@threshold-cd.co.uk. *Classical, jazz, blues, soul, R&B, dance, rock, pop, country, films and shows, easy listening.*

East Croydon

HMV Shop. 137 North End, Croydon CR0 1TN *tel:* 020 8686 5557.

Godalming

Record Corner. Pound Lane, Godalming, Surrey GU7 1BX *tel:* 01483 422006 *also fax. CDs, cassettes, vinyl, mus books, styli, videos.*

Guildford

HMV Shop. 75-79 The Friary Centre, Guildford, Surrey GU1 4YU *tel:* 01483 565650.

Kingston

HMV Shop. Units 11-12, 1st Floor, Bentalls Centre, Clarence St, Kingston KT1 1TR *tel:* 020 8974 8037.

Tower Records. 17 Fife Rd, Kingston KT1 1SB *tel:* 020 8546 2500 *fax:* 020 8974 6993. *CDs and books.*

Richmond

HMV Shop. 70-72 George St, Richmond, Surrey TW9 1HE *tel:* 020 8940 9880 *fax:* 020 8332 6584.

Tyne and Wear

Gateshead

HMV Shop. 22 (68a) Cameron Walk, Metro Centre, Gateshead NE11 9YR *tel:* 0191 460 3883.

Newcastle upon Tyne

HMV Shop. 56 Northumberland St, Newcastle NE1 7AE *tel:* 0191 230 0626.

J G Windows Ltd. 1-7 Central Arcade, Newcastle NE1 5BP *tel:* 0191 232 1356 *fax:* 0191 261 2366. *Records, cassettes, CDs, m/order.*

Virgin Megastore. Monument Mall, 15-21 Northumberland St, Newcastle NE1 7AE *tel:* 0191 230 5959/5956 *fax:* 0191 230 2218.

Sunderland

HMV Shop. 61 High St West, Sunderland, Tyne and Wear SR1 3DP *tel:* 0191 514 1267.

West Midlands

Birmingham

HMV Shop. 134 New St, Birmingham B2 4NP *tel:* 0121 643 7029. *CDs, cassettes and videos.*

HMV Store. 38 High St, Birmingham B4 7SL *tel:* 0121 643 2177. *Records, CDs, cassettes, videos.*

Tower Records. 5 Corporation St, Birmingham B2 4LP *tel:* 0121 616 2677 *fax:* 0121 616 2686. *CDs, videos, books, magazines, accs.*

Virgin Megastore. 98 Corporation St, Birmingham B4 6SX *tel:* 0121 236 2523 *fax:* 0121 236 7229. *CDs, cassettes, computer games, videos and accs.*

Wolverhampton

HMV Shop. 8 The Gallery, Mander Square, Wolverhampton WV1 3NJ *tel:* 01902 429978. *CDs, cassettes and videos.*

West Yorkshire

Bradford

HMV Shop. Unit 2, 18 Broadway, Bradford BD1 1EY *tel:* 01274 394900. *CDs, cassettes and videos.*

Leeds

HMV Shop. 1 Victoria Walk, Headrow Centre, Leeds LS1 6JD *tel:* 0113 245 5548. *Cassettes, CDs and videos.*

Wakefield

HMV Shop. 2 Kirkgate, Wakefield, W Yorks WF1 1SP *tel:* 01924 291281. *CDs, cassettes and videos.*

Wiltshire

Devizes

Heritage Records. 39 Woodland Rd, Patney, nr Devizes, Wilts SN10 3RD *tel:* 01380 840362 *also fax. Second-hand 78s and LPs.*

Salisbury

The Collector's Room (at Sutton's Music Centre). 3 Endless St, Salisbury, Wilts SP1 1DL *tel:* 01722 326153. *Classical and jazz records, cassettes, CDs (new and second-hand).*

Swindon

HMV Shop. 16-17 Regents St, Swindon SN1 4JQ *tel:* 01793 420963.

Worcester

HMV Shop. 88-89 High St, Worcester WR1 2EX *tel:* 01905 24567.

York, City of

York

Banks & Sons (Music) Ltd. 18 Lendal, York YO1 8AU *tel:* 01904 658836 *fax:* 01904 629547 *email:* banksmusic@dial.pipex.com. *Classical recordings, sheet music, hi-tech department, worldwide m/order.*

HMV Shop. 10a Coney St, York YO1 1NA *tel:* 01904 640218 *fax:* 01904 640318. *Cassettes, CDs, videos, laser discs, CDI.*

Scotland

Aberdeen, City of

Aberdeen

HMV Shop. 11-12 Union Bridge, Aberdeen AB11 6BE *tel:* 01224 593535. *Cassettes, CDs, books, magazines, video, laser disc, computer games.*

Virgin Megastore. 133 Union St, Aberdeen AB12 2BH *tel:* 01224 213050/212908 *fax:* 01224 213568.

Dundee, City of

Dundee

HMV Shop. 71-77 Murraygate, Dundee DD1 2EA *tel:* 01382 225383.

Edinburgh, City of

Edinburgh

Bauermeister Booksellers. Record Department, 15-16 George IV Bridge, Edinburgh EH1 1EH *tel:* 0131 226 5561 *fax:* 0131 220 0679. *Cassettes, CDs; classical specialists.*

HMV Shop. 43-44 St James Centre, Edinburgh EH1 3SL *tel:* 0131 556 1236. *CDs, cassettes and videos.*

Virgin Megastore. 125 Princes St, Edinburgh EH2 4BD *tel:* 0131 220 2230 *fax:* 0131 220 1757.

Fife

Dunfermline

Silver Service CD. 24 Touch Wards, Dunfermline, Fife KY12 7TG *tel:* 01383 738159 *email:* silverservicecd@btinternet.com. *CDs, m/order.*

Glasgow, City of

Glasgow

HMV Shop. 154-160 Sauchiehall St, Glasgow G2 3DH *tel:* 0141 332 6631.

HMV Shop. 72 Union St, Glasgow G1 3QS *tel:* 0141 221 1850. *Records, cassettes, CDs, books, videos.*

Tower Records. 217-221 Argyle St, Glasgow G2 8DL *tel:* 0141 204 2500 *fax:* 0141 248 3640.

Virgin Megastore. Unit 4, Lewis Bldg, Argyle St, Glasgow G1 2AQ *tel:* 0141 221 2606 *fax:* 0141 221 2607. *CDs, cassettes and videos.*

Wales

Cardiff County Borough

Cardiff

HMV Shop. 51 Queen St, Cardiff CF1 4AS *tel:* 029 2022 7147. *Records, cassettes, CDs.*

Pembrokeshire

Haverfordwest

Swales Music Centre Ltd. 2-6 High St, Haverfordwest, Pembs SA61 2DJ *tel:* 01437 762059 *fax:* 01437 760872 *email:* musician@swalesmusic.co.uk. *Records, cassettes, CDs, m/order.*

Swansea County

Swansea

HMV Shop. 21-23 Queens Arcade, The Quadrant Centre, Swansea SA1 3QW *tel:* 01792 462094 *fax:* 01792 455138. *LPs, CDs, videos, accs.*

Services

The Queen's Household

Master of the Queen's Music: Malcolm Williamson CBE AO. c/o Campion Press Music Publishers, Sandon, Buntingford, Herts SG9 0QW *tel:* 01763 247287 *fax:* 01763 249984.

Organist, Choirmaster and Composer, HM Chapels Royal: Richard Popplewell MVO FRCO FRCM. St James Palace, London SW1A 1BG *tel:* 020 7930 3007.

Organist and Choirmaster, HM Chapel Royal: Carl Jackson. Hampton Court Palace, East Molesey, Surrey KT8 9AU *tel:* 020 8781 9597 *fax:* 020 8977 4771 *email:* carl_jackson@ccis.org.uk.

Department for Culture, Media and Sport

2-4 Cockspur St, London SW1Y 5DH *tel:* 020 7211 6200 *email:* enquiries@culture.gov.uk. Rt Hon Chris Smith MP, Secretary of State; Rt Hon Alan Howarth CBE MP, Minister for the Arts; Rt Hon Janet Anderson MP, Minister for Tourism, Film and Broadcasting; Rt Hon Kate Hoey MP, Minister for Sport; Robin Young, permanent sec; Paul Bolt, dir of strategy and communications.

The Department for Culture, Media and Sport exercises responsibility for arts, sports, national lottery, libraries, museums, galleries, broadcasting, media, heritage and tourism.

British Council

Performing Arts Dept, 11 Portland Place, London W1N 4EJ *tel:* 020 7389 3005/3010 *fax:* 020 7389 3057. John Kieffer, dir of performing arts. *Promotes educational, cultural and technical co-operation between Britain and other countries. The Council's work is designed to establish long-term and worldwide partnerships and to improve international understanding.*

The Arts Group of the British Council

11 Portland Place, London W1N 4EJ *tel:* 020 7930 8466 *fax:* 020 7389 3199. John Tod, dir; Andrea Rose, head of visual arts; Simon Gammell, head of drama and dance; Alistair Niven, head of literature; Paul Howson, head of film and television; Christopher Wade, head of design group.

Visiting Arts

11 Portland Place, London W1N 4EJ *tel:* 020 7389 3019 *fax:* 020 7389 3016 *email:* office@visitingarts.demon.co.uk. Terry Sandell OBE, dir; Camilla Edwards, deputy dir; Richard Lambert, chmn; Nelson Fernandez, Melissa Naylor, asst dirs. *Visiting Arts is a joint venture of the Arts Councils of England, Wales and Northern Ireland and the Scottish Arts Council, the Crafts Council, the Foreign and Commonwealth Office and the British Council. Visiting Arts is an advisory, consultancy and information organisation which promotes and facilitates the inward flow of foreign arts into England, Scotland, Wales and Northern Ireland in the context of the contribution they can make to cultural relations, cultural awareness and fostering mutually beneficial international arts contacts and activities at national, regional and institutional levels.*

Arts Council of England

14 Great Peter St, London SW1P 3NQ *tel:* 020 7333 0100 *fax:* 020 7973 6590. Gerry Robinson, chmn; Peter Hewitt, chief exec; Hilary Carty, dance dir. Music Department Staff: Hilary Boulding, mus dir; Phill Ward, opera, mus theatre, contemporary mus; Andrew Pinnock, mus educ, early mus, amateur and mus for youth; Genevieve Newton, orch; Rajan Hooper, traditional mus, jazz and non-western mus, recordings; Graeme Wall, new mus. *The Arts Council receives a grant-in-aid from the government, and is incorporated under Royal Charter with the following objects: (a) to develop and improve the knowledge, understanding and practice of the arts; (b) to increase the accessibility of the arts to the public and (c) to advise and co-operate with Government departments, local authorities and other bodies on any matters concerned whether directly or indirectly with the foregoing objects. The members of the Council, who may not exceed 20 in number, are appointed by the Secretary of State for the National Heritage. Funds from the National Lottery for the Arts in England are administered by the Arts Council of England's National Lottery Department, which aims to give the maximum benefit to the public by supporting arts projects which make an important and lasting difference to the quality of life of people throughout England.*

Arts Council of Northern Ireland

MacNeice House, 77 Malone Rd, Belfast BT9 6AQ *tel:* 028 9038 5200 *fax:* 028 9066 1715 *email:* performance@artscouncil-ni.org. Brian Ferran, chief exec; Philip Hammond, dir of performing arts. *The Arts Council of Northern Ireland, funded by the British Government via the Department of Education for Northern Ireland, has functions of subsidy and promotion similar to those of the Arts Council of England.*

Arts Council of Wales

9 Museum Place, Cardiff CF10 3NX *tel:* 029 2037 6500 *minicom:* 029 2039 0027 *fax:* 029 2022 1447 *email:* information@ccc-acw.org.uk. Joanna Weston, chief exec.

Arts Council of Wales, North Wales Office. 36 Prince's Drive, Colwyn Bay LL29 8LA *tel:* 01492 533440 *minicom:* 01492 532288 *fax:* 01492 533677. *Conwy, Denbighshire, Flintshire, Gwynedd, Isle of Anglesey, Wrexham, Montgomeryshire area of Powys.*

Arts Council of Wales, Mid and West Wales Office. 6 Gardd Llydaw, Jackson's Lane, Carmarthen SA31 1QD *tel:* 01267 234248 *fax:* 01267 233084. *Carmarthenshire, Ceredigion, Pembrokeshire, Swansea, Neath Port Talbot, Powys.*

Scottish Arts Council

12 Manor Place, Edinburgh EH3 7DD *tel:* 0131 226 6051 *fax:* 0131 225 9833 *email:* administrator.sac@artsfb.org.uk. Seona Reid, dir; Nod Knowles, mus dir.

Isle of Man Arts Council

10 Villa Marina Arcade, Douglas, Isle of Man IM1 2HN *tel:* 01624 611316 *fax:* 01624 615423. Lynda Cannell, sec; Dawn Lancaster, arts offr.

International Arts Bureau

4 Baden Place, Crosby Row, London SE1 1YW *tel:* 020 7403 6454 (admin); 020 7403 7001 (enq) *fax:* 020 7403 2009 *email:* iab@mcmail.com. Rod Fisher, dir; Valerie Synmoie, mgr. *Established in 1994 to provide a range of monitoring, research, publication and training services for the Arts Council of England, the Regional Arts Boards, the arts constituency and funding system. Free enquiry service on international arts funding, policies, contracts, etc. Mon-Fri 10am-1pm and 2pm-5pm on above number. Publishes* International Arts Navigator *and, for the Arts Council of England, a quarterly* International Arts Digest. *Other publications available, contact for details.*

The Foundation for Sports and the Arts

PO Box 20, Liverpool L13 1HB *tel:* 0151 259 5505 *fax:* 0151 230 0664. Grattan Endicott, sec to the Trustees. *The FSA was established in 1991 by members of the Pool Promoters' Association. Enquiries by telephone or fax.*

London Boroughs Grants

5th Floor, Regal House, London Rd, Twickenham, Middx TW1 3QS *tel:* 020 8891 5021 *fax:* 020 8891 5874. Andy Ganf, principal grants mgr; Paula Ghosh, principal grants offr. *This organisation supports a wide range of arts projects including theatres, arts centres, touring groups, festivals, one-off events, advice and information groups and museums.*

Music Information Centres

British Music Information Centre. 10 Stratford Place, London W1N 9AE *tel:* 020 7499 8567 *fax:* 020 7499 4795 *email:* bmic@bmic.co.uk. Matthew Greenall, dir.

Irish Contemporary Music Centre. 95 Lower Baggot St, Dublin 2, Ireland *tel:* 00 353 1 661 2105 *fax:* 00 353 1 676 2639 *email:* info@cmc.ie. Eve O'Kelly, dir.

Scottish Music Information Centre. 1 Bowmont Gardens, Glasgow G12 9LR *tel:* 0141 334 6393 *fax:* 0141 337 1161 *email:* smic@glasgow.almac.co.uk. Moray Brooksbank, dir; Alasdair Pettinger, info offr; Caitie Faulds, admin. *Exists to document and promote work by Scottish and Scottish-based composers of all periods.*

Welsh Music Information Centre. Ty Cerdd, 15 Mount Stuart Square, Cardiff CF10 5DP. *Written enquiries only.*

Regional Arts Boards

English Regional Arts Boards. 5 City Rd, Winchester, Hants SO23 8SD *tel:* 01962 851063 *fax:* 01962 842033 *email:* info@erab.org.uk. Christopher Gordon, chief exec; Carolyn Nixson, admin. *The ten Regional Arts Boards in England exist to promote and develop the arts and the audience for the arts in their regions. They provide information, help and guidance to all kinds of arts organisations in their area and in many cases can provide financial assistance. English Regional Arts Boards is the representative body for the ten RABs. Its Winchester secretariat provides project management, services and information for the members and acts on their behalf in appropriate circumstances.*

East Midlands Arts Board. Mountfields House, Epinal Way, Loughborough, Leics LE11 0QE *tel:* 01509 218292 *fax:* 01509 262214 *email:* info.ema@artsfb.org.uk. John Buston, chief exec; Penny Hefferan, arts offr, orch mus; Helen Flach, head of perf arts; Karl Chapman, arts offr, contemporary mus; Deborah Duggan, info offr. *Derbys (excluding the High Peak District), Leics, Lincs, Northants, Rutland and Notts. The Board aims to enrich life in the East Midlands by offering the opportunity for everyone to participate in and enjoy the arts.*

Eastern Arts Board. Cherry Hinton Hall, Cambridge CB1 8DW *tel:* 01223 215355 *fax:* 01223 248075 *email:* music@eastern-arts.co.uk. Rosy Greenlees, acting chief exec; Kate Tyrrell, mus offr. *Beds, Cambs, Essex, Herts (other than London borough overlap), Norfolk, Suffolk.*

London Arts Board. 3rd Floor, Elme House, 133 Long Acre, London WC2E 9AF *tel:* 020 7240 1313 *fax:* 020 7670 2400 *email:* andrew.mckenzie @lonab.co.uk. Trevor Phillips, chmn; Andrew McKenzie, principal mus offr. *Covers the area of 32 boroughs of London and the Corporation of London.*

North West Arts Board. Manchester House, 22 Bridge St, Manchester M3 3AB *tel:* 0161 834 6644 *minicom:* 0161 834 9131 *fax:* 0161 834 6969 *email:* nwarts-info@ mcr1.poptel.org.uk. Debra King, perf arts offr (mus). *Cheshire, Greater Manchester, High Peak (Derbys), Lancs, Merseyside.*

Northern Arts Board. 9-10 Osborne Terrace, Jesmond, Newcastle upon Tyne NE2 1NZ *tel:* 0191 281 6334 *fax:* 0191 281 3276 *email:* nab@norab.demon.co.uk. Andrew Dixon, chief exec; Brian Debnam, head of perf arts; Mark Monument, Mark Mulqueen, offrs for perf arts. *Teesside, Cumbria, Durham, Northumberland, Tyne and Wear.*

South East Arts. Union House, Bridge Rd, Tunbridge Wells, Kent TN4 8HF *tel:* 01892 507200 *fax:* 01892 549383. Debra Reay, dir perf arts; Jonathan Dabner, mus offr; Felicity Harvest, chief exec. *Kent, Surrey, E and W Sussex.*

South West Arts. Bradninch Place, Gandy St, Exeter EX4 3LS *tel:* 01392 218188 *fax:* 01392 413554 *email:* info@swa.co.uk. Nicholas Capaldi, chief exec; Ouvrielle Holmes, Sarah Holmes, perf arts admin. *Regional arts development agency for Cornwall, Devon, Dorset (excluding Bournemouth, Christchurch, Poole), Glos, Somerset and the unitary authorities of Bath, Bristol, N E Somerset, N Somerset, S Glos, Torbay and Plymouth.*

Southern Arts Board. 13 St Clement St, Winchester, Hants SO23 9DQ *tel:* 01962 855099 *fax:* 01962 861186 *email:* info@southernarts.co.uk. Robert Hutchison, chief exec; David Everett, mus offr; Jane Bryant, educ and planning offr. *Berks, Bucks, SE Dorset (Bournemouth, Christchurch and Poole), Hants, Isle of Wight, Oxon, Wilts.*

West Midlands Arts. 82 Granville St, Birmingham B1 2LH *tel:* 0121 631 3121 *fax:* 0121 643 7239 *email:* info @west-midlands-arts.co.uk. Sally Luton, chief exec; Val Birchall, mus offr. *Herefordshire, Worcestershire, Staffs, Warwicks and Shrops, Stoke-on-Trent, Telford and Wrekin and the metropolitan districts of Birmingham, Coventry, Dudley, Sandwell, Solihull, Walsall and Wolverhampton.*

Yorkshire Arts. 21 Bond St, Dewsbury, W Yorks WF13 1AX *tel:* 01924 455555 *fax:* 01924 466522 *email:* info@yarts.co.uk. Roger Lancaster, chief exec; Jim Beirne, head of perf arts; Andrew Cleaton, mus offr. *S Yorks, W Yorks, N Yorks, N Lincs, N E Lincs, E Riding and Hull and York cities.*

National Music Council

Francis House, Francis St, London SW1P 1DE *tel:* 020 8347 8618 *also fax*. Russell Jones, chmn; Mark Isherwood, deputy chmn; Jennifer Goodwin, admin.

Founded in 1953, the National Music Council is an organisation dedicated to promoting and representing the interests of those working within the field of music in the United Kingdom. It is also the UK representative on the International Music Council (UNESCO) through which it acts as a voice for British music within Europe and throughout the world.

The Council co-ordinates the publication of a regular newsletter and an annual programme of seminars and meetings thus providing a forum through which shared interests and concerns can be voiced, and the means for concerted action agreed. Membership is open to all organisations with an interest in the development of music in the UK; professional, voluntary and amateur, subsidised and commercial, creative and educational.

The Council is also committed to promoting the advancement of music education and provision. Each year, in collaboration with the Association of County Councils, the Association of District Councils and the Association of Metropolitan Authorities acting through the Council of Local Education Authorities, the National Music Council presents awards to those local authorities and local education authorities that have demonstrated an outstanding commitment to music.

Associations

This list includes musical societies devoted to a named composer or instrument. Organisations for and on behalf of people with disabilities (including organisations for the practice of music therapy) are grouped together in a separate list immediately following this section (*see* **Music and Disability**). The **Musicians' Union** regional offices are listed at the end of this section.

Access to Music. 18 York Rd, Leicester LE1 5TS *tel:* 0116 255 1936 *fax:* 0116 255 1938 *email:* alan@access-to-music.co.uk. John Ridgeon, dir. *Independent mus training organisation currently running foundation courses in contemporary popular mus (2 years, f/t) at various locations around the country. Accredited by the Open College Network in the South East Midlands at level 3. A one year pre-foundation course is also available. Instrumental Music Facilitator Course (30 weeks, p/t) also running aimed at mature musicians who wish to teach mus (accredited as above). For further information on courses contact the mkt dept on 0800 281842.*

Adult Residential Colleges Association (ARCA). PO Box 31, Washbrook, Ipswich, Suffolk IP8 3HP *tel:* 01473 730737 *also fax. Short courses averaging 2 to 7 days. Many member colleges include mus in the range of subjects covered.*

Alan Bush Music Trust. 127 Halton Rd, Sutton Coldfield, W Midlands B73 6NY *tel:* 0121 355 3265 *email:* info@alanbushtrust.org.uk. Michael Hinson, hon sec; Maeve O'Higgins, chair; Rachel O'Higgins, info sec; Paul O'Higgins, treasurer; Catherine Hinson, publicity sec. *Promotes the mus of Alan Bush through information resources, projects and events. Publishes annual newsletter* Clarion.

Alkan Society. 21 Heronswood, Salisbury, Wilts SP2 8DH *tel:* 01722 325771 *also fax.* Peter Grove, hon sec. *Founded in 1977. Publishes a bulletin 3 times pa, also discography. One all-day meeting pa in London.*

Alwyn (William) Foundation. Lark Rise, Dunwich Rd, Blythburgh, Halesworth, Suffolk IP19 9LT *tel:* 01502 478331 *also fax; email:* WAF@innotts.co.uk. Mary Alwyn, archivist. *Promotes the study, performance and recording of the mus and writings of William Alwyn.*

The Alwyn (William) Society. 122 Vernon Ave, Old Basford, Nottingham NG6 0AL *tel:* 0115 978 0863 *fax:* 0115 913 0860. Andrew Palmer, sec; Mary Alwyn, president; Vilem Tausky, patron. *Aims to widen knowledge and encourage the performance of Alwyn's work. Regular newsletters; information on Alwyn's life and work.*

Arnold (Malcolm) Society. 6 Walton St, Barnsley, S Yorks S75 2PE *tel:* 01226 284116 *also fax.* Keith Llewellyn, hon sec. *Exists to promote the mus of Sir Malcolm Arnold. Quarterly newsletter, concert details, reviews and details of recorded mus.*

The Arts Foundation. 2nd Floor, 6 Salem Rd, London W2 4BU *tel:* 020 7229 3813 *fax:* 020 7229 4047. John Kieffer, mgr. *A private, charitable organisation established to foster innovation and patronage in the arts by awarding Fellowships to individual artists. No open applications accepted: nominations only.*

Arts Marketing Association. Bolton's Warehouse, 23 Tenison Rd, Cambridge CB1 2DG *tel:* 01223 578078 *fax:* 01223 578079 *email:* info@a-m-a.co.uk. Tim Baker, chmn. *National body for arts marketeers providing advice, speaker's tours, mentoring, newsletters, jobwatch and an annual conference.*

Associated Board of the Royal Schools of Music. 14 Bedford Square, London WC1B 3JG *tel:* 020 7636 5400 *fax:* 020 7637 0234 *email:* abrsm@abrsm.ac.uk. Richard Morris, chief exec; Philip Mundey, dir exams; Richard Crozier, dir, professional development course; Suzannah Power, head of mkt. *The Associated Board offers a graded system of mus exams from preparatory level to professional diploma. Exams are offered in 35 insts, jazz pno, jazz ens, singing, choral singing, practical musicianship and theory. Over half a million candidates are examined each year world-wide. A Professional Development Course is available for inst and singing teachers, leading to the qualification of CT ABRSM.*

Association for the Advancement of Teacher Education in Music *see* **National Association of Music Educators.**

Association British Choral Directors

REGIONAL & NATIONAL EVENTS

conducting training
workshops
masterclasses
repertoire sessions
discussion forums
open rehearsals

15th Annual Choral Conductors' Convention
August 24-27 2000 Chester UK

CALLING...

choir trainers
choral directors
teachers
organists
animateurs
students
lecturers
composers
singers

Membership 1999/2000
Student – £12 Individual – £25 Joint – £37
Associate/Corporate on request

Further info General Secretary ABCD
46 Albert St Tring HP23 6AU
tel/fax 01442 891633

email
marie.louise.petit@abcd.org.uk

website
www.abcd.org.uk

NEW

Choral Conducting Courses

Beginner Intermediate Advanced

All levels - October 1999 - April 2000 London
4 Sunday afternoons and residential weekend
Tutors - Peter Broadbent Jo McNally Therees Hibbard
Focusing on practical aspects of choral conducting at each level
Cost - £275 including meals & accommodation
Accreditation - Roehampton Institute London Trinity College of Music

Further courses in 2000 across UK

Course outlines, dates, venues, costs & forms from General Secretary NON-MEMBERS WELCOME

ABCD is a registered charity which exists to promote choral music education

Charity registration No. 1016594

Association for Business Sponsorship of the Arts. Nutmeg House, 60 Gainsford St, Butlers Wharf, London SE1 2NY *tel:* 020 7378 8143 *fax:* 020 7407 7527 *email:* absa@dircon.co.uk. Colin Tweedy, chief exec. *National organisation promoting business support for the arts. Manages the Pairing Scheme (formerly Business Sponsorship Incentive Scheme, BSIS), and Business in the Arts (BIA), on behalf of Department for Culture, Media and Sport.*

Association for Business Sponsorship of the Arts (Scotland). 13 Abercrambie Place, Edinburgh EH3 6LB *tel:* 0131 558 1277 *fax:* 0131 558 3370. Alison Hogg, dir. *To provide services and advice to the business and arts communities on business sponsorship; to run the government's Pairing Scheme and Business in the Arts, and promote business support of the arts.*

Association for Business Sponsorship of the Arts (Wales and South West England). 16 Museum Place, Cardiff CF1 3BH *tel:* 029 2030 3023 *fax:* 029 2030 3024. Gavin Backley, dir; Rachel Jones, mgr.

Association of British Choral Directors (ABCD). 46 Albert St, Tring, Herts HP23 6AU *tel:* 01442 891633 *also fax; email:* marie.louise.petit @abcd.org.uk. Marie-Louise Petit, gen sec; Howard Layfield, chair. *The association and forum for choral conds. Promotes educ, training and development for choral conds and teachers in all sectors of activity and all standards. Holds regional events throughout the UK; annual convention each Aug bank holiday w/end.*

Association of British Jazz Musicians. Jazz Services, Africa House, 64-78 Kingsway, London WC2B 6BD *tel:* 020 7405 0737 *fax:* 020 7405 0828 *email:* admin@jazzservices.org.uk. Chris Hodgkins. *Represents the interests of jazz musicians in the UK who are members of the Musicians' Union.*

Association of British Orchestras. Pegasus House, 37-43 Sackville St, London W1X 1DB *tel:* 020 7333 0371 *fax:* 020 7287 9959 *email:* info@abo.org.uk. Libby MacNamara, dir; Fiona Penny, educ development mgr; Alex Knight, project mgr; Alison White, membership mgr. *Representation of the collective interests of professional UK orchs: conferences, seminars, negotiation, training and general advocacy.*

Association of Educational Advisers in Scotland. Cunninghame House, Irvine, KA12 8EE *tel:* 01294 324450 *fax:* 01294 324444. Jan Ward, snr adviser, curriculum development, president.

Association of English Singers and Speakers. 16a Cromwell Ave, Highgate, London N6 5HL *tel:* 020 8347 6889. Jill White, chmn. *Aims to encourage the communication of English words in speech and song with clarity, understanding and imagination.*

Association of Irish Choirs. 4 Drinan St, Cork, Republic of Ireland *tel:* 00 353 21 312296 *fax:* 00 353 21 962457 *email:* cnc@iol.ie. Barbara Heas, admin. *Established in 1980 to promote choral mus and singing. Organises annual summer school and other courses; publishes choral mus; administers the Irish Youth Choir; issues newsletter* In-Choir.

Association of Medical Advisers to the British Orchestras (AMABO) *see* **British Performing Arts Medicine Trust.**

Association of Professional Composers *see* **British Academy of Composers and Songwriters.**

Association of Professional Music Therapists. 26 Hamlyn Rd, Glastonbury, Somerset BA6 8HT *tel:* 01458 834919 *also fax; email:* APMToffice@aol.com. Diana Asbridge, admin. *Deals with the needs of professional mus therapists in relation to standards of practice, employment career structure, training, etc.*

Association of Professional Recording Services LTD (APRS). PO Box 111, Uckfield TN22 5WQ *tel:* 01803 868600 *fax:* 01803 868444 *email:* info@aprs.co.uk. Mark Broad, chief exec. *Trade association for businesses and individuals involved in professional sound recording and associated fields; organises annual international APRS Audio Exhibition in London.*

Association of Teachers and Lecturers (ATL). 7 Northumberland St, London WC2N 5DA *tel:* 020 7930 6441 *fax:* 020 7930 1359 *email:* info@atl.org.uk. Peter Smith, gen sec. *Provides over 150,000 members (5000 mus teachers) with full trade union services. Also curriculum development.*

Association of Teachers of Singing. 146 Greenstead Rd, Colchester, Essex CO1 2SN *tel:* 01206 867462 *also fax.* Norman Tattersall, conference dir; Colin J Schooling, sec and treasurer. *For qualified teachers of singing; holds annual conference in different venues and spring and winter conference in London.*

Association of University Teachers. Egmont House, 25-31 Tavistock Place, London WC1H 9UT *tel:* 020 7670 9700 *fax:* 020 7670 9799 *email:* hq@aut.org.uk. David Triesman, gen sec.

Association of University Teachers (Scotland and Northumbria). 6 Castle St, Edinburgh EH2 3AT *tel:* 0131 226 6694 *fax:* 0131 226 2066 *email:* scotland&ne@aut.org.uk. David Bleiman, asst gen sec; Tony Axon, research offr; Lesley Little, admin offr. *Professional association for academic and related staff in universities.*

Association of Woodwind Teachers. 90 Becmead Ave, Kenton, Middx HA3 8HB *tel:* 020 8907 8428 *also fax;* 07710 520539; 01234 301236 *email:* cbarlowuk@aol.com. Angela Fussell, chmn; Caroline Barlow, sec. *The aims of the association are to promote and encourage high standards of w/wind teaching and to give support and practical help to w/wind teachers both specialist and general. Also encourages professional development through exchange of information and mutual support.*

Association of Workers for Children with Emotional and Behavioural Difficulties. Charlton Court, East Sutton, nr Maidstone, Kent ME17 3DQ *tel:* 01622 843104 *fax:* 01622 844220 *email:* awcebd@mistral.co.uk. Allan Rimmer, admin offr. *Serves all disciplines involved with children with emotional and behavioural difficulties.*

Audio Engineering Society Ltd. PO Box 645, Slough SL1 8BJ *tel:* 01628 663725 *fax:* 01628 667002 *email:* uk@aes.org. Heather Lane, admin. *International society of 11,000 members in the world of audio. Over 700 members in British section.*

Australian Music Centre. 51b Dartmouth Rd, London NW2 4EP *tel:* 020 8208 1541 *also fax; email:* gray-dupuy@mcmail.com. Tony Gray, UK rep. *Object is to promote performance and awareness of Australian mus in Britain. Library of scores and recordings.*

The Bagpipe Society. 25 Baden Rd, Evington, Leicester LE5 5PA *tel:* 0116 273 4453. Tim Garland, publicity offr. *For all types of folk, early and art bagpipes. Regular newsletters, journals, diary of bagpipe events and other publications.*

Baptist Music Network. 19 Limefields Way, East Hunsbury, Northampton NN4 0SA *tel:* 01604 760928. Paul Lavender, chmn and training offr; Lesley Goulbourne, admin. *Offers practical help and encouragement to those involved with mus in churches.*

Barbirolli Society. 2 Cedar Close, Uttoxeter, Staffs ST14 7NP *tel:* 01889 564562 *also fax.* Pauline Pickering, chmn. *Dedicated to keeping alive the art of Sir John Barbirolli through the re-issue of his recordings.*

Beecham (Sir Thomas) Trust. 15 North Pallant, Chichester, W Sussex PO19 1TQ *tel:* 01243 789855. Shirley, Lady Beecham, A M Mackarel Davies, trustees; Christopher R Hopper MVO, chmn. *The provision of scholarships and awards at certain universities and mus institutions throughout the UK.*

Benslow Association. Little Benslow Hills, off Benslow Lane, Hitchin, Herts SG4 9RB *tel:* 01462 459446 *fax:* 01462 440171. Jean Williams, chmn. *The Friends of Benslow Music Trust.*

Benslow Music Trust. Little Benslow Hills, off Benslow Lane, Hitchin, Herts SG4 9RB *tel:* 01462 459446 *fax:* 01462 440171 *email:* BMusicT@aol.com. Helen Marshall, mus mgr. *National centre for residential w/end and midweek mus courses and meeting place for amateur musicians of all standards. Over 100 short courses each year. Aged 16 and over.*

Berkshire Young Musicians Trust. Stoneham Court, 100 Cockney Hill, Reading RG30 4EZ *tel:* 0118 901 2350 *fax:* 0118 901 2351 *email:* david_marcou@bymt-po.ccmail.compuserve.com. David Marcou, principal; Lady Solti, Evelyn Glennie OBE, patrons. *Provides a wide range of mus opportunities in schools, mus centres and at county level.*

The Bliss Trust. c/o Taylor Joynson Garrett, Carmelite, 50 Victoria Embankment, Blackfriars, London EC4Y 0DX *tel:* 020 7353 1234 *fax:* 020 7936 2666. Sarah Faulder, chmn. *To promote understanding and awareness of the mus of Arthur Bliss through performance, recordings, research, academic writing and publication. Awards, prizes and scholarships are offered mainly through centres of learning and educ.*

Boughton (The Rutland) Music Trust. 25 Bearton Green, Hitchin, Herts SG5 1UN *tel:* 01462 434318. Carolyn Boughton, hon sec; Vernon Handley, president; Michael Hurd, mus adviser. *Registered charity established in 1978 to promote the works of Rutland Boughton. Mailing list. Publicity leaflet available.*

Brian (Havergal) Society. 5 Eastbury Rd, Watford WD1 4PT *tel:* 01923 224607 *fax:* 01923 250506 *email:* hbs@havergal.demon.co.uk. Alan Marshall, admin sec. *To further public knowledge of Brian's work by supporting and sponsoring its publication, performance and recording.*

Bridge (Frank) Trust. 14 Barlby Rd, London W10 6AR *tel:* 020 8969 3579 *fax:* 020 8969 3579. John Bishop, admin. *Acts as a centre of information about all aspects of Bridge's mus; publishing and recording programme.*

British Academy of Composers and Songwriters. The Penthouse, 4 Brook St, London W1Y 1AA *tel:* 020 7629 0992 *fax:* 020 7629 0993 *email:* info@britishacademy.com. Chris Green, chief exec. *Represents the interests of composers and songwriters across all genres and advises on professional and artistic matters. Quarterly magazine and other printed information. Administers several major awards and events, including the Ivor Novello Awards.*

British Actors' Equity Association. Guild House, Upper St Martin's Lane, London WC2H 9EG *tel:* 020 7379 6000 *fax:* 020 7379 7001

BRITISH ASSOCIATION OF SYMPHONIC BANDS AND WIND ENSEMBLES

BASBWE is **the** Association for everyone with an interest in Wind Music: players, conductors, composers, teachers and publishers.

BASBWE encourages performances of quality wind music at all levels – school, community and professional.

BASBWE has a proud record of commissioning music from Britain's leading composers.

BASBWE manages the National Concert Band Festival sponsored by Boosey & Hawkes plc.

BASBWE publishes *Winds* magazine, an essential resource of news and reviews.

BASBWE *membership includes:*

- Reduced rates for the annual BASBWE Conference and International Wind Festival
- Quarterly magazine *Winds*
- Affiliation to BASBWE Education Trust
- Network of contacts through the Membership Directory
- Information on wind music and performers from around the world

Dates for your diary:

Third RNCM Manchester International Wind Festival and BASBWE Conference
Royal Northern College of Music April 14-16, 2000

Fourth RNCM Manchester International Wind Festival and BASBWE Conference
Royal Northern College of Music April 6-8, 2001

For more information about BASBWE, Winds, Membership and Subscriptions, please contact Brendon Le Page, Executive Officer,
Wayfaring, Smither's Lane, East Peckham, Tonbridge, TN12 5HT, England.
Tel/fax +44(0)1622 872758 BASBWE@winds.org.uk

EQUITY.....

is the organisation that represents singers from across the industry.

Thousands of concert, session, pop, opera singers and choristers belong to Equity and take advantage of the services and peace of mind this brings them:

singers' rates ◆ singers' agreements ◆ singers' task force ◆ singers' committee ◆ singers' register ◆ singers' newsletter ◆ experienced staff who know about singers' needs and issues ◆ information for agents ◆ pension schemes ◆ free insurance cover for accident, public liability and backstage cover ◆ free legal help ◆ free welfare advice ◆ job information service, and many more.

If you are working professionally as a singer and are not yet a member please call one of our six offices, or see our website for details on joining your union:

www.equity.org.uk
London & S. East: 0207 670 0253
North East: 01142 305 294
Scotland & N Ireland: 0141 248 2472
North West: 0161 832 3183
Midlands: 01926 408 638
Wales & S. West: 02920 387 971

.....EQUITY

BRITISH FEDERATION OF YOUNG CHOIRS

BFYC

Encouraging Choral Singing

The British Federation of Young Choirs organises a wide programme of activities to stimulate and develop singing amongst young people throughout the UK. These include singing days and choral workshops, animation schemes, schools' singing projects, and in-service training for conductors and teachers.

Through its affilation to the European Federation of Young Choirs, BFYC offers its members International Singing Weeks and Conductor Study Tours, contact for overseas travel and exchanges, and participation in the European Youth Choir and Youth Parliament.

For further details about BFYC membership, activities and Choral Service, contact:
The BFYC Office
Devonshire House
Devonshire Square
Loughborough
Leics LE11 3DW
Tel: 01509 211664
Fax: 01509 260630

BFS
The British Flute Society

The British Flute Society is Europe's longest-established flute organisation. Its membership includes professional players, teachers, students and amateurs and its journal, Pan, is recognised worldwide as a highly informative and entertaining flute magazine.

Benefits of membership include:

- Pan magazine every quarter, packed with articles, concert, CD and music reviews and listings of concerts, courses and flute events.
- Reduced entry fees for nationwide B.F.S. flute events, which include concerts, masterclasses and opportunities to meet and play with other flautists.
- Discounts of up to 50% for concerts by major British orchestras throughout the country.
- A network of area representatives to put you in touch with players and flute clubs in your area.
- A 10% discount voucher for new members on music and accessories from members of the Association of Flute Traders.
- Six years membership for the price of five.

For an application form contact
Nick Wallbridge (Membership Secretary),
12 Uplands, Croxley Green, Hertfordshire WD3 4RD.

The British Flute Society is a Registered Charity (No. 326473)

email: equity@easynet.co.uk. Ian McGarry, gen sec. *The union representing British actors, singers, dancers, variety artists, stage mgrs, theatre dirs and designers, broadcasters and others in the entertainment business.*

British Arts Festivals Association. 3rd Floor, Whitechapel Library, 77 Whitechapel High St, London E1 7QX *tel:* 020 7247 4667 *fax:* 020 7247 5010 *email:* bafa@netcomuk.co.uk. Gwyn Rhydderch, co-ord. *Aims to represent a full range of arts festivals. Activities include an annual conference, special interest meetings, arts festivals listings and a website directory.*

British Association for Early Childhood Education (BAECE). 111 City View House, 463 Bethnal Green Rd, London E2 9QY *tel:* 020 7739 7594 *fax:* 020 7613 5330. Mrs B Boon, snr admin offr; Mrs J Rabin, project mgr. *Concerned with all aspects of learning for children aged 0-9. Organises national conferences, seminars and meetings; also publishes a newsletter.*

British Association for Performing Arts Medicine *see* **British Performing Arts Medicine Trust.**

British Association of Christian Bands (Brass). Winyards, Lytton Rd, Woking, Surrey GU22 7BH *tel:* 01483 760904. Norman Gerhold, hon sec; Trevor Austin, hon chmn. *Brings Christian musicians together for fellowship and to learn from experienced conds. Branches in Andover, Nottingham, Tyne and Wear and Faversham.*

British Association of Symphonic Bands and Wind Ensembles (BASBWE). Wayfaring, Smithers Lane, Hale St, Tonbridge, Kent TN12 5HT *tel:* 01622 872758 *also fax; email:* basbwe@winds.org.uk. Brendan Le Page, exec offr; John Myatt, chmn; Guy Woolfenden, chmn elect; Sir Simon Rattle, president. *Promotes interest and activities in wind bands and ens nationwide. Quarterly publication* Winds.

British Choral Institute. 6 Chailey Ave, Rottingdean, Brighton BN2 7GH *tel:* 01273 300894 *fax:* 01273 308394 *email:* britchorinst@fastnet.co.uk. Roy Wales, dir; Christine Wales, admin. *Advisory, promotional, educ and training body for choral singers, conds, choral administrators and organisers, with a special emphasis on developing international choral projects.*

The British Clavichord Society. 3 East Castle Rd, Edinburgh EH10 5AP *tel:* 0131 229 8018 *email:* 100603.2732@compuserve.com. Sheila Barnes, membership sec. *Encourages understanding and enjoyment of the clvd, promoting recitals and organising educ activities. Publishes a newsletter 3 times pa, and a comprehensive* Register *which lists performers, makers, tuners and teachers and is available free to all members.*

British Copyright Council. 29-33 Berners St, London W1P 4AA *tel:* 01986 788122 *fax:* 01986 788847. Janet Ibbotson, sec. *Liaison committee of professional associations, trade unions and collecting societies whose individual members own copyright in original literary, dramatic, musical and artistic works, together with publishers' and performers' organisations.*

British Double Reed Society. 9 Hamlyn Gardens, Church Rd, London SE19 2NX *tel:* 020 8653 3625 *email:* john.wingfield@bdrs.demon.co.uk. Deirdre Dundas-Grant, chmn; David Moore, hon sec. *Society established to further the interests of all involved with the ob and bsn.*

British Federation of Audio. 19 Charing Cross Rd, London WC2H 0ES *tel:* 020 7930 3206 *fax:* 020 7839 4613 *email:* chriscowan@british-audio.org.uk. C I C Cowan, sec. *Trade association for British manufacturers of hi-fi audio equipment.*

British Federation of Brass Bands. 17 Kiln Way, Badgers Dene, Grays, Essex RM17 5JE *tel:* 01375 375831 *fax:* 01375 391246 *email:* bfbb@clara.net. Norman Jones, gen sec; Peter Parkes, president. *The national body representing the interests of br bands throughout the UK.*

British Federation of Festivals. Festivals House, 198 Park Lane, Macclesfield, Cheshire SK11 6UD *tel:* 01625 428297 *fax:* 01625 503229 *email:* liz@festivals.demon.co.uk. Liz Whitehead, chief exec. *Headquarters of the amateur mus, speech and dance festival movement.*

British Federation of Young Choirs (BFYC). Devonshire House, Devonshire Square, Leics LE11 3DW *tel:* 01509 211664 *fax:* 01509 260630 *email:* admin@bfyc.demon.co.uk. Susan Lansdale, chief exec; Andrew Fairbairn, hon sec. *Offers events, courses, training and encouragement to people of all ages involved with choral singing. Choral animateurs employed in Scotland, Northern Ireland, the South East, Midlands, East Anglia and London.*

British Flute Society. 61 Queen's Drive, London N4 2BG *tel:* 020 8802 5984 *fax:* 020 8809 7436. Ann Cherry, sec; Nick Wallbridge, membership sec. *Promotes fl playing from beginner to professional standard. Events held throughout the country. Quarterly journal* Pan.

British Horn Society. c/o 50 Kings Hall Rd, Beckenham, Kent BR3 1LS *tel:* 020 8289 8864 *also fax; email:* mikef@tesco.net. Barry Tuckwell,

British Performing Arts Medicine Trust

- Helping performers back to fitness

Performers need to operate at the peak of fitness in order to maintain high standards of work, yet they frequently suffer from injury, strain or stress, either physical or psychological.

Founded in 1984, The British Performing Arts Medicine Trust is a unique charity set up to promote the treatment and study of performing arts injuries and related medical and psychological conditions. We are here to help performers carry on working with minimum disruption and to maximum effect.

The Trust operates a membership organisation for all those interested in performing arts medicine, the British Association for Performing Arts Medicine (BAPAM).

The British Performing Arts Medicine Trust
196 Shaftesbury Avenue, London WC2H 8JL
Tel: 0171 240 3331 (Admin)
Tel: 0171 240 4500 (Helpline, London)
Tel: 0845 602 0235 (Helpline, all other areas)
E-mail: bpamt@dial. pipex.com

Registered Charity No. 326786

BRITISH SOCIETY FOR MUSIC THERAPY

BSMT

Information
Meetings and conferences
Publications • Membership

Members receive yearly:

- 2 issues of the British Journal of Music Therapy
- 3 issues of the BSMT *Bulletin*
- Reduced admission fees to meetings and conferences
- Details of new books, videos and BSMT publications

The BSMT is a Registered Charity – donations can extend music therapy sessions nationwide, assist musicians during music therapy training and support the profession by helping to fund the Information Service.

BSMT
25 Rosslyn Avenue, East Barnet, Herts, EN4 8DH
Tel and Fax: 020 8368 8879
E-mail: Denize@bsmt.demon.co.uk
website: www.bsmt.org.uk

BRITISH TROMBONE SOCIETY

Promoting the trombone and its repertoire in all musical styles.

President: Mark Nightingale

The BTS presents the greatest trombonists from UK and abroad in concerto performances, recitals, jazz nights, workshops and teaching seminars. The annual Festival is held at a different location each year offering a full day of trombone playing and education, with a massed trombone choir session that everyone can join in.

Membership details and free copy of the BTS magazine *"The Trombonist"* from

BRITISH TROMBONE SOCIETY
PO Box 817 London SE21 7BY
email: http://www.trombone-society.org.uk
Affiliated to the International Trombone Association

The Friends of Cathedral Music

President: Dr George Guest CBE

A message for everyone who is inspired by the sound of a cathedral choir

Our founder, Ronald Sibthorp, started FCM to ginger up low performing standards in cathedral sung services after World War II. Nowadays, cathedral choirs are achieving ever better results and are heard by more and more people, thanks to broadcasting, records and tourism.

FCM's part in this recovery is widely recognised. We now have over 2,500 members; their subscriptions, combined with our invested capital funds, enable us to disburse over £100,000 annually in grants to cathedrals which have requested our help. The grants of up to £15,000 go to help meet collective or individual chorister needs.

In 1999 our grants were:
Hereford, Newcastle and St Woolos Cathedrals – each get £15,000

Manchester Cathedral –	£12,000	St Asaph Cathedral –	£7,000
Rochester Cathedral –	£10,000	Durham Cathedral –	£6,000
St Davids Cathedral –	£8,000	Coventry Cathedral –	£4,000

We need your support!

The subscription to FCM is not fixed, you give what you want to.

For membership application forms write to:
FCM [BMYB], 61 Leigh Gardens, Kensal Rise, London NW10 5HN
E-mail: fcm@netcomuk.co.uk

You will then receive details of our activities and publications

The Friends of Cathedral Music is a registered charity (No: 285121). Founded in 1956, it exists to promote cathedral music and give financial support to cathedral choirs

president; Shirley Hopkins, hon chmn. *Dedicated to the art, craft and fun of hn-playing. Student, amateur and professional membership. Organises festivals, w/shops and publishes* The Horn *magazine.*

British Institute of Organ Studies. Clifford Manor (West Wing), Judges Lane, Newent, Glos GL18 1JY. Jim Berrow, sec; Peter Williams, chmn. *Dedicated to the scholarly study and conservation of historic British orgs, their source materials and repertoire. Operates an advisory service and administers the British Organ Archive, the National Pipe Organs Register and the Historic Organs Certificate Scheme. Regular day and residential conferences and publications.*

The British and International Bass Forum. Studio Ten, Farnham Maltings, Farnham, Surrey GU9 7QR *tel:* 01252 319610 *also fax; email:* bibf@classical-artists.com. David Heyes, admin, ed. *Promotes the db in all aspects of performance and educ. International membership (21 countries). Four magazines per year. Bass-Fest Composition Competition.*

British Kodály Academy. 13 Midmoor Rd, London SW19 4JD *tel:* 020 8946 6528 *fax:* 020 8946 6561 *email:* enquiries@britishkodalyac.demon.co.uk; celiacviic@aol.com. Celia Cviic, treasurer and courses sec; Jane Lee, chmn; Brenda Harris, sec and w/shop sec. *Offers teacher training according to the Kodály concept in mus educ through w/shops and INSET courses throughout the UK. Also w/end courses, diploma courses and an annual summer school.*

British Music Information Centre. 10 Stratford Place, London W1N 9AE *tel:* 020 7499 8567 *fax:* 020 7499 4795 *email:* bmic@bmic.co.uk. Matthew Greenall, dir; Simon Woolf, information mgr. *Scores and recordings collection of 20th C British classical mus: reading and listening facilities available. Free admission; open Mon-Fri, noon-5pm. Concerts, usually Tue and Thu 7.30pm.*

British Music Society. 30 Chester Rd, Watford, Herts WD1 7DQ *tel:* 01923 230111. David Burkett, hon sec; Stephen Trowell, membership enquiries; orders: 7 Tudor Gardens, Upminster, Essex RM14 3DE *tel:* 01708 224795. *Concentrates particularly on promoting an interest in neglected British composers through learned publications, professionally produced recordings and live concerts.*

British Performing Arts Medicine Trust. 196 Shaftesbury Ave, London WC2H 8JL *tel:* 020 7240 4500 (helpline)/240 3331 (admin) *fax:* 020 7240 3335 *email:* bpamt@dial.pipex.com. Eileen Quilter Williams, general admin; Angela Spurrier, asst admin; Yinka Fasawe, helpline co-ord. *Founded in 1984, aims via its helplines, clinics and contacts to put performers in touch with medical expertise, both physical and psychiatric, conventional and alternative practitioners, who may be able to help them overcome or reduce injury and illness.*

The British Phonographic Industry Ltd. 25 Savile Row, London W1X 1AA *tel:* 020 7287 4422 *fax:* 020 7287 2252 *email:* general@bpi.co.uk. John Deacon, dir gen. *Trade association for British record companies.*

British Piano Duo Association. 15 Birchmead Close, St Albans, Herts AL3 6BS *tel:* 01727 858485 *also fax*. Harvey Dagul, president; Isabel Beyer, president. *Encourages the study and performance of the pno duo repertoire on one and two pnos.*

British Radio & Electronic Equipment Manufacturers Association. 19 Charing Cross Rd, London WC2H 0ES *tel:* 020 7930 3206 *fax:* 020 7839 4613. H Peltor CBE, dir. *Trade association for manufacturers in the consumer electronics industry.*

British Recording Media Association. Ambassador House, Brigstock Rd, Thornton Heath, Surrey CR7 7JG *tel:* 020 8665 5395 *fax:* 020 8665 6447 *email:* brma@admin.co.uk. A C Skipper, sec. *Representative organisation for manufacturers of blank audio and video tape and other recording media.*

British Society for Music Therapy. 25 Rosslyn Ave, E Barnet, Herts EN4 8DH *tel:* 020 8368 8879 *also fax; email:* denize@bsmt.demon.co.uk. Denize Christophers, admin. *Promotes the use of mus therapy in the treatment, educ and rehabilitation of children and adults suffering from emotional, physical or mental handicap. Holds meetings and conferences, publishes papers and a journal for members. Membership is open to all interested in mus therapy.*

British Society for Practitioners of Jewish Music. Membership Secretary, 16 Park Farm Close, East End Rd, London N2 0PU *tel:* 020 8883 1773 *also fax*. Viv Bellos, membership secretary; Alex Knapp, chair; Barry Weinberg, treasurer; John Abramson, secretary. *Raises the profile of practitioners in the field of Jewish mus. Provides a practical and intellectual forum for the exchange of information, ideas and resources. Events cover a wide range of topics associated with Jewish mus. Directory of members is available to members.*

British Suzuki Institute. 39 High St, Wheathampstead, Herts AL4 8BB *tel:* 01582 832424 *fax:* 01582 834488 *email:* bsi@suzukimusic.force9.co.uk. Suzanne Porter, gen sec. *Suzuki teacher training in vn, pno, vc and fl. P/t courses lead to Diploma of European Suzuki Association.*

British Trombone Society. PO Box 817, London SE21 7BY *tel:* 020 8658 0405 *also fax* (sec); 020 8340 4109 *also fax* (ed) *email:* cellobone@aol.com (mem sec); lerncurv@aol.com (ed). John Edney, membership sec; Anthony Parsons, ed. *Open to all ages and abilities interested in the trb.*

British Violin Making Association. 114 Mid St, South Nutfield, Redhill, Surrey RH1 4JH *tel:* 01737 822341 *fax:* 01737 823512 *email:* j.topham@btinternet.com. John Topham, sec; Marc Soubeyran, chmn; Florian Leonhard, treasurer. *Aims to promote the craft of vn and bow making in all aspects.*

Calouste Gulbenkian Foundation (UK Branch). 98 Portland Place, London W1N 4ET *tel:* 020 7636 5313 *fax:* 020 7637 3421. Ben Whitaker, dir. *Grant-giving foundation (UK and Ireland only) which also publishes books within the three policy areas of social welfare, arts and educ. Send for free 'Advice for Applicants' before applying.*

Cambridge Society of Musicians. PO Box 107, Manchester M14 7SL *tel:* 0161 225 0445 *fax:* 0161 224 4530 *email:* csm@music-services.demon.co.uk. Lee P Longden, dir; Ian Roche, admin dean; Nicholas Groves, academic dean. *A learned society which elects experienced musicians to membership, and formally qualified musicians to the higher grades of Associateship and Fellowship.*

Careers Research and Advisory Centre (CRAC Ltd). Sheraton House, Castle Park, Cambridge CB3 0AX *tel:* 01223 460277 *fax:* 01223 311708 *email:* enquiries@crac.org.uk. Helen Dickson, mkt mgr; Donald McGregor, chief exec. *CRAC is an independent development agency and registered educ charity founded in 1964. It provides information, informs policy, anticipates developments and identifies practical solutions in careers, educ and guidance and lifelong learning.*

Carreras (José), Friends of. 89 Gordon Rd, Corringham, Essex SS17 7QZ *tel:* 01375 678788 *also fax*. Joan Sheppard, chmn. *Appreciation society; career information. Leukaemia Foundation fundraising. 1000+ members worldwide.*

The Carreras (José) Society. 26 Denbydale Way, Royton, Oldham OL2 5TJ *tel:* 0161 624 5264 *fax:* 0161 287 8234 *email:* jsoc@chantler1.demon.co.uk. Patricia Chantler, organiser. *Artistic appreciation society and support group for the José Carreras International Leukaemia Foundation worldwide membership.*

Cathedral Music, Friends of. Aeron House, Llangeitho, Tregaron, Ceredigion SY25 6SU *tel:* 01974 821614 *also fax; email:* joycooke@aol.com. Michael Cooke, hon sec; Alan Thurlow, chmn. *To assist cathedrals financially in maintaining their mus and to increase public awareness of the unique heritage of cathedral mus.*

Cathedral Organists' Association. Royal School of Church Music, Cleveland Lodge, Westhumble, Dorking RH5 6BW *tel:* 01306 877676 *fax:* 01306 887260 *email:* cl@rscm.com. John Harper, dir. *Association of present and former cathedral organists.*

Catholic Stage Guild. Corpus Christi, 1 Maiden Lane, London WC2E 7NP *tel:* 020 7240 1221. Ann Rutherford, hon sec. *For Catholics engaged in the theatre, films, TV, radio and allied arts including actors, directors, writers, performers, musicians and technicians.*

Cavatina Chamber Music Trust. 52d Maresfield Gardens, London NW3 5RX *tel:* 020 7435 8479 *fax:* 020 7431 2737 *email:* majaro@clara.net. Simon Majaro, Pamela Majaro, trustees. *Aims to preserve the tradition of chmbr mus for young people by performances in schools and private venues and by giving young ens a chance to perform. Also offers a subsidised ticket scheme for selected concerts in major arts venues.*

Cello Club. 12 Pierrepoint Rd, London W3 9JH *tel:* 020 8248 9067 *also fax; email:* celloclub@wbruce.demon.co.uk. William Bruce, dir; Christopher Bunting, president. *A non-profit making national club for young cellists. Members receive three magazines and three newsletters each year on everything to do with the vc world, the opportunity to participate in special vc events and discounts on vc supplies.*

Central Composers' Alliance. 21 Kingsway Rd, Leicester LE5 5TL *tel:* 0116 273 6257. Sir Richard Rodney Bennett, patron; Andrew Downes, president; David Fisher, chmn; Terence Thompson, treasurer; Peter Crump, sec. *An alliance of composers resident in the Midlands and neighbouring counties, or with Midlands connections to promote their mus through performance, recording and other means and to stimulate mutual support among members. Open to all bona fide composers.*

Centre For Creative Communities. Ground Floor, 118 Commercial St, London E1 6NF *tel:* 020 7247 5385 *fax:* 020 7247 5256 *email:* baaa@easynet.co.uk. Jennifer Williams, exec dir. *Organisation devoted to community development through the arts and educ; does not run programmes or give funds.*

Chance for Children Trust. Freepost (SE 6892), London SE25 4BR *tel:* 020 8997 5831 *fax:* 020 8656 0727. Helen Ranger, project organiser. *Mus w/shops for children and young people who have been through a period of trauma.*

Channel 4 Schools. PO Box 100, Warwick CV34 6TZ *tel:* 01926 436444 *fax:* 01926 436446 *email:* info@schools.channel4.co.uk. *Provides a range of television programmes to support mus educ for 5-16 year olds. Available to buy on video and supported by a variety of resources, including teachers' guides, activity books, CD-ROMs and net notes - programme notes available free on the Channel 4 Schools website. Free timetables and brochures contain further information.*

Children's Music Foundation In Scotland. 537 Sauchiehall St, Glasgow G3 7PQ *tel:* 0141 248 1611 *fax:* 0141 248 1989 *email:* childclasscon@compuserve.com. Louise Naftalin, exec dir; Lizanne McKerrell, associate dir. *Organises and promotes Children's Classic Concerts, an award-winning series of concerts specially designed for children's listening in major concert halls throughout Britain. Educ w/shops in conjunction with performances arranged for schools.*

Choir Schools' Association. The Minster School, Deangate, York YO1 7JA *tel:* 01904 624900 *fax:* 01904 632418. Mrs W A Jackson, admin. *Membership includes over 40 schools which educate boy and girl choristers for cathedrals, churches and collegiate chapels. Also administers a Bursary Trust Fund, which aims to ensure that no chorister is denied a place at choir school on financial grounds.*

Christian Copyright Licensing (Europe) Ltd. PO Box 1339, Eastbourne, E Sussex BN21 4YF *tel:* 01323 417711 ext 1 *fax:* 01323 417722 *email:* info@ccli.co.uk. Chris Williams, Judy Kneen, communications. *Issues and administrates the Church Copyright Licence on behalf of over 2500 copyright owners. The licence allows reproduction and recording of the words of copyright worship songs and hymns to churches, schools and Christian organisations for non-commercial use. CCL also issues a Music Reproduction Licence for the photocopying of mus taken from a wide range of mus publications.*

Church Music Society. 17 Fulneck, Pudsey, W Yorks LS28 8NT *tel:* 0113 255 6143 *also fax; email:* simonlin@nascr.net. Simon Lindley, hon sec. *Leading publisher of all kinds of church mus in association with OUP mus dept. Annual lecture and other events.*

Clarinet Heritage Society. 47 Hambalt Rd, London SW4 9EQ *tel:* 020 8675 3877 *email:* stephen.bennett@telia.com. Stephen Bennett, hon sec. *Publishes and records new and rare cl mus and promotes the image of the cl.*

Clarinet and Saxophone Society of Great Britain. 8 Garden Close, Hampton, Middx TW12 3EG *tel:* 020 8390 8307. Susan Moss, membership sec. *Advice and consultancy service; library, discount insurance, quarterly journal, annual conference, teachers' course, regional events.*

Clarinetwise. Pengribyn, Cilrhedyn, Llanfyrnach, Pembs SA35 0AA *tel:* 01239 698602 *fax:* 01239 612200. Jacqueline Browne, events organiser and ed; Michael Collins, president. *W/shops, m/classes, competitions, courses, playing days; quarterly journal. All ages and abilities. Special section and w/shops for teachers and under-14s.*

The Clarsach Society. 22 Durham Rd South, Edinburgh EH15 3PD *tel:* 0131 669 8972 *fax:* 0131 468 1223 *email:* arco@globalnet.co.uk. Alistair Cockburn, admin. *Promotes the teaching and playing of the celtic hp; organises the Edinburgh Harp Festival and publishes mus for celtic hp. 9 area branches throughout the UK. Full mus catalogue available.*

Club for Acts and Actors (*incorporating* The Concert Artistes' Association). 20 Bedford St, London WC2E 9HP *tel:* 020 7836 3172. Barbara Daniels, sec. *Private Members' Club for artistes in all branches of entertainment with opportunities to perform and meet with other professionals. Concert hall may be hired for rehearsals, auditions, etc. Membership is also open to those with a strong interest in the performing arts.*

Commercial Radio Companies Association *formerly* The Association of Independent Radio Companies. 77 Shaftesbury Ave, London W1V 7AD *tel:* 020 7306 2603 *fax:* 020 7470 0062. Paul Brown, chief exec. *Trade body for UK commercial radio, representing commercial radio to Government, the Radio Authority, Copyright Societies and other organisations involved with radio. Acts as a source of advice to members and a clearing house for radio information. CRCA is a founder member of the Association of European Radios (AER).*

Composers' Guild of Great Britain *see* **British Academy of Composers and Songwriters.**

The Concert Artistes' Association *see* **Club for Acts and Actors.**

Confraternity of Polish Artists in Great Britain. 34 Denmark Rd, London W13 8RG *tel:* 020 8567 1565. Miss Maris Morganti-Sta Chów, sec.

Contemporary Music-Making for Amateurs (COMA). Toynbee Studios, 28 Commercial St, Whitechapel, London E1 6LS *tel:* 020 7247 7736 *fax:* 020 7247 7732 *email:* coma@coma.org. Chris Shurety, dir; Gill Redfern, admin; Simon Foxley, mus dir. *Provides opportunities for amateurs of all abilities to take part in contemporary mus-making. Also developing a high-quality contemporary repertoire for amateur ens through commissions and research.*

Corps of Drums Society. 62 Gally Hill Rd, Church Crookham, Hants GU13 0RU *tel:* 01252 614852 *email:* reg@corpsofdrums.softnet.co.uk. Reg Davis, hon sec. *Promotes and preserves the concept and traditions of drum and fife mus, and assists in achieving and maintaining standards of efficiency.*

Covent Garden, The Friends of. Royal Opera House, Covent Garden, London WC2E 9DD *tel:* 020 7212 9267/9268 *fax:* 020 7212 9468 *email:* friends@roh.org.uk. Phyllida Ritter, dir. *Events, open rehearsals, m/classes, magazine, advance booking and regular mailings. 16,000 members support opera and ballet at the ROH.*

Critics' Circle. c/o The Stage Newspaper, 47 Bermondsey St, London SE1 3XT *tel:* 020 7403 1818 ext 106 *fax:* 020 7357 9287. Catherine Cooper, admin; Charles Hedges, sec. *Organisation for critics of the performing arts. Membership by invitation only.*

Crotch (William) Society. c/o Jonathan Rennert, St Michael's Vestry, Cornhill, London EC3V 9DS *tel:* 01737 244604 *fax:* 01737 271128. Jonathan Rennert, hon sec. *Provides information to performers and scholars on the life and mus of the composer, teacher, painter and infant prodigy, Dr William Crotch (1775-1847). No membership.*

Dalcroze Society. 41a Woodmansterne Rd, Coulsdon, Surrey CR5 2DJ *tel:* 020 8645 0714 *also fax.* P Piqué, sec. *Mus educ through movement. Rhythmics, improvisation, ear training and therapy for all age groups. Summer course at Christ Church College, Canterbury in 2000.*

Delius Trust. 16 Ogle St, London W1P 8JB *tel:* 020 7436 4816 *fax:* 020 7637 4307 *email:* delius_trust@compuserve.com. David Lloyd-Jones, chmn; Marjorie Dickinson, sec. *Promotes only the mus of Frederick Delius by giving help towards the cost of performances, recordings and publications.*

Donizetti Society. 146 Bordesley Rd, Morden, Surrey SM4 5LT *tel:* 020 8648 9364. J P Clayton, hon sec. *Promotes interest in the works of Gaetano Donizetti and the mus of his day. Publishes 3 newsletters pa.*

Dvořák Society for Czech and Slovak Music. 69 Grasmere Rd, London N10 2DH *tel:* 020 8883 7362 *fax:* 020 8245 5591. Graham Melville-Mason, chmn. *Czech and Slovak mus. Journal, newsletters, lectures, concerts, record service, library, yearbook, international reciprocal memberships.*

Early Music Network. 31 Abdale Rd, London W12 7ER *tel:* 020 8743 0302 *fax:* 020 8743 0996 *email:* glyn@earlymusicnet.demon.co.uk. Glyn Russ, admin. *To generate the development of early mus through the promotion of live performances, educ and the dissemination of information. Runs biennial competition and showcases for young musicians; produces monthly listings newsletter.*

Eastern Orchestral Board. 10 Stratford Place, London W1N 9AE *tel:* 020 7629 9601 *fax:* 020 7495 4710 *email:* eob@compuserve.com. David Richardson, dir; Stuart Bruce, educ mgr; Jan Ford, mkt mgr; Nancy Buchanan, admin. *A development agency for professional orch mus working with local authorities, orchs and other agencies. Supports concerts, community and educ projects and audience development initiatives.*

Educational Centres Association (ECA). Berkhamsted Centre, 179 High St, Berkhamsted, Herts HP4 3HB *tel:* 01442 875086 *also fax.* Pat Aitchison, mgr sec. *National adult educ network concerned with furthering the development of adult educ locally, nationally and internationally.*

Educational Institute of Scotland. 46 Moray Place, Edinburgh EH3 6BH *tel:* 0131 225 6244 *fax:* 0131 220 3151. Ronald A Smith, gen sec. *Scottish teachers' union. Publishes* Scottish Educational Journal, *minimum 6 pa, free to members.*

Elgar Foundation. The Elgar Birthplace Museum, Crown East Lane, Lower Broadheath, Worcester WR2 6RH *tel:* 01905 333224. Melanie Weatherley, Catherine Sloan, curators. *The country cottage where Elgar was born is now a museum dedicated to the composer's life and work.*

The Elgar Society. 29 Van Diemens Close, Chinnor, Oxon OX9 4QE *tel:* 01844 354096 *fax:* 01844 354459 *email:* jnorris@elgar.sonnet.co.uk. Wendy Hillary, hon sec. *The society exists to foster and encourage a lively interest in and enthusiasm for Elgar's mus as well as to stimulate research into his life and works.*

English Folk Dance and Song Society. Cecil Sharp House, 2 Regents Park Rd, London NW1 7AY *tel:* 020 7485 2206 *fax:* 020 7284 0534. Diana Jewitt, teacher training mgr; Malcolm Taylor, librarian. *Information service; school supply catalogue, project packs; library including tapes and videos. Dance courses.*

English National Opera, Friends of. London Coliseum, St Martin's Lane, London WC2N 4ES *tel:* 020 7845 9441 *fax:* 020 7845 9272 *email:* friends@eno.org. *Provides vital financial support for new productions and enjoys a wide range of opportunities to become closely involved with ENO.*

English Poetry and Song Society. 76 Lower Oldfield Park, Bath, Somerset BA2 3HP *tel:* 01225 313531. Richard Carder, chmn. *EPSS is dedicated to the performance, publication and recording of English Art Songs; newsletter and song lists by living composers; competitions.*

English Regional Arts Boards. 5 City Rd, Winchester, Hants SO23 8SD *tel:* 01962 851063 *fax:* 01962 842033 *email:* info@erab.org.uk. Christopher Gordon, chief exec; Carolyn Nixson, admin. *Information, co-ordination and liaison services for the ten Regional Arts Boards in England and national and international representation of their interests.*

English Sinfonia Friends Association. 1 Wedgwood Court, Stevenage, Herts SG1 4QR *tel:* 01438 350990 *fax:* 01438 350930 *email:* EnglishSinfonia@tesco.net. Karen Foster, mgr; Liz Clark, sec. *Supporters of the English Sinfonia receive regular newsletters, attend rehearsals, hold social events and periodically receive other benefits, including discounts on recordings.*

Enterprise Music Scotland. 37 Dee St, Aberdeen AB11 6DY *tel:* 01224 574422 *fax:* 01224 572315. Ronnie Rae, exec dir. *Established to take over from the Scottish Arts Council the administration of funding, tours co-ordination and development of mus clubs and arts guilds in Scotland.*

European Association of Teachers (EAT). 20 Brookfield, Highgate West Hill, London N6 6AS *tel:* 020 8340 9136. Mary Duce, hon sec (UK section). *As the UK branch of a European organisation, works to promote and examine cross-curricular European knowledge in schools and colleges through FCAA approved tests.*

European Conference of Promoters of New Music. c/o Gaudeamus Foundation, Swammerdamstraat 38, NL-1091 RV Amsterdam, Netherlands *tel:* 00 31 20 694 7349 *fax:* 00 31 20 694 7258 *email:* ecpnm@xs4all.nl. H Heuvelmans, sec; H W Erdmann, president. *The European union of organisations concerned with the promotion of 20th C mus, festivals and concert organisers.*

European Guitar Teacher's Association (UK). 29 Longfield Rd, Tring, Herts HP23 4DG. Sarah Clarke, sec; John Williams, president. *Aims to improve the standard of classical gui educ and the inst's place in the mainstream mus world.*

European Piano Teachers' Association (UK) Ltd (EPTA). 1 Wildgoose Drive, Horsham, W Sussex RH12 1TU *tel:* 01403 267761 *also fax; email:* eptauk@hotmail.com. Frances Bryan, admin; Frank Martin, chmn. *EPTA has 32 regional organisations in the UK, promoting excellence in pno teaching and performance in the UK.*

European String Teachers Association (ESTA). 105 Perryfield Way, Richmond, Surrey TW10 7SN *tel:* 020 8940 4640 *fax:* 020 8940 4300. Marion Seymour, admin. *Aims to raise the standard of str playing and teaching, provide an international forum for the exchange of ideas, promote w/shops, lectures, discussions and sponsor publications.*

Faculty of Church Music. 27 Sutton Park, Blunsdon, Swindon, Wilts SN2 4BB *tel:* 020 8675 0180 *also fax.* Rev G Gleed, registrar. *Promotion of high standards in Church mus through graded exams. Tuition provided in theoretical subjects and for external mus degrees.*

Farnon (Robert) Society. Stone Gables, Upton Lane, Seavington St Michael, Ilminster, Somerset TA19 0PZ *tel:* 01460 242226 *also fax.* David Ades, sec. *RFS supports work of Robert Farnon and leading musicians and composers in the light orch and film mus fields.*

Federation of British Conservatoires. c/o Birmingham Conservatoire, Paradise Circus, Birmingham B3 3HG *tel:* 0121 331 5910 *fax:* 0121 331 5906 *email:* george.caird@uce.ac.uk. George Caird, sec. *The federation has a membership of the major independent conservatoires of mus in the UK.*

Federation of Music Services. 8 High St, Hindon, nr Salisbury, Wilts SP3 6DR *tel:* 01747 820739 *also fax.* Richard Hichman, chief exec; Michael Wearne, chmn. *Aims to offer support and advice to mus services in the provision and development of high-quality specialist mus educ to schools and the wider community; to help mus services to maintain and develop access and opportunity; and to promote the work of mus services.*

Federation of Recorded Music Societies. 67 Galleys Bank, Whitehill, Kidsgrove, Staffs ST7 4DE *tel:* 01782 782419 *email:* the-frms @netcentral.co.uk. Marjorie Williamson, sec. *To promote the development and extension of societies and organisations using recorded mus as part of their activities.*

Fellowship of Makers and Researchers of Historical Instruments. 171 Iffley Rd, Oxford OX4 1EL *email:* jeremy.montagu@music.oxford.ac.uk. Jeremy Montagu, hon sec. *Promotes authenticity in the reconstruction and use of historical insts.*

The Finzi Trust. Hillcroft, Shucknall Hill, Hereford HR1 3SL. Elizabeth Pooley, admin. *Aims to advance 20th C British mus through assisting and promoting festivals, recordings and performances. Limited number of small grants offered to young musicians for training but not for diplomas, degrees or p/grad study.*

The Finzi Trust Friends. Hillcroft, Shucknall Hill, Hereford HR1 3SL. Elizabeth Pooley, admin. *Formed in 1982 to link admirers of Gerald Finzi's mus. Aims to encourage a wider knowledge of his mus. Annual subscription £10.*

Flutewise. 9 Beaconsfield Rd, Portslade, E Sussex BN41 1XA *tel:* 01273 702367 *fax:* 01273 888864 *email:* mail@flutewise.com. James Galway, president; Liz Goodwin, ed and dir. *International organisation for all flautists, especially the young. Quarterly magazine with competitions and prizes. Regular events.*

Galpin Society. 2 Quinton Rise, Oadby, Leicester LE2 5PN *tel:* 0116 271 1808 *also fax.* P Holden, sec and admin. *Founded in 1946 for the publication of original research into the history, construction, development and use of mus insts.*

Gamba Music Club. 32 The Burgage, Market Drayton TF9 1EG *tel:* 01630 653802. Cathy Gaskell, admin. *Issues a directory of viol players, teachers and makers; publishes a selection of viol mus annually.*

Gilbert and Sullivan Society. 1 Nethercourt Ave, Finchley, London N3 1PS. Margaret Bowden, hon sec. *Aims to encourage an interest in the Gilbert and Sullivan operas. Magazine 3 times a year. Research and library facilities.*

Girls' Day School Trust. 100 Rochester Row, London SW1P 1JP *tel:* 020 7393 6666 *fax:* 020 7393 6789. M Oakley, sec.

Girls' Schools Association. 130 Regent Rd, Leicester LE1 7PG *tel:* 0116 254 1619 *fax:* 0116 255 3792 *email:* gsa@dial.pipex.com. Ms S Cooper, gen sec; Mrs W Khan, admin.

Grainger (Percy) Society. 6 Fairfax Cres, Aylesbury, Bucks HP20 2ES *tel:* 01296 428609 *also fax; email:* 101464.2670@compuserve.com. Barry P Ould, sec and mus archivist. *To promote interest in the life and works of the composer Percy Aldridge Grainger (1882-1961).*

Grieg Society of Great Britain. 25 Belgrave Square, London SW1X 8QD *tel:* 01634 714434 *also fax.* David Cornwell, sec; Beryl Foster, chmn. *Promotes interest in Grieg and other Norwegian composers amongst performers and audiences in Britain. Lecture and educ programmes arranged.*

Guild for the Promotion of Welsh Music. 94 Walter Rd, Swansea SA1 5QA *tel:* 01792 464623/464648. Geraint W Walters, chmn. *Promotes the composition, performance, recording and publication of contemporary Welsh mus. Bi-annual journal, plus catalogue of all known contemporary mus due for publication.*

Guild of Church Musicians. St Katharine Cree, 86 Leadenhall St, London EC3A 3DH *tel:* 01883 741854 *also fax fax:* 01883 740570. John Ewington OBE, gen sec. *Examining body to Archbishops of Canterbury and Westminster: Archbishop's Certificate in Church Music. Fully ecumenical.*

Gurney (Ivor) Society. 7 Carlsgate, Hay-on-Wye, Herefordshire HR3 5BS *tel:* 01497 820541; 01452 712871. John Phillips, sec; Anthony Boden, chmn.

Handbell Ringers of Great Britain. 87 The Woodfields, Sanderstead, South Croydon, Surrey CR2 0HJ *tel:* 020 8651 2663 *also fax; email:* hrgb@easynet.co.uk. Sandra Winter, hon sec. *National association for handbell, handchime and belleplate tune ringers.*

Handel at Barn Elms. 14 Oldfield Rd, Bishopdown Farm, Salisbury, Wilts SP1 3GQ *email:* rsoar@aol.com. Richard Soar, convener. *New society acknowledging links with Barn Elms, near Barnes, and promoting interest in Handel's less often performed works.*

Haydn Society of Great Britain. Music Dept, University of Lancaster, Lancaster LA1 4YW *tel:* 01524 593777 *fax:* 01524 847298 *email:* d.mccaldin@lancaster.ac.uk. Denis McCaldin, dir; Stella Birchall, admin. *Promotes the mus of Joseph Haydn and his circle in the form of concerts, recordings and the publication of an annual journal.*

The Headmasters' and Headmistresses' Conference. 130 Regent Rd, Leicester LE1 7PG *tel:* 0116 285 4810 *fax:* 0116 247 1167 *email:* hmc@hmc.org.uk. Vivian Anthony, sec; David Prinie, membership sec. *Association of heads of independent boys' and co-educational schools, with 242 members. Publishes a private members bulletin. Divided into 7 areas, each area meeting regularly to exchange ideas and concerns.*

Headteachers Association of Scotland. University of Strathclyde, Jordanhill Campus, Southbrae Drive, Glasgow G13 1PP *tel:* 0141 950 3298 *fax:* 0141 950 3434 *email:* head.teachers@strath.ac.uk. George S Ross, gen sec. *Exists to promote educ, particularly secondary educ in Scotland and to safeguard and promote the interests of headteachers, deputy heads and assistant heads.*

House of Commons Culture, Media and Sport Committee. Committee Office, 7 Millbank, London SW1P 3JA *tel:* 020 7219 6120/5739/6188 *fax:* 020 7219 6606 *email:* cmscom@parliament.uk. Colin Lee, clerk of the committee. *The committee examines the work of the Department of Culture, Media and Sport and of associated public bodies.*

House of Commons Education and Employment Committee. Committee Office, House of Commons, London SW1P 3JA *tel:* 020 7219 5774/6243/6181/0653 *fax:* 020 7219 0848 *email:* educempcom@parliament.uk. Matthew Hamlyn, clerk of the committee; Tom Healey, second clerk. *Monitors activities of DfEE and associated public bodies.*

Howells (Herbert) Society. 32 Barleycroft Rd, Welwyn Garden City, Herts AL8 6JU *tel:* 01707 335315 *fax:* 01707 880765. Andrew Millinger, sec. *Promotes interest in performances and recordings of the mus of Herbert Howells.*

The Hurdy-gurdy Society. The Old Mill, Duntish, Dorchester, Dorset DT2 7DR *tel:* 01300 345412 *email:* hurdyplay@aol.com; gurdysmith@aol.com. Michael Muskett, sec; Richard Smith, membership sec; Angela Beaumont, publicity sec.

Hymn Society of Great Britain and Ireland. 7 Paganel Rd, Minehead, Somerset TA24 5ET *tel:* 01643 703530 *also fax.* Rev Geoffrey Wrayford, sec. *Society for those interested in the study and application of hymnody.*

Incorporated Association of Organists. 11 Stonehill Drive, Bromyard, Herefordshire HR7 4XB *tel:* 01885 483155 *fax:* 01885 488609. Richard Popple MBE, hon gen sec. *Dedicated to improving org playing at all levels; has over 6000 members worldwide. Publishes* Organists' Review *quarterly.*

Incorporated Association of Preparatory Schools. 11 Waterloo Place, Leamington Spa, Warwicks CV32 5LA *tel:* 01926 887833 *fax:* 01926 888014 *email:* hq@iaps.org.uk. J H Morris, gen sec. *The main professional association for headteachers of independent preparatory and junior schools throughout the British Isles and overseas.*

Incorporated Society of Musicians. 10 Stratford Place, London W1N 9AE *tel:* 020 7629 4413 *fax:* 020 7408 1538 *email:* membership@ism.org. Neil Hoyle, chief exec. *Professional body for all musicians. Legal, financial and professional services; conferences, seminars and publications. Full, associate, student and corporate categories.*

Independent Schools Association. Boys' British School, East St, Saffron Walden, Essex CB10 1LS *tel:* 01799 523619 *fax:* 01799 524892 *email:* isa@dial.pipex.com. T M Ham, gen sec.

Independent Schools Careers Organisation. 12a Princess Way, Camberley, Surrey GU15 3SP *tel:* 01276 21188 *fax:* 01276 691833 *email:* info@isco.org.uk. John Stuart, national dir; Kate Bennett, national info offr. *Provides advice to students, parents and member schools concerning all aspects of HE and careers. Support and training is provided for school staff.*

Independent Schools Information Service (ISIS). Grosvenor Gardens House, 35-37 Grosvenor Gardens, London SW1W 0BS *tel:* 020 7798 1500 *fax:* 020 7798 1501 *email:* national@isis.org.uk. D J Woodhead, dir. *Information for parents about independent schools, including specialist mus and choir schools and mus scholarships.*

Independent Television Commission. 33 Foley St, London W1P 7LB *tel:* 020 7255 3000 *fax:* 020 7306 7806 *email:* publicaffairs@itc.org.uk. Peter Rogers, chief exec; Sarah Thane, programmes and cable dir; Frank Willis, dir of advertising and sponsorship. *Licenses and regulates non-BBC television services including Channels 3, 4 and 5, cable, satellite, digital TV services and additional services.*

Institute of Contemporary Arts. The Mall, London SW1Y 5AH *tel:* 020 7930 0493 *fax:* 020 7873 0051 *email:* christinea@ica.org.uk. Christine Atha, head of educ; Christopher Hewitt, curator of live arts.

Institute of Leisure and Amenity Management (ILAM). Ilam House, Lower Basildon, Reading RG8 9NE *tel:* 01491 874800 *fax:* 01491 874801 *email:* info@ilam.co.uk. Alan Smith, dir. *Professional body representing over 7000 managers throughout the leisure industry. ILAM represents its members both nationally and regionally, offering its own qualification system and a wide range of benefits to members, including educ and training seminars, dissemination of information, publications and conferences.*

Institute of Musical Instrument Technology. PO Box 118, Southsea, Hants PO4 9YP. Jim Masters, hon sec. *Promotes the professional status of members engaged in mus inst design, manufacture and repair.*

International Artist Managers' Association (IAMA). 4 Addison Bridge Place, London W14 8XP *tel:* 020 7610 4884 *fax:* 020 7610 4994 *email:* iama@easynet.co.uk. Richard Steele, exec dir; Patrick Vincent, admin mgr; Wiebke Morgan, membership development mgr. *International professional association for classical mus artist managers and concert agents.*

International Association of Music Libraries. Archives and Documentation Centres, c/o County Library Headquarters, Walton St, Aylesbury, Bucks HP20 1UU *tel:* 01296 382266 *fax:* 01296 382274 *email:* mroll@buckscc.gov.uk. Margaret Roll, gen sec. *Careers information and special students' subscriptions available to those working in, or with interest in, mus librarianship. Interest in any issues regarding/affecting mus librarians in any sphere.*

International Cultural Desk. 3 Bruntsfield Cres, Edinburgh EH10 4HD *tel:* 0131 446 3001 *fax:* 0131 446 3048 *email:* info@icd.org.uk. Hilde Bollen, development mgr; Kerry Jardine, information offr. *Assists the Scottish cultural community to operate more effectively in an international context by providing information and advice. Provides and disseminates information on funding sources, international opportunities and cultural policy development in Europe, and assists with establishing contacts internationally. It is not a funding agency. The Desk publishes* Communication, *a bi-monthly update about forthcoming international opportunities, and* InFocus, *a series of specialised guides with an international focus.*

International Federation of the Phonographic Industry. IFPI Secretariat, 54 Regent St, London W1R 5PJ *tel:* 020 7878 7900 *fax:* 020 7878 7950 *email:* info@ifpi.org. Jason Berman, chair, chief exec; Nic Garnett, dir gen, chief operating offr. *IFPI promotes and defends the copyright interests of its members in sound recordings and mus videos.*

The International Handchime Circle. Hillcroft, Northbrook Ave, Winchester, Hants SO23 0JW *tel:* 01962 856404 *also fax.* Sue Richardson, dir. *Database of affiliated handchime teams in the UK.*

International Piano Teachers' Consultants (IPTEC). 29 Beaumont Rd, Chiswick, London W4 5AL *tel:* 020 8994 4288. Meriel Jefferson, hon sec. *1-day courses. Consultations available in specialist subjects.*

International Shakuhachi Society. Lorien, Wadhurst, Sussex TN5 6PN *tel:* 01892 782045. Dan E Mayers, president; Clive Bell, sec and treasurer. *The society provides information on teachers, methods and recordings to devotees of Shakuhachi worldwide. Also provides Shakuhachi insts and bamboo blanks. Periodically publishes hardback volume,* Annals of the International Shakuhachi Society, *sent free to members.*

International Society for Contemporary Music (ISCM). British Section, c/o spnm, Francis House, Francis St, London SW1P 1DE *tel:* 020 7828 9696 *fax:* 020 7931 9928 *email:* spnm@spnm.org.uk. Gill Graham, admin. *Organises talks, concerts and exhibitions and provides information on the activities of the International Society for Contemporary Music. In 2000 the ISCM world mus day will be held in Luxembourg.*

International Society for Music Education (ISME). International Centre for Research in Music Education, University of Reading, Bulmershe Court, Reading RG6 1HY *tel:* 0118 931 8846 *also fax; fax:* 0118 935 2080 *email:* e.smith@reading.ac.uk. Elizabeth Smith, admin. *Aims to promote mus educ throughout the world as an integral part of general educ through conferences, publications, etc. Membership information and details of the next world conference are available from the above address.*

International Society for the Study of Tension in Performance. School of Music, Kingston University, c/o 28 Emperor's Gate, London SW7 4HS *tel:* 020 7373 7307 *fax:* 020 7373 5440. Carola Grindea, chmn; Gordana Petrovic, sec. *Charitable organisation committed to helping musicians afflicted by physical and psychological problems at ISSTIP/London College of Music 'Performing Arts Clinic'. Publishes ISSTIP journal.*

International Trombone Association. 3 Cumbria Close, Coventry CV1 3PG *tel:* 024 7623 0900 *fax:* 024 7623 0901 *email:* steven@warwickmusic.com. Steven Greenall, UK rep; Paul Hunt, president; Mark Nightingale, 2nd vice president. *The world's largest association for trb players with over 4500 members from across the globe. Members receive reductions at specialist retailers, free ITA CD and the quarterly magazine,* ITA Journal.

Ireland (John) Trust. 35 St Mary's Mansions, St Mary's Terrace, London W2 1SQ *tel:* 020 7723 6376 *fax:* 020 7724 8362. Mrs M Taylor, hon sec.

The Irish Contemporary Music Centre. 95 Lower Baggot St, Dublin 2, Republic of Ireland *tel:* 00 353 1 661 2105 *fax:* 00 353 1 676 2639 *email:* info@cmc.ie. Eve O'Kelly, dir. *Promotes and documents Irish contemporary mus.*

Jazz Services Ltd. Room 518, Africa House, 64 Kingsway, London WC2B 6BD *tel:* 020 7405 0737/47/57 *fax:* 020 7405 0828 *email:* admin @jazzservices.org.uk. Chris Hodgkins, dir; Celia Wood, information. *Promotes the growth and development of jazz within the UK by providing services in marketing, communications, touring, information, educ and jazz newspapers.*

Jewish Music Heritage Trust. PO Box 232, Harrow, Middx HA1 2NN *tel:* 020 8909 2445 *fax:* 020 8909 1030 *email:* jewishmusic@jmht.org. Geraldine Auerbach. *Facilitates the study and performance of Jewish mus. Leading promoter of Jewish mus in Britain having gained recognition on the concert platform in educ and through its information and resourcing services. Artistic Programme: the JMHT organises/promotes Jewish mus on the concert platform, through the London International Jewish Music Festival and other events; also produces recordings of mus of special Jewish interest. Education Programme: JMHT co-founded/sponsors the Joe Loss Lectureship in Jewish Music which is being inaugurated at the School of Oriental and African Studies, University of London; organises triennial London International Conferences on Jewish Music (next Jun 2000, SOAS); also preparing Jewish mus packs for primary schools. Information, Resources and Publications Programme: JMHT produces newsletter, collects and catalogues books, mss and recordings, and gives information to scholars, media and public.*

The John Curwen Society. 5 Bigbury Close, Coventry CV3 5AJ *tel:* 024 7641 3010 *also fax.* John Dowding, dir. *Promotes the New Curwen Method which encourages children to listen attentively to mus, to recognise pitch, rhythm and phrasing, develop a musical memory, and sing at sight with confidence. Recommended for use in primary schools.*

The Josephs (Wilfred) Society. North Lodge, 77 High Rd, Hockley, Essex SS5 4SZ *tel:* 020 7722 7539 *also fax;* 07976 714030 *email:* claudiajosephs@compuserve.com. Matthew Eve, UK chmn, newsletter ed. *Promotes Josephs' performances and broadcasts; helps the remaining unpublished works into print; produces and disseminates recordings. Produces a newsletter 2-3 times a year.*

Karg-Elert Society. 29 Orford Gardens, Twickenham, Middx TW1 4PL *tel:* 020 8894 6859 *also fax.* Anthony Caldicott, chmn; Graham Barber, president; Brian Parsons, sec. *Promotion of the composer and organist Sigfrid Karg-Elert through encouraging research and dissemination of information.*

Kato Havas Association for the New Approach (KHANA). 3 Beacon View, Marple, Stockport SK6 6PX *tel:* 0161 449 7347 *email:* mgbbeaconview@compuserve.com. Gloria Bakhshayesh, admin and treasurer. *Kato Havas vn teaching method. KHANA holds w/shops on the alleviation and prevention of physical tensions and anxiety in str playing. 2 journals pa.*

King (Reginald) Trust. 6 Fairfax Cres, Aylesbury, Bucks HP20 2ES *tel:* 01296 428609 *also fax; email:* 101464.2670@compuserve.com. Barry Peter Ould, archivist. *Promotes interest in the life and mus of Reginald King (1904-1991). Mus and sound archives maintained.*

Klavar Music Foundation of Great Britain. 171 Yarborough Rd, Lincoln LN1 3NQ *tel:* 01522 523117. Michael Magnus Osborn, dir. *Educ Trust. Klavar system correspondence courses for pno, org, gui and pno-accordion. Klavar notation printed mus supplies.*

The Kodály Centre of London. 64 Montpelier Rise, Wembley, Middx HA9 8RQ *tel:* 020 8904 8923 *also fax; email:* david@vinden.freeserve.co.uk. David Vinden, Yuko Vinden, dirs. *Kodály musicianship and teacher training classes comprising solfège musicianship, classroom techniques and methodology, choral direction and folk-song analysis. For class teachers, inst teachers and singers. 3 levels of training carry Trinity College of Music accreditation. Publications include: Harmonic Foundations, the Modes, rhythm flip cards and flash cards.*

The Kodály Institute of Britain. 133 Queen's Gate, London SW7 5LE *tel:* 020 7823 7371 *fax:* 020 7584 7691. Mary Skone-Roberts, admin; Cecilia Vajda, dir. *Adult educ; 1-year p/t courses in musicianship. W/end courses on early childhood mus educ, primary and secondary educ, held in London and Edinburgh. Annual Aug international summer school in Edinburgh. Publications include books, video and audio cassettes.*

The Ladies Association of British Barbershop Singers. 17 Haldane Rd, Caversham, Reading RG4 7PS *tel:* 01189 474156. Jean Olman, membership sec; Sue Horder, convention mgr.

Lake District Summer Music Education Outreach Programme. Stricklandgate House, 92 Stricklandgate, Kendal, Cumbria LA9 4PU *tel:* 01539 733411 *fax:* 01539 724441 *email:* info@ldsm.org.uk. Andrew Lucas, admin. Moving Mountains to Make Music, *Lake District Summer Music's new educ outreach programme, offers a broad range of creative educ opportunities. Running throughout the year, the programme consists of a variety of w/shops, m/classes and community projects in schools and community centres. Projected 1999/2000 programme includes* Everything a pianist ought to know, *mus training needs organisations, a community performance of Peter Maxwell Davies's* Cinderella.

Leighton (Kenneth) Trust. 38 McLaren Rd, Edinburgh EH9 2BN *tel:* 0131 667 3113 *email:* joleighton@ukgateway.net. Mrs J A Leighton, sec. *Promotes British mus in general and Leighton's mus in particular by providing financial assistance for performances (especially by younger performers), recordings and commissions.*

Library Association. 7 Ridgmount St, London WC1E 7AE *tel:* 020 7636 7543 *fax:* 020 7436 7218 *email:* info@la-hq.org.uk. Ross Shimmon, chief exec. *Professional body for library and information managers with 25,000 members UK and overseas.*

Light Music Society. Lancaster Farm, Chipping Lane, Longridge, Preston, Lancs PR3 2NB *tel:* 01772 783646 *fax:* 01772 786026. Ernest Tomlinson, chmn. *Backing group for Library of Light-Orchestral Music. Promotes interest in light mus. Regular newsletter.*

Liszt Society. 9 Burnside Close, Twickenham, Middx TW1 1ET *tel:* 020 8287 5518 *also fax; email:* 100707.47@compuserve.com. Jan Hoare, sec. *The Society, through its publications and holding of events such as recitals, m/classes and soirées, exists to promote interest in and appreciation of the works of Franz Liszt.*

London Piano Circle. 7 Meynell Cres, Hackney, London E9 7AS *tel:* 020 7723 8818 *also fax.* Malcolm Scott, hon organiser. *For proficient amateurs wishing to play in groups, in one another's homes.*

London Suzuki Group. 96 Farm Lane, London SW6 1QH *tel:* 020 7386 8006 *also fax; email:* lsg@pullinger.prestel.co.uk. Christine Livingstone, dir of mus; Nicholas Pullinger, admin. *Charitable organisation of teachers, parents and children committed to the Suzuki approach to mus educ for children aged 3-18.*

Lowland and Border Pipers' Society. 6 Garrioch Cres, Maryhill, Glasgow G20 8RR *tel:* 0141 946 8624. Rona MacDonald, publicity; Andrew Hunter, chmn. *Aims to provide a focus for everyone interested in Scottish bellows-blown pipes through meetings, concerts, sessions, newsletters and a twice yearly magazine.*

Lute Society. Southside Cottage, Brook Hill, Albury, Guildford GU5 9DJ *tel:* 01483 202159 *fax:* 01483 203088 *email:* lutesoc@aol.com. Christopher Goodwin, sec. *Holds 4 meetings pa in central London with lectures and recitals on all aspects of the lute and related insts and their repertoire. Publishes annual journal* The Lute, *quarterly newsletter* Lute News, *performing editions, working drawings of lutes. Holds occasional 1-day w/shops. Lutes available for hire.*

The Massenet Society. Flat 2, 79 Linden Gardens, London W2 4EU *tel:* 020 7229 7060. Stella J Wright, founder and dir. *Founded 1972, the society promotes a greater knowledge and understanding of Massenet's works.*

The Masterclass Music Charitable Trust. The Bursar's Office, Eltham College, Grove Park Rd, London SE9 4QF *tel:* 020 8857 7360 *fax:* 020 8851 9622. Danny Cooper, treasurer; Susannah Wainman, exec dir. *To promote, facilitate and support mus educ with special emphasis on young people in educ, primarily in the UK.*

Mayr + Donizetti Collaboration. 8 Cosway Mansions, Cosway St, London NW1 6UE *tel:* 020 7258 1798 *also fax.* Ian Caddy, John Stewart Allitt, founders. *Promotes the work of the two composers, co-ordinates scholarship and performing material; biographies and editions for sale.*

MCPS (Mechanical-Copyright Protection Society Ltd). Copyright House, 29-33 Berners St, London W1P 4AA *tel:* 020 7580 5544 *fax:* 020 7306 4455 *email:* info@mcps.co.uk. *Represents writers and publishers of mus, licensing their works whenever they are recorded and collecting the mechanical royalties accrued on their behalf. Also at: Elgar House, 41 Streatham High St, London SW16 1ER* tel: *0181 664 4400* fax: *0181 769 8792.*

Metier. Glyde House, Glydegate, Bradford, W Yorks BD5 0BQ *tel:* 01274 738800 *fax:* 01274 391566 *email:* admin@metier.org.uk. Duncan Sones, chief exec; Jane Fear, head of research; Ruth Churchill, head of lifelong learning. *Metier is the National Training Organisation for the arts and entertainment sector. Concerned with vocational training and educ. The core of this work is the development and implementation of National Vocational Qualifications (NVQs) and Scottish Vocational Qualifications (SVQs). Also research into the work force and training from new entrants to continuing professional development and on-line learning.*

The Music Club of London. 78 Bedford Court Mansions, Bedford Ave, London WC1B 3AE *tel:* 020 7636 2946 *also fax.* Mike Coleman, organiser. *Bi-monthly newsletter. Programme of special events, audiences with leading musical personalities and international travel to festivals and important musical events.*

Music Education Council. 54 Elm Rd, Hale, Altrincham, Cheshire WA15 9QP *tel:* 0161 928 3085 *fax:* 0161 929 9648 *email:* ahassan@easynet.co.uk. Anna Hassan, admin. *The major forum for those involved in mus educ and training in the UK.*

Music for Youth. 102 Point Pleasant, London SW18 1PP *tel:* 020 8870 9624 *fax:* 020 8870 9935 *email:* mfy@globalnet.co.uk. Larry Westland CBE, exec dir; Pippa Cleeve, Lucy Riley, asst dirs. *Charity dedicated to providing regional and national platforms for young musicians.*

Music Industries Association. Wix Hill House, Epsom Rd, West Horsley, Surrey KT24 6DZ *tel:* 01483 223326 *fax:* 01483 222743 *email:* office@mia.org.uk. Bob Kelley, sec gen; Lizzie Evans, membership sec; Nick Lobley, commercial mgr. *Trade association representing manufacturers, distributors and retailers of mus insts and accs. Sponsors UK trade and public exhibitions and promotes British involvement in appropriate overseas trade fairs. Publishers of* The Fourth R, Let the Children Play *and* So You Want To Open A Music Shop.

Music Masters' and Mistresses' Association (MMA). Wayfaring, Smithers Lane, East Peckham, Tonbridge, Kent TN12 5HT *tel:* 01622 871576 *also fax; email:* mma.admin@cwcom.net. Katharine Le Page, admin; Debbie Tye, membership sec (*tel:* 01353 660741). *Furthers all aspects of mus in schools. Membership open to those teaching mus in schools, and those wishing to support the development of mus in schools. Regular regional meetings, courses and an annual conference are held. Termly journal, annual yearbook and mus scholarship guide.*

Music, Mind and Movement. 28 Glebe Place, London SW3 5LD *tel:* 020 7352 1666 *also fax; email:* musicmindmovement@btinternet.com. Lucinda Mackworth-Young, Nicola Gaines, Karin Greenhead, dirs. *An association devoted to enhancing the performance and teaching of mus*

and dance through an integrated multi-arts approach. Courses run for performers, teachers and students in the practical application of psychology, eurhythmics, dance through the ages, improvisation and other disciplines related to the performance, teaching and learning of mus and dance. Courses are validated by Trinity College of Music as bearing credit to the ATCL and LTCL (Music Education) or certificate in mus educ.

Music Publishers' Association Ltd. 3rd Floor, Strandgate, 18-20 York Buildings, London WC2N 6JU *tel:* 020 7839 7779 *fax:* 020 7839 7776 *email:* mpa@musicpublishers.co.uk. Sarah Faulder, chief exec; Avril Peyton, publicity and events mgr. *Trade organisation representing mus publishers in the UK, advising and assisting members in the promotion and protection of mus copyright.*

Music Trades Benevolent Society. 8 Darsway, Castle Donington, Derbys DE74 2RZ *tel:* 01332 811320 *also fax.* J M Smith, sec. *Assists mus industry employees and former employees who through accident, illness, and other stresses of life have been caused deep personal hardship.*

Musicians Against Nuclear Arms (MANA). 71 Greenfield Gardens, London NW2 1HU *tel:* 020 8455 1030. Elizabeth Fraser, chair; John Williams, president; Joan R Horrocks, admin. *Organises concerts to assist the peace movement. Professionals, amateurs and non-performing mus lovers welcome. Quarterly newsletter. Annual subscription £7.50 (unwaged £2).*

Musicians Benevolent Fund. 16 Ogle St, London W1P 8JB *tel:* 020 7636 4481 *fax:* 020 7637 4307 *email:* helen.faulkner@mbf.sprint.com. Philip Jones CBE, chmn; Helen Faulkner, sec. *Largest charity in the UK helping professional musicians and their dependants in need.*

Musicians Benevolent Fund, Friends of the. 16 Ogle St, London W1P 8JB *tel:* 020 7636 4481 *fax:* 020 7637 4307 *email:* hilary.pentycross@mbf.sprint.com.uk. Hilary Pentycross. *Supports the Musicians Benevolent Fund (see above).*

Musicians' Social and Benevolent Council. 100a Weston Park, Crouch End, London N8 9PP *tel:* 020 8348 9358. *Assists London-based professional musicians in times of sickness and distress. Mainly funded by contributions from London orchestral and theatre musicians. All donations gratefully received.*

Musicians' Union. 60-62 Clapham Rd, London SW9 0JJ *tel:* 020 7582 5566 *fax:* 020 7582 9805 *email:* info@musiciansunion.org.uk. Dennis Scard, gen sec.

Musicians in Focus. 1 Poets Rd, London N5 2SL *tel:* 020 7354 2050 *fax:* 020 7359 7535 *email:* musiciansinfocus@compuserve.com. Jacqueline Clifton, dir; Alan McCulloch, dir. *Founded in response to a demand for access to mus tech by visually impaired musicians.*

Musicosophia. PO Box 3030, Littlehampton, W Sussex BN17 6GA *tel:* 01273 327712 *also fax;* 01903 786745 *email:* ics@pavilion.co.uk. Catherine Brophy, dir. *Organises courses for listeners, age 6-adult, as part of an international movement for mus lovers. See entry in* **Summer Schools** *for details.*

National Association for Gifted Children. Elder House, Milton Keynes MK9 1LR *tel:* 01908 673677 *fax:* 01908 673679 *email:* nagc@rmplc.co.uk. Peter Carey, dir; Michal Hambourg, mus counsellor. *A national charity helping able and talented children to achieve fulfilment and advising those involved in their upbringing and educ.*

National Association for Music in Higher Education (NAMHE). c/o Royal Northern College of Music, 124 Oxford Rd, Manchester M13 9RD *tel:* 0161 907 5269 *fax:* 0161 273 7611 *email:* g.d.barber@leeds.ac.uk; dKimbell@music.ed.ac.uk. Graham Barber, chmn; David Kimball, membership sec and treasurer. *Professional subject association for mus staff in HE. Membership is arranged through mus depts. It is a forum for debate and exchange of information about teaching methodology and admin matters.*

National Association for Primary Education (NAPE). University of Leicester, Barrack Rd, Northampton NN2 6AF *tel:* 01604 636326 *fax:* 01604 636328 *email:* nationaloffice@nape.org.uk. Thelma Abbott, hon gen sec. *Membership includes parents, teachers, governors, school communities and others who share concern for children's educ from 0-13. Festival of voices held annually in London.*

National Association of Advisory Officers for Special Education. 32a Pleasant Valley, Saffron Walden, Essex CB11 4AP *tel:* 01799 521257 *also fax; email:* xve40@dial.pipex.com. *Links inspectors and advisers with responsibility for special educ provision both in mainstream and special schools and those involved in OFSTED inspections with an SEN brief.*

National Association of Careers and Guidance Teachers. Portland House, 4 Bridge St, Usk, Gwent NP5 1BG *tel:* 01291 672985 *fax:* 01291 672090 *email:* jcnacgt@aol.com. Mrs J G Cook, gen sec. *Professional association for careers teachers and others involved in careers educ and guidance.*

National Association of Choirs. 21 Charmouth Rd, Lower Weston, Bath BA1 3LJ *tel:* 01225 426713. John Robbins, gen sec. *NAC caters exclusively for choirs, providing a wide range of services such as liaison with festivals, insurance, charitable status applications, mus discount, mus loan scheme. Choirs benefit from being placed in groups for local and combined choir activities.*

National Association of Music Educators. 4 Apperley Park, Apperley, Glos GL19 4EB *tel:* 01452 780680 *also fax; email:* musiceducation@name.org.uk. Alison Ley, professional offr. *Represents all those involved in mus educ - advisers, inspectors, teachers; lecturers in schools, FE, conservatoires and teacher educ; publishers and the educ industry; specialist organisations and freelance mus educ consultants. Network of professional support provides national and regional conferences, training days, meetings, w/shops and subject support and advice for teachers and inspectors. Also provides information for parents, governors, headteachers, politicians and the mus industry. Various publications on application as well as quarterly newsletter and biannual magazine.*

National Association of Musical Instrument Repairers. 2 Arthur Cottages, Frimley Rd, Ash Vale, Surrey GU12 5PD *tel:* 01252 518098 *also fax; email:* namir@dickyd.globalnet.co.uk. Richard Dawson. *Individual repairers dedicated to maintaining standards of quality in a particular inst. Enables enquirers to contact a local repairer of the appropriate specialism.*

National Association of Schoolmasters' Union and Women Teachers (NASUWT). Hillscourt Education Centre, Rose Hill, Rednal, Birmingham B45 8RS *tel:* 0121 453 6150 *fax:* 0121 457 6208 *email:* nasuwt@nasuwt.org.uk. Nigel de Gruchy, gen sec.

National Association of Youth Orchestras. Ainslie House, 11 St Colme St, Edinburgh EH3 6AG *tel:* 0131 539 1087 *fax:* 0131 539 1069 *email:* admin@nayo.org.uk. Carol Main, dir; Jenny Brockie, admin. *National association for youth orchs throughout UK. Activities include annual Festival of British Youth Orchestras in Edinburgh and Glasgow, Anglo-German Youth Music Week, British Reserve Insurance Conducting Prize (biennial), British Reserve Insurance Youth Orchestra Awards (annual). Newsletter* Full Orchestra *3 pa, free to members. Marion Semple Weir library of chmbr mus, no hire charges to members. In preparation:* Directory of Youth and Student Orchestras. *For information on the European Association of Youth Orchestras contact Anneke van Nes, Otterswijk 13, NL-7701 PC Dedemsvaart, The Netherlands* tel: *0031 5236 38435.*

National Campaign for the Arts. Francis House, Francis St, London SW1P 1DE *tel:* 020 7828 4448 *fax:* 020 7931 9959 *email:* mail@artscampaign.org. Victoria Todd, dir; Susan Borland, admin. *The independent lobby for all arts interests, including mus and mus in educ. Entire funding from membership fees. New members always welcome.*

National Council for Vocational Qualifications *see* **Qualifications and Curriculum Authority.**

National Early Music Association (NEMA). Southside Cottage, Brook Hill, Albury, Guildford, GU5 9DJ *tel:* 01483 202159 *fax:* 01483 203088 *email:* lutesoc@aol.com. Christopher Goodwin, admin. *Publishes the* Early Music Yearbook *incorporating the* Register of Early Music *and a quarterly magazine* Early Music Performer.

National Federation of Music Societies. 7-15 Rosebery Ave, London EC1R 4SP *tel:* 020 7841 0110 *fax:* 020 7841 0115 *email:* nfms@nfms.demon.co.uk. Robin Osterley, chief exec. *Provides legal, financial, artistic, training, advocacy and lobbying services for 2000 voluntary member mus societies.*

National Harmonica League. Rivendell, High St, Shirrell Heath, nr Southampton, Hants SO32 2JN *tel:* 01329 832178 *fax:* 01329 832178 *email:* 100571.132@compuserve.com. Colin Mort, chmn. *For harmonica enthusiasts; newsletter and events.*

National Institute for Careers Education and Counselling. Sheraton House, Castle Park, Cambridge CB3 0AX *tel:* 01223 460277 *fax:* 01223 311708 *email:* nicec@crac.org.uk. A G Watts, dir. *Carries out applied research and development work related to careers guidance in educ settings and in work and community settings.*

National Institute of Adult Continuing Education. 21 De Montfort St, Leicester LE1 7GE *tel:* 0116 204 4200 *fax:* 0116 285 4514 *email:* niace@niace.org.uk. Louise McGill, snr information offr. *Twice yearly, Jan/Aug, publishes* Time to Learn *at £4.95, detailing a wide range of w/end and 1-week residential courses held at various centres throughout the UK.*

National Junior Music Club of Great Britain. 23 Hitchin St, Biggleswade, Beds SG18 8AX *tel:* 01767 316521 *fax:* 01767 317221 *email:* njm@lindsaymusic.co.uk. Douglas Coombes, mus dir; Rose Miles, membership sec; Carole Lindsay-Douglas, ed. *Termly resource magazine for primary and middle-school teachers. Membership includes right to photocopy for use within own school and preferential fees for courses organised by the club.*

National Music Council. Francis House, Francis St, London SW1P 1DE *tel:* 020 8347 8618 *also fax.* Russell Jones, chmn; Mark Isherwood, deputy chmn; Jennifer Goodwin, admin. *Forum for mus organisations concerned to further the interests of mus and musicians in the UK.*

National Operatic and Dramatic Association (NODA). NODA House, 1 Crestfield St, London WC1H 8AU *tel:* 020 7837 5655 *fax:* 020 7833 0609. Mark Thorburn, chief exec. *Umbrella body for the Amateur Theatre. Services include discounted sales of mus, scripts, make-up, insurance, etc. Also summer school and conferences.*

National Piano Centre. 5 Summerfield Rd, London W5 1ND *tel:* 020 8997 1793 *also fax; email:* info@pianocentre.co.uk. Jonathan Ranger, dir. *Working hands-on collection of the history and development of the pno and mus, in social, artistic and political context through the ages. Courses and training. Resource centre and forum for mus professionals, teachers, students, arts organisations, schools, colleges and individuals. Membership includes meetings, visits, publications, discounts, information and advice.*

National Sound Archive (British Library). 96 Euston Rd, London NW1 2DB *tel:* 020 7412 7440 *fax:* 020 7412 7441 *email:* nsa@bl.uk. A Crispin Jewitt, dir. *Largest reference collection of sound recordings in the UK open to the public, full reference library of associated literature. Information on commercial discs, broadcasting, history of recording. Free listening service; groups from schools, universities and colleges welcome to listen by prior arrangement. Free newsletter.*

National Union of Teachers. Hamilton House, Mabledon Place, London WC1H 9BD *tel:* 020 7388 6191 *fax:* 020 7387 8458. Doug McAvoy, gen sec; Steve Sinnott, deputy gen sec.

National Youth Jazz Association (NYJA). 11 Victor Rd, Harrow, Middx HA2 6PT *tel:* 020 8863 2717 *fax:* 020 8863 8685 *email:* bill.ashton@virgin.net. William Ashton, chmn. *Organises two Sat clinics by the National Youth Jazz Orchestra and w/shops throughout Britain usually in conjunction with a concert by NYJO.*

North West Composers' Association. 41 Parklands Way, Poynton, Cheshire SK12 1AL *tel:* 01625 875389 *also fax; email:* david.f.golightly@btinternet.com. Stuart Scott, sec; Jeremy Pike, chmn. *Comprised of members of the Composers' Guild of Great Britain who live in the north-west region, the association promotes concerts of mus by north-west composers. Aims to increase concert series, be involved in educ w/shops and develop a composers' representative agency.*

Northumbrian Pipers' Society. 7 Halton Drive, Wideopen, Northumberland NE13 6AA *tel:* 0191 236 5724 *email:* seumas@richmond77.freeserve.co.uk. J Richmond, hon sec. *Supports the playing and making of Northumbrian pipes, and the composition of trad Northumbrian mus.*

NUS Ents. PO Box 1199, London SW2 1QH *tel:* 020 7737 2944 *fax:* 020 7924 0890 *email:* waves@mite.co.uk. Nik Kirton, mgr.

Opera and Music Theatre Forum. Pegasus House, 37-43 Sackville St, London W1X 2DL *tel:* 020 7287 7018 *fax:* 020 7287 9959. Jean Nicholson, mgr; Andrew Bennett, chmn. *Represents small and medium-scale opera companies in UK and international links. Information centre for related activities and serves to advance the ideals of its member companies.*

The Operetta Foundation. 27 Cheetham Fold Rd, Hyde, Cheshire SK14 5DU *tel:* 0161 366 1709. Jeffrey Lomas, chmn; Joan Pancott-Lomas, development; John Edwars, finance controller. *Promotes and sponsors operetta.*

Orff Society (UK). 7 Rothesay Ave, Richmond, Surrey TW10 5EB *tel:* 020 8876 1944 *also fax.* Margaret Murray, hon sec. *Through teachers' courses it promotes Orff's creative approach to mus educ, stressing improvisation and using voices, movement and perc insts.*

The Organ Club. 19 St Peter's St, London N1 8JD *tel:* 020 7226 1218. Frederic Symonds, membership sec; Adrian Gunning, president. *A worldwide society for friends of the org, founded in 1926. Monthly visits to hear new and historic insts, bi-monthly journal. Large library housed at RAM, London. Prospectus and subs details available from Frederic Symonds, Rothes Glen Hotel, Rothes, Morayshire AB38 7AQ.*

Organists' Benevolent League. 10 Stratford Place, London W1N 9AE. Martin Neary, president; Richard Lyne, sec. *Charity to provide assistance for organists or their dependants in cases of need.*

PRS (Performing Right Society). Copyright House, 29-33 Berners St, London W1P 4AA *tel:* 020 7580 5544 *fax:* 020 7306 4455 *email:* info@prs.co.uk. *Collects royalties on behalf of mus creators and publishers for the public performance and broadcast of their copyright mus work. Also at: Elgar House, 41 Streatham High St, London SW16 1ER* tel: *0181 664 4400* fax: *0181 769 8792.*

The Phil, Friends of. Philharmonic Hall, Hope St, Liverpool L1 9BP *tel:* 0151 210 3798 *fax:* 0151 210 2902 *email:* rlpsociety@aol.com. Betty Green, admin. *Members are entitled to priority booking, discounts on tickets and free rehearsal passes.*

Philatelic Music Circle. 22 Bouverie Gardens, Kenton, Middx HA3 0RQ *tel:* 020 8907 2790 *also fax; email:* pmcmail@aol.com. Irene Lawford, president and consultant ed; Geoffrey Datson, hon chmn. *For mus stamp collectors. Magazine* The Baton; *holds meetings, exchanges, competitions, exhibitions. A/v programme on loan, library, worldwide membership.*

Piano Trade Suppliers' Association Ltd. 78-80 Borough High St, London SE1 1XG *tel:* 020 7403 2300 *fax:* 020 7403 8140 *email:* d_m_hart@compuserve.com. David M Hart, sec.

Piano Trio Society. Stoneville Cottage, Gretton Fields, Cheltenham, Glos GL54 5HH *tel:* 01242 620736 *also fax.* Colin Taylor, chmn; Christine Talbot-Cooper, admin. *International membership organisation for performers, amateurs, composers, mus publishers, corporate members and mus lovers with a wide-ranging programme of events based on the pno trio medium. Three newsletters a year.*

Pianoforte Tuners' Association. 10 Reculver Rd, Herne Bay, Kent CT6 6LD *tel:* 01227 368808 *also fax.* Mrs V M Addis, sec. *The association has country-wide membership. An examination is required for entry.*

Piobaireachd Society. 20 Otago St, Glasgow G12 8JH *tel:* 0141 334 3587 *fax:* 0141 337 3024 *email:* info@piping.scot.net. Dugald MacNeill, sec.

Pipers' Guild. 121 Hallam Way, West Hallam, Derbys DE7 6LP *tel:* 0115 930 8323 *email:* margent@rmplc.co.uk. Stephanie Payne, sec; Mary Argent, chmn; Betty Roe, president. *Organisation for the making, playing and decorating of bamboo pipes (insts similar to renaissance rcdrs).*

Player Piano Group. 93 Evelyn Ave, Ruislip, Middx HA4 8AH *tel:* 01895 634288. Tony Austin, hon sec. *Concerned with the mus, mechanical and historic aspects of the player pno and the reproducing pno, organising social meetings, quarterly bulletin and occasional public concerts.*

Polish Cultural Institute. 34 Portland Place, London W1N 4HQ *tel:* 020 7636 6032 *fax:* 020 7637 2190. Aleksandra Czapiewska, dir. *Promotes Polish arts in Great Britain in general. Assists in arranging Polish-British contacts.*

Pro Corda Trust (National School for Young Chamber Music Players). Leiston Abbey House, Theberton Rd, Leiston, Suffolk IP16 4TB *tel:* 01728 831354 *fax:* 01728 832500 *email:* procorda@procorda. demon.co.uk. Robert Max, mus dir; Pamela Spofforth MBE, artistic dir emeritus; Mererid Crump, admin; Sir Colin Davis, president. *Courses held during school holidays for young str players and pianists under the direction of distinguished musicians.* See **Summer Schools and Short Courses.**

Professional Association of Teachers (PAT). 2 St James' Court, Friar Gate, Derby DE1 1BT *tel:* 01332 372337 *fax:* 01332 290310/292431 *email:* hq@pat.org.uk. Kay Driver, gen sec; Richard Fraser, communications offr. *Independent trade union and professional association with around 35,000 members from all parts of the UK in both the maintained and independent sectors, teaching at all levels from nursery to FE and HE. PAT is non-party political and is not affiliated to the TUC. A publications list is available.*

Qualifications and Curriculum Authority (QCA). 29 Bolton St, London W1Y 7PD *tel:* 020 7509 5555 *fax:* 020 7509 6666 *email:* watkina@qca.org.uk. Sir William Stubbs, chmn; Sir Dominic Cadbury, dep chmn; Nicholas Tate, chief exec; Tony Knight, principal subject offr; Anna Watkin, subject offr. *A public body brought into being on 1 Oct 1997 by the Education Act 1997. The act gave QCA a core remit to promote quality and coherence in educ and training. QCA brings together the work of the National Council for Vocational Qualifications (NCVQ) and the School Curriculum and Assessment Authority (SCAA) with additional powers and duties. Its remit ranges from the under-fives to higher level vocational qualifications. It is responsible for ensuring that the curriculum and qualifications available to young people and adults are of a high quality, coherent and flexible. As a body committed to enhancing quality in educ, QCA aims to help raise national standards of achievement. This includes promoting greater access to and participation in educ and training, enhancing lifelong learning opportunities, creating ways of giving credible national recognition for all learners, and developing ways of increasing achievements in literacy, numeracy and key skills generally.*

Rachmaninoff Society. 4 Springfield Cottages, New Rd, Rotherfield, E Sussex TN6 3JR *tel:* 0189285 2265. John Lockyer, admin. *Promotes Rachmaninoff as a composer, pianist and conductor. Publishes quarterly newsletter; annual conference in UK.*

Rawsthorne (Alan) Society. RNCM Library, 124 Oxford Rd, Manchester M13 9RD *tel:* 0161 273 6283. Tony Hodges, chmn. *Promotes the mus of Rawsthorne with recordings, live concerts, publications, etc. Publishes* The Creel *annually.*

Reed Organ Society (UK branch). York House, Bluntisham Rd, Colne, Huntingdon, Cambs PE17 3LY *tel:* 01487 842722 *fax:* 01223 330388 *email:* brian.styles@mrc-bsu.cam.ac.uk. Brian C Styles, regional counsellor. *International society with headquarters in the USA. Publishes quarterly journal with historical, restoration and performance articles.*

Royal College of Organists. 7 St Andrew St, London EC4A 3LQ *tel:* 020 7936 3606 *fax:* 020 7353 8244. Gordon Clarke, registrar; Alan Dear, snr

exec; Robin Langley, librarian. *Educ charity of 3200 members for promotion of org playing and choir directing. Exams for Associateship, Fellowship diplomas, choir directing and org teaching diplomas and preliminary certificate. Library and programme of lectures, seminars, short courses, overseas tours, m/classes. Also student section.*

Royal Liverpool Philharmonic Society. Philharmonic Hall, Hope St, Liverpool L1 9BP *tel:* 0151 210 2895 *fax:* 0151 210 2902 *email:* rlpsociety@aol.com. *Promotes the Royal Liverpool Philharmonic Orchestra and Choir, the Merseyside Youth Orchestra as well as managing the Philharmonic Hall itself.*

Royal Musical Association (RMA). 20 Third Acre Rise, Botley, Oxford OX2 9DA *tel:* 01865 862524 *also fax; email:* phillips@patrol.i-way.co.uk. Julian Rushton, president; Geoffrey Lawrence, hon treasurer; Bruce Phillips, sec. *Holds meetings for the presentation of musicological papers and publishes The Journal of the Royal Musical Association, a Research Chronicle, a newsletter and a series of monographs. It hosts one-day meetings, an annual conference and a conference for research students.*

Royal Philharmonic Society. 10 Stratford Place, London W1N 9AE *tel:* 020 7491 8110 *fax:* 020 7493 7463 *email:*admin@rps-uk.demon.co.uk. Rosemary Johnson, gen admin. *Financial support for a season of concerts, lectures and other events. Administers competitions and awards for students in UK; also international Gold Medal and annual RPS Music Awards for outstanding achievement. Membership by application.*

Royal School of Church Music. Cleveland Lodge, Westhumble, Dorking RH5 6BW *tel:* 01306 872800 *fax:* 01306 887260 *email:* cl@rscm.com. Prof John Harper, dir gen. *Training and advisory organisation for the development of church mus. Membership open to all churches, with or without choirs, and to individuals.*

Royal Scottish Country Dance Society. 12 Coates Cres, Edinburgh EH3 7AF *tel:* 0131 225 3854 *fax:* 0131 225 7783. Miss G S Parker, sec. *Aims to preserve and further the practice of trad Scottish country dances and to provide educ and instruction to this end. Has 162 branches throughout the world and more than 500 affiliated groups. Founded 1923.*

Royal Scottish Pipe Band Association. 45 Washington St, Glasgow G3 8AZ *tel:* 0141 221 5414 *fax:* 0141 221 1561. Iain M White, exec offr. *Association of amateur pipe bands. 12 branches running educ classes. Organises contests and championships. Publishes bi-monthly magazine,* The Pipe Band. *Annual summer school in third week of Jul at above address.*

The Royal Society of Musicians of Great Britain. 10 Stratford Place, London W1N 9AE *tel:* 020 7629 6137 *also fax.* Maggie Gibb, sec. *The Society exists to provide help for professional musicians and their families in need as a result of illness, accident or old age.*

The RVW Society. c/o The Chantry, Stoney Lane, Stocklinch, Ilminster, Somerset TA19 9JJ *tel:* 01460 57819 *fax:* 01206 852876 *email:* mason@oup.co.uk. Robin Barber, sec; Stephen Connock, chmn. *Aims to increase knowledge and appreciation of Ralph Vaughan Williams' mus and to encourage performances of lesser known works.*

RVW Trust. 7th Floor, Manfield House, 1 Southampton St, London WC2R 0LR *tel:* 020 7379 6547 *fax:* 020 7240 6333. Bernard Benoliel, admin. *Assists young British composers with premieres and second performances and promotes works by neglected British composers of the past. Also considers applications from the smaller mus festivals who programme mus by young British composers. Does not accept applications towards the cost of recordings, mus insts, degree or summer courses.*

St John's, Smith Square, Friends of. St John's, Smith Square, London SW1P 3HA *tel:* 020 7222 2168 *fax:* 020 7233 1618. Paul Davies, gen mgr. *Mailing list membership, priority booking, concerts (evening and lunchtime), art exhibitions, ticket discounts. Free entry to Thursday lunchtime concert series.*

Schools Music Association of Great Britain (SMA). 71 Margaret Rd, New Barnet, Herts EN4 9NT *tel:* 020 8440 6919 *also fax.* Maxwell Pryce, hon sec and chief exec. *Promotes the mus educ of school pupils and students by encouraging and supporting all who work with them.*

Schubert Institute (UK). 56a Moor Lane, Sherburn-in-Elmet, Leeds LS25 6DN *tel:* 01977 682691 *email:* SIUK@dial.pipex.com. Brian Newbould, chmn; Paul Reid, vice-chmn. *Aims to promote the study of Schubert's life and work and appreciation of his mus. All Schubert lovers welcomed. Affiliated to International Franz Schubert Institute, Vienna. Schubert Institute Research Centre inaugurated May 1997 at University of Leeds.*

Schubert Society of Britain. c/o The General Secretary, German YMCA, 35 Craven Terrace, London W2 3EL *tel:* 020 7723 9276 *fax:* 020 7706 2870 *email:* y-services@g-ymca.ndirect.co.uk. Bernd Hildebrandt, sec. *The Schubert Society presents 'Schubertiades' in London monthly, Oct-May (except Dec), as a forum for young artistes.*

Scottish Amateur Music Association. 18 Craigton Cres, Alva, Clackmannanshire FK12 5DS *tel:* 01259 760249 *email:* secretary@sama.org.uk. Margaret W Simpson, hon sec. *Provides national training courses to help and encourage amateur mus-making in Scotland.*

Scottish Association for Music Education. c/o Music Dept, Fife Council, Auchterderran Centre, Woodend Rd, Cardenden KY5 0NE *tel:* 01592 414600 *fax:* 01592 414641 *email:* gwilson@itasdarc.demon.co.uk. Graeme Wilson, sec and mus adviser; H C Richardson, chmn. *Annual journal produced in Dec (available to members). Also annual conference.*

Scottish Music Education Forum. School of Music, Dept of Aesthetic Education, Northern College, Hilton Place, Aberdeen AB24 4FA *tel:* 01224 283558 *fax:* 01224 283900 *email:* j.p.stephens@norcol.ac.uk. Jonathan Stephens, dir of mus, head of aesthetic educ. *Acts as co-ordinating body, providing a point of contact for those involved in mus and mus educ courses, associations and societies. Membership consists of reps from wide range of mus interests: school, HE, commerce, industry and special interest groups including Scottish trad mus. Aims to promote diversity of mus in Scotland, maintain particular strengths, collate and disseminate information, and identify and promote good practice.*

Scottish Music Information Centre. 1 Bowmont Gardens, Glasgow G12 9LR *tel:* 0141 334 6393 *fax:* 0141 337 1161 *email:* smic@glasgow.almac.co.uk. Alasdair Pettinger, information offr. *Resource and information centre for mus (especially contemporary) by Scottish and Scottish-based composers. Reference, hire and audio libraries; photocopying service, promotional activities.*

Scottish Musicians Benevolent Fund. c/o 10 Manse Rd, Bearsden, Glasgow G61 3PT *tel:* 0141 942 1364 *also fax.* Evelyn Bryson, hon sec and treasurer. *Cares for Scottish professional musicians (and their dependants) in need, ill or convalescing. Regular monthly grants and one-off grants. Membership of a trade union/professional organisation is not necessary.*

Scottish Secondary Teachers' Association. 15 Dundas St, Edinburgh EH3 6QG *tel:* 0131 556 5919 *fax:* 0131 556 1419 *email:* sstateach@aol.com. David Eaglesham, gen sec. *Professional association for secondary teachers in Scotland. Recognised at the Scottish Office Education Dept and represented on the Scottish Joint Negotiating Committee for Teaching Staff in School Education. Publishes bulletins (6 pa) and* Secondary Teacher *(4 pa) for members only.*

Scottish Society of Composers. Mazagon, 4 Glen Rd, Lennoxtown G65 7JX *tel:* 01360 313217 *fax:* 01360 319020. Thomas Wilson CBE, hon president; Neil Butterworth, chmn; Derek Ball, sec and treasurer. *Promotes wider knowledge of contemporary mus in Scotland through international and local liaison, annual awards to musicians, distribution of catalogues of new mus and sponsorship of new mus recording.*

Secondary Heads Association. 130 Regent Rd, Leicester LE1 7PG *tel:* 0116 299 1122 *fax:* 0116 299 1123. John Dunford, gen sec. *Professional association which caters specifically for the principals, deputies and snr mgrs in secondary schools and colleges.*

Seeds Ltd (Christian Creative Resource Service). 30 Grasvenor Ave, Barnet, Herts EN5 2BZ *tel:* 020 8364 9652 *email:* seeds30@aol.com. Neil Ruckman, admin and educ; Chris Norris, chmn.

Sibelius Society. 5 Fitzwilliam Rd, London SW4 0DL *tel:* 020 7627 3086; 020 7583 6357 *fax:* 020 7583 6358 *email:* edward@tallis.u-net.com. E W Clark, president; A Barnett, chmn. *Promotes the works of Sibelius. Quarterly newsletter and awards for best CD and artist. Regular concerts held in London. Promotion activities with the Finnish Embassy.*

The Silvester (Victor) Appreciation Society. 1 Portland Cres, Weymouth, Dorset DT4 0NW *tel:* 01305 784379. Geoff Williams, sec. *Produces 3 newsletters pa.*

Simpson (Robert) Society. 13 Third Ave, London W10 4RS *tel:* 020 8960 1358. Donald Macauley, membership sec. *Promotes study, performance and recording of the mus and writings of Robert Simpson.*

The Sir George Dyson Trust. 14 Barlby Rd, London W10 6AR *tel:* 020 8969 3579 *fax:* 020 8969 3579. John Bishop, admin. *Acts as information centre about all aspects of Dyson's life and mus; has recording and publishing programme.*

Society for Co-operation in Russian & Soviet Studies. 320 Brixton Rd, London SW9 6AB *tel:* 020 7274 2282 *fax:* 020 7274 3230. J Turner, sec. *Reference library of mus scores, encyclopedias and records pertaining to Russian and Soviet mus and composers.*

Society for Music Analysis. Dept of Music, University of Wales, Bangor, Gwynedd LL57 2DG *tel:* 0115 951 4755 *fax:* 0115 951 4756 *email:* sally.britten@nottingham.ac.uk. S Britten, admin; R Pascall, president. *Society for the development of all aspects of mus analysis, especially research and teaching. Open to lecturers, students and all who are interested in analysis.*

Society for Research in the Psychology of Music and Music Education. c/o Dept of Music, The University of Sheffield, Western Bank, Sheffield

S10 2TN. Annette Davison, membership sec. *Aims to encourage the exchange of ideas and to disseminate research findings in the fields of psychology of mus and in mus educ.*

Society of Assistants Teaching in Preparatory Schools. 20 Brycedale Cres, Southgate, London N14 7EY *tel:* 020 8882 0630 *also fax; email:* satips@ford.anglia.ac.uk. June Keyte, editor, Music Broadsheet. *The mus group of an organisation covering all subjects taught in prep schools. It publishes termly broadsheets for members and organises occasional conferences.*

Society of Headmasters and Headmistresses of Independent Schools. Celedston, Rhosesmor Rd, Halkyn, Holywell CH8 8DL *tel:* 01352 781102 *also fax; email:* gensec@shmis.demon.co.uk. I D Cleland, gen sec. *An association of 80 heads of independent secondary schools with VI forms. Most of the schools have boarders and almost all are wholly or partly co-educational. The society represents the smaller independent school offering a balanced educ to pupils of widely varying interests and abilities; also included are two of the specialist mus schools and a ballet school.*

Society of Leisure and Entertainment Consultants and Publishers (SOLCAP). 1 Sandringham Close, Sandringham Park, Tarleton, Lancs PR4 6UZ *tel:* 01772 816046. J B A Sharples, dir. *Represents consultants and publishers in the field of entertainment and the arts, recreation, marketing, leisure and allied interests.*

Society of Producers and Composers of Applied Music (PCAM). Birchwood Hall, Storridge, Malvern, Worcs WR13 5EZ *tel:* 01886 884204 *also fax; email:* bfromer@netcomuk.co.uk. Bob Fromer, admin. *A trade association representing composers, producers and mus production companies who create mus for advertising, television programmes and other a/v applications.*

Society of Recorder Players. 15 Palliser Rd, London W14 9EB *tel:* 020 7385 7321 *email:* secretary@srp.org.uk. A Read, sec. *A national society with international membership offering rcdr players in the UK the opportunity to meet regularly and play in conducted ens. 48 groups meet nationwide, mostly on a monthly basis. Members also receive* The Recorder Magazine *quarterly. The Society issues its own certificate to confirm a candidate's ability to conduct and direct rcdr groups. Annual festival and other events take place throughout the year.*

Society of Schoolmasters and Schoolmistresses. The King's School, Canterbury, Kent CT1 2ES *tel:* 01227 595546. R B Mallion, hon sec. *Gives assistance to necessitous masters and mistresses of all recognised schools, independent or maintained, and their dependants, provided such persons have been continuously engaged in teaching for not less than 10 years.*

Society of Teachers of the Alexander Technique (STAT). 20 London House, 266 Fulham Rd, London SW10 9EL *tel:* 020 7351 0828 *fax:* 020 7352 1556 *email:* info@stat.org.uk. Liz Flint, admin. *The society can provide a list of members who teach in the UK, details of affiliated societies throughout the world and information on the Technique.*

Sonic Arts Network *formerly* **EMAS.** The Jerwood Space, 171 Union St, London SE1 0LN *tel:* 020 7928 7337 *fax:* 020 7928 7338 *email:* rachel@sonicartsnetwork.org. Paul Wright, educ dir; Rachel Spencer, admin. *National association of composers, performers and teachers and others interested in the creative uses of tech in the composition and performance of mus. Campaigns for a national centre for sonic art and initiates educ projects bringing together composers, school pupils and teachers. Also INSET on ways of integrating new tech with other classroom resources.*

The Sorabji Archive. Easton Dene, Bailbrook Lane, Bath BA1 7AA *tel:* 01225 852323 *fax:* 01225 852523 *email:* sorabji-archive@lineone.net; alistair_hinton@compuserve.com. Alistair Hinton, curator and dir. *Makes available to the public the mus and literary collection of Sorabji's works. Includes published, manuscript and new edition scores; articles and essays; reviews of books, mus publications, concerts and recordings; correspondence and discography.*

Sound Sense - The National Development Agency for Community Music. Riverside House, Rattlesden, Bury St Edmunds, Suffolk IP30 0SF *tel:* 01449 736287 *fax:* 01449 737649 *email:* 100256.30@compuserve.com. Kathryn Deane, dir; Clare Adams, admin; Anita Holford, communications offr; Kate Murdoch, projects offr; Margaret Sloan, information offr. *The development agency for participatory, creative mus-making, offering support, advice and training to community musicians and groups as well as other arts and educ organisations. Information services include newsletters, publications, mus and disability advice, help lines and a directory of courses in community mus.*

spnm - promoting new music. Francis House, Francis St, London SW1P 1DE *tel:* 020 7828 9696 *fax:* 020 7931 9928 *email:* spnm@spnm.org.uk. Gill Graham, exec dir; Katy Bignold, admin; Sarah Gibbon, educ consultant. *Contemporary jazz, classical and pop mus, film, dance and other creative media. Educ work with 16-19 year olds and their teachers. Also publishes* new notes *monthly concert listings magazine and* Best *magazine for 16-19 year olds.*

Spohr Society of Great Britain. 123 Mount View Rd, Sheffield S8 8PJ *tel:* 0114 258 5420. C H Tutt, sec; K Warsop, chmn. *Aims to support and promote the mus of Louis Spohr through research, publications and recordings.*

Steel Band Adviser. 60 Greenford Gardens, Greenford, Middx UB6 9LZ *tel:* 020 8578 6485; 07850 650401 *fax:* 020 8578 6485 *email:* terry.noel@btinternet.com. Terry Noel, chmn. *Provides advice on all aspects of steel bands, getting insts, tuition, upkeep of insts.*

Stevens (Bernard) Trust. The Forge, Great Maplestead, Halstead, Essex CO9 2RE *tel:* 01787 460315 *also fax.* Bertha Stevens, sec; Roderick Swanston, chmn; John Cruft, Michael Finnissy, Matthew Greenall, Edwin Roxburgh, Catherine Stevens, Ronald Stevenson, trustees. *Promotes the mus of Bernard Stevens (1916-1983). Recordings, concerts and publications.*

The Stevenson (Ronald) Society. 3 Chamberlain Rd, Edinburgh EH10 4DL *fax:* 0131 229 9298 *email:* medeco@perthalmac.co.uk. P Hutton, chmn; C Scott-Sutherland, treasurer; Ian Colquhoun, sec. *Promotes the mus of Ronald Stevenson; sponsors publication, performance and recording of his work. Annual summer school.*

Stolz (Robert), The Friends of. Red Lion Court, Stalbridge, Sturminster Newton, Dorset DT10 2LR *tel:* 01963 362999. Robert Keys, founder and sec. *Supports and promotes the mus of Robert Stolz, with meetings, bulletins, concerts, lectures and a reference library.*

Strauss (Johann) Society of Great Britain. Flat 12, Bishams Court, Church Hill, Caterham, Surrey CR3 6SE *tel:* 01883 349681. Mrs V E Coates, hon sec. *Promotes the performance, recording, study and deeper appreciation of the mus of the Strauss family and their Viennese contemporaries.*

Strauss (Richard) Society. 39 Tamworth Park, Mitcham, Surrey CR4 1HZ *tel:* 020 8646 7054 *also fax.* Bernard Hughes, chmn; Nigel Coles, treasurer. *Quarterly newsletter. Monthly meetings in Central London. Block opera bookings.*

The Takemitsu Society. c/o 26 Sandown Rd, West Malling, Kent ME19 6NS *tel:* 01732 870414 *email:* takemitsu@postmaster.co.uk. Ms Junko Kobayashi, chmn; Peter Burt, vice-chmn. *Promotes the understanding of the mus of the late Tōru Takemitsu and other contemporary Japanese composers.*

The Tomkins Tate Musical Instrument Trust. 20 Church St, Horwich, Bolton BL6 6AD *tel:* 01204 693187 *also fax; email:* nicky.clark@cwcom.net. Mrs N Clark. *The Trust lends str inst to young people who could not otherwise afford to play. Applications to be made in writing.*

Traditional Music and Song Association of Scotland. 95-97 St Leonard's St, Edinburgh EH8 9QY *tel:* 0131667 5587 *fax:* 0131 662 9153. Elspeth Cowie, national organiser; Fiona Nisbet, admin asst. *National organisation promoting the performance and awareness of trad Scottish mus and song, story-telling and dance. Organises w/shops, m/classes and school curriculum enrichment visits.*

Tureck Bach Research Foundation. Windrush House, Davenant Rd, Oxford OX2 8BX *tel:* 01865 515760 *fax:* 01865 512620 *email:* rosalyn.tureck@st-hildas.ox.ac.uk. Rosalyn Tureck, dir; Dawn Gill, admin asst. *Explores the identities of the fundamental concepts that nourish the arts, sciences and humanities in annual international symposia. Proceedings of each symposium reported in TBRF journal,* Interaction *(vol 1 Dec 1995; vol 2 1998).* Institute for Advanced Musical Studies *held semi-annually; lectures and m/classes for advanced and professional musicians - period and modern insts and musicological studies.*

UK-Japan Music Society. 27 Heron Close, Great Glen, Leicester LE8 9DZ *tel:* 0116 259 3891 *also fax. UK Japan choir meets in London and Leicester. Performances with orch.*

Ulster Society of Organists and Choirmasters. 1b Beverley Hills, Bangor, N Ireland BT20 4NA *tel:* 028 9146 5222. Rodney Bambrick, hon sec. *Provides a forum for church musicians of all denominations; lectures, discussions, recitals, w/shops, org visits, etc.*

United Kingdom Harp Association. 58 Argyle St, London WC1H 8ER *tel:* 020 7837 4954 *fax:* 020 7833 8155 *email:* ukharpassn@aol.com. Hugh Webb, magazine ed. *600 members worldwide. For professional harpists, students, amateurs, hp makers and retailers. Publishes quarterly magazine and directory of members. Also annual awards for student harpists.*

Universities Association for Continuing Education. University of Cambridge Board of Continuing Education, Madingley Hall, Madingley, Cambridge CB3 8AQ *tel:* 01954 280279 *fax:* 01954 280200 *email:* smi20@cam.ac.uk. Michael Richardson, sec. *The association promotes and represents the interests of continuing educ within HE, acts as a forum for the discussion of policy issues, promotes and conducts research and disseminates the results to the general public and interested organisations.*

Universities and Colleges Admissions Service (UCAS). Rosehill, New Barn Lane, Cheltenham, Glos GL52 3LZ *tel:* 01242 227788 *fax:* 01242

221622 *email:* enq@ucas.ac.uk. M A Higgins, chief exec; A P McClaren, deputy chief exec. *UCAS is the central agency through which applicants apply for all f/t u/grad first degrees and most DipHE and HND courses at universities and colleges in the UK.*

Video Performance Ltd. 1 Upper James St, London W1R 3HG *tel:* 020 7534 1400 *fax:* 020 7534 1414. Roger Drage, consultant. *Administers the public performance and broadcast rights in mus videos on behalf of its 700 member companies.*

Viola d'Amore Society of Great Britain. 4 Constable Rd, Felixstowe, Suffolk IP11 7HH *tel:* 01394 285584. Nicholas Neale, publisher (*tel:* 01277 899247); Ian White, Alex Tinlin, composers. *Aims to promote the va d'am, and to use it in performance with other insts. Also publishes original works from the 18th C and supplies them on demand. Tuition available along with advice over proper set-ups of insts and stringing. Also repairs to insts and bows.*

Viola da Gamba Society. 56 Hunters Way, Dringhouses, York YO24 1JJ *tel:* 01904 706959 *also fax; email:* admin@vdgs.demon.co.uk. Caroline Wood, admin. *Publishes annual journal and quarterly newsletter* Music for Viols. *Meetings and conferences. Viols for hire.*

The Voices Foundation. 21 Earls Court Square, London SW5 9BY *tel:* 020 7370 1944 *fax:* 020 7370 1874 *email:* vf@voicefnd.demon.co.uk. Susan Digby, principal; Michael Stocks, dir of curriculum and training. *Educ charity specialising in mus curriculum development in primary schools and the professional development of primary teachers. 1-day w/shops for parents and teachers. 6-day courses for mus specialists and mus curriculum leaders.*

The Wagner Society. 15 David Ave, Wickford, Essex SS11 7BG *tel:* 01268 560833 *also fax; email:* pritchard@shsb.essex.sch.uk. J J Pritchard, chmn. *A charity dedicated to the appreciation and study of Richard Wagner's life and mus.*

Warlock (Peter) Society. 32a Chipperfield House, Cale St, London SW3 3SA *tel:* 020 7589 9595 *also fax; email:* malcolmrudland@ndirect.co.uk. Malcolm Rudland, sec. *To increase awareness and knowledge of the composer.*

Welsh Amateur Music Federation. Ty Cerdd, 15 Mount Stuart Square, Cardiff CF10 5DP *tel:* 029 2046 5700 *fax:* 029 2046 2733. Keith Griffin, dir. *Offers financial assistance, advice and training to amateur mus organisations in Wales. It founded and now administers the National Youth Brass Band of Wales and the National Youth Choir of Wales.*

The Welsh Association of Ladies' Choirs. 11 The Firs, Newton Burrows, Porthcawl, Mid Glamorgan CF36 5AX *tel:* 01656 782970. J L Walker, sec; V Grenfell, chmn. *Works to develop an appreciation of female choral singing within a wider audience; provides a forum for shared experience and increases the friendship and co-operation between individuals and between choirs by arranging massed events.*

Welsh Association of Male Choirs. 98 Glannant Way, Cimla Neath, W Glamorgan, SA11 3YN *tel:* 01639 641061; 01639 637932 *also fax.* J J Watkins, organising sec; J Layton Watkins, admin sec. *Offers a legal advice service and mus and insurance at a discount to members. Also organises festival.*

Welsh Folk Dance Society. Ffynnonlwyd, Trelech, Caerfyrddin, Sir Gaerfyrddin SA33 6QZ *tel:* 01994 484496 *also fax; email:* dafyddevans@welshfolkdance.freeserve.co.uk. Dafydd M Evans, sec. *Formed in 1949 to promote Welsh folk dancing and dance mus.*

Welsh Folk Song Society. Hafan, Cricieth, Gwynedd *tel:* 01766 522096. Buddug Lloyd Roberts, sec. *Annual magazine* Cann Gwerin, *Rhidian Griffiths, Rhiannon Ifans, eds.*

Welsh Jazz Society Ltd. 26 The Balcony, Castle Arcade, Cardiff CF10 2BY *tel:* 029 2034 0591 *fax:* 029 2066 5160 *email:* jazzwale@compuserve.com. Brian Hennessey, mgr dir. *An educ charity devoted to the promotion, educ and presentation of jazz in all its varied forms.*

Welsh Music Information Centre. Ty Cerrd, 15 Mount Stuart Square, Cardiff CF10 5DP *Enquiries only to the address above.*

Welsh National Opera, Friends of. John St, Cardiff CF1 4SP *tel:* 029 2046 4666 *fax:* 029 2048 3050. Maureen Lawrence, admin; Sara Greenwood, asst.

White (Ernest George) Society. 106 Gladstone Rd, South Willesborough, Ashford, Kent TN24 0DD *tel:* 01233 629921 *fax:* 01233 638430. Dorothy Douse, sec. *An educ charity to promote White's voice teaching on the principles described as Sinus Tone Production.*

Whitlock (Percy) Trust. 32 Butcher Close, Staplehurst, Kent TN12 0TJ *tel:* 01580 891128 *also fax.* Malcolm Riley, hon sec. *Holds archive of scores, diaries, photographs, letters, etc.*

Whittaker Centenary Fund. Viking Publications, The Oast House, Goddards Green, Benenden, Cranbrook, Kent TN17 4AR *tel:* 01580 240377. Jonathan Piers-Pollitzer. *To promote the mus of W G Whittaker (1876-1944).*

William Walton Trust. 9 Central Chambers, Wood St, Stratford-upon-Avon CV37 6JQ *tel:* 01789 261573 *fax:* 01789 266467 *email:* wwt@swartists.co.uk. Stephannie Williams, artistic dir; Martin Denny, admin. *The trust aims, through the mus of William Walton, both to encourage educ projects in schools and to develop the potential in young professional musicians at the start of their careers.*

Women in Music. Riverside House, Rattlesden, Bury St Edmunds IP30 0SF *tel:* 01449 736287 *fax:* 01449 737649 *email:* 100256.30 @compuserve.com. Clare Adams, admin. *Celebrates and raises public awareness of women's work in mus. Produces a bi-monthly magazine* Women in Music Now, *and provides information on women's involvement in mus. Administers a commissioning fund.*

Workers' Educational Association. 17 Victoria Park Square, London E2 9PB *tel:* 020 8983 1515 *fax:* 020 8983 4840 *email:* info@nat.wea.org.uk. Robert Lochrie, gen sec. *Adult educ charity with 14 districts and over 700 branches in the UK.*

Workers' Music Association. 240 Perry Rise, Forest Hill, London SE23 2QT *tel:* 020 8699 2250. A F Schuman, chair, hon sec; Aubrey Bowman, president; M Cook, (acting) treasurer. *The association believes that mus has a bearing on social life and is a means of attaining a brighter and better society; publishes mus; annual summer school of mus; London-based choir.*

Worshipful Company of Musicians. 74-75 Watling St, London EC4M 9BJ *tel:* 020 7489 8888 *fax:* 020 7489 1614. S F N Waley, clerk. *Livery Company of the City of London (founded 1500).*

York Early Music Foundation. PO Box 226, York YO30 5ZU *tel:* 01904 645738 *fax:* 01904 612631 *email:* yemf@netcomuk.co.uk. *Charity dedicated to sustaining York Early Music Festival and to promoting complementary activities both locally and nationally. Plans to establish a National Early Music Centre in York, opening scheduled for autumn 1999.*

Young Concert Artists Trust. 23 Garrick St, London WC2E 9AX *tel:* 020 7379 8477 *fax:* 020 7379 8467. Rosemary Pickering, chief exec. *A charity offering career management for young musicians. Annual auditions. Apply to YCAT for application forms and eligibility.*

Young Persons Concert Foundation. PO Box 419, Enfield, Middx EN2 0ZB *tel:* 020 8367 0553; 01923 859388 *fax:* 020 8366 3535. William A J Starling, artistic dir; Sally Needleman, special projects co-ord. *Presents w/shops and concerts (from individual str, w/wind, br and perc sections to full orch) by young professional players from the Foundation Philharmonic Orchestra; free to schoolchildren where sponsorship is available.*

Youth and Music. 28 Charing Cross Rd, London WC2H 0DB *tel:* 020 7379 6722 *fax:* 020 7497 0345 *email:* stagepass@yandm.org.uk. Monica Ferguson, exec dir; Katharine Meadows, company sec; Kate Powell, publications offr; Samantha Hook, mkt offr; Paul Terry, membership sec. *Operates* Stagepass, *a nationwide ticket concessionary scheme for young people. British representative of Jeunesses Musicales. Also World Orchestra, World Choir, international mus camps, etc.*

Musicians' Union Offices

Musicians' Union National Office. 60-62 Clapham Rd, London SW9 0JJ *tel:* 020 7582 5566 *fax:* 020 7582 9805 *email:* info@musiciansunion.org.uk. Dennis Scard, gen sec; Howard Evans, session organiser; Nigel McLune, mus business adviser. Bob Wearn, Andy Knight, asst gen secs.

Musicians' Union London Office and Central London Branch. 60-62 Clapham Rd, London SW9 0JJ *tel:* 020 7582 5566 *fax:* 020 7840 5599. Horace Trubridge, London official.

Musicians' Union Midlands Office. Benson House, Lombard St, Birmingham B12 0QN *tel:* 0121 622 3870 *fax:* 0121 622 5361 *email:* info@musiciansunion.org.uk. Bob Bennett, Midlands district organiser, Birmingham branch sec, br band liaison official and jazz section sec.

Musicians' Union North-East/North-West Office. 40 Canal St, Manchester M1 3WD *tel:* 0161 236 1764 *fax:* 0161 236 0159 *email:* dgl@musiciansunion.org.uk. Elaine Rogers, North-East district organiser; Bill Kerr, North-West district organiser.

Musicians' Union Scottish Office. 11 Sandyford Place, Glasgow G3 7NB *tel:* 0141 248 3723 *fax:* 0141 204 3510. Ian D C Smith, Scottish organiser, Glasgow branch sec; Francesca Howell, admin asst.

Musicians' Union South-East Office and East District Office. 60-62 Clapham Rd, London SW9 0JJ *tel:* 020 7582 5566 *fax:* 020 7582 9805. Alf Clarke, east/south-east district organiser.

Musicians' Union South-West Office. 131 St Georges Rd, Bristol BS1 5UW *tel:* 0117 926 5438 *fax:* 0117 925 3729. Paul Westwell, district organiser.

Music and Disability

Organisations

All Clear Designs Ltd. 3rd Floor, Cooper House, 2 Michael Rd, London SW6 2AD *tel:* 020 7384 2950/1 *fax:* 020 7384 2951 *email:* allclear@easynet.co.uk. James Holme-Siedle, dir. *Specialises in access design and disability equality training, following a format of detailed audits on existing buildings or advice on new designs which produce working documents for the architect and designer. The disability equality training offers customised courses run by disabled trainers for design professionals and staff within a range of organisations.*

Arts Council of England. Library and Enquiry Service, 14 Great Peter St, London SW1P 3NQ *tel:* 020 7333 0100 *minicom:* 020 7973 6564 *fax:* 020 7973 6590 *email:* enquiries@artscouncil.org.uk. Mary Holland, policy offr (disability); Louise Rutkowski, asst mus offr. *Publishes a directory of arts and disability contacts, available from Information Services. Enquiries about the funding of mus-related projects should be made to the mus dept.*

Arts for Health. Manchester Metropolitan University, All Saints, Manchester M15 6BY *tel:* 0161 236 8916 *fax:* 0161 247 6390 *email:* p.senior@mmu.ac.uk. Peter Senior MBE, dir; Kath Beaven, admin. *National centre providing practical consultancy, advice and information to all those interested in using any art form as a complimentary aspect of health care.*

Artsline. 54 Chalton St, Camden, London NW1 1HS *tel:* 020 7388 2227 *fax:* 020 7383 2653 *email:* artsline@dircon.co.uk. *Minicom available. Information and advice service for disabled people on access to arts and entertainments, including participation in the arts in London. Open for enquiries Mon-Fri 9.30am-5.30pm. Produces* Play, *a booklet with details of activities available to disabled children. Also produces other access guides for theatres, cinemas, mus venues and tourist attractions. Runs a multicultural project for disabled people from ethnic minority communities, an access guide to venues with a multicultural focus, Disability Equality Training for arts and entertainment venues in London, a youth project for disabled people aged 16-24 and an access audit service to make buildings more accessible.*

Association of Professional Music Therapists. 26 Hamlyn Rd, Glastonbury, Somerset BA6 8HT *tel:* 01458 834919 *also fax; email:* APMToffice@aol.com. Diana Asbridge, admin. *Deals with the needs of professional mus therapists in relation to standards of practice, employment, career structure, training, etc.*

Beethoven Fund for Deaf Children. PO Box 16975, London NW8 6ZL *tel:* 020 7586 8107 *fax:* 020 7722 7981. Ann Rachlin MBE, founder, chmn, trustee; Kevin Maddison, hon treasurer, trustee; Max Ziff, vice-chmn, trustee. *Charity providing specially-designed insts to help profoundly deaf children to speak. Funds mus speech therapy centres throughout UK for deaf children.*

British Dyslexia Association. 98 London Rd, Reading, Berks RG1 5AU *tel:* 0118 966 8271 (helpline); 0118 966 2677 *fax:* 0118 935 1927 *email:* info@dyslexiahelp-bda.demon.co.uk. *Provides information and advice relating to the effect of dyslexia on reading and writing mus. Also deals with individual enquiries regarding mus difficulties arising from dyslexia.*

British Society for Music Therapy (BSMT). 25 Rosslyn Ave, E Barnet, Herts EN4 8DH *tel:* 020 8368 8879 *also fax; email:* denize@bsmt.demon.co.uk. Nigel Hartley, chmn. *Promotes the use and development of mus therapy in the treatment, educ and rehabilitation of children and adults suffering from emotional, physical or mental handicap. Membership is open to all interested in mus therapy. The Society holds meetings, w/shops and conferences. Publishes a journal (jointly with the Association of Professional Music Therapists) and a bulletin for members.*

British Wireless for the Blind Fund. Gabriel House, 34 New Rd, Chatham, Kent ME4 4QR *tel:* 01634 832501 *fax:* 01634 817485 *email:* margaret@blind.org.uk. Mrs M R Grainger, chief exec. *Provides radios and radio cassette recorders on a free permanent loan basis to registered blind people in need in the UK.*

The Chantry Trust. 1a King's Mews, London WC1N 2JA *tel:* 020 7242 8586 *fax:* 020 7831 7914 *email:* rupertcrew@compuserve.com. Rex Montgomery, founder and admin. *Organisation researching therapeutic benefits of mus in educ for autistic and handicapped children. Grants not available at present, but occasional gifts of books and ms material made to established bodies in similar fields.*

Children Helping Children. Medlar Cottage, Lodge Lane, Keymer, Hassocks, W Sussex BN6 8NA *tel:* 01273 843348 *fax:* 01273 846585. Dona Lee Croft, Vanessa Latarche, dirs; Anthony Abbott, admin. *Fundraising gala concerts by talented, young violinists and pianists to benefit charities working to alleviate the plight of disabled, disadvantaged, potentially terminally ill, abused or neglected children.*

Community Music Wales. 2 Leckwith Place, Canton, Cardiff CF1 8PA *tel:* 029 2038 7620 *also fax; email:* cmw@pop3.poptel.org.uk. Simon Dancey, development offr. *Inspired by the belief that everyone can derive pleasure and satisfaction from playing mus, and that mus projects provide a rich learning environment in which a host of other important skills can be acquired. Resources and expertise in a wide range of mus forms, including mus tech, are made available to people who are typically excluded from opportunities for creative self-expression and personal development for reasons of disability or disadvantage. Also professional training course for community musicians.*

Council for Music in Hospitals (Scotland). 10 Forth St, Edinburgh EH1 3LD *tel:* 0131 556 5848 *fax:* 0131 556 0225. Alison Frazer, dir. *Concerts of live mus given by professional musicians selected for their communication skills. Participation encouraged. Venues include hospitals, hospices, homes for elderly people and day centres.*

Disability Scotland. 5 Shandwick Place, Edinburgh EH2 4RG *tel:* 0131 229 8632 *fax:* 0131 229 5168 *email:* disability.scotland@virgin.net. Robert Pickles, development mgr (Access). *Works with Scottish cultural agencies and institutions to ensure that opportunities are created for people with a disability to become involved in cultural activities.*

Drake Music Project. Christchurch Forum, Trafalgar Rd, London SE10 9EQ *tel:* 020 8305 0580 *fax:* 020 8305 0583 *email:* centralservices @drakemusicproject.com. Adèle Drake, project dir; Brent Barraclough, development dir; Tim Anderson, tech mgr. *Involved in research, including specialist software development. Enables people with severe disabilities to explore the world of mus through w/shops, and trains professionals in related fields. Also London, Scotland, Midlands, Ireland, Newcastle, Manchester and Milton Keynes (partnership project with Scope) co-ords.*

Healing Arts: Isle of Wight. St Mary's, Parkhurst Rd, Newport, Isle of Wight PO30 5TG *tel:* 01983 524081 ext 4253 *fax:* 01983 525157 *email:* healingarts@iowht.swest.nhs.uk. Guy Eades, arts dir. *Co-ordinates an arts programme across the spectrum of health services with particular emphasis on mus in healthcare.*

London Disability Arts Forum. 34 Osnaburgh St, London NW1 3ND *tel:* 020 7916 5484 *fax:* 020 7916 5396 *email:* ldaf@dail.dircon.co.uk. Julie McNamara, co-ord. *Set up to define and promote disability arts, to provide a forum for disabled artists and performers, and to further the participation and representation of disabled people in the arts. Maintains and manages databases of disabled performers in all fields including mus. Hosts mus performances throughout the year.*

MusicSpace Trust. St Matthias Campus, (UWE) Oldbury, Court Rd, Fishponds, Bristol BS16 2UP *tel:* 0117 976 2634 *fax:* 0117 976 2635 *email:* musicspace@uwe.ac.uk. Leslie Bunt, dir. *Provides mus therapy sessions for people of all ages, also w/shops and training sessions, including p/t mus therapy diploma course in conjunction with Bristol University and short introductory courses at the University of the West of England.*

National Association for Special Educational Needs (NASEN). NASEN House, 4-5 Amber Business Village, Amber Close, Amington, Tamworth B77 4RP *tel:* 01827 311500 *fax:* 01827 313005 *email:* welcome@nasen.org.uk. C Gallow, exec office admin. *Promotes the interests of children and young people with special educ needs and supports those who work with them.*

National Disability Arts Forum. Mea House, Ellison Place, Newcastle upon Tyne NE1 8XS *tel:* 0191 261 1628 *fax:* 0191 222 0573 *email:* ndaf@ndaf.org. Geoff Armstrong, dir; Sian Williams, information worker. *Organisation established by disabled people to promote equality of opportunity for disabled people in all aspects of the arts. Particularly concerned with supporting the development of disability arts locally, nationally and internationally.*

National Music and Disability Information Service (NMDIS). Sound Sense, Riverside House, Rattlesden, Bury St Edmunds, Suffolk IP30 0SF *tel:* 01449 736287 *fax:* 01449 737649 *email:* 100256.30@compuserve.com. Sarah Bennett-Day, NMDIS adviser. *NMDIS, run by Sound Sense, gives information and advice on most aspects of mus and disability issues. Publications and quarterly journal available.*

Nordoff-Robbins Music Therapy Centre. 2 Lissenden Gardens, London NW5 1PP *tel:* 020 7267 4496 *fax:* 020 7267 4369 *email:* nrmtc@dircon.co.uk. Pauline Etkin, dir. *Centre houses a clinic which children and adults with a variety of needs can attend for mus therapy. Offers a 2-year Master of Music Therapy training validated by City*

University. Library holds collection of material including documentation of the work of Dr Nordoff and Dr Robbins.

Northern Ireland Music Therapy Trust. Graham House, Knockbracken Healthcare Park, Saintfield Rd, Belfast BT8 8BH *tel:* 028 9070 5854 *also fax.* Karen Diamond, team leader; Michael Swallow OBE, board sec. *Promotes interest in, and the application of, mus therapy throughout Northern Ireland.*

Nottinghamshire Arts Support Service. Eastbourne Centre, Station Rd, Sutton in Ashfield, Notts NG17 5FF *tel:* 01623 466713 *fax:* 01623 466701. John Childs, arts co-ord. *Developing the use of the arts and a variety of creative work within schools.*

Royal Association for Disability and Rehabilitation (RADAR). 12 City Forum, 250 City Rd, London EC1V 8AF *tel:* 020 7250 3222/4119 (minicom) *fax:* 020 7250 0212 *email:* radar@radar.org.uk. *National campaigning and information organisation working with and for physically disabled people with an information dept for general enquiries.*

Royal National Institute for the Blind (RNIB). Music Education Advisory Service, National Education Services, Garrow House, 190 Kensal Rd, London W10 5BT *tel:* 020 8968 8600 *fax:* 020 8960 3593 *email:* szimmermann@rnib.org.uk. Sally-Anne Zimmermann, mus educ adviser. *Offers advice and information on all matters concerning the mus educ of visually impaired children and adults.*

Shape London. c/o The London Voluntary Sector Resource Centre, 356 Holloway Rd, London N7 6PA *tel:* 020 7700 8138/9 *also minicom; fax:* 020 7700 8143. Maggie Woolley, dir. *Arts development agency working with disabled and older people for greater access and involvement in all aspects of the arts. W/shops, projects and events. Offers accredited training courses and placements in all aspects of arts management and practice. Deaf Arts Programme and Ticket Scheme with reduced price tickets and volunteer escorts/drivers. Artists' residencies in schools for deaf and disabled children plus advice, information and consultancy on all aspects of arts and disability.*

Yorkshire and Humberside Association for Music in Special Education. 46 Nunroyd Rd, Leeds LS17 6PF *tel:* 0113 268 4198. Mavis West, sec. *Open to anyone interested in exploring the role of mus with people with special needs; for pleasure, educ and communication, through courses, seminars, w/shops and concerts.*

Professional Training

The courses listed below are mainly designed for able-bodied people who wish to work with people with disabilities.

Anglia Polytechnic University. Division of Music and Performing Arts, East Rd, Cambridge CB1 1PT *tel:* 01223 363271. Helen Odell-Miller, admissions tutor and course dir. *MA and Professional Diploma in Music Therapy cover both university work and placements. Applicants should normally possess a degree or graduate diploma in mus, but graduates of other disciplines with an appropriate level of musicianship will be considered. Some practical experience needed, working with people with learning disabilities and/or mental illness. 15 places on course. 38 weeks f/t Sep-Aug. Fees: £4010.*

Bristol University. Dept of Music, Victoria Rooms, Queens Rd, Clifton, Bristol BS8 1SA *tel:* 0117 954 5032 *fax:* 0117 954 5033 *email:* john.pickard@bristol.ac.uk. John Pickard, lecturer in mus. *2-year p/t diploma in mus therapy. Applicants should possess a mus degree or diploma and be aged 25 or above. 15 places on course. Next course Jan 2000.*

Centre for Music Therapy and Related Practices. Northern College, Hilton Place, Aberdeen AB24 4FA *tel:* 01224 283500 ext 3510 *fax:* 01224 283900 *email:* j.w.robertson@norcol.ac.uk. James Robertson, co-ord of mus therapy practices. *The centre seeks to provide BEd Hons mus students with an insight into the nature and value of mus therapy practices. Central to this will be the opportunity for children with a wide range of needs to receive mus therapy provision. It is also envisaged that this work will be developed on a modular basis for existing teachers and related professionals.*

City University. Music Dept, Northampton Square, London EC1V 0HB *tel:* 020 7477 8284 *fax:* 020 7477 8576 *email:* music@city.ac.uk. Denis Smalley, head of dept. *Offers one research fellowship in mus therapy for graduate mus therapists wishing to pursue theoretical and academic studies in relation to practical clinical work.*

Colchester Institute. Music Dept, Sheepen Rd, Colchester, Essex CO3 3LL *tel:* 01206 718000 *fax:* 01206 763041. Christopher Turner, module leader. *In the final year of the mus BA/BA Hons, there is special honours study entitled Health and Educational Studies for Musicians. There is also an MA in Health and the Arts.*

Goldsmiths, University of London. Dept of Professional and Community Education, Lewisham Way, London SE14 6NW *tel:* 020 7919 7229. Rachel Darnley-Smith, James D'Angelo, course tutors. *Termly introduction to the ways in which various forms of mus and vocal sound phenomena can be used to promote physical and mental health in both clinically diagnosed cases and people who want to reduce stress and release energy blockages. Very suitable for those considering a career in mus therapy or in conducting sound health w/shops.*

Guildhall School of Music and Drama. Silk St, Barbican, London EC2Y 8DT *tel:* 020 7628 2571 *fax:* 020 7256 9438. Sarah Hoskyns, head of mus therapy dept; Jackie Robarts, mus therapy lecturer; Elaine Streeter, mus therapy clinical tutor; Rachel Darnley-Smith, mus therapy group leader. *Diploma in Music Therapy. 1-year p/grad mus therapy course validated by the University of York and recognised by the Dept of Health. Applicants must normally have had 3 years of f/t HE. Applications from mature professional musicians are also welcomed. Some experience with disabled, mentally or physically ill or hospitalised people is essential, as is personal therapy prior to or during the course.*

Nordoff-Robbins Music Therapy Centre. 2 Lissenden Gardens, London NW5 1PP *tel:* 020 7267 4496 *fax:* 020 7267 4369 *email:* admin@nordoff-robbins.org.uk. Pauline Etkin, dir, head of training. *Offers a 2-year Master of Music Therapy training validated by City University. Fees: £4800. Places: max 6 pa. Also one-day conferences for those interested in mus therapy for children and adults and 10-week evening class on Nordoff-Robbins approach to mus therapy.*

Roehampton Institute, London. Dept of Music, Southlands College, 80 Roehampton Lane, London SW15 5SL *tel:* 020 8392 3709 *fax:* 020 8392 3435 *email:* music@roehampton.ac.uk. John Woodcock, Kay Sobey, mus therapy programme conveners. *Introduction to Music Therapy. A short course in the spring term for those in related professions or who are considering training. Graduate Diploma in Music Therapy (1 f/t; 2-3 p/t, recognised by the Association of Professional Music Therapists) is designed to train musicians as therapists with the ability and flexibility to practise professionally with a wide range of clients within the NHS, educ, social services or private sector. Also research MA. Fees: Graduate Diploma in Mus Therapy, £3448 (1 year f/t, home fee), £1367 (p/t year 1), £2081 (p/t, year 2); MA Mus Therapy, £1188.*

Activities and Courses for People with Disabilities

Artsreach. Jacksons Lane Community Centre, 269a Archway Rd, London N6 5AA *tel:* 020 8340 5226 *fax:* 020 8348 2424 *email:* jacksonslane@pop3.poptel.org.uk. Patricia Place, co-ord. *Offers arts-based w/shops (including mus) to special schools and units, integration work in mainstream schools, primarily in the London Boroughs of Barnet, Camden, Islington and Haringay.*

The Bull. 68 High St, Barnet EN5 5SJ *tel:* 020 8449 0048 *fax:* 020 8364 9037. Alison Duthie, dir; Hilary Wetherilt, gen mgr; Esther Hingle, mkt mgr; Martin Hutchings, technical mgr; Adrian Berry, educ offr. *Runs occasional performing arts w/shops for adults with learning difficulties. Regular programme of mus events, including rock, funk, jazz and Klezmer.*

Carousel. Community Base, 113-117 Queen's Rd, Brighton BN1 3XG *tel:* 01273 234734 *fax:* 01273 234735. Liz Hall, admin. *Works to promote the active involvement and participation of people with learning difficulties in the arts (including mus) through w/shops, residencies, special events, performances, exhibitions, and training courses run for volunteers and staff.*

Council for Music in Hospitals (England, Wales and Northern Ireland). 74 Queens Rd, Hersham, Surrey KT12 5LW *tel:* 01932 252809/252811 *fax:* 01932 252966. Diana Greenman, dir. *Over 4000 live concerts pa given by professional musicians for patients in hospitals, nursing homes, hospices and day centres.*

Council for Music in Hospitals (Scotland). 10 Forth St, Edinburgh EH1 3LD *tel:* 0131 556 5848 *fax:* 0131 556 0225. Alison Frazer, dir. *Concerts of live mus given by professional musicians selected for their communication skills. Participation encouraged. Venues include hospitals, hospices, homes for elderly people and day centres.*

Creative Young People Together (CRYPT Foundation). Forum Workspace, Stirling Rd, Chichester, W Sussex PO19 2EN *tel:* 01243 786064. *Residencies in the community arranged for young people (aged 18-30) with disabilities to further their arts skills, including all aspects of mus.*

Drake Music Project. Christchurch Forum, Trafalgar Rd, London SE10 9EQ *tel:* 020 8305 0580 *fax:* 020 8305 0583 *email:* centralservices @drakemusicproject.com. Adèle Drake, project dir; Brent Barraclough, development dir; Tim Anderson, tech mgr. *Weekly mus w/shops to enable children and adults with physical disabilities to produce and play mus by use of computers and electronic tech. Training of teachers, carers and musicians through seminars and in-service training days. Training course available in London, Coventry and Manchester leading to a BTEC Advanced Award. Summer courses and residencies are held in London, Manchester, Scotland, Midlands, Ireland and Sarajevo.*

Ebony Steelband Trust. Acklam Playcentre and Adventure, 6 Acklam Rd, London W10 5QZ *tel:* 020 8960 6424 *fax:* 020 8964 4624 *email:* ebony@omnimail.net. Tony Nunn, project mgr; Pepe Francis, dir. *Classes and w/shops throughout London to provide relief and personal development through the provision of mus therapy. One-to-one sessions are also available. Steelpan tutors are available for all educ establishments.*

English Touring Opera. 250a Kennington Lane, London SE11 5RD *tel:* 020 7820 1131/1141 (minicom and voice) *fax:* 020 7735 7008. Paul Reeve, educ mgr; Nicholas Skilbeck, artistic consultant. *Extensive programme of work for people with disabilities including w/shops and signed performances for people who are deaf or hard of hearing, w/shops for visually impaired people and creative opera projects with adults and young people with disabilities. Also projects and recital programmes in hospitals and hospices.*

Firebird Trust. 27 Newport, Lincoln LN1 3DN *tel:* 01522 522995 *also fax.* Sibyl Burgess, dir. *Large number of w/shops, residencies, research and training projects.*

Heart'n'Soul. c/o Albany Empire, Douglas Way, Deptford, London SE9 4AG *tel:* 020 8694 1632/2988 *email:* heartnsoul@compuserve.com. Mark Williams, dir; Hannah Kent, development mgr; Michael Gaunt, tour mgr; Angela McNicholl, finance and admin mgr. *Theatrical mus company for people with learning disabilities. Touring shows and mus; organised by members within the UK and abroad. Also run Beautiful Octopus Club, providing multimedia entertainment for people with learning disabilities.*

The International Handchime Circle. Hillcroft, Northbrook Ave, Winchester, Hants SO23 0JW *tel:* 01962 856404 *also fax.* Sue Richardson, dir. *Sessions in handchime ringing for the partially sighted and those seeking mus therapy.*

Leeds College of Music. 3 Quarry Hill, Leeds LS2 7PD *tel:* 0113 222 3400 *also fax.* Kate Holdsworth. *Mus-making lessons for disabled people and those with learning difficulties.*

Lewisham Academy of Music. 77 Watson's St, Deptford, London SE8 4AU *tel:* 020 8691 0307 *also fax; email:* lam@dircon.co.uk. Keith Swailes, exec co-ord; John Savage, mus co-ord. *A range of w/shops for people with special needs: Young Music Workshop, ages 5-14; Young Adult Music Workshop, ages 14-25.*

Live Music Now! 4 Lower Belgrave St, London SW1W 0LJ *tel:* 020 7730 2205 *fax:* 020 7730 3641. Virginia Renshaw, dir; Katherine Potter, asst dir. *Brings live mus performances by selected young professional musicians into community venues, especially those for disadvantaged and disabled people.*

Morley College. 61 Westminster Bridge Rd, London SE1 7HT *tel:* 020 7450 9238 *fax:* 020 7928 4074. Robert Hanson, dir of mus; Helen Simpson, mus access co-ord. *Offers two specific courses: Music for People with Learning Difficulties and Music for People with Physical Disabilities. Also aims to integrate disabled people into other classes.*

Music and the Deaf. Kirklees Media Centre, 7 Northumberland St, Huddersfield HD1 1RL *tel:* 01484 425551 *fax:* 01484 425560 *email:* matd@architechs.com. Paul Whittaker, artistic dir. *An organisation to help hearing-impaired people of all ages to explore the world of mus and to develop their own mus skills and interests. W/shops, lectures, residencies, signed song. Various publications available.*

Musicians in Focus. 1 Poets Rd, London N5 2SL *tel:* 020 7354 2050 *fax:* 020 7359 7535 *email:* musiciansinfocus@compuserve.com. Jacqueline Clifton, Alan McCulloch, dirs. *Aims to research and further develop tech for visually impaired musicians. Provides advice and support as well as a permanent facility for w/shops and courses in collaboration with Overtones Studios.*

Richard Attenborough Centre for Disability and the Arts. University of Leicester, PO Box 138, University Rd, Leicester LE1 9HN *tel:* 0116 252 2455 *fax:* 0116 252 5165 *email:* racentre@le.ac.uk. E Hartley, dir. *Organises taught courses and opportunities to participate in creative arts activities, including mus w/shops. Priority is given to people with disabilities.*

Royal National College for the Blind (RNC). College Rd, Hereford HR1 1EB *tel:* 01432 265725 *fax:* 01432 353478. *VIEW* Diploma in Piano Tuning and repairs; A-level music; BTEC First and National Diplomas in Performing Arts; National Diploma in Music Technology.

SHARE Music. 15 Deramore Drive, Belfast BT9 5JQ *tel:* 028 9066 9042 *also fax.* Michael Swallow, dir. *Promotes residential courses in mus and drama with special facilities for people with physical disabilities or sensory impairments.*

SITE at the City Lit. Stukeley St, London WC2B 5LJ *tel:* 020 7831 6908. Janet Wyatt MBE, head of section. *Programme of w/shops and classes for people with learning difficulties. Training course for teachers, musicians and others in Independence Through Education (mus and other arts).*

Strathcona Theatre Company. Unit 13 The Leather Market, Weston St, London SE1 3ER *tel:* 020 7403 9316 *fax:* 020 7403 9587 *email:* stc@strathco.demon.co.uk. Ann Cleary, Ian McCurrach, dirs; Roger Farrell, admin. *Theatre company of people with learning difficulties who devise their own productions.*

Wedgwood Memorial College. Barlaston, Stoke-on-Trent, Staffs ST12 9DG *tel:* 01782 372105 *fax:* 01782 372393 *email:* wedgwood. college@staffordshire.gov.uk. Derek Tatton, principal. *Residential adult educ college which organises regular mus courses for visually impaired people including one on Creative Arts.*

Wingfield Trust. 4 Mortlock Court, 63 Whitta Rd, Manor Park, London E12 5DU. Ms C Woods, gen sec. *Mus activities to assist children and adults with physical or minor learning handicaps to overcome disabilities by learning to play mus insts. The Wingfield Orchestra, made up of able-bodied and disabled people, gives concerts in and around the outskirts of London.*

Manufacturers and Retailers

Acorn (Percussion) Ltd. Unit 33, Abbey Business Centre, Ingate Place, London SW8 3NS *tel:* 020 7720 2243 (24 hrs) *fax:* 020 7627 8883. Richard Benson, dir; Marguerite Vetter, dir of sales. *Manufacturer and supplier of a variety of multicultural and mainstream perc insts for special needs educ and hospitals. Also perc insts for general school use.*

Echo City. 7 Mornington Terrace, Camden, London NW1 7RR *tel:* 020 7387 7962 *fax:* 020 7263 9153 *email:* echocity @mccourt-perring.demon.co.uk. Paul Shearsmith, Giles Perring, members. *Designs, builds and installs sound playgrounds and organises inst building and mus w/shops. Office hours 10am-4pm Mon-Thu.*

Music Education Supplies. 101 Banstead Rd South, Sutton, Surrey SM2 5LH *tel:* 020 8770 3866 *fax:* 020 8770 3554. Ray Mason, dir. *Agents of Sonor school perc and suppliers of Suzuki handchimes and perc, Nordoff-Robbins reed horns, Aulos recorders, books, insts, etc.*

Partially Sighted Society. PO Box 322, Doncaster, S Yorks DN1 2XA *tel:* 01302 323132 *fax:* 01302 368998. *Provides wide-spaced, heavily lined ms and a service for enlarging mus.*

REMAP (Technical Equipment for Disabled People). Hazeldene, Ightham, Sevenoaks, Kent TN15 9AD *tel:* 01732 883818 *fax:* 01732 886238. John Wright, dir. *Registered charity which designs, manufactures and supplies 'one-off' aids and adaptions that are not commercially available.*

Libraries and Museums

The following list is limited to major collections of musical interest with some special collections in larger libraries. An asterisk indicates membership of the **International Association of Music Libraries, Archives and Document Centre**, c/o County Library Headquarters, Walton St, Aylesbury, Bucks HP20 1UU *tel:* 01296 382266 *fax:* 01296 382274.

National Copyright Libraries

These libraries are available for reference only. Application for a reader's ticket is essential.

Aberystwyth. National Library of Wales. Aberystwyth, Ceredigion SY23 3BU *tel:* 01970 632800 *fax:* 01970 615709 *email:* rhidian.griffiths@llgc.org.uk. Rhidian Griffiths, keeper of printed books. *Mss dept rich in 19th C Welsh mus; large coll of printed Welsh mus; Welsh mus catalogue; British mus received under legal deposit since 1912; West European mus.*

Cambridge. Cambridge University Library Music Department. West Rd, Cambridge CB3 9DR *tel:* 01223 333000/72 *fax:* 01223 333160 *email:* music@ula.cam.ac.uk. R M Andrewes, under-librarian, head of mus dept. *Includes Hedli Anderson coll, F T Arnold coll, F A Booth coll, Edith Coates and Harry Powell Lloyd coll, Marion Scott coll, Alfredo Campoli coll, Peter Warlock autograph mss, R J S Stevens diaries and memoirs, W H Weiss papers and diaries, Hans Keller papers, James Hook autograph mss.*

* **Edinburgh.** National Library of Scotland. George IV Bridge, Edinburgh EH1 1EW *tel:* 0131 226 4531 *fax:* 0131 622 4803 *email:* enquiries@nls.uk. *Special colls including Balfour-Handel, Hopkinson-Berlioz, Hopkinson-Verdi; also Scottish mus colls and Grainger mss.*

* **London.** British Library. Music Collections, 96 Euston Rd, London NW1 2DB *tel:* 020 7412 7772 *fax:* 020 7412 7751 *email:* music-library@bl.uk. Hugh Cobbe, head of mus colls; Chris Banks, curator of mus mss. *Over one million items of printed mus received by copyright deposit, purchase or gift. Special colls include Hirsch Music Library, Royal Music Library (including Handel autographs). The large coll of mus mss includes autographs of Bach, Haydn, Mozart, Beethoven, Elgar, Vaughan Williams, Holst, Britten, Tippett, etc; medieval and modern vocal and inst mus, Stefan Zweig coll, Royal Philharmonic coll (on loan).*

* **Oxford.** Bodleian Library, Music Section. Oxford OX1 3BG *tel:* 01865 277063 *fax:* 01865 277182 *email:* music@bodley.ox.ac.uk. P Ward Jones, mus librarian. *Including 10th-20th C mss; former Music School coll, Deneke-Mendelssohn coll, Wight Bequest, Bourne Bequest, Harding coll, former St Michael's College, Tenbury coll.*

British Library Document Supply Centre

* Boston Spa, Wetherby, W Yorks LS23 7BQ *tel:* 01937 546060 *fax:* 01937 546333 *email:* dsc-customer-services@bl.uk. Malcolm Smith, dir. *Acts as a clearing house for all inter-library loans, both nationally and internationally, with a system of 'back-up' libraries, including the National Copyright Libraries and the major regional libraries (see below). In addition it has an extensive stock of its own, including a substantial and comprehensive collection of mus scores (excluding vocal and orch sets). The BLDSC does not lend directly to individuals, but through a network of borrowers comprised of public libraries, university and college libraries, and institutions. Any organisation may apply to join, details from the above address.*

Major Regional Public Libraries

These libraries have major music collections, and also act as regional and national centres for lending. Personal or institutional borrowers are welcome.

* **Birmingham.** Central Music Library. Chamberlain Square, Birmingham B3 3HQ *tel:* 0121 303 2482 *fax:* 0121 233 9702 *email:* john.gough@birmingham.gov.uk. John Gough, head of mus services. *Including coll of British Institute of Organ Studies, material surrounding Birmingham Triennial Festivals including ms score of Mendelssohn's 'Elijah', letters by Elgar, Gounod, Bruch, etc.*

Liverpool. Central Library (Music). William Brown St, Liverpool L3 8EW *tel:* 0151 225 5463. *Including Carl Rosa opera library.*

London. Barbican Music Library. Barbican Centre, London EC2Y 8DS *tel:* 020 7638 0672 *fax:* 020 7638 2249. Robert Tucker, mus librarian. *Includes The Music Performance Research Centre.*

* **London.** Westminster Music Library. 160 Buckingham Palace Rd, London SW1W 9UD *tel:* 020 7641 4292 *fax:* 020 7641 4281. Ruth Walters, Hugh Thomas, mus librarians. *Colls include Oriana Madrigal Soc.*

* **Manchester.** Henry Watson Music Library. Central Library, St Peter's Square, Manchester M2 5PD *tel:* 0161 234 1976 *fax:* 0161 234 1963 *email:* music@libraries.manchester.gov.uk. Martin Thacker. *Including 2000 items of early printed mus and 500 mss; Newman Flower Handel Collection.*

* **Wakefield.** Wakefield Library HQ. Balne Lane, Wakefield, W Yorks WF2 0DQ *tel:* 01924 302229 *fax:* 01924 302245. Steven Dowd, snr librarian. *Yorkshire Libraries Joint Music and Drama Collection: large coll of choral and orch sets.*

Regional Public Libraries

These libraries hold a significant stock of scores, sheet music, books, audio/visual material and collections of local interest. Unless specified otherwise, material is available nationally via the inter-library loan system.

* **London.** Barnet Cultural Services. Hendon Music Library, The Burroughs, London NW4 4BQ *tel:* 020 8359 2882. E M Hart, mus adviser. *Includes colls of recordings of Chopin, Liszt, stage musicals and Japanese ethnic mus.*

* Ealing Public Libraries. Library Support Centre, Ealing Central Sports Ground, Horsenden Lane South, Greenford UB6 8AP *tel:* 020 8810 7664 *fax:* 020 8810 7651. Glynis R Hillier, mus librarian.

* London Borough of Enfield Central Music Library. Cecil Rd, Enfield, London EN2 6TW *tel:* 020 8379 8392 *fax:* 020 8379 8401 *email:* enfield.library@dial.pipex.com. Mike Jones, team leader, mus and a/v services. *Audio specialisation includes J S Bach, jazz artists BAJ-BH.*

Fulham Music Library. 598 Fulham Rd, London SW6 5NX *tel:* 020 8576 5253 *fax:* 020 7736 3741 *email:* info@haflibs.org.uk. Sadie McGarry, mus and a/v librarian. *For details of colls see* Hammersmith Music Library.

* London Borough of Greenwich Libraries. Support Services, Plumstead Library, 232 Plumstead High St, London SE18 1JL *tel:* 020 8317 4466 *fax:* 020 8317 4868. John Conroy, librarian. *Special audio colls of Ravel, Schumann, English folk mus, jazz performers.*

* Hammersmith Music Library. Shepherds Bush Rd, London W6 7AT *tel:* 020 8576 5054 *fax:* 020 8576 5022 *email:* hcr@haflibs.org.uk. Elin Stephens, mus and a/v librarian. *Cassettes, CDs, videos, LPs, mus books, scores and magazines. Audio specialisation: Mendelssohn, Vaughan Williams, jazz artists HP-JEF, folk mus of Iran, Iraq, Jordan, Lebanon and Syria, British poetry. Colls also held at Fulham Music Library and Shepherds Bush Library.*

* London Borough of Islington Libraries. Central Library, 2 Fieldway Cres, London N5 1PF *tel:* 020 7619 6954 *fax:* 020 7619 6902. C Millington, snr librarian a/v services. *Audio specialisation of classical composers GM-KH (excluding Handel and J Haydn), jazz musicians SHB-SM, folk mus of SE Europe and recordings of obsolete mus insts. Loans within Greater London to personal borrowers only.*

London Borough of Southwark Libraries. Dulwich Library, 368 Lordship Lane, London SE22 8NB *tel:* 020 8693 5171 *fax:* 020 8693 5135. Mark Challen, mus and a/v librarian. *CDs, cassettes, videos, scores, and books. Special colls include Berlioz, Messiaen, jazz, SE Asian folk mus, and mus practice records.*

Wandsworth Music Libraries. Balham Music Library, Ramsden Rd, London SW12 8QY *tel:* 020 8871 7195 *fax:* 020 8675 4015. F Daniels, snr mus librarian. *Encompasses Battersea, Balham and Putney mus libraries. Comprehensive stocks of CDs, cassettes, videos (also LPs at Balham), scores and books. Vocal score sets coll at Putney. GLASS coll (Greater London Audio Specialisation Scheme) at Putney. Wandsworth coll in this scheme comprises Prokofiev, Rachmaninoff, film soundtracks, jazz artists LEE-LZ and Scottish folk mus.*

* **Aylesbury.** Buckinghamshire County Library. County Library Headquarters, Walton St, Aylesbury, Bucks HP20 1UU *tel:* 01296 382266 *fax:* 01296 382274 *email:* mroll@buckscc.gov.uk. Margaret Roll, mus librarian. *Vocal sets, sheet mus.*

* **Ballynahinch.** South Eastern Education and Library Board. Library Headquarters, Reference and Information Service, Windmill Hill, Ballynahinch, Co Down BT24 8DH *tel:* 028 9756 6400 *fax:* 028 9756 5072. J W Glenn, principal asst librarian. *Coll of cassettes, CDs, mus scores and books covering all types of mus.*

Blackburn. Blackburn Music Library. Blackburn Central Library, Town Hall St, Blackburn BB2 1AG *tel:* 01254 661221 *fax:* 01254 690539. Catherine Perris, acting mus librarian. *Includes multimedia, a/v, extensive jazz coll.*

* **Bournemouth.** Bournemouth Music Library. Meyrick Rd, Lansdowne, Bournemouth BH1 3DJ *tel:* 01202 553781 *fax:* 01202 291781. Sandrey Date, mus librarian. *Camm coll of (mainly 19th C) full scores, miniature scores, chmbr and inst mus. Wide range of printed mus, books, CDs and videos. Sets of choral and orch works available.*

* **Brighton.** Brighton Music Library. 115 Church St, Brighton BN1 1UD *tel:* 01273 296961 *fax:* 01273 296965/296951. Jane Cox, team librarian (mus). *General range of scores, books, CDs, cassettes, records and videos.*

* **Bristol.** Bristol Music Library. Central Library College Green, Bristol BS1 5TL *tel:* 0117 929 9149 *fax:* 0117 922 6775. Andrew Grinnell, mus and a/v librarian. *Russell coll of Victorian and Edwardian songs. Coll of books, mus and recordings by Bristol authors and musicians. Comprehensive coll of books, journals, scores, sets of choral/orch parts and recordings.*

* **Cardiff.** Cardiff County Library Service: Cardiff Central Library. St David's Link, Frederick St, Cardiff CF1 4DT *tel:* 029 2038 2116 *fax:* 029 2023 8642 *email:* robboddy@cardlib.demon.co.uk. Elizabeth Pinnell, Sheila Basford, mus librarians. *Mackworth and Aylward colls of 17th and 18th C mss and printed mus; currently on long-term loan to University College Cardiff Music Library.*

Chesterfield. Chesterfield Library. County Music and Drama Library, New Beetwell St, Chesterfield, Derbyshire S40 1QN *tel:* 01246 209292 *fax:* 01246 209304 *email:* chesterfield.library@derbyshire.gov.uk. Mrs M Brandram, county mus and drama librarian. *General colls of single copy material, vocal sets, orch sets and playsets. Coke-Steele coll of books, scores and some mss (not yet catalogued but available for consultation by prior arrangement).*

* **Colchester.** Colchester Central Library. Trinity Square, Colchester, Essex CO1 1JB *tel:* 01206 245918 *fax:* 01206 245901 *email:* col.lib@dial.pipex.com. Mrs V Kuphal, snr subject librarian, mus. *Large coll of sets of vocal and orch mus, county mus coll.*

* **Cork.** Cork City Library. Grand Parade, Cork, Republic of Ireland *tel:* 00 353 21 277110 *fax:* 00 353 21 275684 *email:* cork.citylibrary@indigo.ie. Catherine Buckley, mus librarian. *General stock including classical, inst, vocal, choral and orch, pop, country and rock, jazz, blues, light opera, musicals, films, br and military band, Irish traditional and world mus, children's mus. Large coll of audio material and listening facilities. Scores and books.*

* **Devizes.** Wiltshire County Music and Drama Library. Sheep St, Devizes, Wilts SN10 1DL *tel:* 01380 722633 *fax:* 01380 722161. *Books, mus scores, vocal and orch sets, records, cassettes and CDs, chmbr mus sets, miniature scores.*

* **Dorking.** Surrey Performing Arts Library. Vaughan Williams House, West St, Dorking, Surrey RH4 1BY *tel:* 01306 887509; 01306 875453 (enquiries) *fax:* 01306 875074 *email:* p.arts@dial.pipex.com. G Muncy, snr librarian. *Large range of printed and a/v mus reference, information and lending materials. Major regional coll of choral and orch performance material. Charges for the loan of choral and orch sets.*

Dudley. Dudley Library. St James's Rd, Dudley, W Midlands DY1 1HR *tel:* 01384 815554 *fax:* 01384 815543 *email:* dudlib.pls @mbc.dudley.gov.uk. M R Gay, reference librarian.

* **Eastbourne.** Eastbourne Music Library. Grove Rd, Eastbourne, E Sussex BN21 4TL *tel:* 01323 434224 *fax:* 01323 649174. Pauline Kennard, asst in charge. *Nearly 10,000 sound recordings on record, cassette and CD covering all types of mus both classical and popular. Scores, books, Music Master/Gramophone and MPA catalogue on CD-ROM, and song index.*

* **Edinburgh.** Edinburgh City Libraries. Music Library, George IV Bridge, Edinburgh EH1 1EG *tel:* 0131 225 5584 *fax:* 0131 225 8783. Martina McChrystal, principal library offr, mus. *Books, scores, cassettes and CDs for borrowing. Reference material includes periodicals. Scottish mus from all periods is strongly represented. Information files are maintained covering local mus teachers, societies and organisations.*

* **Gloucester.** Gloucester Music and Drama Library. Greyfriars, Gloucester GL1 1TS *tel:* 01452 426982 *fax:* 01452 506241 *email:* glosoff @gloscc.gov.uk. Helen Briggs, snr librarian, mus and drama. *Mus sets, printed mus, books, CDs, cassettes, videos. Inter-library loan. Personal borrowers only. CD-ROMs for reference.*

* **Hatfield.** Performing Arts Library. Central Resources Library, New Barnfield, Travellers Lane, Hatfield, Herts AL10 8XG *tel:* 01707 281533 *fax:* 01707 281514 *email:* fmo34@viscount.org.uk. Di Robb, snr library asst for performing arts. *Fairly large general coll, including sets of vocal scores and orch material primarily for local use, although will consider inter-library loan.*

* **Lincoln.** Lincolnshire County Libraries. Lincoln Central Library, Free School Lane, Lincoln LN1 1EZ *tel:* 01522 510800 *fax:* 01522 575011. A H Mason, librarian (mus and drama). *General public library mus coll with books, scores, sets of vocal and orch mus, CDs.*

Luton. Luton Central Music Library. St George's Square, Luton, Beds LU2 1NG *tel:* 01582 730161 *fax:* 01582 724638. Malcolm J Thatcher, mus librarian. *Scores, books, CDs, cassettes. Archive of Luton Girls' Choir material.*

* **Maidstone.** Kent County Music Library. Kent Arts and Libraries, County Central Library, Springfield, Maidstone, Kent ME14 2LH *tel:* 01622 696511 *fax:* 01622 753338. Miss F Metcalfe, mus librarian. *Wide range of printed mus, books and a/v material. Major coll of performance sets available for loan (charge for societies outside Kent).*

* **Newcastle upon Tyne.** Newcastle Libraries and Information Services. City Library, Princess Square, Newcastle upon Tyne NE99 1DX *tel:* 0191 261 0691 *fax:* 0191 261 1435 *email:* nlis.human@dial.pipex.com. Alan Macfarlane, city library service mgr. *Scores, books, small coll of vocal sets. Cat of printed mus and comprehensive directory coverage. Loan coll of CDs and audio cassettes.*

* **Nottingham.** Nottingham Music Library. Nottingham Central Library, Angel Row, Nottingham NG1 6HP *tel:* 0115 915 2832 *fax:* 0115 915 2830 *email:* music@notlib.demon.co.uk. Malcolm Lewis, head of mus library. *Eric Coates coll. Inter-library loan system.*

* **Plymouth.** Plymouth Music and Drama Library. Central Library, Drake Circus, Plymouth PL4 8AL *tel:* 01752 305914 *also fax.* Andrew Laycock, mus and drama librarian. *Vocal and orch sets. Rev Sabine Baring-Gould coll of folk song mss. Mus scores, playscripts, playsets and books on mus and theatre for loan. Cassettes, CDs, videos. Comprehensive reference stock, including Music Master/Gramophone on CD-ROM, song index.*

* **Preston.** Lancashire County Library. County Library Headquarters, County Hall, PO Box 61, Preston, Lancs PR1 8RJ *tel:* 01772 264051 *fax:* 01772 264880 *email:* thiesa@lb.lancscc.gov.uk. Alison Thies, principal librarian, cultural services. *J A Fuller-Maitland coll (*The

Times *mus critic 1889-1911) includes books, scores, periodicals and mss with special emphasis on English folk mus, Bach and Purcell.*

* **Reading.** Music and Drama Library. Reading Central Library, Abbey Square, Reading RG1 3BQ *tel:* 0118 901 5960. Mrs C Muncy, snr librarian. *Vocal and drama set colls. Books, scores, videos, cassettes and CDs.*
* **Ruthin.** Denbighshire Library and Information Service. c/o Ruthin Library, Record St, Ruthin, Denbighshire LL15 1DS *tel:* 01824 705274/708203 *fax:* 01824 702580. R Arwyn Jones, principal librarian; Llinos Davies, community librarian. *Special coll of Welsh mus.*
* **St Austell.** Cornwall Library - Performing Arts. 2 Carlyon Rd, St Austell, Cornwall PL25 4LD *tel:* 01726 61702 *fax:* 01726 77844. Jonathan L Roberts, principal library offr (arts). *Large general coll of mus scores, including performance sets (vocal and orch); Cornish mus (folk, dance, carols); classical CDs, books on all aspects of mus for lending and reference; videos; sound effects recordings.*
* **Shrewsbury.** Shropshire Music and Drama Library. Lending Library, Castle Gates, Shrewsbury, Shropshire SY1 2AS *tel:* 01743 255341 *fax:* 01743 255309 *email:* lp97@dial.pipex.com. Nicola Dawson, librarian. *General colls including classical, pop, folk and world mus. Inter-library loan.*
* **Sutton.** Sutton Central Library. St Nicholas Way, Sutton, Surrey SM1 1EA *tel:* 020 8770 4765 *fax:* 020 8770 4777. Leigh Allen, information mgr: recreation. *Sets of vocal scores, small coll of orch parts available on loan. Audio specialisation includes recordings of Bruckner, choral recitals, jazz artists GIM-HARD, ethnic folk mus of the USA. Music Master/Gramophone cats on CD-ROM, MPA cat on CD-ROM.*
* **Warwick.** Warwickshire County Council. Barrack St, Warwick CV34 4TH *tel:* 01926 412168 *fax:* 01926 412471 *email:* warcolib@dial.pipex.com. Kathleen Collins, mus and drama librarian. *16,000 mus scores, including vocal sets and sets of part-songs. Books on mus and some orch sets in the schools mus library.*
* **Worcester.** Worcestershire Cultural Services, City Library. Foregate St, Worcester WR1 1DT *tel:* 01905 765310 *fax:* 01905 726664 *email:* worcesterlib@worcestershire.gov.uk. Richard Davies, librarian: mus and drama. *Choral sets, instrumental sets, at Worcester City Library. Sound recordings at all branch libraries; single scores at all branches.*
* **Wrekin.** Telford & Wrekin: Wellington Music and Drama Library. Wellington Library, Walker St, Wellington, Wrekin TF1 1BD *tel:* 01952 248423 *fax:* 01952 256960. Carol Woollard, snr librarian. *General colls including classical, pop, folk and world mus. Inter-library loan.*
* **Yeovil.** Somerset County Library. County Music and Drama Library, King George St, Yeovil, Somerset BA20 1PY *tel:* 01935 472020 *fax:* 01935 429133 *email:* rdtaylor@nildram.co.uk. Roger Taylor, county mus and drama librarian.

Church and Cathedral Libraries

These libraries are private but are usually open to bona fide scholars. Applications for admission are advisable.

London. Lambeth Palace Library. London SE1 7JU *tel:* 020 7928 6222 *fax:* 020 7928 7932. *A few mss (including early 16th C choir books) and some printed books including church mus.*

St Paul's Cathedral Library. London EC4M 8AE *tel:* 020 7246 8325/7236 4128 *fax:* 020 7248 3104. Joseph Wisdom, librarian; Elizabeth Norman, asst librarian. *17th-18th C ms part-books; a number of autograph scores of services and anthems, some by former organists, mainly 19th and 20th C.*

Westminster Abbey Library. East Cloister, London SW1P 3PA *tel:* 020 7222 5152 *fax:* 020 7222 6391 *email:* library@westminster-abbey.org. T A Trowles, librarian. *Includes 16th-19th C mss and printed mus.*

Bristol. Baptist College Library. Duncan House, The Promenade, Clifton, Bristol BS8 3NF *tel:* 0117 946 7050 *fax:* 0117 946 7787. Mrs M E Barker, librarian. *Special coll of Baptist hymn books (mostly words only).*

Bristol. Methodist Church Music Society Library. Wesley College, Henbury Rd, Westbury on Trym, Bristol BS10 7QD *tel:* 0117 959 1200 *fax:* 0117 950 1277. Janet Henderson, librarian. *Coll of hymn books, psalters, etc, and books with special emphasis on hymnody and church mus, 17th-20th C.*

Canterbury. Cathedral Archives and Library. The Precincts, Canterbury CT1 2EH *tel:* 01227 865287 *fax:* 01227 865222 *email:* catlib@ukc.ac.uk (library). Michael Stansfield, archivist; Sheila Hingley, librarian. *Archives: medieval mus mss, 17th-18th C choir mus mss. Library: printed choir mus; mss and printed mus of Canterbury Catch Club.*

Durham. Dean and Chapter Library. The College, Durham DH1 3EH *tel:* 0191 386 2489 *email:* r.c.norris@durham.ac.uk. Roger Norris, deputy chapter librarian. *17th-19th C cathedral choir and organists mss; 17th-19th C printed mus from Bamburgh Castle; Philip Falle coll of 17th C printed mus. 2 weeks notice needed to visit. Open Mon-Fri 2.15-5pm only, closed Aug.*

Hereford. Cathedral Library. Hereford HR1 2NG *tel:* 01432 359880 *fax:* 01432 355929 *email:* library@herefordcathedral.co.uk. J Williams, librarian. *Chained library. 18th-20th C printed and ms mus, including Roger North, Wesley and Elgar mss. Hereford Breviary, with mus, c 1270.*

Lichfield. Cathedral Library. 19a The Close, Lichfield, Staffs *tel:* 01543 306175 *fax:* 01543 306109 *email:* lich.cath@virgin.net. Pat Bancroft, hon mus librarian; Percy M Young. *Cat of 18th-early 19th C mss. Cat of 17th-mid 19th C printed mus in preparation.*

Lincoln. Cathedral Library. Lincoln LN2 1PZ *tel:* 01522 544544 *fax:* 01522 511307. Nicholas Bennett. *Including medieval mss and early printed mus. 17th-19th C ms part books.*

Ripon. Cathedral Library. Ripon, N Yorks HG4 1QT *tel:* 01765 602072 *fax:* 01765 603462. *16th C liturgical printed books; Higgin bequest (now on deposit at Brotherton Library, Leeds University).*

Wimborne. Minster Church of St Cuthburga Library. High St, Wimborne, Dorset BH21 1HT *tel:* 01202 884753. *Chained library of early mus.*

Winchester. Cathedral Library. 5 The Close, Winchester, Hants SO23 9LS *tel:* 01962 853137 *fax:* 01962 841519 *email:* winchester.cathedral.office@dial.pipex.com. John Hardacre, curator. *Coll of 18th and 19th C printed church mus.*

Windsor. St George's Chapel Chapter Library. Windsor Castle, Windsor, Berks SL4 1NJ *tel:* 01753 857942 *also fax.* Eileen Scarff, librarian and archivist. *Including mss of Tallis and William Child.*

Worcester. Cathedral Music Library. Worcester WR1 2LH *tel:* 01905 28854 *fax:* 01905 611139 *email:* worcestercathedral@compuserve.com. *17th-18th C part books, mss and printed church mus.*

York. York Minster Library. Dean's Park, York YO1 7JQ *tel:* 01904 625308/611118 *fax:* 01904 611119. Mrs D M Mortimer, librarian; Mrs A L Hampson, archivist. *Mainly 16th-20th C mss and printed mus, including many rare items such as mss and printed mus by Purcell, the Minster repertoire of the choir from 16th C to present day; some medieval liturgical mus, mainly of the use of York; also coll donated by Marmaduke Fothergill.*

University and College Libraries

Primarily available to staff and students of the institution, but visiting scholars may also be admitted. Applications in writing are advisable.

* **London.** Goldsmiths College Library. New Cross, London SE14 6NW *tel:* 020 7919 7168 *fax:* 020 7919 7165 *email:* lbs0lpm@gold.ac.uk. Peter Morris, asst librarian. *Includes the A L Lloyd coll (scores, books and offprints of folk and traditional mus, especially Eastern Europe), the Ewan MacColl/Peggy Seeger coll (books and scores, especially English and Scottish folksongs) and the Alan Bush coll (scores of 20th C Eastern European mus).*
* Imperial College of Science, Technology and Medicine. Haldane Music Library, London SW7 2AZ *tel:* 020 7594 8812 *fax:* 020 7584 3763 *email:* j.m.smith@ic.ac.uk. Janet M Smith, Haldane librarian. *Haldane mus coll. Recordings, scores, books.*

Jewish Music Resource Centre. c/o School of Oriental and African Studies, University of London, Music Dept, Rm 516, Thornhaugh St, Russell Square, London WC1H 0XG *tel:* 020 7691 3410 *fax:* 020 7637 6182 *email:* ak42@soas.ac.uk. Alexander Knapp, Joe Loss lecturer in Jewish mus.

* King's College London Library. Strand, London WC2R 2LS *tel:* 020 7848 2394 *fax:* 020 7848 1777 *email:* evelyn.cornell@kcl.ac.uk. Evelyn Cornell, mus readers' adviser.

London College of Music and Media. Thames Valley University LRC, St Mary's Rd, London W5 5RF *tel:* 020 8231 2648 *fax:* 020 8231 2631 *email:* colin.steele@tvu.ac.uk. Colin Steele, mus librarian. *Scores, books, journals, LPs, CDs, listening facilities, CD-ROM multimedia.*

London School of Economics. Shaw Library, Houghton St, London WC2A 2AE *tel:* 020 7955 7171 *fax:* 020 7955 7603. Alan D Lowson, Shaw librarian and mus dir. *Books, scores, serials and recordings.*

Morley College Library. 61 Westminster Bridge Rd, London SE1 7HT *tel:* 020 7928 8501 *fax:* 020 7928 4074. Lise Foster, librarian. *Scores, sheet mus, books, records, CDs.*

* Royal Academy of Music Library. Marylebone Rd, London NW1 5HT *tel:* 020 7873 7323 *fax:* 020 7873 7322 *email:* library@ram.ac.uk. Kathy Adamson, acting librarian. *Including Sir Henry Wood library of orch mus, Sir Arthur Sullivan archives, English Bach Society Library, R J S Stevens Library, David Munrow Library, Robert Spencer coll.*

* Royal College of Music Library. Prince Consort Rd, London SW7 2BS *tel:* 020 7591 4325 *fax:* 020 7589 7740 *email:* pthompson@rcm.ac.uk. Pam Thompson, chief librarian. *Includes libraries of Sacred Harmonic Society, Concerts of Ancient Music, Heron-Allen coll.*

Royal College of Organists. 7 St Andrew St, London EC4A 3LQ *tel:* 020 7936 3606 (admin); 020 7936 4321 (lib) *fax:* 020 7353 8244 (admin); 020 7936 3966 (lib) *email:* rco@rco.org.uk. Robin Langley, librarian; Andrew McCrea, asst librarian. *Mainly org mus, recordings and books on the org; non-members for reference only, by prior appointment, during college opening hours.*

School of Oriental and African Studies Library. University of London, Thornhaugh St, Russell Square, London WC1H 0XG *tel:* 020 7323 6105 *fax:* 020 7636 2834 *email:* yyl@soas.ac.uk. Y Yasumura, asst librarian. *Books, sound recordings (and video) of Asian and African mus.*

* Trinity College of Music. The Library, Academic Studies Centre, 10-11 Bulstrode Place, London W1M 5FW *tel:* 020 7487 9656 *fax:* 020 7486 6018 *email:* library@tcm.ac.uk. Kate Sloss, chief librarian. *General book colls include mus educ, 20th C mus and mus therapy. Special colls include: Lionel Tertis coll; Barbirolli coll; Charles Proctor coll; William Lovelock coll; Cherkassky coll; Almeida coll (includes Charles Munch's conducting scores); Alan Cave coll of wind band mus.*

* University of London Library Music Collection. Senate House, Malet St, London WC1E 7HU *tel:* 020 7862 8457 *fax:* 020 7862 8480 *email:* ull@ull.ac.uk. Ruth Darton, mus librarian. *Including library of Royal Musical Association; Tudor Church Music coll, Littleton coll.*

* **Aberdeen.** Aberdeen University Library. Queen Mother Library, Meston Walk, Aberdeen AB24 3UE *tel:* 01224 272592 *fax:* 01224 487048 *email:* r.turbet@abdn.ac.uk. Richard Turbet, mus librarian. *Including libraries of Gavin Greig and Forbes Leith; Stationers' Hall coll (18th-19th C printed mus obtained under copyright).*

Aberystwyth. University of Wales (Hugh Owen Library). Aberystwyth, Dyfed SY23 3DZ *tel:* 01970 622391 *fax:* 01970 622404 *email:* library@aber.ac.uk. R Brinkley, humanities adviser. *Including David de Lloyd mss; Mendelssohn letters and autographs; George Powell bequest (19th C scores and some 18th-19th C mss).*

* **Belfast.** Queen's University. Belfast BT7 1LS *tel:* 028 9033 5020 *fax:* 028 9032 3340 *email:* nrussell@qub.ac.uk. N J Russell, librarian. *Including Bunting mss of Irish folk mus; Hamilton Harty library.*

* **Birmingham.** Barber Music Library. University of Birmingham, Edgbaston, Birmingham B15 2TS *tel:* 0121 414 5852 *fax:* 0121 414 5853 *email:* mulib@bham.ac.uk. Anna Greig, mus librarian. *Including Granville Bantock, Gloria Rose and Shaw-Hellier colls, Elgar diaries.*

* **Birmingham.** Birmingham Conservatoire Library. University of Central England, Paradise Place, Birmingham B3 3HG *tel:* 0121 331 5914/5 *fax:* 0121 331 5906 *email:* conservatoire.library@uce.ac.uk. Robert Allan, faculty librarian. *Birmingham Flute Society coll.*

Bristol. University of Bristol Library. Tyndall Ave, Bristol BS8 1TJ *tel:* 0117 928 9000 *fax:* 0117 925 5334 *email:* library@bris.ac.uk. Michael Leat, asst librarian.

Cambridge. Anglia Polytechnic University Library. East Rd, Cambridge CB1 1PT *tel:* 01223 363271 ext 2302 *fax:* 01223 363271.

Cambridge. Cambridge University Library *see* **National Copyright Libraries.**

Cambridge. Cambridge University Musical Society. c/o University Music School, West Rd, Cambridge CB3 9DP *tel:* 01223 335180/3. Andrew Bennett. *Including approx 400 sets of orch parts.*

Cambridge. Clare College. Cambridge CB3 9AJ *tel:* 01223 333202/333267 *fax:* 01223 357664 *email:* fml1@ula.cam.ac.uk. Roger Schofield, librarian and archivist; Elizabeth A Keith, asst librarian. *Including mss of Cecil Sharp's folksong colls; mss of W C Denis-Browne; mss of F P Haines.*

Cambridge. Gonville and Caius College. Cambridge CB2 1TA *tel:* 01223 332419 *fax:* 01223 332430 *email:* library@cai.cam.ac.uk. J H Prynne, librarian. *Including mss and fragments of mus from the 10th-18th C (mostly 11th-14th C); also papers and materials relating to Charles Wood (1866-1926).*

Cambridge. King's College. Rowe Music Library, Cambridge CB2 1ST *tel:* 01223 331252. Mrs M V Cranmer, librarian. *Including libraries of L T Rowe, A H Mann and A H King; also E J Dent papers.*

Cambridge. Magdalene College. Cambridge CB3 0AG *tel:* 01223 332100 *fax:* 01223 332187. R Luckett, Pepys librarian. *Pepys Library (personal library of Samuel Pepys (1633-1703): mss, ballads, printed mus); library open chiefly during term-time (appointment necessary). Catalogued in R C Latham, ed The Pepys Library at Magdalene College, Cambridge* (11 vols), IV.

Cambridge. Pembroke College. Cambridge CB2 1RF *tel:* 01223 338121 *fax:* 01223 338163 *email:* lib@pem.cam.ac.uk. T R S Allan, librarian. *Including 17th C ms part-mus; 18th C chmbr mus.*

Cambridge. Pendlebury Library of Music. University Music School, West Rd, Cambridge CB3 9DP *tel:* 01223 335182 *fax:* 01223 335067. Andrew Bennett, librarian. *Library of the university mus faculty.*

Cambridge. Peterhouse. Trumpington St, Cambridge CB2 1RD *tel:* 01223 338200 *fax:* 01223 337578. R W Lovatt, Perne librarian. *Including 16th-17th C part-books (permanently deposited at University Library).*

Cambridge. St John's College. Cambridge CB2 1TP *tel:* 01223 338662 *fax:* 01223 337035 *email:* library@joh.cam.ac.uk. *Samuel Butler coll, Rootham compositions.*

Cambridge. Trinity College. Cambridge CB2 1TQ *tel:* 01223 338488 *fax:* 01223 338532 *email:* trin-lib@lists.cam.ac.uk. D J McKitterick, librarian. *Including roll of 15th C English carols, two 15th C Greek mss with mus, lute tablatures of Bacheler, Greaves, Johnson and Taylor, autographs of Gray, Parry and Stanford; early printed mus of Byrd, Mace, Playford and Purcell.*

Cardiff. University of Wales. Music Dept, Corbett Rd, Cardiff CF1 3EB *tel:* 029 2087 4000 ext 4387 *email:* musicliby@cardiff.ac.uk. Gillian Jones, mus librarian. *Mackworth coll: early 18th C printed and mss scores. Aylward coll: printed editions of 18th and 19th C scores.*

* **Cardiff.** Welsh College of Music and Drama Library. Castle Grounds, Cathays Park, Cardiff CF10 3ER *tel:* 029 2034 2854 *fax:* 029 2023 7639 *email:* agusjm@wcmd.ac.uk. Judith Agus, librarian.

* **Colchester.** Colchester Institute Library. Sheepen Rd, Colchester, Essex CO3 3LL *tel:* 01206 718641/718644 *fax:* 01206 718643. Miss J Benfield, subject librarian (mus). *Liturgical mus, wind band and jazz band scores, collected works.*

Durham. University Library. Palace Green Section, Durham DH1 3RN *tel:* 0191 374 3001 *email:* pg.library@durham.ac.uk. Elizabeth Rainey, sub-librarian. *Britten correspondence and related mss, Dame Ethel Smyth mss, medieval liturgical mss, Pratt Green Collection of hymn books and hymnology.*

Edinburgh. Edinburgh University Library: Main Library. George Square, Edinburgh EH8 9LJ *tel:* 0131 650 3384 *fax:* 0131 667 9780 *email:* library@ed.ac.uk. I R M Mowat, university librarian. *General and special book colls include books of Scottish song; special colls include early Scottish mss (surviving leaves of 14th C Inchcolm Antiphoner, and colls of lute and pipe-tunes, etc); English madrigal books; Marjorie Kennedy-Fraser coll of Hebridean folk-song recordings and books on Highland mus and dance; archives of the Scottish Students' Song Book Committee (1901-1991) and Edinburgh Royal Choral Union (1857-). Main mus colls are held in the Reid Music Library (see below).*

* **Edinburgh.** Edinburgh University Library: Reid Music Library. Alison House, 12 Nicolson Square, Edinburgh EH8 9DF *tel:* 0131 650 2436 *fax:* 0131 650 2425 *email:* reid.music.library@ed.ac.uk. J Upton, mus librarian. *Mus section of Edinburgh University Library. Colls of scores, books and periodicals on Western mus. Special colls include Sir Donald Tovey archive; Niecks bequest of books on the theory of mus; Weiss coll of Beethoven literature; Kenneth Leighton mss; Dallapiccola complete scores.*

Edinburgh. School of Scottish Studies. University of Edinburgh, 27 George Square, Edinburgh EH8 9LD *tel:* 0131 650 3060/4159 *fax:* 0131 650 4163. Francesca Hardcastle, librarian; Rhona Talbot, archives asst. *Book colls include Scots and Gaelic song since the 18th C, folk mus and ethnomusicology of Ireland, England, N America and the world. Archives include traditional and national Scottish mus field recordings, the John Levy coll of ethnomusicological recordings (mostly oriental), the Peter Cooke coll of African mus recordings, the Will Forret coll of Scottish national, popular, folk revival mus, and smaller colls (Chilean, Irish, Indian).*

* **Egham.** Royal Holloway, University of London, Music Library. Egham Hill, Egham, Surrey TW20 0EX *tel:* 01784 443560/443759 *fax:* 01784 439441 *email:* c.grogan@rhbnc.ac.uk. C P Grogan. *Includes library of Dom Anselm Hughes.*

* **Exeter.** University Library. Stocker Rd, Exeter EX4 4PT *tel:* 01392 263860 *fax:* 01392 263871 *email:* c.a.whiskin@exeter.ac.uk. Catherine Whiskin. *Including special coll of American mus.*

* **Glasgow.** Royal Scottish Academy of Music and Drama. 100 Renfrew St, Glasgow G2 3DB *tel:* 0141 332 4101 *fax:* 0141 332 5924 *email:* library@rsamd.ac.uk. Gordon Hunt, head of information services.

* **Glasgow.** University Library. Hillhead St, Glasgow G12 8QE *tel:* 0141 330 6797 *fax:* 0141 330 4952 *email:* library@gla.ac.uk (general); m.mackie@lib.gla.ac.uk. Morag Mackie, subject librarian for mus. *Includes Euing Music coll; Drysdale, Farmer, Lamond, McEwen, MacCunn, Zavertal colls. Incorporates Trinity College library and Mearns coll of hymnology.*

Guildford. George Edwards Library. University of Surrey, Guildford, Surrey GU2 5XH *tel:* 01483 300800 ext 3322 *fax:* 01483 259500. Glenda Davies, mus librarian.

Hull. Brynmor Jones Library. The University of Hull, Cottingham Rd, Hull HU6 7RX *tel:* 01482 465250 *fax:* 01482 466205 *email:* libhelp@acs.hull.ac.uk. Richard Heseltine, dir and librarian of academic services.

Lancaster. University Library. Bailrigg, Lancaster LA1 4YH *tel:* 01524 65201 *fax:* 01524 63806. *Including libraries of H F Redlich, Edward Lockspeiser and archive of Jack Hylton.*

Leeds. Brotherton Library. University of Leeds, Leeds LS2 9JT *tel:* 0113 233 5513 *fax:* 0113 233 5561 *email:* library@library.leeds.ac.uk. *Including mss and correspondence of Mendelssohn, Charles Dibdin mss, Novello (mus publishers) mss and correspondence, correspondence of Herbert Thompson (mus critic).*

* **Leeds.** Leeds College of Music. 3 Quarry Hill, Leeds LS2 7PD *tel:* 0113 222 3400 *fax:* 0113 243 8798 *email:* j.glasby@leedscolmusic.ac.uk. Jay Glasby, head of library and learning resources. *Orch and US sets for hire. Scores, books, journals, recordings. Jazz archive available by appointment for reference.*

Leicester. University Library. PO Box 248, University Rd, Leics LE1 9QD *tel:* 0116 252 2042 *fax:* 0116 252 2066 *email:* library@leicester.ac.uk. Evelyn Cornell, information librarian. *General mus section of university library.*

Liverpool. The University of Liverpool Music Library. 82 Bedford St South, PO Box 147, Liverpool L69 3BX *tel:* 0151 794 3105/2684 *fax:* 0151 794 2681 *email:* c.morgan@liv.ac.uk. Colin Morgan, arts librarian. *Russian mus, German mus 1830-1945, French mus 1860-1945, facsimile editions.*

* **Manchester.** John Rylands University Library. Oxford Rd, Manchester M13 9PP *tel:* 0161 275 3751 (main library); 834 5343/6765 (special colls) *fax:* 0161 273 7488 (main library); 834 5574 (special colls) *email:* stephen.pearson@man.ac.uk. Stephen Pearson, subject specialist for mus. *The main library has printed scores and secondary mus material. Special colls include: medieval mus mss; several 18th-19th C British mus scores; Wesley family papers; rare scores and collected editions of the works of Handel and Bach and research notes on Handel and Mahler (Arthur D Walker Music Collection); material relating to Ralph Vaughan Williams (papers of Michael Kennedy).*

Manchester. Royal Northern College of Music Library. 124 Oxford Rd, Manchester M13 9RD *tel:* 0161 907 5243 *fax:* 0161 273 7611 *email:* library@rncm.ac.uk. Rosemary Williamson, librarian. *Including Rawsthorne mss, Horenstein coll, Adolph Brodsky archive, Newmania (memorabilia of Philip Newman), Rothwell coll of wind mus, Dame Eva Turner coll, John Ogden archive, Ida Carroll archive, Thomas Pitfield archive, RNCM coll of historic mus insts.*

* **Nottingham.** Music Library. The Arts Centre, University of Nottingham, University Park, Nottingham NG7 2RD *tel:* 0115 951 4596 *fax:* 0115 951 4756 *email:* robin.phillips@nottingham.ac.uk. Robin Phillips, Jenny Mills, mus librarians. *Approximately 20,000 books and scores, including many collected editions of composers and national mus colls. Also sheet mus and miniature scores. Over 30 current periodical subscriptions.*

* **Oxford.** Bodleian Library *see* **National Copyright Libraries.**

Oxford. Brasenose College Library. Oxford OX1 4AJ *tel:* 01865 277827 *fax:* 01865 277831. J W Davies, fellow librarian. *Includes Heberden bequest of books about mus in Ancient Greece and Rome.*

Oxford. Christ Church Library. Oxford OX1 1DP *tel:* 01865 276169 *email:* library@christ-church.ox.ac.uk. *Includes Henry Aldrich bequest and Richard Goodson bequest.*

* **Oxford.** University Faculty of Music Library. St Aldate's, Oxford OX1 1DB *tel:* 01865 276146/8 *fax:* 01865 286260 *email:* john.wagstaff@music.ox.ac.uk. John Wagstaff, librarian; Julie Crawley, deputy librarian. *Open Mon-Fri 9.30am-5.30pm (term-time), 10am-4.30pm (vacations). General u/grad and research mus coll, including sound and video recordings.*

Reading. International Centre for Research in Music Education. University of Reading, Bulmershe Court, Earley, Reading RH6 1HY *tel:* 0118 931 8821 *fax:* 0118 935 2080 *email:* e.smith@reading.ac.uk. Elizabeth Smith, admin. *An extensive archive of documents relating to the development of mus educ in the UK. Publications of the Music Teaching in Private Practice Initiative. MA in Music Education dissertations. Comprehensive coll of publications and materials for primary and secondary class teaching.*

Reading. University Music Library. 35 Upper Redlands Rd, Reading RG1 5JE *tel:* 0118 931 8413 *fax:* 0118 931 8412. A Margaret Laurie, mus librarian; Sheila M Corrall, librarian. *Finzi coll.*

St Andrews. University Library. North St, St Andrews, Fife KY16 9TR *tel:* 01334 462280 *fax:* 01334 462282 *email:* library@st-and.ac.uk. *Includes Finzi coll of 18th C mus.*

Sheffield. University of Sheffield Music Library. 38 Taptonville Rd, Sheffield, S Yorks S10 5BR *tel:* 0114 222 7330 *fax:* 0114 266 8053 *email:* t.mccanna@sheffield.ac.uk. Tom McCanna, mus librarian.

Southampton. Hartley Library. University of Southampton, University Rd, Highfield, Southampton SO17 1BJ *tel:* 023 8059 5000 ext 2372 *fax:* 023 8059 3007 *email:* ng@soton.ac.uk. N Graffy, arts librarian. *Scores, books, periodicals, CDs.*

* **Totnes.** Dartington College of Arts Library. Totnes, Devon TQ9 6EJ *tel:* 01803 861651 *fax:* 01803 863569 *email:* library@dartington.ac.uk. Dorothy Faulkner, dir, academic services; Richard Taylor, deputy librarian.

* **York.** University Library. Heslington, York YO10 5DD *tel:* 01904 433865 *fax:* 01904 433866 *email:* librl@york.ac.uk. David Griffiths. *Copland coll and Delius coll.*

Libraries of Societies and Institutions

These libraries are for the use of members and staff, but reference facilities are extended to visitors. Applications in writing are advisable.

London. Arts Council of England Reference Library and Enquiry Service. 14 Great Peter St, London SW1P 3NQ *tel:* 020 7973 6517 *fax:* 020 7973 6590 *email:* enquiries@artscouncil.org.uk. Jackie Lomas, Kirsty Brown, April Child, asst information offrs. *Material on arts policy and admin, subsidy and funding of the arts in UK and overseas. Enquiries from 10am-1pm and 2-5pm, Mon-Fri; visits by appointment with library staff only.*

* The BBC Music Library. Broadcasting House, Portland Place, London W1A 1AA *tel:* 020 7765 3724 *fax:* 020 7765 5304. Rachel Ladyman, mgr, research services. *Largest coll of performing material and commercial and private gramophone records. Loans of mus materials for non-broadcast use are made only if no other source exists and are subject to copyright restrictions; the sound recordings coll is for BBC programme purposes only.*

British Film Institute National Library. 21 Stephen St, London W1P 2LN *tel:* 020 7255 1444 *fax:* 020 7436 2338. Ray Templeton, head of BFI national library. *Includes information about film and TV mus and composers.*

British Institute of Recorded Sound *see* British Library National Sound Archive *under* **Specialised Gramophone Record and Tape Libraries.**

British Music Information Centre. 10 Stratford Place, London W1N 9AE *tel:* 020 7499 8567 *fax:* 020 7499 4795 *email:* bmic@bmic.co.uk. Matthew Greenall, dir; Simon Woolf, information mgr. *Reference coll: 20th C mus by British composers; visitors welcome (Mon-Fri 12-5pm). Reading and listening facilities, free of charge.*

Commonwealth Institute. Commonwealth Resource Centre, Kensington High St, London W8 6NQ *tel:* 020 7603 4535 ext 210 *fax:* 020 7603 2807 *email:* info@commonwealth.org.uk. Karen Peters, head of library and information services. *Coll includes mus from most commonwealth countries; loan service for teachers throughout Britain.*

* English Folk Dance and Song Society. Vaughan Williams Memorial Library, Cecil Sharp House, 2 Regent's Park Rd, London NW1 7AY *tel:* 020 7485 2206 *fax:* 020 7284 0523. M H Taylor, librarian; E Bradtke, library asst. *Includes Cecil Sharp bequest; original recordings by many leading folksong collectors.*

Gerald Coke Handel Collection. 40 Brunswick Square, London WC1N 1AZ. *Handel coll. A privately owned library; until further notice written application essential to Gerald Coke Handel Foundation at above address.*

* The Serge Prokofiev Archive. Goldsmiths College, University of London, London SE14 6NW *tel:* 020 7919 7558 *fax:* 020 7919 7255

email: mua01nm@gold.ac.uk. Noëlle Mann, curator. *Property of the Serge Prokofiev Foundation. The archive holds copies of published works, microfilms of mss, books, articles and reviews; sound recordings, photos, documents. Also, unique coll of Prokofiev's correspondence 1921-1936.*

Society for Co-operation in Russian and Soviet Studies. 320 Brixton Rd, London SW9 6AB *tel:* 020 7274 2282 *fax:* 020 7274 3230. Jane Rosen, librarian. *Reference library of mus scores, encyclopaedias and recordings appertaining to Russian and Soviet mus and composers. Fees available on request.*

* **Aldeburgh.** Britten-Pears Library. The Red House, Aldeburgh, Suffolk IP15 5PZ *tel:* 01728 451700 *fax:* 01728 453076 *email:* k.cooke@britten-pears.co.uk. *Mss of Britten and other composers including Bridge, Holst, Tippett, Armstrong Gibbs, Alwyn, Shostakovich. Also special material on English song and English Opera Group Archive, books, printed mus, correspondence, sound recordings, ephemera and photographs. Open for research, by appointment only.*

Cardiff. Welsh Music Information Centre. Ty Cerdd, 15 Mount Stuart Square, Cardiff CF10 5DP *tel:* 029 2046 2855 *fax:* 029 2046 2733. *Mus of Welsh composers, published and unpublished. Written enquiries only.*

Crowthorne. British Institute of Jazz Studies. 17 The Chase, Crowthorne, Berks RG45 6HT *tel:* 01344 775669 *fax:* 01344 780947. Graham Langley, sec. *Library of jazz and blues material: books, periodicals, ephemera, etc; visits by appointment.*

Glasgow. Scottish Music Information Centre. 1 Bowmont Gardens, Glasgow G12 9LR *tel:* 0141 334 6393 *fax:* 0141 337 1161 *email:* smic@glasgow.almac.co.uk. Morag Brooksbank, dir; Alasdair Pettinger, information offr. *Information and documentation centre for Scottish composers and Scottish mus. Scores, recordings, rare books and mss, some available for sale or hire.*

Loughton. National Jazz Foundation Archive. Loughton Central Library, Traps Hill, Loughton, Essex IG10 1HD *tel:* 020 8502 0181 *fax:* 020 8508 5041. David Nathan, archivist. *Archive of printed material for research into jazz. Books, periodicals, concert brochures, photographs, posters, etc.*

Manchester. Chetham's Library. Long Millgate, Manchester M3 1SB *tel:* 0161 834 7961 *fax:* 0161 839 5797. Michael Powell, librarian. *Halliwell-Phillipps coll of proclamations, broadsides, ballads and poems. For reference only.*

Preston. Library of Light-Orchestral Music. Lancaster Farm, Chipping Lane, Longridge, Preston, Lancs PR3 2NB *tel:* 01772 783646 *fax:* 01772 786026. Ernest Tomlinson, chmn. *Standard published sets, ms arrangements; hire and sale.*

Stockport. National Library for the Blind. Far Cromwell Rd, Bredbury, Stockport, Cheshire SK6 2SG *tel:* 0161 355 2045 *fax:* 0161 355 2098 *email:* luba.brown@nlbuk.org. Luba Brown, mus librarian. *Large coll of braille mus on free loan (print and braille cat available); UK source for Library of Congress braille and large-print mus; enlarging service.*

Stratford upon Avon. Shakespeare Centre Library. Henley St, Stratford upon Avon, Warwicks CV37 6QW *tel:* 01789 201813 *fax:* 01789 296083 *email:* library@shakespeare.org.uk. Marian Pringle, snr librarian; Sylvia Morris, deputy librarian. *Mus connected with Shakespeare and RSC productions, including Vaughan Williams, Ilona Sekacz, James Walker, and Guy Woolfenden mus.*

* **Westhumble.** Royal School of Church Music. Cleveland Lodge, Westhumble, Dorking RH5 6BW *tel:* 01306 872800 *fax:* 01306 877260 *email:* jhender@rscm.u-net.com. John Henderson, librarian. *Colles Library, church mus and books. Please enquire for details of access.*

Eton. College Library. Eton College, Windsor, Berks SL4 6DB *tel:* 01753 671221 *fax:* 01753 801507 *email:* collections@etoncollege.org.uk. M C Meredith, librarian. *Includes the Eton Choir Book (c 1500), 18th C ms org books, minor mss of works by Parry, Butterworth, Quilter, Warlock, Britten, Hoddinott, etc.*

Specialised Gramophone Record and Tape Libraries

This list does not include the record collections available at many public libraries.

London. BBC Music Library *see* **Libraries of Societies and Institutions.**

* British Library National Sound Archive. The British Library, 96 Euston Rd, London NW1 2DB *tel:* 020 7412 7440 *fax:* 020 7412 7441 *email:* nsa@bl.uk. Crispin Jewitt, dir. *Largest reference coll of sound recordings in the UK open to the public, full reference library of associated literature. Information on commercial discs and location of recordings around the UK. Groups from schools, universities, colleges welcome to listen by prior arrangement; w/shops, talks and seminars also offered by arrangement.*

BTW Production Music Library. 106 Westpole Ave, Cockfosters, Herts EN4 0BB *tel:* 020 8449 6110 *also fax.* John Borthwick, snr partner. *Mus for TV, radio and a/v productions.*

* Music Performance Research Centre. Barbican Library, Barbican Centre, Silk St, London EC2Y 8DS *tel:* 01730 893611 *also fax; email:* mprc@dial.pipex.com. Margaret Gray, admin. *A/v archive concerned with preservation, rights protection and research of public mus performances by international artists. Also records and houses interviews with performers.*

National Sound Archive *see* **British Library National Sound Archive.**

Cambridge. Cambridge Anthropology Sound Archive. Dept of Social Anthropology, Free School Lane, Cambridge CB2 3RF *tel:* 01223 334599/334402 *email:* socanth-admin@lists.eam.ac.uk. Carole Pegg. *Coll of commercial and field recordings of traditional and other mus from all countries.*

Gloucester. The Traditions Library. 16 Brunswick Square, Gloucester GL1 1UG *tel:* 01452 415110 *email:* peter@folktrax.demon.co.uk. Peter Kennedy, mgr; Beryl Kennedy, mgr. *International traditional mus and customs in print and on studio tape, cassette, CD, film and video.*

St Annes-on-Sea. Long Playing Record Library Ltd. Squires Gate Music Centre, Rear 13 St Andrews Rd South, St Annes-on-Sea, Lancs FY8 1SX *tel:* 01253 782588 *fax:* 01253 782985. Ivan March, mgr. *Commercial lending library for CDs; also specialist suppliers of CDs and tapes to libraries, broadcasting stations, individuals worldwide, specialising in classical mus.*

Museums and Other Collections

Hours of opening may vary considerably and should be checked before a visit is organised. Some collections may be viewed only after written application to the curator.

London. Fenton House. Hampstead Grove, London NW3 6RT *tel:* 020 7435 3471. Mimi S Waitzman, keeper of the insts. *Early keyboard insts, including hpds, clvds and early pnos. Demonstration tours, concert series, and recordings available.*

The Handel House Trust Ltd. 10 Stratford Place, London W1N 9AE *tel:* 020 7495 1685 *fax:* 020 7495 1759 *email:* mail@handelhouse.prestel.co.uk. *Charity engaged in establishing a museum to Handel in his home at 25 Brook St, Mayfair, London W1.*

Horniman Museum and Gardens. 100 London Rd, London SE23 3PQ *tel:* 020 8699 1872 *fax:* 020 8291 5506 *email:* enquiries@horniman.demon.co.uk. Frances Palmer, keeper of mus insts; D W Allen, librarian; Margaret Birley, deputy keeper of mus insts. *Large coll of mus insts from all over world (6000 insts, 1500 on display) including Adam Carse coll, Percy A Bull coll, Wayne coll of concertinas, Alice Schulmann Frank coll of world mus insts and Dolmetsch coll. Library includes sections on mus insts. Also educ service. The Music Room display may be affected by re-development at the Museum. Please call before you visit.*

Museum of London. London Wall, London EC2Y 5HN *tel:* 020 7600 3699 *fax:* 020 7600 1058 *email:* info@museumoflondon.org.uk. Rory O'Connell, curator. *Str, keyboard and wind insts; small coll only, 1950s fittings from Dobell's Jazz shop, printed ephemera on theatres and mus in London, (closed Mon). Small number of paper rolls, vinyl discs, cylinders, c 1900-70s.*

Musical Museum (Charitable Trust). 368 High St, Brentford, Middx TW8 0BD *tel:* 020 8560 8108. Richard Cole, curator. *Keyboards, automatic mus insts, player-pnos, orchestrations, Wurlitzer Fotoplayer, Welte Philharmonic Reproducing Pipe Organ, Aeolian Residence Duo-Art Pipe Organ, etc. Open w/ends Apr-Oct, 2pm-5pm; Weds, Jul-Aug, 2-4pm.*

Royal College of Music. Prince Consort Rd, London SW7 2BS *tel:* 020 7589 3643/7591 4346 (museum); 020 7591 4340 (portraits) *fax:* 020 7589 7740 *email:* museum@rcm.ac.uk. Mrs E P Wells, museum curator; O H Davies, keeper of portraits. *Museum of insts (keyboard, str, wind), including Tagore, Donaldson, Hipkins, Ridley and Hartley colls; 600 insts (500 European, 100 Asian and African). Dept of Portraits and Performance History: paintings, prints, photographs, concert programmes, etc.*

Theatre Museum. Tavistock St, Covent Garden, London EC2E 7PA *tel:* 020 7836 7891 *fax:* 020 7836 5148. Margaret Benton, head of museum. *National museum of performing arts including theatre, mus, pop, melodrama, ballet and opera. Public research facilities.*

Victoria and Albert Museum. Cromwell Rd, South Kensington, London SW7 2RL *tel:* 020 7938 8500/8287 *fax:* 020 7938 8283. James Yorke, asst curator. *Comprehensive exhibition coll of decorative mus insts; mus insts and mus iconography included in National Art Library at the V & A.* Catalogue of Musical Instruments at the Victoria and Albert Museum: Vol 1, Keyboard Instruments *by Howard Schott;* Vol 2 Non-keyboard Instruments *by Anthony Baines, with additions by James Yorke, reprinted 1998 in one volume, £40.*

Belfast. Ulster Museum. Botanic Gardens, Belfast BT9 5AB *tel:* 028 9038 3000 *fax:* 028 9038 3013. Mrs W Glover, curator of ethnography; T Wylie, curator of history. *Small coll of ancient and modern mus insts. Ethnographic mus insts include 2 sets of Chimu pottery pan pipes, 2 Bronze Age hns, 3 pairs of Uillean pipes, 4 hps, 2 fifes, 4 Lambeg drums.*

Birmingham. Museum of Science and Industry. Newhall St, Birmingham B3 1RZ *tel:* 0121 303 1662 *fax:* 0121 233 9210. *Museum closed, access for research purposes only and by appointment. Mechanical mus insts; coll of mus boxes.*

Bradford. Bolling Hall Museum. Bowling Hall Rd, Bradford, W Yorks BD4 7LP *tel:* 01274 723057 *fax:* 01274 726220 *email:* abickley@legend.co.uk. Anthea Bickley, snr keeper, history. *Coll of mus insts dispersed among various museums in Bradford Metropolitan area. Mostly at Cliffe Castle Museum, Keighley.*

Cambridge. Fitzwilliam Museum. Trumpington St, Cambridge CB2 1RB *tel:* 01223 332900 *fax:* 01223 332923 *email:* fitzwilliam-enquiries@lists.cam.ac.uk. Duncan Robinson, dir. *Printed and ms mus, including major colls of Handel, Macfarren, Hadley, and the Fitzwilliam Virginal Book. A few guis, lutes, and keyboard insts, a pitch pipe, and a small coll of unstrung hps.*

Cambridge. University Museum of Archaeology and Anthropology. Downing St, Cambridge CB2 3DZ *tel:* 01223 333516 *fax:* 01223 333503. D W Phillipson, dir and curator; Ms A C Herle, snr asst curator (anthropology). *Coll of insts of anthropological interest.*

Cardiff. Museum of Welsh Life (National Museums and Galleries of Wales). St Fagans, Nr Cardiff CF5 6XB *tel:* 029 2057 3500 *fax:* 029 2057 3490. Emma Lile, research asst. *Str, keyboard and wind insts.*

Carlisle. City Museum and Art Gallery. Tullie House, Castle St, Carlisle, Cumbria CA3 8TP *tel:* 01228 534781 *fax:* 01288 810249 *email:* tullie-house@carlisle-city.gov.uk. Melanie Gardner, keeper of fine and decorative arts. *Str and wind insts, including Andrea Amati vn of 1564 and str insts by Forster family.*

Cheltenham. Holst Birthplace Museum. 4 Clarence Rd, Pittville, Cheltenham, Glos GL52 2AY *tel:* 01242 524846 *fax:* 01242 262334. Helen Brown, Mary Greensted, keepers of visitor services. *Unique coll of Holst material including printed mus, pictures, concert programmes, books, personal possessions. Open to public all year (closed Sun-Mon), small admission charge, enquiries to information offr, Cheltenham Art Gallery, Clarence St, Cheltenham* tel: *01242 237431.*

Chester. Grosvenor Museum. 27 Grosvenor St, Chester CH1 2DD *tel:* 01244 402008 *fax:* 01244 347587 *email:* s.fowler@chestercc.gov.uk. Sophie Fowler, keeper of local and social history. *Unique set of Bressan rcdrs (recording available).*

Douglas. Manx National Heritage. Douglas, Isle of Man IM1 3LY *tel:* 01624 648000 *fax:* 01624 648001 *email:* enquiries@mnh.gov.im. Stephen Harrison, dir. *Str, keyboard and wind insts.*

Edinburgh. Edinburgh University. Collection of Historic Musical Instruments, Reid Concert Hall, Bristo Square, Edinburgh EH8 9AG *tel:* 0131 650 2423 *fax:* 0131 650 2425 *email:* Collection_Historic_Musical_Ins@ed.ac.uk. Arnold Myers, dir and curator; Murray Campbell, asst curator. *University coll of over 2000 historic mus insts spanning 400 years. Open Wed 3-5pm, Sat 10-1pm (Mon-Fri 2-5pm throughout Edinburgh Festival). Closed over Christmas and New Year. Admission free.*

Edinburgh. Russell Collection of Early Keyboard Instruments. St Cecilia's Hall (Edinburgh University), Niddry St, Cowgate, Edinburgh EH1 1LJ *tel:* 0131 650 2805 *fax:* 0131 650 2812 *email:* russell.collection@music.ed.co.uk. Grant O'Brien, curator. *Includes hpds, virginals, spinets, clvds, early pnos and chmbr orgs from 1586-1840.*

Glasgow. Art Gallery and Museum. Kelvingrove, Glasgow G3 8AG *tel:* 0141 287 2700 *fax:* 0141 287 2690. *Coll of historical mus insts.*

Goudhurst. Finchcocks Living Museum of Music. Finchcocks, Goudhurst, Kent TH17 1HH *tel:* 01580 211702 *fax:* 01580 211007. William Dow, curator. *Richard Burnett coll of historic keyboard insts. Open Sun and Bank Holidays Easter-Sep; Wed and Thu in Aug; other times by prior arrangement. Mus tours whenever open.*

Holdenby. Holdenby House. Holdenby, Northants NN6 8DJ *tel:* 01604 770074 *fax:* 01604 770962. Mrs S Maughan, admin. *Non-player pno exhibition, old pnos from 1790. 11 pnos from British Piano Museum. House tours/groups by appointment, min 25.*

Huddersfield. Tolson Memorial Museum. Ravensknowle Park, Wakefield Rd, Huddersfield HD5 8DJ *tel:* 01484 223830 *fax:* 01484 223843. *Br, wind and str insts.*

Ipswich. Christchurch Mansion. Christchurch Park, Ipswich IP4 2BE *tel:* 01473 253246 *fax:* 01473 210328. Jane Sedge, snr asst curator. *Str, wind and keyboard insts. Enquiries and correspondence to Ipswich Museum, see below.*

Ipswich. Ipswich Museum. High St, Ipswich IP1 3QH *tel:* 01473 213761 *fax:* 01473 281274. D L Jones, keeper, human history. *Ethnographic insts.*

Keighley. Cliffe Castle Art Gallery and Museum. Keighley, W Yorks BD20 6LH *tel:* 01535 618230 *fax:* 01535 610536. Anthea Bickley, snr keeper, history. *General coll of mus insts.*

Leicester. Charles Moore Collection of Musical Instruments. Music Department, University of Leicester, University Rd, Leicester LE1 7RH *tel:* 0116 252 2781; 01234 360221 *fax:* 0116 252 2782 *email:* bedfordhs-mkss@bbcnc.org.uk; ap1@leicester.ac.uk. Stephen Weston, curator; Anthony Pither, dir of mus; Margaret Rose, admin asst. *Mainly 18th and 19th C w/wind and br.*

Liverpool. Liverpool Museum. William Brown St, Liverpool L3 8EN *tel:* 0151 478 4262 *fax:* 0151 478 4390. Pauline Rushton, curator of costume and textiles. *Coll of 17th-19th C insts including former Rushworth and Dreaper coll.*

* **Manchester.** Royal Northern College of Music. 124 Oxford Rd, Manchester M13 9RD *tel:* 0161 907 5243 *fax:* 0161 273 7611 *email:* library@rncm.ac.uk. Rosemary Williamson, college librarian. *RNCM coll of historic mus insts.*

Northleach. Keith Harding's World of Mechanical Music. Oak House, High St, Northleach, Glos GL54 3ET *tel:* 01451 860181 *fax:* 01451 861133. Keith Harding. *Demonstrations of antique clocks, mus boxes, automata, reproducing pnos and mechanical mus insts presented as live entertainment. Restoration work done.*

Norwich. Strangers' Hall Museum (Norfolk Museums Service). Charing Cross, Norwich NR2 4AL *tel:* 01603 667229. Helen Rowles, asst. *Str, keyboard, perc and mechanical wind insts. Gramophones, printed and ms mus in store. Viewing by arrangement.*

Oxford. Ashmolean Museum. Beaumont St, Oxford OX1 2PH *tel:* 01865 278000 *fax:* 01865 278042 *email:* sarah.herring@ashmus.ox.ac.uk. *Hill coll of str insts and bows (photographs and measured drawings of str insts available for research).*

Oxford. Bate Collection of Musical Instruments. Oxford University Faculty of Music, St Aldate's, Oxford OX1 1DB *tel:* 01865 276139 *fax:* 01865 276128 *email:* bate.collection@music.oxford.ac.uk. H La Rue, curator; J Archibald, museum asst. *W/wind, br, early keyboards and bow makers w/shop. Open Mon-Fri, 2-5pm, admission free. Open Sat during University full term, 10am-12pm.*

Oxford. University of Oxford, Pitt Rivers Museum. 60 Banbury Rd, Oxford OX2 6PN *tel:* 01865 270927 *fax:* 01865 274725 *email:* pitt@ermine.ox.ac.uk. H La Rue, curator. *Important worldwide coll of more than 6000 mus insts. New gallery Music Makers in the Balfour Building, 60 Banbury Rd, Oxford* tel: *01865 274726. Includes a sound guide and a/v booth.*

St Albans. Organ Museum. 320 Camp Rd, St Albans, Herts AL1 5PE *tel:* 01727 851557 *also fax.* Bill Walker, chmn, trustee; Peter Allen, treasurer, trustee; Colin Hartwell, sec. *Mechanical insts and theatre orgs; open Sun 2.15-4.30pm. Other times by arrangement. Correspondence and enquiries to the Secretary, c/o 326 Camp Rd, St Albans, Herts AL1 5PB.*

Shipley. Victorian Reed Organ and Harmonium Museum. Victoria Hall, Victoria Rd, Saltaire Village, Shipley, W Yorks *tel:* 01274 585601 (after 5pm) *email:* phil@harmoniumservice.demon.co.uk. Phil Fluke, curator. *Private coll of 95 reed orgs. Players encouraged to play. Also mechanical reed orgs. Open to the public Sun-Thu, 11am-4pm.*

Worcester. The Elgar Birthplace Museum. Crown East Lane, Lower Broadheath, Worcester WR2 6RH *tel:* 01905 333224 *also fax.* Melanie Weatherley, Catherine Sloan, curators. *Unique coll of Elgarian material including mss, scores, letters, books, photographs, insts and personal possessions.*

York. York Castle Museum. York YO1 9RY *tel:* 01904 653611 *fax:* 01904 671078. *Social history museum of everyday life. General coll of mus insts, with good w/wind, keyboard and mechanical sections (some on display).*

Early Music

The specialist publications are *Early Music Today, Early Music Review, Early Music, Early Music History, Early Music News, Leading Notes,* and the *Early Music Yearbook,* details of which will be found in the **Music Periodicals** section.

Additional information can be obtained from **The Early Music Network** (31 Abdale Rd, London W12 7ER *tel:* 020 8743 0302 *fax:* 020 8743 0996 *email:* glyn@earlymusicnet.demon.co.uk *website:* www.earlymusic.org.uk), or from the **National Early Music Association** (Southside Cottage, Brook Hill, Albury, Guildford, GU5 9DJ *tel:* 01483 202159 *fax:* 01483 203088 *email:* lutesoc@aol.com *website:* www.brainlink.com/~starmus/unison/nema/nema.html).

Early Music Fora

Border Marches Early Music Forum (BMEMF). 3 Upper Linney, Ludlow, Shropshire SY8 1EF *tel:* 01584 876175. Jenny Sayer, sec. *Medieval to baroque vocal and inst day w/shops held on Sundays, in Leominster, Herefordshire. Occasional sponsoring of early mus concerts.*

East Midlands Early Music Forum (EMEMF). 127 Sheepbridge Lane, Mansfield, Notts NG18 5DT *tel:* 01623 658951 *email:* ememf@compuserve.com. Tony Brett, treasurer, events co-ord. *Quarterly newsletter, w/shops, choral and baroque mus days. What's On diary of early mus concerts, early mus w/shops, courses and summer schools both locally and nationwide. Assists members to make contacts for their own mus-making.*

Midlands Early Music Forum (MEMF). 21 Oakfield Ave, Kingswinford, W Midlands DY6 8HJ *tel:* 01384 295210 *email:* paul@diabolus-in-musica.freeserve.co.uk. Paul Baker, sec. *Regular newsletter, w/shops, social events.*

North East Early Music Forum (NEEMF). 43 Becketts Park Cres, Leeds LS6 3PH *tel:* 0113 278 6886 *fax:* 0113 230 7818 *email:* bmb6jlj@bmb.leeds.ac.uk. Jillian Johnson, hon sec. *Regular one-day w/shops in performance and interpretation, for singers and insts. Residential w/end in Sep.*

North West Early Music Forum (NWEMF). 1 Oak Lea, Standish, Wigan WN6 0SL *tel:* 01257 400018. Rosemary Dewey, sec. *W/shops and summer school for singers and insts.*

South West Early Music Forum (SWEMF). Little Hampden, Hunnacott, Landkey, Barnstaple, Devon EX32 0NW *tel:* 01271 831092. Susan Madgwick, sec. *Promoting interest in early mus through w/shop performances.*

Southern Early Music Forum (SEMF). 108 Howard Drive, Allington Park, Maidstone ME16 0QB *tel:* 01622 762409 *email:* ruth@fox-haunt.demon.co.uk. Tim Samuelson, newsletter ed. *Early mus playing days. Register of contacts for musicians in the South East.*

International Directory

INTERNATIONAL DIRECTORY

Photo: Coneyl Jay

Medieval Image courtesy of the British Museum

THE DUFAY COLLECTIVE

Festival Brežice2000

15.7. – 29.7.2000

A superbe series of Early Music concerts by prominent international artists in the most beautiful halls in Slovenia.

Student Festival
International exchange of music students
August 2000

International Master Classes in Early Music

ARS RAMOVŠ
Institute for Art, Marketing, Promotion, and Investment
SI-1000 Ljubljana, Slovenska cesta 1, Slovenia

Tel (+386 61) 125 33 66
Fax (+386 61) 174 154 1
www.k-ramovs.si
E-mail: info@k-ramovs.si

Agents and Promoters

The agents listed below provide representation for individual artists, ensembles and orchestras; many also promote concerts, concert series and festivals.

Andorra

RIAL Andorra Ltd. 24 Ave de Tarragona, Andorra la Vella, Principality of Andorra *tel:* +376 860686 *fax:* +376 860992 *email:* r.i.a.l@andorra.ad. Pascal Lair, managing director. *Artist management and tour promotion. Classical and jazz.*

Argentina

Conciertos Gama. Corrientes 1665, 3rd Fl Room A, 1042 Buenos Aires, Argentina *tel:* +54 1 374 4257/6288/5403 *fax:* +54 1 112260. Alejandro Szterenfeld. *Artist representation and concert promotion.*

Daniel Artist Management. Dragones 1929, 1428 Buenos Aires, Argentina *tel:* +54 1 788 4308 *fax:* +54 1 786 3305 *email:* lumpui@ba.net. Rosario Bauza de Quesada. *Artist representation and concert promotion.*

Organización de Conciertos Grapa. Juncal 1360, 2A, 1062 Buenos Aires, Argentina *tel:* +54 11 4813 2724 *fax:* +54 11 4813 6383 *email:* elgrap@sinectis.com.ar. Elias Grapa, Nina Grapa, directors. *Artist representation and concert promotion.*

Werner S Wagner. Casilla de Correo 5293, Correo Central, 1000 Buenos Aires, Argentina *tel:* +54 11 4777 7667 *fax:* +54 11 4774 7962. *Artist representation, specialising in opera, conductors, soloists.*

Australia

Adelaide Festival Centre Trust. King William Rd, Adelaide, SA 5000, Australia *tel:* +61 8 216 8600 *fax:* +61 8 212 7849. Andrew Bleby, programme director. *Concert promotion.*

Arts Management Pty Ltd. Station House, Rawson Place, 790 George St, Sydney, NSW 2000, Australia *tel:* +61 2 9212 5066 *fax:* +61 2 9211 7762 *email:* enquiries@artsmanagement.com.au. Virginia Braden, managing director. *Artist representation of conductors, instrumentalists, singers, ensembles, lighting designers, designers and directors.*

Cameron's Management. Suite 5, Edgecliff Court, 2 New McLean St, Edgecliff, Sydney, NSW 2027, Australia *tel:* +61 2 9362 0500 *fax:* +61 2 9363 3317. Judith Alexander, director. *Artist representation of opera and concert singers.*

Jenifer Eddy Artists' Management. The Clivedon Suite 11, 596 St Kilda Rd, Melbourne, Victoria 3004, Australia *tel:* +61 3 9525 2700 *fax:* +61 3 9529 5410 *email:* jeam@compuserve.com. Jenifer Eddy, director; Simon Fletcher, Alexander Furman, Anna Robinson, associate directors. *Representation of singers and conductors.*

Symphony Australia. GPO Box 9994, Sydney, NSW 2001, Australia *tel:* +61 2 9333 1677 *fax:* +61 2 9333 1678 *email:* dixons@symphony.net.au. Derek Watt, managing director; Samuel C Dixon, artistic admin. *Concert promotion.*

Victoria Arts Centre Trust. 100 St Kilda Rd, Melbourne, Victoria 3004, Australia *tel:* +61 3 9281 8000 *fax:* +61 3 9281 8282 *email:* vicartscentre@vact.vic.gov.au. Tim Jacobs, chief executive. *Performing arts centre.*

Weaver Artist Management. PO Box 7670, St Kilda Rd, Melbourne, Victoria 3004, Australia *tel:* +61 3 9481 4729 *fax:* +61 3 9481 4739 *email:* weaver@rainbow.net.au. Jeff Weaver, director; Mark Matthews. *Representation of singers, conductors, directors, instrumentalists, chamber music and ensembles.*

Austria

Agentur Kleinheisterkamp. Rechte Lande 10, A-6820 Frastanz, Austria *tel:* +43 552 252193 *also fax*; +43 664 252 9790. *Artist representation.*

artsprojects. Meytensgasse 14, A-1130 Wien, Austria *tel:* +43 1 876 6728 *fax:* +43 1 876 0755 *email:* k.josel@artsprojects.com. Kristel Josel, general manager. *Representation of instrumentalists and conductors; festival consultancy, chamber music touring.*

Austroconcert International. Gluckgasse 1, A-1010 Wien, Austria *tel:* +43 1 513 2657 *fax:* +43 1 512 6154 *email:* aconcert@magnet.at. Prof Wolfgang Hartl, general manager; Elisabetta Hartl, assistant manager. *Representation of conductors, singers and orchestras.*

Crepaz Music Management. Straubstr 1, A-6060 Hall in Tirol, Austria *tel:* +43 5223 45222 *fax:* +43 5225 45222 20 *email:* info@crepaz-music.com. Christoph Crepaz, managing director; Gerhard Crepaz, festivals and cultural concepts. *Artist representation and concert promotion, specialise in early music, opera, classical and contemporary music.*

Esther Schollum Artists' Management. Guntramsdorferstr 12/2, A-2340 Mödling b. Wien, Austria *tel:* +43 22 364 1004; *mobile:* +43 676 545 4654 *fax:* +43 223 641 0044 *email:* es@art-mgmt.com. *Artist representation.*

Gerhard Schroeder Konzertdirektion. Am Steinbruch 20, A-4020 Linz-Puchenau, Austria *tel:* +43 73 222 1523 *fax:* +43 73 222 1952. *Concert promotion.*

Gerhild Baron International Artists Management. Dornbacher Str 41/111/2, A-1170 Wien, Austria *tel:* +43 1 489 6154 *fax:* +43 1 485 6711 *email:* baron@via.at. Gerhild Baron, managing director; Daniela Wacha, managing assistant; Laura Borsi, organisation. *Artist representation, specialising in concerts and opera.*

Goodmusic Artists' Management and Consulting Künstlervermittlung KEG. Dopschstr 20/3, A-1210 Wien, Austria *tel:* +43 1 259 2027 *fax:* +43 1 259 6124 *email:* johngoodman@goodman.at. John Goodman, general manager. *Artist representation and concert promotion; music theatre; personal and general management.*

Kammermusik-Vereinigung Wien. Ganglbauergasse 38-6, A-1160 Wien, Austria *tel:* +43 1 492 3684 *fax:* +43 1 493 3927 *email:* vonnemann@art-vienna.com. Yossi Gutman, music director; Anna Vonneman, manager. *Artist representation specialising in chamber music.*

Konzertdirektion Schlote GmbH. Danreitergasse 4, A-5020 Salzburg, Austria *tel:* +43 66 262 2174 *fax:* +43 662 629 9645. Joachim and Michael Schlote. *International management for opera, operetta, ballet, drama, musicals, orchestras, and soloists.*

Künstleragentur Dr Raab & Dr Böhm. Plankengasse 7, A-1010 Wien, Austria *tel:* +43 51 20501 *fax:* +43 512 7743 *email:* raab.boehm@magnet.at. Horst Böhm, company director and director of concert division. *International representation of singers, instrumentalists, chamber ensembles and orchestras, conductors.*

Künstleragentur Hollaender-Calix. Grinzinger Allee 46, Haus 2, A-1190 Wien, Austria *tel:* +43 1 320 5317 *fax:* +43 1 328 4733. Ariane Hollaender-Calix, managing director. *Artist representation for opera, operetta and concerts.*

Künstlersekretariat Buchmann GmbH. Schachnerstr 27, A-1220 Wien, Austria *tel:* +43 1 203 6357 *fax:* +43 1 203 7483 *email:* buchmann@m.xpoint.at. *Artist representation and concert promotion.*

Künstlervermittlung Klaus Eisenberger. Peter Jordan Str 8, PO Box 3, A-1183 Wien, Austria *tel:* +43 1 368 1363 *fax:* +43 1 369 2323 *email:* eisenberger@classic-music.at. Klaus Eisenberger, general manager. *Artist representation specialising in chamber music, soloists, early music, contemporary music.*

Martin C Turba Arts Management. Franz-Josef-Kai 7, A-5020 Salzburg, Austria *tel:* +43 66 284 6578 *fax:* +43 66 284 7556 *email:* turba@netway.at. Martin C Turba, director. *Artist representation, specialising in orchestra tours; concert management.*

Mayler Artist Management (MAM). Längenfeldgasse 26/33, A-1120 Wien, Austria *tel:* +43 1 815 3733 *fax:* +43 1 812 7167 *email:* mam-vienna@netway.at. Keith Hoare-Mayler, managing director; Gabriele Kader, artists' manager. *General management and artist representation. Special interest in early music and festival consulting.*

Melos Konzerte Wien. Postfach 71, Salesianergasse 12/11, A-1037 Wien, Austria *tel:* +43 1 714 9196 *fax:* +43 1 714 9191. Christian May, chairman; Martha Maluk, Eleonore Schmidt, artist managers. *Artist management for instrumentalists, conductors, chamber music ensembles. Orchestra tours. Local office in Munich.*

Musikalische Jugend Österreichs-Jeunesse. PO Box 45, Lothringerstr 20, A-1037 Wien, Austria *tel:* +43 1 710 3616 *fax:* +43 1 710 361617 *email:* m.naske@jeunesse.at. Matthias Naske, general manager. *Promotion of concerts for young people. 400 classical concerts a year.*

Musikmanagement MW. Nußdorfer Str 38/19, A-1090 Wien, Austria *tel:* +43 1 317 1871 *fax:* +43 1 317 1872 *email:* m.m.m@appleservice.com. Rudolf Morawitz, director; Daniela Weber, artists department. *Artist representation and concert promotion, especially for orchestras, chamber music, instrument soloists and conductors. Festival consulting.*

Musikverein für Steiermark. Landhausgasse 12, A-8010 Graz, Austria *tel:* +43 31 682 9924 *fax:* +43 31 682 992423. Mag Uta Werner, general secretary. *Concert promotion for symphony orchestras, chamber music, instrumentalists and singers.*

Opera Vladarski Bühnenvermittlung Internationaler Sänger. Reithlegasse 12, A-1190 Wien, Austria *tel:* +43 1 368 6960/1 *fax:* +43 1 368 6962 *email:* opera.vladarski@netway.at. Lotte Vladarski, director. *Artist representation.*

Primusic. Herrengasse 6-8, A-1010 Wien, Austria *tel:* +43 1 532 7124 *fax:* +43 1 532 7140. Thomas Wolfram, managing director. *Artist representation and concert promotion.*

Belgium

Agnes De Hooghe. 81 Rue Basse, B-1180 Bruxelles, Belgium *tel:* +32 2 375 7821 *fax:* +32 2 375 8073 *email:* agnes.de.hooghe@skynet.be. Agnes De Hooghe, artists' manager.

Ariën International Concert and Teaterbureau. De Boeystr 6, B-2018 Antwerp, Belgium *tel:* +32 3 218 6975/6 *fax:* +32 3 230 3523. Albrecht Klora, Pascale Montauban, managers. *Artist representation, specialising in opera singers, instrumentalists, conductors and orchestras.*

Centre of International Cultural Relations. Association for Public Benefit, Torenstraat 13, B-9160 Lokeren, Belgium *tel:* +32 9 348 8000/9010/4993 *fax:* +32 9 348 9974 *email:* j-p.vanavermaet @skynet.be. Jean Pierre Van Avermaet, managing director; Vessela Dyakova, staff member. *Institution dedicated to international cultural exchanges; organisation of concert tours in co-operation with cultural societies and small towns, concerts of Belgian and European artists, and choir festivals in France, Lettony, Poland and Switzerland.*

Joy Mebus Artists' Management. Waterstr 43, B-3770 Zussen (Riemst), Belgium *tel:* +32 1 245 7236 *fax:* +32 1 245 7234 *email:* joy.mebus @ping.be. Joy Mebus, director. *Artist representation.*

Liliane Weinstadt Bureau de Concerts. 69 Rue Langeveld, B-1180 Bruxelles, Belgium *tel:* +32 2 374 2138 *fax:* +32 2 375 7382 *email:* concerts.weinstadt@euronet.be. Liliane Weinstadt, executive director; Luc Van Loocke, managing director. *Artist representation.*

Maestro Music Productions. Leeuwerikstraat 20, B-3680 Maaseik, Belgium *tel:* +32 8 956 7557 *fax:* +32 8 956 1117 *email:* info@ maestro-brosse.be. Eric Langie, general manager; Dirk Brossé, artistic director. *Artist representation and concert promotion.*

Music Management FEW. Rue Grisar, 21, B-1070 Bruxelles, Belgium *tel:* +32 2 520 2009 *fax:* +32 2 520 7150 *email:* F.E.de.Wasseige @cyclone.be. Francois-Emmanuel de Wasseige, manager. *Artist representation and concert promotion, chamber music only.*

Promorga Sprl. Villalaan 26, B-1630 Linkebeek, Belgium *tel:* +32 3 380 9860 *fax:* +32 3 380 8876. Michel Hellawell, manager. *Concert promoter, specialising in Brazilian folk.*

Société Philharmonique de Bruxelles. Rue Baron Horta 11, B-1000 Bruxelles, Belgium *tel:* +32 2 507 8410 *fax:* +32 2 511 7977. Paul Dujardin, general director; Christian Renard, production manager. *Concert organiser.*

Brazil

Gaby Leib Produções Culturais. Rua Otávio Correia 420/6, 22291-180 Urca, Rio de Janiero RJ, Brazil *tel:* +55 21 295 0730 *fax:* +55 21 295 0580 *email:* gabyleib@easyline.com.br. Gabriele Ilse Leib, director. *Artist representation and concert promotion.*

Interarte Produções Artisticas S/C Ltda. Rua Mourato Coelho 299, CJ 04 Sao Paulo SP, Brazil *tel:* +55 11 881 1911 *fax:* +55 11 883 1056 *email:* roring@dialdata.com.br. Roberto Ring, Sergio Melardi, managers. *Artist representation and concert promotion. Festivals and orchestra touring.*

Non Plus Ultra-Artes. Rua Donatucio Dotaviano 55, 13094-310 Campinas, Sao Paulo SP, Brazil *tel:* +55 19 254 2069 *also fax; email:* acangucu@sanet.com.br. Adriana Camargo Cangucu, director. *Concert tour agent.*

Schlochauer & Associados. Consultoria e Representaçoes Ltda, Caixa Postal 21151, 04602-970 Sao Paulo SP, Brazil *tel:* +55 11 247 6631 *fax:* +55 11 547 0715 *email:* hansregi@uol.com.br. Hans Schlochauer, managing director. *Artist representation and concert promotion.*

Studio Serrano. Rua Santa Cristina 127, Santa Teresa, 20241-250, Rio de Janiero RJ, Brazil *tel:* +55 21 508 5220/611 4877 *fax:* +55 21 253 2815/611 4877 *email:* serrano@marlin.com.br. Marne Serrano Caldera, president. *Artist representation and concert promotion.*

Bulgaria

Apollonia Art Foundation & Art Agency. 23a Shipchenski Prohod Blvd, BG-1111 Sofia, Bulgaria *tel:* +359 2 723131 *also fax.* Dimo Dimov, president; Margarita Dimitrova, artistic director. *Artist representation and concert promotion.*

Bulgarian Artistic Agency Sofiaconcert. P Volov Str 3, BG-1527 Sofia, Bulgaria *tel:* +359 2 442914 *fax:* +359 2 445136. Jeanna Mollova, director. *Artist representation.*

Music Agency Festival Concert. 128 Vasil Aprilovstr, PO Box 545, BG-4000 Plovdiv, Bulgaria *tel:* +359 32 556493 *fax:* +359 32 262626. Jivko Jekov, chief officer. *Artist representation and concert promotion.*

Nelly Lalova Management. Udovo Str 10, Bx 2, BG-1463 Sofia, Bulgaria *tel:* +359 2 29 2 8076 *also fax.* Nelly Lalova, managing director. *Artist representation, specialising in soloists, choirs and orchestras.*

Canada

Andrew Kwan Artists Management Inc. 1315 Lawrence Ave East, Suite 515, Toronto, Ont M3A 3R3, Canada *tel:* +1 416 445 4441 *fax:* +1 416 445 7744 *email:* akam@compuserve.com. Andrew J Kwan, director. *Artist representation for instrumentalists and chamber ensembles.*

Ann Summers International. PO Box 188, Sta A, Toronto, Ont M5W 1B2, Canada *tel:* +1 416 362 1422 *fax:* +1 416 359 0043 *email: sumintl@sympatico.ca.* Ann Summers Dossena, president; Rob Spencer, executive assistant. *Artist representation and concert promotion.*

B C Fiedler Management. 55 Maitland St, Penthouse 5, Toronto, Ont M4Y 1C9, Canada *tel:* +1 416 967 1421 *fax:* +1 416 967 1991 *email:* bcf@the-wire.com. Bernie Fiedler, president. *Artist representation and concert promotion.*

Colwell Arts Management. RR 1 New Hamburg, Ont N0B 2G0, Canada *tel:* +1 519 662 3499 *fax:* +1 519 662 2777 *email:* jcolwell@golden.net. Jane Colwell, director; Nancy Ripley, assistant. *Specialist representation for classical singers, instrumentalists and ensembles; national co-ordinator for Piano Six project.*

Cyrann Ltd. 669 Highway 104, Burtts Corner, NB E6L 2B7, Canada *tel:* +1 506 363 2751 *fax:* +1 506 363 2738 *email:* abccjc@nbnet.nb.ca. Annemarie Couturier, entertainment. *Artist representation, specialising in entertainment co-ordination.*

Dean Artists Mangement. 204 St George St, Toronto, Ont M5R 2N6, Canada *tel:* +1 416 969 7300 *fax:* +1 416 969 7969 *email:* deanarts@interlog.com. Bruce Dean, president; Carrol Anne Curry, managing director; Henry Ingram, concerts director. *Artist representation for singers and conductors only.*

Diane Kadota Arts Management. 1014 Homer St, Suite 103, Vancouver, BC, V6B 2W9, Canada *tel:* +1 604 683 8240 *fax:* +1 604 683 7911 *email:* dkam@istar.ca. Diane Kadota. *Represents artists in fields of world music, jazz, New Music, Musique Actuelle.*

Fleming Artists Management. 4102 St Urbain, Montréal (QC), H2W 1V3, Canada *tel:* +1 514 844 7393 *fax:* +1 514 844 9989 *email:* fleming @globale.net. Heidi Fleming, director. *Represents mainly jazz and folk artists.*

Fox, Jones and Associates. 2nd Fl, 243 College St, Toronto, Ont M5T 1R5, Canada *tel:* +1 416 586 1302 *fax:* +1 416 586 0287 *email:* foxjones@inforamp.net. Jeremy Fox, president; Margaret Barkman, manager. *Artist representation.*

Genovese Vanderhoof and Associates. 77 Carlton St, Suite 1103, Toronto, Ont M5B 2J7, Canada *tel:* +1 416 340 2762 *fax:* +1 416 340 6276. Margaret Genovese, Dory Vanderhoof, senior partners. *Management consultants for the performing arts.*

Latitude 45 Arts Promotion. 109 St Joseph Boulevard West, Montreal PQ, H2T 2P7, Canada *tel:* +1 514 276 2694 *fax:* +1 514 276 2696 *email:* lat45arts@aol.com. Barbara Scales, director; Marie-Catherine La Pointe, Francis Beaulieu, assistants. *Artist representation, specialising in contemporary music as well as classical, jazz and theatre.*

Marilyn Gilbert Artists Management. 33 Isabella Street, Suite 112, Toronto, ON, M4Y 2P7, Canada *tel:* +1 416 410 3004 *fax:* +1 416 928 0097 *email:* MGArtists@aol.com. Marilyn Gilbert, director. *Artist representation.*

Novater Artists Inc. PO Box 69, 31 Adelaide St E, Toronto, Ont M5C 2H8, Canada *tel:* +1 416 214 2288 *email:* novater@novater.com. David Julien, artistic director; Judith Alltree, managing director. *Artist representation and concert promotion for classical, jazz and world music.*

Productions Musicales Cibé. 12-3058 Rue des Chatelets, Ste-Foy (QC), G1V 3Z2, Canada *tel:* +1 418 658 3778 *email:* ibrisson@upc.qc.ca. Irene Brisson, manager. *Artist representation for chamber music and solists only. No new artists accepted for 2000.*

Renée Simmons Artists Management. 117 Ava Rd, Toronto, Ont, Canada *tel:* +1 416 782 7712 *fax:* +1 416 256 7657 *email:* ivorene @compuserve.com. Renée Simmons, director. *Artist representation for instrumentalists and chamber ensembles; concert promotion.*

Robert Missen Artists Management. 156 Front St W, Suite 303, Toronto, Ont M5J 2L6, Canada *tel:* +1 416 971 4839 *fax:* +1 416 971 4841 *email:* rmissen@ibm.net. Robert Missen, president. *Artist representation.*

Tanglewood Family Entertainment Group. Unit G, 39 Orfus Road, Toronto, ON, M6A 1L7, Canada *tel:* +1 416 787 8687 *fax:* +1 416 787 8647 *email:* mail@tanglewood.com. Bruce Davidsen, president; Matt Segriff, music director. *Concert promotion.*

Unicorn Artist Management. 2334 Rue Coursol, Montréal (QC), H3J 1C7, Canada *tel:* +1 514 934 1298 *also fax; fax:* +1 514 934 5646. Sylvia Langdon. *Jazz representation.*

VKD International Artists. 2304 Towne Boulevard, Oakville, Ont L6H 5J5, Canada *tel:* +1 905 257 5279 *also fax.* V K DuBois, executive director. *Artist representation.*

Colombia

Ismael Arensburg Artist & Concert Management. Carerra 6a No 67-09 Ofc 103, PO Box 53490, Bogotá 2, Colombia *tel:* +57 1 211 3626; +57 1 310 0345 *fax:* +57 1 310 0452. *Artist representation and concert promotion.*

Sociedad Musical Arthur Rubinstein. Carrera 4 A No 25C17, Ofic. 1502, PO Box 53490, Bogotá, Colombia *tel:* +57 1 283 0920 *also fax.* Mario Fernando López, managing director. *Artist representation and concert promotion for soloists, chamber and symphony.*

Sociedad Musical Daniel. Carrera 6 No 67-09, Ofc 103, PO Box 53490, Bogotá DE, Colombia *tel:* +57 1 211 3626; +57 1 310 0345 *fax:* +57 1 310 0452. Ishmael Arensburg. *Artist representation and concert promotion.*

Costa Rica

Ensemble Musical-Latin American Artists Management. Apartado 979-1007, San José, Costa Rica *tel:* +506 282 7724 *fax:* +506 282 4574 *email:* jantich@una.ac.cr. Jordi Antich, president. *Concert promotion.*

Croatia

Koncertna Direkcija Zagreb. Kneza Mislava 18, 1000 Zagreb, Croatia *tel:* +385 1 4611 709 *fax:* +385 1 4611 807 *email:* kdz@zg.tel.hp. Erika Krpan, director. *Artist representation and concert promotion.*

Koncertna Dvorana Vatroslav Lisinski. Trg Stjepana Radica 4, 10000 Zagreb, Croatia *tel:* +385 1 612 1111 *fax:* +385 1 530023. Lovro Lisicic, general manager; Dubravko Majnaric, programme manager. *Concert promotion.*

Musidon. Petrinjska 2, 10000 Zagreb, Croatia *tel:* +385 1 481 0571/0654 *fax:* +385 1 48 07190. Prof Fred Dosek, manager. *Artist representation.*

Czech Republic

Ars/Koncert Ltd. Tvoz 39, CR-602 00 Brno, Czech Republic *tel:* +420 5 432 33116 *fax:* +420 5 432 33358 *email:* ars@arskoncert.cz. Miroslav Stehlik, general director; Marie Choutková, secretary. *Artist representation, concert promoter, general management of the International Music Festival of Brno, special events.*

Art Productions Praha. Ke Skalkam 2450, CR-106 00 Praha 10, Czech Republic *tel:* +420 2 762221 *also fax.* Jiri Kovac, director. *Concert promotion.*

Czech Artists Agency Dr Bechyne. V Olsinách 114, CZ-100 00 Praha 10, Czech Republic *tel:* +420 2 782 0633 *fax:* +420 2 781 3801 *email:* bechyne@terminal.cz. Václav Bechyne, director. *Artist representation, specialising in orchestras, opera and soloists.*

Czech Arts and Concert Agency Prague LUPULUS. Korunii 60, CR-120 000 Praha 2, Czech Republic *tel:* +420 2 2251 1752 *fax:* +420 2 2251 3782 *email:* lupulus@comp.cz. Dagmar Vlckova, director; Oldrich Vlcek, art director. *Artist representation and concert promotion; festivals.*

Czechkoncert. PO Box 17, Ládvi 108, CR-251 68 Stirin, Czech Republic *tel:* +420 204 672218 *fax:* +420 204 672800 *email:* czechkoncert @ri.ipex.cz. Libor Novácek, director. *Artist representation.*

Eurosound Artist Agency. Modranská 23, CR-147 00 Praha 4, Czech Republic *tel:* +420 2 402 2576 *also fax.* Katerina Novotná, general manager. *Artist representation and concert promotion.*

Jan Drasky Künstlersche Agentur/Art Agency. Ovcí Hájek 2162, CR-15500 Praha 5, Czech Republic *tel:* +420 2 561 0372 *also fax. Artist representation for singers, instrumentalists, conductors, directors and designers. Concert promotion.*

Moravia Artist Management. Anenská 10, CR-602 00 Brno, Czech Republic *tel:* +420 5 4724 4033 *fax:* +420 5 4321 1266 *email:* jsajtar@iol.cz. Dr Jirí Sajtar, director. *Artist representation for classical, jazz, folk music, and brass bands.*

Musart Prag. Kaplická 35, CR-140 00 Praha 4, Czech Republic *tel:* +420 2 438774 *fax:* +420 2 437081 *email:* musart@iol.cz. Zinaida Hortková, director. *Artist representation. Classical, orchestras, opera, ballet, choirs, etc.*

Music Agency Martin Zyka. Dominikánské nám 6/7, CR-602 00 Brno, Czech Republic *fax:* +420 5 422 13421. Martin Zyka. *Artist representation and concert promotion, specialising in orchestras, chamber ensembles and singers.*

Music Agency of the Prague Symphony Orchestra. Kostel Sv Šimona a Judy, Dušní ulice, CR-110 00 Praha 1, Czech Republic *tel:* +420 2 232 1068 *fax:* +420 2 231 9389 *email:* fok@login.cz. Daniel Sobotka, department manager. *Concert promoter.*

Music Art Prague Agency. Moravská 30, CR-120 00 Prague 2, Czech Republic *tel:* +420 2 242 57726 *also fax*; +420 2 251161. Lubomír Cízek, managing director. *Concert promotion.*

Noel Music Agency. PO Box 35, CR-170 04 Praha 74, Czech Republic *tel:* +420 2 573 17883 *fax:* +420 2 548909. Marek Schmidt, production manager. *Artist representation.*

Panart Arts Management. Jungmannova 5, CR-110 00 Praha 1, Czech Republic *tel:* +420 2 249 48533 *also fax.* Tatyána Czechowská. *Artist representation.*

Posh Co. Art. Lublanská 13, Praha 2, CR-120 00, Czech Republic *tel:* +420 2 900 042 06 *also fax; email:* poshp@telecom.cz. Marcela Podaná, assistant artistic director; Bohumil Pospiech, director. *Artist representation for classical, opera, orchestral, jazz, choral, ballet, operetta. Opera and operetta producer.*

Pragokoncert - Czech Arts Agency. Celetná 17, CR-Praha 1, Czech Republic *tel:* +420 2 2481 1690/1659 *fax:* +420 2 232 0353. Ivo Letov, artistic director; Vera Eksteinova, manager. *Artist representation and concert promotion. Jazz, pop and rock artists as well as classical.*

Sonus Artists Management. Pod Smukyrkou 1049, CR-150 00 Praha 5, Czech Republic *tel:* +420 2 526583 *also fax.* Zdenek Vokurka, general director. *Artist representation and concert promotion, specialising in chamber music and singers.*

Denmark

Arte. Hvidkildevej 64, DK-2400 Copenhagen, Denmark *tel:* +45 38 884900 *fax:* +45 38 332083. Mogens Hjorth, managing director. *Artist representation.*

Dr Gösta Schwarck International Concert Management. Dalgas Blvd 48, PO Box 13, DK-2000 Copenhagen F, Denmark *tel:* +45 31 877010 *fax:* +45 31 877011. Dr Gösta Schwarck, managing director. *Artist representation and concert promotion.*

International Personal Management. St Kongensgade 46, DK-1264 Copenhagen K, Denmark *tel:* +45 33 115225 *fax:* +45 33 131950. Steen Wittrock, managing director. *Artist representation and concert promotion.*

Rohr Artists Management. Grøndalsvej 47, DK-2000 Copenhagen F, Denmark *tel:* +45 38 873223 *also fax; email:* rohr.voss@get2net.dk. Joyce Rohr, director. *Artist representation.*

Tivoli Artists Management. Vesterbrogade 3, DK-1630 Copenhagen V, Denmark *tel:* +45 33 750400 *fax:* +45 33 750375 *email:* artistsmanagement@tivoli.dk. Tom Kristensen, manager. *Artist representation.*

Wilhelm Hansen Concert & Theatre Management. Gothersgade 11, 4th Floor, DK-1123 Copenhagen K, Denmark *tel:* +45 33 143710 *fax:* +45 33 144428. Hanne Wilhelm Hansen, manager.

Estonia

Eesti Kontsert. State Concert Institution, 4 Estonia Av, EE-0001 Tallinn, Estonia *tel:* +372 644 2901; +372 644 6255 *fax:* +372 631 4171 *email:* eesti.konsert@concert.ee. Enno Mattisen, general director; Aivar Mäe, vice-director. *Artist representation and concert promotion, specialising in festivals.*

Finland

Allegro Artist Management. Tapiolan Keskustorni Tap-House, 11th Floor, FIN-02100 Espoo, Finland *tel:* +358 9 462007 *fax:* +358 9 525 94200 *email:* allegro.artist@dlc.fi. Pekka K Pohjola, managing director; Vilja Valkeinen, assistant. *Artist representation.*

Fazer Artists' Management Inc. Nervanderinkatu 5 E 46, FIN-00100 Helsinki, Finland *tel:* +358 9 454 2470 *fax:* +358 9 446 841 *email:* tuula.sarotie@fazerartists.fi. Tuula Sarotie, general manager. *Artist representation.*

Festium Oy. Partiotie 34, FIN-00370 Helsinki 37, Finland *tel:* +358 9 556024 *fax:* +358 9 557020. Mirja Salomaa, managing director. *Artist representation and concert promotion.*

FinnConcert. Paivolantie 12, FIN-73770 Sayneinen, Finland *tel:* +358 400 279455 *fax:* +358 176 10285 *email:* someroj@nettilinja.fi. Raija Helena, president. *Artist representation.*

Helsingin Juhlamusiikkipalvelu/JMP Music Ltd. Nöykkiöntie 18, FIN-02320 Espoo, Finland *tel:* +358 9 262 8109 *fax:* +358 9 262 8113. Lassi Marttala, director. *Artist representation and concert promotion.*

Orfeo Oy Ltd. Rauhankatu 7, FIN-00170 Helsinki, Finland *tel:* +358 9 135 8993 *fax:* +358 9 622 73400 *email:* orfeo@pp.kolumbus.fi. Erkki Alste, executive manager; Maarit Mattala, assistant. *Artist representation, specialising in singers.*

PPM Artists Management. PO Box 46, FIN-00511 Helsinki, Finland *tel:* +358 9 877 6720 *fax:* +358 9 877 6721 *email:* ppm@ppm.pp.fi. Tuomas Pulakka, director. *Concert promotion.*

Rockadillo. Ilmarinkatu 12 A 2, FIN-33500 Tampere, Finland *tel:* +358 3 213 1260 *fax:* +358 3 213 1297 *email:* agency@rock.pp.fi. Tapio Korjus, managing director. *Artist representation and concert promotion. Mainly rock, jazz and world music.*

Sibelius Academy Concert Agency. PO Box 86, FIN-00251 Helsinki, Finland *tel:* +358 9 405 4662 *fax:* +358 9 405 4603. Anja Frosen, Vesa Ruotonen, Anna Krohn, managers. *Concert promotion.*

StillArt. Annegatan 6B, FIN-00120 Helsingfors, Finland *tel:* +358 9 641771 *fax:* +358 9 607319. Maj-Britt Still, secretary; Magnus Still, director. *Artist representation and concert promotion, specialising in festival planning.*

WellDone. Sorvaajankatu 9 A 4 krs, FIN-00810 Helsinki, Finland *tel:* +358 0 755 3100 *fax:* +358 0 755 3131 *email:* welldone@welldone.fi. Risto Juvonen, managing director. *Concert promotion.*

France

Agence Artistique Eliane Ribet. Rue Ledion 9, F-75014 Paris, France *tel:* +33 1 45 43 26 07 *fax:* +33 1 45 43 58 25. *Artist representation.*

Agence Artistique Ludmila Lincy. 35 Avenue des Champs-Elysées, F-75008 Paris, France *tel:* +33 1 53 53 97 10 *fax:* +33 1 53 53 97 11. Ludmila Lincy. *Artist representation.*

Agence Bourbon-Briant. 27 Rue de l'Echiquier, F-75010 Paris, France *tel:* +33 1 47 70 42 93 *fax:* +33 1 45 23 41 36. Michel Chouanard. *Represents jazz artists.*

Agency Jacques Thelen. 252 Rue de Faubourg St Honoré, F-75008 Paris, France *tel:* +33 1 45 61 47 47 *fax:* +33 1 45 61 90 70. *Artist representation.*

Artistic Organisation. BP 146, 63 Cours Balguerie, F-33027 Bordeaux Cedex, France *tel:* +33 5 57 87 33 55 *fax:* +33 5 57 87 33 88 *email:* artistic.ccc@wanadoo.fr. Christian Chartier, managing director. *Artist representation of jazz musicians.*

Artists International Management Ltd. 10 Rue des Acacias, F-75017 Paris, France *tel:* +33 1 45 74 16 24 *fax:* +33 1 45 74 33 20 *email:* aim-music@wanadoo.fr. Claude-Franck Boisson, managing director. *Artist representation, specialising in conductors and orchestra tours.*

B/A (Billard Azaïs) Musique. BP 14, 37 Rue de Vilmorin, F-45290 Nogent sur Vernisson, France *tel:* +33 2 38 97 60 04 *fax:* +33 2 38 97 64 06. Julien Azaïs, director. *Artist representation.*

Bureau de Concerts Marcel de Valmalète. 7 Rue Hoche, F-92300 Levallois, France *tel:* +33 1 47 59 87 59 *fax:* +33 1 47 59 87 50. Mme Pochet de Valmalète, general director. *Artist representation and concert promotion.*

Bureau de Concerts Maurice Werner. 7 Rue Richepance, F-75008 Paris, France *tel:* +33 1 47 03 13 60 *fax:* +33 1 49 26 05 07. Maurice Werner, Dominique Werner, directors. *Artist representation, specialising in soloists, conductors and chamber music.*

Bureau International de Concerts. 252 Rue du Faubourg St Honoré, F-75008 Paris, France *tel:* +33 1 45 63 79 55 *fax:* +33 1 45 62 24 17. Camille Kiesgen, president. *Artist representation.*

Class Inc Organisation. 8 Rue Berthollet, F-75005 Paris, France *tel:* +33 1 43 36 82 11 *fax:* +33 1 47 07 86 55. Dorothée Bonhomme. *Concert and event promotion.*

Classical Artist Management. 16 Rue du Regard, F-75006 Paris, France *tel:* +33 1 45 44 49 45 *fax:* +33 1 45 44 48 82. Eliza Jamin, director. *Artist representation and concert and festival promotion.*

Classics International Management (CIM). 54 Av d'Iena, F-75116 Paris, France *tel:* +33 1 47 20 55 53 *fax:* +33 1 47 20 37 51. Jacqueline Guélis, director. *Artist representation of orchestras, soloists, conductors and chamber music.*

Harry Lapp Organisation. 9 Ave de la Liberté, F-67000 Strasbourg, France *tel:* +33 3 88 15 29 29 *fax:* +33 3 88 24 03 16. Harry Lapp. *Concert promotion and artist representation, specialising in classical music, opera, jazz, rock and ballet.*

IMG Artists. 54 Avenue Marceau, F-75008 Paris, France *tel:* +33 1 44 31 44 31 *fax:* +33 1 44 31 44 45 *email:* artistsparis@imgworld.com. Philippe Etourneau, director, artist management; Peter Wiggins, director, vocal division; Giles Demonet, director, orchestra tours. *Artist representation, specialising in conductors, instrumentalists and singers.*

Living Art - Impresariat. 9 Blvd Montmartre, F-75002 Paris, France *tel:* +33 1 42 36 49 44/36 32 *fax:* +33 1 42 33 64 91. Angelika Belamaric, director. *Artist representation for opera singers and conductors only.*

Management Artistique Professionnel. 51 Rue Le Marois, F-75016 Paris, France *tel:* +33 1 46 51 85 56. Alain Gramola, president. *Artist representation and concert promotion.*

Monique Cazeneuve Agence Artistique. 5-7 Av Mac-Mahon, F-75017 Paris, France *tel:* +33 1 43 80 15 86 *fax:* +33 1 46 22 58 76. Monique Cazeneuve. *Artist representation for conductors, instrumentalists and ensembles. Also local tours for international orchestras.*

Musica Gyr. 79 Quai André Citroën, F-75015 Paris, France *tel:* +33 1 45 75 51 88 *fax:* +33 1 45 75 02 73. Santiago Gyr. *Artist representation and concert promotion. Festivals.*

Musicaglotz. 11 Rue Le Verrier, F-75006 Paris, France *tel:* +33 1 42 34 53 40 *fax:* +33 1 40 46 93 77. Michel Glotz, general director. *Artist representation for conductors, instrumentalists and opera singers.*

Musilyre. 1 Square de Châtillon, F-75014 Paris, France *tel:* +33 1 45 42 65 00 *fax:* +33 1 45 42 65 01 *email:* musilyr@club-internet.fr. Véronique

Réaud, manager; Florence Montaigne, assistant. *Representation of baroque artists and concert promotion.*

Organisation Internationale Opéra et Concert. 1 Rue Volney, F-75002 Paris, France *tel:* +33 1 42 96 18 18 *fax:* +33 1 42 96 18 00. Charles Fabius, Dominique Riber, Christophe Delhoume, Diane du Saillant, artists managers; Paule Fabre, Jacqueline Chollet, admin. *Artist representation for conductors, singers and instrumentalists.*

Productions Dominique Werner. 7 Rue Richepance, F-75008 Paris, France *tel:* +33 1 47 03 13 66 *fax:* +33 1 49 26 05 07. Dominique Werner, director. *Artist representation and concert promotion, specialising in orchestras, opera and ballet.*

Germany

Accento-Künstlersekretariat Alte Musik. Kiesseestr 57a, D-37083 Göttingen, Germany *tel:* +49 551 77930 *fax:* +49 551 77932 *email:* accento-loepthien@t-online.de. Wolfgang Loepthien, director. *Representation of early music artists and concert promotion.*

Agentur Kleinheisterkamp. Welzheimerstr 28a, D-70188, Germany *tel:* +49 711 483247 *fax:* +49 711 485796. Trude Kleinheisterkamp; Haus Kleinheisterkamp. *Artist representation for orchestras and chamber orchestras.*

Agentur Ocklenburg Buehnenvermittlung. Hartungstr 15, D-20146 Hamburg, Germany *tel:* +49 40 418656 *fax:* +49 40 410 4668. Guenter Ocklenburg; Wolfgang Schmitt. *Representation of opera singers.*

Art-Concerts GmbH. Widenmayerstr 46a, D-80538 München, Germany *tel:* +49 892 904990 *fax:* +49 892 883111 *email:* mail@art-concerts.de. Franz Abraham, CEO; Florian Zwipf, artistic manager. *Concert promotion.*

Artists International. Am Kreispark 32, D-51379 Leverkusen, Germany *tel:* +49 217 142663 *fax:* +49 217 143981. Linda Abberton, director. *Sponsorship, orchestra touring and special events.*

Artists Management Hartmut Hasse. Aalgrund 8, D-31275 Lehrte, Germany *tel:* +49 517 595 3232 *fax:* +49 517 595 3233 *email:* artists@t-online.de. *Artist representation of singers and conductors.*

Bayerische Konzertdirektion Karl Gensberger. Marienplatz 1, D-80331 München, Germany *tel:* +49 892 27488 *fax:* +49 892 25311 *email:* b.pkreye@t-online.de. Paul Kreye, director. *Artist representation and concert promotion, specialising in choirs, chamber, festivals.*

Beaumier & Strauth. Hochdahlerstr 1a, D-40625 Düsseldorf, Germany *tel:* +49 211 292233 *fax:* +49 211 281104. Carine Strauth. *Artist representation for ensembles, specialising in South American.*

Berliner Konzertagentur Monika Ott. Dramburgerstr 46, D-12683 Berlin, Germany *tel:* +49 30 514 4858 *fax:* +49 30 514 2659 *email:* berlinkonzert.ott@t-online.de. Monika Ott, manager. *Artist representation, specialising in conductors and instrumentalists.*

Bielefelder Konzertdirektion Werner Vollmer. Vormbaumstr 9a, D-33604 Bielefeld, Germany *tel:* +49 521 285565.

Braunschweiger Konzertdirektion. Am Fallersleber Tore, D-38100 Braunschweig, Germany *tel:* +49 531 44115 *fax:* +49 531 46873. Hans Ulrich Schmid, managing director. *Concert promotion.*

C Sauer-Intveen. International Music Management, D-78315 Radolfzell/Bodensee, Germany *tel:* +49 773 258837 *fax:* +49 773 258836. *Artist representation and concert promotion with emphasis on young musicians.*

Christian Lange Personal Artist Management. Ludwig Behrstr 7, D-82327 Tutzing, Germany *tel:* +49 815 81832 *fax:* +49 815 88521. Christian Lange, president. *Artist representation and concert promotion. Festivals.*

Classical Music and Media. Steinlestr 27, D-60596 Frankfurt, Germany *tel:* +49 963 60792 *fax:* +49 963 60793. Medi A Gasteiner-Girth, managing director. *Artist representation and public relations, specialising in conductors and singers.*

Concert Management Classic 2000. Carl von Ossietzkystr 56, D-65197 Wiesbaden, Germany *tel:* +49 611 464619 *fax:* +49 611 464755. Rista Savic.

Concertbüro Nürnberg. Gotzner & Tollrian GmbH, Ludwigstr 53, D-90402 Nürnberg, Germany *tel:* +49 911 333363 *fax:* +49 911 446 9292 *email:* info@cbn-forum.de. Alex Gotzner, Harald Tollrian, managers.

Concertino Agentur Rita de la Chevallerie. Nerotal 24, D-65193 Wiesbaden, Germany *tel:* +49 611 599559 *fax:* +49 611 522263 *email:* concwies@t-online.de. *Artist representation of orchestras, chamber ensembles, soloists, and vocalists.*

Concertino Jutta Jochimsen. Postfach 450210, D-12172 Berlin, Germany *tel:* +49 331 270 9888 *fax:* +49 331 270 9891. *Concert promotion.*

Concerto Winderstein GmbH. Postfach 440446, D-80753 München, Germany *tel:* +49 89 383 8460 *fax:* +49 89 337938 *email:* artists @winderstein.de. Hans-Dieter Goehre, director. *Artist representation and concert promotion.*

Contour, Büro für Concert und Gastspieltourneen GmbH. PO Box 250152, D-40093 Düsseldorf, Germany *tel:* +49 211 934 8486 *fax:* +49 211 345235 *email:* contour@online-club.de. Klaus Winker, manager. *Artist representation of orchestras, choirs, chamber music.*

Crescendo Artists Management. Eckbergstr 27, D-76534 Baden-Baden, Germany *tel:* +49 722 199801 *fax:* +49 722 199802. Alec Band, president, CEO. *Artist representation and concert promotion.*

Daniela Wiehen Artists Management. Falkenried 7, D-20251 Hamburg, Germany *tel:* +49 404 231 3121 *fax:* +49 404 231 3120 *email:* daniela.wiehen@hamburg.netsurf.de. Daniela Wiehen. *Artist representation, specialising in string quartets, soloists, conductors.*

Dr Thomas Parr. Guerickostr 49, D-23666 Lübeck, Germany *tel:* +49 451 606 2121 *also fax; email:* parr@decide.de. Thomas Parr, director. *Management and marketing for theatre, dance and music.*

Elisabeth Meister. Mallertshofener Str 8, D-85716 Unterschleissheim, Germany *tel:* +49 893 177 0924 *fax:* +49 893 177 0925. *Artist representation for conductors.*

Euroconcert GmbH. Im Hotzental 17, D-78234 Engen, Germany *tel:* +49 773 33256 *fax:* +49 773 33259. Werner Walschburger, general manager. *Artist representation and concert promotion.*

Herwald Artists' Management. Straße des Roten Kreuzes 64, D-76228 Karlsruhe, Germany *tel:* +49 721 947 3939 *fax:* +49 721 947 3937 *email:* herwaldartists@t-online.de. Thomas Herwald, director. *Artist representation, specialising in singers and conductors.*

Johannes Adams. Stadtwaldgürtel 44b, D-50931 Köln, Germany *tel:* +49 221 401538 *fax:* +49 221 408243. Johannes Adams. *Artist representation.*

Kikis Kleiner Tourneeservice. KKT GmbH, NeuerKamp 30, D-20357 Hamburg, Germany *tel:* +49 431 3460 *fax:* +49 432 53133 *email:* kkthamburg@aol.com. Kiki Ressler, managing director; Casi Clausen, assistant.

Koko Entertainment. Bruder-Turm-Gasse 4a, Postfach 101063, D-78410 Konstanz, Germany *tel:* +49 753 190880 *fax:* +49 753 190 8888. Dieter Boes, managing director. *Concert promotion.*

Konzert und Werbe GmbH. Julienstr 34, D-45130 Essen, Germany *tel:* +49 201 792059 *fax:* +49 201 779328. Walter Gommers. *Concert promotion.*

Konzertagentur Erika Esslinger. Spittlerstr 6, D-70190 Stuttgart, Germany *tel:* +49 711 283276 *fax:* +49 711 261421 *email:* esslinger@konzertagentur.de. *Artist representation, specialising in chamber and early music.*

Konzertagentur Eva Maria Kaufmann. Pillnitzer Landstr 7, D-01326 Dresden, Germany *tel:* +49 351 268 7212 *fax:* +49 351 264 0585. Eva-Maria Kaufmann, director; Thomas Kaufmann. *Artist representation.*

Konzertagentur Fahrenholtz. Winterleitenweg 17B, D-97082 Würzburg, Germany *tel:* +49 931 784 7230 *also fax.* Wolfgang Fahrenholtz, director. *Artist representation.*

Konzertagentur Ingrid Hellmann. Birnenweg 12, D-06112 Halle/Saale, Germany *tel:* +49 345 560 3041 *fax:* +49 345 560 3654. *Artist representation and concert promotion, specialising in chamber music, soloists, orchestras and ensembles.*

Konzertagentur Jens Gunnar Becker. Grünstr 13, D-58313 Herdecke, Germany *tel:* +49 233 070389 *fax:* +49 233 07507 *email:* becker @beckerkonzert.de. Evelyn Dürwald, assistant. *Artist representation and concert promotion.*

Konzertagentur Jörg Hannemann. Haydnstr 15, D-20249 Hamburg, Germany *tel:* +49 404 807575 *fax:* +49 404 86281. Jörg Hannemann. *Artist representation, specialising in orchestra tours.*

Konzertagentur Marek Lieberberg GmbH. Mörikestr 14, D-60320 Frankfurt/M, Germany *tel:* +49 699 562020 *fax:* +49 695 68199. *Concert promotion.*

Konzertbüro Andreas Braun. Sülzgürtel 86, D-50937 Köln, Germany *tel:* +49 221 942 0430 *fax:* +49 221 942 04319 *email:* braun@angel.de. Andreas Braun, director. *Artist representation for early and chamber music, soloists, singers, choirs, conductors.*

Konzertbüro Richard Weber. Haupstr 66, D-77652 Offenburg, Germany *tel:* +49 781 72041 *fax:* +49 781 23406 *email:* konzertbuero. weber@baden-online.de. Irma Weber, manager. *Artist representation, specialising in Russian folk music and church music.*

Konzertdirektion Andrea Hampl. Prenzlauer Promenade 189, D-13189 Berlin, Germany *tel:* +49 304 782699 *fax:* +49 304 783792 *email:* hampl@konzertdirektion.de. *Artist representation for instrumentalists, chamber music and orchestras.*

Konzertdirektion Dr Rudolf Goette. Colonnaden 70, D-20354 Hamburg, Germany *tel:* +49 403 46018 *fax:* +49 403 42715. Hans Werner Funke, managing director; Egbert Zinner, manager. *Artist representation and concert promotion.*

Konzertdirektion Egbert Zinner. Kirchennalle 22, D-20099 Hamburg, Germany *tel:* +49 402 805 2227 *fax:* +49 402 805 2228 *email: service@musicontact.de.* Egbert Zinner. *Artist representation.*

Konzertdirektion Fischer GmbH. Joh-Phil-Palm-Str 21, D-73614 Schorndorf, Germany *tel:* +49 718 160000 *fax:* +49 718 160 0050. Dieter Fischer. *Artist representation.*

Konzertdirektion Fritz Dietrich. Eckenheimer Landstr 483, D-60435 Frankfurt am Main, Germany *tel:* +49 695 45658/544504 *fax:* +49 695 484107. Fritz Dietrich, manager. *Artist representation.*

Konzertdirektion Hans Adler. Auguste-Viktoria-Str 64, D-14199 Berlin, Germany *tel:* +49 308 959920 *fax:* +49 308 263520 *email:* info @musikadler.de. Witiko Adler, director. *Artist representation and concert promotion.*

Konzertdirektion Hans Ulrich Schmid. Schmiedestr 8, D-30159 Hanover, Germany *tel:* +49 511 366 0739/27 *fax:* +49 511 366 0734. Hans Ulrich Schmid, chairman; Cornelia Schmid, managing director. *Artist representation and orchestra tours.*

Konzertdirektion Heinz Bertsch. Berg-gasse 62, D-72762 Reutlingen, Germany *tel:* +49 712 122799. Heinz Bertsch. *Concert promotion.*

Konzertdirektion Karsten Jahnke. Hallerstr 72, D-20146 Hamburg, Germany *tel:* +49 404 147880 *fax:* +49 404 43597 *email:* karsten-jahnke@t-online.de. Karsten Jahnke, managing director; Hauke Tedsen, managing director and head of artists booking; Matthias Boensel, head of classic marketing. *Concert and tour promotion.*

Konzertdirektion Kurt Collien. Spielbudenplatz 29/30, D-20359 Hamburg, Germany *tel:* +49 40 313901/2 *fax:* +49 40 319 1919. Kurt Collien; Michael K Collien, manager. *Concert promotion.*

Konzertdirektion Meuer. Geislinger Weg 28, D-89522 Heidenheim, Germany *tel:* +49 732 155381 *also fax.* Martha Munz. *Concert promotion.*

Konzertdirektion Praeger & Meier. Torgauer Str. 27, D-28215 Bremen, Germany *tel:* +49 421 375507 *fax:* +49 421 375508. Hannes Nimpuno, managing director.

Konzertdirektion Rainer Haas. Postfach 1240, D-69247 Schonau b Heidelberg, Germany *tel:* +49 622 81375 *fax:* +49 622 88455. *Artist representation for soloists and chamber music. No singers as soloists.*

Konzertdirektion, Tobischek, Rosemarie und Dr Herbert Tobischek. Schiefenberg 34, D-45239 Essen, Germany *tel:* +49 201 840 5175 *fax:* +49 201 840 5176. *Artist representation for conductors, soloists, singers, chamber music and orchestras.*

Konzert-Management Jochum. Rotenbühler Weg 28a, D-66123 Saarbrücken, Germany *tel:* +49 681 397359 *fax:* +49 681 372310. *Artist representation, specialising in pianists, violinists, organists and conductors. Also concert promoter.*

Kulturbüro Köln. Engelbertstr 32, D-50674 Küln, Germany *tel:* +49 221 240 3133 *fax:* +49 221 240 3247. Jürgen Ruppert, director. *Artist representation, specialising in music theatre.*

Künstler Sekretariat am Gasteig. Rosenheimer Str 52, D-81669 München, Germany *tel:* +49 894 82086 *fax:* +49 894 489522 *email:* team@ks-gasteig.de. Elisabeth Söling-Ehlers, Lothar Schacke, directors. *Artist representation.*

Künstlersekretariat Astrid Schoerke. Mönckebergallee 41, D-30453 Hanover, Germany *tel:* +49 511 401048/49 *fax:* +49 511 407435. Astrid Schoerke, director. *Artist representation for conductors, chamber music ensembles and instrumentalists.*

Künstlersekretariat Rolf Sudbrack. Gösselkoppel 54a, D-22339 Hamburg, Germany *tel:* +49 405 382165 *fax:* +49 405 387220. Rolf Sudbrack, CEO. *Artist representation, specialising in chamber music.*

La Vergne Verlag und Musikproduktion. Ulvenbergstr 16, D-64297 Darmstadt, Germany *tel:* +49 615 157761 *fax:* +49 615 1594332. Pasal Amann, general manager. *Artist representation and concert promotion.*

Marguerite Kollo Bühnenvermittlung. Mehringdamm 69, D-10961 Berlin, Germany *tel:* +49 306 932062 *fax:* +49 306 927747. *Artist representation, specialising in opera.*

Michael Herrmann Konzert & Künstleragentur. Thorwaldsenanlage 74, Postfach 3033, D-65195 Wiesbaden, Germany *tel:* +49 611 599998 *fax:* +49 611 599895. *Artist representation and concert promotion.*

MM Konzerte GmbH. Wilhelmstr 8, D-34117 Kassel, Germany *tel:* +49 561 709550 *fax:* +49 561 15081. Uwe Vater, Christian Schaeling. *Concert promotion.*

Monika Bundschu Opern und Konzertagentur. Tal 15, D-80331 München, Germany *tel:* +49 892 916 1663 *fax:* +49 892 916 1667. *Artist representation.*

Music Circus Concertbüro GmbH. Charlottenplatz 17, D-70173 Stuttgart, Germany *tel:* +49 711 221105 *fax:* +49 711 292705. Hans-Peter Haag, director. *Concert promotion.*

Nentwig Internationale Musikagentur. Freiherr vom Steinstr 1, D-63526 Erlensee, Germany *tel:* +49 618 33087 *fax:* +49 618 374339. Dieter Nentwig, manager. *Represents jazz artists and gospel choirs.*

Ocklenburg, Guenter. Hartungstr 15, D-20146 Hamburg, Germany *tel:* +49 404 18656 *fax:* +49 404 104668. Guenter Ocklenburg, Wolfgang Schmitt. *Representation for opera singers.*

Opernagentur. Inge Tennigkeit, Kempener Straße 4, D-40474 Düsseldorf, Germany *tel:* +49 211 516 0060 *fax:* +49 211 516 00616. Inge Tennigkeit, president; Claudia Heckmanns, assistant. *Artist representation for opera singers.*

Opernagentur Lore Blümel. Postfach 1725, D-82159 Gräfelfing, Germany *tel:* +49 89 8 593864 *fax:* +49 89 8 593759. Lore Blümel. *Artist representation.*

Paradise Media. Schwibbogengasse 27a, D-86150 Augsburg, Germany *tel:* +49 821 33336 *fax:* +49 821 33309 *email:* info@paradise.de. Hubert G. Feil. *Artist management, PR and sponsorship.*

Personal Artists Management Gudrun Rohrbach. Sierichstr 99, D-22299 Hamburg, Germany *tel:* +49 404 88147 *fax:* +49 404 801247 *email:* pamhamburg@compuserve.com. *Artist representation for both concert and opera.*

PMI (Paradise Management International). Nachtigallenstr 36, D-63243 Neu-Isenburg, Germany *tel:* +49 610 252696 *also fax.* R Klug, managing director. *Artist representation and concert promotion. Personal management for artists and groups.*

PR2 Classic. Kreuznacherstr 63, D-50968 Köln, Germany *tel:* +49 221 381063 *fax:* +49 221 383955. Gabriele Schiller, director; Ulrike Jessel, Eva Luise Roth, assistants. *Artist representation and PR.*

PROFFessional Promotion. Hamburg Str 80, D-28205 Bremen, Germany *tel:* +49 421 434 0266/7 *fax:* +49 421 434 0268 *email:* tproff@t-online.de. Thomas Proff, director.

Rafael Concerts GmbH. Frauenberg 4, D-97980 Bad-Mergentheim, Germany *tel:* +49 793 197900 *fax:* +49 793 197 9020 *email:* rafael.concerts@t-online.de. Rafael Brown, managing director; Dagmar Strottner, Thomas Martin, project managers; Daniel Pistorius, technical director. *Producer of large-scale operas.*

Reinald Heissler-Remy Theater Agentur. Drakestr 2, PO Box 110931, D-40545 Düsseldorf, Germany *tel:* +49 211 578051 *fax:* +49 211 553498 *email:* remy.agent@t-online.de. Reinald Heissler-Remy; Neill Thornborrow, assistant. *Artist representation, specialising in opera.*

Roschlau, Edith. Agentur für Musiktheater und Konzert, Samuel-Schmidt-Str 7, D-96450 Coburg, Germany *tel:* +49 956 132549 *fax:* +49 956 142 0792. *Artist representation.*

Shooter Promotions and Classics GmbH. Gartenstr 6, D-60594 Frankfurt am Main, Germany *tel:* +49 696 109390 *fax:* +49 696 109 3988 *email:* shooterpromotions@t-online.de. Willi Engelhorn, managing director; Christa Wenzl, tour co-ordinator. *Artist representation and concert promotion, specialising in ballet and dance.*

Sigrid Rostock. Eugen Schönhaarstr 1, D-10407 Berlin, Germany *tel:* +49 30 425 7514 *fax:* +49 30 423 9136. *Artist representation for singers.*

Sonia Simmenauer Impresariat. Falkenried 7, D-20251 Hamburg, Germany *tel:* +49 404 231 3111 *fax:* +49 404 231 3113. Sonia Simmenauer; Swantje Baxmann. *Artist representation, specialising in string quartets.*

Südwestdeutsche Konzertdirektion Erwin Russ. Charlottenplatz 17, D-70173 Stuttgart, Germany *tel:* +49 711 163 5311/6 *fax:* +49 711 163 5330. Michael Russ, CEO. *Artist representation and concert promotion.*

Theater und Konzertagentur. Orlandostr 8, D-80331 München, Germany *tel:* +49 892 904766 *fax:* +49 892 904765. Lydia Storle. *Artist representation.*

Theater und Konzertagentur Hermann and Astrid G Winkler. Grillparzerstr 46, D-81675 München, Germany *tel:* +49 894 705857 *fax:* +49 894 707123. *Artist representation.*

Theateragentur Dr Carl F Jickeli. Nymphenburgerstr 62, D-80335 München, Germany *tel:* +49 891 239 2626 *fax:* +49 891 239 2627. *Artist representation for singers and conductors.*

Theateragentur Glado von May. Hermannstr 32, D-60318 Frankfurt am Main, Germany *tel:* +49 692 83347 *fax:* +49 692 95513. Glado von May, head; Heidi Schäfer, assistant. *Representation of singers (opera and concert) and conductors.*

Theateragentur Hannagret Bueker. Fuhsestr 2, D-30419 Hannover, Germany *tel:* +49 511 271 6910 *fax:* +49 511 271 7873. Hannagret Bueker. *Artist representation.*

Theateragentur Luisa Petrov. Glauburgstr 95, D-60318 Frankfurt am Main, Germany *tel:* +49 695 970377 *fax:* +49 695 974808. Luisa Petrov. *Artist representation, specialising in opera.*

Theateragentur Werner Kühnly. Wörthstr 31, D-70563 Stuttgart, Germany *tel:* +49 711 780 2764 *fax:* +49 711 780 4403. Herta Kühnly, manager; Vermit Tlerin. *Artist representation for opera and concert singers and conductors.*

Theateragentur Wolfgang Stoll. Mitarbeiter Karl-Erich Haase, Martiusstr 3, D-80802 München, Germany *tel:* +49 893 33162 *fax:* +49 893 42674. Karl-Erich Haase. *Artist representation.*

Tourneemanagement Berlin. Immanuelkirchstr 5, D-10405 Berlin, Germany *tel:* +49 30 441 5299 *also fax.* Lutz-Rainer Seidel. *Artist representation.*

Veranstaltungs-Management GmbH. Hardenbergstr 6, D-10623 Berlin, Germany *tel:* +49 303 137007 *fax:* +49 303 127083. Otfried Laur, business manager. *Concert promotion.*

Volker Schmidt-Gertenbach. Rúdower Chaússee 3, D-12489 Berlin, Germany *tel:* +49 30 670 44884 *fax:* +49 30 670 44880. Volker Schmidt-Gertenbach. *Artist representation.*

ZBF Agentur Berlin. Ordensmeisterstr 15, D-12099 Berlin, Germany *tel:* +49 30 757600 *fax:* +49 30 75 760249.

ZBF Agentur Leipzig. Schillerweg 34a, D-04155 Leipzig, Germany *tel:* +49 341 580880 *fax:* +49 341 580 8850.

Zentrale Bühnen-, Fernseh- und Filmvermittlung (ZBF) Generalagentur Bonn. Villemombler Str 76, D-53123 Bonn, Germany *tel:* +49 228 7130. *Artist representation.*

Greece

Cultural Foundation. 15 Amerikis Str, GR-106 72 Athens, Greece *tel:* +30 1 362 6274 *fax:* +30 1 361 9373. Pia Hadjinikos-Angelini, director; Elpida Temarel, secretary. *Concert promotion.*

Lavris Ltd, Cultural Events Agency. 3 Marasli St, GR-106 76 Athens, Greece *tel:* +30 1 72 58510 *fax:* +30 1 72 58513 *email:* lavris@hol.gr. Georgia Iliopoulou, managing director; Mrs Thomi Tsioptsia, production manager. *Artist representation and concert promotion, specialising in contemporary music and dance, jazz and street theatre as well as classical music.*

Hungary

Budapest Artists Management. Somlói ut 39, H-1118 Budapest, Hungary *tel:* +36 1 3186 6790 *also fax.* Ildikó Gedényi, director. *Artist representation for conductors, soloists and chamber music.*

Clemens Concerts Ltd. Attila út 61, H-1013 Budapest, Hungary *tel:* +36 1 212 20 45; +36 20 934 58 23 *fax:* +36 1 375 81 62 *email:* clemens@elender.hu. Pál Kelemen, director; Adam Bikfalvy, manager. *Artist representation and concert promotion.*

Gergely Arts Ltd. Hollán Erno u 25 I/1, H-1136 Budapest, Hungary *tel:* +36 1 129 4064 *also fax;* +36 1 270 0846. Mária Gergely, managing director; Erzsebet Nemeth, manager. *Artist representation.*

Hungarokoncert Oszk International Artists Agency. Városligeti fasor 38, H-1068 Budapest, Hungary *tel:* +36 1 322 0641 *fax:* +36 1 322 5412. László Szirmai, director; D A Starnfeld, Ferenc Szénási, impresarios. *Artist representation and concert promotion.*

Pentaton Artists & Concerts Management Ltd. Rákóczi ut 65, H-1081 Budapest, Hungary *tel:* +36 1 333 2337 *fax:* +36 1 333 2075 *email:* pentaton@elender.hu. Zsófia Zimányi, owner; György Lörinczy, managing director. *Artist representation and concert promotion, including opera and music theatre.*

Premier Theatre and Music Agency. Premier Bt, Jakab L U5, H-6724 Szeged, Hungary *tel:* +36 62 458996 *also fax. Artist representation and concert promotion, including operetta and theatre.*

Sotto Voce. József A sgt 67/A, H-6723 Szeged, Hungary *tel:* +36 20 958 3660 *fax:* +36 1 222 4064 *email:* ervin.bonecz@ac.com. Ervin Bonecz. *Represents, promotes and develops the careers of young and talented artists. Organises masterclasses.*

India

Bombay Madrigal Singers' Organisation. Oak Chambers, 9 Oak Lane, Fort, Bombay 400023, India *tel:* +91 22 267 4218 *fax:* +91 22 265 6556. Adi B Sagar, honorary secretary. *Presentation of artists and concerts.*

Republic of Ireland

International Concert Management/ICM Artists & Tours. 23 Farmleigh Ave, Stillorgan, Co Dublin, Ireland *tel:* +353 1 288 6251 *also fax; email:* icmtours@esatclear.ie. Ashley Pringle, director. *Artist representation and concert promotion. Local and international touring arrangements for orchestras, choirs, ensembles, singers and instrumentalists.*

Israel

Artis Ltd. 17 Ben Yehuda St, 63802 Tel Aviv, Israel *tel:* +972 3 517 0605/9025 *fax:* +972 3 516 0045. Pinhas Postel. *Concert promotion for orchestras, opera, ballet, modern dance, classical music and jazz.*

Bloch Artists Management Inc (Israel). POB 261, Sha'a Rei, Tikvah, DN Efraim, Israel 44810 *tel:* +972 3 936 3114/732 6055 *fax:* +972 3 936 3275/732 5822 *email:* ileneblo@netmedia.net.il. Joel Bloch, director. *Artist representation for conductors, vocalists, opera and oratorio singers.*

International Music Consultants. POB 45401, 61453 Tel Aviv, Israel *tel:* +972 3 604 0766 *fax:* +972 3 604 5916 *email:* WYElias@hotmail.com. William Elias, president.

Shmuel Zemach. 108 Dizengof St, 64397 Tel Aviv, Israel *tel:* +972 3 524 7722 *fax:* +972 3 527 9967 *email:* szemach@internet-zahav.net. *Artist representation and concert promotion.*

Italy

Accademia Romana delle Arti. Largo Josemaria Escrivà 1-00142 Roma, Italy *tel:* +39 06 5196 3475 *fax:* +39 06 5196 8431 *email:* arda@mclink.it. Riccardo Lana, president. *Concert promotion. Organisation of the Rome Festival of Church Music.*

A.C.O.M - Organizzione Concertistica Internazionale. Piazza Buonarroti 29, I-20149 Milano, Italy *tel:* +39 024 800 1924 *also fax;* +39 024 60636 *email:* llpegna@tin.it. Luigi La Pegna. *Artist representation for conductors, soloists, orchestras, choirs, ballet, chamber music, early music, sacred music, etc.*

AMP - Artists' Management and Productions. Corso di Porta Ticinese 89, I-20123 Milano, Italy *tel:* +39 02 8942 0788 *fax:* +39 02 8942 0724 *email:* amp@netitalia.it. Ettore F Volontieri, managing director; Ernesto Palacio, opera department; Dario Betti, consultant; Fiorenza Scholey, special projects. *Artist representation for singers, conductors and soloists.*

Artists Management Company. Via Valverde 32, I-37122 Verona, Italy *tel:* +39 045 852 0718 *fax:* +39 045 852 0434 *email:* amc@ amcmusic.com. Franco Pio Panozzo. *Artist representation for soloists and orchestras.*

Associazione Musica Libera. Via Ciro Menotti 147, I-61100 Pesaro, Italy *tel:* +39 072 141 4341 *also fax; email:* musicalibera@abanet.it. Paolo Giaro, artistic director; Antonio Cioffi, co-director. *Festival and concert promotion for world music and jazz.*

Concerto Management. Via Roma 107, I-84084 Fisciano (SA), Italy *tel:* +39 08 995 8565 *fax:* +39 08 989 1819. Bianca Rosa, managing director; Domenico Spetrini, director. *Artist representation, specialising in orchestras, chamber ensembles and soloists.*

Dell'Amore Management. Via Zeffirino Re 2c, I-47023 Cesena (Forlí), Italy *tel:* +39 054 761 1690 *fax:* +39 054 725895 *email:* amor@linknet.it. Franco Dell'Amore, artistic director; Carla Dell'Amore, admin. *Artist representation and concert promotion for early music, world music and contemporary music.*

Firenze Musica. Via Maggio 35, I-50125 Firenze, Italy *tel:* +39 055 214705 *fax:* +39 055 282631 *email:* rcoletti@dada.it. Raffaella Coletti, Silvia Ponzanelli. *Artist representation.*

Girard, Elisa. Via Luciano Manara 57, I-00153 Roma, Italy *tel:* +39 06 589 9479 *fax:* +39 06 581 0245 *email:* r.girard@uni.net. Fabrizio di Mauro, tour manager; Gaia Giraro, assistant. *Artist representation.*

Giuseppe Pastorello. Viale Trieste 308, I-93100 Caltanisetta, Italy *tel:* +39 09 3455 4688 *fax:* +39 093 459 2025.

Grompone, Aldo. 195 Via Giulia, I-00186 Roma, Italy *tel:* +39 06 687 6495 *fax:* +39 06 686 4605. Alessandra Ferrando, assistant. *Production and promotion for theatre, contemporary music and dance.*

IUMA Management. Via Emanuele Filiberto 125, I-00185 Roma, Italy *tel:* +39 06 7045 2328/7720 1524 *fax:* +39 06 7720 5607 *email:* cfcatena@pelagus.it. Chris F Catena, chairman; Debora Farina, assistant. *Artist representation and concert promotion, specialising in operas, concerts and ballet.*

Laifer Artists International. Via Maddalena 45/c, I-37138 Verona, Italy *tel:* +39 045 562950 *also fax. Artist representation for opera singers.*

Mario Dradi by Opera Art SRL. Via Isolalta Forette, I-37068 Vigasio VR, Italy *tel:* +39 045 664 9911 *fax:* +39 045 664 9912 *email:* madradi@tin.it. Mario Dradi, head; Irene Gall, assistant. *Artist representation for opera singers and conductors; some concert promotion.*

Modena International Music. Via Carlo Zucchi 31/A, I-41100 Modena, Italy *tel:* +39 059 821128 *fax:* +39 059 821132 *email:* mim@mimsrl.it. Francesco Cattini, president. *Artist representation and concert promotion.*

Music Center SnC di Oldani Giuseppe & Co. Viale Legioni Romane 26, I-20147 Milano, Italy *tel:* +39 024 870 2828/0258 *fax:* +39 024 870 0692 *email:* mcenter@planet.it. Giuseppe Oldani, chief executive; Andrea De Amici, consultant. *Artist representation.*

Musical Dorica. Castella Postale nr 29, I-60021 Camerano (An), Italy *tel:* +39 071 801181 *fax:* +39 071 801235. Silvano Frontalini. *Artist representation and concert promotion, specialising in lyric opera, ballet and orchestral music.*

ORIA di Maria Bruzzese, Denise Petriccione. Corso Sempione, 40, I-20154 Milano, Italy *tel:* +39 023 311122 *fax:* +39 023 311140. Maria Bruzzese, Denise Petriccione, partners. *Artist representation.*

Ouverture di Orta Leonardo & C sas. Via Braccianese Claudia 44 Km 20, I-00062 Bracciano (Roma), Italy *tel:* +39 06 998 6602 *fax:* +39 06 998 6603 *email:* ouverture@edl.it. Marzia Maramici, Franziska Kurth, assistants. *Artist representation for opera singers and conductors.*

Preludio. Viale Carducci 18, I-40125 Bologna, Italy *tel:* +39 051 342167 *also fax.* Alessandra Scheda. *Artist representation, specialising in soloists and chamber music.*

Prima International Artists Management Srl. Palazzo Zambeccari, Piazza de Caldenini 2/2, I-40124 Bologna *tel:* +39 051 264056 *fax:* +39 051 230766 *email:* prima@primartists.com. Angelo Gabrielli, Virginio Fedeli, managers. *Artist representation.*

Propoganda Musicale SRL. Via Po 43, I-00198 Roma, Italy *tel:* +39 06 884 2218/2221 *fax:* +39 06 884 2222. Sonia Quercia, Adelano Manfrini. *Artist representation.*

Resia. Via Manzoni 31, I-20121 Milano, Italy *tel:* +39 026 54161/2/3/4 *fax:* +39 026 597851 *email:* resiasrl@tin.it. Patrizia Garrasi, Luisa Panarello, partners. *Artist representation.*

Ricercare. Progetti Artistici Internazionali. Via E Filberto 4, I-20052 Monza, Italy *tel:* +39 039 744703 *fax:* +39 039 744797 *email:* ricercar@askesis.it. Gabriella Castelli, Kim Sommerschield, directors. *Artist representation, specialising in early music.*

Thomas Arndt - International Management. Via Rubattino 6/6, I-00153 Roma, Italy *tel:* +39 06 578 3784 *fax:* +39 06 574 2888. Thomas Arndt.

Walter Beloch Artists Management Srl. Via Melzi d'Eril 26, I-20154 Milano, Italy *tel:* +39 023 310 1922 *fax:* +39 023 313643 *email:* belochartists@iol.it. Walter Beloch, president; Luiz Antonio Polon, Daniela Rodriguez, concert managers. *Artist representation.*

Japan

Camerata Tokyo. Wako Bldg 2F, 14-3 Motoyoyogi, Shibuya-ku, Tokyo 151-0062, Japan *tel:* +81 3 5790 5566 *fax:* +81 3 5790 5562 *email:* camerata@rc4.so-net.ne.jp. Hiroshi Isaka, president. *Artist representation and concert promotion, specialising in chamber music.*

Japan Arts Corp. 2-1-6 Shibuya, Shibuya-ku, Tokyo 150, Japan *tel:* +81 3 3499 8090 *fax:* +81 3 3499 8092. Yasuo Nakato, chairman; Masayuki Sekita, president. *Artist representation and concert promotion.*

Japan Orchestral Society Ltd. 4F Cl-Building, 1-3-6 Ebisu-minami, Shibuya-ku, Tokyo 150, Japan *tel:* +81 3 5721 4621 *fax:* +81 3 5721 4624. Hiroshi Kobayashi, chairman. *Artists' agent and concert promoter, specialising in orchestras, chamber orchestras and soloists.*

Japan Performing Arts Foundation. 4-26-4 Meguro, Meguro-ku, Tokyo 153-0063, Japan *tel:* +81 3 3791 8000. Tadatsugu Sasaki, executive director. *Concert promotion for classical music, opera and ballet (including The Tokyo Ballet).*

Kajimoto Concert Management Company Ltd. Kahoku Building, 8-6-25 Ginza, Chuo-ku, Tokyo 104, Japan *tel:* +81 3 3574 0969 *fax:* +81 3 3574 0980 *email:* kajimoto@music.co.jp. Naoyasu Kajimoto, chairman; Masahide Kajimoto, president. *Artist representation and concert promotion, specialising in international classical artists.*

Kambara Music Office Ltd. Urban Life Building, Room 101, 9-2-14 Akasaka, Minato-ku, Tokyo 107, Japan *tel:* +81 3 3403 8011 *fax:* +81 3 3479 6577. Yoshiro Kambara, president; Masahiro Nishizawa, director. *Artist representation and concert promotion for orchestras, chamber ensembles, instrumentalists and singers, ballet and flamenco dance.*

Nippon Artists Management Inc. 2-11-16-303 Kanda Surugadai, Chiyoda-ku, Tokyo 101, Japan *tel:* +81 3 3293 1951 *fax:* +81 3 3293 1960 *email:* info@nami.co.jp. Yusuke Terada, president. *Artist representation and concert promotion, specialising in solo piano and violin and chamber music.*

Noah Corp Ltd. Shinjuku-ku Shimoochial 1-5-10-1011, Tokyo 161, Japan *tel:* +81 3 5386 7000 *fax:* +81 3 5286 7060.

Ohba Ongaku Jimusho (Ohba Music Promotion). 3-5-3 Nishishinjuku #712, Shinjuku-ku, Tokyo 160-0023, Japan *tel:* +81 3 3344 1922 *fax:* +81 3 3344 1923. Teruko Ohba, president. *Concert promotion.*

Pro Arte Musicae. Otowa 2-2-2-603, Bunkyo-ku, Tokyo 112-0013, Japan *tel:* +81 3 3943 6677 *fax:* +81 3 3943 6659 *email:* pam@proarte.co.jp. Genroh Hara, president. *Artist representation and concert promotion.*

Sautille Company Ltd. Music Office, 2-11-19 Jingumae, Shibuya-ku, Tokyo 150, Japan *tel:* +81 3 3470 2727 *fax:* +81 3 3470 2740 *email:* sautille@red.an.egg.or.jp. Takao Kasahara, executive director. *Artist representation and concert promotion, specialising in baroque and guitar music.*

Station Co Ltd. 2F Sakuma Bldg, 11 Araki-Cho, Shinjuku-Ku, Tokyo 160-0007, Japan *tel:* +81 3 3358 1901 *fax:* +81 3 3353 4830 *email:* lh1m-tmr@asahi-net.or.jp. Mitsuo Tamura, music promoter. *Concert promotion.*

Korea

Fine Artists Management. 219-8 Pulkwang-dong, Eunpyong-ku, Seoul 122-041, Korea *tel:* +82 2 353 7538 *fax:* +82 2 358 6074 *email:* fam410 @nownuri.net. Chung Hoon-sang Thomas, president. *Artist representation and concert promotion.*

Latvia

Baltic Concerts Ltd. Strelnieku iela 9, LV-1010 Riga, Latvia *tel:* +371 783 0501 *also fax.* Gatis Darzins, executive director. *Artist representation and concert promotion, specialising in conductors and orchestras.*

Liechtenstein

Artists Management Company Est. Postfach 1131, Austr 1, FL-9490 Vaduz, Liechtenstein *tel:* +423 75 232 1444 *fax:* +423 75 232 2085.

Andreas von Bennigsen, director; Daniel Zulauf, co-director. *Concert promotion specialising in orchestra tours. Artist representation.*

Luxembourg

Bureau de Concerts Jacques Mauroy. 19 Rue des Primevères, L-2351, Luxembourg *tel:* +35 2 345 3935 *fax:* +35 2 347 5928. Jacques Mauroy, Marianne Gérard. *Artist representation, specialising in soloists, string quartets, chamber and symphony orchestras.*

Malaysia

IMG Artists Asia. Level 61, Tower 2, Petronas Twin Towers, Kuala Lumpur City Centre, 50088 Kuala Lumpur *tel:* +60 603 266 2166 *fax:* +60 603 262 6634 *email:* artistsasia@imgworld.com. *Artist representation.*

Mexico

Conciertos Daniel. Av Horacio 1725-PH, 11510 México D F, Mexico *tel:* +52 5 280 5592 *fax:* +52 5 280 9477. Ernesto de Quesada, manager; Janine de Quesada, manager. *Artist representation.*

Muchi Music Mex. Wisconsin 114, Apt 307, Colonia Nápoles, 03710 México D F, Mexico *tel:* +52 5 563 9961 *also fax; email:* muchi@excite.com. José María Alvarez, executive director; Laura López, associate. *Artist representation and concert promotion, specialising in early music, soloists and conductors.*

Monaco

Bureau de Concerts Pierre-Edouard Ornella. 49 Rue Plati, MC-98000, Monaco *tel:* +377 93 15 04 44 *fax:* +377 93 15 94 84. Pierre-Edouard Ornella, director. *Concert promotion.*

Vivienne H Taylor. Le Soleil D'Or, 20 Blvd Prince Rainier III, MC-98000, Monaco *tel:* +377 93 15 03 81 *fax:* +377 93 25 62 51 *email:* vtaylor@monaco.mc. *Personal representation and administration.*

Netherlands

Amstel Artists Muziek Produkties. Ruysdaelkade 155, NL-1072 AS Amsterdam, Netherlands *tel:* +31 20 679 6553 *email:* amartists@capitolonline.nl. Jelle Kikkert. *Artist representation, baroque/renaissance.*

Ariëtte F C Drost Artists Representative. Prins Bernhardweg 18, NL-6862 ZH Oosterbeek, Netherlands *tel:* +31 26 339 0187 *fax:* +31 26 334 1349. Ariëtte Drost, director. *Artist representation, specialising in singers, opera, oratorio, orchestral and chamber music concerts.*

CNM Centrum Nederlandse Muziek. PO Box 1634, NL-1200 BP Hilversum, Netherlands *tel:* +31 35 624 0957 *fax:* +31 35 621 0570 *email:* cnm@pi.net. J W ten Broeke, managing director. *Promotion of Dutch classical music.*

Concertdirectie Samama & Co BV. Weteringschans 130, NL-1017 XV Amsterdam, Netherlands *tel:* +31 20 421 1611 *fax:* +31 20 421 1747 *email:* concertdirectie@samama.nl. Niels Veenhuijzen, managing director. *Artist representation and concert promotion.*

Concertmanagement Rob Groen. W G Plein 206, NL-1054 SE Amsterdam, Netherlands *tel:* +31 20 616 8096 *fax:* +31 20 616 9652. Rob Groen, managing director.

Euro Stage. Lijnbaansgracht 292-11, NL-1017 RM Amsterdam, Netherlands *tel:* +31 20 620 6556 *fax:* +31 20 623 7951. Peter Ultee, managing director. *Concert promotion, specialising in opera, classical ballet and African music.*

European Conference of Promoters of New Music (ECPNM). Secretariate ECPNM, c/o Gaudeamus Swammerdamstr 38, 1091 RV Amsterdam, Netherlands *tel:* +31 20 694 7349 *fax:* +31 20 694 7258 *email:* ecpnm@xs4all.nl. Henk Heuvelmans, secretary general. *Concert promoter.*

Herzberger Artists. 't Woud 1, NL-3862 PM Nijkerk, Netherlands *tel:* +31 34 247 2255 *fax:* +31 34 247 5275. Marianne Herzberger, director. *Artist representation.*

Impresariaat Jacques Senf & Partners. PO Box 42, NL-3155 ZG Maasland, Netherlands *tel:* +31 10 592 3155 *fax:* +31 10 591 5159 *email:* publi@senf.nl. Jacques Senf, Matthÿs Bongertman, directors. *Artist representation, specialising in shows, musicals, opera, concerts and ballet.*

Impulse Art Management. Singel 308-Sous, NL-1016 AE Amsterdam, Netherlands *tel:* +31 20 626 6944 *fax:* +31 20 622 7118. Martijn Jacobus, director. *Artist representation and concert promotion.*

Interartists BV. Post Box No 38, 1250 AA, Laren, Netherlands *tel:* +31 35 533 5835 *fax:* +31 35 533 5836 *email:* interartists@xs4all.nl. Jeannine Salomons, director; Charlie de la Cousine, artist manager. *Artist management.*

International Music Productions (IMP). Paviljoensgracht 76, NL-2512 BR Den Haag, Netherlands *tel:* +31 70 363 8778 *fax:* +31 70 360 8114 *email:* musicimp@wxs.nl. Michaël Hanekroot. *Artist representation.*

International Society for Contemporary Music. Secretariate ISCM, c/o Gaudeamus Swammerdamstr 38, 1091 RV Amsterdam, Netherlands *tel:* +31 20 694 7349 *fax:* +31 20 694 7258 *email:* iscm@xs4all.nl. Henk Heuvelmans, secretary general. *Concert promoter.*

Ivy Artists bv. PO Box 592, NL-1200 AN Hilversum, Netherlands *tel:* +31 35 628 2270/623 3133 *fax:* +31 35 623 6619 *email:* music@ivyartists.com. Loes Aalders. *Artist representation.*

Marianne Brinks. Graaf Willemlaan 52, NL-1181 EH Amstelveen, Netherlands *tel:* +31 20 643 2043 *fax:* +31 20 640 3961 *email:* mbrinks@xs4all.nl. *Artist representation and director of Delft Chamber Music Festival.*

Marijke Klinkhamer Artists Management. Willemsparkweg 114, NL-1071 HN Amsterdam, Netherlands *tel:* +31 20 675 4061 *fax:* +31 20 675 4771. Marijke Klinkhamer, director. *Artist representation.*

The Office Performing Arts Management. Keizersgracht 261, NL-1016 EC Amsterdam, Netherlands *tel:* +31 20 622 6979 *fax:* +31 20 622 9081 *email:* kantoor@euronet.nl. L Schipper, director. *Concert promotion, music theatre, contemporary music and festivals.*

Pieter G Alferink Artists Management. Apollolaan 181, NL-1077 AT Amsterdam, Netherlands *tel:* +31 20 664 3151 *fax:* +31 20 675 2426 *email:* alferlink@worldonline.nl. Pieter G Alferink, managing director; Helga Blaimschein, associate. *Artist representation, specialising in singers and conductors. Also event management and promotion of concerts and special projects.*

Riaskoff Concert Management. Concertgebouwplein 15, NL-1071 LL Amsterdam, Netherlands *tel:* +31 20 664 5353 *fax:* +31 20 671 5106. Marco Riaskoff, managing director; Jeroen Tersteeg, artists manager. *Artist representation and concert promotion.*

Stadsschouwburg en Concertgebouw De Vereeniging. Postbus 364, 6500 AJ Nijmegen, Netherlands *tel:* +31 24 322 8344 *fax:* +31 24 322 2465 *email:* schouwburg.nijmegen@inter.nl.net. Sandor Joó, general manager. *Concert promotion.*

Supierz Artist Management. Linnaeus-serre 17, NL-3823 DL Amersfoort, Netherlands *tel:* +31 33 455 5656 *fax:* +31 33 455 5433 *email:* supierz@worldaccess.nl. Zdzislaw Supierz, managing director. *Agent and concert promotion for opera, ballet, operetta and folk music.*

Ton Art - Rupert Fäustle. Faes Eliaslaan 39, NL-3742 AS Baarn, Netherlands *tel:* +31 35 543 0202 *fax:* +31 35 543 0442. Rupert Fäustle, general manager. *Music production, A&R consultancy, orchestra tours.*

Norway

Impresario A/S. Tollbugata 3, N-0152 Oslo, Norway *tel:* +47 22 426 379 *fax:* +47 22 332 238. Vibeke Gottschalk, managing director. *Artist representation and concert promotion for orchestras and ballet.*

Oslo Konsertdireksjon As. Bjerkebakken 1, N-0756 Oslo, Norway *tel:* +47 22 522 546 *fax:* +47 22 730 103. Ruth Klungsøyr, director. *Artist representation and concert promotion.*

Pro Arte International Management. John Lunds Plass 1, N-5007 Bergen, Norway *tel:* +47 55 319 435; +47 95 140 074 *fax:* +47 55 960 765. Kjell Wernoe, director. *Artist representation.*

Paraguay

Ruben Franco Producciones. PO Box 1642, Luis Morales 995, Asuncion, Paraguay *tel:* +595 21 227220 *email:* nefertiti90@yahoo.com. Ruben Dario Franco Alcaraz, director. *Artist representation specialising in chamber music and ballet.*

Phillippines

National Philharmonic Society. MCPO Box 2650, Makati, Metro Manila, Phillippines *tel:* +63 2 817 2601/815 2651/810 7988 *fax:* +63 2 815 3483. Redentor L Romero, music director; Theresa Veloso, concert manager. *Concert promotion of chosen artists.*

Poland

Andrzej Szwed Artists' Management. ul Borsucza 64, PL-05-807 Podkowa Lesna, Poland *tel:* +48 22 758 9649/826 5711 *fax:* +48 22 758 9218 *email:* szwedart@supermedia.pl. Andrzej Szwed, director. *Artist representation and concert promotion for conductors, instrumentalists, ensembles, orchestras, choirs and singers.*

The Artists Management of the National Theatre. Plac Teatralny 1, PL-00-950, Warszawa, Poland *tel:* +48 22 826 3001/7001 ext 282; +48 22 692 0755/826 7429 *fax:* +48 22 826 0423/5012. *Artist representation.*

Classic Management Marek Strasz. ul Goscincowa 37, PL-05-092 Lomianki, Warszawa, Poland *tel:* +48 22 751 7633 *fax:* +48 22 751 8633 *email:* mstrasz@ikp.pl. Marek Strasz, president. *Artist representation, specialising in classical and jazz.*

Classical Recordings and Concerts. ul Szpitalna 8/33, 00-031 Warszawa, Poland *tel:* +48 22 828 3495 *fax:* +48 22 828 2161 *email:* musicprod@supermedia.pl. Maria Kmicik Lejman, director. *Concert promotion.*

ESPO Artists Management. ul Pogodna 21 a, k Warszawy, PL-05-077 Wesola, Poland *tel:* +48 22 773 1759 *also fax; email:* igor@profiaudio.com.pl. Igor Pogorzelski, manager. *Promotes Polish music abroad, especially classical music. Organises concerts, marketing, artists promotion, etc. Specialises in chamber and symphony orchestras.*

Jacek Nedzynski Artists Management. Os Jagiellonskie 12/71, PL-61-227 Poznan, Poland *tel:* +48 61 876 5801 *also fax*; +48 60 176 7993. Jacek Nedzynski, director. *Artist representation, specialising in chamber music, dance, instrumentalists and choirs.*

Music Productions. ul Cynamonowa 2/37, PL-02-777 Warszawa, Poland *tel:* +48 22 648 3938 *fax:* +48 22 648 3950 *email:* wojnowak@aol.com. Wojciech Nowak, director. *Concert promotion and classical music recording.*

Polish Concert Agency. ul Koszykowa 24/7, PL-00-553 Warszawa, Poland *tel:* +48 22 621 6332; +48 22 621 3074 *email:* kbk@free.art.pl. *Music promotion.*

Warsaw Artists Management Ltd. Kazimierzowska 47/5, PL-02-572 Warszawa, Poland *tel:* +48 22 646 2829 *fax:* +48 22 487666. Andrzej Haluch, president. *Artist representation and concert promotion.*

Romania

Artexim. Piata Victorei Nr 155, Bl D1 Sc 8 Et 2, 71012 Bucharest, Romania *tel:* +40 1 650 1806/7 *fax:* +40 1 311 0200/659 7523. Mihai Constantinescu, manager. *Artist representation and concert promotion.*

Russia

Art Time Corp. 3-1 Serebrianichesky Lane, 109028 Moscow, Russia *tel:* +7 095 916 1111 *fax:* +7 095 917 4202 *email:* arttime@online.ru. Svetlana Antyukhina, president. *Artist representation and concert promotion.*

Artistic Association Vivaldi's House. Maly Vlasievsky per 4/1, 121002 Moscow, Russia *tel:* +7 095 244 0653 *also fax*. Vladimir Youriev, director. *Concert promotion.*

Nectary Music Company Ltd. PO Box #3, 121359 Moscow, Russia *tel:* +7 095 149 9776 *also fax; email:* nectary@usa.net. Svetlana Zharova, manager; Serge V Drouzhinine, president. *Artist representation and concert promotion, specialising in classical and folk.*

Sovinart. 18 Murmansky Proezd, App 77, 129075 Moscow, Russia *tel:* +7 095 215 7571 *fax:* +7 095 215 2274. Eilina Tikhomirova, general director. *Artist representation.*

Serbia

Sava Centar. Milentija Popovica 9, 11070 Beograd, Serbia *tel:* +381 11 222 2277 *fax:* +381 11 222 1156. George Milutinovic, chief executive. *Concert promotion.*

Yugoconcert. Terazije 41, 11000 Beograd, Serbia *tel:* +381 11 323 9917/916 *fax:* +381 11 324 0478. Eduard Ille, director; Branka Ristic, Miroslav Medak, international department. *Artist representation and concert promotion.*

Slovak Republic

Akord Art Agency. E Culinka, Gessayova 15, 85103 Bratislava, Slovak Republic *tel:* +421 7 815335 *also fax. Artist representation and concert promotion, specialising in brass soloists and ensembles. Also jazz and folk.*

Interartists Bratislava. Bajzova 4, 82108 Bratislava, Slovak Republic *tel:* +421 7 555 77 170 *also fax; email:* interart@netax.sk. Jana Kovácikоvá, director. *Representation for soloists, chamber music, choirs and orchestras.*

Intermedia. Jakubovo nam 12, 811 09 Bratislava, Slovak Republic *tel:* +421 7 363700/363707 *fax:* +421 7 363296. Peter Horak, general manager. *Mainly concert promotion.*

Slovkoncert - Artists Management. Michalska 10, 81536 Bratislava, Slovak Republic *tel:* +421 7 544 34561/34538 *fax:* +421 7 544 32652 *email:* slovkoncert@netlab.sk. Marian Lapsansky, director. *Artist representation, concert promotion and festival organisation.*

Slovenia

Ars Ramovs Institute of Arts, Marketing, Promotion and Investment. Slovenska cesta 1, 1000 Ljubljana, Slovenia *tel:* +386 61 125 3366 *fax:* +386 61 174 1541 *email:* info@k-ramovs.si. Klemen Ramovs, president. *Concert promotion, specialising in early music.*

Brina Jez-Brezavscek. Rutarjeva 5, Ljubljana, Slovenia *tel:* +386 61 213972. Brina Jez-Brezavscek, president; Myriam Zgevec, secretary. *Artist representation and concert promotion, specialising in Slovene composers.*

Cankarjev dom Cultural & Congress Centre. Presernova 10, 1000 Ljubljana, Slovenia *tel:* +386 61 125 8121/212492 *fax:* +386 61 224279/176 7119 *email:* cankarjev.dom@cd-cc.si. Mitja Rotovnik, general director; Monika Kartin, music programme director. *Concert promotion for classical, jazz and entertainment artists.*

JHP Artist Management. Krakovski nasip 6, 1000 Ljubljana, Slovenia *tel:* +386 61 125 7008; +386 41 676089 *fax:* +386 61 125 7194 *email:* jeff013@hotmail.com. Jeff H Pivac, director. *Artist representation and concert promotion for jazz, blues, world music, classical and early music.*

South Africa

Nico Theatre Centre. PO Box 4107, Cape Town 8000, South Africa *tel:* +27 21 410 9800 *fax:* +27 21 215 448 *email:* capab@global.co.za. Michael Maas, CEO; Rudi Basson, marketing director. *Concert promotion for music, opera, ballet, contemporary dance and drama.*

Pim Broere Promotions CC. PO Box 55401, Northlands, Johannesburg 2116, South Africa *tel:* +27 11 788 4690 *fax:* +27 11 788 8274 *email:* pbroere@global.co.za. Pim Broere, manager; Paul Mercer, assistant manager. *Artist representation and concert promotion for classical music, jazz and contemporary dance.*

State Theatre Pretoria. PO Box 566, Pretoria 0001, Transvaal, South Africa *tel:* +27 12 322 1665 *fax:* +27 12 322 3913 *email:* truk @iafrica.com. Alan Joseph, CEO. *Producers of opera, ballet, dance, musical theatre, concerts, and all performing arts disciplines.*

Spain

Arte Tripharia. Apdo 14622, E-28080 Madrid, Spain *tel:* +34 91 522 1715 *fax:* +34 91 521 4742 *email:* arte@mail.com. Rudesindo Soutelo, director. *Artist representation.*

Conciertos Augusto SL. Calle Viento No 15, 2-B Majadahonda, E-28220 Madrid, Spain *tel:* +34 91 634 0205 *fax:* +34 91 634 0250 *email:* conciertosaugusto@eipoint.com. Gonzalo Augusto, director; Monica Royuela, Alicia Idigoras. *Artist representation.*

Donald Scrimgeour. Apartado 905, E-41080 Seville, Spain *tel:* +34 95 434 3802 *fax:* +34 95 434 3807. Donald Scrimgeour. *Artist representation for classical ballet.*

EMJ Art et Musique SL. Playa de Sitges 27, Punta Galea, E-28290 Madrid, Spain *tel:* +34 91 630 3070 *fax:* +34 91 630 2198 *email:* emusique@mad.servicom.es. Elisabeth Michot de Jowers, managing director. *Artist representation and concert promotion for chamber music, ensembles and early music.*

EuroArte Management. Felipe III 4, 1 Izq, E-28012 Madrid, Spain *tel:* +34 91 365 8405 *fax:* +34 91 364 0018 *email:* euroarte@microdelta.es. Luis Vivo, director. *Concert promotion for ballet, opera and special events.*

Euroconcert. Rambla de Catalunya 10, 2n, 4a, E-08007 Barcelona, Spain *tel:* +34 93 318 5158 *fax:* +34 93 412 4114. Antoni Sábat, director. *Artist representation and concert promotion.*

Harmonia Catalunya. C/Montserrat 7, E-08292 Esperarregeura-Barcelona, Spain *tel:* +34 93 777 6060 *fax:* +34 93 777 2165 *email:* harcat@intercom.es. Montserrat Sitja, managing director; Christian Florea, artistic director. *Concert promotion for orchestras, chamber music, singers and soloists.*

Ibermúsica. Costa Rica 32, Bajo B, E-28016 Madrid, Spain *tel:* +34 91 359 5296/0964 *fax:* +34 91 345 2489 *email:* ibermusica@mad.servicom.es. Alfonso Aijón, director. *Concert promotion.*

Mercedes Sanchez del Rio 'Musica Clasica'. C/Cafeto n 5, E-28007 Madrid, Spain *tel:* +34 91 501 9150 *fax:* +34 91 551 6153. *Artist representation for conductors, soloists, orchestras and chamber music.*

Musiespaña. c/ Zurbano 34, 4- Derecha, E-28010 Madrid, Spain *tel:* +34 91 308 4724 *fax:* +34 91 310 1065 *email:* h.oran@musiespana.com. Humberto Orán, director. *Artist representation and concert promotion.*

Organización Espanola de Conciertos "Sanzkonzert". Pau Claris 113, E-08009 Barcelona, Spain *tel:* +34 93 487 3833 *fax:* +34 93 487 7892. Alfonso Sanz Lopez, director. *Artist representation for symphonic and chamber orchestras, opera and ballet.*

Primusic. Fernan Gonzalez 37, E-28009 Madrid, Spain *tel:* +34 91 574 9051 *fax:* +34 91 573 1077. Carmen Prieto. *Artist representation and concert promotion for early and baroque music.*

Sociedad Musical Armonia. Pl del Principe 2 Entlo, E-39003 Santander, Spain *tel:* +34 94 236 1880 *fax:* +34 94 236 1969. Sorin Melinte, president; Belen Alonso, managing director, Ana Fernandez, officer. *Artist representation and concert promotion, specialising in symphony orchestras.*

Tritó Concerts. Carrer dels Arcs 8, E-08002 Barcelona, Spain *tel:* +34 91 302 2722/301 9555 *fax:* +34 91 302 2670. Mapau Roca, general manager. *Artist representation and concert promotion.*

Sweden

Konsertbolaget Scandinavian Artists Management AB. Vasagatan 52, S-111 20 Stockholm, Sweden *tel:* +46 8 245815 *fax:* +46 8 245595. Thomas Boltenstern, managing director; Katarina Boltenstern, Michael Ljung, artist managers. *Artist representation.*

Nordic Artist AB. PO Box 17779, S-11893 Stockholm, Sweden *tel:* +46 8 5626 2050 *fax:* +46 8 5626 2060 *email:* info@nordicartist.se. Johan Englund, managing director; Patrick Froom, producer. *Artist representation and concert promotion.*

Svensk Konsertdirektion AB. Box 5076, S-402 22 Göteborg, Sweden *tel:* +46 3 183 0095 *fax:* +46 3 140 8011. Henrik Lodding, manager; Gunilla Lodding-Ruijsenaars, assistant manager. *Artist representation and concert promotion.*

Svenska Konsertbyran AB (Swedish Concert Bureau). Jungfrugatan 45, S-114 44 Stockholm, Sweden *tel:* +46 8 665 8088 *fax:* +46 8 665 8066 *email:* info@svenskakonsertbyran.se. Kerstin Hammarström, managing director; Ann Braathen, artist manager. *Artist representation.*

Switzerland

Agency Inter Media. Zwinglistr 35, CH-8004 Zürich, Switzerland *tel:* +41 1 241 1739 *fax:* +41 1 242 3297 *email:* zehnder_maria@compuserve.com. Maria Zehnder. *Artist representation and concert promotion, specialising in contemporary music and drums.*

Artists Management Zürich. Rütistr 52, CH-8044 Zürich-Gockhausen, Switzerland *tel:* +41 1 821 8957 *fax:* +41 1 821 0127. Rita Schütz, director. *Artist representation for opera.*

Artists Personal Representative Claudia Bloechlinger. Gatterstr 1b, CH-9010 St Gallen, Switzerland *tel:* +41 71 222 3980 *fax:* +41 71 222 3889. *Artist representation.*

Balmer & Dixon Management AG. Granitweg 2, CH-8006 Zürich, Switzerland *tel:* +41 1 363 6280 *fax:* +41 1 361 9355 *email:* badix @compuserve.com. Ritha Dixon, Rudolf Balmer, directors. *Artist representation and personal management.*

Circolo Musicale. Emilia Tonolla-Rosa Rappresentanza Artisti, Vignon, CH-6558 Lostallo, Switzerland *tel:* +41 91 830 1288 *fax:* +41 91 830 1555 *email:* etonolla@ticino.com. Emilia Tonolla-Rosa, manager. *Artist representation.*

Columbia Artists Management AG. Kapuzinerweg 7, CH-6006 Luzern, Switzerland *tel:* +41 41 420 7758 *fax:* +41 41 420 7759 *email:* camich @cami.mhs.compuserve.com. Beatrice Vesper, manager; Michael Eriskat, artist manager. *Artist representation and orchestra tours.*

Interclassica. 4 Rue Jean Jacques Rousseau, CH-1800 Vevey, Switzerland *tel:* +41 21 922 4016 *fax:* +41 21 922 4018. Martin Tison Engstroem, director; Jean Jacques Indermühle, president. *Artist representation and concert promotion.*

International Booking Agency. Av Florimont 3, CH-1820 Montreux, Switzerland *tel:* +41 21 963 5031 *fax:* +41 21 963 8895. Willy Leiser, director; Christiane de Dompierre, assistant. *Representation for jazz, blues and gospel artists; concert tour producer.*

Internationale Konzertagentur Pio Chesini. Aeschenvorstadt 24, Postfach, CH-4010 Basel, Switzerland *tel:* +41 61 272 2229 *also fax; fax:* +41 61 272 2291.

Konzert-Agentur Suzanne Gfeller GmbH. Homelstr 34, CH-4114 Hofstetten, Switzerland *tel:* +41 61 733 0373 *fax:* +41 61 733 0374 *email:* gfeller@konzert.ch. Gaby Ris, secretary. *Artist representation for soloists and chamber music. No singers as soloists.*

Konzertdirektion Bern. Münzgraben 2, CH-3011 Bern, Switzerland *tel:* +41 31 311 2515 *fax:* +41 31 311 8531 *email:* hambergerbern @swissonline.ch. Rolf Hamberger, director. *Artist management and concert promotion.*

Musa Promotion. Thormannstr. 64, CH-3005 Berne, Switzerland *tel:* +41 31 351 4245 *fax:* +41 31 351 4246. Alexandru Lucianu, director. *Artist representation.*

Music Management. Untere Zelg 30, CH-3145 Berne-Obersherli, Switzerland *tel:* +41 31 849 2323 *fax:* +41 31 849 1719. Dina Thoma-Tennenbaum, president. *Concert promotion.*

Pro Musicis. Rütistr 38, CH-8032 Zürich, Switzerland *tel:* +41 1 251 6533 *fax:* +41 1 252 2914. Silvia Ackermann, director; Andrea Frehner, assistant. *Artist representation for soloists and chamber music.*

Saenger-Sekretariat Heidi Wiedmer. Brambergerstr 30, CH-3176 Neuenegg, Switzerland *tel:* +41 31 741 1845 *also fax. Artist representation for singers.*

Schlaepfer & Partner, ASAM. Hottingerstr 44, Postfach, CH-8030 Zürich, Switzerland *tel:* +41 12 610000 *fax:* +41 12 514342. Ulrich Schlaepfer, director; Judith C Meyer-Franz, manager. *Artist representation.*

Ukraine

National Philharmonia of Ukraine. Volodmyrsky Uzviz 2, Kiev, Ukraine *tel:* +380 44 229 6251 *fax:* +380 44 228 0330. V A Loukashev, general and artistic director. *Promotion of all concerts by National Philharmonia of Ukraine.*

Ukrainian Artists Management. Tchystyakivska St 6-10, Apt 47, 252062 Kiev, Ukraine *tel:* +380 44 442 4561 *also fax; email:* stecuza@culture.kiev.ua. Irena Stecura, director. *Artist representation and concert promotion.*

Uruguay

Martin Vivo, Personal Artist Management. Misiones 1305, Piso 1, 11000 Montevideo, Uruguay *tel:* +598 2 915 1734 *fax:* +598 2 916 2755 *email:* martinv@adinet.com.uy. *Artist representation for conductors and soloists.*

USA

AIM - Artists International Management. PO Box 2146, Morristown, NJ 07962-2146, USA *tel:* +1 973 538 0302 *fax:* +1 973 734 1737 *email:* aimartists@aol.com. Birgit Schmid-Salm, executive director; Vincent L Scwenk, programmes and contracts. *Artist representation.*

Albert Kay Associates Inc. 58 W 58 St, No 31e, New York, NY 10019-2510, USA *tel:* +1 212 593 1640 *fax:* +1 212 759 7329 *email:* slbkayassc@aol.com. Albert Kay, chairman; Jay S Yoo, president; Grace Avrick Lawrence, vice-president. *Artist representation and concert promotion.*

Alkahest Agency Inc. PO Box 12403 Northside Sta, Atlanta GA 30355, USA *tel:* +1 404 315 0709 *fax:* +1 404 636 0844 *email:* alkagency@aol.com. Scott A Bridges, president. *Artist representation.*

American Artists Management Inc. 801 West End Ave, Suite 12A, New York, NY 10025, USA *tel:* +1 212 222 3770 *fax:* +1 212 222 3774 *email:* aami801@aol.com. Sophy Haynes, president. *Artist representation.*

American International Artists. 356 Pine Valley Rd, Hoosick Falls, NY 12090, USA *tel:* +1 518 686 0972 *fax:* +1 518 686 1960 *email:* cbherbst@compuserve.com. Cynthia Herbst, director. *Artist representation, specialising in composers, soloists and ensembles and jazz.*

Amy Blum Publicity/Personal Representation. 144 Village Landing, Suite 190, Fairport, NY 14450, USA *tel:* +1 716 425 1864 *also fax; email:* prmaven352@aol.com. Amy Blum, president. *Artist representation and publicity.*

Andes Management. PO Box 55219, Madison, WI 53705, USA *tel:* +1 608 263 1913 *fax:* +1 608 262 8876 *email:* jfcalder@facstaff.wisc.edu. Javier Calderon. *Artist representation.*

Anthony George Artist Management. 250 W 77 St, New York, NY 10024, USA *tel:* +1 212 580 1306/2405 *fax:* +1 212 721 9144. Anthony George, chief officer. *Artist representation, specialising in opera.*

Arthur H Roach Artists Management. 1749B S Hayes St, Arlington, VA 22202-2714, USA *tel:* +1 703 685 5275 *fax:* +1 703 685 5176 *email:* arthurhr@aol.com. Arthur Roach, director. *Artist representation for opera and oratorio singers. Also contract negotiation.*

Arthur Shafman International Ltd. 163 Amsterdam Ave #121, New York, NY 10023, USA *tel:* +1 212 799 4814 *fax:* +1 212 874 3613 *email:* ashafman@aol.com. Arthur Shafman, president; Jill Joseloff, tour co-ordinator. *Artist representation and concert promotion, specialising in physical theatre, dance, jazz and family entertainment.*

Artists' Alliance Management. 28818 NE Hancock Rd, Camas, WA 98607, USA *tel:* +1 360 834 7022 *fax:* +1 360 834 9680 *email:* manager@crystalrecords.com. Peter Christ, manager. *Artist representation, specialising in woodwind and brass.*

Artists International Management Inc/BFA. The Historic Shuler Theater, 131 N Second St, Raton, NM 87740, USA *tel:* +1 505 445 5528 *fax:* +1 505 445 8572 *email:* aimbfa@raton.com. Marvin Fleming, president/CEO. *Artist representation, specialising in musicals and children's shows.*

Artra Artists Management Inc. 555 W Madison St, Suite 2110, Chicago, IL 60661, USA *tel:* +1 312 648 4100 *fax:* +1 312 648 0600. Robert Bauchens, president; Terryl Jares, vice-president. *Artist representation.*

ArtsPower. 39 S Fullerton Ave, Montclair, NJ 07042, USA *tel:* +1 973 744 0909 *fax:* +1 973 744 3609 *email:* gblackman@artspower.org. Gary Blackman, managing director.

Barbara Serage Artist Management. 7419 Hogarth St, Springfield, VA 22151, USA *tel:* +1 703 941 3445 *fax:* +1 703 941 3909 *email:* bserage451@aol.com. Barbara Serage, president; Vi Carrick, associate. *Artist representation.*

Baylin Artists Management. 110 Pennsylvania, Oreland, PA 19075, USA *tel:* +1 215 887 7870 *fax:* +1 215 887 7873 *email:* bayam@aol.com. Marc Baylin, president. *Artist representation.*

Bennett Morgan & Associates Ltd. 1282 Rt 376, Wappingers Falls, NY 12590, USA *tel:* +1 914 227 6065 *fax:* +1 914 227 4002 *email:* jazzymag@aol.com. Bennett Morgan, Becky Morgan, artists' representatives. *Artist representation: jazz.*

Betsy M Green Associates Inc. 36 Hampshire Rd, Wayland, MA 01778, USA *tel:* +1 508 358 2939 *fax:* +1 508 358 5556 *email:* bmga@aol.com. Betsy M Green, president; Rose Raduziner, executive secretary. *Artist representation, specialising in classical, percussion, piano, world and new music.*

Beverly Wright & Associates. 157 W 57 St, Suite 1100, New York, NY 10019, USA *tel:* +1 212 333 7735 *fax:* +1 212 333 7734 *email:* bevwright@aol.com. Beverly Wright, director. *Artist representation, concert promotion and publicity. Specialises in conductors, composers and instrumentalists and chamber, world and early music.*

Bonnie Fox Artists Management. 1810 Avenida del Mundo, Suite 305, Coronado, CA 92118, USA *tel:* +1 619 435 9273 *fax:* +1 619 435 9140. Bonnie Fox, president. *Artist representation and concert promotion.*

Bravo Artist Management Inc. 14045 Greenwood Ave N#103, Seattle, WA 98133, USA *tel:* +1 206 547 0433 *fax:* +1 206 547 2906 *email:* Bravotpt@aol.com. Lauren Anderson, president. *Artist representation specialising in chamber music and recitals.*

The Bresner Management Inc. Hotel des Artistes, 1 W 67 St, Suite 2E, New York, NY 10023, USA *tel:* +1 212 877 0788 *fax:* +1 212 769 1722. Carol Bresner, president; Lizabeth Skalski, vice-president; Lynn Manuell, international representative.

Bret Adams Ltd. 448 W 44 St, New York, NY 10036, USA *tel:* +1 212 765 5630 *fax:* +1 212 265 2212 *email:* badamsltd@aol.com. Bret Adams, president; Bruce Ostler, Margi Rountree, partners. *Artist representation.*

Bridge Records Inc (Management Division). JAF Box 1864, New York, NY 10116-1864, USA *tel:* +1 914 654 9270 *fax:* +1 914 636 1383 *email:* bridgerec@aol.com. Becky Starobin, director. *Artist representation and recording label, specialising in classical music.*

Cal Performances. 101 Zellerbach Hall, UC Berkeley, Berkeley, CA 94720, USA *tel:* +1 510 642 0212 *fax:* +1 510 643 6707 *email:* calperfs@berkeley.edu. Robert Cole, director; Mark Heiser, general manager; Hollis Ashby, associate director. *Concert promotion for dance, chamber music, theatre, opera, jazz, 20th C classical music, early music.*

California Artists Management. 41 Sutter St, Suite 420, San Francisco, CA 94104-4903, USA *tel:* +1 415 362 2787 *fax:* +1 415 362 2838 *email:* don@calartists.com. Susan Endrizzi, Donald E Osborne, directors. *Artist representation, specialising in early, baroque and chamber music, and vocal ensembles*

Carol Gerson. 145 W 71 St, New York, NY 10023, USA *tel:* +1 212 362 4375 *also fax.* Carol Gerson, president. *Artist representation, specialising in harpsichord, clavichord, forte-piano.*

Casella Artist Management. 250 W 57 St, Suite 1517, New York, NY 10107-1517, USA *tel:* +1 212 245 6008 *fax:* +1 212 245 0637 *email:* maestra@aol.com. Donna Casella, president. *Artist representation for opera singers.*

CBI Artists Associates Inc. 307 E, 89 St, Suite 4-C, New York, NY 10128, USA *tel:* +1 212 427 6479 *fax:* +1 212 831 1605 *email:* cbiartists@hotmail.com. Harold Pomerantz, general director; Diane Bradshaw, artistic director.

CCS International. 3145 Haddington Drive, Los Angeles, CA 90064, USA *tel:* +1 310 836 8081 *fax:* +1 310 836 0438 *email:* ccsconcert@aol.com. Carol Cunning, manager. *Artist representation for chamber music and instrumentalists.*

Century Artists Bureau Inc. 250 W 57 St, Suite 1005, New York, NY 10107-1005, USA *tel:* +1 212 247 3920 *fax:* +1 212 247 3991. Walter Gould, president; Betty Gould, vice-president. *Artist representation, specialising in choral groups.*

Charles Rothschild Prod'ns Inc. 330 E 48 St, New York NY 10017, USA *tel:* +1 212 752 8753 *fax:* +1 212 688 0515. Charles Rothschild, president. *Artist representation and concert promotion.*

Chicago Concert Artists. The Manhattan Suite 906, 431 S Dearborn St, Chicago, IL 60605, USA *tel:* +1 312 663 6434 *fax:* +1 312 663 9416. Carol LaSage, president; Judith Reale, Kimberly K Stewart, artist representatives. *Artist representation for singers, classical guitarists and conductors.*

CHL Artists of Beverley Hills. 9777 Wilshire Blvd, Suite 504, Beverley Hills, CA 90212-1905, USA *tel:* +1 310 278 2158 *fax:* +1 310 278 5801 *email:* chlartists@aol.com. Christopher Ling, president and CEO; Carolyn Nelson, artist repesentative. *Artist representation.*

Classical Concepts International. PO Box 4100, Suite 239, Del Mar, CA 92014, USA *tel:* +1 619 759 0591 *fax:* +1 619 759 0592. Susan Parker, director. *Artist representation, promotion, PR and design.*

Colbert Artists Management Inc. 111 W 57 St, New York, NY 10019, USA *tel:* +1 212 757 0782 *fax:* +1 212 541 5179 *email:* aecolbert@aol.com. Agnes Eisenberger, president; Charlotte Schroeder, vice-president. *Artist representation.*

Columbia Artists Management Inc. 165 W 57 St, New York, NY 10019, USA *tel:* +1 212 841 9500 *fax:* +1 212 841 9552. Ronald Wilford, president. *Artist representation.*

Concert Artists Guild. 850 Seventh Ave, Suite 1205, New York, NY 10019, USA *tel:* +1 212 333 5200 *fax:* +1 212 977 7149 *email:* caguild@aol.com. Carlotta Wilsen, executive director. *Artist representation for winners of the Concert Artists Guild Competition.*

Corbett Arts Management Ltd. 41 Sutter St, Suite 518, San Francisco, CA 94104-4903, USA *tel:* +1 415 982 2505 *fax:* +1 415 982 5295 *email:* info@corbettarts.com. Joanne Corbett-Barnes, president. *Artist* *representation for classical and world music, specialising in conductors, soloists and ensembles.*

Côté Artists' Management Inc. PO Box 20145, New York, NY 10011-9993, USA *tel:* +1 212 255 4252 *fax:* +1 212 255 5183 *email:* coteopera@aol.com. Paul G Côté, president. *Artist representation for opera singers.*

CRS Artists Representative. 724 Winchester Rd, Broomall, PA 19008, USA *tel:* +1 610 544 5920 *fax:* +1 610 544 5921 *email:* crsnews@erols.com. Jack Shusterman, Caroline Hunt, representatives. *Artist representation and concert promotion.*

Curzon & Kedersha Artists Management. 330 E 39 St, Suite 28E, New York, NY 10016, USA *tel:* +1 212 883 0873/877 5257 *fax:* +1 212 769 1835. Pamela Curzon, Julie Kedersha, co-directors. *Artist representation.*

Del Rosenfield Associates Inc. 714 Ladd Rd, Riverdale, Bronx, NY 10471-1204, USA *tel:* +1 718 549 5687 *fax:* +1 718 548 4313 *email:* delrosedra@aol.com. Marydel Rosenfield, president. *Artist representation, general classical and ragtime.*

Dorothy Cone Artists Representatives Inc. 150 W 55 St, New York, NY 10019, USA *tel:* +1 212 765 7412 *fax:* +1 212 765 7443 *email:* dcone@ix.netcom.com. Dorothy Cone, president; Joseph Guiliano, assistant. *Artist representation for opera singers, conductors, stage directors.*

DOTS Int'l. 202 Hillsboro Dr, Silver Spring, MO 20902, USA *tel:* +1 301 681 0860 *fax:* +1 301 681 0857. Ala Kuchinsky, representative. *Artist representation for pianists and orchestras.*

dworkin eliason pARTners. PO Box 248, Bedford Hills, NY 10507, USA *tel:* +1 914 244 3803 *fax:* +1 914 244 3878 *email:* dworkin @worldnet.att.net. Elizabeth Dworkin, Barbara Eliason, partners. *Artist representation, media relations, special projects.*

East & West Artists. 310 Riverside Drive, Suite 313, New York, NY 10025-4101, USA *tel:* +1 212 222 2433 *also fax; email:* acos_ewa @cwix.com. Adolovni Acosta, Bo Lawergren. *Concert promotion and management, specialising in soloists and small ensembles.*

Engdahl Artists International. 315 E 69th St, New York, NY 10021, USA *tel:* +1 212 744 2230 *fax:* +1 212 744 0343. Arlyne Engdahl, James Engdahl, artists' representatives. *Artist representation.*

Esther Prince Management. 340 W 55 St, No 5D, New York, NY 10019, USA *tel:* +1 212 586 7137 *fax:* +1 212 586 6734. Esther Prince, president. *Artist representation.*

Europa Artists Management. 707 Westview Ave, Suite 2W, Philadelphia, PA 19119, USA *tel:* +1 215 848 3456 *also fax; email:* imakellienne@aol.com. Marja Kaisla, managing director. *Artist representation, specialising in chamber ensembles.*

F Sharp Productions Ltd. 157 W 57 St, PH-B, New York, NY 10019, USA *tel:* +1 212 265 6637 *fax:* +1 212 265 6638. Jim DiGiovanni, president; David Sneed, assistant. *Artist representation, specialising in film composers.*

Feuchtenberger Management. 804 Fincastle Drive, Fincastle Estates, Bluefield, VA 24605, USA *tel:* +1 540 326 1491 *also fax; email:* pfeuch@netscope.net. Pat Feuchtenberger, director; Mary Wallace, assistant. *Representation for solo artists.*

Fine Arts Management. 201-A 6th Ave, Brooklyn, NY 11217, USA *tel:* +1 718 857 2757 *fax:* +1 718 857 4582 *email:* arhodes@fineartsmgmt.com. Steven Sobol, director; Amy Rhodes, associate; Zachary Hooper, PR director; Tom Gaitens, computer associate. *Artist representation and computer software.*

Firebird Artists Management Inc. 132 Tregarone Rd, Timonium, MD 21093, USA *tel:* +1 410 560 2142 *fax:* +1 410 560 2173. Gregory Kuperstein, president. *Artist representation for solo instrumentalists, conductors and chamber music.*

Frank Salomon Associates. 201 W 54 St, Suite 1C, New York, NY 10019, USA *tel:* +1 212 581 5197 *fax:* +1 212 581 4029 *email:* salomonf @aol.com. Frank Salomon, president; John Robinson, executive director; Barrie Steinberg, director. *Artist representation for conductors, soloists, ensembles, orchestra tours. Also educational and outreach activities.*

GAMI/Simonds. 24 Church Hill Rd, Washington Depot, CT 06794, USA *tel:* +1 860 354 5295 *fax:* +1 860 354 5298 *email:* gamisim@worldnet.att.net. Laurelle Favreau, Don Verdery, directors. *Artist representation, specialising in classical, chamber, folk and Latin music.*

George M Martynuk Inc. 352 7th Ave, 12th Floor, New York, NY-10001, USA *tel:* +1 212 631 7567 *fax:* +1 212 631 7591 *email:* georgemartynuk@msn.com. George M Martynuk, principal. *Personal management for opera singers; worldwide PR and publicity for opera singers and other classical artists.*

Gina Bachauer International Piano Foundation. PO Box 11664, Salt Lake City, UT 84147, USA *tel:* +1 801 521 9200 *fax:* +1 801 521 9202 *email:* gina@bachauer.com. Susan Kelly, general manager; Paul Pollei, artistic manager; Massimiliano Frani, associate artist manager. *Artist representation and concert promotion.*

The Gordon Artists. 3 Church Lane, Baltimore, MD 21208, USA *tel:* +1 410 484 6410 *fax:* +1 410 484 0653 *email:* lpbernstein@gordontrust.org. Loraine Bernstein, assistant director.

Great Lakes Performing Artist Associates. 505 E Huron, Suite 302, Ann Arbor, MI 48104, USA *tel:* +1 734 665 4029 *fax:* +1 734 665 8594 *email:* au757@detroit.freenet.org. Elizabeth Humes, executive director; Bonnie Long McLaughlin, direct marketing and development. *Representation for artists resident in Great Lakes area.*

Gurtman & Murtha Associates Inc. 450 7th Av #603, New York, NY 10123-0101, USA *tel:* +1 212 967 7350 *fax:* +1 212 967 7341 *email:* jmurtha457@aol.com. Bernard Gurtman, president; James Murtha. *Booking agent.*

Guy Freedman Personal Representative. 42 Stony Run, New Rochelle, NY 10804, USA *tel:* +1 914 632 1292 *also fax.* Guy Freedman, personal represenative; Miriam Lewinger, Kathy Hahn, associates. *Artist representation, specialising in jazz.*

Harwood Management Group Inc. 509 W 110 St, New York, NY 10025, USA *tel:* +1 212 864 0773 *fax:* +1 212 663 1129 *email:* jim @harwood-management.com. Jim Harwood. *Artist representation.*

Hendrickson Artists Management. 885 Third Ave, Suite 2900, New York, NY 10022-4834, USA *tel:* +1 212 829 5533 *fax:* +1 212 829 5534 *email:* wrhmgt@aol.com. William R Hendrickson, executive director. *Representation of vocal artists for opera and symphony concerts and solo recitals.*

Henry Hunt Management. 1270 Lincoln Ave, Suite 100, Pasadena, CA 91103, USA *tel:* +1 626 791 9193 *fax:* +1 626 791 2556. *Artist representation, specialising in organists.*

Herbert Barrett Management Inc. 1776 Broadway, Suite 1610, New York, NY 10019, USA *tel:* +1 212 245 3530 *fax:* +1 212 397 5860 *email:* info@herbarrett.com. Herbert Barrett, president; Nancy Wellman, John Anderson, executive vice-presidents. *Artist representation.*

Hirsch Entertainment Inc. PO Box 250390, Columbia Univ Sta, 1123 Amsterdam Ave, New York, NY 10026, USA *tel:* +1 212 864 0773 *fax:* +1 212 663 1129 *email:* hirschent@juno.com. James Harwood, president. *Artist representation.*

Howard Stokar Management. 870 West End Ave, New York, NY 10025-4918, USA *tel:* +1 212 866 5798 *fax:* +1 212 662 0804 *email:* hstokar@stokar.com. Howard Stokar. *Artist representation for composers.*

Hummingbird Artist Management. 2805 Mataro St, Pasadena, CA 91107, USA *tel:* +1 818 449 1417 *also fax.* Lee Brooks, president. *Artist representation.*

Hunstein Artist Services. 65 W 90 St, Suite 13F, New York, NY 10024, USA *tel:* +1 212 724 2693 *fax:* +1 212 724 9393 *email:* deeanne@ interport.com. DeeAnne Hunstein, director; Don Hunstein, associate. *Artist representation and concert promotion, specialising in chamber music.*

ICA Management. PO Box 1216, Redding, CT 06875-1216, USA *tel:* +1 203 938 3476 *fax:* +1 203 938 8887. Harry de Freese, admin. *Artist representation and concert promotion.*

IMG Artists North America. 825 Seventh Ave, New York, NY 10019, USA *tel:* +1 212 489 8300 *fax:* +1 212 246 1596 *email:* artistsny @imgworld.com. Edna Landau, managing director, senior vice-president. *Artist representation for instrumentalists, singers, conductors, ensembles and dance.*

International Artists Alliance. PO Box 131, Springfield, VA 22150, USA *tel:* +1 703 451 1662 *fax:* +1 703 451 0628. Ernesto Farago, president; Rose Burke, booking agent; Robert Katona, artistic adviser. *Concert promotion.*

International Artists Guild. 323 W 74 St, New York, NY 10023, USA *tel:* +1 212 580 9173 *fax:* +1 212 769 3502 *email:* artguild@interport.net. Bob Katsenbogen, executive director; Henry Gris, vice-president. *Artist representation.*

International Masters of Music. PO Box 5213, Scottsdale, AZ 85261, USA *tel:* +1 602 465 0141 *also fax.* Mary Hazlett, president. *Artist representation, specialising in vocal soloists.*

ITM Artists Management. PO Box 9401, Rancho Santa Fe, CA 92067, USA *tel:* +1 619 259 2503 *fax:* +1 619 259 5508 *email:* iim@aol.com. Michael Tseitlin, president; Nathaly Hosay, general manager. *Artist representation for instrumentalists, chamber music ensembles, orchestras and choirs, and concert promotion.*

Jacques Leiser Artists' Management. The Del Prado, 666 Upas St, Suite 1005, San Diego, CA 92103, USA *tel:* +1 619 293 3177 *fax:* +1 619 293 0088. Jacques Leiser, president. *Artist representation and consultation.*

Jane Davis Inc. 61 Taunton Lake Rd, Newtown, CT 06470, USA *tel:* +1 203 426 9768 *fax:* +1 203 270 7423 *email:* janeinc@aol.com. Jane I Davis, president; Pamela J Titus, vice-president. *Artist representation.*

Jane Music Management Inc. 1060 Park Ave, Suite 9G, New York, NY 10128, USA *tel:* +1 212 534 6191 *fax:* +1 212 534 6311 *email:*

janemgt@aol.com. Jane Deckoff, president. *Artist representation, specialising in recitalists and chamber music.*

Jecklin Associates. 2717 Nichols Lane, Davenport, IA 52803, USA *tel:* +1 319 359 0866; +1 212 490 0605 *fax:* +1 319 359 1266 *email:* jecklin@webtv.net. Lois Jecklin, president; Elaine Brown, admin assistant. *Artist representation for instrumentalists and composers.*

Jeffrey W James Arts Consulting. 316 Pacific St, Massapequa Park, NY 11762, USA *tel:* +1 516 797 9166 *also fax; email:* jamesarts @worldnet.att.net. Jeffrey James, president; John Christie Cotsonas, vice-president. *Artist representation and public relations, specialising in working with composers and creating recording projects.*

JEJ Artists. 2450 East Rock Creek, Bloomington, IN 47401-6822, USA *tel:* +1 812 323 0427 *fax:* +1 812 323 1453 *email:* jjarriel @bluemarble.net. Janet Jarriel, executive director. *Artist representation, specialising in organ, piano, violin and voice.*

JKES Inc. 404 Park Ave S, New York, NY 10016, USA *tel:* +1 212 686 2200 ext 101 *fax:* +1 212 689 9140 *email:* jerrykravat@msn.com. Jerry Kravat, booking agent. *Artist representation.*

Joanne Rile Artists Management Inc. 801 Old York Rd, Suite 212, Jenkintown, Pennsylvania 19046, USA *tel:* +1 215 885 6400 *fax:* +1 215 885 9929 *email:* artists@rilearts.com. Joanne Rile, president and co-director; John R Rile, executive vice-president and co-director. *Artist management for all kinds of classical music groups and soloists.*

John Gingrich Management Inc. PO Box 1515, New York, NY 10023, USA *tel:* +1 212 799 5080 *fax:* +1 212 874 7652 *email:* gingarts @erols.com. John Gingrich, president; Anne Slayden, assistant; David Ezer, associate. *Artist representation, specialising in chamber music and keyboard.*

Joseph H Conlin Concert Management. 853 7th Ave, New York, NY 10019, USA *tel:* +1 212 307 1990 *also fax.* Joseph H Conlin, president.

Jupiter Artists Inc. 155 W 71 St, Suite 2-J, New York, NY 10023, USA *tel:* +1 212 724 4426 *fax:* +1 212 875 0715. Joseph Greene, president. *Artist management and personal representation, specialising in opera and other vocal areas. Also concert promoter.*

Karen McFarlane Artists Inc. 12429 Cedar Rd, Suite 29, Cleveland, Ohio 44106, USA *tel:* +1 216 721 9095 *fax:* +1 216 721 9098 *email:* kmcfar123@aol.com. Karen McFarlane, president. *Artist representation, specialising in organists and Anglican choirs.*

Kirshbaum Delmar & Associates, Inc. 711 West End Ave, Suite 5KN, New York, NY 10025, USA *tel:* +1 212 222 4843 *fax:* +1 212 222 7321 *email:* skirsh711@aol.com. Shirley Kirshbaum, Susan Demler, directors; Pamela Rendsland, booking associate. *Artist management and publicity.*

Komar Management Inc. 1122 Wes St, Oceanside, CA 92054, USA *tel:* +1 760 722 1181 *fax:* +1 760 722 1182. Marilyn Lambson, director. *Artist representation, specialising in piano.*

Lee Jon Associates. 24 Del Rio Blvd, Boca Raton, FL 33432-4734, USA *tel:* +1 800 282 3161 *fax:* +1 561 394 0520. Marjorie Gordon, executive director; Lee Merrill, executive assistant; Jon Ellis, PR director. *Music and programme consultancy, specialising in opera and chamber music.*

Levine Associates Management Inc. 662 Colonial Ave, Pelham, NY 10803, USA *tel:* +1 914 738 1888 *fax:* +1 914 738 6905.

Lieberman, David. 2333 Pontius Ave, Los Angeles, CA 90064, USA *tel:* +1 310 312 1648 *fax:* +1 310 479 3388 *email:* liebermand@aol.com. David Lieberman, artists' representative; Jay Quantrill, operations; Elizabeth A McInerney, admin. *Artist representation, specialising in neo-classical modern dance.*

Liegner Management. PO Box 230 884, New York, NY 10023, USA *tel:* +1 212 496 1515 *fax:* +1 212 787 9449 *email:* liegnermgt@aol.com. Judith Liegner, director. *Artist representation for soloists, choreographers and directors.*

Ligeti Artist Mangement. 415 W 55 St, New York, NY 10019, USA *tel:* +1 212 246 8949 *fax:* +1 212 787 9449 *email:* MRLigeti@aol.com. Peter Ligeti.

Lindy S Martin Personal Management. PO Box 4326, Pinehurst, NC 28374-4326, USA *tel:* +1 910 295 3303 *fax:* +1 910 295 8333 *email:* MSislen950@aol.com. Lindy S Martin, president. *Artist representation specialising in classical guitar.*

Lisa Sapinkopf Artists. 1250 Campus Drive, Berkeley, CA 94708, USA *tel:* +1 510 845 6725 *fax:* +1 510 845 4040 *email:* lsapinkopf@aol.com. Lisa Sapinkopf, director. *Artist representation, specialising in chamber ensembles and orchestras and soloists.*

Living Arts Inc. 250 W 57 St, Suite 2401, New York, NY 10107, USA *tel:* +1 212 765 7777 *fax:* +1 212 397 5205. Peter Klein, president. *Artist representation and concert promotion.*

Lois Scott Management Inc. PO Box 140, Closter, NJ 07624, USA *tel:* +1 201 768 6970 *fax:* +1 201 768 7257 *email:* lsminc@aol.com. Lois Scott, president. *Artist representation and management for the performing arts.*

Lynn Garon. 1199 Park Ave, New York, NY 10128, USA *tel:* +1 212 876 1279 *fax:* +1 212 722 3819 *email:* lynnpg@juno.com. Lynn Garon, CEO. *Composers' services.*

Magna Carta Management. 3359 Kelly Lane SW, Roanoke, VA 24018, USA *tel:* +1 540 776 3454 *also fax.* Sylvia Craft, CEO. *Representation of composers only.*

Manhattan Management Group. 166 W 94 St, Suite 4B, New York, NY 10025, USA *tel:* +1 212 749 4364 *also fax.* D L Jones, artist representative. *Artist representation.*

Marimba Productions. 392 Kirby Ave, Elberon, NJ, USA *tel:* +1 732 870 8600 *fax:* +1 732 870 8610. Sue Giambalvo, administrator. *Artist representation and concert promotion for marimba keyboards and other tuned percussion.*

Mary Ella Collins & Associates Artists Management. 6310 Turner Way, Dallas, TX 75230, USA *tel:* +1 972 661 9074 *fax:* +1 972 661 9514 *email:* mec@mec-sing.com. Mary Ella Collins, president; Tasia Antahades, associate. *Artist representation and management for singers, conductors and stage directors.*

Master Artists. PO Box 13985, Gainesville, FL 32604, USA *tel:* +1 904 376 9055 *fax:* +1 904 372 2049 *email:* artsacad@net-magic.net. Richard A Dickson, president. *Artist representation for soloists and small ensembles.*

Matthew Laifer Artists' Management. 410 W 24 St, Suite 2-i, New York, NY 10011, USA *tel:* +1 212 929 7429 *fax:* +1 212 633 2628 *email:* laiferart@aol.com. Matthew Laifer, manager. *Artist management and personal representation.*

Maxim Gershunoff Attractions Inc. 1401 NE 9th St, Suite 38, Fort Lauderdale, FL 33304-4412, USA *tel:* +1 954 769 9105 *fax:* +1 954 769 9107 *email:* leonmax@aol.com. Leon Van Dyke, Maxim Gershunoff, artist managers. *Artist representation for instrumentalists and conductors; also concert promotion.*

MCM Artists. PO Box 589, Millbrook, NY 12545, USA *tel:* +1 914 677 5881 *fax:* +1 914 677 5912 *email:* mcmltd@aol.com. Thomas Gallant, William Reinert, managing directors. *Artist representation and concert promotion.*

MDR Magenta Artistic Management. PO Box 770, Summit, NJ 07902-0770, USA *tel:* +1 718 231 6842. Joyce Ann Sinno, artist manager. *Artist representation for classical singers.*

Mellon Music Management. Hog Mountain Rd, Fleischmanns, NY 12430, USA *tel:* +1 914 586 3588 *fax:* +1 914 586 2540 *email:* mellon@catskill.net. Barbara Mellon, director. *Artist representation.*

Melody Bunting International. 155 West 72 St #604, New York, NY 10023, USA *tel:* +1 212 799 4949 *fax:* +1 212 580 8698 *email:* melbunting @aol.com. Melody Bunting, owner. *Artist representation.*

Melvin Kaplan Inc. 115 College St, Burlington, VT 05401, USA *tel:* +1 802 658 2592 *fax:* +1 802 658 6089 *email:* melkap@aol.com. Melvin Kaplan, president; Cynthia Seybolt, associate. *Artist representation, specialising in chamber music and soloists.*

Michal Schmidt Artists International Inc. 59 E 54 St, Suite 83, New York, NY 10022, USA *tel:* +1 212 421 8500 *fax:* +1 212 421 8583. *Artist representation for conductors, piano, violin, cello and orchestras.*

Midwest Artist Management. 846 Washtenaw St NE, Grand Rapids, MI 49505-4846, USA *tel:* +1 616 451 2012 *also fax.* Lisa TeRoller. *Artist representation and concert promotion.*

Munro Artists Management. 786 Dartmouth St, South Dartmouth, MA 02748, USA *tel:* +1 508 993 9011 *fax:* +1 508 993 9044 *email:* operamom@aol.com. Martha Munro, president. *Artist representation, specialising in opera.*

Musicians International Inc. 130 E 94 St, Suite 5A, New York, NY 10128, USA *tel:* +1 212 722 5793 *fax:* +1 212 860 2139 *email:* eggw65a @prodigy.com. Richard Epstein, president. *Artist representation and concert promotion.*

Mutual Artists Management Alliance. 30 East End Ave, New York, NY 10028, USA *tel:* +1 212 288 4261. Rolande Young, executive director; Rolande Schrade, Robert Schrade, directors. *Artist representation and concert promotion for artists participating in Sevenars Music Festival.*

ND Artists Management. 7 Ferncliff Rd, Scarsdale, NY 10583, USA *tel:* +1 914 723 0960 *fax:* +1 914 723 1206 *email:* NDartsmgt@msn.com. Nick Darnay, president; Harold Schagrin, Martin Moserowitz, representatives; Jean Acheson, PR director; Shirley Castro, marketing director. *Artist representation. Established artists who specialise in performing and explaining works to audiences during recital and donated 'Community Performances'. Artists also make solo orchestral appearances.*

Neil Funkhouser Artists Management. 105 Arden Street, #2F, New York, NY 10040-1118, USA *tel:* +1 212 304 3796 *fax:* +1 212 304 4507 *email:* neilfunk@aol.com. Neil Funkhouser, president; Scott Levine, associate. *Artist representation of singers, conductors and stage directors.*

New World Classics. 1 Riverdale Ave, Suite 4, Riverdale, NY 10463-4912, USA *tel:* +1 718 549 1673 *fax:* +1 718 549 7186. Kerby Lovallo, director; Satoko Kuroda, manager. *Artist representation.*

Ovation! Management. 6161 N Hamilton, Chicago, IL 60659-4220, USA *tel:* +1 773 338 4182 *fax:* +1 773 338 8331 *email:* ovationmgmt99@hotmail.com. Blanche Artis Lewis, president; Alexander Boas, sales. *Artist representation for singers, dancers, chamber groups, conductors, and instrumentalists.*

Pan American Music International. 6407 Overbrook Ave, Philadelphia, PA 19151, USA *tel:* +1 215 879 9090 *fax:* +1 215 879 9979. Justin Fink, president. *Specialises in Latin-American and Caribbean artists.*

Parker Artists. 382 Central Park West, #9G, New York, NY 10025, USA *tel:* +1 212 864 7928 *fax:* +1 212 864 8189 *email:* tfparker@aol.com. Thomas F Parker, owner. *Artist representation for soloists, conductors and chamber ensembles.*

Parsons Artists Management Inc. 1134 Wade St, Highland Pk, IL 60035, USA *tel:* +1 847 433 7374 *fax:* +1 847 432 8103 *email:* pamgtinc@aol.com. Pamela Parsons, president. *Artist management.*

Performing Artists International. 4417 Dunwick, Suite 300, Fort Worth, TX 76109-2508, USA *tel:* +1 817 924 2225 *fax:* +1 817 924 1399 *email:* afabry@flash.net. Angela Fabry, director. *Artist management for soloists and conductors.*

Performing Artservices Inc. 260 W Broadway, New York, NY 10013, USA *tel:* +1 212 941 8911 *fax:* +1 212 334 5149. Mimi Johnson, director. *Artist representation, specialising in avant-garde contemporary composers.*

Phillip Truckenbrod Concert Artists. PO Box 331060, West Hartford, CT 06133-1060, USA *tel:* +1 860 560 7800 *fax:* +1 860 560 7788 *email:* email@concertartists.com. Phillip Truckenbrod, president; Charles Miller, Raymond Albright, vice-presidents. *Artist representation, specialising in British choirs and concert organists.*

Prima Americas Artists Management Inc (formerly Wolf Artists Management). 788 Columbus Ave, No 15A, New York, NY 10025-5936, USA *tel:* +1 212 531 1514 *fax:* +1 212 531 1610 *email:* americas@primartists.com. Isabel Wolf, president; Nicola Lischi, manager. *Artist representation for singers, conductors and directors.*

Primo Concerts. 7 Elm Place, St Louis, MO 63119, USA *tel:* +1 314 968 9027 *fax:* +1 314 961 7842 *email:* melkaty@aol.com. Mel Jernigan, agent. *Artist representation, specialising in brass, chamber music and Dixieland jazz.*

Pro Piano Management. 85 Jane St, New York, NY 10014, USA *tel:* +1 212 206 8794 *fax:* +1 212 633 1207 *email:* ricard@propiano.com. Ricard de La Rosa, executive director, founder. *Artist representation.*

Professional Women Singers Association. PO Box 884, Planetarium Sta, New York, NY 10024, USA *tel:* +1 212 969 0590 *fax:* +1 212 255 4982 *email:* singerpwsa@aol.com. Carol Flamm, president. *Co-operative organisation of female singers.*

Randsman Artists' Management. 400 W 43 St, Suite 18E, New York, NY 10036, USA *tel:* +1 212 290 2281 *fax:* +1 212 290 2284 *email:* randsman@aol.com. Peter Randsman, president; Rick Lusby, associate. *Artist representation and management for opera singers, conductors and stage directors.*

Raymond Weiss Artist Management Inc. 300 W 55 St, No 5L, New York, NY 10019-5138, USA *tel:* +1 212 581 8478 *fax:* +1 212 581 8479 *email:* rwam@mcimail.com. Raymond Weiss, president emeritus; Jeffrey Dimmerman, president. *Artist representation, specialising in chamber ensembles.*

Reuben Guss Enterprises. 215 W 92 St, New York, NY 10025, USA *tel:* +1 212 580 7401. Reuben Guss, artist manager. *Artist representation; mostly opera.*

Ricard de La Rosa. 85 Jane St, New York, NY 10014, USA *tel:* +1 212 206 8794 *fax:* +1 212 633 1207 *email:* ricard@propiano.com.

Richard Hadden Management. 158 Graham Ave, St Ignace, MI 49781, USA *tel:* +1 906 643 7773 *fax:* +1 906 643 7229. Richard M Hadden, director. *Artist representation.*

Robert Gewald Management Inc. 58 West 58 St, New York, NY 10019, USA *tel:* +1 212 753 0450 *fax:* +1 212 935 3706. Robert M Gewald, president; Joyce Rashti, co-ordinator. *Artist representation.*

Robert Lombardo Associates. 61 W 62 St, Suite 6F, New York, NY 10023, USA *tel:* +1 212 586 4453 *fax:* +1 212 581 5771 *email:* robertjl@ix.netcom.com. Robert Lombardo, president; Michael Rosen, Lewis Ehlers, artist managers. *Artist representation, specialising in opera.*

Rosalie Calabrese Management. Box 20580, New York, NY 10025, USA *tel:* +1 212 663 6620 *fax:* +1 212 663 5941. Verna Fine, associate. *Personal representation for American classical composers.*

Sally Sanfield Artist Management. 31550 Stonewood Court, Farmington Hills, MI 48334, USA *tel:* +1 248 626 0948 *fax:* +1 248 626 0904 *email:* ssanfield@aol.com. Sally Sanfield, director. *Artist representation.*

Sardos Artist Management Corp. 180 West End Ave, New York, NY 10023, USA *tel:* +1 212 874 2559 *fax:* +1 212 721 7815. Rita Sardos, president. *Artist representation, specialising in opera singers, stage directors and conductors.*

Schofer/Gold Associates Ltd. 50 Riverside Drive, New York, NY 10024, USA *tel:* +1 212 877 0776 *fax:* +1 212 874 1020. Marvin Schofer, president. *Artist representation, specialising in conductors and music directors.*

Schwalbe & Partners. 170 E 61st St, #5 N, New York, NY 10021, USA *tel:* +1 212 935 5650 *fax:* +1 212 935 4754 *email:* schwalbe_partners @compuserve.com. Douglas Schwalbe, president; Carrie Sykes, managing partner. *Artist representation.*

Seidel Artists Management. 2092 W Greenleaf Ave, Chicago, IL 60645, USA *tel:* +1 773 761 7001 *fax:* +1 773 761 2025 *email:* seidelam@aol.com. Jean Seidel, executive director. *Artist representation for oratorio, opera, music theatre.*

Sempre Musica. 11260 Overland Ave, Suite 15B, Culver City, CA 90230, USA *tel:* +1 310 287 1031 *fax:* +1 310 815 8133 *email:* sempremus @compuserve.com. Valerie Bernstein, president; Ina Jo Scheid, vice-president. *Artist representation, specialising in chamber and early music, and soloists.*

Sheldon Soffer Management Inc. 130 West 56 St, New York, NY 10019, USA *tel:* +1 212 757 8060 *fax:* +1 212 757 5536 *email:* shelsoffer@aol.com. Sheldon Soffer, president. *Artist representation.*

Shupp Artist Management. 202 Michigan Ave, Port Jefferson, NY 11777, USA *tel:* +1 516 928 1531 *fax:* +1 516 474 5071. Erica Shupp. *Artist representation.*

Siegel Artist Management. 1416 Hinman Ave, Evanston, IL 60201, USA *tel:* +1 847 475 4224 *fax:* +1 847 475 0440 *email:* lizsam@aol.com. Liz Silverstein, associate director; Jane Lawrence Curtiss, director; Jennifer Morris, artist representative. *Artist representation, specialising in dance and theatre, jazz, classical ensembles and soloists.*

Sondra Ross Associates Inc. 2705 McGee Av, Middletown, OH 45044, USA *tel:* +1 513 423 3023 *fax:* +1 513 425 6655 *email:* SondraRoss@aol.com. Sondra Ross, president. *Artist representation.*

Springwood Artist Management. Box 622, Hershey, PA 17033, USA *tel:* +1 717 838 9813 *fax:* +1 717 838 4521 *email:* springwd@aol.com. Roger Gale, director. *Representation for classical vocalists.*

by arrangement with Matthew Sprizzo. 477 Durant Ave, Staten Island, NY 10308, USA *tel:* +1 718 948 5402 *fax:* +1 718 984 8996 *email:* MSprizzo@aol.com. Matthew Sprizzo. *Artist representation for instrumentalists, vocalists, and conductors.*

Stanley Weinstein Arts Management. 408 Charlestown Rd, Hampton, NJ 08827, USA *tel:* +1 908 537 6832 *also fax; email:* stanweinstein@sprintmail.com. Stanley Weinstein, president; Ilene Beckerman, vice-president. *Artist representation for chamber music, special attractions, dance and cabaret artists. Arts management consultancy.*

Stanton Consulting & Management. 45-05 Newtown Rd, Astoria, NY 11103, USA *tel:* +1 718 956 6092 *fax:* +1 718 956 5385. Todd Stanton, president; Douglas Hamilton, Marcia Olivo, senior associates. *Artist representation and concert promotion.*

Steorra Public Relations. 243 West End Ave, Suite 907, New York, NY 10023, USA *tel:* +1 212 799 5783 *fax:* +1 212 799 1121 *email:* steorrapr@aol.com. Lynda Ciolek, president. *Artist representation, specialising in piano, voice, chamber music.*

Sutton Artists Corp. 20 West Park Ave, Suite 305, Long Beach, NY 11561-2019, USA *tel:* +1 516 432 1790 *fax:* +1 516 869 1855. Frank Modica, president. *Artist representation and concert promotion.*

Thea Dispeker Inc. 59 East 54 St, New York, NY 10022, USA *tel:* +1 212 421 7676 *fax:* +1 212 935 3279 *email:* info@dispeker.com. Larry Wasserman, president. *Artist management.*

Tornay Management Inc. 155 West 72 St, New York, NY 10023, USA *tel:* +1 212 580 8696 *fax:* +1 212 580 8698 *email:* stornay@aol.com. Sara Tornay, president. *Artist representation, specialising in vocalists.*

Trawick Artists Management Inc. 1926 Broadway, New York, NY 10023, USA *tel:* +1 212 874 2482 *fax:* +1 212 874 2866. Brenda Trawick, president. *Artist representation.*

Victoria Brandys Artists Management. 3824 S Fraser, Aurora, CO 80014-4022, USA *tel:* +1 303 693 6267 *fax:* +1 303 766 9332 *email:* vbrandys@aol.com. Victoria Brandys, director. *Artist representation, specialising in guitar, piano and world music.*

Vivace Artistic Representation. 110 Union St, Suite 510, Seattle, WA 98101, USA *tel:* +1 206 340 2557 *fax:* +1 206 583 2726. Roz Benaroya, executive director. *Artist representation and concert promotion, specialising in vocal artists and chamber music.*

Vladimir Baranov Inc. 301 East 69 St, No 9-E, New York, NY 10021, USA *tel:* +1 212 496 6452 *also fax.* Faina Baranov, director; Vladimir Baranov, president. *Artist representation for opera singers.*

Warden Associates Inc. 5626 Deer Run Rd, Doylestown, PA 18901, USA *tel:* +1 215 794 3767 *fax:* +1 215 794 8627 *email:* michael@ispa-os.com. Diana Warden, president; Michael Lowell Larsen, vice-president. *Artist representation specialising in opera.*

William Knight. Grant House, 309 Wood St, Burlington, NJ 08016, USA *tel:* +1 609 386 3933 *fax:* +1 609 386 8703. William Knight, president; Nancy Gorman, vice-president. *Artist representation for American vocalists and conductors. No instrumentalists.*

World Artists. 3126 Bolero Drive, Atlanta, GA 30341, USA *tel:* +1 770 939 4343 *fax:* +1 770 908 1231 *email:* lynnmc@mindspring.com. Lynn McConnell. *Artist representation for international folk music and dance. Also Dixieland Jazz.*

WSA Artist Management. PO Box 740564, Dallas, TX 75374, USA *tel:* +1 214 341 1911 *also fax; email:* wsa@scobiemusic.com. Greta Critchlow Scobie, administration director. *Artist representation, specialising in community outreach programmes.*

Young Concert Artists Inc. 250 W 57 St, Suite 1222, New York, NY 10019, USA *tel:* +1 212 307 6655 *fax:* +1 212 581 8894 *email:* yca@yca.org. Susan Wadsworth, director. *Representation for exceptional young artists; artists chosen through international auditions.*

Zajonc/Valenti Management. PO Box 7023, Ann Arbor, MI 48107, USA *tel:* +1 800 650 8742 *fax:* +1 734 662 8733 *email:* zvmgmt@aol.com. Judy Valenti, manager. *Artist representation for traditional and contemporary jazz, folk and musical theatre, ballet and children's entertainment.*

Symphony Orchestras

The orchestras listed below perform regularly and operate on a professional, or mainly professional, basis. The number of performers is shown in parenthesis, and the conductor or musical director is listed, together with the names of the chief administrative staff.

Albania

Symphonic Orchestra of the Theatre of Opera and Ballet. Sheshi 'Skenderbey', Tirana, Albania *tel:* +355 42 26747 *fax:* +355 42 25856/24753 *email:* root@tob.tirana.al.

Armenia

Armenian Philharmonic Orchestra (106). Mesrop Mashtotz 46, Erevan, Armenia *tel:* +37 42 560645 *fax:* +37 42 151055. Loris Tjeknavorian, artistic director, principal conductor; Robert Mirzoyan, manager.

Australia

Adelaide Symphony Orchestra (80). GPO Box 2121, Adelaide SA 5001, Australia *tel:* +61 8 8343 4834 *fax:* +61 8 8343 4808 *email:* aso@aso.com.au. Robert Clarke, managing director; James Koehne, artistic admin.

Canberra Symphony Orchestra (70). GPO Box 1919, Canberra, Act 2601, Australia *tel:* +61 6 247 9191 *fax:* +61 6 247 9026 *email:* info@cso.org.au. Barbara George, general manager.

Melbourne Philharmonic Orchestra. BOX 102, Glen Iris, Vic 3146, Australia *tel:* +61 3 9885 8500 *also fax; email:* ptcoppens@csi.com.

Melbourne Symphony Orchestra (96). GPO Box 9994, Melbourne, Vic 3001, Australia *tel:* +61 3 9626 1110 *fax:* +61 3 9626 1101 *email:* info@mso.com.au. Hiroyuki Iwaki, conductor laureate; Marcus Stenz, chief conductor; Trevor Green, managing director.

Queensland Symphony Orchestra (71). GPO Box 9994, Brisbane, Queensland 4001, Australia *tel:* +61 7 3377 5000 *fax:* +61 7 3377 5001 *email:* qso@qso.com.au. Rodney Jacobson, acting general manager; Muhai Tang, principal conductor; Alan Smith, concert master.

State Orchestra of Victoria (69). 100 St Kilda Rd, Melbourne, Vic 3004, Australia *tel:* +61 3 9281 8279 *fax:* +61 3 9281 8079. Peter Garnick, admin; Stephen Moschner, acting orchestra manager.

Sydney Symphony Orchestra (106). GPO Box 4972, Sydney, NSW 2001, Australia *tel:* +61 2 9334 4644 *fax:* +61 2 9334 4646 *email:* symphony@sso.com.au. Mary Vallentine, managing director; Edo de Waart, chief conductor and artistic director; Mary Jo Capps, director of development; Luke Shaw, orchestra manager; Luke Nestorowicz, director of marketing.

Symphony Australia. GPO Box 9994, Sydney NSW 2001, Australia *tel:* +61 2 9333 1651 *fax:* +61 2 9333 1678 *email:* info@symphony.net.au. Derek Watt, managing director.

Tasmanian Symphony Orchestra (47). GPO Box 9994, Hobart, Tas 7001, Australia *tel:* +61 03 6235 3646 *fax:* +61 03 6235 3651 *email:* tso@tso.com.au. Julie Warn, general manager; David Porcelijn, chief conductor and artistic director.

West Australian Symphony Orchestra (90). GPO Box 9994, Perth, WA 6001, Australia *tel:* +61 8 9326 0011 *fax:* +61 8 9326 0099 *email:* waso@waso.com.au. Rod Lillis, managing director; N Kegie, general manager and artistic admin; E Saunders, general manager: development; M Lekias, general manager: marketing; Vladimir Verbitsky, conductor laureate.

Austria

Austrian Hungarian Haydn Orchestra. Raffaelgasse 20/1/32, A-1200 Wien, Austria *tel:* +43 1 334 6356 *also fax.* Adam Fischer, director.

The Haydn Academy. Wiener Str 14, A-2100 Korneuburg, Austria *tel:* +43 22 627 2662 *also fax.* Anton Gabmayer, director.

Haydn Sinfonietta Wien (45). Bossigasse 76, A-1130 Vienna, Austria *tel:* +43 1 877 5208 *fax:* +43 1 876 462317 *email:* haydn_sinfonietta@netway.at. Manfred Huss, music director.

Mozarteum Orchester (91). Erzbischof-Gebhard Str 10, A-5020 Salzburg, Austria *tel:* +43 66 284 3571 *fax:* +43 66 284 357123. Hubert Soudant, music director; Mag. Erwin Niese, financial director.

Symphonieorchester Vorarlberg/Camerata Bregenz (90). Römerstr 15, A-6900 Bregenz, Austria *tel:* +43 55 744 3447 *fax:* +43 55 744 3448. Christoph Eberle, chief conductor; Bertram Grass, president; Michael Löbl, manager.

Vienna Chamber Orchestra (30-40). Schachnerstr 27, A-1220 Wien, Austria *tel:* +43 1 203 6357 *fax:* +43 1 203 7483 *email:* buchmann@m.xpoint.at. Christian Buchmann, general manager.

Vienna Mozart Orchestra (30). Brucknerstr 4, A-1040 Wien, Austria *tel:* +43 1 505 77660 *fax:* +43 1 505 9720 *email:* concerts@mozart.co.at. Gerald Grünbacher, director, international tours and sales; Manuel Hernandez-Silva, Konrad Leitner, principal conductors.

Wiener Philharmoniker (131). Bösendorferstr 12, A-1010 Wien, Austria *tel:* +43 1 505 6525. Clemens Hellsberg, president; Peter Pecha, general manager.

Wiener Symphoniker (127). Lehágasse 11/ Stg 2, A-1060 Wien, Austria *tel:* +43 1 589 79 *fax:* +43 1 589 7954 *email:* office@wiener-symphoniker.at. Rainer Bischof, general secretary; Vladimir Fedosejev, chief conductor.

Belgium

Collegium Instrumentale Brugense (15-30). Vijversdreef 96, B-8310 Bruges, Belgium *tel:* +32 5 035 3717 *fax:* +32 5 036 2717. Lieve Geerolf, admin; Patrick Peire, music director.

Orchestre National de Belgique (90). Ravenstein Galery 3 Box 10, B-1000 Bruxelles, Belgium *tel:* +32 2 552 0460 *fax:* +32 2 552 0468. Albert Wastiaux, general manager; Gilles Ledure, production; Yuri Simonov, music director.

Orchestre Philharmonique de Liège et de la Communauté Française (94). Rue Forgeur 11, B-4000 Liège, Belgium *tel:* +32 4 223 6360 *fax:* +32 4 223 7065 *email:* opl@skynet.be. Pierre Bartholomée, conductor and artistic manager; Paul-Emile Mottard, manager; Michael Stockhem, concerts manager; Georges Viatour, financial manager.

Orchestre Symphonique de la Monnaie (96). Rue Leopold 4, B-1000 Bruxelles, Belgium *tel:* +32 2 229 1218 *fax:* +32 2 229 1386. Ingrid De Backer, orchestra manager; Antonio Pappano, music director.

Royal Philharmonic Orchestra of Flanders (90). Braziliestraat 15, B-2000 Antwerp 1, Belgium *tel:* +32 3 213 5408 *fax:* +32 3 213 5400 *email:* admin@kfovv. Luc Vanackere, manager; Philippe Herreweghe, music director.

Symphony Orchestra of Flanders (65). Albrecht Rodenbachstraat 44, B-8020 Oostkamp (Brugge), Belgium *tel:* +32 50 84 0587 *fax:* +32 50 84 0687. Dirk Coutigny, general manager; Filip Decruynaere, PR officer; Katrijn De Meyer, accountant; Geert Stubbe, production leader; David Angus, principal conductor.

Brazil

Orquestra Filarmônica do Rio de Janeiro (80). Rua das Marrecas 25, Sala 901, Centro 20031-040 Rio de Janeiro, Brazil *tel:* +55 21 240 7354 *fax:* +55 21 262 4269. Florentino Dias, music director and conductor; Regina Helena Macedo, manager.

Orquestra Sinfônica Brasileira (85). Av Rio Branco 135, Rm 916-920, Rio de Janeiro RJ 20040-006, Brazil *tel:* +55 21 509 5842/252 6330/508 9592 *fax:* +55 21 242 5754. Carlos Alvim Corréa, general manager; Sergio Nepomuceno, admin manager.

Orquestra Sinfônica de Ribeirão Preto *tel:* +55 16 610 8932 *also fax; email:* osrp@artonline.com.br.

Bulgaria

Sofia Philharmonic Orchestra (115). 1 Benkovski Str, BG-1000 Sofia, Bulgaria *tel:* +359 2 883197/883195 *fax:* +359 2 874072 *email:* Sofiaphil@ibn.bg. Emil Tabakov, music director and principal conductor; Bedros Papazian, executive director.

Vratza State Philharmonic Orchestra (55). 1 Christo Botev Square, BG-3000 Vratza, Bulgaria *tel:* +359 9 223434/223261 *fax:* +359 9 260053 *email:* vratzaphil@mbox.digsys.bg. Dimitar Panov, director; Valeri Vatchev, chief conductor.

Canada

Calgary Philharmonic Orchestra (64). 205 Eighth Ave SE, Calgary, Alta T2G 0K9, Canada *tel:* +1 403 571 0270 *fax:* +1 403 294 7424. Hans Graf, music director; Leonard Stone, executive director.

Edmonton Symphony Orchestra (56). Winspear Centre, 9720-102 Avenue NW, Edmonton, AB T5J 4B2, Canada *tel:* +1 780 428 1108 *fax:* +1 780 425 0167 *email:* eso@oanet.com. Grzegorz Nowak, music director; John David Sterne, CEO; Tim Watson, director of artisic operations.

Kingston Symphony (55). PO Box 1616, Kingston, Ont K7L 5C8, Canada *tel:* +1 613 546 9729 *fax:* +1 613 546 8580. Katherine Carleton, general manager; Glen Fast, music director.

Kitchener-Waterloo Symphony (52). Centre in the Square, 101 Queen St, N Kitchener, Ont N2H 6P7, Canada *tel:* +1 519 745 4711 *fax:* +1 519 745 4474. Chosei Komatsu, music director/conductor.

Montréal Chamber Orchestra (14-32). 800 Blvd René-Lévesque O, Suite 450, Montréal, QC H3B 1X9, Canada *tel:* +1 514 871 1224 *fax:* +1 514 871 8967. Wanda Kaluzny, conductor and artistic director; Betty Wallbank, treasurer and finance administrator; Diane Schrenk, president of the board of governors; Carmelita Sideco, president of the board of directors; Evanthia Paraskevopoulos, executive administrator.

Montréal Symphony Orchestra. 85 Ste-Catherine W Suite 900, Montréal, PQ H2X 3P4, Canada *tel:* +1 514 842 3402 *fax:* +1 514 842 0728.

National Arts Centre Orchestra of Canada (46). PO Box 1534, Station B, Ottawa, Ont K1P 5W1, Canada *tel:* +1 613 996 5051 *fax:* +1 613 943 1400. Pinchas Zukerman, music director; Mario Bernardi, conductor laureate; Franz-Paul Decker, principal guest conductor; Christopher Deacon, orchestra managing director.

Newfoundland Symphony Orchestra (55). Arts and Culture Centre, PO Box 1854, Prince Philip Dr, St John's, NF A1C 5P9, Canada *tel:* +1 709 753 6492 *fax:* +1 709 753 0561. Peter Gardner, general and artistic director; Marc David, principal conductor; Sandra Pope, admin assistant; Pamela Murray, income and development manager; Valerie Holden, print and media manager and librarian.

Niagara Symphony (55). 73 Ontario St, Unit 104, St Catharines, Ont L2R 5J5, Canada *tel:* +1 905 687 4993 *fax:* +1 905 687 1149. Michael Reason, music director and principal conductor; Laura Tilley, director of development.

Orchestra London Canada Inc (44). Centennial Hall, 520 Wellington St, London, Ont N6A 3R1, Canada *tel:* +1 519 679 8558 *fax:* +1 519 679 8914. John David Sterne, executive director; Mark Laycock, music director.

Ottawa Symphony Orchestra (90). 501-1390 Prince of Wales Dr, Ottawa, Ont K2C 3N6, Canada *tel:* +1 613 224 4982 *also fax*. Marian Pickering, managing director; David Currie, music director.

Toronto Symphony Orchestra (99). Suite 550, 212 King St West, Toronto, Ont M5H 1K5, Canada *tel:* +1 416 593 7769 *fax:* +1 416 593 6788. Jukka-Pekka Saraste, music director; Loie Fallis, artistic admin.

Vancouver Symphony (73). 601 Smithe St, Vancouver BC V6B 5G1, Canada *tel:* +1 604 684 9100 *fax:* +1 604 684 9264. Larry Blackman, personnel manager; Sergiu Comissiona, music director; Michael Aze, production director.

Victoria Symphony (50). 846 Broughton St, Victoria, BC V8W 1E4, Canada *tel:* +1 604 385 9771 *fax:* +1 604 385 7767. C Stephen Smith, general manager; Lynn Mesher, admin assistant; Peter McCoppin, music director; Brian Jackson, principal Pops conductor; Kees Bakels, principal guest conductor.

Winnipeg Symphony Orchestra (67). 101 555 Main St, Winnipeg, MB R3B 1C3, Canada *tel:* +1 204 949 3950 *fax:* +1 204 956 4271. Bramwell Tovey, artistic director; Howard Jang, executive director; Charles D'Amours, senior development and marketing director; Annemarie Petrov, music admin and operations director; Aileen White, director of marketing and sales.

Chile

Santiago Philharmonic Orchestra (95). PO Box 18, San Antonio 149, Santiago, Chile *tel:* +56 2 638 1515 *fax:* +56 2 633 7214. Andrés Pinto, admin director.

China

Shanghai Symphony Orchestra (90). 105 Hunan Lu, Shanghai 200031, China *tel:* +86 21 6433 3752 *also fax*. Chen Xieyang, music director and principal conductor; Chen Guangxian, general manager; Cai Zhong, personnel manager.

Colombia

Bogotá Philharmonic Orchestra (94). Calle 39 A No 14-57, Aptdo Aéreo 16034, Santa Fé de Bogotá DC, Colombia *tel:* +57 1 288 3466/4453 *fax:* +57 1 288 3162/340 6643 *email:* filarmonicabogota@iname.com. María Cristina Sánchez H, executive manager; Francisco Rettig, chief conductor; Eduardo Carrizosa, assistant conductor; Marco Tulio Chacin, administration manager.

Czech Republic

Brno Philharmonic Orchestra (115). Komenského nám 8, CR-602 00 Brno, Czech Republic *tel:* +420 5 4221 2300/8284 *also fax*. Julius Kessner, director; Boris Pác, concert manager; Aldo Ceccato, principal conductor; Caspar Richter, permanent guest conductor; Enoch Zu Guttenberg, guest conductor.

Czech Philharmonic Orchestra (127). Alsovo Nábrezi 12, CR-110 00 Praha 1, Czech Republic *tel:* +420 2 248 93201 *fax:* +420 2 231 9051 *email:* cfsecr@mbox.vol.cz; cfmark@mbox.vol.cz; cforch@mbox.vol.cz. Ing Jiri Kovár, general director; Vladimir Askhkenazy, chief conductor; Petra Drtinova, artistic manager; Eva Sedlakova, marketing manager.

Czech Symphony Orchestra FISYO (73). Trachtova 2/1130, CR-158 00 Praha 5, Czech Republic *tel:* +420 2 684 9379 *also fax*. Jiri Kauders, director.

Janácek Philharmonic Orchestra (102). 28 Ríjna 124, CR-70200 Ostrava, Czech Republic *tel:* +420 69 661 9996/9914 *fax:* +420 69 661 9997. Jan Haliska, director; Christian Arming, chief conductor.

North Czech Philharmonic Orchestra Teplice (70). U Zámku 1, CR-415 28 Teplice, Czech Republic *tel:* +420 417 29463 *fax:* +420 417 533103 *email:* sev.filharmonie@iol.cz. Jirí Malina, general manager; Charles Olivieri-Munroe, principal conductor.

Prague Symphony Orchestra (110). Námestí Republiky 5, Obecní Dum, CR-110 00 Praha 1, Czech Republic *tel:* +420 2 231 5981/2200 2425 *fax:* +420 2 231 0784 *email:* fok@login.cz. Roman Belor, managing director; Peter Polívka, orchestra manager; Libor Pesek, principal guest conductor; Tadeusz Strugala, permanent guest conductor.

Radio Symphony Orchestra Pilsen (50). Nam Miru 10, CR-320 70 Plzen, Czech Republic *tel:* +420 1 927 2254 *also fax*. Jan Motlík, manager; Jan Chalupecky, conductor; Milos Chaloupka, production.

Denmark

Aalborg Symphony Orchestra (65). Kjellerupsgade 14, DK-9000 Aalborg, Denmark *tel:* +45 98 131955 *fax:* +45 98 130378 *email:* symfoni@pip.dknet.dk. Owain Arwel Hughes, chief conductor.

Aarhus Symfoniorkester (72). Musikhuset, Thomas Jensens Alle, DK-Aarhus C, Denmark *tel:* +45 89 318280 *fax:* +45 86 127466 *email:* aso@post3.tele.dk. Leif Balthzersen, general and artistic director; James Loughran, chief conductor.

Copenhagen Philharmonic Orchestra (74). Ny Kongensgade 13, DK-1472 Kobenhavn K, Denmark *tel:* +45 33 911199 *fax:* +45 33 149034 *email:* cph.phil@get2net.dk. Tomas Vitek, manager; Heinrich Schiff, chief conductor; Giordano Bellincampi, guest conductor.

Danish National Radio Symphony Orchestra (99). Radiohuset, Rosenorns Allé 22, DK-1999 Frederiksberg C, Denmark *tel:* +45 35 203040 *fax:* +45 35 206121 *email:* ron@dr.dk. Per Erik Veng, general manager and artistic director; Gerd Albrecht, chief conductor; Yuri Temirkanov, Michael Schønwandt, principal guest conductors.

Det Kongelige Kapel (104). Postboks 2185, DK-1017 Kobenhavn K, Denmark *tel:* +45 33 696702 *fax:* +45 33 696767. Konges Nytorv; Klas Sjöblom, assistant opera director; Paavo Berglund, chief conductor; Dietfried Bernet, chief guest conductor.

Odense Symfoniorkester (73). Odense Koncerthus, Claus Bergs Gade 9, DK-5000 Odense, Denmark *tel:* +45 66 129357 *fax:* +45 65 910047 *email:* orchestra@odensesymfoni.dk. Jan Wagner, principal conductor; Per Holst, general manager; Marianne Granvig, chief of public relations; Asger Bondo, librarian.

Randers Chamber Orchestra (10-35). Vaerket, Mariagervej 6, DK-8900 Randers, Denmark *tel:* +45 86 412833 *fax:* +45 86 412414 *email:* rbo@post3.tele.dk. Bjarne Mørch Jensen, concert admin; David Riddell, principal conductor and managing director.

Royal Danish Orchestra (99). The Royal Theatre, Tordenskjoldsgade 8, Postboks 2185, DK-1017 Copenhagen, Denmark *tel:* +45 33 696701 *fax:* +45 33 696767 *email:* kgl-teat@inet.uni-c.dk. Elaine Padmore, artistic director; Klas Sjöblom, orchestra manager; Paavo Berglund, principal conductor.

Sønderjyllands Symfoniorkester (64). Skovvej 16, DK-6400 Sonderborg, Denmark *tel:* +45 74 426161 *fax:* +45 74 426106 *email:* lvsb@sonderjyllands-symfoniorkester.

Egypt

Cairo Symphony Orchestra (101). c/o Egyptian Opera House, Geziro, Cairo, Egypt *tel:* +202 342 0601/02/03; +202 339 8157 *fax:* +202 342 0599; +202 339 8186 *email:* opera@frcu.eun.eg. Ahmed Elsaedi, music director and principal conductor; Farouk El Masry, assistant general manager; Ingy Abdel Aziz, executive secretary; Ossama Abdallah, PR; Khaled Abdel-Halim, publicity officer.

Estonia

Estonian National Opera Symphony Orchestra (97). Estonia Ave 4, EE-10148 Tallinn, Estonia *tel:* +372 6 260201 *fax:* +372 6 313080 *email:* info@opera.ee. Paul Himma, general manager; Paul Mägi, artistic director and chief conductor.

Estonian National Symphony Orchestra (98). Estonia Pst 4, EE-0001 Tallinn, Estonia *tel:* +372 2 446597 *fax:* +372 6 314055 *email:* erso@estpak.ee. Ville-Markus Kell, managing director; Arvo Volmer, chief conductor.

Foto: Jörg Hejkal
Architekten: Peter Busmann - Godfrid Haberer BAUTURM Köln

Finland

Finnish Radio Symphony Orchestra (98). PO Box 14, FIN-00024 YLE, Finland *tel:* +358 9 148 04366 *fax:* +358 9 148 03551 *email:* helena.hiilivieta@yle.fi. Jukka-Pekka Saraste, principal conductor; Sakari Oramo, co-principal conductor; Helena Hiilivirta, manager.

Helsinki Philharmonic Orchestra (98). Finlandia Hall, Karamzinikatu 4, FIN-00100 Helsinki, Finland *tel:* +358 9 40241 *fax:* +358 9 406484 *email:* helsinki.philharmonic@fin.hel.fi. Leif Segerstam, chief conductor; Helena Ahonen, general manager.

Tampere Philharmonic Orchestra (83). Yliopistonkatu 55, FIN-33100 Tampere, Finland *tel:* +358 3 243 4411 *fax:* +358 3 243 4400 *email:* orchestra@tampere.fi. Eri Klas, artistic director; Jouni Kaipainen, composer-in-residence; Maritta Hirvonen, general manager.

Vaasa City Orchestra. Vaasanp 12, FN-65100 Vaasa, Finland *tel:* +358 6 325 3761.

France

Orchestre des Champs Elysées (45-70). La Chapelle Royale, 10 Rue Coquillière, F-75001 Paris, France *tel:* +33 1 40 26 58 00 *fax:* +33 1 40 26 38 37 *email:* info@lachappelleroyale.com. Philippe Herreweghe, music director; Stephan Maciejewski, artistic adviser; Nicolas Droin, admin; Rachel Dale, sales.

Orchestre des Concerts Lamoureux (96). 252 Rue du Faubourg Saint Honoré, F-75008 Paris, France *tel:* +33 1 45 63 44 34/60 62 *fax:* +33 1 45 62 05 41. Annie Foultier, admin; Lionel Evans, president; Frédéric Aladjem, general secretary.

Orchestre National Bordeaux-Aquitaine (117). BP 95, F-33025 Bordeaux Cédex, France *tel:* + 33 56 00 84 30; +33 56 48 30 30 (box office) *fax:* +33 56 44 64 85. Thierry Fouquer, general director; Hans Graf, music director.

Orchestre National de France (118). 116 Av du Président Kennedy, F-75786 Paris, Cédex 16, France *tel:* +33 1 42 30 26 03 *fax:* +33 1 42 30 43 33. Charles Dutoit, music director; Hélène Montussac, press and PR.

Orchestre National de Lille (100). 30 Place Mendès France, BP 119, F-59027 Lille Cédex, France *tel:* +33 3 20 12 82 40 *fax:* +33 3 20 78 29 10. Jacqueline Brochen, admin director; Jean-Claude Casadesus, director and conductor.

Orchestre National de Lyon (102). 82 Rue de Bonnel, F-69431 Lyon Cédex 03, France *tel:* +33 4 78 95 95 00 *fax:* +33 4 78 60 13 08. Patrice Armengau, general director; Emmanuel Krivine, music director; David Robertson, music director (from September 2000).

Orchestre de Paris (114). Salle Pleyel, 252 Rue du Faubourg St Honoré, F-75008 Paris, France *tel:* +33 1 45 61 65 60 *fax:* +33 1 42 89 24 49. Michel Prada, president; Georges-François Hirsch, general director; Hewé Burckel de Tell.

Orchestre Philharmonique de Montpelier Languedoc-Roussillon (91). Le Corum, BP 9056, F-34041 Montpelier, France *tel:* +33 67 61 67 21 *fax:* +33 67 61 67 20. Friedemann Layer, music director; Jany Macaby, admin director; René Koering, general director.

Orchestre Philharmonique des Pays de Loire (102). Maison des Arts, 25 Av Montaigne, F-49000 Angers, France *tel:* +33 2 41 24 11 24 *fax:* +33 2 41 87 80 52. Hubert Soudant, music director; Patrice Chéreau, president.

Orchestre Philharmonique de Radio-France (138). 116 Av du Président Kennedy, F-75220 Paris Cédex 16, France *tel:* +33 1 42 30 36 30 *fax:* +33 1 42 30 47 48. Marek Janowski, music director; Eric Montalbetti, artistic delegate.

Orchestre Philharmonique de Strasbourg (Orchestre National) (112). Place de Bordeaux, F-67000 Strasbourg, France *tel:* +33 03 88 15 09 00 *fax:* +33 03 88 15 09 01. Albert Moritz, administration director; Jan Latham-Koenig, music director.

Orchestre Symphonique et Lyrique de Nancy (66). 1 Rue Sainte Catherine, F-54000 Nancy, France *tel:* +33 83 85 33 20 *fax:* +33 83 85 30 66. Jean-Marie Blanchard, general admin; Christopher Bezzone, admin.

Philharmonie de Lorraine (70). 25 Av Robert Schuman, F-57000 Metz, France *tel:* +33 87 55 12 02 *fax:* +33 87 65 69 36. Jacqus Lacombe, music director; Christine Raffin, president.

Republic of Georgia

Chamber Orchestra (21). 48/21 Chavchavadze St, Tbilisi, Republic of Georgia *tel:* +995 32 231683 *fax:* +995 32 952761. Vadim Shubladze, director and conductor; Manana Ivardava, manager.

Germany

Bamberger Symphoniker (112). Mußstr 1, D-96047 Bamberg, Germany *tel:* +49 951 964 7100 *fax:* +49 951 964 7123. Christian Schmölder, business manager; Horst Stein, conductor laureate; Ingo Metzmacher, principal guest conductor.

Bayerisches Staatsorchester (140). Nationaltheater, Max-Joseph-Platz 2, D-80539 München, Germany *tel:* +49 892 185 1000 *fax:* +49 892 185 1003. Peter Jonas, general director; Zubin Mehta, general music director; Roland Felber, managing director; Annette Zühlke, orchestral director; Aldo Volpini, orchestra chairman.

Berlin Philharmonic Orchestra (125). Herbert von Karajan Str, D-10785 Berlin, Germany *tel:* +49 30 254880 *fax:* +49 30 261 4887. Claudio Abbado, music director; Elmar Weingarten, general manager; Helge Grünewald, press and PR.

Dresden Philharmonic (119). Postfach 120424, Kulturplast Am Altmarkt, D-01005 Dresden, Germany *tel:* +49 351 486 6282 *fax:* +49 351 486 6283 *email:* contact@dresdnerphilharmonie.de. Olivier von Winterstein, manager; Marek Janowski, music director (from 2001); Juri Temirkanow, principal guest conductor; Kurt Masur, conductor laureate.

Düsseldorf Symphonic Orchestra (130). Ehrenhof 1, Tonhalle, D-40479 Düsseldorf, Germany *tel:* +49 211 899 3606 *fax:* +49 211 892 9143. Salvador Mas Conde, music director; Elisabeth von Leliwa, press; Thomas Stührk, orchestra manager.

Hamburg Symphony Orchestra (67). Dammtorwall 46, D-20355 Hamburg, Germany *tel:* +49 40 344851 *fax:* +49 40 353788. Miguel Gómez-Martínez, principal conductor; Peter Dannenberg, general manager.

Handelfestspielorchester (104). Opernhaus Halle, Postfach 110554, D-06019 Halle (Saale), Germany *tel:* +49 345 511 0300 *fax:* +49 345 511 0303 *email:* opernhaus@halle.de. Klaus Froboese, general manager; Reinhard Popp, director; Roger Epple, general music director.

Kölner Rundfunk-Sinfonie-Orchester (118). Westdeutscher Rundfunk, D-50600 Köln, Germany *tel:* +49 221 220 2146 *fax:* +49 221 220 2945. Semyon Bychkov, principal conductor.

Leipziger Gewandhausorchester (193). Gewandhaus zu Leipzig, Augustusplatz 8, D-04109 Leipzig, Germany *tel:* +49 341 12 700 *fax:* +49 341 12 70200. Herbert Blomstedt, principal conductor, Master of Chapel.

MDR Sinfonieorchester (168). Springerstr 22-24, D-04105 Leipzig, Germany *tel:* +49 341 300 5505 *fax:* +49 341 300 5532. Hubertus Franzen, admin; Manfred Honeck, Fabio Luisi, Marcello Viotti, principal conductors.

Munich Philharmonic Orchestra (130), Kellerstr 4/III, D-81667 München, Germany *tel:* +49 89 4809 8509 *fax:* +49 89 4809 8513 *email:* mphilhar@compuserve.com. Bernd Gellermann, manager; Roswitha Wetz, artistic admin; Peter Meisel, director of PR; Dieter Girstenbrei, head of admin.

New Westphalian Symphonic Orchestra (137). Castroper Str 12c, D-45665 Recklinghausen, Germany *tel:* +49 236 148860 *fax:* +49 236 148 8666. Johannes Wildner, principal conductor; Norbert Thomas, artist manager.

Philharmonisches Orchester der Landeshauptstadt Kiel (76). Rathausplatz 4, D-24103 Kiel, Germany *tel:* +49 431 901 2895/2856/2853 *fax:* +49 431 901 62889. Ulrich Windfuhr, general music director; Gabriele Koschnitzke, orchestra manager.

Philharmonisches Staatsorchester Hamburg (134). Grosse Theaterstr 34, D-20354 Hamburg, Germany *tel:* +49 40 356 8405 *fax:* +49 40 356 8463. Albin Hänseroth, general manager; Ingo Metzmacher, general music director.

Radio-Sinfonie-Orchester Frankfurt (121). Hessischer Rundfunk, Postfach 101001, Bertramstr 8, D-60320 Frankfurt am Main, Germany *tel:* +49 691 552071 *fax:* +49 691 552720 *email:* rso-frankfurt@hr-online.de. Hugh Wolff, principal conductor; Medi Gasteiner-Girth, orchestra manager.

Staatskapelle Berlin. Staatsoper Unter den Linden, Unter den Linden 5-7, D-10117 Berlin, Germany *tel:* +49 30 203540 (operator); +49 30 2035 4555 (box office) *fax:* +49 30 2035 4206 (admin); +49 30 2035 4483 (box office) *email:* contact@staatsoper-berlin.org. Daniel Barenboim, general music director.

Stadt Augsburg Philharmonic Orchestra (70). Postfach 111949, D-86044 Augsburg, Germany *tel:* +49 821 324 4903 *fax:* +49 821 324 4909. Peter Leonard, general music director; Andreas Finke, admin manager.

SWR Radio-Sinfonieorchester Stuttgart (106). D-70150 Stuttgart, Germany *tel:* +49 711 929 2590/2591 *fax:* +49 711 929 4053 *email:* felix.fischer@swr-online.de. Felix Fischer, orchestra manager; Sir Roger Norrington, chief conductor.

Greece

La Camerata - Orchestra of the Friends of Music (24). Vas Sofias and Kokkali St, 11521 Athens, Greece *tel:* +30 1 728 2341/2 *fax:* +30 1 725 0136 *email:* kamerata@admin.megaron.gr. Emmanuel Hadjiandreou, admin director; Alexander Myrat, artistic director; Julie Theodoropoulou, secretary.

Orchestra of Colours (90). 18 Alexandrou Soutsou, 10671 Athens, Greece *tel:* +30 1 362 8074/8819/8589 *fax:* +30 1 362 1477. George Kouroupos, artistic director; Vicky Galatou, director of admin and production; Miltos Logiades, conductor.

Orchestra of the Greek National Opera (70). 18a Charilaou Trikoupi St, 10679 Athens, Greece *tel:* +30 1 360 0180 *fax:* +30 1 364 8309. Spyros Evangelatus, president; Lukas Karytinos, artistic director; Ilias Vaudouris, chief conductor.

Thessaloniki State Symphony Orchestra (120). Moni Lazariston, Kolokotroni 21, 564 30 Thessaloniki, Greece *tel:* +30 31 602970/606524 *fax:* +30 31 604854. Leonidas Kavakos, artistic director.

Hong Kong

Hong Kong Philharmonic Orchestra (93). Level 8, Administration Building, Hong Kong Cultural Centre, 10 Salisbury Rd, Kowloon, Hong Kong *tel:* +852 2721 2030 *fax:* +852 2311 6229 *email:* webmaster@hkpo.com. David Atherton, music director; Edith Lei, general manager.

Pan Asia Symphony Orchestra (60-80). 1/F Wah Chi Building, 292 Temple St, Kowloon, Hong Kong *tel:* +852 2317 0681 *fax:* +852 2317 1360 *email:* jadeangy@hotmail.com. Yip Wai-Hong, music director; Jade Ang, co-ordinator.

Hungary

Budapest Concert Orchestra MAV (98). Muzeum utca 11, H-1088 Budapest, Hungary *tel:* +36 1 138 2664 *fax:* +36 1 138 4085. Gabor Fenyö, admin director; Tamás Gál, principal conductor.

Budapest Philharmonic Orchestra (152). Andrássy út 22, H-1061 Budapest, Hungary *tel:* +36 1 3319 478 *also fax; email:* radotti@mail.matav.hu. Béla Melis, president.

Budapest Symphony Orchestra (102). Bródy Sándor utca 5-7, H-1088 Budapest, Hungary *tel:* +36 1 328 8326/7161 *fax:* +36 1 328 7161 *email:* kovacsga@bartok.radio.hu. János Szirányi, director; Apor Héthy, managing director; Tamás Vásáry, artistic director.

Hungarian National Philharmonic Orchestra (118). Vörösmarty tér 1, H-1051 Budapest, Hungary *tel:* +36 1 429 1090 *fax:* +36 1 429 1099 *email:* natphilharm@mail.matav.hu. Zoltán Kocsis, music director; Ken-Ichiro Kobayashi, conductor laureate; Géza Kovács, managing director.

MATAV Hungarian Symphony Orchestra (86). 10-12 Páva utca, H-1094 Budapest, Hungary *tel:* +36 1 215 5770/5358 *fax:* +36 1 215 5462 *email:* orchestra@mail.matav.hu. Andras Ligeti, music director; Gregory Laczko Toth, managing director.

Iceland

Iceland Symphony Orchestra (73). Háskólabió, Hagatorg, PO Box 7052, IS-127 Reykjavik, Iceland *tel:* +354 562 2255 *fax:* +354 562 4475 *email:* sinfonia@sinfonia.is. Throstur Olafsson, general manager; Helga Haukdóttir, concert manager; Rico Saccani, conductor and music director.

Republic of Ireland

National Symphony Orchestra of Ireland (88+). The Music Department, Office Block, RTÉ, Donnybrook, Dublin 4, Republic of Ireland *tel:* +353 1 208 2530 *fax:* +353 1 208 2160. Niall Doyle, director of music; Martyn Westerman, general manager; Alexander Anissimov, principal conductor; Gerhard Markson, principal guest conductor; Claire Meehan, concerts manager.

RTÉ Concert Orchestra (44+). The Music Dept, Office Block, RTÉ, Donnybrook, Dublin 4, Republic of Ireland *tel:* +353 1 208 2142 *fax:* +353 1 208 3340 *email:* elliss@rte.ie. Niall Doyle, director of music; Gareth Hudson, executive producer; Proinnsías Ó Duinn, principal conductor; Sam Ellis, orchestra manager; Claire Meehan, concerts manager.

Israel

Haifa Symphony Orchestra (75). PO Box 6746, 18 Derekh Hayam, 37171 Haifa, Israel *tel:* +972 4 836 3131 *fax:* +972 4 837 6355 *email:* hso@netvision.net.il. Stanley Sperber, conductor and music director; Leor Segal, director general.

Israel Chamber Orchestra (35). Amot Mishpat House, 8 Shaul Ha'melech Blvd, Tel Aviv 64733, Israel *tel:* +972 3 696 1167 *fax:* +972 3 691 0104. Idith Zvi, director general; Philippe Entremont, conductor laureate; Salvador Mas Conde, music director.

Italy

Orchestra della Toscana (ORT) (45). Via Ghibellina 101, I-50122 Firenze, Italy *tel:* +39 055 280670/281993 *fax:* +39 055 281640 *email:* ort@dada.it. Giorgio Battistelli, artistic director; Giorgio van Straten, president.

Orchestra Filarmonica Marchigiana (50-70). Vicolo Aranci 2, I-60121 Ancona, Italy *tel:* +39 071 206168 *fax:* +39 071 206730. Gustav Kuhn, artistic director; Giuliano Gasparini, president.

Orchestra Sinfonica Nazionale della RAI (117). Piazza Fratelli Rossaro 15, I-10124 Torino, Italy *tel:* +39 011 4961/810 4949 *fax:* +39 011 817 7410/888300. Sergio Sablich, artistic director; Paolo Robotti, assistant artistic director; Maria Sciavolino, orchestra manager; Cesare Dapino, general manager; Eliahu Inbal, principal conductor; Jeffrey Tate, principal guest conductor.

Rome Philharmonic Orchestra. c/o IUMA Management, Via E. Filiberto 125, I-00185 Roma *tel:* +39 06 7720 1524 *fax:* +39 06 7720 5607 *email:* cfcatena@pelagus.it. Alexander Frey, music director; Chris F Catena, manager; Damiano Capria, admin.

Toscanini Symphony Orchestra (60-100). c/o Fondazione Arturo Toscanini, Via G Tartini 13, I-43100 Parma, Italy *tel:* +39 0521 2741; 274417 (PR); 274421 (general secretary) *fax:* +39 0521 272134 (PR); 785257 *email:* fondazione@toscanini.dsnet.it; dirfond@toscanini.dsnet.it (general manager). Piero Manganoni, chairman; Gianni Baratta, general manager; Patrick Fournillier, music director; Enzo Restagno, artistic adviser.

Japan

Hiroshima Symphony Orchestra (68). Hacchobori 15-10, Naka-ku, Hiroshima 730, Japan *tel:* +81 8 2222 8448 *fax:* +81 8 2222 8447 *email:* hirokyo@hiroshima-cdas.or.jp. Hideto Ohno, managing director; Kazuyoshi Akiyaima, principal conductor.

Japan Philharmonic Symphony Orchestra (83). 1-6-1 Umezato, Suginami-ku, Tokyo 166, Japan *tel:* +81 3 5378 6311 *fax:* +81 3 5378 6161 *email:* j-phil@vcom.or.jp. Kobayashi Ken-ichiro, chief conductor; Hirokami Jun-ichi, principal conductor; Tanabe Minoru, executive director.

Kyoto Symphony Orchestra (87). 103 Izumoji Tatemoto-cho, Kita-ku, Kyoto 603-8134, Japan *tel:* +81 75 222 0331 *fax:* +81 75 222 0332. Uwe Mund, music director; Naoto Otomo, principal conductor; Shunji Kitayama, manager; Junzo Matsunaga, assistant manager; Fumio Kusaka, intendant.

New Japan Philharmonic (99). Sumida Triphony Hall 7 Fl, 1-2-3 Kinshi, Sumida-ku, Tokyo 130-0013, Japan *tel:* +81 3 5610 3820 *fax:* +81 3 5610 3825. Senji Mori, managing director.

NHK Symphony Orchestra (111). 2-16 49 Takanawa, Minato-ku, Tokyo 108-0074, Japan *tel:* +81 3 5793 8111 *fax:* +81 3 3443 0278 *email:* nhksym@blue.ocn.ne.jp. Ken Soga, chairman; Takeshi Hara, deputy chairman.

Osaka Philharmonic Orchestra (95). 1-1-44 Kishinosato, Nishinari-ku, Osaka 557-0041, Japan *tel:* +81 6 656 7711 *fax:* +81 6 656 7714. Takashi Asahina, general music director; Shoji Onodera, secretary general.

Sendai Philharmonic Orchestra (71). 1-3-9 Nishikicho, Aoba-ku, Sendai 980-0012, Japan *tel:* +81 2 2225 3934 *fax:* +81 2 2225 4238. Yuzo Toyama, music director; Saneyuki Yoshi, general manager.

Tokyo Metropolitan Symphony Orchestra (101). c/o Bunka Kaikan, 5-45 Ueno Koen Taito-ku, Tokyo 110-0007, Japan *tel:* +81 3 3822 0727 *fax:* +81 3 3822 0729. Katsumoto Iyama, managing director; Akira Imamura, general manager; Gary Bertini, music director; Jean Fournet, honorary conductor; Eliahu Inbal, Kazuhiro Koizumi, guest conductors.

Korea

Pusan Philharmonic Orchestra (89-98). 848-4 Daeyon 4 Dong, Nam-gu, Pusan, Korea *tel:* +82 51 625 8130 *fax:* +82 51 625 8138. Sung Kwak, music director; Won-Chul Park, general manager.

Latvia

Latvian National Symphony Orchestra (104). Amatu iela 6, LV-1664 Riga, Latvia *tel:* +371 722 9537 *fax:* +371 722 4997 *email:* lnso@mail.bkc.lv. Ilona Brege, managing director; Terje Mikkelsen, chief conductor and artistic director; Janis Kudins, manager of Concert Hall.

Liepaja Symphony Orchestra (73). Graudu 50, LV-3401 Liepaja, Latvia *tel:* +371 342 5538; +371 342 5588 *fax:* +371 348 1478 *email:* lsovija@mail.anet.lv. Imants Resnis, artistic director and chief conductor; Vija Feldmane, manager.

Lithuania

Lithuanian National Symphony Orchestra (101). Ausros Vartu 5, 2001 Vilnius, Lithuania *tel:* +370 2 627047 *fax:* +370 2 622859. Juozas Domarkas, artistic director and chief conductor; Gintautas Kevisas, general director; Eugenijus Janutenas, manager.

Lithuanian State Symphony Orchestra (96). Zygimantu 6, LT-2600 Vilnius, Lithuania *tel:* +370 2 628127 *fax:* +370 2 220966 *email:* lvso@iti.lt. Gintaras Rinkevicius, chief conductor and artistic director; Arunas Simaska, managing director; Jonas Vilimas, deputy managing director.

Luxembourg

Orchestre Philharmonique du Luxembourg (80). BP 2243, Villa Louvigny, L-1022, Luxembourg *tel:* +352 22 990 1205 *fax:* +352 22 9998 *email:* jmauroy@opl.lu; ofrank@opl.lu. Jacques Mauroy, Olivier Frank, managers; David Shallon, chief conductor.

Malaysia

Malaysian Philharmonic Orchestra (105). Level Two, Tower Two, Petronas Twin Towers, Kuala Lumpur City Centre, 50088 Kuala Lumpur, Malaysia *tel:* +603 581 3208 *fax:* +603 581 3216 *email:* johndc@petronas.com.my; sallr@petronas.com.my. Kees Bakels, music director; Chean See Ooi, resident conductor; John A Duffy, general manager; Sally Rogers, orchestra admin.

Mexico

Filarmónica de la Ciudad de México (98). Periférico Sur 5141, Col Isidro Fabela, 14030 México DF, Mexico *tel:* +52 905 606 8933 *fax:* +52 905 606 8401. Jorge Mester, conductor; José Jacinto, general manager.

National Symphony Orchestra of Mexico (120). Regina 52, Centro, 06080 Mexico DF, México *tel:* +52 5 709 8118 *fax:* +52 5 709 3533. Enrique Arturo Diemecke, music director; Javier Cuétara-Priede, general manager; Eduardo Neri-Chaires, artistic manager; Benito Alcocer, artistic manager.

State of Mexico Symphony Orchestra (86). Plaza Fray Andrés de Castro, Edif C Primer Piso, 50000 Toluca, Edo de Mexico *tel:* +52 7 244 5219 *fax:* +52 7 245 6216. Enrique Batiz, music director; Alfredo Higuera Hernandez, admin director.

Moldova

Symphony Orchestra of the National Philharmonic of Moldova (75). 78 Mitropolitul Varlaam Str, 2012 Chisinau, Moldova *tel:* +373 2 224016 *fax:* +373 2 228293. Ion Josan, director general; Ion Uncu, vice-director; Valentin Doni, chief conductor and artistic director; Marc Loznic, music secretary, management.

Netherlands

Barokorkest van de Nederlandse Bachvereniging (20). Postbus 12017, NL-3501 AA Utrecht, Netherlands *tel:* +31 30 252 4010 *fax:* +31 30 251 1639. Maria Hansen, managing director; Jos van Veldhoven, artistic director.

Brabant Philharmonic Orchestra (88). J Van Lieshoutstraat 5, NL-5611 EE Eindhoven, Netherlands *tel:* +31 40 265 5699 *fax:* +31 40 246 3459. Marc Soustrot, chief conductor; Jaap Van Zweden, principal guest conductor; Detlev Weeks, managing director.

The Gelders Orchestra (94). Velperbuitensingel 12, PO Box 1180, NL-6801 BD Arnhem, Netherlands *tel:* +31 26 442 2632 *fax:* +31 26 443 9966. Lawrence Renes, principal conductor; Jan Taat, manager; Benno Brugmans, PR; Dolf Hofs, deputy manager.

Limburgs Symphony Orchestra/Symphony Orchestra of Maastricht (70). Statenstraat 5, NL-6211 TB Maastricht, Netherlands *tel:* +31 43 350 7000 *fax:* +31 43 350 7025 *email:* info@lso.nl. John Floore, managing director; Junichi Hirokami, chief conductor.

Netherlands Ballet Orchestra (80). Muziektheater, Waterlooplein 22, NL-1011 PG Amsterdam, Netherlands *tel:* +31 20 551 8823 *fax:* +31 20 620 8019 *email:* info@balletorkest.nl. Rob Tijsen, manager; Maurits Haenen, deputy manager; Julia Bastiaanse, planning and education; Thierry Fischer, chief conductor; Jan Pieter Koch, artistic director.

Netherlands Chamber Orchestra/Netherlands Philharmonic Orchestra (140). Beurs van Berlage, Damrak 213, NL-1012 ZH Amsterdam, Netherlands *tel:* +31 20 627 1161 *fax:* +31 20 622 9939 *email:* ro@nedpho.nl. Rob Overman, managing director; Herbert Slegers, artistic manager; Hartmut Haenchen, chief conductor; Philippe Entremont, principal guest conductor.

Netherlands Radio Philharmonic (108). Heuvellaan 33, PO Box 125, NL-1200 AC Hilversum, Netherlands *tel:* +31 35 671 4130 *fax:* +31 35 671 4171. Edo de Waart, music director; Rob Overman, manager.

Noord-Nederlands Orchestra. Palmslag 20, NL-9724 CS Groningen, Netherlands *tel:* +31 50 369 5800 *fax:* +31 50 369 5815 *email:* nno@tref.nl. Jan Geert Vierkant, general manager; Klaas Holtman, PR and marketing.

Noordhollands Philharmonisch Orkest (NPO) (70). Klokhuisplein 2A, NL-2011 HK Haarlem, Netherlands *tel:* +31 23 531 9248 *fax:* +31 23 532 8533. Stan Paardekooper, general manager; David Porcelyn, chief conductor.

Radio Symphony Orchestra (93). Heuvellaan 33, PO Box 125, NL-1200 AC Hilversum, Netherlands *tel:* +31 35 671 4140 *fax:* +31 35 671 4171. Eri Klas, chief conductor; Henk Smit, manager.

Residentie Orkest The Hague (104). Spuiplein 150, NL-2511 DG Den Haag, Netherlands *tel:* +31 70 360 7925 *fax:* +31 70 365 1907 *email:* info1@residentieorkest.nl. H van den Akker, general manager; Evgenii Svetlanov, chief conductor; Leo Samama, artistic manager.

Rotterdam Philharmonic Orchestra (114). De Doelen, Kruisstraat 2, NL-3012 CT Rotterdam, Netherlands *tel:* +31 10 217 1760 *fax:* +31 10 404 8023. Paul Zeegers, general manager; Kees Hillen, artistic leader; Valery Gergiev, principal conductor.

Royal Concertgebouw Orchestra (115). Jacob Obrechtstraat 51, NL-1071 KJ Amsterdam, Netherlands *tel:* +31 20 679 2211 *fax:* +31 20 676 3331 *email:* info@concertgebouworkest.nl. Jan Willem Loot, managing director; Riccardo Chailly, chief conductor.

New Zealand

Auckland Philharmonia (63). PO Box 56-024, Auckland 3, New Zealand *tel:* +64 9 638 7073 *fax:* +64 9 630 9687 *email:* apo@clear.net.nz. Lloyd Williams, general manager; John Ure, artistic manager.

Christchurch Symphony Orchestra (110). PO Box 3260, Christchurch 8000, New Zealand *tel:* +64 3 379 3886 *fax:* +64 3 379 3861 *email:* tk@cso.co.nz. Iola Shelley, artistic director; Jan van den Berg, concert master; A H Kunowski, general manager; Sir William Southgate, conductor laureate.

New Zealand Symphony Orchestra (95). PO Box 6640, Wellington 6035, New Zealand *tel:* +64 4 801 3890 *fax:* +64 4 801 3891 *email:* nzso@actrix.gen.nz. Ian Fraser, chief executive; Franz-Paul Decker, conductor laureate; James Judd, music director.

South Pacific Symphony (20-47). PO Box 660, Shortland St, Auckland 1015, New Zealand *tel:* +64 21 901479 *fax:* +64 21 698479 *email:* SPS@southpacifsymph.com. Eliano Matticzzi-Petralia, artistic director.

Norway

Bergen Philharmonic Orchestra (94). Grieghallen, E Griegs pl 1, N-5015 Bergen, Norway *tel:* +47 55 216100 *fax:* +47 55 318534 *email:* post@harmonien.no. Lorentz Reitan, general manager; Simone Young, music director; Tarjei Flotve, orchestra manager.

Kristiansand Symfoniorkester (37). PO Box 777, N-4666 Kristiansand, Norway *tel:* +47 38 022440 *fax:* +47 38 022991 *email:* post@kso.no. Jan Stigmer, artistic director; Öystein Eidsaa, director.

Norwegian Chamber Orchestra (15-40). Stockholmsgata 12, N-0566 Oslo, Norway *tel:* +47 22 046270 *fax:* +47 22 046290. Bernt Lauritz Larsen, managing director; Iona Brown, art director.

Oslo Philharmonic Orchestra (108). PO Box 1607 Vika, Haakon VIIs gt 2, N-0119 Oslo, Norway *tel:* +47 22 014900 *fax:* +47 22 014901. Trond Okkelmo, managing director; Mariss Jansons, music director; Manfred Honeck, principal guest conductor.

Stavanger Symfoniorkester (70). Bjergsted, N-4007 Stavanger, Norway *tel:* +47 51 508830 *fax:* +47 51 508839. Anna-Marie Antonius, managing director; Erik Landmark, general manager.

Trondheim Symfoniorkester (73). Post Box 774 Sentrum, N-7001 Trondheim, Norway *tel:* +47 73 539800 *fax:* +47 73 539801 *email:* post@tso.no. Siri Fristad Mathisen, general and publicity manager; Daniel Harding, chief conductor.

Peru

Orquesta Sinfónica Nacional (78). Avda Javier Prado Este 2465, Lima 41, Peru *tel:* +51 37 7633 *also fax*; +51 225 8882 (telefax). José Carlos Santos, conductor and artistic director; Mina Maggiolo Dibos, assistant conductor; Grimaldo Núñez Maguiña, general manager; Milagros Cerna Campos, secretary.

Poland

Kielce Philharmonic (85). Plac Moniuszki 2b, PL-25-334 Kielce, Poland *tel:* +48 41 368 1140/0501/0502 *fax:* +48 41 368 1191. Szymon Kawalla, general and artistic director and conductor; Leonard Skrobacz, deputy director; Zbigniew Goncerzewicz, assistant conductor; Sylwester Furmanczyk, admin section manager.

Krakow Philharmonic (102). ul Zwierzyniecka 1, PL-31-103 Kraków, Poland *tel:* +48 12 422 4312; +48 12 422 0958 *also fax; email:* pfk@filharmonia.dnd.com.pl. Anna Oberc, managing director; Tomasz Bugaj, artistic director and conductor.

Orchestra of the Grand Theatre - National Opera. Plac Teatralny 1, PL-00-950 Warszawa, Poland *tel:* +48 22 692 0500 *fax:* +48 22 826 0423/5012. Jacek Kaspszyk, director.

Philharmonic Orchestra (80). ul Piotrkowska 243, PL-90-456 Lodz, Poland *tel:* +48 42 637 2652/2653 *fax:* +48 42 636 8232. Katarzyna Nowicka, general manager; Piotr Redel, artistic director.

National Polish Radio Symphony Orchestra (115). Pl Sejmu Slaskiego 2, PL-40032 Katowice, Poland *tel:* +48 32 251 8903; +48 32 255 3261 *fax:* +48 32 257 1384 *email:* nospr@nospr.org.pl. Irena Siodmok, managing director; Antoni Wit, general and artistic director.

State Philharmonic Orchestra (100). ul Pilsudskiego 19, PL-50044 Wroclaw, Poland *tel:* +48 71 342 2001 *fax:* +48 71 342 8980. Marek Pijarowski, conductor and manager; Tadeusz Nesterowicz, assistant manager.

Szymanowski Philharmonic Orchestra (102). ul Zwierzyniecka 1, PL-310103 Kraków, Poland *tel:* +48 12 422 0958; +48 12 422 4312 *also fax; email:* pfk@filharmonia.dnd.com.pl. Anna Oberc, managing director; Tomasz Bugaj, artistic director and conductor.

Warsaw Philharmonic (109). ul Jasna 5, PL-00950 Warszawa, Poland *tel:* +48 22 826 8311 *fax:* +48 22 826 5617 *email:* filharmonia @filharmonia.pl. Kazimierz Kord, artistic manager and chief conductor; Wojciech Nowak, deputy director.

Portugal

Gulbenkian Orchestra (60). Fundaçao Calouste Gulbenkian, Av de Berna 45, P-1067 Lisboa, Portugal *tel:* +351 1 793 5131 *fax:* +351 1 793 7296 *email:* orquestragulbenkian@ip.pt. Muhai Tang, principal conductor; Claudio Scimone, honorary conductor; Michael Zilm, principal guest conductor.

Lisbon Metropolitan Orchestra (40). Travessa da Galé 36, P-1300 Lisboa, Portugal *tel:* +351 1 362 3830 *fax:* +351 1 362 3833. Miguel Graça Moura, artistic director; Cristina Ribeiro, executive director; Manuela Magallaes, marketing director.

Portuguese Symphony Orchestra (110). Fundaçao Sao Carlos, Rua Serpa Pinto 9, P-1200 Lisboa, Portugal *tel:* +1 351 343 1734 *fax:* +1 351 343 1735. Paulo Ferreira de Castro, artistic director of the foundation; Alvaro Cassuto, artistic director and principal conductor.

Romania

Iasi Philharmonic (99). Str Cuza Voda 29, 6600 Iasi, Romania *tel:* +40 32 114601/112100/212620 *fax:* +40 32 214160. Bujor Prelipcean, artistic director; Gheorghe Costin, Camil Marinescu, orchestra conductors; Alexandru Lascae, conductor.

Transylvania State Philharmonic, Cluj-Napoca (106). St Emanuel de Martonne 1, 3400 Cluj-Napoca, Romania *tel:* +40 64 430060/3 *fax:* +40 64 197812 *email:* fila@codec.ro. Emil Simon, general director; Bianca Temes, programme manager; Adrian Pop, artistic adviser.

Russia

Bolshoi Symphony Orchestra (130). Bolshoi Theatre, Teatralnaya Sq 1, Moscow 103009, Russia *tel:* +7 095 292 4421 *fax:* +7 095 292 9032. Mark Ermler, music director and conductor; Sergey Amedian, orchestra manager.

"Klassika" St Petersburg State Symphony Orchestra (72). 48/4 Moika riv. quay, St Petersburg 191186, Russia *tel:* +7 812 219 6569 *also fax*; +7 812 443 5206 *also fax; email:* livchits@peterlink.ru.

Russian National Symphony Orchestra. Studio Moscow, Alexeya Tolstovo St 26-33, 103001 Moscow, Russia *tel:* +7 095 290 6262 *fax:* +7 095 292 6511. Mikhail Pletnev, founder and conductor; Tatyana Sukhacheva, manager.

Russian State Philharmonic Orchestra. 18 Murmansky Proezd, App 77, 129075 Moscow, Russia *tel:* +7 095 233 8996. Valery Poljansky, chief conductor.

St Petersburg Academic Symphony Orchestra. St Petersburg Shostakovich Philharmonia, Mikhailovskaya ul 2, 191011 St Petersburg, Russia *tel:* +7 812 311 7331 *fax:* +7 812 311 2126 *email:* mail@philharmonics.sbp.ru. Anton Getman, general manager; Yuri Temirkanov, artistic director; Alexander Dmitriev, musical director, principal conductor; Vladimir Altshuler, associated principal conductor.

St Petersburg Philharmonic Orchestra (125). St Petersburg Shostakovich Philharmonia, Mikhailovskaya ul 2, 191011 St Petersburg, Russia *tel:* +7 812 311 7331 *fax:* +7 812 311 2126 *email:* mail@philharmonics.sbp.ru. Anton Getman, general manager; Yuri Temirkanov, musical director, principal conductor; Mariss Yansons, associated principal conductor.

Singapore

Singapore Symphony Orchestra (90). 2nd Floor, Victoria Memorial Hall, 11 Empress Pl, Singapore 179558, Singapore *tel:* +65 336 4417 *fax:* +65 336 6382 *email:* ssonet@mbox3.singnet.com.sg. Lan Shui, music director; Liew Chin Choy, general manager.

Slovak Republic

Orchestra of the Slovak National Theatre (107). Gorkého 4, 815 86 Bratislava, Slovak Republic *tel:* +421 7 5443 5085 *fax:* +421 7 5443 5072 *email:* snd@snd.sk.

Slovak Radio Symphonic Orchestra (99). Mytna 1, 810 05 Bratislava, Slovak Republic *tel:* +421 7 431 3475 *fax:* +421 7 431 3386 *email:* milos_jurkovic@slovakradio.sk. R Stankovsky, chief conductor; Milos Jurkovic, managing director; Marian Turner, manager.

The State Philharmonic, Kosice (85). Dom Umenia, Moyzesova 66, 041 23 Kosice, Slovak Republic *tel:* +421 95 622 4514/4509 *also fax; email:* sfk@point.sk. Julius Klein, executive director; Tomás Koutnik, chief conductor.

Slovenia

Slovenian Philharmonic (100). Kongresni Trg 10, PO Box 156, 1000 Ljubljana, Slovenia *tel:* +386 61 213554 *fax:* +386 61 213640 *email:* slo-filharmonija@filharmonija.si. Hojca Henart, director; Marko Letonja, artistic director and conductor.

South Africa

Cape Town Philharmonic Orchestra (85). PO Box 4040, Cape Town 8000, South Africa *tel:* +27 21 418 9190 *fax:* +27 21 418 9187. Bernhard Gueller, principal conductor; Rodney Phillips, chief executive; Anthony Kuhnet, artistic administrator.

Kwa Zulu-Natal Philharmonic Orchestra (70). PO Box 5353, Durban 4000, Natal, South Africa *tel:* +27 31 369 9438 *fax:* +27 31 369 9559 *email:* kznpoce@iafrica.com. Bongani Tembe, chief executive.

New Arts Philharmonic Orchestra Pretoria (NAPOP) (68). PO Box 566, Pretoria 0001, South Africa *tel:* +27 12 322 1665 *fax:* +27 12 322 3913 *email:* orchestra@statetheatre.co.za. Ivan Christian, general manager; Gérard Korsten, principal guest conductor; Graham Scott, artistic director.

Spain

Bilbao Symphony Orchestra (95). Euskalduna Jauregia, Abandoibarra 4, E-48011 Bilbao, Basque Country, Spain *tel:* +34 94 403 52056 *fax:* +34 94 403 5115. Gorka Robles, general manager; Juanjo Mena, artistic director.

City of Palma Symphony Orchestra, Baleares (67). C/Vicente Juan Rosselló 22, E-07013 Palma de Mallorca, Spain *tel:* +34 971 287 565 *fax:* +34 971 287 758. Sebastian Roig, manager; Mariano Isasi, admin; Salvador Brotons, principal conductor.

Le Concert des Nations (20-45). Travesera de Gracia 18-20 2, E-08021 Barcelona, Spain *tel:* +34 93 580 6069 *email:* 101617.3236@compuserve.com. Jordi Savall, music director; Irene Bloc, admin.

Orquesta de Cadaqués (45). Arcs 8, 1er 2a, E-08002 Barcelona, Spain *tel:* +34 93 301 9555 *fax:* +34 93 302 2670 *email:* trito@bcn:servicom.es. Llorenç Caballero, president and artistic director; Maria Pav Roca, general manager.

Orquesta Filarmónica de Gran Canaria (83). Bravo Murillo 21-23, E-35003 Las Palmas de Gran Canaria, Spain *tel:* +34 92 832 0513 *fax:* +34 92 831 4747. Juan Antonio González Ojellón, manager; Manuel Benítez González, artistic co-ordinator; Adrian Leaper, music director.

Orquesta Sinfonica de Euskadi (90). Paseo de Miramón 124, E-20014 San Sebastian, Spain *tel:* +34 94 330 8332 *fax:* +34 94 330 8324 *email:* artistas@orquestadeeuskadi.es. Jesus Aguirre, intendent; Germán Ormazabal Artolazabal, general manager; Gilbert Varga, Mario Venzago, musical directors.

Orquesta Sinfonica de Galicia (85). Auditorio y Palacio de Congresos, E-15004 La Coruna, Spain *tel:* +34 98 125 2021 *fax:* +34 98 127 7499 *email:* osg@lcg.servicom.es. Victor Pablo Perez, artistic director; Enrique Rojas, manager.

Orquesta de Valencia (97). Palau de la Música, Paseo de la Alameda 30, E-46023 Valencia, Spain *tel:* +34 96 337 5020 *fax:* +34 96 337 0988. Miguel Angel Gohez Martínez, conductor; Maria Irene Beneito, president.

Real Orquesta Sinfónica de Sevilla (103). Imagen, 9-2 Derecha, E-41003 Sevilla, Spain *tel:* +34 95 456 1536 *fax:* +34 95 456 1888. Klaus Weise, artistic director and principal conductor; Francisco José Senra Lazo, managing director; José Manuel Delgado Rodriquez, technical director.

Symphony Orchestra of Castille and Leon (75). c/o Santiago 19, 2a, E-47001 Valladolid, Spain *tel:* +34 98 337 0076 *fax:* +34 98 333275. Carlos Rubio, manager; Max Bragado Darman, conductor.

Tenerife Symphony Orchestra (83). Plaza de Espana 1, E-38003 Santa Cruz de Tenerife, Spain *tel:* +34 92 223 9801 *fax:* +34 92 223 9617 *email:* ost@cabtfe.es. Victor Pablo Perez, principal director; Dulce Xerach Perez Lopez, president; Carmen Kemper, manager.

Sweden

Göteborgs Operans Orkester (87). Christina Nilssons Gata, S-41104 Göteborg, Sweden *tel:* +46 3 110 8090 *fax:* +46 3 110 8025 *email:* klas.sjoblom@opera.se. Klas Sjöblom, orchestra director.

Malmö Symphony Orchestra. Föreningsgatan 35, S-205 80 Malmö, Sweden *tel:* +46 4 034 3510 *fax:* +46 40 611 7505 *email:* office@mso.se.

Royal Stockholm Philharmonic Orchestra (101). Hötorget 8, PO Box 7083, S-103 87 Stockholm, Sweden *tel:* +46 8 786 0219 *fax:* +46 8 200548 *email:* lotta.bjelkeborn@konserthuset.se. Lotta Bjelkeborn, press; Alan Gilbert, conductor and artistic advisor.

Swedish National Orchestra (108). Stenhammarsgatam 1, S-412 56 Göteburg, Sweden *tel:* +46 31 778 7800 *fax:* +46 3 120 3502. Neeme Järvi, principal conductor; Sture Carlsson, general manager.

Swedish Radio Symphony Orchestra (103). Berwaldhallen, Swedish Radio Broadcasting Corporation, S-105 10 Stockholm, Sweden *tel:* +46 8 784 5000 *fax:* +46 8 667 3283 *email:* orkestern@bwh.sr.se. Michael Tydén, general manager; Lennart Stenkvist, artist and programme manager; Evgeny Svetlanov, principal conductor (until autumn 2000); Manfred Honeck, principal conductor (from autumn 2000); Eva Bjurenhed, touring manager, Karin Adolfsson, marketing manager.

Switzerland

Basel Sinfonietta (85-120). Postfach, CH-4002 Basel, Switzerland *tel:* +41 61 335 5415 *fax:* +41 61 335 5535 *email:* mail@baselsinfonietta.ch. Thomas Nidecker, manager; C Fahrni, C Waldmann, secretary.

Berner Symphonie-Orchester (105). Münzgraben 2, CH-3000 Berne 7, Switzerland *tel:* +41 31 328 2424 *fax:* +41 31 328 2425. Dmitrij Kitajenko, principal conductor; Margrit Lenz, manager.

Sinfonieorchester Basel (120). Barfüsserplatz 8 Casino Basel, CH-4001 Basel, Switzerland *tel:* +41 61 205 0095 *fax:* +41 61 205 0099 *email:* jf-sinfaniebasel@datacomm.ch. Jürgen Fabritius, director.

Tonhalle-Orchester Zürich (98). Gotthardstr 5, CH-8002 Zürich, Switzerland *tel:* +41 1 206 3440 *fax:* +41 1 206 3436. Trygve Nordwall, executive director; David Zinman, music director and principal conductor; Jürg Keller, director of finance and admin; Etienne Reymond, artistic admin.

Thailand

Bangkok Symphony Orchestra (70). Tejapaibul Building, 5th Floor, 16 Plubplaichi Rd, Bangkok 10330, Thailand *tel:* +66 2 223 08715 *fax:* +66 2 621 5751 *email:* bso_bangkok@hotmail.com. Witaya Tumornsoontorn, general manager; Anthony Camden, artistic director; Veerapahn Vawklang, resident conductor.

Turkey

Istanbul State Symphony Orchestra. Atatürk Kültür Merkezi Taksim, 80090 Istanbul, Turkey *tel:* +90 212 243 1068 *fax:* +90 212 251 0507. Türkmen Güner, director; Ertugrul Köse, vice-director; Erol Erdinç, conductor; Orhan Topcuoglu, programme co-ordinator.

Presidential Symphony Orchestra (110). Talatpasa Bulvari 38, Ankara, Turkey *tel:* +90 312 309 1343 *fax:* +90 312 311 7548. Nedím Tanrikulu, director; Irfaní Özdemír, artistic director.

USA

Arkansas Symphony Orchestra (72). PO 7328, 2417 N Tyler, Little Rock, AR 72217, USA *tel:* +1 501 666 1761 *fax:* +1 501 666 3193 *email:* aso1@alltel.net. William Vickery, executive director; David Itkin, music director.

Atlanta Symphony Orchestra (96). 1293 Peachtree St NE, Suite 300, Atlanta, GA 30309, USA *tel:* +1 404 733 4900 *fax:* +1 404 733 4901. Yoel Levi, music director; J Frank Dans, artistic admin; Allison Vulgamore, president.

Baltimore Symphony Orchestra (97). 1212 Cathedral St, Baltimore, MD 21201, USA *tel:* +1 410 783 8100 *fax:* +1 410 783 8077. John Gidwitz, president; Yuri Temirkanov, music director-designate.

Boulder Philharmonic Orchestra (85). The Dairy Centre for the Arts, 2590 Walnut St, Suite 6, Boulder, CO 80302-5700, USA *tel:* +1 303 449 1976 *fax:* +1 303 443 9203. Theodore Kuchar, music director; William Lightfoot, executive director.

Buffalo Philharmonic Orchestra (80). PO Box 5202, Buffalo, NY 14213, USA *tel:* +1 716 885 0331 *fax:* +1 716 885 9372. Jo Ann Falletta, music director.

Charlotte Symphony Orchestra (76). 211 N College St, Suite 202, Charlotte, NC 28202, USA *tel:* +1 704 332 0468 *fax:* +1 704 332 1963. Peter McCoppin, music director; Janna Hymes-Bianchi, resident conductor; Richard L Early, president and executive director; David Tang, assistant conductor; Anita Strauss-LaRowe, director of development.

Chattanooga Symphony and Opera (up to 90). 630 Chestnut St, Chattanooga, TN 37402, USA *tel:* +1 423 267 8583 *fax:* +1 423 265 6520 *email:* csoa@chattanooga.net. Robert Bernhardt, music director; John Wehrle, executive director; Patty Grove-Currey, PR director.

Cincinnati Symphony Orchestra (97). 1241 Elm St, Cincinnati, OH 45210, USA *tel:* +1 513 621 1919 *fax:* +1 513 621 2132. Steven Monder, executive director; Jesús López-Cobos, music director.

The Cleveland Orchestra (104). Severance Hall, Cleveland, OH 44106, USA *tel:* +1 216 231 7300 *fax:* +1 216 231 0202. Christoph von Dohnányi, music director; Thomas W Morris, executive director.

Colorado Symphony Orchestra (79). 821 17th St, Suite 700, Denver, CO 80202, USA *tel:* +1 303 292 5566 *fax:* +1 303 293 2649. Marin Alsop, music director; Maria Williamson, artistic admin; J Thomas Bacchetti, executive director; Lawrence Loh, associate conductor; Duain Wolfe, chorus director.

Dallas Symphony Orchestra (92). 2301 Flora St, Suite 300, Dallas, TX 75201-2497, USA *tel:* +1 214 871 4000 *fax:* +1 214 871 4049. Eugene Bonelli, president; Andrew Litton, music director.

Detroit Symphony Orchestra (95). 3663 Woodward Av, Detroit, MI 48201-2403, USA *tel:* +1 313 576 5100 *fax:* +1 313 576 5101 *email:* info@detroitsymphony.com. Neeme Jarvi, music director; Louis G Spisto, president; Emil Kang, vice-president of operations.

Florida Philharmonic Orchestra (84). 3401 NW Ninth Av, Fort Lauderdale, FL 33309-5903, USA *tel:* +1 954 561 2997 *fax:* +1 954 561 1390. Elizabeth Hare, executive director; James Judd, music director; Peter Nero, pops director.

Florida West Coast Symphony (80). 709 North Tamiami Trail, Sarasota, FL 34236, USA *tel:* +1 941 953 4252 *fax:* +1 941 953 3059 *email:* marketing@fwcs.com. Gayle A Williams, marketing director; Leif Bjaland, artistic director and conductor; Gretchen Serrie, executive director; Trevor Cramer, general manager.

Fort Worth Symphony Orchestra (72). 330 East Fourth St, Suite 200, Fort Worth, TX 76102, USA *tel:* +1 817 665 6500 *fax:* +1 817 665 6600 *email:* ticks@fwsymphony.org. Ann Koonsman, executive director; John Giordano, music director.

Honolulu Symphony (62). 677 Ala Moana Blvd, Suite 615, Honolulu, HI 96813, USA *tel:* +1 808 524 0815 *fax:* +1 808 524 1507. Samuel Wong, conductor; Michael Tiknis, executive director.

The Houston Symphony (98). 615 Louisiana St, Houston, TX 77002-2798, USA *tel:* +1 713 224 4240 *fax:* +1 713 222 7024 *email:* hso@iwl.net. Christoph Eschenbach, music director; James Berdahl, general manager; David M Wax, executive director.

Indianapolis Symphony Orchestra (88). 45 Monument Circle, Indianapolis, IN 46204-2919, USA *tel:* +1 317 262 1100 *fax:* +1 317 262 1159. Dan Shewman, marketing; Raymond Leppard, music director and conductor.

Jacksonville Symphony Orchestra (52). 300 West Water St, Suite 200, Jacksonville, FL 32202, USA *tel:* +1 904 354 5479 *fax:* +1 904 354 9238. Gary L Good, president; Roger Nierenberg, conductor laureate; Cecil S Cole, orchestra manager.

Knoxville Symphony Orchestra (80). 406 Union Ave, Suite 100, Knoxville TN 37902, USA *tel:* +1 423 523 1178 *fax:* +1 423 546 3766. Rick Lester, executive director; Kirk Trevor, music director and conductor.

Los Angeles Philharmonic (105). 135 N Grand Av, Los Angeles, CA 90012, USA *tel:* +1 213 972 7300 *fax:* +1 213 617 3065. Willem Wijnbergen, executive vice-president/managing director; Esa-Pekka Salonen, music director.

Louisiana Philharmonic Orchestra (71). 305 Baronne St, Suite 600, New Orleans, LA 70112, USA *tel:* +1 504 523 6530 *fax:* +1 504 595 8468 *email:* lpo@gnofn.org. Robert J Stiles, executive director.

The Louisville Orchestra (70). 300 West Main Street, Louisville, KY 40202, USA *tel:* +1 502 587 8681 *fax:* +1 502 589 7870. Tim King, executive director; Geoffrey Woodward, orchestra manager; Uriel Segal, music director.

Milwaukee Symphony Orchestra (88). 330 E Kilbourn Av, Suite 900, Milwaukee, WI 53202, USA *tel:* +1 414 291 6010 *fax:* +1 414 291 7610 *email:* milwaukeesymphony@execpc.com. Steven A Ovitsky, vice-president and executive director; Andreas Delfs, music director; Andrew Sill, assistant conductor.

Minnesota Orchestra (96). 1111 Nicollet Mall, Minneapolis, MN 55403, USA *tel:* +1 612 371 5600 *fax:* +1 612 371 0838 *email:* info@mnorch.org. David J Hyslop, president; Eiji Oue, music director; Stanislaw Skrowaczewski, conductor laureate; Jeffrey Tate, sommerfest conductor; Doc Severinsen, pops conductor.

Nashville Symphony Orchestra (72). 209 10th Av South, Suite 448, Nashville, TN 37203, USA *tel:* +1 615 255 5600 *fax:* +1 615 255 5656. Kenneth Schermerhorn, music director and conductor; Alan Valentine, executive director.

National Symphony Orchestra (100). John F Kennedy Center for Performing Arts, Washington, DC 20566, USA *tel:* +1 202 416 8100 *fax:* +1 202 416 8105. Richard Hancock, executive director; Leonard Slatkin, music director.

New Jersey Symphony Orchestra (76). 2 Central Av, Newark, NJ 07102, USA *tel:* +1 201 624 3713 *fax:* +1 201 624 2115 *email:* information@njsymphony.org. Zdenek Macal, music director; Lawrence Tamburri, executive director; Karen Swanson, general manager.

New World Symphony (83). 541 Lincoln Rd, Miami Beach, FL 33139, USA *tel:* +1 305 673 3330 *fax:* +1 305 673 6749 *email:* email@nws.org. Christopher Dunworth, president; Michael Tilson Thomas, artistic director; David Loebel, conductor-in-residence; Douglas Merilatt, vice-president, artistic operations.

New York Philharmonic (107). 10 Lincoln Centre Plaza, New York, NY 10023-6973, USA *tel:* +1 212 875 5000 *fax:* +1 212 875 5717. Kurt Masur, music director; Welz Kauffman, artistic admin.

North Carolina Symphony Orchestra (65). 2 E South St, Raleigh, NC 27601, USA *tel:* +1 919 733 2750 *fax:* +1 919 733 9920. Gerhardt Zimmermann, music director and conductor; Hiram Black, artistic admin.

Pacific Symphony Orchestra (90). 1231 E Dyer Rd, Suite 200, Santa Ana, CA 92705-5606, USA *tel:* +1 714 755 5788 *fax:* +1 714 755 5789. Louis G Spisto, vice-president and executive director; Carl St Clair, music director; James T Medvitz, director of operations.

Pittsburgh Symphony Orchestra (102). 600 Penn Av, Pittsburgh, PA 15222, USA *tel:* +1 412 392 4900 *fax:* +1 412 392 4909. Mariss Jansons, music director; Robert Moir, artistic admin.

Rochester Philharmonic Orchestra (79). 108 East Av, Rochester, NY 14604, USA *tel:* +1 716 454 2620 *fax:* +1 716 423 2256 *email:* rpo@rpo.org. Christopher Seaman, music director; Richard Nowlin, president and CEO; Jeff Tyzik, principal pops conductor; Peter Bay, principal guest conductor.

St Louis Symphony Orchestra (101). Powell Symphony Hall, 718 N Grand Blvd, St Louis, MO 63103, USA *tel:* +1 314 533 2500 *fax:* +1 314 286 4142. Bruce Coppock, executive director; Hans Vonk, music director and conductor.

St Paul Chamber Orchestra (32). 408 St Peter St, Suite 500, St Paul, MN 55102, USA *tel:* +1 651 292 3248 *fax:* +1 651 292 3281 *email:* info@spcomail.org. Brent Assink, president and managing director; Hugh Wolff, music director.

San Antonio Symphony (77). PO Box 658, San Antonio, TX 78293-0658, USA *tel:* +1 210 554 1000 *fax:* +1 210 554 1008. John Binkley, executive director.

San Diego Symphony (78). 1245 Seventh Av, CA 92101, USA *tel:* +1 619 231 8915 *fax:* +1 619 231 0613. Jung Ho Pak, artistic director; Thomas Gordon, president.

San Francisco Symphony (106). Davies Symphony Hall, San Francisco, CA 94102, USA *tel:* +1 415 552 8000 *fax:* +1 415 431 6857. Herbert Blomstedt, conductor laureate.

San Jose Symphony (89). 495 Almaden Blvd, San Jose, CA 95110, USA *tel:* +1 408 287 7383 *fax:* +1 408 286 6391. Leonid Grin, conductor; Paul Chummers, executive director; Tim Beswick, artistic admin.

Seattle Symphony (89). 200 University St, Seattle, WA 98101, USA *tel:* +1 206 215 4700 *fax:* +1 206 215 4701. Gerard Schwarz, music director; Abraham Kaplan, associate conductor (choral); Adam Stern, associate conductor; Deborah R Card, executive director.

Shreveport Symphony Orchestra (29). 619 Louisana Av, Shreveport, LA 71101, USA *tel:* +1 318 222 7496 *fax:* +1 318 222 7490. Rob Gold, executive director; Dennis Simons, music director; Lucy Medvec, marketing director; Penny Granger, box office; Scott Green, development director; Janice Nelson, operations manager.

Syracuse Symphony Orchestra (67). 411 Montgomery St, Syracuse, NY 13202, USA *tel:* +1 315 424 8222 *fax:* +1 315 424 1131. Fabio Mechetti, music director; David C. Worters, executive director.

Toledo Symphony Orchestra (85). 2 Maritime Plaza, Toledo, OH 43604-1803, USA *tel:* +1 419 241 1272 *fax:* +1 419 321 6890 *email:* tolsymorch@aol.com. Robert Bell, president; Andrew Massey, music director and conductor; Andrew Sewell, associate conductor; Kathleen Carroll, executive vice-president, development.

Utah Symphony (83). 123 W South Temple, Salt Lake City, UT 84101, USA *tel:* +1 801 533 5626 *fax:* +1 801 521 6634 *email:* d.andrews @utahsymphony.org. Donald L Andrews, president; Keith Lockhart, music director; Pavel Kogan, principal guest conductor; Bundit Ungrangsee, associate conductor.

Wichita Symphony Orchestra (85). 225 W Douglas, Suite 207, Wichita, KS 67202, USA *tel:* +1 316 267 5259 *fax:* +1 316 267 1937 *email:* symphony@louverture.com. Mitchell A Berman, general manager; Zuohuang Chen, music director.

Venezuela

Orquesta Sinfónica del Estado Nueva Esparta (70). Paseo Romulo Gallegos, Sector Guaraguao, Final Calle Diaz, Porlamar Estado Nueva Esparta, Venezuela *tel:* +58 95 641282 *also fax*. Ecberth Lucena, music director and conductor; Enmanuel Alfonzo, president.

Opera Companies

This list includes the major international opera companies. Some are touring companies, but many perform substantially at a principal venue. Details of performances are listed in *Opera Now* magazine, also available from Rhinegold Publishing.

Albania

Theatre of Opera and Ballet Tirana. Sheshi 'Skenderbey', Tirana, Albania *tel:* +355 42 27471 *fax:* +355 42 25856/24753 *email:* root@tob.tirana.al. Vasil S Tole, general director.

Argentina

Teatro Colòn. Cerrito 618, 1010 Buenos Aires, Argentina *tel:* +54 1 382 8924/2389 *fax:* +54 1 111232. Kive Staiff, general and artistic director; Carlos M M Elia, admin director.

Australia

National Chamber Opera of Australia. The Great Hall, Sydney University, Paramatta Rd, Sydney, Australia *tel:* +61 2 9266 4800.

Opera Australia. PO Box 291, Strawberry Hills, NSW 2012, Australia *tel:* +61 2 9699 1099 *fax:* +61 2 9699 3184. Donald McDonald, general manager; Moffatt Oxenbould, artistic director; Sharolyn Kimmorley, artistic admin; Noel Stanton, technical director.

Opera Queensland. PO Box 3677, South Brisbane, Queensland 4101, Australia *tel:* +61 7 3875 3030 *fax:* +61 7 3844 5352 *email:* operagold@operagold.org.au. Chris J Mangin, general manager; Jillianne Stoll, head of music; Tom Cullen, artistic admin.

The State Opera of South Australia. PO Box 211, Marleston BC, SA 5033, Australia *tel:* +61 8 226 4790 *fax:* +61 8 226 4791 *email:* stateopera@cobweb.com.au. Stephen Phillips, general director; Mandy MacGillivray, marketing and business affairs manager; Nigel Bray, finance director; Florin Radulescu, head of music.

West Australian Opera. 3rd Floor, His Majesty's Theatre, 825 Hay St, Perth WA, Australia *tel:* +61 8 9321 5869 *fax:* +61 8 9324 1134 *email:* administration@waopera.asn.au. Pamela Foulkes, general manager; Richard Mills, artistic director; Marilyn Phillips, head of music; Michael Herrmann, marketing and development manager; Judy Reid, admin manager.

Austria

Haydn Festival. Schloss Esterháy, A-7000 Eisenstadt, Austria *tel:* +43 2682 61866 *fax:* +43 2682 61805 *email:* office@haydnfestival.at. Walter Reicher, artistic director; Walter Kain, marketing director.

Landestheater Linz. Promenade 39, A-4020 Linz, Austria *tel:* +43 732 761 1100 *fax:* +43 732 761 1105 *email:* landestheater@linz.info.at.

Opernhaus Bühnen Graz. 10 Kaiser Josef-Platz, A-8010 Graz, Austria *tel:* +43 316 8008 *fax:* +43 316 800 8565 *email:* info@buehnen-graz.com. Gerhard Brunner, general manager; Peter Nebel, financial director; Michael Lakner, artistic admin.

Salzburger Landestheater. Schwarzstr 22, A-5020 Salzburg, Austria *tel:* +43 662 871512 *fax:* +43 662 871 51213 *email:* intendanz@theater.co.at. Lutz Hochstraate, artistic director; Diethmar Strasser, artistic manager; Anton Schmidjell, financial director.

Tiroler Landestheater. Rennweg 2, A-6020 Innsbruck, Austria *tel:* +43 512 52074 *fax:* +43 512 52074 333 *email:* tiroler@landestheater. Harøld Mayr, general manager.

Volksoper Wien. Währinger Str 78, A-1090 Wien, Austria *tel:* +43 1 514 443201 *fax:* +43 1 514 443215 *email:* birner-schuschu@oebthu.gv.at. Dominique Mentha, director.

Wiener Kammeroper. Fleischmarkt 24, A-1010 Wien, Austria *tel:* +43 1 512 0100 *fax:* +43 1 512 010010 *email:* wienerkammeroper@via.at. Josef Hussek, general director; Isabella Gabor, vice director; Steffi-Maria Schlinke, drama and PR.

Wiener Openntheater. Myrthengasse 5/11, A-1070 Wien, Austria *tel:* +43 1 526 2136 *also fax.* Sven Hartberger, general manager.

Wiener Staatsoper. Opernring 2, A-1010 Wien, Austria *tel:* +43 1 514440 *fax:* +43 1 514 442330. Ioan Holender, director; Peter Hecht, admin; Elisabeth Sobotka, Irina Kubadinow, press.

Belgium

De Vlaamse Opera (Antwerpen). Van Ertbornstraat 8, B-2018 Antwerpen, Belgium *tel:* +32 3 233 6808 *fax:* +32 3 232 2661. Marc Clémeur, general director; Massimo Zanetti, music director.

De Vlaamse Opera (Gent). Schouwburgstraat 3, B-9000 Gent, Belgium *tel:* +32 9 225 2425 *fax:* +32 9 223 8726. Marc Clémeur, general director; Massimo Zanetti, music director.

L'Opéra Royal de Wallonie. Rue de Dominicains 1, B-4000 Liege, Belgium *tel:* +32 4 221 4720 *fax:* +32 4 221 0201. Jean-Louis Grinda, director general.

Théâtre Royal de la Monnaie. Koninklijke Muntschouwburg Rue Leopoldstraat 4, B-1000 Brussels, Belgium *tel:* +32 2 229 1200 *fax:* +32 2 229 1380. Antonio Pappano, music director; Bernard Foccroulle, general director.

Bulgaria

National Theater-Opera National de Sofia. Blvd Dondukov 30, BG-1000 Sofia, Bulgaria *tel:* +359 2 988 5869/987 7011 *fax:* +359 2 987 7998 *email:* sfopera@geobiz.net. Plamen Katraloff, director; Vladimir Andreev, deputy director; Gueorgui Notev, chief conductor; Emil Boshnakov, artistic director.

Canada

Calgary Opera. 601, 2378 Ave SE, Calgary, AB T2G 5C3, Canada *tel:* +1 403 262 7286 *fax:* +1 403 263 5428 *email:* calopera@lexicom.ab.ca. Bob McPhee, general director; Heather Davies, financial officer; Brenda Ann Marks, development manager; Nini Ann Pili, contributions manager; Fran Pauzé, communications manager; Jacqueline Dawson, production manager.

The Canadian Opera Company. 227 Front St East, Toronto, Ont M5A 1E8, Canada *tel:* +1 416 363 6671 *fax:* +1 416 363 5584. Richard Bradshaw, general director.

Opera Atelier. 87 Avenue Rd, Hazelton Lanes, Box 343, Toronto, Ont M5R 3R9, Canada *tel:* +1 416 925 3767 *fax:* +1 416 925 4895. Joan Bosworth, general manager; M Pynkoski, J Zingg, co-artistic directors.

Opera Lyra Ottawa. 110-2 Daly Ave, Ottawa, Ont K1N 6E2, Canada *tel:* +1 613 233 9200 *fax:* +1 613 233 5431 *email:* lyra@cyberus.ca; John Peltier, finance director; Gerald Morris, communications manager; Ron Ward, production manager; Louise Morez, box office manager.

L'Opéra de Montréal. 260 Blvd de Maisonneuve Ouest, Montréal, QU H2X 1Y9, Canada *tel:* +1 514 985 2222 *fax:* +1 514 985 2219 *email:* odm@total.net. Bernard Uzan, general and artistic director; Michel Beaulac, artistic admin; Élise Côté, fundraising and development director; Patrick-Jean Poirier, communications and marketing director; Michel Gagnon, production director; Margot Provencher, guild director.

Opera Ontario (Opera Hamilton and Kitchener-Waterloo Opera). 110 King St West, 2nd Floor, Hamilton, Ont L8P 4S6, Canada *tel:* +1 905 527 7627; +1 519 578 5573 *fax:* +1 905 527 0014. Kenneth D Freeman, general director; Daniel Lipton, artistic director; Mary Romeo, artistic admin; Christopher Richardson, office manager; Shelley Gadsden, marketing associate.

Opéra de Québec. 1220 Ave Taché, Québec, PQ G1R 3B4, Canada *tel:* +1 418 529 4142 *fax:* +1 418 529 3735. Bernard Labadie, artistic and music director; Grégoire Legendre, general director; Louis Robert, executive assistant and press officer; Lucien Pouliot, accountant.

Pacific Opera Victoria. 1316b Government St, Victoria, BC V8W 1Y8, Canada *tel:* +1 250 385 0222 (box office); +1 250 382 1641(admin) *fax:* +1 250 382 4944 *email:* info@pov.bc.ca. Timothy Vernon, artistic director; David Devan, general manager; Susan Kerschbaumer, marketing manager; Shelley Gadsden, development manager; Kathy Allison, admin assistant.

Vancouver Opera. Suite 500, 845 Cambie St, Vancouver, BC V6B 4Z9, Canada *tel:* +1 604 682 2871 *fax:* +1 604 682 3981 *email:* info@vanopera.bc.ca. Robert J Hallam, general director; David Agler, music director.

Chile

Teatro Municipal. San Antonio 149, Santiago Centro, Chile *tel:* +56 2 369 0282 *fax:* +56 2 633 7214 *email:* tmschile@reuna.cl. Andrés Rodríguez, general and artistic director; Andrés Pinto, director of admin; Gustavo Rivera, finance director; Carlos Bruna, technical director; Cristóbal Giesen, general co-ordinator; Gabor Otvös, principal conductor.

China

Shanghai Opera House. 10 Lane 100, Changshu Rd, Shanghai 200040, China *tel:* +86 216 248 5359 *fax:* +86 216 249 8127 *email:* shgjy@online.sh.ch. He

New Productions

Fidelio Ludwig van Beethoven
Zubin Mehta, Peter Mussbach, Andrea Schmidt-Futterer, Konrad Lindenberg –
Waltraud Meier/Gabriele Schnaut (March), Dorothea Röschmann/Ruth Ziesak (July);
Thomas Moser/Stig Andersen (March 15, 18, July), Rainer Trost, Pavlo Hunka,
Matti Salminen/René Pape (March), Hanno Müller-Brachmann/Eike Wilm Schulte (March)
October 29, November 1, 5, 10, 13, 17, 1999, March 15, 18, 23, July 2, 6, 2000

Ariodante Georg Friedrich Händel
Coproduction with ENO and Welsh National Opera
Ivor Bolton, David Alden, Ian MacNeil, Michael Keegan-Dolan, Paul Taylor/Wolfgang Göbbel –
Ann Murray, Joan Rodgers, Julie Kaufmann; Christopher Robson, Paul Nilon, Umberto Chiummo
January 17, 20, 24, 28, February 1, 5, July 15, 18, 2000

Faust Charles Gounod
Simone Young, David Pountney, Stefanos Lazaridis, Marie Jeanne Lecca –
Angela-Maria Blasi, Heidi Brunner; Marcelo Alvarez, John Tomlinson, Rodney Gilfry
February 28, March 2, 8, 11, 14, 17, July 8, 12, 2000

I puritani Vincenzo Bellini
Marcello Viotti, Jonathan Miller, Isabella Bywater, Clare Mitchell –
Edita Gruberova; Alastair Miles, Paul Groves, Paolo Gavanelli
May 26, 29, June 1, 4, 7, 10, July 3, 7, 2000

Don Carlo Giuseppe Verdi
Zubin Mehta, Jürgen Rose –
Kallen Esperian, Dolora Zajick; Roberto Scandiuzzi, Sergej Larin, Paolo Gavanelli, Paata Burchuladze
July 1, 5, 9, 11, 2000

Rinaldo Georg Friedrich Händel
Harry Bicket, David Alden, Paul Steinberg, Buki Shiff, Pat Collins –
Dorothea Röschmann, Noemi Nadelmann; Axel Köhler, David Daniels, Egils Silins
July 10, 13, 16, 20, 23, 26, 2000

KANON für geschlossene Gesellschaft Ruedi Häusermann, Martin Hägler, Martin Schütz
world premiere – comissioned by the Bavarian State Opera
June 28, 29, 30, July 2, 3, 2000

The Dairy of One Who Disappeared Leoš Janáček
co-production with Lincoln Center New York, Melbourne Festival, Holland Festival,
Bergen Festival, English National Opera, Festival d'Automne Paris
Deborah Warner, Jean Kalman – Ian Bostridge; Julius Drake
July 8, 10, 11, 13, 14, 2000

Other productions in the 1999/2000 repertory: Aida, Ariadne auf Naxos, Il barbiere di Siviglia, La bohème, Carmen, La clemenza di Tito, Don Giovanni, Don Pasquale Elektra, Die Fledermaus, La forza del destino, Die Frau ohne Schatten, Der Freischütz, Hänsel und Gretel, L'italiana in Algeri, Katja Kabanova, Lohengrin, Macbeth, Madama Butterfly, Die Meistersinger von Nürnberg, Le nozze di Figaro, Otello, Parsifal, Der Rosenkavalier, Salome, Simon Boccanegra, Tosca, La traviata, Il trovatore, Die verkaufte Braut, Die Zauberflöte.

Bavarian State Ballett: The Second Detail, Petruschka, Le sacre du printemps, A Cinderella Story, Don Quijote, Apollo, Artifact II, La Bayadère, Chaconne, Emma B., Giselle, Giselle – Mats Ek, Onegin, Swan Lake, Die vier Temperamente, The Unsung.

Academy Concerts, Chamber Concerts, Recitals

Bayerische Staatsoper Staatsintendant Peter Jonas, Generalmusikdirektor Zubin Mehta
Box Office: Maximilianstraße 11, D – 80539 München
Phone: + 49-89-21 85 19 20, **Fax:** + 49-89-21 85 19 03
E-Mail: tickets@st-oper.bayern.de

Information
Phone: + 49-89-21 85 10 24, Fax: + 49-89-21 85 10 23
E-Mail: presse@st-oper.bayern.de
Webside: http://www.bayerische.staatsoper.de

New Productions | Bayerische
1999/2000 | Staatsoper

Zhao-hua, director; Cao Ding, Lin You-Sheng, conductors; Chen Guang-xiam, Zhao Zhi-ming, Li Jian-yei, admins.

Czech Republic

Moravian Theatre Olomouc. Tr Svobody 33, CR-771 07 Olomouc, Czech Republic *tel:* +420 68 522 5727 *fax:* +420 68 522 5781. Václav Kozusnik, director; Martin Dubovic, opera director; Michelle Philippe, chief conductor.

The National Theatre Opera. Národní Divadlo, PO Box 865, CR-112 30 Praha 1, Czech Republic *tel:* +420 2 24 901227 *fax:* +420 2 24 911 524/901 0285 *email:* harvanek@praha.czcom.cz. Zdenek Harvánek, admin; Josef Prudek, artistic director.

Opera Furore. Sevastopolská 14, CR-101 00 Praha 10, Czech Republic *tel:* +420 02 741095/742708 *fax:* +420 02 739064 *email:* via@gts.cz. Jirí Nekvasil, Daniel Dvorák, directors.

Opera Mozart. Sevastopolská 14, CR-101 00 Praha 10, Czech Republic *tel:* +420 2 7174 2623/1403; +420 2 2481 9323 (ticket sales) *fax:* +420 2 7174 1733; +420 2 2481 9324 (ticket sales) *email:* mozart@telecom.cz; festival@mozart.cz (ticket sales).

Orfeo Chamber Opera Company. Armenska 17/6, CR-625 00 Brno, Czech Republic *tel:* +420 05 352110 *fax:* +420 05 529080. Josef Stanek, artistic chief; Anna Erdingerova, admin director.

Statni Opera Praha. Legerova 75, CR-111 21 Praha, Czech Republic *tel:* +420 22 4227 6936 *fax:* +420 22 423 0410/29437. Daniel Dvorák, general manager; Jirí Nekvasil, art director.

Denmark

Den Jyske Opera (Danish National Opera). Musikhuset Aarhus, Thomas Jensens Allé, DK-8000, Arhus C, Denmark *tel:* +45 89 318260 *fax:* +45 86 133710 *email:* post@jyske-opera.dk. Troels Kold, general director; Tonny Borup Mortensen, administration manager; Ritta Løndal, PR; Trine T Sandegaard, sales and marketing.

The Royal Danish Opera. The Royal Theatre, Postbox 2185, DK-1017 Copenhagen K, Denmark *tel:* +45 33 696701 *fax:* +45 33 696767 *email:* admin@kgl-teater.dk. Elaine Padmore, artistic director; Michael Christiansen, theatre director.

Estonia

Estonian National Opera. Estonia Avenue 4, EE-10148 Tallinn, Estonia *tel:* +372 6 260201 *fax:* +372 6 313080 *email:* info@opera.ee. Paul Himma, general manager; Paul Mägi, artistic director and chief conductor; Neeme Kuningas, producer-in-chief; Mai Murdmaa, choreographer-in-chief.

Finland

Finnish National Opera. PO Box 176, Helsinginkatu 58, FIN-00251 Helsinki, Finland *tel:* +358 9 403021 *fax:* +358 9 4030 2305. Juhani Raiskinen, general director; Okko Kamu, music director; Jorma Uotinen, ballet director; John E Westö, admin director; Heidi Almi, press manager.

Joensuun Ooppera. Raimo Paltakari Kirkkokatu 10 B17, FIN-80110 Joensuu, Finland *tel:* +358 1 322 4563 *fax:* +358 1 325 14590 *email:* raimo.paltakari@jnor.joensuu.fi.

Lahden Ooppera. Marja Tikka, Kuhilaankatu 6, FIN-15900 Lahti, Finland *tel:* +358 3 753 5236 *also fax; email:* Marja.Tikka@sci.fi. Mirja Ollikainen, chairman; Eero Pulkkinen, vice-chairman.

Mikkeli Opera. Vuorikatu 3A, FIN-50100 Mikkeli, Finland *tel:* +358 1 516 2063 *fax:* +358 1 5191 2323. Kyöti Kostiainen, chairman; Kimmo Suortamo, producer.

Opera Alueooppera. Irma Rewell, Koulukatu 10C, FIN-65100 Vaasa, Finland *tel:* +358 6 317 3135 *fax:* +358 6 317 9971. Irma Rewell, opera chief; Outi Takkinen, secretary.

Tampere Opera. Vellamonkatu 2, FIN-33100 Tampere, Finland *tel:* +358 3 212 7726 *fax:* +358 3 222 0266 *email:* ooppera@tampere.fi. Jussi Tapola, general director; Saila Lintula, production assistant; Terttu Saarikko, administrative assistant.

Turku Opera. Markku Uotinen, Aninkaistenkatu 9, FIN-20110 Turku, Finland *tel:* +358 0 2231 4563 *fax:* +358 0 2244 4104. Hilkka Urho, executive manager.

Vaasan Opera. Koulukatu 10, FIN-65100 Vaasa, Finland *tel:* +358 6 317 3135 *fax:* +358 6 317 9971. Irma Rewell.

France

Châtelet Théâtre Musical. 2 Rue Edouard Colonne, F-75001 Paris, France *tel:* +33 1 40 28 28 28 *fax:* +33 1 42 36 89 75. Jean-Pierre Brossmann, general director; Jacques Hedouin, admin general.

Le Grand Théâtre de Bordeaux. BP 95, F-33025 Bordeaux Cedex, France *tel:* +33 56 00 85 20 *fax:* +33 56 81 93 66. Thierry Fouquet, general director; Francois Vienne, admin and finance director; Jean-Luc Maeso, general secretary.

L'Opéra d'Avignon. Regie Municipale BP 111, F-84007 Avignon Cedex 1, France *tel:* +33 90 82 42 42 *fax:* +33 90 85 04 23. Raymond Duffaut, director general.

L'Opéra Comique. 5 Rue Favart, F-75002 Paris, France *tel:* +33 1 42 44 45 40 *fax:* +33 1 49 26 05 93. Pierre Medecin, director; Dominique Seridji, admin; Francois Bou, production.

L'Opéra de Lille. 2 Rue des Bons Enfants, F-59800 Lille, France *tel:* +33 3 20 14 99 20 *fax:* +33 3 20 14 99 27. Ricardo Szwarcer, artistic director; Michel Defaut, admin director.

Opéra de Lyon. 1 Place de la Comédie, F-69001 Lyon, France *tel:* +33 72 00 45 00 *fax:* +33 72 00 45 01. Alain Durel, general manager; Louis Langrée, music director; Jean-Marc Péraldi, admin and finance director.

L'Opéra de Marseille. 2 Rue Moliere, F-13001 Marseille, France *tel:* +33 4 91 55 21 12/00 70. Elie Bankhalter, opera director.

Opéras de Montpellier. 11 Blvd Victor Hugo, F-34000 Montpellier, France *tel:* +33 4 67 60 19 80/99 *fax:* +33 4 67 60 19 90. Henri Maier, director general; Renée Panabière, admin.

L'Opéra de Nancy et de Lorraine. 1 Rue Sainte Catherine, F-54000 Nancy, France *tel:* +33 83 85 33 20 *fax:* +33 83 85 30 66. Jean-Marie Blanchard, general director; Christophe Bezzone, admin.

Opéra National du Rhin. 19 Place Broglie BP 320, F-67008 Strasbourg Cedex, France *tel:* +33 3 88 75 48 23 *fax:* +33 3 88 24 09 34 *email:* info@opera-national-du-rhin.com. Rudolf Berger, director general; Lucien Collinet, admin and finance director; Daniel Dollé, assistant to director general; Anne-France Boissenin, communications director.

Opéra de Rennes. BP 3126, F-35031 Rennes Cédex, France *tel:* +33 2 99 78 48 68 *fax:* +33 2 99 78 48 65. Daniel Bizeray, director; Eric Le Bihan, admin.

L'Opéra de Tours. Grand Théâtre de Tours, 34 Rue de la Scellerie, F-37000 Tours, France *tel:* +33 47 05 33 47/37 87. Michel Jarry, director; Luc Cavalier, admin.

L'Opéra de Vichy. Mairie de Vichy, BP 2158, F-03208 Vichy Cedex, France *tel:* +33 4 70 30 17 17. Diane Polya, general and artistic manager.

Théâtre des Champs Elysées. 15 Ave Montaigne, F-75008 Paris, France *tel:* +33 1 49 52 50 00 *fax:* +33 1 49 52 07 41. Dominique Meyer, general director; Francis Lepigeon, deputy director.

Théâtre Municipal. 4-5 Place de la Concorde, F-57000 Metz, France *tel:* +33 87 55 51 87. D Ory, director; Daniel Lucas, admin.

Théâtre de Nîmes. 6 Rue Fresque, F-30000 Nîmes, France *tel:* +33 4 66 36 65 20 *fax:* +33 4 66 21 92 67. Jean Lebeau, director general; Catherine Laugier, secretary general; Luc Favier, admin; Michèle Tellier, financial director; Philippe Sarrat, information director; François Noel, technical director.

Germany

Bayerische Kammeroper. Wengertspfad 2, D-97523 Schwanfeld, Bayern, Germany *tel:* +49 938 48772 *fax:* +49 938 48678.

Bayerische Staatsoper. Nationaltheater, Max-Joseph-Platz 2, D-80539 München, Germany *tel:* +49 892 185 1000 *fax:* +49 892 185 1003. Peter Jonas, general and artistic director; Zubin Mehta, music director; Roland Felber, admin director; Gerd Uecker, opera director; Ulrike Hessler, director of public relations.

Berlin Kammeroper. Koltbusser Damm 79, D-10967 Berlin, Germany *tel:* +49 30 693 1054 *fax:* +49 30 692 5201. Brynmor Llewelyn Jones, artistic director; Dirk Kiefer, executive director.

Bühnen der Landeshauptstadt Kiel. Rathausplatz 4, D-24103 Kiel, Germany *tel:* +49 431 901 2880 *fax:* +49 431 901 2838. Ülrich Windführ, general music director; Kirsten Harms, Raymund Richter, artistic team; Günther Bechert.

Bühnen der Stadt Köln. Offenbachplatz, Postfach 101061, D-50450 Köln, Germany *tel:* +49 221 8300/8216/8314 *fax:* +49 221 8219. Günter Krämer, general director; James Conlon, general music director; Graeme Jenkins, principal guest conductor; Karen Stone, general opera director.

Deutsche Oper Berlin. Richard Wagner Str 10, D-10585 Berlin, Germany *tel:* +49 30 343 8401 *fax:* +49 30 343 84232. Götz Friedrich, general director; Christian Tuielemann, general music director; Alard Rohr, opera director; Sylviane Bayard, ballet director.

Deutsche Oper am Rhein. Heinrich-Heine-Allee 16a, D-40213 Düsseldorf, Germany *tel:* +49 211 89080 *fax:* +49 211 890 8289 *email:* rheinoper@aol.com. Tobias Richter, general director; John Fiore, music director; Werner Hellfritsch, finance director; Tim Coleman, chief dramaturge.

Deutsches National-Theater Weimar. Postfach 3 und 5, D-99401 Weimar, Germany *tel:* +49 364 375 5334 *fax:* +49 364 375 5307. Günther Beelitz, artistic and financial director; George Alexander Albrecht, general music director; Ehrhard Warneke, opera director.

Frankfurt Opera, Städtische Bühnen. Untermainanlage 11, D-6000 Frankfurt am Main 1, Germany *tel:* +49 692 1202 *fax:* +49 692 123 7565.

Martin Steinhoff, general director; Klauspeter Seibel, chief conductor; Hans Peter Doll, artistic consultant.

Hamburgische Staatsoper. Große Theaterstr 34, D-20354 Hamburg, Germany *tel:* +49 40 35680 *fax:* +49 30 356 8456 *email:* pressestelle@hamburgische-staatsoper.de. Albin Hänseroth, managing director; Detlef Meierjohann, manager; John Neumeier, ballet director.

Kammeroper Frankfurt. Sternstra 31, D-60318 Frankfurt am Main, Germany *tel:* +49 69 55 6189 *also fax.* Rainer Pudenz, artistic director; Roland Böer, conductor.

Komischer Oper. Behrenstr 55-57, D-10117 Berlin, Germany *tel:* +49 30 20 2600 *fax:* +49 30 20 260405 *email:* opera@berlin.snafu.de. Albert Kost, director; Harry Kupfer, principal stage director; Yakov Kreizberg, principal conductor; Richard Wherlock, ballet director.

Landesbühnen Sachsen. Meissner Str 152, D-01445 Radebeul, Germany *tel:* +49 351 89540 *fax:* +49 351 895 4201 *email:* landesbühnensachsen@dresden-theater.de. Christian Schmidt, director; Alexander von Brük, music director; Angelika Hentschel, orchestra admin.

Nationaltheater. Mozartstr 9, D-68161 Mannheim, Germany *tel:* +49 621 16800 *fax:* +49 621 21540. Ulrich Schwab, general manager; Jun Märkl, general music director.

Niedersächsisches Staatstheater Hannover. Opernplatz 1, D-30159 Hannover, Germany *tel:* +49 511 168 46161 *fax:* +49 511 368 1768/2536 *email:* info@staatstheater-hannover.com. Hans-Peter Lehmann, theatre director; Andreas Delfs, general music director; Knut Lehmann, general admin.

Oper Leipzig. Augustusplatz 12, Postfach 346, D-04109 Leipzig, Germany *tel:* +49 341 12610 *fax:* +49 341 126 1387 *email:* oper@leipzig-online.de. Udo Zimmermann, director; Bettina Pesch, admin; Michail Jurowski, acting chief conductor; Axel Joliet, artistic admin.

Opernhaus Chemnitz. Theaterplatz 2, D-09111 Chemnitz, Germany *tel:* +49 371 488 4662 *fax:* +49 371 488 4697.

Opernhaus Halle. Postfach 110554, D-06019 Halle (Saale), Germany *tel:* +49 345 51100 *fax:* +49 345 511 0333 *email:* opernhaus@halle.de. Klaus Froboese, general manager; Reinhard Popp, director; Roger Epple, general music director.

Pocket Opera Company. Gertrudstr 21, D-90429 Nürnberg, Germany *tel:* +49 911 329047 *fax:* +49 911 314606. Peter B Wyrsch, artistic director; David Seaman, music director; Doris Gross, project manager; Andrea Molino, music theatre director.

Saarlandisches Staatstheater. Schillenplatz 1, D-66111 Saarbrucken, Germany *tel:* +49 681 30920 *fax:* +49 681 309 2325. Kurt Josef Schildknecht, general director; Helmut Beckamp.

Sächsische Staatsoper Dresden. Theaterplatz 2, D-01067 Dresden, Germany *tel:* +49 351 49110 *fax:* +49 351 491 1691 *email:* presse@semperoper.de. Christoph Albrecht, general director; Roland Beneke, admin director; Semyon Bychkov, chief conductor; Rolf Wollrad, opera director; Hans-Joachim Frey, artistic company director; Matthias Brauer, chorus master.

Schillertheater NRW. Spinnstr 4, D-42283 Wuppertal, Germany *tel:* +49 202 563 4230 *fax:* +49 202 563 8078. Holk Freytag, Ludwig Baum, admin.

Staatsoper Unter den Linden. Unter den Linden 5-7, D-10117 Berlin, Germany *tel:* +49 30 203 54555 (box office); +49 30 203540 (operator) *fax:* +49 30 203 54483 (box office); +49 30 203 54206 (operator) *email:* contact@staatsoper-berlin.org. Georg Quander, director; Daniel Barenboim, general music director; Georg Vierthaler, general director; Achim Dobschall, artistic director; Stephan Adam, PA; Sabine Turner, marketing.

Staatsoperette Dresden. Pimaer Landstr 131, D-01257 Dresden, Germany *tel:* +49 351 207 990/21 *fax:* +49 351 207 9922.

Staatstheater Braunschweig. Postfach 4539, D-38100 Braunschweig, Germany *tel:* +49 531 484 2700 *fax:* +49 531 484 2727 *email:* service@staatstheater-braunschweig.de. Wolfgang Gropper, general director; Jonas Alber, general music director; Thomas Fehrle, admin director; Peter Schanz, artistic director; Ingrid Baumann, operations director; Uwe Schwarz, chief stage manager.

Staatstheater Darmstadt. Postfach 111432, D-64229 Darmstadt, Germany *tel:* +49 615 128111 *fax:* +49 615 128 11226. Gerd-Theo Umberg, director; Michael Obermeier, admin.

Staatstheater Stuttgart. Oberer Schlossgarten 6, Postfach 104345, D-70173 Stuttgart, Germany *tel:* +49 711 203 2520 *fax:* +49 711 203 2514. Klaus Zehelein, opera director; Lothar Zagrosek, general music director; Pamela Rosenberg, opera co-director; Doris Szenczar, head of planning.

Städtische Bühnen Augsburg. Postfach 111949, D-86044 Augsburg, Germany *tel:* +49 821 324 3933 *fax:* +49 821 324 4544. Helge Thoma, director; Peter Leonard, general music director; Erich Payer, ballet director.

Städtische Bühnen Nürnberg. Theater Nürnberg, Richard-Wagner Platz 2-10, D-90443 Nürnberg, Germany *tel:* +49 911 231 3808 *fax:* +49 911 231 3534. Wulf Konold, general director; Phillippe Auguin, general music director.

Städtische Bühnen Regensburg. Bismarckplatz 7, Postfach 110617, D-93047 Regensburg, Germany *tel:* +49 941 507 1422 *fax:* +49 941 507 4429. Marietheres List, artistic admin; Holger von Berg, admin.

Greece

Greek National Opera. 18 Charilaou Tricoupi, GR-106 79 Athens, Greece *tel:* +30 1 363 3105 *fax:* +30 1 360 0224. G Kouroupos, president; L Karytinos, chief conductor.

Opera at the Megaron. The Athens Concert Hall, Vas Sofias Ave, 1 Kokkali St, GR-115 21 Athens, Greece *tel:* +30 1 728 2000 *fax:* +30 1 729 0174. Christos Lambrakis, chairman; Nikos Manolopoulos, general manager; N Tsouchlos, director artistic programmes; H Spanopoulou, marketing director; Y Papatheodorou, press officer; Alexander Mycat, artistic director.

Hungary

The Hungarian State Opera. Andrássy út 22, H-1061, Budapest, Hungary *tel:* +36 1 331 2550 *fax:* +36 1 332 7331 *email:* venczel@opera.jegymester.hu; kissimre@opera.jegymester.hu. Miklós Szinetar, general director; Imre Kiss, general manager; Attila Fülöp, general secretary; Sándor Venczel, financial manager; Andor Lénárd, programme director; Géza Oberfrank, Ervin Lukács, senior music directors.

Iceland

The Icelandic Opera. Ingolfsstraeti, PO Box 1416, 121 Reykjavik, Iceland *tel:* +354 552 7033 *fax:* +354 552 7384 *email:* gardar@opera.is; opera@opera.is.

Republic of Ireland

Abbey Centre. Tirconnel St, Ballyshannon, Co Donegal, Republic of Ireland *tel:* +353 7 251375 *fax:* +353 7 22832. Barney McLaughlin, manager.

An Taibhdhearc. Middle St, Galway, Co Galway, Republic of Ireland *tel:* +353 9 156 2024/563600 *fax:* +353 9 156 3195 *email:* taibh@iol.ie. Aoife Ni Scolat, admin; Padraigh OhEanai, music director; Micheal OhAinnin, chairman.

Opera Ireland. John Player House, 276-288 South Circular Rd, Dublin 8, Republic of Ireland *tel:* +353 1 453 5519/5520 *fax:* +353 1 453 5521 *email:* info@opera-ireland.ie. David Collopy, general manager; Dieter Kaegi, artistic director; Kay Keilthy, admin; Taragh Loughrey-Grant, marketing executive; Donal Sheils, company manager; Paul Foley, production manager.

Opera Theatre Company. Temple Bar Music Centre, Dublin 2, Republic of Ireland *tel:* +353 1 679 4962 *fax:* +353 1 679 4963 *email:* otc@imn.ie. James Conway, director; Gemma Murray, admin; Nick Costello, marketing and education; Jan Duffy, publicity.

Israel

Ambassador Enterprise. 2 Truart Hameri St, 55286 Kiryat Ono, Israel *tel:* +972 3 635 3418 *fax:* +972 3 535 2726 *email:* ambtours@actcom.co.il. Roni Abramson, managing director.

New Israeli Opera. Tel Aviv Performing Arts Centre, 28 Leonardo da Vinci St, POB 33321, Tel Aviv 61332, Israel *tel:* +972 3 692 7803 *fax:* +972 3 695 4886 *email:* opera@netvision.net.il. Hanna Munitz, general director; Asher Fisch, music director.

Italy

L'Arena di Verona. Fondazione Arena di Verona, Piazza Bra 28, I-37121 Verona, Italy *tel:* +39 045 805 1811 *fax:* +39 045 801 1566. Renzo Giacchieri, general director.

Teatro Comunale (Florence). Maggio Musicale Fiorentino, Via Solferino 15, I-50123 Firenze, Italy *tel:* +39 055 27791 *fax:* +39 055 239 6954 *email:* teatro.comunale@infogroup.it (ticket office). Francesco Emani, general manager; Zubin Mehta, principal conductor; Semyon Bychkov, principal guest conductor; Cesare Mazzonis, artistic director; Susanna Colombo, press officer.

Teatro Comunale (Treviso). Corso Del Popolo 31, I-31100 Treviso, Italy *tel:* +39 042 241 0130/254 6355 *fax:* +39 042 258 2285/241 0804. Alfonso Malaguti, director; Giancarlo Gentilini, co-ordinator.

Teatro Comunale di Bologna. Largo Respighi 1, I-40126 Bologna, Italy *tel:* +39 051 52 9901/9958/9999 *fax:* +39 051 52 9934/9905. Felicia Bottino, director; Sindaco di Bologna, president.

Teatro Comunale Giuseppe Verdi. Riva 3 Novembre, I-34121 Trieste, Italy *tel:* +39 040 672 2111 *fax:* +39 040 672 2249. Lorenzo Jorio, director; Gianni Gori, production manager.

Teatro Comunale di Modena. Via del Teatro 8, I-41100 Modena, Italy *tel:* +39 059 225443. Pietro Valenti, theatre director; Aldo Sisillo; Rossana Borghi, admin; Lorena Loschi.

Il Teatro dell'Opera. Piazza B Gigli 8, I-00184 Roma, Italy *tel:* +39 06 481601 *fax:* +39 06 488 1253.

Teatro Massimo. Via R Wagner 2, I-90139 Palermo, Italy *tel:* +39 091 605 3111 *fax:* +39 091 605 3324/5 *email:* infotm@teatromassimo.it. Attilio Orlando, general manager; Marco Betta, artistic director; Antonio Cognata, general secretary.

Teatro Municipale Valli. Piazza Martiri 7, Luglio, Reggio Emilia, Italy *tel:* +39 052 245 8811 *fax:* +39 052 245 8922 *email:* uffstampa @i-teatri.re.it. Elio Canova, president; Bruno Borghi, director; Mario Vighi, marketing, communications manager; Daniela Spallanzani, admin manager; Elisabetta Miselli, box office, group sales.

Teatro Regio (Parma). Via Garibaldi 16, I-43100 Parma, Italy *tel:* +39 052 121 8912/8698 *fax:* +39 052 120 6156. Angela Cauzzi, director; Gianni Tangucci, artistic consultant.

Teatro Regio (Torino). Piazza Castella 215, I-10124 Torino, Italy *tel:* +39 011 88151 *fax:* +39 011 881 5214 *email:* dirarptr@inrete.it. Carlo Majer, artistic director.

Teatro di San Carlo. Via San Carlo 98 F, I-80132 Naploi, Italy *tel:* +39 081 797 2111. Francesco Canessa, general manager; Carlo Mayer, artistic director.

Teatro Sociale. Piazza Folengo 4, I-46100 Mantua, Italy *tel:* +39 037 636 2739 *also fax*. Riccardo Riva Berni, president; Enzio Ricci, artistic director and admin.

Japan

The Japan Opera Foundation. Nishiazabu 28 Mori Building, 4-16-13 Nishiazabu, Minato-ku, Tokyo 106, Japan *tel:* +81 3 5466 3185 *fax:* +81 3 5466 3186. jof@jof.or.jp.

Nissay Theatre. 1-1-1 Yuraku-cho, Chiyoda-ku, Tokyo, Japan *tel:* +81 3 501 3122 *fax:* +81 3 3581 3493 *email:* s.inoue@nissaytheatre.or.jp. Shinji Inoue, executive director.

Oitaken Folk Opera Society. 11-1 Nakakasuga-cho, Oita-shi, Oita-ken 870-0039, Japan *tel:* +81 9 7532 5836 *also fax*. Takanari Kocho, manager; Hisako Kocho, president; Tadayasu Kato, vice-president.

Latvia

Latvian National Opera. Aspazijas Blvd 3, LV-1050 Riga, Latvia *tel:* +371 722 5747/5803/3436 *fax:* +371 722 8240/8930 *email:* opera@latnet.lv. Andrejs Zagars, general manager; Arturs Maskats, artistic co-director.

Lithuania

Lithuanian Opera and Ballet Theatre. Vienuolio 1, Vilnius, Lithuania *tel:* +370 262 0093/0636/0515 *fax:* +370 262 3503 *email:* opera@lithill.lt.

Mexico

Compañiá Nacional de apera. Palacio de Bellas Artes, Ave Hidalgo No 1, Mexico DF 06050, Mexico *tel:* +52 5 521 3668 *also fax; fax:* +52 5 521 6776. Gerado Kleinburg, artistic director; Jose Arean, assistant conductor, artistic manager; Eleonora Velasquez, stage director; Esther Perez, PR; Octavio Sosa, orchestra manager; Mariano Alva, admin.

Monaco

L'Opéra de Monte-Carlo. BP 139, Place du Casino, Monte-Carlo, Monaco *tel:* +37 79 216 2318 *fax:* +37 79 330 0757. John Mordler, director; Marie-Christine Forestier, financial admin; Olivier Lefebvre, communication.

Netherlands

Chassé Theater. PO Box 1135, NL-4801 BC Breda, Netherlands *tel:* +31 76 530 3132/3100 *fax:* +31 76 530 3190. Reg ten Zijthoff, artistic director; Bart Van Mossel, head of programme department.

De Nederlandse Opera. Waterlooplein 22, NL-1011 PG Amsterdam, Netherlands *tel:* +31 20 551 8922 *fax:* +31 20 551 8311 *email:* info@nederlandse-opera.nl. Truze M Lodder, general admin; Pierre Audi, artistic director; Edo de Waart, chief conductor; Peter de Caluwe, artistic admin.

Internationaal Opera Centrum Nederland. Vendelstr 2, NL-1012 XX Amsterdam, Netherlands *tel:* +31 20 420 0562 *fax:* +31 20 420 2505 *email:* info@iocn.nl. Hans Nieuwenhuis, general director; Peter Tra, general admin; Winfried Maczewski, music director.

Nationale Reisopera. Perikweg 97, Postbus 1321, NL-7512 DP Enschede, Netherlands *tel:* +31 53 487 8500 *fax:* +31 53 432 1882 *email:* nationale@reisopera.nl. Louwrens Langevoort, general director; Andreas Heinen, technical director; Bert Eenink, financial director; Ben Coelman, PR.

Opera Zuid. PO Box 104, NL-6200 AC Maastricht, Netherlands *tel:* +31 43 321 0166 *fax:* +31 43 325 7655 *email:* office@operazuid.nl. Jan Nijsten, managing director; Rennie Wright, artistic director.

Stadsschouwburg Eindhoven. Elzentlaan 50, NL-5615 CN Eindhoven, Netherlands *tel:* +31 40 211 1122 *fax:* +31 40 238 4810.

Stadsschouwburg Heerlen. Burgemeester Van Grunsvenplein 145, NL-6411 AS Heerlen, Netherlands *tel:* +31 45 576 8576/571 6607 (tickets) *fax:* +31 45 571 8794. Bas Schoonderwoerd, director; Wim Slooten, accounting; Jos Palmen, chief engineer; Helmi Engelen, operations manager.

New Zealand

The National Opera of Wellington. Opera House, PO Box 6588, Wellington, New Zealand *tel:* +64 4 384 4434 *fax:* +64 4 384 3333 *email:* nat.opera@xtra-co.nz. Patricia Hurley, manager; Bruce Greenfield, artistic admin.

Norway

Bergen Kammeropera. Fjøsangerveien 33A, N-5054 Bergen, Norway. Marit Karaskiewicz, art director; Inke Magnuson, art co-ordinator.

Den Norske Opera. Box 8800, Youngstorget, N-0028 Oslo, Norway *tel:* +47 22 429 475 *fax:* +47 22 334 027. Bjørn Simensen, general manager; Bernt E Bauge, admin director.

Kristiansund Opera. King Olav V St 1, N-6500 Kristiansund, Norway *tel:* +47 7158 9960 *fax:* +47 7158 9961 *email:* opera@oik.no. Olav Grytnes, director; Rune Svendsen, production manager; Kjell Seim, music director.

Opera Bergen. Komediebakken 9, N-5016 Bergen, Norway *tel:* +47 55 323 856 *fax:* +47 55 322 435. Anne Randine Överby, artistic director; Tone Kvam Thorsen, production manager.

Opera Vest. Eduard Griegsplass 1, N-5015 Bergen, Norway *tel:* +47 55 216 120 *fax:* +47 55 216 121 *email:* bit20ens@bgnett.no. Stein Olav Henrichsen, artistic director; Ø Kvinge, producer.

Poland

Grand Theatre-National Opera. Plac Teatralny 1, PL-00-950 Warsaw, PO Box 59, Poland *tel:* +48 22 692 0200 *fax:* +48 22 826 5012/0423 *email:* office@teatrwielki.pl. Waldemar Dabrowski, general director; Jacek Kaspszyk, artistic director; Jerzy Bojar, first deputy general director; Janusz Chojecki, technical director; Stanislaw Leszczynski, deputy artistic director.

Warsaw Chamber Opera. Ul Nowogrodzka 49, PL-00-695 Warszawa, Poland *tel:* +48 82 628 3096; +48 22 293233 *also fax; fax:* +48 223 14764. Stefan Sutowski, artistic director.

Portugal

Fundacao de Sao Carlos. Rua Serpa Pinto 9, P-1200 Lisboa, Portugal *tel:* +35 1 346 8408. Manuel E Machado Macedo, president; Paulo Ferreira de Castro, artistic director; Alfred Barrosi, member of the executive committee.

Slovak Republic

Slovak National Theatre. Gorkého 4, 815 86 Bratislava, Slovak Republic *tel:* +421 7 533 5085 *fax:* +421 7 533 5072. Ondrej Lenárd, artistic director; Miroslav Fischer, general director.

South Africa

Cape Town Opera. PO Box 4107, Cape Town 8000, South Africa *tel:* +27 21 215470 *fax:* +27 21 215448. Angelo Gobbato, director; Charmaine Ferreira, manager; Ronnie Theys, company manager; Alec Beukes, publicity and press manager.

State Theatre Pretoria. Opera, PO Box 566, Pretoria 0001, South Africa *tel:* +27 12 322 1665 *fax:* +27 12 322 3913 *email:* truk@iafrica.com. Johan Maré, admin head.

Spain

Teatre Principal. Carrer La Riera 2-A, E-07003 Palma de Mallorca, Balearic Islands, Spain *tel:* +34 97 1 713346 *fax:* +34 97 1 725542.

Teatro de la Maestranza. Paseo de Colon S/n, E-41001 Sevilla, Spain *tel:* +34 95 4223344 *fax:* +34 95 422 5995 *email:* rrpp@arrakis.es. Jose Luis Castro, managing director; Giuseppe Cuccia, production manager; Francisco Santamaria, admin director; Antonio Moreno, technical director; Rocio Castro, press, PR.

Teatro de la Zarzuela. Jovellanos 4, E-28014 Madrid, Spain *tel:* +34 91 524 5400 *fax:* +34 91 429 7157. Emilio Sagi, artistic director; Miguel Roa, music director; José Luis Morata, general director; Cristina Vázquez, prod director.

Sweden

Drottningholm Slottsteater. PO Box 270500, S-10251 Stockholm, Sweden *tel:* +46 8 665 1400 *fax:* +46 8 665 1473. Per Erik Öhrn, artistic director; Per Forsström, general manager.

Göteborgs Operan. Christina Nilssons Gata, S-41104 Göteborg, Sweden *tel:* +46 3 110 8000 *fax:* +46 3 110 8030 *email:* info@opera.se. Dag Hallberg, general director; Kjell Ingebretsen, artistic director; Anders Hellström, ballet director.

Norrlandsoperan. PO Box 360, S-90108 Umeå, Sweden *tel:* +46 90 154300 *fax:* +46 90 126845 *email:* info@vbm.se. Lars Tibell, general and artistic director; Helen Sundström-Hetta, deputy general director and finance manager; Camilla Fahlander, marketing officer; Björn Björklund, press officer; Eva Lindh-Holmgren, company manager; Anders Andersson, technical admin.

Royal Swedish Opera. Box 16094, S-10322 Stockholm, Sweden *tel:* +46 8 791 4300 *fax:* +46 8 791 4444. Bengt Hall, general manager; Lars Jonasson, financial manager; Claes-Håkan Ahnsjö, opera director; Peiter Jacobsson, ballet director; Staffan Carlweitz, press officer.

Swedish Folkopera. Hornsgatan 72, S-11821 Stockholm, Sweden *tel:* +46 8 616 0750/0700 *fax:* +46 8 844146 *email:* m.aspegren@folkopera.se. Claes Fellbom, artistic director; Kerstin Nerbe, music director; Magnus Aspegren, managing director; Elenor Wolgers, marketing manager.

Switzerland

Grand Théâtre de Genève. Administration 11, Blvd du Théâtre, CH-1211 Genève 11, Switzerland *tel:* +41 22 418 3000 *fax:* +41 22 418 3001. Renée Auphan, general director; François Duchêne, general secretary; Jacques Ayrault, technical director; Guillaume Tourniaire, choirmaster; Marcel Quillévéré, assistant to the director; Guy Demole, president of the board.

Luzerner Theater. Theaterstr 2, CH-6002 Luzern, Switzerland *tel:* +41 41 210 6618/9 *fax:* +41 41 210 3367. Horst Statkus, artistic director; Adrian Balmer, admin director; Jonathan Nott, music director.

Opernhaus Zurich. Falkenstrasse 1, CH-8008 Zurich, Switzerland *tel:* +41 1 268 6400/6666 *fax:* +41 1 268 6401/6555. Alexander Pereira, general director; Franz Welser-Möst, music director; Grischa Asagaroff, artistic director.

Stadtheater St Gallen. Museumstrasse 24, CH-9004 St Gallen, Switzerland *tel:* +41 71 242 0505 *fax:* +41 71 242 0506. Werner Signer, managing director; Peter Schweiger, director of drama.

Theater Basel. Elisabethenstrasse 16, CH-4010 Basel, Switzerland *tel:* +41 61 295 1100 *fax:* +41 61 295 1200 *email:* info@theater-basel.ch. Michael Schindhelm, general manager; Ivo Reichlin, admin director; Albrecht Puhlmann, opera director; Julia Jones, chief conductor.

TML Opera de Lausanne. CP 3972, CH-1002 Lausanne, Switzerland *tel:* +41 21 310 1616/1600 *fax:* +41 21 310 1690. Dominique Meyer, director; Paul Durussel, admin; Bruno Boyer, technical director; Laurence Authier, press and communication; Marie-Laure Chabloz, secretary; Emmanuel de Bougknecht, secretary.

USA

Arizona Opera. 3501 North Mountain Ave, Tucson, AZ 85719, USA *tel:* +1 520 293 4336 *fax:* +1 520 293 5097 *email:* nancy1@azopera.com. Glynn Ross, general director; Lloyd Yunker, admin director; Dean Ryan, music director; Leilani Rothrock, business and finance director; Laura Schairer, marketing director; Monica Burrows, director of PR.

The Atlanta Opera. 1800 Peachtree St NW, Suite 620, Atlanta, Georgia 30309, USA *tel:* +1 404 355 3311/817 8700 *fax:* +1 404 355 3259 *email:* atlopera@mindspring.com. Alfred Kennedy, executive director; William Fred Scott, artistic director.

Austin Lyric Opera. PO Box 984, Austin, TX 78767, USA *tel:* +1 512 472 5927 *fax:* +1 512 472 4143 *email:* frontdesk@austinlyricopera.org. Joseph McClain, general director.

Baltimore Opera Company. 110 W Mount Royal Ave, Suite 306, Baltimore, MD 21201, USA *tel:* +1 410 727 6000 (box office); +1 410 625 1600 (admin) *fax:* +1 410 727 7854; +1 410 625 6474. Michael Harrison, general director; James Harp, artistic admin and chorus master; William Yannuzzi, music director; Peter Johnson, production manager; Joel Purcell, business manager.

Boheme Opera NJ. PO Box 4157, Trenton, NJ 08610, USA *tel:* +1 609 581 9551; +1 609 683 8000 (box office) *fax:* +1 609 581 9553; +1 609 497 0369 (box office). Joseph Pucciatti, artistic director, conductor; Sandra Pucciatti, managing director; Sheila Marrero, development director; Barbara Golomb, admin assistant; Mary Kaye Metcalf, president.

Central City Opera. 621 17th St, Suite 1601, Denver, CO 80293, USA *tel:* +1 303 292 6700 *fax:* +1 303 292 4958 *email:* ccopera@mho.net. Pelham G Pearce, general director; Curt Hancock, artistic admin.

Chautauqua Opera. Chautauqua Institution, Chautauqua, New York 14722, USA *tel:* +1 716 357 6200/6250 *fax:* +1 716 357 9014. Jay Lesenger, artistic director.

The Cincinnati Opera. 1241 Elm St, Cincinnati, OH 45210, USA *tel:* +1 513 621 1919/241 2742 *fax:* +1 513 621 4310. Patricia K Beggs, managing director; Nicholas Muni, artistic director; Thomas Bankston, artistic admin; Glenn L Plott, director of production.

Cleveland Opera. State Theatre, Playhouse Square Centre, 1519 Euclid Avenue, Cleveland, OH 44115-1901, USA *tel:* +1 216 575 0903 *fax:* +1 216 575 1918 *email:* mail@clevelandopera.org. David Bamberger, general director; Carola Bamberger, associate director and marketing director.

Connecticut Opera. 226 Farmington Ave, Hartford, CT 06105, USA *tel:* +1 203 953 3517/27 *fax:* +1 203 293 1715 *email:* connopera@aol.com.

The Dallas Opera. 3102 Oak Lawn Ave, Suite 450, Dallas, TX 75219, USA *tel:* +1 214 443 1043 *fax:* +1 214 443 1060 *email:* opera@computek.net. Plato Karayanis, general director; Graeme Jenkins, music director; George Landis, marketing and communications director; John Gage, production director; Jonathan Pell, artistic admin director; Rebecca Sherman, PR manager.

Des Moines Metro Opera. 106 West Boston Ave, Indianola, IA 50125, USA *tel:* +1 515 961 6221 *fax:* +1 515 961 2994. Jerilee Mace, executive director; Robert Larsen, artistic director; Kristin Varme, marketing and public relations director; Kirkland Gilmer, production manager; Molly Spain, art director; Denise Core, box office; Arlys Kellar, business manager; Robert Montana, admin director.

Florentine Opera Company. 735 N Water St, Suite 1315, Milwaukee, WI 53202 4106, USA *tel:* +1 414 291 5700 *fax:* +1 414 291 5706 *email:* info@florentineopera.org. Dennis W Hanthorn, general director; Joseph Rescigno, artistic adviser.

Florida Grand Opera. 1200 Coral Way, Miami, Fl 33145-2980, USA *tel:* +1 305 854 1643 *fax:* +1 305 856 1042 *email:* info@fgo.org. Robert M Heuer, general director and CEO; Stewart Robertson, music director; Paul P Lapinski, assistant general director; Karl W Hesser, director of artistic admin.

Glimmerglass Opera. PO Box 191, Cooperstown, NY 13326, USA *tel:* +1 607 547 2255 *fax:* +1 607 547 1257 *email:* glimmer@telenet.net. Esther Nelson, general director; Paul Kellogg, artistic director; Stewart Robertson, music director; Nicholas Russell, director of artistic admin; Tara Barnwell, marketing manager; Michael Willis, director of public relations.

Houston Grand Opera. 510 Preston St, Houston, TX 77002, USA *tel:* +1 713 546 0200 *fax:* +1 713 247 0906 *email:* administration@hgo.com. David Gockley, general director; Jim Ireland, general manager.

Indianapolis Opera. 250 E 38th St, Indianapolis, IN 46205, USA *tel:* +1 317 283 3531 *fax:* +1 317 923 5611. James Caraher, artistic director; John C Pickett, executive director; Patty Harvey, director of education; JoEllen Bendall, director of advancement; Dave Lawrence, director of marketing; Stephen Goldberg, production manager.

Kentucky Opera. 101 S 8th St, Louisville, KY 40202-4016, USA *tel:* +1 502 584 4500 *fax:* +1 502 584 7484 *email:* kyopera@ntr.net. Deborah Sandler, general director; H Charles Schmidt, director of production; Robin Stamper, director of music and education; Gerald Farrar, director of special events and PR; Robert Curland, director of sales; Teresa Kinney, director of audience development.

Los Angeles Music Center Opera. 135 North Grand Ave, Los Angeles, CA 90012, USA *tel:* +1 213 972 7219 *fax:* +1 213 687 3490. Peter Hemmings, general director; Christopher Hahn, artistic admin.

Lyric Opera of Chicago. 20 North Wacker Drive, Chicago, IL 60606, USA *tel:* +1 312 332 2244 *fax:* +1 312 419 8345. William Mason, general director; Bruno Bartoletti, artistic director; Danny Newman, PR counsel; Farrell Frentress, director of development; Susan Mathieson, director of marketing and communications.

Madison Opera. 333 Glenway St, Madison, WI 53705-1310, USA *tel:* +1 608 238 8085 *fax:* +1 608 233 3431. Ann Stanke, general director; John De Main, artistic director; Patricia R Helm, marketing director.

The Metropolitan Opera. Lincoln Center, New York, NY 10023, USA *tel:* +1 212 799 3100/362 6000 (tickets). James Levine, artistic director; Joseph Volpe, general manager; Sarah Billinghurst, assistant manager; Jonathan Friend, artistic admin; François Giuliani, press and PR.

Michigan Opera Theatre. Administrative Offices, Lothrop Landing, 104 Lothrop, Detroit, MI 48202, USA *tel:* +1 313 874 7850/7464 *fax:* +1 313 871 7213. David DiChiera, general director; Tom Tomlinson, managing director; Steve Haviaras, marketing director; Laura Wyss, PR director.

The Minnesota Opera. 620 North First St, Minneapolis, MN 55401, USA *tel:* +1 612 333 2700 *fax:* +1 612 333 0869. Kevin Smith, president and general director; Dale Johnson, artistic director.

Mobile Opera Inc. PO Box 66633, Mobile, AL 26660-1633, USA *tel:* +1 334 476 7377 *fax:* +1 334 476 7373 *email:* gendir@aol.com. Jerome Shannon, general director; Carole Jett, executive assistant; Nancy Tomar, box office manager; Beverly Corte, president.

Nevada Opera. PO Box 3256, Reno, NV 89505, USA *tel:* +1 702 786 4046 *fax:* +1 702 786 4063 *email:* Nvopera@aol.com. Frank D Kistler, general director.

New Orleans Opera. 305 Baronne St, Suite 500, New Orleans, LA 70112-1618, USA *tel:* +1 504 529 2278 *fax:* +1 504 529 7668 *email:* newogendir@aol.com; carolnooa@aol.com. Robert Tannebaum, general director; Carol Rausch, education director.

New York City Opera. New York State Theater, 20 Lincoln Center, New York, NY 10023, USA *tel:* +1 212 870 5600 *fax:* +1 212 724 1120. Paul Kellogg, general and artistic director; Sherwin Goldman, executive director.

Opera Carolina. 345 N College St #409, Charlotte, NC 28202, USA *tel:* +1 704 332 7177/372 1000 *fax:* +1 704 332 6448/333 1154 *email:* operacar@charlotte.infi.net. James W Wright, president and general director; Gaetano Staffa, vice president; Steve Dellinger, production manager; Teresa Robertson, director of education and community programmes; Angela Taylor, business manager; Susan Delong, development officer.

Opera Columbus. 177 Naghten St, Columbus, OH 43215, USA *tel:* +1 614 461 0022 *fax:* +1 614 461 0806 *email:* operacols@aol.com. William F Russell, general director.

Opera Company of Philadelphia. 510 Walnut St, Suite 1500, Philadelphia, PA 19106, USA *tel:* +1 215 928 2100/2110 *fax:* +1 215 928 2112 *email:* ostroff@operaphilly.com. Robert Driver, general director; Susan Ashbaker, artistic admin; Don Smith, development and planning director; Gary Gausky, director of finance; Craig Hamilton, public affairs director; Boyd Ostroff, director of production.

Opera Delaware. 824 N Market St #200, Wilmington, DE 19801-3024, USA *tel:* +1 302 658 8063 *fax:* +1 302 658 4991 *email:* opinfo@operadel.org. Leland Kimball, general director.

Opera Memphis. University of Memphis, Campus Box 526331, Memphis, TN 38152-6331, USA *tel:* +1 901 678 2706 *fax:* +1 901 678 3506. Michael Ching, general and artistic director; Karen Tiller, executive director and director of production; Adrienne Clark, marketing director; David Barnwell, box office manager; Sheri Bancroft, education co-ordinator and company manager.

Opera Music Theatre International. 1201 Pennsylvania Avenue NW, Suite 300, Washington DC, 20004, USA *tel:* +1 202 661 4716 *fax:* +1 202 661 4699 *email:* mail@omti.org. James K McCully, general director; Randall R Reade, administrative director.

Opera Pacific. PO Box 28679, Santa Ana, California, CA 92799, USA *tel:* +1 714 428 0500 *fax:* +1 714 428 0508. Martin Hubbard, executive director; John DeMain, artistic director; George Sebastian, general manager.

Opera Roanoke. 541 Luck Ave, Jefferson Centre, Suite 209, Roanoke, VA 24016, USA *tel:* +1 540 982 2742 *fax:* +1 540 982 3601 *email:* opera_roanoke@compuserve.com. Craig Fields, artistic director; William Krause, executive director; Sallee Ebbett, finance manager; Marguerite Collins, production manager, marketing director.

Opera Theatre of Saint Louis. PO Box 191910, St Louis, MO 63119-7910, USA *tel:* +1 314 961 0171 *fax:* +1 314 961 7463. Eric Millner, artistic co-ordinator.

Palm Beach Opera. 415 S Olive Ave, West Palm Beach, FL 33401, USA *tel:* +1 561 833 7888 *fax:* +1 561 833 8294 *email:* pbopera@pbopera.org. Herbert P Benn, general director; Anton Guadagno, artistic director and principal conductor.

Piedmont Opera Theatre. 900 West First St, Winston-Salem, NC 27101, USA *tel:* +1 336 725 7101 *fax:* +1 336 725 7131 *email:* info@piedmontopera.org. Mary Robert, general director; Virginia Hart, marketing director; Victoria Auchincloss, company manager; John Motoc, production manager.

Pittsburgh Opera. 801 Penn Ave, Pittsburgh, PA 15222-3407, USA *tel:* +1 412 281 0912/456 6666 *fax:* +1 412 281 4324 *email:* pghopera@aol.com. Tito Capobianco, artistic director; Mark J Weinstein, executive director.

Portland Opera. 1515 SW Morrison, Portland, OR 97205, USA *tel:* +1 503 241 1401/241 1802 *fax:* +1 503 241 4212. Robert Bailey, general director; Valeria Ramirez, admin director; Kathy Park, director of development; James Fullan, director of public relations; Susan Thompson, director of marketing; John Peter Jeffries, director of production.

San Diego Opera. 18th Floor, Civic Centre Plaza, 1200 Third Ave, San Diego, CA 92101-4112, USA *tel:* +1 619 232 7636 *fax:* +1 619 231 6915 *email:* sdostaff@sdopera.com. Ian D Campbell, general director; Michael Murphy, director of admin; Marianne Flettner, artistic admin.

San Francisco Opera. War Memorial Opera House, San Francisco, CA 94012-4509, USA *tel:* +1 415 565 6431/864 3300 *fax:* +1 415 621 7508. Lotfi Mansouri, general director; Donald C Runnicles, music director; Michael J Savage, managing director; Christina Scheppelmann, artistic admin; Clifford Cranna, music admin.

The Santa Fe Opera. PO Box 2408, Santa Fe, NM 87504-2408, USA *tel:* +1 505 986 5955 *fax:* +1 505 986 5999. John Crosby, general director; Richard Gaddes, associate general director; Brad Woolbright, company manager.

Sarasota Opera. 61 North Pineapple Dr, Sarasota, FL 34236-5716, USA *tel:* +1 941 366 8450 *fax:* +1 941 955 5571 *email:* sarasota@aol.com. Deane C Allyn, executive director; Victor DeRenzi, artistic director.

Seattle Opera. PO Box 9248, Seattle, WA 98109, USA *tel:* +1 206 389 7600/7676/7699 *fax:* +1 206 389 7651. Speight Jenkins, general director; Kathy Magiera, admin director; Melanie Ross, company manager; Cynthia Savage, production director; Linda Prather, marketing director; Tina Ryker, PR director.

Shreveport Opera. 212 Texas St Suite 101, Shreveport, LA 71101-3249, USA *tel:* +1 318 227 9503 *fax:* +1 318 227 9518. Gayle Norton, general manager; Joseph Illick, artistic director.

Skylight Opera Theatre. 158 N Broadway, Milwaukee, WI 53202, USA *tel:* +1 414 291 7800 *fax:* +1 414 291 7815. Joan Lounsbery, managing director; Richard Carsey, artistic director; Paula Suozzi, associate artistic director.

Tacoma Opera. PO Box 7468, Tacoma, WA 98407, USA *tel:* +1 206 627 7789. Anne Farrell, general manager; Marian Scheele, fund development; David Bartholomew, resident stage director.

Toledo Opera. The Valentine Theatre, 406 Adams St, Toledo, OH 43604-1407, USA *tel:* +1 419 255 7464 *fax:* +1 419 255 6344 *email:* info@toledo-opera.com. James Meena, general director and principal conductor; Libbey McKnight, marketing director; Joan Eckermann, education and outreach director; Elizabeth Emmert, development director; Paul Causman, box office manager.

Townsend Opera Players. PO Box 4519, Modesto, CA 95352, USA *tel:* +1 209 523 6426 *fax:* +1 209 579 0532. Erik Buck Townsend, general director; Erika Townsend, operations manager; Bunny Donalson, PR and marketing; Barbara Wesley, membership; Bryan Hoffman, production manager.

Tri-Cities Opera. 315 Clinton St, Binghamton, NY 13905, USA *tel:* +1 607 772 0400 *fax:* +1 607 797 6344 *email:* tco@tier.net. Peyton Hibbitt, Duane Skrabalak, artistic directors; Susan MacLennan, executive director; Peter Sicilian, associate director; Kim Eaton, marketing director.

Utah Opera. 50 West 200 South, Salt Lake City, UT 84101, USA *tel:* +1 801 736 6868 *fax:* +1 801 736 6815 *email:* info@utahopera.org. Anne Ewers, general director; Leslie Peterson, director of operations; John Wehrle, music admin; Denise Simpkins, development resource manager; Judith Carleson, director of PR and marketing; LeGrand Richins, finance director; Michelle Peterson, director of production.

The Virginia Opera. 300 W Franklin St, Suite 101E, Richmond, VA 23220, USA *tel:* +1 804 644 8168 *fax:* +1 804 644 0415. Peter Mark, general and artistic director; Russell P Allen, general manager; Debra Harrison, director of production; Donna Hildebrand, director of finance and admin; Joseph Walsh, artistic admin; Amy Bridge, manager.

The Washington Opera. 2600 Virginia Ave, NW, Suite 104, Washington DC 20037, USA *tel:* +1 202 295 2420 *fax:* +1 202 298 6008. Patricia L Mossel, executive director; Placido Domingo, artistic director; Edward C Purrington, artistic admin; Heinz Fricke, music director; Noel Uzemack, technical director.

Whitewater Opera Company. 1118 E Main St, Richmond, IN 47374, USA *tel:* +1 765 962 7106 *fax:* +1 765 962 7451 *email:* wocop@infocom.com. Charles Combopiano, artistic director; Curtis Tucker, managing director; Nadine L Harris, marketing director, office manager; Jeffry A Harris, development director.

Wolf Trap Opera Company. Wolf Trap Foundation, 1624 Trap Road, Vienna, VA 22182-2063, USA *tel:* +1 703 255 1935 *fax:* +1 703 255 1924 *email:* wtoc@wolf-trap.org. Kim Pensinger Witman, general director; Lisa A Ostrich, admin director.

Choirs and Choruses

The following list includes professional choirs and major choruses who tour internationally and are reputed for their public performances and recording work. Some of the choirs are affiliated to orchestras which may be listed in the **Symphony Orchestra** section.

Australia

Astra Choir (45). PO Box 365, North Melbourne, Vic 3051, Australia *tel:* +61 3 9326 5424 *fax:* +61 3 9329 2272. John McCaughey, director; Bobby Hodge, manager. *10 professional performances a year.*

Melbourne Chorale (200). 110 Keppel St, PO Box 1148, Carlton, Vic 3053, Australia *tel:* +61 3 9347 9885 *fax:* +61 3 9347 7973 *email:* melbchor@vicnet.net.au. Graham Abbott, musical director; Nick Bailey, general manager.

Sydney Philharmonia Choirs (40-120). Pier 4, Hickson Rd, Millers Point, Sydney 2000, Australia *tel:* +61 2 9251 2024 *fax:* +61 2 9251 2117. Jo Jacobs, general manager; Mats Nilsson, musical director. *12 professional performances per year.*

Tasmanian Conservatorium Chorale (70). GPO Box 252-63, Hobart, TAS 7001, Australia *tel:* +61 3 6223 5220 *fax:* +61 3 6226 7318 *email:* belinda.flowers@central.tased.edu.au. Jan Guersen, chair (*tel:* +61 3 6260 2132 *email:* saddco@trumpet.au). *3 amateur performances per year.*

Tasmanian Symphony Orchestra Chorus (5-85). GPO Box 9994, Hobart, Tas 7001, Australia *tel:* +61 03 6235 3646 *fax:* +61 03 6235 3651 *email:* tso@tso.com.au. *Associated with Tasmanian Symphony Orchestra. 10 professional performances a year.*

Austria

Concentus Vocalis Wien (12-48). Vivenotweg 12, A-3411 Weidling, Austria *tel:* +43 22 432 6626 *fax:* +43 22 433 3886. Herbert Böck, musical director. *20 professional performances a year.*

Großer Chor des Landeskonservatorium Tirol (60). Paul Hofhaimer Gasse 6, A-6020 Innsbruck, Austria *tel:* +43 55 523 2862. Günther Simonott, conductor. *2-3 professional performances per year.*

Vienna Boys Choir (Wiener Sängerknaben) (100). Augartenpalais, Ob. Augartenstr 1, A-1020 Wien, Austria *tel:* +43 1 21 63942 *fax:* +43 1 21 639 4253 *email:* office@wsk.at. Norbert Balatsch, artistic director; Manfred Seipt, director of administration; Gerald Wirth, deputy artistic director. *350 performances a year.*

Vienna Male Choral Society (80-90). Bösendorferstr 12, A-1010 Wien, Austria *tel:* +43 1 505 7362 *fax:* +43 1 504 5450. Gerhard Track, music director; Kurt Schuh, president. *Vienna's oldest male voice choir, founded in 1843. Performs and tours worldwide. 2 main concerts a season, numerous others.*

Belgium

Choeur de Chambre de Namur (16-32). Avenue Jean 1er, No 2, B-5000 Namur, Belgium *tel:* +32 8 174 2752 *fax:* +32 8 174 2194 *email:* centredechantchoral.assl@skynet.be. Denis Menier, musical director; Jean-Marc Poncelet, manager. *Diapasson D'Or, Choc Du Monde de la Musique. 25 performances per year.*

Choeur Symphonique de Namur et de la Communauté Française de Belgique (80-120). Avenue Jean 1er, No 2, B-5000 Namur, Belgium *tel:* +32 8 174 2752 *fax:* +32 8 174 2194. Denis Menier, musical director; Jean-Marie Marchal, manager.

Vlaums Radioloon (Flemish Radio Choir) (25). Brusselsestraat 63, B-3000 Leuven, Belgium *tel:* +32 1 629 0319 *fax:* +32 1 631 6670. Johan Duyck, conductor; Kristien van Diest, director. Nicole Rouckhout, secretary. *Only professional Belgian choir (excluding opera choirs), performing music by contemporary Flemish, Belgian and foreign composers. 30 performances per year.*

Bulgaria

Sofia Philharmonic Choir (100). 1 Benkovski Str, BG-1000 Sofia, Bulgaria *tel:* +359 2 883197 *fax:* +359 2 874072. Gueorgui Robev, conductor.

Canada

Calgary Philharmonic Chorus (100). 205 Eighth Ave SE, Calgary, Alta T2G 0K9, Canada *tel:* +1 403 571 0270 *fax:* +1 403 294 7424.

Cape Breton Chorale (50). PO Box 381, Sydney, Nova Scotia, Canada B1P 6H2 *tel:* +1 902 564 0990 *fax:* +1 902 539 6089 *email:* gsmith@eagle.uccb.ns.ca; smitty@fox.nstn.ca. Sister Rita Clare, director. *Several television and radio performances.*

Kitchener Waterloo Philharmonic Choir (110). The Centre in the Square, 101 Queen St North, Kitchener, Ontario N2H 6P7, Canada *tel:* +1 519 578 6885 *fax:* +1 519 578 9230. Howard Dyck, artistic director. *Lieutenant-Governor's Award for the Arts, 1997; CBC National broadcasts 1996-8.*

Toronto Mendelssohn Choir (180). 60 Simcoe St, Suite C501, Toronto, Ont M5J 2H5, Canada *tel:* +1 416 598 0422 *fax:* +1 416 598 2992. Noel Edison, conductor; Eileen Keown, general manager.

Vancouver Chamber Choir (20). 1254 W Seventh Ave, Vancouver BC, V6H 1B6, Canada *tel:* +1 604 738 6822 *fax:* +1 604 738 7832 *email:* vcc@dowco.com. Jon Washburn, artistic and executive director; Violet Goosen, general manager. *Magaret Hillis Award for Choral Excellence. Regular broadcasts and releases. 30-40 performances per year.*

Czech Republic

Kühnuv Mixed Choir (98). Krakovská 10, CR-110 00 Praha 1, Czech Republic *tel:* +420 2 222 10172 *fax:* +420 2 266 365 *email:* his@mbox.vol.cz. Pavel Kühn, choirmaster; Vladimir Breza, secretary. *Frequent performances in Europe and regular recording releases.*

Prague Radio Choir FISYO. Trachtova 2/1130, CR-158 00 Praha 5, Czech Republic *tel:* +420 2 684 6256 *fax:* +420 2 684 9379.

Denmark

The Danish National Radio Choir (75). P2M/OK-red, Radiohuset, Rosenørns Allé 22, DK-1999 Frederiksberg C, Denmark *tel:* +45 3520 6381 *fax:* +45 3520 6121 *email:* gal@dr.dk. Gordon Alsing, executive producer; Per Erik Veng, general manager and artistic director; Stefan Parkman, chief conductor; Stephen Layton, principal guest conductor. *Approximately 50 professional performances per year. Extensive touring and recording.*

Royal Opera Chorus (60). Det Kgl Teater, Tordenskjoldsgade 8, PO Box 2185, DK-1017 Copenhagen, Denmark *tel:* +45 33 696701 *fax:* +45 33 696767. Kaare Hansen, choirmaster; Birgitte Christiansen, administrator.

Tivoli Concert Choir (80-100). Rudersdalsvej 74, DK-2840 Holte, Denmark *tel:* +45 42 425400 *also fax.* Morten Schuldt-Jensen, artistic director. *Resident choir of Tivoli Concert Hall. 8-10 professional concerts a year.*

Estonia

Estonian Philharmonic Chamber Choir (24). Lühike Jalg 9, Tallinn, EE-10130, Estonia *tel:* +372 6 448926 *fax:* +372 6 313179 *email:* epcc @online.ee. Tõnu Kaljuste, principal conductor, artistic director; Tiiu Valper, assistant director. *50 professional performances per year. Tours USA, Canada in February 2000 and the Netherlands in April. Repertoire includes Gregorian chants, Baroque and contemporary music. Won several Grammy Awards.*

Finland

The Finnish Radio Chamber Choir (24). PO Box 14, FIN-00024 Yleisradio, Finland *tel:* +358 9 1480 4375 *fax:* +358 9 1480 2089 *email:* outi.paananen@yle.fi; maret.sarkima@yle.fi. Outi Paananen, producer; Maret Sarkima, assistant; Timo Nuoranne, conductor.

The Jubilate Choir (c 35). Suonionkatu 7B15, FIN-00530 Helsinki, Finland *tel:* +358 9 712 281. Astrid Riska, conductor.

The Polytech Choir (75). PO Box 69, FIN-02151 Espoo, Finland *tel:* +358 9 468 3161 *fax:* +358 9 468 3181 *email:* pk@otax.tky.hut.fi. Tapani Länsiö, conductor; Mikko Kontiainen, chairman. *Male voice choir. 20 performances a year.*

Tampere Philharmonic Choir (100). Turjankatu 6-8 A 13, FIN-33100 Tampere, Finland *tel:* +358 3 255 4594 *also fax; email:* eija.koivusalo@sci.fi. Eija Koivusalo, chairman; Heikki Liimola, conductor. *Founded in 1990. Performs with Tampere Philharmonic Orchestra among others. Winners Cannes Classical Award 1998 and Finnish Janne Award 1999.*

France

A Sei Voci (4-12). 32 Rue Gambetta, F-72300 Sable, France *tel:* +33 2 43 92 76 58 *fax:* +33 2 43 92 76 59 *email:* AseiVoci@csi.com. Bernard Fabre-Garrus, artistic director; Thomas Vasseur, manager. *Researches and performs renaissance polyphonic works. Regular performances and releases.*

Choeur de Radio France (112). 116 Ave du Président Kennedy, F-75220 Paris, Cédex 16, France *tel:* +33 1 42 30 26 97 *fax:* +33 1 42 30 42 35. François Polgar, choir manager.

Choeurs de Lyon - Bernardtetu (80). 149 Rue Garibaldi, F-69431 Lyon, France *tel:* +33 78 95 29 40 *fax:* +33 78 62 29 03. Bernard Tetu, artistic director; Pascaline Maugat, PR contact. *Prix de l'Academie des Beaux Arts, Institut de France.*

Choir of La Chapelle Royale (30). 10 Rue Coquilliere, F-75001 Paris, France *tel:* +33 1 40 26 58 00 *fax:* +33 1 40 26 38 37. *Performs classical and romantic repertoire. Links with Orchestre des Champs Elysées.*

Ensemble Vocal Jean Sourisse, Paris (20-25). 3 Rue Jean Bart, F-75006 Paris, France *tel:* +33 1 42 22 98 17 *also fax; email:* rswyer@worldnet.fr. Jean Sourisse, choirmaster; Claire Lamboley, president. *Regular recording and performing.*

Germany

Chor der Bamberger Symphoniker. Mußstr 1, D-96047 Bamberg, Germany *tel:* +49 951 964 7100 *fax:* +49 951 964 7123. R Beck, director. *Associated with Bamberger Symphoniker.*

Dresdner Kreuzchor (150). Eisenacherstr 21, D-01277 Dresden, Germany *tel:* +49 351 315 3560 *fax:* +49 351 315 3561 *email:* buero@kreuzchor.de. Leiter Roderich Kreile, musical director; Uwe Grüner, manager. *Boys' choir of the Church of the Holy Cross. 90 professional performances per year. Regularly performs with the Dresden Philharmonic Orchestra and the Saxon State Orchestra. Repertoire includes baroque works and contemporary compositions. Also secular music.*

Frankfurter Kantorei (120). Homburger Hohl 18, D-60437 Frankfurt am Main, Germany *tel:* +49 695 093 0041 *fax:* +49 695 093 0042. Winfrid Toll, artistic director; Johannes Kaballo, president.

Kammerchor Stuttgart (16-60). Stuttgarter Musik Podium, Christophstr 5, D-70178 Stuttgart, Germany *tel:* +49 711 239 1390 *fax:* +49 711 239 1399 *email:* smp@n.zgs.de. Mattis Dänhardt, manager; Frieder Bernius, conductor.

Kölner Kammerchor (15-40). c/o Oberborsbacher Str 6, D-51519 Odenthal, Germany *tel:* +49 220 270293 *fax:* +49 220 270294. Peter Neumann, conductor. *Diapason d'Or, 1996.*

Philharmonischer Chor Dresden (110). Postfach 120368, Kulturplast Am Altmarkt, D-01005 Dresden, Germany *tel:* +49 351 486 6282/6365 *fax:* +49 351 486 6283 *email:* philharm@imedia.de. Matthias Geissler. *Founded 1967. Associated with Dresden Philharmonic Orchestra.*

Philharmonischer Chor München (150). Gasteig-Kulturzentrum, Kellerstr 4/III, D-181667 München, Germany *tel:* +49 89 4809 509 *fax:* +49 89 4809 513. *Links with Munich Philharmonic.*

Rheinische Kantorei (16-32). Ostpreussenallee 5, D-41539 Dormagen, Germany *tel:* +49 213 347 7905 *also fax.* Hermann Max, conductor; Matin Kahl, manager. *Several awards for CD recordings including Echo-Klassik 1996 prize for best choral recording of the year.*

Städttischer Musikverein zu Düsseldorf. Ehrenhof 1, Tonhalle, D-40479 Düsseldorf, Germany *tel:* +49 211 794 310 *fax:* +49 211 794 3112. Raimund Wippermann, director. *Associated with Düsseldorf Symphonic Orchestra.*

Hong Kong

Hong Kong Philharmonic Chorus (140). 8/F Admin Building, Hong Kong Cultural Centre, 10 Salisbury Rd, Tsimshatshi, Kowloon, Hong Kong *tel:* +852 2721 2030 *fax:* +852 2311 6229. Wing-sie Yip, director; Amanda Lai, secretary. *Associated with Hong Kong Philharmonic Orchestra.*

Hungary

Children's Choir of the Hungarian Radio and TV (c 80). Bródy Sándor u. 5-7, H-1088 Budapest, Hungary *tel:* +36 1 328 8710/7161 *also fax.* János Szirányi, director; Gabriella Thész, artistic director.

Hungarian National Philharmonic Choir. Vörösmarty tér 1, H-1051 Budapest, Hungary *tel:* +36 1 266 9097 *also fax; email:* natphilharm@mail.matav.hu. Mátyás Antal, artistic director; Géza Kovács, managing director.

Hungarian State Choir (76). Vörösmarty tér 1, H-1051 Budapest, Hungary *tel:* +36 1 266 9097. Mátyás Antal, artistic director.

Mixed Choir of the Hungarian Radio and TV (69). Bródy Sándor u 5-7, H-1088 Budapest, Hungary *tel:* +36 1 328 8710/7161 *also fax.* János Szirányi, director; Kalman Strausz, artistic director.

Iceland

Kór Langholtskirkju (85). Sólheimum 13, IS-104 Reykjavík, Iceland *tel:* +354 520 1300 *fax:* +354 520 1324/520 1301 *email:* klang@kirkjan.is. Jón Stefánsson, conductor. *4-6 performances a year.*

Republic of Ireland

Anúna (12-20). PO Box 4468, Churchtown, Dublin 14, Republic of Ireland *tel:* +353 1 283 5533 *also fax; email:* info@anuna.ie. Michael McGlynn, director and founder.

Galway Baroque Singers (65-70). 14 Montrose House, Whitestrand, Galway, Co Galway, Republic of Ireland *tel:* +353 9 1088 6911460 *also fax.* Audrey Corbett, musical director; Joan Armitage, secretary.

Irish Youth Choir (120). c/o Association of Irish Choirs, Drinan St, Cork, Republic of Ireland *tel:* +353 2 131 2296 *fax:* +353 2 196 2457 *email:* cnc@iol.ie. Barbara Heas, administrator; Geoffrey Spratt, conductor. *Mixed-voice, ages 17-29. Only choir of its type in Ireland.*

RTÉ Philharmonic Choir. The Music Department, Office Block, RTÉ, Donnybrook, Dublin, Republic of Ireland *tel:* +353 1 208 2738 *fax:* +353 1 208 2511. Michael Casey, choral manager; Claire Meehan, concerts manager. *Average 3 concerts per year.*

Israel

Ichud Choir (45). Seminar EFAL, Ramat Efal 52960, Israel *tel:* +972 3 530 1419 *fax:* +972 3 535 7116. Hava Yardeny, administrative co-ordinator; Ron Zahri, conductor and musical director.

Italy

Coro Filarmonico di Pesaro (55). Via Pavoramica Ardizio 95, I-61100 Pesaro, Italy *tel:* +39 072 155468 *also fax.* Roberto Renili, artistic director; Flavio Angelini, president.

Coro Jubilate (40). 3 Via Milano, I-20025 Legnano, Italy *tel:* +39 033 159 4504 *fax:* +39 033 159 7433 *email:* amj@mail.nemo.it. Paolo Alli, director; Carlo Leonardi, president. *Repertoire composed of 15th-20th C polyphonic a cappella mus.*

Schola Gregoriana Mediolaneisis (76). Via Masotto 30, I-201333 Milano, Italy *tel:* +39 027 010 0338 *also fax; fax:* +39 027 010 4245. Giovanni Vianini, director.

Japan

Osaka Philharmonic Choir (c 200). 1-1-44 Kishinosato, Nishinari-ku, Osaka 557-0041, Japan *tel:* +81 6 656 7711 *fax:* +81 6 656 7714. Takashi Asahina, general musical director. *Associated with Osaka Philharmonic Orchestra.*

Latvia

Latvia State Academic Choir (60). Kalku 11a, LV-1050 Riga, Latvia *tel:* +371 722 3839 *also fax; email:* choir.latvia@lmuza.lv. Maris Sirmais, principal conductor. *Associated with Latvian National Symphony Orchestra.*

Moldova

DOINA - State Academic Choir (70). 78 Mitropolitul, Vaarlam str, 277012 Chisinau, Moldova *tel:* +373 2 224016 *fax:* +373 2 228293. Garstea Veronica, chief conductor and artistic director. *40 professional performances a year. Associated with the Moldova National Philharmonic Symphony Orchestra.*

Netherlands

Koninklijk Schledams Mannenkoor Orpheus (65). c/o Akkerpad 63, 3124 AA Schiedam, Netherlands *tel:* +31 10 471 9010. H van der Gaag, secretary; Pim Overduin, director.

Koor van De Nederlands Bachvereniging (20). De Nederlandse Bachvereniging, Postbus 12017, NL-3501 AA Utrecht, Netherlands *tel:* +31 30 252 4010 *fax:* +31 30 251 1639. Maria Hansen, managing director; Jos van Veldhoven, artistic director.

Netherlands Radio Choir (79). Groot Omroepkoor, Postbox 125, NL-1200 AC Hilversum, Netherlands *tel:* +31 35 671 4120 *fax:* +31 35 671 4171 *email:* gok@mco.nl. Martin Wright, principal conductor; Monica H M Damen, managing director. *30 professional performances a year.*

Noord-Nederlands Concertkoor. Palmslag 20, NL-9724 CS Groningen, Netherlands *tel:* +31 50 369 5800 *fax:* +31 50 369 5815 *email:* nno@tref.nl. H Pruiksma, repetiteur; J Lamminga, choirmaster. *Associated with Noord-Nederlands Orchestra.*

Norway

Cathedral Choir of Bergen (55). c/o Bjorgvin Kirkemusikk AS, PO Box 765, N-5807 Bergen, Norway *tel:* +47 55 313 320 *fax:* +47 55 558 140. Magnar Mangersnes, conductor. *15 performances a year.*

Oslo Cathedral Choir (50). Karl Johans gt 11, N-0154 Oslo, Norway *tel:* +47 22 427 758 *fax:* +47 22 411 717. Terje Kvam, conductor; Bente Johnsrud, director.

Oslo Philharmonic Choir (140). PO Box 1607 Vika, Haaton VIIs gt. 2, NO119 Oslo, Norway *tel:* +47 22 014 900 *fax:* +47 22 014 901. Trond Okkelmo, managing director; Tore Erik Mohn, chorus master. *Associated with Oslo Philharmonic Orchestra.*

Skruk (50). v/Fredrik Mork Haskjold, Mork, N-6100 Volda, Norway *tel:* +47 70 076 667 *fax:* +47 70 078 567. Per Oddvar Hildre, conductor; Fredrik Mork Haskoolp, manager.

Poland

Warsaw Philharmonic Choir (102). ul. Jasna 5, PL-00950 Warszawa, Poland *tel:* +48 826 5617/8311 *fax:* +48 826 5617 *email:* filharmonia@filharmonia.pl. Henryk Wojnarowski, choir director, principal conductor. *Associated with Warsaw Philharmonic Orchestra. Nomination for Grammy Award 1996.*

Portugal

Gulbenkian Choir (100). Fundação Calouste Gulbenkian, Ave de Berna 45, P-1067-001 Lisboa, Portugal *tel:* +351 1 793 5131 *fax:* +351 1 793 7296. *Associated with the Gulbenkian Orchestra.*

Romania

Iasi Philharmonic (70). Str Cuza Voda 29, 6600 Iasi, Romania *tel:* +40 32 114601/112100/212620 *fax:* +40 32 214160. Doru Morariu, conductor. *Concerts of religious music and carols, concerts with vocal-symphonic music by Verdi, Mahler, Brahms, Orff, Mozart, Haydn and Romanian composers.*

Transilvania State Philharmonic Choir, Cluj-Napoca (70). St Emanuel de Martonne 1, 3400 Cluj-Napoca, Romania *tel:* +40 64 430060/3 *fax:* +40 64 197812 *email:* fila@codec.ro. Cornel Groza, conductor; Emil Simon, general director. *44 professional performances a year.*

Russia

Glinka State Choir of St Petersburg (70). Moika St, St Petersburg, Russia *tel:* +7 812 314 1073 *fax:* +7 812 110 6913. Vladislav Chernoushenko, artistic director.

Rossica Choir of St Petersburg (26). 12 Warren Drive, Dorridge, Solihull, W Midlands B93 8JY *tel:* +44 1564 776376 *also fax; email:* jean.shearman@virgin.net. Jean Shearman, UK manager; Valentina Kopylova, conductor and director. *Tours throughout Europe. CD* Holy Love *issued by Olympia.*

Spain

Agrupación Coral de Cámara de Pamplona (18-21). C/San Antón 12, E-31001 Pamplona, Spain *tel:* +34 94 822 3405 *fax:* +34 94 822 6803 *email:* koldop@arrakis.es. Koldo Pastor, director; Luis Felipe Sarasa, president. *40-50 performances per year. Specialises in contemporary music.*

La Capella Reial de Catalunya (6-15). Travesera de Gracia 18-20, E-08021 Barcelona, Spain *tel:* +34 93 594 47 60 *fax:* +34 93 580 56 06 *email:* 101617.3236@compuserve.com. Jordi Savall, director; Irene Bloc, administrator. *35 professional performances per year.*

Coral Agora Segovia (45). Pza S Esteban 11, 3 Segovia, Spain *tel:* +34 92 143 4423 *also fax.* José Miguel Arranz, secretary; Marisa Martin, director. *Choral singing and choral conducting course, end of August.*

Coral Polifónica de Santa Cruz de Tenerife. Ap Corveos 57, Laesperanza, 38290 Tenerife, Spain *tel:* +34 922 297209. Francisco Padrón Correa, director; Angeles Cabrera Siverio, assistant director.

Coro Fundación Principe de Asturias (100). Fundación Principe de Asturias, C/General Yagüe 2, E-33004 Oviedo, Spain *tel:* +34 98 525 8755 *fax:* +34 98 524 2104. José Esteban Garcia Miranda, director; Luis Heres Prieto, secretary.

Orfeó Català (90). C/San Francisco de Paula 2, E-08003 Barcelona, Spain *tel:* +34 93 268 1000 *fax:* +34 93 268 4824. Jordi Casas Bayer, director.

Polifonica de Girona (35). c/ Onze de Setembre, 21, E-17007 Girona, Spain *tel:* +34 97 221 5289. Jordi Bernado Figueras, director.

Sweden

Göteburg Symphony Orchestra Chorus (200+). Stenhammarsgatam 1, S-412 56 Göteburg, Sweden *tel:* +46 3 177 877800 *fax:* +46 3 120 3502. *Associated with Swedish National Orchestra.*

Stockholm Bach Choir (30). Adolf Frederiks Church, PO Box 3270, S-10365 Stockholm, Sweden *tel:* +46 8 411 2351 *fax:* +46 8 204912. Anders Öhrwall, conductor.

Swedish Radio Choir (33). Berwaldhallen, Swedish Radio Broadcasting Corporation, 105 10 Stockholm, Sweden *tel:* +46 8 784 5000 *fax:* +46 8 784 1343 *email:* radiokoren@bwh.sr.se. Tónu Kaljuste, principal cond; Michael Tydén, general manager; Gunnar Andersson, artist and programme manager. Eva Bjurenhed, touring manager; Karin Adolfsson, marketing manager. *Professional mixed choir, mostly a capella. Contemporary repertoire. Tours internationally.*

Switzerland

Basler Madrigalisten (16-48). Gundeldingerstr 93, CH-4053 Basel, Switzerland *tel:* +41 61 272 8333 *fax:* +41 61 272 8338. Fritz Näf, conductor; Rita Froesch, managing director. *8-10 professional performances per year.*

Ensemble Vocal de Lausanne (12-70). Avenue du Grammont 11 bis, CH-1007 Lausanne, Switzerland *tel:* +41 21 617 4707 *fax:* +41 21 617 4867 *email:* sjollema@span.ch. Michel Corboz, musical director; Frederik Sjollema, manager. *25 professional performances per year.*

Taiwan

The National Experimental Chorus (80). No 21-1 Chung-Shan South Road, Taipei, Taiwan *tel:* +886 2 2343 1360 *fax:* +886 2 2341 9373. Chen-Long Huang, director; Ching-Chuan Tai, conductor.

Taipei Philharmonic Chorus. B1 28, Lane 233, Tun Hua s Rd, Sec 1, Taipei, Taiwan *tel:* +886 22 773 3691 *fax:* +886 22 773 3692. Dirk DuHei, conductor.

Ukraine

Kiev Chamber Choir (23). vul Laboratorna, 12, 252005 Kiev, Ukraine *tel:* +380 44 252 8828 *also fax; email:* choir@mail.kar.net. Mykola Gobdich, musical director; Alexander Sokolik, general manager. *70 professional performances per year. Winners of many awards.*

USA

Atlanta Symphony Orchestra Chorus (200). 1293 Peachtree St NE, Suite 300, Atlanta, GA 30309, USA *tel:* +1 404 733 4876 *fax:* +1 404 733 4888. Robert Shaw, conductor; Norman Mackenzie, assistant conductor. Nola Frink, choral administrator; Jeffrey Baxter, choral assistant. *Associated with Atlanta Symphony Orchestra. 6 Grammy Awards for 'Best Choral Performance'.*

Chanticleer (12). 650 Fifth St, Suite 311, San Francisco, CA 94107, USA *tel:* +1 415 896 5866 *fax:* +1 415 896 1660 *email:* chanticlee@aol.com. Joseph Jennings, musical director; Philip Wilder, artistic administrator. *Founded in 1978; regular tours and recordings; wide variety of styles.*

Cleveland Orchestra Chorus. Severance Hall, Cleveland, OH 44106, USA *tel:* +1 216 231 7300 *fax:* +1 216 231 0202. *Associated with the Cleveland Orchestra.*

Colorado Symphony Chorus (225). 821 17th St, Suite 700, Denver, CO 80202, USA *tel:* +1 303 292 5566 *fax:* +1 303 293 2649. Duain Wolfe, founder, conductor; Mary Louise Burke, assistant conductor. Eric Israelson, chorus manager.

The Dale Warland Singers (40). 120 N Fourth St, Minneapolis, MN 55401, USA *tel:* +1 612 339 9707 *fax:* +1 612 339 9826. Dale Warland, musical director; Bruce K Taylor, executive director.

Dallas Symphony Chorus (240). 2301 Flora St, Suite 300, Dallas, TX 75201-2497, USA *tel:* +1 214 871 4000 *fax:* +1 214 871 4049. *Official vocal ensemble of the DSO, founded in 1977. Volunteer organisation.*

Handel and Haydn Society (33). 300 Massachusetts Ave, Boston, MA 02115, USA *tel:* +1 617 262 1815 *fax:* +1 617 266 4217 *email:* handelhaydn@aol.com. Mary Deissler, executive director; Christopher Hogwood, artistic director.

Houston Symphony Chorus. 615 Louisiana St, Houston, TX 77002-2798, USA *tel:* +1 713 224 4240 *fax:* +1 713 222 7024. *Associated with Houston Symphony.*

Milwaukee Symphony Chorus. 330 E Kilbourn Ave, Suite 900, Milwaukee, WI 53202, USA *tel:* +1 414 291 6010 *fax:* +1 414 291 7610 *email:* amadeus@execpc.com. *Associated with Milwaukee Symphony Orchestra.*

Music of the Baroque Chorus and Orchestra (26). 100 N LaSalle St, Suite 1610, Chicago, IL 60602, USA *tel:* +1 312 551 1415 *fax:* +1 312 551 1444 *email:* baroque@baroque.org. Thomas Wikman, musical director; Anna-Lise Pasch, concert manager.

Oratorio Singers of Charlotte (130-15). 211 N College St, Suite 202, Charlotte, NC 28202, USA *tel:* +1 704 332 0468 *fax:* +1 704 332 1963 *email:* marshas@charlottesymphony.org. David Tang, director; Marsha Summers, manager; James H Glenn, director, Youth Oratorio. *Associated with Charlotte Symphony Orchestra.*

Pacific Chorale (165). 1221 E Dyer Rd, Suite 230, Santa Ana, CA 92705-5606, USA *tel:* +1 714 662 2345 *fax:* +1 714 662 2395. John Alexander. *Associated with Pacific Symphony Orchestra.*

The Philadelphia Singers (32). 1211 Chestnut St, Suite 200, Philadelphia, PA 19107, USA *tel:* +1 215 751 9494 *fax:* +1 215 751 9490.

Plymouth Music Series of Minnesota (24-110). 1900 Nicollet Ave, Minneapolis, MN 55403, USA *tel:* +1 612 870 0943 *fax:* +1 612 870 9962. Philip Brunelle, artistic director; Frank Stubbs, general manager. *Ensembles and Symphony Chorus.*

Saint Louis Chamber Chorus (36). PO Box 11558, Clayton, St Louis, Missouri, MO 63105 *tel:* +1 314 458 4343 *email:* maltworm@inlink.com. Linda Ryder, executive director; Philip Barnes, artistic director. Stuart McIntosh, assistant conductor. *Oldest independent a cappella choir in Midwest (founded 1955).*

Saint Louis Symphony Chorus (125). Powell Symphony Hall, 718 N Grand Blvd, St Louis, MO 63103, USA *tel:* +1 314 286 4130 *fax:* +1 314 286 4140. Amy Kaiser, director. *Associated with Saint Louis Symphony Orchestra.*

Saint Olaf Choir (75). 1520 St Olaf Ave, Northfield, MN 55057, USA *tel:* +1 507 646 3179 *fax:* +1 507 646 3527. B J Johnson, manager.

San Francisco Symphony Chorus (200). Davies Symphony Hall, San Francisco, CA 94102, USA *tel:* +1 415 552 8000 ext 207 *fax:* +1 415 431 6857 *email:* boals@sfsymphony.org. Gregory Boals, chorus administrator; Vance George, chorus director. *Associated with San Francisco Symphony. 24+ professional performances per year. Twice Grammy winners for best choral recording.*

Seattle Symphony Chorale (130). PO Box 21906, Seattle, WA 98111-3906, USA *tel:* +1 206 215 4700 *fax:* +1 206 215 4701. Abraham Kaplan, leader. *Associated with Seattle Symphony Orchestra.*

Utah Symphony Chorus (130). Department of Music, 1375 E Presidents Cir Rm 204, University of Utah, Salt Lake City, UT 84112-0130, USA *tel:* +1 888 901 7464 *fax:* +1 801 581 5683 *email:* ed.thompson@music.utah.edu. Bennet P Peterson, president; Edgar J Thompson, conductor. Michael D Hutt, associate conductor, accompanist. *Associated with Utah Symphony Orchestra. 2 Grammy nominations.*

Wichita Symphony Orchestra Chorus. 225 W Douglas, Suite 207, Wichita, KS 67202, USA *tel:* +1 316 267 5259 *fax:* +1 316 267 1937 *email:* symphony@louverture.com. *Volunteer choir associated with Wichita Symphony Orchestra.*

Competitions

The competitions listed here are open to international entry and are usually annual. The **Fédération Mondiale des Concours Internationaux de Musique** lists international competitions well in advance. Their booklet is available from 104 Rue de Carouge, CH-1205 Genève, Switzerland *tel:* +41 22 321 3620 *fax:* +41 22 781 1418 *email:* fmcim@iprolink.ch.

Competitions for Performers and Conductors

Australia

The Australian Singing Competition. c/o Gridiger & Co, Solicitors, 67 Castlereagh St, Sydney NSW 2000, Australia *tel:* +61 2 9231 4888 *fax:* +61 2 9221 8201. Vivian Zeltzer, co-ordinator. *Oct. Applications by June. For opera singers and classical musicians. Must be a resident of Australia or New Zealand, aged under 26. Cash prizes of A$25,000 and A$5000. Marianne Mathy Scholarship.*

Sydney International Piano Competition of Australia. PO Box 420, Double Bay, Sydney NSW 2028, Australia *tel:* +61 2 9326 2405 *fax:* +61 2 9326 2604 *email:* sipc@desknet.com.au. Claire Dan, president; Warren Thomson, artistic director. *Quadrennial. Next 29 June-15 July 2000. Presented by the Cladan Cultural Exchange Institute of Australia in association with the University of Sydney and with the co-operation of the Australian Broadcasting Corporation. Ages 17-30. First prize A$25,000 plus concert tours.*

Symphony Australia Young Performers Awards. GPO Box 9994, Sydney NSW 2001, Australia *tel:* +61 2 9333 1682 *fax:* +61 2 9333 1678 *email:* lidbetterk@symphony.net.au. Kate Lidbetter, artist development manager. *Feb-Oct, applications towards end of year. Provides performance opportunities for young singers and instrumentalists. Must have been in continuous residence in Australia for one year and must compete in states of residence. Award of A$7500 plus concert performances and other affiliated prizes and scholarships.*

Austria

Beethoven International Piano Competition. Lothringerstr 18, A-1030 Wien, Austria *tel:* +43 1 5880 6190 *fax:* +43 1 58 806107. Elga Ponzer, general secretary. *Quadrennial. Next May/June 2001, applications by 30 Sept 2000. Ages 17-32. First prize ATS 80,000, a piano and concerts.*

Franz Schubert and the Music of Modernity. Universität für Musik und darstellende Kunst Graz, Leonhardstrasse 15, A-8010 Graz, Austria *tel:* +43 316 389 1900/1210 *fax:* +43 316 389 1901/1710 *email:* franz.schubert@mhsg.ac.at. Susanne Kogler, competition office. *Triennial. Next 23 February-3 March 2000. Applications by 15 November 1999. Categories: piano solo; duo for voice and piano (Lied); string quartet. Female singers and piano soloists aged 32 and under; male singers and instrumentalists aged 34 and under; combined age of string quartet must not exceed 120 by end of 2000. Total prizes: ATS 945,000.*

International Belvedere Hans Gabor Competition for Opera Singers. Fleischmarkt 24, A-1010 Wien, Austria *tel:* +43 1 512 0100 *fax:* +43 1 512 010020 *email:* wienerkammeroper@magnet.at. Isabella Gabor. *11-16 July 2000, applications by 15 June. Young singers of any nationality aged under 32 (male) or under 30 (female). Prize of ATS 50,000.*

International Competition for Choirs Spittal. c/o Kulturamt Burgplatz 1, A-9800 Spittal an der Drau, Austria *tel:* +43 47 623420 *fax:* +43 47 623237 *email:* stadt.spittal@spittal-drau.at. Gabi Obernosterer, cultural officer. *6-9 July 2000, entries by 31 January. Mixed choirs. First prize ATS 20,000.*

International Mozart Competition. Alpenstr 48, A-5020 Salzburg, Austria *tel:* +43 662 6198 2200 *fax:* +43 662 6198 2209 *email:* ulrike.baciu@moz.ac.at. Klaus Ager, rector; Ulrike Baciu, general secretary. *Quadrennial. Next 2003. Singers, pianists, violinists, composers. First prize: ATS 120,000 in each category.*

Belgium

International Guitar Competition. Place du Chef Lieu 9, c/o Le Printemps de la Guitare, B-6040 Charleroi-Jumet, Belgium *tel:* +32 71 350448 *fax:* +32 71 355320 *email:* printemps.guitare@imageweb.be. André Tobie, president. *Biennial. Next 25 September-7 October 2000, closing date 30 June. Ages 32 and under. First prize 300,000 BF and medal.*

International Singing Competition. c/o Opera Royal de Wallonie, Rue des Dominicains 1, B-4000 Liège, Belgium *tel:* +32 41 221 4720 *fax:* +32 41 210201 *email:* direction@orw.be. Cécile Duvivier, secretary. *Biennial. Next 2001. Ages 18-30 (women), 18-35 (men). First prize 200,000 BF. Entry fee 2000 BF.*

Musica Antiqua International Competitions. Festival van Vlaanderen-Brugge, Collaert Mansionstraat 30, B-8000 Bruges, Belgium *tel:* +32 50 332283 *fax:* +32 50 345204 *email:* musica-antiqua@unicall.be. R Dewitte MBE, director. *2-9 August 2000. Closing date 15 April. Competitions for soloists (organ: Bach) and ensembles. Age limit 32 (ensembles), 35 (singers). First prizes: soloists 150,000 BF; ensembles 150,000 BF. Entry fees: 1500 BF soloists; 2000 BF ensembles.*

Queen Elisabeth International Music Competition of Belgium. 20 Rue aux Laines, B-1000 Bruxelles, Belgium *tel:* +32 25 130099 *fax:* +32 25 143297 *email:* info@concours-reine-elisabeth.be. Cécile Ferrière, secretary general. *Next 5-27 May 2000, applications by 15 January 2000. For vocalists (2001, violin). Cash awards, recordings, concerts. Entry fee 2200 BF. First prize 500,000 BF plus engagements and CD recordings.*

Canada

Banff International String Quartet Competition. Banff Centre for the Arts, PO Box 1020, Station 28, Banff, Alta T0L 0C0, Canada *tel:* +1 403 762 6180 *fax:* +1 403 762 6345 *email:* arts_info@banffcentre.ab.ca. *Triennial. Next 2001.*

Calgary International Organ Festival and Competition. 3rd Floor 134-11 Ave SE, Calgary, Alta T2G 0X5, Canada *tel:* +1 403 543 5115 *fax:* +1 403 543 5129 *email:* info@ciof.com. Timothy H Rendell, president; Cathy Nickel, manager, communications. *Quadrennial. Next autumn 2002. Open to organists of any nationality born on or after 4 October 1970. Closing dates early 2002. International selection rounds in North America, Europe and Asia-Pacific. Final round in Calgary with 10 world competitors. Also includes festival with workshops, masterclasses, concerts and silent films. Prizes: Can $25,000 Recital Gold Medal, Can $25,000 Concerto Gold Medal; also Bach, Improvisation and Encore prizes.*

Eckhardt-Gramatté National Music Competition for the Performance of Canadian Music. School of Music, Brandon University, Brandon, MB R7A 6A9, Canada *tel:* +1 204 728 8212 *fax:* +1 204 729 9085 *email:* eckhardt@brandonu.ca. Karen Kempe, admin. *5-7 May 2000 (strings). Rotates between piano, voice and strings. To encourage young performers to perform contemporary and Canadian works. Open to Canadian citizens or residents in Canada, born after 1 January 1970 and before 1 January 1982. First prize $5000 and Canadian recital tour.*

Esther Honens Calgary International Piano Competition. Third Floor, 134 Eleventh Ave SE, Calgary, Alta T2G 0X5, Canada *tel:* +1 403 299 0130 *fax:* +1 403 299 0137 *email:* info@honens.com. Andrew Raeburn, president, Jayme Johnston; manager, marketing, communications; Stephen McHolm, artistic admin. *Quadrennial. Next 9-25 November 2000. Ages 20-30. Cash prizes totalling $66,500; first prize $22,500 and an Artistic and Career Development Programme (3 years).*

Czech Republic

Beethoven's Hradec Interpretation Contest. Administration of Castles, in Hradec nad Moravici, and Radun, Mestecko 2, CR-747 41 Hradec nad Moravici, Czech Republic *tel:* +420 653 911185/6. *June, applications by April. Entrance fee $30 for pno section, $60 for string quartet section. First prize Kc 18,000 for pno, Kc 24,000 for string.*

Concertino Praga. International Radio Competition for Young Musicians, Cêsky Rozhlas, Vinohradská 12, CR-120 99 Praha 2, Czech Republic *tel:* +420 2 2409 4288 *fax:* +420 2 2421 8089 *email:* Jana.Hlinkova@cro.cz. Josef Havel, programme director (Czech Radio); Jana Hlinková, secretary. *November 2000, applications by 30 April. Annual in 3-year cycles. 2000 piano, violin and cello. Aged 18 and under. First prize concert engagements in Prague and Southern Bohemia and live broadcasts.*

Emmy Destinn International Singing Competition. Rudolfov 393, CR-373 71 Ceske Budejovice, Czech Republic *tel:* +420 383 9254 *also fax.* Antonín Kazil. *August, applications by June. Operatic repertoire. Aged 35 and under. First prize comprises concert opportunities and financial award.*

International Singing Contest of Antonin Dvorák. KC Amethyst, I P Pavlova 14, CR-360 01 Karlovy Vary, Czech Republic *tel:* +420 17 322 8707/8708 *fax:* +420 17 322 3753. Marie Drlíková, contest secretary. *3-10 November 2000, applications by 30 June. Category A: women aged under age 23 and men under 24; category B: women aged under 30 and men under 32. Application fees: category A, DM 150; category B, DM 200 (or equivalent in US dollars). First prizes Kc 10,000 (category A) and Kc 25,000 (category B).*

Mezinárodní Sborová Soutez Bedricha Smetany. Smetanovo nám 72, CR-570 01 Litomysl, Czech Republic *tel:* +420 464 612575 *also fax.* Jan Pikna, festival director.

Prague Spring International Music Competition. Hellichova 18, CR-118 00 Praha 1, Czech Republic *tel:* +420 2 533474 *fax:* +420 2 536040 *email:* nedvedova@festival.cz. Jarmila Nedvedová, competition secretary. *6-15 May 2000. Applications by 15 December. Conducting, cello. Open to artists aged 30 and under. Application fees: $100. First prize Kc 200,000.*

Zlata Praha. Ceska Televize, Kavci Hory, CR-140 70 Praha 4, Czech Republic *tel:* +420 6113 4028/4153/4133 *fax:* +420 6121 2891 *email:* ruzena.jezkova@czech-tv.cz. Ruzena Jezkova, head of international relations. *May. Applications by end January. Entry fee DM 300. First prize DM 10,000.*

Denmark

Carl Nielsen International Music Competitions. Odense Koncerthuset, Claus Bergs Gade 9, DK-5000 Odense C, Denmark *tel:* +45 66 120057 *fax:* +45 65 910047 *email:* carlnielsencompetition@odensesymfoni.dk. Marianne Granvig, secretary general. *1-9 June 2000, applications by February. Flute. Aged 30 and under. First prize c $20,000.*

International Organ Competition. Laessoegade 74, DK-5230 Odense M, Denmark *fax:* +45 66 136363 *email:* organcomp@post.tele.dk. Henning Nielsen, admin. *Biennial. Next 17-25 August 2000, applications by 1 April. Age 35 and under. First prize DKK 40,000.*

Nicolai Malko International Competition for Young Conductors. Radiohuset, Rosenorns Allé 22, DK-1999 Frederiksberg C, Denmark *tel:* +45 35 206371 *fax:* +45 35 206121. Gert Herzberg, general secretary. *Triennial. Next June 2001, applications by 1 February 2001. Ages 20-31. First prize $10,000 and engagements.*

Estonia

International Choral Festival Tallinn. Estonian Choral Society, Suur-Karja 23, EE-10148 Tallinn, Estonia *tel:* +372 6 441849 *fax:* +372 6 449147 *email:* kooriyhing@kul.ee. Ants Soots, chairman. *Triennial. Next 19-22 April 2001, closing date 30 October 2000. Mixed, chamber, female and male choirs. First prize EEK 10,000.*

Finland

International Jean Sibelius Violin Competition. PO Box 31, FIN-00101, Helsinki 10, Finland *tel:* +358 9 4114 3443 *fax:* +358 9 2200 2680 *email:* violin-competition@kolumbus.fi. Tuomas Haapanen, chairman; Harri Pohjolainen, competition secretary. *Quinquennial. Next 18 November-2 December 2000, entries by 18 August. Open to violinists born in 1970 or later. First prize 16,000 euros.*

International Sibelius Conductors' Competition. Finlandia Hall, FIN-00100 Helsinki, Finland *tel:* +358 4 0503 0997 *fax:* +358 4 0803 0997 *email:* elina.siltanen@icenet.fi. Elina Siltanen, secretary general. *Quinquennial. Next 14-18 May 2000, closing date 16 December. Ages 35 and under. Repertoire ranges from Mozart to contemporary Finnish works. The finalists are required to conduct a Sibelius symphony. First prize $15,000.*

Lahti International Organ Competition. Kirkkokatu 5, FIN-15110 Lahti, Finland *tel:* +358 3 782 3184 *fax:* +358 3 783 2190 *email:* lof@pp.phnet.fi. *Next 2001.*

Mirjam Helin International Singing Competition. Finnish Cultural Foundation, PO Box 203, FIN-00121 Helsinki, Finland *tel:* +358 9 602144 *fax:* +358 9 640474 *email:* mh@skr.fi. Timo Arjas, executive secretary. *Quinquennial. Next Aug 2004.*

Tampereen Sävel International Choir Contest and Festival. Tullikamarinaukio 2, FIN-33100 Tampere, Finland *tel:* +358 3 3146 6136/6172 *fax:* +358 3 223 0121 *email:* music@tampere.fi. Annamaija Saarela, director. *Biennial. Next 2001, entries by March. Vocal ensembles and choirs. No age limits. First prize 35,000 FM in both competitions.*

France

Competition for Music Lovers. Concours Européen pour les Mélomanes, c/o 32 Rue Carnot, F-92100 Boulogne, France *tel:* +33 1 46 04 80 02 *fax:* +33 1 47 12 09 24. Régine Bessis, president. *18-19 March (Cannes); 26 March, 30 April, 7 May (Paris); winners concert 13 May (Paris). Applicants to be aged over 25 years. Prizes of concerts, workshops, materials and CD total 100,000 FF.*

Florilege Vocal de Tours International Choral Singing Competition. Rue des Minimes, BP 1452, F-37014 Tours Cedex 1, France *tel:* +33 2 47 21 65 26 *fax:* +33 2 47 21 67 71. Christian Balandras, artistic director. *May, applications by November. Annual competition for amateur choirs. First prize 16,000 FF.*

International Competition of French Music. 28 Rue da la Paix, F-78390 Bois D'Arcy, France *tel:* +33 1 34 60 30 96 *fax:* +33 1 34 60 08 53. Désiré N'Kaoua, president. *October. Applications by September. Chamber music ensembles of two or more people; no age limit. Entry fee 450 FF per member. First prize 25,000 FF.*

International Maurice André Trumpet Competition. Association Acanthes, 3 Rue des Couronnes, F-75020 Paris, France *tel:* +33 1 40 33 45 35 *fax:* +33 1 40 33 45 38. *October.*

International Organ Competition. Association Acanthes, 3 Rue des Couronnes, F-75020 Paris, France *tel:* +33 1 40 33 45 35 *fax:* +33 1 40 33 45 38. Colette Morillon, general secretary. *Biennial. Age limit 35.*

International Rostropovich Cello Competition. Association Acanthes, 3 Rue des Couronnes, F-75020 Paris, France *tel:* +33 1 40 33 45 35 *fax:* +33 1 40 33 45 38. Jacqueline Fraisse. *Quadrennial. Next 2001. All nationalities, aged 33 and over. Entrance fee 500 FF. First prize 70,000 FF plus engagements.*

International Singing and Chamber Music Competition. Secrétariat, 8 Rue du Dôme, F-75116 Paris, France *tel:* +33 1 47 04 76 38 *fax:* +33 1 47 27 35 03 *email:* ufam@wanadoo.fr. Christiane de Bayser, president. *Biennial. Chamber music, October-November 2000, applications by 20 September. Voice, June-July, applications by May. Women up to 32 years, men up to 34 years. First prizes 30,000 FF (chamber music), 50,000 FF (voice) plus performances.*

International Young Conductors Competition. 3 Rue Léonel de Moustier, F-25000 Besançon, France *tel:* +33 81 25 05 85 *fax:* +33 81 81 52 15. Yvette Cussey, admin. *September, applications by March. Aged 35 and under. Entry fee 1000 FF. First prize 70,000 FF.*

Jean-Pierre Rampel Flute Competition. Concours Internationaux de la Ville de Paris, Acanthes, 3 Rue des Couronnes, F-75020 Paris, France *tel:* +33 1 40 33 45 35 *fax:* +33 1 40 33 45 38. Claude Samuel, general manager. *Triennial. Next autumn 2001. Ages 30 and under. First prize 70,000 FF.*

Marguerite Long and Jacques Thibaud International Competition. 32 Ave Matignon, F-75008 Paris, France *tel:* +33 1 42 66 66 80 *fax:* +33 1 42 66 06 43 *email:* longthi@club.internet.fr. Mrs Perin, permanent secretary. *Alternates piano and violin. November 2000 (piano), applications by September. Ages 30 and under. First prize 150,000 FF and engagements.*

Maurice André Trumpet Competition. Concours Internationaux de la Ville de Paris, Acanthes, 3 Rue des Couronnes, F-75020 Paris *tel:* +33 1 40 33 45 35 *fax:* +33 1 40 33 45 38. Claude Samuel, general manager. *Autumn 2000. Ages 30 and under. First prize 70,000 FF.*

Olivier Messiaen Competition. Concours Internationaux de la Ville de Paris, Acanthes, 3 Rue des Couronnes, F-75020 Paris, France *tel:* +33 1 40 33 45 35 *fax:* +33 1 40 33 45 38. Claude Samuel, general manager. *Autumn 2000. Ages 30 and under. First prize 70,000 FF.*

Organ Competition. Concours Internationaux de la Ville de Paris, Acanthes, 3 Rue des Couronnes, F-75020 Paris, France *tel:* +33 1 40 33 45 35 *fax:* +33 1 40 33 45 38. Claude Samuel, general manager. *October. Ages 35 and under. First prize 50,000 FF.*

Rostropovitch Cello Competition. Concours Internationaux de la Ville de Paris, Acanthes, 3 Rue des Couronnes, F-75020 Paris, France *tel:* +33 1 40 33 45 35 *fax:* +33 1 40 33 45 38. Claude Samuel, general manager. *1-14 Oct 2001. Ages 33 and under. First prize 70,000 FF.*

Toulouse International Voice Competition. Théâtre du Capitole, F-31000 Toulouse, France *tel:* +33 5 61 62 13 51 *fax:* +33 5 61 62 96 90. George Canet, general secretary. *Biennial. Next 25-30 September 2000, applications by 10 July. Ages 18-33. Application fee 100 FF. First prize 40,000 FF.*

Violin and Bow Making Competition. Concours Internationaux de la Ville de Paris, Acanthes, 3 Rue des Couronnes, F-75020 Paris, France *tel:* +33 1 40 33 45 35 *fax:* +33 1 40 33 45 38. Claude Samuel, general manager. *November-December. No age limit. First prize 25,000 FF (violin making); 10,000 FF (bow making).*

Germany

Brahms International Competition. Hartungstrasse 8, D-20146 Hamburg, Germany *tel:* +49 40 452158 *fax:* +49 40 104 6691. Eckhart Besch, president. *Biennial. Next 2001.*

Carl Orff International Singing Competition. Carl Orff-Stiftung, Herzogstr 57, D-80803 München, Germany *tel:* +49 89 335033 *fax:* +49 89 335937 *email:* carlorffst@aol.com. *June, applications by April.*

8th INTERNATIONAL ORGAN COMPETITION

ODENSE - DENMARK

August 17 - August 25, 2000

3 rounds in the competition
7 concerts by members of the jury
Masterclass

Deadline for application:
April 1, 2000

Secretariat:
Læssøegade 74,
DK-5230 Odense M
Fax: (+45) 6613 6363

Healthy Practice for Musicians

by Elizabeth Andrews

Packed full of practical advice covering every aspect of a musician's physical and mental well-being. The book suggests ways of adapting the performing world to fit you and is a treasure trove for those who, despite the occupational hazards, want to go on doing their job successfully, and look after themselves in an environment that is physically, mentally and chemically as benign as possible.

"I would give this book my full and heartfelt endorsement as one of the most important gifts for all our colleagues."
YEHUDI MENUHIN

HEALTHY PRACTICE FOR MUSICIANS
Hardback. 432 pages
Price: **£19.70**
(inc. UK p&p)

Send your cheque (payable to Rhinegold Publishing Ltd) to:
Book Sales Dept, Rhinegold Publishing Ltd, 241 Shaftesbury Ave, London WC2H 8EH
Tel: 020 7333 1721 • Fax: 020 7333 1769

www.rhinegold.co.uk

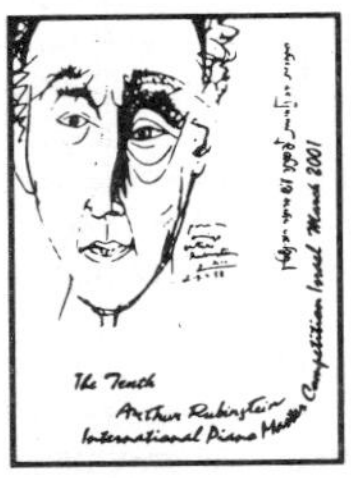

CELEBRATING ITS 10th EDITION
A COMPETITIVE FESTIVAL IN THE ART OF THE PIANO

THE ARTHUR RUBINSTEIN INTERNATIONAL PIANO MASTER COMPETITION TEL AVIV

will be held **from 20 March to 4 April 2001**
in conjunction with
THE ISRAEL PHILHARMONIC ORCHESTRA

ARTHUR RUBINSTEIN's first request on granting the Founder-Director of the Competition his name to the contest and to its main Award was: "look for an artist in your contest, - not for a mere pianist . . . put the highest acceptable repertoire demands before the competitors, and the highest criteria for artistic evaluation to the Jury"
LORIN MAAZEL - " . . . I am most impressed by the criteria that have been established by which the best creative interpretations of music in various styles will be of prime importance . . . "
CLAUDIO ARRAU - " . . . No piano competition in the future will bear a better name . . . "

**** The Competition is open for pianists of all nationalities between 18 and 32 years old.***
**** Applications deadline: 1 October 2000.***

PRIZES

1st Prize - **Arthur Rubinstein Award** - Competition Gold Medal (22 carat gold) bearing the portrait of Arthur Rubinstein, **drawn by Picasso**, and **$25.000**;
2nd Prize - Competition Silver Medal and **$15,000**;
3rd Prize -Competition Bronze Medal and **$10,000**;
4th, 5th and 6th Prizes - **$3,000** each one.
Additional prizes will be announced in our future publications.

The Competition Management undertakes to help promote the artistic carees of its laureates during 2 years after winning the Competition by recommending them to leading orchestras, festivals, concerts managements and recording companies.

Competition Founder / Director: **Jan Jacob Bistritzky**
Artistic Adviser: **Prof. Arie Vardi**
The Competition is a member of the Federation des Concours Internationaux de Musique, Geneve.
For further details please apply to The Arthur Rubinstein International Piano Master Competition.
Secretariat, 12, Huberman St. Tel Aviv 64075 (POB 6018, Tel Aviv 61060) Israel, Telephone: (972-3) 6856684, Fax: (972-3) 6854924
E-mail: competition@arims.org.il Site: http://www.arims.org.il

Soprano, tenor, baritone, bass singers. Ages 33 and under. First prize DM 10,000.

Cologne International Pianoforte Competition. The Tomassoni Foundation, Dagobertstr 38, D-50668 Köln, Germany *tel:* +49 221 912 818112 *fax:* +49 221 131204 *email:* barbara.schmidt@uni-koeln.de. Gerhard Peters, artistic director; Barbara Schmidt, organisation office. *September-October 2001, applications by June. Pianists of all nationalities aged 30 and under. First prize DM 15,000, second prize DM 10,000, third prize DM 5000. Application fee DM 150.*

Cologne International Singing Competition. The Helga and Paul Hohnen Foundation, Dagobertstr 38, D-50668 Köln, Germany *tel:* +49 221 912 818112 *fax:* +49 221 131204 *email:* barbara.schmidt@uni-koeln.de. Gerhard Peters, artistic director; Barbara Schmidt, organisation office. *Next September-October 2002, applications by 15 June. Ages 30 or under. First prize DM 15,000, second prize DM 10,000, third prize DM 5000. Application fee DM 150.*

Cologne International Violin Competition. The Georg Kulenkampff Foundation, Dagobertstr 38, D-50668 Köln, Germany *tel:* +49 221 912 818112 *fax:* +49 221 131204 *email:* barbara.schmidt@uni-koeln.de. Gerhard Peters, artistic director; Barbara Schmidt, organisation office. *September-October, applications by 15 June. Open to violinists of all nationalities aged under 30. First prize DM 15,000. Application fee DM 150.*

Ettlingen International Competition for Young Pianists. Pforzheimerstr 25a, D-76275 Ettlingen, Germany *tel:* +49 7243 101 311/2 *fax:* +49 7243 101 436 *email:* piano.ettlingen@t-online.de. Frank Reich, director of organisations. *Biennial. Next 12-20 August 2000, applications by 9 May. Two age categories: 16 and under, 21 and under. Entrance fee DM 110. First prize, DM 7500 plus concerts.*

Hannover International Violin Competition. Stiftung Niedersachsen, Ferdinandstr 4, D-30175 Hannover, Germany *tel:* +49 511 990540 *fax:* +49 511 314499 *email:* sn.kultur@t-online.de. Krzysztof Wegrzyn, artistic director; Linda Anne Engelhardt, executive director. *Triennial. Next 5-18 November 2000. Applications by June. Ages 16-30. First prize DM 50,000, CD recording, debut concerts and agency guidance for 2 years.*

International Chamber-Choir Competition Marktoberdorf. c/o Bayerische Musikakademie Marktoberdorf, Kurfürstenstr 19, D-87616 Marktoberdorf, Germany *tel:* +49 834 296 1825 *fax:* +49 834 240370 *email:* 100530.317@compuserve.com. Dolf Rabus, director. *Biennial. Next 31 May-6 June 2001, applications by mid-Oct 2000. Mixed and female choirs of 16-36 singers. First prize DM 5000.*

International Friedrich Kuhlau Flute Competition. PO Box 2061, D-29510 Uelzen, Germany *tel:* +49 581 800240 *fax:* +49 581 800220. Hans Rudolf Mentasti, organiser. *Triennial. Next November 2001.*

International J S Bach Competition. Sekretariat Bachwettbewerbe, Thomaskirchhof 16, D-04109 Leipzig, Germany *tel:* +49 341 964410 *fax:* +49 341 964 4195 *email:* jsbach@rzaix530.rz.uni-leipzig.de. Hans-Joachim Schulze, president; Sabine Martin, general secretary. *Next 2000. Org and hpd. Age limit 32 (voice, 34). Entrance fee DM 100. First prize DM 12,000.*

International Karl-Klingler Competition. c/o Hochschule für Musik "Hanns Eisler" Berlin, Charlottenstr 55, D-10117 Berlin, Germany *tel:* +49 302 0309 2487 *fax:* +49 302 0309 2402. Karl-Klingler Wettbewerb. *Next 2003. String quartets. Total age of quartet must not exceed 130. First prize DM 50,000.*

International Music Competition of the ARD. Bayerischer Rundfunk, D-80300 München, Germany *tel:* +49 895 900 2471 *fax:* +49 895 900 3091 *email:* ard.conc@br-mail.de. Renate Ronnefeld, general secretary; Gisela Mauss, secretary. *Annual. 5-22 September 2000, applications by 20 April (instrumentalists); 1 July (voice, duo, quartet). Entry fee DM 150. Age limits: instrument soloists born between 1970-1983; female singers 1970-1980; male singers 1968-1980; duo and trio 1968-1983. Categories: voice, viola, flute (first prize DM 20,000); piano duo (first prize DM 25,000); string quartet (first prize DM 32,000).*

International Pablo Casals Cello Competition. Kronberg Academy, Königsteinerstr 5, D-61476 Kronberg, Germany *tel:* +49 6173 950085 *also fax; email:* ikacello@aol.com. Raimund Trenkler, artistic director; Gabriela Denicke; Oda Cramer von Lane, admin. *1-11 July 2000. Cello competition.*

International Robert Schumann Choral Competition. Münzstr 12, D-08056 Zwickau, Germany *tel:* +49 375 212636 *fax:* +49 375 834130 *email:* kulturbuero@zwickau.de. *Next 2002. Open to female, male and mixed choirs. First prize DM 10,000.*

International Robert Schumann Competition for Piano and Voice. Münzstr 12, D-08056 Zwickau, Germany *tel:* +49 375 212636 *fax:* +49 375 834130 *email:* kulturbuero@zwickau.de. Gerd Nauhaus, chairman. *Quadrennial. Next 15-25 June 2000, applications by 1 April. Ages 30 and under for pianists, 32 and under for singers. First prize DM 15,000, for pianists and singers.*

International Singers' Contest 'Alexander Girardi'. Kulturabteilung der Stadt Coburg, Steingasse 18, D-96450 Coburg, Germany *tel:* +49 956 189 1402 *fax:* +49 956 189 1029. Albrecht Tauer, culture division director. *Next June-July 2001. Opera and operetta competition open to female singers born 1971-83 and male singers born 1969-83. First prize DM 15,000. Entrance fee DM 150.*

International Singing Contest 'New Voices'. Carl-Bertelsmann-Str 256, PO Box 103, D-33311 Gütersloh, Germany *tel:* +49 524 1817372 *fax:* +49 524 1819513 *email:* nadine.lindemann@bertelsmann.de. Nadine Lindemann, contact; Liz Mohn, president. *Biennial. Next autumn 2001, applications by spring. Male singers 32 years; female singers 30 years. First prize DM 15,000.*

International Violin Competition Leopold Mozart. Leopold-Mozart Konservatorium, Maximilianstr 59, D-86150 Augsburg, Germany *tel:* +49 821 324 4892 *fax:* +49 821 313088 *email:* l.mozart.comp@augsburg.de. Kranz Angelika, secretary. *Quadrennial. Next November 2003. Violinists of all nationalities, professional and student. Ages 15-30. Cash prizes, young musician awards, CD recording and concert engagements, audience prize, Mozart prize, extra prizes. Total cash prizes DM 60,000.*

International Young Arts Music Competition. Düsseldorfer Altstadt Herbst gGmbH, Bolkerstraße 57, D-40213 Düsseldorf, Germany *tel:* +49 211 133222 *fax:* +49 211 322203 *email:* info@altstadtherbst.de. Krysia Olbert, organiser. *September, applications by June. Ensembles with 2 to 9 members, aged under 35. First prize DM 12,000.*

Robert Stolz Song Competition. Sekretariat des Wettbewerbs, Landesverband der Tonkünstler und Musiklehrer, eV Steilshooperstr 42, D-22305 Hamburg, Germany *tel:* +49 40 690 1091 *fax:* +49 40 690 1092. *Annual. 9-12 March 2000, applications by 3 February. Entrants must have been born after 1 March 1965. First prize DM 8000.*

Greece

Athens International Choir Festival: Choir Competition. Polifonia Athenaeum, 2 Spartis Str, GR-153 42 Agia Paraskevi, Athens, Greece *tel:* +301 601 4741/601 3713/608 0119 *fax:* +301 600 9204/608 0119 *email:* rama@compulink.gr. Thrassos Cavouras, artistic director. *8-12 November 2000, applications by 29 February 2000. Mixed, male, female, children, chamber and folklore choirs.*

Dimitris Mitropoulos International Competition. 18 Alex Soutsou, GR-10671 Athens, Greece *tel:* +30 1 362 7412 *fax:* +30 1 362 1477. Traute Lutz, chief officer. *Annual. 15 November 2000, applications by 30 April. 2000: conducting for those born after 30 April 1965. 2001: composing. First prize DRS 4,000,000 .*

Maria Callas Grand Prix for Pianists. Athenaeum International Cultural Centre, 3 Adrianou St, GR-105 55 Athens, Greece *tel:* +30 1 321 1949/1955/1987 *fax:* +30 1 321 1196 *email:* athenm@ibm.net. Michel Bichsel. *24 March-3 April 2000, applications by December 1999. Ages 32 and under. Entry fee $100. First prize DRS 3,000,000 and concerts.*

Maria Callas Grand Prix for Singers. Athenaeum International Cultural Centre, 3 Adrianou St, GR-105 55 Athens, Greece *tel:* +30 1 321 1949/1955/1987/1932 *fax:* +30 1 321 1196 *email:* athenm@ibm.net. Michel Bichsez; Anna Koukouraki, general secretary. *Spring 2001, applications by December 2000. Ages 32 and under for males, 30 and under for females. Entry fee $100. First prizes DRS 2,000,000 and engagements in three categories: male, female and oratorio-lied.*

Rhodes International Music Festival: Choir Competition. Polifonia Athenaeum, 2 Spartis Str, GR-153 42 Agia Paraskevi, Athens, Greece *tel:* +30 1 601 4741 *fax:* +30 1 600 9204 *email:* rama@compulink.gr. Thrassos Cavouras, artistic director. *18-21 April 2001, applications by 30 November 2000.*

Hungary

Budapest International Music Competition. Interart Festivalcentre, PO Box 80, Vörösmarty tér 1, H-1366 Budapest 5, Hungary *tel:* +36 1 317 9838/266 3108 *fax:* +36 1 317 9910. Maria Liszkay, manager. *Harpsichord competition. 19 September-1 October 2000, applications by 1 May. First prize $3000.*

Hungarian Television International Conductors Competition. Interart Festivalcentre, PO Box 80, Vörösmarty tér 1, H-1366 Budapest, Hungary *tel:* +36 1 266 3108/317 9838 *fax:* +36 1 317 9910. Maria Liszkay, manager. *Triennial. Next 2001.*

International Choir Competition Béla Bartók. Nemzetközi Kórusverseny Irodája, Hunyadi u 1-3, H-4026 Debrecen, Hungary *tel:* +36 5 241 3977/9812 *fax:* +36 5 241 6040. Zoltan Szabò, secretary. *Annual. July. Member of the European Grand Prix of Choral Singing. 20th C and contemporary choral mus.*

International Chamber Choir Festival and Competition, Pécs. Szent István tér 17, H-7624 Pécs, Hungary *tel:* +36 72 215543 *fax:* +36 72 315679 *email:* nevhaz@mail.c3.hu. *Biennial. Next 14-17 April 2000,* *applications by 15 November 1999. Amateur choirs of not more than 30 members. First prize DM 1500.*

Republic of Ireland

Cork International Choral Festival. PO Box 68, Cork, Republic of Ireland *tel:* +353 21 308308 *fax:* +353 21 308309 *email:* chorfest@iol.ie. John Fitzpatrick, festival director. *26-30 April 2000, entries by 1 November 1999. Amateur choirs (not children's choirs, minimum 20 voices). First prize £2000.*

Guardian Dublin International Piano Competition. City Hall, Dublin 2, Republic of Ireland *tel:* +353 1 677 3066 *fax:* +353 1 671 1385. Ann Fuller, admin. *Triennial. Next 2000, entries by 30 November 1999. Ages 17-30. First prize £10,000 and international engagements.*

Limerick Church Music International Choral Festival. City Hall, Limerick, Republic of Ireland *tel:* +353 61 415799/229914 (H) *fax:* +353 61 415266/418601 *email:* limcorp@iol.ie; dunan@iol.ie. Fergus Quinlivan, director. *24-26 March 2000, entries by 15 February. Choirs and choral groups. First prize cheque and trophy.*

Israel

Arthur Rubinstein International Piano Master Competition. Secretariat, 12 Huberman St, PO Box 6018, 61060 Tel Aviv, Israel *tel:* +972 3 685 6684 *fax:* +972 3 685 4924 *email:* competition@arims.org.il. Jan J Bistritzky, founder and director. *Triennial. Next March-April 2001, entries by October 2000. Ages 18-32. Contact secretariat for further details.*

International Harp Contest. 4 Aharonowitz St, 63566 Tel Aviv, Israel *tel:* +972 3 528 0233 *fax:* +972 3 629 9524 *email:* harzimco@netvision.net.il. Esther Herlitz, director. *12-27 November 2000, applications by 1 May. All nationalities, aged 35 and under. Application fee $150. First prize Concert Grand Harp.*

Italy

Alessandro Casagrande International Piano Competition. Comune di Terni-Vico S Lorenzo 1, I-05100 Terni, Italy *tel:* +39 0744 549 713 *also fax; email:* concasag@tim.it. Riceputi Loredana, secretary. *Biennial. Next 31 May-11 June 2000. Applications by 15 March. Ages 28 and under. Entrance fee 150,000 lira. First prize 15,000,000 lira.*

Arturo Toscanini International Conductors' Competition. c/o Fondazione Arturo Toscanini, Office for International Competitions, Via G Tartini n 13, I-43100 Parma, Italy *tel:* +39 0521 274421 *fax:* +39 0521 272134 *email:* fondazione@toscanini.dsnet.it. Gianni Baratta, general manager; Fulvio Zannoni, secretary. *Triennial. Next 2001. Open to conductors of any nationality aged 35 and under. First prize (The Arturo Toscanini Award) 15,000,000 lire, contracts and diploma.*

Bellini International Voice Competition. Ibla International Music Foundation, 226 E Second St, Suite 5D, New York, NY 10009, USA *tel:* +1 212 387 0111 *fax:* +1 212 388 0102. Salvatore Moltisanti, president. *Annual. June-July, applications by March. Open to singers from all over the world, no age limit. Prize approx $15,000 to sponsor recitals, debut in Europe and/or USA, scholarships and recording for Athena Records.*

Bottega International Competition for Conducting. Corporation for the Civic Theatre of Treviso, Corso del Popolo 31, I-31100 Treviso, Italy *tel:* +39 0422 410130 *fax:* +39 0422 52285.

Carlo Soliva International Music Competition. Istituto Musicale Carlo Soliva, 35 Via Facino Cane, I-15033 Casale Monferrato, Italy *tel:* +39 0142 55760 *also fax.* Pier Narciso Masi, president; Adelaide Bobba, secretary. *Biennial. Next 26 March-1 April 2000, closing date 28 February. Any nationality. Soloists, piano duo and chamber music. First prize 25,000,000 lire for soloists plus 10 concerts, 160,000 lire for duo, 200,000 lire for trio.*

City of Senigallia International Piano Competition. Piazza del Duca, I-60019 Senigallia, Italy *tel:* +39 071 65568 *fax:* +39 071 60942 *email:* senigallia@an.nettuno.it. Domenico Pergolesi, general director; Luigi Mostacci, artistic director. *August, International Meeting of Young Pianists. September, piano competition. IMYP: under 16. Age range for piano competition 15-36. Entry fees, IMYP 150,000 lire; piano competition 200,000 lire. Entries by 30 June. First prize for piano competition 20,000,000 lire.*

Concorso Internazionale per 'Voci Verdiane'. Comune di Busseto, Piazza Giuseppe Verdi 10, I-43011 Busseto (Parma), Italy *tel:* +39 0524 92603/91841 *fax:* +39 0524 92360/92603. Sindaco di Busseto, president. *Annual. July, applications by June. Ages 30 and under (soprano and tenor), 33 and under (mezzo-soprano, baritone, bass). First prize 7,000,000 lire.*

Competition for Young Opera Singers belonging to the European Community. Istituzione Teatro Lirico Sperimentale, di Spoleto 'A Belli', Piazza G Bovio 1, I-06049 Spoleto (PG), Italy *tel:* +39 0743 221645/220440 *fax:* +39 0743 222930 *email:* teatrolirico@mail.caribusiness.it. Lepore Claudio, admin. *15-19 March 2000, applications by 29 February. Singers from European Community countries; sopranos and tenors aged 30 and under; mezzo-sopranos, contraltos, baritones and basses aged 32 and under. Applicants should be citizens of an EU country. Winners will be awarded grants for a 5-month singing course culminating in a performance at the Teatro Lirico Sperimentale, Spoleto amounting to 1,500,000 lire each month.*

Dino Ciani Prize for Young Pianists. Teatro alla Scala, Via Filodrammatici 2, I-20121 Milano, Italy *tel:* +39 02 88791 *fax:* +39 02 887 9424. Riccardo Muti, jury president; Laura Colombo, secretary. *Triennial. Next 2002. Age limit 30. Entry fee $100. First prize 25,000,000 lire, concerts and CD with EMI.*

Ettore Pozzoli International Piano Competition. Via Paradiso 6, I-20038 Seregno, Italy *tel:* +39 0362 222914 *also fax; email:* pozzoli@concorsopozzoli.it. Lia Diotti, secretary. *Biennial. Next Sept 2001. Open to those born after 1 January 1967. First prize 20,000,000 lire and CD recording.*

European Music Competition Città di Moncalieri. Via Carlo Alberto 3/b, I-10024 Moncalieri (TO), Italy *tel:* +39 011 640 8597 *fax:* +39 011 640 3060. *October-November. Applications by 30 September. Ages 8-35 in eight categories. Cash prizes.*

Ferruccio Busoni International Piano Competition. Conservatorio Claudio Monteverdi, Piazza Domenicani 19, I-39100 Bolzano, Italy *tel:* +39 0471 976568 *fax:* +39 0471 973579 *email:* busonibz@tin.it. Mariapia Venturi, secretary. *Annual. 17 August-2 September 2000. Entrance fee. Ages 16-32. First prize 20,000,000 lire and c 60 concerts.*

Gian Battista Viotti International Music and Ballet Competition. Societa del Quartetto, PO Box 127, I-13100 Vercelli, Italy *tel:* +39 0161 252667 *fax:* +39 0161 255575 *email:* gbviotti@net4u.it. Pier M Robbone, co-ordinator. *Annual. October. Applications by September. Entry fee 100,000 lire. Categories of voice, piano, chamber music, cello. Max ages: voice 35, piano 30, chamber music 32, cello 30. First prize 15,000,000 lire and engagements.*

Guido d'Arezzo International Polyphonic Competition. Fondazione 'Guido d'Arezzo', Corso Italia 102, I-52100 Arezzo, Italy *tel:* +39 0575 356203/23835 *fax:* +39 0575 324735 *email:* fondguid@nots.it. Paolo Nicchi, commissioner; Nino Materazzi, executive director; Maria Cristina Cangelli, general secretary. *Last week of August 2000, applications by 15 February. Competition for amateur choirs; special competition for contemporary music. Ages 15 and under for children; no age limit for other categories. First prize 4,000,000 lire for each category; 5,000,000 lire grand prize.*

Ibla International Piano Competition. 226 E Second St, Suite 5D, NYC, NY 10009, USA *tel:* +1 212 387 0111 *fax:* +1 212 388 0102. Salvatore Moltisanti, president. *Annual. June-July. Applications by March. Pianists worldwide. Five categories: adult, young, four hands, concerto and accompanists. Prizes are concert engagements and scholarships, totalling $15,000. Eventual CD recording.*

International Choir Competition of Riva del Garda. Associazione Concorso Corale, Via Maffei, 7, I-38066 Riva del Garda (TN), Italy *tel:* +39 0464 560113 *fax:* +39 0464 520900 *email:* cmr@anthesi.com.

International Classical Guitar Competition. Piazza Garibaldi 16, I-15100 Alessandria, Italy *tel:* +39 0131 251207 *fax:* +39 0131 235507 *email:* pittalug@email.alessandria.alpcom.it. Micaela Pittaluga, president; Maria Luisa Pittaluga, vice-president. *Annual. 25-29 September 2000. Applications by August. For those born after January 1970. First prize 12,000,000 lire, medal, diploma, CD, and concert tour of Italy.*

International Competition for Instrumental and Vocal Performance. Via Aurelia 139, I-18016 San Bartolomeo al Mare (IM), Italy *tel:* +39 0183 400967/888/200 *fax:* +39 0183 403050; +39 0185 771790 *email:* roveredoro@hotmail.com. Luciano Lanfranchi, artistic director. *Annual. July, applications by June. Open to instrumentalists and singers born 1963-1987. First prizes 20,000 lire (soloists) and 35,000 lire (non-soloists).*

5th International String Quartet Competition, Premio Paolo Borciani. c/o Teatro Municipale Valli, Piazza Martiri del 7 Luglio, I-42100 Reggio Emilia, Italy *tel:* +39 0522 458811/458908 *fax:* +39 0522 458822 *email:* direzione@i-teatri.re.it. Elio Canova, president; Francesca Zini, secretary general; Guido A Borciani, artistic director. *11-18 June 2000, entries by 31 January. Dedicated to the memory of Paolo Borciani. Total age of ensembles 120, individuals not aged above 35. 1st prize 36,000,000 lire and an international tour. Entry fee: 150,000 lire.*

Liszt Competition. Conservatorio di Musica 'A Boito', Via del Conservatorio 27, I-43100 Parma, Italy *tel:* +39 0521 282320 *fax:* +39 0521 200398. Mr Falavigna. *Quadrennial. Next 2000. Ages 16-32. Pno.*

Nicolo Paganini International Violin Competition. Comune di Genova, PO Box 586, c/o Ufficio Postale, I-16100 Genova Centro, Italy *tel:* +39 010 5574215 *fax:* +39 010 2469272. Maria Sanfilippo, competition secretary. *Annual. 29 September-8 October 2000, applications by 31 May. Ages 16-33. Entry fee 180,000 lire. First prize 20,000,000 lire and exhibition concert.*

THE 4th
HAMAMATSU
INTERNATIONAL
PIANO
COMPETITION
2000.11.13-11.26
Member of the World Federation of International Music Competitions
■Date : First Stage／11.13～11.17 Second Stage／11.18～11.20
Third Stage／11.21～11.22
Final Stage／11.25～11.26 Presentation of Awards／11.26
■Venue : Preliminary Stages／ACT City Hamamatsu Concert Hall
Final Stage・Presentation of Awards／ACT City Hamamatsu Main Hall
■Organized by City of Hamamatsu／ACT City Hamamatsu Management Foundation
■In cooperation with The Ministry of Foreign Affairs/The Agency for Cultural Affairs/The Shizuoka Prefectural Government/Japan Federation of Musicians/Japanese Society for Rights of Authors, Composers and Publishers(JASRAC)/The Japan Broadcasting Corporation(NHK)/The Asahi Shimbun Hamamatsu Office/The Mainichi Newspapers/The Yomiuri Shimbun Hamamatsu Office/Nihon Keizai Shimbun, Inc./The Sankei Shimbun/Japan Times/The Chunichi Shimbun,Tokai Headquarters/The Shizuoka Shimbun・Shizuoka Broadcasting System/Ongaku no Tomo Sha Corporation/Chopin Corporation
■Judges : NAKAMURA Hiroko(Japan・Chairperson)/Michel BEROFF(France)/Barbara HESSE-BUKOWSKA(Poland)/Alexander JENNER(Austria)/Jerome LOWENTHAL(U.S.A.)/Viktor MERZHANOV(Russia)/NODAIRA Ichiro(Japan)/NOJIMA Minoru(Japan)/Piero RATTALINO(Italy)/Joaquim SORIANO(Spain)/Arie VARDI(Isarel)/ZHOU Guangren(China)
■Eligibility : open to pianists born after 1 January, 1972
■For more information : Secretariat of the Hamamatsu International Piano Competition
Hamamatsu P. O. Box 105, 430-7790 Japan
Tel: (81/53)451-1114 Fax: (81/53)451-1123
e-mail:hipic@city.hamamatsu.shizuoka.jp
http://www.city.hamamatsu.shizuoka.jp/actcity/hipic/index.html

Rodolfo Lipizer International Violin Competition. Via Don Giovanni Bosco 91, I-34170 Gorizia GO, Italy *tel:* +39 0481 34775 *fax:* +39 0481 536710 *email:* lipizer@mail.seta.it. Lorenzo Qualli, president; Elena Lipizer, artistic director. *Annual. Next 9-17 September 2000, entries by 15 May. Violinists of any nationality born after 17 September 1965. First prize 12,000,000 lire and a violin.*

Syrinx International Competition for Flute. c/o Accademia Italiana del Flauto, 43 Via Innocenza X, I-00152 Roma, Italy *tel:* +39 06 581 6225 *fax:* +39 06 588 0429. Gian Luca Morseletto, chief officer. *Biennial. Next 2001. Flautists of all nationalities. First prize 6,000,000 lire and a flute.*

Toti dal Monte International Singing Competition. Ente Teatro Comunale, Corso del Popolo 31, Via Diaz 7, I-31100 Treviso, Italy *tel:* +39 0422 410130 *fax:* +39 0422 582285. Lucio De Piccoli, press officer. *Annual. July. Prizes 2,500,000-3,500,000 lire.*

Umberto Micheli International Piano Competion. c/o Resia SrL, Via Manzoni 31, I-20121 Milano, Italy *tel:* +39 02 654161/2/3/4 *fax:* +39 02 659 7851 *email:* resiasrl@tin.it. Patrizia Garrasi, director general. *Triennial. Next 2001. Concentrates specifically on contemporary music.*

Valentino Bucchi di Roma Capitale International Prize. Via Ubaldino Peruzzi 20, I-00139 Roma, Italy *tel:* +39 06 8720 0121 *fax:* +39 06 8713 1527. Liliana Pannella, president. *Annual. November, applications by 15 September (performance) and 30 September (composition). Categories rotate: 2000 20th C and 2 piano, flute and piccolo, clarinet; violin, viola, cello, double-bass, quartet and strings (performance and composition); voice and choir, music and nature, game and fairy tales (piano performance for children and composition); 2001 flute and piccolo, clarinet (performance and composition); wind instruments for children. Ages 32-35 (performance); 40 (composition). First prize 11,000,000 lire (piano) approx, 30,000,000 lire (2 pianos) approx.*

Vittorio Gui International Chamber Music Competition. Associazione Concorsi e Rassegne Musicali, Teatro Comunale di Firenze, via Solferino, 15, I-50123 Firenze, Italy *tel:* +39 055 2779 446 *also fax; email:* acerm@firenze.net. Massimo Bogianckino, president; Colella Ornella, organising secretary. *Annual. 9-15 October 2000, entries by 5 September. Ages 32 and under (for trio, quartet and quintet the average age must not exceed 32 years). Entry fee 250,000 lire. First prize 15,000,000 lire and concert tour.*

Vittoria Caffa Righetti International Music Competition. Comune di Cortemilia, C.so Einaudi, I-12074 Cortemilia, Italy *tel:* +39 011 661 0589 *fax:* +39 017 381154. Luigi Giachino, artistic manager. *Late September. Applications by early September. Entry fee 60,000 lire. First prize 4,000,000 lire scholarship; other cash prizes.*

Japan

Hamamatsu International Piano Competition. Hamamatsu, PO Box 105, 430-7790, Japan *tel:* +81 53 451 1114 *fax:* +81 53 451 1123 *email:* hipic@city.hamamatsu.shizuoka.jp. Masaru Honma, secretary general. *13-26 November 2000. Open to pianists born after 1 January 1972. Competition is in four stages. First prize 3,000,000 yen, a certificate of merit and a gold medal.*

International Music Competition of Japan. Japan Federation of Musicians, Kaga Bldg 2F, Toranomon 5-2-8, Minato-Ku, Tokyo 105-0001, Japan *tel:* +81 3 3437 6837 *fax:* +81 3 3437 6820. Kenji Kouchi, secretary general. *Triennial.*

Osaka International Chamber Music Competition. C/-Yomiuri Telecasting Corporation, 2-33 Shiromi 2-chome, Chuo-ku, Osaka 540-8510, Japan *tel:* +81 6 947 2184 *fax:* +81 6 947 2198. Kunihiko Tamakoshi, producer. *May, applications by 31 October. Entry fee 20,000 yen. First prize 3,000,000 yen.*

Luxembourg

ICSC International Coloratura Singing Competition - Sylvia Geszty. PO Box 1163, D-75390 Gechingen, Germany *tel:* +49 7056 8024 *fax:* +49 7056 4256. Sylvia Geszty. *Biennial. Next May 2000, entries by 1 March. Ages 32 and under. First round stages held in Warsaw, Bloomington (USA), Luxembourg, London, Berlin, Budapest and Madrid; final takes place in Luxembourg. First prize 16,000 DM.*

Netherlands

César Franck Organ Competition. Santpoorterstr 10, NL-2023 DC Haarlem, Netherlands *tel:* +31 23 525 2706 *fax:* +31 23 525 2766 *email:* nhermans@euronet.nl. Louk Hermans, admin. *Triennial. Next October 2001, entries by 1 June 2001. Open to professional organists.*

IKF International Choir Festival. Plompetorengracht 3, NL-3512 CA Utrecht, Netherlands *tel:* +31 30 231 3174 *fax:* +31 30 231 8137 *email:* snk@euronet.nl. Jos Vranken Jr, music manager. *28 June-5 July 2001. Arnhem.*

International Competition for Early Music Ensembles. 'Van Wassenaer Competition 2000', Willemsparkweg 114, NL-1071 HN Amsterdam, Netherlands *tel:* +31 20 6 266944 *fax:* +31 20 6 227118. Martijn Jacobus, director. *Biennial. Next 15-18 November 2000. Instrumental and vocal ensembles (max 8 persons), repertoire 1600-1800.*

International Competition for Organ Improvisation. Postbus 3333, Stadhuis, NL-2001 DH Haarlem, Netherlands *tel:* +31 23 511 5733 *fax:* +31 23 511 5743. E L S Hendrikse, secretary. *Biennial. Next 2000. No age limit. First prize DFL 10,000.*

International Franz Liszt Piano Competition. Muziekcentrum Vredenburg PO Box 550, NL-3500 AN Utrecht, Netherlands *tel:* +31 30 286 2229 *fax:* +31 30 231 6522 *email:* liszt@vredenburg.nl. Quinten Peelen, office manager. *Triennial. Next March 2002. Ages 15-30. First prize DFL 25,000 plus recitals in the Netherlands and abroad.*

International Gaudeamus Interpreters Competition. Gaudeamus Foundation, Swammerdamstraat 38, NL-1091 RV Amsterdam, Netherlands *tel:* +31 20 694 7349 *fax:* +31 20 694 7258. *Biennial. Next 2001. All instruments and vocal soloists and ensembles (max 12 performers). Special ensembles prize. Ages 35 and under.*

International Kirill Kondrashin Competition For Young Conductors. c/o NOS (Netherlands Broadcasting Corp), PO Box 26444, NL-1202 JJ Hilversum, Netherlands *tel:* +31 35 677 5453 *fax:* +31 35 677 4311 *email:* kondrashin@nos.nl. Max Snijder, manager. *Quadrennial. Next September 2002, entries by April 2002. Conducting. Ages 36 and under. First prize DFL 75,000.*

International Vocal Competition. PO Box 1225, NL-5200 BG's-Hertogenbosch, Netherlands *tel:* +31 73 690 0999 *fax:* +31 73 690 1166. Arthur Oostvogel, managing director. *21 September-1 October 2000, applications by 1 June. Ages 30 and under. First prize 15,000 euros.*

Norway

The Queen Sonja International Music Competition. PO Box 5190, Majorstua, N-0302 Oslo, Norway *tel:* +47 23 367067 *fax:* +47 22 463630 *email:* sonja@nmh.no. Lars Fleten, executive director. *Biennial. Next 2001.*

Poland

Chopin International Youth Piano Competition. Chopin Centre, 87-404 Radomin, Poland *tel:* +48 56 683 9322 *fax:* +48 56 683 2280. *For children and young people. May, Szafarnia.*

Grzegorz Fitelberg International Competition for Conductors. Ul Sokolska 2, PL-40084 Katowice, Poland *tel:* +48 32 596074 *also fax.* Leon Markiewicz, director. *Quadrennial. Next 2003. Age limit 35. First prize $10,000.*

Henryk Wieniawski International Violin Competition. Swietoslawska St 7, PL-61840 Poznan, Poland *tel:* +48 61 852 2642/8992 *fax:* +48 61 852 8991. M Merczynski, director. *Quinquennial. Next 13-27 October 2001, applications by 30 June. Ages 30 and under. First prize $20,000.*

International Frederick Chopin Piano Competition. Frederick Chopin Society in Warsaw, Ostrogski Castle, Okolnik 1, PL-00368 Warszawa, Poland *tel:* +48 22 826 8190/827 5471 *fax:* +48 22 827 9599 *email:* konkurs@chopin.pl. *Quinquennial. Next 4-21 October 2000. Applications by 1 March. Ages 17-28. First prize $25,000 and a gold medal.*

International Festival of Choral Song. Concert Agency 'Rondo', PO Box 77, PL-70334 Szczecin 4, Poland *tel:* +48 91 484 5242 *fax:* +48 91 484 6193 *email:* rondo@ubique.com.pl. Jan Szyrocki, music director; Stanislaw Zaborowski, director. *June, applications by February. Entry fee $200. First prize PZL 6000.*

Stanislaw Moniuszko Vocal Competition. Plac Teatralny1, PL-00950, Warszawa, Poland *tel:* +48 22 692 0642 *fax:* +48 22 692 0742. Maria Foltyn, manager and artistic director. *Triennial. Next 2001. Ages 35 and under. First prize $15,000.*

Portugal

Porto International Music Competition. Avenida da Boavista, 1681 - 2°, Sala 2.10, 4150 Porto, Portugal *tel:* +351 2 606 7258 *fax:* +351 2 606 7471. Fernanda Wandschneider, president; Elzira Coelho, general secretary. *Annual. Only the first 90 entries will be accepted. Contestants to have been born between 1 January 1968 and 1 September 1983. First prize 1,500,000 escudos; second prize 500,000 escudos; third prize 350,000 escudos; fourth prize 150,000 escudos.*

Romania

Constantin Silvestri International Concerto Competition. c/o LSP, 72 Warwick Gardens, London W14 8PP, UK *tel:* +44 20 7603 1396 *also fax; email:* schubert@dial.pipex.com. *In Sinaia, Romania. Next end August 2002. All instruments. Ages 18-28. Prizes: concert tours with professional orchestras and recitals.*

Constantin Silvestri International Conducting Competition. c/o LSP, 72 Warwick Gardens, London W14 8PP, UK *tel:* +44 20 7603 1396 *also fax; email:* schubert@dial.pipex.com. *In Sinaia, Romania. Biennial.*

Next end August 2001. Ages 35 and under. Prizes: concert tours with professional orchestras.

George Enescu International Piano, Violin and Singing Competition. Calea Victoriei nr 155, bl D1 sc 8 et 2, 71012 Bucharest, Romania *tel:* +40 1 650 1806/12 *fax:* +40 1 311 0200 *email:* artexim@com.pcnet.ro. Mihai Constantinescu.

South Africa

UNISA International Music Competitions. University of S Africa, PO Box 392, RSA 0001 Pretoria, South Africa *tel:* +27 12 429 3344/3353 *fax:* +27 12 429 3644 *email:* musicomp@alpha.unisa.ac.za. John Roos, artistic director. *Biennial. Next 20 January-5 February 2000. Ages 32 and under. Application fee $50. First prize $20,000 for violin, cello, piano, voice and organ.*

Spain

Alhambra International Guitar Competition. Manufacturas Alhambra SL, Duquesa de Almodóvar, 17, E-03830 Muro del Alcoy, Alicante, Spain *tel:* +34 965 530011 *fax:* +34 966 516302 *email:* alhambra @tsai.es. D Jaime Julia Abad, manager director; D Yukiharu Inoue, chief officer. *Next 2000. First prize 1,700,000 ptas.*

Cadaqués International Conducting Competition. Carrer dels Arcs 8, 1er 2, E-08002 Barcelona, Spain *tel:* +34 933 019555 *fax:* +34 933 022670 *email:* trito@bcn.servicom.es. Llorenc Caballero, secretary; Maria Pau Roca, co-ordinator. *23-28 July 2000, closing date April. Ages 35 and under. First prize 1,000,000 ptas and orchestra engagements in Spain.*

Dos Hermanas International Clarinet Competition. Secretaria del Concurso Internacional de Clarinete, Ayuntamiento, E-41700 Dos Hermanas, Sevilla, Spain *tel:* +34 95 491 9570/491 9524 *fax:* +34 95 491 9525 *email:* doshermanas@dipusevilla.es. Antonio Moran; Pedro Sanchez. *26 September-1 October 2000, applications by 6 September. Open to clarinettists of all nationalities aged 30 and under on opening date of competition. First prize 1,000,000 ptas, a clarinet and concerts.*

Francisco Tárrega International Guitar Contest. Ayuntamiento de Benicasim, E-12560 Benicasim Castellón, Spain *tel:* +34 964 300962 *fax:* +34 964 303432. S Alcalde, president. *Annual. August-September. Ages 32 and under. First prize 1,350,000 ptas, CD and concerts.*

Francisco Vinas International Singing Contest. Calle Bruc 125, E-08037 Barcelona, Spain *tel:* +34 932 154227; +34 934 578646. Maria Vilardell Vinas, president. *Annual. January, entries by December. Max ages: 35 male, 32 female. Application fee 14,000 ptas. Two categories: opera and oratorio-Lieder. First grand prize for male and female singers 1,300,000 ptas each.*

International Choral Competition. Centro de Iniciativas and Turismo, Calle Emeterio Arrese, 2, PO Box 100, E-20400 Tolosa, San Sebastian, Spain *tel:* +34 943 650414 *fax:* +34 943 698028. *Annual. October 2000. Closing date 15 May. No age limit.*

International Singing Competition Alfredo Kraus. Bravo Murillo 21-23, E-35003 Las Palmas de Gran Canaria, Spain *tel:* +34 928 320513/321747 *fax:* +34 928 314747 *email:* orfigc@orfigc.com. Juan Antonio González Ojellón, manager. *Biennial. Next 2001. Singers of any nationality aged 18-32 (male) or 20-35 (female). First prize 2,000,000 ptas. Entrance fee 10,000 ptas.*

International Voice Competition of Bilbao. Apartado de Correos no 1532, E-48080 Bilbao, Spain *tel:* +34 944 246533 *fax:* +34 944 246454. José Antonio, competition director. *Biennial. Next 25 November-2 December 2000, applications by 16 October 2000. Ages 18-33. First prize 900,000 ptas each for male and female entrants.*

José Iturbi International Piano Competition. Diputación Provincial, Plaza de Manises 4, Servicio de Cultura, E-46003 Valencia, Spain *tel:* +34 963 882500 *fax:* +34 963 882775. *Biennial. Ages 31 and under.*

Julian Gayarre International Singing Competition. Calle Santo Domingo 6, E-31001 Pamplona, Spain *tel:* +34 948 426072/426500 *fax:* +34 948 223906 *email:* iaranazz@cfnavarra.es. Ignacio Aranaz, co-ordinator; Piero Rattalino, artistic director. *Biennial. Next September 2000, applications by 30 June. Ages 35 and under for male, 32 and under for female. First prizes (for male and female) 1,500,000 ptas and engagement.*

Maria Canals International Competition for Musical Performance. Gran Via de les Corts Catalanes 654, E-08010 Barcelona, Spain *tel:* +34 93 318 7731 *also fax*. Elisabeth Martinez, general secretary. *Annual. 2-18 April 2000, applications by 2 February. For piano and voice. Ages 18-32 (pianists), 18-35 (singers). First prize 800,000 ptas and gold medal. Entry fee 22,000 ptas.*

Pablo Sarasate International Violin Competition. Calle Santo Domingo 6, E-31001 Pamplona, Spain *tel:* +34 948 426072/426500 *fax:* +34 948 223906 *email:* iaranazz@cfnavarra.es. Ignacio Aranaz, co-ordinator; Vladimir Spirakov, president. *Biennial. Next 11 September 2001, entries by 30 June. Ages 27 and under. First prize 1,500,000 ptas plus engagements.*

Paloma O'Shea International Santander Piano Competition. Calle Hernán Cortés 3, E-39003 Santander, Spain *tel:* +34 942 311451 *fax:* +34 942 314816 email: ccpianoak@mundivia.es. Annelies Kaufmann, general secretary. *Triennial. Next 27 July-7 August 2002. For ages 29 and under. All participants receive full board and travel expenses. First prize $46,000, concerts, recitals and a recording.*

Pedro Lavirgen International Singing Competition. Ayuntamiento de Priego, Centro Cultural Victor Rubino Chavarri, 14800 Priego de Cordoba, Spain *tel:* +34 957 708410 *fax:* +34 957 708409. Tomás R Delgado Toro. *Next 2000.*

Premio Internacional de Canto Acisclo Fernández. Fundación Jacinto e Innocencio Guerrero de Música, Gran Vía 78, E-28013 Madrid, Spain *tel:* +34 915 476618 *fax:* +34 915 483493 *email:* jeig@adenle.es. *Biennial. Next 2000. Open to all singers and all nationalities born after 1 January 1965. First prize 2,500,000 ptas.*

Premio Internacional de Guitarra. Gran Vía 78, c/o Fundación Jacinto e Inocencio Guerrero, E-28013 Madrid, Spain *tel:* +34 915 476618 *fax:* +34 915 483493. *Biennial. Next 2000. Open to guitar players of any nationality born on or after 1 January 1965. First prize 2,500,000 ptas.*

Premio Internacional de Piano Fundación Guerrero. Gran Vía 78, c/o Fundación Jacinto e Inocencio Guerrero, E-28013 Madrid, Spain *tel:* +34 915 476618 *fax:* +34 915 483493 *email:* jeig@adenle.es. *Biennial. Next 2001. Open to pianists of any nationality aged under 35. First prize 2,500,000 ptas.*

Switzerland

Clara Haskil Piano Competition. PO Box 234, CH-1800 Vevey 1, Switzerland *tel:* +41 21 922 6704 *fax:* +41 21 922 6734 *email:* clara.haskil@smile.ch. Patrick Peikert, director; Christiane Susset, secretary. *Biennial. Next August-September 2001, applications by 1 July. Ages 27 and under. First prize SFR 20,000.*

Géza Anda International Piano Competition. Bleicherweg 18, CH-8002 Zürich, Switzerland *tel:* +41 1 205 1423 *fax:* +41 1 205 1429 *email:* info@gezaanda.org. Ruth Bossart, secretary general. *Triennial. Next 24 June-6 July 2000, entries by 1 March 2000. Ages 32 and under. Entry fee SFR 300. First prize SFR 30,000, concert engagements and management service.*

International Tibor Varga Violin Competition. Association du Festival Tibor Varga, Case Postale 1429, CH-1951 Sion, Switzerland *tel:* +41 27 323 4314 *fax:* +41 27 323 4662 *email:* festivargasion@vtx.ch. Pierre Gillioz, director; Gilbert Varga, artistic director. *Annual. 8-18 August 2000, applications by 1 May. Application fee SFR 100. Ages 15-32. First prize SFR 10,000, total prizes SFR 35,000.*

The Reding-Piette International Competition for Duo Piano. Chateau Perigord II, Monte Carlo, MC-98000, Monaco *tel:* +377 93 30 07 21 *also fax; email: coco@net.neuchatel2000.ch.* Janine Reding, Theo Loosli, competition presidents. *Triennial. Next 23 June-1 July 2001, applications by 20 December 2000. To select young professional piano duos preparing for an international concert career. Ages 30 and under. First prize SFR 25,000.*

Swiss Organ Competition. Place du Prieur, CH-1323 Romainmôtier, Switzerland *tel:* +41 24 453 1718 *fax:* +41 24 453 1150. Marisa Aubert. *September-October 2000, applications by 1 May. No age limit. Repertoire changes every year. First prize SFR 4000.*

USA

Carmel Chamber Music Competition. PO Box 6283, Carmel, CA 93921, USA *tel:* +1 408 624 9541 *fax:* +1 408 625 6927. Amy Anderson, president. *6-7 May 2000, entries by 15 March. Open to non-professional chamber ensembles of 3-6 players, average age under 26. First prize $3000.*

Center for Contemporary Opera International Opera Singers Competition. PO Box 1350, Gracie Sta, New York, NY 10028-0010, USA *tel:* +1 212 308 6728 *fax:* +1 212 308 6744 *email:* conopera @mindspring.com. Richard Marshall, director. *September-October 2000, entries postmarked no later than 15 May. To encourage singers to explore contemporary repertory. Open to all singers who have not attained international careers. Entry fee $35. First prize $2000 and a New York recital.*

Chamber Music America Awards for Excellence in Chamber Music Teaching. 305 Seventh Ave 5th Floor, New York, NY 10001-6008, USA *tel:* +1 212 242 2022 *fax:* +1 212 242 7955. Dean Stein, executive director. *$1000 cash award granted to an individual teacher in charge of a chamber music programme for students aged 6-18.*

Chamber Music America Commissioning Program. 305 Seventh Ave, 5th Floor, New York, NY 10001-6008, USA *tel:* +1 212 242 2022 *fax:* +1 212 242 7955. Dean Stein, executive director. *Awards to enrich the chamber music repertoire and encourage partnerships among ensembles, composers and instrumentalists, made on basis of artistic excellence and demonstrated commitment to the performance of* *contemporary music. Open to members of Chamber Music America. Composers must be American citizens or permanent residents of the USA.*

Chopin Foundation of the United States. 1440 79 St, Causeway, Suite 117, Miami, FL 33141, USA *tel:* +1 305 868 0624 *fax:* +1 305 865 5150 *email:* info@chopin.org. Blanka A Rosenstiel, president. *Quinquennial. Next 4-12 March 2000. Held in advance of the International Chopin Competition in Warsaw. Open to American pianists born between 4 October 1972 and 14 October 1983. Automatic acceptance at International Chopin Piano Competition in Warsaw, $75,000 in cash prizes and concert engagements.*

Cleveland International Piano Competition. c/o The Cleveland Institute of Music, 11021 E Boulevard, Cleveland, OH 44106, USA *tel:* +1 216 791 5000 *fax:* +1 216 791 3063 *email:* ClevePiano@aol.com. Karen Knowlton, executive director. *Biennial. Next August 2001, entries by March. Ages 17-35. First prize $15,000.*

Coleman Chamber Ensemble Competition. 202 S Lake Ave, No 201, Pasadena, CA 91101, USA *tel:* +1 626 793 4191 *fax:* +1 818 787 1294 *email:* krfccma@aol.com. Kathy Freedland, executive director. *29 April 2000, applications by 24 February. Open to non-professional chamber ensembles (strings, wind and brass) under the direction of a coach. Average age of players in each ensemble must be under 26. Total of $11,200 awarded.*

Concert Artists Guild Competition. 850 7th Ave, Suite 1205, New York, NY 10019, USA *tel:* +1 212 333 5200 *fax:* +1 212 977 7149 *email:* caguild@concertartists.org. Mary Madigan, competition director. *20 February 2000. Suggested age limit 35. Open to all solo instrumentalists, chamber groups and singers. First prize includes management by CAG, New York recital, other prizes include recording contracts and engagements.*

The Ducrest International Young Artist Competition. c/o Acadiana Symphony Orchestra, 412 Travis St, Lafayette, LA 70503, USA *tel:* +1 318 232 4277 *fax:* +1 318 237 4712 *email:* symphony@iamerica.net. Geraldine Hubbell, executive director. *19-20 November 2000, Lafayette, Louisiana. Applications by 1 October. Open to artists aged under 30 and not under professional management. First prize $5000 plus appearance with orchestra.*

East and West Artists International Auditions for New York Debut. 310 Riverside Drive, Suite 313, New York, NY 10025-4101, USA *tel:* +1 212 222 2433 *also fax; email:* acos_ewa@cwix.com. Adolovni Acosta, executive director; Bo Lawergren, artistic director. *20-22 October 2000, entries by 1 June. Instrumentalists, singers, ensembles (up to 5 members) who have not given a New York debut recital. Ages 18 and above. Prize, fully sponsored solo debut in Weill Recital Hall at Carnegie Hall.*

Elizabeth Harper Vaughn Concerto Competition. 1200 E Center St, Kingsport, TN 37660, USA *tel:* +1 423 392 8423 *fax:* +1 423 392 8426. Lisa M Baker, manager. *To promote the performance of classical music by young artists. 2000: wind, brass, percussion, harp, guitar. Ages 26 and under. Entry fee $20. First prize $1000 and concert with the Kingsport Symphony Orchestra.*

Ellsworth Smith International Trumpet Solo Competition. The Ohio State University, Columbus, OH 43210, USA *tel:* +1 614 292 0254 *fax:* +1 614 292 1102. William Campbell, School of Music. *Biennial.*

Florida Grand Opera Young Artist Studio and Technical Apprentice Programs. 1200 Coral Way, Miami, FL 33145-2980, USA *tel:* +1 305 854 1643 *fax:* +1 305 856 1042 *email:* info@fgo.org. *Eight-month programme in an environment of continuous performing and intensive training. 10 selected vocalists and an accompanist/coach given chance to perform in Florida Grand Opera Season; production and technical assistants will be assigned to the Opera's technical staff. Vocalist entry fee $10. Entries by August (technical and design), October (singers and accompanists/coaches). Auditions December for following season.*

Friedrich Schorr Memorial Performance Prize in Voice. 110 S Madison St, Adrian, MI 49221-2575, USA *tel:* +1 517 264 3121 *fax:* +1 517 265 3607. David Katz, artistic director. *To choose professional singing artists to take lead roles in productions of opera and oratorio performances. Open to all professional singers. $15,000 of prizes in form of stipends and performances.*

George London Foundation for Singers Awards. 515 East 79th St, Suite 7B, New York, NY 10021, USA *tel:* +1 212 772 2768 *fax:* +1 212 396 9772. Nora London, president. *Annual. March, entries by January. To identify especially talented singers, ages 35 and under, in the early stage of their careers. Open to American and Canadian opera singers who have performed at least one role with a professional company and are contracted for at least one more professional engagement. Contestants are required to perform four arias in contrasting styles and languages. Six prizes of $5000 and five of $1000.*

Gina Bachauer International Piano Competition. PO Box 11664, Salt Lake City, UT 84147, USA *tel:* +1 801 521 9200 *fax:* +1 801 521 9202 *email:* gina@bachauer.com. Paul C Pollei, founder, artistic director; Susan Kelly, general manager. *Quadrennial. Next 2003. Entry fee $100. Ages 18-32. Artists selected at live international auditions. Also junior competition (ages 11-18).*

Heida Hermanns International Young Artists Competition. 61 Unquowa Rd, Fairfield, CT 06430, USA *tel:* +1 203 319 8271 *fax:* +1 203 319 8273 *email:* clavecjn@aol.com. Millette Alexander. *December, entries by October. Open to solo singers and solo string players not under professional management. Ages 19-33 for singers, 18-30 for string players. First prize in each category $3000.*

International Violin Competition of Indianapolis. 47 S Pennsylvania, Suite 401, Indianapolis, IN 46204, USA *tel:* +1 317 637 4574 *fax:* +1 317 637 1302 *email:* ivci@indy.net. Thomas Beczkiewicz, executive director. *Next September 2002, entries by 28 February 2002. Ages 16-29. First prize $30,000, a gold medal, Carnegie Hall recital date and 50 engagements or recitals with major orchestras in N America and Europe.*

Irving M Klein International String Competition. 960 Howard St, San Francisco, CA 94103, USA *tel:* +1 415 278 5780 *fax:* +1 415 512 1042 *email:* imkcomp@aWarehouse.com. M Klein, director; L Chung, manager. *10-11 June 2000, entries by 15 February. Ages 15-23. First prize $10,000 and performances. Entry fee $45.*

Irving S Gilmore International Keyboard Festival. Kalamazoo Center, 100 West Michigan Ave, Kalamazoo MI 49007, USA *tel:* +1 616 342 1166 *fax:* +1 616 342 0968. Irma Vallecillo, artistic director. *Competition renowned for its non-competitive, anonymous selection process. The jury is able to make a careful and detailed appraisal of performance skills without candidates knowing of their participation. The focus of evaluation is changed from the artificial pressure of a competition to varied performances in natural concert settings.*

Joanna Hodges International Piano Competition. College of the Desert, 43-500 Monterey Ave, Palm Desert, California 92260, USA *tel:* +1 760 773 2575 *fax:* +1 760 776 7310. Terri Fleck, admin director. *Spring, entry forms available the preceding winter. Various categories for pianists aged 35 and under. Major prizes include debuts in New York, London, Rome and Vienna.*

Kingsville International Young Performers' Competition. PO Box 2873, Kingsville, TX 78363, USA *tel:* +1 361 592 2374 *fax:* +1 361 592 9551 *email:* youngperf@hotmail.com. J D Tryer, director. *30 March-1 April 2000, entries by 18 January. Entrance fee $30. Ages 25 and under. Piano, strings, wind, percussion. First prize $5000 and a performance with Corpus Christi Symphony Orchestra.*

Kosciuszko Foundation Chopin Piano Competition. 15 E 65 St, New York, NY 10021-6595, USA *tel:* +1 212 734 2130 *fax:* +1 212 628 4552 *email:* thekf@aol.com. Thomas Pniewski, director of cultural affairs. *6-8 April 2000, applications by 3 March. To encourage highly talented musicians to study and play the works of Chopin, Szymanowski and other Polish composers. Open to US citizens, permanent residents or full-time foreign students with valid visa, aged 16-22. First prize $2500.*

Kurt Weill Prize. The Kurt Weill Foundation for Music, 7 East 20th St, New York, NY 10003-1106, USA *tel:* +1 212 505 5240 *fax:* +1 212 353 9663 *email:* kwfinfo@kwf.org. Carolyn Weber, associate director. *Autumn 2001, closing date 30 April 2001. Awarded for distinguished scholarship in 20th C music theatre, including opera. Work must be published within 2 years prior to the deadline. Prize $2500.*

Loren L Zachary Society National Vocal Competition for Young Opera Singers. 2250 Gloaming Way, Beverly Hills, CA 90210, USA *tel:* +1 310 276 2731 *fax:* +1 310 275 8245. Nedra Zachary, director. *28 February-3 March (New York) and 11-14 April (Los Angeles) 2000, applications by 24 January and 16 March respectively. Grand Finals Concert 21 May 2000. To help launch the careers of young opera singers and to help them obtain contracts in European opera houses. Open to female singers aged 21-33, male singers aged 21-35 ready to pursue a professional operatic career. First prize $10,000.*

MacAllister Award for Opera Singers. Indiana Opera Theatre, 7515 E 30, PO Box 1941, Indianapolis, IN 46206, USA *tel:* +1 317 253 1001 *fax:* +1 317 253 2008. Elaine Morgan Bookwater, general director. *Annual. August. US citizens only. Age limit: 25 for college competition, 36 for professionals. First prize $2500 for college competition, $10,000 for professionals. To provide non-restricted funds for opera artists to pursue their careers.*

Marguerite McCammon Voice Competition. Opera Guild of Fort Worth, PO Box 100381, Fort Worth, TX 76185-0381, USA *tel:* +1 817 924 1536 *fax:* +1 817 924 1886 *email:* geopat@ftw.com. Pat Crowley, chairman. *Biennial. Next 2001. Entry fee $25. Open to any singer aged 21-32 (female) or 21-35 (male) working towards a professional opera career. First prize $5000.*

Marian Anderson Award. Marian Anderson Foundation Inc, 1 Lakeside Rd, Danbury, CT 06811, USA *tel:* +1 203 744 4454 *fax:* +1 203 748 3029. June Goodman, admin. *To recognise and advance careers of talented singers of concert and opera. US citizens by recommendation only. First prize $20,000.*

Missouri Southern International Piano Competition. Missouri Southern State College, 3950 E Newman Rd, Joplin, MO 64801-1595, USA *tel:* +1 417 625 9755 *fax:* +1 417 625 9798 *email:* msipc@mail.mssc.edu. Vivian León, director. *Biennial. Next April 2000, entries by 10 January. Age limit: 17 junior division, 18-30 senior division. Overseas students may apply for travel assistance. First prize senior division $10,000 and Carnegie Hall recital debut. First prize junior division $2500.*

Murray Dranoff International Two Piano Competition. Murray Dranoff Foundation, 180 NE 39 St, Miami, Florida 33137, USA *tel:* +1 305 758 8700 *fax:* +1 305 757 0686 *email:* dranoff@mci2000.com. Loretta Dranoff, director. *Biennial. Next 2001. Ages 18-35. First prize $20,000.*

Naftzger Young Artists Auditions and Music Awards. Wichita Symphony Society, 225 W Douglas, Suite 207, Wichita, KS 67202, USA *tel:* +1 316 267 5259 *fax:* +1 316 267 1937 *email:* symphony@louverture.com. Anne Marie Brown, operations manager. *5-6 May 2000, applications by 3 March. Entrance fee $15. For piano, instrument and voice. Open to student residents of Kansas, Oklahoma, Missouri and non-residents enrolled in a college, university or conservatory in Kansas, Oklahoma or Missouri and working towards a music degree. Age limit: 20-28 for voice, 18-26 for other instruments. First prize $5000. Each division prize $2000.*

Opera at Florham Guild Vocal Competition. PO Box 343, Convent Station, NJ 07961, USA *tel:* +1 201 443 8620. Theresa Di Paolo, chairman. *29 April 2000, applications by 27 February. Aims to support the growth of young operatic singers by offering prizes and an opportunity to appear in recital or in one of the company's productions. First prize $3000.*

Oratorio Society of New York Solo Competition. Carnegie Hall Suite 504, 881 Seventh Ave, New York, NY 10019, USA *tel:* +1 212 247 4199. Janet Plucknett, chairman. *March-April, applications by February. To seek out new talent in oratorio solo singing and give a debut platform for competition winners. Open to all singers aged under 40; must not have made formal New York Oratorio debut in reviewed New York concert. Cash prizes and performance contracts. First prize $5000.*

Palm Beach Opera National Vocal Competition. 415 S Olive Ave, West Palm Beach, FL 33401, USA *tel:* +1 561 833 8924 *fax:* +1 561 833 8294 *email:* pbopera@pbopera.org. Valerie Stoelzel, music/education administrator. *27-30 April 2000, entries by 10 February. Entry fee $35. Open to singers aged 18-23 (junior division), 24-30 (advanced division) who are North American and not under professional management. First prize $3000 (junior), $6000 (advanced). Total cash prizes of over $47,500.*

Pro Musicis International Award. 140 W 79 St, No 9F, New York, NY 10024, USA *tel:* +1 212 787 0993 *fax:* +1 212 362 0352. John E Haag, executive director. *May 2001, entries by 1 March. Career development through major recitals in the US, France and Hong Kong for concert soloists prepared to perform for the aged, disabled, infirm and imprisoned. Open to concert soloists of exceptional talent willing to repeat each of their sponsored recitals in Community Service Concerts for individuals in institutions. Eligible instruments rotate. 2001: harp, harpsichord, strings, voice. 2002: guitar, piano, wind. Prizes are major recitals in New York, Los Angeles, Boston, Paris and Hong Kong. Ages 35 and under.*

Pro Piano New York Recital Series. 85 Jane St, New York, NY 10014, USA *tel:* +1 212 206 8794 *fax:* +1 212 633 1207 *email:* classicmus@aol.com; ricard@propiano.com. Ricard de La Rosa, executive director, founder; Chitose Okashira, artistic director. *Pianists, chamber groups with piano. No age limits. Auditions May in New York. Prize includes recording contract.*

Raissa Tselentis Memorial Johann Sebastian Bach International Competitions. PO Box 197, Saratoga Springs, NY 12866, USA *tel:* +1 518 233 1139. James Marra, president, director. *Annual, from 2000. To stimulate interest in the study and performance of works by J S Bach. Piano, voice, organ, guitar, period instruments, choral. Performance by memory. Open to ages 20-45. Entry fee $50. Cash awards and concert appearances.*

San Antonio International Piano Competition. PO Box 39636, San Antonio, TX 78218, USA *tel:* +1 210 655 0766 *fax:* +1 210 822 6056. Virginia Lawrence. *Pno. Triennial. Next autumn 2000, entries by spring. $50 registration fee. Age 20-32 at date of competition. First prize $10,000.*

Stefan and Wanda Wilk Prizes for Research in Polish Music. c/o Polish Music Reference Center, University of Southern California, Los Angeles, CA 90089-0851, USA *tel:* +1 213 740 9369 *fax:* +1 213 740 3217 *email:* polmusic@usc.edu. Maria Anna Harley, director, PMRC. *Entries by 30 September annually for decision by 30 December. For the best unpublished papers reflecting original research in the music of Poland; to stimulate research on Polish music in academic circles outside Poland. No previously published essay may be submitted. First prize $1000 and publication in* Polish Music Journal. *Student prize $500 and publication.*

University of Maryland International William Kapell Piano Competition. University of Maryland, The Rossborough Festival, 4321 Hartwick Rd, Suite 220, College Park, MD 20740, USA *tel:* +1 301 403 8370 *fax:* +1 301 403 8375 *email:* gmoquin@umdacc.umd.edu. George Moquin, executive director. *Biennial. 20-29 July 2000, applications by 15 March 2000. Ages 18-33. Finals with Baltimore Symphony Orchestra. First prize $25,000 and engagements including recital in Alice Tully Hall, Lincoln Center, New York.*

University of Maryland Leonard Rose Cello Competition. University of Maryland, The Rossborough Festival, 4321 Hartwick Rd, Suite 220, College Park, MD 20740, USA *tel:* +1 301 403 8370 *fax:* +1 301 403 8375 *email:* gmoquin@umdacc.umd.edu. George Moquin, executive director. *Quadrennial. Next in 2001, entries by 15 March. Ages 18-30. $50,000 in cash awards. Finals with orchestra. First prize $25,000 and engagements.*

University of Maryland Marian Anderson International Vocal Arts Competition. University of Maryland, The Rossborough Festival, 4321 Hartwick Rd, Suite 220, College Park, MD 20740, USA *tel:* +1 301 403 8370 *fax:* +1 301 403 8375 *email:* gmoquin@umdacc.umd.edu. George Moquin, executive director. *Quadrennial. Next 2003. Ages 21-39. Open to all singers regardless of race, colour, gender or national origin. First prize $20,000 and engagements including recital in Alice Tully Hall, Lincoln Center, New York.*

Van Cliburn International Piano Competition. 2525 Ridgmar Blvd, Suite 307, Fort Worth, TX 76116, USA *tel:* +1 817 738 6536 *fax:* +1 817 738 6534 *email:* cliburn@startext.net. Richard Rodzinski, executive director. *Quadrennial. Next 25 May-10 June 2001, entries by 15 October 2001. Ages 18-30. First prize $20,000, gold medal plus debut recital in Carnegie Hall, concert tours in America, Europe and Asia for approximately 2 years; 2nd, 3rd and further prizes. Free airfare, room and board.*

Vocal Competition. Opera/Columbus, 177 Naghten Street, Columbus, Ohio 43215-2613, USA *tel:* +1 614 461 8101 *fax:* +1 614 461 0806 *email:* lesepstein@aol.com. Les Epstein, director of education. *8-9 January 2000. Applications by early November. Entrants must have lived in Ohio for four months. First prize $2,500 and partial scholarship to American Institute Musical Studies.*

Washington International Competition. 2939 Van Ness St #1219 NW, Washington DC 20008, USA *tel:* +1 202 363 8873. Mildred Henninger. *March, applications by December. Pianists aged 18-32. First prize $7000.*

Young Concert Artists International Auditions. 250 W 57 St, New York, NY 10019, USA *tel:* +1 212 307 6655 *fax:* +1 212 581 8894 *email:* yca@yca.org. Susan Wadsworth, director; Mark Hayman, auditions co-ordinator. *October-January. Entrance fee $35. To discover and launch the US careers of exceptional young solo musicians, string quartets and singers. First prize $5000. Winners are presented in recital in New York, Washington and Boston and given all management services, including concert engagements across the US and all publicity materials.*

Venezuela

Alirio Diaz Guitar Performance Competition. Fundación Vicente Emilio Sojo, Ave Los Mangos No9, Los Chorros 1071, Apartado Postal 70537, Caracas, Venezuela *tel:* +58 2 284 1235 *fax:* +58 2 284 1115 *email:* funves@conicit.ve. *Biennial. Next 2001. Alternating with the Rodrigo Riera Guitar Composition Competition.*

Competitions for Composers

Austria

Competition for Contemporary Music. Wiener Sommer-Seminar für neue Musik, Postfach 345, A-1061 Wien, Austria *tel:* +44 222 5971 292. Konrad Musalek. *31 March 2000. In association with the Vienna Summer-Seminar, composition of works in contemporary style for accordion, cembalo, flute, guitar, mandolin, oboe (also oboe d'amore, english horn), piano, solo or ensemble (in free combination) for a duration of up to 10 minutes. For composers of any age and nationality. Entry fee ATS 500 per work. Three prizes awarded.*

International Mozart Competition. Mirabellplatz 1, A-5020 Salzburg, Austria *tel:* +43 662 88908 203 *fax:* +43 662 88908 55 *email:* ulrike.baciu@moa.ac.at. Klaus Ager, rector; Ulrike Baciu, general secretary. *Quadrennial. Next 2003. Four prizes of ATS 50,000.*

Prix Ars Electronica. ORF/Landesstudio Oberösterreich, Europlatz 3, A-4010 Linz, Austria *tel:* +43 732 6900 ext 24227 *fax:* +43 732 6900 ext 24270 *email:* music.info@prixars.orf.at. Christine Schoepf. *Annual. Festival September, applications by 25 April. Competition for composition of Digital Music. First prize Golden Nica Award $12,930, two distinctions $4300 each.*

Vienna International Composition Competition. c/o Casinos Austria, Dr-Karl-Lueger-Ring 14, A-1015 Wien, Austria *tel:* +43 1 534 4068 *fax:* +43 1 534 4034. Gerhard Skoff, director. *Different theme for competition each year. 2000: children's chamber opera. Applicants must be aged 40 or under, and works must have been written no earlier than four years before the competition deadline. Prize ATS 300,000-400,000.*

Belgium

Queen Elisabeth International Music Competition. 20 Rue aux Laines, B-1000 Bruxelles, Belgium *tel:* +32 2 513 0099 *fax:* +32 2 514 3297 *email:* info@concours-seine-elisabeth. *2001: violin and composition.*

Canada

New Music Festival Canadian Composers Competition. 555 Main St, Ste 101, Winnipeg, MB R3B 1C3, Canada *tel:* +1 204 949 3950 *fax:* +1 204 956 4271. Bramwell Tovey, artistic director; Annemarie Petrov, admin. *January-February. For Canadian citizens, no age restrictions, works must be unpublished and not performed professionally. First prize $4000 and a $4000 commission.*

The Nouvel Ensemble Moderne Forum 2002. 200 Ave Vincent-d'Indy, CP 6128, Succursale Centre-ville, Montréal, PQ H3C 3J7, Canada *tel:* +1 514 343 5962 *fax:* +1 514 343 2443 *email:* carriean@magellan.umontreal.ca. Lorraine Vaillancourt, artistic director; Annick-Patricia, communication director. *Next 2002. Applications from April 2000. Please contact for details.*

Saint-Sauveur Festival of the Arts Composition Competition. 75 Ave de la Gare, Bloc L-1, Saint-Sauveur-des-Monts, Québec, Canada J0R 1R6 *tel:* +1 450 227 0427 *fax:* +1 450 227 2039 *email:* festart@qc.aira.com. Camilla Malashenko, director of competitions. *28 July-13 August 2000, applications by mid-April. Entrance fee Can $50. Music compositon for dance. First prize Can $4000.*

Czech Republic

International Competition for Blind and Partially Sighted Composers. SONS - Czech Blind United, Karlinské nám 12, CZ-186 03 Praha 8, Czech Republic *tel:* +420 2 2481 7393 *fax:* +420 2 2481 8398 *email:* sons_zahrbraillnet.cz. Václav Polásek, chief officer. *Triennial. Next 2002. First prize approximately Kc 10,000.*

International Composers' Competition. Ipos-Artama, Kresomyslova 7, CZ-140 16 Praha 4, Nusle, Czech Republic *tel:* +42 02 6121 56847 *fax:* +42 02 6121 5688 *email:* artama@ipos-mk.cz. Jaroslava Modrochová. *Closing date 30 November. Compositions for womens' and mixed chamber choirs, a capella or maximum 3 instrument accompaniment. Duration 3-4 minutes. Total prize money Kc 20,000.*

Denmark

Thad Jones Competition. Danmarks, Radio P2 Musik, DK-1999 Frederiksberg C, Denmark *tel:* +45 35 206408 *fax:* +45 35 206128. *November, applications by 1 June. International competition for jazz composers and arrangers born after 1 June 1965. First prize $10,000.*

France

Florilège Vocal de Tours Composition Competition. Rue des Minimes, BP 1452, F-37014 Tours Cedex 1, France *tel:* +33 2 47 21 65 26 *fax:* +33 2 47 21 67 71. Pierre-Marie Dizier. *May, entries by March. Compositions for choir a cappella. First prize 10,000 FF.*

International Celtic Harp Festival of Dinan. La Galerie, F-22490 Plouër, France *tel:* +33 96 86 84 94 *fax:* +33 96 86 89 40 *email:* harp@wanadoo.fr. Elisabeth Affolter, director; Myrdhin, artistic director. *15 July 2000, entries by 30 May 2000. Entrance fee 150 FF. Ages 17 or above. Prizes for improvisation and composition. First prize 7000 FF.*

International Composition Competition of the Atelier Musique. Atelier Musique de Ville d'Avray, 10 Rue de Marnes, F-92410 Ville d'Avray, France *tel:* +33 1 47 50 44 28 *fax:* +33 1 47 50 53 90. J Louis Petit. *For choirs and brass quintet. No age limit. Application fee 300 FF. First prize 10,000 FF*

International Electroacoustic Music Competition. Institut International du Musique Electroacoustique de Bourges, Place André Malraux, BP 39, F-18000 Bourges Cedex, France *tel:* +33 2 48 20 41 87 *fax:* +33 2 48 20 45 51 *email:* ime-bourges@gmeb.fr. Françoise Barriere. *June 2000, entries by 20 April.*

International Rostrum of Composers. International Music Council, UNESCO, 1 Rue Miollis, F-75732 Paris Cedex 15, France *tel:* +33 1 45 68 25 50 *fax:* +33 1 43 06 87 98 *email:* imc_cim@compuserve.com. Guy Huot, secretary. *Annual. May-June. Organised by the International Music Council with the support of UNESCO. Radio music producers worldwide select contemporary works for broadcasting. The aim is to foster the exchange of performance of contemporary music between broadcasting organisations. Entries to be submitted by national broadcasting organisations only. First prize: worldwide broadcasts guaranteed for selected works.*

Musical Composition Competition. Secrétariat, 3 Rue Léonel de Moustier, F-25000 Besancon, France *tel:* +33 381 25 05 85 *fax:* +33 381 81 52 15. Yvette Cussey, admin manager. *September 2000, applications by 15 July 2000. Professional composers aged under 40. Symphonic works. Entry fee 700 FF. First prize 25,000 FF.*

Noroit Prize for Acousmatic Musical Composition. Noroit, 9 Rue des Capucins, F-62000 Arras, France *tel:* +33 21 71 30 12 *fax:* +33 21 71 09 94. Bernard Petitot, director. *Biennial. Next 2001. Ages 40 or under.*

Germany

International Competition for Composers. z H Herrn Hinrich Bergmeier, Zur Salzhaube 12, D-31832 Springe, Germany *tel:* +49 5041 971516 *fax:* +49 5041 971517 *email:* bergmeier-hgnm@t-online.de. *May, entries by end of Feb.*

International Competition for Women Composers. GEDOK, PO Box 101324, D-68013 Mannheim, Germany *tel:* +49 621 861631 *fax:* +49 621 407354. Ursula Pawlak. *Next 2002.*

Hungary

First International Composers' Competition: In Memoriam Zoltan Kodaly. Andrassy ut 89, H-1062 Budapest, Hungary *tel:* +36 1 342 8448 *fax:* +36 1 322 9647 *email:* kodalyzm@mail.matav.hu. Marta Vandulek, admin. *Next 2002 (to be confirmed). Open to composers of any nationality. No age limit. Each applicant may send in two works, each of duration 15-20 mins. Orchestral works. Compositions should be scored for standard symphonic instruments with or without chorus and soloists, or a concerto involving one or more solo instruments.*

Italy

Alfredo Casella International Composition Contest. Accademia Musicale Chigiana, Via di Citta 89, I-53100 Siena, Italy *tel:* +39 0577 46152 *fax:* +39 0577 288124. *Entries by 1 Oct. No age limit. First prize 8,000,000 lire and publication by Ricordi.*

Citta di Pescara International Competition of Composition. Kamerton Citta di Pescara 13, I-65131 Pescara Fontanelle, Italy. *Open to composers born after 31 Dec 1961. Aims to promote New Consonant Music and pedagogic music.*

The Ennio Porrino International Piano and Composition Competition. Associazione Amici della Musica di Cagliari, Casella Postale 118, 09100 Cagliari, Italy *tel:* +39 070 42280. *Entries by October for announcement in December.*

European International Competition for Composers (Italy). 226 E Second St, Suite 5D, New York, NY 10009, USA *tel:* +1 212 387 0111 *fax:* +1 212 388 0102. Salvatore Moltisanti, president. *Annual. June-July, entries by March. No age limit, all nationalities. Prizes approx $10,000 to sponsor recitals, debut in Europe and/or USA, scholarships and CD recording.*

Gino Contilli International Competition for Composition. Segreteria dell'Accademia Filarmonica, via Giacinto 4, I-98122 Messina, Italy *tel:* +39 090 343420; +39 090 46432 *also fax; email:* accademia@solnet.it. Giuseppe Uccello, president; Alba Crea, secretary (*tel:* +39 090 715136). *Composition for symphonic music. Ages 45 and under. Applications by September. First prize 5,000,000 lire.*

Guido d'Arezzo International Composition Competition. Fondazione Guido d'Arezzo, Corso Italia 102, I-52100 Arezzo, Italy *tel:* +39 0575 356203 *fax:* +39 0575 324735 *email:* fondguid@krenet.it. Remo Manganelli, commissioner. *Open to composers of all nationalities and ages. Composition for choir (mixed, male, female or vocal ensemble, up to a maximum of 16 voices) and for choir with instruments (1 or more instruments up to a maximum of a model chamber orchestra). First prize 10,000,000 lire.*

International Competition of Classical Guitar Composition 'Michele Pittaluga'. Piazza Garibaldi, I-15100 Alessandria, Italy *tel:* +39 0131 251207 *fax:* +39 0131 235507 *email:* pittalug@email.alessandria.alpcom.it. Marcello Pittaluga, secretary; Micaela Pittaluga, president. *29 September 2000, applications by 15 July. Solo guitar with string quartet or quintet. First prize 5,000,000 lire, performances and publication.*

International Competition for Original Composition for Band. Segretaria Organizzativa, Via Laudati 4, I-06073 Corciano PG, Italy *tel:* +39 075 697 9109 *also fax.* Antonio Pagana, president; Antonietta Trombetta, general secretary. *Entries by July. Compositions may be based on any theme and musical form, with or without inst or vocal soloists. First prize 5,000,000 lire.*

International Goffredo Petrassi Competition for Composers. c/o Fondazione Arturo Toscanini, Via G Tartini n 13, I-43100 Parma, Italy *tel:* +39 0521 274421 *fax:* +39 0521 272134 *email:* fondazione@toscanini.dsnet.it. Gianni Baratta, manager Goffredo Petrassi honorary president; Fulvo Zannoni, secretary. *Triennial. Next 2001. No age limit. For unpublished symphonic composition. First prize 15,000,000 lire.*

International Mario Bernardo Angelo-Comneno Composition Competition. Accademia Angelica, Constantiniana di lettere, arti e scienze, Via delle Balduina 75, I-00136 Roma, Italy *tel:* +39 0635 343557; +39 0774 615465 *also fax.* Manuele Ferrari. *Composition for string quartet. First prize 3,500,000 lire.*

International New Chamber Opera Competition. Teatro Lirico Sperimentale di Spoleto, Piazza G Bovio 1, I-06049 Spoleto, Italy *tel:* +39 0743 221645/220440 *fax:* +39 0743 222930 *email:* teatrolirico@mail.caribusiness.it. Claudio Lepore, manager; Nadia Nigris, assistant. *Next March 2000, entries by 31 December 1999. Open to composers of all nationalities aged 35 and under. For unpublished and unperformed chamber operas with librettos in Italian, German, English, French or Spanish. Duration 45-60 mins. Prizes of 10,000,000 lira, performances in Spoleto and Ricordi publication.*

Luigi Russolo International Competition for Young Composers of Analogic or Digital Electro-acoustic Music. Fondazione Russolo-Pratella, Via G Bagaini 6, I-21100 Varese, Italy *tel:* +39 0332 237245 *fax:* +39 0332 280331. G Franco Maffina, president; Rossana Maggia, PR. *Annual. September, applications by 30 August. For analogic or digital electro-acoustic music, electro-acoustic music with instruments or voice and electro-acoustic music for the radio. Italian and foreign composers aged 35 or under.*

Valentino Bucchi di Roma Capitale International Prize. Valentino Bucchi Foundation, Via Ubaldino Peruzzi 20, I-00139 Roma, Italy *tel:* +39 06 8720 0121/8713 1151 *fax:* +39 06 8713 1527. *Annual. Ages 40 and under. Categories rotate. First prize 25,000,000 lire and publication.*

Japan

Irino Prize (International Composers' Competition). Irino Prize Foundation, 5-22-2 Matsubara, Setagaya-ku, Tokyo 156-0043, Japan *tel:* +81 3 3323 0646 *fax:* +81 3 3325 5468. Reiko Takahashi Irino, president. *July 2000, entries by 30 April. Open to composers of any nationality under the age of 40. 2000 competition for orchestral work. Prize 650,000 Yen.*

Toru Takemitsu Composition Award. Office of the Toru Takemitsu Composition Award, Tokyo Opera City Cultural Foundation, PO Box 2502, 3-20-2 Nishi-Shinjuku, Shinjuku-ku, Tokyo 163-1403, Japan *tel:* +81 3 5353 0770 *fax:* +81 3 5353 0771. *Applications by 29 September 2000 for 2001 competition, 28 September 2001 for 2002 competition. Composers under age of 35 to submit orchestral works of 10-20 mins. First prize 3,000,000 yen and performance in the Tokyo Opera City Concert Hall.*

Netherlands

The International Gaudeamus Music Week. Gaudeamus Foundation, Swammerdamstraat 38, NL-1091 RV Amsterdam, Netherlands *tel:* +31 20 694 7349 *fax:* +31 20 694 7258 *email:* gaud@xs4all.nl. *1-9 September 2000, entries by 31 January. Works may already have been performed but must have been composed not more than three years ago. Orchestral, choir and chamber music. First prize DFL 10,000.*

Norway

Edward Grieg Memorial Competition for Young Composers. The Oslo Grieg Society, Gaustadveien 4b, N-0372 Oslo, Norway *tel:* +47 22 493630 *fax:* +47 22 492311. *Write for information. Closing date 1 March 2000.*

Poland

International Witold Lutoslawski Composers' Competition. Warsaw Philharmonic, 5 Jasna Str, PL-00 950 Warsaw, Poland *tel:* +48 22 8265713 *fax:* +48 22 8265617 *email:* phil@pol.pl. Katarzyna Andrzejowska, secretary. *Composition for symphony orch. No age limits. First prize PZL 3000.*

Kazimierz Serocki International Composers Competition. Polish Society for Contemporary Music, ISCM Polish Section, Ul Mazowiecka 11, PL-00 052 Warsaw, Poland *tel:* +48 22 8276981 *fax:* +48 22 8277804 *email:* iscm_pl@oldg.ant.pl. Grazyna Dziura, executive secretary. *Biennial. Applications by 5 February 2000. Composition for string quartet with one soloist or voice. Duration 15-30 minutes. Enrolment fee $20.*

Spain

Premi Internacional de Composició Musical Ciutat de Tarragona. Plaça de la Font 1, c/o Ajuntament de Tarragona, E-43003 Tarragona, Spain *tel:* +34 977 250923 *fax:* +34 977 296118 *email:* ajtargna@tinet.fut.es. *Entries by 15 November; decision made by 15 December. Composition must be unpublished, unperformed and not previously awarded a prize. First prize 1,500,000 ptas.*

Sweden

Stockholm Electronic Arts Award. EMS, Söder Mälarstrand 61, S-11825 Stockholm, Sweden *email:* pignon@oden.se. Paul Pignon, competition producer. *Entries by June for jury decision in September. Competitors of any age/nationality to enter not more than 1 work. Tapes to be sent as 1/4 inch analogue tape or DAT cassette.*

Switzerland

Fribourg International Competition in Composition of Sacred Music. Fribourg Festival of Sacred Music, Case Postale 292, CH-1701 Fribourg, Switzerland *tel:* +41 26 322 4800 *fax:* +41 26 322 8331 *email:* sacredmusicfr@pingnet.ch. Nicole Renevey, administrator. *Biennial. Next 2001, entries by July 2001. Any age and nationality. First prize cash plus performance at the Fribourg Festival of Sacred Music.*

International Musical Composition Contest 'Queen Marie José'. Box 19 CH-1252, Meinier, Genève, Switzerland. *Biennial. Next November 2000, applications by 31 May. For string quartet (2 violins, viola and cello) and chromatic concert accordion; or string quartet and bandoneon. First prize SFR 15,000.*

USA

ABA Ostwald Composition Contest. Harding Band Bldg, 1103 S, Sixth St, Champaign, IL 61820, USA *tel:* +1 217 333 3025 *fax:* +1 217 244 8810. James Keene, chairman. *Annual. November. To stimulate writing of important new compositions for band. Entry open to all except members of ABA. Works must be original, unpublished and composed within the last year. First prize $8000.*

ALEA III International Composition Prize. Boston University School of Music, 855 Commonwealth Ave, Boston, MA 02215, USA *tel:* +1 617 353 3340 *also fax.* Theodore Antoniou, artistic director. *September, entries by March. Ages 40 and under. Only 1 score per composer. Works must be unpublished and must not have been publicly performed or broadcast before announcement of the prize. First prize $2500.*

Aliénor Harpsichord Composition Awards. PO Box 3529, Augusta, Georgia 30904-1529, USA. *Spring 2000. This is the last competition.*

ASCAP Foundation Grants to Young Composers. 1 Lincoln Plaza, New York, NY 10023, USA *tel:* +1 212 621 6327 *fax:* +1 212 595 3342. Frances Richard, vice-president, director of concert music. *Entries by 15 March. Citizens or permanent residents of the US aged under 30 on closing date. $20,000 given in prizes.*

Biennial Competition for the AGO/ECS Publishing Award in Choral Composition. American Guild of Organists, 475 Riverside Dr, Suite 1260, NY 10115, USA *tel:* +1 212 870 2310 *fax:* +1 212 870 2163 *email:* info@agohq.org. *For unpublished work for SATB and org, duration 4-8 mins. $2000 of prizes, publication and performance. Entrants must be citizens of US, Canada or Mexico.*

Boston Chamber Ensemble Composition Contest. 6 Summer St, Hyde Park MA 02136, USA *tel:* +1 617 361 5975 *fax:* +1 617 364 1944 *email:* ebirdseye@earthlink.net. Elisa Birdseye, executive director. *Entries by July. Compositions for chamber ensembles or orchestras. Entry fee $20. First prize $300.*

Composers' Guild Annual Composition Contest. Box 586, Farmington, UT 84025, USA *tel:* +1 801 451 2275. Ruth Gatrell, president. *Annual. Entries by 31 August. No age limit except in young composers' category (aged under 18 on 31 August). No limit on number of entries. Grand prize $500, first prize in each category $100.*

Delius Composition Contest. c/o Jacksonville University, College of Fine Arts, Jacksonville, FL 32211, USA *tel:* +1 904 745 7371. William McNeiland. *Annual. First week in March, entries by 1 October. For vocal, keyboard and instrument composition. First prize $500.*

Harvey Gaul Composition Contest. Duquesne University School of Music, Pittsburgh, PA 15282, USA *tel:* +1 412 261 0554 *fax:* +1 412 396 5479 *email:* grose@ziplink.net. Gil Rose, music director. *Biennial. Next 2000, applications by 14 April. To encourage composition of new music. Open to US composers. Entrance fee $15. First prize $3000, commission and premiere.*

National Association of Composers USA Young Composers' Competition. 84 Cresta Verde Dr, Rolling Estates, CA 90274, USA *tel:* +1 310 541 8213 *fax:* +1 310 373 3244 *email:* bia@flash.net. Marshall Bialosky, president. *Annual. Entries by 30 October. Ages 18-30. First prize $200 and performances in Los Angeles.*

Pulitzer Prize in Music. Columbia University, 709 Journalism, New York, NY 10027, USA *tel:* +1 212 854 3841. Seymour Topping, admin. *Awarded for 'distinguished musical composition of significant dimension by an American that has had its first performance in the United States this year'. Applications by 3 January.*

Rome Prize Fellowships of the American Academy in Rome. 7 E 60 St, New York, NY 10022-1001, USA *tel:* +1 212 751 7200 *fax:* +1 212 751 7220 *email:* aainfo@aol.com. Programmes Department. *Entries by 15 November. For musical composition. Open to US citizens with a BA or equivalent. First prize $15,000 and one year residency at the American Academy in Rome.*

Second International Guitar Composition Competition Rodrigo Riera. ATT Latin American Music Center, Indiana University School of Music, Bloomington, IN 47405-2200, USA *tel:* +1 812 855 2991 *also fax; email:* lamc@indiana.edu. *Open to composers of any age and nationality to compose pieces for one, two or three guitars of between 8 and 15 minutes duration. Entries by March. Application fee $20. First prize $10,000.*

Sonic Circuits. ACF-SC 332 Minnesota Street E-145, Saint Paul, MN 55101-1300, USA *tel:* +1 651 228 1407 *fax:* +1 651 291 7978 *email:* pblackburn@composersforum.org. Philip Blackburn, program director. *Annual. Applications by 1 July. For works involving electronic technology. Chosen works form part of caravan of curated works which travel the world, receiving multiple performances at various venues.*

University of Louisville Grawemeyer Award for Music Composition. School of Music, University of Louisville, Louisville, Kentucky 40292, USA *tel:* +1 502 852 6907 *fax:* +1 502 852 0520. *Closing date 31 January 2000. Compositions incorporating large musical genre: choral, orchestral, chamber, electronic, opera, etc. First prize $150,000 spread over 5 years. Entries must be sponsored by a professional musical organisation or individual; a composer may not therefore submit his/her own work. Recent winners include Krzysztof Penderecki, Joan Tower, Witold Lutoslawski, Karel Husa, John Adams.*

Washington International Composition Competition. 11920 Canfield Rd, Potomac, MD 20854, USA *tel:* +1 301 762 8334. Wang An-Hing, chairman. *Triennial. Next 2000, applications by November 1999. Work for string quartet. Ages 20-35. First prize $3000.*

Young Composers Awards, National Guild of Community Schools of the Arts. PO Box 8018, Englewood, NJ 07631, USA *tel:* +1 201 871 3337 *fax:* +1 201 871 7639 *email:* almayadas@worldnet.att.net. Lolita Mayadas, executive director. *3 April 2000. To recognise young composers of talent and to encourage young people to write serious music. Open to students aged 13-18, resident in the USA or Canada. First prize $1000.*

Music Festivals

An asterisk denotes membership of the **European Festivals Association** (120b Rue de Lausanne, CH-1202 Genève, Switzerland *tel:* +41 22 732 2803 *fax:* +41 22 738 4012 *email:* geneva@eurofestivals.efa.ch *website:* www.eurofestivals.efa.ch). Additional information on new music festivals may be obtained from the **International Society for Contemporary Music**, British Section, c/o spnm, Francis House, Francis St, London SW1P 1DE, UK *tel:* +44 20 7828 9696 *fax:* +44 20 7931 9928 *email:* spnm@spnm.org.uk, and from the **European Conference of Promoteers of New Music,** c/o Gaudeamus Foundation, Swammerdamstraat 38, NL-1091 RV Amsterdam, Netherlands *tel:* +31 20 694 7349 *fax:* +31 20 694 7258 *email:* ecpnm@xsyall.nl.

Argentina

Encuentros. Fundacióon EIMC/SIMC, C Correos 1008, Correo Central, 1000 Buenos Aires, Argentina *fax:* +54 1 822 1383. *July-September. Contemporary music.*

Australia

Adelaide Festival of Arts. PO Box 8116, Station Arcade, Adelaide, SA 5001, Australia *tel:* +61 8 8216 4444 *fax:* +61 8 8216 4455 *email:* afa@adelaidefestival.net.au. Nicholas Heyward, general manager; Robyn Archer, artistic director. *Biennial. Next 3-19 March 2000. Opera, dance, music, theatre, visual arts, literary.*

Australian Festival of Chamber Music. James Cook University of North Queensland, Townsville, Qld 4811, Australia *tel:* +61 7 781 5131 *fax:* +61 7 781 4411. Theodore Kuchar, artistic director; Annika Shelley, general manager. *Concert season of chamber music and chamber music seminar.*

Australian International Music Festival Sydney. World Projects Australia, PO Box 62, Annandale NSW 2038, Australia *tel:* +61 2 9310 7599 *fax:* +61 2 9310 7299 *email:* wpcaust@ozemail.com.au. Luke Robinson, general manager. *Annual. 24 June-1 July 2000. Brings together best school, university, community musicians, with opportunity to perform at Sydney Opera House and join in a wide variety of music and social activities.*

Melbourne Autumn Music Festival. PO Box 92, Parkville, Vic 3052, Australia *tel:* +61 3 9347 0447 *also fax; email:* mifoh@ariel.its.unimelb.edu.au. David Agg, director. *21-30 April 2000. Mainly Early Music festival featuring soloists, vocal and instrumental ensembles. Over 20 separate events in various venues around Melbourne.*

Perth International Arts Festival. The University of Western Australia, Nedlands, WA 6907, Australia *tel:* +61 8 9386 7977 *fax:* +61 8 9386 2763 *email:* festival@festival.uwa.edu.au. Seán Doran, chief executive and artistic director; Elaine Webster, operations director; Brigid Barry, media relations manager. *26 January-20 February 2000. Oldest and largest arts festival in the southern hemisphere; covers all art forms including music, theatre, dance, literature. Also Festival Fringe on the Rim and OSSIA - the Oz Summer School of International Artists.*

Sydney Festival. 36-38 Young St, Sydney NSW 2000, Australia *tel:* +61 2 8248 6500 *fax:* +61 2 8248 6599 *email:* mail@sydneyfestival.org.au. Leo Schofield, festival director. *January.*

Austria

Allegro Vivo: International Chamber Music Festival Austria (Waldviertel). Festivalbüro, Wiener Str 2, A-3580 Horn, Austria *tel:* +43 2 982 4319 *also fax;* +43 2 2 528 9320 *also fax; email:* office@allegro-vivo.or.at. Mag Robert Berger; Margaret Ley, admin. *Early baroque, classic Viennese, romantic, contemporary music. Concerts, summer academy.*

Attergauer Kultursommer. Attergaustr 31, A-4880 St Georgen im Attergau, Austria *tel:* +43 7 667 8672 *fax:* +43 7 667 8918. Wolfgang Schuster, artistic director. *July-August. Classical and chamber orchestra, recitals.*

Austro-Hungarian Music Festival. 10 Barley Mow Passage, London W4 4PH, UK *tel:* +44 20 8742 3355 *fax:* +44 20 8742 1066 *email:* info@martinrandall.co.uk. Martin Randall, managing director; Sheila Taylor, Emma Duffield. *Annual. 5-12 August 2000. 10 concerts in abbeys, palaces and country homes beside or within easy reach of the Danube, with leading local ensembles and soloists. Sold only as complete package including accommodation and tickets for all concerts.*

* **Bregenzer Festival.** PO Box 311, Festspiel und Kongreßhaus, Platz der Wiener Symphoniker 1, A-6901 Bregenz, Austria *tel:* +43 5 574 4070 *fax:* +43 5 574 407400 *email:* info@bregenzerfestspiele.com. Alfred Wopmann, director; Franz Salzmann, business director. *July-August. Opera, orchestra, chamber music, sacred music, dance, drama.*

* **Carinthian Summer Festival Ossiach-Villach.** Carinthischer Sommer, Stift Ossiach, A-9570 Ossiach, Austria *tel:* +43 4 243 2510 *fax:* +43 4 243 2353 *email:* office@carinthischersommer.at. Gerda Fröhlich, director. *Annual. July-August. Concerts, opera.*

Chopin Festival. Biberstr 4, A-1010 Wien, Austria *tel:* +43 1 512 2374 *fax:* +43 1 512 646375 *email:* icg@netway.at. Theodor Kanitzer, director; Tomasz Olszewski, general secretary. *August at Charterhouse Gaming, Lower Austria. Orchestral, choral music, chamber music, symphony music, recitals.*

Easter Festival "Music of Religions". Studienzentrum fur Neue Musik, Galerie St Barbara, Herzog Otto Str 4, A-6060 Hall in Tirol, Austria *tel:* +43 52 235 6706 *fax:* +43 52 234 5926 *email:* g.st.barbara@tirolkultur.at. Gerhard Crepaz, artistic director; Maria Crepaz, organiser. *9-23 April 2000. Early and classical music, new music, world music, dance, lectures/workshops/ symposia/politics, theatre, exhibitions, liturgies.*

Festival Klangbogen Wien. Festival Management Wien, Rathausstr 4, A-1010 Wien, Austria *tel:* +43 1 4000 84725 *email:* tickets@klangbogen.at. Roland Geyer, music director. *June-September. Opera and operetta, symphony concerts, chamber music, church concerts, recitals, Viennese music. Also Easter festival.*

Franz Liszt Festival. Festivalbüro, Schloß Esterházy, A-7000 Eisenstadt, Austria *tel:* +43 2682 61866 *fax:* +43 2682 61805. Walter Reicher, artistic director. *May.*

Haydn Festival - Eisenstadt. Festivalbüro, Schloß Esterházy, A-7000 Eisenstadt, Austria *tel:* +43 268 261866 *fax:* +43 268 261805 *email:* office@haydnfestival.at. Walter Reicher, artistic director; Wolfgang Kuzmits, marketing. *Annual festival, at the Esterházy Palace: September. Concert season: May-October. Offers internationally renowned solo artists, chamber ensembles, as well as complete orchestras a natural setting in which they may interpret the works of Haydn and others on the original stages.*

Innsbruck Festival of Early Music. Haspingerstr 1, A-6020 Innsbruck, Austria *tel:* +43 512 571032 *fax:* +43 512 563142 *email:* alte.musik@magnet.at. René Jacobs, artistic director; Eva Schintlmeister, managing director. *1 July-31 August 2000. Annual event featuring baroque music (2 operas, 25 concerts) played on period instruments at historic sites.*

International Academy for New Composition. Avantgarde Art Society, Wopfnerstrasse 16, A-6130 Schwaz/Tirol, Austria *tel:* +43 524 265737 *fax:* +43 524 261199. Marianne Penz-van Stappershoef, director. *Annual. New music and audio art.*

* **International Bruckner Festival.** Linzer Veranstaltungsgesellschaft mbH, Brucknerhaus Linz, Untere Donaulände 7, A-4010 Linz, Austria *tel:* +43 732 775230 *fax:* +43 732 7612201. Thomas Daniel Schlee, music director. *September-October. Extensive presentation of works by Anton Bruckner, plus music relating to an annual theme.*

Internationales Kammermusikfest Lockenhaus. Kremerata Musica, Hauptplatz 5, A-7442 Lockenhaus, Austria *tel:* +43 261 62072 *fax:* +43 261 62023. Josef Herowitsch, managing director; Gidon Kremer, artistic director. *29 June-9 July. Music for chamber orchestra and smaller ensembles comprising of work from the baroque masters to the contemporary composers. Concerts held in a baroque church and a medieval castle; open rehearsals and workshops.*

Internationale Sommerakademie Universität 'Mozarteum'. Alpenstr 48, A-5020, Salzburg, Austria *tel:* +43 662 6198 4500 *fax:* +43 662 6198 4509 *email:* michaela.bartsch@moz.ac.at. Michaela Bartsch, student office; Micha Wieser-Hois, director's office. *17 July-26 August 2000. Masterclasses for classical musicians.*

Musikprotokoll. ORF-Steiemark, Marburger Strasse 20, Graz, Austria *tel:* +43 316 470227 *fax:* +43 316 470253. Christian Scheib, director; Rosalinde Vidic, admin. *Contemporary music.*

Salzburg Easter Festival. Herbert-von-Karajan-Pl 9, A-5020 Salzburg, Austria *tel:* +43 662 804 5328 *fax:* +43 662 804 5790. Michael Dewitte, general manager. *15-24 April 2000. Orchestral, choral, opera.*

* **Salzburg Festival.** Postfach 140, A-5010 Salzburg, Austria *tel:* +43 662 80450/8045579 *fax:* +43 662 8045700/8045760 *email:* info@salzburgfestival.at; presse@salzburgfestival.at. Eva Maria Wieser, artistic admin; Regina Wohlfarth, press officer. *Annual. 24 July-31 August 2000. Drama, opera, concerts. Founded in 1920.*

Schubertiade. Gesellschaft mbH, Schweizer Strasse 1, Postfach 100, A-6845 Hohenems, Austria *tel:* +43 557 672091 *fax:* +43 557 675450 *email:* info@schubertiade.at. G Nachbauer, manager. *Annual, 20-28 May, 15-25 June, 30 August-10 September 2000. Chamber music, song recitals, orchestra concerts.*

Styriarte/ Summer Music Festival in Styria. Palais Attems, Sackstr 17, A-8010 Graz, Austria *tel:* +43 316 812941 *fax:* +43 316 877 3836 *email:* styriarte@styria.com. Mathis Huber; Irmgard Heschl, admin. *June-July. Classical and baroque music, chamber and orchestral music, operas, children's orchestral.*

Wien Modern. Wiener Konzerthausgesellschaft, Lothringerstr 20, A-1037 Vienna, Austria *tel:* +43 1 712 46860 *fax:* +43 1 713 1709 *email:* mail@konzerthaus.at. Christoph Lieben-Seutter, secretary general. *November. 20th C music. Interdisciplinary festival. Retrospective of music composed after WWII.*

Wiener Festwochen. Lehárgasse 11, A-1060 Wien, Austria *tel:* +43 1 589 220 *fax:* +43 1 589 2249 *email:* festwochen@festwochen.at. Wolfgang Wais, secretary general; Luc Bondy, theatre director; Klaus-Peter Kehr, music drama director; Hortensia Völckers, dance director. *May-June. Drama, music, dance and exhibitions from all periods, including contemporary.*

Belgium

Bruges Early Music Festival. Collaert Mansionstraat 30, B-8000 Brugge, Belgium *tel:* +32 50 332283 *fax:* +32 50 345204 *email:* musica-antiqua@unicall.be. Robrecht Dewitte, director; Alice Dens, press. *29 July-12 August 2000. International Organ Week: competitions, interpretation classes, recitals. Lunchtime and evening concerts: Musica Sacra - Musica Britannica. Medieval to early romantic period.*

Festival Ars Musica. 89 Rue Royale, B-1000 Bruxelles, Belgium *tel:* +32 2 219 2660 *fax:* +32 2 219 8814 *email:* secretariat@arsmusica.be. Virginie Civrais, general co-ordinator. *March. Annual festival of contemporary music worldwide. Concerts, conferences, masterclasses, pluridisciplinary activities (exhibitions, films), opera.*

Festival des Midis-Minimes. Rue Grisar 21, B-1070 Bruxelles, Belgium *tel:* +32 2 527 3847 *fax:* +32 2 520 7150 *email:* F.E.de.Wasseige@cyclone.be. François-Emmanuel de Wasseige, artistic director. *3 July-1 September 2000. One concert a day except on Saturdays and Sundays. Chamber and baroque music on original instruments.*

* **Festival de Wallonie.** Rue de L'Armée, Grouchy 20, B-5000 Namur, Belgium *tel:* +32 81 733781 *fax:* +32 81 742503 *email:* festival.wallonie@skynet.be. Baudouin Muylle, general secretary. *June-October. 80 classical music concerts.*

* **Flanders Festival.** Kasteel Borluut, Kleine Gentstraat 46, B-9051 Gent, Belgium *tel:* +32 92 439494 *fax:* +32 9 243 9490 *email:* festival@skynet.be; festival-gent@skynet.be. Jan Briers, co-ordinator. *April-October 2000. Concerts and dance.*

International Electro-acoustic Festival. Musiques et Recherches, Place de Ransbeck 3, B-1380 Ohain, Belgium *tel:* +32 23 544368 *fax:* +32 2 351 0094. Vande Gorne Annette, artistic director. *Four-day festival in March. Presents an opportunity to meet electro-acoustic composers.*

Les Nuits de Septembre. Rue des Mineurs 17, B-4000 Liège, Belgium *tel:* +32 42 230214 *fax:* +32 4 2221540 *email:* jmlg@arcadis.be. Philippe Vendrix, director; Claire Ringlet, manager. *September. Early and baroque music.*

Bulgaria

International Festival of Contemporary Music 'Musica Nova-Sofia'. ISCM Bulgarian Section, 149 Evlogy Georgiev Blvd, BG-1504 Sofia, Bulgaria *tel:* +359 2 442780 *fax:* +359 2 432675 *email:* mproducers@bnr.acad.bg; ludens@mail.bol.bg. Simeon Pironkoff, president; Lachesar Karanlakov, secretary general. *10-20 June 2000. Promotion of new music. Chamber, symphonic, stage, dance, electro-acoustic music.*

Thracia Summer Music Festival. Bogomil 25/21, 4000 Plovdiv, Bulgaria *tel:* +359 32 260604/228936 *fax:* +359 32 270270 *email:* thracia@vienna.at. Nayden Todorov, music director; Andrey Andreev, musicologist; Roman Eccher, manager. *August. Concerts in Plovdiv, Sofia, Pasardjik, Tchirpan, Stara Zagora, Haskovo.*

* **Varna Summer International Music Festival.** Varna Municipality, 43 Osmi Primorski Polk Blvd, BG-9000 Varna, Bulgaria *tel:* +359 52 222425 *fax:* +359 52 220101. Plamena Tsoneva, musicologist. *June-August.*

Canada

Banff Arts Festival. The Banff Centre Centre for the Arts, Box 1020, Station 28, Banff, Alberta, T0L 0C0, Canada *tel:* +1 403 762 6180 *fax:* +1 403 762 6345 *email:* arts_info@banffcentre.ab.ca. *June-August. Masterclasses, chamber music, jazz, etc.*

Calgary International Organ Festival. 3rd Floor, 134 - 11 Av, S.E., Calgary, Alberta T26 0X6, Canada *tel:* +1 403 543 5115 *fax:* +1 403 543 5129 *email:* info@ciof.com. Timothy Rendell, president; Cathy Nickel, communications; Scott Dunlop, festival events manager. *Quadrennial. Next 2002. More than 30 events celebrating organ music, including jazz, choral, baroque, rock and classical concerts; silent film festival; m/classes and w/shops; symposia. Finals round of international organ competition featuring world's top ten organists.*

Centara Corporation New Music Festival. 555 Main St, Room 101, Winnipeg, MB R3B 1C3, Canada *tel:* +1 204 949 3950 *fax:* +1 204 956 4271 *email:* wso@wso.mb.ca. Aileen White, marketing director. *28 January-5 February 2000. John Taverner, Distinguished Guest Composer for the year 2000. Strong component of the festival is to perform Canadian and world premieres and to have international composers on-site during the festival.*

CINARS (International Exchange for the Performing Arts). 3575 Blvd Saint-Laurent, #216 Montréal, Québec, Canada H2X 2T7 *tel:* +1 514 842 5866 *fax:* +1 514 843 3168 *email:* arts@cinars.org. Géneviève Gouin. *December. Over 60 presentations of dance, theatre, music and other performing arts disciplines.*

The Elora Festival - A Celebration in Song. PO Box 370, Elora, Ont N0B 1S0, Canada *tel:* +1 519 846 0331 *fax:* +1 519 846 5947 *email:* info@elora.org. Cheryl Ewing, general manager. *14 July-6 August 2000. Choral, classical and contemporary music festival.*

Festival des Arts de Saint-Sauveur. 75 Ave de la Gare, Bloc L-1, Saint-Sauveur-des-Monts, Québec, Canada J0R 1R6 *tel:* +450 227 0427 *fax:* +450 227 2039 *email:* festart@qc.aira.com. Camilla Malashenko, director of competitions. *28 July-13 August 2000. Multi-disciplinary event in music and dance. Features dual competition in choreography and music composition.*

Festival International de Lanaudière. 1500 Base-de-Roc Boulevard, Joliette, PQ J6E 3Z1, Canada *tel:* +1 514 759 7636 *fax:* +1 514 759 3082. François Bédard, general manager. *July-August. Classical.*

Festival International de Musique Actuelle de Vitoriaville. CP 460, Victoriaville, PQ G6P 6T3, Canada *tel:* +1 819 752 7912 *fax:* +1 819 758 4370 *email:* fimav@cdcbf.qc.ca. Michel Levasseur, artistic director. *18-22 May 2000. New music festival, jazz, improvised rock, contemporary and electro-acoustic music.*

Festival International de Musique Baroque de Lamèque. 2-28 Rue de l'Hôpital, Lamèque NB, E8T 1C3, Canada *tel:* +1 506 344 5846 *fax:* +1 506 344 0366 *email:* agaplus@nbnet.nb.ca. Mathieu Duguay, artistic director. *29 July-6 August 2000. Early and baroque music on period instruments.*

Festival Orford. 3165 Chemin du Parc, Orford, Québec J1X 7A2, Canada *tel:* +1 819 843 3981 *fax:* +1 819 843 7274 *email:* arts.orford@sympatico.ca. Isabelle Langlois, communications and promotion. *30 June-12 August 2000. Chamber and symphonic music, dance, opera, sacred music with musicians of international repute such as Emanuel Borok, Yuli Turovsky, Janos Starker. Tickets: CAN $12-25.*

Festival of the Sound. PO Box 750, Parry Sound, Ont P2A 2Z1, Canada *tel:* +1 705 746 2410 *fax:* +1 705 746 5639 *email:* festival@parrysound.net. Margaret Boyd, admin. *July-August. Chamber music.*

Guelph Spring Festival. PO Box 1718, Guelph, Ont N1H 6Z9, Canada *tel:* +1 519 821 3210 *fax:* +1 519 821 3210 *email:* gsf@freespace.net. Simon Wynberg, artistic director; Lynn McGuigan, general manager. *May-June. Classical, jazz, world music, chamber and opera.*

Montréal International Jazz Festival. 822 Sherbrooke E, Montréal, PQ H2L 1K4, Canada *tel:* +1 514 523 3378 *fax:* +1 514 525 5775. Alain Simard, president; Caroline Jamet, vice-president, communications, tourism. *28 June-9 July 2000. Jazz, rhythm and blues, cajun.*

Ottawa International Jazz Festival. PO Box 3104, Sta D, Ottawa, Ont K1P 6H7, Canada *tel:* +1 613 241 2633; +1 888 226 4495 (toll free) *fax:* +1 613 241 5774 *email:* info@jazz.ottawa.com. Estée Barica, executive producer; Catherine O'Grady, executive producer. *21-31 July 2000. Over 450 jazz musicians from all over the world. Includes Afro-Cuban, Latin, swing, big band, bebop, avant-garde, mainstream, traditional, blues.*

Scotia Festival of Music. 6181 Lady Hammond Rd, Halifax, NS B3K 2R9, Canada *tel:* +1 902 429 9267 *fax:* +1 902 425 6785 *email:* scotia.festival@ns.sympatico.ca. Christopher Wilcox, manager and artistic director. *21 May-4 June 2000. Chamber music, masterclasses, lectures, concerts.*

Summer Music from the Comox Valley. PO Box 3056, Courtenay, BC V9N 5N3, Canada *tel:* +1 250 338 7463 *fax:* +1 250 334 2934 *email:* cmyc@island.net. Stacey Wright, general manager. *July-August. Jazz, chamber music, orchestral, music theatre.*

Vancouver Early Music Festival. 1254 West 7th Av, Vancouver, BC V6H 1B6, Canada *tel:* +1 604 732 1610 *fax:* +1 604 732 1602 *email:* staff@earlymusic.bc.ca. José Verstappen, director. *July-August 2000.*

Colombia

VI Festival y Escuela Internacional de Música. Universidad Antonio Nariño, Carrera 38 # 58A-77, Santafé de Bogotá, Colombia *tel:* +57 1 316 8590 *fax:* +57 1 221 3352 *email:* closada@email.gc.cuny.edu. Cristina Losada, admin director. *15 June-13 July 2000. Chamber music, concerts and teaching.*

Côte d'Ivoire

Market for African Performing Arts (MASA). Direction Generale du Masa, 09 BP 2877 Abidjan 09, Cote d'Ivoire *tel:* +225 21 35 20/21 69 10 *fax:* +225 21 35 21/21 95 19 *email:* masa@africaonline.co.ci. Thomas Manou Yablaih, director general; Maiimouna Coulibaly, promotion officer; Joseph Kapet, admin and finance officer. *3-10 March 2001. Festival of music, dance and theatre with performers from all over Africa.*

Croatia

* **Dubrovnik Festival.** PO Box 132, HR-50000 Dubrovnik, Croatia *tel:* +385 59 412288/26351 *fax:* +385 59 27944. Frano Matusic, general manager; Valter Despalj, artistic director. *Theatre ballet, concerts and folklore.*

* **Zagreb Music Biennial International Festival of Contemporary Music.** c/o Hrvatsko Drustvo Skladatelja, Berislaviceva, HR-10000 Zagreb, Croatia *tel:* +385 1 423463 *fax:* +385 1 422850 *email:* hdsl@zg.tel.hr. Ivo Josipovic, director; Sanda Vojkovic, deputy director. *April. Contemporary music.*

Czech Republic

Art Days of the Blind in Moravia. SONS, Czech Blind United, Karlinské nám 12, CR-186 03 Praha 8, Czech Republic *tel:* +420 2 2481 7393 *fax:* +420 2 2481 8398 *email:* sons_zahr@braillnet.cz. Marina Barakova, international dept. *Annual. Spring. Six to nine towns in central Moravia. Seminars, music, recitation, graphic art, handicrafts and theatre performances and workshops.*

* **Brno International Music Festival.** Úvoz 39, CR-602 00 Brno, Czech Republic *tel:* +420 5 4323 3116 *fax:* +420 5 4323 3358 *email:* mhfb@arskoncert.cz. Jitka Runstuková. *16 March-30 April 2000, Easter Festival of Sacred Music. 20 September-8 October, Moravian Autumn Festival: symphony, chamber music, opera. 30 September-4 October, Exposition of New Music: contemporary arts, music, theatre and dance.*

Emmy Destinn Music Festival. Rudolfov 393, CR-373 71 Ceské Budejovice, Czech Republic *tel:* +420 3 839254 *also fax.* Antonín Kazil. *Operatic, oratorio and chmbr mus repertoire.*

Festival Mozart Open. Zatecká St 1, Prague 1 110 00, Czech Republic *tel:* +420 2 2481 9322/3 *fax:* +420 2 2481 9324 *email:* festival@mozart.cz. Jan Dvoisk, director; Viktor Meska, director of ticket sales. *Classical opera, modern chamber opera, classical marionettes and puppet shows, baroque theatre.*

Forfest. Artistic Initiative of Kromeriz, Kojetinska 1425, CR-767 01 Kromeriz, Czech Republic *tel:* +420 6 342 4316 *also fax.* Zdenka Vaculovicová, managing director. *18-25 June 2000. International festival of contemporary arts with spiritual orientation; concerts, exhibitions, workshops, lectures, with local and foreign artists. Colloqui 'Church and Art', portraits of well-known composers, presentations of young composers and creative artists. Chamber music, contemporary classical, sacred, choral, electronic music. Member of European Conference of Promoters of New Music.*

International Jazz Festival Prague. Pragokoncert Arts Agency, Peckova 13, Praha 8, Czech Republic *tel:* +420 2 2481 7272 *fax:* +420 2 2481 8272. Ivo Letov, artistic director. *October 2000. Jazz, from traditional to modern, over four concerts.*

* **International Music Festival Janacek May.** Masna 10, CR-702 00 Ostrava 1, Czech Republic *tel:* +420 6 9612 2300 *fax:* +420 6 9611 4016. Jaromír Javurek, manager and director. *May-June. Symphonic, chamber concerts, recitals. Classical music from 17th C to contemporary. Features top international artists.*

Prague International Choir Festival and Competition. c/o AD International Inc, 136 Lawrenceville-Pennington Rd, Lawrenceville, NJ 08648-1413, USA *tel:* +1 609 896 9330 *fax:* +1 609 896 3450 *email:* adadi@aol.com. *20-26 June 2000. International festival for children and high-school age choirs. Held in Prague.*

* **Prague Spring International Music Festival.** Hellichova 18, CR-118 00 Praha 1, Czech Republic *tel:* +420 2 573 20468/533474 *fax:* +420 2 536040 *email:* festival@login.cz. Oleg Podgorny, director. *12 May-3 Jun 2000. Classical music festival.*

Denmark

Aarhus Festival. Officersbygningen, Vester Allé 3, DK-8000 Aarhus C, Denmark *tel:* +45 89 318270 *fax:* +45 86 191336 *email:* festugeinfo@aarhusfestuge.dk. Lars Seeberg, general secretary; Annita Hornslet, head of programme section. *Annual. 1-9 September 2000. Largest single concentration of cultural events in Scandinavia, including theatre, cabaret, opera, ballet and dance, classical and new music, rock, jazz and folk music. Exhibitions, film and media, sports. Symposia, seminars and events for children.*

Composers' Biennale. c/o Dansk Komponist Forening, Gråbrodretorv 16, 1, DK-1154 Copenhagen K, Denmark *tel:* +45 33 135405 *fax:* +45 33 143219. Mogens Winkel Holm, chairman. *Biennial. Next March 2000. Presentation of contemporary Danish music, organised by Danish Composers' Society.*

Contemporary Music in Suså. Tyvelsevej 26, DK-4171 Glumso, Denmark *tel:* +45 57 648102 *email:* nymususaa@adr.dk. Anne Kristine Smith, director; Hans-Henrik Nordstroem (www.nordstroem.dk), artistic director. *Annual. 26-27 August 2000. At Suså School between Sorø and Naestved. Works by contemporary Danish composers will be performed, including world premieres.*

Copenhagen Choir Festival. Greiff Musik, Gammeltoftsgade 16, kld tv, DK-1355 Kobenhavn K, Denmark *tel:* +45 3313 5580 *fax:* +45 3313 5540 *email:* info@greiff.dk. Anja Reiff, production manager; Nicolaí Gjessing, admin manager. *Annual. 23-27 June 2000. Concerts and workshops.*

Copenhagen Early Music Festival. c/o Greiff Musik, Gammeltoftsgade 16 kld tv, DK-1355 Kobenhavn K, Denmark *tel:* +45 3313 5570/80 *fax:* +45 3313 5540 *email:* info@greiff.dk. Anja Reiff, production manager; Nicolai Gjessing, admin manager. *Annual, summer. Concerts and workshops to promote interest in choral music.*

Copenhagen International Experimental Music Festival. Skraep, Den Anden Opera, Kronprinsensgade 7, DK-1114 Kobenhavn, Denmark *tel:* +45 33 327222; +45 47 982763 *fax:* +45 33 327234; +45 47 982764 *email:* skraep@skraep.dk; otis.winther@get2net.dk. Niels Winther, secretary. *17-20 and 24-27 August 2000. Experimental composition and improvisation.*

Copenhagen Jazz Festival. Kjeld Langes Gade 4A, DK-1367 Kobenhavn K, Denmark *tel:* +45 33 932013 *fax:* +45 33 934413 *email:* cjf@dkb.dk. *July. 10 days of jazz in jazz clubs, concert halls and on the streets and squares of Copenhagen.*

European Youth Music Festival. Ishoej Musikskole, Jaegerbuen 6, DK-2635 Ishoej, Denmark *tel:* +45 43 543025 *fax:* +45 43 542761. *June-July.*

Fanø Musikfestival. Toftestien 21, Sonderho, DK-6720 Fano, Denmark *tel:* +45 75 164429 *fax:* +45 75 164529. Vibeke Schott, director. *3, 11, 18, 24 July and 1, 8, 15, 22 August 2000. Chamber music.*

Frederiksvaerk Music Festival. Gjethuset, Gjethusgade 5, DK-3300 Frederiksvaerk, Denmark *tel:* +45 47 770607. Charlotte Lund Christiansen. *Annual. July. Chamber music concerts, mainly with Danish artists and ensembles, Saturdays at 8pm, Sundays at 4pm. Combined with art exhibition.*

Music Harvest Festival. Det Fynske Musikkonservatorium, Islandsgade 2, DK-5000 Odense, Denmark *tel:* +45 66 110663 *fax:* +45 66 177763. Bertel Krarup, Per Erland Rasmussen, artistic leaders. *Annual. 8-12 November 2000. Held in Odense, concerts and seminars on contemporary music.*

Selsø Summer Concerts. Langs Hegnet 39, DK-2800 Lyngby, Denmark *tel:* +45 45 930778 *also fax; email:* friis.schaeffer@get2net.dk. Mogens Friis, director. *Annual. June-August. Classical music.*

Sorø International Music Festival. Sasserbrovej 10, DK-4173 Fjenneslev, Denmark *tel:* +45 53 609639 *also fax; email:* knudvad@post.tele.dk. Knud Vad, artistic director; Jorgen Birkedal, secretary. *June-September 2000. Classical music, including contemporary.*

Vendsyssel Festival. Perikumvej 18, DK-9800 Hjorring, Denmark *tel:* +45 98 924588 *fax:* +45 98 911354 *email:* info@vendsysselfestival.dk. *Annual. July-August. Concerts in churches, stately homes and art museums in the Vendsyssel area.*

Estonia

International Festival of New Music NYYD. Eesti Kontsert, Estonia Ave 4, 10148 Tallinn, Estonia *tel:* +372 644 6255/2901 *fax:* +372 631 4171 *email:* madis@concert.ee. Madis Kolk, manager. *Biennial. Next 2001. Contemporary music concerts, opera performances, workshops, multidisciplinary events, exhibitions.*

Faroe Islands

Summartónar. Reynagota 12, FR-100 Tórshavn, Faroe Islands *tel:* +298 14815 *fax:* +298 14825 *email:* summar@olivant.fo. Kristian Blak, managing director. *Annual. June-July. Festival of classical and contemporary music. Indoor and outdoor locations all over Tórshavn and the Faroe Islands.*

Finland

April Jazz Espoo. Ahertajantie 6 B, FIN-02100 Espoo, Finland *tel:* +358 9 455 0003 *fax:* +358 9 465172 *email:* espoo.big.band@pp.kolumbus.fi. Martti Lappalainen, general director. *April. International jazz festival.*

Avanti! Summer Sounds. Tallberginkatu 1 B 80, FIN-00180 Helsinki, Finland *tel:* +358 9 694 0091 *fax:* +358 9 694 2208 *email:* avanti @kaapeli.fi. Esa-Pekka Salonen, artistic director; Aila Manninen, managing director. *28 June-2 July 2000. Orchestral and chamber music concerts, baroque and contemporary music.*

Crusell Week. Uudenkaupungin Kultuuritoimisto, Rauhankatu 10, FIN-23500 Uusikaupunki, Finland *tel:* +358 2 8451 5300/5302 *fax:* +358 2 8451 5442.

Espoo International Piano Festival. Espoo Cultural Centre, Kulttuuriaukio, FIN-02100 Espoo, Finland *tel:* +358 09 816 5051 *fax:* +358 09 816 57220 *email:* espoo.kulttuurikeskus@espoo.fi. Osmo Pylvänäinen, director; Erik T Tawaststjerna, Marita Viitasalo, artistic directors. *Biennial. Next 2001. Classical and contemporary piano music, recitals and orchestral concerts, master course.*

Finland Festivals. Uudenmaankatu 36 D 21, FIN-00120 Helsinki, Finland *tel:* +358 9 612 6760 *fax:* +358 9 612 67610 *email:* info@ mail.festivals.fi. Tuomo Tirkkonen, general director; Ritta Kerman, marketing secretary. *Various music festivals, including opera, chamber, jazz, rock, film, dance/theatre and general music. Apply for specific dates.*

* **Helsinki Festival.** Glass Palace, Mannerheimintie 22-24, FIN-00100 Helsinki, Finland *tel:* +358 9 6126 5100 *fax:* +358 9 6126 5161 *email:* info@helsinkifestival.fi. Risto Nieminen, director. *Annual. August-September. Arts festival featuring classical, popular and world music, dance, theatre, visual arts, cinema, and city events.*

Hetta Music Event. Virastotalo, FIN-99400 Enontekiö, Finland *tel:* +358 1 655 6278 *fax:* +358 1 655 6229 *email:* Anneli.Aro@enontekio.fi. Anneli Aro, secretary of culture. *16-24 April 2000. Sacred and baroque music.*

Ilmajoki Music Festival. Ilkantie 17, FIN-60800 Ilmajoki, Finland *tel:* +358 6 424 7049 *fax:* +358 6 424 7171. Lasse Lintala, artistic director; Kari Marjamäki, general director. *Annual. June. Opera, concerts.*

International Kalottjazz and Blues Festival. Tornion Kulttuuritoimisto, Lukiokatu 10, FIN-95400 Tornio, Finland *tel:* +358 1 643 2424 *fax:* +358 1 643 2612 *email:* helena.junes@tornio.fi. Helena Junes, festival director. *29 June-2 July 2000.*

Joensuu Festival. Koskikatu 1, FIN-80100 Joensuu, Finland *tel:* +358 1 3 267 5330 *fax:* +358 1 3 267 5320 *email:* joensuun.laulujuhlat@co.inet.fi. Juha Iso-Aho, executive director. *Annual. June. Classical to rock and pop, ethno and jazz. Dance, theatre, films, exhibitions and seminars.*

Kangasniemi Music Festival. The Cultural Secretary, Kangasniemi Municipality, Otto Mannisen tie 2, FIN-51200 Kangasniemi, Finland *tel:* +358 1 5780 1265 *fax:* +358 1 5780 1292. *July. Classical and vocal music; concerts, courses and competitions for singers and Lied-pianists.*

Kaustinen Folk Music Festival. PO Box 24, FIN-69601 Kaustinen, Finland *tel:* +358 6 860 4111 *fax:* +358 6 860 4222 *email:* folk.fest@kaustinen.inet.fi. Jyrki Heiskanen, programme director. *15-23 July 2000. Largest annual folk music and dance festival in the Nordic countries. Folk, world, traditional, ethnic, folk-dance.*

Korsholm Music Festival. FIN-65610 Mustasaari, Finland *tel:* +358 6 322 2390 *fax:* +358 6 322 2393. Frans Helmerson, artistic director; Ros-Mari Djupsund, executive director. *Late June. Chamber music with Nordic features.*

Kuhmo Chamber Music Festival. Fredikinkatu 77 A 2-4, FIN-00100 Helsinki, Finland *tel:* +358 9 493 902 *fax:* +358 9 493 956 *email:* kuhmo.festival@kajak.fi. Seppo Kimanen, artistic director. *Annual. 16-30 July 2000. Chamber music.*

Lahti Organ Festival. Kirkkokatu 5, FIN-15110 Lahti, Finland *tel:* +358 3 782 3184 *fax:* +358 3 783 2190 *email:* lof@pp.phnet.fi. Erkki Krohn, executive manager. *Annual. 1-6 August 2000. Organ, chamber music, ensembles and choirs.*

Lakeside Blues Festival. Järvenpään Blues-Jazz Diggarit ry, PO Box 143, FIN-04401 Järvenpää, Finland *tel:* +358 9 271 1305 *fax:* +358 9 279 2550 *email:* blues@sci.fi. Jussi 'Auvo' Laaksonen, festival promoter. *Annual. Last week in June. Rhythm and blues.*

Lieska Brass Week. Koski-Jaakonkatu 4, FIN-81700 Lieksa, Finland *tel:* +358 13 520 2055 *fax:* +358 13 520 2044 *email:* brass. week@lieksa.fi. Jouko Harjanne, artistic director; Petri Aarnio, managing director; Anu Mustonen, secretary. *21-30 July 2000. Classical concerts, music courses, competition.*

Mikkeli Music Festival. Vuorikatu 3 A, FIN-50100 Mikkeli, Finland *tel:* +358 1 516 2076 *fax:* +358 1 519 12323 *email:* mikkeli. musicfestival@iwn.fi. Valeri Gergiev, artistic director; Kari Moring, executive director. *June-July. Opera in stage and concert productions, symphony concerts, recitals. Main performers: Orchestra and Choir of Mariinsky (Kirov) Theatre.*

* **Musica Nova Helsinki.** c/o The Helsinki Festival, Glass Palace, Mannerheimintie 22-24, FIN-00100 Helsinki, Finland *tel:* +358 9 6126 5100 *fax:* +358 9 6126 5161 *email:* info@helsinkifestival.fi. Risto Nieminen, director. *3-11 March 2000. Part of Helsinki Festival. Annual festival of contemporary music.*

Naantali Music Festival. Henrikinkatu 1, PO Box 46, FIN-21101 Naantali, Finland *tel:* +358 2 434 5363 *fax:* +358 2 434 5425 *email:* info@naantalinmusiikkijuhlat.fi. Tina Tunturi, executive director; Arto Noras, artistic director. *Annual. 10-21 June 2000. Chamber music and recitals. 18-22 concerts. Main venue medieval abbey of Naantali.*

Northern Accordion, Folkmusic and Folkdance Festival. Tornio Cultural Office, Lukiokatu 10, FIN-95400 Tornio, Finland *tel:* +358 1 643 2424 *fax:* +358 1 643 2612.

Oulainen Music Week. Reservikomppaniankatu 4, FIN-86300 Oulainen, Finland *tel:* +358 8 479 3272 *fax:* +358 8 470172. *October-November.*

Oulu Music Festival. Lintulammentie 1, FIN-90150 Oulu, Finland *tel:* +358 8 336830 *fax:* +358 8 336822. Ismo Sirén, artistic director; Heli Heikkilä-Murto, concert secretary. *March. Full symphonic, chamber orchestra, chamber music, contemporary classical, recitals, children's concerts.*

Pori Jazz Festival. Pohsoisranta 11, FIN-28100 Pori, Finland *tel:* +358 2 626 2200 *fax:* +358 2 626 2225 *email:* festival@porijazz.fi. Jyrki Kangas, artistic director; Olli Kivela, general manager. *Annual. 15-23 July 2000. International jazz festival. Also pop, rock, Latin and classical music.*

Riihimäki Summer Concerts. Kalevankatal, FIN-11101 Riihimäki, Finland *tel:* +358 1 974 1615 *fax:* +358 1 973 2626. Juha Pesonen, artistic director. *June. Recitals and chamber music.*

Sata Häme Accordion Festival. PO Box 37, FIN-39501 Ikaalinen, Finland *tel:* +358 3 440 0224 *fax:* +358 3 450 1365. Kimmo Mattila, artistic director; Terhi Palonen, general director. *Annual. July.*

* **Savonlinna Opera Festival.** Olavinkatu 27, FIN-57130 Savonlinna, Finland *tel:* +358 15 476750 *fax:* +358 15 4767540 *email:* info@operafestival.fi. Paavo Suokko, general director; Jorma Hynninen, artistic director. *Annual. 1-31 July 2000. Opera, recitals, concerts.*

Sysmä Summer Sounds. PO Box 26, FIN-19701 Sysmä, Finland *tel:* +358 3 8431 239 *fax:* +358 3 7172 831. *30 June-9 July 2000.*

Tampere Biennale. Tullikamarinaukio 2, FIN-33100 Tampere, Finland *tel:* +358 3 314 66136 *fax:* +358 3 223 0121 *email:* music@tampere.fi. Annamaija Saarela, director. *Biennial. Next 12-16 Apr 2000. Contemporary Finnish music.*

Tampere Jazz Happening. Tullikamarinaukio 2, FIN-33100 Tampere, Finland *tel:* +358 3 314 66136/66172 *fax:* +358 3 223 0121 *email:* music@tampere.fi. Annamaija Saarela, director. *Annual. 3-5 November 2000. International contemporary jazz festival.*

Tampereen Sävel - Tampere International Choir Festival. Tullikamarinaukio 2, FIN-33100 Tampere, Finland *tel:* +358 3 314 66136 *fax:* +358 3 223 0121 *email:* music@tampere.fi. Annamaija Saarela, director. *Biennial. Next 2001. Chorus review, contest for vocal ensemble, course for choir leaders, concert series.*

Tango Festival in Seinäjoki. Kauppakatu 15 C, FIN-60100 Seinäjoki, Finland *tel:* +358 6 420 1111 *fax:* +358 6 414 2350 *email:* info @tangomarkkinat.fi. Reijo Pitkakoski, managing director. *July 2000. Concentrates mainly on tango music. 12 concerts, street dance, tango singing and dancing contest, etc.*

Time of Music. Musiikin Aika, FIN-44500 Viitasaari, Finland *tel:* +358 1 457 3195 *fax:* +358 1 457 93515 *email:* time.music@festivals.fi. Harri Natunen, manager. *6-12 July 2000. Contemporary music, jazz club, courses.*

Turku Music Festival. Uudenmaankatu 1, FIN-20500 Turku, Finland *tel:* +358 2 251 1162 *fax:* +358 2 231 3316 *email:* info@turkumusicfestival.fi. Martti Rousi, artistic director; Alarik Repo, executive director. *Annual. 11-20 August 2000. Orchestral, early, contemporary and chamber music.*

Vantaa Baroque Week. PO Box 10, FIN-01301 Vantaa, Finland *tel:* +358 9 830 6265 *fax:* +358 9 830 6261. Håkan Wikman, artistic director. *Annual. August. Western European baroque music.*

France

Besançon Festival of Music. 3 bis, Rue Léonel de Moustier, F-25000 Besançon, France *tel:* +33 81 25 05 85 *fax:* +33 81 81 52 15. Yvette Cussey, admin director. *September. Classical and symphonic concerts and recitals.*

Bordeaux Festival d'Été. Grand Théâtre, Service de Location, BP 95, F-33025 Bordeaux Cedex, France *tel:* +33 05 56 00 85 20 *fax:* +33 05 51 81 93 66. Catherine Lillet. *July.*

La Chaise-Dieu Festival. PO Box 150, F-43004 Le Puy-en-Velay, France *tel:* +33 4 71 09 48 28 *fax:* +33 4 71 09 55 58 *email:* festival-la-chaise-dieu @wanadoo.fr. Guy Ramona, director; Cécile Laurent de Stredel, communications. *24 August-3 September 2000. Over 30 concerts of sacred and spiritual music.*

Ensemble Orchestral Contemporain. Centre National de Création Musicale, 9 Rue de Garet, BP 1185, F-69202 Lyon Cedex 01, France *tel:* +33 4 72 07 37 00 *fax:* +33 4 72 07 37 01 *email:* grame@rd.grame.fr.

Festival Aspects des Musiques d'Aujourdhui. Conservatoire National du Region, 1 Rue de Carel, F-14027 Caen, France *tel:* +33 3186 4200 *fax:* +33 3186 1892. Fabrice Greweutti, artistic director; Stephanie Viet, PR. *11-19 March 2000. Contemporary music. Concerts, exhibitions, masterclasses; conferences with Klaus Huber.*

Festival d'Auvers-sur-Oise. Manoir des Colombières, Rue de la Sansonne, F-95430 Auvers-sur-Oise, France *tel:* +33 30 36 70 82 *fax:* +33 30 36 71 55. Pascal Escande, director. *May-June. Vocal, piano, chamber music, opera.*

Festival International d'Art Lyrique et de Musique. Palais de l'Ancien ArchevÛché, F-13100 Aix-en-Provence, France *tel:* +33 4 42 17 34 34 *fax:* +33 4 42 63 13 74. Jean-François Picheral, president; Bernard de Saint-Rapt, admin. *June-July. Chamber music concerts, recitals, public rehearsals, masterclasses.*

Festival International de Musique Baroque et Classique. Office du Tourisme, Place de la Halle, F-21200 Beaune, France *tel:* +33 80 26 21 30 *fax:* +33 80 26 31 39 *email:* blanchard.anne@wanadoo.fr. Anne Blanchard, director. *August 2000. Vocal, medieval, renaissance, baroque, opera.*

Festival International de Musique de Menton. 11 Av Delcassé, F-75008 Paris, France *tel:* +33 1 45 63 25 87 *fax:* +33 1 42 89 44 66. *July-August. Classical, chamber music and recitals.*

Festival Musique en Scène. 9 Rue du Garet, BP 1185, F-69202 Lyon Cedex 01, France *tel:* +33 4 72 07 37 00 *fax:* +33 4 72 07 37 01 *email:* grame@rd.grame.fr. James Giroudon, artistic director. *March. Contemporary music, music theatre, films.*

Festival Synthèse. Institut International de Musique Electroacoustique de Bourges, Place André Malreux - BP 39, F-18001 Bourges, France *tel:* +33 2 48 20 41 87 *fax:* +33 2 48 20 45 51 *email:* ime-bourges @gmeb.fr. Francoise Barrière, director. *Annual. May-June. Electro -acoustic music.*

Jazz Vienne. Bureau du Festival, 21 rue des Célestes, F-38200 Vienne, France *tel:* +33 4 74 78 87 87 *fax:* +33 4 74 78 87 88 *email:* festival @jazzavienne.com. Pierre Budimir, PR; Jacques Lannay, director; Jean-Paul Boutellier, founder. *July. Jazz, world, blues, gospel. Member of European Jazz Festivals Organisation.*

La Tour De France International Festival of Music and the Arts. c/o Mananan Festival Office, Erin Arts Centre, Port Erin, Isle of Man IM9 6LD, UK *tel:* +44 1624 835858 *also fax; fax:* +44 1624 836658. *email:* erinartscentre@enterprise.net. John Bethell, dir. *23-27 Jul 2000. Choral, orchestral, chamber music, opera. Vocal study course with Jeffrey Lawton. Visual art exhibitions.*

Les Estivales. La Charité, 77 Rue Cottier, PO Box 113, F-84204 Carpentras Cédex, France *tel:* +33 4 90 60 4600 *fax:* +33 4 90 60 5285. Joelle Pérault, admin. *July. Theatre, music, dance and variety show.*

Musica International Festival of Contemporary Music. 2 Rue d'Ingwiller, F-67000 Strasbourg, France *tel:* +33 3 88 21 02 21 *fax:* +33 3 88 21 02 88 *email:* musica67@cybercable.fr. J Cloquet, admin; Jean-Dominique Marco, managing director. *Annual. Sep-Oct. Contemporary music.*

* **Orange Festival.** Chorégies d'Orange, PO Box 205, 18 Place Silvain, F-84107 Orange Cédex, France *tel:* +33 490 51 83 83 *fax:* +33 490 34 87 67 *email:* choregies.asso.fr. Thierry Mariani, president; Raymond Duffaut, director. *Annual. July-August. Opera and symphonic concerts.*

Pablo Casals Festival. Bureau du Festival (BP24), Rue Victor Hugo, F-66502 Prades Cédex, France *tel:* +33 68 96 33 07 *fax:* +33 68 96 50 95. Michel Lethiec, artistic director. *Annual. July-August. Chamber music concerts, international music academy, instrumental and chamber music masterclasses, choral session.*

Piano aux Jacobins. 61 Rue de la Pomme, F-31000 Toulouse, France *tel:* +33 5 61 22 40 05 *fax:* +33 5 61 21 74 20 *email:* pianojacobins@hol.fr. Catherine d'Argoubet, artistic director. *Annual. September. Classical and contemporary music. Piano festival.*

Rendez-vous Musique Nouvelle. Centre Culturel, av St Rémy, F-57600 Forbach, France *tel:* +333 87 85 12 31 *also fax; email:* rdvmusiquenouvelle @bplorraine.fr. Claude Lefebvre, artistic director. *10-12 November 2000. Contemporary music. Also stages courses on composition and analysis and has a library of scores.*

Strasbourg International Music Festival. Wolf Musique, 24 Rue de la Mésange, F-67000 Strasbourg, France *tel:* +33 3 88 32 43 10 *fax:* +33 3 88 32 42 38. Harry Lapp, general manager. *June-July. Concerts, operas, recitals, jazz.*

Germany

Art Point. Trombacher Hof, D-55583 Bad Münster a St, Germany *tel:* +49 670 83616 *fax:* +49 670 83653. Signue von Osten.

Art Projekt. International Musikfestival GmbH, Widenmayerstr 41, D-80538 München, Germany *tel:* +49 892 907490 *fax:* +49 892 907 4999 *email:* mail@art-concerts.de. Franz Abraham, CEO. *September. Held in the Falkoner Centre, Copenhagen. Classical music, jazz and various other musical genres.*

Bad Hersfeld Festival. Nachtigallenstr 7, D-36251 Bad Hersfeld, Germany *tel:* +49 662 150670 *fax:* +49 662 164355. *Bach Festival. Easter, organ and choir. Mid June-August, opera and classical music.*

* **Bayreuth Festival.** PO Box 100262, D-95402 Bayreuth, Germany *tel:* +49 921 78780. Wolfgang Wagner, director. *Annual. July-August. Richard Wagner opera festival.*

* **Berlin Festival.** PO Box 301648, Budapester Str 50, D-10787 Berlin, Germany *tel:* +49 30 254890 *fax:* +49 30 254 89111. Dirk Nabering, music director. *Annual. 3-29 September. Mahler Festival. Orchestral, chamber, choral, vocal.*

Berliner Tage für Alte Musik. Postfach 580411, D-10414 Berlin, Germany *tel:* +49 30 447 6082 *also fax; email:* ars.musica@knoware.nl. Arnold Riesthuis, director. *14-22 October 2000. Concerts, instrument market, workshops. Theme: music and politics.*

Choreley. Kultursommer Rheinland-Pfalz, Kaiserstr 26-30, D-55116 Mainz, Germany *tel:* +49 61 31 288380 *fax:* +49 61 31 288388.

Donaueschingen Festival of Contemporary Music. Südwestfunk Baden-Baden, D-76522 Baden-Baden, Germany *tel:* +49 722 192 2247 *fax:* +49 722 192 4362. Armin Köhler, editor. *October. Contemporary music.*

* **Dresdner Musikfestspiele.** Postfach 202723, D-01193 Dresden, Germany *tel:* +49 351 478560 *fax:* +49 351 471 7896 *email:* dmf@musikfestspiele.com. Michael Hampe, director. *Annual. 27 May-June 12 2000. Theme: 'Baroque and Jazz'. Focus on vocal music and guitar. Opera, oratorio, church music, dance. Also Hasse and Strauss.*

Düsseldorfer Altstadt Herbst - The Young Arts Music Festival. Düsseldorfer Altstadt Herbst gGmbH, Bolkerstr 57, D-40213 Düsseldorf, Germany *tel:* +49 211 322332 *fax:* +49 211 322203 *email:* info@altstadtherbst.de. Christiane Oxenfort, Andreas Dahmen, artistic directors and managers. *September-October. To make a new experience out of classical music, bring old and new together, concerts in unfamiliar venues, etc.*

Europa Cantat - European Federation of Young Choirs (EFYC). c/o Bayerische Musikakademie Marktoberdorf, Kurfürstenstr 19, D-87616 Marktoberdorf, Germany *tel:* +49 8342 961826 *fax:* +49 8342 40370 *email:* modmusik@compuserve.com. Dolf Rabus, secretary general. *Triennial singing festival. Next 21-30 July 2000. International singing weeks in various European countries in 2001. European Youth Choir, European Academy for Young Choral Conductors, international study tours for choral conductors.*

Frankfurt Music Festival. Konzerthalle Carl Philipp Emanuel Bach, Collegienstr 8, D-15230 Frankfurt, Germany *tel:* +49 335 663880 *fax:* +49 335 6638877 *email:* c-ph-e-bach@ff.shuttle.de. Wolfgang Jost, director. *3-31 March 2000. Mainly works of Carl Philipp Emanuel Bach but also Eastern European composers. Information and exhibitions.*

Gegenwelten International Festival für Neue Musik. Kulturinstitut Komponistinnen Gestern-heute, Theatrestr 11, D-69117 Heidelberg, Germany *tel:* +49 446 221 166861 *fax:* +49 446 221 182072. Roswitha Sperber, artistic director; Rainer Koehl, executive. *April. Contemporary music and symposium.*

Göttingen Handel Festival. Hainholzweg 3-5, D-37085 Göttingen, Germany *tel:* +49 551 56700 *fax:* +49 551 45395 *email:* info@haendel.org. Benedikt Poensgen. *Annual. 8-13 June 2000. Baroque music and Handel operas.*

Halle Handel Festival. Große Nikolaistr 5, D-06108 Halle, Germany *tel:* +49 345 5009 0222 *fax:* +49 345 5009 0416 *email:* haendel@halle.de. Hanna John, director. *2-13 June 2000. Opera, concerts, oratorio, open-air performances, scientific conference, competitions.*

Heidelberg Castle Festival. Friedrichstr 5, D-69117 Heidelberg, Germany *tel:* +49 622 158 3521 *fax:* +49 622 158 3599. Helmut Hein, director. *28 July-27 August 2000. Opera, musical, plays, concerts.*

International May Festival. c/o Hessisches Staatstheater, PO Box 3247, D-65022 Wiesbaden, Germany *tel:* +49 611 1321 *fax:* +49 611 132337. Achim Thorwald, artistic leader; Marie-Louise Welck, secretary. *May. Opera, drama, ballet, musical, children and youth theatre.*

Inventionen - Berliner Festival Neuer Musik. c/o DAAD, Berliner Künstlerprogramm, Markgrafenstr 37, D-10117 Berlin, Germany *tel:* +49 302 022080 *fax:* +49 302 041267 *email:* beirer.berlin@daad.de; hein@gigant.kgw.tu-berlin.de. Ingrid Beirer, DAAD; Folkmar Hein, TU Berlin. *May-June 2000. 50 years of musique concrète: concerts, electro-acoustic music performances, films.*

* **Kissinger Sommer Festival.** Postfach 2260, Marktplatz 12, D-97672 Bad Kissingen, Germany *tel:* +49 971 807110 *fax:* +49 971 807191. Kari Kahl-Wolfsjäger. *Annual. June-July. Symphony concerts, chamber music, opera, Lieder, jazz.*

* **Ludwigsburg International Festival.** Festspiele Baden-Württemberg, PO Box 1022, D-71610 Ludwigsburg, Germany *tel:* +49 714 193960 *fax:* +49 714 193 9677. Wolfgang Gönnenwein, artistic director; Susanne Dieterich, admin director. *Annual. June-September. Opera, ballet, classical music, jazz.*

Markgräfler Gitarrentage - Müllheim. Stadt Müllheim, Kulturamt, Bismarckstr 3, D-79379 Müllheim, Germany *tel:* +49 76 31 801 132 *fax:* +49 76 31 801 126 *email:* studt@muellheim.de. F D Koch, director; Hucky Eichelmann, artistic director; Birgit Schweir. *29 September-6 October 2000. Guitar festival.*

Metapher Festival for New Vocal Music. Musik der Jahrhunderte, Hasenbergstr 31/2, D-70178 Stuttgart, Germany *tel:* +49 711 629 0510 *fax:* +49 711 629 0515 *email:* 106673.1024@compuserve.com. Christine Fischer, managing director; Hans-Peter Jöhn, Manfred Schreier, artistic directors. *Contemporary vocal music.*

Münchener Biennale - Internationales Festival für neues Musiktheater. Kulturreferat der Landeshauptstadt, Rindermarkt 3-4, D-80313 München, Germany *tel:* +49 89 280 5607 *fax:* +49 89 280 5679 *email:* 100635.2504@compuserve.com. Peter Ruzicka, artistic director. *April 2000. New music theatre including world premieres.*

* **Munich Opera Festival.** Bayerische Staatsoper Nationaltheater, Max-Joseph Platz 2, D-80539 München, Germany *tel:* +49 89 2185 1000 *fax:* +49 89 2185 1003. Peter Jonas, artistic and general director; Ulrike Hessler, PR director. *Annual international opera festival. July 2000. Opera, ballet, concerts, modern dance, exhibitions, multimedia.*

Musica Bayreuth. Ludwigstr 26, D-95444 Bayreuth, Germany *tel:* +49 921 67367 *also fax.* Viktor Lukas, conductor and organist. *May. Classical music and opera.*

Musica Sacra International. c/o Bayerische Musikakademie Marktoberdorf, Kurfürstenstrasse 19, D-87616 Marktoberdorf, Germany *tel:* +49 83 42 961825 *fax:* +49 834 240370 *email:* 100530.317 @compuserve.com. Dolf Rabus, director. *Biennial. Next 9-14 June 2000. Music from the 5 main world religions' choirs, instrumentalists, singers, dancers, combinations of music and other art forms.*

Musik-Biennale Berlin, International Festival of Contemporary Music. Berliner Festspiele GmbH, Budapester Str 50, D-10787 Berlin, Germany *tel:* +49 30 25 4890 *fax:* +49 30 254 89111 *email:* musikbiennale@berlinerfestspiele.de. Heike Hoffmann. *Biennial. Next 9-18 March 2001.*

Musikfestspiele Saarland eV. Rotenbühlerweg 28a, D-66123 Saarbrücken, Germany *tel:* +49 681 397359 *fax:* +49 681 372310. Prof Robert Leonardy, artistic director. *May-June. Theme of Spanish music. Classical concerts, oratorios, Flamenco, Spanish rock music.*

Oleg Kagan Music Festival. Musikfest Kreuth e.V, PO Box 5, D-83708 Kreuth, Germany *tel:* +49 802 91819 *fax:* +49 802 91828 *email:* info@kreuth.de. Rudi Wolf, organisation manager; Peter Baier, press. *Early July 2000. Classical and modern chamber music represented by internationally acclaimed artists.*

* **Rheingau Musik Festival Konzertgesellschaft.** Rheinallee 1, D-65375, Oestrich-Winkel, Germany *tel:* +49 6723 91770 *fax:* +49 6723 917719 *email:* rmf@rheingau-musik-festival.de. Greg Deninger.

* **Schleswig-Holstein Festival.** Postfach 2655, D-23514 Lübeck, Germany *tel:* +49 451 389570 *fax:* +49 451 3895757. Rolf Beck, director; Christoph Eschenbach, artistic director. *July-August. Classical music.*

* **Schwetzinger Festival.** Postfach 106040, D-70049 Stuttgart, Germany *tel:* +49 711 929 3038/+49 6202 4733 *fax:* +49 711 929 4076. Friedmar Lueke, director; Klaus-Peter Kehr, artistic director. *Annual. April-June. Opera, drama, ballet, concerts.*

Stockstaedter Musiktage. Berlinerstr 65, D-64589 Stockstadt-am-Rhein, Germany *tel:* +49 615 884818 *fax:* +49 615 882926. *2-4 June 2000. Festival mainly celebrating early music, performed on period instruments.*

Summer Academy Johann Sebastian Bach, European Music Festival. Johann-Sebastian-Bach-Pl, D-70178 Stuttgart, Germany *tel:* +49 711 619210 *fax:* +49 711 619 2123 *email:* office@bachakademie.de. Christian Eisert, programme planning; Christa Richter, course office. *Annual. 27 August-10 September 2000. Instrumental works of J S Bach. Courses, lectures and concerts.*

Tage Alter Musik Regensburg. Postfach 100903, D-93009 Regensburg, Germany *tel:* +49 941 52687 *fax:* +49 941 53094 *email:* 100721.2242 @compuserve.com. Ludwig Hartmann, Stephan Schmid. *May. Early music from Middle Ages to early romantic on period instruments. Also big exhibition of early instruments.*

Tage für Neue Musik Stuttgart. Musik der Jahrhunderte, Hasenbergstr 31/2, D-70178 Stuttgart, Germany *tel:* +49 711 629 0510 *fax:* +49 711 629 0515 *email:* mdjstuttgart@csi.com. Christine Fischer, managing director; Hans-Peter Jahn, artistic director. *Annual. February. Contemporary music combined with visual arts, video and performances.*

Wittener Tage fur Neue Kammermusik. Kulturforum Witten, Bergerstr 25, D-58452 Witten, Germany *tel:* +49 230 2581 2427/2424 *fax:* +49 230 2581 2499. *April. New chamber music.*

Greece

* **Athens Festival.** c/o Greek National Tourism Organisation, 1 Voukourestiou Str, GR-10564 Athens, Greece *tel:* +30 1 323 0049 *fax:* +30 1 323 5172. Nikiforos Gegos, director. *Annual. June-September. Orchestral, opera, contemporary music, ballet and theatre.*

Hong Kong

Hong Kong Arts Festival. c/o International Programme Office, 35 Little Russell St, London WC1A 2HH, UK *tel:* +44 20 7637 5661 *fax:* +44 20 7323 1151 *email:* joseph.seelig@easynet.co.uk. Joseph Seelig, international programme consultant. *February-March 2000. Features all types, but mainly classical, world music and jazz.*

Hungary

Bartók International Festival. Interart Festivalcenter, H-1366 Budapest PO Box 80, Hungary *tel:* +36 1 317 9838 *fax:* +36 1 317 9910. Beata Schanda, director; Agnes Szell, secretary, manager. *Annual. 7-20 July 2000. 20th C and contemporary music.*

* **Budapest Autumn Festival.** Rákóczi út 65 Vl 66, H-1081 Budapest, Hungary *tel:* +36 1 210 1249/2795 *fax:* +36 1 210 5906 *email:* budfest@elender.hu. Péter Máté, director. *October. Presenting various music, dance, theatre performances, film screening, fine art, photography and computer art, orchestra and chamber concerts, composer competition, conferences, world and Hungarian premieres. Features independent and experimental artists, events, ideas.*

Budapest Farewell Party. Budapest Festival Center, Rákóczi út 65 Vl 66, H-1081 Budapest, Hungary *tel:* +36 1 133 2337/210 2792 *fax:* +36 1 133 2075 *email:* budfest@elender.hu. Zsófia Zimányi, director. *June. Open air programmes.*

Budapest Spring Festival. Budapest Festivalcenter, Ràkóczi ut 65 VI/66, H-1081 Budapest, Hungary *tel:* +36 1 133 2337/210 2792 *fax:* +36 1 133 2075 *email:* budfest@elender.hu. Zsófia Zimányi, director. *March. Opera, ballet, orchestral concerts, jazz, theatre, open air programmes and* Musica Sacra *and* Musica Antiqua *series.*

Esztergom International Guitar Festival and Seminar. Szendrey-Karper László International, Guitar Festival Foundation, PO Box 8, H-2501 Esztergom, Hungary *fax:* +36 3 341 3808. Istvàn Bàrdos, director. *August. Festival, concerts, master courses, guitar competition, exhibition of instruments (guitar).*

International Kodály Festival. POB 188, H-6001 Kecskemét, Hungary *fax:* +36 7 632 0160 *email:* office@kodaly-inst.hu. Peter Erdei, director. *Biennial. Next 2001. Chamber concerts and recitals, introduction of prize-winning young artists. Work of Kodály and contemporary Hungarian music.*

Kecskemét International Kodály Festival. Interart Festivalcenter, PO Box 80, Vörösmarty tér 1, H-1366 Budapest, Hungary *tel:* +36 1 266 3108/317 9838 *fax:* +36 1 317 9910. Maria Liszkay, manager. *July-August.*

Mini Festival. c/o Hungarian Music Society, H-1025 Budapest, Pusztaszeri út 30, Hungary *tel:* +36 1 325 7313 *also fax.* Agghâzy Eszter (*tel:*+36 1 466 0543), admin; Janos Devich, director. *Annual. January. Contemporary music, Hungarian and 2 days for foreign composers. Works performed by Hungarian musicians.*

Pécs Symphony Orchestra International Music Festival. Király utca 19, H-7621 Pécs, Hungary, Hungary *tel:* +36 7 232 4350 *fax:* +36 7 224 2793. Péter Szkladanyi, director. *June-July. Symphonic music, oratorios, organ, chamber music.*

Zemplén Art Festval. Kiskorona u 7, Óbudai Társaskör, H-1036 Budapest *tel:* +36 1 2500288 *fax:* +36 1 3878376 *email:* gandrasi@c3.hu. János Rolla, director. *18-26 August 2000. Chamber and symphonic music, operetta, folk music, theatre, exhibition.*

Iceland

Dark Music Days. Society of Icelandic Composers, Laufásvegi 4, IS-101 Reykjavik, Iceland *tel:* +354 5 524972 *fax:* +354 5 562 6273 *email:* kjol@ismennt.is. Kjartan Olafsson. *January, May, and October 2000. Icelandic music from the 20th C. In connection with 'Reykjavik - Cultural City of Europe 2000'.*

Reykjavik Arts Festival. Laekjargata 3b, PO Box 88, IS-121 Reykjavik, Iceland *tel:* +354 5 612444 *fax:* +354 5 622350 *email:* artfest@artfest.is. Harpa Björnsdottir, executive director; Sveinn Einarsson, artistic director. *Biennial. Next 20 May-8 June 2000. Mostly classical, but also features modern, pop, jazz and world music. Exhibitions, concerts, opera, dance, theatre.*

Skálholt Music Festival. Strönd, IS-225 Bessastadahreppi, Iceland *fax:* +354 5 652985 *email:* sumartonleikar@kirkjan.is. Helga Ingólfsdóttir, director. *Annual. July-August. Baroque and sacred modern music.*

Republic of Ireland

Cork International Choral Festival. PO Box 68, Cork, Republic of Ireland *tel:* +353 21 308308 *fax:* +353 21 308309 *email:* chorfest@iol.ie. Cynthia Morris. *Annual. 26-30 April 2000, 2-6 May 2001. For amateur choirs. Featuring nightly gala concerts, fringe programme, public performances, church visits and the prestigious Fleischmann International Trophy Competition.*

Dublin International Organ and Choral Festival. Liffey House, Tara St, Dublin 2, Republic of Ireland *tel:* +353 16 773066 ext 416 *fax:* +353 16 798991 *email:* organs@dioef.iol.ie. Gerard Gillen, artistic director. *Triennial. Next June 2002. Organ and choral music including international organ competition. National Symphony Orchestra of Ireland with organ. Recitals, workshops, seminars.*

Kilkenny Arts Festival. 92 High St, Kilkenny, Republic of Ireland *tel:* +353 56 63663 *fax:* +353 56 51704 *email:* kaw@iol.ie. Maureen Kennelly. *11-20 August 2000. Classical music, jazz, visual arts, literature, theatre, and children's events.*

Limerick International Band Festival. Shannon Development, The Granary, Michael St, Limerick, Republic of Ireland *tel:* +353 61 410777 *fax:* +353 61 315634 *email:* bandfest@shannon-dev.ie. Caroline Nolan-Diffley, director; Elenora Hogan, project executive. *18-19 March 2000. Drill and Dance Team Competition; Band Recital Competition; Marching Band Parade.*

Music@Drumcliffe. The Cottage, Drinaghan, Ballintrillick, Co Sligo, Ireland *tel:* +353 71 66420 *fax:* +44 1232 745177 *email:* darraghm @hotmail.com. Darragh Morgan, artistic director. *23 July-13 August 2000 (4 consecutive Sundays). Concert series at The Yeats Church, Co Sligo.*

Waterford International Festival of Light Opera. 60 Morrissons Ave, Waterford, Republic of Ireland *tel:* +353 51 375437. Sean Dower, general secretary; Patrick Giles, chairman. *Annual. 16 September-1 October 2000. Competitive 16-day festival of light opera and musicals by amateur operatic and musical societies from Ireland, UK and Europe.*

West Cork Chamber Music Festival. Durrus, Bantry, Co Cork, Republic of Ireland *tel:* +353 27 61105; Box Office: +353 27 61576 *fax:* +353 27 61485 *email:* coomkeen@tinet.ie. Francis Humphrys, festival director; Christopher Marwood, artistic director; Roisin McGuigan, admin. *25 June-2 July 2000. Chamber music festival with over 30 recitals and concerts; masterclasses, poetry, and visual arts exhibitions.*

Wexford Festival Opera. Theatre Royal, Wexford, Republic of Ireland *tel:* +353 53 22400/22144 (box office) *fax:* +353 53 24289/47438 (box office) *email:* info@wexopera.iol.ie. Luigi Ferrari, artistic director; Jerome Hynes, chief executive; Philomena Keeling, admin. *Annual. October-November. Three productions of rare or neglected operas plus over forty other daytime events.*

Israel

Ein Gev Music Festival. 14940 Kibbutz Ein Gev, Israel *tel:* +972 6 665 8039 *fax:* +972 6 665 8888. David Israel, manager. *April. Popular music and jazz.*

* **Israel Festival, Jerusalem.** Jerusalem Theatre, PO Box 4409, Jerusalem 91044, Israel *tel:* +972 2 561 1438 *fax:* +972 2 566 9850. Yossi Tal-Gan, general director; Micah Lewensohn, artistic director. *Annual. May-June. Opera, symphonic and chamber music, contemporary and early music, recitals, traditional and experimental theatre, classical and contemporary dance, ethnic music, jazz, rock, performance art.*

Red Sea Jazz Festival. 6 Rabin Sq, 64951 Tel Aviv, Israel *tel:* +972 3 695 9355 *fax:* +972 3 696 3528 *email:* eilam@netvision.net.il. Dan Gottfried, artistic director. *Annual. Last week in August. 40 concerts featuring top jazz ensembles, masterclasses and evening sessions.*

Zimriya-World Assembly of Choirs. 4 Aharonowitz St, Tel Aviv 63566, Israel *tel:* +972 3 528 0233 *fax:* +972 3 629 9524 *email:* harzimco @netvision.net.il. Esther Herlitz, director. *Triennial. Next July-August 2001. Choral music workshops and concerts.*

Italy

Animato. Viale Gorizia 24/a, I-00198 Roma, Italy *tel:* +39 06 854 6191 *also fax.* Lucia Ronchetti. *September-December. Contemporary music.*

* **Brescia and Bergamo International Piano Festival (Arturo Benedetti Michelangeli).** Direzione Artistica, c/o Teatro Grande, Via Paganora 19/A, I-25121 Brescia, Italy *tel:* +39 03 029 3022 *fax:* +39 03 024 00771 *email:* festivalpianistico@numerica.it. Agostino Orizio, artistic director. *Annual. 25 April-10 June 2000. Classical piano.*

Cervo and Coldinava Academy International Music Festival. Accademia Ambiente e Turismo, Coldinava-S S 28 km 100, I-18020 Pornassio (Imperia), Italy *tel:* +39 01 833 3017/3196 *fax:* +39 01 833 3193. *August, apply by end of June; fees: 400,000 lire. Masterclass in technical and interpretive elements of universal literature for guitar.*

Corsi di Pefezionomento Estiui. Fondazione Accademia Musicale Chigiana, 89 Via di Città, I-53100 Siena, Italy *tel:* +39 05 774 6152 *fax:* +39 05 772 88124.

Festival di Nuova Consonanza. Associazione Nuova Consonanza, Via Simone de Saint Bon 61, I-00195 Roma, Italy *tel:* +39 06 370 0323 *fax:* +39 06 372 0026. *October-December. Contemporary and electronic music, workshops and concerts.*

Festival Opera Barga. Associazione Culturaale Opera Barga, Via della Fornacetta, 11-55051, I-55051 Barga (Lucca), Italy *tel:* +39 05 8372 3250/601 *fax:* +39 05 8372 3250 *email:* operabarga@mclink.it. Nicholas Hunt, president; Daniela Pisano, musical director. *July-August 2000. Baroque and contemporary opera; concerts for small orchestras and ensembles in 18th C theatre.*

Festival Organistico Internazionale Città di Treviso. Via Canova, 48, I-31100 Treviso, Italy *tel:* +39 04 2254 5895 *also fax.* Riccardo Moscatelli, secretary; Andrea Marcon, artistic director. *September-October. International Organ Academy with seminars, lectures, masterclasses. Mainly early music on ten historical organs inside the city walls.*

Festival Pontino. Viale Le Corbusier 379, I-04100 Latina, Italy *tel:* +39 07 7360 5551 *fax:* +39 07 7360 5548 *email:* campus.musica@panservice.it. Riccardo Cerocchi, manager; Goffredo Petrassi, president; Raffaele Pozzi, artistic director. *June-July 2000. Classical and contemporary, including premieres.*

Festival Pucciniano. Biglietteria del Teatro all'Aperto, Belvedere Puccini n 4, I-55048 Torre del Lago Puccini, Italy *tel:* +39 05 8435 9322 *fax:* +39 05 8435 0277. Balderi Marco, artistic manager; Agostini Grazia, ticket office. *July-August. Opera, concerts, lyrical music.*

Festival Spaziomusica. Spaziomusica, Via Liguria 60, I-09127 Cagliari, Italy *tel:* +39 07 040 0844 *fax:* +39 07 048 5439 *email:* smusica@ tiscalinet.it. Franco Oppo, artistic director; Marcello Pusceddu, president. *November-December 2000. Contemporary music. Member of the European Conference of Promoters of New Music.*

* **Festival della Valle d'Itria.** Centro Artistico Musicale, Palazzo Ducale, I-74015 Martina Franca, Italy *tel:* +39 08 05100/05702 *fax:* +39 080 480 5120. Franco Punzi, president; Sergio Segalini, artistic director. *Annual. July-August. Opera and concerts.*

Gubbio Festival. Pza Oderisi 6, I-06024 Gubbio (PG), Italy *tel:* +39 075 922 0230/0693 *fax:* +39 075 927 3409 *email:* info@gubbiofestival.org. Pavel Vernikov, artistic director; Giovanni Sannipoli, festival supervisor. *Annual. July-August. Masterclasses, concerts, seminars, exhibitions, competition.*

Incontri Europei con la Musica. Associazione Musica Aperta, Via Borgo Palazzo 31, I-24125 Bergamo, Italy *tel:* +39 035 242287 *also fax; email:* mabg@unibg.it. Pieralberto Cattaneo. *February-April 2000. Classical, modern and contemporary chamber music. Member of the European Conference of Promoters of New Music.*

International Choral Festival Verona. Associazione Gruppi Corali, St Porta Palio 54a, I-37122 Verona, Italy *tel:* +39 45 810 3216 *fax:* +39 45 819 8483. Lino Pasetto, chairman; Piero Zamboni, vice-chairman; Paola Castellani Vigano, secretary. *5-8 April 2000. Festival and competition of classical, folk, choral, jazz, and swing.*

* **Maggio Musicale Fiorentino.** Teatro Comunale, Via Solferino 15, I-50123 Firenze, Italy *tel:* +39 05 527791/211158 (tickets) *fax:* +39 055 239 6954/277 9410 (tickets) *email:* sovzun@maggiofiorentino.com; tickets@maggiofiorentino.com. Francesco Ernani, general manager; Cesare Mazzonis, artistic director; Susanna Colombo, press officer. *Annual. May-June. Opera, concerts, ballet, exhibitions, films and meetings.*

Musica 2000 Festival. 75 Via G Bruno, I-60127 Ancona, Italy. Corrado Canonici, artistic director. *September. Contemporary music.*

Musica Attuale. Octandre Musica Attuale, PO Box 259, I-40100 Bologna, Italy *tel:* +39 05 1676 8076 *also fax; email:* octamdre@iperbole.bologna.it. *May-August. Lectures, concerts and seminars on contemporary music.*

Pesaro Spring Festival. Via Ciro Menotti 147, I-61100 Pesaro, Italy *tel:* +39 07 2141 4341 *also fax; email:* musicalibera@abanet.it. Paolo Giaro, artistic director. *Annual. May. Festival held at Teatro Rossini, Pesaro. Contemporary, jazz, ethnic, world and computer music.*

Rassegna di Nuova Musica. CP 92, I-62100 Macerata, Italy *tel:* +39 07 3326 1334 *fax:* +39 07 33 26 1499 *email:* macerataopera@mecurio.it. Stefano Scodanibbio, artistic director; Gianfranco Leli, production director. *September-October. Contemporary music.*

* **Ravenna Festival.** Box Office, Teatro Alighieri, Via Mariani, 2, I-48100 Ravenna, Italy *tel:* +39 0544 32577 *fax:* +39 05 44 215840 *email:* info@ravennafestival.org. Cristina Mazzavillani Muti, president. *July.*

* **Rossini Opera Festival.** Via Rossini 37, I-61100 Pesaro, Italy *tel:* +39 07 213 4473 *fax:* +39 07 21 30979 *email:* rof@rossinioperafestival.it. Gianfranco Mariotti, general manager; Luigi Ferrari, artistic director. *Annual. August. Rossini's operas and concerts.*

* **Settembre Musica.** Citta di Torino, Assessorato per le Risorse Culturali e la Comunicazione, Piazza San Carlo 161, I-10123 Torino, Italy *tel:* +39 01 1442 4715/4703 *fax:* +39 01 14 424738 *email:* settembre.musica @commune.turino.it. Laura Tori, co-ordinator. *Annual. September. Classical, contemporary and ethnic music.*

Settimana Musicale Senese. Fondazione Accademia Musicale Chigiana, Via di Città 89, I-53100 Siena, Italy *tel:* +39 05 774 6152 *fax:* +39 05 77 28 8124. *Annual. August.*

* **Settimane Musicali di Stresa - Festival Internazionale.** Via Ruggero Bonghi 4, I-28838 Stresa, Italy *tel:* +39 03 233 1095/0459 *fax:* +39 03 233 3006. Italo Trentinaglia de Daverio, artistic director. *August-September. Symphony concerts, chamber concerts (quartets, violin, cello, piano and organ recitals).*

* **Verona Festival.** Fondazione Arena di Verona, Piazza Brà 28, I-37121 Verona, Italy *tel:* +39 04 580 51811 *fax:* +39 04 580 11566 *email:* ticket@arena.it. *January-May, July-September.*

Japan

Japan International Youth Musicale in Shizuoka. Tokoha Gakuen Educational Institute, 1 22 1 Sena Shizuoka City, Shizuoka Prefecture 420-0911, Japan *tel:* +81 54 261 1356 *fax:* +81 54 261 5601 *email:* music@unv.tokoha.ac.jp. Tsutomu Asaba, director. *Triennial. Next 16-24 July 2000. Workshops and concerts by ensembles from around the world.*

Kitakyushu International Music Festival. 1-1 Otemachi, Kokurakita-ku, Kitakyushu 803-8510, Japan *tel:* +81 93 582 2391 *fax:* +81 93 581 5755. Nobuyoshi Ishimoto, secretary general. *Annual. 3 weeks in October-November (mainly weekends). Chamber music.*

* **Osaka International Festival Society.** New Asahi Building, 2-3-18 Nakanoshima, Kita-ku, Osaka 530-0005, Japan *tel:* +81 6 6227 1061 *fax:* +81 6 6227 1262 *email:* osakafestival@ma.neweb.ne.jp. Michi Murayama, president. *April 2000. Classical music, concertos, piano recitals and Noh play.*

Pacific Music Festival. Pacific Music Festival Organizing Committee, c/o Sapporo Concert Hall, 1-15, Nakajima-Koen, Chuo-Ku, Sapporo, 064-0931 Japan *tel:* +81 11 520 2222 *fax:* +81 11 520 1687 *email:* pmfoc@hi-ho.ne.jp. Toshiko Shoji, admin. *8-30 July 2000. International educational music festival with orchestral and chamber music course and course for voice and keyboard.*

Tokyo International Chamber Music Festival. c/o Japan International League of Artists, Hidaka Bldg 1-34-8 Shinjuku, Shinjuku-ku, Tokyo, Japan *tel:* +81 3 3356 4033 *fax:* +81 3 3356 5780 *email:* jila@tokyo-cci.or.jp. Kazuhiko Hattori, chairman. *July-August 2000. Contemporary, pop, and Japanese traditional music.*

Latvia

First International Music Industry Forum 'Forte Riga'. International Exhibition Co BT1, 3 Smerla iela 338, LV-1006, Riga, Latvia *tel:* +371 2 520724/529918/529948 *fax:* +371 7 821493/540319/540316 *email:* musicforum@mailbox.riga.lv; bt1@mailbox.riga.lv. Gints Putnins, project director. *Music festival, trade fair and conference.*

Lebanon

* **Al Bustan International Festival of Music and the Arts.** c/o PO Box 343, 56 Gloucester Rd, London SW7 4UB, UK *fax:* 020 7937 2633 *email:* festival@albustan.co.uk. Myrna Bustani, president. *23 February-26 March 2000. Classical music including opera, choral, chamber music and orchestral. Also jazz, dance and oriental music. Beirut address: PO Box 3764, Beirut, Lebanon* tel: *+961 4 972903* fax: *+961 4 871569.*

Lithuania

Baltic Music Festival 'Gaida'. Lithuanian Composers Union, Mickeviciaus 29, 2600 Vilnius, Lithuania *tel:* +370 2 223611 *fax:* +370 2 220939 *email:* center@mipc.vno.osf.lt. Gintaras Sodeika, chairman. *Annual. 20-30 October 2000. Contemporary music from countries surrounding the Baltic Sea.*

Festival of Musical Action. Teatro 10-12, 2009 Vilnius, Lithuania *tel:* +370 9 849020 *fax:* +370 2 791603 *email:* tomas@lithill.lt. Tomas Ziburkus.

Jauna Muzika - New Music Festival. PO Box 2489, 2051 Vilnius, Lithuania *tel:* +370 2 263291/225003 *fax:* +370 2 220939. Remigijus Merkelys, chairman. *April. Lithuanian and foreign composers and musicians. Contemporary music with emphasis on music of young composers.*

Mariu Klavyrai - New Music Festival. Lithuanian Composers' Union (Klaipeda Dept), Taikos 19-36, 5802 Klaipeda, Lithuania *tel:* +370 6 213582 *fax:* +370 6 293643. Oleg Sotnikov, artistic director. *Annual. October. Contemporary music.*

Luxembourg

* **Festival Européen de Wiltz-Luxembourg.** Château de Wiltz, L-9516 Wiltz, Luxembourg *tel:* +352 958145 *fax:* +352 958190; +352 959310. Fernand Koenig, artistic director. *July. Classical, opera, drama, ballet, jazz.*

* **Festival International Echternach.** BP 30, L-6401 Echternach, Luxembourg *tel:* +352 728347 *fax:* +352 727112 *email:* musique@pt.lu. Mariette Scholtes, administrative director; Cyprien Katsaris, artistic director. *Annual. May-June 2000. Mainly classical (symphonic, chamber, choral).*

ISCM World Music Days 2000 - Luxembourg. ISCM Luxembourg Section, LGNM, Case Postale 828, L-2018 Luxembourg *tel:* +352 225821 *fax:* +352 225823 *email:* lgnm@lgnm.lu. Marcel Wengler, artistic director. *29 September-8 October 2000. Focus on contemporary music. Also sound installations, video-art, music and film installations and exhibitions will be on show.*

Macedonia

Balkanski Festival Na Narodni Pesni i Igri. Makedonski Prosvetiteli 4, PO Box 94, 96000 Ohrid, Macedonia *tel:* +389 96 263433 *fax:* +389 96 261063; +389 96 32 380. Dragica Siljanoska, manager. *5-10 July 2000. Folk music and dance.*

* **Ohrid Summer Festival.** PO Box 23, 96000 Ohrid, Macedonia *tel:* +389 96 21304/22304 *fax:* +389 96 21133. Vasko Zorovski, programme director. *Jul-Aug. Classical music, early music and renaissance. Orchestras, opera, ballet, chamber music, recitals, theatre.*

Mexico

* **Festival Internacional Cervantino.** Av Alvaro Obregon 273, Col Roma Norte, 06700 Mexico City, Mexico *tel:* +52 5 207 4764 *fax:* +52 5 533 4122 *email:* cofic@rtn.net.mx. Sergio Vela, general director; María González, programming director. *4-22 October 2000. Traditional, fine and contemporary art: dance, opera, music and theatre, academic activities, film cycles and art exhibitions.*

Festival de Música de Cámara de San Miguel de Allende. Bellas Artes, Calle Hernández Macias 75, San Miguel de Allende, Mexico *tel:* +52 415 20936 *fax:* +52 415 20289 *email:* ufartha@atlasinc.on.ca. Carmen Masip de Hawkins, Tom Sawyer, co-directors. *July- August. Classical and chamber music. Masterclasses and ensemble coaching for scholarship students.*

Monaco

* **Printemps des Arts de Monte-Carlo.** 4 Bd des Moulins, MC-98000 (Principauté), Monaco *tel:* +377 93 15 83 03 *fax:* +377 93 50 66 94. Rainier Rocchi. *Annual. April-May. Ballet, vocal recitals, choral music, orchestral, chamber and opera.*

Netherlands

Delft Festival of Chamber Music. PO Box 404, nl-2260 AK Leidschendam, Netherlands *tel:* +31 70 320 2500 *fax:* +31 70 320 2611. Isabelle van Keulen, artistic director. *Annual. August. Chamber music.*

Donemus Foundation - Dutch Music Days. Paulus Potterstraat 16, NL-1017 CZ Amsterdam, Netherlands *tel:* +31 20 676 4436 *fax:* +31 20 673 3588 *email:* donemus@wxs.nl. L J Deuss, manager. *Early December. Dutch, mainly contemporary music.*

Festival on Spiritualism in Contemporary Music/Requiem for a Millennium. Gaudeamus Foundation Contemporary Music Centre, Swammerdamstraat 38, NL-1091 RV, Amsterdam, Netherlands *tel:* +31 20 694 7349 *fax:* +31 20 694 7258 *email:* gaud@xs4all.nl. Arthur van der Drift, Michael van Eekeren. *November.*

Haarlem International Organ Festival. PO Box 3333, NL-2011 DH Haarlem, Netherlands *tel:* +31 23 160574 *fax:* +31 23 160576. Mrs E L S Hendrikse, secretary. *July. Various recitals (organ, choir, instrumental).*

* **Holland Festival.** Kleine-Gartmanplantsoen 21, NL-1017 RP Amsterdam, Netherlands *tel:* +31 20 530 7110 *fax:* +31 20 530 7119 *email:* info @hollandfestival.nl. Juo van Hove, festival director; Jacques van Veen, managing director. *Annual. June. Opera, music theatre and dance.*

* **Holland Festival Early Music Utrecht.** Organisatie Oude Muziek, PO Box 734, NL-3500 AS Utrecht, Netherlands *tel:* +31 30 236 2236 *fax:* +31 30 232 2798 *email:* oom@oudemuziek.nl. Casper Vogel, executive manager; Tineke de Ruiter, production manager. *Annual. August-September. Over 100 concerts, lectures, workshops, masterclasses, exhibitions, information market. Repertoire covers last ten centuries, mainly performed on authentic period instruments or copies.*

International Choir Festival - Arnhem. Stichting SNK, Plompetorengracht 3, NL-3512 CA Utrecht, Netherlands *tel:* +31 30 231 3174 *fax:* +31 30 231 8137 *email:* snk@euronet.nl. Joseph Vranken Jr, music director. *Quadrennial. Next 28 Jun-5 July 2001. All types of choral music.*

International Gaudeaumus Music Week, Amsterdam. Gaudeamus Foundation, Swammerdamstraat 38, NL-1091 RV Amsterdam, Netherlands *tel:* +31 20 694 7349 *fax:* +31 20 694 7258 *email:* gaud@xs4all.nl. H Heuvelmans, director. *Annual. 1-9 September 2000. Amsterdam. Contemporary music. Performances of works by winners of the International Gaudeaumus Composers' Competition Prize (see* **Competitions**). *An international selection of c 40 works in very different musical styles by composers aged 30 and under.*

International Society for Contemporary Music. c/o Gaudeamus, Swammerdamstraat 38, NL-1091 RV Amsterdam, Netherlands *tel:* +31 20 694 7349 *fax:* +31 20 694 7258 *email:* iscm@xs4all.nl. H Heuvelmans, secretary general. *World Music Days 29 September-8 October 2000 in Luxembourg. Contemporary music concerts.*

Orlando Chamber Music Festival. Keizersgracht 261, NL-1016 EC Amsterdam, Netherlands *tel:* +31 20 623 0469 *fax:* +31 20 622 9081. Isabelle Bensa, director. *30 July-13 August 2000. Chamber music concerts, masterclasses, students academy. Youth orchestra.*

North Korea

The April Spring Friendship Art Festival. Pyongyang International Culture Centre, Yonggwang St, Ryonhwa Dong, Central District, Pyongyang City, DPR Korea *tel:* +850 2 381 8653 *fax:* +850 2 381 4777/2100. Jang Chol, president, organising committee. *10-18 April 2000. Open to vocal and instrumental soloists and ensembles as well as professional art troupes, dancers and acrobats.*

Norway

* **Bergen International Festival.** PO Box 183, N-5001 Bergen, Norway *tel:* +47 55 210630 *fax:* +47 55 210640 *email:* info@fib.no. Bergljót Jónsdóttir, festival director. *Annual. May. Music, ballet, dance theatre, classical concerts at the homes of Edvard Grieg, Ole Bull and Harald Saeverud.*

Førde Folk Music Festival. PO Box 395, N-6801 Førde, Norway *tel:* +47 57 721940 *fax:* +47 57 721941 *email:* fordefolk@prodat.no. Hilde Bjørkum, festival director. *6-9 July 2000. Folk music from all over the world. Concerts, workshops, exhibitions, children's events.*

Ilios Festival for Contemporary Music. NY Musik, Nord-Norge, Box 244, N-9401 Harstad, Norway *tel:* +47 77 066047 *also fax.* John Lien, festival director. *February.*

International Biennale of Contemporary Arts. Stavanger Speculum, Sandvigõ 27, N-4007 Stavanger, Norway *tel:* +47 51 846676 *fax:* +47 51 846673. *November. Thematic multimedia festival of contemporary arts including music, dance, theatre, exhibitions, film and conferences.*

* **International Chamber Music Festival, Stavanger.** Sandvigå 27, N-4007 Stavanger, Norway *tel:* +47 51 846670 *fax:* +47 51 846673 *email:* icmf@online.no. Sine Bjørnevik, deputy manager. *Annual. 11-20 August 2000. Chamber music.*

International Church Music Festival. Kristiansand Domkirke, PO Box 321, N-4663 Kristiansand, Norway *tel:* +47 38 120940 *fax:* +47 38 120949 *email:* intkirke@online.no. Andrew Wilder, cathedral organist, artistic director; Nina Schei Ledang, admin. *Annual. 9-17 May 2000. Church music, organ music, chamber music, vocal and instrumental soloists, folk music, art exhibitions, seminars.*

Lillehammer Winter Festival. PO Box 696, N-2601 Lillehammer, Norway *tel:* +47 61 279700 *fax:* +47 61 279701 *email:* kalas@online.no. Olemìc Thomessen, director; Jorgen Damskau, project leader, technics and music. *February. International arts festival with music of all genres, theatre, children's Olympics, snow sculpture, outdoor winter activities and exhibitions of arts and handicrafts.*

Music Factory. Grieghallen, Edvard Griegs Plass 1, N-5015 Bergen, Norway *tel:* +47 55 216120 *fax:* +47 55 216121 *email:* mfactory @bgnett.no. James Clapperton, artistic director. *20-31 May 2000. Approx 12 contemporary music concerts in Bergen. Also dance and opera. Masterclass in composition.*

Nordland Music Festival. PO Box 319, N-8001 Bodo, Norway *tel:* +47 75 522398 *fax:* +47 75 522387. Roar Leinan, director. *July-August. Classical, jazz, rock.*

Nordlyd - Trondheim Contemporary Music Festival. Mellomer 10, N-7042 Trondheim, Norway *tel:* +47 73 524551 *email:* arnujaha @online.no. Arnulf Johansen. *November. Contemporary music.*

North Norway Festival. PO Box 901, N-9401 Harstad, Norway *tel:* +47 77 066599 *fax:* +47 77 067363. *June. Concerts, theatre, dance, art exhibitions, literature and film, seminars and children's festival.*

Oslo Chamber Music Festival. Grev Wedels Plass 2, N-0151 Oslo, Norway *tel:* +47 23 100730 *fax:* +47 23 100731 *email:* kammermusikkfestival@oslo.online.no. *August.*

Peer Gynt Festival. Turist-og Messekontoret, Nedregt 5A, N-2640 Vinstra, Norway *tel:* +47 61 294770 *fax:* +47 61 294771 *email:* peergynt@online.no. Stig R Nyhus, admin. *July-August. Theatre and music festival.*

St Olav Festival of Trondheim. PO Box 2045, N-7001 Trondheim, Norway *tel:* +47 73 929470 *fax:* +47 73 503866. Per Kuistad Uddu, director. *July-August. Church services, concerts, lectures, guided tours, exhibitions, activities for children, chamber music courses and projects in early music.*

Ultima Oslo Contemporary Music Festival. Tollbugt 28, N-0157 Oslo, Norway *tel:* +47 22 429999 *fax:* +47 22 424218 *email:* ultima@notam.uio.no. Ase Hedstrom, festival director; Beate Styri, PR; Howard Gamble, executive director. *Annual. October. Contemporary music, including concerts and performances, sound-installations, multimedia concerts, films, educational arrangements and seminars.*

Vestfold International Festival. PO Box 500, N-3101 Tonsberg, Norway *tel:* +47 33 308850 *fax:* +47 33 308860 *email:* info@vestfoldfest.no. Birger Carlsen, director. *29 June-9 July 2000.*

Poland

Baroque Opera Festival in Warsaw. Warsaw Chamber Opera, Ul Nowogrodzka 49, PL-00695 Warszawa, Poland *tel:* +48 82 628 3096; +48 2 229 3233 *fax:* +48 2 229 3233; +48 2 231 4764. Stefan Sutkowski, artistic director. *Annual. October.*

Days of Organ Music Kraków. c/o State Philharmonic Orchestra Karol Szymanowski, Zwierzyniecka 1, PL 31-103 Kraków, Poland *tel:* +48 12 422 0958 *also fax; fax:* +48 12 422 4312. Jacek Berwaldt, programme deputy head. *17-25 March 2000. Organ recitals, oratorio concerts (Bach anniversary).*

Miedzyzdroje International Choral Song Festival. c/o Rondo Concert Agency, PO Box 77, PL-70334 Szczecin 4, Poland *tel:* +48 91 484 5242 *fax:* +48 91 484 6193 *email:* rondo@ubique.com.pl. Stanislaw Zaborowski, managing director. *June. Choral songs.*

Monteverdi's Opera Festival. Warsaw Chamber Opera, Ul Nowogrodzka 49, PL-00695 Warszawa, Poland *tel:* +48 82 628 3096/629 3233 *fax:* +48 82 629 3233. Stefan Sutkowski, artistic director. *Annual. October. All Monteverdi's stage works.*

The Mozart Festival in Warsaw. Warsaw Chamber Opera, ul Nowogrodzka 49, PL-00695 Warszawa, Poland *tel:* +48 82 628 3096; +48 22 293233 *also fax; fax:* +48 22 314764. Stefan Sutkowski, artistic director. *15 June-26 July annually. Features all Mozart's stage works (24 productions) and a selection of his concert music.*

Music in Old Cracow. Ul Zwierzyniecka 1, PL-31103 Kraków, Poland *tel:* +48 12 421 4566/429 4328 *fax:* +48 12 421 9660 *email:* capellac@ispid.com.pl. Stanislaw Galonski, director. *August. Symphonic, vocal, chamber music, recitals.*

Warsaw Autumn (International Festival of Contemporary Music). c/o Polish Composers' Union, Rynek Starego Miasta 27, PL-00272 Warszawa, Poland *tel:* +48 22 831 1634; +48 22 831 0607 *also fax; email:* festival@warsaw-autumn.waw.pl. Tadeusz Wielecki, director. *Annual. 15-23 September 2000. Contemporary music; symphony and chamber music, solo recitals, electronic and computer music, multimedia project.*

Portugal

* **Estoril Music Festival.** Casa dos Arcos, Estrada Marginal, P-2775 Parede, Portugal *tel:* +351 1 468 5199 *fax:* +351 1 468 5607 *email:* festivaldoestoril@mail.telepac.pt. Piñeiro Nagy, artistic director. *July-August 2000. Symphonic, chamber, recitals, ballet, traditional music from Far East. Theme: 500th Anniversary of Discovery of Brazil.*

Festival Internacional de Música da Póvoa de Varzim. Rua D. Maria I 56, P-4490 Póvoa de Varzim, Portugal *tel:* +351 5 261 4145 *fax:* +351 5 261 2548. J Marques, director. *July 2000. Medieval, renaissance, baroque, classical, romantic, and contemporary music.*

Gulbenkian Contemporary Music Encounters. Calouste Gulbenkian Foundation, Ave de Berna, 45 A, P-1067 Lisboa Codex, Portugal *tel:* +351 1 793 5131 *fax:* +351 1 793 7296 *email:* musica@gulbenkian.pt. Luís Pereira Leal, director; Carlos de Pontes Leca, assistant director. *May. Contemporary music festival often featuring compositions of participating composers.*

Sintra Music Festival. Praça da República 23, P-2710 Sintra, Portugal *tel:* +351 9 234895/243518 *fax:* +351 9 234845. Luís Pereira Leal, director; Ana Alcântara, co-ordinator. *June-July. Classical music in the Sintra Palaces or 'Quintas'.*

Puerto Rico

Festival Casals de Puerto Rico. PO Box 41277, Minillas Sta, San Juan, Puerto Rico *tel:* +787 728 5744 *fax:* +787 723 5843. Krzysztof Penderecki, music director. *June. Symphonic and chamber music.*

Romania

Cluj Modern. Academia de Muzica 'Georghe Dima', Str IC Bratianu nr 25, 3400 Cluj-Napoca, Romania *tel:* +40 6 419 3879 *also fax; email:* amgd@amgd.edu.soroscj.ro. *Biennial. Next 1-6 April 2001. Contemporary music.*

* **George Enescu International Festival.** Artexim, Calea Victoriei nr 155, bl D1 sc 8 et 2, 71012 Bucharest, Romania *tel:* +40 1 650 1806/12 *fax:* +40 1 311 0200 *email:* artexim@com.pcnet.ro. Lawrence Foster, artistic director, Mihai Constantinescu, organiser. *September. Classical music, concert recitals, opera, ballet.*

Russia

Autumn Constellation Festival of Organ Music. Chmelnitzckogo 61-A, 236039 Kaliningrad, Russia *tel:* +7 0112 443451 *fax:* +7 0112 444546. Valeri Aliev, director. *October. Organ music.*

Moscow Conservatory International Summer Music Festival. c/o 41 Ashen Grove, London SW19 8BL, UK *tel:* +44 20 8947 7201 *also fax.* Niel Immelman. *August. For piano, voice and all orchestral instruments. Daily recitals by Moscow Conservatory professors and winners of international competitions.*

Rakhmaninov Festival. Berzhavinskya 5, 392000 Tambov, Russia *tel:* +7 752 221664/1 *fax:* +7 752 222 3009. Aleksey Trunin, director of Tambor Phylarmony. *May-June. Symphonic, chamber music.*

Sviatoslav Richter's December Nights. Volkonkha 12, 121019 Moscow, Russia *tel:* +7 095 202 2464/203 6974 *fax:* +7 095 203 4674. Inna Pruss, co-ordinator, executive director. *December. Chamber music of Schubert, Brahms and Mendelssohn, also includes oratorios, masses and chamber operas.*

Serbia

Belgrade Music Festival (BEMUS). Jugokoncert, Terazije 41/I, 11000 Belgrade, Serbia *tel:* +381 11 323 9917 *fax:* +381 11 324 0478. Eduard Ile, general director. *Annual. October.*

Singapore

Singapore Arts Festival. Festival Secretariat, National Arts Council, 35th Storey, PSA Building, 460 Alexandra Rd, 119963, Singapore *tel:* +65 270 0722 *fax:* +65 273 6880 *email:* nac_foac@nac.gov.sg. Liew Chin Choy, director (artistic programmes). *Biennial. Next 2001. Traditional, classical and contemporary music, drama and theatre.*

Slovak Republic

Expo Music. Incheba J S C, Viedenská cesta 7, 852 51 Bratislava, Slovak Republic *tel:* +421 7 6727 2206 *fax:* +421 7 6727 2201 *email:* sskovajsova@incheba.sk; incheba@incheba.sk. Sona Skovajsova, exhibition manager.

Melos-Ethos International Festival of Contemporary Music. Michalská 10, 815 36 Bratislava, Slovak Republic *tel:* +421 7 5443 1373 *also fax; email:* slovkonc@mbox.bts.sk. Slávka Ferencová, general secretary. *Biennial. Next 2001. Contemporary music concerts and seminars.*

Schlossfestspiele In Zvolen. Jozef Gregor Tajovsky-Theater, Divadelná 3, 960 77 Zvolen, Slovak Republic *tel:* +421 8 552 9698/ 331791 *also fax;* +42 855 331781. Juraj Sarvas, festival director. *June-July. Opera, poetic dance, theatre.*

Slovenia

Festival Brezice. c/o Ars Ramovs Institute of Arts, Marketing, Promotion and Investment, Slovenska cesta 1, 1000 Ljubljana, Slovenia *tel:* +386 61 125 3366 *fax:* +386 61 174 1541 *email:* BreziceFestival@k-ramovs.si. Klemen Ramovs. *July-August. Medieval and baroque music.*

* **International Summer Festival Ljubljana.** Trg Francoske Revolucije 1-2, 1000 Ljubljana, Slovenia *tel:* +386 61 126 4340 *fax:* +386 61 221288 *email:* info@festival-lj.si. Darko Brlek, director. *Annual. June-August. Music (classical, jazz, pop, ethno), dance, theatre, and also music workshops and artistic communion.*

South Africa

Spier Festival. PO Box 16645, Vlaeberg 8018, South Africa *tel:* +27 21 423 3351 *fax:* +27 21 423 0742 *email:* spier@iafrica.com. Brad Jarrett, festival director; Alexanne Tingley, artistic administrator. *Annual. November-March. All genres of music and theatre. Opera season in February.*

Spain

* **Barcelona Summer Festival Grec.** Institut de Cultura de Barcelona, La Rambla 99, E-08002 Barcelona, Spain *tel:* +34 93 301 7775 *fax:* +34 93 301 6100. Ferran Mascarell, general manager; Xavier Alberti, artistic director. *Annual. Classical, flamenco and rock music.*

Contemporary Music Festival of Valencia - ENSEMS. c/Bilbao, 18-5°-9, E-46009 Valencia, Spain *tel:* +34 96 366 1957 *fax:* +34 96 366 1938. Joan Cerveró, artistic director. *May 2000. Contemporary music. Conferences, composers, meetings, installations, etc.*

* **Cuenca Religious Music Festival.** Semanas de Música Religiosa, Apartado 97, E-16080 Cuenca, Spain *tel:* +34 96 917 8857 *also fax; email:* aef@vtx.ch. Ignacio Yepes, music director; Ismael Barambio, executive director. *16-23 April 2000. All types of sacred music.*

Festival de Cadaqués. Arcs 8 1er 2a, E-08002 Barcelona, Spain *tel:* +34 93 301 9555 *fax:* +34 93 302 2670 *email:* trito@bcn.servicom.es. Llorenç Caballero, director. *23 July-15 August 2000. Symphonic and chamber music. Resident orchestra.*

* **Festival Internacional de Música de Torroella de Montgrí.** Apartat 70, E-17257 Torroella de Montgrí, Spain *tel:* +34 97 276 0605 *fax:* +34 97 276 0648 *email:* jjmmtdm@ddgi.es. *Annual. July-August. Orchestral, chamber, vocal, choral and instrumental.*

Festival de Música de Canarias. SOCAEM, S A, León y Castillo, 427-3, E-35007 Las Palmas de Gran Canaria, Spain *tel:* +34 92 824 7442/3 *fax:* +34 92 827 6042 *email:* festival@socaem.com. Rafael Nebot, director; Nora Krozewski, festival secretary. *Annual. 7 January-2 March 2000. Classical and contemporary chamber music concerts and recitals including premieres of works commissioned by the festival. On Gran Canaria, Tenerife and throughout the Canary Islands.*

Festival de Otono de la Comunidad de Madrid. Plaza de Espand 8, E-28008 Madrid, Spain *tel:* +34 91 580 2575/7 *fax:* +34 91 580 2565. Agustín Tend, director. *September-November. Performing arts, contemporary and traditional music.*

* **Granada International Festival of Music and Dance.** Auditorio Manuel de Falla, Paseo de los Mártires s/n, E-18009 Granada, Spain *tel:* +34 95 822 1844 *fax:* +34 95 822 0691 *email:* granadafestival@tsai.es. Maricarmen Palma, admin director. *Annual. June-July. Classical music, recitals, opera, ballet.*

International Festival of Contemporary Music. Centro para la Difusión de la Música Contemporánea, Santa Isabel 52, E-28012 Madrid, Spain *tel:* +34 91 468 2310 *fax:* +34 91 530 8321 *email:* consuelo.diez@cdmc.inaem.es. Consuelo Diez, CDMC director. *Alicante. September 2000. Contemporary Spanish music. Forum for information and exchange on music from around the world.*

International Festival of Primavera Andres Segovia. C/ Fuerte de Navidad 32-6d, E-28004 Madrid, Spain *tel:* +34 91 705 1112 *also fax.* Pablo de la Cruz, artistic director. *Annual. 6-30 May 2000. Guitar in orchestra, chamber and early music. Dedicated to the memory of Andres Segovia.*

International Guitar Festival. Ayuntamiento de Benicasim, E-12560 Benicasim (Castellon), Spain *tel:* +34 96 430 0962 *fax:* +34 96 430 3432 *email:* benicassim@gua.es. Sr Alcolde, president. *August-September. Classical guitar.*

Jornadas de Informatica y Electronica Musical. CDMC, Centro de Arte Reina Sofia, Santa Isabel 52, E-28012 Madrid, Spain *tel:* +34 91 468 2310/2931 *fax:* +34 91 530 8321 *email:* adolfo.nunez@cdmc.inaem.es. Adolfo Nunez, LIEM-CDMC director; Consuelo Diéz, CDMC director. *June-July 2000. Electro-acoustic, contemporary, electronic and computer music. Multimedia and seminars.*

* **Quincena Musical/Musika Hamabostaldia.** Reina Regente 9, E-20003 San Sebastian, Spain *tel:* +34 94 348 1238/9 *fax:* +34 94 343 0702 *email:* udala_quincena@donostia.org. José Antonio Echenique, director. *Annual. August. Opera, ballet, early music, chamber music, contemporary music, symphonic, organ, recitals.*

* **Santander International Festival.** Palacio De Festivales de Cantabria, C/Gamazo s/n, E-39004 Santander, Cantabria, Spain *tel:* +34 94 221 0508 *fax:* +34 94 231 4767 *email:* f_i_santander@mundivia.es. José Luis Ocejo, director. *Annual. August. Over 60 programmed activities. Classical, contemporary, chamber, opera, concert and recital. Classical and contemporary ballet and theatre. Held in Festival Hall of Santander and historical sites throughout the region.*

* **Torroella de Montgri International Music Festival.** Apartat de Correus 70, E-17257 Torroella de Montgri, Spain *tel:* +34 97 276 1098 *fax:* +34 97 276 0648 *email:* jjmmtdm@ddgi.es. *June-August. Orch and chamber music, ethnic music and jazz.*

Sweden

* **Drottningholms Slottsteater Festival.** PO Box 27050, S-10251 Stockholm, Sweden *tel:* +46 8 665 1400 *fax:* +46 8 665 1473. Per Forsstrom, general manager; Per-Erik Óhrn, artistic director. *Annual. Late May to early September. 17th and 18th C opera and ballet (period productions).*

Festival of Electronic Music. EMS Swedish Broadcasting, Svenska Rikskonserter, Soder Malarstrand 61, S-11825 Stockholm, Sweden *tel:* +46 8 658 1990 *fax:* +46 8 658 6909 *email:* ems@ems.srk.se. Ulf Stenberg, director. *November. Electro-acoustic music.*

Göteborg International Organ Academy. Musikhögskolan, Box 210, S-405 30 Göteborg, Sweden *tel:* +46 31 773 52 06/11 *fax:* +46 31 773 52 00 *email:* organ.academy@musik.gu.se. *Biennial festival. Next 7-18 August 2000. Includes concerts, workshops, seminars, lectures, discussions and services.*

Music Festival of Piteå. The Academy of Framnäs, S-943 33 Öjebyn, Sweden *tel:* +46 9 119 6816 *fax:* +46 9 119 6828 *email:* sven-erik.sandlund@mh.luth.se. Ulla-Britt Sandlund. *June-July. Masterclasses.*

Örebro Chamber Music Festival. Solbergavägen 6A, S-71930 Vintrosa, Sweden *tel:* +46 1 929 4927 *fax:* +46 1 929 4997 *email:* orefestspel@swipnet.se. Paul Morgan, chairman. *Annual. August. Instrumental and vocal chamber music with international artists.*

Stockholm International Composer Festival. Stockholm Concert Hall, PO Box 7083, SE-10387 Stockholm, Sweden *tel:* +46 8 786 0200 *fax:* +46 8 200548. Mats Engström, planning manager; Åse Hedström, executive and artistic director.

Stockholm New Music. c/o The Swedish Concert Institute, PO Box 1225, S-111 82 Stockholm, Sweden *tel:* +46 8 791 4600 *fax:* +46 8 676 0018. Martin Martinsson, director; Christina Falk, festival co-ordinator. *Triennial. Next 2002. Festival of contemporary music.*

Vadstena Opera Festival. Bergsgatan 57, S-11231 Stockholm, Sweden *tel:* +46 8 652 6180 *fax:* +48 8 650 8230 *email:* info@vadstena-akademien.org. Anders Wiklund, artistic leader. *July-August 2000. Rare early operas, newly commissioned works and concerts in historic setting of Vadstena's medieval town.*

Switzerland

* **Easter Festival Lucerne.** Hirschmattstr 13, CH-6002 Lucerne, Switzerland *tel:* +41 41 226 4400 *fax:* +41 41 226 4460 *email:* media@LucerneMusic.ch. Michael Haefliger, director; Martin Elbel, communications; Toni J Krein, artistic manager. *March. Classical, sacred and choral music.*

Festival Archipel. 8, Rue de la Coulouvrenière, CH-1204 Genève, Switzerland *tel:* +41 22 329 4242 *fax:* +41 22 329 6868. Jean Prévost, artistic director. *March.*

Fribourg Festival of Sacred Music. CP 292, CH-1701 Fribourg, Switzerland *tel:* +41 26 322 4800 *fax:* +41 26 322 8331 *email:* sacredmusicfr@pihgnet.ch. Nicole Renevey, admin. *Biennial. Next 7-16 July 2000. 12 concerts of early music, medieval, renaissance, baroque, romantic, contemporary. Gregorian chant workshop. Extra-European music concerts. Lectures/interpretation courses.*

* **International Festival of Musique et d'Art Lyrique.** Rue du Théâtre 5, Case Postal 353, CH-1820 Montreux 2, Switzerland *tel:* +41 21 966 8020 *fax:* +41 21 963 2506 *email:* courrier@montreux-festival.com. Christian Chorier, director. *Opera, concerts, recital, baroque music.*

* **International Festival of Music Lucerne.** Hirschmattstr 13, CH-6002 Lucerne, Switzerland *tel:* +41 41 226 4480 *fax:* +41 41 226 4485 *email:* lucernemusic@lucernemusic.ch. Michael Haefliger, director; Martin Elbel, communications; Toni J Krein, art manager. *19 August-16 September 2000. Classical music festival with symphony concerts, chamber music, recitals, choral concerts, serenades, musica nova, composer-in-residence.*

Lucerne Easter Festival. c/o International Festival of Music Lucerne, Hirschmattstr 13, CH-6002 Lucerne, Switzerland *tel:* +41 41 226 4480 *fax:* +41 41 226 4485 *email:* lucernemusic@lucernemusic.ch.

* **Lucerne Piano Festival.** c/o International Festival of Music Lucerne, Hirschmattstr 13, CH-6002 Lucerne, Switzerland *tel:* +41 41 226 4480 *fax:* +41 41 226 4485 *email:* lucernemusic@lucernemusic.ch. Michael Haefliger, director; Martin Elbel, communications; Toni J Krein, art manager. *November 2000. Six piano recitals, accompanying arts programmes.*

Montreux Choral Festival. PO Box 125, CH-1820 Territet-Montreux, Switzerland *tel:* +41 21 966 5555 *fax:* +41 21 966 5569 *email:* montreuxchoralfestival@bluewin.ch. Marcel Baudet, president; Claude Gaulis, communication. *26-30 April 2000. Includes choral work competition and concerts.*

* **Musiksommer Gstaad-Saanenland.** Postfach 382, CH-3780 Gstaad, Switzerland *tel:* +41 33 748 8338 *fax:* +41 33 748 8339 *email:* musiksommer@gstaad.ch. Gidon Kremer, artistic director; Hans-Ueli Tschanz, director. *Annual. July-September. Chamber music, orchestral music, recitals, quartets.*

Sion Summer Music Academy. Académie de Musique de Sion, CP 954, CH-1951 Sion, Switzerland *tel:* +41 27 322 6652 *fax:* +41 27 323 4662 *email:* festivargasion@vtx.ch. Liliane Martin. *July-August.*

Tibor Varga Festival. PO Box 954, CH-1951 Sion, Switzerland *tel:* +41 27 323 4317 *fax:* +41 27 323 4662 *email:* festivargasion@vtx.ch. Gillioz Pierre, director. *Annual. 21 July-14 September 2000. 30 concerts and open-air productions.*

* **Verbier Festival and Academy.** 4 Rue Jean-Jacques Rousseau, CH-1800 Vevey, Switzerland *tel:* +41 21 922 4010 *fax:* +41 21 922 4012 *email:* verbierfestival@music.ch. Martin T:son Engstroem, executive director; Avi Shoshani, artistic director; Miguel Esteban, admin. *Annual. July-August. A summer performing arts community includes symphony, chamber music, recitals, conferences, contemporary theatre and dance.*

Thailand

Thailand Festival of the Arts by Volvo. Asia Music International Ltd, 301-3 Sukhumuit 31, Bangkok 10110, Thailand *tel:* +66 2 662 1836 *fax:* +66 2 258 8156 *email:* huckye@mozart.inet.co.th. Hucky Eichelmann, director; Manatsanan Viengpetchthong, assistant. *Annual. January-February. Classical, jazz, ethnic and cross-cultural music and dance.*

Turkey

* **International Ankara Music Festival.** SCA Music Foundation, Tunali Hilmi Cad 114/43, TR-06680 Ankara, Turkey *tel:* +90 312 427 0855 *fax:* +90 312 467 3159 *email:* scavakfi@ada.com.tr. Mehmet A Basman, president; Elif Mülayim Basman, co-ordinator. *24 April-18 May 2000. Classical music, ballet, jazz.*

* **International Istanbul Music Festival.** Istanbul Foundation for Culture and Arts, Istiklal Caddesi 146 Luvr Apt, Beyoglu, TR-80070 Istanbul, Turkey *tel:* +90 212 251 0541 *fax:* +90 212 249 5667 *email:* music.fest@istfest-tr.org. Cevza Aktüze, director; Ahmet Erenli, assistant director. *Annual. 8 June-2 July 2000. Orchestra, chamber, recitals, vocal, opera, dance, traditional music, young soloists.*

USA

American Landmark Festivals. Federal Hall National Memorial, 26 Wall St, New York, NY 10005, USA *tel:* +1 212 866 2086 *fax:* +1 212 825 6874/864 1665. Francis Heilbut, artistic director. *Regular recitals and concerts presented throughout the year at historic sites in New York.*

Amherst Early Music Festival. 65 West 95th St, #1a, New York, NY 10025, USA *tel:* +1 212 222 3351 *fax:* +1 212 222 1898 *email:* amherst@compuserve.com. Valerie Horst.

Artpark. Box 371, Lewiston, NY 14092, USA *tel:* +1 716 754 9000 *fax:* +1 716 754 2741. David Grapes, executive director. *July-September. Summer festival featuring a wide range of music from classical to popular, dance, opera, jazz, ethnic and music theatre.*

Aspen Music Festival. 2 Music School Rd, Aspen, CO 81611, USA *tel:* +1 970 925 3254 *fax:* +1 970 925 3802 *email:* festival@aspenmusic.org. Robert Harth, president; Edward Sweeney, general manager, CEO; David Zinman, music director. *Annual. 22 June-20 August 2000. Orchestral, chamber music, opera.*

Bellingham Festival of Music. 1300 North State St, Suite 202, Bellingham, WA 98225, USA *tel:* +1 800 335 5550; +1 360 676 5997 *fax:* +1 360 647 3521 *email:* info@bellinghamfestival.org. Andrew Moquin, president. *30 July-13 August 2000. Theme: 'Beethoven in Bellingham'. Chamber music, symphony concerts, recitals; jazz.*

The Berkeley Festival and Exhibition. 101 Zellerbach Hall, University of California, Berkeley, CA 94720, USA *tel:* +1 510 642 0212 *fax:* +1 510 643 6707. Robert Cole, director; Laura Abrams, festival admin; Jean Catino, PR manager; Mary Dixon, director of marketing. *4-11 June 2000. 'Largest early music festival in North America'.*

BONK Festival of New Music. 215 1-2 Comanche Ave, Tampa, Florida 33604, USA *tel:* +1 813 930 8440 *fax:* +1 941 359 4479 *email:* info@bonkfest.org; submissions@bonkfest.org. Robert Constable. *March. Annual forum for avant-garde and experimental music held in venues all over the Tampa Bay area.*

The Boston Early Music Festival. PO Box 2632, Cambridge, MA 02238, USA *tel:* +1 617 661 1812 *fax:* +1 617 267 6539 *email:* bemf@bemf.org. Kathleen Fay, executive director; Stephen Stubbs, Paul O'Dette, artistic directors. *Biennial. Next 12-17 June 2001. 'The French Influence in Europe' including Jean-Baptiste Lully's 'Tragedie Lyrique'. 15 concerts featuring internationally acclaimed early music specialists. Festivals, annual activities, educational programmes, tours.*

Bowdoin Summer Music Festival. Bowdoin College, 6300 College Station, Brunswick, ME 04011-8463, USA *tel:* +1 207 725 3322 *fax:* +1 207 725 3047 *email:* bsmf@blazenetme.net. Lewis Kaplan, artistic director. *June-August 2000. Chamber music festival and school for 200. Piano, strings, woodwind, and composition programme designed for conservatory track students aged 12-30.*

Breckenridge Music Festival. c/o PO Box 1254, Breckenridge, CO 80424, USA *tel:* +1 303 453 2120. Joseph H Kremer, executive director; Susannah Tomann, Pat Keysiak, festival admin. *June-August.*

Britt Festivals, Music and Performing Arts Festival. PO Box 1124, Medford, OR 97501, USA *tel:* +1 541 779 0847 *fax:* +1 541 776 3712 *email:* brittfest@aol.com. Ron McUne, general manager. *June-August. Classical, dance, musical theatre, jazz, folk, country, popular and world music. Concerts take place in outdoor amphitheatre, Jacksonville.*

Central City Opera Festival. 621 17th St, Ste 1601, Denver, CO 80293, USA *tel:* +1 303 292 6700/6500 *fax:* +1 303 292 4958 *email:* ccopera@mho.net. Pelham Pearce, general director. *Annual. June-August. Three operas presented in the Central City Opera House, in the Colorado Rocky Mountains.*

Chautauqua Institution. PO Box 28, Chautauqua, NY 14722, USA *tel:* +1 716 357 6200 *fax:* +1 716 357 9014. Marty Merkley, vice president, director of programming. *24 June-27 August 2000. Symphony, opera, chamber music, theatre, folk, rock and popular music.*

Cincinnati Opera Summer Festival. Cincinnati Music Hall, 1241 Elm St, Cincinnati, OH 45210, USA *tel:* +1 513 621 1919 *fax:* +1 513 621 4310 *email:* cincinnati.opera@ibm.net. Nicholas Muni, artistic director; Patricia K Beggs, managing director. *Annual. June-July. Opera festival.*

Des Moines Metro Opera Summer Festival. 106 West Boston Av, Indianola, IA 50125, USA *tel:* +1 515 961 6221 *fax:* +1 515 961 2994. Robert L Larsen, artistic director; Jerilee M Mace, executive director. *June-July. Sixteen performances of 3 different operas at Blank Performing Arts Center in Indianola.*

Festival Miami. University of Miami, PO Box 248165, Coral Gables, FL 33124, USA *tel:* +1 305 284 3941 *fax:* +1 305 284 3901 *email:* whipp@miami.edu. William Hipp, director. *Annual. Mid September-mid October. Orchestral, choral, jazz, symphonic, chamber, vocal, piano and violin recitals.*

Florida International Festival. PO Box 1310, Daytona Beach, FL 32115-1310, USA *tel:* +1 904 252 1511 ext 487; +1 904 257 7790 (box office) *fax:* +1 904 238 1663 *email:* fifcfce@n-jcenter.com. Dewey Anderson, general manager; Tippen Davidson, festival director; Ellen Barum, PR and marketing. *Biennial. Next 2001. Jazz, dance, country music, chamber, masterclasses. 40 performances, plus free public events.*

Gina Bachauer Piano Festival. PO Box 11664, Salt Lake City, UT 84147, USA *tel:* +1 801 521 9200 *fax:* +1 801 521 9202 *email:* gina@bachauer.com. Paul C Pollei, founder and artistic director; David Pollei, general manager. *June 2000. Masterclasses, concerts, seminars, and junior competition for ages 14-18 organised by the Gina Bachauer International Piano Foundation.*

Glimmerglass Opera Festival. Box 191, Cooperstown, NY 13326, USA *tel:* +1 607 547 5704 *fax:* +1 607 547 6030 *email:* glimmer@telenet.net. Michael Willis, director of PR; Tara Barnwell, marketing manager. *July-August 2000. Operas, recitals, symposia.*

Grand Teton Music Festival. Walk Festival Hall, Teton Village, WY 83025, USA *tel:* +1 307 733 1128 *fax:* +1 307 739 9043 *email:* gtmf@gtmf.org. Joanna Giesek, executive director. *Annual. 4 July-26 August 2000. Symphony orchestra and chamber music. Guest artists and company of 200 orchestral musicians from leading North American orchestras. Educational outreach programmes, pre-concert talks, etc.*

Irving S Gilmore International Keyboard Festival. Kalamazoo Centre, 100 W Michigan, Kalamazoo, MI 49007, USA *tel:* +1 616 342 1166 *fax:* +1 616 342 0968. Irma Vallecillo, artistic director. *April-May. Piano recitals, chamber music, concertos. Mainly classical, plus jazz and contemporary.*

Lake George Opera Festival. PO Box 2172, Glen Falls, NY 12801, USA *tel:* +1 518 793 3858/3859 *fax:* +1 518 793 6719. Susan Danis, general director. *Annual. June-July. Traditional and neglected opera masterpieces, chamber music and special events.*

Massachusetts International Festival for the Arts. 269 Main St, Northampton, MA 01060, USA *tel:* +1 413 584 4425 *fax:* +1 413 586 5368 *email:* tfisk@mifa-net.org. Donald T Sanders, executive artistic director. *January/February; May/June; October/November. Opera, theatre, dance, visual arts, concerts.*

Mostly Mozart Festival. 70 Lincoln Center Plaza, New York, NY 10023, USA *tel:* +1 212 875 5135 *fax:* +1 212 875 5145. Jane Moss, vice-president for programming. *July-August.*

Newport Music Festival. PO Box 3300, Newport, RI 02840, USA *tel:* +1 401 846 1133 *fax:* +1 401 849 1857 *email:* staff@newportmusic.org. Mark P Malkovich III, general director; Mark Malkovich IV, marketing director. *7-23 July 2000. Chamber music of the romantic era with American debut recitals of international artists. Complete chamber music of Saint-Saens every afternoon.*

Norfolk Chamber Music Festival. 135 College St, New Haven, CT 06520, USA *tel:* +1 203 432 1966 *fax:* +1 203 432 2136. Elaine C Carroll, festivals manager. *June-August. Chamber music concerts, student recitals, family activities, string quartets, wind quintets, piano trios, mixed ensembles.*

Opera Theatre of St Louis. PO Box 191910 St Louis, MO 63119-7910, USA *tel:* +1 314 961 0171 *fax:* +1 314 961 7463. *May-June.*

Other Minds Festival. 333 Valencia St, Suite 303, San Francisco, CA 94103, USA *tel:* +1 415 934 8134 *fax:* +1 415 934 8136 *email:* otherminds@otherminds.org. *March 2000. Contemporary music festival, featuring compositions of participating composers.*

Princeton Invitational Choir Festival. c/o AD International Inc, 136 Lawrenceville-Pennington Rd, Lawrenceville, NJ 08648-1413, USA *tel:* +1 609 896 9330 *fax:* +1 609 896 3450 *email:* adadi@aol.com. George Plasko, artistic director. *21-25 June 2001. International festival for children and high-school age choirs.*

The Pro Piano New York Recital Series. 85 Jane St, New York, NY 10014, USA *tel:* +1 212 206 8794 *fax:* +1 212 206 1207 *email:* ricard@propiano.com. Ricard de La Rosa, executive director, founder; Chitose Okashiro, artistic director.

Ravinia Festival. c/o Steans Institute for Young Artists, 400 Iris Lane, Highland Park, IL 60035, USA *tel:* +1 847 266 5106 *fax:* +1 847 266 5063. Miriam Fried, Margo Garrett, faculty chairmen; Diane P Dorn, admin. *11 June-9 September 2000. Programmes for piano, strings and singers. Also dance and pop attractions.*

Riverbend Festival. 537 Market St, Suite 16, PO Box 886, Chattanooga, TN 37401, USA *tel:* +1 423 756 2212 *fax:* +1 423 756 2719 *email:* information@riverbendfestival.com. Richard D Brewer Jr, executive director. *June. Jazz, big band, folk and fusion, acoustic, country, classic, rock and roll, blues and light music.*

Round Top International Festival. PO Drawer 89, Round Top, TX 78954-0089, USA *tel:* +1 409 249 3129 *fax:* +1 409 249 3100 *email:* festinst@fais.net. James Dick, founder and artistic director; Alain G Declert, artistic co-ordinator. *10 June-15 July 2000. Classical, orchestral, chamber, solo. Also presents an early music festival in May and 'August-to-April' series.*

The Santa Fe Opera. PO Box 2408, Santa Fe, NM 87504-2408, USA *tel:* +1 505 986 5900 *fax:* +1 505 986 5999 *email:* boxoff@santafeopera.org. Tom Morris, director of operations. *30 June-26 August 2000. Outdoor summer opera festival: classics, neglected masterpieces, world premieres.*

Sarasota Music Festival. 709 North Tamiami Trail, Sarasota, FL 34236, USA *tel:* +1 941 952 9634 *fax:* +1 941 953 3059. Paul Wolfe, artistic director; Trevor Cramer, admin director. *June. Masterclasses and concerts of a wide range of chamber music.*

Saratoga Performing Arts Center. Saratoga Springs, NY 12866, USA *tel:* +1 518 584 9330 *fax:* +1 518 584 0809 *email:* info@spac.org. Donna Eichmeyer, director of sales and marketing. *Annual. June-September. Summer home of New York City Ballet in July and the Philadelphia Orchestra and Saratoga Chamber Music Festival in August. Also a jazz festival and a variety of contemporary performers.*

Sevenars Concerts. The Academy, South Ireland St and Rte 112, S Worthington, MA 01098, USA *tel:* +1 413 238 5854 *also fax.* Robert and Rolande Schrade, artistic directors. *2nd Sunday in July, August and autumn. Classical, piano chamber music.*

Spoleto Festival USA. PO Box 157, Charleston, SC 29402, USA *tel:* +1 803 722 2764 *fax:* +1 803 723 6383. Nigel Redden, general director; Nunally Kersh, producer. *May-June. Opera, dance, theatre, symphony music, chamber and jazz.*

Summer Festival. Seattle Opera, PO Box 9248, Seattle, WA 98109, USA *tel:* +1 206 389 7676 *fax:* +1 206 389 7651. Speight Jenkins, general director; Tina Ryker, PR director; Linda Prather, director of marketing and communications. *Seminars, lectures and previews.*

Tanglewood Music Festival. Lenox, MA 01240, Boston, MA 02115, USA *tel:* +1 617 266 1492; +1 413 637 5165 (late Jun-Sep) *fax:* +1 617 638 9288; +1 413 637 5288. Caroline Smedvig, PR. *Last week of June to first weekend in September. Classical, popular, contemporary, chamber music and recitals.*

Vermont Mozart Festival. PO Box 512, Burlington, VT 05402, USA *tel:* +1 802 862 7352 *fax:* +1 802 862 2201 *email:* vtmozart@together.net. Laura Cole, executive director; Ellen Gurwitz, associate director. *16 July-6 August 2000. Large orchestra or chamber music.*

Summer Schools and Short Courses

The music courses listed below are held at various times of the year and the course content may vary from year to year. The addresses given here are those of the organising bodies, and are not necessarily the same as the address of the course itself. Financial grants may be offered on scholarship terms. For foreign government grants, enquiries should be made to the appropriate embassy.

Jeunesses Musicales International is a worldwide network for youth and music, organising 45,000 activities for 6,000,000 young people of all nationalities. These activities include youth orchestras, festivals and music camps. A brochure and full details are available from 10 Rue Royale, B-1000 Bruxelles, Belgium *tel:* +32 2 513 9774 *fax:* +32 2 514 4755 *email:* mail@jmi.net *website:* www.jmi.net, or from **Youth and Music**, 28 Charing Cross Rd, London WC2H 0DB, UK *tel:* +44 020 7379 6722.

Australia

National Music Camp Australia. c/o Youth Music Australia, PO Box 810, Darlinghurst NSW 1300, Australia *tel:* +61 2 9380 8899 *fax:* +61 2 9380 8273 *email:* yma@s054.aone.net.au. Carol Hellmers, programme admin. *January; applications by July; fees: $525; age range: 14-23. Provides young Australians with comprehensive approach to excellence in music training performance. Scholarships, grants and awards are available. Also* Words About Music *provides opportunities to learn about broadcasting, music journalism, etc.*

Ronald Dowd National Summer School for Singers. 171 Albion St, Surry Hills, NSW 2010, Australia *tel:* +61 2 9360 4049 *fax:* +61 2 9332 1585. Maggie Niven, executive director; Victor Morris, artistic director. *January, applications by November. Opera mastercourses in Sydney for singers and repetiteurs.*

Austria

Berwang Holiday Music Course (Austria). Willowdown, Megg Lane, Chipperfield, Herts WD4 9JN, UK *tel:* +44 1923 263715 *fax:* +44 1923 268412. *August-September. All ages. Strings, woodwind, singers.*

Eichendorff's Ruh Walter Hermann Sallagar. A-2564 Furth, Austria *tel:* +43 267 488265 *fax:* +43 1 714 1710. *9-16 July 2000, applications by 9 June. Courses in bassoon ensemble and repair,* Fagottissimo. *Age 16 and over. Fees: 700 euros (including board and accommodation).*

International Academy for New Composition and Audio-Art. Josef Wopfnerstr 16, A-6130 Schwaz/Tirol, Austria *tel:* +43 5242 65737 *fax:* +43 5242 61199 *email:* avantgarde.schwaz@tirol.com. Marianne Penz-van Stappershoef. *Annual. August-September, applications by 15 May. Composers' and Audio-Art workshops. Number of participants restricted to eight. International Academy for New Composition and Audio-Art. Fees: ATS 3500.*

Salzburg International Summer Academy Mozarteum. Mirabellplatz 1, A-5020 Salzburg, Austria *tel:* +43 662 88908 400/401 *fax:* +43 662 872659 *email:* michaela.bartsch@moz.ac.at. Michaela Bartsch, students' officer. *Annual. July-August, applications by 1 June. No age limit, although most participants aged 20-30. Masterclasses for voice and instruments. Fees: ATS 7000.*

Salzburg Orff-Schulwerk Course. Orff Institute, Frohnburgweg 55, A-5020 Salzburg, Austria *tel:* +43 662 889 08613/08310 *fax:* +43 662 624 867. *Annual. July.*

Salzkammergut International Music Course. 5 Neville Court, Grove End Rd, London NW8 9DD, UK *tel:* +44 20 7286 4865 *fax:* +44 20 7266 0181 *email:* kenneth.lewis1@virgin.net. Anne Lewis, administrator; Frank Wibaut, artistic/course director; Sir Colin Davis, president. *Mid-July, Landesmusikschule and Schloss Concert Hall, Mondsee, Austria. Apply by 31 March. Limited bursaries may be available. Masterclasses, individual lessons, coaching sessions and concerts for advanced performers in solo and chamber music repertoire. Covers piano, strings, wind and voice (subject to change yearly).*

Vienna Summer-Seminar for Contemporary Music (Composition and Interpretation). Postfach 345, A-1060 Wien, Austria *tel:* +43 222 594 1292. Konrad Musalek. *August, applications by 31 May. Annual meeting of composers, performers, students and other interested people. Information, research and discussions on new music styles and development. Daily concerts, lectures, workshops. ATS 1000.*

Wiener Meisterkurse. Reisnerstrasse 3, A-1030 Wien, Austria *tel:* +43 1 714 8822 *fax:* +43 1 714 8821. Elisabeth Keschmann; Monika Wildauer. *End June-August, applications by 1 June. 2-week master courses with leading professional musicians in flute, guitar, piano, cello; also choral, chamber, opera, conducting and singing. Final concert, diploma. Fees: ATS 5200 (participants), ATS 2700 (listeners).*

Belgium

Antwerp Summer Academy Courses. Ruckers Genootschap, c/o Museum Vleeshuis, Vleeshouwersstraat 38-40, B-2000 Antwerp, Belgium *tel:* +32 3 233 6404/383 1690 *fax:* +32 3 383 1690 *email:* jlambrechtsdouillez@compuserve.com. Mrs J Lambrechts-Douillez. *August, applications by May. Academy for interpretation of music on historic instruments (harpsichord, forte-piano). Course for post-graduates. Fees: 10,000 BF.*

Choir Conducting Masterclass - Frieder Bernius. CIMC, Ave Jean 1er, B-5000 Namur, Belgium *tel:* +32 8 173 5796 *fax:* +32 8 173 7872 *email:* jcwilkens@compuserve.com. *Next 2000. Workshop for choral conductors on Bach 6 motets with professional choir in residence. Fees: c 19,500 BF.*

Harmonium Projekt. Koninklijk Vlaams Muziekconservatorium, Desguinlei 25, B-2018 Antwerp, Belgium *tel:* +32 3 244 1800 *fax:* +32 3 238 9017. J Verdin, professor of music. *April. Four days consisting of lectures, workshops and concerts. Course title: The French and German Repertoire. Fees: 2500 BF.*

Muziekactief. PO Box 45, B-3990 Peer, Belgium *tel:* +32 1 163 2164 *fax:* +32 1 163 4911 *email:* info@musica.be. Bart Demuyt, co-ordinator. *Training programmes for adult amateur and semi-professional musicians. Weekly and evening courses.*

Canada

Acadia Summer Music Institute. Division of Distance & Continuing Education, Acadia University, Wolfville, NS B0P 1X0, Canada *tel:* +1 800 585 6568; +1 902 585 1434 *fax:* +1 902 585 1068 *email:* continuing.education@acadiau.ca. *July-August. Summer music camps in jazz, concert band, strings and piano. All ages and levels.*

Adventures in Summer Music. PO Box 5005, Red Deer, AB T4N 5H5, Canada *tel:* +1 403 342 3526 *fax:* +1 403 347 0399 *email:* jhowdle @rdc.ab.ca. Joyce Howdle, performing arts co-ordinator. *August, applications by 1 August. Introductory, junior, intermediate band workshop, including full band rehearsals, sectionals, options and theory for ages 9-15. For junior and intermediate must have 2-4 years playing experience. Fees: $125 (not including instrument rental).*

Banff Centre for the Arts. Box 1020, Station 28, Banff, Alberta T0L 0C0, Canada *tel:* +1 403 762 6180 *fax:* +1 403 762 6345. Karen Harper, assistant registrar. *Long and short-term residential courses at various times May-August, including a series of short, intensive masterclasses (string, wind, piano), jazz and chamber music. Self-directed programme for professional musicians (partial financial assistance available). Summer courses, 2-4 weeks (May-August), Autumn (September-December), Winter (January-April), applications by early February. Fees: $325 per week. Ages 20-40.*

Camp Musical de Lanaudiere. PO Box 44, Joliette, PQ J6E 3Z3, Canada *tel:* +1 514 755 2496. Nicole Bourassa, executive secretary. *Four sessions June-August, applications by mid-June. Chamber music, choral, and orchestral programmes for ages 9-17 who have studied for a minimum of 2 years. Fees: $495.*

Courtenay Youth Music Centre (CYMC). PO Box 3056, Courtenay, BC V9N 5N3, Canada *tel:* +1 250 338 7463 *fax:* +1 250 334 2934 *email:* cymcreg@island.net; cymc@island.net. Stephanie Spiers, general manager. *July-August. Ages 10-adult. Programmes of jazz, piano, strings, harp, musical theatre, classical guitar, concert band and orchestral for beginners to advanced performers.*

Lake MacDonald Music Centre. Cammac National Office, #2509-1751 Richardson, Montreal, PQ, H3K 1G6, Canada *tel:* +1 514 932 8755 *fax:* +1 514 932 9811 *email:* national@cammac.ca. Raymond Sealey, executive director. *28 June-21 August 2000. All ages, children's* *programme available. One week sessions for amateur musicians - orchestral, early music, jazz, opera and many other courses. Fees: $20-300.*

Le Domaine Forget Academy for Music and Dance. 5 St Antoine, St-Irénée, PQ G0T 1V0, Canada *tel:* +1 418 452 8111 *fax:* +1 418 452 3503 *email:* dforget@cite.net. *4 June-27 August 2000. Courses from brass and medieval music to oriental percussion and jazz. Fees: $370 (1 week)-990 (3 weeks).*

Czech Republic

International Workshop for Conductors. c/o Symphonic Workshops Ltd, 281 Pacific Ave, Toronto, Ont M6P 2P8, Canada *tel:* +1 416 760 9319 *fax:* +1 416 762 6258 *email:* symphwk@interlog.com. Harry M B Hurwitz, director. *Three weeks July-August. Large faculty of internationally known conductors, with the Bohuslav Martinu Philharmonic. Podium time for participants on alternate days as well as daily seminars, practice sessions, plus prize awards. No age limit. Fees: US$2195 (including accommodation).*

Marienbad Workshop. c/o Symphonic Workshops, 281 Pacific Ave, Toronto, Ont M6P 2P8, Canada *tel:* +1 416 760 9319 *fax:* +1 416 762 6258 *email:* symphwk@interlog.com. Harry M B Hurwitz, director. *March. Daily podium time with the Marienbad Chamber Orchestra, Marienbad, Czech Republic, for 8 participants; two concerts and prize awards. No age limit. Fees: US$1750 (including accommodation).*

Opera Workshop for Conductors and Singers. c/o Symphonic Workshops, 281 Pacific Ave, Toronto, Ont M6P 2P8, Canada *tel:* +1 416 760 9319 *fax:* +1 416 762 6258 *email:* symphwk@interlog.com. Harry M B Hurwitz. *June-July 2000. Perform/conduct two complete staged opera productions.*

Practical Course in Conducting (Czech Republic). c/o Symphonic Workshops, 281 Pacific Ave, Toronto, Ont M6P 2P8, Canada *tel:* +1 416 760 9319 *fax:* +1 416 762 6258 *email:* symphwk@interlog.com. Harry M B Hurwitz. *July-August. Podium time with the Kromeriz Orchestra for 30 participants on alternate days in addition to daily seminars, practice sessions, prize awards. No age limit. Beginners also welcome. Fees: US$1995 (including accommodation).*

Prague Rychnov NKN Summer Camp for Strings. Hudební Mladez CR, Krizikova 64, Cr-186 00 Praha 8, Czech Republic *tel:* +420 223 22470 *also fax.* Jana Klimtova, general secretary. *18-28 August 2000, applications by 1 June. String orchestra and chamber music. Teachers from Czech conservatoires. Ages 15-25. Fees: $300.*

Recording Fest. c/o Symphonic Workshops, 281 Pacific Ave, Toronto, Ont M6P 2P8, Canada *tel:* +1 416 760 9319 *fax:* +1 416 762 6258 *email:* symphwk@interlog.com. Harry M B Hurwitz, director. *March; 10 days. Composers' new works played by Moravia Philharmonic Orchestra under established conductor. For conductors, composers, and soloists. Fees: from US$450 for 2 hours recording.*

Repertoire Workshop. c/o Symphonic Workshops, 281 Pacific Av, Toronto, Ont M6P 2P8, Canada *tel:* +1 416 760 9319 *fax:* +1 416 762 6258 *email:* symphwk@interlog.com. Harry M B Hurwitz, director. *June. Daily podium time with the Hradec Kralove Philharmonic Orchestra for 15 participants; two concerts and prize awards. No age limit. Fees: US$1750 (including accommodation).*

Finland

Kuhmo Chamber Music Festival Music Camp. Fredrikinkatu 77 a 2-4, FIN-00100 Helsinki, Finland *tel:* +358 9 493867 *fax:* +358 9 493956 *email:* kuhmo.festival@kajak.fi. Seija Kahkonen, secretary. *19-28 July 2000, applications by 14 April. Workshops, masterclasses, individual tuition. Ages 12-25. Fees: 2800 FM.*

France

Académie International d'Eté de Nice. 24 Blvd de Cimiez, F-06000 Nice, France *tel:* +33 04 93 81 01 23 *fax:* +33 04 93 53 33 91 *email:* academies@expomed.org. Jacques Taddei, president; Hubert Tassey. *July-August. Instrumental, vocal, chamber, composition masterclasses. Fees: from 1950 FF for 1 week to 6850 FF for 4 weeks.*

Centre Acanthes. 3 Rue des Couronnes, F-75020 Paris, France *tel:* +33 1 40 33 45 35 *fax:* +33 1 40 33 45 38. Jacqueline Fraisse, public relations. *July, applications by beginning of May, in Chartreuse de Villeneuve-Lez-Avignon. For composers, instrumentalists, teachers and students interested in contemporary music. Lecture series and composition, instrumental and chamber music workshops. Scholarships available. Fees: 1500 FF.*

Chant Sans Frontieres. 141 Inverness Ave, Westcliff on Sea, Essex SS0 9DU, UK *tel:* +44 1702 349009. Isobel Tedstill. *Early August (tbc), applications by 31 May. 1-week intensive tuition, all aspects of singing; technique, interpretation, presentation by highly experienced tutors, performance opportunity. Age 18 and over. Fees: £156-325 (including full board). Spectators welcome if room available.*

Europa Cantat XIV in France. *see* Europa Cantat, Germany. *Next 21-30 July 2000 in Nevers, France. Closing date February. Festival for choirs, singers and conductors. Special concerts presenting French works, small concerts by the participating choirs and 'open singing' for all participants. Special offers for choral conductors.*

Ferrandou Summer School. c/o Bridge House, Lower St, Cavendish, Suffolk CO10 8AQ, UK *tel:* c/o +44 1787 280140 *fax:* +44 1787 282497 *email:* g-t.cooke@talk21.com. David Wilson-Johnson, director; Tricia Cooke, admin. *Solo and group sessions for singers and pianists of all ages. Based in Ferrandou in the Dordogne Valley.*

Latour De France International Festival of Music and the Arts (France). c/o Mananan Festival Office, Erin Arts Centre, Victoria Square, Port Erin, Isle of Man IM9 6LD, UK *tel:* +44 1624 835858 *fax:* +44 1624 836658 *email:* erinartscentre@enterprise.net. Martin Norbury, admin; John Bethell, director. *23-29 July 2000, applications by 31 March. Fees: £100. Choral and operatic study course for young professional singers.*

Michael Procter Courses. Institut für Kunst, Musik & Sprachen, Rintheimer Straße 50, D-76131 Karlsruhe, Germany *tel:* +49 721 616450 *also fax; email:* InstKMS@aol.com. Michael Procter, director; Pippa Dice, admin. *July 2000. Liturgical performance of early music in the context of monastic life. Held at Abbey St Martin an Mondaye, near Bayeux, Normandy.*

Music at Ladevie. Coopers Farm, Stonegate, Wadhurst, E Sussex TN5 7EH, UK *tel:* +44 1580 200386 *fax:* +44 1580 200866. Paul Roberts, director. *July-August, piano summer school in SW France. Age 17 and over. For professionals and amateurs. Fees: £380-690.*

Roujan Singing Weeks. Cantax House, Lacock, Chippenham, Wiltshire SN15 2JZ, UK *tel:* +44 1249 730468 *also fax.* Andrew van der Beek. *August. Two separate weeks for amateur choral singers in village near Pezenas in the south of France. All ages. Fees: 2250 FF.*

T & M Music and Drama Course. ATEM, Théâtre des Amandiers, 7 Ave Pablo Picasso, F-92022 Nanterre Cedex, France *tel:* +33 1 46 14 70 19 *fax:* +33 1 47 25 17 75 *email:* tem@club-internet.fr. Myriam Henne, assistant. *August-September, applications by 15 May. Music theatre, opera and orchestra workshops. Ages 18 and over. Fees: 1700 FF.*

Germany

Anglo-German Youth Music Week. National Association of Youth Orchestras, c/o The Band of the RAF Regiment, Royal Air Force Cranwell, Sleaford, Lincs NG34 8MB, UK *tel:* +44 7050 622403 *fax:* +44 7020 934902 *email:* malcolm.goodman@nayo.org.uk. Malcolm Goodman, course administrator. *28 July-6 August 2000, Münster, Germany. Annual residential music week, alternately in Germany and the UK. Wide range of orchestral and chamber music with students from other European countries. Full symphony orchestra forming two chamber orchestras. For ages 15-25, with minimum of grade 7 on primary orchestral instrument. Fees: £255.*

Cello Masterclasses. Kronberg Academy, Königsteinerstr 5, D-61476 Kronberg, Germany *tel:* +49 6173 950085 *fax:* +49 6173 950086 *email:* ikacello@aol.com. Raimund Trenkler, artist director; Almut Latscha; Gabriela Denicke, organisation office. *25 September-2 October 2000, applications by 23 August. Ages 30 and under. Cello masterclasses with David Geringas, Bernard Greenhouse and Frans Helmerson. Active participants selected by audition.*

Course in Bayreuth. Bela Bartók Centre for Musicianship, 6 Frognal Court, 158 Finchley Rd, London NW3 5HL, UK tel: +44 171 435 3685 *email:* Agnes.Kory@kcl.ac.uk. Agnes Kory, director. *July/August. 5-day intensive course for musicians, music teachers, music students. Covers general musicianship, history and analysis, and chamber music. Contact for details of dates. Fee: £250.*

Europa Cantat - European Federation of Young Choirs (EFYC). c/o Bayerische Musikakademie Marktoberdorf, Kurfürstenstrasse 19, D-87616 Marktoberdorf, Germany *tel:* +49 8342 961826 *fax:* +49 8342 40370 *email:* modmusik@compuserve.com. Dolf Rabus, secretary general. *Summer. International singing weeks and workshops with well-known conductors throughout Europe. Including European Youth Choir in Germany (ages 25 and under); European Academy for Young Choral Conductors (ages 30 and under); International Study Tour.*

Fortbildungszentrum für Neue Musik. An der Munze 7, D-21335 Luneburg, Germany *tel:* +49 4131 309390 *also fax; email:* erdmann @uni-lueneberg.de. Helmut W Erdmann. *Weekend chamber music course for all instruments, studying classical and contemporary compositions.*

International Association for Music & Education. Heinrich Schütz Allee 33, D-34131 Kassel, Germany *tel:* +49 561 935170 *fax:* +49 561 313772 *email:* iamev@t-online.de. Frank Ebel, executive director. *Over 70 courses throughout the year for experienced, amateur singers from all over Europe.*

International New Music Holiday Courses. Internationales Musikinstitut, Nieder-Ramstädter Str 190, D-64285 Darmstadt, Germany *tel:* +49 6151 132416/17 *fax:* +49 6151 132405 *email:* imd@stadt.darmstadt.de. Wilhelm Schlüter. *Biennial. Next July 2000 in Darmstadt. International vacation courses for composition and interpretation of contemporary music. Fees: DM 1350.*

Internationale Bachakademie. Johann-Sebastian-Bach-Platz, D-70178 Stuttgart, Germany *tel:* +49 7116 19210 *fax:* +49 7116 192123. Christa Richter, course officer; Christian Eisert, programme planning. *August-September, applications by 30 June, in Stuttgart for any age. Conducting and vocal masterclasses and seminars in musicology. Fees: DM 650-750.*

Internationaler Arbeitskreis für Musik. Heinrich-Schütz-Allee 33, D-34064 Kassel, Germany *tel:* +49 5619 35170 *fax:* +49 561 313772. Adolf Lang, secretary general..

Jeunesses Musicales Germany. Marktplatz 12, D-97990 Weikersheim/Tauber, Germany *tel:* +49 793 4280 *fax:* +49 793 48526 *email:* weikersheim@jeunessesmusicales.de. Thomas Rietschel, general secretary. *August-September, applications by July. Many courses throughout year in one of the most beautiful castles in Germany, including international chamber music course for woodwind, strings and piano, with internationally acclaimed teachers. Age range 22-28. Fees: DM 300-700. Grants available.*

Michael Procter Courses. Rintheimer Straße 50, D-76131 Karlsruhe, Germany *tel:* +49 721 616450 *also fax; email:* MicProc@aol.com. Michael Procter, director. *15-23 April 2000. Easter Academy for choral singers, held in Passau, Bavaria. For singers in Renaissance sacred music.*

Musicosophia International. Finkenherd 6, D-79271 Sankt Peter, Germany *tel:* +49 776 0581 *fax:* +49 766 01536. Uwe Fricke, manager; George Balan, founder. *Monthly courses "The Art of Conscious Music Listening" in UK, France, Germany, Italy, Spain and South America. Applications by 2 weeks before course. Ages 6-80. No musical knowledge required. Fees: DM 220 (weekend course), DM 380 (5-day).*

String Chamber Music Course. Landesmusikrat Hessen EV, Eschersheimer Landstr 325, D-60320 Frankfurt Am Main, Germany *tel:* +49 695 67155; +49 696 37111(evenings) *fax:* +49 695 67045. Juan von Haselberg, co-ordinator and organiser. *March and October, applications by 1 March and 13 September respectively. Intensive string chamber music course for serious-minded amateurs and music teachers aged 21-65. Fees: DM 490 (tuition and board).*

Young Artists Festival Bayreuth. Internationales Jugend-Festspieltreffen, Aussere Badstr 7a, D-95448 Bayreuth, Germany *tel:* +49 921 9800444 *fax:* +49 921 98486 *email:* info@das-treffen.de. Sissy Thammer, general director. *August, applications by June, in Bayreuth. Young Artists Festival; choral, orchestral, percussion, chamber music course, opera workshop, song interpretation. Ages 18-25. Fees: DM 950 (including registration and insurance).*

Greece

International Computer Music Conference. c/o Programme of Psychoacoustics, PO Box 308, Aristotle University of Thessaloniki, 54006 Thessaloniki, Greece *tel:* +30 3 199 4760 *fax:* +30 3 199 4769 *email:* ipsa@auth.gr. *September. Workshops and concerts in computer music.*

Hungary

Course in Budapest. Bela Bartók Centre for Musicianship, 6 Frognal Court, 158 Finchley Rd, London NW3 5HL, UK tel: +44 171 435 3685 *email:* Agnes.Kory@kcl.ac.uk. Agnes Kory, director. *July/August. 5-day intensive course for musicians, music teachers, music students. Covers general musicianship, history and analysis, and chamber music. Contact for details of dates. Fees: £250.*

Early Music Days, Sopron. c/o Interart Festivalcenter, PO Box 80, Vörösmarty tér 1, H-1366 Budapest, Hungary *tel:* +36 1 317 9838/266 3108 *fax:* +36 1 317 9910. Mária Liszkay, manager. *24 June-1 July 2000 in Sopron, applications by 15 May. Harpsichord, voice, violin, flute, dance. Fees: DEM 250-400.*

International Bartok Seminar and Festival. c/o Interart Festivalcenter, PO Box 80, Vörösmarty tér 1, H-1366 Budapest, Hungary *tel:* +36 1 317 9838 *fax:* +36 1 317 9910. Magdolna Szávai, secretary. *July, applications by 20 May, in Szombathely. Course for piano, chamber music and conducting, violin, string quartet, singing, musicology, composition.*

International Kodály Seminar. Kodály Institute, H-6001 Kecskemét, Hungary *tel:* +36 7 648 1518 *fax:* +36 7 632 0160 *email:* lkeri@kodaly-inst.hu; office@kodaly-inst.hu. Laura Kéri, registrar. *Next July 2001. Theoretical and practical aspects of the Kodály concept, masterclasses for choral conductors, piano course, interpretation course for singers. Also International Kodály Symposium and Festival.*

International String, Keyboard and Chamber Music Masterclasses. Young European Strings, The Close, Cypress Downs, Templeogue, Dublin 6W, Republic of Ireland *tel:* +353 1 490 5263 *fax:* +353 1 492 0355 *email:* yes@iol.ie. Maria Kelemen, director. *22-29 October 2000. Closing date for applications 30 May. Ages 10-16. Fees (including accommodation and full board): £250 or 317 euros (approx).*

'Pro Musica' International Summer Academy. Gyula Csetenyi, Nagymező utca 1, H-1065 Budapest, Hungary *tel:* +36 1 321 7514 *fax:* +36 1 322 8207. Gyula Csetenyi, artistic director. *August, applications by 15 June. Flute, oboe, clarinet, bassoon, violin, cello, piano and chamber music. Ages 14-30. Fees: US$400 (inclusive of tuition and board).*

Republic of Ireland

Association of Irish Choirs. 4 Drinan St, Cork, Republic of Ireland *tel:* +353 21 312296 *fax:* +353 21 962457 *email:* cnc@iol.ie. Barbara Heas, admin. *3-7 July 2000. Basic, intermediate and advanced choral conducting, vocal training, masterclasses and lectures during an annual summer school for choral conductors and teachers. Other regional courses and choral days. Ages 17 and over. Fees: IR£45-85.*

Blas. The Irish World Music Centre, University of Limerick, Republic of Ireland *tel:* +353 61 202565 *fax:* +353 61 202589 *email:* niall.keegan@ul.ie; sandra.joyce@ul.ie. Sandra Joyce; Niall Keegan. *July 2000, applications by 14 June. 10-day summer school of Irish traditional music and dance with intensive academic and practical content. For ages 16 and above. Accreditation available.*

Ennis IMRO Composition Summer School. AIC, Copyright House, Pembroke Row, Dublin 2, Republic of Ireland *tel:* +353 1708 3924 *fax:* +353 62 89432 *email:* ennis@cmc.ie. Eithne Egar, executive director; Martin O'Leary, tutor. *10-12 July 2000, applications by 30 April. For 3rd level and graduate students. Lectures and tuition by course directors and international guest composer. Performance and recording of students' work by professional musicians. Fees: £145-225.*

Israel

The Israel Jeunesses Musicales International Summer Camp. c/o Jeunesses Musicales, 19 Achad-Ha'am St, Tel Aviv 65151, Israel *tel:* +972 3 560 6069 *fax:* +972 3 560 8345. Meir Wiesel, Neomi Lev, artistic directors. *Annual. July-August, entries by 15 May. Strings, woodwind, piano. Ages 13-18 (camp) and 16-26 (advanced seminar). Fees: $700 and $10 registration.*

Keshet Eilon Violin Mastercourse. Kibbutz Eilon, Western Galilee 22845, Israel *tel:* +972 4 985 8191 *fax:* +972 4 980 6766 *email:* keshetei@bigfoot.com. Gilad Sheba, managing director. *28 July-15 August 2000, applications by 15 April. Ages 25 and under. Course for gifted young violinists of all nationalities. Special project: Archery and the Violin. Private lessons, masterclasses and solo concert experience. Fees: $1500.*

Italy

Accademia Musicale Chigiana. 89 Via di Citta, I-53100 Siena, Italy *tel:* +39 057 746152 *fax:* +39 057 728 8124. *Annual summer schools for young musicians, including masterclasses, seminars, concerts and a festival.*

Corso di Canto Corale di Castiglione del Lago. Cantax House, Lacock, Chippenham, Wiltshire SN15 2JZ, UK *tel:* +44 1249 730468 *also fax.* Andrew van der Beek, admin. *August. Two separate weeks for amateur choral singers in small lakeside town in Umbria. All ages. Fees: 650,000 lire.*

Fondazione Giorgi Cini. Seminari di Musica Antica e Concerti, Isola di S Giorgio Maggiore, I-30124 Venezia, Italy *tel:* +39 041 528 9900 *fax:* +39 041 523 8540. *Annual. July-August in Venice, applications by June.*

Incontri Musicali. Segretaria Corsi, c/o Asolo Musica, Via Robert Browning 141, I-31011 Asolo (TV), Italy *tel:* +39 042 395 0150 *fax:* +39 042 352 9890 *email:* asolomusica@tin.it. Federico Pupo, artistic director. *May-December. A series of courses and masterclasses for music graduates given by professional musicians. Held in Northern Italy Castelfranco, Veneto. Include chamber music, strings, brass, harp, guitar, opera, conducting, piano, organ, woodwind. Candidates must pass entrance exam to qualify for courses. Fees: c 300,000 lire.*

The Inner Voice in Italy. The White House, Aston Hill, Aston Rowant, Watlington, Oxon OX9 5SG, UK *tel:* +44 1844 351561 *fax:* +44 1844 354891 *email:* elisabeth@innervoice.demon.co.uk. Elisabeth Wingfield; Aliya Gordon-Creed. *Residential courses designed to help performers free themselves from problems associated with nerves, lack of self-confidence and the inner critic. Also, courses on the psychology of musical performance, held in England and Italy. Designed for teachers, students and professional singers and musicians.*

International Academy of Sacred Music. c/o IAM, Heinrich Schütz Allee 33, D-34131 Kassel, Germany *tel:* +49 561 935170 *fax:* +49 561 313772

email: iamev@t-online.de. Michael Procter, director. *10-18 June 2000. Annual course for experienced singers. Housed at the Palazzo Giustinian, on the Grand Canal. Performances in great Venetian churches including St Mark's, with music mainly from Venice. Ages 17 and over. Fees: £600.*

Michael Procter Courses. Rintheimer Straße 50, D-76131 Karlsruhe, Germany *tel:* +49 721 616450 *also fax; email:* MicProc@aol.com. Michael Procter, director. *Many courses, mainly for singers in Renaissance sacred music. 2000: 15-23 April - Easter Academy for choral singers, held in Passau, Bavaria; 10-18 June - Venice (Internationaler Arbeitskreis für Music), intensive course for experienced singers on sacred music of Venice; concert, High Mass in St Mark's; late July - Summer Academy for liturgical performance of early music held near Bayeux, Normandy.*

Music, Dance and Didactics Symposium. Coop Co Gi Tur, via Pisacane 6, I-09047 Selargius, Cagliari, Italy *tel:* +39 070 841297 *also fax. Residential courses for renaissance and baroque music, singing, organ, renaissance and baroque dance, international and Sardinian folk dance, music teaching methods (Orff, Kodály). Held in Selargius, Sardinia.*

Professional Training Course for Orchestral Players. c/o Teatro Lirico Sperimentale di Spoleto, Piazza Giovanni Bovio, I-06049 Spoleto, Italy *tel:* +39 074 322 1645/220440 *fax:* +39 074 322 2930 *email:* teatrolirico@mail.caribusiness.it. Claudio Lepore, manager. *July-September, in Spoleto; applications by June. Brass and string (age limits 25 and 27 respectively). No charges for these courses. All applicants must be registered at employment exchange and possess a Diploma from a Conservatoire or officially recognised Institute of Music.*

Spazio Musica Stages Internazionali. Associazione Spazio Musica, Via Parini 10, I-16145 Genova, Italy *tel:* +39 010 317192 *also fax; email:* spmusica@tn.village.it. *July-August, applications by 30 June. Various courses in opera singing, opera conducting, directing, jazz, stage design, oboe, horn, violin, piano, and cello. Fees: 250,000 lire.*

Latvia

Solvita Sejane of the Riga Early Music Centre. Brivibas 85, LV-1001, Riga, Latvia *tel:* +37 1227 5575 *fax:* +37 1227 8060 *email:* musbalt@com.latnet.lv. *July, applications by June. Renaissance music course for singers, instrumentalists and dancers in Edole Castle. Fees: £200.*

Lithuania

Youth Chamber Music Days. Lithuanian Composers' Union, Mickeviciaus 29, 2600 Vilnius, Lithuania *tel:* +370 2 223611 *fax:* +370 2 220939 *email:* center@mipc.vno.osf.lt. Kestutis Bieliukas, artistic director. *May 2000. Weekend in Druskininkai (south Lithuania). Concerts, lectures, workshops with Lithuanian young composers and musicologists.*

Mexico

International Composers Course in Mexico City. Sones Contemporaneas Association, Medellín 251 Colonia Roma Sur, 06760 Mexico DF, Mexico *tel:* +525 584 9241; +527 312 3831 *fax:* +525 564 4002 *email:* rasgado@mail.internet.com.mx. Franco Donatoni, Theo Loevendie, Victor Rasgado, teachers. *February-March. Applications by December. Course open to composers of any age and nationality. Diploma awarded to participants. Apply with 2 recent scores and current CV. Scholarships available.*

Netherlands

Holland Music Sessions. PO Box 250, NL-1860 AG Bergen, Netherlands *tel:* +31 72 582 1300 *fax:* +31 72 582 1299 *email:* hmsinfo@haaf.nl. Frans Wolfkamp, artistic director; Perry Reitsma, general manager. *June-August, apply by 1 February. Age 15-27. Classes in piano, clarinet, piano accompaniment, cello, violin, flute. Also possibilities for auditors. Daily concerts by active participants in several venues, including the Concertgebouw Amsterdam. Fees: DFL 650-7565 (6 weeks including full board, tuition).*

9th International Flute Summer Course 2000 by Wil Offermans. Studio E, Vrolikstraat 195 D, NL-1091 TX Amsterdam, Netherlands *tel:* +31 20 668 2478 *fax:* +31 20 665 1425 *email:* wof@xs4all.nl. *August 2000. Flute course on comtemporary techniques given by Wil Offermans. Open to flute students, flautists and teachers. Technical information as well as cultural and historical references. Group sessions and private lessons. DFL 595 (including board, tuition), with DFL 295 advance payment.*

International Summer Academy for Organists. Townhall, PO Box 3333, NL-2001 DH Haarlem, Netherlands *tel:* +31 23 511 5733 *fax:* +31 23 511 5743. Miss E L S Hendrikse, secretary. *Next July 2000.*

Kirill Kondrashin International Masterclass for Young Conductors. c/o NOS, PO Box 26444, NL-1202 JJ Hilversum, Netherlands *tel:* +31 35 677 5453 *fax:* +31 35 677 4311 *email:* kondrashin@nos.nl. Max Snijder, manager. *23 August-24 September 2000, applications by 24 April. Ages 36 and under. Masterclasses and workshops for conductors.*

Kurt Thomas Summer Course. SNK, Plompetorengracht 3, NL-3512 CA Utrecht, Netherlands *tel:* +31 30 231 3174 *fax:* +31 30 231 8137 *email:* snk@euronet.nl. *Next July 2000, applications by May. Various group sessions for choral conductors. Course concludes with public concert. Fees: DFL 575 (active), DFL 300 (auditors).*

Summer School around Mozart and Dvorak. La Pellegrina, Twijnstraat 42 bis, NL-3511 ZL Utrecht, Netherlands *tel:* +31 30 238 2535 *fax:* +31 30 238 2536 *email:* d.horringa@inter.nl.net. Dirkjam Horringa, director. *August, applications by 1 May. Orchestral and chamber music coaching for strings, wind and piano. All ages. Fees: £300.*

Norway

Chamber Music Seminar. Nordland Akademi, PB 10, N-8490 Melbu, Norway *tel:* +47 76 158 233 *fax:* +47 76 158 210. Tim Challman, co-ordinator, musical events. *July, in Melbu, applications by 30 June. For advanced students to work with professional instructors. Course combined with Clarinet Seminar. All strings, individual and ensemble instrumentalists aged 15 and over. Fees: 1500 NKR.*

Clarinet Seminar. Nordland Akademi, PB 10, N-8490 Melbu, Norway *tel:* +47 76 158 233 *fax:* +47 76 158 210. Tim Challman, co-ordinator, musical events. *July in Melbu, applications by 30 June. For advanced students to work with professional instructors. Course combined with Chamber Music Seminar for professional or advanced level instrumentalists. Fees: 1500 NKR.*

International Festival for Youth and Children's Choirs. Norges Barne og Ungdomskorforbund, Tollbugata 28, N-0157 Oslo, Norway *tel:* +47 22 425 480 *fax:* +47 22 425 499 *email:* nobu@online.no. Kjetil Aamann, artistic director. *Biennial. Next June 2001. Aged 25 and under. Festival organised in collaboration with the Norwegian Children's and Youth Choir Association.*

Ringve Museum International Summer Course in Early Music. PO Box 2045, N-7001 Trondheim, Norway *tel:* +47 73 929 470 *fax:* +47 73 503 866 *email:* gamosand@online.no. *July in Trondheim, applications by 1 May. Early music performance practice. Ages 20-60. Fees: 800-1000 NKR.*

Poland

Summer Courses for Young Composers. ISCM Polish Section, Mazowiecka 11, PL-00 052 Warsaw, Poland *tel:* +48 22 827 6981 *fax:* +48 22 827 7804 *email:* iscm_pl@ddg.art.pl. Grazyna Dziura, executive secretary. *September, applications by 30 June. US$500. Ages 30 and under. Workshops, individual lessons and lectures for young composers.*

Portugal

International Courses for Early Music. Academia de Musica Antiga de Lisboa, Rua Ricardo Espirito Santo, 3-1 Esq, P-1200 Lisboa, Portugal *tel:* +351 1 390 7724 *also fax; email:* musicantiga@mail.telepac.pt. Sofia de Mendia, director. *24-30 April and 7-14 August 2000, applications by 17 March and 1 July. Ages 16 and above. Masterclasses and chamber music, singing, recorder and traverso, violin and viola, cello and gamba, harpsichord. Fees: 30,000 escudos for April; 47,500 escudos for August.*

Romania

Academia de Muzica 'Gheorghe Dima'. Str I C Bratianu 25, 3400 Cluj-Napoca, Romania *tel:* +40 6 419 3879 *also fax; email:* amgd@amgd.edu.sorosciro.ro. Hans Peter Türk, (for Bach Academy); Cristian Misievici, (Canto and Opera). *Bach Academy, November. Chamber Music, May. Canto and Opera, June.*

Spain

Casares Early Music Week. Cantax House, Lacock, Chippenham, Wiltshire SN15 2JZ, UK *tel:* +44 1249 730468 *also fax.* Andrew van der Beek, admin. *April (Holy Week). For choral singers. Held in small town near Estepona in southern Spain. All ages. Fees: 50,000 ptas.*

Concurso Internacional de Guitarra Alhambra. Manufacturas Alhambra, S.L., Duquesa de Almodovar 17, E-03830 Muro de Alcoy, Alicante, Spain *tel:* +34 96 553 0011 *fax:* +34 96 651 6302 *email:* alhambra@tsai.es. Jaime Julia, managing director. *Next 2000.*

Escuela de Musica Segovia. Tejedores 26 - El Carmen, E-40004 Segovia, Spain *tel:* +34 92 143 4423 *also fax; email:* kent@futurnet.es. Jose Miguel Arranz, manager. *Piano, guitar and singing summer courses in July and August for national and international students. Applications by 1 June. Ages 16-30.*

Francisco Viñas International Interpretation Course. Bruch 125, E-08037 Barcelona, Spain *tel:* +34 93 215 4227/457 8646. Maria Vilardell, president. *January-February, in Barcelona. Applications by*

December. Various aspects of vocal interpretation, including operatic performance and acting skills, Lieder, French melodies, piano accompaniment for lied, etc. Open to all voices and nationalities. Fees: 24,000 ptas; listeners 5000 ptas.

Sweden

Masterclasses in the Music Festival of Pitea. The Academy of Framnas, S-943 33 Ojebyn, Sweden *tel:* +46 91 196816 *fax:* +46 91 196828 *email:* sven-erik.sandlund@m.h.luth.se. Ulla-Britt Sandlund, Sven-Erik Sandlund, directors. *June-July.*

Switzerland

Académie de Musique de Sion. Sion Summer Music Academy, CP 1429, CH-1951 Sion, Switzerland *tel:* +41 27 322 6652 *fax:* +41 27 323 4662 *email:* musacademysion@bluewind.ch. Liliane Martin, admin. *July and August. Masterclasses.*

Académie d'Orgue de Fribourg. Derrière-les-Jardins 1, CH-1700 Fribourg, Switzerland *tel:* +41 26 323 4900 *also fax; email:* academie.orgue@melomane.ch. Maurizio Croci, artistic director. *27 April-5 May 2000, applications by 1 March. Masterclasses, conferences and concerts. Theme: JS Bach and French music.*

Camp for Wind Instruments. c/o Jeunesses Musicales, Maison de la Radio, Bd Carl Vogt 66, CP 233, CH-1211 Genève 8, Switzerland *tel:* +41 22 328 7064 *fax:* +41 22 328 5193 *email:* jmusicales@bluewin.ch. Jean Claude Beuchat, artistic director; Christiane Buntschu, general secretary. *July, applications by 31 May, in Couvet. Chamber and wind orchestras. Ages 15 and over. Fees: SFR 300.*

Chamber Music Course. c/o Jeunesses Musicales, Maison de la Radio, CP233, CH-1211 Genève 8, Switzerland *tel:* +41 22 328 7064 *fax:* +41 22 328 5193 *email:* jmusicales@bluewin.ch. Christiane Buntschu, general secretary. *July, applications by June. Ages 10-16. Fees: FF 680 (all inclusive).*

International Improvisation Week. c/o Jeunesses Musicales, Maison de la Radio, Bd Carl Vogt 66, CP 233, CH-1211 Genève 8, Switzerland *tel:* +41 22 328 7064 *fax:* +41 22 328 5193 *email:* jmusicales@bluewin.ch. Christiane Buntschu, general secretary. *July, applications by May. Aged 14 and above. Fees: SFR 520.*

International Orchestral Course. c/o Jeunesses Musicales, Maison de la Radio, Bd Carl Vogt 66, CP 233, CH-1211 Genève 8, Switzerland *tel:* +41 22 328 7064 *fax:* +41 22 328 5193 *email:* jmusicales@bluewin.ch. Magdalena Burdet, secretary. *July, applications by 10 April, in Sornetan. Symphony orchestra and chamber music. Ages 15-25. Fees: SFR 580.*

International Summer Academy of Music Lenk. Stiftung Kulturforderung Lenk, Secretariat, PO Box 342, CH-3775 Lenk, Switzerland *tel:* +41 33 733 4030 *fax:* +41 33 733 2027. Sanmann Monika, manager. *August-September, applications by 30 June. Instrumental, vocal and chamber music masterclasses. Fees: SFR 340-750.*

Internationale Meisterkurse. Konservatorium für Musik, Kramgasse 36, CH-3011 Berne, Switzerland *tel:* +41 31 311 6221 *fax:* +41 31 312 2053. Heinrich Forster, artistic director; Agnes Schneiter. *International Autumn Academy September-October, in Berne, applications by 30 June. Master courses at the Berne Conservatoire. String quartet, violin, horn. For advanced students and young professionals. Fees: SFR 500.*

Margess International of Switzerland. Steinmuristrasse 6B, CH-8123 Ebmatingen, Switzerland *tel:* +41 1 980 0778 *also fax; email:* rosamar@promovis.ch. Nancy Chumachenco, director. *July-August, applications by 1 April. Intensive string and piano. Ages 10-22. Fees: SFR 1600.*

Music Holiday Weeks. c/o Jeunesses Musicales, Maison de la Radio, CP 233, CH-1211 Genève 8, Switzerland *tel:* +41 22 328 7064 *fax:* +41 22 328 5193 *email:* j.musicales@bluewin.ch. Christiane Buntschu, general secretary. *July, applications by April. Ages 12-18. Fees: SFR 960 (all inclusive).*

Music for Strings. c/o Jeunesses Musicales, Maison de la Radio, CP 233, CH-1211 Genève 8, Switzerland *tel:* +41 22 328 7064 *fax:* +41 22 328 5193 *email:* j.musicales@bluewin.ch. Philippe Domont, artistic director. *August, applications by June. Fees: SFR 770 (all inclusive), SFR 490. Aged 19 and over. Chamber music for good musicians.*

Orchestral and Piano Camp for Children. c/o Jeunesses Musicales, Maison de la Radio, Bd Carl Vogt 66, CP 233, CH-1211 Genève 8, Switzerland *tel:* +41 22 328 7064 *fax:* +41 22 328 5193 *email:* j.musicales@bluewin.ch. Christiane Buntschu, general secretary. *July, applications by 10 April, in Geneva. Orchestral and chamber music, jazz, classical improvisation for the pianist. Ages 8-15. Fees: SFR 470.*

Reding-Piette Seminar For Duo Piano Teams. Reding-Piette School, Chateau Perigord, Monte Carlo MC-98000, Monaco *tel:* +377 93 300721; +41 32 730 2427 *also fax; email:* coco@net.neuchatel2000.ch. *Held at Neuchatel. Two-week masterclasses throughout year for piano duo, given by Professor Janine Reding. No age limits. Repertory of original works written for 2 pianos. Possibility of scholarships. Accommodation provided.*

Scuola Teatro Dimitri. CH- 6653 Verscio, Switzerland *tel:* +41 91 796 2544 *fax:* +41 91 796 2982. *Theatrical school where teaching is based primarily on study of movement of the body and theatrical expression.*

Verbier Festival and Academy. 4 JJ Rousseau, CH-1800 Vevey, Switzerland *tel:* +41 21 922 4010 *fax:* +41 21 922 4012 *email:* info@verbierfestival.com. Miguel Esteban, academy director. *21 July-6 August 2000, applications by 15 February. All ages. Workshops for violin, viola, cello, piano, theatre and dance.*

Workshop for Gregorian Chant. c/o Jeunesses Musicales, Maison de la Radio, Bd Carl Vogt 66, CP 233, CH-1211 Genève 8, Switzerland *tel:* +41 22 328 7064 *fax:* +41 22 781 5218. Christiane Buntschu, general secretary. *Biennial. Next 2000.*

Youth Choir of Switzerland. c/o Jeunesses Musicales, Maison de la Radio, CP233, CH-1211 Genève 8, Switzerland *tel:* +41 22 328 7064. Pascal Mayer. *April-May, July.*

USA

American Suzuki Institute Courses. University of WI-SP, Stevens Point, WI 54481-3897, USA *tel:* +1 715 346 3033 *fax:* +1 715 346 3858 *email:* dmartz@uwsp.edu. Dee Martz, director. *30 July-12 August 2000, applications by 9 June. For ages 3 and over. Individual and group lessons, and teacher training using the Suzuki method. Fees: $500 (adult), $475 (student).*

Aspen Music School. Office of Student Services, 2 Music School Rd, Aspen, CO 81611, USA *tel:* +1 970 925 3254 *fax:* +1 970 925 5708 *email:* school@aspenmusic.org. Dean W Harold Laster, student services. *June-August, applications by February. Full range of courses and private lessons; orchestral, opera, vocal concert studies, composition, conducting, chamber music, classical guitar. No age restriction (most aged 18-22). Fees: $2100, tuition; $2300, room and board.*

Baroque Dance and its Music Workshop. Department of Music, Braun Music Center, Stanford University, Stanford, CA 94305-3076, USA *tel:* +1 415 337 7779 *also fax; email:* Dolascetta@earthlink.net. Louise M Pescetta, admin. *17-28 July 2000, closing date 31 May. Annual summer workshop for dancers, dance scholars, choreographers, musicians and theatre specialists. Fees: $475 for 2 weeks; $345 for 1 week.*

Chamber Music Institute Course. PO Box 45776, Seattle, Washington 98145, USA *tel:* +1 206 527 8839 *fax:* +1 206 526 8621 *email:* olymusic@brigadoon.com. Alan Iglitzin, executive director; Meike Kaan, festival manager. *3 weeks in July. Intense chamber music instruction for ages 14-17 in a pastoral setting. Many performance opportunities and individualised coaching. Fees: $40, application; $1500, tuition.*

Education through Music Summer Institute. c/o 641 Excelsior Ave, San Francisco CA 94112, USA *tel:* +1 415 586 2217 *fax:* +1 415 239 2737 *email:* etm@quiknet.com. Trudi Richards. *Mount St Mary's, California. Fees: $310 for 2 weeks; for teachers and children.*

The Festival-Institute at Round Top. PO Drawer 89, Round Top, TX-78954-0089, USA *tel:* +1 409 249 3129 *fax:* +1 409 249 3100 *email:* festinst@fais.net. James Dick, founder/artistic director; Alain G Declert, artistic co-ordinator. *3 June-16 July 2000, applications by 26 February. Ages 18-35. Orchestral and chamber music session. A professional summer institute for advanced study and performance. Scholarships available. Fees: $540.*

Indiana University School of Music. Special Programs, Merrill Hall, 121 Indiana University, School of Music, Bloomington, Indiana 47405, USA *tel:* +1 812 855 6025 *fax:* +1 812 855 9847 *email:* musicsp@indiana.edu. Eric Jon Nichols, director of Outreach. *June-end July 2000. Age 12 and over. Variety of programmes from pre-college academics to adult masterclasses. Fees: $200-2400.*

International String Workshop. 187 Aqua View Rd, Cedarburg, WI 53012, USA *tel:* +1 414 377 7062 *fax:* +1 414 377 7096 *email:* thintz@execpc.com. Tori Hintz, manager. *24 July-6 August 2000, applications by 1 July. In Glasgow, Scotland. String and piano pedagogy, performance, jazz, and conducting. Ages 16-90. Fees US$1795.*

Ithaca College Chamber Music Institute. Ithaca Talent Education, PO Box 669, Ithaca, NY 14851, USA *tel:* +1 607 272 6006 *fax:* +1 607 275 0239. Sanford Reuning, director. *July, applications by April. Ages 12-18. Fees: $1600.*

Ithaca Violoncello Institute. 125 Ridgecrest Rd, Ithaca, NY 14850, USA *tel:* +1 607 273 8896. Einar Holm, director. *Late June-August for 7 weeks. Serious or professionally-minded cellists, aged 16 and over. Fees: c $3000 including tuition, room and board.*

The Kodály Institute at Capital University. Conservatory of Music, Capital University, Columbus, OH 2394, USA *tel:* +1 614 236 6267 *fax:* +1 614 236 6680 *email:* smathias@capital.edu. Sandra Mathias, director. *10-28 July 2000, applications by 1 June. 20th Anniversary. Teacher-training course utilising the Kodály philosophy of music education, levels 1, 2 and 3. Ages 20 and over. OAKE endorsed certification course.*

Magic Mountain Music Farm. 817 West End Av, New York, NY 10025, USA *tel:* +1 212 662 6634; +1 607 263 2304 *fax:* +1 212 662 2916; 607 263 9647. Burton Kaplan, director. *January, March (orchestra excerpts session), May-June, June, July-August, August (orchestra excerpts session). Fees: $40 registration; $1350 tuition, board. For professional string performers and teachers and advanced college and conservatory students. Daily workshops to improve concentration, practising effectiveness, etc.*

Margaret Rowell Cello Symposium. San Francisco Conservatory of Music, 1201 Ortega St, San Francisco, CA 94122, USA *tel:* +1 415 759 3454 *fax:* +1 415 759 3499. Laura Crisp, assistant; Cindy Dove, publications editor. *June. Intensive week-long course for cellists. Co-ordinated by Bonnie Hampton. Morning sessions include ensembles playing and survey of cello technique. Afternoon masterclasses allow for individual attention.*

New Music Miami Festival. School of Music, Florida International University, University Park Campus, Miami, FL 33199, USA *tel:* +1 305 348 2896 *fax:* +1 305 348 4073 *email:* garciao@fiu.edu. Orlando Jacinto Garcia, co-director. *17-19 February 2000. Composers invited to attend masterclasses and forums and hear a performance of one of their works. Master artists: Orlando Jacinto Garcia, Frederick Kaufman, Chinary Ung and Charles Dodge. Fees: $475 plus lodging and travel.*

Phil Mattson Vocal Jazz/Choral Workshops. Southwestern Community College, Creston, IA 50801, USA *tel:* +1 515 782 7081 ext 319. *Workshops for university students and teachers. Fees: $375.45*

Western Wind Summer Workshops in Ensemble Singing. Western Wind Vocal Ensemble, 263 West 86th St, New York, NY 10024, USA *tel:* +1 800 788 2187 *fax:* +1 212 873 2849 *email:* workshops@westernwind.org. Zach Nelson, workshop co-ordinator. *June, July, apply by early June. Workshops for ensembles singing from renaissance to modern jazz for all ages. Fees: $149-399 (tuition), $150-550 (room and board).*

Music Publishers

The following list includes major international publishers of scores and sheet music.

Argentina

Barry Editorial Com Ind SRL. Ave Roque Sáenz Peña 1185 8°N, 1035 Buenos Aires, Argentina *tel:* +54 11 4382 3230/4383 0745 *fax:* +54 11 4383 3946 *email:* barry@satlink.com.

Australia

Alfred Publishing (Australia) Ltd. PO Box 2355, Taren Point, NSW 2229, Australia *tel:* +61 2 9524 0033 *fax:* +61 2 9524 0023.

Allans Publishing Pty. PO Box 4072, Richmond East, Victoria 3121, Australia *tel:* +61 3 4281 600 *fax:* +61 3 428 1811. *Hire for Donemus.*

Boosey & Hawkes Inc. Unit 12/6 Campbell St, AUS-Artarmon, New South Wales 2064, Australia.

Charles Paine Pty Ltd. 8 Ferris St, North Parramatta, NSW, Australia *tel:* +61 2 9890 1388.

Holborne Australasia Pty. PO Box 282, Alexandria, NSW 2015, Australia *tel:* +61 2 9519 9066 *fax:* +61 2 9519 3622 *email:* holborne@ozemail.com.au.

The Really Useful Company (Australia). 1st Floor, 24 Bay St, Double Bay, Sydney 2028, Australia *tel:* +61 2 9363 2499 *fax:* +61 2 9363 1589.

Austria

Bosworth & Co. Postfach 178, A-1201 Wien, Austria.

Doblinger Musikverlag. Dorotheergasse 10, A-1010 Wien, Austria *tel:* +43 1 515 030 *fax:* +43 1 515 0351 *email:* music@doblinger.co.at. Helmuth Pany, general manager.

Josef Weinberger GmbH. Neulerchenfelderstr 3-7, A-1160 Wien, Austria *tel:* +43 1 403 59910 *fax:* +43 1 403 599113 *email:* musik@ weinberger. co.at. Hans J Granzer, managing director; Christian Kobee, assistant manager.

Musikwissenschaftlicher Verlag. Dorotheergasse 10, A-1010 Wien, Austria *tel:* +43 1 515 0343 *fax:* +49 1 515 0351 *email:* music@doblinper.co.at. Herbert Vogg, general manager; Mathilde Eder, confidential clerk.

traunmusik Wien. Postfach 300, A-1021 Wien, Austria *tel:* +43 1 216 575510 *fax:* +43 1 216 575513. Josef P Traun, general manager. *Scores and sheet music of contemporary Austrian composers. Music for education and concerts.*

Universal Edition AG. PO Box 3, A-1015 Wien, Austria *tel:* +43 1 505 8695 *fax:* +43 1 505 2720 *email:* uemusic@uemusic.at. Marion von Hartlieb, director.

Wiener Waldhorn Verein Verlag. Postfach 134, A-1080 Wien, Austria *fax:* +43 22 393705. Roland Horvath, president; Siegfried Schwarel, vice-president; E Seyfried, musical director. *Overseas offices: Oliver Brockway, 53 Oakley St, London SW3 5HB, UK; Marie-France Vigneron, Residence des Alpes, 194 rue du Château du Rentiers F-75013 Paris, France; Daryl Ponder, 4 Oakwood Drive, Milville NJ 08322-1917, USA.*

Belgium

Alamire Music Publishers. PO Box 45, B-3990 Peer, Belgium *tel:* +32 1 163 2164 *fax:* +32 1 163 4911 *email:* info@musica.be. Herman Baeten, managing director. *Facsimile editions of early musical sources; scientific publications; short studies;* Musica Antiqua *magazine; exclusive collection of greeting cards, posters, postcards and miniatures out of ancient musical sources.*

Centre Belge de Documentation Musicale. Rue d'Arlon 75-77, B-1040 Bruxelles, Belgium *tel:* +32 2 230 9430/9437 *also fax; email:* 101573.3644@compuserve.com. Diana von Volborth-Danys, director. *Contemporary Belgian classical scores.*

Canada

Banff Music Limited. PO Box 309, Mount Albert, Ont L0G 1M0, Canada *tel:* +1 905 773 6848 *fax:* +1 905 853 2955 *email:* swain00@ibm.net. Wayne Patton, vice-president; Derek Swain, director.

Diffusion i Média. 4580 Avenue de Lorimier, Montréal, QC H2H 2B5, Canada *tel:* +1 514 526 4096 *fax:* +1 514 526 4487 *email:* dim@cam.org. Jean-François Denis. *Electro-acoustic music CD label 'empreintes DIGITALes'.*

Gamelon Music Publications. PO Box 525, Station P, Toronto, Ont M5S 2T1. Michael Kleniec, manager.

Les Editions Doberman-Yppan. PO Box 2021, St-Nicholas, PQ G7A 4X5, Canada *tel:* +1 418 831 1304 *fax:* +1 418 836 3645 *email:* doberman.yppan@videotron.ca. Paul Gerrits, president. *80 classical guitar, 170 Canadian concert music.*

Leslie Music Supply Inc. 198 Speers Rd, Oakville, Ont L6K 2E9 *tel:* +1 905 844 3109 *fax:* +1 905 844 7637. E Joan Leslie, president; Pat Leslie VanderHeyden, general manager; W J Leslie, accountant. *Selling agent: Roberton Publications, The Windmill, Wendover, Aylesbury, Bucks HP22 6JJ, UK.*

Mayfair Music Publishing. 2600 John St, Unit 220, Markham, Ont L3R 3W3, Canada *tel:* +1 905 475 1848 *fax:* +1 905 474 9870 *email: sales@mayfairmusic.com. Steve Loweth, USA sales manager; Lucie Stubbington, Canada sales manager.*

Sound Ideas. 105 West Beaver Creek Rd, Suite No 4, Richmond Hill, Ont L4B 1C6, Canada *tel:* +1 905 886 5000 *fax:* +1 905 886 6800 *email:* info@sound-ideas.com. Brian Nimens, president; Michael Bell, vice-president.

Czech Republic

Divertimento Ltd. Czech Music Fund, Parizka 13, Stare Mesto, CR-110 00 Praha 1, Czech Republic *tel:* +420 2 24 811258 *fax:* +420 2 24 810614. Vesna Padovic, Vaclav Drevikovsky, Barbara Wheeler, hire librarians.

Edit. Zarubova 493, CR-142 00 Praha 4, Lhotka, Czech Republic *tel:* +420 2 471 4540 *also fax.* Ing Miroslav Sik, managing director; Zdenek Kalina, commercial director; Mgr Veroslav Neumann, artistic director; Zdenek Hertl, chief producer.

Editio Praga a s. Chopinova 4, CR-120 00 Praha, Czech Republic *tel:* +420 2 627 4219/20 *fax:* +420 2 627 4235 *email:* musicpbl@editio-praga.cz. Michael Lochar, director.

H Music Publishing. Mikulovice 131, CR-530 02 Pardubice, Czech Republic *tel:* +420 40 33234 *also fax; email:* h.music.publishing@telecom.cz. Jaroslav Horinka.

Music Cheb. Na vyhlidce 25, CR-350 02 Cheb, Czech Republic *tel:* +420 1 6642 3356 *also fax; email:* jansky@ch.cesnet.cz. Petr Jansky, director.

Muzikus. Prístavní 18, CR-170 00 Praha 7, Czech Republic *tel:* +420 2 808780 *fax:* +420 2 876130 *email:* muzikus@mbox.vol.cz.

Nakladatelstvi A-Z. Tyrsova 22, CR-702 00 Ostrava, Czech Republic. Cejka Karel, editor in chief.

Nakladatelstvi Tempo. U druzstva Tempo 10, CR-142 00 Praha 4, Czech Republic *tel:* +420 2 472 1407 *fax:* +420 2 472 8010. Cervinkova Blanka, editor in chief. *Overseas office: Boosey & Hawkes; Bote & Bock.*

Denmark

Edition Egtved A/s. Mårkaervej 13, DK-2630 Tåstrup, Denmark *tel:* +45 4 399 9400 *fax:* +45 4 399 9407 *email:* egtved@post8.tele.dk. Simon Faber, daily leader; Svend Ulstrup, secretary; Hans-Ulrik Barfoed, music consultant. *Organ and choral music specialists.*

Edition Wilhelm Hansen. Bornholmsgade 1, 1, DK-1266 Copenhagen K, Denmark *tel:* +45 33 117888 *fax:* +45 33 148178 *email:* ewh@ewh.dk. Tine Birger Christensen, managing director; Ole Hansen, promotion. *Scores, songbooks, educational music books, etc. Music Sales Ltd, 8/9 Frith St, London W1V 5TZ, UK.*

Engstrøm & Sødring AS. Borgergade 17, DK-1300 Copenhagen K, Denmark *tel:* +45 33 143228 *fax:* +45 33 143227. Helge Schlenkert, managing director.

The Society for the Publication of Danish Music. Gråbrødrestrœde 18, 1, DK-1165 Copenhagen K, Denmark *tel:* +45 33 135445 *fax:* +45 33 933044 *email:* sales@samfundet.dk. Klaus Ib Jørgensen, president; Niels Prins, administrator, webmaster.

SteepleChase Music/Edition Kontrapunkt. PO Box 35, DK-2930 Klampenborg, Denmark *tel:* +45 39 644244 *fax:* +45 39 645044. Nils Winther, managing director. *Jazz and classical contemporary.*

Finland

Sulasol. Fredrikinkatu 51-53 B, FIN-00100 Helsinki, Finland *tel:* +358 9 413 61100 *fax:* +358 9 4136 1122 *email:* sulasol.co@inet.fi. Matti Apajalahti, executive director; Reijo Kekkonen, publications manager.

Warner Music Finland Oy. PO Box 169, FIN-02101 Espoo, Finland *tel:* +358 9 435 011 *fax:* +358 9 675 531. Marita Kaasalainen, managing director; Mark Fry, promotion/label manager; Timo Kivinen, sales manager; Jari Tiessalo, A&R, executive director, classical.

France

Alphonse Leduc Editions Musicales. 175 Rue Saint-Honoré, F-75040 Paris cedex 01, France *tel:* +33 1 42 96 89 11 *fax:* +33 1 42 86 02 83 *email:* AlphonseLeduc@wanadoo.fr. François Leduc, Mike Warren, sales; Basile Crichton, promotion. *Includes Hamelle, Heugel and Robert*

King. US affiliate and distributor: Robert King Music Sales Inc, 140 Main Street, North Easton, MA 02356, USA.

Breitkopf & Härtel. 20 Rue Jean-Baptiste Pigalle, F-75009 Paris, France *tel:* +33 1 42 81 40 11 *fax:* +33 1 40 16 80 02.

Choudens Editions. 38 Rue Jean Mermoz, F-75008 Paris, France *tel:* +33 1 42 66 62 97 *fax:* +33 1 42 66 62 79.

Delrieu Edition. 26 Av George-Sand, F-75016 Paris, France *tel:* +33 1 48 74 34 83 *fax:* +33 1 48 74 48 37. Pierre Lemoine, chief executive officer.

Editions Henry Lemoine. 41 Rue Bayen, F-75017 Paris, France *tel:* +33 1 56 68 86 65 *fax:* +33 1 56 68 90 66. Pierre H Lemoine, president.

Editions Notissimo. 4 Rue de Brest, F-69002 Lyon, France *tel:* +33 4 78 37 50 04 *fax:* +33 4 78 42 56 53. Michel Girer, director; Ronan Schönberg, sales manager.

Editions Paul Beuscher. 27 Blvd Beaumarchais, F-75004 Paris, France *tel:* +33 1 44 54 36 00 *fax:* +33 1 48 08 08 37.

Editions Ricordi. 22 Rue Chauchat, F-75009 Paris, France *tel:* +33 1 47 70 37 28 *fax:* +33 1 42 47 17 56. Ivanka Stoianova, artistic director.

Editions Salabert. 22 Rue Chauchat, F-75009 Paris, France *tel:* +33 1 48 24 55 60 *fax:* +33 1 42 47 17 56 *email:* salabert@hd.fr. Marcel Landowski, president; Nelly Quérol, secretary.

Gérard Billaudot Editeur SA. 14 Rue de l'Echiquier, F-75010 Paris, France *tel:* +33 1 47 70 14 46 *fax:* +33 1 45 23 22 54. François Derveaux, chairman.

Hamelle. 175 Rue St Honore, F-75040 Paris cedex 01, France *tel:* +33 1 42 96 89 11 *fax:* +33 1 42 86 02 83. Francois Leduc, Mike Warren, sales; Basile Crichton, promotion.

Jobert Societé des Editions. 76 Rue Quincampoix, F-75003 Paris, France *tel:* +33 1 42 72 83 43 *fax:* +33 1 42 72 27 67. Georges Denise.

Musique and Music. 19 Rue Anatole France, F-92800 Puteaux, France *tel:* +33 1 41 97 08 08 *fax:* +33 1 41 97 08 00 *email:* jmmarquaille@musique-music.com. Jean-Michel Marquaille, president.

Studio G Sarl. Les Eversins du Presle, F-69870 Chambost-Allières, France *tel:* +33 4 74 60 12 44 *also fax.* E Mercer, distribution, France.

Germany

Anton Böhm & Sohn. Lange Gasse 26, D-86152 Augsburg, Germany *tel:* +49 821 502840 *fax:* +49 821 502 8433. Thomas Ballinger-Amtmann, manager. *Sacred, secular and organ music.*

Apollo-Verlag Paul Lincke GmbH. Weihergarten 5, D-55116 Mainz, Germany *tel:* +49 613 124 6300 *fax:* +49 613 124 6861 *email:* apollo@schott-musik.de. Christian Sprang, company lawyer.

Art.e Concert Company. Dobbenweg 9, D-28203 Bremen, Germany *tel:* +49 421 430 0223 *fax:* +49 421 430 0229 *email:* artebremen@compuserve.com. Thomas Proff, Jörg Zander, managing directors.

Bärenreiter-Verlag Karl Vötterle GmbH & Co KG. Heinrich-Schütz-Allee 35, D-34131 Kassel-Wilhelmshöhe, Germany *tel:* +49 561 31050 *fax:* +49 561 310 5240 *email:* baerenreiter@baerenreiter.com. Barbara Scheuch-Vötterle; Leonhard Scheuch. *Alkor-Edition Kassel GmbH; Gustav Bosse GmbH & Co KG; Henschel Verlag für Musik GmbH; Johann-Philipp Hinnenthal Verlag; Nagels-Verlag; Süddeutscher Musikverlag GmbH & Co KG.*

Benjamin Anton J GmbH. Werderstr 44, D-20144 Hamburg, Germany *tel:* +49 404 51225 *fax:* +49 404 51803. *D Rahter; N Simrock.*

Blasmusikverlag Schulz GmbH. Am Märzengraben 6, D-79112 Freiburg, Germany *tel:* +49 766 41431/2004 *fax:* +49 766 45123. Klaus Schulz, publisher.

Boosey & Hawkes/Bote & Bock GmbH & Co. Lützowufer 26, D-10787 Berlin, Germany *tel:* +49 30 2500 1300 *fax:* +49 30 2500 1399 *email:* musikverlag@boosey.com. Winifried Jacobs, managing director.

Bosworth & Co. Augustinusstr 9b, D-50226 Frechen; Postfach 4041, D-50216 Frechen, Germany *tel:* +49 223 461348/61397 *fax:* +49 223 465335. Reimar Segebrecht, managing director.

Breitkopf & Härtel. Walkmühlstr 52, D-65195 Wiesbaden, Germany *tel:* +49 611 450080 *fax:* +49 611 450 0859 *email:* info@breitkopf.com. Lieselotte Sievers, Gottfried Möckel, general managers. *Deutscher Verlag für Musik, Leipzig GmbH; Bessel.*

Breitkopf & Härtel (Sales). Obere Waldstr 30, D-65232 Taunusstein, Germany *tel:* +49 612 896 6321 *fax:* +49 612 896 6350 *email:* sales@breitkopf.com. Ulrike Lorenz, sales manager.

Carus-Verlag GmbH. Editorial Offices, Wannenstr 45, D-70199 Stuttgart, Germany *tel:* +49 711 960110 *fax:* +49 711 608247 *email:* info@carus-verlag.com. Waltraud Graulich, managing director; Jo Kunze, sales manager. *Sheet music, CDs, music books.*

Chanterelle Verlag. PO Box 103909, D-69029 Heidelberg, Germany *tel:* +49 622 178 4105 *fax:* +49 622 178 4106 *email:* chanterelle@t-online.de. Michael Macmeeken, owner. *Guitar music.*

Edition Schultheiss. Pasinger Str 38a, D-82152 Planegg b München, Germany *tel:* +49 89 859 9944 *fax:* +49 89 859 3323 *email:* Thomi-Berg@t-online.de. Elisabeth Thomi-Berg, managing director.

Ewoton-International Elmar Wolf GmbH. Mittelfeldstr 4, D-66851 Queidersbach, Germany *tel:* +49 637 192300 *fax:* +49 637 117212.

G Henle Verlag. Forstenrieder Allee 122, D-81476 München, Germany *tel:* +49 897 59820 *fax:* +49 897 598240 *email:* info@henle.de. Martin Bente, general manager; Michael Ingendaay, sales manager. *Overseas address: G Henle USA Inc, 1897 Craig Rd, St Louis, MO 63146, USA.*

Gehann-Musik-Verlag. Lamperter Flur 2, D-55481 Kludenbach, Germany *tel:* +49 676 32195 *fax:* +49 676 32175.

Georg Löffler Publishing (GLM). Kaiser Ludwig Platz 1, D-80336 München, Germany *tel:* +49 89 5440 4534 *fax:* +49 89 5440 4535 *email:* glm@glm.de. Michele Claveau, product manager.

Gerig (Contemporary Music) *see* **Breitkopf.**

Halter Musikverlag. Gablonzerstr 24, D-76185 Karlsruhe, Germany *tel:* +49 721 567272 *fax:* +49 721 562674 *email:* office@halter.de.

Heinrichshofen's Verlag GmbH & Co KG. Liebigstr 16, D-26389 Wilhelmshaven, Germany *tel:* +49 4421 92670 *fax:* +49 4421 202007 *email:* heinrichshofen@t-online.de. Eva Noetzel, president.

Josef Weinberger GmbH. Oeder Weg 26, D-60318 Frankfurt am Main, Germany *tel:* +49 69 955 288 30 *fax:* +49 69 955 288 44 *email:* Weinberger.Musikverlage@t-online.de.

Kantor Publishing. Dobbenweg 9, D-28203 Bremen, Germany *tel:* +49 421 430 0225 *fax:* +49 421 430 021 *email:* artebremen@compuserve.com. Karsten Arndt, managing director.

Karl Heinrich Möseler Verlag. Hoffmann-von-Fallersleben-Str 8, D-38304 Wolfenbüttel, Germany *tel:* +49 533 195970 *fax:* +49 533 195 9720. Jutta Möseler, Dietrich Möseler.

KGA Verlags Service. Postfach 10 21 80, D-3500 Kassel, Germany *tel:* +49 561 930960 *fax:* +49 561 930 9610 *email:* order@baerenreiter.com. *Distributor for Bärenreiter and other publishers.*

Kistner & C.F.W. Siegel & Co. Aggerweg 6, D-51149 Köln, Germany *tel:* +49 2203 180 037 *fax:* +49 2203 180 039. Marianne Feder, owner; Annette Valder, attorney.

Kurt Maas Berklee Publications. Röntgenstr 5, D-82152 Martinsried, Germany *tel:* +49 89 856 2477 *fax:* +49 89 856 2478. Inge Maas, manager.

Leu-Verlag Wolfgang Leupelt. Herweg 34, D-51429 Bergisch Gladbach, Germany *tel:* +49 220 498 1141 *fax:* +49 220 498 1143 *email:* leuverlag@aol.com.

Leuckart FEC Musikverlag. Rheingoldstr 4, D-80639 München, Germany *tel:* +49 89 173928 *fax:* +49 89 176054. Marco Sander, managing director.

Lutz-Musikverlag. Schepp-Allee 17, D-64295 Darmstadt, Germany *tel:* +49 616 284086 *also fax.* Viljem Lutz, Regina Lutz, managers.

Mannheimer Musik-Verlag GmbH. Kunigundenstr 4, D-53179 Bonn, Germany *tel:* +49 228 347989 *fax:* +49 228 856372. Joachim von Roebel, manager.

Max Brockhaus. Mirbachstr 9, D-53173 Bonn, Germany *tel:* +49 228 363789/347989 *fax:* +49 228 856372. Joachim V Roebel.

Melodie der Welt. Gr Friedberger Str 23-27, D-60313 Frankfurt, Germany *tel:* +49 692 998670 *fax:* +49 692 998 6710. Pamela Michel, general manager.

Moeck Verlag & Musikinstrumentenwerk. Inh Dr Hermann Moeck, Hans-Heinrich-Warnke Str 14, D-29227 Celle, Germany *tel:* +49 514 188530 *fax:* +49 514 188 5342. Sabine Haare-Moeck, publishing director; Andrea Höutsch-Bertram, hire material. *Overseas address: Magna Music Distributors Inc, PO Box 338, 74 Amenia Union Rd, Sharon, CT 06069, USA email:* magnamusic@magnamusic.com.

Musik-Gross-Sortiment Görz. Erletstr 14, D-85053 Ingolstadt, Germany *tel:* +49 841 61058/66274 *fax:* +49 841 68771 *email:* musik-goerz@t-online.de. Mrs Gregg, owner; Mrs Kerscher, Mr Paulus, Mr Maierstein, order processors. *Wholesaler: deliver all music publications.*

Musica Vera Musikverlag. Torgauer Str 27, D-28215 Bremen, Germany *tel:* +49 421 374918 *fax:* +49 421 375325 *email:* hn.enterprises@mail.netware.de. Hannes Nimpuno.

Musikverlag G Ricordi & Co. Velaskostr 6, D-85622 Feldkirchen, Germany *tel:* +49 89 903 8851 *fax:* +49 89 903 8859. Roberto Babini Cattaneo, Mimma Guastoni.

Musikverlage Hans Sikorski. Johnsallee 23, Postfach 13-2001, D-20148 Hamburg, Germany *tel:* +49 40 41 41 000 *fax:* +49 40 44 94 68 *email:* webmaster@sikorski.de. Hans-Ulrich Duffek, director; Helmut Peters, head of promotions; Reinhold Seyboth, librarian; Liselotte Schwartz, sales manager.

Oertel (J). Ainmiller Str 42, D-80801 München, Germany *tel:* +49 810 54689.

Otto Wrede Regina-Verlag oHG. Schumannstr 35, D-65193 Wiesbaden, Germany *tel:* +49 611 523118 *fax:* +49 611 520773. Edda Wrede.

Peermusic Classical. Mühlenkamp 43, D-22303 Hamburg, Germany *tel:* +49 40 278 3790 *fax:* +49 40 2783 7940 *email:* classicaleur@peermusic.com. Reinhard Flender, European director; J Glissmann; U zur Nieden, rental material, editorial and promotion. *See also New York office.*

PJ Tonger Musikverlag GmbH & Co. Auf dem Brand 3, D-50996 Köln, Germany *tel:* +49 93 55640 *fax:* +49 93 556411. Peter Tonger, managing director.

Richard Birnbach Musikverlag. Aubinger Str 9, D-82166 Lochham, Germany *tel:* +49 89 875450 *fax:* +49 89 871 4639.

Ries & Erler, Berlin Musikverlag. Wandlenallee 8, D-14052 Berlin, Germany *tel:* +49 30 825 1049 *fax:* +49 30 825 9721 *email:* verlag @rieserler.de. Andreas Meurer, general manager.

Robert Lienau Musikverlag. Strubbergstr 80, D-60489 Frankfurt, Germany *tel:* +49 699 782866 *fax:* +49 699 782 8679. Judith Picard, production manager; Saskia Herchenröder, hire department.

Schott Musik International. Postfach 36 40, D-55026 Mainz; Weihergarten 5, D-55116 Mainz, Germany *tel:* +49 613 12460 *fax:* +49 613 124 6211 *email:* katya.kratzer@schott-musik.de. Peter Hanser-Strecker, Rolf Reisinger, managing directors; Rainer Mohrs, head of editorial department; Helmut Fischer, sales manager. *See also: European American Music Distributors Corp; Schott Japan Company Ltd; Schott Music Publishers (Canada) Ltd, 2 Bloor St West, Toronto, Canada; Schott China Ltd, 111 Connaught Rd Central, Hong Kong.*

Stockhausen-Verlag. Kettenberg 15, D-51515 Kürten, Germany *fax:* +49 2268 1813. *All works of Karlheinz Stockhausen, books, scores and CDs.*

Thomi-Berg Publisher & Sheet Music Distributor. Pasinger Straße 38a, D-82152 Planegg, Germany *tel:* +49 89 859 9944 *fax:* +49 89 859 3323 *email:* Thomi-Berg@t-online.de. Elisabeth Thomi-Berg, managing director.

Tonos Musikverlags GmbH. Robert Edler Haus, Holzhofallee 15, D-64295 Darmstadt, Germany *tel:* +49 6151 39040 *fax:* +49 6151 39 0490 *email:* tonos@aol.com. Marian Golf, Johanna Golf, directors.

Wolfgang G Haas - Musikverlag Köln. Postfach 90 07 48, D-51117 Köln, Germany *tel:* +49 2203 98 883 0 *fax:* +49 2203 98883 50 *email:* info@Haas-Koeln.de.

Zander Records. Dobbenweg 9, D-28203 Bremen, Germany *tel:* +49 421 43002 27/25 *fax:* +49 421 43002 1 *email:* artebremen@compuserve.com. Jörg Zander, managing director; Karsten Arndt, executive director.

Zimmermann GmbH + Co. Strubbergstr 80, D-60489 Frankfurt, Germany *tel:* +49 699 782866 *fax:* +49 699 782 8679 *email:* 101572.1364@compuserve.com. Michael Henne, sales manager; Saskia Herchenröder, hire department.

Hong Kong

Schott China Ltd. 111 Connaught Rd Central, Hong Kong.

Hungary

Editio Musica Budapest Ltd. Vörösmarty tér 1, PO Box 322, H-1370 Budapest, Hungary *tel:* +36 1 318 4228 *fax:* +36 1 338 2732 *email:* musicpubl@emb.hu. István Homolya, managing director.

Republic of Ireland

An Gúm. The Publications Branch, Dept of Education and Science, 44 Sráid Uí Chonaill, Uacht, Dublin 1 *tel:* +353 1 809 5034 *fax:* +353 1 873 1140 *email:* gum@educ.irlgov.ie. Máire Nic Mhoaláin, editor. *Traditional, choral and instrumental music.*

Association of Irish Choirs. Drinan St, Cork, Republic of Ireland *tel:* +353 2 131 2296 *fax:* +353 2 196 2457 *email:* cnc@iol.ie. Barbara Heas, administrator. *Choral music, especially Irish.*

Israel

Israeli Music Publications Ltd. PO Box 7681, Jerusalem 94188, Israel *tel:* +972 2 625 1370 *fax:* +972 2 624 1378 *email:* impltd@galanet.net. Sergey Khanukaev, director of music publications; Victor Licht, assistant manager.

Italy

Bèrben (Edizioni Musical). Via Redipuglia 65, I-60100 Ancona, Italy *tel:* +39 071 204428 *fax:* +39 071 57414 *email:* info@berben.it.

Boccaccini & Spada Editori Srl. Via Arezzo 17, 00040 Pavona di, Albano Laziale (RM), Italy *tel:* +99 06 93 10 217/516 *fax:* +99 06 93 11 903 *email:* p.spada@agora.stm.it. Pietro Spada, administrator.

Casa Ricordi - BMG Ricordi. Via Berchet 2, I-20121 Milano, Italy *tel:* +39 02 88811 *fax:* +39 02 888 112212.

Nuova Carisch SA. Via Campania 12, I-20098 San Giuliano Milanese (Milano), Italy *tel:* +39 029 82211 *fax:* +39 029 822 1200. Adriano Solaro, president; Marco Volontè, managing director.

Japan

Ongaku No Tomo Sha Corp. Kagurazaka 6-30, Shinjuku-ku, Tokyo 162-8716, Japan *tel:* +81 3 3235 2111 *fax:* +81 3 3235 2110. Kazuyuki Nabeshima, head of copyright.

Schott Japan Company Ltd. Kasuga Building, 2-9-3 Iidabashi, Chiyoda-ku, Tokyo 102-0072, Japan *tel:* +81 3 3263 6530 *fax:* +81 3 3263 6672.

Luxembourg

Letzebuerger Vollekslidderverlag ASBL. Rue Sosthene Weis 2, L-2722, Luxembourg *tel:* +35 2 462536 *fax:* +35 2 471440 *email:* direction @ugda.al.lu. Henri Schumacher, president.

Mexico

Ediciones Mexicanas de Musica AC. Avda Juarez 18, Despacho 206, 06050 D F, Mexico *tel:* +52 5 521 5855 *also fax.* Isolda Acevedo Jiménez, manager.

Netherlands

Albersen & Co BV. 182 Groot Hertoginnelaan, NL-2517 EV Den Haag, Netherlands *tel:* +31 70 345 6000 *fax:* +31 70 345 7110 *email:* albersenmuziek@introweb.nl. Herman Albersen, general manager; Michel Krens, sales department.

Amstel Music BV. Middenweg 213, NL-1098 AN Amsterdam, Netherlands *tel:* +31 20 668 0232 *fax:* +31 20 692 2027 *email:* amsmusic@euronet.nl. Johan de Meij, director; Chris Abelen, chief editor.

Beurskens Muziekuitgeverij. 8052, NL-5993 ZG Maasbree, Netherlands *tel:* +31 77 465 1907 *fax:* +31 77 465 3883. Annemie Beurskens, Hans Beurskens, directors.

Donemus Publishing House. Paulus Potterstr 16, NL-1071 CZ Amsterdam, Netherlands *tel:* +31 20 676 4436 *fax:* +31 20 673 3588. L J Deuss, managing director.

Koch Benelux BV Music Publishing. Bredaseweg 108a, NL-4902 NS Oosterhout (NB), Netherlands *tel:* +31 16 247 0999 *fax:* +31 16 247 0888 *email:* kochbnl@xsyall.nl. Rudy Schedler, publishing manager; Ger A M van der Meys, general manager.

XYZ International. Ambachtsweg 42, NL-1271 Am Huizen, Netherlands *tel:* +31 35 524 2104 *fax:* +31 35 524 2336 *email:* emcmusic @strengholt.nl. Pieter A van Zuylen, managing director; Frank Wymenga, export manager.

New Zealand

Catholic Supplies Ltd. 80 Adelaide Rd, Wellington, New Zealand *tel:* +64 4 384 3665 *fax:* +64 4 384 3663 *email:* catholic.supplies@clear.net.nz. Peter D Hoskins, general manager; Barbara L Hoskins, marketing manager; Cecelia M Healion, customer service manager.

Norway

Cantando Musikkforlag. PO Box 1594, N-4093, Stavanger, Norway *tel:* +47 51 894601 *fax:* +47 51 894602 *email:* order@cantando.com. Stefan Bergtsson, manager.

Editio Aap. AasWangsvei 8, N-1613 Fredrikstad, Norway *tel:* +47 69 319795 *also fax; email:* aap@audioattic.com. Frank Nordensten, manager; Katya Meyer, secretary.

Fortissimo Forlag A/S. PO Box 160, N-1459 Fjellstrand, Norway *tel:* +47 66 910891 *fax:* +47 66 910892. Christer Johannesen, director. *Band music and music for wind ensembles.*

Frost Music A/S. PO Box 6062, Etterstad, N-0601, Oslo, Norway *tel:* +47 22 677111 *fax:* +47 22 677241 *email:* frostm@sn.no. Birger Brynjulfsen, business manager; Fred Svendsen, music librarian.

Lyche Musikkforlag A/S. PO Box 624 Stromso, N-3003 Drammen, Norway *tel:* +47 32 245000/5182 *fax:* +47 32 245189. Oyvin Brock, manager.

Musikkverkstedet. Gutzeitsgt 4, N-1610 Frederikstad, Norway *tel:* +47 69 316535 *also fax; email:* forlag@online.no. Radnar Evensen, Christin Z Olsen, proprietors.

Norwegian Music Information Centre. Tollbugt 28, N-0157 Oslo, Norway *tel:* +47 22 429090 *fax:* +47 22 429091 *email:* nmic @notam.uio.no. Jostein Simble, director; Hilde Holboek-Hanssen, head of information.

Østnorsk Musikkforlag. Gullagata 15, N-3513, Hønefoss, Norway *tel:* +47 32 126396 *also fax; email:* hanlien@online.no. Hans Olav Lien, manager. *Publications managed through Cantando Musikkforlag, Norway.*

Warner/Chappell Music Norway A/S. Nydalsvn 15 inng B, PO Box 4523, Torshov, N-0404 Oslo, Norway *tel:* +47 22 580960 *fax:* +47 22 232396 *email:* warner.chappell@os.telia.no. Odd Steenberg, print manager.

Poland

PWM Edition Polskie Wydawnictwo Muzyczne. Al Krasinskiego 11a, PL-31111 Kraków, Poland *tel:* +48 12 422 7328 *also fax; fax:* +48 12 422 7171 *email:* pwm@pwm.com.pl. Leszek Polony, director, chief executive; Grazyna Adamczyk, deputy director, publishing and promotion; Andrzez Grobelski, deputy director, economy.

Portugal

Sintonia SA. Rua Profesor Mira Fernandes, Lote 1, Loja, P-1900 Lisboa, Portugal.

Singapore

Alfred Publishing Co (Singapore) Ltd. Toa Payoh North Post Office, PO Box 841, Singapore 913135, Singapore *tel:* +65 250 8981 *fax:* +65 250 8971 *email:* alfredco@pacific.net.sg. Larry Bong, marketing manager.

Slovak Republic

Hudobny Fond Bratislava. Medená 29, 81102 Bratislava, Slovak Republic *tel:* +421 7 5443 1689 (publishing dept) *fax:* +421 7 5443 2645 (hire library) *email:* hfv@hfv.sk. Hilos Kocian, director; Ivan Valenta, head of publishing department. *Information sheet: Presto.*

South Africa

Peermusic (Pty) Ltd. 62 St Patrick Rd, Upper Houghton, Johannesburg, South Africa *tel:* +28 11 648 5404.

Spain

Catalana d'Edicions Musicals. CEM/SEEMSA, Layetana 23, Planta 1r-D, E-08003 Barcelona, Spain *tel:* +34 93 319 7958 *fax:* +34 93 310 1844. Josep Cruells Solbés, director.

Clivis Publicacions. Dep de Promoció, Mila i Fontanals 14-26 3r 9a, E-08012 Barcelona, Spain *tel:* +34 93 458 8989 *also fax; email:* clivis@grn.es. Elisenda Climent, general manager. *600 works of contemporary Spanish composers.*

Monge y Boceta Asociados Musicales SL. Calle Goya, 103-2 Dcha, E-28009 Madrid, Spain *tel:* +34 91 431 6505/67 *fax:* +34 91 577 9166 *email:* myb@mad.servicom.es.

Multimusic SL. Abdón Terradas 3, 28015 Madrid, Spain *tel:* +34 91 544 7880 *fax:* +34 91 544 6554 *email:* clif@sintoniasa.es. Bartolomé Espadalé, president; Clifton Williams, director.

Nueva Carsich Espana SL. Magallanes 25, E-28015 Madrid, Spain *tel:* +34 91 446 8161 *fax:* +34 91 593 3433.

Sintonia SA. Abdón Terradas 3-5, E-28015 Madrid, Spain *tel:* +34 91 549 2350 *fax:* +34 91 543 9690 *email:* sintonia@sintoniasa.es. Bartolomé Espadalé, president, managing director; Clifton Williams, publishing director. *Overseas address: R Professor Mira Fernandes, LT1-Loma, P-1900 Lisboa, Portugal.*

Tritó S L. Carrer dels Arcs 8 1/2, E-08002 Barcelona, Spain *tel:* +34 93 302 2722/ 93 301 9555 *fax:* +34 93 302 2670 *email:* trito@bcn.servicom.es. Josep Dolcet, director.

Sweden

Edition Reimers. PO Box 15030, S-161 15 Bromma, Sweden *tel:* +46 8 740 0280 *fax:* +46 8 804228.

Edition Suecia. PO Box 27327, S-102 54 Stockholm, Sweden *tel:* +46 8 783 8800 *fax:* +46 8 783 9510 *email:* swedmic@stim.se. Karin Heurling, editor.

Gehrmans Musikförlag. Box 6005, S-102 31 Stockholm, Sweden *tel:* +46 8 610 0600 *fax:* +46 8 610 0625 *email:* order@gehrmans.se. Kettil Skarby, manager; Kristina Hector, orchestra department; Inga Nilsson, sales department; Mona-Lisa Ahlstrand, copyright department.

Scandinavian Songs AB. Box 109, S-182 12 Danderyd, Sweden *tel:* +46 8 755 9970 *fax:* +46 8 755 8870 *email:* ssmg@scandinavian-songs.se. Björn Hakanson, Kaj Lundén-Welden, directors; Niclas Johansson, label manager.

Switzerland

Amadeus. Postfach 473, CH-8405 Winterthur, Switzerland *tel:* +41 52 233 2866 *fax:* +41 52 233 5401.

Bärenreiter Verlag Basel AG. Neuweiler Strasse 15, CH-4015 Basel, Switzerland *tel:* +41 61 307 9666 *fax:* +41 61 307 9660 *email:* baerenreiter_ch@compuserve.com. Peter G Isler, director; Sven Steiner, manager.

Guild Music Ltd. Wiesholz 42b, 8262 Ramsen, Switzerland *tel:* +41 52 743 1600 *fax:* +41 52 743 1553 *email:* guildmusic@bluewin.ch. Silvia Lalkaka, director; Kaikoo C Lalkaka, managing director. *Overseas address: P O Box 5092, Colchester, Essex CO1 1FN, UK.*

Harwood Academic Publishers. Poststr 22, CH-7000 Chur, Switzerland *email:* info@gbhap.com. *Books for students, academics, professionals and the general public on all aspects/periods of music. Also c/o IPD, PO Box 90, Reading, Berks RG1 8JL, UK* tel: *+44 118 956 0080* fax: *+44 118 956 8211. Andrew Hansen, international sales director.*

Hug and Co Musikverlage. Limmatquai 28-30, CH-8022 Zürich, Switzerland *tel:* +41 1 251 6850 *fax:* +41 1 261 6166.

Jecklin & Co AG. Römistr 30 + 42, CH-8024 Zürich, Switzerland *tel:* +41 1 261 7733 *fax:* +41 1 251 4102 *email:* jecklin@bluewin.ch. Hannes Hinnen, general manager.

Ruh Emil Musikverlag. Zurichstr 33, CH-8134 Adliswil, Switzerland *tel:* +41 1 710 6313 *fax:* +41 1 710 6207.

Swiss Music Edition (SME). Postfach 7851, CH-6000 Luzern 7, Switzerland *tel:* +41 41 210 6070 *also fax; email:* Mail@musicedition.ch. Ulrich Gasser, president; Peter Bitterli, secretary.

Taiwan

De Fwo Trading Company Ltd. Nei Hu PO Box 9-59, 11411 Taipei, Taiwan *tel:* +886 22 735 3014 *fax:* +886 22 377 7735 *email:* defwo@ms17.hinet.net. Din-Lie Yung, chairman; Tsun-Li Chang, general manager. *De Wolfe Music, Rouge Music, Hudson Music and De Wolfe/Naxos Classical Music.*

Turkey

Muzikotek Ltd. 4 Gazeteciler Sitesi A 17-4, Levent 80670, Istanbul, Turkey *tel:* +90 212 282 8194 *fax:* +90 212 282 8195. D Baydur, director; F Bezmen, T Kizilirmak, assistants.

USA

Abingdon Press. 201 Eighth Av, Nashville, TN 37203, USA *tel:* +1 615 749 6158 *fax:* +1 615 749 6239 *email:* 72233.172@compuserve.com. Gary Alan Smith, music resources editor.

Accura Music. PO Box 4260, Athens, OH 45701, USA *tel:* +1 740 594 3547 *fax:* +1 740 592 1609 *email:* accuramusic@compuserve.com. Carl Fink, president.

Alfred Publishing Co Inc. PO Box 10003, Van Nuys, CA 91410-0003, USA *tel:* +1 818 891 5999 *fax:* +1 818 891 2182 *email:* customerservice@alfredpub.com. Morton Manus, president; Andrew Surmani, vice-president, marketing; Andrew Higgins, marketing manager; Berry Mooney, sales manager. *Also at: 7 Amber Business Village, Amington, Tamworth, Staffs B77 4RP, UK; PO Box 2355, Taren Point, NSW 2229, Australia; Toa Pnyoh North Post Office, PO Box 841, Singapore 913135; Max-Planck-Str 9, 53577 Neustadt-Fernthal, Germany.*

Alry Publications Etc Inc. PO Box 36542, Charlotte, NC 28236, USA *tel:* +1 704 334 3413 *fax:* +1 704 334 1143 *email:* amyblu@aol.com. Amy Rice Blumenthal, president; Susan Price, Julie Shadrick, assistants.

American International Guitar Pubs/PJN Pubs. 4a Holland Dr, West Hurley, NY 12491, USA *tel:* +1 914 679 9762 *fax:* +1 914 679 0525 *email:* pjnpub@ulster.net. Jared Walker, owner.

Anglo-American Music Publishers. PO Box 161323, Altamonte Springs, FL 32716-1323, USA *tel:* +1 407 464 9454 *also fax.* Eric Fletcher, president.

AR Editions Inc. 801 Deming Way, Madison, WI 53717, USA *tel:* +1 608 836 9000 *fax:* +1 608 831 8200. Patrick Wall, president.

Ashgate Publishing Co. Old Post Rd, Brookfield, VT 05036-9704, USA *tel:* +1 802 276 3162 *fax:* +1 802 276 3651 *email:* info@ashgate.com. James Gerard, president; Barbara Church, international marketing manager.

Boosey & Hawkes Inc. 35 East 21st St, New York, NY 10010-6212, USA *tel:* +1 212 358 5379 *fax:* +1 212 358 5303.

Carl Fischer LLC. 65 Bleecker St, 8 Fl, New York, NY 10012, USA *tel:* +1 212 777 0900 *fax:* +1 212 477 6996. Sandy Feldstein, president.

Cherry Lane Music Co. 10 Midland Av, Port Chester, NY 10573, USA *tel:* +1 914 935 5200 *fax:* +1 914 937 9139. Ted Piechocinoki, senior vice-president; Dan Rosenbaum, vice-president.

Choristers Guild. 2834 West Kingsley Rd, Garland, TX 75041, USA *tel:* +1 972 271 1521 *fax:* +1 972 840 3113 *email:* choristers@choristersguild.org. George Eison, executive director; Kathy Lowrie, music and literary editor; E Wayne Lord, *The Chorister*, editor.

Concordia Publishing House. 3558 South Jefferson Av, St Louis, MO 63118, USA *tel:* +1 314 268 1000 *fax:* +1 314 268 1329 *email:* chporder@cph.org. Rev David A Johnson, director of music and worship; Greg Gastler, marketing manager of music and worship.

Criterion Music Corp. 6124 Selma Av, Hollywood, CA 90028, USA *tel:* +1 323 469 2296 *fax:* +1 323 962 5751. Michael H Goldsen, CEO; Bo Goldsen, president.

Dantalian Inc. 11 Pembroke St, Newton, MA 02158, USA *tel:* +1 617 244 7230 *also fax; email:* dantinfo@dantalian.com. Lora Harvey, chief administrator; James Vincent, manager.

Dover Publications Inc. 31 East 2nd St, Mineola, NY 11501, USA *tel:* +1 516 294 7000 *fax:* +1 516 742 6953; +1 516 873 1401 *email:* dover@inch.com. Ronald Herder, music editor. *Reprints of classical music.*

ECS Publishing. 138 Ipswich St, Boston, MA 02215-3534, USA *tel:* +1 617 236 1935 *fax:* +1 617 236 0261. Robert Schuneman, president.

Edwin F Kalmus & Co Inc. 6403 West Rogers Circle, Boca Raton, FL 33487, USA *tel:* +1 407 241 6340 *fax:* +1 407 241 6347 *email:* efkalmus@aol.com. Lawrence Galison, chairman; Leon Galison, president; Clark McAlister, vice-president.

Elkin Music International. 16 North-East 4th St, Fort Lauderdale, FL 33301, USA *tel:* +1 954 522 3611 *fax:* +1 954 522 3609 *email:* timsloan@elkinmusic.com. Timothy B Sloan, president.

European American Music Distributors Corp. PO Box 850, Valley Forge, PA 19482, USA *tel:* +1 610 648 0506 *fax:* +1 610 889 0242 *email:* eamdc@eamdc.com. Ronald Freed, president. See also *Universal Edition, Austria, and Schott, Germany.*

Faber Music Inc *see* **Boosey and Hawkes.**

G Schirmer Inc. 257 Park Av South, 20th Floor, New York, NY 10010, USA *tel:* +1 212 254 2100 *fax:* +1 212 254 2013 *email:* schirmer @msc-gs.com. Barrie Edwards, president; Susan Feder, vice-president.

GIA Publications. 7404 South Mason Av, Chicago, IL 60638, USA *tel:* +1 708 496 3800 *fax:* +1 708 496 3828 *email:* custserv@giamusic.com. Edward Harris, chief administrator.

Hal Leonard Corporation. 7777 West Bluemound Rd, PO Box 13819, Milwaukee, WI 53213, USA *tel:* +1 414 774 3630 *fax:* +1 414 774 3259. Keith Mardak, president; Dan Bayer, senior vice-president.

Helicon Music Corporation. c/o European American Music Corporation, Valley Forge, PA 19482, USA *tel:* +1 610 648 0506 *fax:* +1 610 889 0242 *email:* eamdc@eamdc.com.

Herman and Apter. 5748 West Brooks Rd, Shepherd, MI 48883-9202, USA *tel:* +1 517 828 6987 *email:* herman.apter@sensible-net.com. Mark Herman, chief administrator; Ronnie Apter. *14 dual-language piano-vocal scores.*

Hildegard Publishing Co. Box 332, Bryn Mawr, PA 19010, USA *tel:* +1 610 649 8649 *fax:* +1 610 649 8677 *email:* sglickman@hildegard.com. Sylvia Glickman, president; Martha Furman Schleifer, senior editor. *Music by women composers.*

Hinshaw Music Inc. PO Box 470, Chapel Hill, NC 27514-0470, USA *tel:* +1 919 933 1691 *fax:* +1 919 967 3399. Roberta M Van Ness, president.

Hope Publishing Co. 380 South Main Pl, Carol Stream, IL 60188, USA *tel:* +1 630 665 3200 *fax:* +1 630 665 2552 *email:* hope@hopepublishing.com. George H Shorney, chairman; William G Shorney, president.

Houston Publishing Inc. 222 South Lebanon St, Lebanon, IN 46052, USA *tel:* +1 317 482 4440 *also fax.* Jim Houston, president; Michelle Skow, administration assistant.

Jazzmuze Inc. 80 Rumson Pl, Little Silver, NJ 07739, USA *tel:* +1 732 747 5227 *fax:* +1 732 747 7822 *email:* wmtodt@aol.com. Joe Utterback, president; William E Todt, vice-president, secretary; Mary Todt, treasurer. *Jazz influenced compositions for classical artists.*

Joseph Patelson MusicHouse Ltd. 160 West 56 St, New York, NY 10019, USA *tel:* +1 212 757 5587 *fax:* +1 212 246 5633. Dan Patelson, president; Carlos Vasquez, business manager; Scott Shade, buyer.

Kendor Music Inc. PO Box 278, Delevan, NY 14042, USA *tel:* +1 716 492 1254 *fax:* +1 716 492 5124 *email:* kendor@wycol.com. Craig Cornwall, president; Jeff Jarvis, chief executive officer; Nadine Gardner, copyright administrator.

Lawson-Gould Music Publishers Inc. 250 West 57 St, Suite 1005, New York, NY 10107, USA *tel:* +1 212 247 3920 *fax:* +1 212 247 3991. Walter Gould, president; Betty Gould, vice-president. *Specialise in choral music.*

Liben Music Publishers. 1191 Eversole Rd, Cincinnati, OH 45230, USA *tel:* +1 513 232 6920 *fax:* +1 513 232 1866 *email:* info@liben.com. Madeline Bennett, chief administrator.

Lorenz Corp. Box 802, 501 East 3rd St, Dayton, OH 45401-0802, USA *tel:* +1 937 228 6118 *fax:* +1 937 223 2042 *email:* order@lorenz.com. Geoffrey R Lorenz, president; Larry F Pugh, music publishing president.

Loux Music Publishing Co. 2 Hawley Lane, Hannacroix, NY 12087-0034, USA *tel:* +1 518 756 2273 *also fax.* Joseph A Loux, Jr, chief administrator. *For recorder, viol, horn - early instruments.*

Ludwig Music Publishing Co Inc. 557 East 140 St, Cleveland, OH 44110, USA *tel:* +1 216 851 1150 *fax:* +1 216 851 1958. Elizabeth Ludwig Fennell, president; Joseph Wahr, general manager; Dick Sakal, sales manager; Frederick Fennell, vice-president. *Distributes through dealers around the world.*

McGinnis & Marx Music Publishers. 236 West 26 St, No 1101, New York, NY 10001-6736, USA *tel:* +1 212 675 1630 *also fax.* Paul Sadowski.

Mark Foster Music Co. PO Box 4012, 28 East Springfield, Champaign, IL 61824-4012, USA *tel:* +1 217 398 2760 *fax:* +1 217 398 2791 *email:* info@markfostermus.com. Jane Menkhaus, president. *Choral titles.*

Mel Bay Publications Inc. #4 Industrial Dr, Pacific, MO 63069, USA *tel:* +1 636 257 3970 *fax:* +1 636 257 5062 *email:* email@melbay.com. William Bay, president; Doug Witherspoon, purchasing and facilities manager.

Merion. c/o Theodore Presser Company, 1 Presser Pl, Bryn Mawr, PA 19010-3490, USA *tel:* +1 610 525 3636 *fax:* +1 610 527 7841.

MJQ Music Inc. 1697 Broadway, New York, NY 10019, USA *tel:* +1 212 582 6667 *fax:* +1 212 582 0627. Paul Schwartz, general manager.

MMB Music Inc. Contemporary Arts Building, 3526 Washington Avenue, St Louis, MO 63103-1019, USA *tel:* +1 314 531 9635 *fax:* +1 314 531 8384 *email:* mmbmusic@mmbmusic. Marcia Lee Goldberg, vice-president, sales/marketing; Norman A Goldberg, president.

Music for Percussion, Inc. 170 North East 33rd St, Fort Lauderdale, FL 33334, USA *tel:* +1 305 563 1844 *fax:* +1 305 563 9006. Bernard Fisher, president. *Percussion music for solo and ensemble, method books.*

Musicdata, Inc. PO Box 12380, Philadelphia, PA 19119-0380, USA *tel:* +1 215 248 3530 *fax:* +1 215 248 3531 *email:* musicdat @voicenet.com/~musicdat. Frank James Staneck, editor and general manager. *Publish* The Music-in-Print Series, *34 volumes of catalogues listing music from over 900 international publishers. Choral, organ, orchestral, string, classical guitar, and woodwind.*

Neil A Kjos Music Co. 4380 Jutland Dr, San Diego, CA 92117, USA *tel:* +1 619 270 9800 *fax:* +1 619 270 3507 *email:* email@kjos.com. Neil A Kjos, president.

Oxford University Press Music Department. 198 Madison Av, New York, NY 10016-4314, USA *tel:* +1 212 726 6050 *fax:* +1 212 726 6444 *email:* mxp@oup-usa.org. Maribeth Anderson Payne, director and executive editor; Christopher Johnson, senior editor and manager.

Paraclete Press. PO Box 1568, Orleans, MA 02653, USA *tel:* +1 508 255 4685 *fax:* +1 508 255 5705. Loretta Jack, sales manager; Paul Tingley, music editor assistant. *Sacred music: sheet music, CDs.*

Paumanok Press. 974 Hardscrabble Rd, Chappaqua, NY 10514, USA *tel:* +1 914 238 9367. Theresa Vorgia, chief administrator. *Publisher of the music of Michael Jeffrey Shapiro.*

Peermusic Classical. 810 Seventh Av, New York, NY 10019, USA *tel:* +1 212 265 3910 *fax:* +1 212 489 2465 *email:* peerclassical@compuserve.com. Todd Vunderink, vice-president, classical; Maggie Heskin, editor; Tobin W Fowler, promotions and publicity. *See also Hamburg office.*

Pro Piano Records. 85 Jane St, New York, NY 10014, USA *tel:* +1 212 206 8794 *fax:* +1 212 633 1207 *email:* ricard@propiano.com. Ricard de La Rosa.

Red Poppy. c/o Lynn Garon, 1199 Park Avenue, New York, NY 10128, USA *tel:* +1 212 876 1279 *fax:* +1 212 722 3891 *email:* lynnpg@juno.com. *Distributed worldwide by G Schirmer Inc.*

Routledge Inc. 29 West 35th St, New York, NY 10001, USA *tel:* +1 212 244 3336 *fax:* +1 212 563 2269. *Also at: 11 New Fetter Lane, London EC4P 4EE, UK.*

Schott Music Corporation. c/o European American Music Distributors Corporation, PO Box 850, Valley Forge, PA 19482-0850, USA *tel:* +1 610 648 0506 *fax:* +1 610 889 0242 *email:* eamdc@eamdc.com.

Seesaw Music Corp. 2067 Broadway, New York, NY 10023, USA *tel:* +1 212 874 1200. Raoul R Ronson, president.

Smith Publications/Sonic Art Editions. 2617 Gwynndale Av, Baltimore, MD 21207, USA *tel:* +1 410 298 6509 *fax:* +1 410 944 5113. Sylvia Smith, editor.

Sound Adventures. PO Box 531, Wellsville, NY 14895, USA *tel:* +1 716 593 1636.

Southern Music Co. PO Box 329, 1100 Broadway, San Antonio, TX 78292, USA *tel:* +1 210 226 8167 *fax:* +1 210 223 4537 *email:* info@southernmusic.com. Arthur Gurwitz, president.

Subito Music Publishing Inc. c/o Theodore Presser Company, 1 Presser Pl, Bryn Mawr, PA 19010-3490, USA *tel:* +1 610 525 3636 *fax:* +1 610 527 7841.

Themes and Variations. 39 Danbury Av, Westport, CT 06880-6822, USA *tel:* +1 203 227 5709 *fax:* +1 203 227 5715 *email:* jwwaxman@aol.com. John W Waxman, chief administrator.

Theodore Presser Co. 1 Presser Pl, Bryn Mawr, PA 19010-3490, USA *tel:* +1 215 525 3636 *fax:* +1 215 527 7841. Arnold Broido, chairman; Thomas Broido, president; George D Hotton, vice-president; Don Direso, treasurer. *Distributed in UK by Alfred A Kalmus, 38 Eldon Way, Paddock Wood, Tonbridge, Kent TN12 6BE, UK.*

Transcontinental Music Publications/New Jewish Music Press. 838 Fifth Av, New York, NY 10021, USA *tel:* +1 212 650 4101 *fax:* +1 212 650 4109 *email:* tmp@vahc.org. Judith B Tischler, director, senior editor; Charles C Sachs, sales administrator; Peter Saxe, marketing manager. *European agent: Mandy Feingers, Israel Music Associates, 49/1 Meir Nagar St, Jerusalem 93803, Israel.*

Viola World Publications. 2 Inlander Rd, Saratoga Springs, NY 12866, USA *tel:* +1 518 583 7177 *also fax; email:* violaworld@aol.com. Alan Arnold, director. *UK office: Music Sales, Bosworth Division, 8-9 Frith St, London W1V 5TV, UK.*

Wayne Leupold Editions Inc. 8510 Triad Dr, Colfax, NC 27235, USA *tel:* +1 336 996 8445 *also fax.*

William Grant Still Music. 4 South San Francisco St, Suite 422, Flagstaff, AZ 86001-5737, USA *tel:* +1 520 526 9355 *fax:* +1 520 526 0321 *email:* wgsmusic@bigplanet.com. Judith Anne Still, proprietor; Lisa M Huffman, marketing; Daniel Headlee, accounting; Celeste Anne Headlee, operations. *UK office: African to American Music Society, c/o Mike Wright, 49 Waltham Avenue, Guildford, Surrey GU2 6QF, UK.*

Willis Music Co. 7380 Industrial Rd, Florence, KY 41042, USA *tel:* +1 606 283 2050 *fax:* +1 606 283 1784 *email:* orderdpt@willis-music.com.

Wiscasset Music Publishing Co. PO Box 380810, Cambridge, MA 02238-0810, USA *tel:* +1 617 492 5720 *fax:* +1 617 492 4031. Betsy Warren-Davis, chief administrator.

World Music Press. PO Box 2565, Danbury, CT 06813-2565, USA *tel:* +1 203 748 1131 *fax:* +1 203 748 3432 *email:* wmpress@aol.com. Judith Cook Tucker, publisher, editor in chief; Claudia Chapman, associate editor, graphic design.

Worldwide Music. PO Box 161323, Altamonte Springs, FL 32716-1323, USA *tel:* +1 407 464 9454. Eris Fletcher, president. *Distribution.*

Ybarra Music. PO Box 665, Lemon Grove, CA 91946, USA *tel:* +1 619 462 6538 *fax:* +1 619 460 4130 *email:* vbraun8368@aol.com. Dick Braun, proprietor. *School orchestra, band and woodwind chamber music.*

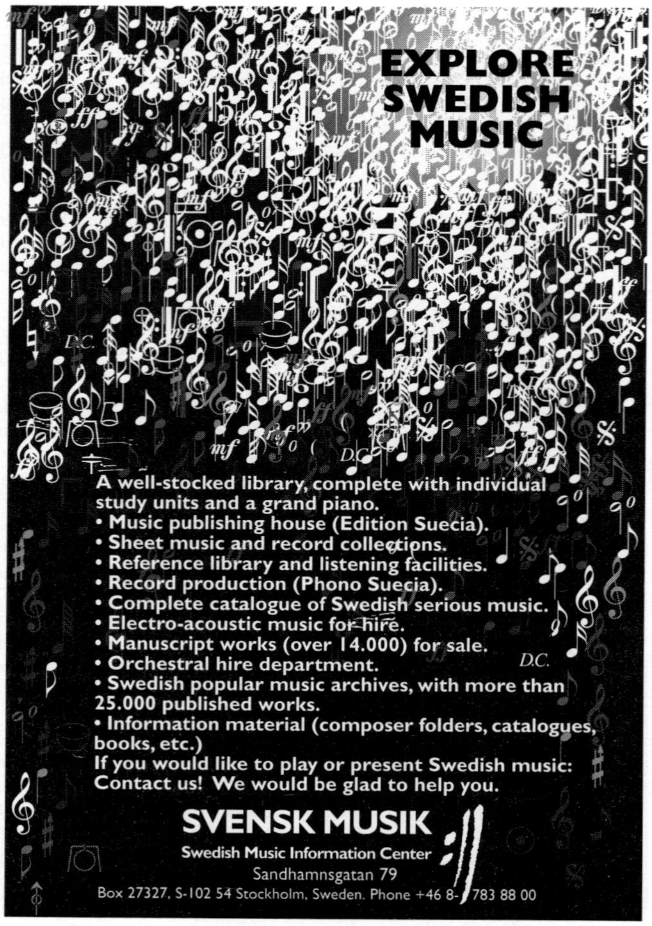

Music Information Centres and Organisations

The entries marked with an asterisk are members of the **International Association of Music Information Centres** (Stiftgasse 29, A-1070 Wien, Austria *tel:* +43 1 521 0455 *fax:* +43 1 521 0499 *email:* office@iamic.at) which is a worldwide network of organisations promoting new music. Music Information Centres are open to the public and have extensive resources: large libraries of sheet music and sound archives, and up-to-date collections of biographical and research material. Many issue publications and recordings, while all serve as a focus of musical activity.

The other organisations listed below also disseminate information about music and musical activities in their respective countries. Many take particular interest in living composers and contemporary music. These may include composers' societies, associations and national music committees of the International Music Council.

Albania

National Music Committee (Albania). Rr 'Sitki Cico', Pallatet 9 kate, Shkalla 2, Ap 4, Tirana, Albania *tel:* +355 42 74127 *fax:* +355 42 25856 *email:* root@tob.tirana.al. Vasil S Tole, president; Fatmir Hysi, general secretary. *Promotes music education, music performance and every form of music. 25 affiliated members.*

Argentina

International Encounters of Contemporary Music Foundation. Casilla de Correo 1008, Correo Central, 1000 Buenos Aires, Argentina *tel:* +54 1 822 1383 *also fax*. Carlos Berberian, president; Alicia Terzian, artistic director; Nidia Corrado, executive secretary. *Devoted to 20th C music composed in the Americas. Organise yearly Festivals of Contemporary Music; commission works to composers, organise seminars for new techniques for composers and interpreters. Prize to young composers of presenting their works to International Rostrum of Composers organised by IMC and at World Music Days (International Society of Contemporary Music).*

National Music Committee (Argentina). Casilla de Correos 5532, Correo Central, 1000 Buenos Aires, Argentina *tel:* +54 1 822 1383 *also fax*; +54 1 832 1436. Alicia Terzian, president; Ada Rissetto, secretary. *Member of IMC (UNESCO). Organises the Argentine Tribune of Composers, The Argentine Music Tribune, Congress of Music Education, concerts, young composers and interpreters competitions. Give prizes to the researchers of ethnic, folk and baroque music of Latin America and 19th C music of Argentina. Participate in international events.*

Australia

* **Australian Music Centre Ltd.** 1st Floor, Argyle Stores, 18 Argyle St, The Rocks, Sydney, Australia *tel:* +61 2 9247 4677 *fax:* +61 2 9241 2873 *email:* info@amcoz.com.au. John Davis, general manager; Harriet Cunningham, marketing manager. *AMC was established to facilitate and encourage the performance and understanding of music by Australian composers throughout the world. The Music Resource Library houses 12,000 works by more than 300 composers. The collection focuses on contemporary Australian music and, in many cases, is the only source for certain works. The Library holds recordings, books and published scores, biographical files on more than 1000 Australian composers, press clippings, reviews and concert programmes, analyses, photographs and an extensive collection of programme notes. Many of these are available for loan, hire or sale.*

Music Council of Australia. PO Box 1432, Neutral Bay, NSW 2089, Australia *tel:* +61 2 9969 2082 *fax:* +61 2 9969 6562 *email:* ozmusico@zeta.org.au. Richard Letts, chairman. *Australian affiliate to UNESCO International Music Council. An advocacy and service body with a membership of 50 national music organisations and individuals. Publishes 2 periodicals:* Music Forum *covers major issues in the situation of music,* Music Alive *is the periodical of its major service programme. Also Community Music Australia, a national network for community music development. Strategy for choral development, school music education and support to talented emerging artists.*

Austria

Austrian Society for Contemporary Music. Stiftgasse 29, A-1070 Wien, Austria *tel:* +43 1 521 0441 *fax:* +43 1 521 0449. Lothar Knessl.

International Music Centre Vienna. Speisinger Str 121-127, A-1230 Wien, Austria *tel:* +43 1 889 0315 *fax:* +43 1 889 0315 77 *email:* office@imz.at. Adrienne Clarkson, president; Monika Gelbman, editor; Franz Patay, secretary general; Katharina Setzer, event manager. *International association of audio-visual producers of arts programmes with an emphasis on classical and contemporary music, jazz, world music and dance. Organises congresses, seminars, workshops and screenings on topical issues. Also organises festivals and competitions for audio-visual dance and music theatre productions. Operates a database for TV programmes and publishes a trilingual trade magazine* Music in the Media.

* **Musik Informations Zentrum Österreich (MICA).** Stiftgasse 29, A-1070 Wien, Austria *tel:* +43 1 521 040 *fax:* +43 1 521 0459 *email:* office@mica.at. Matthias Finkentey, managing director. *Provides detailed information on contemporary Austrian music including a composer database and a jazz database. Also liaises between artists and representatives from the music business and government cultural organisations.*

Musikalische Jugend Österreichs. Generalsekreteriat, Postfach 45, Lothringerstr 20, (im Konzerthausgebäude), A-1037 Wien, Austria *tel:* +43 1 710 3616 *fax:* +43 1 710 361617 *email:* mail@jeunesse.at. Matthias Naske, general secretary; Catharina Jürs, marketing; Albert Seidlinger, press. *Promoting classical music for a youth audience.*

National Music Committee (Austria). Österreichischer Musikrat, Stiftgasse 29, A-1070 Wien, Austria *tel:* +43 1 521 0471 *fax:* +43 1 521 0479. Matthias Finkentey, secretary general. *Platform for musicians in Austria. Member of International Music Council (IMC).*

Österreichische Gesellschaft für Musik. 1 Hanuschgasse 3, A-1010 Wien, Austria *tel:* +43 1 512 3143 *fax:* +43 1 512 4299. Walburga Litschauer, chairman. *Information, promotion (especially of contemporary mus), publications, concerts, symposia, congresses.*

Bangladesh

National Music Committee (Bangladesh). I/1 Purana Paltan, Dacca, Bangladesh. Mustafa Zaman Abbasi, president.

Belgium

Artist Service. Postbus 1, B-8460 Oudenburg, Belgium *tel:* +32 5 933 2116 *also fax; email:* artistserv@club.innet.be. Jean-Paul Steenmans, president. *Publish Music Yearbook for Belgium:* Guidebook for musicians, artists and showbusiness.

* **Centre Belge de Documentation Musicale (CeBeDeM).** Rue d'Arlon 75-77, B-1040 Bruxelles, Belgium *tel:* +32 2 230 9430 *fax:* +32 2 230 9437 *email:* 101573.3644@compuserve.com. Diana von Volborth-Danys, director. *Non-profit-making association which aims to promote the performance of Belgian contemporary classical music. Facilities available include a sheet music library, recording library, reading and listening room, loan department, publishing and reproduction, and promotion department.*

Centre of International Cultural Relations. Torenstr 13, B-9160 Lokeren, Belgium *tel:* +32 9 348 8000 *fax:* +32 9 348 9974 *email:* j-p.vanavermaet@skynet.be. Jean Pierre Van Avermaet, managing director. *Operates an extended database containing musicological information, biographical data and a list of local organisers throughout Europe. Provides translations of mus related texts in Russian, Bulgarian, Dutch, English, German and French.*

International Federation of Jeunesse Musicales. 10 rue Royale, B-1000 Bruxelles, Belgium. Dag Franzen, secretary general.

National Music Committee (Belgium). Palais des Beaux Arts, Rue Royale 10, B-1000 Bruxelles, Belgium *tel:* +32 2 507 8211 *fax:* +32 2 514 3044 *email:* pbapskdir@skynet.be. Mrs M M Spehl-Robeyns, general manager; Mr Vaureffeliu, head of planning. *Rental of concert halls (120-2000 seats).*

Bolivia

National Music Committee (Bolivia). Centre Pedagogico y Cultural de Portales, Av Potosi N-1450, Casilla 544, Cochabamba, Bolivia. Luz Maria Calvo, secretary general.

Brazil

* **CDMC-Brasil/Unicamp (Universidade Estadual de Campinas).** Cx P 6136, 13083-970 Campinas SP, Brazil *tel:* +55 19 289 3965 *fax:* +55 19 289 5806 *email:* cdmusica@obelix.unicamp.br. José Augusto Mannis, director; Sandra Aparecida G Caro Florio, manager. *Collection of over 3000 scores, cassettes and CDs. Database of contemporary Brazilian music.*

National Music Committee (Brazil). Rua Pres Carlos de Campos No 115 B, 2/902, 22231-080 Laranjeiras, Rio de Janeiro RJ, Brazil *tel:* +55 21 553 6222 *fax:* +55 21 553 9963. Maria-Luiza Corker-Nobre, secretary general. *Provides information about Brazilian music life and is publishing a* Complete Guide to the Brazilian Music World *with addresses of all Brazilian institutions, artists, managers, orchestras, etc. The NMC participates at the IMC/UNESCO programmes, particularly the International Rostrum of Composers.*

Sociedade de Cultura Artistica. Rua Nestor Pestana 196, 01303-010 Sao Paulo SP, Brazil *tel:* +55 11 256 0223; +55 11 231 4271 *fax:* +55 11 258 3595 *email:* cultart@dialdata.com.br. Gérald Perret.

Bulgaria

National Music Committee (Bulgaria). Union of Bulgarian Composers, 2 Rue Iv Vazov, BG-1000 Sofia, Bulgaria. Victor Tchoutchkov, secretary general.

Canada

American Federation of Musicians of the United States and Canada. 75 The Donway West, Suite 1010, Don Mills, Ont M3C 2E9, Canada *tel:* +1 416 391 5161 *fax:* +1 416 391 5165 *email:* canoff@afm.org. David Jandrisch, vice-president; Alan Willaert, international representative. *Membership is open to all professional musicians and vocalists in the USA and Canada.*

The Canada Council for the Arts/Conseil des Arts du Canada. PO Box 1047, 350 Albert St, Ottawa, Ont K1P 5V8, Canada *tel:* +1 613 566 4414 *fax:* +1 613 566 4390. *Provides grants and services to professional Canadian artists and arts organisations.*

* **Canadian Music Centre/Centre de Musique Canadienne (CMC).** Chalmers House, 20 St Joseph St, Toronto, Ont M4Y 1J9, Canada *tel:* +1 416 961 6601 *fax:* +1 416 961 7198 *email:* cmc@interlog.com. Elisabeth Bihl, executive director. *Collects, reproduces, promotes, records and distributes the music and recordings of its associate composers. Also operates a free lending library of printed music.*

Conseil Québécois de la Musique (Québec Music Council). 1908, Rue Panet, Bureau 302 , Montreal (Québec) H2L 3A2, Canada tel: +1 514 524 1310 *fax:* +1 514 524 2219 *email:* adm@cqm.qc.ca. Isolde Lagacé, president; Andrée Girard, director; Robert Hyland, assistant director. *The Quebec Music Council was created out of a need for the mus milieu to join forces, in order to better develop and promote Quebec's mus life.The organisation interacts with the different levels of government and is committed to many issues. It also brings promotional projects into operation, such as the Opus awards ceremony.*

International Association of Music Libraries, Archives and Documentation Centres. Carleton University Library, 1125 Colonel By Drive, Ottawa, Ont K1S 5B6, Canada *tel:* +1 613 530 2600 ext 8150 *fax:* +1 613 520 3583 *email:* alison_hall@carleton.ca. Alison Hall, secretary general.

China

National Music Committee (China). 10 Nong Zhanguan Nanli, Beijing 100026, China *tel:* +86 1 065 389265 *fax:* +86 1 065 004524. Liu, Xiao Yin, Ms, secretary general. *The NMC (also Chinese Musicians' Assn) is a non-governmental national organisation of professional musicians across China. 34 branches with over 8000 members. Member of International Music Council/UNESCO. Aims to unite and organise professional musicians in China to promote music compositions and theory; to improve music performing art and music education; to develop the nation's traditional music; to carry out and enhance music exchange with other countries; to defend the rights and interests of members.*

Colombia

* **Centro de Documentación Musical.** Calle 24, No 5-60, 4 Piso, Santafé de Bogotá 1, Colombia *tel:* +57 1 342 2097 *fax:* +57 1 243 5994. Jaime H Quevedo, director; Ana Maria Ochoa, research division. *Classical, contemporary, popular and folk Colombian music on scores, recordings, videotapes, newspaper articles, concert programmes, etc.*

National Music Committee (Colombia). Centro Cultural Gimnasio Moderno, Carrera 9 No 74-99, Santafé de Bogotá, Colombia. Cecilia Casa Ceron, president.

Costa Rica

National Music Committee (Costa Rica). c/o Comision Costarricense de Cooperación con la UNESCO, Apartado Postal 393, 2050 San Pedro de Montes de Oca, San Jose, Costa Rica. Carmen Mendez, permanent secretary.

Cote d'Ivoire

National Music Committee (Cote d'Ivoire). PO Box 49, Abidjan 08, Cote d'Ivoire. Paul Dagri, president.

Croatia

Croatian Composers' Society. Berislaviceva 9, HR 10000 Zagreb, Croatia *tel:* +385 1 423463 *fax:* +385 1 422850. Ivo Josipovic, secretary general; Lidija Parac, admin secretary. *Organises festivals of Croatian music; publishes contemporary and ancient Croatian music.*

Culturelink, c/o Institute for International Relations (IMO). Ul Ljudevita Farkasa Vukotinovica 2, PO Box 303, 10000 Zagreb, Croatia *tel:* +385 1 482 6522 *fax:* +385 1 482 8361 *email:* clink@mairmo.irmo.hr. Biserka Cvjeticanin, co-ordinator; Zrinjka Perusko-Culek; Aleksandra Uzelac, researcher. *Culturelink is an information network established by UNESCO and the Council of Europe. It is devoted to promoting research into cultural development, cultural policies and cultural and artistic co-operation. It also aims to collect, process and disseminate information. The* Culturelink Bulletin *is issued 4 times a year providing updated information on current activities and projects to its members.*

Cuba

National Music Committee (Cuba). Instituto Cubano de la Musica, Calle F y 15 N 452, El Vedado, La Habana, Cuba *tel:* +537 32 7121 *fax:* +537 77 3158. Guido Lopez Gavilan.

Cyprus

National Music Committee (Cyprus). Prince Charles 21, Ayios Dometios, PO Box 4326, Nicosia, Cyprus *tel:* +357 2 462837 *fax:* +357 2 441213. Lenia Serghi, president.

Czech Republic

* **Music Information Centre.** Besední 3, CR-11800 Praha 1, Czech Republic *tel:* +420 2 573 20008 *fax:* +420 2 539720/534234 *email:* his@vol.cz. Miroslàv Pudlák, director; Adam Klemens, editor of Czech Music. *Promotes Czech contemporary music. Publishes the periodical* Czech Music *(in English), a Czech music directory, bulletin and website, and has archives of scores and recordings plus a database of compositions.*

National Music Committee (Czech Republic). Institute of Musicology, Academy of Sciences, Puskinovo nam 9, CR-16000 Praha 6, Czech Republic. Lenka Dohnalova, secretary general.

Democratic Republic of Congo

National Music Committee (Democratic Republic of Congo). 5151 Av President Kasa-Vubu, Zone de Kalamu, PO Box 16505 KIN I, Kinshasa, Democratic Republic of Congo. Basunga Mundele, secretary general.

Denmark

The Danish Cultural Institute. Kultorvet 2, DK-1175 Kobenhavn K, Denmark *tel:* +45 33 135448 *fax:* +45 33 151091 *email:* jr@dankultur.dk. *Disseminates information on Denmark; furthers international cultural exchanges.*

Danish Music Council. Vesterbrogade 24, 4, DK-1620 Kobenhavn V, Denmark *tel:* +45 33 251055 *fax:* +45 33 242242 *email:* sm@musikraad.dk. Lennart Ricard, chairman; Erik Skovgaard Pedersen, secretary general. *Advises and assists public authorities and institutions in music-related matters. Promotes musical life in Denmark and Danish music abroad. National Committee of IMC.*

* **Danish Music Information Centre.** Graabrødre Torv 16, DK-1154 Kobenhavn K, Denmark *tel:* +45 33 112066 *fax:* +45 33 322016 *email:* mic@mic.dk. Anette Faaborg, director; Bendt Viinholt Nielsen, chief librarian; Bodil Høgh, head of projects. *Promotion of Danish music worldwide, plus documentation of all aspects of music and musical life in Denmark. Library of books, printed music and autograph copies, magazines, newspaper cuttings and recordings. Computer database listing more than 10,000 contemporary Danish works.*

Jazzkontakten/Jazzcentret. Borupvej 66, DK-4683 Rønnede, Denmark *tel:* +45 567 1 567 *fax:* +45 567 1 749 *email:* jazzcent@inet.uni2.dk. Arnvid Meyer, president. *The JAZZPAR Project has been established to promote jazz music and includes the world's biggest jazz award.*

Egypt

National Music Committee (Egypt). Gamal-el-Afgany St, Pyramids Av, Giza, Cairo, Egypt. Samha El Kholy.

Equador

National Music Committee (Equador). Conservatorio Nacional de Musica, Calle Madrid No 1159, y Andalucia (La Floresta), Casilla de Correos 3358, Quito, Equador. Eduardo Granja, rector.

Estonia

Estonian Music Council. Suur-Karja 23, EE-10148 Tallinn, Estonia *tel:* +372 644 9931 *also fax; email:* emn@kul.ee. Peep Lassmann, president. *Independent non-governmental organisation which, as the representative body of musicians, connects the music institutions of Estonia. Composed of 32 members. Aims to propagate Estonian music in all forms; to encourage co-operation among Estonian musicians; to protect their rights and to promote and facilitate Estonian representation in international music life.*

National Music Committee (Estonia). Estonian Academy of Music, Vabaduse pst 130, EE-0009 Tallinn, Estonia. Peep Lassmann, president.

Finland

Finland Festivals. Uudenmaankatu 36 D 21, FIN-00120 Helsinki, Finland *tel:* +358 9 612 6760 *fax:* +358 9 612 67610 *email:* info@mail.festivals.fi. Tuomo Tirkkonen, general director; Riitta Kerman, marketing secretary. *Produces and distributes a catalogue containing dates, addresses and a short description of 58 different Finnish festivals.*

* **Finnish Music Information Centre.** Lauttasaarentie 1, FIN-00200 Helsinki, Finland *tel:* +358 9 6810 1313 *fax:* +358 9 682 0770 *email:* info@mic.teosto.fi. Pekka Hako, executive director; Anni Heino, information manager, service co-ordinator. *A non-profit institution which promotes Finnish composers and compositions. The information service publishes brochures, essays and booklets on various aspects of music. Also a library of over 20,000 compositions.*

Finnish Performing Music Promotion Centre (ESEK). Pieni Roobertinkatu 16, FIN-00120 Helsinki, Finland *tel:* +358 9 6803 4040 *fax:* +358 9 6803 4033 *email:* esek@gramex.fi. Leena Hirvonen, secretary general. *Supports Finnish performing music projects and provides information about Finnish artists.*

France

* **Centre de Documentation de la Musique Contemporaine.** Cité de la Musique, 16 Place de la Fontaine aux Lions, F-75019 Paris, France *tel:* +33 1 47 15 49 81 *fax:* +33 1 47 15 49 89 *email:* cdmc@cdmc.asso.fr. Marianne Lyon, director; Corinne Monceau, documentation dept. *Documentation and information on composers, performers, organisations, etc. Scores, recordings, books, theses, articles, reviews of contemporary music.*

Centre d'Information et de Resource pour les Musiques Actuelles. 21 Bis, Rue de Paradis, F-75010 Paris, France *tel:* +33 1 44 83 10 30 *fax:* +33 1 44 83 10 40. Gilles Castagnac, managing director; Joël Bastenaire, co-managing director. *IRMA offers access to databases with over 50,000 contacts, publications, advice and training programmes to all involved in music.*

Comité National de la Musique (CNM). 252 Rue du Faubourg St Honoré, Salle Pleyel, F-75008 Paris, France *tel:* +33 1 45 63 48 58 *also fax.* Pierre Henry, president; Masson-Forestier Jacques, general secretary. *French section of the International Council of Music of UNESCO, including 40 musical unions covering all sectors of music.*

European Association of Conservatoires, Academies de Musique and Musikhochschulen. c/o Conservatoire de Paris, 209 Av Jean Jaurès, F-75019 Paris, France *tel:* +33 1 40 40 46 09 *fax:* +33 1 40 40 46 03 *email:* aecinfo@aecinfo.org. Marc-Olivier Dupin, secretary general.

International Federation of Musicians. 21b Rue Victor Massé, F-75009 Paris, France. Jean Vincent, secretary general.

International Music Council (UNESCO). 1 Rue Miollis, F-75732 Paris Cédex 15, France *tel:* +33 1 45 68 25 50 *fax:* +33 1 43 06 87 98 *email:* imc_cim@compuserve.com. Guy Huot, secretary general. *Exists to support music education, research, contemporary composers, traditional music and young professional musicians, to promote the exchange of amateur and professional musicians, music (written and recorded) and information, and to foster appreciation of music by the public.*

International Music Critics Association. Press Club de France, 11 Avenue d'Lena, F-75016 Paris, France. Antoine Livio, president.

National Music Committee (France). 252 Rue du Faubourg Saint-Honore, F-75008 Paris, France *tel:* +33 1 45 63 48 58. Jacques Masson-Forestier, secretary general; Pierre Henry, president. *Member of International Music Council (IMC). Reports on music education, authors, publishers and performers' rights.*

Georgia

* **Georgian Music Information Centre.** David Agmashenebeli Ave 123, 380064 Tbilisi, Republic of Georgia *tel:* +995 88 32 954861/968678 *fax:* +995 32 958016. Natela Mamaladze, director; Svetlana Kervalishvili, chief editor. *Aims to promote Georgian music in Georgia and abroad. Organises recitals, exchange concerts and festivals of contemporary music. Publishes information bulletin in Georgian and in English.*

Germany

Deutscher Musikrat eV (German Music Council). Weberstr 59, D-53113 Bonn, Germany *tel:* +49 228 20910 *fax:* +49 228 209 1200 *email:* deutscher-musikrat.bonn@t-online.de. Franz Müller-Heuser, president; Marlene Wartenberg, general secretary. *Umbrella organisation for all fields of musical life in Germany. Its main aim is to influence public opinion and the processes of political decision-making in order to secure for music a position appropriate to its social importance and to contribute to the further development of musical culture. Also provides information and statistics on all aspects of musical life in Germany (see* **German Music Information Centre** *below).*

Dresden Centre of Contemporary Music (DZzM). Schevenstr 17, D-01326 Dresden, Germany *tel:* +49 351 264620 *fax:* +49 351 264 6223 *email:* ernesti@zeitmusik.de. Udo Zimmermann, director; Marc Ernesti, PR manager. *Non-profit institution dedicated to the promotion of new music, acting as a music information centre for East Germany. Archives, documentation, department of musicology and Research Centre for Exiled Music. Major festival 'Dresden Days of Contemporary Music' in October.*

Fortbildungszentrum für Neue Musik. An der Münze 7, D-21335 Luneberg, Germany *tel:* +49 413 130 9390 *also fax.* Helmut W Erdmann.

* **German Music Information Centre.** Weberstr 59, D-53113 Bonn, Germany *tel:* +49 228 209 1180 *fax:* +49 228 209 1280 *email:* miz.dmr@t-online.de. Joachim-Felix Leonhard; Margot Wallscheid. *Part of the German Music Council (see above). Provides information on all aspects of music life in Germany. Includes music education and vocational training; promotional facilities; music research and documentation; music in the media, etc. Triennially publishes the* Musik Almanach, *the central reference book with facts and figures on musical life in Germany.*

* **Internationales Musikinstitut Darmstadt (IMD).** Nieder-Ramstädter Str 190, D-64285 Darmstadt, Germany *tel:* +49 615 113 2416/7 *fax:* +49 615 113 2405. Solf Schaefer, director; Wilhelm Schlüter, chief librarian.

Music in Europe/European Association of Concert Agents. c/o Konzertbüro Andreas Braun, Sülzgürtel 86, D-50937 Köln, Germany *tel:* +49 221 942 0430 *fax:* +49 221 942 04319 *email:* braun@angel.de. Andreas Braun, editor. Music in Europe *is the worldwide edition of the European artist list of the European Association of Concert Agents.*

National Music Committee (Germany). Deutscher Musikrat, Weberstr 59, D-53113 Bonn, Germany. Andreas Eckhardt, secretary general.

Ghana

National Music Committee (Ghana). International Centre for African Music and Dance, School of Performing Arts, PO Box 19, Legon, Accra, Ghana. Kwabena Nketia.

Greece

National Music Committee (Greece). 38 Rue Mitropoleos, GR-105 63 Athens, Greece. Apostolos Kostios, secretary general.

Hong Kong

Hong Kong Arts Development Council. 38 Russell St, Soundwill Plaza 11/F, Causeway Bay, Hong Kong *tel:* +852 2 827 8786 *fax:* +852 2 519 9301 *email:* hkadc@hkadc.org.uk. Anita Yu, admin assistant; Lillian Hau, executive officer (music and dance). *Established to plan, promote and support the broad development of the arts and to improve the participation and education in, and knowledge, practice, appreciation, accessibility and informed criticism of the arts, with a view to improving the life of the whole community. Provides grants to arts organisations and artists. The Music and Dance Committee supports applications from dance and music practitioners and places emphasis on projects promoting research and archiving.*

Hungary

* **Hungarian Music Council.** Vorosmarty ter 1, PO Box 47, H-1364 Budapest, Hungary *tel:* +36 1 318 4243 *fax:* +36 1 317 8267 *email:* hmc@a-m.hu. Eva Csebfalvi, secretary general. *Member of the*

IMC/UNESCO. Information available on festivals, competitions, courses, scholarships and music events. Database for choral music and contemporary Hungarian composers, performers and muscial institutions.

* **Hungarian Music Information Centre.** Hungarian Music Council, PO Box 47, H-1364 Budapest, Hungary *tel:* +36 1 317 9598 *fax:* +36 1 317 8267 *email:* hmic@mail.c3.hu. Eszter Vida, director. *Functions under the auspices of the Hungarian Music Council. The centre collects and provides information on all aspects of Hungarian musical life, especially contemporary music. Large collection of contemporary music, scores, recordings and books.*

Iceland

* **Iceland Music Information Centre.** Sídumúli 34, IS-108 Reykjavík, Iceland *tel:* +354 568 3122 *fax:* +354 568 3124. Ásta Hrönn Maack, director; Bergpora Jonsdottir, publications. Adalheidur Porsteindottir, information service; Margaret Porvaldsdottir, library. *Information on Icelandic music, sound recordings and printed material. Music library with sheet music, hire material and catalogues. Information and services to the public and composers. Publication of CDs and sheet music.*

India

National Music Committee (India). 12 K Dubash Marg, Bombay 400 023, India *tel:* +91 22 284 4420/4782 *fax:* +91 204 0806/284 2410 *email:* bom.anparikh@lae.sprintrpg.ems.vsnl.net.in. Arvind Parikh, member of executive committee of IMC.

Iran

National Music Committee (Iran). Iranian Music Centre, Ministry of Culture and Islamic Orientation, Av Hafez - Av Arfa, Salle Vahdat, Teheran, Iran. Ali Moradkhani, director general.

Iraq

National Music Committee (Iraq). Ministry of Culture and Information, PO Box 6150 (Mansour), Baghdad, Iraq. Bassim Hanna Petros, secretary general.

Republic of Ireland

* **Irish Contemporary Music Centre.** 95 Lower Baggot St, Dublin 2, Republic of Ireland *tel:* +353 1 661 2105 *fax:* +353 1 676 2639 *email:* info@cmc.ie. Eve O'Kelly, director. *National archive and resource centre for new music and is used by performers, composers, promoters and members of the public. Library and sound archive contain the only comprehensive collection in existence of music by Irish composers.*

Israel

* **Israel Music Institute.** 144 Hayarkon St, 63451 Tel Aviv, Israel *tel:* +972 3 544 0219/524 6475 *fax:* +972 3 524 5276 *email:* 035245275@doar.net. Paul Landau, director. *Non-profit organisation supported by Israel Ministry of Education and Culture. Aims to publish and promote Israeli music. Information Centre has regular gatherings of composers and musicians and has ties with over 30 countries.*

National Council for Culture and the Arts. Kanfei Nesharim St 22, Ministry of Education and Culture, 91911 Jerusalem, Israel *tel:* +972 2 560 1741 *fax:* +972 2 560 1568. Raaya Simran, music department director. *A government institution supporting musical institutions and professional activities across the country. Commissions new compositions, encouraging the development of new projects. Also holds choir workshops and awards prizes for composers and performers.*

National Music Committee (Israel). Ministry of Education and Culture, Music Department, Jerusalem 91911, Israel. Ofer Turiel, secretary general.

Italy

Centro Ricerche Musicali (CRM). Via Lamarmora 18, I-00185 Roma, Italy *tel:* +39 06 446 4161 *fax:* +39 06 446 7911 *email:* crm.it@usa.net. Laura Bianchini, director; Michelangelo Lupone, art director; Lorenzo Feno, scientific director. *Advanced technology centre for music research in Europe. CRM has made significant contributions to the fields of musical composition, psycho-acoustics, musicology and musical informatics, including the design and construction of original devices for analysis, synthesis and processing in real time. Collaborates with important instrumental groups and musical institutions. Realises complex electro-acoustic works in concerts and workshops, conferences worldwide.*

National Music Committee (Italy). Centro Italiano di Iniziative Musicale, Via Vittoria Colonna 18, I-00193 Roma, Italy. Francesco Agnello, president.

Jamaica

National Music Committee (Jamaica). Ministry of Information and Culture, 2a Devon Rd, Kingston, Jamaica. Pearl Anderson, permanent secretary. Focus on Japan's moden and contemporary music. Also organises exhibitions, concerts, etc.

Japan

* **Documentation Centre of Modern Japanese Music.** 8-14 Azabudai 1-chome, Minato-ku, Tokyo 106, Japan *tel:* +81 3 3224 1584 *fax:* +81 3 3224 1654. Kazuyuki Toyama, director. *Focus on Japan's modern and contemporary music. Also organises exhibitions, concerts, etc.*

The Japan Foundation. Performing Arts Division, Ark Mori Building, 1-12-32 Akasaka, Minato-ku, Tokyo 107-6020, Japan *tel:* +81 3 5562 3530 *fax:* +81 3 5562 3500 *email:* koenka@jpf.go.jp. Fumio Matsunaga, director. *Semi-government organisation designed to promote cultural exchange between Japan and the rest of the world. Award grants towards artists' international travel costs. Occasionally organises Japanese music related events.*

National Music Committee (Japan). c/o Kunitachi College of Music, 5-5-1 Kashiwa-cho, Tachikawa-shi, Tokyo 190, Japan. Jinko Katsumura, secretary general.

Jordan

National Music Committee (Jordan). The National Music Conservatory, PO Box 926687, Amman, Jordan *tel:* +962 6 568 7620/560 5772 *fax:* +962 6 568 7621 *email:* nmc@go.com.jo. Kifah Fakhouri, director of N M Conservatory. *Provides specialist music education through pre-college and college level programmes. Organises annual music season featuring musicians from all over the world. NMC utilizes its expertise to the service of government and non-government bodies in Jordan.*

Kenya

National Music Committee (Kenya). PO Box 43844, Nairobi, Kenya. Wahington Omondi, president.

Latvia

International New Music Centre. Jelgavas 25, LV-1004 Riga, Latvia *tel:* +371 288 28538. Egils Straune, director.

Lebanon

National Music Committee (Lebanon). PO Box 14/5213, Beirut, Lebanon. Tawfik El-Basha, president.

Lithuania

Lithuanian Music Information and Publishing Centre. A Mickeviciaus 29, LT-2600 Vilnius, Lithuania *tel:* +370 2 726986 *also fax; email:* center@mipc.vno.osf.lt. Daiva Parulskiene, head. *Documents and promotes contemporary Lithuanian music. Publishes and distributes scores, runs archives of manuscripts and recordings, provides information on Lithuanian composers and releases promotional CDs.*

Luxembourg

National Music Committee (Luxembourg). 2 Rue Sosthène Weis, L-2722, Luxembourg-Grund *tel:* +35 246 2537 *fax:* +35 247 1440 *email:* direction@ugda.al.lu. Henri Schumacher, president.

Union Europeénne des Musiciens. 2 Rue Sosthène-Weis, L-2722, Luxembourg-Grund *tel:* +35 246 2536 *fax:* +35 247 1440 *email:* direction@ugda.al.lu. Henri Schumacher, president. *European music association.*

Union Grand-Duc Adolphe Asbl (Fédération Nationale de Musique du Grand-Duché de Luxembourg). 2 Rue Sosthène-Weis, L-2722, Luxembourg-Grund *tel:* +35 246 2536 *fax:* +35 247 1440. Henri Schumacher, president. *National Music Federation of Luxembourg.*

Madagascar

National Music Committee (Madagascar). 107 Rue Rainandriamampandry, 1001 Antananarivo, Madagascar. Emilie Radaody-Ralarosy, president.

Mexico

National Music Committee (Mexico). Paseo del Cantil 6, Cantil del Pedregal, Coyoacan, CP 04730, Mexico *tel:* +52 5 665 5280 *fax:* +52 5 666 5143 *email:* madeli@df1.telmex.net.mx. Manuel de Elias, president; Graciela Agudelo, vice president. Juan Trigos, sec; Manuel Zacarías, treasurer.

Moldova

National Music Committee (Moldova). c/o Union of Composers of Moldova, Str 31 August 153, 277 004 Chisinau, Moldova. Ghenadie Ciobanu, president.

Monaco

National Music Committee (Monaco). 8 Rue Louis Notari, 98000 Monte Carlo, Monaco.

Mongolia

National Music Committee (Mongolia). Science and Cultural Building, 5th Floor, Sukhebaatar Sq 3, Ulaanbaatar-11, Mongolia. D Luvsansharav, president.

Netherlands

* **Donemus.** Paulus Potterstraat 16, NL-1017 CZ Amsterdam, Netherlands *tel:* +31 20 676 4436 *fax:* +31 20 673 3588 *email:* donemus@wxs.nl. Bèr Deuss, managing director. *Scores, books, journals, reviews, brochures, CDs, tapes, videos, biographies, etc for Dutch composers since 1945. Also some information on Dutch composers 1890-1945.*

European Association of Artists Managers. Pieter G Alferink Artists Management, Apollolaan 181, NL-1077 AT Amsterdam, Netherlands *tel:* +31 20 664 3151 *fax:* +31 20 675 2426 *email:* alferink@worldonline.nl. Peter G Alferink, president; Irene van Affelen, general secretary. *Non-profit organisation which aims to protect the interests of classical music managers and their artists. Also promotes the exchange of knowledge between its members.*

European Conference of Promoters of New Music. Swammerdamstraat 38, NL-1091 RV Amsterdam, Netherlands *tel:* +31 20 694 7349 *fax:* +31 20 694 7258 *email:* ecpnm@xs4all.nl. Helmut Erdmann, president; Henk Heuvelmans, secretary. *Umbrella organisation for concert and festival organisers and music information centres in the field of contemporary music. Publishes a calendar of new music events. Information services through a bulletin board database.*

* **Gaudeamus Foundation.** Swammerdamstraat 38, NL-1091 RV Amsterdam, Netherlands *tel:* +31 20 694 7349 *fax:* +31 20 694 7258 *email:* gaud@xs4all.nl. Henk Heuvelmans, director. *Centre for contemporary mus. Library of scores, records and CDs, periodicals. General information about contemporary mus; organisation of concerts and festivals.*

International Society For Contemporary Music. Swammerdamstraat 38, N-1091 RV Amsterdam, Netherlands *tel:* +31 20 694 7349 *fax:* +31 20 694 7258 *email:* iscm@xs4all.nl. Henk Heuvelmans, secretary general. *International umbrella organisation with 47 member countries. Annual General Assembly and festival: ISCM World Music Days. Publisher of* World New Music Magazine.

Muziek Netwerk Nederland. Drift 23, NL-3512 BR Utrecht, Netherlands *tel:* +31 30 232 2046 *fax:* +31 30 231 2641. Frans A Vodegál, director. *The electronic information service of and for the Dutch musical world, collecting current bibliographic, educational, commercial and documentary information and aiming to link and integrate related subjects.*

National Music Committee (Netherlands) *see* **Donemus**.

* **Stichting Repertoire Informatiecentrum Muziek (RIM).** Drift 23, NL-3512 BR Utrecht, Netherlands *tel:* +31 30 232 2046 *fax:* +31 30 231 2641 *email:* info@rim.nl. J van Opstal, chairman. *A foundation which aims to promote innovation in the musical repertoire of the Netherlands. Music library of 70,000 works for ensembles, choirs and orchestras. RIM also holds a large collection of educational material, publishers catalogues, professional magazines and other reference material.*

New Zealand

* **The Centre for New Zealand Music Ltd (SOUNZ New Zealand).** PO Box 10 042, Wellington, 39 Cambridge Terrace, Wellington, New Zealand *tel:* +64 4 801 8602 *fax:* +64 4 801 8604 *email:* sounz@actrix.gen.nz. Scilla Askew, executive director; Phillip Collins, information assistant. *Promotes New Zealand composers and their music. Services include: library, website, free newsletter, database (220 composers and 5500 works), catalogues, sales of scores, recordings and reference books. Study guides and workshops of New Zealand music; also promotional CDs. Funded by Creative New Zealand and APRA.*

Nigeria

National Music Committee (Nigeria). Federal Ministry of Culture, National Theatre, Private Mailbag 12524, Lagos, Nigeria. A O Olusesi, assistant director of culture.

North Korea

National Music Committee (North Korea). Pyongyang International Culture Centre, Yong, wang St, Ryonhwa Dong, Central District, Pyongyang City, DPR Korea *tel:* +850 2 18111/381 8653 *fax:* +850 2 381 4777/2100. Kim Won Gyun, president.

Norway

Norwegian IMC Committee. Rikskonsertene, PO Box 2835 Solli, N-0204 Oslo, Norway *tel:* +47 22 838 350 *fax:* +47 22 831 610. Einar Solbu, executive director. *Responsible for the Norwegian representation in the IMC and its European branch, the EMC. Committee advises on music matters and provides information about the Norwegian music organisations that participate in international music life.*

* **Norwegian Music Information Centre (Norsk Musikkinformasjon).** Tollbugata 28, N-0157 Oslo 5, Norway *tel:* +47 22 429 090 *fax:* +47 22 429 091 *email:* info@mic.no. Jostein Simble, director; Hilde Holbaek-Hanssen, head of information. *Provides information on Norwegian music; arranges exhibitions, seminars and courses. Resources include manuscript library, orchestral rental materials, reference library with study and listening rooms, Norwegian jazz archives, archives for folk and popular song, plus other music institutions. Produces a music magazine* Listen to Norway .

Pakistan

National Music Committee (Pakistan). Pakistan National Music Council of the Arts, Block No 6/c, F-7, Markaz, Islamabad, Pakistan. Kishwar Naheed, president.

Peru

National Music Committee (Peru). Peruvian National Committee for UNESCO, Ministry of Education, Piso 9 - Ofcina 301, Apartado Postal 4681, Correo Central, Lima, Peru. Judith Reyes, permanent secretary.

Phillippines

Cultural Center of the Philippines. Cultural Centre of the Philippines Complex, Roxas Blvd, Pasay City 1300, Metro Manila, Philippines *tel:* +632 832 1125 *fax:* +632 832 3683. Baltazar N Endriga, president; Nestor O Jardine, deputy director; Melissa Mant, director, music division. *Showcases Filipino artistic achievements, encourages creation of original works inspired by authentic Filipino themes and traditions. Helps make Filipino art accessible to all sectors of society, in seeking to preserve, promote and enhance the artistic and cultural heritage of the Filipino people. Brings together resident and other artists through CCP Outreach Program and welcomes exhibitions of foreign artists.*

National Music Committee (Philippines). National Commission for Culture and the Arts, 633 Gen Luna St, Intramuros, Manila, Philippines. Vilma S Felipe, president.

Poland

National Music Committee (Poland). Fredry 8 Room 305, PL-00-097 Warszawa, Poland. Jan Steszewski, president.

Polish Cultural Institute. Polish Embassy, 34 Portland Place, London W1N 4HQ *tel:* +44 20 7636 6032 *fax:* +44 20 7637 2190 *email:* pci-lond@pcidir.demon.co.uk. *Promotes Polish art in Britain; assists in arranging Polish-British contacts.*

Portugal

* **Fundaçao Calouste Gulbenkian.** Avenida de Berna 45, P-1067 Lisboa, Portugal *tel:* +351 1 793 5131 *fax:* +351 1 793 7296 *email:* musica@gulbenkian.pt. Luis Pereira Leal, director. *The Foundation supports culture within Portugal and can also provide aid for Portuguese culture in other countries.*

National Music Committee (Portugal). Rua Rosa Araujo 6-3, P-1200 Lisboa, Portugal. Alvaro Salazar, president.

Romania

National Music Committee (Bucarest). Strada Esarçu 2, Sector 1, Bucarest, Romania. Petre Codreanu, secretary.

Russia

International Centre of Culture of the Russian Federation. Ministry of Culture, Kitajgorodskij proezd 7, 103074 Moscow, Russia *tel:* +7 095 220 4620 *fax:* +7 095 925 8723. Suren Shaumian, director general. *Cultural exchange programmes. Organises international festivals, competitions, tours of theatrical companies, music groups and individual performers on a commerical basis.*

National Music Committee (Russia). c/o Pax Sonoris, Krumsky val 8, 117049, Moscow, Russia. Margarita Karatyghina, secretary general.

Saudi Arabia

National Music Committee (Saudi Arabia). United Arab Music, Arab Music Academy, PO Box 4623, Jeddah, Saudi Arabia. Tariq A Hakeem, president.

Senegal

National Music Committee (Senegal). Conservatoire National Douta Seck, PO Box 3111, Dakar, Senegal. Moustapha Ndiaye, president.

Serbia

* **Yugoslav Music Information Centre (SOKOJ -MIC).** Misarska St 12-14, 11000 Beograd, Serbia *tel:* +381 11 324 5192 *also fax; fax:* +381 11 323 6168 *email:* sokojmic@eunet.yu. Ana Kotevska, director; Zorica

Premate, executive editor; Slobodanka Govedarica, librarian and archivist. *Music archive, library.* New Sound, *international magazine for mus. Small concerts in 60 seat hall.*

Slovak Republic

* **Music Information Centre of the Music Fund.** Medená 29, 811 02 Bratislava, Slovak Republic *tel:* +421 7 5443 1380 *fax:* +421 7 5443 3569 *email:* his@his.sk. Olga Smetanová, head of centre; Alena Volná, documentor. *Documents the activity of Slovak composers, musicologists and performers. The information service stores sound recordings, musicological works, press reviews and cuttings.*

National Music Committee (Slovak Republic). c/o SlovKoncert, Michalska 10, 815 36 Bratislava, Slovak Republic. Agnes Zoliomiova, secretary general.

Slovenia

Muzina. Rutarjeva 5, Ljubljana, Slovenia *tel:* +386 61 213972. Brina Jez-Brezavscek. *An association for contemporary music, especially for the promotion of Slovene composers born after 1950.*

South Korea

National Music Committee (South Korea). c/o The Music Association of Korea, Building 1-117, Dongsung-dong, Chongro-gu, Seoul, South Korea. Jai Kook Kwack, secretary general.

Spain

* **Centro de Documeutación de Músicz y Danza.** c/ Torregalindo 10, E-28016 Madrid, Spain *tel:* +34 91 350 8600 *fax:* +34 91 359 1579 *email:* cdmyd@sarenet.es. Antonio Álvarez Cañibano, director. *Directory and database of music and dance resources in Spain.*

Centro Para la Difusión de la Música Contemporánea. Santa Isabel 52, E-28012 Madrid, Spain *tel:* +34 91 468 2310 *fax:* +34 91 530 8321 *email:* consuelo.diez@cdmc.inaem.es. Consuelo Diéz, director. *Aims to create a more favourable atmosphere for new composition, and to help the understanding, enjoyment and study of contemporary music. It programmes and stages music performances. Also the study, examination and experimentation of new music genres and trends, with a focus on Spanish composers. Also involved in promotion, advertising, etc.*

International Society for Contemporary Music. Avda de America 58-5, E-28028 Madrid, Spain *tel:* +34 91 356 3621. Luis De Pablo.

National Music Committee (Spain). Ministry of Culture, INAEM, Plaza del Rey 1, 28004 Madrid, Spain. Tomás Marco, president.

Sweden

International Confederation for Electroacoustic Music. Kocksgaten 1, S-116 23 Stockholm, Sweden. Sten Hanson, president.

International Federation for Choral Music. Klockargårdsv 18, S-135 68 Tyresö, Sweden. Christian Ljunggren, secretary general.

National Music Committee (Sweden). c/o Kungl Musikaliska Akademien, Blaisieholmstorg 8, S-111 48 Stockholm, Sweden. Bengt Holmstrand, secretary general.

* **Swedish Music Information Centre.** Box 27327, 79 Sandhamnsgatan, S-102 54 Stockholm, Sweden *tel:* +46 8 783 8800 *fax:* +46 8 783 9510 *email:* swedmic@stim.se. Roland Sandberg, executive director. *Hire library and mail order service for unpublished, copyright-protected sheet music. Hire library of electro-acoustic music, historical popular sheet music collection, listening room with published sheet music, commercial and tape recordings, literature about Swedish music and musical life, information service about composers and works. Own publishing house: Edition Suecia. Record society: Phono Suecia.*

Switzerland

European Festivals Association. CH-1202 Geneve, Switzerland *tel:* +41 22 738 6873 *fax:* +41 22 738 4012 *email:* geneva@eurofestivals.efa.ch. Tamas Klenjanszky, secretary general. *Aims to promote significance of festivals through common publicity, to maintain and develop high artistic quality of festivals and emphasize their important role in international cultural co-operation.*

European Music Council of International Music Council. Haus der Musik Gönhardweg 32, CH-5000 Aarau, Switzerland *tel:* +41 62 822 9423 *fax:* +41 62 822 9407 *email:* musikrat@aarauonline.ch. Ursula Bally-Fahr, secretary general. *Platform for representatives of the National Music Councils and all organisations involved in the field of music education, creation, performance and heritage from all European countries.*

* **Fondation SUISA pour la musique.** Rue de l'Hôpital 22, Case postale 409, CH-2001 Neuchâtel, Switzerland *tel:* +41 32 725 2536 *fax:* +41 32 724 0472 *email:* info@fondation-suisa.ch. Claude Delley, director. *Encourages the composition of all styles of Swiss music.*

International Confederation of Music Societies. Hammerstr 37, CH-4058 Basel, Switzerland. Hans Schaad, secretary general.

Swiss Council of Music. Haus der Musik Gönhardweg 32, CH-5000 Aarau, Switzerland *tel:* +41 62 822 9423 *fax:* +41 62 822 9407 *email:* musikrat@aarauonline.ch. Jakob Stämpfli, president; Ursula Bally-Fahr, secretary general. *Represents the whole of Swiss musical life in its capacity as an umbrella organisation for all national organisations and associations. Four main issues: Jugend + Musik, cultural policy, music education, and co-operation with European music organisations.*

Swiss Music Edition (SME/EMS). PO Box 7851, CH-6000, Lucerne 7, Switzerland *tel:* +41 41 210 6070 *also fax; email:* sme@centralnet.ch. Ulrich Gasser, president; Peter Bitterli, secretary. *Publishes scores by contemporary Swiss composers. Swiss Music Information Centre on internet details Swiss composers, performers, editors, scores, discs, organisations of live mus.*

World Federation of International Music Competitions. 104 Rue de Carouge, CH-1205 Geneve, Switzerland *tel:* +41 22 321 3620 *fax:* +41 22 781 1418 *email:* fmcim@iprolink.ch. Jacques Haldenwang, secretary general; Lottie Chalut, executive secretary. *Co-ordinates and promotes the activities of 109 major music competitions throughout the world, and publishes an annual calendar of competitions.*

Tunisia

National Music Committee (Tunisia). Ministry of Culture and Information, Rue du 2 Mars 1934, La Kasbah, Tunis, Tunisia. Fehti Zghonda, secretary general.

Turkey

National Music Committee (Turkey). c/o Turkish National Commission for UNESCO, Göreme Sokak No 7, Kavaklidere, Ankara, Turkey.

Ukraine

* **Music Information Centre of the Ukraine Composers Union.** Ul Sofiuska 16/16, 252001 Kiev 1, Ukraine *tel:* +380 44 228 3304 *fax:* +380 44 229 6940. Volodymyr Simonenko, director.

National Music Committee (Ukraine). 32 Puschkin Str, 252 004 Kiev, Ukraine. Nina Gersimova, secretary general.

Uruguay

National Music Committee (Uruguay). Rio Negro 1228, 11100 Montevideo, Uruguay. Tania Siver, delegate.

USA

American Federation of Musicians of the United States and Canada. 1501 Broadway, Suite 600, New York, NY 10036, USA *tel:* +1 212 869 1330 *fax:* +1 212 764 6134 *email:* info@afm.org. Steve Young, president. *Union representing the professional interests of musicians performing all styles of mus. Membership of the Federation is open to all professional musicians and vocalists in the USA and Canada.*

* **American Music Center.** 30 West 26th St, Suite 1001, New York, NY 10010-2011, USA *tel:* +1 212 366 5260 *fax:* +1 212 366 5265 *email:* center@amc.net. Richard Kessler, executive director. *Promotes the creation, performance and appreciation of American contemporary music, through information services, a collection of scores and recordings, grant programmes, and advocacy on behalf of American music.*

Americans for the Arts. 1 E 53 St, New York, NY 10022-4201, USA *tel:* +1 212 223 2787 *fax:* +1 212 980 4857 *email:* info@artsusa.org. Robert Lynch, president. *National organisation for groups and individuals dedicated to advancing the arts and culture across the USA. Founded by the ACA, it represents a broad network of arts supporters, patrons, business leaders and community arts organisations.*

Music Associates of America (MAA). 224 King St, Englewood, NJ 07631, USA *tel:* +1 201 569 2898 *fax:* +1 201 569 7023 *email:* maasturm@sprynet.com. George Sturm, executive director. *An organisation providing administrative and promotional services to music publishers, distributors and composers of concert music.*

National Music Committee (USA). Kingsborough College, Department of Music, 2001 Oriental Boulevard, Brooklyn, NY 11235, USA. Dean Stein, president.

Uzbekistan

National Music Committee (Uzbekistan). c/o National Commission of Uzbekistan for UNESCO, 54 Buyak Ipak Yuli, Tashkent 700 137, Uzbekistan *tel:* +37 12 670 646 *fax:* +37 12 670 546/538 *email:* unesco@natcom.org.az. Zakhid Khaknazarov, president; Tukhtasin Gafurbekov, vice-president. *Research on fundamental problems in music; facilitates and encourages development of composers and music.*

Vietnam

National Music Committee (Vietnam). 32 Nguyen Thai Hoc, Hanoi, Vietnam. Pham Dinh Sau, president.

Zambia

National Music Committee (Zambia). Centre of the Arts, University of Zambia, PO Box 32279, Lusaka, Zambia. M I Mapoma, president.

Index of International Listings by Country

Bangladesh

Belgium

Bolivia

Brazil

Aalborg Symphony Orchestra
Aarhus Symfoniorkester
Copenhagen Philharmonic Orchestra
Danish National Radio Symphony Orchestra
Det Kongelige Kapel
Odense Symfoniorkester
Randers Chamber Orchestra
Royal Danish Orchestra
Sønderjyllands Symfoniorkester
Opera Companies 591
Den Jyske Opera (Danish National Opera)
The Royal Danish Opera
Choirs and Choruses 598
The Danish National Radio Choir
Royal Opera Chorus
Tivoli Concert Choir
Competitions 605
Carl Nielsen International Music Competitions
International Organ Competition
Nicolai Malko International Competition for Young Conductors
Competitions for Composers 617
Thad Jones Competition
Music Festivals 623
Aarhus Festival
Composers' Biennale
Contemporary Music in Suså
Copenhagen Choir Festival
Copenhagen Early Music Festival
Copenhagen International Experimental Music Festival
Copenhagen Jazz Festival
European Youth Music Festival
Fanø Musikfestival
Frederiksvaerk Music Festival
Music Harvest Festival
Selsø Summer Concerts
Sorø International Music Festival
Vendsyssel Festival
Music Publishers 645
Edition Egtved A/s
Edition Wilhelm Hansen
Engstrøm & Sødring AS
The Society for the Publication of Danish Music
SteepleChase Music/Edition Kontrapunkt
Music Information Centres 652
The Danish Cultural Institute
Danish Music Council
Danish Music Information Centre
Jazzkontakten/Jazzcentret

Egypt
Symphony Orchestras 579
Cairo Symphony Orchestra
Music Information Centres 653
National Music Committee (Egypt)

Equador
Music Information Centres 653
National Music Committee (Equador)

Estonia
Agents and Promoters 560
Eesti Kontsert
Symphony Orchestras 579
Estonian National Opera Symphony Orchestra
Estonian National Symphony Orchestra
Opera Companies 591
Estonian National Opera
Choirs and Choruses 598
Estonian Philharmonic Chamber Choir
Competitions 605
International Choral Festival Tallinn
Music Festivals 623
International Festival of New Music NYYD
Music Information Centres 653
Estonian Music Council
National Music Committee (Estonia)

Faroe Islands
Music Festivals 623
Summartónar

Finland
Agents and Promoters 560
Allegro Artist Management
Fazer Artists' Management Inc
Festium Oy
FinnConcert
Helsingin Juhlamusiikkipalvelu/JMP Music Ltd
Orfeo Oy Ltd
PPM Artists Management
Rockadillo
Sibelius Academy Concert Agency
StillArt
WellDone
Symphony Orchestras 581
Finnish Radio Symphony Orchestra
Helsinki Philharmonic Orchestra
Tampere Philharmonic Orchestra
Vaasa City Orchestra
Opera Companies 591
Finnish National Opera
Joensuun Ooppera
Lahden Ooppera
Mikkeli Opera
Opera Alueooppera
Tampere Opera
Turku Opera
Vaasan Opera
Choirs and Choruses 598
The Finnish Radio Chamber Choir
The Jubilate Choir
The Polytech Choir
Tampere Philharmonic Choir
Competitions 605
International Jean Sibelius Violin Competition
International Sibelius Conductors' Competition
Lahti International Organ Competition
Mirjam Helin International Singing Competition
Tampereen Sävel International Choir Contest and Festival
Music Festivals 623
April Jazz Espoo
Avanti! Summer Sounds
Crusell Week
Espoo International Piano Festival
Finland Festivals
Helsinki Festival
Hetta Music Event
Ilmajoki Music Festival
International Kalottjazz and Blues Festival
Joensuu Festival
Kangasniemi Music Festival
Kaustinen Folk Music Festival
Korsholm Music Festival
Kuhmo Chamber Music Festival
Lahti Organ Festival
Lakeside Blues Festival
Lieska Brass Week
Mikkeli Music Festival
Musica Nova Helsinki
Naantali Music Festival
Northern Accordion, Folkmusic and Folkdance Festival
Oulainen Music Week
Oulu Music Festival
Pori Jazz Festival

Jamaica

Japan

Sweden

Switzerland

Indexes

Index of Advertisers

Index of Advertising Artists

Index of Subjects

For your *free editorial entry* in the

British Music Yearbook 2001

Complete this form or a photocopy, and return to:

The Editor, British Music Yearbook, Rhinegold Publishing Ltd, 241 Shaftesbury Avenue, London WC2H 8EH, UK (*tel:* 020 7333 1760 *fax:* 020 7333 1769)

ORGANISATION/INSTITUTION ....

SECTION OF BOOK ....

ADDRESS ....

....

....

....

.... POSTCODE ....

TEL .... FAX ....

EMAIL .... WEBSITE ....

CONTACT .... POSITION ....

OTHER PERSONNEL ....

....

....

COMPREHENSIVE DETAILS (PLEASE INCLUDE FOR ALL ENTRIES) ....

....

....

....

....

....

....

....

....

Performers and **Composers** please use the form on the next page.
Please attach any additional details to support your entry.
Editorial entries are *free*, but are included at the discretion of the editor.

For inclusion in the 2001 edition, please return this form by June 2000.

PLEASE TICK HERE IF YOU WOULD BE INTERESTED IN ADVERTISING IN THE BRITISH MUSIC YEARBOOK ☐

Performers and Composers

For your *free editorial entry* in the

British Music Yearbook 2001

Complete this form or a photocopy, and return to:

The Editor, British Music Yearbook, Rhinegold Publishing Ltd, 241 Shaftesbury Avenue, London WC2H 8EH, UK (*tel:* 020 7333 1760 *fax:* 020 7333 1769)

NAME..

VOICE/INSTRUMENT/COMPOSER..

CONTACT ADDRESS ....

....

....

....

....POSTCODE...

TEL ....FAX...

EMAIL ....WEBSITE..

AGENT(S) ....

COMPREHENSIVE DETAILS: Performers, please list your last six performances (including date, venue, works performed, etc) and include a short CV. Composers, please list your publishers and details of your last six works performed or broadcast. Ensembles, also include personnel details and a description of ensemble. **Please note that no entries can be accepted without these details.**

....

....

....

....

....

....

....

....

Please attach any additional details to support your entry.
Editorial entries are *free*, but are included at the discretion of the editor.

For inclusion in the 2001 edition, please return this form by June 2000.

PLEASE TICK HERE IF YOU WOULD BE INTERESTED IN ADVERTISING IN THE BRITISH MUSIC YEARBOOK ☐